SECOND EDITION

# CORRECTIONS
## IN THE
# COMMUNITY

Edward J. Latessa
Professor and Division Head
Division of Criminal Justice
University of Cincinnati

Harry E. Allen
Professor Emeritus
Administration of Justice Department
San Jose State University

**anderson publishing co.**
2035 Reading Road
Cincinnati, OH 45202
800-582-7295

**Corrections in the Community, Second Edition**

Copyright © 1997, 1999
Anderson Publishing Co.
2035 Reading Rd.
Cincinnati, OH 45202

Phone 800.582.7295 or 513.421.4142
Web Site www.andersonpublishing.com

**Library of Congress Cataloging-in-Publication Data**

Latessa, Edward J.
    Corrections in the community / Edward J. Latessa, Harry E. Allen.
       p.    cm.
    Includes bibliographical references and indexes.
    ISBN 0-87084-238-2 (pbk.)
    1. Corrections--United States.  I. Allen, Harry E.  II. Title.
HV9469.L27  1999
364.6 ' 0973--dc21

99-18634
CIP

Cover design by Tin Box Studio, Inc.
Cover photo credit: © Ian O'Leary/Tony Stone Images

EDITOR  Gail Eccleston
ACQUISITIONS EDITOR  Michael C. Braswell

# Dedication

This book is dedicated to the Latessa children:
Amy, Jennifer, Michael, and Allison

Dad

And to the Allen nephews:
Craig, Forrest, and Hunter, Jr.

Uncle Harry

# Acknowledgments

Writing a book requires a great deal of help and support. We realize that it is a cliché to say that it could not have been possible without the following people, but truer words were never spoken.

There are many people who have allowed us to study and learn about community corrections. They all worked with us over the years, and have contributed immeasurably to our knowledge and experience. In particular we would like to thank the following friends and colleagues:

Nancy Shomaker, Sharon Kennedy, David Dillingham, Allen Ault, George Keiser, Peter Kinziger, Don Andrews, Barry Glick, Arthur Lurigio, Rob Bresciani, Jerry Smith, Carl Wicklund, Linda Smith, Dominic Lisa, Melissa Moon, Brandon Applegate, Steve Holmes, Mario Paparozzi, Paul Gendreau, Ed Kollin, Vince Polito, Bill Kroman, Ute Vilfroy, Dan Peterca, Loretta Ryland, Maria Nemec, Dennis Dimatteo, Grafton Payne, Lauren Maio, Tom Muhleman, Jim Dare, Paul Ringer, Tim Shannon, Mike Walton, Wendy Niehaus, Eric Jefferis, Dena Hanley, Bill King, Dan Joyner, Bill Hamilton, Bruce Gibson, Joe Ellison, Doug Brothers, Gary Yates, Rob Clevenger, Bob Dugan, Larry Muse, Jim Wichtman, Candi Peters, Don Petit, Doug Moorman, Brenda Peters, Glen Lammon, Bob Markin, Neil Tilow, Pam McClain, Larry Williams, Tom Berghausen, Debbie Brooks, Tim Alley, Jim Lawrence, Anne Connell Favend, Mary Spotswood, Merel Pickenpaugh, John Baron, Monda DeWeese, Gene Gallo, Rick Billak, Jim Corfman, Fransaia LoDico, Craig Prysock, Kurt Williams, Marie Scott, Chris Liza, Debbie Rees, John Chin, Jill Goldhart, Randy Gortz, Butch Huyandi, Barb Kaminski, Dan Lombardo, Bob Balboni, Lynn Bielecki, Karen Chapple, Ron Corbett, Joe Hassett, Mindy Hutcherson, Bryan Riley, Tom Berghausen, Bob Swisher, Evalyn Parks, Robert Mecum, Geno Natalucci-Persichetti, Linda Modry, Ed Heller, Ryan Geis, Al Neff, Carole Rapp-Zimmerman, Jack Reil, Sherry Walters, Ed Rhine, Greg Buckholtz, Steve Anderson, Peggy Ritchie-Matsumoto, and Reggie Wilkinson.

At Anderson Publishing we want to thank Kelly Grondin and Bill Simon for sticking with us, and for all their support. The copy editing, proofing, and sundry tasks associated with the production of a book were in the very capable hands of Gail Eccleston. We also want to thank Dennis Gilday for the great job he has done peddling the book, and Carla Hoskinds for putting up with us. Please accept our sincere appreciation and gratitude. We would be remiss not to mention the assistance and support of our friend Mickey Braswell, and the helpful review of the first edition from Dr. John Whitehead at East Tennessee State University.

A number of graduate students at the University of Cincinnati assisted us (and put up with Ed Latessa) while we were finishing this book:

Alex Holsinger, Betsy Fulton, Dana Jones, Shelly Johnson, Jodi Sundt, Chris Lowenkamp, Sheli McDonough, Lois Presser, Amy Stichman, Kim Gentry-Sperber, Martha Henderson, Colleen Kadleck. We wish them well with their careers, and hope they adopt the book!

A special word of thanks to Violet Hall, Charlotte Better, Jason Hanna, and Kristi Wahoff, for all their help and support.

To our colleagues and friends, without whose support and expertise this book would never have been possible: Larry Travis, Frank Cullen, Jim Frank, Jerry Vito, Bob Langworthy, Chris Eskridge, and Clifford Simonsen.

We also have to thank Amy, Jennifer, Michael, and Allison, who reminded us that delinquency prevention begins at home.

Finally, to Sally, who supported, fed, and cared for us. We love you.

EJL & HEA

We would like to thank the following individuals for taking the time to send comments concerning the first edition of *Corrections in the Community*. We attempted to address many of the suggestions that were made, and we are grateful to everyone who took the time to respond.

Rudolph Alexander
Michael Ardis
John Baron
Socorro Benitez
Melissa Blevins
John Boal
Sue Bourke
Pauline Brennan
Pat Brownell
Shirley Carna
Dawn Cecil
Marilyn Chandler Ford
Dae Chang
Todd Clear
Joe Cook
Kevin Courtright

George Coxey
Keith Crew
Concetta Culliver
Carol Davis
Jack Dison
Richard Dittbenner
Temple Doerr
Don Dougherty
Ed Frayley
Jay Garrett
William Gibson
James Gillham
Delores Godley
A. Godwin
Colin Goff
Linda Groome

Nancy Grosselfinger
Elizabeth Grossi
Paul Hahn
Dena Hanley
Kelly Hannah
Cary Heck
Zelma Henriques
Sharon Heuschele
Vincent Holland
Roy Hungerford
David Johnson
Richard Kania
J. Kiedrowski
Kay Kiernan
Tammy King
Allan Krescent
Richard Lawrence
Frank Leonbruno
Karol Lucken
Larry Lunnen
Faith Lutze
Ronald Lyon
Jeff Maahs
Dan Macallair
Mike Markulis
Larry Marshall
Jim Miller
Martin Miller
Geoffrey Moss
Randall Murphy
Jay Newberger
Emmanuel Onyeozili
Ken Orr

William Osborne
John Paitakes
Andrew Pappas
William Parks
Fred Patrick
Robert Pattison
Ronald Robinson
Judith Rumgay
Ronnie Salahu
Nancy Schaefer
Richard Seiter
Sandi Sostak
Charles Stapleton
Rick Steinmann
Richard Stempien
Gale Stevens
Michael Summers
Gregory Talley
Lydia Todd
Sam Torres
Bill Wakefield
Joseph Waldron
Charles West
Paul White
Deborah Williamson
Melissa Winston
Gregory Witkowski
Betsy Witt
John Wozniak
George Yefchak
Suzanne Youngblood
Sherwood Zimmerman

# Preface

Writing a book on a topic as broad and dynamic as community corrections is a very difficult task. It is extremely hard to know when to stop. The field is changing rapidly and, as a result, information and data are quickly outdated. We believe that we have pulled together some of the most recent and salient information available; however, we accept responsibility for any errors or shortcomings. There are several caveats we would like to make concerning this book.

First, as you will undoubtedly note, definitions of terms are often repeated in different chapters. This was done intentionally to aid students by reemphasizing important information.

Second, there are a great many charts and tables with data. Memorizing the numbers is not important, they change daily. What is important are the trends over time. We want students to see patterns of what is happening in community corrections.

Third, you will also become aware of our bias. We believe that we incarcerate too many of our citizens, that this is not good social policy, and that they can be supervised in the community without seriously jeopardizing public safety. We believe that much public treasure is wasted and human misery increased while incarcerating low risk offenders. But, as our good friend Frank Cullen often says, "we are liberal, not stupid." We recognize that some offenders—those who are violent and would likely cause serious harm to others—belong in prison. We do not believe however, that all or even a majority of 1.2 million or so incarcerated fit that description.

Finally, there are many who believe that the ills confronting probation and parole are terminal. We do not believe that to be the case. While there is little doubt that the tasks confronting these correctional sanctions are daunting, we believe that the future of community corrections is bright and filled with promise.

# Table of Contents in Brief

# Table of Contents

# The
# Criminal Justice System

> It is hard to identify the benefits inmates gain from prison, but the harm done there is readily seen. If you want to increase the crime problem, incite men to greater evil, and intensify criminal inclinations and proclivities, then lock violators up in prison for long periods, reduce their outside contacts, stigmatize them and block their lawful employment when released, all the while setting them at tutelage under the direction of more skilled and predatory criminals. I know of no better way to gain your ends than these.
> —Harry E. Allen

Crime is everywhere, in all nations great and small and, in this nation, crime is a violation of criminal statutes passed by elected representatives. The statutes are enforced by a variety of social control agencies specifically designed to fulfill some desired social function. These agencies include law enforcement, prosecution, court, and post-adjudication components that include, among other major units, the probation and parole systems. These varied agencies and actions, along with their philosophical bases and objectives, are usually called the "criminal justice system."

No one imposed this unique blend of agencies on the nation. We invented them ourselves and, if there is something amiss with an agency or mission, it can be changed. One fact about the American criminal justice system is that it is rapidly evolving and changing as a result of the volume of crime, emerging national priorities, available funding, and changing political ideologies. Behaviors thought particularly heinous in one epoch may become regulated, if not accepted, behavior in another. The Great Experiment of Prohibition attempted to protect our national character and youth, increase productivity, lessen collateral problems of idleness and wastrel-like behavior, and improve the moral fiber of those using alcohol, but is no longer a national crusade. As a result, earlier twentieth-century law enforcement efforts lapsed into a phase of tax collection, and controlled-substance, concerned only in large part with keeping alcohol out of the hands of youthful consumers. So it is with the current War on Drugs.

One component of the criminal justice system is corrections, earlier defined as "post-adjudication processing of convicted criminal offenders." This definition, if it were ever adequate, probably best fits the correctional scene of the early twentieth century, when the major sentencing options available to sentencing courts were committing the offender to prison or granting probation. In fact, the study of post-adjudication processing of criminal law offenders was, until about 1969, commonly referred to as "penology."

The field of corrections, like most of the justice system, has undergone rapid change in the last three decades. Programs have been developed to allow prosecutors to suspend prosecution of alleged malefactors provided they became and remained actively involved in seeking personal development and rehabilitation under the "deferred prosecution" program. Pretrial detention of accused law violators is now rare, due to the development of personal recognizance programs that reduced the importance of the bondsman in the pretrial portion of the system. In addition, the tools of technology have grown greatly in the last two decades, expanding probation supervision into conventional probation, intensive supervised probation, house arrest (with or without electronic monitoring), community service, day attendance centers, and restitution programs. There are even probation variations that combine serving a sentence in jail before probation begins, and several probation programs that require a period of imprisonment prior to return to the community under probation supervision! These latter programs, incidentally, are part of the "intermediate sanctions" that have emerged in the last 20 years: offender control programs that fall somewhere between probation and imprisonment.

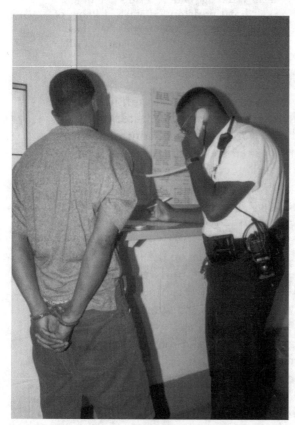

Photo 1.1
Booking in local jail. Photograph by Beth Sanders.

What has corrections become? How can we best define it at the present time? For us, corrections is the social control agency that provides societal protection by providing incarceration and community supervision and rehabilitation services to persons accused or convicted of criminal law violating behavior. This definition includes pretrial diversion programs as well as the more traditional probation and parole services. It also embraces intermediate sanctions as well as alternative early-release programs for inmates in prisons across the nation. In sum, corrections is social control of persons whose behavior has brought them to the attention of the justice system. The missions, objectives, procedures, and even principles of corrections have undergone such rapid change recently that we are forced to expand the traditional definition of corrections to include the most recent developments. In another two decades, our current definition may be thought as outdated as the earlier one. We hope to suggest the emerging dimensions as your reading progresses.

## Corrections in the Community

This textbook describes and explains corrections in the community, or "community corrections." This term refers to numerous and diverse types of supervision, treatment, reintegration, control, and supportive programs for criminal law violators. Community corrections programs, as will be seen later, are designed for offenders at many levels of both the juvenile and criminal justice systems. First, community corrections programs are found in the pre-adjudication level of the justice systems, and include diversion and pretrial release programs, as well as treatment programs provided by private sector agencies, particularly for juveniles (Moon, Applegate & Latessa, 1997; Monroe, 1996; Latessa & Travis, 1991; Farrington, 1994; Tolan & Guerra, 1994).

As correctional clients move further into the justice system, community corrections programs have been developed and designed to minimize their further processing and penetration into the justice system. These pre-imprisonment programs include restitution, community services, active probation, intensive supervised probation, house arrest, and residential community facilities, such as halfway houses. (All these programs are described in detail in later chapters.) One assumption underlying the effort to minimize offender penetration into the justice system is that incarceration is less effective in reintegrating offenders and is unnecessarily expensive for the good attained. Another assumption is that community corrections is more humane, although there is some contemporary debate over whether corrections ought to be humane rather than harsh. Community corrections is no less effective in reducing recidivism than is the prison.[1]

Community corrections continues after incarceration, (and in some cases is combined with incarceration)[2] and among the many programs

Figure 1.1
**What is the Sequence of Events in the Criminal Justice System?**

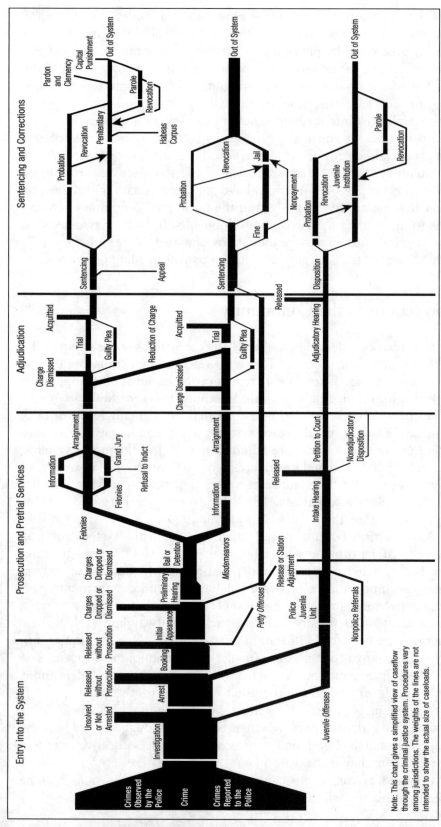

Note: This chart gives a simplified view of caseflow through the criminal justice system. Procedures vary among jurisdictions. The weights of the lines are not intended to show the actual size of caseloads.

Source: Adapted from *The Challenge of Crime in a Free Society.* President's Commission on Law Enforcement and Administration of Justice, 1967.

found at this level are split sentences (jail followed by probation), shock incarceration and shock probation, prison furlough programs, work and educational release, shock parole, and parole programs and services.[3] The various points at which community correction programs have been developed are suggested in Figure 1.1, which identifies the flow of clients into and through the justice system.

The diagram of Figure 1.1 first appeared in President Lyndon Johnson's Crime Commission report, *The Challenge of Crime in a Free Society* (1969). It outlined the basic sequence of events in the criminal justice process. Police, courts, and corrections were thus viewed as elements that were interrelated and interdependent. The idea was to demonstrate the manner in which successful crime prevention was the goal of the entire system. Community corrections fits squarely into this goal: offenders whose criminal behavior is reduced or eliminated through programs in the community will commit fewer if any crimes in the future.[4]

Two major factors should be pointed out in Figure 1.1. First, the major ways out of the system are probation and parole, shown here as system outputs. The second conclusion is that the number of cases flowing through the system decreases as offenders are processed at the various decision points (prosecutor, court, sentencing, and release from prison). Figure 1.2 depicts the flow of offenders through the system.

Figure 1.2
**Outcomes for Arrest for Felony Crime: 1996**

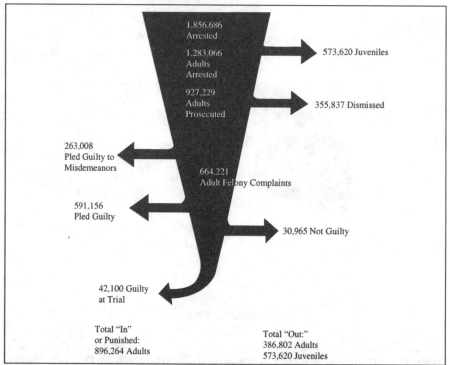

Sources: Federal Bureau of Investigation (1997). *Crime in the United States.* Washington, DC: U.S. Department of Justice. Figure adapted from C. Silberman (1978). *Criminal Violence, Criminal Justice,* pp. 257-261. New York, NY: Random House.

Box 1.1

### Probation and Parole

Probation is a sentence imposed by the court that does not usually involve confinement and imposes conditions to restrain the offender's actions in the community. The court retains authority to modify the conditions of the sentence or to resentence the offender if he or she violates the conditions.

Parole is the release of an offender from confinement prior to expiration of sentence on condition of good behavior and supervision in the community.

The types of sentences imposed for felonies in the United States can be found in Figure 1.3. Non-incarceration sentences were imposed in 29 percent of the cases of convicted felons sentenced in 1994. Another 45 percent were sentenced to prison and all but a scant few of these will be released from prison onto parole supervision. Even a large part of those offenders sentenced to jail may be released onto probation as part of a split-sentence. Community corrections handles a large proportion of the offenders in the nation.

Figure 1.3
**Percentage of Felony Sentences Imposed in State Courts, 1994**

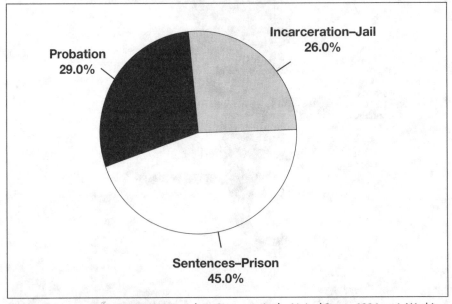

Source: P. Langan and J. Brown (1997). *Felony Sentences in the United States, 1994*, p. 4. Washington, DC: U.S. Bureau of Justice Statistics.

Box 1.2

## Jail

A jail is a confinement facility, usually administered by a local law enforcement agency, intended for adults but sometimes containing juveniles, that holds persons detained pending adjudication and/or persons committed after adjudication for sentences of one year or less. Jails are usually supported by local tax revenues and, as such, are particularly vulnerable to resource reductions.

Additional categories of jail inmates include mentally ill persons for whom there are no other facilities or who are awaiting transfer to mental health authorities, parolees and probationers awaiting hearings, court-detained witnesses and persons charged with contempt of court, federal prisoners awaiting pick up by marshals, and offenders sentenced to state department of corrections for whom there is not yet space but who cannot be released ("hold-backs").

A more detailed picture of the importance of community corrections is found in Table 1.1, which presents data on adult felony arrest disposition in California (California Department of Justice, 1998). In brief, the data show that for every 100 felony arrests made in 1994, 44 offenders were sentenced to jail plus probation and another 6 received probation. About 3 were incarcerated in jail, and 14 were sent to prison, from which they will eventually emerge on a period of mandatory parole supervision. In total, only 3 persons for every 67 convicted of a felony crime in California in 1994 were not clients in the community correctional system!

Table 1.1 clearly shows evidence of the "funnel effect." This funnel results from the attrition that occurs at every stage of the criminal justice process. There is a clear and steady reduction in the number of of-

Box 1.3

## Prison

A state or federal confinement facility having custodial authority over criminal-law violating adults sentenced to confinement for usually more than one year.

Table 1.1
**Sentencing Outcomes for Felony Arrests, California: 1997**

| | |
|---|---|
| Dispositions for Arrested Persons: | |
| Stationhouse Release | 4.4% |
| Prosecutorial Denial of Complaint | 14.9 |
| Complaint Filed | 80.7 |
| | 100.0% |
| | |
| Disposition of Filed Complaint: | |
| Dismissed by Court, Prosecutor | 11.2% |
| Diversion | 2.0 |
| Found Not Guilty at Trial | .2 |
| Guilty and Sentenced | 67.3 |
| | 80.7% |
| | |
| Sentence Disposition: | |
| Probation | 5.7% |
| Jail | 2.6 |
| Jail Plus Probation | 44.2 |
| Prison | 14.0 |
| Other (Fine, Suspended Sentence, etc.) | .7 |
| | 67.2% |

Source: California Department of Justice (1998). *Crime and Delinquency in California, 1997: Advance Release*, p. 4. Sacramento, CA: CDJ.

fenders processed from arrest through imprisonment: 19 percent from arrest to complaints being filed, and another 13 percent from filing to case disposition.

As Table 1.1 indicates for California, 81 out of 100 felony arrests result in prosecution, 67 cases are convicted, and 14 persons are eventually imprisoned (most for a short period of time). Naturally, national figures vary across jurisdictions and severity of offense, but the funnel effect remains pronounced. Community correctional programs, particularly probation and parole, play a major role in the creation of this funnel effect. For example, the Bureau of Justice Statistics (1997) reported that 2,800 of every 100,000 adult residents of the nation were under correctional control at the start of 1995. On the basis of 100,000 adult residents in the nation, 1,621 were on probation (Table 1.2), 359 on parole (Table 1.5), 420 in prison, and 212 in jail. Approximately 2 out of 3 offenders were living in the community on a given day in 1997 (see Figure 1.4).

Table 1.2
**Adults on Probation, 1996**

| Region and jurisdiction | Probation population 1/1/96 | 1996 Entries | 1996 Exits | Probation population 12/31/96 | Percent change in probation population during 1996 | Number on probation on 12/31/96 per 100,000 adult residents |
|---|---|---|---|---|---|---|
| **U.S. total** | 3,077,861 | 1,651,544 | 1,545,937 | 3,180,363 | 3.3% | 1,621 |
| Federal[a] | 35,457 | 18,796 | 19,952 | 34,301 | −3.3% | 17 |
| State | 3,042,404 | 1,632,748 | 1,525,985 | 3,146,062 | 3.4 | 1,603 |
| **Northeast** | 538,941 | 243,971 | 224,307 | 558,605 | 3.6% | 1,434 |
| Connecticut | 54,507 | 37,290 | 35,819 | 55,978 | 2.7 | 2,261 |
| Maine[b] | 8,641 | 2,651 | 3,596 | 7,696 | −10.9 | 815 |
| Massachusetts | 43,680 | 36,436 | 35,258 | 44,858 | 2.7 | 960 |
| New Hampshire | 4,347 | 3,232 | 3,165 | 4,414 | 1.5 | 509 |
| New Jersey | 126,759 | 61,851 | 62,729 | 125,881 | −.7 | 2,098 |
| New York | 168,012 | 47,502 | 34,934 | 180,580 | 7.5 | 1,323 |
| Pennsylvania | 106,823 | 41,643 | 37,934 | 110,532 | 3.5 | 1,206 |
| Rhode Island | 18,850 | 9,385 | 7,789 | 20,446 | 8.5 | 2,708 |
| Vermont | 7,322 | 3,981 | 3,083 | 8,220 | 12.3 | 1,860 |
| **Midwest** | 675,380 | 481,350 | 459,923 | 702,419 | 4.0% | 1,532 |
| Illinois | 109,489 | 72,672 | 66,658 | 115,503 | 5.5 | 1,329 |
| Indiana | 95,267 | 77,962 | 73,639 | 99,590 | 4.5 | 2,294 |
| Iowa | 16,579 | 12,559 | 13,754 | 15,384 | −7.2 | 721 |
| Kansas | 16,547 | 13,805 | 14,620 | 15,732 | −4.9 | 835 |
| Michigan[c] | 141,436 | 117,050 | 112,937 | 148,595 | 5.1 | 2,106 |
| Minnesota[c] | 83,778 | 57,314 | 55,853 | 88,039 | 5.1 | 2,581 |
| Missouri[c] | 41,728 | 23,799 | 20,804 | 44,644 | 7.0 | 1,126 |
| Nebraska | 13,895 | 12,753 | 12,145 | 14,503 | 4.4 | 1,199 |
| North Dakota | 2,320 | 1,581 | 1,380 | 2,521 | 8.7 | 531 |
| Ohio[c] | 103,327 | 65,556 | 64,155 | 102,755 | −.6 | 1,234 |
| South Dakota[c,d] | 3,745 | 4,324 | 4,151 | 3,484 | −7.0 | 660 |
| Wisconsin[c] | 47,269 | 21,975 | 19,827 | 51,669 | 9.3 | 1,354 |
| **South** | 1,248,608 | 629,386 | 594,268 | 1,281,451 | 2.6% | 1,858 |
| Alabama[c,e] | 33,410 | 7,416 | 4,251 | 38,764 | 16.0 | 1,213 |
| Arkansas | 22,397 | 7,828 | 6,192 | 24,033 | 7.3 | 1,299 |
| Delaware[c] | 16,124 | : | : | 16,528 | 2.5 | 3,012 |
| District of Columbia | 10,414 | 5,399 | 6,073 | 9,740 | −6.5 | 2,246 |
| Florida[c] | 243,736 | 156,044 | 147,648 | 249,479 | 2.4 | 2,273 |
| Georgia | 142,954 | 71,241 | 70,038 | 144,157 | .8 | 2,669 |
| Kentucky[c] | 11,499 | 7,503 | 6,171 | 11,689 | 1.7 | 401 |
| Louisiana | 33,753 | 11,920 | 10,298 | 35,375 | 4.8 | 1,135 |
| Maryland | 71,029 | 35,467 | 35,943 | 70,553 | −.7 | 1,864 |
| Mississippi | 9,595 | 3,827 | 3,423 | 9,999 | 4.2 | 510 |
| North Carolina[c] | 97,921 | 54,271 | 49,111 | 102,483 | 4.7 | 1,867 |
| Oklahoma[c] | 27,866 | 13,970 | 13,729 | 28,090 | .8 | 1,161 |
| South Carolina | 39,821 | 15,479 | 13,218 | 42,082 | 5.7 | 1,524 |
| Tennessee | 36,485 | 20,685 | 19,769 | 37,401 | 2.5 | 936 |
| Texas[f] | 421,213 | 192,793 | 188,217 | 425,789 | 1.1 | 3,113 |
| Virginia | 24,264 | 25,543 | 20,187 | 29,620 | 22.1 | 587 |
| West Virginia[c] | 6,127 | : | : | 5,669 | −7.5 | 404 |
| **West** | 579,475 | 278,041 | 247,487 | 603,587 | 4.2% | 1,421 |
| Alaska[e] | 3,481 | 1,699 | 1,420 | 3,760 | 8.0 | 890 |
| Arizona | 40,614 | 12,854 | 10,278 | 43,190 | 6.3 | 1,318 |
| California | 280,545 | 147,585 | 136,111 | 292,019 | 4.1 | 1,269 |
| Colorado[c] | 42,687 | 20,919 | 18,619 | 41,212 | −3.5 | 1,459 |
| Hawaii | 12,957 | 7,082 | 5,801 | 14,238 | 9.9 | 1,623 |
| Idaho[a] | 5,308 | 2,239 | 1,692 | 5,855 | 10.3 | 696 |
| Montana[b] | 4,318 | 1,509 | 1,354 | 4,473 | 3.6 | 692 |
| Nevada[b] | 8,634 | 5,733 | 4,607 | 9,760 | 13.0 | 823 |
| New Mexico | 8,524 | 9,197 | 8,793 | 8,928 | 4.7 | 737 |
| Oregon[g] | 39,725 | 16,878 | 14,311 | 42,292 | 6.5 | 1,766 |
| Utah | 8,562 | 4,125 | 3,576 | 9,111 | 6.4 | 689 |
| Washington[c] | 120,466 | 46,198 | 38,878 | 125,317 | 4.0 | 3,059 |
| Wyoming[c] | 3,654 | 2,023 | 2,047 | 3,432 | −6.1 | 986 |

Note: Counts are subject to revision. Final counts and additional data will be published in *Correctional Populations in the United States, 1996*.
: Not known
[a] Defined as persons received for probation directly from court.
[b] Total entries and exits are estimated.
[c] Because of nonresponse or incomplete data, the population on December 31, 1996, does not equal the population on January 1, 1996, plus entries, minus exits.
[d] Data are for year ending June 30, 1996.
[e] January 1, 1996, population count is estimated.
[f] Data are for year ending August 31, 1996.
[g] Total entries are estimated.

Source: Bureau of Justice Statistics (1997). "Nation's Probation and Parole Population Reached Almost 3.9 Million Last Year," p. 5. Washington, DC: U.S. Department of Justice.

Figure 1.4
**Correctional Populations in the United States: 1997**

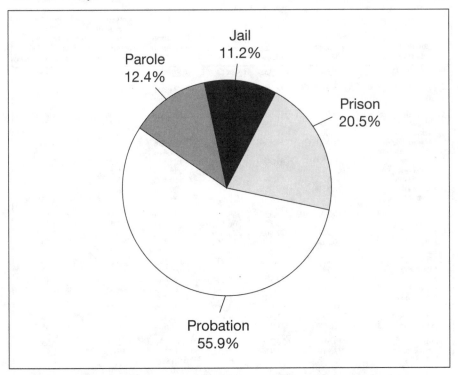

Source: Adapted from J. Brown and A. Beck (1997). "Nation's Probation and Parole Population Reached Almost 3.9 Million Last Year," pp. 1-8. Washington, DC: U.S. Bureau of Justice Statistics.

Box 1.4

### Time Served in Prison

In 1997, the Department of Justice released results from a study of the time offenders serve in confinement for various criminal offenses. The median time served in State prisons was 24 months, about 50 percent of the original sentence imposed by the sentencing court. In general, inmates who had committed violent crimes served a median of 48 months, about twice as long as other offenders. Most incarcerated offenders do not serve long sentence terms. (Mumola & Beck, 1997: 1-11.)

## Probation in America

Approximately 56 percent of the adults under correctional care or custody are on probation, the largest single segment of the community correctional system. Data in Figure 1.5 indicate that 3,180,000 offenders were on probation at the end of calendar year 1997, up about 3 percent from the year before. This is a rate of 1,621 per 100,000 adult residents, as stated above, up 240 percent over the 1985 rate of 510. As shown in Table 1.2, Texas had the highest rate: 3,113 per 100,000 adult residents, and five other states each had a rate of more than 2,500. The Federal system rate was 17 per 100,000. The lowest state rate was Kentucky (401 per 100,000). Probation is fast growing as the major community corrections program; only 11 states had decreases in probation populations in 1996 (Brown & Beck, 1997:5).

Figure 1.5
**Correctional Populations in the United States: 1985 and 1997**

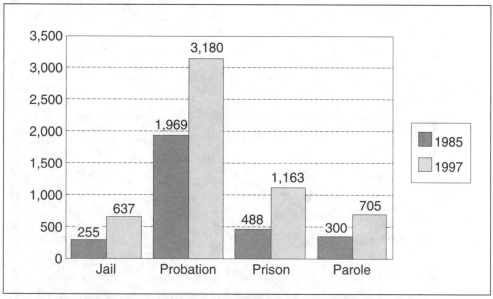

Source: Extrapolated from J. Brown and A. Beck (1997). "Nation's Probation and Parole Population Reached Almost 3.9 Million Last Year," p. 7. Washington, DC: U.S. Bureau of Justice Statistics. In thousands.

In all, it is clear that a greater number of convicted persons are now being placed on probation instead of incarcerated. In most cases, probation agencies monitor the offender's compliance with the conditions of probation release (restitution, community service, payment of fines, house arrest, drug/alcohol rehabilitation, etc.). The crucial roles that probation plays in community corrections and the justice system become even more apparent when institutional and parole population figures are examined.

---

Box 1.5

### Time Served in Prison: California Parolees

Felons in California prisons who exited onto parole in 1992 served an average of 21 months, about the national average. There was a wide range in actual time served, however, as can be seen below. In general, offenders serving sentences for violent offenses served significantly longer sentences.

| Offense: | Months Served: |
|---|---|
| All | 21 |
| | |
| Murder 1st degree | 206 |
| Murder 2nd degree | 125 |
| Attempted murder | 86 |
| Sodomy | 55 |
| Kidnapping | 53 |
| Manslaughter | 49 |
| Rape | 49 |
| Lewd act with child | 39 |
| Robbery | 31 |
| Assault with deadly weapon | 28 |
| Arson | 27 |
| Burglary | 22 |
| Vehicular manslaughter | 22 |
| Escape | 15 |

---

## The U.S. Prison Population

Because the rate of parole in a given state is affected by the size of the prison population, it is necessary to examine the size of the U.S. prison population before considering parole figures. A census of state and federal institutions is conducted each year by the Bureau of Justice Statistics (Beck & Gilliard, 1998). Table 1.3 reflects the prison census of 1997.

Overall, the U.S. prison population rose 150 percent from 1985 to 1997, to an all-time high of 1,218,256 inmates. This is an unprecedented increase over the mid-1980s! Another key comparison is the number of sentenced prisoners per 100,000 population, or the incarceration rate. This statistic makes it possible to compare rates of incarceration across states of different sizes. Nationally, the rate is 436 per 100,000 population. Regionally, the South has the highest incarceration rate (495), with the District of Columbia recording the highest number of prisoners per 100,000 population (1,373). The lowest rate of incarceration was recorded by North Dakota (104).

These figures are important to the parole rates in part because they represent the source of clients for the parole system. Prisoners enter the parole system by a parole board decision or by fulfilling the condition of mandatory release. Typically, at some time between their minimum and maximum sentences, inmates are released from prison and placed on parole. Mandatory releasees enter parole supervision automatically at the expiration of their maximum terms (minus sentence reductions for time credit accumulated for good time, jail time, and other "gain" procedures). Traditionally, this has been the manner in which a parole system operated under the indeterminate sentencing model presently in force in one-half of the states. The "abandon parole" movement began in 1976, and 11 states have changed their statutes to remove the authority of the parole board to release offenders before the expiration of their sentences.

## Parole in America

Adults on parole at year-end 1996 are found in Table 1.4 and totaled 704,709, the highest number ever on parole and an increase of almost 70 percent over 1989. The national rate was 359 per 100,000 adult residents, up 144 percent from the 147 rate in 1983. The parole rate ranged from a high of 1,642 in the District of Columbia, to a low of 6 (Maine). Maine and Virginia have abolished parole, but Connecticut, which had abolished parole, restored it in 1991.

In sum, the parole statistics reveal the relationship between the size of the prison population and the number of parolees. These figures indicate that both the prison and parole populations are dramatically increasing.

Table 1.3

**Prisoners under the Jurisdiction of State or Federal Correctional Authorities, June 30 and December 31, 1996, and June 30, 1997**

| Region and jurisdiction | Total | | | Percent change from— | | Prison incarceration rate, 6/30/97[a] |
| | 6/30/97 | 12/31/96 | 6/30/96 | 6/30/96 to 6/30/97 | 12/31/96 to 6/30/97 | |
|---|---|---|---|---|---|---|
| **U.S. total** | 1,218,256 | 1,180,520 | 1,163,058 | 4.7% | 3.2% | 436 |
| Federal | 110,160 | 105,544 | 103,722 | 6.2% | 4.4% | 35 |
| State | 1,108,096 | 1,074,976 | 1,059,336 | 4.6 | 3.1 | 401 |
| **Northeast** | 167,706 | 166,417 | 165,224 | 1.5 | .8 | 310 |
| Connecticut[b] | 15,608 | 15,007 | 14,975 | 4.2 | 4.0 | 322 |
| Maine | 1,559 | 1,426 | 1,468 | 6.2 | 9.3 | 118 |
| Massachusetts[c] | 11,907 | 11,796 | 11,996 | −.7 | .9 | 301 |
| New Hampshire | 2,153 | 2,062 | 2,050 | 5.0 | 4.4 | 183 |
| New Jersey | 27,766 | 27,490 | 27,753 | 0 | 1.0 | 346 |
| New York | 69,530 | 69,709 | 68,721 | 1.2 | −.3 | 383 |
| Pennsylvania | 34,703 | 34,537 | 33,939 | 2.3 | .5 | 288 |
| Rhode Island[b] | 3,293 | 3,271 | 3,226 | 2.1 | .7 | 203 |
| Vermont[b, d] | 1,187 | 1,119 | 1,096 | 8.3 | 6.1 | 152 |
| **Midwest** | 212,779 | 204,653 | 199,414 | 6.7% | 4.0% | 339 |
| Illinois[d, e] | 40,425 | 38,852 | 38,373 | 5.3 | 4.0 | 340 |
| Indiana | 17,549 | 16,960 | 16,582 | 5.8 | 3.5 | 296 |
| Iowa[d] | 6,636 | 6,342 | 6,176 | 7.4 | 4.6 | 232 |
| Kansas | 7,790 | 7,756 | 7,462 | 4.4 | .4 | 302 |
| Michigan[d] | 43,784 | 42,349 | 41,884 | 4.5 | 3.4 | 454 |
| Minnesota | 5,348 | 5,158 | 5,040 | 6.1 | 3.7 | 114 |
| Missouri | 23,687 | 22,003 | 20,541 | 15.3 | 7.7 | 438 |
| Nebraska | 3,431 | 3,287 | 3,248 | 5.6 | 4.4 | 201 |
| North Dakota | 739 | 722 | 640 | 15.5 | 2.4 | 104 |
| Ohio[a] | 47,248 | 46,174 | 45,314 | 4.3 | 2.3 | 422 |
| South Dakota | 2,177 | 2,059 | 2,049 | 6.2 | 5.7 | 296 |
| Wisconsin | 13,965 | 12,991 | 12,105 | 15.4 | 7.5 | 256 |
| **South** | 484,391 | 469,252 | 467,901 | 3.5% | 3.2% | 495 |
| Alabama | 22,076 | 21,760 | 21,495 | 2.7 | 1.5 | 499 |
| Arkansas | 9,539 | 9,407 | 9,430 | 1.2 | 1.4 | 368 |
| Delaware[b] | 5,313 | 5,110 | 5,148 | 3.2 | 4.0 | 442 |
| Dist. of Columbia[b] | 9,739 | 9,376 | 9,763 | −.2 | 3.9 | 1,373 |
| Florida[d] | 64,713 | 63,763 | 64,333 | .6 | 1.5 | 443 |
| Georgia[d] | 36,329 | 35,139 | 34,808 | 4.4 | 3.4 | 476 |
| Kentucky | 13,858 | 12,910 | 12,652 | 9.5 | 7.3 | 355 |
| Louisiana | 28,382 | 26,779 | 26,673 | 6.4 | 6.0 | 651 |
| Maryland | 22,415 | 22,050 | 22,118 | 1.3 | 1.7 | 417 |
| Mississippi | 14,639 | 13,859 | 13,785 | 6.2 | 5.6 | 505 |
| North Carolina | 32,334 | 30,647 | 30,671 | 5.4 | 5.5 | 385 |
| Oklahoma[e] | 19,931 | 19,593 | 19,134 | 4.2 | 1.7 | 599 |
| South Carolina | 21,021 | 20,446 | 20,814 | 1.0 | 2.8 | 542 |
| Tennessee | 15,827 | 15,626 | 15,634 | 1.2 | 1.3 | 294 |
| Texas | 136,599 | 132,383 | 129,937 | 5.1 | 3.2 | 677 |
| Virginia | 28,673 | 27,655 | 28,827 | −.5 | 3.7 | 412 |
| West Virginia | 3,003 | 2,749 | 2,679 | 12.1 | 9.2 | 163 |
| **West** | 243,220 | 234,654 | 226,797 | 7.2% | 3.7% | 397 |
| Alaska[b] | 3,741 | 3,716 | 3,583 | 4.4 | .7 | 396 |
| Arizona[d] | 23,176 | 22,493 | 22,143 | 4.7 | 3.0 | 484 |
| California | 153,010 | 146,049 | 141,535 | 8.1 | 4.8 | 466 |
| Colorado[e] | 12,840 | 12,438 | 11,742 | 9.4 | 3.2 | 330 |
| Hawaii[b] | 4,491 | 4,011 | 3,693 | 21.6 | 12.0 | 258 |
| Idaho | 4,105 | 3,832 | 3,623 | 13.3 | 7.1 | 339 |
| Montana | 2,295 | 2,293 | 2,162 | 6.2 | .1 | 258 |
| Nevada | 8,617 | 8,439 | 8,064 | 6.9 | 2.1 | 505 |
| New Mexico | 4,692 | 4,724 | 4,528 | 3.6 | −.7 | 258 |
| Oregon[f] | 7,899 | 8,661 | 8,564 | – | – | 226 |
| Utah | 4,154 | 3,972 | 3,643 | 14.0 | 4.6 | 202 |
| Washington | 12,732 | 12,527 | 12,059 | 5.6 | 1.6 | 226 |
| Wyoming | 1,468 | 1,499 | 1,458 | .7 | −2.1 | 304 |

—Not calculated.
[a]The number of prisoners with a sentence of more than 1 year per 100,000 in the resident population.
[b]Prison and jails form an integrated system. Data include total jail and prison population.
[c]The incarceration rate includes an estimated 7,500 inmates sentenced to more than 1 year but held in local jails.
[d]Population figures are based on custody counts.
[e]Population counts for inmates "sentenced to more than 1 year" include an undetermined number of inmates "sentenced to one year or less."
[f]Since January 1, 1997, Oregon no longer has jurisdictional responsibility for inmates with sentences of less than 1 year.

Source: A.J. Beck and D.K. Gilliard (1998). *Prison and Jail Inmates at Midyear 1997*, p.3. Washington, DC: U.S. Bureau of Justice.

Table 1.4
**Adults on Parole, 1996**

| Region and jurisdiction | Parole population 1/1/96 | 1996 Entries | 1996 Exits | Parole population 12/31/96 | Percent change in parole population during 1996 | Number on parole on 12/31/96 per 100,000 adult residents |
|---|---|---|---|---|---|---|
| U.S. total | 679,421 | 421,055 | 395,721 | 704,709 | 3.7% | 359 |
| Federal[a] | 51,461 | 30,518 | 22,846 | 59,133 | 14.9% | 30 |
| State | 627,960 | 390,537 | 372,875 | 645,576 | 2.8 | 329 |
| **Northeast** | 175,207 | 74,605 | 67,564 | 181,856 | 3.8% | 467 |
| Connecticut | 1,233 | 1,505 | 1,655 | 1,083 | −12.2 | 44 |
| Maine | 55 | 2 | 0 | 57 | 3.6 | 6 |
| Massachusetts[b, c] | 5,256 | 3,889 | 3,917 | 4,836 | −8.0 | 104 |
| New Hampshire | 785 | 854 | 573 | 1,066 | 35.8 | 123 |
| New Jersey | 37,867 | 13,530 | 9,850 | 41,547 | 9.7 | 692 |
| New York | 55,568 | 27,064 | 25,495 | 57,137 | 2.8 | 419 |
| Pennsylvania | 73,234 | 26,903 | 25,124 | 75,013 | 2.4 | 819 |
| Rhode Island | 591 | 532 | 548 | 575 | −2.7 | 76 |
| Vermont | 618 | 326 | 402 | 542 | −12.3 | 123 |
| **Midwest** | 86,598 | 60,401 | 60,443 | 87,013 | .5% | 190 |
| Illinois | 29,541 | 22,763 | 22,240 | 30,064 | 1.8 | 346 |
| Indiana | 3,200 | 4,382 | 4,007 | 3,575 | 11.7 | 82 |
| Iowa | 2,340 | 1,964 | 2,104 | 2,200 | −6.0 | 103 |
| Kansas | 6,094 | 4,074 | 4,164 | 6,004 | −1.5 | 319 |
| Michigan | 13,862 | 9,463 | 8,716 | 14,609 | 5.4 | 207 |
| Minnesota | 2,117 | 2,698 | 2,438 | 2,377 | 12.3 | 70 |
| Missouri[b, c] | 13,001 | 4,316 | 5,384 | 12,197 | −6.2 | 308 |
| Nebraska | 661 | 823 | 778 | 706 | 6.8 | 58 |
| North Dakota | 114 | 191 | 201 | 104 | −8.8 | 22 |
| Ohio | 7,432 | 4,785 | 5,886 | 6,331 | −14.8 | 76 |
| South Dakota | 688 | 614 | 577 | 725 | 5.4 | 137 |
| Wisconsin[b] | 7,548 | 4,328 | 3,948 | 8,121 | 7.6 | 213 |
| **South** | 240,478 | 108,639 | 104,231 | 244,475 | 1.7% | 354 |
| Alabama[c] | 7,793 | 1,651 | 4,231 | 5,213 | −33.1 | 163 |
| Arkansas[c] | 4,685 | 5,551 | 5,093 | 5,143 | 9.8 | 278 |
| Delaware[c] | 1,033 | : | : | 1,033 | − | 188 |
| District of Columbia | 6,340 | 2,951 | 2,171 | 7,120 | 12.3 | 1,642 |
| Florida[d] | 11,197 | 3,984 | 5,938 | 9,243 | −17.5 | 84 |
| Georgia[b] | 19,434 | 11,959 | 10,036 | 21,146 | 8.8 | 392 |
| Kentucky | 4,257 | 3,491 | 3,127 | 4,621 | 8.6 | 159 |
| Louisiana | 19,028 | 11,408 | 9,438 | 20,998 | 10.4 | 674 |
| Maryland | 15,748 | 11,080 | 10,582 | 16,246 | 3.2 | 429 |
| Mississippi[b] | 1,510 | 1,107 | 886 | 1,513 | .2 | 77 |
| North Carolina | 18,501 | 10,544 | 16,687 | 12,358 | −33.2 | 225 |
| Oklahoma | 2,356 | 465 | 662 | 2,159 | −8.4 | 89 |
| South Carolina | 5,545 | 1,334 | 1,512 | 5,367 | −3.2 | 194 |
| Tennessee | 8,851 | 3,918 | 3,835 | 8,934 | .9 | 223 |
| Texas[c] | 103,089 | 28,149 | 18,644 | 112,594 | 9.2 | 823 |
| Virginia[b, c] | 10,188 | 10,479 | 10,767 | 9,918 | −2.7 | 197 |
| West Virginia | 923 | 568 | 622 | 869 | −5.9 | 62 |
| **West** | 125,677 | 146,892 | 140,637 | 132,232 | 5.3% | 311 |
| Alaska[b] | 459 | 542 | 378 | 553 | 20.5 | 131 |
| Arizona | 4,109 | 5,314 | 5,638 | 3,785 | −7.9 | 115 |
| California | 91,807 | 126,506 | 121,250 | 97,063 | 5.7 | 422 |
| Colorado | 3,024 | 3,039 | 2,769 | 3,294 | 8.9 | 117 |
| Hawaii | 1,689 | 623 | 579 | 1,733 | 2.6 | 198 |
| Idaho | 619 | 469 | 396 | 692 | 11.8 | 82 |
| Montana[b] | 744 | : | : | 771 | 3.6 | 119 |
| Nevada[b] | 2,863 | : | : | 3,216 | 12.3 | 271 |
| New Mexico | 1,366 | 1,381 | 1,321 | 1,426 | 4.4 | 118 |
| Oregon | 15,019 | 6,893 | 6,112 | 15,800 | 5.2 | 660 |
| Utah | 2,700 | 1,914 | 1,639 | 2,975 | 10.2 | 225 |
| Washington[c] | 875 | 42 | 357 | 560 | −36.0 | 14 |
| Wyoming[b] | 403 | 169 | 198 | 364 | −9.7 | 105 |

Note: Counts are subject to revision. Final counts and additional data will be published in *Correctional Populations in the United States, 1996.*
:Not known.
− Not calculated.
[a]Defined as persons received for probation supervision upon release from prison. Includes supervised release, parole, military parole, special parole, and mandatory release.
[b]Because of nonresponse or incomplete data, the population on December 31, 1996, does not equal the population on January 1, 1996, plus entries, minus exits.
[c]All data are estimated.
[d]The January 1, 1996 count is estimated.

Source: Bureau of Justice Statistics (1997). "Nation's Probation and Parole Population Reached Almost 3.9 Million Last Year," p. 6. Washington, DC: U.S. Department of Justice.

## Summary

This brief consideration of statistics from the major components of the correctional system (probation, prisons, and parole) demonstrates their crucial linkage within the criminal justice system. Imagine what would happen if probation and parole were completely abolished and all convicted persons were required to serve their full prison terms! If this had happened in 1996, the prison population could have been nearly six million! Naturally, the prison system is not equipped to handle such a large number of inmates, nor would it be good social policy to attempt such a foolish venture.

Figure 1.6
**Average Length of Prison Stay (in Months)**

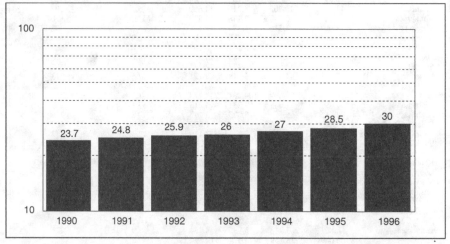

Source: C. Camp and G. Camp (1997). *The 1997 Corrections Yearbook,* p. 47. South Salem, NY: Criminal Justice Institute.

We do not wish to suggest that all offenders could and should be released to community corrections. At least 15 to 25 percent of the prison population are too dangerous or pose too great a threat to community safety to allow their immediate release, even onto "intensive supervised parole" (Allen & Simonsen, 1998:638).

It is the function of probation and its many variants (the so-called "intermediate punishments"), as well as parole, to determine how the population of convicted persons can be managed in a fashion consistent with not only the capacity of the prison population but also the goals of societal protections and offender rehabilitation and reintegration.

In short, the examination of corrections in the community is the theme of this text. We will consider such key issues as: What are the best methods for classifying offenders? For supervising them? What background, education, and training should various community correctional agents possess? How effective are community correctional programs, in terms of public safety? And at what cost? What are the recent innovations in community corrections and intermediate punishments? How effective are these compared to incarceration? The consideration of these (and other) issues will provide readers with the opportunity to form their own opinions and ideas concerning the proper use of community correctional programs, and how to coordinate these in the criminal justice system.

## Review Questions

1.  What is corrections in the community?

2.  What is meant by the funnel effect, and how does it occur?

3.  If probation and parole were completely abolished, what effect would this have on the prison system?

4.  Develop an argument for increased use of community corrections.

5.  How are offenders generally released from prison?

6.  Describe the current distribution of offenders across the main components of the criminal justice system.

## Key Terms

community corrections
criminal justice system
hold-backs
incarceration
intermediate punishments
jail

mandatory release
parole
prison
probation
split sentence

## Recommended Readings

Allen, H.E. and C.E. Simonsen (1998). *Corrections in America*, Englewood-Cliffs, NJ: Prentice-Hall.

Duffee, D.E. and E.F. McGarrell (eds.) (1990). *Community Corrections: A Community Field Approach*, Cincinnati, OH: Anderson Publishing Co.

## Notes

[1]    An evaluation of California's juvenile boot camp program (LEAD) that was coupled with intensive parole aftercare found no significant differences between LEAD parolees and a group of control wards on known criminal activity and severity of reoffense behavior. California Department of the Youth Authority (1997). *LEAD: A Boot Camp and Intensive Parole Program: Final Impact Evaluation.* Sacramento, CA: CDYA.

[2]    For example, in Ohio, the state funds "community-based correctional facilities." These facilities are operated by local community corrections boards, are designed to provide treatment, and often utilize local community services. They are, however, secure facilities. For descriptions of the Florida circumstances, see Karl Lucken (1997). "The Dynamics of Penal Reform." *Crime, Law and Social Change* 26 (4): 367-384.

[3]    Some would argue that many so-called "community" correctional programs are essentially institutional correctional facilities because they are state run. However, we believe that state-operated programs can indeed be considered community correctional programs, provided they include some type of supervision in the community. For a different perspective on this issue see D.E. Duffee (1990). "Community Characteristics: The Presumed Characteristics and Argument for a New Approach." In D.E. Duffee and E.F. McGarrell (eds.) Community Corrections: A Community Field Approach. Cincinnati, OH: Anderson Publishing Co. See also Burke, P.B. (1997). *Policy Driven Responses to Probation and Parole Violations.* Washington, DC: U.S. Department of Justice.

[4]    See E.J. Latessa, L.F. Travis, and A. Holsinger (1997). *Evaluation of Ohio's Community Corrections Act Programs and Community Based Correctional Facilities: Final Report.* Cincinnati, OH: Division of Criminal Justice, University of Cincinnati.

## References

Allen, H.E. and C.E. Simonsen (1998). *Corrections in America.* Englewood Cliffs, NJ: Prentice-Hall.

Beck, A.J. and D.K. Gilliard (1998). *Prison and Jail Inmates at Mid-Year 1997.* Washington, DC: U.S. Bureau of Justice.

Brown, J.M. and A.J. Beck (1997). "Nation's Probation and Parole Population Reached Almost 3.9 Million Last Year." Washington, DC: U.S. Department of Justice.

Bureau of Justice Statistics (1997). *Correctional Populations in the United States, 1995.* Washington, DC: U.S. Department of Justice.

Burke, P.B. (1997). *Policy Driven Responses to Probation and Parole Violations.* Washington, DC: U.S. Department of Justice.

California Department of Justice (1998). *Crime and Delinquency in California, 1997: Advance Release.* Sacramento: CDJ.

California Department of the Youth Authority (1997). *LEAD. A Boot Camp and Intensive Supervision Program: Final Impact Evaluation.* Sacramento, CDYA.

Duffee, D.E. and E.F. McGarrell (eds.) (1990). *Community Corrections: A Community Field Approach.* Cincinnati, OH: Anderson Publishing Co.

Farrington, D. (1994). "Early Developmental Prevention of Juvenile Delinquency." *Criminal Behavior and Mental Health*, 4(3):209-227.

Federal Bureau of Investigation (1997). *Crime in the United States, 1996.* Washington, DC: U.S. Department of Justice.

Langan, P. and J. Brown (1997). *Felony Sentences in the United States, 1994.* Washington, DC: U.S. Bureau of Justice Statistics.

Latessa, E.J. and L.F. Travis (1991). "Halfway House or Probation: A Comparison of Alternative Dispositions." *Journal of Criminal Justice*, 14:1-11.

Latessa, E.J, L.F. Travis, and A. Holsinger (1997). *Evaluation of Ohio's Community Corrections Act Programs and Community Based Correctional Facilities: Final Report.* Division of Criminal Justice, University of Cincinnati.

Lucken, K. (1997). "The Dynamics of Penal Reform.' *Crime, Law and Social Change*, 26(4):367-384.

Monroe, T.M. (1996). "An Alternative to Detention for Juvenile Parole Violators." *Journal for Juvenile Justice and Detention Services*, 11(2):73-76.

Moon, M.M., B.K. Applegate, and E.J. Latessa (1997). "RECLAIM Ohio: A Politically Viable Alternative to Treating Youthful Felony Offenders." *Crime & Delinquency*, 43(4):438-456.

Mumola, C.J. and A.J. Beck (1997). *Prisoners in 1996.* Washington, DC: U.S. Bureau of Justice Statistics.

President's Commission on Law Enforcement and Administration of Justice (1969). *The Challenge of Crime in a Free Society.* Washington, DC: U.S. Government Printing Office.

Silberman, C. (1978). *Criminal Violence, Criminal Justice.* New York, NY: Random House.

Tolan, P. and N. Guerra (1994). *What Works in Reducing Adolescent Violence: An Empirical Review of the Field.* Boulder, CO: Center for the Study and Prevention of Violence, University of Boulder.

# Sentencing and Community Corrections

**2**

## The Sentencing Decision

Defendants at the sentencing stage of the criminal proceeding are those who have not yet been diverted through the correctional funnel (see Chapter 1). They have either pled guilty to or been found guilty of a crime in a jury or bench trial (Gaskins, 1990; Bodapati, Jones & Marquardt, 1995). The judge must now decide how to dispose of their cases, using the wide variety of sentences that range from fines through the intermediate sanctions to imprisonment, or even the death penalty. Making a sentencing decision is often the most complicated and difficult task for the sentencing judge, especially in those states that still retain the indeterminate sentence.

This decision is exacerbated by the nationwide problem of high incarceration rates, despite a two-decade building or renovation binge in every state that has brought the nation 410 new prisons since 1989, and another 61 under construction (Camp & Camp, 1997:64, 66). As shown in Table 2.1, the rates range from as high as 677 per 100,000 population (Texas) to a low of 105 (North Dakota). The United States incarcerates more persons per 100,000 residents that any other major country, with the exception of Russia (Mauer, 1997). Rising rates of gang and gun violence, along with longer determinate sentences, make the sentencing decision even more difficult than ever.

## The Indeterminate Sentence

A basic tenet underlying sentencing in the nineteenth century was a belief in the perfectibility of humans. The American Revolution engen-

Table 2.1
**Ranking of States by Prison Incarceration Rates: 1997**
**(Inmates per 100,000 Residents)**

| Rank | State | Rate | Rank | State | Rate |
|------|-------|------|------|-------|------|
| 1  | Texas          | 677 | 26 | Connecticut    | 322 |
| 2  | Louisiana      | 651 | 27 | Wyoming        | 304 |
| 3  | Oklahoma       | 599 | 28 | Kansas         | 302 |
| 4  | South Carolina | 542 | 29 | Massachusetts  | 301 |
| 5  | Mississippi    | 505 | 30 | Indiana        | 296 |
| 5  | Nevada         | 505 | 30 | South Dakota   | 296 |
| 6  | Alabama        | 499 | 31 | Tennessee      | 294 |
| 7  | Arizona        | 484 | 32 | Pennsylvania   | 288 |
| 8  | Georgia        | 476 | 33 | Hawaii         | 258 |
| 9  | California     | 466 | 33 | Montana        | 258 |
| 10 | Michigan       | 454 | 33 | New Mexico     | 258 |
| 11 | Florida        | 443 | 34 | Wisconsin      | 256 |
| 12 | Delaware       | 442 | 35 | Iowa           | 232 |
| 13 | Missouri       | 438 | 36 | Oregon         | 226 |
| 14 | Ohio           | 422 | 36 | Washington     | 226 |
| 15 | Maryland       | 417 | 37 | Rhode Island   | 203 |
| 16 | Virginia       | 412 | 38 | Utah           | 202 |
| 17 | Alaska         | 396 | 39 | Nebraska       | 201 |
| 18 | North Carolina | 385 | 40 | New Hampshire  | 183 |
| 19 | New York       | 383 | 41 | West Virginia  | 163 |
| 20 | Arkansas       | 368 | 42 | Vermont        | 152 |
| 21 | Kentucky       | 355 | 43 | Maine          | 118 |
| 22 | New Jersey     | 346 | 44 | Minnesota      | 114 |
| 23 | Illinois       | 340 | 45 | North Dakota   | 104 |
| 24 | Idaho          | 339 | 46 | Federal System | 35  |
| 25 | Colorado       | 330 |    |                |     |

Source: D.K. Gilliard and A.J. Beck (1998). *Prison and Jail Inmates at Midyear 1997*, p. 3. Washington, DC: U.S. Bureau of Justice Statistics.

dered a great deal of interest and enthusiasm for reform. The emerging nation threw off the dread yoke of British imperialism, including the harsh and widely hated British laws in place throughout the colonies that relied so heavily on the death penalty. In its place, a more rational system of "corrections" arose; the ideal of certain but humane punishment that was believed to most certainly deter offenders from criminal careers. American entered the "Progressive Era" in which "rational men" would be able to pursue their best interests and maximize gain and reward, while avoiding penalties or pain. This famous principle ("hedonistic calculus") was wholeheartedly accepted as a guiding objective in the question being asked by concerned citizens, lawmakers, and public officials: "Who are offenders and what shall we do with them?"

Under the British codes, they were seen as inherently evil and thus to be punished, killed, or disabled. Under the Progressive Era, the answer that emerged was quite different: They are people out of touch with God and, given a chance to change by thinking about their crime and relationship with God and fellow humans, they will opt to repent and change. The prison was the answer to the policy question of what to do with offenders, and America embraced prisons with its general zeal for humanitarianism and enthusiasm, building huge "fortress" prisons that emphasized reform and repentance. The American penitentiary ("place to do penance") was a contribution to corrections throughout the world.

Yet in the emerging penitentiary and later reformatory movements, there remained the philosophical quandary: What to do with the reformed offender who continued to be held in prison years after actual reformation. Sentencing codes were determinate or "flat" and inmates were expected to serve their sentences to the day. In this philosophical environment, correctional administrators began to innovate.

In the British outpost of Australia, offenders who had been sentenced to exile by transportation to Australia occasionally continued their violent criminal behavior. Transported felons were failures because they had committed crimes in England; when they continued their miscreant behavior in Australia, they were shipped to Norfolk Island, onto a bleak and inhospitable shore some 1,000 miles to the east. These "double failures" of Australia who were subsequently sentenced to death thanked God, but those sentenced to Norfolk Island sank into the deepest depression and sadness. Such was the place that Captain Alexander Maconochie inherited when he was posted as managing officer in 1842.

Maconochie quickly determined that the violence, treachery, and staff-inmate confrontations had to stop, and seized upon what is now known as the "mark" system (also known now as a form of token economy). Assembling the inmates, he promised that there was hope of freedom if any inmate could amass 100 marks (credits). Each inmate was to be billed for food, clothing, and tools; marks were to be assigned for quantity and quality of work. Through hard work and frugal living, inmates could save marks; when an inmate amassed 100 marks, he was free from correctional control, to marry and live on the island, and conduct himself in proper behavior. Assault and violence immediately declined with this innovative and constructive management approach, but the Royal Marines assigned to prison officer duty thought Maconochie was too lenient and molly-coddled offenders. Maconochie was quickly removed, and Norfolk Island slid rapidly back into the slough of despair it was before Maconochie's innovative management.

Fortunately, Maconochie's ideas spread: imprisonment could be used to prepare an offender for a productive life and eventual return to the community under what could be seen as an "indeterminate sentence." The implications of this demonstration were that sentence length should not be an arbitrary or "flat" sentence but one related to the reform and rehabilitation of the inmate. Sir Walter Crofton in Ireland used Maconochie's concepts when he developed what became known as the "Irish" system.

Crofton reasoned that if penitentiaries were places where offenders reflect on their crimes and would decide to stop their criminal activities ("repent"), then there should be some mechanism or scheme to detect when the reform had occurred, as well as releasing the offender when this had happened. Crofton established a three-stage system, each of which would bring the convict closer to freedom within the community. Phase One consisted of solitary confinement and tedious work, such as picking oakum (separating coconut fibers for the purpose of making rope). After six months, the convict could be assigned to public works on a team, each member of which was responsible for the behavior of every other team member (an early use of "peer pressure"). Anyone who misbehaved would cause all team members to be returned to Phase One. The last phase was assignment to a transitional prison permitting unsupervised day work outside the prison. If the inmate's behavior was good and he could find employment in the community, he was given a "ticket of leave," in effect extending the limits of confinement to include placement in the county on "conditional pardon." While the ex-inmate could not leave the county and was required to produce his "ticket" upon demand by law enforcement agents, he was nonetheless free of correctional control for the duration of his sentence. Of course, if his conduct was bad, the ticket could be revoked and the offender returned to prison (Phase One). In effect, Crofton established conditional liberty in the community, what now would be called parole.

By 1870, prison crowding in the United States had become so massive and the related management problems so complex that a conference was deemed necessary. Prison administrators, wardens, religious leaders, concerned leaders, and innovators met in Cincinnati, Ohio in 1870 in the first meeting of what would become the American Correctional Association. Spurred on by Crofton and empowered by eloquent oratory by Zebulon Reed Brockway, the assembly adopted standards and principles that addressed both new types of buildings to be constructed as well as an early release system. In 1876, Brockway initiated parole in the nation by the ticket of leave system. New York quickly passed enabling legislation and parole became a reality.

Other states responded by changing their sentencing structures as well as by authorizing parole as a mechanism for releasing reformed offenders. The resultant sentencing system was the indeterminate sentence, the dominant sentencing structure in the United States until the mid-1970s.

> ### Box 2.1
>
> ### Indeterminate Sentencing
>
> Under the indeterminate sentencing system, the sentencing judge pronounces a minimum and maximum period of incarceration, such as from three to five years ("3 to 5") or 5-10, or 1-20, and so on. Correctional personnel were expected to assist the offenders in changing their behavior and preparing for eventual return to the community, and the parole board was to monitor offender behavior and change. The actual decision on parole readiness and release was detailed to a parole board, charged with protecting society and releasing offenders onto community correctional supervision. The actual conditions of parole were set by the parole board, which retained authority to return non-adjusting offenders to the prison for further treatment and punishment. In essence, the sentencing judge shares sentence length determination with the executive branch in which parole boards are located.

## Rapid Change in Sentencing

By 1930, most states and federal courts were operating under the indeterminate sentencing structure. The wide range of sentence lengths reflected the dominant rehabilitation goal of the correctional system and the belief that once the offender had been rehabilitated, the parole board would detect the change and then order parole release.[1] Parole boards actually determined the length of the sentence served, using their authority of discretionary release.

Following a very long period of relative inactivity (1930-1974), American sentencing laws and practices began to undergo rapid change, a fundamental restructuring of the sentencing process. The causes have been identified (Allen & Simonsen, 1998:116):

1. Prison uprisings (such as at Attica in New York, and others in New Mexico and Florida) indicated that inmates were particularly discontented with the rhetoric of rehabilitation and the reality of the prison environment.

2. The abuse of discretion caused concerns about individual rights, as prosecutors, judges, and parole boards were immune from review and some practiced arbitrary uses of discretion.

3. Court orders and decisions led to a movement that demanded accountability in official decisionmaking and outcomes.

4. The rehabilitation ideal was challenged, both empirically and ideologically, which undermined the rationale of the indeterminate sentence's "parole after rehabilitation" corollary.

5. Experimental and statistical studies of judicial sentencing found substantial disparity and both racial and class discrimination. Such inconsistencies and disparities fostered the conclusion that sentencing practices were unfair.

6. Crime control and corrections became a political football, useful for those seeking election to public office. Such political opportunists led the general public to believe that lenient judges and parole boards were releasing dangerous offenders back into the community, with little concern for public safety.

## New Goals

Although corrections in the 1970s generally reflected the utilitarian goal of rehabilitation, other discussions from the reform movement brought additional correctional goals to the forefront in the 1980s, such as the incapacitation of persons likely to commit future crimes and its variant of selective incapacitation, in which the highest-risk offenders would receive much longer sentences in order to prevent any more criminal activity. The specific deterrence of sentenced offenders—and the general deterrence of those contemplating committing a crime—was legitimized as a social policy goal. One emerging example of this new goal is the "three-strikes" policy states have recently adopted, particularly in California, mandating long-term incarceration (at least 25 years) for those persons convicted of a serious or violent third felony. It will become obvious in later chapters that, as a crime prevention strategy, "three-strikes" focuses on older criminals in the desistance phase of their criminal careers.[2] In fact, since crime is basically a young-person's game (the peak crime age is 17, followed by 16 and 18, respectively), a strategy that focuses on a low-volume crime group cannot do much to attain the goal of a lowering the crime rate.

In addition, retribution as a goal became attractive, inasmuch as it would impose deserved punishment. (Such a "just deserts" strategy looks backward to the offender's personal culpability, focuses on the nature of the act, and considers the harm done.)

> Box 2.2
>
> ### Deterrence
>
> The prevention of criminal behavior through the threat of detection, apprehension, and punishment.
>
> As a policy, deterrence programs can be directed against individuals or the general society. Individual or specific deterrence is designed to prevent a person from committing a crime, and can take such forms as punishment, persuasion, deprivation of liberty, or even death. "Scared Straight" programs that fleetingly mix hardened convicts with impressionable juveniles are believed by some to be a specific deterrent.
>
> A societal deterrence program reminds potential offenders of what might happen to them if they commit legal violations. Driving automobiles while intoxicated, for example, is believed to be prevented or discouraged by a well-planned and coordinated television advertisement, linked to staunch enforcement by local policing agencies and mandatory loss of driving privileges or short periods of incarceration in jail. The death penalty is frequently cited as a general deterrent.

## Reform Options

As a result of the reform movement, sentencing practices were changed, in the belief that such practices would limit disparity and discretion, and establish more detailed criteria for sentencing or new sentencing institutions. These contradictory options included:

1. abolishing plea bargaining;

2. establishing plea-bargaining rules and guidelines;

3. setting mandatory minimum sentences;

4. establishing statutory determinate sentencing;

5. setting voluntary or descriptive sentencing guidelines or presumptive or prescriptive sentencing guidelines;

6. creating sentencing councils;

7. requiring judges to provide reasons for their sentences;

8. setting parole guidelines to limit parole board discretion;

9. abolishing parole;

10. adopting or modifying good-time procedures; and

11. routinizing appellate review of sentences (Allen & Simonsen, 1998:118-119).

Those options represent only the principal steps designed to limit unbridled discretion, make sentencing more fair, enhance justice, and lessen discrimination.

Figure 2.1
**States with Mandatory Prison Term Statutes**

| Key | | | | | | | | | |
|-----|---|---|---|---|---|---|---|---|---|
| **V** Violent Crime | | | **N** Narcotic/drug law violation | | | | | | |
| **H** Habitual offender | | | **G** Handgun/Firearm | | | | | | |

| | V | H | N | G | | V | H | N | G |
|---|---|---|---|---|---|---|---|---|---|
| Federal system | — | — | — | — | Montana | V | — | N | G |
| District of Columbia | — | — | N | G | Nebraska | V | H | — | — |
| | | | | | Nevada | V | H | N | G |
| Alabama | V | H | N | — | New Hampshire | V | — | — | G |
| Alaska | V | H | N | G | New Jersey | V | — | — | G |
| Arizona | V | H | N | G | | | | | |
| Arkansas | V | H | — | G | | | | | |
| California | V | H | N | G | New Mexico | V | H | — | G |
| | | | | | New York | V | H | N | G |
| Colorado | V | H | — | — | North Carolina | V | — | N | G |
| Connecticut | V | — | N | G | North Dakota | V | — | — | G |
| Delaware | V | H | N | G | Ohio | V | H | N | G |
| Florida | V | — | N | G | | | | | |
| Georgia | V | H | N | G | Oklahoma | — | H | N | — |
| Hawaii | V | H | N | — | Oregon | V | — | — | G |
| Idaho | V | H | N | G | Pennsylvania | V | H | — | G |
| Illinois | V | H | N | G | Rhode Island | — | H | N | G |
| Indiana | V | H | N | G | South Carolina | V | H | N | — |
| Iowa | V | — | N | G | | | | | |
| | | | | | South Dakota | V | — | N | — |
| Kansas | — | — | — | G | Tennessee | V | H | N | — |
| Kentucky | — | H | — | G | Texas | V | H | — | — |
| Louisiana | V | H | N | G | Utah | — | — | — | — |
| Maine | V | — | — | G | Vermont | — | — | — | — |
| Maryland | V | H | — | G | | | | | |
| Massachusetts | V | H | N | G | Virginia | — | — | — | G |
| Michigan | V | — | N | G | Washington | V | — | N | G |
| Minnesota | V | — | — | G | West Virginia | V | H | — | G |
| Mississippi | V | H | — | G | Wisconsin | V | — | — | — |
| Missouri | V | — | N | G | Wyoming | V | H | N | — |

Source: Bureau of Justice Statistics (August 1983). *Setting Prison Terms*, p. 3. Washington, DC: Department of Justice.

## Reform Effects

Over the last two decades, the dramatic changes in sentencing structures and practices thus became evident. Discretionary release by a parole board was abolished in at least 14 states, and parole sentencing guidelines had been established in one-half of the others. In 1987, the U.S. Federal Sentencing Guidelines were promulgated, and fewer federal offenders are paroled by the U.S. Parole Commission. Across the country, more offenders are now released on mandatory than under discretionary parole. It is against that background of concern and change that we shall look at the sentencing decision.

---

**Box 2.3**

### Parole Release

Discretionary parole release means that the parole board opted to release an offender before the maximum sentence was met. Mandatory release means the offender had to be released because the maximum sentence (or its equivalent) had been attained. Both imply parole supervision in the community.

---

## Predicting Behavior

If the sentence had no purpose except to punish the offender, as was the case until fairly recently, the judge's job would be easily prescribed by statute. In modern times, however, the sentence is also intended to be the cornerstone for reintegration, incapacitation, and deterrence. Those broadly divergent objectives create a paradox that may force judges to choose between equally unwise alternatives based on the offense rather than the offender. Police, prosecutors, victims, and the public often pressure the sentencing judge to incarcerate certain offenders for long periods (Davis & Smith, 1994; Newman, 1995).

The sentencing decision has a major impediment: it usually requires that judges predict human behavior. As judges ask themselves if specific offenders will respond to prison positively or perhaps benefit more from psychiatric, drug treatment, or counseling while on probation, they have too little factual information to guide them. (Sometimes the sentencing judge is asked to validate a negotiated plea, one part of which may be an agreement on sentence: probation, or some specific and short term of incarceration.) In the final analysis, most judges must rely on a presentence investigation and their own intuition, experience, and imagination to produce the best decision.

---

Box 2.4

### Reintegration

A broad correctional ideology stressing acquisition of legitimate skills and opportunities by criminal offenders, and the creation of supervised opportunities for testing, using, and refining those skills, particularly in community settings.

---

Box 2.5

### Incapacitation

A crime prevention strategy based on specific deterrence that would disable the potential offender from committing another crime by isolating the instant offender. Common forms of incapacitation include transportation to other countries or colonies, committing the offender to an asylum or mental hospital, and life-long imprisonment.

---

## The Presentence Investigation

Most states require a presentence report for offenses for which imprisonment can be more than one year. It is estimated that more than 85 percent of the states prepare some kind of presentence report on felony cases, although there may be extreme variation in the report's quality and usefulness. The presentence report, if properly researched and prepared, can be an extremely valuable document for trial judges in their sentence decisions.[3] It also is useful for probation supervision, institutional classification procedures, parole board deliberations, and correctional research.

The presentence investigation is usually prepared by the court's probation officer or by any available staff of social workers. In some states, private agencies (such as the Salvation Army) are contracted to prepare court presentence evaluations. Privately commissioned presentence investigation reports prepared for the court (Gitchoff & Rush, 1989), as well as creation of local agencies to prepare individualized client-specific sentencing plans that stress non-incarceration sanctions (Macallair, 1994), also assist sentencing judges. The defense attorney usually reviews the report, and may challenge substantive error and points in order to help the judge make a sentencing decision based on information from all sources. Walter C. Reckless (1967:673) pointed out the essential elements of a workable presentence investigation report. He said that a presentence investigation report, when written up and presented to the judge, should include in summary form such information as:

- present offense (including the person's attitudes toward it and his or her role in it);

- previous criminal record, family situation (including tensions and discord and the factors affecting his or her happiness);

- neighborhood environment; school and educational history;

- employment history (especially the skills and the efficiency and stability as a worker);

- associates and participation;

- habits (including alcohol, gambling, promiscuity, and so forth);

- physical and mental health (as reported by various sources and by special examinations); summary and recommendations.

Although most presentence investigations will emphasize such objective facts as employment, age, and school grade completed, it is important that the investigating officer capture such subjective content as defendant remorse, willingness to engage in restitution, and feeling about the crime. Defendants' perspectives on life and their approach to it, as well as attitudes toward the objects and the social relationships of their milieu, are the most crucial items in a presentence investigation. Subjective data, in short, give the more revealing clues as to what has shaped the behavior and criminal activity of the defendant so far and what future possibilities might be.

The presentence investigation report gives the judge a comprehensive and factual overview of offenders, their crime, nature, needs, risk, history, habits, personality, and problems. It also usually contains a recommendation to the court of an appropriate disposition for the case. Judges tend to accept the presentence recommendation at a rate of about 83 percent for probation and 87 percent for imprisonment (Schmolesky & Thorston, 1982).

## Determinate Sentencing

Critics have identified several unwarranted and unwanted problems with indeterminate sentencing, as well as parole board decisionmaking. Reformers, neoclassical theorists, politicians, and organized political action groups with punitive agendas coalesced to attack rehabilitation and parole. The primary substitute for the indeterminate sentence is the determinate sentence, a throw-back to the tradition of "flat time" in our earlier history. A determinate sentence is a fixed period of incarceration imposed on the offender by the sentencing court. The ideology underlying determinate sentencing is retribution, just deserts, incapacitation, and selective incapacitation.[4]

---

**Box 2.6**

### Selective Incapacitation

The doctrine of incapacitation calls for isolating or "social disablement" of the offender by incarcerating those whose criminal behavior is so probable or damaging that nothing short of isolation will protect the public. Unfortunately correctional technology, classification, and prediction do not allow accurate identification of these malefactors before the fact. Two major errors are, first, predicting that an offender will become a "chronic" offender which in fact is not true (the "false positive problem"). If intervention is based on this false fact, considerable social injustice would be done that our Constitutional framers would denounce. The second error is predicting that someone will not be a "high rate" offender when the opposite is true (the "false negative problem"). In brief, the number of errors in prediction usually equals or exceeds the number of correct identifications.

One famous after-the-fact study of chronic offenders in Philadelphia (Wolfgang et al., 1972) found that about 23 percent of all male offenders accounted for 61 percent of all the crimes of that study group, including 61 percent of all homicides, 76 percent of all rapes, 73 percent of all robberies, and 65 percent of all aggravated assaults. The study was done several decades after the fact and to get into the chronic group, the juveniles would have had to log in at least five arrests by age 18, at which time criminal desistence was strong and widespread.

Selective incapacitation is isolating specific chronic offenders for long periods of incarceration for the purpose of reducing the volume of crime. One wag advanced the theory that the nation could attain about a 60 percent drop in the crime rate by imprisoning all 16- to 19-year-olds for three years. While this is a preposterous proposal and is rampant with false positive errors, there is at least a substantial chance of success in crime prevention. At what cost?

# Problems in Setting Prison Terms

In the past, the determination of prison terms was left largely to the courts. Decisions were made within the broad parameters of plea bargaining and statutory limitations. The courts generally established maximum sentences and parole boards determined the actual lengths of confinement according to limits established by the court and by law. In the past two decades, however, control over the sentencing process has become more of a concern to state legislatures. Concerns about disparate sentences and other abuses or perceived abuses of the system have resulted in six basic strategies to formalize legislative control over the sentencing process:

- **Determinate sentencing**—sentencing systems under which parole boards no longer may release prisoners before their sentences (minus good time) have expired;

- **Mandatory prison terms**—statutes through which legislatures require a prison term always to be imposed for convictions for certain offenses or offenders;

- **Sentencing guidelines**—procedures designed to structure sentencing decisions based on measures of offense severity and criminal history;

- **Parole guidelines**—procedures designed to structure parole release decisions based on measurable offender criteria;

- **Good-time policies**—statutes that allow for reducing a prison term based on an offender's behavior in prison; and

- **Emergency crowding provisions**—policies that relieve prison crowding by systematically making inmates eligible for release sooner.

Prison populations are increasing in all but four states (Maine, Vermont, Nebraska, and Oklahoma). Policies for setting prison terms influence the size of prison populations by both the number that are sentenced and the length of time that they stay in prison. As a result, many states have attempted to find ways to modify prison terms and reduce population pressures. Those methods include the following: sentencing guidelines that use available prison capacity as a consideration in setting the length of terms (such as those in Minnesota and Florida); mechanisms for accelerating good time; and direct release of certain prisoners—usually those already close to their release date—under administrative provisions (such as emergency crowding laws, the use of commutation, sentence revisions, and early-release programs).

Sentencing guidelines for structuring the penalty decisions of judges work by providing decisionmakers with criteria and weights on which the sanction decision should be based (Hoffman & DeGostin, 1975). By explicitly stating the factors that are deemed relevant to the sentence decision, and by providing guidance to the sentencer, these guidelines ensure a greater degree of uniformity in criminal penalties. Explicit sentencing guidelines then work to limit the effect of extralegal factors on the sentencing decision.

Such a sentencing structure limits judicial control over sentencing, as the legislature heavily influences the sentence length. Whether there are unforeseen problems in presumptive sentencing remains to be

Figure 2.2
**States Vary by the Amount of Control Over Sentence Served**

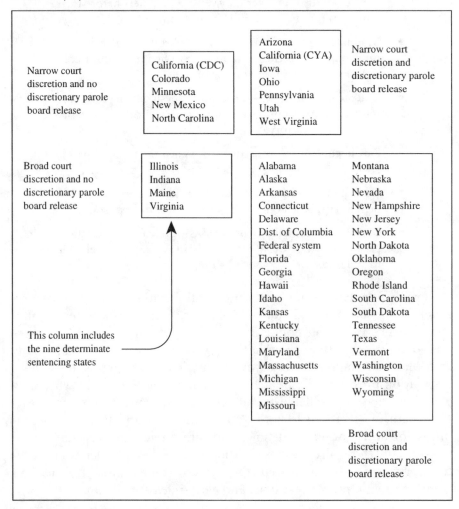

Source: Bureau of Justice Statistics (August 1993). *Setting Prison Terms*, p. 3. Washington, DC: U.S. Department of Justice.

proven, but California's prison population problems may well be due to a corollary of presumptive sentencing: abolition of parole board early release authority that has been used to control prison overcrowding in the past. (California now is the largest single prison system in the world.)

Mandatory prison-term statutes now exist in all states. Those statutes apply for certain crimes of violence and for habitual criminals, and the court's discretion in such cases (regarding, for example, probation, fines, and suspended sentences) has been eliminated by statute. In some states the imposition of a prison term is constrained by sentencing guidelines, such as those shown in Figure 2.3. Guidelines are usually set by a governor's commission, including a cross section of the state population. As noted by a recent study (Coleman & Guthrie, 1988:142):

> A sentencing commission in each state monitors the use of the guidelines and departures from the recommended sentences by the judiciary. Written explanations are required from judges who depart from guideline ranges. The Minnesota Sentencing Guidelines Commission states that 'while the sentencing guidelines are advisory to the sentencing judge, departures from the presumptive sentences established in the guidelines should be made only when substantial and compelling circumstances exist.' Pennsylvania sentencing guidelines stipulate that court failure to explain sentences deviating from the recommendations 'shall be grounds for vacating the sentence and re-sentencing the defendant.' Furthermore, if the court does not consider the guidelines or inaccurately or inappropriately applies them, an imposed sentence may be vacated upon appeal to a higher court by either the defense or the prosecution.

The range and particular format for sentencing guidelines can include such things as specifically worded statutes and grids with a range of judicial options. Similarly, parole guidelines are sometimes closely prescribed, and sometimes wide discretion is afforded to the parole board. The amount of flexibility in such decisions can directly enhance or detract from the efforts to relieve crowded prison conditions. Because most parole decisions are not based on time but on perceived "risk to the community," tighter and tighter criteria make it difficult to manage prison population size by such decisions.

Good-time policies are another way to control behavior in the institutions and to control population pressures as well. The threat of losing up to one-third of their sentences by poor conduct does act as a control over some inmates' behavior. The States also use good time and programming ("earned") time to reduce prison crowding.

Figure 2.3
**Sentencing Guidelines**

---

Offender: _____    Docket number: _____

Judge: _____    Date: _____

Offense(s) convicted of: _____

_____

*Crime score:*
A.  Injury
   0 = No injury
   1 = Injury
   2 = Death        _____ +
B.  Weapon
   0 = No weapon
   1 = Weapon
   2 = Weapon present and used    _____ +
C.  Drugs
   0 = No sale of drugs
   1 = Sale of drugs      _____ =

Crime
score

*Offender score:*
A.  Current legal status
   0 = Not on probation/parole, escape
   1 = On probation/parole, escape    _____ +
B.  Prior adult misdemeanor convictions
   0 = No convictions
   1 = One conviction
   2 = Two or more convictions    _____ +
C.  Prior adult felony convictions
   0 = No convictions
   2 = One conviction
   4 = Two or more convictions    _____ +
D.  Prior adult probation parole revocations
   0 = None
   1 = One or more revocations    _____ +
E.  Prior adult incarcerations (over 60 days)
   0 = None
   1 = One incarceration
   2 = Two or more incarcerations    _____ =

Offender
score

Guideline sentence: _____

Actual sentence: _____

Reasons (if actual sentence does not fall within guideline range): _____

_____

Figure 2.3—*continued*

Crime score

| 4-5 | 4-6 years | 5-7 years | 6-8 years | 8-10 years |
| --- | --- | --- | --- | --- |
| 3 | 3-5 years | 4-6 years | 6-8 years | 6-8 years |
| 2 | 2-4 years | 3-5 years | 3-5 years | 4-6 years |
| 1 | Probation | Probation | 2-4 years | 3-5 years |
| 0 | Probation | Probation | Probation | 2-4 years |
| | 0-1 | 2-4 | 5-7 | 8-10 |

Offender score

The sentencing judge first determines the crime score, typically concerned with the actual crime, injury, weapon used, and drug sale. Points are assigned as above under "Crime Score." Second, the judge scores the offender's prior behavior, using those items identified under "Offender Score." Determining the guideline sentence entails finding the grid cell that corresponded to the crime and offender score, and then imposing a sentence that falls within the suggested range.

Source: J. Kress et al. (1978). *Developing Sentencing Guidelines: Trainers Handbook.* Washington, DC: National Institute of Criminal Justice.

Table 2.2
**Types of Felony Sentences Imposed in State Courts, 1994 (in percent)**

| Crime | Non-Incarceration Probation | Incarceration Jail | Sentences Prison | Percent Total |
| --- | --- | --- | --- | --- |
| Murder | 3 | 2 | 95 | 100 |
| Rape | 12 | 17 | 71 | 100 |
| Robbery | 12 | 11 | 77 | 100 |
| Aggravated Assault | 25 | 27 | 48 | 100 |
| Burglary | 25 | 22 | 53 | 100 |
| Larceny | 45 | 23 | 31 | 100 |
| Drug Trafficking | 29 | 23 | 48 | 100 |
| ALL | 29 | 26 | 45 | 100 |

Source: P.A. Langan and J.M. Brown (1997). *Felony Sentences in the United States, 1994.* Washington, DC: U.S. Bureau of Justice Statistics.

Figure 2.4
**Administrative Reduction of the Amount of Time Spent in Prison**

Key
**B** Reductions for good behavior
**P** Reductions for program participation

| | B | P | | B | P |
|---|---|---|---|---|---|
| Federal system | B | P | Montana | B | P |
| District of Columbia | B | — | Nebraska | B | P |
| | | | Nevada | B | P |
| Alabama | B | P | New Hampshire | B | P |
| Alaska | B | — | New Jersey | B | P |
| Arizona | B | — | | | |
| Arkansas | — | P | | | |
| California | — | P | New Mexico | B | P |
| | | | New York | B | — |
| Colorado | B | P | North Carolina | B | P |
| Connecticut | B | P | North Dakota | B | P |
| Delaware | B | P | Ohio | B | — |
| Florida | B | P | | | |
| Georgia | B | — | Oklahoma | — | P |
| | | | Oregon | B | P |
| Hawaii | — | — | Pennsylvania | — | — |
| Idaho | B | P | Rhode Island | B | P |
| Illinois | B | P | South Carolina | B | P |
| Indiana | B | — | | | |
| Iowa | B | P | South Dakota | B | — |
| | | | Tennessee | — | — |
| Kansas | B | P | Texas | B | P |
| Kentucky | B | P | Utah | — | — |
| Louisiana | — | P | Vermont | B | P |
| Maine | B | P | | | |
| Maryland | B | P | | | |
| | | | Virginia | B | P |
| Massachusetts | B | P | Washington | B | — |
| Michigan | B | P | West Virginia | B | P |
| Minnesota | B | — | Wisconsin | B | P |
| Mississippi | B | P | Wyoming | B | P |
| Missouri | B | P | | | |

Source: Bureau of Justice Statistics (August 1993). *Setting Prison Terms*, p. 6. Washington, DC: U.S. Department of Justice.

Box 2.7

### Sentencing Disparity

Sentencing disparity is the divergence in the types and lengths of sentences imposed for the same crimes, with no evident reason for the differences. It is also known as unequal treatment of similarly situated offenders.

## Three-Strikes Laws

No discussion of sentencing changes would be complete without exploring "three-strikes" sentencing laws. Although sentence enhancement statutes exist in most states (such as habitual or repeat offender laws), legislation that specifically identified a group of repeat offenders for lengthy incapacitation began to bloom in 1993. Currently 24 states and the federal government have enacted so-called three-strikes laws, all designed to remove offenders convicted of repeated serious offenses from society for a long period of time, if not for life (Shichor, 1997). In California, for example, the minimum sentence under the three-strikes legislation is 25 years, with "good time" credits restricted to no more than 20 percent of the sentence imposed: time served will be no less than 20 years. Oregon, Washington, and California citizens have voted for three-strikes laws.

In California, there is substantial evidence that prosecutors use these statutes disproportionately against minority offenders, and some 27,000 of the 147,000 (about 18%) prison inmates are now incarcerated for third (or second) strike offenses. As a result of such legislation, three-strikes cases are more than three times likely to go to jury trial, jails are crowded with pretrial cases, civil court judges have been transferred to criminal dockets, and prison costs are escalating as the inmate population booms and the percentage of inmates age 50 and over ("geriatric inmates") increases. See Figure 2.5. Despite legislation of this sort, there is little evidence that three-strikes laws are contributing significantly to reductions in crime rates, and there is no reason to believe that this sentencing effort will be appreciably different from other attempts to limit discretion.

This review of the changes in sentencing practices and their consequences in the last decade clearly shows the shifts that have taken place. Although discretion in determining sentence length has been somewhat removed from the sentencing judge and parole board, it was reduced by legislatures through their enactment of new sentencing structures. In turn, in many jurisdictions, the prosecutor's discretion was increased.[5] The prison populations will continue to climb as more and more offenders are committed and serve longer and longer sentences (Wooldredge, 1996). American corrections appears to be on a collision course with a standard of human decency: the Eighth Amendment to the U.S. Constitution, which forbids cruel and unusual punishment.

Figure 2.5
**Predicted Prison Population Age 50 and Over Under California's Three-Strikes Law**

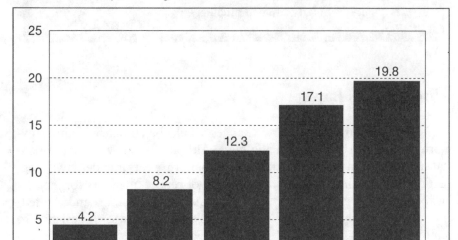

Source: M.A. Jones and J. Austin (1995). *The 1995 NCCD National Prison Population Forecast,* p. 11. San Francisco, CA: National Council on Crime and Delinquency.

## Summary

A discussion of sentencing would be incomplete without identifying policy implications of the increasing demand for deterrence. Some writers now argue that those states that imprison more of the offender population (rather than use community corrections) would have lower crime rates if the proportion of persons sentenced to prison were to increase. Though this may appeal to conservatives who believe that the criminal justice system can affect the rates of crime and serve as a deterrent, the data on the effects of higher imprisonment rates do not bear out the presumed effects. In both the United States and Canada, the rates of crime do not go down with increased imprisonment (Biles, 1979; Clear & Barry, 1983). Instead, the rates of crime go up when the proportion of offenders per 100,000 who are sentenced to prison is raised. We thus may need to start thinking about the continued use of imprisonment to deter others from committing crime, when studies show that it has just the opposite effect (Turk & Shover, 1986).

The past 15 years represent a revolution in sentencing in the United States. Among the changes imposed are the abolition of the parole board's authority to release offenders at their discretion and the adoption of sentencing guidelines for judges. Changes also include shifting to mandatory prison sentences for specified crimes, adoption of presumptive sentences, and other efforts to limit discretion and disparity in sentencing and length of time served in prison.

In addition to the sentencing law changes, sharp increases have occurred in the number of persons incarcerated. Never in the history of the United States have we had so many (1 million) inmates and such a large proportion of the public incarcerated in prisons (Kuhn, 1998). Reasons for the sudden increase are not exactly understood; it is obvious, however, that corrections is once again in crisis and on a collision course with the Eighth Amendment's prohibition against cruel and unusual punishment. The next chapter examines efforts to develop corrections in the community, using the jail as the hub of corrections.

## Review Questions

1.  Describe the development of the indeterminate sentence.

2.  How was the offender viewed during the Progressive Era?

3.  How does the sentencing judge share sentencing with the parole board under the indeterminate sentence?

4.  What factors contributed to the change from the indeterminate to the determinate sentence?

5.  List five options that were proposed as alternatives to the indeterminate sentence.

6.  How can the chronic offender be identified?

## Key Terms

Captain Alexander Maconochie
determinate sentence
good-time policies
incapacitation
indeterminate sentence
mandatory sentences
mark system
presentence investigation report

reintegration
selective incapacitation
sentencing
sentencing disparity
sentencing guidelines
Sir Walter Crofton
three-strikes laws

## Recommended Readings

Irwin, J. and J. Austin (1994). *It's About Time: America's Imprisonment Binge.* Belmont, CA: Wadsworth.

Rothman, D. (1980). *Conscience and Convenience: The Asylum and Its Alternatives in Progressive America.* Boston, MA: Little, Brown.

Morris, N. and M. Tonry (1990). *Between Prison and Probation.* New York, NY: Oxford Press.

## Notes

[1]   Some historians argue that the noble ideals of rehabilitation never really were implemented, and that the "convenience" of punishment won out over the "conscience" of rehabilitation. See D. Rothman (1980). *Conscience and Convenience: The Asylum and Its Alternatives in Progressive America.* Boston, MA: Little, Brown. See also J. Irwin (1980). *Prisons in Turmoil.* Boston, MA: Little, Brown.

[2]   For a discussion of the flaws of the California three-strikes program, see M. Vitiello (1997), "Three Strikes: Can We Return to Rationality?" *Journal of Criminal Law and Criminology,* 87(2):395-481.

[3]   An excellent examination of the presentence report and child sexual molesters can be found in E. Leberg (1997). *Understanding Child Molesters: Taking Charge.* Thousand Oaks , CA: Sage.

[4]   For a view of inmate perception of the goals of sentencing, see P. Van Voorhis, S.L. Browning, and M. Simon (1997). "The Meaning of Punishment: Inmates' Orientation to the Prison Experience." *Prison Journal,* 77(2):135-167.

[5]   Readers can find a review of the lessons learned from sentencing reform efforts in J. Austin, C. Jones, and J. Kramer (1995). *National Assessment of Structured Sentencing: Final Report.* Washington, DC: U.S. Bureau of Justice Statistics.

## References

Allen, H. and C. Simonsen (1998). *Corrections in America.* Englewood Cliffs, NJ: Prentice-Hall.

Beck, A. and T. Bonczar (1994). *State and Federal Prison Population Tops One Million.* Washington, DC: U.S. Department of Justice.

Biles, D. (1979). "Crime and the Use of Prisons." *Federal Probation,* 43(2):39-43.

Bodapati, M.R., M. Jones, and J.W. Marquardt (1995). "The Sentencing Practices of Judges and Juries: A Comparative Analysis Using Texas Drug Offenders." *Journal of Crime and Justice,* 18(2):181-203.

Bureau of Justice Statistics (1983). *Setting Prison Terms*. Washington, DC: U.S. Department of Justice.

Camp, C. and G. Camp (1997). *The Corrections Yearbook, 1997*. South Salem, NY: The Criminal Justice Institute.

Clear, T. and O. Barry (1983). "Some Conceptual Issues in Incapacitating Offenders." *Crime & Delinquency*, 29:529-545.

Coleman, S. and K. Guthrie (1988). *Sentencing Effectiveness in Preventing Crime*. St. Paul, MN: Criminal Justice Statistical Analysis Center.

Davis, R. and B. Smith (1994). "The Effects of Victim Impact Statements on Sentencing Decisions." *Justice Quarterly*, 11:453-512.

Gaskins, C. (1990). *Felony Case Processing in State Courts, 1986*. Washington, DC: U.S. Bureau of Justice Statistics.

Gitchoff, T. and G. Rush (1989). "The Criminological Case Evaluation and Sentencing Recommendation: An Idea Whose Time Has Come." *International Journal of Offender Therapy and Comparative Criminology*, 33:77-83.

Hoffman, P. and L. DeGostin (1975). "An Argument for Self-Imposed Explicit Judicial Sentencing Standards." *Journal of Criminal Justice*, 3:195-206.

Irwin, J. (1980). *Prisons in Turmoil*. Boston, MA: Little, Brown.

Irwin, J. and J. Austin (1994). *It's About Time: America's Imprisonment Binge*. Belmont, CA: Wadsworth.

Jones, M.A. and J. Austin (1995). *The 1995 NCCD National Prison Population Forecast*. San Francisco, CA: National Council on Crime and Delinquency.

Kress, J., L. Wilkins, D. Gottfredson, J. Calpin, and A. Gelman (1978). *Developing Sentencing Guidelines: Trainers Handbook*. Washington, DC: U.S. National Institute of Justice.

Kuhn, A. (1998). "Incarceration Rates: The United States in an International Perspective." *Criminal Justice Abstracts*, 30(2):321-353.

Langan, P.A. and J. Brown (1997). *Felony Sentences in the United States, 1994*. Washington, DC: U.S. Bureau of Justice Statistics.

Leberg, E. (1997). *Understanding Child Molesters: Taking Charge*. Thousand Oaks, CA: Sage.

Macallair, D. (1994). "Disposition Case Advocacy in San Francisco's Juvenile Justice System: A New Approach to Deinstitutionalization." *Crime & Delinquency*, 40:84-95.

Maguire, K. and A. Pastore (eds.) (1994). *Sourcebook of Criminal Justice Statistics, 1993*. Washington, DC: U.S. Department of Justice.

Mauer, M. (1997). *Americans Behind Bars: U.S. and International Uses of Incarceration, 1995*. Washington, DC: The Sentencing Project.

Morris, N. and M. Tonry (1990). *Between Prison and Probation*. New York, NY: Oxford Press.

Newman, D.W. (1995). "Jury Decision Making and the Effect of Victim Impact Statements in the Penalty Phase." *Criminal Justice Policy Review*, 7(3-4):291-300.

Reckless, W. (1967). *The Crime Problem*. New York, NY: Appleton-Century-Crofts.

Rothman, D. (1980). *Conscience and Convenience: The Asylum and Its Alternatives in Progressive America.* Boston, MA: Little, Brown.

Schmolesky, J. and T. Thorston (1982). "The Importance of the Presentence Investigation Report After Sentencing." *Criminal Law Bulletin*, 18:406-441.

Shichor, D. (1997). "Three Strikes as a Public Policy: The Consequences of the New Penology and the McDonaldization of Punishment." *Crime & Delinquency*, 43(4):470-492.

Turk, C. and N. Shover (1986). "Research Note: The Origins of Sentencing Reforms." *Justice Quarterly*, 3:329-342.

Wooldredge, J. (1996). "Research Note: A State-Level Analysis of Sentencing Options and Inmate Crowding in State Prisons." *Crime & Delinquency*, 42(3):456-466.

Wolfgang, M., R. Figlio, and T. Sellin (1972). *Delinquency in a Birth Cohort.* Chicago, IL: University of Chicago Press.

# Sentencing and the Jail

## Contemporary Sentencing Practices

Historically, the American criminal justice system was an adversarial combat between the State and the accused defendant in a criminal trial. The accused denied committing the alleged offense, and the trial jury was charged with determining the fact of innocence or guilt. The presiding judge, using all available information and guided by the presentence investigation report previously ordered from the court's investigators, would then impose sentence on the guilty in the interest of justice and to achieve some recognizable correctional objective. Such objectives could include punishment, rehabilitation, reintegration, retribution, reparation, or deterrence.

Perhaps this model typified the justice system a half-decade ago, but it is atypical of sentencing practices in the 1990s. Some 872,217 persons were convicted of a felony offense in State courts in 1994, including 164,583 for a violent felony (Langan & Brown, 1997). A large number of convictions were for drug possession and trafficking, about 31 percent of the total number of felony convictions and almost double the number of convictions for *all* crimes of violence totaled together (murder, robbery, rape, and aggravated assault). Federal courts convicted 39,624 persons of a felony in 1994. That number represents only 4 percent of the combined state and federal convictions in that year.

Determination of guilt, however, seldom employed a jury in 1994. Instead, most of those convicted (89%) pled guilty for considerations, and the judge usually complied with the negotiated plea that had been struck by prosecutor and defense counsel. Only 11 percent of the total convicted were found guilty through trial, and about one-half of those were convicted by the judge in a bench trial (Langan & Brown, 1997:9). A definition of plea bargaining is found in Box 3.1.

---

Box 3.1

### Plea Bargaining

The exchange of prosecutorial and/or judicial concessions, commonly a lesser charge, the dismissal of other pending charges, a recommendation by the prosecutor for a reduced sentence or a combination thereof, in return for a plea of guilty.

---

Regardless of the avenue of conviction, most (71%) convicted felony offenders were sentenced to incarceration; some 45 percent were imprisoned, and another one in four were sentenced to jail. All but a scant one percent of those receiving non-incarceration sentences were sentenced to probation, along with collateral penalties. See Table 3.1.

Table 3.1
**Felons Sentenced to Collateral Penalties, 1994**

| Collateral Penalty | Percent Sentenced |
|---|---|
| Fine | 21% |
| Restitution | 18 |
| Treatment | 7 |
| Community service | 7 |
| All Other* | 8 |

*Other includes community control, house arrest, work release, drug testing, and loss of driver's license. In total, 41% or more of convicted felons received additional penalties in 1994.

Source: P.A. Langan and J.M. Brown (1997). *Felony Sentences in State Courts, 1994*. Washington, DC: U.S. Bureau of Justice Statistics.

The most frequently imposed collateral penalty was the fine,[1] usually as a condition of probation. Gordon and Glaser (1991) and Green (1996) found the odds of recidivism (subsequent arrest and incarceration) to be significantly less for those offenders given a financial penalty, in contrast to those receiving a jail sentence. Other collateral penalties are discussed below.

> **Box 3.2**
>
> ### Fine
>
> A penalty imposed on a convicted person by the court, requiring that he or she pay a specified sum of money. The fine is a cash payment of a dollar amount assessed by the judge in an individual case or determined by a published schedule of penalties.
>
> Fines may be paid in installments in many jurisdictions in the nation.

## Sentencing Options

In the plea bargaining process, defense counsel may negotiate sentence outcome to avoid incarceration of the accused. Thus the decision to incarcerate may, in part, depend on the outcome of negotiated justice. The two major incarceration outcomes are imprisonment in a penal facility or in a jail. The major alternative to incarceration is probation and such other intermediate punishments as weekend confinement, house arrest, electronic monitoring, fines, restitution and work centers, intensive supervised probation, and so on. These are discussed below.

> **Box 3.3**
>
> ### Jail
>
> A confinement facility, usually administered by a local law enforcement agency, intended for adults but sometimes also containing juveniles, that holds persons detained pending adjudication and/or persons committed after adjudication for sentences of one year or less.

> **Box 3.4**
>
> ### Prison
>
> A confinement facility, usually administered by a state agency, having custodial authority over adults sentenced to confinement for more than one year.

If the decision is to place the offender on probation or other intermediate punishment, usually as a condition of probation, the offender is
typically supervised by an officer of the local probation department.
Conditional freedom under probation requires the probationer to meet
certain conditions of behavior, as is noted in Chapter 5. If the probationer is in danger of substantively violating these conditions, or determined to be in need of additional service or more intensive supervision,
the supervising officer may request that the judge increase the conditions of supervision to include additional restrictions or program participation. The intent of this practice, often called *tourniquet sentencing*, is
to lessen the risk of failure and recidivism, and assist the probationer to
decide to conform to court expectations. The implicit alternative to
nonconforming behavior is incarceration, frequently in the local jail, for
a period of time to be imposed by the judge. To understand tourniquet
sentencing, it is necessary to examine the jail and its roles as a hub of
community corrections.

Box 3.5

**Tourniquet Sentencing**

Tightening or increasing the conditions of probation to encourage the client to conform to legal and supervisory expectations. A probation officer requests the court to order additional
restrictions or to mandate participation in identified programs.
The correctional objective is reintegration or avoidance of
criminal activity. One example of tourniquet sentencing is the
probationer convicted of indecent exposure who continues to
consume alcohol. The court may order participation in Alcoholics Anonymous, as well as house arrest with electronic monitoring, or that the probationer take Antebus, a medication that
generally sickens the person who imbibes alcohol.

Source: The term "tourniquet sentencing" is attributed to Judge Albert
Kramer, District Judge, Quincy, MA. A. Klein (1980). *Earn It: The Story So
Far*. Brandeis University, Waltham, MA.

## The Jail

The local detention facility, usually administered by a county law
enforcement agency, is generally known as the "jail." In 1997, there
were 3,287 jails across the nation, housing a record 637,319 persons.
This is the largest number of Americans ever housed in jails, and represents 212 persons per 100,000 population, up from 68 per 100,000 in
1983 (Gilliard & Beck, 1998:7), a staggering increase. As a nation,

America incarcerates more persons per 100,000 population than any major Western nation, including South Africa. The incarceration rate for African-Americans in the nation exceeds that for South Africa[2] by a ratio of 4:1. Almost two percent of the adult African-American males are in the nation's jails each day.

Photo 3.1
The Cincinnati Workhouse. Courtesy of the Hamilton County Sheriff's Office.

In the United States, the ratio of African-Americans in jails is more than six times that of whites, twice that of Hispanics, and almost four times that of the national average. See Table 3.2. Why African-Americans are overrepresented in correctional facilities is hotly debated, but racism, lack of education, and social class have been identified as explanations.[3] Others also cite the higher arrest rates of African-Americans, and increases in black-on-black crime as explanations.

Table 3.2
**Demographic Characteristics of Local Jail Inmates: 1997**

| Group | Number | Percentage | Number of Inmates per 100,000 Population |
|-------|--------|------------|------------------------------------------|
| Total U.S.: | 567,079 | 100 | 212 |
| White | 230,300 | 41 | 188 |
| Black | 237,900 | 42 | 737 |
| Hispanic | 88,900 | 16 | 304 |
| Other | 10,000 | 2 | 87 |

Source: D.K. Gilliard and A.J. Beck (1998). *Prison and Jail Inmates at Midyear 1997*, p. 7. Washington, DC: U.S. Bureau of Justice Statistics.

Jails incarcerate a wide variety of persons. Jails receive individuals pending arraignment and hold them awaiting trial, conviction, and sentencing. They also re-admit probation, parole, and bail-bond violators, and absconders, as well as temporarily detain juveniles pending transfer to juvenile authorities. Further, they hold mentally ill persons pending their movement to appropriate health facilities, as well as individuals for the military, protective custody and contempt, and for the court as witnesses.[4] In addition, jails release convicted inmates to the community upon completion of sentence, and transfer inmates to state, federal, and other local authorities. They temporarily incarcerate convicted felons sentenced to prisons but for whom there are no bed spaces (Beck, 1995:1). Finally, they relinquish custody of temporary detainees to juvenile and medical authorities (Stephan, 1990:2). It is small wonder that there are more than 23 million entries to and exits from local jails in 1993. The median length of stay in jail in 1989 was three days; jail populations would be even larger if the average stay were longer. The number of jail inmates increased more than 9 percent from 1996 to 1997 (Langan & Brown, 1997).

Photo 3.2
A cell in the Cincinnati Workhouse. Courtesy of the Hamilton County Sheriff's Office.

## Jail Facilities

Between 1985 and 1997, the number of jail inmates increased 110 percent; the total staff increased more than 156 percent, and the number of correctional officers increased 165 percent. The figures reflect responses to the jail crowding and increased arrests for drug offenses and violent crime (including domestic violence), probation and parole violations, greater number of inmates held in local jails because of crowded state or federal facilities, length of sentences, and incarceration in jail of offenders committing felonies that otherwise have been sent to prison. Jails now house more than one-third of all persons incarcerated in the nation.

Since 1987, the number of persons arrested increased some 16 percent but, for some offenses, the gain was even more pronounced. Arrests for simple assault increased by 63 percent, aggravated assault by

43 percent, drug laws by 58 percent, and weapons violations by 10 percent. About one in four of the jail population is charged with or convicted of a drug offense. The estimated number of drug offenders in local jails in 1997 was almost 142,000, representing more than a 500 percent increase since 1983! From 1983 to 1997, the increase of the number of persons charged with drug violations contributed 40 percent of the total growth of jail populations.

On average, felons sentenced to local jails received a mean sentence of 7 months, about the same sentence length as the 1983 national jail census. In addition to those sentenced to jail time, nearly one in eight (almost 80,000) inmates were prisoners being held for state or federal authorities.

The costs of maintaining jail facilities is not cheap. Some $9.6 billion were expended in 1997, and almost one-fourth of that was for capital improvements (adding new beds, buying land, jail construction and renovation, increased security, etc.). Of course, not all jurisdictions provide the same level of funding. For example, the national cost per inmate in 1993 was more than $20,000. The most expensive state costs in 1993 were in New York, at $29,300 per inmate; the least cost was to Mississippi, at $7,000 per inmate. The newly opened federal jails cost $22,773 per inmate, about 50 percent more than the national average. In general, jail expenditures increased 355 percent over the last decade!

Much of the expenditure increase has gone to achieve lower inmate-to-staff ratios. Front-line correctional officers saw their inmate-staff ratio decrease from 5.0 to 3.9, despite the unparalleled gains in number of inmates, reflecting the addition of significant numbers of officers. Yet crowding remains a major problem and has adversely affected services and operations. Primarily, the emphasis has shifted from treatment and programming to containment,[5] requiring diversion of jail resources from programs to security. Among those services most impacted by crowding were mental health and recreational programs. Many jail administrators would welcome having more separate cells or housing for mentally ill inmates, employing more mental health professionals, or contracting for treatment of mentally ill sex offenders.[6] It is in the latter area that community corrections can be of particular assistance to jail managers and administrators.

Alternatives to incarceration have also helped alleviate the effects of jail crowding; 11 percent of jail inmates in 1997 were in alternative programs outside jail facilities. Programs that have been added or implemented include work release centers, electronic monitoring, boot camps, and day reporting centers. These programs typically fall under the jurisdiction of probation departments, although some jurisdictions contract with service providers, as will be seen below.

---

Box 3.6

### Pretrial Release of Felony Defendants, 1992

An estimated 63 percent of the defendants who had State felony charges filed against them in the nation's 75 most populous counties during May 1992 were released by the court prior to the disposition of their case. More received nonfinancial release (35%) than bond release (25%). Almost 1 in 3 were held on bail, not being able to make the bond. Only 6 percent of the arrestees were held without bail, mostly charged with murder, rape, burglary, and robbery.

Among defendants already on pretrial release for a prior case when arrested on the current felony charges, 56 percent were released again. Also released were about 1 in 3 of those arrested while on parole and some 44 percent of those already on probation when arrested on the instant charge.

Overall, about 14 percent failed to appear at their court date. Those who failed to appear in court at least once before had a higher failure-to-appear rate (38%) than other released defendants.[7] At the end of a year, 1 in 12 released arrestees were still fugitives (Reaves and Perez, 1994).

A study of King County, Washington court bail and pretrial detention found continuing racial and ethnic disparities that affected case disposition above and beyond the influence of case-related characteristics (Bridges, 1997).

Source: B. Reaves and J. Perez (1994). *Pretrial Release of Defendants, 1992,* p. 1. Washington, DC: U.S. Department of Justice.

---

## Jail Inmates

Jail inmates do not mirror the general population. For example, males constituted 89 percent of all jail inmates in 1997, but slightly less than 50 percent of the population. White non-Hispanics were 41 percent of the local jail population, followed by non-Hispanic African-Americans (42%) and Hispanics (16%). All other races totaled 2 percent of the jail population. The percentage of African-Americans and Hispanic jail inmates increased measurably since 1983; more than 40 percent of the increase was the result of the increase in the number of persons held for drug offenses (Beck, 1995:1).

An estimated 47 percent of the jail inmates were on probation or parole, out on bail, or under some other criminal justice status at the time of their instant arrest. More than three-quarters of the jail inmates had a prior sentence to probation or incarceration. At least one-third were in jail for a violent offense or had a prior sentence for a violent offense (Beck, 1991:2). Almost 60 percent of the inmates in 1997 were awaiting trial.

Jail inmates are multi-problemed. Not only are most of them engaging in criminal activities, they are beset by numerous social and personal problems along several dimensions. Nearly one in four jail inmates were in jail for a drug offense; one-third of all Hispanics and one-quarter of African-American non-Hispanic inmates were in for a drug violation, compared to less than one-sixth of the white non-Hispanic inmates. More than one-half of all inmates had used crack or cocaine sometime in their lives, and at least one in four were current users of a major drug. More than one-half (57%) were under the influence of drugs (15%) or alcohol (29%) or both (12%) when they committed their offense.

More than four out of 10 of the female and 13 percent of male inmates reported that they had been sexually or physically abused at one time in their life prior to their current incarceration. Finally, four out of 10 jail inmates had grown up in a single-parent household; an additional 11 percent lived in a household without either parent (Beck, 1991:2).

The marital status of jail inmates, despite their age (60% were at least age 25), was diverse. About one-fifth were married and one-quarter were either divorced or separated. More than one-half had never been married.

Educational levels were very low. More than one-half of the jail inmates had failed to complete high school. The percentage who were veterans declined to 16 percent (compared to 21% in 1983), possibly reflecting the decreased percentage of Vietnam-era veterans among jail inmates, as well as the effects of aging on crime patterns.

About two-thirds of the 1989 jail inmates were employed at the time of their arrest, even though 1 in 10 were working part-time. More than 1 in 3 were unemployed. Approximately 81 percent of the inmates had been out of jail or prison for at least one year prior to their arrest, but one in four of those earned less than $3,000 during that year. For those not incarcerated for less than one year, more than one-fifth earned less than $300 per month in income (Beck, 1995:3).

Women in jail were even more disadvantaged. First, the number of women in local jails increased to 60,100 in 1997, up 230 percent from 1983! Almost one-half of this increase resulted from drug violations (Snell, 1992:1). More than 1 in 3 females were in jail in 1989 for drug offenses, an increase from 1 in 8 in 1983. Among convicted female inmates, nearly two-fifths reported that they had committed their first offense under the influence of drugs, and one-quarter reported the drug to be cocaine or crack. Approximately four in 10 used drugs daily. About one in four convicted women reported that they committed their current offense in order to get money to buy drugs, yet only 1 in 5 reported they were under the influence of alcohol at the time of their offense. Some two-thirds of the jailed women had children under the age of 18, and most of these were with either grandparents or father.

Box 3.7

## War on Drugs

The war on drugs is a crime prevention strategy that rose in the mid-1980s from politicians espousing a conservative ideology. It is predicated on protecting the moral fiber of the nation, and particularly American youth, by drying up drugs at their sources, interdicting drug traffic, increasing penalties for drug trafficking and possession, selectively incapacitating drug sellers and users, initiating asset seizure and forfeiture, and taking the profit out of drugs.

Three important effects have been the increase in the number of men and women sent to jail and prisons for drug possession and law violations, massive jail (and prison) construction efforts, and increasing incarceration rates of minorities, particularly African-Americans and Hispanics dealing crack, the drug of choice among the minorities who are sometimes called the *underclass*. Notably absent are reductions in drug availability, large amounts of interdicted drugs, a drop in drug use across the nation, and increased numbers of prevention and abuser treatment programs.

Billions of dollars have been spent in an effort that has led to widespread violence and corruption, and has undermined government throughout the world without achieving its goals of reducing crime and drug abuse. The war has incarcerated disproportionate numbers of minorities (particularly African-Americans) and spawned both a destructive fear of and hostility toward police. The drug war has resulted in America now incarcerating more people per capita that any major Western country in the world, including South Africa. Even the police are put into a situation they cannot win.

There were more drug arrests in 1996 for drug offenses (including drug trafficking) than for *all* murder and nonnegligent manslaughter, rapes, robberies, aggravated assaults, and burglaries, motor vehicle theft, and arson! Since 1984, both the number of adult arrests for drug law violation and the probability of incarceration for those arrests have tripled. More than 60 percent of federal and 22 percent of state prisoners, and 31 percent of the jail inmates, are incarcerated for drug law violations.

The National Center on Addiction and Substance Abuse (1998) reported regular drug use in the month preceding arrest by 76 percent of state prison inmates, 69 percent of federal prison inmates, and 70 percent of jail inmates. From 1980 to 1995, drug law violators accounted for 30 percent of the increase in state prison populations, 68 percent of the federal prisoner population, and 41 percent of the jail inmate popula-

Box 3.7—*continued*

tions. Only 13 percent of the prison populations received drug treatment in 1996.

If present trends continue, the nation will need to increase jail staff by another 60,000 and prison correctional officers by 65,000 over the next five years, as well as building 100,000 jail beds and 325,000 prison cells.

A recent study of mental illness among female jail inmates (Teplin, Abrams & McClelland, 1997) in Chicago found that 80 percent of their representative sample met the criteria for at least one lifetime psychiatric disorder, most commonly drug and alcohol abuse or dependence, and post-traumatic stress disorder. Rates for all psychiatric disorders (particularly depression) were significantly higher than those of the general population. Investigators concluded that few female jail inmates received in-facility treatment, primarily because inmate needs by far exceeded current resources.

Approximately 40 percent of the female inmates grew up in a single-parent household, and an additional 17 percent lived in a household without either parent. Close to one-third of all women in jail had a parent or guardian who abused drugs or alcohol, and 4 in 10 reported that another family member (usually a brother or sister) had been incarcerated.

The drug-crime link among jail inmates is further explained when asking why inmates committed crimes. Of those using drugs in the month before committing the offense for which they were convicted, more than 1 in 4 said they had committed the crime to get money for drugs; more than 1 in 3 robbers and burglars admitted to this motivation in their current offense.[8] Drug use in general (including the use of such major drugs as cocaine, crack, heroin, PCP, LSD, and methadone) was most prevalent among inmates reporting that their parents had abused drugs. These jail inmates also reported substantially younger ages of first drug use. Finally, more than 70 percent of those in jail for a drug charge had served at least one prior sentence of probation or incarceration, frequently for a drug offense. About 1 in 2 convicted jail inmates who were daily users of a major drug in the month before arrest for their current offense had participated in a drug treatment program.[9]

This brief examination of jails and jail inmates suggests a group of offenders with high needs who were frequently victimized as they were growing up. Broken homes, sexual and physical abuse, minority status, parental/guardian abuse of alcohol or drugs, and early onset of drug use characterize a large portion of the jail population. This segment of offenders is not generally likely to receive effective treatment for their major, underlying problems. After the average stay of less than seven months, most will be returned to the community to continue their efforts to break their drug dependencies and, for the most part, these efforts will fail without intensive assistance. Some will fail despite intensive intervention.

## Sentencing Options

Sentencing judges make decisions to incarcerate offenders in jails or prisons, or to place them on probation with its numerous ancillary programs ("in" or "out" decisions). If the decision is to retain the offender in the community under probation or its supplemental programs, the judge increasingly has a large number of supervision and control strategies from which to pick, known as *intermediate sanctions* (Gowdy, 1993; Lynch & Sabol, 1997). Obviously, selected programs are not capriciously imposed but are designed to achieve a correctional objective, such as community protection, reintegration, treatment and rehabilitation, and so on. Court officers, usually probation officers, oversee the implementation of and client compliance with court conditions. If the client appears to be failing at technical conditions (such as no alcohol, or attending Alcoholics Anonymous meetings), the judge may tighten the requirements by imposing mandatory daily attendance. In extreme cases, a request for medical intervention (Antebus for alcohol abusers, or methadone maintenance for heroin addicts) may be issued. If these conditions are not met, or are insufficient for the particular client, the court may further increase the conditions of control by imposing weekend confinement in jail or house arrest. If these are insufficient, the judge may order a short term of jail incarceration to be followed by additional control programs, such as house arrest with electronic monitoring. In extreme cases, the court may order a breath analyzer installed in the offender's residence, as well as in-

---

**Box 3.8**

### Intermediate Sanctions

Intermediate sanctions, ranging from severity from day fines to shock incarceration ("boot camps"), are interventions that fill the sentencing gap between jails and prisons, at one extreme, and probation at the other. Lengthy incarceration periods may be inappropriate for some offenders; for others, probation may be too inconsequential and may not provide the degree of public supervision necessary to ensure public safety. By expanding sentencing options, intermediate sanctions enable the criminal (and juvenile) justice system to tailor punishment more closely to the nature of the crime and the criminal, to maximize offender compliance with court objectives, and hold offenders strictly accountable for their actions.

tensive supervision. Tightening the conditions and restraints is commonly called "tourniquet sentencing." We turn now to a brief description of major ancillary control ("probation-plus") programs, and then explore two scenarios that typify tourniquet sentencing as a process.

## Intermediate Controls

Intermediate punishments are explored in greater detail in Chapter 12. For heuristic purposes, the major intermediate control programs are listed with brief descriptions. The reader will notice that each increases the level of "penal harm" and crime control. For many offenders, such preventive control is necessary for them to begin to deal with their rehabilitation needs.[10] The discussion moves from least to most punishment approaches.

### Fines

The penalties courts impose on offenders require specific sums of money be paid, cash payments of a dollar amount. Judges may impose fines based on a fixed schedule published and used throughout the court, or on an individual basis.

### Day Fines

The general concept of day fines is simple: determining the amount of punishment to be administered to an offender is separated from a consideration of how much money that offender must pay (McDonald, Greene & Worzella, 1995; Tonry, 1997). Judges determine how much punishment an offender deserves; this is then denominated into some unit other than money. The *punishment* units are then translated into monetary units based on how much money the offender makes per day.

In practice, the day fine approach consists of a simple two-step process. First, the court uses a "benchmark" or "unit scale" to sentence the offender to a certain number of day fine units (such as 20, 60, or 120 units) according to the gravity of the offense and without regard to income. To guide the court's choices, benchmarks are typically developed by a planning unit of judges, prosecutors, and defense counselors familiar with the disposition patterns of a court. ("This crime is worth 40 units of punishment.") The value of each unit is then set at a percentage of the offender's daily income, and the total fine amount is determined by simple multiplication. Fine amounts are higher for affluent offenders under the day fine system.[11] Day fines are in widespread use in Europe.

## Community Service

Community service or work orders represent court-ordered non-paid work for a specified number of hours that offenders must perform, usually for some charitable organization or public service such as volunteer hospital orderly, doing interstate and street cleaning, performing maintenance or repair of public housing, or providing service to indigent groups (Anderson, 1998). Professionals such as dentists or doctors can be ordered to provide free services for the indigent, welfare recipients, or probationers.

An interesting version of community service began in 1986 when the Minnesota Department of Corrections established a Sentencing to Service jail program in collaboration with the Minnesota Department of Natural Resources. Certain nondangerous offenders ages 18-25 were sentenced to work on county- and state-operated work teams to beautify forests and recreational trails, and assist in natural resource management work projects. It was found that participating offenders strongly preferred to be working rather than sitting idle in jail cells, and that they tended to work hard and developed a sense of ownership and pride in their assigned work projects. Supervising officers found the workers easier to manage at night, since they were tired and tended to go to bed early. Staff also reported prisoner attitudes improved and conflicts were rare. Initial analysis in 1991 indicated the project is cost-effective and has a potential to return $5 in services for every $1 of expenditure, that some 86 percent successfully completed their programs, and that more than $1 million was saved using this work program, including the approximately 21,000 jail days saved (McLagan, 1992). This program is jail-based community work; most community work orders allow the offender to remain in their homes and report for community service on designated days (such as weekends).

## Restitution

This court-ordered condition of probation requires the offender to repair the financial, emotional, or physical damage done (a reparative sentence) by making financial payment of money to the victim or, alternatively, to a fund to provide services to victims. Restitution programs may also be ordered in the absence of a sentence to probation. Restitution is usually a cash payment by the offender to the victim of an amount considered to offset the loss incurred by the victim (medical expenses, insurance deductibles, time lost from work due to victim's injuries, etc.). Payments may be made in installments in most jurisdictions and sometimes services directly or indirectly benefiting the victim may be substituted for cash payments.

## Day Reporting Centers

Certain persons on pretrial release, probation or parole may be required to appear at a day reporting center on a frequent and regular basis in order to participate in services or activities provided by the center or other community agencies. Failure to report or participate is a violation that could cause revocation of pretrial release, conditional release, or community supervision.

Reports on the national scene indicate that offenders in these programs must not only physically report to their centers but also provide a schedule of planned activities, and participate in designated activities (McDevitt, Domino & Baum, 1997). In addition, offenders must call the centers by phone throughout the day; they can also expect random phone checks by center staff during the day and at home after curfew. In some programs, offenders must contact their respective centers an average of 60 times weekly and, in all but one, take random drug tests (Gowdy, 1993:5).

## Probation

Probation is the conditional freedom granted by a judicial officer to an alleged offender, or adjudicated adult or juvenile, as long as the person meets certain conditions of behavior. Unsupervised probation resembles *sursis*, or "no action by the court as long as there are no further incidents" but, generally, probation includes the requirement to report to a designated person or agency over a period of time.

## Intensive Supervised Probation

These are court-ordered programs of community supervision by probation officers working with very small caseloads to provide intensive supervision. Such programs are usually linked to impromptu (and scheduled) drug and alcohol testing, curfews, restitution, volunteer sponsors, probation fees, and other punitive intrusions (Anderson, 1998). Sometimes (as in Georgia) two officers will share a caseload of 25 probationers.

## House Arrest

House or home arrest is a more intensive program that requires the offender to remain secluded in his or her own home except for work, grocery shopping, community service, or other minor exceptions. Drug and alcohol use or possession in the residence is a violation of house arrest and can result in increased intervention.[12] Frequently, house arrest may be intensified by requiring the offender to wear an electronic device that signals a computer that the offender is at home, or by requiring electronic breath analyzer testing to determine any alcohol use.

## Electronic Monitoring

This program requires an offender to wear a bracelet or anklet that will emit an electronic signal, confirming via telephone contact that the offender is located at a specific, required location. Strict curfews are required and restrictions on visitors may be imposed. Some monitoring systems have the capability of emitting signals that can be picked up by

Photo 3.3
Electronic Monitoring Devices. Photograph by Beth Sanders.

cellular listing posts within a community, to signal to a computer monitor that the offender is moving within the community (not at home). Frequently, the electronic monitoring system is buttressed by scheduled probation officer visits, drug testing, and other surveillance options. Electronic monitoring is used with both pretrial releasees and for convicted offenders on community release. In either case, clients pay for at least part (if not all) of the cost of leasing the monitoring equipment.

Home detention with electronic monitoring is successful with at least 73 percent of participants. Clients most likely to complete home detention successfully lived with a spouse or opposite-gender roommate. Of the 27 percent failures, 13 percent were technical violators and 14 percent were absconders. Those more likely to abscond were sentenced eventually to jail or prison (Gowdy, 1993:6) Three important findings of a national survey of telemonitoring of offenders were:

- The average monitoring term was 79 days. The longer the period of monitoring, the higher the odds for success.

- There were no significant differences in successful terminations among probationers, offenders on parole, or those in community corrections. Successful termination rates varied from 74 percent to 86 percent, and one site reported a 97 percent successful completion rate in 1992.

- Rule violations resulted in incarceration, brief confinement in residential facilities, intensified reporting requirements, stricter curfews, or additional community service (Gowdy, 1993:6-7).

Electronic monitoring is widely used and also highly effective in England (Mortimer & May, 1997).

## Community Residential Centers

Formerly known as halfway houses, community residential centers are nonconfining residential facilities for adjudicated adults or juveniles, or those subject to criminal or juvenile proceedings. They are intended as an alternative to jail incarceration for persons in danger of failing on probation or who need a period of readjustment. Increasingly, correctional and victim services (such as services and treatment for battered women, drunk drivers, mentally ill sex offenders, etc.) are offered in these 24-hour facilities.

## Split Sentences

Frequently, sentencing judges impose both a short term of incarceration in the local jail, to be followed by a term of probation. For example, the split sentence (jail plus probation) is the most frequently imposed sentence for felony convictions in California (Lundgren, 1998).

A variation on "jail plus" is weekend confinement. To lessen the negative impacts of short-term incarceration and allow offenders to retain current employment, as well as keep their dependents off welfare rolls, some jurisdictions permit sentences to be served during non-working weekends. Such weekend confinement allows offenders to check into the jail facility on Friday after work and to leave Sunday morning, sometimes early enough to attend religious services. A "weekender" serving his or her sentence over a number of months would generally be credited with three days of confinement per weekend. Some jurisdictions have so many "weekenders" that specific buildings are set aside for their short-term detention. In larger jurisdictions in which sufficient numbers of offenders work on weekends but not every day during the ordinary work week, those buildings operate all week but at reduced staffing levels.

A third version of split-sentencing jail incarceration revolves around shock incarceration programs that require offenders to serve a short jail term in a quasi-military program similar to military boot camps or basic training. At least 10 local jurisdictions, 30 states, and the Federal Bureau of Prisons have boot camp programs, and another 8 programs have been designated solely for juveniles.

The philosophy behind jail boot camps is simple. Offenders who can be turned around before they graduate to major felony crime can improve their own opportunities and futures. Once in the camp, the participant is subjected to a regimen of military drills and discipline, physical exercise, specialized education and training, and counseling and treatment for alcohol abuse and drug addiction.

Boot camp advocates indicate that the population at greatest risk of graduating to prison is the young male adult who is poorly educated, comes from a low-income background, frequently is a minority member, has little if any work skills, has not had proper role modeling or discipline, and comes from an environment where drug use and trafficking are common.

He or she[13] generally will be returned to community corrections in a few months, having experienced discipline and direction as persons who still have a chance of being diverted from a life of crime and incarceration. Most boot camps focus on chemical abuse and addiction, specific needs of this high-risk group of offenders (Allen & Simonsen, 1998; Grossi, 1997).

These newer community corrections programs are still in the implementation and early evaluation stages. Some (house arrest and restitution, for example) clearly have effective and proven outcomes. Others (particularly boot camp programs) are under initial evaluation, primarily because of their recency but also because differing components of the justice system expect different outcomes. Law enforcement, for example, tends to expect selective incapacitation and punishment as primary outcomes; jail administrators expect rehabilitation and control of participants; clients expect more acceptance and strength to avoid further temptation; probation officers expect more mature adults willing to assume adult employment and living roles. It is, of course, unrealistic to expect a short-term boot camp program to achieve all these objectives and overcome in three months (or so) the years of earlier experiences, poverty, marginal existence, gang influence, and neighborhood structures. The evidence on their effectiveness is still not amassed. But what is evident is that, taken together, intermediate sanctions provide sentencing judges, probation, jail and community agencies with a number of options for addressing crime in the local community among local residents. Making the options best fit the needs remains the challenge for newer practitioners and scholars in the future.

## The Jail as the Center of Corrections

It should be obvious that the jail serves many functions and differing clients in local communities: holding, processing, punishing, and assisting offenders to become law-abiding citizens. We clarify the role of the jail with two scenarios.

## Exhibitionism

Thomas was arrested in Florida for exhibitionism, publicly displaying his genitals before under-aged females. The judge fined him $500, sentenced him to 30 days in jail and 100 hours of community service, and imposed a three-year period of probation, a special condition of which was group therapy for exhibitionism. These conditions were suggested to the court by the presentence investigator. Thomas' underlying problems were the inability to relate to the opposite sex (although Thomas was married at the time of the offense) and alcohol abuse. Clinical evidence offered later was poor self-concept and sense of inadequacy.

Thomas was allowed to serve the 30-day jail sentence as a weekender, completing the sentence in less than four months. Serving his time under these circumstances allowed him to keep his job as an accountant with a larger firm. Thomas perceived group counseling as irrelevant and boring, and had sketchy attendance at mandatory meetings. He also resumed weekend binge drinking when his jail sentence was completed.

Noting the technical violations of Thomas' behavior, his probation officer initiated his arrest and Thomas reappeared before the sentencing judge on a charge of technical probation violations. The sentencing judge tightened the conditions of probation (tourniquet sentencing), imposing mandatory daily attendance at an Alcoholics Anonymous group, and house arrest with electronic monitoring. The judge also told Thomas that he would be sentenced to 6 months in jail if future violations were noted. Thomas conformed his behavior to expectations and served the remainder of the 3 years probation under house arrest and electronic monitoring.

## Drunk Driving

Drunk driving remains one of the most perplexing problems facing this nation. Drunk drivers kill and injure many thousands of people each year, more than the number of homicides in America annually. Billions of dollars of property are damaged, not to mention damage suffered by the families of victims of drunk driving, insurance costs, lost productivity, jail overcrowding, etc. (Langworthy & Latessa, 1993). Proposed solutions range from getting drinking people to their homes without their driving (holding bartenders liable for "overdosing" patrons, taxicab company programs, designated drivers, etc.) to the "ultimate penalty in urban America:" loss of vehicle (denying driving privileges, breath analyzer ignition locks, vehicle seizure, loss of driving privileges in perpetuity, etc.). Social programs are underway that redefine the use of alcohol and its mystique, as well as treat the pathological drinker. Finally, social protest groups such as Mothers Against Drunk Drivers and Students Against Drunk Drivers, as well as law enforcement groups, are striving to decrease pathological behavior by increased penalties (longer sentences, mandatory incarceration, presumptive guilt at increasingly lower blood-alcohol levels, etc.).

Programs that treat drunk drivers fall into one of three categories: (1) long-term treatment designed to cure pathological drinking, (2) programs that prevent the drunk driver (DUI) from driving, and (3) educational programs intended to correct poor judgment. Outcome studies suggest that individualized treatment over an extended time period generate promising results for *chronic drunk drivers* (Langworthy & Latessa, 1993:266; Deyoung, 1997).

Talbert House, Inc. designed the Turning Point Program for Hamilton County, Ohio to provide housing and treatment for multiple-DUI offenders in a chemical dependency treatment program. Clients have multiple DUI offenses, serve at least 30 days in county jail, and then enter a 28-day residence program. The actual program is a comprehensive treatment regimen and includes individualized alcohol treatment, family counseling, and educational services. Clients are not allowed to leave during their 28-day treatment phase. Each client receives assessment and diagnosis to develop and implement an individual treatment plan. The program includes daily educational presentations (e.g., learning about the impact of chemical dependency, how to establish a recovery program), individual and group counseling, promotion of personal change, family treatment, and Alcoholics Anonymous (or Narcotics Anonymous) meetings.

WIZARD OF ID                    BY BRANT PARKER & JOHNNY HART

By permission of Johnny Hart and Creators Syndicate, Inc.

If the client graduates from the in-patient treatment plan, the court is asked for a modified sentence that would include two years of probation, and mandatory after-care including a minimum of 26 group meetings and at least three AA/NA meetings per week. Graduates who did not observe minimum requirements were returned to court and jail. Significant lower recidivism results emerged: ". . . persons who were treated . . . performed better (less likely to be charged with new alcohol-related offense) after their release from custody than those in the comparison group" (Langworthy & Latessa, 1993:273). Particularly significant gains were made by those clients with three or more DUIs.

This scenario depicts the interface of jail inmates with treatment services specifically designed to address their problem behavior, as well as indicates how the jail can be the center of corrections in the community.

## Summary

The jail serves many functions in the criminal justice system, processing millions of offenders each year and containing criminal behavior of those detained and under treatment. The workload of jail personnel, as well as the number of correctional officers and budgets, have grown over the last decade and will continue to grow in the future.

To meet the demands of number of offenders, detention and treatment, jail administrators and county lawmakers have begun to expand the number of alternatives and program options for handling offenders and the mentally ill. New programs include weekend confinement, work release centers, electronic monitoring, boot camps, and day reporting centers. Treatment and counseling services, particularly in the sex offender, chemical abuse, and mental health areas have expanded.

Much remains to be done. New bed spaces will be needed; containment strategies for drug and gang-related crime are sorely needed. Classification methods will require refinement (Wells & Brennan, 1995; Gendreau, Shilton & Clark, 1995); information systems should be improved. New programs and tactics will emerge. As long as the jail contains so many of the failures of society, the jail will need to serve as well as protect.

## *Review Questions*

1.  Compare male and female jail inmates.

2.  Why has the jail population increased so dramatically over the last decade?

3.  What alternatives to incarceration alleviated jail crowding?

4.  Explain the higher jail incarceration rate for African Americans.

5.  What impact has the War on Drugs had on jail populations?

6.  How is the jail the center of community corrections?

## Key Terms

boot camps

collateral punishments

community work orders

day reporting centers

electronic monitoring

fine

intensive supervised probation

intermediate sanctions

jail

plea bargaining

prison

restitution

split sentence

tourniquet sentencing

War on Drugs

## Recommended Readings

Anderson, D.C. (1998). *Sensible Justice: Alternatives to Prison*. New York, NY: New press.

Clear, T. (1994). *Harm in American Penology: Offenders, Victims, and Their Communities*. Albany, NY: State University of New York Press.

Zupan, L.L. (1991). *Jails: Reform and the New Generation Philosophy*. Cincinnati, OH: Anderson Publishing Co.

## Notes

[1]   See M. Gordon and D. Glaser (1991). "The Use and Effects of Financial Penalties in Municipal Courts." *Criminology*, 29:651-676; W. Spelman (1995). "The Severity of Intermediate Sanctions," *Journal of Research in Crime and Delinquency*, 32:107-135. For the federal system, see United States Government Accounting Office (1994). *Sentencing: Intermediate Sanctions in the Federal Criminal Justice System*. Washington, DC: U.S. Government Printing Office.

[2]   We are speaking of the ratio of inmates compared to their proportion in the general population. See M. Mauer (1990). *Young Black Men and the Criminal Justice System*. Washington, DC: Sentencing Project, National Institute of Justice. See also M. Mauer (1995). "The International Use of Incarceration." *The Prison Journal*, 75:113-123; and M. Mauer (1997). *Americans Behind Bars: U.S. and International Use of Incarceration*. Washington, DC: The Sentencing Project, 1997.

[3]   Hewitt, C., A. Shorter, and M. Godfrey (1994). *Race and Incarceration in San Francisco: Two Years Later*. San Francisco: Center on Juvenile and Criminal Justice; M. Tonry (1994a). "Editorial: Racial Disparities in Courts and Prisons." *Criminal Behavior and Mental Health*, 4:158-162; M. Tonry (1994b). "Racial Politics, Racial Disparities, and the War on Crime." *Crime & Delinquency*, 40:475-494; and T.M. Arvanites (1997). "The Direct and Indirect Effects of Race and Poverty on County Incarceration Rates." *Journal of Crime and Justice*, 20(2):87-102.

[4]    The "material" witness detained in jails to ensure presence at trial is a seldom-studied actor in the justice system; hence, little is known about this category of jail inmate.

[5]    McEwen, T. (1995) *National Assessment Program: 1994 Survey Results*. Washington, DC: U.S. Department of Justice, p. 7.

[6]    Rice, M., T. Chaplain, and G. Harris (1994). "Empathy for the Victim and Sexual Arousal Among Rapists and Nonrapists." *Journal of Interpersonal Violence*, 9:435-449; R. Watson and L. Stermac (1994). "Cognitive Group Counseling for Sexual Offenders." *International Journal of Offender Therapy and Comparative Criminology*, 38:259-270; J. Gonsiorek, W. Bera, and D. LeTourneau (1994). *Male Sexual Abuse: A Trilogy of Intervention Strategies*. Thousand Oaks, CA: Sage; and L. Teplin, K.M. Abram, and G.M. McClelland (1997). "Mentally Disordered Women in Jail: Who Receives Services?" *American Journal of Public Health,* 87(4):604-609.

[7]    Federal pretrial arrestees were about as likely to receive pretrial release but exhibit far less misconduct on release. Almost 9 in 10 have no known misconduct and only 3 percent were rearrested for a new offense. B. Reaves and J. Perez (1994). *Pretrial Release of Federal Felony Defendants*. Washington, DC: U.S. Department of Justice.

[8]    For a recent summary of drug data, see Bureau of Justice Statistics (1995). *Drugs and Crime Facts, 1994*. Washington, DC: U.S. Department of Justice.

[9]    Harlow, C.W. (1991). *Drugs and Jail Inmates: 1989*. Washington, DC: U.S. Department of Justice, p. 9. For an excellent approach to treatment of drug abuse, see J. Inciardi, F. Tims, and B. Fletcher (eds.) (1993). *Innovative Approaches in the Treatment of Drug Abuse: Program Models and Strategies*. Westport, CT: Greenwood Press.

[10]    Clear, T. (1994). *Harm in American Penology: Offenders, Victims, and their Communities*. Albany, NY: State University of New York Press. Clear argues that more effective strategies of crime reduction would be rehabilitating the offender, community crime prevention programs, and situational prevention. See also P. Langan (1994). "Between Prison and Probation: Intermediate Sanctions." *Science*, 262:791-793.

[11]    Winterfield, L. and S. Hillsman (1993). *The Staten Island Day-Fine Project*. Washington, DC: U.S. Department of Justice. For the federal system, see United States General Accounting Office (1993) *National Fine Center*. Washington, DC: U.S. General Accounting Office.

[12]    Technical violators among those on intermediate sanctions can be a large component of the offenders. See F. Taxman (1995). "Intermediate Sanctions: Dealing with Technical Violators." *Corrections Today*, 57(1):46-57.

[13]    One boot camp for female misdemeanants can be found in the Santa Clara (San Jose), California Office of the County Sheriff.

## References

Allen, H. and C. Simonsen (1998). *Corrections in America*. Englewood Cliffs, NJ: Prentice-Hall.

Anderson, D.C. (1998). *Sensible Justice: Alternatives to Prison*. New York, NY: New Press.

Arvanites, T.M. (1997). "The Direct and Indirect Effects of Race and Poverty on County Incarceration Rates." *Journal of Crime and Justice*, 20(2):87-102.

Beck, A. (1995). *Profile of Jail Inmates: 1989*. Washington, DC: U.S. Department of Justice.

Bridges, G.S. (1997). *A Study on Racial and Ethnic Disparities in Superior Court Bail and Pretrial Detention Practices in Washington*. Olympia, WA: Washington State Minority and Justice Commission.

Bureau of Justice Statistics (1995). *Drugs and Crime Facts, 1994*. Washington, DC: U.S. Department of Justice.

Clear, T. (1994). *Harm in American Penology: Offenders, Victims, and Their Communities*. Albany, NY: State University of New York Press.

Deyoung, D.J. (1997). "An Evaluation of the Effectiveness of Alcohol Treatment, Driver License Actions, and Jail Terms in Reducing Drunk Driving Recidivism in California." *Addiction*, 92(8):989-997.

Gendreau, P., M.K. Shilton, and P.M. Clark (1995). "Intermediate Sanctions: Making the Right Move." *Corrections Today*, 57(1):26-65.

Gilliard, D.K. and A.J. Beck (1998). *Prison and Jail Inmates at Midyear 1997*. Washington, DC: U. S. Bureau of Justice Statistics.

Gonsiorek, J., W. Bera, and D. LeTourneau (1994). *Male Sexual Abuse: A Trilogy of Intervention Strategies*. Thousand Oaks, CA: Sage.

Gordon, M. and D. Glaser (1991). "The Use and Effects of Financial Penalties in Municipal Courts." *Criminology*, 29:651-676.

Gowdy, V. (1993). *Intermediate Sanctions*. Washington, DC: U.S. Department of Justice.

Green, J.A. (1996). *The Maricopa County FARE Probation Experiment: An Effort to Introduce a Means-Based Monetary Sanction as a Targeted Felony-Level Intermediate Sanction*. New York, NY: Vera Institute of Justice.

Grossi, E.L., ed. (1997). "Prison and Jail Boot Camps," *Journal of Contemporary Criminal Justice*, 13(2):93-205.

Harlow, C.W. (1991). *Drugs and Jail Inmates: 1989*. Washington, DC: U.S. Department of Justice.

Hewitt, C., A. Shorter, and M. Godfrey (1994). *Race and Incarceration in San Francisco: Two Years Later*. San Francisco, CA: Center on Juvenile and Criminal Justice.

Holmes, M.D., H.M. Holsch, and H.C. Daudistel (1996). "Ethnicity, Legal Resources, and Felony Dispositions in Two Southwestern Jurisdictions." *Justice Quarterly*, 13(1):11-30.

Inciardi, J., F. Tims, and B. Fletcher (eds.) (1993). *Innovative Approaches in the Treatment of Drug Abuse: Program Models and Strategies*. Westport, CT: Greenwood Press.

Innes, C. (1990). *Population Density of Local Jails: 1988*. Washington, DC: U.S. Department of Justice.

Klein, A. (1980). *Earn It: The Story So Far*. Waltham, MA: Brandeis University.

Langan, P. (1994). "Between Prison and Probation: Intermediate Sanctions." *Science*, 262:791-793.

Langan, P. and J. M. Brown (1997). *Felony Sentences in State Courts, 1994*. Washington, DC: U.S. Bureau of Justice Statistics.

Langworthy, R. and E. Latessa (1993). "Treatment of Chronic Drunk Drivers: The Turning Point Project." *Journal of Criminal Justice*, 21:265-276.

Lundgren, D. (1998). *Crime and Delinquency in California, 1997: Advance Release*. Sacramento, CA: Department of Justice.

Lynch, J.P. and W.J. Sabol (1997). *Did Getting Tough on Crime Pay?* Washington, DC: Urban Institute.

McDevitt, J., M. Domino, and K. Baum (1997). *Metropolitan Day Reporting Center: An Evaluation*. Boston, MA: Center for Criminal Justice Policy Research, Northeastern University.

McDonald, D., J. Greene, and C. Worzella (1995). *Day Fines in American Courts*. Washington, DC: U.S. Department of Justice.

McEwen, T. (1995). *National Assessment Program: 1994 Survey Results*. Washington, DC: U.S. Department of Justice.

McLagan, J. (1992). "Sentencing to Service." *American Jails*, 5(6):28-32.

Mauer, M. (1995). "The International Use of Incarceration." *The Prison Journal*, 75:113-123.

Mauer, M. (1990). "Young Black Men and the Criminal Justice System." Washington, DC: Sentencing Project, National Institute of Justice.

Mortimer, E. and C. May (1997). *Electronic Monitoring in Practice*. London, UK: U.K. Home Office.

National Center on Addiction and Substance Abuse (1998). *Behind the Bars: Substance Abuse and America's Prison Population*. New York, NY: Columbia University.

Perkins, C., S. Stephan, and A. Beck (1995). *Jail and Jail Inmates 1993-94*. Washington, DC: U.S. Department of Justice.

Reaves, B. and J. Perez (1994). *Pretrial Release of Federal Felony Defendants: 1992*. Washington, DC: U.S. Department of Justice.

Rice, M., T. Chaplain, and G. Harris (1994). "Empathy for the Victim and Sexual Arousal Among Rapists and Nonrapists." *Journal of Interpersonal Violence*, 9:435-449.

Snell, T. (1992). *Women in Jail: 1989*. Washington, DC: U.S. Department of Justice.

Spelman, W. (1995). "The Severity of Intermediate Sanctions." *Journal of Research in Crime & Delinquency*, 32:107-135.

Stephan, J. (1990). *Census of Local Jails: 1988*. Washington, DC: U.S. Department of Justice.

Taxman, F. (1995). "Intermediate Sanctions: Dealing with Technical Violators." *Corrections Today*, 57(1):46-57.

Teplin, L.A., K.M. Abrams, and G.M. McClelland (1996). "Prevalence of Psychiatric Disorders Among Incarcerated Women." *Archives of General Psychiatry,* 53(2):505-512.

Tonry, M. (1997). *Intermediate Sanctions in Sentencing Guidelines.* Washington, DC: U.S. National Institute of Justice.

Tonry, M. (1994a). "Editorial: Racial Disparities in Courts and Prisons." *Criminal Behavior and Mental Health,* 4:158-162.

Tonry, M. (1994b). "Racial Politics, Racial Disparities, and the War on Crime." *Crime & Delinquency,* 40:475-494.

United States Government Accounting Office (1994). *Sentencing: Intermediate Sanctions in the Federal Criminal Justice System.* Washington, DC: U.S. Government Accounting Office.

United States Government Accounting Office (1993). *National Fine Center.* Washington, DC: U.S. Government Accounting Office.

Watson, R. and L. Stermac (1994). "Cognitive Group Counseling for Sexual Offenders." *International Journal of Offender Therapy and Comparative Criminology,* 38:259-270.

Wells, D. and T. Brennan (1995). "Jail Classification: Improving Link to Intermediate Sanctions." *Corrections Today,* 57(1):58-63.

Winterfield, L. and S. Hillsman (1993). *The Staten Island Day-Fine Project.* Washington, DC: U.S. Department of Justice.

Wray, H. (1994). *Restitution, Fines, and Forfeiture.* Washington, DC: U.S. Government Accounting Office.

Zupan, L.L. (1991). *Jails: Reform and the New Generation Philosophy.* Cincinnati, OH: Anderson Publishing Co.

# The Prison Institution

## 4

> He who opens a school door, closes a prison.
>
> —Victor Hugo

## Purposes of Incarceration

Organized society has dealt with criminal offenders in a variety of ways. In earlier ages, when victims were responsible for dealing with their perpetrators, their motivation was *revenge* or *compensation* for loss. Later, when the state began to intervene in the name of the victim, *retribution* became another motivation, the most common form being the death penalty (Allen & Simonsen, 1998:55).

---

**Box 4.1**

### Retribution

Philosophically, this term generally means "getting even" with the perpetrator. Social revenge suggests that individuals cannot exact punishment, but that the state will do so in their name.

Retribution assumes that offenders willfully chose to commit the evil acts, are responsible for their own behavior, are likely to commit similar acts again, and should receive the punishment they so richly deserve. The *just deserts* movement in sentencing reflects the retribution philosophy. For many, it provides a justifiable rationale for the death penalty.

---

The Church appears to have been the first social institution to confine offenders as a form of *punishment* (Johnston, 1973:3), building differing types of institutions to achieve desired objectives. Monastic prisons were designed for long-term incarceration; during the Inquisition, underground cells were utilized for lifetime incarceration of witches, heretics, sorcerers, and other malefactors who sought the more sanguine church-law trials and were subsequently spared the death penalty. The Church also built workhouses and training schools to institutionalize deviants, juvenile offenders, and the unemployed while correcting them.

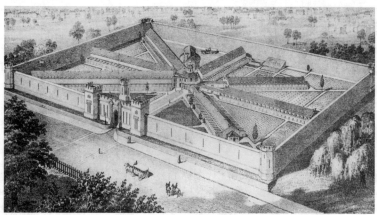

Photo 4.1
American prison: Eastern State Penitentiary. Federal Bureau of Prisons.

The penitentiary was basically an American invention, developed by Philadelphia Quakers who introduced yet another objective of prisons: *reformation.* Underlying the reform movement is the assumption of the perfectibility of human kind who, as rational beings, would reflect on the error of their ways and turn away ("repent") from their former criminal actions. Individual reform is an example of deterrence. The humanitarian emphasis of reformation (Rothman, 1971:62) has made this objective a resilient purpose of incarceration.

Box 4.2

### Prison

A state or federal confinement facility having custodial authority over adults sentenced to confinement for more than one year.

Box 4.3

### Deterrent

Punishment or program designed to discourage commission of a criminal act.

Other objectives have emerged recently, as the populations of American prisons have soared (see Figure 4.1). The newly identified objectives are *incapacitation* and its corollary, *selective incapacitation*. This theory asserts that there is no hope for the individual as far as rehabilitation is concerned ("once a thug, always a thug") and that the only solution is to temporarily isolate, remove, or cripple such persons in some way (Greenwood, 1983; Loeber & Snyder, 1990; Zimring & Hawkins, 1995).

Figure 4.1
**Prisoners in America: 1980-2000 (in thousands)**

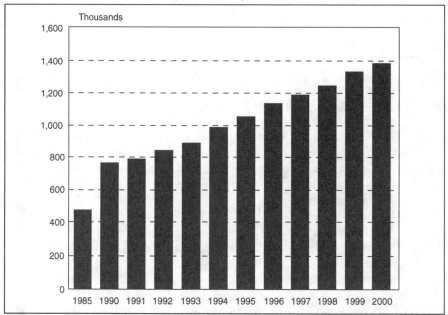

Source: D.K. Gilliard and A.J. Beck (1998). *Prison and Jail Inmates at Midyear 1997*, p. 2. Washington, DC: U.S. Bureau of Justice Statistics. 1997-2000 data estimated.

This theory of imprisonment is sometimes referred to as the "theory of disablement," a euphemism for banishment, death, or mutilation. Currently, the thrust in America is toward using imprisonment for purposes of deterrence and punishment. One result is increased rates of imprisonment in America (see Figure 4.2).

Figure 4.2
**Imprisonment Rates: 1990-1997 (Per 100,000 Residents)**

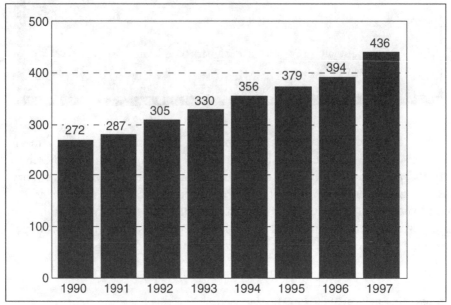

Source: C.J. Mumola and A.J. Beck (1997). *Prisoners in 1996,* p. 1. Washington, DC: U.S. Bureau of Justice Statistics. Data for 1997 estimated.

---

Box 4.4

### Selective Incapacitation

This doctrine of isolating the offender, or causing "social disablement," proposes adopting a policy of incarcerating those whose criminal behavior is so damaging or probable that nothing short of isolation will prevent recidivism. This "nothing-else-works" approach would require correctly identifying those offenders who should receive long-term imprisonment and diverting others into community corrections. Thus we would be able to make maximum use of prison cells, a scarce resource, to protect society from the depredations of such dangerous and repetitive offenders. The "third strike and out" is a continuation of this theme.[1]

Current correctional technology does not permit our correctly identifying those who require incapacitation. Rather, the evidence is that we would probably incarcerate numerous noneligibles (a "false positive" problem) and release to lesser control many of those eligible (a "false negative" problem). Whatever benefits might accrue to this sentencing doctrine have thus far eluded corrections.

In summary, the major purposes of confinement are punishment, deterrence, reformation, incapacitation and, more recently, reintegration into the community. Correctional staff at some prisons favor reformation; others stress punishment and incapacitation. Yet evidence of efforts to achieve all correctional objectives can be found in every institution. Fortunately, some of the latter have been designed to achieve clear-cut objectives and ease the transition to the community. We begin with types of prisons.

By permission of Johnny Hart and Creators Syndicate, Inc.

## Types of Prisons

Existing correctional facilities can be heuristically divided into five security levels (Camp & Camp, 1997:58-59): Maximum (6%), High/Close (7%), Medium (24%), Minimum (21%), Intake (2%) and Community Facilities (20%). Original prisons stressed security above all else, and our earliest prisons were consistently maximum security facilities. Designed for punishment, they were typically surrounded by a wall from 30 to 50 feet high and many feet thick, equipped with towers with armed guards ordered to prevent escape and riot, illuminated by searchlights after dark, and sometimes encircled by electrified wire to further prevent escape.[2] Such monolithic structures were isolated in the countryside, far from cities, and were fortresses that kept offenders in and civilians in the dark about prison operations and procedures. The maximum security walled prison of the nineteenth century was described by Johnston (1973:12):

> In 1825 prisoners arrived in leg shackles from Auburn at a site on the Hudson River, later to be known as Sing Sing, to construct a new prison. The plan was similar: tiny cells back to back on five tiers, with stairways on either end in the center of the very long range. Cell doors were iron with grillework in

the upper portion, and they fastened with gang locks. Cells received small amounts of light coming through a tiny window located nine feet away in the outer wall opposite the cell door. These cells were extremely damp, dark, and poorly ventilated and, like those at Auburn, contained no toilet facilities except buckets. The East House, which alone contained 1,000 cells and continued in use until 1943, was to become the prototype for most American prison cellhouse construction, rather than the earlier Auburn prison from which the system took its name.

For the remainder of the nineteenth century, in this country, the characteristic layout for nearly all prisons was to consist of a central building housing offices, mess hall, and chapel, usually flanked and joined on each side by a multi-tiered cellblock. In the prison enclosure formed by the wall would be shops, hospitals and a power plant . . . . [By 1913,] nearly all the states had built maximum security prisons and little prison building would occur again until the late 1930s.

These great Gothic-style prisons—fearsome and forbidding atmospheres designed to emphasize rejection, guilt, doubt, intimidation, infe-

riority, apathy, and despair— were built in the belief that this kind of setting would contribute to the restoration of prisoners. This belief was discredited by the turn of the twentieth century, when penologists began to seek effective treatment programs. Unfortunately, American corrections is stuck with some 60 of these mega-facilities, built in the last century with economy, isolation, and security in mind. The treatment programs that were adopted in these monstrosities had to be adapted to conform to the architecture. It should have been the other way around: physical plants should have been built to fit prison programs. American corrections is still dominated by the approaches of a century and a half ago, the outmoded archi-

Photo 4.2
Abandoned wing of the Hamilton County Jail. Photograph by Beth Sanders.

tecture of most maximum security facilities, that held more than 117,477 male and female inmates in 1997, some 11 percent of the almost 1.2 million prison inmates in 1997 (Camp & Camp, 1997; Gilliard & Beck, 1998:1).

---

Box 4.5

### Maximum Security Prison

A facility designed, built, and managed so as to minimize escape, disturbances, and violence, while maximizing control over the inmate population. Custody and security are the focal concerns in a maximum security prison. The latest trend is the development of the "super" max prison. These facilities are designed to hold the "worst of the worst" inmates.

---

Photo 4.3
Riverbend Maximum Security Institution. Indiana Department of Corrections.

Classification of prisoners and construction of special treatment programs designed to address the identified treatment needs of individual offenders arose in the 1930s, primarily in conjunction with the creation of the U.S. Bureau of Prisons, the federal prison system. If offenders had identifiable and differing needs that could be addressed in the corrections process in prisons, there had to be some system for designing rehabilitation prisons and classifying inmates by their security needs as well as treatment needs. Both management classification and offender classification contributed to the creation of new and more effective prison units: the medium and minimum security prisons.

> ### Box 4.6
>
> ### Medium and Minimum Security
>
> Medium security institutions are prisons designed, built, and operated to prevent escape, disturbances, and violence. However, they have fewer restrictions on the movement and activities of prison inmates than would be found in maximum security prisons. Usually, there are more treatment options in the medium security institutions. Minimum security facilities allow maximum inmate movement, freedom, and self-determination, while still following methods to avoid escape, violence, and disturbances. Most inmates prefer minimum security facilities. These prisons also allow more opportunity for inmates to move into the community for treatment programs, work release, furloughs, training programs, and graduated integration.

A broad range of innovative correctional programs were launched in the twentieth century, primarily as alternatives to maximum security prisons (see Box 4.6). Most of the construction of the last decade has been for medium security prisons, which now house about one-fourth of the prison inmates. Medium security facilities are usually smaller, have less intrusive security systems and are less overwhelming psychologically, and have less routinized regimen. External fences, sophisticated electronic and television monitoring devices, and creative use of glass and plastic (Foster, 1987:92) improve the atmosphere of the medium security units, while permitting security over inmates.

Other innovations include the creation of the so-called campus design, including attractive residence areas with single rooms (not cells) and dormitories for inmates. The new medium security prisons represent the best of current strategies for correctional facilities in the future.

Minimum security and open institutions are two other major correctional institutions used today, and were designed to serve the needs of rural farm areas and public works. Such facilities range from plantation-style farms to forestry and road camps, and are preferable to the traditional maximum secu-

Photo 4.4
Drug abuse has contributed to prison and jail crowding. Photograph by Beth Sanders.

Box 4.7

### New Prisons: 1989-1996*

The prison construction boom has accelerated since 1989. At least 410 new prison facilities were added (excluding renovations, expansions and extensions of existing prisons, as well as prison camps, community work release units, facilities for offenders convicted of driving under the influence of alcohol and drugs, etc.). Prisons in 1997 by security level (Camp & Camp, 1997:59):

| | |
|---|---|
| Maximum security institutions: | 6% |
| Close security institutions: | 7 |
| Medium security institutions: | 24 |
| Minimum security institutions: | 21 |
| Community: | 20 |
| Multilevel: | 20 |
| Other: | 2 |
| Total: | 100% |

* Excludes 657,759 beds under construction stages (1997).

rity institutions for inmates whose escape and disturbance potential are low. One drawback to such prison facilities is that most inmates placed in them should instead be diverted to community-based corrections for correctional treatment programs. In addition, the fortress-style prisons of yesteryear should be abandoned; only a few institutions are needed to house the estimated 15 to 20 percent of the incarcerated felons (Allen & Simonsen, 1998:231) who need this level of protection and surveillance. It certainly can be argued that we incarcerate too high a proportion of convicted offenders, and this has resulted in prison overcrowding. Of course, the more conservative view is that we do not use prisons enough, and that those we incarcerate are not kept a sufficient length of time.

## Inmate Population Growth

From 1962 until 1969, the American prison population decreased to 187,000, but since that time has escalated to an estimated 1,159,763 inmates in federal and state prisons (Gilliard & Beck, 1998). Another 60,000 sentenced offenders are being held in jails, awaiting transfer to prison when space becomes available, a scarce commodity even though the nation has rapidly expanded its prison stock (see Figure 4.3). We incarcerate 436 persons per 100,000 population (Camp & Camp, 1995:9). Male age and race specific incarceration rates are found in Figure 4.4; female race incarceration rates are shown in Figure 4.5.

Figure 4.3
**New Prisons Opened Each Year: 1990-1996**

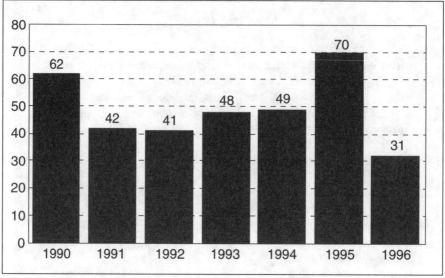

Source: C. Camp and G. Camp (1997). *The 1997 Corrections Yearbook,* p. 64. South Salem, NY: Criminal Justice Institute.

Figure 4.4
**Estimated Incarceration Rates by Race/Ethnicity
Per 100,000 Male Residents: 1985, 1990, 1995**

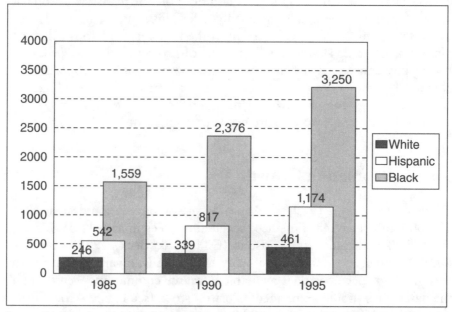

Source: C.J. Mumola and A.J. Beck (1997). *Prisoners in 1996,* p. 9. Washington, DC: U.S. Bureau of Justice Statistics.

The consequent overcrowding of the system means that inmates are double-bunked in cells built for one occupant; packed into make-shift dormitories; and bunked in basements, corridors, renovated hospital facilities, tents, trailers, warehouses, gymnasiums, and other activity areas of American prisons. We incarcerate more citizens than any other major Western country, exceeded only by the Soviet Union.[3] If the present trends continue, there will be more than 1.4 million prison inmates by 2000! The domestic growth in number of female prisoners is shown in Figure 4.5.

Figure 4.5
**Number of Sentenced Female Prisoners By Group (Select Years)**

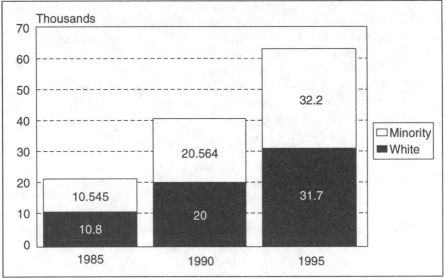

Source: C.J. Mumola and A.J. Beck (1997). *Prisoners in 1996*, p.9. Washington, DC: U.S. Bureau of Justice Statistics.

It is not easy to explain the rapid increase in prison population in the nation, but part of it can be traced to a hardening of public attitudes toward crime (Skovron, Scott & Cullen, 1988) and the War on Crime. The latter has had significant impacts on the number of offenders in prisons, particularly in the sharp increase of drug law violators. This attitude in turn produces more and more "get tough" policies in the criminal justice system, one evidence of which is the return of the chain gang (Allen & Abril, 1997).

The courts are under pressure to deter crime by giving longer sentences, and so they are using probation proportionately less and are themselves pressing for better legislation in the area of probation. Legislators respond by passing more mandatory-sentencing laws, further restricting the judges' options to use probation or reduce the minimum time for parole consideration. Evidently, the policymakers are not aware of the evidence that an increased use of imprisonment is positively correlated with higher—rather than lower—levels of crime. Public safety is not enhanced by greater use of imprisonment (Biles, 1979; Irwin & Austin, 1994; Kuhn, 1998). The public has been badly misinformed about the crime deterrent strength of imprisonment (Zimmerman, Alstyne & Dunn, 1988; Gottfredson & Gottfredson, 1992). Finally, the number of inmates killed in prison has increased sharply from 1990 (Figure 4.6).

---

**Box 4.8**

### Effects of Prison Overcrowding

Despite the fact that the nation has opened or expanded more than 343 prisons in less than 7 years and there are another 657,000 beds under construction, the average prison space available for inmates has dropped by more than 10 percent. Prison crowding is getting worse.

What effect does prison crowding have? One is that fewer programs are available for inmates on a relative basis; another is that recreational opportunities are less. But it is in the health and safety areas that the impact is felt most. For example, the number of prisoners killed per year has substantially increased since 1990, but the rate per 100,000 inmates has remained basically unchanged, as is shown in Figure 4.6 (Camp & Camp, 1997).

The rates of death, suicide, homicides, inmate assaults, and disturbances increase as prison population density increases (population density is measured by square feet of floor space per inmate). This finding holds true regardless of whether a prisoner is confined in maximum, medium, or minimum security.

The incidence of colds, infectious diseases, drug resistant tuberculosis, sexually communicable diseases, psychological disturbances, and psychiatric crises also is related to overcrowding. There were major outbreaks of tuberculosis in American prisons from 1990-94, evidence of overcrowding. The more overcrowded the institution, the higher the incidence of medical problems, and incidences of vandalism. Overcrowded maximum security prisons appear to be the most likely to have the worst impact on prisoner and officer health and safety. Correctional administrators and elected officials must plan to reduce the negative impacts of imprisonment on offenders.

Source: A. Newton (1980). "The Effects of Imprisonment." *Criminal Justice Abstracts*, 12/1:134-151; and M. Silberman (1995). *A World of Violence*. Belmont, CA: Wadsworth.

Box 4.9

## War on Drugs

The War on Drugs is a crime prevention strategy that rose in the late 1980s from politicians espousing a conservative ideology. It is predicated on protecting the moral fiber of the nation, and particularly American youth, by drying up drugs at their sources, interdicting drug traffic, increasing penalties for drug trafficking and possession, selectively incapacitating drug sellers and users, initiating asset forfeiture, and taking the profit out of drugs.

Three important effects have been the increase in the number of women (and men) sent to prison for drug possession and law violations, massive prison construction efforts, and increasing incarceration rates of minorities, particularly Hispanics and [Africans-Americans] dealing crack, the drug of choice among minorities who are sometimes called the *underclass*. Notably absent is a reduction in drug availability, large amounts of interdicted drugs, a drop in drug use across the nation, or increased numbers of prevention and abuser treatment programs.

Billions of dollars have been spent in an effort that has led to widespread violence and corruption and has undermined governments throughout the world without achieving its goals of reducing crime and drug abuse. The war has incarcerated disproportionate numbers of minorities (particularly blacks) and spawned both a destructive fear of and hostility to police. The drug war hysteria has blocked medical research of drugs to prevent pain and has blocked the development of programs to provide sterile needles and help prevent the spread of AIDS. It has resulted in America now incarcerating more people per capita than any other country in the world except Russia. Even the police are put in a position in which they cannot win.

There were almost as many drug arrests in 1996 for drug offenses (including drug trafficking) than for *all* crimes of violence (murders and nonnegligent manslaughters, rapes, robberies, and aggravated assault). Since 1980, the number of incarcerations of adults for drug law violations increased more than *1,000* percent. More than one-half of the increase of prisoners admitted to state prisons can be accounted for by drug offenses. Almost two-thirds of federal prisoners and one-half of state prisoners are incarcerated for drug law violations.

If present trends continue, the nation will need to increase correctional prison staff by almost 50,000 officers in the next five years, as well as build about 1,700 new prison beds per week nationwide.

Source: M. Tonry (1994). "Racial Politics, Racial Disparities, and the War on Crime." *Crime & Delinquency*, 40(4):475-494; H. Allen (1995). "The American Dream and Crime in the Twenty-First Century." *Justice Quarterly*, 12(3):1101-1119; and D. Gilliard and A. Beck (1998). *Prison and Jail Inmates Midyear 1997*, p. 2. Washington, DC: U.S. Bureau of Justice Statistics.

Figure 4.6
**Prisoners Killed While in U.S. Prisons: 1990-1996**

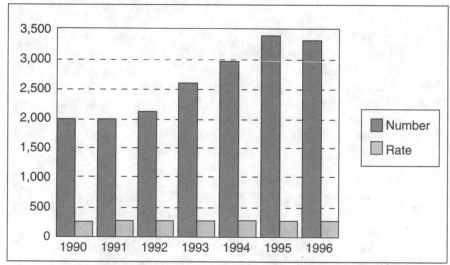

Sources: D.K. Gilliard and A.J. Beck (1998). *Prison and Jail Inmates at Midyear 1997*, p.27. Washington, DC: U.S. Bureau of Justice Statistics, p. 2. C. Camp and G. Camp (1997). *The Corrections Yearbook*, South Salem, NY: Criminal Justice Institute.

Another factor contributing to the increase of the prison population as a whole is the increase in the general population in the 20- to 30-year-old age group. This is seen as the population at risk, as crime is a young person's activity. This group is a direct result of the "baby boom" following World War II, which successively clogged the grade school and high school systems of America in the 1950s and 1960s, and has now affected yet another area: urban crime. Most offenders are afforded rehabilitation-focused treatments at the early onset of criminal behavior; their "high prison commitment years" lag by about a decade.

---

Box 4.10

### Recidivism of Prisoners

Of the 596,400 persons released from prisons in 42 states in 1996, some 33% recidivated. A recidivism study of Wisconsin parolees found almost two-thirds were rearrested and nearly half were reconvicted within three years. Parolees frequently need extensive help in their efforts to reintegrate.

Source: C. Camp and G. Camp (1997). *The Corrections Yearbook*. South Salem, NY: Criminal Justice Institute; Minnesota Office of the Legislative Auditor (1997). *Recidivism of Adult Felons*. St. Paul, MN: MOLA.

Box 4.11

### Drug-Abusing Women Offenders

In recent years, women, particularly women arrested on drug charges, have constituted the fastest growing segment within the criminal justice system. From 1982 to 1991, the number of women arrested for drug offenses increased almost 90 percent. The increasing rate of arrest has been matched by corresponding increases in the number of women under community supervision, in jails, and in prisons. At least 40 percent of the women in prison need drug treatment; in some institutions, the figure may be as high as 80 percent.

Most drug-abusing women offenders started abusing drugs and alcohol at an early age, and many used drugs, particularly cocaine, on a daily basis prior to incarceration. In one study, almost one-half the women inmates reported they had used drugs and/or alcohol at the time of their offense. Almost 1 in 4 have previously been in some community drug/alcohol treatment program, most likely of short duration and limited intensity.

More institutional treatment programs are available than in the past, but have not reduced the gap between those who need and those who receive drug treatment. Many programs do not assess the multiple problems of the drug-abusing inmate and do not address those problems with suitable services. Treatment provided by prison programs generally are of short duration and limited in intensity.

Source: J. Wellisch et al. (1994) *Drug-Abusing Women Offenders: Results of a National Survey*. Washington, DC: U.S. Department of Justice.

These are the incoming prison inmates that are now clogging the nation's prisons. In addition, younger persons (ages 16-24) in the current generation have one of the highest unemployment rates and, in a time of general unemployment, will continue to commit crime disproportionate to their population size. As Allen (1989:7) noted:

> The incarceration rate per 100,000 population increased [322] percent, from 135 in 1978 to [436] in [1997]. Yet the nation's population has only grown by some [26] percent since 1975. Nor has the cause been crime rates, which have remained relatively constant over the last 10 years, a timeframe in which the prison population has grown [over 200 percent]. Existing evidence indicates that elected officials have changed sentencing legislation; this has resulted in a higher proportion of offenders being imprisoned for longer terms of incarceration. There

is evidence that some parole supervision authorities are eager to return parolees to prison settings. Thus America's imprisonment binge is fed not by a swelling of the population or by sharply increased crime rates; it is a function of political decisionmaking that has resulted in even higher and more disproportionate imprisonment of minorities. Prison population information can be found in Table [4.1]. Updated by author.

## The Bricks and Mortar Solution

The public demands more prisons in America. There were 1,515 state and federal adult prisons in America in 1997—1,042 more state and federal adult prisons than there were in 1984. There appears to be no end to the building boom in sight. State corrections budgets in 1997 exceeded $31.5 billion, up 130 percent over 1989. The annual cost of imprisonment of inmates in 1997 ranged from $7,350 in Alabama to $46,920 for one institution in Alaska;[5] in 1996, the average national cost for one year of incarceration was $19,800. Camp and Camp (1997) report average new prison construction costs as between $40,600/bed space. The "bricks and mortar" solution to prison overcrowding is expensive. The average daily costs of imprisonment (1988-97) can be found in Figure 4.7.

Figure 4.7
**Average Daily Cost Per Inmate**

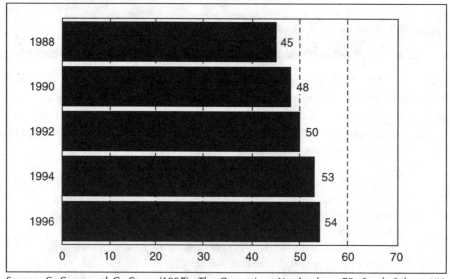

Source: C. Camp and G. Camp (1997). *The Corrections Yearbook,* p. 75. South Salem, NY: Criminal Justice Institute.

Table 4.1
**Prisoners under the Jurisdiction of State or Federal Correctional Authorities, June 30 and December 31, 1996, and June 30, 1997**

| Region and jurisdiction | Total 6/30/97 | Total 12/31/96 | Total 6/30/96 | Percent change from— 6/30/96 to 6/30/97 | Percent change from— 12/31/96 to 6/30/97 | Prison incarceration rate, 6/30/97[a] |
|---|---|---|---|---|---|---|
| **U.S. total** | 1,218,256 | 1,180,520 | 1,163,058 | 4.7% | 3.2% | 436 |
| Federal | 110,160 | 105,544 | 103,722 | 6.2% | 4.4% | 35 |
| State | 1,108,096 | 1,074,976 | 1,059,336 | 4.6 | 3.1 | 401 |
| **Northeast** | 167,706 | 166,417 | 165,224 | 1.5 | .8 | 310 |
| Connecticut[b] | 15,608 | 15,007 | 14,975 | 4.2 | 4.0 | 322 |
| Maine | 1,559 | 1,426 | 1,468 | 6.2 | 9.3 | 118 |
| Massachusetts[c] | 11,907 | 11,796 | 11,996 | −.7 | .9 | 301 |
| New Hampshire | 2,153 | 2,062 | 2,050 | 5.0 | 4.4 | 183 |
| New Jersey | 27,766 | 27,490 | 27,753 | 0 | 1.0 | 346 |
| New York | 69,530 | 69,709 | 68,721 | 1.2 | −.3 | 383 |
| Pennsylvania | 34,703 | 34,537 | 33,939 | 2.3 | .5 | 288 |
| Rhode Island[b] | 3,293 | 3,271 | 3,226 | 2.1 | .7 | 203 |
| Vermont[b, d] | 1,187 | 1,119 | 1,096 | 8.3 | 6.1 | 152 |
| **Midwest** | 212,779 | 204,653 | 199,414 | 6.7% | 4.0% | 339 |
| Illinois[d, e] | 40,425 | 38,852 | 38,373 | 5.3 | 4.0 | 340 |
| Indiana | 17,549 | 16,960 | 16,582 | 5.8 | 3.5 | 296 |
| Iowa[d] | 6,636 | 6,342 | 6,176 | 7.4 | 4.6 | 232 |
| Kansas | 7,790 | 7,756 | 7,462 | 4.4 | .4 | 302 |
| Michigan[d] | 43,784 | 42,349 | 41,884 | 4.5 | 3.4 | 454 |
| Minnesota | 5,348 | 5,158 | 5,040 | 6.1 | 3.7 | 114 |
| Missouri | 23,687 | 22,003 | 20,541 | 15.3 | 7.7 | 438 |
| Nebraska | 3,431 | 3,287 | 3,248 | 5.6 | 4.4 | 201 |
| North Dakota | 739 | 722 | 640 | 15.5 | 2.4 | 104 |
| Ohio[e] | 47,248 | 46,174 | 45,314 | 4.3 | 2.3 | 422 |
| South Dakota | 2,177 | 2,059 | 2,049 | 6.2 | 5.7 | 296 |
| Wisconsin | 13,965 | 12,991 | 12,105 | 15.4 | 7.5 | 256 |
| **South** | 484,391 | 469,252 | 467,901 | 3.5% | 3.2% | 495 |
| Alabama | 22,076 | 21,760 | 21,495 | 2.7 | 1.5 | 499 |
| Arkansas | 9,539 | 9,407 | 9,430 | 1.2 | 1.4 | 368 |
| Delaware[b] | 5,313 | 5,110 | 5,148 | 3.2 | 4.0 | 442 |
| Dist. of Columbia[b] | 9,739 | 9,376 | 9,763 | −.2 | 3.9 | 1,373 |
| Florida[d] | 64,713 | 63,763 | 64,333 | .6 | 1.5 | 443 |
| Georgia[d] | 36,329 | 35,139 | 34,808 | 4.4 | 3.4 | 476 |
| Kentucky | 13,858 | 12,910 | 12,652 | 9.5 | 7.3 | 355 |
| Louisiana | 28,382 | 26,779 | 26,673 | 6.4 | 6.0 | 651 |
| Maryland | 22,415 | 22,050 | 22,118 | 1.3 | 1.7 | 417 |
| Mississippi | 14,639 | 13,859 | 13,785 | 6.2 | 5.6 | 505 |
| North Carolina | 32,334 | 30,647 | 30,671 | 5.4 | 5.5 | 385 |
| Oklahoma[e] | 19,931 | 19,593 | 19,134 | 4.2 | 1.7 | 599 |
| South Carolina | 21,021 | 20,446 | 20,814 | 1.0 | 2.8 | 542 |
| Tennessee | 15,827 | 15,626 | 15,634 | 1.2 | 1.3 | 294 |
| Texas | 136,599 | 132,383 | 129,937 | 5.1 | 3.2 | 677 |
| Virginia | 28,673 | 27,655 | 28,827 | −.5 | 3.7 | 412 |
| West Virginia | 3,003 | 2,749 | 2,679 | 12.1 | 9.2 | 163 |
| **West** | 243,220 | 234,654 | 226,797 | 7.2% | 3.7% | 397 |
| Alaska[b] | 3,741 | 3,716 | 3,583 | 4.4 | .7 | 396 |
| Arizona[d] | 23,176 | 22,493 | 22,143 | 4.7 | 3.0 | 484 |
| California | 153,010 | 146,049 | 141,535 | 8.1 | 4.8 | 466 |
| Colorado[e] | 12,840 | 12,438 | 11,742 | 9.4 | 3.2 | 330 |
| Hawaii[b] | 4,491 | 4,011 | 3,693 | 21.6 | 12.0 | 258 |
| Idaho | 4,105 | 3,832 | 3,623 | 13.3 | 7.1 | 339 |
| Montana | 2,295 | 2,293 | 2,162 | 6.2 | .1 | 258 |
| Nevada | 8,617 | 8,439 | 8,064 | 6.9 | 2.1 | 505 |
| New Mexico | 4,692 | 4,724 | 4,528 | 3.6 | −.7 | 258 |
| Oregon[f] | 7,899 | 8,661 | 8,564 | – | – | 226 |
| Utah | 4,154 | 3,972 | 3,643 | 14.0 | 4.6 | 202 |
| Washington | 12,732 | 12,527 | 12,059 | 5.6 | 1.6 | 226 |
| Wyoming | 1,468 | 1,499 | 1,458 | .7 | −2.1 | 304 |

—Not calculated.
[a]The number of prisoners with a sentence of more than 1 year per 100,000 in the resident population.
[b]Prison and jails form an integrated system. Data include total jail and prison population.
[c]The incarceration rate includes an estimated 7,500 inmates sentenced to more than 1 year but held in local jails.
[d]Population figures are based on custody counts.
[e]Population counts for inmates "sentenced to more than 1 year" include an undetermined number of inmates "sentenced to one year or less."
[f]Since January 1, 1997, Oregon no longer has jurisdictional responsibility for inmates with sentences of less than 1 year.

Source: D.K. Gilliard and A.J. Beck (1998). *Prison and Jail Inmates at Midyear 1997,* p. 3. Washington, DC: U.S. Bureau of Justice Statistics.

Four major points need to be stressed. First, the further the offender is carried into the prison-parole cycle, the more expensive corrections will become. Second, the "bricks and mortar" solution tends to mortgage the future of corrections, taxpayers and our children, saddling the nation with institutions that are not likely to be emptied in the near future.[6] Third, there is considerable evidence that the longer the offender remains in prison, the more likely that incapacitation will result in recidivism (Behan, 1987; Greenfield, 1985; Beck & Shipley, 1987). Finally, the prison construction boom is harmful to corrections since prisons are seldom closed. Prisons built on correctional strategies of 50 years ago are ill-designed to contribute to modern correctional treatments and contemporary standards of integration.

## Alternatives to Prison Overcrowding

There are basically three correctional options for reducing prison populations and overcrowding, and you have already encountered two: the so-called "bricks and mortar" building program and the "front-end" of prison avoidance programming (Chapter 3). The latter includes restitution programs, intensive supervised probation, house arrest, electronic monitoring, shock probation, shock incarceration, intermittent punishment, fines, and other innovative programs of intermediate punishments.[7] In later chapters, we deal with parole and its functions. We now turn to the third correctional option: the "back-end" solutions.

### Back-End Solutions

Back-end solutions to prison overcrowding refers to strategies, programs, and innovations designed to reduce prison populations after offenders arrive in prisons. They can be either "early-out" or "extended limits" options. The former accelerates the speed at which parole boards determine parole eligibility, as well as legislatively enacted prison population caps that would mandate release of certain categories of inmates. The latter allows inmates to leave the institution for approved programs of leave: participation in educational, work, or training programs only available in community settings. We begin with the "early-out" programs and a brief exploration of parole.

Box 4.12

## Solutions to Prison Overcrowding

Due to the prison population crisis across the nation, many states are exploring strategies to reduce the overcrowding. The three basic strategies can be described as "bricks and mortar," "front-end solutions," and "back-end solutions."

"Bricks and mortar" refers to attempts to construct or renovate existing facilities to expand available beds. Even though there are literally billions of dollars in construction, renovation, expansion, and retrofitting going on, no one with any understanding of the comprehensive nature of the problem holds out much hope that the nation can build enough prisons to accommodate the influx of inmates.

"Front-end solutions" refers to those alternative sentences and intermediate punishments that would control offenders without penal commitment. These would include, among others, probation, house arrest, deferred prosecution, electronic monitoring, shock probation, intensive supervised probation, intermittent punishment, jail incarceration, "boot camp" shock incarceration, and other programs.

"Back-end solutions" refers to ways used to reduce prison populations after the offender arrives in prison. These can be viewed as "early-out" or "extended limits" options: parole, shock parole, emergency release (usually court-ordered), expanded good-time credits that count against the minimum sentence, work and educational furlough, prerelease to halfway houses (used extensively by the U.S. Bureau of Prisons, the Federal prison system), and other programs.

Box 4.13

## Parole

Release of an inmate from confinement prior to expiration of sentence on condition of good behavior.

## Early-Out Credits

Many states have indeterminate sentencing structures that require the sentencing judge to pronounce a minimum and maximum term of incarceration (such as "from one to five years of imprisonment"). The actual sentence time that would be served would depend on parole board action after the minimum sentence period (varying from state to state). To determine the minimum period, many parole boards grant time credits[8] against the inmate's minimum sentence. When the minimum term was served (actual time in prison plus earned time credits), inmates would become eligible for release onto parole. Parole boards could credit the offender with time spent in jails prior to conviction, "earned-time" credits for hard work and good behavior in prison, and achievement credits for completion of an academic or training program, or participating in medical programs. California, for example, awarded good time in 1997 at the rate of "1 for 2": one day of reduction for every two days served.

Many parole boards have increased the amount of credits and rates at which credits may be earned. These increases have been designed to assist other correctional components in coping with prison overcrowding (Duffee, 1989:424). Accelerating the rate of earned credits shortens the average length of time inmates are incarcerated and would thus lower the prison population.[9]

---

Box 4.14

### Parole Board

Any correctional person, authority, or board that has the authority to release on parole those adults (or juveniles) committed to confinement facilities, to set conditions for behavior, to revoke from parole, and to discharge from parole. Parole boards also recommend executive clemency through pardon or sentence commutation (shortening), as well as set policies for supervision of parolees.

---

A second example of "early out credits" can be seen in prison population capacity "caps" established by state legislatures (such as in Iowa and Minnesota). In Iowa, the "cap" legislation of 1981 empowered the director of the department of corrections to declare a "state of emergency" in corrections, mandating the Iowa parole board to review for possible release all inmates within three months of the end of their sentence. If, after 90 days, the parole board had not released sufficient number of offenders ("reduced the population below the cap"), then the sentences of all property offenders would be reduced by 90 days, effectively leading to the immediate discharge of all property offenders who are within 90 days of expiration of sentence (Wright, 1984). It is obvious that Iowa decided to resolve its prison crisis by using community corrections (see Table 4.2). More offenders have been placed on probation and released on parole, enabling the Iowa department of corrections to maintain prison populations close to the cap, and using scarce prison beds to incarcerate more dangerous inmates who have offended against the person (rapists, murderers, assaulters, etc.). Those jurisdictions that do not construct early-out escape mechanisms can anticipate possible court-ordered emergency release designed to reduce prison populations and maintain the quality of life and services in the face of the Eighth Amendment's prohibition against cruel and unusual punishment.[15]

Table 4.2
**Correctional Supervision of Convicted Offenders in Iowa (1984-1996)**

| | Correctional Status | | |
|---|---|---|---|
| **Year** | **Probation** | **Prison** | **Parole** |
| 1984 | 11,924 | 2,836 | 1,662 |
| 1987 | 12,745 | 2,863 | 1,966 |
| 1990 | 13,895 | 3,967 | 2,111 |
| 1993 | 14,505 | 5,092 | 1,887 |
| 1996 | 15,384 | 5,906 | 2,200 |

Sources: U.S. Department of Justice (various years). *Probation and Parole.* Washington, DC: U.S. Bureau of Justice Statistics; *Prisoners.* Washington, DC: U.S. Bureau of Justice Statistics; J.M. Brown and A.J. Beck (1998). "Nation's Probation and Parole Population Reached Almost 3.9 Million Last Year." Washington, DC: U.S. Bureau of Justice Statistics.

## Extended Limits Options

One of the earliest programs for releasing prisoners before their full sentences expired was the result of the first *work release* legislation. The work release philosophy, which permits inmates to work on their own in the free community, is an extension of the limits of confinement to include placement in the community, conditional upon good behavior. Technically, work release participants remain inmates and, if misbehaving, can quickly be returned to confinement.

The first work-release statute was passed in Wisconsin in 1913, allowing misdemeanants to continue to work at their jobs while serving short sentences in jail. North Carolina adapted the statute to apply to felony offenders in 1957 (under limited conditions). Maryland, Michigan, and Ohio quickly followed suit.

Figure 4.8
**Inmates Participating in Early Release Programs: 1996**

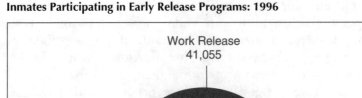

Source: C. Camp and G. Camp (1997). *The Corrections Yearbook*, p. 103. South Salem, NY: Criminal Justice Institute.

In 1965, Congress passed the Federal Prisoner Rehabilitation Act, which provided for work release, furloughs, and community treatment centers for federal prisoners. This act, an excerpt of which follows, served as a model for many states (Academy of Political and Social Sciences, 1969:85):

> The Attorney General may extend the limits of the place of confinement of a prisoner as to whom there is reasonable cause to believe that he will honor this trust, by authorizing him, under prescribed conditions, to:
>
> 1.  visit a specifically designated place or places for a period not to exceed 30 days and return to the same or another institution or facility. An extension of limits may be granted only to permit a visit to a dying relative, attendance at the funeral of a relative, the obtaining of medical services not

otherwise available, the contacting of prospective employers, or for any other compelling reason consistent with the public interest; or

2. work at paid employment or participate in a training program in the community on a voluntary basis while continuing as a prisoner of the institution or facility to which he is committed . . . .

The willful failure of a prisoner to remain within the extended limits of confinement, or to return within the time prescribed, to an institution or facility, designated by the Attorney General, shall be deemed an escapee from the custody of the Attorney General.

Institutional work release is not intended to be a substitute for parole, but it can be a valuable tool for the correctional administrator and the parole officer who must eventually supervise an individual who participated in work release. The work-release program is not really an alternative to incarceration. Rather, it is a chance for offenders to test their work skills and personal control over their behavior in the community. And it allows them to spend the major part of the day away from the institution, sometimes at day attendance centers. Because offenders must still return to the institution or designated alternative facility, the work-release program may be considered only a partial alternative.

Work release can ease the transition into the community, allowing inmates to gain training or employment prior to parole. Both work skill and experience may also be attained. The income derived from work can be used to keep dependents off welfare rolls or augment public assistance families may be receiving. Inmates can reimburse victims; pay restitution, fines, and court costs; and build a nest-egg for their time of release (Duffee, 1989:412). States may also receive payments for room and board, as well as transportation costs, while inmates are on work release. Further, communities become aware of inmates' ability to maintain jobs without creating problems for themselves or others. Association with stable co-workers in the free world may function to provide support and guidance releasees could not find inside the walls (Shichor & Allen, 1977:7-17). The "ability to do a good day's work" both heightens the offender's self-esteem and commands respect from others (Schilling, Ivanof and El-Bassel, 1997). Many Scandinavian prisons have factories attached to them, allowing inmates to work at real-world jobs for equal pay to that earned by the outside worker. Formally established work-release programs have been developed in Australia, the Republic of Korea, Thailand, Malaysia, Singapore, and Sri Lanka. (Mohammed et al., 1987).

Another form of partial release is the furlough. Both work release and the furlough extend the limits of confinement to include unsupervised absences from the institution. Education has been another reason for extensive use of the furlough; it often allows the inmate to attend high school, community college or university programs during the school day, with the inmate returning to a correctional institution on non-school time. Shichor and Allen (1977) noted increasing use of both work release and educational furlough. In 1997, 32 correctional agencies provided work release for some 41,055 inmates.

Major roadblocks to further development of such extension of confinement programs include a few highly publicized and sensational failures, escapes, and low net savings by inmates due to court-ordered and correctionally imposed charges. There are many evaluations of such programs but most are poorly designed. The most exacting and scientifically sound was a true field experiment conducted which found that work release participants, compared to control subjects, did not differ on self-esteem, legal self-concept, perceived opportunity for legitimate activity, or achievement motivation (Waldo, Chiricos & Dobrin, 1973). Katz and Decker (1982) reviewed more than 40 work release evaluations and concluded that the benefits inherent with such programs may have accrued more to the organizations than the inmates. Schichor and Allen conclude that, without effective evaluation, the effectiveness and value of study-release will remain speculation, although Turner and Petersilia (1996) found overall positive results in their study of work release in Washington.

## Boot Camp Programs

Boot camps, frequently called shock incarceration, require offenders to serve a short term in prison in a quasi-military program similar to military boot camps or basic training. Currently 34 states, at least 17 local jurisdictions, and the Federal Bureau of Prisons have boot camp programs. Another 60 programs have been designated solely for juveniles. Both the number of and participants in boot camps have steadily increased since 1988. Some boot camps are only for probationers or parolees, but most handle offenders committed to prison.

Most state programs target young first offenders convicted of violent offenses who are serving their first prison terms and who are usually drug abusers. Participating offenders typically serve 90-120 days in the heavily regimented programs, although the average term is 107 days. In a one-year period, at least 40,000 inmates complete the program (MacKenzie, 1973; MacKenzie & Piquero, 1994; Camp & Camp, 1997).

Figure 4.9
**Boot Camps and Number of Agencies Operating Them (1996)**

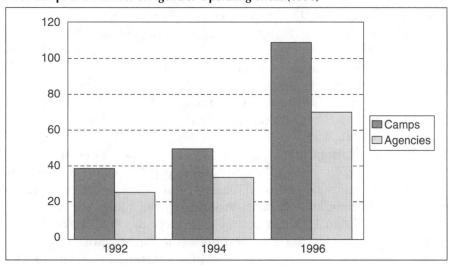

Source: C. Camp and G. Camp (1997). *The Correctional Yearbook*. South Salem, NY: The Criminal Justice Institute, pp. 96, 98, 170, 224.

Almost all inmates who complete the program are released onto community supervision; most of those who do not complete the program are returned to the general prison population to serve their sentences. Most receive intensive supervision at least during the first portion of their community release. Camp and Camp (1997:98) estimate the average daily cost of boot camp at $57.

Boot camps are increasingly popular. Policymakers and politicians, fearing the "Willie Horton" problem of appearing soft on crime (Tonry, 1994), can manipulate the voting public to make them think they are tough on crime. The public thinks offenders lack discipline and self-control and that boot camps will instill these. Correctional administrators stress provision of drug education, reduction in recidivism, and rehabilitation of offenders. Correctional officers can administer direct punishment in terms of excessive exercise ("Gimme 100 push-ups! Run another mile! Carry that 100-pound pole until I tell you to put it down!"). Inmates volunteer for the potential of early release.

Photo 4.6
Boot Camp Program, Maryland Department of Corrections. Used with permission of the American Correctional Association.

Early evaluations of outcomes indicate that boot camps reduce expenditures for the care and custody of inmates and reduce the demand for prison bed space. The New York State Department of Corrections requires participants to undergo treatment and pursue education and training as part of the program. New York estimated it saved $176 million to 1993 by using shock incarceration; Illinois reports a savings of almost $5 million over four years (Karr & Jones, 1994). Some 70 percent of the New York boot camp graduates earned the GED after a short period of study and preparation; they also had lower recidivism rates (Clark et al., 1994).

Other evaluations (MacKenzie & Piquero, 1994) found that, when shock incarceration participants are diverted from prison (rather than from probation-bound offenders), there can be substantial cost savings and lowered prison cell demand. Virginia reports a low recidivism rate: 15 percent (Virginia Department of Corrections, 1992); South Carolina's recidivism rate for women boot camp inmates was 12 percent. Illinois reports recidivism for its graduates after 24 months in the community as 17 percent (Karr & Jones, 1994). Michigan (Hansen, 1993), Louisiana (MacKenzie et al., 1993), and Florida (Florida Department of Juvenile Justice, 1997) do not find lower recidivism rates or costs savings.

Future evaluations of the effectiveness of boot camps in reducing recidivism and costs saving through shorter prison sentences and lessened demand for prison construction will have to focus on true prison-diversion programs, types and intensity of treatment, matching of inmate need with treatment programs, and longer-term follow-up. At present, we can conclude that boot camps are not treatment focused, do not match inmate needs to services, and often do not include community-based follow-up.

Photo 4.7
Boot Camp Program, Maryland Department of Corrections. Used with permission of the American Correctional Association.

# Summary

The primary mission of the correctional system is protection of the public. Programs must be designed with that objective in mind, or they will be doomed to early failure and public rejection. What seems to be needed is a *system* that offers as many alternatives to incarceration as are possible for the individuals who appear to have some hope of benefiting from them and who will present little, if any, danger to the community. The residual population may be required to remain in more secure institutions until new treatments can be found for them. The prison, in a modified form, has a valuable place in a correctional system for the estimated 15 to 20 percent of the convicted offenders who require this level of control. For most convicted offenders, however, the use of either partial or total alternatives to imprisonment is a more reasonable response than is incarceration.

---

Box 4.15

### Tourniquet Sentencing

This strategy involves the sentencing judge selecting a community control program (such as probation) and then increasing the level of control until the offender conforms his or her behavior to the required conditions. An offender placed on probation may later be ordered into house arrest, or be made to participate in electronic monitoring to ensure conformity to regulations. Non-conforming clients can later be placed into community residential treatment centers (such as a halfway house) if necessary. Variations in control would reflect the degree of cooperation of the client with supervising agents.

Source: The term "tourniquet sentencing" is attributed to Judge Albert Kramer, District Judge, Quincy, MA. A. Klein (1980). *Earn It: The Story So Far*. Brandeis University, Waltham, MA.

---

Prisons should be the "last choice" of sentencing judges faced with the difficult decision of how to manage offenders before them, and how best to attain the correctional objective being sought. Judges are increasingly turning to "tourniquet sentencing" as a promising strategy for determining those sanctions.

Whatever good prisons do is difficult to measure, but the damage done is easily detected. If our objective is the protection of society from criminal recidivism, long-term strategies must be developed. If we are determined to control offenders and lower the costs of over-incarceration, it will become necessary to develop a system of community corrections that includes extensive program alternatives and increasing levels of control over the offender in the arms of the law. The process of developing the desired system is discussed in Chapter 15; many of its parts exist in most local communities now. Developing an effective community corrections program will require formulating social policy that requires handling local problems in the community, setting priorities for control of crime, and making resources available to develop and maintain the proposed system. Probation is one of the elements in such a system and the next chapter speaks to its many variations and functions.

## Review Questions

1. What are the main purposes of imprisonment?

2. Differentiate between the three major types of prisons.

3. Why is the "bricks and mortar" solution to prison overcrowding antithetical to corrections in the next century?

4. Define prison overcrowding. What are its negative consequences?

5. How can parole boards reduce prison overcrowding?

6. Explain why prisons in America have become so overcrowded.

7. Contrast work release and educational furlough.

8. What are the problems of the "extended limits" options to imprisonment? How can these be overcome?

9. In general, how effective is work release?

10. What are the alternatives to "bricks and mortar" as a solution to prison overcrowding?

## Key Terms

boot camps
"bricks and mortar"
deterrent
disablement
early-out options
educational furlough
good-time laws
overcrowding
parole
parole boards

prison
prison population cap
reformation
retribution
selective incapacitation
time credits
tourniquet sentencing
War on Drugs
work release

## Recommended Readings

Allen, H.E. and C.E. Simonsen (1998). *Corrections in America*. Upper Saddle River, NJ: Prentice Hall.

American Correctional Association (1990). "Technology and Security," *Corrections Today* 60 (4): 58-93 (theme issue).

Byrne, J. and A. Lurigio (eds.) (1991). *Smart Sentencing? An Examination of the Emergence of the Intermediate Punishment*. Beverly Hills, CA: Sage Publications.

## Notes

[1]     Three-strike laws generally require a flat sentence (such as 25 years) or multiple of the mandatory sentence (whichever is more) with minimum early release credits. California, for example, mandates 25 years or three times the mandatory presumed sentence (whichever is greater) and required 80 percent of the sentence to be served, regardless of time credits. See P. Greenwood, C. Rydell, and A. Abrahamse (1994). *Three Strikes and You're Out: Estimated Benefits and Costs of California's New Mandatory Sentencing Law*. Santa Monica, CA: Rand; V. Schiraldi, P. Sussman, and L. Hyland (1994). *Three Strikes: The Unintended Victims*. San Francisco, CA: Center on Juvenile and Criminal Justice; and M. Ezell and L. Cohen (1997). "Age, Crime and Crime Control Policies." *Studies on Crime and Crime Prevention*, 6(2):169-199.

[2]     All of California's prisons will have been outfitted with electrified barriers by the end of this century.

[3]     M. Mauer (1995). "The International Use of Incarceration." *The Prison Journal*, 75:113-123 (1997).

[4]     Camp, C. and G. Camp (1997). *The Corrections Yearbook, 1994: Adult Corrections*, p. 33. South Salem, NY: The Criminal Justice Institute.

[5]    American Correctional Association (1997). *Directory*. Laurel, MD: ACA:10.

[6]    The "Iron Law of Prison Commitment" states that judicial commitments to prison expand to fill all available bed space, but this is not true. In the last part of the decade of the 1960s, there was unused capacity in many jurisdictions. In addition, commitment to prison can greatly exceed available bed space.

[7]    See the excellent essay on prisons by A. Blumstein (1995). In J. Wilson and J. Petersilia (eds.) *Crime*, pp. 387-419. San Francisco, CA: Institute for Contemporary Studies.

[8]    See E. Chayet (1994). "Correctional 'Good Time' as a Means of Early Release." *Criminal Justice Abstracts*, 26:521-538; and J. Austin, C. Jones, and J. Kramer (1995). *National Assessment of Structured Sentencing*. Washington, DC: U.S. Bureau of Justice Statistics.

[9]    Austin, J. (1994). *The Case for Shorter Prison Terms: The Illinois Experience*. San Francisco, CA: National Council on Crime and Delinquency.

## References

Alexander, J. and J. Austin (1994). *Understanding Why Inmates are Misclassified*. San Francisco, CA: National Council on Crime and Delinquency.

Allen, H.E. (1995). "The American Dream and Crime in the Twenty-First Century." *Justice Quarterly*, 12:1101-1119.

Allen, H.E. (1990). "AIDS and the Prison Community: Trends and Prospects." Paper presented at the annual meeting of the American Society of Criminology, Baltimore.

Allen, H.E. (1989). "Pitfalls in Privatization of Correctional Institutions." Paper presented at the "Stigma '89" meetings, London School of Economics.

Allen, H.E. and J.C. Abril (1997). "The New Chain Gang: Corrections in the Next Century." *American Journal of Criminal Justice*, 22(1):1-12.

Allen, H.E. and C. Simonsen (1998). *Corrections in America*. Upper Saddle River, NJ: Prentice-Hall.

Allen, H.E. and C. Simonsen (1995). *Corrections in America*. Englewood Cliffs, NJ: Prentice-Hall.

American Academy of Political and Social Sciences (1969). "The Continuum of Corrections." *The Future of Corrections (The Annals)*, 38(1).

American Correctional Association (1990). *Directory of Juvenile and Adult Correctional Departments, Institutions, Agencies, and Paroling Authorities*. Laurel, MD: ACA.

American Correctional Association (1995) *Directory*. Laurel, MD: ACA.

American Correctional Association (1990). "On the Outside: Corrections in the Community." *Corrections Today*, 56(2):6-7.

Austin, J. (1994). *The Case for Shorter Prison Terms: The Illinois Experience*. San Francisco, CA: National Council on Crime and Delinquency.

Bear, J. and W. Chambliss (1997). "Generating Fear: The Politics of Crime Reporting," *Crime, Law and Social Change*, 27(2):109-119.

Beck, A. and T. Bonczar (1994). *State and Federal Prison Population Tops One Million*. Washington, DC: U.S. Department of Justice.

Beck, A. and B. Shipley (1987). *Recidivism of Young Parolees*. Washington, DC: U.S. Department of Justice.

Behan, C. (1987). "ROPE: Repeat Offender Program Experiment." *FBI Law Enforcement Bulletin*, 56(8):1-5.

Biles, D. (1979). "Crime and the Use of Prisons." *Federal Probation*, 43(3):39-43.

Blumstein, A. (1995). "Prisons." In J. Wilson and J. Petersilia (eds.) *Crime*, pp. 387-419. San Francisco, CA: Institute for Contemporary Studies.

Brown, S. (1994). "South Carolina's Shock Incarceration for Women." *Corrections Compendium*, 19(2):1-5.

Byrne, J. and A. Lurigio (eds.) (1991). *Smart Sentencing? An Examination of the Emergence of the Intermediate Punishment*. Beverly Hills, CA: Sage Publications.

Camp, C. and G. Camp (1997). *The Corrections Yearbook*. South Salem, NY: Criminal Justice Institute.

Camp, C. and G. Camp (1995). *The Corrections Yearbook, 1994: Adult Corrections*. South Salem, NY: The Criminal Justice Institute.

Camp, D. and Sandhu, H. (1995). "Evaluation of Female Offender Regimented Treatment Program," *Journal of the Oklahoma Criminal Justice Research Consortium*, 2(Aug):50-57.

Chayet, E. (1994). "Correctional 'Good Time' as a Means of Early Release." *Criminal Justice Abstracts*, 26:521-538.

Clark, C., C. Aziz, and D. MacKenzie (1994). "Shock Incarceration." In New York, NY: *Focus on Treatment*. Washington, DC: U.S. Department of Justice.

Duffee, D. (1989). *Corrections: Practice and Policy*. New York, NY: Random House.

Ezell, M. and L. Cohen (1997). "Age, Crime and Crime Control Policies," *Studies on Crime and Crime Prevention*, 6(2):169-199.

Foster, M. (1987). "Security Glazing: New Technology Offers New Options." *Corrections Today*, 51(4):92, 94, 144.

Gilliard, D. and A. Beck (1998). *Prison and Jail Inmates at Midyear 1997*. Washington, DC: U.S. Bureau of Justice Statistics.

Gilliard, D. and A. Beck (1994). *Prisoners in 1993*. Washington, DC: U.S. Department of Justice.

Gottfredson, S. and D. Gottfredson (1992). Incapacitation Strategies and the Criminal Career. Sacramento, CA: California Division of Law Enforcement.

Greenfield, L. (1985). *Examining Recidivism*. Washington, DC: U.S. Department of Justice.

Greenwood, P. (1983). *Selective Incapacitation*. Santa Monica, CA: Rand Corporation.

Greenwood, P., C. Rydell, and A. Abrahamse (1994). *Three Strikes and You're Out: Estimated Benefits and Costs of California's New Mandatory Sentencing Law*. Santa Monica, CA: Rand Corporation.

Grossi, E. (ed.) (1997). "Prison and Jail Boot Camps," *Journal of Contemporary Criminal Justice*, 13(2):93-205.

Hallinan, J. (1995). "Hard Time in Hell. "*San Francisco Chronicle*, June 25:A-10.

Hansen, M. (1993). *Prison Boot Camps: Are They Saving the State Money?* Lansing, MI: Michigan Senate Fiscal Agency.

Hassine, V. (1996). *Life Without Parole*. Los Angeles, CA: Roxbury.

Haynes, H. and M. Geerken (1997). "The Idea of Selective Release." *Justice Quarterly*, 14(2):353-370.

Irwin, J. and J. Austin (1994). *It's About Time*. Belmont, CA: Wadsworth.

Jackson, K. (1998). "Evaluating Correctional Technology," *Corrections Today*, 60(4):58-67,82.

Johnston, N. (1973). *The Human Cage: A Brief History of Prison Architecture*. New York, NY: Walker.

Johnston, N., K. Finkel, and J. Cohen (1994). *Eastern State Penitentiary: Crucible of Good Intentions*. Philadelphia, PA: Philadelphia Museum of Art.

Karr, S. and R. Jones (1994). *Impact Incarceration Program: 1993 Annual Report to the Governor and the General Assembly*. Springfield, IL: Illinois Department of Corrections.

Katz, J. and S. Decker (1982). "An Analysis of Work Release: The Institutionalization of Unsubstantial Reforms." *Criminal Justice and Behavior*, 9:229-250.

Klein, A. (1980). *Earn It: The Story So Far*. Waltham, MA: Brandeis University.

Kuhn, A.C. (1998). "Incarceration Rates: The United States in an International Perspective." *Criminal Justice Abstracts*, 30(2):321-353.

Loeber, R. and H. Snyder (1990). "Rate of Offending in Juvenile Careers: Findings on Constancy and Change in Lambda." *Criminology*, 28:97-110.

MacKenzie, D. and A. Piquero (1994). "The Impact of Shock Incarceration Programs on Prison Crowding." *Crime & Delinquency*, 40:222-249.

MacKenzie, D. and J. Shaw (1993). "The Impact of Shock Incarceration of Technical Violations and New Criminal Activities." *Justice Quarterly*, 10:463-487.

Mauer, M. (1997). *Americans Behind Bars: U.S. and International Use of Incarceration, 1995*. Washington, DC: The Sentencing Project.

Mauer, M. (1995). "The International Use of Incarceration." *The Prison Journal*, 75:113-123.

Mohamed, H., E. Monjardi, C. Yimvilai, and R. Sing (1987). *Corrections in Asia and the Pacific: Record of the Eighth Asian and Pacific Conference of Correctional Administrators*. Canberra: Philip, 1987.

Mumola, C.J. and A. Beck (1997). *Prisoners in 1996*. Washington, DC: U.S. Bureau of Justice Statistics.

Nathan, D. and M. Snedecker (1995). *Satan's Silence: Ritual Abuse and the Making of a Modern American Witch Hunt*. New York, NY: Basic Books.

Newton, A. (1980). "The Effects of Imprisonment." *Criminal Justice Abstracts*, 12/1:134-151.

Paboojian, A. and R. Teske (1997). "Preservice Correctional Officers: What Do They Think About Treatment?" *Journal of Criminal Justice*, 25(5):425-433.

Rothman, D. (1971). *The Discovery of the Asylum*. Boston, MA: Little, Brown.

Shichor, D. and H. Allen (1977). "Study Release: A Correctional Alternative." *Offender Rehabilitation*, 2:7-17.

Schilling, R. A. Ivanof, and N. El-Bassel (1997). "HIV-Related Behaviors in a Transitional Correctional Setting," *Criminal Justice and Behavior*, 24(2):256-277.

Schiraldi, V., P. Sussman, and L. Hyland (1994). *Three Strikes: The Unintended Victims*. San Francisco, CA: Center on Juvenile and Criminal Justice.

Silberman, M. (1995). *A World of Violence*. Belmont, CA: Wadsworth.

Skovron, S.E., J.E. Scott, and F.T. Cullen (1988). "Prison Crowding: Public Attitudes Toward Population Control." *Journal of Research in Crime and Delinquency*, 25:150-169.

Southeimer, H. and T. Duncan (1996). *Assessment of County Intermediate Punishment Programs*. Harrisburg, PA: Pennsylvania Commission on Crime and Delinquency.

Tonry, M. (1994). "Racial Politics, Racial Disparities, and the War on Crime." *Crime & Delinquency*, 40:475-494.

Turner, S. and J. Petersilia (1996). "Work Release in Washington," *Prison Journal*, 76 (2):138-164.

Virginia Department of Corrections (1992). An Evaluation of Southampton Intensive Treatment Center. Richmond, CA: VDOC.

Waldo, G., T. Chiricos, and L. Dobrin (1973). "Community Contact and Inmate Attitudes: An Experimental Assessment of Work Release." *Criminology*, 11(3):345-374.

Walens, S. (1997). *War Stories: An Oral History of Life Behind Bars*. Westport, CT: Praeger.

Wellisch, J., M. Pendergast, and M. Anglin (1994). *Drug-Abusing Women Offenders: Results of a National Survey*. Washington, DC: U.S. Department of Justice.

Wright, D. (1984). "Emergency Prison Release Policies: The Iowa Example." *Prison Journal*, 64:88-96.

Zimmerman, S., D. Alstyne, and C. Dunn (1988). "The National Punishment Survey and Public Policy Consequences." *Journal of Research in Crime and Delinquency*, 25(2):120-149.

Zimring, F. and G. Hawkins (1995). *Incapacitation: Penal Confinement and the Restraint of Crime*. New York, NY: Oxford University Press.

# The Historical
# Development of Probation

5

I can forgive, but I cannot forget, is only another way of saying, I will not forgive. Forgiveness ought to be like a canceled note—
torn in two, and burned up, so that it never
can be shown against one.
—Henry Ward Beecher

Probation represents one of the unique developments within the
criminal justice system. The development of this method of minimizing
offender penetration into the correctional system was a crucial aspect of
the rise of the rehabilitation model in this country. Any study of probation must begin with an analysis of its predecessors. This historical review will help explain how probation, both for adults and juveniles, developed into its current forms and practices.

---

**Box 5.1**

### Definition of Probation: Adults

A sentence not involving confinement that imposes conditions and retains authority in the sentencing court to modify
the conditions of sentence or to resentence the offender if the
offender violates the conditions. Such a sentence should not
involve or require suspension of the imposition or execution of
any other sentence.

---

Therefore, probation is a conditional sentence that avoids incarceration of the offender—it is an alternative disposition available to the
court. While probation is an outcome of the offender's conviction in a
criminal court, it neither confines him or her in an institution nor allows
the offender's release from court authority. Supervision by a probation
officer is almost always a condition of release.

As indicated by the National Advisory Commission on Criminal Justice Standards and Goals (1973a:115-17), probation can also refer to other functions, activities, and services. It is a *status*, given to the convicted offender, that falls somewhere between that of free citizen and incarcerated felon. As a *subsystem* of criminal justice, it refers to the agency or organization that administers the probation process. As a *process*, it refers to those activities that include the preparation of reports for the court, the supervision of probationers, and providing of services for those probationers. These activities are undertaken by the probation officer as a part of his or her regular duty. Finally, as (Reed, 1997) notes, probation can serve to lower prison populations.

The rationale for the use of probation has been clearly stated by Dressler (1962:26):

> . . . the assumption that certain offenders are reasonably safe risks in society by the time they appear in court; it would not facilitate their adjustment to remove them to institutions, and the move might well have the opposite effect. Meantime, the community would have to provide for their dependents. And the effect of such incarceration upon the prisoner's family would be incalculable. If, then, the community would not be jeopardized by a defendant's presence, and if he gave evidence of ability to change to a law-abiding life, it served both society and the individual to give him the chance, conditionally, under supervision and guidance.

Probation is thus clearly tied to the correctional goals of rehabilitation and reintegration, providing potential benefits to the offender as well as the community.

## Precursors of Probation

The use of probation dates back to the mid-nineteenth century, and while its precursors bear some resemblance to their modern-day counterparts, they did not possess all the attributes that are currently associated with probation. Indeed, crucial elements were absent in all predecessors!

## Benefit of Clergy

A common association with the term probation is forgiveness. After all, the word probation derives from Latin, its root meaning "a period of proving or trial" (Dressler, 1962:6). Upon cursory examination, some of these precursors would appear to be far-fetched. Barnes and Teeters (1959:552) cite the early right to sanctuary as one of these early but questionable forms. Under this procedure, cities or places were set aside to which the accused might flee and escape punishment for his or her crime. Another earlier predecessor was the benefit of clergy (United Nations, 1976a:82-83; Dressler, 1962:7-8; Acker and Lanier, 1993:293). This special plea was a part of the feudal power struggle between Church and State in England as Henry II sought to expand his power over the Church by subjecting clerics to the King's Court. The benefit of clergy was a mechanism through which Church functionaries escaped potential persecution. Ordained clerks, monks, and nuns accused of crimes could claim the benefit and have their case transferred to the Bishop's Court.

Dressler (1962:7) describes the process in greater detail:

> When a member of the cloth, suspected of a crime, was brought into King's Court, his bishop could claim the dispensation for him. Thereupon, the charge was read to the cleric, but no evidence was presented against him. Instead, he gave his own version of the alleged offense and brought in witnesses to corroborate his testimony. With all the evidence against the accused expunged and only favorable witnesses testifying, it is hardly astounding that most cases ended in acquittal.

By the fourteenth century, the benefit was extended to nonclerics, providing they were literate. A passage from the Psalms ("Have mercy upon me, O God, according to thy loving kindness, according to the multitude of thy tender mercies blot out my transgressions") was utilized as a literacy test. Since the benefit of clergy was most often used to avoid capital punishment and gain access to the more lenient Bishop's Court, this Psalm became known as the "neck verse." As Dressler indicates (1962:8), the benefit of clergy deteriorated to the point that it became "a clumsy set of rules which operated in favor of all criminals to mitigate in certain cases the severity of the criminal law." It was abolished for commoners in 1827 and for peers in 1841; the American colonies did not use the plea until after the Revolution. Thus, although the benefit of clergy was very unlike probation in terms of actual practice, it can be viewed as a predecessor. As we shall see, opponents of probation have often complained that it is also "too lenient," and that the offender is avoiding a harsher punishment so richly deserved.[1] In the 1990s, opponents of perceived leniency by juvenile courts pushed for waiver to adult felony courts of those juveniles who committed heinous crimes, to increase their punishment. Research indicates that the probability of incarceration decreases and the probability of probation increases when juveniles are bound over to adult court (Stern, 1991). Some 8,500 juveniles are now in prisons for adult felons (American Correctional Association, 1997: xxxi).

## Judicial Reprieve

Of course, other predecessors bear a much closer resemblance to probation. The English courts utilized judicial reprieve—a temporary suspension by the court of either the imposition or execution of a sentence—which was often used to permit the convicted person to apply for a pardon. While designed to suspend the sentence temporarily, it sometimes led to the abandonment of prosecution (United Nations, 1976a:83). Although the defendant remained in the community until a final disposition of the case, judicial reprieve did not involve certain practices of probation, particularly the conditions of release and the supervision by an agent of the court (Dressler, 1962:8).

## Recognizance

More aspects of contemporary probation appear in the practice of recognizance. This practice, also called "binding over," involves the use of "a bond or obligation entered into by a defendant, who thus is bound to refrain from doing, or to do, something for a stipulated period, and to appear in court on a specified date for trial or for final disposition of the case" (Dressler, 1962:9). In England, it was frequently used with petty offenders. If the offender violated the terms of the agreement, the bond would be claimed by the state and the defaulting offender might also be incarcerated.

For this reason, recognizance has been described as containing the "germs of supervision": the suspension of sentence, conditional freedom, and possible revocation. However, unlike probation, recognizance did not provide official supervision by an agent of the court. Therefore, although recognizance (bail) is one method of assuring a defendant's appearance at trial (Clark & Alan, 1996), it also played an important role as a precursor of probation (Eskridge, 1983).

## Filing of Cases

This practice, unique to Massachusetts, involving suspension of the imposition of sentence when: "After [a] verdict of guilty, in a criminal case . . . the court is satisfied that, by reason of extenuating circumstances, or of a question of law in a like case before a higher court, or other sufficient reason, public justice does not require an immediate sentence" (United Nations, 1976a:86). With the consent of both defendant and prosecutor, the judge filed the case and made the offender subject to certain conditions set by the court. But, as Dressler indicates (1962:11), the filing of a case did not constitute final action. The court could later take further action, and could order imprisonment.

Therefore, the filing of cases also contained some aspects of probation: the suspension of sentence, conditional release, and provision for revocation. Again, supervision by an officer of the court was the crucial omission in comparison to probation. With these precursors in mind, let us now look at the major historical creators of probation.

## Founders of Probation

John Augustus of Boston is commonly recognized as the originator of probation (Allen & Simonsen, 1998:185), but there were other contributors to its development both before and after his unique contribution.

Dressler (1962:12-13) cites the 1841 activities of Matthew Davenport Hill of Birmingham, England. In Warwickshire, Hill observed that, in the case of youthful offenders, magistrates often imposed token sentences of one day with the special condition that the defendant remain under the supervision of a guardian. This experiment represented a mitigation of the punishment; no other conditions were imposed and there was no provision for revocation. When Hill became a recorder, he modified this procedure; he suspended the sentence and placed the offender under the supervision of a guardian, under the assumption that "there would be better hope of amendment under such guardians than in the [jail] of the county." Hill's program has some of the same elements as Augustus's method: selected cases, suspended sentences, and if the defendant got into trouble again no sanctions were levied. Hill was not unwilling to take action against repeaters, however: "That the punishment should be such as to show that it was from no weakness, from no mistaken indulgence, from no want to resolution on the part of the court to perform its duty" that the previous sentence had been suspended. Hill also demonstrated his concern for the safety of the community by requesting that the superintendent of police investigate the conduct of persons placed under a guardian's supervision.

This program was an example of the practice of "binding over," discussed earlier. In this country, one of its foremost proponents was Judge Peter Oxenbridge Thatcher of Boston. By 1836, Massachusetts passed legislation promoting the practice of releasing petty offenders upon their recognizance with sureties at any stage of the proceedings.[2]

However, it was a volunteer to the court, John Augustus, who is most often given credit for the establishment of probation in the United States. Augustus first appeared in police court in Boston when he stood bail for a man charged with drunkenness and then helped the offender find a job. The court ordered the defendant to return in three weeks, at which time he demonstrated great improvement. Instead of incarcerating this individual, the judge imposed a one-cent fine and ordered the defendant to pay costs.

From this modest beginning, Augustus proceeded to bail out numerous offenders, supervising them and offering guidance until they were sentenced. Over an 18-year period (from 1841 until his death in 1859), Augustus "bailed on probation" 1,152 men and 794 women (Barnes & Teeters, 1959:554). He was motivated by his belief that "the object of the law is to reform criminals and to prevent crime and not to punish maliciously or from a spirit of revenge" (Dressler, 1962:17). Augustus obviously selected his candidates carefully, offering assistance "mainly to those who were indicted for their first offense, and whose hearts were not wholly depraved, but gave promise of better things." He also considered the "previous character of the person, his age and influences by which he would in the future be likely to be surrounded and, although these points were not rigidly adhered to, still they were the circumstances which usually determined my action" (United Nations, 1976a:90). In addition, Augustus provided his charges with aid in obtaining employment, an education, or a place to live, and also made an impartial report to the court. The task was not without its frustrations, as Augustus noted (Barnes & Teeters, 1959:554):

> While it saves the country and state hundreds and I might say thousands of dollars, it drains my pockets instead of enriching me. To attempt to make money by bailing poor people would prove an impossibility. The first two years of my labor I received nothing from anyone except what I earned by my daily labor.

His records on the first 1,100 individuals whom he bailed out revealed that only one forfeited bond (Dressler, 1962:18). When Augustus died in 1859, he was destitute—an unfitting end for a humanitarian visionary!

## Philosophical Bases of Probation

Probation emerged in the United States during the nineteenth century, a period of considerable social turmoil and conflict. It was a development widely influenced by certain thoughts, arguments, and debates in Europe. In a larger sense, probation is an extension of the Western European philosophical arguments about the functions of criminal law and how offenders should be handled and punished. The punishment philosophy generally advocated by the kings, emperors, and other rulers of Europe focused on the crime, and attempted to treat all crimes equally. They viewed the purposes of criminal law as to punish, to deter others, and to seek revenge and vengeance for violations of the "king's peace." Widespread use of the death penalty, torture, banishment, public humiliations, and mass executions resulted from "disturbing the king's peace."

In the eighteenth century, French philosophers created a controversy by focusing on liberty, equality, and justice. Famous French philosophers and lawyers attempted to redefine the purpose of criminal law in an effort to find some way to make the criminal justice system of their time more attuned to the humanitarian ethos of the Age of Enlightenment. A major figure of the time was Cesare Beccaria, a mildly disturbed Italian genius who only left his country once—when invited to visit Paris to debate the French philosophers.

When Beccaria published his classic work, *An Essay on Crimes and Punishments* (1764), he established the "Classical School" of criminology, which attempted to reorient the law toward more humanistic goals. This would include no torturing of the accused in order to extract confessions, no secret indictments and trials, the right to defense at a trial, improvement of the conditions of imprisonment, and so on. His work focused on the offense and not on the offender. He believed that punishment should fit the crime. His work was widely read throughout Europe, and even attracted the attention of Catherine the Great, the Russian empress, who invited Beccaria to revise Russian criminal law. Unfortunately, he never took her up on her offer.

The philosophical ferment of the period quickly spread to England and, from there, to the colonies. When the United States emerged from the Revolutionary War, the remaining vestiges of the harsher English penal codes were resoundingly abandoned. What emerged was a constitutional system that incorporated the major components of the humanitarian philosophy, along with a populace imbued with the belief in the inherent goodness of humankind and the ability of all persons to rise to their optimal level of perfectibility.

The difference between the earlier approach to handling offenders (harsh punishments openly administered, and corporal and capital punishments) and the emerging reformation emphasis of the last decade of the eighteenth century, were primarily in (1) the way offenders were viewed and (2) the focus and intent of the criminal law. Prior to the Revolutionary War offenders were seen as inherently evil, deserving punishment so that they might "Get right with God." After the Civil War, Americans had generally recognized that humankind was not basically evil. The focus shifted to dealing with individual offenders, rather than focusing on the crime that had been committed. The Civil War further added to the movement toward democracy, the rise of the reformation movement, and to the further individualization of treatment and punishment. Eventually the question arose: Do all offenders need to be imprisoned in order for them to repent and stop their criminal behavior? It was in this philosophical environment that Massachusetts began to answer the question, and the concern was juvenile probation.

## The Growth of Probation

Buoyed by Augustus's example, Massachusetts quickly moved into the forefront of probation development. An experiment in providing services for children (resembling probation) was inaugurated in 1869, under the auspices of the Massachusetts State Board of Health, Lunacy, and Charity (Johnson, 1928:7). A statute enacted in that year provided that, when complaints were made in court against a juvenile under 17 years of age, a written notice must be furnished to the state. The state agent was then given an opportunity to investigate, attend the trial, and to safeguard the interest of the child.

Despite the early work of Augustus and others with adult offenders, probation was more readily supported for juveniles. It was not until 1901 that New York passed the first statute authorizing probation for adult offenders, more than 20 years after Massachusetts passed a law for juvenile probation (Lindner & Savarese, 1984c). Although the development of probation for adults lagged that of juveniles, by 1923, virtually every state had a law authorizing probation for adults. Historical data on select states can be found in Table 5.1. Surprisingly, it was the Federal Government that resisted probation.

## Probation at the Federal Level

Although probation quickly became almost universal in the juvenile justice system, no early specific provision for probation was made for federal offenders, either juvenile or adult. As a substitute, the federal courts suspended sentence in instances where imprisonment imposed special hardships. However, this practice was quickly called into question by several sources.

The major question was a legal one: Did federal judges have the constitutional authority to suspend a sentence indefinitely, or did this practice represent an encroachment upon the executive prerogative of pardon and reprieve and was it, as such, an infringement upon doctrine of separation of powers? This issue was resolved by the U.S. Supreme Court in the *Killits* decision (*Ex parte* U.S. 242 U.S. 27-53, 1916). In a case from the northern district of Ohio, John M. Killits suspended the five-year sentence of a man who was convicted of embezzling $4,700 from a Toledo Bank. The defendant was a first offender with an otherwise good background and reputation, who made full restitution for this offense. The bank officers did not wish to prosecute. The government contended that such action was beyond the powers of the court. A unanimous opinion, delivered by Chief Justice Edward D. White, held that the federal courts had no inherent power to suspend sentence indef-

Table 5.1
**States with Juvenile and Adult Probation Laws: 1923**

| States | Years Enacted Juvenile | Adult |
|---|---|---|
| Alabama | 1907 | 1915 |
| Arizona | 1907 | 1913 |
| Arkansas | 1911 | 1923 |
| California | 1903 | 1903 |
| Colorado | 1899 | 1909 |
| Connecticut | 1903 | 1903 |
| Delaware | 1911 | 1911 |
| Georgia | 1904 | 1907 |
| Idaho | 1905 | 1915 |
| Illinois | 1899 | 1911 |
| Indiana | 1903 | 1907 |
| Kansas | 1901 | 1909 |
| Maine | 1905 | 1905 |
| Maryland | 1902 | 1904 |
| Massachusetts | 1878 | 1878 |
| Michigan | 1903 | 1903 |
| Minnesota | 1899 | 1909 |
| Missouri | 1901 | 1897 |
| Montana | 1907 | 1913 |
| Nebraska | 1905 | 1909 |
| New Jersey | 1903 | 1900 |
| New York | 1903 | 1901 |
| North Carolina | 1915 | 1919 |
| North Dakota | 1911 | 1911 |
| Ohio | 1902 | 1908 |
| Oklahoma | 1909 | 1915 |
| Oregon | 1909 | 1915 |
| Pennsylvania | 1903 | 1909 |
| Rhode Island | 1899 | 1899 |
| Tennessee | 1905 | 1915 |
| Utah | 1903 | 1923 |
| Vermont | 1900 | 1900 |
| Virginia | 1910 | 1910 |
| Washington | 1905 | 1915 |
| Wisconsin | 1901 | 1909 |

Source: Adapted from F.R. Johnson (1928). *Probation for Juveniles and Adults*, pp. 12-13. New York, NY: Century Co.

initely and that there was no reason "to continue a practice which is inconsistent with the Constitution, since its exercise in the very nature of things amounts to a refusal by the judicial power to perform a duty resting upon it and as a consequence thereof, to an interference with both the legislative and executive authority as fixed by the Constitution." However, instead of abolishing this probationary practice, the *Killits* decision actually sponsored its further development. Interested parties interpreted the reversal of the "doctrine of inherent power to suspend sentences indefinitely" to mean that enabling legislation should be passed that specifically granted this power to the judiciary.

At the federal level, the National Probation Association (then headed by Charles Lionel Chute) carried on a determined educational campaign and lobbied for federal legislation. These efforts did not go unopposed, however. For example, prohibitionists feared that the growth of probation would take the sting out of the provisions of the Volstead Act.[3] As Evjen (1975:5) has demonstrated, letters from judges to Chute clearly denounced the practice of probation.

> What we need in this court is not a movement such as you advocate, to create new officials with resulting expense, but a movement to make enforcement of our criminal laws more certain and swift . . . In this county, due to the efforts of people like yourselves, the murderer has a cell bedecked with flowers and is surrounded with a lot of silly people. The criminal should understand when he violates the law that he is going to a penal institution and is going to stay there. Just such efforts as your organization is making are largely responsible for the crime wave that is passing over the country today and threatening to engulf our institutions.

Objections also arose from the Justice Department. For example, Attorney General Harry M. Daugherty wrote that he hoped "that no such mushy policy will be indulged in as Congress turning courts into maudlin reform associations . . . the place to do reforming is inside the walls and not with lawbreakers running loose in society." A memorandum from the Justice Department further revealed this sentiment against probation: "It is all a part of a wave of maudlin rot of misplaced sympathy for criminals that is going over the country. It would be a crime, however, if a probation system is established in the federal courts."

Approximately 34 bills to establish a federal probation system were introduced in Congress between 1909 and 1925. Despite such opposition, a bill passed on its sixth introduction to the House. The bill was sent to President Coolidge who, as a former governor of Massachusetts, was familiar with the functioning of probation. He signed the bill into law on March 4, 1925. This action was followed by an appropriation to defray the salaries and expenses of a limited number of probation officers, to be chosen by civil service (Meeker, 1975; Lindner & Savarese, 1984a; Burdress, 1997).

## Recent Legal Developments

Understanding the development of probation also requires a quick tour through the major and recent cases that deal with adult probation. These concern the nature of probation, revocation, probation conditions, supervision, and remedies.

## Nature of Probation and Revocation

Probation is a privilege, not a right (del Carmen, 1984). This was decided in *United States v. Birnbaum* (1970).[4] Once granted, however, the probationer has an interest in remaining on probation, commonly referred to as an entitlement. The U.S. Supreme Court has ruled that probation cannot be withdrawn (revoked) unless certain basic elements of due process are observed. If a court is considering removing the offender from probation (through a "revocation" hearing), the following rights and procedures must ensue: The probationer must: (1) be informed in writing of the charge against him or her, (2) have the written notice in advance of the revocation hearing, and (3) attend the hearing and be able to present evidence on his or her own behalf. The probationer also has a right (4) to challenge those testifying against him or her, (5) to confront witnesses and cross-examine them, and (6) to have legal counsel present if the charges are complicated or the case is so complex that an ordinary person would not be able to comprehend the legal issues. These rights and procedures were enunciated in *Gagnon v. Scarpelli*, 1972.[5]

## Probation Conditions

The judge usually imposes the conditions that must be observed by the offender while on probation and has absolute discretion and authority to impose, modify, or reject these conditions. Some examples of conditions a judge might impose are routine blood testing to detect narcotics use and abuse; participation in Alcoholics Anonymous if the probationer has an alcohol problem; restitution to victims of the probationer (but probation may not be revoked if the offender cannot make payments because of unemployment: *Bearden v. Georgia*, 1983);[6] and not leaving the court's jurisdiction without prior approval. Many cases have challenged the conditions that courts might impose, but case law has determined any condition may be imposed if it is constitutional, reasonable, clear, and related to some definable correctional goal, such as rehabilitation or public safety. These are difficult to challenge and leave the court with broad power and tremendous discretion in imposing conditions. Such discretion has contributed to the volume of civil rights suits (del Carmen, 1984).

Table 5.2
**Significant Events in the Development of Probation**

| Date | Events |
|---|---|
| Middle Ages | *Parens patriae* established to protect the welfare of the child in England. |
| 1841 | John Augustus becomes the "Father of Probation." |
| 1869 | Massachusetts develops the visiting probation agent system. |
| 1875 | Society of the Prevention of Cruelty to Children established in New York, paving the way for the juvenile court. |
| 1899 | The first juvenile court in America was established in Cook County (Chicago) Illinois. |
| 1901 | New York passes the first statute authorizing probation for adults. |
| 1925 | Congress authorizes probation at the federal level. |
| 1927 | All states but Wyoming have juvenile probation laws. |
| 1943 | Federal Probation System formalizes the Presentence Investigation Report. |
| 1954 | Last state enacts juvenile probation law. |
| 1956 | Mississippi becomes the last state to pass authorizing legislation to establish adult probation. |
| 1965 | Ohio is first state to create "shock probation," which combines prison with probation. |
| 1967 | *In re Gault* decided by the U.S. Supreme Court. |
| 1969 | Jerome Miller is appointed Youth Commissioner in the State of Massachusetts and begins to decarcerate state institutions. |
| 1971 | Minnesota passes the first Community Corrections Act. |
| 1973 | National Advisory Commission on Criminal Justice Standards and Goals endorses more extensive use of probation. |
| 1974 | Congress passes the Juvenile Justice and Delinquency Prevention Act establishing the Federal Office of Juvenile Justice and Delinquency Prevention. |
| | Restorative justice and victim/offender mediation programs begin in Ontario, Canada. |
| 1975 | The State of Wisconsin receives funding from the Law Enforcement Assistance Administration to develop a case classification system. Four years later the Risk/Needs Assessment instruments are designed and implemented. |
| 1980 | American Bar Association issues restrictive guidelines to limit use of preadjudication detention. |
| 1982 | "War on Drugs" begins. |
| 1983 | Electronic monitoring of offenders begins. Georgia establishes the new generation of Intensive Supervised Probation program. |
| 1984 | Congress passes Sentence Reform Act to achieve longer sentences, "just deserts" and equity in sentencing. |
| 1989 | President Bush displays clear plastic bag of crack on prime time television. |
| 1994 | American Bar Association issues proposals to counteract the impact of domestic violence on children. |
| 1998 | National Institute of Corrections begins national correctional training on implementing community restorative justice programs. |

Source: Compiled by authors.

## Supervision

The probation officer is responsible for seeing that the conditions imposed by the court are met and, if not, calling the violations to the attention of the court. As such, the probation officer functions both as a helper and as a supervisor of the probationer. Legal liability is greater for the probation officer than the court; although an agent of the court, the probation officer does not enjoy the absolute immunity from liability that the court enjoys.

Some areas of potential liability for the probation officer include acts taken or protective steps omitted. For example, a probation officer may be liable for failing to disclose a probationer's background to a third party if this results in subsequent serious injury or death. Case decisions have generally held that the probation officer should disclose the past behavior of the probationer if able to reasonably foresee a potential danger to a specific third party. This would include an employer hiring a probationer as an accountant in a bank when the instant crime was embezzlement, or hiring a child molester to work in a grade school position. Insurance for liabilities can be obtained from the American Correctional Association.[7]

As a counselor to probationers, probation officers are often faced with the problem of encouraging their clients to share their problems and needs. Frequently, during the monthly contact, a probationer will reveal involvement in criminal activities. Under these noncustodial circumstances, probation offers are required to warn the probationer against self-incrimination through the *Miranda* warnings[8] or the evidence cannot be used in a court of law. Any discussion with a probationer under detention circumstances must be preceded by the *Miranda* warnings. Litigation is so extensive within the probation area that the probation officer must frequently take an active role as a law enforcement officer rather than a helper, a sad development from the original role John Augustus initiated and correctional personnel usually pursue!

## Remedies

While legal remedies are discussed later in this text, we should point out that probationers can seek redress from violation of their rights through civil suits (tort cases) entered in state courts or, should the issue concern whether their incarceration were legal, through state courts over habeas corpus suits (questioning the legality of their current incarceration from revocation procedures). An increasing avenue for seeking of redress in Section 1983 of Chapter 42 United States Code:

> Every person who under color of any statute, ordinance, regulation, custom, or usage of any State or Territory, subjects or causes to be subjected, any citizen of the United States or any other person within the jurisdiction thereof to the deprivation of any rights, privileges, or immunities secured by the Constitution and laws, shall be liable to the party injured in an action at law, suit in equity, or other proper proceeding for redress.

The important issue here is the general trend toward an increased use of legal avenues to standardize the probation service, to remove capricious and discriminatory activities, and to broaden the rights of probationers.

The field is in flux, and widespread changes are in progress (Kane, 1995; Cornelius, 1997). What will eventually emerge from the litigation and current turmoil will probably be more clearly defined procedures and policies, increased preservice and in-service training of probation officers, refinement of agency procedures and practices, written policies governing supervision and probationer control, and increased innovation in probation. These will be welcome changes in probation practice (Parker, 1997).

Figure 5.1
**Growth of Probation: 1991-1997 (In Millions)**

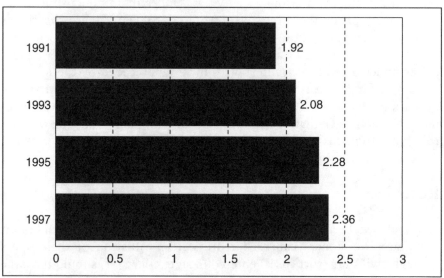

Source: C. Camp and G. Camp (1997). *The Corrections Yearbook,* p. 140. South Salem, NY: Criminal Justice Institute.

## Summary

This chapter has traced the historical, philosophical, and legal developments in the field of probation over the last two centuries. While John Augustus is given credit as the "father" of probation, we have seen that many others played an important part in developing and shaping probation. Major changes are occurring, and probation services will undoubtedly emerge stronger and fairer.

## *Review Questions*

1.  How did the precursors of probation contribute to its development?

2.  Why was probation established much earlier for juvenile offenders than for adult offenders?

3.  Define probation.

4.  Why should probation be the disposition of choice with juvenile offenders?

5.  What are some of the major court cases that have affected juveniles?

6.  How did juvenile court emerge?

7.  What is decarceration and what state led the way in this movement?

## *Key Terms*

benefit of clergy

Cesare Beccaria

decarceration

diversion

filing of cases

John Augustus

judicial reprieve

juvenile court

*Killits* decision

parens patriae

probation

recognizance

restitution

tourniquet sentencing

utilitarianism

## *Recommended Readings*

Dressler, D. (1962). *Practice and Theory of Probation and Parole*. New York, NY: Columbia University Press. A cogent and well-documented analysis of the historical development of probation.

Evjen, V.H. (1975). "The Federal Probation System: The Struggle to Achieve It and Its First 25 Years." *Federal Probation*, 39(2):3-15. A very thorough description of the rise of the Federal probation system.

Lindner, C. and M.R. Savarese (1984). "The Evolution of Probation: Early Salaries, Qualifications and Hiring Practices;" "The Evolution of Probation: The Historical Contributions of the Volunteer;" "The Evolution of Probation: University Settlement and the Beginning of Statutory Probation in New York City;" "The Evolution of Probation: University Settlement and Its Pioneering Role in Probation Work." *Federal Probation*, 48(1-4). This four-part series examines the early rise of probation in the United States.

Rodgers, J.W. and G.L. Mays (1987). *Juvenile Delinquency and Juvenile Justice*. New York, NY: John Wiley. A readable and comprehensive view of the juvenile justice system, its operations and problems.

## *Notes*

[1]    No doubt much of this frustration toward the leniency of probation stems from the fact that probation "lacks the drama of sending a man to a penal institute." In H.E. Barnes and N.D. Teeters (1959). *New Horizons in Criminology*, p. 555. Englewood Cliffs, NJ: Prentice-Hall. See also W.J. Cornelius (1997). *Swift and Sure: Bringing Certainty and Finality to Criminal Punishments*. Irvington-on-Hudson, NY: Bridge Street Press.

[2]    Sureties refers to cash, property, or bond posted by an offender, to be forfeited if he or she fails to conform to such conditions as to appear in court for trial, or to avoid further criminal behavior over a specified time period. It can also refer to a pledge by another responsible person to assure that the accused will appear or behave properly.

[3]    The Volstead Act authorized the enforcement of anti-alcohol legislation—the "Great Experiment" of the Thirteenth Amendment to the U.S. Constitution.

[4]    421 F.2d 993, *cert. denied*, 397 U.S. 1044 (1970).

[5]    411 U.S. 778, 93 S. Ct. 1756 (1972).

[6]    461 U.S. 660 (1983).

[7]    The current mailing address for the American Correctional Association is 4380 Forbes Boulevard, Lanham, MD 20706-4322.

[8]    *Miranda* warnings: 1. That the suspect has the right to remain silent; 2. That any statement he does make may be used as evidence against him; 3. That he has a right to the presence of an attorney; 4. That if he cannot afford an attorney, one will be appointed for him prior to any questioning if he so desires. See *Black's Law Dictionary* (1994), 5th ed., St. Paul, MN: West.

# References

Acker, J.R. and C.S. Lanier (1993). "Capital Murder from Benefit of Clergy of Bifurcated Trials: Narrowing the Class of Offenses Punishable by Death." *Criminal Law Bulletin,* 29(4):291-316.

Allen, H.E. and C.E. Simonsen (1998). *Corrections in America.* Upper Saddle River, NJ: Prentice Hall.

American Bar Association (1980). *Standards Relating to Interim Status: Release, Control and Detention of Accused Juvenile Offenders Between Arrest and Disposition.* Cambridge, MA: Ballinger.

American Bar Association (1970). *Project Standards for Criminal Justice: Standards Relating to Probation.* New York, NY: Institute of Judicial Administration.

American Correctional Association (1997). *Directory of Juvenile and Adult Correctional Departments, Institutions, Agencies and Paroling Authorities.* Lanham, MD: ACA.

American Correctional Association Commission on Accreditation for Corrections (1979). *Manual of Standards for Juvenile Detention Facilities and Services.* Rockville, MD: ACA.

Barnes, H.E. and N.D. Teeters (1959). *New Horizons in Criminology.* Englewood Cliffs, NJ: Prentice-Hall.

Beccaria, C. (1764). *Essay On Crimes and Punishments.* Translated by H. Paulucci (1963). Indianapolis, IN: Bobbs-Merrill.

*Breed v. Jones,* 421 U.S. 519 (1975).

Burdress, L.A. (ed.) (1997). "The Federal Probation and Pretrial Services System." *Federal Probation,* 61(1):5-111.

Camp, C. and G. Camp (1997). *The Corrections Yearbook 1997.* South Salem, NY: Criminal Justice Institute.

Citizens Committee for Children (1982). *Lost Opportunities: A Study of the Promise and Practices of the [New York City] Department of Probation's Family Court.* New York, NY: Citizens Committee for Children.

Clark, J. and H. Alan (1996). *The Pretrial Release Decision Making Process: Goals, Current Practices, and Challenges.* Washington, DC: Pretrial Services Resource Center.

Clear, T.R. and G.F. Cole (1990). *American Corrections.* Pacific Grove, CA: Brooks/Cole.

Clemmer, D. (1940). *The Prison Community.* New York, NY: Rinehart and Company.

Coates, R.B., A.D. Miller, and L.E. Ohlin (1977). *Diversity in a Youth Correctional System: Handling Delinquents in Massachusetts.* Cambridge, MA: Ballinger.

Conrad, J. P. (1987). "Return to John Augustus." *Federal Probation,* 51(4):22-27.

Cornelius, W.J. (1997). *Swift and Sure: Bringing Certainty and Finality to Criminal punishments.* Irvington-on-Hudson: Bridge Street Books.

del Carmen, R. (1984). "Legal Issues and Liabilities in Community Corrections." Paper presented at the meeting of the Academy of Criminal Justice Sciences, Chicago, IL.

del Carmen, R., M. Parker, and F.P. Reddington (1998). *Briefs of Leading Cases in Juvenile Justice.* Cincinnati, OH: Anderson Publishing Co.

Dressler, D. (1962). *Practice and Theory of Probation and Parole.* New York, NY: Columbia University Press.

Eskridge, C. (1983). *Pretrial Release Programming.* New York, NY: Clark Boardman Company.

Evjen, V.H. (1975). "The Federal Probation System: The Struggle to Achieve It and Its First 25 Years." *Federal Probation,* 39(2):3-15.

*Fare v. Michael C.,* 442 U.S. 707 (1979).

Fenwick, C. (1982). "Juvenile Court Intake Decision Making: The Importance of Family Affiliation." *Journal of Criminal Justice,* 10:469-480.

Folks, H. (February 1910). *Juvenile Probation in New York.* Survey, p. 667.

*In re Winship,* 397 U.S. 358 (1970).

Johnson, F.R. (1928). *Probation for Juveniles and Adults.* New York, NY: Century Co.

Kane, R.J. (1995). "A Sentencing Model for Modernizing Sentencing Practices in Massachusetts' 68 District Courts." *Federal Probation,* 59(3):10-15.

*Kent v. United States,* 383 U.S. 54 (1966).

Kindsey, B.B. (1925). "Colorado's Contribution to the Juvenile Court." In H. Lou (ed.) *The Child, the Clinic and the Court,* pp. 108-138. New York, NY: World.

Krajick, K. (1981). "Annual Prison Population Survey: The Boom Resumes." *Corrections Magazine,* 7:16-20.

Krisberg, B., J. Austin, and P.A. Steele (1989). *Unlocking Juvenile Corrections: Evaluating the Massachusetts Department of Youth Services.* San Francisco, CA: The National Council on Crime and Delinquency.

Krisberg, B., J. Austin, K. Joe, and P. Steele (1987). *The Impact of Court Sanctions.* San Francisco, CA: The National Council on Crime and Delinquency.

Kuhl, A. and H.E. Allen (1983). "Social Policies and Practices in Juvenile Corrections: Issues in Criminological Predication." Paper presented at the 9th International Congress on Criminology, Vienna, Austria.

Lindner, C. and M.R. Savarese (1984a). "The Evolution of Probation: Early Salaries, Qualifications and Hiring Practices." *Federal Probation,* 48(1):3-9.

Lindner, C. and M.R. Savarese (1984b). "The Evolution of Probation: The Historical Contributions of the Volunteer." *Federal Probation,* 48(2):2-10.

Lindner, C. and M.R. Savarese (1984c). "The Evolution of Probation: University Settlement and the Beginning of Statutory Probation in New York City." *Federal Probation,* 48(3):3-12.

McCord, W. and J. Sanchez (1983). "The Treatment of Deviant Children: A Twenty-Five Year Follow-Up Study." *Crime & Delinquency,* 29:238-253.

*McKeiver v. Pennsylvania,* 403 U.S. 528 (1971).

McKelvey, B. (1977). *American Prisons: A History of Good Intentions.* Montclair, NJ: Patterson-Smith.

Marshall, F. and G.F. Vito (1982). "Not Without the Tools: The Task of Probation in the Eighties." *Federal Probation*, 46(4):37-40.

Meeker, B.S. (1975). "The Federal Probation System: The Second 25 Years." *Federal Probation*, 39(2):16-25.

National Advisory Commission on Criminal Justice Standards and Goals (1973a). *Corrections*. Washington, DC: U.S. Government Printing Office.

National Advisory Commission on Criminal Justice Standards and Goals (1973b). "Probation: National Standards and Goals." In R.N. Carter and L.T. Wilkins (eds.) *Probation, Parole and Community Services*, pp. 115-147. New York, NY: John Wiley and Sons.

National Center for Juvenile Justice, U.S. Department of Health, Education and Welfare (1970). *Juvenile Court Statistics*. Washington, DC: U.S. Government Printing Office.

National Council on Crime and Delinquency (1961). *Standards and Guides for the Detention of Children and Youth*. New York, NY: National Council on Crime and Delinquency.

National Criminal Justice Information and Statistics Service (1978). *State and Local Probation and Parole Systems*. Washington, DC: U.S. Government Printing Office.

*Nelson v. Heyne*, 491 F.2d 352 (7th Cir. 1974).

Paulsen, M. and C. Whitebread (1974). *Juvenile Law and Procedure*. Reno, NV: National Council of Juvenile Court Judges: Institute of Judicial Administration.

Parker, L.C. (1997). "A Contemporary View of Alternatives to Incarceration in Denmark." *Federal Probation*, 61(2):67-73.

Platt, A. (1969). *The Child Savers*. Chicago, IL: University of Chicago Press.

President's Commission on Law Enforcement and Administration of Justice (1967a). Corrections. Washington, DC: U.S. Government Printing Office.

President's Commission on Law Enforcement and Administration of Justice (1967b). *Juvenile Delinquency and Youth Crime*. Washington, DC: U.S. Government Printing Office.

President's Commission on Law Enforcement and Administration of Justice (1967c). Task Force Report Corrections. Washington, DC: U.S. Government Printing Office.

Rausch, S.P. and C.H. Logan (1982). "Diversion from Juvenile Court: Panacea or Pandora's Box?" Paper presented at the meeting of the American Society of Criminology, Toronto, Canada.

Reed, T. (1997). *Apples to Apples: Comparing the Operational Costs of Juvenile and Adult Correctional Programs in Texas*. Austin, TX: Texas Criminal Justice Policy Council.

Rogers, J.W. and G.L Mays (1987). *Juvenile Delinquency & Juvenile Justice*. New York, NY: John Wiley.

Rothman, D.J. (1979). *Incarceration and Its Alternatives in 20th-Century America*. Washington, DC: National Institute of Law Enforcement and Criminal Justice.

Saari, R. (1974). *Under Lock and Key: Juveniles in Jail and Detention*. Ann Arbor, MI: National Assessment of Juvenile Corrections.

Schur, E. (1971). *Labeling Deviant Behavior: Its Sociological Implications*. New York, NY: Harper and Row.

Shannon, L.W. (1982). *Assessing the Relationship of Adult Career Criminals to Juvenile Careers*. Washington, DC: U.S. Government Printing Office.

Sherrill, M. (1975a, February). "Jerome Miller: Does He Have the Answers . . .?" *Corrections Magazine*, 3(1):24-28.

Sherrill, M. (1975b, February). "Juvenile Corrections in Massachusetts." *Corrections Magazine*, 3(1):3-12.

Sherrill, M. (1975c, February). "Harvard Recidivism Study." *Corrections Magazine*, 3(1):21-23.

Solomon K. and M. Klein (1983). *National Evaluation of the Deinstitutionalization of Status Offender Programs*. Washington, DC: Office of Juvenile Justice and Delinquency Prevention, U.S. Department of Justice.

Stern, I. R. (1991). *Juvenile Waiver: A Policy Brief*. Honolulu, HI: University of Hawaii at Manoa.

Tucker, J. (1982, September). *Federal News Clips: On the Line*. College Park, MD: American Correctional Association.

United Nations (1976a). "The Legal Origins of Probation." In R.N. Carter and L.T. Wilkins (eds.) *Probation, Parole and Community Services*, pp. 81-88. New York, NY: John Wiley and Sons.

United Nations (1976b). "The Origin of Probation in the United States." In R.N. Carter and L.T. Wilkins (eds.) *Probation, Parole and Community Services*, pp. 89-92. New York, NY: John Wiley and Sons.

Whitlack, W.G. (1973). "Practical Aspects for Reducing Detention Home Population." *Juvenile Justice*, 24:17-29.

# Juvenile Probation

When we are out of sympathy with the
young, then I think our work in the world is
over.

—George MacDonald

## The Juvenile Crime Problem

The challenge of crime in the United States remains a major social
problem that has serious and sometimes deadly consequences but, in the
last half-decade, the size of the problem has abated as the nature of
crime has changed. For example, the Federal Bureau of Investigation reports that the volume of crime, while unacceptably high, actually decreased almost 3 percent from 1995 to 1996, and the crime *rate* decreased almost 4 percent (FBI, 1997). Hopefully, this favorable trend
will continue!

The rise in the juvenile crime rate is considered a problematic aspect
of the crime problem. Youth under age 18 now commit almost 1 in 3 of
the most serious crimes in the nation (Table 6.1) and account for more
than one-half of the arrests for arson and at least one-third of the arrests for robbery, burglary, larceny-theft, and motor-vehicle theft. When
arrests for juveniles are compared to those for adults over the last
decade, even more disturbing trends are evident (Table 6.2). Juvenile arrests for violent crimes increased 60 percent (compared to 24 percent
for adults), and 8 percent for property crimes (compared to a *decrease*
of 6 percent for adults!). Huge jumps can be seen in arrests for murder
and non-negligent manslaughter, robbery, aggravated assault, and
arson. Two out of every 10 juvenile murder arrests involve a victim
under age 18 and, of those, 88 percent were under age 14. Unfortunately, homicide victimization is concentrated among minority groups:
the victimization rate for black youth is more than 6 times the rate for
white youth (Snyder, Sickman & Yamagata, 1996:19).

Table 6.1
**Percentage of Juvenile (Under Age 18) Arrests Among All Arrests, 1987 and 1996**

| OFFENSE: | 1987 | 1996 |
|---|---|---|
| Total: | 29 | 31 |
| Violent Crime Index | 15 | 19 |
| Murder | 10 | 15 |
| Forcible Rape | 15 | 17 |
| Robbery | 23 | 32 |
| Aggravated Assault | 12 | 15 |
| Burglary | 34 | 37 |
| Larceny-Theft | 31 | 34 |
| Motor Vehicle Theft | 39 | 42 |
| Arson | 41 | 53 |
| Violent Crimes | 15 | 19 |
| Property Crimes | 32 | 35 |

Source: Federal Bureau of Investigation (1997). *Crime in the United States 1996*, p. 218. Washington, DC: U.S. Department of Justice.

Table 6.2
**Percentage Growth of Arrests: Juvenile and Adults, From 1987 to 1996**

| OFFENSE: | Juvenile | Adult |
|---|---|---|
| Total: | 14 | 2 |
| Murder | 51 | −10 |
| Forcible Rape | −3 | −14 |
| Robbery | 57 | −3 |
| Aggravated Assault | 70 | 39 |
| Burglary | −12 | −22 |
| Larceny-Theft | 14 | −1 |
| Motor Vehicle Theft | 9 | −2 |
| Arson | 36 | −17 |
| Violent Crimes | 60 | 24 |
| Property Crimes | 8 | −6 |

Source: Federal Bureau of Investigation (1997). *Crime in the United States 1996*, p. 218. Washington, DC: U.S. Department of Justice.

Much of these increases are due to the emergence of crack cocaine, juvenile gangs, and violence as major aspects of gang culture (Allen & Simonsen, 1998:318). Unfortunately, these crimes appear to have spread to many youth who are not part of gangs. These crime issues and changes have caused the society as a whole to rethink rehabilitation, to advocate "get-tough" approaches, to waiver in their acceptance of juvenile courts, and to bind juveniles over to prisons for adult felons. There are more than 16,500 inmates in American *prisons* who are under age 18, up from 7,100 in 1986 (American Correctional Association, 1986; 1997). Fortunately, most juvenile offenders who come to the attention of the court will receive treatment and non-incarcerative dispositions.

As was the case with adult offenders, the development of community corrections has led to probation, currently the most frequently used disposition for juvenile offenders. In the United States, almost 57 percent of the cases that reach the juvenile court dispositional stage result in probation (U.S. Bureau of Justice Statistics, 1994a:549).

Probation for juvenile offenders is defined as a legal status created by a court of juvenile jurisdiction. It usually involves (President's Commission, 1967:130):

1.  A judicial finding that the behavior of the child has been such to bring him within the purview of the court;

2.  The imposition of conditions upon his continued freedom; and

3.  The provision of means for helping him meet those conditions and for determining the degree to which he meets them.

Probation thus implies more than indiscriminately giving the child "another chance." Its central thrust is to give him or her positive assistance in adjustment in the free community.

## Historical Background

The historical precursors of juvenile probation are as generally outlined above. The legal underpinnings of modern juvenile probation was established in England during the early Middle Ages, under the principle of *parens patriae*: "The King, being father of His country, must protect the welfare of the children."

As with adult probation, John Augustus is viewed as the "father of juvenile probation" since many of his charges were female juveniles in trouble with the law. His work contributed to the development of the first visiting probation agent systems in Massachusetts (1869) and passage of the first enabling legislation establishing probation for juveniles

(1878). In the same era, the Society for the Prevention of Cruelty to Children (1875) was established. Their proposed policies and activism directly contributed to the first juvenile court in America specifically set up to address the care, treatment, and welfare of juvenile offenders: the Cook County (Chicago), Illinois juvenile court in 1899. See Table 5.1 in Chapter 5.

The Cook County juvenile court emerged from the concerns of a group of compassionate, humanitarian, and wealthy women in Chicago who wished each child to receive the care, custody, and treatment as their natural parents ought to have provided (Lindner & Savarese, 1984a). The juvenile court was one project devised to attain these objectives,[1] and utilized individualized treatment based on extensive diagnosis of the child's personality and needs, with the judge serving as a counselor to the patient (juvenile). It was widely argued that the juvenile court would safeguard presumed superconstitutional rights[2] (the child would receive more than his or her just deserts) and avoid the stigma of criminal conviction through informal court proceedings based on benevolent attention, understanding the juvenile, humanitarian intervention, solicitous care, and regenerative and restorative[3] treatment. To attain these objectives, procedural safeguards guaranteed under the U.S. Constitution were abandoned; the focus was on the child, not the deed. Box 6.1 contains three selected Amendments to the U.S. Constitution that pertain to rights guaranteed to adults.

Photo 6.1
Counseling a juvenile. Courtesy of Talbert House, Inc.

Juvenile court proceedings were informal, conducted in the absence of legal counsel, closed to the public, and individualized to maximize guidance and outcome. To protect and serve the "best interests of the child," records were confidential. Legal challenges were rare.

Juvenile courts were quickly established throughout the various states, federal government, and Puerto Rico. By 1927, all but two states had enacted enabling legislation establishing both juvenile court and probation. The theoretical assumption of juvenile probation was that providing guidance, counseling, resources, and supervision would assist low-risk juveniles to adapt to constructive living, thus avoiding the necessity of institutionalization.

Box 6.1

### Selected Amendments to the U.S. Constitution

**Fourth Amendment:** The right of the people to be secure in their persons, houses, papers, and effects, against unreasonable searches and seizures, shall not be violated, and no warrants shall issue, but upon probable cause, supported by oath or affirmation, and particularly describing the place to be searched, and the person or things to be seized.

**Fifth Amendment:** No person shall be held to answer for a capital, or otherwise infamous crime, unless a presentment or indictment of a Grand Jury, except in cases arising in land or naval forces, or the Militia, when in actual service in time of War or public danger; nor shall any person be subject for the same offense twice put in jeopardy of life or limb; nor shall be compelled in any criminal case to be a witness against himself, nor to be deprived of life, liberty or property, without due process of law; nor shall private property be taken for public use, without just compensation.

**Sixth Amendment:** In all criminal prosecutions, the accused shall enjoy the right to a speedy and public trial, by an impartial jury of the state or district wherein the crime shall have been committed, which district shall have been previously ascertained by law, and to be informed of the nature and the cause of the accusation; to be confronted with the witnesses against him, to have compulsory process for obtaining witnesses in his favor, and to have the Assistance of Counsel for his defense.

The primary goals of probation became to assist juveniles in dealing with their individual problems and social environments. Resolving underlying causes of the youthful offenders would permit their reintegration into the community. It was argued that probation, rather than incarceration, should be the disposition of choice, because:

1. Probation provides for community safety while permitting the youthful offender to remain in the community for reintegration purposes;

2. Institutionalization leads to prisonization, the process of learning the norms and culture of institutional living (Clemmer, 1940). This decreases the ability of the juvenile to function as a law-abiding citizen when released, and thus leads to further involvement as an adult offender;[4]

3. The stigma of incarceration is avoided (Schur, 1971);

4. The negative labeling effects of being treated as a criminal are avoided;

5. Reintegration is more likely if existing community resources are used and the youth continues to engage in social and familial support systems (family, school, peers, extracurricular activities, employment, friends, etc.); and

6. Probation is less expensive than incarceration, arguably more humanitarian, and is at least as effective in reducing further delinquent behavior as is institutionalization.[5]

The "child saving movement" underlying the development of the juvenile court is clearly seen here.[6]

Ed Stein. Reprinted courtesy of the Rocky Mountain News.

# The Legal Rights of Juveniles

It is obvious that the juvenile court, as it developed over the twentieth century, addressed juvenile offenders under civil rather than criminal procedures (civil suits deal with individual wrongs, while criminal prosecutions involve public wrongs). The most important objective of the original creators of the juvenile court was to create a separate court system for delinquent, dependent, and neglected children. Following the doctrine of *parens patriae*, the juvenile court system suspended or ignored the legal rights constitutionally guaranteed to all citizens: the right to trial and against self-incrimination, and other rights. Constitutional rights were thought unnecessary for juveniles, as the court would focus on and uphold the best interests of a child in a civil setting. Many juvenile judges and child advocates perceived inequity and attempted to provide constitutional safeguards. Beginning in the 1960s, questions about juvenile court proceeding fairness and the constitutionally guaranteed rights of juveniles were brought to the U.S. Supreme Court. Significant changes were made. It is necessary to review those decisions to comprehend their impact of juvenile probation.

## Kent v. United States

In 1966, the U.S. Supreme Court was asked to consider the issue of the transfer ("waiver") of a juvenile to the criminal court system.[7] The issue was the legislative waiver of the juvenile court procedures. The Court stated:

> There is much evidence that some juvenile courts . . . lack the personnel, facilities, and the techniques to perform adequately as representatives of the State in a *parens patriae* capacity, at least with respect to children charged with law violation. There is evidence, in fact, that here may be grounds for concern that the child receives the worst of both worlds: that he gets neither the protections accorded to adults nor the solicitous care and regenerative treatment postulated for children (*Kent v. United States*, 1966).

This case portended more important issues on which the Court was asked to rule (Merlo, Benekos & Cook, 1997).

## In re Gault

In 1967, the Court decided its first major issue in the area of juvenile court *procedures*. In Arizona, Gerald Gault, then age 16, allegedly telephoned a neighbor woman and used obscene phrases and words. The use of such language over the telephone violated an Arizona statute. Gerald Gault was subsequently adjudicated a juvenile delinquent after a proceeding in which he was denied basic procedural safeguards otherwise guaranteed to any adult. This landmark decision[8] categorically granted the following to all juveniles charged with delinquent acts that might result in such grievous harm as commitment to a correctional institution:

1.  Right to know the nature of the charges against them, to prepare for trial;

2.  Right to counsel;

3.  Right against self-incrimination; and

4.  Right to confront and cross-examine accusers and witnesses.

The *Gault* decision not only returned procedural rights to juveniles, it also ended the presumption that juvenile courts were beyond the purview and scope of due process protections (Sanborn, 1994).[9]

## In re Winship

This 1970 decision further defined the rights of juveniles. Proof used in a court finding of delinquency must show "beyond a reasonable doubt" that the juvenile committed the alleged delinquent act (Sanborn, 1994), the same proof standard used for adults in criminal trials. The Court specifically found unpersuasive the argument that juvenile proceedings were noncriminal and intended to benefit the child (*In re Winship*, 1970).[10] Currently, juveniles do not have the right to trial by jury (*McKeiver v. Pennsylvania*, 1971).

These three major decisions by the U.S. Supreme Court created the due process model for the juvenile court. The *McKeiver* decision seemed to indicate that the Court was moving away from increased rights for juveniles but, in 1975, the Court ruled (*Breed v. Jones*) that, once tried as a juvenile, that person cannot be tried as an adult on the same charges.[11] In 1979, (*Fare v. Michael C.*), the Court ruled on interrogation, and indicated that a child cannot voluntarily waive his privilege against self-incrimination without first speaking to his parents and without first consulting an attorney.[12] In 1984, the Court distinctly departed from the trend toward increased juvenile rights by reaffirming parens patriae (*Schall v. Martin*, 1984). As Allen and Simonsen (1998:643) note:

> As a result of Supreme Court cases, the juvenile court is now basically a court of law. . . .

Thus far, the procedural rights guaranteed to a juvenile in court proceedings are as follows:

1.  The right to adequate notice of charges against him or her;

2.  The right to counsel and to have counsel provided if the child is indigent;

3.  The right of confrontation and cross-examination of witnesses;

4.  The right to refuse to do anything that would be self-incriminatory;

5.  The right to a judicial hearing, with counsel, prior to transfer of a juvenile to an adult court; and

6.  The right to be considered innocent until proven guilty beyond a reasonable doubt.

Juvenile probation, as seen in court proceedings and used in juvenile courts, is currently vacillating between these two models, and major changes are forthcoming (Rogers & Mays, 1987). On one hand, we see liberal reformers who call for increased procedural and legal safeguards for juveniles; on the other hand, we have a conservative movement that focuses on the victim (Torbert, Gable & Hurst, 1996) and seriousness of the crime (Clear & Cole, 1990).[13] As one conservative put it, "You are just as dead if a 15-year-old shoots you as you are if a 25-year-old does."[14]

## Criticisms of the Juvenile Court and *Parens Patriae*

Criticisms of and disenchantment with the *parens patriae* juvenile court and its procedures (Moore & Wakeling, 1997) have been voiced by such groups as the bar, the judiciary, the federal government, practitioners, private nonprofit organizations, researchers,[15] and voluntary organizations, among others. Such efforts, when coupled with decisions by the U.S. Supreme Court, have focused on four major areas of concern:

1.  Diversion of juveniles;

2.  Status Offenders;

3.  Decriminalization; and

4.  Deinstitutionalization (decarceration).

It is with diversion and deinstitutionalization that juvenile probation is most concerned.

---

Box 6.2

### Status Offenders

A status offender is generally a juvenile who has come into contact with the juvenile authorities based upon conduct that is an offense only when committed by a juvenile. A status offense is conduct that would not be defined as a criminal act when committed by an adult (Maxson & Klein, 1997).

## Diversion of Juveniles

The *Gault*, *Kent*, and *Winship* cases defined those constitutionally guaranteed rights that must be accorded every juvenile, and formed the basis of the due process model noted above. This model requires adherence to minimally guaranteed legal procedures,[16] a voluntary and helping relationship, and the least restrictive environment necessary to treat the juvenile. It also requires a demonstrated need for detention[17] and, absent this, a mandatory noncommitment to an institution (del Carmen, 1984; 1998).

> **Box 6.3**
>
> ### Fourteenth Amendment
>
> All citizens born and naturalized in the United States, and subject to the jurisdiction thereof, are citizens of the United States and of the State wherein they reside. No State shall make or enforce any law which shall abridge the privileges or immunities of citizens of the United States; nor shall any State deprive any person of life, liberty or property, without due process of law, nor deny to any person within its jurisdiction of the equal protection of the law.

The question of whether incarcerated juveniles have a mandatory right to treatment has been addressed in several federal cases. The most significant of these was *Nelson v. Heyne* (1974), which upheld a categorical right to treatment for confined juveniles under the due process clause of the Fourteenth Amendment. The appellate court stated that the *parens patriae* principle of the juvenile court could be justified only if committed delinquent youth receive treatment:

> . . . the right to treatment includes the right to minimum acceptable standards of care and treatment for juveniles and the right to individualized care and treatment. Because children differ in their needs for rehabilitation, individual need for treatment will differ. When a state assumes the place of a juvenile's parents, it assumes as well the parental duties, and its treatments of its juveniles should, so far as can be reasonably required, be what proper parental care would provide. Without a program of individual treatment, the result may be that the juveniles will not be treated, but warehoused (*Nelson v. Heyne*).

Despite the implications of *Nelson*, a nationwide survey of state, local, and privately run juvenile detention facilities in 1994 found serious problem areas ranging from inadequate living space and crowding, to high numbers of injuries to confined juveniles through "alarmingly widespread" suicidal behavior.[18] There appears to be no consensus on which youth are best served by residential (versus community) care, and there are inadequate numbers of controlled experiments to date that allow determination of how outcomes are linked to treatment.[19]

The due process model and the *Nelson* requirements have significantly contributed toward the diversion process of juveniles. Cost is another factor; the American Correctional Association (1997) reports the cost of one juvenile institution as $46,500 and $109,500 for New Jersey and Pennsylvania, respectively. Allen and Simonsen (1998:613) define diversion as:

> The official halting or suspension, at any legally prescribed processing point after a recorded justice system entry, of formal juvenile justice proceedings against an alleged offender, and referral of that person to a treatment or care program administered by a nonjustice agency or to a private agency. Sometimes no referral is given.

Diversion programs function to divert juveniles out of the juvenile justice system, encourage the use of existing correctional facilities and agencies for such offenders, and avoid formal contact with the juvenile court. These programs include remedial education programs,[20] foster homes, group homes, community drug treatment,[21] attendance centers,[22] and local counseling facilities and centers. The effectiveness of such programs are not yet definitively documented, but Rausch and Logan (1982) summarized existing studies and concluded:

> One common component to all rationales for diversion seems to be that less intervention is better than more intervention. Thus, whatever else it involves, diversion necessarily implies an attempt to make the form of social control more limited in scope. Studies of diversion programs, however, indicate that instead of limiting the scope of the system, diversion programs often broaden it. They do this either by intensifying services or by taking in more cases. The latter is referred to as a "widening of the net" effect. Police and court intake personnel are often reluctant to simply ignore them or turn them loose. When provided with a formal channel for diversion, police and court intake officers have been directing to this channel many individuals who otherwise would have been left alone or released at the intake stage.

## Deinstitutionalization

The concept of deinstitutionalization, also known as decarceration, is recent; 1969 is considered its inception. In that year, Jerome Miller began deinstitutionalization of incarcerated juvenile offenders in Massachusetts. Asserting that the era of confinement of children in larger correctional facilities was over and that an era of more humane, decent, and community-based care for delinquents had begun, Miller closed the major juvenile institutions. Confined charges were placed in small homes, using other, already existing community-based correctional programs and services (Sherrill, 1976a & 1975b).

Initial program evaluations found the community-based juvenile group did worse in terms of recidivism (74% vs. 66%) than earlier juveniles[23] processed through the correctional units (McCord & Sanchez, 1983). However, closer analysis of the data revealed that, when community-based programs were properly implemented, recidivism rates were equal or slightly lower than the institutional group.

Photo 6.2
Juvenile Community Service Program. Photograph by Bill Sherlock. Used with permission of the American Correctional Association.

Other states (particularly Hawaii) have followed Massachusetts' lead. Utah closed a 350-bed training school and placed the 290 youth in community-based programs modeled on Massachusetts' program. Again, researchers concluded there was no evidence that public safety had been compromised. There was strong evidence that Utah saved considerable money when compared to past correctional practices (Krisberg, Austin, Joe & Steele, 1987). McMahon (1992) argues that decarceration is possible.

Recently, Ohio began a program entitled RECLAIM Ohio (Reasoned and Equitable Community and Local Alternatives to Incarceration of Minors). This statewide initiative is designed to assist counties in providing community services to adjudicated juvenile offenders. Essentially, local juvenile courts are given an allocation of funds to use for community-based alternatives. In turn, they must pay for all youths who are incarcerated in a state institution from their allocation. Preliminary results indicated that they are successfully reducing the commitment rate of juveniles to state facilities (Latessa, Moon & Applegate, 1995). A statewide study of RECLAIM Ohio (Latessa, Turner, Moon &

Applegate, 1998) found sharply reduced commitments to the state institutions within the Department of Youth Services (previously operating at some 160% of capacity). Local programs implemented in the pilot phase were able to reduce commitments 42 percent below expected commitments ("base expectancy"), while the newer second phase programs reduced commitments by 36 percent. Local juvenile courts were strengthened; private sector service providers increased their participation; and cooperation across prosecutor, court and court services increased. Failure rates were not unusually high and the percentage of youth participating in RECLAIM who were eventually committed to state institutions has remained low. Project RECLAIM is a constructive example of coordination and use of community corrections to avoid sending youth the secure institutions.

---

**Box 6.4**

### Selective Incapacitation

This doctrine of isolating the juvenile offender, or "social disablement," proposes a policy of incarcerating those whose criminal behavior is so damaging or probable that nothing short of isolation will prevent recidivism. This "nothing-else-works" approach would require correctly identifying those offenders who would be eligible for long-term incarceration, and diverting others into correctional alternatives. Thus we would be able to make maximum effective use of detention cells, a scarce resource, to protect society from the depredations of such dangerous and repetitive offenders.

Current correctional technology does not permit correctly identifying those who require incapacitation. Rather, the evidence is that we would probably incarcerate numerous non-dangerous juveniles (a "false-positive" problem). Yet there is evidence of effectiveness of some prediction scales to identify low-rate juvenile offenders for selective early release (Hayes & Geerken, 1997). This would be selective "decapacitation"! Whatever benefits might accrue to this sentencing doctrine have thus far eluded corrections.

Yet chronic repeat offenders (those with five or more arrests by age 18), who make up a very small proportion of all offenders, commit a very high proportion of all crimes. More research into correct classification of juvenile and adult offenders is needed.

Those favoring placement of juveniles in secure institutions cite the public's fear of violent youth crime as a rationale for incarcerating young offenders. They also argue that "getting those thugs" off the streets prevents further offending (selective incapacitation), provides the structure and control necessary for treatment and educational programs (rehabilitation), and prevents other juveniles from committing serious offenses (general deterrence). Deinstitutionalization advocates counter that many incarcerated juveniles were not committed for serious violent offenses, institutionalization is costly, the deterrence evidence is almost non-existent, the evidence of effective rehabilitation in correctional facilities is weak, and community alternatives are just as effective. Finally, opponents of institutionalization argue that local community alternatives, when coupled with child advocates, can substantially reduce commitments to state juvenile correctional institutions.[24]

## The Future of Juvenile Probation

Several conclusions are suggested by this review of current trends and developments. It is obvious that juvenile justice and juvenile probation are in a period of rapid change, and that juvenile policy is vacillating between the old *parens patriae* and the newer due process model. Further, the roles and functions of the juvenile probation officer are undergoing change and enlargement. The various state juvenile systems and jurisdictions are moving toward diversion, waiver of juvenile offenders into the criminal justice arena, removal of the status offender from juvenile court jurisdiction, and deinstitutionalization of juveniles. In addition, faced with the legal constraints, requirements for treatment of incarcerated youth, and the high costs of juvenile institutions, probation officers are facing emerging and divergent demands. Finally, to divert and refer juveniles to social services, there must be increased community and private service programs and agencies to provide local community services to juveniles. States can encourage these developments with subsidies and legislation that enable local and county community corrections (Harris, 1996). In other chapters, we explore privatization of juvenile services, technologies applied to juvenile supervision (electronic monitoring, classification devices, specialized service providers, and so on), and newer supervision strategies, such as house arrest, day attendance centers, intensive supervised probation, and specialized caseloads. Reintegrative and restorative approaches are being implemented across the nation, including restitution, victim-offender mediation, compensation, and community work orders. The issues surrounding crowding, changing faces of probation clients, and training needs can be found in later chapters.

Since juvenile probation services, as agents of court supervision for young offenders, depend on the philosophy of the juvenile court, court administrators, and referral agencies, a patchwork of temporizing procedures, responses and programs is emerging. With a shortfall in resources facing almost every court agency, innovation and strategic planning are required. There is no quick fix for the quandary of juvenile probation and corrections, and we conclude this section by pointing out that new demands will continue to emerge.

## Summary

Since the early beginnings of juvenile court, correctional reformers have sought ways to effectively deal with the juvenile crime problem. This chapter has examined the development of juvenile court and the role of juvenile probation in the processing and treatment of youthful offenders.

### Review Questions

1. Why was probation established across the nation much earlier for juveniles than for adult offenders?

2. Why should probation be the disposition of choice with juvenile offenders?

3. Identify and describe three major court cases that have affected juveniles.

4. What is deinstitutionalization, and what state led the way in this movement?

5. Argue the case for binding over serious juvenile offenders as adults; against this practice.

### Key Terms

decarceration
deinstitutionalization
diversion
Fourteenth Amendment

juvenile court
parens patriae
selective incapacitation
status offender

## Recommended Readings

Krisberg, B. (1997). *The Impact of the Justice System on Serious, Violent, and Chronic Juvenile Offenders.* San Francisco: National Council on Crime and Delinquency.

Schissel, B. (1997). *Blaming Children: Youth Crime, Moral Panic and the Politics of Hate.* Halifax, CN: Fernwood Publishing.

Simonsen, C.E. (1997). *Juvenile Justice in America.* Englewood Cliffs, NJ: Prentice-Hall.

Whitehead, J.T. and S.P. Lab (1996). *Juvenile Justice,* Second Edition. Cincinnati, OH: Anderson Publishing Co.

## Notes

[1]    Chicago courts continue to innovate to handle juvenile offenders. See U.S. Bureau of Justice Statistics (1994b). *Night Drug Courts: The Cook County Experience.* Washington, DC: U.S. Bureau of Justice Statistics. For a critical view of the Illinois juvenile justice system, see Randall Berger, "Illinois Juvenile Justice: An Emerging Dual System." *Crime & Delinquency,* 40(1):54-68.

[2]    Critics argue that this has not happened. See Barry Feld (1993). "Criminalizing the American Juvenile Court." In Michael Tonry (ed.) *Crime and Justice: A Review of Research,* pp. 197-280. Chicago, IL: University of Chicago Press.

[3]    Mark Umbreit (1994). *Victim Meets Offender: The Impact of Restorative Justice and Mediation.* Monsey, NY: Criminal Justice Press. See also G. Bazemore and M. Umbreit (1995). "Rethinking the Sentencing Function in Juvenile Court: Retributive or Restorative Responses to Youth Crime." *Crime & Delinquency,* 41(3):296-316.

[4]    The perceived relationship between juvenile delinquency and adult criminality has been seriously challenged by recent research. Arguing that evidence is not sufficient to establish accurate predictions about whether juvenile delinquents would eventually become adult offenders, Lyle Shannon also found that the relationship that does exist can in large part be explained by the effects of processes within the juvenile and criminal justice systems, as well as the continued delinquent behavior of the juvenile. See L.W. Shannon (1982). *Assessing the Relationship of Adult Career Criminals to Juvenile Careers.* Washington, DC: U.S. Government Printing Office.

[5]    See K. Solomon and M. Klein (1983). *National Evaluation of the Deinstitutionalization of Status Offender Programs.* Washington, DC: U.S. Department of Justice.

[6]    Not all scholars agree that the moving force behind early juvenile court development was benevolent. For example, A.M. Platt believes that the rationale for saving the youth was part of a larger social movement that attempted to strengthen the position of corporate capitalism in the United States. He argues that the juvenile court was a means of preserving the existing class system. See A.M. Platt (1977). *The Child Savers: The Invention of Delinquency.* Chicago, IL: University of Chicago Press.

[7]     Leona Lee (1994). "Factors Determining Waiver to a Juvenile Court." *Journal of Criminal Justice*, 22(4):329-340. See also Eric Jenson and L. Metzger, "A Test of the Deterrent Effect of Legislative Waiver on Violent Juvenile Crime." *Crime & Delinquency*, 40(1):96-104; and A. Merlo, P. Benekos, and W. Cook (1997). "'Getting Tough' on Youth: Legislative Waiver as Crime Control." *Juvenile and Family Court Journal*, 48(3):1-15.

[8]     *In re Gault*, 387 U.S. 1 (1967). See also J. Sanborn (1994). "Remnants of Parens Patria in the Adjudicatory Hearing." *Crime & Delinquency*, 40(4):594-615; and C. Manfredi (1998). *The Supreme Court and Juvenile Justice*. Lawrence, KS: University Press of Kansas.

[9]     See also Joseph Sanborn (1994). "Constitutional Problems of Juvenile Delinquent Trials." *Judicature*, 78(2):81-88.

[10]     Historical data identifying main sources of the growth of juvenile prosecutions in London Court (1790-1820) can be found in Peter King and Joan Noel (1994). "The Origins of the Problem of Juvenile Delinquency: The Growth of Juvenile Prosecution in London." In L. Knafla et al., *Criminal Justice History: An International Volume*, pp. 17-41. Westport, CT: Greenwood Press.

[11]     This would be a grievous case of double jeopardy. See also Sanborn, *supra* note 11.

[12]     In *Fare v. Michael C.* (1979), a juvenile murder suspect consented to an interrogation after he was denied the opportunity to consult with his probation officer. The U.S. Supreme Court ruled that there is no constitutional mandate to allow a suspect to speak with his probation officer. The Court indicated that the trial court judge should take into consideration the totality of the circumstances of the youth's waiver of his or her rights. Factors such as age, maturity, intelligence, and experience should be taken into consideration.

[13]     Randall Berger (1994). "Illinois Juvenile Justice: An Emerging Dual System." *Crime & Delinquency*, 40(1):54-68. Cohn is more pessimistic: Alvin Cohn (1994). "The Future of Juvenile Justice Administration: Evolution v. Revolution." *Juvenile and Family Court Journal*, 45(3):51-63.

[14]     See Joseph Sheley, Zina McGee, and James Wright (1994). *Weapons-Related Victimization in Selected Inner-City High School Samples*. Washington, DC: Bureau of Justice Statistics. Linda Bastian and Bruce Taylor (1994). *Young Black Male Victims*. Washington, DC: Bureau of Justice Statistics.

[15]     Michael Jones and Barry Krisberg (1994). *Images and Reality: Juvenile Crime, Youth Violence and Public Policy*. San Francisco, CA: National Council on Crime and Delinquency; and M. Moore and S. Wakeling (1997). *Juvenile Justice: Shoring Up the Foundations*. Chicago: University of Chicago Press.

[16]     Sanborn, *supra* note 11.

[17]     Gordon Bazemore (1994). "Understanding the Response to Reform Limiting Discretion: Judges' Views on Restrictions on Detention Intake." *Justice Quarterly*, 11(2):429-452.

[18]   Abt Associates (1994). *Conditions of Confinement: Juvenile Detention and Corrections Facilities*. Washington, DC: Office of Juvenile Justice and Delinquency Prevention.

[19]   United States Government Accounting Office (1994). *Residential Care: Some High-Risk Youth Benefit but More Study is Needed*. Washington, DC: U.S. Government Accounting Office.

[20]   An example of this is Project READ, San Jose State University.

[21]   Elizabeth Mauser, Kit Van Stelle, and Paul Moberg "The Economic Impacts of Diverting Substance-Abusing Offenders into Treatment." *Crime & Delinquency*, 40(4):568-588.

[22]   J. McDevitt, M. Domino, and K. Brown (1997). *Metropolitan Day Reporting Center: An Evaluation*. Boston: Center for Criminal Justice Policy Research, Northeastern University.

[23]   Similar finding emerged when Maryland's Montrose Training School was closed. Denise Gottfredson and William Barton (1993). "Deinstitutionalization of Juvenile Offenders." *Criminology*, 31(4):591-610.

[24]   Dan Macallair (1994). "Disposition Case Advocacy in San Francisco Juvenile Justice System: A New Approach to Deinstitutionalization," *Crime & Delinquency*, 40(1):84-95. See also Dan Macallair (1993). "Reaffirming Rehabilitation in Juvenile Justice." *Youth and Society*, 25(1):104-125.

## References

Abt Associates (1994). *Conditions of Confinement: Juvenile Detention and Corrections Facilities*. Washington, DC: Office of Juvenile Justice and Delinquency Prevention.

Allen, H.E. and C.E. Simonsen (1998). *Corrections in America*. Upper Saddle River, NJ: Prentice Hall.

American Correctional Association (1997). *Directory of Juvenile and Adult Correctional Departments, Institutions, Agencies and Paroling Authorities*. Lanham, MD: ACA.

American Correctional Association (1986). *Directory of Juvenile and Adult Correctional Departments, Institutions, Agencies and Paroling Authorities*. College Park, MD: ACA.

Bazemore, G. (1994). "Understanding the Response to Reform Limiting Discretion: Judges' Views on Restrictions on Detention Intake." *Justice Quarterly*, 11(2):429-452.

Bazemore, G. and M. Umbreit (1995). "Rethinking the Sentencing Function in Juvenile Court: Retributive or Restorative Response to Youth Crime." *Crime & Delinquency*, 41(3):296-316.

Berger, R. (1994). "Illinois Juvenile Justice: An Emerging Dual System." *Crime & Delinquency*, 40(1):54-68.

*Breed v. Jones*, 421 U.S. 519 (1975).

Clear, T.R. and G.F. Cole (1990). *American Corrections*. Pacific Grove, CA: Brooks/Cole.

Clemmer, D. (1940). *The Prison Community*. New York, NY: Rinehart and Company.

Cohn, A. (1994). "The Future of Juvenile Justice Administration: Evolution v. Revolution." *Juvenile and Family Court Journal*, 45(3):51-63.

del Carmen, R. (1984). "Legal Issues and Liabilities in Community Corrections." Paper presented at the annual meeting of the Academy of Criminal Justice Sciences, Chicago, IL.

del Carmen, R., M. Parker, and F. Reddington (1998), *Briefs of Leading Cases in Juvenile Justice*. Cincinnati, OH: Anderson Publishing Co.

*Fare v. Michael C.*, 442 U.S. 707 (1979).

Federal Bureau of Investigation (1997). *Crime in the United States, 1996*. Washington, DC: U.S. Department of Justice.

Gottfredson, D. and W. Barton (1993). "Deinstitutionalization of Juvenile Offenders." *Criminology*, 31(4):591-610.

Government Accounting Office (1994). *Residential Care: Some High Risk Youth Benefit but More Study is Needed*. Washington, DC: U.S. Government Accounting Office.

Harris, K. (1996). "Key Differences Among Community Corrections Acts in the United States: An Overview." *Prison Journal*, 76(2):192-238.

*In re Gault*, 387 U.S. 1 (1967).

*In re Winship*, 397 U. S. 358 (1970).

Hayes, H. and M. Geerken (1997). "The Idea of Selective Release." *Justice Quarterly*, 14(2):353-370.

*Kent v. United States*, 383 U.S. 54 (1966).

King, P. and J. Noel (1994). "The Origins of the Problem of Juvenile Delinquency: The Growth of Juvenile Prosecution in London." In L. Knafla (ed.) *Criminal Justice History: An International Volume*. Westport, CT: Greenwood Press.

Krisberg, B. (1997). "The Impact if the Justice System on Serious, Violent and Chronic Juvenile Offenders." San Francisco, CA: National Council on Crime and Delinquency.

Krisberg, B., J. Austin, K. Joe, and P. Steele (1987). *The Impact of Court Sanctions*. San Francisco, CA: National Council on Crime and Delinquency.

Latessa, E.J., M.M. Moon, and B.K. Applegate (1995). *Preliminary Evaluation of the Ohio Department of Youth Services RECLAIM Ohio Pilot Project*. Cincinnati, OH: University of Cincinnati.

Latessa, E.J., M. Turner, M. Moon, and B. Applegate (1998). *A Statewide Evaluation of the RECLAIM Ohio Initiative*. Cincinnati, OH: University of Cincinnati.

Lee, L. (1994). "Factors Determining Waiver to a Juvenile Court." *Journal of Criminal Justice*, 22(4):329-340.

Lindner, C. and M.R. Savarese (1984a). "The Evolution of Probation: Early Salaries, Qualifications and Hiring Practices." *Federal Probation*, 48(1):3-9.

Macallair, D. (1994). "Disposition Case Advocacy in San Francisco Juvenile Justice System: A New Approach to Deinstitutionalization." *Crime & Delinquency*, 40(1):84-95.

Macallair, D. (1993). "Reaffirming Rehabilitation in Juvenile Justice." *Youth and Society*, 25(1):104-125.

McMahon, M. (1992). *The Persistent Prison? Rethinking Decarceration and Penal Reform*. Toronto, CN: University of Toronto Press.

Maxson, C. and M. Klein (1997). *Responding to Troubled Youth*. New York, NY: Oxford University Press.

Mauser, E., K. Van Stelle, and P. Moberg (1994). "The Economic Impacts of Diverting Substance-Abusing Offenders into Treatment." *Crime & Delinquency*, 40(4):568-588.

McCord, J. and J. Sanchez (1983). "The Treatment of Deviant Children: A Twenty-Five Year Follow-Up Study." *Crime & Delinquency*, 29(2):238-253.

*McKeiver v. Pennsylvania*, 403 U.S. 528 (1971).

Merlo, A., P. Benekos, and W. Cook (1997). "'Getting Tough' with Youth: Legislative Waiver as Crime Control." *Juvenile and Family Court Journal*, 48(3):1-15.

Moore, M. and S. Wakeling (1997). "Juvenile Justice: Shoring Up the Foundations," in M. Tonry (ed.) *Crime and Justice: A Review of Research*, pp. 253-301. Chicago, IL: University of Chicago Press.

*Nelson v. Heyne*, 491 F.2d 352 (7th Cir. 1974).

Platt, A.M. (1977). *The Child Savers: The Invention of Delinquency*. Chicago, IL: University of Chicago Press.

President's Commission on Law Enforcement and Administration of Justice (1967). *Juvenile Delinquency and Youth Crime*. Washington, DC: U.S. Government Printing Office.

Rausch, S.P. and C.H. Logan (1982). "Diversion from Juvenile Court: Panacea or Pandora's Box?" Paper presented at the annual meeting of the American Society of Criminology, Toronto, Canada.

Rogers, J. and G. Mays (1987). *Juvenile Delinquency and Juvenile Justice*. New York, NY: John Wiley.

Sanborn, J. (1994). "Constitutional Problems of Juvenile Delinquency Trials." *Judicature*, 78(2):81-88.

Sanborn, J. (1994). "Remnants of Parens Patria in the Adjudicatory Hearing." *Crime & Delinquency*, 40(4):599-615.

Schur, E. (1971). *Labeling Deviant Behavior: Its Sociological Implications*. New York, NY: Harper and Row.

*Schall v. Martin*, 467 U.S. 253, 104 S. Ct. 2403, 81 L.Ed.2d 207 (1984).

Shannon, L.W. (1982). *Assessing the Relationship of Adult Career Criminals to Juvenile Careers*. Washington, DC: U.S. Government Printing Office.

Sheley, J., Z. McGee, and J. Wright (1995). *Weapons-Related Victimization in Selected Inner-City High School Samples*. Washington, DC: Bureau of Justice Statistics.

Sherrill, M. (1975a, February). "Jerome Miller: Does He Have the Answers . . .?" *Corrections Magazine*, 1(2):24-28.

Sherrill, M. (1975b, February). "Harvard Recidivism Study." *Corrections Magazine*, 1(2):21-23.

Snyder, H., M. Sickman, and E. Yamagata (1996). *Juvenile Offenders and Victims*. Washington, DC: U.S. Office of Juvenile Justice and Delinquency Prevention.

Solomon, K. and M. Klein (1983). *National Evaluation of the Deinstitutionalization of Status Offender Programs*. Washington, DC: Office of Juvenile Justice and Delinquency Prevention, U.S. Department of Justice.

Torbert, P., R. Gable, and H. Hurst (1996). *State Responses to Serious and Violent Juvenile Crime*. Washington, DC: U.S. Office of Juvenile Justice and Delinquency Prevention.

Umbreit, M. (1994). *Victim Meets Offender: The Impact of Restorative Justice and Mediation*. Monsey, NY: Criminal Justice Press.

U.S. Bureau of Justice Assistance (1994a). *Drug Night Courts*. Washington, DC: USBJS.

U.S. Bureau of Justice Statistics (1994b). *Night Drug Courts: The Cook County Experience*. Washington, DC: USBJS.

Whitehead, J.T. and S.P. Lab (1996). *Juvenile Justice*, Second Edition. Cincinnati, OH: Anderson Publishing Co.

# The Development of Parole in America

... to ascertain, by experiment, the effect of establishing a system of reward and punishment not founded merely upon the prospect of immediate pain or immediate gratifications, but [on] ... the hope of obtaining or the fear of losing *future and distant advantages* ... The great object of a good system for the government of convicts should be that of teaching them to look forward to the future and remote effects of their own conduct, and to be guided in their actions by their reason, instead of merely by their animal instincts and desires.

—Report on the Select Committee
on Transportation

Parole is the most frequently used mechanism by which offenders may be released from a correctional institution after completion of a portion of the sentence (see Figure 7.1). Contemporary parole also includes the concepts of supervision by state, release on condition of good behavior while in the community, and return to prison for failing to abide by these conditions or for committing a new crime. As we shall see, earlier parole practices did not include all of these elements.

## The Roots of American Parole

Parole from prison, like the prison itself, is primarily an American innovation.[1] It emerged from a philosophical revolution and a resulting tradition of penal reform established in the late eighteenth century in the newly formed United States. As with many other new ideas that emerged in early America, parole had its roots in the practices of English and European penal systems.

Figure 7.1
**Adults Exiting from Prison: 1996**

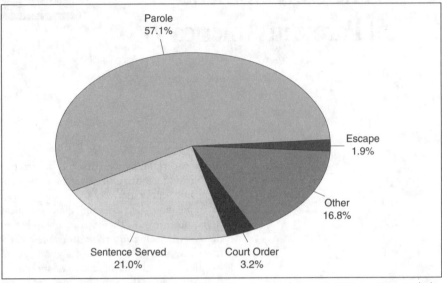

Source: American Correctional Association (1997). *Directory.* Lanham, MD: ACA, p. xxxiv. Excludes 3,777 inmates who died in prison.

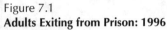

### Retribution

Philosophically, this earlier policy generally meant getting even with the perpetrator. *Social revenge* suggests that individuals cannot exact punishment, but the state will do so in their name.

Retribution assumes that offenders willfully chose to commit their evil acts, are responsible for their own behavior, are likely to commit similar acts again, and should receive the punishment they so richly deserve. Retribution requires the state to make the offender suffer for the sake of suffering.

There has been a rebirth of retribution during the last decade, as seen in minimum mandatory prison sentences, abolition of parole releases in some states, habitual offender statutes, and the "three-strikes" laws.

Early punishment for offenses were often what Langbein (1976:35-63) called "blood punishments." Capital and corporal punishment were accepted penal practices in Europe and the United States well into the nineteenth century. This was so, in part, because the technology and economy of these principally rural societies were unable to process and control large inmate populations, and also because these societies had strong traditions of corporal punishment that were rooted in the Old Testament.[2]

In the late seventeenth and early eighteenth centuries, two massive social changes occurred that altered the direction of Western civilization and, consequently, had an impact on criminal law and penalties. The first was the Enlightenment, which gave rise to a conception of the human being as a rational and ultimately perfectible being and, along with this, a belief in basic human equality.[3] Second, urbanization and the earliest movements toward industrialism simultaneously changed the nature of social interactions and created a new social class, the urban working class.

The writing of such thinkers as Locke, Voltaire, Beccaria, and Montesquieu both created and reflected a changing conception of man and the social order. These writers believed that government or society existed because individuals allowed it to exist. In other words, a "social contract" governed society. In order to be secure in their persons and possessions, free and equal individuals banded together and surrendered certain of their freedoms to the government on conditions that it protect them from their enemies.

Among those enemies were criminals. The state assumed the responsibility of controlling crime and, by administering justice, punishing offenders. Individuals surrendered their "rights" to seek revenge and to commit crimes or avenge themselves. The social contract was the product of rational, free individuals. And since rational and free people had control of their own fates, they could be held responsible for their actions.

A crime was considered a "breach of contract," an offense against all parties to the social contract and not just the injured party. This state of affairs enabled the establishment of a central body of law (such as the Common Law in England), and centralized control of enforcement. Finally, rational individuals, presumed to have prior knowledge of the law and its penalties, were expected to perceive that it was in their own interest not to violate the law and suffer the penalties. Deterrence was the rationale of the criminal law and its sanctions, which were severe so as to enhance the deterrent effect of the law (Beccaria, 1764). (In fact, more than 200 offenses carried the death penalty in England at one time. During the reign of Henry VIII, some 74,000 major and minor thieves were sent to the gallows. Under his daughter Elizabeth I, 300 to 400 at a time were hanged, attracting large crowds where pickpockets flourished—even though pick pocketing was an offense punishable by death (Rennie, 1978:6-7).

---

Box 7.2

### Deterrence

The prevention of criminal behavior through the threat of detection, apprehension, and punishment.

As a policy, deterrence programs can be directed against individuals or the general society. Individual or specific deterrence is designed to prevent a person from committing a crime by inducing fear. It can take such forms as punishment, persuasion, deprivation of liberty, or even death. "Scared Straight" programs that fleetingly mix hardened convicts with impressionable juveniles are believed by some to be a specific deterrent.

A societal deterrence program reminds potential offenders of what might happen to them if they commit legal violations. Driving automobiles while intoxicated, for example, is believed to be prevented or discouraged by a well-planned and coordinated television advertisement, linked to staunch enforcement by local policing agencies and mandatory loss of driving privileges or short periods of incarceration in jail. The death penalty is frequently cited as a general deterrent.

---

Since the criminal law in colonial America developed from the English Common Law, it was also very harsh. Judges and magistrates in the English system had the option to impose a variety of penalties less severe than death, such as branding, maiming, the stocks, fines, or any combination of these. As a reaction against cruel punishments, the "benefit of clergy" was developed to mitigate punishment for clerics and the wealthy. Initially designed to separate church and state, the "benefit" was eventually extended to all literate British citizens, even to those who could feign literacy (Clear, 1978:6-7; Briggs, Harrison & McInnes, 1996).

The reluctance of juries to convict and judges to impose sentences that were perceived to be disproportionate to the severity of most offenses did much to detract from the deterrent effect of the law. In addition, the inequity evident in sentencing, coupled with the potential and actual practices of abuses of the power to suspend sentences altogether, led to calls for reform in the English eighteenth-century criminal code, particularly for a reduction in the severity of penalties. A gradual shift in the conception of humankind and concomitant re-evaluation of the effectiveness and severity of punishment contributed significantly to the origins of parole as it exists today (Fogel, 1975:30-35).

Other writers, however, felt that poverty and lack of education, or heredity and biological inferiority, were the factors that gave rise to crime. The shifting conception of mankind as being at least partly at the mercy of forces beyond their control reduced the degree to which they could be held responsible for criminal actions, and paved the way for a reduction in the severity of many penalties. These changes in the philosophical conception of crime and punishment brought a new factor into the determination of sentences. Instead of imposing uniformly harsh sanctions for nearly all offenders, judges began to mitigate penalties for those "unfortunates" whom they "deemed to be worthy."

In England, orders of transportation were thought to be a severe punishment. In the eighteenth century, banishment, a common penalty for the aristocracy or nobility for centuries, was imposed on the common offender for the first time. The judge would order the common offender transported to the colonies rather than to the gallows or pillory. The criminal would be allowed to go at liberty in the new land, sometimes for a period of indenture (Pisciotta, 1982), on the condition of not returning to England for a specified time period (such as 10 years), if at all (Hawkins, 1971:Chapter 1). The concept of transportation thus avoids the extreme harshness of existing criminal law while at the same time serving incapacitative purposes of those penalties. The serious felony offender, of course, was still sentenced to death.

---

**Box 7.3**

### Incapacitation

A crime prevention strategy based on specific deterrence that would disable the potential offender from committing another crime by isolating the instant offender. Common forms of incapacitation include transportation to other countries or colonies, committing the offender to an asylum or mental hospital, and life-long imprisonment.

A contemporary version of this strategy is "selective incapacitation," a policy that would reserve prison beds for the most hardened, rapacious, and dangerous offenders. It would also require the use of community corrections for less severe offenders.

Two major problems with selective incapacitation are the inability of corrections to devise classification devices that would accurately predict which offenders would repeat (recidivate) or would not commit another crime. The second problem is more intractable: the widespread, but erroneous belief that *all* offenders are dangerous and cannot be controlled in the community. The latter has been a major impediment to the creation of community corrections.

While transportation was a partial solution to England's crime problem and, for a time helped to settle and develop the new lands (the colonies, however, had no similar outlet for their offenders, with the exception of casting them into the wilderness, with usually the same results as the death penalty), it was only a temporary one. As a result of the American Revolution, England was forced to transport her convicts elsewhere (Campbell, 1994), and for a time they were sent to Australia; until, eventually, even Australia closed its doors to English convicts.[4]

Criminologists commonly accept punishment by transportation as the principal forerunner of parole (Hawkins, 1971). They argue that transportation was an organized, uniform process by which thousands of convicts were punished in a manner short of execution or corporal punishment, as it was a system wherein offenders eventually obtained their freedom. In addition, transportation did not necessarily involve a period of incarceration.

## The Rise of Early Prison Reform

The Treaty of Paris in 1783 acknowledged the creation of the first republic in Western civilization since the fall of the Roman Empire. The United States of America, free from the English monarchy and founded on the teachings of the Enlightenment, became a fertile ground for the development of a new system of criminal justice.

While the influence of English Common Law, with its harsh penalties, was strong in the new republic, even stronger were anti-British sentiment and the desire to abandon the oppressive regime of the English king. American reformers moved away from the archaic, tyrannical sanctions of colonial law and toward a more humane and rational penalty of incarceration.[5] It was argued that fair, simple laws, backed by certain and humane punishment, would eradicate crime.

Chief among the reform groups were the Quakers (Offutt, 1995). The Act of 1789 established imprisonment as the penalty for most crimes in Pennsylvania (American Correctional Association, 1979:79). In a nation that had newly acquired independence, what more fitting penalty could be found than the deprivation of liberty? When Patrick Henry uttered his now-famous line, "Give me liberty or give me death," little did he know that he had identified the perfect penalty for crime. The prison replaced the penalty of death and yet denied liberty to its inmates. Much to the dismay of these first reformers, their efforts were not rewarded by a reduction in crime. Rather, the first penal institutions were dismal failures (Rothman, 1971:62):

> The faith of the 1790s now seemed misplaced; more rational
> codes had not decreased crime. The roots of deviancy went

deeper than the certainty of punishment. Nor were the institutions fulfilling the elementary task of protecting society, since escapes and riots were commonplace occurrences.

The search for the causes of crime continued. The reformers still believed that offenders were rational people who would strive to improve themselves, but the manner in which they could be convinced to obey the law was still unknown. In a time of rapid social change and movement from an agrarian to an industrial society, environmental factors came to be viewed as criminogenic: cities, poverty, and idleness were believed to be the hotbeds of crime.

The proposed solution that emerged was: remove the offender from bad environments and teach benefits of industry and morality. Offenders needed to be shown the error of their ways. Criminal law was required to do more than punish and deter; it should change the prisoner into a productive citizen. Punishment should serve to allow the prisoner to repent, to be trained, and to be reformed into a good citizen. A place to repent was thus needed, and prisons were developed to fulfill that need.

The original basis of the prison was the reformation of the offender, and the ideal of reformation placed high value on discipline and regimentation. In short, in the newly created free society, incarceration itself was punishment, and while incarcerated, the goal was to reform the prisoner. Offenders were expected to obey strict rules of conduct to work hard at assigned tasks (Johnson, 1994). In this milieu, it was believed, the offender would learn the benefit of discipline and industry.

---

Box 7.4

### Positivism

A major school in criminology that argues that most offenders do not exercise free will and resulting criminal behavior arises from social, biological, or psychological forces over which the offender has little or no control. This school led to a search for the causes of crime that lay within the offender or the social setting in which the offender lived, and provides the theoretical basis for both prevention and treatment programs.

---

The founders of the penitentiaries were mindful that the prison was a means to an end; their successors were not (Rothman, 1971:245-256). Reformation of inmates came to be identified solely with confinement, and custody eventually grew to be the ultimate goal of incarceration (Rothman, 1971:238). Furthermore, inmates posed significant threats to the security of the penitentiaries. Prison officials resorted to severe corporal punishments in order to maintain control within the prison—a penalty the development of prisons was supposed to replace.

The second generation of prison officials also saw another way of keeping the inmates out of trouble. American industry in the middle 1800s was labor-intensive, and prison populations were ideal sources of cheap labor. Inmate labor was expected to generate the money necessary to run the prisons, and prison administrators were thus receptive to offers to hire entire populations. This situation led to grossly underpaid prison labor, antagonism from unemployed free citizens, and the emergence of the labor contractor as major force in institutional administration.[6] A Report from the Massachusetts General Court Joint Special Committee on Contract Convict Labor (1880:16) illustrates the problem.

> In the State Prison, contracts have been made which have no clause [giving] the State power to annul [them] . . . Such bargains are bad, and, carried out to the fullest extent with large contracts, may naturally be expected to lead to a condition of affairs that has existed in other States given ground to the popular assertion that contractors, and not the State, control the prison.

## Early Practices in Other Nations

The first operational system of conditional release was started by the governor of a prison in Spain in 1835. Up to one-third of a prison sentence could be reduced by good behavior and a demonstrated desire to do better (Carter, McGee & Nelson, 1975:200). A similar system was enacted in Bavaria in the 1830s, and many prison reformers in France in the 1840s advocated the adoption of similar conditional release systems. In fact, the term "parole" comes from the French parole d'honneur, or "word of honor," which characterized the French efforts to establish parole release. Prisoners would be released after showing good behavior and industry in the prison,[7] and on their word of honor that they would obey the law.

Despite the fact that these efforts predate those of Alexander Maconochie, it is he who is usually given credit as being the father of parole. In 1840, Captain Maconochie was put in charge of the English penal colony in New South Wales at Norfolk Island, about 1,000 miles off the coast of Australia. To this colony were sent the criminals who were "twice condemned." They had been shipped from England to Australia, and then from Australia to Norfolk (Allen & Simonsen, 1998:58). Conditions were allegedly so bad at Norfolk Island that men reprieved from the death penalty wept and those who were to die thanked God (Barry, 1957:5). The conditions on Norfolk Island were so unbearable that suicide became a means of escape and an act of solidarity. Hughes (1987:468) describes it in vivid terms:

> A group of convicts would choose two men by drawing straws: one to die, the other to kill him. Others would stand by as witnesses. There being no judge to try capital offenses on Norfolk Island, the killer and witnesses would have to be sent to Sidney for trial—an inconvenience for the authorities but a boon to the prisoners, who yearned for the meager relief of getting away from the "ocean of hell," if only to a gallows on the mainland. And in Sidney there was some slight chance of escape. The victim could not choose himself; everyone in the group apparently, had to be equally ready to die, and the benefits of his death had to be shared equally by all survivors.

It was under these conditions that Maconochie devised an elaborate method of granted conditional release. Maconochie's plan was based on five basic principles (Barnes & Teeters, 1959:419):

1. Release should not be based on the completing of a sentence for a set period of time, but on completion of a determined and specified quantity of labor. In brief, time sentences should be abolished, and task sentences substituted.

2. The quantity of labor a prisoner must perform should be expressed in a number of "marks" which he must earn, by improvement of conduct, frugality of living, and habits of industry, before he can be released.

3. While in prison he should earn everything he receives. All sustenance and indulgences should be added to his debt of marks.

4. When qualified by discipline to do so, he should work in association with a small number of other prisoners, forming a group of six or seven, and the whole group should be answerable for the conduct of labor of each member.

5. In the final stage, a prisoner, while still obliged to earn his daily tally of marks, should be given a proprietary interest in his own labor and be subject to a less rigorous discipline, to prepare him for release into society.

Under his plan, prisoners were awarded marks and moved through stages of custody until finally granted release. His system involved *indeterminate sentencing*, with release based upon the number of marks earned by prisoners for good conduct, labor, and study. The five stages, based upon the accumulation of marks, each carried increased responsibility and freedom, leading to a ticket of leave or parole resulting in a conditional pardon and, finally, to full restoration of liberty.

Maconochie has been described as a zealot (Hughes, 1987); however, his reforms made life bearable at Norfolk Island, and can be described as revolutionary in comparison to the horrible conditions that existed there before his arrival. While Maconochie's reforms transposed Norfolk Island from one of despair to one of hope, it was short lived. Petty bureaucrats, and a general mistrust of Maconochie's ideas led to his recall as Commandant in 1843.

Sir Walter Crofton, director of the Irish prison system in the 1850s, built upon foundations laid by Maconochie. He decided that a transitional stage between prison and full release was needed, and developed a classification scheme based upon a system in which the prisoner progressed through three stages of treatment. The first was segregated confinement with work and training provided to the prisoner. This was followed by a transition period from confinement to freedom, during which the prisoner was set to work on public projects with little control being exercised over him. If he performed successfully in this phase, he was released on "license" (Clare & Kramer, 1976:69-70; Maguire, Peroud & Dison, 1996).

Release on license was constrained by certain conditions, violations of which would result in reimprisonment. While on license, prisoners were required to submit monthly reports and were warned against idleness and associating with other criminals. Prisoners on license, then, had to report, could be reimprisoned for violating the conditions of release, and had not been pardoned. These distinctions from earlier systems of release were large steps toward modern parole.

## Early American Practices

Convicts sentenced to prison in America in the early 1800s received definite terms; a sentence of five years meant the offender would serve five years in prison. This strict sentencing structure led to overcrowded prisons and widespread problems in the institutions. It was not uncommon for a governor to grant pardons to large numbers of inmates in order to control the size of prison populations. In some states, this pardoning power was even delegated to prison wardens (Sherrill, 1977:5).

This method of rewarding well-behaved prisoners with reductions in sentence was first formalized in 1817 by the New York State legislature. In that year, the first "good-time" law was passed. This law authorized a 25 percent reduction in length of term for those inmates serving five years or more who were well behaved and demonstrated industry in their prison work. By 1869, 23 states had good-time laws, and prison administrators supported the concept as a method of keeping order and controlling the population size (Sherrill, 1977:6).

Box 7.5

## Pardon

An act of executive clemency that absolves the offender in part or in full from the legal consequences of the crime and conviction.

Probably the most famous example is President Gerald Ford's pardon of President Richard Nixon for his role in the Watergate crimes.

Executive clemency can include gubernatorial action that results in the release of an inmate from incarceration, as well as pardoning current and former inmates. In 1996, clemency was awarded to 74 inmates; an additional 307 former and 40 current inmates were pardoned across 32 states (Camp & Camp, 1997:52).

The liberal use of the pardoning power was continued in those states that did not have good-time laws, and the mass pardon was not uncommon even in those states that already allowed sentence reductions for good behavior. These developments are important because they represent the first large-scale exercise of sentencing power by the executive branch of government, the branch in which parole boards would eventually be located.

Box 7.6

## Parole Board

Any correctional person, authority, commission, or board that has legal authority to parole those adults (or juveniles) committed to confinement facilities, to set conditions for behavior, to revoke from parole, and to discharge from parole.

Parole boards also can usually recommend shortening a prisoner's sentence (commuting sentences), recommend pardons to a Governor, set parole policies and, in some jurisdictions, recommend reprieve from execution. An example of parole policy would be a "zero tolerance" policy for parolees whose urine samples indicate recent use of illicit drugs, usually resulting in certain return to confinement.

Another philosophical base for American parole was the indenture system established by the New York House of Refuge. Although not called parole, for all intents and purposes a parole system was already operational for juveniles committed to the House of Refuge in New

York. The House of Refuge had developed a system of indenture whereby youths were released from custody as indentured servants of private citizens. Unfortunately, this system permitted corruption.[8]

To combat these abuses, the New York House of Refuge developed a system supervising the indentured. A committee was formed that selected youths for indenture, defined the conditions under which they served their indentureships, and established rules both for the superintendent of the House of Refuge and for the persons to whom youths were indentured.

There was no formal mechanism for releasing the youths from custody, but they were able to work off their contracts and thus obtain their freedom. Their masters could break the contracts and return the youths to the House of Refuge at any time. In essence, a parole system was operating.

In addition to these forms of release from custody before the expiration of the maximum term, the concept of supervising released offenders had also been operationalized. It is important to note, however, that supervision of released prisoners prior to the creation of parole in America only required providing assistance and not crime control duties.[9]

In 1845, the Massachusetts legislature appointed a state agent for discharged convicts and appropriated funds for him to use in assisting ex-prisoners in securing employment, tools, clothes, and transportation. Other states followed this example and appointed agents of their own. As early as 1776, however, charitable organizations, such as the Philadelphia Association for the Alleviation of Prisoners' Miseries, were already providing aid to released convicts (Sellin, 1970:13). By the late 1860s, dissatisfaction with prisons was widespread and a concerted effort to establish a formal parole release and supervision system began. In 1867, prison reformers Enoch Wines and Louis Dwight reported that "There is not a state prison in America in which reformation of the convicts is the one supreme object of discipline, to which everything else is made to bend" (Rothman, 1971:240-243).

In 1870, the first meeting of the American Prison Association was held in Cincinnati, Ohio.[10] Reform was the battle cry of the day, and the meeting took on an almost evangelical fervor (Fogel, 1975:30-31). Both Sir Walter Crofton and American warden F.B. Sanborn advocated the Irish system (Lindsey, 1925:20).

Armed with the success of the meeting, the focus of prison reformers shifted from incarceration as the answer to crime and, instead, concentrated on the return of offenders to society. Prisons remained central, but they were now seen almost as a necessary evil, not as an end in themselves. Prison reformers everywhere began to advocate adoption and expansion of good-time laws, assistance to released prisoners, the adoption of the ticket of leave system, and parole. In 1869, the New York State legislature passed an act creating the Elmira Reformatory and an indeterminate sentence ". . . until reformation, not exceeding five years."

---

Box 7.7

### Indeterminate Sentencing

Originally, the indeterminate sentence had no minimum length of period of incarceration. Later, legislatures changed this practice to require a minimum period of incarceration.

Indeterminate sentences typically require a minimum and maximum period (1 to 3 years, 2 to 10 years, 10 to 25 years, etc.). Offenders ordinarily will be released during some point in the spread of years pronounced by the sentencing judge.

Both the minimum and maximum terms can be reduced by certain credits allowable under legal statute and practice. These include time spent in jail awaiting trial or sentence; good-time credits for behaving while in prison; and program credits frequently awarded for completion of institutional programs (attaining the equivalent of a high-school diploma, active involvement in Alcoholic Anonymous, basic welding classes, etc.).

---

This law created the reformatory as a separate institution for young offenders, expressly designed to be an intermediate step between conviction and return to a law-abiding life. The administrators of the reformatory were empowered to release inmates upon demonstration of their reformation. Such release was conditional, and released offenders were to be supervised by a state agent (Lindsey, 1925:21-23).

With the passage of this law, parole in the United States became a reality. It soon spread to other jurisdictions, and by 1944, every jurisdiction in the nation had a parole authority (Hawkins, 1971:64). Table 7.1 illustrates the rapid growth of parole in the United States up to the year 1900. Between 1884 and 1900, parole was adopted in 20 states. The rapid growth of parole, however, was fraught with difficulties and criticism.

## The Spread of Parole

Parole release was adopted by the various state jurisdictions much more rapidly than was the indeterminate sentence. By 1900, some 20 states had adopted parole; by 1944, every jurisdiction had a parole system (See Table 7.2). The expansion of parole has been characterized as being a process of imitation (Lindsey, 1925:21-23), yet a great deal of variation in the structure and use of parole was observed.[11]

Table 7.1
**States with Parole Laws by 1900**

| State | Year Enacted |
|---|---|
| Alabama | 1897 |
| California | 1893 |
| Colorado | 1899 |
| Connecticut | 1897 |
| Idaho | 1897 |
| Illinois | 1891 |
| Indiana | 1897 |
| Kansas | 1895 |
| Massachusetts | 1884 |
| Michigan | 1895 |
| Minnesota | 1889 |
| Nebraska | 1893 |
| New Jersey | 1895 |
| New York | 1889 |
| North Dakota | 1891 |
| Ohio | 1896 |
| Pennsylvania | 1887 |
| Utah | 1898 |
| Virginia | 1898 |
| Wisconsin | 1889 |

Source: Adapted from E. Lindsey (1925). "Historical Origins of the Sanction of Imprisonment for Serious Crime." *Journal of Criminal Law and Criminology,* 16:9-126.

Table 7.2
**Significant Developments in Parole**

| Date | Development |
|---|---|
| 1776 | Colonies reject English Common Code and begin to draft their own codes. |
| 1840 | Maconochie devises mark system for release of prisoners in Australian penal colony, a forerunner of parole. |
| 1854 | Crofton establishes ticket-of-leave program in Ireland. |
| 1869 | New York State legislature passes enabling legislation and establishes indeterminate sentencing. |
| 1870 | American Prison Association endorses expanded use of parole. |
| 1876 | Parole release adopted at Elmira Reformatory, New York. |
| 1931 | Wickersham Commission criticizes laxity in early parole practice. |
| 1944 | Last state passes enabling legislation for parole. |
| 1976 | Maine abolishes parole. |
| 1984 | Federal system abolishes parole as an early release mechanism. |
| 1996 | Ohio becomes 11th state to abolish parole. |

Source: Compiled by authors.

The growth and expansion of modern parole was assisted by a number of factors. One of the most important was the tremendous amount of support and publicity that prison reformers gave the concept at the National Congress on Penitentiary and Reformatory Discipline. Its inclusion in the congress's Declaration of Principles, coupled with the publicity of Alexander Maconochie's work in New South Wales, provided the necessary endorsement of correctional experts.

In addition, it was quickly recognized that a discretionary release system solved many of the problems of prison administration. A major factor in favor of parole was that it supported prison discipline. A number of writers pointed out that by placing release in the inmate's own hands, the inmate would be motivated both to reform and to comply with the rules and regulations of the prison.[12] Finally, parole provided a safety valve to reduce prison populations, which were generally overcrowded (Wilcox, 1929:345-354).

A third contributory factor was that the power to pardon was being liberally exercised in a number of states. The effect of liberal pardoning policies was to initiate parole even though it was not yet authorized by law.

These early parole systems were controlled by state legislators that, in general, rigidly defined which prisoners could be paroled. Most legislation authorizing parole release restricted it to first offenders convicted of less serious crimes. Through the passage of time and a gradual acceptance of the idea of discretionary early release, the privilege was eventually extended to serious offenders.

Early parole systems were primarily operated by persons with a direct interest in the administration of prisons. So the decisions on parole release and those who acted as parole officers were institution-based. Eligibility was strictly limited, at the inception of parole, and only gradually expanded to include more serious offenders. Supervision of released inmates was nominal, and the seeds of corruption and maladministration were present.

## Early Public Sentiments

The decade between 1925 and 1935 was a turbulent time, including both the economic boom (and the Prohibition Era) as well as the Great Depression. Crime—particularly as sensationalized in the mass media—appeared to be rampant. As crime rates increased, the public felt more and more that crime was "public enemy number one."[13] This period also saw the rise of attempt by the federal government to stem interstate crimes, particularly kidnapping, bootlegging, bank robbery, and a host of newly enacted legislation that considerably widened the net of crime the government would seek to prevent and prosecute. Two significant events, reflecting public concern about crime,[14] were the establishment of the maximum security federal prison on Alcatraz, and a crusade headed by J. Edgar Hoover, chief of the Federal Bureau of Investigation, against interstate crime. His pronouncements assumed a political nature, as he strongly advocated neoclassical responses to crime: long-term prison sentences, abolition of parole, increased incarceration of offenders, and use of the death penalty, etc.[15]

Both the releasing and supervision functions of parole were sharply and roundly criticized. The major concern of these criticisms was the failure of parole to protect the public safety. The Report of the Advisory Commission on Penal Institutions, Probation and Parole to the Wickersham Commission in the 1931 summarized the problems with parole, stating:

Parole is defective in three main respects:

1. In the chasm existing between parole and preceding institutional treatment.

2. In the manner in which persons are selected for parole.

3. In the quality of supervision given to persons on parole.

In short, parole was seen as failing to be effective in attaining the promised and lofty goals. The primary arguments were that convicted criminals were being set loose on society, inadequately supervised, and unreformed. The concept of parole and the general ideology of reform were not yet under attack; it was the means and not the ends that were being criticized.

The decade of the 1930s saw the publication of two documents concerning parole, the 1931 Wickersham Commission Report, noted above, and, in 1939, the Attorney General's Survey of Release Procedures (Hawkins, 1971:47). As with the reports of Wines and Dwight and the International Prison Congress of over 50 years earlier, the 1931 and 1939 documents pointed to flaws in the operation of American corrections and advocated reforms to improve both prisons and parole services.[16]

Simultaneously, the correctional medical model was on the rise. This criminogenic approach was based on a belief that human beings are basically moral, and that crime is deviation from humankind's basic behavior inclinations. Unlike the earlier views that humans were, at heart, bestial, but restrained their primitive drives because reason informed them that by doing so they would be safe, the idea that humans are basically good led to the inevitable conclusion that there must be something fundamentally wrong with those who were bad. The job of corrections should then be to diagnose the problems, prepare and administer the treatment programs, and make offenders well again. Offenders committed crimes when social, personal, or psychological forces and factors overwhelmed them. Hence, the instillation of new habits, the threat of deterrent sanctions, and the giving of religious instruction dealt only with the symptoms of a deeper disorder. The real causes of crime remained deep within the personality structure of the offender. If the prisons were to be hospitals, the parole board was to release the patient when "well"—that is, when able to deal with all phases of everyday life. This development had significant implications for parole.

---

**Box 7.8**

### Parole

Release of an inmate from confinement to expiration of sentence on condition of good behavior and supervision in the community. This is also referred to as post-incarceration supervision, or in the case of juveniles, aftercare.

---

Between the adoption of parole release in Elmira in 1876 and the enactment of enabling legislation for parole in Mississippi in 1944, the concept of parole faced two critical challenges. The first involved the issue of legality of executive control over sentencing and indeterminate sentences. The second centered on the administration of parole systems. Toward the end of the first quarter of the twentieth century, a new behavioral technology came into its own and grew to be predominant goal of corrections and sentencing. The rehabilitative ideal gave new legitimacy to parole, endorsing discretion.

## Legal Challenges to Parole

The basic legal challenge raised against parole was that the placing of control over sentence length and criminal penalties in the hands of a parole board was unconstitutional. The specific arguments varied across individual lawsuits, but they were basically of two types. First, the questions of infringement on the principle of the separation of powers clauses of the federal and state constitutions were raised in several states (Lindsey, 1925:40-52).

These suits claimed that parole release was an impairment of judicial sentencing power, an improper delegation of legislative authority to set penalties, and usurpation of the executive branch's power of clemency (Hawkins, 1971:47). For the most part, parole authorities emerged victorious from these court battles, and those constitutional questions of parole were laid to rest.

A further rationale behind challenges to the constitutionality of parole release were based on the Eighth Amendment prohibition against cruel and unusual punishment. Although the issue was weighty, most criminal penalties were limited by legislatively set maximum terms. The most common judicial response to these arguments was that indeterminate sentences could be interpreted as sentences that would not extend the maximum terms as set by the legislature or judge, thereby rendering moot the issue of cruelty by virtue of uncertainty (Hawkins, 1971:49).

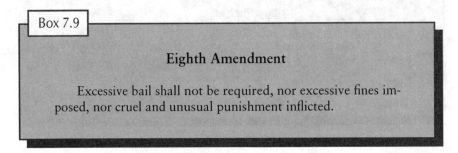

Box 7.9

### Eighth Amendment

Excessive bail shall not be required, nor excessive fines imposed, nor cruel and unusual punishment inflicted.

## Administrative Challenges

We have seen that, in the late nineteenth and early twentieth centuries, parole practices were criticized for failing to protect the public. The basic arguments were that parole authorities were not following procedures that would lead to the release of only deserving inmates, and that the lack of subsequent parole supervision placed the community in danger. Such were the complaints reflected by the Wickersham Commission and the Attorney General's Survey. These were not the only critical voices.[17]

One salient argument, supported by ample evidence, was that parole had become a commonplace method of reducing prison populations. In several states, most inmates were released immediately upon expiration of their minimum terms. Only those inmates whose conduct records within prison showed a failure to conform were held longer. The problem was defined as inadequate or improper release decisionmaking.

Blanket release policies were felt to be inappropriate for several reasons. First, because parole boards failed to consider risk, and parole supervision was inadequate, such wholesale release practices were felt to endanger public safety. Second, since most parole boards were dominated by prison officials, it was believed that too much weight was attached to prison conduct and the needs of the prison administration. Finally, failure to consider reformation efforts of the inmate, or the prison, worked to hamper the success of prisons in reforming criminals.

Proposed solutions were varied and involved beefing-up parole supervision staffs and increasing post-release surveillance of parolees. It was believed that these actions could enhance public protection. Additionally, there were calls for professional parole boards comprised of trained, salaried, full-time decisionmakers who would be removed from the pressures of day-to-day prison administration and its needs, and were skilled in identifying those inmates who were reformed.

These proposals arose at about the same time behavioral sciences expanded into the world of public policy. Psychology and sociology were beginning to develop practical components in addition to their traditional theoretical bases. The new professions of clinical psychologist, social worker, and criminologist were developing. An ability to predict, change, and control undesirable human behavior was promised.[18] Corrections and parole seemed ideal places in which these professions could have their most positive impact. The dawn of the rehabilitative model was at hand, and this model caused radical changes in the practice and organization of the American parole system, as will be seen in later chapters.

## Summary

Although the early beginnings of parole can be traced to Europe and Australia, the process as it is known today is almost exclusively an American invention. Once embraced by early reformers, parole quickly spread and, by 1944, every state jurisdiction had a parole system. In spite of the growth, parole was not without its detractors. Early criticism of parole included a suspicion of the way in which prisoners were selected for release, concern over a lack of community supervision, and extensive abuse by prison authorities. Many of the criticisms leveled at parole continue today, and these issues will be discussed in greater detail in later chapters.

## *Review Questions*

1. Contrast the punishment model with the reform model of corrections.

2. How did Maconochie contribute to the development of parole?

3. How did parole develop in the United States?

4. What were the early criticisms of parole in America?

5. What were three elements of corruption that emerged in American corrections between 1790 and 1930?

6.  Contrast the view of criminals offered by Maconochie with that of J. Edgar Hoover.

7.  How did the decade from 1925 to 1935 affect attitudes of the American public toward parole?

## Key Terms

| | |
|---|---|
| American Prison Association | parole |
| conditional release | parole board |
| determinate sentence | penal colony |
| deterrence | penitentiary |
| good time | positivism |
| incapacitation | reformatory regime |
| indeterminate sentence | retribution |
| mark system | selective incapacitation |
| pardon | transportation |

## Recommended Readings

Hughes, R. (1987). *The Fatal Shore*. New York, NY: Alfred A. Knopf. This is the definitive book on the history of Australia as a penal colony, and the beginning roots of parole as developed by Captain Maconochie.

Murphy, J.W. and J.E. Dison (eds.) (1990). *Are Prisons Any Better? Twenty Years of Correctional Reform*. Newbury Park, CA: Sage.

Rothman, D.J. (1980). *Conscience and Convenience: The Asylum and Its Alternatives in Progressive America*. Boston, MA: Little, Brown. A fastidious discussion of the modern effort to reform the programs that have dominated criminal justice in the twentieth century.

Rothman, D.J. (1971). *The Discovery of the Asylum: Social Order and Disorder in the New Republic*. Boston, MA: Little, Brown. This book presents an excellent history of the use of punishments and corrections in early colonial America.

## Notes

[1]   Various forms of conditional release from incarceration were developed in other countries before an American state adopted a parole system. However, the core elements of a parole system administrative board making release decisions and granting conditional, supervised release with the authority to revoke it—were first created by legislation in New York State (1869).

[2]    For a recent view of the impacts of conservative Christian beliefs on punishment of offenders, see Harold Gramich and Anne McGill (1994). "Religion, Attribution Style, and Punitiveness Toward Offenders." *Criminology*, 32(1):23-46. In the area of impact of evangelical and fundamentalist religion on the death penalty, see Harold Gramich, John Cochran, Robert Burish, and M'Lou Kimpel (1993). "Religion, Punitive Justice, and Support for the Death Penalty." *Justice Quarterly*, 10(2):289-314. For contrasting evidence, see M. Sandys and E. McGarrell (1997). "Beyond the Bible Belt: The Influences (or Lack Thereof) of Religion on Attitudes Toward the Death Penalty." *Journal of Crime and Justice* 20 (1): 179-190.

[3]    For an excellent reading of the movement as it relates to the study of crime, see Y. Rennie (1978). *The Search for Criminal Man*. Lexington, MA: Lexington Books, D.C. Heath.

[4]    For an excellent description of transportation to Australia, see Robert Hughes (1987). *The Fatal Shore: The Epic of Australia's Founding*. New York, NY: Knopf. Pre-transportation detention usually was in hulks, dilapidated and unseaworthy naval vessels. See Charles Campbell (1994). *The Intolerable Hulks: British Shipboard Confinement*. Bowie, MD: Heritage Books.

[5]    For a conflicting interpretation of the political purposes intended for prisons, see A.M. Durham (1990). "Social Control and Imprisonment During the American Revolution: Newgate of Connecticut." *Justice Quarterly*, 7:293-323.

[6]    For a review of the contemporary issues in the prison privatization movement, see David Shichor (1993). "The Corporate Context of Private Prisons." *Crime, Law and Social Change*, 20(2):113-138.

[7]    See Ellen Chayet (1994). "Correctional 'Good Time' As a Means of Early Release." *Criminal Justice Abstracts*, 26(3):521-538.

[8]    It was not uncommon for juveniles to be indentured without a careful investigation of those who would hold the indenture contracts. Thus, juveniles were sometimes indentured to criminals, and the conditions of their indentureships were virtually uncontrolled.

[9]    The first legislatively authorized "parole officer" position was established in 1937 in Massachusetts. The officer was charged with assisting released convicts to obtain shelter, tools, and work. The legislation made no mention of any surveillance duties.

[10]    For a history of the American Correctional Association, see A. Travisono and M. Hawkes (1995). *Building a Voice: The American Correctional Association, 125 Years of History*. Landham, MD: ACA.

[11]    See E. Lindsey (1925). "Historical Sketch of the Indeterminate Sentence and Parole System." *Journal of Criminal Law and Criminology*, 16:9-126. Lindsey writes, "There has been considerable modification and variation in various phases of the system as it has spread from one state to another. Methods of administration are also widely different." For an update on parole practices, see John Runda, Edward Rhine, and Robert White (1994). *The Practice of Parole*. Lexington, KY: Council of State Government.

[12]    Perhaps chief among these were E.C. Wines and T.W. Dwight who, in 1867, published a report to the New York Prison Association that was entitled, *Prisons and Reformatories of the United States and Canada*. Albany. Other state committees echoed

the call for a parole system. See Report of the Massachusetts General Court Joint Special Committee on Contract Convict Labor (1880). Boston.

[13]　For a remarkably similar view of contemporary corrections and public fears, see J.W. Murphy and J. Dison (eds.) (1990). *Are Prisons Any Better? Twenty Years of Correctional Reform*. Newbury Park, CA: Sage.

[14]　On media influence on citizen perception and fear of crime, see Melissa Barlow, David Barlow and Theodore Chiricos (1995). "Economic Conditions and Ideologies of Crime in the Media: A Content Analysis of Crime News," *Crime & Delinquency*, 43(1):3-19; Richard Bennett and Jeanne Flavin (1994). "Determinants of the Fear of Crime: The Effects of Cultural Setting." *Justice Quarterly*, 11(3):357-381; and John Wright, Francis Cullen, and Michael Blankenship (1995). "The Social Construction of Corporate Violence: Media Coverage of the Imperial Food Products Fire." *Crime & Delinquency*, 41(1):20-36; and T. Chiricos, S. Escholz, and M. Gertz (1997). "Crime News and Fear of Crime." *Social Problems*, 44(3):343-357.

[15]　But see C. DeLoach (1995). *Hoover's FBI: The Inside Story by Hoover's Trusted Lieutenant*. Washington, DC: Regenery.

[16]　The authors of these reports were joined by others. Reformers wanted full-time, paid parole authorities who had to meet certain qualifications and who were as far removed as possible from political patronage. See W. Colvin (1922). "What Authority Should Grant Paroles?" *If a Board, How Should It Be Composed? Journal of Criminal Law and Criminology*, 12:545-548.

[17]　Field, H.E. (1931). "The Attitudes of Prisoners as a Factor in Rehabilitation." *The Annals*, 157, 162.

[18]　Predicting post-release behavior is difficult. See Stephen Gottfredson and Don M. Gottfredson (1994). "Behavioral Prediction and the Problem of Incapacitation." *Criminology*, 32(3):441-474.

## References

Allen, H.E. and C.E. Simonsen (1998). *Corrections in America*. Upper Saddle River, NJ: Prentice-Hall.

American Correctional Association (1974). "Development of Modern Correctional Concepts and Standards." In E. Edelfonso (ed.) *Issues in Corrections*, pp. 76-100. Beverly Hills, CA: Glencoe.

Barlow, M., D. Barlow, and T. Chiricos (1995). "Economic Conditions and Ideologies of Crime in the Media: A Content Analysis of Crime News." *Crime & Delinquency*, 43:3-19.

Barnes, H.E. and N.D. Teeters (1959). *New Horizons in Criminology*. Englewood Cliffs, NJ: Prentice-Hall.

Barry, J.V. (June 1957). "Captain Alexander Maconochie." *The Victorian Historical Magazine*, 27:1-18.

Beccaria, C. (1764). *On Crimes and Punishments*. Translated by H. Paulucci (1963). Indianapolis, IN: Bobbs-Merrill.

Bennett, R. and J. Flavin (1994). "Determinants of the Fear of Crime: The Effects of Cultural Setting." *Justice Quarterly*, 11:357-381.

Briggs, J., C. Harrison, and A. McInnes (1996). *Crime and Punishment in England: An Introductory History*. New York, NY: St. Martin's Press.

Camp, C. and G. Camp (1997). *The Corrections Yearbook*. South Salem, NY: Criminal Justice Institute.

Campbell, C. (1994). *The Intolerable Hulks: British Shipboard Confinement*. Bowie, MD: Heritage Books.

Carter, R.M., R.A. McGee, and K.E. Nelson (1975). Corrections in America. Philadelphia, PA: J.B. Lippincott.

Chayet, E. (1994). "Correctional 'Good Time' As a Means of Early Release." *Criminal Justice Abstracts*, 26:521-538.

Chiricos, T., S. Escholz, and M. Gertz (1997). "Crime, News and Fear of Crime." *Social Problems,* 44(3):342-357.

Clare, P.K. and J.H. Kramer (1976). *Introduction to American Corrections*. Boston, MA: Holbrook Press.

Clear, T.R. (1978). *A Model for Supervising the Offender in the Community*. Washington, DC: National Institute of Corrections.

Colvin, W. (1922). "What Authority Should Grant Paroles? If a Board, How Should It be Composed?" *Journal of Criminal Law and Criminology*, 12:545-548.

DeLoach, C. (1995). *Hoover's FBI: The Inside Story by Hoover's Trusted Lieutenant*. Washington, DC: Regenery.

Durham, A.M. (1990). "Social Control and Imprisonment During the American Revolution: Newgate of Connecticut." *Justice Quarterly*, 7:293-323.

Field, H.E. (1931). "The Attitudes of Prisoners as a Factor in Rehabilitation." *The Annals*, 157, 162.

Fogel, D. (1975). *We are the Living Proof . . .* Cincinnati, OH: Anderson Publishing Co.

Gramich, H. and A. McGill (1994). "Religion, Attribution Style, and Punitiveness Toward Offenders." *Criminology*, 32:23-46.

Gramich H., J. Cochran, J. Burish, and M. Kimpel (1993). "Religion, Punitive Justice, and Support for the Death Penalty." *Justice Quarterly*, 10:289-314.

Hawkins, K.O. (1971). "Parole Selection: The American Experience." Unpublished doctoral dissertation, University of Cambridge, England.

Hughes, R. (1987). *The Fatal Shore*. New York, NY: Alfred A. Knopf.

Johnson, E. (1994). "Opposing Outcomes of the Industrial Prison: Japan and the United States Compared." *International Criminal Justice Review,* 4(1):52-71.

Langbein, J.H. (1976). "The Historical Origins of the Sanction of Imprisonment for Serious Crime." *Journal of Legal Studies*, 5:35-63.

Lindsey, E. (1925). "Historical Origins of the Sanction of Imprisonment for Serious Crime." *Journal of Criminal Law and Criminology*, 16:9-126.

Maguire, J.W. and J. Dison (eds.) (1996). *Automatic Conditional Release: The First Two Years*. London, UK: Her Majesty's Stationery House.

Murphy, J.W. and J. Dison (eds.) (1990). *Are Prisons Any Better? Twenty Years of Correctional Reform.* Newbury Park, CA: Sage.

National Commission of Law Observance and Enforcement (1939). George W. Wickersham, Chairman. *Report on Penal Institutions, Probation and Parole.* Washington, DC: U.S. Government Printing Office.

Offutt, W. (1995). *Of "Good Laws" and "Good Men:" Law and Society in the Delaware Valley, 1680-1710.* Chicago, IL: University of Chicago Press.

Pisciotta, A. (1982). "Saving the Children: The Promise and Practice of *Parens Patria, 1838-1898.*" *Crime & Delinquency,* 28(3):410-425.

Rennie, Y. (1978). *The Search for Criminal Man.* Lexington, MA: D.C. Heath.

Report on the Commissioners to Examine the Various Systems of Prison Discipline, and Propose an Improved Plan, cited in Harry E. Barnes's A History of the Penal, Reformatory and Correctional Institutions of the State of New Jersey-Analytical and Documentary (n.d.).

Report of the Massachusetts General Court Joint Special Committee on Contract Convict Labor (1880). Boston, MA: State of Massachusetts.

Rothman, D.J. (1971). *The Discovery of the Asylum: Social Order and Disorder in the New Republic.* Boston, MA: Little, Brown.

Runda, J., E. Rhine, and R. White (1994). *The Practice of Parole.* Lexington, KY: Council of State Government.

Sandys, M. and E. McGarrell (1997). "Beyond the Bible Belt: The Influence (or Lack Thereof) of Religion on Attitudes Toward the Death Penalty," *Journal of Crime and Justice,* 20(1):179-190.

Sellin, T. (Spring-Summer 1970). "The Origin of the Pennsylvania System of Prison Discipline." *The Prison Journal,* 50:13, 15-17.

Sherrill, M.S. (1977, September). "Determinate Sentencing: History, Theory, Debate." *Corrections Magazine,* 3:3-13.

Shichor, D. (1993). "The Corporate Context of Private Prisons." *Crime, Law and Social Change,* 20:113-138.

Travisono, A. and M. Hawkes (1995). *Building a Voice: The American Correctional Association, 125 Years of History.* Landham, MD: ACA.

Wilcox, C. (1929). "Parole: Principles and Practice." *Journal of Criminal Law and Criminology,* 20:345-354.

Wines, E.C. and T.W. Dwight (1867). *Prisons and Reformatories of the United States and Canada.* Albany, NY: New York Prison Association.

Wright, J., F.T. Cullen, and M. Blankenship (1995). "The Social Construction of Corporate Violence: Media Coverage of the Imperial Food Products Fire." *Crime & Delinquency,* 41:20-36.

# Granting Probation

Free administration decisionmaking based on individual characteristics of the offender has given way to the offender's relative success at plea bargaining . . . Nowadays it is likely that the prosecutor has communicated the plea bargaining agreement to the probation officer, and the latter's recommendation takes into consideration the prosecutor's agreement with the offender.

—Herbert Callison

As we have already learned, probation is the most widely used correctional sanction. While the imposition of probation is an important part of our sentencing structure, it is important to remember that probation is a privilege, not a right (*Gagnon v. Scarpelli*, 1972). It is an "act of grace" extended by the sentencing judge who presided over the trial (although a few states permit the jury that determined guilt to award or recommend probation). Of all the principal groups of offenders under correctional control in America—probationers, jail inmates, prison inmates, and parolees—the largest group is probationers. The United States Bureau of Justice Statistics (1997a) found that 58 percent of all convicted offenders were on probation, 13 percent were on parole, 20 percent were in prison, and 9 percent were in jail. Numerically, in 1996, there were 3,180,363 probationers supervised by at least 20,000 caseload supervision staff, with a national average caseload of about 125 offenders per officer (see Figure 8.1). Perhaps not surprising, California reported the highest caseload size; between 800 and 1,000 per officer! In Texas, which has the largest number of individuals on probation (425,789) and parole (112,594), 3.9 percent of ALL adults in Texas were on probation or parole!

Table 8.1 illustrates the frequency with which probation was imposed at sentencing by crime of conviction. What is the process by which so large a proportion of offenders is placed on probation?

Figure 8.1
**Average Caseload Size, Regular Supervision Caseload**

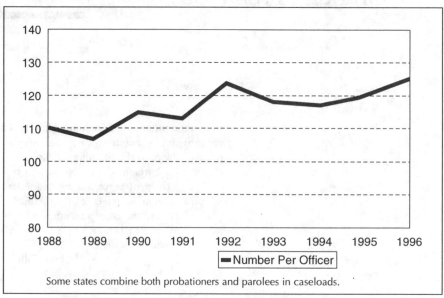

Some states combine both probationers and parolees in caseloads.

Source: C. Camp and G. Camp (1997). *The Corrections Yearbook, 1997.* South Salem, NY: Criminal Justice Institute, Inc.

## Objectives and Advantages of Probation

As the reader will recall from Chapter 5, both state and federal jurisdictions enacted statutes that permit the granting of probation, as well as define certain categories of offenses for which probation may not be granted. These acts could include all crimes of violence, crimes requiring a life sentence, armed robbery, rape or other sex offenses, use of a firearm in a crime, or multiple-convicted offenders.

Yet, despite the existence of legislatively defined exclusion, granting probation is a highly individualized process that usually focuses on the criminal rather than the crime. The following are the general objectives of probation:

1. Reintegrate amenable offenders.

2. Protect the community from further antisocial behavior.

3. Further the goals of justice.

4. Provide probation conditions (and services) necessary to change offenders and to achieve the above objectives.

While probation granting is individualized, judges and corrections personnel generally recognize the advantages of probation:

1. Use of community resources to reintegrate offenders who are thus forced to face and hopefully resolve their individual problems while under community supervision.

2. Fiscal savings over imprisonment.

3. Avoidance of prisonization, which tends to exacerbate the underlying causes of criminal behavior.

4. Keeping offenders' families off local and state welfare rolls.

5. A relatively successful process of correcting offenders behavior (60 to 90 percent success rates have been reported).[1]

6. A sentencing option that can permit "selective incapacitation."

---

**Box 8.1**

### Running On Empty

Year after year, the correctional system of America is forced to deal with increasingly larger volumes of intakes. Never in the history of this nation have so many people been in the correctional system. The numbers are skyrocketing and now total more than 5.4 million persons, or one out of every 37 adults in the United States.

The crime rate in the nation has not skyrocketed. It remains about where it was a decade past. Politicians and the general public are misinformed about the nature of crime, and are attempting to solve social problems through the justice system.

Perhaps the most alarming figure is that almost one out of every three African-American men in the United States is under correctional supervision.

We must learn to punish less expensively and for shorter periods of time. Alternatively, we must develop more effective systems of crime prevention and treatment.

---

Probation, the most frequent disposition for offenders and widely recognized for its advantages (Dawson, 1990:1), has also received strong endorsement from numerous groups and commissions, including the prestigious National Advisory Commission on Criminal Justice Standards and Goals (1973), the General Accounting Office (1982), and the American Bar Association (1970). The National Advisory Commission recommended that probation be used more extensively, and the ABA

Box 8.2

## Prisonization

Prisonization refers to the socialization process by which the inmate learns the prison culture, a cluster of folkways and mores that indoctrinates the new inmate into the inmate world of prisons. Prisonization rules reward non-conforming behavior, reduce inmate change, and reinforce the inmates' commitment to a life of crime. It is also believed to interfere with the ability of the inmate to function as a law-abiding citizen following release.

endorsed probation as the presumed sentence of choice for almost all felonies. Others have argued (Finn, 1984) universal use of probation would reduce prison populations. It is important to remember that prison space is a limited and, some would say, scarce resource. The economics of corrections are such that probation is essential if the system is going to effectively manage its finite resources (Clear, Clear & Burrell, 1989). Figure 8.2 illustrates the cost per offender for probation supervision. Even when we consider specialized supervision (e.g., intensive, electronic) the daily supervision still averages less than $4 per day. When is probation and appropriate sentence and how is it granted?

Figure 8.2
**Average Daily Cost per Probationer by Supervision Type**

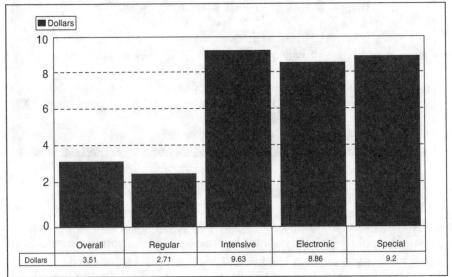

| | Overall | Regular | Intensive | Electronic | Special |
|---|---|---|---|---|---|
| Dollars | 3.51 | 2.71 | 9.63 | 8.86 | 9.2 |

Source: C. Camp and G. Camp (1997). *The Corrections Yearbook, 1997*. South Salem, NY: Criminal Justice Institute, Inc.

# Granting Probation

Sentencing is a complicated process, and sentencing judges frequently find that the disposition of the case (sentence) has already been determined—by the prosecutor, not the judge! This is because, prior to the determination of guilt, the prosecuting attorney and defense counsel have engaged in plea bargaining. During this interaction, any (or even all) of the following trial elements may have been negotiated:

1. The defendant's pleading guilty to a lesser crime but one that was present in the illegal behavior, for which the penalty is considerably more lenient.

2. The frequency of the crime ("number of counts") to which the defendant will plead guilty.

3. The number of charges that will be dropped.

4. Whether the prosecutor will recommend that the defendant receive probation or be sentenced to incarceration in jail or prison.

5. The recommended length of time (months or years) of incarceration.

6. If sentence will be consecutive or concurrent.

It appears that the judiciary tend to accept and acquiesce to the negotiation outcomes (Glaser, 1985; Dixon, 1995). However, in many cases, judges still decide the sentence, one alternative of which may be probation.

---

Box 8.3

### Selective Incapacitation

Selective incapacitation refers to a crime control policy of identifying high-risk offenders for incarceration on the premise that, while imprisoned, such offenders would be incapable of committing further criminal acts, and may be deterred from illegal behavior when released.

---

The process of granting probation begins after the offender either pleads guilty (frequently for favorable personal considerations) or is adjudicated guilty following a trial. For those offenders whose crime falls within the list of probation-eligible offenses, or in those states where mandated by law, a presentence investigation will be ordered. One of the major functions of a presentence investigation report is to assist the court in determining the most appropriate sentence.

Based on observations of the defendant at trial—including demeanor, body language, evidence of remorse, and behavior—as well as the recommendation in presentence reports and the prosecutor's recommendation for sentence, judges attempt to determine the appropriate sentence for a particular individual. Judges are aware that individualized justice demands that the sentence fit not only the crime but also the criminal.[2]

Box 8.4

### Sentencing: Concurrent or Consecutive?

If the offender is to be sentenced for more than one crime and receives a *concurrent* sentence, the offender would start serving time for all his crimes, beginning on the day of arrival in prison. If a *consecutive* sentence is imposed, the offender generally must serve the minimum sentence for the first crime before beginning to serve time for the second offense. Offenders obviously prefer the concurrent over the consecutive sentence option, since they would be eligible for release from prison much earlier!

As one might expect, probation tends to be granted more prevalently for nonviolent offenders. Table 8.1 shows that in general offenders convicted of non-violent crimes (e.g., drug possession, fraud/forgery) were more likely to received probation than those convicted of violent offenses (e.g., murder, rape). The only exception was aggravated assault, where 25 percent received probation.

Table 8.1
**Type of State and Federal Felony Sentences in the United States**

| Crime of Conviction | Percent of Convicted Felons Receiving Straight Probation Sentence |
|---|---|
| Murder | 3% |
| Rape | 12 |
| Robbery | 12 |
| Aggravated Assault | 25 |
| Drug Trafficking | 27 |
| Possession of Drugs | 34 |
| Burglary | 25 |
| Auto Theft | 28 |
| Fraud/Forgery | 41 |

Source: P.A. Langan and J.M. Brown (1997). "Felony Sentences in the United States, 1994." *Bureau of Justice Statistics Bulletin.*

A number of factors can influence the sentencing decision, such as the nature of the offense, the demeanor of the offender, the harm done the victim, judicial and community attitudes, and many other considerations. Many of these factors are brought forth in a document call the presentence investigation report or PSI.

Perhaps the most important criteria is the recommendation of the probation officer who composes the PSI. The role of the presentence report recommendation is a major factor, for the extent of concurrence between the probation officer's recommendations and the judge's sentencing decision is quite strong. Liebermann, Schaffer, and Martin (1971) found that, when probation was recommended, judges followed that recommendation in 83 percent of the cases; Carter (1966) found an even stronger agreement: 96 percent of the cases. Liebermann et al. (1971) also found that, when the recommendation was for imprisonment, the judge agreed in 87 percent of the cases. Macallair (1994) found that defense-based disposition reports for juveniles that recommended probation alternatives consistently lowered commitments to state correctional facilities. So what is the PSI?

---

Box 8.5

### Hanging Tough or Cooperating?

There is considerable evidence that forcing the prosecutor (and thus the court) into trial, rather than pleading guilty for considerations, will invite a much longer sentence. One study (Peterson & Hagan, 1984) found that ordinary drug dealers who demand a trial and the full panoply of guaranteed rights receive prison sentences that average 36 months longer than those who cooperate and plead guilty. For big drug dealers, the average prison sentence is more than 126 months longer.

---

## The Presentence Investigation Report

One of the primary responsibilities of probation agencies is investigation. This includes gathering information about probation and technical violations, facts about arrest, and, most importantly, completing the presentence investigation report for use in sentencing hearings.

The concept of the presentence investigation report (PSI) developed with probation.[3] Judges originally used probation officers to gather background and personal information on offenders to "individualize" punishment.[4] In 1943, the Federal Probation System formalized the presentence investigation report as a required function of the federal probation process. The PSI can have a great deal of significance in the sentencing process, since 80 to 90 percent of defendants plead guilty and the judge's only contact with the offender is during sentencing ("The Presentence Report," 1970). The judge's knowledge of the defendant is usually limited to the information contained in the presentence report. As Walsh concludes (1985:363), "judges lean heavily on the professional advice of probation."

Box 8.6

### Presentence Report

The document resulting from an investigation undertaken by a probation agency or other designated authority, at the request of a criminal court, into the past behavior, family circumstances, and personality of an adult who has been convicted of a crime, in order to assist the court in determining the most appropriate sentence.

The equivalent document for the juvenile court is usually known as the "predispositional report."

In a recent study of the acceptance of the PSI recommendation, Latessa (1993) examined 285 cases in Cuyahoga County, Ohio (which includes the city of Cleveland). He found that judges accepted the recommendation of the probation department in 85 percent of the cases when probation was recommended, and in 66 percent when prison was the recommendation.

The importance of the PSI to a probation agency is illustrated by U.S. Department of Justice estimates that over one million probation presentence investigations are submitted annually (Allen & Simonsen, 1989:147). In 1994, the number of presentence investigation reports exceeded 1.3 million. In terms of the agency workload, almost one-half (45%) of the agencies that conduct presentence investigations reported that more than 25 percent of their workloads were devoted to these reports.

Recent introduction of Federal Sentencing Guidelines have increased the importance of the presentence investigation and the role and responsibility of the probation officer, particularly at the federal level (Dierna, 1989; Jaffe, 1989; McDonald & Carlson, 1993).

## Functions and Objectives

The primary purpose of the PSI is to provide the sentencing court with succinct and precise information upon which to base rational sentencing decisions. Judges usually have a number of options available to them: they may suspend sentence, impose a fine, require restitution, incarcerate, impose community supervision, and so on. The PSI is designed to aid the judge in making the appropriate decision, taking into consideration the needs of the offender as well as the safety of the community.

Over the years, many additional important uses have been found for the presentence report. Basically, these functions include:[5]

1.  Aiding the court in determining sentence.

2.  Assisting correctional authorities in classification and treatment in release planning.

3.  Giving the parole board useful information pertinent to consideration of parole.

4.  Aiding the probation officer in rehabilitation efforts during probation.

5.  Serving as a source of information for research.

In those jurisdictions in which probation and parole services are in the same agency, the PSI can be used for parole supervision purposes.

A presentence investigation report includes more than the simple facts about the offender, as is seen below. If it is to fulfill its purpose, it must include all objective historical and factual information that is significant to the decision-making process, an assessment of the character and needs of the defendant and the community, and a sound recommendation with supporting rationale that follows logically from the evaluation (Bush, 1990). A reliable and accurate report is essential, since judges tend to agree with and frequently impose the disposition recommended by the investigator (Carter & Wilkins, 1967). The officer completing the report should make every effort to ensure that the information contained in the PSI is reliable and valid. Information that has not been validated should be indicated.

## Content, Format, and Style

The presentence investigation report is not immune from a lack of consistency across jurisdictions, but there seem to be some common elements that illustrate the uses and content of the PSI. A survey of 147 probation agencies across the nation (Carter, 1976) revealed that the cover sheets contained 17 pieces of identical information in more than 50 percent of the agencies surveyed. The information that appears most often across the various jurisdictions is included in Table 8.2.

Table 8.2
**Common Elements Contained in Presentence Reports**

| | | | |
|---|---|---|---|
| 1. | Name of Dependent | 10. | Plea |
| 2. | Name of Jurisdiction | 11. | Date of Report |
| 3. | Offense | 12. | Sex |
| 4. | Lawyer | 13. | Custody or Detention |
| 5. | Docket Number | 14. | Verdict |
| 6. | Date of Birth | 15. | Date of Disposition |
| 7. | Address | 16. | Marital Status |
| 8. | Name of Sentencing Judge | 17. | Other Identifying Numbers |
| 9. | Age | | |

Source: R.N. Carter (1976). "Prescriptive Package on Pre-Sentence Investigations." Unpublished draft. Washington, DC: Law Enforcement Assistance Administration.

While the content requirements for a presentence investigation vary from jurisdiction to jurisdiction, there appear to be some common areas that are included and these generally consist of the following:

1. Offense
   Official Version
   Defendant's Version
   Codefendant Information
   Statement of Witnesses, Complainants, and Victims

2. Prior Record
   Juvenile Adjudications
   Adult Record

3. Personal and Family Data
   Defendant
   Parents and Siblings
   Marital Status
   Employment
   Education
   Health (physical, mental, and emotional)
   Military Service
   Financial Condition
   Assets
   Liabilities

4. Evaluation
   Alternative Plans
   Sentencing Data

5. Recommendations

Basically, these areas reflect the recommendation of Carter (1976:9), who states that "in spite of the tradition of 'larger' rather than 'shorter,' there is little evidence that more is better." At a minimum, the PSI should include the five basic areas outlined above. This permits flexibility by allowing for expansion of a subject area and increased detail of circumstances as warranted. On the other hand, a subsection may be summarized in a single narrative statement.

Carter believes it is not necessary to know everything about an offender. Indeed, there is some evidence that in human decisionmaking, the capacity of individuals to use information effectively is limited to five or six items of information. Quite apart from the questions of the reliability, validity, or even relevance of the information, are the time and workload burdens of collecting and sorting masses of data for decisionmaking. The end result may be information overload and impairment of efficiency. Figure 8.3 is a sample outline of a presentence report from the Montgomery County Adult Probation Department (Dayton, Ohio).

The PSI contains information related to the present character and behavior of the offender. One has to question the need for detailed information on family members with whom an adult offender has had no contact in many years. On the other hand, this type of information may be crucial to a young defendant who lives at home and has experienced difficulties getting along with other members of the family. The probation officer must use professional judgment in completing and detailing the presentence report. The Federal Probation System has delineated some simple guidelines to be followed in composing the report ("The Presentence Investigation Report," 1978:7):

1. *Brevity.* Avoid repetition. For clarity and interest, use short sentences and paragraphs, not, however, at the expense of completeness.

2. *Use of "label" terms.* Generalized terms should be avoided as they have different meanings to different people.

3. *Verbation style.* Use caution in verbation reporting. Use direct quotations only if it gives a better picture of the defendant or situation. Quotation marks are used for exact words of person, not an interpretation. Do not take language out of context.

4. *Sources of information.* Verify the facts contained in presentence report. Clearly label any unverified information. Immeasurable harm may result from unverified information presented as fact.

5. *Technical words and phrases.* Use technical words and phrases only if they have wide usage and a common meaning.

Figure 8.3
**The Montgomery County Common Pleas Court Adult Probation Department Presentence Report**

Prosecutor:                                    Defense Attorney:

_____ I. Case Information _____

A.  Case No.:                         C.  Jail Status:
       Referred:                             Amount of Bond:
       Disposition:                          Days in Custody:

B.  Name                              D.  Urinalysis Ordered Yes___ No___
       Alias(es):                           Urine(s) Collected:
       Address:                             Result(s) Positive:
                                            Result(s) Negative:
       Phone:                               Probation Officer:

    Date of Birth:                    E.  Codefendant Status:

    Social Security No.:              F.  Restitution:

_____ II. Charge Information _____

A.  Current Adjudicated Charge(es)/
       O.R.C./Penalty:
                                      D.  Other Pending Cases/Detainers:

                                      E.  Prior Felonies:
B.   Indicated Charge:
                                      F.  Repeat Offender Status:

C.  Original Jurisdiction:            G.  Eligibility for Conditional Probation:

_____ III. Client Information _____

A.  Physical
       Sex_____ Race_____ Height_____
       Weight_____ Eyes_____ Hair_____
       Present Health _____

B.  Social
       Marital Status _____
       No. of Dependents _____
       Custody of Children if Sentenced _____
       _____
       Employment Status _____
       Last Grade Completed _____
       Social Service Involvement _____
       Past _____
       _____
       Present _____
       _____
       Limitations:
                        Rec. Bailiff_____ Date/Time_____

Figure 8.3—*continued*

Part I. The Offense

Part II. Criminal Record Section

A.    Juvenile

B.    Adult

Part III. Employment/Other Pertinent Data

Part IV. Recommendation

Reasons:

1.

2.

3.

4.

Respectfully Submitted,

_____

Team Supervisor_____

Source: The Montgomery County Adult Probation Department.

6.  *Style and format.* A simple, direct, lucid style is effective. The report need not be elaborate nor seek a dramatic effect.

7.  *Writing the report.* Dictate the presentence report at the earliest possible time following the investigation. The longer the delay, the greater the chance of overlooking significant observations.

A thorough PSI is not complete without a plan of supervision for those individuals selected for probation. If this type of information is developed while preparing the PSI, supervision can begin on day one, not several weeks into the probation period. During the development of the PSI, special attention is also given to seeking innovative alternatives to traditional sentencing dispositions (jail, fines, prison, or probation). Recently, there has been increased attention given the victim (Umbreit, 1994; Roy, 1994). Many probation department's now include as part of their PSI report a section pertaining the victim. An example of a victim statement from the Montgomery County is presented in Figure 8.4.

Figure 8.4
**Victim Impact Statement**

| |
|---|
| Judge: |
| Case No.: |
| Name of Defendant: |
| Disposition Date: |
| A.  Economic Loss |
| B.  Physical Injury |
| C.  Change in Personal Welfare or Familial Relationships |
| D.  Psychological Impact |
| E.  Comments |

Source: The Montgomery County Adult Probation Department.

## When to Prepare a PSI Report

It is best to prepare a presentence report after guilt has been determined. This is so for several reasons. First, if the PSI is completed beforehand and the defendant were acquitted, then an invasion of privacy has occurred, and because certain information may come from the defendant, it may be awkward if discussions with a probation officer precede the actual trial. Second, material contained in a PSI is not admissible at trial, but there is always the chance that it may come to the attention of the court before guilt has been determined. This, of course, could bias the outcome and could lead to a mistrial or appeal. Finally, there are economic reasons. A presentence report takes time and resources to complete. It makes little sense to expend resources on a PSI that may never be used. Though there may be exceptions—for example, a defense attorney may believe that having a completed PSI prior to the trial will be in the best interest of the client—the general rule is to complete the PSI only after a determination of guilt.

Carter (1978) believes that a PSI should be prepared in every case in which a sentence of confinement could be a year or longer, where the court has a sentencing option, and in all cases that the court so requests.

## Disclosure and Confidential Nature of the PSI Report

Disclosure of the presentence report to defense counsel has been debated for some time. A 1963 survey found that 56.8 percent of the judges in the sample never divulged any information from a PSI to a defendant or defense attorney (Higgins, 1964). Several court cases have resolved much of the debate in favor of disclosure of the report to the defendant.[6] Currently 16 jurisdictions mandate disclosure.

The disclosure of the report provides the defendant with the opportunity to identify inaccurate, incomplete, or otherwise misleading information. There is also a fundamental due process consideration. Sentencing is a critical state in the criminal justice system; due process enables mistakes to be corrected and rights to be protected.

The arguments against disclosure center around the concern of protecting confidential sources (Zastrow, 1971; Dubois, 1981). Rule 32 of the Federal Rules of Criminal Procedures ("The Presentence Investigation Report," 1978) provides explicit protection for this concern. The rules state that the court shall, upon request, permit counsel and defendant to read the PSI (exclusive of exempted information and recommendations). The three types of information that the court may exempt are:

1. Diagnostic option which, if revealed, might seriously disrupt a program of rehabilitation and treatment. [This could be necessary when the knowledge of psychiatric diagnosis or prognosis might interfere with a defendant's receptivity to treatment.]

2. Sources of information obtained upon promise of confidentiality. [Not all of the information provided by the confidential sources is protected, but only that information that would in any way reveal the identity of the source.]

3. Any other information which, if disclosed, might result in harm, physical or otherwise, to the defendant or other persons. [Some defendants have had a close relationship with dangerous associates or have had serious family difficulties. If unfavorable information about the defendant or other persons were divulged and there might be a risk of retaliation, such information would also be exempt from disclosure.]

If the court believes that information contained in a presentence report may be harmful to the defendant as well as others, then the court must provide, in writing, a summary of the factual information. As a rule, the presentence report is a confidential document (Shockley, 1988) and is not available to anyone without permission of the court.

## Evaluation and Recommendation

Two of the most important sections of the presentence investigation report are the evaluation and the recommendation. Although the research evidence is mixed, there appears to be a high correlation between the probation officer's recommendation and the judge's decision (Hagan, 1975; Walsh, 1985). There is also some evidence that the sections most widely read by the judge are the PSI evaluation and recommendation.

The evaluation should contain the probation officer's professional assessment of the objective material contained in the body of the report. Having gathered all the facts, the probation officer must now consider the protection of the community and the need of the defendant.

First, the probation officer should consider the offense. Was it situational in nature, or indicative of persistent behavior? Was violence used? Was a weapon involved? Was it a property offense or a personal offense? Was there a motive?

Second, the community must be considered. For example, does the defendant pose a direct threat to the safety and welfare of others? Would a disposition other than prison deprecate the seriousness of the crime? Is probation a sufficient deterrent? What community resources are available?

Finally, the probation officer has to consider the defendant and his or her special problems and needs, if any. What developmental factors were significant in contributing to the defendant's current behavior? Was there a history of antisocial behavior? Does the defendant acknowledge responsibility or remorse? Is the defendant motivated to change? What strengths and weaknesses does the defendant possess? Is the defendant employable or supporting any immediate family? The probation officer should also provide a statement of sentencing alternatives available to the court. This does not constitute a recommendation, but rather informs the court which services are available should the defendant be granted probation.

A sound recommendation is the responsibility of the probation officer. Some of the alternatives may include:

| | |
|---|---|
| probation | fine |
| work release | house arrest/electronic monitoring |
| incarceration | community service |
| split sentence | psychiatric treatment |
| shock probation | day fines |
| halfway house | victim mediation |
| day reporting | shock incarceration |
| restitution | no recommendation |

If commitment were recommended, the probation officer would indicate any problems that may need special attention on the part of the institutional staff. In addition, if the defendant were considered a security risk, the investigator would include escape potential, as well as any threats made to or received from the community or other defendants.

Regardless of the recommendation, the probation officer has the responsibility to provide supporting rationale that will assist the court in achieving its sentencing goals.

## Psychiatric and Psychological Reports

Occasions arise during a presentence investigation report when a probation officer and mental health professionals interact. While it is not possible to delineate the full range of possible involvements of the mental health professionals with probation officers, Robert Mills (1980:177-179) has listed some of the primary relationships as follows:

1.  Referral for hospitalization or other treatment as a sentencing alternative. In some cases, the mental condition of the defendant, in relation to his offense(s), warrants a diagnostic evaluation for possible psychiatric treatment. Such an evaluation can be made a condition of probation, or the judge may place the implementation of the referral in the hands of a probation officer without specifying probation.

2.  Psychiatric/psychological consultation is requested by the probation officer as part of the presentence investigation. This is probably the most common use of psychiatric/psychological resources. The probation officer, confronted with a family counseling situation, a sexual perversion, a drug addiction, or some other problem for which referral to a community service agency seems indicated, requests an evaluation for the purpose of verifying diagnostic and treatment recommendations and sometimes providing an intake report to a prescribed agency. In this case, the psychiatric report would be incorporated as a part of his PSI to the court.

3.  A sentencing judge desires a prediction of an offender's probable response to incarceration. There are offenders whose adjustment is so precarious that the imposition of a jail sentence may precipitate a negative outcome which exceeds the requirements of justice. For example, a depressed defendant could become suicidal. In another instance, a frail-looking 18-year-old was diverted to a halfway house for sentence because of the likelihood of homosexual attack in a jail where adequate safeguards against such attacks were not deemed sufficient.

4.  Evaluation of "outside" psychiatric evaluation for the sentencing judge, when such evaluations are offered to the court by defense attorneys. While it may appear presumptuous for a probation officer to get involved in "second guessing" mental health professionals, it is certainly

within a judge's discretion to request clarification on psychiatric formulations through consultation with the officers of his court. Where courts maintain their own psychiatric staff, consultation or re-examination of the defendant by the internal staff members would be preferable. However, the probation officer's familiarity with the network of mental health agencies and with treatment methods make him a valuable resource to judges, especially in those instances when the court does not employ its own internal treatment staff.

## The Sentencing Hearing

While procedures vary across jurisdictions, most criminal courts will conduct a sentencing hearing independent of the trial or determination of guilt. The role of the defense counsel may be important at this phase of the decision-making process. Some common strategies of defense counsel include having a private presentence investigation conducted at the defendant's expense (Gitchoff & Rush, 1989; Greenwood & Turner, 1993); filing a sentencing memorandum with the court that points out the strengths and mitigating factors that counsel sees as worthy of the court's attention; advising the defendant on how to interact with the PSI investigator (be cooperative, provide names and addresses of persons who will be able to speak on his or her behalf, give own version of the offense, etc.); and challenging any inaccurate, incomplete, or misleading findings in the court's PSI.

**DOONESBURY**                                          by Garry Trudeau

## Privately Commissioned Presentence Reports

Recently, privately commissioned presentence reports have been offered as supplements or alternatives to the probation department's report (Hoelter, 1984; Granelli, 1983). As Gitchoff (1980:1) has pointed out, "the sentencing function performed by judges is the most difficult and distasteful of their judicial role." Indeed since the vast majority of offenders plead guilty, the most important function of the defense attorneys may be at the time of sentencing. The failure of many defense attorneys to adequately prepare for sentencing forces most judges to rely on the probation department's report as the sole source of information on which to base a decision. Because most attorneys are not trained in behavioral science, retaining a "correctional expert" has been suggested as a more plausible approach and, although there are ethical issues involved (Evans & Scott, 1983), it appears that a social scientist can serve an important role in the sentencing process.

By permission of Johnny Hart and Creators Syndicate, Inc.

The private PSI may provide additional information about the defender, but it is more likely to provide a more tailored sentencing alternative. Criminologists who have prepared private PSIs suggest a number of specially designed alternatives including: restitution, counseling, community service, and residential treatment (Rodgers, Gitchoff & Paur, 1979). Private PSIs are allowable in many states, including California, Ohio, and the Federal Courts.

In general, private PSIs are expensive and not widespread in practice. Where they are prepared, they tend to be duplicative of much of the information available in the court-ordered PSI; yet they also generally contain a more detailed alternative disposition plan. There are no empirical evaluations of the effects of private PSIs on dispositional outcomes in those cases in which they were available. Anecdotal materials suggest that they have some positive impact on a judge's decision to place the offender on probation. Private PSIs are not without their critics. Kulis (1983) argues that the private sector should have no role in the quasi-judicial sentencing process. He is also critical of the cost of private PSIs, which he believes contributes to a dual system of justice; one for those that can afford it and one for everyone else.

## Factors Related to Sentencing Decisions

As mentioned previously, the PSI involves a great deal of a probation department's time and resources. The presentence report is the primary comprehensive source of information about the defendant that is available to the sentencing judge. Although most judges agree that the PSI is a valuable aid in formulating sentencing decisions, there appear to be some differences of opinion about the value of the recommendations section of the report.[7]

Several studies have attempted to identify those factors that appear to be of primary importance to sentencing judges. Carter's 1976 survey found that the two most significant factors were the defendant's prior criminal record and the current offense. An earlier study by Carter and Wilkins (1967) found that the most important factors for judges in making a decision to grant probation included the defendant's educational level, average monthly salary, occupational level, residence, stability, participation in church activities, and military record. But, again, when factors were ranked according to their importance in the sentencing decision, the current offense and the defendant's prior record, number of arrests, and number of commitments were ranked most important. Welch and Spohn (1986) also concluded that prior record clearly predicts the decision to incarcerate, however, their research suggests that a wide range of indicators have been used to determine "prior record," but that the safest choice to use is prior incarceration.

In another study, Rosecrance (1988:251) suggests that the PSI report serves to maintain the myth that criminal courts dispense individualized justice. His conclusions are, "that present offense and prior criminal record are the factors that determine the probation officer's final sentencing recommendation." Rosecrance (1985) also believes that probation recommendations are designed to endorse pre-arraigned judicial agreements, and that probation officers structure their recommendations in the "ball park" in order to gain judicial acceptance. Rogers (1990) argues, however, that the presentence investigation individualizes juvenile justice.

Photo 8.1
Probation officer explaining conditions of probation. Photograph by Beth Sanders.

In a more recent study, Latessa (1993) examined both the factors that influenced the probation officers recommendation, as well as the actual judicial decision. He found that offenders were more likely to be recommended for prison if: they were repeat offenders, committed more serious offenses, there was a victim involved, and they had a prior juvenile record. The factors that influenced the actual sentencing decision included: the recommendation, drug history, mental health history, seriousness of offense, and having been incarcerated previously in a state prison. Latessa concluded that in this jurisdiction sentencing factors are based mainly on offense and prior record factors, and other relevant information, such as the presence of a victim. It is important to note that demographic factors, such as race, sex, and age did not play a factor in either the recommendations or the decisions of the judges.

## Conditions of Probation

When probation is granted, the court may impose certain reasonable conditions on the offender, which the probation officer is expected to monitor in the supervision process. These must not be capricious, and may be both general (required of all probationers) or specific (required of an individual probationers). General conditions include obeying laws, submitting to searchers, reporting regularly to the supervising officer, notifying the officer of any change in job or residence, and not being in possession of a firearm, associating with known criminals, refraining from excessive use of alcohol, or not leaving the court's jurisdiction for long periods of time without prior authorization. Services provided by probation jurisdictions can be found in Figure 8.5.

Figure 8.5
**Specific Probation Programs Provided**

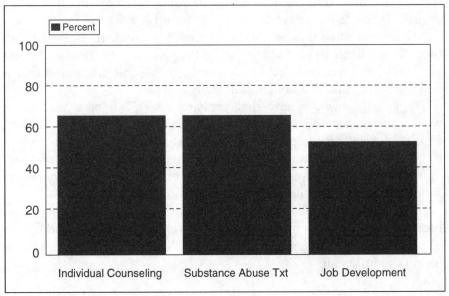

Source: C. Camp and G. Camp (1997). *The Corrections Yearbook, 1997*. South Salem, NY: Criminal Justice Institute, Inc.

Specific conditions are generally tailored to the needs of the offender or philosophy of the court. For reintegration or other such purposes, the court may impose conditions of medical or psychiatric treatment; residence in a halfway house or residential center; intensive probation supervision, electronic surveillance, house arrest, community service, active involvement in Alcoholics Anonymous; participation in a drug abuse program; restitution or victim compensation; no use of psychotropic drugs (such as cocaine or marijuana); observing a reasonable curfew; no hitchhiking; staying out of bars and poolrooms (particularly if the probationer is a prostitute); group counseling; vocational training; or other court-ordered requirements. Such required conditions are specifically designed to assist the probationer in the successful completion of probation. An example of the standard conditions of probation from the Federal Courts are presented in Figure 8.6.

## Probationer Fees

As part of the conditions of probation, many jurisdictions have included probation fees as part of the probation experience. These fees are levied for a variety of services including the preparation of presentence reports, electronic monitoring, ignition interlock devices, work release programs, drug counseling, and regular probation supervision (Ring, 1988). The fees range anywhere from $5 to $40 per month, usually with a sliding scale for those unable to pay. The imposition of supervision fees has increased dramatically over the years, with only 10 states reported user fees in 1980, at least 25 states by 1986, and by 1996, 41 states had authorized the imposition of some form of supervision fee (Baird, Holien & Bakke, 1986; Camp & Camp, 1997).

The critics of probation fees argue that it is unfair to assess a fee to those most unable to pay. Others argue that probationer fee's will result in a shift from treatment and surveillance to fee collection, and that it will turn probation officers into bill collectors.

Others however, believe that probation fees can be a reasonable part of the probation experience (Wheeler, Macan, Hissong & Slusher, 1989; Wheeler, Rudolph & Hissong, 1989). Harlow and Nelson (1982:65) point out that successful fee programs serve a dual purpose, "both an important revenue source and an effective means of communicating to the offender the need to pay one's own way."[8]

It appears that probation fees are rapidly becoming a fixture in probation. Not only is it a means of raising revenue and offsetting the costs of supervision, treatment and surveillance, but it can also be used as a form of punishment.

Figure 8.6

---

PROB 7A
(Rev. 10/89)    **Conditions of Probation and Supervised Release**

## UNITED STATES DISTRICT COURT

### FOR THE

_____

Name _____    Docket No. _____

Address _____

Under the terms of your sentence, you have been placed on probation/supervised release (strike one) by the Honorable _____, United States District Judge for the District of _____ . Your term of supervision is for a period of _____ , commencing _____ .

While on probation/supervised release (strike one) you shall not commit another Federal, state, or local crime and shall not illegally possess a controlled substance. Revocation of probation and supervised release is mandatory for possession of a controlled substance.

## CHECK IF APPROPRIATE:

☐ As a condition of supervision, you are instructed to pay a fine in the amount of _____ ; it shall be paid in the following manner _____ .

☐ As a condition of supervision, you are instructed to pay restitution in the amount of _____ to _____ ; it shall be paid in the following manner _____ .

☐ The defendant shall not possess a firearm or destructive device. Probation must be revoked for possession of a firearm.

☐ The defendant shall report in person to the probation office in the district to which the defendant is released within 72 hours of release from the custody of the Bureau of Prisons.

☐ The defendant shall report in person to the probation office in the district of release within 72 hours of release from the custody of the Bureau of Prisons.

**It is the order of the Court that you shall comply with the following standard conditions:**

(1)    You shall not leave the judicial district without permission of the Court or probation officer;

(2)    You shall report to the probation officer as directed by the Court or probation officer, and shall submit a truthful and complete written report within the first five days of each month;

(3)    You shall answer truthfully all inquiries by the probation officer and follow the instructions of the probation officer;

(4)    You shall support your dependents and meet other family responsibilities;

Figure 8.6—*continued*

(5)    You shall work regularly at a lawful occupation unless excused by the probation officer for schooling, training, or other acceptable reasons;

(6)    You shall notify the probation officer within 72 hours of any change in residence or employment;

(7)    You shall refrain from excessive use of alcohol and shall not purchase, possess, use, distribute, or administer any narcotic or other controlled substance, or any paraphernalia related to such substances, except as prescribed by a physician;

(8)    You shall not frequent places where controlled substances are illegally sold, used, distributed, or administered;

(9)    You shall not associate with any persons engaged in criminal activity, and shall not associate with any person convicted of a felony unless granted permission to do so by the probation officer;

(10)    You shall permit a probation officer to visit you at any time at home or elsewhere, and shall permit confiscation of any contraband observed in plain view by the probation officer;

(11)    You shall notify the probation officer within 72 hours of being arrested or questioned by a law enforcement officer;

(12)    You shall not enter into any agreement to act as an informer or a special agent of a law enforcement agency without the permission of the Court;

(13)    As directed by the probation officer, you shall notify third parties of risks that may be occasioned by your criminal record or personal history or characteristics, and shall permit the probation officer to make such notifications and to confirm your compliance with such notification requirement.

**The special conditions ordered by the Court are as follows:**

Upon a finding of violation of probation or supervised release, I understand that the Court may (1) revoke supervision or (2) extend the term of supervision and/or modify the conditions of supervision.

These conditions have been read to me. I fully understand the conditions, and have been provided a copy of them.

(Signed) _____     _____
　　　　　　　　　　　Defendant　　　　　　　　　　　Date

_____     _____
U.S. Probation Officer/Designated Witness　　　　Date

# Restitution and Community Service

Two recent but related trends in the conditions the court may impose are restitution and community work orders. Restitution requires the offender to make payment (perhaps monetary) to a victim to offset the damages done in the commission of the crime. If the offenders cannot afford to repay at least a part of the loss suffered by the victim, it is possible to restore the victim's losses through personal services. Probation with restitution thus has the potential for being a reparative sentence and Galaway (1983) argues that it should be the penalty of choice for property offenders. Restitution can lessen the loss of the victim, maximize reconciliation of the offender and community, and marshal community support for the offender, perhaps through enlisting a community sponsor to monitor and encourage the offender's compliance. A good example of this can be seen in California, where in 1982 voters passed a Victim's Bill of Rights. Part of this initiative was a Crime Victim Restitution Program that enables the court to order offenders to repay victims and the community through restitution or community service.

By permission of Johnny Hart and Creators Syndicate, Inc.

Community work orders as conditions of probation appear to be increasingly used in conjunction with probation, particularly if there are no direct victim losses or the nature of the crime demands more than supervised release. Examples of community work orders would include requiring a dentist convicted of driving while intoxicated to provide free dental services to a number of indigents, or ordering a physician to provide numerous hours of free medical treatment to jail inmates, perhaps on Saturday mornings. Juveniles may frequently be ordered to work for community improvements through litter removal, cutting grass, painting the homes of the elderly or public buildings, or driving shut-ins to market or to visit friends and relatives. Both restitution and community work orders can serve multiple goals: offender punishment, community reintegration, and reconciliation. The four reasons most commonly cited for using community service are:

1.  It is a punishment that can fit many crimes.

2.  The costs of imprisonment are high and are getting higher.

3.  Our jails and prisons are already full.

4.  Community service requires an offender to pay with time and energy.

The specific probation programs offered across the nation can be seen in Figure 8.7.

Figure 8.7
**Specific Probation Programs Provided (in percent)**

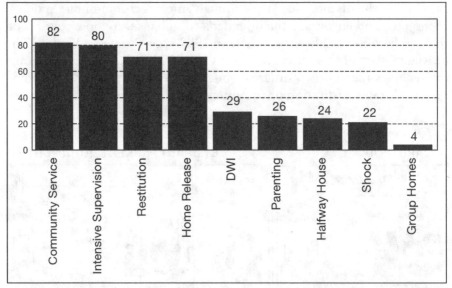

Source: C. Camp and G. Camp (1995). *The Corrections Yearbook, 1994: Probation and Parole,* p. 32. South Salem, NY: The Criminal Justice Institute.

## Alternative Probation Procedures

In addition to the most frequent procedures described above, there are six other variations of granting probation that need to be discussed before we consider the legal process of revoking probation of those who cannot or will not abide by court-imposed conditions of liberty in the community:

1.  prosecutorial probation,

2.  court probation without adjudication,

3.  shock probation,

4.  intermittent incarceration,

5. split sentences, and

6. modification of sentence.

While probation most frequently is imposed by a trial judge after a guilty plea or trial, it may also replace the trial completely, in which case it is called "probation without adjudication." In practice, the process embraces two separate programs, one operated by the prosecutor (a form of deferred prosecution) and the other by the judge in those limited number of jurisdictions in which state legislation permits a bifurcated process (determining guilt, followed by adjudication as a felon). Both result in probation but are vastly different.

## Deferred Prosecution Probation

Part of the broad power accorded a prosecutor in the United States is the ability to offer the accused deferred prosecution. In those programs in which the prosecutor grants deferred prosecution, the accused will generally be asked to sign a contract accepting moral (but usually not legal) responsibility for the crime and agreeing to make victim restitution, to undergo specific treatment programs (Alcoholics Anonymous, methadone maintenance, psychotherapy, etc.), to report periodically to a designated official (usually a probation officer), and to refrain from other criminal acts during the contract period. If these conditions are satisfied, the prosecutor dismisses (*nolle pros*) the charge. If the accused does not actively participate and cooperate in the program the prosecutor can, at any time during the contract period, carry the case forward to trial. Deferred prosecution can, although it is infrequent, lead to a unique probation organization within the office of the prosecutor.

## Probation by Withholding Adjudication

This process refers to a judge's optional authority that is available in those states (such as Florida) where statutes permit a bifurcated process: first determine guilt and then declare the defendant a convicted felon. By refraining from the declaration of a guilty felon, the judge can suspend the legal process and place the defendant on probation for a specific time period, sometimes without supervision being required (a "summary" or nonreporting probation). Thus the judge gives the offender a chance to demonstrate his or her ability and willingness to adjust and reform. The offenders know that they can still be returned to court for adjudication of guilt and sentencing, and frequently imprisonment.

The advantages of this option fit squarely in the general philosophy of probation. Not only is treatment in the community emphasized, but the collateral benefits are considerable (Allen, Friday, Roebuck & Sagarin, 1981:361-362):

> (The judge) places him or her on probation without requiring him to register with local law enforcement agencies as a previously convicted felon; without serving notice on prospective employers of a previous conviction; without preventing the offender from holding public office, voting, or serving on a jury; without impeding the offender from obtaining a license that requires "reputable character;" without making it more difficult than others to obtain firearms; in short, without public or even private degradation.

## Shock Probation

In 1965, Ohio became the first of at least 14 states that enacted an early release procedure generally known as "shock probation." Shock probation combined the leniency of probation with a short period of incarceration in a penal institution. The assumptions and features underlying this innovative program were described by the then director of the Ohio Adult Parole Authority (Allen & Simonsen, 1995:229). It was:

1.  A way for the courts to impress offenders with the seriousness of their actions without a long prison sentence.

2.  A way for the courts to release offenders found by the institution to be more amenable to community-based treatment than was realized by the courts at time of sentence.

3.  A way for the courts to arrive at a just compromise between punishment and leniency in appropriate cases.

4.  A way for the courts to provide community-based treatment for rehabilitable offenders while still observing their responsibilities for imposing deterrent sentences where public policy demands it.

5.  [A way to afford] the briefly incarcerated offender a protection against absorption into the "hard rock" inmate culture.

Vito and Allen (1981) note that shock probation is a program of judicial reconsideration of the original sentence. Convicted defendants, originally sentenced to prison for varying numbers of years may, through their own motion or that of their legal counsel or even through direct motion by the court, be recalled to court and have the remainder of their sentences suspended and be placed on probation. When granted release to the community on probation, these offenders are supervised by probation officers under the same rules and regulations that apply to other probationers, including the possibility of probation revocation. Both the eligibility requirements and sentence length are fixed by statute, although the sentencing judge may shorten the period of supervision in the community.

The effectiveness of shock probation has been evaluated by a number of researchers, the most sophisticated of which was by Vito (1978). Effectiveness—as measured by a variety of failure indicators—ranges from a success rate of 78 percent to 91 percent. Farmer (1981) reported that, of the 13,012 offenders released under shock probation in Ohio from 1966 until 1979, only 1,389 (10.6%) were reinstitutionalized. There is some evidence that combining shock probation with intensive supervision will further improve effectiveness (Latessa & Vito, 1988). There is also evidence that shock probation is an effective means of reducing prison populations (Kozuh, Guenther, Plattsmier & Buckmaster, 1980).

Shock probation has also been acclaimed (Reid, 1976) as a program that permits the offender a reduction in the time he or she would have spent in prison; a chance to be quickly reintegrated into the community; a mechanism by which to maintain family and community ties; an opportunity to avoid prisonization; a speedy judicial review of sentence; and an early release mechanism that both reduces prison population and the costs of imprisonment (Vito, 1978).

Critics have argued that shock probation combines philosophically incompatible objectives: punishment and leniency. Other criticisms (Reid, 1976) are that the defendant is further stigmatized by the incarceration component of shock probation, and the existence of a shock probation sentence may encourage the judiciary to rely less on probation than previously. But the most damaging criticism is by Vito and Allen (1981:74):

> . . . the fact of incarceration is having some unknown and unmeasurable effect upon [the more unfavorable] performance of shock probationers. . . . It could be that the negative effects of incarceration are affecting the performance of shock probationers.

Vito has drawn some conclusions about shock probation based on his long-term work in this area (1984:26-27):

1. The level of reincarceration rates indicate that the program has some potential.

2. If shock probation is utilized, it should be used with a select group of offenders who cannot be considered as good candidates for regular probation.

3.  The period of incarceration must be short in order to achieve the maximum deterrent effect while reducing the fiscal cost of incarceration.

4.  In this time of severe prison overcrowding, the use of shock probation can only be justified as a diversionary measure to give offenders who would otherwise not be placed on probation a chance to succeed.

The overall effects and effectiveness of shock probation remain unknown. Until more research is conducted, perhaps the best tentative conclusion is that the program is no worse than probation and incarceration, is less costly than imprisonment, and may be just as effective in preventing recidivism as is probation.

## Combining Probation and Incarceration

There are a number of alternatives to placing an offender on probation, other than shock probation, that include a period of incarceration (Parisi, 1980). The U.S. Department of Justice (Bureau of Justice Statistics, 1983) notes:

> Although the courts continue to use (probation) as a less severe and less expensive alternative to incarceration, most courts are also given discretion to link probation to a term of incarceration—an option selected with increasing frequency.

Combinations of probation and incarceration include:

> Split sentences: where the court specifies a period of incarceration to be followed by a period of probation (Parisi, 1981).

> Modification of sentence: where the original sentencing court may reconsider an offender's prison sentence within a limited time and change it to probation.

> Intermittent incarceration: where an offender on probation may spend weekends or nights in jail (Bureau of Justice Statistics, 1983).

It is not known how frequently sentencing judges use these options. However, they appear to be gaining popularity, particularly with jail and prison populations at an all-time high. See Figure 8.8.

Figure 8.8
**Correctional Populations in the United States: 1983, 1993 and 1997**

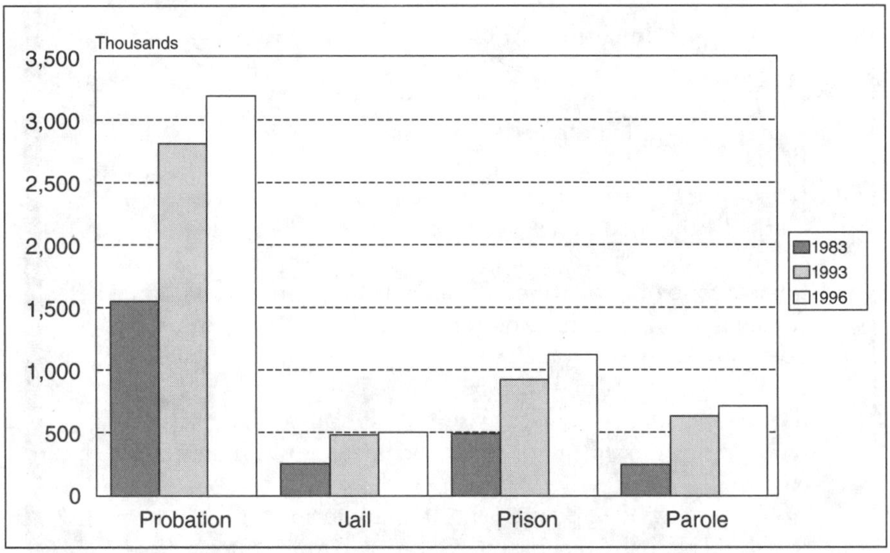

Source: U.S. Department of Justice (1997). *Nation's Probation and Parole Populations Reached Almost 3.9 Million.*

## Probation Revocation

Once placed on probation, offenders are supervised and assisted by probation officers who are increasingly using existing community agencies and services to provide individualized treatment based on the offender's needs. Assuming the offender meets the court-imposed conditions, makes satisfactory progress in resolving underlying problems, and does not engage in further illegal activities, probation agencies may request the court to close the case. This would terminate supervision of the offender and probation. Probation may also be terminated by the completion of the period of maximum sentence, or by the offender having received "maximum benefit from treatment."

In supervising a probationer, officers should enforce the conditions and rules of probation pragmatically, considering the client's particular and individual needs, legality of decisions they must make while supervising clients (Watkins, 1989), the clarity of anticipation by probationer of assistance from the supervising officer (and expectations of the probationer), and the potential effects of enforcing rules on a client's future behavior and adjustment (Koontz, 1980). Many clients have drug problems, and must be tested for drug use. See Figure 8.9.

Box 8.7

## Modifications of Conditions of Sentence

Probation officers supervise clients assigned by sentencing courts and, during the period of community release, may find that certain probationers refuse to abide by the court-imposed rules, or that their clients' personal circumstances change so markedly that additional court direction may be needed.

If the client has difficulty accepting the legitimacy of community control, probation officers may recommend additional surveillance or treatment options. These range from imposing house arrest to electronic monitoring, or daily surveillance by the officer. Clients may also be required to reside in a residential setting, such as a halfway house, or appear daily at a day reporting program, until their behavior or circumstances change.

Increasing the requirements for conformity to court-ordered liberty is frequently referred to as "tourniquet sentencing." Conditions may be relaxed as behavior improves.

Figure 8.9
**Percentage of Drug Tests Resulting in Probation or Parole Revocations During 1996**

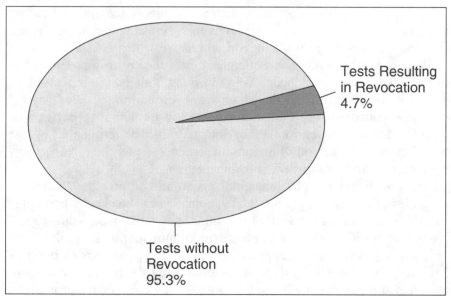

Source: C. Camp and G. Camp (1997). *The Corrections Yearbook, 1997*. South Salem, NY: The Criminal Justice Institute, Inc.

Probationers vary in their ability to comply with imposed conditions, some of which may be unrealistic, particularly those that require extensive victim restitution or employment during an economic period of high unemployment (Smith, Davis & Hillenbrand, 1989). Some probationers are also indifferent or even hostile, unwilling or psychologically unable to cooperate with their probation supervisor or the court. Others commit technical violations of court orders that are not per se new crimes but are seen as harbingers of future illegal activity. In these circumstances, probation officers must deal with technical probation violations.

Probation officers, charged with managing such cases, may determine that technical violators need a stern warning or that court-imposed conditions should be tightened (or relaxed, depending on individual circumstances). These determinations may lead to an offender's reappearance before the court for a warning or redefinition of conditions. Judges and probation officers, ideally, collaborate in such cases to protect the community or increase the probability of successful reintegration. Offenders are frequently returned to probation, and supervision and treatment continue.

If the warning and new conditions are not sufficient, or the offender repetitively violates conditions of probation, or is arrested for an alleged new crime, a probation revocation hearing may be necessary. If the probationer is not already in jail for the alleged new crime, a warrant may be issued for his or her arrest. Reasons for probation revocation in 1996 can be seen in Figure 8.10.

Figure 8.10
**Reason for Return to Custody of Probationers During 1996**

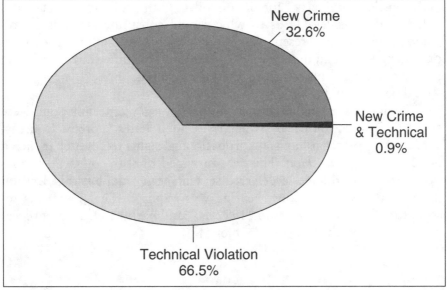

Source: C. Camp and G. Camp (1997). *The Corrections Yearbook, 1997*. South Salem, NY: The Criminal Justice Institute, Inc.

It is also clear that technical violations can be a major source of failures on probation, and that the rates can vary considerably from jurisdiction to jurisdiction. Figure 8.11 illustrates this point with data from a recent recidivism study conducted in Ohio. As part of this study recidivism rates were compared for probation agencies across the state, by the size of the county. Probation departments in the medium and small counties were more likely to use technical violations for probation revocation and incarceration than the larger counties.

---

**Box 8.8**

### Technical Violation of Probation

A technical violation refers to an infraction of a court order, often in the form of a probation condition. It generally is not considered a new crime per se, but can be used by the probation officer to bring an offender back in front of the judge. An example of a technical violation would be the failure of a probationer to meet with his or her probation officer as scheduled. Technical violations can lead to the revocation of probation and the imposition of incarceration or another sanction.

---

A probation revocation hearing is a serious process, posing potential "grievous loss of liberty" for the offender. Both probation officers and judges vary considerably as to what would constitute grounds for revoking probation and resentencing to imprisonment. Punitive probation officers may contend that technical violations are sufficient for revoking probation; judges may believe that the commission of a new crime would be the only reason for revocation.

The due process rights of probationers at a revocation hearing were generally ignored until 1967, when the United States Supreme Court issued an opinion regarding state probationers' rights to counsel at such a hearing (*Mempa v. Rhay*). This case provided right to counsel if probation were revoked under a deferred sentencing statute, but this decision did not specify that a court hearing was required. That issue was resolved in *Gagnon v. Scarpelli* (1972), a landmark case in due process procedures in probation (see Chapter 5).

Figure 8.11
**Reason for Subsequent Incarceration for Probationers by County Size**

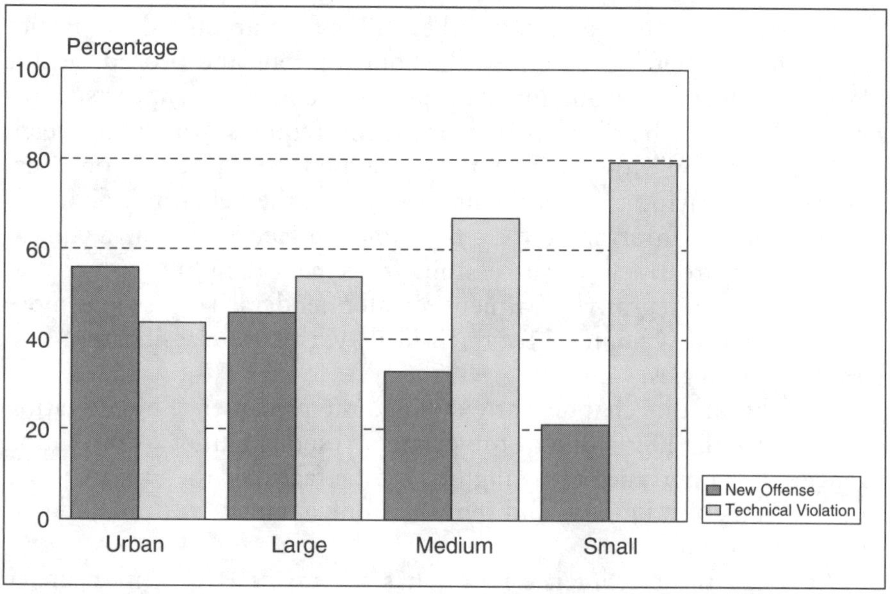

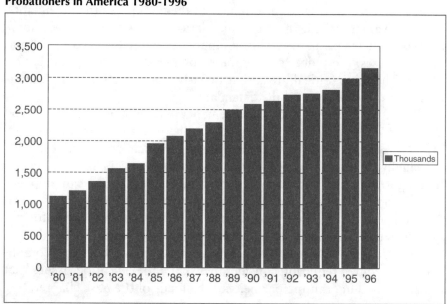

Source: E.J. Latessa, L.F. Travis, and A. Holsinger (1997). *Evaluation of Ohio's Community Corrections Act Programs by County Size.* Cincinnati, OH: Division of Criminal Justice, University of Cincinnati.

Figure 8.12
**Probationers in America 1980-1996**

Source: U.S. Department of Justice (1997). *Nation's Probation and Parole Populations Reached Almost 3.9 Million Last Year.*

## Summary

Probation continues to serve the bulk of adult offenders (Figure 8.12). This chapter has described the court options and procedures for placing offenders on probation, as well as some issues in supervising offenders. It should be obvious that probation requires a judge to weigh "individualization" of treatment as opposed to "justice" or "just deserts." Underlying this perplexing problem is the belief in individualized treatment. Unfortunately, at this time we lack sufficient technical knowledge of treatment to successfully implement the philosophy of individualized, reintegrative treatment for all offenders. This issue is more fully explored in Chapter 11, which deals with case classification and treatment strategies.

In addition, this chapter has examined the presentence investigation report. Since the PSI is one of the primary responsibilities of probation agencies, its importance is highlighted by the fact that the vast majority of defendants plead guilty, and that their only contact with the judge is during sentencing.

Although the presentence report has several functions, its primary purpose is to aid the judge in determining sentence. The five major components of the presentence report include: (1) current offense, (2) prior record, (3) personal history, (4) evaluation, and (5) recommendation.

Preparation of the presentence report is usually made after guilt has been established. This ensures that the facts about the defendant are accurate and reliable. Several types of information are exempt, but the court must provide a written summary of the findings to the defendant.

The evaluation and the recommendation are two extremely important components of the PSI. This is supported by the fact that in the majority of cases, the judge follows the recommendation of the probation officer. The three critical areas that must be considered include: the offense, the community, and the defendant.

Recently, there has been a movement to submit privately prepared presentence reports. These reports have generally augmented the court-ordered PSI with special attention given to sentencing alternatives.

Finally, probation officer monitoring of clients' behavior suggests that tightening the conditions of probation supervision can improve community safety and increase probation effectiveness. Only when clients repeatedly violate the conditions of their probation, when tourniquet sentencing has failed to deter, is probation revoked.

Granting probation and supervising probation clients are complicated procedures requiring considerable skill and dedication, issues that are also raised in granting parole, and the focus of the next chapter.

## Review Questions

1. Describe the distribution of offenders under correctional control.

2. What are the general objectives of probation?

3. Describe the advantages of probation.

4. How is justice individualized?

5. What functions does the presentence investigation serve?

6. Debate: The presentence investigation report should be disclosed to the offender.

7. Identify and define five supervision conditions that might be included in the PSI recommendation.

8. List five conditions of probation that are generally required of all probationers.

9. What are three grounds for revoking probation and sentencing to incarceration?

10. Describe the procedures in a sentencing hearing.

11. List five possible sentencing recommendations that can be made.

## Key Terms

concurrent sentencing
conditions of probation
consecutive sentencing
individualized justice
presentence investigation report
prisonization
private presentence report
probation

probationer fees
restitution
revocation
selective incapacitation
sentencing hearing
shock probation
split sentence

## Recommended Readings

del Carmen, R.V. (1985). "Legal Issues and Liabilities in Community Corrections." In L.F. Travis (ed.) *Probation, Parole and Community Corrections*, pp. 47-70. Prospect Heights, IL: Waveland. This chapter does an excellent job of summarizing the legal issues surrounding probation, including release, conditions, and supervision.

Gowdy, V. (1993). *Intermediate Sanctions*. Washington, DC: U.S. Department of Justice. An excellent overview of the range of and issues surrounding intermediate punishments.

Johnson, H.A. (1996). *History of Criminal Justice*, Second Edition. Cincinnati, OH: Anderson Publishing Co. This book provides a history of criminal justice, and probation and examines the philosophy of individualized justice.

Rothman, D.J. (1980). *Conscience and Convenience: The Asylum and Its Alternatives in Progressive America*. Boston, MA: Little, Brown. Chapter 3 provides a critical assessment of the early use of probation and the development of the presentence investigation.

## Notes

[1]    While some dispute the effectiveness of probation (Petersilia, 1985), other researchers (McGaha et al., 1987; G.F. Vito, 1986) have found probation generally to be effective. This issue is discussed in greater detail in Chapter 14.

[2]    There is some evidence that sentencing is in part influenced by judges' personal goals, such as potential for promotion to a higher court. M.A. Cohen (1992). "The Motives of Judges: Empirical Evidence from Antitrust Sentencing." *International Review of Law and Economics*, 12:13-30.

[3]    For a thorough discussion of the early development of the presentence investigation report see "The Presentence Report: An Empirical Study of Its Use in the Federal Criminal Process" (1970). *Georgetown Law Journal*, 58:12-27.

[4]    See E. Sieh (1993). "From Augustus to the Progressives: A Study of Probation's Formative Years." *Federal Probation*, 57(3):67-72.

[5]    These functions are adapted from the Administrative Office of the U.S. Courts (1978). *The Presentence Investigation Report*. Washington, DC: U.S. Government Printing Office. See also T.B. Marvell (1995). "Sentencing Guidelines and Prison Population Growth." *The Journal of Criminal Law and Criminology*, 85:696-707.

[6]    Several cases in which the disclosure issue has been tested include: *Kent v. United States*, 383 U.S. 541 (1966); *Baker v. United States*, 287 F.2d 5 (9th Cir. 1961); and *Gardner v. Florida*, 20 Cr.L. 3083 (1977).

[7]    For example, in Cincinnati, Ohio, a single probation department serves both the Municipal Court and the Court of Common Pleas, yet each court requires a different presentence investigation report. The Court of Common Pleas does not permit probation officer recommendations to be included in the report, but the Municipal Court requires one.

[8]    For a description of the Texas Program, see P. Finn and D. Parent (1992). *Making the Offender Foot the Bill: A Texas Program*. Washington, DC: U.S. Department of Justice.

# References

Allen, H.E., P. Friday, J. Roebuck, and E. Sagarin (1981). *Crime and Punishment*. New York, NY: The Free Press.

Allen, H.E. and C.E. Simonsen (1995). *Corrections in America*. Englewood Cliffs, NJ: Prentice-Hall.

Allen, H.E. and C.E. Simonsen (1989). *Corrections in America*. New York, NY: Macmillan.

Allen, H.E. and C.E. Simonsen (1981). *Corrections in America*. New York, NY: Macmillan.

American Bar Association Project on Standards for Criminal Justice (1970). "Standards Relating to Probation." Approved Draft.

*Baker v. United States*, 287 F.2d 5 (9th Cir. 1961).

Baird, C.S., D.A. Holien, and J.A. Bakke (1986). *Fees for Probation Services*. Washington, DC: National Institute of Corrections.

Bureau of Justice Statistics (1997a). *Correctional Populations in the United States*. Washington, DC: U.S. Department of Justice.

Bureau of Justice Statistics (1997b). *Nation's Probation and Parole Population Reached Almost 3.9 Million Last Year*. Washington, DC: U.S. Department of Justice.

Bush, E.L. (1990). "Not Ordinarily Relevant? Considering the Defendant's Children at Sentencing." *Federal Probation*, 54(1):15-22.

Callison, H.G. (1983). *Introduction to Community Based Corrections*. New York, NY: McGraw-Hill.

Camp, C. and G. Camp (1997). *The Corrections Yearbook*. South Salem, NY: The Criminal Justice Institute.

Carter, R.M. (1978). *Presentence Report Handbook: Prescriptive Package*. Washington, DC: Law Enforcement Assistance Administration.

Carter, R.M. (1976). "Prescriptive Package on Pre-Sentence Investigations." Unpublished draft. Washington, DC: Law Enforcement Assistance Administration.

Carter, R.M. (1966). "It Is Respectfully Recommended . . ." *Federal Probation*, 30(2):38-40.

Carter, R.M. and L.T. Wilkins (1967). "Some Factors in Sentencing Policy." *Journal of Criminal Law, Criminology and Police Science*, 58(4):503-514.

Clear, T.R., V.B. Clear, and W.D. Burrell (1989). *Offender Assessment and Evaluation: The Presentence Investigation Report*. Cincinnati, OH: Anderson Publishing Co.

Cohen, M.A. (1992). "The Motives of Judges: Empirical Evidence from Antitrust Sentencing." *International Review of Law and Economics*, 12:13-30.

Dawson, J.M. (1990). *Felons Sentenced to Probation in State Courts*. Washington, DC: U.S. Department of Justice.

del Carmen, R.V. (1985). "Legal Issues and Liabilities in Community Corrections." In L.F. Travis (ed.) *Probation, Parole and Community Corrections*, pp. 47-70. Prospect Heights, IL: Waveland.

Dierna, J.S. (1989). "Guideline Sentencing: Probation Officer Responsibilities and Inter-agency Issues." *Federal Probation*, 53(3):3-11.

Dixon, J. (1995). "The Organizational Context of Criminal Sentencing." *American Journal of Sociology*, 100:1157-1198.

Dubois, P.L. (1981). "Disclosure of Presentence Reports in the United States District Courts." *Federal Probation*, 45(1):3-9.

Evans, S.S. and J.E. Scott (1983). "Social Scientists as Expert Witnesses: Their Use, Misuse and Sometimes Abuse." *Law and Policy Quarterly*, 5:181-214.

Farmer, G. (1981). "Letter to the Editor." *International Journal of Offender Therapy and Comparative Criminology*, 25:75-76.

Finn, P. (1984). "Prison Crowding: The Response of Probation and Parole." *Crime & Delinquency*, 30:141-153.

Finn, P. and D. Parent (1992). *Making the Offender Foot the Bill: A Texas Program*. Washington, DC: U.S. Department of Justice.

*Gagnon v. Scarpelli*, 411 U.S. 778, 93 S. Ct. (1972).

Galaway, B. (1983). "Probation as a Reparative Sentence." *Federal Probation*, 46(3):9-18.

*Gardner v. Florida*, 20 Cr. L. 3083 (1977).

General Accounting Office (1982). *Federal Parole Practices*. Washington, DC: GAO.

Gilliard, D. and A. Beck (1994). *Prisoners in 1993*. Washington, DC: U.S. Department of Justice.

Gitchoff, T.G. (1980). *Expert Testimony of Sentencing. American Jurisprudence Proof of Facts*, 21:1-9. Rochester, NH: Lawyers Cooperative Publishers, 1980.

Gitchoff, T.G. and G.E. Rush (1989). "The Criminological Case Evaluation of Sentencing Recommendation: An Idea Whose Time Has Come." *International Journal of Offender Therapy and Comparative Criminology*, 33(1):77-83.

Glaser, D. (1985). "Who Gets Probation and Parole: Case Study Versus Actuarial Decision-Making." *Crime & Delinquency*, 31:367-378.

Gowdy, V. (1993). *Intermediate Sanctions*. Washington, DC: U.S. Department of Justice.

Granelli, J.S. (1983, May). "Presentence Reports Go Private." *National Law Journal*, 15:1-23.

Greenwood, P.W. and S. Turner (1993). "Private Presentence Reports for Serious Juvenile Offenders: Implementation Issues and Impacts." *Justice Quarterly*, 10:229-243.

Hagan, J. (1975). "The Social and Legal Construction of Criminal Justice: A Study of the Presentence Report." *Social Problems*, 22:620-637.

Harlow, N. and K.E. Nelson (1982). *Management Strategies for Probation in an Era of Limits*. Washington, DC: National Institute of Corrections.

Higgins, J. (1964). "Confidentiality of Presentence Reports." *Albany Law Review*, 28:31-47.

Hoelter, H. (1984). "Private Presentence Reports: Boon or Boondoggle?" *Federal Probation*, 48(3):66-69.

Jaffe, H.J. (1989). "The Presentence Report, Probation Officer Accountability, and Recruitment Practices: Some Influences of Guideline Sentencing." *Federal Probation*, 53(3):12-14.

Johnson, H.A. (1996). *History of Criminal Justice*. Cincinnati, OH: Anderson Publishing Co.

*Kent v. United States*, 383 U.S. 541 (1966).

Koontz, J.B (1980). "Pragmatic Conditions of Probation." *Corrections Today*, 42:14-44.

Kozuh, J., R. Guenther, R. Plattsmier, and D. Buckmaster (1980). *1980 TAPC Shock Probation Survey*. Austin, TX: Adult Probation Commission, Division of Information Services.

Kulis, C.J. (1983). "Profit in the Private Presentence Report." *Federal Probation*, 47(4):11-16.

Langan, P.A. and J.M. Brown (July 1997). "Felony Sentences in the United States, 1994." *Bureau of Justice Statistics Bulletin*, U.S. Department of Justice, Office of Justice Programs.

Latessa, E.J. (1993). *An Analysis of Pre-Sentencing Investigation Recommendations and Judicial Outcome in Cuyahoga County Adult Probation Department*. Cincinnati, OH: Department of Criminal Justice, University of Cincinnati.

Latessa, E.J. and G.F. Vito (1988). "The Effects of Intensive Supervision on Shock Probationers." *Journal of Criminal Justice*, 16:319-330.

Liebermann, E., S. Schaffer, and J. Martin (1971). *The Bronx Sentencing Project: An Experiment in the Use of Short-Form Presentence Report for Adult Misdemeanants*. New York, NY: Vera Institute of Justice.

Macallair, D. (1994). "Disposition Case Advocacy in San Francisco's Juvenile Justice System: A New Approach to Deinstitutionalization." *Crime & Delinquency*, 40:84-95.

McDonald, D.C. and K.E. Carlson (1993). *Sentencing in the Federal Courts: Does Race Matter?* Washington, DC: U.S. Bureau of Justice Statistics.

McGaha, J., M. Fichter, and P. Hirschburg (1987). "Felony Probation: A Re-Examination of Public Risk." *American Journal of Criminal Justice*, 12:1-9.

Marvell, T.B. (1995). "Sentencing Guidelines and Prison Population Growth." *The Journal of Criminal Law and Criminology*, 85:696-707.

*Mempa v. Rhay*, 389 U.S. 128 (1967).

Mills, R.B. (1980). *Offender Assessment*. Cincinnati, OH: Anderson Publishing Co.

National Advisory Commission on Criminal Justice Standards and Goals (1973). *Corrections*. Washington, DC: U.S. Government Printing Office.

Parisi, N. (1981). "A Taste of the Bars." *Journal of Criminal Law and Criminology*, 72:1109-1123.

Parisi, N. (1980). "Combining Incarceration and Probation." *Federal Probation*, 46(2):3-10.

Peterson, R. and J. Hagan (1984). "Changing Conceptions of Race: Toward an Account of Anomalous Findings of Sentencing Research." *American Sociological Review*, 49:56-70.

Petersilia, J. (1985). "Probation and Felony Offenders." *Federal Probation*, 49(2):4-9.

The Presentence Report: An Empirical Study of Its Use in the Federal Criminal Process (1970). *Georgetown Law Journal*, 58:12-27.

The Presentence Investigation Report (1978). *Federal Rules of Criminal Procedure*, Rule 32 (Appendix A). Washington, DC: Administrative Office of the United States Courts, Publication No. 105.

Reid, S.T. (1976). *Crime and Criminology*. Hinsdale, IL: Dryden Press.

Ring, C.R. (1988). *Probation Supervision Fees: Shifting Costs to the Offender*. Boston, MA: Massachusetts Legislative Research Bureau.

Rodgers, T.R., T.G. Gitchoff, and I.O. Paur (1979). "The Privately Commissioned Pre-Sentence Report: A Multidisciplinary Approach." *Criminal Justice Journal*, 2:271-279.

Rogers, J.W. (1990). "The Predispositional Report: Maintaining the Promise of Individualized Justice." *Federal Probation*, 54(1):43-57.

Roy, S. (1994). "Victim Offender Reconciliation Program for Juveniles in Elkhard County, Indiana: An Exploratory Study." *Justice Professional*, 8(2):23-35.

Rosecrance, J. (1988). "Maintaining the Myth of Individualized Justice: Probation Presentence Reports." *Justice Quarterly*, 5:235-256.

Rosecrance, J. (1985). "The Probation Officers' Search for Credibility: Ball Park Recommendations." *Crime & Delinquency*, 31:539-554.

Rothman, D.J. (1980). *Conscience and Convenience: The Asylum and Its Alternatives in Progressive America*. Boston, MA: Little, Brown.

Shockley, C. (1988). "The Federal Presentence Investigation Report: Sentence Disclosure Under the Freedom of Information Act." *Administrative Law Review*, 40(1):79-119.

Sieh, E. (1993). "From Augustus to the Progressives: A Study of Probation's Formative Years." *Federal Probation*, 57(3):67-72.

Smith, B.E., R.C. Davis, and S.W. Hillenbrand (1989). *Improving Enforcement of Court-Ordered Restitution*. Chicago, IL: American Bar Association.

Travisono, A.P. (1990). "Crime Victims Seeking Fairness, Not Revenge: Toward Restorative Justice." *Federal Probation*, 53(3):52-57.

Umbreit, M.S. (1994). *Victim Meets Offender: The Impact of Restorative Justice and Mediation*. Monsey, NY: Criminal Justice Press.

U.S. Department of Justice (1994). *Probation and Parole Populations Reach New Highs*. Washington, DC: U.S. Department of Justice (September 11).

Vito, G.F. (1986). "Felony Probation and Recidivism: Replication and Response." *Federal Probation*, 50(4):17-25.

Vito, G.F. (1984). "Development in Shock Probation: A Review of Research Findings and Policy Implications." *Federal Probation*, 48(2):22-27.

Vito, G.F. (1978). "Shock Probation in Ohio: A Comparison of Attributes and Outcomes." Unpublished doctoral dissertation, Ohio State University.

Vito, G.F. and H.E. Allen (1981). "Shock Probation in Ohio: A Comparison of Outcomes." *International Journal of Offender Therapy and Comparative Criminology*, 25:70-75.

Walsh, A. (1985). "The Role of the Probation Officer in the Sentencing Process." *Criminal Justice and Behavior*, 12:289-303.

Watkins, J.C. (1989). "Probation and Parole Malpractice in a Noninstitutional Setting: A Contemporary Analysis." *Federal Probation*, 53(3):29-34.

Welch, S. and C. Spohn (1986). "Evaluating the Impact of Prior Record on Judges' Sentencing Decisions: A Seven-City Comparison." *Justice Quarterly*, 3:389-407.

Wheeler, G.R., T.M. Macan, R.V. Hissong, and M.P. Slusher (1989). "The Effects of Probation Service Fees on Case Management Strategy and Sanctions." *Journal of Criminal Justice*, 17:15-24.

Wheeler, G.R., A.S. Rudolph, and R.V. Hissong (1989). "Do Probationers' Characteristics Affect Fee Assessment, Payment and Outcome?" *Perspectives*, 3(3):12-17.

Zastrow, W.G. (1971). "Disclosure of the Presentence Investigation Report." *Federal Probation*, 35(4):20-23.

# Granting Parole

## 9

The most vivid disagreements over the matter of rights were caused by the ticket-of-leave system. There were only three ways in which the law might release a man from bondage. The first, though the rarest, was an absolute pardon from the governor, which restored him all rights including that of returning to England. The second was a conditional pardon, which gave the transported person citizenship within the colony but no right of return to England. The third was the ticket-of-leave.

—Robert Hughes

Most inmates do not serve their entire prison sentence, but are released from correctional institutions in a variety of ways, among them pardon and conditional release—more commonly called parole. At present, approximately 60 percent of those released from prison are released to parole supervision[1] (see Figure 9.1). Contemporary parole may be defined as the release of an offender from correctional institutions after they have served a portion of their sentence, under conditions that facilitate reintegration to society, while placing the ex-offender under the continued custody of the state and with the possibility of reincarceration in the event of misbehavior.[2]

As was noted in Chapter 6, parole was originally implemented as a method of releasing reformed inmates at the ideal time. The primary focus of parole was the rehabilitation and eventual reintegration of the offender to society, although it also functioned to incapacitate violent and dangerous offenders whose probability of reoffending was believed to be unacceptably high. But it also serves as a decompression period that helps the offender make the adjustment between the institution and the outside world. As such, parole is an integral component of the indeterminate sentence.

The indeterminate sentence serves as both the philosophical and operational foundation of parole. Sanctions are determined by the legislature, in establishing minimum and maximum terms; by the sentencing judge, in determining the specific sentencing range; and by correctional and parole officials, in determining how long individuals will be incarcerated. Under indeterminate sentencing, judges have little impact upon the actual length of time the inmate will serve once the sentence is pronounced.

Figure 9.1
**Adults Exiting from Prison: 1996**

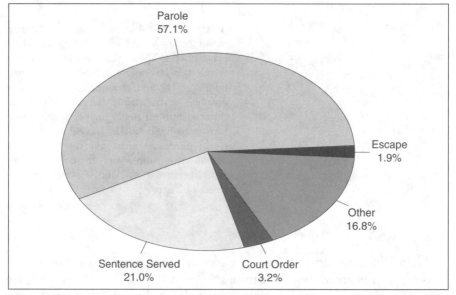

Source: American Correctional Association (1997). *Directory*, p. xxxiv. Lanham, MD: ACA. Excludes 3,777 inmates who died in prison.

## Overview of the Parole Process

The parole process begins in the courtroom when the judge sentences an individual to a prison determinate or indeterminate sentence. The latter includes fixing a term by stating the minimum and maximum length of time the individual is to serve. At the expiration of a certain portion of that sentence, less credit granted for good behavior and performance of duties, an individual becomes eligible for parole. The amount of the sentence that must be served and the amount of credit that can be given for good behavior and performance of duties vary from state to state. In Nebraska, an individual sentenced to a three-to-five-year term can become eligible for parole at the end of two years and five months if they have behaved "properly" within the institution.[3] This does not mean that a release will actually occur; it only means that the individual is eligible to be released. There are a number of states that have mandatory parole release statutes that state that at the expiration of a certain portion of the sentence, inmates must be released onto parole, unless the inmate chooses not to be released. A small number of inmates refuse to be released onto parole because they do not want to be subject to a parole officer's supervision and consequently they choose to serve their entire prison sentence ("max out").

---

**Box 9.1**

### Good Time Credits

Statutes in almost every state allow for the reduction of a prison term based on an offender's behavior in prison ("good time"), or for participation and completion of certain educational or treatment programs ("program time"). Reduction in time is awarded; such awards reduce the date to the parole board or minimum sentence, and maximum time to be served.

Good time credits are earned by a formula established within correctional settings, sometimes set into law but usually decided by institutional administrators in collaboration with the parole board. In California, the award is four months for each eight months served (four for 8, or 1:2). If an offender is serving a 3-year sentence (36 months) and earns maximum good time, that offender will be in prison no more than 24 months.

Some jurisdictions award time for pretrial detention and post-conviction jail time while awaiting transport to prison. There are more than 31,500 jail inmates who have been sentenced to prison but are being held back pending availability of prison space and transport to prison. These inmates generally earn "jail credits" at a 1:1 ratio, and will bring those credits to the parole board, further reducing the maximum time they will serve as prison inmates.

Finally, to encourage participation in institutional work and rehabilitation programs, credits may be awarded for participation in and completion of specific programs: welding, masonry, car repair, GED, drug treatment, etc. The awards across jurisdictions vary, but usually approximate the "good time credit" ratio.

Thus an inmate sentenced to three years in prison but detained four months on a pretrial basis and held four months in jail after sentencing before being transported to prison would bring eight months of jail time credit and would generally receive an additional four months for good time, the equivalent of serving one year against the term of punishment. If the offender participates in and graduates from a drug treatment program within the first 12 months, that offender will usually serve less than 16 months before being released as having served the maximum sentence ("max out"): 36 months.

Regardless of whether these individuals wish to max out or receive parole, institutional officers compile information concerning their personal characteristics and backgrounds. Treatment progress is continually updated and, at some point in time, the staff begins working with offender's friends, family, and employers to develop a release plan.

---

Box 9.2

### Discretionary and Mandatory Release

Discretionary release is parole of an inmate from prison prior to the expiration of maximum sentence, according to the boundaries set by the legislature and sentence. Discretionary release is associated with the indeterminate sentence and implies that the offender is ready for release and continued treatment within the community.

Mandatory release is the *required* release of the offender by the parole board because the statutes mandate release of any inmate who has served the equivalent of the maximum sentence. Mandatory release implies that the parole board refused to release an inmate prior to attainment of maximum sentence imposed by the court. Mandatory release means the time served behind prison walls, when added to time credits for jail time, good time and earned time, total the sentence imposed by the sentencing court. About one in three inmates leave prison under mandatory release.

---

The information, along with the presentence and institutional progress reports, is periodically brought to the attention of the releasing authority, usually a parole board. Some states review inmates' progress on a yearly basis, even though they are not eligible for release. In accordance with the eligibility guidelines and an interview with the offender, the parole board decides whether to release the offender on parole. If the decision is to deny release, a future rehearing date is usually set. If a release is to be effected, the parole board then determines when and where the release is to be made. A contract, usually including very specific conditions of parole, is also established. Once a release has been achieved, inmates (now called parolees) come under the supervision of parole officers.

## Current Operations

Parole is a complex procedure and has many functions and processes that differ from one jurisdiction to another. Traditionally, parole includes five basic functions:

1. Selecting and placing prisoners on parole;

2. Establishing conditions of supervision (frequently case-specific);

3. Aiding, supervising, assisting, and controlling parolees in the community;

4. Returning parolees to prison if the conditions of parole are not met; and

5. Discharging parolees when supervision is no longer necessary or when sentence is completed.

Parole, unlike probation, is an administrative process located within the executive branch of every state, as well as the federal government. This may soon change, however, for 12 states (Arizona, California, Florida, Kansas, Maine, Minnesota, New Mexico, North Carolina, Ohio, Oregon, Virginia, and Washington) and the federal prison system has virtually eliminated the discretionary release power of these parole boards. Two of these states (Maine and Virginia) have abolished both their parole boards and parole supervision. Connecticut abolished parole in 1981 but reinstated it nine years later, after prison costs surged.[4] Thirty other jurisdictions have developed various systemwide parole guidelines that have restricted the discretionary powers of the parole boards.[5] The operation of parole, obviously, is not all uniform.[6]

Box 9.3

### Parole Board Members

Governors appoint parole board members in 41 jurisdictions, usually with the advice and consent of the state legislature. The most frequent term is four years, and most states stagger the terms of office of members, to achieve continuity of parole boards regardless of changes in the governor's mansion or philosophy. Five-, six-, and seven-year terms are found in Alabama, Arizona, Georgia, and so on. Ohio parole board members serve an indefinite term. In Utah, parole board members are appointed by the Board of Corrections and serve six-year terms.

There are no *statutory* qualifications for parole board membership in 29 jurisdictions, but the other 22 jurisdictions have qualifications that speak to length of time and experience in corrections (or such related field as welfare, religion, or law enforcement). Seven jurisdictions set the minimal educational level as at least a bachelor's degree.

State parole systems vary widely in terms of their organizational makeup and administrative process.[7] Most parole boards are independent state agencies that only administer parole. Depending on the state, there are anywhere from 3 to 19 members on a parole board (Camp & Camp, 1997:181). Only 22 states have any statutory requirements for specific qualifications for parole board members, and even those are usually stated in such broad terms as "possessing good character" or "judicious temperament." The governor is directly responsible for parole board appointments in 45 states; Wisconsin and Ohio appoint parole board members from a civil service list. In 1967, the President's Commission on Law Enforcement and Administration of Justice recommended that parole board members be appointed solely on the basis of competence.

## Parole Selection Process

In most jurisdictions, individual cases are assigned to individual members of the parole board. They review each case and make initial recommendations. These recommendations are usually accepted, although occasionally the board as a whole may seek to obtain more details. While there are some jurisdictions that make the final release decision solely on the basis of written reports, most states conduct some type of a formal hearing. The hearing may be with one member of the parole board, the assembled board as a whole (*en banc*), or handled by a hearing examiner with no members of the board present. Occasionally, prison staff are also interviewed. Some states send the board members and/or hearing examiners to the institutions to conduct the hearings, while others bring those to be interviewed to the board/examiners.

Parole selection guidelines differ widely from state to state. The U.S. Supreme Court has consistently held parole to be a privilege and, consequently, held that a full complement of due process rights do not need to be afforded at parole-granting hearings (*Greenholtz v. Inmates of the Nebraska Penal and Correctional Complex*, 99 S. Ct. 2100 (1979). As a result, the states have been given the opportunity to establish whatever inmate privileges they feel are appropriate at parole-granting hearings.

Inmates are permitted the use of counsel in 21 states and are allowed to present witnesses in 19 states. The rationale for the parole decision must be formally articulated in 11 parole jurisdictions. Most states have established regulations as to the amount of time an inmate is required to serve prior to parole eligibility. In 16 states, eligibility is obtained upon completion of the minimum sentence. In 10 states, as well as the federal system, eligibility is achieved upon completion of one-third of the maximum sentence. Other states use the number of prior felony convictions and length of prior sentences to calculate eligibility rules. Even in the states that use the same eligibility guidelines, there is such a wide variation in the length of the minimum and maximum prison terms handed down for the same offense that, in reality, there are literally as many variations in eligibility as there are parole jurisdictions.[8] In addition to time factors, some states restrict the use of parole for those convicted of various serious personal offenses, such as first degree murder, kidnapping, aggravated rape,[9] etc.

If an inmate does not meet parole standards, the sentence is continued, and a date set for the next parole review. If parole is approved, the individual is prepared for release to the parole field service authority. Just how long an inmate must wait to hear the verdict varies greatly. The inmate receives word immediately in many jurisdictions. In others, and in those jurisdictions where no hearings are held, inmates are notified by the prison staff or by mail. Receipt by the inmate of formal written notification varies from immediately in several states to as long as three to four weeks in New Jersey.

---

**Box 9.4**

### Flopped

*Flopped* is inmate argot for being denied early release by the parole board for failing to meet parole board standards or expectations. When flopped, the inmate is usually given a "next review date" by the board, and his or her case will be heard again at that time. Frequently the board suggests treatments, programs or goals the offender is expected to complete before the next review (learning to read and write, AA involvement, Life Skills, etc.)

---

The parole-granting hearing is a very significant event for inmates. Regardless of the outcome, the result will greatly affect their lives. They realize that a single inappropriate word or action could jeopardize their freedom for years to come. Yet despite the significance of the decision, Mitford (1971) found that the California Youth Authority averaged less than 17 minutes per case. The national average is probably between 12 and 15 minutes per case. This means that parole boards are hearing approximately 15 to 20 cases per day.

It is difficult to determine exactly how long a parole board deliberates because they operate in relative secrecy. Hearings are at least partially closed, and decision-making criteria are not really known to outsiders. Indeed, a major problem in the parole process is a reluctance on the part of most parole boards to clearly articulate standards and guidelines for release. As Porter (1958:227) has stated, there is nothing more cruel, inhumane, and frustrating than serving a prison term without knowledge of what will be measured and what rules determine release readiness.[10] This discretionary use (and occasional abuse) of power has come under close scrutiny and criticism by both academicians and politicians, and some have called for abolition of both parole and indeterminate sentence. At press time, New York is considering abolishing parole.

## Shock Parole

On January 1, 1974, a new criminal code became law in the state of Ohio. Part of this new code was designed to provide for the early release of inmates by placing them on parole after six months of incarceration. This type of release is called shock parole and is limited for use with first offenders—the basic penological theory behind its use is that of deterrence. Hopefully, the first offender will be "shocked" by the harsh realities of prison life and inspired to avoid criminal behavior upon release. At the same time, it attempts to perform a rehabilitative function by avoiding the possible negative effects of incarceration by releasing the first offender as soon as possible. These offenders can be released on parole, after serving six months in prison, provided that (Vaughan, 1980:22):

- The offense for which the prisoner was sentenced was an offense other than murder or aggravated murder.

- The prisoner has not previously been convicted of any felony for which, pursuant to sentence, he was confined for 30 days or more in a penal or reformatory institution in this state or in the United States.

- The prisoner is not a dangerous offender (psychopathic) as defined in the Revised Code.

- The prisoner does not need further confinement in a penal or reformatory institution for his correction or rehabilitation.

- The history, character, condition, and attitudes of the prisoner indicate that he is likely to respond affirmatively to early release on parole and is unlikely to commit another offense.

The discretionary authority to release an inmate on shock parole rests entirely with the parole board. Hearings on shock cases are held in the same manner as regular parole hearings.

Early research on the program (Vaughan et al., 1976:271-284) examined the factors related to the parole board's decision to release an

inmate on shock parole. It was discovered that among 1,980 shock candidates from 1974, one was most likely to be granted shock parole if
one: (1) were female, (2) were nonblack, (3) were younger, (4) were better educated, (5) were incarcerated for embezzlement, (6) received a
lower maximum sentence, (7) had less prior criminal involvement as indicated by total time previously served in jails and prisons. However, it
is not possible to reach any definite conclusion about motives of the parole board on the basis of this evidence. It is possible that these factors
are related to a single important variable, such as severity of present offense, and should not be interpreted in an attempt to find the ultimate
causes of shock parole decisionmaking. Many states now utilize shock
incarceration that leads to parole in the community (MacKenzie &
Shaw, 1993).

The research also compared the on-parole performance of shock
and regular parolees in an effort to examine the effectiveness of the program. Vaughan et al. (1976:271-284) conducted a four-month follow-
up investigation on the performance of 56 shock and 60 regular
parolees released in July 1974 and used arrest and parole violation as
indicators of recidivism. They discovered that 14 percent of shock cases
and 22 percent of the regular parolees had been arrested. It was also reported that 2 percent of the shock cases and 6 percent of the regular
parolees violated their conditions of release. Due to the small size of the
sample and the preliminary nature of the study, the authors caution that
"no final conclusions can be drawn at this time concerning the relative
adjustment of shock parolees compared to 'regular' parolees."

Despite such tentative findings and negative public attitudes, an
early release mechanism like shock parole can provide certain benefits if
it is properly administered (Vaughan, 1993). In time of nationwide
overcrowding in correctional institutions, shock parole can send a definite message to the nondangerous offender and help decrease the staggering financial cost of incarceration. It can also cause a number of
problems since it gives the parole board another measure of discretionary power over the inmate. It is clear shock parole is an innovation
that bears further analysis and investigation.

## Factors Influencing Parole Decisions

In theory, parole decisions should be based upon the factors outlined
in state statutes. In practice, however, it appears that parole boards are
influenced by a wide variety of criteria, not all of which are articulated
by law. Furthermore, some states do not have any legal guidelines.

In his study of 325 males and 34 females facing a parole decision in
a Midwest state in 1968, Scott (1974) examined the factors that influenced the parole decision. He determined that the seriousness of the

crime, a high number of prison disciplinary reports, age (older inmates), a low level of education, a marital status of single, and (surprisingly) a good institutional record were factors that lengthened an inmate's sentence. Prior record and race were determined to have no effect upon the parole decision.

However, in his study of 243 inmates in an eastern facility, Carroll (1976) found that race did play a significant role in this determination. A number of factors that were not related to the parole decision for white prisoners were important for blacks. Blacks who participated in treatment programs or were older were more likely to be released. The supposition is that these blacks were perceived as nonmilitant and therefore less likely to cause problems upon release.

For the purposes of this analysis, we will explore the release criteria that influenced parole boards, as suggested by Dawson (1966):

- Factors for granting parole based upon the probability of recidivism.

- Factors for granting parole other than probability of recidivism.

- Factors for denying parole other than probability of recidivism.

## Probability of Recidivism

Perhaps the most basic aspect of the decision-making process is estimating the probability that an individual will violate the law if and when released on parole.[11] This is known as the recidivism factor. Parole boards, as quasipolitical entities, are extremely sensitive to the public criticism that may arise when parolees violate parole, especially if they commit a serious offense. Just how parole boards determine the probability of recidivism is unclear. As early as 1928, Burgess (1928) advocated the need to develop methodologically sound prediction tables for potential parolees that were based upon socioeconomic data. Since this observation, many such scales and tables have been developed (Babst, Inciardi & Jarman, 1970; Bromley & Gathercole, 1969; Gottfredson, Babst & Ballard, 1958; Glaser, 1962; Wilkins & Mac-Naughton-Smith, 1964; Gottfredson & Gottfredson, 1993). For more than 50 years, the value of prediction devices has been recognized as a means of standardizing parole release and more accurately assessing recidivism probability. At least one-half of all parole boards use formal risk assessment (Burke, 1997).[12]

## Factors for Granting Parole Other Than Probability of Recidivism

There are occasions when inmates are granted parole despite the parole board's belief that they possess a relatively high probability of recidivism. In instances when offenders are believed not likely to commit a crime of a serious nature, the parole board may vote to grant parole. This factor is often accompanied by a determination that the inmate will gain little additional benefit from further institutionalization. For example, although an inmate may be an alcoholic with a long record of public intoxication arrests, the parole board may grant a release because it feels that the individual is relatively harmless, and that continued institutionalization will very likely have little further impact upon the alcoholism problem. Compassionate release of inmates dying of cancer and AIDS also fall under this category (Pagliaro & Pagliaro, 1992).[13]

Occasionally, situations arise when inmates have but only a short period of time to serve before the completion of their sentences. When such circumstances arise, parole boards frequently parole these individuals, despite what may be a high perceived probability of recidivism, in order to provide even a brief period of supervisory control and, more importantly, to assist the parolee in the environmental decompression and social reintegration process.

An additional criterion that may swing a parole board, despite an apparent high recidivism probability, is the length of time served. If an inmate has failed to respond to institutional treatment but has served a relatively long sentence, the parole board may grant parole under the conviction that these individuals have paid their dues, and that perhaps they will succeed on parole to avoid being sent back. Occasionally, the maturation process will play an important role. When lengthy sentences are mandated for young persons, the parole board may affect an early release, noting the general process of maturation that will enable these individuals to adopt more acceptable patterns of behavior once released.

## Factors for Denying Parole Other Than Probability of Recidivism

There are circumstances when individuals may not be granted a release despite a relatively low recidivism probability. For example, when inmates have demonstrated occasional outbursts of violent and assaultive behavior, parole boards tend to be somewhat reluctant to grant release. As previously noted, parole boards are extremely sensitive to public criticism, and while the probability of a violent attack may be very small, the seriousness of the incident would likely attract considerable media attention. Consequently, release in such a situation will often be denied. Community attitudes and values often play major roles in overriding the re-cidivism probability factors. For example, murderers have traditionally been good parole risks in terms of likelihood of parole success. However, whether and how quickly they should be paroled is often a function of community attitudes. If a community attitude is unfavorable, parole is likely to be denied, for the release of such an inmate might expose the pa-role board to bitter public criticism, and most parole boards prefer to keep an inmate in prison rather than incur the public's anger.

There are also occasions when parole is used as a tool to support and maintain institutional discipline. Individuals may possess very high poten-tial for success on parole, but continually violate institutional rules and regulations. In these situations, parole will frequently be denied. Occa-sionally, an inmate with a drug abuse problem may be counseled by the parole board to enroll in an existing drug-dependency program, sending a clear message to the inmate population that such rehabilitation programs are appropriate and functional for release. In this way, parole can be viewed as an incentive for good behavior and a sanction against inappro-priate conduct. There are even situations when parole may be denied so as to benefit the inmate. Circumstances occasionally arise when inmates are making rapid progress in academic pursuits, or may be receiving and responding to necessary medical and/or psychological treatment. The pa-role board may temporarily postpone such a case for a few months to give these individuals the opportunity to complete their high school work, for example, or recover from medical treatment they are undergoing.

---

Box 9.5

### Parole Board Functions

The most visible function of a parole board is the discre-tionary release of an inmate from confinement prior to the expi-ration of sentence, on condition of good behavior in the com-munity. This is commonly known as the parole release decision. But parole boards have extensive authority to undertake a vari-ety of other functions seldom acknowledged in the justice area.

**Setting Policy.** The parole board enunciates and refines broad policy governing specific areas of parole, such as direc-tives to community supervision officers on offenders whose drug tests show illicit drug use. Some policies require the offi-cer to hold a revocation hearing under *Morrissey v. Brewer;* other jurisdictions may only suggest that officers tighten up the conditions of parole ('motivational' jail time, house arrest, or NA). When parole boards establish a "zero tolerance" pol-icy, a large portion of drug-abusing parolees may be returned to prison.

Box 9.5—*continued*

**Modification of Presumed Release Date.** If an offender is given a presumed release date, it usually is based on conformity to institutional rules. When inmates persistently violate those, a decision may be made to delay release ("extend the time") based on institutional behavior. In effect, the parole board reinforces control of prison inmates and encourages participation in institutional programs.

**Commutation of Sentence.** Inmates serving life sentences or double-life or life-plus-a-day or minimum sentences of several hundred years have few hopes of ever leaving the facility alive. It is possible, however, to petition the executive branch for commutation, a reduction in sentence length. A parole board, whose recommendation for commutation is seriously considered by the Governor, usually hears the initial plea. "Lifers" who receive commutations usually leave the penal institution shortly thereafter.

**Revocation from Parole.** If a supervising officer requests a hearing for revocation of parole under Morrissey and the hearing officer finds reasonable cause, the case will be heard by the parole board (or its authorized designee), and the offender's grant of parole maybe revoked. The offender is then returned to prison to serve additional time.

**Pardon.** Only the executive branch may grant a pardon, absolving the offender in part or full from the legal consequences of the crime and conviction. Governors usually receive such petitions after they have been considered by the parole board, generally authorized to advise the Governor on these matters.

**Reprieve.** A reprieve is a stay in imposition of sentence, typically associated with death row inmates nearing their execution date. Parole boards, sometimes in conjunction with the Governor's Cabinet, may recommend reprieve to a Governor.

**Incapacitation.** Some offenders have demonstrated a pattern of violent and dangerous criminal behavior that continues unabated in prison. By denying parole and thus forcing such inmates to serve longer prison sentences, parole boards protect the public through disabling future violent crime. This function is seldom recognized.

Finally, there are situations when the parole board may feel that individuals are good risks but ineligible for release because they have not served the minimum terms as fixed by the sentencing judge. Some have expressed a concern over the fact that the courts occasionally err in handing down sanctions more severe than are necessary. Correctional officials, after more careful observation and evaluation than the courts could originally consider, may clearly document greater progress than the court expected. Nevertheless, as previously noted, state parole statutes may mandate a minimum time to be served (calculated as a percentage of the minimum or maximum sentence) that even the parole board cannot ignore. Such inmates may be released, however, under work furlough programs.

Some state jurisdictions (Wisconsin and Michigan, for example) adopted an early-decision model called the Mutual Agreement Program (MAP). In a MAP contract system, shortly after the offender enters the institution, correctional officials, parole officials, and individual offenders meet to develop a program plan that clearly details the areas in which the offender has to improve, and the extent of the improvement needed, in order to be granted parole and, once paroled, to be release from supervision. The MAP plan also involves the establishment of an exact date of release if the contract is met. This serves to eliminate the uncertainty factor so prominent in traditional parole and, furthermore, provides offenders with the opportunity to participate in the development of treatment plan tailored to their own specific needs. No state is now known to use the MAP process.

## Parole Board Release Decisions

All persons who are eligible for parole are not automatically granted a release. Occasionally, parole boards will not release individuals who could be safely released. This is partially, a desire by parole boards to minimize the number of persons who are classified as good risks and released, but whom the board feel are in reality bad risks and expected to fail on parole. Failed parole is a problem the boards seek to minimize (Wiggins, 1984).

At present, however, criminologists have not been able to predict well. In fact, prediction accuracy has a rather dismal track record (Smykla, 1984; Monahan, 1981; Gottfredson & Gottfredson, 1994), although Gendreau (1996) has pointed the way to effective prediction studies in the future. As a result, there is now a general tendency to overpredict dangerousness, and this results in more persons being classified as bad risks,[14] fewer persons being granted parole, and an increase in prison populations (Monahan, 1981). Although such tendencies have come under intense criticism, overprediction of dangerousness continues (Morris, 1974; Smykla, 1984). This is probably due to the perception that overprediction is viewed as having smaller short-term costs. In the short-run, it may be cheaper to incarcerate larger numbers of offenders than to permit a few dangerous persons to roam the streets and commit crimes. Such an approach is quite costly in the long-run, however, as more and more persons are housed and cared for within the prison system. Furthermore, there are indications that after the extended prison sentences are served, the former inmates will commit more serious crimes more frequently than they would have prior to their incarceration.

While the courts have ruled that parole cannot be denied on the basis of race, religion, or national origin,[15] they have really not become involved in parole board policies and practices. This is due in large part to the fact that the Supreme Court has defined parole as a privilege rather than a right (*Greenholz*, 1979). Consequently, there is no constitutional mandate that there even be any formal parole release guidelines, no right to obtain access to institutional files, and no right to counsel at the hearing. Indeed, there is no constitutional requirement that there even be a formal hearing. The state is under no constitutional obligation to articulate the reason for denial of parole and there is no right of appeal, except as given by an individual state.

Most states have adopted laws and/or administrative policies that outline parole procedures. Some allow inmates access to their files and permit the presence of legal counsel. As of 1977, the U.S. Parole Commission[16] and 23 states offered inmates the opportunity to internally appeal parole release hearing decisions (O'Leary & Hanrahan, 1977:42-47). Up to this point, however, the courts have continued to refuse to become involved in any type of review of a negative parole board decision. Many feel that the time will soon come when the courts will mandate basic rules of procedures for parole hearings, and perhaps even become actively involved in actual appellate reviews. If the latter were to occur, the parole decision, at this point an administrative matter, could become a judicial matter. In other words, indeterminate sentences, which are now a joint venture between the judiciary and the executive branch, could become the sole possession of the judiciary or the legislative branch.

Figure 9.2
**Parolees in America 1987-1997 (in thousands)**

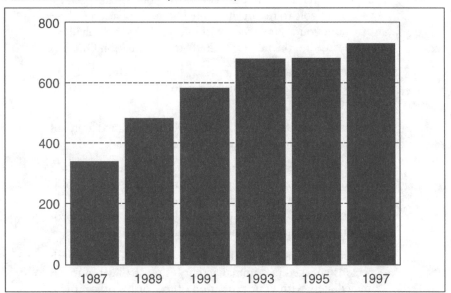

Source: J. Brown and A. Beck (1997). *Nation's Probation and Parole Population Reached Almost 3.9 Million Last Year*, p. 7. Washington, DC: U.S. Bureau of Justice Statistics. Data for 1997 are estimated.

## Conditions of Parole

Parole is in essence a contract between the state and the offender. If the offender is able to abide by the terms of the contract, freedom is maintained. If a violation of these conditions occurs, or if a parolee is charged with a new crime, the parole board may revoke parole and return the offender to prison. The offender must abide by the contract, and stay under parole supervision for the period of time outlined by the parole board. While every state has its own policies and procedures, parole usually lasts more than two but less than seven years. Some states in fact permit discharge from parole after a very short time, as long as the offender has diligently adhered to the pre-release contract. While the exact content of the contracts varies from state to state and from individual to individual, the following federal guidelines[17] cover the majority of the conditions that are usually adopted:

- You shall go directly to the district showing on this CERTIFICATE OF PAROLE (unless released to the custody of other authorities). Within three days after your arrival you shall report to your parole advisor if you have one, and to the United States Probation Officer whose name appears on this certificate. If in an emergency you are unable to get in touch with your parole advisor, or your probation officer or his office, you shall communicate with the [United States Parole Commission, 550 Friendship Blvd., Suite 420, Chevy Chase, MD 20815-7286].

- If you are released to the custody of other authorities, and after your release from physical custody of such authorities, you are unable to report the United States Probation Officer to whom you are assigned within three days, you shall report instead to the nearest United States Probation Officer.

- You shall not leave the limits of this CERTIFICATE OF PAROLE without written permission from the probation officer.

- You shall notify your probation officer immediately of any change in your place of residence.

- You shall make a complete and truthful written report (on a form provided for that purpose) to your probation officer between the first and third day of each month, and on the final day of parole. You shall also report to your probation officer at other times as he directs.

- You shall not violate any law. Nor shall you associate with persons engaged in criminal activity. You shall get in touch immediately with your probation officer or his office if you are arrested or questioned by a law enforcement officer.

- You shall not enter into any agreement to act as an "informer" or special agent for any law-enforcement agency.

- You shall work regularly, unless excused by your probation officer, and support your legal dependents, if any, to the best of your ability. You shall report immediately to your probation officer any change in employment.

- You shall not drink alcoholic beverages to excess. You shall not purchase, possess, use, or administer marijuana or narcotics or other habit forming or dangerous drugs, unless prescribed or advised by a physician. You shall not frequent places where such drugs are illegally sold, dispensed, used, or given away.

- You shall not associate with persons who have a criminal record unless you have permission of your probation officer.

- You shall not have firearms (or other dangerous weapons) in your possession without the written permission of your probation officer, following prior approval of the United States Board of Parole.

- You shall, if ordered by the Board pursuant to Section 4203, Title 18, U.S.C., as amended October 1970, reside in and/or participate in a treatment program of a Community Treatment Center operated by the Bureau of Prisons, for a period not to exceed 120 days.

The U.S. Parole Commission's authority and reach is rapidly declining.[18] See Figure 9.3.

## Parole Revocation

In 1972, the U.S. Supreme Court established procedures for parole revocation with the case of *Morrissey v. Brewer*, 408 U.S. 471 (1972). In this case, the Supreme Court said that once parole is granted, it is no longer just a privilege but a right. Consequently, the Court ruled that parolees should be granted certain due process rights in any parole revocation proceeding. While the Court did not grant a full array of due process rights in *Morrissey*, it did advance the mandate of fundamental fairness. The Court required the following minimum due process rights in the event of a parole revocation proceeding.

- Parolee given advanced written notification of the inquiry, its purpose, and alleged violation.

- A disclosure to the parolee of the evidence against him or her.

Figure 9.3
**Oregon Parole Board Conditions of Parole**

---

GENERAL/SPECIAL PAROLE AND POST-PRISON SUPERVISION CONDITIONS

Parole/Post-Prison Supervision is subject to all listed General Conditions and the designated Special Conditions. Prior to release the Board may modify the conditions at any time. After parole/post-prison supervision has commenced, conditions may be added upon your signed consent or after opportunity to be heard, orally or in writing.

Parole may be revoked for violation of any of these conditions and/or you may be returned when parole is not in your best interest or the best interest of society.

The Board may, at its discretion, sanction violations of Post-Prison Supervision Conditions; sanctions may include returning you to the Department of Corrections custody.

As used in this exhibit, the following words have the following meanings: "Offender" means persons released to parole or post-prison supervision. "Parole Officer" shall also mean the supervisory authority under the post-prison supervision system.

GENERAL CONDITIONS

1. Pay supervision fees, fines, restitution, or other fees ordered by the Board.

2. Not use or possess controlled substances except pursuant to a medical prescription.

3. Submit to testing of breath or urine for controlled substance or alcohol use if the offender has a history of substance abuse or if there is a reasonable suspicion that the offender has illegally used controlled substances.

4. Participate in a substance abuse evaluation as directed by the supervising officer and follow the recommendations of the evaluator if there are reasonable grounds to believe there is a history of substance abuse.

5. Remain in the State of Oregon until written permission to leave is granted by the Department of Corrections or a county community corrections agency.

6. If physically able, find and maintain gainful full-time employment, approved schooling, or a full-time combination of both. [Any waiver of this requirement must be based on a finding by the court stating the reasons for the waiver.]

7. Change neither employment nor residence without prior permission from the Department of Corrections or a county community corrections agency.

8. Permit the supervising officer to visit the offender or the offender's residence or work site, and report as required and abide by the direction of the supervising officer.

9. Consent to the search of person, vehicle, or premises upon the (required) *request* of a representative of the supervising officer if the supervising officer has reasonable grounds to believe that evidence of a violation will be found, and submit to fingerprinting or photographing, or both, when requested by the Department of Corrections or a county community corrections agency for supervision purposes.

Figure 9.3—*continued*

---

10. Obey all laws, municipal, county, state, and federal.

11. Promptly and truthfully answer all reasonable inquiries by the Department of Corrections or a county community corrections agency.

12. Not possess weapons, firearms, or dangerous animals.

### SPECIAL CONDITIONS

1. Offender shall be evaluated by a mental health evaluator and follow all treatment recommendations.

2. Offender shall follow a psychiatric or psychotropic medication monitoring program with a physician per the physician's instructions.

3. Offender shall have no contact with minor females and shall not frequent any place where minors are likely to congregate (e.g., playgrounds, school grounds, arcades) without prior written approval from their supervising officer.

4. Offender shall have no contact with minor males and shall not frequent any place where minors are likely to congregate (e.g., playgrounds, school grounds, arcades) without prior written approval from their supervising officer.

5. Offender shall submit to random polygraph tests as part of a sex offender surveillance program. Failure to submit to the tests may result in return to Department of Corrections custody. Specific responses to the tests shall not be the basis for return to Department of Corrections custody.

6. Offender shall enter and complete or be successfully discharged from a recognized and approved sex offender treatment program which may include polygraph and/or plethysmograph testing and a prohibition on possession of printed, photographed, or recorded materials that the offender may use for the purpose of deviant sexual arousal.

7. Offender shall pay court-ordered restitution to the clerk of the court of the county of sentencing (ORS 137.106, OAR 255-65-005).

8. When criteria applies, the Department of Corrections may notify the community of the sex offender's status pursuant to ORS 181.507-509, OAR 291-28-010 to 291-28-030.

9. Offender shall not use intoxicating beverages.

10. Other: Special conditions may be imposed that are not listed above when the Board of Parole and Post-Prison Supervision determines that such conditions are necessary.

11. Offender shall have no contact with those listed below:

---

The authors are indebted to Lawrence Travis for providing this document.

- The opportunity to be heard in person and present witnesses and documentary evidence.

- The right to confront and cross-examine adverse witnesses.

- A neutral and detached hearing body.

- A written statement by the hearing body as to the evidence relied upon and reasons for revoking parole.

The *Morrissey* case also established a dual state procedure, including a preliminary inquiry at the time of the alleged parole violations as well as a formal revocation hearing. Left unanswered, however, was the right to counsel, and whether or not the Exclusionary Rule should apply to revocation cases. One year later, in the case *Gagnon v. Scarpelli*, 411 U.S. 778 (1971), the Court held that parolees do have a limited right to counsel in revocation proceedings and that the hearing body must determine, on a case-by-case basis, whether counsel should be afforded. While it need not be granted in all cases, ". . . Counsel should be provided where, after being informed of his right, the . . . parolee requests counsel, based on a timely and colorable claim that he had not committed the alleged violation or, if the violation is a matter of public record or uncontested, there are substantial reasons in justification or mitigation that make revocation inappropriate."

The Exclusionary Rule issue remains unanswered. While illegally seized evidence cannot be used in a criminal trial, many states do permit such evidence to be used in parole revocation cases, where the standard is "probable cause." To date, the courts have generally upheld this practice.[19]

## Problems with Parole Board Discretionary Power

Beginning in the 1970s, dramatic shifts began in the field of corrections. Dissatisfied with high recidivism rates, many states opted to amend the traditional indeterminate sentencing model and adopt some of the aspects of a determinate or fixed sentencing model (see Table 9.1). The use of the indeterminate sentence in the United States represented a grand experiment in controlling if not eliminating criminal behavior. Indeterminate sentencing, in which the judge sets limits within legislatively determined minimum and maximum sentences (e.g., one to seven years for burglary), would focus upon the individual criminal and his or her needs, rather than establishing a fixed penalty for certain types of crime. It sought to maximize the possibility of criminal rehabilitation through the use of various educational, vocational, and psychological treatment programs in the institution, and the use of parole board that would release the inmate on parole at the optimum moment when change had occurred.

Through this "medical model of corrections," it was argued that such parole board decisionmaking would offer several benefits:

- It would provide an incentive for rehabilitation by linking it to release from prison.

- This incentive would also apply as a mechanism to control the prison population, ensuring inmate discipline and safety.

- Another latent function of parole would be to provide a mechanism to control the size of the prison population.

- Similarly, the parole board would share the responsibility for societal protection with the judiciary through its control over prison release procedures. The board could also serve as a check and balance to judicial discretion by reducing sentencing disparities (such that inmates who committed the same crime would serve approximately the same amount of actual time in prison).

However, a number of factors combined to question the efficacy and fairness of medical model. Penologists, such as Martinson (1974) and MacNamara (1977), reviewing the outcome of research reports on correctional rehabilitation programs, concluded that the medical model failed to cure criminals, reduce recidivism, or protect the public.[20] Others (Morris, 1974) argued that the medical model harmed the inmates because the program participation was tied to, and dependent upon such participation. From the inmates' point of view, the decisions of the board were arbitrary, capricious, prejudicial, unpredictable, and not subject to external review by any other governmental body (Irwin, 1977). In fact, a number of studies (see Goodstein, 1980) have indicated that inmate frustration over failure to obtain release on parole is a factor that contributes to prison violence (Hassine, 1996).

## Parole Board Decision-Making Guidelines: The U.S. Parole Commission

Concerns over some of these issues led a number of jurisdictions, including the Federal Parole System, to adopt parole release guidelines. The U.S. Parole Commission developed its system of parole decision-making guidelines in 1974. The major complaint against parole board decisionmaking has been, and remains, the great amount of discretionary power. The parole decision-making guidelines propose to structure this discretionary power to promote equity and fairness,[21] and also to reduce sentencing disparity. The task was to make the decisions of the parole board less arbitrary and more explicit.

Table 9.1
**Sentencing Models by State**

| State | Type of Sentencing | Mandatory Sentencing | Mandatory Offenses |
|---|---|---|---|
| Alabama | Determinate | Yes | Repeat felony |
| Alaska | Determinate, presumptive | Yes | Murder, kidnapping, firearms, repeat felony |
| Arizona | Determinate, presumptive | Yes | Firearms, prior felony convictions |
| Arkansas | Determinate | Yes | Robbery, deadly weapons |
| California | Determinate, presumptive | No | |
| Colorado | Determinate, presumptive | No | |
| Connecticut | Determinate | Yes | Sex assault with firearm, burglary, repeat felony, assault on elderly |
| Delaware | Determinate | Yes | Murder, kidnapping, prison assault, robbery, narcotics, deadly weapons, habitual criminal, obscenity, others |
| Florida | Indeterminate | Yes | Drugs |
| Georgia | Determinate | Yes | Armed robbery, burglary, drugs |
| Hawaii | Indeterminate | No | |
| Idaho | Determinate | Yes | Firearms, repeat extortion, kidnap or rape with bodily injury |
| Illinois | Determinate | Yes | Major offenses, specified felonies and offenses, repeaters, weapons |
| Indiana | Determinate, presumptive | Yes | Repeat felony, violent crime, deadly weapons |
| Iowa | Indeterminate | Yes | Forcible felonies, firearms, habitual offenders, drugs |
| Kansas | Indeterminate | Yes | Sex offense, firearms |
| Kentucky | Indeterminate | No | |
| Louisiana | Indeterminate | Yes | Drugs, violent crime |
| Maine | Determinate | No | |
| Maryland | Determinate, guidelines | Yes | Repeat violent offenders, handgun |
| Massachusetts | Indeterminate | Yes | Firearms, auto theft, drug trafficking |
| Michigan | Indeterminate | Yes | Murder, armed robbery, treason, firearms |
| Minnesota | Guidelines | No | |
| Mississippi | Determinate | Yes | Armed robbery, repeat felony |
| Missouri | Determinate | Yes | Dangerous weapons, repeat felony |
| Montana | Indeterminate | Yes | Firearms |

Table 9.1—*continued*

| State | Type of Sentencing | Mandatory Sentencing | Mandatory Offenses |
|---|---|---|---|
| Nebraska | Indeterminate | No | |
| Nevada | Determinate | Yes | 2nd degree murder, 1st degree kidnapping, sexual assault, firearms, repeat felony |
| New Hampshire | Indeterminate | Yes | Firearms |
| New Jersey | Determinate, presumptive | Yes | Sexual assault, firearms |
| New Mexico | Determinate, presumptive | Yes | Firearms |
| New York | Indeterminate | Yes | Specified violent and nonviolent felonies |
| North Carolina | Determinate, presumptive | Yes | Armed robbery, 1st degree burglary, repeat felony with firearm |
| North Dakota | Determinate | Yes | Firearms |
| Ohio | Indeterminate | Yes | Rape, drug trafficking |
| Oklahoma | Determinate | No | Repeat felony |
| Oregon | Indeterminate, guidelines | Yes | Drugs |
| Pennsylvania* | Indeterminate, guidelines | Yes | Selected felonies with firearms, within 7 years of prior convictions, in or near public transportation |
| Rhode Island | Indeterminate | No | |
| South Carolina | Determinate | Yes | Armed robbery, drugs, bomb threat |
| South Dakota | Indeterminate | No | |
| Tennessee | Determinate, indeterminate | Yes | Specified felonies, firearms, repeat felony |
| Texas | Determinate | Yes | Repeat felony, violent offenses |
| Utah | Indeterminate | No | |
| Vermont | Indeterminate | Yes | Drugs, violent crime |
| Virginia | Determinate | No | |
| Washington | Indeterminate | Yes | Firearms, rape, repeat felony |
| West Virginia | Indeterminate | Yes | Firearms in felony |
| Wisconsin | Indeterminate | No | |
| Wyoming | Indeterminate | No | |

*Pennsylvania updated as of December 1982.

Sources: Richard S. Morelli, Craig Edelman, and Roy Willoughby (September, 1981). "A Survey of Mandatory Sentencing in the U.S." Pennsylvania Commission on Crime and Delinquency; Criminal Courts Technical Assistance Project (January, 1982). "Judicial and Executive Discretion in the Sentencing Process: Analysis of Felony State Code Provisions." Washington, DC: American University; Michael Kanvensohn (December, 1979). "A National Survey of Parole-Related Legislation." San Francisco, CA: Uniform Parole Reports.

---

Box 9.6

### Presumptive Sentencing

One alternative to limiting sentencing disparity is the presumptive sentencing system, a variation of the determinate sentence. In presumptive sentencing, the state legislature sets minimum, average, and maximum terms, allowing the judge to select a term based on the characteristics of the offender and any aggravating or mitigating circumstances proven in court. The sentence imposed will be the time served, less any credits against that sentence that the offender earns (jail time, good time, and program time). California has a presumptive sentencing structure that provides three options to the sentencing judge, as seen here for the crime of burglary.

1. aggravating circumstances: 7 years
2. presumptive (average) sentence: 5 years
3. mitigating circumstances: 3 years

Ordinarily, the judge would decide if the offender should be placed on probation or imprisoned (the "in-out" decision). Assuming imprisonment to be the answer, the judge would impose the average or presumed term of 5 years, unless mitigating circumstances were present at the time of the offense (such as the offender being under the influence of a controlled substance at the time of the offense, or had a weak personality and was easily led into committing crime for peer approval, etc.). If mitigating circumstances were proven, the judge would impose the least sentence (3 years). On the other hand, if aggravating circumstances were proven in court, the judge *must* impose the highest sentence (7 years). Examples of aggravating circumstances are gross bodily harm to the victim, prior incarceration in prison, victim extremely vulnerable (blind, frail, paraplegic, over 60 years of age, and so on).

---

A central portion of these guidelines is based upon the salient factor scoring scale (Hoffman & Adelberg, 1980; Hoffman, 1994). Figure 9.4 is a copy of the scale[22] recently used by the U.S. Board of Parole Examiners.

The scale consists of six items. With each case, the examiner assigns a score to each item. The sum of the six items ranges from 0 to 10; the higher the score, the better the prospects for success on parole. This predictive score is then collapsed into eight categories. The task completed, the examiner then consults the guidelines as detailed in Figure 9.5, which indicates the amount of prison time an offender should serve with a certain record and who has been convicted of an offense of a given severity. In sum, the examiner uses the information from Figure 9.5 to rank severity of the present offense and the parole prognosis (salient factor score) of the individual offender. Note that, for offenders who commit serious crimes, no limits are established for time to be served. In this fashion, the guidelines system attempts to structure the discretionary power of the parole board while at the same time maintaining equity and fairness (Hoffman, 1983).

Figure 9.4
**Salient Factor Score (SFS/81)**

A.  PRIOR CONVICTIONS/ADJUDICATIONS (ADULT OR JUVENILE)
    None .......................... = 3
    One ........................... = 2
    Two or three ............. = 1
    Four or more ........... = 0

B.  PRIOR COMMITMENTS OF MORE THAN 30 DAYS
    (ADULT OR JUVENILE)
    None ......................... = 2
    One or two ............... = 1
    Three or more .......... = 0

C.  AGE AT CURRENT OFFENSE/PRIOR COMMITMENTS
    Age at commencement of the current offense:
    26 years of age or more .............. = 2*
    20-25 years of age ...................... = 1*
    19 years of age or less ................ = 0
    *EXCEPTION: If five or more prior commitments of more than thirty days (adult or juvenile), place an x here _____ and score this item ............................................................................. = 0

D.  RECENT COMMITMENT-FREE PERIOD (THREE YEARS)
    No prior commitment of more than thirty days (adult or juvenile), or released to the community from last such commitment at least three years prior to the commencement of the current offense ..................................................................................... = 1
    Otherwise ............................................................................. = 0

E.  PROBATION/PAROLE/CONFINEMENT/ESCAPE STATUS VIOLATOR THIS TIME
    Neither on probation, parole, confinement, or escape status at the time of the current offense; nor committed as a probation, parole, confinement, or escape status violator at this time ........ = 1
    Otherwise ............................................................................. = 0

F.  HEROIN/OPIATE DEPENDENCE
    No history of heroin or opiate dependence ........ = 1
    Otherwise ........................................................... = 0

TOTAL SCORE ...................................................................................

Figure 9.5
**Parole Jurisdictions Using Electronic Monitoring Devices: 1988-1998**

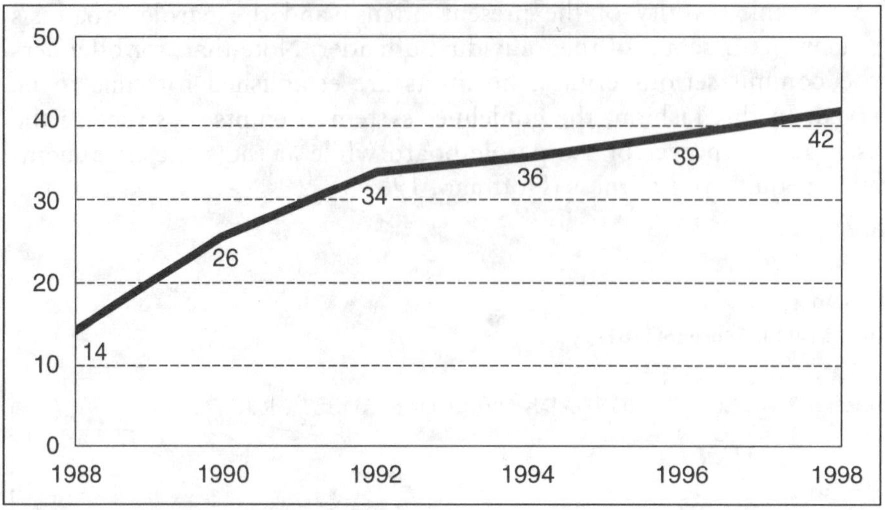

Source: C. Camp and G. Camp (1997). *The Corrections Yearbook,* p. 164. South Salem, NY: Criminal Justice Institute. Data for 1998 are estimated.

However, board examiners are permitted to deviate from the guidelines. As Hoffman and Adelberg (1980:45) point out, the use of a salient factor score with a guidelines system does not mean the elimination of clinical judgment. The examiners can shorten or lengthen the amount of time specified by the guidelines when, in their judgment, the case at hand appears to merit such consideration. However, when such a step is taken, the examiner is required to state the specific factors present that led to such a judgment. Only 12 percent of the cases were outside the guidelines in 1992 (Hoffman, 1994). Again, the emphasis is upon the articulation of those factors that influence parole board decisionmaking.

However, research indicates that guidelines appear to have some effect in reducing sentencing disparity among inmates. Gottfredson (1979) collected data on sentence length and time served (presumptive release date) for 4,471 adult cases appearing before the Parole Commission between October 1977 and May 1978. He then grouped the offenders with similar offense severity rating and similar prior records as ranked by the Commission and the salient factor score categories. Statistical analysis revealed that for every category of equally situated offenders, the variations in decisions made by the Commission are less disparate than the judicial decisions. The use of parole board decisionmaking guidelines attempts to deal with the traditional problems of the parole process. They do not represent a panacea, but they are an alternative to either the typical method, outright abolition, or the use of determinate sentencing. There is evidence of more widespread adoption and use of formal risk assessment, as well as toward structural revocation decisionmaking (Runda et al., 1994).

---

Box 9.7

### Sentencing Guidelines

In an attempt to limit if not remove sentencing disparity, many jurisdictions have implemented a set of guidelines to help judges decide what sentence ought to be imposed, given the seriousness of the offense and the characteristics of the offender. Guidelines are based on past experience by a large number of sentencing judges, and represent average sentences imposed by sentencing peers in similar cases. Obviously, inasmuch as the determinations are guidelines, judges are *not* required to impose the recommended sentence (but at least must state in writing why they are deviating from the recommended range).

One such guideline to determine sentence length is from Minnesota. Across the top of the guideline grid is a score for the characteristics the offender brings to the sentencing hearing: number of prior juvenile adjudications, adult convictions for misdemeanors and felonies, number of time the offender has been previously incarcerated, employment status and educational attainment, and so on. Obviously, the higher the score, the worse the criminal history and longer the recommended sentence length.

The severity of the offense is found on the left side of the grid, ranked from the least severe to highest offense. After the judge calculates the criminal history score, she or he locates the offense category and reads across to see what other judges have done in terms of sentence length. The sentencing judge then imposes a sanction within the suggested range. Obviously, such a guidelines must be revalidated frequently.

---

## Abolition of Parole?

While some criminologists and practitioners have been content to alter various aspects and procedures of the parole process, others have called for its complete abolition. The states of Maine and Virginia, as previously discussed, have, for all intents and purposes, abolished parole; the state of New York may be next.

Whatever the change, one should be aware of the argument by Sigler (1978:335): "I say that as long as we use imprisonment in this county, we will have to have someone, somewhere, with the authority to release people from imprisonment. Call it parole, call it what you will. It's one of those jobs that has to be done." As seen in Table 9.2, the attack on parole release has been ongoing for more than 20 years.

Table 9.2
**Significant Events in the Abolition of Parole**

| | |
|---|---|
| 1976 | Maine abolishes parole. |
| 1978 | California abolishes indeterminate sentencing and discretionary parole release. |
| 1980 | Minnesota abolishes parole. |
| 1983 | Florida abolishes parole. |
| 1984 | Washington abolishes parole. |
| 1986 | Congress abolishes parole at the Federal level. |
| 1990 | Delaware abolishes parole. |
| 1993 | Kansas abolishes parole. |
| 1994 | Arizona and North Carolina abolish parole. |
| 1995 | Virginia abolishes parole. |
| 1996 | Ohio abolishes parole. |

Source: Compiled by authors.

One example of hysteria in sentencing can be seen in the development of "three strikes" sentencing statutes in several states. They have the potential to reduce violent crime by repeat offenders by selective incapacitation of up to 25 years, but at multiple-billion dollar costs for prison construction, operations, and maintenance. Further, locking up second and third time offenders for long periods of time will not (1) address the successive waves of juveniles and young offenders who will take the place of those incarcerated for 25 years, nor (2) ameliorate the etiological causes of crime (poverty, racism, drug abuse, blocked opportunities, etc.), or (3) be accurate enough to isolate the truly dangerous from the truly stupid. "Three-strikes" sentencing assumes offenders operate as rational persons in a middle-class background and are driven by free-will to commit crimes. Most criminals are neither so simplistic nor pure. Parole boards are a better option and their return is likely to emerge in the future of corrections. At least 22 states and the federal government have enacted these laws since 1993 (Campaign for An Effective Crime Policy, 1996). California has used these statutes more extensively than other states, and at least 27,000 offenders have been sentenced to at least twice to three times the sentence they would have received, absent the se "enhancement" laws. One untoward outcome is that geriatric inmates (those over age 50) will become an increasing proportion of California's prison population, leading one wag to refer to the California prison system as the largest "old-age home" in the nation!

# Summary

There is considerable contemporary discussion relative to the value of parole. Indeed, there are those who oppose the indeterminate sentencing mode in general and wish to see parole abolished in particular. Concerns over these issues, and the perceived ineffectiveness of the present parole system, have led jurisdictions to either abolish parole altogether or dramatically adjust the entire parole process. Of all community programs, parole faces perhaps the greatest challenge. There are new indications, however, that pragmatism in the form of simple economics may renew an interest in parole. As our jail and prison populations swell above capacity, criminal justice planners and politicians will be forced to either continue to construct new facilities or develop alternative models. Parole emerges as a relatively inexpensive alternative model and, perhaps more importantly, one that is already in place. There is a need, though, to improve the parole process and supervision so as to overcome the deficiencies detailed above. Intermediate sanctions undoubtedly will increase in the parole area.

Even if this apparent renewed interest in parole phases out, and parole as we know it is abolished in a stampede toward the determinate sentencing model, the need to assist inmates in their transition from the institution to the free community will remain. The problems facing released inmates are usually temporal or material: obtaining employment, suitable housing, financial aid, alcohol and drug abuse, etc. Parole supervision will require assistance.

As parole moves toward structuring release and revocation decisions to remove unwanted discrepancies, and jurisdictions consider abolition of parole as a release mechanism (whether assisted by guidelines or from clinical experience), two facts remain. First, parole has always served as a "release valve" or mechanism to prevent (or lower) prison overcrowding, a fact sadly ignored by policymakers and politicians. Second, discretionary parole has within it the authority to retain dangerous persons whose behavior would lead reasonable persons, citizens, and experienced correctional practitioners alike, to protect society by not paroling dangerous offenders. If the nation is to avoid the even more extreme of hiking sentences by multiples of current statutory terms, parole authorities should have the ability to protect the public by selective incapacitation of those who have several convictions for crimes against the person (murder, rape, aggravated assault, robbery, etc.). Of course it is important to remember that parole board members are human, and as such they cannot be expected to be infallible. Some inmates invariably are released who should not be, and others are kept far longer than necessary.

## Review Questions

1.  Debate the following resolution: Discretionary parole from prison should be abolished.

2.  What functions do parole boards serve?

3.  If parole boards could not release offenders into the community, would they be abolished? Why or why not?

4.  How do sentencing guidelines work? Parole guidelines?

5.  How can parole boards use and implement intermediate sanctions?

6.  How can three strike laws affect corrections?

## Key Terms

flopped
good-time credits
jail credits
mandatory release
Mutual Agreement Programming
pardon
parole board

parole conditions
parole guidelines
program credits
revocation
sentencing guidelines
shock incarceration
shock parole

## Recommended Readings

Donziger, Steven, ed. (1996). *The Real War on Crime.* New York, NY: HarperCollins.

Hassine, V. (1996). *Life Without Parole.* Los Angeles, CA: Roxbury.

Klofas, J. and S. Stojkovic, eds. (1997). *Crime and Justice in the Year 2010.* Belmont, CA: Wadsworth.

## Notes

[1]    American Correctional Association (1997). *Directory.* Laurel, MD: ACA:xxxiv.

[2]    This is an extrapolation of the definition developed in the Attorney General's Survey of Release Procedures. Washington, DC: U.S. Government Printing Office, 1939, p. 4.

3    The offender's mandatory release date in Nebraska is calculated as follows:

For all odd-numbered maximum terms MR=(MAX-1)/2+11 months
For all even-numbered minimum terms MR=Max/2+5 months

4    Editors (1995). "APPA and APAI Go On the Offensive for Parole." *American Probation and Parole Association Perspectives*, 19(3):12.

5    Runda, J., E. Rhine, and R. Wetter (1994). *The Practice of Parole Boards*. Lexington, KY: Council of State Governments.

6    Such intrastate variations may also be true within states. For example, Sutton recently observed that the decision to place an individual in prison or not, and the length of the sentence per se, may be more a function of the county where the sentence was handed down than the nature of the offense. See Paul L. Sutton (1981). *Criminal Sentencing in Nebraska: The Feasibility of Empirically Based Guidelines*. Williamsburg, VA: National Center for State Courts, 1981. But see M. Turner, F. Cullen, and J. Sundt (1997). "Public Tolerance for Community-Based Sanctions." *Prison Journal*, 77(1):6-26.

7    Rhine, E., W. Smith, and R. Jackson (1992). *Paroling Authorities: Recent History and Current Practices*. Laurel, MD: American correctional Association.

8    Florida Office of Program Policy Analysis and Government Accountability (1996). *Information Brief of Control Release Workload of the Florida Parole Commission*. Tallahassee: FOPPAGA.

9    English, K., C. Colling, and S. Pullen (1996). *How Are Adult Felony Sex Offenders Managed on Probation and Parole: A National Assessment*. Denver, CO: Colorado Department of Public Safety.

10    Tinklenberg, J., H. Steiner, and W. Huckaby (1996). "Criminal Recidivism Predicted from Narratives of Violent Juvenile Offenders." *Child Psychiatry and Human Development*, 27(2):69-79.

11    Oregon Intermediate Sanctions for Female Offenders Policy Group (1995). *Intermediate Sanctions for Females*. Salem, OR: Oregon Department of Corrections.

12    Sutton, *supra* note 6.

13    Hammett, T., L. Harrold, and M. Gross (1994). *1992 Update: HIV/AIDS in Correctional Facilities: Issues and Options*. Washington, DC; U.S. Department of Justice. See also T. Hammett, L. Harrold, and J. Epstein (1994). *Tuberculosis in Correctional Facilities*. Washington, DC: U.S. Department of Justice. See also P. Pagliaro and A. Pagliaro (1992). "Sentenced to Death: HIV Infections and AIDS in Prison – Current and Future Concerns." *Canadian Journal of Criminology*, 34(2):201-214.

14    Monahan, J. and H. Steadman (eds.) (1994). *Violence and Mental Disorder: Developments in Risk Behavior*. Chicago, IL: University of Chicago Press.

15    See *Block v. Potter*, 631 F.2d 233 (3d Cir. 1980); *Candelaria v. Griffin*, 641 F.2d 868 (10th Cir. 1980); *Farris v. U.S. Board of Parole*, 384 F.2d 948 (7th Cir. 1973).

[16]    Gottfredson, S. and D. Gottfredson (1994). "Behavioral Prediction and the Problem of Incapacitation." *Criminology*, 32:441-474.

[17]    Hoffman, P. (1994). "Twenty Years of Operational Use of a Risk Prediction Instrument: The United States Parole Commission's Salient Factor Score." *Journal of Criminal Justice*, 22:477-494.

[18]    Violators of federal statutes sentenced after November 1, 1987 do not fall under the authority of the U.S. Parole Commission but are instead sentenced under the new federal sentencing guidelines, a form of determinate sentencing that emphasizes just deserts. Sentencing guidelines were developed by the U.S. Sentencing Commission and are quite similar to the system used under the Parole Commission.

[19]    See *State v. Malone*, 403 So.2d 1234 (Sup. Ct. of La., September 8, 1981); *United States ex rel. Santos v. New York State Board of Parole*, 441 F.2d 1216 (2d Cir. 1971), *cert. denied*, 423 U.S. 827 (1975); *People v. Anderson*, 536 P.2d 302 (Colo. Sup. Ct., 1975). But see Cornelius, W. (1997). *Swift and Sure: Bringing Certainty and Finality to Criminal Punishment*. Irvington-on-Hudson, NY: Bridge Street Books.

[20]    The weight of evidence has shifted against the "nothing works in corrections" argument. See Chapter 14, and P. Gendreau (1996). "The Principles of Effective Intervention with Offenders." In A. Harland (ed.) (1995). *Choosing Correctional Options that Work: Defining the Demand and Evaluating the Supply*. Thousand Oaks, CA: Sage.

[21]    As defined by Gottfredson, Hoffman, Sigler, and Wilkins (1980:7), equity and fairness means that "similar persons are dealt with in similar ways in similar situations. Fairness thus implies the idea of similarity and of comparison."

[22]    This scale was constructed through the use of a random sample of federal prisoners (N=2,497) released in 1970. A two-year follow-up period was used for each case and all three major types of release were utilized (parole, mandatory release, and expiration of sentence). An additional sample of 2,149 offenders released during 1971-72 was used to validate the factors on the scale (Hoffman & Adelberg, 1980:44). In addition, this scale was revalidated (Hoffman & Beck, 1980) using a sample of federal prisoners released in 1976 (N=1,260).

## References

American Correctional Association (1997). *Directory*. Laurel, MD: ACA.

Babst, D.V., J.A. Inciardi, and D.R. Jarman (1970). *The Uses of Configural Analysis in Parole Prediction Research*. New York, NY: Narcotics Control Commission.

*Block v. Potter*, 631 F.2d 233 (3d Cir. 1980).

Bromley, E. and C.E. Gathercole (1969). "Boolean Predication Analysis: A New Method of Prediction Index Construction." *British Journal of Criminology*, 17:287-292.

Burgess, E.W. (1928). "Factors Determining Success or Failure on Parole." In B. Harmo, E.W. Burgess, and C.L. Landeson (eds.) *The Workings of the Indeterminate Sentence Law and the Parole System in Illinois*. Springfield, IL: Illinois State Board of Parole.

Burke, P. (1997). *Policy Driven Responses to Probation and Parole Violators*. Washington, DC: U.S. National Institute of Justice.

Camp, C. and G. Camp (1997). *The Corrections Yearbook*. South Salem, NY: The Criminal Justice Institute.

Campaign for an Effective Crime Policy (1996). *The Impact of "Three Strikes and You're Out" Laws: What Have We Learned?* Washington, DC: CFECP.

*Candelaria v. Griffin*, 641 F.2d 868 (10th Cir. 1980).

Carroll, L. (1976). "Racial Bias in the Decision to Grant Parole." *Law and Society Review*, 11:93-107.

Cornelius, W. (1997). *Bringing Certainty and Finality to Criminal Punishments*. Irvington-on-Hudson, NY: Bridge Street Books.

Criminal Courts Technical Assistance Project (1982). *Judicial and Executive Discretion in the Sentencing Process: An Analysis of Felony State Code Provisions*. Washington, DC: American University.

Dawson, R.O. (1966). "The Decision to Grant or Deny Parole: A Study of Parole Criteria in Law and Practice." *Washington University Law Quarterly*, (June):248-285.

Editors (1995). "APPA and APAI Go On the Offensive for Parole." *American Probation and Parole Association Perspectives*, 19(3):12.

*Farris v. U.S. Board of Parole*, 384 F.2d 948 (7th Cir. 1973).

*Gagnon v. Scarpelli*, 411 U.S. 788 (1972).

Gendreau, P. (1996). "The Principles of Effective Intervention with Offenders." In A. Harland (ed.) *Choosing Correctional Options That Work: Defining the Demand and Evaluating the Supply*. Thousand Oaks, CA: Sage.

Gendreau, P., C. Coggin, and T. Little (1996). *Predicting Adult Offender Recidivism: What Works!* Ottawa, CN: Solicitor General Canada.

Glaser, D. (1962). "Prediction Tables as Accounting Devices for Judges and Parole Boards." *Crime & Delinquency*, 8:239-258.

Goodstein, L. (1980). "Psychological Effects of the Predictability of Prison Release: Implications for the Sentencing Debate." *Criminology*, 18:363-384.

Gottfredson, D.M., D.V. Babst, and K.B. Ballard (1958). "Comparison of Multiple Regression and Configural Analysis Techniques for Developing Base Expectancy Tables." *Journal of Research in Crime and Delinquency*, 5:72-80.

Gottfredson, D.M., P.B. Hoffman, M.H. Sigler, and L. Wilkins (1980). "Making Parole Policy Explicit." In S.M. Talarico (ed.) *Criminal Justice Research*, pp. 2-20. Cincinnati, OH: Anderson Publishing Co.

Gottfredson, M.R. (1979). "Parole Guidelines and the Reduction of Sentencing Disparity: A Preliminary Study." *Journal of Research in Crime and Delinquency*, 16:218-331.

Gottfredson, S. and D. Gottfredson (1994). "Behavioral Prediction and the Problem of Incapacitation." *Criminology*, 32:441-474.

Gottfredson, S. and D. Gottfredson (1993). "The Long-Term Predictive Utility of the Base Expectancy Score." *Howard Journal of Criminal Justice*, 32:276-290.

*Greenholtz v. Inmates of the Nebraska Penal and Correctional Complex*, 442 U.S. 1 (1979).

Hammett, T. and M. Gross (1994). *1992 Update: HIV/AIDS in Correctional Facilities: Issues and Options*. Washington, DC: U.S. Department of Justice.

Hammett, T., L. Harrold, and J. Epstein (1994). *Tuberculosis in Correctional Facilities*. Washington, DC: U.S. Department of Justice.

Hassine, V. (1996). *Life Without Parole*. Los Angeles, CA: Roxbury.

Hoffman, P. (1994). "Twenty Years of Operational Use of a Risk Prediction Instrument." *Journal of Criminal Justice*, 22:477-494.

Hoffman, P. and S. Adelberg (1980). "The Salient Factor Score: A Nontechnical Overview." *Federal Probation*, 45(1):185-188.

Hoffman, P. and J.L. Beck (1980). "Revalidating the Salient Factor Score: A Research Note." *Journal of Criminal Justice*, 8:185-188.

Irwin, J. (1977). "Adaptation to Being Corrected: Corrections from the Convict's Perspective." In R.G. Legar and J.R. Stratton (eds.) *The Sociology of Corrections*, pp. 276-300. New York, NY: John Wiley and Sons.

Irwin, J. and J. Austin (1997). *It's About Time: America's Imprisonment Binge*. Belmont, CA: Wadsworth.

Kanvensohn, M. (1979). "A National Survey of Parole-Related Legislation." *Uniform Parole Reports*. San Francisco, California.

Koppell, H. (1983). *Sentencing Practices in 13 States*. Washington, DC: U.S. Department of Justice.

MacKenzie, D. and J. Shaw (1993). "The Impact of Shock Incarceration on Technical Violations and New Criminal Activities," *Justice Quarterly*, 10:463-487.

MacNamara, D.E.J. (1977). "The Medical Model in Corrections: Requiescat in Pax." *Criminology*, 14:435-438.

McCleary, R. (1978). *Dangerous Men*. Beverly Hills, CA: Sage.

Martinson, R. (1974). "What Works? Questions and Answers About Prison Reform." *Public Interest*, 25(Spring):22-25.

Minnesota Sentencing Guidelines Commission (1983). *Report to the Legislature*. St. Paul, Minnesota.

Mitford, J. (1971). "Kind and Unusual Punishment in California." *Atlantic Monthly*, 227(March):79-87.

Monahan, J. (1981). *Predicting Violent Behavior: An Assessment of Clinical Techniques*. Beverly Hills, CA: Sage Publications.

Monahan, J. and H. Steadman (eds.) (1994). *Violence and Mental Disorder: Developments in Risk Assessment*. Chicago, IL: University of Chicago Press.

Morelli, R.S., C. Edelman, and R. Willoughby (1981). *A Survey of Mandatory Sentencing in the U.S. Pennsylvania Commission on Crime and Delinquency*.

Morris, N. (1974). *The Future of Imprisonment*. Chicago, IL: University of Chicago Press.

*Morrissey v. Brewer*, 408 U.S. 471 (1972).

O'Leary, V. and K. Hanrahan (1977). *Parole Systems in the United States: A Detailed Description of Their Structure and Procedure*, Third Edition. Hackensack, NJ: National Council on Crime and Delinquency.

P. Pagliaro and A. Pagliaro (1992). "Sentenced to Death: HIV Infections and AIDS in Prison – Current and Future Concerns." *Canadian Journal of Criminology*, 34(2):201-214.

Porter, E.M. (1958). "Criteria for Parole Selection." In Proceedings of the American Correctional Association, pp. 109-112. New York, NY: American Correctional Association.

Runda, J., E. Rhine, and R. Wetter (1994). *The Practice of Parole Boards*. Lexington, KY: Council of State Governments.

Scott, J. (1974). "The Use of Discretion in Determining the Severity of Punishment for Incarcerated Offenders." *Journal of Criminal Law and Criminology*, 65:214-224.

Sigler, M. (1978). "Abolish Parole?" In G. Killinger and P.R. Cromwell (eds.) *Corrections in the Community*, pp. 325-335. St. Paul, MN: West.

Smykla, J.O. (1984). "Prediction in Probation and Parole: Its Consequences and Implications." Paper presented at the Annual Meeting of the Academy of Criminal Justice Sciences, Chicago, Illinois.

*State v. Malone*, 403 So.2d 1234 (Sup. Ct. of La., September 8, 1981).

Sutton, P.L. (1981). *Criminal Sentencing in Nebraska: The Feasibility of Empirically Based Guidelines*. Williamsburg, VA: National Center for State Courts.

Turner, M.G., J.L. Sundt, B.K. Applegate, and F.T. Cullen (1995). "Three Strikes and You're Out Legislation: A National Assessment." *Federal Probation*, 59(3):16-35.

*People v. Anderson*, 536 P.2d 302 (Colo. Sup. Ct. 1975).

U.S. Department of Justice, Probation and Parole Populations Reach New Highs (September 11, 1994).

*United States ex rel. Santos v. New York State Board of Parole*, 441 F.2d 1216 (2d Cir. 1971), *cert. denied*, 423 U.S. 827 (1975).

Vaughan, D. (1993). "Listening to the Experts: A National Study of Correctional Administrators' Responses to Prison Crowding." *Criminal Justice Review*, 18(1):12-25.

Vaughan, D. (1980). "Shock Probation and Shock Parole: The Impact of Changing Correctional Ideology." In D.M. Peterson and C.W. Thomas (eds.) *Corrections: Problems and Prospects*, pp. 216-237. Englewood Cliffs, NJ: Prentice-Hall.

Vaughan, D., J.E. Scott, R.H. Bonde, and R.C. Kramer (1976). "Shock Parole: A Preliminary Evaluation." *International Journal of Criminology and Penology*, 4:271-284.

Wiggins, M.E. (1984). "False Positives/False Negatives: A Utility Cost Analysis of Parole Decision Making." Paper presented at the Annual Meeting of the Academy of Criminal Justice Sciences, Chicago, Illinois.

Wilkins, L.E. and P. MacNaughton-Smith (1964). "New Prediction and Classification Methods in Criminology." *The Journal of Research in Crime and Delinquency*, 1:19-32.

# Roles of Probation
# and Parole Officers

**10**

> . . . **A** parole officer can be seen going off to his/her appointed rounds with Freud in one hand and a .38 Smith and Wesson in the other hand. It is by no means clear that Freud is as helpful as the .38 in most areas where parole officers venture . . . Is Freud backup to the .38? Or is the .38 carried to support Freud?
>
> —David Fogel

As Fogel (McCleary, 1978:10-11) succinctly indicates, the role of the probation or parole officer (PO)[1] has traditionally been viewed as a dichotomy (American Correctional Association, 1995). The supervision role involves both maintaining surveillance (societal protection) over as well as *helping* or treating the offender (counseling, rehabilitation, reintegration). Supervising officers are often left to their own devices with regard to which role would be most appropriate in supervising their caseloads (Figure 10.1). This dilemma is likely to remain with us even though calls from several quarters of the criminal justice system point toward coming changes in the role of the supervising officer (Clear & Latessa, 1993). This chapter describes and outlines the boundaries of this role conflict as it has developed over time, the problems associated with it, and the ways that probation and parole officers are educated.

## Responsibilities of Probation and Parole Agencies

To begin, it is necessary to examine what duties and responsibilities are held in common by probation and parole agencies. O'Leary (1974) has argued that parole resembles probation in several ways. With both, information is gathered and presented to a decision-making authority (either a judge or a parole board). This authority has the power to release (parole) or suspend the sentence (probation) of the offender. In turn, the liberty that the offender enjoys is subject to certain conditions that are imposed by the decision-making authority. If these conditions are not obeyed, the offender may be sentenced, or returned, to prison (Oregon Department of Corrections, 1992).

Figure 10.1
**Average Caseloads for Probation and Parole Agencies**

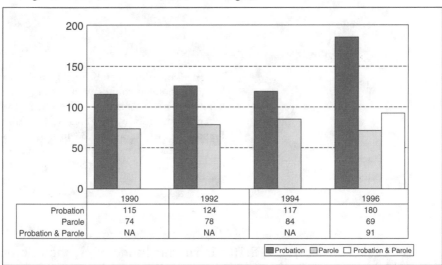

| | 1990 | 1992 | 1994 | 1996 |
|---|---|---|---|---|
| Probation | 115 | 124 | 117 | 180 |
| Parole | 74 | 78 | 84 | 69 |
| Probation & Parole | NA | NA | NA | 91 |

■ Probation  ☐ Parole  ☐ Probation & Parole

Source: C. Camp and G. Camp (1997). *The Corrections Yearbook, 1997.* South Salem, NY: The Criminal Justice Institute, Inc. Prior to 1996 agencies providing combined probation and parole caseloads were not separated.

On the other hand, parole differs from probation in distinct ways. The offender on parole has served a portion of his or her sentence in a correctional facility. The decision to release the offender from prison is usually an administrative one, made by the parole board. The decision to grant probation lies entirely with the court. As Wallace (1974:950) has written, "Probation is more than a process; it connotes an organization, basically a service agency, designed to assist the court and to perform particular functions in the administration of criminal justice."

Despite these differences, probation and parole agencies share one particular and significant function: They provide supervision of offenders in the community. The basic question remains: What is the purpose of supervision? To Wallace, the function of supervision, drawn from the social work field, is based upon the casework model. Supervision is the basis of a treatment program. The officer uses all the information available about the offender to make diagnosis of that person's needs and to design a treatment plan. One example of a treatment plan for probationers, emphasizing the need for reintegration, was suggested by the President's Task Force on Corrections (1967:30):

> . . . developing the offender's effective participation in the
> major social institutions of the school, business and church . . .
> which offer access to a successful career.

Yet, providing treatment is only on aspect of supervision. In addition, the PO is expected to maintain surveillance of those offenders who make up the caseload.

A classic definition of surveillance was provided by the National Conference of Parole (Studt, 1978:65):

> Surveillance is that activity of the parole officer which utilizes watchfulness, checking, and verification of certain behavior of a parolee without contributing to a helping relationship with him.

Although these statements indicate that the treatment and surveillance roles of the probation/parole officer are almost diametrically opposed, several authors have indicated that they coexist as a part of the agency's mission. Some authors—such as Glaser (1969), McCleary (1978), and Studt (1978)—have noted that the PO has two missions: to rehabilitate the offenders who are amenable to treatment, while simultaneously protecting society from those who prove to be dangerous.

In his study of parole officers at work, McCleary (1978:112) discovered that parole officers typically reviewed their caseload to identify the presence of "dangerous men." This term refers to the offender who is irrational or unpredictable. The dangerous man does not respond in a rational manner to the threats or promises made by the PO. It is this responsibility that leads the parole officer to label him or her dangerous and, as such, a prime candidate for surveillance. Despite this evidence, other scholars have suggested that parole officers perceive their role in different ways because of their particular view of the job as well as the appropriate role that they perceive should follow.[2] From this perspective, it is the PO's perception of the purpose of supervision that determines which of the two goals is most appropriate in a given client's case.

Carlson and Parks (1979:155-157) have listed four major responsibilities of a probation or parole agency:

- **Surveillance:** While the term "surveillance" usually means simply "watching" in a police sense it should be pointed out that a helping purpose is also intended. When surveillance is properly carried out, the client is continually sensitized to the possible results of a course of action that has made him vulnerable in the past. Just as an alcoholic or narcotics addict who is trying to change his life derives support from frequent contact with others who have successfully conquered their problems, so also can many clients derive beneficial results from frequent meetings with the probation officer.

- **Investigation:** The investigation function includes reporting violative behavior, or actual violation on the part of probationers, and gathering facts about arrests and reporting suspicions to supervisors.

- **Concrete Needs Counseling:** This type of counseling includes the following areas: employment, education, training, housing, clothing, financial, medical, dental, legal, and transportation.

- **Emotional Needs Counseling:** The services that a probation officer provides depend on the needs of clientele they serve. These needs can include: marital/family relationships, companions, emotional stability, alcohol and drug usage, mental ability and sexual behavior.

## Role Typologies

In one of the first studies of types of officers, Ohlin and his associates (1956:211-225) developed the following typology of PO styles:

- The punitive officer, who perceives himself as the guardian of middle-class morality; he attempts to coerce the offender into conforming by means of threats and punishment, and emphasizes control, the protection of the community against the offender, and the systematic suspicion of those under supervision.

- The protective officer, who vacillates literally between protecting the offender and protecting the community. His tools are direct assistance, lecturing, and, alternately, praise and blame. He is perceived as ambivalent in his emotional involvement with the offender and others in the community as he shifts back and forth in taking sides with one against the other.

- The welfare officer, who has as his ultimate goal the improved welfare of the client, achieved by aiding him in his individual adjustment within limits imposed by the client's capacity. Such an officer believes that the only genuine guarantee of community protection lies in the client's personal adjustment, since external conformity will only be temporary and, in the long run, may make a successful adjustment more difficult. Emotional neutrality permeates his relationship. The diagnostic categories and treatment skills which he employs stem from an objective and theoretically based assessment of the clients needs and capacities.

Glaser (1969:293) later extended this typology to include, as a fourth category, the passive officer, who sees his job as a sinecure requiring only minimum effort. For example, Erickson (1977:37) has satirically offered the following gambit to officers who wish to "fake it" and have an "ideal, trouble-free caseload:"

> "I'm just so busy—never seem to have enough time." A truly professional execution of this ploy does require some preparation. Make sure that your desktop is always inundated with a potpourri of case files, messages, memos, unopened mail, and professional literature . . . Have your secretary hold all your calls for a few days and schedule several appointments for the same time. When, after a lengthy wait, the probationer is finally ushered into your presence, impress him (or her) with the volume of your business . . . Always write while conversing with the subject, and continue to make and receive telephone calls. Interrupt your dialogue with him to attend to other important matters, such as obtaining the daily grocery list from your wife or arranging to have your car waxed. Apologize repeatedly and profusely for these necessary interruptions and appear to be distracted, weary, and slightly insane. Having experienced the full treatment, it is unlikely that the probationer will subsequently try to discuss with you any matters of overwhelming concern. He could even feel sorrier for you than he does for himself. You should henceforth be able to deal with him on an impersonal basis, if indeed he tries to report anymore at all.

The complete typology is presented in tabular form in Figure 10.2. The key distinction in this figure is the manner in which the supervising officer personally views the purpose of the job of supervision. Personal preference and motivations of the PO will often determine the style of supervision that is followed.

Figure 10.2
**Typology of PO Supervision Styles**

|  |  | **Emphasis on Control** | |
|---|---|---|---|
|  |  | HIGH | LOW |
| **Emphasis on Assistance** | HIGH | Protective Officer | Welfare Officer |
|  | LOW | Punitive Officer | Passive Officer |

Source: F.C. Jordan and J.M. Sasfy (1974). *National Impact Program Evaluation: A Review of Selected Issues and Research Findings Related to Probation and Parole*, p. 29. Washington, DC: Mitre Corporation.

A similar typology was developed by Klockars (1972:550-552), based on the working philosophy of the officer. The first style that he presented is that of the "law enforcer." Such officers are primarily motivated by: (1) the court order and obtaining offender compliance with it, (2) the authority and decision-making power of the PO, (3) officer responsibility for public safety, and (4) police work—the PO as police officer of the agency.

The second category is that of the "time server." This individual feels that the job has certain requirements to be fulfilled until retirement—"I don't make the rules; I just work here." The third type is the "therapeutic agent," a supervising officer who accepts the role of administrator of a form of treatment (usually casework oriented) to help the offender.

Finally, the "synthetic officer" attempts to blend treatment and law enforcement components by "combining the paternal, authoritarian, and judgmental with the therapeutic." The synthetic officer attempts to solve what Miles (1965a) terms criminal justice (offender is wrong but responsible for own behavior) with treatment (casework, offender is sick) goals. In sum, Klockar's typology rounds out the original scheme developed by Ohlin et al. (1956) by providing an example through which the PO can integrate the best of each possible role.

Czajkoski (1973) expanded on the law enforcement role of the officer's job by outlining the quasi-judicial role of the probation officer. He develops his thesis on five lines of functional analysis. The first line examines the plea bargaining, Czajkoski cites Blumberg's (1974) argument that the probation officer serves to "cool the mark" in the confidence game of plea bargaining by assuring the defendant of how wise it was to plead guilty. In this fusion, the PO certifies the plea bargaining process—a task that can significantly undermine the helping/counseling role of the PO.

The second line of quasi-judicial functioning by the probation officer occurs at the intake level. For example, at the juvenile level, the officer is often asked which cases are appropriate for judicial processing. Like the prosecutor, this function permits the probation officer to have some control over the intake of the court.

The third quasi-judicial function of the probation officer concerns setting the conditions of probation, a power the judge often gives the probation officer. This often leads to discretionary abuses, since indefinite conditions (often moralistic or vague in terms of offender's behavior) can become a vehicle for maintaining the moral status quo as interpreted by the probation officer. In addition, probation conditions can become substitutions for, or even usurp, certain formal judicial processes. For example, the monetary obligations[3] of the probationer (such as supporting dependents) can be enforced by the probation officer, rather than by a court that is specifically designed to handle such matters (Schneider, Griffith & Schneider, 1982).

The fourth quasi-judicial role is concerned with probation violation procedures. Czajkoski contends that such procedures are highly discretionary, especially in view of the vague and all-encompassing nature of the probation conditions, which are usually not enforced until the officer has reason to believe that the probationer is engaged in criminal activity. Petersilia and Turner (1993) noted that increased surveillance increases the incidence of technical violations, jail terms, and incarceration rates, as well as program and court costs.

The final quasi-judicial role of the probation officer concerns the ability to administer punishment. Since the officer may restrict the liberty of his or her charge in several ways, this is tantamount to punishment. In this fashion, Czajkoski highlights some of the actions officers take that relate to his or her function as a quasi-judicial official, and illustrates more ways in which the PO uses discretionary power in judicial-like ways.

Tomaino (1975) also attempts to reveal some of the hidden functions of probation officers. Figure 10.3 summarizes the Tomaino typology. Once again, concern for control is contrasted with concern for rehabilitation. To Tomaino, the key probation officer role is the "Have It Make Sense" face. This role attempts to integrate the often-conflicting concerns of societal protection and offender rehabilitation. Accordingly, Tomaino recommends that the officer stress goals, not offender personality traits, to ". . . organize legitimate choices through a collaborative relationship which induces the client to act in accord with presocial expectations." Perhaps, as Lindner (1975) suggests, the probation officer can create a learning situation for the offender and induce a desire for change.

A different but related role for the probation officer is also presented by Arcaya (1973), who stresses the counseling aspect of probation. Arcaya recommends that the officer adopt a "dwelling presence" in which he or she openly accepts the ambiguity of feelings and responsibilities attached to probation work and uses it to develop an awareness of the officer's own humanity within the client. To accomplish this objective, the officer should blend "active listening" (putting aside all preconceptions and thus permitting the probationer to define himself) and "responsive talking" (a dialogue with the probationer to conceptualize and situate the offender's world in the knowledge that the client can serve as his or her own best advisor). In this fashion, the officer can develop a style of empathetic understanding that goes beyond any original preconceptions of the offender's background, crime, or even social status, a role that requires skill and training.

Figure 10.3
**The Five Faces of Probation Supervision**

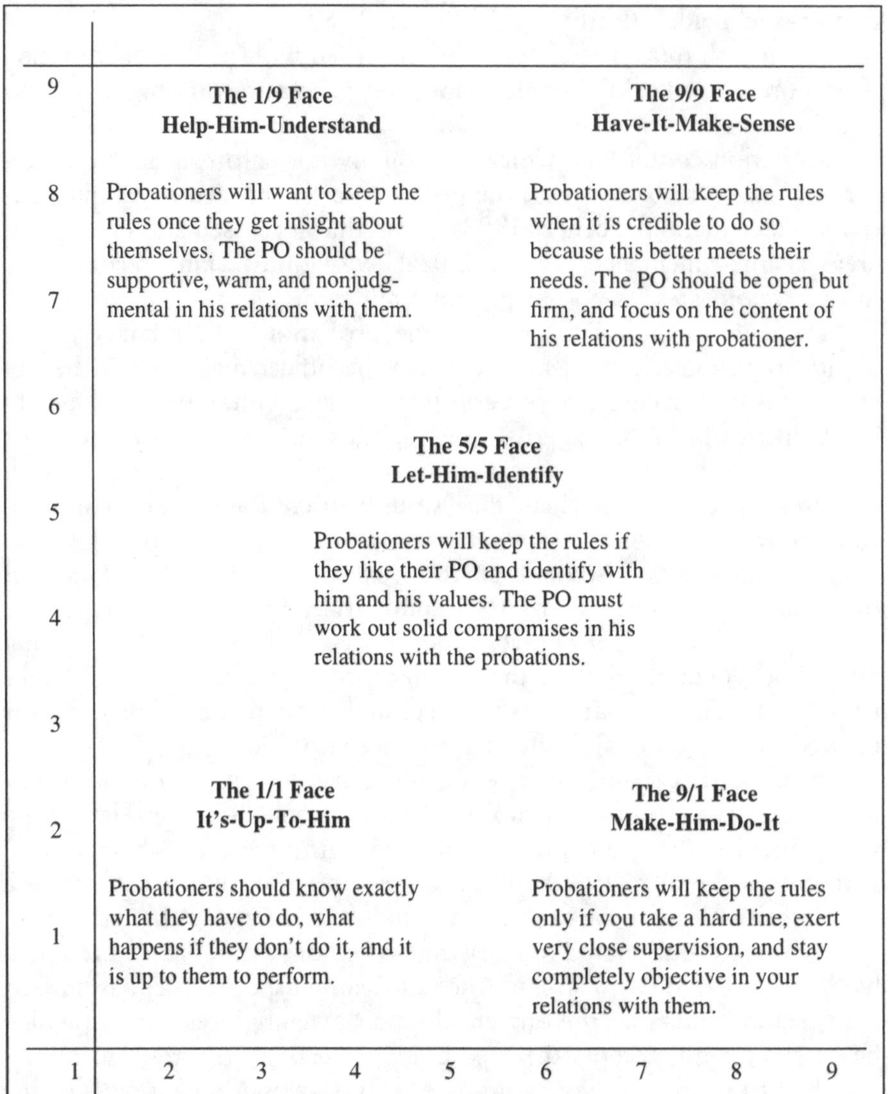

|  | | |
|---|---|---|
| 9 | **The 1/9 Face**<br>**Help-Him-Understand** | **The 9/9 Face**<br>**Have-It-Make-Sense** |
| 8<br><br>7 | Probationers will want to keep the rules once they get insight about themselves. The PO should be supportive, warm, and nonjudgmental in his relations with them. | Probationers will keep the rules when it is credible to do so because this better meets their needs. The PO should be open but firm, and focus on the content of his relations with probationer. |
| 6<br><br>5<br><br>4 |  **The 5/5 Face**<br>**Let-Him-Identify**<br><br>Probationers will keep the rules if they like their PO and identify with him and his values. The PO must work out solid compromises in his relations with the probations. | |
| 3<br><br>2<br><br>1 | **The 1/1 Face**<br>**It's-Up-To-Him**<br><br>Probationers should know exactly what they have to do, what happens if they don't do it, and it is up to them to perform. | **The 9/1 Face**<br>**Make-Him-Do-It**<br><br>Probationers will keep the rules only if you take a hard line, exert very close supervision, and stay completely objective in your relations with them. |
| 1 | 2    3    4    5    6    7    8    9 | |

Source: L. Tomaino (1975). "The Five Faces of Probation." *Federal Probation*, 39(4):43.

Unlike the previous authors, Smith and Berlin (1974) consider the role of probationer as an involuntary client. They feel the probationer qualifies as an involuntary client because of the "degree of injury to self resulting from disregarding the conditions established by the agency." In view of this occurrence, Smith and Berlin suggest that the probation officer adopt the role of "community resource agent" to bring the offender into contact with the agency and community resources designed to satisfy those needs.

In sum, these authors indicate that the supervising officer has a range of choices concerning the style of supervision to be followed and the ultimate goal of the entire probation/parole process. There is a strong emphasis here upon blending the need for control with the need for counseling. The officer must choose which style to adopt based upon the individual client (severity of the offense, amenability to treatment) and the nature of the situation. Supervising officers clearly have the discretionary power to either enforce the law (i.e., conditions of supervision) or offer help and treatment. No doubt, the world view of the PO also plays a crucial role in this decision.

## Characteristics of Effective Change Agents

What are the characteristics of effective probation and parole officers? Andrews (1979) suggests that effective change agents have several characteristics. First, they are able to develop a quality interpersonal relationship with the probationer or parolee. Warmth, genuineness, and flexibility characterize such relationships. Second, they are able to model behavior in concrete and vivid ways. Third, they are a source of not simply punishment, but of reinforcement for positive behavior. Finally, an effective change agent engages in disapproval with strong, emphatic statements of disagreement about an offender's negative attitudes and behaviors. Unfortunately, as Shichor (1978:37) points out, such characteristics are in sharp contract to current probation and parole practices that are more oriented toward "people processing than people changing."

## The Self-Image of Probation and Parole Officers

How do probation and parole officers see themselves and their work? The following studies focused upon agents to secure their views concerning what the appropriate goals of supervision should be and, within the criminal justice system, where such agents primarily identify with their allegiance.

In an early study, Miles (1965b) surveyed all 116 probation and parole officers on duty in Wisconsin on a single day. In addition, 48 officers were interviewed and accompanied into the field by the researchers. On the basis of these data, Miles discovered that a majority of these officers basically identified with the field of corrections (61.5%). The clear majority of individuals identified themselves as probation officers when dealing with judges (81%), social agencies (69%), and potential client employers (79%). These officers emphasized their identification with correctional work and did not wish to have this primary link absorbed by another area (for example, social work).

The survey also uncovered what is considered to be the basic dilemma of probation in terms of its primary goal: offender rehabilitation versus societal protection. Apparently, experienced officers cited societal protection as the primary responsibility, while seeking to maximize the client's potentialities in a nontherapeutic manner. On the other hand, the inexperienced officer is more concerned with the therapeutic function. It appears that this dilemma may be resolved with the passage of time, by the novice officers either resigning their positions in frustration or adjusting their conceptions to meet those of the more experienced majority. Miles concluded that, until legislature of the various states provide precise definitions of the functions of probation and parole officers, the dilemma of what is the fundamental goal will not be resolved. Some jurisdictions (such as Georgia) have bifurcated these roles in intensive supervision (Erwin & Bennett, 1987).

In a similar study, Sigler and Benzanson (1970) conducted a survey of a random sample of New Jersey probation officers in an attempt to learn about their role perceptions. The authors randomly selected 130 of the 522 probation officers serving the New Jersey's 21 countries and achieved a response rate of 55.4 percent. In every situation, the probation officer asserted his or her desire to be identified with the field of probation. The clear implication from this survey is that probation officers believe that probation is a separate profession and should not be confused or identified with other criminal justice agencies or functions.

In a similar study, von Laningham, Taber, and Dimants (1966) sent questionnaires to 417 adult probation officers in selected probation services across various regions, levels of urbanization, and levels of education, and received a response rate of 85.1 percent. The subjects were asked to rate the appropriateness of 52 tasks performed by probation officers. As a result, seven categories were ranked by the respondents according to their perceived degree of conformity to the proper role of the PO (von Laningham et al., 1966:101-104).

- **Referral Function.** Probation officer refers his or her client to other community resources for help or assistance.

- **Advice and Guidance.** Providing fairly direct advice or guidance for day-to-day living.

- **Court Consultant.** A well-established role in which the probation officer interprets for the court the social and personal factors of the client for decision-making purposes.

- **Psychotherapy.** Utilizes the techniques based largely upon psychological orientation and is concerned with deep-seated emotional problems. Only agreed upon for use with the "unduly suspicious," "reckless risk-taking," or alcoholic probationer.[4]

- **Law Enforcement.** Detecting and apprehending violators. Only considered appropriate for two examples—checking to see if an alcoholic probationer is attending AA or if a probationer has made court appearances without your knowledge.

- **Environmental Manipulation.** Attempt to directly influence the persons and organizations important in the probationer's adjustment. In this case, only one example was considered appropriate—speaking to a loan company on a probationer's behalf.

- **Conduct Establishment and Enforcement.** The use of the officers authority to attempt to coerce the probationer into behaving in accordance with the prevailing moral system of the community as perceived by the officer.

These ratings give some identification of the functions of the probation officer considered most proper by practitioners in the field. The ranking order evident in this study, particularly the importance placed on the referral and guidance functions, is particularly noteworthy. A survey of probation and parole agencies in 1997 revealed remarkably similar service functions for probation and parole officers, shown in Figures 10.4 and 10.5 (Camp & Camp, 1997).

Figure 10.4
**Services Provided by Probation and Parole Agencies**

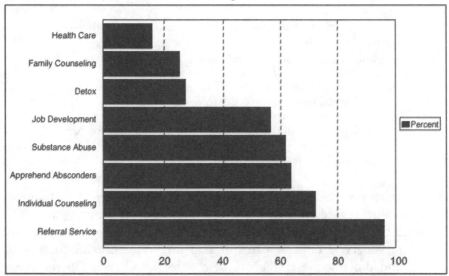

Source: C. Camp and G. Camp (1997). *The Corrections Yearbook, 1997*. South Salem, NY: The Criminal Justice Institute, Inc.

Figure 10.5
**Programs Administered by Probation and Parole Agencies**

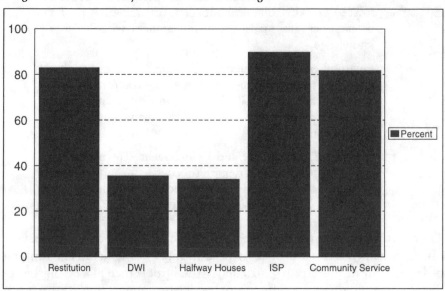

Source: C. Camp and G. Camp (1997). *The Corrections Yearbook, 1997.* South Salem, NY: The Criminal Justice Institute, Inc.

Similarly, Dembo (1972) tested three dimensions of parole officer orientation by surveying 94 New York State parole officers with between four and five years of on-the-job experience. The three dimensions were (1972:194-196):

- **Conception of the Parolee.** The divergent ways that officers see their clients . . . viewing the parolee as essentially anti-social . . . or as an individual in a positive sense.

- **View of Parole Purpose.** The distinction between police and social work approaches to deviant behavior.

- **Belief in Method of Law Enforcement.** The use of parole rules to deter crime and literal enforcement of their intent imply a punitive orientation toward the parolee.

The results revealed the presence of two distinct groups of parole officers[5] with regard to their belief in the efficacy of reintegration. The parole officers who had high reintegration scores were liberal, either preferred to supervise difficult cases or had no preferences as to type of client, and did not prefer the use of control on clients. On the other hand, officers who had low reintegration scores tended to be conservative; preferred to handle low-risk cases; were dissatisfied with the political factors of the job,[6] the long hours, and the constant crisis situations encountered in their work; and possessed high control attitudes.

Dembo's study appears to indicate, once again, that the role assumed by the PO and the underlying view of the proper function of supervision are related to the personal attitudes and beliefs of the officers themselves.

To test their view of the officer-client relationship, Studt (1978) interviewed 11 agents and 125 parolees in order to examine the interaction between the purpose of supervision as viewed by the client, as well as the officer. She focused on three dimensions of the client's experience: (1) the kinds of help provided by the agent, (2) the usefulness of supervision to the parolee, and (3) the kinds of events that cause "trouble" and may terminate parole for the parolee.

On the first measure, type of help provided, Studt (1978:169) discovered that the more practical and specific the agent's action (i.e., helping the parolee find a job), the more likely this action would be remembered by the client as helpful. Conversely, the more the officer directs his efforts toward what the client considers a "personal affair" (i.e., "managing their social life"), the more probable the client will remember it as help given, but the less likely it will be remembered as help received. It would seem that these parolees favor a less intrusive form of supervision based on the treatment rather than the surveillance model.

With regard to the usefulness of the parole period, Studt (1978:173) discovered that parolees were not hesitant to admit that the experience had been useful in several ways. Specifically, the parolees felt that the agents were most useful when they needed someone "higher up to go to bat for them" and to "kick around pros and cons when making decisions." The officers' responses on this point were also supportive of the treatment model. They felt that they were most useful when they "kept him working steadily" or when the parolee "needed help with personal problems."

As one would expect, the officer and client perceptions of the disadvantages of parole differed sharply. Parolees clearly felt that the personal problems for which they needed help were a direct result of the fact that they were on parole. On the other hand, officers were apt to state that the parolee was better off than persons with similar problems because the agent was there to help, or that client complaints were excuses and rationalizations for their own inadequacies.

Studt also encountered vast differences between the officer and client perceptions of what constitutes "trouble" on parole. The officers were likely to make a causal connection between living conventionally (i.e., middle-class lifestyle) and the ability to avoid crime.[7] Parolees tended to think of "success" on parole as simply "not committing crime." It is clear that the parolees were voicing their objections to the technical conditions of parole,[8] the violation of which could result in a prison term, and which typically are aimed at the urban, lower-class lifestyle.[9]

In sum, Studt found that parolees view their officers as helpful when they contribute to their survival in the community, but they do not accept either the officer's responsibility for supervising their personal lifestyles or the relevance of what they felt were overly intrusive conditions of parole.

In a more recent study, Allen (1985) interviewed 87 federal probationers concerning their attitudes toward probation. When asked their opinions on the purpose of probation, most ranked rehabilitation highest, followed closely by deterrence. The study also supported the notion that they perceived probation officers as helpful and assistance oriented.

Overall, the studies examined reveal that POs are aware of the surveillance/treatment dichotomy that exists with regard to style of supervision. A number of factors (age, education, years of job experience) are related to or influence the PO's style and method of supervision. Yet, in general, there is a distinct lack of consensus over which style of supervision should dominate.

Table 10.1
**Tasks Performed by at least 40 Percent of the Respondents on a Weekly or Daily Basis**

| Skills | Percent |
| --- | --- |
| COURT | |
| Attends court hearings with client | 58.6% |
| Takes court notes on court proceedings of clients | 47.2% |
| Confers with State's Attorney about cases | 64.2% |
| | |
| SUPERVISION—CASELOAD MANAGEMENT | |
| Meets with minor in office, home, and at school | 57.1% |
| Listens to complaints and problems | 72.9% |
| Asks minors about any general problems and disturbances | 56.5% |
| Inquires about police contacts | 44.3% |
| Consults teachers, therapists, significant others, community services agencies | 44.3% |
| Intervenes in crisis situations | 42.9% |
| Counsels parents | 47.8% |
| Confers with dean of students or school counselors | 47.8% |
| | |
| CASE NOTING | |
| Accounts for the entire history of the case | 65.7% |
| | |
| MONTHLY STATISTICS | |
| Documents all intakes, transfers, terminations, etc. | 44.9% |
| | |
| STAFFINGS | |
| Confers with other staff on informal basis about cases | 60.8% |

Source: L.R. Colley, R.G. Culbertson, and E.J. Latessa (1987). "Juvenile Probation Officers: A Job Analysis," p. 5. *Juvenile and Family Court Journal.*

While most studies of probation officers have been conducted in urban areas, it is important to note what appear to be differences in the roles and tasks performed between urban and rural probation officers. Rural officers perform a wider range of tasks than urban officers, and are less specialized (Colley, Culbertson & Latessa, 1986).

In a similar study of job tasks, Colley and her associates (1987) surveyed 70 juvenile probation officers in Illinois. Table 10.1 illustrates the tasks performed by at least 40 percent of the sample. It should be remembered that the variety of officer behavior found by Colley and her associates is replicated across the probation and 35,000 probation and parole officers who supervise their clients on a daily basis (Figure 10.6). When viewed in light of their average starting salaries (Figure 10.7), one glimpses the dedication of most PO staff!

Figure 10.6
**Employees of Probation and Parole Agencies as of January 1, 1997**

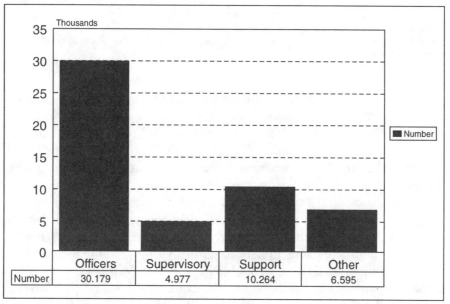

| Number | Officers | Supervisory | Support | Other |
|---|---|---|---|---|
| | 30.179 | 4.977 | 10.264 | 6.595 |

Source: C. Camp and G. Camp (1997). *The Corrections Yearbook, 1997.* South Salem, NY: The Criminal Justice Institute, Inc.

## Social Work or Law Enforcement?

The split between treatment and surveillance has attracted a great deal of attention, but very little in terms of empirical studies. Most authors seem to interpret role conflict as somehow tragic, intractable, and overwhelming. The most common solution has been to advocate that one orientation must be emphasized over all others (Gettinger, 1981). Simply put, is it the role of the probation or parole officer or that of the helper or the cop?[10]

Figure 10.7
**Average Probation and Parole Staff Salaries on January 1, 1997**

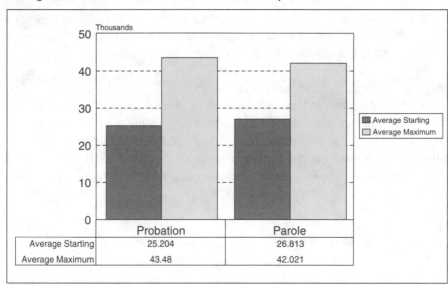

| | Probation | Parole |
|---|---|---|
| Average Starting | 25.204 | 26.813 |
| Average Maximum | 43.48 | 42.021 |

Source: C. Camp and G. Camp (1997). *The Corrections Yearbook, 1997.* South Salem, NY: The Criminal Justice Institute, Inc.

The roots of role conflict often are attributed to inconsistencies that exist in the three main functions of supervision: to enforce the legal requirements of supervision (the "law enforcement" role), to assist the offender in establishing a successful community adjustment (the "social worker" role), and to carry out the polices of the supervision agency (the "bureaucrat" role). The existence of this role conflict has been seen as a major source of staff burnout (Lindquist & Whitehead, 1986; Whitehead, 1989). Others have recommended abandoning one of the roles, either social work (Barkdull, 1976) or law enforcement (Stanley, 1976). Interestingly, no one seems to believe seriously that the bureaucratic role can ever be eliminated (Rosecrance, 1987; Lipsky, 1980; Takagi, 1967).

Several authors have addressed the consequences of this dilemma with regard to parole and probation. Blumberg (1974:154-158) has written that probation officers suffer from "civil service malaise" due to their lack of genuine professional status in the court organization. He also argues that probation officers have no "service ideal" because their primary allegiance is to the organization rather than their clients. Studt (1978:189-190) concludes that the community will not provide the agency with the resources necessary to reintegrate offenders; that the agency's technology will emphasize surveillance to alert the community to dangerous persons; and that the officers will focus on the nature of the lifestyle of their clientele. In addition, this problem will lead clients to be selective about the kinds of help they might seek from the agency and to view the agency's offer of help as hypocritical.

One critic of surveillance is Conrad (1979:21), who writes:

> We can hardly justify parole services on the basis of the sur-
> veillance model. What the parole officer can do, if it should be
> done at all, can better be done by the police. The pushing of
> doorbells, the recording of "contacts," and the requirement of
> monthly reports all add up to expensive pseudoservices. At
> best they constitute a costly but useless frenzy of activity. But
> more often than not, I suspect, they harass and humiliate the
> parolee without gaining even the illusion of control.

Figure 10.8
**Traditional Justice**

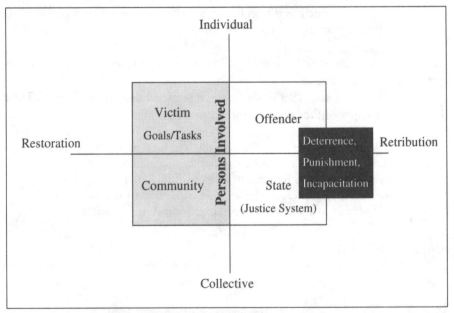

Source: A.H. Crow (1998). "Restorative Justice and Offender Rehabilitation: A Meeting of the
Minds." *Perspectives*, 22:30-31.

Can this dilemma be resolved? Several potential solutions have been
offered from various quarters. Fogel et al. ("A Swinging to the Right?",
1981:34) have suggested that Fogel's "justice model" (1975) might be
applied to probation:

> The probation office is neither a cop nor a counselor; he/she is
> an officer of the court. As such, he/she is responsible for moni-
> toring compliance with the demands of justice . . . [and] ensur-
> ing that the essence of probation is carried out.

They recommend that the officer should adopt a "compliance orientation," strictly carrying out the sanctions imposed by the court. A con-

tract should be developed among the court, the probation officer, and the client "so that all parties know exactly what to expect and have some recourse if the rights and obligations specified in the sentence fail to be carried out."

Not all persons associated with probation, however, agree with this contention. The California Probation, Parole and Correctional Association ("A Swinging to the Right?", 1981:34) has stated:

> Decisions constantly must be made between the relative risk of law violation at the present time and the probable long-term gain if a probationer is to be allowed the opportunity to develop an improved lifestyle. The role of the probation officer is complicated by his dual orientation . . . yet he must resist being stereotyped as a member of either camp if he is to be effective in planting the seeds of change.

Here the treatment-surveillance dichotomy is viewed as a strength, rather than a weakness.

Clear and Latessa (1993:442) have a somewhat different view. They believe that role conflict is common to professions.

> College professors face the age-old conflict of research and teaching; lawyers confront the conflicting demands of client advocacy and case management; even ministers must consider whether they represent the interest of deities to the world or the needs of lost souls (and requisite bodies) in the world.

Figure 10.9
**Offender Rehabilitation**

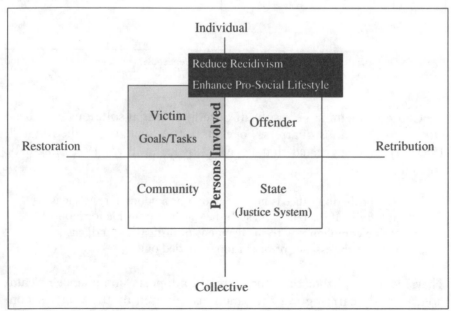

Source: A.H. Crow (1998). "Restorative Justice and Offender Rehabilitation: A Meeting of the Minds." *Perspectives,* 22:30-31.

Figure 10.10
**Restorative Justice**

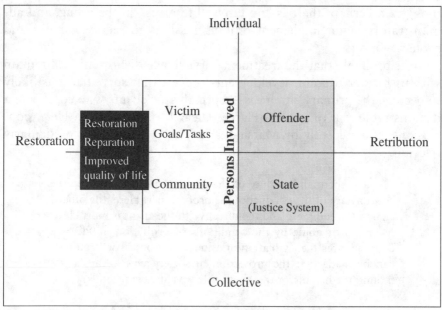

Source: A.H. Crow (1998). "Restorative Justice and Offender Rehabilitation: A Meeting of the Minds." *Perspectives*, 22:30-31.

Certainly, probation or parole officers have no monopoly on role conflict. Many feel that the true "professional" finds a way of integrating various role expectations, balancing them and weighing the appropriateness of various expressions of the roles. There is even some evidence that the roles of "social worker" and "law enforcer" are not incompatible, and that organizational policy can have a direct impact on the attitudes and behavior of probation and parole officers (Clear & Latessa, 1993).

A recent development in PO work is the increased level of assault by clients, leading to demand for arming or increased firepower (or both) of POs. The exact number of critical incidents is unknown, as there is no state of federal bank that tracks the dangers faced by probation, parole, and even pretrial persons. With the emerging emphasis on supervision and surveillance within community corrections, the potential for crisis will increase. Camp and Camp (1995) report more than 10,700 assaults by inmates on prison correctional staff in 1993; about one in five required medical attention. Another study of the extent of serious assault on community correctional personnel (Bigger, 1993) found 1,818 incidents since 1980, probably only the tip of the iceberg. Not only is there a need for a central information bank that would track critical incidents, there is a need for in-service training and orientation that would lessen the incipient danger. Brown (1993) suggested that PO safety could be enhanced by physical training as well as being mentally

prepared for such crises, including crisis rehearsal, understanding the continuum of force, kinesics (using force), and positive thinking ("self-thought"). Perhaps there is "no farewell to arms" in the offing, and administrators might implement training sessions to reduce liability and protect workers.[11]

It is probable that the treatment-surveillance dichotomy will remain with us forever. Recent developments suggest that surveillance is likely to become the primary emphasis—especially for clients who constitute a demonstrable risk to society (Harris, Clear & Baird, 1989). Here, conclusions made recently by Marshall and Vito (1982:37) are particularly relevant.

> . . . It is the manifest duty of the probation officer to keep the court aware of the conduct of the probationer. Here, the official charge to the officer and the directive to the client is most clear: Maintain or abide by the conditions of probation or face the consequences (i.e., violation and incarceration). The argument can be made that the protection of society was always paramount; the helping or treatment role was always secondary.

In a recent study of probation and parole officer attitudes in two states, Stichman, Fulton, Latessa, and Travis (1997) found that officers who had strong support for treatment strategies also placed more importance on control tasks. Conversely, they found that officers with more control attitudes led to placing more importance on treatment tasks. One explanation for this finding is that, as Morris (1978) states, control and treatment in corrections is a false dichotomy. In probation and parole agencies, control of offenders is always important, even if treatment is strongly supported. For example, for an officer to determine whether an offender is attending treatment and changing his or her behavior will require the officer to monitor the offender's behavior and compliance with the conditions of supervision. Stichman, Fulton, Latessa, and Travis (1998) also found that officers' attitudes and orientations may not have a significant effect on their own performance or on the performance of their clients. It may be possible that, similar to Clear and Latessa's (1993) findings that regardless of their own preferences, officers are able to perform the tasks that their organizational policy requires. The effect of officer attitudes and orientations on offender outcome is a very important question, and merits further study.

A final word about PO work, job performance, and satisfaction. Most POs find their work satisfying and their roles challenging, although many would hope for better work conditions, leadership, and quality of work. The federal probation system, which provides both probation and parole services, has begun to explore how to achieve better management through "total quality management" (TQM), widely implemented in corporate settings. TQM has certain management principles:

- leadership;

- customer-driven quality;

- continuous improvement of the work process;

- employee empowerment;

- blaming the system (not the people);

- ownership; and

- partnership.

Perhaps the quality of PO work would improve even more if administrators would implement team building through quality circles and self-managed teams.[12]

## Beyond Punishment and Treatment: The Restorative Role

Recently, there have been those who have argued that both retributive punishment (Braithwaite, 1989; Wilkins, 1991; Garland, 1990), and treatment responses (Byrne, 1989; Reiss, 1986) are practically and conceptually incomplete. Bazemore and Umbreit (1995:301) believe that both punitive and treatment interventions place offenders in a passive role—as the objects of treatment or services on the one hand, and punishment and surveillance on the other. They offer as a new paradigm for supervision—a restorative model that shifts the focus of offender accountability from the state to the victim. Table 10.2 illustrates both the current system and a model of restorative justice.

With a restorative model, focus shifts from punishment, or even individual treatment, to accountability and restoring the community. Table 10.3 shows the differences in the messages espoused by the treatment, punishment, and restorative models. Recently, several states, including Vermont and Ohio have begun to systematically introduce restorative into the correctional system. A public survey conducted in Vermont (Perry & Gorczyk, 1997) found that the public supports community based sentences, but that they want accountability from the offender. Specifically, they want the following from offenders:

- Full acceptance of responsibility of the crime;

- Acknowledgement of guilt;

- Full restitution;

- A commitment never to repeat; and

- Some good to come from it.

Table 10.2
**Current and Restorative Assumptions**

| Current System | Restorative Justice |
| --- | --- |
| Crime is an act against the state, a violation of the law, and abstract idea | Crime is an act against another person and the community |
| The criminal justice system controls crime | Crime control lies primarily in the community |
| Offender accountability defined as taking punishment | Accountability defined as assuming responsibility and taking action to repair harm |
| Crime is an individual act with individual responsibility | Crime has both individual and social dimensions of responsibility |
| Punishment is effective<br>  a. threat of punishment deters crime<br>  b. punishment changes behavior | Punishment alone is not effective in changing behavior and is disruptive to community harmony and good relationships |
| Victims are peripheral to the process | Victims are central to the process of resolving a crime |
| The offender is defined by deficits | The offender is defined by capacity to make reparations |
| Focus on establishing blame or guilt, on the past (did he/she do it?) | Focus on problem solving, on liabilities/obligations, on the future (what should be done?) |
| Emphasis on adversarial relationship | Emphasis on dialogue and negotiation |
| Imposition of pain to punish and deter/prevent | Restitution as a means of restoring both parties; goal of reconciliation/ restoration |
| Community on sideline, represented abstractly by state | Community as facilitator in restorative process |

Source: G. Bazemore and M. Umbreit (1995). "Rethinking the Sanctioning Function in Juvenile Court: Retributive or Restorative Responses to Youth Crime." *Crime & Delinquency,* 41:303. Adopted from Zehr, 1990. Reprinted by permission of Sage Publications, Inc.

Table 10.3
**"The 'Messages' of Sanctions"**

|  | Individual Treatment | Retributive Punishment | Restorative Accountability |
|---|---|---|---|
| Offender | You are "sick" or disturbed and your behavior is not your fault. We will provide treatment or services in your best interests. | You are a bad person who willfully chose to commit an offense. We will punish you with swiftness and severity proportionate to the seriousness of the crime. | Your actions have consequences; you have wronged someone or the community through your offense. You are responsible for your crime and capable of restoring the victim or repaying the damages. |
| Victim | Our fundamental concern is the needs of the offender. | The first concern of the system is to make offenders suffer the consequences of their crime. You will benefit because the offender will be punished. | The system believes you are important and will do its best to ensure that the offender repays the debt incurred to you from the crime. |
| Community | We will do our best to rehabilitate offenders through providing appropriate treatment and services. Highly trained professionals will solve the problem. Leave it to us. | We will do our best to punish offenders to teach them that crime will not be tolerated. Threats are the best way to control behavior. | Requiring offenders to repay victims and the public for their crimes receives highest priority in the justice system. We need the help of the community. The community is a key player in holding offenders accountable. |

Source: G. Bazemore and M. Umbreit (1995). "Rethinking the Sanctioning Function in Juvenile Court: Retributive or Restorative Responses to Youth Crime." *Crime & Delinquency*, 41:303. Adopted from Schneider, 1985.

Figures 10.8 through 10.10 compare three justice paradigms, Traditional Justice, Offender Rehabilitation, and Restorative Justice. With the Traditional model the emphasis is on deterrence, punishment, and incapacitation. The Offender Rehabilitation model focuses on reducing recidivism through the successful treatment of the offender. Finally, Restorative Justice attempts to restore the harm that has been done through reparation and improved quality of life for the community. Table 10.4 illustrates some of the differences among the three paradigms. It should be noted that some believe that the restorative justice model can be supplemented by key principles from the rehabilitation model, and combined to create a new model of justice and supervision (Rhine, Neff & Natalucci-Persichetti, 1998). Whether this can be effectively accomplished is still open to debate.

Despite the growing call for a shift to a more restorative justice model, there are some critics. Levrant (1998) raises a number of potential concerns related to restorative justice programs. She divides these issues into three categories: staffing, programming, and clientele. Staff issues revolve around the problem of motivation and support of staff for reparative efforts. Vermont, for example, found staff resistance and differing philosophies of punishment an obstacle in program implementation (Dooley, 1996). Programmatic issues stem from the problems associated with changing the underlying manner in which programs operate. Despite efforts to the contrary, most programs remain offender-oriented, and continue to ignore the other criminal justice clientele. Restorative programs may also be easier to implement in communities that are better able to organize, thus possibly eliminating some of the more disadvantaged communities (where crime most often occurs). Clientele issues include the possibility of net-widening, especially because of the increased willingness for victims and offenders involved in minor crimes to mediate the conflict (Niemeyer & Shichor, 1996). Finally, there is some evidence that many victims and offenders are unwilling to participate in these programs (Umbreit, 1992).

## Education and Training of Probation and Parole Officers

During the past 30 years, several national commissions and studies have recommended formal education as a means of significantly improving the delivery of justice in this country (President's Commission, 1967; American Bar Association, 1970; National Advisory Commission, 1973a; *National Manpower Survey of the Criminal Justice System*, 1978; Sherman, 1978). Graduate-level education and frequent in-service training for probation and parole officers have also been advocated for many years. The emerging philosophy now requires undergraduate degree education as a prerequisite for quality probation and parole service, and continuous in-service training as a means of maintaining and improving both service and skills (President's Commission, 1967; Loughery, 1975; National Advisory Commission, 1973b; Senna, 1976).

Photo 10.1
Training session. Photograph by Betsy Fulton.

Table 10.4
**Comparison of Restorative Justice, Offender Rehabilitation, and Criminal Justice Models**

| Criteria | Restorative Justice | Offender Rehabilitation | Criminal Justice System |
|---|---|---|---|
| Primary focus of attention | Victims & Community | Higher-risk offenders | The criminal offense |
| Goals | Safe communities with improved quality of life for all citizens, restoration of victims and community; reparation of harm | Safe communities with improved quality of life for all citizens, rehabilitate offenders and reduce probability of re-offending | Safe communities with improved quality of life for all citizens, deterrence, retribution, and incapacitation |
| Role of Government | Limited | Moderate | Extensive |
| Principle Methods Used | Personal Interactions | Cognitive/Behavioral Interventions | Surveillance and isolation of offenders from community |
| Community Members Involved | Victim, offender, community members, community agencies | Primarily offenders, criminal justice agencies, and select community agencies | Offenders and criminal justice agencies, and personnel |
| Flow of Resources | From offenders to victims to community | From offenders, victims and community to treatment programs | From victims and community to criminal justice services |

Source: A.H. Crow (1998). "Restorative Justice and Offender Rehabilitation: A Meeting of the Minds." *Perspectives,* 22:32.

Since 1959, the National Probation and Parole Association has recommended that all probation and parole officers should hold at least a bachelor's degree, supplemented by at least one year of graduate study or full-time field experience. This recommendation reflects the assumption that an educated officer is more competent and mature and thus in a better position to efficiently perform the varied functions of probation and parole. However, it was not until the 1967 President's Commission on Law Enforcement and Administration of Justice Task Force Report, which led to the Law Enforcement Education Program, that federal funds were made available for higher education of justice system personnel, including a college education for probation and parole officers. In 1970, the American Bar Association (1970:92) reaffirmed the National Probation and Parole Association's minimum standards, and suggested that probation and parole officers should hold a master's degree. It is also important to note that the American Correctional Association Accreditation Guidelines for Probation and Parole (1981) require entry-level probation and parole officers to possess a minimum of a bachelor's degree. They consider this an important guideline for accreditation.

From the data in Table 10.5, it can be seen that more than 80 percent of the jurisdictions in this country require at least a bachelor's degree for initial employment of parole officers. A more recent survey concerning the educational requirements for probation officers is in Table 10.6. Again, the majority of jurisdictions require a four-year college degree. A 1987 survey of Texas probation officers (Philips, 1987) found that more

Table 10.5
**Entry-Level Requirements for Parole Officers**

| Jurisdiction | Preservice Education Requirements | Other Requirements |
|---|---|---|
| Alabama | BS in social psychology, criminal justice or related area | Six weeks of law enforcement training prior to achieving permanent status |
| Alaska | BS; not specific | None |
| Arizona | High school degree | None |
| Arkansas | BS in criminology, sociology, or related area | None |
| California | Some college; not specific | Experience in custody, treatment, and supervision of human services |
| Colorado | BS in behavioral science | Ability to work with clients, public, agency; written and oral communication skills |
| Connecticut | BS | College and experience |
| Delaware | BS in behavioral sciences or related area | None |
| Florida | BS; not specific | Pass examination |
| Georgia | BS; not specific | Passing score on competitive examination |
| Hawaii | BS; not specific | None |
| Idaho | Some college; social science or criminal justice | Experience in related field |
| Illinois | BS in law enforcement or human services | Pass civil service examination |
| Indiana | Some college; 15 hours in social work, psychology, sociology, guidance, or criminal justice | Four-year full-time paid experience (college training may be substituted for three years of experience) |
| Iowa | Some college; not specific | Merit examination, two years of experience in casework |
| Kansas | Some college; humanities | None |
| Kentucky | BS; not specific | None |
| Louisiana | BS; not specific | None |
| Maine | BS; not specific, but social science preferred | None |
| Maryland | BS; not specific | None |
| Massachusetts | BS; not specific | No criminal record |
| Michigan | BS in criminal justice, social work, psychology, sociology | Interview, personal investigation |
| Minnesota | BS in behavioral science or related area | None |
| Mississippi | Master's degree in criminal justice behavioral sciences | Three years of experience in job-related field |
| Missouri | BS in social work, psychology, behavioral science | Nine hours of college work in criminology or corrections, or internship |
| Montana | BS in behavioral science | None |
| Nebraska | Not specific, but prefer criminal justice, behavioral science | Valid driver's license |

Table 10.5—*continued*

| Jurisdiction | Preservice Education Requirements | Other Requirements |
|---|---|---|
| Nevada | BS in behavioral science/social science | One year of experience to reach full journeyman level |
| New Hampshire | BS in sociology, criminology, behavioral science | Prior experience in probation, parole, or social welfare work |
| New Jersey | Not specific | Valid New Jersey driver's license |
| New Mexico | BS in corrections, social work, penology, or related field | None |
| New York | Not specific | Three years of experience in social work setting (may substitute graduate school) |
| North Carolina | Not specific, but prefer sociology, criminal justice, or corrections | None |
| North Dakota | Not specific | State civil service |
| Ohio | BS in behavioral science, counseling, and interview skills | Valid driver's license |
| Oklahoma | BS in counseling, sociology, psychology, law enforcement, education | None |
| Oregon | BS in behavioral science | Two years of experience in a related or social service or rehabilitation setting; one year must be in a correctional setting |
| Pennsylvania | Not specific | Valid driver's license |
| Rhode Island | High school degree | Physical examination |
| South Carolina | BS in sociology, psychology, social science, or criminal justice | Experience; parole officer II one year plus degree; parole officer III, two years plus degree; parole officer IV, three years plus degree |
| South Dakota | BS in criminal justice or other social science | None |
| Tennessee | BS in behavioral science | Must be twenty-five years old |
| Texas | Not specific | Two years of full-time paid experience in people-oriented area |
| Utah | Not specific | None |
| Vermont | Not specific | Eighteen months of experience in pertinent field |
| Virginia | BS in behavioral science | Two years of related experience or equivalent qualification |
| Washington | BS in social services | One year of experience in social work, police work, or related area |
| West Virginia | BS in sociology, psychology, penology, criminal justice, related area | None |
| Wisconsin | Not available | None |
| Wyoming | BS in criminal justice, social sciences | Two years of experience counseling to reach full agent status |
| District of Columbia | behavioral science | Two years of experience in related field |
| Federal | Master's degree; not specific | Two years of experience |

Source: E.J. Latessa and H.E. Allen (1982). *Management Issues in Parole*. San Jose, CA: San Jose State University Foundation.

Table 10.6
**Entry-Level Requirements for Probation Officers**

| Jurisdiction | Preservice Education Requirements |
|---|---|
| Alabama | BS in social science, criminal justice or related area |
| Alaska | BS in social science, criminal justice or related field |
| Arizona | BS; not specific |
| Arkansas | BS or 60 credits and 2 yrs. experience in criminal justice, social work, or education |
| California | Varies; set by counties |
| Colorado | BS in behavioral science |
| Connecticut | BS in appropriate field |
| Delaware | BS in social or behavioral sciences or equivalent education and experience |
| Florida | BS and 1 yr. experience in human service |
| Georgia | BS; not specific |
| Hawaii | Master's degree in criminal justice or social work or BS and related experience |
| Idaho | Knowledge of criminal justice system |
| Illinois | BS; not specific |
| Indiana | BS; not specific |
| Iowa | BS in social science or 2 yrs. college and 2 yrs. related experience or combination of education and experience equal to 4 yrs. |
| Kansas | BS in criminal justice, political science, psychology or social work, or 60 credit hours and 2 yrs. experience |
| Kentucky | BS; not specific |
| Louisiana | BS and 2-4 yrs. experience or 3-4 yrs. experience and 30 credit hrs. |
| Maine | BS and 6 mos. experience in related field |
| Maryland | BS with 30 credits in social science |
| Massachusetts | BS and 1 yr. experience or master's degree |
| Michigan | BS in criminal justice, social work, or related field |
| Minnesota | No college required |
| Mississippi | Master's degree in related field or BS with 1 yr. experience or high school diploma with experience equal to education requirement |
| Missouri | BS in criminal justice, sociology, psychology or social work |
| Montana | BS in criminal justice or related field and 2 yrs. experience in criminal justice |

Table 10.6—*continued*

| Jurisdiction | Preservice Education Requirements |
| --- | --- |
| Nebraska | BS preferred in criminal justice or social science |
| Nevada | BS in behavioral science or law enforcement and 1 yr. experience, or high school diploma and 5 yrs. experience or combination of education and experience |
| New Hampshire | BS in sociology, psychology, criminal justice, or social science |
| New Jersey | BS in social or behavioral science |
| New Mexico | BS including 15 credits in corrections, counseling, social work, penology, or related field |
| New York | BS with minimum of 30 credits in social or behavioral sciences |
| North Carolina | BS in criminal justice or related field |
| North Dakota | BS in criminal justice or related field |
| Ohio | Varies by counties |
| Oklahoma | BS including 24 hrs. in social or behavioral sciences |
| Oregon | BS in behavioral science or related field and 2 yrs. counseling experience |
| Pennsylvania | BS; not specific |
| Rhode Island | BS in criminal justice social work, social science, or related field or combination of experience and education |
| South Carolina | BS degree preferred; combination or education and experience may be substituted |
| South Dakota | BS or comparable experience |
| Tennessee | BS; not specific |
| Texas | BS and 1 yr. experience or Master's degree |
| Utah | BS in criminal justice or related field or 4 yrs. experience or combination of education and experience |
| Vermont | BS or AS and 2 yrs. paraprofessional experience |
| Virginia | BS in social science or combination education and experience |
| Washington | BS in social science or related fields |
| West Virginia | BS; not specific |
| Wisconsin | College degree not required |
| Wyoming | BS in criminal justice, social sciences, counseling, or related field |
| Federal | BS in social science or related field and 1 yr. experience |

Source: Adapted from "Survey" (1987). *Corrections Compendium,* October:9-13.

than 92 percent had a bachelor's degree or higher. Similarly, results from Illinois reported that more than 84 percent of probation officers had a four-year college degree or higher (Colley, Culbertson & Latessa, 1987a).

In addition, many jurisdictions require specific areas of college study, as well as various levels of training and experience. While there is some consensus as to the level of education needed (bachelor's degree), the exact content of undergraduate study is still a matter of some debate. Generally speaking, however, aspiring probation and parole personnel would better prepare themselves for agency entry by enrolling in various criminal justice, sociology, social work, and psychology courses. In Texas, nearly 40 percent of probation officers reported criminal justice or criminology as their major in college (Philips, 1987). Myren (1975) points out that care must be taken in academic programs to prepare generalists who would have the skills to manage the system, establish policy, and perform most of the client-related tasks. Increasingly, this seems to be the prevailing philosophy among probation and parole administrators, and many academic programs have responded by developing a broad interdisciplinary curriculum. There is also a growing interest among educators in many fields and disciplines to guarantee all students a common core of learning (Scully, 1977; Fish, 1978).

There is also some evidence that a comprehensive approach to training and development can effectively instill in officers the supervision attitudes that are most conducive to promoting offender change (Stichman, Fulton, Travis & Latessa, 1997).

## Summary

In summary, the conflict between counseling and surveillance is simply part of the job of the PO and a duality that makes their positions in the criminal justice system vital, unique, and necessary. While some see role conflict as a reason for eviscerating some of the less salient tasks, others believe that the profession can find a way of integrating and balancing various role expectations.

The need for college-educated staff has been advocated for many years and is becoming a reality. There has come to be a general acceptance of formal education as a perquisite of quality probation and parole service, and of in-service development as a means of maintaining and improving that service. This need has been identified and encouraged by several national commissions and organizations, as well as by numerous individual writers and researchers. A decade from now, the entry-level educational requirement may be a master's degree.

## Review Questions

1. What are the four primary responsibilities of a probation or parole agency?

2. What are the quasi-judicial roles of probation officers?

3. How does a probation/parole officer serve a law enforcement role? A social work role?

4. List those tasks that a probation or parole officer can undertake to assist an offender, and those to control an offender.

5. List the seven categories of tasks ranked by probation officers in the von Langingham study.

6. According to Andrews, what are the characteristics of effective agents of change?

## Key Terms

conditions of probation          punitive officer
investigation                    surveillance
protective officer               welfare officer

## Recommended Readings

Conrad, J. (1979). "Who Needs a Doorbell Pusher?" *The Prison Journal*, 59, 17-26. Building upon his experience as a probation officer, a noted scholar gives his opinions on the role of supervision.

Ditton, J. and R. Ford (1994). *The Reality of Probation: A Formal Ethnography of Process and Practice.* Aldershot, UK: Avebury.

McCleary, R. (1978). *Dangerous Men: The Sociology of Parole.* Beverly Hills, CA: Sage Publications. Based on participant observation, this is an in-depth examination of a parole agency and the supervision styles of its officers.

Parent, D., D. Wentworth, and P. Burke (1994). *Responding to Probation and Parole Violators.* Washington, DC: U.S. National Institute of Justice.

Ward, R.H. and V.J. Webb (1981). *Quest for Quality.* New York, NY: University Publications. This is the report of the Joint Commission on Criminology and Criminal Justice Education and Standards. It examines the issues surrounding the education of criminal justice professionals.

## Notes

[1]    Throughout this chapter, when the abbreviation PO is utilized, it is meant to designate both probation and parole officers. Their views with regard to their role, as well as the dilemmas that they face, are so intimately related that this abbreviation will not misrepresent the opinions, findings, and conclusions of the various authors.

[2]    Nowhere is the dichotomy of rehabilitation-casework versus surveillance-control more evident than between juvenile and adult probation officers. Juvenile officers support the former by a wide margin, but felony probation officers, particularly males, are more likely to endorse law enforcement strategies. R. Sluder and F. Reddington (1993). "An Empirical Examination of Work Ideologies of Juvenile and Adult Probation Officers." *Journal of Offender Rehabilitation*, 22:115-137.

[3]    Most probationers satisfy financial obligations as ordered by the court. G. Allen and H. Treger (1994). "Fines and Restitution Orders: Probations' Perceptions." *Federal Probation*, 58(2):34-40.

[4]    See U.S. Federal Judicial Center, Court Education Division (1994). *Handbook for Working with Mentally Disordered Offenders*. Washington, DC: USFJC.

[5]    R. Sluder and F. Reddington, *supra* note 2.

[6]    For the politicization of probation, see R. Aday (1994). "Continuity and Change: Probation and Politics in Contemporary Britain." *International Journal of Offender Therapy and Comparative Criminology*, 38(1):33-45. For a discussion of the effects of politics on corrections in general, see M. Tonry (1994). "Racial Politics, Racial Disparities, and the War on Crime." *Crime & Delinquency*, 40:465-494.

[7]    Blumberg also spoke to this tendency of the PO. Blumberg feels that supervision provides as "unanticipated job bonus"—experiencing the life of the client vicariously, which is often "a stark, heady contrast to the conventional and pedestrian style of life of the minor civil servant." See A.S. Blumberg (1974). *Criminal Justice*. New York, NY: New Viewpoints, 159.

[8]    Drug testing as a condition of both probation and parole is explored in Council of State Governments and American Probation and Parole Association (1992). *A Comprehensive Review of State-by-State Probation and Parole Drug Testing State Laws*. Lexington, KY: CSG.

[9]    Simon, J. (1993). *Poor Discipline: Parole and Social Control of the Underclass, 1890-1990*. Chicago, IL: University of Chicago Press.

[10]    For a discussion of law enforcement officers as agents of reintegrative surveillance, see S. Guarino-Ghezzi (1994). "Reintegrative Police Surveillance of Juvenile Offenders: Forging an Urban Model." *Crime & Delinquency*, 40:131-153.

[11]    Vaughn, M. (1994). "Police Liability for Abandonment in High Crime Areas and Other High Risk Situations." *Journal of Criminal Justice*, 22:407-424.

[12]    Janes, R. (1993). "Total Quality Management: Can It Work in Federal Probation?" *Federal Probation*, 57(4):28-33; F. Chavaria (1994). "Building Synergy in Probation." *Federal Probation*, 58(3):18-22.

# References

Aday, R. (1994). "Continuity and Change: Probation and Politics in Contemporary Britain." *International Journal of Offender Therapy and Comparative Criminology*, 38(1):33-45.

Allen, G.F. (1985). "The Probationers Speak: Analysis of Probationers' Experiences and Attitudes." *Federal Probation*, 49(3):67-75.

Allen, G. and H. Treger (1994). "Fines and Restitution Orders: Probations' Perceptions." *Federal Probation*, 58(2):34-40.

American Bar Association (1970). *Standards Relating to Probation*. New York, NY: American Bar Association.

American Correctional Association (1995). *Field Officer Resources Guide*. Laurel, MD: ACA, 1994.

American Correctional Association (1981). *Standards for Adult Probation and Parole Field Services*. Rockville, MD: Commission on Accreditation for Corrections, ACA.

Andrews, D.A. (1979). *The Dimensions of Correctional Counseling and Supervision Process in Probation and Parole*. Toronto: Ontario Ministry of Correctional Services.

Arcaya, J. (1973). "The Multiple Realities Inherent in Probation Counseling." *Federal Probation*, 37(4):58-63.

Barkdull, W. (1976). "Probation: Call It Control and Mean It." *Federal Probation*, 40(4):3-8.

Bazemore, G. and M. Umbreit (1995). "Rethinking the Sanctioning Function in Juvenile Court: Retributive or Restorative Responses to Youth Crime." *Crime & Delinquency*, 41:296-316.

Bigger, P. (1993). "Officers in Danger." *APPA Perspectives*, 17(4):14-20.

Blumberg, A.S. (1974). *Criminal Justice*. New York, NY: New Viewpoints.

Braithwaite, J. (1989). *Crime, Shame and Reintegration*. New York, NY: Cambridge University Press.

Brown, P. (1993). "Probation Officer Safety and Mental Conditioning." *Federal Probation*, 57(4):17-21.

Byrne, J.M. (1989). "Reintegrating the Concept of Community into Community-Based Corrections." *Crime & Delinquency*, 35:471-499.

Camp, C. and G. Camp (1997). *The Corrections Yearbook 1997*. South Salem, NY: The Criminal Justice Institute Inc.

Camp, C. and G. Camp (1995). *The Corrections Yearbook 1995: Probation and Parole*. South Salem, NY: The Criminal Justice Institute.

Carlson, E.W. and E.C. Parks (1979). *Critical Issues in Adult Probation*. Washington, DC: National Institute of Law Enforcement and Criminal Justice.

Clear, T.R. and E.J. Latessa (1993). "Probation Officer Roles in Intensive Supervision: Surveillance Versus Treatment." *Justice Quarterly*, 10:441-462.

Chavaria, F. (1994). "Building Synergy in Probation." *Federal Probation*, 58(3):18-22.

Colley, L., R.G. Culbertson, and E.J. Latessa (1987). "Juvenile Probation Officers: A Job Analysis." *Juvenile and Family Court Journal*, 38(3):1-12.

Colley, L., R.G. Culbertson, and E.J. Latessa (1986). "Probation Officer Job Analysis: Rural-Urban Differences." *Federal Probation*, 50(4):67-71.

Conrad, J. (1979). "Who Needs a Door Bell Pusher?" *The Prison Journal*, 59:17-26.

Corrections Compendium (October, 1987). *Survey*, pp. 9-13.

Council of State Governments and American Probation and Parole Association (1992). *A Comprehensive Review of State-by-State Probation and Parole Drug Testing State Laws*. Lexington, KY: CSG.

Crowe, A.H. (1998) "Restorative Justice and Offender Rehabilitation: A Meeting of the Minds." *Perspectives*, 3:28-40.

Czajkoski, E.H. (1973). "Exposing the Quasi-Judicial Role of the Probation Officer." *Federal Probation*, 37(2):9-13.

Dembo, R. (1972). "Orientation and Activities of the Parole Officer." *Criminology*, 10:193-215.

Ditton, J. and R. Ford (1994). *The Reality of Probation: A Formal Ethnography of Process and Practice*. Aldershot, UK: Avebury.

Dooley, M. J. (1996). "Reparative Probation Boards." In B. Fulton (ed.) *Restoring Hope Through Community Partnerships: The Real Deal in Crime Control*, pp. 185-192. Lexington, KY: American Probation and Parole Association.

Erickson, C.L. (1977). "Faking It: Principles of Expediency as Applied to Probation." *Federal Probation*, 41(3):36-39.

Erwin, B. and L. Bennett (1987). "New Dimensions in Probation: Georgia's Experience with Intensive Probation Supervision (ISP)." *Research in Brief*, 2/2.

Fish, E.B. (1978, May 3). "Harvard Tightens Up Curriculum Ends 'General Education' Program." *New York Times*, p. 1.

Fogel, D. (1975). *We Are the Living Proof* . . . Cincinnati, OH: Anderson Publishing Co.

Fulton B., A. Stichman, L. Travis, and E. Latessa (1997). "Moderating Probation and Parole Officer Attitudes To Achieve Desired Outcomes." *The Prison Journal*, 77: 295-312.

Garland, D. (1990). *Punishment and Modern Society: A Study in Social Theory*. Chicago, IL: University of Chicago Press.

Gettinger, S. (1981, April). "Separating the Cop from the Counselor." *Corrections Magazine*, 7:34-41.

Glaser, D. (1969). *The Effectiveness of a Prison and Parole System*. Indianapolis, IN: Bobbs-Merrill.

Guarino-Ghezzi, S. (1994). "Reintegrative Police Surveillance of Juvenile Offenders: Forging an Urban Model." *Crime & Delinquency*, 40:131-153.

Harris, P.M., T.R. Clear, and S.C. Baird (1989). "Have Community Supervision Officers Changed Their Attitudes Toward Their Work." *Justice Quarterly*, 6:233-246.

Janes, R. (1993). "Total Quality Management: Can It Work in Federal Probation?" *Federal Probation*, 57(4):28-33.

Jordan, F.C. and J.M. Sasfy (1974). *National Impact Program Evaluation: A Review of Selected Issues and Research Findings Related to Probation and Parole.* Washington, DC: Mitre Corp.

Klockars, C.B. (1972). "A Theory of Probation Supervision." *Journal of Criminal Law, Criminology and Police Science*, 63:550-557.

Latessa, E.J. and H.E. Allen (1982). *Management Issues in Parole.* San Jose, CA: San Jose State University Foundation.

Levrant, S. (1998). *Restorative Justice: Emerging Paradigm or Fleeting Panacea.* Masters Thesis. Cincinnati: Division of Criminal Justice, University of Cincinnati.

Lindner, C. (1975). "The Juvenile Offender's Right to Bail," *Probation and Parole*, 7(3):64-68.

Lindquist, C.A. and J.T. Whitehead (1986). "Correctional Officers as Parole Officers: An Examination of a Community Supervision Sanction." *Criminal Justice and Behavior*, 13:197-222.

Lipsky, M. (1980). *Street Level Bureaucracy.* New York, NY: Russell-Sage.

Loughery, D. (1975). "College Education: A Must for Probation Officers?" *Crime and Corrections*, 3:1-7.

Marshall, F. and G.F. Vito (1982). "Not Without the Tools: The Task of Probation in the Eighties." *Federal Probation*, 46(4):37-40.

McCleary, R. (1978). *Dangerous Men: The Sociology of Parole.* Beverly Hills, CA: Sage Publications.

Miles, A.P. (1965a). "The Reality of the Probation Officer's Dilemma." *Federal Probation*, 29(1):18-22.

Miles, A.P. (1965b). "Wisconsin Studies the Function of Probation and Parole." *American Journal of Corrections*, 25:21-32.

Morris, N. (1978). *Conceptual Overview and Commentary on the Movement Toward Determinacy. Determine Sentencing: Reform or Regression?* Washington, DC: U.S. Government Printing Office.

Myren, R. (1975). "Education for Correctional Careers." *Federal Probation*, 39(2):51-58.

National Advisory Commission on Criminal Justice Standard and Goals (1973a). *Criminal Justice System*, Washington, DC: U.S. Government Printing Office.

National Advisory Commission on Criminal Justice Standard and Goals (1973b). *Corrections*. Washington, DC: U.S. Government Printing Office.

*National Manpower Survey of the Criminal Justice System* (1978). Washington, DC: U.S. Government Printing Office.

"National Probation and Parole Association Standards for Selection of Probation and Parole Personnel" (1959). In D. Dressler (ed.) *Practice and Theory of Probation and Parole*, pp. 221. New York, NY: Columbia University.

Niemeyer, M. and D. Shichor (1996). "A Preliminary Study of a Large Victim/Offender Reconciliation Program." *Federal Probation*, 60(3):30-34.

Ohlin, L.E., H. Piven, and M.D. Pappenfort (1956). "Major Dilemmas of the Social Worker in Probation and Parole." *National Probation and Parole Association Journal*, 2:21-25.

O'Leary, V. (1974). "Parole Administration." In D. Glaser (eds.) *Handbook of Criminology*, pp. 909-948. New York, NY: Rand McNally.

Oregon Department of Corrections (1992). *From Community Supervision to Prison: A Study of Felony Probation and Parole Revocations.* Salem, OR: ODOC.

Parent, D., D. Wentworth, and P. Burke (1994). *Responding to Probation and Parole Violators.* Washington, DC: U.S. National Institute of Justice.

Perry, J. and J. Gorczyk (1997). "Restructuring Corrections: Using Market Research in Vermont." Corrections Management Quarterly, 1(3):26-35.

Petersilia, J. and S. Turner (1993). "Intensive Probation and Parole." In M. Tonry (ed.) *Crime and Justice: A Review of Research*, 17:281-336.

Philips, P.W. (1987). *Task Analysis Report on the Job of Adult Probation Officer.* Sam Houston, TX: Criminal Justice Research Center, Sam Houston State University.

President's Commission on Law Enforcement and Administration of Justice (1967). *Task Force Report: Corrections.* Washington, DC: U.S. Government Printing Office.

Reiss, A. (1986). "Why are Communities Important in Understanding Crime?" In A. Reiss and M. Tonry (eds.) *Communities and Crime*, pp. 1-33. Chicago, IL: University of Chicago Press.

Rhine, E.E., A.R. Neff, and G. Natalucci-Persichetti (1998). "Restorative Justice, Public Safety and the Supervision of Juvenile Offenders." *Correctional Management Quarterly*, 2(3):16-28.

Rosecrance, J. (1987). "Getting Rid of the Prima Donnas: The Bureaucratization of a Probation Department." *Criminal Justice and Behavior*, 14:138-155.

Schneider, A. (1985). *Guide to Juvenile Restitution.* Washington, DC: U.S. Department of Justice, Office of Juvenile Justice and Delinquency Prevention.

Schneider, P.R., W.R. Griffith, and A.L. Schneider (1982). "Juvenile Restitution as a Sole Sanction or Condition of Probation: An Empirical Analysis." *Journal of Research in Crime & Delinquency*, 19:47-65.

Scully, M.G. (1977). "Many Colleges Reappraising Their Undergraduate Curricula." *Chronicle of Higher Education*, 13:1.

Senna, J. (1976). "The Need for Professional Education in Probation and Parole." *Crime & Delinquency*, 22:67-74.

Sherman, L. (1978). *The Quality of Police Education.* San Francisco, CA: Jossey-Bass.

Shichor, D. (1978) "The People Changing Versus People Processing Organizational Perspective: The Case of Correctional Institutions." *LAE-Journal of the American Criminal Justice Association*, 4(3):37-44.

Sigler, J.A. and T.E. Benzanson (1970). "Role Perceptions Among New Jersey Probation Officers." *Rutgers Camden Law Journal*, 2:256-260.

Simon, J. (1993). *Poor Discipline: Parole and Social Control of the Underclass, 1890-1990.* Chicago, IL: University of Chicago Press.

Sluder, R. and F. Reddington (1993). "An Empirical Examination of Work Ideologies of Juvenile and Adult Probation Officers." *Journal of Offender Rehabilitation*, 22:115-137.

Smith, A.B. and Berlin, L. (1974). "Self-Determination in Welfare and Corrections: Is There a Limit?" *Federal Probation*, 38(4):3-6.

Stanley, D. (1976). *Prisoners Among Us: The Problem of Parole*. Washington, DC: Brookings Institute.

Stichman, A.J., B. Fulton, E. Latessa, and F. Travis (1998). *Probation Officer Attitudes and Offender Performance: Is There a Link?*. Paper presented at the Academy of Criminal Justice Sciences, Albuquerque, NM.

Stichman, A.J., B. Fulton, E. Latessa, and F. Travis (1997). *From Preference to Performance: Exploring the Relationship Between Role Definition and Role Performance Among Probation Officers*. Paper presented at the Academy of Criminal Justice Sciences, Louisville, KY.

Studt, E. (1978). *Surveillance and Service in Parole*. U.S. Department of Justice: National Institute of Corrections.

"A Swinging to the Right?" (1981, March). *Corrections Magazine*, 7:34.

Takagi, P. (1967). *Evaluation and Adaptations in a Formal Organization*. Berkeley, CA: University of California.

Tomaino, L. (1975). "The Five Faces of Probation." *Federal Probation*, 39(4):41-46.

Tonry, M. (1994). "Racial Politics, Racial Disparities, and the War on Crime." *Crime & Delinquency*, 40:465-494.

Umbreit, M.S. (1992). *Mediating Victim-Offender Conflict: From Single-Site to Multi-Site Analysis in the U.S.* In H. Messmer and H.U. Otto, *Restorative Justice on Trial: Pitfalls and Potentials of Victim-Offender Mediation—International Research Perspectives*, pp. 431-444, Boston, MA: Kluwer Academic Publishers.

U.S. Federal Judicial Center, Court Education Division (1994). *Handbook for Working with Mentally Disordered Offenders*. Washington, DC: USFJC.

Vaughn, M. (1994). "Police Liability for Abandonment in High Crime Areas and Other High Risk Situations." *Journal of Criminal Justice*, 22:407-424.

von Laningham, D.E., M. Taber, and R. Dimants (1966). "How Adult Probation Officers View Their Responsibility." *Crime & Delinquency*, 12:97-104.

Wallace, J.A. (1974). "Probation Administration." In D. Glaser (ed.) *Handbook of Criminology*, pp. 949-969. New York, NY: Rand McNally.

Ward, R.H. and V.J. Webb (1981). *Quest for Quality*. New York, NY: University Publications.

Whitehead, J.W. (1989). *Burnout in Probation and Corrections*. New York, NY: Praeger.

Wilkins, L.T. (1991). *Punishment, Crime and Market Forces*. Brookfield, VT: Dartmouth Publishing Co.

Zehr, H. (1990). *Changing Lenses: A New Focus for Crime and Justice*. Scottsdale, PA: Herald Press.

# Strategies for Classifying, Managing, and Servicing Offenders

He stands erect by bending over the fallen.
He rises by lifting others.
—Robert Green Ingersoll

## Introduction

In terms of community safety, the most significant responsibility of a probation or parole agency is supervising offenders. Underlying this duty are the dual objectives of protecting the community and helping the offenders. As we have already learned, these objectives are not always compatible.

Depending upon the jurisdiction in which the agency is located, offenders placed on probation and parole may have committed almost any type of criminal offense, and may range from first-time offenders to career criminals. The number of offenders placed on probation or released on parole will also vary considerably over time, depending upon political and fiscal climates in the jurisdiction, existing law in the jurisdiction, size of the prison overpopulation, and the prevailing philosophy toward the use of probation and parole. Figure 11.1 shows the growth of offenders under correctional control from 1980, extrapolated to 2000 A.D. Currently, there are some 3.1 million offenders on probation, and more than 700,000 on parole. Prisons hold more than 1 million inmates, while on a given day jails hold over 600,000 residents (some awaiting trial and some serving sentences).

The bulk of probation and parole clients are under regular supervision (see Figure 11.2), although about 1 in 9 are under some other management program, such as intensive supervision, electronic monitoring, house arrest, halfway house, or other programs. Two trends emerging over time are the increased number of clients under correctional control (Bureau of Justice Statistics, 1997), and the increasing use of alternatives to regular supervision (Camp & Camp, 1997). The implications of these supervision strategies are explored below.

Figure 11.1
**Offenders Under Correctional Control: 1980-2000**

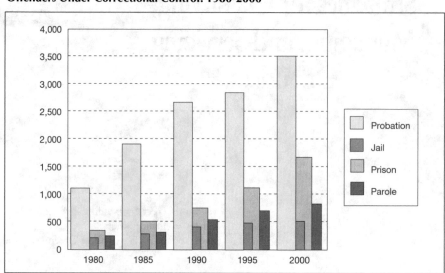

Source: C. Camp and G. Camp (1997). *The Corrections Yearbook 1997*. South Salem, NY: The Criminal Justice Institute, Inc. Year 2000 data are estimates.

Figure 11.2
**Supervised Offenders Under Different Types of Supervision as of January 1, 1997**

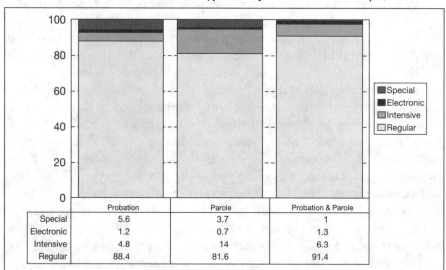

| | Probation | Parole | Probation & Parole |
|---|---|---|---|
| Special | 5.6 | 3.7 | 1 |
| Electronic | 1.2 | 0.7 | 1.3 |
| Intensive | 4.8 | 14 | 6.3 |
| Regular | 88.4 | 81.6 | 91.4 |

Source: C. Camp and G. Camp (1997). *The Corrections Yearbook 1997*. South Salem, NY: The Criminal Justice Institute, Inc.

In addition, there is likely to be variation among probationers and parolees with respect to the type and extent of conditions imposed upon them by the court or the parole board. Finally, individuals being supervised will vary considerably in the types of problems they face (family difficulties, educational or employment needs, mental illness, alcohol or drug abuse). As with other major responsibilities of a probation or parole agency, supervision necessitates an organizational structure that will enable the agency to protect the community efficiently and effectively, and to provide the necessary support to aid the offender. What strategies are available to the supervising agency and the individual probation officer?

Considering the complexity involved in complying with these duties, it is obvious that the agency will be faced with a number of critical management problems and alternatives from which to choose. Many of these which will be discussed separately, are, in reality, closely intertwined. They are not "either/or" alternatives. In fact, many strategies can easily be mixed into a variety of combinations.

This chapter addresses the broad area of service delivery and the ways in which probation and parole agencies handle offenders assigned for supervision. The philosophical models of treatment delivery are examined, as well as the planning process of supervision, different levels of caseload size, ways in which offenders are classified and assessed, and new developments in the area of contracting for services and managing community resources.

## Caseload Assignment Models

Offenders are assigned to a probation department by the court, to a parole department by the parole board, and to other community correctional agencies, such as halfway houses, by both.[1] Since the vast majority of offenders supervised in the community are first placed on probation or parole, we will examine the ways in which offenders are individually assigned to probation or parole officers.

How cases are individually assigned to available probation and parole officers varies from jurisdiction to jurisdiction. Carter and Wilkins (1976:391-401) have developed a useful typology of caseload models that includes the major variations in assignment strategies. Underlying their typology is the assumption that the offender population will vary considerably across any characteristic in question (Sigler & Williams, 1994).

The first model is called the conventional model and it ignores the differences and similarities among offenders; cases are randomly assigned to available probation and parole officers. Because of the random distribution of the offender population among caseloads, each officer handles a mixture that is generally a miniature reproduction of the entire offender population including, of course, wide variation in personal characteristics. With the conventional caseload model, then, probation or parole officers must be able to supervise any type of offender who happens to be assigned to their caseload, usually a difficult situation.

Closely related to the conventional model is what is called the numbers game model. This type may also ignore differences and similarities across offenders. The object of this model is to numerically balance all caseloads within the department. This balancing may or may not take the personal characteristics of individual offenders into account because the numbers game model can be approached in two ways. First, the number of cases to be supervised can simply be divided by the number of officers available to the department. For example, if a probation department has 10 probation officers and 800 probationers, every officer will handle a caseload of 80. Alternatively, the department can select an "ideal size" for each caseload and divide the number of offenders by the ideal size, yielding the number of necessary officers. Under this method, if a department has 800 probationers and has selected 50 as its ideal size caseload, then it must provide 16 probation officers. Variations of the numbers game model may also be used with the others models discussed below.

The third assignment model is called the conventional model with geographic considerations. This one differs from the conventional model in one important respect: the caseload is restricted to residents in one type of geographic area (urban, suburban, or rural). Given the travel time necessary to supervise an entirely rural caseload, the size of a rural caseload is generally smaller than suburban or urban caseloads. Such caseloads, however, are not differentiated on the basis of the personal characteristics of the offenders, except to the extent that the characteristics of urban, suburban, and rural offenders may vary. In a large urban area, probation and parole departments may have satellite offices. When this is the case, geographic distinctions may be based on the side of town an offender resides.

The other two assignment techniques recognize the presence of important similarities and differences among offenders. The more elementary of these techniques is called the single-factor specialized caseload model. This groups offenders together on the basis of one single characteristic that they all share. Examples include drug and or alcohol abuse, mental retardation, sex, age, type of offense, and high potential for violent behavior ("risk"). Despite the existence of a shared characteristic, offenders on each single-factor specialized caseload may vary widely on other characteristics. For example, a caseload restricted to offenders between the ages of 18 and 21 may still include individuals who differ considerably on such variables as type of offense or potential risk to community.

Finally, the most complex assignment model, the vertical model, classifies offenders by two or more factors or characteristics. Often this classification is accomplished by using one of the various prediction devices that estimates the chances of a particular offender's succeeding or failing while under supervision. Prediction devices take a wide variety of individual characteristics into account and stress the similarities among individuals. Once all offenders in the agency are screened according to their probability of success, this classificatory scheme can then be used to create caseloads composed of offenders who have roughly the same chances of success or failure. This model is called vertical because it divides the range of offender characteristics into vertical slices in order to create caseloads.

Caseload size can be varied across both the single-factor and the multifactor classifications. For example, the size of caseloads, when based in the vertical model, are usually varied; it can be decreased in those composed of offenders with a high risk of failure, or increased for those composed of low-risk offenders.

Today, many departments employ workload formulas to determine caseload size. This technique takes into account the fact that not all offenders are the same and some will require more attention than others. Here, cases are screened according to a number of factors, such as risk. Table 11.1 shows an example of a monthly work unit ledger from the Montgomery County Adult Probation Department (Dayton, Ohio). In this particular department, a standard workload is 250 units, based on 107.5 available hours per month. A high-risk case is equal to 4 units, while a PSI is equal to 14. Each type of case and activity is given a weight, based on a time study that was used as the basis for their formula. This is an excellent example of how work can be equally distributed across a department by taking into account differences between offenders and certain activities.

Another creative example of how one probation department handles its caseloads can be seen in the Lucas County Adult Probation Department (Toledo, Ohio). Here, all cases are screened according to risk (high, medium, and low). In addition, there are screening devices to identify alcoholics, drug abusers, sex offenders, and offenders with high mental health needs. One probation officer, along with a team of volunteer probation officers, handles all of the low-risk offenders. High-risk offenders that do not require the assistance of a specialist are supervised in a "High-Risk Unit." Those special needs offenders are placed in one of the four specialty units (e.g., alcohol, mental health). The caseloads for the high-risk and specialty units are considerably smaller. Offenders without these needs that fall in the medium-risk category are supervised by regular treatment officers. In addition, this department has an intensive supervision unit that handles offenders of all types, provided they have been diverted from a state penal institution. PSIs are conducted by a separate unit. Using this scheme, Lucas County is able to siphon off a considerable number of low-risk, minimum supervision cases and divert their attention to offenders that require more specialized treatment or increased surveillance.

Once the general strategy for managing offenders is established, the officers must deliver needed services to their clients. The remainder of this chapter discusses different strategies employed by probation and parole agencies to deliver those services to offenders under supervision. Although we discuss these strategies separately, they are not mutually exclusive, and "pure" types are seldom found in actual supervision practices.

Table 11.1
**Work Units Monthly Ledger Summary**

| | | |
|---|---|---|
| (Team) | | (Month/Year) |

| SUPERVISION CLASSIFICATION | INVESTIGATIONS | WORK UNITS |
|---|---|---|

OFFICER  MAX  MED  MIN  NEW  ITS  UNS  CURT  TLC  INS  INC  PATH  PSI  SHCK  MISC

TOTALS

| | |
|---|---|
| MAX — Maximum Supervision | 4 wk units |
| INS — Intercounty Transfer | 1 wk unit |
| MED — Medium Supervision | 2 wk units |
| PATH — Pay Thru | 1 wk unit |
| MIN — Minimum Supervision | 1 wk unit |
| PSI — Bond or Jail | 14 wk units |
| NEW — Not Yet Classified | 5 wk units |
| SHCK — Shock Report | 2 wk units |
| ITS — Intensive Treatment | 8 wk units |
| UNS — Unsupervised-Court | ½ wk units |
| MISC — Affidavit, Victim | 1 wk unit |
| CURT — Courtesy Supervision | 1 wk unit |
| TLC — Treatment in Lieu of Conviction | 1 wk unit |

(Supervisor)

Adopted from the Montgomery County Adult Probation Department.

# Casework Supervision versus Brokerage Supervision

The two major orientations or approaches to supervision are case-work and brokerage. We will examine each approach, the assumption underlying its use, its advantages and disadvantages, and the major operational concerns. We are discussing "pure" types as though the approaches were mutually exclusive, as if a department would adopt either a caseload or a brokerage approach, but could not combine any feature of the two. In reality, the two approaches are so mixed that it would be unusual if any two departments exhibited precisely the same approach as extreme positions. Most departments adopt positions somewhere along the continuum.

## Casework Supervision

The traditional approach to probation and parole supervision has been the casework approach. Casework is not synonymous with social work; rather it is just one of the three major specialties of social work (the others are community organization and group work). Many definitions of casework and social casework have been offered. Bowers (1950:127) has provided this frequently cited definition:

> Social casework is an area in which knowledge of the science of human relations and skills in relationships are used to mobilize capacities in the individual and resources in the community appropriate for better adjustment between the client and all or any part of his total environment.

Meeker (1948:51-52) has elaborated further:

> The modern emphasis in social casework is upon discovering the positive potential within the individual and helping him exploit his own capabilities, while at the same time revealing external resources in his social and economic environment which will contribute to his ability to assume the mature responsible obligations of a well-adjusted individual.

It is apparent that the basic element in casework is the nature of the relationship between the caseworker and the individual in trouble. It is also obvious from these definitions that casework emphasizes changing the behavior of the offender through the development of a supportive one-to-one relationship. Because of the closeness, this approach views the caseworker as the sole, or at least the primary, agent of treatment for the client.

By following a casework approach, the supervising officer will also follow the basic assumptions of social work. Trecker (1955:8-9) divides these assumptions into four categories: people, behavior problems, the social worker, and the relationship between society and the offender. One of the assumptions about offenders is that ". . . people can and do change in their behavior when they are given the right help at the right time and in the right amount."[2] With respect to behavior problems, it is assumed that, because people's problems are complex and intertwined with the person's total living situation, treatment of those problems must be individualized. The primary treatment agent is assumed to be the social worker, and his or her most important tool is the quality of the relationship created with the client. Finally, it is assumed that the client must be motivated to participate in the treatment process; consequently, a key element of the working relationship between the social worker and the client must be the development of the client's desire to change his or her behavior.

Photo 11.1
Probation officer with an offender. Courtesy of Talbert House, Inc.

A common thread running through these assumptions is the idea that the offender must enter the casework relationship voluntarily, or at least willingly. The relationship involved in correctional supervision, however, does not usually rest on the offender's voluntary participation, but rather on the authority of the probation or parole officer. Under the casework approach, then, it is important to resolve the conflict between the voluntary self-determination of the offender and the authority inherent in the supervising officer's position.

Many authors characterize the authority of the probation or parole officer as an important tool that can be used in the treatment process. Mangrum (1978:219) refers to the use of "coercive casework" and states, "While it is true that effective casework is not something done to or for the client, but with him, it is also true that sometimes it is a matter of some action which *gets his attention or holds him still* long enough for him to recognize that there is motivation from within . . ." (emphasis added). Studt (1954:24) notes that it is important for the offender to learn that ". . . authority is power to help as well as power to limit . . ." Hardman (1959:249-255) feels that authority, if properly used by the probation officer, can be an extremely powerful tool in the social service. He believes that all individuals, including probationers, entertain both positive and negative feelings toward authority, and that a primary responsibility of the caseworker is to help the client understand and accept those conflicting feelings and to learn new ways of controlling and expressing them.

Casework is so extensively used in probation and parole supervision that it is considered the "norm" as a service provision strategy. It basically follows the medical model of corrections in which the supervising officer, through a one-to-one relationship, diagnoses the offender, formulates a treatment strategy, implements that strategy and, finally, evaluates the offender in light of the treatment.

Following this approach, the probation or parole officer attempts to bring about a mutual interaction with the offender in an effort to promote a psychological and social atmosphere that will enable the offender to be more self-accepting and to interact more acceptably with others. In other words, through the use of this close, helping relationship, the officer attempts to change (positively) the behavior of the offender. Because of the close relationship required by the casework approach, the officer is the primary agent of treatment.

Casework is a way of working with individuals. It is consciously planned to help the offender become better adjusted to the demands of social living. The activities that define "casework" are twofold: (1) the officers are dealing with offenders as individuals, and (2) they are consciously controlling what they do so that their activities contribute to the offenders' welfare. Casework is not characterized either by a particular kind of activity on the part of the probation or parole officer, or a particular situation of the offender. For example, while counseling is a large part of casework, it is not the only treatment available. While figuring out what has to be done next, the supervising officer may "cool off" the offender by having him or her jailed on a technical violation. This next step could involve working with the offender's family or, in the case of a juvenile, working with their teacher. Each such activity is a part of casework in the correctional field.

Thus, casework in probation and parole follows the traditional medical model and remains intact in most probation and parole agencies. In reality, however, the supervising officer does not have the time or energy to devote to individual cases. Perhaps the most basic criticisms of the casework approach are that the probation and/or parole officer tries to be all things to all people, and does not adequately mobilize the community and its support systems. In addition, large caseloads, staff shortages, and endless report writing leave supervising officers unable to perform all the tasks called for by casework. Coupled with the trend away from the medical model, probation and parole administrators have initiated both the brokerage approach and community resource management teams.

## Brokerage Supervision

Almost diametrically opposed to the casework approach is the brokerage approach, in which the supervising officer is not concerned primarily with understanding or changing the behavior of the offender, but rather with assessing the concrete needs of the individual and arranging for the probationer or parolee to receive services that directly address those needs. Since the officer is not seen as the primary agent of treatment or change, there is significantly less emphasis placed on the development of a close, one-on-one relationship between the officer and the offender. With the brokerage approach, the supervising officer functions primarily as a manager or broker of resources and social services that are already available from other agencies. It is the task of the probation or parole officer to assess the service needs of the offender, locate the social service agency that addresses those needs as its primary function, refer the offender to the appropriate agency, and follow up referrals to make sure the offender has actually received the services. Under the brokerage approach, it can be said that the officer's relationship with community service agencies is more important than the relationship with an individual client. Both the brokerage and casework approaches share the importance of the offenders' participation in developing their own supervision plans.

The National Advisory Commission on Criminal Justice Standards and Goals (1973:320) recommended that the probation system should "redefine the role of probation officer from caseworker to community resource manager." The Commission report (1973:322-323) characterized this approach in the following way:

> To carry out his responsibilities as a community resource manager, the probation officer must perform several functions. In helping a probationer obtain needed services, the probation officer will have to assess the situation, know available resources, contact the appropriate resource, assist the probationer to obtain the services, and follow up on the case. When the probationer encounters difficulty in obtaining a service he needs, the probation officer will have to explore the reason for the difficulty and take appropriate steps to see that the service is delivered. The probation officer will have to monitor and evaluate the services to which the probationer is referred.

The Commission also addresses the problems of the individual probation officer's providing services that may be available elsewhere. They encouraged (1973:32) the reliance of probation departments on other social service agencies by suggesting that:

> Probation systems should not attempt to duplicate services already created by law and supposedly available to all persons. The responsibility of the system and its staff should be to enable the probationer to cut through the barriers and receive assistance from social institutions that may be all too ready to exclude him.

With its emphasis on the management of community resources, the brokerage approach requires intimate knowledge of the services in the community and the conditions under which each service is available. It may not be feasible for each officer to accumulate and use this vast amount of information about all the possible community service sources.

It has been frequently suggested, therefore, that the brokerage of community services might be more easily handled if individual probation or parole officers were to specialize in gaining knowledge about and familiarity with an agency or set of agencies that provide related services. For example, one officer might become extremely knowledgeable about all community agencies that offer services for individuals with drug-related problems, while another officer might specialize in all agencies that handle unemployed or underemployed individuals. Regardless of whether officers decide to specialize or would prefer to handle all types of community agencies, the essential requirements under the brokerage approach are for the supervising officer to develop a comprehensive knowledge of the resources already available in the community and to use those resources to the fullest extent for the benefit of clients.

Closely related to the brokerage approach is the role of advocate. Several authors have recently stressed the advocacy role for probation officers.[3] Recognizing the fact that some of the services the offenders need will not be available in the community, these authors suggest that, rather than trying to supply those needed services themselves, probation and parole officers should concentrate on working with community agencies to develop the necessary service. This will ensure that these services will be available not only to probation or parole clients, but also to other individuals within the community who might require them.[4]

---

**Box 11.1**

### Static versus Dynamic Risk Predictors

Static risk predictors refer to those factors or characteristics of an offender that cannot change. An example would be criminal history. The number of prior arrests, age at first arrest, number of times incarcerated, etc., are good predictors of risk. However, once in place they cannot change. Dynamic risk predictors are those factors or characteristics of an offender that contribute to their risk, but are changeable. For example, peer associations, substance abuse, criminal thinking, lack of employment, etc. These factors also help predict reoffending, and provide the probation or parole officer with areas to target.

---

The essential tasks of the brokerage orientation to probation and parole are the management of available community resources and the use of those services to meet the needs of offenders. There is little emphasis on the quality of the relationship that develops between the officer and the offenders; rather, more emphasis is placed upon the close working relationship between the officer and the staff members of community social service agencies. Counseling and guidance are considered inappropriate activities for the probation and parole officer; no attempt is made to change the behavior of the offender. The primary function of the officer is to assess the concrete needs of each offender and make appropriate referral to existing community services. Should the needed service not be available in the community, it is the responsibility of the officer to encourage the development of that service.

In contrast to the medical model, the brokerage approach is based upon the reintegration model, which emphasizes the needs of correctional clients for specialized services that can best be provided by established community agencies. As a rehabilitation device, brokerage replaces the casework approach. The brokerage task requires the assessment of client needs and the linkage of available community services with those needs.

Obviously, a pure brokerage approach has its drawbacks. Besides the lack of a strong relationship between the probation or parole officer and the offender, community services may not be readily available. This is often the case in more rural communities, and even if these service agencies are available, they may not be willing to accept an offender population. As a rule, there appear to be more offenders in need of specialized treatment than there is program space available. Cutbacks in government funding has also resulted in fewer programs, which raises the question: "How can a probation or parole officer be a broker if the services are not available?"

This discussion of casework and brokerage—the major orientations for probation and parole supervision and service provision—has highlighted the essential tasks of each approach and has emphasized their differences. Another major issue in supervision is one of form.

## Case Management Classification Systems

As mentioned previously, case classification screening devices have become an integral part of probation and parole agencies. While the use of classification and prediction model in probation and parole is not a new development (Kratcoski, 1985), they have become more popular (Clear & Gallagher, 1985; Clear, 1988). In the case of parole, case screening is usually done by the parole board.[5] Given the widespread use of some form of guidelines, or prediction devices, the parole officer usually has a very good idea of the type of case he or she is receiving. With probation, much of this information is gathered with the PSI report, or during the first visit between the probation officer and the offender. Perhaps the best way to explain the concept of case management classification is to recognize that each case needs to be supervised. Some offenders pose a greater risk[6] to the community (Champion, 1994) or have more needs, whether they be emotional, physical, or mental. Some offenders accept, indeed even welcome, the added support and help, others do not, and may be resistant or hostile to supervision. It will help the probation officer to have this information before supervision actually begins. Not only can they develop a more tailored supervision plan, but they can also begin to identify the special services or programs that might be of assistance to this offender.

## The Evolution of Classification

For our purposes, risk refers to the probability that an offender will reoffend. Thus, high-risk offenders have a greater probability of reoffending than do low-risk offenders. How is offender risk determined? This is obviously a very important question, since it can affect public protection, and the way and manner in which an offender is supervised (or whether they are even released) in the community.

The prehistory of risk assessment in criminal justice refers to the use of "gut feelings" to make decisions about the risk of an offender. With this process, information is collected about the offender, usually through an interview or file review. The information is then reviewed and a general assessment or global prediction is made: "In my professional opinion. . . ." The problems with this approach are considerable, and have been delineated by Wong (1997) and Kennedy (1998):

- Predictions are subject to personal bias;
- Predictions are subjective and often unsubstantiated;
- Decision rules are not observed;
- Can lead to bias decisions;
- It is difficult to distinguish levels of risk; and
- Information is overlooked or overemphasized.

The first generation of formal classification instruments was pioneered by Bruce, Harno, Burgess, and Landesco in 1928. The development of a standardized and objective instrument was brought about by the request of the Illinois Parole Board, which wanted to make more informed decisions about who to release on parole. Bruce and his colleagues reviewed the records of nearly 6,000 inmates. Table 11.2 illustrates the factors found by Bruce et al. (1928) in their risk prediction instrument. While many of these categories seem out-of-date today, the Burgess scale was one of the first attempts to develop an actuarial instrument to predict offender risk. There are several pros and cons to this approach (Wong, 1997; Kennedy, 1998):

Pros—
- Objective and accountable
- Covers important historic risk factors
- Easy to use, and reliable
- Distinguishes levels of risk of reoffending

Cons—
- Consists primarily of static predictors
- Does not identify target behaviors
- Not capable of measuring change in the offender

Table 11.2
**Factors in the Bruce, Harno, Burgess, and Landesco Scale**

General Type of Offense (e.g., fraud, robbery, sex, homicide)
Parental & Marital Status (parents living, offender married)
Criminal Type (first timer, occasional, habitual, professional)
Social Type (e.g., farm boy, gangster, hobo, ne'er-do-well, drunkard)
Community Factor (where resided)
Statement of Trial Judge and Prosecutor (recommended or protests leniency)
Previous Record
Work Record (e.g., no work record, casual, regular work)
Punishment Record in Prison
Months Served Prior to Parole
Intelligence Rating
Age when Paroled
Psychiatric Prognosis
Psychiatric Personality Type (egocentric, socially inadequate, emotionally unstable)

Source: A.A. Bruce, A.J. Harno, E.W. Burgess, and J. Landesco (1928). *The Workings of the Indeterminate-Sentence Law and the Parole System in Illinois.* State of Illinois.

The second generation of risk prediction recognized that risk is more than simply static predictors. The best example can be seen in the Wisconsin Case Management Classification System. First developed and used in Wisconsin in 1975, the Client Management Classification System (CMC) is designed to help identify the level of surveillance for each case, as well as determine the needs of the offender and the resources necessary to meet them. With adequate classification, limited resources can be concentrated on the most critical cases—those of high risk (Wright, Clear & Dickson, 1984). Following Wisconsin's development of the CMC, the National Institute of Corrections (NIC, 1983) adopted it as a model system and began advocating and supporting its use throughout the country. It has been proven satisfactory in many jurisdictions, including Austin, Texas (Harris, 1994).

The foundation of the system is a risk/needs assessment instrument that is completed on each probationer at regular intervals. Cases are classified into high, medium, or low risk/needs. In turn, these ratings are used to determined the level of supervision required for each case. Tables 11.3 and 11.4 illustrates the Wisconsin risk and needs assessment components of this system.

Once an offender is classified into a risk/needs level, a more detailed assessment of that case can be made with a profiling interview that helps to determine the relationship between the officer and the offender. This element of the system is called the Client Management Classification System, and is comprised of four unique treatment modalities:

- **Selective Intervention.** This group is designed for offenders who enjoy relatively stable and prosocial lifestyles (e.g., employed, established in community, and minimal criminal records). Such offenders have typically experienced an isolated and stressful event or neurotic problem. With effective intervention, there is a higher chance of avoiding future difficulty. The goals of treatment for these individuals include the development of appropriate responses to temporary crises and problems, and the re-establishment of pro-life patterns.

- **Environmental Structure.** The dominant characteristics of offenders in this group consist of deficiencies in social, vocational, and intellectual skills. Most of their problems stem from their inability to succeed in their employment or to be comfortable in most social settings, an overall lack of social skills and intellectual cultivation/ability. The goals for these persons include: (a) developing basic employment and social skills; (b) selecting alternatives to association with criminally oriented peers; and (c) improving social skills and impulse controls.

- **Casework/Control.** These offenders manifest instabilities in their lives as evidenced by failures in employment and domestic problems. A lack of goal-directedness is present, typically associated with alcohol and drug problems. Offense patterns include numerous arrests, although marketable job skills are present. Unstable childhoods, family pressure, and financial difficulties are typically present. The goals appropriate for this group include promoting stability in their professional and domestic endeavors, and achieving an improved utilization of the individual's potential along with an elimination of self-defeating behavior and emotional/psychological problems.

- **Limit Setting.** Offenders in this group are commonly considered to be successful and career criminals because of their long-term involvement in criminal activities. They

Table 11.3
**Risk Assessment**

File _____ of _____

CLIENT NAME _____    CASE NUMBER _____
                Last                First        MI
OFFICER _____    UNIT LOCATION _____
                Last                Social Security Number

DATE

**ARRESTED WITHIN (5) YEARS PRIOR TO ARREST FOR CURRENT OFFENSES**
**(exclude traffic):**

**0** No            **4** Yes

**NUMBER OF PRIOR ADULT INCARCERATIONS IN A STATE OR FEDERAL INSTITUTION:**

**0** No            **3** 1 - 2            **6** 3 and above

**NUMBER OF PRIOR ADULT PROBATION/PAROLE SUPERVISIONS**

**0** None          **4** One or more

**NUMBER OF PRIOR PROBATION/PAROLE REVOCATIONS RESULTING IN IMPRISONMENT**
**(Adult or Juvenile):**

**0** None          **4** One or more

**AMOUNT OF TIME EMPLOYED IN LAST 12 MONTHS:**

**0** More than 7 months    **1** 5 to 7 months    **2** Less than 5 months    **0** Not applicable

**NUMBER OF PRIOR FELONY CONVICTIONS (or Juvenile Adjudications):**

**0** None          **2** One            **4** Two or more

**0** None          **3** One            **6** Two or more            **7** Three or more

**AGE AT ARREST LEADING TO FIRST FELONY CONVICTION (or Juvenile Adjudication):**

**0** 24 and over    **2** 20 - 23        **4** 19 and under

**AGE AT ADMISSION TO INSTITUTION OR PROBATION FOR CURRENT OFFENSE:**

**0** 30 and over    **3** 18 - 29        **6** 17 and under

**0** 30 and over    **4** 18 - 29        **7** 17 and under

## RATE THE FOLLOWING BASED ON PERIOD SINCE LAST RE-ASSESSMENT

**ALCOHOL USAGE PROBLEMS**

**0** No interference with functioning    **2** Occasional abuse; some disruption of functioning    **4** Frequent abuse; serious disruption; needs treatment

**0** No interference with functioning    **2** Occasional abuse; some disruption of functioning    **3** Frequent abuse; serious disruption; needs treatment

**OTHER DRUG USAGE PROBLEMS**

**0** No interference with functioning    **2** Occasional abuse; some disruption of functioning    **4** Frequent abuse; serious disruption; needs treatment

**0** No interference with functioning    **1** Occasional abuse; some disruption of functioning    **2** Frequent abuse; serious disruption; needs treatment

**ASSOCIATIONS**

**0** Mainly with non-criminally oriented individuals    **5** Mainly with negative individuals

**TYPE OF ARRESTS (indicate most serious, excluding traffic)**

**0** None          **2** Technical PV only    **4** Misdemeanor arrest(s)    **8** Felony arrest

**ATTITUDE**

**0** No adverse difficulties/ motivated to change    **2** Periodic difficulties/ uncooperative/dependent    **5** Frequent hostile/negative criminal orientation

**Scale:** Max—17 and above
        Med—9-16
        Min—8 and below

**TOTAL**

Table 11.4
**Assessment of Client Needs**

File _____ of _____

CLIENT NAME _____     CASE NUMBER _____
　　　　　　　 Last　　　　　　　　First　　　MI

OFFICER _____     UNIT LOCATION _____
　　　　　 Last　　　　　　　Social Security Number

DATE [ ][ ][ ][ ][ ]

**EMOTIONAL AND MENTAL STABILITY**
**0** No symptoms of emotional and/or mental instability
**2** Symptoms limit but do not prohibit adequate functioning
**3** Symptoms prohibit adequate functioning and/or has Court or Board imposed condition
**8** Severe symptoms requiring continual attention and/or explosive, threatening and potentially dangerous to others and self

[ ][ ][ ][ ][ ]

**DOMESTIC RELATIONSHIP**
**0** Stable/supportive relationship
**3** Some disorganization or stress but potential for improvement
**7** Major disorganization or stress

[ ][ ][ ][ ][ ]

**ASSOCIATIONS**
**0** No adverse relationships
**2** Associations with occasional negative results
**4** Associations frequently negative
**6** Associations completely negative

[ ][ ][ ][ ][ ]

**DRUG ABUSE**
**0** No disruption of functioning
**2** Occasional substance abuse; some disruption of functioning and/or has Court or Board conditions
**7** Frequent abuse; serious disruptions; needs treatment

[ ][ ][ ][ ][ ]

**ALCOHOL USAGE**
**0** No disruption of functioning
**2** Occasional abuse; some disruption of functioning and/or has Court or Board conditions
**7** Frequent abuse; serious disruptions; needs treatment

[ ][ ][ ][ ][ ]

**EMPLOYMENT**
**0** Satisfactory employment, no difficulties reported; or homemaker, student, retired, or disabled
**2** Underemployed
**4** Unsatisfactory employment; or unemployed but has adequate job skills/motivation
**5** Unemployed and virtually unemployable; needs motivation/training

[ ][ ][ ][ ][ ]

**ACADEMIC/VOCATIONAL SKILLS/TRAINING**
**0** Adequate skills, able to handle everyday requirements
**2** Low skill level causing minor adjustment problems
**6** No identifiable skills and/or minimal skill level causing serious adjustment problems

[ ][ ][ ][ ][ ]

**FINANCIAL MANAGEMENT**
**0** No current difficulties
**1** Situational or minor difficulties
**5** Chronic/severe difficulties

[ ][ ][ ][ ][ ]

**ATTITUDES**
**0** No adverse difficulties/ motivated for change
**2** Periodic difficulties/ uncooperative/dependent
**4** Frequently hostile/negative/ criminal orientation

[ ][ ][ ][ ][ ]

**RESIDENCE**
**0** Suitable living arrangement
**2** Adequate living, i.e., temporary shelter
**4** Nomadic and/or unacceptable

[ ][ ][ ][ ][ ]

**MENTAL ABILITY (INTELLIGENCE)**
**0** Able to function independently
**1** Some need for assistance; potential for adequate adjustment
**3** Deficiencies severely limit independent functioning

[ ][ ][ ][ ][ ]

**HEALTH**
**0** Sound physical health; seldom ill
**1** Handicap or illness; interferes with functioning on a recurring basis
**2** Serious handicap or chronic illness; needs frequent medical care

[ ][ ][ ][ ][ ]

**SEXUAL BEHAVIOR**
**0** No apparent dysfunction
**2** Real or perceived situations or minor problems
**6** Real or perceived chronic or severe problems

[ ][ ][ ][ ][ ]

**OFFICER'S IMPRESSION OF NEEDS**
**0** Low
**3** Medium
**5** Maximum

[ ][ ][ ][ ][ ]

**Scale:** Max—26 and above
　　　　Med—13-25
　　　　Min—12 and below

**TOTAL** [ ][ ][ ][ ][ ]

generally enjoy "beating the system," they frequently act for material gain, and they show little remorse or guilt. Because of their value system, they easily adapt to prison environments and return to crime upon release. Goals for this group are problematic, but include changing the offender's basic attitudes and closely supervising his behavior within the community.

The information for the CMC is based on a structured interview with the offender. After a case has been classified, an individual treatment plan is developed. Results from the CMC have found that approximately 40 percent of probation caseloads are Selective Intervention, 15 percent are Environmental Structure, 30 percent are Casework Control, and 15 percent are Limit Setting.

Despite the advantages of the CMC, there are several shortcomings. One is that fact that risk and needs are separately assessed and not fully integrated. Another problem with this system is that the CMC component is time consuming to administer and the scoring is somewhat involved. In practice, many probation departments that use this instrument rely more heavily on the risk component, which is comprised of mainly static predictors.

---

Box 11.2

### Actuarial versus Clinical Prediction

Actuarial or statistical prediction involves examining a group of offenders and identifying the factors associated with recidivism (or some other measure of outcome). With statistical prediction, offenders with a certain set of characteristics have a range of probabilities associated with success or failure. So for example, if we have 100 high-risk offenders, and our classification instrument indicated that the probability of failure for high-risk offenders is 75 percent, we are relatively confident that 75 out of 100 of those offenders will recidivate (assuming no intervention). Of course, we are predicting to the group and not the individual, so we do not know which 75 will fail. With clinical prediction, a trained professional gathers information and then uses his or her professional experience and judgment to render an opinion about the likelihood that an individual will fail or succeed. The evidence is very strong that actuarial or statistical prediction is more accurate than clinical prediction.

The latest generation of classification instruments have successfully combined risk and needs, and are relatively easy to use. One example is the Level of Service Inventory-Revised (LSI-R) designed by Andrews and Bonta (1995). The LSI-R is based on a social learning theory, and has been extensively tested and validated across North America. Figure 11.3 shows recidivism results from 956 male inmates whose risk was assessed using the LSI-R. The LSI-R consists of 58 items in eight areas. Information is collected primarily through a structured interview process. A sample of some of the LSI-R categories is in Table 11.5. There is also a juvenile version called the Youthful-Level of Service Inventory (Hoge & Andrews, 1996).

Figure 11.3
**The Level of Service Inventory—Revised and Recidivism**

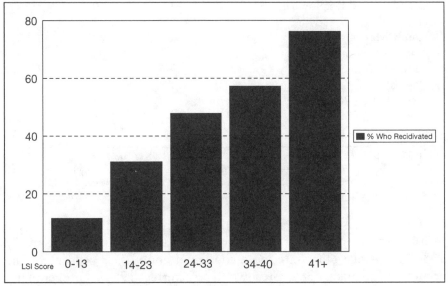

Source: J. Bonta (1993). *A Summary of Research Findings on the LSI.*

There are also classification systems designed to identify certain types of offenders, such as the mentally disordered, or to classify and recommend levels of intervention. One example of the latter is the Offender Profile Index developed by the National Association of State Alcohol and Drug Abuse Directors (Inciardi, McBride & Weinman, 1993). The OPI is a broad classification instrument appropriate for determining which type of drug abuse treatment intervention is most appropriate. Five profiles are produced by the OPI:

- Long-term residential treatment;
- Short-term residential treatment;
- Intensive outpatient treatment;

- Regular outpatient;

- Urine monitoring only.

The OPI is not designed to replace more comprehensive and clinically oriented treatment plans and case studies. However, for probation and parole agencies with large numbers of cases, the OPI can be a valuable tool in case management and appropriate treatment referral.

Table 11.5
**Areas of the Level of Service Inventory-Revised**

| Area | Number of Items in Area |
|------|-------------------------|
| Criminal History | 10 |
| Education and Employment | 10 |
| Financial | 2 |
| Family/Marital | 4 |
| Accommodation | 3 |
| Leisure and Recreation | 2 |
| Companions | 5 |
| Alcohol/Drug Programs | 9 |
| Emotional and Personal | 5 |
| Attitudes and Orientations | 4 |

Copyright © 1995, Multi-Health Systems Inc., 908 Niagara Falls Blvd., North Tonawanda, NY 14120-2060; (800) 456-3003. Reproduced by permission. (The LSI-R is a quantitative survey of attributes of offenders and their situations. The LSI is composed of 54 items. Items are scored in either a "yes-no" format, or in a "0-3" rating format.)

Offender classification is not without its critics. Some argue that the instruments are nothing more than "educated guesses" (Smykla, 1986:127), while others are more concerned about their proper use and accuracy (Wilbanks, 1985; Greenwood & Zimring, 1985). Another major concern centers around the use of a risk instrument in one jurisdiction that has been developed and validated in another. Just because a risk instrument is accurate in one jurisdiction does not necessarily mean it will be effective in predicting outcome in another (Collins, 1990; Kratcoski, 1985; Wright, Clear & Dickson, 1984; Sigler & Williams, 1994). As Travis has stated, "Ideally, a risk classification device should be constructed based on the population on which it is to be used" (Travis, 1989).

Clear (1988:2) maintains that the implementation of these prediction instruments have two main advantages:

> First, they improve the reliability of decisions made about offenders—in a sense they make correctional officials more predictable. Second, they provide a basis on which corrections personnel can publicly justify both individual decisions and decision-making policies. In both cases, the advantage is grounded in the powerful appearance of 'scientific' decision-making.

There are a number of reasons that classification and assessment of offenders is important:

- Guides and helps structure decisionmaking;

- Reduces bias;

- Improves the placement of offenders for treatment and public safety;

- Helps manage offenders in a more effective manner;

- Aids in legal challenges; and

- Helps better utilize resources.

## Principles of Offender Classification

Andrews, Bonta, and Hoge (1990:20) have identified four principles of effective classification:

- **Risk**—Predicting future criminal behavior, and matching levels of treatment/services to the risk level of the offender;

- **Need**—Matching offenders to programs that address their criminogenic needs;

- **Responsivity**—Delivering intervention in a style and mode that is consistent with the ability and learning style of the offender, and recognizing that individuals may be more responsive to certain staff; and

- **Professional Discretion**—Having considered risk, need, and responsivity, decisions are made as appropriate under present conditions.

Through the work of a number of researchers, our understanding of classification and assessment, and the important role it plays in community corrections is becoming more apparent (Andrews, 1983 & 1989; Bonta & Montiuk, 1985; Gendreau, Goggin & Little, 1996; Jones, 1996; Kennedy & Serin, 1997).

Despite these concerns, the latest generation of classification instruments allow the probation or parole department an effective and fairly simple means of classifying and managing offenders. It is important to remember that instruments such as the CMC or LSI-R can be important and useful tools in assisting the community correctional agency and the supervising officer in case management. They will not solve all the problems faced by probation and parole agencies, nor will they fully replace the sound judgment and experience of well-trained probation and parole officers (Schumacher, 1985; Klein, 1989).

> **Box 11.3**
>
> ### Criminogenic Needs and Promising Targets
>
> Criminogenic needs refers to those crime producing factors associated with criminal behavior. The new generation of risk assessment tools measures these needs. Some of the promising need factors which should be identified by researchers include the following:
>
> Changing antisocial attitudes
> Changing antisocial feelings
> Reducing antisocial peer associations
> Promoting familial affection and communication
> Promoting familial monitoring and supervision
> Increasing self-control and problem-solving skills
> Reducing chemical dependencies

## Standards of Classification

Travis and Latessa (1996) have identified 10 elements of effective classification and assessment. They include:

- **Purposeful.** Generally, the purpose of classification and assessment is to insure offenders are treated differentially within a system so as to insure safety, adequate treatment, and understanding.

- **Organizational Fit.** Organizations and agencies have different characteristics, capabilities, and needs.

- **Accuracy.** How well does the instrument correctly assess outcome? Is the offender correctly placed within the system? Basically, reliability and validity are the key elements to accuracy. Glick, Sturgeon, and Venator-Santiago (1998:73) explain reliability and validity thus: Reliability may be defined as hitting the same spot on a bull's eye all the time. If your system is reliable but not valid, you may be hitting the target consistently, but not the right spot.

- **Parsimony.** This refers to the ease of use, the economy of composition, and achieving accuracy with the least number of factors. In other words, short and simple.

- **Distribution.** How well does the system disperse cases across classification groups? If all offenders fall into the same group, there is little distribution.

- **Dynamism.** Is the instrument measuring dynamic risk factors that are amenable to change? Dynamic factors also allow you to measure progress and change in the offender. It also facilitates reclassification.

- **Utility.** To be effective, classification systems must be useful. This means that the staff achieve the purposes of classification and the goals of the agency.

- **Practicality.** Closely related to utility is the practical aspect of classification. The system must be practical and possible to implement. A process that is 100 percent accurate but impossible to apply in an agency does not help that agency. Similarly, a system that is easy to use, but does not lead to better decisions is of no value.

- **Justice.** An effective classification and assessment process should produce just outcomes. Offender placement and service provision should be based upon offender differences that are real and measurable, and yield consistent outcomes, regardless of subjective impressions.

- **Sensitivity.** This is really a goal of the classification process. If all elements are met, the most effective classification and assessment process is sensitive to the differences of offenders. At the highest level, this would mean individualizing case planning.

---

**Box 11.4**

### Responsivity Factors

Recognizing differences in offenders that effect their engagement in treatment and their ability to learn is part of assessing responsivity. Some responsivity considerations include:

  Level of psychological development
  Motivation and readiness to change
  Anxiety/Psychopathy
  Social support for services
  Mental disorders
  Age
  Ethnicity/race
  Gender
  Intelligence

## Contracting for Services

As indicated in Chapter 11, recent events have called for a change in the role of the probation and parole officer. In addition to the increased demands of the surveillance aspect of supervision, other changes in this field have been geared toward enhancing the social service aspect of the probation or parole officer's role. The use of various types of contracts is one example of this development.

Contracts for a wide variety of client and administrative activities are particular to the unique responsibilities of community corrections (Jensen et al., 1987). These include:

- Residential programs (including halfway houses, house arrest, restitution centers and facilities for juveniles, such as group or foster homes).

- Counseling and treatment programs for both general client groups and targeted offenders such as drug addicts and alcoholics.

- Administrative services for data processing, recordkeeping, evaluations, and so forth.

- Programs for victims of crime and crisis intervention. These would include traditional counseling services as well as programs designed to aid victims as they struggle with the criminal justice system and to help them file for victim compensation.

- Programs that conduct private pre-sentence investigation and develop sentencing alternatives for offenders.

- Dispute resolution, mediation programs, and pretrial services.

- Testing, ranging from employment/educational to urinalysis for drug or alcohol abuse. Data on the number of probationers and parolees drug tested in 1996) are found in Figure 11.4.

Recently, stricter punishment policies have brought offenders that are "new" to the criminal justice system, such as drunk drivers, spouse abusers, and persons who fail to pay child support. Crowded jail facilities cannot handle these offender categories and it is unlikely that they will find room for such offenders in the future. As a result, many jurisdictions have turned to private providers to handle these "specialized" groups. For example, in Ohio, anyone convicted of drunk driving must serve three days of incarceration. Many local jails cannot handle the number of new offenders. In order to deal with this problem, Hamilton County, the county in which Cincinnati, Ohio is located, contracted with a local private multi-service community-based agency called Talbert House to run a drunk drivers' intervention program. This program allows convicted drunk drivers to spend a weekend in a program that emphasizes education. The program is also cost effective because it requires participants to pay a fee.

Figure 11.4
**Probationers and Parolees Drug Tested in 1996**

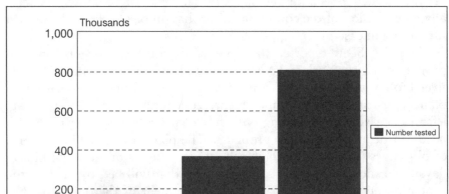

Source: C. Camp and G. Camp (1997). *The Corrections Yearbook 1997*. South Salem, NY: The Criminal Justice Institute, Inc.

Contracting can be an effective way to provide services. For example, many probation and parole agencies contract with local halfway houses for beds. It is much more cost-effective to "lease" the bed space than to build and operate a halfway house. Contracting also gives the agency the flexibility of being able to terminate the contract if the service fails to meet expectations or is no longer needed.

Many of these programs represent an attempt to treat some offenders in a nontraditional fashion and provide close ties between them and community programs. Such innovations can, when used with a particular type of client (such as mentally disordered offenders or drunk drivers), help offenders and relieve the burden of heavy caseloads upon a probation department. Their use could also permit a probation department to deploy its resources in a more efficient manner.

## Contracting with the Client

Another type of contract directly focuses upon the offender and the agency in an attempt to fully spell out the obligations of each party during the supervision period. As defined by Ankersmit (1976:28), setting the contract simply means reaching an agreement with the offender as to what goals he or she will work toward achieving. The basic idea is to use this device as a central point in the planning process, specifically including the probationer in this process. The contract, in this case, is between the supervising officer and the offender. The offender might agree to seek employment, pay child support, and study for a GED. The supervising officer agrees to help the offender meet his or her goals and to provide needed assistance and support. This type of "contract" is actually an extension of the conditions of probation or parole, and can be a useful tool in case planning.

In 1978, Scott reported that the use of contract categories helped programs in New York and Michigan. In New York, the Mutual Objectives Probation Programming specifically identified the clients' program plans in such areas as employment, education, vocational training, leisure-time activities, dealing with financial problems, meeting health needs, or dealing with other problems. The plans are stated in the form of objectives (i.e., enroll in high school equivalency program within 30 days), and the agreement specifies the help that will be provided by the probation department to assist in the attainment of the objective. The New York contract also indicated the anticipated date of probation termination, which may have provided additional incentive. Scott reported (1978:57) that evaluations of this program revealed that it was associated with the decreased use of the local county jails, decreased commitments to state prison, and shorter periods of probation supervision.

In Michigan, the Mutual Objectives Program focuses upon the establishment of contracts that closely resemble traditional special conditions of probation. Terms often outlined payment of fines, court costs, or restitution; education and vocational training; extra reporting agreements; or participation in drug, alcohol, or psychiatric treatment programs. Scott also reported preliminary evaluative evidence that the Michigan program contributed to reduced commitment rates to state prisons.

Scott clearly outlines some additional advantages, as well as disadvantages, associated with probation contracting. First, the probationer is intimately involved in supervision planning from the very beginning of this process. As a result, the sentencing judge is provided with additional information on program plans and on the motivations of the offender. Probationers have clear specifications of what is expected of them, including the possibility of early termination. In addition, the probation officer is provided with clearly specified objectives for supervision, and has a better idea of how to proceed with supervision plans. The hope is that contractual programming will result in a more efficient approach to probation management.

In short, it appears that contracting offers an opportunity to establish a system that strengthens and goes beyond the traditional standard special conditions of supervision. It can provide several benefits to both the offender and the department, and can lead to the efficient management of community services.

Box 11.5

### Motivation to Change

Some of the latest work in the area of responsivity involves the measurement of an offender's motivation or readiness to change by Prochaska and DiClemente (1986). Four stages of change have been identified: precontemplation, contemplation, action, and maintenance. In the precontemplation stage, the individual is not even considering the possibility of change. The contemplation stage is characterized by ambivalence, while in the action stage the offender has made a commitment to change and is engaging in actions to bring it about. Finally, individuals in the maintenance stage are working to sustain the changes they have made and are actively working to prevent relapse.

## Supervision Planning

Regardless of the approach used by an agency to deliver service, an essential ingredient to successful supervision is planning (Ellsworth, 1988). This includes the identification of the needs and problems of the offender, identifying the resources available and arranging for them, and evaluating the effectiveness of the supervision activities. The probation and parole populations under supervision today are different than those supervised 20 years ago. Not only are we seeing higher-risk offenders on probation due to prison and jail crowding, but the offender population is growing older (McCarthy & Langworthy, 1987; Burnett & Kitchen, 1989). With these changes comes a need to improve our planning of the actual supervision task.

## Federal Supervision Planning Example

Perhaps the best example of supervision planning comes from the federal probation system,[7] and is part of its overall classification process. This process involves the establishment of an appropriate supervision level, defined as either high or low activity. Introduced in 1981, the Classification and Supervision Planning System determines the degree of risk of recidivism in an individual case and establishes an appropriate level of supervision activity.

The first step in this system is the classification of the offender into a supervision level. Two actuarial devices are used in the system—the risk prediction scale (which follows in this chapter), for persons on probation, and the salient factor score (see Chapter 9), for persons on parole. Here we will focus on the scale for probationers.

Using the risk scale in Table 11.6, the probation officer determines the level of supervision from a choice of two: low activity and high activity.

Table 11.6
**Risk Prediction Scale**

Automatic Component: Automatically places an individual in low-activity supervision if two conditions are satisfied.

  A.  Offender has a 12th-grade education or better; and

  B.  The individual has a history free of opiate usage.

If the two conditions are not met, the remaining items are scored.

  C.  Twenty-eight years of age, or older, at time of offense (7 points)
       If not, score as 0.

  D.  Arrest-free period of five or more consecutive years (4 points)
       If not, score as 0.

  E.  Few prior arrests (none, one, or two=10 points)
       If not, score as 0.

  F.  History free of opiate usage (9 points)
       If not, score as 0.

  G.  At least four months of steady employment immediately prior to arraignment for present offense (3 points)
       If not, score as 0.

| Risk Score | Minimum Supervisor Level | Maximum Personal Contacts | Collateral Contacts | Contacts |
|---|---|---|---|---|
| Automatic Assignment or 20-33 | Low Activity | 1 per quarter | 1 per quarter | Unlimited |
| 0-19 | High Activity | 1 per month | No maximum | Unlimited |

Source: Adopted from the Classification and Supervision Planning System (January, 1981). Washington, DC: Probation Division, Administrative Office, U.S. Courts.

Persons in the low-activity supervision level, as reflected in their histories, have usually experienced relative success in establishing personal stability. This level is analogous to minimum supervision where sustained control is seldom necessary. Persons in the high-activity supervision level usually experienced difficulty in establishing and maintaining personal stability. Probation officers direct the greater proportion of their efforts toward persons in the high-activity supervision level. The federal system sets no upper limit on the number of contacts given a person in a month's time; however, a minimum of once a month is required.

With the approval of a supervisor, a probation officer may override the prediction supervision level from low activity to high activity. There are three conditions that justify and override:

I.  Aggravated Offense Circumstances
    A.  Violence
        1.  present offense or prior record involving violence
        2.  use of weapons in the commission of crime
    B.  Notoriety of offense
        1.  violation of trust by high-ranking public official
        2.  value of crime greater than $50,000
        3.  endangering national security
    C.  Continuing criminal conspiracy
        1.  wholesale drug distributor
        2.  member of organized crime
        3.  major corporate offender

II.  Special Conditions
    A.  Court or parole commission ordered special supervision
    B.  Drug aftercare program ordered

III.  Exceptional Case Circumstances

    (Exceptional case circumstances are significant social problems characterized by aggravated personal distress that, if left unresolved, would likely subject the community or offender to harm) [Classification and Supervision Planning System, 1981:6].

The classification process is concluded with the establishment of an appropriate level of supervision activity.

The next step in this process involves the development of a supervision plan that identifies significant problems and the methods to be used in resolving these problem areas.

As with all good supervision planning, a critical element is the participation of the offender, since behavior changes only after there are perceived advantages to changing old behavior patterns (Classification and Supervision Planning System, 1981:8).

The three basic interrelated components of the federal system are:

- Identifying supervision problems;

- Setting objectives; and

- Developing the supervision plan.

Supervision problems can be defined as those circumstances that limit the offender's ability or desire to function within the requirements of probation and parole, and which the supervising officer anticipates are directly linked to supervision outcome. An example of a supervision problem from the federal probation system (1981:9) is outlined in Table 11.7.

Table 11.7
**Supervision Problem: An Example**

| Supervision Problems | |
|---|---|
| Health: | This offender has a documented history of heroin addiction dating back 7 years and has two previous convictions for selling drugs to support a $100-a-day habit. |
| Family: | Recently separated from his wife and two children but would like to be reunited with them. Several reports of wife abuse have been recorded. |
| Employment: | Unemployed—occasional construction laborer. |

For each supervision problem, a corresponding supervision objective is developed.

**Supervision Objectives**

Assist offender to locate and maintain employment. Abstain from drug use, stabilize marital relationship.

After problems and objectives have been identified, the supervising officer formulates a plan for achieving those objectives. The methods selected are based on such considerations as the nature of the problem, the abilities and expertise of the officer, the availability of effective community resources, the attitude of the offender, and the exercise of authority necessary to insure the offender's participation.

The federal classification system requires that the plan specify whether a referral will be made to community resources, or whether the officer will be the primary provider of services. If community resources were used, the officer must indicate how he or she intends to complement the work of that agency. The federal probation system does not allow an officer to delegate total responsibility for supervision of an offender to any other agency.

A well thought-out initial supervision plan is the cornerstone of supervision activities. The plan need not be lengthy, but it should specify actions to be taken by the supervising officer, the responsibilities of the offender, and the role of any community resources. Time frames for achieving the supervision objectives should be stated whenever it is reasonable to do so. Several examples of supervision plans from the Federal Classification and Supervision Planning System (1981:22) are as follows:

EXAMPLE 1:

Supervision Plan

Although there are no significant supervision problems which can be clearly identified at the time, we do want to determine if Mr. Edwards has a problem with compulsive gambling. Monthly personal contacts will be addressed to that end. Additionally, until we better understand his financial circumstances, monthly collateral contact will be made at his home and with relevant police officials.

EXAMPLE 2:

Supervision Plan

Mr. Harris has a record of several minor convictions for drunk driving (3), and assault and battery (2), where the complainant was his wife. Although denied by Harris, alcohol abuse may be a significant underlying problem. Semi-monthly personal contact will explore the alcohol issue through direct confrontation and observation with Harris and interaction with the family. A referral to Alcoholics Anonymous may become necessary. The relationship of alcohol abuse to poor work performance and/or attendance will be explored with his employer, who is aware of Mr. Harris' probation status.

The payment of the court-imposed fine of $2,000 may present a problem since considerable liabilities and pressing debts exist. This will be discussed in the next office visit.

EXAMPLE 3:

Supervision Plan

Although a low-activity case, Mrs. Walters has a number of problems, most of which are economic in nature, including dependency on welfare, four residential moves in the past fourteen months, and two children experiencing school problems.

We have contacted the New Start Community Agency (637-2345), a United Way funded agency in her community. They are familiar with the family circumstances and are willing to assign a counselor to work with her and the family. We will discuss a referral to New Start and with Mrs. Walters. The focus of this agency is to teach her a skill with the ultimate goal to enter her in the labor force, rendering welfare unnecessary. Two personal contacts will be made per quarter to encourage her involvement with New Start. Collateral contacts with the agency will be made as necessary.

In addition to the supervision plan, the Federal Probation Division requires semiannual case reviews. This review includes an evaluation of the dynamics of the offender's supervision problems as they have emerged in the previous six months. The review highlights the degree of progress achieved in meeting precisely established objectives and specifies the number and type of contacts during the period under review. Finally, the officer identifies new problems and revises the supervision plan to meet the current situation.

Undoubtedly, supervision planning varies from agency to agency, and often from officer to officer; however, the Federal Supervision Planning System presented above represents one model in caseload management. Regardless of the process of the format, there are common elements involved in supervision planning: recognizing problems, selecting objectives, developing a strategy, implementing that strategy, and, finally, evaluating the effectiveness of the entire process.

One important resource for the community correctional agency is the use of volunteers. If used properly, these individuals can serve as an important asset for a community correctional agency.

## Use of Volunteers

Community correctional programs operate under a basic philosophy of reintegration: connecting offenders with legitimate opportunity and reward structures, and generally uniting the offender within the community. It has become quite apparent that the correctional system cannot achieve this without assistance, regardless of the extent of resources available. Reintegration requires the assistance and support of the community.

This concept is certainly not a new one. The John Howard Association, the Osborne Association, and other citizen prisoners' aid societies have provided voluntary correctional-type services for many years. The volunteer movement developed in this country in the early 1820s, when a group of citizens known as the Philadelphia Society for Alleviating the Misery of Public Prisons began supervising the activities of inmates upon their release from penal institutions. This practice was later adopted by John Augustus, a Boston shoemaker, who worked with well over 2,000 misdemeanants in his lifetime (see Chapter 5).

Volunteerism is alive and well in corrections.[8] Judge Keith Leenhouts of the Royal Oak (Michigan) Municipal Court resurrected the concept some 20 years ago, and continues to serve as a driving force behind this now relatively accepted, and still growing, movement. In addition to the many local programs in existence, there are several national programs supporting volunteerism, such as VISTO (Volunteers in Service to Offenders), VIP (Volunteers in Probation), and the American Bar

Association-sponsored National Volunteer Aide Program. Although exact numbers are not known, it is safe to say that there are thousands of volunteers serving more than 3,000 jurisdictions nationwide.

Proponents of the volunteer concept consider it to be one of the most promising innovations in the field, claiming that it can help alleviate the problem of excessive probation and parole caseloads, and contribute to rehabilitation and reintegration goals for the offender (Greenberg, 1988; Latessa, Travis & Allen, 1983). A good illustration of the effective use of volunteers can be see in Lucas County (Toledo, Ohio). Here, probationers are screened according to risk. All "low-risk" probationers are assigned to one probation officer who, with the help of volunteers, supervises more than 1,000 clients.

Volunteers can range from student interns to older persons with time to devote. Some volunteers are persons that have a specific skill or talent to contribute, while others give their time and counsel.

## Scope of Services

Volunteerism generally refers to situations where individual citizens contribute their talents, wisdom, skills, time, and resources within the context of the justice system, without receiving financial remuneration. Volunteer projects operate on the premise that certain types of offenders can be helped by the services a volunteer can offer, and that such services can be provided at a minimal tax dollar cost and can result in significant cost savings.

By drawing upon the time, talents, and abilities of volunteers to assist in service delivery, community supervision officers can serve to broaden the nature of the services offered. Any community consists of persons who possess a diverse supply of skills and abilities that can be effectively tapped by volunteer programs. The National Center of Volunteers in Courts has reported that some 155 volunteer roles have actually been filled by volunteer persons in different jurisdictions. Scheier (1973) developed a list of more than 200 potential volunteer services including:

| | |
|---|---|
| addiction program volunteer | intake volunteer |
| case aide | newsletter editor |
| clerical courtroom assistance | presentence investigator |
| diagnostic home volunteer | recreation volunteer |
| educational aide | test administrator and scorer |
| foster parent | vocational service aide |
| fund raiser | volunteer counselor |

In addition to the direct service offered, volunteers can supply a number of support services (Lucas, 1987). Volunteers often assist program operations in an administrative capacity. For example, the well-known Royal Oak, Michigan program has been supervised by a full-time volunteer for quite some time. The VISTO program in Los Angeles County (California) has likewise utilized volunteers to fill some of its clerical needs, such as handling supplies, photocopying, answering recruitment correspondence, and routine office contacts, as well as participating in research projects. In addition, many volunteers serve on advisory boards. Many non-profit community agencies, such as halfway houses, rely on volunteers to serve on their boards of directors. There can be little doubt that volunteers can serve as a means of amplifying time, attention, and the type of services given to clients by the system. However, it is also important that an agency not become over-reliant on volunteers, to the extent that they do not hire enough professional officers and staff.

## Summary

This chapter has discussed one of the most important aspects of probation and parole: supervision of the offender. We have noted that assignment of offenders to a probation or parole officer for supervision can follow several models. Some offenders are randomly assigned to caseloads, others are assigned based on geography or special problems, while yet others are classified through the use of prediction devices.

Once assignment is complete, the approach or philosophy of supervision usually centers around casework and brokerage. Casework follows a belief that the supervising officer should be the primary agent of change and thus "all things to all people." The brokerage approach assumes that the best place for treatment is in the community, and that the primary task of the probation or parole officer is to arrange for and manage community resources. While casework is the norm, in reality most probation and parole officers and agencies use techniques for both approaches.

Perhaps due to the prevalence of the casework approach, the tasks of supervision have traditionally been performed by a single officer. This has begun to change, as many agencies begin to recognize the team approach as a viable alternative to the single officer model.

This chapter has also addressed case management classification and supervision planning, and provided examples of the latest attempts to accomplish the many facets of community supervision.

Finally, the use of volunteers is not a new concept. Volunteers play an important role in community corrections.

## Review Questions

1. What are the assumptions of casework? Brokerage?

2. What are the limitations of casework in probation?

3. List three ways that caseloads are assigned.

4. How can risk/needs assessments be used in probation?

5. What are the 10 standards to good classification?

6. What are the four principles of classification?

7. Give an example of a responsivity characteristic?

8. What is the difference between a static and a dynamic predictor?

9. How can volunteers be used in probation?

## Key Terms

actuarial prediction                    numbers game
case management                        responsivity
classification system                   role reversal
contracting                            single-factor assignment
conventional model                     supervision planning

## Recommended Readings

Andrews, D.A. and J. Bonta (1994). *The Psychology of Criminal Conduct.* Cincinnati, OH: Anderson Publishing Co.

Auerbach, B.J. and T.C. Castellano (1998). *Successful Community Sanctions and Services for Special Offenders: Proceedings of the 1994 Conference of the International Community Corrections Association.* Lantham, MD: American Correctional Association.

Dell'Apa, F., W.T. Adams, J.D. Jorgenson, and H.R. Sigurdson (1976). "Advocacy, Brokerage, Community: The ABC's of Probation and Parole." *Federal Probation,* 40(4):37-44.

Harlan, A.T. (1996). *Choosing Correctional Options that Work.* Thousand Oaks, CA: Sage.

Hoge, R.D. and D.A. Andrews (1996). *Assessing the Youthful Offender: Issues and Techniques.* New York, NY: Plenum Press.

Meeker, B. (1948). "Probation is Casework." *Federal Probation*, 12(2):51-52.

Van Voorhis, P. (1994). *Psychological Classification of the Adult Male Prison Inmate.* Albany, NY: State University of New York.

## Notes

[1]    Parole board refers to all agencies (commissions, board of charities, board of prison terms, and so on) whose duty it is to release inmates to the community, under supervision, prior to the expiration of the original sentence length.

[2]    This point is eloquently argued by F.T. Cullen (1994). "Social Support as an Organizing Concept for Criminology." *Justice Quarterly*, 11:527-560.

[3]    For a good example of advocacy in probation and parole, see Frank Dell'Apa et al. (1976). "Advocacy, Brokerage, Community: The ABC's of Probation and Parole." *Federal Probation*, 40:37-44; and Claude T. Mangrum (1975). *The Professional Practitioner in Probation*, pp. 43-44. Springfield, IL: Charles C Thomas.

[4]    For recent discussions of advocacy, see D. Macallair (1994). "Disposition Case Advocacy in San Francisco's Juvenile Justice System: A New Approach to Deinstitutionalization." *Crime & Delinquency*, 40:84-95; D. Macallair (1993). "Reaffirming Rehabilitation in Juvenile Justice." *Youth and Society*, 25:104-125.

[5]    P. Hoffman (1994). "Twenty Years of Operational Use of a Risk Prediction Instrument: The United States Parole Commission's Salient Factor Score." *Journal of Criminal Justice*, 22:447-494. But see J. Proctor (1994). "Evaluating a Modified version of the Federal Prison System's Classification Model: An Assessment of Objectivity and Predictive Validity." *Criminal Justice and Behavior*, 21:256-272.

[6]    Champion, D. (1994). *Measuring Offender Risk: A Criminal Justice Sourcebook.* Westport, CT: Greenwood Press; P. Van Voorhis (1994). *Psychological Classification of the Adult Male Prison Inmate.* Albany, NY: State University of New York Press.

[7]    Much of the material in this section is adopted from Classification and Supervision Planning System (1981) Washington, DC: Probation Division; Administrative Office of the United States Courts.

[8]    American Correctional Association (1993). *Community Partnerships in Action.* Laurel, MD: ACA. See also American Correctional Association (1993). *Standards for Administration of Correctional Agencies.* Laurel, MD: ACA.

# References

American Correctional Association (1993). *Community Partnerships in Action*. Laurel, MD: ACA.

American Correctional Association (1987). *Standards for Administration of Correctional Agencies*. Laurel, MD: ACA.

Andrews, D.A. (1989). "Recidivism is Predictable and Can Be Influenced: Using Risk Assessments to Reduce Recidivism." *Forum on Correctional Research*, 1(2): 11-17

Andrews, D.A. (1983). The Assessment of Outcome in Correctional Samples. In M.K. Lambert, E.R. Christensen, and S.S. DeJulio (eds.) *The Measurement of Psychotherapy Outcome in Research and Evaluation*. New York, NY: Wiley.

Andrews, D.A. and J. Bonta (1995). *LSI-R The Level of Service Inventory—Revised*. Toronto, CN: Multi-Health Systems, Inc.

Andrews, D.A., J. Bonta, and R.D. Hoge (1990). "Classification for Effective Rehabilitation Rediscovering Psychology." *Criminal Justice and Behavior*, 17: 19-52.

Ankersmit, E. (1977). "Setting the Contract in Probation." *Federal Probation*, 41(2):28-33.

Auerbach, B.J. and T.C. Castellano (1998). *Successful Community Sanctions and Services for Special Offenders: Proceedings of the 1994 Conference of the International Community Corrections Association*, Lantham, MD: American Correctional Association.

Bonta, J. (1996). Risk-Needs Assessment and Treatment. In A.T. Harlan, *Choosing Correctional Options that Work: Defining the Demand and Evaluating the Supply*, pp. 33-68. Thousand Oaks, CA: Sage Publications.

Bonta, J. and D.A. Andrews (1993). "The Level of Supervision Inventory: An Overview." *IARCA Journal*, 5(4):6-8.

Bonta, J. and L.L. Motiuk (1985). "Utilization of an Interview-Based Classification Instrument: A Study of Correctional Halfway Houses." *Criminal Justice and Behavior*, 12: 333-352.

Bowers, S. (1950). "The Nature and Definition of Social Casework." In C. Kasius (eds.) *Principles and Techniques in Social Casework*, pp. 126-139. New York, NY: Family Services Association of America.

Bruce, A.A., A.J. Harno, E.W. Burgess, and J. Landesco (1928). *The Workings of the Intermediate-Sentence Law and the Parole System in Illinois*. State of Illinois.

Bureau of Justice Statistics (1997). *Correctional Populations in the United States*. Washington, DC: U.S. Department of Justice.

Burnett, C. and A. Kitchen (1989). "More Than a Case Number: Older Offenders on Probation." *Journal of Offender Counseling, Services and Rehabilitation*, 13:149-160.

Camp, C. and G. Camp 1997). *The Corrections Yearbook 1997*. South Salem, NY: The Criminal Justice Institute.

Carter, R.M. and L.T. Wilkins (1976). "Caseloads: Some Conceptual Models." In R.M. Carter and L.T. Wilkins (eds.) *Probation, Parole and Community Corrections*, pp. 391-401. New York, NY: John Wiley and Sons.

Champion, D. (1994). *Measuring Offender Risk: A Criminal Justice Sourcebook*. Westport, CT: Greenwood Press.

Classification and Supervision Planning System (1981). Washington, DC: Probation Division, Administrative Office, U.S. Courts.

Clear, T.R. (1988). "Statistical Prediction in Corrections." *Research in Corrections*, 1:1-39.

Clear, T.R. and K.W. Gallagher (1985). "Probation and Parole Supervision: A Review of Current Classification Practices." *Crime & Delinquency*, 31:423-444.

Collins, P.M. (1990). "Risk Classification and Assessment in Probation: A Study of Misdemeanants." Unpublished master's thesis, University of Cincinnati, Cincinnati, OH.

Cullen, F.T. (1994). "Social Support as an Organizing Concept for Criminology." *Justice Quarterly*, 11:527-560.

Dell'Apa, F., W.T. Adams, J.D. Jorgensen, and H.R. Sigurdson (1976). "Advocacy, Brokerage, Community: The ABC's of Probation and Parole." *Federal Probation*, 40(4):37-44.

Ellsworth, T. (1988). "Case Supervision Planning: The Forgotten Component of Intensive Probation Supervision," *Federal Probation*, 52(4):28-32.

Gendreau, P., C. Goggin, and T. Little (1996). *Predicting Adult Offender Recidivism: What Works?* Ottawa, CN: Solicitor General Canada.

Glick, B., W. Sturgeon, and C.R. Venator-Santiago (1998). *No Time to Play: Youthful Offenders in Adult Correctional System*. Lantham, MD: American Correctional Association.

Gordon, D.A. and J. Arbuthnot (1988). "The Use of Paraprofessionals to Deliver Home-Based Family Therapy to Juvenile Delinquents." *Criminal Justice and Behavior*, 15:364-378.

Greenberg, N. (1988). "The Discovery Program: A Way to Use Volunteers in the Treatment Process." *Federal Probation*, 52(4):39-45.

Greenwood, P.W. and F.E. Zimring (1985). *One More Chance: The Pursuit of Promising Intervention Strategies for Chronic Juvenile Offenders*. Santa Monica, CA: The Rand Corporation.

Hardman, D.G. (1959). "Authority in Casework: A Bread-and-Butter Theory." *National Probation and Parole Association Journal*, 5:249-255.

Harlan, A.T. (1996). *Choosing Correctional Options that Work*. Thousand Oaks, CA: Sage.

Harris, P. (1994). "Client Management Classification and Prediction of Probation Outcome." *Crime & Delinquency*, 40:154-174.

Hoffman, P. (1994). "Twenty Years of Operational Use of a Risk Prediction Instrument: The United States Parole Commission's Salient Factor Score." *Journal of Criminal Justice*, 22:447-494.

Hoge, R.D. and D.A. Andrews (1996). *Assessing the Youthful Offender: Issues and Techniques*. New York, NY: Plenum Press.

Hoge, R.D. and D.A. Andrews (1996). *The Youthful Level of Service/Case Management Inventory*.

Inciardi, J.A., D.C. McBride, and B.A. Weinman (1993). *The Offender Profile Index: A Users's Guide.* Washington, DC: National Association of State Alcohol and Drug Abuse Directors.

Jensen, C. (1987). *Contracting for Community Corrections Services.* Washington DC: U.S. Department of Justice, National Institute of Corrections.

Jones, P.R. (1996). "Risk Prediction in Criminal Justice." In A.T. Harlan, *Choosing Correctional Options that Work: Defining the Demand and Evaluating the Supply,* pp. 33-68. Thousand Oaks, CA: Sage Publications.

Kennedy, S. (1998). *Effective Interventions with Higher Risk Offenders.* Longmont, CO: National Institute of Corrections.

Kennedy, S. and Serin, R. (1997). "Treatment Responsivity: Contributing to Effective Correctional Programming." *The ICCA Journal on Community Corrections,* 7(4):46-52.

Klein, A.R. (1989, Winter). "The Curse of Caseload Management." *Perspectives,* 13:27-28.

Kratcoski, P.C. (1985). "The Functions of Classification Models in Probation and Parole: Control or Treatment-Rehabilitation?" *Federal Probation,* 49(4):49-56.

Latessa, E.J., L.F. Travis, and H.E Allen (1983). "Volunteers and Paraprofessionals in Parole: Current Practices." *Journal of Offender Counseling Services and Rehabilitation,* 8:91-105.

Lucas, W.L. (1987). "Perceptions of the Volunteer Role." *Journal of Offender Counseling, Services and Rehabilitation,* 12:141-146.

Macallair, D. (1994). "Disposition Case Advocacy in San Francisco's Juvenile Justice System: A New Approach to Deinstitutionalization." *Crime & Delinquency,* 40:84-95.

Macallair, D. (1993). "Reaffirming Rehabilitation in Juvenile Justice." *Youth and Society,* 25:104-125.

McCarthy, B.R. and R.H. Langworthy (1987). "Older Offenders on Probation and Parole." *Journal of Offender Counseling, Services and Rehabilitation,* 12:7-25.

Mangrum, C.T. (1975). *The Professional Practitioner in Probation.* Springfield, IL: Charles C Thomas.

Meeker, B. (1948). "Probation is Casework." *Federal Probation,* 12(2):51-52.

National Advisory Commission on Criminal Justice Standards and Goals (1973). *Corrections.* Washington, DC: U.S. Government Printing Office.

Proctor, J. (1994). "Evaluating a Modified Version of the Federal Prison System's Classification Model: An Assessment of Objectivity and Predictive Validity." *Criminal Justice and Behavior,* 21:256-272.

Prochaska, J.O. and C.C. DiClemente (1986). *Toward a Comprehensive Model of Change.* In W.R. Miller and S. Rollnick (eds). *Motivational Interviewing: Preparing People to Change Addictive Behavior.* New York, NY: Guilford Press.

Scheier, I. (1970). "The Professional and the Volunteer: An Emerging Relationship." *Federal Probation,* 34(2):8-12.

Schumacher, M.A. (1985). "Implementation of a Client Classification and Case Management System: A Practitioner's View." *Crime & Delinquency,* 31:445-455.

Scott, R.J. (1978). "Contract Programming in Probation: Philosophical and Experimental Bases for Building a Model." *The Justice System Journal*, 4:49-70.

Sigler, R. and J. Williams (1994). "A Study of the Outcomes of Probation Officers and Risk-Screening Instrument Classifications." *Journal of Criminal Justice*, 22:495-502.

Smykla, J.O. (1986). "Critique Concerning Prediction in Probation and Parole: Some Alternative Suggestions." *International Journal of Offender Therapy and Comparative Criminology*, 30-31, 125-139.

Studt, E. (1954). "Casework in the Correctional Field." *Federal Probation*, 17(3):17-24.

Travis, L.F. (1989). *Risk Classification in Probation and Parole. Risk Classification Project*, University of Cincinnati, Cincinnati, OH.

Travis, L.F. and E.J. Latessa (1996). *Classification and Needs Assessment Module. In Managing Violent Youthful Offenders in Adult Institutions Curriculum.* Longmont, CO: National Institute of Corrections.

Trecker, H.B. (1955). "Social Work Principles in Probation." *Federal Probation*, 19(1):8-9.

Van Voorhis, P. (1994). *Psychological Classification of the Adult Male Prison Inmate.* Albany, NY: State University of New York Press.

Wilbanks, W.L. (1985). "Predicting Failure on Parole." In D. Farrington and R. Tarling (eds.) *Prediction in Criminology*, pp. 78-94. Albany, NY: SUNY Press.

Wong, S. (1997). *Risk Assessing the Risk of Violent Recidivism.* Presentation at the American Probation and Parole Association, Boston, MA.

Wright, K.N., T.R. Clear, and P. Dickson (1984). "Universal Applicability of Probation Risk Assessment Instruments." *Criminology*, 22:113-134.

# Intermediate Sanctions: Intensive Supervision, Electronic Monitoring, Day Reporting, and House Arrest

## 12

If punishment makes not the will supple it hardens the offender.

—John Locke

The effects of our actions may be postponed but they are never lost. There is an inevitable reward for good deeds and an inescapable punishment for bad. Mediate this truth, and seek always to earn good wages from destiny.

—Wu Ming Fu

## Intermediate Sanctions

No discussion of contemporary probation would be complete without examining the development and application of intermediate sanctions. Faced with overcrowded prison and jail systems, criminal justice professionals and policymakers are being forced to search for alternative ways to sanction and control criminal offenders.

A host of intermediate sanctions designed to treat the criminal offender in the community is being developed and implemented. The intermediate punishments described in this chapter include electronic monitoring, house arrest, community service, day reporting centers, day fines, and intensive supervision. The purposes of these intermediate punishments are to provide correctional alternatives to confinement.

> ### Box 12.1
>
> ### Intermediate Sanctions
>
> Intermediate sanctions, ranging in severity from day fines to "boot camps," are interventions that are beginning to fill the sentencing gap between prison at one extreme and probation at the other. Lengthy prison terms may be inappropriate for some offenders; for others probation may be too inconsequential and may not provide the degree of public supervision necessary to ensure public safety. By expanding sentencing options, intermediate sanctions enable the criminal justice system to tailor punishment more closely to the nature of the crime and the criminal. An appropriate range of punishments makes it possible for the system to hold offenders strictly accountable for their actions.
>
> Source: V. Gowdy (1993). *Intermediate Sanctions*, p. 1. Washington, DC: U.S. Department of Justice.

The U.S. Department of Justice (1990:3) defines intermediate sanctioning as "a punishment option that is considered on a continuum to fall between traditional probation and traditional incarceration." Intermediate sanctions were largely developed out of the need to relieve the prison crowding[1] and satisfy the general publics' desire for new correctional alternatives. Thus, policymakers began to experiment with programs to punish, control, and reform offenders in the community. Figure 12.1 shows the percentage of probationers under different types of sanctions. Over eleven percent are under "special probation" supervision. Two major issues confronting intermediate sanctions are: (1) offender diversion and (2) public safety.

Figure 12.1
**Probationers and Parolees Under Different Types of Supervision in 1996**

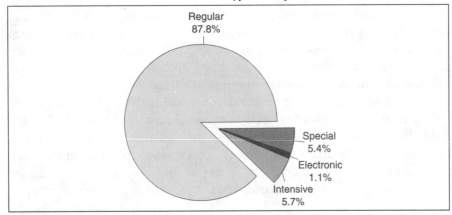

Source: C. Camp and G. Camp (1997). *The Corrections Yearbook 1997*. South Salem, NY: Criminal Justice Institute, Inc.

## The Need for Intermediate Sanctions

The American Correctional Association (1990:5) reports that "crowding has reached the top of most legislative agendas across the country. Most states are beginning to acknowledge that they will not be able to build their way out of the crises. Alternatives to long-term confinement are a necessity." Rosenthal (1989:1) contends that "the prohibitive costs of constructing and operating jails and prisons make it fiscally impossible to build our way out of the current corrections crises, even if public sentiment continues to favor a 'get tough on crime' posture." Camp and Camp (1995) report average construction costs at between \$28,200 and \$80,004 per bed; the national annual incarceration expense for a single prisoner averages \$19,000 but may range as high as \$46,921 (American Correctional Association, 1995).

---

**Box 12.2**

### Types of ISPs

ISPs are usually classified as prison diversion, enhanced probation, and enhanced parole. Each has a different goal.

**Diversion** is commonly referred to as a "front door" program because its goal is to limit the number of offenders entering prison. Prison diversion programs generally identify incoming, lower-risk inmates to participate in an ISP in the community as a substitute for a prison term.

**Enhancement** programs generally select already sentenced probationers and parolees and subject them to closer supervision in the community than regular probation or parole. People placed in ISP enhanced probation or enhanced parole programs show evidence of failure under routine supervision or have committed serious offenses deemed to be too serious for supervision on routine caseloads.

Treatment and service components in the ISP's included drug and alcohol counseling, employment, community service, and payment of restitution. On many of these measures, ISP offenders participated more than did control members; participation in such programs was found to be correlated with a reduction in recidivism. . . .

Source: J. Petersilia and S. Turner (1993). *Evaluating Intensive Supervision of Probation/Parole: Results of a Nationwide Experiment*, pp. 2, 7. Washington, DC: U.S. Department of Justice.

Despite the ever-increasing cost of incarceration, it is necessary for alternative sanctions to gain public, legislative, and judicial support (Finn, 1991). To earn sufficient support, an option to confinement must "be perceived as reasonably safe; address the public's desire for punishment through community control, nonpaid labor, and victim restitution; and offer an opportunity for positive change by providing treatment and employment skills" (American Correctional Association, 1990:2).

## Intensive Supervision

The most widely used community-based intermediate sanction that attempts to meet the above criteria is intensive supervision. Intensive supervision is most often viewed as an alternative to incarceration. Persons who are sentenced to intensive probation supervision are supposed to be those offenders who, in the absence of intensive supervision, would have been sentenced to imprisonment. However, intensive supervision is hardly a new idea. Previous programs of intensive supervision carried the common goal of maintaining public safety, but varied from the "new generation" of intensive supervision programs in very fundamental ways (Latessa, 1986).

Early versions of intensive supervision were based on the idea that increased client contact would enhance rehabilitation while allowing for greater client control. For example, California's Special Intensive Parole Unit experiments in the 1950s and the San Francisco Project in the 1960s were designed as intensive supervision, but they emphasized rehabilitation as the main goal. Later, with rehabilitation still as the main objective, experiments were "undertaken to determine the 'best' caseload size for the community supervision, despite the illogic of the proposition that a magical 'best' number could be found" (McCarthy, 1987:33). Nevertheless, the failure of these experiments to produce results fueled two decades' worth of cynicism about the general utility of community-based methods.

Burkhart (1986) and Pearson (1987) contend that today's intensive supervision programs emphasize punishment of the offender and control of the offender in the community at least as much as they do rehabilitation. Further, contemporary programs are designed to meet the primary goal easing the burden of prison overcrowding.

Figure 12.2 illustrates the differences between the objectives of the original experiments with intensive supervision, and the so called "new generation" programs. The early models were successful at accomplishing smaller caseloads and delivering more contacts and services; however, reductions in recidivism never materialized. Similarly, the more recent programs have reduced caseloads and significantly increased control and surveillance but have not had an appreciable impact directly on prison populations.[2]

Figure 12.2
**Models of ISP Programs**

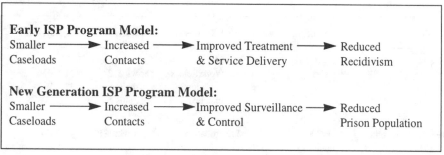

**Early ISP Program Model:**
Smaller ⟶ Increased ⟶ Improved Treatment ⟶ Reduced
Caseloads      Contacts      & Service Delivery      Recidivism

**New Generation ISP Program Model:**
Smaller ⟶ Increased ⟶ Improved Surveillance ⟶ Reduced
Caseloads      Contacts      & Control      Prison Population

Today, no two jurisdictions define intensive supervision in exactly the same way. However, one characteristic of all ISP programs is that they provide for very strict terms of probation. As Jones (1991:1) points out: "Their common feature is that more control is to be exerted over the offender than that described as probation in that jurisdiction and that often these extra control mechanisms involve restrictions on liberty of movement, coercion into treatment programs, employment obligations, or all three." This increased level of control is usually achieved through reduced caseloads, increased number of contacts, and a range of required activities for participating offenders that can include victim restitution, community service, employment, random urine and alcohol testing, electronic monitoring, and payment of a probation supervision fee.

Intensive supervision programs vary in terms of the number and type of contacts per month, caseload size, type of surveillance conducted, and services offered. In addition, programs vary depending upon whether they are staffed by specially trained officers or regular probation officers, and whether an officer "team" approach is used.

In 1986, Byrne conducted a survey on the use of intensive supervision in the United States. Byrne's interstate comparison found that "the numbers of direct personal contacts required ranged from two per month to seven per week. Some programs have specified no curfew checks while others specified three curfew checks per week" (Pearson, 1987:15). Ideally, supervising officers provide monitoring with a reduced caseload of about 15 offenders per officer. Yet, most officers carry caseloads of nearly 25 offenders. Offender entry into an intensive supervision program may be the decision of the sentencing judge, a parole board, a prison release board, or probation agency.

Table 12.1 shows some of the variation among selected ISP programs. The types of clients served, the number of contacts made each month, and the recidivism rates vary greatly from program to program.

Table 12.1
**Intensive Supervision Probation/Parole**

| Author & Year | Site | Sample | Control Groups | Contacts | Recidivism |
|---|---|---|---|---|---|
| Jolin & Stipak (1991) | Oregon | N=70 Drug Users | 100 on EM 100 on Work Release Stratified random sample matched on risk | 5 counseling per wk & 3 self-help per wk., plus curfew & EM | 47% ISP 32% EM 33% WR |
| Erwin (1987) | Georgia | N=200 randomly selected from ISP | N=200 probationers N=97 prison releasees Matched samples | 5 per wk. ISP | 40% ISP 35.5% Probation 57.8% Prison |
| Pearson (1987) | New Jersey | N=554 parolees | N=510 | 20 per mo. | 24.7% ISP 34.6% CG |
| Byrne & Kelly (1989) | Massachusetts | N=227 High-Risk Probationers | N=834 ISP Eligible Offenders plus a 35% random sample of all offenders under supervision (N=2543) | 10 mo. ISP 2 mo. Probation | 56.6% ISP 60.9% Probation |
| Latessa (1993) | Ohio | All offenders in specialized ISP Units Alcohol=140 Drug=121 Sex=64 Mental=76 | N=424 regular probationers randomly selected | 6 mo. Alcohol & Drug 4.5 mo. Sex & Mental Health 1 mo. comparison | 42% Alcohol 59% Drug 22% Sex 27% MH 46% Probation |
| Latessa (1992) | Ohio | N=82 ISP randomly selected | N=101 randomly selected from regular probation | 7.5 mo. ISP 2.2 mo. Prob | 28% ISP 21% Probation |
| Latessa (1993) | Ohio | N=317 ISP N=502 High Risk ISP | N=424 randomly selected from regular probation | 4 mo. ISP 3 mo. High Risk 2 mo. Prob | 35% ISP 43% High 34% Probation |
| Fallen et al. (1981) | Washington | N=289 Low Risk parolees | N=102 matched parolees | 4 per mo. | 32.9% ISP 46.9% CG |
| Petersilia & Turner (1993) | Contra-Costra | N=170 | Randomly selected offenders placed in prison, probation, or parole | 12 per mo. | 29% ISP 27% CG |
| Petersilia & Turner (1993) | Los Angeles | N=152 | Randomly selected offenders placed in prison, probation, or parole | 24 per mo. | 32% ISP 30% CG |
| Petersilia & Turner (1993) | Seattle | N=173 | Randomly selected offenders placed in prison, probation, or parole | 12 per mo. | 46% ISP 36% CG |
| Petersilia & Turner (1993) | Ventura | N=166 | Randomly selected offenders placed in prison, probation, or parole | 24 per mo. | 32% ISP 53% CG |

Table 12.1—*continued*

| Author & Year | Site | Sample | Control Groups | Contacts | Recidivism |
|---|---|---|---|---|---|
| Petersilia & Turner (1993) | Atlanta | N=50 | Randomly selected offenders placed in prison, probation, or parole | 20 per mo. | 12% ISP 4% CG |
| Petersilia & Turner (1993) | Macon | N=50 | Randomly selected offenders placed in prison, probation, or parole | 20 per mo. | 42% ISP 38% CG |
| Petersilia & Turner (1993) | Santa Fe | N=58 | Randomly selected offenders placed in prison, probation, or parole | 20 per mo. | 48% ISP 28% CG |
| Petersilia & Turner (1993) | Dallas | N=221 parolees | Randomly selected offenders placed in prison, probation, or parole | 16 per mo. | 39% ISP 30% CG |
| Petersilia & Turner (1993) | Houston | N=458 parolees | Randomly selected offenders placed in prison, probation, or parole | 10 per mo. | 44% ISP 40% CG |

Source: Compiled by authors.

Many ISP programs have revealed an increase in technical violations for ISP offenders as compared to offenders placed in other sentencing options, but no significant increase in the new offense rate (Erwin, 1987; Petersilia & Turner, 1993; Wagner & Baird, 1993). Most evaluations however, suggest that increased contact alone does not make a difference in terms of overall recidivism rates. In a recent study of ISP in Ohio, Latessa, Travis, and Holsinger (1997) found that offenders in ISP programs were less likely to be rearrested than offenders under other forms of correctional supervision; however, they were more likely to be subsequently incarcerated. They attributed this higher failure rate to revocations for probation violations. Latessa and his colleagues also concluded that ISP programs in Ohio were saving the state over the cost of incarceration.

As it is currently designed, ISP fails to produce significant reductions in recidivism, or alleviate prison overcrowding. This does, however, appear to be a relationship between greater participation in treatment programs and lower failure rates (Petersilia & Turner, 1993; Johnson & Hunter, 1992, Jolin & Stipak, 1992; Paparozzi, n.d.; Pearson, 1987). This is one of the important issues facing intensive supervision. In a recent article summarizing the state of ISP, Fulton, Latessa, Stichman, and Travis (1997:72) summarize the findings concerning ISP:

- ISPs have failed to alleviate prison crowding;

- Most ISP studies have found no significant differences between recidivism rates of ISP offenders and offenders with comparison groups;

- There appears to be a relationship between greater participation in treatment and employment programs and lower recidivism rates;

- ISPs appear to be more effective than regular supervision or prison in meeting offenders needs;

- ISPs that reflect certain principles of effective intervention are associated with lower rates of recidivism;

- ISP does provide an intermediate punishment; and

- Although ISPs are less expensive than prison, they are more expensive than originally thought.

## Issues in Intensive Supervision

Intensive supervision, as a technique for increasing control over offenders in the community (and thereby reducing risk), has gained wide popularity.[3] A 1988 survey found that 45 states had or were developing intensive supervision programs. As of 1990, all states, plus the federal system, had some kind of intensive supervision program in place. This widespread acceptance has provided states with the needed continuum of sentencing options, so that offenders are being held accountable for their crimes while, at the same time, public safety is being maintained. This popularity of intensive supervision has generated much research, thereby raising several issues.

Current issues largely revolve around the effectiveness of intensive supervision. Yet, measures of success vary depending on the stated goals and objectives each program set out to address.[4] For instance, the goals of a treatment oriented program differ from the goals of a program that places emphasis on offender punishment and control. However, it is possible to isolate two overriding themes of recent intensive supervision programs that raise several issues. First, "intensive probation supervision is expected to divert offenders from incarceration in order to alleviate prison overcrowding,[5] avoid the exorbitant costs of building and sustaining prisons, and prevent the stultifying and stigmatizing effects of imprisonment" (Byrne, Lurigio & Baird, 1989:10). Second, ISP is expected to promote public safety through surveillance strategies, while promoting a sense of responsibility and accountability through probation fees, restitution, and community service activities (Byrne, Lurigio & Baird, 1989). These goals generate issues regarding the ability of ISP programs in reducing recidivism, diverting offenders from prison, and ensuring public safety.

The debate over control versus treatment has raged for many years. Recently, there has been a new movement, initiated by the American Probation and Parole Association, to develop a more balanced approach to ISP supervision (Fulton, Stone & Gendreau, 1994; Fulton, Gendreau, and Paparozzi, 1996). This approach continues to support strict conditions and supervision practices, but within the context of more services, and higher quality treatment. Indeed, it appears that if ISP is going to live up to its promises, a new model must be developed.

## Day Reporting Centers

Unlike many other intermediate sanction alternatives, day reporting is of very recent vintage. While day reporting was used earlier in England, the first day reporting program in the United States was opened in Massachusetts in 1986 (McDevitt, 1988). This inaugural program was designed as an early release from prison and jail placement for inmates approaching their parole or discharge date. Participants in the program were required to report to the center each day (hence the name, "Day Reporting"), prepare an itinerary for their next day's activities, and report by telephone to the center throughout the day (Larivee, 1990). By 1992, there were six day reporting centers in operation in Massachusetts with average daily populations ranging from 30 to more than 100 offenders.

Parent (1990) reported that by the late 1980s, day reporting programs were operational in six states, and many more states were considering the option. The characteristics of these programs, and the clients they served varied considerably. As McDevitt and Miliano (1992:153) noted, "Although all centers have similar program elements, such as frequent client contact, formalized scheduling, and drug testing, the operations of different DRCs (day reporting centers) are quite varied. Therefore, it is difficult to define specifically what a day reporting center is; each center is unique."

Larivee (1990), in describing the development of day reporting centers in Massachusetts, noted that these centers were created for the purpose of diverting offenders from confinement in local jails. Offenders live at home, but must report once each day to the center, and are in telephone contact with the center four times each day. By 1990, there were seven centers serving eight counties and the state department of corrections. An evaluation of the Massachusetts day reporting centers reported that more than two-thirds of day reporting clients successfully completed programs and only two percent were returned to prison or jail for new crimes or escape (Curtin, 1990). An earlier evaluation of the Hampden County center (the first opened) reported more than 80 percent successful completion of the program and only one percent arrested for a new crime while in the program. Larivee concluded about the Massachusetts day reporting centers, "Every client in a day reporting center program would otherwise be incarcerated; additionally, no client is held in the center longer than he or she would be kept in jail . . . Only 4 percent of the clients were arrested for a new crime or escape, and none committed a violent offense."

Parent (1990) reported an assessment of 14 day reporting centers known to be in operation in 1989. Only three of the centers were operated by public agencies, with the other 11 being administered by private, non-profit organizations. The programs ranged in capacity from 10 offenders to 150, with most being able to accommodate 50 or fewer. A survey of these centers revealed that successful completion of programs varied greatly by center, and by type of client. Probation and parole violators and those who had been denied discretionary parole release had successful completion rates of about one-third or less, while offenders received from institutional work release programs or diverted from jail had completion rates in excess of two-thirds (Parent, 1990:27). The survey also reported a range in center costs from less than $8 per day per offender to more than $50 per day. The mean cost was nearly $15 per day.

In 1993, Parent, et al. (1995) replicated this survey, this time contacting 114 day reporting centers operating in 22 states. Fifty-four of these programs responded to the survey. Most of these responding programs indicated that they had opened after 1991. Most centers were still operated by private, non-profit organizations, and there was still a wide variety in services, programming, and contact requirements. Newer centers, however, more likely to be operated by public agencies than were the older ones.

When asked to identify the goals of their Day Reporting Center, respondents to the survey identified four purposes of the programs. The most important purpose, according to respondents, was to provide offenders with access to treatment services. Second most important was to reduce jail and prison crowding. Additional program goals included building political support for the program and the provision of surveillance/public safety.

The survey revealed wide variation in Day Reporting Center organizations, populations, costs, and effectiveness. Most centers were operated at the local level by agencies affiliated with the courts. Newer Day Reporting Centers were likely to serve a pre-imprisonment population, while the older centers primarily supervised offenders released from incarceration. Day Reporting Center populations included pretrial releasees, offenders diverted from imprisonment, probation and parole violators, and newly released prison and jail inmates. As Parent, et al. observed (1995:22), "The average negative termination rate for all such programs is 50 percent, with a wide distribution that ranges from 14 to 86 percent." They found that characteristics of the day reporting programs were correlated with higher rates of negative termination. The survey did not provide any information specifically concerning the rearrest rates of program participants. Rather, "negative termination" refers to offenders removed from the program for rule violations, which would include the commission of a new crime.

Centers operated by private agencies were more likely to have high negative termination rates than were those operated by public agencies. Those centers that offered more services, and those using curfews had higher rates of negative terminations. Finally, policies towards violations of center rules were related to rates of negative termination. As would be expected, those centers with stricter policies and fewer alternatives within the program were more likely to experience high rates of negative terminations. It may also be that changes in day reporting populations to include a variety of offender types, and an increase in the number of expectations and conditions placed on these offenders (drug testing, mandatory treatment attendance, curfews, etc.) combined to increase the likelihood of program failure. A final correlate of higher rates of negative terminations was line staff turnover. Programs that experienced higher rates of staff turnover also had higher rates of negative terminations. However, ". . . it is not clear which characteristic influences the other," as Parent, et al. note.

Day reporting programs offered a variety of services to program participants. Most centers offered job skills, drug abuse education, group and individual counseling, job placement, education, life-skills training, and drug treatment. While most services were provided in-house, it was common for drug treatment programs to be offered by providers not located at the Day Reporting Center. A recent trend in these centers noted in the survey as the tendency for the newer, public programs to co-locate social service programs with the day reporting program. The most common in-house programs (those offered at more than three-quarters of the Day Reporting Centers) were job seeking skills, group counseling, and life-skills training.

The costs of these services are usually paid by the Day Reporting Center. For some programs, other agencies pay the costs of services such as drug treatment, transitional housing, and education and job placement assistance. Seldom are offenders required to pay for services. The costs of operation ranged from about $10 per offender day to more than $100 per offender day, with the average daily cost per offender being slightly more than $35. Public centers were found to generally have lower daily operating costs, and costs increased with the stringency of surveillance/supervision requirements. Costs of day reporting were found to be more than intensive probation supervision, but less than residential treatment or incarceration.

Figure 12.3
**Ohio Day Reporting Study: Rearrest Rates**

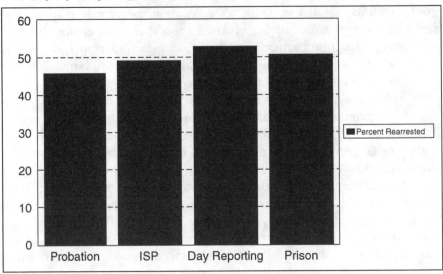

Source: E.J. Latessa, L.F. Travis, A. Holsinger, and J. Hartman (1998). *Evaluation of Ohio's Pilot Day Reporting Program: Final Report.* Cincinnati, OH: Division of Criminal Justice, University of Cincinnati.

Unfortunately, there have not been many empirical studies of day reporting centers. In a recent study, Latessa, Travis, Holsinger, and Hartman (1998) examined five pilot day reporting programs in Ohio. Offenders from the day reporting programs were compared to offenders supervised under regular probation, intensive program, and those released from prison. The rearrest and incarceration rates for each group are presented in Figures 12.3 and 12.4. The rates of rearrest for the day reporting group were slightly higher than those reported for the other groups. The incarceration rates indicate that the day reporting group performed slightly better than those offenders supervised under intensive supervision, worse than those on regular probation, and similar to those released from prison. Noteworthy, the authors also found that the quality of the treatment provided by the five day reporting centers in this study was judged to be poor.

## Day Fines

The fine is a common and widely accepted punishment imposed on misdemeanor and some less serious felony offenders (Zimmerman, et al. 1991). A fine is a penalty imposed by a court that requires the offender to pay a specific amount of money. The fine is a cash payment of a dollar amount assessed by the judge on an individual basis or determined by a published schedule of penalties. Fines may be paid in installments in many jurisdictions, or by use of the offender's credit card.

Figure 12.4
**Ohio Day Reporting Study: Incarceration Rates**

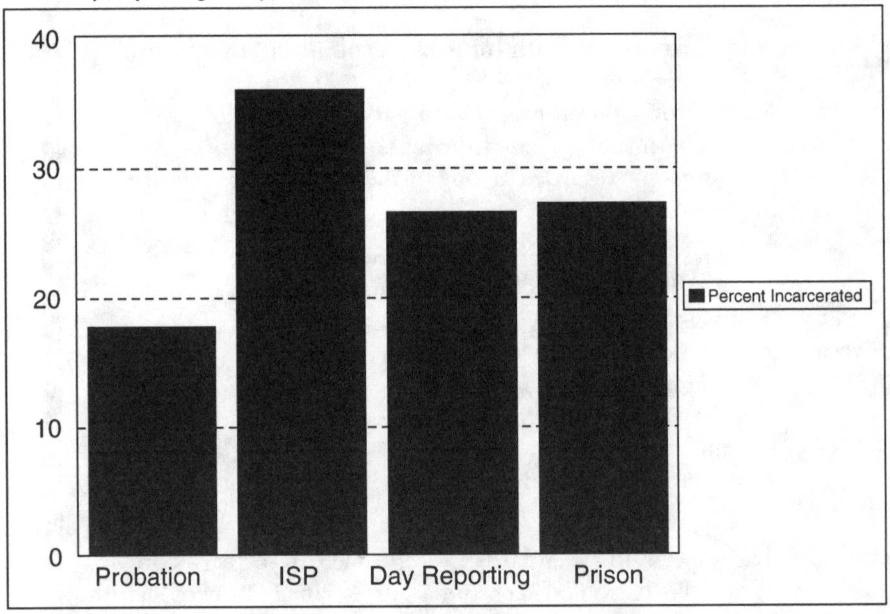

Source: E.J. Latessa, L.F. Travis, A. Holsinger, and J. Hartman (1998). *Evaluation of Ohio's Pilot Day Reporting Program: Final Report*. Cincinnati, OH: Division of Criminal Justice, University of Cincinnati.

Monetary assessments are typically given to low-risk offenders, and the amount of this financial sanction tends to increase with the severity of the crime. Judges tend to employ rational discretion in these areas. Surprisingly, most fines are collected in large part if not in whole, and there is substantial evidence that the chance of further arrest and incarceration are significantly less for those assessed a fine than for those receiving a jail term, when the investigator controls for offender attributes and offense.[6]

Fines are an ancient and widely used penal measure, and noncustodial sanctions are not new in American sentencing. Sentencing judges on the Federal level imposed fines in 21 percent of their felony cases in 1993. State judges imposed fines in 16 percent of their felony dispositions (Maguire & Pastore, 1994:533,541). What is new is a variation on financial sanctions known as the *day fine*, so called because the amount of the fine is tied to an offender's daily earnings, a practice common in European and some South American countries. In the United States, this is not a common practice, for fines have traditionally been based on the offense rather than the individual offender's ability to pay. With the movement toward intermediate punishments, day fines have been enthusiastically incorporated into sentencing systems and by judges, who are increasingly interested in a graduated progression of intermediate penalties: punishment based on an offender's ability to pay.

## Box 12.3

### Georgia's Experience with Intensive Probation Supervision

While probation programs with varying degrees of supervision have been implemented throughout the country, Georgia's ISP is widely regarded as one of the most stringent in the nation. Standards include:

- Five face-to-face contacts per week;
- 132 hours of mandatory community service;
- Mandatory curfew;
- Weekly checks of local arrest records;
- Automatic notification of arrest elsewhere via the State Crime Information Network listing; and
- Routine and unannounced alcohol and drug testing.

The supervision standards are enforced by a team consisting of a Probation Officer and a Surveillance Officer. The team supervises 25 probationers. In some jurisdictions, a team of one Probation Officer and Two Surveillance Officers supervises 40 probationers. The standards are designed to help offenders direct their energies toward productive activities, to assume responsibilities, and to become law-abiding citizens. Most offenders chosen for the ISP program were already sentenced to prison, presented an acceptable risk to the community, and had not committed a violent offense. A risk assessment instrument was used to screen select offenders. While the majority of those selected fell into the category of non-violent property offenders, a large number of individuals convicted of drug- and alcohol-related offenses were included as the program developed. Some of these offenses also involved violence.

Of the original 2,322 people in the program between 1982 and 1985, 370 (or 16%) absconded or had their probation revoked. The remaining 1,952 were successfully diverted from prison; many were still under some form of probationary supervision. The highest rate of success (87%) was seen in drug-related criminal offenders, and Georgia reduced the percentage of felons incarcerated from 37 percent to 27 percent. Georgia achieved a cost savings of nearly $6,000 per offender served.

Source: B.S. Erwin (1987). *Evaluation of Intensive Probation Supervision in Georgia*. Atlanta, GA: Georgia Department of Correction.

As sentencing judges become more familiar and comfortable with the day-fine approach, more will impose financial penalties that can be adjusted to individual circumstances and cases. Day fines have the additional potential of raising total collected fine revenues, and have been implemented not only in Staten Island, New York but in numerous other jurisdictions across the country.[7]

---

Box 12.4

### Meta-analysis

This is a research and statistical technique that allows researchers to pull together the data from many studies to look for effects. This permits the researcher to examine hundreds of studies and thousands of cases, and to determine the average effect size of an intervention or sanction. This technique has been used in many fields, such as medicine, education, and criminal justice.

---

## Home Detention

House arrest, usually conjuring up images of political control and fascist repression, is court-ordered home detention in this nation, confining offenders to their households for the duration of sentence (Meecham, 1986). Introduced in 1984 in Florida, home detention rapidly spread throughout a nation searching for punitive, safe, and secure alternatives to incarceration (Maxfield & Baumer, 1990). The sentence is usually in conjunction with probation but may be imposed by the court as a separate punishment (as in Florida). Florida's Community Control program (FCCP) was designed to provide a safe diversion alternative, and help address the problem of prison population escalation and associated high costs (Flynn, 1986).

Participants may be required to make victim compensation, perform community work service, pay probation fees, undergo drug and alcohol testing and, in some instances, wear electronic monitoring equipment to verify their presence in the residence. (In some jurisdictions, house arrest is used on a pretrial basis,[8] as an isolated sentence, in conjunction with probation or parole, or with a prerelease status such as education or work furlough.) House arrest only allows the offender to leave her or his residence for specific purposes and hours approved by the court or supervising officer, and being absent without leave is a technical violation of conditions that may result in resentencing to jail or prison (Government Accounting Office, 1990).

Box 12.5

## The Talbert House Day Reporting Center

Talbert House, Inc., a private, non-profit organization, administers a day reporting program in Cincinnati, Ohio. The program began in 1994. The objective of the program was to provide an alternative disposition for probationers facing revocation, which combines high levels of supervision and service delivery. The philosophy of the program emphasizes surveillance and compliance with probation supervision requirements. There are seven characteristics or components of the program:

1. Reporting seven days each week;
2. Development and monitoring of daily itineraries;
3. Electronic monitoring;
4. Regular, random urinalysis;
5. Breath testing;
6. Close monitoring of income to insure payments of court financial requirements; and
7. Community service work through the Hamilton County Probation Department.

The program operates with a staff of three, including two caseworkers and a manager. Day reporting is ordered as a condition of probation for all referrals. The program excludes those with a history of substance abuse, repeat violent crimes or assaultive behavior, sexual offenses against minors, a long-standing association with organized crime, or a conviction for arson. Additionally, clients are required to consent to treatment prior to acceptance to the program.

Cases referred to the center are given a risk/needs assessment which includes Michigan Alcohol Scores Testing (MAST). Offenders must report to the center seven days each week, provide urine and breath tests as requested, and, if unemployed, must participate in employment-seeking activities. Offenders meet with center staff each afternoon to participate in program activities until 5:00 p.m., when they leave to return home or go to other arranged treatment activities. Offenders stay in the program between one to six months, based on judicial stipulation. The program currently serves about 10 offenders per day. The center provides in-house treatment including individual and group counseling by appropriately licensed/registered staff. Other services include chemical dependency, case management, introduction to AA and NA, life

Box 12.5—*continued*

skills education, HIV education, budgeting, and nutrition. Additional services available to offenders include education, parenting, financial management, community service, mental health services, and leisure. The goals of the programs are identified as:

1.  Provide a community sanction option for probation violators;
2.  Identify problems facing offenders that may lead to criminality;
3.  Provide on-site or community referral to treat those problems; and
4.  Provide for public safety through intensive supervision, accountability, and retribution.

Home detention is a punitive sentence and was designed in most cases to relieve institutional overcrowding. For many offenders it is their "last chance" to escape from being committed to prison. In addition to surveillance of the offender, home detention is viewed as a cost avoidance program, a "front-end" solution to prison overcrowding, and a flexible alternative for certain offenders (such as a pregnant offender until time of delivery). The use of telemonitoring devices, discussed below as "Electronic Monitoring Programs," can significantly increase the correctional surveillance of offenders.

The most significant critical argument[9] against home detention is that, by making a non-incarcerative control mechanism available to corrections, many petty offenders are brought under correctional control who would best be handled by diversion, fines, or mental health services. In general, such inclusive actions are viewed as "net widening," which occurs when offenders are sentenced to community control who might otherwise have received a lesser or even no sentence.

The National Council on Crime and Delinquency conducted an evaluation of the FCCP and concluded that the impact on prison crowding, offender behavior, and State correctional costs have been positive. With an estimated prison diversion rate of 54 percent, community control is cost-effective despite the combined effect of net widening and the punishments imposed on almost 10 percent of FCCP participants for technical violations. Furthermore, the new offense rate for community control offenders is lower than for similar offenders sentenced to prison and released without supervision. For every 100 cases diverted from prison, Florida saved more than $250,000 (Wagner & Baird, 1993).

Home detention is expected to receive increased endorsement in the remainder of this decade and may become the sentence of choice for many nonviolent offenders in lieu of jail, prison, or even formal probation.

## Electronic Monitoring

Home detention has a long history as a criminal penalty but its new popularity with correctional authorities is due to the advent of electronic monitoring, a technological link thought to make the sanction both practical and affordable. See Figure 12.5.

Figure 12.5
**Electronic Monitoring Devices Used to Monitor Probationers and Parolees, 1995-1997**

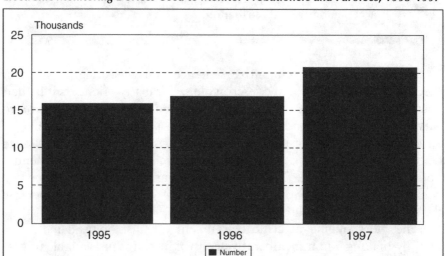

Source: C. Camp and G. Camp (1997). *The Corrections Yearbook 1997*. South Salem, NY: The Criminal Justice Institute, Inc.

The concept of electronic monitoring is not new, having been proposed in 1964 by Schwitzgebel as "electronic parole," and initially used to monitor the location of mental patients.[10] The first studies of home detention enforced by electronic monitoring began in 1986 and, by early 1992, there were at least 40,000 electronic monitors in use (Gowdy, 1993). It is used almost everywhere in the justice system after arrest. See Figure 12.6.

Figure 12.6
**Key Decision Points Where Electronic Monitoring (EM) is Being Used**

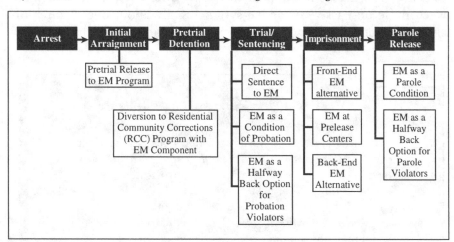

Source: Bureau of Justice Assistance (February, 1989). *Electronic Monitoring in Intensive Probation and Parole Programs.* Washington, DC: U.S. Department of Justice, p. 2.

According to the Bureau of Justice Assistance (1989:3), the goals and objectives of electronic monitoring are to:

- Provide a cost-effective community supervision tool for offenders selected according to specific program criteria;

- Administer sanctions appropriate to the seriousness of the offense;

- Promote public safety by providing surveillance and risk control strategies indicated by the risk and needs of the offenders; and

- Increase the confidence of legislative, judicial, and releasing authorities in ISP designs as a viable sentencing option.

Electronic monitoring can be active or passive. In active monitoring, a transmitter attached to the offender's wrist or ankle sends signals relayed by a home telephone to the supervising office during the hours the offender is required to be at home. Under passive monitoring, a computer program is used to call the offender randomly during the hours designated for home confinement. The offender inserts

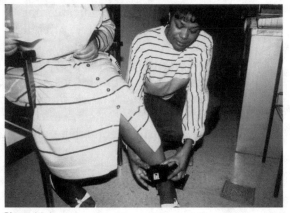

Photo 12.1
Demonstration of an electronic monitoring transmitter. Photograph by Ray Berger. Used with permission of the American Correctional Association.

the wristlet or anklet into a verifier to confirm her or his presence in the residence. There does not appear to be any difference in recidivism between those on passive or active systems. Only about one in three offenders on home detention wear monitoring devices (Petersilia, 1987).

---

**Box 12.6**

### How Day Fines Work

The general concept is simple: determining the amount of punishment to be administered to an offender is separated from a consideration of how much money that offender must pay. Judges determine how much punishment an offender deserves; this is then denominated into some unit other than money. These *punishment units* are then translated into monetary units based on how much money the offender makes per day.

Practically speaking, the day-fine approach consists of a simple, two-step process. First, the court uses a "unit scale" or "benchmark" to sentence the offender to a certain number of day-fine units (for example, 15, 60, or 120 units) according to the gravity of the offense and without regard to income. To guide the court's choices, benchmarks or unit scales are typically developed by a planning unit of judges, prosecutors, and defense counselors familiar with the disposition patterns of a court.

The value of each unit is then set at a percentage of the offender's daily income, and the total fine amount is determined by simple multiplication.

Source: L. Winterfield and S. Hillsman (1993). *The Staten Island Day-Fine Project*, p. 1. Washington, DC: U.S. Department of Justice.

---

National surveys indicate that electronic monitoring was initially (1987) used for property offenders on probation but that a much broader range of offenders was being monitored (1989) than in the past. Monitoring has been expanded to include not only probationers but also to follow up persons after incarceration, to control those sentenced to community corrections, and to monitor persons before trial or sentencing.

The 1989 survey on telemonitoring of offenders noted certain favorable findings:

- Most jurisdictions using electronic monitoring tested some offenders for drug use, and many routinely tested all. Some sites charged for the testing; more than 66 percent charged offenders for at least part of the cost of leasing the monitoring equipment.

- The average monitoring term in 1989 was 79 days. The longer the period of monitoring, the higher the odds of success. The chances of termination do not vary by type of offense, except that those committing major traffic violations committed *fewer* technical violations and new offenses.

- There were no significant differences in successful terminations among probationers, offenders on parole, or those in community corrections. All had successful terminations rates ranging between 74 and 86 percent. [West Palm Beach, Florida reported a 97 percent successful completion rate in 1992.]

- Rule violations resulted in reincarceration, brief confinement at a residential facility, intensified office reporting requirements, stricter curfews, or additional community service (Gowdy, 1993).

Recent evaluations in Oklahoma; Florida; Los Angeles, California; England and Wales;[11] Lake County, Illinois;[12] and Texas[13] indicate continuing success of electronic monitoring of correctional offenders, a technology that no doubt will be improved and expanded in the coming decade. Figure 12.7 shows the program termination from an electronic monitoring program operating in Cleveland, Ohio (Latessa, 1991). This program also gave program participants an exit survey. Table 12.2 shows offender responses to selected questions.

Figure 12.7
**Program Termination from Electronic Monitoring Program**

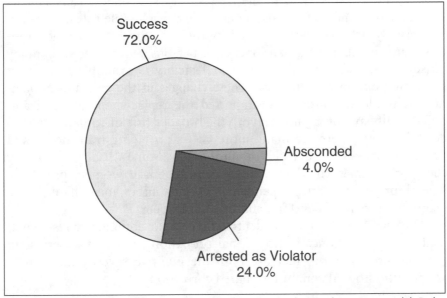

Source: E.J. Latessa (1991). *Report on Electronic Monitoring for the Cuyahoga County Adult Probation Department.* Cincinnati, OH: Department of Criminal Justice, University of Cincinnati.

## Community Residential Centers

Formerly known as "halfway houses," community residential centers (CRCs) are a valuable adjunct to community control and treatment services. Originally designed as residences for homeless men, they are now seen as a key nucleus of community-based correctional networks of residential centers, drug-free and alcohol-free living space, pre-release guidance centers, and private sector involvement with multiple-problemed offenders in need of intensive services. They also serve as noninstitutional residence facilities for a number of different classes of offenders, most of whom are high-need and pose medium-to-high risk to community corrections.

Community residential centers for criminal offenders have a long history in the United States (Hartmann et al., 1994). See Chapter 13. In the past, the typical use of community residential facilities was as "halfway houses." These programs were designed as transitional placements for offenders to ease the movement from incarceration to life in the free society. In time, some programs developed as alternatives to incarceration, so that the "halfway" aspect could mean either halfway *into* prison, or halfway *out* of prison.

CRCs are nonconfining residential facilities for adjudicated adults or juveniles, or those subject to criminal or juvenile proceedings. They are intended as an alternative to confinement for persons not suited for probation or for those who need a period of readjustment to the community after imprisonment.

Between 1950 and 1980, the numbers and use of such halfway houses grew considerably. In the past 15 years, residential placements for criminal offenders have also undergone considerable role expansion. Increasingly, the population served by these programs has come to include large numbers of probationers and persons awaiting trial. In many jurisdictions, placement in a residential facility is available as a direct sentencing option to the judge. These changes in the role and population of residential programs supported the replacement of the traditional "halfway house" notion with the broader title of community residential center. There are many more CRCs providing transitional and extensive services for juveniles than for adults. Some CRCs specialize by client or treatment modality: women only, abused women, prerelease federal furloughers, drug-dependent, alcohol abusers, mentally ill, court diagnostic program, developmentally disabled, etc.

DuPont (1985) explicitly identified a role for community residential facilities as an adjunct to traditional probation or parole supervision. Such facilities serve to increase both the punitive severity and public safety of traditional community-based corrections.

Table 12.2
**Results from Exit Interview with Electronic Monitoring Participants**

| | |
|---|---|
| Before this program have you ever served time in prison or jail? | |
| No | 44% |
| Yes | 56% |
| Do you think the program is better or worse than being in jail? | |
| Worse | 5% |
| Neither better nor worse | 13% |
| Better | 82% |
| To what extent did you find the transmitter comfortable or uncomfortable to wear? | |
| Uncomfortable | 25% |
| Neither comfortable nor uncomfortable | 44% |
| Comfortable | 31% |
| Since you have been on the monitoring program, how well do you get along with the people with whom you live? | |
| Better | 22% |
| About the same as before | 72% |
| Worse | 6% |
| While you were on the monitoring program, did you find that you had more or less money than you did before? | |
| Less money | 30% |
| About the same | 33% |
| More money | 37% |
| Since being on the monitoring program, do you find you have more or fewer friends? | |
| Fewer friends | 42% |
| About the same number of friends | 50% |
| More friends | 8% |
| Do you have the same friends now that you had when you began the monitoring program? | |
| Same friends | 65% |
| Different friends | 35% |
| Did you find the monitoring program better or worse than you expected it would be? | |
| Better | 44% |
| About as I expected it would be | 48% |
| Worse | 8% |
| Did anyone ask what the transmitter was? | |
| No | 30% |
| Yes | 70% |
| Were you able to violate any of the rules of the program without being caught by the monitoring equipment and/or the Probation Officer? | |
| No | 87% |
| Yes | 13% |

Source: E. Latessa (1991). "Report on Electronic Monitoring for Cuyahoga County Adult Probation Department." Cincinnati, OH: Department of Criminal Justice, University of Cincinnati.

---

**Box 12.7**

### Community Service

Community service requires that the offender complete some task that helps the community. It is considered a form of restitution, with labor rather than money being supplied. Common jobs include cleaning neighborhoods, working at nursing homes, painting schools, and doing assorted chores for the elderly. Community service can be a sentence in and of itself, or can be included with other sanctions, such as probation.

One high profile case was Zsa Zsa Gabor, who was required to do community service after being convicted of slapping a Los Angeles police officer.

---

In an era when both correctional costs and populations grow yearly, planners, practitioners, and policymakers have supported a wide range of correctional alternatives. As Guynes (1988) observed, one effect of prison and jail crowding was a dramatic increase in the probation and parole populations. Further, Petersilia (1985), among others, suggests that these larger supervision populations are increasingly comprised of more serious and more dangerous offenders. Community residential facilities have come to be seen as an important option for the management and control of these growing and more dangerous offender populations.

Hicks (1987) observed that the use of residential placement as an alternative to incarceration or traditional community supervision has engendered some change in operations and philosophy. She terms it a movement "toward supervision rather than treatment." Thus in some cases, residential facilities provide little more than a place to live and access to community resources. The emphasis in these programs is upon custody and control rather than counseling and correction.

Unable or unwilling to underwrite the costs of prison for large numbers of convicted offenders, several jurisdictions have supported community residential facilities. As Hicks (1987:7) notes, ". . . budget weary legislators often view halfway houses as an inexpensive lunch." Residential programs, they hope, will provide public safety as well as incarceration, but at a fraction of the cost. As substitute prisons, however, the atmosphere of these programs has changed.

Traditional halfway houses still continue, where staff and programs are designed for the provision of direct services to residents. These programs continue to provide counseling, substance abuse treatment, educational and vocational training, and a variety of social services. In other, newer programs, especially those operated by corrections departments, the atmosphere is closer to that of a minimum security prison than a rehabilitative community.

As the foregoing discussion illustrates, it is not possible to describe the average residential facility. Diversity in population, program, size, and structure is the rule. It is, unfortunately, also not possible to know for certain how many such facilities are in operation today, or the number of offenders served by them. Hicks (1987:2) observed, "There are no national figures, only educated guesses . . ."

---

**Box 12.8**

### Utah's Use of Electronic Monitoring

Utah has restricted electronic monitoring to ISP because of the intrusiveness of the technology as well as the scarcity of correctional resources. Utah began using electronic monitoring for ISP sentenced sex offenders in January 1985. Sex offenders were sentenced to ISP with electronic monitoring as a special condition by the Board of Pardons to be enforced by parole officers. Later, the selection criteria broadened to include high-risk parolees, and finally, probationers who were ordered by the courts to participate.

Utah uses electronic monitoring as a supplement to curfew enforcement. Utah has tried three types of equipment—one intermittent and two continuous monitoring devices. Currently, a continuous signal monitoring system is used. The continuous signal system was determined to be more cost-effective.

A parole officer assisted by a correctional technician operates the program. Staff of a community correctional center in Salt Lake currently monitor the host unit for alarms and play a role in the primary response to an alarm. If the center is unable to verify that an offender is at his/her residence, a parole officer is paged. Parole officers have vehicles and other necessary equipment with which to respond to alarms. Backup is provided by other parole officers in the field or law enforcement officers.

Program data reflect a high violation rate for offenders on electronic monitoring. This result is not surprising given the high violation rate reported in standard ISP and the increase in the level of surveillance provided by EM. Data on the intermittent signal monitoring program indicate that the average time under the system was 9.7 months. Of the original participants; 28 percent committed a new offense, either while on the program or during the follow-up period.

Source: Bureau of Justice Assistance (February, 1989). *Electronic Monitoring in Intensive Probation and Parole Programs*, p. 17. Washington, DC: U.S. Department of Justice.

Box 12.9

### Electronically Monitored House Arrest

One study of the use of electronically monitored home detention focused not on persons already convicted but on defendants awaiting trial. The research site was Marion County (Indianapolis), Indiana, and only defendants who did not qualify for release on recognizance, and could not raise bail, and could not secure a bondsman were considered for pretrial home detention. The pretrial program's goal was to ensure defendant's presence in court while relieving jail congestion. Fewer than 25 percent of referred detainees passed screening; most failed the "suitable residence with telephone" criterion for inclusion in the project.

Alleged crimes among defendants accepted for home pretrial detention included theft, DUI, forgery, habitual traffic offenses, disorderly conduct, and drug law violations.

Home detention with electronic monitoring was successful for 73 percent of participants. Defendants most likely to complete home detention successfully lived with a spouse or opposite-gender roommate. Of the 27 percent failures, 13 percent were technical violators, and 14 percent were absconders. Those most likely to abscond were sentenced eventually to jail or prison.

Source: V. Gowdy (1993). *Intermediate Sanctions*, p. 6. Washington, DC: U.S. Department of Justice.

Given the lack of reliable data, it is possible to estimate that there are in excess of at least 1,000 residential facilities in operation today (Huskey, 1992:71). Further, it appears that the number of facilities has grown as much as 50 percent in the past decade.

It is not possible to estimate the number of offenders served by these facilities with any certainty. Length of residence is typically short, on the order of three to four months, meaning that a facility with 50 beds may serve 150 to 200 individuals annually. Based on the probability that a halfway house would serve three to four times as many residents as it had beds in each year, Allen and his colleagues (1976:6) estimated that roughly 10,000 beds equaled 30,000 to 40,000 residents each year. Further, many of those in residential facilities are included in the totals of other correctional population counts such as the number of prison or furloughed inmates, or persons under parole supervision. Still, it is clear that the total number of residents in these facilities each year is substantial.[14]

---

**Box 12.10**

### Community Residential Facility

Rush (1992) defines a residential facility as:

A correctional facility from which residents are regularly permitted to depart, unaccompanied by any official, for the purposes of using community resources, such as schools or treatment programs, and seeking or holding employment.

This definition is free of any reference to incarceration which was implicit in the term "halfway." Further, it does not necessitate the direct provision of any services to residents within the facility, and clearly identifies the program with a correctional mission. Thus, unlike the traditional "halfway house," the community residential facility serves a more diverse population and plays a broader correctional role. Traditional halfway houses are included within the category of residential facilities, but their ranks are swelled by newer adaptations, such as community corrections centers, pre-release centers, restitution centers, and the like.

---

Despite the long tradition of residential community correctional programs, the research literature is both sparse and inconclusive. There appear to be a number of reasons that residential programs have been largely ignored by correctional researchers.

First, residential facilities represent a relatively small part of the correctional system and, as mentioned above, it is often difficult to distinguish between residential facilities that serve only correctional clientele and those that serve a broader constituency. Second, many programs are operated by private entities, and are either unwilling or unable to facilitate research. Third, generalization is a problem since these programs are often markedly different from locale to locale, both in terms of the treatment offered, and the types of clients they accept. Finally, in evaluation research, it is often difficult to develop an adequate comparison group or to conduct a follow-up of residents. Despite these obstacles, there have been some notable attempts to evaluate the effectiveness of residential programs.

---

Box 12.11

### Day Reporting Centers

Certain persons on pretrial release, probation, or parole are required to appear at day reporting centers on a frequent and regular basis in order to participate in services or activities provided by the center or other community agencies. Failure to report or participate is a violation that could cause revocation of conditional release or community supervision.

Reports indicate that offenders in these programs must not only physically report to their centers daily but also provide a schedule of planned activities, and participate in designated activities. In addition offenders must call the centers by phone throughout the day; they can also expect random phone checks by center staff both during the day and at home following curfew. In some programs, offenders must contact their respective centers an average of 60 times weekly and, in all but one, take random drug tests.

Source: V. Gowdy (1993). *Intermediate Sanctions.* Washington, DC: U.S. Department of Justice, p. 5.

---

Latessa and Travis (1991) evaluated CRC treatment programs for adult offenders sentenced to probation and found that, in comparison with other similarly situated offenders, CRC clients exhibited more prior involvement in alcohol- and drug-treatment, and suffered from more psychiatric problems. Hence the study group was higher-need, higher-risk, and more likely to recidivate. The center's clients received more services and treatment in almost every area examined. Even though prior criminal histories would have predicted higher failure rates, the center's clients did as well as the comparison group in terms of re-offending. Employment services and enrolling in an educational program reduced recidivism. Clearly, for high-risk offenders, residential centers that provide specific client-needed services can be valuable assets in offender control and outcome, particularly for community control clients whose technical violations are a result of high needs otherwise unaddressed within the community. While further research is required to better understand the relationships, the data from the Latessa and Travis study and others tend to support the following observations:

- Residential community correctional groups display greater service needs than do regular probation or parole groups.

- Many of these needs, such as psychiatric and drug/alcohol abuse history, are related both to positive adjustment and to new criminal convictions. Offenders in residential facilities are more likely to receive a variety of treatment and counseling services.

- Based on group characteristics at intake, an a priori assumption that CRC groups would demonstrate a higher rate of recidivism and lower social adjustment seems reasonable.

- Generally, no such difference in outcome has been observed, and residential groups have received considerably more treatment interventions. This may indicate that program participation is beneficial for this group.

It appears that residential community correctional facilities will continue to grow and develop new programs. In large part this will be a response to the crowding of local and state correctional institutions.

## Shock Incarceration Programs

Technically, shock incarceration programs, or boot camps as they are commonly known, are institutional correctional programs, not community-based ones. However, they are considered intermediate sanctions, and are a distant cousin to shock probation programs (see Chapter 8).[15] The most recent shock incarceration programs, or boot camps as they are more commonly called, appeared first in Georgia (1983) and Oklahoma (1984). The concept spread quickly and, since 1983, 50 boot camp prisons have opened in 41 state correctional jurisdictions, and handled over 21,000 inmates in 1996 (Camp & Camp, 1997:96), in addition to many programs developed and being considered in cities and counties (Santa Clara, California, for example), and for juveniles (MacKenzie et al., 1993).

While labeled a recent innovation, the basic elements of boot camp were present in the Elmira Reformatory in 1876, designed by Zebulon Reed Brockway. In its current developments, boot camp combines elements of military basic training and traditional correctional philosophy, particularly rehabilitation. Although there is no generic boot camp since individual programs vary in form and objectives, the typical boot camp is targeted at young, nonviolent offenders.[16] Once in the camp, the participant is subjected to a regimen of: (1) military drills and discipline, (2) physical exercise, (3) hard physical labor, (4) specialized education and training, and (5) counseling and treatment for substance abuse and addiction.

Most boot camp programs require the inmates to volunteer, offering as an incentive an incarceration period of a few months, compared to the much longer periods they would have spent in prison or on probation. Generally, a state boot camp graduate is released to parole, intensive supervision, home confinement, or some type of community corrections.

The philosophy behind the prison boot camps is simple. Offenders who can be turned around before they commit a major crime can improve their own opportunities for living a successful life free of incarceration. Traditional prisons generally have not been viewed as successful in rehabilitating offenders.

Box 12.12

### Ohio's Shock Incarceration Program: Camp Reams

Camp Reams began in 1991 and has a capacity for 100 prisoners. It is a 90-day program for adult males between the ages of 18 and 30, with a sentence of less than five years. All prisoners are selected from inmates already sent to the Ohio penal system.

Every morning the prisoners get up at 5 a.m. for personal hygiene, physical training, and breakfast. Prisoners are then assigned a work gang from 8 a.m. to 2 p.m., Monday through Friday. When they return to camp, there is another physical training session. Following dinner, programming is scheduled and includes adult basic education, GED, religion, etc. Physical training and work assignments are done regardless of weather.

Participation in the program by the prisoners is completely voluntary. A prisoner can drop out of the program at any time. Prisoners can also be removed from the program if they violate the rules. Boot camp is a one-time option. An offender who ends up back in the system does not get a second chance to go through boot camp.

Box 12.12—*continued*

A total of 2,193 prisoners have been admitted to the program since its inception; 1,182 have graduated. Camp Reams estimates the cost per prisoner at $75 per day.

The average prisoner comes to the program with a sixth-grade reading level. Prisoners can earn reduction in sentence by obtaining a GED. Prisoners who come in with a high school or college education work as tutors with other prisoners. If a prisoner completes 50 hours as a tutor, it will reduce his sentence by two months. If prisoners come in with a 4th-grade reading level and leave at a sixth-grade level, they also receive a two-month reduction in sentence.

Once the inmate has completed the 90-day boot camp program, they enter ITD (Intermediate Transitional Detention) at Alvis House in Columbus. The first 30 days of ITD is restricted to the program. Prisoners then work their way into the community for education and employment. Parole supervision is the third and final phase of the boot camp program.

General Rules for Boot Camp Participants at Camp Reams:

1. Always put forth 100 percent effort.

2. Obey all rules given to you.

3. Always acknowledge orders by saying SIR, YES SIR; SIR, NO SIR, or MA'AM, YES MA'AM; MA'AM, NO MA'AM.

4. Always say SIR/MA'AM, EXCUSE ME SIR/MA'AM when passing staff from the front and SIR/MA'AM by your leave when passing staff from the rear.

5. When addressing staff, always ask permission to speak.

6. After receiving orders, take one step back, say AYE, AYE, SIR/MA'AM, do an about face and say, AHH-HHHHHHH!! while leaving.

7. When encountering visitors, do not speak unless authorized by staff.

8. Never gape at visitors, continue with assignments.

9. When a sergeant or above enters a bay, call the bay to attention.

10. Read and understand all rules and regulations of S.I.P.

Source: *Prisoner Handbook*, Camp Reams Shock Incarceration Program.

According to boot camp advocates, the population at greatest risk of entering prison is the young adult who is poorly educated, comes from a low-income background, has not had proper role models or discipline, has little or no work skills, and is subjected to an environment in which drug use and drug trafficking are common. Because many misdirected young persons have become productive citizens after exposure to military training, the boot camp endeavors to provide this same discipline and direction to persons who still have a chance of being diverted from a life of crime and incarceration.

The boot camp concept appeals to diverse elements of the justice system. For the offender, it offers a second chance. He or she[17] generally will be returned to the community in a much shorter period without the stigma of having been in prison. For the judge, it is a sentencing option that provides sanctions more restrictive than probation but less restrictive than a conventional prison. For the correctional system, it allows the placement of individuals outside the traditional prison environment and reduces costs and crowding by moving the persons through the system in less time.

Box 12.13

### Shock Incarceration

[R]esearch indicates that although there is a common core of military-type drill and discipline within these programs, there are also wide variations in their operations, activities, time served, number served, release procedures, and aftercare. The rigorous physical exercise, military drill and discipline, as well as the housing barracks and other noninstitutional characteristics, distinguish correctional boot camps from traditional prisons and jails.

Michael Russell, Acting Director,
National Institute of Justice, 1993

The boot camp concept also appeals to groups with diverse views on the objectives of corrections. For those who believe that corrections should focus more on rehabilitation, the shorter sentence, structured environment, supervision after release, and emphasis on training and treatment can be found in the boot camp. For those who believe that prisons should serve as punishment and a deterrent, the highly disciplined environment, military-style drills, physical exercise, and work within a correctional setting exist in the boot camp. Although boot camps are most often associated with prisons, probation and parole agencies also operate boot camps. According to Camp and Camp (1997:170) 16 probation and parole agencies operated 23 boot camps, and served more than 3,200 offenders in 1996.

Figure 12.8
**Juvenile Boot Camps Rates of Recidivism\* Following Release from Confinement**

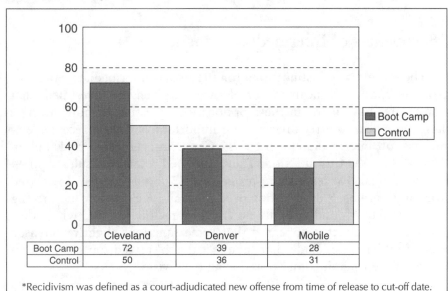

| | Cleveland | Denver | Mobile |
|---|---|---|---|
| Boot Camp | 72 | 39 | 28 |
| Control | 50 | 36 | 31 |

\*Recidivism was defined as a court-adjudicated new offense from time of release to cut-off date.

Source: M.D. Peters, D. Thomas, and C. Zamberlan (1997). *Boot Camps for Juvenile Offenders Program Summary*. Office of Juvenile Justice and Delinquency Prevention, U.S. Dept. of Justice.

Results from studies of the effectiveness of boot camp programs in reducing recidivism have not been positive. Some programs have abandoned the military-style training and incorporated educational, wilderness, job corps, and industrial components (Gowdy, 1993). Figure 12.8 shows the results from a study of three boot camps for juveniles. The Denver and Mobile sites show no reductions in recidivism, while the Cleveland program actually increased recidivism! Some other findings from boot camp evaluations make the following conclusions:

- Low- or moderate-risk juvenile and adult offenders who are subjected to high level of supervision (boot camps) actually do worse than those left on traditional probation (Altschuler & Armstrong, 1994).

- High percentage of minority youth are served by boot camps: conclusion is that boot camp model fails to connect with this population.

- Some evidence that the rate of recidivism declined in boot camp programs for adults where offenders spent 3 hours or more per day in therapeutic activity and had some type of aftercare (MacKenzie & Souryal, 1994).

- In general, studies have found similar recidivism rates for those who completed boot camps and comparable offenders who spent long periods of time in prison.

## Effectiveness of Intermediate Sanctions

There are many justifications for the use of intermediate sanctions as an alternative to incarceration. However, given the investment that many states have made in these options, the question of how effective they are in reducing recidivism is an important one. In a recent meta-analysis of intermediate sanctions, Gendreau, Goggin, and Fulton (1996) addressed this question. They examined research results from 44 ISP programs, 16 restitution programs, 13 boot camps, 13 scared straight programs, 9 drug testing programs, and 6 electronic monitoring programs. They found virtually no effect on recidivism, and where they did find some effect it appeared that some sanctions slightly increased recidivism! They conclude that "the 'get tough' revolution has been an abject failure when it comes to reducing recidivism."

## Summary

Intermediate sanctions have become a vital component of contemporary corrections. Two developments have led to a search for innovative and cost-effective programs; prison and jail crowding, and the development of new technologies, such as electronic monitoring and readily available drug testing. Not only are institutions crowded; probation, parole, and community corrections are also impacted by the waves of offenders caught in the arms of the law.

Our review of intermediate sanctions provides both insight into the reasons for the volume of clients, but also promising programs and strategies for managing the risks posed by different types of offenders who need differing treatments and supervision. Day reporting centers will continue to expand as their usefulness becomes better documented. Change will continue. This is an exciting time for corrections as a field and for students wishing to impact on the futures of clients and the safety of communities.

## Review Questions

1. Explain the difference between fines and day fines.

2. Why are boot camps so popular among the general public?

3. What roles do CRCs play in corrections?

4. What are the two basic types of electronic monitoring programs?

5. What are some of the limitations of electronic monitoring programs?

6. What do we know about the effectiveness of intensive supervision programs?

7. Why are day reporting programs gaining popularity?

## Key Terms

boot camp programs
day fines
day reporting centers
electronic monitoring
fines
home detention

intensive supervised probation
meta-analysis
net widening
shock incarceration
tourniquet sentencing

## Recommended Readings

Byrne, J.M., A. Lurigio, and J. Petersilia (1993). *Smart Sentencing*. Beverly Hills, CA: Sage.

Fulton, B., S. Stone, and P. Gendreau (1994). *Restructuring Intensive Supervision Programs: Applying "What Works."* Lexington, KY: American Probation and Parole Association.

Goldkamp, J. (1993). "Judicial Responsibility for Pretrial Release Decision-making and the Information Role of Pretrial Services." *Federal Probation*, 57(1):28-34.

Petersilia, J. (1998). *Community Corrections: Probation, Parole, and Intermediate Sanctions*. New York, NY: Oxford Press.

## Notes

[1]     Blumstein argues that the nation has not to date been able to meet the demand for additional prisons to build their way out of the crowding crisis. A. Blumstein (1995). "Prisons." In J. Wilson and J. Petersilia (eds.) (1995). *Crime*, pp. 387-419. San Francisco, CA: Institute for Contemporary Studies.

[2]     Not all new generation ISP programs have abandoned the treatment approach. See T. Clear and E.J. Latessa (1993). "Probation Office's Roles in Intensive Supervision versus Treatment." *Justice Quarterly*, 10:441-462. The American Probation and Parole Association is working with several states to modify their ISP programs from a control/surveillance orientation to one more treatment focused.

[3]     J. Byrne and F. Taxman (1994). "Crime Control Policy and Community Corrections Practice." *Evaluation and Program Planning* 17:227-233. See also F. Cullen, P. Van Voorhis and J. Sundt, "Prisons in Crisis: The American Experience." In R. Matthews and P. Francis (eds.) (1996). *Prisons 2000: An International Perspective on the Current State and Future of Imprisonment*. New York, NY: Macmillan.

[4]     Fulton, B., S. Stone, and P. Gendreau (1994). *Restructuring Intensive Supervision Programs: Applying 'What Works'.* Lexington, KY: American Probation and Parole Association.

[5]     For example, J.T. Whitehead, et al. found that intensive probation in Tennessee resulted in both diversion and net widening. They argued that if diversion is the only objective of intensive probation then the efforts might be misguided. See J.T. Whitehead, L.S. Miller and L.B. Myers (1995). "The Diversionary Effectiveness of Intensive Supervision and Community Corrections Programs." In J. Smykla and W. Selke (eds.) *Intermediate Sanctions: Sentencing in the 1990s*, pp. 135-151. Cincinnati, OH: Anderson Publishing Co.

[6]     Margaret Gordon and Daniel Glaser (1991). "The Use and Effects of Financial Penalties in Municipal Courts." *Criminology*, 29(4):651-676.

[7]     Day-fine sentences are being implemented in Maricopa County, Arizona, and in Oregon, Iowa, and Connecticut.

[8]     A discussion of the issues can be found in J. Goldkamp (1993). "Judicial Responsibility for Pretrial Release Decisionmaking and the Information Role of Pretrial Services." *Federal Probation*, 57(1):28-34. See also J. Rosen (1993). "Pretrial Services—A Magistrate Judge's Perspective," *Federal Probation*, 57(1):15-17, and E. McCann and D. Weber (1993). "Pretrial Services: A Prosecutor's View." *Federal Probation*, 57(1):18-22.

[9]     See in particular S. Rackmill (1994). "An Analysis of Home Confinement as a Sanction." *Federal Probation*, 58(1):45-52.

[10]     R.K. Schwitzgebel, R.L. Schwitzgebel, W.N. Pahnke, and W.S. Hurd (1964). "A Program of Research in Behavioral Electronics." *Behavioral Scientist*, 9(3):233-238. See also R.K. Gable (1986). "Application of Personal Telemonitoring to Current Problems in Corrections." *Journal of Criminal Justice*, 14(2):173-182; and J.R. Lilly, R. Ball, and W. Lotz (1986). "Electronic Jail Revisited." *Justice Quarterly*, 3(3):353-361.

[11]    George Mair, Evaluating Electronic Monitoring in England and Wales. Paper presented at the annual meeting of the American Society of Criminology, San Francisco, November 18, 1989. See also J.R. Lilly (1990). "Tagging Revisited." *The Howard Journal*, 29(4):229-245; and National Association for the Care of Offenders and the Prevention of Crime (1989). *The Electronic Monitoring of Offenders*. London, NACRO.

[12]    Keith Cooprider (1992). "Pretrial Bond Supervision: An Empirical Analysis with Policy Implications," *Federal Probation*, 56(3):41-49.

[13]    Richard Enor, Clifford Block and James Quinn, et al. (1992). *Alternative Sentencing: Electronically-Monitored Correctional Supervision*. Briston, IN: Wyndham Hall.

[14]    Estimating the size of the community corrections residential facility population is hazardous at best. In her 1987 article, however, Hicks reported interviews with representatives of California, Texas, and the Federal Bureau of Prisons. These officials estimated that by 1988, the combined total of offenders served in residential facilities for these three jurisdictions would exceed 7,000. Given that these numbers do not include probationers or misdemeanants in all three jurisdictions, a conservative extrapolation yields an estimated 70,000 offenders in residential facilities during 1988. This represents about 10 percent of the prison population for that year.

[15]    Shock probation originated in Ohio in 1965, and was designed to give first-time young adult offenders a "taste of the bars." Offenders were to be sentenced to prison, and then within 30-120 days be released on probation. It was assumed that the physical and psychological hardships of prison life would "shock" the offender straight.

[16]    The bulk of the following section is drawn from Government Accounting Office, Prison Boot Camps. Washington, DC: U.S. Department of Justice, 1993.

[17]    One boot camp program for female misdemeanants can be found in the Santa Clara (San Jose), California Office of the Sheriff.

## *References*

Allen, H.E., R.P. Seiter, E.W. Carlson, H.H. Bowman, J.J. Grandfield, and N.J. Beran (1976). *National Evaluation Program Phase I: Residential Inmate Aftercare the State of the Art Summary*. Columbus, OH: Program for the Study of Crime & Delinquency, Ohio State University.

Altschuler, D.M. and T.L. Armstrong (1994). *Intensive Aftercare for High-Risk Juveniles: A Community Care Model. Program Summary*. Washington, DC: Office of Juvenile Justice and Delinquency Prevention, Office of Justice Programs, U.S. Dept. of Justice.

American Correctional Association (1995). *Directory*. Laurel, MD: ACA.

American Correctional Association (1990). *Intermediate Punishment: Community-based Sanctions*. Baltimore, MD: United Book Press.

Blumstein, A. (1995). "Prisons." In J. Wilson and J. Petersilia (eds.) *Crime*, pp. 387-419. San Francisco, CA: Institute for Contemporary Studies.

Bureau of Justice Assistance (1989). *Electronic Monitoring in Intensive Probation and Parole Programs*. Washington, DC: U.S. Department of Justice.

Burkhart, W.R. (1986). "Intensive Probation Supervision: an Agenda for Research and Evaluation." *Federal Probation*, 50(2):75-77.

Byrne, J.M. and L. Kelly (1989). "Restructuring Probation as an Intermediate Sanction: An Evaluation of the Massachusetts Intensive Probation Supervision Program." *Final Report to the National Institute of Justice*. Washington, DC: U.S. Department of Justice.

Byrne, J.M., A.J. Lurigio, and C. Baird (1989). "The Effectiveness of the New Intensive Supervision Programs." *Research in Corrections*, 2.

Byrne, J.M., A.J. Lurigio, and J. Petersilia (1993). *Smart Sentencing*. Beverly Hills, CA: Sage.

Byrne, J.M. and F. Taxman (1994). "Crime Control Policy and Community Corrections Practice." *Evaluation and Program Planning*, 17:227-233.

Camp, C. and G. Camp (1997). *The Corrections Yearbook 1997*. South Salem, NY: Criminal Justice Institute.

Camp, C. and G. Camp (1995). *The Corrections Yearbook: Probation and Parole, 1995*. South Salem, NY: Criminal Justice Institute.

Clear, T. and E.J. Latessa (1993). "Probation Office's Roles in Intensive Supervision versus Treatment." *Justice Quarterly*, 10:441-462

Cooprider, K. (1992). "Pretrial Bond Supervision: An Empirical Analysis with Policy Implications." *Federal Probation*, 56(3):41-49.

Cullen, F., P. Van Voorhis, and J. Sundt (1996). "Prisons in Crisis: The American Experience." In R. Matthews and P. Francis (eds.) *Prisons 2000: An International Perspective on the Current State and Future of Imprisonment*. New York, NY: Macmillan.

Curtin, E. (1990). "Day Reporting Centers," in A. Travisino (ed.), *Intermediate Punishment: Community-based Sanctions*, pp. 72-73. Laurel, MD: American Correctional Association.

DuPont, P. (1985). *Expanding Sentencing Options: A Governor's Perspective*. Washington, DC: National Institute of Justice.

Enor, R., C. Block, and J. Quinn (1992). *Alternative Sentencing: Electronically-Monitored Correctional Supervision*. Bristol, IN: Wyndham Hall.

Erwin, B.S. (1987). *Final Report: Evaluation of Intensive Probation Supervision in Georgia*. Atlanta, GA: Georgia Department of Corrections.

Fallen, D., C. Apperson, J. Holt-Milligan, and J. Roe (1981). *Intensive Parole Supervision*. Olympia, WA: Department of Social and Health Services, Analysis and Information Service Division, Office of Research.

Finn, P. (1991). "State-by-State Guide to Enforcement of Civil Protection Orders." *Response to the Victimization of Women & Children*, 14(78):3-12.

Flynn, L. (1986). "House Arrest." *Corrections Today*, 48(5):64-68.

Fulton, B., P. Gendreau, M. Paparozzi (1996). "APPA's Prototypical Intensive Supervision Program: ISP As It Was Meant To Be." *Perspectives*, 19(2):25-41.

Fulton, B, E.J. Latessa, A. Stichman, and L.F. Travis (1997). "The State of ISP: Research and Policy Implications." *Federal Probation*, 61(4):65-75.

Fulton, B, S. Stone, and P. Gendreau (1994). *Restructuring Intensive Supervision Programs: Applying "What Works."* Lexington, KY: American Probation and Parole Association.

Gable, R.K. (1986). "Application of Personal Telemonitoring to Current Problems in Corrections." *Journal of Criminal Justice*, 14:173-182.

Gendreau, P., C. Goggin, and B. Fulton (1996). *Intensive Supervision in Probation and Parole*. In C.R. Hollin (ed). *Handbook of Offender Assessment and Treatment*. Chichester, UK: John Wiley & Son.

Goldkamp, J. (1993). "Judicial Responsibility for Pretrial Release Decisionmaking and the Information Role of Pretrial Services." *Federal Probation*, 57(1):28-34.

Gordon, M. and D. Glaser (1991). "The Use and Effects of Financial Penalties in Municipal Courts." *Criminology*, 29:651-676.

Gowdy, V. (1993). *Intermediate Sanctions*. Washington, DC: U.S. Department of Justice.

Government Accounting Office (1993). *Prison Boot Camps*. Washington, DC: U.S. Department of Justice.

Government Accounting Office (1990). *Intermediate Sanctions*. Washington, DC: USGAO.

Guynes, R. (1988). *Difficult Clients, Large Caseloads Plague Probation, Parole Agencies*. Washington, DC: U.S. Department of Justice.

Harland, A. (ed.) (1996) *Choosing Correctional Options That Work: Defining the Demand and Evaluating the Supply*. Thousand Oaks, CA: Sage.

Hartmann, D., P. Friday, and K. Minor (1994). "Residential Probation: A Seven-Year Follow-Up Study of Halfway House Discharges." *Journal of Criminal Justice*, 22:503-515.

Hicks, N. (1987). "A New Relationship: Halfway Houses and Corrections." *Corrections Compendium*, 12(4):1,5-7.

Huskey, B. (1992). "The Expanding Use of Community Reintegration Centers." *Corrections Today*, 54(8):70-74.

Johnson, G. and R. Hunter (1992). *Evaluation of the Specialized Drug Offender Program for the Colorado Judicial Department*. Boulder, CO: University of Colorado, Center for Action Research.

Jolin, A. and B. Stipak (1992). "Drug Treatment and Electronically Monitored Home Confinement: An Evaluation of a Community-Based Sentencing Option." *Crime & Delinquency*, 38:158-170.

Jolin, A. and B. Stipak (1991). *Clackamas County Community Corrections Intensive Drug Program: Program Evaluation Report*. Oregon City, OR: Clackamas County Community Corrections Division.

Jones, M. (1991). "Intensive Probation Supervision in Georgia, Massachusetts, and New Jersey." *Criminal Justice Research Bulletin*, 6(1):1-9.

Klein, M. (1988). *Alternative Sentencing:* Cincinnati, OH: Anderson Publishing Co.

Larivee, J. (1990). "Day Reporting Centers: Making Their Way from the U.K. to the U.S.," *Corrections Today*, (October):86-89.

Latessa, E. (1993a). *An Evaluation of the Lucas County Adult Probation Department's IDU and High Risk Groups.* Cincinnati, OH: Department of Criminal Justice, University of Cincinnati.

Latessa, E. (1993b). *Profile of the Special Units of the Lucas County Adult Probation Department.* Cincinnati, OH: Department of Criminal Justice, University of Cincinnati.

Latessa, E. (1992). *A Preliminary Evaluation of the Montgomery County Adult Probation Department's Intensive Supervision Program.* Cincinnati, OH: Department of Criminal Justice, University of Cincinnati.

Latessa, E. (1986). "Cost Effectiveness of Intensive Supervision." *Federal Probation,* 50(2):70-74.

Latessa, E. (1986). "Cost Effectiveness of Intensive Supervision." *Federal Probation,* 50(2):70-74.

Latessa, E. and L.F. Travis (1991). "Halfway Houses or Probation: A Comparison of Alternative Dispositions." *Journal of Crime and Justice,* 14:53-75.

Latessa, E., L. Travis, B. Fulton, and A. Stichman (1998). *Evaluating the Prototypical ISP: Results from Iowa and Connecticut.* Cincinnati: Division of Criminal Justice, University of Cincinnati.

Latessa, E., L.F. Travis, and A. Holsinger (1997). *Evaluation of Ohio's Community Corrections Act Programs and Community Based Correctional Facilities Final Report.* Cincinnati: Division of Criminal Justice, University of Cincinnati.

Latessa, E., L.F. Travis, A. Holsinger, J. Hartman (1998). *Evaluation of Ohio's Pilot Day Reporting Program Final Report.* Cincinnati, OH: Division of Criminal Justice, University of Cincinnati.

Lilly, J.R. (1990). "Tagging Revisited." *The Howard Journal,* 29:229-245.

Lilly, J.R., R. Ball, and R. Lotz (1986). "Electronic Jail Revisited." *Justice Quarterly,* 3:353-361.

McCann, E. and D. Weber (1993). "Pretrial Services: A Prosecutor's View." *Federal Probation,* 57(1):18-22.

McCarthy, B.R. (ed.) (1987). *Intermediate Punishments: Intensive Supervision, Home Confinement, and Electronic Surveillance.* Monsey, NY: Willow Tree Press.

McDevitt, J. (1988) *Evaluation of the Hampton County Day Reporting Center.* Boston, MA: Crime and Justice Foundation.

McDevitt, J. and R. Miliano (1992). "Day Reporting Centers: An Innovative Concept in Intermediate Sanctions." In J. Byrne, et al. (eds.) *Smart Sentencing,* pp. 153-165. Newbury Park, CA: Sage.

MacKenzie, D., J. Shaw, and V. Gowdy (1993). *An Evaluation of Shock Incarceration in Louisiana.* Washington, DC: U.S. Department of Justice.

MacKenzie, D. and C. Souryal (1994). *Multisite Evaluation of Shock Incarceration.* Washington, DC: National Institute of Justice, Office of Justice Programs, U.S. Dept. of Justice.

Maguire, K. and A. Pastore (eds.) (1994). *Sourcebook of Criminal Justice Statistics 1994.* Washington, DC: U.S. Department of Justice.

Mair, G. (1989). "Evaluating Electronic Monitoring in England and Wales." Paper presented at the annual meeting of the American Society of Criminology, San Francisco, California.

Maxfield, M. and T. Baumer (1990). "Home Detention with Electronic Monitoring: Comparing Pretrial and Postconviction Programs." *Crime & Delinquency*, 36:521-536.

Meecham, L. (1986). "House Arrest: The Oklahoma Experience." *Corrections Today*, 48:102-110.

Morris, N. and M. Tonry (1990). *Between Prison and Probation: Intermediate Punishments in a Rational Sentencing System*. Oxford: Oxford University Press.

National Association for the Care of Offenders and the Prevention of Crime (1989). *The Electronic Monitoring of Offenders*. London, NACRO.

Netherlands Ministry of Justice (1993). *Dutch Penal Law and Policy: Alternative Sanctions for Juveniles in the Netherlands*. The Hague: NMJ.

Orchowsky, S., N. Merritt, and K. Browning (1994). *Evaluation of the Virginia Department of Correction's Intensive Supervision Program: Executive Summary*. Richmond, VA: Virginia Department of Criminal Justice Services.

Paparozzi, M. (n.d.). An Evaluation of the New Jersey Board of Parole's Intensive Supervision Program. Unpublished Report.

Parent, D. (1996). "Day Reporting Centers: An Evolving Intermediate Sanction," *Federal Probation*, 60(4):51-54.

Parent, D. (1990). *Day Reporting Centers for Criminal Offenders—A Descriptive Analysis of Existing Programs*. Washington, DC: National Institute of Justice.

Parent, D., J. Byrne, V. Tsarfaty, L. Valade, and J. Esselman (1995). *Day Reporting Centers: Volume 1*. Washington, DC: National Institute of Justice.

Pearson, F.S. (1987). *Research on New Jersey's Intensive Supervision Program*. New Brunswick, NJ: Administrative Office of the Courts.

Peters, M., D. Thomas, and C. Zamberlan (1997). *Boot Camps for Juvenile Offenders Program Summary*. Washington, DC: Office of Justice Programs, Office of Juvenile Justice and Delinquency Program, U.S. Dept. of Justice.

Petersilia, J. (1998). *Community Corrections: Probation, Parole, and Intermediate Sanctions*. New York, NY: Oxford Press.

Petersilia, J. (1987). *Expanding Options for Criminal Sentencing*. Santa Monica, CA: Rand Publications.

Petersilia, J. (1985). *Probation and Felon Offenders*. Washington, DC: U.S. Department of Justice.

Petersilia, J. and S. Turner (1993). *Evaluating Intensive Supervised Probation/Parole Results of a Nationwide Experiment*. Washington, DC: U.S. Department of Justice.

Petersilia, J. and S. Turner (1990). *Intensive Supervision for High-Risk Probationers*. Santa Monica, CA: Rand Publications.

Rackmill, S. (1994). "Prisoner Handbook, Camp Reams Shock Incarceration Program: An Analysis of Home Confinement as a Sanction." *Federal Probation*, 58(1):45-52.

Rosen, J. (1993). "Pretrial Services—A Magistrate Judge's Perspective." *Federal Probation*, 57(1):15-17.

Rosenthal, C. (1989). "Opportunities in Community Corrections." *Criminal Justice Papers*, Illinois, Volume 5.

Rush, G. (1992). *The Dictionary of Criminal Justice*. Guilford, CT: Duskin.

Schwitzgebel, R.K., R.L. Schwitzgebel, W.N. Pahnke, and W.S. Hurd (1964). "A Program of Research in Behavioral Electronics." *Behavioral Scientist*, 9:233-238.

U.S. Department of Justice (1990). *Survey of Intermediate Sanctions*. Washington, DC: U.S. Government Printing Office.

Wagner, D. and C. Baird (1993). *Evaluation of the Florida Community Control Program*. Washington, DC: U.S. Department of Justice.

Whitehead, J.T., L.S. Miller, and L.B. Myers (1995). "The Diversionary Effectiveness of Intensive Supervision and Community Corrections Programs." In J. Smykla and W. Selke (eds.) *Intermediate Sanctions: Sentencing in the 1990s*, pp. 135-151. Cincinnati, OH: Anderson Publishing Co.

Winterfield, L. and S. Hillsman (1993). *The Staten Island Day-Fine Project*. Washington, DC: U.S. Department of Justice.

Zimmerman, S., B. Rivera, and M. Seis (1991). "An Indirect Assessment of Public Tolerance for Day Fines." Paper presented at the annual meeting of the Academy of Criminal Justice Sciences, Nashville, TN.

# Community Residential
# Correctional Programs

## 13

> [Community Residential Centers] play a
> vital role in the criminal justice system. They
> provide additional sentencing options for the
> court, protect public safety, provide individ-
> ualized and intensive service aimed at reduc-
> ing recidivism, and are cost-effective.
> —Bobbie L. Huskey

Community residential programs for criminal offenders have a long
history in the United States (Latessa & Travis, 1992; Hartmann et al.,
1994) Until very recently, the typical residential community correctional
facility was known as a "halfway house," a transitional residence for
criminal offenders (Wilson, 1985).

---

**Box 13.1**

### Halfway House

Community-based residential facility for offenders who
are either about to be released from an institution or who, immediately after release, are in the initial stages of return to society. In the last three decades, some halfway houses have been
designed as alternatives to jail or prison incarceration, primarily for probationers. Halfway now could mean halfway *into* or
*out* of prison.

---

This chapter places such programs in the larger context of corrections in the community, explaining the historical factors that contributed to the emergence of the halfway house movements; models of
halfway houses; and their current operations and practices, effectiveness, costs, and futures. We begin with an explanation of the birth of
the halfway house over time.

## Historical Development of the Halfway House in America

The halfway house concept began first in England and Ireland during the early 1800s, advocating transitional residences for criminal offenders. It spread quickly across the ocean; in 1817, the Massachusetts Prison Commission recommended establishing a temporary residence to house destitute offenders after release from prison (Cohn, 1973:2):

> The convicts who are discharged are often entirely destitute. The natural prejudice against them is so strong that they find great difficulty in obtaining employment. They are forced to seek shelter in the lowest receptacles; and if they wish to lead a new course of life, are easily persuaded out of it; and perhaps driven by necessity to the commission of fresh crimes. It is intended to afford a temporary shelter in this building, if they choose to accept it, to such discharged convicts as may have conducted themselves well in prison, subject to such regulations as the directors may see fit to provide. They will here have a lodging, rations from the prison at a cheap rate, and . . . a chance to occupy themselves in their trade, until some opportunity offers of placing themselves there they can gain an honest livelihood in society. A refuge of this kind, to this destitute class, would be found, perhaps, humane and political.

The Commission making this recommendation believed that ex-inmates needed an accepting transitional house immediately after release and a supportive environment to assist in the process of establishing a law-abiding and independent existence. It was also motivated by the intention to reduce the unacceptably high rate of recidivism among newly released inmates (Seiter & Carlson, 1977). Unfortunately, the Massachusetts Legislature feared that ex-prisoners might "contaminate" each other if housed together, neutralizing their newly instilled crime resistance learned in prison.

The concept, however, found fertile ground in other locations and under private sponsorship. In 1845, the Isaac T. Hooper Home in New York City opened under the auspices of the Quakers, and today operates as the Women's Prison Association and Hooper Home, serving female clients. Perhaps the most significant halfway house program in this earlier era was Hope House, established by Maud and Ballington Booth in 1896, in New York City. Supported both financially and morally by the Volunteers of America, other Hope Halls opened across the nation (Chicago, San Francisco, New Orleans, etc.). This earlier movement and Hope Halls in particular did not last. Parole was introduced and implemented widely in the early 1900s, as a means for controlling and helping ex-inmates after release from prison. The belief in likely and malevolent contamination from association with other parolees continued. The Great Depression weakened financial support for these privately operated homes, already under-funded. Phase I of the development of the halfway house ended shortly thereafter, not to revive until the 1950s.

The rebirth of the halfway house movement resulted, in part, from a growing awareness of the ineffectiveness of institutional corrections. High recidivism rates were interpreted as indications of ineffectiveness of prison as a venue for rehabilitation. The growing dissatisfaction with prisons was buttressed by new evidence that parolees face problems in the transition from imprisonment to a free society, evidence of the need for supportive services in the transition to community life. In 1954, numerous halfway houses opened in America (such as Crenshaw House in Los Angeles, and Dismas House in St. Louis, under the direction of Father Charles Dismas), England, and Canada. Private and religious groups pioneered in both the historical and revival phases of development of the halfway house.

Photo 13.1
A modern halfway house. Courtesy of Connecticut Halfway Houses, Inc.

Earlier in the revival phase, most houses used individualized treatment, counseling, employment referrals, and substance abuse counseling, reflecting the general correctional philosophy found within the prison: the medical model. Persons not yet committed to predatory criminal lifestyles, younger, and more malleable offenders were believed ideal clients for the medical model. Then Attorney General Robert Kennedy suggested in 1961 that federal funds be used to establish publicly operated halfway houses for juvenile and youthful offenders, leading to the establishment of the Prisoner Rehabilitation Act of 1965. This legislation authorized the Bureau of Prisons to establish community-based residences for adult and youthful pre-release offenders, as well as to transfer federal prisoners to privately sponsored halfway houses. In

1968, the Law Enforcement Assistance Administration began to provide substantial funds for establishing non-federal houses, a thrust that continued until 1980.

---

**Box 13.2**

### Federal Prisoner Rehabilitation Act

The Attorney General may extend the limits of the place of confinement of a prisoner as to whom there is reasonable cause to believe he will honor this trust, by authorizing him, under prescribed conditions, to . . .

1.  visit a specifically designated place for a period not to exceed 30 days and return to the same or another institution or facility. An extension of limits may be granted only to permit a visit to a dying relative, attendance at the funeral of a relative, the obtaining of medical services not otherwise available, the contacting of prospective employees, or for any other compelling reason consistent with the public interest; or

2.  work at paid employment or participate in a training program in the community on a voluntary basis while continuing as a prisoner of the institution or facility to which he is committed. . . .

---

Perhaps the most significant event in Phase II was the development of the International Halfway House Association (IHHA) in 1964.[1] This group, motivated by the absence of state and local support for halfway houses, established a voluntary professional organization of halfway house administrators and personnel (Wilson, 1985). IHHA (now known as the International Community Correctional Association) conducted numerous training workshops, sponsored training programs and conferences, and affiliated with the American Correctional Association.[2] The organization grew from 40 programs in 1966 to over 1,800 in 1982,[3] and now holds annual conferences that deal with "what works" in correctional intervention. Under the direction of the current executive director, Peter Kinziger, the ICCA has become a leader in promoting effective intervention in correctional treatment. As a result of these and related efforts, few cities and counties run their own residential treatment centers, and state programs that operate halfway houses usually contract with private-sector, non-profit halfway houses to provide services.

Box 13.3

### Day Reporting Centers

Community centers to which adults and sometimes juveniles report in lieu of incarceration or as a condition of probation. A variety of community or in-house programs may be offered, including individual and group counseling, job readiness training, Alcoholics Anonymous 12-Step Programs, drug abuse education, and so on. Participants usually return to their individual homes at night.

### Restitution Centers

Community residential centers for offenders ordered by the court to make financial payments to victims. Offenders may also be remanded as a condition of probation. The offender must seek and obtain employment, make restitution to victims, reimburse the center for room and board, and set aside any residual earnings for use after release. Center programs usually require curfews, strict alcohol and drug abstinence, and participation in community or in-house programs.

### Work Furlough Centers

Residential facility for sentenced offenders released from a correctional institution for work during the day. Residents typically spend nights and weekends in the facility and must participate in available community or in-house programs. Participants are generally charged a per diem fee for services, room, and board.

## Uses of Halfway Houses

Over the last 40 years, as suggested above, the numbers, roles, and uses of halfway houses increased considerably. There has been considerable role expansion in residential placements of adult (and juvenile) offenders. For the most part, the increase has been in the services provided to new groups: probationers, the accused awaiting trial, and offenders directly sentenced for treatment, ordered by a judiciary eager to secure services and supervision for offenders. Judges are usually unwilling to incarcerate clients likely to give up criminal behavior if a supportive and facilitating community environment could be provided in which the offenders remediate their needs and improve their functioning. These changes in roles, sentencing alternatives, clients, and use of halfway houses have rendered "halfway house" an obsolete term, one that has been replaced by the more accurate "community corrections residential facility." Rush (1992) defines such facilities as:

> A correctional facility from which residents are regularly permitted to depart, unaccompanied by any official, for the purposes of using community resources, such as school or treatment programs, and seeking or holding employment. This definition not only deletes the term "halfway" but also defines a correctional mission for the facility. The definition does not require centers to provide direct services to clients. Halfway houses are thus subsumed under the larger umbrella term, further reflecting the more diverse populations served, as well as broader correctional mission and such newer programs as day, restitution, and work-release centers.

Another major factor influencing the development and use of community residential centers in the United States has been a shift in the ideology of corrections, from rehabilitation to "reintegration," a term introduced by the President's Commission on Law Enforcement and Administration of Justice in 1967.

Box 13.4

### Reintegration

A broad correctional ideology stressing acquisition of legitimate skills and opportunities by criminal offenders, and the creation of supervised opportunities for testing, using, and refining those skills, particularly in community settings.

This correctional philosophy places priority on keeping offenders in the community whenever possible, rather than commitment to prison. It also stresses the role of the community in corrections. Thus the new ideology, new developments stressing community placement in local correctional programs, and existing halfway houses contributed to an accelerating expansion of community correctional residential programs. This thrust was further expanded by three factors:[4] (1) widespread correctional acceptance of the reintegration mission, (2) success of the reintegration movement in the mental health field, and (3) the lower costs of halfway houses as compared to prisons. Prison overcrowding in the 1980s and early 1990s, resulting from the War on Drugs, further accelerated the shift (Allen & Simonsen, 1992).

---

Box 13.5

### Community Residential Centers

Community residential centers (CRCs) are nonconfining residential facilities to adjudicated adults or juveniles, or those subject to criminal or juvenile proceedings. They are intended as an alternative for persons not suited to probation or who need a period of readjustment to the community after imprisonment.

There are more CRCs providing transitional and extensive services for juveniles than adults. Some CRCs specialize by client or treatment modality: for example, women only, abused women, prerelease federal furloughers, drug-dependent or alcohol abusers, the mentally ill, those identified by the court diagnostic program, or the developmentally disabled.

---

From 1980 through the present, prison inmates have increased dramatically, with now nearly 1,200,000 (Bureau of Justice Statistics, 1997), creating a lack of prison capacity and extensive prison overcrowding. The primary reason for the burgeoning prison population is believed to be the "War on Drugs," reflecting both the conservative emphases on retributive justice and the nation's unwillingness to address the causes of crime (Allen, 1995). Three major results of this development have been (1) an increase in the number of offenders placed on probation and parole, (2) an increase in the seriousness and dangerousness of offenses of those placed into traditional community-based supervision,[5] and (3) a heightened demand for community residential treatment facilities to provide transitional placement for offenders and to respond to such special needs populations as narcotics and drug abusers, offenders driving under the influence of alcohol or drugs, and mental health clients. Community residential facilities and programs expanded and changed to address these new demands, required programs, and heightened supervision levels (Huskey, 1992). Before addressing programs for these clients, it is necessary to understand the models on which the programs operate. Figure 13.1 shows the number of halfway houses in operation in 30 states and the Federal Government between 1994 and 1997. The number of inmates served in these facilities are presented in Figure 13.2. These data indicate that in 1997 nearly 15,000 inmates were served.

Figure 13.1
**Halfway Houses in Operation 1994-1997**

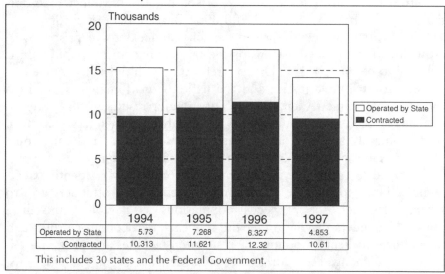

|  | 1994 | 1995 | 1996 | 1997 |
|---|---|---|---|---|
| Operated by State | 89 | 98 | 63 | 79 |
| Contracted | 526 | 510 | 521 | 485 |

This includes 30 states and the Federal Government.

Source: C. Camp and G. Camp (1997). *The Corrections Yearbook 1997*. South Salem, NY: The Criminal Justice Institute, Inc.

Figure 13.2
**Inmates Located at Halfway Houses 1994-1997**

|  | 1994 | 1995 | 1996 | 1997 |
|---|---|---|---|---|
| Operated by State | 5.73 | 7.268 | 6.327 | 4.853 |
| Contracted | 10.313 | 11.621 | 12.32 | 10.61 |

This includes 30 states and the Federal Government.

Source: C. Camp and G. Camp (1997). *The Corrections Yearbook 1997*. South Salem, NY: The Criminal Justice Institute, Inc.

## Models of Community Residential Programs

It should be remembered that Phase II of the development of community residential programs has been underway for more than 30 years. Thus, the models under which halfway houses and related community programs operate have also undergone significant change. We start by examining an earlier model in a less complex environment.

Figure 13.3
**Alternative Models of Halfway Houses**

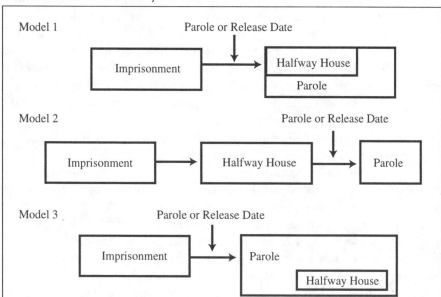

Source: E. Latessa and H. Allen (1982). "Halfway Houses and Parole: A National Assessment." *Journal of Criminal Justice,* 10:153-163.

In 1976, Allen et al. studied halfway houses and probation. These researchers developed three alternative models of halfway houses, based on referral service. This trichotomy is useful in depicting how halfway houses interface with the criminal justice system, as well as the advantages and services these programs offer to their clients. The trichotomy can be found in Figure 13.3 (Latessa & Allen, 1982).

---

**Box 13.6**

### Model

A picture or representation showing the parts of a system. Models suggest the ways that segments of the criminal justice system (courts, probation, prisons, etc.) fit together and interrelate. One implication of a model is that change in one part of the system will have an impact on the other parts of the system. A simplified demonstration of this is seen when law enforcement agencies increase arrests; judicial personnel, probation officers, and jail facilities face increased workloads.

Model 1 is the standard and most frequent pattern of referral to halfway house programs. In this model, an inmate granted a conditional release (such as parole, shock probation, or shock parole) enters a halfway house during the initial parole period. This model provides services to parolees who need support during their period of release. The length of residency in the halfway house may be specified before referral but usually is a shared decision to be made collaboratively by the supervision officer, house staff, and client. Typically, this decision is based on such factors as resident's readiness to leave the house, employment, savings, and alternative residential plan. After leaving the house, the offender generally continues on parole supervision.

Model 2 is similar to the first in that inmates' release plans call for placement in a halfway house as the initial phase of their release process. Unlike the first, however, halfway house residency occurs prior to formal granting of parole and subsequent supervision as a parolee. Typically, these inmates have been scheduled for a definite release date before moving from the prison to the halfway house. These clients remain *inmates*, serving the remainder of their sentences in residency at a halfway house. Halfway house residency provides needed and significant services in the prison-community transition. Additional benefits include continuation of jurisdiction by the referring correctional agency, ability to return the inmate to incarceration without formal violation of parole, development of a more positive attitude toward the halfway house by the resident, and less expensive after-care service that can be more legitimately compared to imprisonment, rather than the costs of parole.[6] The U.S. Bureau of Prisons was a leader in initiating this model for using halfway houses, and continues to use this model on a pre-release basis.[7]

The third model of halfway house use, also based on the reintegration model of corrections, differs by time of placement into the program. With Model 3, offenders on probation and inmates granted parole are assigned to the community without initially residing in a halfway house. If such clients may be reverting to criminal behavior or encounter unanticipated problems that might be resolved by program services of or a period of residency in a halfway house, the supervising agency may remand the offender to the residential setting for a short period. If and when conditions warrant, the client could then be returned to a lower level of supervision. It should be noted here that some residential correctional programs are large and can provide services and programs at many points in the supervision process, as will be explored below. Model 3 appears to best suggest the organization and practices of multi-service agencies in larger urban settings.

In addition to the models described above, halfways houses take on a wide range of functions and services depending on their size, mission, and resources. Figure 13.4 illustrates a continuum of types of programs based on the services they provide. Some halfway houses provide shelter, food, and minimal counseling and referral services. These programs are considered supportive halfway houses. Examples of these types of programs might include shelters and drop-in centers. Halfway houses that offer a full range of services can be considered interventive programs. These are programs that offer a full range of treatment services. Most programs fall somewhere in the middle.

---

**Box 13.7**

### Bureau of Prisons and Halfway Houses

The goal of BOP's halfway house program is to provide federal prison inmates a transition back to the communities where they will live upon release from federal custody. Besides subsistence and housing, BOP guidelines state that halfway house operators are required to offer inmates job counseling, academic and vocational training, family reconciliation services, access to substance abuse programs, post-release housing referrals, and community adjustment services. . . . In 1990, BOP reported it had contracts with 273 operators; this includes both profit and nonprofit operators. According to BOP's figures, halfway house contracts ranged from 1 to 150 beds for a total of 5,012 beds as of October 1990. Halfway house operators are reimbursed based on a daily rate for each inmate. The daily rates ranged from approximately $12 to $85 and averaged $33. In comparison, BOP averaged $49 for each inmate in a federal prison during 1990.

Source: U.S. Government Accounting Office, 1991.

---

Figure 13.4
**Types of Halfway Houses Based on Services**

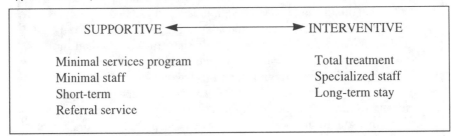

SUPPORTIVE ◄————————► INTERVENTIVE

| | |
|---|---|
| Minimal services program | Total treatment |
| Minimal staff | Specialized staff |
| Short-term | Long-term stay |
| Referral service | |

It should be obvious that roles of halfway houses as residential probation and after-care centers within the correctional process are varied in both operation and focus. Although all three models acknowledge the need for a residential setting at some point in the transition back to the community, there are various approaches and strategies for meeting these needs. To understand the range of alternatives, we will examine a rural community residential treatment center, as well as a larger urban counterpart.

## Rural Community Programs

Rural correctional programs serve a wide range of offenders and are themselves diverse. Whereas the "Mom and Pop" stereotype possibly typical of the earliest developments of rural community corrections has surely died,[8] what has emerged is an increasingly diversified pattern of local programs that solidly reflect the concept of "residential community corrections programs."[9] See, for example, Hilltop House (Durango, Colorado), Portage House (Stevens Point, Wisconsin), Re-Entry House (western upper peninsula in Michigan).

---

Box 13.8

### Rural Community Corrections

Community corrections in its rural expression is the remnant of the grassroots folkart of the original concept. Rural programs are generally not larger than 40 beds (a LARGE rural program) and are concerned about the importation of offenders regularly into their community, the meeting of the next payroll, the expense of travel to training as opposed to the cost of training itself. The rural program generally is not faced with the challenge of adequately accessing and implementing brokerages to existing treatment in their community; we are worried about how to create, fund and perpetuate treatment. Our "community" may be a town of 12,000 serving a catchment area of several hundred miles. Our worries are not typically of gang behavior between "Crips and Bloods." They may, however, include the American Indian in any of its numerous tribal groups, the rural hispanic or black, all in the delicately interwoven and overwoven social fabric of the lineages of a rural community. Every individual job truly means the future of our programs. The failure of one client can affect the future political support of our program; a single incident cannot only destroy a program but also the potential efforts of any program to replace it (Berry, 1990:6-7).

Community residential correctional programs in rural settings face differing challenges. They are smaller, and fewer employment opportunities and educational alternatives exist in local areas for their offender clients. Residents are drawn from a small pool of eligible offenders. These programs face and must overcome community suspicion that the center's existence may attract recalcitrant offenders who will move their base of criminal activities to the local area, the "importation" reaction. Decreased societal tolerance for certain offender types (such as rapists, child molesters, and drug pushers), coupled with concerns over public safety and demands for increased supervision have great potential to restrict treatment, job and educational placement, access to existing treatment programs, and funding from community sources. Many facilities must work hard to interface with referral sources (probation and parole agencies, for example), and develop liaisons with other services offered by mental health, drug, alcohol, sexual abuse, and court agencies.

These opportunities and challenges face Hilltop House,[10] a 28-bed private, nonprofit agency providing residential services to male offenders, and outpatient services to delinquents and victims referred from local, state, and federal sources. In its earliest days, this small program would close in the winter and re-open in the spring, housing not more than 12 clients referred from one judicial district. It now serves a much wider catchment area, working with six district court judges.

Photo 13.2
Substance abuse group. Courtesy of Talbert House, Inc.

Hilltop House began to grow in this environment, even though encountering the conservative political swing that demanded longer sentences, less diversion, and specialized programs to assist the higher-need clients the justice system was processing. This demand was met by:

- Developing liaisons with other court referral units and probation officers.

- Working with non-incarcerated populations (such as misdemeanant offenders, persons driving under the influence, self-referred persons with drug and alcohol abuse problems, youth referred by their parents, and so on).

- Developing new service programs in the areas of incest treatment and domestic violence, and urinalysis collection and testing for a county youth home, private schools, social services, employers, individuals, and parents.

- Developing a sexual abuse treatment team, using workers from a number of agencies and providing service to offenders, their non-offending spouses, victims, and other adults who had been molested as children (AMACs). This multi-agency approach was expanded to include juvenile restitution, a program using many volunteers as mediators and providing subsidized employment and monitored restitution payments, as well as group therapy to reconcile victims and their offenders, and develop empathy among juvenile offenders.

Hilltop House appears to serve the specific needs of the community, develop resources to plan and initiate specialized services, and maximize the therapeutic gains for clients, victims, and citizens. Individuals who resolve conflicts, personal problems, challenges, development problems, and the impacts of being victimized, are more likely to become constructive citizens and lower the crime rate in their community.

---

Box 13.9

### America's Community Residential Centers

A national survey of CRCs in 1991 found more than 1,000 agencies. The most common type of residential programs were a combination of drug treatment and work release centers. The three most frequent types of services provided to clients were job development, drug testing, and counseling. In descending order, their clients were prison pre-releasees, inmates, and probationers. In 1991 alone, more than 16,000 offenders were diverted from incarceration. The rate of program completion is high (more than 70%), and the failure rate (rearrest while in program) was only 3 percent! (Huskey, 1992:70).

---

## Metropolitan Residential Programs

Residential community correctional programs for offenders that are located in urban areas are more numerous and diverse than those in rural areas. In addition, many of the largest programs make extensive use of existing community services, especially if these are needed adjuncts to a treatment plan for an individual client. Treatment generally falls into two categories: individual and group. Individual or one-to-one counseling is probably the most frequently encountered program, available to all offenders and specifically intended to assist individual offenders in dealing with their particular problem or readjustment issue. Three major forms of group treatment are group counseling, group psychotherapy, and guided group interaction. For programs intended to address a specific sub-population with a common problem, a particular treatment model may be offered. Those with alcohol problems may be required to undergo urinalysis, participate in Alcoholics Anonymous, and receive individual and group counseling. Figure 13.5 shows an example of a Halfway House Intake Form.

Programs for drug abusers might include methadone maintenance, weekly and unscheduled urinalysis, transactional analysis, Narcotics Anonymous, and residence in a therapeutic community. Ideally, the offender's entire lifestyle would be changed, and longer-term treatment would be needed.

It should be noted that in 1995, more than 50 percent of all male arrestees tested positive for at least one drug (*Drug Use Forecasting*, 1995), and about one in four reported using a major drug (PCP, heroin, crack, cocaine, or LSD) in that month (Bureau of Justice Statistics, 1995). The rate for convicted female jail inmates was just as high: more than one-half had used drugs in the month prior to the current offense, and approximately 40 percent used drugs daily. According to the U.S. Department of Justice (Greenfield & Minor-Harper, 1991), for women in prison, the use rates were 39 percent (in the prior month) and 24 percent (daily use of major drugs). Alcohol and drug abuse underlies much criminal behavior, and such clients have high needs for treatment that community residential correctional facilities can meet.[11]

---

**Box 13.10**

### Alcoholics and Treatment

Many community corrections center programs focus on Alcoholics Anonymous as part of the overall abstinence program. This may mean requiring residents to memorize the 12 steps of AA, demonstrate understanding of the program, design a post-release plan, chair an AA meeting, and participate in the affairs of the program. The latter might include house chores (vacuuming, cleaning restrooms, shoveling snow, cleaning ashtrays, etc.), attending house meetings, remaining sober and clean, working outside the program, and seeking specialized treatment. If the resident's family unit is not broken, reconciliation counseling might be required. If appropriate, the resident might be required to participate in meetings of Adult Children of Alcoholics (ACAs), or child sexual abuse and domestic violence programs. When alcohol is the underlying cause of criminal behavior, an individually designed, monitored, and supportive program may sharply reduce criminal activity.

Figure 13.5
**Halfway House Intake Form (Form A-2)**

## GENERAL INFORMATION

**1.**

(First)    (Middle)    (Last)    Client Name

**2.** ☐☐☐☐☐☐ Client T.H. ID #

**3.** ☐☐☐-☐☐-☐☐☐☐ Client SS #

**4.** ☐ Admission Status:
(1) New Admission
(2) Re-Admission (within fiscal year)
(3) Re-Admittance after Escape/Absconding
(within fiscal year)
(4) Legal Status Altered

**5.** ☐☐/☐☐/☐☐ Date of Birth (mo/day/yr)

**6.** ☐ Sex (1) Male    (2) Female

**7.** ☐ Race
(AI) American Indian    (OR) Oriental
(BL) Black    (WH) White
(HI) Hispanic    (Specify) Other _____

**7a.** ☐ Appalachian    (1) Yes    (2) No

**8.** ☐ Current Marital Status
(1) Single    (4) Married
(2) Divorced    (5) Separated
(3) Widowed    (6) Common Law

**9.** ☐☐ Number of Dependents (financial responsibility other than self)

**10.** ☐☐ Number of Children

**11.** ☐ Legal Responsibility for Children?    (1) Yes (2) No

**12.** ☐☐☐☐☐ Zip Code of Last Community Address

**13.** ☐ Homeless Before Arrest?    (1) Yes (2) No

**14.** ☐ Place to Live When Discharged?    (1) Yes (2) No

**15.** ☐ Primary Source of Income (at present)
(1) Public Assistance    (5) Family
(2) Investments    (6) No Income
(3) Full-Time Employment    (7) Other _____
(4) Part-Time Employment

**15a.** ☐☐☐☐☐ Total Income Last Year (Nearest Dollar)

**16.** ☐☐☐☐☐ Court Costs Owed (Nearest Dollar)

**17.** ☐☐☐☐☐ Restitution Owed (Nearest Dollar)

## CRIMINAL HISTORY

Note: When answering questions 19-30, if the information is not available from the referral source, use client-reported answers.

**18.** ☐☐☐☐.☐☐☐ Ohio Revised Code for which convicted.

**19.** ☐☐ Number of prior felony convictions (adult/juvenile).

**20.** ☐☐ Number of prior adult felony commitments in a state or federal institution (when sentenced).

**21.** ☐☐ Age at admission to institution (or probation) for current offense.

**22.** ☐☐ Number of offenses (including current offense) committed while under parole/probation supervision.

**23.** ☐☐ Number of offenses (including current offense) involving drugs/alcohol.

**24.** ☐☐ Number of prior arrests during the past five years, prior to incarceration.

**25.** ☐☐ Number of offenses (including current offense) for auto theft.

**26.** ☐☐ Number of offenses (including current offense) involving serious injury to the victim.

**27.** ☐☐ Number of offenses (including current offense) involving the use of a weapon.

**28.** ☐ Has this individual been previously convicted for the same offense? (1) Yes   (2) No

**29.** ☐ Was the current conviction for multiple crimes? (1) Yes   (2) No

**30.** ☐ Was the offender employed at the time of arrest? (1) Yes   (2) No

Figure 13.5—*continued*

## EDUCATION AND EMPLOYMENT HISTORY

31. ☐☐  Years of education attained (last grade completed).

32. ☐  Highest diploma/degree received and name major subject area where applicable.
(1) None
(2) G.E.D.
(3) High School
(4) College        Associate/Major      _____
                   Bachelor/Major       _____
                   Master's/Major       _____
                   Doctoral/Major       _____

33. ☐☐  Years of vocational training.

34. ☐  Certification of vocational training awarded
(1) Yes _____ Trade
(2) No

### Enter 1 for YES  2 for NO for Questions 35-37

35. ☐  Physical/Health impairments (e.g., amputee, paraplegic, deaf, blind, serious illness, debilitating effect of age)

36. ☐  Mental capacity impairment (e.g., diagnosed mental retardation, diagnosed borderline MR)

37. ☐  Behavioral impairment (e.g., mental and/or emotional condition or disorders that require the treatment of a qualified mental health professional).

38. ☐☐  Number of jobs held in the last two years in the community prior to incarceration.

39. ☐☐  Longest stay on the job in the last two years in the community (number of months).

## CLIENT/STAFF ASSISTANCE ASSESSMENT

### Enter 1 for YES  2 for NO for Questions 40-55

40. ☐  Does client feel he/she needs assistance while in residency?

41. ☐  Does this individual need employment assistance?

42. ☐  Does this individual need assistance in academic or vocational training?

43. ☐  Does this individual need assistance in financial management?

44. ☐  Does individual need assistance in the area of domestic relations (e.g., marriage, family, etc.)?

45. ☐  Does this individual need assistance in the area of emotional or mental health?

46. ☐  Is this individual currently required to take medication for any psychological condition?

47. ☐  Does this individual need assistance for a substance abuse (alcohol/drug) problem?

48. ☐  Does this individual need assistance with securing suitable living arrangements?

49. ☐  Does this individual need assistance for a learning disability?

50. ☐  Has medication ever been prescribed for a psychological condition (e.g., nerves)?

51. ☐  Has client had prior psychiatric hospitalization?

52. ☐  Has client ever attempted suicide?

53. ☐  Was client ever a victim of child abuse?

54. ☐  Was client ever a victim of domestic violence?

55. ☐  Was client ever a victim of sexual abuse or incest?

## DRUG/ALCOHOL HISTORY

56. ☐☐  # times client had prior drug/alcohol treatment.

57. ☐☐  # months prior outpatient treatment.

58. ☐  Successful?  (1) Yes  (2) No  (3) NA

59. ☐☐  # months prior inpatient treatment.

60. ☐  Successful?  (1) Yes  (2) No  (3) NA

61. ☐☐  # months prior Halfway House treatment.

62. ☐  Successful?  (1) Yes  (2) No  (3) NA

63. ☐  Has client participated in a halfway house **program** before this occasion?
(1) Yes          (2) No

64. ☐☐  Longest period of drug/alcohol abstinence in community (months) **or** (99) No problem

Staff member completing form

_____

Date  _____

Rev. 061992

Many urban communities across the nation face the problem of finding treatment opportunities that permit reintegration of high-need offenders, such as described above. Increasingly, these counties are turning to private sector, non-profit residential programs for assistance. Figure 13.6 suggests how such residential and community programs can interface with traditional justice agencies in provision of services.

Figure 13.6
**A Reintegration Model**

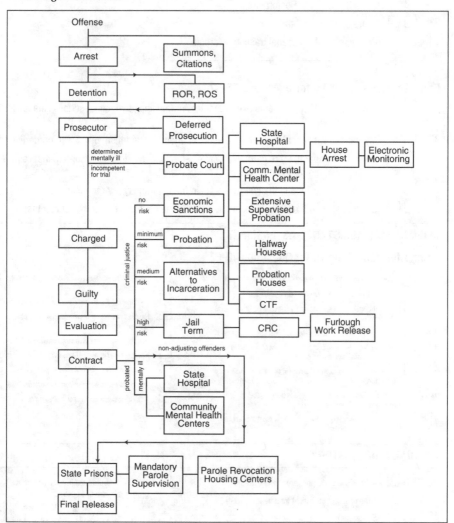

Source: H. Allen and C. Simonsen (1995). *Corrections in America*, p. 665. Englewood Cliffs, NJ: Prentice-Hall.

At the court level, programs can be found that assist judges in working with the mental heath system. Many offenders are referred to the courts as a result of their mental health problems (Michaels et al., 1992). Program staff may provide judges with options regarding clients, conduct assessments, and serve as liaison between the criminal justice and mental health system. One promising program increasingly popular at this level is the Crisis Care Center, a program that runs a 24-hour crisis intervention and suicide prevention program. Inside the facility, staff-run group counseling session for survivors of suicide attempts, survivors of incest, support groups for offenders with learning disabilities, and drug and alcohol abuse prevention programs.

Another group of problem offenders are those with both mental illness and substance abuse problems. County community health boards and criminal courts can both use services for these offenders. Some types of programs would include the "Narcotic Out-Patient and Residential Program for Rehabilitation of Drug Addicts" that would run a therapeutic community for drug addicts, and a "Narcotics Addiction Program" that would run a residential youth treatment program for adolescents ages 13-17. Typically, the service programs in such a Center might include day treatment, residential, and case management services. The Center might charge by the hour, and most clients would receive services through Medicaid payments; others would have insurance, or make direct payment. This set of dually diagnosed offenders is being increasingly recognized as forming a significant client population in need of very specialized services.

At the probation department level, probationers might be referred to the Drug and Family Counseling Center for counseling revolving around methadone maintenance and family services. Increasingly across the nation, proponents of the reintegration model argue that substance abuse and chemical dependency is a disease with its own symptoms, needs for treatment, and particular need for involving family members of clients.

The Female Chemical Dependency Center would provide comprehensive services to women referred through probation agencies. Programs in the Center would include self-esteem development, parenting issues, Batterers Anonymous, substance abuse services, women's health issues, chemical dependence counseling, and case management services to probation departments (Hamm & Kite, 1991).

Day centers are facilities to which probationers report during ordinary working hours, to undertake job readiness training, to learn how to fill out employment applications, schedule time and money, improve working habits and relating to others, and understand and facilitate behaviors with the opposite gender. Job referrals and application coaching, including videotaping of mock employment interviews, are frequently found in these programs.

Restitution centers are facilities receiving court-ordered remand of offenders who must reside in the Center, work, make restitution to their victims, meet in victim-offender reconciliation, learn to appreciate the impacts of their criminal behavior on victims, and save money for use on their return to the community. Nominal room and board fees (such as $15/day) are routinely charged to residents, who usually must agree to have paychecks made payable to themselves and the Restitution Center. The Center disburses payments according to court orders.

Courts are increasingly using split-sentencing to dispose of misdemeanor and felony offenses, requiring a term of incarceration in the county jail, to be followed by a number of years or term on probation. Jail-related programs found at this level include work-release programs, DUI driver intervention programs, and residential treatment programs for men and women convicted and incarcerated for driving under the influence of alcohol and drugs.

Work-release programs, in lieu of jail incarceration, are frequently found in Centers providing 24-hour supervision, job readiness and referral services, and counseling services. Residents are required to work (or locate jobs), pay room and board charges, pay off court costs and fines, observe curfews, and remain at the Center during non-work hours. Residents may also be required to participate in in-house as well as community programs.

Drunk driving intervention programs are designed to provide education and assessment through individual and large group activities and counseling. If used in conjunction with probation, written assessment of progress would provide feedback to probation officers supervising such cases. Many of these programs are 72-hour weekend residential programs in lieu of incarceration, and may run from Thursday night to Sunday morning.

Those released from a mandatory jail sentence for driving under the influence (DUI) may be required as part of the split-sentence to reside for up to 30 days in a residential treatment program for men and women who were in jail for multiple DUI convictions. The residential program not only protects the community from these drivers while they are in residence, but delivers treatment to the clients for their disease. Habitual drunk drivers learn how to control their drinking, self-assessment, behavior control, time management, alternative recreational patterns, identifying and resolving familial problems, and parenting skills. Residents may also be referred to Alcoholics Anonymous as part of the residential phase of their community correctional program.

Perhaps the best example of a comprehensive multi-service agency is Talbert House, Inc. operating out of Cincinnati, Ohio. Talbert House began in 1965 with one halfway house for men. Today it has over 21 programs, and serves more than 12,000 clients per year.[12] Table 13.1 describes the five community residential treatment programs offered by Talbert House. Two of the programs are designed specifically to serve female offenders. Community residential correctional programs of these types exist across the nation and will increase in number and importance in the coming years. The private sector providing these programs, facilities and centers will grow as cities and counties, facing fiscal and policy crises, accept and introduce these programs in their local areas.

## Effectiveness of Community Residential Programs

The question of the effectiveness of halfway houses, along with other community corrections programs, is addressed in Chapter 14. A brief summary statement is included here to place both phases of the halfway house movements in perspective.

Evaluation of effectiveness of halfway houses and, more recently, residential community correctional programs, requires that they be considered across three dimensions: humaneness, recidivism, and cost studies (Latessa & Allen, 1982). There is little doubt that halfway houses, during both phases, were and are more humanitarian that imprisonment. Halfway houses programs were established in part to address the devastating economic and psychological effects of prisons and prisonization of most inmates. Prison crowding, gross idleness of inmates, absence of meaningful

Photo 13.3
Mental health program. Courtesy of Talbert House, Inc.

work and vocational training, unhealthy and unsafe physical plants, prison rape, and gang conflicts within prisons make prisons less than the pinnacle of humanitarianism (Donnelly & Forschner, 1987). Halfway houses are more humane, although the conservative punishment emphases in the last two decades raises policy questions about whether American correctional policy ought to be so (Latessa & Allen, 1982).

The weight of evidence to date demonstrates that halfway houses are cost effective in terms of expenditure of public funds when compared to institutional placement. Further, their programs achieve some if not all stated objectives, including the maintenance of offenders' community ties and making community resources available to offender clients (Dowell et al., 1985).

**Table 13.1**
**Description of Community Residential Treatment Programs**

| | Cornerstone | Beekman Work Release Center | Pathways | Talbert House for Women | McMillan House for Young Men |
|---|---|---|---|---|---|
| Location (Cincinnati, OH) | 2216 Vine St. | 2438 Beekman St. | 334 McGregor St. | 3123 Woodburn Ave. | 1105 McMillan St. |
| Number of Beds Available | 48 | 57 | 20 | 20 | 20 |
| Total Number of Staff | 26 | 20 | 13 | 13 | 13 |
| Number of Professional Staff | 8 | 8 | 5 (plus 2 shared) | 5 (plus 2 shared) | 5 (plus 2 shared) |
| Gender of Clients | Male | Male | Female | Female | Male |
| Age of Clients | 18 and older | 18 and older | 18 and older | 18 and older | age 16-22 |
| **Referral Sources** | | | | | |
| Federal Bureau of Prisons | X | | | X | |
| Federal Probation | X | | | X | |
| Ohio Parole Authority | X | | X | X | X |
| Hamilton County Municipal Court | X | | X | X | X |
| Hamilton County Common Pleas Court | X | X | X | X | X |
| Any Ohio Common Pleas Court | X | | X | X | X |
| DRC for Furlough | X | X | | | |
| **Services Offered** | | | | | |
| Employment and Education Assistance | X | X | X | X | X |
| Chemical Dependency Assessment and Treatment | X | X | X | X | X |
| Financial Management | X | X | X | X | X |
| Personal and Social Development Assistance | X | X | X | X | X |
| Parenting Education | X | X | X | X | X |
| Discharge/Aftercare Planning | X | | X | X | X |
| Self-Esteem Building | | | X | | X |
| Relationship Formation | | | X | | X |
| Structured Sober Leisure Activity | | | X | X | |
| Life Skills | | | X | | |
| ABE and GED Classes | | | X | X | |
| **Level of Supervision** | | | | | |
| Traditional Community Residential | X | | X | X | X |
| Work Release Supervision | X | X | X | X | X |

Source: E.J. Latessa, R.H. Langworthy, and A.D. Thomas (1995). *Community Residential Treatment Program Evaluation for Talbert House, Inc.* Cincinnati, OH: Department of Criminal Justice, University of Cincinnati.

---

**Box 13.11**

### Humaneness of Halfway Houses

[B]ecause of the difficulty of assessing humaneness and behavioral changes, most researchers tend to ignore these variables to pursue more quantifiable data. However, anyone who has worked in or around halfway houses has seen positive changes of the lives of many who enter these programs.

—George Wilson

---

The issue of recidivism is much more complex, particularly with regard to halfway houses. The diversity of halfway houses, as well as the range of types of offenders they serve (parolees, probationers, pretrial detainees, work releasees, and furloughees, not to mention state, county, and federal offenders) make it difficult to develop adequate comparison groups for follow-up studies.[13] The recidivism studies of CRC residents that exist indicate success with about 71 percent of the clients, and in-program rearrest rates of 2 to 17 percent (Huskey, 1992). Follow-up recidivism studies of alcohol-abusing clients show success rates ranging from 70 to 80 percent; driving-under-the-influence rates can be significantly reduced with residential treatment, significantly raising the DUI survival rates (Langworthy & Latessa, 1993; Langworthy & Latessa, 1996). For clients who graduate from CRC programs, success rates can be as high as 92 percent (Friday & Wertkin, 1995). On the whole, follow-up recidivism studies indicate that halfway house residents perform no worse than offenders who receive other correctional sanctions. There is also some evidence that offenders placed in halfway houses have more needs than other offenders (Latessa & Travis, 1991). Latessa (1998) has examined a number of halfway houses across the country. He has several criticisms that are noteworthy:

- Many halfway houses fail to adequately assess offenders, and there are few distinctions made between offenders based on risk;

- In general, qualifications of staff are low, and there is a great deal of staff turnover;

- Most halfway houses offer a wide range of "eclectic" treatment, with little if any theoretically based treatment models in place; and

- Despite some notable exceptions, most halfway houses can be classified as one step above "three hots and a cot."

Box 13.12

**Community-Based Correctional Facilities**

In one of the more unique attempts to provide residential treatment programs, Ohio has developed a correctional alternative called Community-Based Correctional Facilities or CBCFs. Currently there are 12 operating CBCFs in Ohio, and several more in the planning stages. The size of the facilities ranges from 54 to 200 offenders, and several serve both males and females. Funding for the CBCFs is provided by the state, however, the operation and management of the CBCF is left to a local judicial corrections board. In some instances, the local courts operate the facilities, and in other cases, private providers are retained. The CBCFs are secure facilities, however, treatment is the primary focus. Ohio has also developed similar juvenile programs called Community Correctional Facilities.

## The Future of Residential Community Corrections

Predicting future correctional trends is difficult due to possible national policy changes, economic fluctuations, crime trends, and public sentiment. One thing is evident: public sentiment for increasing punishment of offenders in the hope of lessening crime[14] remains strong. Thus it is reasonable to expect increased numbers of offenders in jails and prisons, and on probation, parole, and other community correctional programs.

Despite the increased use of punishment, the future of residential community correctional programs appears promising. Probation populations are at an all-time high, and approximately 95 percent of prison inmates will return to the community. Halfway houses and other community-based programs will be needed to assist in their reintegration. Early release programs, such as work and educational furlough and pre-parole release, will also increase, furthering the demand for services of halfway houses and related programs.

It is also likely that local units of government will increasingly turn to private-sector providers for correctional (and perhaps law enforcement) programs, contracting with larger numbers of halfway houses to provide lower-cost and diverse services that government cannot otherwise fund. To do less would decrease reintegration services and increase the possibility of offenders returning to prisons for committing new crimes in local communities. Indeed, one of the issues facing community corrections is the increased privatization of services and programs.

While non-profit providers have always been the mainstay of traditional halfway houses, the influx of for-profit providers will likely change the face of this industry. Figure 13.7 shows the average daily cost per inmate of halfway houses. These data clearly show that programs operated by contractors are lower cost than those operated by the states.

Figure 13.7
**Halfway House Daily Costs Per Inmate 1991-1996**

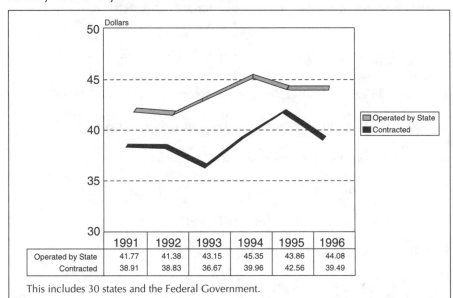

| | 1991 | 1992 | 1993 | 1994 | 1995 | 1996 |
|---|---|---|---|---|---|---|
| Operated by State | 41.77 | 41.38 | 43.15 | 45.35 | 43.86 | 44.08 |
| Contracted | 38.91 | 38.83 | 36.67 | 39.96 | 42.56 | 39.49 |

This includes 30 states and the Federal Government.

Source: C. Camp and G. Camp (1997). *The Corrections Yearbook 1997*. South Salem, NY: The Criminal Justice Institute, Inc.

Halfway houses and related programs will also need to increase the quality and effectiveness,[15] of programs to serve the demands of clients, communities, and corrections. To do this, they will need to maintain relationships with justice agencies, strengthen community ties and acceptance, adopt treatment models that have demonstrated effectiveness, and assist in insuring the safety of the community in reintegrating offenders. Future research will also be needed to address the roles and effectiveness of community residential correctional programs. Fortunately, there is a movement underway to improve the effectiveness of community correctional programs. This movement is being supported by the National Institute of Corrections[1] and the International Community Corrections Association, and is based on the work of scholars such as Paul Gendreau, Don Andrews, Francis Cullen, and others. Through their research we continue to learn about "what works" with offenders.

## Summary

Halfway houses have been part of the correctional scene since the early 1800s. Originally designed to assist offenders who had been released from prison, today, many halfway houses serve as both halfway "in" and halfway "out" facilities. Often called community residential correctional programs, these facilities include both privately and publicly operated programs, and range from "three hots and cot," to programs designed to meet all of an offender's treatment needs.

## *Review Questions*

1.  Why did Phase I of the halfway house movement die in the 1930s?

2.  Explain the revival of the halfway house movement in the 1950s.

3.  Define residential community correctional center.

4.  Why are prisons overcrowded?

5.  What are the advantages of halfway houses?

6.  What is "substance abuse?" Is it a disease?

7.  Define "reintegration" and show how halfway houses can lower crime.

8.  What are some of Latessa's criticisms of halfway houses?

## *Key Terms*

"ACAs"

"AMACs"

CBCFs

crisis care center

dually diagnosed offenders

halfway house

"importation"

reintegration

residential community correctional
    program

restitution center

work furlough

## Recommended Readings

Allen, H.E., E. Carlson, E. Parks, and R. Seiter (1978). *Program Models: Halfway Houses.* Washington, DC: U.S. Department of Justice.

Latessa, E.J. and L.F. Travis (1992). "Residential Community Correctional Programs." In J.M. Byrne and A. Lurigio (eds.) *Smart Sentencing? An Examination of the Emergence of Intermediate Sentencing*, pp. 166-181. Beverly Hills, CA: Sage.

Wilson, G. (1985). "Halfway House Programs for Offenders." In Lawrence F. Travis (ed.) *Probation, Parole and Community Corrections*, pp. 151-164. Prospect Heights, IL: Waveland.

## Notes

[1]    This organization is now known as the International Community Corrections Association, publishes the *ICCA Journal*, and sponsors local, state, regional, national, and international conferences and training programs concerned with halfway houses and community alternatives. Contract ICCA Central Office, P.O. Box 1987, LaCrosse, WI 54602.

[2]    The American Correctional Association, 4380 Forbes Boulevard, Lanham, MD20706-4322.

[3]    The National Institute of Corrections lists more than 1,200 programs in its *1989 Directory of Residential Community Corrections Facilities in the United States*. The *Directory* does not list all small programs, particularly in rural areas. National Institute of Corrections, 1860 Industrial Circle, Suite A, Longmont, CA 80501.

[4]    Harry E. Allen, Eric Carlson, Evalyn Parks, and Richard Seiter. *Program Models: Halfway Houses* (Washington, DC: U.S. Department of Justice, 1978).

[5]    Joan Petersilia, Susan Turner, James Kahan, and Joyce Peterson (1985). *Granting Felons Probation: Risks and Alternatives*, p. 15. Santa Monica, CA: Rand.

[6]    This question is explored in more detail in Nancy Hicks (October, 1987). "Halfway Houses and Corrections." *Corrections Compendium*, 12:1-7. See also G. Wilson (1985). "Halfway House Programs for Offenders." In Lawrence F. Travis (ed.) *Probation, Parole and Community Corrections*, pp. 158-159. Prospect Heights, IL: Waveland; E. Latessa and Lawrence F. Travis (1992). "Residential Community Correctional Programs." In J.M. Byrne and A. Lurigio (eds.) *Smart Sentencing? An Examination of the Emergence of Intermediate Sentencing*, pp. 166-181. Beverly Hills, CA: Sage; and E. Latessa and Harry E. Allen (1982). "Halfway Houses and Parole: A National Assessment." *Journal of Criminal Justice*, 10:153-163.

[7]    Harold Valentine (1991). *Prison Alternatives: Crowded Federal Prisons Can Transfer More Inmates to Halfway Houses*. Washington, DC: U.S. Government Accounting Office. The Bureau of Prisons under utilizes their contracted bedspace, further exacerbating their prison overcrowding problem.

[8]    This nostalgic view of warm-hearted older rural Americans trying to help the less successful, down-trodden and sodden of the Depression years by feeding any who ask, putting transients to work chopping wood or hauling water, and allowing the more needy to sleep in the barn has many adherents. No doubt this pattern of early philanthropic assistance was found in many sites, and continues in isolated locales. These "Mom and Pop" programs, often unofficial, were undoubtedly major sources of humanitarian assistance to the needy in some if not most of the nation during the early Twentieth Century, providing "three hots and a cot." If they exist today, they are an endangered species.

[9]    See *IARCA Journal* for a description of some more successful programs in rural America and urban England (Leeds Alternative to Care and Custody Scheme, and Roundabout Group). *IARCA Journal*, 3 (July, 1990).

[10]    See Thomas Berry (July, 1990). "Rural Community Corrections and the Challenge: Providing Comprehensive Services." *IARCA Journal*, 3:6-7.

[11]    Barbara Owen found that alcohol frequently accompanied drug use among parolees in California, leading to most parole violations. Barbara Owen (1991). "Normative Aspects of Alcohol and Parole Performance." *Drug Problems*, 18:453-476. See also, R. Langworthy and Edward Latessa (1993). "Treatment of Chronic Drunk Drivers: The Turning Point Project." *Journal of Criminal Justice*, 21:265-276.

[12]    Talbert House offers a wide variety of programs in four general areas: mental health services, community residential treatment programs, substance abuse, and family and community outreach.

[13]    It is important to note that studies that do not employ a control group make it very difficult to gauge the effectiveness of programs, at least in terms of recidivism.

[14]    Judging from victimization studies, the crime rate in the nation has been dropping for almost the last 17 years. Yet the public, in part manipulated by politicians and agencies with vested interests in maintaining concern over crime, has come to believe that public safety will be enhanced by "locking up criminals and throwing away the prison keys." This assumption is at least debatable and could be patently wrong.

[15]    There is some evidence that staff attributes within programs influence program effectiveness and recidivism. Staff selection and training, as well as program developments, could be improved by matching personality and attitudinal attributes. See J. Johnson and J. Bonta (1985). "Characteristics of Staff and Programs in Correctional Halfway Houses." *Journal of Offender Counseling, Services and Rehabilitation*, 9:39-51.

[16]    For more information about this movement, write: NIC at 320 1st St. NW, Washington, DC 20534.

# References

Allen, H.E. (1995). "The American Dream and Crime in the Twenty-First Century." *Justice Quarterly*, 12:427-445.

Allen, H.E., E. Bowman, E. Carlson, E. Parks, and R. Seiter (1976). "Halfway Houses in the United States: An Analysis of the State of the Art." Paper presented at the International Halfway House Association, Guilford, England.

Allen, H.E., E. Carlson, E. Parks, and R. Seiter (1978). *Program Models: Halfway Houses*. Washington, DC: U.S. Department of Justice.

Allen, H.E. and C. Simonsen (1992). "Prison Overcrowding and the Conservative Ideology Revisited." Paper presented at the annual meeting of the Academy of Criminal Justice Sciences, Pittsburgh.

Allen, H.E. and C. Simonsen (1995). *Corrections in America*. Englewood Cliffs, NJ: Prentice-Hall.

Berry, T. (1990). "Rural Community Corrections and the Challenge: Providing Comprehensive Services." *IARCA Journal*, 3(July):6-7.

Bureau of Justice Statistics (1995). *Correctional Populations in the United States*. Washington, DC: U.S. Department of Justice.

Camp, C. and G. Camp (1997). *The Corrections Yearbook*. South Salem, NY: The Criminal Justice Institute.

Cohn, J. (1973). *A Study of Community-Based Correctional Needs in Massachusetts*. Boston, MA: Massachusetts Department of Corrections.

Donnelly, P. and B.E. Forschner (1987). "Predictors of Success in a Co-Correctional Halfway House: A Discriminant Analysis." *Journal of Crime and Justice*, 10:1-22.

Dowell, D., C. Klein, and C. Krichmar (1985). "Evaluation of a Halfway House for Women." *Journal of Criminal Justice*, 13:217-226.

*Drug Use Forecasting 1995 Annual Report on Adult and Juvenile Arrestees*. Washington, DC: National Institute of Justice.

Friday, P. and R. Wertkin (1995). "Effects of Programming and Race on Recidivism: Residential Probation," in J. Smykla and W. Selke (eds.) *Intermediate Sanctions: Sentencing in the 1990s*, pp. 209-217. Cincinnati, OH: Anderson Publishing Co.

Greenfield, L. and S. Minor-Harper (1991). *Women in Prison*. Washington, DC: U.S. Department of Justice.

Hamm, M. and J. Kite (1991). "The Role of Offender Rehabilitation in Family Violence Policy: The Batterers Anonymous Experiment." *Criminal Justice Review*, 16:227-248.

Hartmann, D., P. Friday, and K. Minor (1994). "Residential Probation: A Seven-Year Follow-up Study of Halfway House Discharges," *Journal of Criminal Justice*, 22(6):503-515.

Hicks, N. (1987). "Halfway Houses and Corrections." *Corrections Compendium*, 12(October):1-7.

Huskey, B. (1992). "The Expanding Use of CRCs." *Corrections Today*, 54(8):70-74.

Johnson, J. and J. Bonta (1995). "Characteristics of Staff and Programs in Correctional Halfway Houses." *Journal of Offender Counseling, Services and Rehabilitation*, 9:39-51.

Langworthy, R. and E.J. Latessa (1996). "Treatment of Chronic Drunk Drivers: A Four-Year Follow-Up of the Turning Point Project." *Journal of Criminal Justice*, 24:273-281.

Langworthy, R. and E.J. Latessa (1993). "Treatment of Chronic Drunk Drivers: The Turning Point Project." *Journal of Criminal Justice*, 21:265-276.

Latessa, E.J. (1998). *Public Protection Through Offender Risk Reduction: Putting Research Into Practice*. Washington, DC: National Institute of Corrections.

Latessa, E.J. and H.E. Allen (1982). "Halfway Houses and Parole: A National Assessment." *Journal of Criminal Justice*, 10:153-163.

Latessa, E.J., R.H. Langworthy, and A.D. Thomas (1995). *Community Residential Treatment Program Evaluation for Talbert House Inc*. Cincinnati, OH: Division of Criminal Justice, University of Cincinnati.

Latessa, E.J. and L.F. Travis (1992). "Residential Community Correctional Programs." In J.M. Byrne and A. Lurigio (eds.) *Smart Sentencing? An Examination of the Emergence of Intermediate Sentencing*, pp. 166-181. Beverly Hills, CA: Sage.

Latessa, E.J. and L.F. Travis (1991). "Halfway House or Probation: A Comparison of Alternative Dispositions." *Journal of Crime and Justice*, 14(1):53-76.

Michaels, D., D. Zoloth, and P. Alcabes (1992). "Homelessness and Indicators of Mental Illness Among Inmates in New York City's Correctional System." *Hospital and Community Psychiatry*, 32:150-154.

National Institute of Corrections (1989). *1989 Directory of Residential Community Corrections Facilities in the United States*. Longmont, CO: National Institute of Corrections.

Owen, B. (1991). "Normative Aspects of Alcohol and Parole Performance." *Drug Problems*, 18:453-476.

Petersilia, J., S. Turner, J. Kahan, and J. Peterson (1985). *Granting Felons Probation: Risks and Alternatives*. Santa Monica, CA: Rand.

President's Commission on Law Enforcement and Administration of Justice (1967). *Corrections*. Washington, DC: U.S. Government Printing Office.

Rush, G. (1992). *The Dictionary of Criminal Justice*. Guilford, CT: Duskin.

Seiter R. and E. Carlson (1977). "Residential Inmate Aftercare: The State of the Art." *Offender Rehabilitation*, 4:78-94.

Valentine, H. (1991). *Prison Alternatives: Crowded Federal Prisons Can Transfer More Inmates to Halfway Houses*. Washington, DC: U.S. Government Accounting Office.

Wilson, G. (1985). "Halfway House Programs for Offenders." In L.F. Travis (ed.) *Probation, Parole and Community Corrections*, pp. 151-164. Prospect Heights, IL: Waveland.

# The Effectiveness
# of Corrections
# in the Community

> With few and isolated exceptions, the re-
> habilitative efforts that have been reported
> so far have not had an appreciable effect on
> recidivism.
>
> —Robert Martinson

> The data have continued to accumulate, tes-
> tifying to the potency of offender rehabilita-
> tion programs.
>
> —Paul Gendreau

After examining more than two decades of correctional research, Martinson's (1974) now famous conclusion had a tremendous impact on the field of corrections. Whatever the limitations of the Martinson study, and there were many, the conclusion drawn by many was that treatment or rehabilitation is not effective.[1] Thus, what became known as the "nothing works" doctrine, led to renewed efforts to demonstrate the effectiveness of correctional programs.[2]

The effectiveness of community-based correctional programs has been debated and studied for many years. As more and more offenders have been diverted or released to the community, the question of effectiveness has become increasingly important. Many critics of both probation and parole point to discretionary abuses, the arbitrary nature of the indeterminate sentence, the disparity in sentencing practices by judges, the failure of rehabilitation and supervision, and the inadequate delivery of services. In an attempt to offset some of these criticisms, mandatory and determinate sentencing systems have been imposed, sentencing tribunals have been formed, parole boards have adopted and implemented decision-making guidelines, probation and parole departments have tested new and innovative service delivery strategies, and intermediate punishments have been developed. But these, too, are open to attack and are frequently criticized.

Much has been written about the effectiveness of probation and parole. We know that the use of discretionary parole release has declined dramatically over the last few years. In 1977, 72 percent of those released from prison were released on discretionary parole, while in 1989 only 39 percent were so paroled. However, more than 80 percent of those released from prison received supervision in the community (Jankowski, 1990). On any given day in 1997, two out of three offenders were living in the community (Bureau of Justice Statistics, 1997). We also know that there is an ever-increasing number of offenders placed on probation and parole, resulting in large caseloads and workloads for probation and parole departments.

There is also an acute shortage of residential programs and halfway houses. We continually experiment with service systems components—such as brokerage, casework, house arrest, day-reporting, electronic monitoring, intensive and specialized caseloads, and volunteer-paraprofessionals—but, again, we know little about the actual effectiveness of these strategies in community corrections. In short, there have been nearly as many innovative programs and reported results as there are probation and parole agencies. The question of effectiveness remains and, since it is so essential, it should be closely examined.

Perhaps the most limiting aspect of effectiveness studies has been the neglect given to other performance measures. By simply comparing recidivism rates, researchers have ignored some of the main effects that community correctional programs are designed to achieve. The quality of contacts and services provided the probationers and parolees need to be adequately defined and gauged, as does the effect of officer style and attitude on outcome. There are also few cost-benefit or cost-effectiveness studies. The importance of this type of information should not be overlooked. These types of studies can help community correctional agencies make more efficient selections in terms of the resources they will employ and the strategies to be used to deliver those resources. Petersilia (1991) distinguishes between "passive" research designs and "active" ones. She argues that passive

Photo 14.1
Drug abuse is a contributing factor to outcome supervision. Photograph by Beth Sanders.

designs only look at the program in operation and ignore the selection of participants and levels of treatment.

Finally, a list of effectiveness indicators should include the degree of humaneness that community supervision affords the offender and his or her family, and the impact of these alternatives on reducing prison populations and overcrowded conditions in jails and prisons. We have come to realize that we cannot incarcerate everyone that breaks the law.[4] Yet, probation and parole are often an afterthought, particularly when it comes to resource allocation.

There is little doubt that recidivism, no matter how it may be defined, should remain a main criteria; however, the need to measure additional outcome indicators appears obvious. Indeed, there has been a great deal of criticism directed at the research conducted in the area of correctional programming. This chapter will examine some of those criticisms as well as address what is generally known about the effectiveness of probation and parole.

## Limitations of Effectiveness Studies

Evaluating the effectiveness of community corrections is not easy even under the best of circumstances. First, political, ethical, and programmatic reasons may not permit random assignment of clients to membership in the treatment or control group. Nonrandom assignment forces the evaluator to statistically make the groups comparable, an honored tradition in empirical research but one that delivers results that are hard to communicate to policymakers and program directors (and sometimes to other researchers).

Even in the best of circumstances in achieving random assignment, for the same reasons mentioned above, treatment or program effects "bleed over" to the control group or the intended treatment is inappropriately or unevenly applied. This makes difficult the determination of whether the treatment group members received needed treatment, and whether the control group remained "treatment free." After all, no program and no client exist in a vacuum; historical accidents can effect both groups, or one group more than another, or accidentally reinforce negative treatment effects in one group or another.

Another major problem in evaluating treatment effectiveness in community corrections is that it is *rare* to have only one treatment in operation at a time. For example, an offender ("Bob") may be sentenced initially to probation and restitution. The victim-offender interaction and mediation may have very positive effects on Bob's attitudes and behavior. His drinking problem, however, may lead the probation officer to recommend that the court tighten the conditions of probation to include mandatory daily participation in Alcoholics Anonymous

(AA), from which Bob derives much immediate and long-term benefit. Former antisocial friends may become reacquainted with Bob, and misdemeanor crime may occur. Alerted by Bob's subsequent arrest, the PO may have Bob (a failure?) assigned to individual counseling that includes relapse prevention techniques that assist him in identifying high-risk situations and coping with them. After three years of probation, when the victim's losses have been compensated, and with Bob securely employed in a job with a future and now voluntarily participating in AA, it is impossible to determine which of the *treatment program elements* will have been most effective in turning Bob around, and his reintegration. Was it probation supervision? quality of PO supervision? mediation and remorse associated with restitution? AA support and direction? relapse prevention techniques? employment? or some combination of treatment elements? Since "probation" is a generic term that can refer to a combination of treatment and intermediate sanctions ("punishing smarter"), what element should be recognized as the "best intervention?"

Finally, we need to deal with the question of whether Bob should be labeled a "success" or "failure" in corrections. Defining "failure" may mean using outcome indicators: arrest, reconviction or probation revocation, or incarceration (jail or prison). If the research design defines "success" as the absence of arrest, Bob *failed:* he was arrested. Yet the overall picture indicates that the arrest was just one critical incident in the long-range process of reintegration, one that Bob and his probation officer managed to overcome. Yet that single arrest incident in the three-year period would, from the perspective of reintegration, *misclassify* the probationer into the "failure" category. The bulk of evidence, however, clearly indicates that Bob was a *success*!

Thus the analyses that follow should be seen in light of these three major problems: research design and implementation, difficulty in separating effects of various treatment programs, and definition of outcome. With these limitations in mind, let us now turn to the question of effectiveness of treatment. As we do this, keep firmly in mind the argument by Gendreau (1995): ". . . programs that [included principles of effective intervention] reduced recidivism in the range of 25-70% with an average of about 50%. . . ."

## Correctional Effectiveness

While the debate over correctional effectiveness will surely continue for some time, those attempting to evaluate and measure the worth of various strategies and programs found in corrections face a most difficult dilemma-defining "effectiveness."

## Measuring Outcome and Recidivism

A large part of the problem lies in the desire on the part of researchers and practitioners alike to define failure or success in clear-cut, "either/or" terms. Unfortunately, very few programs can be categorized in definitive terms. There is a strong need to view success or failure on a continuum, rather than as a win or lose dichotomy. For example, an offender may complete a sentence of probation yet have erratic employment and numerous technical violations. This individual is certainly not as successful as one who finishes probation, gains upward mobility in a job, makes restitution, supports a family, and incurs no new charges of any type; still, both these cases may be classified as successes. There is also a great deal of difference between the offender who is caught on a minor charge or a technical violation, and one who commits a serious new felony. For example, in California there is evidence that the number of parolees being revoked for technical violations is increasing dramatically (Austin, 1987). Some consider a new arrest a failure, while others count only those that are incarcerated.[3]

---

Box 14.1

### Parole Violation

A parolee can be returned to prison for committing a new criminal act or failing to conform to the conditions of parole. The latter is frequently known as a technical parole violation: a rule violation that is not a criminal act but is prohibited by the conditions of the parole agreement. The latter might include persistent consumption of alcohol, failure to observe curfew, refusal to make victim restitution, failure to file required reports, and so on. Approximately 22 percent of the males and 14 percent of the females on parole in 1984 were returned to custody for parole violation.

In 1978, approximately 18 percent of offenders admitted to California prisons were parole violators. By 1988, that figure had increased to 47 percent. By 1996, without policy changes, the figure could exceed 85,000 violators. California now leads the nation in parole violations.

California parolees are not the most dangerous in the nation, however. Drug use accounts for more than one-half of the violations, and there are few intermediate punishments for parole officers to use. Prison treatment programs for drug abuse are generally insufficient, and community resistance to implementing treatment centers is considerable. Finally, more than 5 percent of the male felons participated recently in pre-release programming. Major policy changes are under consideration in this area.

In addition to this problem, there is no consensus on the indicators of effectiveness. While most agree that recidivism should be a primary performance measure, there is no agreement on its definition nor on the indicators to be used for its measurement. Indeed, one study of parole supervision found that the nature of the outcome criteria had a significant effect upon the interpretation of results (Gottfredson, Mitchell-Herzfeld & Flanagan, 1982). Researchers tend to define recidivism in terms that fit the available data, yet we know official sources are inadequate at best. Community follow-up and appropriate comparison groups are the exception rather than the rule when examining the recidivism of probationers and parolees. There is also some evidence that the amount of time given to the follow-up period may have a significant effect on the reported recidivism rates (Hoffman & Stone-Meierhoefer, 1980).

Correctional outcome, which is usually operationalized as recidivism has some inherent limitations. The indicators used to measure recidivism, length of follow-up, and external and internal factors affect recidivism rates. Indeed, the best way to insure a low recidivism rate is to define it very narrowly (e.g., incarceration in a state penal institution and to utilize a very short follow-up period).

Too often, arrest (and only arrest) is used as a primary indicator when measuring recidivism, and consequently, program success or failure. Certainly arrest may serve as an indicator of post-program (or post-release) performance, but in and of itself arrest has many limitations. Some of the other factors that are overlooked when considering the impact of a correctional program or criminal sanction, even when arrest is being used, are time until arrest; offense for which an offender was arrested (type of offense as well as severity level); whether or not the offender was convicted; if convicted, what the resulting disposition was.

An example of this can be seen from the results of a recent study of community corrections in Ohio. Figure 14.1 show the results from a three-year follow-up of offenders supervised in the community between 1991 and 1993. Four groups were used for this study; offenders supervised under regular probation and intensive probation, those who were released from a community-based correctional facility (CBCF) and those released from prison. In this graph, the *rearrest* rates of the group groups are presented. These data indicate that the ISP and CBCF groups performed better than the regular probation and the prison groups (i.e., lower recidivism rates), at least when measured by rearrest. However, when we examine Figure 14.2 we see a somewhat different picture of recidivism. In this example, the *incarceration* rates for the same four groups are presented. Here we see that the ISP and CBCF groups had the highest failure rates (when defined as subsequent incarceration). Of course what this figure does not show is that the majority of those ISP and CBCF offenders who were incarcerated were as a result of a technical violation. Regular probationers who received a technical violation were often placed in ISP or a CBCF and, since the majority of the offenders in the Prison group were released without parole supervision, they were not subject to revocation.

Figure 14.1
**Offenders Supervised Under Community Corrections in Ohio:**
**Percent Rearrested During a Three-Year Follow-up**

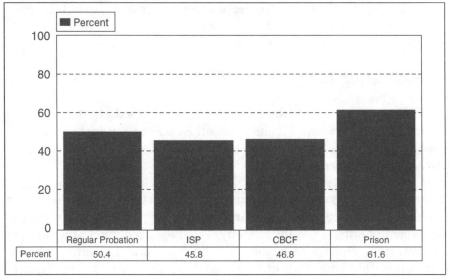

| | Regular Probation | ISP | CBCF | Prison |
|---|---|---|---|---|
| Percent | 50.4 | 45.8 | 46.8 | 61.6 |

Source: E.J. Latessa, L.F. Travis, and A. Holsinger (1997). Evaluation of Ohio's Community Corrections Act Programs and Community Based Correctional Facilities.

Figure 14.2
**Offenders Supervised Under Community Corrections in Ohio:**
**Percent Incarcerated in a Penal Institution During a Three-Year Follow-up**

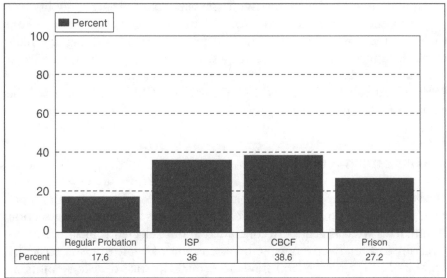

| | Regular Probation | ISP | CBCF | Prison |
|---|---|---|---|---|
| Percent | 17.6 | 36 | 38.6 | 27.2 |

Source: E.J. Latessa, L.F. Travis, and A. Holsinger (1997). Evaluation of Ohio's Community Corrections Act Programs and Community Based Correctional Facilities.

Despite these limitations, recidivism remains the most important measure of public protection. When legislators and other public officials ask if a program works, recidivism is what they are generally referring to. Outcome studies provide much of our knowledge about the effectiveness of correctional programs in reducing recidivism. Unfortunately, outcome studies focus on the results of intervention, and provide little, if any useful information about why a program is or is not effective. Besides the measurement of outcome, another factor that can influence recidivism rates is the quality of a program.

## Measuring Program Quality

Few would argue that the quality of a correctional intervention program has no effect on outcome. Nonetheless, correctional researchers have largely ignored the measurement of program quality. Traditionally, quality has been measured through process evaluations. This approach can provide useful information about a program's operations; however, these types of evaluations often lack the "quantifiability" of outcome studies. Previously, researchers' primary issue has been the development of criteria or indicators by which a correctional program can be measured. While traditional audits and accreditation processes are one step in this direction, thus far they have proven to be inadequate. For example, audits can be an important means to ensure if a program is meeting contractual obligations or a set of prescribed standards, however, these conditions may not have any relationship to effective intervention. It is also important to note that outcome studies and assessment of program quality are not necessarily mutually exclusive. Combining outcome indicators with assessments of program quality can provide a more complete picture of an intervention's effectiveness. Fortunately, there has been considerable progress in identifying the hallmarks of effective programs (Andrews, Zinger, Hoge, Bonta, Gendreau & Cullen, 1990; Cullen & Applegate, 1998; Gendreau & Paparozzi, 1995; Gendreau & Ross, 1979, 1987; Palmer, 1995). This issue will be examined later in this chapter.

## Parole Effectiveness

What is actually known about the effectiveness of probation and parole, and what should future research priorities be? The next section summarizes what is generally concluded about selected topic areas of interest in parole effectiveness. This discussion of topic areas is basically organized along the general flow of criminal justice decision points as they relate to parole; however, most of the findings also pertain to probation, particularly those on supervision and innovative programs.

## Preinstitutional Factors

For at least four decades, researchers have attempted to distinguish the factors that relate to parole success. The rationale offered for such ambitious endeavors vary, but for the most part, they represent attempts to develop prediction instruments and to provide decisionmakers (especially parole boards and judges) with information for more successful judgments.

After reviewing all available literature, one is immediately aware of the confusion and contradictions that much of this research has generated. For almost every study and factor presented as a "successful indicator" or "stable predictor," there is another refuting the finding. The folly of presenting the "ideal" parolee as a "middle-aged white male with no prior record and an annual income over $50,000" is obvious. The studies that have identified significant factors are often methodologically flawed, or limited in their generalizability.

Some studies have attempted to relate supervision success to such nebulous concepts as "self-esteem" or to other equally unmeasurable personality constructs. Gendreau (1995:29) argues that programs that focus on noncriminogenic needs (self-esteem, anxiety, or depression) have not reduced recidivism. One study (Syrotvik, 1978) attempted to correlate birth order with parole success. The author concluded that a first-born was more likely to succeed. We do not know if this applies to both males and females, if the results differ with family size, or if "only child" has an effect on outcome. It also suggests little if any policy direction.

Numerous variables have been associated with parole outcome. Pritchard (1979) reviewed 71 studies and concluded that five variables were the most stable predictors or parole outcome; conviction for auto theft, prior convictions, age at first arrest, history of opiate use, and history of alcohol use. Other researchers have found similar, but somewhat different factors (Gottfredson, 1977; Bonham, Janeksela, Bardo & Iacovetta, 1984; Lunden, 1987).

Some studies have shown race to be a significant factor, but are refuted by others showing no racial differences in outcome (the male age/race specific imprisonment rates for 1993 are seen in Figure 14.3). The three variables that appear consistently associated with parole effectiveness are age (the over-40 group does better), type of offense (with repeat property offenders more likely to fail than personal offenders, especially murderers), and number of prior arrests (the greater the number of prior arrests, the higher the probability of failure on parole).

While prediction has a long history in parole (Hakeem, 1945), recently, prediction in criminal justice has increasingly used more statistically sophisticated methods, especially multivariate statistical techniques. In spite of these advancements, there is little evidence that more sophisticated techniques improve the predictability of parole success beyond that achieved by simpler methods (Alystyne & Gottfredson, 1978). Gottfredson and Gottfredson (1994) argue that little prediction advantage is realized by attention to more sophisticated behavioral outcome criteria.

Figure 14.3
**Male Age/Race Specific Imprisonment Rates: 1991**

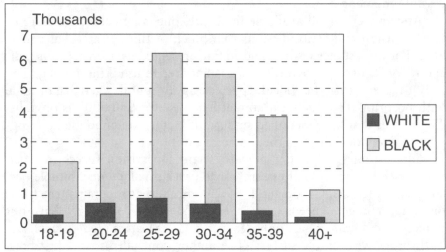

Source: Bureau of Justice Statistics (1994). *Prisoners 1993*. Washington, DC: U.S. Department of Justice. Per 100,000 residents in each age/race group.

In spite of the difficulties posed by predictive instruments, a number of states have developed and implemented decision-making guidelines designed to limit discretion, structure decisionmaking, and provide more "objective" criteria that will lead to better predictions in future success or failure. (For a more thorough discussion of these guidelines, see Chapter 9). There is also mounting evidence that "level of risk" is correlated with outcome (Gendreau & Ross, 1987; Hoffman & Beck, 1985).

Andrews (1994) has identified a major set of risk factors that influence the probability of an offender recidivating:

1.   Antisocial/procriminal attitudes, values, and beliefs

2.   Procriminal associates and isolation from anticriminal others

3.   Temperamental and personality factors conducive to criminal activity including:
     Psychopathy
     Weak socialization
     Impulsivity
     Restless/aggressive energy
     Egocentricism

Below average verbal intelligence
A taste for risk
Weak problem-solving/self regulation skills

4. A history of antisocial behavior and criminal history
   Evident from a young age
   In a variety of settings
   Involving a number and variety of different acts

5. Family factors that include criminality and a variety of psychological problems in the family or origin including:
   Low levels of affection, caring and cohesiveness
   Poor parental supervision and discipline practices
   Outright neglect and abuse

6. Low levels of personal educational, vocational, or financial achievement

## Institutional Factors

Several aspects of the institutional experience are thought to be related to parole and its effectiveness, such as length of time incarcerated, prison behavior, institutional programs, and parole conditions imposed as conditions of release. See Figure 14.4.

Figure 14.4
**Placement and Successful Terminations During 1996 for Probationers and Parolees**

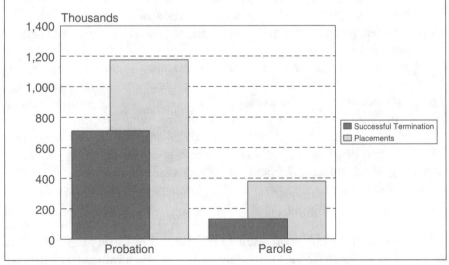

Source: C. Camp and G. Camp (1997). *The Corrections Yearbook 1997*. South Salem, NY: The Criminal Justice Institute, Inc.

Early research that examined the effects of the amount of time served in prison on parole have generally concluded that the shorter the amount of time served, the greater the likelihood of successful parole (Gottfredson, Gottfredson & Garofalo, 1977; Eichman, 1965). Although none of these studies found a "magic" number for time served, most studies centered around a two-year incarceration period as a cutoff point. A recent study of 3,995 parolees from 22 states (Beck, 1987), however, found that time served in prison had no consistent impact on recidivism rates.

Most researchers, however, have concluded that longer prison terms have an adverse effect upon parolee chances of success, implying that the negative aspects of prisonization seem to intensify with time. For example, in his study of shock probationers, Vito (1978) concluded that even a short period of incarceration has a negative impact. The question that remains unanswered by this research is: Are there any characteristics of inmates who have served more time that are also associated with an unfavorable parole outcome?

Existing research on the effectiveness of institutional programs and prison behavior has been limited in its scope. Most such programs are analyzed in relation to institutional adjustment, disciplinary problems, and impact of program participation on the parole-granting process. The few evaluations that included a parole period usually show little if any positive effects with regard to recidivism. Most research that has examined prison behavior has not found a relationship between prison behavior and success on parole (von Hirsch & Hanrahan, 1979; Morris, 1978). However, a study by Gottfredson and Adams (1982), found that there is some relation between institutional infractions and infractions while on parole, after controlling for a prior risk. Overall, however, there has not been a great deal of attention given to the relationship between institutional programs, prison behavior, and subsequent success or failure on parole.

Two areas that have received some attention are work and education programs for offenders. Although the literature on education programs is inconclusive, the evidence does seem to suggest that educational programs[5] can positively affect inmate behavior and recidivism (Linden & Perry, 1982; Ayers, Duguid, Montague & Wolowidnyk, 1980; Roberts & Cheek, 1994; Eskridge & Newbold, 1994). A recent study by MacKenzie and Hickman (1998:17,23) examined 12 correctional education programs for adult offenders. Of the twelve studies, eight produced results suggesting that correctional education may have a positive impact on the rate of recidivism. They also concluded that while there were some inconsistencies in the findings, the preponderance of evidence suggested that vocational education programs were effective in reducing recidivism.

Likewise the literature on work programs[6] does not convincingly demonstrate reduced recidivism (Zeisel, 1982; Vito, 1985b). Gendreau and Ross (1987:380; MacKenzie & Hickman, 1998), however, provide some principles that should be followed with regard to work programs: (1) they must enhance practical skills, (2) develop interpersonal skills and minimize prisonization, and (3) ensure that work is not punishment alone.

---

**Box 14.2**

**Vocational and Academic Indicators of Parole Success**

Schumaker et al. (1990) reported on the effects of in-prison vocational and academic coursework for 760 inmates who were followed on parole for 12 months. Their employment information and criminal activity rates (technical violations and new arrests) were gathered. The vocational/academic groups generally had the lowest criminal activity rates and the highest employment rates. Those who had earned a General Education Diploma had the lowest criminal activity rate, and the control group who did not participate in vocation/academic programming had the highest criminal activity rate.

Source: R. Schumaker, D. Anderson and S. Anderson (1990). "Vocational and Academic Indicators of Parole Success." *Journal of Correctional Education,* 41:8-13.

---

With regard to the imposition of parole conditions, a nationwide survey of 52 parolee field supervision agencies, Allen and Latessa (1980) found 49 had residency requirements as a condition of parole, and 47 had an employment requirement. The Travis and Latessa (1984) survey found similar results. In spite of the widespread requirement of parole conditions, the literature produced only three studies that were directly related to the imposition of these conditions and parole effectiveness. Although two studies (Beasley, 1978; Morgan, 1993) showed a relationship between stability of residency and parole success, the lack of research in this area makes generalization difficult.

## Parole Release

Primarily in response to the supporters of determinate sentencing,[7] researchers have increasingly turned their attention to evaluating the success of parole supervision.

Critics of parole supervision rely on two basic arguments to support their views. The first is that parole supervision simply is not effective in reducing recidivism (Citizens' Inquiry on Parole and Criminal Justice, 1975; Wilson, 1977) The second, more philosophical argument is that supervision is not "just" (von Hirsch & Hanrahan, 1979). A more plausible conclusion is that the evidence is mixed; that parole supervision is effective in reducing recidivism rates among parolees (Flanagan, 1985).

Several studies have compared parolees to mandatory releases, but they have failed to control for possible differences in the selection of the groups (Martinson & Wilks, 1977). Other studies that have been controlled for differences have reported favorable results (Lerner, 1977; Gottfredson, 1975), and yet other studies have reported less positive results (Waller, 1974; Nuttal et al., 1977; Jackson, 1983). In one study, Gottfredson, Mitchell-Herzfeld, and Flanagan (1982:292) concluded that "much of our data does indicate an effect for parole supervision, an effect that varies by offender attributes, and an effect that appears not to be very large." The existing evidence seems to be in favor of parole supervision, although there is no clear consensus as to its effectiveness.

Even the most outspoken critics of parole agree that the agencies responsible for the task of supervision are often understaffed, their officers undertrained, underpaid, and overworked. They are inundated with excessively large caseloads, workloads, and paperwork. Community services are either unavailable or unwilling to handle parolees, and as a consequence parole officers are expected to be all things to all people. As indicated in Chapter 7, they are also expected to perform the dual roles of surveillance-policeman and rehabilitator-treatment agent.

There is some evidence that, by shortening the amount of time on parole, we could save a considerable amount of money and time, and not seriously increase the risk of failure. Most data seem to indicate that the majority of failures on parole occur during the first two years (Hoffman & Stone-Meierhoefer, 1980; Flanagan, 1982) and drop significantly thereafter. There is also some evidence that early release into the community and from parole incurs no higher risk to the community and, in fact, is justifiable on cost considerations (Holt, 1975), a conclusion echoed by MacKenzie and Piquero (1994:244-245). It is also important to note that easing the offender back into the community through community residential centers and furlough programs can facilitate the early release process. The definition and purpose of community residential centers and furloughs are found in Box 14.3 and Box 14.4, respectively.

A Washington State (1976) 10-year follow-up of parolees found that the first year of parole was critical, with more than one-half of those paroled returning to prison during this time period (see Figure 14.5 for revocation rates). In this study, there were more failures in the second, than in first, six months after release. It was also found that those convicted of murder and manslaughter were less likely to recidi-

Box 14.3

### America's Community Residential Centers

Community residential centers (also known as halfway houses) are residential facilities where probationers, furloughees, and parolees may be placed when they are in need of a more structured setting. The primary purpose of a halfway house is to limit an offender's freedom while encouraging reintegration into society through employment, education, treatment, habilitation, restitution, training, compliance with financial sanctions, and other activities designed to rehabilitate the offender and deter future crime (Ohio Community Corrections Organization, 1993).

vate, and that property offenders—especially those convicted of burglary, auto theft, and forgery—had the highest failure rate. As expected, younger parolees did significantly worse than those over 40 years of age. Blacks did slightly worse than whites after the first six months, and Native Americans did significantly worse than all other groups.

Box 14.4

### Furloughs

Furlough is a phased re-entry program designed to ease the offender's transition from prison to the community. Furloughs include escorted or unescorted leaves from confinement, granted for designated purposes and time periods (funerals, dying relatives, etc.), before the formal sentence expires. Primarily used for employment, vocational training, or education, furlough in effect extends the limits of confinement to include temporary residence in the community during the last months of confinement. Furloughees are frequently required to reside in community residential centers. Furloughs allow parole boards to observe the offender's behavior in the community and may lead to faster release from parole supervision for those adjusting favorably. Because furloughees are closely screened and supervised in the community, failure rates appear to be low. For example, Ohio reports a 9 percent return to prison rate for calendar 1992 (Ohio Community Corrections Organization).[8]

Figure 14.5
**Reason for Return to Custody During 1996 for Probationers and Parolees**

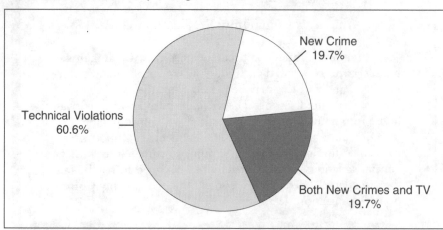

Source: C. Camp and G. Camp (1997). *The Corrections Yearbook 1997*. South Salem, NY: The Criminal Justice Institute, Inc.

In order to summarize, we have selected data from a national study of parole recidivism (Beck, 1987). These data confirm two important points with regard to parole effectiveness; (1) recidivism rates vary depending upon the definition of recidivism, and (2) the type of offense and age are important factors in determining parole success. Other findings included the following:

- Approximately 10 percent of the persons paroled accounted for 40 percent of the subsequent arrest offenses.

- About one-fifth of the subsequent arrests occurred in states other than the original paroling state.

- An estimated 37 percent of the parolees were rearrested while still on parole.

- Recidivism rates were highest in the first 2 years after an offender's release from prison. Within 1 year, 32 percent of those paroled had been arrested; within 2 years, 47 percent had been rearrested.

- Recidivism was higher among men, blacks, and persons who had not completed high school than among women, whites, and high school graduates.

- Almost three-quarters of those paroled for property offenses were rearrested for a serious crime compared to about two-thirds of those paroled for violent offenses.

- Approximately one-third of both property offenders and violent offenders were rearrested for a violent crime upon release from prison.

- The longer the parolee's prior arrest record, the higher the rate of recidivism—over 90 percent of the parolees with six or more previous adult arrests were rearrested compared to 59 percent of the first-time offender.

- The earlier the parolee's first adult arrest, the more likely the chances for rearrest—79 percent of those arrested and charged as an adult before the age of 17 were rearrested, compared to 51 percent of those first arrested at the age of 20 or older.

- Time served in prison had no consistent impact on recidivism rates—those who had served 6 months or less in prison were about as likely to be arrested as those who had served more than 2 years.

Table 14.1
**Age of Parolees and Likelihood of Failure**

| Age at time of prison release | Rate of return to prison by years after release from prison | | | | | | |
|---|---|---|---|---|---|---|---|
| | YEARS | | | | | | |
| | 1 | 2 | 3 | 4 | 5 | 6 | 7 |
| 18-24 years old | 21% | 34% | 41% | 45% | 48% | 49% | 50% |
| 25-34 | 12 | 21 | 28 | 33 | 37 | 41 | 43 |
| 35-44 | 7 | 14 | 18 | 22 | 26 | 30 | 34 |
| 45+ | 2 | 4 | 6 | 8 | 10 | 11 | 12 |
| All Ages | 14 | 23 | 29 | 34 | 37 | 40 | 42 |

Source: Adopted from A.J. Beck (1987). "Recidivism of Young Parolees." Bureau of Justice Statistics.

## Special Topic: Women

In spite of the recent focus on and attention given to the female offender,[9] research on women on parole has been relatively sparse. Findings are not surprising: Female property offenders do worse on parole, and first offenders do better; non-alcohol users do significantly better; black female offenders committed more personal offenses than did their white counterparts; and males (especially blacks) were more likely than females to recidivate. An interesting finding was that males, when compared to females, were more likely to receive parole. One reason offered for this is that females tended to be incarcerated for more serious offenses than were males.

The problem with most of these findings is that they tell us little, if anything, about the effectiveness of parole with women. All of the studies had methodological weaknesses; in addition, they lacked a strong conceptual base. Further, these studies gave little indication of how to deal more effectively with female parolees. While female parolees represent a small percentage of the total parole population, all indications are that this figure is growing dramatically.

## Special Topic: Murderers

Murderers, like female parolees, represent a small percentage of the total parole population. Unlike females, however, murderers on parole have been the focus of a great deal of research over the years.

Studies of parole success by type of offense repeatedly indicate that those who commit murder are among the best parole risks (Neithercutt, 1972). The reasons for this conclusion vary; the explanation most frequently offered is that most murderers tend to be first offenders who have committed crimes of passion. Another reason cited is age; since most convicted murderers spend a great amount of time incarcerated, they tend to be older (and more mature) when released, usually after the high-crime-risk years of 16 to 29.

In a study of murderers that had been given a death sentence, and then had that sentence commuted when *Furman v. Georgia* was overturned, Vito, Wilson and Latessa (1991) found that 43.5 percent of the death row inmates in Ohio were paroled and that 25 percent were returned to prison (recidivated). These results were very similar to those found in Texas, where 19 percent of the paroled *Furman* cases recidivated (Marquart & Sorensen, 1988), and in Kentucky, which had a 29 percent failure rate (Vito & Wilson, 1988).

Overall, studies examining murderers were found to present consistent findings and conclusions over time.

## Special Topic: Determinate Sentencing

As suggested previously, parole has been attacked on a number of fronts, including its ineffectiveness in preventing recidivism and as undermining the deterrent effect of incarceration. Central in the criticisms of parole is concern with the parole-granting process, and the arbitrary and capricious manner in which decisionmaking occurs. Because of its association with indeterminate sentence, and the widely publicized failure of the medical model, a number of states have enacted legislation either to abolish or severely curtail the function of parole. Since 1975, when Maine became the first, 10 states have enacted determinate sentencing. One state, Colorado, changed to determinate sentencing in 1979 and then went back to indeterminate sentencing in 1985 (Report to the Nation on Crime and Justice, 1985:91). Virginia abolished parole as a release mechanism in 1994 (American Correctional Association, 1994). A majority of state prisoners in 1995 served presumptive sentences (Greenfield, 1995).

---

**Box 14.5**

### Estimated Time to Serve

As we go to press, Congress is considering a proposal to require prison inmates to serve a larger percentage of their sentences. If the current average sentence remained the same for violent offenders and the required policy were to be to serve 85 percent of the current sentence, the predicted times served would be increased by:

- for new admissions, 26 months;

- for prisoners now present, 84 months;

- for releases, an average of 33 months longer in prison.

Based on current sentences, the estimated time predicted to be served would be:

| Percent of sentence served | Prison admissions | Prisoners present | Prison releases |
| --- | --- | --- | --- |
| Current | 62 months | 100 months | 43 months |
| 75% | 78 months | 162 months | 67 months |
| 85% | 88 months | 188 months | 76 months |
| 100% | 104 months | 216 months | 89 months |

Source: L. Greenfield (1995). *Prison Sentences and Time Served for Violence.* Washington, DC: U.S. Department of Justice.

---

The two basic alternatives have been to replace the indeterminate sentencing entirely, or to reform it. Thus far, most legislation has focused on the former. The type of sentencing legislation selected has varied from state to state, but generally includes presumptive sentencing, use of mandatory minimum sentences (Greenfield, 1995), determinate discretionary sentencing, or use of sentencing guidelines. Several states that have moved toward presumptive sentencing still include parole as a component of the system, most notably California (see Chapter 1), which has mandatory periods of parole supervision. The California statute has been termed the "purest determinate sentencing scheme yet adopted," and the statute clearly states that the purpose of sentencing is imprisonment, not rehabilitation. Although the statute abolished the parole-release function of the parole board, parole supervision was retained. Other states adopting this type of legislation, such as Indiana, have also retained parole supervision, but with a one-year maximum for supervision. Despite these changes, the effectiveness and impact of the new determinate sentencing acts are still being debated. Research has revealed some interesting and somewhat contradictory findings.

One of the predicted effects of the determinate sentence is an increase in existing prison populations. This seems to be especially true in California. A report of the California Department of Corrections reveals that the number of male felons received from court in January-June 1978 under the new determinate sentencing statute increased 22 percent over the same period in 1977 (Ryan & Pannel, 1979). California has the largest prison population in the country (126,000 in 1995), and the largest prison construction program ever developed.

Research from other states have revealed a mixed bag of effectiveness. In Maine, determinate sentencing has failed to reduce sentencing disparity (Anspach & Monsen, 1989). Some argue that determinacy has failed in Maine, and that judges in Maine have more control over sentencing than anywhere else in the nation (Tonry, 1987:21).

In Minnesota, Miethe and Moore (1985) found that sentencing disparity was reduced by determinate sentencing; however, socioeconomic factors were still finding their way into the sentencing decision indirectly through sources not governed by the sentencing guidelines. Unwarranted disparity in the Minnesota guidelines still exists (Stolzenberg & D'Alessio, 1994).

Goodstein and Hepburn (1986) examined determinate sentencing in Illinois and found mixed success. While released certainty was maximized, they concluded that this was due in large measure to prison crowding, which forced prison officials to release inmates after they served the minimum period allowed by law.[10] They also concluded that longer sentences were given to more serious offenders, and shorter sentences to less serious ones.

In sum, it appears that the attacks on parole will continue, and that states will continue to examine their sentencing practices. However, many practitioners and legislators, when faced with the possibility of abolishing parole, seem to believe that release under supervision is more palatable than release without it. Even Martinson and Wilks (1977:26-27), outspoken opponents of the rehabilitative model, have concluded that, "The evidence seems to indicate that the abolition of parole supervision would result in substantial increases in arrest, conviction, and return to prison."

Table 14.2
**Failure Rates of Parolees**

| Percent of Young Parolees Who within 6 Years of Release from Prison Were— | | | |
|---|---|---|---|
| | Rearrested | Reconvicted | Reincarcerated |
| All Parolees: | 69% | 53% | 49% |
| Sex: | | | |
|     Male | 70% | 54% | 50% |
|     Female | 52 | 40 | 36 |
| Race: | | | |
|     White | 64% | 49% | 45% |
|     Black | 76 | 60 | 56 |
|     Hispanic | 71 | 50 | 44 |
|     Other | 75 | 65 | 63 |
| Education: | | | |
|     Less than 12 yrs. | 71% | 55% | 51% |
|     High School Grad | 61 | 46 | 43 |
|     Some College | 48 | 44 | 31 |
| Paroling Offense: | | | |
|     Violent Offense | 64% | 43% | 39% |
|       Murder | 70 | 25 | 22 |
|       Robbery | 64 | 45 | 40 |
|       Assault | 72 | 51 | 47 |
| Property Offense | 73 | 60 | 56 |
|     Burglary | 73 | 60 | 56 |
|     Forgery/Fraud | 74 | 59 | 56 |
|     Larceny | 71 | 61 | 55 |
| Drug Offense | 49% | 30% | 25% |

Source: Adopted from A.J. Beck (1987). "Recidivism of Young Parolees." Bureau of Justice Statistics.

# Probation Effectiveness

As with parole, the quality of probation research is dubious. Unlike parole, which is found on state and federal levels, probation still remains primarily a local governmental function. The fact that probation can be found at local, state, and federal levels; that there are municipal and county probation departments; and that probation serves both misdemeanants and felons, combined with the problems discussed previously, make research in probation very difficult to conduct. Indeed, much of the research has been limited to only the several probation departments to which researchers have been welcome. This event gives us a limited sense of the true picture of probation.

As with parole, the research on probation effectiveness will be divided into sections. However, unlike our presentation of parole, the research on probation will be divided into four groups: studies that compare the performance of offenders receiving alternative dispositions; studies that simply measure probation outcome without comparison with any other form of sanction; studies that measure probation outcome and then attempt to isolate the characteristics which tend to differentiate between successful and nonsuccessful outcomes; and studies that examine the cost effectiveness of probation.

## Probation versus Alternative Dispositions

To examine the effectiveness of probation compared to other dispositions we looked at six studies. Three of the studies compared recidivism rates of individuals placed on probation with individuals sentenced to incarceration. Babst and Mannering's study (1965) compared similar types of offenders who were imprisoned or placed on probation. The sample consisted of 7,614 Wisconsin offenders who were statistically comparable in original disposition, county commitment, type of offense committed, number of prior felonies, and marital status. Parolees were followed for two years, and probationers were followed for two years or until discharge from probation, whichever came first. Violations were defined as the commission of a new offense or the violation of probation/parole rules. The findings of this study showed that, for offenders with no prior felony convictions, the violation rate was 25 percent for probationers and 32.9 percent for parolees. For offenders with one prior felony conviction, violation rates were 41.8 percent for probationers and 43.9 percent for parolees; for offenders with two or more felonies, the rates were 51.8 percent for probationers and 48.7 percent for parolees. With respect to the difference in violation rates for first offenders (which was statistically significant at the .05 level), Babst and Mannering note that this finding could be a result of the fact that parolees are a more difficult group to supervise or could actually show that, at least for first offenders, incarceration does more harm than good.

Another study done in Wisconsin (Wisconsin Division of Corrections, 1965) compared the performance of burglars, who had no previous felony convictions, sentenced to prison or placed on probation. While this study also attempted to investigate the characteristics associated with successful and nonsuccessful probationers and parolees, we will simply report at this point that the violation rate (based on a two-year follow-up, using the same definition of violation rate as Babst and Mannering, above) for burglars placed on probation was 23 percent, and for burglars who were incarcerated and then placed on parole was 34 percent. Thus, it appears that, as with the Wisconsin study, probation was more successful than parole.

Box 14.6

## Probationers Rearrested for a Felony Within Three Years

State courts in 32 counties across 17 states sentenced 79,000 felons to probation in 1986. Within 3 years of sentencing, while still on probation, 43 percent were rearrested for a felony. An estimated 18 percent of the arrests were for a violent crime (murder, rape, robbery, or aggravated assault); 33 percent were for a drug offense (drug trafficking or drug possession).

Of each 100 felony probationers tracked for three years:

- 26 went to prison,

- 10 went to jail, and

- 10 absconded.

These findings are based on a follow-up survey of felons on probation, using a sample that represented a fourth of the total 306,000 felons sentenced to probation in 1986. The survey used state criminal history files and probation files to obtain information. It was not based on a nationally representative sample; 39 percent of the follow-up cases were from a single state (California). Nevertheless, based on 12,370 sample cases representing 79,043 felons placed on probation in the counties and states studied, the follow-up represents the largest survey of its kind ever done.

Source: Bureau of Justice Statistics National Update (1994). Washington, DC: U.S. Department of Justice, p. 10.

The Pennsylvania Program for Women and Girl Offenders (1976) compared recidivism rates between all women placed on state probation or released on state parole during a two-year period. Recidivism was defined as any technical violation of probation or parole or any new criminal charge. The findings showed that, overall, women placed on probation had a 35.6 percent recidivism rate. When only women with no prior convictions were considered, the probationers had a 24 percent recidivism rate, and the parolees had a 23.1 percent rate. The differences between these rates were not statistically significant.

Vito (1978) compared regular probationers with shock probationers (who served at least 30 days in prison). He found that shock probationers had a 40 percent higher probability of failure than those released to regular supervision. Vito and Allen (1981:16) concluded:

> . . . the fact of incarceration is having some unknown and un-
> measurable effect upon (the more unfavorable) performance of
> shock probationers. . . . It could be that the negative effects of in-
> carceration are affecting the performance of shock probationers.

Whereas these four studies compared probation with some form of
incarceration, a California study (California Department of Justice,
1969) compared violation rates among offenders placed on probation,
offenders sentenced to probation following a jail term, and offenders
given straight jail sentences. The study examined the performance of a
cohort of offenders, all of whom had an equal exposure of one full year
in the community. For the probation group, cohort status was gained
on the date of the beginning of the probation period; for the group receiving jail sentences, cohort status began on the date of release from
jail. To evaluate the relative effectiveness of these dispositions, three violation levels were used: "none" or no known arrest for a technical violation or a new offense, "minor" or at least an arrest and perhaps a conviction resulting in a jail sentence of less than 90 days or probation of
one year or less, and "major," signifying at least a conviction resulting

---

**Box 14.7**

### Shock Probation

Shock probation (also known as "reconsideration of sentence" or "shock therapy") is a program allowing sentencing
judges to reconsider the offender's original sentence to imprisonment and then recall the inmate for a sentence to probation
within the community under conditions deemed appropriate.
It is presumed that a short term of incarceration would
"shock" the offender into abandoning criminal activity and
into pursuit of law-abiding behavior. It can be seen as an alternative disposition for sentencing judges who wish to control
probationer behavior through deterrence and tourniquet sentencing. It is a last-ditch program used by some judges in the
difficult decision of how best to protect the public while maximizing offender reintegration. In more recent years, it has become a "front end" solution to prison overcrowding.

Vito (1985a) found reincarceration rates to range from 10
to 26 percent across many studies; Boudouris and Turnbull
(1985) found a rearrest/revocation rate of 39 percent in Iowa
over a longer follow-up period. The latter also found that sex
and substance abuse offenders were most responsive to shock
incarceration, and that the cost-savings of sentencing offenders to shock probation would be substantial.

in a jail sentence of not less than 90 days or a term of probation exceeding one year. Since each case was followed for only one year, the final outcome of a violation occasionally did not occur until after the year was over. If it could be inferred that the disposition or sentence was the result of an arrest that did occur within the follow-up year, the action was included in the violation rate.

The findings of this study are illustrated in Table 14.3. Those offenders receiving jail sentences without the benefit of probation services have the worst record of recidivism.

Table 14.3
**Violation Levels of Sentenced Offenders in California**

| Sentence | Violations | | |
| --- | --- | --- | --- |
| | None | Minor | Major |
| Probation only | 64.7% | 23.7% | 11.6% |
| Jail, then probation | 50.3 | 31.7 | 18.0 |
| Jail only | 46.6 | 29.5 | 23.9 |

Source: California Department of Justice (1969).

These studies illustrate that, as a disposition, probation appears to be more effective than incarceration, even for a short period of time. This may be due, in part, to the fact that probationers immediately return to the community, their jobs, and their families.

Finally, an Alaska Study (Alaska Department of Health and Social Services, 1976) utilized an experimental design to compare the performance of misdemeanants offenders receiving probation supervision with offenders officially on probation but not required to report to the probation unit. The groups were created by random assignment to the experimental group (under supervision) or the control group (no supervision) and were followed for periods ranging from two months to slightly more than two years. Performance was assessed by means of recidivism, defined as the conviction for a new offense. The findings of the study showed that 22 percent of the experimental group members and 24 of the control group members had been convicted of new offenses during the follow-up period.

Given the paucity of research and the caution with which recidivism data must be approached, it is nearly impossible, not to mention inappropriate, to attempt to draw any definitive conclusions from these studies about the effectiveness of probation compared to other alternative dispositions. Nonetheless, it appears from the limited research that has been conducted that the following tentative conclusions can be reached. Of the studies that compared probation to incarceration, it tentatively appears that probation may have a significant impact on first offenders. It may also be suggested that the severity of violations appears to increase in proportion to the severity of the disposition. It does not appear that the provision of probation supervision for misdemeanants is more effective than an unsupervised probation period.

## Probation Outcome

There were a number of studies that reported recidivism rates only for probationers. Thirteen of these were reviewed, but one should remember that definitions of failure, follow-up periods, and the types of offenders differ significantly from one study to another. Table 14.4 includes the author, types of instant offenses committed by the probationers in the study, and the definition of failure used in the study, the length of follow-up, and the failure rates.

These summary descriptions illustrate many of the problems associated with attempting to assess probation effectiveness. The type of offenders constituting the samples (as represented by instant offenses) vary, as do the definitions used in each study to characterize failure. Four studies computed failure rates while offenders were on probation, and the length of follow-up periods ranged from several months to many years.

Most of the studies reviewed here stated that their purpose was to assess "probation effectiveness;" however, unlike the five studies examined earlier, none of these studies defined a base (such as a failure rate for comparable parolees or offenders on summary probation) against which to compare findings in order to support a claim that probation is an effective alternative for rehabilitating offenders.

In one of the more critical studies of probation effectiveness, Petersilia (1985) examined 1,672 felony probationers from two counties in California over a 40-month period. She found that over 67 percent were re-arrested and 51 percent were convicted for a new offense. Petersilia concluded that felony probationers posed a significant risk to the community. Critics of the Petersilia study quickly pointed out that two urban counties in California are not representative of the rest of the states or the country. Two replication studies, one in Kentucky (Vito, 1986) and one in Missouri (McGaha, Fichter & Hirschburg, 1987) found quite different results. In both Kentucky and Missouri, felony probationers were re-arrested at about one-third of the rate as those in California.

Morgan (1993) studied 266 adult felony probationers in Tennessee to determine factors associated with favorable probation outcome and those that would predict success. She found that only 27 percent of the probationers failed and that females, married probationers, and those with higher levels of education were most likely to succeed. Factors significantly related to probation *failure* were prior felonies, prior probation, prior institutional commitment, and probation sentence length (the longer the sentence, the more likely the failure).

Table 14.4
**Studies Reporting Recidivism Rates for Probationers**

| Study | Instant Offense | Failure | Follow-Up | Failure Rate (%) |
|-------|-----------------|---------|-----------|------------------|
| Caldwell (1951) | Internal revenue laws (72%) | Convictions | Post-probation 5½-11½ yrs. | 16.4 |
| England (1955) | Bootlegging (48%) & forgery | Convictions | Post-probation 6-12 yrs. | 17.7 |
| Davis (1955) | Burglary, forgery & checks | Two or more violations (technical & new offense) | To termination 4-7 yrs. | 30.2 |
| Frease (1964) | Unknown | Inactive letter, Bench warrant & revocation | On probation 18-30 mos. | 20.2 |
| Landis et al. (1969) | Auto theft, forgery & checks | Revocation (technical & new offense) | To termination | 52.5 |
| Irish (1972) | Larceny & burglary | Arrests or convictions | Post-probation Minimum 4 yrs. | 41.5 |
| Missouri Div. Probation & Parole (1976) | Burglary, larceny & vehicle theft | Arrests & convictions | Post-probation 6 mos.- 7 yrs. | 30.0 |
| Kusuda (1976) | Property | Revocation | To termination 1-2 yrs. | 18.3 |
| Comptroller General (1976) | Unknown | Revocation & post-release conviction | Post-probation 20 mo. average | 55.0 |
| Irish (1977) | Property | Arrests | Post-probation 3-4 yrs. | 29.6 |
| Petersilia (1985) | Felony probationers | Arrests | Tracked over 40 mos. | 65.0 |
| McGaha, Fichter & Hirschburg (1987) | Felony probationers | Arrests | Tracked over 40 mos. | 22.3 |
| Vito (1986) | Felony probationers (excluding drug offenses) | Arrests | Tracked over 40 mos. | 22.0 |

Source: Adapted and updated from H.E. Allen, E.W. Carlson, and E.C. Parks (September, 1979). *Critical Issues in Adult Probation: Summary*, p. 35. National Institute of Law Enforcement and Criminal Justice.

---

Box 14.8

### Probation as a Correctional Alternative

Morgan reviewed the probation outcome literature through 1991 and concluded that probation is effective as a correctional alternative. Failure rates ranged from 14 to 60 percent for a group that had already committed crime; success rates vary from 40 to 86 percent.

Factors more frequently associated with failure on probation included age, sex, marital status, low income, prior criminal record, and employment status. Those most likely to fail were unemployed or underemployed young males with a low income and prior criminal record. The reconviction offenses of those who failed were more likely to be minor misdemeanors rather than felonies. Probationers who were adequately employed, married with children, and had lived in their area for at least two years were most often successful when placed on probation.

Source: K. Morgan (1993). "Factors Influencing Probation Outcome: A Review of the Literature." *Federal Probation*, 57:23-29.

---

One suggested reason for these differences is the effects of budget cuts on probation staffs in California. Caseloads of over 300 are commonplace, and there is virtually no enforcement of probation conditions (Snider, 1986). In spite of the reasons, it is important to note that the effectiveness of felony probation is still very much in debate.

The review of these 13 studies demonstrates that little progress has apparently been made over the past few years toward an adequate assessment of probation. The conclusions drawn by the authors of these studies, however, appear to suggest that there exists an unwritten agreement or rule of thumb that probation can be considered to be effective, and that a failure rate above 30 percent indicates it is not effective. This tendency is suggested by the comments in Table 14.5.

## Probation Outcome and Statistics

In addition to measuring the effectiveness of probation, a number of studies have also attempted to isolate characteristics that could be related to offender rehabilitation. Table 14.6 presents a summary of the major factors that were found in each study to be statistically correlated with failure. Keeping in mind the methodological differences among the

Table 14.5
**Evaluations of Effectiveness of Probation**

| Year | Author | Failure Rate | Comments |
|------|--------|--------------|----------|
| 1951 | Caldwell | 16% | [P]robation is an effective method of dealing with federal offenders . . . |
| 1955 | England | 18% | A reconviction rate of less than one-fifth or one-quarter . . . is an acceptable performance for a probation service. |
| 1976 | Missouri | 30% | Probation is an effective and efficient way of handling the majority of offenders in the State of Missouri. |
| 1976 | Comptroller | 55% | [P]robation systems we reviewed were achieving limited success in protecting society and rehabilitating offenders. |
| 1977 | Irish | 30% | [S]upervision program is effectively accomplishing its objective. |
| 1985 | Petersilia | 65% | Felony probation does present a serious threat to public safety. |
| 1986 | Vito | 22% | Felony probation supervision appears to be relatively effective in controlling recidivism . . . |
| 1987 | McGaha et al. | 22% | In Missouri, it does not appear that the current use of felony probation poses a high risk to the security of the community. |
| 1991 | Whitehead | 40% | [C]alls for drastically reduced use of probation for felony offenders are only partially in order. |
| 1994 | Morgan | 27% | [I]nadequate employment and unemployment are major impediments to achieving successful probation adjustment and . . . outcome. |
| 1997 | Mortimer and May | 18% | Electronic monitoring and probation orders yield comparable success rates. |

Source: Adapted and updated from H.E. Allen, E.W. Carlson and E.C. Parks (September 1979). *Critical Issues in Adult Probation: Summary,* p. 36. National Institute of Law Enforcement and Criminal Justice; J. Petersilia (1985). "Probation and Felony Offenders." *Federal Probation,* 49(2):4-9; G. Vito (1986). "Felony Probation and Recidivism: Replication and Response." *Federal Probation,* 50(4):17-25; J. McGaha, M. Fichter and P. Hirschburg (1987). "Felony Probation: A Re-Examination of Public Risk." *American Journal of Criminal Justice,* 12:1-9; J.T. Whitehead (1991). "The Effectiveness of Felony Probation: Results from an Eastern State." *Justice Quarterly,* 8:525-543; K. Morgan (1993). "Factors Influencing Probation Outcome: A Review of the Literature." *Federal Probation,* 57(2):23-29. E. Mortimer and C. May (1997). *Electronic Monitoring in Practice.* London, UK: U.K. Home Office.

Table 14.6
**Studies Reporting Factors Related to Probationer Recidivism**

| Study | Previous Criminal History | Youth | Status Other Than Married | Not Employed | Low Income (Below $400) | Education Below 11th Grade | Abuse of Alcohol or Drugs | Property Offender | On-Probation Maladjustment | Imposition of Conditions |
|---|---|---|---|---|---|---|---|---|---|---|
| Caldwell (1951) | Significant correlation | Significant correlation | Significant correlation | Significant correlation | Significant correlation | Significant correlation | | * | | |
| England (1955) | Significant correlation | Significant correlation | Significant correlation | Significant correlation | Significant correlation | Significant correlation | | * | | Significant correlation |
| Davis (1955) | Significant correlation | Significant correlation | | | | | | Significant correlation | Significant correlation | |
| Frease (1964) | Significant correlation | | Significant correlation | | ! | Significant correlation | Significant correlation | | | Significant correlation |
| Landis (1969) | Significant correlation | Significant correlation | Significant correlation | Significant correlation | Significant correlation | Significant correlation | Significant correlation | | Significant correlation | |
| Irish (1972) | Significant correlation | Significant correlation | Significant correlation | Significant correlation | Significant correlation | Significant correlation | Significant correlation | Significant correlation | * | |
| MO Div. of Prob. & Parole | Significant correlation | Significant correlation | Significant correlation | Significant correlation | + | Significant correlation | Significant correlation | Significant correlation | | |
| Kusuda (1976) | | Significant correlation | Significant correlation | Significant correlation | ! | * | Significant correlation | * | | |
| Comptroller General (1976) | | | | | | | | * | | |
| Irish (1977) | Significant correlation | | Significant correlation | Significant correlation | | | | * | Significant correlation | |
| Petersilia (1985) | Significant correlation | Significant correlation | Significant correlation | | | | | Significant correlation | | |
| Benedict (1998) | Significant correlation | Significant correlation | Significant correlation | | | Significant correlation | Significant correlation | | Significant correlation | Significant correlation |

* In these studies, instant & post-probation offenses committed by probationers were predominantly "property;" however, a correlation between property offenses & re-cidivism was not investigated.

! Correlation only with income between $100 and $400; those who make less than $100 & those who made above $400 both had an equal probability of success.

+ Correlation only with income between $100 and $700; those who made less than $100 or above $700 both had an equal probability of success.

Source: Adapted from H.E. Allen, E.W. Carlson and E.C. Parks (September 1979). *Critical Issues in Adult Probation: Summary*, p. 37. National Institute of Law Enforcement and Criminal Justice.

studies in terms of definition of failure and specification of follow-up period, it appears that the one characteristic most commonly found to be associated with failure is the probationer's previous criminal histories. Other factors frequently cited are: the youthfulness of the probationer, marital status other than married, unemployment, and educational level below the eleventh grade.

Factors such as employment and education are dynamic factors that are correlated with outcome. Since these are areas that can be addressed during supervision, one can reasonably view these factors positively; we have a clear indication of offender needs, and they can be improved. On the other hand, a question remains as to whether probation and parole officers are addressing these needs adequately. When probation and parole agencies fail to meet offender needs that are correlated with outcome, the result is often higher failure rates.

## Cost Effectiveness

While the public has demanded tougher sentences, it has become increasingly apparent that the cost associated with more incarceration and prison construction are astronomical. Estimates place the cost of constructing a maximum security prison at approximately $80,000 per bed, and the annual cost of maintenance and housing inmates at more than $19,800 (Camp & Camp, 1997:75). The acute shortage of prison space, despite the opening of 410 new prisons since 1988, and an additional 172,642, beds in 1996 and 1997 alone (Camp & Camp, 1997:67), has made incarceration a scarce resource. Many states are faced with severe budget deficits, and legislators and the public are reluctant to vote for new prison construction. Yet there is also ample evidence that once prisons are built they are filled. In addition, 31 states are under court order to increase services or reduce or limit their prison populations or the population in a specific prison (American Correctional Association, 1995:xx). Because of the increasingly high cost associated with incarceration, researchers have begun to focus on the cost effectiveness of alternatives.

In light of these factors, and in addition to the research aimed at measuring effectiveness in terms of recidivism, there have been attempts to demonstrate cost effectiveness of probation. Typically, with criminal justice agencies, costs are usually divided into three types: processing, program, and client-centered. Processing costs include monies spent in identifying and selecting individuals for a given program. Program costs are expenditures associated with incarceration and include direct costs, such as loss of earning, and indirect costs, such as psychological effects upon of alienation/prisonization, social stigma, and other detrimental effects upon the prisoner's marriage and family (Nelson, 1975).

Similarly, the benefits generated by probation could include savings to society through the use of diversion, wages, and taxes generated by the participants, and reduced crime or recidivism rates (Vito & Latessa, 1979:3). In addition there are the costs associated with failure, such as the monetary loss and grief experienced by the victims.

The studies that provided the most thorough financial comparisons were those that treated the cost-benefit analysis as their primary focus, and considered direct and indirect costs and benefits.

In one of the most comprehensive studies of probation costs, Frazier (1972) attempted to develop realistic cost information on probation and incarceration for the purpose of comparison.

---

Box 14.9

### Substance Abuse Programs

General estimates indicate that as many as 80 percent of all offenders have some form of substance abuse problem (particularly alcohol and drugs). Mauser et al. (1994) estimate total annual societal losses at $144 billion, not including pain and suffering of victims and family members, costs of crimes to victims, diminished health of substance abusers, or use of medical resources. As a result, the justice system has responded with specialized probation caseloads and counseling, community substance abuse programs, chemical dependency counseling, etc. Halfway houses offer residential settings for delivery of substance abuse and family counseling, life skills and crisis management training, and so on. Jail programs include Alcoholics Anonymous and Narcotics Anonymous, Sober Living Programs, and transfer to specialized care treatment centers. In addition, Treatment Alternatives Programs (TAP) have been developed to divert substance abusers from the justice system.

Despite the stereotypical belief that nothing works, recidivism rates for program graduates are low, ranging from 10-15 percent for probation-ordered treatment to 17 to 36 percent for jail programs. Mauser et al. (1994) argue that the benefits of TAP are greater than the short-term costs of the program and there is less recidivism among TAP completers. Savings were found in the reduction of the number of jail days served, the number of arrests, and costs to victims of crimes.

---

A number of estimates were used to compare the indirect costs associated with incarceration. These factors included the average wage and average months employed per year, the average taxes paid on gross wages, and the cost of welfare support for children whose wage-earning

Box 14.10

### Drug Court Treatment

One of the most promising responses to the flood of drug cases coming to criminal court has been the Miami Treatment Drug Court. Since 1989, the judge has assumed a "hands on" approach to managing third-degree drug felony drug possession defendants who had no prior convictions. Defendants were offered a treatment program in lieu of prosecution, with the proviso that frequent reports were made to the judge and appearances would be made in court.

The treatment program phased from detoxification (Phase I) to counseling (Phase II) through educational/vocational assessment and training (Phase III). Graduation was the final Phase. Each client must appear in court at an appointed time, with the record of progress and participation, and would be encouraged or admonished by the judge. "Jail as a motivator" might be imposed on absent or contemptuous clients. Outpatient treatment at four clinics was required. Thus this is a judge-supervised outpatient drug treatment program operating in the community.

Favorable outcomes were observed for 67 percent of the program participants: no rearrest. The median number of days to first rearrest was significantly lengthened for drug program participants, and the rate of failure to appear in court was sharply lower for drug court cases than other felony drug cases. Drug court treatment appeared to particularly benefit defendants with some college education and those older than 25 years of age. Defendants with prior robbery arrests and prior failure to appear records had higher probabilities of being rearrested. There is no evidence of increased threat to public safety.

Defendants who completed the treatment program had a significantly lower rate of recidivism than defendants eligible but who did not participate in the diversion program, a finding similar to that in Maricopa County, Arizona (Hepburn et al., 1994). The Miami drug court represents a promising merger of court, community, and treatment efforts.

Source: J. Goldcamp (1994). "Miami's Treatment Drug Court for Felony Misdemeanants." *The Prison Journal*, 73:110-166.

parent had been incarcerated. These figures were based upon data collection from a representative sample of 115 inmates, and were then extended to the entire inmate population in Texas for 1970. The total indirect costs of incarceration were estimated to be $5,938,447.

---

**Box 14.11**

### House Arrest and Electronic Monitoring

House arrest requires offenders to remain within the confines of their residences and obey a curfew, and is generally used with probation but can be used as a "stand alone" program for pretrial defendants, for convicted offenders as an alternative to incarceration, and for intensive probation and parole supervision. Supervising officers verify the presence of participants by telephone or face-to-face checks. Evaluations indicate that the impact on prison crowding, offender behavior, and state correctional costs have been favorable. Only 10 percent of Florida participants received additional punishment for technical violations, and the reoffense rate for community control offenders is lower than for similar offenders sentenced to prison (Wagner & Baird, 1993).

Electronic monitoring provides technological verification of the offender's whereabouts, and is used to monitor house arrestees and curfew observation. It is also used to follow up parolees, control those sentenced to community corrections, and monitor pretrial defendants. Recent technological developments allow for on-site testing for alcohol consumption. Home detention with electronic monitoring was successful for 73 percent of participants in a pretrial release program. Defendants most likely to complete home detention lived with a spouse or opposite-gender roommate. Of the 27 percent failures, about one-half were technical violators and the other half absconded. Electronic monitoring programs with probationers, offenders on parole, and those in community corrections report successful termination rates ranging from 74 to 86 percent, although rates as high as 97 percent have been achieved (Gowdy, 1993).

---

Frazier (1972) then combined the indirect with the direct cost of incarceration (defined as all costs included in the yearly budget of the Department of Corrections) to obtain a 1970 figure of $28,331,702. The savings generated by probation were then illustrated through the use of an example. If a felon were convicted, given a five-year sentence, incarcerated for three years, and then placed on parole for two years, the total costs would be $6,927. However, if the same felon were placed on probation, the costs would only equal $1,370—a cost avoidance or savings of $5,557 over the five-year period. The authors concluded that if 3,000 inmates were diverted, a one-year savings of $5,715,000 could be generated.

In sum, the Texas study is an excellent example of the high quality of information that can be generated by the cost-benefit analysis. The only apparent shortcoming is the failure to compare the cost of recidivism in the two systems. The recidivism rate of probationers versus parolees would take on more meaning under this type of comparison (Vito & Latessa, 1979).

There have been several other cost-benefit analyses, however, that tend to include cost comparisons as part of a large research effort, and thus are plagued by errors of omission, and incomplete costs or benefit identifications (Erwin, 1984; Pearson, 1985; Wetter, 1985; Latessa, 1985; Latessa, 1986; System Sciences, 1982). Despite their limitations, these studies also support the contention that probation is a cost-effective alternative to incarceration. In one recent study that included cost effectiveness as part of a larger research effort, Latessa, Travis and Holsinger (1997) compared the cost of four correctional options (regular probation, ISP, Community Based Correctional Facilities, and Prison). Figure 14.6 shows the average cost per offender by each of the correctional alternatives. This shows that probation and ISP are clearly cheaper alternatives to residential and institutional options. They went on to conclude:

- Compared to incarceration, placement in ISP or CBCFs program produces savings and revenues between $4,500 and $5,000 per offender when compared to imprisonment.

- ISP and CBCF programs were more expensive than regular probation, but substantially less expensive than imprisonment.

- If only half of the offenders served in the community had been incarcerated, the state realized a savings of $49 million.

- Offenders in the ISP and CBCFs paid over $3.4 million in court costs, fines, and restitution, and $1.7 million in the value of community service and labor over a three year period.

Figure 14.6
**Average Cost Per Day Per Offender in Ohio**

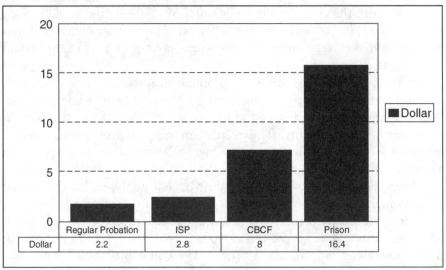

| | Regular Probation | ISP | CBCF | Prison |
|---|---|---|---|---|
| Dollar | 2.2 | 2.8 | 8 | 16.4 |

Source: E.J. Latessa, L.F. Travis, and A. Holsinger (1997). Evaluation of Ohio's Community Corrections Act Programs and Community Based Correctional Facilities, Cincinnati Division of Criminal Justice, University of Cincinnati.

## What Works in Correctional Intervention?

As discussed earlier in this chapter, the importance of evaluating correctional programs, especially those operating in the community, has never been more pronounced. Vast sums are being spent on correctional programming, and the public is demanding programs that work. The critical questions the remainder of this chapter will address is "what works"?, what do we know about program effectivness?, and what harm is done when we fail to develop effective programs?

One of the most important areas of contemporary concern for correctional officials is the design and operation of effective correctional intervention programs. This is particularly relevant since there is consistent evidence that the public supports rehabilitation programs for offenders (Applegate, Cullen & Fisher, 1997). Furthermore, survey research also reveals strong support for public protection as an important goal of corrections (Applegate et al., 1997). Consequently, disagreements arise, focusing on what the best methods may be to achieve these and other correctional goals. On one side are advocates for more punitive policies such as an increased use of incarceration, punishing smarter (e.g., boot camps), or simply increasing control and monitoring if the offender is supervised in the community. Those advocating these strategies of crime control do so on the basis of the often interrelated goals of punishment—deterrence, retribution, and incapacitation. The limits of these approaches have been outlined and debated by others (Currie 1985, Bennett, DiIulio & Walters, 1996). The ultimate effect of most of these policies has been described as "penal harm" (Clear, 1994).

As Cullen and Applegate (1998) imply, the most disheartening aspect of these "get tough" policies is their dismissal of the importance of programming that is designed to rehabilitate offenders. Cullen and Applegate further question whether the penal harm movement's rejection of rehabilitation is sound public policy. As many states have found, simply locking up offenders and "throwing away the key" has proven to be a very expensive approach to crime control. This approach is also very limited, since the vast majority of offenders will one day return to society. Many will return at best unchanged, and at worst with many more problems and intensified needs for service (Petersilia, 1992). For those advocating incapacitation, one must also ask what should be done with offenders while incarcerated? Some scholars, such as Cullen and Applegate do not believe that incapacitation and rehabilitation are mutually exclusive. Furthermore, since the vast majority of offenders are supervised in the community at differing degrees of intensity, it is even more important that we develop programs that work toward reducing recidivism.

Many of the "intermediate sanctions" that have been developed over the past few years are but a few examples of "programs" that often fail to live up to their expectations, particularly in terms of reductions in recidivism (Latessa, Travis & Holsinger, 1997; Petersilia, 1997). These results are often attributed to policies that emphasize control and surveillance over treatment and service delivery (Fulton, Latessa, Stichman & Travis, 1997).

Despite the punitive movement, there is increasing evidence that correctional treatment can be effective in reducing recidivism among offenders (Andrews, Zinger, Hoge, Bonta, Gendreau & Cullen, 1990; Gendreau & Andrews, 1990; Cullen & Gendreau, 1989; Van Voorhis, 1987). Nonetheless, some scholars remain unconvinced (Antonowicz & Ross, 1994; Lab & Whitehead, 1988; Logan & Gaes, 1993). The debate surrounding treatment effectiveness has been on going since Martinson's proclamation that "nothing works," with many still clinging to this mantel, despite evidence to the contrary. Principle among the reasons for disbelief in the potential effectiveness of correctional programming is the failure to measure outcome properly, and the lack of quality programs.

Gendreau (1995) has examined hundreds of correctional and rehabilitation programs that attempt to intervene with offenders. Others have conducted similar studies (Lipsey & Wilson, 1997) and have come to the same conclusion; rehabilitation can be effective in reducing recidivism. For example, citing the work of Lipsey (1992), Gendreau (1995) found that 64 percent of the offender rehabilitation studies (that had control groups) reported reductions in favor of the treatment group; the average reduction in recidivism was 10 percent. When the studies were categorized by the general type of program (employment, relapse prevention, etc.), reductions in recidivism averaged 18 percent.

Gendreau and Paparozzi (1995) also found that, when rehabilitation programs incorporated at least some of eight principles of effective intervention, those programs reduced recidivism in the range of 25-70 percent, with the average about 50 percent. His principles of effective intervention are as follows:

1. Programs have intensive services that are behavioral in nature, that occupy 40-70 percent of the offender's time in a program and are from 3-9 months in duration. [Behavioral means using positive reinforcers to strengthen behavior, such as rewarding "doing good" with attendance at sports events, praise, and approval.] Further, behavioral strategies are essential to effective service delivery.

2. Behavioral programs target the criminogenic needs of high-risk offenders, such as antisocial attitudes, peer associations, and chemical dependencies.

3. Programs incorporate responsivity between offender, therapist, and program. Simply said, treatment program should be delivered in a manner that facilitates the offender's learning new prosocial skills.

4. Program contingencies and behavioral strategies are enforced in a firm but fair manner; positive reinforcers are greater than punishers by at least 4:1.

5. Therapists relate to offenders in interpersonally sensitive and constructive ways and are trained and supervised accordingly. Treatment is systematically delivered by competent therapists and treaters.

6. Program structure and activities disrupt the delinquency network by placing offenders in situations (with people and in places) where prosocial activities predominate.

7. Provide relapse prevention in the community by such tactics as planning and rehearsing alternative prosocial responses, anticipating problem situations, training significant others (family and friends) to provide reinforcement for prosocial behavior, and establishing a system for booster sessions.

8. A high level of advocacy and brokerage as long as the community agency offers appropriate services.

Similarly, Gendreau lists those principles of ineffective intervention:

- Counseling for everyone

- Nondirective, relationship-oriented therapy

- Radical nonintervention

- Traditional medical model approaches

- Intensive services directed to low-risk offenders

- Intensive services oriented to non-crime-producing needs

One example of a program that was not effective in reducing recidivism is found in Box 14.12. In a recent review of substance abuse treatment by Lightfoot (1997), she identified the effective and ineffective types of treatment. Table 14.7 illustrates her findings. Interestingly, the types of effective and ineffective treatment models for substance abusers mirrors the findings from studies of other offender types.

---

Box 14.12

### Acupuncture Treatment for Drug-Dependent Offenders

Acupuncture is defined as "the Chinese medical art of inserting fine needles into the skin to relieve pain or disability" (Wensel, 1990:5). A number of advocates claim that acupuncture can be an effective remedy for drug addiction (Smith, et al., 1982 & 1984; Smith et al., 1984).

In 1992 Latessa and Moon published the results from a study they conducted on a outpatient drug treatment program for felony probationers. The program participants were randomly divided into three groups; an experimental group, which received acupuncture on a regular basis, a control group, which did not receive acupuncture, and a placebo group, which received an acupuncture-like simulation. They concluded that, "With regard to outcome there is no evidence that acupuncture had any appreciable effect on program completion, arrests, convictions, or probation outcome" (1992:330).

Source: E.J. Latessa and M.M. Moon (1992). "The Effectiveness of Acupuncture in an Outpatient Drug Treatment Program." *Journal of Contemporary Criminal Justice*, 8:317-331.

---

Gendreau concludes that many programs in the past and present lack most of the effective components listed above. When these are present, reductions in recidivism are high. His arguments suggest that the "nothing works in corrections" position is not only premature, it is inaccurate. A program focused on behavioral change, organized with the principles of effective treatment in mind in the various components and subsystems of community-based corrections could significantly improve how we handle and rehabilitate offenders. Rehabilitation does appear to work, but it also seems that the programs that meet the above principles are more effective than those that do not. One important question however, is how do we determine the degree to which a program meets the principles of effective intervention? Gendreau and Andrews (1994) accomplished this through the development of an instrument known as the Correctional Program Assessment Inventory (CPAI).

Table 14.7
**Review of Drug Treatment Effectiveness by Lightfoot**

What treatment types were effective in quasi-experimental and/or controlled studies:

⇒  Social-Learning Based Treatments
⇒  Aversion Therapy:  Electrical/Chemical Counter-conditioning
⇒  Covert Sensitization
⇒  Contingency Management/Contingency Contracting
⇒  Broad Spectrum Therapies
⇒  Individualized Behavior Therapy
⇒  Community Reinforcement
⇒  Behavior Self-Control Thinking
⇒  Relapse Prevention

What treatment types showed no clear evidence of effectiveness from controlled studies:

⇒  Acupuncture
⇒  Education
⇒  Lectures
⇒  Bibliotherapy
⇒  Self-help
⇒  Alcoholics Anonymous
⇒  Narcotics Anonymous
⇒  Al-Anon
⇒  Adult Children of Alcoholics
⇒  Psycho-therapy
⇒  Supportive
⇒  Confrontational
⇒  Pharmacotherapies

Source: Lightfoot, L. (1997). *What Works in Drug Treatment*. Presented at the International Community Corrections Association annual meeting.

The CPAI is a tool that has been used for assessing correctional intervention programs. The CPAI assesses a program on six primary areas: (1) program implementation and leadership; (2) offender assessment and classification; (3) characteristics of the program; (4) characteristics and practices of the staff; (5) evaluation and quality control; and (6) miscellaneous items such as ethical guidelines and levels of support. One advantage of the CPAI is that is allows researchers to quantify the degree to which a program meets the principles of effective intervention. Each section of the CPAI is scored as either "very satisfactory" (70% to 100%), "satisfactory" (60% to 69%), "satisfactory but needs improvement" (50% to 59%) or "unsatisfactory" (less than 50%).

To date, researchers from the University of Cincinnati have assessed 77 correctional programs across the country. The types of programs assessed include residential facilities, halfway houses, ISPs, work release centers, therapeutic communities, day reporting programs, school based programs, boot camps, substance abuse treatment programs, and a variety of special programs for offenders. Figure 14.7 shows the percentages of programs that scored in each category. Only 11.7 percent of the programs assessed scored in the "very satisfactory" range, while 60 percent scored either "satisfactory but needs improvement," or "unsatisfactory" category. These results indicate that many programs are not meeting the principles of effective intervention.

Figure 14.7
**Percentage of Programs in Each CPAI Category**

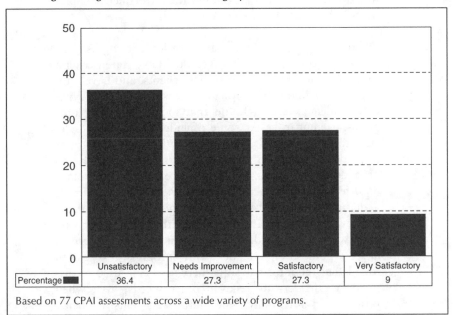

| Percentage ■ | Unsatisfactory | Needs Improvement | Satisfactory | Very Satisfactory |
|---|---|---|---|---|
| | 36.4 | 27.3 | 27.3 | 9 |

Based on 77 CPAI assessments across a wide variety of programs.

Source: Cincinnati, OH: Division of Criminal Justice, University of Cincinnati.

Although there was a great deal of variation between (and within) programs, Latessa and Holsinger (1998) have summarized some of the major strengths and weakness in each of the CPAI areas across the 77 programs they assessed:

- **Program Implementation and Leadership.** Strengths: Effective programs have strong leadership and involvement of the program director. For the most part we have found qualified and experienced program directors, who were involved in designing the program. They tend to be involved in the hiring and training of staff, and in many instances they provide some direct services to offenders. It is also important for the support of a program that the values and goals of the program be consistent with existing values in the community or institution in which it resides, and that there be a documented need for the program. Support for the program also depends on perceptions of cost-effectiveness. We usually find that most correctional programs meet these conditions. Weaknesses: There are two flaws that are common in this area. Effective programs are based on strong theoretical models that are derived from the treatment literature. Regardless, many of the correctional intervention programs we examined were basically designed with little regard for the empirical research on what works with the type of offenders they were serving. In addition, effective programs are usually begun on a pilot basis to work out the logistics. Thus far we have found few programs that piloted their treatment components before full implementation.

- **Offender Assessment and Classification.** Strengths: The vast majority of programs we studied have stated criteria for admissions, receive appropriate clients, and have a rational legal/clinical basis for the exclusion of certain types of offenders. We also found that in general, most programs attempt to assess some offender characteristics related to risk and need. Weaknesses: While many programs did indeed attempt to assess offenders regarding risk and need, doing so did not involve the incorporation of a standardized, objective, actuarial instrument. The absence of actuarial risk/needs assessment instruments was particularly evident in programs that deal with juvenile offenders. Even when a standardized assessment is being performed at some point in the offender's entry/progress, it is seldom found that the information gathered is being used to distinguish offenders by risk. In other words, even when proper (and potentially beneficial) assessments are being performed, the information is not influencing the decision making process, let alone service delivery. In addition, it is generally found that staff assessments of offenders are based on a quasi-clinical approach that does not result in a summary score. Likewise, it has been very rare to find that programs are routinely measuring with standardized instruments responsivity characteristics, such as levels of motivation, intelligence, or psychological development.

- **Characteristics of the Program.** Strengths: Effective intervention programs focus the vast majority of their efforts on targeting criminogenic needs and behaviors. In general we have found that many correctional intervention programs target these behaviors (although we still find programs that provide intensive services and treatment in non-crime producing areas, such as self-esteem). Another common strength was that many programs have criteria for program completion, and upon discharge many offenders are routinely referred to programs and services that help meet their needs. Weaknesses: Offenders typically have not been spending a significant percentage of their time in structured programs. In addition, the amount of services and treatment provided has not been varying by risk and need levels. Yet another characteristic of an effective program is the use of a treatment model that has been found to be effective. Since programs are rarely designed around a theoretical model, was not surprising to find a lack of a consistently applied treatment model in place. In general, the major shortcomings found when considering the "Characteristics of Program" portion of the CPAI include: lack of programmatic structure; incomplete or non-existent treatment manuals; few rewards to encourage program participation and compliance; the ineffective use of punishment; staff being allowed to design their own interventions regardless of the treatment literature base; a host very obvious and definable, yet ineffective treatment models. This area of the CPAI also examines the extent to which matching occurs between offenders and staff, offenders and programs, and staff and programs. Even when matching is found to occur, it is uncommon to observe it being based on specific responsivity criteria. In addition, it is very rare to find a program that includes family and/or friends of the offender in the treatment process. Finally, many programs failed to provide aftercare services or booster sessions.

- **Characteristics and Practices of the Staff.** Strengths: Although there is a great deal of variation from program to program with regarding staff quality, for the most part we found educated and experienced staff working with offenders. Often staff were selected on personal characteris-

tics such as life experience, fairness, firmness, and prob-
lem-solving skills. We also found that staff usually had
input in the structure of the programs, and that on-going
training was provided. Weaknesses: Staff turnover was
often a problem with some types of correctional programs
(e.g., halfway houses), and we rarely found staff who had
received sufficient training on the interventions and treatments utilized by the program. Clinical supervision was
not routinely provided, and staff were rarely assessed on
service delivery skills.

- **Evaluation and Quality Control.** Programs that study
  themselves tend to be more effective than programs that
  do not. Data provides insight into program and offender
  performance, helps identify who is successful and who is
  not, and allows adjustments to be made. Strengths: File review and case audits were usually conducted. Weaknesses:
  Periodic, objective, and standardized assessment of offenders to see if criminogenic factors were being reduced
  was uncommon. In short, most programs do not develop
  meaningful performance measures (to measure either program or offender performance over time). We also found
  that the majority of programs were not tracking offenders
  after they have left the program, and formal evaluations
  involving comparison groups were the exception.

- **Other Items.** Strengths: Most of the programs we examined score well in this area. In general, offender records
  are complete and are kept in a confidential file. Changes
  that jeopardize programs, funding, or community support
  are rare. Weaknesses: Some programs do not have ethical
  guidelines for intervention, and public agencies tend not
  to have advisory boards, while those operated by non-
  profits do.

While these results indicate that the majority of correctional programs
assessed are not fully meeting the principles of effective intervention,
they also provide some useful information on how to improve the quality of correctional interventions.

## The Harm of Ineffective Programs

This chapter has outlined what many of the pertinent issues have
been when evaluating program effectiveness. It has become apparent
that the way recidivism is measured may need to be reconsidered in
order to more fully understand the essence of a program's crime-reduc-

Box 14.13

## Sex Offender Treatment: Does it Work?

The typical justice response to sex offenders involves punishment and incapacitation by eliminating offender access to victims. Since almost all sex offenders return to the community, incapacitation without treatment does not reduce reoffending. In Vermont, the cost of a relapse (justice and victim services) is estimated to be over $138,000.

McGrath (1994) provides a synopsis of 68 outcome studies and clearly shows that treatment in the community is effective, particularly more recent programs that use relapse prevention treatment models delivered in group therapy sessions. Typical treatment goals include accepting responsibility for the offense, developing empathy with the victim, improving social competence, controlling deviant sexual arousal, and developing relapse prevention skills. More recent treatment programs (since 1980) appear to be more effective.

Re-offending rates for treated offenders are 80 percent *less* than for untreated offenders; persons who complete treatment programs (versus dropping out) are 77 percent *less* likely to recidivate. Sex offenders treated in relapse prevention (versus behavioral change) groups are 73 percent *less* likely to re-offend. Finally, the re-offending rate for sex offenders treated since 1980 is 6 *percent*. Furby et al. (1989) argue it is no more than 10 percent but argue for longer follow-up periods after treatment.

McGrath concludes that results from the 68 sex offender outcome studies reviewed show that treatment works, is cost effective, and can be provided in communities under probation control.

Source: R. McGrath (1995). "Sex Offender Treatment: Does it Work?" *American Probation and Parole Association Perspectives,* 19:24-26.

ing potential. Further, and perhaps more importantly, measuring other indicators or program performance, such as program quality if often neglected. The result of allowing ineffective correctional strategies to continue is quite likely to be harmful, which manifests itself in several ways. First, the undermining of confidence and support. When faced with the existence of ineffective correctional treatment strategies, judges, legislators, and the public lose confidence in correctional efforts, which in turn undermines support for effective programs. In the realm of public opinion regarding correctional sanctions, some bad apples may indeed spoil the entire bushel—programs that are effectively reducing recidivism

Box 14.14

### Probation Supervision of the Mentally Disordered Offender

Despite claims by mental health advocates that "people with mental illness pose no more of a crime threat than do other members of the general public," (National Mental Health Association, 1987), strong evidence suggests that this is not the case. However, for the correctional system, the issue of whether the mentally ill are more "dangerous" than members of the general public is not a particularly relevant question. For mentally ill individuals who have been convicted of an offense, a more appropriate question is whether they pose more of a risk than *other* offender groups being supervised in the community?

In a recent study, Latessa (1996) compared arrest, conviction, and probation outcome data for several groups under probation supervision. The probation groups included: sex offenders, drug offenders, high-risk offenders, regularly supervised offenders, and mentally disordered offenders. He found that mentally disordered offenders performed as well, and in some cases better, than other probation groups. He concluded that mentally ill offenders can and are being supervised in the community without increasing risk to public safety.

Source: E.J. Latessa (1996). "Offenders with Mental Illness on Probation," *Community Corrections in America: New Directions and Sounder Investments for Persons with Mental Illness and Co-Disorders*. Washington, DC: National Institute of Corrections and the National Coalition for Mental and Substance Abuse Health Care in the Justice System.

based on what we know works can be harmed by programs that are not. In short, if ineffective strategies continue to flourish the risk of returning to a "nothing works" doctrine will undoubtedly increase. Second, there is a tendency to seek "quick fix" solutions that have no empirical support. The result has often been programs that promise a quick fix to the problem of criminal behavior, or what Cullen (*Personal Communication*, n.d.) refers to as correctional "quackery." There is no panacea approach to changing offender behavior. Those searching for a "magic pill" for reducing crime and changing human behavior will not only be disappointed, but will at best perpetuate the myth that there is some simple solution, and at worst erode faith in the potential for effective intervention. Finally, offenders get all the blame. Perhaps the greatest harm that is perpetuated is that which is done to the offender. When we use programs that are not effective, the offender receives the blame, not the program. Too often we hear judges say that they have already sent the offender to some program, and that they have failed. This "failure" is then used to justify even harsher punishments. Sending an offender to a program that does not adequately meet the principles of effective intervention should not be expected to change criminal behavior. Blaming the offender absolves us from designing and operating high quality and effective intervention programs.

## Summary

During the past few years there have been a number of meta-analysis studies that have focused on the positive results of correctional treatment programs (Gendreau & Ross, 1987; Van Voorhis, 1987; Garrett, 1985; Palmer, 1991). Meta-analysis refers to a type of research method that examines other studies on a specific subject or topic. These studies have been very critical of the "nothing works" doctrine put forth by Martinson and others (Whitehead & Lab, 1989). However, as Palmer (1991:331) states:

> . . . . the research designs of many individual studies that comprised the meta-analyses and literature reviews were much less than excellent and were in that respect open to valid questions.

Even though there appear to be programs and interventions that are effective, the research conducted to date has been hampered by many constraints and limitations and, as a result, is less than adequate.

Part of this dilemma rests with the concept of effectiveness. While, as noted above, most would agree that recidivism should be a primary performance measure, there is no consensus on its definition or the indicators to be used for its measurement. Other performance measures of effectiveness, especially those examining the management or supervisory aspects of parole and probation, and the quality of correctional programs are often ignored by researchers.

## *Review Questions*

1. What are some of the indicators of effectiveness used in correctional research?

2. Why is it so difficult to predict recidivism?

3. List some of the factors that are related to outcome for parolees.

4. How does probation compare to other correctional alternatives with regard to outcome?

5. List the principles of effective intervention.

6. What are the six major risk factors identified by Andrews?

7. What are the six areas of the Correctional Program Assessment Inventory?

8. What percentage of correctional program can be classified as "very satisfactory"?

## Key Terms

cost effectiveness

determinate sentencing

length of follow-up

outcome measures

parole conditions

parole violation

program quality

recidivism

## Recommended Readings

Champion, D.J. (1988). *Felony Probation, Problems and Prospects*. New York, NY: Praeger.

Furby, L., M. Weinrott, and L. Blackshaw (1989). "Sex Offender Recidivism: A Review." *Psychological Bulletin*, 105:3-30.

Gendreau, P. (1996). "The Principles of Effective Intervention with Offenders." In A. Harland (ed.) *Choosing Correctional Options that Work: Defining the Demand and Evaluating the Supply*. Thousand Oaks, CA: Sage.

Gendreau, P. and R.R. Ross (1987). "Revivification of Rehabilitation: Evidence from the 1980s." *Justice Quarterly*, 4:349-407.

Lipsey, M. (1992). "Juvenile Delinquency Treatment: A Meta-Analytic Inquiry into the Variability of Effects." In T. Cook, H. Cooper, D. Cordray, H. Hartmann, L. Hedges, R. Light, T. Louis, and F. Mosteller (eds.) *Meta-Analysis for Explanation*, pp. 83-127. New York, NY: Russell Sage Foundation.

Martinson, R. (1974). "What Works?—Questions and Answers About Prison Reform." *The Public Interest*, 35:22- 54.

## Notes

[1]  For a discussion of the limitations and criticism of the Martinson study see T. Palmer (1975). "Martinson Revisited."Journal of Research in Crime and Delinquency, 12:133-152. S. Adams (1976). "Evaluation: A Way Out of Rhetoric." In *Rehabilitation, Recidivism, and Research*. National Council on Crime and Delinquency, 41- 62, 75-92.

[2]  Francis T. Cullen eloquently argues that rehabilitation reduces recidivism across programs by about 50 percent when interventions are based on principles of effective treatment. F.T. Cullen (1994). "Social Support as an Organizing Concept for Criminology." *Justice Quarterly*, 11:52-59.

[3]  For a discussion of the various alternative definitions of recidivism see D.J. Champion (1988). Felony Probation, Problems and Prospects. New York, NY: Praeger, pp. 95-97; and T. Palmer (1995). "Programmatic and Nonprogrammatic Aspects of Successful Intervention: New Directions for Research." *Crime & Delinquency*, 41:101-131.

[4]  Gendreau, P. and M. Paparozzi (1995). "Examining What Works in Community Corrections." *Corrections Today*, 56(8):28-30.

[5]  See the excellent collection of articles by G. Vito (ed.) (1994). "Education in Correctional Settings." *The Prison Journal*, 74:395-473.

[6]  For a synopsis of inmate participation in institutional work programs, see C. Camp and G. Camp (1995). *The Corrections Yearbook, 1994: Adult Corrections*. South Salem, NY: The Criminal Justice Institute, pp. 53-55.

[7]  California adopted a determinate sentencing system in 1977 that, despite literally hundreds of revisions, is deemed seriously flawed. See N. Holt (1995). "California's Determinate Sentencing: What Went Wrong?" *American Probation and Parole Association Perspectives*, 19(3):19-23.

[8]  It is important to note that reported success rates that do not provide more information on the source of the findings, research design used, length of follow-up, definitions of failure, and so forth, make it very difficult to gauge the effectiveness of programs, at least in terms of recidivism.

[9]  See for example the special theme issue by B. Bloom, R. Immarigeon and B. Owens (1995). "Women in Prisons and Jails." *The Prison Journal*, 75:131-272; and M. Morash, R. Haarr, and L. Rucker (1994). "A Comparison of Programming for Women and Men in U.S. Prisons in the 1980s." *Crime & Delinquency*, 41:101- 131.

[10]  For a discussion of credit-based early release from prison onto parole, see E. Chayet (1994). "Correctional 'Good Time' as a Means of Early Release." *Criminal Justice Abstracts*, 226:521-538. A discussion of the impact of good time laws on prison population in Illinois can be found in J. Austin (1994). *The Case for Shorter Prison Terms: The Illinois Experience*. San Francisco, CA: National Council on Crime and Delinquency.

# References

Adams, S. (1976). "Evaluation: A Way Out of Rhetoric. Rehabilitation, Recidivism, and Research." *National Council on Crime and Delinquency*, 7(2):75-92.

Alaska Department of Health and Social Services (1976). *Misdemeanants Probation Project*. Juneau, AK: Division of Corrections.

Allen, H.E., E.W. Carlson, and E.C. Parks (1979). *Critical Issues in Adult Probation*. Washington, DC: National Institute of Law Enforcement and Criminal Justice.

Allen, H.E. and E.J. Latessa (1980). *Parole Effectiveness in the United States: An Assessment*. San Jose, CA: San Jose State University Research Foundation.

Alstyne, D. and M.R. Gottfredson (1978). "A Multidimensional Contingency Table Analysis of Parole Outcome: New Methods and Old Problems in Criminological Prediction." *Journal of Research in Crime and Delinquency*, 15:172-193.

American Correctional Association (1995). *Directory*. Laurel, MD: ACA.

American Correctional Association (1994). "Virginia Legislature Abolishes Parole." *On the Line*, 17(5):2.

Andrews, D.A. (1994). *An Overview of Treatment Effectiveness: Research and Clinical Principles*, Ottawa, CN: Dept. of Psychology, Carleton University.

Andrews, D.A., I. Zinger, R. Hoge, J. Bonta, P. Gendreau, and F.T. Cullen (1990). "Does Correctional Treatment Work? A Clinically Relevant and Psychologically Informed Meta-Analysis," *Criminology*, 28:369-404.

Anspach, D.F. and H.S. Monsen (1989). "Determinate Sentencing, Formal Rationality, and Khadi Justice in Maine: An Application of Weber's Typology." *Journal of Criminal Justice*, 17:471-485.

Antonowicz D.H. and R.R. Ross (1994). "Essential Components of Successful Rehabilitation Programs for Offenders." *International Journal of Offender Therapy and Comparative Criminology*, 38:97-104.

Applegate, B.K., F.T. Cullen, and B.S. Fisher (1997). "Public Support for Correctional Treatment: The Continuing Appeal of the Rehabilitative Ideal." *The Prison Journal*, 77:237-258.

Austin, J. (1987). *Success and Failure on Parole in California: A Preliminary Evaluation*. Washington, DC: U.S. Department of Justice.

Ayers, D.J., S. Duguid, C. Montague, and S. Wolowidnyk (1980). *Effects of the University of Victoria Program: A Post-Release Study*. Ottawa, CN: Ministry of the Solicitor General of Canada.

Babst, D.V. and J.W. Mannering (1965). "Probation versus Imprisonment for Similar Types of Offenders." *Journal of Research in Crime and Delinquency*, 2:60-71.

Beasley, W. (1978). "Unraveling the Process of Parole: An Analysis of the Effects of Parole Residency on Parole Outcome." Paper presented at the meeting of the American Society of Criminology, Atlanta, GA.

Beck, A.J. (1987). *Recidivism of Young Parolees*. Washington, DC: Bureau of Justice Statistics Special Report.

Benedict, W., L. Huff-Corzine, and J. Corzine (1998). "'Clean Up and Go Straight': Effects of Drug Treatment on Recidivism Among Felony Probationers." *American Journal of Criminal Justice*, 22(2):169-187.

Bennett, W. J., J.J. DiIulio, Jr., and J.P. Walters (1996). *Body Count: Moral Poverty . . . and How to Win America's War Against Crime and Drugs*, New York, NY: Simon and Schuster.

Bloom, B., R. Immarigeon, and B. Owen (eds.) (1995). "Women in Prisons and Jails." *The Prison Journal*, 75:131-272.

Bonham, G., G. Janeksela, J. Bardo, and R. Iacovetta (1984). "Predicting Parole Outcome Via Discriminant Analysis." *Justice Quarterly*, 1:329-341.

Boudouris, J. and B. Turnbull (1985). "Shock Probation in Iowa." *Journal of Offender Counseling, Services and Rehabilitation*, 9(4):53-67.

Bureau of Justice Statistics (1997). *Correctional Populations in the United States*. Washington, DC: U.S. Department of Justice.

Caldwell, M.G. (1951). "Review of a New Type of Probation Study Made in Alabama." *Federal Probation*, 15(2):3-11.

California Department of Justice (1969). *Superior Court Probation and/or Jail Sample: One Year Follow-Up for Selected Counties*. Sacramento, CA: Division of Law Enforcement, Bureau of Criminal Statistics.

Camp, C. and G. Camp (1997). *The Corrections Yearbook, 1997*. South Salem, NY: The Criminal Justice Institute.

Champion, D.J. (1988). *Felony Probation, Problems and Prospects*. New York, NY: Praeger.

Chayet, E. (1994). "Correctional 'Good Time' as a Means of Early Release." *Criminal Justice Abstracts*, 26:521-538.

Citizens' Inquiry on Parole and Criminal Justice (1975). *Prison Without Walls: Report on New York Parole*. New York, NY: Praeger.

Clear, T.R. (1994). *Harm in American Penology: Offenders, Victims, and Their Communities*. Albany State University of New York Press.

Comptroller General of the United States (1976). *State and County Probation: Systems in Crisis, Report to the Congress of the United States*. Washington, DC: U.S. Government Printing Office.

Cullen, F.T. (n.d.). *Personal Communication*.

Cullen, F.T., and B.K. Applegate (1998). *Offender Rehabilitation*, Brookfield, MA: Ashgate Darthmouth.

Cullen, F.T. and P. Gendreau (1989). *The Effectiveness of Correctional Rehabilitation: Reconsidering the "Nothing Works" Debate*. In L. Goodstein and D. MacKenzie (eds.) *American Prisons: Issues in Research and Policy*, pp. 23-44. New York, NY: Plenum.

Currie, E. (1985). *Confronting Crime: An American Dilemma*, New York, NY: Pantheon.

Eichman, C. (1965). "The Impact of the Gideon Decision Upon Crime and Sentencing in Florida: A Study of Recidivism and Socio-Cultural Change." Unpublished master's thesis, Florida State University, Tallahassee, FL.

England, R.W. (1955). "A Study of Postprobation Recidivism Among Five Hundred Federal Offenders." *Federal Probation*, 19(3):10-16.

Erwin, B. (1984). *Georgia's Intensive Supervision Program: First Year Evaluation*. Atlanta, GA: Department of Offender Rehabilitation.

Eskridge, C. and G. Newbold (1994). "Corrections in New Zealand." *Federal Probation*, 57(3):59-66.

Flanagan, T.J. (1985). "Questioning the 'Other' Parole: The Effectiveness of Community Supervision of Offenders." In L.F. Travis (ed.) *Probation, Parole and Community Corrections*, pp. 167-184. Prospect Heights, IL: Waveland.

Flanagan, T.J. (1982). "Risk and the Timing of Recidivism in Three Cohorts of Prison Releasees." *Criminal Justice Review*, 7:34-45.

Frazier, R.L. (1972). "Incarceration and Adult Felon Probation in Texas: A Cost Comparison." Unpublished master's thesis, Institute of Contemporary Corrections and the Behavioral Sciences, Sam Houston State University, Huntsville, TX.

Frease, D.E. (1964). *Factors Related to Probation Outcome*. Olympia, WA: Washington Department of Institutions, Board of Prison Terms and Paroles.

Fulton, B., E.J. Latessa, A. Stichman, and L.F. Travis (1997). "The State of ISP: Research and Policy Implications," *Federal Probation*, 61(4):65-75.

Furby, L., M. Weinrott, and L. Blackshaw (1989). "Sex Offender Recidivism: A Review." *Psychological Bulletin*, 105:3-30.

Garrett, C.J. (1985). "Effects of Residential Treatment on Adjudicated Delinquents: A Meta-Analysis." *Journal of Research in Crime and Delinquency*, 22:287-308.

Gendreau, P. (1995). "The Principles of Effective Intervention with Offenders." In A. Harland (ed.) (in press) Choosing Correctional Options that Work: *Defining the Demand the Evaluating the Supply*. Thousand Oaks, CA: Sage.

Gendreau, P. and D. Andrews (1994). *The Correctional Program Assessment Inventory* (5th ed.) Saint John, CN: University of New Brunswick.

Gendreau, P. and D. Andrews (1990). Tertiary Prevention: What the Meta-Analysis of the Offender Treatment Literature Tells us About "What Works." *Canadian Journal of Criminology*, 32:173-184.

Gendreau, P. and M. Paparozzi (1995). "Examining What Works in Community Corrections." *Corrections Today*, (February): 28-30.

Gendreau, P. and R.R. Ross (1987). "Revivification of Rehabilitation: Evidence from the 1980s." *Justice Quarterly*, 4:349-407.

Gendreau, P. and R.R. Ross (1979). "Effective Correctional Treatment: Bibliography for Cynics." *Crime & Delinquency*, 25:463-489.

Goldcamp, J. (1994). "Miami's Treatment Drug Court for Felony Misdemeanants." *The Prison Journal*, 73:110-166.

Goodstein, L. and J. Hepburn (1986). "Determinate Sentencing in Illinois: An Assessment of its Development and Implementation." *Criminal Justice Policy Review*, 1:305-327.

Gottfredson, D. (1977). "Assessment Methods." In S.L. Radzinowicz and M.E. Wolfgang (eds.) *Crime and Justice: The Criminal Under Restraint*, pp. 79-111. New York, NY: Basic Books.

Gottfredson, D. (1975). "Some Positive Changes in the Parole Process." Paper presented at the meeting of the American Society of Criminology.

Gottfredson, D., M. Gottfredson, and M. Adams (1982). "Prison Behavior and Release Performance." *Law and Policy Quarterly*, 4:373-391.

Gottfredson, M. and J. Garofalo (1977). "Time Served in Prison and Parolee Outcomes Among Parolee Risk Categories." *Journal of Criminal Justice*, 5:1-12.

Gottfredson, S. and D. Gottfredson (1994). "Behavioral Prediction and the Problem of Incapacitation." *Criminology*, 32:441-474.

Gottfredson, M., S. Mitchell-Herzfeld, and T. Flanagan (1982). "Another Look at the Effectiveness of Parole Supervision." *Journal of Research in Crime and Delinquency*, 18:277-298.

Gowdy, V. (1993). *Intermediate Sanctions*. Washington, DC: U.S. Department of Justice.

Greenfield, L. (1995). *Prison Sentences and Time Served for Violence*. Washington, DC: U.S. Department of Justice.

Hakeem, M. (1945). "Prediction of Criminality." *Federal Probation*, 9(3):31-38.

Hepburn, J., C. Johnston, and S. Rogers (1994). *Do Drugs, Do Time: An Evaluation of the Maricopa County Demand Reduction Program*. Washington, DC: National Institute of Justice.

Hoffman, P.B. and J.L. Beck (1985). "Recidivism Among Released Federal Prisoners: Salient Factor Score and Five Year Follow-Up." *Criminal Justice and Behavior*, 12:501-507.

Hoffman, P.B. and B. Stone-Meierhoefer (1980). "Reporting Recidivism Rates: The Criterion and Follow-Up Issues." *Journal of Criminal Justice*, 8:53-60.

Holt, N. (1975). *Rational Risk Taking: Some Alternatives to Traditional Correctional Programs*. Proceedings: Second National Workshop on Corrections and Parole Administration, Louisville, Kentucky.

Irish, J.F. (1972). *Probation and Its Effects on Recidivism: An Evaluative Research Study of Probation in Nassau County, New York*. New York, NY: Nassau County Probation Department.

Jackson, P.G. (1983). *The Paradox of Control: Parole Supervision of Youthful Offenders*. New York, NY: Praeger.

Jankowski, L. (1990). "Probation and Parole 1989." Washington, DC: *Bureau of Justice Statistics Bulletin*.

Kusuda, P.H. (1976). "Probation and Parole Terminations." Madison, WI: Wisconsin Division of Corrections.

Lab, S. and J. Whitehead (1988). "An Analysis of Juvenile Correctional Treatment," *Crime & Delinquency*, 28:60-85.

Landis, J.R., J.K. Mercer, and C.E. Wolff (1969). "Success and Failure of Adult Probationers in California." *Journal of Research in Crime and Delinquency*, 6:34-40.

Latessa, E.J. (1996). "Offenders with Mental Illness on Probation." *Community Corrections in America: New Directions and Sounder Investments for Persons with Mental Illness and CoDisorders*. Washington, DC, National Institute of Corrections and the National Coalition for Mental and Substance Abuse Health Care in the Justice System.

Latessa, E.J. (1986). "The Cost Effectiveness of Intensive Supervision." *Federal Probation*, 50(2):70-74.

Latessa, E.J. (1985). *The Incarceration Diversion Unit of the Lucas County Adult Probation Department Report Number Six*. Cincinnati, OH: University of Cincinnati.

Latessa, E.J. and A. Holsinger (1998). "The Importance of Evaluating Correctional Programs: Assessing Outcome and Quality," *Corrections Management Quarterly*.

Latessa, E.J. and M.M. Moon (1992). "The Effectiveness of Acupuncture in an Outpatient Drug Treatment Program." *Journal of Contemporary Criminal Justice*, 8:317-331.

Latessa, E.J., L.F. Travis, and A. Holsinger (1997). *Evaluation of Ohio's Community Corrections Act Programs and Community Based Correctional Facilities*, Cincinnati, OH: Division of Criminal Justice, University of Cincinnati.

Lerner, M. (1977). "The Effectiveness of a Definite Sentence Parole Program." *Criminology*, 15:32-40.

Linden, R. and L. Perry (1982). "The Effectiveness of Prison Education Programs." *Journal of Offender Counseling, Services and Rehabilitation*, 6:43-57.

Lightfoot, L. (1997). "Treating Substance Abuse and Dependence in Offenders: A Review of Methods and Outcome." Paper presented at the International Community Corrections Association meeting, Cleveland, OH.

Lipsey, M. (1992). "Juvenile Delinquency Treatment: A Meta-Analytic Inquiry into the Variability of Effects." In T. Cook, H. Cooper, D. Cordray, H. Hartmann, L. Hedges, R. Light, T. Louis, and F. Mosteller (eds.) *Meta-Analysis for Explanation*, pp. 83-127. New York, NY: Russell Sage Foundation.

Lipsey, M. and D. Wilson (1997). "Effective Interventions for Serious Juvenile Offenders," in R. Loeber and D. Farrington (eds.) *Serious and Violent Juvenile Offenders: Risk Factors and Successful Interventions*, pp. 313-345. Thousand Oaks, CA: Sage.

Logan, C.H. and G.G. Gaes (1993) "Meta-Analysis and the Rehabilitation of Punishment," *Justice Quarterly*, 10:245-263.

Lunden, R. (1987). *Risk and Recidivism Among Massachusetts Parolees: An Update*. Massachusetts Parole Board Research and Planning Unit.

McGaha, J., M. Fichter, and P. Hirschburg (1987). "Felony Probation: A Re-Examination of Public Risk." *American Journal of Criminal Justice*, 12:1-9.

McGrath, R. (1995). "Sex Offender Treatment: Does it Work?" *American Probation and Parole Association Perspectives*, 19:24-26.

MacKenzie, D. and L.J. Hickman (1998). *What Works in Corrections? An Examination of the Effectiveness of the Type of Rehabilitation Programs Offered by Washington State Department of Corrections*. Report to the State of Washington Legislature Joint Audit and Review Committee, College Park, MD: Dept. of Criminology and Criminal Justice, University of Maryland.

MacKenzie, D. and A. Piquero (1994). "The Impact of Shock Incarceration Programs on Prison Crowding." *Crime & Delinquency*, 40:222-249.

Martinson, R. (1974). "What Works?—Questions and Answers About Prison Reform." *The Public Interest*, 35:22- 54.

Martinson, R. and J. Wilks (1977). "Save Parole Supervision." *Federal Probation*, 42(3):23-27.

Marquart, J.W. and J.R. Sorensen (1988). "Institutional and Post-Release Behavior of Furman-Commuted Inmates in Texas." *Criminology*, 26:667-693.

Mauser, E., K. van Stelle, and D. Moberg (1994). "The Economic Impact of Diverting Substance-Abusing Offfenders into Treatment." *Crime & Delinquency*, 40(4):568-588.

Miethe, T.D. and C.A. Moore (1985). "Socioeconomic Disparities Under Determinate Sentencing Systems: A Comparison of Preguideline and Postguideline Practices in Minnesota." *Criminology*, 23:337-363.

Missouri Division of Probation and Parole (1976). *Probation in Missouri, July 1, 1968 to June 30, 1970: Characteristics, Performance, and Criminal Reinvolvement.* Jefferson City, Missouri.

Morash, M., R. Haarr, and L. Rucker (1994). "A Comparison of Programming for Women and Men in U.S. Prisons in the 1980s." *Crime & Delinquency*, 40:197-221.

Morgan, K. (1993). "Factors Influencing Probation Outcome: A Review of the Literature." *Federal Probation*, 57(2):23-29.

Morris, N. (1978). "Conceptual Overview and Commentary on the Movement Toward Determinacy." In *Determinate Sentencing: Proceedings of the Special Conference on Determinate Sentencing*. Washington, DC: National Institute of Law Enforcement and Criminal Justice.

Mortimer, E. and C. May (1997). *Electronic Monitoring in Practice*. London, UK: U.K. Home Office.

National Mental Health Association (1987). *Stigma: A Lack of Awareness and Understanding*. Alexandria, VA: National Mental Health Association.

Neithercutt, M. (1972). "Parole Violation Patterns and Commitment Offense." *Journal of Research in Crime and Delinquency*, 9:87-98.

Nelson, C.W. (1975). "Cost-Benefit Analysis and Alternatives to Incarceration." *Federal Probation*, 39(4):45-50.

Nuttal, C.P. and Associates (1977). *Parole in England and Wales*. Home Office Research Studies No. 38. London: Her Majesty's Stationery Office.

Ohio Community Corrections Organization (1993). *Ohio's Community Corrections Bench Book*. Columbus, OH: OCCO.

Palmer, T. (1995). "Programmatic and Nonprogrammatic Aspects of Successful Intervention: New Directions for Research." *Crime & Delinquency*, 41:101-131.

Palmer, T. (1991). "The Effectiveness of Intervention: Recent Trends and Current Issues." *Crime & Delinquency*, 37:330-346.

Palmer, T. (1975). "Martinson Revisited." *Journal of Research in Crime and Delinquency*, 12:133-152.

Pearson, F. (1985). "New Jersey's Intensive Supervision Program: A Progress Report." *Crime & Delinquency*, 31:393-410.

Pennsylvania Program for Women and Girl Offenders, Inc. (1976). *Report on Recidivism of Women Sentenced to State Probation and Released from SCI Muncy 1971-73.* Philadelphia, PA.

Petersilia, J. (1997). *Probation in the United States.* In M. Tonry (ed.) *Crime and Justice: A Review of Research*, Vol. 22 (149-200), Chicago, IL: University of Chicago Press.

Petersilia, J. (1992) "California's Prison Policy: Causes, Costs, and Consequences," *The Prison Journal*, 72: 8-36.

Petersilia, J. (1991). "The Value of Corrections Research: Learning What Works." *Federal Probation*, 55(2):24-26.

Petersilia, J. (1985). "Probation and Felony Offenders." *Federal Probation*, 49(2):4-9.

Pritchard, D.A. (1979). "Stable Predictors of Recidivism: A Summary." *Journal of Criminology*, 17(May):15-21.

*Report to the Nation on Crime and Justice*, Second Edition (1988). Washington, DC: Bureau of Justice Statistics.

Roberts, R. and E. Cheek (1994). "Group Intervention and Reading Performance in a Medium Security Prison Facility." *Journal of Offender Rehabilitation*, 20:97-116.

Ryan, M. and W. Pannel (1979). *Some Experience with Uniform Determinate Sentencing Act: July 1977-June 1978.* California Department of Corrections.

Schumaker, R., D. Anderson, and S. Anderson (1990). "Vocational and Academic Indicators of Parole Success." *Journal of Correctional Education*, 41:8-13.

Sims, B. and M. Jones (1997). "Predicting Success or Failure on Probation: Factors Associated With Felony Probation Outcomes," *Crime & Delinquency*, 43:314-327.

Snider, R.M. (1986). "The High Risks of Felony Probation." *California Lawyer*, (March):33-37.

Stolzenberg, L. and S. D'Alessio (1994). "Sentencing and Unwarranted Disparity: An Empirical Assessment of the Long-Term Impact of Sentencing Guidelines in Minnesota." *Criminology*, 32:301-310.

Syrotvik, J.M. (1978). "The Relationship Between Birth Order and Parole Outcome." *Canadian Journal of Criminology*, 29:456-458.

System Sciences (1982). *Executive Summary National Evaluation Program—Phase II Intensive Evaluation of Probation.* Bethesda, MD.

Tonry, M. (1987). "Sentencing Guidelines and their Effects." In A. von Hirsch, K. Knapp, and M. Tonry (eds.) *The Sentencing Commission and its Guidelines*, pp. 16-46. Boston, MA: Northeastern University Press.

Travis, L. and E. Latessa (1984). "A Summary of Parole Rules—Thirteen Years Later: Revisited Thirteen years Later." *Journal of Criminal Justice*, 12:591-600.

Van Voorhis, P. (1987). "Correctional Effectiveness: The High Cost of Ignoring Success." *Federal Probation*, 51(1):56-62.

Vito, G. (ed.) (1994). "Education in Correctional Settings." *The Prison Journal*, 74:395-473.

Vito, G. (1986). "Felony Probation and Recidivism: Replication and Response." *Federal Probation*, 50(4):17-25.

Vito, G. (1985a). "Developments in Shock Probation: A Review of Research Findings and Policy Implications." *Federal Probation*, 50(1):22-27.

Vito, G. (1985b). "Putting Prisoners to Work: Policies and Problems." *Journal of Offender Counseling Services and Rehabilitation*, 9:21-34.

Vito, G. (1978). "Shock Probationer in Ohio: A Comparison of Attributes and Outcomes." Unpublished doctoral dissertation, Ohio State University, Columbus.

Vito, G. and H.E. Allen (1981). "Shock Probation in Ohio: A Comparison of Outcomes." *International Journal of Offender Therapy and Comparative Criminology*, 25:70-75.

Vito, G. and E.J. Latessa (1979). "Cost Analysis in Probation Research: An Evaluation Synthesis." *Journal of Contemporary Criminal Justice*, 1:3-4.

Vito, G. and D.G. Wilson (1988). "Back from the Dead: Tracking the Progress of Kentucky's Furman-Commuted Death Row Population." *Justice Quarterly*, 5:101-111.

Vito, G., D.G. Wilson, and E.J. Latessa (1991). "Comparison of the Dead: Attributes and Outcomes of Furman-Commuted Death Row Inmates in Kentucky and Ohio." In R.M. Bohm (ed.) *The Death Penalty in America: Current Research*, pp. 101-111. Cincinnati, OH: Anderson Publishing Co.

von Hirsch, A. and K. Hanrahan (1979). *The Question of Parole: Retention, Reform, or Abolition*. Cambridge, MA: Ballinger.

Waller, I. (1974). *Men Released from Prison*. Toronto, CN: University of Toronto Press.

Wagner, D. and C. Baird (1993). *Evaluation of the Florida Community Control Program*. Washington, DC: U.S. Department of Justice.

Washington Department of Social and Health Sciences (1976). *Who Returns? A Study of Recidivism for Adult Offenders in the State of Washington*. Olympia, WA.

Wensel, L.O. (1990). *Acupuncture in Medical Practice*. Reston, VA: Reston Publishing.

Wetter, R.E. (1985). *Descriptive Analysis of the Intensive Supervision Program*. Frankfort, KY: Office of Administrative Services Planning and Evaluation Branch, Kentucky Corrections Cabinet.

Whitehead, J.T. (1991). "The Effectiveness of Felony Probation: Results from an Eastern State." *Justice Quarterly*, 8:525-543.

Whitehead, J.T. and S.P. Lab (1989). "A Meta-Analysis of Juvenile Correctional Treatment." *Journal of Research in Crime and Delinquency*, 26:276-295.

Wilson, R. (1977). "Supervision (the other parole) Also Attacked." *Corrections* Magazine, 3(3):56-59.

Wisconsin Division of Corrections (1965). *A Comparison of the Effects of Using Probation Versus Incarceration for Burglars with No Previous Felony Convictions*, Madison.

Zeisel, H. (1982). "Disagreement Over the Evaluation of the Controlled Experiment." *American Journal of Sociology*, 88:378-389.

# The Future of Corrections in the Community

Show people that there are programs nationwide where violent or habitual felons are assured prison beds only because many of the nuisance shoplifters, technical probation violators, or petty thieves are being punished in other meaningful ways. Make the public understand that dangerous offenders will still be put in prison; that intermediate sanctions are necessary to reintegrate offenders so they have a better chance of becoming successful citizens and not continuing lives of crime.

—M. Castle
Governor of Delaware

## Introduction

As the nation prepares to enter the twenty-first century, it is legitimate to ask what corrections will look like by the year 2000, and what changes one might find. Both are legitimate questions and offer opportunities to effect closure in the area of corrections in the community. We start by looking once again at where we are, and then where we might be by the year 2000. Data on the current status of corrections can be found in Table 15.1. In 1997, there were 5.55 million people under correctional supervision, approximately one in 38 adult Americans. About 57 percent of those were on probation and another 13 percent were on parole, or 70 percent under corrections in the community. The other 30 percent were incarcerated in jails and prisons. Taken together, we incarcerate more adult residents in this nation (645 per 100,000 residents) than any other major western country, except Russia (690) (Kuhn, 1998). The incarceration rate of African-American males is four times that of Russia (3,250 to 690), formerly a totalitarian country now undergoing democratization. This high rate is due in large part to policies that encourage the use of incarceration and, some would say, over-use of incarceration for property and drug offenders.

Table 15.1
**Correctional Populations in the Future**

| Correctional Program | 1983 | 1995 | 2000* |
|---|---|---|---|
| Probation | 1,583,000 | 3,194,000 | 3,682,000 |
| Jail | 224,000 | 515,000 | 724,000 |
| Prison | 424,000 | 1,073,000 | 1,441,500 |
| Parole | 246,000 | 768,000 | 824,500 |
| | 2,477,000 | 5,550,000 | 6,672,000 |

*Straight line projections from current trends.

The use of imprisonment, of course, varies greatly by group. Although African-Americans make up about 12 percent of the total population, they represent more than one-half of the jail and prison group. This turns out to be about one in 12 adult African-American men aged 14 to 54; there are more African-Americans under incarceration than the total number of African-American men of any age enrolled in college throughout the nation. No doubt this higher rate reflects the differential rate of involvement of African-Americans in violent crimes; it also reflects effects of the War on Drugs, a "crass attempt to purchase the votes of affluent white Americans" (Cullen et al., 1996).[1] The War on Drugs cannot reasonably have any effect on the sale, distribution, or use of illicit controlled substances (GAO, 1997). The War on Drugs will continue well into the twenty-first century (Zimring & Block, 1997).

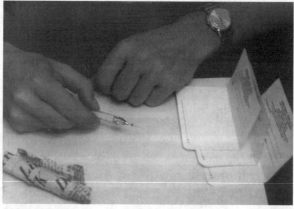

Photo 15.1
The "War on Drugs." Courtesy of Talbert House, Inc.

Figures on the correctional scene in the year 2000 can be found in Figure 15.1, projections of the future using current trends. Short-term projections are usually fairly accurate when straight-line projections are used. We estimate that future correctional populations will total almost 6.7 million offenders, or about one in 30 adult residents in America. As before, the bulk of offenders will be handled on probation or will be under parole supervision. The incarcerated group will surge to more than 2 million, most of those being incarcerated in prison. The increase in incarcerated offenders will continue unabated well into the twenty-first century. How correctional agencies will find the resources to manage this level of crisis will be a major question. See Figure 15.1 for a graphic depiction of the growth and relative distributions of the major correctional components.

Figure 15.1
**Adults Under Community Supervision or Incarcerated, 1985 and 1996**

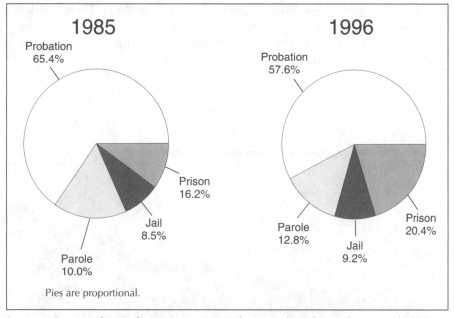

Source: J. Brown and A. Beck (1997). *Nation's Probation and Parole Population Reached Almost 3.9 Million Last Year*, p. 7. Washington, DC: U.S. Bureau of Justice Statistics.

As dire as these projections are, there are major developments and trends under way that can significantly improve both the protection of the public and reintegration of the offender. Far better would be the implementation of more fundamental structural transformations in underclass communities and among those locked out from participation in the American dream, and addressing racism and injustice before America resegregates along racial and class lines (Allen, 1995). The dominant conservative political ideology[2] makes this option less likely, and major change in this area will certainly not be addressed into well into the twenty-first century. The future of change in corrections lies in implementing and expanding intermediate sanctions through "transformative rationality" (Musheno et al., 1989:137), the sustaining over time of broad policy principles while simultaneously adapting those polices to local situations.

## Intermediate Sanctions

The reader should be familiar with intermediate sanctions from Chapters 8 and 12, and will recall that these are correctional interventions that fill the sentencing gap between probation and prison (Allen & Simonsen, 1998:200). Their dominant characteristic is that they allow increased surveillance and control over the offender: they have been advanced as a means of avoiding prison crowding and reintegrating offenders. These are depicted in Figure 15.2, and range across 13 distinct programs, each increasingly punitive and controlling. Some of these programs, of course, are themselves composed of different technologies and usefulness, and many permit effective treatment.

Figure 15.2
**A Range of Sentencing Options: Ranked by Level of Punishment**

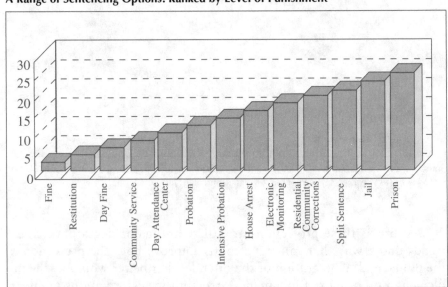

Source: Adapted from J. Byrne (1990). "The Future of Intensive Probation Service." *Crime & Delinquency*, 36:29.

## Public Acceptance

The public tends to perceive corrections as being a choice between "mere" probation and imprisonment,[3] a false dichotomy that implies that public safety is met only when major offenders and miscreants are locked away, out of sight and for long periods of time. It should be apparent at this point that public protection does not mean only prison or that anything short of incarceration will endanger public safety. Castle (1989:1) argued:

1. Nationwide, about 1 in [38] persons is under the control of correctional authorities.

2. [In the 1980s], national per capita expenditures grew 21 percent, but correctional expenditures grew 65 percent.

3. The nations's prison population doubled during the 1980s [and will double again by 1999] . . . If you include the jail population, that's [two] million people behind bars.

4. The growth of America's prison population is over 10 times that of the general population.

5. It would take the total state tax collected from 15 Delaware residents to pay for just 1 resident for only 1 year.

Policymakers in the State of Delaware, convinced that it was not possible to build their way out of the prison crowding problem and that the public held strong preferences for reintegration of offenders,[4] decided to develop and expand community corrections. Their policy priorities were: (1) to remove violent offenders from the community, (2) to restore the victims to the preoffense status by restitution and compensation, and (3) to rehabilitate offenders. The result was a continuum of programs comprising five levels of increasingly restrictive and punitive sanctions that included cost control mechanisms. The system was designed to allow offenders to earn their way out of prison by good behavior, work, and conformity to rules, or to worm their way into the prison system by repeated criminal activity and nonconformity to supervision rules. The system is spread over five "levels."

- Level 5 is full incarceration with complete institutional control.

- Level 4 is quasi-incarceration in which an offender is supervised from 9 to 23 hours a day in such programs as community treatment centers, electronically monitored house arrest, attendance centers, and residential drug treatment centers.

- Level 3 is intensive, direct supervision over 1-8 hours per day, during which offenders are subject to curfew checks, employment checks, and frequent monitoring for attendance in treatment programming.
- Level 2 is "normal" field supervision, generally probation, with from 0 to 1 hour of supervision per day.
- Level 1 is the lowest level of supervision.

The system allows the sentencing judge wide latitude in sentencing both their offender and the offense.

## Creating Change

Prisons, of course, will continue to play a vital role in corrections in future years, yet may be called upon to play decreasingly important functions as they cease to be the central element of corrections. This will require an agenda for change, and the most effective way would be to encourage local communities to address better ways to manage crime and criminals in their own communities. This in turn would require leadership at the state governmental level to sentence "smarter," not just tougher. Is there a politician existing in today's political environment who believes taking a "soft" approach to crime will help in winning an election? The problem to be addressed is not "softer or harsher," but a recognition that what is needed is a philosophy for organizing corrections.

Before describing the prescriptive approach to organizing a system that will incarcerate the truly dangerous, make victims whole, and rehabilitate the changeable, it is necessary to identify the coming crisis in corrections that will contribute to the major changes. The crisis is only in part the overcrowding of prisons, and the fiscal hurdle of finding funds to support institutional corrections, even if this might mean decreasing allocations to other functions of government. After all, education, welfare,[5] and the economic infrastructure can be and have been choked off in the interest of retribution and disabling offenders (Allen, 1995). Rather, the crisis is in the philosophical basis of corrections.

When the "nothing works in corrections" argument arose, many scholars and practitioners who should have known better abandoned the rehabilitation model. Corrections lost its organizing theme or premise. Now that the abandonment of rehabilitation has been recognized as both premature and erroneous, the stage is set for a considerable and acrimonious battle over the "conscience" or purpose of handling offenders. Unfortunately, that will not occur until we are in the twenty-first century, and will probably by triggered at that time by students and powerful constituents (senior citizens, parents, school administrators, etc.) tired of increased taxes and decreased services, outcomes of increasing neglect by policymakers and politicians. The "Great Debate" is imminent but probably will not erupt in this millennium.

We choose to focus on booth camp programs to identify and discuss the dimensions of the crisis to come. Since their inception in 1983, boot camp programs have been implemented in at least 66 jail, prison and probation/parole agencies. At least 22 were scheduled to come on line in 1997. Advocates of this politically popular program point to alleged benefits of book camp ("will make a man[6] out of that kid," "teach the offender discipline," "build up physical and moral fiber," "nothing works like punishment," and so on). Some programs have extensive program components, such as learning to read and write, obtaining a general education diploma (GED), learning survival skills, and breaking drug dependency. At least 14,000 offenders *graduated* from boot camps in 1996 (Camp & Camp, 1997:96). Few scholars or practitioners, however, openly admit that the primary purpose of the program has a quite different objective: managing prison population growth by facilitating early release of basically drug-problemed but low-risk offenders who, if community corrections were more developed and coordinated, should never have been imprisoned. Boot camps have become and probably will remain a permanent part of the correctional scene.

More than 100 evaluations of boot camp programs have been conducted and, by the end of 1997, 72 books, articles and national surveys on adult and juvenile, as well as misdemeanant and felony programs, had been published in the United States, alone. With rare exceptions, most evaluations did not find reduced recidivism; some show that gains made during program participation quickly evaporate ("wash out") after the offender is released back into the community. Although well intentioned and mostly staffed by an enthusiastic and optimistic cadre, boot camps have a fatal flaw: they fail to treat effectively.

Treatment can be defined as the diagnosis of an offender's needs, the design of a specific program to address these concrete and criminogenic needs, the application of that program by competent staff supervised by experienced professionals, routine review of the adequacy of delivery of the service and redesign of the individual's program until it is effective, and graduated release into the community with supervision and assistance. Treatment also requires follow-up of the graduates over time and documentation of outcome, the latter to help "fine-tune" treatments for incoming offenders. Said differently, "treatment" requires diagnosis, classification, delivery of the intervention, and case monitoring and long-term follow-up. We know of no boot camp program in the nation that meets these basics of treatment.

Contemporary community corrections is called upon (see below) to do more with less, to be more effective, and to protect through service and surveillance. Meeting this challenge will require *more* resources, trained professionals, competent administrators, and demonstrated effectiveness. It is no longer enough to be "well meaning." A new breed of correctional practitioner, theorist, manager and specialist is needed. And vital to achieving the new community corrections is the recognition that "more of the same" is no longer acceptable.

Lest the reader misunderstand, we are not berating boot camp programs per se, but identifying the basic philosophical problem that underlies community corrections in particular, but is also applicable to institutional corrections. The need is for vision, mission, and training. Competence, focus, diagnosis, classification and individualized treatment must be incorporated as part of the mission. Students entering corrections who can dedicate themselves to accepting the challenge of crime n a free society would be warmly welcomed.

## Establishing a Community Correctional System

The first step is deciding on the goals of the correctional system (incapacitation, restitution, rehabilitation, and so on), and their priority. Second, a commission should be established, possibly by legislative act, to devise a workable scheme to gain control of prison population and resource problems. The commission should serve as the open forum for debate and research on intermediate sanctions, as well as implementing an accountability system. The commission might best be charged with defining the scope and continuum of acceptable sanctions, as well as accepting testimony from concerned groups and activists. The Commission might be best served by calling for a moratorium on prison construction.[7] Third, public opinion leaders, such as legislators, jurists, and media leaders, should be informed of proposed changes and made part of the developmental process. The judiciary should be charged and empowered to develop sentencing standards and guidelines for possible adoption across jurisdictions. Monitoring of the program, sentencing compliance, concerns, and effectiveness should be coordinated through the commission as part of accountability for the system. This was the basic process used for the highly successful Delaware system.

## Conclusion

The nation cannot build itself out of current prison and management crises, but states and local jurisdictions can manage and control not only the prison populations but also the costs and integrity of the justice system that deals with post-offense corrections. By developing a logical set of sentencing policies with clear goals and a wide range of sentencing options and sanctions, the nation would begin to address public safety on a more sound foundation. In addition, an aggressive public education and information initiative is necessary for public acceptance. In the long run, corrections must hold offenders accountable to the public and the legal system for their criminal behaviors, and politicians must be held accountable to the public for their actions.

Many issues face community corrections; risk management and handling of special need populations, officer safety and work conditions, and the appropriate use of technology, such as drug testing and electronic monitoring. We have confidence that the field will rise to the challenge. We base this faith on our knowledge of the professionals who work in and will come to the field. Because of these dedicated individuals, the future of corrections in the community is bright, and the achievement of a logical, coherent and safe system for handling criminal offenders is attainable. In doing this, we must remember that corrections is above all else a human issue, that change is not easy, and that partners in change are necessary. Corrections has a bright future.

## Recommended Readings

Ambrosio, T. and V. Schiraldi (1997). *From Classrooms to Cell Blocks. A National Perspective*. Washington, DC: Justice Policy Institute.

Klofas, J. and S. Stojkovic (1995). *Crime and Justice in the Year 2010*. Belmont, CA: Wadsworth.

Muraskin, R. and A.R. Roberts (1996). *Visions for Change: Crime and Justice in the Twenty-First Century*. Upper Saddle River, NJ: Prentice-Hall.

## Notes

[1]    This statement is not meant to imply that nonwhites are not concerned about drugs and crime. Surveys indicate that both white and nonwhite Americans are concerned about drug abuse and the effects of drugs on communities.

[2]    Jacobs and Helms found that shifts in the incarceration rate are related to the strength of the Republican party and whether it were an election year. D. Jacobs and R. Helms (1996). "Toward a Political Model of Incarceration." *American Journal of Sociology*, 102(2):323-351.

[3]    Those interested in the death penalty and public opinion should see H. Bedeau (1997). *The Death Penalty in America: Current Controversies*. New York, NY: Oxford University Press.

[4]    Applegate, B., F. Cullen, and B. Fisher (1997). "Public Support for Correctional Treatment: The Continuing Appeal of the Rehabilitative Ideal." *Prison Journal*, 77(3):237-258; Stalans, A. and A. Lurigio, eds. (1996). "Public Opinion on Justice in the Criminal Justice System." *American Behavioral Scientist*, 39(4):365-513.

[5]    There is a clear and negative impact of welfare on crime, particularly cash and public housing programs. For bibliotherapy, see J. Zang (1997). "The Effect of Welfare Programs on Criminal Behavior." *Economic Inquiry*, 35(1):120-137; and Cullen, F., P. Gendreau, and G. Jarjoura (1997). "Crime and the Bell Curve: Lessons from Intelligent Criminology." *Crime & Delinquency*, 43(4):387-411.

[6]    Most boot camp participants are male (13,600 of 14,700 graduates in 1996) but there are at least 21 boot camps for females.

[7]    Ambrosio, T. and V. Schiraldi (1997). *From Classrooms to Cell Blocks: A National Perspective*. Washington, DC: Justice Policy Institute.

## *References*

Allen, H. (1995). "The American Dream and Crime in the 21st Century." *Justice Quarterly*, 12:427-444.

Allen, H. and C. Simonsen (1998). *Corrections in America*. Upper Saddle River, NJ: Prentice-Hall.

Ambrosio, T. and V. Schiraldi (1997). *From Classrooms to Cell Blocks: A National Perspective*. Washington, DC: Justice Policy Institute.

Applegate, B., F. Cullen, and B. Fisher (1997). "Public Support for Correctional Treatment: The Continuing Appeal of the Rehabilitative Ideal." *Prison Journal*, 77(3):237-258.

Brown, J. and A. Beck (1997). *Nation's Probation and Parole Population Reached Almost 3.9 Million Last Year*. Washington, DC: U.S. Bureau of Justice Statistics.

Byrne, J. (1990). "The Future of Intensive Probation Service." *Crime & Delinquency*, 36(1):3-32.

Camp, C. and G. Camp (1977). *The Corrections Yearbook, 1997*. South Salem, NY: The Criminal Justice Institute.

Castle, M. (1989). *Alternative Sentencing: Selling It to the Public*. Washington, DC: U.S. Department of Justice.

Chesney-Lind, M. (1997). *The Female Offender: Girls, Women and Crime*. Thousand Oaks, CA: Sage.

Cullen, F., P. Van Voorhis, and J. Sundt (1996). "Prisons in Crisis: The American Experience." In R. Matthews and F. Francis (eds.) *Prisons 2000: An International Perspective on the Current State and Future of Imprisonment*, pp. 21-52. New York, NY: Macmillan.

Cullen, F., P. Gendreau, and G. Jarjoura (1997). "Crime and the Bell Curve: Lessons from Intelligent Criminology." *Crime & Delinquency*, 43(4):387-411.

General Accounting Office (1997). *Drug Control: Observations on Elements of the Federal Drug Control Strategy*. Washington, DC: USGAO.

Jacobs, D. and R. Holmes (1996). "Toward a Political Model of Incarceration." *American Journal of Sociology*, 102(2):323-357.

Klofas, J. and S. Stojkovic (1995). *Crime and Justice in the Year 2010*. Belmont, CA: Wadsworth.

Kuhn, A. (1998). "Incarceration Rates: The United States in an International Perspective." *Criminal Justice Abstracts,* 30(2):321-353.

Mauer, M. (1995). "The International Use of Incarceration." *The Prison Journal,* 75:113-123.

Muraskin, R. and A.R. Roberts (1996). *Visions for Change: Crime and Justice in the Twenty-First Century*. Upper Saddle River, NJ: Prentice-Hall.

Musheno, M., D. Palumbo, S. Maynard-Moody, and J. Levine (1989). "Community Corrections as an Organizational Innovation: What Works and Why." *Journal of Research in Crime and Delinquency,* 26:136-167.

Palumbo, D., M. Musheno, and M. Hallett (1994). "The Political Construction of Alternative Dispute Resolution and Alternatives to Incarceration." *Evaluation and Program Planning,* 17(2):197-203.

Stalans, L. and A. Lurigio (eds.) (1996). "Public Opinion of Justice in the Criminal Justice System." *American Behavioral Scientist,* 39(4):365-513.

Tonry, M. (1994). "Racial Politics, Racial Disparities, and the War on Crime." *Crime & Delinquency,* 40:475-494.

Zhang, J. (1997). "The Effect of Welfare Programs on Criminal Behavior: A Theoretical and Empirical Analysis." *Economic Inquiry,* 35(1):120-137.

Zimring, F. and M. Block (1997). *Two Views on Imprisonment Policies*. Washington, DC: U.S. Institute of Justice.

# Glossary

The authors are grateful to the Law Enforcement Assistance Administration for the publication of the *Dictionary of Criminal Justice Data Terminology,* from which many of the following terms and definitions have been extracted. It is in the spirit of that effort to standardize criminal justice terminology that we have decided to include this section. We hope that students, especially those new to the field, will take the time to read and absorb the meanings of these tools of the trade. To obtain more detailed information about the terms in this glossary, write to U.S. Department of Justice, National Criminal Reference Service, Washington, DC 20531.

Abscond (corrections). To depart from a geographical area or jurisdiction prescribed by the conditions of one's probation or parole, without authorization.

Abscond (court). To intentionally absent or conceal oneself unlawfully in order to avoid a legal process.

Acquittal. A judgment of a court, based either on the verdict of a jury or a judicial officer, that the defendant is not guilty of the offense(s) for which he or she has been tried.

Adjudicated. Having been the subject of completed criminal or juvenile proceedings, and convicted, or adjudicated a delinquent, status offender, or dependent.

Adjudication (criminal). The judicial decision terminating a criminal proceeding by a judgment of conviction or acquittal or by a dismissal of the case.

Adjudication (juvenile). The juvenile court decision, terminating an adjudicatory hearing, that the juvenile is a delinquent, status offender, or dependent, or that the allegations in the petition are not sustained.

Adjudication hearing. In juvenile proceedings, the fact-finding process wherein the juvenile court determines whether or not there is sufficient evidence to sustain the allegations in a petition.

Adult. A person who is within the original jurisdiction of a criminal, rather than a juvenile, court because his or her age at the time of an alleged criminal act was above a statutorily specified limit.

Alias. Any name used for an official purpose that is different from a person's legal name.

471

Alternative facility. An alternative place of limited confinement that may be an option for certain kinds of offenders. Such facilities may include treatment settings for drug-dependent offenders, minimum security facilities in the community that provide treatment and services as needed, work/study-release centers, and halfway houses or shelter-type facilities. All of these are less secure than the traditional jail but offer a more stimulating environment for the individual.

Appeal. A request by either the defense or the prosecution that a case be removed from a lower court to a higher court in order for a completed trial to be reviewed by the higher court.

Appearance. The act of coming into a court and submitting to the authority of that court.

Appearance, first (initial appearance). The first appearance of a juvenile or adult in the court that has jurisdiction over his or her case.

Appellant. A person who initiates an appeal.

Arraignment. The appearance of a person before a court in order that the court may inform the individual of the accusation(s) against him or her and enter his or her plea.

Arrest. Taking a person into custody by authority of law for the purpose of charging him or her with a criminal offense or initiating juvenile proceedings, terminating with the recording of a specific offense.

Arson. The intentional destruction or attempted destruction, by fire or explosive, of the property of another or of one's own property with the intent to defraud.

Assault. Unlawful intentional inflicting, or attempted or threatened inflicting, of injury upon another.

Assault, aggravated. Unlawful intentional causing of serious bodily injury with or without a deadly or unlawful intentional attempting or threatening of serious bodily injury or death with a deadly weapon.

Assault, simple. Unlawful intentional threatening, attempted inflicting, or inflicting of less than serious bodily injury, in the absence of a deadly weapon.

Assault with a deadly weapon. Unlawful intentional inflicting, or attempted or threatened inflicting, or injury or death with the use of a deadly weapon.

Assault on a law enforcement officer. A simple or aggravated assault, in which the victim is a law enforcement officer engaged in the performance of his or her duties.

Assigned council. An attorney, not regularly employed by a government agency, assigned by the court to represent a particular person(s) in a particular criminal proceeding.

**Attorney/lawyer/counsel.** A person trained in the law, admitted to practice before the bar of a given jurisdiction, and authorized to advise, represent, and act for other persons in legal proceedings.

**Backlog.** The number of pending cases that exceeds the court's capacity, in that they cannot be acted upon because the court is occupied in acting upon other cases.

**Bombing incident.** The detonation or attempted detonation of an explosive or incendiary device with the willful disregard of risk to the person or property of another, or for a criminal purpose.

**Bondsman-secured bail.** Security service purchased by the defendant from a bail bondsman. The fee for this service ranges upward from 10 percent and is not refundable. The bail bondsman system, which permits a private entrepreneur to share with the court the decision on pretrial release, has been criticized for many years and is becoming obsolete in more progressive jurisdictions.

**Booking.** A police administrative action officially recording an arrest and identifying the person, the place, the time, the arresting authority, and the reason for the arrest.

**Burglary.** Unlawful entry of a structure, with or without force, with intent to commit a felony or larceny.

**Camp/ranch/farm.** Any of several types of similar confinement facilities, usually in a rural location, which contain adults or juveniles committed after adjudication.

**Case.** At the level of police or prosecutorial investigation, a set of circumstances under investigation involving one or more persons; at subsequent steps in criminal proceedings, a charging document alleging the commission of one or more crimes; a single defendant; in juvenile or correctional proceedings, a person who is the object of agency action.

**Case (court).** A single charging document under the jurisdiction of a court; a single defendant.

**Caseload (corrections).** The total number of clients registered with a correctional agency or agent during a specified time period, often divided into active and inactive or supervised and unsupervised, thus distinguishing between clients with whom the agency or agent maintains contact and those with whom it does not.

**Caseload (court).** The total number of cases filed in a given court or before a given judicial officer during a given period of time.

Caseload, pending. The number of cases at any given time that have been filed in a given court, or are before a given judicial officer, but have not reached disposition.

Cash bail. A cash payment for a situation in which the charge is not serious and the scheduled bail is low. The defendant obtains release by paying in cash the full amount, which is recoverable after the required court appearances are made.

CCH. An abbreviation for computerized criminal history.

Charge. A formal allegation that a specific person(s) has committed a specific offense(s).

Charging document. A formal written accusation, filed in a court, alleging that a specified person(s) has committed a specific offense(s).

Check fraud. The issuance or passing of a check, draft, or money order that is legal as a formal document, signed by the legal account holder but with the foreknowledge that the bank or depository will refuse to honor it because of insufficient funds or a closed account.

Chief of police. A local law enforcement officer who is the appointed or elected head of a police department.

Child abuse. Willful action or actions by a person causing physical harm to a child.

Child neglect. Willful failure by the person(s) responsible for a child's well-being to provide for adequate food, clothing, shelter, education, and supervision.

Citation (to appear). A written order issued by a law enforcement officer directing an alleged offender to appear in a specific court at a specified time in order to answer a criminal charge.

Citizen dispute settlement. The settlement of interpersonal disputes by a third party or the courts. Charges arising from interpersonal disputes are mediated by a third party in an attempt to avoid prosecution. If an agreement between the parties cannot be reached and the complainant wishes to proceed with criminal processing, the case may be referred to court for settlement.

Commitment. The action of a judicial officer ordering that an adjudicated and sentenced adult, or adjudicated delinquent or status offender who has been the subject of a juvenile court disposition hearing, be admitted into a correctional facility.

Community facility (nonconfinement facility, adult or juvenile). A correctional facility from which residents are regularly permitted to depart, unaccompanied by any official, to use daily community resources such as schools or treatment programs, or to seek or hold employment.

Community service. A period of service to the community as a substitute for, or in partial satisfaction of, a fine. This disposition is generally a condition of a suspended or partially suspended sentence or of probation. The offender volunteers his or her services to a community agency for a certain number of hours per week over a specified period of time. The total number of hours, often assessed at the legal minimum wage, is determined by the amount of the fine that would have been imposed or that portion of the fine is suspended.

Complaint. A formal written accusation made by any person, often a prosecutor, and filed in a court, alleging that a specified person(s) has committed a specific offense(s).

Complaint denied. The decision by a prosecutor to decline a request that he or she seek an indictment or file an information or complaint against a specified person(s) for a specific offense(s).

Complaint granted. The decision by a prosecutor to grant a request that he or she seek an indictment or file an information or complaint against a specified person(s) for a specific offense(s).

Complaint requested (police). A request by a law enforcement agency that the prosecutor seek an indictment or file an information or complaint against a specified person(s) for a specific offense(s).

Conditional diversion. At the pretrial stage, suspension of prosecution while specific conditions are met. If conditions are not satisfied during a specified time period, the case is referred for continued prosecution.

Conditional release. The release of a defendant who agrees to meet specific conditions in addition to appearing in court. Such conditions may include remaining in a defined geographical area, maintaining steady employment, avoiding contact with the victim or with associates in the alleged crime, avoiding certain activities or places, participating in treatment, or accepting services. Conditional release is often used in conjunction with third-party or supervised release.

Confinement facility. A correctional facility from which the inmates are not regularly permitted to depart each day unaccompanied.

Convict. An adult who has been found guilty of a felony and who is confined in a federal or state confinement facility.

Conviction. A judgment of a court, based either on the verdict of a jury or a judicial officer or on the guilty plea of the defendant, that the defendant is guilty of the offense(s) for which he or she has been tried.

Correctional agency. A federal, state, or local criminal justice agency, under a single administrative authority, of which the principal functions are the investigation, intake screening, supervision, custody, confinement, or treatment of alleged or adjudicated adult offenders, delinquents, or status offenders.

Correctional day programs. A publicly financed and operated nonresidential educational or treatment program for persons required, by a judicial officer, to participate.

Correctional facility. A building or part thereof, set of buildings, or area enclosing a set of buildings or structures operated by a government agency for the custody and/or treatment of adjudicated and committed persons, or persons subject to criminal or juvenile justice proceedings.

Correctional institution. A generic name proposed in this terminology for those long-term adult confinement facilities often called "prisons," "federal or state correctional facilities," or "penitentiaries," and juvenile confinement facilities called "training schools," "reformatories," "boys ranches," and the like.

Correctional institution, adult. A confinement facility having custodial authority over adults sentenced to confinement for more than a year.

Correctional institution, juvenile. A confinement facility having custodial authority over delinquents and status offenders committed to confinement after a juvenile dispassion hearing.

Corrections. A generic term that includes all government agencies, facilities, programs, procedures, personnel, and techniques concerned with the investigation, intake, custody, confinement, supervision, or treatment of alleged or adjudicated adult offenders, delinquents, or status offenders.

Count. Each separate offense, attributed to one or more persons, as listed in a complaint, information, or indictment.

Counterfeiting. The manufacture or attempted manufacture of a copy or imitation of a negotiable instrument with value set by law or convention, or the possession of such a copy without authorization, with the intent to defraud by claiming the copy's genuineness.

Court. An agency of the judicial branch of government, authorized or established by statute or constitution, and consisting of one or more judicial officers, which has the authority to decide on controversies in law and dispute matters of fact brought before it.

Court of appellate jurisdiction. A court that does not try criminal cases but does hear appeals.

Court of general jurisdiction. Of criminal courts, a court that has jurisdiction to try all criminal offenses, including all felonies and that may or may not hear appeals.

Court of limited jurisdiction. Of criminal courts, a court of which the trial jurisdiction either includes no felonies or is limited to less than all felonies and which may or may not hear appeals.

Credit card fraud. The use or attempted use of a credit card in order to obtain goods or services with the intent to avoid payment.

Crime (criminal offense). An act committed or omitted in violation of a law forbidding or commanding it for which an adult can be punished, upon conviction, by incarceration and other penalties or a corporation penalized, or for which a juvenile can be brought under the jurisdiction of a juvenile court and adjudicated a delinquent or transferred to adult court.

Crime Index offenses (index crimes). A UCR classification that includes all Part I offenses with the exception of involuntary (negligent) manslaughter.

Crimes against businesses (business crimes, commercial crimes). A summary term used by the National Crime Panel reports, including burglary and robbery (against businesses).

Crimes against households (household crimes). A summary term used by the National Crime Panel reports, including burglary (against households), household larceny, and motor vehicle theft.

Crimes against persons. A summary term used by UCR and the National Crime Panel reports, but with different meanings:

> UCR
> Murder
> Nonnegligent (voluntary) manslaughter
> Negligent (involuntary) manslaughter
> Forcible rape
> Aggravated assault
>
> National Crime Panel
> Forcible rape
> Robbery (against person)
> Aggravated assault
> Simple assault
> Personal larceny

Crimes against property (property crime). A summary term used by UCR, both as a subclass of the Part I offenses and as a subclass of Crime Index offenses, but with different meanings: As a subset of UCR Part I offenses:

> Robbery
> Burglary
> Larceny-theft
> Motor vehicle theft
> As a subset of UCR Crime Index offenses

> Burglary
> Larceny-theft
> Motor vehicle theft

Crimes of violence (violent crime). A summary term used by UCR and the National Crime Panel, but with different meanings: As a subset of UCR Index Crimes:

> Murder
> Nonnegligent (voluntary) manslaughter
> Forcible rape
> Robbery
> Aggravated assault
> As a subset of National Crime Panel crimes against persons
> Forcible rape
> Robbery (against persons)
> Aggravated assault
> Simple assault

Criminal history record information. Information collected by criminal justice agencies on individuals, consisting of identifiable descriptions and notations of arrests, detentions, indictments, informations, or other formal criminal charges, and any disposition(s) arising therefrom, including sentencing, correctional supervision, and release.

Criminal justice agency. Any court with criminal jurisdiction and any other government agency or subunit that defends indigents, or of which the principal functions or activities consist of the prevention, detection, and investigation of crime; the apprehension, detention, and prosecution of alleged offenders; the confinement or official correctional supervision of accused or convicted persons; or the administrative or technical support of the above functions.

Criminal proceedings. Proceedings in a court of law undertaken to determine the guilt or innocence of an adult accused of a crime.

Culpability. The state of mind of one who has committed an act that makes him or her liable to prosecution for that act.

Defendant. A person against whom a criminal proceeding is pending.

Defense attorney. An attorney who represents the defendant in a legal proceeding.

Delinquency. Juvenile actions or conduct in violation of criminal law and, in some contexts, status offenses.

Delinquent. A juvenile who has been adjudicated by a judicial officer of a juvenile court as having committed a delinquent act, which is an act for which an adult could not be prosecuted in a criminal court.

Delinquent act. An act committed by a juvenile for which an adult could not be prosecuted in a criminal court, but for which a juvenile can be adjudicated in a juvenile court.

De novo. Anew, afresh, as if there has been no earlier decision.

Dependency. The legal status of a juvenile over whom a juvenile court has assumed jurisdiction because the court has found his or her care by parent, guardian, or custodian to fall short of a legal standard or proper care.

Dependent. A juvenile over whom a juvenile court has assumed jurisdiction because the court has found his or her care by parent, guardian, or custodian to fall short of a legal standard of proper care.

Detention. The legally authorized holding in confinement of a person subject to criminal or juvenile court proceedings until the point of commitment to a correctional facility or release.

Detention center. A government facility that provides temporary care in a physically restricting environment for juveniles in custody pending court disposition.

Detention facility. A generic name proposed in this terminology as a cover term for those facilities that hold adults or juveniles in confinement pending adjudication, adults sentenced for one year or less of confinement, and in some instances post-adjudicated juveniles, including facilities called "jails," "county farms," "honor farms," "work camps," "road camps," "detention centers," "shelters," "juvenile halls," and the like.

Detention facility, adult. A confinement facility of which the custodial authority is 48 hours or more and in which adults can be confined before adjudication or for sentences of one year or less.

Detention facility, juvenile. A confinement facility having custodial authority over juveniles confined pending and after adjudication.

Detention hearing. In juvenile proceedings, a hearing by a judicial officer of a juvenile court to determine whether a juvenile is to be detained, to continue to be detained, or to be released, while juvenile proceedings are pending in his or her case.

Diagnosis or classification center. A functional unit within a correctional institution, or a separate facility, that holds persons held in custody in order to determine to which correctional facility or program they should be committed.

Dismissal. A decision by a judicial officer to terminate a case without a determination of guilt or innocence.

Disposition. The action by a criminal or juvenile justice agency that signifies that a portion of the justice process is complete and jurisdiction is relinquished or transferred to another agency or that signifies that a decision has been reached on one aspect of a case and a different aspect comes under consideration, requiring a different kind of decision.

Disposition, court. The final judicial decision, which terminates a criminal proceeding by a judgment of acquittal or dismissal or which states the specific sentence in the case of a conviction.

Disposition hearing. A hearing in juvenile court, conducted after an adjudicatory hearing and subsequent receipt of the report of any predisposition investigation, to determine the most appropriate disposition of a juvenile who has been adjudicated a delinquent, a status offender, or a dependent.

Disposition, juvenile court. The decision of a juvenile court, concluding a disposition hearing, that a juvenile be committed to a correctional facility, placed in a care or treatment program, required to meet certain standards of conduct, or released.

Diversion. The official halting or suspension, at any legally prescribed processing point after a recorded justice system entry, of formal criminal or juvenile justice proceedings against an alleged offender, and referral of that person to a treatment or care program administered by a nonjustice agency or a private agency, or no referral.

Driving under the influence of alcohol (drunk driving). The operation of any vehicle after having consumed a quantity of alcohol sufficient to potentially interfere with the ability to maintain safe operation.

Driving under the influence of drugs. The operation of any vehicle while attention or ability is impaired through the intake of a narcotic or an incapacitating quantity of another drug.

Drug law violation. The unlawful sale, transport, manufacture, cultivation, possession, or use of a controlled or prohibited drug.

Early release. Release from confinement before the sentence has been completed. Early release to supervision means less jail time and, with more rapid turnover, low jail populations and capacity requirements. Early release may come about through parole, time off for good behavior or work performed, or modification of the sentence by the court. The last procedure is usually associated with sentences to jail with a period of probation to follow. Although there are some objections to its use, "probation with jail" is a common disposition in some jurisdictions. More often than not, these sentences are in lieu of a state prison term.

**Embezzlement.** The misappropriation, misapplication, or illegal disposal of legally entrusted property with intent to defraud the legal owner or intended beneficiary.

**Escape.** The unlawful departure of a lawfully confined person from a confinement facility or from custody while being transported.

**Expunge.** The sealing or purging of arrest, criminal, or juvenile record information.

**Extortion.** Unlawful obtaining or attempting to obtain the property of another by the threat of eventual injury or harm to that person, the person's property, or another person.

**Felony.** A criminal offense punishable by death or by incarceration in a state or federal confinement facility for a period of which the lower limit is prescribed by statute in a given jurisdiction, typically one year or more.

**Field citation.** Citation and release in the field by police as an alternative to booking and pretrial detention. This practice reduces law enforcement costs as well as jail costs.

**Filing.** The commencement of criminal proceedings by entering a charging document into a court's official record.

**Finding.** The official determination of a judicial officer or administrative body regarding a disputed matter of fact or law.

**Fine.** The penalty imposed on a convicted person by a court requiring that he or she pay a specified sum of money. The fine is a cash payment of a dollar amount assessed by the judge in an individual case or determined by a published schedule of penalties. Fines may be paid in installments in many jurisdictions.

**Forgery.** The creation or alteration of a written or printed document that, if validly executed, would constitute a record of a legally binding transaction, with the intent to defraud by affirming it to be the act of an unknowing second person. Defining features: Making or altering a written or printed document or record. Act being falsely attributed to an unknowing second person. Intent being to deprive illegally a person of property or legal rights.

**Fraud.** An element of certain offenses consisting of deceit or intentional misrepresentation with the aim of illegally depriving a person of property or legal rights.

Fugitive. A person who has concealed himself or herself or fled a given jurisdiction in order to avoid prosecution or confinement.

Group home. A nonconfining residential facility for adjudicated adults or juveniles or those subject to criminal or juvenile proceedings, intended to reproduce as closely as possible the circumstances of family life and at the minimum, providing access to community activities and resources.

> RECOMMENDED CONDITIONS OF USE. Classify government facilities fitting this definition as community facilities.

> ANNOTATION. Group home is variously defined in different jurisdictions. Most of the facilities known by this name are privately operated, though they may be financed mainly from government funds. Classification problems unique to private facilities have not been dealt with in this terminology, although most recommended standard descriptors for publicly operated facilities are also applicable to the private sector. See correctional facility for recommended standard descriptors. The data collection questionnaire for the LEAA series "Children in Custody" defines group home as one that allows juveniles extensive contact with the community, such as through jobs and schools, but none or less than one-half are placed there on probation or "aftercare/parole." It is distinguished from halfway house in this series by the percentage of residents on probation or parole.

Halfway house. A nonconfining residential facility for adjudicated adults or juveniles or those subject to criminal or juvenile proceedings, intended as an alternative to confinement for persons not suited for probation or needing a period of readjustment to the community after confinement.

> RECOMMENDED CONDITIONS OF USE. Classify government facilities fitting this definition as community facilities.

> ANNOTATION. Halfway house is variously defined in different jurisdictions. Most of the facilities known by this name are privately operated, though they may be financed mainly from government funds. Classification problems unique to private facilities have not been dealt with in this terminology, although most recommended standard descriptors for publicly operated facilities are also applicable to the private sector. See correctional facility for recommended standard descriptors. The data collection questionnaire for the LEAA series "Children in Custody" defines halfway house as having 50 percent or more juveniles on probation or aftercare/parole, allowing them extensive contact with the community, such as through "jobs and schools." It is distinguished from group home in this series by the percentage of residents on probation or parole.

Hearing. A proceeding in which arguments, evidence, or witnesses are heard by a judicial officer or administrative body.

Hearing, probable cause. A proceeding before a judicial officer in which arguments, evidence, or witnesses are presented and in which it is determined whether there is sufficient cause to hold the accused for trial or whether the case should be dismissed.

Homicide. Any killing of one person by another.

Homicide, criminal. The causing of the death of another person without justification or excuse.

> Equivalent Terms
> UCR term—for police-reporting level
> Dictionary term Criminal homicide
> Criminal homicide
> Murder (often used as cover term for murder and nonnegligent manslaughter)
> Murder
> Nonnegligent manslaughter
> Voluntary manslaughter
> Equivalent terms
> Negligent manslaughter
> Involuntary manslaughter
> (Included in negligent manslaughter)
> Vehicular manslaughter

Homicide, excusable. The intentional but justifiable causing of the death of another or the unintentional causing of the death of another by accident or misadventure, without gross negligence. Not a crime.

Homicide, justifiable. The intentional causing of the death of another in the legal performance of an official duty or in the circumstances defined by law as constituting legal justification. Not a crime.

Homicide, willful. The intentional causing of the death of another person, with or without legal justification.

Indictment. A formal written accusation made by a grand jury and filed in a court alleging that a specified person(s) has committed a specific offense(s).

Information. A written formal accusation, filed in a court by a prosecutor, that alleges a specific person has committed a specific offense.

Infraction. An offense punishable by fine or other penalty, but not by incarceration.

**Inmate.** A person in custody in a confinement facility.

**Institutional capacity.** The officially stated number of inmates or residents that a correctional facility is designed to house, exclusive of extraordinary arrangements to accommodate overcrowded conditions.

**Intake.** The process during which a juvenile referral is received and a decision is made by an intake unit to file a petition in juvenile court, to release the juvenile, to place the juvenile under supervision, or to refer the juvenile elsewhere.

**Intake unit.** A government agency or agency sub-unit that receives juvenile referrals from police, other government agencies, private agencies, or persons and screens them, resulting in closing of the case, referral to care or supervision, or filing of a petition in juvenile court.

**Jail.** Confinement facility, usually administered by a local law enforcement agency, intended for adults but sometimes also containing juveniles, that holds persons detained pending adjudication and/or persons committed after adjudication for sentences of one year or less.

**Jail (sentence).** The penalty of commitment to the jurisdiction of a confinement facility system for adults, of which the custodial authority is limited to persons sentenced to one year or less of confinement.

**Judge.** A judicial officer who has been elected or appointed to preside over a court of law, whose position has been created by statute or by constitution and whose decisions in criminal and juvenile cases may only be reviewed by a judge or a higher court and may not be reviewed de novo.

**Judgment.** The statement of the decision of a court that the defendant is convicted or acquitted of the offense(s) charged.

**Judicial officer.** Any person exercising judicial powers in a court of law.

**Jurisdiction.** The territory, subject matter, or person over which lawful authority may be exercised.

**Jurisdiction, original.** The lawful authority of a court or an administrative agency to hear or act upon a case from its beginning and to pass judgment on it.

**Jury, grand.** A body of persons who have been selected and sworn to investigate criminal activity and the conduct of public officials and to hear the evidence against an accused person(s) to determine whether there is sufficient evidence to bring that person(s) to trial.

**Jury, trial (petit jury; jury).** A statutorily defined number of persons selected according to law and sworn to determine certain matters of fact in a criminal action and to render a verdict of guilty or not guilty.

**Juvenile.** A person subject to juvenile court proceedings because a statutorily defined event was alleged to have occurred while his or her age was below the statutorily specified limit of original jurisdiction of a juvenile court.

> ANNOTATION. Jurisdiction is determined by age at the time of the event, not at the time of judicial proceedings, and continues until the case is terminated. Thus a person may be described in a given data system as a juvenile because he or she is still subject to juvenile court proceedings, even though his or her actual age may be several years over the limit. Conversely, criminal process data systems may include juveniles if the juvenile court has waived jurisdiction. Although the age limit varies in different states, it is most often the eighteenth birthday. The variation is small enough to permit nationally aggregated data to be meaningful, although individual states should note their age limited communications with other states. UCR defines a juvenile as anyone under eighteen years of age. See youthful offender.

**Juvenile court.** A cover term for courts that have original jurisdiction over persons statutorily defined as juveniles and alleged to be delinquents, status offenders, or dependents.

**Juvenile justice agency.** A government agency, or sub-unit thereof, of which the functions are the investigation, supervision, adjudication, care, or confinement of juveniles whose conduct or condition has brought or could bring them within the jurisdiction of juvenile court.

**Juvenile record.** An official record containing, at a minimum, summary information pertaining to an identified juvenile concerning juvenile court proceedings, and, if applicable, detention and correctional processes.

**Kidnapping.** Unlawful transportation of a person without his or her consent or without the consent of his or her guardian, of a minor.

**Larceny (larceny-theft).** Unlawful taking or attempted taking of property, other than a motor vehicle, from the possession of another.

**Law enforcement agency.** A federal, state, or local criminal justice agency of which the principal functions are the prevention, detection, and investigation of crime and the apprehension of alleged offenders.

**Law enforcement agency, federal.** A law enforcement agency that is an organization unit, or sub-unit, of the federal government.

**Law enforcement agency, local.** A law enforcement agency that is an organization unit, or sub-unit, of local government.

Law enforcement agency, state. A law enforcement agency that is an organization unit, or sub-unit, of state government.

Law enforcement officer (peace officer, police officer). An employee of a law enforcement agency who is an officer sworn to carry out law enforcement duties or is a sworn employee of a federal prosecutorial agency who primarily performs investigative duties.

Law enforcement officer, federal. An employee of a federal law enforcement agency who is an officer sworn to carry out law enforcement duties or is a sworn employee of a federal prosecutorial agency who primarily performs investigative duties.

Law enforcement officer, local. An employee of a local law enforcement agency who is an officer sworn to carry out law enforcement duties or is a sworn employee of a local prosecutorial agency who primarily performs investigative duties.

Law enforcement officer, state. An employee of a state law enforcement agency who is an officer sworn to carry out law enforcement duties or is a sworn employee of a state prosecutorial agency who primarily performs investigative duties.

Level of government. The federal, state, regional, or local county or city location of administrative and major funding responsibility of a given agency.

Manslaughter, involuntary (negligent manslaughter). Causing the death of another by recklessness or gross negligence.

Manslaughter, vehicular. Causing the death of another by grossly negligent operation of a motor vehicle.

Manslaughter, voluntary (nonnegligent manslaughter). Intentionally causing the death of another with reasonable provocation.

Misdemeanor. An offense usually punishable by incarceration in a local confinement facility for a period of which the upper limit is prescribed by statute in a given jurisdiction, typically limited to one year or less.

Model Penal Code. A generalized modern codification of that which is considered basic to criminal law, published by the American Law Institute in 1962.

Monitored release. Recognizance release with the addition of minimal supervision or service; that is, the defendant may be required to keep a pretrial services agency informed of his or her whereabouts, and the agency reminds the defendant of court dates and verifies the defendant's appearance.

Motion. An oral or written request made by a party to an action, before, during, or after a trial, that a court issue a rule or order.

Motor vehicle theft. Unlawful taking, or attempted taking, of a motor vehicle owned by another with the intent to deprive the owner of it permanently or temporarily.

Murder. Intentionally causing the death of another without reasonable provocation or legal justification, or causing the death of another while committing or attempting to commit another crime.

Nolo contendere. A defendant's formal answer in court to the charges in a complaint, information, or indictment in which the defendant states that he or she does not contest the charges and which, though not an admission of guilt, subjects the defendant to the same legal consequences as does a plea of guilty.

Offender (criminal). An adult who has been convicted of a criminal offense.

Offender, alleged. A person who has been charged with a specific criminal offense(s) by a law enforcement agency or court but has not been convicted.

Offense. An act committed or omitted in violation of a law forbidding or commanding it.

Offenses, Part I. A class of offenses selected for use in UCR, consisting of those crimes that are most likely to be reported, that occur with sufficient frequency to provide an adequate basis for comparison, and that are serious crimes by nature and/or volume.

ANNOTATION. The Part I offenses are:
1. Criminal homicide
   a. Murder and nonnegligent (voluntary) manslaughter
   b. Manslaughter by negligence (involuntary manslaughter)
2. Forcible rape
   a. Rape by force
   b. Attempted forcible rape
3. Robbery
   a. Firearm
   b. Knife or cutting instrument
   c. Other dangerous weapon
   d. Strongarm
4. Aggravated Assault
   a. Firearm
   b. Knife or cutting instrument
   c. Other dangerous weapon
   d. Hands, fist, feet, etc.,—aggravated injury
5. Burglary
   a. Forcible entry
   b. Unlawful entry—no force
   c. Attempted forcible entry
6. Larceny-theft (larceny)

7.  Motor vehicle theft
    a.  Autos
    b.  Trucks and buses
    c.  Other vehicles

**Offenses, Part II.** A class of offenses selected for use in UCR, consisting of specific offenses and types of offenses that do not meet the criteria of frequency and/or seriousness necessary for Part I offenses.

ANNOTATION. The Part II offenses are:
Other assaults (simple,* nonaggravated)
Arson*
Forgery* and counterfeiting*
Fraud*
Embezzlement*
Stolen property: buying, receiving, possessing
Vandalism
Weapons: carrying, possessing, etc.
Prostitution and commercialized vice
Sex offenses (except forcible rape, prostitution, and commercialized vice)
Narcotic drug law violations
Gambling
Offenses against the family and children
Driving under the influence*
Liquor law violations
Drunkenness
Disorderly conduct
Vagrancy
All other offenses (except traffic law violations)
Suspicion*
Curfew and loitering law violations (juvenile violations)
Runaway* (juveniles)

Terms marked with an asterisk (*) are defined in this glossary, though not necessarily in accord with UCR usage. UCR does not collect reports of Part II offenses. Arrest data concerning such offenses, however, are collected and published.

**Pardon.** An act of executive clemency that absolves the party in part or in full from the legal consequences of the crime and conviction.

ANNOTATION. Pardons can be full or conditional. The former generally applies to both the punishment and the guilt of the offender and blots out the existence of guilt in the eyes of the law. It also removes his or her disabilities and restores civil rights. The conditional pardon generally falls short of the remedies of the full pardon, is an expression of guilt, and does not obliterate the conviction. (U.S. Supreme Court decisions to pardons and their effects are directly contradictory, and thus state laws usually govern pardons.)

Parole. The status of an offender conditionally released from a confinement facility, prior to the expiration of his or her sentence, and placed under the supervision of a parole agency.

Parole agency. A correctional agency, which may or may not include a parole authority and of which the principal function is the supervision of adults or juveniles placed on parole.

Parole authority. A person or a correctional agency that has the authority to release on parole those adults or juveniles committed to confinement facilities, to revoke parole, and to discharge from parole.

Parolee. A person who has been conditionally released from a correctional institution before the expiration of his or her sentence and who has been placed under the supervision of a parole agency.

Parole violation. A parolee's act or a failure to act that does not conform to the conditions of his or her parole.

Partial confinement. An alternative to the traditional jail sentence, consisting of "weekend" sentences, that permit offenders to spend the work week in the community, with their families, and at the jobs; furloughs, which enable offenders to leave the jail for a period of a few hours to a few days for specific purposes—to seek employment, take care of personal matters or family obligations, or engage in community service; or work/study release, under which offenders work or attend school during the day and return to the detention facility at night and on weekends.

Penalty. The punishment annexed by law or judicial decision to the commission of a particular offense, which may be death, imprisonment, fine, or loss of civil privileges.

Percentage bail. A publicly managed bail service arrangement that requires the defendant to deposit a percentage (typically 10 percent) of the amount of bail with the court clerk. The deposit is returned to the defendant after scheduled court appearances are made, although a charge (usually 1 percent) may be deducted to help defray program costs.

Person. A human being, or a group of human beings considered a legal unit, which has the lawful capacity to defend rights, incur obligation, prosecute claims, or be prosecuted or adjudicated.

Personally secured bail. Security that is put up by the defendant or the defendant's family. This arrangement is generally out of reach of the less affluent defendant.

Petition (juvenile). A document filed in juvenile court alleging that a juvenile is a delinquent, a status offender, or a dependent and asking that the juvenile be transferred to a criminal court for prosecution as an adult.

Petition not sustained. The finding by a juvenile court in an adjudicatory hearing that there is not sufficient evidence to sustain an allegation that a juvenile is a delinquent, status offender, or dependent.

Plea. A defendant's formal answer in court to the charges brought against him or her in a complaint, information, or indictment.

Plea bargaining. The exchange of prosecutorial and/or judicial concessions, commonly a lesser charge, the dismissal of other pending charges, a recommendation by the prosecutor for a reduced sentence or a combination thereof, in return for a plea of guilty.

Plea, final. The last plea to a given charge, entered in a court record by or for a defendant.

Plea, guilty. A defendant's formal answer in court to the charges in a complaint, information, or indictment, in which the defendant states that the charges are true and that he or she has committed the offense as charged.

Plea, initial. The first plea to a given charge, entered in a court record by or for a defendant.

Plea, not guilty. A defendant's formal answer in court to the charges in a complaint, information, or indictment, in which the defendant states that he or she is not guilty.

Police department. A local law enforcement agency directed by a chief of police or a commissioner.

Police officer. A local law enforcement officer employed by a police department.

Population movement. Entries and exits of adjudicated persons, or persons subject to judicial proceedings, into or from correctional facilities or programs.

Predisposition report. The document resulting from an investigation by a probation agency or other designated authority, which has been requested by a juvenile court, into the past behavior, family background, and personality of a juvenile who has been adjudicated a delinquent, a status offender, or a dependent, in order to assist the court in determining the most appropriate disposition.

Presentence report. The document resulting from an investigation undertaken by a probation agency or other designated authority, at the request of a criminal court, into the past behavior, family circumstances, and personality of an adult who has been convicted of a crime, in order to assist the court in determining the most appropriate sentence.

Prior record. Criminal history record information concerning any law enforcement, court, or correctional proceedings that have occurred before the current investigation of, or proceedings against, a person; or statistical description of the criminal histories of a set of persons.

Prison. A confinement facility having custodial authority over adults sentenced to confinement for more than one year.

Prisoner. A person in custody in a confinement facility or in the personal custody of a criminal justice official while being transported to or between confinement facilities.

Prison (sentence). The penalty of commitment to the jurisdiction of a confinement facility system for adults, whose custodial authority extends to persons sentenced to more than one year of confinement.

Privately secured bail. An arrangement similar to the bail bondsman system except that bail is provided without cost to the defendant. A private organization provides bail for indigent arrestees who meet its eligibility requirements.

Probable cause. A set of facts and circumstances that would induce a reasonably intelligent and prudent person to believe that an accused person had committed a specific crime.

Probation. The conditional freedom granted by a judicial officer to an alleged offender, or adjudicated adult or juvenile, as long as the person meets certain conditions of behavior. One requirement is to report to a designated person or agency over some specific period of time. Probation may contain special conditions, as discussed in the conditions of suspended sentence. Probation often includes a suspended sentence but may be used in association with the suspension of a final judgment or a deferral of sentencing.

Probation agency (probation department). A correctional agency of which the principal functions are juvenile intake, the supervision of adults and juveniles placed on probation status, and the investigation of adults or juveniles for the purpose of preparing presentence or predisposition reports to assist the court in determining the proper sentence or juvenile court disposition.

Probationer. A person required by a court or probation agency to meet certain conditions of behavior who may or may not be placed under the supervision of a probation agency.

Probation officer. An employee of a probation agency whose primary duties include one or more of the probation agency functions.

Probation (sentence). A court requirement that a person fulfill certain conditions of behavior and accept the supervision of a probation agency, usually in lieu of a sentence to confinement but sometimes including a jail sentence.

Probation violation. An act or a failure to act by a probationer that does not conform to the conditions of his or her probation.

**Prosecutor.** An attorney employed by a government agency or subunit whose official duty is to initiate and maintain criminal proceedings on behalf of the government against persons accused of committing criminal offenses.

**Prosecutorial agency.** A federal, state, or local criminal justice agency whose principal function is the prosecution of alleged offenders.

**Pro se (in propria persona).** Acting as one's own defense attorney in criminal proceedings: representing oneself.

**Public defender.** An attorney employed by a government agency or subdivision, whose official duty is to represent defendants unable to hire private counsel.

**Public defender's office.** A federal, state, or local criminal justice agency or subunit of which the principal function is to represent defendants unable to hire private counsel.

**Purge (record).** The complete removal of arrest, criminal, or juvenile record information from a given records system.

**Rape.** Unlawful sexual intercourse with a person, by force or without legal or factual consent.

**Rape, forcible.** Sexual intercourse or attempted sexual intercourse with a person against his or her will, by force or threat of force.

**Rape, statutory.** Sexual intercourse with a person who has consented in fact but deemed, because of age, to be legally incapable of consent.

**Rape without force or consent.** Sexual intercourse with a person legally of the age of consent but who is unconscious or whose ability to judge or control his or her conduct is inherently impaired by mental defect or intoxicating substances.

**Recidivism.** The repetition of criminal behavior; habitual criminality.

> ANNOTATION. In statistical practice, a recidivism rate may be any of a number of possible counts of instances of arrest, conviction, correctional commitment, and correctional status changes, related to the numbers of repetitions of these events within a given period of time. Efforts to arrive at a single standard statistical description of recidivism have been hampered by the fact that the term's correct referent is the actual repeated criminal or delinquent behavior of a given person or group; yet the only available statistical indicators of that behavior are records of such system events as rearrests, reconvictions, and probation or parole valuations or revocations. It is recognized that these data reflect agency decisions about events and may or may not closely correspond with actual

criminal behavior. Different conclusions about degrees of correspondence between system decisions and actual behavior consequently produce different definitions of recidivism, that is different judgments of which system event repetition rates best measure actual recidivism rates. This is an empirical question, and not one of definition to be resolved solely by analysis of language usage and system logic. Resolution has also been delayed by the limited capacities of most criminal justice statistical systems, which do not routinely make available the standardized offender-based transaction data (OBTD) that · may be needed for the best measurement of recidivism. Pending the adoption of a standard statistical description of recidivism and the ability to implement it, it is recommended that recidivism analyses include the widest possible range of system events that can correspond with actual recidivism and that sufficient detail of offenses charged be included to enable discrimination among degrees of gravity of offenses. The units of count should be clearly identified and the length of community exposure time of the subject population stated.

Recidivism is measured by (1) criminal acts that resulted in a conviction by a court, when committed by individuals who have been released from correctional supervision or who have been released from correctional supervision within the previous three years, and by (2) technical violations of probation or parole in which a sentencing or paroling authority took action that results in an adverse change in the offender's "legal status."

Neither of these formulations is endorsed as adequate for all purposes. Both limit the measure and concept of recidivism to populations that are or have been under correctional supervision. Yet the ultimate significance of data concerning the repetition of criminal behavior often depends on the comparison of the behavior of unconfined or unsupervised offenders with the behavior of those with correctional experience.

Referral to intake. In juvenile proceedings, a request by the police, parents, or other agency or person that a juvenile intake unit take appropriate action concerning a juvenile alleged to have committed a delinquent act or status offense or to be dependent.

Release from detention. The authorized exit from detention of a person subject to criminal or juvenile justice proceedings.

Release from prison. A cover term for all lawful exits from federal or state confinement facilities primarily intended for adults serving sentences of more than one year, including all conditional and unconditional releases, deaths, and transfers to other jurisdictions, excluding escapes:

Transfer of jurisdiction
Release on parole
Conditional release
Release while still under jurisdiction of correctional agency, before ex-
piration of sentence

Discretionary
Release date determined by parole authority

Mandatory
Release date determined by statute
Discharge from prison
Release ending all agency jurisdiction
Unconditional release

Discretionary
Pardon, commutation of sentence

Mandatory
Expiration of sentence
Temporary release
Authorized, unaccompanied temporary departure for educational, em-
ployment, or other authorized purposes
Transfer of jurisdiction
Transfer of jurisdiction of another correctional agency or a court
Death
Death from homicide, suicide, or natural causes
Execution
Execution of sentence of death

In some systems release on "parole" represents only discretionary conditions release. It is recommended that mandatory conditional release be included, as both types describe conditional releases with subsequent parole status.

Release on bail. The release by a judicial officer of an accused person who has been taken into custody, upon the accused's promise to pay a certain sum of money or property if he or she fails to appear in court as required, a promise that may or may not be secured by the deposit of an actual sum of money or property.

Release on own recognizance. The release, by a judicial officer, of an accused person who has been taken into custody, upon the accused's promise to appear in court as required for criminal proceedings.

Release, pretrial. A procedure whereby an accused person who has been taken into custody is allowed to be free before and during his or her trial.

Release to third party. The release, by a judicial officer, of an accused person who has been taken into custody, to a third party who promises to return the accused to court for criminal proceedings.

Residential treatment center. A government facility that serves juveniles whose behavior does not necessitate the strict confinement of a training school, often allowing them greater contact with the community.

Restitution. Usually a cash payment by the offender to the victim of an amount considered to offset the loss incurred by the victim or the community. The amount of the payment may be scaled down to the offender's earning capacity, and/or payments may be made in installments. Sometimes services directly or indirectly benefiting the victim may be substituted for cash payment.

Restorative justice. Any victim-centered approach that views crime as a violation against individuals, their families and communities, and seeks to repair the harm done by the crime through mediation, reparation and empowerment of both victim and offender. Violators are held accountable for the offense and required to repair all or part of the damage, while being restored to the community.

Retained counsel. An attorney, not employed or compensated by a government agency or sub-unit or assigned by the court, who is privately hired to represent a person(s) in a criminal proceeding.

Revocation. An administrative act performed by a parole authority removing a person from parole, or a judicial order by a court removing a person from parole or probation, in response to a violation by the parolee or probationer.

Revocation hearing. An administrative and/or judicial hearing on the question of whether or not a person's probation or parole status should be revoked.

Rights of defendant. Those powers and privileges that are constitutionally guaranteed to every defendant.

Robbery. The unlawful taking or attempted taking of property that is in the immediate possession of another, by force or the threat of force.

Robbery, armed. The unlawful taking or attempted taking of property that is in the immediate possession of another, by the use or threatened use of a deadly or dangerous weapon.

Robbery, strongarm. The unlawful taking or attempted taking of property that is in the immediate possession of another by the use or threatened use of force, without the use of a weapon.

Runaway. A juvenile who has been adjudicated by a judicial officer of a juvenile court as having committed the status offense of leaving the custody and home of his or her parents, guardians, or custodians without permission and failing to return within a reasonable length of time.

Seal (record). The removal, for the benefit of the subject, of arrest, criminal, or juvenile record information from routinely available status to a status requiring special procedures for access.

Security. The degree of restriction of inmate movement within a correctional facility, usually divided into maximum, medium, and minimum levels.

Security and privacy standards. A set of principles and procedures developed to ensure the security and confidentiality of criminal or juvenile record information in order to protect the privacy of the persons identified in such records.

Sentence. The penalty imposed by a court on a convicted person, or the court decision to suspend imposition or execution of the penalty.

Sentence, indeterminate. A statutory provision for a type of sentence to imprisonment in which, after the court has determined that the convicted person shall be imprisoned, the exact length of imprisonment and parole supervision is afterward fixed within statutory limits by a parole authority.

Sentence, mandatory. A statutory requirement that a certain penalty shall be imposed and executed upon certain convicted offenders.

Sentence, suspended. The court decision postponing the pronouncement of sentence upon a convicted person or postponing the execution of a sentence that has been pronounced by the court.

Sentence, suspended execution. The court decision setting a penalty but postponing its execution.

Sentence, suspended imposition. The court decision postponing the setting of a penalty.

Shelter. A confinement or community facility for the care of juveniles, usually those held pending adjudication.

Sheriff. The elected or appointed chief officer of a county law enforcement agency, usually responsible for law enforcement in unincorporated areas and for operation of the county jail.

Sheriff, deputy. A law enforcement officer employed by a county sheriff's department.

Sheriff's department. A law enforcement agency organized at a county level, directed by a sheriff, that exercises its law enforcement functions at the county level, usually within unincorporated areas, and operates the county jail in most jurisdictions.

Speedy trial. The right of the defendant to have a prompt trial.

State highway patrol. A state law enforcement agency whose principal functions are the prevention, detection, and investigation of motor vehicle offenses and the apprehension of traffic offenders.

State highway patrol officer. An employee of a state highway patrol who is an officer sworn to carry out law enforcement duties, primarily traffic code enforcement.

State police. A state law enforcement agency whose principal functions may include maintaining statewide police communication, aiding local police communication, aiding local police in criminal investigation, training police, guarding state property, and patrolling highways.

State police officer. An employee of a state police agency who is an officer sworn to carry out law enforcement duties, sometimes including traffic enforcement duties.

Stationhouse citation. An alternative to pretrial detention, whereby the arrestee is escorted to the precinct police station or headquarters rather than the pretrial detention facility. Release, which may occur before or after booking, is contingent upon the defendant's written promise to appear in court as specified on the release form.

Status offender. A juvenile who has been adjudicated by a judicial officer of juvenile court as having committed a status offense, which is an act or conduct that is an offense only when committed or engaged in by a juvenile.

Status offense. An act or conduct that is declared by statute to be an offense, but only when committed or engaged in by a juvenile, and that can be adjudicated only by a juvenile court.

Subjudicial officer. A judicial officer who is invested with certain judicial powers and functions but whose decisions in criminal and juveniles cases are subject to de novo review by a judge.

Subpoena. A written order issued by a judicial officer requiring a specified person to appear in a designated court at a specified time in order to serve as a witness in a case under the jurisdiction of that court or to bring material to that court.

Summons. A written order issued by a judicial officer requiring a person accused of a criminal offense to appear in a designated court at a specified time to answer the charge(s). The summons is a request or instruction to appear in court to face an accusation. As an alternative to the arrest warrant, it is used in cases on which complaints are registered with the magistrate or prosecutor's office.

Supervised release. A type of release requiring more frequent contact than monitored release does. Typically, various conditions are imposed and supervision is aimed at enforcing these conditions and providing services as needed. Some form of monetary bail also may be attached as a condition of supervised release, especially in higher-risk cases.

**Suspect.** A person, adult or juvenile, considered by a criminal justice agency to be one who may have committed a specific criminal offense but who has not been arrested or charged.

**Suspended sentence.** Essentially a threat to take more drastic action if the offender again commits a crime during some specified time period. When no special conditions are attached, it is assumed that the ends of justice have been satisfied by conviction and no further action is required, as long as the offender refrains from involvement in new offenses. Suspended sentences may be conditioned on various limitations as to mobility, associates, or activities or on requirements to make reparations or participate in some rehabilitation program.

**Suspicion.** Belief that a person has committed a criminal offense, based on facts and circumstances that are not sufficient to constitute probable cause.

**Theft.** Larceny, or in some legal classifications, the group of offenses including larceny, and robbery, burglary, extortion, fraudulent offenses, hijacking, and other offenses sharing the element of larceny.

**Third-party release.** A release extending to another person the responsibility for ensuring the defendant's appearance in court. This may be a person known to the defendant or a designated volunteer. Third-party release may be a condition of unsecured bail, with the third party as a cosigner.

**Time served.** The total time spent in confinement by a convicted adult before and after sentencing, or only the time spent in confinement after a sentence of commitment to a confinement facility.

**Training school.** A correctional institution for juveniles adjudicated to be delinquent or status offenders and committed to confinement by a judicial officer.

**Transfer hearing.** A preadjudicatory hearing in juvenile court in order to determine whether juvenile court jurisdiction should be retained or waived for a juvenile alleged to have committed a delinquent act(s) and whether he or she should be transferred to criminal court for prosecution as an adult.

**Transfer to adult court.** The decision by a juvenile court, resulting from a transfer hearing, that jurisdiction over an alleged delinquent will be waived and that he or she should be prosecuted as an adult in a criminal court.

**Trial.** The examination of issues of fact and law in a case or controversy, beginning when the jury has been selected in a jury trial, the first witness is sworn, or the first evidence is introduced in a court trial and concluding when a verdict is reached or the case is dismissed.

**Trial, court (trial, judge).** A trial in which there is no jury and a judicial officer determines the issues of fact and law in a case.

Trial, jury. A trial in which a jury determines the issues of fact in a case.

UCR. An abbreviation for the Federal Bureau of Investigation's Uniform Crime Reporting program.

Unconditional discharge. As a posttrial disposition, essentially the same as unconditional diversion. No savings are obtained in criminal justice processing costs, but jail populations may be reduced; conditions of release are imposed for an offense in which the defendant's involvement has been established.

Unconditional diversion. The cessation of criminal processing at any point short of adjudication with no continuing threat of prosecution. This type of diversion may be voluntary referral to a social service agency or program dealing with a problem underlying the offense.

Unsecured bail. A form of release differing from release on recognizance only in that the defendant is subject to paying the amount of bail if he or she defaults. Unsecured bail permits release without a deposit or purchase of a bondsman's services.

Venue. The geographical area from which the jury is drawn and in which trial is held in a criminal action.

Verdict. In criminal proceedings, the decision made by a jury in a jury trial, or by a judicial officer in a court trial, that a defendant is either guilty or not guilty of the offense(s) for which he or she has been tried.

Verdict, guilty. In criminal proceedings, the decision made by a jury in jury trial, or by a judicial officer in a court trial, that the defendant is guilty of the offense(s) for which he or she has been tried.

Verdict, not guilty. In criminal proceedings, the decision made by a jury in a jury trial, or by a judicial officer in a court trial, or by a judicial officer in court trial, that the defendant is not guilty of the offense(s) for which he or she has been tried.

Victim. A person who has suffered death, physical or mental suffering, or loss of property as the result of an actual or attempted criminal offense committed by another person.

Warrant, arrest. A document issued by a judicial officer that directs a law enforcement officer to arrest a person who has been accused of an offense.

Warrant, bench. A document issued by a judicial officer directing that a person who has failed to obey an order or notice to appear be brought before court.

Warrant, search. A document issued by a judicial officer that directs a law enforcement officer to conduct a search for specified property or persons at a specific location, to seize the property or person, if found, and to account for the results of the search to issuing judicial officer.

Witness. A person who directly perceives an event or thing or who has expert knowledge relevant to a case.

Youthful offender. A person, adjudicated in criminal court, who may be above the statutory age limit for juveniles but is below a specified upper age limit, for whom special correctional commitments and special record sealing procedures are made available by statute.

# Corrections-Related Web Sites

**The American Bar Association's "Facts about the American Criminal Justice System" page**
*http://www.abanet.org/media/factbooks/crimjust.html*

**The American Correctional Association**
*http://www.corrections.com/aca/*

**The American Jail Association**
*http://www.corrections.com/aja/*

**The American Probation and Parole Association**
*http://www.csg.org/appa/*

**The Center for Community Alternatives**
*http://www.dreamscape.com/ccacny/ccahome.htm*

**The Correctional Education Association**
*http://www.metalab.unc.edu/icea/*

**Correctional Services of Canada**
*http://www.csc-scc.gc.ca/*

**The Family and Corrections Network**
*http://www.fcnetwork.org/*

**The Federal Judicial Center**
*http://www.fjc.gov/*

**The Federal Judiciary**
*http://www.uscourts.gov/*

**The International Community Corrections Association**
*http://www.cssnet.com/icca/*

**The Justice Information Center**
*http://www.ncjrs.org/*

**The National Center on Institutions and Alternatives**
*http://www.igc.org/ncia/*

**The National Criminal Justice Association**
*http://www.sso.org/ncja/*

**The National Institute of Corrections Information Center**
*http://www.nicic.org/*

**The National Juvenile Detention Association**
*http://www.corrections.com/njda/index.html*

**The Office of International Criminal Justice**
*http://www.oicj.acsp.uic.edu/spearmint.tocKV.cfm*

**The Prison Issues Desk**
*http://www.igc.apc.org/prisons/*

**The Sentencing Project**
*http://www.sentencingproject.org/*

**The U.S. Department of Justice's Federal Bureau of Prisons, National Institute of Corrections**
*http://www.bop.gov/*

**The U.S. Parole Commission**
*http://www.doj.gov/uspc/parole.htm*

**The U.S. Sentencing Commission**
*http://www.ussc.gov/*

# Name Index

Page numbers followed by "n" indicate that the name appears or is included in a reference.

# Subject Index

Page numbers followed by "n" indicate that the name appears or is included in a reference.

# About the Authors

Harry E. Allen is Professor Emeritus in the Administration of Justice Department at San Jose State University, since 1997. Before joining San Jose State University in 1978, he served as Director of the Program for the Study of Crime and Delinquency at Ohio State University. Previously, he served as Executive Secretary of the Governor's Task Force on Corrections in the state of Ohio, after teaching at Florida State University's School of Criminology.

Professor Allen is the author or co-author of numerous articles, chapters, essays and texts, including *Corrections in America* with Clifford Simonsen. He has been very active in professional associations and is the only criminologist to have served as president of both the American Society of Criminology and the Academy of Criminal Justice Sciences. He received the Herbert Bloch Award for service to the American Society of Criminology and the Founder's Award for contributions to the Academy of Criminal Justice Sciences. He is a Fellow in both the Western and the American Societies of Criminology. Currently, he is working on the ninth edition of *Corrections in America* and is enrolled in a degree program at the Pacific School of Religion.

Edward J. Latessa was born in Youngstown, Ohio, to Amelia and Edward. He was a student of Harry Allen's at The Ohio State University, where he received his Ph.D. in Public Administration in 1979. He joined the faculty at the University of Cincinnati in 1980, where he currently holds the rank of Professor and Head of the Division of Criminal Justice. In 1979-80 he was on the faculty at the University of Alabama at Birmingham. Professor Latessa has written extensively in the area of community corrections, and he has co-authored four books. Dr. Latessa has directed more than 50 funded research projects, including studies of day reporting centers, juvenile justice programs, drug courts, intensive supervision programs, halfway houses, and drug and alcohol programs. In 1989-90, Ed Latessa served as President of the Academy of Criminal Justice Sciences. His work has been recognized by a number of organizations: he is a Fellow in and has received the Founder's Award from ACJS; he received the Simon Dinitz Award from the Ohio Community Corrections Organization; and he was recently awarded the prestigious Peter P. Lejins Award for Research from the American Correctional Association. He also serves as a consultant to a number of correctional agencies, including the National Institute of Corrections. In his spare time he serves as the father of four children.

# J.K. LASSER'S®

# YOUR INCOME TAX 2019

Prepared by the

## J.K. LASSER INSTITUTE™

WILEY

**Staff for This Book**

*J.K. Lasser Editorial*

Elliott Eiss, Member of the New York Bar, *Contributing Editor*
Barbara Weltman, Member of the New York Bar, *Contributing Editor*
Angelo C. Jack, *Production Manager*
William Hamill, *Copyediting and Proofreading*
Index by WordCo Indexing Services

**John Wiley & Sons, Inc.**

John Wiley & Sons, Inc.
111 River Street
Hoboken, NJ 07030

ISBN   978-1-119-53271-2  (paper)
ISBN   978-1-119-53267-5  (ePDF)
ISBN   978-1-119-53270-5  (ePub)

Printed in the United States of America

C10005802_111318

Eighty-Second Edition

# How To Use *Your Income Tax 2019*

**Tax alert symbols.** Throughout the text of *Your Income Tax*, these special symbols alert you to advisory tips about filing your federal tax return and tax planning opportunities:

*Filing tip or Filing Instruction* ........................... A **Filing Tip** or **Filing Instruction** helps you prepare your 2018 return.

*Planning Reminder* ................................... A **Planning Reminder** highlights year-end tax strategies for 2018 or planning opportunities for 2019 and later years.

*Caution* ............................................... A **Caution** points out potential pitfalls to avoid and areas where IRS opposition may be expected.

*Law Alert* ........................................... A **Law Alert** indicates recent changes in the tax law and pending legislation before Congress.

*Court Decision* ...................................... A **Court Decision** highlights key rulings from the Tax Court and other federal courts.

*IRS Alert* ............................................ An **IRS Alert** highlights key rulings and announcements from the IRS.

## Visit *jklasser.com* for FREE download of *e-Supplement*

You can download a free *e-Supplement* to *Your Income Tax 2019* at *jklasser.com*. The *e-Supplement* will provide an update on tax developments from the IRS and Congress, including a look ahead to 2019.

On the homepage at *jklasser.com*, you will find free tax news, tax tips and tax planning articles.

The federal income tax law, despite efforts at simplification, remains a maze of statutes, regulations, rulings, and court decisions written in technical language covering thousands and thousands of pages. For 82 years, *J.K. Lasser's™ Your Income Tax* has aided and guided millions of taxpayers through this complex law. Every effort has been made to provide a direct and easy-to-understand explanation that shows how to comply with the law and at the same time take advantage of tax-saving options and plans.

The 2019 edition of *Your Income Tax*—our 82nd edition—continues this tradition. To make maximum use of this tax guide, we suggest that you use these aids:

**Contents Chapter by Chapter.** The contents, on pages *v–xxv*, lists the chapters in Your Income Tax. References direct you to sections within a particular chapter. Thus a reference to *21.1* directs you to *Chapter 21* and then to section 1 within that chapter. Section and page references are provided in the index at the back of the book.

**What's New for 2018.** Pages *xxvii–xxx* alert you to tax developments that may affect your 2018 tax return.

**Key Tax Numbers for 2018.** Pages *xxxi–xxxiii*.

**Tax-Saving Opportunities.** Page *xxxiv*.

**Filing tax basics.** Pages *1–8* alert you to filing requirements, filing addresses for IRS Service Centers, and a calendar with 2019 filing deadlines.

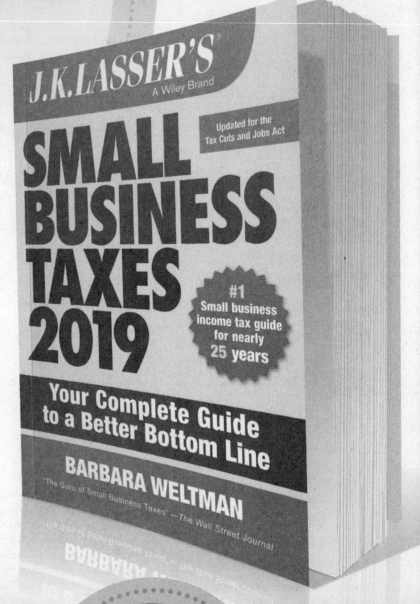

# Contents | Chapter by Chapter

Contents Chapter by Chapter

## Dividend and Interest Income **79**

## Reporting Property Sales **107**

## Retirement and Annuity Income

**170**

## IRAs

**210**

## Income From Real Estate Rentals and Royalties

## Loss Restrictions: Passive Activities and At-Risk Limits  **280**

## Other Income  **310**

## PART 3 • CLAIMING DEDUCTIONS

### Deductions Allowed in Figuring Adjusted Gross Income

### Claiming the Standard Deduction or Itemized Deductions

### Charitable Contribution Deductions

## Itemized Deduction for Interest Expenses — 373

## Deductions for Taxes — 391

## Other Itemized Deductions — 440

## Travel and Meal Expense Deductions — 443

## PART 4 • PERSONAL TAX COMPUTATIONS — 463

## Dependents — 465

## Educational Tax Benefits — 600

## Special Tax Rules for Senior Citizens and the Disabled — 619

**Other Taxes**      **659**

**Gift and Estate Tax Planning Basics**      **667**

**PART 6 • BUSINESS TAX PLANNING**      **675**

**Income or Loss From Your Business or Profession**      **677**

## Retirement and Medical Plans for Self-Employed — 707

## Claiming Depreciation Deductions — 718

## PART 7 • FILING YOUR RETURN AND WHAT HAPPENS AFTER YOU FILE 765

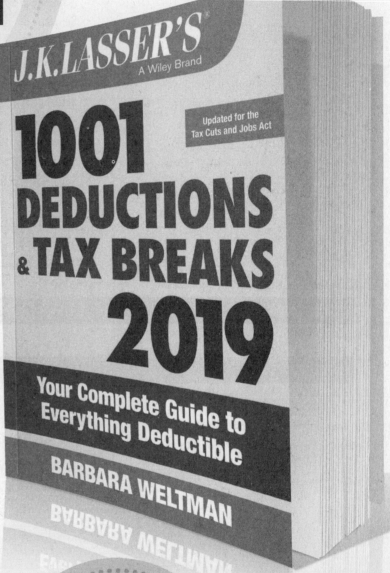

# What's New for 2018

For an update on tax developments and a free download of the *e-Supplement* to this book, visit us online at *jklasser.com*.

**NOTE:** Many of the 2018 items in the table below reflect changes brought about by the Tax Cuts and Jobs Act, such as changes to the tax rate brackets, the standard deductions, AMT, mortgage interest deductions, deductions for state and local taxes, the child tax credit and the new credit for other dependents.

## Tax News for 2018

| Item— | Highlight— |
|---|---|
| **New look for Form 1040** | For 2018, all taxpayers must use Form 1040; Forms 1040A and 1040EZ have been eliminated. Form 1040 has been redesigned and is supplemented by new Schedules 1 through 6 *(page 8)*. |
| **Tax rate brackets and preferential rates for capital gains/qualified dividends** | The rate brackets for 2018 ordinary income are 10%, 12%, 22%, 24%, 32%, 35% and 37%. The top bracket of 37% applies if taxable income exceeds $500,000 for single taxpayers and heads of households, $600,000 for married persons filing jointly and qualifying widows/widowers, and $300,000 for married taxpayers filing separate returns *(1.2)*.<br><br>Qualified dividends *(4.2)* and long-term capital gains *(5.3)* may escape tax entirely under the 0% rate, or be subject to capital gain rates of 15% or 20% depending on filing status, taxable income, and how much of the taxable income consists of qualified dividends and eligible long-term gains *(5.3)*. The 20% capital gain rate applies when taxable income exceeds $425,800 for singles, $452,400 for heads of households, $479,000 for married persons filing jointly and qualifying widows/widowers, and $239,500 for married persons filing separately. The 0%, 15%, and 20% rates do not apply to long-term gains subject to the 28% rate (collectibles and taxed portion of small business stock) or the 25% rate for unrecaptured real estate depreciation *(5.3)*. |
| **Individual health care mandate and premium tax credit** | For 2018, you are required to have minimum essential health coverage through an employer plan, a government program, or other plan, or pay a penalty *(38.5)*, unless you are exempt from this requirement *(38.6)*. The penalty amount for 2018 is the higher of (1) 2.5% of household income above your filing threshold, or (2) $695 per person in your household ($347.50 per dependent child under age 18), up to a maximum of $2,085. The mandate does not apply after 2018.<br><br>To help those of modest means pay premiums for coverage obtained from a government exchange (Marketplace), there's a premium tax credit *(25.13)*. Eligibility for this advanceable, refundable tax credit depends on your household income and other factors. The credit continues to be available even though the individual mandate ends after 2018.<br><br>If you claimed the credit in advance when you obtained coverage for 2018, you have to reconcile what you already applied toward your premiums with what you are actually entitled to; the difference is reported on your tax return *(25.13)*. If you did not receive the credit in advance but are eligible for a credit, you can claim it on your return.<br><br>If you do not claim the premium tax credit and qualify for Trade Adjustment Assistance (TAA), you may qualify for the health coverage tax credit of 72.5% of premiums *(25.14)*. |
| **Standard deductions** | The basic standard deduction for 2018 *(13.1)* is $24,000 for married persons filing jointly and qualifying widows/widowers, $18,000 for heads of households, or $12,000 for single taxpayers or married persons filing separately. These amounts are nearly double what they were for 2017.<br><br>The additional standard deduction *(13.4)* for being 65 or older or blind is $1,600 if single or head of household ($3,200 if 65 and blind). If married filing jointly, the additional standard deduction is $1,300 if one spouse is 65 or older or blind, $2,600 if both spouses are at least 65 (or one is 65 and blind, or both are blind and under age 65). |
| **Personal exemption deductions suspended** | You can no longer claim a personal exemption deduction for yourself, your spouse, or your dependents. |
| **Child tax credit and credit for other dependents** | For 2018, the child tax credit has been significantly increased. The credit amount is up to $2,000 per qualifying child under age 17. This credit is refundable, within limits. What's more, the income limits on eligibility for the credit have been increased *(25.2, 25.3)*.<br><br>There is also a new nonrefundable credit up to $500 for a qualifying dependent who is not a qualifying child *(25.4)*. |

## Tax News for 2018

| Item— | Highlight— |
| --- | --- |
| State and local taxes | There is a cap of $10,000 on the itemized deduction for state and local taxes (income or sales tax, plus real estate taxes) *(16.1)*.<br><br>The IRS has proposed regulations to thwart states from using workarounds to permit residents to get higher charitable deductions from their state and local tax payments *(14.3, 16.1)*. |
| Self-employment tax and deduction for portion of self-employment tax; Social Security wage base | For 2018, the tax rate on the employee portion of Social Security is 6.2% on wages up to $128,400, so Social Security tax withholdings should not exceed $7,960.80. Medicare tax of 1.45% is withheld from all wages regardless of amount.<br><br>On Schedule SE for 2018, self-employment tax of 15.3% applies to earnings of up to $128,400 after the earnings are reduced by 7.65%. The 15.3% rate equals 12.4% for Social Security (6.2% employee share and 6.2% employer share) plus 2.9% for Medicare. If net earnings exceed $128,400, the 2.9% Medicare rate applies to the entire amount *(45.3–45.4)*. One half of the self-employment tax may be claimed as an above-the-line deduction on Schedule 1 of Form 1040 *(45.3–45.4)*. |
| IRA and Roth IRA contribution phaseout; rollover limits | For 2018, the contribution limit for traditional IRAs *(8.2)* and Roth IRAs *(8.20)* is unchanged at $5,500, or $6,500 for those age 50 or older.<br><br>The deduction limit for 2018 contributions to a traditional IRA is phased out *(8.4)* for active plan participants with modified AGI (MAGI) between $63,000 and $73,000 for a single person or head of household, or between $101,000 and $121,000 for married persons filing jointly and qualifying widows/widowers. The phaseout range is MAGI between $189,000 and $199,000 for a spouse who is not an active plan participant and who files jointly with a spouse who is an active plan participant.<br><br>The 2018 Roth IRA contribution limit is phased out *(8.20)* for a single person or head of household with MAGI between $120,000 and $135,000, and for married persons filing jointly and qualifying widows/widowers with MAGI between $189,000 and $199,000.<br><br>If you converted your traditional IRA to a Roth IRA in 2018, you cannot undo it; the conversion is permanent *(8.10)*. |
| Qualified business income deduction | If you are a sole proprietor or have an interest in a partnership, limited liability company, or S corporation, you may be eligible for a deduction of up to 20% of qualified business income *(40.24)*. This deduction is a personal deduction, not a business deduction, and can be claimed whether you itemize or take the standard deduction. |
| First-year expensing | For qualifying property placed in service in 2018, first-year expensing *(42.3)* is allowed up to a limit of $1 million, and the limit begins to phase out if the total cost of qualifying property exceeds $2.5 million *(42.3)*. |
| Bonus depreciation | Bonus depreciation allows a 100% writeoff for the cost of qualifying property acquired and placed in service after September 27, 2018 *(42.18)*. |
| IRS mileage allowance | The IRS standard business mileage rate for 2018 is 54.5 cents a mile *(43.1)*.<br><br>The rate for medical expense *(17.9)* and moving expense for certain military personnel *(12.3)* deductions is 18 cents a mile.<br><br>For charitable volunteers *(14.4)*, the mileage rate is unchanged at 14 cents a mile. |
| Vehicle depreciation limit | For a vehicle placed in service in 2018 and used over 50% for business, bonus depreciation increases the first-year depreciation limit by $8,000 to $18,000. However, if you elect not to have bonus depreciation apply, or you are not eligible for the bonus, the first-year depreciation limit is $10,000 *(43.5)*. |
| Health savings accounts (HSAs) | The definition of a high-deductible health plan, which is a prerequisite to funding an HSA, means a policy with a minimum deductible for 2018 of $1,350 for self-only coverage and a maximum out-of-pocket cap on co-payments and other amounts of $6,650. These limits are doubled for family coverage ($2,700/$13,300) *(41.10)*.<br><br>The contribution limit for 2018 is $3,450 for self-only coverage and $6,900 for family coverage *(41.11)*. |

## Tax News for 2018

| Item— | Highlight— |
|---|---|
| Adoption expenses | For 2018, the limit on the adoption credit as well as the exclusion for employer-paid adoption assistance is $13,810. The benefit phaseout range is modified adjusted gross income between $207,140 to $247,140 *(25.9)*. |
| Earned income tax credit | For 2018, the maximum credit amount is $3,461 for one qualifying child, $5,716 for two qualifying children, $6,431 for three or more qualifying children, and $519 for taxpayers who have no qualifying child *(25.7)*. The phaseout ranges for the credit have been adjusted for inflation *(25.8)*. |
| Alternative minimum tax (AMT) exemption and tax brackets | The AMT exemptions, exemption phaseout thresholds, and the dividing line between the 26% and 28% AMT brackets are adjusted for inflation. The 2018 AMT exemptions (prior to any phaseout) are $109,400 for married couples filing jointly and qualifying widows/widowers, $70,300 for single persons and heads of households, and $54,700 for married persons filing separately. *See 23.1* for exemption phaseout rules and AMT calculation details.<br><br>All nonrefundable personal credits for may be claimed against the AMT as well as the regular tax *(23.3)*. |
| Eligibility for saver's credit | The adjusted gross income brackets for the 10%, 20%, and 50% credits are increased for 2018. No credit is allowed when AGI exceeds $31,500 for single taxpayers, $47,250 for heads of households, and $63,000 for married persons filing jointly. ABLE account contributions can now qualify for the credit *(25.12)*. |
| Mortgage interest | The deduction for mortgage interest on a principal residence and second residence is limited to acquisition debt up to $750,000 ($375,000 for married persons filing separately) for loans acquired after December 15, 2017 *(15.2)*.<br><br>No deduction is allowed for interest on home equity debt, regardless of when the loan was obtained. However, this bar does not apply to the extent proceeds are used to buy, build, or substantially improve the home that secures the loan *(15.3)*. |
| Charitable contributions | Cash contributions are limited to 60% of adjusted gross income (AGI) in 2018 (compared with 50% in 2017) *(14.17)*. |
| Casualty and theft losses | For 2018, only casualty and theft losses of personal-use property occurring in a federally declared disaster are deductible *(18.1)*. The usual $100 and 10%-of-AGI limits continue to apply. |
| Deduction limits for long-term care premiums | The maximum amount of age-based long-term care premiums that can be included as deductible medical expenses for 2018 (subject to the AGI floor; *see 17.1*) is $420 if you are age 40 or younger at the end of 2018; $780 for those age 41 through 50; $1,560 for those age 51 through 60; $4,160 for those age 61 through 70; and $5,200 for those over age 70 *(17.15)*. |
| Tax breaks that expired at the end of 2017 but could be extended retroactively for 2018 | Numerous tax breaks that expired at the end of 2017 had not been extended for 2018 when this book was completed, but it remains possible that Congress might retroactively authorize an extension in late 2018 or early 2019 legislation. These provisions include:<br>The above-the-line deduction for tuition and fees *(33.12)*.<br>The itemized deduction for mortgage insurance premiums *(15.5)*.<br>The exclusion for canceled principal residence indebtedness *(11.8)*.<br>The tax credit for home insulation, storm windows, and other energy improvements *(25.15)*.<br>*See* the *e-Supplement* at *jklasser.com* for a legislation update. |
| Foreign earned income and housing exclusions | The maximum foreign earned income exclusion for 2018 is $103,900 *(36.1)*. The limit on housing expenses that may be taken into account in figuring the housing exclusion is generally $31,170, but the limit is increased by the IRS for high cost localities *(36.4)*. |
| Annual gift tax exclusion; Gift tax and estate tax exemption | The annual gift tax exclusion increases to $15,000 per donee for 2018 gifts of cash or present interests *(39.2)*. The basic exemption amount for 2018 gift tax and estate tax purposes is $11,180,000 *(39.4, 39.9)*. The top tax rate remains at 40% *(39.9)*. |

## Tax News for 2018

| Item— | Highlight— |
| --- | --- |
| **529 plans and ABLE accounts** | Distributions from 529 plans to pay tuition in primary and secondary school up to $10,000 is not a taxable distribution *(33.6)*.<br><br>Distributions from 529 plans can be rolled over tax free to ABLE accounts (up to annual contribution limits). Also annual contributions to ABLE accounts can be increased under certain circumstances *(34.12)*. |
| **Tax-free exchanges** | The opportunity to postpone tax on gain through a tax-free exchange is restricted to real property. For exchanges in 2018 and beyond, the tax-free exchange rule does not apply to exchanges of personal property (e.g., the trade in of a truck used for business) *(6.1)*. |
| **Kiddie tax** | Children with unearned income above $2,100 pay tax on it using the tax rates applicable to trusts and estates. The tax on this unearned income is no longer figured using the top rates of the parents *(24.3)*. |
| **Tax breaks no longer allowed** | The Tax Cuts and Jobs Act suspended or repealed certain tax rules. The following are not applicable to 2018 returns:<br>Personal and dependency exemptions<br>Moving expense deduction (other than for certain military personnel)<br>Exclusion for bicycle commuting<br>Miscellaneous itemized deductions subject to the 2%-of-adjusted-gross-income floor<br>Phaseout of itemized deductions |

## Key Tax Numbers for 2018

### Standard Deduction   (13.1)

| | |
|---|---|
| Joint return/Qualifying widow/widower | $ 24,000 |
| Head of Household | $ 18,000 |
| Single | $12,000 |
| Married filing separately | $12,000 |
| Dependents--minimum deduction  (13.5) | $ 1,050 |

Additional deduction if age 65 or older, or blind  (13.4)

| | |
|---|---|
| Married-per spouse, filing jointly or separately | $ 1,300 ($2,600 for age and blindness) |
| Qualifying widow/widower | $ 1,300 ($2,600 for age and blindness) |
| Single or head of household | $ 1,600 ($3,200 for age and blindness) |

### Long-term Care Premiums   (17.15)

Limit on premium allowed as medical expense

| | |
|---|---|
| Age 40 or under | $ 420 |
| Over 40 but not over 50 | $ 780 |
| Over 50 but not over 60 | $ 1,560 |
| Over 60 but not over 70 | $ 4,160 |
| Over 70 | $ 5,200 |

### IRA Contributions

| | |
|---|---|
| Traditional IRA contribution limit  (8.2) | $ 5,500 |
| Additional contribution if age 50 or older but under 70½ | $ 1,000 |

Deduction phaseout for active plan participant  (8.4)

| | |
|---|---|
| Single or head of household | $ 63,000 – $ 72,000 |
| Married filing jointly, two participants | $ 101,000 – $ 121,000 |
| Married filing jointly, one participant | |
| Participant spouse | $ 101,000 – $ 121,000 |
| Non-participant spouse | $ 189,000 – $ 199,000 |
| Married filing separately, live together, either participates | $ 0 – $ 10,000 |
| Married filing separately, live apart all year | |
| Participant spouse | $ 63,000 – $ 73,000 |
| Non-participant spouse | no phaseout |

## Key Tax Numbers for 2018

| | |
|---|---|
| Roth IRA contribution limit *(8.20)* | $ 5,500 |
| Additional contribution if age 50 or older | $ 1,000 |
| Contribution limit phaseout range | |
| Single, head of household | $ 120,000–$ 135,000 |
| Married filing separately, live apart all year | $ 120,000–$ 135,000 |
| Married filing jointly, or qualifying widow/widower | $ 189,000–$ 199,000 |
| Married filing separately, live together at any time | $ 0–$ 10,000 |

### Elective deferral limits

| | |
|---|---|
| 401(k), 403(b), 457 plans *(7.16)* | $ 18,500 |
| Salary-reduction SEP *(8.16)* | $ 18,500 |
| SIMPLE IRA *(8.17)* | $ 12,500 |
| Additional contribution if age 50 or older ("catch-up" contributions) | |
| 401(k), 403(b), governmental 457 and SEP plans *(7.16, 8.16)* | $ 6,000 |
| SIMPLE IRA *(8.17)* | $ 3,000 |

### Education

| | |
|---|---|
| American Opportunity credit limit-per student *(33.8)* | $2,500 |
| Lifetime Learning credit limit-per taxpayer *(33.9)* | $2,000 |
| Phaseout of American Opportunity credit *(33.8)* | |
| Married filing jointly | $ 160,000–$ 180,000 |
| Single, head of household, or qualifying widow/widower | $80,000–$ 90,000 |
| Phaseout of Lifetime Learning credit *(33.9)* | |
| Married filing jointly | $ 114,000–$ 134,000 |
| Single, head of household, or qualifying widow/widower | $ 57,000–$ 67,000 |
| Student loan interest deduction limit *(33.13)* | $2,500 |
| Phaseout of deduction limit | |
| Married filing jointly | $135,000–$165,000 |
| Single, head of household, or qualifying widow/widower | $65,000–$80,000 |
| Coverdell ESA limit *(33.10)* | $2,000 |
| Phaseout of limit | |
| Married filing jointly | $190,000–$220,000 |
| All others | $95,000–$110,000 |

## Key Tax Numbers for 2018

Tuition and fees deduction (if extended to 2018 by Congress; *(33.12)*)

| | |
|---|---|
| Tuition and fees deduction: tier 1 limit income cut-off | $4,000 |
| • Married filing jointly | $130,000 |
| • Single, head of household, or qualifying widow/widower | $65,000 |
| Tuition and fees deduction: tier 2 limit income cut-off | $2,000 |
| • Married filing jointly | $160,000 |
| • Single, head of household, or qualifying widow/widower | $80,000 |

### Capital gain rates—assets held over one year    *(5.3)*

| | |
|---|---|
| If taxable income is no more than $77,200 for married filing jointly and surviving spouses, $51,700 for heads of households, or $38,600 for singles and married filing separately: | 0% |
| If taxable income is above the threshold for the zero rate but no more than the threshold for the 20% rate | 15% |
| If taxable income exceeds $479,000 for married filing jointly and surviving spouses, $452,400 for heads of households, $425,800 for singles, and $239,500 for married filing separately: | 20% |
| Collectibles gain-maximum rate | 28% |
| Unrecaptured Section 1250 gain on depreciated real estate-maximum rate | 25% |

### Qualified dividends tax rate    *(4.2)*

| | |
|---|---|
| *See* the taxable income breakpoints for capital gain rates above | 0%, 15%, or 20% |

### IRS mileage rates

| | |
|---|---|
| Business *(43.1)* | 54.5 cents/mile |
| Medical *(17.9)* and moving for military personnel *(12.3)* | 18 cents/mile. |
| Charitable volunteers *(14.4)* | 14 cents/mile |

### Exclusion for employer provided transportation    *(3.8)*

| | |
|---|---|
| Free parking, transit passes, and van pooling | $260/month |

## Tax-Saving Opportunities for 2018

| Objective— | Explanation— |
|---|---|
| Realizing long-term capital gains | Long-term capital gains are taxed at lower rates than short-term gains and regular income. See *Chapter 5* for basic capital gain rules. See Chapters 30 and 31 for discussions of special investment situations. |
| Earning qualifying dividends | Qualified dividends *(4.2)* are subject to the reduced tax rates for long-term capital gains. |
| Earning tax-free income | You can earn tax-free income by—<br>1. Investing in tax-exempt securities. However, before you invest, determine whether the tax-free return will exceed the after-tax return of taxed income *(30.10)*.<br>2. Taking a position in a company that pays tax-free fringe benefits, such as health and life insurance protection. For a complete discussion of tax-free fringe benefits, *see Chapter 3*.<br>3. Seeking tax-free education benefits with scholarship arrangements, qualified tuition programs and Coverdell ESAs; *see Chapter 33*.<br>4. Taking a position overseas to earn excludable foreign earned income; *see Chapter 36*.<br>5. Investing in Roth IRAs; *see Chapter 8*. |
| Deferring income | You can defer income to years when you will pay less tax through—<br>1. Deferred pay plans, which are discussed in *Chapter 2*.<br>2. Qualified retirement plans such as 401(k) plans *(Chapter 7)*, self-employed plan *(Chapter 41)*, and traditional IRA and Roth IRA plans *(Chapter 8)*.<br>3. Transacting installment sales when you sell property; *see 5.21*.<br>4. Investing in U.S. Savings EE bonds or I-bonds *(4.28–4.29, 30.12–30.13)*. |
| Income splitting | Through income splitting you divide your income among several persons or taxpaying entities that will pay an aggregate tax lower than the tax that you would pay if you reported all of the income. Although the tax law limits income-splitting opportunities, certain business and family income planning through the use of trusts and custodian accounts can provide tax savings; *see* Chapters 24 and 39. |
| Tax-free exchanges | You can defer tax on appreciated property by transacting tax-free exchanges of realty *(6.1, 31.3)*. |
| Buying a personal residence | Homeowners are favored by the tax law.<br>1. If you buy a home, condominium, or cooperative apartment, you may deduct mortgage interest *(15.2)* and taxes *(16.4)*. When you sell your principal residence, you may be able to avoid tax on gains of up to $250,000 if single and up to $500,000 if married filing jointly; *see Chapter 29*.<br>2. Homeowners can borrow on their home equity and deduct interest expenses within limits *(15.3)*. |
| Take advantage of special personal tax breaks for education | The tax law provides several breaks for education expenses; *see Chapter 33*, which discusses scholarships, grants, tuition plans, savings bond tuition plans, education credits, Coverdell Education Savings Accounts, and student loan interest deduction. |
| Take advantage of special tax breaks for health care expenses | The tax law provides several breaks for health care expenses. Employer-provided health and accident plans, including flexible spending arrangements, are discussed in *Chapter 3*. Health savings accounts (HSAs) can be used to save for health care expenses on a tax-free basis *(3.2, 41.10)*. ABLE accounts can be set up for individuals who become disabled before age 26 persons and be used to build up a fund from which tax-free distributions for qualified expenses can be made *(34.12)*. You may be able to qualify for the premium tax credit to help offset the cost of premiums for coverage obtained through the government Marketplace *(25.13)*. |
| Take advantage of personal tax credits | See *Chapter 25* for personal tax credits such as the premium tax credit, child tax credit, dependent care credit, saver's credit and adoption credit that can reduce your tax liability. |

# PART 1

# Filing Basics

In this part, you will learn these income tax basics:

- Whether you must file a return
- When and where to file your return
- Which tax form to file
- What filing status you qualify for
- When filing separately is an advantage for married persons
- How to qualify as head of household
- How filing rules for resident aliens and nonresident aliens differ
- How to claim personal exemption deductions for yourself, your spouse, and your dependents.

## Do You Have to File a 2018 Tax Return?

| If you are— | You must file if gross income for 2018 is at least |
|---|---|
| **Single** | |
| Under age 65 (on January 1, 2019) | $ 12,000 |
| Age 65 or older (on or before January 1, 2019) | 13,600 |
| **Married and living together at the end of 2018** | |
| Filing a joint return—both spouses under age 65 (on January 1, 2019) | $24,000 |
| Filing a joint return—one spouse age 65 or older (on or before January 1, 2019) | 25,300 |
| Filing a joint return—both spouses age 65 or older (on or before January 1, 2019) | 26,600 |
| Filing a separate return for 2018 (regardless of age) | $5 |
| **Married and living apart at the end of 2018** | |
| Filing a joint or separate return (regardless of age) | $5 |
| **Head of a household maintained for a child or other relative** *(1.12)* | |
| Under age 65 (on January 1, 2019) | $18,000 |
| Age 65 or older  (on or before January 1, 2019) | 19,600 |
| **Widowed in 2016 or 2017 and have a dependent child** *(1.11)* | |
| Under age 65 (on January 1, 2019) | 24,000 |
| Age 65 or older (on or before January 1, 2019) | 25,300 |

**Age 65.** Whether you are age 65 or older is generally determined as of the end of the year, but if your 65th birthday is on January 1, 2019, you are treated as being age 65 at the end of 2018.

**Marital status.** For 2018 returns, marital status is generally determined as of December 31, 2018. Thus, if you were divorced or legally separated during 2018, you are not considered married for 2018 tax purposes, and you must use the filing threshold for single persons unless you qualify as a head of household *(1.12)*, or you remarried in 2018 and are filing a joint return with your new spouse.

If your spouse died in 2018 and you were living together on the date of death, use the filing threshold shown for married persons living together at the end of 2018. If you were not living together on the date of death, you must file a 2018 return if you have gross income of at least $5, unless you remarried during 2018 and are filing jointly with your new spouse.

**Same-sex marriages.** Lawfully married same-sex couples are treated as married for all federal tax purposes. The IRS recognizes your marriage to a same-sex spouse if the marriage was legally entered into in one of the 50 States, the District of Columbia, Puerto Rico, U.S. territory or possession, or foreign country *(1.1)*.

**Gross income.** Gross income is generally all the income that you received in 2018, except for items specifically exempt from tax.

*Include* wages and tips *(Chapter 2)*, self-employment income *(Chapter 45)*, taxable scholarships *(Chapter 33)*, taxable interest and dividends *(Chapter 4)*, capital gains *(Chapter 5)*, taxable pensions and annuities *(Chapter 7)*, rents *(Chapter 9)*, and trust distributions *(Chapter 11)*. Home sale proceeds that are tax free *(Chapter 29)* and tax-free foreign earned income *(Chapter 36)* are considered gross income for purposes of the filing test.

*Exclude* tax-exempt interest *(Chapter 4)*, tax-free fringe benefits *(Chapter 3)*, qualifying scholarships *(Chapter 33)*, and life insurance *(Chapter 11)*. Also exclude Social Security benefits unless (1) you are married filing separately and you lived with your spouse at any time during 2018, or (2) 50% of net Social Security benefits plus other gross income and any tax-exempt interest exceeds $25,000 ($32,000 if married filing jointly). If 1 or 2 applies, the taxable part of Social Security benefits (as determined in *34.3*) is included in your gross income.

**Other situations when you must file.** Even if you are not required to file under the gross income tests, you must file a 2018 return if:

- You are self-employed and you owe self-employment tax because your net self-employment earnings for 2018 are $400 or more *(Chapter 45)*, or
- You (or your spouse if filing jointly) received HSA or Archer MSA distributions *(Chapter 41)*, or
- You are entitled to a refund of taxes withheld from your wages *(Chapter 26)* or a refund based on any of these credits: the premium tax credit, the earned income credit for working families, the additional child tax credit *(Chapter 25)*, or the American Opportunity credit *(Chapter 38)*, or
- You owe any special tax such as alternative minimum tax *(Chapter 23)*, the Additional Medicare Tax or the Net Investment Income Tax *(Chapter 28)*, IRA penalties *(Chapter 8)*, household employment taxes *(Chapter 38)*, and FICA on tips *(Chapter 26)*, or
- You received advance payments of the premium tax credit *(25.12)*, or you owe the individual responsibility penalty *(38.5)*.

## Filing Tests for Dependents: 2018 Returns

The income threshold for filing a tax return is generally lower for an individual who may be claimed as a dependent than for a nondependent. You are a "dependent" if you are the qualifying child or qualifying relative of another taxpayer, and the other tests for dependents at *(21.1)* are met. If you are the parent of a dependent child who had only investment income subject to the "kiddie tax" *(24.3)*, you may elect to report the child's income on your own return for 2018 instead of filing a separate return for the child; see *(24.4)* for the election rules.

If, under the tests at *(21.1)*, you may be claimed as a dependent by someone else, use the chart below to determine if you must file a 2018 return. Include as unearned income taxable interest and dividends, capital gains, pensions, annuities, unemployment compensation, taxable Social Security benefits, and distributions of unearned income from a trust. Earned income includes wages, tips, self-employment income, and taxable scholarships or fellowships *(Chapter 33)*. Gross income is the total of unearned and earned income.

For married dependents, the filing requirements in the chart assume that the dependent is filing a separate return and not a joint return *(Chapter 1)*. Generally, a married person who files a joint return may not be claimed as a dependent by a third party who provides support.

For purposes of the following chart, a person is treated as being age 65 (or older) if his or her 65th birthday is on or before January 1, 2019. Blindness is determined as of December 31, 2018.

*Filing Instruction*

**File for Refund of Withholdings**

Even if you are not required to file a return under the income tests on this page, you should file to obtain a refund of federal tax withholdings.

### File a Return for 2018 If You Are a—

**Single dependent.** Were you either age 65 or older or blind?

❏ **No.** You must file a return if any of the following apply.
- Your unearned income was over $1,050.
- Your earned income was over $12,000.
- Your gross income was more than the larger of—
  - $1,050, or
  - Your earned income (up to $11,650) plus $350.

❏ **Yes.** You must file a return if any of the following apply.
- Your unearned income was over $2,650 ($4,250 if 65 or older and blind).
- Your earned income was over $13,600 ($15,200 if 65 or older and blind).
- Your gross income was more than the larger of—
  - $2,650 ($4,250 if 65 or older and blind), or
  - Your earned income (up to $11,650) plus $1,950 ($3,550 if 65 or older and blind).

**Married dependent.** Were you either age 65 or older or blind?

❏ **No.** You must file a return if any of the following apply.
- Your unearned income was over $1,050.
- Your earned income was over $12,000.
- Your gross income was at least $5 and your spouse files a separate return and itemizes deductions.
- Your gross income was more than the larger of—
  - $1,050, or
  - Your earned income (up to $11,650) plus $350.

❏ **Yes.** You must file a return if any of the following apply.
- Your unearned income was over $2,350 ($3,650 if 65 or older and blind).
- Your earned income was over $13,300 ($14,600 if 65 or older and blind).
- Your gross income was at least $5 and your spouse files a separate return and itemizes deductions.
- Your gross income was more than the larger of—
  - $2,350 ($3,650 if 65 or older and blind), or
  - Your earned income (up to $11,650) plus $1,650 ($2,950 if 65 or older and blind).

## Where to File Your 2018 Form 1040

If you filed a paper federal tax return for 2017 and are filing a paper Form 1040 for 2018, check the 2018 Form 1040 instructions to *see* if the IRS filing address for your residence has changed. If the IRS makes late changes to the table below, the changes will be in the *e-Supplement* at *jklasser.com*.

When you file, include your complete return address and if you are enclosing numerous attachments with your return, make sure that you include enough postage.

You can use a private delivery service designated by the IRS to meet the "timely mailing is timely filing/paying" rule *(46.2)*. Only the specific services from FedEx, DHL Express, and UPS that the IRS has designated qualify; the Form 1040 instructions has a list of these services.

## Where Do You File Form 1040?

| IF you live in... | THEN use this address if you: | |
|---|---|---|
| | Are requesting a refund or are not enclosing a check or money order... | Are enclosing a check or money order... |
| Alabama, Georgia, Kentucky, New Jersey, North Carolina, South Carolina, Tennessee, Virginia | Department of the Treasury Internal Revenue Service Kansas City, MO 64999-0002 | Internal Revenue Service P.O. Box 931000 Louisville, KY 40293-1000 |
| Alaska, Arizona, California, Colorado, Hawaii, Idaho, Nevada, New Mexico, Oregon, Utah, Washington, Wyoming | Department of the Treasury Internal Revenue Service Fresno, CA 93888-0002 | Internal Revenue Service P.O. Box 7704 San Francisco, CA 94120-7704 |
| Arkansas, Illinois, Indiana, Iowa, Kansas, Michigan, Minnesota, Montana, Nebraska, North Dakota, Ohio, Oklahoma, South Dakota, Wisconsin | Department of the Treasury Internal Revenue Service Fresno, CA 93888-0002 | Internal Revenue Service P.O. Box 802501 Cincinnati, OH 45280-2501 |
| Connecticut, District of Columbia, Maryland, Pennsylvania, Rhode Island, West Virginia | Department of the Treasury Internal Revenue Service Ogden, UT 84201-0002 | Internal Revenue Service P.O. Box 37910 Hartford, CT 06176-7910 |
| Delaware, Maine, Massachusetts, Missouri, New Hampshire, New York, Vermont | Department of the Treasury Internal Revenue Service Kansas City, MO 64999-0002 | Internal Revenue Service P.O. Box 37008 Hartford, CT 06176-7008 |
| Florida, Louisiana, Mississippi, Texas | Department of the Treasury Internal Revenue Service Austin, TX 73301-0002 | Internal Revenue Service P.O. Box 1214 Charlotte, NC 28201-1214 |
| A foreign country, U.S. possession or territory*, or use an APO or FPO address, or file Form 2555, 2555-EZ, or 4563, or are a dual-status alien | Department of the Treasury Internal Revenue Service Austin, TX 73301-0215 | Internal Revenue Service P.O. Box 1303 Charlotte, NC 28201-1303 |

*If you live in American Samoa, Puerto Rico, Guam, the U.S. Virgin Islands, or the Northern Mariana Islands, see Pub. 570.

## Filing Deadlines (on or before)

**January 15, 2019** — Pay the balance of your 2018 estimated tax. If you do not meet this date, you may avoid an estimated tax penalty for the last quarter by filing your 2018 return and paying the balance due by January 31, 2019.

*Farmers and fishermen:* File your single 2018 estimated tax payment by January 15, 2019. If you do not, you may still avoid an estimated tax penalty by filing a final tax return and paying the full tax by March 1, 2019.

**January 31, 2019** — Make sure you have received a Form W-2 from each employer for whom you worked in 2018.

**April 15 or 17, 2019** — Unless you live in Maine or Massachusetts, you have until Monday, April 15, 2019, to file your 2018 return and pay the balance of your 2018 tax liability. If you live in Maine or Massachusetts, you have until Wednesday, April 17, 2019, to file and pay your tax because Patriots' Day (a legal holiday in these states) falls on Monday April 15, and Emancipation Day, a legal holiday in the District of Columbia, falls on Tuesday, April 16. 2019.

If you cannot meet the April 15 or April 17 deadline for your 2018 return, you may obtain an automatic six-month filing extension to October 15 by filing Form 4868 (electronically or on paper). However, even if you get an extension, interest will still be charged for taxes not paid by the original deadline (April 15 or 17) and late payment penalties will be imposed unless at least 90% of your tax liability is paid by the original deadline or you otherwise show reasonable cause. If you cannot pay the full amount of tax you owe when you file your return, you can file Form 9465 to request an installment payment arrangement.

If on the April 15/17 deadline you are a U.S. citizen or resident alien living and working outside the U.S. or Puerto Rico, or in military service outside the U.S. or Puerto Rico, you have an automatic two-month extension (you don't have to request an extension), until June 17, 2019, for filing your 2018 return and paying any balance due . However, despite the extension to June 17, interest is still charged on payments made after the original due date.

Pay the first installment of your 2019 estimated tax on or before your April 15 or April 17 due date.

**June 17, 2019** — Pay the second installment of your 2019 estimated tax. You may amend an earlier estimate at this time.

You have until this date to file your 2018 return and pay any balance due if on April 15 (April 17 if you live in Maine or Massachusetts) you were a U.S. citizen or resident living and working outside the U.S. or Puerto Rico, or in military service outside the U.S. or Puerto Rico; however, interest will be charged on payments made after the original due date. If you qualify for this out- of- the-country extension but cannot file by June 17, you may obtain an additional four-month filing extension until October 15 by filing Form 4868; this additional extension to October 15 is for filing but not for payment, so interest will be charged for taxes not paid by June 17 and late payment penalties could be imposed.

If you are a nonresident alien who did not have tax withheld from your wages, file Form 1040NR by this date and pay the balance due.

**September 16, 2019** — Pay the third installment of your 2019 estimated tax. You may amend an earlier estimate at this time.

**October 15, 2019** — File your 2018 return if you received an automatic six-month filing extension using Form 4868. Also file your 2018 return and pay the balance due if on April 15 (April 17 if you live in Maine or Massachusetts) you were a U.S. citizen or resident living and working outside the U.S. or Puerto Rico, or in military service outside the U.S. or Puerto Rico, and by June 17 you obtained an additional four-month filing extension by filing Form 4868.

**December 31, 2019** — If self-employed, a qualified retirement plan for 2019 must be set up by this date.

**January 15, 2020** — Pay the balance of your 2019 estimated tax.

**April 15, 2020** — File your 2019 return and pay the balance of your tax. Pay the first installment of your 2020 estimated tax by this date.

**15th day of the 4th month after the fiscal year ends** — File your fiscal year return and pay the balance of the tax due. If you cannot meet the filing deadline, apply for an automatic four-month filing extension on Form 4868.

## 2019

### JANUARY
| S | M | T | W | T | F | S |
|---|---|---|---|---|---|---|
|   |   | 1 | 2 | 3 | 4 | 5 |
| 6 | 7 | 8 | 9 | 10 | 11 | 12 |
| 13 | 14 | 15 | 16 | 17 | 18 | 19 |
| 20 | 21 | 22 | 23 | 24 | 25 | 26 |
| 27 | 28 | 29 | 30 | 31 |   |   |

### FEBRUARY
| S | M | T | W | T | F | S |
|---|---|---|---|---|---|---|
|   |   |   |   |   | 1 | 2 |
| 3 | 4 | 5 | 6 | 7 | 8 | 9 |
| 10 | 11 | 12 | 13 | 14 | 15 | 16 |
| 17 | 18 | 19 | 20 | 21 | 22 | 23 |
| 24 | 25 | 26 | 27 | 28 |   |   |

### MARCH
| S | M | T | W | T | F | S |
|---|---|---|---|---|---|---|
|   |   |   |   |   | 1 | 2 |
| 3 | 4 | 5 | 6 | 7 | 8 | 9 |
| 10 | 11 | 12 | 13 | 14 | 15 | 16 |
| 17 | 18 | 19 | 20 | 21 | 22 | 23 |
| 24 | 25 | 26 | 27 | 28 | 29 | 30 |
| 31 |   |   |   |   |   |   |

### APRIL
| S | M | T | W | T | F | S |
|---|---|---|---|---|---|---|
|   | 1 | 2 | 3 | 4 | 5 | 6 |
| 7 | 8 | 9 | 10 | 11 | 12 | 13 |
| 14 | 15 | 16 | 17 | 18 | 19 | 20 |
| 21 | 22 | 23 | 24 | 25 | 26 | 27 |
| 28 | 29 | 30 |   |   |   |   |

### MAY
| S | M | T | W | T | F | S |
|---|---|---|---|---|---|---|
|   |   |   | 1 | 2 | 3 | 4 |
| 5 | 6 | 7 | 8 | 9 | 10 | 11 |
| 12 | 13 | 14 | 15 | 16 | 17 | 18 |
| 19 | 20 | 21 | 22 | 23 | 24 | 25 |
| 26 | 27 | 28 | 29 | 30 | 31 |   |

### JUNE
| S | M | T | W | T | F | S |
|---|---|---|---|---|---|---|
|   |   |   |   |   |   | 1 |
| 2 | 3 | 4 | 5 | 6 | 7 | 8 |
| 9 | 10 | 11 | 12 | 13 | 14 | 15 |
| 16 | 17 | 18 | 19 | 20 | 21 | 22 |
| 23 | 24 | 25 | 26 | 27 | 28 | 29 |
| 30 |   |   |   |   |   |   |

### JULY
| S | M | T | W | T | F | S |
|---|---|---|---|---|---|---|
|   | 1 | 2 | 3 | 4 | 5 | 6 |
| 7 | 8 | 9 | 10 | 11 | 12 | 13 |
| 14 | 15 | 16 | 17 | 18 | 19 | 20 |
| 21 | 22 | 23 | 24 | 25 | 26 | 27 |
| 28 | 29 | 30 | 31 |   |   |   |

### AUGUST
| S | M | T | W | T | F | S |
|---|---|---|---|---|---|---|
|   |   |   |   | 1 | 2 | 3 |
| 4 | 5 | 6 | 7 | 8 | 9 | 10 |
| 11 | 12 | 13 | 14 | 15 | 16 | 17 |
| 18 | 19 | 20 | 21 | 22 | 23 | 24 |
| 25 | 26 | 27 | 28 | 29 | 30 | 31 |

### SEPTEMBER
| S | M | T | W | T | F | S |
|---|---|---|---|---|---|---|
| 1 | 2 | 3 | 4 | 5 | 6 | 7 |
| 8 | 9 | 10 | 11 | 12 | 13 | 14 |
| 15 | 16 | 17 | 18 | 19 | 20 | 21 |
| 22 | 23 | 24 | 25 | 26 | 27 | 28 |
| 29 | 30 |   |   |   |   |   |

### OCTOBER
| S | M | T | W | T | F | S |
|---|---|---|---|---|---|---|
|   |   | 1 | 2 | 3 | 4 | 5 |
| 6 | 7 | 8 | 9 | 10 | 11 | 12 |
| 13 | 14 | 15 | 16 | 17 | 18 | 19 |
| 20 | 21 | 22 | 23 | 24 | 25 | 26 |
| 27 | 28 | 29 | 30 | 31 |   |   |

### NOVEMBER
| S | M | T | W | T | F | S |
|---|---|---|---|---|---|---|
|   |   |   |   |   | 1 | 2 |
| 3 | 4 | 5 | 6 | 7 | 8 | 9 |
| 10 | 11 | 12 | 13 | 14 | 15 | 16 |
| 17 | 18 | 19 | 20 | 21 | 22 | 23 |
| 24 | 25 | 26 | 27 | 28 | 29 | 30 |

### DECEMBER
| S | M | T | W | T | F | S |
|---|---|---|---|---|---|---|
| 1 | 2 | 3 | 4 | 5 | 6 | 7 |
| 8 | 9 | 10 | 11 | 12 | 13 | 14 |
| 15 | 16 | 17 | 18 | 19 | 20 | 21 |
| 22 | 23 | 24 | 25 | 26 | 27 | 28 |
| 29 | 30 | 31 |   |   |   |   |

## 2020

### JANUARY
| S | M | T | W | T | F | S |
|---|---|---|---|---|---|---|
|   |   |   | 1 | 2 | 3 | 4 |
| 5 | 6 | 7 | 8 | 9 | 10 | 11 |
| 12 | 13 | 14 | 15 | 16 | 17 | 18 |
| 19 | 20 | 21 | 22 | 23 | 24 | 25 |
| 26 | 27 | 28 | 29 | 30 | 31 |   |

### FEBRUARY
| S | M | T | W | T | F | S |
|---|---|---|---|---|---|---|
|   |   |   |   |   |   | 1 |
| 2 | 3 | 4 | 5 | 6 | 7 | 8 |
| 9 | 10 | 11 | 12 | 13 | 14 | 15 |
| 16 | 17 | 18 | 19 | 20 | 21 | 22 |
| 23 | 24 | 25 | 26 | 27 | 28 | 29 |

### MARCH
| S | M | T | W | T | F | S |
|---|---|---|---|---|---|---|
| 1 | 2 | 3 | 4 | 5 | 6 | 7 |
| 8 | 9 | 10 | 11 | 12 | 13 | 14 |
| 15 | 16 | 17 | 18 | 19 | 20 | 21 |
| 22 | 23 | 24 | 25 | 26 | 27 | 28 |
| 29 | 30 | 31 |   |   |   |   |

### APRIL
| S | M | T | W | T | F | S |
|---|---|---|---|---|---|---|
|   |   |   | 1 | 2 | 3 | 4 |
| 5 | 6 | 7 | 8 | 9 | 10 | 11 |
| 12 | 13 | 14 | 15 | 16 | 17 | 18 |
| 19 | 20 | 21 | 22 | 23 | 24 | 25 |
| 26 | 27 | 28 | 29 | 30 |   |   |

### MAY
| S | M | T | W | T | F | S |
|---|---|---|---|---|---|---|
|   |   |   |   |   | 1 | 2 |
| 3 | 4 | 5 | 6 | 7 | 8 | 9 |
| 10 | 11 | 12 | 13 | 14 | 15 | 16 |
| 17 | 18 | 19 | 20 | 21 | 22 | 23 |
| 24 | 25 | 26 | 27 | 28 | 29 | 30 |
| 31 |   |   |   |   |   |   |

### JUNE
| S | M | T | W | T | F | S |
|---|---|---|---|---|---|---|
|   | 1 | 2 | 3 | 4 | 5 | 6 |
| 7 | 8 | 9 | 10 | 11 | 12 | 13 |
| 14 | 15 | 16 | 17 | 18 | 19 | 20 |
| 21 | 22 | 23 | 24 | 25 | 26 | 27 |
| 28 | 29 | 30 |   |   |   |   |

### JULY
| S | M | T | W | T | F | S |
|---|---|---|---|---|---|---|
|   |   |   | 1 | 2 | 3 | 4 |
| 5 | 6 | 7 | 8 | 9 | 10 | 11 |
| 12 | 13 | 14 | 15 | 16 | 17 | 18 |
| 19 | 20 | 21 | 22 | 23 | 24 | 25 |
| 26 | 27 | 28 | 29 | 30 | 31 |   |

### AUGUST
| S | M | T | W | T | F | S |
|---|---|---|---|---|---|---|
|   |   |   |   |   |   | 1 |
| 2 | 3 | 4 | 5 | 6 | 7 | 8 |
| 9 | 10 | 11 | 12 | 13 | 14 | 15 |
| 16 | 17 | 18 | 19 | 20 | 21 | 22 |
| 23 | 24 | 25 | 26 | 27 | 28 | 29 |
| 30 | 31 |   |   |   |   |   |

### SEPTEMBER
| S | M | T | W | T | F | S |
|---|---|---|---|---|---|---|
|   |   | 1 | 2 | 3 | 4 | 5 |
| 6 | 7 | 8 | 9 | 10 | 11 | 12 |
| 13 | 14 | 15 | 16 | 17 | 18 | 19 |
| 20 | 21 | 22 | 23 | 24 | 25 | 26 |
| 27 | 28 | 29 | 30 |   |   |   |

### OCTOBER
| S | M | T | W | T | F | S |
|---|---|---|---|---|---|---|
|   |   |   |   | 1 | 2 | 3 |
| 4 | 5 | 6 | 7 | 8 | 9 | 10 |
| 11 | 12 | 13 | 14 | 15 | 16 | 17 |
| 18 | 19 | 20 | 21 | 22 | 23 | 24 |
| 25 | 26 | 27 | 28 | 29 | 30 | 31 |

### NOVEMBER
| S | M | T | W | T | F | S |
|---|---|---|---|---|---|---|
| 1 | 2 | 3 | 4 | 5 | 6 | 7 |
| 8 | 9 | 10 | 11 | 12 | 13 | 14 |
| 15 | 16 | 17 | 18 | 19 | 20 | 21 |
| 22 | 23 | 24 | 25 | 26 | 27 | 28 |
| 29 | 30 |   |   |   |   |   |

### DECEMBER
| S | M | T | W | T | F | S |
|---|---|---|---|---|---|---|
|   |   | 1 | 2 | 3 | 4 | 5 |
| 6 | 7 | 8 | 9 | 10 | 11 | 12 |
| 13 | 14 | 15 | 16 | 17 | 18 | 19 |
| 20 | 21 | 22 | 23 | 24 | 25 | 26 |
| 27 | 28 | 29 | 30 | 31 |   |   |

## The New Form 1040 and 1040 Schedules

For 2018, all taxpayers will use a redesigned Form 1040. Forms 1040A and 1040EZ have been eliminated. Form 1040 is still a two-page form but it has substantially fewer lines than in prior years. This is because many entries that used to be made directly on Form 1040 now have to be entered first on one of the six new schedules (Schedules 1-6), with the totals from the schedules then entered on Form 1040. As shown below, you will have to use one or more of the new schedules to report various types of income or loss, above-the-line deductions, nonrefundable tax credits, and certain refundable tax credits, tax payments, and tax liabilities.

You will continue to use the familiar schedules from prior years where applicable, such as Schedule A (itemized deductions), Schedule B (taxable interest and ordinary dividends), Schedule C (profit or loss from a sole proprietor's business) Schedule D (capital gains and losses), Schedule E (supplemental income or loss from rental real estate, royalties, partnerships, S corporations, estates or trusts), Schedule EIC (qualifying children for earned income credit), Schedule F (profit or loss from farming), Schedule H (household employment taxes), Schedule SE (self-employment tax), and Schedule 8812 (additional child tax credit).

## Which new schedules do you need to use?

The following table shows many, but not all, of the items that must be reported on the new Form 1040 schedules. See the instructions for the schedules for further details.

| Use— | For— |
| --- | --- |
| Schedule 1 | Reporting various types of income, including business income or loss (from Schedule C), capital gain or loss (from Schedule D), unemployment compensation, alimony received, sales of business property (from Form 4797), taxable refunds of state or local taxes, gambling winnings, prizes and awards, and taxable distributions from an HSA, Coverdell ESA, QTP, or ABLE account. Reporting above-the-line deductions ("adjustments to income") such as for traditional IRA contributions, self-employed retirement plan contributions, student loan interest, alimony paid, educator expenses, HSA contributions, deductible part of self-employment tax (from Schedule SE), self-employed health insurance, or business expenses if you are a qualifying reservist, performing artist, or fee-basis government official (from Form 2106). |
| Schedule 2 | Reporting liability for AMT (from Form 6251), or a repayment of excess advance payments of the premium tax credit (from Form 8962). |
| Schedule 3 | Reporting nonrefundable credits other than the child tax credit or the credit for other dependents, both of which are claimed directly on Form 1040. For example, use Schedule 3 to report the credit for child and dependent care (from Form 2441), education credits (from Form 8863), saver's credit (from Form 8880), adoption credit (from Form 8839), general business credit (from Form 3800), or foreign tax credit (from Form 1116 if required). |
| Schedule 4 | Reporting liability for "other taxes" such as self-employment tax (from Schedule SE), household employment taxes (from Schedule H), early distribution penalties from IRAs and qualified retirement plans, Additional Medicare Tax (from Form 8959), Net Investment Income Tax (from Form 8960), and the health care individual responsibility penalty tax. |
| Schedule 5 | Reporting other payments and refundable credits other than the earned income credit, the additional child tax credit, and the American Opportunity credit, which are claimed directly on Form 1040. For example, use Schedule 5 to show your estimated tax payments, payments made with a filing extension, and the net premium tax credit (from Form 8962). |
| Schedule 6 | Reporting a foreign address if you have one, or identifying a third party designee. |

# CHAPTER 1

# Filing Status

Your filing status determines the tax rates that will apply *(1.2)* to your taxable income when you file your return. Filing status also determines the standard deduction you may claim *(13.1)* if you do not itemize deductions and your ability to claim certain other deductions, credits, and exclusions.

This chapter explains the five different filing statuses: single, married filing jointly, married filing separately, head of household, and qualifying widow/widower. If you are married, filing a joint return is generally advantageous, but there are exceptions discussed in *(1.3)*. If you are unmarried and are supporting a child who lives with you, you may qualify as a head of household *(1.12)*, which will enable you to use more favorable tax rates than those allowed for single taxpayers. If you were widowed in either 2017 or 2016 and in 2018 a dependent child lived with you, you may be able to file as a qualifying widow/widower for 2018, which allows you to use joint return rates *(1.11)*.

Special filing situations, such as for children, nonresident aliens, and deceased individuals, are also discussed in this chapter.

*Planning Reminder*

**Getting Married Can Raise Your Taxes**

The so-called marriage penalty is faced by couples whose joint return tax liability exceeds the combined tax they would pay if they had remained single. This is generally the case where each spouse earns a substantial share of the total income. Legislation has substantially reduced the marriage penalty by allowing married couples filing jointly a standard deduction *(13.1)* that is double the amount allowed to a single person, and by allowing joint filers a 12% bracket *(1.2)* that is twice as wide as that for a single person.

On the other hand, if one spouse has little or no income, there generally is a marriage bonus or singles penalty, as the couple's tax on a joint return is less than the sum of the tax liabilities that would be owed if they were single.

## 1.1 Which Filing Status Should You Use?

Your filing status generally depends on whether you are married at the end of the year, and, if unmarried, whether you maintain a household for a qualifying dependent. The five filing statuses are: single, married filing jointly, married filing separately, head of household, and qualifying widow or widower. The filing status you use determines the tax rates that apply to your taxable income *(1.2)*, as well as the standard deduction you may claim *(13.1)* if you do not itemize deductions. Certain other deductions, credits, or exclusions are also affected by filing status. For example, if you are married, certain tax benefits are only allowed if you file jointly, but in certain cases, more deductions overall may be allowed if you file separately *(1.3)*.

If you are married at the end of the year, you may file jointly *(1.4)* or separately *(1.3)*. If you lived apart from your spouse for the last half of 2018 and your child lived with you, you may qualify as an "unmarried" head of household *(1.12)* for 2018, which allows you to apply more favorable tax rates than you could as a married person filing separately.

If you are unmarried at the end of the year, your filing status is single unless you meet the tests for a head of household or qualifying widow/widower. Generally, you are a head of household *(1.12)* if you pay more than 50% of the household costs for a dependent child or relative who lives with you, or for a dependent parent, whether or not he or she lives with you. For 2018, you generally are a qualifying widow/widower *(1.11)* if you were widowed in 2016 or 2017 and in 2018 you paid more than 50% of the household costs for you and your dependent child. The tax rates for heads of household and for qualifying widows/widowers are more favorable than those for single taxpayers *(1.2)*.

Marital status determined at the end of the year. If you are divorced or legally separated during the year under a final decree of divorce or separate maintenance, you are treated as unmarried for that whole year, assuming you have not remarried before the end of the year. For the year of the divorce or legal separation, file as a single person unless you care for a child or parent and qualify as a head of household *(1.12)*.

If at the end of the year you are living apart from your spouse, or you are separated under a provisional decree that has not yet been finalized, you are not considered divorced. If you care for a child and meet the other head of household tests *(1.12)*, you may file as an unmarried head of household. Otherwise, you must file a joint return or as a married person filing separately.

If at the end of the year you live together in a common law marriage that is recognized by the law of the state in which you live or the state where the marriage began, you are treated as married.

If your spouse dies during the year, you are treated as married for that entire year and may file a joint return for you and your deceased spouse, assuming you have not remarried before year's end *(1.10)*.

**Same-sex marriage.** Lawfully married same-sex couples are treated as married for all federal tax purposes. The IRS recognizes your marriage to a same-sex spouse if the marriage was legally entered into in one of the 50 States, the District of Columbia, Puerto Rico, U.S. territory or possession, or foreign country. However, registered domestic partnerships, civil unions, and similar relationships that are recognized by state law (or foreign law) but that are not treated as marriages under state law are not treated as marriages for federal tax purposes.

As a married couple, you and your spouse must file your federal return using a filing status of married filing jointly *(1.4)* or married filing separately *(1.3)*. However, if you lived apart for the last six months of 2018 and one of you maintained a home for a child or other qualifying relative, that spouse may be able to file as a head of household *(1.12)*.

At IRS.gov, the IRS has tax details for same-sex couples ("Answers to Frequently Asked Questions for Individuals of the Same Sex Who Are Married Under State Law", at www.irs.gov/uac/answers-to-frequently-asked-questions-for-same-sex-married-couples). These question-and-answer guidelines reflect Revenue Ruling 2013-17 (9/16/13), which was issued after the Supreme Court declared in its Windsor decision (6/26/13) that the provision in the Defense of Marriage Act (DOMA) that had prohibited same-sex marriages from being recognized for federal tax purposes was unconstitutional on equal protection grounds.

## 1.2 Tax Rates Based on Filing Status

The most favorable tax brackets apply to married persons filing jointly and qualifying widows/widowers *(1.11)*, who also use the joint return rates. The least favorable brackets are those for married persons filing separately, but filing separately is still advisable for married couples in certain situations *(1.3)*. See *Table 1-1* for a comparison of the 2018 tax rate brackets.

If you have children and are unmarried at the end of the year, do not assume that your filing status is single. If your child lives with you in a home you maintain, you generally may file as a head of household *(1.12)*, which allows you to use more favorable tax rates than a single person. If you were widowed in either of the two prior years and maintain a household for your dependent child, you generally may file as a qualified widow/widower, which allows you to use favorable joint return rates *(1.11)*.

If you are married at the end of the year but for the second half of the year you lived with your child apart from your spouse, and you and your spouse agree not to file jointly, you may use head of household tax rates, which are more favorable than those for married persons filing separately.

**What is your top tax bracket and effective tax rate?** Under the Tax Cuts and Jobs Act, there are seven tax rates that can apply to ordinary income, the same number of rates as under pre-2018 law, but five of the new rates are lower. For 2018, your top marginal tax rate for ordinary income (such as salary, interest income, or short-term capital gains) can be 10%, 12%, 22%, 24%, 32%, 35% or 37%, depending on your taxable income *(22.1)*. Rates on qualified dividends *(4.2)* and net capital gain *(5.3)* can be either 0%, 15%, 20%, 25%, or 28%, depending on the amount of your other income and type of asset sold; *see* below.

The 2018 rate brackets that apply to income other than net capital gain or qualified dividends are shown below in *Table 1-1*. If your top bracket is 22%, for example, this means that each additional dollar of ordinary income will be taxed at 22% for regular income tax purposes; 22% is your "marginal" tax rate. However, because the rate brackets are graduated, your effective tax rate may be significantly lower than your top (marginal) rate. For example, if in 2018 you are single with taxable income of $40,530, all of which is ordinary income, your marginal rate is 22%, but the first $9,525 is taxed at 10%, the next $29,175 ($38,700 – $9,525) is taxed at 12%, and only the last $1,830 ($40,530 – $38,700) is taxed at 24%. The total tax on $40,530 is $4,856, which represents an "effective rate" of 11.98% ($4,856/$40,530 taxable income), reflecting the fact that most of your taxable income is taxed in the 10% and (especially) the 12% brackets.

If you have substantial employee compensation and/or self-employment net earnings in excess of the applicable threshold for your filing status *(28.2)*, you will be subject to an additional 0.9% Medicare tax on the excess earnings.

### Table 1-1 Taxable Income Brackets for 2018 Ordinary Income

| | 10% bracket for 2018 applies to taxable income up to— | 12% bracket for 2018 applies to taxable income up to— | 22% bracket for 2018 applies to taxable income up to— | 24% bracket for 2018 applies to taxable income up to— | 32% bracket for 2018 applies to taxable income up to— | 35% bracket for 2018 applies to taxable income up to— | 37% bracket for 2018 applies to taxable income over— |
|---|---|---|---|---|---|---|---|
| Married filing jointly or Qualifying widow/widower | $19,050 | $77,400 | $165,000 | $315,000 | $400,000 | $600,000 | $600,000 |
| Single | 9,525 | 38,700 | 82,500 | 157,500 | 200,000 | 500,000 | 500,000 |
| Head of household | 13,600 | 51,800 | 82,500 | 157,500 | 200,000 | 500,000 | 500,000 |
| Married filing separately | 9,525 | 38,700 | 82,500 | 157,500 | 200,000 | 300,000 | 300,000 |

The tax rate on qualified dividends *(4.2)* and net capital gain *(5.3)* is generally lower than your top bracket rate on ordinary income. Depending on your top rate bracket for ordinary income *(Table 1-1)*, the rate applied to net capital gain and to most qualified dividends is either 0%, 15%, or 20% *(5.3)*. This does not include 28% rate gains or unrecaptured Section 1250 gains *(5.3)*, which are not eligible for the 0%, 15% and 20% rates. For unrecaptured Section 1250 gains, the rate cannot exceed 25%; for 28% rate gains the maximum rate is 28%.

If your top bracket is 10% *(Table 1-1)* and you do not have 28% or unrecaptured Section 1250 gains, you do not owe any tax on your net capital gain *(5.3)* or on your qualified dividends *(4.2)*; the rate is zero (0%). This is also true if your top bracket is 12%, except that a small amount of income that would otherwise be taxed near the top of the 12% bracket does not qualify for the 0% rate. Specifically, the 0% rate on net capital gain and qualified dividends applies for 2018 if taxable income is no more than $77,200 if you are married filing jointly or a qualifying widow or widower, $38,600 if you are single or married filing separately, or $51,700 if you are a head of household. Note that the $77,200, $38,600, and $51,700 endpoints for the 0% rate are $100 or $200 less than the endpoints for the 12% ordinary income bracket as shown in *Table 1-1*. For taxpayers whose taxable income exceeds the above ceiling ($77,200, $38,600, or $51,700), some net capital gains (except for 28%/unrecaptured Section 1250 gains) and qualified dividends may escape tax under the 0% rate, while others are subject to the 15% or 20% rate *(5.3)*.

If you are subject to the additional Medicare tax on net investment income because your modified adjusted gross income exceeds the threshold for your filing status, you will have to pay an additional 3.8% tax on some or all of the net investment income *(28.3)*.

Use the proper table or worksheet to compute regular income tax liability. To actually compute your 2018 regular income tax, you will look up your tax in the Tax Table *(22.2)* or use the Tax Computation Worksheet *(22.3)* if you do not have net capital gains or qualified dividends. If you have 2018 net capital gain or qualified dividends, use the Qualified Dividends and Capital Gain Tax Worksheet or the Schedule D Tax Worksheet. Depending on your income, you may also be liable for the additional Medicare taxes. Chapter 22 explains these alternatives.

**AMT.** If you are subject to alternative minimum tax (AMT) on Form 6251, you generally apply either a 26% or 28% rate to your AMT taxable income (as reduced by the applicable AMT exemption), but the favorable regular tax rates for net capital gains and qualified dividends also apply for AMT purposes *(23.1)*.

## 1.3 Filing Separately Instead of Jointly

Filing a joint return saves taxes for a married couple where one spouse earns all, or substantially all, of the taxable income. If both you and your spouse earn taxable income, you should figure your tax on joint and separate returns to determine which method provides the lower tax.

Although your tax rate *(1.2)* will generally be higher on a separate return, filing separately may provide an overall tax savings (for both of you together) where filing separately allows you to claim more deductions. On separate returns, larger amounts of medical expenses or casualty losses may be deductible because lower adjusted gross income floors apply. Unless one spouse earns substantially more than the other, separate and joint tax rates are likely to be the same, regardless of the type of returns filed. The Mike & Fran Palmer Example below illustrates how filing separately can save a married couple taxes in some cases.

**Suspicious of your spouse's tax reporting?** If you suspect that your spouse is evading taxes and may be liable on a joint return, you may want to file a separate return. By filing separately, you avoid liability for unpaid taxes due on a joint return, plus interest and penalties.

If you do file jointly and the IRS tries to collect tax due on the joint return from you personally, you may be able to avoid liability under the innocent spouse rules *(1.7)*. If you are no longer married to or are separated from the person with whom you jointly filed, you may be able to elect separate liability treatment *(1.8)*.

*Planning Reminder*

**Changing From Separate to Joint Return**

If you and your spouse file separate returns (including a return as a head of household if eligible *(1.12)*), you can file an amended return (Form 1040X) to change to a joint return. You generally have three years from the original due date (without extensions) of the separate returns to file the amended return.

However, if you file separate returns and either of you has received a notice of deficiency from the IRS, you cannot file a Tax Court petition in order to switch from separate returns to a joint return. The IRS and Tax Court have held that this rule applies not just to spouses who filed as married filing separately, but also where one of the spouses mistakenly files as head of household. The Eighth Circuit Court of Appeals, as well as the Fifth and Eleventh Circuits take a more favorable view. For example, the Eighth Circuit in 2015 reversed the Tax Court and held that the prohibition against changing to a joint return after a notice of deficiency and Tax Court petition applies to married persons filing separately, but not to a spouse who has filed as head of household.

**Standard deduction restriction on separate returns.** Keep in mind that if you and your spouse file separately, both of you must either itemize or claim the standard deduction, which for 2018 is $12,000 for married persons filing separately *(13.3)*. Thus, if for 2018 your spouse itemizes deductions on Schedule A of Form 1040, your standard deduction is zero; you do not have the option of claiming the $12,000 standard deduction and must itemize your deductions on Schedule A even if they are much less than $12,000.

---

### EXAMPLE

Mike Palmer's 2018 adjusted gross income (AGI) is $84,775, and Fran, his wife, has AGI of $60,000. Fran has unreimbursed medical expenses of $15,105 **(17.1)** before taking into account the 7.5% of AGI floor **(17.1)**; Mike's unreimbursed medical expenses are $1,000. Personal property that Mike owned in his own name was damaged in a storm that was designated as a federal disaster **(18.1)**, and he has a casualty loss of $20,078 prior to taking into account the $100 floor and the 10% of AGI floor **(18.13)**. Mike has deductible mortgage interest expenses of $5,000 and Fran has $1,900. Mike's deductible state and local taxes are $2,399; Fran's are $1,000. Mike made deductible charitable contributions of $2,996 and Fran, $500.

As the example worksheet below shows, filing separate returns saves Mike and Fran an overall $2,504, because they can deduct more on separate returns. If they filed jointly, their deductible medical expenses and casualty loss would be substantially lower than the total they can claim on separate returns.

| Item | Mike (Separately) | Fran (Separately) | Joint Return |
|---|---|---|---|
| 1. AGI | $ 84,775 | $ 60,000 | $ 144,775 |
| 2. Medical expenses | 1,000 | 15,105 | 16,105 |
| Less 7.5% of AGI *(17.1)* | 6,358 | 4,500 | 10,858 |
| *Allowable medical* | 0 | 10,605 | 5,247 |
| 3. Taxes | 2,399 | 1,000 | 3,399 |
| 4. Mortgage interest | 5,000 | 1,900 | 6,900 |
| 5. Casualty loss | 20,078 | 0 | 20,078 |
| Less $100 and 10% of AGI *(18.12)* | 8,578 | | 14,578 |
| *Allowable casualty* | 11,500 | | 5,500 |
| 6. Charitable contributions | 2,996 | 500 | 3,496 |
| 7. Total itemized (Lines 2–6) | 21,895 | 14,005 | 24,542 |
| 8. Taxable income (Line 1 minus Line 7) | 62,880 | 45,995 | 120,233 |
| 11. Income tax for 2018 (Tax on Line 8) | 9,772 | 6,054 | 18,330 |
| Total tax filing separately (Line 11) | | | 15,826 |
| *Savings from filing separately* | | | 2,504 |

---

**Certain benefits require joint return and some benefits harder to claim if filing separately.** If married, you must file jointly to claim certain tax benefits, and other tax breaks are much harder to claim on separate returns. For example, you must file jointly to claim the following education-related benefits: the American Opportunity credit or Lifetime Learning credit *(33.7)*, the tuition and fees deduction (if extended by Congress) *(33.12)*, the premium tax credit (unless a spouse is a victim of domestic violence) *(25.12)*, and the deduction for student loan interest *(33.13)*. You also must file jointly to deduct a contribution to an IRA for a nonworking spouse *(8.3)*.

Some benefits are allowed on separate returns only if you live apart from your spouse for all or part of the year. The adoption credit, dependent care credit and the earned income credit *(Chapter 25)*, must be claimed on a joint return unless you live apart for the last six months of the year. If you want to take advantage of the $25,000 rental loss allowance *(10.2)* or the credit for the elderly and disabled *(Chapter 34)*, you must file jointly unless you live apart for the whole year.

IRA contributions are restricted on separate returns. Roth IRA contributions generally may not be made by a married person filing separately because of an extremely low phase-out range *(8.20)*. Similarly, deductions for traditional IRA contributions are restricted on separate returns where the spouses live together at any time during the year and either is an active plan participant *(8.4)*.

In figuring whether you are subject to alternative minimum tax (AMT), your exemption amount is half that allowed to a joint return filer *(23.1)*.

If you receive Social Security benefits, 85% of your benefits are subject to tax on a separate return unless you live apart the entire year *(34.3)*. Similarly, for purposes of figuring Medicare Part B and Part D premiums, harsher premium surcharge rules apply to married persons filing separately who live together at any time during the year *(34.10)*.

## 1.4 Filing a Joint Return

If you are married *(1.1)* at the end of the year, you may file a joint return with your spouse. Same-sex marriages that are legally entered into are recognized for all federal tax purposes; *see 1.1*.

You may not file a 2018 joint return if you were divorced or legally separated under a decree of divorce or separate maintenance that is final by the end of the year. You may file jointly for 2018 if you separated during the year under an interlocutory (temporary or provisional) decree or order, so long as a final divorce decree was not entered by the end of the year. If during the period that a divorce decree is interlocutory you are permitted to remarry in another state, the IRS recognizes the new marriage and allows a joint return to be filed with the new spouse. However, courts have refused to allow a joint return where a new marriage took place in Mexico during the interlocutory period in violation of California law.

**Would you be better off filing separately instead of jointly?** Filing jointly saves taxes for many married couples, but if you and your spouse both earn taxable income, in some cases overall tax liability is reduced by filing separately. This is particularly true where one spouse has deductible expenses that could be claimed on a separate return but not on a joint return because of floors based on adjusted gross income *(1.3)*.

Once you file jointly, you cannot switch to separate returns for that year after the due date for the return has passed. The only exception is for the executor of a deceased spouse, who has one year from the due date (plus extensions) to change to a separate return for the deceased *(1.14)*. Once you file separately, you generally may file an amended return to change to a joint return; *see* the Planning Reminder in *(1.3)*.

**Both spouses generally liable on joint return but "innocent" spouse may be relieved of liability.** When you and your spouse file jointly, each of you may generally be held individually liable for the entire tax due, plus interest and any penalties. The IRS may try to collect the entire amount due from you even if your spouse earned all of the income reported on the joint return, or even if you have divorced under an agreement that holds your former spouse responsible for the taxes on the joint returns you filed together. However, there are exceptions to this joint liability rule for "innocent" spouses and for divorced or separated persons.

You may be able to obtain innocent spouse relief where tax on your joint return was understated without your knowledge because your spouse omitted income or claimed erroneous deductions or tax credits. In such a case, you may claim innocent spouse relief on Form 8857 within two years from the time the IRS begins a collection effort from you for taxes due on the return *(1.7)*.

If you are divorced, legally separated, living apart or the spouse with whom you filed jointly has died, you may be able to avoid tax on the portion of a joint return deficiency that is allocable to your ex-spouse by claiming separate liability relief on Form 8857 *(1.8)* within two years of the time the IRS begins collection efforts against you. In some cases, it may be easier to qualify for relief under the separate liability rules than under the innocent spouse rules because innocent spouse relief may be denied if you had "reason to know" that tax was understated on the joint return, whereas the IRS must show that you had "actual knowledge" of the omitted income or erroneous deductions or credits to deny a separate liability election.

**Signing the joint return.** Both you and your spouse must sign the joint return. Under the following rules, if your spouse is unable to sign, you may sign for him or her.

If, because of illness, your spouse is physically unable to sign the joint return, you may, with the oral consent of your spouse, sign his or her name on the return followed by the words "By _____, Husband (or Wife)." You then sign the return again in your own right and attach a signed and dated statement with the following information: (1) the type of form being filed, (2) the tax year, (3) the reason for the inability of the sick spouse to sign, and (4) that the sick spouse has consented to your signing.

To sign for your spouse in other situations, you need authorization in the form of a power of attorney, which must be attached to the return. IRS Form 2848 may be used.

If your spouse does not file, you may be able to prove you filed a joint return even if your spouse did not sign and you did not sign as your spouse's agent where:

- You intended it to be a joint return—your spouse's income was included (or the spouse had no income).
- Your spouse agreed to have you handle tax matters and you filed a joint return.
- Your answers to the questions on the tax return indicate you intended to file a joint return.
- Your spouse's failure to sign can be explained.

> **EXAMPLE**
> The Hills generally filed joint returns. In one year, Mr. Hill claimed joint return filing status and reported his wife's income as well as his own; in place of her signature on the return, he indicated that she was out of town caring for her sick mother. She did not file a separate return. The IRS refused to treat the return as joint. The Tax Court disagreed. Since Mrs. Hill testified that she would have signed had she been available, her failure to do so does not bar joint return status. The couple intended to make a joint return at the time of filing.

## 1.5 Nonresident Alien Spouse

If you are married and at the end of the year one of you is a U.S. citizen or resident alien *(1.18)* and the other spouse is a nonresident alien *(1.16)*, a joint return may be filed only if both of you make a special election to treat the nonresident alien spouse as a US. resident, which means you will both be taxed on your worldwide income. The same rule applies if one spouse is a "dual status" taxpayer for the year. Thus, if you are a U.S. citizen and your spouse is a nonresident alien at the beginning of the year who becomes a resident during the year, the special election must be made to file jointly. The election is made by attaching a signed statement to the joint return, indicating your intent to be treated as full-year U.S. residents. If you and your spouse make the election, you must keep books and records of your worldwide income and give the IRS access to such books and records.

If the election is not made, you may be able to claim your nonresident alien spouse as an exemption on a return filed as married filing separately, but only if the spouse had no income and could not be claimed as a dependent by another taxpayer *(21.2)*.

Once the election is made to treat a nonresident alien spouse as a U.S. resident, the election applies to later years unless you revoke it, or it is suspended or terminated under IRS rules. A revocation before the due date of the return is effective for that return. An election is suspended if neither spouse is a citizen or resident for any part of the taxable year. If an election is suspended it may again become effective if either spouse becomes a U.S. citizen or resident. If either spouse does not keep adequate records or provide the necessary information on world-wide income to the IRS, the election is terminated. An election

*Filing Tip*

**Spouse in Combat Zone**

If your spouse is in a combat zone or a qualified hazardous duty area *(35.4)*, you can sign a joint return for your spouse. Attach a signed explanation to the return.

*Filing Tip*

**Election To File a Joint Return**

Where a U.S. citizen or resident is married to a nonresident alien, the couple may file a joint return if both elect to be taxed on their worldwide income. The requirement that one spouse be a U.S. citizen or resident need be met only at the close of the year. Joint returns may be filed in the year of the election and all later years until the election is terminated.

also terminates if you legally separate under a decree of divorce or separate maintenance; the termination applies as of the beginning of the year in which the separation occurs. The election automatically terminates in the year following the year of the death of either spouse. However, if the survivor is a U.S. citizen or resident and has a qualifying child, he or she may be able to use joint return rates as a qualifying widow or widower *(1.11)* in the two years following the year of the spouse's death. Once the election is terminated, neither spouse may ever again make the election to file jointly.

## 1.6 Community Property Rules

If you live in Arizona, California, Idaho, Louisiana, Nevada, New Mexico, Texas, Washington, or Wisconsin, the income and property you and your spouse acquire during the marriage is generally regarded as community property. Community property means that each of you owns half of the community income and community property, even if legal title is held by only one spouse. But note that there are some instances in which community property rules are disregarded for tax purposes; these instances are clearly highlighted in the pertinent sections of this book.

**Form 8958 required if filing separately.** If the community property rules apply for tax purposes and you and your spouse file separate returns instead of filing jointly, then on your separate returns each of you must report half of your combined community income and deductions in addition to your separate income and deductions. You must attach Form 8958 to your separate Form 1040 to show how the allocations between you were made.

**Separate property may still be owned.** Property owned before marriage generally remains separate property; it does not become community property when you marry. Property received during the marriage by one spouse as a gift or an inheritance from a third party is generally separate property. In some states, if the nature of ownership cannot be fixed, the property is presumed to be community property.

In some states, income from separate property may be treated as community property income. In other states, income from separate property remains the separate property of the individual owner.

**Divorce or separation.** If you and your spouse divorce, your community property automatically becomes separate property. A separation agreement or a decree of legal separation or of separate maintenance may or may not end the marital community, depending on state law.

**Community income rules may not apply to separated couples.** If a husband and wife in a community property state file separate returns, each spouse must generally report one-half of the community income. However, a spouse may be able to avoid reporting income earned by his or her spouse if they live apart during the entire calendar year and do not file a joint return.

To qualify, one or both spouses must have earned income for the year and none of that earned income may be transferred, directly or indirectly, between the spouses during the year. One spouse's payment to the other spouse solely to support the couple's dependent children is not a disqualifying transfer. If the separated couple qualifies under these tests, community income is allocated as follows:

- Earned income (excluding business or partnership income) is taxed to the spouse who performed the personal services.
- Business income (other than partnership income) is treated as the income of the spouse carrying on the business.
- Partnership income is taxed to the spouse entitled to a distributive share of partnership profits.

**Innocent spouse rules apply to community property.** As discussed above, community property rules may not apply to earned income where spouses live apart for the entire year and file separate returns. In addition, a spouse who files a separate return may be relieved of tax liability on community income that is attributable to the other spouse if he or she does not know (or have reason to know) about the income and if it would be inequitable under the circumstances for him or her to be taxed on such income. Even if you fail to qualify for such relief because you knew (or had reason to know) about the income, the IRS may relieve you of liability if it would be inequitable to hold you liable.

The IRS may disregard community property rules and tax income to a spouse who treats such income as if it were solely his or hers and who fails to notify the other spouse of the income before the due date of the return (including extensions).

Relief from liability on joint return. If you file jointly, you may elect to avoid liability under the innocent spouse rules *(1.7)* and the separate liability rules *(1.8)*. In applying those rules, items that would otherwise be allocable solely to your spouse will not be partly allocated to you merely because of the community property laws.

**Death of spouse.** The death of a spouse dissolves the community property relationship, but income earned and accrued from community property before death is community income.

**Moving from a community property to a common law (separate property) state.** Most common law states (those which do not have community property laws) recognize that both spouses have an interest in property accumulated while residing in a community property state. If the property is not sold or reinvested, it may continue to be treated as community property. If you and your spouse sell community property after moving to a common law state and reinvest the proceeds, the reinvested proceeds are generally separate property, which you may hold as joint tenants or in another form of ownership recognized by common law states.

**Moving from a common law to a community property state.** Separate property brought into a community property state generally retains its character as separately owned property. However, property acquired by a couple after moving to a community property state is generally owned as community property. In at least one state (California), personal property that qualifies as community property is treated as such, even though it was acquired when the couple lived in a common law state.

# 1.7    Innocent Spouse Rules

Unless you qualify for relief, you are personally liable for any tax due on a joint return you have filed, whether you are still married to the spouse with whom you filed the joint return or you have since divorced or separated.

If you are still married and living with the same spouse, the only way to avoid personal liability on the joint return is to qualify as an innocent spouse under the rules in this section, or to apply for equitable relief from the IRS *(1.9)*.

If you are divorced, legally separated, living apart, or your spouse has died, you may either seek relief under the innocent spouse rules below or you may be able to claim separate liability treatment *(1.8)* or seek equitable relief *(1.9)* from the IRS.

**Qualifying tests for innocent spouse relief.** You must satisfy all of the following conditions to qualify for innocent spouse relief:

1. The tax shown on the joint return was understated due to the omission of income by your spouse, or erroneous deductions or credits claimed by your spouse. This means that your actual tax liability is more than the amount shown on the joint return. Innocent spouse relief is not available if the right amount of tax was reported on the return but it was not paid. However, where tax was underpaid, you may request equitable relief *(1.9)*.

2. When signing the joint return, you did not know and had no reason to know that tax on the return was understated.
   In considering whether you had "reason to know" of the tax understatement, the IRS and Tax Court will ask whether a reasonable person in similar circumstances would have known of it. All facts and circumstances will be taken into account including your education level, business experience, involvement in the activity that gave rise to the understatement, and whether you failed to ask about items on the joint return or about omissions from the return that a reasonable person would have questioned.
   Although the "knowledge" test can be a significant hurdle, partial relief may be available. If you knew or had reason to know that there was "some" tax understatement on the return but were unaware of the extent of the understatement, innocent spouse relief is available for the liability attributable to the portion of the understatement that you did not know about or have reason to know about.

*IRS Alert*

**Registered Domestic Partners Must Split Income**

Registered domestic partners in California, Nevada, and Washington are subject to the federal income tax community property rules. Each registered domestic partner must report half of the combined community property income (as determined by state law) on his or her federal tax return, whether from earnings for personal services or income from property.

For federal tax purposes, registered domestic partners are not considered married *(1.1)* and may not file joint returns. They must file as single taxpayers unless eligible for head of household status.

Legally married same-sex couples are treated as married for all federal tax purposes; *see 1.1.*

*Caution*

**Knowledge May Bar Innocent Spouse Relief**

The IRS may try to defeat your claim for innocent spouse relief on the grounds that you knew, or should have known, that tax was understated on the joint return.

*Law Alert*

**IRS Must Notify Non-Electing Spouse**

After the filing of Form 8857, the IRS is required to notify the non-electing spouse (or former spouse) of an electing spouse's request for relief and allow the non-electing spouse an opportunity to participate in the determination. If the IRS makes a preliminary determination granting full or partial relief to the electing spouse, the non-electing spouse may file a written protest and obtain an Appeals Office conference.

*Caution*

**Actual Knowledge Bars Relief**

Separate liability relief generally allows you to avoid liability for the portion of a tax deficiency that is allocable to the other spouse. Such relief is unavailable, however, to the extent that you had actual knowledge of the omitted income or deducted item that gave rise to the tax deficiency.

3. Taking all the circumstances into account, it would be inequitable to hold you liable for the tax. The IRS and courts will consider the extent to which you benefitted from the tax underpayment, beyond receiving normal support. Thus, it is possible to be held liable for a tax understatement that you did not know about or have reason to know about, on the grounds that you benefitted from the underpayment in the form of a high standard of living. The IRS will also consider whether you later divorced or were deserted by your spouse.

4. You file Form 8857 to request innocent spouse relief.

**Request for relief must be filed on Form 8857.** You must file Form 8857 to request innocent spouse relief. You must provide details concerning your finances and your involvement in preparing the joint returns for which relief from liability is sought. The request must be made no later than two years from the date that the IRS first begins collection activity against you for tax due on the joint return, such as (1) by reducing a current refund by an amount the IRS says you owe on the prior joint return, or (2) garnishing your wages to recover tax the IRS says you owe on the joint return. If the request is not made by the end of that two-year period, you will not be granted innocent spouse relief even if you meet the above qualification tests. However, for equitable relief, the two-year deadline for filing a request is extended to 10 years *(1.9)*.

**Tax Court appeal.** If the IRS denies your request for innocent spouse relief, you have 90 days to petition the Tax Court for review. If you petition the Tax Court, the non-electing spouse has the right to intervene in the proceeding.

## 1.8    Separate Liability Relief for Former Spouses

If the IRS attempts to collect the taxes due on a joint return from you and you have since divorced or separated, you may be able to avoid or at least limit your liability by filing Form 8857 to request separate liability relief. If you qualify, you will be liable only for the part of the tax liability (plus interest and any penalties) that is allocable to you. If a tax deficiency is entirely allocable to your former spouse under the rules discussed below, you will not have to pay any part of it. However, you may not avoid liability for any part of a tax deficiency allocable to the other spouse if you had actual knowledge of the income or expense item that gave rise to the tax deficiency that the IRS is trying to collect. See below for details of the knowledge test.

Furthermore, you may not avoid liability to the extent that certain disqualified property transfers were made between you and the other spouse. Relief may be completely denied for both spouses if transfers were made as part of a fraudulent scheme.

As with innocent spouse relief *(1.7)*, separate liability relief applies only to tax understatements where the proper tax liability was not shown on the joint return. If the proper liability was shown but not paid, equitable relief *(1.9)* may be requested.

**Are you eligible for separate liability relief?** You may request separate liability relief on Form 8857 if, at the time of filing:

1. You are divorced or legally separated from the spouse with whom you filed the joint return, or

2. You have not lived with your spouse (with whom you filed the return) at any time in the 12-month period ending on the date you file the election, or

3. The spouse with whom you filed the joint return has died.

You must be prepared to explain to the IRS which items giving rise to the tax understatement are allocable to you and which are allocable to the other spouse. However, you do not have to actually compute your separate liability on Form 8857.

**Deadline for relief request.** To request separate liability relief, you must file Form 8857 no later than two years after the IRS begins collection activities against you.

**Actual knowledge of the item allocable to the other spouse bars relief.** If you request separate liability treatment and the IRS shows that at the time you signed the joint return you had actual knowledge of an erroneous item (omitted income or improper deduction or credit) that would otherwise be allocated to the other spouse, you may not avoid liability for the portion of a deficiency attributable to that item. However, if you signed the return under duress, separate liability is not barred despite your knowledge because a return signed under duress is not considered to be a joint return. You are not liable for tax due on that return and you will be treated as filing separately.

The actual knowledge test is intended by Congress to be more favorable to the taxpayer than the "had reason to know" test under the innocent spouse rules *(1.7)*. Congressional committee reports state that the IRS is required to prove that an electing spouse had actual knowledge of an erroneous item and may not infer such knowledge. According to the Tax Court, the IRS must prove actual knowledge by a "preponderance of the evidence." If the IRS proves actual knowledge of an erroneous item, that item is treated as allocable to both spouses, so the IRS can collect that portion of the deficiency from either spouse.

Where income attributable to your spouse was omitted from your joint return, you will be considered to have "actual knowledge" of it, and separate liability relief will not be allowed, if you knew your spouse received the income, even if you did not know whether the correct taxable amount was reported on the return; *see* Example 1 below.

In the case of a disallowed deduction, the Tax Court requires the IRS to prove that you had actual knowledge of the "factual circumstances" that made the item nondeductible in order for relief to be denied. In one case, the Tax Court denied relief to a spouse who prepared the joint returns on which unsubstantiated Schedule C deductions attributable to her former husband's business were claimed. She had "actual knowledge" because she had access to the business records and knew the extent of the substantiation available for the deductions when she prepared the returns.

In cases involving limited partnership tax-shelter deductions, the IRS may be unable to prove that the spouse claiming relief had disqualifying knowledge, but relief may still be partially denied if he or she received a tax benefit from the deductions; *see* Example 3 below.

---

### EXAMPLES

1. Cheshire knew that her husband had received an early retirement distribution. She knew that the distribution had been deposited into their joint account and used to pay off a mortgage, buy a truck, pay other family expenses and provide start-up capital for the husband's business. Cheshire's husband falsely told her that a CPA had determined that most of his retirement distribution was not taxable. After they divorced, Cheshire requested separate liability election to avoid tax on the unreported income. She claimed that she was entitled to relief because she did not know that the taxable amount of the retirement distribution had been misstated on their joint return. The Tax Court held that she could not obtain relief because she knew about the retirement distribution. It is immaterial that she did not know that the reporting of the distribution on the tax return was incorrect. The Court of Appeals for the Fifth Circuit affirmed. The District of Columbia Circuit has also denied a wife's claim for relief because she had actual knowledge of her husband's retirement income.

2. You file a joint return on which you report wages of $150,000 and your husband reports $30,000 of self-employment income. The IRS examines your return and determines that your husband failed to report $20,000 of income, resulting in a $9,000 deficiency. You file a claim for separate liability relief with the IRS after obtaining a divorce.

   Assume that the IRS proves that you had actual knowledge of $5,000 of the unreported income but not the other $15,000. You are liable for 25% of the deficiency, or $2,250, allocable to the $5,000 of income that you knew about ($2,250 = $5,000 ÷ $20,000 × $9,000). Your former spouse is liable for the entire deficiency since the unreported income was his. The IRS can collect the entire deficiency from him, or can collect $2,250 from you and the balance from him.

3. Mora's husband arranged an investment in a cattle-breeding tax shelter partnership. He put the partnership in both of their names, although Mora did not sign any of the partnership papers. On their joint returns, they claimed partnership losses which turned out to be inflated; deductions were based on overvalued cattle. After their divorce, the IRS disallowed the partnership losses and Mora elected separate liability relief. The IRS refused, claiming that she participated in making the investment so the claimed losses were allocable to her as well as her husband. The Tax Court held

that Mora was not involved in making the investment and so the partnership losses are allocable to the husband unless Mora knew the factual basis for the denial of the deductions or she received a tax benefit from the deductions. She did not know about the overvaluation of the cattle, which was the factual basis for the IRS' denial of the deductions. In fact, the IRS conceded that neither spouse understood the nature of their investment or the basis of the deductions. This may often be the case where passive investors claim deductions passed through to them by a limited partnership. For this reason, the IRS argued that the "knowledge of the factual basis" test makes it too easy for limited partnership investors to obtain relief. The Tax Court responded that the law does not distinguish between passive and active investments and there is no policy reason for the courts to create a distinction. Furthermore, although the husband also lacked knowledge of the factual basis for the disallowance of the losses, he cannot avoid liability for the deficiency since the erroneous deductions would be allocable to him on a separate return.

Despite Mora's "win" on the actual knowledge issue, she remained partially liable for the deficiency because she received a tax benefit from the erroneous deductions. Under the tax benefit rule discussed below, the deductions first offset the income that would have been reported by the husband had he filed a separate return. The balance of the deductions benefitted Mora by reducing her separate return income. If she benefitted from 25% of the deductions, she would remain liable for 25% of the deficiency.

**Allocating tax liability between spouses.** Generally, if you claim separate liability relief, you are liable only for the portion of the tax due on the joint return that is allocable to you, determined as if you had filed a separate return. If erroneous items (omitted income or improper deductions or credits) are allocable to the other spouse but you had actual knowledge of the items as discussed above, you cannot avoid liability and the IRS remains able to collect the tax due from either of you. Where deductions are allocable to the other spouse and you are not barred from relief by the actual knowledge test, you can still be held partially liable if you received a tax benefit from the deductions; *see* the discussion of the tax benefit rule below.

In general, the allocation of a tax deficiency depends on which spouse's "items" gave rise to the deficiency. The items may be omitted income or disallowed deductions or credits. Items are generally allocated to the spouse who would have reported them on a separate return. If a deficiency is based on unreported income, the deficiency is allocated to the spouse who earned the income. Income from a jointly owned business is allocated equally unless you provide evidence that more should be allocated to the other spouse. Similarly, if a deficiency is based on the denial of personal deductions, the deficiency is allocated equally between you unless you show that a different allocation is appropriate. A deficiency based on the denial of business deductions is allocated according to your respective ownership shares in the business. If the IRS can show fraud, it can reallocate joint return items.

On Form 8857, you do not have to figure the portion of the deficiency for which you are liable. The IRS will figure your separate liability (and any related interest and penalties).

### EXAMPLES

1. After you obtain a divorce, the IRS examines a joint return you filed with your former husband and assesses a tax deficiency attributable to income he failed to report. If you did not know about the omitted income and timely elect separate liability treatment, you are not liable for any part of the tax deficiency, which is entirely allocable to your former husband who earned the income. You are not liable even if the IRS is unable to collect the tax from your former husband and you have substantial assets from which the tax could be paid.

2. The IRS assesses a joint return deficiency attributable to $35,000 of income that your former spouse failed to report and $15,000 of disallowed deductions that you claimed. Both of you may make the separate liability election and limit your respective liabilities.

> If you claim relief, your liability will be limited to 30% of the deficiency, as your disallowed deductions of $15,000 are 30% of the $50,000 of items causing the deficiency. If your former husband makes the claim, he will be liable for the remaining 70% of the deficiency (his $35,000 of unreported income is 70% of the $50,000 of items causing the deficiency).
>
> If either of you does not make a relief claim, the non-requesting person could be held liable for 100% of the deficiency unless innocent spouse relief is available or the IRS grants equitable relief.

**Tax benefit rule limits relief based on erroneous deductions or credits.** The tax benefit limitation is an exception to the general rule that allocates items between the spouses as if separate returns had been filed. If you received a tax benefit from an erroneous deduction or credit that is allocable to the other spouse, you remain liable for the proportionate part of the deficiency. You are treated as having received a tax benefit if the disallowed deduction exceeded the income that would have been reported by the other spouse on a hypothetical separate return.

**Transfers intended to avoid tax.** You may be held liable for more than your allocable share of a deficiency if a disqualified asset transfer was made to you by your spouse with a principal purpose of avoiding tax. Transfers made to you within the one-year period preceding the date on which the IRS sends the first letter of proposed deficiency are presumed to have a tax avoidance purpose unless they are pursuant to a divorce decree or decree of separate maintenance. You may rebut the presumption by showing that tax avoidance was not the principal purpose of the transfer. If the tax avoidance presumption is not rebutted, the transfer is considered a disqualified transfer and the value of the transferred asset adds to your share of the liability as otherwise determined under the above election rules.

If the IRS proves that you and your former spouse transferred assets between you as part of a fraudulent scheme, neither of you will be allowed to claim separate liability relief; both of you will remain individually liable for the entire joint return deficiency.

> ### EXAMPLE
>
> On a joint return, you report wages of $100,000 and your husband reports $15,000 of self-employment income. You divorce the following year. The IRS examines the return and disallows a $20,000 business expense deduction claimed by your former husband, resulting in a $5,600 tax deficiency. You elect separate liability relief. Of the $20,000 deduction, $15,000 is allocable to your former husband as that amount offset his entire income. The $5,000 balance offset your separate income and thereby gave you a tax benefit. Your former husband will be liable for 75% of the deficiency ($4,200) and you will be liable for the 25% balance ($1,400).
>
> If your former husband had reported income of $30,000 instead of $15,000, you would not be liable for any part of the deficiency under the tax benefit rule. The deduction is attributed entirely to his income, so the entire deficiency is allocated to him.
>
> These allocations assume that the IRS does not show that you had "actual knowledge" (see above) of the deductions attributable to your former husband. To the extent you had such knowledge, the deductions are allocable to both of you, so both of you remain liable for that part of the deficiency.

**Appeal to Tax Court.** You may petition the Tax Court if the IRS disputes your claim or your allocation of liability. The petition must be filed within 90 days of the date on which the IRS mails a determination to you by registered or certified mail if the IRS mailing is within six months of the filing of the election. If an IRS notice is not mailed within the six-month period, a Tax Court petition may be filed without waiting for an IRS response or, if you do wait, you have until 90 days after the date the IRS mails the notice to file the petition.

The IRS may not take any collection action against you during the 90-day period and if the Tax Court petition is filed, the suspension lasts until a final court decision is made.

## 1.9 Equitable Relief

The IRS may grant equitable relief for liability on a joint return where innocent spouse relief *(1.7)* and separate liability *(1.8)* are not available. For example, separate liability relief and innocent spouse relief are not available where the proper amount of tax was reported on a joint return but your spouse failed to pay the tax owed. If you signed a correct return on which tax was owed and, without your knowledge, your spouse used the funds intended for payment of the tax for other purposes, the IRS may grant you equitable relief. A request for equitable relief is made on Form 8857. The IRS may also grant equitable relief in cases where the proper amount of tax was understated on the joint return if it would be inequitable to hold you liable.

**Threshold conditions you must meet for relief.** Each of the following conditions must be met before the IRS will even consider granting you equitable relief:

1. You filed a joint return for the year that relief is sought.
2. Relief is not available under the innocent spouse *(1.7)* or separate liability *(1.8)* rules.
3. No assets were transferred between you and your spouse as part of a fraudulent scheme.
4. Your spouse did not transfer assets to you for the purpose of tax avoidance. If there was such a transfer, relief can be granted only to the extent income tax liability exceeds the value of these assets.
5. You did not file or fail to file the return with fraudulent intent.
6. The income tax liability for which you are seeking relief is attributable to the other spouse (with whom the joint return was filed). There are exceptions to this requirement if community property law applies, you have nominal ownership of property subject to a deficiency, the other spouse misappropriated funds intended for payment of the tax without your knowledge, or you did not challenge the treatment of items on the joint return because of prior abuse that made you fear retaliation by the other spouse.

**Deadline for requesting equitable relief.** If the IRS claims that you are liable for unpaid tax on the joint return, you may submit a claim for equitable relief until the statute of limitations on IRS collections expires, which generally is 10 years after the tax has been assessed.

**Relief granted in streamlined determination.** If you meet the threshold requirements (shown above) for obtaining equitable relief, the IRS will grant relief in a streamlined determination if you are no longer married, you would face economic hardship if relief were not granted, and you did not know or have reason to know that tax was understated on the joint return or that the tax shown would not be paid. Streamlined relief will not be denied even if you had such knowledge or reason to know, if you were subjected to abuse by the other spouse or you were unable to challenge how items were treated on the joint return or why the tax due was not paid because the other spouse controlled the household finances. If the conditions for streamlined relief are met, the other factors normally taken into account (discussed below) will not be considered.

**Factors the IRS will consider.** If the threshold conditions are satisfied and you do not qualify for streamlined relief as just discussed, you must convince the IRS that equitable relief is appropriate. The IRS will consider all the facts and circumstances.

The following is a nonexclusive list of factors that the IRS will take into account (Revenue Procedure 2013-34) in determining whether to grant equitable relief: whether you are separated or divorced from the spouse with whom you filed the joint return, whether you would suffer economic hardship (i.e., be unable to meet basic living expenses), whether you received any significant benefit from the unpaid tax or item giving rise to the deficiency (beyond normal support), whether you knew or had reason to know that tax was understated on the joint return or that the tax would not be paid, whether you were obligated to pay the outstanding tax liability by a divorce decree or other legally binding agreement, whether you have made a good faith effort to comply with the tax laws in later years, and whether you were in poor health (physical or mental) when you signed the joint return or you requested relief.

*Court Decision*

**Equitable Relief for Interest and Penalties Based on Own Income**

The Tax Court held that a business owner was entitled to equitable relief for late-filing and late-payment penalties and most of the interest assessed by the IRS although the underlying tax liability was attributable to his own income. The taxpayer had relied on his spouse to handle the books for the business and deal with their accountant. She had the accountant prepare their 2003 joint return and the taxpayer signed it, but she never mailed the return, for reasons unknown. After she died in 2005, the taxpayer discovered that the return had not been filed, and in September 2006 he filed a 2003 return reporting his income (the wife had no 2003 income) but did not pay the tax due on the return.

The taxpayer asked the Tax Court for equitable relief from the IRS' interest charges and penalties but not for the tax on the underpayment itself, which he had the legal obligation to pay. The Court noted that the IRS' own guidelines (Revenue Procedure 2013-34) allow equitable relief to be granted where the other spouse's fraud was responsible for the nonpayment of tax, even though the liability was attributable to the requesting spouse (threshold condition 6 *(1.9)*). Here, the taxpayer's wife misled him into thinking that the return had been filed and the tax paid. It would be inequitable to hold him liable for the late filing and payment penalties and for the portion of interest that accrued while he reasonably believed that the tax had been paid (the interest from the due date of the 2003 return until he signed and filed the return in September 2006).

In considering whether to grant equitable relief, the IRS has expanded the weight that it gives to abuse of the spouse seeking relief by the other spouse (with whom the joint return was filed), or the other spouse's financial control. If you are requesting equitable relief and were the victim of physical or psychological abuse, or were unable to challenge how items were treated on the joint return or why taxes were not paid because the other spouse controlled the family finances, the abuse or lack of financial control may mitigate other factors that might otherwise weigh against granting equitable relief (Revenue Procedure 2013-34). For example, ordinarily, if you knew or had reason to know that income was omitted from the joint return, or that the other spouse would not or could not pay the tax due on the return, such "knowledge or reason to know" would be a factor weighing against your request for equitable relief. However, if you were abused or unable to challenge the tax treatment or nonpayment because the other spouse controlled the finances, this will favor the granting of relief even if you knew or had reason to know that there was a tax understatement or that the tax would not be paid.

**Appeal to Tax Court.** If the IRS denies your request for equitable relief, you may petition the Tax Court for review of the IRS decision. The petition must be filed with the Tax Court no later than the 90th day after the date that the IRS mails its final determination notice to you.

## 1.10 Death of Your Spouse in 2018

If your spouse died in 2018, you are considered married for the whole year. If you did not remarry in 2018, you may file a 2018 joint return for you and your deceased spouse. Generally, you file a joint return with the executor or administrator. But you alone may file a joint return if you are otherwise entitled to file jointly and:

1. The deceased did not file a separate return, and
2. Someone other than yourself has not been appointed as executor or administrator before the due date for filing the return. An executor or administrator appointed after the joint return is filed may revoke the joint return within the one-year period following the due date.

If you do file jointly, you include on the return all of your income and deductions for the full year and your deceased spouse's income and deductions up to the date of death *(1.14)*.

For 2019 and 2020, you may be able to file as a qualifying widow/widower if a dependent child lives with you *(1.11)*.

**Joint return barred.** As a surviving spouse, you may not file a joint return for you and your deceased spouse if:

1. You remarry before the end of the year of your spouse's death. In this case you may file jointly with your new spouse. A final return for the deceased spouse must be filed by the executor or administrator using the filing status of married filing separately.
2. You or your deceased spouse has a short year because of a change in annual accounting period.
3. Either of you was a nonresident alien at any time during the tax year; but *see 1.5*.

**Executor or administrator may revoke joint return.** If an executor or administrator is later appointed, he or she may revoke a joint return that you alone have filed by filing a separate return for the decedent. Even if you have properly filed a joint return for you and the deceased spouse (as just discussed), the executor or administrator is given the right to revoke the joint return. But a state court held that a co-executrix could not refuse to sign a joint return where it would save the estate money.

To revoke the joint return, the executor must file a separate return within one year of the due date (including extensions). The executor's separate return is treated as a late return; interest charges and a late filing penalty apply. The joint return that you filed is deemed to be your separate return. Tax on that return is recalculated by excluding items belonging to your deceased spouse.

 *Filing Instruction*

**Reporting Income of Deceased Spouse**

If your spouse died during the year and you are filing a joint return, include his or her income earned through the date of death.

 *Planning Reminder*

**Possible Estate Insolvency**

If you will be appointed executor or administrator and are concerned about estate insolvency, it may be advisable to hedge as follows: (1) File separate returns. If it is later seen that a joint return is preferable, you have three years to change to a joint return. (2) File jointly but postpone being appointed executor or administrator until after the due date of the joint return. In this way, the joint return may be disaffirmed if the estate cannot cover its share of the taxes.

**Signing the return.** A joint return reporting your deceased spouse's income should list both of your names. Where there is an executor or administrator, the return is signed by you as the surviving spouse and the executor or administrator in his or her official capacity. If you are the executor or administrator, sign once as surviving spouse and again as the executor or administrator. Where there is no executor or administrator, you sign the return, followed by the words "filing as surviving spouse."

**Surviving spouse's liability.** If a joint return is filed and the estate cannot pay its share of the joint income tax liability, you, as the surviving spouse, may be liable for the full amount. Once the return is filed and the filing date passes, you can no longer change the joint return election and file a separate return unless an administrator or executor is appointed after the due date of the return.

In that case, as previously discussed, the executor may disaffirm the joint return.

## 1.11   Qualifying Widow/Widower Status for 2018 If Your Spouse Died in 2017 or 2016

If your spouse died in either 2017 or 2016 and you meet the following three requirements, your 2018 filing status is qualifying widow or widower, which allows you to use the same tax rate brackets as married persons filing jointly.

1. You have not remarried as of the end of 2018. If you did remarry in 2018, you may file a 2018 joint return with your new spouse.

2. You are entitled to claim as your dependent *(21.1)* for 2018 a child, stepchild, or adopted child who lived with you during 2018 and you paid over half the cost of maintaining your home. The child must live with you for the entire year, not counting temporary absences such as to attend school or take a vacation. A foster child is not considered your child for purposes of these rules.

3. You were entitled to file jointly in the year of your spouse's death, even if you did not do so.

If you meet all these tests and do not itemize deductions (Schedule A, Form 1040), use the standard deduction for married couples filing jointly *(13.1)*. To figure your regular income tax liability, you generally use the IRS Tax Table or Tax Computation Worksheet *(22.2)* for qualifying widows or widowers, the same one used by married couples filing jointly.

**Spouse's death before 2016.** If your spouse died before 2016 and you did not remarry by the end of 2018, you may be able to use head of household rates for 2018 if you maintain a home for a child or other qualified person under the rules discussed in *1.12.*

## 1.12   Qualifying as Head of Household

You can file as "head of household" for 2018 if you are unmarried at the end of 2018 and you maintained a household for your child, parent, or other qualifying person. You must be a U.S. citizen or resident *(18.1)* for the entire year. Tax rates are lower for a head of household than for a person filing as single *(1.2)* and the standard deduction is higher *(13.1)*. If you are married but for the last half of 2018 you lived apart from your spouse, you may be treated as unmarried and able to qualify for head of household tax rates and standard deduction, which are more favorable than those for a married person filing separately; *see* Test 1 below.

**Head of household tests.** You must meet both of these tests to qualify as a head of household:

1. You were unmarried at the end of the year or you are treated as unmarried (Test 1 below).

2. You paid more than half of the year's maintenance costs for the home of a qualifying person (Test 2 below). A qualifying person other than your parent must live with you in that same house for over half the year, disregarding temporary absences. A qualifying parent does not have to live with you.

Details of the tests are in the following paragraphs.

 *Filing Tip*

**Advantages of Head of Household Status**

Tax rate brackets are more favorable for a head of household than for a person filing as single. The standard deduction is also higher. For a married person who lived apart from his or her spouse during the last half of the year, qualifying as a head of household allows use of tax rate brackets that are more favorable than those for married persons filing separately *(1.2)*.

**Test 1: Are you unmarried?** You are "unmarried" for 2018 head of household purposes if you are any one of the following:

- Single as of the end of 2018.
- A widow or widower and your spouse died before 2018. If a dependent child lives with you, *see 1.1*1 to determine if you may use the even more advantageous filing status of qualifying widow/widower. If your spouse died in 2018, you are treated as married for the entire year and cannot qualify as a 2018 head of household, but a joint return may be filed *(1.10)*.
- Legally separated or divorced under a final court decree as of the end of 2018. A custody and support order does not qualify as a legal separation. A provisional decree (not final), such as a support order pendente lite (while action is pending) or a temporary order, has no effect for tax purposes until the decree is made final.
- Married but living apart from your spouse. You are considered unmarried for 2018 head of household purposes if your spouse was not a member of your household during the last six months of 2018, you file separate 2018 returns, and in 2018 you maintained a household for more than half the year for a dependent child, stepchild, or adopted child. A foster child qualifies if he or she was placed with you by an authorized placement agency, or by a court judgment, decree, or order. You must be able to claim the child as your dependent, but you are treated as meeting this test if you are the custodial parent who waives the right to the exemption to the noncustodial parent *(21.7)*. You are not considered to be "living apart" if you and your spouse lived under the same roof during the last six months of the year.
- Married to an individual who was a nonresident alien during any part of 2018 and you do not elect to file a joint return reporting your joint worldwide income *(1.5)*.

**Test 2: Did you maintain a home for a qualifying person?** You must pay more than half the costs of maintaining a home for a qualifying person.

*Qualifying person.* A child or relative can be your qualifying person for head of household purposes only if he or she is a qualifying child or a qualifying relative under the rules for dependents *(21.1)*. However, you may be eligible for head of household status even if you are unable to actually claim the person as your dependent. For example, an unmarried child who meets the definition of a qualifying child *(21.1)* but who cannot be claimed as your dependent because of one of the additional tests *(21.1)* is nonetheless a qualifying person for head of household purposes. If, under the special rules for divorced or separated parents *(21.7)*, you are the custodial parent and you waive your right to treat your child as a dependent in favor of the other parent, you may claim head of household status; the other parent may not.

A married child must be your dependent to be a qualifying person for head of household purposes unless the only reason you cannot treat the child as your dependent is that you are the dependent of another taxpayer *(21.1)*.

Your parent or any other qualifying relative can be your qualifying person for head of household purposes only if you can treat that person as your dependent *(21.1)*. However, you are not eligible for head of household status if the relative is your dependent only because (1) you have a multiple support agreement granting you the right to the exemption (even though there is no exemption allowed in 2018) *(21.6)* or (2) he or she is your qualifying relative under the member-of-household test *(21.4)*.

*Maintaining a household.* For a qualifying person other than your parent, the home that you maintain must be the principal residence for both of you for more than half the year, disregarding temporary absences; *see* Example 2 below. If the qualifying person is your parent, it does not matter where he or she lives, so long as you pay more than half of the household costs.

You must pay for more than half of the rent, property taxes, mortgage interest, utilities, repairs, property insurance, domestic help, and food eaten in the home. Do not consider the rental value of the lodgings provided to the qualifying person or the cost of clothing, medical expenses, education, vacation costs, life insurance, or transportation you provide, or the value of your work around the house.

 *Planning Reminder*

**Special Separate Household Rule for Parent**

If your dependent parent is the qualifying person, you may claim head of household status even if he or she does not live with you. You must pay over half of your parent's household expenses, whether your parent lives alone, with someone else, or in a senior citizens' residence.

*Caution*

**Meeting Member-of-Household Test Insufficient**

Under the qualifying relative rules, you may be able to treat as your dependent a friend or distant relative that you support in your home under the "member of household" test *(21.4)*. Even if the "member of household" test is met, head of household status is not allowed; a person who qualifies as your dependent under the "member of household" test is not a qualifying person for head of household purposes.

*Temporary absences disregarded.* In determining whether you and a qualifying person lived in the same home for more than half the year, temporary absences are ignored if the absence is due to illness, or being away at school, on a business trip, on vacation, serving in the military, or staying with a parent under a child custody agreement. The IRS requires that it be reasonable to expect your qualifying child or relative to return to your household after such a temporary absence, and that you continue to maintain the household during the temporary absence. Under this rule, you would lose the right to file as head of household if your qualifying person moved into his or her own permanent residence before the end of the year.

> **EXAMPLES**
>
> 1. Your mother lived with your sister in your sister's apartment, which cost $12,000 to maintain in 2018. Of this amount, you contributed $7,000 and your sister $5,000. Your mother's only income is from Social Security and she did not contribute any funds to the household. You qualify as head of household for 2018 because you paid over half the cost of maintaining the home for your mother, who qualifies as your dependent (she is a "qualifying relative"; 21.1). A child or dependent relative other than your parent would have to live with you to enable you to file as head of household.
>
> 2. Doctors advised McDonald that her mentally ill son might become self-sufficient if he lived in a separate residence, but one nearby enough for her to provide supervision. She took the advice and kept up a separate home for her son that was about a mile from her own home. She frequently spent nights at his home and he at hers. The Tax Court agreed with the IRS that McDonald could not file as head of household since her principal residence was not the same as her son's.

## 1.13 Filing for Your Child

The income of your minor child is not included on your return unless you make a special election to report a child's investment income *(24.4)*. A minor is considered a taxpayer in his or her own right. If the child is required to file a return but is unable to do so because of age or for any other reason, the parent or guardian is responsible for filing the return.

A tax return must be filed for a dependent child who had more than $1,050 of investment income and no earned income (for personal services) for 2018. If your child had only earned income (for personal services) and no investment income, a tax return must be filed if the earned income exceeded $12,000. See page 4 for further filing threshold rules.

If the child is unable to sign the return, the parent or guardian should sign the child's name in the proper place, followed by the words, "by [signature], parent [or guardian] for minor child." A parent is liable for tax due on pay earned by the child for services, but not on investment income.

A child who is not required to file a return should still do so for a refund of taxes withheld.

 *Caution*

**Kiddie Tax May Apply to Investment Income**

If your child has 2018 investment income exceeding $2,100, the excess is taxed at the rates applicable to trusts and estates under the "kiddie tax" rules as revised by the Tax Cuts and Jobs Act.. The kiddie tax applies to children under age 18, and also to children who at the end of the year are either age 18 or full-time students under age 24 if their earned income is no more than 50% of their total support for the year. See Chapter 24 for kiddie tax details.

**Social Security numbers.** A parent or guardian must obtain a Social Security number for a child before filing the child's first income tax return. The child's Social Security number must also be provided to banks, brokers, and other payers of interest and dividends to avoid penalties and backup withholding *(26.12)*. To obtain a Social Security number, file Form SS-5 with your local Social Security office. If you have applied for a Social Security number but not yet received it by the filing due date, write "applied for" on the tax return in the space provided for the number.

Whether or not you are filing a return for a child, you must obtain and report on your return a Social Security number for a child whom you are claiming as a dependent *(21.1)*.

**Wages you pay your children.** You may deduct wages paid to your children in your business. Keep records showing that their activities are of a business rather than personal nature.

**Withholding for children.** Children with wages are generally subject to withholding and should file Form W-4 with their employer. An exemption from withholding may be claimed only in limited cases. The child must certify on Form W-4 that he or she had no federal tax liability in the prior year and expects no liability in the current year for which the withholding exemption is sought. For example, a child who expected to be claimed as another taxpayer's dependent for 2018 could claim an exemption from withholding on Form W-4 only if he or she expected to have investment income of $350 or less and total income (expected investment income plus wages) of $1,050 or less; the $350 and $1,050 amounts are subject to change annually.

Wages you pay to your own children under age 18 for working in your business are not subject to FICA taxes (Social Security and Medicare) *(26.9)*.

## 1.14 Return for Deceased

When a person dies, another tax-paying entity is created—the decedent's estate. Until the estate is fully distributed, it will generally earn income for which a return must be filed. For example, Carlos Perez dies on June 30, 2018. The wages and bank interest he earned through June 30 are reported on his final income tax return, Form 1040 for 2018, which is due by April 15, 2019. Interest earned on his bank account after June 30 is attributed to the estate, or to the account beneficiary if the right to the account passes by law directly to the account beneficiary. Income received by the estate is reported on Form 1041, the income tax return for the estate, if the estate has gross income of $600 or more. If Carlos was married, his surviving spouse could file a joint return *(1.10)* for 2018 and include all of Carlos's earnings through June 30. If she jointly owned the bank account with Carlos, the interest after as well as before June 30 could be reported on their joint return.

**What income tax returns must be filed on behalf of the deceased?** If the individual died after the close of the taxable year but before the income tax return was filed, the following must be filed:

1. Income tax return for the prior year;
2. Final income tax return, covering earnings in the period from the beginning of the taxable year to the date of death; and
3. Estate income tax return, covering earnings in the period after the decedent's death.

If the individual died after filing a return for the prior tax year, then only 2 and 3 are filed.

> **EXAMPLE**
>
> Steven Jones, a resident of New York, died on January 31, 2019, before he could file his 2018 tax return. His 2018 income tax return must be filed by April 15, 2019, unless an extension is obtained. A final income tax return to report earnings from January 1, 2019, through January 31, 2019 (date of death), will have to be filed by April 15, 2020. Jones's estate will have to file an income tax return on Form 1041 to report earnings and other income that were not earned by Jones before February 1, 2019, unless the gross income of the estate is under $600.

**Who is responsible for filing?** The executor, administrator, or other legal representative is responsible for filing all returns. For purposes of determining whether a final income tax return for the decedent is due, the annual gross income test at page 3 is considered in full. You do not prorate it according to the part of the year the decedent lived. A surviving spouse may assume responsibility for filing a joint return for the year of death if no executor or administrator has been appointed and other tests are met *(1.10)*. However, if a legal representative has been appointed, he or she must give the surviving spouse consent to file a joint return for the year of the decedent's death. In one case, a state court held that a co-executrix could not refuse consent and was required to sign a joint return where it would save the estate money.

 *Planning Reminder*

**Promptly Closing the Estate**

To expedite the closing of the decedent's estate, an executor or other personal representative of the decedent may file Form 4810 for a prompt assessment. Once filed, the IRS has 18 months to assess additional taxes. The request does not extend the assessment period beyond the regular limit, which is three years from the date the return was filed. Form 4810 must be filed separately from the final return.

*Filing Instruction*

## IRD Not Included on Decedent's Final Return

Do not report on the decedent's final return income that is received after his or her death, or accrues after or because of death if the decedent used the accrual method. This income is considered "income in respect of a decedent," or IRD *(11.16)*. IRD is taxed to the estate or beneficiary receiving the income in the year of the receipt. On the decedent's final return, only deductible expenses paid up to and including the date of death may be claimed. If the decedent reported on the accrual basis, those deductions accruable up to and including the date of death are deductible. If the decedent mailed or delivered a check for payment of a deductible item, a deduction is allowable on the decedent's last return, even though the check was not cashed or deposited by the recipient until after the decedent's death. If the check was not honored by the bank, the item is not deductible.

**How do you report the decedent's income and deductions?** You follow the method used by the decedent during his or her life, either the cash method or the accrual method, to account for the income up to the date of death. The income does not have to be put on an annual basis. Each item is taxed in the same manner as it would have been taxed had the decedent lived for the entire year.

If the decedent owned U.S. Savings Bonds, *see 4.29*.

When one spouse dies in a community property state *(1.6)*, how should the income from the community property be reported during the administration of the estate? The IRS says that half the income is the estate's and the other half belongs to the surviving spouse.

Deductible expenses paid (or accrued under the accrual method) by the decedent before death are claimed on the final return.

**Medical expenses of the decedent.** If the estate pays the decedent's personal medical expenses (not those for the decedent's dependents) within one year of the date of death, the expenses can be deducted on the decedent's final return, subject to the adjusted gross income floor *(17.7)*. However, the expenses are not deductible for income tax purposes if they are deducted for estate tax purposes. To deduct such medical expenses on the decedent's final return, a statement must be attached to the final return affirming that no estate tax deduction has been taken and that the rights to the deduction have been waived.

**Partnership income.** The death of a partner closes the partnership tax year for that partner. The final return for the partner must include his or her distributive share of partnership income and deductions for the part of the partnership's tax year ending on the date of death. Thus, if a partner dies on July 26, 2018, and the partnership's taxable year ends December 31, 2018, the partner's final 2018 return must include partnership items for January 1, 2018, through July 26, 2018. Partnership items for the balance of 2018 must be reported by the partner's executor or other successor in interest on the estate's income tax return.

**Exemptions allowed on a final return.** These are generally the same exemptions the decedent would have had if he or she had not died *(21.1)*. You do not reduce the exemptions because of the shorter taxable year.

**Estimated taxes.** No estimated tax need be paid by the executor after the death of an unmarried individual; the entire tax is paid when filing the final tax return. But where the deceased and a surviving spouse paid estimated tax jointly, the rule is different. The surviving spouse is still liable for the balance of the estimated tax unless an amended estimated tax voucher is filed. Further, if the surviving spouse plans to file a joint return *(1.10)* that includes the decedent's income, estimated tax payments may be required; *see Chapter 27*.

Where the estate has gross income, estimated tax installments are not required on Form 1041-ES for the first two years after the decedent's death.

**Signing the return.** An executor or administrator of the estate signs the return. If it is a joint return, *see 1.10*.

**When a refund is due on a final return.** The decedent's final return may also be used as a claim for a refund of an overpayment of withheld or estimated taxes. Form 1310 may be used to get the refund, but the form is not required if you are a surviving spouse filing a joint return for the year your spouse died. If you are an executor or administrator of the estate and you are filing Form 1040, 1040A, or 1040EZ for the decedent, you do not need Form 1310, but you must attach to the return a copy of the court certificate showing your appointment as personal representative.

**Itemized deduction for IRD subject to estate tax.** Items of gross income that the decedent had a right to receive but did not receive before death (or accrue if under the accrual method) are subject to income tax when received by the estate or beneficiary. This "income in respect of a decedent," or IRD, is also included in the decedent's estate for estate tax purposes. If estate tax is paid, an individual beneficiary may claim an itemized deduction for an allocable share of the estate tax paid on IRD items; *see 11.17* for deduction details.

## 1.15 Return for an Incompetent Person

A legal guardian of an incompetent person files Form 1040 for an incompetent whose gross income meets the filing tests on page 3. Where a spouse becomes incompetent, the IRS says the other spouse may file a return for the incompetent without a power of attorney, if no legal guardian has been appointed. For example, during the period an individual was in a mental hospital, and before he was adjudged legally incompetent, his wife continued to operate his business. She filed an income tax return for him and signed it for him although she had no power of attorney. The IRS accepted the return as properly filed. Until a legal guardian was appointed, she was charged with the care of her husband and his property.

The IRS has accepted a joint return filed by a wife in her capacity as legal guardian for her missing husband. However, the Tax Court has held that where one spouse is mentally incompetent, a joint return may not be filed because the incompetent spouse was unable to consent to a joint return; an appeals court agreed.

## 1.16 How a Nonresident Alien Is Taxed

A nonresident alien is generally taxed only on income from U.S. sources. A nonresident alien's income that is effectively connected with a U.S. business and capital gains from the sale of U.S. real property interests are subject to tax at regular graduated U.S. rates, the same as for a U.S. citizen *(1.2)*. Other capital gains are not taxed unless a nonresident alien has a U.S. business or is in the U.S. for 183 days during the year. Generally, investment income of a nonresident alien from U.S. sources that is not effectively connected with a U.S. business is subject to a 30% tax rate (or lower rate if provided by treaty).

Nonresident aliens who are required to file must do so on Form 1040NR. If you are a nonresident alien, get a copy of IRS Publication 519, U.S. Tax Guide for Aliens. It explains how nonresident aliens pay U.S. tax.

**Dual status.** In the year a person arrives in or departs from the U.S., both resident and nonresident status may apply.

Certain restrictions apply to dual status taxpayers. For example, a joint return may not be filed, unless you and your spouse agree to be taxed as U.S. residents for the entire year.

For details on filing a return for a dual status year, *see* IRS Publication 519 and the instructions to Form 1040NR.

*Caution*

**Who Is a Resident?**

An alien's mere presence in the U.S. does not make him or her a "resident." An alien is generally treated as a "resident" only if he or she is a lawful permanent resident who has a "green card" or meets a substantial presence test *(1.18)*.

> **EXAMPLE**
>
> On May 11, 2018, Leon Marchand arrived on a non-immigrant visa and was present in the U.S. for the rest of the year. From January 1 to May 10, 2018, he is a nonresident; from May 11 to the end of the year, he is a resident, under the 183-day test (1.18). Since he is a U.S. resident on the last day of the year, he files Form 1040 and reports on it the income received during the period he was a resident, as well as income received during the period of nonresidency that was effectively connected with a U.S. business. He writes "Dual-Status Return" across the top of the Form 1040. The income for the nonresident portion of the year should be shown on a statement attached to the Form 1040. Form 1040NR (or, if eligible, Form 1040NR-EZ) can be used as the statement; mark "Dual-Status Statement" across the top of the Form 1040NR (or 1040NR-EZ).

## 1.17 How a Resident Alien Is Taxed

A resident alien *(1.18)* is taxed on worldwide income from all sources, just like a U.S. citizen. The exclusion for foreign earned income may be claimed if the foreign physical presence test is satisfied or if the bona fide residence test is met by an individual residing in a treaty country *(36.5)*. A resident alien may generally claim a foreign tax credit *(36.14)*. A resident alien's pension from a foreign government is subject to regular U.S. tax. A resident alien working in the United States for a foreign government is not taxed on the wages if the foreign government allows a similar exemption to U.S. citizens.

*Planning Reminder*

**Is 2018 Your First Year of Residency?**

If you were not a resident during 2017 but in 2018 you satisfy both the lawful resident (green card) test and the 183-day presence test, your residence begins on the earlier of the first day you are in the U.S. while a lawful permanent resident or the first day of physical presence.

## 1.18 Who Is a Resident Alien?

The following tests determine whether an alien is taxed as a U.S. resident. Intent to remain in the U.S. is not considered.

You are treated as a resident alien and taxed as a U.S. resident for 2018 tax purposes if you meet either of the following tests:

1. You have been issued a "green card," which grants you the status of lawful permanent resident. If you were outside the U.S. for part of 2018 and then became a lawful permanent resident, *see* the rules below for dual tax status.

2. You meet a 183-day substantial presence test. Under this test, you are treated as a U.S. resident if you were in the U.S. for at least 31 days during the calendar year and have been in the U.S. for at least 183 days within the last three years (the current year and the two preceding calendar years). The 183-day test is complicated and there are several exceptions.

To determine if you meet the 183-day test for 2018, the following cumulative times are totaled. Each day in the U.S. during 2018 is counted as a full day. Each day in 2017 counts as ⅓ of a day; each day in 2016 counts as 1/6 of a day. Note that you must be physically present in the U.S. for at least 31 days in the current year. If you are not, the 183-day test does not apply.

Other exceptions to the substantial presence test are: commuting from Canada or Mexico; keeping a tax home and close contacts or connections in a foreign country; having a diplomat, teacher, trainee, or student status; being a professional athlete temporarily in the U.S. to compete in a charitable sports event; or being confined in the U.S. for certain medical reasons. These exceptions are explained in the following paragraphs.

**Commute from Mexico or Canada.** If you regularly commute to work in the U.S. from Mexico or Canada, commuting days do not count as days of physical presence for the 183-day test.

**Tax home/closer connection exception.** If you are in the United States for less than 183 days during 2018, show that you had a closer connection with a foreign country than with the U.S., and keep a tax home there for the year, you generally will not be subject to tax as a U.S. resident even if you meet the substantial presence test. Under this exception, it is possible to have a U.S. abode and a tax home in a foreign country. A tax home is usually where a person has his or her principal place of business; if there is no principal place of business, it is the place of regular abode. Proving a tax home alone is not sufficient; the closer connection relationship must also be shown.

To claim the closer connection exception, you must file Form 8840 explaining the basis of your claim. The tax home/closer connection exception does not apply to an alien who is present for 183 days or more during a year or who has applied for a "green card." A relative's application is not considered as the alien's application.

**Exempt-person exception.** Days of presence in the U.S. are not counted under the 183-day test if you are considered an exempt person such as a teacher, trainee, student, foreign-government-related person, or professional athlete temporarily in the U.S. to compete in a charitable sports event.

To exclude days of presence as a teacher, trainee, student, or professional athlete, you must file Form 8843 with the IRS.

A foreign-government-related person is any individual temporarily present in the U.S. who (1) has diplomatic status or a visa that the Secretary of the Treasury (after consultation with the Secretary of State) determined represents full-time diplomatic or consular status; or (2) is a full-time employee of an international organization; or (3) is a member of the immediate family of a diplomat or international organization employee.

A teacher or trainee is any individual other than a student who is temporarily present in the U.S. under a "J" or "Q" visa and who substantially complies with the requirements for being so present.

A student is any individual who is temporarily present in the U.S. under either an "F," "J," "M," or "Q" visa and who substantially complies with the requirements for being so present.

The exception generally does not apply to a teacher or trainee who has been exempt as a teacher, trainee, or student for any part of two of the six preceding calendar years. However, if during the period you are temporarily present in the U.S. under an "F," "J," "M," or "Q" visa and all of your compensation is received from outside the U.S., you may qualify for the exception if you were exempt as a teacher, trainee, or student for less than four years in the six preceding calendar years. The exception also does not apply to a student who has been exempt as a teacher, trainee, or student for more than five calendar years, unless you show that you do not intend to reside permanently in the U.S. and that you have substantially complied with the requirements of the student visa providing for temporary presence in the U.S.

**Medical exception.** If you plan to leave but cannot physically leave the U.S. because of a medical condition that arose in the U.S., you may be treated as a nonresident, even if present here for more than 183 days during the year. You must file Form 8843 to claim the medical exception.

**Tax treaty exceptions.** The lawful permanent residence test and the substantial physical presence test do not override tax treaty definitions of residence. Thus, you may be protected by a tax treaty from being treated as a U.S. resident even if you would be treated as a resident under either test.

**Dual tax status in first year of residency.** If you first became a lawful permanent resident of the U.S. (received a green card) during 2018 and were not a U.S. resident during 2017, your period of U.S. residency begins with the first day in 2018 that you are present in the U.S. with the status of lawful permanent resident. Before that date, you are a nonresident alien. This means that if you become a lawful permanent resident during 2018 and remain a resident at the end of the year, you have a dual status tax year. On Form 1040, you attach a separate statement showing the income for the part of the year you are a nonresident. Form 1040NR (or 1040NR-EZ) may be used as the statement. Write "Dual-Status Return" across the top of the Form 1040 and "Dual-Status Statement" across the top of the Form 1040NR (or 1040NR-EZ).

To figure tax for a dual status year, *see* IRS Publication 519 and the instructions to Form 1040NR.

You also may have a dual status year if you were not a U.S. resident in 2017, and in 2018 you are a U.S. resident under the 183-day presence test. Your period of U.S. residency starts on the first day in 2018 for which you were physically present; before that date you are treated as a nonresident alien. However, if you meet the 183-day presence test (but not the green card test) and also spent 10 or fewer days in the U.S. during a period in which you had a closer connection to a foreign country than to the U.S., you may disregard the 10-day period. The purpose of this exception is to allow a brief presence in the U.S. for business trips or house hunting before the U.S. residency period starts.

If you are married at the end of the year to a U.S. citizen or resident alien, you and your spouse may elect to be treated as U.S. residents for the entire year by reporting your worldwide income on a joint return. You must attach to the joint return a statement signed by both of you that you are choosing to be treated as full-year U.S. residents.

---

### EXAMPLES

1. Manuel Riveras, who has never before been a U.S. resident, lives in Spain until May 16, 2018. He moves to the U.S. and remains in the U.S. through the end of the year, thereby satisfying the physical presence test. On May 16, he is a U.S. resident. However, for the period before May 16, he is taxed as a nonresident.

2. Same facts as in Example 1, but Riveras attends a meeting in the U.S. on February 2 through 8. On May 16, he moves to the U.S.; May 16, not February 2, is the starting date of the residency. During February, he had closer connection to Spain than to the U.S. Thus, his short stay in February is an exempt period.

**First-year choice.** If you do not meet either the green card test or the 183-day substantial presence test for the year of your arrival in the U.S. or for the immediately preceding year, but you do meet the substantial presence test for the year immediately following the year of your arrival, you may elect to be treated as a U.S. resident for part of the year of your arrival. To do this, you must (1) be present in the U.S. for at least 31 consecutive days in the year of your arrival; and (2) be present in the U.S. for at least 75% of the number of days beginning with the first day of the 31-consecutive-day period and ending with the last day of the year of arrival. For purposes of this 75% requirement, you may treat up to five days of absence from the U.S. as days of presence within the U.S.

Do not count as days of presence in the U.S. days for which you are an exempt individual as discussed earlier.

You make the first-year election to be treated as a U.S. resident by attaching a statement to Form 1040 for the year of your arrival. A first-year election, once made, may not be revoked without the consent of the IRS.

If you make the election, your residence starting date for the year of your arrival is the first day of the earliest 31-consecutive-day period of presence that you use to qualify for the choice. You are treated as a U.S. resident for the remainder of the year.

**Last year of residence.** You are no longer treated as a U.S. resident as of your residency termination date. If you do not have a green card but are a U.S. resident for the year under the 183-day presence test, and you leave the U.S. during that year, your residency termination date is the last day you are present in the U.S., provided that: (1) after leaving the U.S. you had a closer connection to a foreign country than to the U.S. and had your tax home in that foreign country for the rest of the year, and (2) you are not treated as a U.S. resident for any part of the next calendar year.

If during the year you give up your green card (lawful permanent resident status) and meet tests (1) and (2), your residency termination date is the first day that you are no longer a lawful permanent resident. If during the year you meet both the green card test and the 183-day presence test and meet tests (1) and (2), your residency termination date is the later of the last day of U.S. presence or the first day you are no longer a lawful permanent resident. If tests (1) and (2) are not met, the residency termination date is the last day of the calendar year. In the year of your residency termination date, the filing rules for dual status taxpayers in this section apply.

For the year you give up your residence in the United States, you must file Form 1040NR (or Form 1040NR-EZ if eligible) and write "Dual-Status Return" across the top. Attach Form 1040 (or other statement) to show the income for the part of the year you are a resident; across the top write "Dual-Status Statement." See the instructions to Form 1040NR and IRS Publication 519 for filing the dual status return.

## 1.19 Certificate of Tax Compliance for Alien Leaving the United States

Current law generally requires an alien who plans on leaving the U.S. to go to an IRS office before departure to obtain a "sailing" or "departure" permit, technically known as a "certificate of compliance." Diplomats, employees of international organizations or foreign governments, students, industrial trainees and exchange visitors are generally exempt from the permit requirement; *see* Publication 519 for other exceptions. If an exception does not apply, Form 1040-C must be filed to report the income received and expected to be received for the year. In some cases, a shorter Form 2063 may be filed instead of Form 1040-C. If the Form 1040-C (or Form 2063) shows that there will be a tax due, the IRS will generally issue a certificate of compliance without requiring you to pay the tax or posting a bond for it so long as the IRS determines that your departure will not jeopardize collection of the tax. See Publication 519 for further details.

*Planning Reminder*

**Departure Permit**

An alien planning to leave the U.S. may have to obtain a "certificate of compliance" on Form 1040-C (or Form 2063) from the IRS to certify that his or her U.S. tax obligations have been satisfied; *see* Publication 519 for exceptions and further details.

# 1.20  Expatriation Tax

U.S. citizens who have renounced their citizenship and long-term U.S. residents who end their residency are considered expatriates subject to special tax rules. You are considered a long-term resident for purposes of these rules if you give up lawful permanent residency ("green card") after holding it for at least eight of the prior 15 years. Form 8854 must be filed to establish that you have expatriated for tax purposes. The IRS warns that until Form 8854 is filed and the appropriate actions are taken to notify the State Department or Department of Homeland Security of the expatriation, you are not relieved of the obligation to file U.S. tax returns and report your worldwide income as a citizen or resident of the United States. On Form 8854, expatriations after June 16, 2008 have different tax consequences than expatriations after June 3, 2004 and before June 17, 2008.

If you expatriated in 2018 or before 2018 but after June 16, 2008, you are generally subject to a "mark-to-market" tax on Form 8854 if any of the following is true: (1) your average annual net income tax liability for the five years ending before the date of expatriation exceeds an annual ceiling, which is $165,000 for expatriations occurring in 2018, or (2) your net worth on the date of expatriation was $2 million or more, or (3) you fail to certify on Form 8854 under penalty of perjury that you complied with all U.S. federal tax obligations for the five years preceding the expatriation date.

Under the "mark-to market" tax, you are treated as if you had sold all of your assets (but *see* below for deferred compensation items and interests in nongrantor trusts) for their fair market value on the day before the expatriation date, and any net gain on the deemed sale is taxable for the year of the deemed sale to the extent it exceeds an annual floor, which is $711,000 for deemed sales in 2018. Losses are taken into account and the wash sale rules do not apply. An election can be made on Form 8854 to defer payment of the tax on the deemed sales until the assets are sold (or death, if sooner) provided a bond or other security is provided to the IRS. The election is made on a property-by-property basis. Interest will be charged for the deferral period. If the deferral election is made, Form 8854 must be filed annually.

Deferred compensation items and interests in nongrantor trusts are not subject to the mark-to-market tax, but are generally subject to a withholding tax of 30% when distributed to you. IRAs and certain other tax-deferred accounts are treated as if they were completely distributed on the day before the expatriation date, but early distribution penalties do not apply.

See the Form 8854 instructions for further details.

**Expatriation after June 3, 2004, and before June 17, 2008.** If you expatriated after June 3, 2004, but before June 17, 2008, you were subject to tax on U.S. source income for the following 10 years if any of the following applied to you:   (1) your average annual net income tax liability for the five years ending before the date of expatriation exceeded $139,000 if you expatriated in 2008, $136,000 if you expatriated in 2007, $131,000 if you expatriated in 2006, $127,000 if you expatriated in 2005, or $124,000 if you expatriated in 2004, or (2) your net worth on the date of expatriation was $2 million or more, or (3) you failed to certify on Form 8854 under penalty of perjury that you complied with all U.S. federal tax obligations for the five years preceding the expatriation date.

If your expatriation was in 2008 but before June 17, 2008, these rules can still apply to you for 2018, which will be the last year of the 10-year period. U.S. source income and gains are subject to regular individual tax rates unless the tax would be higher under the 30% tax on investment income not connected with a U.S. business. Form 8854 must be filed for the 10-year period. See the Form 8854 instructions and Publication 519 for further details.

# PART 2

# Reporting Your Income

In this part, you will learn what income is taxable, what income is tax free, and how to report income on your tax return.

Pay special attention to—

- Form W-2, which shows your taxable wages and provides other important information on fringe benefits received *(Chapter 2)*.

- Tax-free fringe benefit plans available from your employer *(Chapter 3)*.

- Reporting rules for interest and dividend income *(Chapter 4)*.

- Reporting gains and losses from sales of property *(Chapter 5)*.

- Rules for tax-free exchanges of like-kind property *(Chapter 6)*.

- Planning for retirement distributions. Lump-sum distributions from employer plans may qualify for special averaging or tax-free rollover *(Chapter 7)*.

- IRA contributions and distributions. Penalties for distributions before age 59½ and after age 70½ may be avoided by advance planning *(Chapter 8)*.

- Restrictions on rental losses where a rented residence is used personally by you or by family members during the year *(Chapter 9)*.

- Passive activity restrictions. Losses from rentals or passive business operations are generally not allowed, but certain real estate professionals are exempt from the loss restrictions, and for others, a special rental loss allowance of up to $25,000 may be available *(Chapter 10)*.

- Reporting refunds of state and local taxes. A refund of previously deducted taxes is generally taxable unless you had no benefit from the deduction *(Chapter 11)*.

- Cancellation of debts. When your creditor cancels debts you owe, you generally have taxable income, but there are exceptions for debts discharged while you are bankrupt or insolvent *(Chapter 11)*.

- Damages received in court proceedings. Learn when these are tax free and when taxable *(Chapter 11)*.

- How life insurance proceeds are taxed *(Chapter 11)*.

# CHAPTER 2

# Wages, Salary, and Other Compensation

Except for tax-free fringe benefits *(Chapter 3)*, tax-free foreign earned income *(Chapter 36)* and tax-free armed forces and veterans' benefits *(Chapter 35)*, practically everything you receive for your work or services is taxed, whether paid in cash, property, or services. Your employer will generally report your taxable compensation on Form W-2 and other information returns, such as Form 1099-R for certain retirement payments. Do not reduce the amount you report as taxable compensation on your return by withholdings for income taxes, Social Security taxes, union dues, or U.S. Savings Bond purchases. Your Form W-2 does not include in taxable pay your qualifying salary-reduction contributions to a retirement plan, although the amount may be shown on the form.

Attach Copy B of Form W-2 to your return; do not attach Forms 1099 unless there are withholdings.

Unemployment benefits are fully taxable. The benefits are reported to the IRS on Form 1099-G. You do not have to attach your copy of Form 1099-G to your return.

Income and expenses from self-employment are discussed in *Chapter 40*.

### Table 2-1  Understanding Your Form W-2 for 2018 Wages and Tips

| Amount in— | What You Should Know— |
| --- | --- |
| Box 1 | Taxable wages and tips. Your taxable wages, tips, and other forms of taxable compensation *(2.1)* are listed in Box 1. Taxable fringe benefits will also be included in Box 1 and may be shown in Box 14. |
| Box 2 | Federal income tax withholdings. Enter the amount of federal income tax withheld from your pay on Line 16 of Form 1040. |
| Boxes 3, 4, and 7 | Social Security withholdings. Wages subject to Social Security withholding are shown in Box 3. Tips you reported to your employer are shown separately in Box 7. The total of Boxes 3 and 7 should not exceed $128,400, the maximum Social Security wage base for 2018. Social Security taxes withheld from wages and tips are shown in Box 4 and should not exceed the maximum 2018 7 Social Security tax of $7,960.80 ($128,400 × 6.2% rate). If you worked for more than one employer in 2018 and total Social Security tax withholdings exceeded $7,960.80 you claim the excess as a tax payment on your tax return; *see 26.8*.<br><br>Elective salary deferrals to a 401(k), SIMPLE, salary-reduction SEP, or 403(b) plan, as well as employer payments of qualified adoption expenses, are included in Box 3 and subject to Social Security withholding even though these amounts are not includible in Box 1 taxable wages. Amounts deferred under a nonqualified plan or a 457 plan are included in Box 3 in the year that the deferred amounts are no longer subject to a substantial risk of forfeiture. |
| Boxes 5–6 | Medicare tax withholdings. Wages, tips, elective salary deferrals, and other compensation subject to Social Security tax (Boxes 3 and 7) are also subject to a 1.45% Medicare tax, except that there is no wage base limit for Medicare tax. Thus, the Medicare wages shown in Box 5 are not limited to the $128,400 maximum for Boxes 3 and 7. In Box 6, total Medicare withholdings are reported. For employees with wages and tips over $200,000, the Box 6 total includes the 0.9% Additional Medicare Tax *(28.2)* |
| Box 8 | Allocated tips. If you worked in a restaurant employing at least 10 people, your employer will report in Box 8 your share of 8% of gross receipts unless you reported tips at least equal to that share *(26.7)*. The amount shown here is not included in Boxes 1, 3, 5, or 7, but you must add it to wages on Line 1 of Form 1040. |
| Box 10 | Dependent care benefits. Reimbursements from your employer for dependent care expenses and the value of employer-provided care services under a qualifying plan *(3.5)* are included in Box 10. Amounts in excess of $5,000 are also included as taxable wages in Boxes 1, 3, and 5. Generally, amounts up to $5,000 are tax free, but you must determine the amount of the exclusion on Form 2441. The tax-free amount reduces expenses eligible for the dependent care credit; *see* Chapter 25. |
| Box 11 | Nonqualified plan distributions. Distributions shown in Box 11 are from a nonqualified deferred compensation plan, or a nongovernmental Section 457 plan *(7.20)*. Do not report these distributions separately since they have already been included as taxable wages in Box 1. |
| Box 12 | Elective deferrals to retirement plans. Elective salary deferrals to a 401(k) plan or SIMPLE 401(k) (including any excess over the annual deferral limit; *see 7.16*) are shown in Box 12 with Code D. For example, if you made elective pre-tax salary deferrals of $4,500 to a 401(k) plan, your employer would enter D 4500.00 in Box 12. Code E is used for deferrals to a 403(b) tax-sheltered annuity plan *(7.19)*, Code F for deferrals to a salary-reduction simplified employee pension *(8.16)*, Code G for deferrals (including non-elective as well as elective) to a governmental or nongovernmental Section 457 plan *(7.20)*, Code H for elective deferrals to a pension plan created before June 25, 1959, and funded only by employee contributions, and Code S for salary-reduction deferrals to a SIMPLE IRA *(8.18)*.<br><br>Designated Roth contributions *(7.18)* to a 401(k) plan are reported in Box 12 with Code AA. If the designated Roth contributions are to a 403(b) plan, they will be reported with Code BB, and if they are to a governmental Section 457 plan, Code EE will be used.<br><br>Cost of employer-sponsored health coverage. Your employer may show in Box 12, using Code DD, the total cost of your 2018 health plan coverage. Reporting is optional for certain employers and certain contributions, such as salary-reduction FSA contributions *(3.3)* and HSA contributions *(3.2)*, are not reportable. Any amount reported here is not taxable; it is provided for informational purposes only.<br><br>Reimbursements under qualified small employer health reimbursement arrangements (QSEHRAs). If you were reimbursed for health costs under a QSEHRA *(3.3)*, your employer will show the total amount of permitted reimbursements in Box 12 using Code FF.<br><br>Travel allowance reimbursements. If you received a flat mileage allowance from your employer for business trips *(20.33)*; or a per diem travel allowance to cover meals, lodging, and incidentals *(20.32)*; and the allowance exceeded the IRS rate, the amount up to the IRS rate (the nontaxable portion) is shown in Box 12 using Code L. The excess is included as taxable wages in Box 1.<br><br>Group-term life insurance over $50,000. The cost of taxable coverage over $50,000 is shown in Box 12 using Code C. It is also included in Box 1 wages, Box 3 Social Security wages, and Box 5 Medicare wages and tips.<br><br>If you are a retiree or other former employee who received group-term coverage over $50,000, any uncollected Social Security tax is shown using Code M and uncollected Medicare tax using Code N. The uncollected amount must be reported as an "Other Tax" on Line 62 of Schedule 4 of Form 1040; write "UT" next to it.<br><br>Nontaxable sick pay. If you contributed to a sick pay plan, an allocable portion of benefits received is tax free and is shown using Code J. |

## Table 2-1   Understanding Your Form W-2 for 2018 Wages and Tips

| Amount in— | What You Should Know— |
|---|---|
| Box 12 | Uncollected Social Security and Medicare taxes on tips. If your employer could not withhold sufficient Social Security on tips, the uncollected amount is shown using Code A. For uncollected Medicare tax, Code B is used. This amount must be reported on Line 62 of Schedule 4 of Form 1040 (other taxes); write "UT" next to it. |
| | Excess golden parachute payments. If you received an "excess parachute payment as wages," Code K identifies the 20% penalty tax on the excess payment that was withheld by the employer. This withheld amount is included in Box 2 (federal income tax withheld), but you also must add it as an additional tax on Line 62 of Schedule 4 of Form 1040; identify as "EPP". |
| | Moving expense reimbursements. For members of the U.S. Armed Services, reimbursements of qualifying moving expenses are excludable from income (2.1); the excludable reimbursements are shown with Code P. For all others, employer reimbursements of moving expenses are taxable starting in 2018 under the Tax Cuts and Jobs Act (2.1) and are included in Box 1 wages, and subject to Social Security (Box 3) and Medicare tax (Box 5) withholdings. |
| | Employer contributions to health savings account (HSA) or Archer MSA. Total employer contributions to an HSA are shown with Code W; this includes any contributions you elected to make under a Section 125 cafeteria plan (3.6). Total employer contributions to an MSA are shown with Code R. Contributions exceeding the excludable limit (Chapter 3) are included as taxable wages in Boxes 1, 3, and 5. |
| | Employer-financed adoption benefits. Total qualified adoption expenses paid or reimbursed by your employer (3.6) plus any pre-tax contributions you made to an adoption plan account under a cafeteria plan (3.15) are shown with Code T. |
| | Nonstatutory stock option exercised. If you exercised a nonstatutory stock option, Code V shows the taxable "spread" (excess of fair market value of stock over exercise price). The income should be included in Boxes 1, 3 (up to the $128,400 Social Security wage ceiling), and 5. |
| | Deferrals and income under Section 409A nonqualified deferred compensation plan. Current year deferrals plus all earnings under a 409A plan may be shown (its optional) with Code Y. Code Z shows amounts included as income in Box 1; this income is subject to a penalty plus interest on Form 1040 (2.7). |
| Box 13 | Statutory employee. If this box is checked you report your wage income and deductible job expenses on Schedule C (40.6). Your earnings are not subject to income tax withholding, but are subject to Social Security and Medicare taxes. |
| | Retirement plan. This box is checked if you were an active participant in an employer plan at some point during the year. As an active participant, you are subject to the phaseout rules for IRA deductions) (8.4). |
| Box 14 | Taxable fringe benefits and miscellaneous payments. Your employer may use Box 14 to report fringe benefits or deductions from your pay, such as state disability insurance taxes, union dues, educational assistance, health insurance premiums, or voluntary after-tax contributions to profit-sharing or pension plans. If your employer included in Box 1 the lease value of a car (3.7) provided to you, this value must also be shown in Box 14 or on a separate statement. |
| Boxes 17 and 19 | State and local taxes. State and local tax withholdings shown in Boxes 17 and 19 may be deductible as itemized deductions (16.3). |

| a Employee's social security number | | | |
|---|---|---|---|
| 08-X1X0X1X | OMB No. 1545-0008 | Safe, accurate, FAST! Use | Visit the IRS website at www.irs.gov/efile |

| b Employer identification number (EIN) | 1 Wages, tips, other compensation 57,800.00 | 2 Federal income tax withheld 10,000.00 |
|---|---|---|
| c Employer's name, address, and ZIP code **Finkle Construction Company** **5532 Glasgow Plaza** **City, State XX111** | 3 Social security wages 63,580.00 | 4 Social security tax withheld 3,941.96 |
| | 5 Medicare wages and tips 63,580.00 | 6 Medicare tax withheld 921.91 |
| | 7 Social security tips | 8 Allocated tips |
| d Control number **0X1 - XX - 1X00** | 9 Verification code | 10 Dependent care benefits |
| e Employee's first name and initial   Last name   Suff. | 11 Nonqualified plans | 12a See instructions for box 12 5,780.00 |
| | 13 Statutory employee ☐  Retirement plan ☒  Third-party sick pay ☐ | 12b |
| **Mary Moll** | 14 Other | 12c |
| **176 Garden Road** **City, State 1XXX1** | | 12d |
| f Employee's address and ZIP code | | |

| 15 State  Employer's state ID number | 16 State wages, tips, etc. | 17 State income tax | 18 Local wages, tips, etc. | 19 Local income tax | 20 Locality name |
|---|---|---|---|---|---|
| **State  11-X1X0X1X** | 57,800.00 | 2,980.00 | 57,800.00 | 1,734.00 | City |

Form **W-2** Wage and Tax Statement   **2018**   Department of the Treasury—Internal Revenue Service

**Copy B—To Be Filed With Employee's FEDERAL Tax Return.**
This information is being furnished to the Internal Revenue Service.

## 2.1 Salary and Wage Income

The key to reporting your pay is Form W-2, sent to you by your employer. It lists your taxable wages, which may include not only your regular pay, but also other taxable items, such as taxable fringe benefits. *Table 2-1* explains how employee pay benefits and tax withholdings are reported on Form W-2.

Your employer reports your taxable pay under a simple rule. Unless the item is specifically exempt from tax, you are taxed on practically everything you receive for your work whether paid in cash, property, or services. Benefits that the law specifically excludes from tax are discussed in *Chapter 3*. The most common tax-free benefits are employer-paid premiums for health and accident plans, medical expense reimbursements, and group-term life insurance coverage up to $50,000.

Your employer will include in Box 1 of your Form W-2 the total wages, tips, and other compensation, before payroll deductions, that were paid to you during the year. Box 1 may include, in addition to regular wages and tips, the following types of taxable compensation:

- Bonuses (including signing bonuses)
- Taxable fringe benefits *(Chapter 3)*
- Per diem or mileage allowances exceeding the IRS rate *(20.32–20.33)*
- Expense allowances or business expense reimbursements under a non-accountable plan *(20.34)*
- Moving expense reimbursements, unless you are a qualifying member of the U.S. Armed Forces; *see* this new law rule below.
- Awards or prizes not exempt under 3.11
- Cost of group-term life insurance over $50,000 *(3.4)*
- Cost of accident and health insurance premiums paid by an S corporation for 2%-or-more shareholder-employees
- Deferred income that is currently taxable under a Section 409A nonqualified deferred compensation plan *(2.7)*

Compensation reported in Box 1 of Form W-2 must be reported as wages on Line 1 of Form 1040. Other types of income must also be reported as wages on your return although they are not included in Box 1 of Form W-2, such as non-excludable dependent care *(3.5)* or adoption *(3.6)* benefits, tips not reported to your employer or allocated tips *(26.8)*, disability pension shown on Form 1099-R if you are under your employer's minimum retirement age, or excess salary deferrals to an employer retirement plan *(7.16)*.

**Reimbursed moving expenses.** Under the Tax Cuts and Jobs Act, all employees other than qualifying members of the U.S. Armed Forces are taxed on reimbursements of moving expenses, effective for 2018 through 2025. Qualifying members of the U.S. Armed Forces are also the only taxpayers allowed to deduct unreimbursed moving expenses under the new law *(12.3)*.

Members of the U.S. Armed Forces on active duty can exclude reimbursed moving expenses from income if they move pursuant to a military order and incident to a permanent change of station. The moving expenses must be reimbursed under an accountable plan, and they must be expenses that the Armed Forces member could claim as an above-the-line deduction had they not been reimbursed *(12.3)*. The excludable moving expense reimbursements are shown in Box 12 of Form W-2 with Code P. *See 12.3* for details on deductible moving expenses for Armed Forces members and reimbursements.

**Withholdings for retirement plans.** Amounts withheld from wages as your contribution to your pension or profit-sharing account are generally taxable as compensation unless they are tax-deferred elective deferrals under the limits allowed for Section 401(k) plans *(7.16)*, simplified employee pension plans *(8.16)*, SIMPLE IRAs *(8.18)*, or tax-sheltered annuity plans *(7.19)*. Elective deferrals are reported in Box 12 of Form W-2.

Wages withheld for compulsory forfeitable contributions to a nonqualified pension plan are not taxable if these conditions exist:

1. The contribution is forfeited if employment is terminated prior to death or retirement.
2. The plan does not provide for a refund of employee contributions and, in the administration of the plan, no refund will be made. Where only part of the contribution is subject to forfeiture, the amount of withheld contribution not subject to forfeiture is taxable income.

You should check with your employer to determine the status of your contributions.

*Law Alert*

**Reimbursed Moving Expenses Taxable**

Under the Tax Cuts and Jobs Act, the exclusion for reimbursements of qualified moving expenses applies only to certain members of the U.S. Armed Forces *(2.1)*.

*Caution*

**Severance Pay Taxable**

You must pay tax on severance pay received upon losing a job. The severance pay is taxable even if you signed a waiver releasing your former employer from potential future damage claims. The waiver does not change the nature of the payments from taxable pay to tax-free personal injury damages *(11.7)*. The severance pay is also subject to Social Security and Medicare taxes *(26.8)*.

*Filing Instruction*

**Tips Must Be Reported**

Tips you receive are taxable income. You must report tips to your employer so your employer can withhold FICA and income tax from your regular pay to cover the tips *(26.8)*.

**Assigning your pay.** You may not avoid tax on income you earned by assigning the right to payment to another person. For example, you must report earnings that you donate to charity, even if they are paid directly by your employer to a charity. If you claim itemized deductions, you may claim a contribution deduction for the donation; *see Chapter 14*. Assignments of income-generating intellectual property are held taxable to the assignee. However, if the assignor retained power or control of the property, the assignor could be held liable for the tax according to the 8th Circuit.

The IRS allowed an exception for doctors working in a clinic. The doctors were not taxed on fees for treating patients with limited income (teaching cases) where they were required to assign the fees to a foundation.

**Gifts from employers.** A payment may be called a gift but still be taxable income. Any payment made in recognition of past services or in anticipation of future services or benefits is taxable as wages even if the employer is not obligated to make the payment. However, there are exceptions for employee achievement awards *(3.11)*.

To prove a gift is tax free, you must show that the employer acted with pure and unselfish motives of affection, admiration, or charity. This is difficult to do, given the employer-employee relationship. A gift of stock by majority stockholders to key employees has been held to be taxable.

**Employee leave-sharing plan.** Some companies allow employees to contribute their unused leave into a "leave fund" for use by other employees who have suffered medical emergencies or are disaster victims. If you use up your regular leave and benefit from additional leave that has been donated to the plan, you are taxed on the benefit; it is reported as wages on your Form W-2 and subject to withholding taxes. If you are donating the leave, you are not taxed on the value.

**"Golden parachute" payments.** Golden parachute arrangements are agreements to pay key employees additional compensation upon a change in company control. If you receive such a payment, part of it may be deemed to be an "excess payment" under a complex formula in the law. You must pay a 20% penalty tax on the "excess" amount in addition to regular income tax on the total. The 20% penalty should be identified on Form W-2 with Code K in Box 12; *see Table 2-1*.

If the golden parachute payment is made to a non-employee, the company will report it in Box 7 (non-employee compensation) of Form 1099-MISC. If you are self-employed, report the total compensation on Schedule C *(40.6)* and compute self-employment tax on Schedule SE *(45.3)*. Any "excess parachute payment" should be separately labeled in Box 13 of Form 1099-MISC. Multiply the Box 13 amount by 20% and report it as an "other tax" on Line 62 of Schedule 4 of Form 1040; label it "EPP."

## 2.2 Constructive Receipt of Year-End Paychecks

As an employee, you use the cash-basis method of accounting. This means that you report all income items in the year they are actually received and deduct expenses in the year you pay them.

You are also subject to the "constructive receipt rule," which requires you to report income not actually received but which has been credited to your account, subject to your control, or put aside for you. Thus, if you received a paycheck at the end of 2018, you must report the pay on your 2018 return, even though you do not cash or deposit it to your account until 2019. This is true even if you receive the check after banking hours on the last business day of the year and cannot cash or deposit it until the next year. The Tax Court has also ruled that receipt by an agent (e.g., an attorney) is constructive receipt by the principal.

If your employer does not have funds in the bank and asks you to hold the check before depositing it, you do not have taxable income until the check is cashed. If services rendered in 2018 are paid for by check dated for 2019, the pay is taxable for 2019.

The IRS has ruled that an employee who is not at home on December 31 to take delivery of a check sent by certified mail must still report the check in that year. However, where an employee was not at home to take certified mail delivery of a year-end check that she did not expect to receive until the next year, the Tax Court held that the funds were taxable when received in the following year.

*Court Decision*

**Tax on Assigned Contingent Fee**

An attorney who took a medical malpractice case on a contingent fee basis agreed to split the net fee with his ex-wife pursuant to their divorce agreement. After a favorable settlement, the attorney's take was approximately $40,000 after expenses, half of which went to his ex-wife. Each paid tax on his or her share. The attorney argued that his partial assignment of the fee could shift the tax liability because collection was contingent on the outcome of the lawsuit. However, the IRS and the Tax Court held that the attorney was liable for the tax on the entire contingent fee, and an appeals court agreed. The attorney transferred only the right to receive income. Although his fee was contingent upon the successful outcome of the case, once the fee materialized, it was indisputably compensation for his personal services.

## 2.3    Pay Received in Property Is Taxed

Your employer may pay you with property instead of cash. You report the fair market value of the property as wages.

> **EXAMPLE**
>
> For consulting services rendered, Kate Chong receives a check for $10,000 and property with a fair market value of $5,000. She reports $15,000 as wages.

If you receive your unrestricted company stock as payment for your services, you include the value of the stock as pay in the year you receive it. However, if the stock is nontransferable or subject to substantial risk of forfeiture, you do not have to include its value as pay until the restrictions no longer apply *(2.18)*. You must report dividends on the restricted stock in the year you receive the income.

If you receive your employer's note that has a fair market value, you are taxed on the value of the note less what it would cost you to discount it. If the note bears interest, report the full face value. But do not report income if the note has no fair market value. Report income on the note only when payments are made on it.

A debt canceled by an employer is taxable income.

Salespeople employed by a dealer have taxable income on receipt of "prize points" redeemable for merchandise from a distributor.

## 2.4    Commissions Taxable When Credited

Earned commissions are taxable in the year they are credited to your account and subject to your drawing, whether or not you actually draw them.

Do not report commissions that were earned in 2018 on your 2018 return if they cannot be computed or collected until a later year.

> **EXAMPLE**
>
> Arno Jeffers earns commissions based on a percentage of the profits from realty sales. In 2018 he draws $10,000 from his account. However, at the end of 2018 the full amount of his commissions is unknown because profits for the year have not been figured. In January 2019, his 2018 commissions are computed to be $15,000, and the $5,000 balance is paid to him. The $5,000 is taxable in 2019 even though earned in 2018.

**Advances against unearned commissions.** Under standard insurance industry practice, an agent who sells a policy does not earn commissions until premiums are received by the insurance company. However, the company may issue a cash advance on the commissions before the premiums are received. Agents have claimed that they may defer reporting the income until the year the premiums are earned. The IRS, recognizing that in practice companies rarely demand repayment, requires that advances be included in income in the year received if the agent has full control over the advanced funds. A repayment of unearned commissions in a later year *(2.8)* is deductible on Schedule A, provided you itemize deductions for that year.

Salespeople have been taxed on commissions received on property bought for their personal use. In one case, an insurance agent was taxed on commissions paid to him on his purchase of an insurance policy. In another case, a real estate agent was taxed on commissions he received on his purchase of land. A salesman was also taxed for commissions waived on policies he sold to friends, relatives, and employees.

**Kickback of commissions.** An insurance agent's kickback of his or her commission is taxable where agents may not under local law give rebates or kickbacks of premiums to their clients. The commissions are income and may not be offset with a business expense deduction; illegal kickbacks may not be deducted.

However, in one case, a federal appeals court allowed an insurance broker to avoid tax when he did not charge clients the basic first-year commission. The clients paid the broker the net premium (gross premium less the commission), which he remitted to the insurance company.

*Caution*

**Earned Commissions Credited to Your Account**

You may not postpone tax on earned commissions credited to your account in 2018 by not drawing them until 2019 or a later year. However, where a portion of earned commissions is not withdrawn because your employer is holding it to cover future expenses, you are not taxed on the amount withheld.

The IRS and Tax Court held that the commissions were taxable despite the broker's voluntary waiver of his right to them. He could not deduct them because his discount scheme violated state anti-rebate law (Oklahoma). On appeal, the broker won. The Tenth Circuit Court of Appeals held that since the broker never had any right to commissions under the terms of the contracts he structured with his clients, he was not taxed on the commissions. The court cautioned that if the broker had remitted the full premium (including commission) to the insurance company and then reimbursed the client after having received the commission from the company, the commission probably would have been taxable.

## 2.5    Unemployment Benefits

All unemployment benefits received in 2018 are taxable. You should receive Form 1099-G, showing the amount of the payments. Report the payments on Line 19 of Schedule 1 of Form 1040.

Supplemental unemployment benefits paid from company-financed funds are taxable as wages and not reported as unemployment compensation. Such benefits are usually paid under guaranteed annual wage plans made between unions and employers.

Unemployment benefits from a private or union fund to which you voluntarily contribute dues are taxable as "other" income on Schedule 1 of Form 1040, but only to the extent the benefits exceed your contributions to the fund. Your contributions to the fund are not deductible.

Workers' compensation payments *(2.13)* are not taxable.

Taxable unemployment benefits include federal trade readjustment allowances (1974 Trade Act), airline deregulation benefits (1978 Airline Deregulation Act), and disaster unemployment assistance (1974 Disaster Relief Act).

**Repaid supplemental unemployment benefits.** If you had to repay supplemental unemployment benefits to receive trade readjustment allowances (1974 Trade Act), taxable unemployment benefits are reduced by repayments made in the same year. If you repay the benefits in a later year, the benefits are taxed in the year of receipt and a deduction may be claimed in the later year. If the repayment is $3,000 or less, an "above-the-line" deduction is allowed; add it to your other adjustments to income on Line 36 of Schedule 1 of Form 1040; label it "sub-pay TRA." If the repayment exceeds $3,000, you have the choice between the above-the-line deduction or a credit *(2.8)*.

## 2.6    Strike Pay Benefits and Penalties

Strike and lockout benefits paid out of regular union dues are taxable as wages unless the payment qualifies as a gift, as discussed below. However, if you have made voluntary contributions to a strike fund, benefits you receive from the fund are tax free up to the amount of your contributions and are taxable to the extent they exceed your contributions.

**Strike benefits as tax-free gifts.** Here are factors indicating that benefits are gifts: Payments are based on individual need; they are paid to both union and non-union members; and no conditions are imposed on the strikers who receive benefits.

If you receive benefits under conditions by which you are to participate in the strike and the payments are tied to your scale of wages, the benefits are taxable.

> ### EXAMPLE
> A striking union pilot claimed that strike benefits were tax-free gifts because they were funded by assessments paid by other union pilots who were not on strike. The IRS and Tax Court held that the benefits were taxable. They were not gifts because they were not motivated by a "detached and disinterested generosity." The union was promoting its own self-interest by giving pilots an incentive to support the strike. The non-striking pilots contributed to the strike fund as an obligation of union membership. The strikers were eligible for benefits only if they agreed to perform any strike activities requested by the union, did not fly for airlines in dispute with the union, and did not take actions that could adversely affect the outcome of the dispute.

**Caution**

**Law Violation Not Deductible**

No deduction is allowed for a fine or penalty paid to a government for the violation of a law.

**Caution**

**Penalty and Interest on Nonqualified Deferred Compensation**

If deferred pay is currently taxable under the rules of Code Section 409A, you must also pay a 20% penalty and interest at a rate 1% higher than the regular underpayment rate.

**Strike pay penalties.** Pay penalties charged to striking teachers are not deductible. State law may prohibit public school teachers from striking and charge a penalty equal to one day's pay for each day spent on strike. For example, when striking teachers returned to work after a one-week strike, a penalty of one week's salary was deducted from their pay. Although they did not actually receive pay for the week they worked after the strike, they earned taxable wages. Furthermore, the penalty is not deductible. No deduction is allowed for a fine or penalty paid to a government for the violation of a law.

## 2.7 Nonqualified Deferred Compensation

The rules for determining whether tax may be deferred under a nonqualified deferred compensation plan are governed by Code Section 409A. Section 409A applies generally to amounts deferred after 2004. Amounts deferred before 2005 are "grandfathered," and thus generally exempt, but they become subject to Section 409A (unless excluded under IRS rules) if the plan is materially modified after October 3, 2004.

**Plans subject to and excluded from Section 409A.** Unless an exception applies, Code Section 409A applies to all nonqualified deferred plans, including arrangements between an independent contractor and a service recipient, and a partner and partnership, under which the service provider has a legally binding right during a year to compensation that is not actually or constructively received, and which is payable in a later year. The law does not apply to qualified retirement plans (such as 401(k) plans), Section 403(b) tax-deferred annuities, SIMPLE accounts, simplified employee pensions, and Section 457 plans; these are excluded from the definition of "nonqualified deferred compensation plans." Also excluded are welfare benefit plans such as vacation, sick leave, and disability programs.

The IRS has allowed exceptions for short-term deferrals, incentive stock options, employee stock purchase plan options, and certain stock appreciation rights, tax equalization payments, separation payments, reimbursement arrangements, and fringe benefits. For details, *see* the IRS final regulations (T.D. 9321, 2007-19 IRB 1123).

**Section 409A requirements.** Plans subject to Section 409A must meet detailed requirements pertaining to the timing of deferral elections and the availability of distributions. For example, a deferral election generally must be made prior to the beginning of the year during which the services will be provided, but special rules apply to short-term deferrals and deferrals with respect to forfeitable rights. Distributions before separation from service are generally allowed only if the participant is disabled or has an unforeseeable emergency, the distribution is used to satisfy a domestic relations order, the distribution is on a specific date or under a fixed schedule specified in the plan, or there has been a change in the ownership or effective control of the corporation or in the ownership of a substantial portion of the assets.

If the Section 409A requirements are not met at any time during a taxable year, all amounts deferred under the plan for all years are currently includible in a participant's gross income to the extent that the amounts are not subject to a substantial risk of forfeiture and were not previously included in gross income.

**Reporting of Section 409A plan deferrals and earnings on your tax return.** Your employer may include 2018 plan deferrals in Box 12 of your Form W-2 using Code Y (reporting is optional). If deferrals are reported, Code Y should also be used to show earnings in 2018 on all deferrals, whether for 2018 or prior years. If any amounts are taxable because the Section 409A requirements have not been met, the taxable amount should be reported as taxable wages in Box 1 of Form W-2, and also shown in Box 12 using Code Z.

If you are not an employee, current year Section 409A deferrals of at least $600 and earnings on current and prior year deferrals may be reported in Box 15a of Form 1099-MISC. If any amounts are taxable because the Section 409A requirements have not been met, the taxable amount is reported in Box 15b and also included as non-employee compensation in Box 7 of Form 1099-MISC; this amount is generally subject to self-employment tax.

If there is a taxable amount, a penalty also must be paid equal to 20% of the includible compensation, plus interest at a rate that is 1% higher than the regular underpayment rate. The penalty and interest must be added to Line 62 on Schedule 4 of Form 1040, and identified as "NQDC".

**Financial health triggers and offshore rabbi trusts.** Section 409A blocks the benefit of two funding arrangements that set aside assets to secure the payment of promised deferred compensation. If a nonqualified deferred compensation plan provides that assets will be restricted to payment of deferrals if the employer's financial condition deteriorates, the setting aside of the assets will be considered a transfer of restricted property to the participants, taxable under the Section 83 rules *(2.17)*. This is so even if the assets nominally remain available to satisfy the claims of the employer's general creditors.

Also, a Section 83 transfer *(2.17)* is generally deemed to occur when assets to pay nonqualified deferred compensation are set aside in an offshore rabbi trust. Section 409A treats the funding of an offshore trust as a transfer of property to the participants, taxable under the Section 83 rules *(2.17)*, unless substantially all of the services relating to the deferred compensation were performed in the foreign jurisdiction where the assets are held. A Section 83 transfer is deemed to occur whether or not the offshore assets are nominally available to satisfy the claims of the employer's general creditors.

If deferrals are includible in a participant's income because of the financial health trigger or offshore trust provisions, there is an additional 20% penalty plus interest at 1% more than the regular rate.

**Rabbi trusts.** If IRS tests are met, employer contributions to a domestic "rabbi trust" are not taxed until distributions from the trust are received or made available. The trust must be irrevocable and the trust assets must be subject to the claims of the employer's creditors in the event of insolvency or bankruptcy. Employees and their beneficiaries must have no preferred claim on the trust assets.

Offshore rabbi trusts are subject to Section 409A, as discussed above.

## 2.8 Did You Return Wages Received in a Prior Year?

Did you return income in 2018 such as salary or commissions that you reported in a prior taxable year under a "claim of right," meaning that it appeared you had an unrestricted right to the income in the earlier year? If the repayment of wages exceeds $3,000, you may claim a tax credit, based upon a recomputation of the prior year's tax (see below), or, if you itemize deductions on Schedule A (Form 1040), you can claim the repayment as an "other" itemized deduction *(19.1)*.

However, if the repayment is $3,000 or less, you are not allowed to claim the tax credit or any deduction. For years before 2018, a repayment of $3,000 or less was deductible as a miscellaneous itemized deduction that was subject to the 2% of adjusted gross income floor, but this option has been repealed by the Tax Cuts and Jobs Act; miscellaneous expenses that had been subject to the 2% floor are no longer deductible under the new law.

**Option of tax credit or deduction for repayments over $3,000.** If your repayment of wages exceeded $3,000, you may either (1) claim the repayment as an "other itemized deduction" (Line 16 of Schedule A *(19.1)*), assuming you itemize deductions on Schedule A rather than claim the standard deduction *(13.1)* or (2) claim a tax credit, based upon a recomputation of the prior year's tax; *see* the Filing Instruction on this page.

**Repayment of supplemental unemployment benefits.** Where repayment is required to qualify for trade readjustment allowances, you may deduct the repayment from gross income. Claim the deduction as an "above-the-line" deduction on Line 36 of Schedule 1 of of Form 1040, and to the left of the line write "sub-pay TRA." The deduction is allowed even if you do not itemize. If repayment exceeds $3,000, you have the choice of a deduction or claiming a tax credit based on a recomputation of your tax for the year supplemental unemployment benefits were received, as explained in the Filing Instruction on this page.

**Repayment of disallowed travel expenses.** If a "hedge" agreement between you and your company requires you to repay salary or travel expenses if they are disallowed to the company by the IRS, you may claim a deduction in the year of repayment. According to the IRS, you may not recalculate your tax for the prior year and claim a tax credit under the rules of Section 1341. However, an appeals court rejected the position taken by the IRS and allowed a tax recomputation under Section 1341 to an executive who returned part of a disallowed salary under the terms of a corporate by-law.

 *Filing Instruction*

**Repayment of Wages Exceeding $3,000**

If you repay wages of more than $3,000, a special law (Code Section 1341) allows you to recompute your tax for the prior year as if the wages had not been reported. The difference between the actual tax paid in the prior year and the recomputed tax may be claimed as a tax credit for the year of repayment; write "IRC 1341" next to the line where the credit is claimed (see the Form 1040 instructions). In some cases, you might pay less tax for the year of repayment, if you claim the repayment as an "other" itemized deduction (Line 16, Schedule A, Form 1040), rather than claiming the credit. Choose either the credit or the itemized deduction, whichever gives you the larger tax reduction.

## 2.9 Waiver of Executor's and Trustee's Commissions

Commissions received by an executor for services performed are taxable as compensation. An executor may waive commissions without income or gift tax consequences by giving a principal legatee or devisee a formal waiver of the executor's right to commissions within six months after the initial appointment or by not claiming commissions at the time of filing the usual accountings.

The waiver may not be recognized if the executor takes any action that is inconsistent with the waiver. An example of an inconsistent action would be the claiming of an executor's fee as a deduction on an estate, inheritance, or income tax return.

A bequest received by an executor from an estate is tax free if it is not compensation for services.

## 2.10 Life Insurance Benefits

Company-financed insurance gives employees benefits at low or no tax cost.

**Group life insurance.** Group insurance plans may furnish not only life insurance protection but also accident and health benefits. Premium costs are low and tax deductible to the company while tax free to you unless you have nonforfeitable rights to permanent life insurance, or, in the case of group-term life insurance, your coverage exceeds $50,000 *(3.4)*. Even where your coverage exceeds $50,000, the tax incurred on your employer's premium payment is generally less than what you would have to pay privately for similar insurance.

It may be possible to avoid estate tax on the group policy proceeds if you assign all of your ownership rights in the policy, including the right to convert the policy, and if the beneficiary is other than your estate. Where the policy allows assignment of the conversion right, in addition to all other rights, and state law does not bar the assignment, you are considered to have made a complete assignment of the group insurance for estate tax purposes.

The IRS has ruled that where an employee assigns a group life policy and the value of the employee's interest in the policy cannot be ascertained, there is no taxable gift. This is so where the employer could simply have stopped making payments. However, there is a gift by the employee to the assignee to the extent of premiums paid by the employer. The gift may be a present interest qualifying for the annual gift tax exclusion *(39.2)*.

**Split-dollar insurance.** Where you want more insurance than is provided by a group plan, your company may be able to help you get additional protection through a split-dollar insurance plan. Under the basic split-dollar plan, your employer purchases permanent cash value life insurance on your life and pays all or part of the annual premium. At your death, your employer is entitled to part of the proceeds equal to the premiums he or she paid. You have the right to name a beneficiary to receive the remaining proceeds which, under most policies, are substantial compared with the employer's share. Equity split-dollar arrangements allow employees to retain the right to the cash surrender value in excess of the premiums paid by the employer.

In final regulations applicable to split-dollar arrangements entered into or materially modified after September 17, 2003, the IRS has provided two sets of rules, depending on whether the employee or the employer owns the insurance policy (T.D. 9092, 2003-46 IRB 1055). If the employee is the owner, the employer's premium payments will be treated as loans and the imputed interest will be taxed to the employee. If the employer owns the policy, the employee will be taxed on the value of the life insurance protection, the policy cash value that the employee has access to, and the value of any other economic benefits received from the policy.

In addition, the Section 409A rules for nonqualified deferred compensation plans *(2.7)* may also apply to certain types of split-dollar arrangements. Notice 2007-34 contains IRS guidance on applying the Section 409A rules and explaining the effect of modifications to a split-dollar arrangement.

*Caution*

**Charitable Split-Dollar Insurance**

In a charitable split-dollar insurance plan, you give money to a charity, which invests in a life insurance policy and splits the proceeds with your beneficiaries. Taxpayers have attempted to deduct the initial "donations," but the tax law was changed to disallow the deduction.

## 2.11 Educational Benefits for Employees' Children

**Private foundations.** The IRS has published guidelines for determining whether educational grants made by a private foundation established by an employer to children of employees constitute scholarships. An objective, nondiscriminatory program must be adopted. If the guidelines are satisfied, employees are not taxed on the benefits provided to their children. Advance approval of the grant program must be obtained from the IRS.

IRS guidelines require that:

- Grant recipients must be selected by a scholarship committee that is independent of the employer and the foundation. Former employees of the employer or the foundation are not considered independent.

- Eligibility for the grants may be restricted to children of employees who have been employed for a minimum of up to three years, but eligibility may not be related to the employee's position, services, or duties.

- Once awarded, a grant may not be terminated if the parent leaves his job with the employer, regardless of the reason for the termination of employment. If a one-year grant is awarded or a multi-year grant is awarded subject to renewal, a child who reapplies for a later grant may not be considered ineligible because his parent no longer works for the employer.

- Grant decisions must be based solely upon objective standards unrelated to the employer's business and the parent's employment such as prior academic performance, aptitude tests, recommendations from instructors, financial needs, and conclusions drawn from personal interviews.

- Recipients must be free to use the grants for courses that are not of particular benefit to the employer or the foundation.

- The grant program must not be used by the foundation or employer to recruit employees or induce employees to continue employment.

- There must be no requirement or suggestion that the child or parent is expected to render future employment services.

- A percentage test generally must be met. The number of grants awarded in a given year to children of employees must not exceed (1) 25% of the number of employees' children who were eligible, applied for the grants, and were considered by the selection committee in that year; or (2) 10% of the number of employees' children who were eligible during that year, whether or not they applied. Renewals of grants are not considered in determining the number of grants awarded.

If all of the above tests other than the percentage test are met, the educational grant program can still qualify if the facts and circumstances indicate that the primary purpose of the program is to provide educational benefits rather than to compensate the employees.

**Educational benefit trusts and other plans.** A medical professional corporation set up an educational benefit plan to pay college costs for the children of "key" employees. Children enrolled in a degree program within two years of graduating from high school could participate in the plan. If an eligible employee quit for reasons other than death or permanent disability, his or her children could not longer receive benefits except for expenses actually incurred before termination. The company made annual contributions to a trust administered by a bank. According to the IRS, amounts contributed to the trust were a form of pay to qualified employees, because the contributions were made on the basis of the parents' employment and earnings records, not on the children's need, merit, or motivation. However, the employees could not be taxed when the funds were deposited because the children's right to receive benefits was conditioned upon each employee's future performance of services and was subject to a substantial risk of forfeiture. Tax is not incurred until a person has a vested right to receive benefits; here, vesting did not occur until a child became a degree candidate and incurred educational expenses while his or her parent was employed by the corporation. Once the child's right to receive a distribution from the plan became vested, the parent of the child could be taxed on the amount of the distribution. The company could deduct the same amount.

The Tax Court and appeals court have upheld the IRS position in similar cases.

 *Caution*

**Primary Purpose Determination**

If all guidelines other than the percentage test are satisfied, the IRS will determine whether the primary purpose of the program is to educate the children. If it is, the grants will be considered scholarships or fellowships; if it is not, the grants are taxed to the parent-employees as extra compensation.

## 2.12 Sick Pay Is Taxable

Sick pay received from an employer is generally taxable as wages unless it qualifies as workers' compensation (2.13). Payments received under accident or health plans are generally tax free (3.3), unless they constitute excess reimbursements (17.4). Payments from your employer's plan for certain serious permanent injuries are tax free (3.3).

Disability pensions are discussed in 2.14.

Sick pay received from your employer is subject to income tax withholding as if it were wages. Sick pay from a third party such as an insurance company is not subject to withholdings unless you request it on Form W-4S.

## 2.13 Workers' Compensation Is Tax Free

You do not pay tax on workers' compensation payments for job-related injuries or illness. However, your employer might continue paying your regular salary but require you to turn over your workers' compensation payments. Then you are taxed on the difference between what was paid to you and what you returned.

> **EXAMPLE**
>
> John Wright was injured while at work and was out of work for two months. His company continues to pay his weekly salary of $775. He also receives workers' compensation of $200 a week from the state, which is tax free. He gives the $200 weekly payments to his employer. The balance of $575 a week is considered taxable wages.

To qualify as tax-free workers' compensation, the payments must be made under the authority of a law (or regulation having the force of a law) that provides compensation for on-the-job injury or illness. Payments made under a labor agreement do not qualify as tax-free workers' compensation.

A retirement pension or annuity does not qualify for tax-free treatment if benefits are based on age, length of service, or prior plan contributions. Such benefits are taxable even if retirement was triggered by a work-related injury or sickness.

State law may impose a penalty for unreasonable delay in paying a worker's compensation award. If the penalty is considered to have the remedial purpose of facilitating the injured employee's return to work, the IRS may treat the penalty as part of the original tax-free compensation award.

**Survivors of fallen state and federal public safety officers.** Survivor benefits paid to families of police officers, firefighters, paramedics, and other public safety workers killed in the line of duty are excluded from gross income. The exclusion applies to (1) survivor benefits paid by the federal Bureau of Justice Assistance to families of fallen public safety officers, and (2) state-paid benefits to survivors of public safety officers who died as a result of injuries sustained in the line of duty, but the exclusion does not apply to state benefits that would have been paid even if the death had not been sustained in the line of duty.

**Effect of workers' compensation on Social Security.** In figuring whether Social Security benefits are taxable (34.2), workers' compensation that reduces Social Security or equivalent Railroad Retirement benefits is treated as a Social Security (or Railroad Retirement) benefit received during the year. Thus, the workers' compensation may be indirectly subject to tax (34.2).

> **EXAMPLES**
>
> 1. Kane, a federal district judge, suffered from sleep apnea, a condition characterized by a cessation of breathing during sleep, which was aggravated by the stress of his judicial work. He received a retirement disability payment of $65,135.
>
>    A federal appeals court held that the payment was taxable because it was paid under a statute which did not specifically require that the payments be for work-related injuries. Here, the federal law under which the judge received his payments provided benefits for all permanent disabilities, whether or not job related.

*Court Decision*

**Is Sick Leave Tax-Free Workers' Compensation?**

According to the Tax Court, sick leave may qualify as tax-free workers' compensation if it is paid under a specific workers' compensation statute or similar government regulation that authorizes the sick leave payment for job-related injuries or illness; *see* Examples 2, 3, and 4 (2.13).

*Caution*

**Job-Related Injury or Illness**

Not all payments for job-related illness or injury qualify as tax-free workers' compensation. Unless the statute or regulation authorizing your disability payment restricts awards to on-the-job injury or illness, your payment is taxable. Even if your payments are in fact based upon job-related injury or illness, they are taxed if other individuals can receive payments from the plan for disabilities that are not work related; *see* Example 1 (2.13).

2. A teacher, injured while working, received full salary during a two-year sick leave. She argued that the payments, made under board of education regulations, were similar to workers' compensation and thus tax free. The IRS disagreed; the regulations were not the same as a workers' compensation statute. The Tax Court supported the teacher. The payments were made because of job-related injuries and were authorized by regulations having the force of law.

3. The IRS claimed that a police officer in Lynbrook, N.Y., was subject to tax on line-of-duty disability pay because the payment was under a labor agreement with the Police Benevolent Association (PBA). The Tax Court supported the police officer's claim that the payments were authorized by a specific New York State law requiring full salary for job-related police injuries. The PBA agreement did not affect the officer's rights to those state law payments. Lynbrook treated the case as a workers' compensation claim and in fact received reimbursement from the state workers' compensation board for the payments made to the officer.

4. A Los Angeles sheriff injured on the job retired on disability and, under the Los Angeles workers' compensation law, was allowed to elect sick pay in lieu of the regular workers' compensation amount because the sick pay was larger. The IRS argued that the sheriff had merely received taxable sick pay because he would have received the same amount as sick pay if his injuries had been suffered in a personal accident. However, the Tax Court allowed tax-free treatment. The sick leave was paid under a workers' compensation law that applied solely to work-related injuries. The fact that sick leave may also have been available to other employees under other laws does not mean that it may not be included as an option under a workers' compensation statute.

The IRS announced that it does not agree with the Tax Court's decision allowing full tax-free treatment. According to the IRS, benefits up to the regular workers' compensation amount should be tax free but excess amounts should be taxed.

## 2.14   Disability Pay and Pensions

Disability pensions financed by your employer are taxable wages unless they are for severe permanent physical injuries that qualify for tax-free treatment *(3.3)*, they are tax-free workers' compensation *(2.13)*, or they are tax-free government payments as discussed in this section.

Taxable disability pensions are reported as wages until you reach the minimum retirement age under the employer's plan. After reaching minimum retirement age, payments are reported as a pension *(7.24)*.

If you receive little or no Social Security and your other income is below a specified threshold, you may be eligible to claim a tax credit for disability payments received while you are under the age of 65 and permanently and totally disabled *(34.7)*.

**State short-term disability payments.**   Some states provide or require employers to provide short-term disability pay to workers who are temporarily unable to work due to a non-work related illness or injury, or pregnancy. For federal tax purposes, payments from such plans are taxable to the extent they were financed by your employer or are a substitute for unemployment benefits. For example, payments from the Rhode Island program are not taxable, and payments from California are not taxable unless they are a substitute for unemployment benefits. State disability payments from New York, New Jersey, and Hawaii are taxable to the extent of employer contributions.

**Injury or sickness resulting from active military service.**   Disability pensions for personal injuries or sickness resulting from active service in the armed forces are taxable if you joined the service after September 24, 1975.

Military disability payments are tax free if before September 25, 1975, you were entitled to military disability benefits or if on that date you were a member of the armed forces (or reserve unit) of the U.S. or any other country or were under a binding written commitment to become a member. A similar tax-free rule applies to disability pensions from the following government agencies if you were entitled to the payments before September 25, 1975, or were a member of the service (or committed to joining) on that date: The Foreign Service, Public Health Service, or National Oceanic and Atmospheric Administration. The exclusion for pre–September 25, 1975, service applies to disability pensions based upon percentage of disability. However, if a disability pension was based upon years of service, you do not pay tax on the amount that would be received based upon percentage of disability.

 *Law Alert*

**Disabled Combat Vets Entitled to Refunds of Improper Withholdings**

Lump-sum severance payments to veterans who separate from service because of combat-related injuries are tax free, but for decades, income taxes were improperly withheld from such lump-sum payments because of a glitch in the Defense Department's (DOD) computer payment system. Many affected veterans were unaware that their benefits were improperly reduced. The Combat-Injured Veterans Tax Fairness Act of 2016 requires the DOD to notify affected veterans and to provide instructions for filing an amended return to claim a refund for the improper withholdings. If the regular three-year period for claiming a refund *(47.2)* has already expired, the new law provides an extended deadline: the veteran has one year from the date that the DOD provides the required notice to file a refund claim for the withholdings.

The DOD is required by the new law to modify its payment system to ensure that tax is not withheld from tax-free severance payments.

**VA pensions.** Disability pensions from the Department of Veterans Affairs (VA) are tax free. If you retire from the military and are later given a retroactive award of VA disability benefits, the retirement pay received prior to the award (other than a lump-sum readjustment payment upon retirement) is retroactively made tax free to the extent of the VA disability determination. You may have more than the normal three-year period *(47.2)* to file a refund claim for any tax you paid on the amount that was retroactively determined to be a VA disability benefit. The refund deadline is extended for one year beginning on the date of the VA determination. However, a refund claim within the extended one-year period cannot be made for tax years that began more than five years before the date of the VA determination.

**Social Security disability benefits.** Disability benefits from the Social Security Administration (SSA) are treated as regular Social Security retirement benefits that may be taxable *(34.2)*.

In one case, a veteran who received disability benefits from the SSA as well as a disability pension from the Department of Veterans Affairs (VA) for cancer caused by exposure to Agent Orange during the Vietnam War tried to exclude both benefits from income. The IRS did not dispute the exclusion for the VA payments, but it held that the SSA disability benefits were subject to tax as if they were Social Security retirement benefits. The Tax Court and the Second Circuit Court of Appeals rejected the taxpayer's argument that his SSA disability benefits were excludable as amounts received for personal injuries/sickness resulting from active military service. The Second Circuit held that the military service exclusion is not applicable for SSA disability payments because they are a wage-replacement benefit based on the number of quarters of Social Security coverage, and are payable whether or not the disability arose from military service.

**Disability pay of federal public safety officers.** Disability benefits paid to federal public safety officers by the federal Bureau of Justice Assistance are tax free.

**Pension based on combat-related injuries.** Tax-free treatment applies to payments for combat-related injury or sickness that is incurred as a result of any one of the following activities: (1) as a direct result of armed conflict; (2) while engaged in extra-hazardous service, even if not directly engaged in combat; (3) under conditions simulating war, including maneuvers or training; or (4) that is caused by an instrumentality of war, such as weapons.

**Terrorist attacks or United States military actions.** Tax-free treatment applies to disability payments received by any individual for injuries incurred as the direct result of a terrorist attack against the United States or its allies. The exclusion also applies to disability income received as a direct result of a military action involving U.S. Armed Forces in response to aggression against the United States or its allies.

*Law Alert*

**Terrorist Attacks**

Tax-free treatment applies to disability payments resulting from terrorist attacks inside as well as outside the United States.

## 2.15 Stock Appreciation Rights (SARs)

Stock appreciation rights, or SARs, enable employees to receive the benefit of an increase in value of the employer's stock between the date the SARs are granted and the date they are exercised. When the SARs are exercised, cash or stock may be delivered as payment for the post-grant appreciation. For example, when your employer's stock is worth $30 a share, you get 100 SARs exercisable within five years. Two years later, when the stock price has increased to $50 a share, you exercise the SARs and receive $2,000 ($5,000 value at exercise minus $3,000 value at grant).

If IRS tests are satisfied, you are not taxed until you exercise the SARs and the post-grant appreciation is received. The situation has been complicated by the enactment of Code Section 409A *(2.7)*, which restricts deferrals of income under nonqualified deferred compensation plans. However, the IRS has provided an exception to the Section 409A rules for SARs issued with an exercise price equal to the stock's fair market value when the rights are granted.

## 2.16 Stock Options

Employees receiving statutory stock options do not incur regular income tax liability either at the time the option is granted or when the option is exercised. However, the option spread is generally subject to AMT *(23.2)*. Statutory options include incentive stock options (ISOs) and options under an employee stock purchase plan (ESPP). Employees receiving nonstatutory (nonqualified) stock options generally must include the option spread in income for the year the option is exercised unless the stock does not become vested until a later year.

**Incentive stock options (ISOs).** A corporation may provide its employees with incentive stock options to acquire its stock (or the stock of its parent or subsidiaries). For regular income tax purposes, ISOs meeting tax law tests are not taxed when granted or exercised. Income or loss is not reported until you sell the stock acquired from exercising the ISO. However, for purposes of the alternative minimum tax (AMT), the excess of the fair market value of the stock at exercise over the option price is treated as an adjustment that may substantially increase AMT income. The AMT adjustment applies for the year of exercise or if later, the year in which your rights to the stock are transferrable or no longer subject to a substantial risk of forfeiture; *see* the Caution on this page.

To qualify as an ISO, the option must be exercisable within 10 years of the date it is granted and the option price must be at least equal to the fair market value of the stock when the option is granted. If the fair market value of stock for which ISOs may first be exercised in a particular year by an employee exceeds $100,000 (valued at date of grant), the excess is not considered a qualifying ISO. An ISO may be exercised by a former employee within three months of the termination of employment; if exercised after three months, income is realized under the rules for nonqualified options, discussed later in this section.

**AMT consequences of exercising ISO.** Although you do not realize taxable income for regular tax purposes when you exercise an ISO, you may incur a substantial liability for alternative minimum tax (AMT) *(23.2)*. See the Caution on this page.

**Form 3921 for ISO.** You should receive Form 3921 (or equivalent statement) from the corporation for the year you exercise an ISO. Form 3921 shows the dates on which the ISO was granted and exercised, the exercise price per share, the fair market value per share on the exercise date, and the number of shares acquired when the option was exercised. Keep the Form 3921 in your records and use it to figure the gain or loss when you sell the shares; see " Gain or loss on sale of ISO stock," below. The Form 3921 entries can also be used to figure the AMT adjustment; *see* the Form 6251 instructions.

**Gain or loss on sale of ISO stock.** If the stock acquired by the exercise of the ISO is held for more than one year after acquisition and more than two years after the ISO was granted, you have long-term capital gain or loss *(5.3)* on the sale, equal to the difference between the selling price of the stock and the option price you paid when you exercised the ISO. If you sell to comply with conflict-of-interest requirements, the holding period rules are considered satisfied.

If you sell before meeting the one-year and two-year holding period tests, a gain on the sale is generally treated as ordinary wage income to the extent of the option spread (bargain element)—the excess of the value of the stock when you exercised the ISO over the option price. Any gain in excess of the spread is reported as capital gain. In figuring the capital gain, cost basis for the stock is increased by the amount treated as wages. If the fair market value of the stock declines between the date the option was exercised and the date the stock is sold, the amount that must be treated as wages is generally reduced. The ordinary income (wages) is limited to the actual gain on the stock sale where the gain is less than the option spread at exercise. However, the reduction to ordinary income does not apply on a sale of the stock to a related person or if replacement shares are purchased within the wash sale period *(30.6)* because the reduction applies only if a loss "would be" recognized if sustained (actual loss is not required for limitation to apply so long as a loss "would be" recognized).

If you have a loss on the sale of stock acquired by exercising an ISO, it is a capital loss and there is no ordinary wage income to report.

 *Caution*

**Possible AMT Liability for ISO**

If you exercise an incentive stock option and your rights in the acquired stock are transferable and not subject to a substantial risk of forfeiture, then on your tax return for the year of exercise you must treat the "bargain element" as an adjustment for alternative minimum tax purposes *(23.2)* unless you sell the stock by the end of that year. The bargain element is the excess of the fair-market value of the stock when the option was exercised over the option price. You must report an AMT adjustment based on the value of the stock when the option was exercised, even if the value later declines substantially. You avoid the AMT adjustment if you sell the stock in the same year the option was exercised. If your rights in the stock are restricted in the year you exercise the option, the AMT adjustment applies for the year the restrictions are lifted. See 23.2 for further details.

**Employee stock purchase plans (ESPPs).** These plans allow employees to buy their company's stock, usually at a discount. A discount cannot exceed 15% (option price must be at least 85% of fair market value). The plan must be nondiscriminatory and meet tax law tests on option terms. Options granted under qualified plans are not taxed until you sell the shares acquired from exercising the option.

If you sell the stock more than one year after exercising the option and also more than two years after the option was granted, gain on the sale is capital gain unless the option was granted at a discount. If at the time the option was granted the fair market value of the stock exceeded the option price (which must be no less than 85% of fair market value), then when you sell the stock, gain is ordinary wage income to the extent of that discount. Any excess gain is long-term capital gain. A loss on the sale is long-term capital loss.

If you sell the acquired stock before meeting the one-year and two-year holding period tests, you must report as ordinary wage income the option spread—the excess of the value of the stock when you exercised the option over the option price. This amount must be reported as ordinary income even if it exceeds the gain on the sale (which would occur if the sale price were lower than the exercise price). Add the ordinary income amount to your cost basis for the stock. If the increased basis is less than the selling price, the difference is capital gain. You have a capital loss if the increased basis exceeds the selling price.

For the year that you sell stock acquired at a discount under an ESPP, you should receive Form 3922 (or equivalent statement from the corporation). Form 3922 shows the dates the option was granted and exercised, the fair market value per share on the grant date and also the exercise date, the exercise price per share, and the number of shares sold.

**Nonstatutory (nonqualified) stock options.** A nonstatutory stock option (also called a nonqualified option) can in some cases be considered nonqualified deferred compensation subject to the requirements of Code Section 409A *(2.7)*. Under IRS regulations, the Section 409A rules apply if the exercise price can be less than the value of the underlying stock when the option is granted or the option permits any other deferral feature.

If the Section 409A rules do not apply, the amount of income to include and the time to include it depends on whether the option has a readily ascertainable fair market value when the option is granted. It is very rare for a nonstatutory option to be actively traded on an established securities market or to meet the other tests in IRS regulations for having a readily ascertainable fair market value.

In the usual case where there is no readily ascertainable fair market value for the option at the time it is granted, no income is realized on the receipt of the option. Income will not be realized until the year the option is exercised, or if later, the year your rights to the stock become vested. If the stock is not vested when you exercise the option, income is deferred until the vesting year under the restricted property rules *(2.17)*. In the year that you become vested in the stock, you must report as ordinary wage income the value of the stock (as of the vesting date), minus the amount you paid.

If you receive vested stock when the option is exercised, you are taxed on the difference between the fair market value of the stock when you exercise the option and the option price. For example, in 2018, you exercise a nonstatutory stock option to buy 1,000 shares of your employer's stock at $10 a share when the stock has a value of $30 a share. Your rights to the stock are vested when you buy it. When you exercise the option you are treated as receiving wages of $20,000, equal to the option spread ($30,000 value – $10,000 cost). This income is subject to withholding taxes that you will have to pay out-of-pocket at the time of exercise unless the withholding can be taken from regular cash wages. The taxable spread will be reported as wages on Form W-2 and will be separately identified in Box 12, using Code V. Your cost basis for the shares is increased by the ordinary income reported for exercising the option. If you hold the shares for more than one year after exercising the option and then sell them for $35,000 ($35 a share × 1,000 shares), you will have a $5,000 long-term capital gain ($35,000 – $30,000 basis ($10,000 cost plus $20,000 taxed as wages at exercise)).

If in a rare case a nonstatutory stock option has an ascertainable fair market value, the value of the option less any amount you paid is taxable under the restricted property rules *(2.17)* as ordinary wage income in the first year that your right to the option is freely transferable or not subject to a substantial risk of forfeiture. However, a Section 83(b) election *(2.17)* may not be made for the nonstatutory option. For other details and requirements, *see* IRS Regulation Section *1.83*-7.

Nonstatutory stock options may be granted in addition to or in place of incentive stock options. There are no restrictions on the amount of nonstatutory stock options that may be granted.

*Caution*

**Tax Due on Option Exercise**

Determine the amount of cash you will need to make the purchases and meet your tax liability before you exercise a nonqualified option and receive vested stock. If you receive vested stock when you exercise the option, you will realize wage income equal to the excess of the value of the stock over the option price. In addition to the cash to buy the stock, you will need cash to pay the tax on the wage income. The tax is due even if you plan to hold onto the stock before selling.

### EXAMPLES

1. You are granted an option to buy 1,000 shares from your employer's ESPP for $20 a share at a time when the market price is $22 a share. You exercise the option 14 months later when the value of the stock is $23 a share. You sell the stock for $30 a share 18 months after exercising the option. You meet the one-year and two-year holding period tests but because the option was granted at a discount, part of the gain on the sale is treated as ordinary income.

   | | |
   |---|---|
   | Selling price ($30 × 1,000 shares) | $30,000 |
   | Less: Cost of stock ($20 × 1,000 shares) | 20,000 |
   | Gain | 10,000 |
   | Less: Ordinary wage income<br>($22,000 value at grant – $20,000 option price) | 2,000 |
   | Capital gain<br>($30,000 sales price – basis of $22,000<br>($20,000 cost + $2,000 treated as wages)) | $8,000 |

2. Same facts as in Example 1, except that you sold the stock only six months after you exercised the ESPP option. Since the one-year holding period test was not met, $3,000 of your $10,000 gain is taxed as ordinary wage income. The $3,000 ordinary income equals the option spread between the $23,000 value of the stock when you exercised the option and the $20,000 option price. You also have a $7,000 short-term capital gain: $30,000 sales price – $23,000 basis ($20,000 cost + $3,000 treated as wages).

## 2.17 Restricted Stock

If in return for performing services you buy or receive company stock (or other property) subject to restrictions, special tax rules apply. Unless you make the Section 83(b) election discussed below, you do not have to pay tax on the stock until the first year in which it is substantially vested, which is the year that the stock either becomes transferable or is not

**Caution**

### Likelihood of Enforcement Required for Substantial Risk of Forfeiture

The IRS will take into account both the likelihood that a forfeiture event will occur and the likelihood that the forfeiture will be enforced in determining if there is a "substantial risk of forfeiture" under the restricted property rules.

**Law Alert**

### Election to Defer Income on Qualified Equity Grants

Under the Tax Cuts and Jobs Act, eligible employees of privately-held companies may defer the recognition of income for up to five years when they exercise stock options or settle restricted stock units (RSUs) (Code Section 83(i). The deferral election may not be made by more-than-1% owners, the four highest compensated officers, the CEO, or the CFO. The corporation must not have had any readily traded stock on an established securities market during any preceding year, and a written plan must give at least 80% of all U.S. employees stock options or RSUs with the same rights.

**Planning Reminder**

### Electing Immediate Tax on Restricted Stock

If you expect restricted stock to appreciate, consider making an election (Section 83(b) election) to be immediately taxed on the value of the restricted stock, minus your cost. If you make the election, any appreciation in value that has accrued since the election was made will not be taxable when the stock becomes substantially vested. Tax on appreciation will not be due until the stock is sold.

subject to a substantial risk of forfeiture. A risk of forfeiture exists where your rights are conditioned upon the future performance of substantial services. In the year the property becomes substantially vested, you must report as compensation (wages) the difference between the amount, if any, that you paid for the stock and its value at the time the risk of forfeiture is removed. The valuation at the time the forfeiture restrictions lapse is not reduced because of restrictions imposed on the right to sell the property. However, restrictions that will never lapse do affect valuation.

SEC restrictions on insider trading are considered a substantial risk of forfeiture, so that there is no tax on the receipt of stock subject to such restrictions. However, the SEC permits insiders to immediately resell stock acquired through exercise of an option granted at least six months earlier. As the stock acquired through such options is not subject to SEC restrictions, the executive is subject to immediate tax upon exercise of an option held for at least six months.

If the stock is subject to a restriction on transfer to comply with SEC pooling-of-interests accounting rules, the stock is considered to be subject to a substantial restriction.

**Non-employees.** The tax rules for restricted property are not limited to employees. They also apply to independent contractors who are compensated for services with restricted stock or other property.

**Sale of property that is not substantially vested.** If you sell restricted property in an arm's-length transaction before it has become substantially vested and you did not make the Section 83(b) election discussed below, gain on the sale (amount realized minus what you paid) must be reported as compensation income for the year of the sale. If the sale is to a related person or is otherwise not at arm's length, compensation must be reported not only for the year of sale but also for the year the original property becomes substantially vested, as if you still held it. In the later year, the compensation income equals the fair market value of the stock minus the total of the amount you paid for it and the compensation reported on the earlier sale.

**Election to include value of restricted stock in taxable pay when stock is received (Section 83(b) election).** Although restricted stock is generally not taxable until the year in which it is substantially vested, you may elect to be taxed in the year you receive it on the unrestricted value (as of the date the stock is received), less any payment you made. This is called a Section 83(b) election, which must be made by filing a signed statement with the IRS (at the Service Center where you file your return) no later than 30 days after the date the stock is transferred to you. Also give a copy of the statement to the employer or other party for whom you provided the services.

The statement must specify that you are making the election under Section 83(b) and include the following: your name, address, Social Security number, the year for which you are making the election, a description of the stock and the restrictions on the stock, the date you received the stock, the fair market value of the stock at receipt (ignoring restrictions unless they never lapse), your cost, if any, for the stock, and a statement that you have provided a copy of the statement to your employer or other party for whom the services were provided. The IRS has provided a sample election statement in Revenue Procedure 2012-29 that you can use to make the election.

You do not have to attach a copy of the statement to your tax return for the year in which the stock was transferred to you; this was required for pre-2015 transfers, but the IRS deleted the requirement because it prevented the return from being e-filed.

If you make the election, you recognize ordinary income (wages) based on the value of the stock when it is received, but thereafter you are treated as an investor and later appreciation in value is not taxed as pay when your rights to the stock become vested. When you sell the stock, your basis for figuring capital gain or loss is your cost basis increased by the amount of income you reported as pay under the Section 83 (b) election. If you forfeit the stock after the election is made, a capital loss *(5.4)* is allowed for your cost minus any amount realized on the forfeiture. The election may not be revoked without the consent of the IRS.

# CHAPTER 3

# Fringe Benefits

Employer-furnished fringe benefits are exempt from tax if the tests discussed in this chapter are met.

The most common tax-free benefits are accident and health plan coverage, including employer contributions to health savings accounts (HSAs), group-term life insurance plans, dependent care plans, education assistance plans, tuition reduction plans, adoption benefit plans, cafeteria plans, and plans providing employees with discounts, no-additional-cost services, or employer-subsidized meal facilities.

Highly compensated individuals may be taxed on certain benefits from such plans if nondiscrimination rules are not met.

## Table 3-1  Are Your Fringe Benefits Tax Free?

| Fringe benefit— | Tax Pointer— |
| --- | --- |
| Adoption benefits | Employer payments to a third party or reimbursements to you in 2018 for qualified adoption expenses are generally tax free up to a limit of $13,810 The exclusion for 2018 starts to phase out if modified adjusted gross income (MAGI) exceeds $207,140 and is completely phased out if MAGI is $247,140 or more *(3.6)*. |
| Athletic facilities | The fair market value of athletic facilities, such as gyms, swimming pools, golf courses, and tennis courts, is tax free if the facilities are on property owned or leased by the employer (not necessarily the main business premises) and substantially all of the use of the facilities is by employees, their spouses, and dependent children. Such facilities must be open to all employees on a nondiscriminatory basis in order for the company to deduct related expenses. |
| Child or dependent care plans | The value of day-care services provided or reimbursed by an employer under a written, nondiscriminatory plan is tax free up to a limit of $5,000, or $2,500 for married persons filing separately. Expenses are excludable if they would qualify for the dependent care credit; *see* Chapter 25. On your tax return, you must report employer-provided benefits to figure the tax-free exclusion. Tax-free employer benefits reduce eligibility for the dependent care tax credit *(3.5)*. |
| De minimis (minor) fringe benefits | These are small benefits that are administratively impractical to tax, such as occasional supper money and taxi fares for overtime work, company parties or picnics, and occasional theater or sporting event tickets *(3.10)*. |
| Discounts on company products and services | Services from your employer that are usually sold to customers are tax free if your employer does not incur additional costs in providing them to you *(3.16)*. Merchandise discounts and other discounted services are also eligible for a tax-free exclusion *(3.17)*. |
| Education plans | An up-to-$5,250 exclusion applies to employer-financed undergraduate and graduate courses *(3.7)*. |
| Employee achievement awards | Achievement awards are taxable unless they qualify under special rules for length of service or safety achievement *(3.12)*. |
| Group-term life insurance | Premiums paid by employers are not taxed if policy coverage is $50,000 or less *(3.4)*. |
| Health and accident plans including HSAs | Premiums paid by an employer are tax free. For 2018, employer contributions to a health savings account, or HSA, on behalf of an eligible employee are generally not taxed up to $3,450 for self-only coverage or $6,900 for family coverage *(3.2)*. Health benefits paid from an employer plan are also generally tax free (3.1–3.4). |
| Interest-free or low-interest loans | Interest-free loans received from your employer may be taxed *(4.31)*. |
| Moving expense reimbursements | Starting in 2018, employer reimbursements of moving expenses to an employee are taxable, with one exception: reimbursements of qualifying moving costs are tax free to members of the U.S. Armed Forces on active duty who move pursuant to a military order and incident to a permanent change of station *(2.1, 12.3)*. |
| Retirement planning advice | Employer-provided retirement income planning advice and information are tax free to employees (and their spouses) so long as the employer maintains a qualified retirement plan. The exclusion does not apply to tax preparation, accounting, legal, or brokerage services. |
| Transportation benefits | Within limits, employer-provided parking benefits, transit passes, and bicycle commuting reimbursements are tax free; *see 3.8*. |
| Tuition reductions | Tuition reductions for courses below the graduate level are generally tax free. Graduate students who are teaching or research assistants are not taxed on tuition reduction unless the reduction is compensation for teaching services *(3.7)*. |
| Working condition benefits | Benefits provided by your employer that would be deductible if you paid the expenses yourself are a tax-free working condition fringe benefit. These include business use of a company car or employer-provided cell phone *(3.9)*. |

## 3.1 Tax-Free Health and Accident Coverage Under Employer Plans

You are not taxed on contributions or insurance premiums your employer makes to a health, hospitalization, or accident plan to cover you, your spouse, your dependents, and your children under age 27 (as of the end of the year) whether or not they can be claimed as your dependents. Tax-free treatment for a spouse applies to same-sex as well as opposite sex spouses. A domestic partner is not a spouse; you must pay tax on employer-paid coverage for a domestic partner.

If you obtain coverage by making pre-tax salary-reduction contributions under your employer's cafeteria plan *(3.15)*, the salary reductions are treated as employer contributions that are tax free to you. If you are temporarily laid off and continue to receive health coverage, the employer's contributions during this layoff period are tax free. If you are retired, you do not pay tax on insurance paid by your former employer. Medical coverage provided to the family of a deceased employee is tax free since it is treated as a continuation of the employee's fringe-benefit package. If you are age 65 or older, Medicare premiums paid by your employer are not taxed. If you retire and have the option of receiving continued coverage under the medical plan or a lump-sum payment covering unused accumulated sick leave instead of coverage, the lump-sum amount is reported as income at the time you have the option to receive it. If you elect continued coverage, the amount reported as income may be deductible as medical insurance if you itemize deductions *(17.5)*.

**Disability coverage.** If your employer pays the premiums for your disability coverage (short term or long term) and does not report the payment as compensation income on your Form W-2, or if you pay the premiums with pre-tax salary-reduction contributions, your coverage is tax free but any benefits you subsequently receive from the plan upon becoming disabled will be includible in your gross income *(3.3)*. If you pay the premiums with after-tax contributions or your employer makes contributions that are included on your Form W-2, any disability benefits you receive from the plan will not be taxable to you.

**Health Reimbursement Arrangements (HRAs).** Employer contributions to health reimbursement arrangements (HRAs) are not taxed to the employees. The contributions must be paid by the employer and not provided by salary reduction. HRA contributions can be used to reimburse the medical costs of employees, their spouses, and their dependents, and unused expenses may be carried forward to later years *(3.3)*.

**Long-term care coverage.** You are not taxed on contributions your employer makes for long-term care coverage that would pay you benefits in the event you become chronically ill *(17.15)*. However, long-term care coverage may not be offered to you through a cafeteria plan *(3.15)* and reimbursements of long-term care expenses may not be made through a flexible spending arrangement *(3.16)*.

**Continuing coverage for group health plans (COBRA coverage).** Employers are subject to daily penalties unless they offer continuing group health and accident coverage to employees who leave the company voluntarily or involuntarily (unless for gross misconduct) and to spouses and dependent children who would lose coverage in the case of divorce or the death of the employee. Federal COBRA continuing coverage rules apply to employers with 20 or more employees but smaller employers may be required under state law to provide comparable continuing coverage under "mini-COBRA" laws.

Generally, an employer may charge you premiums for continuing coverage that are as much as 102% of the regular plan premium for the applicable (family or individual) coverage.

## 3.2 Health Savings Accounts (HSAs) and Archer MSAs

If you are covered by a qualifying high-deductible health plan (HDHP), your employer may make tax-free contributions to a health savings account (HSA) on your behalf. Earnings accumulate tax free within an HSA and distributions are tax free if used to pay your qualified medical expenses, or those of your spouse or dependents. If your employer does not make the maximum tax-free contribution to your HSA, you can make a deductible contribution, so long as the total does not exceed the annual contribution limit (see below).

 *Filing Instruction*

**Proof of Medical Coverage**

To avoid a tax penalty under the individual mandate provision of the Affordable Care Act, you must indicate on your tax return that you had minimum essential health insurance coverage for the entire year or you qualify for an exemption *(38.5)*. If you are covered by an employer plan, your employer must give you Form 1095-C (or you receive Form 1095-B from the insurer) showing the months of your coverage.

*Filing Tip*

**Above-the-Line Deduction for HSA Contributions**

If you are an eligible employee, contributions you make to your HSA are reported on Form 8889 and deducted on Line 25 of Schedule 1 of Form 1040; *see 3.2* for contribution limits. The deduction is "above the line," so it is allowed even if you claim the standard deduction.

If you are self-employed, you may claim the "above-the-line" HSA deduction subject to the same limits; *see* Chapter 41 for further details.

Archer MSAs are an older type of medical savings plan that HSAs are intended to replace. If your employer set up an Archer MSA on your behalf before 2008, or you became eligible to participate after 2007 in a pre-2008 plan, your employer may continue to contribute to the account. If you work for an eligible small employer with a high-deductible plan, your employer may make tax-free contributions to an Archer MSA on your behalf. A rollover can be made from an Archer MSA to a new health savings account (HSA) that accepts rollovers. If the Archer MSA is retained, withdrawals will be tax free if used to pay qualified medical expenses for you, your spouse, or your dependents.

## Health Savings Account (HSA)

You may set up an HSA only if you are covered by a qualifying high-deductible health plan (HDHP, *see* details below), you are not enrolled in Medicare, and you are not the dependent of another taxpayer. Generally, you must have no coverage other than HDHP coverage, but there are exceptions. You are allowed to have separate coverage for vision, dental, or long-term care, accidents, disability, per diem insurance while hospitalized, insurance for a specific disease or illness, car insurance (or similar insurance for owning or using property), or insurance for workers' compensation or tort liabilities. Preventive care is also exempt from the deductible requirement.

As an eligible employee, you, your employer, or both may contribute to your HSA. The same maximum annual contribution limit applies (see below) regardless of the number of contributors. Your employer may allow you to make pre-tax salary-reduction contributions to an HDHP and HSA as an option under a "cafeteria" plan *(3.13)*.

**High-deductible health plan (HDHP).** An HDHP must have a minimum annual deductible and an annual out-of-pocket maximum. For 2018, the minimum plan deductible was $1,350 for self-only coverage and $2,700 for family coverage. Out-of-pocket costs for 2018 were limited to $6,650 for self-only coverage and $13,300 for family coverage.

For 2019, the minimum plan deductibles are staying at $1,350 for self-only coverage and $2,700 for family coverage. The cap on out-of- pocket costs increases to $6,750 for self-only coverage and $13,500 for family coverage. The limit for out-of- pocket costs covers plan deductibles, co-payments and other out-of-pocket expenses, but not premiums.

In the case of family coverage, the terms of the HDHP must deny payments to all family members until the family as a unit incurs annual covered expenses in excess of the minimum annual deductible ($2,700 for 2018). Thus, a plan is not a qualified HDHP for 2018 if it allows payment of an individual family member's medical expenses exceeding $1,350 (the minimum deductible for self-only coverage) but the family as a whole does not have expenses over $2,700.

However, the minimum annual HDHP deductible does not apply to preventive care benefits. The plan can qualify as an HDHP even if it pays for preventive care without a deductible or after a small deductible (below the regular HDHP minimum). The IRS has provided a safe harbor list of preventive care benefits, including annual physicals, routine prenatal and well-child care, immunizations, tobacco cessation and obesity programs, and screening services for a broad range of conditions including cancer (such as breast, cervical, prostate, ovarian, and colorectal cancer) and cardiovascular disease. Prescription drugs qualify for the preventive care safe harbor if taken by asymptomatic patients with risk factors for a disease, or by recovering patients to prevent the recurrence of a disease.

By law, prescription drug coverage, other than coverage meeting the preventive care safe harbor, is not a permitted exception to the high-deductible requirement. This is a problem for employees whose employers offer separate prescription drug plans that provide first-dollar drug coverage with either a flat dollar or percentage co-payment. HSA contributions cannot be made for individuals with an HDHP and such a prescription drug plan because the prescription drug benefits are not subject to the HDHP minimum annual deductible.

**Maximum annual HSA contribution for employees.** For 2018, the maximum HSA contribution for an employee with self-only coverage is $3,450, and for an employee with family coverage, the maximum contribution for 2018 is $6,900. For employees who are age 55 or older by the end of 2018 but not enrolled in Medicare, an additional "catch-up" contribution of $1,000 may be made. The applicable limit must be reduced by any contributions to an Archer MSA.

For 2019, the self-only contribution limit increases slightly to $3,500, and the limit for family coverage increases to $7,000, plus the additional $1,000 catch-up for those age 55 or older; the $1,000 catch-up is fixed by statute.

If you become eligible under an HDHP, contributions are allowed for the months prior to your enrollment in the HDHP, provided you are eligible in December of that year. However, the contributions for the months prior to your enrollment will be included in your income and subject to a 10% penalty if you do not remain eligible for the 12 months following the end of the first eligibility year, unless you are disabled (or die).

All employer contributions must be reported on Form 8889, which you attach to your Form 1040. Contributions by your employer up to the above limit are tax free and are not subject to withholding for income tax or FICA (Social Security and Medicare) purposes. All employer contributions to an HSA are reported in Box 12 of Form W-2 with Code W. Contributions exceeding the excludable limit are also reported in Box 1 of Form W-2 as taxable wages. If you do not remove an excess contribution (and any net income) by the due date for your return (including extensions), the excess is subject to a 6% penalty; *see* the instructions to Forms 8889 and 5329.

If your employer contributes less than the limit, you may contribute to your HSA but the same overall limit applies to the aggregate contributions. Contributions you make are reported on Form 8889 and deductible "above the line" from gross income on Line 25 of Schedule 1 of Form 1040. You must attach Form 8889 to your Form 1040.

## Archer MSAs

Most employers have replaced Archer MSAs (medical savings accounts) with HSAs. However, an Archer MSA that is not rolled over to a new HSA may continue to be funded.

To contribute, you must have coverage under a high-deductible health plan and must work for a "small employer," one that had an average of 50 or fewer employees during either of the two preceding years. For 2018, self-only coverage under a high-deductible health plan, the minimum deductible was $2,300, the maximum deductible was $3,450, and the plan limit on out-of-pocket expenses (other than premiums) was $4,550. For 2018 family coverage, the deductible had to be at least $4,550 and no more than $6,850, and the limit on out-of-pocket expenses (other than premiums) was $8,400. All of these limits are subject to an inflation adjustment for 2019; *see* the ***e-Supplement*** at ***jklasser.com***.

Generally, you are not eligible for an Archer MSA if you have any other health insurance in addition to the high-deductible plan coverage, except for policies covering only disability, vision or dental care, long-term care, or accidental injuries, or plans that pay a flat amount during hospitalization.

**Employer contribution limits.** Your employer's contributions to your Archer MSA are tax free up to an annual limit of 65% of the plan deductible if you have individual coverage and 75% of the deductible for family coverage. The limit is reduced on a monthly basis if you are not covered for the entire year. For example, if for all of 2018 you were covered by a qualifying family coverage high-deductible plan with a $6,850 annual deductible (this is the maximum deductible for 2018), the maximum tax-free contribution is $5,138 (75% of $6,850). If you had coverage for only 10 months, the limit would be $4,282 (10/12 × $5,138). All employer contributions to your Archer MSA are reported in Box 12 of Form W-2 (Code R). If the contributions exceed the tax-free limit, the excess is reported in Box 1 of Form W-2 as taxable wages. You must report all employer contributions on Form 8853, which you attach to your Form 1040.

If your employer makes any contributions to your account, you may not make any contributions for that year. In addition, if you and your spouse have family coverage under a high-deductible plan and your spouse's employer contributes to his or her Archer MSA, you cannot contribute to your Archer MSA. If your employer (or spouse's employer) does not contribute, you may make deductible contributions up to the above employer contribution limits. You report your contributions on Form 8853 and claim your deduction on Line 36 of Form 1040; label it "MSA." Contributions exceeding the annual limit are subject to a 6% penalty.

 *Planning Reminder*

**One-Time Transfer From IRA to HSA**

You can make a one-time tax-free transfer from your IRA or Roth IRA to your HSA. A qualifying transfer is not taxable or subject to the 10% penalty for distributions before age 59½. Generally, only one IRA/Roth IRA transfer to an HSA is allowed during your lifetime, but if a transfer is made to a self-only HDHP, and later in the same year you obtain family HDHP coverage, a second transfer from an IRA or Roth IRA may be made in that year. The transfer (or transfers) count towards the annual HSA contribution limit for that year, so if the transfer exceeds the annual HSA contribution limit, the excess is taxable (and possibly subject to the pre-59½ penalty). If you want to transfer amounts from more than one IRA or Roth IRA to an HSA, you have to first roll the funds into a single IRA/Roth IRA and then make the transfer from that account.

To be tax free, the transfer must be directly to the HSA trustee or custodian. Furthermore, you must remain HSA-eligible (have qualifying HDHP coverage) for 12 months following the date of the distribution; otherwise, the distribution is taxable (and possibly subject to the pre-59½ penalty) in the year that you cease to be eligible. Changing from family-HDHP coverage to a self-only HDHP during the 12-month testing period is not considered a cessation of HSA eligibility.

## 3.3 Reimbursements and Other Tax-Free Payments From Employer Health and Accident Plans

Several types of payments from a health or accident plan are tax free to you even if your employer paid the entire cost of your coverage:

1. Reimbursements of your medical expenses; *see* below.
2. Payments for permanent physical injuries; *see* below.
3. Distributions from a health savings account (HSA) or Archer MSA if they are used to pay for qualified medical expenses; *see* below.
4. Payments you receive when you are chronically ill from a qualifying long-term-care insurance contract; but if payments are made on a per diem or other periodic basis, the exclusion may be limited. For 2018, payments of up to $360 per day are tax free regardless of actual expenses. If the payments exceed $360 per day, you are only taxed to the extent that the payments exceed your qualifying long-term-care expenses. **See *17.1*5** for further details.

Payments that are not within the above tax-free categories, such as disability benefits, are not taxable to you if you paid all of the premiums with after-tax contributions. If your contributions were made on a pre-tax basis, benefits received from the plan are taxable. For example, disability benefits are taxable if you paid premiums paid under a cafeteria plan *(3.14)* with pre-tax contributions that were excluded from your income. If your employer paid all the premiums and you were not taxed on your employer's payment, any benefits you receive from the plan are fully taxable. If both you (with after-tax contributions) and your employer contributed to the plan, only the amount received that is attributable to your employer's payments is taxable.

### Tax-Free Reimbursements for Medical Expenses

Reimbursements of medical expenses *(17.2)* that you paid for yourself, your spouse, or any dependents and your children under age 27 are tax free, provided you incurred the expenses after the plan was established. Payment does not have to come directly to you to be tax free; it may go directly to your medical care providers.

Tax-free reimbursements may be from a health-care flexible spending arrangement (FSA) *(3.16)*. Reimbursements made under a qualifying health reimbursement arrangement (HRA) also qualify for tax-free treatment; *see* below.

Tax-free treatment applies only for reimbursed expenses, not amounts you would have received anyway, such as sick leave that is not dependent on actual medical expenses. If your employer reimburses you for premiums you paid, the reimbursement is tax free so long as your payment was from after-tax funds. If you paid premiums with pre-tax salary reductions, a "reimbursement" from the employer will be taxable to you because the salary reductions are treated as your employer's payment, not yours.

Reimbursements for cosmetic surgery do not qualify for tax-free treatment, unless the surgery is for disfigurement related to congenital deformity, disease, or accidental injury.

Reimbursements for your dependents' medical expenses are tax free. This exclusion applies not only to reimbursed expenses of persons claimed as dependents *(21.1)* on your return, but also to expenses of qualifying children or relatives who cannot be claimed as your dependents because: (1) they are claimed by the other parent under the special rules for divorced/separated parents *(21.7)*, (2) their gross income exceeds the limit for qualifying relatives ($4,150 for 2018), (3) they file a joint return with their spouse, or (4) you are the dependent of another taxpayer and thus are barred from claiming any dependents on your return.

A qualifying dependent does not include a live-in mate where the relationship violates local law.

If the reimbursement is for medical expenses you deducted in a previous year, the reimbursement may be taxable. **See *17.4*** for the rules on reimbursements of deducted medical expenses.

If you receive payments from more than one policy and the total exceeds your actual medical expenses, the excess is taxable if your employer paid the entire premium; *see* the Examples in *17.4*.

*Caution*

**Reimbursed Cosmetic Surgery**

An employer's reimbursement of expenses for cosmetic surgery is taxable unless the employee had surgery to correct disfigurement from an accident, disease, or congenital deformity.

**Health Reimbursement Arrangements (HRAs).** Employers can set up health reimbursement arrangements (HRAs) that are integrated with a group health plan. The HRA reimburses out-of-pocket medical expenses of employees, their spouses, children under age 27 and their dependents. Former employees including retired employees, and spouses and dependents of deceased employees can be covered. Self-employed individuals are not eligible. An HRA must be funded solely by employer contributions and not by salary reductions or after-tax contributions from employees.

Employees are not taxed on HRA reimbursements for medical expenses that may be claimed as itemized deductions *(17.2)*, including premiums. Over-the-counter medicines or drugs other than insulin do not qualify for tax-free reimbursement from an HRA unless they are prescribed by a physician. For contributions and reimbursements *(3.1)* to be tax free, employees must not receive cash or any benefit (taxable or nontaxable) from an HRA other than reimbursement for medical expenses. If the reimbursement limit is not fully used up by the end of a coverage year, the unused limit can be carried forward to a subsequent year. Nondiscrimination rules apply to self-insured HRAs.

**Qualified Small Employer Health Reimbursement Arrangements (QSEHRAs).** If your employer is a "small employer" (no more than 49 full-time and full-time-equivalent employees) that does not offer a group health plan, you may be offered reimbursements of your premiums for personally obtained health coverage and other out-of-pocket medical expenses (that may be claimed as itemized deductions *(17.2)*) through a qualified small employer health reimbursement arrangement (QSEHRA). A QSEHRA is funded solely by the employer (no salary reductions permitted) and must meet certain nondiscrimination requirements. Reimbursements are tax-free up to an annual limit. For 2018, the maximum amount of excludable reimbursements under a QSEHRA is $5,050 for self-only coverage, or $10,250 for family coverage; these amounts may get an inflation increase for 2019; *see* the *e-Supplement* at *jklasser.com*. The dollar limit is prorated for your period of coverage. Thus, if you obtained family coverage starting July 1, 2018, your excludable reimbursement for 2018 is limited to $5,125 (6/12th of $10,250). You must provide proof of coverage to your employer.

A QSEHRA is not treated as a group health plan. If you obtain health coverage through a government marketplace and are eligible for the premium tax credit *(25.12)*, the credit amount is reduced by reimbursements through a QSEHRA; you must disclose to the marketplace the amount that you could be reimbursed for under a QSEHRA if you are applying for advance payment of the credit.

Your employer must provide you with a written notice about your eligibility for reimbursement and the terms of your employer's QSEHRA. The notice generally must be provided at least 90 days before the start of the year for which the QSEHRA is provided, or 90 days before the first eligibility date for employees not eligible at the beginning of the year. The notice must state that you may be liable for the individual responsibility penalty, and that your reimbursements under the QSEHRA may become taxable, if you do not have minimum essential health coverage *(38.5)*. In addition, the notice must include the requirement (noted above) that you disclose your QSEHRA coverage to a government marketplace when applying for advance payment of the premium tax credit.

**Self-employed health plan that includes spouse.** If a self-employed person hires his or her spouse and provides family coverage under a health plan purchased in the name of the business, the employee-spouse may be reimbursed tax free for medical expenses incurred by both spouses and their dependent children.

**Executives taxed in discriminatory self-insured medical reimbursement plans.** Although reimbursements from an employer plan for medical expenses of an employee and his or her spouse and dependents are generally tax free, this exclusion does not apply to certain highly compensated employees and stockholders if the plan is self-insured and it discriminates on their behalf. A plan is self-insured if reimbursement is not provided by an unrelated insurance company. If coverage is provided by an unrelated insurer, these discrimination rules do not apply. If a self-insured plan is deemed discriminatory, rank-and-file employees are not affected; only highly compensated employees are subject to tax.

 *Law Alert*

**Qualified Small Employer Health Reimburement Arrangements (QSEHRAs)**

Employers with less than 50 employees and without a group health plan may offer tax-free reimbursements of premiums and other medical costs to employees under a qualified small employer health reimbursement arrangement (QSEHRA).. *See* the nearby text for details.

Highly compensated participants subject to these rules include employees owning more than 10% of the employer's stock, the highest paid 25% of all employees (other than employees who do not have to be covered under the law), and the five highest paid officers.

If highly compensated employees are entitled to reimbursement for expenses not available to other plan participants, any such reimbursements are taxable to them. For example, if only the five highest paid officers are entitled to dental benefits, any dental reimbursements they receive are taxable. However, routine physical exams may be provided to highly compensated employees (but not their dependents) on a discriminatory basis. This exception does not apply to testing for, or treatment of, a specific complaint.

If highly compensated participants are entitled to a higher reimbursement limit than other participants, any excess reimbursement over the lower limit is taxable to the highly compensated participant. For example, if highly compensated employees are entitled to reimbursements up to $5,000 while all others have a $1,000 limit, a highly compensated employee who receives a $4,000 reimbursement must report $3,000 ($4,000 received minus the $1,000 lower limit) as income.

A separate nondiscrimination test applies to plan eligibility. The eligibility test requires that the plan benefit: (1) 70% or more of all employees or (2) 80% or more of employees eligible to participate, provided that at least 70% of all employees are eligible. A plan not meeting either test is considered discriminatory unless proven otherwise. In applying these tests, employees may be excluded if they have less than three years of service, are under age 25, do part-time or seasonal work, or are covered by a union collective bargaining agreement. A fraction of the benefits received by a highly compensated individual from a nonqualifying plan is taxable. The fraction equals the total reimbursements to highly compensated participants divided by total plan reimbursements; benefits available only to highly compensated employees are disregarded. For example, assume that a plan failing the eligibility tests pays total reimbursements of $50,000, of which $30,000 is to highly compensated participants. A highly compensated executive who is reimbursed $4,500 for medical expenses must include $2,700 in income:

$$\frac{30,000}{50,000} \times 4,500 = 2,700$$

Taxable reimbursements are reported in the year during which the applicable plan year ends. For example, in early 2019 you are reimbursed for a 2018 expense from a calendar-year plan. If under plan provisions the expenses are allocated to the 2018 plan year, the taxable amount should be reported as 2018 income. If the plan does not specify the plan year to which the reimbursement relates, the reimbursement is attributed to the plan year in which payment is made.

## Tax-Free Payments for Permanent Physical Injuries

Payments from an employer plan are tax free if they are for the permanent loss of part of the body, permanent loss of use of part of the body, or for permanent disfigurement of yourself, your spouse, your children under age 27 (as of the end of the year), or your dependent. An appeals court held that severe hypertension does not involve loss of a bodily part or function and thus does not qualify for the exclusion.

To be tax free, the payments must be based on the kind of injury and have no relation to the length of time you are out of work or prior years of service. If the employer's plan does not specifically allocate benefits according to the nature of the injury, the benefits are taxable even if an employee is in fact permanently disabled.

**Disability payments from profit-sharing plan.** The Tax Court has held that a profit-sharing plan may provide benefits that qualify for the exclusion for permanent disfigurement or permanent loss of bodily function. The plan must clearly state that its purpose is to provide qualifying tax-free benefits, and a specific payment schedule must be provided for different types of injuries. Without such provisions, payments from the plan are treated as taxable retirement distributions.

*Filing Tip*

**Permanent Physical Injuries**

An employer's payment for permanent disfigurement or permanent loss of bodily function is tax free if the payment is based solely on the nature of the injury. Whether or not you qualify for this exclusion, you may deduct as an itemized deduction any unreimbursed medical expense you have in connection with these injuries subject to the adjusted gross income floor *(17.1)*.

> **EXAMPLE**
> After he loses a foot in an accident, Marc Jones receives $50,000 as specified in his employer's plan. The payment is tax free as it does not depend on how long Jones is out from work.

## HSA or Archer MSA Payments

**Tax-free distributions from a health savings account (HSA).** Distributions from an HSA *(3.2)* are tax free if used to pay qualified medical expenses for you, your spouse, or your dependents. Qualified medical expenses are unreimbursed costs eligible for the itemized deduction *(17.2)* on Schedule A of Form 1040. Over-the-counter medicines other than insulin that do not require a prescription qualify for HSA purposes if they are actually prescribed by a physician. Medical expenses are "qualified" only if incurred after the HSA has been established. A distribution is taxable to the extent it is not used to pay qualified medical expenses. A taxable distribution is also subject to a 20% penalty unless you are disabled or are age 65 or older. Distributions will be reported to you on Form 1099-SA and you must report them on Form 8889, which you attach to Form 1040. On Form 8889, you determine if any part of the distribution is taxable and, if it is, that amount must be included as "Other income" on Line 21 Schedule 1 of Form 1040. The 20% penalty from Form 8889, if any, is entered on the line for "Other Taxes" on Form 1040.

A non-spouse beneficiary who inherits an HSA after the death of the account owner generally must include in income the fair market value of the assets as of the date of death. However, the beneficiary is not subject to the 20% penalty for taxable distributions. If the beneficiary is the account owner's spouse, he or she becomes the owner of the HSA and will be taxed only on distributions that are not used for qualified medical expenses.

**Tax-free distributions from Archer MSA.** If you work for a small-business employer and have a qualifying Archer MSA *(3.2)*, earnings accumulate in the account tax free. Withdrawals are tax free if used to pay deductible medical costs for you, your spouse, or dependents. Withdrawals used for a non-qualifying purpose are taxable and a taxable distribution before age 65 or becoming disabled is also subject to a 20% penalty. *See 41.13* for further details.

## 3.4 Group-Term Life Insurance Premiums

You are not taxed on your employer's payments of premiums of up to $50,000 on your life under a group-term insurance policy. You are taxed only on the cost of premiums for coverage of over $50,000 as determined by the IRS rates shown in the table below. On Form W-2 your employer should include the taxable amount as wages in Box 1 and separately label the amount in Box 12 with Code C. You may not avoid tax by assigning the policy to another person.

If two or more employers provide you with group-term insurance coverage, you get only one $50,000 exclusion. You must figure the taxable cost for coverage over $50,000 by using the IRS rates below.

Regardless of the amount of the policy, you are not taxed if, for your entire tax year, the beneficiary of the policy is a tax-exempt charitable organization or your employer.

**Your payments reduce taxable amount.** If you pay part of the cost of the insurance, your payment reduces dollar for dollar the amount includible as pay on Form W-2.

**Retirees.** If your former employer provides you with over $50,000 of group-term life insurance coverage, the cost of the coverage over $50,000 is generally taxable to you as if you were an employee. However, if you retired because of a total and permanent disability and remain covered by your company's plan, you are not taxed even if coverage exceeds $50,000.

There are also exceptions for coverage under plans in existence on January 1, 1984. If you retired on or before that date (normal retirement or disability), were covered by the plan when you retired, and are still covered by it, your current coverage is tax free even if coverage is over $50,000. If you were age 55 or older on January 1, 1984, and retired after that date, and were employed during 1983 by the employer providing the current coverage or a predecessor employer, you are not taxed on the cost of your current coverage.

*Filing Instruction*

**Uncollected Social Security and Medicare of Former Employees**

If you receive coverage as a former employee, you must pay with Form 1040 your share of Social Security and Medicare taxes on group-term life insurance over $50,000. The taxable amounts are shown in Box 12 of Form W-2, with Codes M (Uncollected Social Security tax) and N (Uncollected Medicare tax).

However, even if the above tests for tax-free coverage are met, you may be taxed under the rule below for discriminatory plans if you retired after 1986 and were a key employee.

**Key employees taxed under discriminatory plans.** The $50,000 exclusion is not available to key employees unless the group plan meets nondiscrimination tests for eligibility and benefits. For 2018, key employees include those who during the year were: (1) more-than-5% owners; (2) more-than-1% owners earning over $150,000; and (3) officers with compensation over $175,000. If the plan discriminates, a key employee's taxable benefit is based on the larger of (1) the actual cost of coverage or (2) the amount for coverage using the IRS rate table below.

The nondiscrimination rules also apply to former employees who were key employees when they separated from service. The discrimination tests are applied separately with respect to active and former employees.

**Group-term life insurance for dependents.** Employer-paid coverage for your spouse or dependents is a tax-free *de minimis* fringe benefit *(3.10)* if the policy is $2,000 or less. For coverage over $2,000, you are taxed on the excess of the cost (determined under the IRS table below) over your after-tax payments for the insurance, if any.

---

**EXAMPLE**

In 2018, Lynda Jackson's company pays all the premiums on $200,000 of group-term life insurance it provides for her for the entire year. Lynda is age 52 at the end of 2018. The taxable value of the coverage is based on the $150,000 coverage in excess of the $50,000 exclusion. As shown in the rate table below, the premium used to determine the taxable coverage is $0.23 for every $1,000 of coverage over $50,000. The taxable amount for the year is $414 ($0.23 × 12 months × 150).

If Lynda had paid $120 towards the coverage, the taxable amount would be reduced to $294 ($414 − $120).

---

**Permanent life insurance.** If your employer pays premiums on your behalf for permanent nonforfeitable life insurance, you report as taxable wages the cost of the benefit, less any amount you paid. A permanent benefit is an economic value that extends beyond one year and includes paid-up insurance or cash surrender value, but does not include, for example, the right to convert or continue life insurance coverage after group coverage is terminated. Where permanent benefits are combined with term insurance, the permanent benefits are taxed under formulas found in IRS regulations.

**Table 3-2   Taxable Premiums for Group-Term Insurance Coverage Over $50,000**

| Age—* | Monthly cost for each $1,000 of coverage over $50,000— |
|---|---|
| Under 25 | $0.05 |
| 25–29 | 0.06 |
| 30–34 | 0.08 |
| 35–39 | 0.09 |
| 40–44 | 0.10 |
| 45–49 | 0.15 |
| 50–54 | 0.23 |
| 55–59 | 0.43 |
| 60–64 | 0.66 |
| 65–69 | 1.27 |
| 70 and over | 2.06 |

*Age is determined at end of year.

## 3.5 Dependent Care Assistance

The value of qualifying day-care services provided by your employer under a written, nondiscriminatory plan is generally not taxable up to a limit of $5,000, or $2,500 if you are married filing separately. The same tax-free limits apply if you make pre-tax salary deferrals to a flexible spending account for reimbursing dependent care expenses *(3.15)*. Note that the maximum exclusion is $5,000/$2,500 regardless of the number of dependents for whom care is provided. However, you may not exclude from income more than your earned income. If you are married and your spouse earns less than you do, your tax-free benefit is limited to his or her earned income. If your spouse does not work, all of your benefits are taxable unless he or she is a full-time student or is disabled. If a full-time student or disabled, your spouse is treated as earning $250 a month if your dependent care expenses are for one dependent, or $500 a month if the expenses are for two or more dependents.

Expenses are excludable from income only if they would qualify for the dependent care credit; *see Chapter 25*. If you are being reimbursed by your employer, the exclusion is not allowed if dependent care is provided by a relative who is your dependent (or your spouse's dependent) or by your child under the age of 19. You must give your employer a record of the care provider's name, address, and tax identification number. The identifying information also must be listed on your return.

If the plan does not meet nondiscriminatory tests, benefits provided for highly-compensated employees are not excludable from their income.

**Reporting employer benefits on your return.** Your employer will show the total amount of your dependent care benefits in Box 10 of your Form W-2. Any benefits over $5,000 will also be included as taxable wages in Box 1 of Form W-2 and as Social Security wages (Box 3) and Medicare wages (Box 5).

You must report the benefits on Part III of Form 2441, where you determine both the tax-free and taxable (if any) portions of the employer-provided benefits. If any part is taxable, that amount must be included on Line 1 of Form 1040 as wages and labeled "DCB."

Follow IRS instructions for identifying the care provider (employer, babysitter, etc.) on Part I of Form 2441.

The tax-free portion of employer benefits reduces expenses eligible for the dependent care credit *(Chapter 25)*.

## 3.6 Adoption Benefits

If your employer pays or reimburses you in 2018 for qualifying adoption expenses under a written, nondiscriminatory plan, up to $13,810 per qualifying child may be tax free. Employer-provided adoption assistance may be for any child under age 18, or a person physically or mentally incapable of self-care. The exclusion applies to adoption fees, attorney fees, court costs, travel expenses, and other expenses directly related to a legal adoption. Expenses for adopting your spouse's child and the costs of a surrogate-parenting arrangement do not qualify. If you have other qualifying adoption expenses, you may also be able to claim a tax credit up to a separate $13,810 limit; both the exclusion and the credit may be claimed for the same adoption if they are not for the same expenses. The exclusion and the credit are subject to similar limitations, including a phaseout based on income. See Chapter 25 for a full discussion of the credit.

The full $13,810 exclusion limit is available for the adoption of a "special needs" child even if actual adoption expenses are less than $13,810. A "special needs" designation is made when a state determines that adoption assistance is required to place a child (U.S. citizen or resident) with adoptive parents because of special factors, such as the child's physical condition or ethnicity.

If you are adopting a child who is not a U.S. citizen or resident when the adoption effort begins, the exclusion is available only in the year the adoption becomes final. For example, if in 2018 your employer pays for expenses of adopting a foreign child but the adoption has not become final by the end of the year, you must report the employer's payment as wage income for 2018. You will claim the exclusion on Form 8839 in the year the adoption is final.

*Caution*

**Tax-Free Exclusion for Employer-Provided Dependent Care**

You cannot assume that your employer-provided dependent care benefit is completely tax free merely because your employer has not included any part of it in Box 1 of Form W-2 as taxable wages. Although up to $5,000 of benefits are generally tax free, the tax-free amount is reduced where you or your spouse earn less than $5,000 or where you file separately from your spouse. You must show the amount of your qualifying dependent care expenses and figure the tax-free exclusion on Form 2441.

*Filing Tip*

**Claiming Credit and Exclusion**

If you paid adoption expenses that were not reimbursed by your employer, and the adoption was final by the end of the year, you may be able to claim the adoption credit; *see 25.14*.

**Reporting employer benefits and claiming the exclusion on your return.** You must file Form 8839 to report your employer's payments and to figure the tax-free and taxable portions of the benefits. The employer's payments will be included in Box 12 of Form W-2 (Code T). This total includes pre-tax salary reduction contributions that you made to a cafeteria plan *(3.14)* to cover such expenses.

If you are married, you generally must file a joint return to exclude the benefits as income. However, if you are legally separated or if you lived apart from your spouse for the last six months of the year, the exclusion may be available on a separate return; *see* Form 8839 for details.

On 2018 tax returns, the allowable exclusion begins to phase out if your modified adjusted gross income (MAGI) exceeds $207,140. If MAGI is $247,140 or more (including the employer's adoption assistance and adding back certain tax-free income from foreign sources), the phaseout is complete and all of the employer-paid adoption assistance is taxable. Figure the tax-free amount on Form 8839.

## 3.7    Education Assistance Plans

If your employer pays for job-related courses, the payment is tax free to you provided that the courses do not satisfy the employer's minimum education standards and do not qualify you for a new profession. If these tests are met, the employer's education assistance is a tax-free working condition fringe benefit *(3.9)*.

Even if not job related, your employer's payment for courses is tax free up to $5,250, provided the assistance is under a qualifying Section 127 plan meeting nondiscriminatory tests. Graduate courses qualify for the exclusion as well as undergraduate courses. The Section 127 exclusion covers tuition, fees, books, and equipment, plus supplies that you cannot keep at the end of the course. Lodging, meals, and transportation are not covered by the exclusion. Sports or hobby-type courses qualify only if the courses are related to your business or are required as part of a degree program.

**Tuition reductions.** Employees and retired employees of educational institutions, their spouses, and their dependent children are not taxed on tuition reductions for undergraduate courses provided the reduction is not payment for teaching or other services. However, an exclusion is allowed for tuition reductions under the National Health Services Corps Scholarship Program and the Armed Forces Health Professions Scholarship Program despite the recipient's service obligation. Widows or widowers of deceased employees or of former employees also qualify. Officers and highly paid employees may claim the exclusion only if the employer plan does not discriminate on their behalf. The exclusion applies to tuition for undergraduate education at any educational institution, not only the employer's school.

Graduate students who are teaching or research assistants at an educational institution are not taxed on tuition reductions for courses at that school if the tuition reduction is in addition to regular pay for the teaching or research services or the reduction is provided under the National Health Services Corps Scholarship Program or the Armed Forces Health Professions Scholarship Program. The graduate student exclusion for tuition reductions applies only to teaching and research assistants, and not to faculty or other staff members (or their spouses and dependents) who take graduate courses and also do research for or teach at the school. However, if the graduate courses are work related, a tuition reduction for faculty and staff may qualify as a tax-free working condition fringe benefit *(3.9)*.

## 3.8    Company Cars, Parking, and Transit Passes

The costs of commuting to a regular job site are not deductible *(20.2)*, but employees who receive transit passes or travel to work on an employer-financed van get a tax break by not having to pay tax on some or all of such benefits. Where a company car is provided, the value of personal use is generally taxable, as discussed below.

**Company cars.** The use of a company car is tax free under the working condition fringe benefit rule *(3.9)* to the extent you use the car for business. If you use the car for personal driving, your company has the responsibility of calculating taxable income, which generally

*Planning Reminder*

**Education Assistance May Be Fully or Partially Tax Free**

Education assistance from an employer plan for job-related courses can be completely tax free, while payments for courses that are not job related can be tax free up to $5,250 if under a qualifying Section 127 plan; *see 3.7.*

is based on IRS tables that specify the annual lease value of various priced cars. You are also required to keep for your employer a mileage log or similar record to substantiate your business use; your employer should specify what you need to provide.

Regardless of personal use, you are not subject to tax for a company vehicle that the IRS considers to be of limited personal value. These are ambulances or hearses; flatbed trucks; dump, garbage, or refrigerated trucks; one-passenger delivery trucks (including trucks with folding jump seats); tractors, combines, and other farm equipment; or forklifts. Also not taxable is personal use of school buses, passenger buses (seating at least 20), and moving vans where such personal use is restricted. Exclusions are also allowed for commuting use of a clearly marked police, fire, or public safety officer vehicle by officers required to be on call at all times, and for officially authorized uses of unmarked vehicles by law enforcement officers.

**Demonstration cars.** The value of a demonstration car used by a full-time auto salesperson is tax free as a working condition fringe benefit if the use of the car facilitates job performance and if there are substantial personal-use restrictions, including a prohibition on use by family members and for vacation trips. Furthermore, mileage outside of normal working hours must be limited and personal driving must generally be restricted to a 75-mile radius around the dealer's sales office.

**Chauffeur services.** If chauffeur services are provided for both business and personal purposes, you must report as income the value of the personal services. For example, if the full value of the chauffeur services is $30,000 and 30% of the chauffeur's workday is spent driving on personal trips, then $9,000 is taxable (30% of $30,000) and $21,000 is tax free.

If an employer provides a bodyguard-chauffeur for business security reasons, the entire value of the chauffeur services is considered a tax-free working condition fringe benefit if: (1) the automobile is specially equipped for security and (2) the bodyguard is trained in evasive driving techniques and is provided as part of an overall 24-hour-a-day security program. If the value of the bodyguard-chauffeur services is tax free, the employee is still taxable on the value of using the vehicle for commuting or other personal travel.

**How your employer reports taxable automobile benefits.** Social Security and Medicare tax must be withheld. Income tax withholding is not required, but your employer may choose to withhold income tax. If income tax is not withheld, you must be notified of this fact so that you may consider the taxable benefits when determining whether to make estimated tax installments; *see Chapter 27*. Whether or not withholdings are taken, the taxable value of the benefits is entered on your Form W-2 in Box 14 or on a separate Form W-2 for fringe benefits.

A special IRS rule allows your employer to include 100% of the lease value of using the car as income on your Form W-2, even if you used the car primarily for business. Your employer must specifically indicate on Form W-2 (Box 14) or on a separate statement if 100% of the lease value has been included as income on your Form W-2. If your employer does this on your 2018 Form W-2, you may not claim an offsetting deduction for the value of your business use of the car. Under prior law, a deduction for the business value of the car, plus any unreimbursed car operating expenses, may have been available as a miscellaneous itemized deduction on Schedule A, but it was subject to the 2% of AGI floor. However, under the Tax Cuts and Jobs Act, this possibility is no longer available; the deduction for employee job expenses subject to the 2% floor has been repealed for 2018 through 2025 *(19.1)*.

**Company planes.** Under rules similar to those for company cars, employees who use a company airplane for personal trips are taxable on the value of the flights, as determined by the employer using IRS tables.

## Qualified Transportation Benefits

Your employer may provide you with transportation benefits that are tax free within certain limits. There are two categories of qualified benefits: (1) transit passes and commuter transportation in a van, bus, or similar highway vehicle are considered together, and (2) parking.

*Planning Reminder*

**Year-End Benefits**

Your employer may decide to treat fringe benefits provided during the last two months of the calendar year as if they were paid during the following year. For example, if your employer makes this election for a company car provided to you in 2018, only the value of personal use from January through October is taxable to you for 2018; the value of your personal use in November and December is treated as taxable pay for 2019. If your employer elects this special year-end rule, you should be notified near the end of the year or when you receive Form W-2.

*Planning Reminder*

**Transportation Benefits**

If your employer offers you the choice of receiving parking, transit pass, or van pooling benefits instead of cash salary as part of a "cafeteria" plan *(3.13)* and you elect the benefits rather than the cash, you are not taxed, provided the value does not exceed the monthly tax-free limit.

*Law Alert*

**Bicycle Commuting Reimbursements Now Taxable**

The Tax Cuts and Jobs Act has suspended (for 2018 through 2025) the prior law exclusion for up to $20 of qualified bicycle reimbursements per month.

For 2018, benefits from each category are excludable from your income so long as the $260 monthly limit (see below) is not exceeded. If the benefits exceed the $260 monthly limit, the excess is treated as wages subject to income tax, Social Security, and Medicare tax.

For years before 2018, qualifying bicycle commuting reimbursements were tax free up to $20 per month, but the Tax Cuts and Jobs Act repealed this exclusion for tax years 2018 through 2025.

Transit pass/commuter transportation benefits and parking benefits may be provided through a salary-reduction arrangement. An irrevocable salary-reduction election may be made prospectively for a monthly amount of benefits. The salary reduction for any month may not exceed the total limit for both categories. Unused salary reductions may be carried over to later months and from year to year. However, if you leave the company before using the carryover, the unused amount is forfeited; you cannot get a refund.

**Exclusion limit.** The same monthly exclusion limit applies to (1) the combined value of qualified employer-provided transit passes plus commuting in an employer's van or bus, and (2) qualified parking benefits. For 2018, the maximum monthly exclusion for each of these categories is $260 per month. If the value of benefits for any month does not equal the exclusion limit, the unused amount is lost and may not be carried over to other months. For 2019, the monthly cap for each benefit may be increased above $260 by an inflation adjustment; *see* the **e-Supplement** at *jklasser.com*.

Details on what constitutes qualified transit pass/van pool, and parking benefits are in the following paragraphs.

**Qualified transit passes and van/bus transportation.** For purposes of the exclusion, qualifying transit passes include tokens, fare cards, or vouchers for mass transit or private transportation businesses using highway vehicles seating at least six passengers. A cash reimbursement for a transit pass is taxable if vouchers (or similar items) are readily available to the employer for distribution to employees. "Ready availability" is determined under tests in IRS regulations. Cash advances are taxable.

Qualifying van or bus pool vehicles must seat at least six passengers and be used at least 80% of the time for employee commuting; on average, the number of employees must be at least half the seating capacity.

The exclusion applies only to regular employees. For partners, more than 2% S corporation shareholders, and independent contractors who are provided transit passes, the IRS allows up to $21 per month as a tax-free *de minimis* benefit. If the monthly value exceeds $21, the full value is taxable and not just the excess over $21.

**Qualified parking benefits.** The value of employer-provided parking spots or subsidized parking qualifies for the exclusion (up to the monthly limit) if the parking is on or near the employer's premises, or at a mass transit facility such as a train station or car pooling center. For purposes of determining if the value of the parking exceeds the monthly limit ($260 per month in 2018), the IRS tells employers to value parking benefits according to the regular commercial price for parking at the same or nearby locations. For example, if an employer in a rural or suburban location provides free parking for employees and there are no commercial parking lots in the area, the employee parking is tax free. Where free parking is available to both business customers and employees, the employee parking is considered to have "zero" value unless the employee has a reserved parking space that is closer to the business entrance than the spaces allotted to customers.

If the value of the right of access to a parking space for a month exceeds the monthly exclusion limit ($260 per month in 2018), an employee will be taxed on the excess even if he or she actually uses the space for only a few days during the month.

If the employee pays a reduced monthly price for parking, there is a taxable benefit for that month only if the price paid plus the monthly exclusion amount is less than the value of the parking.

Commuter parking benefits for self-employed partners, independent contractors, or more-than-2% S corporation shareholders do not qualify for the monthly exclusion but may qualify as a tax-free *de minimis* benefit *(3.10)*.

## 3.9   Working Condition Fringe Benefits

An employer-provided benefit that would be deductible by you as a job expense if you paid for it yourself (and the miscellaneous itemized deduction subject to the 2% of adjusted gross income floor had not been suspended) *(19.1)* is a tax-free working condition fringe benefit. These benefits include:

**Company car or plane.** The value of a company car or plane is tax free to the extent that you use it for business; *see 3.8* for more on company cars.

**Employer-provided cell phone.** The cost of an employer-provided cell phone is a tax-free working condition benefit if your employer has substantial business reasons for giving you the phone. The phone qualifies if the employer needs to reach you at all times for work-related emergencies or you need to call clients when away from the office or outside of normal business hours. On the other hand, the value of the phone is taxable if it is a goodwill gesture or intended as additional compensation; these are not considered substantial business reasons.

**Employer-paid subscriptions or memberships.** For example, if your employer pays for your subscriptions to business-related publications, or reimburses you for membership dues in professional associations, these are tax-free working condition benefits.

**Product testing.** This is a limited exclusion for employees who test and evaluate company manufactured goods away from company premises.

**Employer-provided education assistance.** Employer-paid undergraduate and graduate courses may be a tax-free working condition fringe benefit if the courses maintain or improve your job skills but are not needed to meet your employer's minimum educational requirements and do not prepare you for a new profession.

**Job-placement assistance.** According to the IRS, job placement services are tax free so long as they are geared to helping you find a job in the same line of work and you do not have an option to take cash instead of the benefits. The employer must also have a business purpose for providing such assistance, such as maintaining employee morale or promoting a positive business image.

For tax-free treatment, there is no nondiscrimination requirement; different types of job placement assistance may be offered, or no assistance at all, in the case of discharged employees with readily transferable skills. Tax-free benefits include the value of counseling on interviewing skills and resume preparation. Executives may be given secretarial support and the use of a private office during the job search.

Job placement benefits that you receive as part of a severance pay arrangement are taxable to the extent that you could have elected to receive cash. If your severance benefits are reduced because you get job placement assistance, you are taxed on the difference between the reduced and unreduced severance amounts.

## 3.10   *De Minimis* Fringe Benefits

Small benefits that would be administratively impractical to tax are considered tax-free *de minimis* (minor) fringe benefits. Examples are personal use of an employer-provided cell phone (see below), occasional meal money or local transportation fares given to employees working overtime, employer-provided coffee, tea, doughnuts, or soft drinks, personal use of company copying machines, company parties, or tickets for the theater or sporting events.

**Personal use of employer-provided cell phone.** If your employer gives you a phone for substantial business reasons, the value of the phone is a tax-free working condition fringe benefit *(3.9)*. In such a case, your personal use of the phone is tax free as a *de minimis* benefit.

**Company eating facility.** The value of meals provided to employees on workdays at a subsidized eating facility is a tax-free *de minimis* fringe benefit if the facility is located on or near the business premises and the annual revenue from meal charges equals or exceeds the facility's direct operating costs. Revenue is treated as equal to operating costs for meals that are tax-free to employees under the employer convenience test *(3.13)*.

*IRS Alert*

**Local Lodging Excludable**

As discussed in *20.6*, the value of local lodging provided by an employer for a bona fide business purpose is a tax-free working condition fringe benefit.

Highly compensated employees or owners with special access to executive dining rooms may not exclude the value of their meals as a *de minimis* fringe benefit; however, the meals may be tax free if meals must be taken on company premises for business reasons *(3.13)*.

**Commuting under unsafe circumstances.** If you are asked to work outside your normal working hours and due to unsafe conditions your employer provides transportation such as taxi fare, the first $1.50 per one-way commute is taxable but the excess over $1.50 is a tax-free *de minimis* benefit. This exclusion is not available to certain highly compensated employees and officers, corporate directors, or owners of 1% or more of the company.

Even when working their regular shift, hourly employees eligible for overtime who are not considered highly compensated are taxed on only $1.50 per one-way commute if their employer pays for car service or taxi fare because walking or taking public transportation to or from work would be unsafe. The excess value of the transportation over $1.50 is tax free. These rules can apply to day-shift employees who work overtime as well as night-shift employees working regular hours so long as transportation is provided because of unsafe conditions.

## 3.11 Employer-Provided Retirement Advice

If your employer maintains a qualified retirement plan, the value of retirement planning information and advice provided to you by the employer is not taxable. The exclusion is not limited to information pertaining to the employer's particular retirement plan. It applies to information for you and your spouse on general retirement income planning, as well as information on how the employer's plan fits within your overall plan.

Highly compensated employees qualify for the exclusion if similar services are provided to all employees who normally receive information updates on the employer's retirement plan.

The exclusion does not apply to related services that may be provided by the employer, such as brokerage services, tax preparation, accounting, or legal services; the value of such services is taxable.

## 3.12 Employee Achievement Awards

Achievement awards are taxable unless they meet special rules for awards of tangible personal property (such as a watch, television, or golf clubs) given to you in recognition of length of service or safety achievement. The Tax Cuts and Jobs Act specifies that the following items are not "tangible personal property" and thus are taxable: cash awards, gift cards, gift certificates (unless they entitle the employee to select from an approved employer list of items of tangible personal property), vacations, meals, lodging, tickets to sports or theater events, stocks, bonds, other securities, or similar items.

As a general rule, if your employer is allowed to deduct the cost of a tangible personal property award, you are not taxed. The employer's deduction limit, and therefore the excludable limit for you, is $400 for awards from nonqualified plans and $1,600 for awards from qualified plans or from a combination of qualified and nonqualified plans. If your employer's deduction is less than the item's cost, you are taxed on the greater of: (1) the difference between the cost and your employer's deduction, but no more than the award's fair market value; or (2) the excess of the item's fair market value over your employer's deduction. Deduction tests for achievement awards are discussed in *40.6*. Your employer must tell you if the award qualifies for full or partial tax-free treatment.

An award will not be treated as a tax-free safety achievement award if employee safety achievement awards (other than those of *de minimis* value) during the year have already been granted to more than 10% of employees (not counting managers, administrators, clerical employees, or other professional employees). An award made to a manager, administrator, clerical employee, or other professional employee for safety achievement does not qualify for tax-free treatment.

Tax-free treatment also does not apply when you receive an award for length of service during your first five years of employment or when you previously received such an award during the current year or in the four preceding years, unless the prior award qualified as a *de minimis* fringe benefit.

*Planning Reminder*

**Occasional Overtime Meal Money or Cab Fare**

If you work overtime and occasionally receive meal money or cab fare home, the amount is tax free. The IRS has not provided a numerical standard for determining when payments are "occasional."

*Caution*

**Underpriced Award Items**

If the value of an achievement award item is disproportionately high compared to the employer's cost, the IRS may conclude that the award is disguised compensation, in which case the entire value would be taxable.

## 3.13 Employer-Furnished Meals or Lodging

The value of employer-furnished meals is not taxable if furnished on your employer's business premises for the employer's convenience. The value of lodging is not taxable if, as a condition of your employment, you must accept the lodging on the employer's business premises for the employer's convenience.

**Business premises test.** The IRS generally defines business premises as the place of employment, such as a company cafeteria in a factory for a cook or an employer's home for a household employee. The Tax Court has a more liberal view, extending the area of business premises beyond the actual place of business in such cases as these:

- A house provided a hotel manager, although located across the street from the hotel. The IRS has agreed to the decision.
- A house provided a motel manager, two blocks from the motel. However, a court of appeals reversed the decision and held in the IRS' favor.
- A rented hotel suite that is used daily by executives for a luncheon conference.

*Remote camp in foreign country.* Lodging in certain foreign "camps" is considered to be furnished on the business premises of the employer. To qualify, lodging must be provided to employees working in remote foreign areas where satisfactory housing is not available on the open market, it must be located as near as practicable to where they work, and it must be in a common area or enclave that is not available to the public and which normally accommodates at least 10 employees.

 *Court Decision*

**House One Block Away**

Two federal courts held that a school superintendent received tax-free lodging where the home was one block away from the school and separated by a row of other houses. This met the business premises test. The IRS announced that it would continue to litigate similar cases arising outside the Eighth Circuit in which the case arose. The Eighth Circuit includes the states of Arkansas, Iowa, Minnesota, Missouri, Nebraska, and North and South Dakota.

**EXAMPLES**

1. A Las Vegas casino operator provided free cafeteria meals to employees, who were required to remain on casino premises during their entire shift. A federal appeals court (Ninth Circuit) held that the casino's "stay-on-premises" requirement constituted a legitimate business reason for the meals and thus all of the employee meals were tax free under the employer convenience test. The court refused to second guess the casino's business decision that a "stay-on-premises" policy was necessary for security and logistics reasons. Once that policy was adopted, the casino employees had no choice but to eat on the premises. The IRS responded to the decision by announcing that it would not challenge "employer convenience" treatment in similar cases where employees are precluded from obtaining a meal off-premises within a normal meal period.

2. A waitress who works from 7 a.m. to 4 p.m. is furnished two meals a day without charge. Her employer encourages her to have her breakfast at the restaurant before working, but she is required to have her lunch there. The value of her breakfast and lunch is not taxable under IRS regulations because it is furnished during her work period or immediately before or after the period. But say she is also allowed to have free meals on her days off and a free supper on the days she works. The value of these meals is taxable; they are not furnished during or immediately before or after her work period.

3. A hospital maintains a cafeteria on its premises where all of its employees may eat during their working hours. No charge is made for these meals. The hospital furnishes meals to have the employees available for emergencies. The employees are not required to eat there. Since the hospital furnishes the meals in order to have employees available for emergency call during meal periods, the meals are not income to any of the hospital employees who obtain their meals at the hospital cafeteria.

4. To assure bank teller service during the busy lunch period, a bank limits tellers to 30 minutes for lunch and provides them with free meals in a cafeteria on the premises so they can eat within this time period. The value of the meals is tax free.

**Convenience of employer test.** The employer convenience test requires proof that an employer provides the free meals or lodging for a business purpose other than providing extra pay. In the case of meals, the employer convenience test is deemed to be satisfied for all meals provided on employer premises if a qualifying business purpose is shown for more than 50% of the meals. If meals and lodging are described in a contract or state statute as extra pay, this does not bar tax-free treatment provided they are also furnished for other substantial, noncompensatory business reasons; for example, you are required to be on call 24 hours a day, or there are inadequate eating facilities near the business premises.

*Planning Reminder*

**Meal Exclusion**

You may be able to avoid tax on meals that you receive on your employer's premises even if your meals do not satisfy the employer convenience test. If more than half of the employees to whom meals are furnished on the employer's business premises are furnished the meals for the employer's convenience, all of the on-premises meals are treated as being furnished for the employer's convenience.

*Caution*

**Housing as Job Requirement**

If housing is provided to some employees with a certain job and not others, the IRS may hold that the lodging is not a condition of employment. For example, the IRS taxed medical residents on the value of hospital lodging where other residents lived in their own apartments.

*Caution*

**Partners Are Not Employees**

The IRS does not consider partners or self-employed persons as employees and so does not allow them to exclude the value of partnership-provided meals and lodging.

**Meal charges.** Your company may charge for meals on company premises and give you an option to accept or decline the meals. However, by law, the IRS must disregard the charge and option factors in determining whether meals that you buy are furnished for noncompensatory business reasons. If such business reasons exist, the convenience-of-employer test is satisfied. If such reasons do not exist, the value of the meals may be tax free as a *de minimis* benefit *(3.10)*; otherwise, the value of the meal subsidy provided by the employer is taxable.

Where your employer provides meals on business premises at a fixed charge that is subtracted from your pay whether you accept the meals or not, the amount of the charge is excluded from your taxable pay. If the meal is provided for the employer's convenience, as in the previous Examples, the value of the meals received is also tax free. If it is not provided for the employer's convenience, the value is taxable whether it exceeds or is less than the amount charged.

**Lodging must be condition of employment.** This test requires evidence that the lodging is necessary for you to perform your job properly, as where you are required to be available for duty at all times. The IRS may question the claim that you are required to be on 24-hour duty. For example, at one college, rent-free lodgings were provided to teaching and administrative staff members, maintenance workers, dormitory parents who supervised and resided with students, and an evening nurse. The IRS ruled that only the lodgings provided to the dorm parents and the nurse met the tax-free lodging tests because, for the convenience of the college, they had to be available after regular school hours to respond to emergencies.

If you are given the choice of free lodging at your place of employment or a cash allowance, the lodging is not considered to be a condition of employment, and its value is taxable.

If the lodging qualifies as tax free, so does the value of employer-paid utilities such as heat, electricity, gas, water, sewerage, and other utilities. Where these services are furnished by the employer and their value is deducted from your salary, the amount deducted is excluded from taxable wages on Form W-2. But if you pay for the utilities yourself, you may not exclude their cost from your income.

> **EXAMPLE**
>
> Tyrone Jones is employed at a construction project at a remote job site. His pay is $1,500 a week. Because there are no accessible places near the site for food and lodging, the employer furnishes meals and lodging for which it charges $400 a week, which is taken out of Jones's pay. Jones reports only the net amount he receives—$1,100 a week. The value of the meals and lodging is a tax-free benefit.

**Groceries.** An employer may furnish unprepared food, such as groceries, rather than prepared meals. Courts are divided on whether the value of the groceries is excludable from income. One court allowed an exclusion for the value of nonfood items, such as napkins and soap—as well as for groceries—furnished to a doctor who ate at his home on the hospital grounds so that he would be available for emergencies.

**Cash allowances.** A cash allowance for meals and lodging is taxable.

**Faculty lodging.** Teachers and other employees (and their spouses and dependents) of an educational institution, including a state university system or academic health center, do not have to pay tax on the value of school-provided lodging if they pay a minimal rent. The lodging must be on or near the campus. The minimal required rent is the smaller of: (1) 5% of the appraised value of the lodging; or (2) the average rental paid for comparable school housing by persons who are neither employees nor students. Appraised value must be determined by an independent appraiser and the appraisal must be reviewed annually.

For purposes of the 5% minimum rent rule, academic health centers include medical teaching hospitals and medical research organizations with regular faculties and curricula in basic and clinical medical science and research.

**Peace Corps and VISTA volunteers.** Peace Corps volunteers working overseas may exclude subsistence allowances from income under a specific code provision. The law does not provide a similar exclusion for the small living expense allowances received by VISTA volunteers.

## Table 3-3   Are Your Meals and Lodging Tax Free?

| Yes— | No— |
|---|---|
| Hotel executives, managers, housekeepers, and auditors who are required to live at the hotel. | Your employer gives you a cash allowance for your meals or lodgings. |
| Domestics, farm laborers, fishermen, canners, seamen, servicemen, building superintendents, and hospital and sanitarium employees who are required to have meals and lodging on employer premises. | You have a choice of accepting cash or getting the meals or lodging. For example, under a union contract you get meals, but you may refuse to take them and get an automatic pay increase. |
| Restaurant and other food service employees who have meals furnished during or immediately before or after working hours. | A state hospital employee is given a choice. He or she may live at the institution rent free or live elsewhere and get extra pay each month. Whether he or she stays at the institution or lives outside, the extra pay is included in his or her income. |
| Employees who must be available during meal periods for emergencies. | A waitress, on her days off, is allowed to eat free meals at the restaurant where she works. |
| Employees who, because of the nature of the business, must be given short meal periods. | |
| Workers who must use company-supplied facilities in remote areas. | |
| Park employees who voluntarily live in rent-free apartments provided by a park department in order to protect the park from vandalism. | |

### EXAMPLE

Carol Eng, a professor, pays annual rent of $12,000 for university housing appraised at $200,000. The average rent for comparable university housing paid by non-employees and non-students is $14,000. She does not have to pay any tax on the housing since her rental payments are at least 5% of the appraised housing value (5% of $200,000, or $10,000). If her rent was $9,000, she would have to report income of $1,000 ($10,000 minimum required rent − $9,000).

## 3.14   Minister's Housing or Housing Allowance

By statute, a duly ordained minister pays no tax on the rental value of a home provided as part of his or her pay. If a minister is provided with a cash allowance rather than a home itself, the allowance is generally tax free if used to pay rent, to make a down payment to buy a house, to pay mortgage installments, or for utilities, interest, tax, and repair expenses of the house. However, the exclusion for a cash allowance is limited to the fair rental value of the home, including furnishings and appurtenances such as a garage, plus the cost of utilities. A rabbi or cantor is treated the same as a minister for purposes of the allowance or in-kind housing exclusion.

The Tax Court has held that the parsonage exclusion is allowed for expenses of a second home as well as for a principal residence. However, the Eleventh Circuit appeals court reversed the Tax Court, concluding that the exclusion can apply only to one home.

The church or local congregation must officially designate the part of the minister's compensation that is a rental or housing allowance. To qualify for tax-free treatment, the designation must be made in advance of the payments. Official action may be shown by an employment contract, minutes, a resolution, or a budget allowance.

*Caution:* When this book was completed, the constitutionality of the cash housing allowance exclusion was being challenged in federal court; *see* the Court Decision on this page.

 *Filing Tip*

**Mortgage Interest and Taxes**

If you itemize deductions on Schedule A (Form 1040), deduct payments for qualifying home mortgage interest *(15.1)* and real estate taxes *(16.6)* on your home even if you use a tax-free housing allowance to finance the payments.

*Court Decision*

**Appeals Court to Decide Constitutionality of Cash Housing Allowance**

When this book was completed, the Seventh Circuit Court of Appeals was reviewing a decision of a Wisconsin federal district court that held that the law allowing ministers and other religious leaders to exclude from income cash housing allowances (Code Section 107(2)) is unconstitutional. According to the district court, Code Section 107(2) violates the Establishment Clause of the U.S. Constitution because it does not have a secular purpose and a "reasonable observer" would view it as endorsing religion; it demonstrates a preference for ministers over secular employees who have similar housing needs. The federal government joined religious groups in appealing to the Seventh Circuit, claiming that the district court decision would impose new tax burdens on ministers and thereby harm many churches and their communities.. See the *e-Supplement* at *jklasser.com* for an update on the litigation.

**Who qualifies for the exclusion?** Tax-free treatment is allowed to ordained ministers, rabbis, and cantors who receive in-kind housing or housing allowances as part of their compensation for ministerial duties. Retired ministers qualify if the housing or allowance is furnished in recognition of past services.

The IRS has allowed the exclusion to ministers working as teachers or administrators for a parochial school, college, or theological seminary which is an integral part of a church organization. A traveling evangelist was allowed to exclude rental allowances from out-of-town churches to maintain his permanent home. Church officers who are not ordained, such as a "minister" of music (music director) or "minister" of education (Sunday School director), do not qualify.

The IRS has generally barred an exclusion to ordained ministers working as executives of nonreligious organizations even where services or religious functions are performed as part of the job. The Tax Court has focused on the duties performed. A minister employed as a chaplain by a municipal police department under church supervision was allowed a housing exclusion, but the exclusion was denied to a minister-administrator of an old-age home that was not under the authority of a church and a rabbi who worked for a religious organization as director of inter-religious affairs.

**Allowance subject to self-employment tax.** Although a qualifying housing allowance is not treated as taxable income, the exempt amount is included as self-employment income for Social Security and Medicare purposes; *see Chapter 45*. If you do not receive a cash allowance, report the rental value of the parsonage as self-employment income. Rental value is usually equal to what you would pay for similar quarters in your locality. Also include as self-employment income the value of house furnishings, utilities, appurtenances supplied—such as a garage—and the value of meals furnished that meet the rules in *3.13*.

**Business expenses allocable to tax-free housing not deductible.** A minister may deduct business expenses allocable to taxable compensation, but not expenses allocable to a tax-free housing allowance or in-kind housing. If part of a minister's salary is designated as a housing allowance, and the minister also has self-employment earnings from the exercise of his ministry, a double allocation is required, first between salary income and self-employment income, and then between the taxable and tax free parts of salary.

**For example, in one case a minister had self-employment income comprising 21.56% of his annual income.** Of the rest, 53.85% was a tax-free housing allowance and 46.15% was taxable salary. The Tax Court agreed with the double allocation required by the IRS. Since the minister did not provide evidence as to which expenses were generated by which type of income, the Court allocated expenses on a pro rata basis, applying the ratio of salary and self-employment income to total income. Since the self-employment income was 21.56% of total income (including the allowance), 21.56% of the expenses were deductible on Schedule C. The remaining expenses were treated as job-related costs deductible, if at all, as miscellaneous itemized expenses on Schedule A. However, because 53.85% of the minister's salary was a tax-free housing allowance, 53.85% of the expenses were nondeductible. The balance (46.15% of the expenses) could be claimed on Schedule A as a miscellaneous itemized deduction subject to the 2% of adjusted gross income floor *(19.3)*.

## 3.15 Cafeteria Plans Provide Choice of Benefits

"Cafeteria plans" is a nickname for plans that give an employee a choice of selecting either cash or at least one qualifying nontaxable benefit. You are not taxed when you elect qualifying nontaxable benefits, although cash could have been chosen instead. A cafeteria plan may offer tax-free benefits such as group health insurance or life insurance coverage, long-term disability coverage, dependent care or adoption assistance, medical expense reimbursements, or group legal services. Long-term care insurance may not be offered through a cafeteria plan under current law.

Employees may be offered a premium-only plan (POP), which allows them to purchase group health insurance coverage or life insurance on a pre-tax basis using salary-reduction contributions.

Health savings accounts (HSAs) and their related high-deductible health plans (HDHPs) may be offered as options by a cafeteria plan *(3.2)*. If so, employees may elect to have contributions made to an HSA and an HDHP on a pre-tax salary-reduction basis.

A cafeteria plan may also offer benefits that are nontaxable because they are attributable to after-tax employee contributions. For example, employees may be offered the opportunity to purchase disability benefits (short term or long term) with after-tax contributions. If a covered employee subsequently receives disability benefits that are attributable to after-tax contributions, the benefits will be tax free. On the other hand, the plan may allow employees to elect paying for disability coverage on a pre-tax basis and, in this case, any benefits from the plan attributable to the pre-tax contributions will be taxable when received.

Under a flexible spending arrangement (FSA), employees may be allowed to make tax-free salary-reduction contributions to a medical or dependent care reimbursement plan *(3.16)*.

A qualified cafeteria plan must be written and not discriminate in favor of highly compensated employees and stockholders. If the plan provides for health benefits, a special rule applies to determine whether the plan is discriminatory. If a plan is held to be discriminatory, the highly compensated participants are taxed to the extent they could have elected cash. Furthermore, if key employees *(3.4)* receive more than 25% of the "tax-free" benefits under the plan, they are taxed on the benefits. Employers averaging 100 or fewer employees who agree to contribute a fixed amount towards benefits are treated as meeting the nondiscrimination tests under special rules for "simple" cafeteria plans.

**Wellness program's cash rewards and reimbursements of premiums are taxable.** A cafeteria plan may allow employees to make pre-tax salary-reduction contributions to a wellness program that provides health benefits such as screenings, as well as benefits that are not qualifying medical expenses, such as gym memberships or other cash rewards. In a legal memorandum, IRS Chief Counsel concluded that the coverage purchased with the salary reduction is tax free, assuming there are screenings and other health benefits sufficient for the wellness program to be treated as a health and accident plan *(3.1)*, and the health screenings and similar benefits are tax-free reimbursements of medical expenses *(3.2)*. However, any cash rewards or other benefits received from the program that are not medical care are includible in the employee's income as wages, unless they are excludable as *de minimis* benefits *(3.10)*. A T-shirt qualifies as a tax-free *de minimis* benefit, but payment or reimbursement of gym membership fees is a cash benefit that is not excludable as a *de minimis* fringe benefit. The gym fees and any other benefits or rewards not otherwise excludable from income are treated as wages subject to employment taxes. Similarly, any reimbursement of an employee's salary-reduction contributions to the wellness program are includible in the employee's income as wages subject to employment taxes.

## 3.16 Flexible Spending Arrangements

A flexible spending arrangement (FSA) allows employees to get reimbursed for medical or dependent care expenses from an account they set up with pre-tax dollars. Under a typical FSA, you agree to a salary reduction that is deducted from each paycheck and deposited in a separate account. The salary-reduction contributions are not included in your taxable wages reported on Form W-2. As expenses are incurred, you are reimbursed from the account. Reimbursements used to pay qualified medical expenses are excluded from your income even though the contributions to your account were also not taxed to you.

The tax advantage of an FSA is that your salary-reduction contributions are not subject to federal income tax or Social Security taxes, allowing your medical or dependent care expenses to be paid with pre-tax rather than after-tax income. The salary deferrals are also exempt from most state and local taxes; check with the administrator of your employer's plan.

In the case of a health FSA, paying medical expenses with pre-tax dollars allows you to avoid the adjusted gross income (AGI) floor *(17.1)* that limits itemized deductions for medical costs.

However, to get these tax advantages, you must assume some risk. Under a "use-it-or-lose-it" rule, if your qualifying out-of-pocket expenses for the year are less than your contributions, the balance of the contributions will be forfeited unless your employer allows a carryover or gives you an additional 2½ months to spend the funds, as discussed below.

**FSA election to contribute generally irrevocable.** An election to set up an FSA for a given year must be made before the start of that year. You elect how much you want to contribute during the coming year and that amount will be withheld from your pay in monthly installments.

Once the election for a particular year takes effect, you may not discontinue contributions to your account or increase or decrease a coverage election unless there is a change in family or work status that qualifies under IRS regulations.

**Carryover or grace period may be offered by employers to ease the use-it-or-lose-it deadline.** The use-it-or-lose-it rule in IRS regulations discourages employees from making "excessive" salary-reduction contributions. Generally, salary-reduction contributions made in one year cannot be used to pay expenses incurred after the end of that year. Any unused account balance as of the end of the year must be forfeited to the employer.

However, the use-it-or-lose-it rule has been strongly criticized over the years, and in response to pressure from Congress, the IRS has given employers some options that can ease the impact of the use-it-or-lose-it rule. Depending on the type of plan, a limited carryover or a grace period for unused contributions may be offered. Keep in mind that the law does not require a carryover or grace period. These are options that the IRS allows an employer to offer after amending the plan document.

1. Carryover of up to $500 for unused health FSA expenses. If a health FSA permits a carryover, the grace period (below) may not also be offered. Only health FSAs may offer a carryover; no carryover is allowed for dependent care FSAs.

   An employer that elects to allow a health FSA carryover (by amending the plan) may choose to allow up to the $500 carryover limit (the IRS maximum), but the limit may be set at less than $500. For any year, the carryover cannot exceed the lower of your unused expenses from the prior year or the carryover cap set by the employer (not to exceed the IRS limit of $500); you may not accumulate or "bank" your carryovers.

2. Grace period of up to 2½-months. The grace period can be for a health FSA or a dependent care FSA. However, for a health FSA, either the grace period or the carryover may be offered, not both.

The grace period allows contributions that have not been used by the end of the year to be applied to qualified expenses incurred in the following year if they are within the grace period. For example, assume that a calendar-year plan has been amended to allow a grace period of two months and fifteen days (the IRS limit). Employees with unused health FSA funds at the end of 2018 may use them to reimburse qualified medical expenses incurred during the grace period beginning January 1 and ending March 15, 2019. If the expenses incurred by March 15, 2019, do not cover the unused amount from 2018, the balance will be forfeited to the employer.

The end-of-year balance of health FSA funds may only be applied to health expenses incurred during the grace period and not to dependent care or other expenses. Similarly, unused dependent care FSA amounts may be used only for dependent care expenses incurred during the grace period. During the grace period, unused amounts may not be cashed out or converted to any other benefit (taxable or nontaxable). The employer may allow additional time following the end of the grace period to submit reimbursement claims for qualified expenses paid during the plan year and the grace period. For example, many calendar-year plans allow up to March 31 for submitting reimbursement claims.

**Health FSA.** There is an annual limit on salary-reduction contributions to a health FSA. The maximum salary-reduction contribution that could be made to a health FSA for 2018 was $2,650. For 2019, the $2,650 limit might get an inflation increase; *see* the *e-Supplement* at *jklasser.com*. A plan must apply the annual dollar limit to remain a qualified cafeteria plan; otherwise, all plan benefits are includible in the employees' gross income. The annual limit is the maximum salary-reduction contribution that the plan can allow, but employers may set a lower limit.

*IRS Alert*

**2½-Month Grace Period For Unused Expenses**

Employers have an opportunity to relax the use-it-or-lose-it deadline for both health-care and dependent care FSAs by allowing a grace period for unused expenses. However, for a health FSA, the grace period is an alternative to a carryover of up to $500; an employer can offer one but not both. For a dependent care FSA, an employer may allow the grace period but not the carryover. If the grace period is adopted, FSA funds that are unused at the end of a plan year can be applied to expenses incurred within the first 2½ months of the following year.

The annual limit applies per person and not per household. If you and your spouse each work and both of you are offered health FSA coverage, you may each elect to make salary-reduction contributions up to the annual limit, provided the employer allows that much. This is true even if you and your spouse work for the same employer.

Funds from a health FSA may generally be used to reimburse you for expenses that you could claim as a medical expense deduction *(17.2)* such as the annual deductible under your employer's regular health plan, co-payments you must make to physicians or for prescriptions, and any other expenses that your health plan does not cover. These may include eye examinations, eyeglasses, routine physicals, and orthodontia work for you and your dependents. Over-the-counter medications such as cold remedies, pain relievers, and allergy medications can be reimbursed tax free from an FSA only if a physician provides a prescription for the medication; this restriction does not apply to insulin. The restriction on over-the-counter medications has been criticized in Congress and numerous proposals have been made to repeal it, but no change had been made at the time this book was completed; for any developments, *see* the *e-Supplement* at *jklasser.com*.

A health FSA may not be used to reimburse you for premiums paid for other health plan coverage, including premiums for coverage under a plan of your spouse or dependent. Premiums are not reimbursable under a FSA regardless of whether the premiums were paid with pre-tax or after-tax funds. In addition, expenses for long-term care services cannot be reimbursed under a health FSA. You may not receive tax-free reimbursements for cosmetic surgery expenses unless the surgery is necessary to correct a deformity existing since birth or resulting from a disease or from injury caused by an accident. Nonqualifying reimbursements are taxable.

At any time during the year, you may receive reimbursements up to your designated limit, even though your payments into the FSA account up to that point may add up to less. For example, if you elect to make salary-reduction contributions of $100 per month to a health-care FSA and you incur $500 of qualifying medical expenses in January, you may get the full $500 reimbursement even though you have paid only $100 into the plan. Your employer may not require you to accelerate contributions to match reimbursement claims.

Your employer may allow the 2½ month grace period or a carryover of up to $500 for unused health FSA expenses, but not both, as discussed earlier.

**Employees on medical or family leave.** Employees who take unpaid leave under the Family and Medical Leave Act (FMLA) to deal with medical emergencies or care for a newborn child may either continue or revoke their coverage during FMLA leave. If the coverage continues, the maximum reimbursement selected by such an employee must be available at all times during the leave period. If the coverage is terminated, the employee must be reinstated under the FSA after returning from the leave, but no reimbursement claims may be made for expenses incurred during the leave.

**Dependent care FSA.** You may contribute to a dependent care FSA if you expect to have expenses qualifying for the dependent care tax credit *(25.4)*, but if you contribute to a dependent care FSA, any tax-free reimbursement from the account reduces the expenses eligible for the credit *(25.5)*. If you are married, both you and your spouse must work in order for you to receive tax-free reimbursements from an FSA, unless your spouse is disabled or a full-time student *(3.5)*.

The maximum tax-free reimbursement under the FSA is $5,000, but if either you or your spouse earns less than $5,000, the tax-free limit is the lesser earnings. If your spouse's employer offers a dependent care FSA, total tax-free reimbursements for both of you are limited to $5,000. Furthermore, if you are considered a highly compensated employee, your employer may have to lower your contribution ceiling below $5,000 to comply with nondiscrimination rules.

You must use Part III of Form 2441 to figure how much of your reimbursement is tax free and how much must be included in your income. Unlike health FSAs, an employer may limit reimbursements from a dependent care FSA to your account balance. For example, if you contribute $400 a month to the FSA and in January you pay $1,500 to a day-care center for your child, your employer may choose to reimburse you $400 a month as contributions are made to your account.

 *Filing Instruction*

**Dependent Care Reimbursements Affect Credit**

Reimbursements received tax free from your dependent care FSA reduce the expense base for figuring the dependent care credit; *see* Chapter 25.

Your employer may allow a 2½ month grace period for unused dependent care FSA contributions (but not a carryover), as discussed earlier.

## 3.17 Company Services Provided at No Additional Cost

Employees are not taxed on the receipt of services usually sold by their employer to customers where the employer does not incur additional costs in providing them to the employees. Examples are free or low-cost flights provided by an airline to its employees; free or discount lodging for employees of a hotel; and telephone service provided to employees of telephone companies. These tax-free fringes also may be provided to the employee's spouse and dependent children; retired employees, including employees retired on disability; and widows or widowers of deceased or retired employees. Tax-free treatment also applies to free or discount flights provided to parents of airline employees. Benefits provided by another company under a reciprocal arrangement, such as standby tickets on another airline, may also qualify as tax free.

The employer must have excess service capacity to provide the service and not forego potential revenue from regular customers. For example, airline employees who receive free reserved seating on company planes must pay tax on the benefit because the airline is foregoing potential revenue by reserving seating that could otherwise be sold.

**Line of business limitations.** If a company has two lines of business, such as an airline and a hotel, an employee of the airline may not receive tax-free benefits provided by the hotel. However, there are exceptions. An employee who provides services to both business lines may receive benefits from both business lines. Benefits from more than one line in existence before 1984 may also be available under a special election made by the company for 1985 and later years. Your employer should notify you of this tax benefit.

## 3.18 Discounts on Company Products or Services

The value of discounts on company products is a tax-free benefit if the discount does not exceed the employer's gross profit percentage. For example, if a company's profit percentage is 40%, the maximum tax-free employee discount for merchandise is 40% of the regular selling price. If you received a 50% discount, then 10% of the price charged customers would be taxable income. The employer has a choice of methods for figuring profit percentage.

Discounts on services that are not tax free under *3.17* for no-additional-cost services qualify for an exclusion, limited to 20% of the selling price charged customers. Discounts above 20% are taxable. An insurance policy is treated as a service. Thus, insurance company employees are not taxed on a discount of up to 20% of the policy's price.

Some company products do not qualify for the exclusion. Discounts on real estate and investment property such as securities, commodities, currency, or bullion are taxable. Interest-free or low-interest loans given by banks or other financial institutions to employees are not excludable. Such loans are subject to tax under the rules discussed at *4.31*.

For highly compensated employees, the exclusions for discounts on company products and services are subject to the nondiscrimination rules discussed in the Caution on this page.

 *Caution*

**Highly Compensated Employees**

Highly compensated employees can receive tax-free company services only if the same benefits are available to other employees on a nondiscriminatory basis. For 2018, highly compensated employees include employees owning more than a 5% interest in 2018 or 2017, and employees who in 2017 had compensation over $120,000. Employers have the option of including only the top-paid 20% in the over-$120,000 category.

# CHAPTER 4

# Dividend and Interest Income

Dividends and interest that are paid to you are reported by the payer to the IRS on Forms 1099.

You will receive copies of:

- Forms 1099-DIV, for dividends
- Forms 1099-INT, for interest
- Forms 1099-OID, for original issue discount

Dividends paid by most domestic corporations and many foreign corporations are subject to the same preferential tax rates as net long-term capital gains *(4.2)*.

Report the amounts shown on the Forms 1099 on your tax return. The IRS uses the Forms 1099 to check the income you report. If you fail to report income reported on Forms 1099, you will receive a statement asking for an explanation and a bill for the tax deficiency. If you receive a Form 1099 that you believe is incorrect, contact the payer for a corrected form.

Do not attach your copies of Forms 1099 to your return. Keep them with a copy of your tax return.

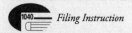

*Filing Instruction*

### So-Called Dividends That Are Really Interest

Distributions from the following financial institutions are called "dividends," but are actually interest reported on Form 1099-INT: dividends from credit unions, cooperative banks, savings and loan associations, building and loan associations, and mutual savings banks.

## 4.1 Reporting Dividends and Mutual Fund Distributions

Dividends paid to you out of a corporation's earnings and profits are taxable as ordinary income. The corporation will report dividends on Form 1099-DIV (or equivalent statement). Mutual fund dividends and distributions are also reported on Form 1099-DIV (or similar form). Corporate dividends and mutual fund distributions of $10 or more are reported on Form 1099-DIV (or equivalent) whether you receive them in cash or they have been reinvested at your request.

**Form 1099-DIV.** Form 1099-DIV gives you a breakdown of the dividends and distributions paid to you during the year. If you were a shareholder of record in a mutual fund or real estate investment trust (REIT) during October, November, or December of 2018 and entitled to a dividend declared in one of those months, but the dividend was not paid to you until January 2019, it will be reported to you on the 2018 Form 1099-DIV, as if it had been paid before the end of the year *(4.10)*. The company or fund may send a statement that is similar to Form 1099-DIV. You do not have to attach the Form 1099-DIV (or similar statement) to your tax return.

*Box 1a.* Ordinary dividends taxed to you are shown in Box 1. These are the most common type of distribution, payable out of a corporation's earnings and profits. Your share of a mutual fund's ordinary dividends is also shown on Form 1099-DIV; short-term capital gain distributions are included in the Box 1a total.

*Box 1b.* Part of the Box 1a amount may be qualified dividends. Qualified dividends reported in Box 1b are generally taxed at the same favorable rates (zero, 15% or 20%) as net capital gains. *See 4.2* for further details on qualified dividends.

*Boxes 2a–2d.* Capital gain distributions (long term) from a mutual fund (or real estate investment trust) are shown in Box 2a. Box 2b shows the portion of the Box 2a amount, if any, that is unrecaptured Section 1250 gain from the sale of depreciable real estate. Box 2c shows the part of Box 2a that is Section 1202 gain from small business stock eligible for an exclusion *(5.7)*. Box 2d shows the amount from Box 2a that is 28% rate gain from the sale of collectibles. If any amount is reported in Box 2b, 2c, or 2d, you must file Schedule D with Form 1040 *(5.3)*.

*Box 3.* Nontaxable distributions that are a return of your investment are shown in Box 3; see "Return of capital distributions" below.

*Box 4.* If you did not give your taxpayer identification number to the payer, backup withholding at a 28% rate *(26.10)* is shown in Box 4.

*Box 5.* Your share of expenses from a non–publicly offered mutual fund is shown in Box 5 , which is included in Box 1a. Due to the suspension of miscellaneous itemized deductions subject to the 2%-of-adjusted-gross income floor, they are not deductible.

☐ CORRECTED (if checked)

| PAYER'S name, street address, city or town, state or province, country, ZIP or foreign postal code, and telephone no.<br><br>Very Mutual Fund<br>155 East 38th Street<br>City, State 010X0 | 1a Total ordinary dividends<br>$ 500 | OMB No. 1545-0110<br>**2018**<br>Form **1099-DIV** | **Dividends and Distributions** |
|---|---|---|---|
| | 1b Qualified dividends<br>$ 435 | | |
| | 2a Total capital gain distr.<br>$ 375 | 2b Unrecap. Sec. 1250 gain<br>$ | **Copy B**<br>**For Recipient** |
| PAYER'S TIN   X1-01X0110    RECIPIENT'S TIN   00X-1X-0X00 | 2c Section 1202 gain<br>$ | 2d Collectibles (28%) gain<br>$ | |
| RECIPIENT'S name<br>Noelle Ballesteros | 3 Nondividend distributions<br>$ | 4 Federal income tax withheld<br>$ | This is important tax information and is being furnished to the IRS. If you are required to file a return, a negligence penalty or other sanction may be imposed on you if this income is taxable and the IRS determines that it has not been reported. |
| Street address (including apt. no.)<br>21 Chauncy Street | 5 Section 199A dividends<br>$ | 6 Investment expenses<br>$ | |
| City or town, state or province, country, and ZIP or foreign postal code<br>City, State 111X0 | 7 Foreign tax paid<br>$ | 8 Foreign country or U.S. possession | |
| | 9 Cash liquidation distributions<br>$ | 10 Noncash liquidation distributions<br>$ | |
| FATCA filing requirement ☐ | 11 Exempt-interest dividends<br>$ | 12 Specified private activity bond interest dividends<br>$ | |
| Account number (see instructions) | 13 State 14 State identification no. | 15 State tax withheld<br>$<br>$ | |

Form **1099-DIV**   (keep for your records)    www.irs.gov/Form1099DIV   Department of the Treasury - Internal Revenue Service

*Boxes 6 and 7.* The foreign tax shown in Box 6 (imposed by the country shown in Box 7) may be claimed as a tax credit on Form 1116 or as an itemized deduction on Schedule A (36.13s).

*Boxes 8 and 9.* Cash and noncash liquidation distributions are shown in these boxes.

**Nominee distribution—joint accounts.** If you receive dividends on stock held as a nominee for someone else, or you receive a Form 1099-DIV that includes dividends belonging to another person, such as a joint owner of the account, you are considered to be a "nominee recipient." If the other owner is someone other than your spouse, you should file a separate Form 1099-DIV showing you as the payer and the other owner as the recipient of the allocable income. For 2018 dividends, give the owner a copy of Form 1099-DIV by January 31, 2019, so the dividends can be reported on his or her 2018 return. File the Form 1099-DIV, together with a Form 1096 ("Transmittal of Information Return"), with the IRS by February 28, 2019; the deadline is April 1, 2019, if filing electronically.

On your Schedule B (Form 1040 or 1040A), you list on Line 5 the ordinary dividends reported to you on Form 1099-DIV. Several lines above Line 6, subtract the nominee distribution (the amount allocable to the other owner) from the total dividends. Thus, the nominee distribution is not included in the taxable dividends shown on Line 6 of Schedule B or Schedule 1.

**Return of capital distributions.** A distribution that is not paid out of earnings is a nontaxable return of capital, that is, a partial payback of your investment. The company will report the distribution in Box 3 of Form 1099-DIV as a nontaxable distribution. You must reduce the cost basis of your stock by the nontaxable distribution. If your basis is reduced to zero by a return of capital distributions, any further distributions are taxable as capital gains, which you report on Schedule D of Form 1040.

*Planning Reminder*

**Dividends on Life Insurance Policies**
Dividends on a life insurance policy (other than a modified endowment contract) are actually a refund of your premiums and are not taxed until they exceed the total premiums paid.

# 4.2 Qualified Corporate Dividends Taxed at Favorable Capital Gain Rates

Dividends paid out of current or accumulated earnings of a corporation are taxable *(4.5)*. Stock dividends on common stock *(4.6)* are generally not taxable, but other types of stock dividends are taxed *(4.8)*.

Dividends from most domestic corporations and many foreign corporations are treated as "qualified dividends," which are subject to the same favorable rates as net capital gain (the excess of net long-term capital gains over net short-term losses *(5.3)* ). The rate on your qualified dividends is either zero, 15% or 20%, depending on your taxable income *(5.3)*. More than one of these favorable rates may apply to your qualified dividends depending on their amount and your other income. Although the zero rate is intended to benefit taxpayers with modest incomes, taxpayers with substantial dividends/gains whose top bracket would be 22% or higher (assuming there were no capital gain rates) may pay no tax (zero rate) on a portion of their qualified dividends/net capital gains, provided their ordinary income (such as salary and interest) is low; *see* the Examples in *5.3*.

The benefit of the reduced rates is obtained as part of the computation of tax liability on the "Qualified Dividends and Capital Gain Tax Worksheet" in the instructions for Form 1040, or, if required, on the Schedule D Tax Worksheet *(5.3)*.

On Form 1099-DIV for 2018, the amount of qualified dividends eligible for the capital gain rate will be shown in Box 1b. To be eligible, the dividend must be received on stock you held at least 61 days during the 121-day period beginning 60 days before the ex-dividend date. The ex-dividend date is the first date following the declaration of a dividend on which the purchaser of the stock is not entitled to receive the dividend *(4.9)*. When counting the number of days you held the stock, include the day you disposed of the stock but not the day you acquired it. You cannot count towards the 61-day test any days on which your position in the securities was hedged, thereby diminishing your risk of loss.

Some dividends from a mutual fund or exchange-traded fund (ETF) may be reported as qualified distributions on Form 1099 although they are not actually qualified distributions and cannot be reported as such on your return. Both you and the fund must hold the underlying security for the required 61-day period. The fund may report a dividend as qualifying without taking into account whether you purchased or sold your shares during the year, so you must determine whether you have met the 61-day holding period test for the shares on which the dividends were paid. When counting the number of days you held the shares, include the day you disposed of the shares but not the day you acquired them.

Generally, distributions on preferred stock instruments do not qualify for qualified dividend treatment because the instruments are hybrid securities that are treated as debt and not stock. Payments on such hybrid instruments are considered interest rather than dividends and thus are not eligible for the reduced tax rate. If the preferred instrument is treated as stock, the reduced rate does not apply to dividends attributable to periods totaling less than 367 days unless the 61-day holding period (discussed above) is met. If the dividends are attributable to periods of more than 366 days, the stock must be held at least 91 days in the 181-day period starting 90 days before the ex-dividend date.

**Some dividends are actually interest.** Distributions that are called dividends but are actually interest income, such as payments from credit unions and mutual savings banks, are not eligible for the reduced dividend rate. Similarly, certain dividends from exchange-traded funds (ETFs) and from mutual funds represent interest earnings and are not eligible for the reduced rate. Dividends paid by a real estate investment trust (REIT) generally are not eligible, but the reduced rate does apply to REIT distributions that are attributable to corporate tax at the REIT level or which represent qualified dividends received by the REIT and passed through to shareholders.

Dividends from foreign corporations qualify for the reduced rate if the corporation is traded on an established U.S. securities market, incorporated in a U.S. possession, or certain treaty requirements are met.

If your broker loans out your shares as part of a short sale, substitute payments in lieu of dividends may be received on your behalf while the short sale is open. Such substitute payments are not considered dividends and should be included in Box 8 of Form 1099-MISC and reported by you as "Other income" on Line 21 of Schedule 1 of Form 1040.

Tax-deferred retirement accounts such as traditional IRAs and 401(k) plans do not benefit from the reduced dividend rate. Distributions from such retirement plans are taxable as ordinary income even if the distribution is attributable to dividends that otherwise meet the tests for qualified dividends.

## 4.3 Dividends From a Partnership, S Corporation, Estate, or Trust

Dividends you receive as a member of a partnership, stockholder in an S corporation, or as a beneficiary of an estate or trust may be qualified dividends eligible for the reduced capital gain rate of zero, 15%, or 20% *(4.2)*.

A distribution from a partnership or S corporation is reported as a dividend only if it is portfolio income derived from nonbusiness activities. Your allowable share of the dividend will be shown on the Schedule K-1 you receive from the partnership or S corporation.

## 4.4 Real Estate Investment Trust (REIT) Dividends

Dividends from a real estate investment trust (REIT) are shown on Form 1099-DIV. Ordinary dividends reported in Box 1a are taxable at ordinary income rates except for the portion, if any, shown in Box 1b that qualifies for the zero, 15% or 20% capital gain rate. Dividends reported in Box 2a as capital gain distributions are reported by you as long-term capital gains regardless of how long you have held your trust shares. A loss on the sale of REIT shares held for six months or less is treated as a long-term capital loss to the extent of any capital gain distribution received before the sale plus any undistributed capital gains. However, this long-term loss rule does not apply to sales under periodic redemption plans.

*Legislative Alert*

**REIT Dividends May Create a QBI Deduction**

You may be able to claim a deduction of up to 20% of qualified REIT dividends. This is a component of the qualified business income (QBI) deduction. *See 40.24.*

## 4.5 Taxable Dividends of Earnings and Profits

You pay tax on dividends only when the corporation distributing the dividends has earnings and profits. Publicly held corporations will tell you whether their distributions are taxable. If you hold stock in a close corporation, you may have to determine the tax status of its distribution. You need to know earnings and profits at two different periods:

1. Current earnings and profits as of the end of the current taxable year. A dividend is considered to have been made from earnings most recently accumulated.

2. Accumulated earnings and profits as of the beginning of the current year. However, when current earnings and profits are large enough to meet the dividend, you do not have to make this computation. It is only when the dividends exceed current earnings (or there are no current earnings) that you match accumulated earnings against the dividend.

The tax term "accumulated earnings and profits" is similar in meaning to the accounting term "retained earnings." Both stand for the net profits of the company after deducting distributions to stockholders. However, "tax" earnings may differ from "retained earnings" for the following reason: Reserve accounts, the additions to which are not deductible for income tax purposes, are ordinarily included as tax earnings.

### EXAMPLES

1. During 2018, Corporation A paid dividends of $25,000. At the beginning of 2018 it had accumulated earnings of $50,000. It lost $25,000 during 2018. You are taxed on your dividend income in 2018 because the corporation's net accumulated earnings and profits exceed its dividends.

2. At the end of 2017, Corporation B had a deficit of $200,000. Earnings for 2018 were $100,000. In 2018, it paid stockholders dividends of $25,000. The dividends are taxed in 2018; earnings exceeded the dividends.

## 4.6 Stock Dividends on Common Stock

If you own common stock in a company and receive additional shares of the same company as a dividend, the dividend is generally not taxable (see **Chapter 30**) for the method of computing cost basis of stock dividends **(30.3)** and rights and sales of such stock **(30.4)**.

**Exceptions to tax-free rule.** A stock dividend on common stock is taxable **(4.8)** when (1) you may elect to take either stock or cash; (2) there are different classes of common stock, one class receiving cash dividends and another class receiving stock; or (3) the dividend is of convertible preferred stock.

**Fractional shares.** If a stock dividend is declared and you are only entitled to a fractional share, you may be given cash instead. To save the trouble and expense of issuing fractional shares, many companies directly issue cash in lieu of fractional shares or they set up a plan, with shareholder approval, for the fractional shares to be sold and the cash proceeds distributed to the shareholders. Your company should tell you how to report the cash payment. According to the IRS, you are generally treated as receiving a tax-free dividend of fractional shares, followed by a taxable redemption of the shares by the company. You report on Form 8949 and Schedule D **(5.8)** capital gain or loss equal to the excess of the cash over the basis of the fractional share; long- or short-term treatment depends on the holding period of the original stock. In certain cases, a cash distribution may be taxed as an ordinary dividend and not as a sale reported on Form 8949 (and Schedule D); your company should tell you if this is the case.

**Stock rights.** The rules that apply to stock dividends also apply to distributions of stock rights. If you, as a common stockholder, receive rights to subscribe to additional common stock, the receipt of the rights is not taxable provided the terms of the distribution do not fall within the taxable distribution rules **(4.8)**.

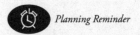 *Planning Reminder*

**Dividend Reinvestment in Company Stock**

Your company may allow you either to take cash dividends or automatically reinvest the dividends in company stock. If you elect the stock plan, and pay fair market value for the stock, the full cash dividend is taxable.

If the plan lets you buy the stock at a discount, the amount of the taxable dividend is the fair market value of the stock on the dividend payment date plus any service fee charged for the acquisition. The basis of the stock is also the fair market value at the dividend payment date. The service charge may be claimed as an itemized deduction subject to the 2% of adjusted gross income floor **(19.1)**. If at the same time you also have the option to buy additional stock at a discount and you exercise the option, you have additional dividend income for the difference between the fair market value (as of the dividend payment date) of the optional shares and the discounted amount you paid for the shares.

 *Filing Tip*

**Stock Splits Are Not Taxed**

The receipt of stock under a stock split is not taxable. Stock splits resemble the receipt of stock dividends, but they are not dividends. They do not represent a distribution of surplus as in the case of stock dividends. Although you own more shares, your ownership percentage has not changed. The purpose of a stock split is generally to reduce the price of individual shares in order to increase their marketability. The basis of the old holding is divided among all the shares in order to find the basis for the new shares **(30.3)**.

## 4.7 Dividends Paid in Property

A dividend may be paid in property such as securities of another corporation or merchandise. You report as income the fair market value of the property. A dividend paid in property is sometimes called a dividend in kind.

**Corporate benefit may be treated as constructive dividend.** On an audit, the IRS may charge that a benefit given to a shareholder-employee should be taxed as a constructive dividend. For example, the Tax Court agreed with the IRS that a corporation's payment for a license that gave the sole shareholder the right to buy season tickets to Houston Texans football games was a constructive dividend to the shareholder.

> **EXAMPLE**
>
> You receive one share of X corporation stock as a dividend from the G company of which you are a stockholder. You received the X stock when it had a market value of $25; you report $25, the value of the property received. The $25 value is also your basis for the stock.

## 4.8 Taxable Stock Dividends

The most frequent type of stock dividend is not taxable: the receipt by a common stockholder of a corporation's own common stock as a dividend *(4.6)*.

**Taxable stock dividends.** The following stock dividends are taxable:

- Stock dividends paid to holders of preferred stock. However, no taxable income is realized where the conversion ratio of convertible preferred stock is increased only to take account of a stock dividend or split involving the stock into which the convertible stock is convertible.
- Stock dividends elected by a shareholder of common stock who had the choice of taking stock, property, or cash. A distribution of stock that was immediately redeemable for cash at the stockholder's option was treated as a taxable dividend.
- Stock dividends paid in a distribution where some shareholders receive property or cash and other shareholders' proportionate interests in the assets or earnings and profits of the corporation are increased.
- Distributions of preferred stock to some common shareholders and common stock to other common shareholders.
- Distributions of convertible preferred stock to holders of common stock, unless it can be shown that the distribution will not result in the creation of disproportionate stock interests.

**Constructive stock dividends.** You may not actually receive a stock dividend, but under certain circumstances, the IRS may treat you as having received a taxable distribution. This may happen when a company increases the ratio of convertible preferred stock.

## 4.9 Who Reports the Dividends

**Stock held by broker in street name.** If your broker holds stock for you in a street name, dividends earned on this stock are received by the broker and credited to your account. You report on your 2018 return all dividends credited to your account in 2018. The broker is required to file an information return on Form 1099 (or similar form) showing all such dividends.

If your statement shows only a gross amount of dividends, check with your broker if any of the dividends represented nontaxable returns of capital.

**Dividends on stock sold or bought between ex-dividend date and record date.** Record date is the date set by a company on which you must be listed as a stockholder on its records to receive the dividend. However, in the case of publicly traded stock, an ex-dividend date, which usually precedes the record date by several business days, is fixed by the exchange to determine who is entitled to the dividend.

*If you buy stock before the ex-dividend date,* the dividend belongs to you and is reported by you. If you buy on or after the ex-dividend date, the dividend belongs to the seller.

*If you sell stock before the ex-dividend date,* you do not have a right to the dividend. If you sell on or after the ex-dividend date, you receive the dividend and report it as income.

The dividend declaration date and date of payment do not determine who receives the dividend.

**Nominees or joint owners.** If you receive ordinary dividends on stock held as a nominee for another person, other than your spouse, give that owner a Form 1099-DIV and file a copy of that return with the IRS, along with a Form 1096 ("Transmittal of U.S. Information Return"). The actual owner then reports the income. List the nominee dividends on Schedule B (Form 1040) along with your other dividends, and then subtract the nominee dividends from the total.

---

### EXAMPLE

You receive Form 1099-DIV showing dividends of $960 including a $200 nominee distribution. You prepare a Form 1099-DIV for the actual owner showing the $200 distribution, and file a copy of the form with the IRS, plus Form 1096. When you file your Form 1040, report the nominee distribution along with other ordinary dividends on Schedule B and then subtract it from the total.

| Dividend Income | Amount |
| --- | --- |
| Mutual Fund | $ 310 |
| Computer Inc. | 450 |
| Utility Inc. | 200 |
| Subtotal | $ 960 |
| Less: Nominee distribution | (200) |
| Net dividends | $ 760 |

---

Follow the same procedure if you receive a Form 1099-DIV for an account owned jointly with someone other than your spouse. Give the other owner a Form 1099-DIV, and file a copy with the IRS, along with a Form 1096. The other owner then reports his or her share of the joint income. On your return, you list the total dividends shown on Forms 1099-DIV and subtract from the total the nominee dividends reported to the other owner.

## 4.10 Year Dividends Are Reported

Dividends are generally reported on the tax return for the year in which the dividend is credited to your account or when you receive the dividend if paid by check.

Dividends received from a corporation in a year after the one in which they were declared, when you held the stock on the record date, are taxed in the year they are received; *see* Example 4 below.

---

### EXAMPLES

1. A corporation declares a dividend payable on December 31, 2018. It follows a practice of paying dividends by checks that are mailed so that stockholders do not receive them until January 2019. You report this dividend on your 2019 return.

2. On December 31, 2018, a mutual fund declares a dividend payable to shareholders of record as of that date. You receive it in January 2019. The dividend is taxable in 2018, when declared, and not 2019, when received, under the special rule for dividends declared by a mutual fund in the last three months of the year.

3. On December 31, 2018, a dividend is credited by a corporation to a stockholder's account and made immediately available. The dividend is taxable in 2018 as the crediting is considered constructive receipt by you in 2018, even if you do not receive it until 2019.

4. You own stock in a corporation. In April 2018, the corporation declared a dividend, but it provided that the dividend will be paid when it gets the cash. It finally pays the dividend in September 2019; the dividend is taxable in 2019.

---

 *Caution*

**Year-End Dividend From Mutual Fund**

A dividend declared in October through December by a mutual fund or REIT that is payable to shareholders of record on a date within those three months is taxable in the year it is declared, even if it is not paid until January of the following year.

*Filing Tip*

**Insurance Premium Refund**

Dividends on insurance policies are actually returns of premiums you previously paid. They are not subject to tax until they exceed the net premiums paid for the contract.

## 4.11 Distribution Not Out of Earnings: Return of Capital

A return of capital or "nontaxable distribution" reduces the cost basis of the stock. If your shares were purchased at different times, reduce the basis of the oldest shares first. When the cost basis is reduced to zero, further returns of capital are taxed as capital gains on Schedule D. Whether the gain is short term or long term depends on the length of time you have held the stock. The company paying the dividend will usually inform you of the tax treatment of the payment.

**Life insurance dividends.** Dividends on insurance policies are not true dividends. They are returns of premiums you previously paid. They reduce the cost of the policy and are not subject to tax until they exceed the net premiums paid for the contract. Interest paid or credited on dividends left with the insurance company is taxable. Dividends on VA insurance are tax free, as is interest on dividends left with the VA.

Where insurance premiums were deducted as a business expense in prior years, receipts of insurance dividends are included as business income. Dividends on capital stock of an insurance company are taxable.

## 4.12 Reporting Interest on Your Tax Return

You must report all taxable interest. Forms 1099-INT, sent by payers of interest income, give you the amount of interest to enter on your tax return. Although they are generally correct, you should check for mistakes, notify payers of any error, and request a new form marked "corrected." If tax was withheld *(26.10)*, claim this tax as a payment on your tax return. The IRS will check interest reported on your return against the Forms 1099-INT sent by banks and other payers. If you earn over $1,500 of taxable interest, you list the payers of interest on Part I of Schedule B if you file either Form 1040 or Form 1040A. Form 1040EZ may not be used if your taxable interest exceeds $1,500. You must also list tax-exempt interest on your return even though it is not taxable.

You must report interest that has been shown on a Form 1099-INT in your name although it may not be taxable to you. For example, you may have received interest as a nominee or as accrued interest on bonds bought between interest dates. In these cases, list the amounts reported on Form 1099 along with your other interest income on Schedule B (Form 1040 or Form 1040A). On a separate line, label the amount as "Nominee distribution," or "Accrued interest" *(4.15)*, and subtract it from the total interest shown. Accrued interest is discussed below. Nominee distributions are discussed below under "Joint Accounts."

If you received interest on a frozen account *(4.13)*, include the interest from Form 1099 on Schedule B i(Form 1040). On a separate line, write "frozen deposits" and subtract the amount from the total interest reported.

You generally do not have to list the payers of interest if your interest receipts are $1,500 or less. However, complete Part I of Schedule B if you have to reduce the interest shown on Form 1099 by nontaxable amounts such as accrued interest, tax-exempt interest, nominee distributions, frozen deposit interest, amortized bond premium, or excludable interest on savings bonds used for tuition.

**Joint accounts.** Form 1099-INT will be sent to the joint owner whose name and Social Security number was reported to the bank (or other payer) on Form W-9 when the account was opened. If you receive a Form 1099-INT for interest on an account you own with someone other than your spouse, you should file a nominee Form 1099-INT with the IRS to indicate that person's share of the interest, together with Form 1096 ("Transmittal of Information Return"). Give a copy of the Form 1099-INT to the other person. When you file your own return, you report the total interest shown on Form 1099-INT and then subtract the other person's share so you are taxed only on your portion of the interest; *see* the Example below.

Do not follow this procedure if you contributed all of the funds and set up the joint account merely as a "convenience" account to allow the other person to automatically inherit the account when you die. In this case, you report all of the interest income.

*Caution*

**Reporting Foreign Accounts**

If in 2018 you had a financial interest in or signature authority over a financial account in a foreign country, you must file Schedule B even if you are not otherwise required to file it. In Part III of Schedule B, you must disclose your interest in the foreign account and are directed to the instructions for FinCEN Form 114 (FBAR) to determine if you must file that form (if yes, it must be filed electronically), and to indicate in Part III of Schedule B if the FBAR is required. There are penalties for not filing a required FBAR. Regardless of whether you must file a FBAR, you may have to file Form 8938 to disclose your ownership of specified foreign financial assets. Penalties also apply for failure to file a required Form 8938. See 48.7 for details on the FBAR and Form 8938 filing requirements.

**EXAMPLE**

Your Social Security number is listed on a bank account owned jointly with your sister. You each invested 50% of the account principal and have agreed to share the interest income. You receive a Form 1099-INT for 2018 reporting total interest of $1,700 on the account. By January 31, 2019, prepare and give to your sister another Form 1099-INT that identifies you as the payer and her as the recipient of her share, or $850 interest. Send a copy of the Form 1099-INT and a Form 1096 to the IRS no later than February 28, 2019 (April 1, if filing electronically). Your sister will report the $850 interest on her return. On your Form 1040, report the full $1,700 interest on Line 1 of Schedule B, along with your other interest income. Above Line 2, subtract the $850 belonging to your sister to avoid being taxed on that amount; label the subtraction "Nominee distribution."

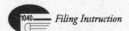 *Filing Instruction*

**Tax-Exempt Interest**

Tax-exempt interest, such as from municipal bonds, must be reported on your return although it is not subject to regular income tax. Tax-exempt interest is shown in Box 8 of Form 1099-INT and any portion that is subject to AMT *(23.3)* is shown in Box 9. Report the Box 8 amount on Line 8b of Form 1040.

**Savings certificates, deferred interest.** The interest element on certificates of deposit and similar plans of more than one year is treated as deferred interest original issue discount (OID) and is taxable on an annual basis. The bank notifies you of the taxable OID amount on Form 1099-OID. If you discontinue a savings plan before maturity, you may have a loss deduction for forfeited interest, which is listed on Form 1099-INT or Form 1099-OID *(4.16)*.

Tax on interest can be deferred in some cases on a savings certificate with a term of one year or less. Interest is taxable in the year it is available for withdrawal without substantial penalty. Where you invest in a six-month certificate before July 1, the entire amount of interest is paid by the end of the year and is taxable in that year (the year of payment). However, when you invest in a six-month certificate after June 30, only interest actually paid or made available for withdrawal before the end of the year without substantial penalty is taxable in the year of issuance. The balance is taxable in the year of maturity. You can defer interest to the following year by investing in a six-month certificate after June 30, provided the payment of interest is specifically deferred to the year of maturity by the terms of the certificate. Similarly, interest may be deferred to the following year by investing in certificates of up to one year, provided that the crediting of interest is specifically deferred until the year of maturity.

**Accrued interest on a bond bought between interest payment dates.** Interest accrued between interest payment dates is part of the purchase price of the bond. This amount is taxable to the seller as explained in *4.15*. If you purchased a bond and received a Form 1099-INT that includes accrued interest on a bond, include the interest on Line 1 of Schedule B, Form 1040, and then on a separate line above Line 2 subtract the accrued interest from the Line 1 total.

**Custodian account of a minor (Uniform Transfers to Minors Act).** The interest is taxable to the child if his or her name and Social Security number were provided to the payer on Form W-9. However, if the child has net investment income for 2018 over $2,100, the "kiddie tax" probably applies, in which case the excess over $2,100 is subject to tax at the rates for trusts and estates under new law rules provided by the Tax Cuts and Jobs Act *(24.2)*.

## 4.13 Interest on Frozen Accounts Not Taxed

If you have funds in a bankrupt or insolvent financial institution that freezes your account by limiting withdrawals, you do not pay tax on interest allocable to the frozen deposits. The interest is taxable when withdrawals are permitted. Officers and owners of at least a 1% interest in the financial institution, or their relatives, may not take advantage of this rule and must still report interest on frozen deposits.

On Part I of Schedule B (Form 1040), report the full amount shown on Form 1099-INT, even if the interest is on a "frozen" deposit. Then, on a separate line, subtract the amount allocable to the frozen deposit from the total interest shown on the Schedule; label the subtraction "frozen deposits." Thus, the interest on the frozen deposit is not included on the line of your return showing taxable interest.

**Refund opportunity.** If you reported interest on a frozen deposit on a tax return for a prior year, you generally have three years to file a refund claim for the tax paid on the interest *(47.2)*.

*Filing Tip*

**Lost Deposits**

If you lose funds because of a financial institution's bankruptcy or insolvency, and you can reasonably estimate such a loss, you may deduct the loss as a nonbusiness bad debt, as a casualty loss, or as a miscellaneous itemized deduction *(18.5).*

*Filing Tip*

**Accrued Interest**

When you buy bonds between interest payment dates and pay accrued interest to the seller, this interest is taxable to the seller. The accrued interest is included on the Form 1099-INT you receive, but you should subtract it from your taxable interest; *see* Example 1 in *4.15.*

## 4.14 Interest Income on Debts Owed to You

You report interest earned on money that you loan to another person. If you are on the cash basis, you report interest in the year you actually receive it or when it is considered received under the "constructive receipt rule." If you are on the accrual basis, you report interest when it is earned, whether or not you have received it.

*See 4.31* for minimum interest rates required for loans and 4.18 when OID rules apply.

Where partial payment is being made on a debt, or when a debt is being compromised, the parties may agree in advance which part of the payment covers interest and which covers principal. If a payment is not identified as either principal or interest, the payment is first applied against interest due and reported as interest income to the extent of the interest due.

Interest income is not realized when a debtor gives you a new note for an old note where the new note includes the interest due on the old note.

If you give away a debtor's note, you report as income the collectible interest due at the date of the gift. To avoid tax on the interest, the note must be transferred before interest becomes due.

## 4.15 Reporting Interest on Bonds Bought or Sold

When you buy or sell bonds between interest dates, interest is included in the price of the bonds. If you are the buyer, you do not report as income the interest that accrued before your date of purchase. The seller reports the accrued interest. Reduce the basis of the bond by the accrued interest reported by the seller. The following Examples illustrate these rules.

### EXAMPLES

1. Purchase. On April 30, you buy for $5,200 a $5,000 corporate bond bearing interest at 5% per year, payable January 1 and July 1. The purchase price of the bond included accrued interest of $88.33 for the period January 1–April 30.

   | | |
   |---|---|
   | Interest received on 7/1 | $125.00 |
   | *Less:* Accrued interest | $83.33 |
   | Taxable interest | $41.67 |

   Form 1099 sent to you includes the $83.33 of accrued interest. On Schedule B of Form 1040, you report the total interest of $125 received on July 1 and then on a separate line subtract the accrued interest of $83.33. Write "Accrued Interest" on the line where you show the subtraction.

   Your basis for the bond is $5,117 ($5,200 – $83.33) for purposes of figuring gain or loss on a later sale of the bond.

2. Sale. On April 30, you sell for $5,200 a $5,000 5% bond with interest payable January 1 and July 1. The sales price included interest of $83.33 accrued from January 1–April 30. Your cost for the bond was $5,000. On your return, you report interest of $83.33 and capital gain of $117.

   | | |
   |---|---|
   | You receive | $ 5,200.00 |
   | Less: Accrued interest | $83.33 |
   | Sales proceeds | $ 5,116.67 |
   | Less: Your cost | $5000.00 |
   | Capital gain | $ 116.67, or $117 |

**Redemptions, bankruptcy, reorganizations.** On a redemption, interest received in excess of the amount due at that time is not treated as interest income but as capital gain.

**EXAMPLE**

You hold a $5,000 9% bond with interest payable January 1 and July 1. The company can call the bonds for redemption on any interest date. In May, the company announces it will redeem the bonds on July 1. But you may present the bond for redemption beginning with June 1 and it will be redeemed with interest to July 1. On June 1 you present the bond and receive $5,225: $5,000 principal, $187.50 interest to June 1, and $37.50 extra interest to July 1. The $37.50 is treated as a capital gain; the $187.50 is interest.

Taxable interest may continue on bonds after the issuer becomes bankrupt, if a guarantor continues to pay the interest when due. The loss on the bonds will occur only when they mature and are not redeemed or when they are sold below your cost. In the meantime, the interest received from the guarantor is taxed.

Bondholders exchanging their bonds for stock, securities, or other property in a tax-free reorganization, including a reorganization in bankruptcy, have interest income to the extent the property received is attributable to accrued but unpaid interest; *see* Internal Revenue Code Section 354(a)(2)(B).

**Bonds selling at a flat price.** When you buy bonds with defaulted interest at a "flat" price, a later payment of the defaulted interest is not taxed. It is a tax-free return of capital that reduces your cost of the bond. This rule applies only to interest in default at the time the bond is purchased. Interest that accrues after the date of your purchase is taxed as ordinary income.

## 4.16 Forfeiture of Interest on Premature Withdrawals

Banks usually impose an interest penalty if you withdraw funds from a savings certificate before the specified maturity date. You may lose interest if you prematurely withdraw funds in order to switch to higher paying investments, or if you need the funds for personal use. In some cases, the penalty may exceed the interest earned so that principal is also forfeited to make up the difference.

If you are penalized, you must still report the full amount of interest credited to your account. However, on Form 1040, you may deduct the full amount of the penalty, forfeited principal as well as interest. The deductible penalty amount is shown in Box 2 of Form 1099-INT sent to you. You may claim the deduction even if you do not itemize deductions. On Schedule 1 of Form 1040, enter the deduction on Line 30, marked "Penalty on early withdrawal of savings."

**Loss on redemption before maturity of a savings certificate.** If you redeem a long-term (more than one year) savings certificate for a price less than the stated redemption price at maturity, you are allowed a loss deduction for the amount of original issue discount (OID) reported as income but not received. The deductible amount is shown in Box 3 of Form 1099-OID. Claim the deduction on Line 30 of Schedule 1 of Form 1040. The basis of the obligation is reduced by the amount of the deductible loss.

Do not include in the computation any amount based on a fixed rate of simple or compound interest that is actually payable or is treated as constructively received at fixed periodic intervals of one year or less.

## 4.17 Amortization of Bond Premium

Bond premium is the extra amount paid for a bond in excess of its principal or face amount when the value of the bond has increased due to falling interest rates. The premium is included in your basis in the bond but if the bond pays taxable interest, you may elect to amortize the premium by deducting it over the life of the bond. Amortizing the premium annually is usually advantageous because it gives an annual deduction to offset the interest income from the bond. Basis of the bond is reduced by the amortized premium. If you claim amortization deductions and hold the bond to maturity, basis is reduced by the entire amortized premium and you have neither gain nor loss at redemption.

 *Caution*

**CD Early Withdrawal**

If you are penalized for making an early withdrawal from a certificate of deposit, you may lose part of your interest or principal. You must report the full amount of interest credited to your account, but you may deduct the full amount of the penalty (whether forfeited principal or interest) on Line 30 of Schedule 1 of Form 1040.

*Planning Reminder*

## Amortized Premium Reduces Basis

You reduce the cost basis of the bond by the amount of the premium taken as a deduction.

If you hold the bond to maturity, the entire premium is amortized and you have neither gain nor loss on redemption of the bond. If before maturity you sell the bond at a gain (selling price exceeds your basis for the bond), you realize long-term capital gain if you held the bond long term. A sale of the bond for less than its adjusted basis gives a capital loss.

*Filing Tip*

## How To Deduct Amortized Premium

You may not have to deduct the amortized premium because you are reporting the net amount of interest income (interest income reduced by the allocable premium amortization), as shown by the payer on Form 1099-INT. If you are reporting the total interest income and want to offset it by the amortizable premium, you must show the reduction on Schedule B (Form 1040). Report the full interest from the bond on Line 1 of Schedule B, along with the rest of your interest income. On a separate line, subtract the amortized premium from a subtotal of the other interest. Label the subtraction "ABP Adjustment."

You may not claim a deduction for a premium paid on a tax-exempt bond. However, you must still reduce your basis in the bond by the annual amortization amount. The amortized amount also reduces the amount of tax-exempt interest that you report on your return *(4.24)*.

Dealers in bonds may not deduct amortization but must include the premium as part of cost.

**Capital loss alternative to amortizing premium.** If you do not elect to amortize the premium on a taxable bond, you will realize a capital loss when the bond is redeemed at par or you sell it for less than you paid for it. For example, you bought a $1,000 corporate bond for $1,300 and did not amortize the $300 premium; you will realize a $300 capital loss when the bond is redeemed at par: $1,000 proceeds less $1,300 cost basis ($1,000 face value plus $300 premium). You could realize a capital gain if you sell the bond for more than the premium price you paid.

**Determining the amortizable amount for the year.** For a taxable "covered" bond issued by a corporation, the amount of premium amortization allocable to the interest payments will be reported by the payer in Box 11 of Form 1099-INT unless (1) the interest reported in Box 1 has been reduced to reflect the offset of the interest by the allocable premium amortization, or (2) you provided written notice to the payer that you did not want to amortize the bond premium. For example, if the taxable interest from a "covered" corporate bond is $40 and the amount of bond premium amortization allocable to the interest is $4, the payer may either report the net interest of $36 in Box 1 and $0 in Box 11, or report the $40 of interest income in Box 1 and the $4 of allocable premium amortization in Box 11.

For a U.S. Treasury bond that is "covered," Box 12 of Form 1099-INT will show the amount of bond premium amortization allocable to the interest paid during the year, unless the net amount of interest is reported in Box 3 to reflect the offset of the interest by the allocable amortization.

If a taxable bond is "noncovered," the payer is required to report only the gross amount of interest in Box 1 of Form 1099-INT.

The annual amortizable premium is based on the constant yield method (this has been the method for all bonds issued after September 27, 1985). The constant yield method is also an option for reporting market discount *(4.20)*. See IRS Publication 550 for details on figuring the amortizable premium or consult a tax professional for making the complex computations.

For taxable bonds subject to a call before maturity, the amortization computation is based on the earlier call date if that results in a smaller amortization deduction.

**Electing amortization—either in or after the year you acquire a bond.** An election to amortize premium on a taxable bond does not have to be made in the year you acquire the bond. Attach a statement to the tax return for the first year to which you want the election to apply. If the election is made after the year of acquisition, the premium allocable to the years prior to the year of election is not amortizable; the unamortized amount is included in your cost basis for the bond and will result in a capital loss when the bond is redeemed at par or sold prior to maturity for less than basis.

**How to deduct amortized premium on taxable bonds.** The premium amortization for such bonds offsets your interest income from the bonds; *see* the Filing Tip in this section. Any excess of the allocable premium over interest income may be fully deducted as a miscellaneous deduction (not subject to the 2% floor) on Line 16 of Schedule A (Form 1040). However, the miscellaneous deduction is limited to the excess of total interest inclusions on the bonds in prior years over total bond premium deductions in the prior years.

**Effect of amortization election on other taxable bonds you acquire.** If you elect to amortize the premium for one bond, you must also amortize the premium on all similar bonds owned by you at the beginning of the tax year, and also to all similar bonds acquired thereafter. An election to amortize may not be revoked without IRS permission. If you file your return without claiming the deduction, you may not change your mind and make the election for that year by filing an amended return or refund claim.

**Callable bonds.** On taxable bonds, amortization is based either on the maturity or earlier call date, depending on which date gives a smaller yearly deduction. This rule applies regardless of the issue date of the bond. If the bond is called before maturity, you may deduct as an ordinary loss the unamortized bond premium in the year the bond is redeemed.

**Convertible bonds.** A premium paid for a convertible bond that is allocated to the conversion feature may not be amortized; the value of the conversion option reduces basis in the bond.

**Premium on tax-exempt bonds.** You may not take a deduction for the amortization of a premium paid on a tax-exempt bond. However, you must still reduce your basis in the bond each year by the amortized amount. The amortization for the year also reduces the amount of tax-exempt interest otherwise reportable on Line 2b of Form 1040. If the tax-exempt bond is a "covered" security, the payer of the bond must report in Box 13 of Form 1099-INT the amount of premium amortization that is allocable to the annual interest payments, unless the tax-exempt interest reported in Box 8 of the Form 1099-INT is the net amount (Box 9 if the tax-exempt interest is subject to alternative minimum tax), reflecting the offset of the interest paid by the allocable premium.

When you dispose of the bond, you reduce the basis of the bond by the amortized premium for the period you held the bond amount. If the bond has call dates, the IRS may require the premium to be amortized to the earliest call date.

## 4.18 Discount on Bonds

There are two types of bond discounts: original issue discount and market discount.

**Market discount.** Market discount arises when the price of a bond declines because its interest rate is less than the current interest rate. For example, a bond originally issued at its face amount of $1,000 declines in value to $900 because the interest payable on the bond is less than the current interest rate. The difference of $100 is called market discount. The tax treatment of market discount is explained in *4.20*.

**Original issue discount (OID).** OID arises when a bond is issued for a price less than its face or principal amount. OID is the difference between the principal amount (redemption price at maturity) and the issue price. For publicly offered obligations, the issue price is the initial offering price to the public at which a substantial amount of such obligations were sold. All obligations that pay no interest before maturity, such as zero coupon bonds, are considered to be issued at a discount. For example, a bond with a face amount of $1,000 is issued at an offering price of $900. The $100 difference is OID.

Generally, part of the OID must be reported as interest income each year you hold the bond, whether or not you receive any payment from the bond issuer. This is also true for certificates of deposit (CDs), time deposits, and similar savings arrangements with a term of more than one year, provided payment of interest is deferred until maturity. OID is reported to you by the issuer (or by your broker if you bought the obligation on a secondary market) on Form 1099-OID *(4.19)*.

**Exceptions to OID.** OID rules do not apply to: (1) obligations with a term of one year or less held by cash-basis taxpayers *(4.21)*; (2) tax-exempt obligations, except for certain stripped tax-exempts *(4.26)*; (3) U.S. Savings Bonds; (4) an obligation issued by an individual before March 2, 1984; and (5) loans of $10,000 or less from individuals who are not professional money lenders, provided the loans do not have a tax avoidance motivation.

 *Filing Tip*

**When OID May Be Ignored**

You may disregard OID that is less than one-fourth of one percent (.0025) of the principal amount multiplied by the number of full years from the date of original issue to maturity. On most long-term bonds, the OID will exceed this amount and must be reported.

### EXAMPLES

1. A 10-year bond with a face amount of $1,000 is issued at $980. One-fourth of one percent (.0025) of $1,000 times 10 is $25. As the $20 OID is less than $25, it may be ignored for tax purposes.
2. Same facts as in Example 1, except that the bond is issued at $950. As OID of $50 is more than the $25, OID must be reported under the rules explained at *4.19*.

**Bond bought at premium or acquisition premium.** You do not report OID as ordinary income if you buy a bond at a premium. You buy at a premium where you pay more than the total amount payable on the bond after your purchase, not including qualified stated interest. When you dispose of a bond bought at a premium, the difference between the sale or redemption price and your basis is a capital gain or loss *(4.17)*.

If you do not pay more than the total due at maturity, you do not have a premium, but there is "acquisition premium" if you pay more than the adjusted issue price. This is the issue price plus previously accrued OID but minus previous payments on the bond other than qualified stated interest. The acquisition premium reduces the amount of OID you must report as income; *see 4.19*.

## 4.19 Reporting Original Issue Discount on Your Return

The issuer of the bond (or your broker) will make the Original Issue Discount (OID) computation and report in Box 1 of Form 1099-OID the OID for the actual dates of your ownership during the calendar year. In most cases, the entire OID must be reported as interest income on your return. However, the amount shown in Box 1 of Form 1099-OID may have to be adjusted if you bought the bond at an acquisition premium and generally must be adjusted if you bought the bond at a premium, the bond is indexed for inflation, the obligation is a stripped bond or stripped coupon (including zero coupon instruments backed by U.S. Treasury securities), or if you received Form 1099-OID as a nominee for someone else. Your basis in the bond is increased by the OID included in income.

If you did not receive a Form 1099-OID, contact the issuer or check IRS Publication 1212 for OID amounts.

**Treasury inflation-indexed securities.** You must report as OID any increase in the inflation-adjusted principal amount of a Treasury inflation-indexed security that occurs while you held the bond during the tax year. This amount should be reported to you in Box 1 of Form 1099-OID, but this amount must be adjusted if during the year you bought the bond after original issue or sold it. The adjusted amount of OID must be computed using the coupon bond method discussed in IRS Publication 1212.

Periodic interest (non-OID) paid to you during the year on a Treasury inflation-indexed security may be reported to you either in Box 2 of Form 1099-OID or in Box 3 of Form 1099-INT.

**Premium.** If you paid a premium *(4.18)* for a bond originally issued at discount, you do not have to report any OID as income. Report the amount shown on Form 1099-OID and then subtract it as discussed in the Filing Tip in this section.

**Acquisition premium.** If you pay an acquisition premium *(4.18)* and the payer reports the gross amount of OID in Box 1 of Form 1099-OID, that amount will not be correct because such premium reduces the amount of OID you must report as interest income. However, for a newly acquired bond, the payer may either (1) report in Box 1 a net amount of OID that reflects the offset of OID by the amortized acquisition premium for the year, or (2) report the gross amount of OID in Box 1 and show in Box 6 the acquisition premium amortization for the year; the Box 6 amount reduces the OID that you must report as interest income.

If you are reporting less than the full Box 1 amount of OID, report the full amount and then reduce it, as discussed in the Filing Tip in this section.

**Stripped bonds or coupons.** The amount that is shown in Box 1 of Form 1099-OID may not be correct for a stripped bond or coupon *(4.22)*. If it is incorrect, adjust it following the rules in Publication 1212.

**Nominee.** If you receive a Form 1099-OID for an obligation owned by someone else, other than your spouse, you must file another Form 1099-OID for that owner. The OID computation rules shown in IRS Publication 1212 should be used to compute the other owner's share of OID. You file the other owner's Form 1099-OID and a transmittal Form 1096 with the IRS, and give the other owner a copy of the Form 1099-OID. On your own tax return, report the amount shown on the Form 1099-OID you received and then reduce it, as discussed in the Filing Tip in this section.

 *Filing Tip*

**Reporting OID and Recomputed OID**

If you are reporting the full amount of OID from Box 1 of Form 1099-OID, include the amount as interest on Form 1040. However, if you are reporting less OID than the amount shown in Box 1 of Form 1099-OID, you must adjust the reportable amount on Schedule B (Form 1040). Include the full amount shown in Box 1 of Form 1099-OID on Line 1 of Schedule B, along with other interest income. Make a subtotal of the Line 1 amounts and subtract from it the OID you are not required to report. Write "OID Adjustment" on the line where you show the subtraction. Label the subtraction "Nominee Distribution" if that is the reason for the reduction.

Your basis for the obligation is increased by the taxable OID for purposes of figuring gain on a sale or redemption *(4.23)*.

**Periodic interest reported on Form 1099-OID.** If in addition to OID there is regular interest payable on the bond, such interest will be reported in Box 2 of Form 1099-OID. However, for a Treasury inflation-indexed security, the interest may be reported in Box 3 of Form 1099-INT. Report the full amount as interest income if you held the bond for the entire year. If you acquired the bond or disposed of it during the year, figure the interest allocable to your ownership period *(4.15)*.

**REMICS.** If you are a regular interest holder in a REMIC (real estate mortgage investment conduit), Box 1 of Form 1099-OID shows the amount of OID you must report on your return and Box 2 includes periodic interest other than OID. If you bought the regular interest at a premium or acquisition, the OID shown on Form 1099-OID must be adjusted as discussed above. If you are a regular interest holder in a single-class REMIC, Box 2 also includes your share of the REMIC's investment expenses. These expenses should be listed in a separate statement and are deductible on Schedule A as a miscellaneous itemized deduction subject to the 2% of adjusted gross income floor *(19.1)*.

## 4.20 Reporting Income on Market Discount Bonds

Market discount arises where the price of a bond declines below its face amount because it carries an interest rate that is below the current rate of interest.

When you realize a profit on the sale of a market discount bond, the portion of the profit equal to the accrued discount must be reported as ordinary interest income rather than as capital gain. Alternatively, an election may be made to report the accrued market discount annually instead of in the year of disposition; *see* below for "Reporting discount annually".

These tax reporting rules do not apply to the following bonds, which are excluded from the "market discount bond" category: (1) bonds with a maturity date of up to one year from date of issuance; (2) certain installment obligations, (3) U.S. Savings Bonds, and (4) tax-exempt bonds bought before May 1, 1993; at disposition, all the gain on these older tax-exempts is capital gain.

Furthermore, you may treat as zero any market discount that is less than one-fourth of one percent (.0025) of the redemption price multiplied by the number of full years after you acquire the bond to maturity. Such minimal discount will not affect capital gain on a sale.

**Deferral of interest deduction and ordinary income at disposition if you borrow to buy or carry market discount bonds.** If you do not elect to report the accrued market discount annually as interest income (see below for "Reporting discount annually"), and you took a loan to buy or carry a market discount bond, your interest deductions may be limited. If your interest expense exceeds the income earned on the bond (including OID income, if any), the excess may not be currently deducted to the extent of the market discount allocated to the days you held the bond during the year. The allocation of market discount is based on either the ratable accrual method or constant yield method; *see* below.

In the year you dispose of the bond, you may deduct the interest expenses that were disallowed in prior years because of the above limitations.

You may choose to deduct disallowed interest in a year before the year of disposition if you have net interest income from the bond. Net interest income is interest income for the year (including OID) less the interest expense incurred during the year to purchase or carry the bond. This election lets you deduct any disallowed interest expense to the extent it does not exceed the net interest income of that year. The balance of the disallowed interest expense is deductible in the year of disposition.

**How to figure accrued market discount.** If the election to report market discount annually is not made, gain on a market discount bond is taxed as ordinary interest income to the extent of the market discount accrued to the date of sale. There are two methods for figuring the accrued market discount. The basic method, called the ratable accrual method, is figured by dividing market discount by the number of days in the period from the date you bought the bond until the date of maturity. This daily amount is then multiplied by the number of days you held the bond to determine your accrued market discount; *see* Example 1 below.

Instead of using the ratable accrual method to compute accrual of market discount, you may elect to figure the accrued discount for any bond under an optional constant yield (economic accrual) method. If you make the election, you may not change it. The constant yield method initially provides a smaller accrual of market discount than the ratable method, but it is more complicated to figure. It is generally the same as the constant yield method used in IRS Publication 1212 to compute taxable OID *(4.19)*. For accruing market discount, treat your acquisition date as the original issue date and your basis for the market discount bond (immediately after you acquire it) as the issue price when applying the formula in Publication 1212.

**Reporting discount annually.** Rather than report market discount in the year you sell the bond, you may elect, in the year you acquire the bond, to report market discount currently as interest income. You may use either the ratable accrual method, as in Example 3 below, or the elective constant yield method discussed earlier. If you notified the payer that you are electing to report the market discount currently, the payer may include the annual accrued discount in Box 5 of Form 1099-OID. Attach to your timely filed return a statement that you are making the election and describe the method used to figure the accrued market discount. Your election to report annually applies to all market discount bonds that you later acquire. You may not revoke the election without IRS consent. If the election is made, the interest deduction deferral rule discussed earlier does not apply. Furthermore, the election could provide a tax advantage if you sell the bond at a profit and you can benefit from lower tax rates applied to net long-term capital gains.

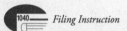
*Filing Instruction*

**Discount Bonds Held to Maturity**

If you do not report the discount annually and hold a bond until maturity, the discount is reported as interest income in the year of redemption. However, you have the option of reporting the market discount annually instead of at sale.

---

### EXAMPLES

1. You buy a taxable bond at a market discount of $200. There are 1,000 days between the date of your purchase and the maturity date. The daily accrual rate is 20 cents. You hold the bond for 600 days before selling it for a price exceeding what you paid for the bond. Under the ratable accrual method, up to $120 of your profit is market discount taxable as interest income (600 × $0.20).

2. You paid $9,100 for a $10,000 bond maturing in 2018. If you hold the bond to maturity, you will receive $10,000, giving you a gain of $900, equal to the market discount. The entire $900 market discount will be taxable as interest income in 2018 when the bond is redeemed.

3. In 2018, you buy a bond at a $200 discount. There are 1,000 days between the date of your purchase and the maturity date, so that daily accrual is 20 cents. You elect to report the market discount currently using the ratable accrual method. If you held the bond for 112 days in 2018, on your 2018 return you report $22 as interest income (112 × $0.20).

---

**Partial principal payments.** If the issuer of a bond (acquired by you after October 22, 1986) makes a partial payment of the principal (face amount) and you did not elect to report the discount annually, you must include the payment as ordinary interest income to the extent it does not exceed the accrued market discount on the bond. See IRS Publication 550 for options on determining accrued market discount. A taxable partial principal payment reduces the amount of remaining accrued market discount when figuring your tax on a later sale or receipt of another partial principal payment.

**Market discount on a bond originally issued at a discount.** A bond issued at original issue discount may later be acquired at a market discount because of an increase in interest rates. If you acquire at a market discount a bond with OID, the market discount is the excess of: (1) the issue price of the bond plus the total original issue discount includible in the gross income of all prior holders of the bond over (2) what you paid for the bond.

**Exchanging a market discount bond in corporate mergers or reorganizations.** If you hold a market discount bond and exchange it for another bond as part of a merger or other reorganization, the new bond is subject to the market discount rules when you sell it.

However, under an exception, market discount rules will not apply to the new bond if the old market discount bond was issued before July 19, 1984, and the terms and interest rates of both bonds are identical.

## 4.21 Discount on Short-Term Obligations

Short-term obligations (maturity of a year or less from date of issue) may be purchased at a discount from face value. If you are on the cash basis, the discount on short-term obligations other than tax-exempt obligations must be reported as interest income in the year the obligations are sold or redeemed unless you elect to include the accrued discount in income currently.

> **EXAMPLE**
>
> In May 2017, you paid $970 for a short-term note with a face amount of $1,000. In January 2018, you receive payment of $1,000 on the note. On your 2018 tax return, you report $30 as interest.

**Discount must be currently reported by dealers and accrual-basis taxpayers.** Discount allocable to the current year must be reported as income by accrual-basis taxpayers, dealers who sell short-term obligations in the course of business, banks, regulated investment companies, common trust funds, certain pass-through entities, and for obligations identified as part of a hedging transaction. Current reporting also applies to persons who separate or strip interest coupons from a bond and then retain the stripped bond or stripped coupon; the accrual rule applies to the retained obligation.

For short-term nongovernmental obligations, OID is generally taken into account instead of acquisition discount, but an election may be made to report the accrued acquisition discount. See IRS Publication 550 for details.

Basis in the obligation is increased by the amount of acquisition discount (or OID for nongovernmental obligations) that is currently reported as income.

**Interest deduction limitation for cash-basis investors.** A cash-basis investor who borrows funds to buy a short-term discount obligation may not fully deduct interest on the loan unless an election is made to report the accrued acquisition discount as income. If the election is not made, the interest you paid during the year is deductible only to the extent it exceeds (1) the portion of the discount allocated to the days you held the bond during the year, plus (2) the portion of interest not taxable for the year under your method of accounting. Any interest expense disallowed under this limitation is deductible in the year in which the obligation is disposed of.

The interest deduction limitation does not apply if you elect to include in income the accruable discount under the ratable accrual method or constant yield method *(4.20)*. The election applies to all short-term obligations acquired during the year and also in all later years.

**Gain or loss on disposition of short-term obligations for cash-basis investors.** If you have a gain on the sale or exchange of a discounted short-term governmental obligation (other than tax-exempt local obligations), the gain is ordinary income to the extent of the ratable share of the acquisition discount received when you bought the obligation. Follow the computation shown in the discussion of Treasury bills *(4.27)* to figure this ordinary income portion. Any gain over this ordinary income portion is short-term capital gain; a loss would be a short-term capital loss.

Gain on short-term nongovernmental obligations is treated as ordinary income up to the ratable share of OID. The formula for figuring this ordinary income portion is similar to the formula for short-term governmental obligations *(4.27)*, except that the denominator of the fraction is days from original issue to maturity, rather than days from acquisition. A constant yield method may also be elected to figure the ordinary income portion. Gain above the computed ordinary income amount is short-term capital gain *(Chapter 5)*. For more information, *see* IRS Publication 550.

 *Filing Tip*

**Discount on Short-Term Government Obligations**

For short-term governmental obligations (other than tax-exempts), the acquisition discount is accrued in daily installments under the ratable method, unless an election is made to use the constant yield method.

*Caution*

**Recomputing Form 1099-OID Amount**

Do not report the amount shown in Box 1 of Form 1099-OID for a stripped bond or coupon; that amount must be recomputed under complicated rules described in IRS Publication 1212. *See 4.19* for reporting the recomputed OID on your return.

 *Caution*

**Reporting Zero Coupon Bond Discount**

Zero coupon bond discount is reported annually as interest over the life of the bond, even though interest is not received. This tax cost tends to make zero coupon bonds unattractive to investors, unless the bonds can be bought for IRA and other retirement plans that defer tax on income until distributions are made.

The value of zero coupon bonds fluctuates sharply with interest rate changes. This fact should be considered before investing in long-term zero coupon bonds. If you sell zero coupon bonds before the maturity term at a time when interest rates rise, you may lose part of your investment.

## 4.22 Stripped Coupon Bonds and Stock

Brokers holding coupon bonds may separate or strip the coupons from the bonds and sell the bonds or coupons to investors. Examples include zero-coupon instruments sold by brokerage houses that are backed by U.S. Treasury bonds.

The U.S. Treasury also offers its version of zero coupon instruments, with the name STRIPS, which are available from brokers and banks.

Brokers holding preferred stock may strip the dividend rights from the stock and sell the stripped stock to investors.

*If you buy a stripped bond or coupon,* the spread between the cost of the bond or coupon and its higher face amount is treated as original issue discount (OID). This means that you annually report a part of the spread as interest income. For a stripped bond, the amount of the original issue discount is the difference between the stated redemption price of the bond at maturity and the cost of the bond. For a stripped coupon, the amount of the discount is the difference between the amount payable on the due date of the coupon and the cost of the coupon. The rules for figuring the amount of OID *(4.19)* to be reported annually are in IRS Publication 1212.

*If you strip a coupon bond,* interest accrual and allocation rules prevent you from creating a tax loss on a sale of the bond or coupons. You are required to report interest accrued up to the date of the sale and also add the amount to the basis of the bond. If you acquired the obligation after October 22, 1986, you must also include in income any market discount that accrued before the date you sold the stripped bond or coupons. The method of accrual depends on the date you bought the obligation; *see* IRS Publication 1212. The accrued market discount is also added to the basis of the bond. You then allocate this basis between the bond and the coupons. The allocation is based on the relative fair market values of the bond and coupons at the date of sale. Gain or loss on the sale is the difference between the sales price of the stripped item (bond or coupons) and its allocated basis. Furthermore, the original issue discount rules apply to the stripped item which you keep (bond or coupon). Original issue discount for this purpose is the difference between the basis allocated to the retained item and the redemption price of the bond (if retained) or the amount payable on the coupons (if retained). You must annually report a ratable portion of the discount.

## 4.23 Sale or Retirement of Bonds and Notes

Gain or loss on the sale, redemption, or retirement of debt obligations issued by a government or corporation is generally capital gain or loss.

A redemption or retirement of a bond at maturity must be reported as a sale on Form 8949 and Schedule D of Form 1040 *(5.8)* although there may be no gain or loss realized.

The accrued amount of OID is reported annually as interest income *(4.19)* and added to basis; this includes the accrued OID for the year the bond is sold. If the bonds are sold or redeemed before maturity, you realize capital gain for the proceeds over the adjusted basis (as increased by accrued OID) of the bond, provided there was no intention to call the bond before maturity. If at the time of original issue there was an intention to call the obligation before maturity, the entire OID that has not yet been included in your income is taxable as ordinary income; the balance is capital gain.

Market discount on bonds is taxable under the rules in *4.20*.

**Tax-exempts.** *See 4.26* for discount on tax-exempt bonds.

**Obligations issued by individuals.** If you hold an individual's note for over $10,000, accrued OID must be reported annually *(4.19)* and added to basis, unless the note was issued before March 2, 1984. Gain on your sale of the note is subject to the rules discussed above for corporate and government OID bonds.

If the note is $10,000 or less (when combined with other prior outstanding loans from the same individual), OID is not reported annually provided you are not a professional lender and tax avoidance was not a principal purpose of the loan. On a sale of the note at a gain, your ratable share of the OID is taxed as ordinary income; any balance is capital gain. A loss is a capital loss.

**EXAMPLE**

On February 8, 2016, you bought a 10-year, 5% corporate bond at original issue for $7,600. If you hold the bond to maturity, you will receive $10,000 (the stated redemption price). At the time of original issue, there was no intention to call the bond before maturity. You sell the bond for $9,040 on February 12, 2018. Assume that for 2016, 2017 and the period in 2018 prior to the sale, you accrue $334 of OID, which you report as interest income on your 2016-2018 returns. Your basis in the bond is increased by the accrued OID to $7,934 ($7,600 + $334). On the sale, you have a long-term capital gain of $1,106 ($9,040 - $7,934).

If at original issue there had been an intention to call the bond before maturity, a gain of up to $2,066 (total OID of $2,400 ($10,000-$7,600) minus $334 of OID reported as interest income) would be taxed as ordinary income. Since this is more than the actual gain of $1,106, the entire $1,106 is ordinary income.

## 4.24  State and City Interest Generally Tax Exempt

Generally, you pay no tax on interest on bonds or notes of states, cities, counties, the District of Columbia, or a possession of the United States. This includes bonds or notes of port authorities, toll road commissions, utility services activities, community redevelopment agencies, and similar bodies created for public purposes. Bonds issued after June 30, 1983, must be in registered form for the interest to be tax exempt. Interest on federally guaranteed obligations is generally taxable, but *see* exceptions in *4.25*.

Check with the issuer of the bond to verify the tax-exempt status of the interest.

**Tax-exempt interest must be reported on your return.** If you are required to file a federal return, you must report the amount of your tax-exempt interest although it is not taxable. On Form 1040, you list the tax-exempt interest on Line 2b.

**Private activity bonds.** Interest on so-called private activity bonds is generally taxable *(4.25)*, but there are certain exceptions. For example, interest on the following "qualified bonds" is tax exempt even if the bond may technically be in the category of private activity bonds: qualified student loan bonds; exempt facility bonds, including New York Liberty bonds, Gulf Opportunity Zone bonds, Midwestern disaster and Hurricane Ike area bonds, and enterprise zone facility bonds; qualified small issue bonds; qualified mortgage bonds and qualified veterans' mortgage bonds; qualified redevelopment bonds; and qualified 501(c)(3) bonds issued by charitable organizations and hospitals. Check with the issuer for the tax status of a private activity bond.

**AMT treatment.** Tax-exempt interest on qualified private activity bonds issued after August 7, 1986 and before 2009, or on bonds issued after 2010, is generally treated as a tax preference item subject to alternative minimum tax (AMT, *23.2*), but there are exceptions. The AMT does not apply to interest on qualified 501(c)(3) bonds, New York Liberty bonds, Gulf Opportunity Zone bonds, Midwestern disaster and Hurricane Ike disaster area bonds, and exempt facility, qualified mortgage, and qualified veterans' bonds issued after July 30, 2008.

The interest on any qualified bond issued in 2009 or 2010 is not subject to AMT.

## 4.25  Taxable State and City Interest

Interest on certain state and city obligations is taxable. These taxable obligations include federally guaranteed obligations, mortgage subsidy bonds, private activity bonds, and arbitrage bonds.

**Federally guaranteed obligations.** Interest on state and local obligations issued after April 14, 1983, is generally taxable if the obligation is federally guaranteed, but there are exceptions allowing tax exemptions for obligations guaranteed by the Federal Housing Administration, Department of Veterans Affairs, Bonneville Power Authority, Federal Home Loan Mortgage Corporation, Federal National Mortgage Association, Government National Mortgage Corporation, Resolution Funding Corporation, and Student Loan Marketing Association.

**Mortgage revenue bonds.** Interest on bonds issued by a state or local government after April 24, 1979, may not be tax exempt if funds raised by the bonds are used to finance home mortgages. There are exceptions for certain qualified mortgage bonds and veterans' bonds. Check on the tax-exempt status of mortgage bonds with the issuing authority.

**Private activity bonds.** Generally, a private activity bond is any bond where more than 10% of the issue's proceeds are used by a private business whose property secures the issue, or if at least 5% of the proceeds (or $5 million if less) are used for loans to parties other than governmental units. Interest on such bonds is generally taxable, but there are exceptions *(4.24)*. Check on the tax status of the bonds with the issuing authority.

## 4.26 Tax-Exempt Bonds Bought at a Discount

Original issue discount (OID) on tax-exempt obligations is not taxable, and on a sale or redemption, gain attributed to OID is tax exempt. Gain attributed to market discount is capital gain or ordinary income depending on whether the bond was purchased before May 1, 1993, or on or after that date; *see* below.

**Original issue discount tax-exempt bond.** This arises when a bond is issued for a price less than the face amount of the bond. The discount is considered tax-exempt interest. Thus, if you are the original buyer and hold the bond to maturity, the entire amount of the discount is tax free. On a disposition of a tax-exempt bond issued after September 3, 1982, and acquired after March 1, 1984, you must add to basis accrued OID before determining gain or loss. OID must generally be accrued using a constant yield method; *see* IRS Publication 1212.

**Market discount tax-exempts.** A market discount arises when a bond originally issued at not less than par is bought at below par because its market value has declined. If before May 1, 1993, you bought at a market discount a tax-exempt bond which you sell for a price exceeding your purchase price, the excess is capital gain. If the bond was held long term, the gain is long term. A redemption of the bond at a price exceeding your purchase price is similarly treated.

However, for market discount tax-exempt bonds purchased after April 30, 1993, market discount is treated as ordinary income *(4.20)*. If you do not report the accrued market discount as taxable interest income each year you own the bond, any gain when you sell the bond is treated as interest income to the extent of the market discount *(4.20)*.

**Stripped tax-exempt obligations.** OID is not currently taxed on a stripped tax-exempt bond or stripped coupon from the bond if you bought it before June 11, 1987. However, for any stripped bond or coupon you bought or sold after October 22, 1986, OID must be accrued and added to basis for purposes of figuring gain or loss on a disposition. Furthermore, if you bought the stripped bond or coupon after June 10, 1987, part of the OID may be taxable; *see* Publication 1212 for figuring the tax-free portion.

## 4.27 Treasury Bills, Notes, and Bonds

Interest on securities issued by the federal government is fully taxable on your federal return. However, interest on federal obligations is not subject to state or local income taxes. Interest on Treasury bills, notes, and bonds is reported on Form 1099-INT.

**Treasury bonds and notes.** Treasury notes have maturities of two, three, five, seven or 10 years. Treasury bonds have maturities of 30 years. Interest on notes and bonds is paid every six months and is taxable when received on your federal return. Treasury bonds and notes are capital assets; gain or loss on their sale, exchange, or redemption is reported as capital gain or loss on Form 8949 and Schedule D *(Chapter 5)*. If you purchased a federal obligation below par (at a discount), *see 4.19* for the rules on reporting original issue discount. If you purchased a Treasury bond or note above par (at a premium), you may elect to amortize the premium *(4.17)*. If you do not elect to amortize and you hold the bond or note to maturity, you have a capital loss.

**Treasury inflation-protected securities (TIPS).** These pay interest semiannually at a fixed rate on a principal amount that is adjusted to take into account inflation or deflation. The interest is taxable when received and any increase in the inflation-adjusted principal amount while you hold the bond must be reported as original issue discount (OID) *(4.19)*. Your basis in the bond is increased by the OID included in income. On a sale or redemption before maturity, any gain is generally capital gain, but if there was an intention to call before maturity, gain is ordinary income to the extent of the previously unreported OID *(4.23)*.

**Treasury bills.** These are short-term U.S. obligations with maturities of four weeks, 13 weeks, 26 weeks, or 52 weeks. On a bill held to maturity, you report as interest income the difference between the discounted price and the amount you receive on a redemption of the bills at maturity.

Treasury bills are capital assets and a loss on a disposition before maturity is taxed as a capital loss. If you are a cash-basis taxpayer and have a gain on a sale or exchange, ordinary income is realized up to the amount of the ratable share of the discount received when you bought the obligation. This amount is treated as interest income and is figured as follows:

$$\frac{\text{Days T-bill was held}}{\text{Days from acquisition to maturity}} \times \text{Acquisition discount (redemption value at maturity } minus \text{ your cost)}$$

Any gain over this amount is capital gain; *see* the Example below. Instead of using the above fractional computation for figuring the ordinary income portion of the gain, an election may be made to apply the constant yield method. This method follows the OID computation rules shown in IRS Publication 1212 for obligations issued after 1984, except that the acquisition cost of the Treasury bill would be treated as the issue price in applying the Publication 1212 formula.

> **EXAMPLE**
>
> You buy at original issue a 26-week $10,000 Treasury bill (182-day maturity) for $9,900. You sell it 95 days later for $9,950. Your entire $50 gain ($9,950 – $9,900) is taxed as interest income as it is less than the $52 treated as interest income under the ratable daily formula:
>
> $$\frac{\text{95 days held}}{\text{182 days from acquisition to maturity}} \times \text{\$100 discount} = \text{\$52}$$

Accrual-basis taxpayers and dealers who are required to currently report the acquisition discount element of Treasury bills using either the ratable accrual method or the constant yield method *(4.20)* do not apply the above formula on a sale before maturity. In figuring gain or loss, the discount included as income is added to basis.

**Interest deduction limitation.** Interest incurred on loans used to buy Treasury bills is deductible by a cash-basis investor only to the extent that interest expenses exceed the following: (1) the portion of the acquisition discount allocated to the days you held the bond during the year; and (2) the portion of interest not taxable for the year under your method of accounting. The deferred interest expense is deductible in the year the bill is disposed of. If an election is made to report the acquisition discount as current income under the rules for governmental obligations *(4.21)*, the interest expense may also be deducted currently. The election applies to all future acquisitions.

## 4.28    Interest on United States Savings Bonds

Savings Bond Tables: The *e-Supplement* at www.*jklasser.com* will contain redemption tables showing the 2018 year-end values of Series EE bonds and Series I bonds.

**EE Bonds.** Series EE bonds may be cashed for what you paid for them plus an increase in their value over their 30-year maturity period. See the discussion of the interest accrual and redemption rules for U.S. Savings Bonds *(30.12)*.

The increase in redemption value is taxable as interest, but you do not have to report the increase in value each year on your federal return. You may defer *(4.29)* the interest income until the year in which you cash the bond or the year in which the bond finally matures, whichever is earlier. But if you want, you may report the annual increase by merely including it on your tax return. If you use the accrual method of reporting, you must include the interest each year as it accrues. Savings bond interest is not subject to state or local taxes.

 *Planning Reminder*

**Tax Deferral: T-Bill Maturing Next Year**

If you are a cash-basis taxpayer, you may postpone the tax on Treasury bill interest by selecting a Treasury bill maturing next year. Income is not recognized until the date on which the Treasury bill is paid at maturity, unless it has been sold or otherwise disposed of earlier.

If you initially choose to defer the reporting of interest and later want to switch to annual reporting, you may do so. You may also change from the annual reporting method to the deferral method. *See 4.2*9 for rules on changing reporting methods.

**Series I bonds.** "I bonds" are inflation-indexed bonds issued at face amount *(30.13)*. As with EE bonds, you may defer the interest income (the increase in redemption value each year is interest) until the year in which the bond is redeemed or matures in 30 years, whichever is earlier *(4.29)*.

**Education funding.** If you buy EE or I bonds to pay for educational expenses and you defer the reporting of interest *(4.29)*, you may be able to exclude the accumulated interest from income when you redeem the bonds *(33.4)*.

**Bonds registered only in name of child.** Interest on U.S. savings bonds bought for and registered in the name of a child will be taxed to the child, even if the parent paid for the bonds and is named as beneficiary. Unless an election is made to report the increases in redemption value annually, the accumulated interest will be taxable to the child in the year he or she redeems the bond, or if earlier, when the bond finally matures. The kiddie tax *(24.2)* may apply to a portion of the annually reported interest or to interest on redeemed bonds. For example, if a child under age 18 has 2018 investment income over $2,100, the excess is taxed at the tax rates applicable to trusts and estates *(24.2)*. To avoid kiddie tax, savings bond interest may be deferred *(4.29)*.

**Bonds must be reissued to make gift.** Assume you have bought I or EE bonds and had them registered in joint names of yourself and your daughter. The law of your state provides that jointly owned property may be transferred to a co-owner by delivery or possession. You deliver the bonds to your daughter and tell her they now belong to her alone. According to Treasury regulations, this is not a valid gift of the bonds. The bonds must be surrendered and reissued in your daughter's name. For the year of reissue, you must include in your income all of the interest earned on the bonds other than interest you previously reported.

If you do not have the bonds reissued and you die, the bonds are taxable to your estate. Ownership of the bonds is a matter of contract between the United States and the bond purchaser. The bonds are nontransferable. A valid gift cannot be accomplished by manual delivery to a donee unless the bonds also are surrendered and registered in the donee's name in accordance with Treasury regulations.

**Series E bonds.** There are no Series E bonds still earning interest. The last E bonds, those issued in June 1980, reached final maturity in June 2010, 30 years from the date of issue.

**Series HH.** These bonds were available after 1979 and before September 1, 2004, in exchange for E or EE bonds, or for Freedom Shares. They were issued at face value and pay semiannual interest that is taxable when received. They mature in 20 years.

**Series H.** These bonds were available before 1980 and they reached final maturity 30 years later. If you obtained Series H bonds in an exchange for Series E bonds, and you did not report the E bond interest annually, the accumulated interest on the E bonds became taxable when the H bonds were redeemed or, if earlier, when the H bonds reached final maturity 30 years from issue.

## 4.29 Deferring United States Savings Bond Interest

You do not have to make a special election on your tax return in order to defer the interest on Series EE or I savings bonds. You may simply postpone reporting the interest until the year you redeem the bond or the year in which it reaches final maturity, whichever is earlier. If you choose to defer the interest, you may decide in a later year to begin reporting the increase in redemption value each year as interest, but this election applies to all the EE and I bonds you own. You may also switch from annual reporting to the deferral method. You must use the same method—deferral or annual reporting—for all of your EE and I bonds. These options are discussed in this section.

*Planning Reminder*

**Election for Children Not Subject to Kiddie Tax**

If your child has net investment income under the annual threshold ($2,100 for 2018) for the kiddie tax *(24.2)*, making the election to report the interest annually may be advisable. For example, a dependent child may claim a standard deduction for 2018 of at least $1,050 *(13.5)*. If the election to report the savings bond interest currently was made for 2018, up to $1,050 of the interest would be offset by the standard deduction, assuming the child had no other income.

*Filing Tip*

**Form 1099-INT When Savings Bond Is Cashed**

When you cash in an EE or I bond, you receive Form 1099-INT that lists as interest the difference between the amount received and the amount paid for the bond. The form may show more taxable interest than you are required to report because you have regularly reported the interest or a prior owner reported the interest. Report the full amount shown on Form 1099-INT on Schedule B if you file Form 1040, along with your other interest income. Enter a subtotal of the total interest and then, on a separate line, reduce the subtotal by the savings bond interest that was previously reported and identify the reduction as "Previously Reported U.S. Savings Bond Interest." The interest is exempt from state and local taxes.

**Changing from deferral to annual reporting.** If you have deferred reporting of interest (the annual increases in redemption value) and want to change to annual reporting starting with your 2018 return, you must report on your 2018 return all interest accrued through 2018 on all your EE and I bonds. Then, starting in 2019, you report the interest accruing each year on all of your bonds, including bonds you acquired after the 2018 election. Suppose you do not change from the deferral method to the annual method on your 2018 return and later wish you had. If the due date of the return has passed, it is too late to make the election. You may not file an amended return for 2018 to report the accrued interest. You have to wait until next year's return to make the election.

**Changing from annual reporting to deferral.** If you have been reporting annual increases in redemption value as interest income, you may change your method and elect to defer interest reporting until the bonds mature or are redeemed. You make the election by attaching a statement to your federal income tax return for the year of the change; *see* IRS Publication 550 for details.

**Co-Owners.** How to report interest on a Series EE or I bond depends on how it was bought or issued:

1. You paid for the entire bond: Either you or the co-owner may redeem it. You are taxed on all the interest, even though the co-owner cashes the bond and you receive no proceeds. If the other co-owner does cash in the bond, he or she will receive a Form 1099-INT reporting the accumulated interest. However, since that interest is taxable to you, the co-owner should give you a nominee Form 1099-INT, as explained in the rules for joint accounts in *4.12*.

2. You paid for only part of the bond: Either of you may redeem it. You are taxed on that part of the interest which is in proportion to your share of the purchase price. This is so even though you do not receive the proceeds.

3. You paid for part of the bond, and then had it reissued in another's name. You pay tax only on the interest accrued while you held the bond. The new co-owner picks up his or her share of the interest accruing afterwards.

**Changing the form of registration.** Changing the form of registration of an I or EE bond may result in tax. Assume you use your own funds to purchase a bond issued in your name, payable on your death to your son. Later, at your request, a new bond is issued in your son's name only. The increased value of the original bond up to the date it was redeemed and reissued in your son's name is taxed to you as interest income.

As shown in the Examples below, certain changes in registration do not result in an immediate tax.

**Transfer to a spouse.** If you have been deferring interest on U.S. Savings Bonds, and then you transfer them to your spouse or ex-spouse as part of a divorce-related property settlement, you will be taxed on the interest deferred before the transfer date *(6.7)*.

**Transfer to a trust.** If you transfer U.S. Savings Bonds to a trust giving up all rights of ownership, you are taxed on the accumulated interest to date of transfer. If, however, you are considered to be the owner of the trust and the interest earned before and after the transfer is taxable to you, you may continue to defer reporting the interest.

**Transfer to a charity.** Tax on the accumulated interest is not avoided by having the bonds reissued to a philanthropy. The IRS held that by having the bonds reissued in the philanthropy's name, the owner realized taxable income on the accumulated bond interest.

**Transfer of savings bond at death.** If an owner does not report the bond interest annually and dies before redeeming the bond, the income tax liability on the interest accumulated during the deceased's lifetime becomes the liability of the person who acquires the bond, unless an election is made to report the accrued interest in the decedent's final income tax return *(1.14)*. If the election is not made on the decedent's final return, the new owner may choose to report the accumulated interest annually, or defer reporting it until the bond is redeemed or reaches final maturity, whichever is earlier. If the election is made on the decedent's final return, the new owner is taxable only on interest earned after the date of death.

 *Caution*

**E Bonds and Certain EE Bonds No Longer Earn Interest**

All E bonds have reached final maturity and no longer earn interest. EE bonds stop earning interest when they reach final maturity, 30 years from their issue date *(30.12)*. All deferred interest is taxable in the year of final maturity.

 *Filing Tip*

**Deduction for Estate Tax Paid on Interest**

Where an estate tax has been paid on bond interest accrued during the owner's lifetime, the new bondholder may claim the estate tax as a miscellaneous itemized deduction in the year that he or she pays tax on the accumulated interest. The deduction is not subject to the 2% of adjusted gross income floor *(11.17)*.

## 4.30 Minimum Interest Rules

The law requires a minimum rate of interest to be charged on loan transactions unless a specific exception covers the transaction. Where minimum interest is not charged, the law imputes interest as if the parties agreed to the charge.

The rules are complicated and have been subject to several revisions. There are different minimum interest rates and reporting rules depending on the nature of the transaction. The following discussion provides the important details for understanding the rules. For specific cases and computations, we suggest that you consult IRS regulations for details not covered in this book.

There are two broad classes of transactions:

**Loans.** These are generally covered by Internal Revenue Code Section 7872. Below-market or low-rate interest loans are discussed in *4.31*.

**Seller-financed sales of property.** These are covered by either Internal Revenue Code Section 1274 or Section 483. Seller-financed sales are discussed in *4.32*. If parties fail to charge the minimum required interest rate, the same minimum rate is imputed by law.

## 4.31 Interest-Free or Below-Market-Interest Loans

For many years, the IRS tried to tax interest-free or below-market-interest loans. However, court decisions supported taxpayers who argued that such loans did not result in taxable income or gifts. To reverse these decisions, the IRS convinced Congress to pass a law imposing tax on interest-free or low-interest loans made by individuals and businesses. If you make an interest-free or low-interest loan to a relative, you may have to report imputed interest income that you do not actually receive ("phantom income"), and also be subject to gift tax, although there are exceptions that shield many gift loans from the imputed interest rules; *see* below for the $10,000 and $100,000 gift loan exceptions.

**How the imputed interest rules work.** If interest at least equal to the applicable federal rate set by the IRS is not charged, the law generally treats a below-market-interest loan as two transactions:

1. The law assumes that the lender has transferred to the borrower an amount equal to the "foregone" interest element of the loan. In the case of a loan between individuals, such as a parent and child, the lender is subject to gift tax on this element; in the case of a stockholder borrowing from a company, the element is a taxable dividend; in the case of a loan made to an employee, it is taxable pay.

   Note: For gift tax purposes *(39.2)*, a term loan is treated as if the lender gave the borrower the excess of the amount of the loan over the present value of payments due during the loan term. Demand loans are treated as if the lender gave the borrower annually the amount of the foregone interest.

2. The law assumes that imputed interest equal to the applicable federal rate is paid by the borrower to the lender, who must report it as interest income. In other words, the lender must report as income an amount (the imputed interest) that is not actually received. The borrower may be able to claim a deduction for the interest if the loan is used to buy a home and the loan is secured by the residence *(15.1)*, or the loan is used to buy investment property *(15.10)*.

With gift loans and demand loans between individuals, the above transfers between the lender and borrower are treated as made on the last day of the borrower's taxable year.

An IRS "blended annual rate" may be used to figure the imputed interest on certain demand loans; *see* below.

**Blended annual rate for demand loans.** Where a demand loan is in effect for the entire calendar year, a "blended annual rate" issued by the IRS to simplify reporting may be used to compute the imputed interest. For 2018, the blended rate is 2.03% (Revenue Ruling 2018-19). The blended rate may be used for a gift loan to an individual or for a business loan, such as an interest-free loan to an employee, so long as it is payable on demand and is of a fixed principal amount that remains outstanding for the entire calendar year. If the loan was not outstanding for the entire year or if the loan balance fluctuated, the regular imputed interest rules apply, as the blended rate is not available.

**Charging the applicable federal rate avoids the imputed interest rules.** Gift loans qualifying for the $10,000 and $100,000 exceptions (below) are not subject to imputed interest rules. For other loans, the rules imputing income to you as the lender may be avoided by charging interest at least equal to the applicable federal rate. Applicable federal rates are set by the IRS monthly and published in the Internal Revenue Bulletin; you can also get the rates from your local IRS office. For a term loan, the applicable rate is the one in effect as of the day on which the loan is made, compounded semiannually. The short-term rate applies to loans of three years or less; the mid-term rate to loans over three and up to nine years; the long-term rate applies to loans over nine years. For a demand loan, the applicable federal rate is the short-term rate in effect at the start of each semiannual period (January and July).

**Different computations for different types of loans.** There are two general classes of loans: (1) Gift loans, whether term or demand, and nongift demand loans, and (2) nongift term loans.

The distinction is important for figuring and reporting imputed interest. For example, in the case of nongift term loans, the imputed interest element is treated as original issue discount *(4.19)*.

**Gift loans and nongift loans payable on demand.** As a lender, you are taxable on the "foregone interest," that is, the interest that you would have received had you charged interest at the applicable federal rate over any interest actually charged. The borrower may be able to claim an interest deduction if the funds are used to buy investment property *(15.10)*.

**Nongift term loans.** A term loan is any loan not payable on demand. As a lender of a nongift term loan, you are taxable on any excess of the loan principal over the present value of all payments due under the loan. The excess is treated as original issue (OID) which you report annually as interest income *(4.19)*.

**Reporting imputed interest.** Imputed interest is generally treated as transferred by the lender to the borrower and retransferred by the borrower to the lender on December 31 in the calendar year of imputation and is reported under the regular accounting method of the borrower and lender.

> **EXAMPLE**
>
> On January 1, 2018, Jones Company makes a $200,000 interest-free demand loan to Frank, an executive. The loan remains outstanding for the entire 2018 calendar year. Jones Company has a taxable year ending September 30. Frank is a calendar year taxpayer. For 2018 the imputed compensation payment to Frank and the imputed interest payment to the corporation are treated as made on December 31, 2018.

## Certain Loans Are Exempt From Imputed Interest Rules

**The $10,000 gift loan exception.** In the case of a gift loan to an individual, no interest is imputed to any day on which the aggregate outstanding amount of all loans between the parties is $10,000 or less, provided the loan is not attributed to the purchase or carrying of income-producing assets. If the exception applies, there are no income tax or gift tax consequences to the loan.

*Planning Reminder*

**Gift Loans up to $100,000**

If you give a child or other individual an interest-free or below-market-interest loan, such as to buy a home or start a business, the amount of interest imputed to you may be limited or completely avoided provided (1) the total outstanding loan balance owed to you by the borrower at all times during the year does not exceed $100,000, and (2) avoidance of federal tax is not a principal purpose of the interest arrangement.

If the above tests are met, and the borrower's net investment income is $1,000 or less, there is no imputed interest. The imputed amount cannot exceed the net investment income and net investment income of $1,000 or less is treated as zero.

**The $100,000 gift loan exception.** No interest is imputed on an interest-free or low-interest loan to an individual of up to $100,000 if the borrower's net investment income is $1,000 or less. Under the exception, imputed interest cannot exceed the borrower's net investment income, and net investment income of $1,000 or less is treated as zero; *see* the following Example. The exception applies only if avoiding federal tax is not a main purpose of the interest arrangement.

> **EXAMPLE**
>
> On January 1, 2018, you make a $100,000 interest-free loan to your son, payable on demand, which he uses for a down payment on a home. This is the only outstanding loan between you and your son. Your son's net investment income for 2018 is $650. Since the loan does not exceed $100,000, and your son's net investment income does not exceed $1,000, you do not have to report the "foregone interest" as interest income. Under the $100,000 gift loan exception, imputed interest is limited to the borrower's net investment income and net investment income of $1,000 or less is treated as zero.
>
> If your son's net investment income were $2,650 instead of $650, you would have to report the foregone interest as imputed interest income. Using the IRS blended annual rate for 2018 of 2.03%, the imputed interest would be $2,030 ($100,000 × 2.03%), which you must report as income since it is well below your son's net investment income of $2,650.
>
> For gift tax purposes, the foregone interest is a taxable gift. Using the IRS blended annual rate, the foregone interest of $2,030 ($100,000 × 2.03%) is a taxable gift, but if this was your only gift to your son in 2018, there would be no gift tax, and you would not have to file a gift tax return because of the annual gift tax exclusion of $15,000 per donee *(39.2)*.

**Exceptions for compensation-related loans.** For compensation-related and corporate-shareholder loans, the imputed interest rules do not apply to any day on which the total amount of outstanding loans between the parties is $10,000 or less, provided the principal purpose of the loan is not tax avoidance. Certain low-interest loans given to employees by employers to buy a new residence in a new job location are exempt from the imputed interest requirements.

**Exception for loans to continuing care facilities.** If you pay a refundable fee when moving into a qualified continuing care facility under a continuing care contract (as defined in Code Section 7872 (h)), the fee is not treated as a "loan" subject to the imputed interest rules if you or your spouse is age 62 or older at the end of the year.

## 4.32 Minimum Interest on Seller-Financed Sales

The law requires minimum interest charges for seller-financed sales. If the minimum rate is not charged, the IRS imputes interest at the minimum applicable rate requiring both buyer and seller to treat part of the purchase price as interest even though it is not called interest in the sales contract. Generally, interest at the applicable federal rate (AFR) must be charged; *see* the chart at the end of this section for minimum required rates. For example, investment property is sold on the installment basis for $100,000 and the parties fail to charge adequate interest. Assume the IRS imputes interest of $5,000. For tax purposes, $95,000 is allocated to the sale of the property and the principal amount of the debt; the balance is imputed interest of $5,000, taxable to the seller and deductible by the buyer if allowed under the rules of *Chapter 15*.

**Two statute classes.** The minimum or imputed interest rules are covered by two Internal Revenue Code statutes: Sections 1274 and 483. Under both, the same minimum interest rates apply but the timing of interest reporting is different, as discussed below.

Section 483 applies to any payment due more than six months after the date of sale under a contract which calls for some or all payments more than one year after the date of sale. If the sales price cannot exceed $3,000, Section 483 does not apply. Transactions within Section 483 are sales or exchanges of: (1) principal residences; (2) any property if total payments, including interest and any other consideration to be received by the seller, cannot exceed $250,000; (3) farms if the total price is $1 million or less; and (4) sales of land between family members to the extent the aggregate sales price of all sales between the same parties in the same year is $500,000 or less.

If the selling price exceeds the respective $250,000, $1 million, or $500,000 amount listed in (2) through (4) above, the sale is subject to Section 1274 reporting rules provided some or all payments are due more than six months after the date of sale. Section 1274 also applies to all other transactions where neither the debt instrument nor the property being sold is publicly traded as long as some payments are deferred more than six months.

**Timing of interest reporting.** One important practical difference between the two statutes covering minimum interest involves the timing of the reporting and deducting of interest.

Under Section 483, a seller and lender use their regular reporting method for imputed interest. For a cash-basis seller, interest is taxed when received; a cash-basis buyer deducts interest when paid if a deduction is allowable. However, if too much interest is allocated to a payment period, the excess interest is treated as prepaid interest, and the deduction is postponed to the year or years interest is earned. Section 483 also describes imputed interest as unstated interest.

Under Section 1274, the interest element is generally reported by both buyer and seller according to the OID accrual rules, even if they otherwise report on the cash basis. Where the seller financing is below an annual threshold ($4,165,300 for a 2018 sale on or after April 30, 2018, or $4,167,600 if before April 30, 2018), the parties can elect the cash method to report the interest regardless of the OID and accrual rules if: (1) the seller-lender is on a cash-basis method and is not a dealer of the property sold and (2) the seller and buyer jointly elect to use the cash method. The cash-basis election binds any cash-basis successor of the buyer or seller. If the lender transfers his interest to an accrual-basis taxpayer, the election no longer applies; interest is thereafter taxed under the accrual method rules. The OID rules also do not apply to a cash basis buyer of personal-use property; here, the cash basis debtor deducts only payments of interest required by the contract, assuming a deduction is allowed under the home mortgage rules discussed in *Chapter 15*.

**Figuring applicable federal rate (AFR).** There is no imputed interest if the sales contract provides for interest that is at least equal to the AFR. See *Table 4-1* below for determining the AFR.

**Assumptions of loans.** The imputed interest rules of Sections 1274 and 483 do not generally apply to debt instruments assumed as part of a sale or exchange, or if the property is taken subject to the debt, provided that neither the terms of the debt instrument nor the nature of the transactions are changed.

*Important:* In planning deferred or installment sales, review Treasury regulations to the Internal Revenue Code Sections 483 and 1274 for further examples and details.

 *Caution*

**Buyer's Personal-Use Property**

If adequate interest is not charged on an installment sale of personal-use property, such as a residence to be used by the buyer, imputed interest rules do not apply to the buyer. Thus, the buyer may not deduct the imputed interest. The buyer's deduction is limited to the payment of interest stated in the contract if a deduction is allowed under the home mortgage interest rules in *Chapter 15*.

## Table 4-1    Minimum Interest Rate for Seller Financing

| Type— | Description— |
|---|---|
| Applicable federal rates | The IRS determines the AFR rates which are published at the beginning of each month in the Internal Revenue Bulletin. There are three AFR rates depending on the length of the contract: <br><br> • Short-term AFR—A term of three years or less. <br><br> • Mid-term AFR—A term of over three years but not over nine years. <br><br> • Long-term AFR—A term of over nine years. <br><br> The imputed interest rules do not apply if the interest rate provided for in the sales contract is at least the lesser of (1) the lowest AFR in effect during the three-month period ending with the month in which a binding written sales contract is entered into, or (2) the lowest AFR in effect during the three-month period ending with the month of sale. <br><br> If insufficient interest is charged, the total unstated interest is allocated to payments under an OID computation. |
| 9% safe harbor rate | If seller financing does not exceed an annual limit, the minimum required interest is the lower of 9% compounded semiannually and the applicable federal rate (AFR). For sales in 2018, the seller financing limit is $5,831,500, for sales on or after April 30, 2018, or $5,834,700 for sales before April 30, 2018. The amount of seller financing is the stated principal amount under the contract. If the seller-financed amount exceeds the annual limit, the minimum interest rate is 100% of the AFR. The limit for the 9% safe harbor is indexed annually for inflation. <br><br> The 9% safe harbor provides a benefit only if it is less than the AFR, but in recent years the AFR has been much lower than 9%. Thus, until prevailing interest rates substantially increase, charging interest at the AFR will be sufficient to avoid application of the minimum interest rules. <br><br> IRS regulations allow the parties to use an interest rate lower than the AFR if it is shown that the borrower could obtain a loan on an arm's-length basis at lower interest. |
| Seller-financed sale-leaseback transactions | Interest equal to 110% of AFR must be charged. |
| Sales of land between family members | To the extent that the sales price does not exceed $500,000 during a calendar year, the minimum required interest rate is the lower of 6% compounded semiannually and the applicable federal rate (AFR). As with the 9% safe harbor discussed above, the 6% rate safe harbor provides a benefit only if it is less than the AFR, which has been well below 6% in recent years. To prevent multiple sales from being used to avoid the $500,000 limit, the $500,000 ceiling applies to all land sales between family members during the same year. To the extent that the $500,000 sales price limit is exceeded, the general 9% or 100% of AFR rules apply. |

# CHAPTER 5

# Reporting Property Sales

Long-term capital gains are generally taxed at lower rates than those imposed on ordinary income. Depending on your taxable income, some or all of your long-term capital gains may qualify for a 0% rate and thus completely avoid tax *(5.3)*. If the 0% rate does not apply, your long-term gains are subject to maximum rates of 15% or 20% depending on your income, or, for certain assets, a maximum rate of 25% or 28% *(5.3)*, but regular tax rates apply if they result in a lower tax than the maximum rate.

If you sell property and will receive payments in a year (or years) after the year of sale, you may report the sale as an installment sale on Form 6252 and spread the tax on your gain over the installment period *(5.21)*.

Sales of business assets and depreciable rental property are reported on Form 4797. Most assets used in a business are considered Section 1231 assets, and capital gain or ordinary loss treatment may apply depending upon the result of a netting computation made on Form 4797 for all such assets sold during the year *(44.8)*.

Special types of sale situations are detailed in other chapters.

*See Chapter 29* for the exclusion of gain on the sale of a principal residence.

*See Chapter 32* for figuring gain or loss on the sale of mutual fund shares.

*See Chapter 6* for tax-free exchanges of property.

*See Chapter 30* for sales of stock dividends, stock rights, wash sales, short sales, and sales by traders in securities.

## 5.1 General Tax Rules for Property Sales

1. Property is classified according to its nature and your purpose for holding it; *see* 5.2, *Table 5-1*, and holding period rules at 5.3 and 5.9–5.12.

2. Sales of capital assets must generally be reported on Form 8949, with Part I used for short-term gains and losses and Part II for long-term gains and losses *(5.8)*. However, in some cases you do not need Form 8949 and may report your transactions directly on Schedule D; *see* 5.8. If you file Form 8949, you must check a box to indicate whether you received a Form 1099-B from a broker showing your basis in securities sold. If you are reporting more than one sale of securities, you may need to file multiple Forms 8949 depending on how basis was reported on Form 1099-B. Total amounts for sales price and basis are transferred from Form 8949 to Schedule D of Form 1040. On Schedule D you net short-term and long-term transactions to figure your net gain or loss for the year and, if you have net long-term gain, you are directed to the appropriate IRS worksheet for computing your tax liability taking into account the favorable capital gain rates, as discussed in the next paragraph. Filing Form 8949 or Schedule D may not be necessary if your only capital gains are from a mutual fund or REIT *(32.8)*.

3. If you sell property at a gain, the applicable tax rate depends on the classification of the property (see *Table 5-1*) and, in the case of capital assets, the period you held the property before sale. A capital gain is long term if you held the asset for more than one year, short-term if you held it for one year or less. Short-term capital gains that are not offset by short- or long-term losses are subject to regular income tax rates.

   If you have net capital gain for the year (net long-term gain over net short-term loss if any), your gains are subject to favorable capital gain rates. Depending on your taxable income and the amount and source of your long-term gains, the gains may be completely tax free under the 0% rate or subject to a maximum rate of 15%, 20%, 25%, or 28% where that maximum rate is less than the otherwise applicable regular tax rate *(5.3)*.

   If you do not have 28% rate gains or unrecaptured Section 1250 gains subject to a maximum 25% rate, you compute your tax liability taking into account the 0%, 15% and 20% capital gain rates on the Qualified Dividends and Capital Gain Tax Worksheet in the Form 1040 instructions. If you have either 28% gain or unrecaptured Section 1250 gain, use the Schedule D Tax Worksheet in the Schedule D instructions to compute your tax liability.

4. Loss deductions are allowed on the sale of investment and business property but losses are not deductible on the sale of personal assets; *see Table 5-1*. Capital loss deductions in excess of capital gains are limited to $3,000 annually, $1,500 if married filing separately; *see* the details on the capital loss limitations later in this Chapter (5.4 – 5.5).

*Caution*

**Loss on Sale of Personal-Use Assets**

You may not deduct a capital loss on the sale of property held for personal use, such as a car or vacation home. The loss is not deductible.

Losses on the sale of property held for investment, such as stock or mutual fund shares, are fully deductible against capital gains but any excess loss is subject to the $3,000 limit *(5.4)*.

## 5.2 How Property Sales Are Classified and Taxed

The tax treatment of gains and losses is not the same for all types of property sales. Tax reporting generally depends on your purpose in holding the property, as shown in *Table 5-1*.

**When capital gain or loss treatment does not apply.** Certain sales do not qualify for capital gain or loss treatment. Business inventory and property held for sale to customers are not capital assets. Depreciable business and rental property are not capital assets, but you may still realize capital gain after following a netting computation for Section 1231 assets *(44.8)*.

Although assets held for personal use, such as a car or home, are technically capital assets, you may not deduct a capital loss on their sale.

Certain other assets held for investment or personal use are excluded by law from the capital asset category. These include copyrights, literary or musical compositions, letters, memoranda, or similar property that: (1) you created by your personal efforts or (2) you acquired as a gift from the person who created the property or for whom the property was prepared or produced.

Although musical compositions and copyrights in musical works that you personally created (or you acquired as a gift from the creator) are generally excluded from the capital asset category, you can make an election on a timely filed (including extensions) Form 8949 for the year the musical composition or copyright is sold to treat the sale as a sale of a capital asset.

**Table 5-1   Capital or Ordinary Gains and Losses From Sales and Exchanges of Property**

| If you sell— | Your gain is— | Your loss is— | Reported on— |
|---|---|---|---|
| Stocks, mutual funds, bonds, land, art, gems, stamps, and coins held for investment are capital assets. | Capital gain. Holding period determines short-term or long-term gain treatment (5.3). Security traders may report ordinary income and loss under a mark-to-market election (30.15). | Capital loss. Capital losses are deductible from capital gains with only $3,000 of any excess deductible from ordinary income, $1,500 if married filing separately (5.4). | Form 8949 and Schedule D (5.8). However, if the only amounts you have to report on these forms are mutual fund capital gain distributions, then you may report the distributions directly on Form 1040A or Form 1040 (Table 32-1, "Reporting Mutual Fund Distributions for 2018," in Chapter 32). Form 4797 for gains and losses of a trader in securities who makes the mark-to-market election (30.15). |
| Business inventory held for sale to customers. Also, accounts or notes receivable acquired in the ordinary course of business or from the sale of inventory or property held for sale to customers, or acquired for services as an employee. | Ordinary income. Such property is excluded by law from the definition of capital assets. | Ordinary loss. Ordinary loss is not subject to the $3,000 deduction limit imposed on capital losses. However, passive loss restrictions, discussed in Chapter 10, may defer the time when certain ordinary losses are deductible. | Schedule C if self-employed; Schedule F if a farmer; Form 1065 for a business operated as a partnership; Form 1120 or 1120S for an incorporated business. |
| Depreciable residential rental property or trucks, autos, computers, machinery, fixtures, or equipment used in your business. | Capital gain or ordinary income. Section 1231 determines whether gain is taxable as ordinary income or capital gain (44.8). Where an asset such as an auto or residence is used partly for personal purposes and partly for business or rental purposes, the asset is treated as two separate assets for purposes of figuring gain or loss (44.9). | Ordinary loss if there is a net Section 1231 loss (44.8). However, if you are considered to be an investor in a passive activity, see 10.12 and 10.13. | Form 4797 for Section 1231 transactions. |
| Personal residence, car, jewelry, furniture, art objects, and coin or stamp collection held for personal use. | Capital gain. See the holding period rules that determine short-term or long-term gain treatment and the preferential tax rates applied to net long-term capital gains (5.3). Where an asset such as an auto or residence is used partly for personal purposes and partly for business or rental purposes, the asset is treated as two separate assets for purposes of figuring gain or loss (44.9). All or part of a profit from a sale of a principal residence may be excludable from income; see Chapter 29. | Not deductible. Losses on sales of assets held for personal use are not deductible although profits are taxable. | Form 8949 and Schedule D |

*Filing Tip*

**Holding Periods for Capital Assets**

The time you own a capital asset determines short-term or long-term treatment when you sell. The short-term holding period is a year or less, the long-term period more than one year *(5.9–5.12)*.

Also excluded from the capital asset category are letters, memoranda, or similar property prepared or produced for you by someone else. U.S. government publications obtained from the government for free or for less than the normal sales price do not qualify as capital assets.

Under the Tax Cuts and Jobs Act, for dispositions after 2017, a patent, invention, model or design, secret formula or process is excluded from the capital asset category if held by: (1) the person whose personal efforts created the property, or (2) a person who acquired it as a gift from the person who created the property.

Stock is generally treated as a capital asset, but losses on Section 1244 stock of qualifying small businesses may be claimed as ordinary losses on Form 4797, rather than on Schedule D as capital losses, which are subject to the $3,000 deduction limit ($1,500 if married filing separately) *(30.11)*.

Traders in securities may elect to report their sales as ordinary income or loss rather than as capital gain or loss *(30.14)*.

**Small business/empowerment zone business stock exclusion.** Gains on the sale of qualifying small business stock held for more than five years may be excluded from income *(5.7)*.

**Deferral of gains reinvested in qualified Opportunity Zones.** The Tax Cuts and Jobs Act allows taxable gain from the sale of any property to be deferred if the gain is reinvested in a qualified Opportunity Zone within 180 days of the sale *(5.7)*.

**Like-kind exchanges of business or investment real property.** Exchanges of like-kind business or investment real estate are subject to special rules that allow gain to be deferred, generally until you sell the property received in the exchange *(6.1)*. When property received in a like-kind exchange is held until death, the unrecognized gain escapes income tax forever because the basis of property in the hands of an heir is generally the fair market value of the property at the date of death *(5.17)*. A loss on a like-kind exchange is not deductible.

**Stock redemption allocation to covenant not to compete.** If you sell company stock back to your employer and you are subject to a covenant not to compete with the company for a period of time, any portion of the purchase price for the stock that is allocated to the covenant in the contract is taxed to you as ordinary income and not capital gain.

## 5.3 Capital Gains Rates and Holding Periods

Form 8949 is used for reporting sales of capital assets. On Form 8949, you separate your sales into short-term and long-term categories. Assets held for one year or less are in the short-term category and assets held for more than one year are in the long-term category. The totals from Form 8949 are entered on Schedule D (Form 1040). See the Example in *5.8*, which includes filled-in samples of Form 8949 and Schedule D.

The computation of tax liability using the favorable long-term capital gain rates is not made directly on Schedule D, but on worksheets in the IRS instructions. Mutual fund and REIT investors may be able to apply the favorable rates on the "Qualified Dividends and Capital Gain Tax Worksheet" included in the Form 1040 instructions, without having to file Form 8949 or Schedule D (see *Table 32-1*, "Reporting Mutual Fund Distributions for 2018," in *Chapter 32*).

**Held for a year or less.** Details for sales of capital assets held for a year or less are reported in Part I of Form 8949 unless you are able to report them directly on Schedule D and you choose to do so. The total sales prices and total cost basis shown on Form 8949 for short-term transactions, along with any adjustments for such transactions, are transferred to Part I of Schedule D, where the net short-term gain or loss for the year is determined. A net short-term capital gain is subject to regular tax rates. On Part III of Schedule D, a net short-term loss from Part I offsets a net long-term gain, if any, from Part II of Schedule D. A net short-term loss in excess of net long-term gain is deductible up to the $3,000 capital loss limit *(5.4)*.

**Held for more than a year.** Details for sales of capital assets held for more than a year are reported in Part II of Form 8949, unless you are able to report them directly on Schedule D and you choose to do so. The total sales prices and total cost basis for all the long-term transactions shown on form 8949, along with any adjustments for such transactions, are transferred to Part II of Schedule D, where the net long-term gain or loss for the year is determined. A net long-term capital loss offsets a net short-term gain, if any, from Part I of Schedule D. If you have a net long-term capital gain on Part II and also a net short-term capital loss on Part I of Schedule D, the short-term loss offsets the net long-term gain. The offsets are made on Part III of Schedule D. If the net short-term loss exceeds the net long-term gain, the excess short-term loss is deductible up to the $3,000 capital loss limit *(5.4)*. If you have a net long-term gain in excess of a net short-term capital loss (if any), the excess is called net capital gain and it is this amount to which the favorable capital gain rates may apply, as discussed below.

## Reduced Rates on Net Capital Gain

Net capital gain is the excess of your net long-term capital gain over your net short-term capital loss. The net capital gain is subject to maximum tax rates that are generally lower than the rates that would apply if it were ordinary income. Qualified dividends *(4.2)* are subject to the same favorable rates as net capital gain. To get the benefit of the favorable rates for net capital gain and qualified dividends, you must compute your regular income tax liability on IRS worksheets.

If you have a net capital gain for 2018 that does not include a 28% rate gain or unrecaptured Section 1250 gain (see below), you should compute your 2018 regular tax liability on the "Qualified Dividends and Capital Gain Tax Worksheet" in the Form 1040 instructions. On the Worksheet, you take into account the favorable capital gain rates, as applicable, and the regular tax rates on the rest of your taxable income. The Worksheet must be used to figure your regular income tax liability instead of the regular IRS Tax Table *(22.2)* or Tax Computation Worksheet *(22.3)* in order to benefit from the maximum capital gain rates.

If you have a net capital gain that includes either a net 28% rate gain or unrecaptured Section 1250 gain, you must compute your regular income tax liability on the "Schedule D Tax Worksheet" in the Schedule D instructions to benefit from the maximum capital gain rates applicable to those assets.

On both the Qualified Dividends and Capital Gain Tax Worksheet and the Schedule D Tax Worksheet, net capital gain eligible for the maximum capital gain rates is reduced by any gains that you elect to treat as investment income on Form 4952 to increase your itemized deduction for investment interest *(15.10)*.

**The 0%, 15%, and 20% rates.** Your qualified dividends *(4.1)* and net capital gain (net long-term gains in excess of net short-term losses) are generally subject to a 0%, 15%, or 20% rate, or a combination of these rates, depending on your taxable income, filing status, and the amount of your ordinary income. *Table 5-2* below shows the 2018 brackets for the 0%, 15%, and 20% rates, as provided in the Tax Cuts and Jobs Act.

*Note:* The 0%, 15% and 20% rates do not apply to any portion of net capital gain that is 28% rate gain (from collectibles and Section 1202 exclusion) or unrecaptured Section 1250 gain (from post-1986 real estate depreciation); these are subject, respectively, to maximum rates of 28% and 25%. The 28% and 25% rates are discussed below. Also keep in mind that if your MAGI exceeds the threshold for the 3.8% tax on net investment income *(28.3)*, the effective rate on some or all of your gains (depending on MAGI) will be increased.

Different rates apply to qualified dividends and net capital gain of children subject to the "kiddie tax"; *see* below.

For 2017 and earlier years, the 0% rate applied up to the exact endpoint of the 15% (second lowest) ordinary income bracket. However, under the Tax Cuts and Jobs Act, the 2018 endpoints of the 0% rate bracket, as shown in *Table 5-2*, do not correspond exactly to the endpoints for the 12% ordinary income rate bracket, the second lowest bracket for ordinary income (see *Table 1-1* in *1.2*). For joint filers (and qualifying widows/widowers), the 0% rate bracket for net capital gain and qualified dividends ends $200 below the

 *Law Alert*

### 0%, 15%, and 20% Rates Apply to Most Long-term Gains

If you have a net capital gain (net long-term gain over net short-term loss if any), the net gain may avoid tax under the 0% rate or be taxed at 15% or 20%, depending on your income. However, the 0%, 15%, and 20% rates do not apply to 28% rate gains from collectibles or 25% unrecaptured Section 1250 gains (real estate depreciation); *see 5.3*. Qualified dividends *(4.2)* may also be tax free under the 0% rate, and if the 0% rate does not apply, they are taxed at either 15% or 20%, depending on your income.

The effective tax rate on capital gains and qualified dividends, as well as on other investment income, increases by 3.8% for higher-income taxpayers subject to the additional tax on net investment income *(28.3)*.

endpoint of the 12% ordinary income bracket, and for other taxpayers the endpoint of the 0% rate bracket is $100 below the endpoint of the 12% ordinary income bracket. It is possible that Congress will eliminate the differential between the top of the 0% capital gain rate bracket and the top of the 12% ordinary income bracket; *see* the *e-Supplement* at *jklasser.com* for an update, if any.

## Do your qualified dividends and net capital gain fall within the 0% rate bracket?

If your 2018 taxable income, including your qualified dividends and net capital gain, is within the 0% rate bracket shown in *Table 5-2*, and none of your net capital gain is 28% rate gain or 25% rate unrecaptured Section 1250 gain, then all of your net capital gain and qualified dividend income is tax free. Perhaps surprisingly, you may be able to benefit from the 0% rate even if your total taxable income is above the endpoint of the 0% rate bracket and it appears, at least at first glance, that you are subject to the 15% or even the 20% rate on your qualified dividends and net capital gain.

The extent to which you can benefit from the 0% rate depends on your taxable income, your filing status, which determines the top of your 0% rate bracket, and the amount of your qualified dividends and net capital gain, which in turn determines the amount of your "ordinary income." On the IRS worksheets used to figure tax liability (the "Qualified Dividends and Capital Gain Tax Worksheet," or the "Schedule D Tax Worksheet," as applicable), your taxable income is reduced by your qualified dividends and net capital gain (other than 28% rate gain and unrecaptured Section 1250 gain). The resulting amount is treated as ordinary income and if it is less than the top of the 0% rate bracket for your filing status *(Table 5-2)*, your qualified dividends and net capital gain (other than 28% rate gain and unrecaptured Section 1250 gain) are tax free under the 0% rate to the extent that they "fill up" the rest of the 0% rate bracket.

For example, if you are single and for 2018 you have taxable income of $47,850, including $2,000 of qualified dividends and $12,000 of eligible net capital gain, your ordinary income for purposes of the 2018 worksheet computation is $33,850 ($47,850–$14,000), and since the top of the 0% rate bracket for single taxpayers is taxable income of $38,600 *(Table 5-2)*, there is still $4,750 left within the 0% rate bracket ($38,600-$33,850 ordinary income). The 0% rate applies to $4,750 of your gains/dividends, and the $9,250 balance ($14,000 – $4,750) is taxed at 15%.

| *Table 5-2* | Rates and Brackets for 2018 Net Capital Gain and Qualified Dividends | | | |
|---|---|---|---|---|
| | Married filing jointly and qualifying widow/widower | Single | Head of Household | Married filing separately |
| 0% rate applies if taxable income is: | $1 through $77,200 | $1 through $38,600 | $1 through $51,700 | $1 through $38,600 |
| 15% rate applies if taxable income is: | $77,201 through $479,000 | $38,601 through $425,800 | $51,701 through $452,400 | $38,601 through $239,500 |
| 20% rate applies if taxable income is: | $479,001 and over | $425,801 and over | $452,401 and over | $239,501 and over |

If the ordinary income (taxable income minus the net capital gain and qualified dividends) is equal to or more than the top of your 0% rate bracket ($38,600, $51,700, or $77,200, as shown in *Table 5-2*), the 0% rate will not apply to any of your qualified dividends and eligible gains; *see* Example 3 below.

---

### EXAMPLES

1. Arlen and Alice Able file a joint return for 2018 and report taxable income of $65,428. This includes qualified dividends of $3,298 and a long-term gain of $6,702 from the sale of stock. The 0% rate applies to the qualified dividends and long-term gain to the extent that they fit within the 0% rate bracket after taking into account the Ables' "ordinary" income. On the Qualified Dividends and Capital Gain Tax Worksheet, their ordinary income is considered to be $55,428 ($65,428 taxable income − $10,000 ($3,298 qualified dividends + $6,702 long-term gain)). Since the top, or end-point, of the 0% rate bracket for 2018 joint returns is taxable income of $77,200 *(Table 5-2)*, the 0% rate can apply to dividends/gains of up to $21,772 ($77,200 − $55,428 ordinary income) and as $21,772 exceeds the Ables' $10,000 of qualified dividends and long-term gain, the entire $10,000 is tax free under the 0% rate.

2. Same facts as in Example 1, except Arlen and Alice have taxable income of $77,600. On the Qualified Dividends and Capital Gain Tax Worksheet, ordinary income is $67,600 ($77,600 taxable income− $10,000 qualified dividends and long-term gain). After taking into account the ordinary income, there is still room for another $9,600 before the endpoint of the 0% rate bracket is reached ($77,200). Thus, $9,600 of their dividends/gain ($77,200 top of the 0% rate bracket − $67,600 ordinary income) are tax free under the 0% rate. The $400 balance of dividends/gain ($10,000 − $9,600) is taxed at the 15% capital gain rate on the Qualified Dividends and Capital Gain Tax Worksheet.

3. Same facts as in Example 1, except Arlen and Alice's taxable income is $90,000. Since the ordinary income of $80,000 ($90,000 taxable income − $10,000 qualified dividends and long-term gain) exceeds the $77,200 top of the 0% rate bracket, none of the dividends/gains are eligible for the 0% rate. The entire $10,000 is taxed at 15%.

---

**28% rate gains from sales of collectibles and small business or empowerment zone business stock eligible for exclusion.** Long-term gains on the sale of collectibles such as art, antiques, precious metals, gems, stamps, and coins are considered "28% rate gains." If you sell qualified small business stock eligible for an exclusion (Section 1202 exclusion *(5.7)*), the taxable portion of the gain is also treated as a 28% rate gain. The 28% rate transactions are reported first in Part II (long-term capital gains and losses) of Form 8949 and then transferred to Schedule D, unless you are able to directly report them on Schedule D. If taking into account all your transactions you have both a net long-term capital gain for the year and a net capital gain (excess of net long-term gain over net short-term loss if there is one), you have to complete the "28% Rate Gain Worksheet" in the Schedule D instructions. On the Worksheet, 28% rate gains are reduced by any long-term collectibles losses and net short-term capital loss for the current year, and any long-term capital loss carryover from the previous year.

A net 28% rate gain from the 28% Rate Gain Worksheet is entered on Line 18 of Schedule D and then on the "Schedule D Tax Worksheet" in the Schedule D instructions. The Schedule D Tax Worksheet is used to figure the regular tax on all of your taxable income (not just on your net capital gain and qualified dividends). The effect of the worksheet computation is to tax 28% rate gain at either the 28% rate or at the regular rates on ordinary income, whichever results in the lower tax.

**Unrecaptured Section 1250 gain on sale of real estate.** Long-term gain that is attributable to real estate depreciation is not taxable at the 0%, 15% or 20% capital gain rate. Gain attributable to pre-1987 depreciation may be recaptured as ordinary income *(44.2)*. To the extent your gain is attributable to post-1986 depreciation, the gain is considered "unrecaptured Section 1250 gain." Unrecaptured Section 1250 gain is figured on the "Unrecaptured Section 1250 Gain Worksheet" in the Schedule D instructions. The worksheet computation reduces unrecaptured Section 1250 gain by a net loss, if any, from the 28% rate group.

The net unrecaptured Section 1250 gain from the worksheet is entered on Line 19 of Schedule D and then on the Schedule D Tax Worksheet, where tax liability on all of your taxable income is computed. The effect of the computation on the Schedule D Tax Worksheet is to tax unrecaptured Section 1250 gain at either a 25% rate or at the regular rates on ordinary income, whichever results in the lower tax.

**Capital gain distributions from mutual funds.** Your fund will report long-term capital gain distributions on Form 1099-DIV. See Chapter 32 for details on how to report the distributions.

**Capital gain from Schedule K-1.** Net capital gain or loss from a pass-through entity such as a partnership, S corporation, estate, or trust is reported to you on a Schedule K-1. Report net short-term gain or loss in Part I of Schedule D and net long-term gain or loss in Part II of Schedule D.

**Kiddie tax rates on net capital gain and qualified dividends.** Beginning in 2018, the Tax Cuts and Jobs Act provides that a child subject to the kiddie tax *(24.2)* who has net investment income exceeding $2,100 is taxed on the excess using the tax rates applicable to trusts and estates. Here are the 2018 trust and estate rate brackets for net capital gain and qualified dividends that apply to the kiddie tax. See Chapter 24 for kiddie tax details.

| | |
|---|---|
| 0% rate applies if taxable income is: | $1 through $2,600 |
| 15% rate applies if taxable income is: | $2,601 through $12,700 |
| 20% rate applies if taxable income is: | $12,701 and over |

## 5.4 Capital Losses and Carryovers

Capital losses are fully deductible against capital gains on Schedule D, and if losses exceed gains, you may deduct the excess from up to $3,000 of ordinary income on Form 1040. Net losses over $3,000 are carried over to future years. On a joint return, the $3,000 limit applies to the combined losses of both spouses *(5.5)*. The $3,000 limit is reduced to $1,500 for married persons filing separately.

Although qualified dividends *(4.1)* are subject to the same rates as net capital gain, the dividends are not reported as long-term gains on Part II of Form 8949 or Schedule D and thus are not offset by capital losses in determining whether you have a net capital gain or loss for the year.

In preparing your 2018 Schedule D, remember to include any capital loss carryovers from your 2017 return. Use the carryover worksheet in the 2018 Schedule D instructions for figuring your short-term and long-term loss carryovers from 2017 to 2018. Short-term carryover losses are entered on Line 6 of Part I and long-term carryover losses are entered on Line 14, Part II.

**Losses from wash sales not deductible.** You cannot deduct a loss from a wash sale of stock or securities unless you are a dealer in those securities. A wash sale occurs if within 30 days before or after your sale at a loss, you acquire substantially identical securities or purchase an option to acquire such securities *(30.6)*. A disallowed wash sale loss should be reported in Box 1g of Form 1099-B.

Report a wash sale on Part 1 (short-term) or Part II (long-term) of Form 8949 and enter code "W" in column (f) to identify the wash sale loss. In column (g) enter the disallowed loss as a positive amount.

**Death of taxpayer cuts off carryover.** If an individual dies and on his or her final income tax return net capital losses, including prior year carryovers, exceed the $3,000 or $1,500 limit, the excess may not be deducted by the individual's estate. If the deceased individual was married, his or her unused individual losses may not be carried over by the surviving spouse *(5.5)*.

## 5.5 Capital Losses of Married Couples

On a joint return, the capital asset transactions of both spouses are combined and reported on one Schedule D. A carryover loss of one spouse may offset capital gains of the other spouse on a jointly filed Schedule D. Where you and your spouse separately incur net

*Filing Tip*

**Keep Records of Loss Carryovers**

If you have capital losses for 2018 in excess of the deductible limit, keep a copy of your 2018 Form 1040 and Schedule D to figure your loss carryover when you file your 2019 Schedule D; there will be a carryover worksheet in the 2019 Schedule D instructions. IRS Publication 550 for 2018 also will have a worksheet you can use to figure your loss carryovers from 2018 to 2019.

capital losses, $3,000 is the maximum capital loss deduction that may be claimed for the combined losses on your joint return. This limitation may not be avoided by filing separate returns. If you file separately, the deduction limit for each return is $1,500. Neither of you may deduct any of the other's losses on a separate return.

### EXAMPLE

In 2018, you individually incurred net long-term capital losses of $5,000 and your spouse incurred net long-term capital losses of $4,000. If you file separate returns, the maximum amount deductible from ordinary income on each return is $1,500. The balance must be carried forward to 2019.

If you had net losses below the $1,500 limit, you could not claim any part of your spouse's losses on your separate return.

**Death of a spouse.** The IRS holds that if a capital loss is incurred by a spouse on his or her own property and that spouse dies, the loss may be deducted only on the final return for the spouse (which may be a joint return). The surviving spouse may not claim any unused loss carryover on a separate return and the decedent's estate may not deduct the unused carryover.

### EXAMPLE

In 2015, Alex Smith realized a substantial net long-term capital loss on separately owned property, which was reported on a 2015 joint return filed with his wife, Anne. Part of the excess loss (over the $3,000 limit) was carried over to the couple's 2016 joint return. In 2017, before the carryover loss was used up, Alex died. Anne could claim the unused carryover, up to the $3,000 limit, on a joint return filed for 2017, the year of Alex's death. However, there is no loss carryover to 2018 or later years for the balance. Although the loss was originally reported on a joint return, Anne may claim only her allocable share of the loss on her individual returns for years after 2017, the year of Alex's death. However, since the 2015 loss was on property owned solely by Alex, no part of the loss is allocable to Anne.

## 5.6 Losses May Be Disallowed on Sales to Related Persons

A loss on a sale to certain related taxpayers may not be deductible, even though you make the sale at an arm's-length price, the sale is involuntary (for example, a member of your family forecloses a mortgage on your property), or you sell through a public stock exchange and related persons buy the equivalent property; *see* Examples 1 and 2 in this section.

If you have a nondeductible related party loss, identify it by entering code "L" in column (f) of Form 8949 (Part I or Part II as appropriate), and enter it as a positive amount in column (g).

**Related parties.** Losses are not allowed on sales between you and your brothers or sisters (whether by the whole or half blood), parents, grandparents, great-grandparents, children, grandchildren, or great-grandchildren. Furthermore, no loss may be claimed on a sale to your spouse; the tax-free exchange rules discussed in *Chapter 6* apply *(6.7)*.

A loss is disallowed where the sale is made to your sister-in-law, as nominee of your brother. This sale is deemed to be between you and your brother. But you may deduct the loss on sales to your spouse's relative (for example, your brother-in-law or spouse's step-parent) even if you and your spouse file a joint return.

The Tax Court has allowed a loss on a direct sale to a son-in-law. In a private ruling, the IRS allowed a loss on a sale of a business to a son-in-law where it was shown that his wife (the seller's daughter) did not own an interest in the company. Losses have been disallowed upon withdrawal from a joint venture and from a partnership conducted by members of a family. Family members have argued that losses should be allowed where the sales were motivated by family hostility. The Tax Court ruled that family hostility may not be considered; losses between proscribed family members are disallowed in all cases.

 *Filing Tip*

**Carryovers From Joint or Separate Returns**

If you or your spouse has a capital loss carryover from a year in which separate returns were filed, and you are now filing a joint return, the carryovers from the separate returns may be combined on the joint return. If you previously filed jointly and are now filing separately, any loss carryover from the joint return may be claimed only on the separate return of the spouse who originally incurred the loss *(5.5)*.

Losses are barred on sales between an individual and a controlled partnership or controlled corporation (where that individual owns more than 50% in value of the outstanding stock or capital interests). In calculating the stock owned, not only must the stock held in your own name be taken into account, but also that owned by your family. You also add (1) the proportionate share of any stock held by a corporation, estate, trust, or partnership in which you have an interest as a shareholder, beneficiary, or partner; and (2) any other stock owned individually by your partner.

Losses may also be disallowed in sales between controlled companies, a trust and its creator, a trust and a beneficiary, a partnership and a corporation controlled by the same person (more than 50% ownership), or a tax-exempt organization and its founder. An estate and a beneficiary of that estate are also treated as related parties, except where a sale is in satisfaction of a pecuniary bequest. Check with your tax counselor whenever you plan to sell property at a loss to a buyer who may fit one of these descriptions.

**Related buyer's resale at profit.** Sometimes, the disallowed loss may be saved. When you sell to a related party who resells the property at a profit, he or she gets the benefit of your disallowed loss. Your purchaser's gain is not taxed to the extent of your disallowed loss; *see* Example 4 below.

### EXAMPLES

1. You sell 100 shares of A Co. stock to your brother for $1,000. They cost you $5,000. You may not deduct your $4,000 loss.

2. The stock investments of a mother and son were managed by the same investment counselor. But neither the son nor mother had any right or control over the other's securities. The counselor followed separate and independent policies for each. Without the son's or his mother's prior approval, the counselor carried out the following transactions: (1) on the same day, he sold at a loss the son's stock in four companies and bought the same stock for the mother's account; and (2) he sold at a loss the son's stock in a copper company, and 28 days later bought the same stock for his mother. The losses of the first sale were disallowed, but not the losses of the copper stock sale because of the time break of 28 days. However, the court did not say how much of a minimum time break is needed to remove a sale-purchase transaction from the rule disallowing losses between related parties.

3. You own 30% of the stock of a company. A trust in which you have a one-half beneficial interest owns 30%. Your partner owns 10% of the stock of the same company. You are deemed the owner of 55% of the stock of that company (30%, plus one-half of 30%, plus 10%) and may not deduct a loss on the sale of property to that company since your deemed ownership exceeds 50%.

4. Smith bought securities in 2010 that cost $10,000. In 2013, he sold them to his sister for $8,000. The $2,000 loss was not deductible by Smith. His sister's basis for the securities is $8,000. In 2018, she sells them for $9,000. The $1,000 gain is not taxed because it is washed out by part of the brother's disallowed loss. If she sold the securities for $11,000, then only $1,000 of the $3,000 gain would be taxed.

 *Law Alert*

**Section 1202 Exclusion**

The exclusion applies to gain on the sale of qualified small business stock held over five years. The excludable percentage is 50% of the gain if the property was acquired before February 18, 2009, and 75% of the gain for qualified stock acquired after February 17, 2009, and before September 28, 2010. A full 100% exclusion is allowed for gain on the sale of qualified stock bought after September 27, 2010, and held over five years.

## 5.7 Special Treatment of Gain on Sale of Small Business Stock or Qualified Opportunity Zone Investment

To encourage investments in certain "small" businesses, the tax law provides special tax benefits.

**Exclusion of gain on small business stock (Section 1202 exclusion).** If you sell qualified small business stock (QSB stock) after holding it more than five years, 50%, 75% or even 100% of the gain is excludable from your income, depending on when you acquired it. To qualify as QSB stock, the stock must be stock in a C corporation (not S corporation) that was originally issued after August 10, 1993. The gross assets of the corporation must have been no more than $50 million at all times after August 9, 1993, and before issuance of the stock, as well as immediately after issuance of the stock. You must have acquired the stock at its original issue, as a gift or inheritance from a qualifying transferor, or in a conversion of other qualified stock. The C corporation must have met an active business requirement for substantially the entire time you held the stock. The active business test generally requires that the C corporation used at least 80% of its assets (by value) in the active conduct of at least one qualified trade or business, which is any business not specifically excluded by the law. However, many types of businesses are excluded from the "qualified" category. These are: (1) service businesses in the fields of health, law, accounting, financial services, brokerage, consulting, actuarial science, engineering, architecture, performing arts, or sports, (2) any business whose principal asset is the skill or reputation of one or more of its employees, (3) restaurants, hotels, motels or similar businesses, (4) insurance, banking, financing, leasing or similar businesses, (5) farming, and (6) oil, gas, and extraction businesses that can use percentage depletion. If you acquired the QSB stock before February 18, 2009, 50% of the gain is excludable from income. If you acquired the QSB stock after February 17, 2009, and before September 28, 2010, the exclusion is 75%. The 100% exclusion applies to the gain on a sale of QSB stock acquired after September 27, 2010, if the over-five-year holding period was met.

If you qualify for the exclusion, report the sale in Part II of Form 8949. Enter code "Q" in column (f) and enter the excluded amount as a negative adjustment in column (g). If you have a net capital gain (net long-term gain in excess of net short-term loss, if any) on Schedule D, include the taxable portion of the QSB stock gain on the 28% Rate Gain Worksheet in the Schedule D instructions *(5.3)*.

There is an annual and lifetime limit on the Section 1202 exclusion for QSB stock from any one issuer. The amount of gain from any one issuer that is eligible for the exclusion in 2018 is limited to the greater of (1) 10 times your basis in the qualified stock that you disposed of during 2018, or (2) $10 million ($5 million if married filing separately) minus any gain on stock from the same issuer that you excluded in prior years.

*Will there be an exclusion or rollover option for Empowerment Zone business stock sold in 2018?* The law authorizing the designation of an area as an Empowerment Zone expired at the end of 2017, and without an extension of the law, there will be no Empowerment Zone designations in effect for 2018. Without the extension, the prior-law increase in the QSB exclusion from 50% to 60% for sales of qualifying Empowerment Zone business stock acquired before February 18, 2009, would not be allowed for 2018 sales. Failure to extend the law also would mean that the option to defer gains on sales of qualifying Empowerment Zone assets held over one year if replacement property was purchased within 60 days would not be available for 2018 sales. See the *e-Supplement* at *jklasser.com* for an update, if any, on an extension of the law allowing empowerment zone designations.

**New Law: Deferral and possible exclusion for gain reinvested in a Qualified Opportunity Fund (QOF).** The Tax Cuts and Jobs Act authorizes States to designate certain low-income communities as qualified Opportunity Zones; the IRS must certify the designations. Taxpayers who realize gain on the sale of any property (wherever located) to an unrelated party may defer the gain if, within 180 days of the sale, they reinvest the gain in a Qualified Opportunity Fund (QOF). A QOF is an interest in a corporation or partnership organized to invest in a designated Opportunity Zone (QOZ) and which holds at least 90% of its assets in QOZ property (QOZ stock, partnership interest, or property used in a QOZ business).

The election to defer is made on Form 8949 for the year of the sale to the unrelated party. However, the deferred gain may eventually have to be included in income, depending on how long the QOF investment is held.

If the QOF investment is sold before 2027, the originally deferred gain (i.e. the amount reinvested in the QOF) generally will have to be reported as income for the year of the sale, but the reportable amount will depend on how long the QOF investment is held. Basis in the QOF investment is treated as zero ($0) if the investment is held under five years, so in this case, all of the originally deferred gain will have to be reported as income in the year the QOF investment is sold, plus the appreciation if any (excess of the sales price over the investment in the QOF). If the QOF investment is sold after being held at least five years but under seven years, the zero basis is increased by 10% of the originally deferred gain, so only 90% of the deferred gain will have to be included in income for the year the investment is sold, plus the appreciation if any. If the QOF investment is held at least seven but under 10 years before it is sold, the basis is increased by 15% of the deferred gain and 85% of the deferred gain will have to be includible in income.

 *Law Alert*

**Deferral and Exclusion Opportunity for Capital Gain Reinvested in a Qualified Opportunity Fund**

The Tax Cuts and Jobs Act allows gain from the sale of any property sales to an unrelated party to be deferred if it is reinvested within 180 days in a qualified opportunity fund (QOF), which is generally a corporation or partnership organized to invest in a low-income community that has been designated as a qualified Opportunity Zone by a State with the approval of the IRS. Depending on how long the QOF investment is held, some or all of the deferred gain will have to be reported as income in the year the investment is sold, but if the investment has not been sold by December 31, 2026, it must be reported as 2026 income. See the discussion of the QOF rules in the nearby text.

*Law Alert*

**New Law Repeals SSBIC Rollover Option**

For sales after 2017, the Tax Cuts and Jobs Act repeals the election to defer taxable gain from the sale of publicly traded securities if the sale proceeds are used within 60 days to buy common stock or a partnership interest in a "specialized small business investment company," or SSBIC.

If the QOF investment is not sold by December 31, 2026, some or all of the originally deferred gain will have to be recognized as 2026 income, depending on the holding period as of December 31, 2026. Basis in the investment will be treated as zero if the holding period as of the end of 2026 is under five years, and that zero basis will be increased by 10% of the originally deferred gain if the investment was held at least five but less than seven years, or by 15% if the investment was held at least seven years. The gain recognized for 2026 will be treated as basis for purposes of figuring gain or loss when the investment is later sold. However, if the QOF investment is sold after a holding period of at least 10 years, an election may be made to treat the date-of-sale fair market value as the basis of the investment. Where the QOF investment has appreciated in value, this election will allow all of the appreciation to be excluded from income.

See IRS Publication 550 for further information on QOF investments.

## 5.8    Reporting Capital Asset Sales on Form 8949 and on Schedule D

You generally must report sales and other dispositions of capital assets on Form 8949, but in some cases (see below), you can report your transactions directly on Schedule D without having to report them on Form 8949. You report on Form 8949/Schedule D sales of securities, redemptions of mutual fund shares, worthless personal loans, sales of stock rights and warrants, sales of land held for investment, and sales of personal residences where part of the gain does not qualify for the home sale exclusion *(29.1)*.

Although capital gain distributions from mutual funds and REITs are generally reported as long-term capital gains on Line 13 of Schedule D, investors who receive such distributions but have no other capital gains or losses to report may generally report the distributions directly on Form 1040 without having to file Schedule D; *see 32.8* for details.

The favorable maximum capital gain rates *(5.3)* apply to net capital gain (net long-term capital gain in excess of net short-term capital loss) from Schedule D, and also to qualified dividends *(4.2)*. Although qualified dividends are subject to the same favorable maximum rates as net capital gain, they are not entered as long-term gains in Part II of Schedule D. The favorable rates are applied to qualified dividends when tax liability is computed on either the Qualified Dividends and Capital Gain Tax Worksheet or the Schedule D Tax Worksheet. You must use the applicable worksheet to obtain the benefit of the favorable maximum capital gain rates for your net capital gain and qualified dividends. The Schedule D Tax Worksheet in the Schedule D instructions is used only if you have a net 28% rate gain or unrecaptured Section 1250 gain *(5.3)*. If you do not have a net 28% rate gain or unrecaptured Section 1250 gain, use the Qualified Dividends and Capital Gain Tax Worksheet in the Form 1040 instructions.

**Basis of "covered" securities reported on Form 1099-B.** When you sell a "covered" security, the broker must report your basis in the security in Box 1e of the Form 1099-B sent to you and the IRS. Box 3 should be checked where the basis is being reported to the IRS. In general, a covered security is stock acquired after 2010, mutual fund shares acquired after 2011, stock acquired after 2011 in a dividend reinvestment plan eligible for the average basis method, futures contracts entered into after 2013, certain bonds acquired after 2013 (described in the Form 1099-B instructions) and certain bonds acquired after 2015, including variable rate and inflation-indexed bonds (see further details in the Form 1099-B instructions).

Even if you sell a "noncovered" security, the broker may report basis in Box 1e and if so, Box 3 should be checked to indicate that basis is being reported to the IRS. For a noncovered security, Box 5 should have been checked whether or not basis is reported. If the broker does not check Box 5 for a noncovered security, penalties can be assessed against the broker for not correctly completing Boxes 1b (date acquired), 1e(basis), 1f(accrued market discount), 1g (disallowed wash sale loss) and 2 (short-term or long-term gain or loss or ordinary income).

If during the year you have sold more than one security with the same broker, each transaction is generally reported on a separate Form 1099-B (or equivalent statement); there is an exception for futures, option and foreign currency contracts that may be reported on an aggregate basis.

If in the same transaction both covered and noncovered securities were sold, each type should be reported on a separate Form 1099-B (or equivalent statement). If some covered securities were held short term and others long term (over a year), the short-term transactions should be reported separately from the long-term transactions.

**Can you report directly on Schedule D?** You do not need to report certain transactions on Form 8949. You can aggregate the transactions reported on Forms 1099-B that show (in Box 3) that basis was reported to the IRS and report them directly on Schedule D if you do not have to adjust the basis, the amount of gain or loss, or the type of capital gain or loss (short-term or long-term). Check the Form 8949 instructions for other requirements. You may choose to report the transactions separately on Form 8949 even if direct reporting on Schedule D is allowed. If you qualify for direct reporting and choose to do so, the aggregated short-term transactions are entered on Line 1a of Schedule D and the aggregated long-term transactions are reported on Line 8a of Schedule D.

**Loss on the sale of a personal residence.** You cannot deduct a loss on the sale (or exchange) of a capital asset held for personal use, such as a loss on the sale of your principal residence or a vacation home. Although the loss is not deductible, you must report the transaction on Form 8949 and Schedule D if you received a Form 1099-S. On Form 8949, enter code "L" (the code for a nondeductible loss) in column (f), and then enter the loss as a positive adjustment in column (g). In column (h), the gain or loss will be "0," since the adjustment in column (g) offsets the loss.

**Reporting transactions first on Form 8949 and then entering totals on Schedule D.** Use Part I of Form 8949 for short-term capital gains and losses (assets held one year or less) and Part II for long-term capital gains and losses (assets held more than one year). You may have to file more than one Part I or Part II, or multiple copies of both, depending on whether and how your transactions were reported on Form 1099-B ("Proceeds From Broker and Barter Exchange Transactions"). In Parts I and II of Form 8949, you must check a box to indicate whether your basis for sold securities was reported to the IRS by your broker on Form 1099-B. When reporting short-term transactions in Part I, check Box A if Form 1099-B shows that basis was reported to the IRS; check Box B if Form 1099-B shows that basis was not reported to the IRS; and check Box C if you did not receive Form 1099-B for the transactions. In Part II of Form 8949 for long-term transactions, you check Box D if Form 1099-B shows that basis was reported to the IRS, Box E if Form 1099-B shows that basis was not reported to the IRS; and Box F if you did not receive Form 1099-B for the transaction. If you need to check more than one type of box in either Part I or Part II, as when you have some Box A and some Box B or C transactions in Part I, or some Box D and some Box E or F transactions in Part II, you must complete a separate Part I or Part II for each type of box.

In the columns of Form 8949, you report transaction details. You report the sale proceeds in column (d) and your basis in column (e). Report your gain or loss in column (h).

If you did not receive a Form 1099-B (or substitute statement) for a securities transaction, enter in column (d) of Form 8949 the net proceeds. That is, reduce the gross proceeds by your selling expenses such as broker fees, commissions and state and local transfer taxes. Similarly, if you sold real estate and did not receive a Form 1099-S (or substitute statement), you should enter the net proceeds (gross proceeds minus your selling expenses) in column (d) of Form 8949.

If you received a Form 1099-B for a securities transaction, the net proceeds (gross proceeds minus commissions, fees and transfer taxes) should have been reported in Box 1d, but in Box 6 ("Reported to the IRS"), the "gross proceeds" box should be checked. If securities were sold because of the exercise of an option, the broker may report in Box 1d of Form 1099-B either the gross proceeds or reduce the proceeds by any option premiums; a box in Box 6 will be checked to indicate if the gross proceeds or net proceeds have been reported.

*Caution*

**Sale Details Reported to IRS by Brokers on Form 1099-B**

If you sold stocks, bonds, commodities, regulated futures contracts or other financial instruments through a broker in 2018, or you exchanged property or services through a barter exchange, the sale is reported to the IRS on Form 1099-B. You are sent Copy B of Form 1099-B or a substitute statement. In Box 1e of Form 1099-B, the broker must report your basis for "covered" securities, which includes stock acquired after 2010, mutual fund shares acquired after 2011, and certain bonds acquired after 2013 (or after 2015 in some cases). If basis is shown in Box 1e, Box 3 should be checked, indicating that the basis has been reported to the IRS. For a "noncovered" security, such as stock acquired before 2011, the broker may omit basis from Box 1e if Box 5 is checked, indicating that a "noncovered" security was sold. Alternatively, the broker may report basis for a noncovered security in Box 1e even though Box 5 is checked, and in this case Box 3 (basis reported to IRS) will also be checked.

You report basis for the asset in column (e) of Form 8949 and Schedule D. The IRS can use the basis information from Box 1e of Form 1099-B to check your computation of gain or loss on Form 8949 and Schedule D.

If a "covered" security was sold, the basis will be reported in Box 1e of Form 1099-B, and even if a "noncovered" security was sold (if so, Box 5 will be checked), basis may be shown in Box 1e.

On Form 8949, report the sales proceeds and basis as shown on Form 1099-B, and if you have to adjust the amounts shown, follow the Form 8949 instructions for entering the adjustment in column (g) and the adjustment code in column (f).

If you received a Form 1099-S for a real estate sale, the gross proceeds are shown in Box 2. Selling expenses are not taken into account on the form and neither is basis. On Form 8949, enter in column (d) the gross proceeds shown on the Form 1099-S and enter your basis in column (e). You must enter your selling expenses as a negative adjustment in column (g) of Form 8949, with code "E" entered in column (f).

Form 8949 must be attached to Schedule D. The totals from columns (d), (e), (g) and (h) of Form 8949 are transferred to the appropriate lines of Schedule D, depending on which Box was checked on Form 8949 (Box A, B, C, D, E, or F).

The Example below for John and Karen Taylor and accompanying worksheets illustrate how transactions are entered on Form 8949 and Schedule D.

## EXAMPLE

For 2018, John and Karen Taylor file a joint return. They report two short-term transactions in Part I of Form 8949 and three long-term transactions in Part II of Form 8949. On Part I, they check Box A to indicate that for each transaction they received a Form 1099-B that reported their basis. In Part II, they check Box E, indicating that the Forms 1099-B they received did not report basis. For each sale, the broker reported on Form 1099-B the net proceeds (gross sales price minus broker's commissions on the sale and state and local transfer taxes, if any), and the Taylors report that net sales price in column (d) of Form 8949. The totals from columns (d), (e), and (h) of John and Karen's Form 8949 are transferred to the applicable lines of their Schedule D, as shown below. They also report on Schedule D capital gain distributions received in 2018 from their mutual funds as well as a long-term loss carryover from 2017.

1.  Sale of stock (short-term gain)—The Taylors bought 200 shares of XL Research Co. stock on July 20, 2017, for $2,400. They sold the stock on May 11, 2018, for $3,360.

2.  Sale of mutual fund shares (short-term loss)—The Taylors bought 100 shares of the XYZ Mutual Fund on November 9, 2017, for $3,500. They sold the shares on February 12, 2018, for $2,500.

3.  Sale of stock (long-term gain)—The Taylors bought 100 shares of Acme Steel stock on October 20, 2009, for $6,000. On April 25, 2018, they sold the 100 shares for $13,000.

4.  Sale of stock (long-term loss)—The Taylors bought 200 shares of Zero Computer Co. stock for $5,000 on July 10, 2007. On March 16, 2018, they sold the shares for $2,000.

5.  Sale of mutual fund shares (long-term gain)—The Taylors bought 1,435 shares of the ABC Mutual Fund between 2010 and 2016. On July 23, 2018, they sold 500 of the shares for $21,500. The average basis (32.9) for their shares, shown on their sale confirmation from the Fund, is $24.50 per share. Thus, their basis for the 500 sold shares is $12,250 (500 × $24.50).

6.  Capital gain distributions—The Taylors received capital gain distributions of $1,050 in December 2018 from mutual funds (32.4, 32.8).

7.  Long-term capital loss carryover—The Taylors had a long-term capital loss carryover of $950 from their 2017 return.

Because the Taylors do not have a net 28% rate gain or unrecaptured Section 1250 gain, they are directed by Line 20 of Schedule D to use the Qualified Dividends and Capital Gain Tax Worksheet in the Form 1040 instructions to compute their regular income tax liability. If they did have a net 28% rate gain or unrecaptured Section 1250 gain, the Taylors would use the Schedule D Tax Worksheet in the Schedule D instructions to figure their tax.

***Tax computation on the Qualified Dividends and Capital Gain Tax Worksheet.*** In the following pages, we show how John and Karen report their transactions on Form 8949 and Schedule D, and how their 2018 tax liability is figured on the Qualified Dividends and Capital Gain Tax Worksheet. On the Worksheet, John and Karen will figure the tax on their 2018 taxable income, taking into account the favorable rates (5.3) for net capital gain and qualified dividends. Assume that the taxable income on their 2018 joint return is $83,000. In addition to their net capital gain of $13,310 from Line 16 of Schedule D (net long-term gain of $13,350 less net short term loss of $40), the Taylors have $1,200 of qualified dividends (4.2) from Line 3a of Form 1040 that are eligible for the favorable capital gain rates (5.3). The qualified dividends are added to their net capital gain on the Qualified Dividends and Capital Gain Tax Worksheet (Lines 2-4 of the Worksheet).

Under this set of facts, of their $14,510 in combined qualified dividends ($1,200) plus net capital gain ($13,310), the Taylors will avoid tax completely on $8,710. The $8,710 is eligible for the 0% rate for qualified dividends/net capital gain (5.3): $8,710 is the excess of $77,200, the top of the 0% rate bracket for 2018 joint filers (5.3) over $68,490, their "ordinary income" ($68,490 = $83,000 taxable income minus $14,510 qualified dividends plus net capital gain). The balance of their qualifying dividends and net capital gain, or $5,800, is taxed at the 15% capital gain rate, for a tax of $870. The tax on the ordinary income of $68,490 is $7,836 (using the IRS 2018 Tax Table).The Taylors' total tax liability of $8,706 ($870 plus $7,836) is $1,439 less than the liability of $10,145 that would apply (shown on Line 26 of the Worksheet) if the law did not provide favorable rates for net capital gain and qualified dividends.

## Sample Form 8949—Sales and Other Dispositions of Capital Assets
*(This sample is subject to change; see the e-Supplement at www.jklasser.com)*

| Form **8949** | **Sales and Other Dispositions of Capital Assets** | OMB No. 1545-0074 |
|---|---|---|
| Department of the Treasury<br>Internal Revenue Service | ▶ Go to *www.irs.gov/Form8949* for instructions and the latest information.<br>▶ File with your Schedule D to list your transactions for lines 1b, 2, 3, 8b, 9, and 10 of Schedule D. | 20**18**<br>Attachment<br>Sequence No. **12A** |

| Name(s) shown on return | Social security number or taxpayer identification number |
|---|---|
| John and Karen Taylor | X11-01-11X0 |

*Before you check Box A, B, or C below, see whether you received any Form(s) 1099-B or substitute statement(s) from your broker. A substitute statement will have the same information as Form 1099-B. Either will show whether your basis (usually your cost) was reported to the IRS by your broker and may even tell you which box to check.*

**Part I** — **Short-Term.** Transactions involving capital assets you held 1 year or less are generally short-term (see instructions). For long-term transactions, see page 2.

**Note:** You may aggregate all short-term transactions reported on Form(s) 1099-B showing basis was reported to the IRS and for which no adjustments or codes are required. Enter the totals directly on Schedule D, line 1a; you aren't required to report these transactions on Form 8949 (see instructions).

You *must* check Box A, B, *or* C below. **Check only one box.** If more than one box applies for your short-term transactions, complete a separate Form 8949, page 1, for each applicable box. If you have more short-term transactions than will fit on this page for one or more of the boxes, complete as many forms with the same box checked as you need.

- ☑ **(A)** Short-term transactions reported on Form(s) 1099-B showing basis was reported to the IRS (see **Note** above)
- ☐ **(B)** Short-term transactions reported on Form(s) 1099-B showing basis **wasn't** reported to the IRS
- ☐ **(C)** Short-term transactions not reported to you on Form 1099-B

**1**

| (a)<br>Description of property<br>(Example: 100 sh. XYZ Co.) | (b)<br>Date acquired<br>(Mo., day, yr.) | (c)<br>Date sold or disposed of<br>(Mo., day, yr.) | (d)<br>Proceeds<br>(sales price)<br>(see instructions) | (e)<br>Cost or other basis.<br>See the **Note** below<br>and see *Column (e)*<br>in the separate<br>instructions | (f)<br>Code(s) from<br>instructions | (g)<br>Amount of<br>adjustment | (h)<br>Gain or (loss).<br>Subtract column (e)<br>from column (d) and<br>combine the result<br>with column (g) |
|---|---|---|---|---|---|---|---|
| 200 shares-XL Research Company | 7/20/2017 | 5/11/2018 | 3,360 | 2,400 | | | 960 |
| 100 shares- XYZ Mutual Fund | 11/9/2017 | 2/12/2018 | 2,500 | 3,500 | | | (1,000) |
| | | | | | | | |
| | | | | | | | |
| | | | | | | | |
| | | | | | | | |
| | | | | | | | |
| | | | | | | | |
| | | | | | | | |
| | | | | | | | |
| | | | | | | | |
| | | | | | | | |
| **2 Totals.** Add the amounts in columns (d), (e), (g), and (h) (subtract negative amounts). Enter each total here and include on your Schedule D, **line 1b** (if **Box A** above is checked), **line 2** (if **Box B** above is checked), or **line 3** (if **Box C** above is checked) ▶ | | | 5,860 | 5,900 | | | (40) |

**Note:** If you checked Box A above but the basis reported to the IRS was incorrect, enter in column (e) the basis as reported to the IRS, and enter an adjustment in column (g) to correct the basis. See *Column (g)* in the separate instructions for how to figure the amount of the adjustment.

**For Paperwork Reduction Act Notice, see your tax return instructions.**     Cat. No. 37768Z     Form **8949** (2018)

## Sample Form 8949—Sales and Other Dispositions of Capital Assets

*(This sample is subject to change; see the e-Supplement at www.jklasser.com)*

Form 8949 (2018)      Attachment Sequence No. **12A**    Page **2**

| Name(s) shown on return. Name and SSN or taxpayer identification no. not required if shown on other side | Social security number or taxpayer identification number |
|---|---|
| **John and Karen Taylor** | **X11-01-11XO** |

*Before you check Box D, E, or F below, see whether you received any Form(s) 1099-B or substitute statement(s) from your broker. A substitute statement will have the same information as Form 1099-B. Either will show whether your basis (usually your cost) was reported to the IRS by your broker and may even tell you which box to check.*

**Part II**    **Long-Term.** Transactions involving capital assets you held more than 1 year are generally long-term (see instructions). For short-term transactions, see page 1.

**Note:** You may aggregate all long-term transactions reported on Form(s) 1099-B showing basis was reported to the IRS and for which no adjustments or codes are required. Enter the totals directly on Schedule D, line 8a; you aren't required to report these transactions on Form 8949 (see instructions).

You **must** check Box D, E, **or** F below. Check only one box. If more than one box applies for your long-term transactions, complete a separate Form 8949, page 2, for each applicable box. If you have more long-term transactions than will fit on this page for one or more of the boxes, complete as many forms with the same box checked as you need.

- ☐ **(D)**
- ☑ **(E)**
- ☐ **(F)**

**1**

| (a)<br>Description of property<br>(Example: 100 sh. XYZ Co.) | (b)<br>Date acquired<br>(Mo., day, yr.) | (c)<br>Date sold or<br>disposed of<br>(Mo., day, yr.) | (d)<br>Proceeds<br>(sales price)<br>(see instructions) | (e)<br>Cost or other basis.<br>See the **Note** below<br>and see *Column (e)*<br>in the separate<br>instructions | (f)<br>Code(s) from<br>instructions | (g)<br>Amount of<br>adjustment | (h)<br>Gain or (loss).<br>Subtract column (e)<br>from column (d) and<br>combine the result<br>with column (g) |
|---|---|---|---|---|---|---|---|
| 100 shares- Acme Steel | 10/20/2009 | 4/25/2018 | 13,000 | 6,000 | | | 7,000 |
| 200 shares- Zero Computer Company | 7/10/2007 | 3/16/2018 | 2,000 | 5,000 | | | (3,000) |
| 500 shares- ABC Mutual Fund | "various" | 7/23/2018 | 21,500 | 12,250 | | | 9,250 |
| | | | | | | | |
| | | | | | | | |
| | | | | | | | |
| | | | | | | | |
| | | | | | | | |
| | | | | | | | |
| | | | | | | | |
| | | | | | | | |
| **2 Totals.** Add the amounts in columns (d), (e), (g), and (h) (subtract negative amounts). Enter each total here and include on your Schedule D, **line 8b** (if **Box D** above is checked), **line 9** (if **Box E** above is checked), or **line 10** (if **Box F** above is checked) ▶ | | | 36,500 | 23,250 | | | 13,250 |

**Note:** If you checked Box D above but the basis reported to the IRS was incorrect, enter in column (e) the basis as reported to the IRS, and enter an adjustment in column (g) to correct the basis. See *Column (g)* in the separate instructions for how to figure the amount of the adjustment.

Form **8949** (2018)

## Sample Schedule D—Capital Gains and Losses

*(This sample is subject to change; see the e-Supplement at www.jklasser.com)*

| SCHEDULE D (Form 1040) | **Capital Gains and Losses** | OMB No. 1545-0074 |
|---|---|---|
| Department of the Treasury Internal Revenue Service (99) | ▶ Attach to Form 1040 or Form 1040NR.<br>▶ Go to *www.irs.gov/ScheduleD* for instructions and the latest information.<br>▶ Use Form 8949 to list your transactions for lines 1b, 2, 3, 8b, 9, and 10. | 20**18**<br>Attachment Sequence No. **12** |

| Name(s) shown on return | Your social security number |
|---|---|
| John and Karen Taylor | X11-01-11X0 |

### Part I   Short-Term Capital Gains and Losses—Generally Assets Held One Year or Less  (see instructions)

| See instructions for how to figure the amounts to enter on the lines below.<br><br>This form may be easier to complete if you round off cents to whole dollars. | (d)<br>Proceeds<br>(sales price) | (e)<br>Cost<br>(or other basis) | (g)<br>Adjustments<br>to gain or loss from<br>Form(s) 8949, Part I,<br>line 2, column (g) | (h) Gain or (loss)<br>Subtract column (e)<br>from column (d) and<br>combine the result<br>with column (g) |
|---|---|---|---|---|
| **1a** Totals for all short-term transactions reported on Form 1099-B for which basis was reported to the IRS and for which you have no adjustments (see instructions). However, if you choose to report all these transactions on Form 8949, leave this line blank and go to line 1b . | | | | |
| **1b** Totals for all transactions reported on Form(s) 8949 with **Box A** checked . . . . . . . . . . . | 5,860 | 5,900 | | (40) |
| **2** Totals for all transactions reported on Form(s) 8949 with **Box B** checked . . . . . . . . . . . | | | | |
| **3** Totals for all transactions reported on Form(s) 8949 with **Box C** checked . . . . . . . . . . . | | | | |

| | | |
|---|---|---|
| **4** Short-term gain from Form 6252 and short-term gain or (loss) from Forms 4684, 6781, and 8824 . . | **4** | |
| **5** Net short-term gain or (loss) from partnerships, S corporations, estates, and trusts from Schedule(s) K-1 . . . . . . . . . . . . . . . . . . . . . . . . . . . . . . | **5** | |
| **6** Short-term capital loss carryover. Enter the amount, if any, from line 8 of your **Capital Loss Carryover Worksheet** in the instructions . . . . . . . . . . . . . . . . . . . . . . | **6** ( ) | |
| **7** **Net short-term capital gain or (loss).** Combine lines 1a through 6 in column (h). If you have any long-term capital gains or losses, go to Part II below. Otherwise, go to Part III on the back . . . . . . | **7** | (40) |

### Part II   Long-Term Capital Gains and Losses—Generally Assets Held More Than One Year  (see instructions)

| See instructions for how to figure the amounts to enter on the lines below.<br><br>This form may be easier to complete if you round off cents to whole dollars. | (d)<br>Proceeds<br>(sales price) | (e)<br>Cost<br>(or other basis) | (g)<br>Adjustments<br>to gain or loss from<br>Form(s) 8949, Part II,<br>line 2, column (g) | (h) Gain or (loss)<br>Subtract column (e)<br>from column (d) and<br>combine the result<br>with column (g) |
|---|---|---|---|---|
| **8a** Totals for all long-term transactions reported on Form 1099-B for which basis was reported to the IRS and for which you have no adjustments (see instructions). However, if you choose to report all these transactions on Form 8949, leave this line blank and go to line 8b . | | | | |
| **8b** Totals for all transactions reported on Form(s) 8949 with **Box D** checked . . . . . . . . . . . | | | | |
| **9** Totals for all transactions reported on Form(s) 8949 with **Box E** checked . . . . . . . . . . . | 36,500 | 23,250 | | 13,250 |
| **10** Totals for all transactions reported on Form(s) 8949 with **Box F** checked . . . . . . . . . . . | | | | |

| | | |
|---|---|---|
| **11** Gain from Form 4797, Part I; long-term gain from Forms 2439 and 6252; and long-term gain or (loss) from Forms 4684, 6781, and 8824 . . . . . . . . . . . . . . . . . . . . | **11** | |
| **12** Net long-term gain or (loss) from partnerships, S corporations, estates, and trusts from Schedule(s) K-1 | **12** | |
| **13** Capital gain distributions. See the instructions . . . . . . . . . . . . . . . . . . | **13** | 1,050 |
| **14** Long-term capital loss carryover. Enter the amount, if any, from line 13 of your **Capital Loss Carryover Worksheet** in the instructions . . . . . . . . . . . . . . . . . . . . . | **14** ( 950 ) | |
| **15** **Net long-term capital gain or (loss).** Combine lines 8a through 14 in column (h). Then go to Part III on the back . . . . . . . . . . . . . . . . . . . . . . . . . . . . | **15** | 13,350 |

For Paperwork Reduction Act Notice, see your tax return instructions.          Cat. No. 11338H          Schedule D (Form 1040) 2018

## Sample Schedule D—Capital Gains and Losses

*(This sample is subject to change; see the e-Supplement at www.jklasser.com)*

---

Schedule D (Form 1040) 2018 Page **2**

**Part III**    **Summary**

**16**    Combine lines 7 and 15 and enter the result . . . . . . . . . . . . . . . . . . | **16** | 13,310

- If line 16 is a **gain,** enter the amount from line 16 on Schedule 1 (Form 1040), line 13, or Form 1040NR, line 14. Then go to line 17 below.
- If line 16 is a **loss,** skip lines 17 through 20 below. Then go to line 21. Also be sure to complete line 22.
- If line 16 is **zero,** skip lines 17 through 21 below and enter -0- on Schedule 1 (Form 1040), line 13, or Form 1040NR, line 14. Then go to line 22.

**17**    Are lines 15 and 16 **both** gains?
     ☑ **Yes.** Go to line 18.
     ☐ **No.** Skip lines 18 through 21, and go to line 22.

**18**    If you are required to complete the **28% Rate Gain Worksheet** (see instructions), enter the amount, if any, from line 7 of that worksheet . . . . . . . . . . . . . ▶ | **18** |

**19**    If you are required to complete the **Unrecaptured Section 1250 Gain Worksheet** (see instructions), enter the amount, if any, from line 18 of that worksheet . . . . . . . . . ▶ | **19** |

**20**    Are lines 18 and 19 **both** zero or blank?
     ☑ **Yes.** Complete the **Qualified Dividends and Capital Gain Tax Worksheet** in the instructions for Form 1040, line 11a (or in the instructions for Form 1040NR, line 42). **Don't** complete lines 21 and 22 below.

     ☐ **No.** Complete the **Schedule D Tax Worksheet** in the instructions. **Don't** complete lines 21 and 22 below.

**21**    If line 16 is a loss, enter here and on Schedule 1 (Form 1040), line 13, or Form 1040NR, line 14, the **smaller** of:

- The loss on line 16; or
- ($3,000), or if married filing separately, ($1,500)    }   . . . . . . . . . . . . . . . . | **21** | (        )

**Note:** When figuring which amount is smaller, treat both amounts as positive numbers.

**22**    Do you have qualified dividends on Form 1040, line 3a, or Form 1040NR, line 10b?

     ☐ **Yes.** Complete the **Qualified Dividends and Capital Gain Tax Worksheet** in the instructions for Form 1040, line 11a (or in the instructions for Form 1040NR, line 42).

     ☐ **No.** Complete the rest of Form 1040 or Form 1040NR.

Schedule D (Form 1040) 2018

## Sample Qualified Dividends and Capital Gains Worksheet

*(This sample is subject to change; see the e-Supplement at jklasser.com)*

**Qualified Dividends and Capital Gain Tax Worksheet—Line 11a**

2018 Form 1040—Line 11a
*Keep for Your Records*

| **Before you begin:** | ✓ See the earlier instructions for line 11a to see if you can use this worksheet to figure your tax. |
| | ✓ Before completing this worksheet, complete Form 1040 through line 10. |
| | ✓ If you don't have to file Schedule D and you received capital gain distributions, be sure you checked the box on line 13 of Schedule 1. |

| | | | |
|---|---|---|---|
| 1. | Enter the amount from Form 1040, line 10. However, if you are filing Form 2555 or 2555-EZ (relating to foreign earned income), enter the amount from line 3 of the Foreign Earned Income Tax Worksheet .................... | 1. | **83,000** |
| 2. | Enter the amount from Form 1040, line 3a* ........ | 2. | 1,200 |
| 3. | Are you filing Schedule D?* | | |
| | ☑ **Yes.** Enter the **smaller** of line 15 or 16 of Schedule D. If either line 15 or 16 is blank or a loss, enter -0-. | 3. | 13,310 |
| | ☐ **No.** Enter the amount from Schedule 1, line 13. | | |
| 4. | Add lines 2 and 3 ............................. | 4. | 14,510 |
| 5. | If filing Form 4952 (used to figure investment interest expense deduction), enter any amount from line 4g of that form. Otherwise, enter -0- .......... | 5. | - 0 - |
| 6. | Subtract line 5 from line 4. If zero or less, enter -0- ................... | 6. | 14,510 |
| 7. | Subtract line 6 from line 1. If zero or less, enter -0- ................... | 7. | 68,490 |
| 8. | Enter: | | |
| | $38,600 if single or married filing separately, | | |
| | $77,200 if married filing jointly or qualifying widow(er), | 8. | 77,200 |
| | $51,700 if head of household. | | |
| 9. | Enter the smaller of line 1 or line 8 ................. | 9. | 77,200 |
| 10. | Enter the smaller of line 7 or line 9 ................. | 10. | 68,490 |
| 11. | Subtract line 10 from line 9. This amount is taxed at 0% .............. | 11. | 8,710 |
| 12. | Enter the smaller of line 1 or line 6 ................ | 12. | 14,510 |
| 13. | Enter the amount from line 11 ..................... | 13. | 8,710 |
| 14. | Subtract line 13 from line 12 ..................... | 14. | 5,800 |
| 15. | Enter: | | |
| | $425,800 if single, | | |
| | $239,500 if married filing separately, | 15. | 479,000 |
| | $479,000 if married filing jointly or qualifying widow(er), | | |
| | $452,400 if head of household. | | |
| 16. | Enter the smaller of line 1 or line 15 ................ | 16. | 83,000 |
| 17. | Add lines 7 and 11 ............................ | 17. | 77,200 |
| 18. | Subtract line 17 from line 16. If zero or less, enter -0- ................ | 18. | 5,800 |
| 19. | Enter the smaller of line 14 or line 18 .............. | 19. | 5,800 |
| 20. | Multiply line 19 by 15% (0.15) ............... | 20. | 870 |
| 21. | Add lines 11 and 19 ..................... | 21. | 14,510 |
| 22. | Subtract line 21 from line 12 ................ | 22. | - 0 - |
| 23. | Multiply line 22 by 20% (0.20) .......... | 23. | - 0 - |
| 24. | Figure the tax on the amount on line 7. If the amount on line 7 is less than $100,000, use the Tax Table to figure the tax. If the amount on line 7 is $100,000 or more, use the Tax Computation Worksheet .............. | 24. | 7,836 |
| 25. | Add lines 20, 23, and 24 ...................... | 25. | 8,706 |
| 26. | Figure the tax on the amount on line 1. If the amount on line 1 is less than $100,000, use the Tax Table to figure the tax. If the amount on line 1 is $100,000 or more, use the Tax Computation Worksheet .............. | 26. | 10,145 |
| 27. | **Tax on all taxable income.** Enter the **smaller** of line 25 or 26. Also include this amount on the entry space on Form 1040, line 11a. If you are filing Form 2555 or 2555-EZ, don't enter this amount on the entry space on Form 1040, line 11a. Instead, enter it on line 4 of the Foreign Earned Income Tax Worksheet .............. | 27. | 8,706 |

*\* If you are filing Form 2555 or 2555-EZ, see the footnote in the Foreign Earned Income Tax Worksheet before completing this line.*

## 5.9 Counting the Months in Your Holding Period

The period of time you own a capital asset before its sale or exchange determines whether capital gain or loss is short term or long term.

These are the rules for counting the holding period:

1. A holding period is figured in months and fractions of months.

2. The beginning date of a holding month is generally the day after the asset was acquired. The same numerical date of each following month starts a new holding month regardless of the number of days in the preceding month. If you acquire an asset on the last day of a month, a holding month ends on the last day of a following calendar month, regardless of the number of days in each month.

3. The last day of the holding period is the day on which the asset is sold.

---

**EXAMPLES**

1. On September 19, 2018, you buy stock. The holding months begin on September 20, October 20, November 20, and December 20, etc., and end on October 19, November 19, December 19, etc. A sale on or after September 20, 2019, would result in long-term gain or loss.

2. You buy stock on July 31, 2018. A holding month ends on August 31, September 30, October 31, November 30, December 31, January 31, February 28 (or 29 in a leap year), etc.

---

## 5.10 Holding Period for Securities

Rules for counting your holding period for various securities transactions are as follows:

**Stock sold on a public exchange.** The holding period starts on the day after your purchase order is executed (trade date). The day your sale order is executed (trade date) is the last day of the holding period, even if delivery and payment are not made until several days after the actual sale (settlement date).

---

**EXAMPLES**

1. On June 3, you sell a stock at a profit. Your holding period ends on June 3, although proceeds are not received until June 6.

2. You sell stock at a gain on a public exchange on Monday, December 31, 2018. The gain must be reported on your 2018 return even though the proceeds are received in 2019. The installment sale rule does not apply; see 5.21.

---

**Stock subscriptions.** If you are bound by your subscription but the corporation is not, the holding period begins the day after the date on which the stock is issued. If both you and the company are bound, the date the subscription is accepted by the corporation is the date of acquisition, and your holding period begins the day after.

**Tax-free stock rights.** When you exercise rights to acquire corporate stock from the issuing corporation, your holding period for the stock begins on the day of exercise, not on the day after. You are deemed to exercise stock rights when you assent to the terms of the rights in the manner requested or authorized by the corporation. An option to acquire stock is not a stock right.

**FIFO method for stock sold from different lots.** If you purchased shares of the same stock on different dates and cannot determine which shares you are selling, the shares purchased at the earliest time are considered the stock sold first; this is called the FIFO (first-in, first-out) method (30.2).

**Commodities.** If you acquired a commodity futures contract, the holding period of a commodity accepted in satisfaction of the contract includes your holding period of the contract, unless you are a dealer in commodities.

 *Planning Reminder*

**Long-Term Holding Period of More Than a Year**

To obtain the benefit of favorable long-term capital gains rates (5.3), you must hold an asset more than a year before selling it.

**Employee stock options.** When an employee exercises a stock option, the holding period of the acquired stock begins on the day after the option is exercised. If an employee option plan allows the exercise of an option by giving notes, the terms of the plan should be reviewed to determine when ownership rights to the stock are transferred. The terms may affect the start of the holding period for the stock.

**Wash sales.** After a wash sale, the holding period of the new stock includes the holding period of the old stock for which a loss has been disallowed *(30.6)*.

**Other references.** For the holding period of stock dividends, *see 30.3*; for short sales, *see 30.5*; and for convertible securities, *see 30.7*.

> **EXAMPLE**
>
> You purchased 100 shares of ABC stock on May 3, 1995, 100 shares of ABC stock on May 1, 1997, and 300 shares of ABC stock on September 2, 1998. In 2018, you sell 250 shares of ABC stock, and are unable to determine when those particular shares were bought. Using the "first-in, first-out" method, 100 shares are from May 3, 1995, 100 shares from May 1, 1997, and 50 shares are from September 2, 1998 (30.2).

## 5.11 Holding Period for Real Estate

Your holding period starts on the day after the date of acquisition. The acquisition date is the earlier of: (1) the date title passes to you or (2) the date you take possession and you assume the burdens and privileges of ownership under the contract of sale; taking possession under an option agreement does not start your holding period. In disputes involving the starting and closing dates of a holding period, you may refer to the state law that applies to your sale or purchase agreement. State law determines when title to property passes.

If you convert a residence to rental property and later sell the home, the holding period includes the time you held the home for personal purposes.

**Year-end sale.** The date of sale is the last day of your holding period even if you do not receive the sale proceeds until the following year. For example, you sell land held for investment at a gain on December 31, 2018, receiving payment in January 2019. Your holding period ends on December 31, although the sale is reported in 2019 when the proceeds are received. Note that the December 31 gain transaction can be reported on your 2018 return by making an election to "elect out" of installment reporting *(5.23)*. If you had a loss on the sale, it is reported as a loss for 2019, when the proceeds are received.

## 5.12 Holding Period: Gifts, Inheritances, and Other Property

**Gift property.** If, in figuring a gain or loss, your basis for the property under 5.17 is the same as the donor's basis, you add the donor's holding period to the period you held the property. If you sell the property at a loss using as your basis the fair market value at the date of the gift *(5.17)*, your holding period begins on the day after the date of the gift.

**Inherited property.** The law gives an automatic holding period of more than one year for property inherited from someone who died before or after 2010. Report the transaction in Part II of Form 8949 ("Long-Term") and enter "INHERITED" in column (b) as the date of acquisition.

If property was inherited from someone who died in 2010 and the executor elected on Form 8939 to apply modified carryover basis rules *(5.17)*, the holding period for property subject to those rules includes the period that the deceased held it; *see* Publication 4895 (Rev. October 2011) and Revenue Procedure 2011-41.

Where property is purchased by the executor or trustee and distributed to you, your holding period begins the day after the date on which the property was purchased.

**Partnership property.** When you receive property as a distribution in kind from your partnership, the period your partnership held the property is added to your holding period. But there is no adding on of holding periods if the partnership property distributed was inventory and was sold by you within five years of distribution.

---

*Planning Reminder*

**Year-End Sales**

Tax reporting for year-end sales of real estate is different from that for publicly traded securities. Gain on a sale of realty at the end of 2018 may be deferred under the installment sale rules *(5.22)* if payments will be received in 2019 or later years. Gain on a sale of publicly traded securities at the end of 2018 must be reported on your 2018 return although you receive payment in 2019.

*Filing Tip*

**Selling Inherited Property**

When you sell property that you inherited from someone who died before or after 2010 (and usually in 2010 as well, *see 5.17*), report the sale as long-term gain or loss on Form 8949 and Schedule D even if you actually held the property for less than one year. The law automatically treats inherited property as if it were held for more than one year.

**Involuntary conversions.** When you have an involuntary conversion and elect to defer tax on gain, the holding period for the qualified replacement property generally includes the period you held the converted property. A new holding period begins for new property if you do not make an election to defer tax.

## 5.13 Calculating Gain or Loss

In most cases, you know if you have realized an economic profit or loss on the sale or exchange of property. You know your cost and selling price. The difference between the two is your profit or loss. The computation of gain or loss for tax purposes is similarly figured, except that the basis adjustment rules may require you to increase or decrease your cost and the amount-realized rules may require you to increase the selling price. As a result, your gain or loss for tax purposes may differ from your initial calculation.

When reporting a sale on Form 8949, follow the form instructions for reporting sale proceeds, basis, and selling expenses *(5.8)*.

*Planning Reminder*

**Records for Rental Property Improvements**

Keep records of permanent improvements and legal fees for rental property. These increase your basis and lower any potential gain when you sell the property.

---

### EXAMPLE

You sell rental property to a buyer who pays you cash of $50,000 and assumes your $35,000 mortgage. You bought the property for $55,000 and made $12,000 of permanent improvements. You deducted depreciation of $7,250. Selling expenses were $2,000. Your gain on the sale is $23,250, figured as follows:

| | | | |
|---|---|---|---|
| 1. | Amount realized (5.14) | | |
| | Cash | $50,000 | |
| | Mortgage assumed by buyer | 35,000 | |
| | | $85,000 | |
| 2. | Minus selling expenses* | 2,000 | |
| 3. | Net proceeds | 83,000 | |
| 4. | Original cost | 55,000 | |
| 5. | Plus improvements | 12,000 | |
| | | $67,000 | |
| 6. | Minus depreciation | 7,250 | |
| 7. | Adjusted basis | 59,750 | |
| 8. | Gain: Subtract Line 7 from Line 3 | $23,250 | |

---

### Table 5-3    Figuring Gain or Loss on Form 8949 and Schedule D

| | | |
|---|---|---|
| 1. | Amount realized or total selling price *(5.14)*, minus selling expenses*. | $ _____ |
| 2. | Cost or other unadjusted basis *(5.16)*. | $ _____ |
| 3. | Plus: Improvements; certain legal fees *(5.20)*. | $ _____ |
| 4. | Minus: Depreciation, casualty losses *(5.20)*. | $ _____ |
| 5. | Adjusted basis: 2 plus 3 minus 4 *(5.20)*. | $ _____ |
| 6. | Gain or loss: Subtract 5 from 1. | $ _____ |

*Selling expenses on Form 8949 and Schedule D.* As discussed in *5.8*, the Form 8949 instructions require you to report the net proceeds (gross proceeds minus your selling expenses) if you did not receive a Form 1099-B or Form 1099-S for your transaction. If you sold securities and received a Form 1099-B on which the net proceeds shown does not include all of your selling expenses, you enter on Form 8949/Schedule D the proceeds shown on Form 1099-B and then enter the additional selling expenses as a negative adjustment. If you sold real estate for which you received a Form 1099-S, selling expenses are not shown on that form; enter on Form 8949/Schedule D the proceeds shown on Form 1099-S and then enter the additional selling expenses as a negative adjustment.

## 5.14 Amount Realized Is the Total Selling Price

Amount realized is the tax term for the total selling price. It includes cash, the fair market value of additional property received, and any of your liabilities that the buyer agrees to pay. The buyer's note is included in the selling price at fair market value. This is generally the discounted amount that a bank or other party will pay for the note.

**Sale of mortgaged property.** The selling price includes the amount of the unpaid mortgage. This is true whether or not you are personally liable on the debt, and whether or not the buyer assumes the mortgage or merely takes the property subject to the mortgage. The full amount of the unpaid mortgage is included, even where the value of the property is less than the unpaid mortgage. Computing amount realized on foreclosure sales is discussed in **Chapter 31 (31.9)**.

If, at the time of the sale, the buyer pays off the existing mortgage or your other liabilities, you include the payment as part of the sales proceeds.

*Caution*

**Mortgaged Property**

When you sell mortgaged property, you must include the unpaid balance of the mortgage as part of the sales price received, in addition to any cash.

> ### EXAMPLES
>
> 1. You sell property subject to a mortgage of $60,000. The seller pays you cash of $30,000 and takes the property subject to the mortgage. The sales price or "amount realized" is $90,000.
>
> 2. A partnership receives a nonrecourse mortgage of $1,851,500 from a bank to build an apartment project. Several years later, the partnership sells the project for the buyer's agreement to assume the unpaid mortgage. At the time, the value of the project is $1,400,000 and the partnership basis in the project is $1,455,740. The partnership figures a loss of $55,740, the difference between basis and the value of the project. The IRS figures a gain of $395,760, the difference between the unpaid mortgage and basis. The partnership claims the selling price is limited to the lower fair market value and is supported by an appeals court. The Supreme Court reverses, supporting the IRS position. That the value of property is less than the amount of the mortgage has no effect on the rule requiring the unpaid mortgage to be part of the selling price. A mortgagor realizes value to the extent that his or her obligation to repay is relieved by a third party's assumption of the mortgage debt.

## 5.15 Finding Your Cost

In figuring gain or loss, you need to know the "unadjusted basis" of the property sold. This term refers to the original cost of your property if you purchased it. The general rules for determining your unadjusted basis are in **5.16**. Basis for property received by gift or inheritance is in **5.17**; rules for surviving joint tenants are in **5.18**. Keep in mind that you have to adjust this figure for improvements to the property, depreciation, or losses **(5.20)**.

## 5.16 Unadjusted Basis of Your Property

To determine your tax cost for property, first find in the following section the unadjusted basis of the property, and then increase or decrease that basis **(5.20)**.

**Property you bought.** Unadjusted basis is your cash cost plus the value of any property you gave to the seller. If you assumed a mortgage or bought property subject to a mortgage, the amount of the mortgage is part of your unadjusted basis.

Purchase expenses are included in your cost, such as commissions, title insurance, recording fees, survey costs, and transfer taxes.

If you buy real estate and reimburse the seller for property taxes he or she paid that cover the period after you took title, and you include the payment in your itemized deduction for real estate taxes **(16.4)**, do not add the reimbursement to your basis. However, if you did not reimburse the seller, you must reduce your basis by the seller's payment.

*Filing Tip*

**Basis of Mutual Fund Shares**

To figure gain or loss on the sale of mutual fund shares where purchases are made at various times, you may use an averaging method to determine the cost basis of the shares sold **(32.10)**.

> ### EXAMPLE
>
> You bought a building for $120,000 in cash and a purchase money mortgage of $60,000. The unadjusted basis of the building is $180,000.

If at the closing you also paid property taxes attributable to the time the seller held the property, you add such taxes to basis.

**Property obtained for services.** If you paid for the property by providing services, the value of the property, which is taxable compensation, is also your adjusted basis.

**Property received in taxable exchange.** Your unadjusted basis for the new property is generally equal to the fair market value of the property received. See below for tax-free exchanges.

> ### EXAMPLE
>
> You acquire real estate for $35,000. When the property has a fair market value of $40,000, you exchange it for machinery also worth $40,000. You have a gain of $5,000 and the basis of the machinery is $40,000.

**Property received in a tax-free exchange.** The computation of basis is made on Form 8824. If the exchange is completely tax free *(6.1)*, your basis for the new property will be your basis for the property you gave up in the exchange, plus any additional cash and exchange expenses you paid. If the exchange is partly nontaxable and partly taxable because you received "boot" *(6.3)*, your basis for the new property will be your basis for the property given up in the exchange, decreased by any cash received and by any liabilities on the property you gave up, and increased by any cash and exchange expenses you paid, liabilities on the property you received, and gain taxed to you on the exchange. Gain is taxed to the extent you receive "boot," in the form of cash or a transfer of liabilities that exceeds the liabilities assumed in the exchange; *see* **6.3** for a discussion on taxable boot. The Example in *6.3* illustrates the basis computation.

**Property received from a spouse or former spouse.** Tax-free exchange rules apply to transfers of property to a spouse, or to a former spouse where the transfer is incident to a divorce *(6.7)*. The spouse receiving the property takes a basis equal to that of the transferor. Certain adjustments may be required where a transfer of mortgaged property is made in trust. The tax-free exchange rule applies to transfers between spouses after July 18, 1984.

If you received property before July 19, 1984, under a prenuptial agreement in exchange for your release of your dower and marital rights, your basis is the fair market value at the time you received it.

 *Planning Reminder*

**Carryover Basis From Spouse or Ex-Spouse**

If you receive a gift of property from your spouse or you receive property from a former spouse in a divorce settlement, your basis for the property is generally the same as the spouse's basis *(6.7)*.

> ### EXAMPLES
>
> 1. You exchange investment real estate, which cost you $100,000, for other investment real estate. Both properties have a fair market value of $125,000 and neither property is mortgaged. You pay no tax on the exchange. The unadjusted basis of the new property received in the exchange is $100,000.
>
> 2. Same facts as in Example 1, but you receive real estate worth $115,000 and cash of $10,000. On this transaction, you realize gain of $25,000 (amount realized of $125,000 less your basis of $100,000), but only $10,000 of the gain is taxable, equal to the cash "boot" received. Your basis for the new property is $100,000, figured this way:
>
> | | |
> |---|---|
> | Basis of old property | $100,000 |
> | Less: Cash received | 10,000 |
> | | 90,000 |
> | Plus: Gain recognized | 10,000 |
> | Basis of new property | $100000 |

**New residence purchased under tax deferral rule of prior law.** If you sold your old principal residence and bought a qualifying replacement under the prior law deferral rules, your basis for the new house is what you paid for it, less any gain that was not taxed on the sale of the old residence.

**Property received as a trust beneficiary.** Generally, you take the same basis the trust had for the property. But if the distribution is made to settle a claim you had against the trust, your basis for the property is the amount of the settled claim.

If you received a distribution in kind for your share of trust income after June 1, 1984, your basis is the basis of the property in the hands of the trust. If the trust elects to treat the distribution as a taxable sale, your basis is generally fair market value. For distributions before June 2, 1984, the basis of the distribution is generally the value of the property to the extent allocated to distributable net income.

---

**EXAMPLE**

A building with an adjusted basis of $100,000 is destroyed by fire. The owner receives an insurance award of $200,000, realizing a gain of $100,000. He buys a building as a replacement for $150,000. Of the $100,000 gain, $50,000 is taxable, while the remaining $50,000 is deferred. Taxable gain is limited to the portion of the insurance award not used to buy replacement property ($200,000 – $150,000). The basis of the new building is $100,000:

| | |
|---|---|
| Cost of the new building | $150,000 |
| Less: deferred gain | 50,000 |
| Basis | $100,000 |

---

**Property acquired with involuntary conversion proceeds.** If you acquire replacement property *(18.23)* with insurance proceeds from destroyed property, or a government payment for condemned property, basis is the cost of the new property decreased by the amount of the gain that is deferred *(18.24)*. If the replacement property consists of more than one piece of property, basis is allocated to each piece in proportion to its respective cost.

## 5.17 Basis of Property You Inherited or Received as a Gift

Special basis rules apply to property you received as a gift or that you inherited. Gifts from a spouse are subject to the rules discussed in *6.7*. If you are a surviving joint tenant who received full title to property upon the death of the other joint tenant, *see 5.18*.

### Basis of Property Received as Gift

If the fair market value of the property equaled or exceeded the donor's adjusted basis *(5.20)* at the time you received the gift, your basis for figuring gain or loss when you sell it is the donor's adjusted basis plus all or part of any gift tax paid; *see* the gift tax rule below. Additional adjustments to basis (plus or minus) may be required for the period you held the property *(5.20)*.

If on the date of the gift the fair market value of the property was less than the donor's adjusted basis, there are two basis rules, one for determining if you have a gain, and another for determining if you have a loss. For purposes of figuring gain when you sell the property, your basis is the donor's adjusted basis, and your basis for figuring loss is the fair market value on the date of the gift. Additional adjustments to basis (plus or minus) may be required for the period you held the property *(5.20)*.

Depending on your selling price, it is possible that you will have neither gain nor loss when you sell. This happens when you figure a loss when using the donor's basis as your basis (the basis rule for determining if you have a gain), and you figure a gain when using the fair market value of the property at the time of the gift as your basis (the basis rule for determining if you have a loss); *see* Line 3 of Example 1 below.

**Did the donor pay gift tax?** If the donor paid a gift tax *(39.2)* on the gift to you, your basis for the property is increased under these rules:

1.  For property received after December 31, 1976, the basis is increased by an amount that bears the same ratio to the amount of gift tax paid by the donor as the net appreciation in the value of the gift bears to the amount of the gift after taking into

*Caution*

**Basis for Gift**

The basis of gift property you receive generally depends on the donor's basis. Make sure you get this information from the donor.

account the annual gift tax exclusion *(39.2)* that applied in the year of the gift. The increase may not exceed the tax paid. Net appreciation in the value of any gift is the amount by which the fair market value of the gift exceeds the donor's adjusted basis immediately before the gift. See Example 3 below.

2. For property received after September 1, 1958, but before 1977, basis is increased by the gift tax paid on the property but not above the fair market value of the property at the time of the gift.

---

### EXAMPLES

1. Assume that in 2008 you received a gift of stock from your father that you sold in 2018. His adjusted basis was $1,000.

   The basis you use to determine gain or loss depends on whether the fair market value of the stock on the date of the gift equaled or exceeded your father's $1,000 adjusted basis. If it did, your basis is your father's $1,000 basis and you will realize a gain if your selling price exceeds $1,000, as on Line 1 below, or a loss if the selling price is below $1,000, as on Line 4.

   If the value of the stock on the date of the gift was less than $1,000 (father's basis) then you use your father's basis to figure if you have a gain and the date-of-gift value to figure if you have a loss. Thus, you have a gain if you sell for more than $1,000, as on Line 5 below; a loss if you sell for less than the date-of-gift value, as on Line 2; or neither gain nor loss if you sell for more than the date-of-gift value but no more than $1,000 (father's basis), as on Line 3.

   | | If value of the gift at receipt was— | And you sold it for— | Your basis is— | Your gain is— | Your loss is— |
   |---|---|---|---|---|---|
   | 1. | $3,000 | $2,000 | $1,000 | $1,000 | none |
   | 2. | 700 | 500 | 700 | none | $ 200 |
   | 3. | 300 | 500 | * | none | none |
   | 4. | 1,500 | 500 | 1,000 | none | 500 |
   | 5. | 500 | 1,200 | 1,000 | 200 | none |

   *On Line 3 of the Example, where you sell for more than the date-of-gift value but for no more than the donor's basis, there is neither gain nor loss. To *see* if you have a gain, you use the donor's $1,000 basis as your basis, but on a sale for $500, you have a loss ($500) and not a gain. To *see* if you have a loss, you use the $300 date-of-gift value of the stock as your basis, but on a sale for $500, you have a gain ($200) and not a loss. Thus, you have neither gain nor loss under the basis rules, which require you to use the donor's basis for determining if you have a gain and the date-of-gift value for determining if you have a loss.

2. In 1975, your father gave you rental property with a fair market value of $78,000. The basis of the property in his hands was $60,000. He paid a gift tax of $15,000 on the gift. The basis of the property in your hands is $75,000 ($60,000 + $15,000).

3. In 2001, your father gave you rental property with a fair market value of $178,000. His basis in the property was $160,000. He paid a gift tax of $44,560 on a taxable gift of $168,000, after claiming the $10,000 annual exclusion. The basis of the property in your hands is your father's basis increased by the gift tax attributable to the appreciation. Gift tax attributable to the appreciation is:

$$\frac{\text{Appreciation}}{\text{Gift minus annual exclusion}} \times \text{Gift tax paid}$$

$$\frac{\$18,000}{\$168,000} \times \$44,560 = \$4,774$$

   Your basis for figuring gain or loss or depreciation is $164,774 ($4,774 + $160,000 father's basis).

*Filing Tip*

**No Gain or Loss**

When you sell property that you received as a gift, it is possible that you may realize neither gain nor loss. You have neither gain nor loss if you sell for more than the date-of-gift value but not more than the donor's adjusted basis.

**Depreciation on property received as a gift.** If the property is depreciable *(Chapter 42)*, your basis for computing depreciation deductions is the donor's adjusted basis *(5.20)*, plus all or part of the gift tax paid by the donors as previously discussed.

To figure gain or loss when you sell the property, you must adjust basis for depreciation you claimed and make other adjustments required for the period you hold the property *(5.20)*. If accelerated depreciation is claimed and you sell at a gain, you are subject to the ordinary income recapture rules *(44.1)*.

## Basis of Inherited Property

Your basis for property inherited from someone who died before or after 2010 is generally the fair market value of the property on the date of the decedent's death. If the executor of the decedent's estate elected to use an alternate valuation date (within six months after the date of death), your basis is the fair market value on the alternate valuation date. If the decedent died in 2010, your basis may be the fair market value, but *see* below for the exception where the executor filed Form 8939.

If the property increased in value while the decedent owned the property, the "step-up" in basis to its fair market value can provide a substantial tax break. If your basis is the value at the decedent's death or at the alternate valuation date, then, when you sell the property, you completely avoid income tax on the appreciation in value that occurred while the decedent owned it.

If you inherit property that was reported on an estate tax return (Form 706) filed after July 31, 2015, the executor is generally required to report the value of the estate assets to the IRS on Form 8971 and Schedule A, and if the property you inherit increased estate tax liability, you will face a penalty if you claim a basis for the property that exceeds the value shown on your copy of Schedule A. See below for details of this basis consistency rule.

If you owned the property jointly with the deceased, *see 5.18*.

If you inherit appreciated property that you (or your spouse) gave to the deceased person within one year of his or her death, your basis is the decedent's basis immediately before death, not its fair market value.

If the inherited property is subject to a mortgage, your basis is the value of the property, and not its equity at the date of death. If the property is subject to a lease under which no income is to be received for years, the basis is the value of the property—not the equity.

You might be given the right to buy the deceased person's property under his or her will. This is not the same as inheriting that property. Your basis is what you pay—not what the property is worth on the date of the deceased's death.

If property was inherited from an individual who died after 1976 and before November 7, 1978, and the executor elected to apply a carryover basis to all estate property, your basis is figured with reference to the decedent's basis. The executor must inform you of the basis of such property.

**Community property.** Upon the death of a spouse in a community property state, one-half of the fair market value of the community property is generally included in the deceased spouse's estate for estate tax purposes. The surviving spouse's basis for his or her half of the property is 50% of the total fair market value. For the other half, the surviving spouse, if he/she receives the asset, or the other heirs of the deceased spouse have a basis equal to 50% of the fair market value.

**Did executor of decedent who died in 2010 elect modified carryover basis rules on Form 8939?** If you inherited property from a person who died in 2010, you get a full stepped-up basis (to fair market value on date of death or alternate valuation date), provided the executor did not elect to file Form 8939. Under the Tax Relief, Unemployment Insurance Reauthorization, and Job Creation Act of 2010, the executors of estates of individuals dying in 2010 were allowed to opt out of estate tax entirely (no estate tax at all applied even if the gross estate exceeded the $5 million exemption) provided an election was made on Form 8939 to apply modified carryover basis rules under which the heirs generally received a stepped-up basis only for the first $1.3 million in assets, plus an additional $3 million for property passing to a surviving spouse. Executors had to make the modified carryover basis election on Form 8939 by January 17, 2012. Further details on the modified carryover basis rules are in Publication 4895 (Rev. October 2011) and Revenue Procedure 2011-41.

If the executor of a 2010 estate did not elect on Form 8939 to apply the modified carryover basis rules, the regular stepped-up basis rules apply.

**Farm or closely-held business property.** If for estate tax purposes the executor of the estate valued qualifying real estate based on its use as a farm or use in a closely-held business, rather than at its fair market value, that farm or business value is the basis for the heirs. If you inherit such property, contact the executor for the special valuation.

**Basis consistency requirement may apply to you if you inherit property reported on estate tax return filed after July 31, 2015.** Legislation was enacted in 2015 in an attempt to ensure that the values reported for property on a federal estate tax return (Form 706) are used by the estate beneficiaries as their basis for the assets they inherit. Congress was concerned that some beneficiaries understate their gain when they sell inherited property, or overstate a loss (for investment property), by claiming a basis for the property that is more than the fair market value reported by the executor on the estate tax return. Similarly, deductions for depreciation or amortization could be inflated by using a basis higher than the estate tax value of the property.

*Reporting by executor to the IRS and beneficiaries on Form 8971 and Schedule A.* An executor who files an estate tax return generally must report the value of the property included in the gross estate to the IRS on Form 8971 and Schedule A no later than 30 days after the date the estate tax return is filed, or if earlier, 30 days after the filing due date with extensions. Executors are subject to penalties for failure to file timely and correct Forms 8971 and Schedules A. The penalty amounts generally depend on how late the filing is; details are in the Form 8971/Schedule A instructions.

However, the Form 8971 and Schedule A requirements do not apply if the gross estate (plus adjusted gifts) was under the filing threshold for Form 706 and the sole reason for filing the estate tax return was to make a portability election that allows the decedent's unused estate tax exemption to be preserved for the decedent's surviving spouse *(39.9)*. Also, the reporting requirements do not apply if the estate tax return is filed solely to make a generation-skipping transfer election.

Certain property included in the gross estate is exempt from reporting. This includes (1) cash bequests, but not coins or bills with numismatic value, (2) income in respect of a decedent *(11.16)*, (3) small items of tangible personal property (generally household and personal effects) that do not require an estate tax appraisal, and (4) property sold by the estate and therefore not distributed to a beneficiary.

Where reporting is required, the executor must submit to the IRS a separate Schedule A for each beneficiary receiving property from the estate, and give each beneficiary (within the above 30-day deadline) a copy of his/her Schedule A. Schedule A provides information about the beneficiary and the property he or she has inherited (e.g., the beneficiary's name and tax identification number, description of the property, and its valuation). If the executor has not yet determined which beneficiary will receive an item of property as of the due date of the Form 8971 and Schedule(s) A, that property must be reported on a Schedule A for each beneficiary who might receive it. In this case, the same property will be reported on multiple Schedules A, and when the property is actually distributed, or the property is used to fund the distributions of multiple beneficiaries, the executor may file a supplemental Form 8971 and corresponding Schedules A to each of the affected beneficiaries.

*Potential penalty for beneficiary.* You will receive a copy of your Schedule A from the executor, but not a copy of the Form 8971 and Schedules A prepared for other beneficiaries. Column C of Schedule A will indicate if the property you inherited increased the estate tax liability payable by the estate. If it did ("Y" will be entered in this column), there is a notice on your Schedule A warning you that you are subject to the basis consistency requirement. This means that you are required to use as your basis the estate tax value for that property, which is shown in Column E of the Schedule A. If you claim a basis that exceeds the estate tax value when reporting a sale or other taxable event (such as depreciation), you are subject to a 20% "accuracy-related" penalty *(48.6)*. If the value reported to you in Column E subsequently changes (such as when a valuation dispute is settled), the executor must send you (and the IRS) an updated Schedule A within 30 days after the adjustment.

 *Law Alert*

**Beneficiary Can Be Penalized for Claiming Basis Higher Than Estate Tax Value**

A beneficiary who sells inherited property and understates the tax due on the sale may be subject to a 20% penalty if the understatement results from claiming a basis for the property that exceeds the value reported by the executor on the estate tax return.. The penalty applies to property included in an estate tax return filed after July 31, 2015, provided that inclusion of the property in the estate increased the estate tax liability.

If you are a surviving spouse and received property that qualified for the marital deduction, that property did not increase the estate tax liability ("N" should be entered in Column C) and the basis consistency rule and potential penalty do not apply.

## 5.18  Joint Tenancy Basis Rules for Surviving Tenants

If you are a surviving joint tenant, your basis for the property you inherit depends on (1) how much of the value was includible in the deceased tenant's gross estate, and this depends on whether the joint tenant was your spouse or someone other than your spouse, and (2) how much of the tax basis of the property is treated as your contribution, and this amount also depends on whether the joint tenant was your spouse or someone other than your spouse.

These rules apply only to jointly owned real estate or other physical property and jointly owned investment accounts, and not to inherited retirement accounts (inherited IRA, or inherited account from a 401(k) plan or other qualified retirement plan).

*Caution:* If you inherited property from a person who died in 2010 and the executor elected on Form 8939 to apply the modified carryover basis rules *(5.17)*, basis will be determined under that election.

**Qualified joint interest rule for survivor of spouse who died after 1981.** A "qualified joint interest" rule applies to a joint tenancy with right of survivorship where the spouses are the only joint tenants, and to a tenancy by the entirety between a husband and wife.

Where the surviving spouse is a U.S. citizen, the qualified joint interest rules provide that one-half of the fair market value of the property is includible in the decedent's gross estate. This is true regardless of how much each spouse contributed to the purchase price. Fair market value is fixed at the date of death, or six months later if an estate tax return is filed and the optional alternate valuation date is elected.

The qualified joint interest rules do not apply if the surviving spouse is not a U.S. citizen on the due date of the estate tax return. In this case, the basis rule is generally the same as the rule discussed below for unmarried joint tenants.

*Surviving spouse's basis.* Under the qualified joint interest rules, the surviving spouse's basis equals the total of these two amounts: (1) 50% of the amount included in the decedent's gross estate (either 50% of the date-of-death value, or 50% of the alternate valuation date value if an estate tax return was filed for the decedent and alternate valuation was elected), plus (2) 50% of the adjusted basis *(5.20)* for the property; *see* Example 1 below.

In the typical case, no estate tax return is due because the value of the estate is below the filing threshold, so under (1) above, the surviving spouse always takes into account 50% of the fair market value of the property at the date of death, since alternate valuation is not available where no estate tax return is filed.

If depreciation deductions for the property were claimed before the date of death, the surviving spouse must reduce basis by his or her share (under local law) of the depreciation; *see* Example 2 below.

*Planning Reminder*

**Spousal Joint Tenancies Created Before 1977**

If spouses jointly own property and one spouse dies, the surviving spouse generally receives a stepped-up basis equal to 50% of the date-of-death value. The IRS at one time took the position that the 50% stepped-up basis rule applied to pre-1997 spousal joint tenancies. However, after the Tax Court and two federal appeals courts allowed a surviving spouse a 100% stepped-up basis if the spousal joint tenancy was created before 1977 and the surviving spouse did not contribute to the purchase price (see Example 4 in *5.18*), the IRS decided to follow the Tax Court decision.

### EXAMPLES

1. John and his spouse Jennifer jointly bought a house for $50,000 in 1979. John paid $45,000 of the purchase price and Jennifer, $5,000. Over the years, they made $60,000 in improvements to the house. In 2018, John died when the house was worth $300,000. One-half of the date-of-death value, or $150,000, is includible in John's estate tax return (or would be if an estate tax return were due) although he contributed 90% of the purchase price. Under the qualified joint interest rule, Jennifer's basis for the house is $205,000 figured as follows:

| | |
|---|---|
| One-half of adjusted basis ($50,000 cost plus $60,000 improvements × 50%) | $55,000 |
| Inherited portion (50% of $300,000 date-of-death value) | 150,000 |
| Jennifer's basis | $205,000 |

2. Same facts as in Example 1 except that the home was rental property for which $30,000 of depreciation deductions had been allowed before John's death. Under local law, Jennifer had a right to 50% of the income from the property and, thus, a right to 50% of the depreciation. Her basis for the property is $190,000: $205,000 as shown in Example 1, reduced by $15,000, her share of the depreciation.

3. Assume that in addition to their jointly owned home, John and Jennifer also jointly owned an investment account holding mutual funds and stocks. When John dies in 2018, their cost basis for the investments, including reinvested dividends, is $100,000, and the value of the investments on the date of his death is $250,000. Jennifer's basis for the investment account is $175,000, equal to (1) 50% of the $250,000 value of the account on the date of John's death, plus (2) 50% of their $100,000 basis in the account.

4. The Gallensteins purchased farm property in 1955 as joint tenants; Mr. Gallenstein provided all the funds. When he died in 1987, Mrs. Gallenstein claimed that 100% of the property was includible in her husband's gross estate and she had a stepped-up basis for that full amount. The IRS argued that under the rules for estates of spouses dying after 1981, she received a stepped-up basis for only 50% of the date-of-death value. The federal appeals court for the Sixth Circuit (Kentucky, Michigan, Ohio, and Tennessee) agreed with Mrs. Gallenstein. The appeals court held that pre-1977 spousal joint tenancies were not affected when the law was changed to provide a 50% estate tax inclusion and 50% stepped-up basis for spousal deaths after 1981. For pre-1977 spousal joint tenancies, the prior law rule continues to apply: 100% of the date-of-death value of jointly held property is included in the estate of the first spouse to die unless it is shown that the survivor contributed towards the purchase. In this case, where Mrs. Gallenstein's deceased husband had paid the entire purchase price, her basis was 100% of the value of the property and she realized no taxable gain when she sold the property at a price equal to that stepped-up basis.

   The Tax Court and the Fourth Circuit Appeals Court (Maryland, North Carolina, South Carolina, Virginia, and West Virginia) agreed with the Sixth Circuit's approach of allowing a 100% stepped-up basis for a pre-1977 spousal joint interest where the deceased spouse had paid the entire purchase price. The IRS acquiesced to the Tax Court decision and no longer litigates the issue.

 *Planning Reminder*

**Joint Property Held With Non-Spouse**

If you own property with someone other than your spouse, then at the other owner's death your basis for the property equals your share of the cost basis plus the portion of the property's value that was includible in the gross estate of the deceased owner.

**Unmarried joint tenants.** If you are a surviving joint tenant who owned property with someone other than your spouse, your basis for the inherited property is your basis for your share before the joint owner died plus the fair market value of the decedent's share at death (or on the alternate valuation date if the estate uses the alternate date). Even if the estate is too small to require the filing of an estate tax return, you may still include the decedent's share of the date-of-death value in your basis. However, if no estate tax return is required, you may not use the alternate valuation date basis.

### EXAMPLE

You and your sister bought a home in 1990 for $120,000. She paid $72,000, and you paid $48,000. Title to the house was held by both of you as joint tenants. Your sister died in 2018 when the house was worth $250,000. Since your sister paid 60% of the cost of the house, 60% of the value at her death, $150,000, is included in her estate tax return (or would be included if an estate tax return was due). Your basis for the house is now $198,000, equal to the $48,000 you originally paid plus the $150,000 fair market value of your sister's 60% share at her death.

**Exception for pre-1954 deaths.** Where property was held in joint tenancy and one of the tenants died before January 1, 1954, no part of the interest of the surviving tenant is treated, for purposes of determining the basis of the property, as property transmitted at death. The survivor's basis is the original cost of the property.

**Survivor of spouse who died before 1982.** The basis rule for a surviving spouse who held property jointly (or as tenancy by the entirety) with a spouse who died before 1982 is generally the same as the above rule for unmarried joint tenants. However, special rules applied to qualified joint interests and eligible joint interests are discussed below.

**EXAMPLE**

Spouses owned rental property as tenants by the entirety that they purchased for $30,000. The husband furnished two-thirds of the purchase price ($20,000) and the wife furnished one-third ($10,000). Depreciation deductions taken before the husband's death were $12,000. On the date of his death in 1979, the property had a fair market value of $60,000. Under the law of the state in which the property is located, as tenants by the entirety, each had a half interest in the property. The wife's basis in the property at the date of her husband's death was $44,000, computed as follows:

| | |
|---|---:|
| Interest acquired with her own funds | $ 10,000 |
| Interest acquired from husband (2/3 of $60,000) | 40,000 |
| | $50,000 |
| Less: Depreciation of ½ interest not acquired by reason of death (½ of $12,000) | 6,000 |
| Wife's basis at date of husband's death | $ 44,000 |

If she had not contributed any part of the purchase price, her basis at the date of her husband's death would be $54,000 ($60,000 fair market value less $6,000 depreciation). This basis would be increased by any additions or improvements made to the property by the wife since the husband's death, and reduced by any depreciation (5.20).

**Qualified joint interest and eligible joint interest where spouse died before 1982.** Where, after 1976, a spouse dying before 1982 elected to treat realty as a "qualified joint interest" subject to gift tax, such joint property was treated as owned 50–50 by each spouse, and 50% of the value was included in the decedent's estate. Thus, for income tax purposes, the survivor's basis for the inherited 50% half of the property is the estate tax value; the basis for the other half is determined under the gift rules *(5.17)*. Personal property is treated as a "qualified joint interest" only if it was created or deemed to have been created after 1976 by a husband and wife and was subject to gift tax.

Where death occurred before 1982 and a surviving spouse materially participated in the operation of a farm or other business, the estate could have elected to treat the farm or business property as an "eligible joint interest," which means that part of the investment in the property was attributed to the surviving spouse's services and that part was not included in the deceased spouse's estate. Where such an election was made, the survivor's basis for income tax purposes includes the estate tax value of property included in the decedent's estate.

## 5.19  Allocating Cost Among Several Assets

Allocation of basis is generally required in these cases: when the property includes land and building; the land is to be divided into lots; securities or mutual fund shares are purchased at different times; stock splits; and in the purchase of a business.

**Purchase of land and building.** To figure depreciation on the building, part of the purchase price must be allocated to the building. The allocation is made according to the fair market values of the building and land. The amount allocated to land is not depreciated.

**Purchase of land to be divided into lots.** The purchase price of the tract is allocated to each lot, so that the gain or loss from the sale of each lot may be reported in the year of its sale. Allocation is not made ratably, that is, with an equal share to each lot or parcel. It is based on the relative value of each piece of property. Comparable sales, competent appraisals, or assessed values may be used as guides.

**Securities.** *See 30.2* for details on methods of identifying securities bought at different dates. *See 30.3* for allocating basis of stock dividends and stock splits and 30.4 for allocating the basis of stock rights.

**Mutual fund shares.** *See 32.1*0 for determining the basis of mutual fund shares where purchases were made at different times.

**Purchase price of a business.** *See 44.9* for allocation rule.

## 5.20 How To Find Adjusted Basis

After determining the unadjusted cost basis for property *(5.16–5.19)*, you may have to increase it or decrease it to find your adjusted basis, which is the amount used to figure your gain or loss on a sale *(5.13)*.

1. Additions to basis. You add to unadjusted basis the cost of these items:

2. All permanent improvements and additions to the property and other capital costs. Increase basis for capital improvements such as adding a room or a fence, putting in new plumbing or wiring, and paving a driveway. Also include capital costs such as the cost of extending utility service lines, assessments for local improvements such as streets, sidewalks, or water connections, and repairing your property after a casualty (for example, repair costs after a fire or storm).

3. Legal fees. Increase basis by legal fees incurred for defending or perfecting title, or for obtaining a reduction of an assessment levied against property to pay for local benefits.

4. Sale of unharvested land. If you sell land with unharvested crops, add the cost of producing the crops to the basis of the property sold.

5. Decreases to basis. You reduce cost basis for these items:

6. Return of capital, such as dividends on stock paid out of capital or out of a depletion reserve when the company has no available earnings or surplus *(4.11)*.

7. Losses from casualties and thefts. Decrease basis by insurance awards, by payments in settlement of damages to your property, and by deductible casualty/theft losses not covered by insurance.

8. Depletion allowances *(9.15)*.

9. Depreciation, first-year expensing deduction, amortization, and obsolescence on property used in business or for the production of income. In some years, you may have taken more or less depreciation than was allowable.

   If you claim less than what was allowable, you must deduct from basis the allowable amount rather than what was actually claimed. You may be able to file an amended return to claim the full allowable depreciation for a year. If IRS rules do not allow the correction on an amended return, you can change your accounting method in order to claim the correct amount of depreciation; *see* IRS Publication 946 for details.

10. If you took more depreciation than was allowable, you may have to make the following adjustments: If you have deducted more than what was allowable and you received a tax benefit from the deduction, you deduct from basis the full amount of the depreciation. But if the excess depreciation did not give you a tax benefit, because income was eliminated by other deductions, the excess is not deducted from basis.

11. Amortized bond premium *(4.17)*.

12. Canceled debt excluded from income. If you did not pay tax on certain cancellations of debt because of bankruptcy or insolvency, or on qualifying farm debt or business real property, you reduce basis of your property for the amount forgiven *(11.8)*.

13. Investment credit. Where the full investment credit was claimed in 1983 or later years, basis is reduced by one-half the credit.

 *Court Decision*

**Improvements Covered by Note**

In an unusual case, the owner of office condominiums financed substantial improvements to the units by giving promissory notes to a contracting company that he controlled. Before paying off the notes he sold the units. He included the cost of the improvements in basis to figure his gain on the sale, but the IRS, with the approval of a federal district court, held that this was improper. The court held that as a cash-basis taxpayer, he could not include the face amount of the notes in the basis of the condominiums until the notes were paid.

> **EXAMPLE**
>
> Your vacation home, which cost $175,000, was damaged by fire in 2010 when it was worth $400,000. You deducted the uninsured casualty loss of $100,000 and spent $50,000 to repair the property. In 2019, you sell the house for $600,000. To figure your profit, increase the original cost of the house by the $50,000 of repairs and then reduce basis by the $100,000 casualty loss deduction to get an adjusted basis of $125,000 ($175,000 + $50,000 – $100,000). Your gain on the sale is $475,000 ($600,000 – $125,000).

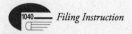

*Filing Instruction*

**Payments from Prior Installment Sales**

If you reported a pre-2018 sale on the installment method, use Form 6252 to report any 2018 payments on the sale.

## 5.21 Tax Advantage of Installment Sales

If you sell property at a gain in 2018 and you will receive one or more payments in a later year or years, you may use the installment method to defer tax unless the property is publicly traded securities or you are a dealer of the property sold. If you report the sale as an installment sale on Form 6252, your profit is taxed as installments are received. You may elect not to use the installment method if you want to report the entire profit in the year of sale; *see* Example 1 below and *5.23*.

Losses may not be deferred under the installment method.

**How the installment method works.** For each year you receive installment payments, report the allocable gain for that year on Form 6252. Installment income from the sale of a capital asset is then transferred to Schedule D. If your gain in the year of sale is long-term capital gain, gain in later years is also long term; short-term treatment in the year of sale applies also to later years. Interest payments you receive on the deferred sale installments are reported with your other interest income on Form 1040, not on Form 6252.

Installment income from the sale of business or rental property is figured on Form 6252 and then entered on Form 4797. If you make an installment sale of depreciable property, any depreciation recapture *(44.1)* is reported as income in the year of disposition. The recaptured amount is first figured on Form 4797 and then entered on Form 6252. On Form 6252, recaptured income is added to basis of the property for purposes of figuring the gross profit ratio for the balance of gain to be reported, if any, over the installment period *(44.6)*.

Installment sales of business or rental property for over $150,000 may be subject to a special tax if deferred payments exceed $5 million *(5.31)*.

---

### EXAMPLES

1. In October 2018, you sell vacant land for $100,000 that you bought in 1999 for $44,000. Selling expenses were $6,000. You receive a $20,000 payment by the end of 2018, and will receive payments of $20,000 in 2019 and 2020, and $40,000 in 2021, plus interest of 4% compounded semiannually. Your gross profit is $50,000 ($100,000 contract price less $44,000 cost and $6,000 selling expenses). For installment sale purposes, your gross profit percentage, which is the percentage of each payment that you must report, is 50% ($50,000 profit ÷ $100,000 contract price). When the buyer makes the installment note payments, you report the following:

   | In | You report | |
   |---|---|---|
   | | Payment of: | Income of: |
   | 2018 | $20,000 | $10,000 |
   | 2019 | 20,000 | 10,000 |
   | 2020 | 20,000 | 10,000 |
   | 2021 | 40,000 | 20,000 |
   | Total | $100,000 | $50,000 |

   In 2018, you file Form 6252 to figure your gross profit and gross profit percentage. You report only $10,000 as long-term gain on Line 11 of Schedule D; *see* the sample Schedule D at *5.8*. If you do not want to use the installment method, you make an election to report the entire gain of $50,000 on Form 8949 for 2018 *(5.23)*.

   The buyer's interest payments are separately reported as interest income on Form 1040.

2. On December 17, 2018, you sell a building for $150,000, realizing a profit of $25,000. You take a note payable in January 2019. You report the gain on Form 6252 with your 2019 return. Receiving a lump-sum payment in a taxable year after the year of sale is considered an installment sale.

**Year-end sales of publicly traded stock or securities.** You have no choice about when to report the gain from a sale of publicly traded stock or securities made at the end of 2018. Any gain must be reported on your 2018 Form 1040, even if the proceeds are not received until early 2019. The sale is not considered an installment sale.

**Farm property.** A farmer may use the installment method to report gain from the sale of property that does not have to be inventoried under his method of accounting. This is true even though such property is held for regular sale.

**Dealer sales.** Generally, dealers must report gain in the year of sale for personal property regularly sold on an installment plan or real estate held for resale to customers. However, the installment method may be used by dealers of certain time share units (generally time shares of up to six weeks per year) and residential lots, but only if an election is made to pay interest on the tax deferred by using the installment method. The rules for computing the interest are in Code Section 453 (l) (3). The interest is reported as an "Other tax" on Line 62 of Form 1040.

## 5.22 Figuring the Taxable Part of Installment Payments

On the installment method, a portion of each payment other than interest represents part of your gain and is taxable. The interest (including imputed interest *(5.27)* if any) is reported as interest income on your return and does not enter into the calculation of taxable installment payments on Form 6252.

On Form 6252, the taxable part of your installments payments is based on the gross profit percentage or ratio, which is figured by dividing gross profit by the contract price. The contract price is the same as the selling price unless an adjustment is made for an existing mortgage assumed or "taken subject to" by the buyer; *see* below for the mortgage adjustment to contract price. By following the line-by-line instructions to Form 6252, you get the gross profit percentage. Selling price, gross profit, and contract price are explained in the following paragraphs.

Interest equal to the applicable federal rate must generally be charged on a deferred payment sale. Otherwise, the IRS treats part of the sale price as interest *(4.32)*.

> ### EXAMPLE
>
> On December 12, 2018, you sell unmortgaged real estate for $100,000. The property had an adjusted basis of $56,000. Selling expenses are $4,000. You receive installment payments of $25,000 in 2018, 2019, 2020, and 2021, plus interest at 5%, compounded semiannually. The gross profit percentage of 40% is figured as follows:
>
> | | |
> |---|---:|
> | Selling price (contract price) | $100,000 |
> | Less: Installment sale basis | |
> |     (adjusted basis plus selling expenses) | 60,000 |
> | Gross profit | $40,000 |
>
> $$\frac{\text{Gross profit}}{\text{Contract price}} = \frac{\$40,000}{\$100,000} = 40\% \text{ (gross profit percentage)}$$
>
> In 2018 (year of sale), you report a profit of $10,000 (40% of $25,000 payment) on Form 6252. Interest received with the payment is separately reported as interest income on your Form 1040. Similarly, in each of the following three years, a profit of $10,000 is reported so that by the end of four years, the entire $40,000 profit will have been reported.

**Selling price.** Include cash, fair market value of property received from the buyer, the buyer's notes (at face value), and any outstanding mortgage on the property that the buyer assumes or takes subject to. If, under the contract of sale, the buyer pays off an existing mortgage or assumes liability for any other liens on the property, such as taxes you owe, or pays the sales commissions, such payments are also included in the selling price. Notes of a third party given to you by the buyer are valued at fair market value. Interest, including minimum interest imputed under the rules in *4.32*, is not included in the selling price.

**Caution**

**Year-End Sales of Securities**

Gain on a 2018 year-end sale of publicly traded securities cannot be deferred to 2019, even if you do not receive payment until early January 2019.

**Caution**

**Foreclosures**

If your property is foreclosed, the amount of the mortgage is treated as sales proceeds even if you do not receive anything on the sale.

*Caution*

### Recapture of Depreciation or First-Year Expensing Deduction

The entire amount of ordinary income recapture *(44.1–44.3)* is reported in the year of sale on Form 4797, even though you report the sale on the installment basis. An installment sale does not defer the reporting of the recaptured depreciation. You also add the recaptured amount to the basis of the sold asset on Line 12 of Form 6252 to compute the amount of the remaining gain to be reported on each installment. See the instructions to Form 6252.

**Installment sale basis.** You need to know your installment sale basis to figure your gross profit. Installment sale basis is the total of the adjusted basis of the property *(5.20)*, selling expenses, such as brokers' commissions and legal fees, and recaptured depreciation income, if any *(44.1)*.

**Gross profit and gross profit percentage.** Gross profit is the selling price minus your installment sale basis. Divide the gross profit by the contract price (see next paragraph) to get the gross profit percentage. Each year, you multiply this percentage by your payments to determine the taxable amount under the installment method.

**Contract price where the buyer takes subject to or assumes an existing mortgage.** The selling price includes the amount of your existing mortgages that the buyer assumes or takes the property subject to. To figure the gross profit percentage, first reduce the selling price by the mortgages. The reduced amount is the contract price. You then divide your gross profit by the contract price to get the gross profit percentage.

However, if the mortgage exceeds your installment sale basis (total of adjusted basis of the property, selling expenses, and depreciation recapture), you are required to report the excess as a payment received in the year of sale and also increase the contract price by that excess amount. Where the mortgage equals or exceeds your installment sale basis, the contract price will be the same as the gross profit, and the gross profit percentage will be 100%; *see* Example 3 below.

In a wraparound mortgage transaction, the buyer does not assume the seller's mortgage or take the property subject to it, but instead makes payments that cover the seller's outstanding mortgage liability. At one time, the IRS treated a wraparound mortgage transaction as an assumption of a mortgage by the buyer and required a reduction of the selling price by the mortgage to compute the contract price. The Tax Court rejected the IRS position, and the IRS acquiesced in the decision. Currently, the IRS does not require a reduction of selling price for a wraparound mortgage in the Form 6252 instructions or in Publication 537; *see* Example 4 below.

---

### EXAMPLES

1. You sell a building for $300,000. The building was secured by an existing mortgage of $50,000 that you pay off at the sale closing from the buyer's initial payment. The contract price is $300,000.

2. Same facts as in Example 1, but the buyer will pay $250,000 and assume the mortgage of $50,000. The contract price is $250,000 ($300,000 – $50,000).

3. You sell a building for $90,000. The buyer will pay you $10,000 annually for three years (plus 5% interest) and assume an existing mortgage of $60,000. The adjusted basis of the property is $45,000. Selling expenses are $5,000. The total installment sale basis is $50,000 ($45,000 plus $5,000). The mortgage exceeds this basis by $10,000 ($60,000 – $50,000). This $10,000 excess is included in the contract price and treated as a payment made in the year of sale. The contract price is $40,000:

| | |
|---|---|
| Selling price (including $60,000 mortgage) | $90,000 |
| Less: Mortgage | 60,000 |
| Total amount to be received from buyer (other than interest) | $30,000 |
| Add: Excess of mortgage ($60,000) over installment sale basis ($50,000) | 10,000 |
| Contract price | $40,000 |
| Selling price | $90,000 |
| Less: Installment sale basis | 50,000 |
| Gross profit | $40,000 |
| Gross profit percentage ($40,000 gross profit ÷ $40,000 contract price) | 100% |

> Since the gross profit percentage is 100%, 100% of each annual payment must be reported as taxable gain from the sale. The $10,000 excess of the mortgage over installment basis is treated as a payment in the year of sale, and so 100% (the gross profit percentage) of it must be reported as taxable gain for that year.
>
> 4. Abel sells real property, encumbered by a mortgage of $900,000, for $2 million. Installment sale basis (adjusted basis plus selling costs) is $700,000. The buyer pays $200,000 cash and gives an interest-bearing wraparound mortgage note for $1.8 million. Abel remains obligated to pay off the $900,000 mortgage. The gross profit ratio is 65% ($1,300,000 gross profit ÷ $2,000,000 contract price). In the year of sale, Abel reports the $200,000 cash, of which 65%, or $130,000, is taxable income.

**Change of selling price.** If the selling price is changed during the period payments are outstanding, the gross profit percentage is refigured on the new selling price. The adjusted profit ratio is then applied to payments received after the adjustment.

### EXAMPLE

Jones sold real estate in 2016 for $100,000. His basis, including selling expenses, was $40,000, so his gross profit was $60,000. The buyer agreed to pay, starting in 2016 (year of sale), five annual installments of $20,000 plus 5% interest. As the gross profit percentage was 60% ($60,000 ÷ $100,000), Jones reported profit of $12,000 (60% of $20,000) on the installments received in 2016 and 2017.

In early 2018, the parties renegotiated the sales price, reducing it from $100,000 to $85,000, and reducing payments for 2018, 2019 and 2020 to $15,000. Jones's original profit of $60,000 is reduced to $45,000 ($85,000 revised sales price less $40,000 basis). Of the $45,000 profit, $24,000 has already been reported: $12,000 was reported in 2016 and an additional $12,000 in 2017. To get the revised profit percentage, Jones must divide the $21,000 of profit not yet received ($45,000 less $24,000) by the remaining sales price of $45,000 ($85,000 less $40,000 in total installments in 2016 and 2017). The revised profit percentage is 46.67% ($21,000 ÷ $45,000). In 2018, 2019, and 2020, Jones reports profit of $7,000 on each $15,000 installment (46.67% of $15,000).

**Payments received during the year.** Payments include cash, the fair market value of property or services received, and payments on the buyer's notes. Payments do not include receipt of the buyer's notes or other evidence of indebtedness, unless payable on demand or readily tradable. "Readily tradable" means registered bonds, bonds with coupons attached, debentures, and other evidences of indebtedness of the buyer that are readily tradable in an established securities market. This rule is directed mainly at corporate acquisitions. A third-party guarantee (including a standby letter of credit) is not treated as a payment received on an installment obligation.

If the buyer has assumed or taken property subject to a mortgage that exceeds your installment sale basis (adjusted basis plus selling expenses plus depreciation recapture, if any), you include as a payment in the year of the sale the excess of the mortgage over the installment basis; *see* the Johnson Example below.

*Caution*

**Extension of Pledge Rule**

If a loan arrangement gives you the right to repay the debt by transferring an installment obligation, you are treated as if you had directly pledged the obligation as security for the debt. As a result, the loan proceeds are treated as a payment on the installment obligation, which will increase installment income for the year of the "deemed pledge."

### EXAMPLE

Johnson sells a building for $160,000, subject to a mortgage of $60,000. Installments plus interest are to be paid over five years. His adjusted basis in the building was $30,000 and his selling expenses were $10,000, so his installment sale basis is $40,000 and his gross profit is $120,000 ($160,000 – $40,000). The contract price is also $120,000, the selling price of $160,000 less $40,000, the part of the mortgage that did not exceed the installment sale basis.

The $20,000 excess of the $60,000 mortgage over the installment sale basis of $40,000 is part of the contract price and is also treated as a payment received in the year of sale. Since the mortgage exceeds Johnson's installment sale basis, he is treated as having recovered his entire basis in the year of sale, and all installment payments will be taxable, as his gross profit ratio is 100%: gross profit of $120,000 ÷ contract price of $120,000. In the year of sale, Johnson must report as taxable gain 100% of the installment payment received, plus the $20,000 difference between the mortgage and his installment sale basis.

**Pledging installment obligation as security.** If, as security for a loan, you pledge an installment obligation from a sale of property of more than $150,000 (excluding farm property, personal-use property and timeshares and residential lots), the net loan proceeds must be treated as a payment on the installment obligation. The net loan proceeds are treated as received on the later of the date the loan is secured and the date you receive the loan proceeds. These pledging rules do not apply if the debt refinances a debt that was outstanding on December 17, 1987, and secured by the installment obligation until the refinancing. If the refinancing exceeds the loan principal owed immediately before the refinancing, the excess is treated as a payment on the installment obligation. See the Form 6252 instructions.

## 5.23 Electing Not To Report on the Installment Method

If any sale proceeds are to be received after the year of sale, you must file Form 6252 and use the installment method unless you "elect out" by making a timely election to report the entire gain in the year of sale. If you want to report the entire gain in the year of sale, do not file Form 6252. Include the entire gain on Form 8949 or Form 4797 by the due date for filing your return (plus extensions) for the year of sale. If you timely file your return without making the election, you can do so on an amended return filed no later than six months after the original due date (without extensions); write "Filed pursuant to section *301.9100*-2" at the top of the amended return.

**Election out is generally irrevocable.** If you "elect out" of the installment method by reporting the entire gain in the year of sale, you may change to the installment method on an amended return only with the consent of the IRS. In private rulings, the IRS has granted permission to revoke an election out that was inadvertent, such as where the taxpayer's accountant was instructed to use the installment method but the accountant mistakenly reported the entire gain in the year of sale.

In one case, where the sales price was payable over 12 years, the accountant who was preparing the taxpayers' joint return erroneously determined that the installment method would not be beneficial to them, so he "elected out" of the installment method by reporting the entire gain as income in the year of the sale. The taxpayers were not aware that the accountant did this. When the accountant prepared their return for the following year, he realized he made a mistake and that installment sale reporting would have been beneficial. On behalf of the taxpayers, the accountant filed a request with the IRS to revoke the "election out," and the IRS agreed in a private ruling. The election out was based on the accountant's erroneous computation and the taxpayers were unaware of the error.

If the IRS is not convinced that the election out was inadvertent, it will likely refuse permission to retroactively allow the change to the installment method, on the grounds that a revocation of the election would involve hindsight and result in tax avoidance. For example, in one case, a seller "elected out" in a year in which he planned to deduct a net operating loss carryforward from an installment sale gain. In a later year, the IRS substantially reduced the loss. The seller then asked the IRS to allow him to revoke the "election out" so he could use the installment method. The IRS refused in a private ruling, claiming that the seller asked for the revocation to avoid tax. The installment sale would defer gain to a later year, which is a tax avoidance purpose.

## 5.24 Restriction on Installment Sales to Relatives

The installment sale method is not allowed where you sell depreciable property to a controlled business, or to a trust in which you or your spouse is a beneficiary. All payments to be received over the installment period are considered received in the year of sale.

Further, if you sell property to a relative on the installment basis, and the relative later resells the property, you could lose the benefit of installment reporting. Generally, you are taxed on your relative's sale if it is within two years of the original sale.

**Two-year resale rule for property.** If you make an installment sale of property to a related party, you are taxed on a second sale by the related party only if it occurs within two years of the initial installment sale and before all payments from the first installment sale are made. However, the two-year limitation does not apply if the property is marketable securities.

*Caution*

**Installment Sale to Relative**

If you sell property on the installment basis to a relative who later resells the property, you could lose the benefit of installment reporting.

Related parties include a spouse, child, grandchild, parent, grandparent, brother or sister, controlled corporation (50% or more direct or indirect ownership), any S corporation in which you own stock or partnership in which you are a partner, a trust in which you are a beneficiary, or a grantor trust of which you are treated as the owner. You are treated as owning stock held by your spouse, brothers, sisters, children, grandchildren, parents, and grandparents.

For the year of the related party sale, you must report as additional installment sale income: (1) the proceeds from the related party's sale or the contract price from the initial installment sale, whichever is less, minus (2) installment payments received from the related party as of the end of the year. The computation is made in Part III of Form 6252.

The two-year period is extended during any period in which the buyer's risk is lessened by a put on the property, an option by another person to acquire the property, or a short sale or other transaction lessening the risk of loss.

 *Caution*

**IRS Notice of Related Party Transfer**
Where you transfer property to a related party, the IRS has two years from the date you notify it that there has been a second disposition to assess a deficiency with respect to your transfer.

### EXAMPLE

In 2018, Jones Sr. sells unmortgaged land to his son for $300,000, payable in five equal annual installments starting that year, plus 4% interest. The father's installment sale basis is $120,000, so his gross profit is $180,000 and his gross profit percentage is 60% ($180,000 profit / $300,000 contract price). In 2018 (the year of sale), Jones Sr. receives the first $60,000 payment and reports on his 2018 return $36,000 ($60,000 × 60%) as installment sale income. The next year, in 2019, the son makes the required $60,000 payment to his father and then sells the land to a third party for $400,000. Under the two-year resale rule, the father must report additional income for 2019. The father is considered to have received $180,000 on the son's resale, and he must report a total of $144,000 as installment sale income for 2019:

| | |
|---|---|
| Lesser of sale proceeds from resale ($400,000) or original contract price ($300,000) | $300,000 |
| Minus: total payments from son by end of 2019 | 120,000 |
| Treated as received by father from resale | 180,000 |
| Plus: payment from son in 2019 (resale year) | 90,000 |
| Total amount treated as received by father for 2019 | 240,000 |
| Multiply by 60% gross profit percentage | .60 |
| Father's total installment sale income for 2019 | $144,000 |

The father will not be taxed on payments from the son after 2019, apart from interest, since he has already reported all of the payments ($300,000) due on the initial sale ($60,000 payment was reported for 2018 and $240,000 for 2019).

**Exceptions to related-party rule.** There are exceptions to the related-party rule. Second dispositions resulting from an involuntary conversion of the property will not be subject to the related-party rule so long as the first disposition occurred before the threat or imminence of conversion. Similarly, transfers after the death of the person making the first disposition or the death of the related person (who acquired the property in the first disposition) are not treated as second dispositions. Also, a sale or exchange of stock to the issuing corporation is not treated as a first disposition. Finally, you may avoid tax on a related party's second sale by satisfying the IRS that neither the initial nor the second sale was made for tax avoidance purposes. The non-tax-avoidance exception is considered met if the second disposition by the related party is an installment sale with payment terms that are substantially equal to or longer than those for the original installment sale; there must not be significant deferral of gain from the original sale.

**Sales of depreciable property to related party.** Installment reporting is not allowed for sales of depreciable property made to a controlled corporation or partnership (50% control by seller) and between such controlled corporations and partnerships. In figuring control of a corporation, you are considered to own stock held by your spouse, children, grandchildren, brothers or sisters, parents, and grandparents. Installment reporting is also disallowed on a sale to a trust in which you or a spouse is a beneficiary unless your interest is considered a remote contingent interest whose actuarial value is 5% or less of the trust property's value. On these related-party sales, the entire gain is reported in the year of sale, unless the seller convinces the IRS that the transfer was not motivated by tax avoidance purposes.

On a sale of depreciable property to a related party, if the amounts of payments are contingent (for example, payments are tied to profits), the seller must make a special calculation. He or she must treat as received in the year of sale all noncontingent payments plus the fair market value of the contingent payments if such value may be reasonably ascertained. If the fair market value of the contingent payments may not be reasonably calculated, the seller recovers basis ratably. The purchaser's basis for the acquired property includes only amounts that the seller has included in income under the basis recovery rule. Thus, the purchaser's basis is increased annually as the seller recovers basis.

## 5.25 Contingent Payment Sales

Where the final selling price or payment period of an installment sale is not fixed at the end of the taxable year of sale, you are considered to have transacted a "contingent payment sale." Special rules apply where a maximum selling price may be figured under the terms of the agreement or there is no fixed price but there is a fixed payment period, or there is neither a fixed price nor a fixed payment period.

**Stated maximum selling price.** Under IRS regulations, a stated maximum selling price may be determined by assuming that all of the contingencies contemplated under the agreement are met. When the maximum amount is later reduced, the gross profit ratio is recomputed.

> **EXAMPLE**
>
> Smith sells stock in Acme Co. for a down payment of $100,000 plus an amount equal to 5% of the net profits of Acme for the next nine years. Smith's basis for the stock is $200,000. The contract provides that the maximum amount payable, including the $100,000 down payment but exclusive of interest, is $2,000,000. The selling price and contract price is $2,000,000. Gross profit is $1,800,000. The gross profit ratio is 90% ($1,800,000 ÷ $2,000,000). Thus, $90,000 of the first payment is reportable as gain and $10,000 as a recovery of basis.

**Fixed period.** When a stated maximum selling price is not determinable but the maximum payment period is fixed, basis—including selling expenses—is allocated equally to the taxable years in which payment may be received under the agreement. If, in any year, no payment is received or the amount of payment received is less than the basis allocated to that taxable year, no loss is allowed unless the taxable year is the final payment year or the agreement has become worthless. When no loss is allowed in a year, the basis allocated to the taxable year is carried forward to the next succeeding taxable year.

**No stated maximum selling price or fixed period.** If the agreement fails to specify a maximum selling price and payment period, the IRS may view the agreement as a rent or royalty income agreement. However, if the arrangement qualifies as a sale, basis (including selling expenses) is recovered in equal annual increments over a 15-year period commencing with the date of sale. If in any taxable year no payment is received or the amount of payment received (exclusive of interest) is less than basis allocated to the year, no loss is allowed unless the agreement has become worthless. Excess basis not recovered in one year is reallocated in level amounts over the balance of the 15-year term. Any basis not recovered at the end of the 15th year is carried forward to the next succeeding year, and to the extent unrecovered, carried forward from year to year until basis has been recovered or the agreement is determined to be worthless. The rule requiring initial level allocation of basis over 15 years may not apply if you prove to the IRS that a 15-year general rule will substantially and inappropriately defer recovery of basis.

In some cases, basis recovery under an income forecast type of method may also be allowed.

*Caution*

**Contingent Sales**

An example of a contingent sale in which the selling price cannot be determined by the end of the year of the sale is a sale of your business where the selling price includes a percentage of future profits. You and your tax advisor should consult the technical rules in IRS Regulation Section 15A.453-1(c) for details on reporting such sales.

**EXAMPLE**

Brown sells property for 10% of the property's gross rents over a five-year period. Brown's basis is $5,000,000. The sales price is indefinite and the maximum selling price is not fixed under the terms of the contract; basis is recovered ratably over the five-year period.

| Year | Payment | Basis recovered | Gain |
|------|---------|-----------------|------|
| First | $ 1,300,000 | $ 1,000,000 | $ 300,000 |
| Second | 1,500,000 | 1,000,000 | 500,000 |
| Third | 1,400,000 | 1,000,000 | 400,000 |
| Fourth | 1,800,000 | 1,000,000 | 800,000 |
| Fifth | 2,100,000 | 1,000,000 | 1,100,000 |

## 5.26 Using Escrow and Other Security Arrangements

When you sell property on the installment basis, the remaining sales proceeds (plus interest) may be placed in an escrow account pending the possible occurrence of an event such as the approval of title or your performance of certain contractual conditions. If the escrow account is irrevocable or there are no escrow restrictions preventing you from receiving immediate payment, the IRS does not allow installment reporting. It considers the buyer's obligation paid in full when the balance of the proceeds is deposited into the unrestricted escrow account. If in a year after the year of the installment sale an escrow account is set up as a substitute for unpaid notes or deeds of trust, the IRS considers the escrow funds as payment in full, assuming there are no substantial restrictions on your right to the proceeds.

**EXAMPLES**

1. Anderson sold stock and mining property for almost $5 million. He agreed to place $500,000 in escrow to protect the buyer against his possible breaches of warranty and to provide security for certain liabilities. The escrow agreement called for Anderson to direct the investments of the escrow fund and receive income from the fund in excess of $500,000.

   The IRS claimed that in the year of sale Anderson was taxable on the $500,000 held in escrow on the ground that Anderson's control of the fund rendered the fund taxable immediately. Anderson argued he was only taxable as the funds were released to him, and the Tax Court agreed. The fund was not under his unqualified control. He might never get the fund if the liabilities materialized. Although Anderson had a free hand with investment of the money, he still lacked ultimate ownership.

2. Rhodes sold a tract to a buyer who was willing to pay at once the entire purchase price of $157,000. But Rhodes wanted to report the sale on the installment basis over a period of years. The buyer refused to execute a purchase money mortgage on the property to allow the installment sale election (required under prior law) because he wanted clear and unencumbered title to the tract. As a solution, Rhodes asked the buyer to turn over the purchase price to a bank, as escrow agent, which would pay the sum over a five-year period.

   The escrow arrangement failed to support an installment sale. Rhodes was fully taxable on the entire price in the year of the sale. The buyer's payment was unconditional and irrevocable. The escrow arrangement involved no genuine conditions that could defeat Rhodes's right to payment, as the buyer could not revoke, alter, or end the arrangement.

3. In January, an investor sold real estate for $100,000. He received $10,000 as a down payment and six notes, each for $15,000, secured by a deed of trust on the property. The notes, together with interest, were due annually over the next six years. In July, the buyer deposited the remainder of the purchase price with an escrow agent and got the seller to cancel the deed of trust.

   The agreement provides that the escrow agent will pay off the buyer's notes as they fall due. The buyer remains liable for the installment payments. The escrow deposit is irrevocable, and the payment schedule may not be accelerated by any party under any circumstances. According to the IRS, the sale, which initially qualified as an installment sale, is disqualified by the escrow account.

## 5.27 Minimum Interest on Deferred Payment Sales

The tax law requires a minimum amount of interest to be charged on deferred payment sales. The rules for imputing interest on sales are discussed in *4.32*. Imputed interest is included in the taxable income of the seller. Imputed interest is deductible by the buyer if the property is business or investment property, but not if it is used substantially all the time for personal purposes.

## 5.28 Dispositions of Installment Notes

A sale, a gift, an exchange or other transfer or cancellation of mortgage notes or other obligations received in an installment sale has tax consequences. If you sell or exchange the notes or if you accept less than face value in satisfaction of the obligation, gain or loss results to the extent of the difference between the basis of the notes and the amount realized. For example, if in satisfaction of an installment note, the buyer gives you other property worth less than the face value of the note, you have gain (or loss) to the extent your amount realized exceeds (or is less than) your basis in the installment note. The basis of an installment note or obligation is the face value of the note less the income that would be reported if the obligation were paid in full; *see* Example 2 below.

Gain or loss is long term if the original sale was entitled to long-term capital gain treatment. This is true even if the notes were held short term. If the original sale resulted in short-term gain or ordinary income, the sale of the notes gives short-term gain or ordinary income, regardless of the holding period of the notes.

Suppose you make an installment sale of your real estate, taking back a land contract. Later a mortgage is substituted for the unpaid balance of the land contract. The IRS has ruled that the substitution is not the same as a disposition of the unpaid installment obligations. There is no tax on the substitution.

**Gift of installment obligation.** If the installment obligations are disposed of other than by sale or exchange, such as when you make a gift of the installment obligations to someone else, gain or loss is the difference between the basis of the obligations and their fair market value at the time of the disposition. If an installment obligation is canceled or otherwise becomes unenforceable, the same rule for determining gain or loss applies. However, no gain or loss is recognized on a gift to a spouse *(6.7)*.

### EXAMPLES

1. You sell a lot for $200,000 that cost you $100,000. In the year of the sale, you received $50,000 in cash and the purchaser's notes for the remainder of the selling price, or $150,000. A year later, before the buyer makes a payment on the notes, you sell them for $130,000 cash:

| | |
|---|---|
| Selling price of property | $200,000 |
| Cost of property | 100,000 |
| Total profit | $100,000 |
| Profit percentage, or proportion of each payment returnable as income, is 50% ($100,000 total profit ÷ $200,000 contract price) | |
| Unpaid balance of notes | $150,000 |
| Amount of income reportable if notes were paid in full (50% of $150,000) | 75,000 |
| Adjusted basis of the notes | $75,000 |

    Your profit on the sale of the notes is $55,000 ($130,000 – $75,000). It is capital gain if the sale of the lot was taxable as capital gain.

2. You sell a lot on the installment basis for $200,000 that cost you $120,000. In the year of sale, you received $20,000 in cash and the buyer's note for $180,000. Your gross profit percentage is 40% ($80,000 total profit ÷ $200,000 contract price).

Two years later, the buyer is facing financial difficulties and is unable to make payments on the $180,000 note. In satisfaction of the installment note, the buyer agrees to give you two other parcels of real estate, each worth $50,000. By accepting less than the $180,000 face value of the note in satisfaction of the obligation, you realize an $8,000 capital loss; the difference between the amount you realize and your basis in the installment obligation is figured as follows:

| | |
|---|---|
| Amount realized ($50,000 for each parcel) | $100,000 |
| Face value of note | 180,000 |
| Less: Amount of income reportable if note was paid in full given 40% profit percentage (40% of $180,000 = $72,000) | 72,000 |
| Basis in installment note | $108,000 |

The difference between the $100,000 amount realized and $108,000 basis gives you an $8,000 loss. Assuming your profit on the original sale was long-term capital gain, the loss would be deducted as a long-term capital loss.

A gift of installment obligations to a person other than a spouse or to a charitable organization is treated as a taxable disposition. Gain or loss is the difference between the basis of the obligations and their fair market value at the time of the gift. If the notes are donated to a qualified charity, you may claim a contribution deduction for the fair market value of the obligations at the time of the gift.

**Transfer at death.** A transfer of installment obligations at the death of the holder of the obligation is not taxed as a disposition. As the notes are paid, the estate or beneficiaries report income in the same proportion as the decedent would have, had he or she lived. A transfer of installment obligations to a revocable trust is also not taxed. However, the estate is subject to tax if the obligation is canceled, becomes unenforceable, or is transferred to the buyer because of the death of the obligation holder.

# 5.29 Repossession of Personal Property Sold on Installment

When a buyer defaults and you repossess personal property, either by a voluntary surrender or a foreclosure, you may realize gain or loss. The method of calculating gain or loss is similar to the method used for disposition of installment notes *(5.28)*. Gain or loss is the difference between the fair market value of the repossessed property and your basis for the installment obligations satisfied by the repossession. This rule is followed whether or not title was kept by you or transferred to the buyer. The amount realized is reduced by costs incurred during the repossession. The basis of the obligation is face value less unreported profit.

If the property repossessed is bid in at a lawful public auction or judicial sale, the fair market value of the property is presumed to be the purchase or bid price, in the absence of proof to the contrary.

Gain or loss in the repossession is reported in the year of the repossession.

Repossession gain or loss keeps the same character as the gain or loss realized on the original sale. If the sale originally resulted in a capital gain, the repossession gain is also a capital gain.

Your basis in the repossessed property is its fair market value at the time of repossession.

**Real property.** Repossessions of real property are discussed in *Chapter 31 (31.12)*.

### EXAMPLE

In December 2017, you sell home furniture for $4,500—$900 down and $300 a month plus 3% interest beginning January 2018. You reported the installment sale on your 2017 tax return. The buyer defaulted after making three monthly payments.

You foreclosed and repossessed the property in 2018; the fair market value on the repossession date was $4,200. The legal costs of foreclosure and the cost of moving the furniture back to your home was $400. The gain on the repossession in 2018 is computed as follows:

| | | |
|---|---:|---:|
| Fair market value of property repossessed | | $ 4,200 |
| Basis of the buyer's notes at time of repossession: | | |
| Selling price | $ 4,500 | |
| Less: Payments made | 1,800 | |
| Unpaid balance of notes at repossession | $ 2,700 | |
| Less: Unrealized profit (assume gross profit percentage of 331/3 × $2,700) | $ 900 | |
| Basis of obligation ($2,700-$900) | | 1,800 |
| Gain on repossession | | $ 2,400 |
| Less: Repossession costs | | 400 |
| Taxable gain on repossession | | $ 2,000 |

## 5.30 Boot in Like-Kind Exchange Payable in Installments

An exchange of like-kind property is tax free unless boot is received. "Boot" may be cash or notes. If you transfer property subject to a mortgage and the amount of the mortgage you give up exceeds the mortgage you assume on the property received, that excess is boot *(6.3)*. Boot is taxable, and if payable in installments, the following rules apply. Contract price is reduced by the fair market value of like-kind property received. Gross profit is reduced by gain not recognized. "Payment" does not include like-kind property.

The same treatment applies to certain tax-free reorganizations that are not treated as dividends, to exchanges of certain insurance policies, exchanges of the stock of the same corporation, and exchanges of United States obligations.

*Planning Reminder*

**Taxable Boot Received in Exchange**

If you make an exchange of like-kind property and also receive cash or other property that is payable in one or more future years, you may report the gain using the installment method.

### EXAMPLE

In 2018, property with an installment sale basis (basis plus selling expenses) of $400,000 is exchanged for like-kind property worth $200,000, plus installment obligations of $800,000, of which $100,000 is payable in 2019, plus interest. The balance of $700,000 plus interest will be paid in 2020. The contract price is $800,000 ($1 million selling price less $200,000 like-kind property received). The gross profit is $600,000 ($1 million less $400,000 installment sale basis). The gross profit ratio is 75% (gross profit of $600,000 ÷ contract price of $800,000). Like-kind property is not treated as a payment received in the year of exchange, so no gain is reported in 2018. In 2019, gain of $75,000 will have to be reported (75% gross profit ratio × $100,000 payment), and in 2020 there will be a gain of $525,000 (75% of $700,000 payment).

## 5.31 "Interest" Tax if Sales Price Exceeds $150,000 With Over $5 Million Debt

If property is sold on the installment basis for more than $150,000, and the balance of installment obligations outstanding at the end of the year exceeds $5 million, an interest charge is imposed on the tax-deferred amount. The special tax applies to non-dealer sales of business or rental property (real estate or personal property) for over $150,000. Farm property and personal-use property, such as a residence, are exempt from the tax.

**How to report interest tax.** The interest charge is an additional tax. The method of computing the interest tax is complicated; the rules are in Internal Revenue Code Section 453A. In general, you compute the ratio of the face amount of outstanding installment obligations in excess of $5 million to the face amount of all outstanding installment obligations. This ratio is multiplied by the year-end unrecognized gain on the obligation, your top tax rate (ordinary income or capital gain) for the year, and also by the IRS interest rate for the last month of the year.

The interest is not deductible. It is reported on Line 62, Schedule 4 of Form 1040; identify it with code "453A(c)".

**Dealer sale of time shares and residential lots.** The installment method can be used to report income from sales of certain time-share rights (generally time shares of up to six weeks per year) or residential lots if the seller elects to pay interest on the tax deferred under the installment method. The rules for computing the interest are in Code Section 453(l)(3). The interest is reported on Line 62, Schedule 4 of Form 1040; identify it with code "453(l)(3)".

## 5.32 Worthless Securities

If you owned stock or a bond as an investor (not as a securities dealer) that became completely worthless in 2018, you may deduct your cost basis for the security as a capital loss, subject to the deduction limit of $3,000 ($1,500 if married filing separately) in excess of capital gains *(5.4)*. The worthless security is treated as sold on the last day of the year, which determines whether the loss is a short-term or long-term capital loss. Report the worthless security in the short-term or long-term section of Form 8949, as applicable (see below). Capital loss treatment applies unless ordinary loss treatment is available for worthless Section 1244 stock *(30.11)*.

A loss of worthless securities is deductible only in the year the securities become completely worthless. If you abandon the securities, the securities are treated as completely worthless under an IRS regulation; *see* below. The loss may not be deducted in any other year. You may not claim a loss for a partially worthless security. However, if there is a market for it, sell the security and deduct the capital loss.

Because it is sometimes difficult to determine the year in which a security becomes completely worthless, the law allows you to file a refund claim within seven years from the due date of the return for the proper year (the year the security actually became completely worthless), or if later, within two years from the date you paid the tax for that year.

To support a deduction for 2018, you must show:

1. The security had some value at the end of 2017. That is, you must be ready to show that the stock did not become worthless in a year prior to 2018. If you learn that the security did become worthless in a prior year, file an amended return for that year; *see* the Filing Tip on this page.

2. The security became totally worthless in 2018. You must be able to present facts fixing the time of loss during this year. For example, the company went bankrupt, stopped doing business, and is insolvent. Despite evidence of worthlessness, such as insolvency, the stock may be considered to have some value if the company continues to do business, or there are plans to reorganize the company. No deduction may be claimed for a partially worthless corporate bond or stock.

If you are making payments on a negotiable note you used to buy the stock that became worthless and you are on the cash-basis method, your payments are deductible losses in the years the payments are made, rather than in the year the stock became worthless.

If the security is a bond, note, certificate, or other evidence of a debt incurred by a corporation, the loss is deducted as a capital loss, provided the obligation is in registered form or has attached interest coupons. A loss on a worthless corporate obligation is always deemed sustained on the last day of the year, regardless of when the company failed during the year.

If the obligation is not issued with interest coupons or in registered form, or if it is issued by an individual, the loss is treated as a bad debt. If you received the obligation in a business transaction, the loss is fully deductible. You may also make a claim for a partially worthless business bad debt. If it is a nonbusiness debt, the loss is a capital loss and no claim may be made for partial worthlessness *(5.33)*.

 *Filing Tip*

**Refund Deadline for Worthless Stock**

You can take advantage of a special seven-year statute of limitations to claim a refund due to a worthless security or bad debt. An amended return for the year the security or debt became worthless can be filed within seven years from the date your original return for that year had to be filed, or, if later, within two years from the date you paid the tax.

For example, if you have held securities that you learn became worthless in 2011, you still have until April 15, 2019, to file for a refund of 2011 taxes by claiming a deduction for the worthless securities on an amended return (Form 1040X) for 2011.

### Selling Before the Security Becomes Worthless

To claim a deduction for worthless stock or bonds, you must be able to prove that the security became completely worthless in the year for which you are claiming the deduction. Sometimes you can avoid the problem of proving worthlessness by selling while there is still a market for the security. For example, a company you own stock in is on the verge of bankruptcy in 2019, but there is some doubt about the complete worthlessness of its securities. You might sell the securities for whatever you can get for them and claim the loss on the sale as a capital loss on your 2019 return. Sell to an unrelated buyer to avoid the loss disallowance rule *(5.6)*. If there is no market for the security, you can abandon it to claim a deduction for worthlessness; *see 5.32* for the abandonment rule.

*Caution*

### Accounts and Notes Receivable

If you report income and expenses using the cash method, you may not claim a bad debt deduction for accounts and notes receivable on unpaid goods or services that you have not included as gross income *(40.6)*. If your client or customer fails to pay your bill for services rendered, you do not have a deductible bad debt because you do not have a "basis" in the debt to deduct.

**When to deduct worthless stock.** If at the end of 2018 a company is in financial trouble but you are not sure whether its condition is hopeless, it is advisable to claim the deduction for 2018 to protect your claim. If you claim the deduction for 2018 and it turns out that complete worthlessness did not occur until a later year, you can claim the deduction for the proper year and then file an amended return for 2018 to eliminate the deduction.

Another option in fixing the timing of your loss deduction is to abandon the securities, as discussed below.

**Abandoned securities treated as worthless.** The IRS treats abandoned securities as totally worthless under a regulation that took effect for abandonments after March 12, 2008. To abandon a security, you must permanently surrender and relinquish all rights in the security and receive no payment in exchange for the security. Make sure that the security is removed from your account. The IRS will determine whether there has been an abandonment based on all the facts and circumstances. Under the general timing rule for worthless securities, the loss on abandonment is treated as resulting from a sale of a capital asset on the last day of the year in which the abandonment occurs.

**Report a worthless security as a long-term or short-term loss on Form 8949.** If securities became worthless during 2018, they are treated as if they were sold on the last day of the year for purposes of determining your holding period, regardless of when worthlessness actually occurred. If a sale on the last day of the year provides you with a short-term (one year or less) holding period, report the loss as a short-term capital loss in Part I of Form 8949. Use Part II of Form 8949 for a long-term loss.

> **EXAMPLE**
>
> You bought 100 shares of Z Co. stock on July 1, 1999. On March 20, 2018, the stock is considered wholly worthless. The loss is deemed to have been incurred on December 31, 2018. The loss is reported as a long-term capital loss on Form 8949; the holding period is from July 2, 1999 to December 31, 2018. Label the loss as "Worthless" across the columns for date sold and sales price. The long-term loss from Form 8949 will be transferred to Schedule D, where net capital gain or loss for the year is determined.

**Ordinary loss on Small Business Investment Company (SBIC) stock.** On Form 4797, investors may take ordinary loss deductions for losses on the worthlessness or sale of SBIC stock. The loss may also be treated as a business loss for net operating loss purposes. However, a loss realized on a short sale of SBIC stock is deductible as a capital loss. A Small Business Investment Company is a company authorized to provide small businesses with equity capital. Do not confuse investments in these companies with investments in small business stock (Section 1244 stock) *(30.11)*.

**S corporation stock.** If an S corporation's stock becomes worthless during the taxable year, the basis in the stock is adjusted for the stockholder's share of corporate items of income, loss, and deductions before a deduction for worthlessness is claimed.

**Bank deposit loss.** If you lose funds in a bank that becomes insolvent, you may claim the loss as a nonbusiness bad debt *(5.33)*, a casualty loss *(18.5)*, or in some cases, an investment expense *(19.16)*. These options are discussed in *Chapter 18 (18.5)*.

## 5.33 Tax Consequences of Bad Debts

When you lend money or sell on credit and your debtor does not repay, you may deduct your loss. The type of deduction depends on whether the debt was incurred in a business or personal transaction. This distinction is important because business bad debts receive favored tax treatment.

**Business bad debt.** You may deduct partially or totally worthless business debts. A business bad debt is fully deductible from gross income on Schedule C if you are self-employed, or on Schedule F if your business is farming; *see* IRS Publication 535 for details.

**Nonbusiness bad debt.** To be deductible, a nonbusiness bad debt must be totally worthless; you may not deduct a partially worthless nonbusiness debt. A nonbusiness bad debt for 2018 is reported as a short-term capital loss on Form 8949 with Box C checked (to indicate that you did not receive a Form 1099-B). Enter "0" as the proceeds in column (d)). Enter your basis in the debt in column (e). You must attach a statement that describes the debt, your relationship to the debtor, your efforts to collect the debt, and your reasons for concluding that it had become worthless. As a short-term capital loss, a nonbusiness bad debt is deductible only from capital gains, if any, and $3,000 of ordinary income ($1,500 if married filing separately). Any excess is deductible as a capital loss carryover to 2019 and later years *(5.4)*.

**Examples of nonbusiness bad debts:**
- You enter into a deal for profit that is not connected with your business; for example, debts arising from investments are nonbusiness bad debts.
- You make a personal loan to a family member or friend with a reasonable hope of recovery and you are not in the business of making loans. You must be able to show that this is a bona fide loan and not a gift. Put the loan in writing and spell out repayment terms.
- You are assigned a debt that arose in the assignor's business. The fact that he or she could have deducted it as a business bad debt does not make it your business debt. A business debt must arise in your business.
- You pay liens filed against your property by mechanics or suppliers who have not been paid by your builder or contractor. Your payment is considered a deductible bad debt when there is no possibility of recovering reimbursement from the contractor and a judgment obtained against him or her is uncollectible.
- You lose a deposit on a house when the contractor becomes insolvent.
- You loan money to a corporation in which you are a shareholder, and your primary motivation is to protect your investment rather than your job; *see* below.
- You had an uninsured savings account in a financial institution that went into default.
- You are held secondarily liable on a mortgage debt assumed but not paid by a buyer of your home. Your payment to the bank or other holder of the mortgage is deductible as a bad debt if you cannot collect it from the buyer of the home.

**Guarantor or endorsement losses as bad debts.** If you guarantee a loan and must pay it off after the principal debtor defaults, your payment is deductible as a business bad debt if you had a business reason for the guarantee. For example, to protect a business relationship with a major client, you guarantee the client's loan. Your payment on the guarantee qualifies as a business bad debt. If, as a result of your payment, you have a legal right to recover the amount from the client (right of subrogation or similar right), you may not claim a bad debt deduction unless that right is partially or totally worthless.

A loss on a guarantee may be a nonbusiness bad debt if you made the guarantee to protect an investment, such as where you are a main shareholder of a corporation and guarantee a bank loan to the company. No deduction is allowed if you guaranteed the loan as a favor to a relative or friend.

**Loans by shareholders.** It is a common practice for stockholders to make loans to their corporations or to guarantee loans made to the company by banks or other lenders. If the corporation fails and the stockholder is not repaid or has to make good on the guarantee, tax treatment of the bad debt depends on whether the stockholder is an employee who made the loan to protect his or her job.

If the dominant motivation for the loan was to maintain employment, the bad debt is not deductible; employee business expenses are not deductible for 2018 and later years under the Tax Cuts and Jobs Act.

If the dominant motivation for the loan was to protect the stockholder's investment in the company and not his or her job, the bad debt is generally a nonbusiness bad debt deductible on Form 8949/Schedule D as a short-term capital loss.

If the stockholder is in the business of lending money and the loan was made in that capacity, the bad debt would be a business bad debt, deductible on Schedule C by a sole proprietor.

 *Filing Instruction*

**Nonbusiness Bad Debt**

If a nonbusiness bad debt became totally worthless in 2018, claim it as a short-term capital loss in Part I of Form 8949. Attach a statement describing the loan, your relationship to the debtor, how you tried to collect it, and why you decided it was worthless.

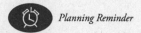

**Debt Worthless Before Due**

You do not have to wait until the debt is due in order to deduct a bad debt. Claim the deduction for the year that you can prove worthlessness occurred.

## 5.34 Four Rules To Prove a Bad Debt Deduction

To determine whether you have a bad debt deduction, read the four rules explained below. Pay close attention to the fourth rule, which requires proof that the debt became worthless in the year the deduction is claimed. Your belief that your debt is bad, or the mere refusal of the debtor to pay, is not sufficient evidence. There must be an event, such as the debtor's bankruptcy, to fix the debt as worthless.

**Rule 1.** You must have a valid debt. There must be a valid loan and not a gift, as in the case of an informal loan to a friend or relative. You have no loss if your right to repayment is not fixed or depends upon some event that may not happen. Thus, advances to a corporation already insolvent are not valid debts. Nor are advances that are to be repaid only if the corporation has a profit. Voluntary payment of another's debt is also nondeductible. If usurious interest was charged on a worthless debt, and under state law the debt was void or voidable, the debt is not deductible as a bad debt. However, where the lender was in the business of lending money, a court allowed him to deduct the unpaid amounts as business losses.

If advances are made to a company that has lost outside borrowing sources and is thinly capitalized, with heavy debt-to-equity ratio, this indicates that the advances are actually capital contributions and not loans.

**Rule 2.** A debtor-creditor relationship must exist at the time the debt arose. You have a loss if there was a promise to repay at the time the debt was created and you had the right to enforce it. If the advance was a gift and you did not expect to be repaid, you may not take a deduction.

**Rule 3.** The funds providing the loan or credit were previously reported as income or part of your capital. If you are on the cash basis, you may not deduct salary, rent, or fees that have not been paid to you as a bad debt. On the cash basis, you do not include these items in income until you are paid.

**Rule 4.** You must show that the debt became worthless during the year for which you are claiming the deduction. To prove that a debt became worthless in 2018, you must show:

First, that the debt had some value at the end of the previous year (2017), and that there was a reasonable hope and expectation of recovering something on the debt. Your personal belief unsupported by other facts is not enough.

Second, that an identifiable event occurred in 2018—such as a bankruptcy proceeding—that caused you to conclude the debt was worthless. In the case of a business debt that has become partially worthless, you need evidence that the debt has declined in value. Additionally, reasonable collection steps must have been undertaken. That you cancel a debt does not make it worthless. You must still show that the debt was worthless when you canceled it. You do not have to go to court to try to collect the debt if you can show that a court judgment would be uncollectible.

Third, that there is no reasonable hope the debt may have some value in a later year. You are not required to prove that there is no possibility of ever receiving some payment on your debt.

**Effect of statute of limitations.** A debt is not deductible merely because a statute of limitations has run against the debt. Although the debtor has a legal defense against your demand for payment, he or she may still recognize the obligation to pay. A debt is deductible only in the year it becomes worthless. What if your debtor recognized his or her moral obligation to pay in spite of the expiration of the statute of limitations, but dies before paying? Your claim would be defeated if the executor raises the statute of limitations. You have a bad debt deduction in the year you made the claim against the estate.

## 5.35 Family Bad Debts

The IRS views loans to relatives, especially to children and parents, as gifts, so that it is rather difficult to deduct family bad debts.

To overcome the presumption of a gift when you advance money to a relative, take the same steps you would in making a business loan. Take a note, set a definite payment date, and require interest and collateral. If the relative fails to pay, make an attempt to collect. Failure to enforce collection of a family debt is viewed by the courts as evidence of a gift, despite the taking of notes and the receipt of interest.

**Is a former spouse's default on child support a basis for a bad debt deduction?** If you pay support for your children when your former spouse defaults on court-ordered support payments, can you claim your expenses as a nonbusiness bad debt deduction on the grounds that your position is similar to a guarantor who pays a creditor when the principal debtor defaults? The IRS does not agree with such a claim and will disallow the deduction; its position is supported by the Tax Court.

The federal appeals court for the Ninth Circuit left open the possibility that such a claim may have merit if the spouse who did not receive the required child support can show: (1) what she or he spent on the children; and (2) that the former spouse's obligation to support was worthless in the year the deduction is claimed.

The Tax Court has subsequently reiterated its position that defaulted child support payments are not a basis for a bad debt deduction. Following these Tax Court decisions, the IRS also announced its continuing opposition to the Ninth Circuit's suggestion that a deduction may be possible. The IRS holds that since the support obligation of the defaulting spouse is imposed directly by the divorce court, the other parent who pays support to make up for the arrearage has no "basis" to support a bad debt deduction.

Periodically, legislation has been proposed to allow a bad debt deduction for unpaid child support, but none of the proposals have been enacted into law.

 *Caution*

**Formalize Loan With Relative**

To protect against a possible IRS claim that your loan was a gift and not a loan, put the loan in writing with repayment terms as if the debtor were a third party.

# CHAPTER 6

# Tax-Free Exchanges of Property

You may exchange investment or business real property for "like-kind" property without incurring a tax in the year of exchange if you meet the rules detailed in this chapter. Gain may be taxed upon a later disposition of the replacement property because the basis of the replacement property is usually the same as the basis of the property surrendered in the exchange. Thus, if you exchange property with a tax basis of $10,000 for property worth $50,000, the basis of the property received in exchange is fixed at $10,000, even though its fair market value is $50,000. The gain of $40,000 ($50,000 – $10,000), which is not taxed at the time of the exchange, is technically called "unrecognized gain." If you later sell the property for $50,000, you will realize a taxable gain of $40,000 ($50,000 – $10,000).

Where property received in a tax-free exchange is held until death, the unrecognized gain escapes income tax forever because basis of the property in the hands of an heir is generally the value of the property at the date of death. If the exchange involves the transfer of boot, such as cash or other property, gain on the exchange is taxable to the extent of the value of boot.

You may not make a tax-free exchange of U.S. real estate for foreign real estate.

Tax-free exchanges between related parties may become taxable if either party disposes of the exchanged property within a two-year period.

## 6.1 Like-Kind Exchanges of Real Property

You do not realize gain or loss on the "like-kind" exchange of business or investment real property (Code Section 1031). By making a qualifying exchange, you can defer the gain. On the other hand, a loss is also generally deferred; a loss on a qualifying exchange is not deductible unless you give up "unlike" property (not like-kind); *see* below.

For exchanges completed after 2017, only real property held for business or investment is eligible for like-kind treatment under the Tax Cuts and Jobs Act. Exchanges of personal property are no longer eligible. Thus, exchanges of depreciable tangible personal property, such as business airplanes, cars or trucks, or construction equipment, are now taxable transfers. However, the new law includes a transition rule to allow like-kind treatment for exchanges of personal property begun but not completed by the end of 2017, assuming the exchange qualified under the prior-law rules for personal property; the 45-day identification deadline *(6.3)* and 180-day completion deadline *(6.3, 6.4)* must be met.

For tax-free gain treatment, you must trade real property held for business use or investment for like-kind business or investment real property. If the properties are not simultaneously exchanged, the time limits for deferred exchanges *(6.3)* must be satisfied. The entire gain is deferred only if you do not receive any "boot"; gain is taxed to the extent of boot received *(6.2)*. Where gain on a qualifying exchange is deferred and not immediately taxed, it may be taxable in a later year when you sell the property because your basis for the new property (called "replacement property") is generally the same as the basis for the property you traded (called "relinquished property") *(5.16–5.20)*.

If you make a qualifying like-kind exchange with certain related parties, tax-free treatment may be lost unless both of you keep the exchanged properties for at least two years *(6.5)*.

**What is "like-kind" real property?** The term like-kind refers to the nature or character of the property, that is, whether real estate is traded for real estate. It does not refer to grade or quality, that is, whether the properties traded are new or used, improved or unimproved. This means that land may be traded for a building, farm land for city lots, commercial property for residential rental property, or a leasehold interest of 30 years or more for an outright ownership in realty. These are all considered like-kind exchanges of real estate. However, real property in the United States and foreign real property are not (by statute) like-kind.

 *Law Alert*

**Tax Deferral for Like-Kind Exchanges Preserved Only for Real Estate**

In recent years, proposals were made to eliminate entirely the tax-deferral benefits of like-kind exchanges (Code Section 1031), or to limit them, such as by putting a cap on the amount of capital gain that could be deferred on an exchange. Real estate interests fought hard to preserve like-kind exchanges, claiming that repeal would have a devastating impact on real estate investors and developers. The Tax Cuts and Jobs Act preserves like-kind exchanges for real property, while eliminating deferral treatment for exchanges of personal property.

---

### EXAMPLES

1. Jones, a real estate investor, purchased Parcel A for investment in 1999 for $5,000. In 2011, he exchanged it for another parcel, Parcel B, which had a fair market value of $50,000. The gain of $45,000 was not taxed in 2011.

2. Same facts as above, except that in 2018 Parcel B still has a fair market value of $50,000 and Jones sells it for that price. His taxable gain in 2018 is $45,000. The "tax-free" exchange rules have the effect of deferring tax on the appreciation on Parcel A until the property received in exchange for it is sold.

3. Same facts as in 1 above, but the value of Parcel B was $3,000 in 2011. Jones could not deduct the loss in 2011. Jones' basis in Parcel B is $5,000, the same as the basis of Parcel A. If Jones sells Parcel B in 2018 for $3,000, he may deduct a loss of $2,000.

---

**Personal use safe harbor for rental residence.** An IRS safe harbor (Revenue Procedure 2008-16) allows rental real estate used occasionally as a vacation home to be treated as investment property so that it can be exchanged without endangering tax-deferred treatment.

To qualify, the relinquished residence has to be owned for at least 24 months immediately before the exchange, and, in each of the two 12-month periods immediately preceding the exchange, the residence must be rented at a fair rental for at least 14 days and personal use by the owner and his or her relatives cannot exceed the greater of 14 days or 10% of the days for which the residence is rented at a fair rental in the 12-month period.

**Caution**

**Exchanging Depreciable Realty May Be Subject to Depreciation Recapture**

Recapture provisions supersede tax-free exchange rules. Thus, if you exchange a depreciable building placed in service before 1987, depreciation may be recaptured as ordinary income, so check the consequences of any "recapture" element. For example, if you exchange the building for land, the recaptured amount is fully taxable as ordinary income; *see 44.2*.

Parallel requirements apply to the replacement residence. The replacement residence must be owned for at least 24 months after the exchange and, within each of the two 12-month periods following the exchange, it must be rented at a fair rental for 14 days or more and the taxpayer's personal use (including use by relatives) cannot exceed the greater of 14 days or 10% of the fair rental days during the 12-month period.

If a taxpayer expects to meet the fair rental and personal use tests for the replacement residence and based on that expectation reports the exchange on his or her return as a tax-deferred exchange, but it turns out that the tests are not met, an amended return must be filed to report the exchange as a taxable sale.

**Losses.** If a loss is incurred on a like-kind exchange, the loss is not deductible, whether you receive only like-kind property or "unlike" property together with like-kind property. However, a deductible loss may be incurred if you give up unlike property as part of the exchange; the loss equals any excess of the adjusted basis of the unlike property over its fair market value.

**Reporting an exchange.** You must file Form 8824 to report an exchange of like-kind property. If you figure a recognized gain on Form 8824, you also must report the gain on Schedule D (investment property) or on Form 4797 (business property).

If in addition to the like-kind property you gave up "unlike" property (other than cash), you figure the gain or loss on the unlike property on Lines 12-14 of Form 8824 and report it as if it were from a regular sale. If the fair market value of the unlike property exceeds its adjusted basis, the gain should be reported on Form 8949 and Schedule D (if investment property) or Form 4797 (business property). If the adjusted basis of the unlike property exceeds its fair market value, the loss is deductible on Form 8949/Schedule D or Form 4797 as if the exchange were a regular sale.

If your exchange is with a related party *(6.6)*, Form 8824 must be filed not only for the year of the exchange but also for the two years following the year of the exchange.

**Property not within the tax-free trade rules.** In addition to exchanges of personal property, which do not qualify for like-kind treatment after 2017 (see new law discussion above) the following exchanges are ineligible:

- Real property used for personal purposes (but exchanges of principal residences may qualify as tax free under different rules; *see Chapter 29*)
- Foreign real estate
- Property held for sale
- Inventory or stock-in-trade
- Securities
- Notes
- Partnership interest; *see below*

See also *31.3* for tax-free exchanges of realty and 6.11 for tax-free exchanges of insurance policies.

**Exchange of partnership interests.** Exchanges of partnership interests in different partnerships are not within the tax-free exchange rules. If you have an interest in a partnership that has elected to be excluded from the application of partnership rules, your interest is treated as an interest in each partnership asset, not as an interest in the partnership.

**Real estate or personal property in foreign countries.** You may not make a tax-free exchange of U.S. real estate for foreign real estate; by law they are not considered like-kind property. However, if your real estate is condemned, foreign and U.S. real estate are treated as like-kind property for purposes of making a tax-free reinvestment *(18.23)*.

## 6.2 Receipt of Cash and Other Property—"Boot"

If, in addition to like-kind *(6.1)* property, you receive cash or other property (unlike kind), gain is taxable up to the amount of the cash and the fair market value of any unlike property received. The additional cash or unlike property is called "boot." If a loss was incurred on the exchange, the receipt of boot does not permit you to deduct the loss unless it is attributable to unlike-kind property you gave up in the exchange.

## EXAMPLE

Jones owns an apartment house held for investment that has a fair market value of $220,000, subject to an $80,000 mortgage. His adjusted basis is $100,000. In 2018, Jones exchanges his building for Smith's apartment building (also held for investment), which has a fair market value of $250,000, is subject to a $150,000 mortgage, and has an adjusted basis of $175,000. Jones and Smith each assume the mortgage on the building received. Jones also receives from Smith $40,000 in cash. Smith and Jones each pay $5,000 in exchange expenses.

The Sample Forms 8824 for Jones and Smith on the previous page show how they report the exchange. On Line 15, they show the boot received; their taxable gain on Line 22 is limited to this boot.

For Jones, the Line 15 boot is $35,000:

| | |
|---|---|
| Cash received | $40,000 |
| Less: Exchange expenses | 5,000 |
| Boot received by Jones | $35,000 |

Jones does not have to include the $80,000 in mortgage liabilities transferred to Smith as boot on Line 15 because it does not exceed the $150,000 of mortgage liabilities he assumed from Smith.

For Smith, the Line 15 boot is $25,000:

| | |
|---|---|
| Mortgage transferred | $150,000 |
| Less: Mortgage assumed | (80,000) |
| Less: Cash paid | (40,000) |
| Net amount received by Smith | 30,000 |
| Less: Exchange expenses | 5,000 |
| Boot received by Smith | $25,000 |

On Line 18, Jones and Smith increase their basis for the buildings they gave up by the net amount paid to the other party, if any.

For Jones, the Line 18 total of $170,000 includes:

| | | |
|---|---|---|
| Adjusted basis of building traded | | $100,000 |
| Plus: Net mortgage assumed: | | |
| Mortgage assumed | $150,000 | |
| Less: Mortgage transferred | 80,000 | 70,000 |
| | 70,000 | $170,000 |

For Smith, the Line 18 total of $175,000 includes:

| | | |
|---|---|---|
| Adjusted basis of building traded | | $175,000 |
| Plus: Net amount paid: | | |
| Mortgage assumed | $80,000 | |
| Plus: Cash paid | 40,000 | |
| Less: Mortgage transferred | (150,000) | 0 |
| | (30,000) | $175,000 |

The liabilities Smith assumed and the cash he paid are not included on Line 18 as an adjustment to basis because their total of $120,000 does not exceed the $150,000 of liabilities he transferred to Jones.

Line 22 of the Sample Forms 8824 shows the taxable gain Jones and Smith must report for 2018 on Schedule D. Line 25 shows the basis of the buildings Jones and Smith received in the exchange.

## Sample Form 8824 for Jones (see the Example beginning on the previous page)

Form 8824 (2018)

| Name(s) shown on tax return. Do not enter name and social security number if shown on other side. | Your social security number |
|---|---|
| John Jones | X00-01-XX11 |

### Part III — Realized Gain or (Loss), Recognized Gain, and Basis of Like-Kind Property Received

**Caution:** If you transferred **and** received **(a)** more than one group of like-kind properties or **(b)** cash or other (not like-kind) property, see **Reporting of multi-asset exchanges** in the instructions.

**Note:** Complete lines 12 through 14 **only** if you gave up property that was not like-kind. Otherwise, go to line 15.

| | | | |
|---|---|---|---:|
| 12 | Fair market value (FMV) of other property given up . . . . . | **12** | |
| 13 | Adjusted basis of other property given up . . . . . . . . | **13** | |
| 14 | Gain or (loss) recognized on other property given up. Subtract line 13 from line 12. Report the gain or (loss) in the same manner as if the exchange had been a sale . . . . . . . . . | **14** | |
| | **Caution:** If the property given up was used previously or partly as a home, see **Property used as home** in the instructions. | | |
| 15 | Cash received, FMV of other property received, plus net liabilities assumed by other party, reduced (but not below zero) by any exchange expenses you incurred. See instructions . . . | **15** | 35,000 |
| 16 | FMV of like-kind property you received . . . . . . . . . . | **16** | 250,000 |
| 17 | Add lines 15 and 16 . . . . . . . . . . . . . . . . | **17** | 285,000 |
| 18 | Adjusted basis of like-kind property you gave up, net amounts paid to other party, plus any exchange expenses **not** used on line 15. See instructions . . . . . . . . . . | **18** | 170,000 |
| 19 | **Realized gain or (loss).** Subtract line 18 from line 17 . . . . . . . | **19** | 115,000 |
| 20 | Enter the smaller of line 15 or line 19, but not less than zero . . . . . . . . . | **20** | 35,000 |
| 21 | Ordinary income under recapture rules. Enter here and on Form 4797, line 16. See instructions | **21** | - 0 - |
| 22 | Subtract line 21 from line 20. If zero or less, enter -0-. If more than zero, enter here and on Schedule D or Form 4797, unless the installment method applies. See instructions . . . . . | **22** | 35,000 |
| 23 | **Recognized gain.** Add lines 21 and 22 . . . . . . . . . | **23** | 35,000 |
| 24 | Deferred gain or (loss). Subtract line 23 from line 19. If a related party exchange, see instructions | **24** | 80,000 |
| 25 | **Basis of like-kind property received.** Subtract line 15 from the sum of lines 18 and 23 . . | **25** | 170,000 |

## Sample Form 8824 for Smith (see the Example beginning on the previous page)

Form 8824 (2018)

| Name(s) shown on tax return. Do not enter name and social security number if shown on other side. | Your social security number |
|---|---|
| Al Smith | X00-1X-XX11 |

### Part III — Realized Gain or (Loss), Recognized Gain, and Basis of Like-Kind Property Received

**Caution:** If you transferred **and** received **(a)** more than one group of like-kind properties or **(b)** cash or other (not like-kind) property, see **Reporting of multi-asset exchanges** in the instructions.

**Note:** Complete lines 12 through 14 **only** if you gave up property that was not like-kind. Otherwise, go to line 15.

| | | | |
|---|---|---|---:|
| 12 | Fair market value (FMV) of other property given up . . . . . | **12** | |
| 13 | Adjusted basis of other property given up . . . . . . . . | **13** | |
| 14 | Gain or (loss) recognized on other property given up. Subtract line 13 from line 12. Report the gain or (loss) in the same manner as if the exchange had been a sale . . . . . . . . . | **14** | |
| | **Caution:** If the property given up was used previously or partly as a home, see **Property used as home** in the instructions. | | |
| 15 | Cash received, FMV of other property received, plus net liabilities assumed by other party, reduced (but not below zero) by any exchange expenses you incurred. See instructions . . . | **15** | 25,000 |
| 16 | FMV of like-kind property you received . . . . . . . . . . | **16** | 220,000 |
| 17 | Add lines 15 and 16 . . . . . . . . . . . . . . . . | **17** | 245,000 |
| 18 | Adjusted basis of like-kind property you gave up, net amounts paid to other party, plus any exchange expenses **not** used on line 15. See instructions . . . . . . . . . . | **18** | 175,000 |
| 19 | **Realized gain or (loss).** Subtract line 18 from line 17 . . . . . . . | **19** | 70,000 |
| 20 | Enter the smaller of line 15 or line 19, but not less than zero . . . . . . . . . | **20** | 25,000 |
| 21 | Ordinary income under recapture rules. Enter here and on Form 4797, line 16. See instructions | **21** | - 0 - |
| 22 | Subtract line 21 from line 20. If zero or less, enter -0-. If more than zero, enter here and on Schedule D or Form 4797, unless the installment method applies. See instructions . . . . . | **22** | 25,000 |
| 23 | **Recognized gain.** Add lines 21 and 22 . . . . . . . . . | **23** | 25,000 |
| 24 | Deferred gain or (loss). Subtract line 23 from line 19. If a related party exchange, see instructions | **24** | 45,000 |
| 25 | **Basis of like-kind property received.** Subtract line 15 from the sum of lines 18 and 23 . . | **25** | 175,000 |

**Assumption of mortgages.** If you transfer mortgaged property and the other party assumes the mortgage, the amount of the assumed mortgage is part of your boot, as if you had received cash equal to the liability. If both you and the other party assume mortgages on the exchanged properties, the party giving up the larger debt treats the excess as taxable boot. The party giving up the smaller debt does not have boot; *see* also *31.3*. If you pay cash to the other party, or give up unlike-kind property, add this to the mortgage you assume in figuring which party has given up the larger debt.

**Form 8824.** The computation of boot, gain (or loss), and basis of the property received is made on Form 8824. Form 8824 must be filed for the year in which you transfer like-kind property. If the other party to the exchange is related to you, Form 8824 must also be filed for each of the two years following your transfer *(6.5)*.

## 6.3 Time Limits and Security Arrangements for Deferred Exchanges

Assume you own property that has appreciated in value. You want to sell it and reinvest the proceeds in other property, but you would like to avoid having to pay tax on the appreciation. You can defer the tax on the gain if you are able to arrange an exchange for like-kind *(6.1)* property.

The problem is that it may be difficult to find a buyer who has property you want in exchange, and the time for closing the exchange is restricted. If IRS tests are met, intermediaries and security arrangements may be used without running afoul of constructive receipt rules that could trigger an immediate tax.

**Deferred exchange distinguished from a reverse exchange.** A deferred exchange is one in which you first transfer investment or business property and then later receive like-kind investment or business property *(6.1)*. If before you receive the replacement property you actually or constructively receive money or unlike property as full payment for the property you have transferred, the transaction will be treated as a sale rather than a deferred exchange. In that case, you must recognize gain (or loss) on the transaction even if you later receive like-kind replacement property. In determining whether you have received money or unlike property, you may take advantage of certain safe harbor security arrangements that allow you to ensure that the replacement property will be provided to you without jeopardizing like-kind exchange treatment; *see* below for the safe harbor security tests.

A reverse exchange is one in which you acquire replacement property before you transfer the relinquished property. The like-kind exchange rules generally do not apply to reverse exchanges. However, the IRS has provided safe harbor rules that allow like-kind exchange treatment to be obtained if either the replacement property or the relinquished property is held in a qualified exchange accommodation arrangement (QEAA) *(6.4)*.

**Time limits for completing deferred exchanges.** You enerally have up to 180 days to complete an exchange, but the period may be shorter. Specifically, property will not be treated as like-kind property if received (1) more than 180 days after the date you transferred the property you are relinquishing or (2) after the due date of your return (including extensions) for the year in which you made the transfer, whichever is earlier. Furthermore, the property to be received must be identified within 45 days after the date on which you transferred property.

If the transaction involves more than one property, the 45-day identification period and the 180-day exchange period are determined by the earliest date on which any property is transferred. When the identification or exchange period ends on a Saturday, Sunday, or legal holiday, the deadline is not advanced to the next business day (as it is when the deadline for filing a tax return is on a weekend or holiday).

**How to identify replacement property.** You must identify replacement property in a written document signed by you and delivered before the end of the 45-day identification period to the person handling the transfer of the replacement property or to any other person involved in the exchange other than yourself or a related party. The identification may also be made in a written agreement. The property must be unambiguously described by a legal description or street address.

**Caution**

**Deducting a Loss**

You may deduct a loss incurred on an exchange if it is attributable to unlike property transferred in the exchange. The loss is recognized to the extent that the basis of the unlike property (other than cash) transferred exceeds its fair market value. However, a loss is not recognized if the unlike property is received together with the like-kind property in the exchange. Such a loss is not deductible.

**Caution**

**Strict Time Limits**

No extensions of time are allowed if the 45-day or 180-day statutory deadline for a deferred exchange cannot be met. If extra time is needed for finding suitable replacement property, it is advisable to delay the date of your property transfer because the transfer date starts the 45-day identification period.

You may identify more than one property as replacement property. However, the maximum number of replacement properties that you may identify without regard to the fair market value is three properties. You may identify any number of properties provided the aggregate fair market value at the end of the 45-day identification period does not exceed 200% of the aggregate fair market value of all the relinquished properties as of the date you transferred them. If, as of the end of the identification period, you have identified more than the allowable number of properties, you are generally treated as if no replacement property has been identified.

If property is valued at no more than 15% of the total value of a larger item of property that it is transferred with, the smaller property is considered "incidental" and does not have to be separately identified.

**Avoiding constructive receipt.** In a deferred exchange, you want financial security for the buyer's performance and compensation for delay in receiving property. To avoid immediate tax, you must not make a security arrangement that gives you an unrestricted right to funds before the deal is closed. As discussed next, certain safe harbor security arrangements may be used without endangering like-kind exchange treatment.

**Safe harbor tests for deferred exchange security arrangements.** If one of the following safe harbors applies to your security arrangement, you are not treated by the IRS as having actually or constructively received cash or unlike property prior to receiving the like-kind replacement, so tax-deferred exchange treatment may be obtained.

The first two "safe harbors" cover escrow accounts, mortgages and other security arrangements with your transferee. The third allows the use of professional intermediaries who, for a fee, arrange the details of the deferred exchange. The fourth allows you to earn interest on an escrow account.

1. The transferee may give you a mortgage, deed of trust, or other security interest in property (other than cash or a cash equivalent), or a third-party guarantee. A standby letter of credit may be given if you are not allowed to draw on such standby letter except upon a default of the transferee's obligation to transfer like-kind replacement property.

2. The transferee may put cash or a cash equivalent in a qualified escrow account or a qualified trust. The escrow holder or trustee must not be related to you. Your rights to receive, pledge, borrow, or otherwise obtain the cash must be limited. For example, you may obtain the cash after all of the replacement property to which you are entitled is received. After you identify replacement property, you may obtain the cash after the later of (1) the end of the identification period and (2) the occurrence of a contingency beyond your control that you have specified in writing. You may receive the funds after the end of the identification period if within that period you do not identify replacement property. In other cases, there can be no right to the funds until the exchange period ends.

3. You may use a qualified intermediary if your right to receive money or other property is limited (as discussed in safe harbor rule 2, above). A qualified intermediary (QI) is an unrelated party who, for a fee, acts to facilitate a deferred exchange by entering into an agreement with you for the exchange of properties pursuant to which the intermediary acquires your property from you and transfers it, acquires the replacement property, and transfers the replacement property to you. Typically, the QI transfers your property to the buyer in exchange for cash and uses the cash to purchase the replacement property that will be transferred to you.

There are restrictions on who may act as an intermediary. You may not employ any person as an intermediary who is your employee or is related to you or your agent or has generally acted as your professional adviser, such as an attorney, accountant, investment broker, real estate agent, or banker, in a two-year period preceding the exchange. Related parties include family members and controlled businesses or trusts (*5.6*), except that for purposes of control, a 10% interest is sufficient under the intermediary rule. The performance of routine financial, escrow, trust, or title insurance services by a financial institution or title company within the two-year period is not taken into account. State laws that may be interpreted as fixing an agency relationship between the transferor and transferee or fixing the transferor's right to security funds are ignored.

In a simultaneous exchange, the intermediary is not considered the transferor's agent.

4. You are permitted to receive interest or a "growth factor" on escrowed funds if your right to receive the amount is limited as discussed under safe harbor rule 2.

*IRS Alert*

**Safe Harbor If Exchange Fails Due to Qualified Intermediary's Default**

The IRS has provided relief if you hire a qualified intermediary (QI) to facilitate an exchange but are unable to meet the deadlines for relinquishing or receiving replacement property solely because the QI defaults on its obligations due to bankruptcy or receivership proceedings. By meeting the requirements of Revenue Procedure 2010-14, you can use a safe harbor that allows you to avoid having to report gain from the failed exchange until payments attributable to the relinquished property are received. A safe harbor gross profits ratio method is provided for reporting the gain.

> **EXAMPLE**
>
> You and Jones agree to enter a deferred exchange under the following terms and conditions. On May 18, 2018, you transfer to Jones real estate that has been held for investment; it is unencumbered and has a fair market value of $100,000. On or before July 2, 2018 (the end of the 45-day identification period), you must identify like-kind replacement property. On or before November 14, 2018 (the end of the 180-day exchange period), Jones is required to buy the property and transfer it to you. At any time after May 18, 2018, and before Jones has purchased the replacement property, you have the right, upon notice, to demand that he pay you $100,000 instead of acquiring and transferring the replacement property. However, you identify replacement property, and Jones purchases and transfers it to you. According to the regulations, you have an unrestricted right to demand the payment of $100,000 as of May 18, 2018. You are therefore in constructive receipt of $100,000 on that date. Thus, the transaction is treated as a taxable sale, and the transfer of the real property does not qualify as a tax-free exchange. You are treated as if you received the $100,000 for the sale of your property and then purchased replacement property.

**Escrow account earnings are generally exempt from imputed interest rules.** Under final IRS regulations, it is possible for a taxpayer who has an escrow arrangement with a qualified intermediary to be taxed on imputed interest, but there is a $2 million exemption that is expected to apply to the majority of exchange arrangements with small business exchange facilitators. Under the regulations, when a qualified intermediary holds exchange funds (cash, cash equivalents, or relinquished property) in escrow for a taxpayer under a deferred exchange agreement prior to the acquisition of replacement property, the exchange funds are treated as a loan from the taxpayer to the qualified intermediary unless the agreement provides that all of the earnings (such as bank interest) on the exchange funds will be paid to the taxpayer.

However, even when the intermediary retains the escrow earnings, as is typically the case with small nonbank exchange facilitators, the imputed interest rules do not apply if the deemed loan does not exceed $2 million and the loan does not extend beyond six months. If the loan exceeds $2 million or lasts more than six months, the taxpayer must report imputed interest. For example, a taxpayer transfers property to a qualified intermediary who transfers it to a purchaser in exchange for $2.1 million cash, which the intermediary deposits in a money market account for three months until the intermediary withdraws the funds and purchases replacement property identified by the taxpayer. Assuming that the taxpayer is not entitled to the earnings under the exchange agreement, the taxpayer is treated as having made a $2.1 million loan to the intermediary. The amount of the imputed interest taxable to the taxpayer is based on the lower of (1) the short-term applicable federal rate in effect on the day the deemed loan was made, compounded semiannually, or (2) the rate on a 91-day Treasury bill issued on or before the date of the deemed loan. The IRS could increase the $2 million exempt amount in future guidance.

## 6.4 Qualified Exchange Accommodation Arrangements (QEAAs) for Reverse Exchanges

The like-kind exchange rules *(6.1)* generally do not apply to a so-called reverse exchange in which you acquire replacement property before you transfer relinquished property. However, if you use a qualified exchange accommodation arrangement (QEAA), the transfer may qualify as a like-kind exchange.

Under a QEAA, either the replacement property or the relinquished property is transferred to an exchange accommodation titleholder (EAT) who is treated as the beneficial owner of the property for federal income tax purposes. If the property is held in a QEAA, the IRS will accept the qualification of property as either replacement property or relinquished property, and the treatment of an EAT as the beneficial owner of the property for federal income tax purposes.

The QEAA rules allow taxpayers to structure "parking transactions" in which the replacement property is acquired by the EAT before the transfer of the relinquished property. However, the QEAA safe harbor does not apply if the taxpayer transfers property to an EAT and receives that same property back as replacement property for other property of the taxpayer.

 *Caution*

**Parking Transactions**

Property transferred to you by the exchange accommodation titleholder (EAT) cannot be treated as property received in an exchange if you previously owned it within 180 days of its transfer to the EAT.

The IRS has set numerous technical requirements for QEAAs. Property is held in a QEAA only if you have a written agreement with the EAT, the time limits for identifying and transferring the property are met, and the qualified indicia of ownership of property are transferred to the EAT.

The EAT must meet all the following requirements: (1) Hold qualified indicia of ownership (see below) at all times from the date of acquisition of the property until the property is transferred within the 180-day period (see below); (2) be someone other than you, your agent, or a person related to you or your agent; (3) be subject to federal income tax. If the EAT is treated as a partnership or S corporation, more than 90% of its interests or stock must be owned by partners or shareholders who are subject to federal income tax.

The IRS defines qualified indicia of ownership as either legal title to the property, other indicia of ownership of the property that are treated as beneficial ownership of the property under principles of commercial law (for example, a contract for deed), or interests in an entity that is disregarded as an entity separate from its owner for federal income tax purposes (for example, a single member limited liability company) and that holds either legal title to the property or other indicia of ownership.

There are time limits for identifying and transferring property under a QEAA. No later than 45 days after the transfer of qualified indicia of ownership of the replacement property to the EAT, you must identify the relinquished property in a manner consistent with the principles for deferred exchanges *(6.3)*. If qualified indicia of ownership in replacement property have been transferred to the EAT, then no later than 180 days after that transfer, the replacement property must be transferred to you either directly or indirectly through a qualified intermediary *(6.3)*. If the EAT receives qualified indicia of ownership in the relinquished property, then no later than 180 days after that transfer, the relinquished property must be transferred to a person other than you, your agent at the time of the transaction, or a person who is related to you or your agent.

*Note:* For further details on the IRS' guidelines for QEAAs, *see* IRS Publication 544 and Revenue Procedure 2000-37, as modified by Revenue Procedure 2004-51 (parking transactions).

## 6.5    Exchanges Between Related Parties

A like-kind exchange between related persons may be disqualified if either party disposes of the property received in the exchange within two years after the date of the last transfer that was part of the exchange. Unless an exception applies, any gain deferred on the original exchange becomes taxable when the original like-kind property is disposed of by either party within the two-year period. If a loss was deferred on the original exchange, the loss becomes deductible if allowed under the rules in *5.6*.

Indirect dispositions of the property within the two-year period, such as transfer of stock of a corporation or interests in a partnership that owns the property, may also be treated as taxable dispositions.

**Related parties.** Related persons falling within the two-year rule include your children, grandchildren, parent, brother, or sister, controlled corporations or partnerships (more than 50% ownership), and a trust in which you are a beneficiary. A transfer to a spouse is not subject to the two-year rule unless he or she is a nonresident alien.

**Plan to avoid two-year rule.** If you set up a prearranged plan under which you first transfer property to an unrelated party who within two years makes an exchange with a party related to you, the related party will not qualify for tax-free treatment on that exchange.

**Exceptions.** No tax will be incurred on a disposition made after the death of either related party; in an involuntary conversion provided the original exchange occurred before the threat of the conversion; or if you can prove that neither the exchange nor the later disposition was for a tax avoidance purpose.

## 6.6    Property Transfers Between Spouses and Ex-Spouses

Under Section 1041, all transfers of property between spouses are treated as tax-free exchanges, other than transfers to a nonresident alien spouse, certain trust transfers of mortgaged property, and transfers of U.S. Savings Bonds; these exceptions are discussed

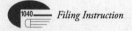
*Filing Instruction*

**Filing Form 8824**

The IRS requires related parties who exchange property to file Form 8824 for the year of the exchange and also for the two years following the exchange. If either party disposes of the property received in the original exchange in any of these years, the gain deferred on the original exchange must be reported in the year of disposition.

The two-year period is suspended for a holder of exchanged property who has substantially diminished his or her risk of loss, such as by use of a put or short sale.

below. Section 1041 applies to transfers during marriage as well as to property settlements incident to a divorce. In a Section 1041 transfer, there is no taxable gain or deductible loss to the transferor spouse. The transferee-spouse takes the transferor's basis in the property, and so appreciation in value will be taxed to the recipient on a later sale. This basis rule applies to all property received after July 18, 1984, under divorce or separation instruments in effect after that date.

A transfer is "incident to the divorce" if it occurs either within one year after the date the marriage ceases or, if later, is related to the cessation of the marriage, such as a transfer authorized by a divorce decree. A Treasury regulation provides that any transfer pursuant to a divorce or separation instrument occurring within six years of the end of the marriage is considered to be "related to the cessation of the marriage," and therefore as "incident to a divorce." Transfers made pursuant to the divorce or separation instrument that are more than six years after the end of the marriage, or transfers made within the six-year period that are not pursuant to the divorce or separation instrument, are considered related to the cessation of the marriage if they were made to effect the division of property owned by the spouses at the time of the cessation of the marriage. For example, a transfer not made within the six-year period qualifies if it is shown that an earlier sale was hampered by legal or business disputes such as a fight over the property value.

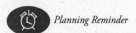

*Planning Reminder*

**Recipient Spouse Bears Tax Consequences of Transferred Property**

Under the tax-free exchange rules, the transferor-spouse does not have taxable gain or deductible loss on the transfer of property, even if cash is received for the property or the other spouse (or former spouse) assumes liabilities or gives up marital rights as part of a property settlement. The spouse who receives property may incur tax on a later sale because his or her basis in the property is the same as the transferor-spouse's basis; *see* the Examples in *6.6*. Because the transferee bears the tax consequences of a later sale, he or she should consider the potential tax on the appreciation in negotiating a marital settlement. In a marital settlement, the transferee spouse can lessen the tax burden by negotiating for assets that have little or no unrealized appreciation.

---

### EXAMPLES

1. In a property settlement accompanying a divorce, a husband plans to transfer to his wife stock worth $250,000 that cost him $50,000. In deciding whether to agree to the transfer, the wife should be aware that her basis for the stock will be $50,000. if she sells the stock for $250,000, she will have to pay tax on a $200,000 gain. This tax cost should be accounted for in arriving at the settlement.

2. Basis of the property in the hands of the transferee-spouse is not increased even if cash is paid as part of the transfer. For example, a husband received a house originally owned by the wife as part of a marital settlement. Her basis for the house was $32,200. He paid her $18,000 cash as part of the settlement and when he later sold the house for $64,000, he argued that his basis for purposes of computing profit was $50,200—the wife's $32,200 basis plus his $18,000 cash payment. The IRS refused to consider the cash payment as part of basis, and the Tax Court agreed that the carryover basis rule applies.

---

**Nonresident alien.** The tax-free exchange rule does not apply to transfers to a nonresident alien spouse or former spouse.

**Transfers of U.S.** Savings Bonds. The IRS has ruled that the tax-free exchange rules do not apply to transfers of U.S. Savings Bonds. For example, if a husband has deferred the reporting of interest on EE bonds and transfers the bonds to his ex-wife as part of a divorce settlement, the deferred interest is taxed to him on the transfer. The wife's basis for the bonds is the husband's basis plus the income he realizes on the transfer. When she redeems the bonds, she will be taxed on the interest accrued from the date of the transfer to the redemption date.

**Payment for release of community property interest in retirement pay.** The Tax Court allowed tax-free treatment for a payment made to a wife for releasing her community property claim to her husband's military retirement pay. The IRS had argued that the tax-free exchange rules discussed in this section did not apply to the release of rights to retirement pay that would otherwise be subject to ordinary income tax. The Tax Court disagreed, holding that the tax-free exchange rule applies whether the transfer is for relinquishment of marital rights, cash, or other property.

**Transfers in trust.** The tax-free exchange rules generally apply to transfers in trust for the benefit of a spouse or a former spouse if incident to a divorce. However, gain cannot be avoided on a trust transfer of heavily mortgaged property. If the trust property is mortgaged, the transferor spouse must report a taxable gain to the extent that the liabilities assumed by the transferee spouse plus the liabilities to which the property is subject (even if not assumed) exceed the transferor's adjusted basis for the property. If the transferor realizes a taxable gain under this rule, the transferee's basis for the property is increased by the gain.

**Sole proprietorship sale to spouse.** Tax-free exchange rules may apply to a sale of business property by a sole proprietor to a spouse. The buyer spouse assumes a carryover basis even if fair market value is paid. The transferor is not required to recapture previously claimed depreciation deductions or investment credits. However, the transferee is subject to the recapture rules on premature dispositions or if the property ceases to be used for business purposes.

**Transfer of nonstatutory options or nonqualified deferred compensation.** According to the IRS, if a vested interest in nonstatutory (nonqualified) stock options or nonqualified deferred compensation is transferred to a former spouse as part of a property settlement, the transferor-spouse (the employee) does not have to report any income; the Section 1041 tax-free exchange rules apply. When the transferee-spouse later exercises the options or receives the deferred compensation, he or she will be taxed on the option spread *(2.17)* or the deferred compensation as if he or she was the employee. Income tax withholding and FICA tax withholding (Social Security and Medicare taxes) is generally required from the payments made to the transferee-spouse.

**Divorce-related redemptions of stock in closely held corporation.** When a married couple own all (or most) of the stock in a closely held corporation, the corporation may redeem the stock of one of the spouses as part of an overall divorce settlement. Does the transferring spouse avoid tax on the redemption under the Section 1041 tax-free exchange rules?

If the redemption of one of the spouses' stock is treated as a transfer to a third party on behalf of the other spouse, Section 1041 applies and the transferor-spouse would escape tax on the redemption. However, there has been much confusion and litigation as to the standards for determining whether a redemption is "on behalf of" the non-transferor spouse, and whether different tests should apply for determining the tax treatment of each spouse. Court decisions have generally supported tax-free treatment for a spouse whose stock is redeemed under the terms of the couple's divorce or separation instrument, or where the other (non-transferring) spouse requests or consents to the redemption. However, the courts are divided on the issue of whether the non-transferor spouse, who is left in control of the corporation, has realized a constructive dividend as a result of the redemption. See Example 2 below for the disputed positions taken by Tax Court judges in the Read case.

In response to the inconsistent standards used by the courts (see the Examples below), the IRS amended its regulations to provide a specific rule for determining which spouse will be taxed on the redemption. The regulation allows tax-free exchange treatment under Section 1041 to the transferor-spouse (whose stock was redeemed) only if under applicable law the redemption is treated as resulting in a constructive dividend to the nontransferor-spouse. If constructive dividend treatment does not apply to the nontransferor-spouse, the form of the redemption transaction is followed and the transferor-spouse taxed on the redemption. The IRS regulation adopts the position of some of the dissenting judges in the Read case; *see* Example 2 below. The spouses are allowed to provide in a divorce or separation agreement that the redemption will be taxable to the nontransferor-spouse even if the redemption would not result in a constructive dividend to that spouse under applicable law. Alternatively, they can provide that the transferor will be taxed on the redemption although the redemption would otherwise be treated as a constructive dividend to the nontransferor-spouse.

**Basis of property received before July 19, 1984, or under instruments in effect before that date.** The tax-free exchange rules do not apply to property received before July 19, 1984, from your spouse (or former spouse if the transfer was incident to divorce). Your basis for determining gain or loss when you sell such property is its fair market value when you received it. The same fair market value basis rule applies to property received after June 18, 1984, under an instrument in effect on or before that date unless a Section 1041 election was made to have the tax-free exchange rules apply. For property subject to such an election, your basis is the same as the transferor-spouse's adjusted basis.

*Court Decision*

**Interest on Marital Property Settlements**

Parties may agree to pay interest on property transfers relating to divorce settlements when payments are to be made over time. The actual property transfer is generally a tax-free exchange. According to the Tax Court, the interest is separate and apart from the property transferred. The deductibility of the interest paid depends on the nature of the property transferred. Interest allocated to residential property, for instance, is deductible as residential mortgage interest; interest allocated to investment property is deductible as investment interest subject to the net investment income limit. See Chapter 15.

*Planning Reminder*

**Transfers to Third Parties**

If you transfer property to a third party on behalf of your spouse or former spouse where the transfer is required by a divorce or separation instrument, or if you have your spouse's or former spouse's written request or consent for the transfer, the transfer is tax free to you under Section 1041. The transfer is treated as if made to your spouse or former spouse, who then retransfers the property to the third party. A written request or consent must specifically state that the tax-free exchange rules of Code Section 1041 are intended, and you must receive it before filing the tax return for the year of the transfer. As discussed in the Examples in *6.6*, a divorce-related stock redemption may qualify for Section 1041 treatment as a transfer "on behalf of" the other spouse.

**EXAMPLES**

1. A federal district court and the Ninth Circuit Court of Appeals held that, under Section 1041, a wife was not taxable on the redemption of her stock by the couple's closely held corporation where the redemption was pursuant to their divorce agreement and incorporated into the divorce decree. The Ninth Circuit viewed the transfer as if the husband had received the stock directly from the wife and then transferred it to the company.

   After the Ninth Circuit held that the redemption was not taxable to the wife, the IRS argued in a separate case against the nonredeeming husband that he received a taxable constructive dividend. However, the Tax Court disagreed, holding that there was no dividend to the husband because under state law he was merely a guarantor; he was not primarily and unconditionally obligated to buy the stock. The IRS did not appeal the Tax Court decision.

   In this unusual situation, the IRS is in the position of being unable to collect tax on the redemption proceeds from either the transferor or transferee spouse.

2. After William and Carol Read divorced, William, pursuant to their divorce decree, elected to have their controlled corporation purchase all of Carol's stock. A Tax Court majority held that her transfer was on behalf of William and qualified for Section 1041 non-recognition treatment.

   The Tax Court majority also held that William realized a constructive dividend on the corporation's redemption of Carol's stock. However, the majority relied on a concession by William and did not specify a legal standard for determining whether he should be taxed. Concurring judges suggested that constructive dividend treatment for William followed automatically from the holding that Carol's stock transfer was on his behalf and thus within Section 1041. There were four dissenting opinions, all of which held that under traditional law for constructive dividends, there is no constructive dividend unless William had a "primary and unconditional obligation" to buy the shares, an obligation the corporation satisfied by making the redemption. Most of the dissenters argued that William did not have such an obligation and should not be taxed. They further argued that if William was not obligated to buy the shares, Section 1041 does not apply and thus Carol realized capital gain on the redemption of her shares. Other dissenting judges held that a spouse can never avoid taxable gain under Section 1041 on a redemption incident to divorce.

3. The Eleventh Circuit Court of Appeals allowed tax-free treatment to a redemption of a wife's stock, following the Tax Court majority in Read (Example 2 above). The redemption was on behalf of her ex-husband. The redemption was required by their divorce decree and it left him in control of 98% of the corporation's stock. He had guaranteed the corporation's 10-year promissory note to her, and the terms of the note specifically said that the guarantee was in his interests.

   Furthermore, although the corporation's note did not provide for interest, interest income was not imputed to the wife. Imputed interest does not apply where the underlying transfer is not taxable under Section 1041.

## 6.7 Tax-Free Exchanges of Stock in Same Corporation

Gain on the exchange of common stock for other common stock of the same corporation is not taxable. The same rule generally applies to an exchange of preferred stock of the same corporation, but not if "nonqualified" preferred with special redemption rights or a varying dividend rate is received. Loss realized on a qualifying exchange is not deductible. The exchange may take place between the stockholder and the company or between two stockholders.

An exchange of preferred stock for common, or common for preferred, in the same company is generally not tax free, unless the exchange is part of a tax-free recapitalization. In such exchanges, the company should inform you of the tax consequences.

**Convertible securities.** A conversion of securities under a conversion privilege is tax free *(30.7)*.

## 6.8   Joint Ownership Interests

The change to a tenancy in common from a joint tenancy is tax free. You may convert a joint tenancy in corporate stock to a tenancy in common without income-tax consequences. The transfer is tax free even though survivorship rights are eliminated. Similarly, a partition and issuance of separate certificates in the names of each joint tenant is also tax free.

A joint tenancy and a tenancy in common differ in this respect. On the death of a joint tenant, ownership passes to the surviving joint tenant or tenants. But on the death of a tenant holding property in common, ownership passes to his or her heirs, not to the other tenant or tenants with whom the property was held.

A tenancy by the entirety is a form of joint ownership recognized in some states and can be only between a husband and wife.

**Dividing properties held in common.** A division of properties held as tenants in common may qualify as tax-free exchanges.

For example, three men owned three pieces of real estate as tenants in common. Each man wanted to be the sole owner of one of the pieces of property. They disentangled themselves by exchanging interests in a three-way exchange. No money or property other than the three pieces of real estate changed hands, and none of the men assumed the others' liability. The transactions qualified as tax-free exchanges and no gain or loss was recognized.

**Receipt of boot.** Exchanges of jointly owned property are tax free as long as no "boot," such as cash or other property, passes between the parties *(6.2)*.

## 6.9   Setting up Closely Held Corporations

Tax-free exchange rules facilitate the organization of a corporation. When you transfer property to a corporation that you control solely in exchange for corporate stock in that corporation (but not nonqualified preferred stock), no gain or loss is recognized on the transfer. For control, you alone or together with other transferors (such as partners, where a partnership is being incorporated) must own at least 80% of the combined voting power of the corporation and 80% of all other classes of stock immediately after the transfer to the corporation. If you receive securities in addition to stock, the securities are treated as taxable "boot." The corporation takes your basis in the property, and your basis in the stock received in the exchange is the same as your basis in the property. Gain not recognized on the organization of the corporation may be taxed when you sell your stock, or the corporation disposes of the property.

**Transfer of liabilities.** When assets subject to liabilities are transferred to the corporation, the liability assumed by the corporation is not treated as taxable "boot," but your stock basis is reduced by the amount of liability. The transfer of liabilities may be taxable when the transfer is part of a tax avoidance scheme, or the liabilities exceed the basis of the property transferred to the corporation.

> **EXAMPLE**
>
> You transfer a building worth $500,000, which cost you $100,000, to your newly organized corporation in exchange for all of its outstanding stock. You realize a $400,000 gain ($500,000 − $100,000) that is not recognized. Your basis in the stock is $100,000 (same as your basis in the building); the corporation's basis in the building also is $100,000. The following year, you sell all of your stock to a third party for $500,000. The $400,000 gain that had been deferred is now recognized.

## 6.10   Tax-Free Exchanges of Insurance Policies

Certain types of insurance policies can be exchanged tax free. These are:

- Life insurance policy for another life insurance policy, endowment policy, or an annuity contract.
- Life insurance policy, an endowment policy, or an annuity contract for a qualified long-term care policy.

*Caution*

**Consider Taxable Transfer**

Before making a property transfer to a closely held corporation, consult an accountant or an attorney on the tax consequences. There may be instances when you have potential losses or you desire the corporation to take a stepped-up basis that would make tax-free treatment undesirable.

- Endowment policy for another endowment policy that provides for regular payments beginning no later than the date payments would have started under the old policy, or in exchange for an annuity contract.
- Annuity contract for another annuity contract with identical annuitants.
- These exchanges are not tax free:
- Endowment policy for a life insurance policy, or for another endowment policy that provides for payments beginning at a date later than payments would have started under the old policy.
- Annuity contract for a life insurance or endowment policy.
- Transfers of life insurance contracts where the insured is not the same person in both contracts. The IRS held that a company could not make a tax-free exchange of a key executive policy where the company could change insured executives as they leave or join the firm.

**Endorsement of annuity check for another annuity is taxable.** Cashing out a commercial annuity or nonqualified employee contract and investing it in another annuity does not qualify as a tax-free exchange. The IRS denied tax-free exchange treatment to a taxpayer who tried to complete a direct exchange of a non-qualified annuity contract but was foiled by the insurance company holding the contract. The taxpayer had asked the insurance company to issue a check directly to another insurer as consideration for a new annuity contract, intending the transaction to be treated as a tax-free exchange under Section 1035. The insurer refused and instead issued a check to the taxpayer. The taxpayer did not deposit the check, but instead endorsed it to the second insurance company to obtain the new annuity contract.

The IRS ruled that endorsing the check over to the second insurance company as consideration for the new contract was not a tax-free exchange. Instead, the taxpayer had to include in gross income the portion of the check that was allocable to income on the contract. If this had been a tax-sheltered 403(b) annuity or a qualified employee annuity, a distribution from the policy could have been rolled over tax-free to another such annuity, or even to another eligible retirement plan such as an IRA or qualified employer trust. However, in the case of a non-qualified annuity, there is no rollover provision for amounts distributed from the contract.

*Note:* Tax-free exchange treatment may be allowed if you surrender an annuity contract or insurance policy of an insurer in serious financial difficulty, and roll over the proceeds in a new policy or contract with a different insurer; *see* the Planning Reminder in this section *(6.11)*.

**IRS scrutiny of partial exchanges of annuity contracts.** The IRS has been concerned that a direct transfer of a portion of the cash surrender value of an existing annuity contract for another annuity contract, followed by a withdrawal from or surrender of either the original annuity contract or the new contract, could be used to reduce the tax on earnings that would otherwise be due on a non-annuity distribution. The IRS has guidelines for determining whether the direct transfer of a portion of the cash surrender value of an existing annuity contract to another contract is a tax-free exchange. The rules apply whether or not the two contracts are issued by the same or different companies. Revenue Procedure 2011-38 allows tax-free exchange treatment for a direct transfer of a portion of the cash surrender value of an existing annuity contract for a second annuity contract if no amount, other than an amount received as an annuity for 10 or more years or during one or more lives, is received under either the original or new contract during the 180-day period starting on the transfer date. If tax-free exchange treatment is allowed under these guidelines, the two annuity contracts will be treated separately and the IRS will not require that they be aggregated even if the same insurance company issued both. If the 180-day test is not met, the IRS will determine if the amount received under either contract within the 180 days should be treated as a distribution taxable to the extent of earnings, or as boot *(6.2)* in a tax-free exchange.

*Planning Reminder*

**Financially Troubled Insurer**

If your annuity contract or insurance policy is with an insurance company that is in a rehabilitation, conservatorship, insolvency, or a similar state proceeding, you may surrender the policy and make a tax-free reinvestment of the proceeds in a new policy with a different insurance company. The transfer must be completed within 60 days. If a government agency does not allow you to withdraw your entire balance from the troubled insurance company, you must assign all rights to any future distributions to the issuer of the new contract or policy. See IRS Revenue Procedure 92-44.

# CHAPTER 7

# Retirement and Annuity Income

For employees, coverage in a qualified employer retirement plan is a valuable fringe benefit, as employer contributions are tax free within specified limits. Certain salary-reduction plans allow you to make elective deferrals of salary that are not subject to income tax. An advantage of all qualified retirement plans is that earnings accumulate tax free until withdrawal.

Along with tax savings opportunities come technical restrictions and pitfalls. For example, retirement plan distributions eligible for rollover are subject to a mandatory 20% withholding tax if you receive the distribution instead of asking your employer to make a direct trustee-to-trustee transfer of the distribution to an IRA or another qualified employer plan.

This chapter discusses tax treatment of annuities and employer plan distributions, including how to avoid tax penalties, such as for distributions before age 59½. These distribution rules also generally apply to plans for self-employed individuals; retirement plans for self-employed individuals are discussed further in *Chapter 41*.

IRAs are discussed in *Chapter 8*.

A tax credit is available to low-to-moderate income taxpayers who make traditional or Roth IRA contributions, electives deferrals to a 401(k) or other employer plan, and voluntary after-tax contributions to a qualified plan. The credit is discussed in *Chapter 25*.

## Table 7-1  Key to Tax-Favored Retirement Plans

| Type— | General Tax Considerations— | Tax Treatment of Distributions— |
|---|---|---|
| Company qualified plan | A company qualified pension or profit-sharing plan offers these benefits:<br><br>1. You do not realize current income on your employer's contributions to the plan on your behalf.<br>2. Income earned on funds contributed to your account compounds tax free.<br>3. Your employer may allow you to make voluntary after-tax contributions. Although these contributions may not be deducted, income earned on the voluntary contributions is not taxed until withdrawn. | If you collect your retirement benefits as an annuity over a period of years, the part of each payment allocable to your investment is tax free and the rest is taxable *(7.25)*.<br><br>If you receive a lump-sum payment from the plan, the distribution is generally taxable except to the extent of after-tax contributions you made. Taxable distributions before age 59½ are generally subject to penalties, but there are exceptions *(7.13)*. However, you can avoid immediate tax by making a rollover to a traditional IRA or to another company plan *(7.5)*. If the lump-sum distribution includes company securities, unrealized appreciation on those securities is not taxed until you finally sell the stock *(7.8)*. If you were born before January 2, 1936, and receive a lump sum, tax on employer contributions and plan earnings may be reduced by a special averaging rule *(7.3)*. |
| Plans for self-employed | You may set up a qualified self-employed retirement plan if you earn self-employment income through your performance of personal services. You may deduct contributions up to limits discussed in *Chapter 41*; income earned on assets held by the plan is not taxed.<br><br>You must include employees in your plan under rules explained in *Chapter 41*.<br><br>Other retirement plan options, such as a SEP or SIMPLE plan, are also discussed in *Chapter 41*. | You may not withdraw plan funds until age 59½ unless you are disabled or meet other exceptions at *7.13*. Qualified distributions to self-employed persons or to beneficiaries at death may qualify for favored lump-sum treatment *(7.2)*.<br><br>Distributions from a SEP are subject to traditional IRA rules *(8.8)*. Distributions from a SIMPLE-IRA also are subject to traditional IRA rules, but a 25% penalty (instead of 10%) applies to pre-age-59½ distributions in the first two years *(8.18)*. |
| IRA and Roth IRA | Anyone who has earned income may contribute to a traditional IRA, but the contribution is deductible only if certain requirements are met. Your status as a participant in an employer retirement plan and your income determine whether you may claim a deduction up to the annual contribution limit (for 2018, $5,500, or $6,500 if age 50 or older), a partial deduction, or no deduction at all. See Chapter 8 for these deduction limitations.<br><br>Income earned on IRA accounts is not taxed until the funds are withdrawn.<br><br>This tax-free buildup of earnings also applies where you make nondeductible contributions to a Roth IRA under the rules in *Chapter 8*. | Traditional IRA distributions are fully taxable unless you have previously made nondeductible contributions *(8.9)*. A taxable withdrawal before age 59½ is subject to a 10% penalty, but there are exceptions if you are disabled, have substantial medical expenses, pay medical premiums while unemployed, or receive payments in a series of substantially equal installments; *see* the details on these and other exceptions *(8.12)*. Starting at age 70½, you must receive minimum annual distributions to avoid a 50% penalty *(8.13)*.<br><br>Distributions from a Roth IRA of contributions are tax free. Distributions of earnings are also tax free after you are over age 59½ and have held the account for at least five years *(8.24)*. |
| Simplified Employee Plan (SEP) | Your employer may set up a SEP and contribute to an IRA more than you can under regular IRA rules *(8.15)*. You are not taxed on employer contributions of up to 25% of your compensation (but no more than $55,000 for 2018). Elective deferrals of salary may be made to qualifying plans set up before 1997 *(8.16)*. | Withdrawals from a SEP are taxable under the rules explained above for IRAs. |
| Deferred salary or 401(k) plans | If your company has a profit-sharing or stock bonus plan, the tax law allows the company to add a cash or deferred pay plan that can operate in one of two ways: (1) Your employer contributes an amount for your benefit to your trust account. (2) You agree to take a salary reduction or to forego a salary increase. The reduction is placed in a trust account for your benefit and is treated as your employer's contribution, which is tax free within an annual limit *(7.18)*. Income earned on your trust account accumulates tax free until it is withdrawn. | Withdrawals are penalized unless you have reached age 59½, become disabled, or meet other exceptions *(7.13)*. If you were born before January 2, 1936, and receive a qualifying lump sum *(7.3)*, or you receive a qualifying lump sum as the beneficiary of a plan participant born before January 2, 1936 *(7.4)*, tax on the lump sum may be computed using a special averaging rule. |

## 7.1 Retirement Distributions on Form 1099-R

On Form 1099-R, payments from pensions, annuities, IRAs, Roth IRAs, SIMPLE IRAs, insurance contracts, profit-sharing, and other qualified corporate and self-employed plans are reported to you and the IRS. Social Security benefits are reported on Form SSA-1099; *see Chapter 34* for the special rules to apply in determining the taxable portion of Social Security benefits.

*Here is a guide to the information reported on Form 1099-R. A sample form is on the next page.*

**Box 1.** The total amount received from the payer is shown here without taking any withholdings into account.

If an exchange of insurance contracts was made, the value of the contract will be shown in Box 1, but if the exchange qualified as tax free, a zero taxable amount will be shown in Box 2a and Code 6 will be entered in Box 7.

**Boxes 2a and 2b.** The taxable portion of distributions from employer plans and insurance contracts may be shown in Box 2a. The taxable portion does not include your after-tax contributions to an employer plan or insurance premium payments.

If the payer cannot figure the taxable portion, the first box in 2b should be checked ("Taxable amount not determined"); Box 2a should be blank. You will then have to figure the taxable amount yourself. A 2018 payment from a pension or an annuity is only partially taxed if you contributed to the cost and you did not recover your entire cost investment before 2018. See the discussion of commercial annuities *(7.21)* or employee annuities *(7.25)* for details on computing the taxable portion if you have an unrecovered investment.

The payer of a traditional IRA distribution will probably not compute the taxable portion, and in this case, the total distribution from Box 1 should be entered as the taxable portion in Box 2a, with a check in Box 2b for "Taxable amount not determined". The total distribution amount is fully taxable unless you have made nondeductible contributions, in which case Form 8606 is used to figure the taxable portion of the distribution *(8.9)*. Form 8606 is also used to figure the taxable part, if any, of a nonqualified distribution from a Roth IRA *(8.24)*.

If the payment is from an employer plan and the "total distribution" box has been checked in 2b, *see* the discussion of possible rollover options *(7.2, 7.5)*. If you were born on or before January 1, 1936, 10-year averaging is available for a lump sum *(7.2)*. The taxable amount in Box 2a should not include net unrealized appreciation (NUA *(7.8)*) in any employer securities included in the lump sum or the value of an annuity contract included in the distribution.

**Box 3.** If the payment is a lump-sum distribution, you were born before January 2, 1936, and you participated in the plan before 1974, or if you are the beneficiary of such a person, you may treat the amount shown in Box 3 as capital gain subject to a 20% rate *(7.3)*.

**Box 4.** Any federal income tax withheld is shown here. Do not forget to include it along with your other income tax withholdings on Form 1040. If Box 4 shows any withholdings, attach Copy B of Form 1099-R to your Form 1040.

**Box 5.** If you made after-tax contributions to your employer's plan, or paid premiums for a commercial annuity or insurance contract, your contribution is shown here, less any such contributions previously distributed. IRA or SEP contributions (see *Chapter 8*) are not shown here.

**Box 6.** If you received a qualifying lump-sum distribution that includes securities of your employer's company, the total net unrealized appreciation (NUA) is shown here. Unless you elect to pay tax on it currently *(7.8)*, this amount is not taxed until you sell the securities. If you did not receive a qualifying lump sum, the amount shown here is the net unrealized appreciation attributable to your after-tax employee contributions, which are also not taxed until you sell the securities *(7.8)*.

**Box 7.** In Box 7, the payer will indicate if the distribution is from a traditional IRA, SEP, or SIMPLE and enter codes that are used by the IRS to check whether you have reported the distribution correctly, including the penalty for distributions before age 59½.

If you are at least age 59½, Code 7 should be entered; this indicates that you received a "normal" distribution not subject to the 10% early distribution penalty *(7.13)*. If Code 1 is entered, this indicates that you were under age 59½ at the time of the distribution and,

---

*Filing Instruction*

**Conversion of Traditional IRA to Roth IRA**

If you converted a traditional IRA (or a SEP or SIMPLE IRA) to a Roth IRA, the total amount converted will be included in Box 1 and Box 2a of Form 1099-R, but in Box 2b, the "Taxable amount not determined" box will be checked. A conversion to a Roth IRA is fully taxable except for any portion allocable to nondeductible contributions *(8.22)*.

as far as the payer knows, no exception to the early distribution penalty applies. However, the fact that Code 1 is entered does not mean that a penalty exception is not available. For example, you may qualify for the medical expense exception *(7.13)* or you may have made a tax-free 60-day rollover instead of having your employer make a direct rollover *(7.5)*.

Code 2 will be entered in Box 7 if you are under age 59½ and the payer knows that you do qualify for an exception to the early distribution penalty, such as the exception for separation of service after age 55 for an employer-plan distribution, or the distribution is part of a series of substantially equal payments. Code 3 will be used if the disability exception applies. If you are the beneficiary of a deceased employee, the early distribution penalty does not apply to your distribution; Code 4 should be entered to indicate that the exception for beneficiaries applies.

If the employer made a direct rollover, Code G will be entered; however, Code H is used for a direct rollover from a designated Roth account to a Roth IRA.

If an annual IRA contribution was recharacterized from one type of IRA to another *(8.21)*, either Code N or R will be entered. For example, on Form 1099-R for 2018, Code N is entered if the original contribution and recharacterization were both made in 2018, and Code R is entered if the original contribution was for 2017 and the recharacterization was in 2018.

If you contributed to a 401(k) plan and are a highly compensated employee, your employer may have made a corrective distribution to you in 2018 of contributions (and allocable income) that exceed allowable nondiscrimination ceilings. In this case, the employer will enter Code 8 if the corrective distribution is taxable in 2018, Code P if taxable in 2017.

If you receive a lump-sum distribution that qualifies for special averaging, Code A will be entered. See the sample Form 1099-R below and the discussion of the special averaging rules *(7.3)*.

**Box 8.** If the value of an annuity contract was included as part of a lump sum you received, the value of the contract is shown here. It is not taxable when you receive it and should not be included in Boxes 1 and 2a. For purposes of computing averaging on Form 4972, this amount is added to the ordinary income portion of the distribution *(7.3)*.

**Box 9.** If several beneficiaries are receiving payment from an employer plan total distribution, the amount shown in Box 9a is your share of the distribution. Box 9b may show your after-tax contributions to your employer's plan

**Box 10.** A distribution from a designated Roth account allocable to an in-plan Roth rollover is reported here.

**Boxes 12–15.** The payer may make entries in these boxes to show state or local income tax withholdings.

See the Andrew Kellogg Example *(7.3)*

*Filing Tip*

**Lump-Sum Distribution**

If you are paid a distribution that qualifies for lump-sum averaging *(7.3)*, Code A will be entered in Box 7 of Form 1099-R.

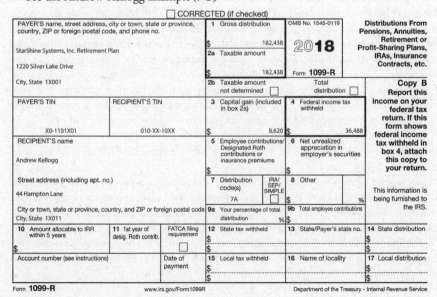

## 7.2 Lump-Sum Distributions

If you are entitled to a lump-sum distribution from a qualified company or self-employed retirement plan, you may avoid current tax by asking your employer to make a direct rollover of your account to an IRA or another qualified employer plan. If the distribution is made to you, 20% will be withheld, but it may still be possible to make a tax-free rollover within 60 days *(7.5)*.

If you receive a lump sum and do not make a rollover, the taxable part of the distribution (shown in Box 2a of Form 1099-R) must be reported as ordinary pension income on your return unless you were born before January 2, 1936, and qualify for special averaging, as discussed in *7.3*. Your after-tax contributions and any net unrealized appreciation (NUA *(7.8)*) in employer securities that are included in the lump sum are recovered tax free; they are not part of the taxable distribution.

A taxable distribution before age 59½ is subject to a 10% penalty in addition to regular income tax, unless you qualify for an exception *(7.13)*.

**Spousal consent to lump-sum distribution.** If you are married, you may have to obtain your spouse's consent to elect a lump-sum distribution *(7.9)*.

**Withholding tax.** An employer must withhold a 20% tax from a lump-sum distribution that is paid to you and not rolled over directly by the employer to a traditional IRA or another employer plan *(7.5)*.

**Beneficiaries.** If you are the surviving spouse of a deceased plan participant (employee or self-employed) and receive a lump-sum distribution from his or her account, you can roll over the distribution to another qualified employer plan or to your own IRA. If you are a nonspouse beneficiary of a lump-sum distribution, you may instruct the plan to make a direct trustee-to-trustee transfer to an IRA that must be treated as an inherited IRA *(7.6)*.

If you are the beneficiary of a deceased employee who was born before January 2, 1936, you may elect special averaging or capital gain treatment for a lump-sum distribution of the account *(7.4)*, unless the distribution is disqualified.

**Court ordered lump-sum distribution to a spouse or former spouse.** If you are the spouse or former spouse of an employee and you receive a distribution under a qualified domestic relations order (QDRO), you may be eligible for a tax-free rollover or, in some cases, special averaging treatment *(7.10)*.

## 7.3 Lump-Sum Options If You Were Born Before January 2, 1936

If you were born before January 2, 1936, and receive a qualified lump-sum distribution (defined below) from your employer's plan, you may be able to figure your tax on the distribution using the 10-year averaging method. If you participated in the plan before 1974, you may be able to apply a 20% capital gain rate to the pre-1974 part of a qualifying lump-sum distribution if 20% is lower than the averaging rate or your regular rate. The averaging and capital gain elections are allowed only once; if you previously used averaging (10-year or prior law 5-year averaging) for a lump-sum distribution received as a plan participant after 1986, you are barred from electing averaging again for a current lump-sum distribution. You may also be disqualified from making the averaging and capital gain elections because you did not participate in the plan for more than five years or because rollovers were previously made to or from the same employer plan; see "Disqualified distributions" below.

If you receive a lump-sum distribution as the beneficiary of a deceased plan participant who was born before January 2, 1936, you generally may elect averaging or capital gain treatment for the distribution unless it is disqualified as discussed below. Note that although a distribution made in the first five years of plan participation is a disqualification event for the participant while alive, this rule does not apply to you as the beneficiary; you can elect averaging or capital gain treatment for an otherwise qualifying distribution regardless of how long the deceased was a plan participant.

**Lump-sum distribution defined.** A lump-sum distribution is the payment within a single taxable year of a plan participant's entire balance from an employer's qualified plan. If the employer has more than one qualified plan of the same kind (profit-sharing, pension, stock bonus), you must receive the balance from all of them within the same year. A series of payments may qualify as a lump-sum distribution provided you receive them within the same tax year.

The account balance does not include deductible voluntary contributions you made after 1981 and before 1987; these are not treated as part of a lump-sum distribution and thus are not eligible for 10-year averaging *(7.4)* or the 20% capital gain election; *see* below.

If you receive more than one lump sum during the year that is eligible for averaging, you must make the same choice for all of them. If you deferred tax for one lump sum in 2018 by rolling it over, you may not claim averaging on your 2018 return for another lump sum.

If you make a rollover to an IRA, you cannot change your mind and cancel the IRA account in order to apply special averaging. The rollover election is irrevocable, according to an IRS regulation that has been upheld by the Tax Court. If an IRA rollover account is revoked, the entire distribution is taxable as ordinary income.

**Disqualified distributions.** Even if you receive a lump-sum distribution and meet the age test, averaging and capital gain treatment are not allowed if any of the following are true: (1) you rolled over any part of the lump-sum distribution to an IRA or an employer qualified plan; (2) you received the distribution during the first five years that you participated in the plan; (3) you previously received a distribution from the same plan and you rolled it over tax free to an IRA or another qualified employer plan; (4) you elected 10-year or five-year averaging or capital gain treatment for any other lump-sum distribution after 1986; (5) after 2001, you rolled over to the same plan a distribution from a traditional IRA (other than a conduit IRA, an IRA that held a only a prior distribution and earnings on the distribution), a 403(b) plan *(7.19)*, or a governmental 457 plan *(7.20)*; or (6) after 2001 you rolled over to the same plan a distribution that you received as a surviving spouse from the qualified plan of your deceased spouse.

**Electing averaging for a qualifying lump sum.** If you were born before January 2, 1936, and you received a lump-sum distribution that is not disqualified from averaging as discussed above, you may elect on Form 4972 to compute the tax on a lump-sum distribution received using a 10-year averaging method based on 1986 tax rates for single persons. Follow the IRS instructions to Form 4972 for applying the 10-year averaging method. If you received more than one qualified lump sum, you may elect averaging for one of the distributions only if you elect averaging for all.

If you were born after January 1, 1936, you may not elect averaging for a lump-sum distribution of your account balance. However, you may elect averaging as the beneficiary of a deceased plan participant who was born before January 2, 1936.

The amount eligible for averaging is the taxable portion of the distribution shown in Box 2a of Form 1099-R. You may also elect to add to the Box 2a amount any net unrealized appreciation in employer securities (shown in Box 6) included in the lump sum. If you are receiving the distribution as a beneficiary of a plan participant who died before August 21, 1996, follow the instructions to Form 4972 for claiming a death benefit exclusion that reduces the Box 2a taxable portion.

If the distribution includes capital gain (Box 3 of Form 1099-R) and you want to apply the special 20% capital gain rate (see below), you should subtract the capital gain in Box 3 from the taxable amount in Box 2a and apply averaging to the balance of ordinary income.

The tax computed on Form 4972 is reported on Schedule 2 of Form 1040 as an additional tax. It is completely separate from the tax computed on your other income reported on Form 1040.

See the Andrew Kellogg Example and the Sample Form 4972 below.

**Capital gain treatment for pre-1974 participation.** The portion of a qualifying lump-sum distribution attributable to pre-1974 participation is eligible for a 20% capital gain rate if you were born before January 2, 1936, and the distribution is not disqualified.

 *Caution*

**Averaging Not Allowed for Those Born After January 1, 1936**

If you were born after January 1, 1936, a lump-sum distribution from your plan is not eligible for averaging.

## Sample Form 4972—Lump-Sum Distributions
*(This sample is subject to change; see the e-Supplement at jklasser.com)*

| Form **4972** | **Tax on Lump-Sum Distributions** | OMB No. 1545-0193 |
|---|---|---|
| | **(From Qualified Plans of Participants Born Before January 2, 1936)** | **20**18 |
| Department of the Treasury Internal Revenue Service (99) | ▶ Go to *www.irs.gov/Form4972* for the latest information. <br> ▶ Attach to Form 1040, Form 1040NR, or Form 1041. | Attachment Sequence No. **28** |

**Name of recipient of distribution**
Andrew Kellogg

**Identifying number**
101-XX-10XX

### Part I — Complete this part to see if you can use Form 4972

| | | | Yes | No |
|---|---|---|---|---|
| 1 | Was this a distribution of a plan participant's entire balance (excluding deductible voluntary employee contributions and certain forfeited amounts) from all of an employer's qualified plans of one kind (for example, pension, profit-sharing, or stock bonus)? If "No," **don't** use this form . . . . . . . . . . . | **1** | ✓ | |
| 2 | Did you roll over any part of the distribution? If "Yes," **don't** use this form . . . . . . . . . . | **2** | | ✓ |
| 3 | Was this distribution paid to you as a beneficiary of a plan participant who was born before January 2, 1936? | **3** | | ✓ |
| 4 | Were you **(a)** a plan participant who received this distribution, **(b)** born before January 2, 1936, **and (c)** a participant in the plan for at least 5 years before the year of the distribution? . . . . . . . . . <br> If you answered "No" to both questions 3 **and** 4, **don't** use this form. | **4** | ✓ | |
| 5a | Did you use Form 4972 after 1986 for a previous distribution from your own plan? If "Yes," **don't** use this form for a 2018 distribution from your own plan . . . . . . . . . . . . . . . . . | **5a** | | ✓ |
| b | If you are receiving this distribution as a beneficiary of a plan participant who died, did you use Form 4972 for a previous distribution received as a beneficiary of that participant after 1986? If "Yes," **don't** use this form for this distribution . . . . . . . . . . . . . . . . . . . . . . . . . | **5b** | | |

### Part II — Complete this part to choose the 20% capital gain election (see instructions)

| | | | |
|---|---|---|---|
| 6 | Capital gain part from Form 1099-R, box 3 . . . . . . . . . . . . . . . . | **6** | 8,620 |
| 7 | Multiply line 6 by 20% (0.20) . . . . . . . . . . . . . . . . . . ▶ | **7** | 1,724 |
| | If you also choose to use Part III, go to line 8. Otherwise, include the amount from line 7 in the total on Form 1040, line 11; Form 1040NR, line 42; or Form 1041, Schedule G, line 1b. Be sure to check box **2** on Form 1040, line 11, or check box **b** on Form 1040NR, line 42. | | |

### Part III — Complete this part to choose the 10-year tax option (see instructions)

| | | | |
|---|---|---|---|
| 8 | If you completed Part II, enter the amount from Form 1099-R, box 2a, minus box 3. If you didn't complete Part II, enter the amount from box 2a. Multiple recipients (and recipients who elect to include net unrealized appreciation (NUA) in taxable income), see instructions . . . . . . | **8** | 173,818 |
| 9 | Death benefit exclusion for a beneficiary of a plan participant who died before August 21, 1996 . | **9** | - 0 - |
| 10 | Total taxable amount. Subtract line 9 from line 8 . . . . . . . . . . . . . . | **10** | 173,818 |
| 11 | Current actuarial value of annuity from Form 1099-R, box 8. If none, enter -0- . . . . | **11** | - 0 - |
| 12 | Adjusted total taxable amount. Add lines 10 and 11. If this amount is $70,000 or more, **skip** lines 13 through 16, enter this amount on line 17, and go to line 18 . . . . . . . . . . | **12** | 173,818 |
| 13 | Multiply line 12 by 50% (0.50), but **don't** enter more than $10,000 . . **13** | | |
| 14 | Subtract $20,000 from line 12. If line 12 is $20,000 or less, enter -0- . . . . . . **14** | | |
| 15 | Multiply line 14 by 20% (0.20) . . . . . . . . . . . . **15** | | |
| 16 | Minimum distribution allowance. Subtract line 15 from line 13 . . . . . . | **16** | |
| 17 | Subtract line 16 from line 12 . . . . . . . . . . . . . . . . . | **17** | 173,818 |
| 18 | Federal estate tax attributable to lump-sum distribution . . . . . . . . . | **18** | - 0 - |
| 19 | Subtract line 18 from line 17. If line 11 is zero, **skip** lines 20 through 22 and go to line 23 . . . | **19** | 173,818 |
| 20 | Divide line 11 by line 12 and enter the result as a decimal (rounded to at least three places) . . . . . . . . . . . . . . . . **20** | . | |
| 21 | Multiply line 16 by the decimal on line 20 . . . . . . . . **21** | | |
| 22 | Subtract line 21 from line 11 . . . . . . . . . . . **22** | | |
| 23 | Multiply line 19 by 10% (0.10) . . . . . . . . . . . . . . . . | **23** | 17,382 |
| 24 | Tax on amount on line 23. Use the Tax Rate Schedule in the instructions . . . . . . . | **24** | 3,012 |
| 25 | Multiply line 24 by 10.0. If line 11 is zero, **skip** lines 26 through 28, enter this amount on line 29, and go to line 30 . . . . . . . . . . . . . . . . . . . . . . | **25** | 30,120 |
| 26 | Multiply line 22 by 10% (0.10) . . . . . . . . . . **26** | | |
| 27 | Tax on amount on line 26. Use the Tax Rate Schedule in the instructions . . . . **27** | | |
| 28 | Multiply line 27 by 10.0 . . . . . . . . . . . . . . | **28** | |
| 29 | Subtract line 28 from line 25. Multiple recipients, see instructions . . . . . . ▶ | **29** | 30,120 |
| 30 | **Tax on lump-sum distribution.** Add lines 7 and 29. Also include this amount in the total on Form 1040, line 11 (check box **2**); Form 1040NR, line 42 (check box **b**); or Form 1041, Schedule G, line 1b . . . . . . . . . . . . . . . . . . . . . . . ▶ | **30** | 31,844 |

**For Paperwork Reduction Act Notice, see instructions.**    Cat. No. 13187U    Form **4972** (2018)

If you were born after January 1, 1936, you may not treat any portion of a lump-sum distribution as capital gain. You may not apply the flat 20% rate to the pre-1974 portion of the lump-sum distribution on Form 4972, or include any part of it as capital gain on Schedule D.

On Form 1099-R, the plan paying the lump-sum distribution shows the capital gain portion in Box 3. The ordinary income portion is Box 2a (taxable amount) minus Box 3. If you elect to treat the pre-1974 portion as capital gain subject to a flat rate of 20% on Form 4972, the tax on the balance of the distribution may be figured under the averaging method, or it may be reported as regular pension income on Form 1040, Line 4b. The 20% rate for the capital gain portion is fixed by law, and applies regardless of the tax rate imposed on your other capital gains. Alternatively, you may elect to treat the capital gain portion as ordinary income eligible for averaging on Form 4972. You may not elect to report any portion of the pre-1974 portion of the lump-sum distribution as long-term capital gain on Schedule D.

Under the one-time election rule, if you elect to apply the averaging and/or 20% capital gain rule for a current distribution, you may not elect averaging or capital gain treatment for any later distribution.

> ### EXAMPLE
>
> Andrew Kellogg was born in 1935. In 2018, he retired from StarShine Systems, Inc., where he had worked since 1970. He received a lump-sum distribution of $182,438, before withholdings. The Form 1099-R provided by the company (see page 173) shows in Box 3 the capital gain portion of $8,620, attributable to pre-1974 participation. The mandatory withholding tax of 20% *(7.2)*, here $36,488, is shown in Box 4.
>
> On Form 4972, Andrew applies the special 20% rate to the capital gain portion for a tax of $1,724. He then figures the tax on the $173,818 ordinary income part of the distribution under the 10-year averaging method, using the tax rate schedule in the instructions to Form 4972. As shown on the sample Form 4972 on page 176, Andrew's total tax on the distribution is $31,844, the sum of the $30,120 tax under 10-year averaging and the $1,724 tax on the capital gain portion. In Andrew's case, the special 20% capital gains rate is advantageous because it results in a lower tax than if the capital gain were treated as ordinary income subject to the averaging computation. The tax would be $32,360 if the special capital gain rate was not elected.

**Community property.** Only the spouse who has earned the lump sum may use averaging. Community property laws are disregarded for this purpose. If a couple files separate returns and one spouse elects averaging, the other spouse is not taxed on the amount subject to the computation.

> ### EXAMPLE
>
> A husband in a community property state receives a lump-sum distribution of which the ordinary income portion is $10,000. He and his wife file separate returns. If averaging is not elected, $5,000, or one-half, is taxable on the husband's return and the other $5,000 on his wife's return. However, if he elects the averaging method, only he reports the $10,000 on Form 4972.

## 7.4   Lump-Sum Payments Received by Beneficiary

If you receive a qualifying lump-sum distribution as the beneficiary of a deceased employee or self-employed plan participant who was not your spouse, you may instruct the plan to make a direct trustee-to-trustee transfer to an IRA that must be treated as an inherited IRA. If you are the surviving spouse, you can roll over the distribution to another qualified employer plan or to your own IRA.

**Was the plan participant born before January 2, 1936?** If you are the beneficiary of a deceased employee who was born before January 2, 1936, and receive a qualifying lump-sum distribution of that person's account, you may elect special averaging or capital gain treatment for the lump-sum unless the distribution is disqualified as discussed in *7.3*. Your age is irrelevant. If the deceased employee was in the plan for less than five years, you may still elect averaging as his or her beneficiary, although less than five years of

*Filing Tip*

**Pre-1974 Capital Gain Portion of Distribution**

If you were born before January 2, 1936, and a portion of your lump-sum distribution is attributable to plan participation before 1974 *(7.3)*, you may treat it as ordinary income eligible for averaging, or you may elect to treat it as capital gain taxable at a flat 20% rate; choose the method on Form 4972 that gives the lower overall tax.

**Lump Sums to Multiple Beneficiaries**

A lump-sum distribution to two or more beneficiaries may qualify for averaging and capital gain treatment, so long as the plan participant was born before January 2, 1936. Each beneficiary may separately elect the averaging method for the ordinary income portion, even though other beneficiaries do not so elect. Follow the Form 4972 instructions for multiple recipients.

participation would have disqualified *(7.3)* the distribution from lump-sum treatment had the distribution been received by the employee. If the participant was born before January 2, 1936, and had participated in the plan before 1974, you may elect a 20% capital gain rate for the pre-1974 portion of the distribution and apply the averaging method to the balance *(7.3)*. You may not claim averaging or capital gain treatment for a lump-sum distribution if the plan participant was born after January 1, 1936.

Form 4972 is used to compute tax under the averaging method or to make the 20% capital gain election *(7.3)*. Follow the Form 4972 instructions to claim the up-to-$5,000 death benefit exclusion where the plan participant died before August 21, 1996. Any federal estate tax attributable to the distribution reduces the taxable amount on Form 4972.

A lump sum paid because of an employee's death may qualify for capital gain and averaging treatment, although the employee received annuity payments before death.

An election may be made on Form 4972 only once as the beneficiary of a particular plan participant. If you receive more than one lump-sum distribution as beneficiary for the same participant in the same year, you must treat them all the same way. Averaging must be elected for all of the distributions on a single Form 4972 or for none of them.

Payment received by a second beneficiary (after the death of the first beneficiary) is not entitled to lump-sum treatment.

**Distribution to trust or estate.** If a qualifying lump sum is paid to a trust or an estate, the employee, or, if deceased, his or her personal representative, may elect averaging.

> **EXAMPLE**
>
> Gunnison's father was covered by a company benefit plan. The father died, as did Gunnison's mother, before benefits were fully paid out. Gunnison received a substantial lump sum. He argued that he collected on account of his father's death. The IRS disagreed.
>
> The Tax Court and an appeals court sided with the IRS. Gunnison was entitled to the payment following his mother's death, not his father's death. For special lump-sum treatment, the payout must arise solely on account of the death of the covered employee.

## 7.5 Tax-Free Rollovers From Qualified Plans

A rollover allows you to make a tax-free transfer of a distribution from a qualified retirement plan to another qualified plan that accepts rollovers or to a traditional IRA. For rollover purposes, a 403(b) plan *(7.19)*, or a state or local government 457 plan *(7.20)* is treated as a qualified retirement plan. If a rollover is made to a traditional IRA, later distributions received from the IRA are taxable under the IRA rules *(8.8)*. A tax-free rollover can be made from a qualified retirement plan to a SIMPLE IRA after the first two years of participation in the SIMPLE IRA *(8.18)*.

The rollover rules below and in *7.6* apply whether you are an employee or are self employed.

**Eligible rollover distributions.** Almost all taxable distributions received from a qualified corporate or self-employed pension, profit-sharing, stock bonus, or annuity plan are eligible for tax-free rollover. Exceptions include substantially equal periodic payments over your lifetime or over a period of at least 10 years, hardship distributions, and minimum distributions *(7.11)* required after age 70½; *see* below for the list of ineligible distributions.

**Rollover of after-tax contributions.** When you are entitled to take distributions, after-tax contributions that you have made to the plan may be rolled over to a traditional IRA or to a Roth IRA. A trustee-to-trustee transfer of after-tax contributions may also be made to a qualified defined contribution plan, a defined benefit plan, or a 403(b) tax-sheltered annuity that separately accounts for the after-tax amount.

The IRS has provided a method for making a direct rollover of after-tax contributions to a Roth IRA while directly rolling the pre-tax portion of the account (pre-tax contributions plus the earnings on all contributions) to a traditional IRA; see "Allocating a direct rollover between pre-tax and after-tax contributions" in *7.6*.

**Rollover options: direct rollover or personal rollover.** If you want to make a tax-free rollover of an eligible rollover distribution, you should instruct your employer to directly roll over the funds to a traditional IRA you designate or to the plan of your new employer. You could also choose to have the distribution paid to you, and within 60 days you could make a tax-free rollover yourself. However, to avoid the 20% mandatory withholding tax, you must elect to have the plan make a direct rollover. If an eligible rollover distribution is paid to you, the 20% withholding tax applies. Before a distribution is made, your plan administrator must provide you with written notice concerning the rollover options and the withholding tax rules. *See 7.6* for further details on the direct rollover and personal rollover alternatives.

**Rollover of distribution from designated Roth account.** An eligible rollover distribution from a designated Roth account may be rolled over to a Roth IRA. A qualified (nontaxable) distribution from a designated Roth account may be rolled over to another designated Roth account in a different plan, but only in a direct rollover *(7.6)*. For further details on distributions from designated Roth accounts, including rollovers, *see 7.18*.

**Rollover from qualified retirement plan to traditional IRA after age 70½.** Starting with the year you reach age 70½, you may no longer make contributions to a traditional IRA. However, if you are over age 70½ and you expect to receive an eligible rollover distribution from your employer's plan (including a plan for self-employed participants), you may avoid tax on the distribution by instructing your plan administrator to make a direct rollover of the distribution to a traditional IRA *(7.6)*. If you receive the distribution from the employer, a 20% tax will be withheld. You may then make a tax-free rollover within 60 days of the distribution; *see* the discussion of "personal rollovers" *(7.6)*. After the year of the rollover, you must receive a required minimum distribution from the IRA *(8.13)*.

**Beneficiaries.** See the discussion of rollover options open to beneficiaries *(7.6)*.

**Distributions that are not eligible for rollover.** Any lump-sum or partial distribution from your account is eligible for rollover except for the following:

- Hardship distributions from a 401(k) plan or 403(b) plan *(7.17)*.
- Payments that are part of a series of substantially equal payments made at least annually over a period of 10 years or more or over your life or life expectancy (or the joint lives or joint life and last survivor expectancies of you and your designated beneficiary).
- Minimum required distributions after attaining age 70½ or retiring *(7.11)*.
- Corrective distributions of excess 401(k) plan contributions and deferrals.
- Dividends on employer stock.
- Life insurance coverage costs.
- Loans that are deemed to be taxable distributions because they exceed the limits discussed in *7.14*.

For all of the above taxable distributions that are ineligible for rollover, you may elect to completely avoid withholding on Form W-4P *(26.9)*.

## 7.6 Direct Rollover or Personal Rollover

If you are an employee or a self-employed person entitled to an eligible rollover distribution *(7.5)* from a qualified plan, you may choose a direct rollover, or if you actually receive the distribution you may make a personal rollover within 60 days. To avoid withholding, choose a direct rollover. You must receive a written explanation of your rollover rights from your plan administrator before an eligible rollover distribution is made.

**Rollover to Roth IRA.** An eligible rollover distribution from a qualified employer plan, 403(b) plan, or governmental 457 plan may be rolled over to a Roth IRA, but the rollover is not tax free. A rollover to a Roth IRA, like a conversion from a traditional IRA, is a taxable distribution except to the extent it is allocable to after-tax contributions *(8.23)*.

### Direct Rollover From Employer Plan

If you choose to have your plan administrator make a direct rollover of an eligible rollover distribution to a traditional IRA or another eligible employer plan, you avoid tax on the

*Planning Reminder*

**Direct Rollover to Roth IRA**

A distribution from a qualified employer plan, 403(b) plan, or governmental 457 plan can be rolled over to a Roth IRA, but the rollover is a taxable distribution except to the extent it is allocable to after-tax contributions *(8.22)*.

payment and no tax will be withheld. If you are changing jobs and want a direct rollover to the plan of the new employer, make sure that the plan accepts rollovers; if it does not, choose a direct rollover to a traditional IRA.

When you select the direct rollover option, your plan administrator may transfer the funds directly by check or electronically to the new plan, or you may be given a check payable to the new plan that you must deliver to the new plan.

In choosing a direct rollover to a traditional IRA, the terms of the plan making the payment will determine whether you may divide the distribution among several IRAs or whether you will be restricted to one IRA. For example, if you are entitled to receive a lump-sum distribution from your employer's plan, you may want to split up your distribution into several traditional IRAs, but the employer may force you to select only one. After the direct rollover is made, you may then diversify your holdings by making tax-free trustee-to-trustee transfers to other traditional IRAs.

You may elect to make a direct rollover of part of your distribution and to receive the balance. The portion paid to you will be subject to 20% withholding and is not eligible for special averaging. Withholding is generally not required on distributions of less than $200.

A direct rollover will be reported by the payer plan to the IRS and to you on Form 1099-R, although the transfer is not taxable. The direct rollover will be reported in Box 1 of Form 1099-R, but zero will be entered as the taxable amount in Box 2a. In Box 7, Code G should be entered.

### EXAMPLE

When Tom retires, he has a 401(k) plan account with a $200,000 balance, $40,000 of which is from after-tax contributions and $160,000 of which is pre-tax, consisting of pre-tax contributions, employer matching contributions, and earnings on all contributions including the after-tax contributions. Tom wants to make a tax-free rollover of his after-tax contributions to a Roth IRA and a tax-free rollover of the balance to a traditional IRA. He can do this by specifically instructing the 401(k) plan administrator to directly roll over the $160,000 pre-tax amount to a traditional IRA and the $40,000 after-tax amount to a Roth IRA.

**Allocating a direct rollover between pre-tax and after-tax contributions.** If you have made after-tax contributions as well as pre-tax elective deferrals to the plan, the IRS has provided guidelines that allow you to transfer only the after-tax contributions to a Roth IRA, in what amounts to a tax-free conversion, while moving the pre-tax portion of the account to a traditional IRA in a tax-free rollover. These rules, in IRS Notice 2014-54, apply to distributions from 401(k) plans, 403(b) plans, and governmental Section 457 plans. Final regulations apply the Notice 2014-54 allocation rules to distributions from designated Roth accounts (T.D. 9769, 2016-23 IRB 1020).

The guidelines allow you to make a direct rollover to more than one plan and to select which funds (pre-tax or after-tax) are going into which plan, provided both of these conditions are met: (1) all the transfers are scheduled to be made at the same time, apart from reasonable delays to facilitate plan administration, and (2) you inform the plan administrator of your allocation prior to the time of the direct rollovers.

## Personal Rollover After Receiving a Distribution

If you do not tell your plan administrator to make a direct rollover of an eligible rollover distribution, and you instead receive the distribution yourself, you will receive only 80% of the taxable portion (generally the entire distribution unless you made after-tax contributions); 20% will be withheld. Withholding does not apply to the portion of the distribution consisting of net unrealized appreciation from employer securities that is tax-free *(7.8)*. Remember to include the withheld 20% on your tax return as federal income tax withheld (on Line 16 of Form 1040), so that it can be treated as a credit against the tax otherwise owed.

Although you receive only 80% of the taxable eligible rollover distribution, the full amount before withholding will be reported as the gross distribution in Box 1 of Form 1099-R. To avoid tax you must roll over the full amount within 60 days to a traditional IRA or another eligible employer plan. However, to roll over 100% of the distribution you will have to use other funds to replace the 20% withheld. If you roll over only the 80% received, the 20% balance will be taxable; *see* the John Anderson Example below. For the taxable part that is not rolled over, you may not use special averaging or capital gain treatment even if you meet the age test *(7.3)*. In addition, if the distribution was made to you before you reached age 59½, the taxable amount will be subject to a 10% penalty unless you are disabled, separating from service after reaching age 55, or have substantial medical expenses; *see* the full list of exceptions below *(7.13)*.

### EXAMPLE

John Anderson plans to retire in June 2019 at age 52. Assume that at that time he is due a lump-sum distribution of $100,000 from a qualified plan of his company. If he instructs his plan administrator to make a direct rollover of the entire amount to a traditional IRA or to an eligible employer plan, there is no tax withholding, and the $100,000 is transferred tax free.

Now assume that John decides not to choose a direct rollover because he is planning to use the funds to invest in a business. The plan will pay him $80,000 and withhold a tax of $20,000 that John will apply to his tax liability when he files his 2019 return (by reporting the $20,000 as federal income tax withheld). But, say, a month later John changes his mind about the investment and now wants to roll over his benefits to a traditional IRA. He must make the rollover within 30 days because 30 days of the 60-day rollover period have already passed. Furthermore, to avoid tax on the entire distribution, he must deposit $100,000 in the traditional IRA, even though $20,000 tax has been withheld. If he does not have the $20,000, he must borrow the $20,000 and deposit it in the IRA. If he rolls over only $80,000, he must report $20,000 as a taxable distribution on his 2019 return and since the distribution was made before he reached age 59½, the 10% penalty for early withdrawals will apply; based on these facts, John does not qualify for a penalty exception *(7.13)*.

If a distribution includes your voluntary after-tax contributions to the qualified plan, they are tax free to you if you keep them. However, after-tax contributions may be rolled over to a qualified plan or a 403(b) plan that separately accounts for the after-tax amounts.

A rollover may include salary deferral contributions that were excludable from income when made, such as qualifying deferrals to a 401(k) plan. The rollover may also include accumulated deductible employee contributions (and allocable income) made after 1981 and before 1987. If a qualified retirement plan has invested in a life insurance contract that is distributed to you as part of a lump-sum retirement distribution, you may be able to roll over the life insurance contract to the qualified plan of a new employer, but not to a traditional IRA. The law bars investment of IRA funds in life insurance contracts.

You may not claim a deduction for your rollover.

**Multiple rollover accounts allowed.** You may wish to diversify a distribution in different investments. There is no limit on the number of rollover accounts you may have. A lump-sum distribution from a qualified plan may be rolled over to several traditional IRAs.

**Reporting a personal rollover on your return.** When you receive a distribution that could have been rolled over, the payer will report on Form 1099-R the full taxable amount before withholding, although 20% has been withheld. However, if you make a rollover yourself within the 60-day period, the rollover reduces the taxable amount on your tax return. For example, if in 2018 you were entitled to a $100,000 lump-sum distribution and received $80,000 after mandatory 20% withholding and then within 60 days you rolled over the full $100,000 into a traditional IRA, report $100,000 as a pension payment on line 4a of Form 1040, but enter zero as the taxable amount and write "Rollover" next to the line. If you roll over only part of the distribution, the amount of the lump sum not rolled over is entered as the taxable amount. Remember to include the 20% withholding on the line for federal income tax withheld.

IRS may waive 60-day deadline for personal rollover on equitable grounds. Generally, a personal rollover must be completed by the 60th day following the day on which you receive a distribution from the qualified plan. However, the IRS has discretion to waive the 60-day deadline and permit more time for a rollover where failure to complete a timely rollover was due to events beyond your reasonable control.

You may be able to use a self-certification procedure provided by the IRS to obtain a waiver of the 60-day deadline if you have one or more of 11 acceptable reasons for being late. The self-certification guidelines, which also apply to rollovers from traditional IRAs, as well as the other IRS waiver guidelines, are discussed in *8.10*.

**Extension of 60-day rollover period for frozen deposits.** If you receive a qualifying distribution from a retirement plan and deposit the funds in a financial institution that becomes bankrupt or insolvent, you may be prevented from withdrawing the funds in time to complete a rollover within 60 days. If this happens, the 60-day period is extended while your account is "frozen." The 60-day rollover period does not include days on which your account is frozen. Further, you have a minimum of 10 days after the release of the funds to complete the rollover.

## Rollover by Beneficiary

**Surviving spouse.** If you are your deceased spouse's beneficiary, you have the same rollover options that your spouse would have had for a distribution. You may choose to have the plan make a direct rollover to your own traditional IRA. The advantage of choosing the direct rollover is to avoid a 20% withholding tax. If the distribution is paid to you, 20% will be withheld. You may make a rollover within 60 days, but to completely avoid tax, you must include in the rollover the withheld amount, as illustrated in the John Anderson Example above. If you receive the distribution but do not make the rollover, you will be taxed on the distribution, except for any amount allocable to after-tax contributions. If your spouse was born before January 2, 1936, you may be able to use special averaging *(7.4)* to compute the tax on the distribution. You are not subject to the 10% penalty for early distributions *(7.13)* even if you are under age 59½.

You can roll over the distribution to a Roth IRA but the rollover is taxable under the rules for conversions from traditional IRAs *(8.22)*.

You may also roll over a distribution from your deceased spouse's account to your own qualified plan, 403(a) qualified annuity, 403(b) tax-sheltered annuity, or governmental section 457 plan. However, if you were born before January 2, 1936, are still working, and want to preserve the option of electing averaging or capital gain treatment (for pre-1974 participation) for a later distribution from your employer's qualified plan *(7.3)*, you should not roll over your deceased spouse's account to your employer's qualified plan. If the rollover is made to your employer's qualified plan, a lump-sum distribution from the plan will not be eligible for averaging or capital gains treatment.

**Rollover of distribution received under a divorce or support proceeding.** In a qualified domestic relations order (QDRO) meeting special tax law tests, a state court may give you the right to receive all or part of your spouse's or former spouse's retirement benefits. If you are entitled to receive an eligible rollover distribution, you can instruct the plan to make a direct rollover *(see* above) to a traditional IRA or to your employer's qualified plan if it accepts rollovers. If the distribution is paid to you, 20% withholding will apply. You may complete a rollover within 60 days under the rules for personal rollovers discussed earlier. If you do not make the rollover, the distribution you receive is taxable. If only part of the distribution is rolled over, the balance is taxed as ordinary income in the year of receipt. In figuring your tax, you are allowed a prorated share of your former spouse's cost investment, if any. If your spouse or former spouse was born before January 2, 1936, and you receive a lump-sum distribution that would have been eligible for special averaging *(7.3)* had he or she received it, you may use the averaging method to figure the tax on the distribution. You are not subject to the 10% penalty for early distributions *(7.13)* even if you are under age 59½.

**Nonspouse beneficiaries.** If you are entitled as a nonspouse beneficiary to receive a distribution from a qualified plan, 403(b) plan, or governmental 457 plan, the plan must allow you to roll it over to an IRA in a trustee-to-trustee transfer. The IRA must be treated as an inherited IRA subject to the required minimum distribution (RMD) rules for nonspouse beneficiaries *(8.14)*. This means that you will have to begin receiving RMDs from the inherited IRA by the end of the year following the year of the plan participant's death *(8.14)*.

---

*Law Alert*

**Nonspouse Beneficiary Rollover to Inherited IRA**

A qualified plan must allow a nonspouse beneficiary to make a trustee-to-trustee transfer to an IRA that is treated as an inherited IRA.

## 7.7    Rollover of Proceeds From Sale of Property

A lump-sum distribution from a qualified plan may include property, such as non-employer stock; *see 7.8* for employer securities. If you plan to roll over the distribution, you may find that a bank or other plan trustee does not want to take the property. You cannot get tax-free rollover treatment by keeping the property and rolling over cash to the new plan. If you sell the property, you may roll over the sale proceeds to a traditional IRA as long as the sale and rollover occur within 60 days of receipt of the distribution. If you roll over all of the proceeds, you do not recognize a gain or loss from the sale; the proceeds are treated as part of the distribution. If you make a partial rollover of sale proceeds, you must report as capital gain the portion of the gain that is allocable to the retained sale proceeds.

If you receive cash and property, and you sell the property but only make a partial rollover, you must designate how much of the rolled-over cash is from the employer distribution and how much from the sale proceeds. The designation must be made by the time for filing your return (plus any extensions) and is irrevocable. If you do not make a timely designation, the IRS will allocate the rollover between cash and sales proceeds on a ratable basis; the allocation will determine tax on the retained amount.

## 7.8    Distribution of Employer Stock or Other Securities

If you are entitled to a distribution from a qualified plan that includes employer stock (or other employer securities), you may be able to take advantage of a special exclusion rule. If you withdraw the stock from the plan as part of a lump-sum distribution and invest the stock in a taxable brokerage account instead of rolling it over to a traditional IRA, tax on the "net unrealized appreciation," or NUA, may be deferred until you sell the stock. To defer tax on the full NUA, the employer stock must be received in a lump-sum distribution, as discussed below. If the distribution is not a lump sum, a less favorable NUA exclusion is available, but only if you made after-tax contributions to buy the shares; *see* below.

**Lump-sum distribution.** If you receive appreciated stock or securities as part of a lump-sum distribution, net unrealized appreciation (increase in value since purchase of securities) is not subject to tax at the time of distribution unless you elect to treat it as taxable.

For purposes of the NUA exclusion, a lump-sum distribution is the payment within a single year of the plan participant's entire balance from all of the employer's qualified plans of the same kind (all of the employer's profit-sharing plans, or all pension or stock bonus plans). The distribution must be paid to: (1) a participant after reaching age 59½, (2) an employee-participant who separates from service (by retiring, resigning, changing employers, or being fired), (3) a self-employed participant who becomes totally and permanently disabled, or (4) a beneficiary of a deceased plan participant. If there is any plan balance at the end of the year, there is no lump sum and the NUA exclusion is not available.

Assuming you do not waive the NUA exclusion, you are taxed (at ordinary income rates) only on the original cost of the stock when contributed to the plan. Tax on the appreciation is delayed until the shares are later sold by you at a price exceeding cost basis and the gain attributable to the NUA will be taxed at long-term capital gain rates *(5.3)*.

The NUA in employer's securities is shown in Box 6 of the Form 1099-R received from the payer. It is not included in the taxable amount in Box 2a.

If, when distributed, the shares are valued at below the cost contribution to the plan, the fair market value of the shares is subject to tax. If you contributed to the purchase of the shares and their value is less than your contribution, you do not realize a loss deduction on the distribution. You realize a loss only when the stock is sold for less than your cost or becomes worthless *(5.32)* at a later date. If a plan distributes worthless stock, you may deduct your contributions to the stock as a miscellaneous itemized deduction subject to the 2% of adjusted gross income floor.

*Court Decision*

**Stock Purchased With Cash Withdrawal Cannot Be Rolled Over**

A taxpayer withdrew cash from his qualified self-employment retirement accounts and used most of the net distribution (after withholdings) to buy stock, which was then transferred to an IRA within 60 days of the withdrawal. He treated the entire distribution as a tax-free rollover but the IRS and Tax Court held it was taxable. The transfer of stock to the IRA was not a tax-free rollover; only the cash distribution itself could be rolled over. A negligence penalty was also imposed.

A direct rollover from the accounts to an IRA would have been tax free; the stock could then have been purchased through the new IRA.

*Planning Reminder*

**Deferring Tax on NUA**

If you receive a lump-sum distribution that includes appreciated employer securities, you may defer the tax on the net unrealized appreciation (NUA) in the securities.

**EXAMPLES**

1. Shares valued below your cost contribution. You contributed $500 and your employer contributed $300 to buy 10 shares of company stock having at the time a fair market value of $80 per share. When you retire, the fair market value of the stock is $40 per share, or a total of $400. You do not realize income on the distribution, and you do not have a deductible loss for the difference between your cost contribution and the lower fair market value. Your contribution to the stock is its basis. This is $50 per share. If you sell the stock for $40 per share, you have a capital loss of $10 per share. However, if you sell the stock for $60 per share, you have gain of $10 per share.

2. Appreciated shares. You receive 10 shares of company stock that was purchased entirely with the employer's funds. Your employer's cost was $50 a share. At the time of a lump-sum distribution, the shares are valued at $80 a share. Your employer's contribution of $50 a share, or $500, is included as part of your taxable distribution. The appreciation of $300 (the NUA) is not included, assuming you do not elect to be taxed currently on the appreciation. The cost basis of the shares in your hands is $500 (the amount currently taxable to you). The holding period of the stock starts from the date of distribution. However, if you sell the shares for any amount exceeding $500 and up to $800, your profit is long-term capital gain regardless of how long you held the shares. If you sell for more than $800, the gain exceeding the original NUA of $300 is subject to long-term capital gain treatment only if the sale is long term from the date of distribution. Thus, if within a month of the distribution you sold the shares for $900, $300 would be long-term gain; $100 would be short-term gain.

**Election to waive tax-free treatment.** You may elect to include the NUA in employer stock or securities as ordinary income. You might consider making this election when the NUA is not substantial or you want to accelerate income to the current year by taking into account the entire lump-sum distribution. Make the election to include the unrealized appreciation as ordinary income by reporting it on Line 4b (taxable pensions and annuities) of Form 1040. If you were born before January 2, 1936, and are claiming averaging or capital gain treatment on Form 4972 *(7.3)*, follow the form instructions for adding the unrealized appreciation to the taxable distribution.

**Distribution not a lump sum.** If you receive appreciated employer securities in a distribution that does not meet the lump-sum tests above, you report as ordinary income the amount of the employer's contribution to the purchase of the shares and the appreciation allocated to the employer's cost contribution. You do not report the amount of appreciation allocated to your own after-tax contribution to the purchase. In other words, tax is deferred only on the NUA attributable to your after-tax employee contributions. Net unrealized appreciation is shown in Box 6 of Form 1099-R. Cost contributions must be supplied by the company distributing the stock.

**EXAMPLE**

A qualified plan distributes 10 shares of company stock with an average cost of $100, of which the employee contributed $60 and the employer, $40. At the date of distribution, the stock had a fair market value of $180. The portion of the NUA attributable to the employee's contribution is $48 (60% of $80); the employer's portion is $32 (40% of $80). The employee reports $72 as income: the employer's cost of $40 and the employer's share of NUA, or $32. For purposes of determining gain or loss on a later sale, the employee's basis for each share is $132, which includes the employee contribution of $60 and the $72 reported as taxable income.

## 7.9 Survivor Annuity for Spouse

If you have been married for at least a year as of the annuity starting date, the law generally requires that payments to you of vested benefits be in a specific annuity form to protect your surviving spouse. All defined benefit and money purchase pension plans must provide benefits in the form of a qualified joint and survivor annuity (QJSA) unless you, with the written consent of your spouse, elect a different form of benefit. A qualified joint and survivor annuity must also be provided by profit-sharing or stock bonus plans if you elect a life annuity payout or the plan does not provide that your nonforfeitable benefit is payable in full upon your death either to your surviving spouse, or to another beneficiary if there is no surviving spouse or your spouse consents to the naming of the non-spouse beneficiary.

Under a QJSA, you receive an annuity for your life and then your surviving spouse receives an annuity for his or her life that is at least 50% of the amount payable during your joint lives. Most plans allow you to choose among several options that will provide your surviving spouse with more than 50% of your lifetime benefit after your death. You may waive the QJSA only with your spouse's consent. Without the consent, you may not take a lump-sum distribution or a single life annuity ending when you die. A single life annuity pays higher monthly benefits during your lifetime than the qualified joint and survivor annuity, and a larger QJSA benefit for your surviving spouse means a greater reduction to your lifetime benefit. If benefits begin under a QJSA and you divorce the spouse to whom you were married as of the annuity starting date, that former spouse will be entitled to the QJSA survivor benefits if you die unless there is a contrary provision in a QDRO *(7.13)*.

The law also requires that a qualified pre-retirement survivor annuity (QPSA) be paid to your surviving spouse if you die before the date vested benefits first become payable or if you die after the earliest payment date but before retiring. The QPSA is automatic unless you, with your spouse's consent, agree to a different benefit.

Your plan should provide you with a written explanation of these annuity rules within a reasonable period before the annuity starting date, as well as the rules for electing to waive the joint and survivor annuity benefit and the pre-retirement survivor annuity.

**Plan may provide exception for marriages of less than one year.** The terms of a plan may provide that a QJSA or QPSA will not be provided to a spouse of the plan participant if the couple has been married for less than one year as of the participant's annuity starting date (QJSA) or, if earlier, the date of the participant's death (QPSA).

**Cash out of annuity.** If the present value of the QJSA is $5,000 or less, your employer may "cash out" your interest without your consent or your spouse's consent by making a lump-sum distribution of the present value of the annuity before the annuity starting date. After the annuity starting date, you and your spouse must consent to a cash-out. Written consent is required for a cash-out if the present value of the annuity exceeds $5,000. Similar cash-out rules apply to a QPSA.

*Planning Reminder*

**Spouse Must Consent in Writing to Your Waiver**

Your spouse must consent in writing to your waiver of a required annuity and the selection of a different type of distribution. A spouse's consent must be witnessed by a plan representative or notary public. An election to waive the qualified joint and survivor annuity may be made during the 180-day period ending on the annuity starting date. An election to waive the qualified pre-retirement survivor annuity may be made any time after the first day of the plan year in which you reach age 35. A waiver is revocable during the time permitted to make the election.

## 7.10 Court Distributions to Former Spouse Under a QDRO

As a part of a divorce-related property settlement, or to cover alimony or support obligations, a state domestic relations court can require that all or part of a plan participant's retirement benefits be paid to a spouse, former spouse, child, or other dependent. Administrators of pension, profit-sharing, or stock bonus plans are required to honor a qualified domestic relations order (QDRO) that meets specific tax law tests. For example, the QDRO generally may not alter the amount or form of benefits provided by the plan, but it may authorize payments after the participant reaches the earliest retirement age, even if he or she continues working. A QDRO may provide that a spouse is entitled to all, some, or none of the spousal survivor benefits payable under the plan.

**QDRO distributions to spouse or former spouse.** If you are the spouse or former spouse of an employee or self-employed plan participant and you receive a distribution pursuant to a QDRO, the distribution is generally taxable to you. However, if the distribution would have been eligible for rollover by your spouse or former spouse, you may make a tax-free rollover to a traditional IRA or to a qualified plan *(7.5)*.

To create a valid QDRO, the court order must contain specific language. The recipient spouse (or former spouse) must be assigned rights to the plan participant's retirement benefits plan, and must be referred to as an "alternate payee" in the court decree. The decree must identify the retirement plan and indicate the amount and number of payments subject to the QDRO. Both spouses must be identified by name and address. If the required information is not clearly provided in the decree, QDRO treatment may be denied and the plan participant taxed on the retirement plan distributions, rather than the spouse who actually receives payments.

*Caution*

**RMDs from Multiple Accounts Generally Cannot Be Combined**

If you have more than one qualified employee retirement plan account, such as 401(k) plan accounts with two employers, you must take a required minimum distribution (RMD) from each plan; you cannot combine the separate RMDs and take the total from one of the accounts. Similarly, if you have a 401(k) plan and a tax-sheltered annuity account (403(b) plan *(7.19)*, you must take the RMD from each plan. However, if you have more than one tax-sheltered annuity account, these accounts can be combined for RMD purposes; the total RMD for all the accounts can be taken from any one of the tax-sheltered annuities, or from more than one as you choose.

If you also have traditional IRAs, the IRA RMDs *(8.13)* cannot be combined with your employer plan RMDs. That is, RMDs from your employer retirement plans cannot be taken from the IRAs, and your IRA RMDs *(8.13)* cannot be taken from the employer plans. However, if you must receive RMDs from multiple traditional IRAs, the separately determined RMDs may be combined and taken from any one of the IRAs or from more than one of the IRAs in any combination; *see* Step 3 at *8.13*.

If you do not make a rollover, and your spouse or former spouse (the plan participant) was born before January 2, 1936, a distribution to you of your entire share of the benefits may be eligible for special averaging, provided the distribution, if received by your spouse (or former spouse), would satisfy the lump-sum distribution tests *(7.3)*. If the distribution qualifies, you may use Form 4972 to claim 10-year averaging, and possibly the 20% capital gain election *(7.3)*. Transfers from a governmental or church plan pursuant to a qualifying domestic relations order are also eligible for special averaging or rollover treatment.

**Distributions to a child or other dependent.** Payments from a QDRO are taxed to the plan participant, not to the dependent who actually receives them, where the recipient is not a spouse or former spouse.

## 7.11 When You Must Begin Receiving Required Minimum Distributions (RMDs)

The longer you can delay taking retirement distributions from your company plan or self-employed plan, the greater will be the tax-deferred buildup of your retirement fund. To cut off this tax deferral, the law requires minimum distributions to begin no later than a specified date in order to avoid an IRS penalty. The required beginning date rules apply to distributions from all qualified corporate and self-employed qualified retirement plans, qualified annuity plans, and Section 457 plans of tax-exempt organizations and state and local government employers. The rules also apply to distributions from tax-sheltered annuities *(7.19)* but only for benefits accrued after 1986; there is no mandatory beginning date for tax-sheltered annuity benefits accrued before 1987.

You do not have to figure your required minimum distributions (RMDs). If you are not receiving an annuity, your plan administrator will determine the minimum amount that must be distributed to you each year from your account balance, based upon IRS regulations. The rules for figuring the minimum amount (the RMD) are similar to the rules for traditional IRAs *(8.13)*.

If you do not receive your RMD for a year, a penalty tax applies unless the IRS waives it. The penalty is 50% of the difference between what was received and what should have been received. The IRS may waive the penalty tax if you file Form 5329 and on an attached statement explain that a reasonable error caused the underpayment and the shortfall was or will be corrected.

**Required beginning date.** Unless you are a more-than-5% owner for the plan year ending in the calendar year in which you reach age 70½, your required beginning date is generally the later of these dates: (1) April 1 following the year in which you reach age 70½ or (2) April 1 following the year in which you retire. For example, if you retired in 2014 and will reach age 70½ in March 2019, your first RMD, the RMD for 2019, may be received from the plan in 2019, or if it isn't, it must be received by April 1, 2020. The RMD for 2020 (your second RMD) must be received by December 31, 2020.

A more-than-5% owner must begin distributions by April 1 following the year in which he or she reaches age 70½, and an IRS regulation permits a plan to apply this deadline to all employees. That is, the plan may require all employees, and not just more-than-5% owners, to begin required minimum distributions no later than April 1 of the year after the year in which age 70½ is attained, even if they are still working. Being a more-than-5% owner means that you own over 5% of the capital or profits interest in the business.

If you reach age 70½ in 2019, are not a more-than-5% owner in 2019, and do not retire until 2021, your first RMD from the plan will not have to be received until April 1, 2022 (i.e., April 1 of the year after the year of retirement), assuming the plan does not require all employees to take the first RMD by April 1 of the year after the year of reaching age 70½.

## 7.12 Payouts to Beneficiaries

As the beneficiary of a qualified plan account (corporate or self-employed plan), including a 403(b) tax-sheltered annuity or Section 457 plan, your distribution options depend on the terms of the plan. You may prefer the option of receiving payments over your life expectancy, but the plan may require that you receive a lump-sum distribution or allow installment payments over only a limited number of years.

Although IRS final regulations generally allow beneficiaries to use a life expectancy distribution method, the IRS rules represent the longest permissible payment period. Qualified plans are allowed to require a shorter period and most do.

If you receive a lump-sum distribution, you generally may make a tax-free rollover to another plan, but the rollover options are more restricted for nonspouse beneficiaries than for surviving spouses as discussed below.

If the plan participant was born before January 2, 1936, and you receive a qualifying lump sum, you may be able to claim special averaging *(7.4)*.

**Surviving spouse.** If you are a surviving spouse and receive a distribution that would have been eligible for rollover had your spouse received it, you may make a tax-free rollover to the qualified plan of your employer or to your own traditional IRA. If you make a rollover to a traditional IRA, subsequent withdrawals are subject to the regular IRA distribution rules *(8.8)*.

If you do not make a rollover and the payer plan gives you the option of taking distributions over your life expectancy as allowed by the IRS rules, you may be able to delay the commencement of distributions for several years. If your spouse died before the year in which he or she attained age 70½, and you are the sole designated beneficiary of the account as of September 30 of the year following the year of death, you do not have to begin receiving required minimum distributions (RMDs) until the end of the year in which your spouse would have attained age 70½. This is an exception to the general rule that requires RMDs under the life expectancy method to begin by the end of the year following the year in which the plan participant died.

**Nonspouse beneficiary.** If you are the designated beneficiary of a deceased plan participant who was not your spouse, you are allowed to roll over a distribution, but only by means of a direct trustee-to-trustee transfer to an IRA that is set up as an inherited IRA *(7.6)*. If the transfer is to a Roth IRA, you are taxed as if you made a conversion from a traditional IRA *(8.22)*. If you do not make such a trustee-to-trustee transfer, you must receive distributions as required under the terms of the deceased participant's plan. Most plans allow distributions to be received over the beneficiary's life expectancy, with the first distribution due by December 31 of the year following the year of the plan participant's death.

## 7.13 Penalty for Distributions Before Age 59½

A 10% penalty (the IRS calls this an "additional tax") generally applies to taxable distributions made to you before you reach age 59½ from a qualified corporate or self-employed retirement plan, qualified annuity plan, or tax-sheltered annuity plan (403(b) plan *(7.19)*), but there are several exceptions. For example, the penalty does not apply to distributions made to you after separation from service if the separation occurs during or after the year in which you reach age 55. A full list of exceptions is shown below.

If no exception applies, the penalty is 10% of the taxable distribution. If you make a tax-free rollover *(7.5)*, the distribution is not taxable and not subject to the penalty. If a partial rollover is made, the part not rolled over is taxable and subject to the penalty.

The penalty generally does not apply to Section 457 plans of tax-exempt employers or state or local governments *(7.20)*. However, if a direct transfer or rollover is made to a governmental Section 457 plan from a qualified plan, 403(b) annuity, or IRA, a later distribution from the Section 457 plan is subject to the penalty to the extent of the direct transfer or rollover.

If you make an in-plan rollover to a designated Roth account *(7.18)* from your 401(k) plan, 403(b) plan or governmental 457 plan, the 10% penalty may apply to a distribution received from the designated Roth account within five years of the rollover.

A similar 10% penalty applies to IRA distributions before age 59½ *(8.12)*. The penalty is 25% if a distribution before age 59½ is made from a SIMPLE IRA in the first two years of plan participation *(8.18)*. The 10% penalty generally applies to pre–age 59½ distributions from nonqualified annuities *(7.21)*.

*Caution*

## Penalty Exception for Substantially Equal Payments

The substantially equal payments exception to the 10% early distribution penalty is generally revoked if qualifying payments are not received for at least five years. For example, you separate from service when you are age 57 and you begin to receive a series of qualifying substantially equal payments. When you are age 61, you stop the payments or modify the payment schedule so that it no longer qualifies. Unless the IRS permits an exception, the 10% penalty applies to the payments received before age 59½ because the five-year test was not met.

There are a few differences between the penalty exceptions shown below for qualified corporate and self-employed plan distributions and the exceptions for IRA distributions *(8.12)*. There is no qualified plan exception for higher education expenses as there is for IRAs. On the other hand, the exception for distributions after separation from service at age 55 (or over) applies only to qualified plans and not to IRAs.

**Exceptions to the penalty.** The following distributions from a qualified employer plan are exempt from the 10% penalty, even if made to you before age 59½. If the plan administrator knows that an exception applies, a code for the exception will be entered in Box 7 of Form 1099-R on which the distribution is reported.

- *Rollovers.* Distributions that you roll over tax free under the "direct rollover" or "personal rollover" rules *(7.6)* are not subject to the early distribution penalty.

- *Disability.* Distributions made on account of your total disability do not subject you to the early distribution penalty.

- *Separation from service at age 55 or older.* The early distribution penalty does not apply to distributions after separation from service if you are age 55 or over in the year you retire or leave the company. If you reach age 55 in the same year you separate from service, the distribution must be received after the separation from service but you do not have to turn age 55 before receiving the distribution; the exception applies so long as the distribution is received after the separation from service and you reach age 55 before the end of the same year. You cannot separate from service before the year you reach age 55, wait until the year you reach age 55, and then take a distribution; the penalty will apply because in the year of separation you were not at least age 55.

  As discussed below, the age test is reduced from 55 to 50 for qualified public safety employees (police, fire fighting, emergency medical services).

  Note that the age 55 separation from service exception does not apply to IRA distributions. If you separate from service after age 55 and rollover a distribution to an IRA, the penalty exception will not apply to a distribution received before age 59½ from that IRA. This happened to an attorney who left his law firm at age 56 and rolled over funds from the law firm's pension plan to an IRA. The next year he withdrew about $240,000 from the IRA and was hit with the 10% penalty by the IRS. The Tax Court upheld the 10% penalty and also imposed a penalty for substantially understating tax *(48.6)*. The Seventh Circuit affirmed. The appeals court was sympathetic to the taxpayer's argument that it made no sense to impose the 10% early distribution penalty on the IRA distribution when he could have taken the distribution from his law firm's plan at age 56 with no penalty, but that is how Congress wrote the law. The Courts cannot change the rules that allow the age 55 exception only for qualified plan distributions and not IRAs. The Seventh Circuit also upheld the substantial understatement penalty; the taxpayer had no authority for claiming that the penalty exception applied to his IRA distribution.

- *Public safety employees separated from service at age 50 or later.* The early distribution penalty does not apply to distributions received by public safety officers who separate from service in or after the year of reaching age 50. The penalty exception applies to state and local public safety officers (police, fire, emergency medical), as well as to federal law enforcement officers, customs and border protection officers, federal firefighters, and air traffic controllers. The exception applies whether the distribution is from a defined benefit pension plan or a defined contribution plan such as the federal Thrift Savings Plan (TSP).

- *Medical costs.* Distributions are not subject to the early distribution penalty to the extent that you pay deductible medical expenses exceeding the threshold for medical expense deductions *(17.1)*, whether or not an itemized deduction for medical expenses is actually claimed for the year.

- *Substantially equal payments.* The early distribution penalty does not apply to distributions received after your separation from service that are part of a series of substantially equal payments (at least annually) over your life expectancy, or over the joint life expectancy of yourself and your designated beneficiary. If you claim the exception and begin to receive such a series of payments but then before age 59½ you receive a lump sum or change the distribution method and you are not totally disabled, a recapture penalty tax will generally apply. The recapture tax also applies to payments received before age 59½ if substantially equal payments are not received for at least five years. The recapture tax applies the 10% penalty to all amounts received before age 59½, as if the exception had never been allowed, plus interest for that period. However, the IRS allows taxpayers who have been receiving substantially equal payments under the fixed amortization or fixed annuitization method to switch without penalty to the required minimum distribution method; *see* Revenue Ruling 2002-62 for details. In private rulings, the IRS has allowed the annual distribution amount to be reduced without penalty after the account is divided in a divorce settlement.

- *Beneficiaries.* If you are the beneficiary of a deceased plan participant, you are not subject to the 10% penalty, regardless of your age or the participant's age.
- *Qualified reservist distribution.* If you are a member of the reserves called to active military duty for over 179 days, or indefinitely, distributions received during the active duty period that are attributable to elective deferrals (401(k) or 403(b) plan) are not subject to the early distribution penalty. Furthermore, a qualified reservist distribution may be recontributed to an IRA within two years after the end of the active duty period; a recontribution is not deductible.
- *IRS levy.* Involuntary distributions that result from an IRS levy on your plan account are not subject to the early distribution penalty.
- *QDRO.* Distributions paid to an alternate payee pursuant to a qualified domestic relations court order (QDRO) are not subject to the early distribution penalty.
- *TEFRA designations.* Distributions made before 1984 pursuant to a designation under the 1982 Tax Act (TEFRA).

**Financial hardship distributions or distributions used for college or home-buying costs are subject to the penalty.** The 10% penalty generally applies to a hardship distribution that you receive before age 59½ from a 401(k) plan *(7.17)* or 403(b) tax-sheltered annuity plan *(7.19)*. For example, there is no penalty exception for distributions you take to deal with a casualty loss, to pay tuition costs or to buy a principal residence. However, as noted above, a hardship distribution used to pay medical costs may qualify for an exception if your medical expenses exceed the floor for claiming an itemized deduction *(17.1)*.

Note that for IRA distributions, a penalty exception may apply for a distribution used to pay tuition costs or buy a principal residence *(8.12)*.

**Corrective distributions from 401(k) plans.** If you are considered a highly compensated employee and excess elective deferrals or excess contributions are made on your behalf, a distribution of the excess to you is not subject to the penalty.

**Filing Form 5329 for exceptions.** If your employer correctly entered a penalty exception code in Box 7 of Form 1099-R, you do not have to file Form 5329 to claim the exception. You also do not have to file Form 5329 if you made a tax-free rollover of the entire taxable distribution. You must file Form 5329 if you qualify for an exception, other than the rollover exception, that is not indicated in Box 7 of Form 1099-R.

## 7.14 Restrictions on Loans From Company Plans

Within limits, you may receive a loan from a qualified company plan, annuity plan, 403(b) plan, or government plan without triggering tax consequences. The maximum loan you can receive without tax is the lesser of 50% of your vested account balance or $50,000, but the $50,000 limit is subject to reductions where there are other loans outstanding; *see* below. Loans must be repayable within five years, unless they are used for buying your principal residence. Loans that do not meet these guidelines are treated as taxable distributions from the plan. If the plan treats a loan as a taxable distribution, you should receive a Form 1099-R with Code L marked in Box 7.

*If your vested accrued benefit is $20,000 or less, you are not taxed if the loan, when added to other outstanding loans from all plans of the employer, is $10,000 or less.* However, as a practical matter, your maximum loan may not exceed 50% of your vested account balance because of a Labor Department rule that allows only up to 50% of the vested balance to be used as loan security. Loans in excess of the 50% cap are allowed only if additional collateral is provided.

*If your vested accrued benefit exceeds $20,000, then the maximum tax-free loan depends on whether you borrowed from any employer plan within the one-year period ending on the day before the date of the new loan.* If you did not borrow within the year, you are not taxed on a loan that does not exceed the lesser of $50,000 or 50% of the vested benefit.

 *Law Alert*

**Special Loan Relief for Victims of Hurricanes Harvey, Irma, or Maria, or California Wildfires**

For taxpayers who lived in areas damaged in 2017 by Hurricane Harvey (or Tropical Storm Harvey), Hurricane Irma, Hurricane Maria, or the California wildfires and who suffered an economic loss as a result of these disasters, the allowable limit on loans from employer retirement plans is increased to the lesser of $100,000 or 100% of the account balance (up from the regular limit, the lesser of $50,000 or 50% of the account balance). The higher loan limit applies to loans received from September 29, 2017 (February 9, 2018, if in a California wildfire area), through December 31, 2018.

There is also a one-year suspension for payments due on plan loans. The suspension applies to loan payments otherwise due during the period beginning on the qualified beginning date in 2017 for the particular disaster, and ending December 31, 2018.

*See* IRS Publication 976 for further details on retirement plan relief for victims of the 2017 disasters.

*Law Alert*

## More Time Allowed to Roll Over Unpaid Loan When Leaving Job

If you leave your company before your loan is paid off, the company will reduce your vested account balance by the outstanding debt and report the defaulted amount (the "loan offset") as a taxable distribution on Form 1099-R. However, tax on the loan offset can be deferred if you can come up with the funds to make a timely rollover *(7.6)* of the amount to an IRA or another eligible employer retirement plan.

For example, if your vested account balance is $100,000, and the outstanding loan is $25,000 when your employment ends, your account balance is reduced to $75,000. You could choose a direct rollover *(7.6)* of the $75,000 balance, deferring tax on that amount. The $25,000 loan offset will be reported on Form 1099-R as a taxable distribution.

The Tax Cuts and Jobs Act gives more time to come up with the funds to complete a rollover of the loan offset. Before the new law, tax on the loan offset could be deferred by rolling it over within 60 days of the loan offset. Under the Tax Cuts and Jobs Act, the rollover deadline for loan offsets after 2017 is extended to the due date, including extensions, for filing the tax return for the year the loan offset occurred (the year for which it is treated as a distribution). This extended rollover deadline applies only where the loan offset results from a termination of employment or the employer's termination of the plan.

In the above example, note that if you elected to receive the account balance following the loan offset, rather than choosing a direct rollover to another eligible plan, $20,000 would be withheld (20% of the full $100,000) and you would receive only $55,000 ($100,000 − $25,000 loan offset − $20,000 withheld), but the full $100,000 would be treated as a taxable distribution *(7.6)*. In that case, if the entire $100,000 were not rolled over, you would be taxed on the portion not rolled over. Under the new law, the deadline for completing the rollover is the due date, including extensions, for filing the return for the year of the loan offset.

Also note that to the extent a rollover is not made, the 10% early distribution penalty would apply if you were under age 59½ at the time of the loan offset, unless a penalty exception were available *(7.13)*.

If there were loans within the one-year period, the $50,000 limit must be further reduced. The loan, when added to the outstanding loan balance, may not exceed $50,000 less the excess of (1) the highest outstanding loan balance during the one-year period (ending the day before the new loan) over (2) the outstanding balance on the date of the new loan. This reduced $50,000 limit applies where it is less than 50% of the vested benefit; if 50% of the vested benefit is the smaller amount, that would be the maximum tax-free loan.

> ### EXAMPLE
>
> Your vested plan benefit is $200,000. Assume that in December 2018 you borrow $30,000 from the plan. On November 1, 2019, when the outstanding balance on the first loan is $20,000, you want to take another loan without incurring tax.
>
> You may borrow an additional $20,000 without incurring tax: The $50,000 limit is first reduced by the outstanding loan balance of $20,000—leaving $30,000. The reduced $30,000 limit is in turn reduced by $10,000, the excess of $30,000 (the highest loan balance within one year of the new loan) over $20,000 (the loan balance as of November 1).

**Repayment period.** Generally, loans within the previously discussed limits must be repayable within five years to avoid being treated as a taxable distribution. However, if you use the loan to purchase a principal residence for yourself, the repayment period may be longer than five years; any reasonable period is allowed. This exception does not apply if the plan loan is used to improve your existing principal residence, to buy a second home, or to finance the purchase of a home or home improvements for other family members; such loans are subject to the five-year repayment rule.

**Level loan amortization required.** To avoid tax consequences on a plan loan, you must be required to repay using a level amortization schedule, with payments at least quarterly. According to Congressional committee reports, you may accelerate repayment, and the employer may use a variable interest rate and require full repayment if you leave the company.

Giving a demand note does not satisfy the repayment requirements. The IRS and Tax Court held the entire amount of an employee's loan to be a taxable distribution since his demand loan did not require level amortization of principal and interest with at least quarterly payments. It did not matter that the employee had paid interest quarterly and actually repaid the loan within five years.

If required installments are not made, the entire loan balance must be treated as a "deemed distribution" from the plan under IRS regulations. However, the IRS allows the plan administrator to permit a grace period of up to one calendar quarter. If the missed installment is not paid by the end of the grace period, there is at that time a deemed distribution in the amount of the outstanding loan balance.

Under IRS regulations, loan repayments may be suspended for up to one year (or longer if you are in the uniformed services) if you take a leave of absence during which you are paid less than the installments due. However, the installments after the leave must at least equal the original required amount and the loan must be repaid by the end of the allowable repayment period (five years if not used to buy a principal residence). For example, on July 1, 2018, when his vested account balance is $80,000, Joe Smith takes out a $40,000 non–principal residence loan, to be repaid with interest in level monthly installments of $825 over five years. He makes nine payments and then takes a year of unpaid leave. When he returns to work he can either increase his monthly payment to make up for the missed payments or resume paying $825 a month and on June 30, 2023, repay the entire balance owed in a lump sum.

If loan payments are suspended while you are serving in the uniformed services, the loan payments must resume upon returning to work and the loan repayment period (five years from the date of the loan unless the loan was used to buy your principal residence) is extended by the period of suspension.

**Spousal consent generally required to get a loan.** All plans subject to the joint and survivor rules *(7.11)* must require spousal consent in order to use your account balance as security for the loan in case you default. Check with your plan administrator for consent requirements.

**Interest deduction limitations.** If you want to borrow from your account to buy a first or second residence and you are not a "key" employee *(3.4)*, you can generally obtain a full interest deduction by using the residence as collateral for the loan *(15.2)*. Your account balance may not be used to secure the loan. Key employees are not allowed any interest deduction for plan loans.

If you use a plan loan for investment purposes and are not a key employee, and the loan is not secured by your elective deferrals (or allocable income) to a 401(k) plan or tax-sheltered annuity, the loan account interest is deductible up to investment income *(15.10)*. Interest on loans used for personal purposes is not deductible, unless your residence is the security for the loan.

# 7.15 Tax Benefits of 401(k) Plans

If your company has a profit-sharing or stock bonus plan, it has the opportunity of giving you additional tax-sheltered pay. The tax law allows the company to add a cash or deferred pay plan, called a 401(k) plan.

Your company may offer to contribute to a 401(k) plan trust account on your behalf if you forego a salary increase, but in most plans, contributions take the form of salary-reduction deferrals. Under a salary-reduction agreement, you elect to contribute a specified percentage of your wages to the 401(k) plan instead of receiving it as regular salary. In addition, your company may match a portion of your contribution. A salary-reduction deferral is treated as a contribution by your employer that is not taxable to you if the annual contribution limits are not exceeded.

Employers have the option of amending their 401(k) plans to allow employees to designate part or all of their elective contributions as Roth contributions *(7.18)*.

**Salary-reduction deferrals.** Making elective salary deferrals allows you to defer tax on salary and get a tax-free buildup of earnings within your 401(k) plan account until withdrawals are made.

The tax law sets a maximum annual limit on salary deferrals to a 401(k) plan. For 2018, the maximum deferral was $18,500, plus an additional $6,000 for plan participants age 50 or older if the plan permitted the extra "catch-up" contribution. If these limits are increased for 2019, the adjusted amounts will be reported in the *e-Supplement* at *jklasser. com*. The maximum annual deferral is lower for employees of "small" employers who adopt a SIMPLE 401(k); *see* below. Note that the terms of your employer's plan may limit your maximum deferral to a percentage of your compensation, so you may be unable to defer the maximum annual limit allowed by the tax law.

Elective deferrals within the annual limit are generally pre-tax contributions, so they are not subject to income tax withholding. However, pre-tax contributions are subject to Social Security and Medicare withholdings. If the plan allows, you may apply part or all of the annual deferral limit (including catch-up amount if applicable) to after-tax Roth contributions in a designated Roth account *(7.18)*.

Your employer may not require you to make elective deferrals in order to obtain any other benefits, apart from matching contributions. For example, benefits provided under health plans or other compensation plans may not be conditioned on your making salary deferrals to a 401(k) plan.

**Distributions.** Withdrawals from a 401(k) plan before age 59½ are restricted *(7.17)*. Mandatory 20% withholding applies to a lump sum as well as other distributions that are eligible for rollover if the distribution is paid to you and not directly rolled over to another plan *(7.6)*. For those born before January 2, 1936, a lump-sum distribution may be eligible for averaging *(7.3)*.

 *Law Alert*

**Automatic 401(k) Plan Coverage**

Employers are encouraged to automatically enroll employees in a 401(k) plan. Unless employees affirmatively opt out, a specified percentage of their pay is contributed to the plan. Even though the employees do not make affirmative elections to contribute, such plans are qualified provided that the employees are given advance notice of their right either to receive cash or have the designated amount contributed by the employer to the plan.

Employers are granted protection from nondiscrimination restrictions if they have automatic enrollment plans that include mandatory matching or non-elective employer contributions.

**Nondiscrimination rules.** The law imposes strict contribution percentage tests to prevent discrimination in favor of employees who are highly compensated. If these tests are violated, the employer is subject to penalties and the plan could be disqualified unless the excess contributions (plus allocable income) are distributed back to the highly compensated employees within specified time limits.

**SIMPLE 401(k).** Nondiscrimination tests are eased for employers who adopt a 401(k) plan with SIMPLE contribution provisions. A SIMPLE 401(k) may be set up only by employers who in the preceding year had no more than 100 employees with compensation of at least $5,000. An employer who contributes to a SIMPLE 401(k) must report on a calendar-year basis and may not maintain another qualified plan for employees eligible to participate in the SIMPLE plan.

If the SIMPLE contribution requirements are met, the plan is considered to meet 401(k) nondiscrimination requirements. Employee elective deferrals may not exceed an annual limitation, which was $12,500 for 2018. The plan may also allow additional contributions by participants who are age 50 or older by the end of the year. The limit on the additional contribution was $3,000 for 2018. The limits for 2019 will be reported in the *e-Supplement* at *jklasser.com*.

The employer must either match the employee deferral, up to 3% of compensation, or contribute 2% of compensation for all eligible employees, whether or not they make elective deferrals. All contributions are nonforfeitable. No other type of contribution is allowed. In figuring the 3% or 2% employer contribution, compensation is subject to an annual compensation ceiling; for 2018, the compensation limit was $275,000.

**Partnership plans.** Partnership plans that allow partners to vary annual contributions are treated as 401(k) plans by the IRS. Thus, elective deferrals are subject to the annual limit *(7.16)* and the special 401(k) plan nondiscrimination rules apply.

## 7.16 Limit on Salary-Reduction Deferrals

Elective deferrals to a 401(k) plan must not exceed the annual tax-free ceiling *(7.15)*; otherwise, the plan could be disqualified. If you also participate in a 403(b) tax-sheltered annuity plan *(7.19)*, a salary-reduction SEP established before 1997 *(8.16)*, or you have a self-employed 401(k) plan to which elective deferrals can be made *(41.4)*, the annual limit applies to the total salary reductions for all the plans and any excess deferral should be withdrawn as discussed below. Because of percentage-of-compensation limitations in your employer's plan, you may be unable to make deferrals up to the annual tax-free ceiling. Also, certain highly compensated employees may be unable to take advantage of the maximum annual tax-free ceiling because of restrictions imposed by nondiscrimination tests.

Both the regular annual deferral limit ($18,500 for 2018) and the "catch-up" contribution limit for those age 50 or older ($6,000 for 2018) are subject to cost-of-living increases; *see* the *e-Supplement* at *jklasser.com* for whether the limits will be increased for 2019.

To avoid the strict nondiscrimination tests for employee elective deferrals and employer matching contributions, an employer may make contributions to a SIMPLE 401(k) *(7.15)*.

An employer may make matching or other contributions, provided the total contribution for the year, including the employee's pre-tax salary deferral and any employee after-tax contributions, does not exceed the annual limit for defined contribution plans, which for 2018 was the lesser of 100% of compensation or $55,000.

**Withdrawing excess deferrals.** A single plan must apply the annual limit on salary deferrals to maintain qualified status. If your deferrals to the plan for a year exceed the annual limit, the excess, plus allocable earnings, must be distributed to you or the plan risks disqualification. If you participated in more than one plan and the deferrals to all of the plans exceeded the limit, you should withdraw the excess, plus the allocable income, from any of the plans, by April 15 of the year following the year of the excess deferral.

Whether the excess deferrals were made to one or several plans, you must report the excess as wages on Line 1 of Form 1040 for the year of the deferral. If you withdraw the excess by April 15 of the following year, it is not taxable again when you receive it.

**Caution**

**Reduced Deferral Limit for Highly Compensated Employees**

To avoid discrimination problems an employer may set a lower limit for elective salary deferrals by highly compensated employees than the generally applicable ceiling.

If, after contributions are made, the plan fails to meet the nondiscrimination tests, the excess contributions will either be returned to the highly compensated employees or kept in the plan but recharacterized as after-tax contributions. In either case, the excess contribution is taxable. Form 1099-R will indicate the excess contribution.

However, if the withdrawal of the excess is not received by the April 15 date, the excess is taxed again when received. The withdrawal of allocable earnings is always taxable in the year of the distribution. If a withdrawal of an excess deferral to a salary-reduction SEP (set up before 1997 *(8.16)*) is not withdrawn by the April 15 date, it is treated as a regular IRA contribution that could be subject to the penalty for excess IRA contributions *(8.7)*.

Excess deferrals (and earnings) distributed by the April 15 date are not subject to the 10% early distribution penalty *(7.13)* even if you are under age 59½.

For the year in which the excess deferral and allocable earnings are distributed to you, the plan will send you a Form 1099-R. Box 7 will include a code designating the year for which the excess is taxable.

## 7.17 Withdrawals From 401(k) Plans Restricted

By law, you may not withdraw funds attributable to elective salary-reduction contributions to a 401(k) plan unless (1) you no longer work for the employer maintaining the plan; (2) you have reached age 59½; (3) you have become totally disabled; (4) you can show financial hardship; (5) you are eligible for a qualified reservist distribution *(7.13)*; (6) you are the beneficiary of a deceased employee; or (7) the plan is terminated and no successor defined contribution plan (other than an employee stock ownership plan) is maintained by the employer. If a distribution is allowed and all of your plan contributions were pre-tax elective salary deferrals, the entire distribution is taxable unless it is rolled over to an eligible plan *(7.5)*.

Under IRS rules, it is difficult to qualify for hardship withdrawals; *see* below. If you do qualify, the withdrawal is taxable, and if you are under age 59½, it is subject to the 10% early distribution penalty unless you meet a penalty exception *(7.13)*.

The hardship provision and age 59½ withdrawal allowance do not apply to certain "pre-ERISA" money purchase pension plans (in existence June 27, 1974).

An "involuntary" distribution resulting from an IRS levy on a 401(k) plan account is taxable to the employee (assuming only "pre-tax" contributions) but is not subject to the 10% penalty on pre-age 59½ distributions *(7.13)*.

**Withdrawals before age 59½.** Withdrawals for medical disability, financial hardship, or separation from service are subject to the 10% penalty for early distributions unless you meet one of the exceptions *(7.13)*.

**Loans.** If you are allowed to borrow from the plan, loan restrictions *(7.14)* apply.

**Qualifying for hardship withdrawals.** IRS regulations restrict hardship withdrawals of pre-tax salary deferrals. If you qualify under the following restrictive rules you may withdraw your elective deferrals. Income allocable to elective deferrals may be withdrawn as part of a hardship distribution only in limited circumstances. If the plan so provides, income may be withdrawn if it was credited to your account by a cut-off date that is no later than the end of the last plan year ending before July 1, 1989. Keep in mind that any hardship distribution you are allowed to take is a taxable distribution, and if you are under age 59½, it is subject to the 10% early distribution penalty unless you meet a penalty exception *(7.13)*.

The IRS requires you to show an immediate and heavy financial need that cannot be met with other resources.

Financial need includes the following expenses (this list may be expanded by the IRS in rulings):

- Purchase of a principal residence for yourself (but not mortgage payments);
- Tuition, related fees and room and board for the next 12 months of post-secondary education for yourself, your spouse, children, or other dependents;
- Medical expenses previously incurred for yourself, your spouse, or dependents or expenses incurred to obtain medical care for such persons;
- Preventing your eviction or mortgage foreclosure; and
- Paying funeral expenses for a family member.

 *Planning Reminder*

**Avoiding Withholding on Hardship Distribution**

A hardship distribution from a 401(k) plan is not eligible for rollover *(7.5)* to an IRA or an eligible employer plan. Your employer will not apply 20% withholding to the distribution, as mandatory withholding applies only to rollover-eligible distributions *(7.5)*. However, the withholding rules for nonperiodic distributions apply. You can completely avoid withholding by checking a box on Form W-4P; if you do not do this, 10% will be withheld *(26.9)*.

Even if you can show financial need, you may not make a hardship withdrawal if you have other resources to pay the expenses. You do not have to provide your employer with a detailed financial statement, but you must state to your employer that you cannot pay the expenses with: compensation, insurance, or reimbursements; liquidation of your assets without causing yourself hardship by virtue of the liquidation; stopping your contributions, including salary deferrals, to the plan; other distributions or nontaxable loans from plans of any employer; or borrowing from a commercial lender. Your spouse's assets, as well as those of your minor children, are considered to be yours unless you show that they a re not available to you. For example, property held in trust for a child or under the Uniform Transfers (or Gifts) to Minors Act is not treated as your property.

Under a special rule, you are considered to lack other resources if you have taken all available distributions from all plans of the employer, including nontaxable loans, and you suspend making any contributions to any of the employer's qualified and nonqualified deferred compensation plans for at least six months after receipt of the hardship distribution. Furthermore, all of the employer's plans must provide that for the year after the year of the hardship distribution, elective contributions must be limited to the excess of the annual salary deferral limitation over the elective contributions made for the year of the hardship distribution.

## 7.18 Designated Roth Account Within 401(k), 403(b), or Governmental 457 Plans

Employers with a 401(k) plan may allow employees to irrevocably designate all or part of their elective salary deferrals (including catch-up contributions if age 50 or older) as after-tax Roth contributions. Similarly, a 403(b) plan *(7.19)* or a governmental 457 plan *(7.20)* may allow employees to make elective deferrals to a designated Roth account. The plan must be amended to allow for designated Roth contributions. The annual tax-free ceiling on elective salary-reduction deferrals, including the additional catch-up amount for those age 50 or older *(7.16)*, applies to the combined total of pre-tax elective deferrals and designated Roth contributions. The Roth contributions, being after-tax, are treated as taxable wages subject to withholding.

The major incentive for employees to choose designated Roth contributions is to obtain tax-free treatment for distributions under the qualified distribution rules applicable to Roth IRAs; *see* below for details of the "qualified" and "nonqualified" distribution rules.

The option to make designated Roth contributions can benefit employees who might otherwise be unable to make annual contributions to a Roth IRA. Subject to 401(k) nondiscrimination tests, there are no income limitations on the right to make Roth 401(k) contributions, whereas contributions to a Roth IRA are barred if adjusted gross income exceeds an annual threshold *(8.20)*.

Plans must segregate designated Roth contributions from regular pre-tax 401(k), 403(b), or governmental 457 plan elective deferrals and maintain separate accounts for employees with both types of contributions. Only Roth elective deferrals may be contributed to the designated Roth account. If the employer makes matching contributions, they may not be made to the designated Roth account. Gains, losses, and other credits or charges, as well as contribution and withdrawals, must be allocated between the accounts on a reasonable and consistent basis. Designated Roth contributions are subject to the 401(k) nonforfeitability and distribution restrictions and also to the nondiscrimination tests for pre-tax elective contributions.

**In-plan Roth rollovers.** Employers may (but do not have to) allow employees to roll over amounts from their 401(k), 403(b), or governmental 457(b) plan to a designated Roth account within the same plan. An in-plan Roth rollover is taxable except to the extent attributable to after-tax contributions; this is the same rule as for a conversion of a traditional IRA to a Roth IRA. The taxable amount will be reported on Form 1099-R in Box 2a. If a direct rollover was made, Code G will be entered in Box 7.

 *Law Alert*

**In-Plan Conversion From 401(k) to Roth 401(k) May Be Permitted**

Employers with 401(k), 403(b), or governmental 457 plans have the option of allowing employees to roll over distributions of vested amounts to a designated Roth account within the same plan. An in-plan Roth rollover is taxable unless attributable to after-tax contributions.

**Qualified distributions from designated Roth account are tax free.** The rules for determining tax treatment of distributions from designated Roth accounts generally follow the rules for Roth IRA distributions *(8.24)*. There is a two-part test for determining if a distribution from a designated Roth account is a qualified distribution, and therefore totally tax free:

(1.) it is received at least five years after the year in which the employee's first designated Roth contribution was made, and

(2.) one of the following is true: (a) the distribution is made to an employee age 59½ or older, (b) the distribution is made because the employee is disabled, or (c) the distribution is made to a beneficiary after the employee's death.

If these tests are met, you are not taxed on the earnings part of the distribution or the part attributable to your investment (your designated Roth contributions). For purposes of the five-year participation test, the five-year period begins on the first day of the year for which the first designated Roth contribution is made. For example, if you made your first designated Roth contribution in 2014, then 2014 was year one of the five-year period, which ends December 31, 2018. A distribution in 2019 or later will be a qualified distribution if you are age 59½ or older or you are disabled when you receive it, or if the distribution is paid to your beneficiary after your death.

A distribution from a designated Roth account that is not a qualified distribution under the above tests is taxable to the extent it is allocable to earnings. For example, assume you receive a nonqualified distribution of $10,000 from your designated Roth account when the account balance is $20,000, consisting of $18,800 of designated Roth contributions and $1,200 of earnings. Of the $10,000 distribution, $600 is allocable to earnings and is taxable ($1,200 total earnings/$20,000 account balance × $10,000 distribution = $600). The $9,400 balance is allocable to your designated Roth contributions (basis) and is nontaxable ($18,800 designated Roth contributions/$20,000 account balance × $10,000 distribution = $9,400).

**Required minimum distributions.** The required minimum distribution rules apply to designated Roth accounts and thus you generally must begin to receive minimum annual distributions from the account by the later of April 1 after the year in which you reach age 70½ or April 1 following the year in which you retire; see *7.11* for details. However, if before your required beginning date you make a rollover *(7.5)* from your designated Roth account to a Roth IRA, you will not have to take any required minimum distributions from the Roth IRA *(8.19)*.

**Rollovers from designated Roth account.** An eligible rollover distribution *(7.5)* from a designated Roth account may be rolled over to a Roth IRA *(8.19)*. The nontaxable portion (your basis) of a distribution may be rolled over to another designated Roth account with a different employer, but the rollover must be made by means of a direct rollover *(7.6)*, rather than a personal rollover within 60 days of receiving the distribution. If a direct rollover is not made and you receive the distribution, you may roll over the entire amount to a Roth IRA within the 60-day period, but you cannot roll over the portion allocable to your designated Roth contributions (your basis) to another designated Roth account.

If an employee receives a nonqualified distribution (*see* above) and part of it is rolled over, the rollover is allocated first to the earnings portion of the distribution. For example, assume you receive a nonqualified distribution of $28,000 that is eligible for rollover from your designated Roth account. Also assume that of the $28,000 distribution, $22,000 is allocable to your designated Roth contributions and the other $6,000 is earnings on the account. You can avoid tax on the earnings by rolling over at least $6,000 within 60 days of receipt. If $14,000 is rolled over to a Roth IRA within 60 days, the $14,000 is treated as consisting of the $6,000 of earnings and $8,000 of designated Roth contributions (basis). The entire distribution of $28,000 is tax free because the only part of it that could be taxed is the $6,000 of earnings (the rest is your investment), and that $6,000 is treated as having been rolled over.

## 7.19 Annuities for Employees of Tax-Exempts and Schools (403(b) Plans)

If you are employed by a state or local government public school, or by a tax-exempt (501(c)(3)) religious, charitable, scientific, or educational organization, or are on the civilian staff or faculty of the Uniformed Services University of the Health Sciences (Department of Defense), you may be able to arrange for the purchase of a nonforfeitable tax-sheltered annuity. Tax-sheltered annuities may also be purchased by self-employed ministers and by non-tax-exempt employers of ordained or licensed ministers or chaplains. Another name for a tax-sheltered annuity is a 403(b) plan. A 403(b) plan may invest funds for employees in mutual fund shares as well as in annuity contracts.

The purchase of the annuity or mutual fund shares is generally made through pre-tax elective deferrals made through salary-reduction contributions. Your plan may allow you to allocate some of your elective deferral limit to Roth contributions or to make non-Roth after-tax contributions, and the employer may make non-elective contributions.

Caution: As the following contribution rules for tax-sheltered annuities have been stated in general terms, we suggest that you also consult your employer or the issuer of the contract. IRS Publication 571 has detailed examples.

**Limit on tax-free contributions.** Tax-free salary reductions are limited to the annual ceiling for elective deferrals, and the plan may permit additional deferrals for participants who are age 50 or older *(7.16)*.

If, in addition to a tax-sheltered annuity, you make salary deferrals to a 401(k) plan, SIMPLE plan, or simplified employee pension plan, the annual salary-reduction limit applies to the total deferrals *(7.16)*. If you defer more than the annual limit, the excess is taxable. Further, if a salary-reduction deferral in excess of the annual limit is made and the excess is not distributed to you by April 15 of the following year, the excess will be taxed twice—not only in the year of deferral but again in the year it is actually distributed. To avoid the double tax, any excess deferral plus the income attributable to such excess should be distributed no later than April 15 of the year following the year in which the excess deferral is made *(7.16)*.

The annual salary-reduction ceiling is generally increased by $3,000 for employees of educational organizations, hospitals, churches, home health service agencies, and health and welfare service agencies who have completed 15 years of service. However, the extra $3,000 annual deferral may not be claimed indefinitely. There is a lifetime limit of $15,000 on the amount of extra deferrals allowed. Furthermore, the extra deferrals may not be claimed after lifetime elective deferrals to the plan exceed $5,000 multiplied by your years of service, minus prior-year elective deferrals. Publication 571 has a worksheet for figuring the limit on elective deferrals, including the extra amount under the 15-year rule.

The employee's salary reduction plus any after-tax contributions and any non-elective contributions made by the employer for the year are tax free only if they do not exceed the annual limit on contributions to a defined contribution plan, which for 2018 was the lesser of 100% of compensation or $55,000.

**Roth contributions and in-plan rollover to designated Roth account.** Your plan may allow you to contribute some of the elective deferral limit to a designated Roth account *(7.18)*. These Roth contributions are part of your taxable pay and not excludable from income (they are after-tax contributions). In addition, as noted in *7.18*, your employer may allow you to make an in-plan rollover from your 403(b) plan to a designated Roth IRA within the same plan.

**Distributions from tax-sheltered annuities.** Distributions attributable to salary reduction contributions to a 403(b) tax-sheltered annuity are allowed only when an employee reaches age 59½, has experienced a severance from employment, becomes disabled, suffers financial hardship, becomes eligible for a qualified reservist distribution *(7.13)*, or dies. The hardship distribution rules are the same as for 401(k) plans *(7.17)*. Annuity payments are taxed under the general rules for employees *(7.24)*. Payments are fully taxable if the only contributions to the plan were salary reduction contributions excluded from income (pre-tax contributions) under the annual limits discussed earlier in this section.

Non-annuity distributions from a tax-sheltered annuity do not qualify for special averaging *(7.3)*, but a tax-free rollover of a distribution may be made to another tax-sheltered annuity or traditional IRA unless the distribution is not eligible under the rollover rules *(7.5)*. An eligible rollover distribution *(7.5)* from a 403(b) plan may also be rolled over to a qualified plan or governmental Section 527 plan. If you do not choose to have the payer of the distribution make a direct rollover, mandatory 20% withholding will be applied. You may then personally make a rollover within 60 days, but you would have to include the withheld amount in the rolled-over amount to avoid tax on the entire distribution. *See 7.6* for further rollover and withholding details.

**Required minimum distributions (RMDs).** Benefits accruing after 1986 are subject to the required beginning date rules and a penalty may be imposed for failure to take required minimum distributions *(7.11)*. Benefits accrued before 1987 are not subject to the required minimum distribution rules until the year you reach age 75.

## 7.20 Government and Exempt Organization Deferred Pay Plans

Federal government civilian employees may make salary-reduction contributions to the Federal Thrift Savings Plan. Employees of state and local governments and of tax-exempt organizations may be able to make salary-reduction contributions to a Section 457(b) deferred compensation plan.

**Federal Thrift Savings Plan (TSP).** Federal employees may elect to make salary-reduction deferrals (pre-tax contributions) to the Thrift Savings Plan (TSP) up to the elective deferral limit for 401(k) plans *(7.15)*. Deferrals are not taxed until distributed from the plan. The deferred amount is counted as wages for purposes of computing Social Security taxes and benefits.

The TSP offers employees a Roth option. This allows employees to contribute part or all of the regular deferral limit to a designated Roth account, instead of to the basic pre-tax deferral account. Roth TSP contributions are after-tax contributions, so they are included in taxable pay. Qualified distributions from the Roth TSP are tax free *(7.18)*. The government does not allow employees to roll over funds from their traditional (pre-tax) TSP account into a Roth TSP.

Distributions from the Thrift Savings Plan that are attributable to pre-tax deferrals are generally fully taxable. However, lump-sum distributions are eligible for tax-free rollover treatment *(7.5)*. If you receive a distribution before age 59½, you are subject to the 10% penalty for early distributions unless an exception applies *(7.13)*. As noted above, employees with a Roth TSP are not taxed on qualified distributions from the account *(7.18)*.

**Section 457(b) plan contributions.** State and local governments and tax-exempt organizations other than churches may set up Section 457(b) deferred compensation plans. Non-governmental 457(b) plans are sometimes referred to as "Top Hat" plans, because they are only open to highly-compensated employees, managers and executives; rank-and-file employees may not participate.

Employees eligible to participate in a 457(b) plan may annually defer compensation up to the elective deferral limit, which for 2018 was $18,500 *(7.15)*. Generally, deferrals from all your plans must be aggregated to stay within the annual limit *(7.16)*, but the deferral limit for a 457(b) plan is separate from the deferral limit for other plans. Thus, if you participate in a 457(b) plan and also a 403(b) or 401(k) plan, you do not aggregate the 457(b) deferrals with the deferrals from the other plan. In addition to the annual deferral limit ($18,500 for 2018), employees in state and local government 457(b) plans who are 50 years of age or older may be permitted by the plan to defer an additional "catch-up" amount, which for 2018 was $6,000. The age-50-or -older catch-up is not allowed in non-governmental 457(b) plans.

As discussed in *7.18*, a governmental 457(b) plan may allow you to designate some or all of your salary-deferral limit as after-tax Roth contributions, or to make an in-plan rollover to a designated Roth IRA account within the same plan.

A Section 457(b) plan (whether governmental or non-governmental) may also provide for another type of "catch-up" increase for employees in the last three years before the year in which they reach normal retirement age under the terms of the plan. However, this catch-up increase only applies if the employee has "unused deferral limits" from prior years, so employees who deferred the maximum amount into their plan for every prior year that they were eligible cannot take advantage of it. For employees within three years of normal retirement age who have unused deferral limits from prior years, this catch-up provision allows them to increase the regular deferral limit by the unused deferral limits, up to the regular deferral limit for the current year, which means that it may be possible to double the regular deferral limit for a given year (which for 2018 would be $18,500 × 2=$37,000), depending on the amount of the prior unused deferrals. For employees in a governmental 457(b) plan that allows both the age-50-or-older catch-up and the last- three-years catch-up, the catch-up providing the larger deferral may be used, but not both.

Deferred compensation (and allocable income) under a non-governmental (tax-exempt organization) 457(b) plan is not taxed until paid or otherwise made available under the terms of the plan. Amounts deferred (and earnings) under state or local government 457(b) plans are taxed only when paid. All distributions are taxed as ordinary income.

**Distributions from Section 457(b) plans.** Distributions of deferred amounts to employees or beneficiaries generally may not be made before the employee stops working for the employer, retires, dies, or if earlier, when the employee turns age 70½. The plan may (but does not have to) permit a distribution to an employee or beneficiary who faces an "unforeseeable" emergency. Under IRS regulations, an unforeseeable emergency means severe financial hardship resulting from a sudden illness or accident of the employee or a dependent, the loss of property due to a casualty, or other extraordinary and unforseeable event beyond the employee's control, such as imminent foreclosure or eviction from a primary residence, or having to pay medical costs or funeral expenses. The regulations specifically prohibit payments from the plan to purchase a home or pay for a child's college tuition. If the employee can obtain funds by ceasing deferrals to the plan or by liquidating assets without causing himself or herself severe financial hardship, payment from the plan is not allowed. In one case, an employee covered by a state governmental 457 plan wanted to take a withdrawal from the plan to help pay off substantial credit card debt. IRS Chief Counsel concluded that credit card debt is usually not an unforeseeable emergency, but it would qualify if the debt was incurred to pay medical costs or similar expense beyond the employee's control.

Eligible rollover distributions *(7.5)* from a governmental 457(b) plan may be rolled over tax free to a traditional IRA, another governmental 457(b) plan, a qualified plan (such as a 401(k)plan), or a 403(b) plan. An eligible distribution from a governmental 457(b) plan may also be rolled over to a Roth IRA, subject to the rules for a taxable conversion *(7.6)*. Rollovers of eligible distributions from other plans may also be made to governmental 457(b) plans.

A distribution from a non-governmental 457(b) plan may not be rolled over tax free to a traditional IRA, a qualified plan, or a 403(b) plan. The only rollover option is to roll it over to a new employer with a non-governmental 457(b) plan, assuming that the plan accepts rollovers. Because rollovers from non-governmental 457(b) plans generally may not be made, employees who anticipate a separation from service should carefully review the terms of their employer's plan to determine their distribution options in order to avoid unintended tax consequences.

*See 7.11* for required minimum distribution (RMD) rules after age 70½.

Note: Check with your employer for other details on Section 457(b) contributions and distribution rules.

*Caution*

**Unforeseen Emergency Distributions**

If you can show severe financial hardship arising from a sudden illness or accident, or loss of property due to events beyond your control, and you are unable to obtain funds elsewhere, you may make a withdrawal from your employer's Section 457 plan. However, the need to buy a home or pay college expenses does not qualify as an unforeseeable emergency.

## 7.21 Figuring the Taxable Part of Commercial Annuities

Tax treatment of a distribution depends on whether you receive it before or after the annuity starting date, and on the amount of your investment. A cash withdrawal before age 59½ from an annuity contract is generally subject to a 10% penalty, but there are exceptions; the penalty is discussed at the end of this section. If your annuity is from an employer plan, *see 7.24.*

The annuity starting date is the later of (1) the first day of the first period for which you receive a payment, or (2) the date on which the obligation under the contract becomes fixed. If your right to an annuity is fixed on June 1, 2019, and your monthly payments start on December 1, 2019, for the period starting November 1, 2019, then November 1, 2019 is your annuity starting date.

**Payments before the annuity starting date.** Withdrawals from a commercial annuity contract before the annuity starting date are taxable to the extent that the cash value of the contract (ignoring any surrender charge), immediately before the distribution, exceeds your investment in the contract at that time. Loans under the contract or pledges are treated as cash withdrawals.

There is an exception for contracts purchased before August 14, 1982. Withdrawals from such contracts before the annuity starting date are taxable only to the extent they exceed your investment. Loans are tax free and are not treated as withdrawals subject to this rule. Where additional investments were made after August 13, 1982, cash withdrawals are first considered to be tax-free distributions of the investment before August 14, 1982. If the withdrawal exceeds this investment, the balance is fully taxable to the extent of earnings on the contract, with any excess withdrawals treated as a tax-free recovery of the investment made after August 13, 1982.

**Payments on or after the annuity starting date.** If the withdrawal is a regular (not variable) annuity payment, the part of the annuity payment that is allocated to your cost investment is treated as a nontaxable return of the cost; the balance is taxable income earned on the investment. You may find the taxable part of your annuity payment by following the six steps listed below under "Taxable Portion of Commercial Annuity Payments." If you have a variable annuity, the computation of the tax-free portion is discussed following Step 6.

Payments on or after the annuity starting date that are not part of the annuity, such as dividends, are generally taxable, but there are exceptions. If the contract is a life insurance or endowment contract, withdrawals of earnings are tax free to the extent of your investment, unless the contract is a modified endowment contract.

**Value of refund feature.** Your investment in the contract is reduced by the value, if any, of the refund feature.

Your annuity has a refund feature when these three requirements are present: (1) the refund under the contract depends, even in part, on the life expectancy of at least one person; (2) the contract provides for payments to a beneficiary or the annuitant's estate after the annuitant's death; and (3) the payments to the estate or beneficiary are a refund of the amount paid for the annuity.

The value of the refund feature is figured by using a life expectancy multiple that may be found in Treasury Table III or Table VII, depending on the date of your investment; the tables are in IRS Publication 939.

Where an employer paid part of the cost, the refund is figured on only the part paid by the employee.

The refund feature is considered to be zero if (1) for a joint and survivor annuity, both annuitants are age 74 or younger, the payments are guaranteed for less than 2½ years, and the survivor's annuity is at least 50% of the first annuitant's (retiree's) annuity or (2) for a single-life annuity without survivor benefits, the payments are guaranteed for less than 2½ years and you are age 57 or younger if using the new (unisex) annuity tables, age 42 or younger if male and using the old annuity tables, or age 47 or younger if female and using the old annuity tables.

*Filing Tip*

**Surrender of Contract**

Payments on a complete surrender of the annuity contract or at maturity are taxable only to the extent they exceed your investment.

Also subtract from cost any tax-free recovery of your investment received before the annuity starting date, as previously discussed.

## Taxable Portion of Commercial Annuity Payments

If the payer of the contract does not provide the taxable amount in Box 2a of Form 1099-R, you can compute the taxable amount of your commercial annuity using the following steps.

**Step 1: Figure your investment in the annuity contract.** If you have no investment in the contract, annuity income is fully taxable; therefore, ignore Steps 2 through 6.

| If your annuity is— | Your cost is— |
|---|---|
| Single premium annuity contract | The single premium paid. |
| Deferred annuity contract | The total premiums paid. |
| A gift | Your donor's cost. |
| An employee annuity | The total of your after-tax contributions to the plan plus your employer's contributions that you were required to report as income *(7.26)*. |
| With a refund feature | The value of the refund feature. |

From cost, you subtract the following items:

- Any premiums refunded, and rebates or dividends received on or before the annuity starting date.
- Additional premiums for double indemnity or disability benefits.
- Amounts received under the contract before the annuity starting date to the extent these amounts were not taxed; *see* above.
- Value of a refund feature; *see* below.

**Planning Reminder**

**Life Expectancy Tables**

The life expectancy tables for figuring your expected return are in IRS Publication 939.

**Step 2: Find your expected return.** This is the total of all the payments you are to receive. If the payments are to be made to you for life, your expected return is figured by multiplying the amount of the annual payment by your life expectancy as of the nearest birthday to the annuity starting date. The annuity starting date is the first day of the first period for which an annuity payment is received. For example, on January 1 you complete payment under an annuity contract providing for monthly payments starting on July 1 for the period beginning June 1. The annuity starting date is June 1. Use that date in computing your investment in the contract under Step 1 and your expected return.

If payments are for life, you find your life expectancy in IRS tables included in IRS Publication 939. If you have a single life annuity for which you made any investment after June 30, 1986, use IRS Table V from Publication 939, shown in *Table 7-2* below. *Table 7-2* also shows IRS Table I, which generally is used if the entire investment was before July 1, 1986, but you may elect to use Table V *(7.24)*. When using the single life table, your age is the age at the birthday nearest the annuity starting date. If you have a joint and survivor annuity and after your death the same payments are to be made to a second annuitant, the expected return is based on your joint life expectancy. Use Table II in IRS Publication 939 to get joint life expectancy if the entire investment was before July 1, 1986. Use Table VI if any investment was made after June 30, 1986. If your joint and survivor annuity provides for a different payment amount to the survivor, you must separately compute the expected return for each annuitant; this method is explained in Publication 939. Adjustments to the life expectancy multiple are required when your annuity is payable quarterly, semiannually, or annually *(7.24)*.

If the payments are for a fixed number of years or for life, whichever is shorter, find your expected return by multiplying your annual payments by a life expectancy multiple found in Table IV if your entire investment was before July 1, 1986, or Table VIII if any investment was made after June 30, 1986.

If payments are for a fixed number of years (as in an endowment contract) without regard to your life expectancy, find your expected return by multiplying your annual payment by the number of years.

Note: There is more information on the life expectancy tables in the following section *(7.24)*.

**Step 3: Divide the investment in the contract (Step 1) by the expected return (Step 2).** This will give you the tax-free percentage of your yearly annuity payments. The tax-free percentage remains the same for the remaining years of the annuity, even if payments increase due to a cost-of-living adjustment. A different computation of the tax-free percentage applies to variable annuities; *see* below.

If your annuity started before 1987, and you live longer than your projected life expectancy (shown in the IRS table), you may continue to apply the same tax-free percentage to each payment you receive. Thus, you may exclude from income more than you paid. However, if your annuity starting date is after 1986, your lifetime exclusion may not exceed your net cost, generally your unrecovered investment as of the annuity starting date, without reduction for any refund feature. Once you have recovered your net cost, further payments are fully taxable.

If your annuity starting date is after July 1, 1986, and you die before recovering your net cost, a deduction is allowed on your final tax return for the unrecovered cost. If a refund of the investment is made under the contract to a beneficiary, the beneficiary is allowed the deduction if he or she does not claim the standard deduction. The deduction is claimed as a miscellaneous itemized deduction that is not subject to the 2% of adjusted gross income floor *(19.1)*.

**Step 4: Find your total annuity payments for the year.** For example, you received 10 monthly payments of $1,000 as your annuity began in March. Your total payments are $10,000, the monthly payment multiplied by 10.

**Step 5: Nontaxable portion—multiply the percentage in Step 3 by the number of payments from Step 4.** The result is the nontaxable portion (or excludable amount) of your annuity payments.

**Step 6: Taxable portion for the year—subtract the amount in Step 5 from the amount in Step 4.** The result is the portion of your annuity payments that is subject to tax for the year.

Note: See the Bill Jones example in *7.22*, which shows how to figure the taxable and nontaxable portions for a single life annuity.

---

### EXAMPLES of Variable Annuities *(see text below the examples)*

1. Andrew Taylor's total investment of $12,000 for a variable annuity was made after June 30, 1986. The annuity starting date was June 1, 2018. The annuity payments began July 1, 2018, in varying annual installments for life. Andrew's age (nearest birthday) on the June 1 starting date was 65. To figure the tax-free part of each annual payment, he uses a life expectancy multiple of 20.0, the amount shown in Table V (see *Table 7-2* below) for a person age 65. The amount of each payment excluded from tax is:

| | |
|---|---|
| Investment in the contract | $12,000 |
| Multiple (from Table V) | 20.0 |
| Amount of each payment excluded from tax ($12,000 ÷ 20) | $600 |

   If the first annual payment is $920, then 320 ($920 − $600) will be included in Andrew's 2018 income.

## Table 7-2  Life Expectancy Tables from IRS Publication 939

### TABLE I  Investments Before July 1, 1986

| Male | Female | Multiples | Male | Female | Multiples | Male | Female | Multiples |
|------|--------|-----------|------|--------|-----------|------|--------|-----------|
| 6 | 11 | 65.0 | 41 | 46 | 33.0 | 76 | 81 | 9.1 |
| 7 | 12 | 64.1 | 42 | 47 | 32.1 | 77 | 82 | 8.7 |
| 8 | 13 | 63.2 | 43 | 48 | 31.2 | 78 | 83 | 8.3 |
| 9 | 14 | 62.3 | 44 | 49 | 30.4 | 79 | 84 | 7.8 |
| 10 | 15 | 61.4 | 45 | 50 | 29.6 | 80 | 85 | 7.5 |
| 11 | 16 | 60.4 | 46 | 51 | 28.7 | 81 | 86 | 7.1 |
| 12 | 17 | 59.5 | 47 | 52 | 27.9 | 82 | 87 | 6.7 |
| 13 | 18 | 58.6 | 48 | 53 | 27.1 | 83 | 88 | 6.3 |
| 14 | 19 | 57.7 | 49 | 54 | 26.3 | 84 | 89 | 6.0 |
| 15 | 20 | 56.7 | 50 | 55 | 25.5 | 85 | 90 | 5.7 |
| 16 | 21 | 55.8 | 51 | 56 | 24.7 | 86 | 91 | 5.4 |
| 17 | 22 | 54.9 | 52 | 57 | 24.0 | 87 | 92 | 5.1 |
| 18 | 23 | 53.9 | 53 | 58 | 23.2 | 88 | 93 | 4.8 |
| 19 | 24 | 53.0 | 54 | 59 | 22.4 | 89 | 94 | 4.5 |
| 20 | 25 | 52.1 | 55 | 60 | 21.7 | 90 | 95 | 4.2 |
| 21 | 26 | 51.1 | 56 | 61 | 21.0 | 91 | 96 | 4.0 |
| 22 | 27 | 50.2 | 57 | 62 | 20.3 | 92 | 97 | 3.7 |
| 23 | 28 | 49.3 | 58 | 63 | 19.6 | 93 | 98 | 3.5 |
| 24 | 29 | 48.3 | 59 | 64 | 18.9 | 94 | 99 | 3.3 |
| 25 | 30 | 47.4 | 60 | 65 | 18.2 | 95 | 100 | 3.1 |
| 26 | 31 | 46.5 | 61 | 66 | 17.5 | 96 | 101 | 2.9 |
| 27 | 32 | 45.6 | 62 | 67 | 16.9 | 97 | 102 | 2.7 |
| 28 | 33 | 44.6 | 63 | 68 | 16.2 | 98 | 103 | 2.5 |
| 29 | 34 | 43.7 | 64 | 69 | 15.6 | 99 | 104 | 2.3 |
| 30 | 35 | 42.8 | 65 | 70 | 15.0 | 100 | 105 | 2.1 |
| 31 | 36 | 41.9 | 66 | 71 | 14.4 | 101 | 106 | 1.9 |
| 32 | 37 | 41.0 | 67 | 72 | 13.8 | 102 | 107 | 1.7 |
| 33 | 38 | 40.0 | 68 | 73 | 13.2 | 103 | 108 | 1.5 |
| 34 | 39 | 39.1 | 69 | 74 | 12.6 | 104 | 109 | 1.3 |
| 35 | 40 | 38.2 | 70 | 75 | 12.1 | 105 | 110 | 1.2 |
| 36 | 41 | 37.3 | 71 | 76 | 11.6 | 106 | 111 | 1.0 |
| 37 | 42 | 36.5 | 72 | 77 | 11.0 | 107 | 112 | 0.8 |
| 38 | 43 | 35.6 | 73 | 78 | 10.5 | 108 | 113 | 0.7 |
| 39 | 44 | 34.7 | 74 | 79 | 10.1 | 109 | 114 | 0.6 |
| 40 | 45 | 33.8 | 75 | 80 | 9.6 | 110 | 115 | 0.5 |
| | | | | | | 111 | 116 | 0.0 |

### TABLE V  Investments After June 30, 1986

| Age | Multiple | Age | Multiple | Age | Multiple |
|-----|----------|-----|----------|-----|----------|
| 5 | 76.6 | 42 | 40.6 | 79 | 10.0 |
| 6 | 75.6 | 43 | 39.6 | 80 | 9.5 |
| 7 | 74.7 | 44 | 38.7 | 81 | 8.9 |
| 8 | 73.7 | 45 | 37.7 | 82 | 8.4 |
| 9 | 72.7 | 46 | 36.8 | 83 | 7.9 |
| 10 | 71.7 | 47 | 35.9 | 84 | 7.4 |
| 11 | 70.7 | 48 | 34.9 | 85 | 6.9 |
| 12 | 69.7 | 49 | 34.0 | 86 | 6.5 |
| 13 | 68.8 | 50 | 33.1 | 87 | 6.1 |
| 14 | 67.8 | 51 | 32.2 | 88 | 5.7 |
| 15 | 66.8 | 52 | 31.3 | 89 | 5.3 |
| 16 | 65.8 | 53 | 30.4 | 90 | 5.0 |
| 17 | 64.8 | 54 | 29.5 | 91 | 4.7 |
| 18 | 63.9 | 55 | 28.6 | 92 | 4.4 |
| 19 | 62.9 | 56 | 27.7 | 93 | 4.1 |
| 20 | 61.9 | 57 | 26.8 | 94 | 3.9 |
| 21 | 60.9 | 58 | 25.9 | 95 | 3.7 |
| 22 | 59.9 | 59 | 25.0 | 96 | 3.4 |
| 23 | 59.0 | 60 | 24.2 | 97 | 3.2 |
| 24 | 58.0 | 61 | 23.3 | 98 | 3.0 |
| 25 | 57.0 | 62 | 22.5 | 99 | 2.8 |
| 26 | 56.0 | 63 | 21.6 | 100 | 2.7 |
| 27 | 55.1 | 64 | 20.8 | 101 | 2.5 |
| 28 | 54.1 | 65 | 20.0 | 102 | 2.3 |
| 29 | 53.1 | 66 | 19.2 | 103 | 2.1 |
| 30 | 52.2 | 67 | 18.4 | 104 | 1.9 |
| 31 | 51.2 | 68 | 17.6 | 105 | 1.8 |
| 32 | 50.2 | 69 | 16.8 | 106 | 1.6 |
| 33 | 49.3 | 70 | 16.0 | 107 | 1.4 |
| 34 | 48.3 | 71 | 15.3 | 108 | 1.3 |
| 35 | 47.3 | 72 | 14.6 | 109 | 1.1 |
| 36 | 46.4 | 73 | 13.9 | 110 | 1.0 |
| 37 | 45.4 | 74 | 13.2 | 111 | 0.9 |
| 38 | 44.4 | 75 | 12.5 | 112 | 0.8 |
| 39 | 43.5 | 76 | 11.9 | 113 | 0.7 |
| 40 | 42.5 | 77 | 11.2 | 114 | 0.6 |
| 41 | 41.5 | 78 | 10.6 | 115 | 0.5 |

## Table 7-3  Multiple Adjustment Table

| If the number of whole months from the annuity starting date to the first payment date is— | 0–1 | 2 | 3 | 4 | 5 | 6 | 7 | 8 | 9 | 10 | 11 | 12 |
|---|---|---|---|---|---|---|---|---|---|---|---|---|
| And payments under the contract are to be made: | | | | | | | | | | | | |
| Annually | +0.5 | +0.4 | +0.3 | +0.2 | +0.1 | 0.0 | 0.0 | −0.1 | −0.2 | −0.3 | −0.4 | −0.5 |
| Semiannually | +0.2 | +0.1 | 0.0 | 0.0 | −0.1 | −0.2 | | | | | | |
| Quarterly | +0.1 | 0.0 | −0.1 | | | | | | | | | |

2. Assume that, after receiving the 2018 payment of $920 in Example 1, Andrew receives $500 in 2019 and $1,200 in 2020. None of the $500 received in 2019 is taxable, as $600 is excludable from each annual payment (Example 1). Andrew may also elect to recompute his annual exclusion starting with the 2020 payment. The exclusion is recomputed as follows:

| | |
|---|---|
| Amount excludable in 2019 | $600 |
| Amount received in 2019 | 500 |
| Difference | $100 |
| Multiple as of 1/1/20 (see Table V in Table 7-2 for age 67) | 18.4 |
| Amount added to previously determined annual exclusion ($100 ÷ 18.4 = $5.43) | $5.00 |
| Revised annual exclusion for 2020 and later years ($600 + $5) | $605 |
| Amount taxable in 2020 ($1,200 − $605) | $595 |

**Variable annuities.** If you have a variable annuity that pays different benefits depending on cost-of-living indexes, profits earned by the annuity fund, or similar fluctuating standards, the tax-free portion of each payment is computed by dividing your investment in the contract (Step 1 above) by the total number of payments you expect to receive. If the annuity is for a definite period, the total number of payments equals the number of payments to be made each year multiplied by the number of years you will receive payments. If the annuity is for life, you divide the amount you invested in the contract by a multiple obtained from the appropriate life expectancy table; *see* Step 2. The result is the tax-free amount of annual annuity income.

If you receive a payment that is less than the nontaxable amount, you may elect when you receive the next payment to recalculate the nontaxable portion. The amount by which the prior nontaxable portion exceeded the payment you received is divided by the number of payments you expect as of the time of the next payment. The result is added to the previously calculated nontaxable portion, and the sum is the amount of each future payment to be excluded from tax. A statement must be attached to your return explaining the recomputation; *see* Andrew Taylor, Example 2 above.

## Penalty on Premature Withdrawals From Deferred Annuities

Withdrawals before the annuity starting date may be taxable or tax free, depending on whether investments were made before or after August 13, 1982, as discussed at the beginning of *7.21*.

Withdrawals before age 59½ are also generally subject to a penalty of 10% of the amount includible in income. A withdrawal from an annuity contract is penalized unless:

1. You have reached age 59½ or have become totally disabled.

2. The distribution is part of a series of substantially equal payments, made at least annually over your life expectancy or over the joint life expectancies of you and a beneficiary. If you can avoid the penalty under this exception and you change to a nonqualifying distribution method within five years or before age 59½, such as where you receive a lump sum, a recapture tax will apply to the payments received before age 59½.

3. The payment is received by a beneficiary or estate after the policyholder's death.

4. Payment is from a qualified retirement plan, tax-sheltered annuity, or IRA; in this case the penalty rules for qualified plans *(7.13)* or IRAs *(8.8)* apply.

5. Payment is allocable to investments made before August 14, 1982.

6. Payment is from an annuity contract under a qualified personal injury settlement.

7. Payment is from a single-premium annuity where the starting date is no more than one year from the date of purchase (an "immediate" annuity).

8. Payment is from an annuity purchased by an employer upon the termination of a qualified retirement plan and held until you separated from service.

 *Filing Tip*

**Form 5329**

If no exception to the early withdrawal penalty applies, you compute the 10% penalty in Part I of Form 5329. In the rare case that you were receiving payments as of March 1, 1986 under a specific schedule pursuant to your written election, and you are still under age 59½ and receiving payments under that election, and no penalty exception applies, the penalty rate is 5% instead of 10%. Attach an explanation to Form 5329 if you are applying the 5% rate.

## 7.22 Life Expectancy Tables

IRS unisex actuarial tables must be used if you made any investment in a commercial annuity contract after June 30, 1986. Generally, life expectancies are longer under the unisex tables than under the prior male-female tables. The unisex life expectancy table for single life annuities is IRS Table V from Publication 939, shown above in *Table 7-2*. The unisex table for ordinary joint life and last survivor annuities is Table VI, in IRS Publication 939.

If your entire investment was before July 1, 1986, you use the older male/female tables. The tables, IRS Tables I through IV, are in Publication 939. Table I, shown above in *Table 7-2*, is for single life expectancies. Table II, for ordinary joint life and last survivor annuities, is in Publication 939.

You may make an irrevocable election to use the unisex tables for all payments received under the contract, even if you did not make an investment after June 30, 1986.

If you invested in the contract both before July 1, 1986, and after June 30, 1986, and you are the first person to receive annuity payments under the contract, you may make a special election to use the prior tables for the pre–July 1986 investment and the unisex tables for the post–June 1986 investment. See IRS Publication 939 for further information. Treasury Regulation *1.72*-6(d) has examples showing how to figure the post–June 1986 and pre–July 1986 investments.

**Birthday nearest annuity starting date.** In looking up single life or joint life expectancy in the applicable table, use your age (and the age of a joint annuitant) at the birthday nearest to the annuity starting date. The number in the table next to this age is the life expectancy multiple used to figure the tax-free and taxable portions of a monthly annuity; *see* the following Examples.

**Adjustments for nonmonthly payments.** An adjustment is required when your annuity payments are received quarterly, semiannually, or annually; *see* Example 3 below.

---

### EXAMPLES of Single Life Annuities

1. Bill Jones had his 66th birthday on April 14, 2018. On May 1, 2018, he received his first monthly annuity check of $1,000. This covered his annuity payment for April. Bill's annuity starting date was April 1, 2018, and his entire investment was before July 1, 1986.

   Looking at Table I in *Table 7-2* under "Male" at age 66 (age on birthday nearest April 1 starting date), Bill finds the multiple 14.4. (He does not have to adjust that multiple because the payments are monthly.) Bill multiplies the 14.4 by $12,000 ($1,000 a month for a year) to find his expected return of $172,800. Assume there is no refund feature and Bill's net investment (Step 1 at *7.21*) is $129,600. He divides his expected return into the net investment ($129,600 ÷ $172,800) and gets his exclusion percentage of 75%. Until Bill recovers his net investment, he receives tax free 75% of his annuity payments and is taxable on 25%. In 2018, Bill receives $8,000 ($1,000 in May through December) and reports $2,000 as the taxable amount:

   | | |
   |---|---|
   | Amount received | $8,000 |
   | Amount excludable (75%) | 6,000 |
   | Taxable portion | $2,000 |

   For 2019, Bill will receive annuity payments for the full year. The amount received will be $12,000, the amount excludable will be $9,000, and the taxable portion will be $3,000. The excludable and taxable portions will remain the same in later years until Bill has excluded his net investment of $129,600. After that, the annuity payments will be fully taxable.

2. Same facts as in Example 1 except there was an investment after June 30, 1986, and Table V is used. Looking at Table V (in *Table 7-2*) under age 66, Bill finds the multiple 19.2. The same multiple applies to males and females. Multiplying the 19.2 by

$12,000 gives an expected return of $230,400. Using a net investment of $129,600, the exclusion percentage is 56.25% ($129,600 ÷ $230,400). For 2018, Bill reports annuity income as follows:

| | |
|---|---|
| Amount received | $8,000 |
| Amount excludable (56.25%) | 4,500 |
| Taxable portion | $3,500 |

For 2019, $12,000 is received. The amount excludable will be $6,750 (56.25% × $12,000), and the taxable portion, $5,250. The same treatment will apply in later years until Bill has excluded his net investment of $129,600. Thereafter, all payments will be fully taxable.

3. You receive quarterly annuity payments. Your first payment comes on January 15, covering the first quarter of the year. Since the period between the starting date of January 1 and the payment date of January 15 is less than one month, you adjust the life expectancy multiple as shown in *Table 7-3* above by adding 0.1. If the life expectancy multiple from the IRS table was 14.4, the adjusted multiple is 14.5.

## 7.23 When You Convert Your Endowment Policy

When an endowment policy matures, you may elect to receive a lump sum, an annuity, an interest option, or a paid-up life insurance policy. If you elect—

**A lump sum.** You report the difference between your cost (premium payments less dividends) and what you receive.

**An annuity before the policy matures or within 60 days after maturity.** You report income in the years you receive your annuity *(7.21)*. Use as your investment in the annuity contract the cost of the endowment policy less premiums paid for other benefits such as double indemnity or disability income. If you elect the annuity option more than 60 days after maturity, you report income on the matured policy as if you received the lump sum; *see* above rule. The lump sum is treated as the cost investment in the annuity contract.

**An interest option before the policy matures.** You report only the interest as it is received, provided you do not have the right to withdraw the policy proceeds. If you have the right to withdraw the proceeds, you are treated as in constructive receipt; the difference between your cost and what you receive would be taxed as if you had received a lump sum.

**Paid-up insurance.** You report the difference between the present value of the paid-up life insurance policy and the premium paid for the endowment policy. In figuring the value of the insurance policy, you do not use its cash surrender value, but the amount you would have to pay for a similar policy with the company at the date of exchange. Your insurance company can give you this figure. The difference is taxed at ordinary income tax rates.

Tax-free exchange rules apply to the policy exchanges listed in *6.12*.

Gain on the sale of a life insurance policy is partly ordinary income and partly capital gain; *see 11.2*0.

The proceeds of a veteran's endowment policy paid before the veteran's death are not taxable.

## 7.24 Reporting Employee Annuities

Tax treatment of employee annuity payments from a qualified employee plan, qualified employee annuity, or tax-sheltered annuity *(7.19)* depends on the amount of your contributions and your annuity starting date. These rules are discussed in *7.25–7.27*. If payments are from a nonqualified employee plan, you must use the rules for commercial annuities *(7.21)*.

## Credit or Deduction for Repaying Pension Overpayment Over $3,000

If you pay tax on a pension distribution and in the next year the plan determines that there was an overpayment, which you repay, and the repayment exceeds $3,000, you may claim whichever of the following would provide a lower tax for the year of repayment: (1) a miscellaneous itemized deduction, assuming you itemize deductions on Schedule A rather than taking the standard deduction *(13.1)*, or (2) a tax credit based on a recomputation of the prior year's tax *(2.8)*.

No deduction or credit is allowed if the repayment is $3,000 or less. For years before 2018, a repayment of $3,000 or less was potentially deductible as a miscellaneous itemized deduction subject to the 2% AGI floor, but the Tax Cuts and Jobs Act has suspended the itemized deduction for miscellaneous expenses subject to the 2% AGI floor for 2018 through 2025 *(19.1)*.

*Filing Instruction*

## Simplified Method Mandatory

If your annuity starting date was in 2018, you must use the simplified method *(7.25)* to figure the taxable part of your 2018 payments, unless on the annuity starting date you were age 75 or older and your payments are guaranteed for at least five years.

**Fully taxable payments if you have no investment in the plan.** If you did not contribute to the cost of a pension or employee annuity, and you did not report as income your employer's contributions, you are fully taxed on payments after the annuity starting date.

An employee is taxed on the full value of a nonforfeitable annuity contract that the employer buys him or her if the employer does not have a qualified pension plan. Tax is imposed in the year the policy is purchased. A qualified plan is one approved by the IRS for special tax benefits.

**Disability pension before minimum retirement age.** Disability payments received before you reach the minimum retirement age (at which you would be entitled to a regular retirement annuity) are fully taxable as wages. After minimum retirement age, payments are treated as an annuity *(7.25)*.

**Partially taxable payments if you have an investment in the plan.** If you and your employer both contributed to the cost of your annuity, the part of each payment allocable to your investment is tax free and the balance is taxable. You generally must use the simplified method to figure the tax-free portion allocable to your investment *(7.25)*. For withdrawals before the annuity starting date, *see 7.27*.

## 7.25 Simplified Method for Calculating Taxable Employee Annuity

If you have an investment in the plan and your annuity starting date was in 2018, you must use the simplified method explained below to figure the tax-free portion of your annuity payments from a qualified employer plan, qualified employee annuity, or 403(b) tax-sheltered annuity. The only exception is if you are age 75 or older on your annuity starting date and are entitled to guaranteed annuity payments for at least five years; in that case you must use the six-step method *(7.23)* for commercial annuities rather than the simplified method.

A beneficiary receiving a survivor annuity may use the simplified method.

**If your annuity started in 2018.** If your annuity started in 2018, and your annuity is for your life only, you figure the tax-free portion of your annuity by using the "number of expected monthly payments" shown for your age in Table I shown below.

Use Table II if your annuity benefits are payable for the lives of more than one annuitant, such as where you started to receive payments in 2018 under a joint and survivor annuity for you and your spouse. Combine your age with the age of your survivor annuitant. If you are the primary annuitant and there is more than one survivor annuitant, combine your age and the youngest survivor annuitant's age when using Table II. If there is no primary annuitant and the annuity is payable to you and other survivor annuitants, the ages of the oldest and youngest are combined. Disregard a survivor annuitant whose entitlement to payment is contingent on something other than the primary annuitant's death.

**If your annuity started before 2018.** If your annuity started before 2018 and you have been using the simplified method to report your annuity payments, continue to do so, using the applicable number of expected monthly payments from either Table I or Table II, as discussed in Step 2 and shown below.

**Figuring taxable and tax-free payments under the simplified method.** Under the simplified method, a level tax-free portion is determined for each monthly payment with the following steps:

1. Step 1. Figure your investment in the contract as of the annuity starting date. Include premiums you paid and any after-tax contributions you made to the employer's pension plan *(7.26)*. If you are the beneficiary of an employee (or former employee) who died before August 21, 1996, also include the death benefit exclusion of up to $5,000 as part of the investment in the contract.

2. Step 2. Divide the investment from Step 1 by the number of expected monthly payments shown in Table I or Table II below, using your age on the annuity starting date. The result is the tax-free recovery portion of each monthly payment.

However, multiply this amount by three (3 months) to get the tax-free portion if payments are made quarterly rather than monthly. The tax-free portion remains the same after the employee's death if a spouse or other beneficiary receives payments under a joint and survivor annuity.

Use Table I if your annuity is based on your life only. Also use Table I for a multiple-lives annuity with a starting date before 1998, taking into account only the primary annuitant's age as of the starting date.

Use Table II if your annuity benefits are payable for the lives of more than one annuitant and the annuity starting date was after December 31, 1997. The ages of the annuitants are combined as discussed earlier under "If your annuity started in 2018".

3. Step 3. Multiply the tax-free recovery amount from Step 2 by the number of monthly payments received during the year; this is the total tax-free payment for the year.

However, in almost all cases, your total tax-free recovery under the simplified method for all years is limited to your investment in the plan from Step 1. Unless your annuity starting date was before 1987, you need to keep track of your annual tax-free cost recoveries. Once you, or you and your survivor annuitant, have recovered the full investment, further payments will be fully taxable. The tax-free amount for any year under the Step 3 computation cannot exceed the excess of your investment from Step 1 over the prior year cost recoveries. If the full investment has not been recovered when the last annuitant dies, the unrecovered investment is allowed on his or her final income tax return as a miscellaneous itemized deduction if deductions are itemized on Schedule A (rather than taking the standard deduction) on that return *(19.1)*.

If the annuity starting date was before 1987, the total exclusion for all years is not limited to the investment. You may continue to take your monthly exclusion for life, and if there is a survivor annuitant, he or she can continue to take the exclusion for as long as annuity payments are received.

4. Step 4. Subtract the Step 3 tax-free payment from the total annuity received this year; this is the taxable annuity you must report on Form 1040 or Form 1040A. If the payer of the annuity shows a higher taxable amount on Form 1099-R, use the amount figured here.

## Table I

| Age of primary annuitant at annuity starting date | Number of expected monthly payments | |
| --- | --- | --- |
| | Annuity starting date before November 19, 1996 | Annuity starting date after November 18, 1996 |
| 55 and under | 300 | 360 |
| 56–60 | 260 | 310 |
| 61–65 | 240 | 260 |
| 66–70 | 170 | 210 |
| 71 and over | 120 | 160 |

## Table II

| Combined ages of annuitants at annuity starting date | Number of expected monthly payments |
| --- | --- |
| 110 and under | 410 |
| 111–120 | 360 |
| 121–130 | 310 |
| 131–140 | 260 |
| 141 and over | 210 |

**EXAMPLE**

Fred Smith, age 57, retires and beginning August 1, 2018, he receives payments under a joint and 50% survivor annuity with his wife Betty, also age 57. Fred receives an annuity of $1,500 per month and Betty will receive a survivor annuity of $750 per month after Fred's death. Fred's investment in the plan was $29,000. To figure the tax-free portion of each payment, Fred divides his $29,000 investment by 360, the number of expected monthly payments shown in Table II for two annuitants with a combined age of 114 years; the result is $80.56. Thus, the tax-free portion of each $1,500 payment is $81 and the balance of each payment, or $1,419 ($1,500 – $81), is taxable. On his 2018 return, Fred reports $7,095 as taxable annuity payments (5 payments × $1,419). In 2019, Fred will receive 12 monthly payments of $1,500, a total of $18,000, of which $972 will be excludable (12 × $81) and $17,028 will be taxable ($18,000 – $972).

In subsequent years, Fred will continue to exclude $81 of each monthly payment from income and report the rest as taxable until the full $29,000 investment is recovered. If Fred dies before the monthly exclusions total $29,000, Betty will also exclude $81 from each of her payments of $750 until the total plan investment of $29,000 is recovered. Once the $29,000 investment is recovered, all subsequent payments will be fully taxable to Betty. If Betty dies before the full investment is recovered, and itemized deductions are claimed on her final income tax return, an itemized deduction will be allowed on the final return for the unrecovered investment *(19.1)*.

## 7.26 Employee's Cost in Annuity

For purposes of figuring the tax-free recovery of your investment under the general rules *(7.21)* or the simplified method *(7.25)*, include the following items paid as of the annuity starting date as your cost in an employee annuity:

- Premiums paid by you or by after-tax withholdings from your pay.
- Payments made by your employer and reported as additional pay.

Reduce the total by any refunded premiums that you received by the annuity starting date, or, if later, the date of your first payment.

## 7.27 Withdrawals From Employer's Qualified Retirement Plan Before Annuity Starting Date

You generally may not make completely tax-free withdrawals from your employer's qualified retirement plan, qualified employee annuity plan, or 403(b) plan before the annuity starting date, even if your withdrawals are less than your investment. On a withdrawal before the annuity starting date, you must pay tax on the portion of the withdrawal that is allocable to employer contributions and income earned on the contract; the portion of the withdrawal allocable to your investment is recovered tax free. However, if one of the exceptions below applies, the tax-free recovery may be increased.

To compute the tax-free recovery under the general rule, multiply the withdrawal by this fraction:

$$\frac{\text{Your total investment}}{\text{Your vested (nonforfeitable) account balance or accrued benefit}}$$

Your investment and vested benefit are determined as of the date of distribution.

**Exceptions.** More favorable investment recovery rules are allowed in the following cases:

1. Employer plans in effect on May 5, 1986. If on May 5, 1986, your employer's plan allowed distributions of employee contributions before separation from service, the above pro-rata recovery rule applies only to the extent that the withdrawal exceeds the total investment in the contract on December 31, 1986.

   For example, assume that as of December 31, 1986, you had an account balance of $9,750, which included $4,000 of your own contributions. If the plan on May 5, 1986, allowed pre-retirement distributions of employee contributions, you may receive prior to your annuity starting date withdrawals up to your $4,000 investment without incurring tax.

*Caution*

**Favorable Recovery Rules**

Both of the favorable cost recovery rules discussed under "Exceptions" in this section *(7.27)* are complicated and you should consult your plan administrator to determine if the exceptions apply and how to make the required calculations.

2. Separate accounts for employee contributions. A defined contribution plan (such as a profit-sharing plan) is allowed to account for after-tax employee contributions (and earnings on the contributions) separately from employer contributions (and earnings on the employer contributions). If separate accounting is maintained, the tax-free part of the withdrawal is increased because the account balance used as the denominator in the fractional computation includes only the employee's after-tax contributions and allocable earnings, without regard to the employer contributions (and allocable earnings).

## 7.28 Special Rules for Victims of Hurricanes Harvey, Irma, Maria, and California Wildfires

Congress provided special retirement plan relief to taxpayers who lived in an area affected by Hurricane Harvey (or Tropical Storm Harvey), Hurricane Irma, Hurricane Maria, or the 2017 California wildfires, and who suffered an economic loss as a result of the disaster. Qualified disaster distributions of up to $100,000 before 2019 from 401(k) plans and other qualified employer plans, tax-sheltered annuity plans (403(b) plans), qualified annuity plans or governmental 457 plans, may be included in income ratably over three years if you do not want to include it all in the year of receipt. The 10% penalty for qualified distributions before age 59½ (*7.13*) does not apply to qualified distributions. You also have the option of repaying qualified distributions within three years of receipt, in which case the distributions are not taxed (and therefore not subject to the 10% early distribution penalty).

The above rules also apply to qualified disaster distributions from traditional IRAs, SEPs, SIMPLE IRAs, and Roth IRAs; *see 8.26* for further details on the qualified disaster distribution rules.

As noted in *7.14* (*see* the Law Alert), the maximum loan limits from qualified retirement plans were increased, and a one-year suspension on loan repayments was provided, to victims of Hurricane Harvey (or Tropical Storm Harvey), Hurricane Irma, Hurricane Maria, or the California wildfires.

# CHAPTER 8

# IRAs

There are several types of IRAs: Traditional IRAs, Roth IRAs, SIMPLE IRAs, and SEPs. You may personally set up a traditional or Roth IRA with your bank or broker. SIMPLE IRAs *(8.18)* and SEPs *(8.15)* are available only if your employer offers such plans. For 2018, the contribution limit for both traditional *(8.2)* and Roth IRAs *(8.20)* is $5,500, or $6,500 for individuals who are age 50 or older at the end of the year. There is no deduction for Roth IRA contributions, which are allowed only if you have earned income and only if your modified adjusted gross income (MAGI) is within specified limits. If you have earnings, you may make traditional IRA contributions, which are either fully deductible, partly deductible, or not deductible at all, depending on whether you (and your spouse) have retirement coverage where you work and if so, whether your MAGI subjects you to the deduction phaseout rules *(8.4)*.

Traditional IRA distributions are generally fully taxable and, if made before age 59½, subject to a penalty; *see 8.12* for penalty exceptions. Minimum annual distributions from a traditional IRA must begin after you reach age 70½ *(8.13)*.

Although contributions to a Roth IRA are not deductible, the Roth IRA has a major tax advantage: tax-free withdrawals of earnings may be made after a five-year waiting period if you are over age 59½ *(8.24)*. Tax-free withdrawals of contributions may be made at any time. A traditional IRA may also be converted to a Roth IRA; conversions are taxable. *See* the discussion of annual Roth IRA contributions *(8.20)* and conversions *(8.22)*.

Low-to-moderate-income taxpayers may be able to claim a tax credit on Form 8880 for contributions to a traditional IRA, Roth IRA, SIMPLE IRA, or salary-reduction SEP *(25.11)*.

# 8.1 Starting a Traditional IRA

If you have earnings, you may contribute to a traditional IRA up to an annual limit *(8.2)*. The contribution may be deductible *(8.4)* or nondeductible *(8.6)*. Earnings within the IRA accumulate tax free until withdrawals are made *(8.8)*.

You also may set up a traditional IRA by rolling over a distribution received from a qualified employer plan. For example, if you receive a lump-sum payment from a qualified employer plan upon retirement, changing jobs, or becoming totally disabled, you may make a tax-free rollover to a traditional IRA *(7.8)*. If you have a traditional IRA, you can roll it over or make a direct transfer to a different traditional IRA *(8.10)*.

Your employer can set up a "deemed IRA" as a separate account under a qualified retirement plan. As long as the separate account otherwise meets IRA requirements, you can make voluntary employee contributions that will be treated as IRA contributions subject to the regular IRA rules. The separate account can be treated as a traditional IRA or Roth IRA *(8.19)*.

**Roth IRAs.** Annual contributions to a Roth IRA and conversions of traditional IRAs to Roth IRAs are discussed at *8.19–8.22*.

**Restrictions on traditional IRAs.** You may withdraw funds from a traditional IRA at any time, but if you take money out before the date you reach age 59½ or become disabled, you are subject to a penalty unless an exception applies *(8.12)*. Pledging the account as collateral is treated as a taxable distribution from the account *(8.8)*. Starting with the year you reach age 70½, you may no longer make traditional IRA contributions *(8.2)*, and you must start to withdraw *(8.13)* from the account. All traditional IRA withdrawals are fully taxable except for amounts allocable to nondeductible contributions *(8.8–8.9)*. Special averaging for lump-sum distributions *(7.4)* does not apply to IRA distributions. Excess contributions *(8.7)* are penalized.

If your IRA loses value because of poor investments, you may not deduct the loss.

**Types of traditional IRAs.** You may set up an IRA as:

1. An individual retirement account with a bank, savings and loan association, federally insured credit union, or other qualified person as trustee or custodian. An individual retirement account is technically a trust or custodial account. Your contribution may be invested in vehicles such as certificates of deposit, mutual funds, and certain limited partnerships.

2. An individual retirement annuity by purchasing an annuity contract (including a joint and survivor contract for the benefit of you and your spouse) issued by an insurance company; no trustee or custodian is required. The contract, endorsed to meet the terms of an IRA, is all that is required. It must provide for flexible premiums up to the annual contribution limit, so that if your compensation changes, your payment may also change. As borrowing or pledging of the contract is not allowed under an IRA, the contracts will not contain loan provisions. Endowment contracts that provide life insurance protection may not be used as individual retirement annuities.

You may set up one type of IRA one year and choose another form the next year. You also may split your contribution between two or more investment vehicles. For example, you are eligible to contribute $5,500 for 2018 if under age 50. You may choose to put $2,750 into an individual retirement annuity and $2,750 into an individual retirement account with a bank, mutual fund, or brokerage firm.

**Self-directed IRA.** If you wish to take a more active role in managing your IRA investments, you may set up a "self-directed" IRA using an IRS model form. The model trust (Form 5305) and the model custodial account agreement (Form 5305-A) meet the requirements of an exempt individual retirement account and so do not require a ruling or determination letter approving the exemption of the account and the deductibility of contributions made to the account. If you use this method, you still have to find a bank or other institution or trustee to handle your account or investment. Investments in a self-directed IRA are subject to restrictions; *see* the Caution in *8.1*.

**SIMPLE IRA.** If you work for a company with 100 or fewer workers, your employer may set up a SIMPLE IRA to which you may make salary reduction contributions *(8.17)*.

 *Caution*

## IRA Fees and Brokerage Commissions

Fees paid to set up or manage an IRA, and annual account maintenance fees, are not considered IRA contributions if they are separately billed. For years before 2018, such fees were deductible as a miscellaneous itemized deduction subject to the 2% of adjusted gross income floor. Under the Tax Cuts and Jobs Act, investment fees and all other miscellaneous expenses subject to the 2% floor have been eliminated for 2018-2025 *(19.1)*. However, broker's commissions, if any, that are paid when you make investments for your IRA are considered IRA contributions subject to the annual contribution limit ($5,500, or $6,500 if age 50 or older for 2018).

 *Planning Reminder*

## Do You Have to File a Form When You Contribute to a Traditional IRA?

You do not have to file any forms with your tax return when you set up or make deductible contributions to a traditional IRA. Form 8606 must be attached to Form 1040 or Form 1040A if you make nondeductible contributions to a traditional IRA *(8.6)*. The trustee or issuer of your IRA will report your contribution to the IRS on Form 5498, and you should receive a copy.

 *Caution*

## Restrictions on Collectibles Investments

If you have a self-directed traditional IRA and you invest in collectibles, such as art works, gems, stamps, antiques, rugs, metals, guns, or certain coins, you will have to pay a tax on your investment. The investment is treated as a taxable distribution to you in the year you make it. Coins are treated as collectibles, except for state-issued coins or certain U.S. minted gold, silver, and platinum coins. There is also an exception for gold, silver, platinum, or palladium bullion held by the IRA trustee, provided the fineness of the metal meets commodity market standards. If bullion is stored with a company other than the IRA trustee, the investment is subject to the deemed distribution rule for collectibles.

**Contributions allowed up until filing due date.** To make deductible or nondeductible IRA contributions for a year, you have until the regular filing due date (without extensions) of the return for that year. Since the deadline for 2018 returns is April 15, 2019 (page 6), you have until the April 15 due date to make your contribution for 2018. For a contribution to count as a 2018 contribution, it must be made by the April 15 due date, even if you get an extension to file your 2018 return *(46.3)*. If you make a contribution between January 1 and April 15, 2019, make sure the IRA trustee or custodian designates it as a 2018 contribution (and not as a 2019 contribution) if that is what you intend. If you are short of cash, you may borrow the funds to make the contribution without jeopardizing a deduction *(8.2)*. If an IRA deduction entitles you to a refund, you can file your return early, claim the IRA deduction, and if you receive the refund in time, apply it towards an IRA contribution before the due date.

## 8.2 Contribution Limit for Traditional IRAs

You may make contributions to a traditional IRA for 2018 of up to $5,500, or $6,500 if you are age 50 or older at the end of 2018, provided that (1) you have at least $5,500/$6,500 of earned income (compensation) in 2018, such as wages, salary, or net self-employment earnings, and (2) you have not reached age 70½ by the end of the year. If your earned income is less than $5,500 ($6,500 if age 50 or older), the contribution limit is 100% of your pay or net earned income if self-employed. If you have more than one traditional IRA, the limit applies to total contributions to all of the IRAs for the year.

If you are married filing jointly, you may each contribute up to $5,500 (or $6,500 if age 50 or older) to an IRA for 2018, as long as your combined earned income covers the contributions *(8.3)*.

Contributions for 2018 may be made up to the filing deadline of April 15, 2019; this is the deadline even if you obtain a filing extension for your 2018 return.

**Contribution limit increased by $1,000 if age 50 or older.** If you are age 50 or older by the end of 2018, an additional contribution of up to $1,000 may be made for 2018, increasing your contribution limit to the lesser of $6,500 (up from the general limit of $5,500) or your compensation. If you are an active participant in an employer retirement plan, the $6,500 limit is subject to the phaseout rule *(8.4)*.

**Deduction limit.** Contributions up to the $5,500 or $6,500 limit (or up to your compensation if less) are fully deductible on your 2018 return if neither you nor your spouse is an active participant in an employer plan or self-employed retirement plan. The deduction limit is phased out for active plan participants with modified adjusted gross income (MAGI) over an annual threshold. For 2018, the MAGI phaseout threshold for single persons is $63,000. The phaseout threshold on a 2018 joint return is generally $101,000 *(8.3)*, but a more favorable $189,000 phaseout threshold applies to a jointly filing spouse who is not a plan participant *(8.4)*. *See* 8.4 for details on the deduction phaseout rules for active plan participants.

> ### EXAMPLE
>
> A trader whose sole income was derived from stock dividends and gains in buying and selling stocks contributed to an IRA. The IRS disallowed the deduction on the grounds that his income was not earned income.
>
> If you live in a community property state, the fact that one-half of your spouse's income is considered your income does not entitle you to make contributions to an IRA. Your contribution must either be based on pay earned through your services or, if you file jointly, it must be allowed under the spousal IRA rules *(8.3)*.

**Contributions must be based on compensation.** Traditional IRA contributions, whether deductible or nondeductible, must generally be based on taxable compensation received for rendering personal services, such as salary, wages, commissions, tips, fees, bonuses, jury fees, or net earnings from self-employment (less retirement plan contributions on behalf of the self-employed). If you elect the foreign earned income exclusion *(36.1)*, the excluded

*IRS Alert*

**IRA Contribution Limit Hasn't Changed Since 2013**

Because of low inflation, there has not been a cost-of-living increase to the basic IRA contribution limit since 2013, when the limit increased from $5,000 to $5,500 (or compensation if less). The additional $1,000 "catchup" contribution limit for those age 50 or older at the end of the year is set by statute and is not subject to inflation adjustments. See the *e-Supplement* at *jklasser.com* to find out whether the 2018 limit of $5,500/$6,500 gets an inflation increase for 2019.

*Planning Reminder*

**IRA Contribution Based on Tax-Free Combat Pay**

Members of the armed services serving in a combat zone *(35.4)* can contribute to either a traditional IRA or a Roth IRA *(8.20)* based on their tax-free combat pay. Without this law, members of the military who did not have any earnings apart from the combat zone pay could not make IRA contributions, which otherwise must be based on taxable compensation.

income may not be the basis of an IRA contribution. There is one type of pay that may be counted for IRA purposes although it is nontaxable, and that is nontaxable combat pay *(35.4)*. In addition, taxable alimony may be treated as compensation for IRA purposes. An IRA contribution (deductible or nondeductible) may not be based upon:

1. Investment income such as interest, dividends, or profits from sales of property;

2. Deferred compensation, pensions, or annuities; or

3. Income earned abroad for which the foreign earned income exclusion is claimed.

**Working for spouse.** If you work for your spouse, you may make an IRA contribution provided you actually perform services and receive an actual payment of wages. A wife who worked as a receptionist and assistant to her husband, a veterinarian, failed to meet the second test. Her husband did not pay her a salary. Instead, he deposited all income from his business into a joint bank account held with his wife. In addition, no federal income tax was withheld from her wages. In a ruling, the IRS held that the wife could not set up her own IRA, even though she performed services; she failed to receive actual payment. Depositing business income into a joint account is neither actual nor constructive payment of the wife's salary. Furthermore, any deduction claimed for the wife's wages was disallowed.

**Self-employed may make IRA contributions.** IRA contributions may be based on net self-employment earnings *(45.1)*. For IRA purposes, net earnings from Schedule C are reduced by deductible contributions made on your behalf to qualified plans and SEPs *(41.5)* and by the deduction for one-half of self-employment tax liability *(45.3)*. If you have a net loss for the year, you may not make an IRA contribution unless you also have wages.

If you have more than one self-employed activity, you must aggregate profits and losses from all of your self-employed businesses to determine if you have net income on which to base an IRA contribution. For example, if one self-employed business produces a net profit of $15,000 but another a net loss of $20,000, you may not make an IRA contribution based on the net profit of $15,000 since you have an overall loss. This netting rule does not apply to salary or wage income. If you are an employee who also has an unprofitable business, you may make an IRA contribution based on your salary.

If you have a self-employed retirement plan from your business, you are considered an active participant in a retirement plan for purposes of the adjusted gross income phaseout rules *(8.4)*.

**Taxable alimony treated as compensation.** A divorced spouse with little or no earnings may treat taxable alimony as compensation, giving a basis for deductible IRA contributions. If you are divorced, you generally may make an IRA contribution for 2018 equal to 100% of the taxable alimony you received in 2018, up to the $5,500 limit ($6,500 if age 50 or older). However, if you are an active participant in an employer plan and your adjusted gross income exceeds the $63,000 threshold for unmarried individuals, *see 8.4* for the phaseout of the deduction limit. Taxable alimony is alimony paid under a decree of divorce or legal separation, or a written agreement incident to such a decree; *see Chapter 37.* It does not include alimony payments made under a written agreement that is not incident to such a decree.

**No contributions to traditional IRA allowed for those age 70½ or older.** Even if you still have earnings, you may not make contributions to a traditional IRA for the year in which you reach age 70½, or for any later year. For example, if you were born in the last six months of 1947 or the first six months of 1948, you reach age 70½ during 2018 and therefore may not make any traditional IRA contributions (deductible or nondeductible) for 2018 or for any later year.

If you have a nonworking spouse under age 70½, you may contribute to his or her IRA, even though no contribution may be made to your own traditional IRA because you have reached age 70½ *(8.3)*.

**Qualified reservist repayments.** If you were called to active duty as a member of the reserves for over 179 days, or indefinitely, and took a distribution from your IRA during your active duty period, the distribution may be repaid to an IRA within the two-year

*Planning Reminder*

**Roth IRA Contributions after Age 70½**

Contributions to a traditional IRA may not be made for the year in which you reach age 70½ or for later years, but contributions to a Roth IRA may be made even if you are over age 70½, provided you have compensation *(8.2)* to support the contribution and your income is within the annual limit allowed under the Roth IRA contribution rules *(8.20)*.

period beginning on the day after the end of the active duty period. The repayment is allowed regardless of the regular IRA contribution limit for the year of repayment. The repaid amount is not deductible. The qualified reservist repayment must be reported as a nondeductible IRA contribution *(8.6)* on Line 1 of Form 8606.

## 8.3 Contributions to a Traditional IRA If You Are Married

If both you and your spouse earned compensation *(8.2)* in 2018 of at least $5,500 and you are both under age 50 at the end of the year, each of you may make a contribution of up to $5,500 to a traditional IRA for 2018 by April 15, 2019. Under the spousal IRA rule (see below), the $5,500 per spouse contribution limit applies even if only one of you has compensation, provided you file jointly and your combined taxable compensation is at least $11,000. An additional contribution of up to $1,000 can be made for each spouse who is age 50 or older by the end of the year so long as there is compensation to cover it and the spouse for which the contribution is made is under age 70½; no IRA contribution is allowed for an individual who is age 70½ or older at the end of the year.

Contributions for 2018 are fully deductible up to the $5,500 limit ($6,500, if applicable) if neither you nor your spouse was covered by an employer retirement plan during the year. If either one of you was an active plan participant *(8.5)*, you are both considered active participants, and a deduction may be limited or disallowed *(8.4)* depending on your modified adjusted gross income (MAGI). However, if you file jointly and only one of you was an active plan participant, a more favorable MAGI phaseout rule applies to the nonparticipant spouse, so that the spouse without coverage may be able to claim a deduction even if the participant spouse may not. The deduction phaseout rules are discussed below.

**Spousal IRA contribution on joint return for nonworking or low-earning spouse.** If you file a joint return for 2018, and you and your spouse are both under age 50 at the end of the year, you may each contribute up to $5,500 to a traditional IRA as long as your combined taxable compensation *(8.2)* is at least $11,000. If you are both age 50 or older by the end of 2018, the contribution limit for each of you is raised to $6,500, so long as your combined taxable compensation is at least $13,000. If one spouse is under age 50 and one is age 50 or older at the end of 2018, the total contribution limit is $12,000 ($5,500 for the spouse under age 50 plus $6,500 for the spouse age 50 or more), provided your combined taxable compensation is at least $12,000. This spousal IRA rule allows a spouse with minimal earnings to "borrow" compensation from his or her spouse in order to reach the maximum contribution limit. In figuring a couple's combined compensation for purposes of the "borrowing" rule, the higher earning spouse's compensation is reduced by his or her deductible IRA contribution and by any regular contributions made by the higher earning spouse to a Roth IRA for the year.

**Deduction phaseout rule for spouses filing jointly for 2018.** If neither you nor your spouse is an active participant in an employer plan *(8.5)* in 2018, the phaseout rules do not apply and each of you may deduct contributions up to the $5,500 or $6,500 (if age 50 or older) limit if you each have compensation *(see 8.2)* of at least that much.

If either you or your spouse was an active participant *(8.4)* in an employer retirement plan during 2018, the phaseout rule may limit or completely disallow an IRA deduction. However, even if one or both of you were active participants in an employer plan, the phaseout rule does not apply and you may each deduct contributions up to the $5,500/$6,500 limit (or compensation if less) if your 2018 joint return modified adjusted gross income (MAGI) *(8.4)* is $101,000 or less.

If both of you were active plan participants for 2018, the deduction limit is phased out over a $20,000 range once your joint return MAGI exceeds $101,000. Thus, no deduction is allowed for either of you if your 2018 joint return MAGI is $121,000 or more.

If you were not an active plan participant in 2018 but your spouse was, a different phaseout rule applies to each of you. Your spouse, as an active plan participant, is subject to the deduction phaseout if MAGI on the joint return is between $101,000 and $121,000; your spouse gets no deduction if joint MAGI is $121,000 or more. However, as the nonparticipant spouse, your deduction limit is not subject to phaseout unless MAGI on the joint return is over $189,000. Your deduction is phased out if joint MAGI is between $189,000 and $199,000, and no deduction is allowed if MAGI is $199,000 or more.

*See 8.4* for an example of how the reduced deduction limit is figured if MAGI is within the above phaseout ranges.

> **EXAMPLE**
>
> Rhonda and Elliot Richards, both under age 50, file a joint return for 2018. Rhonda had salary income of $78,000 in 2018. Elliot was a full-time student and had no compensation. Rhonda may contribute up to $5,500 to her own traditional IRA for 2018. Even though Elliot did not work in 2018, a contribution of up to $5,500 may also be made to his traditional IRA for 2018. Since Rhonda's earnings exceeded $11,000, $5,500 of her earnings may be credited to Elliot for contribution purposes.
>
> If Rhonda and Elliot's modified adjusted gross income (MAGI) *(8.4)* for 2018 does not exceed $101,000, contributions for each of them up to the $5,500 limit are fully deductible on their joint return. If MAGI on their 2018 joint return exceeded $101,000 and if Rhonda was an active participant in her employer's retirement plan during 2018, her deduction would be phased out over a MAGI range of $101,000–$121,000. Under the special rule for spouses who are not active participants, Elliot would be allowed a full $5,500 deduction for 2018 so long as the joint return MAGI was $189,000 or less. See the phaseout rules in the next paragraph..

**Deduction phaseout rule for married persons filing separately for 2018.** If you are married, live together at any time during 2018, file separately for 2018, and either of you was an active participant in an employer plan, the other spouse is also considered an active participant. Both of you are subject to the $0 to $10,000 MAGI deduction phaseout range *(8.4)*.

If you live apart for all of 2018, you each figure IRA deductions as if single. Thus, the more favorable deduction phaseout range of $63,000 to $73,000 applies if you are covered by an employer retirement plan *(8.4)*. If you are not covered, you may claim a full deduction on your separate return.

**Contribution for nonworking or low-earning spouse under age 70½.** If in 2018 you were age 70½ or over and had taxable compensation, and your spouse is under age 70½ at the end of the year, you may contribute to a spousal IRA for 2018 if you file a joint return and your spouse had little or no compensation; *see* the spousal IRA rules above. The entire contribution must be allocated to your nonworking spouse. No contribution may be made to your own traditional IRA for the year in which you reach age 70½, or any later year. However, you may contribute to a Roth IRA even if you are over age 70½, provided your compensation is within the Roth IRA limits *(8.20)*.

## 8.4 Restrictions on Traditional IRA Deduction for Active Participants in Employer Plans

If you are covered by an employer retirement plan, including a self-employed plan, you may be unable to make deductible IRA contributions to a traditional IRA. When you have coverage, your right to claim a full deduction, a limited deduction, or no deduction at all depends on your modified adjusted gross income (MAGI). If you are married, and your spouse has employer plan coverage for 2018 you are also considered to have coverage in most cases. However, if you file jointly and do not individually have employer plan coverage, a special MAGI phaseout rule may allow you to deduct IRA contributions even if a deduction for your spouse is limited or barred.

The deduction phaseout rules do not apply, regardless of your income, if you are unmarried and do not have employer plan coverage, or if you are married and neither of you has coverage. An IRA deduction of up to $5,500 ($6,500 if age 50 or older at end of year) for 2018 is allowed as long as you have compensation *(8.2)* of at least $5,500 ($6,500 if age 50 or older) and you have not reached age 70½ by the end of the year.

*Planning Reminder*

**Phaseout Rule for Nonparticipant Spouses**

If you are not covered by an employer retirement plan but your spouse is, and you file a joint return for 2018, your individual deduction limit is not subject to the phaseout rule unless modified adjusted gross income (MAGI) on the joint return exceeds $189,000 (phaseout complete at $199,000 or more). For your spouse, who is covered by an employer plan, a deduction for 2018 is phased out if modified adjusted gross income on the joint return is between $101,000 and $121,000.

*Caution*

**No Contribution Allowed if Age 70½ or Older**

You cannot deduct any contributions to a traditional IRA for 2018 (or any later year) if you are age 70½ or older at the end of 2018. Nondeductible contributions to a traditional IRA *(8.6)* also are barred if you are age 70½ or older at the end of the year, but a Roth IRA contribution may be allowable depending on your income *(8.20)*.

**Are you an active plan participant?** Generally, you are considered to be "covered" by a retirement plan if you are an active participant in the plan for any part of the plan year ending within your taxable year. If you are an employee, your Form W-2 for 2018 should indicate whether you are covered for the year; if you are, the "Retirement plan" box within Box 13 of Form W-2 should be checked. Active participation *(8.5)* in a self-employed qualified plan or SEP *(Chapter 41)* is treated as employer plan coverage for purposes of the IRA deduction phaseout rules.

---

### EXAMPLE

Sara Wartes, a college teacher, quit her job in 1988 and withdrew all of the contributions she had made to her employee pension plan. The Tax Court held that Sara could not claim an IRA deduction in that year. Sara was an active participant in the college plan during 1988 and under the phaseout rules based upon adjusted gross income, no IRA deduction was allowed. The court noted that the active participation test is not applied at the end of the year. Participation in a company plan at any time during the year triggers the deduction phaseout rules. This is true even where a person has forfeitable benefits.

---

**You are not an active plan participant but your spouse is.** Even if you were not an active participant in an employer retirement plan at any time in 2018, your IRA deduction limit for 2018 may be phased out because of your spouse's coverage. However, if you file jointly, your own deduction is not limited unless modified adjusted gross income (MAGI) on the 2018 joint return exceeds $189,000. For your spouse who has employer plan coverage, the rule is different: the phaseout threshold for his or her 2018 deduction is joint MAGI of $101,000, assuming you file jointly.

As a nonparticipant, you are not allowed any deduction if MAGI on your joint return is $199,000 or more. A deduction for your spouse as an active participant is completely phased out if joint return MAGI for 2018 is $121,000 or more.

Stricter phaseout rules apply to married persons filing separately if they live together at any time during the year. If you lived with your spouse at any time during 2018 and either of you was an active plan participant in 2018, you are both subject to the $0 – $10,000 MAGI phaseout range on separate returns. Neither of you may claim an IRA deduction if the MAGI on your separate return is $10,000 or more.

If you are married filing separately and you lived apart for all of 2018, your spouse's plan participation does not affect your IRA deduction. Take into account only your own participation, if any, and if you are an active participant, your IRA deduction under the phaseout rules is figured as if you were single, so for 2018, the deduction limit is phased out if MAGI is between $63,000 and $73,000; *see* Worksheet 8-2. If you are not an active participant, you may claim the full deduction limit of $5,500, or $6,500 if age 50 or older, assuming you have compensation *(8.2)* of at least that much.

## Figuring Your 2018 IRA Deduction Under the Phaseout Rules

If you are an active plan participant for 2018, or you file a joint return for 2018 and your spouse is an active participant for 2018, the full deduction limit (lesser of $5,500/$6,500 (age 50 or older at end of year) or your compensation; *see 8.2*) is available to you only if your modified adjusted gross income (MAGI) does not exceed the applicable phaseout threshold for your status. Use Worksheet 8-1 to figure your MAGI and then *see Table 8-1* for the 2018 phaseout thresholds and phaseout ranges. As shown in *Table 8-1*, the deduction limit for active plan participants is phased out over the first $10,000 of MAGI exceeding the threshold unless you are married filing jointly or a qualifying widow/widower, in which case the phaseout range doubles to $20,000.

If your MAGI exceeds your phaseout threshold but does not exceed the phaseout endpoint, you can figure your deduction limit by applying the steps of Worksheet 8-2. If you are married and both you and your spouse are contributing to traditional IRAs for 2018, you should separately figure your deduction limits, as your phaseout threshold and phaseout range may be different from that of your spouse. The Examples below Worksheet 8-2 illustrate the computation of the deduction limit.

## *Table 8-1* Can You Deduct Traditional IRA Contributions for 2018?

| If you are | MAGI phaseout threshold is | MAGI phaseout range is | No deduction if MAGI is |
|---|---|---|---|
| Single, head of household, or qualifying widow/widower and you are NOT an active plan participant, or Married filing jointly or separately and NEITHER you nor your spouse are active plan participants | There is no phaseout regardless of your income. You may deduct contributions up to the full deduction limit *(8.2)*. If married filing jointly, *see* the spousal contribution rule at *8.3* if one spouse has little or no compensation | | |
| Single or head of household and you are an active plan participant | $63,000 | over $63,000 and under $73,000 | $73,000 or more |
| Married filing jointly and both you and your spouse are active plan participants. The same phaseout threshold and phaseout range applies to each of you. | $101,000 | over $101,000 and under $121,000 | $121,000 or more |
| Married filing jointly and one of you is an active plan participant and one of you is not. Although you file jointly, you and your spouse have different phaseout thresholds and phaseout ranges. | Plan-participant spouse: $101,000 | over $101,000 and under $121,000 | $121,000 or more |
| | Non-participant spouse: $189,000 | over $189,000 and under $199,000 | $199,000 or more |
| Qualifying widow or widower and you are an active plan participant | $101,000 | over $101,000 and under $121,000 | $121,000 or more |
| Married filing separately, you lived with your spouse at any time during the year and either one of you is an active plan participant. The same unfavorable phaseout rule applies to each of you on your separate returns. | $ 0 | over $0 and under $10,000 | $10,000 or more |
| Married filing separately, you lived apart from your spouse for the entire year and one of you is an active plan participant and the other is not. | Plan-participant spouse: $63,000 | over $63,000 and under $73,000 | $73,000 or more |
| | Non-participant spouse: There is no phaseout regardless of your income. On your separate return, you may deduct contributions up to the full deduction limit *(8.2)*. | | |

## Worksheet 8-1  Figuring Your MAGI for Purposes of the Phaseout of the Traditional IRA Deduction Limit

In most cases, your modified adjusted gross income (MAGI) will be the same as the actual AGI reported on your tax return, but it may be higher because certain deductions and exclusions allowed in figuring AGI must be added back when figuring MAGI. You can use the following steps to figure your MAGI.

1. Enter the AGI reported on your return, assuming no deduction for
   traditional IRA contributions is claimed ........................................... 1. _____

2. Enter any deductions claimed for:
   - a. student loan interest *(33.13)* .................................................. 2a. _____
   - b. qualified tuition and fees, provided Congress extends the
     deduction to 2018 *(33.12)* ...................................................... 2b. _____
   - c. foreign housing expenses if self-employed *(36.4)*; ................... 2c. _____
   - d. Total of (a)—(c) .................................................................... 2d. _____

3. Enter any exclusions claimed for:
   - a. employer-provided adoption assistance *(3.6)* .......................... 3a. _____
   - b. interest on U.S. Savings Bonds used for tuition *(33.4)* ............ 3b. _____
   - c. foreign earned income *(36.1)* ............................................... 3c. _____
   - d. employer-provided foreign housing expenses *(36.4)* ............... 3d. _____
   - e. Total of (a)—(d) .................................................................... 3e. _____

4. Add Lines 1, 2d and 3e. This is your MAGI for traditional IRA
   deduction purposes. ...................................................................... 4. _____

## Worksheet 8-2  Phaseout of IRA Deduction Limit for 2018*

1. Enter your MAGI for 2018; *see* Worksheet 8-1. If married filing jointly,
   this is the MAGI for both of you on the joint return. ......................... 1. _____

2. Enter your phaseout threshold—either $0, $63,000, $101,000, or
   $189,000 as shown in *Table 8-1*. .................................................. 2. _____

3. Subtract Line 2 from Line 1. This is your excess MAGI.
   If your excess MAGI is equal to or more than your $10,000 or $20,000
   phaseout range, as shown in *Table 8-1*, you are not allowed any IRA
   deduction; 100% of the deduction limit is phased out. Do not complete
   Lines 4–6. ...................................................................................... 3. _____

4. If you are married filing jointly and you are an active plan participant or
   a qualifying widow or widower, multiply Line 3 by 27.50% if you were
   under age 50 at the end of 2018, or by 32.50% if you were age 50 or
   older at the end of 2018.
   All others, multiply Line 3 by 55% if you were under age 50 at the end
   of 2018, or by 65% if you were age 50 or older at the end of 2018.
   This is the phased out portion of the deduction limit. ....................... 4. _____

5. Subtract Line 4 from the maximum deduction limit of $5,500 if you
   were under age 50 at the end of 2018, or from $6,500 if you were age
   50 or older at the end of 2018. If your taxable compensation *(8.2, 8.3)*
   is under the $5,500 or $6,500 limit, subtract Line 4 from that lesser
   compensation amount. ................................................................... 5. _____

6. If Line 5 is not a multiple of $10, round it up to the next highest multiple
   of $10. If the result is under $200, increase it to $200. This is your
   deductible limit for 2018 traditional IRA contributions. ................... 6. _____

**\*NOTE**: Use this worksheet only if you or your spouse is an active participant in an employer retirement plan for 2018 and your MAGI is within the phaseout range shown in *Table 8-1*. If you were married and both you and your spouse contributed (or will contribute by the filing deadline) to a traditional IRA for 2018, and either one of you is an active plan participant, you should separately complete this worksheet, as you may have different phaseout thresholds and deduction limits.

**Nondeductible contributions.** Any contributions exceeding the amount allowed under the above rules may be treated as nondeductible IRA contributions *(8.6)*. Alternatively, the excess may be contributed to a Roth IRA if allowed under the Roth IRA rules *(8.20)*.

**Figuring your IRA deduction if you receive Social Security benefits.** If you or your spouse *(8.3)* is an active participant in an employer plan and either of you receives Social Security benefits, you need to make an extra computation before you can figure whether an IRA deduction is allowed. First follow the rules discussed in *34.3* to determine if part of your Social Security benefits would be subject to tax, assuming no IRA deduction were claimed. If none of your benefits would be taxable, you follow the regular rules above for determining IRA deductions. If part of your Social Security benefits would be taxable, MAGI for IRA purposes is increased by the taxable benefits. The allowable IRA deduction is then taken into account to determine the actual amount of taxable Social Security. IRS Publication 590-A has worksheets for making these computations.

*Planning Reminder*

**Roth IRA vs. Deductible IRA**

Even if you qualify for a full IRA deduction, you may want to consider making a nondeductible contribution to a Roth IRA *(8.20)*. For example, you may be willing to give up the current tax deduction in order to create a Roth IRA from which distributions will be completely tax free after you reach age 59½ and a five-year waiting period has passed. If you choose to make a deductible contribution to a traditional IRA, distributions from the traditional IRA will be taxable. You may also prefer the Roth-IRA advantage of not having to take minimum distributions starting at age 70½, as is required with traditional IRAs *(8.13)*.

## EXAMPLES

1. Rob Porter is single and under age 50 at the end of 2018. He is an active participant in an employer retirement plan. His salary for 2018 is $61,865 and his MAGI for 2018 is $64,343. His MAGI exceeds the $63,000 phaseout floor for single persons by $1,343. The maximum deductible contribution Rob can make to a traditional IRA for 2018 is $4,770, figured as follows:

   | | | |
   |---|---|---|
   | 1. | MAGI for 2018 | $64,343.00 |
   | 2. | Phaseout threshold for single taxpayers | 63,000.00 |
   | 3. | Excess MAGI (Line 1– Line 2) | 1,343.00 |
   | 4. | 55% of Line 3 is phased out | 738.65 |
   | 5. | $5,500 minus Line 4 | 4,761.35 |
   | 6. | Since Line 5 is not a multiple of $10, round it up to the next highest multiple of $10. This is Rob's deductible limit for 2018. | 4,770.00 |

2. Ted and Lynn Baker are both under age 50 at the end of 2018 and they file a 2018 joint return. They report wages of $48,000 for Ted and $53,000 for Lynn. Their modified adjusted gross income (MAGI) for 2018 is $104,020. Ted and Lynn are both active participants in employer retirement plans in 2018 and so they are both subject to the $101,000 phaseout threshold. Each of them may make a deductible contribution of up to $4,670 to a traditional IRA for 2018, figured as follows:

   | | | |
   |---|---|---|
   | 1. | MAGI for 2018 | $104,020.00 |
   | 2. | Phaseout threshold for married couples filing jointly | 101,000.00 |
   | 3. | Excess MAGI (Line 1 – Line 2) | 3,020.00 |
   | 4. | 27.50% of Line 3 is phased out | 830.50 |
   | 5. | $5,500 minus Line 4 | 4,669.50 |
   | 6. | Since Line 5 is not a multiple of $10, round it up to the next highest multiple of $10. This is the deductible limit for both Ted and Lynn. On their 2018 joint return, they can each deduct IRA contributions of up to $4,670, for a total maximum deduction of $9,340. | $4,670.00 |

3. Assume the same facts as in Example 2 except that only Lynn was an active participant in an employer plan. Ted and Lynn must figure their deduction limitations separately using different phaseout thresholds.

   For Lynn, the same $4,670 deduction limit applies as in Example 2. The $101,000 phaseout threshold applies, her excess MAGI is $3,020 ($104,020 MAGI on joint return – $101,000 threshold), and her deduction limit as shown in Example 2 is $4,670.

   For Ted, the special $189,000 threshold for nonparticipant spouses applies. Since joint return MAGI is well below the $189,000 threshold, he is not affected by the phaseout rules and may deduct IRA contributions up to the $5,500 ceiling for 2018.

   On their 2018 joint return, they may deduct IRA contributions of $10,170: $4,670 for Lynn and $5,500 for Ted.

4. Assume the same facts as in Example 2 except that Lynn was age 51 at the end of 2018. Ted and Lynn will have different deduction limitations. They are both subject to the $101,000 phaseout threshold because both are active plan participants. However, since Lynn is at least age 50 at the end of the year, her maximum deduction limit prior to any phaseout is $6,500, while the limit for Ted (under age 50) is $5,500. This means that the phaseout percentage on Line 4 is different for Lynn, as well as the deduction limit on Line 6.

For Ted, the deduction limit is $4,670 as shown in Example 2.
For Lynn, the deduction limit is $5,520, figured as follows:

| | | |
|---|---|---|
| 1. | MAGI for 2018 | $104,020.00 |
| 2. | Phaseout threshold for married couples filing jointly | 101,000.00 |
| 3. | Excess MAGI (Line 1-Line 2) | 3,020.00 |
| 4. | 32.50% of Line 3 is phased out | 981.50 |
| 5. | $6,500 minus Line 4 | 5,518.50 |
| 6. | Since Line 5 is not a multiple of $10, round it up to the next highest multiple of $10. This is Lynn's deductible limit for 2018. | $5,520.00 |

On their 2018 joint return, they may deduct IRA contributions of $10,190: $4,670 for Ted and $5,520 for Lynn.

## 8.5 Active Participation in Employer Plan

Active participants in an employer retirement plan are subject to the phaseout rules for deducting contributions *(8.4)*. When a married couple files jointly and only one of the spouses was an active plan participant for the taxable year, a more favorable phaseout range applies to the non-participant spouse than to the spouse who was an active participant *(8.4)*.

An employer retirement plan means:

1. A qualified pension, profit-sharing, or stock bonus plan, including a qualified self-employed retirement plan, SIMPLE IRA, or simplified employee pension (SEP) plan;
2. A qualified annuity plan;
3. A tax-sheltered annuity; and
4. A plan established for its employees by the United States, by a state or political subdivision, or by any agency or instrumentality of the United States or a state or political subdivision, but not eligible state Section 457 plans.

**Form W-2.** If your employer checks the "Retirement plan" box within Box 13 of your 2018 Form W-2, this indicates that you were an active participant in your employer's retirement plan during the year. If you want to make a contribution before you receive your Form W-2, check the following guidelines and consult your plan administrator for your status.

**Type of plan.** Under any type of plan, if you are considered an active participant for any part of the plan year ending with or within your taxable year, you are treated as an active participant for the entire taxable year. Because of this plan year rule, you may be treated as an active participant even if you worked for the employer only part of the year. Under IRS guidelines, it is possible to be treated as an active participant in the year of retirement and even in the year after retirement if your employer maintains a fiscal year plan.

The plan year rule works differently for defined benefit pension plans than for defined contribution plans such as profit-sharing plans, 401(k) plans, money purchase pension plans, and stock bonus plans. These rules are discussed below.

If you are married, and either you or your spouse is treated as an active participant for 2018, *see 8.3* for the effect on the other spouse.

*Caution*

**Active Participant Status**

You are treated as an active participant in a 401(k) plan, profit-sharing plan, stock bonus plan, or money-purchase pension plan if contributions are made or allocated to your account for the plan year that ends with or within your tax year. Under this rule, you may be considered an active participant for a year during which no contributions by you or your employer are made to your account; *see* the Examples in this section.

**EXAMPLES**

1. Pat O'Neil joins a company in February 2018 that has a 401(k) plan (a type of defined contribution plan) with a plan year starting July 1 and ending the following June 30. He is not eligible to participate in the plan year ending June 30, 2018. After he becomes eligible to participate in the second half of 2018, he elects to defer 6% of his remaining 2018 salary to the 401(k) plan for the plan year ending June 30, 2019. Although he makes elective deferrals to the plan during 2018, he is not considered an active participant for 2018 because his contributions were made for the plan year ending in 2019. He will be considered an active participant in 2019 even if he decides not to defer any part of his 2019 salary for the plan year ending June 30, 2020. Since his elective deferrals during 2018 are made for the plan year ending June 30, 2019 and that plan year ends within his 2019 tax year, Pat is treated as an active participant for 2019.

2. Clarise Jones's employer has a defined benefit pension plan with a plan year starting July 1 and ending the following June 30. She is not excluded from participating. If she retired during September 2018, she is considered an active participant for 2018 because she was eligible to participate during the plan year ending June 30, 2018. She will also be considered an active participant for 2019. Although her retirement in September 2018 is only a few months into the plan year starting July 1, 2018, and ending June 30, 2019, she will still be eligible to participate during part of that plan year (from July 1, 2018, until retirement in September 2018), and since the 2018–2019 plan year ends within her 2019 tax year, she will be considered an active participant for 2019.

**Defined benefit pension plans.** You are treated as an active participant in a defined benefit pension plan if, for the plan year ending with or within your taxable year, you are eligible to participate in the plan. Under this rule, as long as you are eligible, you are treated as an active participant, even if you decline participation in the plan or you fail to make a mandatory contribution specified in the plan. Furthermore, you are treated as an active participant even if your rights to benefits are not vested.

**Defined contribution plan.** For a defined contribution plan, you are generally considered an active participant if "with respect to" the plan year ending with or within your taxable year (1) you make elective deferrals to the plan; (2) your employer contributes to your account; or (3) forfeitures are allocated to your account. If any of these events occur, you are treated as an active participant for that taxable year, even if you do not have a vested right to receive benefits from your account.

## 8.6 Nondeductible Contributions to Traditional IRAs

If you are not allowed to deduct any IRA contributions for 2018 because of the phaseout rule *(8.4)*, you may make nondeductible contributions of up to $5,500 ($6,500 if age 50 or over at the end of 2018) where you have compensation of at least that much and are not age 70½ older by the end of the year. If the deduction limit is reduced under the phaseout rules *(8.4)*, you may make a nondeductible contribution to the extent the maximum contribution limit of $5,500 or $6,500 (where compensation is at least that much) exceeds the reduced deductible limit *(8.4)*.

If you make contributions to a traditional IRA during the year, you may not know whether your active participation status *(8.5)* and modified adjusted gross income (MAGI) will permit you to claim a deduction under the phaseout rules in *(8.4)*. You can make your contribution and wait until you file your return to determine if you are eligible for a deduction. Assume that you make a contribution and after the end of the year you determine that you are eligible for only a portion of the deductible amount under the phaseout rule *(8.4)*. In that case, you can leave the nondeductible portion in a nondeductible traditional IRA (reporting it on Form 8606), or you may recharacterize *(8.21)* the nondeductible contribution as a Roth IRA contribution assuming you qualify to contribute to a Roth IRA *(8.20)*. On the other hand, you may decide to withdraw the nondeductible contribution as discussed below.

 *Planning Reminder*

**Roth IRA Alternative**

A Roth IRA is a nondeductible IRA that offers significant tax and retirement planning advantages. Contributions up to the annual limit for a Roth IRA may be made if modified adjusted gross income is below the annual phaseout threshold *(8.20)*. In general, after the five-year period beginning with the first taxable year for which a Roth IRA contribution was made, tax-free withdrawals may be made if you are age 59½ or older, you are disabled or you have qualifying first-time home-buyer expenses. If you have a traditional IRA, you can also obtain the advantages of a Roth IRA by making a conversion to a Roth IRA. The conversion is taxable except to the extent that it is attributable to nondeductible contributions *(8.22)*.

**Roth IRA alternative.** If you are not barred from making Roth IRA contributions *(8.20)* because of your income level, the Roth IRA has advantages over the nondeductible traditional IRA. Although both types of plans allow earnings to accumulate tax free until withdrawal, the Roth IRA has advantages at withdrawal. After a five-year period, completely tax-free withdrawals of earnings as well as contributions may be made from a Roth IRA if you are age 59½ or older, you are disabled, or you withdraw no more than $10,000 for first-time home-buyer expenses *(8.24)*. Even within the first five-year period, contributions (but not earnings) may be withdrawn tax free from a Roth IRA. On the other hand, withdrawals from a nondeductible traditional IRA are partially taxed if any deductible contributions to any traditional IRA were previously made. Even if only nondeductible contributions had been made, earnings from traditional IRAs are taxed at withdrawal. Furthermore, contributions after age 70½ may be made only to a Roth IRA, and mandatory required minimum distributions are not required from a Roth IRA, as they are from a traditional IRA. See the discussion of Roth IRAs in this chapter *(8.19–8.25)*.

**Form 8606.** If you made a nondeductible contribution to a traditional IRA for 2018, you must report it on Form 8606 unless you withdraw the contribution as discussed below. You must list on Form 8606 the value of all of your IRAs as of the end of the year, including amounts based on deductible contributions. If you are married and you and your spouse both make nondeductible contributions, you must each file a separate Form 8606. A $50 penalty may be imposed for not filing Form 8606 unless there is reasonable cause. Furthermore, if you overstate the amount of designated nondeductible contributions made for any taxable year, you are subject to a $100 penalty for each such overstatement unless you can demonstrate that the overstatement was due to reasonable cause. You may file an amended return for a taxable year and change the designation of IRA contributions from deductible to nondeductible or nondeductible to deductible.

**Withdrawing nondeductible contributions.** If you make a contribution to a traditional IRA contribution for 2018 and later realize it is not deductible, you may recharacterize the contribution by transferring it (plus allocable income if any) to a Roth IRA, assuming your income is within the annual Roth IRA contribution limit *(8.21)*.

If you do not want (or are ineligible) to recharacterize the traditional IRA contribution to a Roth IRA, you may make a tax-free withdrawal of the contribution by the filing due date (plus extensions), instead of designating the contribution as nondeductible on Form 8606. To do this, you must also withdraw the earnings allocable to the withdrawn contribution and include the earnings as income on your 2018 return. You might want to make the withdrawal if you incorrectly determined that a contribution would be deductible and you do not want to leave nondeductible contributions in your account. However, making the withdrawal could subject you to bank penalties for premature withdrawals, or other withdrawal penalties imposed by the IRA trustee. Furthermore, if you are under age 59½, the 10% premature withdrawal penalty applies to the withdrawn earnings unless one of the exceptions *(8.12)* is available.

## 8.7 Penalty for Excess Contributions to Traditional IRAs

If you contribute more than the allowable amount to a traditional IRA, whether deductible or nondeductible, the excess contribution may be subject to a penalty tax of 6%. The penalty tax is cumulative. That is, unless you correct the excess, you will be subject to another penalty on the excess contribution in the following year. The penalty tax is not deductible. The penalty is figured in Part III of Form 5329, which must be attached to Form 1040.

The 6% penalty may be avoided by withdrawing the excess contribution by the due date for your return, including extensions, plus any income earned on it. The withdrawn excess contribution is not taxable provided no deduction was allowed for it. The withdrawn earnings must be reported as income on your return for the year in which the excess contribution was made. The earnings should be reported to you as a taxable distribution on Form 1099-R. If you are under age 59½ (and not disabled) when you receive the income, the 10% premature withdrawal penalty applies to the income. Similar rules apply to withdrawals of excess employer contributions to a simplified employee pension plan *(8.15)* made by the due date for your return.

*Planning Reminder*

**Form 8606 for Traditional IRA Distributions**

Keep a copy of each Form 8606 filed showing nondeductible contributions and keep a separate record of deductible contributions. When you make withdrawals from a traditional IRA, the portion of each withdrawal allocable to nondeductible contributions is not taxed. You may not completely avoid tax even if you withdraw an amount equal to your nondeductible contributions. The tax-free portion of the withdrawal is figured on Form 8606. See the rules for figuring tax on withdrawals *(8.9)*.

If an excess contribution for 2018 is not withdrawn by the due date (plus extensions) for your 2018 return, but you filed by the due date (with extensions), the IRS allows the withdrawal to be made no later than October 15, 2019, provided the related earnings are reported on an amended return that explains the withdrawal; *see* the Form 5329 instructions for details. If the withdrawal is not made, the 6% penalty will apply to your 2018 return but it may be avoided for 2019 by withdrawing the excess by the end of 2019. Instead of withdrawing the excess contribution during 2019, you may also avoid or at least reduce a penalty for 2019 by making an IRA contribution for 2019 that is less than the maximum allowable amount. That is, you reduce the 2019 IRA contribution by the excess contribution for the prior year; *see* IRS Publication 590-A and Form 5329 for details.

If you deducted an excess contribution in an earlier year for which total contributions were no more than the maximum deductible amount for that year, you may make a tax-free withdrawal of the excess by filing an amended return by the deadline *(47.2)* to correct the excess deduction. However, the 6% penalty tax applies for each year that the excess was still in the account at the end of the year.

See IRS Publication 590-A for further information on correcting excess contributions made in a prior year.

**Roth IRAs.** A similar 6% penalty applies on Form 5329 to excess contributions to a Roth IRA; *see* Form 5329 and IRS Publication 590-A for further details.

## 8.8 Distributions From Traditional IRAs

If all of your contributions to all of your traditional IRAs were deductible, any distribution from any of your traditional IRAs will be taxable unless you roll it over or redeposit it within 60 days *(8.10)*. If you made both deductible and nondeductible contributions to your traditional IRAs (any of them), withdrawals allocable to the deductible contributions plus earnings are taxable and the balance allocable to the nondeductible contributions is tax free *(8.9)*.

In addition to regular income tax, taxable distributions are also subject to these age-related restrictions:

- Distributions before age 59½ are subject to a 10% tax penalty, unless you are totally disabled, meet exceptions for paying medical costs, receive annual payments under an annuity-type schedule or you qualify for another exception *(8.12)*.

- After you reach age 70½, you must start to receive annual distributions from your traditional IRAs under a life-expectancy calculation. The required beginning date, the date by which the first required minimum distribution (RMD) must be received, is April 1 of the year after the year in which you reach age 70½. For example, if you reach age 70½ during 2018, you must take a required minimum distribution (RMD) for 2018; the RMD for 2018 may be received in 2018 or in 2019 but no later than April 1, 2019. Failure to take the annual required minimum distribution could result in penalties *(8.13)*.

**QCDs are not taxable distributions.** If you are age 70½ or older and you tell your IRA trustee to directly transfer up to $100,000 of deductible contributions and earnings from your IRA to a qualified charitable organization, this is treated as a qualified charitable distribution (QCD) that is not taxable to you and it offsets the required minimum distribution *(8.13)* you must receive for the year; *see* below for QCD details.

**Conversion to Roth IRA.** A conversion of a traditional IRA to a Roth IRA is generally treated as a fully taxed distribution from the traditional IRA *(8.22)*.

**Loan treated as distribution.** If you borrow from your IRA account or use it as security for a loan, you generally are considered to have received your entire interest. Borrowing will subject the account or the fair market value of the contract to tax at ordinary income rates as of the first day of the taxable year of the borrowing. Your IRA account loses its tax-exempt status. If you use the account or part of it as security for a loan, the portion that is pledged is treated as a distribution. However, under the rollover rules, a short-term loan may be made by withdrawing IRA funds and redepositing them in an IRA within 60 days, subject to the once-a-year rollover rule *(8.10)*.

**IRS seizure of IRA treated as distribution.** The Tax Court has held that an IRS levy of an IRA to cover back taxes is a taxable distribution to the account owner, even though the funds are transferred directly from the account to the IRS and not actually received by the owner. Where the owner is under age 59½, the 10% penalty for early withdrawals *(8.12)* does not apply to involuntary distributions attributable to an IRS levy.

**How to report IRA distributions on your 2018 return.** All IRA distributions are reported to you and to the IRS on Form 1099-R *(7.1)*. Form 1099-R must be attached to your return only if federal tax has been withheld. You can avoid withholding by instructing the payer not to withhold using Form W-4P or a substitute form *(26.9)*.

If you have never made nondeductible contributions, your IRA withdrawals are fully taxable and should be reported on Line 4b of Form 1040. If you have made deductible and nondeductible contributions, complete Form 8606 to figure the nontaxable and taxable portions *(8.9)*. Then you report the total IRA withdrawal on Line 4a of Form 1040 and enter only the taxable portion on Line 4b.

If you have an individual retirement annuity, your investment in the contract is treated as zero so all payments are fully taxable. Distributions from an endowment policy due to death are taxed as ordinary income to the extent allocable to retirement savings; to the extent allocable to life insurance, they are considered insurance proceeds.

Proceeds from U.S. retirement bonds (which were issued by the Treasury before May 1982) are taxable in the year the bonds are redeemed. However, you must report the full proceeds in the year you reach age 70½ even if you do not redeem the bonds.

See below for reporting qualified charitable distributions (QCDs).

## Qualified Charitable Distribution by IRA Owner Age 70½ or Older

If you are at least age 70½, you can avoid tax on transfers made directly from your traditional IRA to an eligible charity, up to an annual exclusion limit of $100,000. A QCD counts towards the required minimum distribution *(8.13)* that you must receive from your IRAs for the year. You cannot claim a charitable deduction for the amount of the QCD excluded from income.

To be a qualified charitable distribution (QCD) eligible for the exclusion, the transfer must be made directly by the trustee of your traditional IRA to a qualifying charity that is eligible to receive tax-deductible donations (this excludes a "supporting organization" or donor-advised fund). The QCD rules apply only to traditional IRAs, and not to distributions from SIMPLE IRAs, qualified employer plans, 403(b) plans, or SEPs (including salary-reduction SEPs set up before 1997). If your spouse is also at least age 70½ and instructs the trustee of his or her traditional IRA to make a qualifying direct transfer, you can each claim the up-to-$100,000 exclusion; thus, on a joint return, up to $200,000 is potentially excludable.

Because a QCD is not included in adjusted gross income (up to the $100,00 limit), the exclusion may help you limit the taxability of Social Security benefits *(34.3)*, limit exposure to the 3.8% tax on net investment income *(28.3)*, increase deductibility of unreimbursed medical expenses *(17.1)*, and preserve eligibility for the $25,000 loss allowance under the passive loss rules *(10.2)*

*You must obtain a timely acknowledgment.* Make sure that you get a timely written acknowledgment from the charity. You need the same type of acknowledgment that you have to get to substantiate a donation exceeding $250 under the charitable contribution deduction rules *(14.14)*.

*Have you made nondeductible IRA contributions?* If you authorize a QCD and there were any nondeductible contributions to any of your traditional IRAs, the transfer is deemed to come first out of the part of the distribution that otherwise would be taxable (without the QCD rules)—that is, the amount equal to your deductible contributions plus earnings. The part of the distribution equal to the deductible contributions plus earnings is the amount eligible for the QCD exclusion, up to the $100,000 limit; anything over $100,000 is includible in income, as would any other traditional IRA distribution. Any balance of the transfer (above the amount allocable to deductible contributions plus earnings) is deemed to be a transfer of nondeductible contributions and is nontaxable, but it is not part of the QCD. You must file Form 8606 *(8.9)* to report a distribution of nondeductible contributions and to figure your remaining basis in the IRAs: your pre-distribution basis is reduced by the portion of the distribution that is not considered part of the QCD because it is allocable to nondeductible contributions.

*How to report a QCD.* A QCD must be reported on your return as an IRA distribution on Line 4 of Form 1040. The total transfer is shown on Line 4a). If the entire transfer is a QCD excludable from income, enter "0" on Line 4b as the taxable amount. A transfer in excess of the $100,000 QCD exclusion limit must be included on Line 4b as a taxable IRA distribution. If part of the transfer was allocable to nondeductible contributions reported on Form 8606, that part is not taxable and is not entered on Line 4b. Enter "QCD" next to Line 4b to indicate that you are claiming the QCD exclusion.

If you are able to itemize deductions *(13.1)* on Schedule A (Form 1040), any portion of the transfer allocable to nondeductible contributions can be claimed as a charitable contribution. No charitable deduction is allowed for the excludable part of the QCD (deductible contributions plus earnings).

## 8.9 Partially Tax-Free Traditional IRA Distributions Allocable to Nondeductible Contributions

If you ever made a nondeductible contribution to a traditional IRA, you must file Form 8606 to report a 2018 distribution from any of your traditional IRAs, even if the distribution is from an IRA to which only nondeductible contributions were made. All of your traditional IRAs are treated as one contract. If you receive distributions from more than one traditional IRA in the same year, they are combined for reporting purposes on Form 8606.

When you have made nondeductible as well as deductible contributions to traditional IRAs, any distribution from any of the traditional IRAs will be treated partly as a tax-free return of cost basis in the nondeductible contributions, and partly as a taxable distribution of deductible contributions and earnings. In other words, the part of your withdrawal that is allocable to your nondeductible contributions is tax-free; any balance is taxable. You may not claim that you are withdrawing only your tax-free contributions, even if your withdrawal is less than your nondeductible contributions. The six steps below reflect the IRS method used on Form 8606 to figure the nontaxable and taxable portions of the IRA distributions.

The rule requiring you to combine nondeductible and deductible IRAs when making IRA withdrawals does not apply to withdrawals from a Roth IRA; do not combine your traditional and Roth IRAs. Roth IRAs are treated separately. After a five-year period, withdrawals after age 59½ from a Roth IRA are completely tax-free *(8.24)*.

A bank or other payer of a distribution from a traditional IRA will not indicate on Form 1099-R whether any part of a distribution is a tax-free return of basis allocable to nondeductible contributions. It is up to you to keep records that show the nondeductible contributions you have made. IRS instructions require you to keep copies of all Forms 8606 on which nondeductible contributions have been designated, as well as copies of (1) your tax returns for years you made nondeductible contributions to traditional IRAs; (2) Forms 5498 showing all IRA contributions and showing the value of your IRAs for each year you received a distribution; and (3) Form 1099-R (or previously used Form W-2P) showing IRA distributions. According to the IRS, you should keep such records until you have withdrawn all IRA funds.

**Figuring the taxable portion of a traditional IRA distribution.** If you received a distribution from a traditional IRA in 2018 and have ever made nondeductible contributions to any of your traditional IRAs, follow Steps 1–6 to determine the tax-free and taxable portions of the 2018 distribution. These steps assume that you did not convert a traditional IRA to a Roth IRA during 2018. If you did convert a traditional IRA to a Roth IRA, follow the instructions to Form 8606.

1. Total traditional IRA withdrawals during 2018.
2. Total nondeductible contributions to all traditional IRAs made by the end of 2018. Tax-free withdrawals of nondeductible contributions in prior years reduce the total. If you made any contributions to traditional IRAs for 2018 (including a contribution for 2018 made between January 1 and April 15, 2019) that may be partly nondeductible because your modified adjusted gross income is within the deduction phaseout range shown in *8.4* for active plan participants, you should include the contributions in the Step 2 total.

3. Add Step 1 to the value of all your traditional IRAs (and if any, the value of all SIMPLE IRAs and SEP IRAs) as of the end of 2018. If you received an IRA distribution within the last 60 days of 2018 that was rolled over to another IRA within the 60-day rollover period *(8.10)* but not until 2019, add the 2019 rollover to the 2018 year-end balance.

4. Divide Step 2 by Step 3. This is the tax-free percentage of your IRA withdrawal.

5. Multiply the Step 4 percentage by Step 1. This amount is tax free.

6. Subtract Step 5 from Step 1. This amount must be reported as a taxable IRA distribution on your 2018 return.

---

**EXAMPLE**

Nick James has one traditional IRA. His only contributions were from 2001 through 2007, when he made deductible IRA contributions of $8,000 and nondeductible contributions of $6,000 as follows

| Year | Deductible | Nondeductible |
|------|------------|---------------|
| 2001 | $2,000 | 0 |
| 2002 | 2,000 | 0 |
| 2003 | 2,000 | 0 |
| 2004 | 1,000 | $1,000 |
| 2005 | 1,000 | 1,000 |
| 2006 | 0 | 2,000 |
| 2007 | 0 | 2,000 |
| | $8,000 | $6,000 |

On November 19, 2018, Nick withdraws $5,000 from the traditional IRA. Assume that on December 31, 2018, Nick's total IRA account balance, including earnings, is $27,500, and that the November withdrawal was his first ever IRA withdrawal. On Form 8606 for 2018, Nick figures that $923 of the $5,000 IRA withdrawal is tax free and $4,077 is taxable.

| | | |
|---|---|---|
| Step 1. | IRA withdrawal in November 2018 | $5,000 |
| Step 2. | Nondeductible contributions for all years | 6,000 |
| Step 3. | IRA balance at end of 2018 ($27,500) plus Step 1 withdrawal ($5,000) | 32,500 |
| Step 4. | Tax-free percentage:$6,000 (Step 2) ÷ $32,500 (Step 3) | 18.46% |
| Step 5. | Tax-free withdrawal:18.46% (Step 4) × $5,000 (Step 1) | 923 |
| Step 6. | Taxable withdrawal: $5,000 (Step 1) – $923 (Step 5) | $4,077 |

The total $5,000 withdrawal should be reported on Line 4a of Form 1040, and the taxable $4,077 portion should be entered on Line 4b (Form 1040).

---

**Law Alert**

**Deducting a Loss Based on Unrecovered Basis No Longer Allowed**

Under pre-2018 law, a loss on a traditional IRA investment was sometimes deductible if the taxpayer's basis in nondeductible contributions was not recovered after the entire account was distributed. The loss could only be claimed as a miscellaneous itemized deduction subject to the 2% of adjusted gross income floor, so if the standard deduction was claimed, or the loss on the IRA, when added to other miscellaneous expenses, did not exceed the 2% floor, the loss deduction could not be claimed. The Tax Cuts and Jobs Act suspended for 2018 through 2025 the itemized deduction for all miscellaneous expenses that had been subject to the 2% floor, so deducting a loss for the unrecovered basis in an IRA is not possible in 2018 *(13.2)*.

**Deductible IRA loss based on unrecovered nondeductible contributions.** According to the IRS, a loss is allowed if all IRA funds have been distributed and you have not recovered your basis in nondeductible contributions. However, because the loss is treated as a miscellaneous itemized deduction subject to the 2% of adjusted gross income floor, no deduction is allowed for 2018 through 2025 due to the suspension of this deduction.

## 8.10 Tax-Free Direct Transfer or Rollover From One Traditional IRA to Another

You may switch how your traditional IRA funds are invested without incurring tax on a distribution by rolling over a distribution to another IRA within 60 days of receiving it, although another option, a direct transfer, is a more advantageous way of changing IRA investments, as discussed below.

Distributions from inherited IRAs are subject to separate rules. A surviving spouse beneficiary who withdraws funds from an inherited IRA can do a 60-day rollover (see below), but a nonspouse beneficiary cannot roll over a withdrawal. However, a nonspouse beneficiary as well as a surviving spouse beneficiary can make a direct trustee-to-trustee transfer to another traditional IRA *(8.14)*.

**Direct transfer from one IRA to another.** A direct transfer is made by instructing the trustee (or custodian) of a traditional IRA to transfer all or part of your account to another IRA trustee (or custodian). Direct transfers are tax free because you do not receive the funds. With a direct transfer, there is no risk of missing the 60-day deadline for rolling over a withdrawal into a new IRA. There is also no need to worry about making multiple transfers within the same 12-month period if you use direct transfers. The tax law does not require a waiting period between direct transfers, whereas rollovers are subject to a once-a-year limitation, as discussed below.

For example, assume you have a traditional IRA at Bank "A" and decide to switch your account to Mutual Fund "ABC." The mutual fund provides you with transfer request forms that you complete and return to the fund, which will then forward the forms to the bank; the bank will process the request and then transfer the funds to the fund to complete the direct transfer. You are not taxed on the transfer from the bank to the mutual fund because the IRA funds were not paid to you, and the direct transfer is not considered a rollover subject to the once-a-year rollover limitation. This means that if within one year you become unhappy with the performance of Mutual Fund "ABC," you may make another tax-free direct transfer of your IRA to Fund "XYZ" or to Bank "B."

In some cases, the old IRA trustee may issue you a check payable to the new trustee that you must give to the new trustee. As long as the check is to the new trustee and not to you, this is considered a direct transfer and not a rollover.

**Rollover within 60 days.** If you withdraw funds from your traditional IRA, you have 60 days to make a tax-free rollover to another traditional IRA. The amount you receive from your old IRA must be transferred to the new plan by the 60th day after the day you received it. Amounts not rolled over within the 60-day period must be treated as a taxable distribution for the year you received the distribution (not the year in which the 60-day period expired, if that is later) unless the IRS waives the 60-day deadline (see below). If the distribution is taxed and you were under age 59½ when the distribution was made, the 10% penalty for an "early" distribution applies unless a penalty exception *(8.12)* is available.

The IRS may waive the 60-day rollover deadline on equitable grounds if a distribution cannot be rolled over on time because of events beyond your reasonable control, such as illness, natural disaster, or a financial institution's error; *see* the IRS waiver guidelines below.

There are two other possible grounds for an extension of the 60-day rollover deadline. An extension is allowed if your distribution is "frozen" and cannot be withdrawn from an insolvent or bankrupt financial institution. The deadline is extended to 120 days if a distribution is taken to buy or build a qualifying "first home" and the deal falls through. These extensions are discussed below.

*Caution: one-year waiting period between rollovers.* Once you complete a rollover between traditional IRAs, you must wait one year before you can make another tax-free rollover; *see* below.

**IRS may waive 60-day rollover deadline on equitable grounds.** You may be able to obtain a waiver of the 60-day rollover deadline in one of three ways:

1. You qualify for an automatic waiver. The IRS will automatically waive the deadline if: (a) you deposited the rollover funds with a financial institution within the 60-day period, (b) you followed all of the institution's rollover procedures but the rollover account was not established on time solely because of the institution's error, and (c) the funds were actually deposited in a valid rollover account within one year of the start of the 60-day period.

2. You use the self-certification procedure for a waiver where you missed the 60-day deadline because of one or more of 11 reasons recognized by the IRS, as described below.

3. You apply for a waiver by requesting a private letter ruling and showing that your failure to meet the 60-day deadline was due to reasons beyond your reasonable control. However, a $10,000 user fee must be submitted with the ruling request.

 *Planning Reminder*

**60-Day Loan From IRA**

You can take advantage of the rollover rule to borrow funds from your IRA if you need a short-term loan to pay your taxes or other expenses. As long as you redeposit the amount in an IRA within 60 days you are not taxed on the withdrawal; the redeposit is considered a tax-free rollover. You may roll over the funds to a different IRA from the one from which the withdrawal was made. Keep in mind that only one tax-free rollover can be made within a 12-month period. Thus, if you use a 60-day rollover for a short-term loan (or any other reason), a second withdrawal from the same IRA or from any of your other traditional IRAs within one year would be taxable *(8.10)*.

**Self-certification procedure for getting waiver of 60-day deadline.** The IRS has provided rules (Revenue Procedure 2016-47) that extend the time for completing a rollover if you "self-certify" that you meet specified conditions. The IRS could later question your eligibility, but the procedure allows you and the IRA trustee that receives your transfer after the 60-day period to treat it as a valid rollover.

*Conditions for self-certification.* You can use this procedure if you give a written certification (see below) to the IRA trustee that you meet all of the following three conditions:

1. You were not previously denied a waiver request for a rollover of this distribution by the IRS.

2. You have a good reason for missing the 60-day deadline. There are 11 acceptable reasons:

    • An error was made by the financial institution making the distribution or receiving the rollover transfer.

    • You misplaced and never cashed the distribution check.

    • You deposited the distribution in an account you mistakenly thought was an eligible retirement plan.

    • Your principal residence was severely damaged.

    • A member of your family died.

    • You or a member of your family was seriously ill.

    • You were incarcerated.

    • You were subject to restrictions imposed by a foreign country.

    • There was a postal error.

    • The distribution was made on account of an IRS levy and the proceeds have been returned to you.

    • The party making the distribution delayed providing information required by the receiving IRA despite your efforts to obtain it.

3. You completed the rollover as soon as practicable. This test is considered met if you satisfy a 30-day safe harbor, which applies when the funds are rolled over within 30 days after you are no longer subject to the condition that prevented a timely rollover.

Written self-certification must be given to the new IRA trustee. To make the self-certification, you must give the IRA trustee (the trustee of the IRA to which you are making the late transfer) a signed letter stating that you intended to make the rollover within 60 days of receiving the distribution but were unable to do so because of one or more of the 11 reasons shown above (condition 2), and that conditions 1 and 3 were also met. You can use the model letter in the Appendix to Rev. Proc. 2016-47, or a letter that is substantially similar. Keep a copy of the certification with your records.

Unless the IRA trustee has actual knowledge that you are not eligible for the self-certification, the trustee may rely on your written notification for purposes of accepting the late transfer as a timely rollover and reporting it as a rollover on Form 5498 ("IRA Contribution Information"). On Form 5498, the IRA trustee will report the amount of the late rollover for which self-certification was made in Box 13a ("Postponed Contribution"), and in Box 13c ("Code"), code "SC" will be entered.

Caution: the IRS may question your self-certification. This self-certification process does not require you to provide documentation to the IRA trustee about the circumstance that made you eligible for the waiver. You may report the transfer on your return as a valid rollover (therefore not taxable) unless the IRS has informed you otherwise. However, if you are audited and the IRS questions the waiver, then it is up to you to prove that you met the conditions for the self-certification.

Note that even if you do not self-certify, the IRS could grant a waiver for equitable reasons on an audit of your return.

**Frozen deposits in insolvent financial institutions.** The 60-day limit for completing a rollover is extended if the funds are "frozen" and may not be withdrawn from a bankrupt or insolvent financial institution. The 60-day period is extended while the account is frozen and you have a minimum of 10 days after the release of the funds to complete the rollover.

If a government agency takes control of an insolvent bank, you might receive an "involuntary" distribution of your IRA account from the agency. According to the IRS and Tax Court, such a payment is subject to the regular IRA distribution rules. For example, a couple received payment for their $11,000 IRA balance from the Maryland Deposit Insurance Fund after the bank in which the funds were invested became insolvent. The Tax Court held that the payment was taxable, even though the distribution was from a state insurance fund and not from the bank itself. Furthermore, since they were under age 59½, the 10% penalty for early distributions *(8.12)* was imposed, even though the distribution was involuntary. The tax and penalty could have been avoided by making a rollover of the distribution within 60 days, but this was not done.

**120-day rollover period after failure to acquire "first-time" home.** A "first-time" homebuyer may be able to limit or avoid a 10% penalty for a distribution before age 59½ by using the funds within 120 days to help buy, build, or rebuild a principal residence *(8.12)*. If the requirements of the exception cannot be met because the planned purchase or construction of the home falls through, the law allows the taxpayer to return the distribution to an IRA within 120 days after receiving the distribution. The recontribution is not taken into account for purposes of the once-a-year rollover limit discussed above. The extension of the tax-free rollover period from 60 days to 120 days is automatic if the requirements are met; a waiver of the 60-day deadline (as discussed above) from the IRS is not required. For example, a taxpayer withdrew IRA funds to buy a home and would have qualified as a "first-time" homebuyer, but his offer was rejected by the seller and approximately 72 days after the IRA withdrawal he put the amount of the distribution back into his IRA. The IRS in a private ruling held that the recontribution to the IRA was timely under the special 120-day rollover rule.

## Only One IRA Rollover is Allowed Within Any 12-Month Period

If you receive an IRA distribution and within 60 days of receiving it you rolled it over to the same IRA or to another IRA, you cannot roll over another distribution from any of your IRAs within the 12-month period starting on the date you received the first distribution. A second tax-free rollover within the 12-month period is not allowed even if the proceeds of the second distribution are redeposited into the same IRA from which the distribution was made. Note that if you receive a distribution and roll it over at a later date within the 60-day rollover period, the 12-month period begins on the date that the distribution was received, not the later rollover date.

For purposes of the one-rollover-per year limitation, all of your traditional IRAs, Roth IRAs, SEPs and SIMPLE IRAs are aggregated as if they were one IRA. Only one rollover from any of these accounts is allowed within a 12-month period. Thus, if you make a rollover from one traditional IRA to another, you cannot make a rollover between Roth IRAs within the same 12-month period. Similarly, if a rollover is made from one Roth IRA to another, you cannot make a rollover from one traditional IRA to another within the same 12-month period. However, conversions from a traditional IRA to a Roth IRA are not limited; *see* below.

If within 12 months of making an IRA-to-IRA rollover you receive an IRA distribution and attempt to roll it over, the distribution will be taxable to the extent it is allocable to pre-tax contributions plus earnings (there is no tax on any portion allocable to after-tax contributions), and if you are under age 59½, the 10% early distribution penalty will apply unless you qualify for a penalty exception *(8.12)*. Furthermore, the failed rollover will be treated as an excess contribution subject to a 6% penalty unless it is withdrawn *(8.7)*.

**Conversions to Roth IRA are not limited.** A rollover or a direct transfer from a traditional IRA to a Roth IRA is treated as a taxable distribution *(8.22)* and thus it is not subject to the one-per-year limit on tax-free rollovers. Within the same 12-month period, you can make one or several taxable conversions of traditional IRAs to Roth IRAs and still make one tax-free IRA rollover.

**Direct transfers are not limited.** You can make a trustee-to-trustee from one IRA to another in order to change your IRA investment as often as you would like without limitation. Since the funds do not pass through your hands, a trustee-to-trustee transfer is not a "rollover" and therefore is not subject to the one-rollover-per year limitation. If you receive a check for a distribution from the transferring IRA trustee that is payable to the receiving IRA trustee (not to you) and you deliver the check to the new trustee, this is considered a trustee-to-trustee transfer.

**Recharacterizations not counted as rollovers.** If you make a timely recharacterization of a traditional IRA contribution to a Roth IRA, or a Roth IRA contribution to a traditional IRA, the recharacterization is not treated as a rollover for purposes of the one-rollover-a-year limit *(8.21)*.

> **EXAMPLE**
>
> On July 10, 2018, you received a distribution from traditional IRA-1. You rolled it over to traditional IRA-2 on August 29, 2018 (within the 60-day rollover period). Under the one-rollover-per-year rule, you cannot make a tax-free rollover of any other IRA distribution (whether from a traditional, Roth, SEP, or SIMPLE IRA) in the 12-month period starting on July 10, 2018 and ending on July 9, 2019. The one-year period starts on July 10, 2018, the date you received the distribution, not on August 29 when you rolled it over.
>
> If you want to change IRA investments in the 12-month period ending July 9, 2019, you can do so by authorizing a direct transfer between IRA trustees, as direct transfers are not limited. In addition, a conversion of a traditional IRA to a Roth IRA is not affected by the rollover limitation and can be made at any time; *see* above.

## 8.11   Transfer of Traditional IRA to Spouse at Divorce

If you receive your former spouse's IRA pursuant to a divorce decree or written instrument incident to the decree, the transfer is not taxable to either of you. From the date of transfer the account is treated as your IRA. If you are legally separated, a transfer of your spouse's IRA to you is tax free if made under a decree of separate maintenance or written instrument incident to the decree. The transferred account is then treated as your IRA.

**How to make a divorce-related transfer.** If you are required to transfer IRA assets from your account to your spouse or former spouse by a decree of divorce or separate maintenance, or a written instrument incident to such a decree, use one of these transfer methods to avoid being taxed on the transfer: (1) change the name on the IRA from your name to the name of your spouse or former spouse if you are transferring your entire interest in the IRA, or (2) direct your IRA trustee to transfer the IRA assets directly to the trustee of a new or existing IRA in the name of your spouse or former spouse.

If you simply withdraw money from your IRA and pay it to your spouse, you will be treated as having received a taxable distribution from your IRA. If you are under age 59½, you will be subject to the 10% early distribution penalty (unless an exception applies; *see 8.12*) as well as regular tax on the withdrawal.

**QDRO transfer of spouse's employer plan benefits to your IRA.** If you receive your share of your spouse's or former spouse's benefits from an employer plan under a qualified domestic relations order (QDRO), you can make a tax-free rollover to a traditional IRA or another eligible retirement plan so long as it would have been eligible for rollover had your spouse received it *(7.12)*. If you roll over only part of a qualifying QDRO distribution, you figure the tax on the retained portion by taking into account a prorated share of your former spouse's cost investment.

## 8.12   Penalty for Traditional IRA Withdrawals Before Age 59½

If you receive a taxable distribution from a traditional IRA *(8.8)* before you are age 59½, you have to pay a 10% penalty in addition to regular tax on the distribution, unless you qualify for a penalty exception specified in the tax law. There is no general exception for financial hardship. Although you may be forced in tough economic times to tap your IRA to cover living expenses, or you face a family emergency, you will be able to avoid the early distribution penalty only if you fit within one of the designated penalty exceptions, such as for disability, paying substantial medical expenses, or higher education expenses.

Here is the list of allowable penalty exceptions: (1) you take the distribution because you are totally disabled, (2) you pay medical expenses exceeding the applicable percentage of adjusted gross income (*see 17.1*), (3) you receive unemployment compensation for at least 12 consecutive weeks and pay medical insurance premiums, (4) you pay qualified higher education expenses, (5) the distribution is $10,000 or less and used for qualified first-time home-buyer expenses, (6) you receive a qualified reservist distribution, (7) the distribution is one of a series of payments being made under one of several annuity-type methods, (8) the distributions are made to you as a beneficiary of a deceased IRA owner, or (9) the distribution was due to an IRS levy on your IRA. These exceptions are further discussed below.

Also note that a qualifying rollover *(8.10)* of an IRA distribution is not subject to tax and therefore not subject to the 10% penalty even if you are under age 59½.

The penalty is 10% of the taxable IRA distribution. For example, if before age 59½ you withdraw $3,000 from your traditional IRA, you must include the $3,000 as part of your taxable income and, in addition, pay a $300 penalty tax. If part of a pre-59½ distribution is tax free because it is allocable to nondeductible contributions *(8.9)* or rolled over to another IRA *(8.10)*, the 10% penalty applies only to the taxable portion of the distribution.

If you do not owe the penalty because you qualify for an exception, you may have to file Form 5329, depending on whether the payer of the distribution correctly marked the exception in Box 7 of Form 1099-R. If the plan administrator knows that you qualify for an exception and indicates this by entering a code in Box 7 of Form 1099-R, you do not have to file Form 5329. For example, if the distribution was made to you as the beneficiary of a deceased IRA owner and the payer has correctly entered Code 4 ("Death") in Box 7, you do not have to file Form 5329 to claim the beneficiary exception. Similarly, if the plan administrator knows that you qualify for the annuity-method exception and enters Code 2 in Box 7 ("Early distribution, exception applies"), you do not have to file Form 5329. If the annuity method or beneficiary exception applies but Code 2 is not entered in Box 7 of Form 1099-R, you must file Form 5329 to claim the penalty exception.

If you qualify for the disability exception, the medical expenses exception, or the higher education expenses exception (see below), it is unlikely that the payer will know of that fact and thus Code 2 ("Early distribution, exception applies") will probably not be marked in Box 7 of Form 1099-R. In this case, you must file Form 5329 to claim the exception: On Line 2 of Part I (Form 5329), you would enter exception number 3 for the disability exception, number 5 for the medical expenses exception, or number 8 for the higher education expenses exception; *see* the Form 5329 instructions for any changes to these exception numbers.

If part of your distribution is eligible for a penalty exception, you must enter on Form 5329 the exception number (from the instructions) and figure the 10% penalty on the nonqualifying part. The penalty is entered on Line 59 of Form 1040 ("Additional Tax on IRAs, Other Qualified Plans, etc.").

**Beneficiaries.** Beneficiaries are exempt from the pre–age 59½ penalty. If the IRA owner was not your spouse and you liquidate the account and receive the proceeds, or if you receive annual payments as a beneficiary under the inherited IRA rules *(8.14)*, any distributions you receive before age 59½ are not subject to the early distribution penalty, although they are subject to regular income tax.

If you inherit an IRA from your deceased spouse and elect to treat it as your own IRA as discussed in *8.14*, you are not eligible for the beneficiary exception; distributions from the account before you reach age 59½ will be subject to the penalty unless another exception applies. The beneficiary exception applies if the account is maintained in the name of your deceased spouse and you are receiving the distribution according to the rules for a spousal beneficiary *(8.14)*.

**Disability exception.** To qualify for the disability exception, you must be able to show that you have a physical or mental condition that can be expected to last indefinitely or result in death and that prevents you from engaging in "substantial gainful activity" similar to the type of work you were doing before the condition arose.

In one case, a 53-year-old stockbroker claimed that his IRA withdrawal of over $200,000 should be exempt from the 10% penalty because he suffered from mental depression. However, the Tax Court upheld the IRS imposition of the penalty because he continued to work as a stockbroker.

**Caution**

## Medical Expenses Exception

The medical expense exception to the early distribution penalty applies only to the extent that in the year you receive the distribution, you pay deductible medical costs *(17.2)* in excess of the AGI floor for claiming itemized medical expenses *(17.1)*. If the deductible medical expenses are not paid in the year the distribution is received, the exception is not available.

**Planning Reminder**

## Annuity-Schedule Penalty Exceptions

If you are planning a series of payments to avoid the 10% early distribution penalty, keep in mind that payments under this exception must continue for at least five years, or until you reach age 59½, whichever is the longer period.

**Caution**

## Timing Problem for Higher Education Costs

Qualified higher education expenses must be paid in the same year that the distribution is received for the penalty exception to apply. This timing rule turns the penalty exception into a tax trap when a tuition payment made at the end of the year is "reimbursed" by an IRA withdrawal at the beginning of the following year, or an IRA distribution is taken at the end of the year to cover a tuition payment due at the start of the next year.

**IRS Alert**

## Division of IRA in Divorce

The IRS in private rulings has allowed a reduction in the scheduled payments from an IRA if part of the IRA is transferred to an ex-spouse as part of a divorce settlement. The reduction in payments is not treated by the IRS as a "modification" that triggers the penalty.

**Medical expense exception.** If you withdraw IRA funds in a year in which you pay deductible medical costs *(17.1)*, part of the distribution may avoid the pre–age 59½ penalty. The penalty does not apply to the part of the distribution equal to the expenses over your AGI floor *(17.1)*). The distribution must be received in the same year that the medical expenses are paid. The medical costs must be eligible for the itemized medical deduction *(17.2)*, but the IRA penalty exception applies whether you itemize or claim the standard deduction.

Unemployed person's medical insurance exceptions. There is no general penalty exception for being unemployed. However, if you are unemployed and received unemployment benefits under Federal or state law for at least 12 consecutive weeks, you may make penalty-free IRA withdrawals to the extent of medical insurance premiums paid during the year for you, your spouse, and your dependents. The withdrawals may be made in the year the 12-week unemployment test is met, or in the following year. However, the penalty exception does not apply to distributions made more than 60 days after you return to the work force.

Self-employed persons who are ineligible by law for unemployment benefits may be treated as meeting the 12-week test, and thus eligible for the exception, under regulations to be issued by the IRS.

Higher education expenses exception. A penalty exception is allowed for IRA distributions that do not exceed higher education expenses, including graduate school costs, for you, your spouse, your or your spouse's children, or your or your spouse's grandchildren that you paid during the year of the IRA distribution. Eligible expenses include tuition, fees, books, supplies, and equipment that are required for enrollment or attendance, plus room and board for a person who is at least a half-time student.

The penalty exception applies only if the withdrawal from the IRA and the payment of the qualified higher education expenses occur within the same year. For example, in one case, a taxpayer under age 59½ took IRA distributions in 2001 to pay credit card debt incurred in 1999 and 2000 to pay qualified higher education expenses for those years. Another taxpayer under age 59½ took IRA distributions in 2002 and used them to pay qualified expenses incurred in 2003 and 2004. In both cases, the Tax Court agreed with the IRS that the penalty exception was not available because the IRA withdrawals were not made in the same year that the qualified higher education expenses were incurred.

**First-time home-buyer expense exception.** A penalty exception is allowed for up to $10,000 of qualifying "first-time" home-buyer expenses. You are a qualifying first-time home-buyer if you did not have a present ownership interest in a principal residence in the two-year period ending on the acquisition date of the new home. If you are married, your spouse also must have had no such ownership interest within the two-year period. The penalty does not apply to IRA distributions that are used within 120 days to buy, construct, or reconstruct a principal residence for you, your spouse, child, grandchild, or ancestor of you or your spouse. Qualifying home acquisition costs include reasonable settlement, financing, or other closing costs. If you qualify, the exception applies only for $10,000 of home-buyer expenses. This is a lifetime cap per IRA owner and not an annual limit.

If you take a distribution, intending to use it for home acquisition costs that would qualify for the first-time buyer exception, but the transaction falls through, you have 120 days from the date you receive the distribution to roll it back to an IRA *(8.10)*.

**IRS levy.** The 10% penalty does not apply to an "involuntary" distribution due to an IRS levy on your IRA.

**Qualified reservist distribution.** If you are a member of the reserves called to active military duty for over 179 days, or indefinitely, distributions received during the active duty period are not subject to the early distribution penalty. Furthermore, a qualified reservist distribution may be recontributed to the plan within two years after the end of your active duty period without regard to the regular limits on IRA contributions *(8.2)*. A recontribution is not deductible.

## Table 8-2  Joint Life and Last Survivor Life Expectancy
### (see "Required minimum distribution method" above)

| Beneficiary \ Self | 30 | 31 | 32 | 33 | 34 | 35 | 36 | 37 | 38 | 39 | 40 | 41 | 42 | 43 | 44 | 45 | 46 | 47 | 48 | 49 | 50 | 51 | 52 | 53 | 54 | 55 | 56 | 57 | 58 | 59 |
|---|---|---|---|---|---|---|---|---|---|---|---|---|---|---|---|---|---|---|---|---|---|---|---|---|---|---|---|---|---|---|
| 30 | 60.2 | 59.7 | 59.2 | 58.8 | 58.4 | 58.0 | 57.6 | 57.3 | 57.0 | 56.7 | 56.4 | 56.1 | 55.9 | 55.7 | 55.5 | 55.3 | 55.1 | 55.0 | 54.8 | 54.7 | 54.6 | 54.5 | 54.4 | 54.3 | 54.2 | 54.1 | 54.0 | 54.0 | 53.9 | 53.8 |
| 31 | 59.7 | 59.2 | 58.7 | 58.2 | 57.8 | 57.4 | 57.0 | 56.6 | 56.3 | 56.0 | 55.7 | 55.4 | 55.2 | 54.9 | 54.7 | 54.5 | 54.3 | 54.1 | 54.0 | 53.8 | 53.7 | 53.6 | 53.5 | 53.4 | 53.3 | 53.2 | 53.1 | 53.0 | 53.0 | 52.9 |
| 32 | 59.2 | 58.7 | 58.2 | 57.7 | 57.2 | 56.8 | 56.4 | 56.0 | 55.6 | 55.3 | 55.0 | 54.7 | 54.4 | 54.2 | 53.9 | 53.7 | 53.5 | 53.3 | 53.2 | 53.0 | 52.9 | 52.7 | 52.6 | 52.5 | 52.4 | 52.3 | 52.2 | 52.1 | 52.1 | 52.0 |
| 33 | 58.8 | 58.2 | 57.7 | 57.2 | 56.7 | 56.2 | 55.8 | 55.4 | 55.0 | 54.7 | 54.3 | 54.0 | 53.7 | 53.4 | 53.2 | 52.9 | 52.7 | 52.5 | 52.3 | 52.2 | 52.0 | 51.9 | 51.7 | 51.6 | 51.5 | 51.4 | 51.3 | 51.2 | 51.2 | 51.1 |
| 34 | 58.4 | 57.8 | 57.2 | 56.7 | 56.2 | 55.7 | 55.3 | 54.8 | 54.4 | 54.0 | 53.7 | 53.3 | 53.0 | 52.7 | 52.4 | 52.2 | 52.0 | 51.7 | 51.5 | 51.4 | 51.2 | 51.0 | 50.9 | 50.8 | 50.6 | 50.5 | 50.4 | 50.3 | 50.3 | 50.2 |
| 35 | 58.0 | 57.4 | 56.8 | 56.2 | 55.7 | 55.2 | 54.7 | 54.3 | 53.8 | 53.4 | 53.0 | 52.7 | 52.3 | 52.0 | 51.7 | 51.5 | 51.2 | 51.0 | 50.8 | 50.6 | 50.4 | 50.2 | 50.0 | 49.9 | 49.8 | 49.7 | 49.5 | 49.4 | 49.4 | 49.3 |
| 36 | 57.6 | 57.0 | 56.4 | 55.8 | 55.3 | 54.7 | 54.2 | 53.7 | 53.3 | 52.8 | 52.4 | 52.0 | 51.7 | 51.3 | 51.0 | 50.7 | 50.5 | 50.2 | 50.0 | 49.8 | 49.6 | 49.4 | 49.2 | 49.1 | 48.9 | 48.8 | 48.7 | 48.6 | 48.5 | 48.4 |
| 37 | 57.3 | 56.6 | 56.0 | 55.4 | 54.8 | 54.3 | 53.7 | 53.2 | 52.7 | 52.3 | 51.8 | 51.4 | 51.1 | 50.7 | 50.4 | 50.0 | 49.8 | 49.5 | 49.2 | 49.0 | 48.8 | 48.6 | 48.4 | 48.2 | 48.1 | 47.9 | 47.8 | 47.7 | 47.6 | 47.5 |
| 38 | 57.0 | 56.3 | 55.6 | 55.0 | 54.4 | 53.8 | 53.3 | 52.7 | 52.2 | 51.7 | 51.3 | 50.9 | 50.4 | 50.1 | 49.7 | 49.4 | 49.1 | 48.8 | 48.5 | 48.2 | 48.0 | 47.8 | 47.6 | 47.4 | 47.2 | 47.1 | 47.0 | 46.8 | 46.7 | 46.6 |
| 39 | 56.7 | 56.0 | 55.3 | 54.7 | 54.0 | 53.4 | 52.8 | 52.3 | 51.7 | 51.2 | 50.8 | 50.3 | 49.9 | 49.5 | 49.1 | 48.7 | 48.4 | 48.1 | 47.8 | 47.5 | 47.3 | 47.0 | 46.8 | 46.6 | 46.4 | 46.3 | 46.1 | 46.0 | 45.8 | 45.7 |
| 40 | 56.4 | 55.7 | 55.0 | 54.3 | 53.7 | 53.0 | 52.4 | 51.8 | 51.3 | 50.8 | 50.2 | 49.8 | 49.3 | 48.9 | 48.5 | 48.1 | 47.7 | 47.4 | 47.1 | 46.8 | 46.5 | 46.3 | 46.0 | 45.8 | 45.6 | 45.5 | 45.3 | 45.1 | 45.0 | 44.9 |
| 41 | 56.1 | 55.4 | 54.7 | 54.0 | 53.3 | 52.7 | 52.0 | 51.4 | 50.9 | 50.3 | 49.8 | 49.3 | 48.8 | 48.3 | 47.9 | 47.5 | 47.1 | 46.7 | 46.4 | 46.1 | 45.8 | 45.5 | 45.3 | 45.1 | 44.8 | 44.7 | 44.5 | 44.3 | 44.2 | 44.0 |
| 42 | 55.9 | 55.2 | 54.4 | 53.7 | 53.0 | 52.3 | 51.7 | 51.1 | 50.4 | 49.9 | 49.3 | 48.8 | 48.3 | 47.8 | 47.3 | 46.9 | 46.5 | 46.1 | 45.8 | 45.4 | 45.1 | 44.8 | 44.6 | 44.3 | 44.1 | 43.9 | 43.7 | 43.5 | 43.3 | 43.2 |
| 43 | 55.7 | 54.9 | 54.2 | 53.4 | 52.7 | 52.0 | 51.3 | 50.7 | 50.1 | 49.5 | 48.9 | 48.3 | 47.8 | 47.3 | 46.8 | 46.3 | 45.9 | 45.5 | 45.1 | 44.8 | 44.4 | 44.1 | 43.8 | 43.6 | 43.3 | 43.1 | 42.9 | 42.7 | 42.5 | 42.4 |
| 44 | 55.5 | 54.7 | 53.9 | 53.2 | 52.4 | 51.7 | 51.0 | 50.4 | 49.7 | 49.1 | 48.5 | 47.9 | 47.3 | 46.8 | 46.3 | 45.8 | 45.4 | 44.9 | 44.5 | 44.2 | 43.8 | 43.5 | 43.2 | 42.9 | 42.6 | 42.4 | 42.1 | 41.9 | 41.7 | 41.5 |
| 45 | 55.3 | 54.5 | 53.7 | 52.9 | 52.2 | 51.5 | 50.7 | 50.0 | 49.4 | 48.7 | 48.1 | 47.5 | 46.9 | 46.3 | 45.8 | 45.3 | 44.8 | 44.4 | 44.0 | 43.6 | 43.2 | 42.8 | 42.5 | 42.2 | 41.9 | 41.6 | 41.4 | 41.2 | 40.9 | 40.7 |
| 46 | 55.1 | 54.3 | 53.5 | 52.7 | 52.0 | 51.2 | 50.5 | 49.8 | 49.1 | 48.4 | 47.7 | 47.1 | 46.5 | 45.9 | 45.4 | 44.8 | 44.3 | 43.9 | 43.4 | 43.0 | 42.6 | 42.2 | 41.8 | 41.5 | 41.2 | 40.9 | 40.7 | 40.4 | 40.2 | 40.0 |
| 47 | 55.0 | 54.1 | 53.3 | 52.5 | 51.7 | 51.0 | 50.2 | 49.5 | 48.8 | 48.1 | 47.4 | 46.7 | 46.1 | 45.5 | 44.9 | 44.4 | 43.9 | 43.4 | 42.9 | 42.4 | 42.0 | 41.6 | 41.2 | 40.9 | 40.5 | 40.2 | 40.0 | 39.7 | 39.4 | 39.2 |
| 48 | 54.8 | 54.0 | 53.2 | 52.3 | 51.5 | 50.8 | 50.0 | 49.2 | 48.5 | 47.8 | 47.1 | 46.4 | 45.8 | 45.1 | 44.5 | 44.0 | 43.4 | 42.9 | 42.4 | 41.9 | 41.5 | 41.0 | 40.6 | 40.3 | 39.9 | 39.6 | 39.3 | 39.0 | 38.7 | 38.5 |
| 49 | 54.7 | 53.8 | 53.0 | 52.2 | 51.4 | 50.6 | 49.8 | 49.0 | 48.2 | 47.5 | 46.8 | 46.1 | 45.4 | 44.8 | 44.2 | 43.6 | 43.0 | 42.4 | 41.9 | 41.4 | 40.9 | 40.5 | 40.1 | 39.7 | 39.3 | 38.9 | 38.6 | 38.3 | 38.0 | 37.8 |
| 50 | 54.6 | 53.7 | 52.9 | 52.0 | 51.2 | 50.4 | 49.6 | 48.8 | 48.0 | 47.3 | 46.5 | 45.8 | 45.1 | 44.4 | 43.8 | 43.2 | 42.6 | 42.0 | 41.5 | 40.9 | 40.4 | 40.0 | 39.5 | 39.1 | 38.7 | 38.3 | 38.0 | 37.6 | 37.3 | 37.1 |
| 51 | 54.5 | 53.6 | 52.7 | 51.9 | 51.0 | 50.2 | 49.4 | 48.6 | 47.8 | 47.0 | 46.3 | 45.5 | 44.8 | 44.1 | 43.5 | 42.8 | 42.2 | 41.6 | 41.0 | 40.5 | 40.0 | 39.5 | 39.0 | 38.5 | 38.1 | 37.7 | 37.4 | 37.0 | 36.7 | 36.4 |
| 52 | 54.4 | 53.5 | 52.6 | 51.7 | 50.9 | 50.0 | 49.2 | 48.4 | 47.6 | 46.8 | 46.0 | 45.3 | 44.6 | 43.8 | 43.2 | 42.5 | 41.8 | 41.2 | 40.6 | 40.1 | 39.5 | 39.0 | 38.5 | 38.0 | 37.6 | 37.2 | 36.8 | 36.4 | 36.0 | 35.7 |
| 53 | 54.3 | 53.4 | 52.5 | 51.6 | 50.8 | 49.9 | 49.1 | 48.2 | 47.4 | 46.6 | 45.8 | 45.1 | 44.3 | 43.6 | 42.9 | 42.2 | 41.5 | 40.9 | 40.3 | 39.7 | 39.1 | 38.5 | 38.0 | 37.5 | 37.1 | 36.6 | 36.2 | 35.8 | 35.4 | 35.1 |
| 54 | 54.2 | 53.3 | 52.4 | 51.5 | 50.6 | 49.8 | 48.9 | 48.1 | 47.2 | 46.4 | 45.6 | 44.8 | 44.1 | 43.3 | 42.6 | 41.9 | 41.2 | 40.5 | 39.9 | 39.3 | 38.7 | 38.1 | 37.6 | 37.1 | 36.6 | 36.1 | 35.7 | 35.2 | 34.8 | 34.5 |
| 55 | 54.1 | 53.2 | 52.3 | 51.4 | 50.5 | 49.7 | 48.8 | 47.9 | 47.1 | 46.3 | 45.5 | 44.7 | 43.9 | 43.1 | 42.4 | 41.6 | 40.9 | 40.2 | 39.6 | 38.9 | 38.3 | 37.7 | 37.2 | 36.6 | 36.1 | 35.6 | 35.1 | 34.7 | 34.3 | 33.9 |
| 56 | 54.0 | 53.1 | 52.2 | 51.3 | 50.4 | 49.5 | 48.7 | 47.8 | 47.0 | 46.1 | 45.3 | 44.5 | 43.7 | 42.9 | 42.1 | 41.4 | 40.7 | 40.0 | 39.3 | 38.6 | 38.0 | 37.4 | 36.8 | 36.2 | 35.7 | 35.1 | 34.7 | 34.2 | 33.7 | 33.3 |
| 57 | 54.0 | 53.0 | 52.1 | 51.2 | 50.3 | 49.4 | 48.6 | 47.7 | 46.8 | 46.0 | 45.1 | 44.3 | 43.5 | 42.7 | 41.9 | 41.2 | 40.4 | 39.7 | 39.0 | 38.3 | 37.6 | 37.0 | 36.4 | 35.8 | 35.2 | 34.7 | 34.2 | 33.7 | 33.2 | 32.8 |
| 58 | 53.9 | 53.0 | 52.1 | 51.2 | 50.3 | 49.4 | 48.5 | 47.6 | 46.7 | 45.8 | 45.0 | 44.2 | 43.3 | 42.5 | 41.7 | 40.9 | 40.2 | 39.4 | 38.7 | 38.0 | 37.3 | 36.7 | 36.0 | 35.4 | 34.8 | 34.3 | 33.7 | 33.2 | 32.8 | 32.3 |
| 59 | 53.8 | 52.9 | 52.0 | 51.1 | 50.2 | 49.3 | 48.4 | 47.5 | 46.6 | 45.7 | 44.9 | 44.0 | 43.2 | 42.4 | 41.5 | 40.7 | 40.0 | 39.2 | 38.5 | 37.8 | 37.1 | 36.4 | 35.7 | 35.1 | 34.5 | 33.9 | 33.3 | 32.8 | 32.3 | 31.8 |

## Annuity Schedule Payments Avoid 10% Penalty

You may avoid the penalty if you are willing to receive annual distributions under one of the three IRS-approved annuity-type methods discussed in this section. Before arranging an annuity-type schedule, consider these points: all of the payments will be taxable (unless allocable to nondeductible contributions (8.9)), and if you do not continue the payments for a minimum number of years, the IRS will impose the 10% penalty for all taxable payments received before age 59½, plus interest charges. The minimum payout period rules do not apply to totally disabled individuals or to beneficiaries of deceased IRA owners.

The payments must continue for at least five years, or until you reach age 59½, whichever period is longer. Thus, if you are in your 40s, you would have to continue the scheduled payments until you are age 59½. If you are in your mid-50s, the minimum payout period is not as serious a burden, as you only need to continue the scheduled payments for at least five years, starting with the date of the first distribution, provided that the period ends after you reach age 59½.

During this minimum period, the arranged annuity-type schedule generally may not be changed unless you become disabled. For example, taking a lump-sum distribution of your account balance before the end of the minimum payout period would trigger the retroactive penalty, plus interest charges. The penalty is triggered even if the change in distribution methods is made after you reach age 59½. However, the IRS may allow a reduction in payments during the minimum period, such as where part of an IRA has been transferred to an ex-spouse following a divorce. Also, as discussed below, the IRS allows a one-time irrevocable switch from the fixed amortization method or fixed annuitization method to the required minimum distribution method. After the minimum payout period, you can discontinue the payments or change the method without penalty.

**Three approved payment methods.** If you would like to take advantage of this penalty exception, you may apply one of the following three payout methods that have been approved by the IRS. With each method, you must receive at least one distribution annually. Under Method 1, the payment changes annually based on the value of the account. Under Methods 2 and 3 the annual payment is generally fixed when the payments begin, but in private rulings the IRS has approved payment schedules that from inception recalculate the amount to be withdrawn each year. Methods 2 and 3 require the assistance of a tax professional and financial advisor to plan the series of payments. The IRS allows taxpayers receiving payments under Method 2 or 3 to reduce the required annual amount without penalty by switching to Method 1.

1. *Required minimum distribution method.* This is the easiest method to figure but provides smaller annual payments than the other methods. Figure the annual withdrawal by dividing your account balance by your life expectancy or by the joint life and last survivor expectancy of you and your beneficiary.

   For example, assume that in 2018 you are age 50 and need to begin receiving distributions from your IRA, which has a balance of $100,000 at the beginning of the year. If you use your single life expectancy, you may take a penalty-free payment of $2,924 in 2018 ($100,000 account balance ÷ 34.2 life expectancy). Single life expectancy is shown in *Table 8-5*, Beneficiary's Single-Life Expectancy Table *(8.14)*.

   If instead of using your single life expectancy you used the joint life and last survivor expectancy of you and your beneficiary, the annual penalty-free amount would be smaller given the longer joint life expectancy. For example, if your beneficiary was age 45, your joint life and last survivor life expectancy would be 43.2 years (using ages 50 and 45), and the penalty-free withdrawal $2,315 ($100,000 account balance ÷ 43.2). See *Table 8-2* for a sample section of the IRS joint life and last survivor life expectancy table. The full IRS table showing joint life and last survivor life expectancy is in IRS Publication 590-B and can also be obtained from your IRA trustee.

2. *Fixed amortization method.* Under this method, you amortize your IRA account balance like a mortgage, using the same life expectancy as under Method 1 (your single life expectancy or the joint life and last survivor expectancy of you and your beneficiary). The interest rate used must be no more than 120% of the federal mid-term rate for either of the two months immediately preceding the month in which distributions begin. In private rulings, the IRS has approved proposed payment schedules that annually recalculate the payments to be received under the fixed amortization method. *See* Revenue Ruling 2002-62 for further details on this method.

3. *Fixed annuitization method.* This method is similar to the fixed amortization method, but an annuity factor from a mortality table is used. Revenue Ruling 2002-62 provides the mortality table to be used. The maximum interest rate used cannot exceed 120% of the federal mid-term rate for either of the two months immediately preceding the month in which distributions begin. In private rulings, the IRS has approved proposed payment schedules that annually recalculate the payments to be received under the fixed annuitization method.

## 8.13   Mandatory Distributions From a Traditional IRA After Age 70½

The tax law requires that by April 1 of the year following the year in which you reach age 70½, you have to start receiving on an annual basis minimum distributions from your traditional IRAs under a schedule that meets IRS tests. The distributions will be fully taxable unless some of your IRA contributions were nondeductible *(8.8)*. You cannot avoid tax on a required minimum distribution (RMD) by rolling it over to another account. However, by authorizing a qualified charitable distribution (QCD), you can satisfy your RMD requirement while avoiding tax on the distribution *(8.8)*.

If you do not receive the required minimum amount, a penalty tax of 50% applies (unless the IRS waives it) to the difference between the amount that should have been received and the amount you did receive. Assume that, under the rules discussed below, your RMD is $3,818, but you do not receive it. You would be subject to a penalty of $1,909 (50% of $3,818), assuming the IRS does not waive it. If you received an RMD of only $3,000, you would have to pay a penalty of $409, 50% of the $818 shortfall, unless the IRS waives the penalty.

If you are subject to a penalty, you should figure it on Form 5329, which must be attached to Form 1040. You can request a waiver of the penalty on Form 5329 if the failure to receive the proper amount was due to a reasonable error and you have or have or will make up for the shortfall; follow the Form 5329 instructions.

Keep in mind that the RMD rules govern only the minimum amount you must receive each year. You are not limited to that amount; you may withdraw more than the RMD or the entire account if you wish. Whatever you receive will be taxable except to the extent that it is allocable to nondeductible contributions.

IRA owners and beneficiaries figure required minimum distributions (RMDs) differently. The RMD rules for account owners of traditional IRAs are discussed in this section *(8.13)*. Beneficiaries of traditional IRAs also must receive annual RMDs unless their entire share of the account is received by the end of the year after the year of the owner's death. However, beneficiaries must use different rules to figure their RMDs *(8.14)*.

Roth IRA owners *(8.19)* are not subject to RMD rules, but beneficiaries of Roth IRAs are *(8.24)*.

**Deadline for receiving your first required minimum distribution (RMD).** Your "required beginning date," the date by which you must receive your first RMD, is April 1 of the year following the year in which you reach age 70½. However, it may be advantageous to take your first RMD during the year in which you reach age 70½ rather than delaying it until January 1-April 1 of the following year. For example, if you reach age 70½ in 2019, and you do not receive your first RMD (the RMD for 2019) during 2019, you have until April 1, 2020, to receive it. However, keep in mind that your second RMD, and the RMD for each year after that, must be received by December 31 of the applicable year. This means that if you delay the first RMD until 2020 (but no later than April 1), you will have to take two distributions in 2020, one by April 1 (the RMD for 2019) and the other by December 31 (the RMD for 2020). This could substantially increase your 2020 taxable income.

### Figuring Your Required Minimum Distribution (RMD)

The trustee or custodian of your traditional IRA must calculate the amount of your required minimum distribution or offer to do so. If you are required to receive a required minimum distribution (RMD) for 2018, the trustee or custodian should have reported the amount to you by January 31, 2018, or offered to calculate it upon your request. If you are required to receive an RMD for 2019, the IRA trustee or custodian must tell you what your RMD is by January 31, 2019, or offer to calculate it for you upon your request. The calculation is based on final IRS regulations.

To calculate the RMD for yourself, you can use Steps 1–3 below, which are based on the final IRS regulations.

If the IRA trustee or custodian calculates the RMD, the calculation may be based on the Uniform Lifetime Table (*Table 8-3* below), which assumes that your beneficiary is 10 years younger than you are. However, if your sole beneficiary is your spouse who is

 *IRS Alert*

**QLACs—Longevity Annuities in IRAs Are Exempt From RMD Rules**

IRS regulations issued in 2014 (T.D. 9673) allow qualified longevity annuities (QLACs) to be bought within traditional IRAs. Without such regulations, annuities that delayed the onset of payments beyond age 70½ could not be used in IRAs because of the required minimum distribution (RMD) requirements. The benefit of a QLAC is that the annuity balance is excluded from the prior-year account balance used to figure your annual RMDs (under the rules in section *8.13*), thereby reducing the amount of the RMDs. An annuity qualifies as a QLAC if the terms delay the onset of RMDs until no later than age 85, and the cost of the QLACs does not exceed the lesser of 25% of the account balance or an annual limit, which for 2018 is $130,000.. The 25%/dollar cost limit is an aggregate limit on the cost of all QLACs in all your IRA accounts, not on each IRA separately. The $130,000 cost limit might be increased for 2019 by an inflation adjustment; *see* the *e-Supplement* at *jklasser.com*.

 *Planning Reminder*

**Qualified Charitable Distributions (QCDs) Satisfy RMD Requirement**

You can make a qualified charitable distribution (QCD) by authorizing a direct transfer from your traditional IRA to a qualifying charity. A QCD counts towards the RMD that you must otherwise receive and include in income for the year. If you have one traditional IRA, the QCD is excluded from your income so long as it does not exceed $100,000. The $100,000 limit is an annual exclusion limit regardless of the number of your traditional IRAs, so if you have several traditional IRAs and you authorize a QCD from each of them, the total tax-free limit for all of them is $100,000 annually. If your spouse is also at least age 70½, he or she can also make QCDs up to the annual $100,000 exclusion limit. See 8.8 for further QCD details.

**Uniform Lifetime Table**

To figure your required minimum distribution (RMD) for the year you become age 70½ and later years, use the Uniform Lifetime Table unless the exception for younger spouses applies.

more than 10 years younger than you, your RMD can be reduced by using the Joint Life and Last Survivor Expectancy Table (see *Table 8-4*). If this more-than-10-years-younger spousal exception applies and your IRA trustee or custodian does not use the Joint Life and Last Survivor Expectancy Table in calculating your RMD, you can do so yourself by calculating the RMD under Steps 1–3 below.

**Steps for figuring your required minimum distribution (RMD).** For each of your traditional IRAs, figure the required minimum distribution (RMD) you must receive using the following steps. Keep in mind that once you have separately determined the RMD for each IRA, the IRS allows you to withdraw the total RMD for the year from any of the accounts in any combination you choose.

**Step 1: Find the account balance of your IRA as of the previous December 31.** The account balance to be used for figuring a required minimum distribution (RMD) is the account balance as of the end of the year before the year for which you are figuring the RMD. Thus, if you reach age 70½ during 2019, the account balance to be used for figuring your first required minimum distribution (RMD), the RMD for 2019, is the account balance as of December 31, 2018. Use the year-end 2018 balance to figure your 2019 RMD even if this is your first RMD and you delay taking it until the first quarter of 2020 (January 1–April 1, 2020).

The year-end account balance must be adjusted if toward the end of the year there is an outstanding rollover. For example, if in December of 2018 you withdrew funds from your IRA and you rolled the funds back to the same IRA or a different one within 60 days *(8.10)* but not until early in 2019, the rollover amount must be included as part of the December 31, 2018 account balance of the receiving IRA, even though it was not actually in either account on that date.

**Step 2: Divide the account balance (Step 1) by the applicable life expectancy.** Your life expectancy under the IRS rules is taken from the Uniform Lifetime Table unless your sole beneficiary is your spouse who is more than 10 years younger than you are. The Uniform Lifetime Table *(Table 8-3)* provides a joint life expectancy for you and a "deemed" beneficiary who is exactly 10 years younger than you are. Your beneficiary's actual age does not matter. The life expectancy period from the uniform table applies even if you have not named a beneficiary as of your required beginning date (April 1 of the year after the year you reach age 70½). Furthermore, you continue to use the Uniform Lifetime Table even if you change your beneficiary or beneficiaries after starting to receive RMDs, unless the change results in the naming of your spouse as sole beneficiary for the entire year and you qualify to use the Joint Life and Last Survivor Expectancy Table *(Table 8-4)* because your spouse is more than 10 years younger than you are.

Your "deemed" life expectancy from the Uniform Lifetime Table is the number of years listed next to your age on your birthday in the year for which you are making the computation. For example, if you are figuring your RMD for 2019, and you are age 71 on your birthday in 2019, your life expectancy from the table, based on age 71, is 26.5 years. When you figure your RMD for 2020, you will use a life expectancy of 25.6 years, the life expectancy from the Uniform Lifetime Table for someone age 72.

**Exception for younger spouses.** If the sole beneficiary of your IRA is your spouse and he or she is more than 10 years younger than you are, do not use the Uniform Lifetime Table (*Table 8-3* below) to get your life expectancy for Step 2. Use the actual joint life expectancy of you and your spouse, which will allow you to spread out RMDs over an even longer period. See *Table 8-4*, which has a sample section of the Joint Life and Last Survivor Expectancy Table from IRS Publication 590-B.

This rule applies only if your spouse meets the age test and is the sole beneficiary of your entire interest in the IRA at all times during the calendar year for which the RMD is being figured. If your spouse is named beneficiary during the year or he or she is one of several beneficiaries on the account, the Uniform Lifetime Table must be used for that year. Your spouse would not meet the sole beneficiary test. However, if you are married on January 1 of a year and during the year you divorce or your spouse dies, you are considered married for the entire year and may use the spousal exception to figure that year's RMD using the joint life table *(Table 8-4)*.

If this exception for younger spouse beneficiaries applies, find your joint life expectancy from the IRS table corresponding to both of your ages on your birthdays for the year of the computation. For example, if you are age 71 on your birthday in 2019 and your spouse on his or her birthday in 2019 is age 58, use a joint life expectancy of 28.6 years (see *Table 8-4*) to figure your RMD for 2018. This is longer than the 26.5-year distribution period provided by the Uniform Lifetime Table *(Table 8-3)* for a 71-year-old, which means that your RMD will be somewhat lower.

**Step 3: If you have more than one traditional IRA, total the required minimum distributions (RMDs) for all the accounts.** After separately figuring the required minimum distribution (RMD) for each of your IRAs under Step 2, total the amounts. This is the minimum you must receive for the year; you are, of course, free to withdraw more than that. Although you must calculate the RMD separately for each account, you do not have to make withdrawals from each of them. The total RMD from all accounts may be taken from any one account, or more than one account if you prefer. For example, if you have five bank IRAs, you may take the entire RMD from the bank where you have the largest balance, or from any other combination of banks; *see* Example 3 below. The entire distribution is taxable unless part is allocable to nondeductible IRA contributions *(8.9)*.

---

### EXAMPLES

1. Joe Blake reaches age 70½ in March 2019. He has one traditional IRA. Joe's first required minimum distribution (RMD), the RMD for 2019, must be withdrawn from his traditional IRA during 2019 or in 2020 by April 1, 2020 (see "Deadline for receiving your first required minimum distribution (RMD)" above).

   As of December 31, 2018, Joe's IRA balance was $200,000. The 2018 year-end balance is used to compute the RMD for 2019 even if that RMD is not received until the first quarter of 2020 (by the April 1 deadline). Joe's beneficiary is his wife, who is age 63 on her birthday in 2019. On his birthday in September 2019, Joe is age 71. Here is how Joe figures his required minimum distribution (RMD) for 2019:

   Step 1. Account balance of $200,000 as of December 31, 2018.

   Step 2. Based on Joe's age of 71 (as of his birthday in 2019), the life expectancy from the Uniform Lifetime Table *(Table 8-3)* is 26.5 years. The table assumes that Joe has a beneficiary who is age 61 (10 years younger than he is). The fact that his wife is age 63 does not matter.

   Step 3. Divide Step 1 by Step 2: $200,000 ÷ 26.5 = $7,547. This is the RMD for 2019 that Joe may receive any time in 2019 or in early 2020, but no later than April 1, 2020.

   To figure his RMD for 2020, Joe will divide his 2019 year-end balance by 25.6 years, the life expectancy from the Uniform Lifetime Table (for someone age 72 (his age on his birthday in 2020); that RMD must be received by December 31, 2020.

2. Same facts as Example 1, except that Joe's wife is age 56 on her birthday in 2019. Because Joe's wife is more than 10 years younger than Joe, he uses the joint life and last survivor expectancy table. Based on their ages of 71 and 56 (on their birthdays in 2019), the joint life expectancy from the table (see *Table 8-4*) is 30.1 years. Joe's RMD for 2019 is $6,645 ($200,000 ÷ 30.1).

3. Cynthia Lowell has two traditional IRAs. She reaches age 70½ on January 15, 2019 and thus must receive her first RMD, the RMD for 2019, either in 2019 or in 2020 by April 1, 2020. The beneficiary of IRA-1 is Cynthia's brother, who is age 61 on his birthday in 2019; the account balance of IRA-1 as of December 31, 2018 is $100,000. The beneficiary of IRA-2 is her husband, who is age 74 on his birthday in 2019; the account balance of IRA-2 at the end of 2018 is $50,000.

   To figure her RMD for 2019, Cynthia uses the IRS' Uniform Lifetime Table *(Table 8-3)*. The ages of her beneficiaries do not affect the computation.

   IRA-1: The RMD is $3,774. This is the account balance of $100,000 divided by 26.5, the life expectancy from the Uniform Lifetime Table for a person age 71 (Cynthia's age on her birthday in 2019).

   IRA-2: The RMD is 1,887, the account balance of $50,000 divided by 26.5, the life expectancy from the Uniform Lifetime Table, using age 71.

   Cynthia's total RMD for 2019 from both IRAs is $5,661, which may be withdrawn from either one or both of the IRAs.

## Table 8-3   Uniform Lifetime Table*

| IRA Owner's Age | Distribution Period | IRA Owner's Age | Distribution Period | IRA Owner's Age | Distribution Period |
|---|---|---|---|---|---|
| 70 | 27.4 | 85 | 14.8 | 100 | 6.3 |
| 71 | 26.5 | 86 | 14.1 | 101 | 5.9 |
| 72 | 25.6 | 87 | 13.4 | 102 | 5.5 |
| 73 | 24.7 | 88 | 12.7 | 103 | 5.2 |
| 74 | 23.8 | 89 | 12.0 | 104 | 4.9 |
| 75 | 22.9 | 90 | 11.4 | 105 | 4.5 |
| 76 | 22.0 | 91 | 10.8 | 106 | 4.2 |
| 77 | 21.2 | 92 | 10.2 | 107 | 3.9 |
| 78 | 20.3 | 93 | 9.6 | 108 | 3.7 |
| 79 | 19.5 | 94 | 9.1 | 109 | 3.4 |
| 80 | 18.7 | 95 | 8.6 | 110 | 3.1 |
| 81 | 17.9 | 96 | 8.1 | 111 | 2.9 |
| 82 | 17.1 | 97 | 7.6 | 112 | 2.6 |
| 83 | 16.3 | 98 | 7.1 | 113 | 2.4 |
| 84 | 15.5 | 99 | 6.7 | 114 | 2.1 |
| | | | | 115 and over | 1.9 |

*Use this table unless your spouse is your sole IRA beneficiary and he or she is more than 10 years younger than you are. If the exception for younger spouse beneficiaries applies, use the IRS' joint life and last survivor expectancy table with the actual ages of both spouses; *see Table 8-4*, which will provide a longer life expectancy distribution period than the above table provides).

## 8.14   Inherited Traditional IRAs

Although inheritances are generally tax free *(11.4)*, distributions that you receive as a beneficiary of a traditional IRA are taxable. However, if the account owner made nondeductible contributions to the account, distributions allocable to those contributions on Form 8606 are tax free under the rules at *8.9*. Taxable distributions that you receive as a beneficiary before you reach age 59½ are not subject to the 10% penalty for early distributions *(8.12)*.

*Surviving spouses.* A surviving spouse who is the sole beneficiary of a deceased spouse's IRA may elect to treat the account as his or her own IRA by designating himself or herself as the account owner. By becoming the IRA owner, the surviving spouse determines his or her required minimum distributions (RMDs) under the regular owner rules *(8.13)*, rather than under the beneficiary rules discussed in this section. A surviving spouse (whether or not the sole beneficiary) who does not become owner of the deceased spouse's IRA and who receives a distribution from the IRA may roll it over within 60 days to his or her own IRA *(8.10)*. These rules for surviving spouse beneficiaries are discussed further at the end of this section *(8.14)*.

## Table 8-4  Joint Life and Last Survivor Expectancy Table
### (for use by owners whose spouses are more than 10 years younger)*

| Spouse \ Self | 70 | 71 | 72 | 73 | 74 | 75 | 76 | 77 | 78 | 79 | 80 | 81 | 82 | 83 | 84 | 85 | 86 | 87 | 88 | 89 | 90 |
|---|---|---|---|---|---|---|---|---|---|---|---|---|---|---|---|---|---|---|---|---|---|
| 35 | 48.7 | 48.7 | 48.7 | 48.6 | 48.6 | 48.6 | 48.6 | 48.6 | 48.6 | 48.6 | 48.5 | 48.5 | 48.5 | 48.5 | 48.5 | 48.5 | 48.5 | 48.5 | 48.5 | 48.5 | 48.5 |
| 36 | 47.8 | 47.7 | 47.7 | 47.7 | 47.7 | 47.7 | 47.6 | 47.6 | 47.6 | 47.6 | 47.6 | 47.6 | 47.6 | 47.6 | 47.6 | 47.5 | 47.5 | 47.5 | 47.5 | 47.5 | 47.5 |
| 37 | 46.8 | 46.8 | 46.8 | 46.7 | 46.7 | 46.7 | 46.7 | 46.7 | 46.6 | 46.6 | 46.6 | 46.6 | 46.6 | 46.6 | 46.6 | 46.6 | 46.6 | 46.6 | 46.6 | 46.6 | 46.6 |
| 38 | 45.9 | 45.9 | 45.8 | 45.8 | 45.8 | 45.7 | 45.7 | 45.7 | 45.7 | 45.7 | 45.7 | 45.7 | 45.6 | 45.6 | 45.6 | 45.6 | 45.6 | 45.6 | 45.6 | 45.6 | 45.6 |
| 39 | 44.9 | 44.9 | 44.9 | 44.8 | 44.8 | 44.8 | 44.8 | 44.8 | 44.7 | 44.7 | 44.7 | 44.7 | 44.7 | 44.7 | 44.7 | 44.6 | 44.6 | 44.6 | 44.6 | 44.6 | 44.6 |
| 40 | 44.0 | 44.0 | 43.9 | 43.9 | 43.9 | 43.8 | 43.8 | 43.8 | 43.8 | 43.8 | 43.7 | 43.7 | 43.7 | 43.7 | 43.7 | 43.7 | 43.7 | 43.7 | 43.7 | 43.7 | 43.7 |
| 41 | 43.1 | 43.0 | 43.0 | 43.0 | 42.9 | 42.9 | 42.9 | 42.9 | 42.8 | 42.8 | 42.8 | 42.8 | 42.8 | 42.8 | 42.7 | 42.7 | 42.7 | 42.7 | 42.7 | 42.7 | 42.7 |
| 42 | 42.2 | 42.1 | 42.1 | 42.0 | 42.0 | 42.0 | 41.9 | 41.9 | 41.9 | 41.9 | 41.8 | 41.8 | 41.8 | 41.8 | 41.8 | 41.8 | 41.8 | 41.8 | 41.8 | 41.7 | 41.7 |
| 43 | 41.3 | 41.2 | 41.1 | 41.1 | 41.1 | 41.0 | 41.0 | 41.0 | 40.9 | 40.9 | 40.9 | 40.9 | 40.9 | 40.9 | 40.8 | 40.8 | 40.8 | 40.8 | 40.8 | 40.8 | 40.8 |
| 44 | 40.3 | 40.3 | 40.2 | 40.2 | 40.1 | 40.1 | 40.1 | 40.0 | 40.0 | 40.0 | 40.0 | 39.9 | 39.9 | 39.9 | 39.9 | 39.9 | 39.9 | 39.9 | 39.9 | 39.8 | 39.8 |
| 45 | 39.4 | 39.4 | 39.3 | 39.3 | 39.2 | 39.2 | 39.1 | 39.1 | 39.1 | 39.1 | 39.0 | 39.0 | 39.0 | 39.0 | 39.0 | 38.9 | 38.9 | 38.9 | 38.9 | 38.9 | 38.9 |
| 46 | 38.6 | 38.5 | 38.4 | 38.4 | 38.3 | 38.3 | 38.2 | 38.2 | 38.2 | 38.1 | 38.1 | 38.1 | 38.1 | 38.0 | 38.0 | 38.0 | 38.0 | 38.0 | 38.0 | 38.0 | 38.0 |
| 47 | 37.7 | 37.6 | 37.5 | 37.5 | 37.4 | 37.4 | 37.3 | 37.3 | 37.2 | 37.2 | 37.2 | 37.2 | 37.1 | 37.1 | 37.1 | 37.1 | 37.1 | 37.0 | 37.0 | 37.0 | 37.0 |
| 48 | 36.8 | 36.7 | 36.6 | 36.6 | 36.5 | 36.5 | 36.4 | 36.4 | 36.3 | 36.3 | 36.3 | 36.2 | 36.2 | 36.2 | 36.2 | 36.2 | 36.1 | 36.1 | 36.1 | 36.1 | 36.1 |
| 49 | 35.9 | 35.9 | 35.8 | 35.7 | 35.6 | 35.6 | 35.5 | 35.5 | 35.4 | 35.4 | 35.4 | 35.3 | 35.3 | 35.3 | 35.3 | 35.2 | 35.2 | 35.2 | 35.2 | 35.2 | 35.2 |
| 50 | 35.1 | 35.0 | 34.9 | 34.8 | 34.8 | 34.7 | 34.6 | 34.6 | 34.5 | 34.5 | 34.5 | 34.4 | 34.4 | 34.4 | 34.3 | 34.3 | 34.3 | 34.3 | 34.3 | 34.3 | 34.2 |
| 51 | 34.3 | 34.2 | 34.1 | 34.0 | 33.9 | 33.8 | 33.8 | 33.7 | 33.6 | 33.6 | 33.6 | 33.5 | 33.5 | 33.5 | 33.4 | 33.4 | 33.4 | 33.4 | 33.4 | 33.3 | 33.3 |
| 52 | 33.4 | 33.3 | 33.2 | 33.1 | 33.0 | 33.0 | 32.9 | 32.8 | 32.8 | 32.7 | 32.7 | 32.6 | 32.6 | 32.6 | 32.5 | 32.5 | 32.5 | 32.5 | 32.5 | 32.4 | 32.4 |
| 53 | 32.6 | 32.5 | 32.4 | 32.3 | 32.2 | 32.1 | 32.0 | 32.0 | 31.9 | 31.8 | 31.8 | 31.8 | 31.7 | 31.7 | 31.7 | 31.6 | 31.6 | 31.6 | 31.6 | 31.5 | 31.5 |
| 54 | 31.8 | 31.7 | 31.6 | 31.5 | 31.4 | 31.3 | 31.2 | 31.1 | 31.0 | 31.0 | 30.9 | 30.9 | 30.8 | 30.8 | 30.8 | 30.7 | 30.7 | 30.7 | 30.7 | 30.7 | 30.6 |
| 55 | 31.1 | 30.9 | 30.8 | 30.6 | 30.5 | 30.4 | 30.3 | 30.3 | 30.2 | 30.1 | 30.1 | 30.0 | 30.0 | 29.9 | 29.9 | 29.9 | 29.8 | 29.8 | 29.8 | 29.8 | 29.8 |
| 56 | 30.3 | 30.1 | 30.0 | 29.8 | 29.7 | 29.6 | 29.5 | 29.4 | 29.3 | 29.3 | 29.2 | 29.2 | 29.1 | 29.1 | 29.0 | 29.0 | 29.0 | 28.9 | 28.9 | 28.9 | 28.9 |
| 57 | 29.5 | 29.4 | 29.2 | 29.1 | 28.9 | 28.8 | 28.7 | 28.6 | 28.5 | 28.4 | 28.4 | 28.3 | 28.3 | 28.2 | 28.2 | 28.1 | 28.1 | 28.1 | 28.0 | 28.0 | 28.0 |
| 58 | 28.8 | 28.6 | 28.4 | 28.3 | 28.1 | 28.0 | 27.9 | 27.8 | 27.7 | 27.6 | 27.5 | 27.5 | 27.4 | 27.4 | 27.3 | 27.3 | 27.2 | 27.2 | 27.2 | 27.2 | 27.1 |
| 59 | 28.1 | 27.9 | 27.7 | 27.5 | 27.4 | 27.2 | 27.1 | 27.0 | 26.9 | 26.8 | 26.7 | 26.6 | 26.6 | 26.5 | 26.5 | 26.4 | 26.4 | 26.4 | 26.3 | 26.3 | 26.3 |
| 60 |  | 27.2 | 27.0 | 26.8 | 26.6 | 26.5 | 26.3 | 26.2 | 26.1 | 26.0 | 25.9 | 25.8 | 25.8 | 25.7 | 25.6 | 25.6 | 25.5 | 25.5 | 25.5 | 25.4 | 25.4 |
| 61 |  |  | 26.3 | 26.1 | 25.9 | 25.7 | 25.6 | 25.4 | 25.3 | 25.2 | 25.1 | 25.0 | 24.9 | 24.9 | 24.8 | 24.8 | 24.7 | 24.7 | 24.6 | 24.6 | 24.6 |
| 62 |  |  |  | 25.4 | 25.2 | 25.0 | 24.8 | 24.7 | 24.6 | 24.4 | 24.3 | 24.2 | 24.1 | 24.1 | 24.0 | 23.9 | 23.9 | 23.8 | 23.8 | 23.8 | 23.7 |
| 63 |  |  |  |  | 24.5 | 24.3 | 24.1 | 23.9 | 23.8 | 23.7 | 23.6 | 23.4 | 23.4 | 23.3 | 23.2 | 23.1 | 23.1 | 23.0 | 23.0 | 22.9 | 22.9 |
| 64 |  |  |  |  |  | 23.6 | 23.4 | 23.2 | 23.1 | 22.9 | 22.8 | 22.7 | 22.6 | 22.5 | 22.4 | 22.3 | 22.3 | 22.2 | 22.2 | 22.1 | 22.1 |
| 65 |  |  |  |  |  |  | 22.7 | 22.5 | 22.4 | 22.2 | 22.1 | 21.9 | 21.8 | 21.7 | 21.6 | 21.6 | 21.5 | 21.4 | 21.4 | 21.3 | 21.3 |
| 66 |  |  |  |  |  |  |  | 21.8 | 21.7 | 21.5 | 21.3 | 21.2 | 21.1 | 21.0 | 20.9 | 20.8 | 20.7 | 20.7 | 20.6 | 20.5 | 20.5 |
| 67 |  |  |  |  |  |  |  |  | 21.0 | 20.8 | 20.6 | 20.5 | 20.4 | 20.2 | 20.1 | 20.1 | 20.0 | 19.9 | 19.8 | 19.8 | 19.7 |
| 68 |  |  |  |  |  |  |  |  |  | 20.1 | 20.0 | 19.8 | 19.7 | 19.5 | 19.4 | 19.3 | 19.2 | 19.2 | 19.1 | 19.0 | 19.0 |
| 69 |  |  |  |  |  |  |  |  |  |  | 19.3 | 19.1 | 19.0 | 18.8 | 18.7 | 18.6 | 18.5 | 18.4 | 18.3 | 18.3 | 18.2 |
| 70 |  |  |  |  |  |  |  |  |  |  |  | 18.5 | 18.3 | 18.2 | 18.0 | 17.9 | 17.8 | 17.7 | 17.6 | 17.6 | 17.5 |
| 71 |  |  |  |  |  |  |  |  |  |  |  |  | 17.7 | 17.5 | 17.4 | 17.3 | 17.1 | 17.0 | 16.9 | 16.9 | 16.8 |
| 72 |  |  |  |  |  |  |  |  |  |  |  |  |  | 16.9 | 16.7 | 16.6 | 16.5 | 16.4 | 16.3 | 16.2 | 16.1 |
| 73 |  |  |  |  |  |  |  |  |  |  |  |  |  |  | 16.1 | 16.0 | 15.8 | 15.7 | 15.6 | 15.5 | 15.4 |
| 74 |  |  |  |  |  |  |  |  |  |  |  |  |  |  |  | 15.4 | 15.2 | 15.1 | 15.0 | 14.9 | 14.8 |
| 75 |  |  |  |  |  |  |  |  |  |  |  |  |  |  |  |  | 14.6 | 14.5 | 14.4 | 14.3 | 14.2 |
| 76 |  |  |  |  |  |  |  |  |  |  |  |  |  |  |  |  |  | 13.9 | 13.8 | 13.7 | 13.6 |
| 77 |  |  |  |  |  |  |  |  |  |  |  |  |  |  |  |  |  |  | 13.2 | 13.1 | 13.0 |
| 78 |  |  |  |  |  |  |  |  |  |  |  |  |  |  |  |  |  |  |  | 12.6 | 12.4 |
| 79 |  |  |  |  |  |  |  |  |  |  |  |  |  |  |  |  |  |  |  |  | 11.9 |

\* This is a sample of the Joint Life and Last Survivor Expectancy Table shown in IRS Publication 590-B. Use this table to figure your required minimum distribution only if your spouse is your sole beneficiary and he or she is more than 10 years younger than you are; see "Exception for younger spouses" in 8.13. Find your age (as of your birthday for the year you are making the computation) on the horizontal line and your spousal beneficiary's age in the vertical column. For example, if you are age 74 and your spousal beneficiary is 63, the life expectancy factor is 24.5 years. If your age or your spouse's age is not shown here, refer to IRS Publication 590-B.

*Caution*

**Nonspouse Beneficiaries Cannot Make a Rollover**

If you inherit a traditional IRA from someone other than your spouse, and receive a distribution from the account, you are not allowed to roll it over within 60 days. Once a distribution is paid to you, tax on it cannot be avoided. If you want to change investments without incurring tax, you can use a trustee-to-trustee transfer to send all or some of the funds in the inherited IRA to another investment firm. A trustee-to-trustee transfer is not treated as a taxable distribution and is not a prohibited rollover because you do not take possession of the funds *(8.10)*. Make sure that the transferred funds remain in the name of the deceased account owner; *see 8.14.*

*Nonspouse beneficiaries.* A nonspouse beneficiary may not elect to be treated as the owner or make a rollover. However, the IRS allows a nonspouse beneficiary to make a trustee-to-trustee transfer of the IRA to another financial institution as long as the IRA into which the funds are moved is set up and maintained in the name of the deceased IRA owner for the benefit of the nonspouse beneficiary. Whether or not the account is transferred, a nonspouse beneficiary must receive required minimum distributions (RMDs) under the beneficiary rules below. The financial institution holding the account will change the Social Security number on the account from the deceased owner's number to the number of the beneficiary for purposes of tracking RMDs. However, a nonspouse beneficiary must make sure that the deceased owner's name remains on the account. Putting the account in the nonspouse beneficiary's name would be treated by the IRS as a prohibited rollover, resulting in a taxable distribution, as if the beneficiary had received a total distribution of his or her share of the IRA. For example, if Jane Smith dies on March 4, 2018, and her brother John is her IRA beneficiary, the account should be retitled to indicate that Jane has died and that the IRA is now being held for the benefit of (FBO) John as beneficiary, with wording such as this: "Jane Smith, deceased March 4, 2018 , IRA FBO John Smith, Beneficiary."

> ### EXAMPLE
>
> Todd Johnson died in 2018 at age 73 after receiving the 2018 required minimum distribution (RMD) from his traditional IRA. Todd's IRA beneficiary is Fred, his son. Fred must begin receiving RMDs from his father's IRA starting in 2019, the year after the year of Todd's death. Fred will use his life expectancy as of 2019 and the account balance as of the end of 2018 (the year of Todd's death) to figure his first RMD, the RMD for 2019. On his birthday in 2019, Fred is age 47. As shown in *Table 8-5*, the life expectancy for a 47-year-old is 37 years. Using the rules discussed below for owner deaths after the required beginning date, Fred figures his RMD for 2019 by dividing the account balance at the end of 2018 by his 37-year life expectancy. If the 2018 year-end account balance was $100,000, Fred's RMD for 2019 is $2,703 ($100,000 ÷ 37), which he must receive by December 31, 2019. Of course, Fred may withdraw more than $2,703 in 2019; this is simply the minimum he must receive to avoid a penalty under the RMD rules. Fred's withdrawal, whether it is the RMD or more, will be taxable as ordinary income.
>
> Fred will figure his second RMD, the RMD for 2020, by dividing the account balance at the end of 2019 by his remaining life expectancy. Fred's remaining life expectancy in 2020 is 36 years, one year less than the initial 37-year life expectancy determined in 2019 (when he was 47 as explained in the preceding paragraph). Thus, Fred will divide his 2019 year-end balance by 36 years (37 − 1) to figure his RMD for 2020. If the account balance at the end of 2019 is $105,000, Fred's RMD for 2020 will be $2,917 ($105,000 ÷ 36). Fred must receive the $2,917 RMD by December 31, 2020.
>
> To figure his RMD for each subsequent year, Fred will continue to decrease his life expectancy by one year, so that for the 2021 RMD, his life expectancy will be 35 years, for the 2022 RMD it will be 34 years, and so on. For each year for which an RMD is being figured, Fred will divide his remaining life expectancy into the account balance as of the end of the prior year.

**Beneficiaries must receive required minimum distributions (RMDs) annually.** Beneficiaries of a traditional IRA must receive a required minimum distribution (RMD) from the inherited account for each year after the year of the IRA owner's death. This includes a surviving spouse who elects to receive distributions from an inherited traditional IRA as a beneficiary rather than treating the IRA as her or his own.

If you are the "designated beneficiary" as determined under the final IRS regulations discussed below, RMDs may be spread over your life expectancy (see *Table 8-5*). You must receive the first RMD by the end of the year following the year of the IRA owner's death. The RMD for each subsequent year must be received by December 31 of that year. If the RMD for a year is not received, you are subject to a penalty tax of 50% on the difference between the required minimum amount and the amount actually received, unless the IRS waives the penalty. Of course, you are not limited to the RMD. You may withdraw more than the annual RMD amount or even withdraw your entire interest in the account should you want the funds. Keep in mind that whatever you receive will be taxable except to the extent that it is allocable to nondeductible contributions made by the deceased account owner.

## Who Is the Designated Beneficiary?

The maximum life expectancy period over which required minimum distributions (RMDs) may be extended generally depends on the identity of the "designated beneficiary" as of September 30 of the year following the year of the owner's death. Any individual who is a beneficiary as of the date of the owner's death can be a "designated" beneficiary, whether he or she is selected as beneficiary by the IRA owner or is selected under the terms of the plan, but for purposes of determining the maximum period over which RMDs can be paid, there can be only one "designated beneficiary" for each inherited traditional IRA. Where multiple individuals are co-beneficiaries, the oldest beneficiary is treated as the designated beneficiary unless the IRA is split into separate accounts; *see* the rules for multiple beneficiaries below.

Under the final IRS regulations, the determination of the designated beneficiary is not made until September 30 of the year following the year of the IRA owner's death. However, despite the September 30 rule, an exception allows multiple individual beneficiaries to separate their accounts and use their individual life expectancies to figure their RMDs, provided the separate accounts are established by December 31 of the year following the year of the owner's death; *see* the discussion of the separate account rule below.

A beneficiary named through an estate, either under the owner's will or by state law, cannot be a designated beneficiary for RMD purposes. An estate or a charity cannot be a designated beneficiary. Trust beneficiaries may qualify if certain tests are met, as discussed below.

The delay in determining the designated beneficiary does not mean that new beneficiaries can be added after the owner's death. However, after the account owner's death and prior to the September 30 determination date, a beneficiary named as of the date of death can be eliminated by means of the beneficiary's qualified disclaimer or distribution of the beneficiary's benefit. A beneficiary's interest can be cashed out by the September 30 determination date, leaving the balance to other co-beneficiaries named by the owner. For example, if a charity and an individual are named as co-beneficiaries, and the charity's interest is cashed out by the September 30 determination date, the remaining beneficiary can use his or her life expectancy to figure RMDs.

**Qualified disclaimer.** A qualified written disclaimer made no later than nine months after the IRA owner's death can be used by an older primary beneficiary to pass all or part of an IRA to a younger contingent beneficiary. The disclaimer, made by the September 30 determination date, leaves the younger beneficiary as the designated beneficiary, thereby allowing required minimum distributions to be spread out over his or her longer life expectancy. Of course, a younger primary beneficiary may also disclaim in favor of an older contingent beneficiary. An estate may not disclaim its interest in order to create a designated beneficiary.

One of the requirements for a qualified disclaimer is that the person making the disclaimer must not have accepted the property prior to the disclaimer. The IRS in Revenue Ruling 2005-36 held that this rule does not prevent a beneficiary from making a disclaimer after taking the RMD for the year of the death (where the owner dies before receiving it). The act of taking the RMD is treated as an acceptance of that portion of the property, plus the income attributable to the distribution. However, after receiving the RMD, the beneficiary may make a qualified disclaimer (by the nine-month deadline) of all or part of the balance of the account, except for the income allocable to the RMD. The disclaimed amount and the income allocable to the disclaimed amount must either be paid outright to the successor beneficiary entitled to receive it following the disclaimer or be segregated in a separate IRA for the benefit of that beneficiary. See Revenue Ruling 2005-36 for further details.

*Caution*

**Estate as Beneficiary**

If you name your estate as beneficiary of your IRA and you die before your required beginning date, the entire account must be withdrawn by the estate beneficiary (or beneficiaries who inherit through the estate) by the end of the fifth year following the year of your death. If you die on or after the required beginning date, the account can be distributed over the balance of your single life expectancy, determined by your age in the year of death. *See Table 8-5*, "Beneficiary's Single Life Expectancy Table."

*Caution*

**Inherited IRAs Not Exempt in Bankruptcy**

The Supreme Court unanimously held that funds held in an inherited IRA are not "retirement funds", and thus are not exempt from creditors under the federal bankruptcy law. Although contributory IRAs (traditional and Roth) are exempt from creditors up to a limit, and IRAs set up by rollovers from 401(k) plans are fully exempt, similar bankruptcy protection does not apply to inherited IRAs. Although the beneficiary seeking the bankruptcy exemption might invest the funds and preserve the account for his or her own future retirement, the beneficiary did not set aside the funds for retirement. In support of its conclusion that inherited IRAs are not "retirement" funds", the Court pointed out that the beneficiary may not add contributions to the inherited account, required minimum distributions must be taken based on life expectancy without regard to retirement, and withdrawals can be taken at any time for any purpose without penalty, as there is no pre-age 59½ penalty for beneficiaries (Clark, U.S. Supreme Court, 6/12/14).

## Table 8-5 Beneficiary's Single Life Expectancy Table

| Age | Life expectancy | Age | Life expectancy |
|---|---|---|---|
| 0 | 82.4 | 56 | 28.7 |
| 1 | 81.6 | 57 | 27.9 |
| 2 | 80.6 | 58 | 27.0 |
| 3 | 79.7 | 59 | 26.1 |
| 4 | 78.7 | 60 | 25.2 |
| 5 | 77.7 | 61 | 24.4 |
| 6 | 76.7 | 62 | 23.5 |
| 7 | 75.8 | 63 | 22.7 |
| 8 | 74.8 | 64 | 21.8 |
| 9 | 73.8 | 65 | 21.0 |
| 10 | 72.8 | 66 | 20.2 |
| 11 | 71.8 | 67 | 19.4 |
| 12 | 70.8 | 68 | 18.6 |
| 13 | 69.9 | 69 | 17.8 |
| 14 | 68.9 | 70 | 17.0 |
| 15 | 67.9 | 71 | 16.3 |
| 16 | 66.9 | 72 | 15.5 |
| 17 | 66.0 | 73 | 14.8 |
| 18 | 65.0 | 74 | 14.1 |
| 19 | 64.0 | 75 | 13.4 |
| 20 | 63.0 | 76 | 12.7 |
| 21 | 62.1 | 77 | 12.1 |
| 22 | 61.1 | 78 | 11.4 |
| 23 | 60.1 | 79 | 10.8 |
| 24 | 59.1 | 80 | 10.2 |
| 25 | 58.2 | 81 | 9.7 |
| 26 | 57.2 | 82 | 9.1 |
| 27 | 56.2 | 83 | 8.6 |
| 28 | 55.3 | 84 | 8.1 |
| 29 | 54.3 | 85 | 7.6 |
| 30 | 53.3 | 86 | 7.1 |
| 31 | 52.4 | 87 | 6.7 |
| 32 | 51.4 | 88 | 6.3 |
| 33 | 50.4 | 89 | 5.9 |
| 34 | 49.4 | 90 | 5.5 |
| 35 | 48.5 | 91 | 5.2 |
| 36 | 47.5 | 92 | 4.9 |
| 37 | 46.5 | 93 | 4.6 |
| 38 | 45.6 | 94 | 4.3 |
| 39 | 44.6 | 95 | 4.1 |
| 40 | 43.6 | 96 | 3.8 |
| 41 | 42.7 | 97 | 3.6 |
| 42 | 41.7 | 98 | 3.4 |
| 43 | 40.7 | 99 | 3.1 |
| 44 | 39.8 | 100 | 2.9 |
| 45 | 38.8 | 101 | 2.7 |
| 46 | 37.9 | 102 | 2.5 |
| 47 | 37.0 | 103 | 2.3 |
| 48 | 36.0 | 104 | 2.1 |
| 49 | 35.1 | 105 | 1.9 |
| 50 | 34.2 | 106 | 1.7 |
| 51 | 33.3 | 107 | 1.5 |
| 52 | 32.3 | 108 | 1.4 |
| 53 | 31.4 | 109 | 1.2 |
| 54 | 30.5 | 110 | 1.1 |
| 55 | 29.6 | 111+ | 1.0 |

**Multiple individual beneficiaries can split IRA into separate accounts.** If a traditional IRA has several beneficiaries as of the September 30 determination date, all of whom are individuals, the general rule under the regulations is that the oldest beneficiary is considered to be the designated beneficiary, and that person's life expectancy, which will be shorter than that of the other beneficiaries, is the period over which all the beneficiaries must receive required minimum distributions (RMDs). This result can be avoided by splitting the IRA into separate IRAs, one for each beneficiary, with each beneficiary getting his or her separate share of the account, as listed in the IRA document. Each beneficiary can then spread distributions over his or her individual life expectancy. Keep in mind that non-spouse beneficiaries may not do a rollover (as discussed at the beginning of *8.14*), so nonspouse beneficiaries must use trustee-to-trustee transfers to set up the separate accounts, rather than withdrawing funds and redepositing them into separate accounts, which would be a prohibited rollover, resulting in a taxable distribution of the beneficiary's entire share of the IRA.

If the IRA account owner did not split the account into separate IRAs, the regulations allow the beneficiaries to do so by December 31 of the year after the year of the owner's death. If the account is split in the year following the year of the owner's death by the December 31 date, each beneficiary may compute RMDs (for the year following the year of the owner's death and also for later years) using his or her own life expectancy, which, depending on a particular beneficiary's age, could be much more advantageous than having to use the life expectancy of the oldest beneficiary. For example, if the IRA owner dies in 2019 and the beneficiaries split the account into separate accounts by December 31, 2020 (the year after the year of the owner's death), then each beneficiary would compute his or her RMD for 2020 by following the regular rules for beneficiaries, as shown above in the Todd and Fred Johnson example. That is, each beneficiary would figure his or her RMD for 2020 (their first RMD) by finding their life expectancy, based on his/her age in 2020, in *Table 8-5* (Single Life Expectancy Table), and dividing that life expectancy into his or her share of the account balance as of the end of 2019 (the year of the owner's death). For each subsequent year that initial life expectancy is reduced by one year, and the reduced life expectancy is divided into the account balance as of the end of the preceding year to figure that year's RMD.

Although the regulations allow the beneficiaries to use their individual life expectancies if the IRA is split by December 31 of the year after the year of the owner's death, it is advisable for the beneficiaries to split the account into separate accounts by the September 30 determination date or soon afterwards, and not to wait until the last minute, in order to avoid the possibility that a problem may arise that could prevent the splitting of the account by the December 31 deadline.

**Estate or charity is named beneficiary or there is individual and non-individual beneficiary for same account.** If as of the September 30 determination date there is a non-individual beneficiary other than a qualifying trust, or there is a non-individual beneficiary as well as one or more individual beneficiaries, the owner is treated as not having a designated beneficiary. If the owner's death was on or after his or her required beginning date (April 1 of the year after the year age 70½ is reached), the regulations require RMDs to be made over the owner's remaining life expectancy. Use the owner's life expectancy as of his or her birthday in the year of death and reduce it by one year for each subsequent year. For example, assume an 80-year-old IRA owner received his RMD for 2018 in mid-2018 and then died later in the year, leaving the IRA to his estate. The owner's life expectancy in 2018 was 10.2 years (*Table 8-5* life expectancy for 80-year old), and that would be reduced by one, to 9.2 years, to figure the RMD for 2019 that the estate must receive. If the account balance at the end of 2018 was $200,000, the RMD for 2019 would be $21,739 ($200,000 ÷ 9.2).

The 5-year rule applies if the owner died before the required beginning date (April 1 of the year after the year age 70½ is reached) without a designated beneficiary. Under the 5-year rule, the entire account must be distributed by the end of the fifth year following the year of death. No distribution has to be received before that fifth year. For example, if a 68-year old IRA owner dies in 2018, leaving his IRA to his estate, the entire account must be distributed by the end of 2023.

If a charity or the IRA owner's estate is a co-beneficiary of the IRA along with one or more individuals, there is an advantage to the individual beneficiaries of having the interest of the charity or estate paid out in full before September 30 of the year after the year of the IRA owner's death. This would leave only the individual beneficiary or beneficiaries as of the September 30 determination date. A single individual beneficiary could then use his or her own life expectancy to figure RMDs. Multiple individual co-beneficiaries have until the end of that year (December 31 of the year after the year of the owner's death) to split the inherited IRA into separate accounts, thereby allowing them to base RMDs on their own life expectancies.

**Trust as beneficiary.** If a trust is named the beneficiary of the account, the trust beneficiaries may be treated as designated beneficiaries if certain tests are met. The trust must be valid under state law and be irrevocable or become irrevocable upon the account owner's death. The beneficiaries who are entitled to receive the trust's interest in the inherited IRA must be identifiable from the trust instrument. Documentation of the trust beneficiaries must be provided to the IRA trustee or plan administrator. The deadline under the regulations for providing the documentation is October 31 of the year following the year of the owner's death. However, even if the required conditions are met, the regulations do not allow separate accounts to be created for the trust beneficiaries. All of the trust beneficiaries must receive RMDs over the life expectancy of the oldest beneficiary.

If the required conditions are not met, then the owner is treated as not having a designated beneficiary and the rules discussed above for an estate or charity apply. That is, the IRA must be paid out either: (1) under the five-year rule if the IRA owner died before the required beginning date, or (2) over the remaining life expectancy of the deceased owner if death was on or after the required beginning date.

If a trust is a co-beneficiary of an IRA along with one or more individuals, and the interest of the trust is distributed before the September 30 determination date, the individual beneficiaries may be able to use their own life expectancies in figuring RMDs, as discussed above where a charity or the owner's estate is a co-beneficiary.

**Beneficiary's death before September 30 determination date.** If an individual named as a beneficiary by the account owner dies after the owner but before the September 30 date for determining the designated beneficiary, that individual continues to be treated as a designated beneficiary under the final regulations. This means that the remaining life expectancy of the deceased beneficiary must be used by his or her successor beneficiary, whether that successor was named by the original beneficiary or under the terms of the original beneficiary's estate.

Did IRA Owner Die Before His/Her Required Beginning Date or On or After the Required Beginning Date?

The distribution period for beneficiaries may depend on whether the IRA owner died before his or her required beginning date, or on or after the required beginning date, which is April 1 of the year that the owner reached or would have reached age 70½ *(8.13)*.

**Owner's death on or after required beginning date.** If an owner dies on or after the required beginning date (April 1 of the year after the year the owner reaches age 70½), and there is a designated beneficiary, required minimum distributions (RMDs) are generally payable over the beneficiary's life expectancy. However, if on the date of the owner's death the designated beneficiary is older than the owner, the final regulations allow the beneficiary to receive RMDs over the owner's remaining life expectancy rather than over the beneficiary's shorter life expectancy. If there is no "designated" beneficiary, as when the owner's estate is named as the beneficiary, RMDs are based upon the deceased owner's remaining life expectancy.

If the owner did not receive his or her RMD for the year of death, the beneficiary must receive that amount in the year of death or as soon as possible in the next year. The beneficiary must receive the RMD that the owner was required to receive for the year of death (under the owner RMD rules, 8.13); the owner's age as of his or her birthday in the year of death is used to figure the RMD even if the owner died earlier in the year.

The first RMD to a designated beneficiary must be received by the beneficiary in the year following the year of the owner's death. The RMD is figured by dividing the year-end account balance for the year of death by the designated beneficiary's life expectancy in the year following the year of death, taken from the Beneficiary's Single Life Expectancy Table *(Table 8-5)*. To figure the RMDs for later years, a nonspouse designated beneficiary reduces his or her initial life expectancy by one for each succeeding year, and that reduced life expectancy is divided into the account balance as of the end of the prior year. The Example at the beginning of *8.14* (Todd and Fred Johnson) illustrates how a nonspouse beneficiary's RMD computations are made. If the sole designated beneficiary is the surviving spouse of the deceased owner, the surviving spouse recalculates life expectancy each year based on his or her attained age; see "surviving spouse as sole beneficiary" below.

Successor beneficiaries. If the designated beneficiary dies before receiving the balance of the inherited IRA, the successor beneficiary may not start a new RMD schedule based upon his or her own life expectancy. The successor must use the remaining life expectancy of the designated beneficiary. For example, assume a 47-year-old designated beneficiary figures his first RMD (for the year after the year of the IRA owner's death) using his initial life expectancy of 37 years (*Table 8-5* for 47-year-old), and he dies after receiving two more RMDs. The successor beneficiary "steps into the shoes" of the designated beneficiary and continues to reduce the designated beneficiary's life expectancy each year just as the designated beneficiary would have. Thus, the successor beneficiary would use a remaining life expectancy of 34 years to figure his or her first RMD and would continue to reduce it by one each year until the IRA is completely distributed or the declining life expectancy is used up.

**Owner's death before required beginning date.** If an owner dies before the required beginning date and there is an individual designated beneficiary, the period for receiving required minimum distributions (RMDs) is generally the life expectancy of the designate d beneficiary. The computation of required minimum distributions under the life expectancy method is explained above under "Owner's death on or after required beginning date." The life expectancy method is the "default" rule under the final regulations, so the designated beneficiary automatically gets the benefit of the life expectancy method unless he or she elects the five-year rule.

For an individual designated beneficiary, there is no advantage to electing the five-year rule. Under the five-year rule, the entire account must be distributed by the end of the fifth year after the year of the owner's death. The beneficiary is allowed but not required to take any distribution for any year prior to that fifth year. For example, if the IRA owner dies in 2018 at age 58 (before required beginning date), and the designated beneficiary elects the five-year rule, he or she must receive the entire account by December 31, 2023; no distribution must be received before 2023. Even if the beneficiary plans to withdraw the entire account within the five-year period, that result can be achieved with the life expectancy method, which provides the flexibility to spread distributions over the longer life expectancy period, while allowing the beneficiary to accelerate distributions however he or she wishes, including taking the entire account at any time within a few years after the owner's death.

As noted above, the five-year rule is mandatory if the owner dies before the required beginning date and there is no designated beneficiary, as is the case where the owner's estate is the beneficiary.

## Special Rules for Surviving Spouses

A surviving spouse may take advantage of rules not available to nonspouse beneficiaries.

**Surviving spouse's rollover or election to treat IRA as his or her own.** A surviving spouse who is the sole beneficiary of an IRA with unlimited withdrawal rights may elect to treat the IRA as his or her own by retitling the IRA in his or her name. If the surviving spouse contributes to the IRA or does not receive a timely RMD under the beneficiary rules (December 31 of the year after the year of the deceased owner's death), the surviving spouse is deemed to have made the election. The final regulations confirm that to make the election, the surviving spouse must take the RMD for the year of the owner's death (if any) to the extent that the owner did not receive it.

A surviving-spouse beneficiary may make a spousal rollover from the deceased spouse's IRA, either by authorizing a direct transfer (trustee-to-trustee) to an IRA in the surviving spouse's name, which is the preferable method, or by rolling over a distribution within 60 days of receiving it to his or her own IRA *(8.10)*. However, if the deceased IRA owner did not receive the RMD for the year of death, the surviving spouse must receive and pay tax on that RMD; that amount cannot be rolled over (or directly transferred).

If the surviving spouse elects to treat the inherited IRA as his or her own or makes a spousal rollover, the surviving spouse is then subject to the same rules as any IRA owner. The surviving spouse should immediately name a new beneficiary for the IRA. The regular distribution rules apply, including the 10% penalty for taxable distributions received before age 59½ *(8.8)*. If the surviving spouse is under age 70½, RMDs may be delayed until April 1 of the year following the year in which he or she reaches age 70½, at which time his or her RMDs will be based on the Uniform Lifetime Table for owners *(8.13)*.

 *Planning Reminder*

**Surviving Spouse Under Age 70½**

If you inherit your spouse's traditional IRA and you are under age 70½, you may delay the start of required minimum distributions by treating the IRA as your own.

**Surviving spouse as sole beneficiary.** If the surviving spouse does not elect to treat an inherited IRA as his or her own, and does not make a spousal rollover, the surviving spouse must receive required minimum distributions (RMDs) as a beneficiary. A surviving spouse who is under age 59½ and needs the funds from the IRA may prefer this option because withdrawals, although taxable (unless allocable to nondeductible contributions made by the deceased spouse), are not subject to the 10% penalty for pre-59½ distributions *(8.12)*.

If the surviving spouse is the sole designated beneficiary, RMDs are based on his or her life expectancy from the Beneficiary's Single Life Expectancy Table *(Table 8-5)*. Each year, life expectancy is recalculated using the spouse's attained age during the year. A spousal beneficiary is the only beneficiary who may recalculate life expectancy. Others must reduce their life expectancy from *Table 8-5* for the year after the year of the owner's death by one year in each succeeding year.

If a surviving spouse is the sole designated beneficiary and the deceased spouse died before the year in which he or she would have reached age 70½, the surviving spouse does not have to begin receiving RMDs until the year that the deceased spouse would have reached age 70½.

Even if a surviving spouse begins receiving RMDs under the beneficiary rules, the surviving spouse may make a spousal rollover to his or her own IRA at any time *(8.10)*, but the rollover cannot include the RMD for the year of the rollover; the RMD must be received and reported as income as it is not eligible for rollover. As noted earlier, it is advisable to make a spousal rollover by authorizing a direct trustee-to-trustee transfer, rather than taking a distribution and doing a 60-day rollover *(8.10)*, as the direct transfer avoids concerns over missing the 60-day deadline and it is not treated as a rollover subject to the once-a-year rollover limitation.

## 8.15    SEP Basics

A simplified employee pension plan (SEP) set up by an employer allows the employer to contribute to an employee's IRA account more money than is allowed under regular IRA rules. For 2018, your employer generally could contribute and deduct up to 25% of your compensation or $55,000, whichever is less (the $55,000 limit may be increased for 2019 by an inflation adjustment). Your employer's SEP contributions are excluded from your pay and are not included on Form W-2 unless they exceed the limit. If contributions exceed the limit, the excess is included in your gross income and a 6% penalty tax may be imposed unless the excess (plus allocable income) is withdrawn by the due date of the return, plus extensions *(8.7)*. If you are under age 59½, the 10% early distribution penalty may apply to the withdrawal of income earned on the excess contributions *(8.12)*.

**Self-employed plans.** Self-employed individuals may set up a SEP as an alternative to a self-employed retirement plan; *see Chapter 41*.

**Eligibility.** A SEP must cover all employees who are at least age 21, earn over $600 (this amount may get an inflation adjustment for 2019), and who have worked for the employer at any time during at least three of the past five years. Union employees covered by union agreements may generally be excluded.

**SEP salary-reduction arrangements.** If a qualifying small employer set up a salary-reduction SEP before 1997, employees may contribute a portion of their pay to the plan instead of receiving it in cash *(8.16)*.

**SEP distributions.** Distributions from a SEP, including salary-reduction SEPs established before 1997, are subject to the regular distribution rules for traditional IRAs *(8.8)*.

## 8.16    Salary-Reduction SEP Set Up Before 1997

Qualifying small employers may offer employees the option of deferring a portion of their salary to an IRA. There are two types of salary-reduction IRAs, with different eligibility and contribution rules: (1) salary-reduction SEPs established before 1997 and (2) "SIMPLE" IRA accounts established after 1996.

*Caution*

**Employees Over Age 70½**

An employee over age 70½ may still participate in an employer SEP plan. Minimum distributions from the plan must begin as discussed in *7.13*.

After 1996, an employer may establish a SIMPLE plan but not a salary-reduction SEP. Rules for SIMPLE IRAs established after 1996 are at *8.17–8.18*. A salary-reduction SEP that was established before 1997 may continue to receive contributions under the prior law rules discussed below, and employees hired after 1996 may participate in the plan, subject to those rules.

**Salary-reduction SEPs established before 1997.** Salary reductions are allowed for a year only if the employer had no more than 25 employees eligible to participate in the SEP at any time during the prior taxable year. Furthermore, at least 50% of the eligible employees must elect the salary-reduction option, and the deferral percentage for highly compensated employees may not exceed 125% of the average contribution of regular employees.

If salary reductions are allowed, the maximum salary-reduction contribution for 2018 was $18,500 ($24,500 for participants age 50 or older if the plan permitted the extra deferral), although a lower limit may be imposed by the plan terms. These are the same limits as for 401(k) plans *(7.18)*. Deferrals over $18,500 ($24,500 if extra deferral for participants age 50 or older was allowed) are taxable, and if not timely distributed to the employee, can be taxed again when distributed from the plan. The deferral limits for 2019 will be in the *e-Supplement* at *jklasser.com*.

If an employee contributes to both a SEP and a 401(k) plan, the annual limit applies to the total salary reductions from both plans. If an employee makes salary-reduction contributions to a SEP and also to a tax-sheltered annuity plan *(7.21)*, the annual limit generally applies to the total salary reductions to both plans. In some cases, employees with at least 15 years of service may be able to defer an additional $3,000 to the tax-sheltered annuity plan *(7.21)*.

## 8.17 Who Is Eligible for a SIMPLE IRA?

A SIMPLE IRA is a salary-reduction retirement plan that qualifying small employers may offer their employees. For 2018, the maximum salary-reduction contribution was $12,500, or $15,500 for participants age 50 or older (by the end of 2018) if the plan allowed the additional contributions. See the *e-Supplement* at *jklasser.com* for the 2019 limits. Employers are required to make matching contributions or a flat contribution *(8.18)*.

**Qualifying employers.** A SIMPLE IRA may be maintained only by an employer that (1) in the previous calendar year had no more than 100 employees who earned compensation of $5,000 or more and (2) does not maintain any other retirement plan (unless the other plan is for collective bargaining employees). A self-employed individual who meets these tests may set up a SIMPLE IRA, as discussed in *Chapter 41*. A simple IRA must be maintained on a calendar-year basis.

In determining whether the 100-employee test is met for the prior year, all employees under the common control of the employer must be counted. For example, Joe Smith owned two businesses in 2018, a computer rental company with 80 employees and a computer repair company with 60 employees. If they all earned at least $5,000, they all count towards the 100 limit, so if Joe decides in 2019 to set up a retirement plan for his businesses, a different type of plan must be used. He may not establish a SIMPLE IRA for either business under the 100-employee limit.

If a SIMPLE IRA is established but the employer in a later year grows beyond the 100-employee limit, the employer generally has a two-year "grace period" during which contributions may continue to be made.

**Eligible employees.** In general, an employee must be allowed to contribute to a SIMPLE IRA for a year in which he or she is reasonably expected to earn $5,000 or more, provided at least $5,000 of compensation was received in any two prior years, whether or not consecutive. If the employer owns more than one business (under common control rules) and sets up a SIMPLE IRA for one of them, employees of the other business must also be allowed to participate if they meet the $5,000 compensation tests. Employees who are covered by a collective bargaining agreement may be excluded if retirement benefits were the subject of good-faith negotiations.

 *Planning Reminder*

**401(k) SIMPLE Plans**

An employer with a 401(k) plan that reports on the calendar year may avoid the regular 401(k) nondiscrimination tests by following the contribution rules for SIMPLE IRAs *(7.17)*.

The employer may lower or eliminate the $5,000 compensation requirement in order to broaden participation in the plan. No other conditions on eligibility, such as age or hours of work, are permitted.

**Deadline for setting up a SIMPLE IRA.** An employer generally may establish a SIMPLE IRA effective on any date between January 1 and October 1 of a year. If the employer (or a predecessor employer) previously maintained a SIMPLE IRA, a new SIMPLE IRA may be effective only on January 1 of a year. A new employer that comes into existence after October 1 of a year may establish a SIMPLE IRA for that year if the plan is established as soon as administratively feasible after the start of the business.

The employer may use a model SIMPLE IRA approved by the IRS to set up a SIMPLE IRA. Form 5304-SIMPLE allows employees to select a financial institution to which the contributions will be made. With Form 5305-SIMPLE, the employer selects the financial institution to which contributions are initially deposited, but employees have the right to subsequently transfer their account balances without cost or penalty to another SIMPLE-IRA at a financial institution of their own choosing. Use of the IRS model forms is optional; other documents satisfying the statutory requirements for a SIMPLE IRA may be used.

**SIMPLE IRA contributions and distributions.** Contributions and distributions to SIMPLE IRAs are subject to limitations *(8.18)*.

# 8.18 SIMPLE IRA Contributions and Distributions

The only contributions that may be made to a SIMPLE IRA are elective salary-reduction contributions by employees and matching or non-elective contributions by employers. All contributions are fully vested and nonforfeitable when made.

Regardless of compensation, eligible employees *(8.17)* may elect each year to make salary-reduction contributions to the plan up to the annual SIMPLE IRA limit *(8.17)*. Salary-reduction contributions are excluded from the employee's taxable pay on Form W-2 and not subject to federal tax withholding. They are subject to FICA withholding for Social Security and Medicare tax.

Eligible employees must be given notice by the employer of their right to elect salary-reduction contributions and at least 60 days to make the election. After the first year of eligibility, the election to defer for the upcoming year is made during the last 60 days (at minimum) of the prior calendar year. If the employer uses model IRS Form 5304-SIMPLE or 5305-SIMPLE, a notification document is included.

If an employee contributes to a SIMPLE IRA and also to a 401(k) plan, 403(b) or salary-reduction SEP of another employer for the same year, the salary-reduction contributions to the SIMPLE IRA count toward the overall annual limit on tax-free salary-reduction deferrals *(7.17)*. Deferrals over the annual limit are taxable and must be removed to avoid being taxed again when distributed from the plan *(7.18)*.

**Employer contributions.** Each year, the employer must make either a matching contribution or a fixed "non-elective" contribution. If the employer chooses matching contributions, the employee's elective salary-reduction contribution generally must be matched, up to a limit of 3% of the employee's compensation. For up to two years in any five-year period, the 3% matching limit may be reduced to as low as 1% for each eligible employee.

Instead of making either the 3% or reduced (between 1% and 3%) limit matching contribution, the employer may make a "non-elective" contribution equal to 2% of each eligible employee's compensation. If this option is chosen, the 2% contribution must be made for eligible employees whether or not they elect to make salary-reduction contributions for the year. The 2% contribution is subject to an annual compensation limit, which for 2018 was $275,000. Thus, for 2018, the maximum 2% non-elective contribution was $5,500 (2% of $275,000) even if an employee earned more than $275,000. The 3% matching contribution is not subject to the annual compensation limit, but only to the annual salary-reduction limit *(8.17)*. The employer must notify eligible employees of the type of contribution it will be making for the upcoming year prior to the employees' 60-day election period for making elective salary-reduction contributions. The employer must make the matching or non-elective contributions by the due date for filing the employer's tax return (plus extensions) for the year.

**Planning Reminder**

**Employer's Intended Contributions**

The IRS model notification included with Form 5304-SIMPLE or 5305-SIMPLE requires the employer to tell employees how much the employer will be contributing for the upcoming year.

**Planning Reminder**

**Rollover to SIMPLE IRA from Other Retirement Plans**

A tax-free rollover contribution may not be made to a SIMPLE IRA from a qualified employer plan or traditional IRA until after the end of the two-year period starting with the date the employee initially participates in the SIMPLE IRA. A rollover from one SIMPLE IRA to another SIMPLE IRA can be made in the initial two years of participation, as well as afterwards.

**Distributions from a SIMPLE IRA.** A distribution from a SIMPLE IRA is fully taxable unless a tax-free rollover or trustee-to-trustee transfer is made. The penalty for distributions before age 59½ *(8.12)* is increased to 25% from 10%, assuming no penalty exception applies, if the distribution is received during the two-year period starting with the employee's initial participation in the plan. After the first two years, the regular 10% penalty applies.

In the initial two-year period, a tax-free rollover or direct trustee-to-trustee transfer *(8.10)* of a SIMPLE IRA may be made to another SIMPLE IRA. After two years of participation, a tax-free rollover or direct transfer may be made to a traditional IRA, qualified plan, 403(b) plan, or state or local government 457 plan, as well as to a SIMPLE IRA. The mandatory distribution rules that apply to regular IRAs after age 70½ also apply to SIMPLE IRAs *(8.13)*.

**Caution**

**Increased Pre–Age 59½ Penalty**

In the first two years of SIMPLE IRA participation, the penalty for distributions before age 59½ is increased from 10% to 25%.

## 8.19 Roth IRA Advantages

As with traditional IRAs, earnings accumulate within a Roth IRA tax free until distributions are made. The key benefit of the Roth IRA is that tax-free withdrawals of contributions may be made at any time and earnings may be withdrawn tax free after a five-year holding period by an individual who is age 59½ or older, is disabled, or who pays qualifying first-time home-buyer expenses.

A Roth IRA can provide attractive retirement planning and estate planning opportunities. Although annual contributions to a traditional IRA are barred once you reach age 70½ *(8.2)*, contributions to a Roth IRA are allowed after age 70½, provided you have taxable compensation for the year and your modified adjusted gross income does not exceed the annual limitation under the phaseout rule *(8.20)*. Also, the minimum required distribution rules that apply to traditional IRAs after age 70½ *(8.13)* do not apply to Roth IRAs. Thus, a Roth IRA can remain intact after age 70½ and continue to grow tax free. The balance of the account not withdrawn during the owner's lifetime generally may be paid out to the beneficiaries tax free over their life expectancies, thereby providing a substantial tax-deferred buildup within the plan over an extended period *(8.24)*.

A Roth IRA is funded by making annual nondeductible contributions (subject to the income phaseout rule at *8.20*), by converting a traditional IRA, SEP or SIMPLE IRA, or rolling over a distribution from an employer plan, but the conversion or rollover to the Roth IRA is treated as a taxable transfer, as discussed at *(8.21)*.

Your employer can set up a "deemed Roth IRA" as a separate account under a qualified retirement plan. As long as the separate account otherwise meets the Roth IRA rules, you can make voluntary employee contributions that will be subject only to the Roth IRA rules. A deemed IRA can also be set up as a traditional IRA *(8.1)*.

## 8.20 Annual Contributions to a Roth IRA

You may make a nondeductible Roth IRA contribution, regardless of your age, for a year in which you have taxable compensation for personal services and your modified adjusted gross income (MAGI) does not exceed the upper end of the phaseout range for your filing status. The maximum contribution to a Roth IRA, prior to any phaseout, is the same as the traditional IRA limit. For 2018, the limit is $5,500 if you are under age 50, or $6,500 if you are age 50 or older at the end of the year, assuming taxable compensation is at least much; the 2018 phaseout rule for Roth IRA contributions is explained below. A Roth IRA contribution is not reported on your tax return.

If you decide to contribute to a traditional IRA to get a tax deduction, you can in a later year transfer the funds to a Roth IRA by making a taxable conversion *(8.22)*. If you initially contribute to a traditional IRA, you have until the filing deadline to "recharacterize" the contribution as a Roth IRA contribution, and similarly, if you initially contribute to a Roth IRA, you can recharacterize it as a traditional IRA contribution; *see 8.21* for the recharacterization rules. You can contribute to both a Roth IRA and a traditional IRA for the same year, but the annual contribution limit ($5,500/$6,500 for 2018) applies to the combined contributions, as discussed further below.

The Roth IRA rules do not replace the traditional IRA nondeductible contribution rules *(8.6)*. For an individual who is unable to contribute to a Roth IRA because the

**Caution**

**Roth IRA Contribution Deadline**

The deadline for making Roth IRA contributions for 2018 is April 15, 2019, the regular due date for your 2018 return. This is the contribution deadline even if you obtain a filing extension for your 2018 return.

**Contributions After Age 70½**

You can contribute to a Roth IRA even if you are over 70½ years of age, provided you have taxable compensation and are not subject to the MAGI phaseout.

contribution limit is phased out, and who is unable to make deductible traditional IRA contributions because of the phaseout rules for active plan participants *(8.4)*, nondeductible contributions may still be made to a traditional IRA *(8.6)*.

**Contributing to Roth IRA and traditional IRA for the same year.**  If you contribute to both a traditional IRA and Roth IRA for the same year, total contributions for the year to both types of IRAs may not exceed the lesser of (1) the annual limit ($5,500/$6,500 for 2018), or (2) your taxable compensation. This overall limit is applied first to the traditional IRA contributions and then to the Roth IRA contributions. Thus, the maximum contribution limit for 2018 to a Roth IRA is: (1) $5,500, or $6,500 if you are age 50 or older, or, if less, your taxable compensation, minus (2) deductible *(8.4)* or nondeductible *(8.6)* contributions to traditional IRAs. However, this maximum contribution limit may be reduced, as discussed below, by the MAGI phaseout rule for annual Roth IRA contributions.

**Contribution deadline.**  Contributions to a Roth IRA for a year may be made by the filing due date, without extensions. For 2018 contributions, the deadline is April 15, 2019.

**Spousal contribution on joint return for nonworking or low-earning spouse.**  If you are married filing jointly, you generally may contribute to a Roth IRA for each spouse up to the annual limit ($5,500 for spouse under age 50 or $6,500 for spouse age 50 or older at end of 2018) so long as your combined taxable compensation is at least $11,000 if both of you are under age 50 at the end of 2018, $12,000 if one of you is age 50 or older at the end of 2018, or $13,000 if both of you are age 50 or older at the end of 2018. This is the same spousal contribution rule as for traditional IRAs *(8.3)*; the lower-earning spouse is allowed to "borrow" compensation of the higher-earning spouse for contribution purposes. However, the Roth IRA contribution limit may be reduced because of the MAGI phaseout rules, discussed below.

**Roth IRA contribution limit may be phased out because of your MAGI.**  The 2018 Roth IRA contribution limit of $5,500 or $6,500 (or if less, your taxable compensation) is phased out if your 2018 modified adjusted gross income (MAGI) is:

- Over $189,000 and under $199,000, if you are married filing jointly, or a qualifying widow/widower.
- Over $120,000 and under $135,000, if you are single, head of household, or married filing separately and you lived apart for the entire year.
- Over $0 and under $10,000, if you are married filing separately and you lived with your spouse at any time during the year.

If your MAGI (see computation below) exceeds your Roth IRA phaseout threshold of $120,000, $189,000, or $0, and is within the phaseout range of $10,000 (if married filing jointly, a qualifying widow/widower, or married filing separately and you lived with your spouse at any time in the year), or $15,000 (if single or head of household), your contribution limit is reduced by a phaseout percentage; *see* Worksheet 8-3 below. If MAGI equals or exceeds the applicable $135,000, $199,000, or $10,000 phaseout endpoint, no Roth IRA contribution for 2018 is allowed. The MAGI phaseout rule applies to Roth IRA contributions regardless of whether you are covered by an employer retirement plan, unlike the deductible traditional IRA phaseout rules *(8.4)*, which apply only to active plan participants.

For 2019, the $120,000 and $189,000 phaseout thresholds may be increased by an inflation adjustment; *see* the *e-Supplement* at *jklasser.com* for an update.

Note that the Roth IRA phaseout ranges are considerably higher than the phaseout ranges for deductible contributions to a traditional IRA *(8.4)*, unless you are married filing separately and lived with your spouse at any time during the year. If you could claim a deduction for a traditional IRA contribution, consider whether the present tax benefit from the deduction is outweighed by the value of being able to obtain tax-free distributions from a Roth IRA in the future (*see 8.24* for the Roth IRA distribution rules).

Worksheet 8-3 below can be used to figure the reduced contribution limit for 2018 under the phaseout rules, and the example below that worksheet illustrates the computation.

## Worksheet 8-3    Phaseout of Roth IRA Contribution Limit for 2018

1.    Enter your 2018 MAGI (see MAGI definition below). If married filing jointly, this is the combined MAGI for both of you.    _____

2.    Enter the phaseout threshold for your status: $120,000, $189,000, or 0; *see* above.    _____

3.    Subtract Line 2 from Line 1. This is your excess MAGI.    _____

4.    Enter the following phaseout range for your status:

   • $10,000 if married filing jointly, or a qualifying widow or widower, or married filing separately and you with your spouse at any time in 2018, or

   • $15,000 if you are single, head of household, or married filing separately and you lived apart for the entire year    _____

5.    Divide Line 3 by Line 4 and enter the result as a decimal rounded to at least three places. This is your phaseout percentage. If Line 3 equals or exceeds Line 4 (decimal here on Line 5 is 1.000 or more), the phaseout is 100% and you are not allowed any Roth IRA contribution for 2018; do not complete Lines 6-11.  If the decimal here is under 100%, go to Line 6.    _____

6.    Enter the annual contribution limit of $5,500, or $6,500 if you are age 50 or older at the end of 2018. However, if your 2018 taxable compensation from work is less than $5,500/$6,500, enter that lesser amount.
      If married filing jointly, and your own taxable compensation is under the annual $5,500 or $6,500 limit, you can enter the $5,500 or $6,500 limit here if the combined taxable compensation for you and your spouse is at least $11,000 if both of you are under age 50 at the end of 2018, $12,000 if one of you is age 50 or older at the end of 2018, or $13,000 if both of you are age 50 or older at the end of 2018; *see* the spousal contribution rule discussed earlier.    _____

7.    Multiply Line 5 by Line 6. This is the phased out part of the contribution limit.    _____

8.    Subtract Line 7 from Line 6. If the result is not a multiple of $10, round it up to the next highest multiple of $10. If the result is under $200, increase it to $200.    _____

9.    Enter any contributions made to your traditional IRAs for 2018. These reduce the Roth IRA contribution limit.    _____

10.    Subtract Line 9 from Line 6    _____

11.    Enter the lesser of Line 8 or Line 10. This is your maximum 2018 Roth IRA contribution.    _____

**Figuring MAGI.** For purposes of determining if your Roth IRA contribution limit is reduced by the phaseout rule, MAGI may be higher than the actual AGI reported on your return because certain deductions and exclusions must be added back to AGI. On the other hand, if you convert a traditional IRA to a Roth IRA (or rollover funds from employer plan to a Roth IRA), the transfer is generally fully taxable *(8.22)*, but the amount included in AGI is subtracted from AGI to figure MAGI for Roth IRA purposes. Specifically, compute MAGI as follows:

(1) Start with the AGI reported on your return but subtract any income from a conversion to a Roth IRA or a rollover to a Roth IRA from an employer plan.

(2) Increase the Step 1 AGI by the following deductions or exclusions from income that you claimed:

Any deductions claimed for: traditional IRA contributions *(8.4)*, student loan interest *(33.14)*, qualified college tuition and fees, if extended to 2018 by Congress *(33.13)*, or foreign housing expenses if self employed *(36.4)*, and

Any exclusions claimed for: employer-provided adoption assistance *(3.6)*, interest on U.S. Savings Bonds used for tuition *(33.4)*, foreign earned income *(36.1)*, or employer-provided foreign housing expenses *(36.4)*.

**Excess contributions.** If Roth IRA contributions exceed the allowable limit, the excess contribution is subject to a 6% penalty tax unless you withdraw the excess, plus any earnings on the excess contribution, by the filing due date including extensions. The earnings must be reported as income for the year the contribution was made. If you timely file your 2018 return (by April 15, 2019) without withdrawing an excess contribution made in 2018, the IRS will give you until October 15, 2019 to make the withdrawal, and an amended return must be filed for 2018 to report the earnings on the withdrawn contributions; *see* the instructions to Form 5329.

---

**EXAMPLE**

In 2018, Mark Davis is under age 50 and single. His 2018 salary is $118,000 and his modified adjusted gross income (MAGI) is $123,000, $3,000 more than the $120,000 phaseout threshold for a single person's 2018 Roth IRA contribution. Mark did not make any contributions to a traditional IRA for 2018.

Following the steps of Worksheet 8-2, Mark determines that he can contribute up to $4,400 to a Roth IRA for 2018. Of the $5,500 contribution limit, 20% is phased out ($3,000 excess MAGI divided by the $15,000 phaseout range for single persons). Thus, the $5,500 contribution limit is reduced by 20%, or $1,100. Mark may contribute $4,400 ($5,550 – $1,100) to a Roth IRA for 2018.

If Mark was age 50 or over in 2018, the $6,500 contribution limit would be reduced by $1,300 to $5,200 (20% phaseout percentage × $6,500 limit = $1,300 reduction).

| | | |
|---|---|---|
| 1. | MAGI | $ 123,000 |
| 2. | Phaseout threshold | 120,000 |
| 3. | Excess MAGI | 3,000 |
| 4. | Phaseout range for single person | 15,000 |
| 5. | Phaseout percentage (Line 3 / Line 4) | .20 |
| 6. | $5,500 annual contribution limit | 5,500 |
| 7. | 20% (Line 5) × $5,500 (Line 6) is phased out | 1,100 |
| 8. | Line 6 minus Line 7 | 4,400 |
| 9. | Contributions to traditional IRA for 2018 | 0 |
| 10. | Line 6 minus Line 9 | 5,500 |
| 11. | Lesser of Line 8 or Line 10. This is Mark's Roth IRA contribution limit for 2018 | 4,400 |

# 8.21 Recharacterizing a Traditional IRA Contribution to a Roth IRA and Vice Versa

You may be able to change an annual contribution from a traditional IRA contribution to a Roth IRA contribution, or an annual Roth IRA contribution to a traditional IRA contribution, by making a trustee-to-trustee transfer. This is called a recharacterization. A new law bars a recharacterization of a conversion made after 2017 to a Roth IRA *(8.23)*, but you can still recharacterize annual contributions from one type of IRA (traditional or Roth) to the other.

For example, you make a contribution to a traditional IRA early in the year with the expectation of being able to claim a deduction for your contribution *(8.4)*, but it turns out that your MAGI is much higher than expected, such as when you receive large year-end capital gain distributions, and you realize that no deduction would be allowed under the phaseout rule, or that only part of your contribution would be deductible. In this situation, you could recharacterize all or part of the contribution (the part that would not be deductible) by transferring it (plus allocable income) to a Roth IRA, provided the contribution is not barred by the Roth IRA phaseout rule *(8.20)*. For example, if you are single, a 2018 deduction for a traditional IRA contribution (up to $5,500 if under age 50 or $6,500 if age 50 or more at end of year) begins to phase out when your 2018 MAGI exceeds $63,000 and is completely phased out if MAGI is $73,000 or more *(8.4)*, but the limit for a 2018 Roth IRA contribution does not begin to phase out until MAGI reaches $120,000, with a complete phaseout at $135,000 or more *(8.20)*.

On the other hand, if you initially contribute to a Roth IRA, you could decide to recharacterize and switch the contribution to a traditional IRA. This could be the case if you initially contribute to a Roth IRA and it turns out that your MAGI for the year would allow you to claim a full traditional IRA deduction.

**Effect of a recharacterization.** When you recharacterize a contribution, the IRA which receives the recharacterized amount is treated as if it had received the original contribution (and the earnings transferred over in the recharacterization) on the date of the original contribution. A recharacterization is not counted as a rollover for purposes of the one-rollover-per-year limit *(8.10)*.

**How to recharacterize and deadline for completing transfer.** You make an election to recharacterize a contribution by notifying the trustees of both IRAs of your intention. If you are changing trustees, you authorize a trustee-to-trustee transfer from the first IRA (to which the contribution was originally made) to the second IRA (the transferee IRA). If the account is remaining with the same trustee, instruct the trustee that you are electing to treat the contribution as having been made to the second IRA rather than the first. The transfer must include any net income allocable to the original contribution; an allocable loss would reduce the amount that must be transferred.

The election and the transfer itself must be completed on or before the due date, including extensions, for filing your tax return for the year of the original contribution. If you miss this deadline, but you timely filed the return, the IRS allows you six months from the original due date (without extensions) to complete a recharacterization, which in the case of a 2018 return, would allow until October 15, 2019. If you take advantage of this extension and recharacterize after a timely filing, you must file an amended return *(47.1)* to report the recharacterization.

When you recharacterize an IRA contribution (traditional to Roth or Roth to traditional), you must attach a statement to your return to explain the recharacterization. See the instructions to Form 8606 for the details to be included in the statement. Form 8606 does not have to be filed unless you recharacterized only part of a traditional IRA contribution and some of the contribution left in the traditional IRA is nondeductible, or you partially recharacterized a Roth IRA contribution and a portion of the contribution transferred to the traditional IRA is nondeductible.

## 8.22 Converting a Traditional IRA to a Roth IRA

A conversion of a traditional IRA to a Roth IRA is a taxable transfer, unlike a tax-free direct transfer or rollover *(8.10)* to a traditional IRA. If you converted a traditional IRA to a Roth IRA in 2018, the entire transfer must be reported as 2018 income unless after-tax contributions were made to any of your traditional IRAs (see "How to report a 2018 conversion to a Roth IRA," below).

You can convert a traditional IRA to a Roth IRA regardless of your income or filing status. A conversion may be made by directing the trustee of your traditional IRA to make a trustee-to-trustee transfer of your IRA to a new Roth IRA trustee, or by keeping the account with the same trustee but instructing the trustee to change the registration of the account from a traditional IRA to a Roth IRA. You may also make a conversion by receiving a distribution from your traditional IRA and rolling it over to a Roth IRA; the rollover must be completed within 60 days from the time you receive the distribution.

A conversion to a Roth IRA is not treated as a rollover for purposes of the one-rollover-per-year rule *(8.10)*.

**Conversion from SEP or SIMPLE IRA.** You may also convert a SEP *(8.15)* to a Roth IRA. A SIMPLE IRA *(8.18)* may be converted to a Roth IRA if more than two years have passed since you began participation in the SIMPLE IRA.

**Rollover from employer plan to Roth IRA.** The tax treatment of a rollover to a Roth IRA from a 401(k) plan or other qualified employer plan, a 403(b) plan, or a governmental 457 plan, is similar to that of a conversion from a traditional IRA. That is, the rollover is a taxable distribution except to the extent that it is a return of your after-tax contributions, if any.

**Required minimum distributions (RMDs) may not be converted to a Roth IRA.** If you are age 70½ or older, you may not convert to a Roth IRA amounts that represent the required minimum distribution (RMD) from a traditional IRA *(8.13)*. Similarly, the RMD from an employer plan *(7.11)* may not be rolled over to a Roth IRA. Only the amount exceeding the RMD is eligible for conversion or rollover.

**How to report a 2018 conversion to a Roth IRA.** If you converted a traditional IRA, SEP, or SIMPLE IRA to a Roth IRA in 2018, you have to report the conversion on Form 8606 and the entire amount must be reported as a taxable distribution on your 2018 return, except to the extent that it is allocable to after-tax contributions in all of your traditional IRAs. If you converted all of your traditional, SEP and SIMPLE IRAs to Roth IRAs in 2018, report the conversions on Part II of Form 8606; after-tax contributions in all your traditional IRAs, if any, reduce the taxable amount to be reported on your 2018 return. If you made after-tax contributions to any of your traditional IRAs and in 2018 you converted only part of your traditional IRAs, SEPs and SIMPLE IRAs to Roth IRAs, a prorated portion of the converted amount is treated as allocable to the after-tax contributions and that is the nontaxable portion of the conversion. You figure the tax-free percentage on Part 1 of Form 8606 by dividing the after-tax contributions by the sum of the year-end value of all the IRAs plus the conversion amount. Multiplying the resulting percentage by the conversion amount gives you the tax-free part of the conversion. The balance is the taxable part of the conversion. The 10% penalty for pre-age-59½ distributions *(8.12)* does not apply to the taxable part of the conversion. *See* the instructions to Parts I and II of Form 8606 for details on reporting conversions to Roth IRAs.

If you withdrew funds from a traditional IRA towards the end of 2018 and complete a rollover to a Roth IRA in early 2019 within 60 days of withdrawal, this is treated as a 2018 conversion (and thus generally fully taxable on your 2018 return) and not a 2019 conversion.

## 8.23 Conversions Made After 2017 to a Roth IRA Cannot Be Recharacterized

The Tax Cuts and Jobs Act has ended a valuable planning opportunity that was allowed under prior law—the ability to convert a traditional IRA to a Roth IRA *(8.22)* and still have an opportunity to reconsider the move. With a recharacterization, you could undo the conversion if the value of the Roth IRA dropped substantially after the date of the

conversion and you did not want to have to include the conversion date value in income, or you simply were unable to pay the tax due on the conversion *(8.22)*.

This option is no longer available. The ability to in effect "undo" the conversion by recharacterizing all or part of it back to a traditional IRA is no longer allowed for a conversion made in 2018 or later years. In other words, a conversion made in 2018 (or later) is irrevocable. Similarly, the new law prohibits the recharacterization of a rollover made after 2017 from an employer retirement plan *(8.22)* to a Roth IRA.

However, a conversion made in 2017 (or rollover over from an employer plan in 2017) was not affected by the new law and could have been recharacterized, but the deadline for doing so generally ended October 15, 2018. The deadline for recharacterizing a 2017 conversion (or employer plan rollover) to a Roth IRA was generally the filing due date for 2017 returns with extensions (if any), but taxpayers without an extension who reported a conversion as taxable income on their 2017 returns by the regular April 17, 2018, due date had until October 15, 2018, to complete a recharacterization. In this case, an amended return for 2017 must be filed; *see* below.

If a timely recharacterization was made for a 2017 conversion by the above deadline, the IRS disregards the conversion to the Roth IRA and treats the contribution as if it had been made to the transferee traditional IRA (to which recharacterization was made) on the date of the conversion. The recharacterized contribution is not treated as an IRA rollover for purposes of the one-rollover-per-year rule *(8.10)*.

If you timely recharacterized only part of the amount converted in 2017, the non-recharacterized amount should have been reported on Form 8606, Part II, and as a taxable IRA distribution on your 2017 return; *see* the 2017 Form 8606 instructions.

What if you made a conversion in 2017 but missed the October 15, 2018, deadline to recharacterize; can you get a further extension from the IRS? A regulation gives the IRS authority to grant an extension if an "innocent" mistake was made and you act in good faith by promptly asking the IRS for the additional time after discovering the error (Reg. Sec. 301.9100-3). However, it is extremely unlikely that the IRS will grant extensions beyond the extension for timely filers; that is, to October 15, 2018, for 2017 returns.

**Amended return may be required if a 2017 conversion was timely recharacterized.** If you converted a traditional IRA to a Roth IRA during 2017 (or rolled over funds from an employer plan to a Roth IRA in 2017) and you recharacterized the transfer in 2017 or in early 2018 and then filed your 2017 return by April 17, 2018 (the regular due date for a 2017 return), there was no income to report on the 2017 conversion. If you did not recharacterize prior to filing and you filed a timely 2017 return on which you reported a taxable conversion, and then recharacterized by the October 15, 2018, deadline, you must file an amended return for 2017. For example, by April 17, 2018 (the regular due date for a 2017 return), you filed your 2017 return, which included a taxable conversion made in 2017, and then by October 15, 2018, you recharacterized the converted amount back to a traditional IRA. You must file an amended return for 2017 to report the recharacterization and claim a refund for the tax paid on the conversion. The amended return must be filed within the regular amendment period, generally three years *(47.1)*. On the amended return, write "Filed pursuant to Section *301.9100-2*."

**Reconverting to a Roth IRA after a recharacterization of a 2017 conversion.** If a traditional IRA was converted to a Roth IRA in 2017 and then transferred back to a traditional IRA in a timely 2018 recharacterization, a reconversion of the recharacterized amount was allowed once 30 days had passed since the date of the recharacterization. A reconversion after the 30-day period is treated as a new conversion in 2018 and may not be recharacterized; the conversion is irrevocable under the Tax Cuts and Jobs Act.

## 8.24 Distributions From a Roth IRA

A distribution from a Roth IRA is tax free if it is a qualified distribution, as discussed below. Even if a distribution is not a qualified distribution, it is tax free to the extent it does not exceed your regular Roth IRA contributions *(8.20)* and conversion contributions *(8.22)*. The part of a nonqualified distribution allocable to earnings is taxable, but distributions

*Law Alert*

**New Law Ends Ability to Recharacterize a Conversion to Roth IRA**

The Tax Cuts and Jobs Act bars you from "undoing" (recharacterizing) a conversion to a Roth IRA, or a rollover to a Roth IRA from an employer retirement plan, made in 2018 or later years. It was possible to recharacterize a conversion made during 2017, but the recharacterization had to be completed by October 15, 2018; *see* **8.23**.

The new law only bars recharacterizations of conversions to Roth IRAs from traditional IRAs, SEPs or SIMPLE IRAs, and recharacterizations of rollovers from employer plans to Roth IRAs. You may still recharacterize annual IRA contributions for 2018 or later years. As discussed in **8.21**, you may recharacterize an annual contribution made to a traditional IRA as a contribution to a Roth IRA, or you may recharacterize an annual contribution to a Roth IRA as a contribution to a traditional IRA.

**Filing Instruction**

### File Form 8606 to Report a Nonqualified Distribution

If you receive a nonqualified distribution, you must file Form 8606. On Part III of Form 8606, you report the nonqualified distribution and figure the taxable portion, if any, as explained in *8.24*.

are considered to be from contributions first and then from earnings; *see* the "Ordering rules for nonqualified distributions" below for the allocation between contributions and earnings. You must report Roth IRA distributions on Form 8606.

You may make a tax-free direct transfer from one Roth IRA to another. A tax-free rollover of a Roth IRA distribution may be made to another Roth IRA if you complete the rollover within 60 days, but the rollover is subject to the one-rollover-per-year limit *(8.10)*.

You do not have to receive minimum required distributions from a Roth IRA after you reach age 70½ as you would from a traditional IRA *(8.13)*. No Roth IRA distributions at all are required during your lifetime. After your death, your beneficiaries will be subject to a minimum distribution requirement *(8.25)*.

**Qualified Roth IRA distributions are tax free.** Two tests must be met for a Roth IRA distribution to be "qualified," and thus completely tax free: (1) the distribution must be made after the end of the five-year period beginning with the first day of the first taxable year for which any Roth IRA contribution was made and (2) one of the following conditions must be met:

- you are age 59½ or older when the distribution is made,
- you are disabled,
- you use the distribution to pay up to $10,000 of qualifying first-time home-buyer expenses as discussed below, or
- you are a beneficiary receiving distributions following the death of the account owner *(8.25)*.

**Five-year holding period for qualified distributions.** In order to receive tax-free withdrawals of earnings from a Roth IRA, you must satisfy the five-year holding period and also be at least age 59½, be disabled, be a beneficiary, or pay qualifying first-time home-buyer expenses. The five-year holding period begins with January 1 (assuming you are a calendar-year taxpayer) of the first year for which any Roth IRA contribution is made.

For purposes of determining qualified distributions, you have only one five-year period regardless of the number of Roth IRAs you have. Once you satisfy the five-year test for one Roth IRA, you also meet it for all subsequently established Roth IRAs. For example, if you converted a traditional IRA to a Roth IRA during 1998 (the first year Roth IRA contributions were allowed), or made a regular Roth IRA contribution for 1998 at any time between January 1, 1998, and April 15, 1999, your five-year holding period began January 1, 1998. If in a later year you converted *(8.22)* a traditional IRA to a Roth IRA, or made a regular Roth IRA contribution to a different account *(8.20)*, that new Roth IRA does not get its own five-year holding period. In this case, the five-year period for all your Roth IRAs began January 1, 1998, and ended December 31, 2002. If your first Roth IRA contribution was a regular contribution for 2014 (made by April 15, 2015) or a conversion made during 2014, the five-year period for all your Roth IRAs ends December 31, 2018.

If you receive a Roth IRA distribution after the end of your five-year holding period, and you also meet one of the other qualified distribution requirements such as being age 59½ or older, the distribution is completely tax free. If you receive a distribution before satisfying both the five-year holding period requirement and one of the other qualified distribution requirements, and the withdrawal exceeds your contributions, the excess (i.e., earnings) is taxable and possibly subject to the 10% penalty for pre–age 59½ distributions *(8.12)*. Under the ordering rules discussed below, Roth IRA distributions are treated as being made first from contributions and then from earnings.

**Ordering rules for nonqualified distributions.** Even if a distribution does not meet the tests for a qualified distribution and thus is not automatically completely tax free, it may still be fully or partly tax free because a nonqualified distribution is not taxable to the extent of your Roth IRA contributions. All of your Roth IRAs are treated as one account for purposes of determining if contributions or earnings have been withdrawn. If a distribution does not exceed total contributions to all of your Roth IRAs, it is not taxable. The taxable part of a nonqualified distribution is figured on Part III of Form 8606.

**Planning Reminder**

### Meeting the Five-Year Holding Test

For a withdrawal of earnings from a Roth IRA to be tax free, the five-year holding period test must be met and the taxpayer must be at least age 59½ or meet one of the other conditions for a qualified distribution. For example, a taxpayer whose first Roth IRA contribution was for 2013 satisfied the five-year test at the end of 2017 so a distribution received after age 59½ in 2018 (or later) is a tax-free qualified distribution.

Where you have made regular annual contributions and also conversion contributions from a traditional IRA or rollover contributions from an employer plan to a Roth IRA, the regular contributions are considered to be withdrawn first. Allocate a distribution to your contributions and then to earnings in this order:

1. Regular Roth IRA contributions. This is the total of all of your annual contributions for all years.

2. Conversion contributions and rollover contributions. Conversion contributions and rollover contributions are considered to be withdrawn in the order in which they were made. For example, if you made a conversion in 2009 and another conversion in 2010, you allocate the distribution first to the 2009 conversion and then to the 2010 conversion. If part of a conversion or rollover contribution was not taxable (because it was allocable to nondeductible or after-tax contributions in the converted or rolled-over account), the taxable part of the conversion or rollover is deemed withdrawn before the nontaxable part. Assume that the 2009 conversion was partly taxable and partly nontaxable, and the same was true for the 2010 conversion. You would first allocate the distribution to the taxable part of the 2009 conversion, then to the nontaxable part of the 2009 conversion, then to the taxable part of the 2010 conversion, and finally, to the nontaxable part of the 2010 conversion.

   Taking into account the taxable part of a conversion or rollover contribution before the nontaxable part (if any) of the contribution may be important for purposes of determining whether the 10% early distribution penalty applies to the withdrawal before age 59½ of a conversion or rollover contribution within five years of the conversion/rollover (*see* below).

3. Earnings. Earnings on Roth IRA contributions are considered to be withdrawn last, after all contributions are taken into account. If a distribution is not a qualified distribution, and it exceeds the contributions under (1) and (2) above, the withdrawn earnings are subject to tax and, if you are under age 59½, to the 10% early distribution penalty, unless a penalty exception applies *(8.12)*.

**Potential 10% early distribution penalty on withdrawal within five years of conversion or rollover.** If you receive a Roth IRA distribution before age 59½ and within the prior five years you made a conversion from a traditional IRA or rollover from an employer plan, you may be subject to the regular 10% early distribution penalty *(8.12)*. Do not confuse this potential 10% penalty on conversions or rollovers with the 10% penalty that applies before age 59½ to a nonqualified distribution that is allocable to taxable earnings (category 3 under the "Ordering rules" above).

The 10% penalty applies only if all of the following are true: (1) you are under age 59½ when you receive the Roth IRA distribution, (2) you converted or rolled over an amount to a Roth IRA within the five-year period preceding the current Roth IRA distribution, (3) the Roth IRA distribution is allocable to the taxable portion of any conversion or rollover made within the five-year period, and (4) you do not qualify for a penalty exception, such as for first-time homebuyer expenses or higher education costs, or being disabled *(8.12)*.

For purposes of determining the five-year period under test 2, every conversion or rollover is considered made on January 1 of the year in which it occurred, regardless of its actual date. Thus, there is a separate five-year period for each conversion or rollover you have made. For any conversion (or rollover) made in 2013, the five-year period began January 1, 2013, and ended December 31, 2017, so a 2018 Roth IRA distribution cannot be penalized on account of a 2013 conversion (or rollover) even if the 2018 distribution is before age 59½. The 10% penalty could apply to a 2018 distribution if it is allocable to a conversion or rollover made in 2014 through 2018.

Even if there were conversions or rollovers within the five-year period, the penalty applies only to the extent that the current distribution from the Roth IRA is allocable to the taxable portion of any of those conversions or rollovers, as determined by the ordering rules above; *see* category 2 of the ordering rules. Note that under the ordering rules, the entire Roth IRA distribution may be tax free because it is allocable to your contributions- either regular annual contributions (category 1) or your conversion or rollover contributions (category 2). But even if the distribution is entirely tax free, the 10% penalty applies to an early distribution that is allocable to the category 2 conversions or rollovers that were taxable when made, assuming a penalty exception *(8.12)* is not available.

*Caution*

**Early Withdrawal Within 5 Years of Conversion to Roth IRA**

The 10% penalty *(8.12)* for pre–age 59½ distributions may apply if within five years of making a conversion to a Roth IRA, a distribution from any Roth IRA is received. The penalty applies to the portion of the withdrawal allocable to the conversion amount that was taxable in the year of the conversion. This is so even if the withdrawal is tax free under the ordering rule for Roth IRA distributions.

*Caution*

**Some Distributions Partly Taxable to Beneficiary**

If you inherit a Roth IRA and receive a distribution before the end of the owner's five-year holding period for qualified distributions *(8.24)* the part of the distribution that represents a return of the owner's contributions under the ordering rules *(8.24)* is tax free, but the part of the distribution that is allocable to earnings must be included in your taxable income. However, even if you receive a taxable distribution and are under age 59½, you are not subject to the 10% early distribution penalty.

After the end of the owner's five-year holding period, all distributions you receive from the account are tax free.

Follow the instructions to Form 5329 to figure whether you owe the penalty on any of your Roth conversions or rollovers.

**Distribution used for up to $10,000 of first-time home-buyer expenses.** A Roth IRA distribution is "qualified", and therefore tax free, if you meet the five-year holding period and the distribution is used for up to $10,000 of qualifying "first-time" home-buyer expenses. The $10,000 limit is a lifetime cap per IRA owner, not an annual limitation. Expenses qualify if they are used within 120 days of the distribution to pay the acquisition costs of a principal residence for you, your spouse, your child, or your grandchild, or an ancestor of you or your spouse. The residence does not have to be your "first" home. A qualifying first-time home-buyer is considered to be someone who did not have a present ownership interest in a principal residence in the two-year period ending on the acquisition date of the new home. If the home-buyer is married, both spouses must satisfy the two-year test. Eligible acquisition costs include buying, constructing, or reconstructing the principal residence, including reasonable settlement, financing, and closing costs.

## 8.25 Distributions to Roth IRA Beneficiaries

If you are the surviving spouse of the Roth IRA owner and you are the owner's sole Roth IRA beneficiary, you may elect to treat the inherited account as your own Roth IRA. If you treat the account as your own, you do not have to take distributions from the account at any time, since a Roth IRA owner is not subject to minimum distribution requirements. If you take some distributions, you are not locked into a specific distribution schedule unless you agree to that schedule.

Surviving spouses who do not elect to treat an inherited Roth IRA as their own, and beneficiaries other than surviving spouses, must receive required minimum distributions (RMDs). If there is an individual designated beneficiary under the final IRS regulations as of September 30 of the year following the year of the Roth IRA owner's death *(8.14)* RMDs are generally payable over the life expectancy of the designated beneficiary; *see* the Single Life Expectancy table *(Table 8-5) (8.14)* If there is more than one individual beneficiary, they may split the inherited account into separate accounts by December 31 of the year following the year of the Roth IRA owner's death, allowing each beneficiary to use his or her own life expectancy in figuring RMDs *(8.14)* For each year that a RMD is required, the beneficiary must divide the account balance as of the end of the prior year by the applicable life expectancy to figure the amount of the RMD *(8.14)* Although it is unlikely, the plan document may require distributions under the five-year rule, which requires that the entire account be distributed by December 31 of the fifth year following the year of the owner's death but does not require any distributions prior to that date. The plan may allow a choice between the life expectancy rule and the five-year rule, in which case the life-expectancy rule clearly provides more flexibility. Of course, a beneficiary who is receiving RMDs under the life-expectancy method may choose to receive more than the minimum amount required under the life expectancy rule.

Failure to take an RMD will result in a penalty unless the IRS waives it. A penalty tax of 50% applies to the difference between the RMD and the amount you received.

**When distributions to beneficiary must start under life expectancy rule.** For a nonspouse beneficiary to use the life expectancy rule, RMDs must begin by the end of the year following the year of the Roth IRA owner's death. This is also the starting date for a surviving spouse who is a co-beneficiary of the account along with other individuals.

If you are the surviving spouse and are sole beneficiary of the Roth IRA, you may elect to treat the Roth IRA as your own and if you do, you do not have to receive any RMDs. If you do not treat it as your own and your spouse had not reached age 70½ when he or she died, you may delay the start of RMDs until December 31 of the year your spouse would have reached age 70½.

If there is no designated beneficiary under the IRS rules, such as where the Roth IRA owner's estate is the beneficiary *(8.14)* the entire account must be paid out by the end of the fifth year following the year of the owner's death.

**Five-year holding period for tax-free treatment.** The same five-year holding period for receiving fully tax-free distributions that applied to the account owner *(8.24)* also applies to you as the beneficiary. The five-year holding period began on January 1 of the year for which the owner's first Roth IRA contribution was made. If you receive distributions before the end of the five-year holding period, the distributions are "nonqualified," which means that they will be tax free to the extent that they are a recovery of the owner's Roth IRA contributions and taxable to the extent they are earnings under the "ordering rules" at *8.24* If you receive a nonqualified distribution, you must report it and figure the taxable portion, if any, on Part III of Form 8606. Distributions you receive after the end of the owner's five-year holding period are "qualified" distributions *(8.24)* and thus are completely tax free.

## 8.26 Special IRA Rules for Victims of Hurricanes Harvey, Irma, Maria, and California Wildfires

Taxpayers who lived in areas affected by Hurricane Harvey (or Tropical Storm Harvey), Hurricane Irma, Hurricane Maria, or the California wildfires in 2017, and who suffered an economic loss as a result of these disasters, may use favorable reporting and repayment rules for qualified retirement plan distributions of up to $100,000 that are received before 2019. These rules apply to distributions from traditional IRAs, SEPs, SIMPLE IRAs, and Roth IRAs, as well as to distributions from eligible employer retirement plans *(7.28)*

In general, qualified distributions up to the $100,000 limit may be included in income over three years if you do not want to report them in the year of receipt. The 10% penalty for IRA distributions before age 59½ *(8.12)* does not apply to qualified distributions; neither does the 25% penalty for SIMPLE IRA distributions in the first two years of plan participation *(8.18)* You also have the option of repaying qualified distributions within three years of receipt, in which case the distributions are not taxed. You must file Form 8915B to report a qualified disaster distribution or repayment.

**Qualified distributions.** Distributions of up to $100,000 (see below) qualify for the special rules provided (1) your primary residence was located in the disaster area on the date shown below, (2) you received the distribution after the specified date shown below and before 2019 and (3) and you suffered an economic loss as a result of the disaster. Here are the applicable dates:

- For Hurricane Harvey or Tropical Storm Harvey, your principal residence was located in Texas or Louisiana on August 23, 2017, and the distribution was made after August 22, 2017, and before January 1, 2019.

- For Hurricane Irma, your principal residence on September 4, 2017 was located in Florida, Georgia, South Carolina, the U.S. Virgin Islands or Puerto Rico, and the distribution was made after September 3, 2017, and before January 1, 2019.

- For Hurricane Maria, your principal residence was located in Puerto Rico or the U.S. Virgin Islands on September 16, 2017, and the distribution was made after September 15, 2017, and before January 1, 2019.

- For the 2017 California wildfire disasters, your principal residence was located in California at any time between October 8, 2017 and December 31, 2017, and the distribution was made after October 7, 2017, and before January 1, 2019.

You are considered to have an economic loss due to one (or more) of the above disasters if your real or personal property was damaged or destroyed, you were laid off from work, or had a loss because you were displaced from your home. The amount of the distribution you received does not have to be tied to your actual economic loss or your need for the funds.

Note that if tests (1) through (3) above are met, any distribution you receive from an eligible plan in the applicable period can be designated as a qualified distribution, even if you would have received it had the disaster not occurred, such as a periodic pension payment or a required minimum distribution.

**$100,000 limit.** Qualified hurricane-related distributions meeting tests (1) through (3) above are subject to an overall limit of $100,000, and qualified California wildfire distributions are subject to a separate $100,000 limit. Within each category (hurricanes or wildfires), the limit is $100,000 regardless of how many plans you receive distributions from. For example, if in 2018 you took distributions from your traditional IRA and your 401(k) plan that total over $100,000, you would allocate the $100,000 limit between the plans on Form 8915B. If in 2017 you received a qualified distribution of $50,000 and in 2018 you received a qualified distribution of $125,000, only $50,000 of the 2018 distribution can be treated as qualified on Form 8915B for 2018. Note that if you are under age 59½, the early distribution penalty *(8.12, 8.18)* will apply to distributions exceeding the $100,000 limit, unless a penalty exception is available.

**Three-year reporting and repayment rule for qualified distributions.** Unless you elect to report the entire amount in the year of receipt, a qualified distribution is included in income in equal amounts over three years. For example, if you received a qualified distribution of $75,000 from your traditional IRA in 2018, you would include $25,000 as income on your 2018 return, and $25,000 on your returns for 2019 and 2020. You must report a qualified distribution on Form 8915B whether you use the three-year rule or elect to include it all in the year of receipt. As noted above, qualified distributions are not subject to the early distribution penalty *(8.12, 8.18)*, but distributions in excess of the $100,000 limit may be.

You generally have the option of repaying part or all of a qualified distribution to any eligible retirement plan within three years from the day after the date you receive it. Note that the repayment may be made to any eligible plan and not just to the plan from which the distribution was taken, so, for example, the qualified distribution could have been taken from your pension plan but you can repay it to your IRA. Repayments must be reported on Form 8915B. However, certain qualified distributions cannot be repaid. If you are a non-spouse beneficiary, you may not repay a distribution from the plan *(8.14, 7.12)*. You cannot repay a required minimum distribution or a periodic payment from an employer retirement plan that is being received over 10 or more years, or over your life expectancy or the joint life expectancies of you and your beneficiary.

If you report a qualified distribution using the three-year method and in the second year you make a repayment that exceeds the one-third amount otherwise reportable for that year, no income from the distribution will have to be reported for the second year, and you may carry forward the excess repayment to the third year or carry it back to the first year on an amended return; *see* the following example. See the Form 8915B instructions for further details on reporting a repayment.

---

### EXAMPLE

Arthur Taxpayer lived in Texas in 2017 and suffered economic loss due to Hurricane Harvey. In December 2017, he withdrew $90,000 from his traditional IRA. The withdrawal met the tests for a qualified distribution, and on Form 8915B Arthur included one- -third of the distribution, or $30,000, as income for 2017. In November 2018, Arthur repaid $45,000 to his IRA. Since the repayment exceeds the $30,000 required to be included in 2018 income under the three-year rule, Arthur will not have to report any income from the distribution on his 2018 return. Here are Arthur's options for reporting the excess $15,000 repayment.

1. Arthur may carry forward the $15,000 excess repayment for 2018 ($45,000 repayment -$30,000 includible under the three-year rule) to 2019, reducing his 2019 income from the distribution to $15,000 ($30,000 otherwise reportable minus $15,000 carryover), or

2. Arthur may report $30,000 as income on his 2019 return (the full $30,000 due under the three-year rule), and carry back the $15,000 excess repayment to 2017. He would file an amended return for 2017 to reduce the amount of income attributable to the qualified distribution to $15,000, from the $30,000 reported on his original 2017 return.

# CHAPTER 9

# Income From Real Estate Rentals and Royalties

Use Schedule E of Form 1040 to report real estate rental income and expenses. You must also file Form 4562 with your 2018 return to claim depreciation deductions for buildings you placed in service during the year.

Use Schedule C instead of Schedule E if you provide substantial services for the convenience of the tenants, such as maid service. That is, Schedule C is used to report payments received for the use and occupancy of rooms or other areas in a hotel, motel, boarding house, apartment, tourist home, or trailer court where services are provided primarily for the occupant.

If you rent out an apartment or room in the same building in which you live, you report the rent income less expenses allocated to the rental property *(9.4)*.

The law prevents most homeowners from deducting losses (expenses in excess of income) on the rental of a personal vacation home or personal residence if the owner or close relatives personally use the premises during the year. Tests based on days of personal and rental use determine whether you may deduct losses *(9.7)*.

Rental losses may also be limited by the passive activity rules discussed in *Chapter 10*. Real estate professionals may avoid the passive restrictions on rental income. An investor who actively manages property may deduct rental losses of up to $25,000 under an exception to the passive activity loss restrictions.

Use Schedule E to report royalties, but if you are a self-employed author, artist, or inventor, report royalty income and expenses on Schedule C.

Business rentals of equipment, vehicles, or similar personal property are reported on Schedule C, not Schedule E.

*Filing Tip*

**Married Owners Can File Schedule E for Qualified Joint Venture**

If you and your spouse are sole owners of a rental real estate business that you both materially participate in, and you file jointly, you can elect to be treated as a qualified joint venture (QJV) on Schedule E; *see 40.6*. You do not each file a separate Schedule E to report your respective share of the income and expenses. Instead, on Line 1 of Schedule E, each of your individual QJV interests is reported as a separate property, and on Line 2 you check the QJV box for each of the QJV property interests. For each separate property interest, enter on Lines 3-22 (income and expenses) the applicable share of the QJV income, deductions or loss.

Electing QJV status does not change the rule that exempts rental real estate income from self-employment tax *(45.1)*. The passive loss rules *(10.1)* also continue to apply.

*Caution*

**Security Deposits**

Distinguish advance rentals, which are income, from security deposits, which are not. Security deposits are amounts deposited with you solely as security for the tenant's performance of the terms of the lease, and as such are usually not taxed, particularly where local law treats security deposits as trust funds. If the tenant breaches the lease, you are entitled to apply the sum as rent, at which time you report it as income. If both you and your tenant agree that a security deposit is to be used as a final rent payment, it is advance rent. Include it in your income when you receive it.

## 9.1 Reporting Rental Real Estate Income and Expenses

On the cash basis, you report rent income on your tax return for the year in which you receive payment or in which you "constructively" receive it, such as where payment is credited to your bank account.

On the accrual basis, you report income on your tax return for the year in which you are entitled to receive payment, even if it is not actually paid. However, you do not report accrued income if the financial condition of the tenant makes collection doubtful. If you sue for payment, you do not report income until you win a collectible judgment.

**Schedule E reporting.** Use Schedule E (Form 1040) to report rental real estate income and expenses unless you are providing substantial services for tenants that go beyond the provision of utilities, trash collection, and cleaning of public areas. For example, if you operate a hotel or motel, and provide cleaning services such as maid service and changing linens, you should use Schedule C (Profit or Loss from Business *(40.6)*) rather than Schedule E.

**Advance rentals.** Advance rentals or bonuses are reported in the year received, whether you are on the cash or accrual basis.

Tenant's payment of landlord's expenses. The tenant's payment of your taxes, interest, insurance, mortgage amortization (even if you are not personally liable on the mortgage), repairs, or other expenses is considered additional rental income to you. If your tenant pays your utility bills or your emergency repairs and deducts the amount from the rent payment, you must include as rental income the full rental amount, not the actual net payment. However, you can claim an offsetting deduction for expenses, such as repairs, that would have been deductible had you paid them.

**Tenant's payment to cancel lease.** A tenant's payment for canceling a lease or modifying its terms is considered rental income in the year you receive it regardless of your method of accounting. You may deduct expenses incurred because of the cancellation or modification and any unamortized balance of expenses paid in negotiating the lease.

Insurance. Insurance proceeds for loss of rental income because of fire or other casualty are rental income.

**Improvements by tenants.** You do not realize taxable income when your tenant improves the leased premises, provided the improvements are not substitute rent payments. Furthermore, when you take possession of the improvements at the time the lease ends, you do not realize income. However, you may not depreciate the value of the improvements as the basis to you is considered zero.

**Property or services.** If you receive property or services instead of money, include the fair market value of such property or services as rental income.

If you agree upon a specified price for services rendered, that price is generally treated as the fair market value.

**Rental losses.** Rental income may be offset by deductions claimed for depreciation, mortgage interest, and repair and maintenance costs. However, if these expenses exceed rental income, the resulting loss is subject to the passive activity loss restrictions. If you do not qualify as a real estate professional *(10.3)*, you generally may not deduct rental losses from other income (nonpassive income such as salary, interest, and dividends) under the passive loss rules. Rental losses may offset only other rental and passive activity income; excess losses are carried forward to later years until there is passive income to offset or the property is disposed of *(10.13)*. However, if you perform some management role, you may deduct from other income real estate rental losses of up to $25,000, provided your adjusted gross income does not exceed $100,000 *(10.2)*. These restrictions on passive losses make rental income attractive, since the rental income can be offset by the passive losses. See Chapter 10 for details on the passive loss restrictions.

Application of the passive activity loss rules and exceptions assumes that the property is not considered a residence under the personal-use rules *(9.7)*. If a rented property is treated as a residence, rental expenses are deductible from rental income *(9.9)* but a loss is not allowed for that property.

## 9.2    Checklist of Rental Deductions

The expenses in this section are deductible from rental income on Schedule E of Form 1040 in determining your profit.

**Real estate taxes but not assessments for local improvements.**  Deductible real estate taxes do not include special assessments for paving, sewer systems, or other local improvements; these assessments are added to the cost of the land. However, you can deduct as real estate taxes assessments that merely maintain or repair local benefits, and which do not increase the value of your property. *See 16.4* through *16.7* for details on real estate tax deductions.

**Construction period interest and taxes.**  These expenses generally have to be capitalized and depreciated *(16.4)*.

**Depreciation of a rental building.**  You may start claiming depreciation in the month the building is ready for tenants. For example, you bought a house in May 2018 and spent June and July making repairs. The house was ready to rent in August and you began advertising for tenants. On your 2018 return you can begin depreciation as of August, even if a tenant did not move in until September or some later month. The month the building is ready for tenants is the month that determines the first-year depreciation write-off under the mid-month convention. *See 9.5* for the monthly depreciation rates for residential rental property. Rates for nonresidential buildings are at *42.13*.

**Depreciation for furniture and appliances.**  Furniture, carpeting, and appliances such as stoves and refrigerators used in residential rental property are considered five-year property for MACRS depreciation purposes. Furniture used in office buildings is considered seven-year property. *See 42.5* for MACRS rates.

**Management expenses.**  Include fees paid to a company for collecting the rent.

**Maintenance expenses.**  Include heating, repairs, lighting, water, electricity, gas, telephone, coal, and other service costs *(9.3)*.

**Salaries and wages.**  Include payments to superintendents, janitors, elevator operators, and service and maintenance personnel.

**Traveling expenses to look after the properties.**  If you travel "away from home" to inspect or repair rental property, be prepared to show that this was the primary purpose of your trip, rather than vacationing or other personal purposes. Otherwise, the IRS may disallow deductions for round-trip travel costs.

**Legal expenses for dispossessing tenants.**  But expenses of long-term leases are capital expenditures deductible over the term of the lease.

**Interest paid on mortgages and other indebtedness.**  But deductible interest does not include expenses paid to obtain a mortgage such as mortgage commissions and abstract or recording fees. Such costs are capital expenses that can be amortized over the life of the mortgage. For a mortgage obtained in 2018, amortization is claimed on Part VI of Form 4562 ("Depreciation and Amortization") and amortization for expenses of pre-2018 mortgages is claimed on Schedule E as an "Other expense."

**Commissions paid to collect rentals.**  But commissions paid to secure long-term rentals must be deducted over the life of the lease. Commissions paid to acquire the property are capitalized as an addition to basis.

**Premiums for fire, liability, and plate glass insurance.**  If payment is made in one year for insurance covering a period longer than one year, you amortize and deduct the premium over the life of the policy, even though you are on a cash basis.

**Tax return preparation.**  You may deduct as a rental expense the part of a tax preparation fee allocable to Part 1 of Schedule E (income or loss from rentals or royalties). You may also deduct, as a rental expense, a fee paid to a tax consultant to resolve a tax underpayment related to your rental activities.

**Charging below fair market rent.**  If you rent your property to a friend or relative for less than the fair rental value, you may deduct expenses and depreciation only to the extent of the rental income *(9.8)*.

*Law Alert*

**Qualified Business Income (QBI) Deduction for Certain Rental Activities**

If your rental activities are considered to be a trade or business, you may be eligible for a personal deduction of up to 20% of your qualified business income (QBI). The deduction does not reduce rental income. The QBI deduction is explained in *9.17*.

*Court Decision*

**Co-Tenant's Deduction for Real Estate Taxes**

The Tax Court may allow a co-tenant to deduct more than his or her proportionate share of real estate taxes. According to the court, the deduction test for real estate taxes is whether the payment satisfies a personal liability or protects a beneficial interest in the property. In the case of co-tenants, nonpayment of taxes by the other co-tenants could result in the property being lost or foreclosed. To prevent this, a co-tenant who pays the tax is protecting his or her beneficial interest and, therefore, is entitled to deduct the payment of the full tax, provided the payment is from his or her own funds.

In several cases, the Tax Court limited the taxpayer's deduction for taxes to his or her proportionate share, despite payment of the entire amount of taxes, because the taxpayer could not prove that the payment came from his own separate funds. The Tax Court has taken a similar approach when a joint obligor on a mortgage pays more than his or her share of the mortgage interest in order to avoid default.

**Co-tenants.** One of two tenants-in-common may deduct only half of the maintenance expenses even if he or she pays the entire bill. A tenant-in-common who pays all of the maintenance expenses of the common property is entitled to reimbursement from the other co-tenant, so one-half of the bill is not his or her ordinary and necessary expense. Each co-tenant owns a separate property interest in the common property that produces separate income for each. Each tenant's deductible expense is that portion of the entire expense that each separate interest bears to the whole, and no more.

As noted in the Court Decision in this section, a different rule may apply to a co-tenant's payment of real estate taxes (or mortgage interest).

**Costs of canceling lease.** A landlord may pay a tenant to cancel an unfavorable lease. The way the landlord treats the payment depends on the reason for the cancellation. If the purpose of the cancellation is to enable the landlord to construct a new building in place of the old, the cancellation payment is added to the basis of the new building. If the purpose is to sell the property, the payment is added to the cost of the property. If the landlord wants the premises for his or her own use, the payment is deducted over the remaining term of the old lease. If the landlord gets a new tenant to replace the old one, the cancellation payment is also generally deductible over the remaining term of the old lease.

> **EXAMPLE**
>
> Handlery Hotels, Inc., had to pay its lessee $85,000 to terminate a lease on a building three years before the lease term expired. Handlery entered into a new 20-year lease on more favorable terms with another lessee. Handlery amortized the $85,000 cancellation payment over the three-year unexpired term of the old lease. The IRS claimed that the payment had to be amortized over the 20-year term of the new lease because it was part of the cost of obtaining the new lease. A federal district court agreed with the IRS, but an appeals court sided with Handlery. Since the unexpired lease term is the major factor in determining the amount of the cancellation payment, the cost of cancellation should be amortized over that unexpired term.

## 9.3 Distinguishing Between a Repair and an Improvement

Maintenance and repair expenses are not treated in the same way as expenses for improvements and replacements. Only maintenance and incidental repair costs are deductible against rental income. Improvements that add to the value or prolong the life of the property or adapt it to new uses are capital improvements. Capital improvements may not be deducted currently but may be depreciated *(42.12)*. If you make improvements to property before renting it out, add the cost of the improvements to your basis in the property. A safe harbor under final IRS regulations (see below) may allow you to claim a current deduction for an expense that would otherwise have to be treated as an improvement.

A repair keeps your property in good operating condition. For example, repairs include painting, fixing gutters or floors, fixing leaks, plastering, and replacing broken windows. However, putting a recreation room in an unfinished basement, paneling a den, putting up a fence, putting in new plumbing or wiring, and paving a driveway are all examples of depreciable capital improvements *(42.12)*. Putting on a new roof is generally a depreciable capital improvement; however, the Tax Court has allowed current deductions for roof replacements intended to prevent leaks; *see* Example 2 below.

Repairs may not be separated from capital expenditures when both are part of an improvement program; *see* Example 3 below.

**IRS regulations distinguish repairs from improvements.** Under final IRS regulations, an expense that results in the betterment, restoration, or adaptation to a new and different use of property is treated as an improvement that must be capitalized (and depreciated) unless a special safe harbor (see below) allows a current deduction. For example, the regulations affirm the long-held IRS position that replacing a roof is a restoration that is treated as an improvement to the building structure and as such it must be capitalized. An example of a betterment is the installation of bolts to a building located in an earthquake prone area

*Planning Reminder*

**Repairs and Improvements**

What if repairs and improvements are unconnected and not part of an overall improvement program? Assume you repair the floors of one story and improve another story by putting in new windows. You probably may deduct the cost of repairing the floors provided you have separate bills for the jobs. To safeguard the deduction, schedule the work at separate times so that the two jobs are not lumped together as an overall improvement program.

to add structural support and resistance to seismic forces. An example of an adaptation is making modifications to a manufacturing building so it can be used as a showroom.

The regulations also identify specific building systems, called "units of property" or UOPs, and require that an improvement to a particular UOP must be depreciated rather than deducted currently. These UOPs include the HVAC (heating, ventilation, air conditioning), plumbing, electrical, fire protection, security and gas distribution systems.

**Safe harbors under the IRS regulations.** The final regulations provide safe harbors that may allow a current deduction. There are three safe harbors: a *de minimis* safe harbor, a safe harbor for small taxpayers, and a safe harbor for routine maintenance. To the extent that a safe harbor applies, a current deduction is allowed, although the expense might otherwise be considered a depreciable improvement. The *de minimis* safe harbor and small taxpayer safe harbor are annual elections made on a statement attached to your return; they are not a change in accounting method.

1. *De minimis safe harbor.* This safe harbor allows you to deduct amounts up to $2,500 per item or invoice. Thus, a low-cost purchase (such as a small appliance or window replacement) is fully deductible if it costs $2,500 or less. To elect the *de minimis* safe harbor, the IRS requires that you attach a statement to your return and you must apply the safe harbor to all items purchased during the year that are within the $2,500 limit.

    There is also a $5,000 *de minimis* safe harbor (per item or invoice), but this applies only to taxpayers that have an applicable financial statement (AFS), which generally applies to companies required to file financial statements with the SEC or obtain certified audited financial statements.

2. *Safe harbor for small taxpayers.* This safe harbor allows small taxpayers (average annual gross receipts of no more than $10 million in the three prior years) to elect an overall exemption from the capitalization rules for repairs, maintenance, and improvements, but the benefit is limited. The safe harbor applies separately to each building you own, but only buildings with an unadjusted basis of up to $1 million qualify. For each such building, the safe harbor allows a current deduction only if your expenses do not exceed the lesser of $10,000 or 2% of the unadjusted basis of the building. This limit applies to the total expenses during the year for repairs, maintenance, and improvements to that building. Thus, for a building with a $250,000 unadjusted basis, the expense limit is $5,000 (2% × $250,000).

    To the extent that the annual expenses fall within the $10,000/2% ceiling, a deduction is allowed for amounts that would otherwise be considered improvements. To claim the safe harbor, you must file an election on a timely filed original tax return for that year, including extensions. For a building owned by a partnership or S corporation, the election must be made by the entity and not by the shareholders or partners.

    If the total expenses for the year for repairs, maintenance, and improvements exceed the $10,000/2% limit, the safe harbor is not allowed for any of the expenses, and the general rules for determining whether an item is a repair or an improvement apply. This means that a low-cost item may be deductible under the *de minimis* safe harbor, or an expense may be allowed under the routine maintenance safe harbor.

3. *Safe harbor for routine maintenance.* This safe harbor allows you to deduct an expense that is for keeping the property in efficient operating condition if it is reasonably expected that the expense will have to be performed more than once over a 10-year period. An IRS example of a qualifying expense is maintenance of an HVAC system at the manufacturer's recommended schedule of once every four years, including inspection, cleaning, and repair or replacement of component parts.

**EXAMPLES**

1. The cost of painting the outside of a rental building and the cost of papering and painting the inside are repair costs and may be deducted. A change in the plumbing system is generally a capital expenditure that must be depreciated under MACRS *(42.13)* unless a current deduction is allowed under the small taxpayer safe harbor of the final regulations (*see* above).

2. Campbell owned a one-story house that she rented to a tenant. She paid $8,000 to repair the roof after the tenant complained of leaks. The contractor she employed removed the existing layers of roof and replaced them with fiberglass and asphalt; no structural changes were made. The Tax Court allowed Campbell to deduct the full amount of the payment to the contractor as an ordinary and necessary repair because the roof replacement merely restored the property to a leak-free condition and did not add to the value of the home.

The Tax Court also allowed an owner of a commercial building with a leaky roof to fully deduct the $52,000 cost of stripping the roof layers, replacing them, and spraying the new ones with foam to prevent future leaks. These were repairs intended to keep the property in working condition and did not extend the life of the building.

3. You buy a dilapidated business building and have it renovated and repaired before renting it to commercial tenants. The total cost comes to about $130,000, of which $17,800 is allocable to the repairs. The cost of the repairs is generally not deductible because the entire project is a capital expenditure. According to the IRS, when a general improvement program is undertaken, you may not separate repairs from improvements. Both become an integral part of the overall betterment and are a capital investment, although a portion could be characterized as repairs when viewed independently.

## 9.4 Reporting Rents From a Multi-Unit Residence

If you rent out an apartment or room in a multi-unit residence in which you also live, you report rent receipts and deduct expenses allocated to the rented part of the property on Schedule E of Form 1040 whether or not you itemize deductions. You deduct interest and taxes on your personal share of the property as itemized deductions on Schedule A of Form 1040 if you itemize deductions. If you or close relatives personally use the rented portion during the year and expenses exceed income, loss deductions may be barred under the personal-use rules *(9.7)*.

**Court Decision**

**Rented Rooms That Are Not Separate Dwelling Units**

A rental loss was denied to an owner of a two-story, four-bedroom house when he rented out two bedrooms to separate tenants after he lost his job. Although individual locks were placed on the doors of the rented bedrooms, the tenants and the owner shared access to the kitchen, bathroom, and other parts of the house. The Tax Court held that the rented rooms were not separate and distinct from the rest of the house that the owner used. The house was a single dwelling unit shared by the owner and tenants and under the personal-use rules *(9.7)*, the owner could not claim a rental loss.

### EXAMPLE

You buy a three-family house in March 2018. You occupy one floor as your personal residence and starting in June 2018, when the other two floors are ready for tenants, you rent out the two floors. The house cost you $300,000 ($270,000 for the building and $30,000 for the land). Two-thirds of the basis of the building is subject to depreciation, or $180,000 (2/3 of $270,000). For a building placed in service in June, the depreciation rate is 1.970%, as shown in *Table 9-1*, so your depreciation deduction is $3,546 (1.970% $180,000). Assuming you paid property taxes of $6,000, mortgage interest of $3,900, and repairs of $3,000, this is how you deduct expenses for 2018:

| | Total | Personal portion deductible as itemized deductions | Rental portion deductible on Schedule E | Not deductible |
|---|---|---|---|---|
| Taxes | $ 6,000 | $ 2,000 | $ 4,000 | |
| Interest | 3,900 | 1,300 | 2,600 | |
| Repairs | 3,000 | | 2,000 | $ 1,000 |
| Depreciation | 3,546 | | 3,546 | |
| | $ 16,446 | $ 3,300 | $ 12,146 | $ 1,000 |

The taxes and interest allocated to personal use are deductible on Schedule A of Form 1040 if you itemize deductions. The taxes are subject to the overall limit of $10,000 that can be claimed for state and local property taxes plus state income or sales taxes *(16.1)*. Repairs allocated to your apartment are nondeductible personal expenses.

Even if a loss is not barred by the personal-use rules *(9.7)*, a loss shown on Schedule E is subject to the passive loss restrictions discussed in *Chapter 10*. The loss, if it comes within the $25,000 allowance *(10.2)* or the exception for real estate professionals *(10.3)*, may be deducted from any type of income. If your only passive activity losses are rental losses of $25,000 or less from actively managed rental real estate and your modified adjusted gross income is $100,000 or less, you do not have to use Form 8582 to deduct losses under the $25,000 allowance *(10.12)*. If you are not a qualifying real estate professional and cannot claim the allowance, the loss may be deducted only from passive activity income.

## 9.5 Depreciation on Converting a Home to Rental Property

When you convert your residence to rental property, you may depreciate the building. You figure depreciation on the lower of:

- Fair market value of the building at the time you convert it to rental property; or
- Your adjusted basis at the time of the conversion. This is your original cost for the building, exclusive of land, plus permanent improvements and other capital costs, and minus items that represent a return of your cost, such as casualty or theft loss deductions claimed on prior tax returns.

You claim MACRS depreciation based on a 27½-year recovery period, which extends to 28 or 29 years due to the mid-month convention. The specific rate for the year of conversion is the rate for the month in which the property is ready for tenants. For example, you move out of your home in May and make some minor repairs. You advertise the house for rent in June. Depreciation starts in June because that is when the home is ready for rental, even if you do not actually obtain a tenant until a later month. Under a mid-month convention, the house is treated as placed in service during the middle of the month. This means that one-half of a full month's depreciation is allowed for that month. In *Table 9-1*, the monthly depreciation rates for the year the property is placed in service and later years are shown. The table incorporates the mid-month convention.

 *Planning Reminder*

**Obtain Appraisal**

Have an appraiser estimate the fair market value of the house when it is rented. The appraisal will help support your basis for depreciation or a loss deduction on a sale if your return is examined.

### EXAMPLE

In 2002, you bought a house for $125,000, of which $100,000 is allocated to the house; the $25,000 balance is allocated to the land. In June 2018, you move out of the house and rent it to tenants. At that time, the fair market value of the house exclusive of the land is $150,000. The depreciable basis of the house is the adjusted basis of $100,000, as it is less than the $150,000 value. The depreciation rate for placing the house in service in June is 1.970%, as shown in *Table 9-1*. Thus, your 2018 depreciation deduction is $1,970 ($100,000 × 1.970%). Your 2019 depreciation deduction (your second year of depreciation) will be $3,636 ($100,000 × 3.636% rate for year 2).

**Depreciating a rented cooperative apartment.** If you rent out a co-op apartment, you may deduct your share of the total depreciation claimed by the cooperative corporation. The method for computing your share depends on whether you bought your co-op shares as part of the first offering. If you did, follow these steps: (1) Ask the co-op corporation officials for the total real estate depreciation deduction of the corporation, not counting depreciation for office space that cannot be lived in by tenant-shareholders. (2) Multiply Step 1 by the following fraction: number of your co-op shares divided by total shares outstanding. The result is your share of the co-op's depreciation, but you may not deduct more than your adjusted basis.

The computation is more complicated if you bought your co-op shares after the first offering. You must compute your depreciable basis as follows: Increase your cost for the co-op shares by your share of the co-op's total mortgage. Reduce this amount by your share of the value of the co-op's land and your share of the commercial space not available for occupancy by tenant-stockholders. Your "share" of the co-op's mortgage, land value, or commercial space is the co-op's total amount for such items multiplied by the fraction in Step 2 above, that is, the number of your shares divided by the total shares outstanding. After computing your depreciable basis, multiply that basis by the depreciation percentage for the month your apartment is ready for rental.

**Basis to use when you sell a rented residence.** For purposes of figuring gain, you use adjusted basis at the time of the conversion, plus subsequent capital improvements, and minus depreciation and casualty loss deductions. For purposes of figuring loss, you use the lower of adjusted basis and fair market value at the time of the conversion, plus subsequent improvements and minus depreciation and casualty losses. You may have neither gain nor loss to report; this would happen if you figure a loss when using the above basis rule for gains and you figure a gain when using the basis rule for losses.

**Depreciation on a vacant residence.** If you move from your house before it is sold, you generally may not deduct depreciation on the vacant residence while it is held for sale. The IRS will not allow the deduction, and, according to the Tax Court, a deduction is possible only if you can show that you held the house expecting to make a profit on an increase in value over and above the value of the house when you moved from it. That is, you held the house for sale on the expectation of profiting on a future increase in value after abandoning the house as a residence.

**Table 9-1   Depreciation for Residential Rental Property: Use the Row for the Month the Residence Is Ready for Rental in the First Rental Year**

| Year | Month property placed in service | | | | | | | | | | | |
|---|---|---|---|---|---|---|---|---|---|---|---|---|
| | 1 | 2 | 3 | 4 | 5 | 6 | 7 | 8 | 9 | 10 | 11 | 12 |
| 1 | 3.485% | 3.182% | 2.879% | 2.576% | 2.273% | 1.970% | 1.667% | 1.364% | 1.061% | 0.758% | 0.455% | 0.152% |
| 2–9 | 3.636 | 3.636 | 3.636 | 3.636 | 3.636 | 3.636 | 3.636 | 3.636 | 3.636 | 3.636 | 3.636 | 3.636 |
| 10 | 3.637 | 3.637 | 3.637 | 3.637 | 3.637 | 3.637 | 3.636 | 3.636 | 3.636 | 3.636 | 3.636 | 3.636 |
| 11 | 3.636 | 3.636 | 3.636 | 3.636 | 3.636 | 3.636 | 3.637 | 3.637 | 3.637 | 3.637 | 3.637 | 3.637 |
| 12 | 3.637 | 3.637 | 3.637 | 3.637 | 3.637 | 3.637 | 3.636 | 3.636 | 3.636 | 3.636 | 3.636 | 3.636 |
| 13 | 3.636 | 3.636 | 3.636 | 3.636 | 3.636 | 3.636 | 3.637 | 3.637 | 3.637 | 3.637 | 3.637 | 3.637 |
| 14 | 3.637 | 3.637 | 3.637 | 3.637 | 3.637 | 3.637 | 3.636 | 3.636 | 3.636 | 3.636 | 3.636 | 3.636 |
| 15 | 3.636 | 3.636 | 3.636 | 3.636 | 3.636 | 3.636 | 3.637 | 3.637 | 3.637 | 3.637 | 3.637 | 3.637 |
| 16 | 3.637 | 3.637 | 3.637 | 3.637 | 3.637 | 3.637 | 3.636 | 3.636 | 3.636 | 3.636 | 3.636 | 3.636 |
| 17 | 3.636 | 3.636 | 3.636 | 3.636 | 3.636 | 3.636 | 3.637 | 3.637 | 3.637 | 3.637 | 3.637 | 3.637 |
| 18 | 3.637 | 3.637 | 3.637 | 3.637 | 3.637 | 3.637 | 3.636 | 3.636 | 3.636 | 3.636 | 3.636 | 3.636 |
| 19 | 3.636 | 3.636 | 3.636 | 3.636 | 3.636 | 3.636 | 3.637 | 3.637 | 3.637 | 3.637 | 3.637 | 3.637 |
| 20 | 3.637 | 3.637 | 3.637 | 3.637 | 3.637 | 3.637 | 3.636 | 3.636 | 3.636 | 3.636 | 3.636 | 3.636 |
| 21 | 3.636 | 3.636 | 3.636 | 3.636 | 3.636 | 3.636 | 3.637 | 3.637 | 3.637 | 3.637 | 3.637 | 3.637 |
| 22 | 3.637 | 3.637 | 3.637 | 3.637 | 3.637 | 3.637 | 3.636 | 3.636 | 3.636 | 3.636 | 3.636 | 3.636 |
| 23 | 3.636 | 3.636 | 3.636 | 3.636 | 3.636 | 3.636 | 3.637 | 3.637 | 3.637 | 3.637 | 3.637 | 3.637 |
| 24 | 3.637 | 3.637 | 3.637 | 3.637 | 3.637 | 3.637 | 3.636 | 3.636 | 3.636 | 3.636 | 3.636 | 3.636 |
| 25 | 3.636 | 3.636 | 3.636 | 3.636 | 3.636 | 3.636 | 3.637 | 3.637 | 3.637 | 3.637 | 3.637 | 3.637 |
| 26 | 3.637 | 3.637 | 3.637 | 3.637 | 3.637 | 3.637 | 3.636 | 3.636 | 3.636 | 3.636 | 3.636 | 3.636 |
| 27 | 3.636 | 3.636 | 3.636 | 3.636 | 3.636 | 3.636 | 3.637 | 3.637 | 3.637 | 3.637 | 3.637 | 3.637 |
| 28 | 1.97 | 2.273 | 2.576 | 2.879 | 3.182 | 3.485 | 3.636 | 3.636 | 3.636 | 3.636 | 3.636 | 3.636 |
| 29 | | | | | | | 0.152 | 0.455 | 0.758 | 1.061 | 1.364 | 1.667 |

## 9.6 Renting a Residence to a Relative

The tax law distinguishes between a rental of a unit used by a close relative as a principal residence and a rental of a unit that is not the relative's principal residence, such as a second home or vacation home. It is easier to deduct a rental loss on the principal residence rental.

If you rent a unit at a fair market rental price to a close relative who uses it as his or her principal residence, your relative's use is not considered personal use by you that could bar a loss deduction under the personal-use test (9.7). A relative's use of the unit as a second or vacation home is attributed to you in applying the personal-use test (9.7), even if you receive a fair market value rent.

Close relatives who come within these rules are: brothers and sisters, half-brothers and half-sisters, spouses, parents, grandparents, children, and grandchildren.

Fair market rental is the amount a person who is not related to you would be willing to pay. The most direct way to determine fair market rental is to ask a real estate agent in your neighborhood for comparative rentals.

> ### EXAMPLE
> Barranti inherited a residence from her grandmother. The house was in a state of disrepair. A real estate agent estimated the fair market rental rate for the house to be between $700 and $750 per month. Barranti rented the house to her brother for $500 a month while he repaired the structure. After a year, he moved out and Barranti sold the house and claimed a rental loss and a loss on the sale. The Tax Court disallowed both losses. The below-market rental to Barranti's brother was treated as her own personal use of the house, preventing the rental loss deduction. The below-market rental was also treated as evidence that Barranti held the property for personal purposes and therefore she could not deduct the loss on the sale either.

## 9.7 Personal Use and Rental of a Residence During the Year

The number of personal-use days and fair-market-rental days for your residential unit determines how you must report rental income and expenses. If you rent the property for 15 or more days and your personal use of the unit exceeds the 14-day/10% test described below, the unit is treated as a residence rather than rental property, and in this case, some of your rental expenses are deductible only to the extent of the rental income from the property (9.9).

Personal-use days include not only your days of personal use but may also include rental days to family members listed at 9.6 and use days under co-ownership agreements. See 9.8 for details on personal-use days.

**Dwelling units subject to the 14-day/10% test.** The daily-use tests apply to any "dwelling unit" you rent out that is also used as a residence during the year by yourself or other family members. A dwelling unit may be a house, apartment, condominium, cooperative, house trailer, mini motor home, boat, or similar property with basic living accommodations, including any appurtenant structure such as a garage. A dwelling unit does not include property used exclusively as a hotel, motel, inn, or similar establishment.

The hotel/motel/inn exception applies only to property that is used exclusively in such a business. The exception does not apply to the dual-use portion of a hotel, inn, or bed and breakfast. In one case, the Tax Court agreed with the IRS that the owners of a three-floor bed-and-breakfast could not claim business expense deductions for depreciation or interest on the areas that were used both in the B&B business as well as by them personally. The lobby, registration area, office, kitchen, and laundry room were used 75% of the time for the business and 25% of the time for personal purposes. Because these areas were not used solely for operating the B&B, they could not qualify for the hotel exception. The dual-use areas were treated as part of the owners' dwelling unit for purposes of the 14-day/10% personal-use test.

**14-day/10% personal-use test determines if unit is treated as a residence.** A daily-use test determines whether your use of the unit during the taxable year is treated as residential use.

You are considered to have used the unit as a residence if your personal-use days during the year, determined according to the rules for counting personal-use and rental days *(9.8)*, exceeded 14 days, or, if greater, 10% of the days on which the unit was rented to others at a fair market rental price.

If the property is treated as used as a residence because your personal use exceeds the greater of 14 days or 10% of the fair market rental days, and you have a rental loss, a deduction for some of your allocable rental deductions will be limited, as the expenses are offset against rental income following a specific order; *see* Rule 2 below and Steps 1-3 in *9.9*.

**Rule 1: If your personal use does not meet the 14-day/10% test.** If your personal-use days do not exceed 14 days or 10% of the fair market rental days, whichever is more, the property is treated as rental property and not property used as a residence. You report the rental income and expenses on Schedule E (Form 1040) and the rental deductions are not limited to rental income by the personal-use test. However, a loss deduction is subject to the passive activity loss restrictions *(10.1)*. The passive loss rules generally prevent you from deducting a passive rental loss against nonpassive income, but if you are an "active participant" with modified adjusted gross income of no more than $100,000, you may deduct expenses up to $25,000 *(10.2)*, and if you qualify as a real estate professional and materially participate *(10.3)*, a full loss is allowed against nonpassive income.

Another consequence of not meeting the 14-day/10% personal use test is that you lose part of the mortgage interest deduction because the unit is not a qualified second home for mortgage interest purposes if personal use does not exceed the greater of 14 days or 10% of the fair market rental days. The mortgage interest allocable to the rental use *(9.9)* is deductible against rental income on Schedule E, but the balance is nondeductible personal interest.

**Rule 2: If your personal use exceeds the 14-day/10% test and you rent the unit for 15 or more days during the year.** If you are considered to have used the unit as a residence because your personal use of the property exceeds the greater of 14 days or 10% of the fair market rental days, and you rent the property for at least 15 days during the year, you cannot deduct a rental loss on Schedule E. Your rental expenses and depreciation are deductible on Schedule E only to the extent of rental income, following the allocation rules of Steps 1-3 in *9.9*. Expenses that are not deductible in the current year under this limitation may be carried forward and will be deductible up to rental income in the following year. The deduction limit is irrelevant if your rental income exceeds expenses. When you have a profit, you report the rental income and claim all of the deductible rental expenses on Schedule E.

**Rule 3: If your personal use exceeds the 14-day/10% test but you rent the unit for less than 15 days during the taxable year.** If your personal use of the property exceeds the greater of 14 days or 10% of the fair market rental days, and you rent it for fewer than 15 days in the taxable year, do not report the rental income on your tax return (it is not gross income) and the only deductions allowed are those you would be allowed anyway as a homeowner. That is, if you itemize deductions on Schedule A, you deduct allowable mortgage interest *(15.1)*, real estate taxes *(16.1)*, and casualty losses *(18.1)*. No other rental expenses such as depreciation and maintenance expenses are deductible.

### EXAMPLES

1. In 2018, you rented out your condominium unit in Florida at a fair market rental for 260 days. The property is considered used as a residence if your personal use exceeds the greater of 14 days or 10% of the days it is rented to others at a fair market value. Here, under the "greater of" test, 10% of the 260 fair market value days, or 26 days, exceeds 14 days, so if your personal use exceeds 26 days, the condominium is considered a residence subject to the deduction limitation rules under Rule 2 above and Steps 1-3 in *9.9*.

   If you only used the unit for 26 days (10% of the rental days) or less, you are not treated as using the property as a residence under the 14-day/10% test. You may treat the unit for the taxable year as rental property and your expenses are not limited to rental income (under Steps 1-3 in *9.9*). You may deduct a loss, if any, subject to the passive activity rules *(10.1)*. However, if personal use did not exceed 26 days, the mortgage interest allocable to the personal-use days would be nondeductible personal interest.

2. Assume the same unit as in Example 1 but you rented the unit for 130 days. The unit would be treated as a residence if your personal use exceeded 14 days, since under the "greater of" test, 14 days is greater than 10% of the rental days (10% of 130 days or 13 days). If you used the unit personally for 14 days or less, you may treat the unit as a rental property.

## 9.8 Counting Personal-Use Days and Rental Days for a Residence

In applying the 14-day/10% personal-use test *(9.7)*, personal-use days are:

- Days you used the residence for personal purposes other than days primarily spent making repairs or getting the property ready for tenants. If you use a residence for personal purposes on a day you rent it at fair market value, count that day as a personal day, not a rental day, in applying the 14-day/10% test.

- Days on which the residence is used by your spouse, children, grandchildren or great-grandchildren, parents, brothers, sisters, grandparents, or great-grandparents. However, if such a relative pays you a fair rental value to use the home as a principal residence, the relative's use is not considered personal use by you. If you rent a vacation home to such relatives, their use is considered personal use by you even if they pay a fair rental value amount; *see* Example 1 below. The same rules apply if the use of the residence is by a family member of a co-owner of the property.

- Days on which the residence is used by any person under a reciprocal arrangement that allows you to use some other dwelling during the year.

- Days on which you rent the residence to any person for less than fair market value.

- Days that a co-owner of the property uses the residence, unless the co-owner's use is under a shared-equity financing agreement discussed later in this section.

An owner is not considered to have personally used a home that is used by an employee if the value of such use is tax-free lodging required as a condition of employment *(3.13)*.

**Shared-equity financing agreements for co-owners.** Use by a co-owner is not considered personal use by you if you have a shared-equity financing agreement under which: (1) the co-owner pays you a fair rent for using the home as his or her principal residence; and (2) you and your co-owner each have undivided interests for more than 50 years in the entire home and in any appurtenant land acquired with the residence.

Any use by a co-owner that does not meet these two tests is considered personal use by you if, for any part of the day, the home is used by a co-owner or a holder of any interest in the home (other than a security interest or an interest under a lease for fair rental) for personal purposes. For this purpose, any other ownership interest existing at the time you have an interest in the home is counted, even if there are no immediate rights to possession and enjoyment of the home under such other interest. For example, you have a life estate in the home and your friend owns the remainder interest. Use by either of you is personal use.

**Rental of principal residence prior to sale.** You are not considered to have made any personal use of a principal residence that you rent or try to rent at a fair rental for (1) a consecutive period of 12 months or more or (2) a period of less than 12 months that ends with the sale or exchange of the residence. For example, you move out of your principal residence on May 31, 2018, offering it for rental as of June 1. You rent it from June 15 until mid-November, when you sell the house. Under the special rental period rule, your use of the house from January 1 until May 31, 2018, is not counted as personal use. This means that deductions for the rental period are not subject to the rental income limitation (Steps 1-3 in *9.9*).

*Planning Reminder*

**Shared-Equity Financing Agreements**

As an investor, you can help finance the purchase of a principal residence for a family member or other individual. The rental income you receive for your ownership share in the property may be offset by deductions for your share of the mortgage interest, taxes, and operating expenses you pay under the terms of the agreement, as well as depreciation deductions for your percentage share. Rental losses are subject to the passive loss restrictions in *Chapter 10*.

The other co-owner living in the house may claim itemized deductions for payment of his or her share of the mortgage interest and taxes.

### EXAMPLES

1. A son rented a condominium in Florida to his parents, who split their time between the Florida apartment and the home they owned in Illinois. Although the parents paid a fair amount for the Florida condo, the son's rental deductions were limited by the IRS and the Tax Court to interest and real estate taxes that did not exceed the rental income. The

parents' rental days were attributed to the son under the 14 day/10% rental day limit since the home in Illinois, and not the Florida apartment, was their principal residence.

2. You and your neighbor Joe are co-owners of a vacation condominium. You rent the unit out whenever possible; Joe uses the unit for two weeks every year. As Joe owns an interest in the unit, both of you are considered to have used the unit for personal purposes during those weeks.

3. You and your neighbor Tom are co-owners of a house under a shared-equity financing agreement. Tom lives in the house and pays you a fair rental price. Even though Tom has an interest in the house, the days he lives there are not counted as days of personal use by you because Tom rents the house as a main home under a shared-equity financing agreement.

4. You rent a beach house to Jane. Jane rents her house in the mountains to you. You each pay a fair rental price. You are using your house for personal purposes on the days that Jane uses it because your house is used by Jane under an arrangement that allows you to use her house.

## 9.9 Allocating Expenses of a Residence to Rental Days

When you rent out your home or other dwelling unit *(9.7)* for part of the year at fair market value and also use it personally on some days during the taxable year, expenses are allocated between personal and rental use. The deductible rental portion equals your total expenses for the year multiplied by this fraction:

$$\frac{\text{Days unit is rented for fair market rental price}}{\text{Total days of rental and personal use}}$$

The days a unit is held out for rent but not actually rented are not counted as rental days in the numerator of the fraction. Any day for which the unit is rented at a fair rental price is counted as a rental day for allocation purposes even if in fact you use it for personal purposes on that day.

**Mortgage interest and real estate taxes.** There is a conflict of opinion between the IRS and some courts over the issue of whether the above fractional formula applies also to interest and taxes. According to the IRS, it does. According to the Tax Court and two federal appeals courts, it does not; interest and taxes are allocated on a daily basis. Thus, if a house is rented for 61 days in 2018, 16.71% (61/365) of the deductible interest and taxes is deducted first from the rental income. This Tax Court rule allows a larger amount of other expenses to be deducted from rental income than is allowed under the IRS application of the formula; *see* the Examples below. However, where the $10,000 overall limitation on state and local taxes comes into play, then the IRS method may be more favorable.

**Claiming expenses on Schedule E if personal use limits a loss deduction.** If your personal use of a residence exceeds the 14-day /10% test *(9.7)*, the residence was rented for at least 15 days during the year, and the allocable rental expenses (including depreciation) exceed rental income, you cannot deduct the net loss from other income. Some of the expenses will not be currently deductible. The allocable rental expenses are deducted from rental income in a specific order:

1. The rental portion of the following expenses is fully deductible on Schedule E of Form 1040, even if the total exceeds rental income: deductible home mortgage interest *(15.1)*, real estate taxes *(16.4)*, deductible casualty and theft losses *(Chapter 18)*, and directly related rental expenses. Directly related rental expenses are rental expenses not related to the use or maintenance of the residence itself, such as office supplies, rental agency fees, advertising, and depreciation on office equipment used in the rental activity.

2. If there is any rental income remaining after the income is reduced by the expenses in Step 1, the balance is next offset by the rental portion of operating expenses for the residence itself, such as utilities, repairs, and insurance. Do not include depreciation on the rental part of the home in this group.

3. If any rental income remains after Step 2, depreciation on the rental portion of the residence may be deducted from the balance.

Step 1 expenses, as well as the expenses from Steps 2 and 3 that offset rental income, are deducted on the applicable lines of Schedule E. Operating expenses from Step 2 and depreciation from Step 3 that exceed the balance of rental income are carried forward to the next year as rental expenses for the same property. In the next year, the carried-over expenses are deductible only to the extent of rental income from the property for that year, following Steps 1–3, whether or not your personal use of the residence exceeds the 14-day/10% test *(9.7)* for that carryover year.

If you itemize deductions, you claim the personal-use portion of deductible mortgage interest, real estate taxes, and disaster-related casualty and theft losses on Schedule A of Form 1040. Business casualty losses for the rental portion are not limited to those sustained in disaster areas.

**Interest expenses.** If you personally use a rental vacation home for more than the greater of 14 days or 10% of the fair market rental days *(9.7)*, the residence may be treated as a qualifying second residence under the mortgage interest rules *(15.1)*. The interest on a qualifying second home is not subject to disallowance under the passive activity restrictions; the rental is not treated as a passive activity *(10.1)*. As shown in Step 1 above, the portion of the deductible mortgage interest allocable to the rental portion is deducted from rental income (along with taxes) before other expenses.

 *Filing Tip*

**Carryover of Disallowed Expenses**

If your deductions for operating expenses and depreciation are limited by the personal-use rules, the disallowed amounts may be carried over to the following year.

---

### EXAMPLES

1.  You rent out your vacation home for July and August of 2018 (62 days), receiving rent of $4,000 (a fair market rental). You use the home yourself for 124 days during the year. Your annual expenses are mortgage interest of $4,200, real estate taxes of $3,900, and maintenance costs (including utilities and insurance) of $4,500. Depreciation (based on 100% rental use) is $3,940. Since your personal use (124 days) exceeds 14 days (the greater of 14 days or 10% of the 62 fair market rental days *(9.7)*) and your rental expenses exceed the rental income, you may deduct expenses only up to the amount of rental income under Steps 1-3 above. Assume the vacation home is a qualifying second home *(15.1)*, so that all the interest is deductible under the mortgage interest rules. Under the IRS allocation method, one-third of all the expenses (62 rental days divided by 186 total days of use), including the interest and taxes, are deducted on Schedule E in this order:

| | | |
|---|---:|---:|
| Rental income | | $ 4,000 |
| Less Step 1 expenses: | | |
| Interest (1/3 of $4,200) | $1,400 | |
| Taxes (1/3 of $3,900) | 1,300 | 2,700 |
| | | $ 1,300 |
| Less Step 2 expenses: | | |
| Maintenance (1/3 of $4,500, or $1,500, but the offset cannot exceed the $1,300 balance of rental income) | | 1,300 |
| | | $ 0 |

Step 3 Depreciation: 1/3 of $3,940, or $1,313, is allocable to the rental, but none is deductible because there is no remaining rental income.

The $200 of maintenance expenses and the $1,313 of depreciation that are not deductible for 2018 because of the rental income limitation may be carried forward to 2019.

Under the Tax Court's method of allocating interest and taxes, 16.99% (62/365) of the interest and taxes, or $1,376 (16.99% × $8,100) is deductible from rental income, rather than the $2,700 (one-third) required by the IRS method, so more rental income is left that can be offset by maintenance expenses and depreciation.

The interest and taxes allocable to your personal use are deductible as itemized deductions provided you claim itemized deductions on Schedule A of Form 1040; the taxes are subject to the overall $10,000 limit for state and local taxes *(16.1)*.

If the vacation home were not a qualifying second residence as discussed in *15.1*, the interest would not be deducted with taxes from the $4,000 of rental income, but would be treated as an operating expense and deducted along with the maintenance expenses.

2. The Boltons paid interest and property taxes totaling $3,475 on their vacation home. Maintenance expenses (not including depreciation) totaled $2,693. The Boltons stayed at the home 30 days and rented it for 91 days, receiving rents of $2,700. Because the personal use for 30 days exceeded the 14-day limit *(9.7)*, the Boltons could deduct rental expenses only up to the gross rental income of $2,700, reduced by interest and taxes allocable to rental. In figuring the amount of interest and taxes deductible from rents, they divided the number of rental days, or 91, by 366, the number of days in the year. This gave them an allocation of 25%. After subtracting $869 for interest and taxes (25% of $3,475) from rental income, they deducted $1,831 ($2,700 – $869) of maintenance expenses from rental income.

The IRS argued that 75% of the Boltons' interest and tax payments had to be allocated to the rental income. The IRS used an allocation fraction with a denominator of 121 days, the total days of use (30 personal and 91 rental days). Thus, the IRS allocated 75% (91/121) of the interest and taxes, or $2,606, to gross rental income of $2,700. This allocation allowed only $94 maintenance expenses to be deducted ($2,700 – $2,606).

The Tax Court sided with the Boltons and an appeals court (the Ninth Circuit) agreed. The IRS method of allocating interest and taxes to rental use is bizarre. Interest and taxes are expenses that accrue ratably over the year and are deductible even if a vacation home is not rented for a single day. Thus, the allocation to rental use should be based on a ratable portion of the annual expense by dividing the number of rental days by the number of days in a year.

The Tenth Circuit appeals court also supports the Tax Court allocation method.

**Court Decision**

**Allocation of Taxes and Interest**

The IRS position on allocating mortgage interest and real estate taxes to rental income is not as favorable as the position adopted by the Tax Court and several appeals courts where overall state and local taxes are below the $10,000 limitation. But the IRS position may be more favorable for those with state and local taxes exceeding this limitation.

## 9.10 IRS May Challenge Loss Claimed on Temporary Rental of Residence Before Sale

If you are unable to sell your home and must move, it may be advisable to put it up for rent. This way you may be able to deduct maintenance expenses and depreciation on the unit even if it remains vacant. However, the IRS has disallowed loss deductions for some rentals preceding a sale on the ground that there was no "profit motive" for the rental *(40.10)*. For example, where minimal efforts are made to rent out a vacation home in anticipation of an eventual sale, the IRS may claim, as in Example 1 below, that the home was not converted to rental property held for the production of income. Where the IRS determines that you lacked a profit motive for renting the property, it will limit your deduction for rental expenses to the amount of the rental income, and the expenses in excess of rental income cannot be carried forward to a later year. Courts have allowed loss deductions in certain cases.

**EXAMPLES**

1. A married couple bought an oceanfront condominium in 2004 for $875,000, planning to use it as a seasonal home. After the tragic death of their daughter in 2006, they stopped staying at the property and in 2008 they removed most of their belongings from the unit and entered into a one-year contract with a realty company located in their oceanfront community, intending to rent out the condo and eventually sell it at a profit. However, they could not rent out the property and because of the collapsing real estate market in Florida in 2009, they could not sell the property. They changed realtors and sold the home for a $160,000 loss in 2010. The taxpayers claimed rental expenses on their 2009 and 2010 returns and claimed that the loss on the 2010 sale was a fully deductible ordinary loss.

The IRS disallowed deductions for the rental expenses and disallowed any loss deduction on the sale. The Tax Court agreed with the IRS. Although the couple clearly abandoned personal use of the condo in 2008, they did not convert it to a profit-motivated rental property. The realty company's efforts were limited to featuring the condo in an office portfolio and telling prospective buyers that it was available for rent. The taxpayers did change realtors, but beyond putting it on a multiple listing service, there is no evidence that the second agent did anything to rent out the condo.

Nor is there evidence that they took any other steps to rent it. The minimal efforts taken did not constitute a bona fide attempt to rent out the condo and therefore did not convert it to property held for the production of income. Thus, "rental" expenses are not allowed, and the loss on the sale was a nondeductible personal loss.

2. The IRS and Tax Court disallowed a loss deduction for rental expenses under the "profit-motive rules" *(40.10)* where a principal residence was rented for 10 months until it could be sold. According to the Tax Court, the temporary rental did not convert the residence to rental property. Since the sales effort was primary, there was no profit motive for the rental. Thus, no loss could be claimed; rental expenses were deductible only to the extent of rental income. The favorable side of the Tax Court position: Since the residence was not converted to rental property, the owners could under prior law rules defer tax on the gain from the sale by buying a new home. An appeals court reversed the Tax Court and allowed both tax deferral and a loss deduction. The rental loss was allowed since the old home was rented almost continuously until sold for a fair rental price.

3. In 1976, a couple bought a condo apartment in Pompano Beach, Florida. In 1983, they decided to move and listed the unit for either sale or rent with a local real estate broker. Sale of the unit was difficult because of the saturation of the Florida real estate market. Rental of the unit was also difficult because the condominium association's rules barred the rental of condominium units on a seasonal basis. The unit remained unrented until it was sold in 1986 for a substantial gain. In 1984, the couple deducted a $9,576 rental loss ($7,596 for maintenance expenses and $1,980 for depreciation). The IRS disallowed the deduction as not incurred in a bona fide rental activity. The Tax Court allowed the deduction. The couple made an honest and reasonable effort to rent the condominium. Lack of rental income was caused by a slack rental market and the condominium association rules prohibiting short-term rentals.

## 9.11 Reporting Royalty Income

Royalties are payment for use of patents or copyrights or for the use and exhaustion of mineral properties. Royalties are taxable as ordinary income and are reported on Schedule E (Form 1040). Depletion deductions relating to the royalties are also reported on Schedule E. If you own an operating oil, gas, or mineral interest, or are a self-employed writer, investor, or artist, you report royalty income, expenses, and depletion on Schedule C.

### Examples of Royalty Income

- License fees received for use, manufacture, or sale of a patented article.
- Renting fees received from patents, copyrights, and depletable assets (such as oil wells).
- Authors' royalties including advance royalties if not a loan.
- Royalties for musical compositions, works of art, etc.
- Proceeds of sale of part of your rights in an artistic composition or book, for example, sale of motion picture or television rights.
- Royalties from oil, gas, or other similar interests *(9.16)*. To have a royalty, you must retain an economic interest in the minerals deposited in the land you have leased to the producer. You usually have a royalty when payments are based on the amount of minerals produced. However, if you are paid regardless of the minerals produced, you have a sale that is taxed as capital gain if the proceeds exceed the basis of the transferred property interest. Bonuses and advance royalties that are paid to you before the production of minerals are taxable as royalty income and are entitled to an allowance for depletion. However, bonuses and advance royalties for gas and oil wells and geothermal deposits are not treated as gross income for purposes of calculating percentage depletion. If the lease is terminated without production and you received a bonus or advance royalty, you report as income previously claimed depletion deductions. You increase the basis of your property by the restored depletion deductions.

 *Planning Reminder*

**Passive Income Exception**

Certain working oil and gas interests are exempt from the passive activity loss restrictions *(10.10)*.

## 9.12 Production Costs of Books and Creative Properties

Freelance authors, artists, and photographers may deduct their costs of producing original works in the years that the expenses are paid or incurred. If you qualify, the uniform capitalization rules that generally apply to property that you produce for resale *(40.3)* do not apply to the expenses.

You qualify for current expense deductions if you are self-employed and you personally create literary manuscripts, musical or dance scores, paintings, pictures, sculptures, drawings, cartoons, graphic designs, original print editions, photographs, or photographic negatives or transparencies. However, the exception to the uniform capitalization rules does not apply to, and thus current deductions are not allowed for, expenses relating to motion picture films, videotapes, printing, photographic plates, or similar items.

If you conduct business as an owner-employee of a personal service corporation and you are a qualifying author, artist, or photographer, the corporation may claim current deductions related to your expenses in producing books or other eligible creative works. You and your relatives must own substantially all of the corporation's stock.

**Caution**

**Hobby Loss Restrictions**

Authors and artists with expenses exceeding income may be barred by the IRS from claiming loss deductions *(40.10)*.

## 9.13 Deducting the Cost of Patents or Copyrights

If you create an artistic work or invention for which you get a government patent or copyright, you may depreciate your costs over the life of the patent or copyright. Basis for depreciation includes all expenses that you are required to capitalize in connection with creating the work, such as the cost of drawings, experimental models, stationery, and supplies; travel expenses to obtain material for a book; fees to counsel; government charges for patent or copyright; and litigation costs in protecting or perfecting title.

If you purchased the patent or artistic creation, depreciate your cost over the remaining life of the patent or copyright. If your cost for a patent is payable annually as a fixed percentage of the revenue derived from use of the patent, the depreciation deduction equals the royalty paid or incurred for that year. However, if a copyright or patent is acquired in connection with the acquisition of a business, the cost is amortizable over a 15-year period as a Section 197 intangible *(42.18)*.

If you inherited the patent or rights to an artistic creation, your cost is the fair market value either at the time of death of the person from whom you inherited it *(5.17)* or the alternate valuation date if elected by the executor. You get this cost basis even if the decedent paid nothing for it. Figure your depreciation by dividing the fair market value by the number of years of remaining life.

If your patent or copyright becomes valueless, you may deduct your unrecovered cost or other basis in the year it became worthless.

## 9.14 Intangible Drilling Costs

Intangible drilling and development costs (IDCs) refer to drilling and development costs of items with no salvage value, including wages, fuel, repairs, hauling, and supplies incident to and necessary for the preparation and drilling of wells for the production of oil or gas, and geothermal wells. For wells you are developing in the United States, you can elect to deduct the costs currently as business expenses or treat them as capital expenses subject to depreciation or depletion.

**Electing current business deduction.** The election to deduct IDCs as a current business expense must be made on your income tax return for the first tax year in which you pay or incur the costs. As a sole proprietor, you deduct the IDCs as "other expenses" on Schedule C (Form 1040).

*Prepayments.* Tax-shelter investors may deduct prepayments of drilling expenses only if the well is "spudded" within 90 days after the close of the taxable year in which the prepayment is made. The prepayment must also have a business purpose, not be a deposit, and not materially distort income. The investor's deduction is limited to his or her cash investment in the tax shelter. For purposes of this limitation, an investor's cash investment includes loans that are not secured by his or her shelter interest or the shelter's assets and loans that are not arranged by the organizer or promoter. If the above tests are not met, a deduction may be claimed only as actual drilling services are provided.

**Caution**

**Drilling Expense Prepayments**

Prepayments of drilling expenses are deductible by tax-shelter investors only if the well is "spudded" within 90 days after the close of the taxable year in which the prepayment was made, and the deduction is limited to the original amount of the investment.

**Amortizing intangible drilling costs.** If you do not elect to deduct IDCs as current business expenses, you may amortize them on Form 4562, Depreciation and Amortization, over a 60-month period, beginning with the month they were paid or incurred. If you elect 60-month amortization, there is no AMT adjustment; *see* below.

**Recapture of intangible drilling costs for oil, gas, geothermal, or mineral property.** Upon the disposition of oil, gas, geothermal, or other mineral property placed in service after 1986, ordinary income treatment applies to previously claimed deductions for intangible drilling and development costs for oil, gas, and geothermal wells, and to mineral development and exploration costs. Depletion deductions *(9.15)* are also generally subject to this ordinary income treatment upon disposition of the property.

**AMT and intangible drilling costs.** If you are an independent producer or royalty owner and elect to deduct IDCs as a current business expense on Schedule C, you may qualify for an exception to the AMT preference rules for IDCs, but the exception is limited. If your IDC preference (figured under the regular AMT rules) exceeds 40% of your alternative minimum taxable income, figured without regard to the AMT net operating loss deduction, the excess over 40% must be included as a preference item; *see* the instructions on Form 6251. The AMT adjustment can be completely avoided by electing 60-month amortization for the IDCs.

# 9.15 Depletion Deduction

Properties subject to depletion deductions are mines, oil and gas wells, timber, and exhaustible natural deposits.

Two methods of computing depletion are: (1) cost depletion and (2) percentage depletion. If you are allowed to compute under either method, you must use the one that produces the larger deduction. In most cases, this will be percentage depletion. For timber, you must use cost depletion.

**Cost depletion.** The cost depletion of minerals is computed as follows: (1) divide the total number of units (such as tons or barrels) remaining in the deposit to be mined into the adjusted basis of the property; and (2) multiply the unit rate found in Step 1 by the number of units for which payment is received during the taxable year if you are on the cash basis, or by the number of units sold if you are on the accrual basis.

Adjusted basis is the original cost of the property, less depletion allowed, whether computed under the percentage or cost depletion method. It does not include nonmineral property such as mining equipment. Adjusted basis may not be less than zero.

Timber depletion is based on the cost of timber (or other basis in the owner's hands) and does not include any part of the cost of land. Depletion takes place when standing timber is cut. Depletion must be computed by the cost method, not by the percentage method. However, instead of claiming the cost depletion method, you may elect to treat the cutting of timber as a sale subject to capital gain or loss treatment. For further details, *see* IRS Publication 535.

**Percentage depletion.** Percentage depletion is based on a certain percentage rate applied to annual gross income derived from the resource. In determining gross income for percentage depletion, do not include any lease bonuses, advance royalties, or any other amount payable without regard to production. A deduction for percentage depletion is allowed even if the basis of the property is already fully recovered by prior depletion deductions. The percentage to be applied depends upon the mineral involved; the range is from 5% up to 22%. For example, the maximum 22% depletion deduction applies to sulfur, uranium, and U.S. deposits of lead, zinc, nickel, mica, and asbestos. A 15% depletion percentage applies to U.S. deposits of gold, silver, copper, iron ore, and shale.

**Taxable income limit.** For properties other than oil and gas, the percentage depletion deduction may not exceed 50% of taxable income from the property computed without the depletion deduction. In computing the 50% limitation, a net operating loss deduction is not deducted from gross income. A 100% taxable income limit applies to oil and gas properties *(9.16)*.

**Oil and gas property.** Percentage depletion for oil and gas wells was repealed as of January 1, 1975, except for small independent producers and royalty owners *(9.16)*.

## 9.16    Oil and Gas Percentage Depletion

Small independent producers and royalty owners generally are allowed to deduct percentage depletion at a 15% rate for domestic oil and gas production. The deduction is subject to a taxable income limit.

The 15% rate applies to a small producer exemption that equals the gross income from a maximum daily average of 1,000 barrels of oil or 6 million cubic feet of natural gas, or a combination of both. Gross income from the property does not include advance royalties or lease bonuses that are payable without regard to the actual production.

The depletable natural gas quantity depends on an election made annually by independent producers or royalty owners to apply part of their 1,000-barrel-per-day oil limitation to natural gas. The depletable quantity of natural gas is 6,000 cubic feet times the barrels of depletable oil for which an election has been made. The election is made on an original or amended return or on a claim for credit or refund. For example, if your average daily production is 1,200 barrels of oil and 6.2 million cubic feet of natural gas, your maximum depletable limit is 1,000 barrels of oil, which you may split between the oil and gas. You could claim depletion for 500 barrels of oil per day and for 3 million cubic feet of gas per day: 3 million cubic feet of gas is the equivalent of the remaining 500 barrels of oil limit (500 barrels × 6,000 cubic feet depletable gas quantity equals 3 million cubic feet of gas).

**Ineligible retailers and refiners.** Percentage depletion cannot be claimed by a producer who owns or controls a retail outlet for the sale of oil, natural gas, or petroleum products unless gross sales of oil and gas products are $5 million or less for the tax year, or if all sales of oil or natural gas products occur outside the United States and none of the taxpayer's domestic production is exported. Bulk sales of oil or natural gas to industrial or utility customers are not to be treated as retail sales.

Percentage depletion also is not allowed to a refiner who refines (directly or through a related person) more than 75,000 barrels of crude oil on any day during the year. The limit is based on average (rather than actual) daily refinery runs for the tax year.

**Figuring average daily domestic production.** Average daily production is figured by dividing your aggregate production during the taxable year by the number of days in the taxable year. If you hold a partial interest in the production (including a partnership interest), production rate is found by multiplying total production of such property by your income percentage participation in such property.

The production over the entire year is averaged regardless of when production actually occurred. If average daily production for the year exceeds the 1,000-barrel or 6-million-cubic-feet limit, the exemption must be allocated among all the properties in which you have an interest.

**Taxable income limits on percentage depletion.** The percentage depletion deduction for a small producer or royalty owner may not exceed the lesser of (1) 100% of the taxable income from the property before the depletion allowance or the deduction for production activities, or (2) 65% of your taxable income from all sources computed without regard to the depletion deduction allowed under the small producer's exemption, the deduction for production activities, any net operating loss carryback, and any capital loss carryback. Any amount not deductible because of the 65% limit can be carried over and added to the next year's depletion allowance.

**Limitations where family members or related businesses own interests.** The daily exemption rate is allocated among members of the same family in proportion to their respective production of oil. Similar allocation is required where business entities are under common control. This affects interests owned by you, your spouse, and minor children; by corporations, estates, and trusts in which 50% of the beneficial interest is owned by the same or related persons; and by a corporation that is a member of the same controled group.

**Depletion for marginal production.** For independent producers and royalty owners with production from "marginal" wells, the 15% depletion rate could be increased by 1% for each whole dollar that the "reference price" (the average annual wellhead price as estimated by the IRS) of domestic crude oil for the previous year was below $20 per barrel. However, despite relatively low oil prices in recent years, the reference price has been substantially over $20 per barrel, and therefore the basic 15% rate has applied for marginal production every year from 2001 through 2018, and this is likely to remain the case for the foreseeable future.

## 9.17 Qualified Business Income Deduction for Real Estate Activities

If your real estate activities constitute a trade or business, you may be eligible for a deduction of up to 20% of qualified business income (QBI) (the QBI deduction is explained in *40.26*). It appears that if you are actively engaged in the real estate activity (e.g., you make decisions about leases, collect rents, coordinate repairs, and hire contractors), you may be considered to be in a trade or business for purposes of the QBI deduction. Owning even a single property can constitute a trade or business, although renting out your vacation home may not rise to the level of a trade or business.

Merely owning rental property does not automatically constitute a trade or business. For example, if you have triple net lease on your property, which makes the tenant responsible for operating expenses, you may be viewed as a mere investor and not in a trade or business. The determination of trade or business is made on a case by case basis. Being a real estate professional for purposes of the passive activity loss rules *(10.3)* does not impact this determination.

**Limitation.** If your taxable income in 2018 is more than $315,000 on a joint return or $157,500 on any other return, a limitation curtails the deduction. For purposes of the limitation explained in *40.26*, a key component for real estate trades or businesses is the unadjusted basis immediately after acquisition (UBIA) of qualified tangible property; 2.5% of UBIA of qualified tangible property is part of the limitation. UBIA is tangible property subject to depreciation held by a business at the end of the year and used during the year for the production of QBI. The unadjusted basis means the original cost of the property, without any depreciation. For the property to be taken into account, it must still be in use by the business and the depreciable period of the property has not ended. The depreciable period begins the first year the property is placed in service and ends on the later of:

- 10 years, or
- The last day of the applicable recovery period (e.g., 39 years for commercial property; 27 years for residential realty).

> **EXAMPLE**
>
> Harold built a 10-unit apartment building in 2007 at a cost of $1 million, and it constitutes a trade or business for him. In figuring his QBI deduction for 2018, he can take $25,000 into account ($1 million × 2.5%). While 10 years has passed, he is still using and depreciating the building.
>
> **Multiple properties.** If you are considered to be in a trade or business, then the deduction is figured for each activity, unless you elect to aggregate them *(40.26)*. Thus, if you own properties through separate limited liability companies, you compute the deduction for each one and then total them for a single entry on line 10 of Form 1040.

 *Law Alert*

**Qualified Business Income (QBI) Deduction for Real Estate Businesses**

Because many real estate businesses do not entail wages, a special rule was added by the Tax Cuts and Jobs Act to the limitation on the QBI deduction for real estate activities, based on the cost of property. In other words, high-income owners may qualify for a QBI deduction based on a percentage of the cost of their property.

# CHAPTER 10

# Loss Restrictions: Passive Activities and At-Risk Limits

The passive activity laws were intended to discourage tax-shelter investments, but their reach goes beyond tax shelters to cover all real estate investors and persons who invest in businesses as "silent partners" or who are not involved full time in the business. The passive activity rules prevent an investor from deducting what the law defines as a passive loss from salary, self-employment income, interest, dividends, sales of investment property, or retirement income. Such losses are deductible only from income from other passive activities. Losses disallowed by the passive activity rules are suspended and carried forward to later taxable years and become deductible only when passive income is realized or substantially all of the activity is sold.

Casualty and theft losses are not passive losses unless they are of the type usually occurring in a business, such as shoplifting theft losses.

On your tax return, passive income items and allowable deductible items are reported as regular income and deductions. For example, rental income and allowable deductions are reported on Schedule E. However, before you make these entries, you may have to prepare Form 8582, which identifies your passive income and losses and helps you to determine whether passive loss items are deductible.

At-risk rules generally limit losses for an activity to your cash investment and loans for which you are personally liable, as well as certain nonrecourse financing for real estate investments. *See 10.17.*

# 10.1 Rental Activities Generally Treated as Passive

Rental activities (real estate or personal property) are automatically treated as passive unless you qualify as a real estate professional *(10.3)* or the rentals by law are excluded from the rental category and are instead considered to be business activity (see below). If "automatic" passive activity treatment applies, you may not deduct a rental loss against nonpassive income such as salary or investment income unless you can take advantage of the up-to-$25,000 allowance that applies to rental real estate losses *(10.2)*. Even where rental income or loss is not automatically treated as passive because you qualify as a real estate professional or because the activity is excluded from the rental category and treated as a business (see the list below), income or loss will still be "passive" unless you materially participate *(10.6)* in the business activity.

A loss that is not currently deductible due to the passive loss restrictions is suspended and carried forward indefinitely until there is passive income to offset, or until you dispose of your entire interest in the activity *(10.13)*

**What is a rental activity?** Except for activities specifically excluded from the rental category (see the list of rentals treated as businesses below), rentals include all activities in which a customer pays for the use of tangible property (real estate or personal property). Such activities include rentals of apartments and commercial office space (whether long- or short-term); long-term rentals of office equipment, automobiles, and/or a vessel under a bareboat charter or a plane under a dry lease (no pilot or captain and no fuel); and net-leased property. A property is under a net lease if the deductions (other than rents and reimbursed amounts) are less than 15% of rental income or where the lessor is guaranteed a specific return or is guaranteed against loss of income.

**Rentals treated as business activity.** Although rental activities are generally treated as "passive," the following six activities are excluded from the category of rental activity and thus losses from these activities are not deductible under the $25,000 rental real estate loss allowance *(10.2)*. The fact that these activities are not treated as rentals does not mean that the passive activity rules are inapplicable. Income or loss from these activities will still be treated as passive income or loss if you fail to meet one of the business material participation tests *(10.6)*.

> **EXAMPLE**
>
> The Toups purchased a cottage in Callaway Gardens, a vacation resort south of Atlanta, Georgia. The unit was rented for short-term periods of seven days or less during the year to resort guests. The resort's operator was the sole managing and rental agent. Over a three-year period, they deducted net losses of $46,848. Under the seven-days-or-less rule, the activity was not a rental activity. It was treated as a business activity subject to the material participation tests. The IRS disallowed the losses as passive activity losses because the Toups were passive investors who did not materially participate in the activity. The Toups argued that they materially participated, spending more than 300 hours each year preparing an annual budget and cash flow analysis and meeting with other owners to set rental fees and inspect the grounds.
>
> The Tax Court sided with the IRS. The losses were passive because the Toups did not materially participate in the resort operation. They had nothing to do with running the resort on a day-to-day basis. Their activity was merely that of investors.

1. The average period of customer use of the property is seven days or less. Short-term rentals of vacation units, autos, DVDs/videocassettes, tuxedos, and hotel and motel rooms are not considered rental activities if the average period of customer use is seven days or less. You figure the average period of customer use for the year by dividing the aggregate number of days in all rental periods that end during the tax year by the number of rentals. Each period during which a customer has a continuous or recurring right to use the property is treated as a separate rental.

   A loss from a **seven-day-or-less real estate rental activity** is *not* eligible for the up-to-$25,000 loss allowance *(10.2)*. Since it is not treated as a real estate rental activity, it may not be included in the election to aggregate rental real estate activities under the real estate professional rules *(10.3)*.

 *Planning Reminder*

**Short-Term Vacation Home Rentals**

If you rent out a vacation unit for an average rental period of seven days or less at a loss, the loss is treated as a business (not rental) loss that you can deduct from nonpassive income if you meet one of the material participation tests *(10.6)*. If you do not materially participate, the loss is treated as a passive loss, deductible only from passive income. The loss does not qualify for the up-to-$25,000 rental loss allowance *(10.2)* because the property is not treated as rental property.

2. The average period of customer use of the property is more than seven days but is 30 days or less, and you provide significant personal services. Personal services include only services performed by individuals and do not include (a) services necessary to permit the lawful use of the property; (b) construction or repair services that extend the useful life of the property for a period substantially longer than the average period of customer use; and (c) services that are provided with long-term rentals of high-grade commercial or residential real property such as cleaning and maintenance of common areas, routine repairs, trash collection, elevator service, and security guards.

   Note: For purposes of Exceptions 1 and 2, if more than one class of property is rented as part of the same activity, average period of customer use is figured separately for each class. The average period of customer use (as explained in Exception 1) is multiplied by the ratio of gross rental income from that class to the total rental income from the activity; *see* the Form 8582 instructions.

3. Regardless of the average period of customer use, extraordinary personal services are provided so that rental is incidental. In a rare case, it may be possible to avoid the passive loss disallowance rule by showing that "extraordinary personal services" were provided to tenants who rented the space primarily to obtain these services. IRS regulations give as examples the use by patients of a hospital's room and board facilities, which is incidental to the medical services provided, and the use by students of school dormitories, which is incidental to the teaching services provided.

   In one case, an attorney and her husband, a medical doctor, convinced the Tax Court that they met the "personal services" exception by providing legal support services to law firms who leased office space from their LLC. The attorney supervised three clerical employees in providing legal support services to the tenant firms, which included client intake, answering phones and taking messages, conducting legal research, typing briefs and memoranda, binding briefs, photocopying, taking dictation, express mailing, process serving, filing documents at the courthouse and state capital, maintaining a file room, law library, and conference facilities, and providing coffee service. Her husband provided consulting services to the attorneys, reviewing medical malpractice cases, serving as an expert medical witness, helping the attorneys prepare for accreditation reviews of health-care organizations, and providing quality assurance trainings.

   Before the Tax Court, the tenant firms testified that these support services, particularly the legal research, were unique and that they would not have moved into the LLC's building without them. The Tax Court held that the LLC's leasing activity was not a rental activity under the extraordinary services exception, but the taxpayers still had to prove that they "materially participated" in the leasing/support activities to avoid passive loss disallowance for the rental losses. They did so by showing that at least 500 hours were spent working on the activity *(10.6)*.

4. Rental is incidental to a nonrental activity. A rental of property is excluded from the rental activity category if the property is held mainly for investment or for use in a business. A rental is considered incidental to an investment activity if the principal purpose of holding the property is to realize gain from its appreciation and the gross rental income from the property for the year is less than 2% of the unadjusted basis or fair market value of the property, whichever is less; *see* the Example below (Kyle Gail).

   A rental is incidental to a business activity if (1) you own an interest in the business during the year, (2) the rented property was predominately used in that business during the current year or during at least two of the immediately preceding five tax years, and (3) gross rental income from the property is less than 2% of the lower of the unadjusted basis of the property or its fair market value. Under test (2), a rental may qualify for the exception although it is not rented to the related business in the current year, so long as it was used in the business in two or more of the preceding five years.

5. Providing property to a partnership or S corporation that is not engaged in rentals. If you own an interest in a partnership or S corporation and you contributed property to it as an owner, the contributed property is not considered a rental activity. For example, if as a partner you contribute property to a partnership, your distributive share of partnership income will not be considered as income from a rental activity. However, this exception will not apply if the partnership is engaged in a rental activity.

6. The property is generally allowed for the non-exclusive use of customers during fixed business hours, such as operating a golf course. The customers are treated as licensees, not lessees.

> **EXAMPLE**
>
> Kyle Gail owns unimproved land with a fair market value of $400,000 and an unadjusted basis of $300,000. He holds it for the principal purpose of realizing gain from its appreciation. To help reduce the cost of holding the land, he leases it to a rancher for grazing purposes at an annual rental of $3,500. The gross rental income of $3,500 is less than 2% of the lower of the fair market value or the unadjusted basis of the land. The rental of the land is not a rental activity.

**Rental of dwelling unit meeting personal use test is not a passive activity.** If you rented out a residential unit that you personally used as a home during the year for more than the greater of 14 days or 10% of the number of days that it was rented to others at a fair market rental price *(9.7)*, the rental is not a passive activity. However, if you had a net loss from the rental, some rental expenses are not deductible on Schedule E under the allocation rules of *9.9*.

**Grouping rental and nonrental business activities.** Where you conduct rental as well as nonrental business activities, you may not group a rental activity with a nonrental activity, unless they form an appropriate economic unit and one of the activities is considered insubstantial in relation to the other. No guidelines are provided for determining what is "substantial" or "insubstantial."

Under an exception, a rental of property to a business may be grouped together with the business, although one activity is not insubstantial to the other, provided each business owner has the same proportionate ownership in the rental activity and the activities are an appropriate economic unit.

**Real property rentals and personal property rentals.** An activity involving the rental of realty and one involving the rental of personal property may not be treated as a single activity, unless the personal property is provided in connection with the real property or the realty is provided in connection with the personal property.

# 10.2 Rental Real Estate Loss Allowance of up to $25,000

If you are not a real estate professional *(10.3)* but you actively participate by performing some management role in a real estate rental venture, you may deduct up to $25,000 of a real estate rental loss against your regular, nonpassive income such as wages. Your rental loss is still "passive," but the allowance lets you deduct the loss (up to $25,000) as if it were a nonpassive loss. The allowance is phased out if your modified adjusted gross income (MAGI) is between $100,000 and $150,000. You generally take the allowance into account on Schedule E, but Form 8582 is sometimes required *(10.12)*.

If you are married filing separately, you are not eligible for the special loss allowance unless you lived apart for the entire year, and in that case, the allowance is limited to $12,500; *see* below. The allowance applies only to real estate rentals not excluded from the rental category by the rules at *10.1*. For example, short-term vacation home rentals averaging seven days or less do not qualify for the allowance. The allowance applies only to real estate rentals, not to any rentals of equipment or other personal property.

A trust may not qualify for the $25,000 allowance. Thus, you may not circumvent the $25,000 ceiling or multiply the number of $25,000 allowances by transferring rental real properties to one or more trusts.

**Married filing separately.** If you file separately and at any time during the taxable year live with your spouse, you are not allowed to claim any allowance. If you are married but live apart from your spouse for the entire year and file a separate return, the $25,000 allowance and the adjusted gross income phaseout range are reduced by 50%. Thus, the maximum allowance on your separate return is $12,500 and this amount is phased out by 50% of MAGI over $50,000. Therefore, if your MAGI exceeds $75,000, no allowance is allowed.

**Active participation test must be met.** To qualify for the allowance, you must meet an active participation test. Having an agent manage your property does not prevent you from meeting the test, but you must show that you or your spouse participates in management

*Planning Reminder*

**Rental of Personal Residence**

Renting a personal residence is not treated as a passive rental activity if you personally use the home for more than the greater of (1) 14 days or (2) 10% of the days the home is rented for a fair market rental amount *(9.7)*. On Schedule E, you may claim a full deduction for the rental portion of real estate taxes and mortgage interest, assuming the home is a principal residence or qualifying second home under the mortgage interest rules *(15.1)*.

*See 9.9* for limitations on deductions of other rental expenses.

**Planning Reminder**

**Proving Management Activities**

To take advantage of the $25,000 loan allowance, make sure you have proof of active management, such as approving leases and repairs.

decisions, such as selecting tenants, setting rental terms, and reviewing expenses. The IRS may not recognize your activity as meeting the test if you merely ratify your manager's decisions. You (together with your spouse) must also have at least a 10% interest in the property. Limited partners are not considered active participants and do not qualify for the allowance.

If a decedent actively participated in property held by an estate, the estate is deemed to actively participate for the two years following the death of the taxpayer.

> ### EXAMPLES
>
> 1. You live in New York and own a condominium in Florida that you rent through an agent. You set the rental terms and give final approval to any rental arrangement. You also have final approval over any repairs ordered by the agent. You are an active participant and may claim the $25,000 rental allowance.
>
> 2. A married couple who owned a time-share interest in an ocean-front condominium rented the condo during their allotted period to vacationers. They claimed a rental loss that the IRS held did not qualify for the up-to-$25,000 allowance. Since the average rental period for their unit was seven days or less, the rentals were excluded from the category of rental activity; *see 10.1.*

**Figuring the $25,000 allowance.** First match income and loss from all of your passive rental real estate activities in which you actively participate. A net loss from these activities is then applied against net passive income (if any) from other activities and if there is a remaining loss, that loss is deductible under the $25,000 allowance. Keep in mind that rental income or loss from renting a personal residence is disregarded in figuring the $25,000 allowance if the rental is not a passive activity, and it is not a passive activity if your personal use of the home during the year exceeds the greater of 14 days or 10% of the days the home is rented at a fair market rental amount *(9.7)*. The allowance may not be used against carryover losses from prior taxable years when you were not an active participant.

> ### EXAMPLE
>
> David Chung is single and has a $90,000 salary, $15,000 income from a limited partnership, and a $26,000 loss from rental real estate in which he actively participated. The $26,000 loss is first reduced by the $15,000 of passive income from the partnership. Since he actively participated in the rental real estate activities, the remaining balance of the $11,000 rental loss can be deducted from his nonpassive salary income. David's loss allowance is not subject to phaseout (see below) because his modified adjusted gross income (MAGI) is under $100,000. The partnership income and rental loss, which are passive, are disregarded in figuring MAGI.

**Phaseout of the allowance.** The maximum loss allowance of $25,000 ($12,500 if married filing separately and living apart for the entire year) is reduced by 50 cents for every dollar of modified adjusted gross income (MAGI) over $100,000 (or $50,000 if married filing separately).

**Modified adjusted gross income (MAGI).** For purposes of the allowance phaseout, MAGI is adjusted gross income shown on your return, but you should disregard:

- Any passive activity income or loss.
- Any loss allowed for real estate professionals *(10.3)*.
- Taxable Social Security and railroad retirement payments *(34.3)*. For example, if your adjusted gross income on Form 1040 is $90,000, and that includes $5,000 of taxable Social Security benefits, your modified adjusted gross income is $85,000 for purposes of the allowance phaseout.
- Deductible IRA contributions *(Chapter 8)*.
- Deductible tuition and fees, if this deduction is extended for 2018 *(33.13)*.
- The deduction on Form 1040 for one-half of self-employment tax liability *(45.3)*.
- Deductible student loan interest *(33.13)*.
- Overall loss from a publicly traded partnership (PTP)(see instructions to Form 8582).

- Excluded interest on U.S. savings bonds used for paying tuition in the year the bonds are redeemed. If you are allowed to exclude the interest from income for regular tax purposes *(33.4)*, the interest must still be included for purposes of the allowance phaseout.
- Employer-provided adoption assistance that is a tax-free fringe benefit *(Chapter 3)*. The assistance must be included in MAGI for purposes of applying the allowance phaseout rule.

A rental loss that is carried over because it exceeds the allowance may be deductible in a later year if you continue to meet the active participation test.

 *Filing Tip*

**Rental Allowance Based on Income**

If you are single or married filing jointly, the rental loss allowance is phased out when your modified adjusted gross income is over $100,000. For every dollar of income over $100,000, the loss allowance is reduced by 50 cents. When your modified adjusted gross income reaches $150,000, the allowance is completely phased out.

| If modified AGI is– | Loss allowance is– |
|---|---|
| Up to $100,000 | $25,000 |
| 110,000 | 20,000 |
| 120,000 | 15,000 |
| 130,000 | 10,000 |
| 140,000 | 5,000 |
| 150,000 or more | 0 |

---

### EXAMPLES

1. In 2018, Liz Blake had $120,000 in salary, $5,000 of partnership income from a limited partnership, and a $31,000 loss from a rental building in which she actively participates. For purposes of the phaseout rule, the $5,000 limited partnership income and the $31,000 rental loss are disregarded in figuring MAGI because they are passive. The $31,000 rental loss is reduced by the $5,000 of passive partnership income, and of the $26,000 balance, only $15,000 is deductible under the rental loss allowance; $10,000 of the allowance is phased out.. The remaining $11,000 loss ($26,000 -$15,000) must be carried over to 2019. Her deduction and carryover are computed as follows:

| | |
|---|---|
| Modified adjusted gross income for 2018 | $ 120,000 |
| Less: phaseout threshold (MAGI not subject to phaseout) | $ 100,000 |
| Amount subject to phaseout | $ 20,000 |
| Phaseout percentage | 50% |
| Portion of allowance phased out | $ 10,000 |
| Maximum rental allowance | $ 25,000 |
| Less: Phased out part of allowance | $ 10,000 |
| Deductible rental loss for 2018 under the allowance after phaseout | $ 15,000 |
| Passive loss from rental real estate | $ 31,000 |
| Less: Passive income from partnership | $ 5,000 |
| Passive activity loss | $ 26,000 |
| Less: Deductible rental loss allowance for 2018 | $ 15,000 |
| Carryover loss to 2019 | $ 11,000 |

2. Assume the facts of Example 1, and then in 2019 Liz's modified adjusted gross income is below the phaseout range for the loss allowance and she continues to actively participate in the rental building. Her rental loss for 2019 is $5,000. Under the allowance, she may deduct a rental loss of $16,000 for 2019 (the $5,000 loss for 2019 plus the $11,000 carryover loss from 2018 under Example 1).

---

**Real estate allowance for tax credits.** On Form 8582-CR, a deduction equivalent of up to $25,000 may allow a credit that otherwise would be disallowed. You must meet the active participation test in the year the credit arose. The $25,000 allowance is generally subject to the regular MAGI phaseout rule. The special allowance applies to low-income housing and rehabilitation credits even if you do not meet the active participation test.

The deduction equivalent of a credit is the amount which, if allowed as a deduction, would reduce your tax by an amount equal to the credit. For example, a tax credit of $1,000 for a taxpayer in the 25% bracket equals a deduction of $4,000 and would come within the $25,000 allowance provided you actively participated. In the 25% bracket, the equivalent of a $25,000 deduction is a tax credit of $6,250 ($25,000 × 25%). Thus, if you have a rehabilitation credit of $7,000 and you are in the 25% bracket, the $25,000 allowance may allow you to claim $6,250 of the credit, while the balance of the credit would be carried forward to the following year.

If in one year you have both losses and tax credits, the $25,000 allowance applies first to the losses, then to tax credits from rental real estate with active participation, then to tax credits for rehabilitation or low-income housing placed in service before 1990, and finally to tax credits for low-income housing placed in service after 1989.

**The allowance and net operating losses.** If losses are allowed by the $25,000 allowance but your nonpassive income and other income are less than the loss, the balance of the loss may be treated as a net operating loss and may be carried back and forward; *see 40.18* for further details.

## 10.3 Real Estate Professionals

Real estate rental activities are automatically passive *(10.1)* for all taxpayers except qualifying real estate professionals. You qualify as a real estate professional if you meet both parts of Test 1 below. If you qualify under Test 1, any rental real estate activity in which you materially participate (Test 2) is not a passive activity. Income or loss from the rental real estate is reported as nonpassive on Schedule E (Form 1040).

You need reliable records to substantiate your hours worked in real property businesses in order to qualify as a real estate professional (Test 1 below), as well as to substantiate your participation in your rental real estate activities (Test 2).

**Test 1: Qualifying as a real estate professional.** There are two parts to Test 1, and you must meet both of them for the tax year for you to qualify:

1. More than 50% of your personal services in all of your businesses must be performed in real property businesses in which you materially participate *(10.6)*. For this purpose, a real property business means any real property development, redevelopment, construction, reconstruction, acquisition, conversion, rental operation, management, leasing, or brokerage trade or business. Real estate financing is not included. Personal services performed as an employee are not treated as performed in a real estate business unless you are considered a "more than 5% owner" in the employer. That is, you must own more than 5% of the outstanding stock or more than 5% of total combined voting powers of all stock issued by the corporation. In a noncorporate employer such as a partnership, you must own more than a 5% capital or profit interest.

2. More than 750 hours of your services are in real property businesses in which you materially participate *(10.6)*. You must be able to establish that you materially participate (under the tests at *10.6*) in a real property business in order to count your work in that business towards the 750-hour threshold.

   In one case, a taxpayer claimed that when he was not at his full-time job he was "on call" for working on his four rental properties because he could have been called to do work at any time on the properties, and he argued that the "on call" hours should count towards the 750-hour test. Without the "on call" hours, he could substantiate only 645.5 hours of work on the rentals. The Tax Court held that even if the taxpayer was "on call," on call hours do not count towards the 750-hour test, since the law requires that the taxpayer actually perform over 750 hours of service.

For purposes of determining hours of material participation under (1) and (2) above, each interest in rental real estate property is treated as a separate activity unless you elect to treat all of your interests as one rental activity. The election to aggregate can make it easier to prove material participation as discussed below. If, under the rules in *10.1*, you group a rental real estate activity with a business activity, that rental activity is not treated as rental real estate for purposes of the real estate professional rules.

For a married couple filing jointly, both the "50% of services test" and the "750 hours test" must be met by one of the spouses individually, without regard to the other spouse's services.

Attorneys who specialize in real estate practice while participating in a rental business may not treat the legal practice as material participation for purposes of qualifying as real estate professionals.

A closely held C corporation qualifies under the real estate professional rules if in a taxable year more than 50% of the gross receipts of the corporation are from a real property business in which the corporation materially participates *(10.15)*.

*Planning Reminder*

**Tax Break for Real Estate Professionals**

Proving professional status and material participation allows you to avoid passive loss limitations. You may improve your ability to meet the material participation tests in *10.6* by aggregating your rental real estate activities. However, you may not want to aggregate activities if you have passive losses from non–real estate activities and have rental income from an operation that, if treated as passive income, could be offset by the losses.

Also be aware that if you elect to aggregate your rental real estate activities as one activity and later sell one of the rental properties, you will probably be unable to deduct suspended losses from that property because of the rule that requires "substantially all" of your interest in an activity (here, the combined activity) to be disposed of in order to deduct suspended losses *(10.13)*.

**Test 2: Rental real estate activity material participation.** If you qualify as a real estate professional under Test 1 above, you must still show that you materially participate *(10.6)* in your rental real estate activity/activities to avoid passive activity treatment. If you have more than one rental real estate activity and elect to aggregate (see below), total participation in all of the activities is combined in applying the material participation tests in *10.6*. If an election to aggregate has not been made, material participation must be determined separately for each rental property.

**Election to aggregate rental real estate activities.** For purposes of Test 2 (rental real estate material participation), you may elect to aggregate all of your rental real estate activities for any year you qualify under Test 1 as a real estate professional. You elect to aggregate by attaching a statement to your original tax return for the year. The required election statement must contain a declaration that you are a qualifying real estate professional and are treating all of your rental real estate activities as a single activity under Internal Revenue Code Section 469(c)(7)(A). The election is binding for all future years in which you qualify as a real estate professional, even if there are intervening years in which you do not qualify. In the nonqualifying years, the election has no effect. You may not revoke the election in a later year unless there has been a material change in circumstances that you explain in a statement attached to your original return for the year of revocation. That the election no longer gives you a tax advantage is not a basis for a revocation.

If the election to aggregate is made and there is net income for the aggregated activity, the income may be offset by prior-year suspended losses from any of the aggregated rental real estate activities regardless of which of the rental activities produced the income.

 *Caution*

**Consistent Treatment Required**

Once you treat activities separately or group them together as a single activity, the IRS generally requires you to continue the same treatment in later taxable years. You can re-group activities only if the original treatment was "clearly inappropriate" or has become clearly inappropriate because of a material change in circumstances.

---

### EXAMPLE

Kosonen owned seven rental properties. In 1994, he worked on all his properties a total of 877 hours, which qualified him as a real estate professional. But he could not meet the material participation test for each of the individual properties. If he could aggregate the activities, the material participation test would be met for the combined activity, which would be treated as nonpassive, allowing him to deduct his net rental losses against nonpassive income.

On his 1994 return, he reported the losses from all the activities as an aggregate deduction and treated it as nonpassive. The IRS disallowed the deduction because he had not made a specific election to aggregate. Kosonen argued that by claiming on his return the total of his losses, he had put the IRS on notice that he was aggregating his rental activities.

The Tax Court disagreed. A specific election is required to put the IRS on notice that a taxpayer is a qualifying real estate professional making the election to aggregate rental activities. Reporting the net losses on his return as an aggregate active (nonpassive) loss was not enough because Kosonen could also have reported his net losses as active if he had materially participated in each of the seven activities and had not elected to aggregate.

---

**Late elections.** If you do not make the election to aggregate on your original return, Revenue Procedure 2011-34 allows you to make a late election on an amended return if you (1) had reasonable cause for not meeting the original deadline; (2) took positions on your tax returns as if the election to aggregate had been timely made—consistent filing is required for all years including and following the year the requested aggregation is to be effective; and (3) timely filed all the returns that would have been affected by the election had it been timely made. Returns filed within six months of the original due date (without extensions) are treated as timely filed for this purpose.

If you meet tests 1–3, you should attach a statement to an amended return for the most recent tax year and mail it to the IRS service center where your current year return will be filed. The statement must include the required aggregation declaration that you are a qualified real estate professional and are making the election to aggregate pursuant to Code Section 469(c)(7)(A). It must also declare that tests 1–3 have been met and explain what the reasonable cause was for not making a timely election. The statement must be dated and signed under penalties of perjury. At the top, write "FILED PURSUANT TO REV. PROC. 2011-34." Even if the IRS grants relief to make the late election, the IRS can later challenge whether you met the real estate professional and material participation tests, or whether the eligibility requirements of Revenue Procedure 2011-34 were met.

**Rental loss allowance may apply to nonqualifying rental activity.** A real estate professional may also be able to claim all or part of the $25,000 rental loss allowance *(10.2)*. For example, you are a real estate professional and meet the material participation test for one rental real estate activity but not for another and do not elect to aggregate. Losses from the nonqualifying activity can qualify for the rental allowance. Furthermore, suspended prior year losses from the qualifying activity may also be deductible under the rental loss allowance, as illustrated in the Example below.

**Interests in S corporations and partnerships.** Your interest in rental real estate held by a partnership or an S corporation is treated as a single interest in rental real estate if the entity grouped its rental real estate as one rental activity. If not, each rental real estate activity of the entity is treated as a separate interest in rental real estate. However, you may elect to treat all interests in rental real estate, including the rental real estate interests held by an S corporation or partnership, as a single rental real estate activity.

If you hold a 50% or greater interest in the capital, income, gain, loss, deduction, or credit in a partnership or S corporation for the taxable year, each interest in rental real estate held by the entity is treated as a separate interest in rental real estate, regardless of the entity's grouping of activities. However, you may elect to treat all interests in rental real estate, including your share of the rental real estate interests held by the entities, as a single rental real estate activity.

> ### EXAMPLE
>
> Jane Morton owns a rental building in Manhattan and a rental building in Newark. In 2018, she qualifies as a real estate professional. She has not previously elected to treat the two buildings as one activity (such an election would be binding for 2018), and does not make an election to aggregate on her 2018 return. She materially participates in the operations of the Manhattan building, which has $100,000 of disallowed passive losses from prior years and a $20,000 loss for 2018. She does not materially participate in the operation of the Newark building, which has $40,000 of rental income for 2018. Jane also has $50,000 of 2018 income from other nonpassive sources.
>
> Because Jane materially participates in operating the Manhattan building, the $20,000 loss from the building for 2018 is treated as nonpassive and offsets $20,000 of the $50,000 nonpassive income from other sources.
>
> Jane can also use $40,000 of the $100,000 prior year suspended losses from the Manhattan building to offset the $40,000 of passive rental income for 2018 from the Newark building. Of the $60,000 remaining suspended loss, $25,000 may be deducted under the rental loss allowance provided Jane's MAGI is under $100,000, the phaseout threshold for the allowance *(10.2)*. Assuming she qualifies for the full $25,000 allowance, the rental loss allowance is deducted from the $30,000 of remaining nonpassive income ($50,000 nonpassive income – $20,000 offset by nonpassive loss from Manhattan building), leaving Jane with $5,000 of nonpassive income for 2018 ($30,000 nonpassive income – $25,000 allowance). The balance of suspended losses from the Manhattan building of $35,000 ($60,000 – $25,000 rental allowance) may be carried forward and used in 2019 to offset income from the Newark building or passive income from other sources.

**Limited partners.** Generally, a person who has a limited partnership interest *(10.11)* in rental real estate must establish material participation by participating for more than 500 hours during the year (Test 1 in *10.6*) or meeting Test 5 or Test 6 in *10.6*. These material participation tests also generally apply if an election is made to aggregate limited partnership interests in rental real estate with other rental real estate interests. However, the requirement that material participation can be established only under Tests 1, 5, or 6 may be avoided under a *de minimis* exception, which applies if the election to aggregate is made and less than 10% of the gross rental income for the taxable year from all rental real estate activities is attributed to limited partnership interests. In such a case, you may make the election to aggregate all rental real estate activities and determine material participation for the aggregated activity under any of the seven material participation tests *(10.6)*.

## 10.4 Participation May Avoid Passive Loss Restrictions

To avoid passive activity treatment of income and loss from a business investment, you must show material participation in that activity. The word "activity" does not necessarily relate to one specific business. If you invest in several businesses, you may be able to treat all or some of those activities as one activity or treat each separately.

Determining aggregate or separate treatment for your activities is discussed in *10.5* and material participation tests are discussed in *10.6*.

For a rental activity, material participation tests apply only if you are trying to qualify for the passive activity exception for real estate professionals *(10.3)*. For other rental real estate operators or investors, an "active" participation test that requires only certain management duties may allow you to deduct rental losses of up to $25,000 *(10.2)*.

## 10.5 Classifying Business Activities as One or Several

If you are in more than one activity, determining aggregate or separate treatment is important for:

- Deducting suspended losses when you dispose of an activity. If the activity is considered separate from the others, you may deduct a suspended loss incurred from that activity when you dispose of it. If it is not separate from the others, the suspended loss is deductible only if you dispose of substantially all of your investment *(10.13)*.
- Applying the material participation rules *(10.6)*. If activities are separate and apart from each other, the material participation tests are applied to each activity separately. If the activities are aggregated as one activity, material participation in one activity applies to all.
- Determining if you meet the 10% interest requirement for active participation *(10.2)*.

**Grouping activities together.** You may use any reasonable method under the facts and circumstances of your situation to determine if several business activities should be grouped together or treated separately. To be grouped together, the IRS says that the activities should be "an appropriate economic unit" for measuring gain or loss. For making this determination, the IRS sets these general guidelines: (1) similarities and differences in types of business; (2) the extent of common control; (3) geographic location; (4) the extent of common ownership; and (5) interdependencies among the activities. Interdependency is measured by the extent to which several business activities buy or sell among themselves, use the same products or services, have the same customers and employees, or use a single set of books and records.

**You must report new groupings and regroupings to the IRS.** You must file a statement with your return for the first year in which you originally group two or more activities together. The statement must identify the activities (including, if applicable, the employer identification number (EIN)) and must specifically state that the grouped activities are an appropriate economic unit as discussed in the previous paragraph. You also must file a statement with your return for any year in which you add a new activity to an existing group, or for any year in which you regroup activities. When activities are regrouped, the statement must explain how a material change in the facts and circumstances has made the original grouping "clearly inappropriate." See the instructions to Form 8582 and Revenue Procedure 2010-13 for further details on these disclosure requirements.

**Rental activities.** Rental activities may not be grouped with business activities unless one of the exceptions discussed in *10.1* applies.

 *IRS Alert*

**Regrouping Due to Net Investment Income Tax (NII Tax)**

The IRS may allow a one-time election to regroup your activities for the first taxable year that you become subject to the 3.8% NII tax *(28.3)*. This regrouping is also binding for all future tax years. See the instructions to Form 8582 for the eligibility requirements and other election details.

> ### EXAMPLE
> Lance Jones has a significant interest in a bakery and a movie theater at a shopping mall in Baltimore and in a bakery and a movie theater in Philadelphia. The IRS does not explain what constitutes a significant interest. In grouping his activities into appropriate economic units based on the relevant facts and circumstances, Jones could: (1) group the theaters and bakeries into a single activity; (2) place the two theaters into one

group and the bakeries into a second group; (3) put his Baltimore businesses into one group and his Philadelphia businesses in another group; or (4) treat the two bakeries and two movie theaters as four separate activities.

Once he chooses a grouping, he must consistently use that grouping for all future years unless a material change makes the grouping inappropriate. His decision is also subject to IRS review and, if questioned, he must show the factual basis for his grouping.

**IRS may regroup activities.** The IRS may regroup your activities if your grouping does not reflect one or more appropriate economic units and a primary purpose of the grouping is to circumvent the passive loss rules.

### EXAMPLE

Five doctors operate separate medical practices and also invest in tax shelters that generate passive losses. They form a partnership to operate X-ray equipment. In exchange for the equipment contributed to the partnership, each doctor receives limited partnership interests. The partnership is managed by a general partner selected by the doctors. Partnership services are provided to the doctors in proportion to their interests in the partnership and service fees are set at a level to offset the income generated by the partnership against individual passive losses. Under these facts, the IRS will not allow the medical practices and the partnership to be treated as separate activities as this would circumvent the passive loss limitations by generating passive income from the partnership to offset the tax-shelter losses. The IRS will require each doctor to treat his or her medical practice and interests in the partnership as a single activity.

**Partnerships and S corporations.** A partnership or S corporation must group its activities under the facts and circumstances test. Once a partnership or S corporation determines its activities, the partners or shareholders are bound by that decision and may not regroup them. The partners and shareholders then apply the facts and circumstances test to combine the partnership or S corporation activities with, or separate them from, their other activities.

**Special rule for certain limited partners and limited entrepreneurs.** A limited entrepreneur is a person with an ownership interest who does not actively participate in management. A limited entrepreneur or limited partner in films, videotapes, farming, oil and gas, or the renting of depreciable property generally may combine each such activity only with another of such activities in the same type of business, and only if he or she is a limited entrepreneur or partner in both. Grouping of such activities with other activities in the same type of business in which he or she is not a limited partner or entrepreneur is allowed if the grouping is appropriate under the general facts and circumstances test.

## 10.6 Material Participation Tests for Business

The IRS has seven tests for determining material participation in a business. Some tests require only a minimum amount of work, such as 500 hours a year, and others only 100 hours. You need to meet only one of the seven tests to qualify as a material participant. If you do, then the income and loss from that business is treated as nonpassive.

The tests apply whether you do business as a sole proprietor or in an S corporation or partnership. Losses and credits passed through S corporations and partnerships are subject to passive activity rules.

If you are a limited partner, the law presumes that you are not a material participant in the activities of the limited partnership, but IRS regulations provide a limited opportunity to show that you materially participate. Only three of the seven material participation tests are available to you; *see 10.11*.

The impact of the IRS participation rules on your tax position will depend on whether the particular activity produces income or loss. If you have passive activity losses from other activities, you may prefer to have a profitable business activity treated as a passive activity in order to offset the income by the losses from passive activities. On the other hand, if the business activity operates at a loss and you do not have passive income from other sources, you may want to meet the material participation test for that business activity

*Caution*

**Overcoming Investor Status**

The IRS will not recognize time spent as an investor as "participation" unless you can show you are involved in daily operations or management of the activity. According to the IRS, this requires you to be at the business site on a regular basis. Even if you do appear daily, the IRS may ignore such evidence if there is an on-site manager or you have full-time business obligations at another site. Activity of an investor includes the studying and reviewing of financial reports for your own use that are considered unrelated to management decisions. If you invest in a business that is out of state or a distance from your home, you may also find it difficult to prove material participation.

in order to claim current loss deductions. IRS strategy in reviewing your activities would be the opposite. If your return were under audit, an agent would attempt to prevent you from treating income from a business activity as passive. For example, the IRS, by applying Tests 5 and 6, can prevent a retired person from treating post-retirement income from a prior business or profession as passive income that could offset passive losses from another activity. If you realize a loss in one passive activity, Test 4 may prevent you from generating passive income by merely reducing your participation in another activity.

**Material participation results in nonpassive treatment.** There are two key terms: material participation and significant participation. If you materially participate by meeting one of the seven IRS tests, your activity is not a passive activity. For example, under Test 1, work for more than 500 hours in an activity is considered material participation. Under Test 4, significant participation is work for more than 100 hours but less than 500 hours at an activity in which you do not otherwise materially participate. The IRS applies a significant participation rule to convert passive activity income into nonpassive income and to convert several significant participation activities into material participation if the total participation in those activities exceeds 500 hours; *see* Test 4.

## IRS Tests for Material Participation

If you meet one of the following tests for the year in question, you are considered to have materially participated in that activity, and therefore the activity is considered nonpassive for that year. Tests 5 and 6 prevent retired individuals from treating post-retirement income as passive income.

Rules for limited partners and members of LLCs and LLPs are at *10.11*. For participation rules for personal service and closely held corporations, *see 10.15*.

**Work by you or your spouse that counts as participation.** Apart from the exceptions listed below, any work you do in a business in which you have an ownership interest is treated as "participation." If you are married, work by your spouse in the activity during the tax year is generally treated as your participation. This is true even if your spouse does not own an interest in the business or if you file separately. However, this favorable spousal participation rule does not apply if you and your spouse elect to treat your jointly owned business as a qualified joint venture, thereby requiring each of you to report your respective shares of the business income, deductions, credits, gains, and losses on Schedule E; *see 9.1* and the Schedule E instructions.

Do not count the following types of work as participation:

1. Work that is not of a type customarily done by an owner of an activity, if one of the principal reasons for the performance of the work is to avoid the passive loss rules (see the Example below).
2. An investor's review of financial statements or analysis that is unrelated to day-to-day management or operation of the activity.

---

**EXAMPLE**

An attorney owns an interest in a professional football team for which he performs no services. He anticipates a net loss from the football activity and to qualify as a material participant, he hires his wife to work 15 hours a week as an office receptionist for the team. Although a spouse's participation in an activity generally qualifies as participation by both spouses, the receptionist work here does not qualify as participation because (1) it is not the type of work customarily done by an owner of a football team and (2) the attorney hired his spouse to avoid disallowance of a passive loss.

---

**Test 1.** You participate in the activity for more than 500 hours during the tax year.

**Test 2.** Your participation in the activity for the tax year constitutes substantially all of the participation in the activity of all individuals including non-owners for the year.

**Test 3.** You participate in the activity for more than 100 hours during the tax year, and your participation is at least as great as that of any other person including non-owners for that year.

 *Planning Reminder*

**Proof of Material Participation**

Material participation must be determined on an annual basis. Show proof of your participation by keeping an appointment book, calendar, or log of the days and time spent in the operation. If you want to treat contacts by phone as material activity, keep a log of phone calls showing the time and purpose of the calls.

> **EXAMPLE**
>
> Joan Brown and Pat Collins are partners in a moving van business that they conduct entirely on weekends with the help of two employees. They both work for eight hours each weekend. Although neither partner participates for more than 500 hours (Test 1) and do not meet Test 2, they are both treated as material participants under Test 3 because they each participate for more than 100 hours and no one else participates more.

**Test 4.** You are active in several enterprises but each activity does not in itself qualify as material participation. However, if you spend more than 100 hours in each activity and the total hours of these more-than-100-hour activities exceeds 500, you are treated as a material participant in each of these activities. This test is referred to as the "significant participation" test.

> **EXAMPLES**
>
> 1. Mike Smith is a full-time accountant with ownership interests in a restaurant and shoe store. He works 150 hours in the shoe store and 360 hours in the restaurant. Under the significant participation test (Test 4), Smith is considered a material participant in both activities, as the total hours of both exceed 500.
> 2. Carl Young invests in five businesses. In activity (a) he works 110 hours; in activity (b), 100 hours; in activity (c), 125 hours; in activity (d), 120 hours; and in activity (e), 140 hours. He does not qualify under the significant participation test (Test 4). Although his total hours in the five activities exceed 500, activity (b) is ignored in the total count because the hours did not exceed 100. The total of the four other activities is 495.
> 3. Assume that Young worked one hour more for activity (b). It and all of the other activities would be considered as meeting the significant material participation test. The total hours are 596. Assuming that activity (a) totaled 125 hours and activity (b) remained at 100 hours or less, he would meet the test for all of the activities except for activity (b), which did not exceed 100 hours. The total of the four qualified activities is 510 hours.

**Test 5.** You materially participated in the activity for any five tax years during the 10 tax years preceding the tax year in question. The five tax years do not have to be consecutive. Thus, if you are retired but meet the five-out-of-10-year participation test, you are currently considered a material participant, with the result that net income from the activity is treated as nonpassive, rather than passive. If you retired from a personal service profession, an even stricter rule applies; *see* Test 6.

**Test 6.** In a personal service activity, you materially participated for any three tax years preceding the tax year in question. The three years do not have to be consecutive. Examples of personal services within this test are the professions of health, law, engineering, architecture, accounting, actuarial science, the performing arts, consulting, or any other trade or business in which capital is not a material income-producing factor.

**Test 7.** Under the facts and circumstances test, you participate in the activity on a regular, continuous, and substantial basis. According to the IRS, you do not come within this test if you participate less than 100 hours in the activity.

**_Caution_**

**Retired Farmers**

Retired or disabled farmers are treated as materially participating in a farming activity if they materially participated for five of the eight years preceding their retirement or disability. A surviving spouse is also treated as materially participating in a farming activity if the real property used in the activity meets the estate tax rules for special valuation of farm property passed from a qualified decedent and the surviving spouse actively manages the farm.

## 10.7 Tax Credits of Passive Activities Limited

You may generally not claim a tax credit from a passive activity unless you report and pay taxes on income from a passive activity. Furthermore, the tax allocated to that income must be at least as much as the credit. If the tax credit exceeds your tax liability on income allocable to passive activities, the excess credit is not allowed. Use Form 8582-CR to figure the allowable credit. Suspended credits are not allowed when property is disposed of. The credits may be used only when passive income is earned.

**EXAMPLE**

Ben Wall has a $1,000 credit from a passive activity. He does not report income from any passive activity. He may not claim the credit because no part of his tax is attributed to passive activity income. The credit is suspended until he has income from a passive activity and he incurs tax on that income. All or part of the credit may then be claimed to offset the tax. If he disposed of his interest before using a suspended credit, the credit may no longer be claimed but the election to reduce basis, discussed below, could be made.

**Credits for real estate activities.** More favorable tax credit rules apply to real estate activities *(10.2)*.

**Basis adjustment for suspended credits.** If the basis of property was reduced by tax credits, you may elect on Form 8582-CR to add back a suspended credit to the basis when your entire interest in an activity is disposed of. If the property is disposed of in a transaction that is not treated as a fully taxable disposition *(10.13)*, then no basis adjustment is allowed.

**EXAMPLE**

Mark places in service rehabilitation credit property and claims an allowable credit of $50, which also reduces basis by $50. However, under the passive loss rule, he is prevented from claiming the credit. In a later year, he disposes of his entire interest in the activity, including the property whose basis was reduced. He may elect to increase basis of the property by the amount of the original basis adjustment.

## 10.8 Determining Passive or Nonpassive Income and Loss

The purpose of the passive loss rules is to prevent you from deducting passive losses from nonpassive income. Passive losses are losses from business activities in which you do not materially participate *(10.6)* or losses from rental activities that are not deductible under the $25,000 allowance *(10.2)* or which do not qualify you as a real estate professional *(10.3)*. In some cases passive income may be recharacterized as nonpassive income *(10.9)*.

Where you do not materially participate in a business activity, passive income or loss is determined on Form 8582 by matching income and expenses of that activity. Portfolio income (see below) earned by the activity or any pay that you earn is not included to determine passive income or loss.

**Portfolio income.** Portfolio income is nonpassive income and broadly defined as income that is not derived in the ordinary course of business of the activity. Portfolio income includes interest, dividends, annuities, and royalties from property held for investment. However, interest income on loans and investments made in the business of lending money or received on business accounts receivable is generally not treated as portfolio income; *see 10.9* for special recharacterization rules. Similarly, royalties derived from a business of licensing property are not portfolio income to the person who created the property or performed substantial services or incurred substantial costs.

Portfolio income also includes gains from the sale of properties that produce portfolio income or are held for investment.

Expenses allocable to portfolio income, including interest expenses, do not enter into the computation of passive income or loss.

**Sale of property used in activity.** Gain or loss realized on the sale of property used in the activity is generally treated as passive income/loss if at the time of disposition the activity was passive. Under this rule, if you have a gain that you are reporting on the installment method, the treatment of installment payments depends on your status at the time of the initial sale. If you were not a material participant in the year of sale, installment payments in a later year are treated as passive income, even if you become a material participant in the later year. However, an exception to the year-of-sale status rule applies to certain sales of property formerly used in a passive activity *(10.16)*.

 *Filing Tip*

**Portfolio Income Accounting**

You cannot deduct passive losses from portfolio income. The tax law broadly defines "portfolio income" to include nonbusiness types of income including interest, dividends, and profits on the sale of investment property.

Although gain on the sale of property is generally passive income if the activity is passive at the time of sale, there is an exception that could recharacterize the gain as nonpassive income if the property was formerly used in a nonpassive activity *(10.16)*.

**Compensation for personal services is not passive activity income.** The term "compensation for personal services" includes only (1) wages, salaries and other earned income, including certain payments made by a partnership to a partner and representing compensation for the services of the partner; (2) amounts included in gross income involving the transfer of property in exchange for the performance of services; (3) amounts distributed under qualified plans; (4) amounts distributed under retirement, pension, and other arrangements for deferred compensation of services; and (5) Social Security benefits includible in gross income.

Passive activity gross income also does not include (1) income from patent, copyright, or literary, musical, or artistic compositions, if your personal efforts significantly contributed to the creation of the property; (2) income from a qualified low-income housing project; (3) income tax refunds; and (4) payments on a covenant not to compete.

**Passive activity deductions.** On Form 8582, you can offset passive income of an activity with deductible expenses that are related to the activity, such as real property taxes. Deductible expenses from prior years that were disallowed by the passive loss rules and carried forward to the current year are added to the current year deductions. The following are not considered passive activity deductions:

- Casualty and theft losses if similar losses do not recur regularly in the activity.
- Charitable deductions.
- State, local, and foreign income taxes.
- Carryovers of net operating losses or capital losses.
- Expenses clearly and directly allocable to portfolio income.
- Loss on the sale of property producing portfolio income.
- Loss on the sale of your entire interest in a passive activity to an unrelated party; the loss is allowed in full *(10.13)*.

**Interest deductions.** Interest expenses attributable to passive activities are treated as passive activity deductions and are not subject to the investment interest limitations. For example, if you have a net passive loss of $100, of which $40 is attributable to interest expenses, the entire $100 is a passive loss; the $40 is not subject to the investment interest limitation *(15.10)*. Similarly, income and loss from a passive activity·is generally not treated as investment income or loss in figuring the investment interest limitation.

If you rent out a vacation home that you personally use for more than the greater of 14 days or 10% of the fair market rental days *(9.7)*, you may treat the residence as a qualified second residence under the mortgage interest rules *(15.1)*. Interest on such a qualifying second home is generally fully deductible, and the deductible interest *(15.1)* is not treated as a passive activity deduction. The rental portion of the interest is deducted on Schedule E of Form 1040 and the personal-use portion on Schedule A if itemized deductions are claimed *(9.9)*.

**Self-charged management fees or interest.** For an individual with interests in several business entities, the payment of management fees by one of the entities to another is in effect a payment by the owner to himself. However, if the taxpayer materially participates in the entity providing the management services but not in the entity that pays the fees, the passive loss rules prevent the "self-charged" expense from offsetting the nonpassive fee income. IRS final regulations allow a netting deduction only for self-charged interest but not for any other self-charged expense.

> **EXAMPLE**
>
> As an employee of his S corporation, Hillman provided real estate management services to rental real estate partnerships in which he had invested. On his personal return, he reported the management fees as passed-through S corporation income and deducted his allocable share of the fee payments by the partnership. The IRS disallowed the deduction: Since Hillman materially participated in the S corporation but not the partnerships, the fee payments by the partnerships were passive activity expenses that could not be deducted against the S corporation's nonpassive fee

income. The fact that IRS regulations allow a deduction for self-charged interest does not mean that other self-charged passive expenses should also be deductible.

The Tax Court agreed with Hillman that there is no difference between interest and other self-charged expenses. The legislative history indicates a Congressional intent to allow deductions for self-charged expenses because they do not result in a net accretion to the taxpayer's wealth.

However, the Fourth Circuit, while sympathetic to Hillman's situation, reversed the Tax Court. Nothing in the tax law allows self-charged expenses to be deducted against nonpassive income. Although there is no reason why management fees should be distinguished from interest, the legislative history on self-charged expenses specifically mentioned only interest as an exception to the general statutory rule. The Congressional Committee reports that gave the IRS discretion to provide a deduction for other self-charged expenses did not limit that discretion. Unless the IRS changes its regulations, relief must come from Congress. The Fourth Circuit noted that while the denial of a deduction in this situation appears harsh, the deduction is not completely lost; the fee payments may be carried forward to later years as a passive expense.

After the Fourth Circuit ruled against him, Hillman went back to the Tax Court and tried an alternative argument in an attempt to deduct the management fees paid by the partnerships. He argued that the fees were nonpassive deductions that could offset the nonpassive income from the S corporation because the payment of the fees, by itself, constituted a separate business distinguishable from the passive rental activities of the partnerships. The Tax Court disagreed. The management fees were incurred in connection with the rental activities and thus were passive deductions. The Tax Court again acknowledged the unfairness of denying a deduction for the "self-charged" fees. Hillman's plight is lamentable, but as the Fourth Circuit ruled, relief can only come from Congress if the IRS does not liberalize its regulation on self-charged expenses.

## 10.9  Passive Income Recharacterized as Nonpassive Income

There is an advantage in treating income as passive income when you have passive losses that may offset the income. However, the law may prevent you from treating certain income as passive income. The conversion of passive income to nonpassive income is technically called "recharacterization." This may occur when you do not materially participate in the business activity, but are sufficiently active for the IRS to consider your participation as significant. Recharacterization may also occur when you rent property to a business in which you materially participate, rent nondepreciable property, or sell development rental property.

**Significant participation.** The IRS compares income and losses from all of your activities in which you work more than 100 hours but less than 500 and that are not considered material participation under the law. If you show a net aggregate gain, part of your gain is treated as nonpassive income according to the computation illustrated in the following Example.

**Net interest income from passive equity-financed lending.** Gross income from "equity-financed lending activity" is treated as nonpassive income to the extent of the lesser of the equity-financed interest income or net passive income. An activity is an "equity-financed lending activity" for a tax year if (1) the activity involves a trade or business of lending money and (2) the average outstanding balance of the liabilities incurred in the activity for the tax year does not exceed 80% of the average outstanding balance of the interest-bearing assets held in the activity.

**Incidental rental of property by development activity.** Where gains on the sale of rental property are attributable to recent development, passive income treatment may be lost if the sale comes within the following tests: (1) the rental started less than 12 months before the date of disposition; and (2) you materially participated or significantly participated in the performance of services enhancing the value of the property. The 12-month period starts at the completion of the development services that increased the property's value.

 *Caution*

**"Recharacterization" of Passive Income**

Gain on the sale of property used in a passive activity may be recharacterized as nonpassive income if the property was formerly used in a nonpassive activity *(10.16)*.

---

**EXAMPLE**

Carol Warren invests in three business activities—A, B, and C. She does not materially participate in any of the activities during the year but participates in Activity A for 105 hours, in Activity B for 160 hours, and in Activity C for 125 hours. Her net passive income or loss from the three activities is:

|  | A | B | C | Total |
|---|---|---|---|---|
| Passive activity gross income | $600 | $700 | $900 | $2,200 |
| Passive activity deductions | (200) | (1,000) | (300) | (1,500) |
| Net passive activity income | $400 | ($300) | $600 | $700 |

Carol's passive activity gross income from significant participation passive activities of $2,200 exceeds passive activity deductions of $1,500. A ratable portion of her gross income from significant participation activities with net passive income for the tax year (Activities A and C) is treated as gross income that is not from a passive activity. The ratable portion is figured by dividing:

1. The excess of her passive activity gross income from significant participation over passive activity deductions from such activities (here $700) by

2. The net passive income of only the significant participation passive activities having net passive income (here $1,000). The ratable portion is 70%.

Thus, $280 of gross income from Activity A ($400 × 70%) and $420 of gross income from Activity C ($600 × 70%) is treated as nonpassive gross income. This adjustment prevents $700 from being offset by passive losses from another activity.

---

 *Caution*

**Property Rented to Nonpassive Activity (Self-Rental Property)**

You may not generate passive income by renting property to a business in which you materially participate. See "Self-rental rule: Renting to your business" in this section.

**Self-rental rule: Renting to your business.** If you rent a building to your business, the rental income, normally treated as passive income, may be recharacterized by the IRS as nonpassive income where you also have losses from other rentals. Recharacterization prevents you from deducting the rental losses against the net rental income. Although not specifically written into the law, the recharacterization rules are incorporated in IRS regulations. For the recharacterization rule to apply, you must "materially participate" in the business that rents the property from you; *see* the following Examples. The Tax Court and several federal appeals courts have upheld the IRS recharacterization rule.

---

**EXAMPLES**

1. Krukowski, an attorney who operated two businesses through wholly owned C corporations, claimed that the IRS' recharacterization regulations were arbitrary and capricious. He rented personally owned buildings to the corporations, one of which ran a health club and the other the attorney's law firm. He reported net income of $175,149 from the rental to the law firm and a $69,100 net loss from the rental to the health club. He deducted the loss from the income and reported net rental income of $106,049. The IRS disallowed the loss offset by recharacterizing the rental income he received from the law firm as nonpassive income. Recharacterization could be applied under the regulations because the time spent by the attorney in the law firm was material participation. The attorney had to report rental income of $175,149; the health club rental loss was treated as a "suspended" passive loss.

   Before the Tax Court, the attorney claimed that the recharacterization rule was arbitrary and contrary to the passive loss statute. The Court disagreed. The law authorizes the IRS to write regulations interpreting the law. Further, Congressional committee reports contemplate that the IRS would define nonpassive income in such a way as to prevent a taxpayer from offsetting active business income with passive business losses.

   The Seventh Circuit Court of Appeals affirmed the Tax Court. The IRS was given authority by Congress to enact the self-rental rule as a way of eliminating tax shelters. Three other appeals courts, the First, Fifth, and Ninth Circuits, have also upheld the IRS regulation.

---

2. Carlos argued that he could avoid the IRS' self-rental rule by grouping together *(10.5)* as a single rental activity two rental properties. He operated a steel company and a restaurant through wholly owned S corporations. He leased one of his personally owned buildings to the steel company and another to the restaurant. He had substantial rental income from the steel company lease but a loss on the restaurant lease because the restaurant did not pay the agreed upon rent. On his tax returns for 1999 and 2000, Carlos grouped both properties together as a single activity and on Schedule E netted the loss from the restaurant rental against the net income from the steel company rental.

3. Applying the self-rental rule, the IRS required the income from the steel company rental to be reported, while disallowing the losses from the restaurant rental. The income from the steel company rental that would otherwise be treated as passive was recharacterized as nonpassive income since Carlos materially participated in the steel company. After the recharacterization, there was no passive income to be offset by the passive losses from the restaurant rental. The passive losses can be carried forward.

The Tax Court rejected Carlos's argument that his grouping of passive income and loss within a single activity precluded application of the self-rental recharacterization rule. To allow netting in this situation would defeat Congressional intent that a taxpayer not be able to use self-rentals as a means of sheltering nonpassive income from an active business with passive losses.

**Rental of property with an insubstantial depreciable basis.** This rule prevents you from generating passive rental income with vacant land or land on which a unit is constructed that has a value substantially less than the land. If less than 30% of the unadjusted basis *(5.16)* of rental property is depreciable, and you have net passive income from rentals (taking into account carried-over passive losses from prior years), the net passive income is treated as nonpassive income.

### EXAMPLES

1. A limited partnership buys vacant land for $300,000, constructs improvements on the land at a cost of $100,000, and leases the entire property. After the rental period, the partnership sells the property for $600,000, realizing a gain. The unadjusted basis of the depreciable improvements of $100,000 is only 25% of the basis of the property of $400,000. The rent and the gain allocated to the improvements are treated as nonpassive income.

2. Shirley offset a passive rental loss from an investment in a limited partnership, LP, which was a substantial owner of a general partnership, GP, against rental income from an investment in a joint venture, JV. JV had leased to GP land on which GP constructed a shopping center. The IRS held that the rental income from JV was nonpassive rental income within the 30% test and could not be offset by the passive rental loss. The Tax Court agreed and also rejected Shirley's attempt to aggregate her investment activities in JV and LP as one activity. The operations of each group, JV, LP, and GP, were separate and not owned by the same person. She was not the direct owner of any of the units. Further, the aggregation rule does not apply to property falling within the 30% test.

**Licensing of intangible property.** Your share of royalty income in a partnership, S corporation, estate, or trust is treated as nonpassive income if you invested after the organization created the intangible property, performed substantial services, or incurred substantial costs in the development or marketing of it. *See* Publication 925 for further details.

## 10.10 Working Interests in Oil and Gas Wells

Working interests are not treated as passive activities provided your liability is not limited. This is true whether you hold your interest directly or through an entity. As long as you have unlimited liability, the working interest is not a passive activity even if you do not materially participate in the activity. A working interest is one burdened with the financial

**Planning Reminder**

**Limited Liability for Oil or Gas Well**

A working interest in an oil or gas well is exempt from the passive activity restrictions if your liability is unlimited. The following forms of loss protection are disregarded and, thus, are not treated as limiting your liability: protection against loss by an indemnification agreement; a stop-loss agreement; insurance; or any similar arrangement or combination of agreements.

**Planning Reminder**

**Publicly Traded Partnerships (PTPs)**

A PTP is a partnership whose interests are traded on established securities exchanges or are readily tradable in secondary markets. PTPs that are not treated as corporations for tax purposes are subject to special rules that allow losses to be used only to offset income from the same PTP. See the instructions to Form 8582.

risk of developing and operating the property, such as a share in tort liability (for example, uninsured losses from a fire); some responsibility to share in additional costs; responsibility for authorizing expenses; receiving periodic reports about drilling, completion, and expected production; and the possession of voting rights and rights to continue operations if the present operator steps out.

**Limited liability.** If you hold a working interest through any of the following entities, the entity is considered to limit your liability and you are subject to the passive loss rules: (1) a limited partnership interest in a partnership in which you are not a general partner; (2) stock in a corporation; or (3) an interest in any entity other than a limited partnership or corporation that, under applicable state law, limits the liability of a holder of such interest for all obligations of the entity to a determinable fixed amount.

Working interests are considered on a well-by-well basis. Rights to overriding royalties or production payments, and contract rights to extract or share in oil and gas profits without liability for a share of production costs, are not working interests.

## 10.11 Partners and Members of LLCs and LLPs

As a general partner, your share of partnership income or loss during the partnership year ending within your tax year is passive or nonpassive, depending on whether you materially participated under any of the seven IRS tests *(10.6)* in the partnership activities during the year. Limited partners have a reduced ability to show material participation as discussed below. On Schedule K-1 of Form 1065, the partnership will identify each activity it conducts and specify the income, loss, deductions, and credits from each activity.

> **EXAMPLE**
> Don Bailey is a general partner of a fiscal year partnership that ends on March 31, 2018. During that fiscal year he was inactive. Since he did not materially participate, his share of partnership income or loss for 2018 is passive activity income or loss, even if he becomes active from April 1, 2018, to the end of 2018.

Not treated as passive income are payments for services and certain guaranteed payments made in liquidation of a retiring or deceased partner's interest unless attributed to unrealized receivables and goodwill at a time the partner was passive.

Gain or loss on the disposition of a partnership interest may be attributed to different trade, investment, or rental activities of the partnership. The allocation is made according to a complicated formula included in IRS regulations.

**Payments to a retired partner.** Gain or loss is treated as passive only to the extent that it would be treated as such at the start of the liquidation of the partner's interest.

**Limited partners.** Under IRS regulations, a limited partner has only a limited opportunity to establish material participation. A limited partner may use only three of the seven tests to establish material participation and thereby avoid passive treatment for the partnership income or loss:

1. The limited partner participates for more than 500 hours during the tax year; *see* Test 1 *(10.6)* or
2. The limited partner materially participated in the partnership during prior years under either Test 5 or Test 6 *(10.6)*

To determine material participation in rental real estate activities under the special rules for real estate professionals, a limited partner must meet Test 1, Test 5, or Test 6 *(10.6)* but *see* the *de minimis* exception at *10.3*

A limited partner is not considered to be an "active participant" and thus does not qualify for the $25,000 rental loss allowance *(10.2)*

*Who is a limited partner?* The current regulations treat a partner other than a general partner as a limited partner if his or her liability is limited under state law. However, the focus would shift from limited liability to management rights under regulations that the IRS proposed in 2011 but had not finalized when this book was completed. The IRS acknowledged that a new test for determining limited partner status is necessary given the emergence of LLCs and changes in state law that allow limited partners to make management decisions while retaining limited liability. Under the proposed regulations, a taxpayer's interest in an entity that is classified as a partnership is treated as a limited partnership interest if the taxpayer does not have rights to manage the partnership under both the governing agreement and under the law of the jurisdiction in which the partnership was organized. A taxpayer who is treated as a limited partner under this definition would have to establish material participation under Test 1, 5, or 6 as noted above. A taxpayer who has management rights and who is not treated as a limited partner would be able to establish material participation under any of the seven material participation tests described in *10.6*. The *e-Supplement* at *jklasser.com* will report any change in the status of the proposed regulations.

**LLC and LLP members.** The Tax Court and the Court of Federal Claims rejected IRS attempts to treat LLC and LLP members as limited partners under the regulations that focus on limited liability. These court decisions allowed an LLC or LLP member to apply any of the IRS' seven tests for material participation *(10.6)*.

The IRS acquiesced after the result in the Court of Federal Claims case and announced that it would no longer litigate similar cases. This was followed by the release of the 2011 proposed regulations discussed above.

## 10.12 Form 8582 and Other Tax Forms

The purpose of Form 8582 is to assemble in one place items of income and expenses from passive activities in order to determine the effect of the passive loss rules on these items. Note that if you actively participate in a rental real estate activity and therefore qualify for the special loss allowance of up to $25,000, you may not have to complete Form 8582; *see* the conditions under "Schedule E" below.

After Form 8582 is completed, the income and allowable deductions are reported as regular income and deductions in appropriate schedules attached to your tax return. For example, net profits of a self-employed person who is not active in the business are reported on Schedule C, sales of capital assets of a passive activity are reported on Form 8949 and Schedule D, your share of partnership income and allowable deductions is reported on Schedule E, and rental income and allowable deductions are reported on Schedule E.

**Forms 8949 & Schedule D or Form 4797.** Gains or losses from the sale of assets from a passive activity or from the sale of a partial interest that is less than "substantially all" of your entire interest in a passive activity are reported on Form 8949/Schedule D (capital assets) or on Form 4797 (business property). The gain is also entered on Form 8582. Losses must first be entered on Form 8582 to *see* how much, if any, is allowable under the passive loss restrictions before an amount can be entered as a loss on Form 8949/Schedule D or Form 4797.

*Partial dispositions.* A disposition of an insubstantial part of your interest in the activity does not allow a deduction of suspended passive losses from prior years. When you dispose of your entire interest in a passive activity to a nonrelated party in a fully taxable transaction, your losses for the year plus prior year suspended losses from the activity are fully deductible. The same rule applies to a partial disposition only if you are disposing of substantially all of the activity and you have proof of the current year and prior year suspended losses allocable to the disposed-of portion. You net the gain or loss from the disposition with the net income or loss from current year operations and any prior year suspended passive losses. If the netting gives you an overall gain, you enter the gain from the sale, the current year income or loss, and any prior year unallowed losses on the appropriate lines of the Worksheets attached to Form 8582; *see* the Form 8582 instructions. If you have an overall loss after the netting, you do not file Form 8582; all losses including prior year unallowed losses are reported on the normally used forms and schedules (Schedule E, Form 8949 and Schedule D, or Form 4797).

**Schedule E.** If you have a net profit from rental real estate or other passive activity reported on Schedule E and you also have losses from other passive activities, the income reported on Schedule E is also entered on Form 8582.

If you have a net loss on Schedule E (on Line 21) from a rental real estate activity subject to the passive activity rules, the loss generally must be entered on Form 8582. If a loss is allowable after application of the passive loss limits, the allowable amount from Form 8582 is entered on Line 22 of Schedule E as your deductible rental loss.

You do not have to complete Form 8582 if you qualify for the rental real estate loss allowance of up to $25,000 (you actively participated in the rental activity; *see 10.2* ) and you meet all of these conditions:

- Your only passive activities are rental real estate activities and you have no suspended prior year passive losses from these or any other passive activities;
- You have no credits related to passive activities;
- Your overall net loss from the rental real estate activities is $25,000 or less ($12,500 or less if married filing separately and you lived apart from your spouse all year);
- Your modified adjusted gross income is $100,000 or less ($50,000 or less if married filing separately and you lived apart from your spouse all year); and
- You do not own any interest in a rental real estate activity as a limited partner or beneficiary of a trust or estate.

If you meet the above conditions, your rental real estate losses are not limited by the passive activity rules and you do not need to complete Form 8582. Enter the loss from Line 21 of Schedule E as the deductible rental real estate loss on Line 22.

If you have a loss from a passive interest in a partnership, trust, estate, or S corporation, you first determine on Form 8582 whether the loss is deductible on Schedule E.

**Schedule F.** A passive activity farm loss is entered on Form 8582 to determine the deductible loss. If only part of the loss is allowed, only that portion is claimed on Schedule F. A net profit from passive farm activities is also entered on Form 8582 to offset losses from other passive activities.

**Other tax forms.** Other forms tied to Form 8582 are Form 4797 (sale of business assets or equipment), Form 4835 (farm rental income), and Form 4952 (investment interest deductions). For further details *see* Form 8582 and its instructions.

## 10.13 Suspended Losses Allowed on Disposition of Your Interest

Losses and credits that may not be claimed in one year because of the passive activity limitations are suspended and carried forward to later years. The carryover lasts indefinitely, until you have passive income against which to claim the losses and credits. No carryback is allowed. What if you have suspended losses from a business and in a later year you materially participate in the business so it is no longer a passive activity? If the activity is not passive in the current year, and you have net income from the activity for the year, you can offset that income with the suspended losses. Any remaining suspended losses continue to be carried forward to future years. Generally, you may deduct in full your remaining suspended losses when you sell your entire interest in the activity; *see* below.

### EXAMPLE

In 2017, Nick Milo was not a material participant in a business activity and his share of losses was $10,000, which was suspended because he had no passive income. In 2018, he becomes a material participant in the business and his share of income is $1,000. He may apply $1,000 of the suspended loss to offset that income and the remaining $9,000 will be carried over to 2019 as a suspended passive loss.

**Allocation of suspended loss.** If your suspended loss is incurred from several activities, you allocate the loss among the activities using the worksheets accompanying Form 8582. The loss is allocated among the activities in proportion to the total loss. If you have net income from significant participation activities (*see* Test 4 *(10.6)*), such activities may be treated as one single activity in making the allocation; *see* the instructions to Form 8582.

**Disposition of entire interest in passive activity.** If you sell your entire interest in an activity to a nonrelated person in a fully taxable transaction, you can claim any suspended passive losses from the activity. On a qualifying disposition, the suspended losses plus any current year income or loss from the activity are combined with the gain or loss from the sale; *see* the Examples below and follow the instructions to Form 8582 for reporting the net gain or loss.

A "fully taxable transaction" is one in which you recognize all the realized gain or loss. In some cases, it may be unclear if a fully taxable transaction has occurred. The IRS treats an abandonment of property as a qualifying disposition that releases suspended losses.

IRS Chief Counsel has held that there is a fully taxable disposition when you sell at a gain rental property that previously had been your principal residence and the gain is not taxable under the home sale exclusion *(29.1)*. A taxpayer had $30,000 in suspended passive losses from three years of rentals when the home was sold to an unrelated party for a $100,000 gain. Since gain or loss on a disposition must be "recognized" for there to be a "fully taxable transaction," the issue before the IRS was whether tax-free home sale gain is "recognized." Chief Counsel held that the taxpayer's home sale gain was realized and recognized; it was simply excluded from income because of the specific exclusion provision. The $30,000 in suspended losses were deductible in the year of sale. Since the $100,000 home sale gain was excluded from income, it was not considered passive income from the rental property and did not offset the $30,000 of suspended losses.

IRS Chief Counsel has also held that a foreclosure on rental real estate subject to recourse debt is a fully taxable transaction, even though the taxpayer avoids tax on the cancellation of his debt because he is insolvent *(11.8)*. A foreclosure is treated as a sale for tax purposes *(31.9)*; here, the taxpayer realized a $25,000 gain on the foreclosure. He also had cancellation of debt income of $75,000, which was not taxed because of the insolvency exclusion. Chief Counsel concluded that since a foreclosure is a taxable sale, a foreclosure of property constituting the taxpayer's interest in the rental property qualifies as a fully taxable transaction under the passive activity disposition rules. This is so whether or not the taxpayer avoids tax on cancellation of debt income due to the insolvency exclusion.

---

### EXAMPLES

1. Jill Stein has a 5% interest in a limited partnership with an adjusted basis of $42,000. In 2018, she sells her interest in the partnership to an unrelated person for $50,000. For 2018, she has a current year passive loss from the partnership (shown on Schedule K-1) of $3,000. She also has $2,000 of suspended passive losses from prior years that have been carried forward to 2018. Jill's $8,000 gain from the sale of her interest is combined on Form 8582 with the current year loss and suspended losses giving her an overall gain of $3,000, figured as follows:

   | | |
   |---|---|
   | Sales price | $50,000 |
   | Less: Adjusted basis | $42,000 |
   | Gain | $8,000 |
   | Less: Current year loss | $3,000 |
   | Less: Suspended losses | $2,000 |
   | Overall gain | $3,000 |

2. Assume that Jill's suspended losses from prior years were $10,000 instead of $2,000. She has an overall loss of $5,000 after combining the gain from the sale of $8,000, the current year loss of $3,000, and the suspended losses of $10,000.

   Since there is an overall loss after combining the gain and losses, Jill does not file Form 8582. The current year loss plus the suspended losses are reported as nonpassive losses on Schedule E and the gain from the disposition on Form 8949 and Schedule D.

3. Assume in Example 1 that Jill sold her interest for $30,000 instead of $50,000. She would have a $12,000 loss on the sale ($42,000 adjusted basis less $30,000 sales price). Combining the loss with the current year loss of $3,000 and the $2,000 of suspended losses, she has an overall loss of $17,000.

Since there is an overall loss, Jill does not file Form 8582. The current year loss plus the suspended losses are reported as nonpassive losses on Schedule E. The $12,000 loss on the sale is reported on Form 8949 and Schedule D as a capital loss. Under the regular rules for capital losses, the loss will offset capital gains for 2018 and any excess will be deductible only up to $3,000 *(5.4)*. Assuming the $3,000 limit applies, Jill has a $9,000 capital loss carryover to 2019.

**Partial disposition.** If you dispose of substantially all of your interest in an activity, you may treat the part disposed of as a separate activity, thereby allowing the deduction of suspended losses. You must show: (1) the amount of prior year suspended deductions and credits allocable to that part of the activity, and (2) the amount of gross income and any other deductions and credits allocable to that part of the activity for the year of disposition.

If the part disposed of is less than substantially all of your interest, suspended losses are not allowed. Gain or loss will be treated as part of the net income or loss from the activity for the year.

**Gifts.** When a passive activity interest is given away, you may not deduct suspended passive losses. The donee's basis in the property is increased by the suspended loss if he or she sells the property at a gain. If a loss is realized by the donee on a sale of the interest, the donee's basis may not exceed fair market value of the gift at the time of the donation.

**Death.** On the death of an investor in a passive interest, suspended losses are deductible on the decedent's final tax return, to the extent the suspended loss exceeds the amount by which the basis of the interest in the hands of the heir is increased.

> ### EXAMPLE
> An owner dies holding an interest in a passive activity with a suspended loss of $8,000. After the owner's death, the heir's stepped-up basis for the property (equal to fair market value) is $6,000 greater than the decedent's basis. On the decedent's final return, $2,000 of the loss is deductible ($8,000 − $6,000).

*Filing Tip*

**Installment Sale of Your Interest**

If you sell your passive activity interest at a profit and have suspended losses, you may deduct a percentage of the losses each year during the installment period *(10.13)*.

**Installment sales.** If you sell your entire interest in a passive activity at a profit on the installment basis, suspended losses are deducted over the installment period in the same ratio as the gain recognized each year bears to the gain remaining to be recognized as of the start of the year. For example, if you realize a gain of $10,000 and report $2,000 of gain each year for five years, in the year of sale you report 20% of your total gain under the installment method, and 20% of your suspended losses are also allowed. In the second year, you report $2,000 of the remaining $8,000 gain and 25% of the remaining losses ($2,000 ÷ $8,000) are allowed.

## 10.14 Suspended Tax Credits

If you have tax credits that were barred under the passive activity rules, they may be claimed only in future years when you have tax liability attributable to passive income. However, in the year you dispose of your interest, a special election may be available to decrease your gain by the amount of your suspended credit; *see* below.

> ### EXAMPLE
> Dan Brown places in service rehabilitated credit property qualifying for a $50 credit, but the credit is not allowed under the passive loss rules. However, his basis is still reduced by $50. In a later year, Brown makes a taxable disposition of his entire interest in the activity and in the rehabilitation property. Assuming that no part of the suspended $50 credit has been used, Brown may elect on Form 8582-CR to increase his basis in the property by the unused $50 credit.

**Basis election for suspended credits.** If you qualify for an investment credit (under transition rules) or a rehabilitation credit, you are required to reduce the basis of the property even if you are unable to claim the credit because of the passive activity rules. If this occurs and you later dispose of your entire interest in the passive activity, including the property whose basis was reduced, your gain will be increased by virtue of the basis reduction although you never benefitted from the credit. To prevent this, you may reduce the taxable gain by electing to increase the pre-transfer basis of the property by the amount of the unused credit. The election is made on Form 8582-CR.

## 10.15 Personal Service and Closely Held Corporations

To prevent avoidance of the passive activity rules through use of corporations, the law imposes restrictions on income and loss offsets in closely held C corporations and personal service corporations.

Unless the material participation tests discussed in this section are met, the activities of a personal service corporation or a closely held corporation are considered passive activities, subject to the restrictions on loss deductions and tax credits. For purposes of these passive activity rules, a closely held C corporation is a corporation in which more than 50% in value of the stock is owned by five or fewer persons during the last half of the tax year.

A personal service corporation is a C corporation the principal activity of which is the performance of personal services by the employee-owners. Personal services in a personal service corporation are services in the fields of health, law, engineering, architecture, accounting, actuarial sciences, performing arts, or consulting. An employee-owner is any employee who on any day in the tax year owns any stock in the corporation. If an individual owns any stock in a corporation which in turn owns stock in another corporation, the individual is deemed to own a proportionate part of the stock in the other corporation. Further, more than 10% of the corporation's stock by value must be owned by owner-employees for the corporation to be a personal service corporation.

**Form 8810 must be used.** Personal service corporations and closely held corporations use Form 8810 to figure the amount of the passive activity loss or credit that is allowed on the corporation's tax return for the year.

**Material participation.** A personal service corporation or closely held corporation is treated as materially participating in an activity during a tax year only if either:

1. One or more stockholders are treated as materially participating in the activity and they directly or indirectly hold in the aggregate more than 50% of the value of the corporation's outstanding shares; or

2. The corporation is a closely held corporation and in the 12-month period ending on the last day of the tax year, the corporation had at least one full-time manager, three full-time employees, none of whom own more than 5% of the stock, and business deductions exceeded 15% of gross income from the activity.

A stockholder is treated as materially participating or significantly participating in the activity of a corporation if he or she satisfies one of the seven tests for material participation *(10.6)*. For purposes of applying the significant participation test (Test 4 at *10.6*), an activity of a personal service or closely held corporation will be treated as a significant participation activity for a tax year only if:

1. The corporation is not treated as materially participating in the activity for the tax year; and

2. One or more individuals, each of whom is treated as significantly participating in the activity directly or indirectly, hold in the aggregate more than 50% of the value of the outstanding stock of the corporation. Furthermore, in applying the seven participation tests, all activities of the corporation are treated as activities in which the individual holds an interest in determining whether the individual participates in an activity of the corporation; and the individual's participation in all activities other than activities of the corporation is disregarded in determining whether his or her participation in an activity of the corporation is treated as material participation under the significant participation test (Test 4).

**Closely held corporation's computation of passive loss.** Even if a closely held corporation does not meet the material participation tests above, it still qualifies for a slight break from the passive loss restrictions. On Form 8810, a closely held corporation may use passive activity deductions to offset not only passive activity gross income but also net active income. Generally, net active income is taxable income from business operations, disregarding passive activity income and expenses, and also disregarding portfolio income and expenses *(10.8)*. Passive activity losses cannot offset portfolio income.

If a corporation stops being closely held, its passive losses and credits from prior years are not allowable against portfolio income but continue to be allowable only against passive income and net active income.

Tax liability on net active income may be offset by passive activity credits.

## 10.16 Sales of Property and of Passive Activity Interests

Gain on the sale or disposition of property is generally passive or nonpassive, depending on whether your activity is passive or nonpassive in the year of sale or disposition. Thus, gain on the sale of property used in a rental activity is generally treated as passive income, as is the gain on property used in a nonrental business if you did not materially participate in the business in the year of sale. On the other hand, gain on the sale of property is generally nonpassive if the property was used in a business that you materially participated in during the year of sale. However, exceptions described below may change this treatment.

Where you transact an installment sale, treatment of gain in later years depends on your status in the year of sale. For example, if you were considered a material participant in a business, all gain is treated as nonpassive income, including gain for later installments. If you were in a rental activity or were not a material participant in a nonrental business, the gain is treated as passive income, unless the exceptions in this section apply.

**Gain on substantially appreciated property formerly used in nonpassive activity.** Even if an activity is passive in the year that you sell substantially appreciated property, gain on the sale is treated as nonpassive unless the property was used in a passive activity for either 20% of its holding period or the entire 24-month period ending on the date of the disposition. Property is substantially appreciated if fair market value exceeds 120% of its adjusted basis.

**Property used in more than one activity in a 12-month period preceding disposition.** You are required to allocate the amount realized on the disposition and the adjusted basis of the property among the activities in which the property was used during a 12-month period preceding the disposition. For purposes of this rule, the term "activity" includes personal use and holding for investment. The allocation may be based on the period for which the property is used in each activity during the 12-month period. However, if during the 12-month period the value of the property does not exceed the lesser of $10,000 or 10% of the value of all property used in the activity at the time of disposition, gain may be allocated to the predominant use.

> **EXAMPLE**
>
> Joe Smith sells equipment for $8,000. During the 12-month period that ended on the date of the sale, 70% of Smith's use of the equipment was in a passive activity. Immediately before the sale, the fair market value of all property used in the passive activity, including the equipment, was $200,000. The equipment was predominantly used in the passive activity during the 12-month period ending on the date of the sale. The value of the equipment, $8,000, did not exceed the lesser of $10,000 or 10% of the $200,000 value of all property used in the activity immediately before the sale. Thus, the amount realized and the adjusted basis are allocated to the passive activity.

**Disposition of partnership and S corporation interests.** Gain or loss from the disposition of an interest in a partnership and S corporation is generally allocated among the entity's activities in proportion to the amount that the entity would have allocated to the partner or shareholder for each of its activities if the entity had sold its interest in the activities on the "applicable valuation date" chosen by the entity, either the date of the disposition or the beginning of the entity's taxable year in which the disposition occurs.

Gain is allocated only to appreciated activities. Loss is allocated only to depreciated activities. The entity may select either the beginning of its tax year in which the holder's disposition occurs or the date of the disposition as the applicable valuation date.

**Claiming suspended loss on disposition of interest in passive activity.** A fully taxable sale of your entire interest or of substantially all of your interest to a nonrelated person will allow you to claim suspended loss deductions from the activity *(10.13)*.

**Dealer's sale of property similar to property sold in the ordinary course of business.** IRS regulations set down complex tests that determine whether the result of the sale is treated as passive or nonpassive income or loss.

## 10.17 At-Risk Limits

The at-risk rules prevent investors from claiming losses in excess of their actual tax investment by barring them from including nonrecourse liabilities as part of the tax basis for their interest. Almost all ventures are subject to the at-risk limits. Real estate placed in service after 1986 is subject to the at-risk rules as well, but most real estate nonrecourse financing can qualify for an exception *(10.18)*.

> **EXAMPLE**
>
> Crystal Parker invests cash of $1,000 in a venture and signs a nonrecourse note for $8,000. In 2018, her share of the venture's loss is $1,200. The at-risk rules limit her deduction to $1,000, the amount of her cash investment; as she is not personally liable on the note, the amount of the liability is not included as part of her basis for loss purposes.

Losses disallowed under the at-risk rules are carried over to the following year *(10.21)*.

**Form 6198.** If you have amounts that are not at risk, you must file Form 6198 to figure your deductible loss. A separate form must be filed for each activity. However, if you have an interest in a partnership or S corporation that has more than one investment in any of the following four categories, the IRS allows you to aggregate all of the partnership or S corporation activities within each category. For example, all partnership or S corporation films and videotapes may be treated as one activity in determining amounts at risk; *see* the instructions to Form 6198.

1. Holding, producing, or distributing motion picture films or videotapes;
2. Exploring for or exploiting oil or gas properties;
3. Exploring for, or exploiting, geothermal deposits (for wells commenced on or after October 1, 1978); and
4. Farming. For this purpose, farming is defined as the cultivation of land and the raising or harvesting of any agricultural or horticultural commodity—including raising, shearing, breeding, caring for, or management of animals. Forestry and timber activities are not included, but orchards bearing fruits and nuts are within the definition of farming. Certain activities carried on within the physical boundaries of the farm may not necessarily be treated as farming.

In addition to the previous categories, the law treats as a single activity all leased depreciable business equipment (Section 1245 property) that is placed in service during any year by a partnership or S corporation.

*Caution*

**At-Risk Rules Limit Loss Deductions**

The purpose of at-risk rules is to keep you from deducting losses from investments in which you have little cash invested and no personal liability for debts.

*Filing Tip*

**Form 6198**

If you have invested an amount for which you are not at risk, such as a nonrecourse loan, you generally must file Form 6198 to figure a deductible loss. However, nonrecourse financing for real estate that secures the loan is treated as an at-risk investment in most cases *(10.18)*.

Exempt from the at-risk rules are C corporations which meet active business tests and are not in the equipment leasing business or any business involving master sound recording, films, videotapes, or other artistic, literary, or musical property. For details on the active business tests, as well as a special at-risk exception for equipment leasing activities of closely held corporations, *see* IRS Publication 925.

The at-risk limitation applies only to tax losses produced by expense deductions that are not disallowed by reason of another provision of the law. For example, if a prepaid interest expense is deferred under the prepaid interest limitation *(15.14)*, the interest will not be included in the loss subject to the risk limitation. When the interest accrues and becomes deductible, the expense may be considered within the at-risk provision. Similarly, if a deduction is deferred because of farming syndicate rules, that deduction will enter into the computation of the tax loss subject to the risk limitation only when it becomes deductible under the farming syndicate rules.

**Effect of passive loss rules.** Where a loss is also subject to the at-risk rules, you apply the at-risk rules first. If the loss is deductible under the at-risk rules, the passive activity rules then apply. On Form 6198 (at risk), you figure the deductible loss allowed as at risk and then carry the loss over to Form 8582 to determine the passive activity loss.

## 10.18 What Is At Risk?

The following amounts are considered at risk in determining your tax position in a business or investment:

- Cash;
- Adjusted basis of property that you contribute; and
- Borrowed funds for which you are personally liable for repayment.

Personal liability alone does not assure that the borrowed funds are considered at risk. The lender generally must have no interest in the venture other than as a creditor and must not be related to a person (other than the borrower) with an interest in the activity other than that of a creditor. Under final IRS regulations, a lender or person related to the lender is considered to have an interest other than that of a creditor only if the person has a capital interest in the activity or an interest in the net profits of the activity. However, even if the lender has such an interest, a loan after May 3, 2004, for which you are personally liable is treated as at risk if: (1) the loan is secured by real estate used in the activity and (2) the loan, were it nonrecourse, would be qualified nonrecourse financing, as discussed below.

At-risk basis is figured as of the end of the year. Any loss allowed for a year reduces the at-risk amount as of the start of the next year. Therefore, if a loss exceeds your at-risk investment, the excess loss will not be deductible in later years unless you increase your at-risk investment; *see* the Example below and *10.21*.

### EXAMPLE

Julie Kahn, an investor, pays a promoter of a book purchase plan $45,000 for a limited partnership interest. The promoter is the general partner. Kahn pays $30,000 cash and gives a note for $15,000 on which she is personally liable. Her amount at risk is $30,000; the $15,000 personal liability note is not counted because it is owed to the general partner.

**Qualified nonrecourse financing for real estate considered at risk.** Generally, you are not considered at risk for nonrecourse financing, that is, loans for which you are not personally liable, unless the loan is secured by property not used in the activity. However, you are considered to be at risk for qualified nonrecourse financing. This is financing from an unrelated commercial lender or government agency for which no one is personally liable and which is secured by real estate used in the activity. The debt obligation must not be convertible to an ownership interest. In determining whether the financing is secured only by real property used in the activity, you can ignore security that is property valued at less than 10% of the total value of all property securing the financing, as well as property that is incidental to the activity of holding real property. Loans from the seller or promoter do not qualify. Third-party nonrecourse debt from a related lender, other than the seller or promoter, may also be treated as at risk, providing the terms of the loan are commercially reasonable and on substantially the same terms as loans involving unrelated persons.

**Pledges of other property.** If you pledge personally owned real estate used outside the activity to secure a nonrecourse debt and invest the proceeds in an at-risk activity, the proceeds may be considered part of your at-risk investment. The proceeds included in basis are limited by the fair market value of the property used as collateral (determined as of the date the property is pledged as security) less any prior (or superior) claims to which the collateral is subject.

**Partners.** A partner is treated as at-risk to the extent that basis in the partnership is increased by the share of partnership income. That partnership income is then used to reduce the partnership's nonrecourse indebtedness will have no effect on a partner's amount at risk. If the partnership makes actual distributions of the income in the taxable year, the amount distributed reduces the partner's amount at risk. A buy-sell agreement, effective at a partner's death or retirement, is not considered for at-risk purposes.

## 10.19 Amounts Not At Risk

The following may not be treated as part of basis for at-risk purposes in determining your tax position in a business or investment:

- Liabilities for which you have no personal liability, but an exception applies to certain real estate financing *(10.18)*.
- Liabilities for which you have personal liability, but the lender also has a capital or profit-sharing interest in the venture; but *see* the exception in *10.18*.
- Recourse liabilities convertible to a nonrecourse basis.
- Money borrowed from a relative listed in *5.6* who has an interest in the venture, other than as a creditor, or from a partnership in which you own more than a 10% interest.
- Funds borrowed from a person whose recourse is solely your interest in the activity or property used in the activity.
- Amounts for which your economic loss is limited by a nonrecourse financing guarantee, stop-loss agreement, or other similar arrangement.
- Investments protected by insurance or loss reimbursement agreement between you and another person. If you are personally liable on a mortgage but you separately obtain insurance to compensate you for any mortgage payments, you are at risk only to the extent of the uninsured portion of the personal liability. You may, however, include as at risk any amount of premium paid from your personal assets. Taking out casualty insurance or insurance protecting you against tort liability is not considered within the at-risk provisions, and such insurance does not affect your investment basis.

*Caution*

**Lender Has Interest**

Even if you are personally liable for a debt, you may not be considered at risk if the lender has an interest in the activity other than as a creditor *(10.18)*.

**Limited partner's potential cash call.** Under the terms of a partnership agreement, limited partners may be required to make additional capital contributions under specified circumstances. Whether such a potential cash call increases the limited partner's at-risk amount has been a matter of dispute.

In one case, the IRS and Tax Court held that a limited partner was not at risk with respect to a partnership note where, under the terms of the partnership agreement, he could be required to make additional capital contributions if the general partners did not pay off the note at maturity. The possibility of such a potential cash call was too uncertain; the partnership might earn profits to pay off the note and even if there were losses, the general partners might not demand additional contributions from the limited partners.

However, a federal appeals court reversed, holding that the limited partner was at risk because his obligation was mandatory and "economic reality" insured that the general partners would insure their rights by requiring the additional capital contribution.

In another case, limited partners relied upon the earlier favorable federal appeals court decision to argue that they were at risk where they could be required by the general partners to make additional cash contributions, but only in order to cover liabilities or expenses that could not be paid out of partnership assets. So long as the partnership was solvent, the limited partners could "elect out" of the call provision. Because of this election, the Tax Court held that the limited partners' obligation was contingent, rather than unavoidable as in the earlier federal appeals court case. Thus, the cash call provision did not increase their at-risk amount.

---

**EXAMPLES**

1. Some commercial feedlots in livestock feeding operations may reimburse investors against any loss sustained on sales of the livestock above a stated dollar amount per head. Under such "stop-loss" orders, an investor is at risk only to the extent of the portion of his or her capital against which he or she is not entitled to reimbursement. Where a limited partnership makes an agreement with a limited partner that, at the partner's election, his or her partnership interest will be bought at a stated minimum dollar amount (usually less than the investor's original capital contribution), the partner is considered at risk only to the extent of his or her investment exceeding the guaranteed repurchase price.

2. A TV film promoter sold half-hour TV series programs to individual investors. Each investor gave a cash down payment and a note for which he or she was personally liable for the balance. Each investor's note, which was identical in face amount, terms, and maturity date, was payable out of the distribution proceeds from the film. Each investor also bought from the promoter the right to the unpaid balance on another investor's note. The promoter arranged the distribution of the films as a unit and was to apportion the sales proceeds equally among the investors.

   The IRS held that each investor is not at risk on the investment evidenced by the note. Upon maturity, each may receive a payment from another investor equal to the one that he or she owes.

3. A gold mine investment offered tax write-offs of four times the cash invested. For $10,000 cash, an investor bought from a foreign mining company a seven-year mineral claim lease to a gold reserve. Under the lease, he could develop and extract all of the gold in the reserve. At the same time, he agreed to spend $40,000 to develop the lease before the end of the year. To fund this commitment, the investor authorized the promoter to sell an option for $30,000 to a third party who was to buy all the gold to be extracted. The $30,000 along with the $10,000 down payment was to be used to develop the reserve. The promoter advised the investor that he could claim a $40,000 deduction for certain development costs.

   The IRS ruled that $30,000 was not deductible because the amount was not "risk capital." The investor got $30,000 by selling an option that could be exercised only if gold were found. If no gold were found, he would be under no obligation to the option holder. The investor's risk position for the $30,000 was substantially the same as if he had borrowed from the option holder on a nonrecourse basis repayable only from his interest in the activity.

   The Tax Court struck down a similar plan on different grounds. Without deciding the question of what was at risk, the court held that the option was only a right of first refusal. Thus, $30,000 was taxable income to the investor in the year of the arranged sale.

4. David Krepp, an investor, purchases cattle from a rancher for $10,000 cash and a $30,000 note payable to the rancher. Krepp is personally liable on the note. In a separate agreement, the rancher agrees to care for the cattle for 6% of Krepp's net profits from the cattle activity. Krepp is considered at risk for $10,000; he may not increase the amount at risk by the $30,000 borrowed from the rancher.

---

## 10.20 At-Risk Investment in Several Activities

If you invest in several activities, each is generally treated separately when applying the at-risk limitation on Form 6198. You generally may not aggregate basis, gains, and losses from the activities for purposes of at-risk limitations. Thus, income from one activity may not be offset by losses from another; the income from one must be reported while the losses from the other may be nondeductible because of at-risk limitations.

However, you may aggregate activities that are part of a business you actively manage. Activities of a business carried on by a partnership or S corporation qualify if 65% or more of losses for the year are allocable to persons who actively participate in management.

The law allows partnerships and S corporations to treat as a single activity all depreciable equipment (Section 1245 property) that is leased or held for lease and placed in service in any tax year. Furthermore, you may aggregate all partnership or S corporation activities within the four categories of films and videotapes, oil and gas properties, geothermal properties, and farms *(10.17)*.

## 10.21 Carryover of Disallowed Losses

A loss disallowed in a current year by the at-risk limitation may be carried over and deducted in the next taxable year, provided it does not fall within the at-risk limits or the passive loss limits in that year. The loss is subject to an unlimited carryover period until there is an at-risk basis to support the deduction. This may occur when additional contributions are made to the business or when there is income from the business which has not been distributed.

Gain from the disposition of property used in an at-risk activity is treated as income from the activity. In general, the reporting of gain will allow a deduction for losses disallowed in previous years to be claimed in the year of disposition.

## 10.22 Recapture of Losses Where At Risk Is Less Than Zero

To prevent manipulation of at-risk basis after a loss is claimed, there is a special recapture rule. If the amount at risk in an activity is reduced to below zero because of a distribution or a change in the status of a loan from recourse to nonrecourse, income may be realized to the extent of the negative at-risk amount. The taxable amount may not exceed the amount of losses previously deducted.

The recaptured amount is not treated as income from the activity for purposes of determining whether current or suspended losses are allowable. Instead, the recaptured amount is treated as a deduction allocable to that activity in the following year. *See* IRS Publication 925 for further details.

 *Filing Tip*

**Carryover Losses**

Losses disallowed by at-risk rules are carried over and may be deductible in a later year.

# CHAPTER 11

# Other Income

This chapter discusses various types of payments you may receive; some are taxable and others are not taxable. Examples of taxable items include:

- State tax refunds if the tax was claimed as an itemized deduction and the refunded amount provided a tax benefit *(11.5)*.
- Prizes, gambling winnings, and awards *(11.2–11.3)*.
- Cancellations of debt, but there are several exceptions, such as for debts discharged in a bankruptcy proceeding or while you are insolvent *(11.8)*.
- Your share of partnership, S corporation, trust, or estate income or loss, as reported on Schedules K-1 *(11.9–11.15)*.
- Examples of nontaxable items include:
- Gifts and inheritances *(11.4)*.
- Compensatory damages for physical injury or sickness *(11.7)*.
- Life insurance proceeds *(11.18)*.

## 11.1  Prizes and Awards

Prizes and awards are taxable income except for an award or prize that meets all these four tests:

1. It is primarily in recognition of religious, charitable, scientific, educational, artistic, literary, or civic achievement.

2. You were selected without any action on your part.

3. You do not have to perform services.

4. You assign the prize or award to a government unit or tax-exempt charitable organization. You must make the assignment before you use or benefit from the award. You may not claim a charitable deduction for the assignment.

**Prize taxed at fair market value.** A prize of merchandise is taxable at fair market value. For example, where a prize of first-class steamship tickets was exchanged for tourist-class tickets for a winner's family, the taxable value of the prize was the price of the tourist tickets. What is the taxable fair market value of an automobile won as a prize? In one case, the Tax Court held that the taxable value was what the recipient could realize on an immediate resale of the car.

**Employee achievement awards.** Awards from an employer are generally taxable (as part of regular pay on form W-2) but there is an exception for certain awards of tangible personal property given for length of service or safety achievement. An award in the form of cash, a gift certificate or equivalent item does not qualify for the exclusion, but other types of tangible personal property, such as a watch, or golf clubs are generally not taxable up to a limit of $1,600 for a qualified plan award or $400 for a non-qualified plan award *(3.12, 20.25)*.

**Olympic medals.** Cash awards paid by the U.S. Olympic Committee to athletes winnings medals at the Olympic and Paralympic games after 2015 are tax free, as well as the value of the medal itself (value of gold, silver or bronze content). However, the exclusion does not apply to athletes with adjusted gross income exceeding $1 million, $500,000 if married filing separately. If the exclusion applies, the nontaxable amount must still be reported as income, but an offsetting deduction is allowed *(12.2)*.

## 11.2  Lottery and Sweepstake Winnings

Sweepstake, lottery, and raffle winnings are taxable as "other income" on Form 1040. The cost of tickets is deductible only to the extent you report winnings, and only if you itemize deductions rather than claim the standard deduction. If you itemize on Schedule A, a deduction for the cost of tickets may be claimed as an "other" itemized deduction *(19.1)*. For example, if you buy state lottery tickets and win a 2018 drawing, you may deduct on Schedule A the cost of your losing tickets in 2018 up to the amount of your winnings.

When a minor wins a state lottery and the prize is held by his or her parents as custodians under the Uniform Transfers to Minors Act, the prize is taxed to the minor in the year the prize is won.

**Installment payments.** If lottery or sweepstakes winnings or casino jackpots are payable in installments, you pay tax only as installments are received. If within 60 days of winning a prize you have an option to choose a discounted lump-sum payment instead of an annuity, and you elect the annuity, you are taxed as the annuity payments are received. Merely having the cash option does not make the present value of the annuity taxable in the year the prize is won.

## 11.3  Gambling Winnings and Losses

**Gambling winnings are taxable but losses are limited.** If you are not a professional gambler, gambling winnings must be reported as "other income" on Form 1040. According to the IRS and Tax Court, you cannot reduce the winnings by your losses for the year and report only the net win (if any) as income on your tax return. Slot machine players determine if they have a win or loss at the end of a playing session; *see* below for a proposed session safe harbor for slot players.

To deduct losses from gambling, you must itemize deductions on Schedule A (not claim the standard deduction), and even if you itemize, the losses are deductible only up

**Court Decision**

**Assignment of Future Lottery Payments**

Courts have agreed with the IRS that a lump sum received for assigning the rights to future state lottery payments is taxed as ordinary income, not capital gain. The right to receive annual lottery payments is not a capital asset.

**Filing Tip**

**Winnings Paid in Installments**

If you received lottery installments in 2018, these are treated as gambling winnings, and if you itemize deductions, you may deduct any gambling losses incurred in 2018 up to the amount of the installments as a miscellaneous itemized deduction.

to the amount of your gambling winnings. The deduction, not to exceed the gambling income reported on Form 1040, is claimed as an "other" itemized deduction on Schedule A*(19.1)*. Keep records that document your gambling losses in case your itemized deduction is questioned by the IRS.

You may not deduct a net gambling loss for the year (losses exceeding gains) even though a particular state says gambling is legal. Nor does it matter that your business is gambling. You may not deduct a net loss from wagering transactions even if you are a professional gambler (see below).

**Professional gamblers.** According to the Supreme Court, a gambler is engaged in the business of gambling if he or she gambles full time to earn a livelihood and not merely as a hobby.

A professional gambler reports winnings and expenses (wagers and other gambling-related expenses) on Schedule C. However, the Tax Court and federal appeals courts have consistently held that wagers on gambling transactions are deductible only to the extent of wagering gains even if the gambling activity is a business. The statute that specifically bars a deduction of gambling losses in excess of gambling winnings trumps the general statute allowing full deductibility for ordinary and necessary business expenses.

For 2017 and earlier years, a professional's gambling-related expenses other than the cost of actual wagers were not limited to gambling winnings under a Tax Court decision that held that expenses such as transportation and lodging costs (casino gambling), tournament entry fees and gambling-related publications were fully deductible business expenses on Schedule C. However, the Tax Cuts and Jobs Act reverses this result for 2018 and later years. Under the new law, transportation and other gambling-related expenses are treated as "losses from wagering transactions," and thus they, together with the cost of wagers, are deductible by a professional gambler only to the extent of gambling winnings.

> **EXAMPLE**
>
> Tschetschot, a professional gambler, argued that her losses from poker tournaments should not be limited to her winnings because tournament poker, unlike traditional poker, is not "gambling" but a sports and entertainment activity like a golf or tennis tournament. Her tournaments were distinguishable from "wagering activities," she argued, because tournament players have a limited monetary stake in the form of a buy-in entrance fee, they receive the same number of chips, and the highest-place finishers receive cash prizes in predetermined amounts. The Tax Court, however, held that despite the differences between tournament play and other types of poker, the basic nature of the game remains a wagering activity, as bets are still played on each hand and each betting round has consequences. The Court also held that it is not unconstitutional to treat gambling losses differently from losses in sports tournaments, but it implied that Congress might want to reconsider the restriction on gambling losses given the increased acceptance of gambling in our society and improvements in the IRS' ability to accurately track winnings and losses.

**Certain winnings reported to the IRS on Form W-2G.** A payer must report a win from slot machine play or bingo of $1,200 or more (not reduced by the wager) to you and the IRS on Form W-2G. For keno the threshold is $1,500 (reduced by the wager), and for poker tournament winnings the threshold is winnings over $5,000 (reduced by the wager or buy-in). For lotteries, sweepstakes, horse racing, and other wagers, a Form W-2G is required for winnings of $600 or more that are at least 300 times the amount of the wager *(26.7)*.

If you have more than one reportable win from slot machines, bingo, or keno on the same calendar day or "gaming day," the gaming establishment may (this is optional) combine the winnings on one Form W-2G instead of reporting each win separately. A "gaming day" is the 24-hour period ending when business is slowest or the establishment closes down.

**Slot machine win or loss determined on a session by session basis.** The IRS and Tax Court have followed a "per session" rule for determining whether a slot machine player has realized a win or a loss. That is, whether a player has a win or loss is determined for each "session" of play at the end of that session. A session win is taxable income, which a recreational gambler must include as "other income" on Schedule 1 (Form 1040). A session loss is only deductible as an "other itemized deduction" on Schedule A (if you itemize rather than claim the standard deduction), and the itemized deduction for total session losses cannot exceed the total winnings and other gambling income that you report as income.

However, there has been no single standard for determining what a "session" of slot machine play is. In the absence of a specific standard, the IRS uses a facts and circumstances test to determine a session.

In 2015, the IRS proposed an optional safe harbor that taxpayers could use to define a "session of play" for purposes of calculating wins or losses from electronically tracked slot play (Notice 2015-21). If finalized, the safe harbor would help eliminate disputes, but in 2017 the IRS stated that it was still considering whether to finalize or modify the safe harbor and that it would not take effect until it is finalized and an effective date announced in a future revenue procedure. At the time this book was completed, the IRS had not yet made a decision on the safe harbor ; *see* the *e-Supplement* at *jklasser.com* for an update, if any.

Even if the safe harbor is finalized as proposed, it would not change the rule that prevents a non-professional gambler from netting gains from winning sessions against losses from losing sessions in figuring the winnings to be reported as "other income." The winnings would still have to be reported as income, without taking into account the losses. The losses would have to be claimed separately, if at all, as an "other itemized deduction." Therefore, it would still be necessary to maintain records to substantiate losses claimed as an itemized deduction.

Here are the major components of the proposed safe harbor in Notice 2015-21:

1. A taxpayer determines gain or loss from electronically tracked slot machines at the end of each session of play, which begins when the first wager on an electronically tracked slot machine is placed and ends when the last wager on an electronically tracked slot machine is made at the same casino by the end of the same calendar day (12:00 a.m. to 11:59 p.m.).

2. The taxpayer has a gain if the payouts from a session of play exceed the amount wagered during that session. A taxpayer has a loss if the amount wagered is more than the payouts during that session.

3. The session of play does not end if the taxpayer stops and resumes play within the same gaming establishment during the calendar day. However, moving to a new gaming establishment during the same calendar day begins a new session.

---

**EXAMPLES OF IRS PROPOSED OPTIONAL SAFE HARBOR**

1. A taxpayer begins play at an electronically tracked slot machine using her Player's Card in Casino X at 3 p.m. and plays for two hours. At 5 p.m., the taxpayer leaves Casino X and meets friends for dinner, and later returns to Casino X and resumes electronically tracked slot play from 10 p.m. until 2 a.m. Under the proposed optional safe harbor, the slot play from 3 p.m. to 5 p.m. and the play from 10 p.m. through 11:59 p.m. constitute a single session of play, so all wins and net losses during those periods are combined to figure gain or loss for the session. If payouts exceed wagers from 3–5 p.m. by $300, and wagers exceed payouts by $75 from 10–11:59 p.m., there is a $225 gain for that session ($300 − $75). The play from midnight to 2 a.m. is another session because it occurs on the next calendar day; this is true even if the play is at the same slot machine that was being played before midnight. Thus, if the taxpayer has an overall loss for the play from midnight to 2 a.m., the loss would be from a different session and would not reduce the $225 gain from the session that ended at 11:59 p.m.

2. Same facts as Example 1, except that from 7 p.m. to 8 p.m., the taxpayer plays electronically tracked slots in Casino Y. The taxpayer has three separate playing sessions: the play from 3–5 p.m. and 10–11:59 p.m. at Casino X is one session, the play from 7–8 p.m. at Casino Y is another session, and the play from midnight to 2 a.m. at Casino X is another session.

---

## 11.4  Gifts and Inheritances

Gifts and inheritances you receive are not taxable. However, distributions taken from an inherited traditional IRA *(8.14)*, and distributions from inherited qualified plan accounts such as 401(k) and profit-sharing plan accounts *(7.12)*, are taxable, except for amounts attributable to nondeductible contributions made by the deceased account owner. Income earned from gift or inherited property after you receive it is taxable.

*Planning Reminder*

**Gifts You Make**

You may have to file a gift tax return if your gifts to an individual within the year exceed the annual gift tax exclusion, which for 2018 is $15,000 *(39.2)*.

Describing a payment as a gift or inheritance will not necessarily shield it from tax if it is, in fact, a payment for your services *(2.1)*.

A sale of an expected inheritance from a living person is taxable as ordinary income.

---

**EXAMPLES**

1. An employee is promised by his employer that he will be remembered in his will if he continues to work for him. The employer dies but fails to mention the employee in his will. The employee sues the estate, which settles his claim. The settlement is taxable.

2. A nephew left his uncle a bequest of $200,000. In another clause of the will, the uncle was appointed executor, and the bequest of the $200,000 was described as being made in lieu of all commissions to which he would otherwise be entitled as executor. The bequest is considered tax-free income. It was not conditioned upon the uncle performing as executor. If the will had made the bequest contingent upon the uncle's acting as executor, the $200,000 would have been taxed.

3. An attorney performed services for a friend without expectation of pay. The friend died and in his will left the attorney a bequest in appreciation for his services. The payment was considered a tax-free bequest. The amount was not bargained for.

4. A lawyer agreed to handle a client's legal affairs without charge; she promised to leave him securities. Twenty years later, under her will, the lawyer inherited the securities. The IRS taxed the bequest as pay. Both he and the client expected that he would be paid for legal services. If the client meant to make a bequest from their agreement, she should have said so in her will.

---

## 11.5 Refunds of State and Local Income Tax Deductions

A refund of state or local income tax is not taxable if you did not previously claim the tax as an itemized deduction (Schedule A, Form 1040) in a prior year. For example, if you claimed the standard deduction on your 2017 federal return and in 2018 when you filed your 2017 state tax return you received a refund for state tax withheld from your 2017 wages, or for state estimated tax payments made in 2017, the refund is not taxable on your 2018 federal return. If you did claim a deduction for the tax in a prior year, you generally must include a refund in income to the extent that the refunded amount lowered your tax in the earlier year; this is the "tax benefit" rule.

**Taxable part of refund of state/local income taxes or state/local general sales taxes.** If in 2018 you received a refund for state or local income tax that you claimed as an itemized deduction for a prior year, the taxable portion of the refund depends on the amount of the state/local general sales tax that you could have deducted in lieu of the state/local income tax *(16.3)*. In general, the full amount of the refund is taxable for 2018 if it is less than the excess of the state/local income tax claimed as a deduction in the prior year over the state/local general sales tax that you could have but did not deduct. If the refund is more than the excess, the amount subject to tax is limited to the excess. However, the actual taxable portion could be even lower due to the standard deduction limit; *see* below.

For example, on your 2017 federal return, you claimed an itemized deduction for $11,000 in state/local income taxes, as this exceeded your payment of $10,000 in state/local general sales taxes. If in 2018 you received a $750 refund of 2017 state income tax, the entire refund might be taxable (could be less depending on the standard deduction limit), since it is less than the $1,000 excess of the state/local income taxes over the state/local general sales taxes that could have been deducted for 2017. However, if the refund had been $2,500 instead of $750, no more than $1,000 of the refund would be includible in 2018 income (actual $11,000 deduction for state/local income taxes minus $10,000 in state sales tax that could have been deducted), with a further reduction possible under the standard deduction limit.

Similarly, if in 2017 you deducted state/local general sales taxes in lieu of state/local income taxes, and you received a sales tax refund in 2018, the IRS generally requires you to include the entire sales tax refund as income on your 2018 return if it is less than the excess of your 2017 sales tax deduction over the income tax deduction that could have been deducted. The amount subject to tax could be further reduced because of the standard deduction limit discussed below.

### Table 11-1  2017 Standard Deduction
(For Determining Whether Recovery in 2018 of 2017 Itemized Deductions Is Taxable on your 2018 Form 1040)

| If you were— | 2017 standard deduction was— |
| --- | --- |
| Married filing jointly | $ 12,700 |
| Single | 6,350 |
| Head of household | 9,350 |
| Married filing separately | 6,350 |
| Qualifying widow or widower | 12,700 |
| Single age 65 or over | 7,900 |
| Single and blind | 7,900 |
| Single age 65 or over and also blind | 9,450 |
| Married filing jointly with: | |
| • One spouse age 65 or over | 13,950 |
| • Both spouses age 65 or over | 15,200 |
| • One spouse blind under age 65 | 13,950 |
| • Both spouses blind under age 65 | 15,200 |
| • One spouse age 65 or over and also blind | 15,200 |
| • One spouse age 65 or over and other spouse blind and under age 65 | 15,200 |
| • One spouse age 65 or over and also blind; other spouse blind and under age 65 | 16,450 |
| • Both spouses age 65 or over and also blind | 17,700 |
| Qualifying widow or widower age 65 or over | 13,950 |
| Qualifying widow or widower and blind | 13,950 |
| Qualifying widow or widower age 65 or over and also blind | 15,200 |
| Head of household age 65 or over | 10,900 |
| Head of household and blind | 10,900 |
| Head of household age 65 or over and also blind | 12,450 |
| Married filing separately age 65 or over* | 7,600 |
| Married filing separately and blind* | 7,600 |
| Married filing separately age 65 or over and also blind* | 8,850 |

*If on your 2017 return you claimed your spouse as an exemption *(21.1)*, add $1,250 if he or she was either blind or age 65 or older; add $2,500 if he or she was both blind and age 65 or older.

If your itemized deductions in the earlier year were subject to the overall reduction for higher income taxpayers that applied prior to 2018 *(13.7)*, figure what your itemized deductions would have been without the recovered amount. The difference between that amount and your actual itemized deductions under the overall reduction is generally the amount of the recovery that you must report as income, although the taxable amount can be lower if the standard deduction limit discussed below applies.

 *Planning Reminder*

**Refund of State and Local Tax**

A state and local tax refund received in 2018 is taxable on your 2018 federal return only if you claimed the refunded tax as an itemized deduction for a prior year, and only to the extent that your itemized deductions for that prior year exceeded the standard deduction you could have claimed.

To help you figure the taxable portion of 2017 itemized deductions recovered in 2018, 2017 standard deduction amounts are shown in *Table 11-1*.

**If AMT applied in year of deduction.** If the refunded state tax was claimed as an itemized deduction but you were subject to the alternative minimum tax (AMT) for that year, the deduction was not allowable for AMT purposes *(23.2)*. The refund is taxable only if the deduction gave you a tax benefit in the prior year. To determine if there was a tax benefit, you must recompute regular tax liability and AMT for the prior year after increasing your income by the refunded amount. If the recomputation does not increase your total tax, there was no tax benefit and the refund is not taxable. If your total tax increases by any amount, the deduction gave you a tax benefit and the refund is taxable to the extent that the deduction reduced your tax in the prior year.

**Standard deduction limit.** The taxable portion of a refunded state tax cannot exceed the standard deduction limit. You include in income the lesser of the refund or the excess of your itemized deductions for the prior year over the standard deduction that could have been claimed.

The standard deduction limit applies to your total recoveries where you had other recoveries in addition to a refund of state tax *(11.6)*.

> **EXAMPLE**
>
> On your 2017 return, you filed as a single taxpayer. You claimed itemized deductions of $6,600, of which $4,100 was for state and local income taxes, $1,750 was for mortgage interest, and $750 was for charitable contributions. Your deductions exceeded by $250 the $6,350 standard deduction you could have claimed for 2017 as a single person under age 65. You were not subject to alternative minimum tax.
>
> In 2018, you received from the state a $750 refund of your 2017 state income tax. The $4,100 deduction you claimed on your 2017 return for state and local income tax exceeded your 2017 state and local general sales taxes by more than the $750 refund amount. However, because of the standard deduction limit, you only have to report $250 of the refund as income on your 2018 Form 1040. The taxable recovery is limited to the $250 difference between the claimed itemized deductions of $6,600 and the $6,350 standard deduction for 2017.
>
> If you had a negative taxable income in 2017, the taxable recovery figured under the above rule is reduced by the negative amount. If you had a negative taxable income of $100 in 2017, only $150 of the refund would be taxable in 2018.

**Allocating a refund recovery.** If in 2018 you received a refund of state or local income taxes and also a recovery of other deductions, and only part of the total recovery is taxable, you allocate the taxable amount of the recovery according to the ratio between the state income tax refund and the other recovery. You do this by first dividing the state income tax refund by the total of all itemized deductions recovered. The resulting percentage is then applied to the taxable recovery to find the amount to report as the taxable state income tax refund on Schedule 1 of Form 1040; other taxable recoveries are reported on as "other income" on Schedule 1 of Form 1040.

> **EXAMPLE**
>
> In 2018, you received a refund of state income taxes of $500 and also recovered $2,000 of other expenses that you claimed as itemized deductions on your 2017 return. You figure that only $1,500 of the $2,500 recovery is taxable because your total 2017 itemized deductions were $1,500 more than the standard deduction you could have claimed. As a taxable state income tax refund is reported separately from other taxable recoveries on Form 1040, you must figure how much of the $1,500 taxable recovery is attributed to the refund of state income taxes. By dividing the state income tax refund by the amount of the total recovery, you find that 20% is attributed to the refund ($500/$2,500). Thus, 20% of the taxable recovery, or $300 (20% of $1,500), is reported as a taxable state income tax refund on Form 1040, and the balance of $1,200 is reported as "other income." If you received a Form 1099-G reporting the state income tax refund, attach a statement to your Form 1040 explaining that you are reporting as income less than the actual state income tax refund ($500) shown on Form 1099-G as a result of the allocation between the state income tax refund and the other recovered deductions.

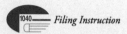
*Filing Instruction*

**Negative Taxable Income**

If your taxable income was a negative amount in the year in which the recovered item was deducted, you reduce the recovery includible in income by the negative amount. For example, if the taxable recovery would be $1,700 but you had a negative taxable income of $500 for the year the deduction was claimed, only $1,200 is taxable.

Refund of state tax paid in installments over two tax years. If you pay estimated state or local income taxes, your last tax installment may be in the year you receive a refund. In this case, you allocate the refund between the two years; *see* the following Example.

> **EXAMPLE**
>
> Your estimated state income tax for 2017 was $4,000, which you paid in four equal installments. You made your fourth payment in January 2018. No state income tax was withheld during 2017. You included the state estimated tax payments made in 2017 ($3,000) in the itemized deductions claimed on your 2017 Form 1040. In 2018, when you filed your 2017 state income tax return, you received a state income tax refund of $400.
>
> You must allocate the $400 refund between 2017 and 2018. As you paid 75% ($3,000 ÷ $4,000) of the estimated tax in 2017, 75% of the $400 refund, or $300, is treated as a recovery of taxes paid in 2017. On your 2018 return, you include $300 as a taxable refund of state income tax on Schedule 1 of Form 1040. You also attach a statement explaining that the $300 amount is less than the $400 refund shown on the Form 1099-G received from the state in 2018 because of the allocation required for the estimated tax installment made in January 2018.
>
> If you itemize deductions on your 2018 Form 1040, then in figuring your 2018 deduction for state income taxes *(16.1)*, you reduce the $1,000 paid in January 2018 by $100 (25% of $400 refund), which is the portion of the refund attributed to your January 2018 payment of estimated state income tax. Your 2018 deduction for state income taxes will include the January net amount of $900 plus any estimated state income taxes paid in 2018 for 2018, any state income tax withheld during 2018, and any state income tax for 2017 that you paid in 2018 when you filed your 2017 state return.
>
> Note: If the $300 refund allocated to 2017 in the previous Example was more than the excess of your 2017 itemized deductions over the 2017 standard deduction you could have claimed, you report only that excess as income on your 2018 Form 1040.

## 11.6 Other Recovered Deductions

The rules in the preceding section *(11.5)* for determining whether a refund of state sales tax is taxable also apply to the recovery of other items for which you claimed a tax deduction, such as a refund of real estate taxes *(16.1)*, adjustable rate mortgage interest *(15.1)*, reimbursement of a deducted medical expense *(17.4)*, a reimbursed casualty loss *(18.2)*, a return of donated property that was claimed as a charitable deduction *(14.1)*, and a payment of debt previously claimed as a bad debt *(5.33)*.

**Unused tax credit in prior year.** If you recover an item deducted in a prior year in which tax credits exceeded your tax, you refigure the prior year tax to determine if the recovery is taxable. Add the amount of the recovery to taxable income of the prior year and refigure the earlier year tax based on the increased taxable income. If the recomputed tax, after application of the tax credits, exceeds the actual tax for the earlier year, include the recovery in income to the extent the recovery reduced your tax in the prior year. The recovery may reduce an available credit carryforward to the current year.

**Alternative minimum tax in the prior year.** If you were subject to the alternative minimum tax (AMT) in the year the recovered deduction was claimed, recompute your regular and AMT tax for the prior year based on the taxable income you reported plus the recovered amount. If inclusion of the recovery does not change your total tax, you do not include the recovery in income. If your total tax increases by any amount, the recovered deduction gave you a tax benefit and you must include the recovery in income to the extent the deduction reduced your tax in the prior year. The recovery may reduce a carryforward of a tax credit based on prior year AMT.

**Recovery of previously deducted items used to figure carryover.** A deductible expense may not reduce your tax because you have an overall loss. If in a later year the expense is repaid or the obligation giving rise to the expense is canceled, the deduction of that expense will be treated as having produced a tax reduction in the earlier year if it increased a carryover that has not expired by the beginning of the taxable year in which the forgiveness occurs. For example, you are on the accrual basis and on your 2017 return you deducted rent that had not yet been paid. The rent obligation is forgiven in 2018. The 2017 rent deduction is treated as having produced a reduction in 2017 tax, even if it resulted in no tax savings for 2017, if it figured in the calculation of a net operating loss that has not expired or been used by the beginning of 2018, the year of forgiveness. The same rule applies to other carryovers such as the investment credit carryover.

---

**EXAMPLE**

You filed a joint return for 2017 and claimed itemized deductions of $13,800, which exceeded your standard deduction of $12,700. You were not subject to the alternative minimum tax on your 2017 joint return. In 2018, you received the following recoveries of amounts deducted on your 2017 return:

| | |
|---|---|
| Medical expenses | $ 200 |
| State income tax refund | 400 |
| Interest expense | 325 |
| Total | $ 925 |

The $400 state income tax refund was less than the difference between the state income tax you deducted and your state general sales taxes. The total recovery of $925 is taxable on your 2018 return. It is less than $1,100, the excess of your 2017 itemized deductions over the allowable standard deduction ($13,800 − 12,700). On Form 1040, you report $400 on the line for taxable refunds of state income tax, and the balance of $525 is reported as "other income."

If the total recovery had been $2,500 instead of $925, $1,100 would be taxable (the excess of $13,800 in itemized deductions over the $12,700 standard deduction for 2017). The $1,400 balance would be tax free.

---

## 11.7 How Legal Damages Are Taxed

By statute, compensatory damages for personal physical injury or physical sickness are tax free, whether fixed by a court or in a negotiated settlement. Damages for nonphysical personal injuries, such as for discrimination, back pay, or injury to reputation, are taxable; a limited exception for certain emotional distress damages may be available as discussed below. Damages for lost profits, breach of contract, or interference with business operations are taxable.

These are the general rules, but damages that would otherwise be taxable can be tax free if received as part of a judgment or settlement relating to a physical injury or sickness. The law excludes from income compensatory damages received "on account of" physical injuries or sickness, so if this "account of" test is met, all compensatory damages are tax free, including amounts for lost wages or emotional distress (see below). Interest added to an award is taxable, even if the award is tax-free damages for physical injury or sickness.

**Emotional distress.** The law that provides an exclusion for damages received on account of a physical illness or sickness specifically provides that emotional distress by itself is not treated as a physical injury or sickness. To be tax free, damages for emotional distress must be attributable to a physical injury or sickness. For example, if you are injured in an accident and receive damages for emotional distress, or damages for emotional distress are included in the damages received in a wrongful death action, the emotional distress damages are tax free because they are deemed to be received "on account of" a physical injury; *see* Example 1 below.

If emotional distress damages are due to an injury other than a physical injury or sickness, as in a discrimination action, the damages are taxable with one exception: Damages up to the amount of actual medical care expenses attributable to emotional distress are tax free. That is, if you can prove actual expenditures for medical care to deal with emotional distress, that portion of the damages is tax free.

Apart from the medical expenses exception, damages for emotional distress are taxable when received for a personal injury other than a physical injury or sickness. Keep in mind that emotional distress, including its physical symptoms, is not treated as a physical injury or sickness, and so in an action for wrongful termination of employment or discrimination, emotional distress damages are taxable, even where the damages cover physical symptoms of emotional distress such as insomnia, headaches, and stomach disorders, although no tax would be due on actual medical costs incurred to deal with those physical symptoms. The Tax Court has held that depression falls within the category of emotional distress; *see* Example 2 below.

---

### EXAMPLES

1. A wrongful death recovery clearly is attributable to a physical injury. The IRS in several private rulings held that where a claim for intentional infliction of emotional distress is part of a wrongful death action, any recovery of compensatory damages is excludable from gross income. In these rulings, the estates of individuals killed in an accident initially brought claims for wrongful death and intentional infliction of emotional distress and a court awarded compensatory damages, prejudgment interest and punitive damages. The exact nature of the accident was not disclosed in the rulings, but it was apparently severe enough that local legislators passed a law to provide compensation to claimants for all their wrongful death and physical injury claims, including emotional distress. The law voided all prior court proceedings. The original defendant paid into a government fund from which damages to the claimants were paid.

    The IRS ruled that all recoveries of compensatory damages from the government fund were for wrongful death, including amounts for emotional distress, and thus excludable as being received on account of a personal physical injury. The only exception is for amounts equal to medical expenses incurred to treat emotional distress that were previously deducted in prior years. Any damages reimbursing the previously deducted expenses are taxable.

2. The Tax Court has held that depression and physical symptoms of depression are a form of emotional distress. In one case, a taxpayer received a settlement after she was fired and brought a wrongful termination case against her former employer. She had suffered from depression, and her symptoms got worse after she lost her job, including insomnia and sleeping too much, migraines, nausea, vomiting, weight gain, acne and pain in her back, shoulder, and neck. In the Tax Court, the taxpayer argued that the exacerbation of her depression symptoms as a result of her termination was a physical injury or sickness, and so her damages should not be taxed. The Tax Court disagreed, reiterating prior holdings that depression falls within the category of emotional distress, which by itself is not considered a physical injury or sickness for which the exclusion from income is allowed.

    The Court rejected the taxpayer's claim that her depression symptoms should be treated like the multiple sclerosis symptoms in the Domeny case discussed in the next paragraph. Unlike in Domeny, the taxpayer here was not determined to be too ill to work by a physician and she did not show that the physical symptoms of her depression were severe enough to rise to the level of a physical disorder.

The National Taxpayer Advocate has argued that it is confusing and unfair to allow tax-free treatment for emotional distress damages that are attributable to physical injury or sickness while imposing tax on emotional distress damages for non-physical injuries such as employer discrimination. She has urged Congress to change the law and allow tax-free treatment for all awards for emotional distress, mental anguish, and pain and suffering.

**Damages for wrongful termination.** If damages are received from a former employer for wrongful termination, the damages are usually taxable as compensation, but any amount for a workplace-related physical injury or illness are excludable from income. Unless the terms of a settlement or verdict specifically allocate damages to a physical illness or injury, it may be difficult to show that you are entitled to the exclusion. But the Tax Court was convinced in the following case.

Domeny was working as a fund-raiser for nonprofit organizations when she was diagnosed with multiple sclerosis (MS) in 1996. She managed her symptoms without medication but in 2000 she took a job with an autism center where she could spend less time on her feet. The position involved fund-raising, grant writing and community development. Domeny had a strained relationship with her supervisor, who restricted her duties. The stress caused

 *Caution*

**Deducting Legal Fees**

You may not deduct legal fees incurred in obtaining tax-free damages for physical injury or physical sickness. If you recover taxable damages, you may be able to deduct legal fees, as discussed in this section (11.7).

her MS symptoms to flare up. In November 2004 she discovered that her supervisor was embezzling funds and she reported this to the center's board of directors, who promised her that they would take action but did not. She felt uncomfortable about having to raise funds from parents while knowing that her supervisor was embezzling funds. This situation continued for months, during which time her distress increased and her MS symptoms intensified. In March 2005, she went to her physician, complaining of vertigo, leg pain, numbness in both feet, burning behind her eyes and extreme fatigue. Her physician told her to stay home from work for two weeks but when Domeny notified the center, she was fired.

Domeny sued the center, alleging numerous discrimination and civil rights violations. The center agreed to settle and paid her a total of $33,308 of which $8,187.50 was treated as Form W-2 wages and $8,187.50 as attorney fees. The $16,933 balance was reported on Form 1099-MISC as nonemployee compensation. Domeny did not include the $16,933 on her 2005 return on the grounds that it was to compensate her for the worsening of her physical condition caused by working in a hostile work environment, and the fact that her condition prevented her from returning to work until more than a year after her termination.

The Tax Court agreed that the $16,933 payment was excludable from Domeny's income. Even though the settlement agreement did not specify why the payment was made, the inference was clear that the center was recognizing Domeny's complaint that a hostile and stressful work environment aggravated her physical illness. The fact that the settlement was segregated into three portions suggested that the center knew that part of the settlement was to compensate for physical illness. The center knew about Domeny's illness before her termination, and her only claim was that she was fired after her work environment had caused the flareup in her MS symptoms.

**Punitive damages.** Punitive damages are taxable, even if they relate to a physical injury or sickness. An exception in the law allows an exclusion from income for punitive damages awarded under a state wrongful death statute if the punitive damages are the only damages that may be awarded.

**Restitution for wrongful incarceration.** Wrongfully incarcerated individuals may exclude from income any civil damages, restitution, or other monetary awards received in connection with the incarceration. There is no cap on the exclusion. If in recent years such payments were received and included in income, a refund can be claimed by filing an amended return on Form 1040X; "Incarceration Exclusion PATH Act" should be written at the top of the form.

**Holocaust restitution payments.** There is a broad exclusion from gross income for Holocaust restitution payments. Tax-free treatment applies to payments received by persons persecuted by Nazi Germany or any Nazi-controlled or allied country, as well as to payments received by heirs or estates of such persecuted persons. Persecution on the basis of race, religion, physical or mental disability, or sexual orientation is covered.

Excludable restitution includes compensation for assets that were stolen or lost before, during, or immediately after World War II and to life insurance issued by European insurers immediately before and during the war. Tax-free treatment also applies to interest earned on escrow accounts and funds established in settlement of Holocaust victim claims against European banks or corporations.

**Legal fees.** If your damages are tax free, you may not deduct your litigation costs. If your damages are taxable, including the contingency fee portion of a taxable recovery (see below) you may be able to deduct your legal fees. A business expense deduction may be claimed on Schedule C for legal fees to recover taxable business income. An above-the-line deduction (directly from gross income) is allowed for legal fees in employment discrimination suits, certain other unlawful discrimination cases, and federal False Claims Act cases paid in connection with a court judgment or settlement after October 22, 2004. The deduction cannot exceed the amount of the judgment or settlement you are including for the year. The above-the-line deduction is claimed on Schedule 1 of Form 1040 *(12.2)*.

For 2018 and later years, you cannot deduct legal fees that are not eligible for the above-the-line deduction or allowed as a Schedule C deduction. Under prior law, a taxpayer who itemized deductions could include the legal fee as a miscellaneous itemized deductions on Schedule A subject to the 2% of adjusted gross income floor, but the Tax Cuts and Jobs Act suspends this miscellaneous itemized deduction for 2018 through 2025 *(19.1)*.

**Attorney's contingent fee paid from taxable award.** If you receive taxable damages, such as back pay in an employment dispute, and a percentage goes directly to your attorney under a contingent fee agreement, can you exclude from your income the contingent fee payment, so that you are only taxed on the net amount you receive?

The answer from the Supreme Court is no. The Supreme Court held in its 2005 Banks decision that the contingency-fee portion of a taxable damages award or settlement generally must be included in the litigant's gross income. The Court's decision did not resolve whether attorney fees paid pursuant to a statutory fee-shifting provision must be included in income, but it suggested that such statutory fees might in some cases be excludable. However, a subsequent Tax Court decision held that the attorney-fee portion of a taxable settlement was includible in the litigant's income where attorney fees were awarded under a California fee-shifting statute. Since the Supreme Court had not decided that issue, the Tax Court relied on its own prior decisions and precedent of the Ninth Circuit (where appeal would lie), which required inclusion of the fee portion of a settlement where a contingency-fee obligation was satisfied by a fee-shifting statute.

*Note:* If the contingency-fee portion of a taxable award in an unlawful employment discrimination case must be included in gross income under the Supreme Court decision, you may be able to offset the inclusion of the fees by an above-the-line deduction, as discussed above.

## 11.8 Cancellation of Debts You Owe

If a debt is canceled or forgiven other than as a gift or a bequest, a debtor who is personally liable on the loan (recourse debt) generally must include the canceled amount in gross income. Exclusions are allowed for discharges of farm or business real estate debt and debts of insolvent and bankrupt persons.

For years before 2018, a discharge of up to $2 million of qualified principal residence indebtedness (as part of a mortgage restructuring or foreclosure) was excluded from income. When this book was completed, legislation to extend this exclusion to discharges occurring in 2018 had not been enacted; *see* the text below and the *e-Supplement* at *jklasser.com* for an update if any.

Details on the various exclusions are provided below. If you qualify for one of the exclusions, you generally must reduce certain "tax attributes" (such as the basis of property) by the amount excluded. The reduction of tax attributes is made on Form 982.

Form 1099-C. You should receive Form 1099-C from a federal government agency, credit union, or bank that cancels or forgives a debt you owe of $600 or more. The IRS receives a copy of the form. Generally, the amount of canceled debt shown in Box 2 of Form 1099-C must be reported as "other income" on Form 1040, unless one of the exclusions discussed below applies.

**Mortgage loan "workouts" and repayment discounts.** If your lender agrees to a "workout" that restructures your loan and reduces the principal balance of your debt, or you are allowed a discount for paying off your loan early, the debt reduction or discount is generally considered cancellation of debt income if you retain the collateral *(31.10)*. If it is considered a cancellation of debt, report it as "other income" on Schedule 1 of Form 1040 unless you can exclude the debt from income under the exclusion for qualified principal residence indebtedness or one of the other exclusions. As noted below, some states treat a loan used to buy a principal residence as nonrecourse debt, and in that case, any forgiveness of the loan does not give rise to cancellation of debt income.

**Foreclosure, repossession, or voluntary conveyance.** If a lender forecloses on a loan secured by your property (such as your home mortgage) or repossesses the property secured by the loan (such as your car), or you voluntarily convey the property to the lender, the transaction is treated as a sale on which you realize gain or loss, as explained in *31.9*.

Apart from the gain or loss on the deemed sale, if you are personally liable on the loan (recourse debt) and the amount of the debt canceled by the lender exceeds the fair market value of the property, you have cancellation of debt income that must be reported as ordinary income unless one of the exclusions discussed below applies. The lender will report fair market value of the property in Box 7 Form 1099-C.

 *Caution*

**Cancellation of Credit Card Debt**

If debt on your personal (non-business) credit card was canceled, you must report the canceled amount as income unless you were insolvent immediately before the cancellation or the cancellation occurred in a Title 11 bankruptcy case.

**State law may treat home mortgage debt as nonrecourse.** Some states have "anti-deficiency" statutes that treat a loan used to purchase a principal residence as a "nonrecourse" loan. In these states, a lender has no recourse against a homeowner for a deficiency judgment following a foreclosure or lender-approved short sale. Where a mortgage debt subject to one of these state laws is forgiven, the taxpayer does not realize cancellation of debt income, as the income rule applies only to the cancellation of recourse debts for which there is personal liability.

Such state anti-deficiency laws would assume even greater significance if Congress does not extend to 2017 and beyond the exclusion for discharges of up to $2 million of qualified principal residence indebtedness.

**Cancellation of student loans.** The cancellation of a student loan results in taxable income unless one of the following exceptions applies.

If a loan by a government agency (federal, state, or local), by a government-funded loan program of an education organization, or by a qualified hospital organization is canceled because you worked for a period of time in certain geographical areas in certain professions, such as practicing medicine in rural areas or teaching in inner-city schools, then the canceled amount is not taxable. The IRS has ruled that the exception also applies to law school graduates who have student loan indebtedness forgiven under the Loan Repayment Assistance program if they work for a specified period of time in law-related public service positions in government or with tax-exempt charitable organizations. If a loan from an educational organization is canceled because you work for that organization, the exclusion from gross income does not apply; the cancellation is taxable unless some other exclusion applies.

There is also a special exclusion for healthcare professionals who have student loans forgiven or repaid to them because they work in underserved communities. This exclusion applies to loans forgiven or repaid under (1) the National Health Services Corps Loan Repayment Program, (2) state loan repayment programs eligible for funding under the Public Health Service Act, or (3) any state loan repayment or forgiveness program that is intended to increase the availability of healthcare services in underserved areas as determined by the state.

The Tax Cuts and Jobs Act has added an exclusion for a discharge of student loan debt in 2018 or later years if the discharge is due to the student's total and permanent disability, or the student's death. This exclusion applies to loans made by a government agency (federal, state, or local), by a government-funded loan program of an education organization, or by a qualified hospital organization, as well to certain "private education" loans.

There is no exception under current law for student loan debt that is canceled under an income-based repayment program, generally after 20–25 years of payments. For the year the loan balance is forgiven, that amount is taxable income.

**Will there be an exclusion for discharges of qualified principal residence indebtedness in 2018 and later years?** For years before 2018, the discharge of up to $2 million of qualified principal residence indebtedness ($1 million if filing separately) was excluded from gross income. Qualified debt was any debt you incurred in acquiring, constructing, or substantially improving your principal residence and which was secured by your principal residence. It also included debt secured by your principal residence that refinanced debt incurred to acquire, construct, or substantially improve your principal residence, but only to the extent of such refinanced debt. The 2 million/$1 million limit was a lifetime limit, applying to the total cancellations of qualifying debt from 2007 (when the exclusion took effect) through 2017.

When this book was completed, Congress had not yet extended the exclusion to discharges of qualified principal residence indebtedness after 2017, and it appeared unlikely that a retroactive extension for 2018 would be provided. If there is no extension, an exclusion would apply to a 2018 discharge of qualifying indebtedness only if it were pursuant to a written arrangement that was entered into before January 1, 2018. An update, if any, will be in the *e-Supplement* at *jklasser.com*.

**Debts canceled in bankruptcy.** Debt canceled in a Title 11 bankruptcy case is not included in your gross income if the cancellation is granted by the court or under a plan approved by the court. Instead, certain losses, credits, and basis of property must be reduced by the amount excluded from income. These losses, credits, and basis of property are called "tax attributes." The amount of canceled debt is used to reduce the tax attributes in the order listed below:

1. Net operating losses and carryovers—dollar for dollar of debt discharge;

2. Carryovers of the general business credit—33⅓ cents for each dollar of debt discharge;

3. AMT minimum tax credit as of the beginning of the year immediately after the taxable year of the discharge—33⅓ cents for each dollar of debt discharge;

4. Net capital losses and carryovers—dollar for dollar of debt discharge;

5. Basis of depreciable and nondepreciable assets—dollar for dollar of debt discharge (but not below the amount of your total undischarged liabilities). Basis of property held at the beginning of the year is reduced in a specific order and within each category, in proportion to adjusted basis. See Publication 4681 for details.

6. Passive activity loss and credit carryovers—dollar for dollar of debt discharge for passive losses; 33⅓ cents for each dollar of debt discharge in the case of passive credits; and

7. Foreign tax credit carryovers—33⅓ cents for each dollar of debt discharge.

After these reductions, any remaining balance of the debt discharge is disregarded. On Form 982, you may make a special election to first reduce the basis of any depreciable assets before reducing other tax attributes in the order above. Realty held for sale to customers may be treated as depreciable assets for purposes of the election. The election allows you to preserve your current deductions, such as a net operating loss carryover or capital loss carryover, for use in the following year. The election also will have the effect of reducing your depreciation deductions for years following the year of debt cancellation. If you later sell the depreciable property at a gain, the gain attributable to the basis reduction will be taxable as ordinary income under the depreciation recapture rules *(44.1)*.

**Debts discharged while you are insolvent.** If your debt is canceled outside of bankruptcy while you are insolvent, the cancellation does not result in taxable income to the extent of the insolvency. Insolvency means that liabilities exceed the fair market value of your assets immediately before the discharge of the debt. IRS Publication 4681 has a worksheet you can use to determine whether you were insolvent immediately before the debt discharge and the extent of the insolvency. The IRS and Tax Court hold that in determining whether liabilities exceed the value of assets at the time of a debt discharge, a taxpayer must include assets that are shielded from creditors under state law. This is true even though for federal bankruptcy purposes creditor-exempt assets do not have to be counted in determining whether an individual seeking bankruptcy protection is insolvent.

If liabilities do exceed the value of assets, the discharged debt is not taxed to the extent of your insolvency and is applied to the reduction of tax attributes on Form 982 in the same manner as to a bankrupt individual. If the canceled debt exceeds the insolvency, any remaining balance is treated as if it were a debt cancellation of a solvent person and, thus, it is taxable unless another exclusion is available as discussed in this section.

*See* the Example below for the IRS approach to figuring insolvency upon a debt cancellation.

**Partnership debts.** When a partnership's debt is discharged because of bankruptcy, insolvency, or if it is qualified farm debt or business real estate debt that is canceled, the discharged amount is allocated among the partners. Bankruptcy or insolvency is tested not at the partnership level, but separately for each partner. Thus, a bankrupt or insolvent partner applies the allocated amount to reduce the specified tax attributes as previously discussed. A solvent partner may not take advantage of the rules applied to insolvent or bankrupt partners, even if the partnership is insolvent or bankrupt.

**S corporation debts.** The tax consequences of a debt discharge are determined at the corporate level. A debt discharge that is excludable from the S corporation's income because of insolvency or bankruptcy does not pass through to the shareholders and thus does not increase the shareholders' basis.

 *Court Decision*

**Credit Card Insurance Payments Taxable**

Insurance can be purchased to cover a portion of credit card debt in the event you become unemployed or disabled, or you die. The Tax Court held that insurance payments of an unemployed credit card holder's debt were a taxable cancellation of debt to the extent the payments exceeded the premiums paid.

> **EXAMPLE**
>
> In 2014, Jones borrowed $1,000,000 from Chester and signed a note payable for that amount. Jones was not personally liable on the note, which was secured by an office building valued at $1,000,000 that he bought from Baker with the proceeds of Chester's loan. In 2018, when the value of the building declined to $800,000, Chester agreed to reduce the principal of the loan to $825,000. At the time, Jones held other assets valued at $100,000 and owed another person $50,000.
>
> To determine the extent of Jones's insolvency, the IRS compares the value of Jones's assets and liabilities immediately before the discharge. According to the IRS, his assets total $900,000: the building valued at $800,000 plus other assets of $100,000. His liabilities total $1,025,000: the other debt of $50,000 plus the liability on the note, which the IRS considered to be $975,000, equal to the $800,000 value of the building and the discharged debt of $175,000. Jones is insolvent by $125,000 ($1,025,000 in liabilities less $900,000 in assets). As $175,000 was the amount of the discharged debt and Jones was insolvent to the extent of $125,000, only $50,000 is treated as taxable income in 2018.
>
> Jones claims the insolvency exception on Form 982 by checking the box on Line 1b and entering the excludable $125,000 on Line 2. In Part II of Form 982, Jones must reduce his "tax attributes," as discussed above under the bankruptcy rules. The $50,000 debt cancellation that is not excludable under the insolvency rule must be reported as "other" income on Schedule 1 of Form 1040.

**Purchase price adjustment for solvent debtors.** If you buy property on credit and the seller reduces or cancels the debt arising out of the purchase, the reduction is generally treated as a purchase price adjustment (reducing your basis in the property). Since the reduction is not treated as a debt cancellation, you do not realize taxable income on the price adjustment. This favorable price adjustment rule applies only if you are solvent and not in bankruptcy, you have not transferred the property to a third party, and the seller has not transferred the debt to a third party, such as with the sale of your installment contract to a collection company.

**Qualified farm debt.** A solvent farmer may avoid tax from a discharge of indebtedness by an unrelated lender, including any federal, state, or local government agency, if the debt was incurred in operating a farm business. This relief is available only if 50% or more of your total gross receipts for the preceding three taxable years was derived from farming. The excluded amount first reduces tax attributes such as net operating loss carryovers and business tax credits, next reduces basis in all property other than farmland, and then reduces the basis in land used in the farming business. See IRS Publication 4681 for details.

**Business real estate debt.** A solvent taxpayer may elect on Form 982 to avoid tax on a discharge of qualifying real property business debt. Such a discharge may occur where the fair market value of the property securing the debt has fallen in value. The debt must have been incurred or assumed in connection with business real property and must be secured by such property. A debt incurred or assumed after 1992 must be incurred or assumed to buy, construct, or substantially improve real property used in a business, or to refinance such acquisition debt (up to the refinanced amount). Debt incurred after 1992 to refinance a pre-1993 business real property debt (up to the refinanced amount) also qualifies. The debt must be secured by the property. Discharges of farm indebtedness do not qualify but may be tax free under the separate rules discussed earlier.

The maximum amount that can be excluded from income is the excess of the outstanding loan principal (immediately before the discharge) over the fair market value (immediately before the discharge) of the real property securing the debt, less any other outstanding qualifying real property business debts secured by the property. The excludable amount also may not exceed the taxpayer's adjusted basis for all depreciable real property held before the discharge. On Line 4 of Form 982, you reduce your basis in all your depreciable real property by the excluded amount.

**Effect of basis reduction on later disposition of property.** A reduction of basis is treated as a depreciation deduction so that a profitable sale of the property at a later date may be subject to the rules of recapture of depreciation (44.1).

---

*Filing Instruction*

**Price Adjustments Not Taxed**

If you bought property on credit and the seller cancels or reduces your purchase-related debt, this is a price adjustment, not a taxable cancellation of debt.

## 11.9 Schedule K-1

Although partnerships, S corporations, trusts, and estates are different types of tax entities, they share a common tax-reporting characteristic. The entity itself generally does not pay income taxes. As a partner, shareholder, or beneficiary, you report your share of the entity's income or loss. The entity files a Schedule K-1 with the IRS that indicates your share of the income, deductions, and credits passed through from the entity. You will receive a copy of the Schedule K-1, which you should keep for your records; it does not have to be attached to your tax return.

To ensure that Schedule K-1 income is being reported, IRS computers match the information shown on the schedules with the tax returns of partners, S corporation shareholders, and beneficiaries.

## 11.10 How Partners Report Partnership Profit and Loss

A partnership files Form 1065, which informs the IRS of partnership profit or loss and each partner's share on Schedule K-1. The partnership pays no tax on partnership income; each partner reports his or her share of partnership net profit or loss and special deductions and credits, whether or not distributions are received from the partnership, as shown on Schedule K-1. Income that is not distributed or withdrawn increases the basis of a partner's partnership interest.

Your share reported to you on Schedule K-1 (Form 1065) is generally based on your proportionate capital interest in the partnership, unless the partnership agreement provides for another allocation.

Your partnership must give you a copy of Schedule K-1 (Form 1065), which lists your share of income, loss, deduction, and credit items, and where to report them on your return. For example, your share of income or loss from a business or real estate activity is reported on Schedule E and is subject to passive activity adjustments, if any. Interest and dividends are reported on Schedule B, royalties on Schedule E, and capital gains and losses on Schedule D. Your share of charitable donations is claimed on Schedule A if you itemize deductions. Tax preference items for alternative minimum tax purposes are also listed.

**Health insurance premiums.** A partnership that pays premiums for health insurance for partners has a choice. It may treat the premium as a reduction in distributions to the partners. Alternatively, it may deduct the premium as an expense and charge each partner's share as a guaranteed salary payment taxable to the partner. The partner reports the guaranteed payment shown on Schedule K-1 as nonpassive income on Schedule E and may deduct 100% of the premium as an adjustment to income (above-the-line deduction) on Schedule 1 of Form 1040 *(12.2)*.

**Guaranteed salary and interest.** A guaranteed salary that is fixed without regard to partnership income is taxable as ordinary wages and not as partnership earnings. If you receive a percentage of the partnership income with a stipulated minimum payment, the guaranteed payment is the amount by which the minimum guarantee exceeds your share of the partnership income before taking into account the minimum guarantee. Interest on capital is reported as interest income.

**Self-employment tax.** As a general partner, you pay self-employment tax on your net partnership income, including guaranteed salary and other guaranteed payments. The self-employment tax is explained in *Chapter 45*. Limited partners do not pay self-employment tax, unless guaranteed payments are received *(45.2)*.

**Special allocations.** Partners may agree to special allocations of gain, income, loss, deductions, or credits disproportionate to their capital contributions. The allocation should have a substantial economic effect to avoid an IRS disallowance. The IRS will not issue an advance ruling on whether an allocation has a substantial economic effect. If the allocation is rejected, a partner's share is determined by his or her partnership interest.

To have substantial economic effect, a special allocation must be reflected by adjustments to the partners' capital accounts; liquidation proceeds must be distributed in accordance with the partners' capital accounts, and following a liquidating distribution, the partners must be liable to the partnership to restore any deficit in their capital.

 *Filing Instruction*

**Partnership Elections**

The partnership, not the individual partners, makes elections affecting the computation of partnership income such as the election to defer involuntary conversion gains, to amortize organization and start-up costs, and to choose depreciation methods, including first-year expensing. An election to claim a foreign tax credit is made by the partners.

If there is a change of partnership interests during the year, items are allocated to a partner for that part of the year he or she is a member of the partnership. Thus, a partner who acquires an interest late in the year is barred from deducting partnership expenses incurred prior to his entry into the partnership. If the partners agree to give an incoming partner a disproportionate share of partnership losses for the period after he or she becomes a member, the allocation must meet the substantial economic effect test to avoid IRS disallowance.

See IRS regulations to Code Section 704 and Form 1065 instructions for further details.

**Reporting transfers of interest to IRS.** If you transfer a partnership interest that includes an interest in partnership receivables and appreciated inventory, you must report the disposition to the partnership within 30 days, or, if earlier, by January 15 of the calendar year after the year of the transfer. The partnership in turn files a report with the IRS on Form 8308. You must also attach a statement to your income tax return describing the transaction and allocating basis to the receivables and inventory items. The IRS wants to keep track of such dispositions because partners have to pay ordinary income tax on the portion of profit attributable to the receivables and inventory.

Within 30 days of your transfer, provide the partnership with a statement that includes the date of the exchange and identifies the transferee (include Social Security number if known). You can be penalized for failure to notify the partnership. You and your transferee should receive a copy of the Form 8308 that the partnership will send to the IRS along with its Form 1065.

## 11.11 When a Partner Reports Income or Loss

You report your share of the partnership gain or loss for the partnership year that ends in your tax reporting year. If you and the partnership are on a calendar-year basis, you report your share of the 2018 partnership income on your 2018 income tax return. If the partnership is on a fiscal year ending March 31, for example, and you report on a calendar year, you report on your 2018 return your share of the partnership income for the whole fiscal year ending March 31, 2018—that is, partnership income for the fiscal year April 1, 2017, through March 31, 2018.

If a Section 444 election of a fiscal year is made on Form 8716, a special tax payment must be computed for each fiscal year and if the computed payment exceeds $500, it must be paid to the IRS. The tax payment is figured and reported on Form 8752. The tax does not apply to the first tax year of a partnership's existence but Form 8752 must still be filed. In later years, a refund of prior payments is available to the extent the prior payments exceed the payment required for the current fiscal year. For example, if the required payment was $12,000 for the fiscal year July 1, 2017–June 30, 2018, and the required payment for the fiscal year starting July 1, 2018, is $10,000, a $2,000 refund may be claimed on Form 8752. Refunds of prior year payments also are available if the fiscal-year election is terminated and a calendar year adopted or if the partnership liquidates.

## 11.12 Partnership Loss Limitations

Your share of partnership losses may not exceed the adjusted basis of your partnership interest. If the loss exceeds basis, the excess loss may not be deducted until you have partnership earnings to cover the loss or contribute capital to cover the loss. The basis of your partnership interest is generally the amount paid for the interest (either through contribution or purchase) less withdrawals plus accumulated taxed earnings that have not been withdrawn. You also have a basis in loans to the partnership for which you are personally liable.

A partner's basis is not increased by accrued but unpaid expenses such as interest costs and accounts payable unless the partnership uses the accrual accounting method. However, basis is increased by capitalized items allocable to future periods such as organization and construction period expenses.

Partners are subject to the "at-risk" loss limitation rules. These rules limit the amount of loss that may be deducted to the amount each partner personally has at stake in the partnership, such as contributions of property and loans for which the partner is personally liable. See the discussion of the "at-risk" rules in *Chapter 10 (10.17)*. Furthermore, if the IRS determines that a tax-shelter partnership is not operated to make a profit, deductions

*Law Alert*

**Qualified Business Income (QBI) Deduction for 2018 Income**

If you receive income from a partnership, you may be eligible for a deduction of up to 20% of qualified business income (QBI) (*see 40.24*). If the partnership is on a fiscal year, you take into account all items from 2018; no allocation for the portion of the year from January 1, 2018, is required.

may be disallowed even where there is an "at-risk" investment. Finally, any loss not barred by these limitations may be disallowed under the passive activity rules discussed in *Chapter 10*.

## 11.13 Tax Audits of Partnerships

For audits of partnership returns for tax years beginning after December 31, 2017, the Bipartisan Budget Act of 2015 (BBA) provides a "centralized audit system" that allows the IRS to audit large partnerships (more than 100 partners) at the partnership level. Any adjustments to the partnership return are handled at the partnership level, unless the partnership opts to push out the deficiency to its partners (certain notices are required and revised Schedule K-1s will be issued for this purpose). This means that if, in effect, there is an underpayment, the partnership pays the adjustment using the highest individual or corporate tax rate, plus penalties and interest. If the opposite occurs, the adjustment is taken into account by the partnership as a reduction in non-separately stated income or an increase in non-separately stated loss. Partnerships with up to 100 partners may elect out of the BBA rules (T.D. 9829, 2018-4 IRB 307).

The BBA replaces the prior-law rules, commonly referred to as the TEFRA audit rules, under which audits (for tax years beginning before 2018) are conducted at the partnership level for partnerships with over 10 partners but any additional tax resulting from the partnership-level audit are assessed and collected against the individual partners. The 10-partner TEFRA exception applies if all the partners are individuals (but not nonresident aliens), estates of deceased partners, or C corporations. A husband and wife (and their estates) are treated as one partner.

New rules specify who can be the partnership's representative under the BBA audit system (T.D. 9839, 2018-38 IRB 325).

When this book was completed, the IRS had provided some guidance on the new BBA audit system, but given the complexity of the rules and the number of changes that must be made to partnership agreements, several practitioner groups asked Congress to delay the implementation of the new system. *See* the *e-Supplement* at *jklasser.com* for an update.

## 11.14 Stockholder Reporting of S Corporation Income or Loss

S corporations are subject to tax reporting rules similar to those applied to partnerships. However, shareholders who work for the corporation are treated as employees for payroll tax purposes. The IRS and the courts require that S corporation shareholders receive reasonable compensation on which Social Security and Medicare taxes (FICA) must be paid. Self-employment tax does not apply to a shareholder's salary or similar receipts from the S corporation.

Your company must give you a copy of Schedule K-1 (Form 1120S), which lists your share of income or loss, deductions, and credits that must be reported on your return. It also includes information needed to figure the qualified business income (QBI) deduction, which is a personal deduction of up to 20% of QBI.

Your share of business income or loss is reported on Schedule E and is subject to passive activity adjustments, if any. Interest and dividends from other corporations are reported on Schedule B, capital gains and losses on Schedule D, Section 1231 gains or losses on Form 4797, and charitable donations on Schedule A. Tax preference items for alternative minimum tax purposes are also listed.

Health insurance premiums paid by an S corporation for more-than-2% stockholders are treated as wages, deductible on Form 1120S by the corporation and reported to the stockholder on Form W-2. A more-than-2% shareholder who reports premiums as wages may deduct the premiums as an adjustment to income (above-the-line deduction) on Schedule 1 of Form 1040 *(12.2)*.

**Allocation to shareholders.** The following items are allocated to and pass through to the shareholders based on the proportion of stock held in the corporation:

- Gains and losses from the sale and exchange of capital assets and Section 1231 property, as well as interest and dividends on corporate investments and losses. Investment interest expenses subject to the rules discussed in *Chapter 15 (15.10)* also pass through.

 *Law Alert*

**Qualified Business Income (QBI) Deduction for S Corporation Shareholders**

You may be eligible for the new qualified business income (QBI) deduction for your share of items from the S corporation. See *(40.24)*.

- Tax-exempt interest. Tax-exempt interest remains tax free in the hands of the stockholders but increases the basis of their stock. Dividends from other companies may qualify for the exclusion.
- First-year expense deduction (Section 179 deduction).
- Charitable contributions made by the corporation.
- Foreign income or loss.
- Foreign taxes paid by the corporation. Each stockholder elects whether to claim these as a credit or deduction.
- Tax preference items.
- Recovery of bad debts and prior taxes.

If your interest changed during the year, your pro rata share must reflect the time you held the stock.

**Passive activity rules limit loss deductions.** Losses allocated to you may be disallowed under the passive activity rules discussed in *Chapter 10*.

**Basis adjustments.** Because of the nature of S corporation reporting, the basis of each shareholder's stock is subject to change. Basis is increased by the pass-through of income items and by loans to the S corporation for which the shareholder is personally liable. Basis is reduced by the pass-through of loss items and the receipt of certain distributions. Because income and loss items pass through to stockholders, an S corporation has no current earnings and profits. An income item will not increase basis, unless you actually report the amount on your tax return. The specific details and order of basis adjustments are listed in the instructions to Schedule K-1 of Form 1120S.

> ### EXAMPLES
>
> 1. A calendar-year corporation incurs a loss of $10,000. Smith and Jones each own 50% of the stock. On May 1, Smith sells all of his stock to Harris. For the year, Smith was a shareholder for 120 days, Jones for 365 days, and Harris for 245 days. The loss is allocated on a daily basis; the daily basis of the loss is $27.3973 ($10,000 divided by 365 days). The allocation is as follows:
>    Smith: $1,644 ($27.3973 × 120 days × 50% interest)
>    Jones: $5,000 ($27.3973 × 365 days × 50% interest)
>    Harris: $3,356 ($27.3973 × 245 days × 50% interest)
> 2. Same facts as in Example 1, except that on May 1, Smith sells only 50% of his stock to Harris. The allocation for Smith accounts for his 50% interest for 120 days and his 25% interest for the remainder of the year.
>    Smith: $3,322 ($27.3973 × 120 days × 50% plus $27.3973 × 245 days × 25%)
>    Jones: $5,000 (as above)
>    Harris: $1,678 ($27.3973 × 245 days × 25%)

## 11.15 How Beneficiaries Report Estate or Trust Income

Trust or estate income is treated as if you had received the income directly from the original source instead of from the estate or trust. This means your share of the trust's capital gain income remains capital gain to you, ordinary income is fully taxed, and tax-exempt income remains tax free. Tax preference items of a trust or estate are apportioned between the estate or trust and beneficiaries, according to allocation of income.

Your share of the trust or estate income, deductions and credits is reported to you (and the IRS) by the fiduciary on Schedule K-1 of Form 1041. You do not file Schedule K-1 with your return; keep it for your records. The instructions to Schedule K-1 indicate where to report the trust or estate items on Form 1040. For example, you report capital gains from Schedule K-1 on Schedule D, along with your other capital gains. You report Schedule K-1 income or loss from real estate or business activities) on Schedule E, subject to the passive activity restrictions discussed in *Chapter 10*.

**Reporting rule for revocable grantor trusts.** A grantor who sets up a revocable trust or keeps certain powers over trust income or corpus must report all of the trust income, deductions, and credits. This rule applies if a grantor retains a reversionary interest in the trust that is valued at more than 5% of the trust (valued at the time the trust is set up) *(39.6)*. If a grantor

*Planning Reminder*

**Basis Limits Loss Deductions**

Deductible losses may not exceed your basis in S corporation stock and loans to the corporation. If losses exceed basis, the excess loss is carried over and becomes deductible when you invest or lend an equivalent amount of money to the corporation. This rule may allow for timing a loss deduction. In a year in which you want to deduct the loss, you may contribute capital or make an additional loan to the corporation. If a carryover loss exists when an S election terminates, a limited loss deduction may be allowed.

*Law Alert*

**Qualified Business Income (QBI) Deduction for Beneficiaries**

You may be eligible for the new qualified business income (QBI) deduction for your share of items from a trust or estate. See 40.24.

is also a trustee of a revocable trust and all the trust assets are in the United States, filing Form 1041 is not necessary. The grantor simply reports the trust income, deductions, and credits on his or her Form 1040. See the Form 1041 instructions for reporting requirements.

## 11.16 Reporting Income in Respect of a Decedent (IRD)

If you receive income that was earned by but not paid to a decedent before death, such as wages, IRA and qualified plan distributions, accrued savings bond interest, lottery prize winnings, or installment sale proceeds, you are said to have "income in respect of a decedent," or IRD. You report the IRD on your return. Where the purchaser of a deferred annuity contract dies before the annuity starting date, payments to a beneficiary in excess of the purchaser's investment are IRD that the beneficiary must report as income, whether payable in a lump sum or as periodic payments.

If the decedent's estate paid federal estate tax that was attributable to the IRD you received, you may claim an itemized deduction for the estate tax paid on that income *(11.17)*.

## 11.17 Deduction for Estate Tax Attributable to IRD

A beneficiary who receives income in respect of a decedent (IRD) on which federal estate tax was paid can claim an itemized deduction for the amount of the allocable federal estate tax. The deduction is allowed to the IRD recipient only for the year in which the recipient reports the IRD income, assuming the beneficiary claims itemized deductions (and not the standard deduction) for that year. No deduction is allowed for state death taxes paid on IRD. If you receive IRD, ask the executor of the decedent's estate for the amount of federal estate tax paid and the portion of the estate that the IRD represented to help you compute the deduction. The deduction is claimed as an "other itemized deduction" on Schedule A (Form 1040).

However, if the IRD you receive is long-term capital gain, such as an installment payment on a sale transacted before a decedent's death, the estate tax attributed to the capital gain item is not claimed as an itemized deduction. The deductible amount is treated as if it were an expense of sale and, thus, reduces the amount of gain, but not below zero.

> ### EXAMPLE
>
> When Jim Bennett died, he was owed a fee of $10,000. He also had not collected accrued bond interest of $5,000. Ed Bennett, Jim's nephew and the sole heir, will collect both items and pay income tax on them. These items are called "income in respect of a decedent." Assume that Jim left a substantial taxable estate and that estate tax of $6,000 was paid on the $15,000 *(39.9)*. Ed collects the $10,000, which he reports on his income tax return. If he itemizes deductions, he may deduct $4,000, computed as follows:
>
> $$\frac{\$10,000}{\$15,000} \times \$6,000 = \$4,000$$
>
> When Ed collects the $5,000, he may deduct the balance, or $2,000 ($6,000 − $4,000), if he itemizes deductions for that year.

## 11.18  How Life Insurance Proceeds Are Taxed to a Beneficiary

Life insurance proceeds received upon the death of the insured are generally tax free. However, in some cases, life insurance proceeds may be includible in a decedent's taxable estate, and if the taxable estate is substantial enough to be subject to estate tax, the beneficiary may actually receive a reduced amount *(39.8)*. Interest paid on proceeds left with the insurer is taxable.

Read the following cases to find how your insurance receipts are taxed.

 *Filing Instruction*

**Consistent Reporting by Beneficiaries**

Beneficiaries of trusts and estates must report items consistently with the Schedule K-1 provided by the trust or estate. If an item is treated inconsistently and a statement identifying the inconsistency is not attached to the beneficiary's return, the IRS may make a summary assessment for additional tax without issuing a deficiency notice.

**A lump-sum payment of the full face value of a life insurance policy: The proceeds are generally tax free.** The tax-free exclusion also covers death benefit payments made under endowment contracts, workers' compensation insurance contracts, employers' group insurance plans, or accident and health insurance contracts.

Insurance proceeds may be taxable where the policy was transferred for valuable consideration. Exceptions to this rule are made for transfers among partners and corporations and their stockholders and officers.

**Installment payments spread over your life under a policy that could have been paid in a lump sum: Part of each installment attributed to interest may be taxed.** Divide the face amount of the policy by the number of years the installments are to be paid. The result is the amount that is received tax free each year.

If the policy guarantees payments to a secondary beneficiary if you should die before receiving a specified number of payments, the tax-free amount is reduced by the present value of the secondary beneficiary's interest in the policy. The insurance company can give you this figure.

**Installment payments for a fixed number of years under a policy that could have been paid in a lump sum.** Divide the full face amount of the policy by the number of years you are to receive the installments. The result is the amount that is received tax free each year.

> ### EXAMPLE
>
> Fran is the beneficiary of her husband's $100,000 life insurance policy. She elects to take installment payments for 10 years. Each year she may receive tax-free principal of $10,000 ($100,000 ÷ 10).

**Installment payments when there is no lump-sum option in the policy:** You must find the discounted value of the policy at the date of the insured's death and use that as the principal amount. The insurance company can give you that figure. After you find the discounted value, you divide it by the number of years you are to receive installments. The result is the amount that is tax free. The remainder is taxed.

> ### EXAMPLE
>
> Alice is the beneficiary of her husband's life insurance policy. She is entitled to $10,000 a year for life. Her life expectancy is 20 years. There is no lump sum stated in the policy. Say the discounted value of the wife's rights is $120,000. The principal amount spread to each year for the wife is $6,000 ($120,000 ÷ 20). Subtracting $6,000 from each annual $10,000 payment gives her taxable income of $4,000.

**Payments to you along with other beneficiaries under the same policy, by lump-sum or varying installments.** *See* the following Example for the way multiple beneficiaries may be taxed.

> ### EXAMPLE
>
> The beneficiaries of an insured's life insurance policy are his surviving wife, daughter, and nephew. The wife is entitled to a lump sum of $120,000. The daughter and nephew are each entitled to a lump sum of $70,000. Under the installment options, the wife chooses to receive $10,000 a year for the rest of her life. (She has a 20-year life expectancy.) The daughter and the nephew each choose a yearly payment of $10,000 for 10 years. This is how each yearly installment is taxed:
>
> Wife: The principal amount spread to each year is $6,000 ($120,000 ÷ 20-year life expectancy). Subtracting $6,000 from the yearly $10,000 payment gives the wife taxable income of $4,000.
>
> Daughter and Nephew: Both are taxed the same way. The principal amount spread to each of the 10 years is $7,000 ($70,000 ÷ 10-year installment period). Subtracting this $7,000 from the yearly $10,000 installment gives the daughter and the nephew taxable income of $3,000 each.

**Planning Reminder**

### Accelerated Death Benefits

A person who is terminally ill may withdraw without tax life insurance proceeds to pay medical bills and other living expenses. For policies lacking an accelerated benefits clause, a terminally ill individual may sell a life insurance policy to a viatical settlement company without incurring tax *(17.16)*.

*Caution*

### Surrender of Policy for Cash

If the cash received on the surrender of a policy exceeds the premiums paid less dividends received, the excess is taxed as ordinary income (not capital gain). If you take, instead, a paid-up policy, you may avoid tax *(6.12)*. You get no deduction if there is a loss on the surrender of a policy.

Tax may be avoided by a terminally ill individual on the surrender of a policy under an accelerated death benefit clause or on a sale of the policy to a viatical settlement company *(17.16)*.

## 11.19 A Policy with a Family Income Rider

Payments received under a family income rider are taxed under a special rule. A family income rider provides additional term insurance coverage for a fixed number of years from the date of the basic policy. Under the terms of a rider, if the insured dies at any time during the term period, the beneficiary receives monthly payments during the balance of the term period, and then at the end of the term period, receives the lump-sum proceeds of the basic policy. If the insured dies after the end of the term period, the beneficiary receives only the lump sum from the basic policy.

When the insured dies during the term period, part of each monthly payment received during the term period includes interest on the lump-sum proceeds of the basic policy (which is held by the company until the end of the term period). That interest is fully taxed. The balance of the monthly payment consists of an installment (principal plus interest) of the proceeds from the term insurance purchased under the family income rider. You may exclude from this balance a prorated portion of the present value of the lump sum under the basic policy. The lump sum under the basic policy is tax free when you eventually receive it.

The rules here also apply to an integrated family income policy and to family maintenance policies, whether integrated or with an attached rider.

In figuring your taxable portions, ask the insurance company for its interest rate and the present value of term payments.

## 11.20 Selling or Surrendering Life Insurance Policy

Surrendering or selling a life insurance policy results in ordinary income, long-term gain, or a combination of both, depending on the type of policy and type of transaction. In Revenue Ruling 2009-13, the IRS presents three situations that illustrate the tax consequences of selling or surrendering a whole life or term insurance contract.

**Situation 1 — surrender of whole life insurance contract.** On January 1 of Year 1, Tom Taxpayer bought a whole life insurance policy on his life, with the proceeds payable to a family member. Tom retained the right to change the beneficiary, take out a policy loan, or surrender the contract for its cash surrender value.

After 89½ months, on June 15 of Year 8, Tom surrenders the contract for its cash surrender value of $78,000. As of the surrender date, Tom had paid total premiums of $64,000, $10,000 of which was the cost of the insurance protection received as of that date. The $78,000 cash surrender value reflected the subtraction of the $10,000 insurance cost.

On the surrender, Tom recognizes income of $14,000, the $78,000 received minus the total premiums paid of $64,000.

The Tax Code does not specify whether income recognized upon the surrender of a life insurance contract, as opposed to a sale, is treated as ordinary income or as capital gain. However, relying on a 1964 ruling (Revenue Ruling 64-51), the IRS holds that the proceeds received by an insured upon the surrender of a life insurance policy constitute ordinary income to the extent such proceeds exceed the cost of the policy. Thus here the $14,000 of income recognized on the surrender of the insurance contract is ordinary income and not capital gain.

**Situation 2 — sale of whole life insurance contract.** Same facts as in Situation 1 except that on June 15 of Year 8, Tom sold the contract for $80,000 to an unrelated person. To figure gain on the sale, the $80,000 amount realized must be reduced by Tom's adjusted basis in the insurance contract. To figure Tom's basis, the $64,000 of total premiums he paid must be reduced by $10,000, the cost of the insurance protection he received before the sale. Therefore, his adjusted basis is $54,000, and his gain on the sale is $26,000 ($80,000 proceeds minus $54,000 basis).

Part of the $26,000 gain is ordinary income and part is capital gain. The Supreme Court has held that under the "substitute for ordinary income" doctrine, income that has been earned but not yet recognized by a taxpayer cannot be converted into capital gain by a sale or exchange. In the case of a sale of a life insurance policy, the portion of the gain that would have been ordinary income if the policy had been surrendered (i.e., the inside buildup under the contract) is ordinary income. However, any income over that amount can qualify for capital gain treatment.

Here, $14,000 of the $26,000 gain is ordinary income representing the inside buildup under the contract ($78,000 cash surrender value minus $64,000 total premiums paid). The remaining $12,000 of income is long-term capital gain.

**Situation 3 — sale of term life insurance contract.** Assume that Tom had entered into a 15-year level premium term contract with no cash surrender value, rather than the whole life contract in Situations 1 and 2. Monthly premiums were $500 and total premiums paid were $45,000 when the policy was sold after 89.5 months to an unrelated party for $20,000.

In this case, as in Situation 2, the adjusted basis of the contract for purposes of determining gain or loss is the total premiums paid minus charges for the provision of insurance before the sale. The cost of insurance protection in this case amounted to $44,750 ($500 × 89.5 months), so Tom's adjusted basis is $250 ($45,000 total premiums minus $44,750).

Tom's gain on the sale is $19,750 ($20,000 sale proceeds minus $250 basis). Because the term insurance contract had no cash surrender value, and thus no inside buildup to which ordinary income treatment could apply, the entire $19,750 is long-term capital gain.

## 11.21 Jury Duty Fees

Fees that you receive for serving on a jury must be reported as "other income" on Form 1040.

If you are an employee and are required to turn over the jury duty fees to your employer because you continue to receive your regular salary while serving on the jury, you can offset the "other income" with a deduction. The deduction is claimed as an adjustment to income (above-the-line deduction) on Schedule 1 of Form 1040; write "Jury Pay" and the amount next to the entry.

## 11.22 Foster Care Payments

You may generally exclude from gross income payments received from a state or local government or a certified placement agency for providing foster care services in your home. However, payments are taxable to the extent they are received for the care of more than five individuals age 19 or older.

In one case, taxpayers who owned two homes were denied the exclusion for payments they received under a state program on the grounds that the home where they provided the foster care services to disabled adults was not "their home." The Tax Court held that a taxpayer's home for purposes of the exclusion is where the taxpayer resides and experiences the routines of private life such as sharing meals, time, and holidays with family. The taxpayers worked in the home where they provided the services but they did not "live" there and so the exclusion was not allowed.

**Exclusion for difficulty-of-care payments.** The exclusion also generally applies to difficulty-of-care payments, which are designated by a state as extra compensation for providing additional care required by handicapped foster individuals in your home. However, difficulty-of-care payments must be reported as income to the extent they are for more than 10 qualified foster individuals under age 19, or more than 5 qualified foster individuals age 19 or older.

*Exclusion for difficulty-of-care payments applies to qualified Medicaid waiver payments.* States provide payments to care givers as additional compensation for providing nonmedical support services to a handicapped Medicaid recipient in the care giver's home. Such payments are considered "Medicaid waiver payments." The IRS changed its position in 2014 and now allows care providers to exclude Medicaid waiver payments as difficulty-of care payments even if the provider is related to the care recipient (Notice 2014-7). Prior IRS policy denied an exclusion for home care provided to biological relatives.

In several letter rulings, the IRS concluded that Notice 2014-7 allows states to treat payments made to individual care providers under in-home supportive care programs as excludable difficulty-of-care payments. Thus, the state did not have to report the payments to the care providers as wages subject to tax.

# Claiming Deductions

In this part, you will learn how you may be able to reduce your tax liability by claiming deductions directly from gross income, and whether or not you have such deductions, by either the standard deduction or itemized deductions. Your tax liability may be lowered by—

- So-called "above-the-line" deductions that you may claim directly from gross income in arriving at adjusted gross income. These are allowed even if you claim the standard deduction. *See Chapter 12.*
- The standard deduction or itemized deductions. The new tax law has substantially increased the standard deduction and cut back or eliminated previously allowed itemized deductions, so even though you may have itemized deductions in prior years, the standard deduction may now be more advantageous for you *(Chapter 13)*. However, read the chapters on itemized deductions *(Chapters 14–20)* to *see* that you have not overlooked itemized deductions for charitable donations, interest expenses, state and local taxes, medical expenses, casualty and theft losses from a federally declared disaster, and miscellaneous expenses. Each itemized deduction is subject to specific restrictions and limitations.
- The qualified business income (QBI) deduction *(40.24)*.
- Other deductions are discussed in the following chapters:
  *Chapter 40* Business expenses
  *Chapter 9* Rental expenses
  *Chapter 43* Automobile expenses

# CHAPTER 12

# Deductions Allowed in Figuring Adjusted Gross Income

Adjusted gross income (AGI) is the amount used in figuring the 7.5% adjusted gross income floor for medical expense deductions *(17.1)*, the 10% floor for personal casualty and theft losses *(18.8)* and the charitable contribution percentage limitations *(14.17)*.

AGI generally also determines the thresholds for the phaseouts of the child tax credit and the credit for other dependents *(Chapter 25)*.

If you follow the instructions and order of the tax return, you will arrive at adjusted gross income automatically. But if you are planning the tax consequences of a transaction in advance of preparing your return, *see* the explanation of how to figure adjusted gross income (AGI) *(12.1)*.

There is an advantage in being able to claim deductions directly from gross income ("above-the-line") in arriving at adjusted gross income, since such deductions are allowed even if you claim the standard deduction rather than itemizing deductions on Schedule A of Form 1040. Another advantage of such deductions is that they also reduce state income tax for taxpayers residing in states that compute tax based on federal adjusted gross income. This chapter will explain the deductions that qualify for the direct deduction from gross income.

## 12.1  Figuring Adjusted Gross Income (AGI)

Adjusted gross income is the difference between gross income in Step 1 and the deductions listed in Step 2.

**Step 1.** Figure gross income. This is all income received by you from any source, such as wages, salary, tips, gross business income, income from sales and exchanges of property, interest and dividends, rents, royalties, annuities, pensions, etc. But because of exclusions allowed by the tax law, gross income does not include such items as tax-free interest from state or local bonds *(4.24)*, tax-free parsonage allowance *(3.13)*, tax-free insurance proceeds *(11.18–11.20)*, gifts and inheritances *(11.4)*, certain home sale gains *(29.1)*, Social Security benefits that are not subject to tax *(34.3)*, Supplemental Security Income (SSI) *(21.5, 34.2)*, tax-free scholarship grants *(33.1)*, tax-free meals and lodging *(3.13)*, and other tax-free fringe benefits *(Chapter 3)*.

**Step 2.** Deduct from your 2018 gross income only the following items:

- Repayment of supplemental unemployment benefits required because of receipt of trade readjustment allowances *(2.9)*
- Forfeiture-of-interest penalties because of premature withdrawals *(4.16)*
- Capital loss deduction up to $3,000 *(5.4)*
- Traditional IRA contributions *(8.4)*
- Rent and royalty expenses *(9.2)*
- Educator expenses *(12.2)*
- Tuition and fees—but only if Congress extends the deduction to 2018 *(12.2)*
- 50% of self-employment tax liability *(12.2)*
- Health savings account (HSA) contributions *(12.2)*
- Health insurance premiums if self-employed *(12.2)*
- Jury duty pay turned over to your employer *(12.2)*
- Performing artist's qualifying expenses *(12.2)*
- Reforestation expenses *(12.2)*
- Reservists' travel costs *(12.2)*
- State and local official expenses *(12.2)*
- Moving expenses for certain military personnel *(12.3)*
- Student loan interest *(33.6)*
- Alimony payments *(37.1)*
- Business expenses *(40.7)*
- Net operating losses *(40.19)*
- Self-employed retirement plan contributions for yourself *(41.5)*
- Archer MSA contributions *(41.13)*

**Step 3.** The difference between Steps 1 and 2 is adjusted gross income.

## 12.2  Claiming Deductions from Gross Income

Many deductions taken directly from gross income in arriving at adjusted gross income are first claimed on Form 1040 schedules devoted to a specific activity, and then the net gain or loss amount for that activity is entered on Form 1040. This includes business deductions claimed on Schedule C *(Chapter 40)*, capital losses claimed on Schedule D *(Chapter 5)*, and real estate rental expenses claimed on Schedule E *(Chapter 9)*.

Other expenses are claimed as "adjustments to income" on Schedule 1 of Form 1040, and then entered on Form 1040 as a reduction to gross income. These adjustments are sometimes referred to as "above-the-line" deductions, as they reduce gross (total) income regardless of whether you claim the standard deduction or itemized deductions.

Here are the adjustments to income (above-the-line deductions) that may be available on Form 1040 for 2018:

**Educator expenses.** If you were a teacher, instructor, counselor, principal, or aide in a private or public elementary or secondary school (kindergarten through grade 12) for at least 900 hours during the school year in 2018, you generally may deduct up to $250 of out-of-pocket costs for books and classroom supplies. Professional development expenses qualify for the deduction, subject to the $250 limit. Eligible supplies include computer equipment (including related software and services), other equipment, and supplementary materials used in the classroom. For courses in health or physical education, supplies must be related to athletics to qualify. Home schooling expenses do not qualify. If you are married filing jointly and you and your spouse both qualify as educators, each of you may deduct up to $250 of your qualified costs, for a $500 maximum on your joint return.

If eligible expenses exceed the $250 limit, the excess is not deductible for 2018 through 2025, even if you itemize deduction *(19.1)*.

The $250 deduction limit may have to be reduced or eliminated completely if certain tax-free amounts are received during the year. The deduction is reduced by tax-free interest on savings bonds used for tuition *(33.4)*, as well as by tax-free distributions from qualified tuition programs *(33.5)* and Coverdell education savings accounts *(33.12)*.

For 2019, the deduction limit may be raised above $250 by an inflation adjustment; *see* the *e-Supplement* at *jklasser.com*.

**Deduction for tuition and fees expired at the end of 2017.** When this book was completed, the deduction for tuition and fees had not been extended to 2018 by Congress, and it was unclear if there would be an extension. *See* the *e-Supplement* at *jklasser.com* for an update.

If there is an extension, you may deduct on Form 8917 up to $4,000 of qualifying college tuition and fees that you paid in 2018 if your MAGI does not exceed $65,000 for single and head of household filers and $130,000 for joint returns. A deduction of up to $2,000 is allowed for single and head of household filers with MAGI exceeding $65,000 but not $80,000 and for joint filers with MAGI exceeding $130,000 but not $160,000 *(33.13)*.

**Overnight travel costs of Reservists and National Guard members.** Armed Forces Reservists and National Guard members who travel over 100 miles and stay overnight to attend Reserve and Guard meetings may deduct their travel expenses as an above-the-line-deduction to the extent of the Federal Government per diem rate for that locality *(35.8)*.

**Expenses of performing artists.** If you are a performing artist, you may be able to deduct job expenses from gross income, but only if your income is extremely low. You must have:

1. Two or more employers during the year in the performing arts with at least $200 of earnings from at least two of them.

2. Expenses from acting or other services in the performing arts that exceed 10% of gross income from such work; and

3. Adjusted gross income (before deducting these expenses) that does not exceed $16,000.

If you are married, a joint return must be filed to claim the deduction, unless you lived apart from your spouse during the whole year. The $16,000 adjusted gross income limitation (AGI) applies to your combined incomes. If both spouses are performing artists, the $16,000 adjusted income limit applies to the combined incomes, but each spouse must separately meet the two-employer test and 10% expense test for his or her job expenses to be deductible on the joint return.

Clearly, the $16,500 AGI limit is so low that few taxpayers will qualify for the above-the-line deduction. The $16,500 AGI limit has been in the law since 1986. If you qualify, you report the performing artist expenses on Form 2106 (or Form 2106-EZ where eligible) and enter the total on Schedule 1 of Form 1040, instead of on Schedule A.

If you do not meet tests 1-3 above, the expenses are not deductible even if you itemize deductions, as job expenses are not deductible in 2018 through 2025 under the Tax Cuts and Jobs Act *(19.1)*.

**State and local officials.** State and local officials paid on a fee basis may deduct from gross income unreimbursed business expenses *(20.1)*.

**Health savings account (HSA) deduction.** If you are self-employed and have coverage under a high-deductible health plan, are not entitled to Medicare benefits, and are not the dependent of another taxpayer, you generally can deduct contributions to an HSA within the limits discussed in *41.10*. If you are an employee, and your employer has contributed less than the applicable limit to an HSA on your behalf, you may contribute the balance and deduct it from gross income *(3.2)*.

**Moving expenses if an Armed Forces member.** For 2018 and later years, moving expenses are deductible only by certain members of the U.S. Armed Forces *(12.3)*.

**50% of self-employment tax.** After you figure your self-employment tax liability for 2018 on Schedule SE, you may deduct 50% of it as an adjustment to income (*see 45.3–45.4*).

**Contributions to self-employed SEP, SIMPLE, and qualified plans.** *See* Chapter 41 for details on deducting these retirement plan contributions.

**Self-employed health insurance deduction.** If you were self-employed with a net profit in 2018, you may deduct from gross income 100% of premiums you paid in 2018 for medical and dental insurance, and qualified (*see* below) long-term-care insurance, for yourself, your spouse, your dependents, and your children who at the end of the year are under age 27 (whether or not your dependents). The instructions to Form 1040 and IRS Publication 535 (Business Expenses) have worksheets for figuring the self-employed health insurance deduction.

You are treated as self-employed for purposes of the 100% deduction if you are a general partner with net earnings, a limited partner receiving guaranteed payments, or a more-than-2% shareholder in an S corporation from which you received wages.

As a sole proprietor, you may claim the 100% above-the-line deduction whether the policy is purchased in your own name or the name of the business. If you are a more than 2% shareholder-employee of an S corporation, the IRS position is that the S corporation must "establish" the health plan, but the plan can be considered "established" by the S corporation even if you obtain the policy in your own name, so long as (1) the corporation makes the premium payments to the insurance company or the corporation reimburses you for premiums you pay, and (2) the premiums are reported as wages on your Form W-2 and on your tax return. Similarly, if you are a partner, a health plan in your name is considered "established" by the partnership if (1) the partnership pays the premiums or you pay them and are reimbursed by the partnership, and (2) the partnership reports the premiums as guaranteed payments on Schedule K-1 (Form 1065) and you include the payments as income on your tax return.

Medicare premiums qualify for the 100% deduction, since they provide insurance that constitutes medical care. As with other health insurance premiums, premiums paid for Medicare coverage of your spouse, dependents, and children who at the end of the year are under age 27 may be included in the 100% deduction

If you have a qualified long-term-care policy, the 100% deduction applies to the premiums that would be deductible as an itemized deduction under the medical expense rules. This amount depends on the age of each person covered, as shown in *17.15*. For example, if in 2018 you paid long-term care premiums for yourself and your spouse, and both of you are age 57 at the end of 2018, premiums of up to $1,560 for each of you are includible in the 100% deduction, assuming the policy is a qualifying long-term care policy *(17.15)*.

*Restrictions on the 100% deduction.* The 100% deduction may not exceed your net profit from the business under which the health premiums are paid, minus the deductible part of your self-employment tax liability and your deductible contributions to self-employed, SEP, or SIMPLE, and qualified retirement plans.

The 100% health insurance deduction may not be claimed for any month that you were eligible to participate in an employer's subsidized health plan, including a plan of your spouse's employer or a plan of the employer of your dependent or child under age 27 at the end of the year. If the deduction would be barred for any month because of such eligibility and you have long-term-care coverage that is not employer subsidized, you may claim the 100% deduction for the portion of the long-term-care premiums that is deductible for your age *(17.15)*.

***Are you entitled to the premium tax credit?*** There is a deduction complication if you are also entitled to the premium tax credit for purchasing health insurance on a government exchange *(25.12)*. The computations are interrelated because the amount of the credit affects the computation of the above-the-line deduction and the credit is based in part on adjusted gross income, which reflects the allowable deduction. Publication 974 (Premium Tax Credit) has worksheets for making the computations. If you or your professional tax preparer use tax preparation software, the software will make the circular computations to figure the deduction and the credit.

Penalty on early savings withdrawals *(4.16)*. If you lost interest because you made an early redemption of a savings certificate, the penalty shown on Form 1099-INT or 1099-OID is an above-the-line deduction.

**Alimony paid.** You can deduct alimony that you paid to your former spouse provided that he or she reports the payments as taxable income; *see Chapter 37*.

**Traditional IRA contribution.** The deductible limits, including the phaseout rules for individuals covered by employer retirement plans, are explained in *8.3–8.4*.

**Student loan interest.** You may be able to deduct interest you pay on a qualified student loan, up to a $2,500 limit, subject to a phaseout based on modified adjusted gross income *(33.13)*.

**Attorney fees in employment discrimination cases.** Attorney fees and court costs in actions involving unlawful discrimination claims are deductible as an adjustment to income on Schedule 1 of Form 1040 (with the label "UDC") if they were paid with respect to settlements or judgments occurring after October 22, 2004. The deduction may not exceed the amount included in income as a result of the judgment or settlement *(11.7)*.

**Archer MSA contribution.** If you are self-employed or employed by a qualifying small business and have high-deductible health coverage, a deduction for contributions to an Archer MSA account may be deductible. The deduction is figured on Form 8853 and then entered on Schedule 1 of Form 1040 with the label "MSA" *(41.13)*.

**Jury duty pay turned over to employer.** If you receive your regular pay while on jury duty and turn over your jury duty fees to your employer, report the fees as "Other income" on Schedule 1 of Form 1040 and claim an offsetting adjustment to income (label it "Jury pay"), also on Schedule 1.

**Repayment of supplemental unemployment benefits.** You may claim a deduction from gross income for the repayment or in some cases a tax credit *(2.9)*. Claim the deduction as an adjustment to income on Schedule 1 of Form 1040 and on the adjacent dotted line write the amount and label it "subpay TRA" (trade readjustment allowances).

**Reforestation amortization.** If you do not have to file Schedule C or F to report income from a timber activity, an amortization deduction for qualifying reforestation expenses may be claimed over an 84-month period; *see* Code Section 194 for details. On Schedule 1 of Form 1040, the amortization deduction should be labeled "RFST."

**Costs incurred in obtaining whistleblower award from the IRS.** You may claim an above-the-line deduction for costs you incurred, including attorneys' fees, in connection with obtaining a whistleblower award from the IRS as an informant, up to the amount of the award reported as income. Label the deduction on Schedule 1 of Form 1040 as "WBF."

**Nontaxable Olympic and Paralympic medals and prize money.** Olympic and Paralympic athletes are not taxed on the value of the medals won and prize money received from the U.S. Olympic Committee unless they have adjusted gross income exceeding $1,000,000, or $500,000 if married filing separately *(11.1)*. The prize money and the value of medals won must be reported as "Other income" on Schedule 1 of Form 1040 even if the athlete qualifies for the exclusion. However, where the exclusion applies, an adjustment to income offsets the income on Schedule 1 of Form 1040, with the label "USOC."

## 12.3 Moving Costs Are Deductible Only by Qualifying Members of the U.S. Armed Forces

Under the Tax Cuts and Jobs Act, the only taxpayers who may deduct unreimbursed moving expenses for 2018 and later years are members of the U.S. Armed Forces on active duty who move pursuant to a military order and incident to a permanent change of station. These qualifying Armed Forces members are also the only taxpayers who may exclude employer allowances or reimbursements for eligible moving expenses *(2.1)*.

Qualifying Armed Forces members report deductible moving expenses on Form 3903. The excess of deductible moving expenses over excludable government allowances or reimbursements, as shown on Form 3903, is entered as an adjustment to income on Schedule 1 of Form 1040.

If you are a qualifying member of the U.S. Armed Forces, you may claim the following moving expenses on Form 3903:

1. Traveling costs of yourself and members of your household en route from your old to the new locality. Here, you include the costs of transportation and lodging for yourself and household members while traveling to your new residence. This includes lodging before departure for one day after the old residence is unusable and lodging for the day of arrival at the new locality.

   If you use your own car, you may either deduct your actual costs of gas, oil, and repairs (but not depreciation) during the trip or take a deduction based on the IRS standard mileage rate. For 2018, the IRS standard mileage rate for moving expenses is 18 cents per mile; the rate may change for 2019; *see* the *e-Supplement* at *jklasser.com*. Also add parking fees and tolls. Meal expenses are not a deductible moving expense.

2. The actual cost of moving your personal effects and household goods. This includes the cost of packing, crating, and transporting furniture and household belongings, in-transit storage up to 30 consecutive days, insurance costs for the goods, and the cost of moving a pet or shipping an automobile to your new residence. You may also deduct expenses of moving your personal effects from a place other than your former home, but only up to the estimated cost of such a move from your former home.

**Nondeductible expenses.** Meal expenses while traveling to your new residence are not deductible.

You may not deduct the cost of pre-move house-hunting trips, temporary living expenses, or expenses of selling, purchasing, or leasing the old or new residence, such as attorneys' fees, real estate fees, mortgage penalties, expenses for trips to sell your old house, a loss on the sale of the house, or costs of settling an unexpired lease. If you have to pay a fee to get out of your apartment lease when you move, the fee is not a deductible moving expense. If you have self-employment income and part of your apartment was a qualifying home office, you may be able to claim an allocable part of the lease cancellation fee as a home office deduction; *see 40.12*.

Other nondeductible costs include the cost of travel incurred for a maid, nurse, chauffeur, or similar domestic help (unless the person is also your dependent), the cost of transporting furniture that you purchased en route from your old home, expenses of refitting rugs and drapes, forfeited tuition, car tags or driver's license for the state you move to, or forfeited club membership fees.

# CHAPTER 13

# Claiming the Standard Deduction or Itemized Deductions

Claim the standard deduction if it exceeds your allowable itemized deductions for mortgage interest, property taxes, medical costs, and charitable donations. Given the large increase in the standard deduction under the Tax Cuts and Jobs Act of 2017, and the corresponding reduction in certain itemized deductions *(13.2)*, many taxpayers who itemized deductions in earlier years will find that, for 2018, the standard deduction provides a larger deduction than itemizing does.

Generally, a single person and a married person filing separately may claim a 2018 standard deduction of $12,000; a head of household, $18,000; and a married couple filing jointly or a qualifying widow/widower, $24,000. Larger standard deductions are allowed to individuals who are age 65 or older or blind, and lower standard deductions are allowed to dependents with only investment income.

Before deciding whether to itemize or claim the standard deduction, read Chapters 14 through 19 to *see* that you have not overlooked any itemized deductions. To itemize, you report your deductions on Schedule A. Under the Tax Cuts and Jobs Act of 2017, there is no longer a reduction to overall itemized deductions for taxpayers with adjusted gross income over a specified threshold.

## Table 13-1 Itemized Deductions and the Standard Deduction for 2018

| Item— | Basic Rule— | Limitations— |
|---|---|---|
| Standard deduction | The basic standard deduction depends on your filing status and age and is adjusted annually for inflation. For 2018, the basic standard deduction is:<br>• $24,000 if you are married filing jointly or<br>• a qualifying widow or widower.<br>• $12,000 if you are single.<br>• $18,000 if you are a head of household.<br>• $12,000 if you are married filing separately.<br><br>An additional standard deduction is allowed for being age 65 or older or blind (13.4). | A married person filing separately may not use the standard deduction if his or her spouse itemizes deductions (13.3). The standard deduction may not be claimed by a nonresident or dual-status alien or on a return filed for a short taxable year caused by a change in accounting period. For a dependent with only unearned income in 2018, the standard deduction is limited to $1,050; this amount is increased for dependents with earned income (13.5). |
| Itemized deductions | You should itemize deductions on Schedule A of Form 1040 if your deductions exceed the standard deduction for your filing status. | Each separate itemized deduction is subject to limitations. For example, the total deduction for state and local taxes (including income taxes as well as real estate taxes) is limited to $10,000. Medical expenses are deductible only to the extent they exceed 7.5% of your AGI. See Chapters 14 through 19 for further itemized deduction limitations. There is no longer an overall reduction to itemized deductions for higher-income taxpayers, as there was for pre-2018 years; this phaseout has been repealed. |
| Charitable Contributions | If you itemize, you may deduct donations to religious, charitable, educational, and other philanthropic organizations that have been approved to receive deductible contributions (14.1). | The contribution deduction is generally limited to 60% of adjusted gross income for cash donations(14.17). Lower ceilings apply to most property donations and contributions to foundations. See Chapter 14 for details on charitable contributions. |
| Interest expenses | If you itemize, you may deduct interest on qualified home acquisition mortgages, points, and interest on loans to carry investments. | Interest on investment loans is deductible only to the extent of net investment income (15.10). Interest on personal and consumer loans is not deductible. Interest on home mortgages is deductible if certain tests are met (15.1). See Chapter 15 for details on interest deductions. |
| Taxes | If you itemize, you can deduct real estate taxes and state and local income taxes, or you may be able to elect to deduct general sales taxes in lieu of the income taxes (16.3). | Under the Tax Cuts and Jobs Act, there is the amount of state and local taxes that can be claimed as an itemized deduction is capped at $10,000 ($5,000 if married filing separately). The $10,000/$5,000 limit applies to the combined total of state and local income taxes or sales taxes, and property taxes (16.1). |
| Medical and dental expenses | If you itemize, you may be able to deduct medical and dental expenses that you paid for yourself, your spouse, and your dependents (17.1). A checklist of deductible medical items is provided in (17.2). With the exception of insulin, drugs are deductible only if they require a prescription by a physician. | Qualified medical and dental expenses are deductible for 2018 only to the extent they exceed 7.5% of adjusted gross income; the 7.5% floor applies regardless of your age (17.1). |
| Casualty and theft losses | You may deduct personal casualty and theft losses only if they are attributable to a federal-declared disaster (18.1). | Each individual disaster-related loss must exceed $100 and the total of all losses other than net disaster losses during the year must exceed 10% of adjusted gross income (18.12). See Chapter 18 for casualty and theft loss details. |

## 13.1 New Law Increases the Standard Deduction for 2018 and Cuts Back Itemized Deductions

The standard deduction is an "automatic" deduction based on your filing status that you may claim regardless of your actual expenses. Claim the standard deduction if it exceeds your allowable itemized deductions. The standard deduction reduces adjusted gross income (AGI).

One of the key features of the Tax Cuts and Jobs Act is a major increase in the standard deduction, starting with 2018 returns; see "Basic standard deduction" below. The new law also reduces or eliminates certain itemized deductions that were allowed under prior law *(13.2)*. The effect of these new law changes is to greatly increase the number of taxpayers who will claim the standard deduction, as opposed to itemizing deductions. However, depending on your individual circumstances, your allowable itemized deductions for medical/dental expenses, state and local taxes, home mortgage interest, charitable contributions, casualty and theft losses from federally-declared disasters and certain miscellaneous expenses may exceed your standard deduction, in which case you can claim those itemized deductions on Schedule A of Form 1040.

If you are married filing separately and your spouse itemizes deductions on his or her return, you must itemize on your return, even if the standard deduction exceeds your itemized deductions *(13.3)*.

**Basic standard deduction.** You can claim the basic standard deduction if you are under age 65 and not blind. For 2018, the basic standard deduction is:

- $24,000 if married filing jointly or a qualifying widow/widower;
- $18,000 if filing as a head of household; and
- $12,000 if single or married filing separately.

Compare the above 2018 amounts to the substantially lower basic standard deduction amounts that were allowed for 2017: $12,700 for married filing jointly or a qualifying widow/widower, $9,350 for a head of household, and $6,350 for single or married filing separately.

If you are married filing separately, you must itemize deductions and may not claim any standard deduction if your spouse itemizes on a separate return *(13.3)*.

The 2018 basic standard deduction amounts ($12,000, $18,000, or $24,000) will be subject to an inflation adjustment for 2019; *see* the *e-Supplement* at *jklasser.com*.

Additional standard deduction if age 65 or older or blind. For taxpayers age 65 or over, or taxpayers of any age who are blind, the basic standard deduction is increased by an additional amount *(13.4)*.

 *Filing Instruction*

**Net Qualified Disaster Loss Increases Standard Deduction**

A net qualified disaster loss that was sustained in 2018 increases the standard deduction you can claim on your 2018 return. Qualifying losses are losses that you sustain in 2018 *(18.2)* from Hurricane Harvey, Tropical Storm Harvey, Hurricane Irma, Hurricane Maria, or the 2017 California Wildfires, or from a federally declared disaster that occurred in 2016. Congress may add certain 2018 disasters to this list; any update will be in the *e-Supplement* at *jklasser.com*.

The loss must be figured on Form 4684 *(18.1)* where it is subject to a $500 reduction. A net qualified disaster loss from Form 4684 is entered on Schedule A (Form 1040) as an "Other Itemized Deduction," where it is combined with your otherwise allowable standard deduction. *See* the instructions to Form 4684 and Schedule A for further details.

---

### EXAMPLE

Ben Green is age 25 and single. In 2018 he has salary income of $47,775 and receives interest income *(32.4)* of $198. He makes a tax deductible contribution of $5,500 to a traditional IRA *(8.2)*. To figure his taxable income for 2018, Ben reduces his adjusted gross income of $42,473 by the $12,000 standard deduction because it exceeds his allowable itemized deductions for the year. Note that no personal exemption is allowed in calculating taxable income; the deduction for exemptions has been repealed *(21.1)*.

Gross income:

| | | |
|---|---:|---:|
| Salary | $47,775 | |
| Interest income | 198 | $47,973 |
| Deduction from gross income: | | |
| IRA (8.4) | | 5,500 |
| | | |
| Adjusted gross income | | $42,473 |
| Less: Standard deduction | | 12,000 |
| | | |
| Taxable income | | $30,473 |

**Dependents.** Individuals under age 65 (or who are blind) who may be treated as dependents by other taxpayers are limited to a $1,050 standard deduction for 2018, unless they have earned income *(13.5)*. An additional deduction is allowed to dependents who are 65 or older or blind *(13.4)*.

**Dual-status alien.** You are generally not entitled to any standard deduction if for part of the year you are a nonresident and part of the year a resident alien. However, a standard deduction may be claimed on a joint return if your spouse is a U.S. citizen or resident and you elect to be taxed on your worldwide income *(1.5)*.

## 13.2 Can You Itemize Your Deductions?

As discussed in *13.1*, the standard deduction is substantially higher in 2018 than in prior years, and some itemized deductions have been reduced or eliminated. Nevertheless, if your allowable itemized deductions for medical expenses, charitable donations, state and local taxes, mortgage interest, investment interest, casualty and theft losses from federally declared disasters, and certain miscellaneous expenses, exceed your standard deduction, you elect to itemize by claiming the deductions on Schedule A of Form 1040.

If you are married filing separately and your spouse itemizes deductions, you must itemize, even if the standard deduction exceeds your itemized deductions; see *(13.3)*.

**Changes to itemized deductions under the Tax Cuts and Jobs Act.** The Tax Cuts and Jobs Act made major changes to itemized deductions, starting with 2018 returns. Most of these changes cap or eliminate itemized deductions that could be claimed on pre-2018 returns. There are also a few positive changes. Here is a summary of the changes to itemized deductions for 2018; *see* Chapters 14 through 19 for itemized deduction details.

1. Your deduction for state and local income taxes (or sales taxes) and real estate taxes is limited to a combined, total deduction of $10,000, or $5,000 if married filing separately *(16.1)*.

2. You can no longer deduct job expenses or other miscellaneous expenses, such as tax preparation expenses, that had been deductible after a 2% of AGI floor *(19.1)*.

3. Mortgage interest on home acquisition debt incurred after December 15, 2017, is deductible on up to $750,000 of indebtedness ($375,000 if married filing separately), down from the prior-law debt limit of $1 million or $500,000 if married filing separately *(15.2)*.

4. You can no longer deduct interest on home equity debt, which means any debt that is not used to buy, build, or substantially improve a qualified residence secured by the debt *(15.3)*.

5. You can no longer deduct personal casualty or theft losses unless they are attributable to a federally declared disaster *(18.1)*.

On the other hand, the new law has a few positive aspects:

1. For medical and dental expenses, the same favorable AGI threshold that applied for 2017 also applies to 2018 expenses; the floor remains 7.5% of AGI for all taxpayers regardless of age. However, starting in 2019, the floor will increase to 10% of AGI for all taxpayers *(17.1)*.

2. The limit on cash charitable contributions increases to 60% of AGI *(14.17)*.

3. Overall itemized deductions are no longer subject to a reduction for higher-income taxpayers *(13.7)*.

 *Filing Instruction*

**Changing an Election**

If you filed your return using the standard deduction and want to change to itemized deductions, or you itemized and want to change to the standard deduction, you may do so within the three-year period allowed for amending your return. If you are married and filing separately, both of you must consent to and make the same change; you each must either itemize or claim the standard deduction.

## 13.3 Spouses Filing Separate Returns

If you and your spouse file separate returns *(1.3)* for 2018, and neither of you is a qualifying head of household *(1.12)*, both of you must either itemize deductions or claim the standard deduction. You must both make the same election; when one of you itemizes the other is not entitled to any standard deduction. That is, if your spouse has itemized deductions exceeding the 2018 standard deduction of $12,000 *(13.1)* and elects to itemize on his or her separate return, you must also itemize on your separate return, even if your itemized deductions are less than $12,000 and you would therefore be better off claiming the $12,000 standard deduction.

On a separate return, each spouse may deduct only those itemized expenses for which he or she is liable and pays. This is true even if one spouse pays expenses for the other. For example, if a wife owns property, then the interest and taxes imposed on the property are her deductions, not her husband's. If he pays them, neither one may deduct them on separate returns. The husband may not because they were not his liability. The wife may not because she did not pay them. This is true also of casualty or theft losses where the property was owned by only one of the spouses.

**No restrictions if divorced or legally separated.** Following a divorce or legal separation under a decree of divorce or separate maintenance, you and your former spouse are free to compute your tax as you each *see* fit, without reference to the way the other files. Both of you are treated as single. If you have itemized deductions, you may elect to claim them, and your former spouse is not required to itemize. Head of household tax rates may be available if certain requirements are met *(1.12)*.

**Head of household possibility if you live apart from your spouse.** If you are separated but do not have a decree of divorce or separate maintenance at the end of 2018, and you file separately from your spouse, then as stated above, both of you must either itemize or claim the standard deduction of $12,000 for 2018. However, you may file your 2018 return as a head of household *(1.12)* and may choose between a standard deduction of $18,000 (if under age 65 and not blind) and itemizing your deductions if you are married and live apart from your spouse and meet the following conditions:

- Your spouse was not a member of your household during the last six months of 2018.
- You paid over half of the costs of maintaining a home that for more than half of 2018 was the principal residence for you and a qualifying dependent. See Test 2 at *1.12* for details.

If you meet these tests and file as a head of household, you may claim the standard deduction or itemize deductions regardless of what your spouse does. If you elect not to itemize, your 2018 standard deduction as a head of household is $18,000 if you are under age 65 and not blind. If you are age 65 or over or blind, your standard deduction is increased by $1,600 *(13.4)*. The filing status of your spouse remains married filing separately. He or she must itemize deductions if you itemize. If you claim the $18,000 standard deduction for a head of household (or $19,600 if age 65 or older, or blind), your spouse can either itemize or claim the $12,000 standard deduction for married persons filing separately (or $13,300 if he or she is age 65 or older, or blind).

## 13.4 Standard Deduction If 65 or Older or Blind

A larger standard deduction is provided for persons who are age 65 or over or who are blind. The larger deduction for blindness is allowed regardless of age.

For purposes of the 2018 standard deduction, blindness and age are determined as of December 31, 2018. However, if your 65th birthday is January 1, 2019, the IRS treats you as reaching age 65 on the last day of 2018, allowing you to claim on your 2018 return the additional standard deduction for those age 65 or older.

If you are age 65 or older or blind for 2018, you may claim an additional standard deduction of $1,600 if you file as a single person or head of household, or $1,300 if your filing status is married filing jointly, married filing separately, or qualifying widow/widower. Keep in mind that if you are married filing separately, you are only allowed to claim the standard deduction if your spouse also claims the standard deduction on his or her own return *(13.3)*.

You can use Worksheet 13-1 to figure your standard deduction for 2018.

 *Filing Instruction*

**Total or Partial Blindness**

For 2018, an additional standard deduction of $1,300 or $1,600 *(13.4)* is allowed to a person who is completely blind as of December 31, 2018. If you are partially blind at the end of the year, you may claim the additional deduction if you obtain a letter from an ophthalmologist or optometrist certifying that you cannot *see* better than 20/200 in your better eye with lenses or that your field of vision is 20 degrees or less. Keep a copy of this letter. If your eye doctor believes that your vision will never improve beyond these limits, the certification should state that fact.

## Worksheet 13-1  Standard Deduction if 65 or Older or Blind

**Check applicable boxes**

|  | 65 or older | Blind |
|---|:---:|:---:|
| Yourself | ☐ | ☐ |
| Your spouse if you file a joint return | ☐ | ☐ |
| Your spouse if you file separately and can claim an exemption for your spouse *(21.2)* | ☐ | ☐ |

Total checks _____

1.     Enter your basic standard deduction for 2018:
   - Married filing jointly or qualifying widow/widower—$24,000
   - Head of household—$18,000
   - Single or married filing separately—$12,000     $ _____

2.     Multiply the number of checks above by:
   - $1,600 if you are single or head of household
   - $1,300 if you are married filing jointly, married filing separately, or a qualifying widow/widower     _____

3.     Add Lines 1 and 2. This is your standard deduction for 2018.     _____

## 13.5  Standard Deduction for Dependents

If someone can treat you as their dependent for 2018 under the tests at *21.1*, your standard deduction is determined under the following rules. You may elect to itemize deductions if these exceed the allowable standard deduction. If you are married and your spouse itemizes on a separate return, you must itemize *(13.3)*.

**Dependent under age 65 and not blind.** Your standard deduction for 2018 is the greater of (1) $1,050, or (2) your earned income plus $350, but no more than the basic standard deduction for your filing status *(13.1)*. Thus, if you can be treated as a dependent for 2018 and you do not have earned income or your earned income is $700 or less, you may claim a standard deduction of $1,050 for 2018.

**Caution**

### Determine Dependency Status First

The reduced standard deduction rules apply to you if you may be treated as a dependent on another tax return, such as by your parents. If you can be treated as a dependent (under the rules at *21.1*), it does not matter whether or not you actually are treated as a dependent by that other taxpayer.

> **EXAMPLES**
>
> 1. Susan, age 17, qualifies as a dependent of her parents for 2018 *(21.1)*. For 2018, she has earned income of $595 and interest income of $40. Her standard deduction is $1,050 because $1,050 is more than the total of her earned income ($595) and $350, or $945.
>
> 2. Assume that Susan's earned income is $2,000 rather than $595. Her standard deduction for 2018 is $2,350, the total of her earned income ($2,000) and $350, because that total exceeds the $1,050 minimum.

**Dependents age 65 or older or blind.** Your standard deduction for 2018 consists of two parts. First, you can deduct the greater of $1,050 or your earned income plus $350, but no more than the basic standard deduction for your filing status *(13.1)*. You then add $1,300 if you are married filing jointly or married filing separately, or $1,600 if single or head of household. Double the $1,300 or $1,600 amount if you are age 65 or older and also blind.

**EXAMPLE**

For 2018, Beth, a 67-year old widow, can be treated as a dependent *(21.1)* of her daughter Jane.. For 2018, Beth has interest income of $400, wages of $2,000, and Social Security benefits of $14,000 that are exempt from tax under the rules discussed at *(34.3)*. Beth's standard deduction is $3,950: $2,350 plus $1,600. Under Step 1 of Worksheet 13-2 below, Beth has a deduction of $2,350, equal to her wages of $2,000 plus $350, as this exceeds the $1,050 minimum. In Step 4 of Worksheet 13-2, the deduction is increased by $1,600, the additional deduction for a single person over age 65. Beth's taxable income is zero. Although her gross income of $2,400 is below the filing threshold (*see* filing tests for dependents on page 4), she should file a tax return to obtain a refund of income tax withheld from her wages.

---

### Worksheet 13-2   Standard Deduction if a Dependent for 2018

1.  Enter the larger of:
    - $1,050, or
    - Your earned income* in 2018 plus $350                                $ _____

2.  Enter your basic standard deduction:
    - Married filing jointly —$24,000
    - Head of household—$18,000
    - Single or married filing separately—$12,000                          $ _____

3.  Enter the smaller of Line 1 or 2                                         $ _____

4.  If you are age 65 or older or blind *(13.4)*, enter:
    - $1,600 if you are single or head of household
    - $1,300 if you are married filing jointly or separately
    - If both age 65 or older and blind, the $1,600 or $1,300
      amount is doubled to $3,200 or $2,600, respectively.                   $ _____

5.  Add Lines 3 and 4. This is your standard deduction for 2018.             $ _____

---

*Earned income. Include pay for services and taxable scholarships (33.1). Include net earnings from self-employment and then subtract the deductible part of self-employment tax liability (45.3) when figuring earned income. However, if your gross income (earned and unearned) for 2018 is $4,150 or more, you are treated as a dependent for purposes of this standard deduction rule only if you are the qualifying child of another taxpayer (21.1).

## 13.6   Prepaying or Postponing Itemized Expenses

Before the end of the year, check your records for payments of deductible itemized expenses. If you find that your payments up to that time are slightly less than the allowable standard deduction *(13.1, 13.4)* for that year, accelerating payment of an expense that you would otherwise pay in the following year could allow you to itemize. For example, at the end of 2018, you may make an additional charitable contribution, or pay a state or local tax bill that is not due until 2019 but which would be deductible for 2018 under the overall $10,000 limit (or $5,000 if married filing separately) for state and local taxes *(16.1)*. There is no tax advantage to prepaying state or local taxes if your payments earlier in the year already exceed the overall $10,000/$5,000 itemized deduction limit, or if you are either subject to AMT or a deduction for the prepayment will make you subject to AMT for 2018 *(23.2)*.

If making a year-end payment would not increase your deductions enough to itemize, you would get no tax benefit from the payment. By postponing the payment until the next year, you may make it easier to itemize on that year's return. However, given the substantial increase in the standard deduction under the new law *(13.1)*, you may find that it makes no difference if you prepay or postpone expenses, as your standard deduction still exceeds the expenses that could be itemized.

## 13.7   Itemized Deductions No Longer Reduced for Higher-Income Taxpayers

For years before 2018, taxpayers with adjusted gross income (AGI) exceeding an annual threshold had to reduce their overall itemized deductions. This reduction no longer applies; the Tax Cuts and Jobs Act repeals the reduction starting with 2018 returns.

 *Planning Reminder*

**Prepaying Deductible Expenses May Allow You To Itemize**

As the end of the year approaches, check your records for payments of deductible itemized expenses. If these payments are slightly less than the allowable standard deduction for the year, making a year-end payment of a deductible expense that you would otherwise pay in the following year might allow you to itemize.

# CHAPTER 14

# Charitable Contribution Deductions

You can help your favorite philanthropy and at the same time receive a tax benefit if you are able to itemize deductions *(13.2)*. For example, if you are in the 24% tax bracket and itemize deductions, a donation of $1,000 reduces your taxes by $240.

For cash donations of any amount, your deduction will be disallowed if you do not have a canceled check or account statement, or a written receipt from the charity, to substantiate your contribution.

For donations of $250 or more, you must receive a written acknowledgement from the organization that indicates whether you received goods or services in return for your donation. You need the acknowledgment as well as a canceled check for a cash donation of $250 or more *(14.14)*.

If you claim deductions for property valued at more than $500, you must substantiate the contribution on Form 8283 and attach it to Form 1040. If the value you claimed for the property exceeds $5,000, you generally must obtain a written appraisal *(14.15)*.

If you donated a car (or other vehicle) valued at over $500, you also must attach Copy B of Form 1098-C to your return. Your deduction is generally limited to the gross sales proceeds received by the charity on a sale of the vehicle, even if you could substantiate a higher fair market value *(14.7)*.

There are deduction ceilings depending on the type of donation and the nature of the charity, and an annual ceiling based on adjusted gross income *(14.17)*.

## 14.1 Deductible Contributions

Charitable contributions are not deductible if you claim the standard deduction *(13.1)*. You must itemize deductions on Schedule A of Form 1040 to deduct your charitable donations. If you itemize, you may deduct donations to religious, charitable, educational, and other philanthropic organizations approved by the IRS to receive deductible contributions; *see* the listing below. If you are unsure of the tax status of a philanthropy, ask the organization about its status, or check the IRS list of tax-exempt organizations (irs.gov/eoselectcheck). Donations to the federal, state, and local government are also deductible.

**Substantiating your donations.** Keep a canceled check or receipt from the charity as proof of your donations. For donations of $250 or more, you need to obtain a written acknowledgment that notes any benefits or goods that you received in exchange *(14.14)*.

For a donated car, other motor vehicle, boat, or airplane valued at over $500, you must obtain an acknowledgment on Form 1098-C (or equivalent substitute) that you must attach to your return *(14.7)*.

**Year-end donations.** You deduct donations on the tax return filed for the year in which you paid them in cash or property. A contribution by check is deductible in the year you give the check, even if it is cashed in the following year. A check mailed and dated at the end of 2018 is deductible for 2018. A check postdated until 2019 is not deductible until 2019. A pledge or a note is not deductible until paid. Donations made through a credit card are deductible in the year the charge is made, so if you donate online or by phone towards the end of 2018, the donation is deductible on your 2018 return, even though you do not pay the credit card bill until 2019. Donations made through a pay-by-phone bank account are not deductible until the payment date shown on the bank statement.

**Delivering securities.** If you are planning to donate appreciated securities near the end of the year, make sure that you consider these delivery rules in timing the donation. If you unconditionally deliver or mail a properly endorsed stock certificate to the donee or its agent, the gift is considered completed on the date of delivery or mailing, provided it is received in the ordinary course of the mails. If you deliver the certificate to your bank or broker as your agent, or to the issuing corporation or its agent, your gift is not complete until the stock is transferred to the donee's name on the corporation's books. This transfer may take several weeks, so, if possible, make the delivery at least three weeks before the end of the year to assure a current deduction. If you plan to donate mutual fund shares to a charity towards the end of the year, contact the fund company to ensure that the transfer of shares to the name of the charity can be completed by the end of the year.

**Debts.** You may assign to a charity a debt payable to you. A deductible contribution may be claimed in the year your debtor pays the charity.

**Limits on deduction.** Depending on the nature of the organization and the donated property, a deduction ceiling of 60%, 30%, or 20% of adjusted gross income applies. In general, the deduction ceiling is 60% for cash contributions and 30% for contributions of appreciated property held long term *(14.17)*. Where donations in one year exceed the percentage limits, a five-year carryover of the excess may be allowed *(14.18)*.

## Organizations Qualifying for Deductible Donations

**The following types of organizations may qualify to receive deductible contributions:**

- A domestic nonprofit organization, trust, community chest, fund, or foundation that is operated exclusively for one of the following purposes:
- Religious. Payments for pew rents, assessments, and dues to churches and synagogues are deductible.
- Charitable. In this class are organizations such as Boy Scouts, Girl Scouts, American Red Cross, Community Funds, Cancer Societies, CARE, Salvation Army, Y.M.C.A., and Y.W.C.A.
- Scientific, literary, and educational. Included in this group are hospitals, research organizations, colleges, universities, and other schools that do not maintain racially discriminatory policies; and leagues or associations set up for education or to combat crime, improve public morals, and aid public welfare.

*Law Alert*

**Direct Transfer From IRA to Charity**

If you are an IRA owner age 70½ or older at the end of the year, you can have the trustee of your traditional IRA make a direct transfer to a qualified charity. If the total of all such qualified charitable distributions (QCDs) for the year does not exceed $100,000, the transfers are not taxable to you *(8.8)*. A QCD is not deductible as a charitable contribution, but it offsets the required minimum distribution that otherwise would have been due from your traditional IRA *(8.13)*.

- Prevention of cruelty to children or animals.
- Fostering amateur sports competition. However, the organization's activities may not provide athletic facilities or equipment.
- Domestic nonprofit veterans' organizations or auxiliary units.

**A domestic fraternal group operating under the lodge system.** The contributions must be used exclusively for religious, charitable, scientific, literary, or educational purposes; or for the prevention of cruelty to children or animals.

**Nonprofit cemetery and burial companies.** Contributions must benefit the whole cemetery, not only your plot.

**Legal services corporations established under the Legal Services Corporation Act.** Such corporations provide legal assistance to financially needy people in noncriminal proceedings.

**The United States, a U.S.** possession, Puerto Rico, a state, city, or town or Indian tribal government. The gift must be for public purposes. The gift may be directed to a government unit, or it may be to a government agency such as a state university, a fire department, a civil defense group, or a committee to raise funds to develop land into a public park. Donations may be made to the Social Security system (Federal Old Age and Survivors Insurance Trust Fund). Donations may be made to the federal government to help reduce the national debt; checks should be made payable to "Bureau of the Public Debt."

## 14.2 Nondeductible Contributions

The following types of contributions are not deductible:

1. Donations to or on behalf of specific individuals, even if needy or worthy. Generally, scholarships for specific students, or gifts to organizations to benefit only certain groups, are not deductible. However, the IRS in private rulings has allowed deductions for scholarship funds that are limited to (1) members of a particular religion, so long as that religion is open to all on a racially nondiscriminatory basis, or (2) are open only to male students.

2. Payments to political campaign committees or political action committees.

3. Payments to an organization that devotes a substantial part of its activities to lobbying, trying to influence legislation, or carrying on propaganda or whose lobbying activities exceed certain limits set by the law, causing the organization to lose its tax-exempt status. The IRS has disallowed contributions to a civic group opposing saloons, nightclubs, and gambling places, although the group also aided libraries, churches, and other public programs.

4. Gifts to organizations such as:

    Fraternal groups—except when they set up special organizations exclusively devoted to charitable, educational, or other approved purposes.

    Professional groups such as those organized by accountants, lawyers, and physicians—except when they are specially created for exclusive charitable, educational, or other philanthropic purposes. The IRS will disallow unrestricted gifts made to state bar associations, although such organizations may have some public purposes. Some courts have allowed deductions for donations to bar associations on the ground that their activities benefit the general public. However, an appeals court disallowed deductible donations to a bar association that rates candidates for judicial office.

    Clubs for social purposes—fraternities and sororities are generally in this class. Unless an organization is exclusively operated for a charitable, religious, or other approved purpose, you may not deduct your contribution, even though your funds are used for a charitable or religious purpose.

5. Donations to civic leagues, chambers of commerce, business leagues, or labor unions.

6. Contributions to a hospital or school operated for profit.

7. Purchase price of church building bond. To claim a deduction, you must donate the bond to the church. The amount of the deduction is the fair market value of the bond when you make the donation. Interest on the bond is income each year, under the original issue discount rules *(4.19)*, where no interest will be paid until the bond matures.

8. Donations of blood to the Red Cross or other blood banks.

9. Contributions to foreign charitable organizations or directly to foreign governments. Thus, a contribution to the State of Israel was disallowed.

*Caution*

**Foreign Charities**

You may deduct donations to domestic organizations that distribute funds to charities in foreign countries, as long as the U.S. organization controls the distribution of the funds overseas. An outright contribution to a foreign charitable organization is not deductible. Some exceptions to this ban are provided by international treaties. For example, if you have income from Canadian, Mexican, or Israeli sources, contributions to certain organizations in those countries are deductible subject to limitations. For details, *see* IRS Publication 526

*Law Alert*

**Contributions to Donor-Advised Funds**

No deduction can be claimed for a contribution to a donor-advised fund if the sponsoring organization is a war veteran's organization, fraternal society, veteran's organization, or a non-functionally integrated Type III supporting organization.

**Donation of services.** You may not deduct the value of your time when you provide volunteer services for charity. But you can deduct unreimbursed expenses incurred during such work *(14.4)*.

**Free use of property.** You may not deduct the rental value of property you allow a charity to use without charge. That is, if you allow a charity rent-free use of an office in your building, you may not deduct the fair rental value. You also have no deduction when you lend money to a charity without charging interest.

To raise money for a charity, supporters of the organization may donate rental time for their vacation home, to be auctioned off to the public. No deduction is allowed for donating the rental time *(14.10)*.

**Seating rights at college sports events.** The Tax Cuts and Jobs Act disallows a deduction for a payment to a college or university that gives the payer the right to purchase tickets to athletic events, effective for payments made after 2017; *see* the nearby Law Alert.

**Parents' support payments of children serving as Mormon missionaries.** According to the Supreme Court, support payments made by parents directly to their children who serve as missionaries are not deductible because the church does not control the funds.

## 14.3 Contributions That Provide You With Benefits

A contribution to a qualifying organization *(14.1)* is generally deductible only to the extent that you intend to give more than the value of benefits you receive and actually do so.

If you contribute $75 or less and receive benefits, the organization may tell you the value of the benefits. If your contribution exceeds $75, the organization by law must give you a written statement that estimates the value of the benefits provided to you and instructs you to deduct only the portion of your contribution that exceeds the benefits. However, the disclosure statement does not have to be provided to you if you receive only token benefits, or if you receive from a religious organization only "intangible religious benefits."

> **EXAMPLES**
>
> 1. You contribute $200 to a philanthropy and receive a book that you have seen on sale for prices ranging between $18 and $25. The charity estimates the value at $20. As the estimate is between the typical retail prices, it is acceptable to the IRS. Although the book sold at a price as high as $25, you may treat the $20 estimate as fair market value and claim a deduction of $180.
>
> 2. A charitable organization sponsors an art auction and provides a catalogue that lists the items being auctioned and estimates of fair market value. The catalogue lists the value of a vase at $100. At the auction, you bid and pay $500 for the vase. Because you were aware of the estimate before the auction and paid more for the vase, you may deduct $400.

**Dues.** Dues paid to a qualified tax-exempt organization are deductible to the extent they exceed the value of benefits from the organization, such as monthly journals, use of a library, or the right to attend luncheons and lectures. As discussed above, you generally must be provided with an estimate of any benefits you received if your donation exceeds $75.

If dues are paid to a social club with the understanding that a specified part goes to a qualifying charity *(14.1)*, you may claim a charitable deduction for dues earmarked for the charity. If the treasurer of your club is actually the agent of the charity, you take the deduction in the year you give him or her the money. If the treasurer is merely your agent, you may take the deduction only in the year the money is remitted to the charity.

**Benefit tickets.** Tickets to theater events, tours, concerts, and other entertainments are often sold by charitable organizations at prices higher than the regular admission charge. The difference between the regular admission and the higher amount you pay is deductible as a charitable contribution. If you decline to accept the ticket or return it to the charity for resale, your deduction is the price you paid.

 *Law Alert*

**Payments Giving Right To Buy Athletic Stadium Tickets No Longer Deductible**

The Tax Cuts and Jobs Act disallows a deduction for payments made after 2017 to a public or nonprofit college or university that give you the right to buy tickets at the school's athletic events. This includes contributions that give you the right to buy seating in stadium skyboxes, suites, or special viewing areas. Prior to the Tax Cuts and Jobs Act, the IRS allowed a deduction for 80% of a contribution paid in exchange for sports seating rights; the nondeductible 20% was considered to be the fair market value of the right to purchase tickets. Payments for actual tickets have always been nondeductible.

 *Caution*

**Tuition or Other Benefits Received**

Except for certain token benefits and memberships that are disregarded for tax purposes, you may not deduct a contribution to a qualified charity to the extent that you receive goods, services, or financial benefits in exchange *(14.3)*.

The IRS does not allow a deduction for tuition payments to a religious school for the education of your children if secular courses that lead to a recognized degree are provided, unless the payments exceed the usual tuition charged for a secular education in your area. The Tax Court and Ninth Circuit Court of Appeals agree with this IRS position.

Fees paid to a tax-exempt rest home in which you live, or to a hospital for the care of a particular patient, are not deductible if any benefit is received from the contribution. A gift to a retirement home, over and above monthly fees, is not deductible if your accommodations are dependent on the size of your gift.

*Caution*

**Bingo and Lotteries**

You may not deduct the cost of raffle tickets, bingo games, or tickets for other types of lotteries organized by charities.

**The charity should explain to you how much is deductible.** The charity must provide an explanation if you paid more than $75; *see* the discussion above.

If the ticket is at or below its normal cost, no deduction is allowed unless you decline the ticket or return it to the charity.

If tickets were purchased for a charity-sponsored series of events and the average cost of a single event is equal to or less than the cost of an individual performance, then a deduction for a returned ticket is based upon the time the ticket was held. Generally, you may deduct only your cost. However, if you have held the ticket for more than a year, you may deduct the price the charity will charge on resale of the ticket.

> **EXAMPLE**
>
> A couple claimed a full deduction for regular-price tickets to a high-school fund-raising event that they did not attend. They argued that they were entitled to the deduction because they received no benefit from their ticket purchase. The IRS disallowed the deduction and the Tax Court agreed, holding that a donor receives a benefit by merely having the right to attend the event. To claim a deduction for the price of the tickets the couple should have returned them to the charity.

**No deduction for donation that gives the right to buy athletic stadium tickets.** If you contribute to a public or nonprofit college or university and receive the right to buy preferential seating at the school's athletic complexes, you may not deduct any part of the contribution. The Tax Cuts and Jobs Act disallows the deduction for 2018 and later years; *see 14.2.*

**No deduction when state and local tax credits are received.** In an effort to allow their residents to continue to enjoy a federal tax benefit from the payment of state and local taxes (SALT) in excess of the $10,000 cap (*see 16.1*), some states have enacted or are considering the enactment of a workaround. Where such action permits residents to receive a state and local tax credit for payments to an entity that is eligible to receive tax deductible contributions, the IRS has said it will propose regulations that require the reduction of any federal charitable contribution deduction by the amount of the state and local tax credit the taxpayer receives or expects to receive (unless it is *de minimis*, as explained below). In effect, the IRS views the workaround as a quid pro quo.

> **EXAMPLE**
>
> If a state grants a 70% state tax credit and the taxpayer pays $1,000 to an eligible entity, the taxpayer receives a $700 state tax credit. The taxpayer must reduce the $1,000 contribution by the $700 state tax credit, leaving an allowable contribution deduction of $300 on the taxpayer's federal income tax return.
>
> Under a *de minimis* rule, no reduction in the federal charitable contribution deduction is required if the tax credit received is no more than 15% of the payment amount or of the fair market value of the property transferred.

**No deduction for house donated to fire department.** Some homeowners planning to tear down their homes to make way for constructing new ones have donated the homes to a fire department and claimed a charitable contribution deduction. The fire department uses the home for training exercises in extinguishing fires. The homeowner's goal is to avoid the costs of demolishing the house while claiming a charitable deduction for the value of the home. However, the IRS and Tax Court have held in such cases that the donated homes have minimal value and disallowed the claimed deductions. A federal appeals court sided with the IRS and Tax Court in barring a charitable deduction where a couple donated their house but not the land, with the understanding that the fire department would use it for training exercises and burn it down within a short period of time. The demolition of the home by the fire department was a benefit to the taxpayers and under the "quid-pro-quo" test, no deduction could be claimed because they could not show that the fair market value of the house exceeded the estimated $10,000 in demolition and debris removal costs that would have been incurred had there been no donation. The donated home had only a minimal value because it could not be used by the fire department for residential purposes but only for training exercises.

> **EXAMPLE**
>
> A taxpayer who makes a $1,000 contribution to an eligible entity is not required to reduce the $1,000 deduction on the taxpayer's federal income tax return if the state or local tax credit received or expected to be received is no more than $150.

## Token Items and Membership Benefits That Do Not Reduce Your Deduction

**Token items.** Popular fund-raising campaigns, such as those for museums, zoos, and public TV, offer token items such as calendars, tote bags, tee shirts, and other items carrying the organization's logo. You are allowed a full deduction for your contribution if the item is considered to be of insubstantial value under IRS guidelines.

The charity must tell you how much of your contribution is deductible in the solicitation that offers the token item. If the items are insubstantial in value, the charity should tell you that your payment is fully deductible. For example, if in 2018 you contributed at least $54, and the offered items cost the charity no more than $10.80, the value of the benefits is ignored and a full 2018 deduction is allowed. A full deduction for 2018 is also allowed if the items were worth no more than 2% of the contribution or $108, whichever is less. The $54, $10.80, and $108 amounts change annually for inflation.

Newsletters or program guides that are not of commercial quality are treated as token items having no fair market value or cost if their primary purpose is to inform members about the organization's activities, and they are not available to nonmembers by paid subscription or through newsstand sales.

Publications with articles written for compensation and advertising are treated as commercial-quality publications for which the organization must figure value to determine if a full deduction is allowed under the "insubstantial value" test. Professional journals, whether or not they have such articles and advertising, will generally be treated as commercial-quality publications that must be valued.

**Membership benefits.** If you contribute $75 or less for an annual membership in a qualified charity *(14.1)* and you receive only the following benefits, the benefits can be disregarded and you may deduct your entire payment:

1. Privileges that can be exercised frequently, such as free or discounted parking or admission to organization events, or discounts on gift shop or online merchandise, or

2. Admission to events that are open only to members and the organization's reasonably projected cost per person for each event excluding overhead (as of the time the membership package is offered) is no more than the annual limit for "low cost articles." For 2018, the "low cost article" limit is $10.80.

## 14.4 Unreimbursed Expenses of Volunteer Workers

If you work without pay for an organization listed at *14.1*, and you itemize deductions, you may deduct as a charitable contribution your unreimbursed expenses in providing the services, such as the out-of-pocket costs of driving your car (gas, oil, parking, tolls) to and from the place of charitable operations. On a trip away from home *(20.6)* for the organization, you can deduct your unreimbursed travel expenses, including transportation (air, rail, bus, taxi and car costs), meals and lodging.

To qualify for the deduction, the expenses must be incurred for a domestic organization that authorizes you to travel. You may not deduct the value of your donated services.

**Substantiating expenses under $250.** The IRS does not have a recordkeeping regulation that is specific to unreimbursed volunteer expenses under $250. The Tax Court held in a 2011 case that volunteer expenses of under $250 are subject to the rules for cash gifts of less than $250 *(14.14)*, even though the terms of the cash gift regulation are a bad fit for volunteer expenses. The regulation requires a cash donor *(14.14)* to have canceled checks or receipts from the charity, or in lieu of either, other reliable written records showing the name of the charity and the date and amount of the contribution. These

*Filing Tip*

**Estimated Value of Benefits**

You may rely on a written estimate from the organization of the value of any benefits given to you unless it seems unreasonable. Although the value of benefits received generally reduces your deductible contribution, certain token items and membership benefits do not reduce the amount of your deduction.

requirements were not written with volunteer expenses in mind, as a volunteer's out-of-pocket expenses (supplies, for example) will generally be paid to third parties rather than to the charity itself. In the case before it, the Tax Court held that a volunteer was in substantial compliance with the IRS rules for expenses of less than $250 because she had records showing the name of the payees, and the dates and amounts of payment, the same information that would be on canceled checks from the charity.

*Note:* Under 2008 proposed regulations, the substantiation requirements for volunteer expenses of under $250 would be waived, but the proposal has not been adopted.

**Substantiating expenses of $250 or more.** To deduct an unreimbursed expense of $250 or more, such as for a plane ticket or a luncheon you hosted on behalf of the organization, you need, in addition to records substantiating the amount of the expense, a written acknowledgment from the charity *(14.14)*. The acknowledgment must describe your services, and state whether you were provided any goods or services by the charity. If so, an estimate of their value must be given unless the benefits are "intangible religious benefits." The acknowledgment must be obtained by the date you file your return, but if you file after the due date (or extended due date if you get an extension), the acknowledgment must be obtained by the filing due date, including extensions. For 2018 returns, the due date (prior to an extension) is April 15, 2019.

**Car expenses.** If you used your car (or other motor vehicle) to provide volunteer services for a charity, you may deduct either the actual vehicle operating costs (such as gas and oil) that are directly related to your volunteer services, or you may claim a flat mileage rate of 14 cents per mile. The 14-cents-per-mile rate is set by statute and not subject to annual cost-of-living increases. Parking fees and tolls are deductible whether you claim actual expenses or the flat mileage rate.

**Other deductible volunteer expenses.** In addition to car expenses, you may claim the following unreimbursed expenses:

- Uniform costs required in serving the organization.
- Cost of telephone calls, and cost of materials and supplies you furnished such as stamps or stationery.
- Travel expenses, including meals and lodging on overnight trips away from home as an official delegate to a convention of a church, charitable, veteran, or other similar organization. If you are a member but not a delegate, you may not deduct travel costs, but you may deduct expenses paid for the benefit of your organization at the convention.
- All related expenses in hosting a fund-raiser are deductible, from the invitations to the food and drink.

> **EXAMPLE**
>
> In the course of doing volunteer work for a charity in 2018, Jill Patton drove her car 1,000 miles. If Jill itemizes deductions on her 2018 return, she may include a charitable contribution deduction of $140 (14 cents a mile), plus tolls and parking.

The IRS does not allow a deduction for "babysitting" expenses of charity volunteer workers. Although incurred to make the volunteer work possible, babysitting costs are a nondeductible personal expense.

**Recreational purposes may bar travel expense deduction.** To claim a charitable deduction for travel expenses of a research project for a charitable organization, you must show the trip had no significant element of personal pleasure, recreation, or vacation.

> **EXAMPLES**
>
> 1. Al Jones sails from one Caribbean island to another and spends eight hours a day counting whales and other forms of marine life as part of a project sponsored by a charitable organization. According to the IRS, he may not claim a charitable deduction for the cost of the trip.

2. Sara Smith works on an archaeological excavation sponsored by a charitable organization for several hours each morning, with the rest of the day free for recreation and sightseeing. According to the IRS, she may not deduct the cost of the trip.

3. Myra Scott, a member of a chapter of a local charitable organization, travels to New York City and spends the entire day at the required regional meeting. According to the IRS, she may deduct her travel expenses as a charitable donation, even if she attends a theater in the evening.

## 14.5 Support of a Student in Your Home

A limited charitable deduction is allowed for support of an elementary or high-school student in your home under an educational program arranged by a charitable organization. If the student is not a relative or your dependent, you may deduct as a charitable contribution your support payments up to $50 for each month the student stays in your home. For this purpose, 15 days or more of a calendar month is considered a full month. You may not deduct any payments received from the charitable organization if any reimbursements are received for the student's maintenance. The only exception is that if you prepay a "one-time" expense such as a hospital bill or vacation for the child at the request of the child's parents or the sponsoring charity, and you are later reimbursed for part of your payment, you may deduct your unreimbursed expenses.

To support the deduction, be prepared to show a written agreement between you and the organization relating to the support arrangement. Keep records of amounts spent for such items as food, clothing, medical and dental care, tuition, books, and recreation in order to substantiate your deduction. No deduction is allowed for depreciation on your house.

## 14.6 What Kind of Property Are You Donating?

If you itemize deductions, a deduction for the fair market value of donated property may generally be claimed, but the tax law does not treat all donations of appreciated property in the same way. Whether the full amount of the fair market value of the property is deductible depends on the type of property donated, your holding period, the nature of the philanthropy, and the use to which the property is put by the philanthropy. For donations of motor vehicles, boats, or airplanes valued at over $500, special deduction restrictions and substantiation restrictions apply *(14.7)*.

Save records to support the market value and cost of donated property. Get a receipt or letter from the charitable organization acknowledging and describing the gift. You must get a receipt for donations of property valued at $250 or more *(14.14)*. Lack of substantiation may disqualify an otherwise valid deduction.

If the total claimed value for all of your property donations exceeds $500, you must report the donations on Form 8283 *(14.15)*, which you attach to Schedule A, Form 1040. If the claimed value of a donated item (or group of similar items) exceeds $5,000, you generally must base the valuation on a written appraisal from a qualified appraiser; *see* *14.15* for details on the appraisal requirements.

**Figuring value.** When donating securities listed on a public exchange, fair market value is readily ascertainable from newspaper listings of stock prices. It is the average of the high and low sales price on the date of the donation.

To value other property, such as real estate or works of art, you will need the services of an experienced appraiser. Fees paid to an appraiser are not deductible as a charitable contribution, nor are they deductible under any other provision of the Tax Code for 2018 and later years; *see* the nearby Law Alert.

**Fair market value deductible for appreciated intangible personal property (such as securities) and real estate held long term.** Fair market value is deductible where you have held such property long term (longer than one year) and you give it to a publicly supported charity or to a private foundation that qualifies as a 50% limit organization, but you may not deduct more than 30% of adjusted gross income *(14.17)*. A five-year

*Law Alert*

**Appraisal Fees not Deductible**

A fee paid for an appraisal of donated real estate or art is not deductible as a charitable contribution and no other deduction is available. For years after 2017, the Tax Cuts and Jobs Act disallows an itemized deduction for appraisal fees; for years before 2018, the fees could be claimed as a miscellaneous itemized deduction subject to the 2% floor *(19.1)*.

carryover for the excess is allowed *(14.18)*. If the donation exceeds the 30% ceiling, you may consider a special election that allows you to apply the 50% ceiling *(14.19)*.

A contribution of appreciated securities or real estate held long term has two tax advantages that reduce the real cost of making the contribution:

1. Your taxes are reduced by the deduction for the fair market value of the property. For example, you donate appreciated stock that is selling at $1,000. You are in the 24% federal tax bracket. The deduction for the donation reduces your taxes by $240.

2. You avoid the tax you would have paid on a sale of the stock. Assume that your cost for the stock was $400 that your regular top bracket is 24%, and that gain on the sale would be taxed at the 15% capital gain rate *(5.3)*. On a sale at $1,000, you would pay tax of $90 (15% capital gain rate on $600 profit). By donating the stock, you save that $90 plus $240 from the $1,000 charitable deduction ($1,000 × 24% bracket), for a total tax savings of $330. Your "cost" for donating the $1,000 asset is $670 ($1,000 – $330).

The IRS ruled that you may not claim a deduction on donated stock if you retain the voting rights, even though the charity has the right to receive dividends and sell the stock. The right to vote is considered a substantial interest and is crucial in protecting a stockholder's investment.

If you are planning a year-end donation of securities, keep in mind that the gift is generally not considered complete until the properly endorsed securities are mailed or delivered to the charity or its agent *(14.1)*.

**Deduction limited to cost for appreciated property not held long term and ordinary income property.** This is property that, if sold by you at its fair market value, would not result in long-term capital gain. The deduction for donations of this kind is restricted to your cost for the property. Examples include: stock and other capital assets held by you for one year or less, inventory items donated by business, farm crops, Section 306 stock (preferred stock received as a tax-free stock dividend, usually in a closely held corporation), and works of art *(14.9)*, books, letters, and memoranda donated by the person who prepared or created them. For example, a former Congressman claimed a charitable deduction for the donation of his papers. His deduction was disallowed. His papers were ordinary income property, and since his cost basis in the papers was zero, he could claim no deduction. Depreciable business property is considered ordinary income property to the extent that depreciation would be recaptured as ordinary income on a sale *(44.1–44.3)*. If the cost of the property was fully deducted under first-year expensing *(42.3)*, you have no cost basis and you may not claim a deduction.

*Caution*

**Tangible Personal Property**

When you donate appreciated collectibles and artwork (other than taxidermy property) held long term, you get a full deduction for the fair market value of the property if the items are used in connection with the charity's main activity or tax-exempt purpose.

If the charity sells your property, your deduction is limited to your basis in the property (what you paid for it, rather than its appreciated value). Protect a deduction for fair market value by obtaining a letter from the charity stating that it intends to use your gift in connection with its tax-exempt purposes.

> **EXAMPLE**
>
> Bob James holds stock that cost him $1,000. It is now worth $1,500. If he holds it for one year or less and donates it to a philanthropy, his deduction would be limited to $1,000. He would get no tax benefit for the appreciation of $500. On the other hand, if he holds the stock over a year before donating it, he could claim a deduction for the full market value of the stock.

**Use of property by charity determines whether fair market value or cost is deductible for appreciated tangible personal property held long term.** If you donate appreciated tangible personal property held long term, such as works of art *(14.9)*, jewelry, furniture, books, equipment, fixtures (severed from realty), and antique cars, the deduction limit depends on how the charitable organization uses the property. If the property is used by the organization for purposes related to its tax-exempt purpose or function, you may deduct the fair market value.

If the organization puts the property to a use that is unrelated to its tax-exempt purpose or function, the deduction is limited to your cost basis because the fair market value must be reduced by the amount of long-term capital gain that would have been realized if the property had been sold at fair market value. If the charity sells your gift to obtain cash for its exempt purposes, your donation is treated as being put to an unrelated use by the charity, and your deduction must be reduced by the long-term gain element unless on the date of the donation you could reasonably anticipate that the property would not be sold (or put to another nonrelated use). A certification of exempt use from the charity is required if you claim a deduction exceeding $5,000 and the charity sells the property within three years; *see* below.

If the donation of tangible personal property is to a 50% deduction limit organization such as a church or college, and you must reduce the deduction as an unrelated gift, the reduced gift is then subject to the 50% annual deduction ceiling discussed in *14.17*. If the organization's use of the property is related to its tax-exempt charitable purposes, and it is a 50% limit organization, you may deduct the property's fair market value subject to the 30% of adjusted gross income deduction ceiling *(14.17)*. Alternatively, you may elect to deduct up to 50% of adjusted gross income by reducing the deduction by the long-term gain *(14.19)*.

**Deductions of appreciated tangible personal property exceeding $5,000 may be reduced or recaptured on sale by charity within three years.** Special certification rules apply to donations of appreciated tangible personal property for which you claim a deduction of more than $5,000:

1. If the charity sells or otherwise disposes of the property during the year that you donated it, your deduction is limited to your cost basis unless the charity provides a written certification of exempt use to the IRS on Form 8282, and gives you a copy. The certification, signed by an officer under penalty of perjury, must either state that the charity's use of the property was substantial and furthered its tax-exempt purpose or function, or state that a related and substantial use of the property was intended at the time of the donation but it became impossible or unfeasible to implement such intent.

2. If you deduct more than your basis in the property and the charity sells it (or otherwise disposes of it) after the year of contribution but within three years of the contribution, and the charity does not provide the IRS and you with the required certification described in (1) above, you must recapture part of your original deduction. In the year of the sale, you must report as ordinary income the excess of the deduction claimed over your cost basis for the property at the time of the donation. Report the recaptured amount as "other income" on Schedule 1 of Form 1040.

> **EXAMPLE**
>
> On October 17, 2018, you contribute to a college a painting worth $7,500 that you held long term. The college displays it in a library where art students may study it. The college's use of the painting is related to its tax-exempt educational purposes and you may deduct fair market value.
>
> However, assume that the college sells the painting in 2019 and uses the proceeds for its educational purposes. Because you claimed a value for the painting that exceeded $5,000, the college must report the sale to the IRS on Form 8282 and give you a copy. There is no effect on your deduction if the college on Form 8282 certifies its exempt use or its intended exempt use. Without the required certification, the recapture rule would apply (rule 2 above) and you would have to report the excess of your $7,500 deduction over your cost basis for the paintings as income for 2019. The same result would apply if the college disposed of the painting in 2020 or in 2021 by October 16, 2021, the end of the three-year recapture period.

**Donating mortgaged property.** A donation of mortgaged property may produce a taxable gain as well as a deduction. Before you give mortgaged property to a charity, have an attorney review the transaction. You may deduct the excess of fair market value over the amount of the outstanding mortgage. However, you may realize a taxable gain. The IRS and Tax Court treat the transferred mortgage debt as cash received in a part-gift, part-sale subject to the rules for bargain sales of appreciated property *(14.8)*. You will realize a taxable gain if the transferred mortgage exceeds the portion of basis allocated to the sale part of the transaction. This is true even if the charity does not assume the mortgage.

**Donating capital gain property to private non-operating foundations.** You generally may not deduct the full fair market value of gifts of capital gain property to private non-operating foundations that are subject to the 20% deduction ceiling for non–50% limit

**Caution**

**Recapture of Deduction for Property Sold Within Three Years**

If you donate appreciated tangible personal property held long term, for which you claim a deduction exceeding $5,000, and it is sold by the charity by the end of the year of the contribution, the deduction is limited to your cost basis (you may not deduct fair market value) unless the charity makes a qualifying written certification (*see* adjacent text) to the IRS and gives you a copy.

If you deduct more than your basis for the property and the charity sells the property after the year of the contribution but within three years of the contribution, and the charity does not provide the required certification, you must recapture part of the previously claimed deduction.

organizations *(14.17)*. (Capital gain property is property that, if sold by you at fair market value, would result in long-term capital gain.) The deduction must be reduced by the long-term gain that would have been realized if the property had been sold at fair market value. In other words, your deduction is limited to your cost basis.

An exception is available for certain contributions of stock to a private non-operating foundation; *see* below.

**Stock donation to private non-operating foundation.** A deduction for fair market value is allowed on a donation to a non-operating private foundation of appreciated publicly traded stock held long term. To qualify, there must be readily available market quotations on an established securities market for the stock on the date of the contribution. If you or family members donated more than 10% of a corporation's stock, the fair market value deduction is allowed only for the first 10%. Under the family aggregation rule, your contributions of stock in a particular publicly traded corporation are aggregated with those of your spouse, brothers, sisters, parents and grandparents, children, grandchildren, and great-grandchildren to all private non-operating foundations, whether the foundations are related or not. If the 10% limit is exceeded, the excess contributions are subject to the cost basis deduction limitation.

The IRS has ruled that for purposes of applying the 10% limit, you must take into account previous stock contributions that the private foundation sold before the new contributions were made. Once publicly traded stock is donated to a private foundation, it must be counted toward the 10% limit, even if it is later disposed of. Furthermore, the value of each contribution at the time it is made is the value taken into account for applying the 10% limitation; prior contributions are not revalued each time there is a new contribution.

> **EXAMPLE**
>
> John Hill donates to a college land held over a year that is worth $250,000 and subject to a $100,000 mortgage. His basis for the land is $150,000. Hill's charitable contribution deduction is $150,000 ($250,000 − $100,000). He also is considered to have made a bargain sale for $100,000 (transferred mortgage debt) on which he realized $40,000 long-term capital gain.
>
> $$\frac{\$100{,}000 \text{ (amount of mortgage)}}{\$250{,}000 \text{ (fair market value)}} = 40\%$$
>
> Basis allocated to sale: 40% of $150,000, or $60,000
>
> | | |
> |---|---|
> | Amount realized | $100,000 |
> | Allocated basis | 60,000 |
> | Gain | $ 40,000 |

**Patents and other intellectual property.** If you donate patents or other intellectual property to charity, such as trademarks, trade names, trade secrets, know-how, and certain copyrights and software, you can claim an initial charitable contribution deduction for your cost basis in the property (assuming that is less than its fair market value). Additional deductions may be claimed in the year of the donation and in later years, based on a percentage of the income that the charity realizes from the property.

The additional deductions are allowed on a sliding scale percentage basis for the 10-year period beginning on the date of the contribution. In order to obtain the additional deductions, you must accompany the donation with a written statement to the charity that includes your name, address, and taxpayer identification number, a description of the intellectual property, and the date of the contribution. The statement must specify that you intend to treat the contribution as a qualified intellectual property contribution and will claim additional deductions for the allowable annual percentage of the charity's income from the property.

For each year that the charity realizes net income from the property in the 10-year period beginning on the date of the contribution, the charity must report the income to the IRS on Form 8899. A copy of Form 8899 is sent to you and the income shown may be used as the basis for claiming an additional contribution deduction.

For further details, *see* the instructions to Form 8899 and IRS Publication 526.

**U.S.** Saving Bonds. You may not donate U.S. Saving Bonds, such as EE bonds or I bonds, because you may not transfer them. They are nonnegotiable. You must first cash the bonds and then give the proceeds to the charity, or surrender the bonds and have new ones registered in the donee's name. When you do this, you have to report the accrued interest on your tax return. Of course, you will then get a charitable deduction for the cash gift if you itemize deductions for that year.

**Gift of installment obligations.** You may deduct your donation of installment notes to a qualified philanthropy. However, if you received them on your sale of property that you reported on the installment basis, you may realize gain or loss on the gift of the notes *(5.28)*. The amount of the contribution is the fair market value of the obligation, not the face amount of the notes.

## 14.7 Cars, Clothing, and Other Property Valued Below Cost

If you donate property whose value has declined below your cost, your deduction generally is limited to the fair market value. However, the rules for cars, trucks, boats, and airplanes are more complicated. Strict substantiation requirements apply to prevent donors from claiming inflated deductions for donated vehicles where the charity actually received much less on a sale to raise cash; *see* below.

If you are planning a donation of stock or other investment or business property worth less than your basis *(5.20)*, consider selling the property and then donating the proceeds. If you donate the property, your deduction is limited to the fair market value and you cannot deduct a loss. If you first sell the property, you can claim a loss on the sale and then claim a charitable contribution on your donation of the sale proceeds; *see* the Example below.

> **EXAMPLE**
>
> Betty Dunn owns securities that cost $20,000 several years ago but have declined in value to $5,000. A donation of these securities gives a charitable contribution deduction of $5,000. If Betty sold the securities for $5,000, she could claim a long-term capital loss *(5.3)* of $15,000. She could then donate the sales proceeds and claim a $5,000 charitable deduction for the cash contribution.

**Clothing or household items.** You can claim a deduction for used clothing or household items only if they are in good used condition or better. Household items include furniture or furnishings, linens, appliances or electronics, but not antiques, art, collections, or jewelry. Your deduction for "good condition" clothing or household items is limited to their fair market value, which is usually much less than your original cost. Prices paid in thrift shops for similar items are an indication of fair market value. If you have photographs of the donated items, or a statement describing them from the charity, this would help support your valuation should the IRS later question your deduction. If an item is valued at over $500 in a qualified appraisal that you attach to your return, a deduction is allowed even if the item is not in good used condition or better.

**Cars, other motor vehicles, boats, and airplanes.** You must obtain a timely written acknowledgment from the charity to substantiate a deduction for a car or other motor vehicle, boat, or airplane with a claimed value of over $500. The required acknowledgment must be on Form 1098-C or an equivalent statement from the charity. Copy B of the Form 1098-C (or equivalent acknowledgment) must be attached to your return; if you do not attach the form to your return, the IRS will disallow your deduction. If you e-file your return, attach the Copy B as a PDF attachment if your software program allows this; otherwise you must attach Copy B of Form 1098-C to Form 8453 and mail the forms to the IRS. You also must attach Form 8283 if your total deduction for all property donations exceeds $500 *(14.15)*. Vehicles held primarily for sale, such as dealer inventory, are not subject to the acknowledgment rules or the deduction restrictions in the following paragraphs *(14.12)*.

If the charity sells the vehicle for more than $500 to a buyer other than a needy individual (see below) without having put it to a significant intervening use, or without materially improving it, your deduction is limited to the gross sales proceeds. You must be sent the Form 1098-C (or equivalent substitute) within 30 days of the sale. The charity must certify in Box 4a that the sale was made in an arm's-length transaction to an unrelated party. The amount of the gross proceeds (not reduced by expenses or fees) will be shown in Box 4c.

If the charity intends to significantly use the vehicle in furtherance of its regularly conducted activities or to materially improve it before selling it, Form 1098-C (or other acknowledgment) must be provided to you within 30 days of the donation. In Box 5a, the charity must certify its intent and in Box 5c it must certify a detailed description of the planned use or improvement, including the intended duration of such use or improvement. If Box 5a is checked, you may take a deduction equal to the fair market value of the vehicle on the date of contribution.

Fair market value is also deductible if the charity checks Box 5b to certify that the donated vehicle will be given to a needy individual, or sold to such to an individual for significantly less than fair market value, in furtherance of the organization's charitable purpose. You must be given Form 1098-C (or equivalent acknowledgment) with Box 5b checked within 30 days of the donation.

Copy B of Form 1098-C states that the deduction may not exceed the gross sales proceeds unless Box 5a or 5b is checked. If fair market value is deductible because Box 5a or 5b is checked, value may be based on an established used-vehicle-pricing guide, provided the amount is for a comparable model in similar condition and sold in the same area.

In Boxes 6a–6c of Form 1098-C, the charity indicates whether any goods or services were provided to the donor and, if so, they are described and a good faith estimate of their fair market value is shown. The deduction must be reduced by the value of the goods/services provided, with one exception. If the only benefits provided to the donor are intangible religious benefits (such as admission to a religious ceremony), Box 6c will be checked and the deduction does not have to be reduced by such benefits.

*If the claimed value of the vehicle is at least $250 but not over $500.* If the claimed value of a car, other motor vehicle, boat, or airplane (but not dealer property) is at least $250 but not over $500, the contribution is not acknowledged on Form 1098-C (or equivalent), but you must obtain a written acknowledgment meeting the general substantiation rules *(14.14)* by the due date for filing.

If the charity sells the donated vehicle (other than a sale to a needy person in furtherance of charitable purposes) without a significant intervening use or material improvement, and the gross sale proceeds are $500 or less, IRS guidelines allow a deduction to be claimed for fair market value if that exceeds the proceeds, but no more than $500 can be deducted. For example, if the gross sale proceeds are $400 but the donor can substantiate a fair market value of $450, a deduction of $450 would be allowed, provided a qualified acknowledgment *(14.14)* is obtained. If the donor could substantiate a fair market value exceeding $500, the deduction would be limited to $500.

## 14.8 Bargain Sales of Appreciated Property

A sale of appreciated property to a charity for less than fair market value allows you to claim a charitable deduction while receiving proceeds from the sale. However, the sale is divided into two parts—the sale and the gift—and you must pay a tax on the part of the gain attributed to the sale.

To compute gain on the sale, you allocate the adjusted basis of the property between the sale and the gift following these steps:

1. Divide the sales proceeds by the fair market value of the property. If the property is mortgaged, include the outstanding debt as sale proceeds; *see* the John Hill example in *14.6*.

2. Apply the Step 1 percentage to the adjusted basis of the property. This is the portion of basis allocated to the sale.

3. Deduct the resulting basis of Step 2 from the sales proceeds to find the gain.

You may deduct the excess of the fair market value over the sales proceeds if the property is capital gain property (gain is long-term capital gain) for which full market value would be deductible on a straight donation (no sale) under the rules in *14.6*. Thus, if the property is securities or real estate held long term or long-term tangible personal property related to the charity's exempt function, you may deduct the excess of the fair market value over the sale proceeds; *see* Example 1 below. However, if a deduction for the property (assuming no sale) would be reduced to cost basis as discussed in *14.6*, your charitable deduction on the bargain sale is also reduced; *see* Example 2 below. This reduction affects sales of capital assets held short term; ordinary income property; tangible personal property not related to the charity's exempt function; depreciable personal property subject to recapture; and sales of capital gain property to private non-operating foundations.

### EXAMPLES

1. Lana Briggs sells stock she held over a year to a university for $12,000 when the fair market value is $20,000. The $12,000 sales price equals Lana's adjusted basis in the stock. On the sale, she recouped her investment and donated the appreciation in value of $8,000 ($20,000 value – $12,000 basis), which she may deduct. At the same time, she realized taxable gain of $4,800 computed as follows: The percentage of basis applied to the sale is 60% ($12,000 sale proceeds ÷ $20,000 fair market value). Thus, 60% of the $12,000 basis, or $7,200, is allocated to the sale. Gain on the sale equals the $12,000 sale proceeds less the $7,200 allocated basis, or $4,800.

2. Joel Marx sells to his church stock that he held short term for his basis of $4,000. At the time of the sale, the stock is worth $10,000. Using Steps 1-3 above and the allocation method in Example 1, 40% ($4,000 sale proceeds ÷ $10,000 fair market value) of his $4,000 basis, or $1,600, is allocated to the sale. Thus, he has a short-term capital gain of $2,400 ($4,000 sale proceeds – $1,600 allocated basis). Furthermore, his deductible charitable contribution is also $2,400, equal to the 60% of basis allocated to the gift (60% of $4,000 = $2,400).

**Basis allocation applies even if a deduction is barred by the annual ceiling.** The basis allocation rules for determining gain on a bargain sale apply even if the annual deduction ceilings *(14.17)* bar a deduction in the year of the donation and in the five-year carryover period.

### EXAMPLE

The Hodgdons contributed real estate valued at $3.9 million but subject to mortgage debt of $2.6 million. The IRS treated the mortgage debt as sales proceeds and figured gain based on the difference between the debt and the portion of basis allocated to the sale element. The Hodgdons claimed that the basis allocation rule, which increased the amount of their gain, should not apply. Earlier in the year, they had made another donation that used up their charitable deduction ceiling for that year as well as for the following five-year carryover period. The Tax Court held that the basis allocation rule applied because a charitable deduction was "allowable," even if the contribution did not actually result in a deduction in the carryover period.

## 14.9 Art Objects

You may claim a charitable deduction for a painting or other art object donated to a charity. The amount of the deduction depends on (1) whether you are the artist; (2) if you are not the artist, how long you owned it; and (3) the type of organization receiving the gift.

*If you owned the art work short term,* your deduction is limited to cost, under the rules applying to donations of ordinary income property *(14.6)*.

*If you owned the art work long term (14.6), your deduction depends on the way the charity uses the property.* If the charity uses it for its exempt purposes, you may deduct the fair market value. However, if the charity's use is unrelated to its exempt purposes, your deduction is reduced by 100% of the appreciation. A donation of art work to a general fund-raising agency would be reduced because the agency would have no direct use for it. It would have to sell the art work and use the cash for its exempt purposes.

**Caution**

### Donations of Personal Creative Works

If you are the artist, your deduction is limited to cost regardless of how long you held the art work or to what use the charity puts it. In the case of a painting, the deduction would be the lower of the cost for canvas and paints and the fair market value.

**Filing Instruction**

### Appraisal Required

To claim a deduction of over $5,000 for any type of property, including art, you must have a written appraisal from a qualified appraiser and the donation must be described on Form 8283, which you file with your return *(14.15)*. If you claim a deduction for art of $20,000 or more you must attach to Form 8283 a copy of the signed appraisal.

Deductions of over $5,000 for art donations (as well as other types of appreciated tangible personal property) may be limited or recaptured if the charity disposes of the property within three years *(14.6)*.

---

### EXAMPLES

1. You give your college a painting that you have owned for many years. Its cost was $1,000 but it is now worth $10,000. The school displays the painting in its library for study by students. This use is related to the school's educational purposes. Your donation is deductible at fair market value. If, however, the school told you it was going to sell the painting and use the proceeds for general education purposes, its use would not be considered related. Your deduction would be reduced by the $9,000 appreciation to $1,000.

   If a deduction for fair market value is allowed, sale by the charity within three years of the donation will trigger a recapture of a deduction, unless the charity makes a qualifying certification *(14.6)*.

2. You donate to the Community Fund a collection of first edition books held for many years and worth $5,000. Your cost is $1,000. Since the charity is a general fund-raising organization, its use of your gift is not related. Your deduction would be $1,000 ($5,000 less $4,000).

3. You contribute to a charity antique furnishings you owned for years. The antiques cost you $500 and are now worth $5,000. The charity uses the furnishings in its office in the course of carrying on its functions. This is a related use. Your contribution deduction is $5,000.

---

**Appraisals.** Be prepared to support your deduction with detailed proof of cost, the date of acquisition, and how value was appraised. *See* the discussion of appraisal requirements later in this chapter *(14.15)*.

The IRS has its own art advisory panel to assess whether the fair market value claimed for donated art works is reasonable. The appraisal fee is not deductible for 2018 through 2025; *see* the Caution in *14.6*.

**Requesting advance valuation of art from the IRS.** To avoid a later dispute, you may ask the IRS for an advance valuation of art that you have had appraised at $50,000 or more. A request for an IRS Statement of Value (SOV) may be submitted for income tax, gift tax, or estate tax purposes. The IRS has the discretion to value items appraised at less than $50,000 if the SOV request includes at least one item appraised at $50,000 or more, and the IRS determines that the valuation is in the best interest of efficient tax administration.

A request for an SOV must be submitted to the IRS before filing the tax return reporting the donation. The request must include a copy of an appraisal for the item of art and a $6,500 fee, which pays for an SOV for up to three items of art. There is an additional charge of $300 for each item of art over three. It takes the IRS between six and 12 months to issue an SOV.

If the IRS agrees with the value reported on the appraisal, the IRS will issue an SOV approving the appraisal. If the IRS disagrees, the IRS will issue an SOV indicating its own valuation and stating the reasons it disagrees with the appraised amount. Regardless of whether you agree with the IRS appraisal, the SOV must be attached to and filed with the return reporting the donation. If you file the return before the SOV is issued, a copy of your request for the SOV must be attached to your return and on receipt of the SOV, an amended return must be filed with the SOV attached. For further SOV details, *see* IRS Publication 561 and Revenue Procedure 96-15, as well as the "Art Appraisal Services" page at IRS.gov.

**Donating a fractional interest in an art collection.** You may deduct the value of a donated partial interest in an art collection, such as where you give a museum the right to exhibit the works for a specific period during the year. The deduction is allowed even if the museum does not take possession of the art works, provided it has the right to take possession. However, if you made a fractional donation after August 17, 2006, and later donate an additional fractional interest in the same property, the deduction for the later contribution is based on the fair market value of the property at the time of the initial fractional contribution where that is less than the value at the time of the later contribution. Furthermore, if you do not transfer your entire remaining interest to the same charity within 10 years of the initial fractional donation, or, if earlier, the date of your death, your charitable contributions will have to be recaptured, plus interest, and a penalty equal to 10% of the recaptured amount will be imposed. See Publication 526 for further details.

**Keeping a reversionary interest.** The IRS may challenge a charitable deduction where you retain some control over the donated property. However, if the possibility of the property reverting back to you is considered to be remote, a deduction may be allowed. For example, a taxpayer who donated her art collection to a museum was allowed to claim a charitable deduction even though she retained the right to decide where and how the art would be displayed. The parties agreed that if there were disputes concerning the art displays, they would be settled by a mutually acceptable museum curator. If the museum breached a condition, it had a period of time to cure the violation. If the museum did not timely cure a violation, ownership of the art collection would revert back to the donor. The IRS allowed the deduction; the retained rights were fiduciary in nature and the possibility of the art reverting to the donor was so remote as to be negligible.

## 14.10 Interests in Real Estate

No deduction is allowed for the rental value of property you allow a charity to use free of charge. This is the case even if the property is used directly in furtherance of the organization's charitable purpose; *see* the Example below.

If you donate an undivided fractional part of your entire interest, a deduction will be allowed for the fair market value of the proportionate interest donated.

A donation of an option is not deductible until the year the option to buy the property is exercised.

> ### EXAMPLE
>
> To help a charity raise money, one owner allowed the charity to auction off a week's stay in his vacation home, and the highest bidder paid the charity a fair rental. The IRS ruled that not only was the owner's donation not deductible, but the one week stay by the bidder was considered personal use by the owner for purposes of figuring deductions for rental expenses. True, if the owner had directly rented the property to the bidder, the bidder's payment of a fair rental value would have been counted as a rental day and not a personal use day. However, the donation for charitable use is not a business rental, and the bidder's rental payment to the charity is not considered a payment to the owner.
>
> Furthermore, the bidder's use of the home pushed the owner over the personal-use ceiling, which in turn prevented him from deducting a rental loss. A rental loss may not be claimed if personal use of a home exceeds the greater of 14 days and 10% of the number of days the home is rented at fair rental value (9.7). Here, the owner personally used the home for 14 days and rented the home for 80 days. The rental expenses exceeded rental income. If the bidder's use of the home was not considered his personal use, the owner could have deducted the loss because his personal use did not exceed the 14-day limit (which was more than 10% of the 80 rental days). However, by adding the bidder's seven days of use to the owner's 14 days, the resulting 21 days of personal use exceeded the 14-day ceiling.

**Remainder interest in home or farm.** You may claim a charitable deduction for a gift of the remainder value of a residence or farm donated to a charity, even though you reserve the use of the property for yourself and your spouse for a term of years or life. Remainder gifts generally must be made in trust. However, where a residence or farm is donated, the remainder interest must be conveyed outright, not in trust. A remainder interest in a vacation home or in a "hobby" farm is also deductible. There is no requirement that the home be your principal residence or that the farm be profitable.

 *Law Alert*

**Recapture of Deductions for Certain Fractional Interests**

If a fractional interest in art or other tangible personal property *(14.6)* is donated after August 17, 2006, and the charity does not receive complete ownership of the item within 10 years of the initial contribution, or, if earlier, the death of the donor, all prior charitable deductions for the property will have to be recaptured, and interest charges plus a 10% penalty will be imposed.

 *Caution*

**Donating Vacation Home Use Not Advisable**

To raise funds, a charitable organization may ask contributors who own vacation homes to donate use of the property, which the charity then auctions off to the public. Be warned that if you offer your home in this way you will not only be denied a charitable deduction for your generosity, but you may jeopardize your deduction for rental expenses. A deduction is not allowed for giving a charity the free use of your property. *See* the Example on this page.

 *Caution*

**IRS Scrutiny of Easement Deductions**

The IRS has been challenging deductions claimed for conservation easements and has won court support in several court cases. If you are considering making such a donation, consult with an experienced tax practitioner to make sure you meet the stringent deduction requirements.

In Notice 2017-10, the IRS designated certain syndicated conservation easement promotions offered to investors in pass-through entities as tax-avoidance transactions. In these transactions, the promoters tell the investors that they can claim charitable deductions that are at least two-and-a-half times their investment. Because of the questionable nature of these promotions, the IRS is treating them as "listed transactions," which means that participating taxpayers must disclose them each year on Form 8886 *(48.6)*; *see* Notice 2017-10 for further details.

**Qualified conservation contributions.** A deduction may be claimed for the contribution of certain partial interests in real property to government agencies or publicly supported charities for exclusively conservational purposes. Qualified conservation contributions include: (1) your entire interest in real property other than retained rights to subsurface oil, gas, or other minerals; (2) a remainder interest; or (3) an easement, restrictive covenant, or similar property restriction granted in perpetuity. The contribution must be in perpetuity and further at least one of the following "conservation purposes"—preservation of land areas for the general public's outdoor recreation, education, or scenic enjoyment; preservation of historically important land areas or structures; or the protection of plant, fish, or wildlife habitats or similar natural ecosystems.

If an easement is donated and the property is subject to a mortgage, the mortgagee's interest must be subordinated to the charity's conservation easement at the time it was granted. In one case, the Tenth Circuit Court of Appeals agreed with the Tax Court and the IRS that a land conservancy's easement rights on mortgaged property were not protected in perpetuity when the prior owner's deed of trust was not subordinated to the easement at the time it was granted. A deduction was disallowed although the prior owner signed a subordination agreement two years after the donation. If the donors had defaulted on their promissory note between the time of the donation and the signing of the subordination agreement, the prior owner could have brought foreclosure proceedings and eliminated the conservation easement. The Appeals Court held that failure to meet the subordination requirement when the easement was granted could not be excused; the likelihood of a default by the donor was not so remote as to be negligible.

To meet the requirement that the conservation purpose of the easement be protected "in perpetuity", there must be legally enforceable restrictions that prevent you from using your retained interest in the property in a way contrary to the intended conservation purpose. The donee organization must be prohibited from transferring the contributed interest except to other organizations that will hold the property for exclusively conservational purposes.

The Fourth Circuit Court of Appeals agreed with the Tax Court and the IRS that the "in perpetuity" test was not met where a donation agreement allowed the donor to substitute other property to be subject to the easement. A deduction was denied even though the charity would have to agree to any substitution and the conservation purposes of the easement would have to be protected after the substitution. IRS regulations allow a change in the property subject to the easement only where continued use of the original property for conservation purposes becomes impossible or impractical.

If you retain an interest in subsurface oil, gas, or minerals, surface mining must generally be specifically prohibited. However, where the mineral rights and surface interests are separately owned, a deduction will be allowed if the probability of surface mining is so remote as to be considered negligible. The exception does not apply if you are related to the owner of the surface interest or if you received the mineral interest (directly or indirectly) from the surface owner.

The Tax Court has held that the written acknowledgment requirement for donations of $250 or more *(14.14)* can be met by the written agreement conveying a conservation easement, "taken as a whole." Thus, even where the easement agreement does not specifically state whether the donor received goods or services in exchange as required by the acknowledgment rule *(14.14)*, the overall terms of the agreement can indicate that no goods or services were received.

Contributions valued at over $5,000 must be supported by a written appraisal from a qualified appraiser *(14.15)*.

**Historic building façade easements.** A donation of a façade easement with respect to a certified historic structure in a registered historic district, other than one listed in the National Register, is allowed only if the easement preserves the entire exterior, including the space above as well as the front, rear, and sides of the building. The easement must bar exterior changes inconsistent with the historical character of the building. A written agreement between the donor and the donee must certify that the donee is a qualifying historic preservation organization with the resources and commitment to enforce the easement.

*Law Alert*

**Higher Deduction Limit for Conservation Contributions**

The deduction for qualified conservation contributions is allowed up to 50% of adjusted gross income, or up to 100% of adjusted gross income for a qualified farmer or rancher *(14.17)*.

The donor must attach to his or her tax return a qualified appraisal of the easement, photographs of the building exterior, and a description of all zoning laws and similar restrictions on development.

If a deduction of over $10,000 is claimed for a façade easement, a $500 fee must be paid or no deduction will be allowed. The fee may be paid electronically or sent to the IRS with Form 8283-V. The $500 fee may be claimed as a miscellaneous itemized deduction, subject to the 2% of adjusted gross income floor *(19.16)*

Reduction for prior rehabilitation credit. The deduction for a historic building easement must be reduced if a rehabilitation tax credit *(31.8)* was claimed for the building in the five years preceding the donation.

## 14.11 Life Insurance

You may deduct the value of a life insurance policy if the charity is irrevocably named as beneficiary and you make both a legal assignment and a complete delivery of the policy. A deduction may be disallowed where you reserve the right to change the beneficiary.

The amount of your deduction generally depends on the type of policy donated. Your insurance company can furnish you with the information necessary to calculate your deduction. In addition, you may deduct premiums you pay after you assign the policy.

**Deducting premium payments on donated policy.** If you assign a life insurance policy to a charity and continue to pay the premiums, you generally may deduct your premium payments as a charitable contribution. However, in states where charities do not have an "insurable interest" in the donor's life, the IRS may challenge income tax and gift tax deductions for the premium payments. The IRS took this position in a private ruling interpreting New York law. In response, New York amended its insurance code to allow individuals to buy a life insurance policy and immediately transfer it to a charity. The IRS then revoked the earlier ruling but it did not announce a change in its position. Thus, the IRS may challenge premium deductions of donors in other states where a charity's insurable interest is not clearly provided by state law.

## 14.12 Business Inventory

Self-employed business owners generally may not deduct more than cost for donations of inventory. If a charitable deduction is claimed, costs incurred in a year prior to the year of donation must be removed from opening inventory and excluded from the cost of goods sold when figuring business gross profit for the year of the contribution.

No contribution deduction is allowed for a gift of merchandise that was produced or acquired in the year donated. Instead, the cost is added to the cost of goods sold to figure gross profit for the year of the contribution. Business deductions are not subject to the percentage limitation applied to donations.

## 14.13 Donations Through Trusts

Outright gifts are not the only way to make deductible gifts to charities. You may transfer property to a charitable lead trust or a charitable remainder trust to provide funds for charity.

A charitable lead trust involves your transfer of property to a trust directed to pay income to a charity you name, for the term of the trust, and then to return the property to you or to someone else. A charitable remainder trust is one that provides income for you or another beneficiary for life, after which the property passes to a charity.

Trust arrangements require the services of an experienced attorney who will draft the trust in appropriate form and advise you of the tax consequences.

**Deductions for gifts of income interests in trust.** Current law is designed to prevent a donor from claiming an immediate deduction for the present value of trust income payable to a charity for a term of years. In limited situations, you may claim a deduction if either: (1) You give away all of your interests in the property to qualifying *(14.1)* organizations. For example, you put your property in trust, giving an income interest for 20 years to a

 *Caution*

**Split-Dollar Insurance Arrangements**

No deduction is allowed for giving a charitable organization money with the understanding that it will be used to pay premiums on life insurance, annuities, or endowment contracts for your benefit or that of a beneficiary designated by you.

*Planning Reminder*

**Life Income Plans**

A charitable organization may offer a life income plan (pooled income fund) to which you transfer property or money in return for a guaranteed income for life. After your death, the charity has full control over the property. If you enter such a plan, ask the organization for the amount of the deduction that you may claim for the value of your gift.

church and the remainder to a college. A deduction is allowed for the value of the property. Or (2) you create a unitrust or annuity trust, and are taxed on the income. A unitrust for this purpose provides that a fixed percentage of trust assets is payable to the charitable income beneficiary each year. An annuity trust provides for payment of a guaranteed dollar amount to the charitable income beneficiary each year. A deduction is allowed for the present value of the unitrust or annuity trust interest.

Because income remains taxable to the grantor, alternative (2) will probably not be chosen, unless the income of the trust is from tax-exempt securities. If such a trust is created, a tax may be due if the donor dies before the trust ends or is no longer the taxable owner of trust income. The law provides for recapture of part of the tax deduction, even where the income was tax exempt.

**Charitable remainder trusts.** A charitable deduction is allowable for transfers of property to charitable remainder trusts only if the trust meets these requirements: The income payable for a noncharitable income beneficiary's life or a term of up to 20 years must be guaranteed under a unitrust or annuity trust. If a donor gives all of his or her interests in the property to the charities, the annuity or unitrust requirements need not be satisfied. IRS tables determine the value of the allowable charitable deduction for a gift in trust.

## 14.14 Records Needed To Substantiate Your Contributions

The type of records you must keep to substantiate your donations generally depends on their amount and whether you are contributing cash or property.

**Cash contributions.** A deduction is not allowed for a cash contribution, regardless of amount, unless you have a receipt or bank record to substantiate it. This includes donations made by check, credit card, electronic fund transfer, or gift card redeemable for cash. You need an e-mail or other written receipt, a canceled check, bank copy of both sides of a canceled check, electronic fund transfer receipt, monthly account statement, or credit card statement that shows the name of the organization and the date and amount of the contribution. Maintaining a diary or log is not sufficient substantiation. If you volunteer your services to a charity, you need similar records to substantiate a deduction for your out-of-pocket expenses of under $250 *(14.4)*.

For a contribution of $250 or more, a canceled check, e-mail, or receipt showing the name of the organization and the date and amount of your contribution is not enough. You must timely obtain a written acknowledgment from the charity, as described below.

For a contribution made by payroll deduction, you need to keep a pay stub, Form W-2, or other employer-furnished document showing the amount withheld as a donation, along with a pledge card or similar document from the charity. If the amount withheld from a single paycheck is $250 or more, the pledge card must include a statement to the effect that no goods or services were provided in return for the contribution.

**Noncash contributions under $250.** As proof of your donation, you need a dated receipt from the organization that provides a reasonably detailed description of the property. However, if it is impractical to obtain a receipt, as where you deposit canned food at a charity's drop site, you can satisfy the recordkeeping requirement with a contemporaneous notation that documents the contribution.

**You need a written acknowledgment from the charity for cash or noncash contributions of $250 or more.** A written acknowledgment is mandatory to prove cash or noncash contributions of $250 or more; *see* below for content details. The acknowledgment requirement does not apply if the donation is less than $250, but if the contribution exceeds $75, you must be given a disclosure statement (see below) from the charity estimating the value of any benefits you received in return for the donation.

The IRS exempts from the acknowledgment requirement grantors of a charitable lead trust, charitable remainder annuity trust, or charitable remainder unitrust. Since a specific charity does not have to be designated as beneficiary at the time the trust transfer is made, there may be no organization available to provide an acknowledgment.

A separate acknowledgment rule applies if you are deducting over $500 for a motor vehicle, boat, or airplane. You must attach Copy B of Form 1098-C to your return *(14.7)*.

**Content of acknowledgment.** An acknowledgment for a donation of $250 or more may be a letter, e-mail, computer-generated form, or postcard. If you gave cash, the amount of the donation must be shown. If you gave property, the property must be described in the acknowledgment, but the charity does not have to value it. If the acknowledgment does not show the date of the contribution, you need a dated bank record or receipt.

The acknowledgment must state whether or not you have received any goods or services from the charity in exchange for the contribution. If you have, the receipt must include a statement describing such benefits and estimating their value. However, "token" items and certain membership benefits, as described in *14.3*, do not have to be described or valued. There is also an exception if the contribution is to a religious organization and the only benefits received are "intangible" religious benefits, such as admission to religious ceremonies; these do not have to be described or valued, but the statement must indicate that they are the sole benefits provided.

**Deadline for 2018 donation acknowledgments.** For a 2018 contribution, the deadline for obtaining an acknowledgment is the date you file your 2018 return, but no later than the filing due date of April 15, 2019 or, if you obtain a filing extension, the extended due date. Keep the acknowledgment with your records; it does not have to be attached to your return.

**Payments throughout the year.** For purposes of the $250 threshold for an acknowledgment, each contribution made during the year is separately considered. Thus, for small donations (each under $250) made during the year, you do not have to obtain an acknowledgment even if they total $250 or more.

If contributions are made by payroll deductions from your wages, the amount withheld from each paycheck is treated separately. An acknowledgment is not required unless withholding on a single paycheck is at least $250. A pay stub or Form W-2 from the employer indicating the amount of a single withholding over $249 is considered a valid "acknowledgment"; a pledge card or other document from the charity must state that you have not received benefits in exchange for the payroll deduction contribution.

**A charity must provide a disclosure statement if you contribute more than $75 and receive benefits.** If you contribute more than $75 but less than $250 to a charity, the charity is required to give you a "disclosure" statement that estimates the value of any benefits you received, such as concert tickets or books. The statement must instruct you to deduct only the excess of your contribution over the value of the benefits. Certain "token" items and membership benefits, and "intangible" religious benefits, can be disregarded; *see Table 14-1*. If a required disclosure statement is not provided when contributions are solicited, it must be provided when you make a contribution exceeding $75.

**Noncash contributions.** For donations of property, the amount of the deduction claimed determines the records you must keep. For a noncash contribution of under $250, you need as proof of your donation a dated receipt from the organization that provides a reasonably detailed description of the property. However, if it is impractical to obtain a receipt, as where you deposit canned food at a charity's drop site, you can satisfy the recordkeeping requirement with a contemporaneous notation that documents the contribution.

For a noncash contribution of $250 or more, you must obtain a written acknowledgment from the charity as described above. The acknowledgment must indicate if you received benefits in exchange for your contribution; *see* the above discussion for acknowledgment details.

To claim a deduction for more than $500 but no more than $5,000, you need, in addition to the written acknowledgment, records that show when and how you got the property (purchase, gift, inheritance), your cost or other basis for the property, and the fair market value; you must report this information on Form 8283 *(14.15)*.

For a deduction over $5,000, you need the written acknowledgment and in most cases you also need an appraisal from a qualified appraiser. You must summarize the appraisal on Form 8283 but generally do not have to attach it to your return. *see 14.15*.

## 14.15 Form 8283 and Written Appraisal Requirements for Property Donations

You must attach Form 8283 to your Form 1040 for 2017 if you claim a total deduction of over $500 for all of your donations of property. The IRS may disallow your deduction if you fail to attach Form 8283. In Part I of Form 8283, you must identify the charity, describe the donated property, provide the value of the property on the date of the donation and indicate how you valued it (such as by appraisal, catalog for a collectible, or thrift shop value for clothing or household furniture). For each item valued at over $500, you also have to indicate how and when you acquired the property, and your cost or other basis.

If you are claiming a deduction exceeding $5,000 for an item, or for a group of similar items (such as paintings, buildings, coins, stamps, or books), you generally need a written appraisal from a qualified appraiser. The appraiser must sign a declaration in Part III of Section B of Form 8283 that he or she is unrelated to you and meets the other requirements for qualified appraisers. The appraisal must be made no earlier than 60 days before your donation, and you must receive it by the due date (including extensions) of the return on which you claim the deduction.

Failure to obtain a qualified appraisal can cost you a deduction even if the value you claim for the property on Form 8283 is a fair value. In one case, the Tax Court sided with the IRS in completely disallowing deductions for property worth about $18.5 million because the donor (a real estate broker and certified real estate appraiser) appraised the properties himself. The Tax Court, although sympathetic to the donor, held that even though the contributions were not overvalued on Form 8283, and may well have been undervalued, the deductions had to be completely disallowed because a timely appraisal from an independent qualified appraiser had not been obtained.

You do not need an appraisal for a car, boat, or airplane if your deduction is limited to the gross proceeds from its sale *(14.17)*, or for publicly traded securities, non-publicly-traded securities of $10,000 or less, intellectual property *(14.6)*, or business inventory.

Whether or not a written appraisal is required for property valued at over $5,000, you must describe the property, value it, and provide your cost and other acquisition details on Form 8283 in Section B, Part 1.

The appraisal itself should be kept with your records and does not have to be attached to your return except in two situations: If you are claiming a deduction of $20,000 or more for art, you must attach a complete copy of the appraisal to Form 8283 and you may be asked by the IRS to submit a color photograph (8" × 10") or a slide (4" × 5") of the art. If the claimed deduction exceeds $500,000, the qualified appraisal must be attached to your return (assuming no exception to the appraisal requirement). See the Form 8283 instructions for further details on the appraisal requirements.

**Donee acknowledgment.** For property donations exceeding $5,000, the donee organization must acknowledge the receipt of the property in Section B, Part IV of Form 8283. If the organization sells or otherwise disposes of the property within three years of the donation, it must file Form 8282 with the IRS and give you a copy.

**Penalty for overvaluation.** You may be penalized for a substantial overvaluation of donated property *(14.16)*.

**Appraisal fees.** A fee paid to an appraiser is not considered a charitable deduction, and no other itemized deduction is allowed for 2018 or later years *(14.6, 14.9)*.

## 14.16 Penalty for Substantial Overvaluation of Property

If the IRS disallows a portion of your claimed deduction for appreciated property on the grounds that you have overvalued it, you may be subject to a penalty as well as additional tax. Depending on the extent of the overvaluation, a 20% or 40% penalty may apply. No penalty is imposed unless the overvaluation results in a tax underpayment exceeding $5,000.

**20% penalty.** If the claimed value of donated property is 150% or more of the correct value, the penalty is 20% of the tax underpayment resulting from the overvaluation, provided the underpayment exceeds $5,000.

**Caution**

**Charity Reports Transfer Within Three Years**

If you reported a property donation exceeding $5,000 on Form 8283 and the charity sells or otherwise disposes of the property within three years after your gift, it must notify the IRS on Form 8282 and send you a copy. The sale might trigger the recapture of a deduction claimed for a contribution of tangible personal property exceeding $5,000 *(14.6)*. Reporting on Form 8282 is not required by the charity for a particular item if in Part II, Section B, of Form 8283 you indicated that the appraised value of that item was not more than $500. Similar items such as a collection of books by the same author, stereo components, or place settings of silverware may be treated as one item. Reporting is also not required on Form 8282 for donated property that the organization uses or distributes without consideration, if this use furthers the organization's tax-exempt function or purpose.

### Table 14-1 What You Need To Substantiate Your Donations

| For each individual contribution of— | You need— |
| --- | --- |
| Cash | Regardless of amount, you need a canceled check, bank copy of a canceled check, account statement, electronic fund transfer receipt, credit card statement, e-mail, or written receipt from the charity showing the name of the organization and the date and amount of the contribution.<br>In addition, for a donation of $250 or more, you need a written acknowledgment as described below. |
| Less than $250 | For a cash donation, you need a bank record, e-mail, or receipt as described above. For a noncash donation, you need a receipt from the charity unless it is impractical to obtain one, as when you have deposited canned food in an organization's drop site. The receipt must show the name of the organization and the date and amount of the contribution and provide a reasonably detailed description of the property, which for securities includes their type and whether they are publicly traded.<br>In addition, if you contributed over $75 and received benefits, the charity is required to give you a "disclosure" statement that estimates the value of any benefits you received, such as concert tickets or books. The statement will tell you to deduct only the excess of your contribution over the value of the benefits. If a required disclosure statement is not provided when contributions are solicited, it must be provided when you make a contribution exceeding $75.<br>The disclosure statement is not required if the only benefits you receive are "token items" or membership benefits that can be disregarded *(14.3)*. Nor is it required where you contribute to a religious organization and the only benefits you receive are "intangible religious benefits." An example of an intangible religious benefit would be admission to religious ceremonies. A Congressional committee report also suggests that tuition for wholly religious education that does not lead to a recognized degree would qualify. |
| $250 or more | You need a written acknowledgment for all donations of $250 or more. For each cash donation of $250 or more, you need a written acknowledgment from the charity that indicates whether you were given any goods or services in exchange for your contribution *(14.14)*. You may not rely on a canceled check, a receipt (including e-mail) or credit card statement to document a cash contribution of $250 or more. A written acknowledgment is also required for a donation of property if you are claiming a deduction of $250 or more, but the charity does not have to value the property, just describe it. If you received any goods or services from the charity in exchange for the contribution, the acknowledgment must estimate their value unless you receive only "token" items or "intangible religious benefits" as discussed in the preceding paragraph. The deadline for obtaining acknowledgments is the date you file your return. If you file after the filing due date or extended due date, get the acknowledgment by the due date or extended due date. Keep the acknowledgment from the charity with your tax records; do not attach it to your tax return.<br>If your total deduction for all property donations exceeds $500, you must report each of the contributions on Form 8283 (not just those valued over $500). If you are not allowed to deduct fair market value for a property donation under the rules at *14.6*, you must attach a statement to Form 8283 explaining the reduction for the appreciation.<br>For each deduction of property for which you are claiming a value over $5,000, you need a written appraisal from a qualified appraise r*(14.15)*. |
| More than $500 in the case of a donated car, other motor vehicle, boat, or airplane | Special acknowledgment rules apply where the claimed value of the vehicle exceeds $500 *(14.7)*. |

**40% penalty.** If the claimed value of donated property is 200% or more of the correct value, the penalty is 40% of the tax underpayment resulting from the overvaluation, provided the underpayment exceeds $5,000.

**Reasonable cause exception for relying on appraisal.** The 20% penalty (but not the 40%) may be avoided under a reasonable cause exception if you relied on a qualified appraisal prepared by a qualified appraiser and, in addition, you made a good faith investigation of the value of the property.

## 14.17 Ceiling on Charitable Contributions

Unless you make donations that are very substantial in relation to your adjusted gross income (Line 7, Form 1040), you do not have to be concerned with the deduction ceilings discussed in this section. For cash contributions to churches, colleges, and other 50% limit organizations (see the list below), the deduction ceiling is 60% of adjusted gross income, but a 30% limit applies to cash contributions to organizations that are not 50% limit organizations, such as veterans' organizations (see below).

For property donations, the deduction limit is generally 30% of adjusted gross income, although it sometimes is 50% or even 20%. As discussed below, the specific limit depends on whether it the property donation is made to a "50% limit organization," whether it is capital gain property, and whether the special 50% or 100% limit for qualified conservation contributions applies.

Where you have made contributions subject to different ceilings, the ceilings are applied in a specific order, and the amount deductible under a particular ceiling may be reduced by contributions subject to other ceilings; see IRS Publication 526 for details.

If your deduction is limited by any of the ceilings, a five-year carryover is allowed for the excess, but the carryover period is extended to 15 years for qualified conservation contributions *(14.18)*.

**Volunteer expenses.** The deduction ceiling for unreimbursed expenses you incur doing volunteer work for a charity *(14.4)* is 50% of adjusted gross income if your services were for a 50% limit organization such as a church or college (see the list below), or 30% of adjusted gross income if the services were on behalf of an organization other than a 50% limit organization.

**30% or 20% limit for contributions for the use of an organization.** If a donation is treated as for the use of, rather than directly to, any organization, it is deductible under a 30% or 20% of adjusted gross income ceiling. A contribution is "for the use of" an organization if it is held in a legally enforceable trust or similar arrangement. Such contributions include a deductible charitable unitrust or annuity trust income interest, as well as a charitable remainder trust transfer if the trust provides that after the death of the income beneficiary, the property is to be held in the trust for the benefit of the charity, rather than distributed to the charity *(14.13)*.

The 20% ceiling applies to contributions of capital gain property (capital assets held over one year) that are for the use of any organization, including 50% limit organizations.

The 30% ceiling applies to contributions of non-capital gain property, such as cash, ordinary income property, and capital assets held short term, that are for the use of any organization, including 50% limit organizations.

Deductible expenses for supporting a student in your home *(14.5)* are considered to be for the use of a charitable organization and thus subject to the 30% ceiling.

### Contributions to 50% Limit Organizations

Organizations in the 50% limit category include churches, schools, publicly supported charities, and certain private foundations; *see* the list below. In addition, the United States, any state or political subdivision of a state, the District of Columbia, Puerto Rico, a U.S. possession or political subdivision of a U.S. possession, or an Indian tribal government or any of its subdivisions is treated as a 50% limit organization.

 *Law Alert*

**Deduction Limit on Cash Contributions to 50% Limit Organizations Increased to 60% of AGI**

For cash contributions made in 2018 and later years to churches, colleges, publicly supported charities, or other 50% limit organizations (*see* the list in *14.17*), the Tax Cuts and Jobs Act increases the deductible limit to 60% of adjusted gross income. For 2017 and prior years, a 50% of adjusted gross income limit applied to such cash contributions. If you make other contributions in addition to cash contributions eligible for the 60% limit, *see* IRS Publication 526 for how to apply the various adjusted gross income ceilings.

The following charitable organizations are 50% limit organizations:

- Churches, synagogues, mosques, and other religious organizations.
- Schools, colleges, and other educational organizations that normally have regular faculties and student bodies in attendance on site.
- Hospitals and medical research organizations associated with hospitals.
- Government-supported or publicly supported foundations for state and municipal universities and colleges.
- Religious, charitable, educational, scientific, or literary organizations that receive a substantial part of their financial support from the general public or a government unit. Libraries, museums, drama, opera, ballet and orchestral societies, community funds, the American Red Cross, the Heart Fund, and the United Way are in this category. Also included are organizations to prevent cruelty to children or animals, or to foster amateur sports (provided they do not provide athletic facilities or equipment).
- Private operating foundations.
- Private non-operating foundations that distribute their contributions annually to qualified charities within 2½ months after the end of their taxable year.
- Private non-operating foundations that pool donations and allow donors to designate the charities to receive their gifts, if the foundation pays out all income within 2½ months after the end of the tax year.
- Organizations that normally receive more than one-third of their support from the general public or governmental units.

**60% ceiling.** Cash contributions to 50% limit organizations are deductible up to 60% of adjusted gross income under the Tax Cuts and Jobs Act; *see* the Law Alert at the beginning of this section.

**50% ceiling.** Contributions to 50% limit organizations of ordinary income property (such as inventory or a work of art you created), including capital assets held short term, are deductible up to 50% of adjusted gross income. If you make contributions subject to this 50% ceiling and in the same year you make cash contributions subject to the above 60% ceiling, *see* IRS Publication 526 for how the ceilings interact.

**30% ceiling for capital gain property held long term.** If you donate property to a 50% limit organization and you would have realized long-term capital gain had you sold it at fair market value, the deduction ceiling is generally 30% of adjusted gross income.

The 30% ceiling applies where the fair market value of the property is deductible under the rules discussed in *14.6*. This includes donations of appreciated securities and real estate held long term. It also includes donations of appreciated tangible personal property (such as furniture or art) held long term where the organization's use of your gift is directly related to its tax-exempt charitable purposes.

However, you may elect to apply the 50% ceiling instead of the 30% ceiling to such property donations if you reduce the fair market value of the property by the appreciation *(14.19)*.

If you donate tangible personal property held long term that is not used by the organization for its tax-exempt charitable purposes, so that your deduction must be reduced for the appreciation *(14.6)*, the reduced amount is deductible under the 50% ceiling, not the 30% ceiling.

In addition, the 30% ceiling does not apply to qualified conservation contributions; *see* below.

Note: If you make contributions subject to the 30% ceiling for long-term capital gain property and in the same year you make contributions subject to the 60% or 50% ceilings (*see* above), *see* IRS Publication 526 for how to apply the different ceilings.

## Contributions to Non–50% Limit Organizations

If a contribution is made to a qualifying organization that is not in the above list of 50% limit organizations, a deduction ceiling of 30% or 20% of adjusted gross income applies. Organizations in this category include veterans' organizations, fraternal societies,

**Appreciated Securities and Real Estate**

When you contribute appreciated securities or real estate that you have held for more than a year to a church, college, or other organization treated as a 50% limit organization, your deduction for the property donation is limited to 30% of your adjusted gross income unless you elect to reduce the fair market value of the property by the appreciation. This election lets you elect the 50% ceiling *(14.19)*.

**Advance Valuation of Art From IRS**

To protect against the possibility of a valuation dispute that could lead to a penalty where you are claiming a deduction of at least $50,000 for a work of art, you may request a valuation from the IRS prior to the time you file. *See* the guidelines for obtaining the IRS valuation *(14.9)*.

*Filing Instruction*

**Carryover for Excess Contributions**

If you contribute cash and property in the same year, your deductions may be subject to different limits, such as 60% of adjusted gross income for the cash and 30% for the property *(14.17)*. See IRS Publication 526 for applying the ceilings.

If your donation exceeds the limits, you may carry over the excess for five years. A 15-year-carryover period applies for qualified conservation contributions *(14.18)*.

nonprofit cemeteries and private non-operating foundations that do not meet the payout requirements for 50% limit organizations.

The 30% limit applies to contributions of cash, ordinary income property, and capital gain property held short term. The 20% limit applies to contributions of capital gain property held long term (more than one year). However, the actual ceiling may be less than 30% or 20% of adjusted gross income where in the same year you have made contributions to 50% limit organizations. In that case, *see* IRS Publication 526 for the rules on applying the deduction ceilings.

## Qualified Conservation Contributions

The deduction limit for a qualified conservation contribution *(14.10)* is 50% of your adjusted gross income reduced by the deduction for other donations. The 50% ceiling applies instead of the usual 30% or 20% limit for capital gain property. For a qualified farmer or rancher the limit is 100% rather than 50% of adjusted gross income. The 100% limit applies if over 50% of gross income is from farming or ranching. The special 50% and 100% limits for qualified conservation contributions are applied after other contributions are taken into account; *see* IRS Publication 526.

## 14.18 Carryover for Excess Donations

If you make donations that are not deductible because they exceed the 60%, 50%, 30%, or 20% of adjusted gross income ceilings *(14.17)*, you may carry the excess over the next five years. A 15-year carryforward applies for donations of qualified conservation contributions subject to the special 50% and 100% of adjusted gross income ceilings *(14.17)*.

In each carryover year, the original percentage ceiling applies. For example, where contributions of appreciated long-term intangible personal property or real estate (or tangible personal property put to a related use by the charity) exceed the 30% ceiling for capital gain property *(14.17)*, the excess remains subject to the 30% ceiling in the carryover years.

Where you have both current year contributions and carried-over deductions from a prior year, you must first figure your deduction for contributions in the current year under the applicable ceilings before taking into account the carried-over contributions. See IRS Publication 526 for the rules on applying the various deduction ceilings in the carryover year.

## 14.19 Election To Reduce Fair Market Value by Appreciation

Although the 30% ceiling generally applies to long-term intangible property (such as securities) and real estate contributed to 50% limit organizations *(14.17)*, you may elect the 50% ceiling, provided you reduce the fair market value of the property by 100% of the appreciation on all such donations during the year. The reduction also applies to donations of tangible personal property related in use to the organization's charitable function. In most cases, this election should be made only where the amount of appreciation is negligible. Where there is substantial appreciation, the increase in the deduction may not make up or exceed the required 100% reduction, which allows you to claim a deduction only for your cost basis in the property. If the election is made in a year in which there are carryovers of capital gain property subject to the 30% ceiling, the carryovers are subject to reduction; *see* IRS Publication 526.

The election of the 50% ceiling is made by attaching a statement to your original return or amended return filed by the original due date. Even where no formal electing statement is made, claiming a deduction without the appreciation in order to come within the 50% ceiling is treated as an election. A formal or "informal" election is not revocable unless a material mistake is shown. A revocation based on a reconsideration of tax consequences is not considered sufficient grounds.

# CHAPTER 15

# Itemized Deduction for Interest Expenses

On Schedule A of Form 1040, you may deduct three types of interest charges:

- Interest on qualifying home acquisition loans *(15.2)* and home equity loans that qualify as home acquisition loans *(15.3)*
- Points *(15.7)*
- Investment interest, but only up to the amount of net investment income *(15.9)*.

Premiums paid in 2018 for qualified mortgage insurance on a principal or second residence will be deductible as interest only if Congress extends the law authorizing the deduction *(15.5)*.

Interest on personal loans (such as loans to buy autos and other personal items and credit card finance charges) is not deductible with the exception of qualifying student loan interest; *see Chapter 33*.

Interest on loans for business purposes is fully deductible on Schedule C. Interest on loans related to rental property is fully deductible from rental income on Schedule E. Whether interest is a business, investment, or a personal expense generally depends upon the use made of the money borrowed, not on the kind of property used to secure the loan. However, interest on a loan secured by a first or second home may be deductible as home equity mortgage interest regardless of the way you use the loan.

Interest on a loan used to finance an investment in a passive activity is subject to the limitations discussed in *Chapter 10*. However, if you rent out a second home that qualifies as a second residence, the portion of mortgage interest allocable to rental use is deductible as qualified mortgage interest and is not treated as a passive activity expense.

## 15.1 Deduction for Home Mortgage Interest

If you itemize deductions, you generally may deduct on Schedule A (Form 1040) interest on home acquisition debt that is secured by a first or second home (see two-residence limit, below). This includes interest on home equity debt that also qualifies as home acquisition debt. However, there are limits on the amount of acquisition debt that can support an interest deduction. Home acquisition debt is debt used to buy, construct, or substantially improve the residence that secures the loan *(15.2)*.

For 2018 and later tax years, the Tax Cuts and Jobs Act made two changes to the mortgage interest deduction rules: (1) the limit on home acquisition debt is lowered except for debt that is "grandfathered," and (2) no deduction is allowed for interest on home equity debt that does not otherwise qualify as acquisition debt.

The new law lowers the limit on acquisition debt from $1 million ($500,000 if married filing separately), to $750,000 ($375,000 if married filing separately). The reduced limit applies to acquisition debt incurred after December 15, 2017. Acquisition debt incurred on or before December 15, 2017, is "grandfathered," so the prior law limit of $1 million ($500,000 if married filing separately) still applies to these loans for purposes of deducting interest on your returns for 2018 and later years.

If you refinance grandfathered debt (debt obtained before 12/16/17), the refinanced debt remains grandfathered to the extent of the loan balance at the time of refinancing; *see 15.2*.

Examples showing how to apply the grandfather rules and the new $750,000 ($375,000) limit for non-grandfathered acquisition debt are in *15.2*.

Although the Tax Cuts and Jobs Act generally prohibits a deduction for interest on a home equity loan for years after 2017, this does not mean that interest on a home equity loan or home equity line of credit is never deductible. As discussed in *15.3*, if a home equity loan is used to buy, construct, or substantially improve a first or second residence that the loan is secured by, the loan falls within the definition of home acquisition debt, so if the applicable limit on acquisition debt has not been reached, the interest on the home equity loan falling within the limit can still be deducted. The Examples in *15.3* illustrate how the new law rules for home equity debt work, including how the grandfather rules apply to some home equity loans but not others.

**Acquisition loan must be secured by residence.** To deduct interest on a home acquisition debt *(15.2)* or a home equity loan that qualifies as home acquisition debt *(15.3)*, the loan must be secured by your main home or a second home, and the home that secures the loan must be the home that you use the loan to buy, construct, or substantially improve. For the loan to be "secured," it must be recorded or satisfy similar requirements under state law. For example, if a relative gives you a loan to help you purchase a home, the relative must take the legal steps required to record the loan with local authorities; otherwise, you may not deduct interest that you pay on the loan. The IRS held in a private ruling that interest paid by a homeowners' association on a loan to rebuild the common area is not deductible by the individual homeowners where their residences are not pledged as collateral.

**Two-residence limit for qualifying mortgage debt.** The rules for deducting interest on qualifying home acquisition debt or home equity debt apply to loans secured by your principal residence and one other residence. A residence may be a condominium or cooperative unit, houseboat, mobile home, or house trailer that has sleeping, cooking, and toilet facilities. If you own more than two houses, you decide which residence will be considered your second residence. You do not have to live in the second residence to designate it as a qualifying home. However, a home that you rent out during the year may be designated as a second residence only if your personal use exceeds the greater of 14 days or 10% of the rental days. In counting rental days, include days that the home is held out for rental or listed for resale. In counting days of personal use, use by close relatives generally qualifies as your personal use *(9.6)*.

A married couple filing jointly may designate as a second residence a home owned by either spouse.

**Law Alert**

**Limit on Home Acquisition Debt Obtained After December 15, 2017**

Under the Tax Cuts and Jobs Act, the maximum amount of home acquisition debt on which mortgage interest may be deducted for 2018 and later years is $750,000 ($375,000 if married filing separately). This limit applies only to loans obtained after December 15, 2017. For loans obtained on or before December 15, 2017, the prior-law limit of $1 million ($500,000 if married filing separately) continues to apply.

**Caution**

**Mortgage Interest Reported on Form 1098**

Banks and other lending institutions report mortgage interest payments of $600 or more to the IRS on Form 1098 or a similar statement. You should receive a copy of Form 1098 (or similar statement) for 2018 by January 31, 2019. The lender will report in Box 1 of Form 1098 the mortgage interest it received from you in 2018. Deductible points *(15.7)* paid on the purchase of a principal home are included in Box 2 of Form 1098. Mortgage insurance premiums *(15.5)* of $600 or more may be shown in Box 5 of Form 1098.

If a married couple files separately, each spouse may generally deduct interest on debt secured by one residence. However, both spouses may agree in writing to allow one of them to deduct the interest on a principal residence plus a designated second residence.

Interest on debt secured by a residence other than your principal or second home may still be deductible, but only if you use the proceeds for investment or business purposes *(15.11)*.

**Mortgage interest paid on your principal residence with assistance from Hardest Hit Fund.** An IRS safe harbor (Notice 2018-63, amplifying Notice 2017-40) allows you to claim a deduction for mortgage interest and for real estate taxes *(16.4)* even though tax-free assistance has been received from a State Housing Finance Agency (State HFA) using funds from the Treasury Department's HFA Hardest Hit Fund. For 2018 through 2021 (at the end of which the safe harbor is scheduled to expire), Notice 2018-63 allows homeowners to first allocate home mortgage payments made during the year to mortgage interest, and then use any reasonable method to allocate the balance of payments to real property taxes, mortgage insurance premiums, home insurance premiums, and mortgage principal.

**Interest on mortgage credit certificates.** Under special state and local programs, you may be able to obtain a "mortgage credit certificate" to finance the purchase of a principal residence or to borrow funds for certain home improvements. A tax credit for interest paid on the mortgage may be claimed. The credit is computed on Form 8396 and claimed on Schedule 3 of Form 1040 ("Nonrefundable credits"). The credit equals the interest paid multiplied by the certificate rate set by the governmental authority, but the maximum annual credit is $2,000. If you claim the credit, your home mortgage interest deduction is reduced by the amount of the current year credit claimed on Form 8396. If you buy a home using a qualifying mortgage credit certificate and sell that home within nine years, you may have to recapture part of the tax credit on Form 8828.

*Planning Reminder*

**Mortgage Interest on a Third Home**

Interest on debt secured by a residence other than your principal or second home is not deductible as home mortgage interest, but an interest deduction may still be allowed if you use the proceeds for investment or business purposes *(15.11)*.

> **EXAMPLE**
>
> You pay $5,000 interest for a mortgage issued under a qualifying mortgage credit certificate. Under its terms, you are allowed a tax credit of $750. You may claim the balance of your mortgage interest, or $4,250 ($5,000 – $750), as home mortgage interest if you itemize deductions. If the allowable credit exceeds tax liability, a three-year carryover is allowed for the excess credit.

## 15.2 Home Acquisition Loans

A qualifying "home acquisition loan" is a loan used to buy, build, or substantially improve your principal residence or second home (*see 15.1* for the two-residence limit), and that is secured by the home being bought, constructed, or substantially improved. To be considered a substantial improvement, an improvement must add to the value of the home or prolong its useful life. Repairs do not qualify. You may deduct the interest paid in 2018 (and later years) on all your home acquisition debt, provided the total debt does not exceed the limit allowed by the Tax Cuts and Jobs Act.

**Limit on home acquisition debt.** If you have home acquisition debt that you obtained before December 16, 2017, you may deduct the interest you pay on the entire amount so long as the total acquisition debt does not exceed $1 million ($500,000 if you are married filing separately). This is the limit that applied before the Tax Cuts and Jobs Act, and under the "grandfather rule" in the new law, the $1 million limit (or $500,000 if married filing separately) continues to apply to the grandfathered debt for 2018 and later years *(15.1)*.

For home acquisition debt obtained after December 15, 2017, the Tax Cuts and Jobs Act lowers the ceiling to $750,000 ($375,000 if married filing separately). However, two "grandfather" rules allow the prior-law loan limit of $1 million limit (or $500,000 if married filing separately) to apply to debt obtained after December 15, 2017:

*Law Alert*

### Higher Loan Limit on "Grandfathered" Loans

Under the Tax Cuts and Jobs Act, home acquisition loans of up to $1million ($500,000 if married filing separately) are "grandfathered" if they were obtained before December 16, 2017, so interest on such loans up to the $1million (or $500,000) limit is still deductible for 2018 and later years. A refinancing of such a loan also benefits from the grandfathered loan limit. The limit on acquisition debt obtained after December 15, 2017, other than a refinancing of grandfathered debt, is $750,000 ($375,000 if married filing separately). *See 15.2* for details and Examples.

1. The first exception is a transition rule for acquisition debt taken out to buy a home under a binding written contract that was in effect before December 16, 2017, provided the home purchase closing was on or before April 1, 2018.

2. The second grandfather exception applies if, after December 15, 2017, you refinance acquisition debt that was originally obtained by that date. The $1 million debt limit (or $500,000 if married filing separately) continues to apply to the loan balance on the date of refinancing; *see* Example 2 below. This refinancing exception lasts until the end of the term of the original loan. If the original loan is not being amortized over its term, the refinancing exception lasts until the first refinancing term ends, but no more than 30 years from the date of that first refinancing.

When you have grandfathered home acquisition debt from before December 16, 2017 (no more than $1 million, or $500,000 if married filing separately), and you take out new loans subject to the $750,000 limit ($375,000 if married filing separately), the grandfathered debt reduces the $750,000 (or $375,000) limit available for the new loans. In other words, interest is only deductible on the new debt to the extent that the grandfathered debt has not used up the entire $750,000 (or $375,000) limit.

**Use IRS worksheets if debt limit exceeded.** If your total debt exceeds the home acquisition debt limit (grandfathered limit or new law limit), you must use IRS worksheets included in Publication 936 to figure the amount of your deductible interest. You need to divide the debt limit by the average mortgage balance to get the deductible percentage of interest paid. Publication 936 provides options for figuring your average balance.

**Unmarried co-owners.** Unmarried co-owners do not have to allocate the applicable acquisition debt limit (*see* above) between them. For example, you and a co-owner (not your spouse) buy a principal residence in 2018 using a $500,000 home acquisition loan for which you are both liable and that is secured by the residence. On your individual returns, you may each deduct your share of the total interest paid on the $500,000 debt. If the loan were for more than $750,000, each of your deductions would be based on the $750,000 limit for home acquisition debt obtained after December 15, 2017; the allowable deduction must be figured using the IRS worksheets in Publication 936. Prior to a 2015 Ninth Circuit Appeals Court decision, the IRS had taken the position, and the Tax Court agreed, that unmarried co-owners had to allocate the debt limit between them (at that time the limit was $1.1 million, $1 million for acquisition debt and $100,000 for home equity debt). The Ninth Circuit allowed each co-owner to deduct interest on the full debt limit and the IRS announced in 2016 that it would follow the Ninth Circuit opinion (2016-31 IRB 193; acquiescence to Voss v. Commissioner, 796 F.3d 1051 (9th Cir. 2015).

**Family member may be treated as beneficial/equitable owner entitled to deduction.** A taxpayer who is not a legal owner of the property on the deed and who has no legal obligation to make mortgage payments may be allowed a deduction for payments of mortgage interest if he or she can show a beneficial or equitable ownership interest in the residence. This requires a showing that the taxpayer has assumed the benefits and burdens of ownership. The Tax Court considers the following factors as evidence that the benefits and burdens of ownership have been assumed:

1. The right to possess the property and enjoy its use, rents, or profits;
2. A duty to maintain the property;
3. Being responsible for insuring the property;
4. Bearing the property's risk of loss;
5. Being obligated to pay the property's taxes, assessments, or charges;
6. Having the right to improve the property without the legal owner's consent;
7. Having the right to obtain legal title at any time by paying the balance of the purchase price.

### EXAMPLES

1. Tom and Traci are married and file joint returns. In 2016 they obtained an $875,000 first mortgage to buy their principal residence. On their 2016 and 2017 joint returns, they deducted all of their mortgage interest payments; the loan was less than the $1 million home acquisition debt limit, so interest payments on the full debt were deductible.

> For 2018, interest on the full loan remains deductible. Because their loan was obtained before December 16, 2017, their debt is "grandfathered," and since it is under the grandfathered loan limit of $1 million, Tom and Traci may continue to deduct all of their mortgage interest payments.
>
> 2. In 2018, when the loan in Example 1 has a balance of $825,000, Tom and Traci refinance the debt, taking out a new first mortgage for the same amount. The refinanced debt is treated as grandfathered acquisition debt, subject to the $1 million limit, and thus interest on the entire $825,000 refinanced debt is deductible.
>
>    However, if they refinanced the debt in 2018 for $900,000, the refinanced debt would be treated as grandfathered acquisition debt only to the extent of the loan balance at the time of refinancing, or $825,000. For 2018, interest may be deducted on up to $825,000 of the debt. Interest on the excess $75,000 debt ($900,000 - $825,000) cannot be deducted because, even if the debt is used for substantial home improvements, thereby qualifying it as home acquisition debt, it is subject to the new law limit of $750,000 (for debt obtained after December 15, 2017, that isn't grandfathered debt), and the $750,000 limit is reduced to zero by the $825,000 of grandfathered debt.
>
> 3. Andrew obtains a first mortgage of $850,000 in 2018 to buy his principal residence. Because the debt is acquired after December 15, 2017, and it is not used to refinance grandfathered debt, Andrew may deduct interest on only $750,000 of the debt on his 2018 return. As discussed above, the deduction must be figured using the IRS worksheets in Publication 936.

 *Court Decision*

**Family Financing of Residence**

The Tax Court allowed a taxpayer to deduct mortgage interest payments on a loan that his brother obtained when the taxpayer's poor credit rating prevented him from obtaining a mortgage loan. The taxpayer's brother bought the house but allowed the taxpayer and his wife to live there on the condition that they make the mortgage payments directly to the bank.

The IRS disallowed the taxpayer's deduction for the mortgage interest on the grounds that he was not liable for the mortgage debt; his brother was. However, the Tax Court allowed the deduction, holding that the taxpayer was the beneficial (equitable) owner of the home and that he was legally obligated to his brother to pay off the mortgage.

As discussed in *15.2*, the Tax Court has taken a similar approach in other cases to allow a mortgage interest deduction to a family member who could show that he or she was the beneficial owner of the home.

In several cases, the Tax Court concluded that a family member who was not a legal owner had assumed the benefits and burdens of ownership and thus became an equitable owner who could deduct mortgage interest payments; *see* the Court Decision sidebar in this section for an example.

In another case, the Tax Court allowed an interest deduction to a son who moved in with his mother on her California ranch after her divorce. She was unable to pay the mortgage and property taxes, and he agreed to pay them in exchange for her oral agreement to give him an ownership interest in the property. In 2010 the son paid $35,880 in interest on the mortgage, which he deducted. In 2013, his name was added to the legal title of the property. The IRS disallowed the 2010 deduction on the grounds that the son was not a legal owner obligated to make the payments until 2013. The Tax Court, however, allowed the deduction. Under California law, it is presumed that the legal owner, here the mother, is the sole beneficial owner, but the son was able to overcome this presumption by testifying credibly that they had an agreement that indicated an intent contrary to what was reflected in the deed. Moreover, he assumed the benefits and burdens of ownership by paying the mortgage and property taxes, as well as the insurance, cable bill, maintenance costs, and property improvements. He also bore a substantial risk of loss for his payments. Based on all the facts and circumstances, the Tax Court concluded that the son was an equitable owner of the property in 2010, and thereby entitled to a deduction for his mortgage interest payments.

**Was your debt incurred in buying, constructing, or substantially improving a qualifying first or second residence?** In some cases, you may treat a loan as home acquisition debt even though you do not actually use the loan proceeds to buy, build, or substantially improve the home. For example, if you buy a home for cash and within 90 days you take out a mortgage secured by the home, the mortgage is treated as home acquisition debt to the extent it does not exceed the home's cost; it does not matter how you use the mortgage loan proceeds.

When you build a home, construction expenses incurred before the loan may qualify as home acquisition debt for a 24-month period; *see 15.4*. Similarly, if substantial improvements to a home are begun but not completed before a loan is obtained, the loan will be treated as acquisition debt (assuming the debt is secured by the home) to the extent of improvement expenses made within 24 months before the loan. If the loan is obtained within 90 days after an improvement is completed, the loan is treated as acquisition debt (assuming the debt is secured by the home) to the extent of improvement expenses made within the period starting 24 months before completion of the improvement and ending on the date of the loan.

Interest on a mortgage to buy or build a home other than your principal residence or qualifying second home *(15.1)* is treated as nondeductible personal interest. If a nonqualifying home is rented out, the part of the mortgage interest that is allocable to the rental activity is treated as passive activity interest subject to the limitations discussed in *Chapter 10*; the interest allocable to your personal use is nondeductible personal interest.

**Cooperatives.** In the case of housing cooperatives, debt secured by stock as a tenant-stockholder is treated as secured by a residence. The cooperative should provide you with the proper amount of your deductible interest. If the stock cannot be used to secure the debt because of restrictions under local law or the cooperative agreement, the debt is still considered to be secured by the stock if the loan was used to buy the stock. For further details on allocation rules, *see* IRS Publication 936.

**Mortgage interest paid after house destroyed.** If your principal residence or second home *(15.1)* is destroyed and the land is sold within a reasonable period of time following the destruction, the IRS treats the property as a residence for purposes of deducting interest payments on the mortgage during the period between the destruction of the residence and the sale of the land. In one case, the IRS allowed the interest deduction where a sale of land took place 26 months after the destruction of a home by a tornado.

If the destroyed residence is reconstructed and reoccupied within a reasonable period of time following the destruction, the property will continue to be treated as a residence during that period, and the interest payments on the mortgage on the property will be deductible. The IRS allowed an interest deduction where reconstruction began 18 months after, and was completed 34 months after, destruction of the home.

## 15.3 Home Equity Loans

Under the Tax Cuts and Jobs Act, a mortgage interest deduction cannot be claimed on Schedule A for interest paid on home equity debt unless the loan otherwise qualifies as home acquisition debt, starting with 2018 returns. If the debt is "only" home equity debt, no mortgage interest deduction is allowed.

As discussed in *15.2*, home acquisition debt is debt that is secured by your principal residence or second home and used to buy, build, or substantially improve that residence. If a home acquisition loan was obtained before December 16, 2017, the loan is "grandfathered" under the new law and the prior-law loan limit of $1 million ($500,000 if married filing separately) continues to apply. If the loan was obtained after December 15, 2017, and it is not used to refinance a grandfathered debt, the limit on acquisition debt for years after 2017 is $750,000 ($375,000 if married filing separately).

It is the use of the loan proceeds that determines if the loan qualifies and not how the loan is labeled. If a home equity loan or home equity line of credit (HELOC) is used to renovate a room in your main home or build an addition to the home, or to buy a second residence, the loan qualifies as home acquisition debt, assuming the loan is secured by the residence (first or second home) that is improved or purchased. If home equity debt qualifies as acquisition debt and the limit on acquisition debt has not already been reached, interest on the home equity debt falling within the limit is deductible for 2018 and later years; *see* the Examples below.

However, if the loan is not used to buy, build, or substantially improve your principal residence or second home, the interest is not deductible as home mortgage interest for 2018 and later years regardless of the amount of the loan, because the loan does not qualify as home acquisition debt. Thus, none of the interest on a home equity loan used to pay credit card debt, student loans, college tuition, medical bills, or other personal expenses is deductible for 2018 or later years, regardless of when the loan was obtained. Interest on such home equity loans was generally deductible for 2017 and prior years up to a debt limit of $100,000 ($50,000 if married filing separately), but the limit could not exceed the excess of the fair market value of your principal residence and second home (if any) over the amount of acquisition debt. This deduction for home equity loans used to pay personal living expenses is no longer available.

**Loans used for investment or business purposes.** The mortgage interest restrictions on home equity loans do not apply to loan proceeds used to buy or improve investment or business property. For example, if you use a home equity loan secured by your principal residence to buy investment securities, the interest deduction is figured on Form 4562 and claimed on Schedule A as investment interest *(15.9)*, not as mortgage interest. If you use a mortgage secured by your home to buy rental real estate, the interest paid is a rental expense deductible on Schedule E *(9.2)*. If you are self-employed and use the mortgage loan proceeds to buy property used in your business, the interest is deductible on Schedule C *(40.6)*.

### EXAMPLES

1. Jim and Joni are married and file joint returns. In 2015 they obtained an $825,000 first mortgage to buy their principal residence; the loan is secured by the residence. In 2016, they took out a home equity line of credit (HELOC) secured by the residence and borrowed $70,000 which they used to renovate their kitchen and bathrooms. Interest on both loans was deductible for 2015-2017. The HELOC qualifies as home acquisition debt because it was secured by the principal residence and used to substantially improve it. Since both the first mortgage and the HELOC were obtained before December 16, 2017, both loans are "grandfathered" under the new law as acquisition debt subject to the $1 million debt limit. Since the total grandfathered debt is less than the $1 million limit, Jim and Joni may deduct the interest paid in 2018 on both loans.

2. Same facts as Example 1 except that Jim and Joni open the HELOC and use the $70,000 loan to renovate their home in 2018, not 2016. Assume the balance of the first mortgage is $800,000 as of January 1, 2018. The $800,000 balance is grandfathered debt as it was acquired before December 16, 2017, and as it is under the $1million debt limit, interest is fully deductible on that loan. However, none of the interest on the HELOC loan is deductible for 2018. True, the HELOC loan qualifies as acquisition debt, as it was secured by their principal residence and used to substantially improve it (renovating the kitchen and bathrooms). However, it is not grandfathered debt because it was not obtained before December 16, 2017, and therefore it cannot count towards the $1 million grandfathered limit. As new acquisition debt, the $70,000 loan is subject to the $750,000 limit, and since the $800,000 mortgage "uses up" the entire $750,000 limit, Jim and Joni cannot deduct any of the interest they pay on the HELOC loan in 2018.

3. Same facts as Example 2, except that the balance of the first mortgage has been reduced to $660,000 as of January 1, 2018. In this case, Jim and Joni may deduct the interest paid in 2018 on both loans. Although the HELOC debt is not grandfathered (because it was obtained after December 15, 2017), it qualifies as home acquisition debt subject to the $750,000 limit and since the total acquisition debt of $730,000 ($660,000 + $70,000) is below $750,000, Jim and Joni may deduct the interest they pay in 2018 on both loans.

4. Same facts as Example 1 except that in 2016, Jim and Joni used the $70,000 HELOC loan to pay their son's college tuition and some medical bills, instead of renovating their home. Although the $70,000 loan was obtained before December 16, 2017, it is not grandfathered debt because it does not qualify as home acquisition debt; Jim and Joni did not use it to buy, build, or substantially improve their residence. Since the HELOC loan does not qualify as home acquisition debt, it is treated only as home equity debt, and interest on home equity debt is not deductible under the Tax Cuts and Jobs Act for 2018 and later years.

5. Karl and Kathryn are married and file jointly. In 2018 they obtain a first mortgage of $550,000 to buy their principal residence. Later in 2018, they take a $100,000 home equity loan, secured by their principal residence, and use it to buy a vacation home. Although the home equity loan was used to buy a second home, the loan does not qualify as home acquisition debt because it was secured by the principal residence and not by the vacation home it was used to buy. Karl and Kathryn can deduct the interest paid in 2018 on the $550,000 mortgage, as it is well under the $750,000 limit, but none of the interest on the $100,000 home equity loan is deductible.

 *Law Alert*

**Interest on Certain Home Equity Loans Still Deductible**

Under the Tax Cuts and Jobs Act, interest on a home equity loan or equity line of credit is deductible as home mortgage interest for 2018 and later years only if the loan is used to buy, build, or substantially improve a residence (first or second home) that secures the loan. Such loans qualify as home acquisition loans and the interest paid is deductible subject to the acquisition loan limits *(15.2)*.

If you claimed mortgage interest deductions before 2018 (under the prior law rules) for a home equity loan used to pay personal living expenses, such as a loan used to pay off credit cards or student debt, and you are still paying off the loan, the interest is not deductible for 2018 or later years. *See 15.3* for details and Examples.

6. Assume instead that Karl and Kathryn take a $300,000 first mortgage loan secured by the vacation home being purchased. The $300,000 loan now qualifies as home acquisition debt subject to the $750,000 loan limit. Because the $300,000 vacation home loan and the $550,000 principal residence loan total more than $750,000, some of the interest paid by Karl and Kathryn in 2018 is not deductible; they should use the worksheets in IRS Publication 936 to figure their average balance and deductible home mortgage interest, based on a loan limit of $750,000.

## 15.4 Home Construction Loans

Interest on a home construction loan may be fully deductible for a period of up to 24 months while the home is under construction. For the 24-month period starting with the commencement of construction, the loan is considered home acquisition debt subject to the $1 million ceiling or the $750,000 ceiling, depending on when the loan was obtained *(15.2)*, provided that the loan is secured by the lot on which construction is taking place and the home is a principal residence or second home when it is actually ready for occupancy. In one case, the Tax Court allowed an interest deduction under the 24-month construction period rule even though the home was never built; *see* Example 4 below.

According to the IRS, if construction begins before a loan is obtained, the loan is treated as acquisition debt to the extent of construction expenses within the 24-month period before the date of the loan. In determining the date of the loan for purposes of this 24-month rule, you can treat the date of a written loan application as the loan date, provided you receive the loan proceeds within 30 days after loan approval.

Interest incurred on the loan before construction begins is treated as nondeductible personal interest (see Example 1 in this section). If construction lasts more than 24 months, interest after the 24-month period also is treated as nondeductible personal interest.

Interest on loans taken out within 90 days after construction is completed may qualify for a full deduction. The loan is treated as acquisition debt to the extent of construction expenses within the last 24 months before the residence was completed, plus expenses through the date of the loan (*see* Example 2 below). For purposes of the 90-day rule, the loan proceeds generally are treated as received on the loan closing date. However, the date of a written loan application is treated as the loan date if the loan proceeds are actually received within 30 days after loan approval. If a loan application is made within the 90-day period and it is rejected, and a new application with another lender is made within a reasonable time after the rejection, a loan from the second lender will be considered timely even if more than 90 days have passed since the end of construction.

---

**EXAMPLES**

1. On October 17, 2017, you borrow $100,000 to buy a residential lot. The loan is secured by the lot. You begin construction of a principal residence on April 10, 2018, and use $250,000 of your own funds for construction expenses. The residence is completed November 27, 2019.

   The interest paid before the 24-month qualifying construction period began on April 10, 2018 is nondeductible personal interest. The $100,000 loan is treated as acquisition debt for the construction period (April 10, 2018--November 27, 2019), and the interest paid during that period is fully deductible *(15.2)*.

2. Same facts as in Example 1, but on February 10, 2020, you take out a $300,000 mortgage on the completed house to raise funds. You use $100,000 of the loan proceeds to pay off the $100,000 loan on the lot and keep the balance.

   All of the interest on the $300,000 loan is fully deductible because the loan qualifies as acquisition debt; $100,000 of the debt is treated as acquisition debt used for construction, since it was used to refinance the original 2017 debt to purchase the lot. The $200,000 balance is also treated as a construction loan under the 90-day rule. It was borrowed within 90 days after the residence was completed (November 27, 2019), and it reimbursed construction expenses of at least $200,000 incurred within 24 months before the completion date.

3. On January 9, 2018, you purchased a residential lot and began building a home on the lot using $90,000 of your personal funds. The home was completed on October 31, 2018. On November 28, 2018, you took out a loan of $72,000 that was secured by the home. The debt may be treated as acquisition debt taken out to build the home since it was taken out no later than 90 days after the home was completed, and expenditures of at least $72,000 were made within the period of 24 months before the home was completed.

4. Rose and his wife took out a $1.2 million loan and in March 2006 bought beach-front property in Fort Myers, Florida. The loan was secured by the property. They tore down the existing home, intending to build a new vacation home on the site. However, they needed a construction permit from the Florida Department of Environmental Protection and to get it, they had to submit plans, surveys and drilling samples in order to show that their proposed home would meet hurricane and flood standards and not harm turtle habitats. They finally obtained their construction permit in February 2008, but by that time the Florida real estate market was in decline, and they could not get financing to start building. In June 2009 they sold the property at a loss of $825,000.

The Roses claimed that their mortgage interest payments in 2006 and 2007 were deductible under the 24-month construction period rule. They argued that their demolition of the old house, clearing the site and their preparatory work for the intended home in surveying and drawing up plans as part of the permit process should be treated as "construction". The IRS countered that there was no construction since the physical building process never began.

The Tax Court allowed the deductions. The demolition and site clearing work, as well as the planning and preparatory work as part of the permit process, were necessary components of the overall process of construction. The deductions are not barred by the fact that the Roses sold the property before completing a residence that was ready for occupancy. The IRS regulation does not specifically address the situation where the residence under construction never becomes ready for occupancy. Each tax year must stand on its own and as things stood in 2006 and 2007, it was impossible for the Roses to know that they would be unable to complete their planned residence because of events beyond their control.

 *Law Alert*

**Deduction for Mortgage Insurance Premiums Expired at End of 2017**

The law authorizing the deduction for mortgage insurance premiums expired at the end of 2017. See the *e-Supplement* at *jklasser. com* for an update on whether Congress extended the deduction to 2018.

## 15.5 Mortgage Insurance Premiums and Other Payment Rules

Payments to the bank or lending institution holding your mortgage may include interest, principal payments, taxes, and insurance premiums. You may deduct eligible home mortgage interest *(15.2, 15.3)*, taxes *(16.4)*, and, possibly, mortgage insurance premiums *(see* below).

In the year you sell your home, check your settlement papers for interest charged up to the date of sale; this amount is deductible.

**Mortgage insurance premiums.** The law that authorized a deduction for mortgage insurance premiums expired at the end of 2017, and Congress had not extended it to 2018 when this book was completed. If the law is not extended, no deduction will be allowed for any mortgage insurance premiums paid in 2018. Also, since the IRS generally requires prepayments of premiums to be allocated over the shorter of 84 months or the mortgage term and treats prepayments as paid over the allocation period (unless the mortgage insurance is from the Department of Veterans Affairs or the Rural Housing Service), no deduction will be allowed for a pre-2018 payment that is allocable to 2018 if Congress does not extend the law.

If the law is extended, a deduction for qualified mortgage insurance premiums (taking into account the prepayment/allocation rule) will be deductible as home mortgage interest for 2018 as long as it is not disallowed under the phaseout rule. The deduction is phased out by 10% for every $1,000, or fraction of $1,000, of adjusted gross income (AGI) exceeding $100,000 or, if married filing separately, by 10% for every $500 of AGI over $50,000. The deduction is completely phased out if AGI exceeds $109,000, or $54,500 if married filing separately. See the *e-Supplement* at *jklasser.com* for a legislation update.

**Mortgage interest paid on your principal residence with assistance from Hardest Hit Fund.** An IRS safe harbor (Notice 2018-63, amplifying Notice 2017-40) allows you to claim a deduction for mortgage interest and for real estate taxes *(16.4)* even though tax-free assistance has been received from a State Housing Finance Agency (State HFA) using funds from the Treasury Department's HFA Hardest Hit Fund. For 2018 through 2021 (at the end of which the safe harbor is scheduled to expire), Notice 2018-63 allows homeowners to first allocate home mortgage payments made during the year to mortgage interest, and then use any reasonable method to allocate the balance of payments to real property taxes, mortgage insurance premiums, home insurance premiums, and mortgage principal.

**Interest on mortgage credit certificates.** Under special state and local programs, you may be able to obtain a "mortgage credit certificate" to finance the purchase of a principal residence or to borrow funds for certain home improvements. A tax credit for interest paid on the mortgage may be claimed. The credit is computed on Form 8396 and claimed on Schedule 3 of Form 1040 ("Nonrefundable credits"). The credit equals the interest paid multiplied by the certificate rate set by the governmental authority, but the maximum annual credit is $2,000. If you claim the credit, your home mortgage interest deduction is reduced by the amount of the current year credit claimed on Form 8396. If you buy a home using a qualifying mortgage credit certificate and sell that home within nine years, you may have to recapture part of the tax credit on Form 8828.

*Filing Tip*

**Joint Liability on Mortgage**

If you do not personally receive a Form 1098 but a person (other than your spouse with whom you file a joint return) who is also liable for and paid interest on the mortgage received a Form 1098, you deduct your share of the interest and attach a statement to your Schedule A showing the name and address of the person who received the form. If you are the payer of record on a mortgage on which there are other borrowers entitled to a deduction for the interest shown on the Form 1098 you received, provide them with information on their share of the deductible amount.

The Tax Court has allowed a joint obligor to deduct his or her payment of another obligor's share of the mortgage interest if the payment is made to avoid the loss of the property, and payment is made with his or her separate funds.

> **EXAMPLE**
>
> You pay $5,000 interest for a mortgage issued under a qualifying mortgage credit certificate. Under its terms, you are allowed a tax credit of $750. You may claim the balance of your mortgage interest, or $4,250 ($5,000 – $750), as home mortgage interest if you itemize deductions. If the allowable credit exceeds tax liability, a three-year carryover is allowed for the excess credit.

**Prepayment penalty.** A penalty for prepayment of a home mortgage is deductible as home mortgage interest provided the penalty is not for specific services provided by the mortgage holder.

**Mortgage assistance payments.** You may not deduct interest paid on your behalf under Section 235 of the National Housing Act.

**Delinquency charges for late payment.** According to the IRS, a late payment charge is deductible as mortgage interest if it was not for a specific service provided by the mortgage holder. In one case, the Tax Court agreed with the IRS that delinquency charges imposed by a bank were not interest where they were a flat percentage of the installment due, regardless of how late payment was. The late charges were primarily imposed by the bank to recoup costs related to collection efforts, such as telephone calls, letters, and supervisory reviews. They were also intended to discourage untimely payments by imposing a penalty.

**Graduated payment mortgages.** Monthly payments are initially smaller than under the standard mortgage on the same amount of principal, but payments increase each year over the first five- or 10-year period and continue at the increased monthly amount for the balance of the mortgage term. As a cash-basis taxpayer, you deduct the amount of interest actually paid even though, during the early years of the mortgage, payments are less than the interest owed on the loan. The unpaid interest is added to the loan principal, and future interest is figured on the increased unpaid mortgage loan balance. The bank, in a year-end statement, will identify the amount of interest actually paid. (An accrual-basis taxpayer may deduct the accrued interest each year.)

**Reverse mortgage loan.** Homeowners who own their homes outright may in certain states cash in on their equity by taking a "reverse mortgage loan." Typically, 80% of the value of the home is paid by a bank to a homeowner in a lump sum or in installments. Principal is due when the home is sold or when the homeowner dies; interest is added to the loan and is payable when the principal is paid. The IRS has ruled that an interest deduction may be claimed by a cash-basis home-owner only when the interest is paid, not when the interest is added to the outstanding loan balance. A deduction is subject to the limits for interest on home equity loans *(15.3)*.

**Redeemable ground rents.** In a ground rent arrangement, you lease rather than buy the land on which your home is located. Ground rent is deductible as mortgage interest if: (1) the land you lease is for a term exceeding 15 years (including renewal periods) and is freely assignable; (2) you have a present or future right to end the lease and buy the entire interest; and (3) the lessor's interest in the land is primarily a security interest. Payments to end the lease and buy the lessor's interest are not deductible ground rents.

## 15.6 Interest on Refinanced Loans

When you refinance home acquisition debt *(15.2)* for the same amount as the remaining principal balance on the old loan, there is no change in the tax treatment of interest. In other words, if interest was fully deductible on the old loan, then it is fully deductible on the new loan.

As discussed in *15.2*, if you refinance home acquisition debt that was obtained before December 16, 2017, for more than the existing balance, the refinanced debt is considered "grandfathered" acquisition debt to the extent of the loan balance at the time of refinancing; as "grandfathered" debt, that amount is subject to the $1 million limit for acquisition debt. The refinanced amount in excess of the existing balance is considered acquisition debt only if it is used to buy, build, or substantially improve your first or second home *(15.2)*, and interest on that debt is deductible for 2018 and later years only if the debt falls within the $750,000 limit, the limit on acquisition debt under the Tax Cuts and Jobs Act for non-grandfathered loans obtained after December 15, 2017.

Interest paid on home acquisition loans in excess of the applicable ceiling (either $1 million or $750,000; *(15.2)*) is generally treated as nondeductible personal interest unless the proceeds are used for business or investment purposes *(15.3, 15.11)*.

### Points Paid on Refinancing

The IRS does not allow a current deduction for points on a refinanced mortgage. According to the IRS, the points must be deducted ratably over the loan period, unless part of the new loan is used for improvements to a principal residence. Thus, if you pay points of $2,400 when refinancing a 20-year loan on your principal residence, the IRS allows you to deduct only $10 a month, or $120 each full year.

A federal appeals court rejected the IRS allocation rule where points are paid on a long-term mortgage that replaces a short-term loan; *see* the Court Decision in this section *(15.7)*.

If part of a refinancing is used for home improvements to a principal residence, the IRS allows a deduction for a portion of the points allocable to the home improvements.

> **EXAMPLE**
>
> In June 2018, Craig Smith refinances the mortgage on his principal residence when the loan balance is $80,000. The new loan is for $100,000, payable over 15 years starting in July 2018. He uses $80,000 to pay off the old $80,000 balance and the remaining $20,000 is used for home improvements. Assume that at the closing of the new loan, Smith pays points of $2,000 from his separate funds. In 2018, the year of payment, he may deduct 20% of the points, or $400, the amount allocable to the 20% of the loan used for home improvements. He may also deduct the ratable portion of the $1,600 balance of the points, which must be deducted over the period of the new loan. The ratable portion is $53 ($1,600 ÷ 180-month loan term × 6 months in 2018). Thus, Craig's total deduction for points in 2018 is $453 ($400 + $53).

**Mortgage ends early.** If you are ratably deducting points on a refinanced loan and you refinance again with a different lender, or the mortgage ends early because you prepay it or the lender forecloses, you can deduct the remaining points in the year the mortgage ends *(15.7)*.

*Court Decision*

**Current Deduction for Points on Refinancing**

Huntsman replaced a three-year loan used to purchase his principal residence with a 30-year mortgage. He deducted $4,400 of points paid on the new mortgage. The IRS and the Tax Court held that the points had to be deducted over the 30-year loan term.

The Federal Appeals Court for the Eighth Circuit disagreed and allowed a full deduction in the year the points were paid. The first loan was temporary and merely a step in obtaining permanent financing for the purchase of the principal residence.

The IRS has announced that in areas outside of the Eighth Circuit, it will continue to disallow full deductions in the year of payment for points paid on refinancings. The Eighth Circuit includes only these states: Minnesota, Iowa, North and South Dakota, Nebraska, Missouri, and Arkansas. In these states, the IRS will not challenge deductions for points on refinancing agreements similar to Huntsman's that replace short-term financing with long-term permanent financing.

In a later case, the Tax Court held that the Huntsman exception does not apply where a borrower refinances a long-term mortgage to take advantage of lower interest rates; the points must be deducted over the term of the new mortgage.

## 15.7 "Points"

Lenders sometimes charge "points" in addition to the stated interest rate. The points increase the lender's upfront fees, but in return borrowers generally are charged a lower interest rate over the loan term. Points are either treated as a type of prepaid interest *(15.13)* or as a nondeductible service fee, depending on what the charge covers. If the points qualify as interest, they are deductible over the term of the loan unless they are paid on the purchase or improvement of your principal residence, in which case they are deductible in the year they are paid, as discussed below. If you pay points on a loan to purchase or improve a second home, you must deduct the points ratably over the term of the loan.

Points are treated as interest if your payment is solely for your use of the money and is not for specific services performed by the lender that are separately charged. Whether a payment is called "points" or a "loan origination fee" does not affect its deductibility if it is actually a charge for the use of money. The purpose of the charge—that is, for the use of the money or the services rendered—will be controlling. For example, you may not deduct points that are fees for services, such as appraisal fees, preparation of a mortgage note or deed of trust, settlement fees, notary fees, abstract fees, commissions, and recording fees.

If you are selling property and you assume the buyer's liability for points, do not deduct the payment as interest but include it as a selling expense that reduces the amount realized on the sale.

### Deduction for Points on Purchase or Improvement of Principal Residence

Points are generally treated as prepaid interest *(15.13)* that must be deducted over the period of the loan. However, there is an exception for points you pay on a loan to buy, build, or improve your principal residence. The points on such loans are deductible in the year paid if these tests are met: (1) the loan is secured by your principal residence; (2) the charging of points is an established business practice in the geographic area in which the loan is made; (3) the points charged do not exceed the points generally charged in the area; (4) the amount of points is computed as a percentage of the loan and specifically earmarked on the loan closing statement as "points," "loan origination fees," or "loan discount"; and (5) you pay the points directly to the lender; see "Points withheld from the principal," below.

**Points paid by seller are deductible by buyer.** The seller's payment is treated as an adjustment to the purchase price that the seller gives to you as the buyer and that you then turn over to the lender to pay off the points. You may fully deduct the points in the year paid if you meet the tests in the preceding paragraph. Otherwise, deduct them over the term of the loan. You must reduce your cost basis for the home by the seller-paid points.

**Points withheld from the principal.** Points withheld from the principal of a loan used to buy, build, or improve your principal residence are deductible as if you paid them directly to the lender if, at or before closing, you have made a down payment, escrow deposit, or earnest money payment that is at least equal to the amount of points withheld. These payments must have been from your own funds and not from funds that have been borrowed from the lender as part of the overall transaction.

**Points on second home.** If you pay points on a mortgage secured by a second home or a vacation home, the points are not fully deductible in the year of payment; you must claim the deduction ratably over the loan term.

**Points paid on refinancing.** The IRS does not allow a current deduction for points on a refinanced mortgage *(15.6)*.

**Deduct balance of points if mortgage ends early.** If you are deducting points over the term of the loan because a full first-year deduction is not allowed, you are allowed to deduct the balance in the year the mortgage ends, such as when you prepay the loan, or the lender forecloses. If the mortgage ends early because you refinance the mortgage with a

**Caution**

**Service Fees Are Not Deductible Points**

You may not deduct as points amounts that are for specific lender services. To be deductible, points on the purchase of a principal residence must be prepaid interest for the use of the loan money.

**Filing Tip**

**Amortize Points Starting in Second Year**

A married couple purchased a principal residence and paid points late in the year. For the year of the purchase, their standard deduction exceeded their itemized deductions. The IRS ruled that claiming the standard deduction for the year the points are paid would not entirely forfeit the deduction for points. The points may be amortized starting in the second year. Assuming that they itemize deductions starting in the second year, the allocable portion of the points may be deducted each year over the remaining loan term.

different lender, you may deduct the balance of the points. For example, if you refinanced your mortgage in 2006 and paid points, those points had to be amortized over the loan term *(15.6)*. If in 2018 you refinance again with a different lender and pay points again, the balance of the points from the 2006 loan are deductible on your 2018 return, and the points on the new loan must be amortized over the loan term. If you refinanced with the same lender, the balance of the points from the 2006 loan must be deducted over the term of the new loan.

## 15.8 Cooperative and Condominium Apartments

**Cooperative apartments.** If you are a tenant-stockholder of a cooperative apartment, you may deduct your portion of:

- Mortgage interest paid by the cooperative on its debts to buy the land, or buy, build or improve the housing complex, provided the apartment is your first or second home *(15.1)*. This includes your pro rata share of the permanent financing expenses (points) of the cooperative on its mortgage covering the housing project.
- Real estate taxes paid by the cooperative *(16.6)*. However, if the cooperative does not own the land and building but merely leases them and is required to pay real estate taxes under the terms of the lease, you may not deduct your share of the tax payment.

In some localities, such as New York City, rent control rules allow tenants of a building converted to a cooperative to remain in their apartments even if they do not buy into the co-op. A holdover tenant may prevent some co-op purchasers from occupying an apartment. The IRS ruled that the fact that a holdover tenant stays in the apartment will not bar the owner from deducting his or her share of the co-op's interest and taxes.

**Condominiums.** If you own an apartment in a condominium, you have a direct ownership interest in the property and are treated, for tax purposes, just as any other property owner. You may deduct your payments of real estate taxes and mortgage interest. You may also deduct taxes and interest paid on the mortgage debt of the project allocable to your share of the property. The deduction of interest from condominium ownership is also subject to the two-residence limit *(15.1)*. If your condominium is used part of the time for rental purposes, you may deduct expenses of maintenance and repairs and claim depreciation deductions subject to certain limitations *(9.7)*.

## 15.9 Investment Interest Limitations

Interest paid on margin accounts and debts to buy or carry other investments is deductible on Schedule A up to the amount of net investment income. If you do not have investment income such as interest, you may not deduct investment interest. Investment income for purposes of the deduction generally does not include net capital gains or qualified dividends, but you may elect to include them in order to increase your investment interest deduction. If you make the election, the elected amount will not be eligible for the favorable capital gain rates; see "Computing the Deduction" below. Investment interest in excess of net investment income may be carried forward and deducted from next year's net investment income.

You compute the deduction for investment interest on Form 4952, which must be attached along with Schedule A to Form 1040. Deductible investment interest is not subject to the reduction of overall itemized deductions for higher-income taxpayers *(13.7)*.

**What is investment interest?** It is all interest paid or accrued on debts incurred or continued to buy or carry investment property such as interest on securities in a margin account. However, interest on loans to buy tax-exempt securities is not deductible *(15.10)*.

Investment interest does not include interest on qualifying home acquisition debt *(15.2)* or home equity debt *(15.3)*, production period interest that is capitalized *(16.4)*, or interest related to a passive activity *(10.8)*.

Investment property includes property producing portfolio income (interest, dividends, or royalties not realized in the ordinary course of business) under the passive activity rules

 *Caution*

**Points Reported to the IRS**

Points you paid in 2018 on the purchase of your principal residence will be reported to the IRS by the lender on Form 1098 if they meet the five tests for a deduction listed in *15.8*. Seller-paid points are also included on Form 1098. Form 1098 is used by the IRS to check on the deduction you claim for points on Schedule A. Points paid on an improvement loan for your principal residence also are deductible if they meet the tests; they are not shown on Form 1098.

**Caution**

**Interest on Loans To Buy Market Discount Bonds and Treasury Bills**

Limits apply to the deduction for interest on loans used to buy or carry market discount bonds *(4.20)* and Treasury bills *(4.27)*.

discussed in *Chapter 10*, and property in activities that are not treated as passive activities, even if you do not materially participate, such as working interests in oil and gas wells.

**Passive activity interest is not investment interest.** Interest expenses incurred in a passive activity such as rental real estate *(10.1)*, or a limited partnership or S corporation in which you do not materially participate *(10.6)*, are taken into account on Form 8582 when figuring net passive income or loss. This includes interest incurred on loans used to finance your investment in a passive activity. Do not treat passive activity interest as investment interest on Form 4952.

However, interest expenses allocable to portfolio income (non–business activity interest, dividends, or royalties) from a limited partnership or S corporation are investment interest and not passive interest. The investment interest will be listed separately on Schedule K-1 received from the partnership or corporation.

## Computing the Deduction

Deductible investment interest is limited to net investment income. Net investment income is the excess of investment income over investment expenses. The key terms investment income and investment expenses are defined below.

**Investment income.** Investment income is generally gross income from property held for investment, such as interest, dividends, other than qualified dividends, annuities, and royalties. Income or expenses considered in figuring profit or loss of a passive activity *(10.8)* is not considered investment income or expenses. Property subject to a net lease is not treated as investment property, as it is within the passive activity rules.

*Do you have net capital gains?* If you have net capital gains (net long-term capital gains exceeding net short-term losses) from the sale of investment property such as stocks or mutual fund shares, or capital gain distributions from mutual funds, such gains and distributions are not treated as investment income unless you specifically elect to include them in investment income on Form 4952. You may elect to include all or part of them. The same election rule applies to qualified dividends *(4.1)* that are subject to net capital gain tax rates. An election must be made on Form 4952 to include qualified dividends in investment income. If you make this election, you may not apply preferential capital gain rates *(5.3)* to the amount of the net capital gains (and capital gain distributions) or qualified dividends treated as investment interest on Form 4952. If you make the election on Form 4952, the elected amount is subtracted from net capital gains when applying the capital gain tax rates on the IRS worksheets *(5.3)*.

**Caution**

**Electing To Treat Long-Term Gains or Dividends as Investment Income**

If you elect on Form 4952 to treat net capital gains *(5.3)* or qualified dividends *(4.2)* as investment income in order to increase your investment interest deduction, that amount is not eligible to be taxed at favorable capital gain rates *(5.3)*.

**Investment expenses.** If you have deductible expenses, other than interest, directly connected with the production of investment income, they reduce investment income on Form 4952; *see* the form instructions.

**Net investment income.** Reducing investment income by investment expenses gives you net investment income. Your deduction for investment interest expenses is limited to this amount; any excess interest expense you had in 2018 may be carried over to 2019, as discussed below.

**Where to enter the deduction on your return.** The deduction figured on Form 4952 is generally entered on Schedule A as investment interest. However, if the interest is attributable to royalties, you may have to enter the interest on Schedule E; follow the Form 4952 instructions. Furthermore, there is an additional complication if you have investment interest for an activity for which you are not "at risk" *(10.18)*. After figuring the investment interest deduction on Form 4952, you must enter the portion of the interest that is attributable to the at-risk activity on Form 6198. The amount carried over to Form 6198 is subtracted from the investment interest deduction claimed on Form 4952.

**Carryover to 2019 and future years.** Investment interest in excess of net investment income for 2018 may be carried forward to 2019 and future years until it can be claimed. A carryover will be added to the current year investment interest and be deductible to the extent the total does not exceed net investment income.

**EXAMPLE**

For 2018, Larry Jones has $10,000 of interest income. He has investment expenses, other than interest, of $3,200. His investment interest expense from securities margin account loans is $8,000. Jones also has income of $2,000 from a passive partnership investment.

Jones's net investment income is $6,800: $10,000 of interest income less $3,200 of non-interest investment expenses. The passive activity income from the partnership is not included in investment income.

Jones's investment interest deduction for 2018 is limited to the $6,800 of net investment income. The $1,200 of investment interest in excess of net investment income ($8,000 – $6,800) is carried forward to 2019.

## 15.10 Debts To Carry Tax-Exempt Obligations

When you borrow money in order to buy or carry tax-exempt bonds, you may not deduct any interest paid on your loan. Application of this disallowance rule is clear where there is actual evidence that loan proceeds were used to buy tax-exempts or that tax-exempts were used as collateral. But sometimes the relationship between a loan and the purchase of tax-exempts is less obvious, as where you hold tax-exempts and borrow to carry other securities or investments. IRS guidelines explain when a direct relationship between the debt and an investment in tax-exempts will be inferred so that no interest deduction is allowed. The IRS will not infer a direct relationship between a debt and an investment in tax-exempts in these cases:

1. The investment in tax-exempts is not substantial. That is, it is not more than 2% of the adjusted basis of the investment portfolio and any assets held in an actively conducted business.

2. The debt is incurred for a personal purpose. For example, an investor may take out a home mortgage instead of selling his tax-exempts and using the proceeds to finance the home purchase. Interest on the mortgage is deductible subject to certain limitations *(15.1)*.

3. The debt is incurred in connection with the active conduct of a business and does not exceed business needs. But if a person reasonably could have foreseen when the tax-exempts were purchased that he or she would have to borrow funds to meet ordinary and recurrent business needs, the interest expenses are not deductible.

The guidelines infer a direct relationship between the debt and an investment in tax-exempts in this type of case: An investor in tax-exempts has outstanding debts not directly related to personal expenses or to his or her business. The interest will be disallowed even if the debt appears to have been incurred to purchase other portfolio investments. Portfolio investments include transactions entered into for profit, including investments in real estate, that are not connected with the active conduct of a business; *see* the Example below.

**EXAMPLE**

An investor owning $360,000 in tax-exempt bonds purchased real estate in a joint venture, giving a purchase money mortgage and cash for the price. He deducted interest on the mortgage. The IRS disallowed the deduction, claiming the debt was incurred to carry tax-exempts. A court allowed the deduction. A mortgage is the customary manner of financing such a purchase. Furthermore, since the purchase was part of a joint venture, the other parties' desires in the manner of financing had to be considered.

## 15.11 Earmarking Use of Loan Proceeds For Investment or Business

The IRS has set down complex record keeping and allocation rules for claiming interest deductions on loans used for business or investment purposes, or for passive activities. The rules deal primarily with the use of loan proceeds for more than one purpose and the commingling of loan proceeds in an account with unborrowed funds. The thrust of the

 *Caution*

**Tax-Exempt Income From Mutual Fund**

You may not deduct interest on loans used to buy or carry tax-exempt securities. If you receive exempt-interest dividends from a mutual fund during the year, you may deduct interest on a loan used to buy or carry the mutual fund shares only to the extent that the proceeds can be allocated to taxable dividends you also receive.

rules is to base deductibility of interest on the use of the borrowed funds. The allocation rules do not affect mortgage interest deductions on loans secured by a qualifying first or second home *(15.1)*.

Keep separate accounts for business, personal, and investment borrowing. For example, if you borrow for investment purposes, keep the proceeds of the loan in a separate account and use the proceeds only for investment purposes. Do not use the funds to pay for personal expenses; interest is not deductible on personal loans other than qualifying student loans *(Chapter 33)*. Furthermore, do not deposit loan proceeds in an account funded with unborrowed money, unless you intend to use the proceeds within 30 days of the deposit. By following these directions, you can identify your use of the proceeds with a specific expenditure, such as for investment, personal, or business purposes, and the interest on the loan may be treated as incurred for that purpose. The 30-day rule is discussed below.

**The IRS treats undisbursed loan proceeds deposited in an account as investment property, even though the account does not bear interest.** When proceeds are disbursed from the account, the use of the proceeds determines how interest is treated; *see* Examples 1 and 2 below.

**30-day disbursement rule.** If you deposit borrowed funds in an account with unborrowed funds, a special 30-day rule allows you to treat payments from the account as made from the loan proceeds. Where you make more than one disbursement from such an account, you may treat any expenses paid within 30 days before or after deposit of the loan proceeds as if made from the loan proceeds. Thus, you may allocate interest on the loan to that disbursement, even if earlier payments from the account have been made; *see* Example 3 below. If you make the disbursement after 30 days, the IRS requires you to allocate interest on the loan to the first disbursement; *see* Example 4 below. Furthermore, if an account includes only loan proceeds and interest earned on the proceeds, disbursements may be allocated first to the interest income and then to the loan proceeds.

**Allocation period.** Interest is allocated to an expenditure for the period beginning on the date the loan proceeds are used or treated as used and ending on the earlier of either the date the debt is repaid or the date it is reallocated.

Accrued interest is treated as a debt until it is paid, and any interest accruing on unpaid interest is allocated in the same manner as the unpaid interest is allocated. Compound interest accruing on such debt, other than compound interest accruing on interest that accrued before the beginning of the year, may be allocated between the original expenditure and any new expenditure from the same account on a straight-line basis. That is done by allocating an equal amount of such interest expense to each day during the taxable year. In addition, you may treat a year as twelve 30-day months for purposes of allocating interest on a straight-line basis.

**Payments from a checking account.** A disbursement from a checking account is treated as made at the time the check is written on the account, provided the check is delivered or mailed to the payee within a reasonable period after the writing of the check. You may treat checks written on the same day as written in any order. A check is presumed to be written on the date appearing on the check and to be delivered or mailed to the payee within a reasonable period thereafter. However, the presumption may not apply if the check does not clear within a reasonable period after the date appearing on the check.

**Change in use of property.** You must reallocate interest if you convert debt-financed property to a different use; for example, when you buy a business auto with an installment loan, interest paid on the auto is business interest, but if during the year you convert the auto to personal use, interest paid after the conversion is personal interest.

**Order of repayment.** If you used loan proceeds to repay several different kinds of debt, the debts being repaid are assumed to be repaid in the following order: (1) personal debt; (2) investment debt and passive activity debt other than active real estate debt; (3) debt from a real estate activity in which you actively participate; (4) former passive activity debt; and (5) business debt. *See* Example 5 below. Payments made on the same day may be treated as made in any order.

### EXAMPLES

1. On January 1, you borrow $10,000 and deposit the proceeds in a non–interest-bearing checking account. No other amounts are deposited in the account during the year and no part of the loan is repaid during the year. On April 1, you invest $2,000 of the proceeds in a real estate venture. On September 1, you use $4,000 to buy furniture.

   From January 1 through March 31, interest on the entire undisbursed $10,000 is treated as investment interest. From April 1 through August 31, interest on $2,000 of the debt is treated as passive activity interest and interest on $8,000 of the debt is treated as investment interest. From September 1 through December 31, interest on $4,000 of the debt is treated as personal interest; interest on $2,000 is treated as passive activity interest; and interest on $4,000 is treated as investment interest.

2. On September 1, you borrow money for business purposes and deposit it in a checking account. On October 15, you disburse the proceeds for business purposes. Interest incurred on the loan before the disbursement of the funds is treated as investment interest expense. Interest starting on October 15 is treated as business interest. However, you may elect to treat the starting date for business interest as of the first of the month in which the disbursement was made—that is, October 1—provided all other disbursements from the account during the same month are similarly treated.

3. On September 1, you borrow $5,000 to invest in stock and deposit the proceeds in your regular checking account. On September 10, you buy a TV and sound system for $2,500 and on September 11 invest $5,000 in stock, using funds from the account. As the stock investment was made within 30 days of depositing the loan proceeds in the account, interest on the entire loan is treated as incurred for investment purposes.

4. Same facts as in Example 3, but the TV and sound system were bought on October 1 and the stock on October 31. As the stock investment was not made within 30 days, the IRS requires you to treat the purchase of the TV and the stereo for $2,500 as the first purchase made with the loan proceeds of $5,000. Thus, the 50% of loan interest that is allocated to the TV and sound system is nondeductible.

5. On July 12, Smith borrows $100,000 and immediately deposits the proceeds in an account. He uses the proceeds as follows:

   | | |
   |---|---|
   | August 31 | $40,000 for passive activity |
   | October 5 | $20,000 for rental activity |
   | December 24 | $40,000 for personal use |

   On January 19 of the following year, Smith repays $90,000. Of the repayment, $40,000 is allocated as a repayment of the personal expenditure, $40,000 of the passive activity, and $10,000 of the rental activity. The outstanding $10,000 is treated as debt incurred in a rental activity.

## 15.12 Year To Claim an Interest Deduction

As a cash-basis taxpayer, you deduct interest in the year of payment except for prepayments of interest *(15.13)*. Giving a promissory note is not considered payment. Increasing the amount of a loan by interest owed, as with insurance loans, is also not considered payment and will not support a deduction. However, an accrual-basis taxpayer generally deducts interest in the year the interest accrues *(40.3)*.

Here is how a cash-basis taxpayer treats interest in the following situations:

*On a life insurance loan, where proceeds are used for a deductible (nonpersonal) purpose, you claim a deduction in the year in which the interest is paid.* You may not claim a deduction when the insurance company adds the interest to your debt. You may not deduct your payment of interest on an insurance loan after you assign the policy.

*On a margin account with a broker, interest is deductible in the year in which it is paid or your account is credited after the interest has been charged.* But an interest charge to your account is not payment if you do not pay it in cash or the broker has not collected dividends, interest, or security sales proceeds that may be applied against the interest due. Note that the interest deduction on margin accounts is subject to investment interest limitations *(15.9)*.

*For partial payment of a loan used for a deductible (nonpersonal) purpose, interest is deductible in the year the payment is credited against interest due.* When a loan has no provision for allocating payments between principal and income, the law presumes that a partial payment is applied first to interest and then to principal, unless you agree otherwise. Where the payment is in full settlement of the debt, the payment is applied first to principal, unless you agree otherwise. Where there is an involuntary payment, such as that following a foreclosure sale of collateral, sales proceeds are applied first to principal, unless you agree to the contrary. *See* also *15.11* for the effect of payments on the allocation of debt proceeds.

**Note renewed.** You may not deduct interest by merely giving a new note. You claim a deduction in the year the renewed note is paid. The giving of a new note or increasing the amount due is not payment. The same is true when past due interest is deducted from the proceeds of a new loan; this is not a payment of the interest.

## 15.13 Prepaid Interest

If you prepay interest on a loan used for investment or business purposes you may not deduct interest allocable to any period falling in a later taxable year. The prepaid interest must be deducted over the period of the loan, whether you are a cash-basis or accrual-basis taxpayer.

Points paid on the purchase of a principal residence are generally fully deductible in the year paid *(15.7)*. Points paid on refinancing generally are not deductible *(15.6)*. With the exception of deductible points *(15.7)*, prepayments of mortgage interest are not deductible; interest must be spread to the years to which it applies. You can only deduct the interest that qualifies as home mortgage interest *(15.1)* for that particular year.

**Treatment of interest included in a level payment schedule.** Where payments of principal and interest are equal, a large amount of interest allocated to the payments made in early years of a loan will generally not be considered prepaid interest. However, if the loan calls for a variable interest rate, the IRS may treat interest payments as consisting partly of interest, computed under an average level effective rate, and partly of prepaid interest allocable to later years of the loan. An interest rate that varies with the "prime rate" does not necessarily indicate a prepaid interest element.

When you borrow money for a deductible purpose and give a note to the lender, the amount of your loan proceeds may be less than the face value of the note. The difference between the proceeds and the face amount is interest discount. For loans that do not fall within the OID rules *(4.18)*, such as loans of a year or less, interest is deductible in the year of payment if you are on the cash basis. If you use the accrual basis, the interest is deductible as it accrues. For loans that fall within OID rules, your lender should provide a statement showing the interest element and the tax treatment of the interest.

*Planning Reminder*

**Business or Investment Loans**

If you prepay business or investment loan interest, you must spread the interest deduction over the period of the loan. In the year of payment, you may deduct only the interest allocable to that year.

# CHAPTER 16

# Deductions for Taxes

If you itemize deductions on Schedule A, you may deduct your payments of state and local income taxes (or state and local general sales taxes in lieu of state and local income taxes), state and local real property taxes, and state and local personal property taxes, but for 2018 and later years, the total deduction for all of such taxes may not exceed $10,000 ($5,000 if you are married filing separately). *(16.1)*.

Subject to the $10,000 (or $5,000) limit, you can increase your deduction for state and local taxes by making a year-end prepayment of estimated tax liability. You also may be able to increase withholdings from your pay to increase your deduction.

If you pay transfer taxes on the sale of securities or investment real estate, the taxes are not deductible. However, they reduce the sales price when figuring your profit or loss.

Taxes paid in operating a business are generally deductible, except for sales taxes, which are added to the cost of the property.

Foreign real property taxes are no longer deductible, but an itemized deduction for foreign income taxes is allowed.

## 16.1    Overall Limit on Deduction for State and Local Taxes

The Tax Cuts and Jobs Act imposes an overall limit on the amount of state and local taxes (referred to as SALT) that can be claimed as an itemized deduction on Schedule A (Form 1040). Starting with your 2018 return, you cannot deduct more than $10,000 ($5,000 if you are married filing separately) for the following taxes, in any combination:

- State and local income taxes. You have the option to deduct state and local general sales taxes in lieu of state and local income taxes *(16.3)*.
- State and local real property taxes *(16.4)*, and
- State and local personal property taxes.

Note that if you are married filing jointly, your deduction limit for total state and local taxes in (1) through (3) above is the same $10,000 limit allowed to a single taxpayer.

There is no dollar limit for state and local real property and personal property taxes that you pay or incur with respect to property used in your business or investment property, such as residential rental property. Thus, state and local taxes imposed on business property are deductible on your Schedule C *(40.6)*, and property taxes imposed on residential rental property are deductible on Schedule E *(9.2)*. These business/investment property taxes are not subject to the $10,000 limit ($5,000 if married filing separately).

However, the new law as written does not exempt state and local income taxes from the $10,000/$5,000 limit if they are paid or incurred in a business or investment activity. If Congress changes this result, it will be reported in the *e-Supplement* at *jklasser.com*.

Foreign real property taxes are no longer deductible. Foreign income taxes are still allowed as an itemized deduction and they are not subject to the $10,000 limit ($5,000 if married filing separately). However, a tax credit may be a better alternative to the deduction *(16.10)*.

## 16.2    Nondeductible Taxes

**Transfer taxes.** Transfer taxes paid on the sale of securities or investment real estate are not separately deductible; but when you report the sale on Form 8949, transfer taxes along with other selling expenses will decrease your gain or increases your loss; *see 5.8*.

A transfer tax (which may be called an excise tax in some states) on the sale of a personal residence is not deductible as a real estate tax; it is imposed on the transaction and not on the value of the property. Transfer taxes are added to cost basis by the buyer or treated as an expense of sale by the seller.

**Gasoline taxes.** State and local taxes on gasoline used for personal purposes are not deductible. If you travel for business, the taxes are deductible as part of your gasoline expenses.

## 16.3    State and Local Income Taxes or General Sales Taxes

On Schedule A (Form 1040), you may deduct either your payments of state and local income taxes or your payments of state and local general sales taxes, but whichever you choose, the deduction is subject to the overall $10,000/$5,000 limit on state and local taxes discussed in *16.1*. On Line 5a of Schedule A, you may claim state and local income taxes or general sales taxes but not both; check the box on Line 5a if you elect to include state and local general sales taxes instead of income taxes.

**State and local income taxes.** Subject to the overall $10,000/$5,000 limit on state and local taxes *(16.1)*, you may deduct on Schedule A (Form 1040) for 2018 state and local income taxes withheld from your pay during 2018 and estimated state and local taxes you paid in 2018, including the last installment of state and local estimated tax for 2017 if you paid it in January 2018. Also deduct any balance of your 2017 state and local taxes that you may have paid in 2018 when you filed your 2017 state/local tax return. If in 2019 you pay additional state/local income tax on your 2018 income (such as paying the last 2018 installment of state/local estimated tax in 2019, or paying the balance due on your 2018 state/local return when you file it in 2019), that payment will be deductible on your 2019 tax return.

*Caution*

**State Workarounds May not Work**

In an effort to enable residents to get a federal tax break from their SALT payments, some states have enacted or are considering enactment of workarounds. For example, New York enacted a measure to allow state tax credits for a portion of tax payments as a way to allow residents to claim a charitable contribution deduction. Unfortunately, the IRS has said that where there's a quid pro quo (other than a de minimis amount), no charitable contribution deduction is allowed. *See 14.3*.

*Law Alert*

**State and Local Taxes Deduction Limited**

The Tax Cuts and Jobs Act limits your itemized deduction for state and local taxes to $10,000 ($5,000 if married filing separately). The $10,000/$5,000 limit is an overall limit that applies to the total of your state and local property taxes (real estate or personal property) and state and local income taxes, or general sales taxes in lieu of income taxes.

*Filing Tip*

**State Income Tax Paid in 2018 For 2017**

In figuring your 2018 itemized deduction for state and local income taxes paid, remember to include tax that you paid in 2018 if you had a balance due when you filed your 2017 state and local tax returns.

## Table 16-1 Checklist of Taxes

| Type of tax— | Deductible as itemized deduction for 2018— |
|---|---|
| Admission | No |
| Alcoholic beverage | No |
| Assessments for local benefits | No |
| Automobile license fees not qualifying as personal property tax | No |
| Cigarette | No |
| Customs duties | No |
| Driver's license | No |
| Estate—federal or state | No* |
| Excise—federal or state, for example, on telephone service | No |
| Foreign income tax | Yes (16.10) |
| Gasoline—federal | No |
| Gasoline and other motor fuel—state and local | No |
| Gift taxes—federal and state | No |
| Income—federal (including alternative minimum tax) | No |
| Income—state or local | Yes (but see limit in 16.1) |
| Inheritance tax | No |
| Mortgage tax | No |
| Personal property—state or local | Yes (but see limit in 16.1) |
| Poll | No |
| Real estate (state, local) | Yes (but see limit in 16.1) |
| Regulatory license fees (dog licenses, parking meter fees, hunting and fishing licenses) | No |
| Social Security | No |
| Tolls | No |
| Transfer taxes on securities and real estate | No |

* But see the exception for miscellaneous itemized deduction for estate tax paid on "income in respect of a decedent" (11.17).

## Table 16-2  Who Claims the Deduction for Real Estate Taxes?

| If the tax is paid by— | Then it is deductible by— |
| --- | --- |
| You, for your spouse | Neither, if your spouse has title to the property, and you each file a separate return. This is true even if the mortgage requires you to pay the taxes. The tax is deductible on a joint return. |
| You, as owner of a condominium | You deduct real estate tax paid on your separate unit. You also deduct your share of the tax paid on the common property. |
| Your cooperative apartment or corporation | You deduct your share of real estate tax paid on the property; *see 15.9.* But if the organization leases the land and building and pays the tax under the terms of the lease, you may not deduct your share. |
| A life tenant | A court allowed the deduction to a widow required to pay the taxes under a will for the privilege of occupying the house during her life. |
| A tenant | The tenant of a business lease may deduct the payment of tax as additional rent, not tax. The tenant of a personal residence may not deduct the payment as either a tax or rent expense, unless placed on the real estate assessment rolls so that the tax is assessed directly against him or her; *see 16.6.* |
| You, as a local benefit tax to maintain, repair, or meet interest costs arising from local benefits | You deduct only that part of the tax that you can show is for maintenance, repair, or interest on maintenance expenses. If you cannot make the allocation, no deduction is allowed. If the benefit increases the value of the property, you add the non-deductible assessment to the basis of the property. |
| You, where your property was foreclosed for failure to pay taxes | You may not deduct the taxes paid out of the proceeds of the foreclosure sale if your interest in the property ended with the foreclosure. |
| Tenant by the entirety or joint tenant | A tenant who is jointly and severally liable for the tax may deduct it if it is paid with his or her separate funds. If a husband and wife own real estate as joint tenants or as tenants by the entirety, taxes paid by either of them may be deducted on their joint return, or if they file separately, by the spouse who pays the tax from his or her own funds. |
| Tenant in common | When property is owned as a tenancy in common, the IRS allows a tenant to deduct only his or her share of the tax, even if the entire tax was paid. However, the Tax Court may allow a co-tenant to deduct the full amount if the tax is paid from his or her separate funds and the payment protects against the possibility of foreclosure in the event the other co-tenants failed to pay their share of the taxes *(9.2)*. |
| A mortgagee | No deduction. If tax is paid before the foreclosure, it is added to the loan. If paid after the foreclosure, it is added to the cost of property. |

State income taxes may be claimed only as itemized deductions, even if attributed solely to business income. That is, state income taxes are not a deductible business expense on Schedule C *(40.6)*.

To increase your itemized deductions on your 2018 return, consider prepaying state income taxes before the end of 2018. The prepayment is deductible provided the state tax authority accepts prepayments and state law recognizes them as tax payments. The IRS has ruled, however, that prepayments are not deductible if you do not reasonably believe that you owe additional state tax. Do not make prepayments if you expect to be subject to alternative minimum tax, since state and local taxes are not deductible for AMT purposes *(23.2)*.

If you report on the accrual basis and you contest a tax liability, claim the deduction in the year of payment.

You may deduct on your federal return state and local income taxes allocable to interest income that is exempt from federal tax but not from state and local income tax. However, state and local taxes that are allocated to other federal exempt income are not deductible. For example, state income tax allocated to a cost-of-living allowance exempt from federal income tax is not deductible as a state tax.

The IRS has held that mandatory employee contributions to state disability or worker's compensation funds in California, New Jersey, New York, Rhode Island and Washington, and mandatory contributions to the Alaska, California, New Jersey, and Pennsylvania state unemployment funds, are deductible as state income taxes. In addition, mandatory contributions to state family leave programs, such as in New Jersey and California, are deductible as state income taxes.

However, employee contributions to a private or voluntary disability plan in California, New Jersey, or New York have been held by the IRS to be nondeductible.

Note: If you get a refund of state income taxes that you claimed as an itemized deduction, you may have to report it as income *(11.5)*.

**State and local general sales taxes option.** If you elect to deduct state and local general sales taxes in lieu of state and local income taxes, you have two ways to figure the sales tax deduction. You can figure deductible state and local general sales taxes using your credit card receipts and other records of non-business purchases for the year. Alternatively, you can use the IRS' optional tables and worksheet in the Schedule A instructions or the Sales Tax Deduction Calculator at IRS.gov.

Generally, you can only deduct sales taxes to the extent that the rate is the same as the general sales tax rate. However, sales taxes on food, clothing, medical supplies, and motor vehicles are deductible as general sales taxes even if the rate paid is less than the general sales tax rate.

If you paid sales taxes on the purchase or lease of a motor vehicle used for personal purposes (car, motorcycle, SUV, truck, van, or off-road vehicle) at a rate that is higher than the general sales tax rate, you may only include up to the general sales tax rate.

You may also include sales taxes paid at the general sales tax rate on the purchase of (1) a home, including a mobile or prefabricated home, or on a substantial addition to a home or a major home renovation, (2) a boat, or (3) an aircraft. See the Schedule A instructions for restrictions on taxes paid on the purchase of a home or major home renovation.

## 16.4 Deducting Real Estate Taxes

Your payments of state and local real estate taxes on your non-business property are deductible on Schedule A (Form 1040), subject to the overall $10,000/$5,000 limit on state and local taxes *(16.1)*. The tax must be based on the assessed value of the property and the assessment must be based on a uniform rate imposed for public purposes. *See 16.5* for deductible and nondeductible assessments for local benefits. Foreign real estate taxes are not deductible for 2018 or later years.

The monthly mortgage payment to a bank or other mortgage holder generally includes amounts allocated to real estate taxes, which are paid to the taxing authority on their due date. Mortgage payments allocated to real estate taxes are deductible in the year you make the payments only if the mortgage holder actually pays the taxes to the tax authority by the end of that year. Typically, banks will furnish you with a year-end statement of disbursements to taxing authorities, indicating dates of payment. *See 16.5–16.7* for further details on real estate taxes.

**Who may deduct real property taxes.** A person who pays a property tax must have an ownership interest in the property to deduct the payment. *Table 16-2* below summarizes who may deduct payments of real property taxes.

**Real estate tax paid on your principal residence with assistance from Hardest Hit Fund.** An IRS safe harbor (Notice 2018-63, amplifying Notice 2017-40) allows you to claim a deduction for real estate taxes paid and for mortgage interest *(15.1)* on your principal residence although you received tax-free assistance from a State Housing Finance Agency (State HFA) using funds from the Treasury Department's HFA Hardest Hit Fund. For 2018 through 2021 (at the end of which the safe harbor is scheduled to expire), Notice 2018-63 allows homeowners to first allocate home mortgage payments made during the year to mortgage interest, and then use any reasonable method to allocate the balance of payments to real property taxes, mortgage insurance premiums, home insurance premiums, and mortgage principal. Any allocation to state or local property taxes is subject to the overall limit of $10,000/$5,000 for state and local taxes *(16.1)*.

 *Filing Tip*

**Refund Credited to State Estimated Tax**
If you were entitled to a refund on your 2017 state tax return and you credited the overpayment towards your 2018 estimated state tax, do not forget to include the credited amount with other 2018 payments of state and local income tax if you itemize deductions for 2018 on Schedule A.

 *Filing Tip*

**Cooperative Apartments**
Tenant-stockholders of a cooperative housing corporation may deduct their share of the real estate taxes paid by the corporation. However, no deduction is allowed if the corporation does not own the land and building but merely leases them and pays taxes under the lease agreement *(15.9)*.

## 16.5  Assessments

**Assessments by homeowner's association not deductible as taxes.** Assessments paid to a local homeowner's association for the purpose of maintaining the common areas of the residential project and for promoting the recreation, health, and safety of the residents are not deductible as real property taxes because they are not imposed by a state or local government.

**Assessments for government services.** If property is used solely as your residence, you may not deduct charges for municipal water bills (even if described as a "tax"), sewer assessments, assessments for sanitation service, or title registration fees. A permit fee to build or improve a personal residence is added to the cost basis of the house.

Assessments for local benefits are deductible if they cover maintenance or repairs of streets, sidewalks, or water or sewer systems, or interest costs on such maintenance. However, assessments for construction of streets, sidewalks, or other local improvements that tend to increase the value of your property are not deductible as real estate taxes. You add such assessments to your cost basis for the property.

If you are billed a single amount, you may deduct the portion allocable to assessments for maintenance or repairs. The burden is on you to support the allocation.

## 16.6  Tenants' Payment of Taxes

You generally may not deduct on Schedule A (Form 1040) a portion of your rent as property taxes. This is so even where state or local law identifies a portion of the rent as being tied to tax increases.

Tenants have been allowed a deduction for property taxes in the following cases: In Hawaii tenants with leases of 15 years or more were allowed to deduct the portion of the rent representing taxes. In California, homeowners on leased land who placed their names on the county tax rolls and who paid the taxes directly to the county were allowed to claim a deduction.

In New York, liability for tax is placed directly on the tenant and the landlord is a collecting agent for paying over the tax to the taxing authorities. However, since the landlord also remains liable for the tax, the IRS ruled that the tenant's payment is in reality rent that cannot be deducted as a payment of real estate tax.

> **EXAMPLE**
>
> A municipal rent control ordinance allowed landlords to charge real property tax increases to the tenants as a monthly "tax surcharge." The ordinance stated that the surcharge was not to be considered rent for purposes of computing cost-of-living rental increases. The IRS ruled that the tenant may not deduct the "tax surcharge" as a property tax. The tax is imposed on the landlord, not on the tenant. The city ordinance, which permitted the landlord to pass on the tax increases to a tenant, did not shift liability for the property taxes from the landlord to the tenant. For federal tax purposes, the surcharge is merely an additional rental payment by the tenant. Similarly, "rates tax" or "renters' tax" imposed on tenants was ruled to be nondeductible because the tax is imposed on the person using the property rather than the property itself.

## 16.7  Allocating Taxes When You Sell or Buy Realty

When property is sold, the buyer and seller apportion the real estate taxes imposed on the property during the "real property year." A "real property year" is the period that a real estate tax covers. This allocation is provided for you in a settlement statement at the time of closing. If you want to figure your own allocations, your local tax authority can give you the "real property year" of the taxes you plan to apportion. If you are the seller and itemize deductions, you can claim on Schedule A the portion of the tax covering the beginning of the real property year through the day before the sale. If you are the buyer and itemize deductions, you can claim on Schedule A the part of the tax covering the date of the sale through the end of the real property year, even if the seller paid the entire tax prior to your purchase. Keep in mind that the deduction is subject to the overall $10,000/$5,000 limit on state and local taxes *(16.1)*,

### EXAMPLE

Your home is located in East County, which has a real property year starting April 1 and ending the following March 31. On May 2, 2018, you pay the $1,000 tax for the real property year ending March 31, 2019. You sell your home on July 10, 2018. You deduct $274 (100/365 of $1,000), since there are 100 days in the period beginning April 1, 2018 and ending July 9, 2018. The buyer deducts $726 (265/365 of $1,000), since there are 265 days in the period beginning with the date of sale on July 10, 2018, and ending March 31, 2019.

The allocation of taxes between the buyer and seller is mandatory for a property year during which both the seller and buyer own the property, whether or not your contract provides for an allocation. However, you do not allocate taxes for a real property year that begins after the date of sale. The buyer gets the deduction for all of the tax for that year because he or she owns the property for the entire real property year. There also is no allocation for a real property year that ends before the date of sale. The seller gets the deduction for that year's tax because the seller owned the property for that entire real property year.

**Form 1099-S.** If Form 1099-S is filed by the mortgage lender or real estate broker responsible for the closing, Box 6 will show the buyer's share of the real estate tax paid in advance by the seller. For example, Smith sells her house in Green County, where the real estate tax is paid annually in advance. In the year of sale she paid $1,200 in real estate taxes. Assuming that the home is sold at the end of the ninth month of the real property tax year, the amount of the real estate tax allocable to the buyer is $300 ($100 per month × 3 months). This amount, which is shown as paid by the seller in advance on an HUD-1 ("Settlement Statement") form provided at the closing, is reported as the buyer's share of the real estate tax in Box 6 of Form 1099-S.

**Seller's deduction in excess of the allocated amount is taxed.** If, in the year before the sale, the seller deducts an amount for taxes in excess of the allocated amount, the seller must report the excess as income in the year of the sale. This may happen when the seller is on the cash basis and pays the tax in the year before the sale.

### EXAMPLE

A real property tax of $1,000 is due and payable on November 30 for the following calendar year. On November 30, 2017, Keith Jones, who uses the cash basis and reports on a calendar year, pays the 2018 tax. On June 27, 2018, he sells the real property. Under the apportionment rule, Jones is allowed to deduct only $485 (177/365 of $1,000, since there are 177 days in the period from January 1 through June 26, 2018) of the tax for the 2017 real property tax year. But Jones has already deducted the full amount on his 2017 return. Therefore, he reports as "other income" for 2018 (Line 21 of Schedule 1, Form 1040), that part of the tax deduction that he was not entitled to under the apportionment.

**Buyer may not deduct payment of seller's back taxes.** If you agree to pay the seller's delinquent taxes as part of your purchase, the back taxes paid are added to your cost of the property. The amount realized on the sale by the seller is increased by your payment of the back taxes.

**Seller's payment upon buyer's failure to pay.** If a buyer is obligated to pay taxes under a land contract but fails to pay, the owner who pays the tax may deduct the payment if the tax is assessed to him or her.

**Buyer of foreclosed property.** If you buy realty at a tax sale and you do not receive immediate title to the property under state law until after a redemption period, you may not be able to deduct payment of realty taxes for several years.

*IRS Alert*

**Form 1099-S for Sale of Principal Residence**

The lender or real estate agent responsible for the closing does not have to report the sale of your principal residence on Form 1099-S if (1) the sales price is $250,000 or less, or $500,000 or less if you are married filing jointly, and (2) you certify in writing under penalty of perjury that you have met the tests for excluding from income the full gain on the sale *(29.1)*.

*Filing Instruction*

**Buyer's Share of Real Estate Tax**

If you sold a house in 2018 and received Form 1099-S, check Box 6 for the amount of real estate tax that you paid in advance and that is allocable to the buyer. The buyer may deduct this amount. You subtract it from the amount you paid when claiming your 2018 itemized deduction for real estate taxes.

## 16.8  Automobile License Fees

You may not deduct an auto license fee based on weight, model, year, or horsepower. But you may include a fee based on the value of the car as a state or local personal property tax (Line 5 of Schedule A) if these three tests are met: (1) the fee is an ad valorem tax, based on a percentage of value of the property; (2) it is imposed on an annual basis, even though it is collected more or less frequently; and (3) it is imposed on personal property. This third test is met even though the tax is imposed on the exercise of a privilege of registering a car or for using a car on the road. A deduction for state/local personal property tax is subject to the overall limit of $10,000/$5,000 for state and local taxes *(16.1)*.

The majority of state motor vehicle registration fees are not ad valorem taxes and do not qualify for the deduction. Various states and localities impose ad valorem or personal property taxes on motor vehicles that may qualify for the deduction. Contact a state or local authority to determine whether a license fee qualifies.

## 16.9  Taxes Deductible as Business Expenses

That a tax is not deductible as an itemized deduction does not mean you may not deduct it elsewhere on your return. For example, you may generally deduct property taxes incurred as a cost of doing business on Schedule C. Here are some other examples:

If you pay excise taxes on merchandise you sell in your business, you deduct the tax as a business expense. If you pay Social Security taxes (FICA) on your employees' wages, you deduct the tax as a business expense on Schedule C. If you pay sales tax on business property, you add the tax to the cost of the property for depreciation purposes. If the tax is paid on nondepreciable property, the tax is included in the currently deductible cost. If you pay sales tax on a deductible business meal, the tax is deductible as part of the meal costs, subject to the 50% cost limit *(20.24)*.

*Note:* If you are not a material participant in the business, your Schedule C expenses are subject to passive activity limitations; *see Chapter 10*.

**Above-the-line deduction for 50% of self-employment tax.** One-half of the self-employment tax figured on Schedule SE is deductible as an above-the-line adjustment to gross income on Line 27 of Schedule 1, Form 1040 *(45.3)*. This is not a business expense and is not deductible on Schedule C.

## 16.10  Foreign Taxes

**If you itemize deductions on Schedule A (Form 1040), you may include your payment of foreign income taxes and excess profits taxes.** Where you pay foreign income or excess profits tax, you have an election of either claiming the tax as an itemized deduction or as a tax credit. Claiming the credit may provide a larger tax savings *(36.13)*.

*Filing Tip*

**Value Portion of Auto License Fee**

If an automobile license fee is based partly on value and partly on weight or other tests, the tax attributed to the value is deductible as an ad valorem tax and is deductible as a personal property tax on Line 7 of Schedule A.

# CHAPTER 17

# Medical and Dental Expense Deductions

If you have unreimbursed medical expenses in 2018 that exceed 7.5% of your adjusted gross income *(17.1)*, you may be able to deduct some of your expenses, assuming that you are able to claim itemized deductions that exceed your standard deduction *(13.1)*.

A different rule applies if you are self employed and paid health insurance premiums. As a self-employed person, you do not have to itemize your premiums; you can claim 100% of the premiums as an above-the-line deduction directly from gross income *(12.2)*.

Carefully review the list of deductible expenses in this chapter so that you do not overlook any deductible expenses. Include payments of doctors' fees, health-care premiums, prescription medicines, travel costs for obtaining medical care, and eligible home improvements.

If you are married, both you and your spouse work, and one of you has substantial medical expenses, filing separate returns may result in a lower overall tax.

Qualifying long-term-care expenses may be treated as medical expenses subject to the AGI floor, including a specified deductible amount of premiums paid for a qualifying long-term-care contract *(17.15)*.

Deductible contributions to health savings accounts (HSAs) and Archer MSAs may be available to individuals covered by high deductible health plans; *see Chapters 12 and 41*.

Deductible medical expenses are not subject to the reduction of itemized deductions that applies to certain higher income taxpayers *(13.7)*.

*Caution*

**Only Unreimbursed Expenses Are Deductible**

You may not deduct medical expenses for which you have been reimbursed by insurance or other awards *(17.4)*. Furthermore, reimbursement of medical expenses deducted in prior tax years may be taxable income *(11.6)*.

## 17.1  Medical and Dental Expenses Must Exceed AGI Threshold

The tax law provides only a limited opportunity to deduct unreimbursed medical and dental costs for you, your spouse *(17.5)*, and your dependents *(17.6)*. Although a wide range of expenses are potentially deductible *(Table 17-1)* if you itemize expenses on Schedule A of Form 1040, your deduction may be completely disallowed or severely limited because of the adjusted gross income (AGI) floor. For 2018, only expenses that exceed 7.5% of your AGI may be claimed. The 7.5% floor applies regardless of your age. AGI is the amount shown on Line 7 of your Form 1040 *(12.1)*.

*Caution:* For years after 2018, the deduction floor is scheduled to increase to 10% of AGI for all taxpayers.

*See* the *e-Supplement* at *jklasser.com* for an update, if any.

> **EXAMPLES**
>
> 1. Frank Ryan's adjusted gross income (AGI) *(12.1)* for 2018 is $50,000. His unreimbursed expenses in 2018 are $2,875 for doctor and dentist visits, $845 for prescribed *(17.2)* drugs and medicines, and $3,250 for medical insurance premiums. Assuming that Frank itemizes deductions for 2018 on Schedule A (Form 1040), he may deduct medical/dental expenses of $3,220 after taking into account the 7.5% AGI floor:
>
> | | |
> |---|---|
> | Doctor and dentist fees | $ 2,875 |
> | Premiums | 3,250 |
> | Drugs | 845 |
> | Total | $ 6,970 |
> | Less: 7.5% of adjusted gross income (7.5% of $50,000) | 3,750 |
> | Medical and dental expense deduction for 2018 | $3,220 |
>
> 2. Same facts as in Example 1 except that Frank's AGI for 2018 is $100,000, not $50,000. Here, Frank may not claim any medical/dental deduction because his expenses of $6,970 do not exceed $7,500, (7.5% × $100,000 AGI).

**Do your expenses count as paid in 2018?**  On your 2018 return, you may deduct expenses paid in 2018 in cash or by a check you mail in 2018 (unless the check is postdated to 2019) for yourself, your spouse *(17.6)*, or your dependents *(17.7)*. The 2018 deduction includes payments made in 2018 for medical services provided before 2018. If you paid medical or dental expenses by credit card in 2018, the deduction is allowed for 2018, although you do not pay the charge bill until 2019. If you pay expenses online, the payment date shown on your online bank statement governs. If you borrow to pay medical or dental expenses, you claim the deduction in the year you use the loan proceeds to pay the bill, even if you do not repay the loan until a later year.

## 17.2  Allowable Medical and Dental Care Costs

In determining whether you have paid deductible medical expenses exceeding the AGI floor *(17.1)*, include the cost of diagnosis, cure, mitigation, treatment, or prevention of disease, or any treatment that affects a part or function of your body *(Table 17-1)*. Also include qualifying costs you paid for your spouse *(17.5)* and your dependents *(17.6)*.

Expenses that are solely for cosmetic reasons are not deductible. Also, expenses incurred to benefit your general health are not deductible even if recommended by a physician *(17.3)*.

Medicine and drugs. To be deductible, medicines and drugs other than insulin must be obtainable solely through a prescription by a doctor. Insulin is deductible even though a prescription may not be required. You may not deduct the cost of over-the-counter medicines and drugs, such as aspirin and other cold remedies, even if you have a doctor's prescription for them.

Marijuana is not deductible even if prescribed by a doctor in a state allowing the prescription.

A prescribed drug brought in or shipped into the U.S. from another country is not deductible unless the FDA (Food and Drug Administration) allows that drug to be legally imported by individuals.

**Diagnostic tests.** The IRS treats unreimbursed diagnostic procedures as deductible medical expenses (subject to the AGI floor), even if you had no symptoms of illness and you underwent the test without a physician's recommendation. For example, the cost of an annual physical performed by a doctor and related laboratory tests is a medical expense, whether or not you were feeling ill. Similarly, a full body scan is a deductible diagnostic procedure, whether or not a physician recommended it. Where a procedure does not have a nonmedical function, a physician's recommendation is not necessary. It also does not matter if a less expensive alternative to the full body scan is available. Finally, a home pregnancy test qualifies as a medical expense even though its purpose is not to detect disease but to test for the healthy functioning of the body.

**Health insurance premiums.** Premiums you pay for health insurance covering yourself, your spouse *(17.5)* and your dependents *(17.6)* generally qualify for a deduction, *see 17.8* for limitations.

**Vitamins and nutritional or herbal supplements.** The IRS does not allow a deduction for the cost of vitamins, nutritional or herbal supplements, or "natural" medicines unless a medical practitioner recommends them as treatment for a specific medical condition diagnosed by a physician. Otherwise, they are considered to be for maintaining your general health rather than for medical care.

**Stop-smoking programs.** The cost of smoking cessation programs is a deductible medical expense, as well as nicotine withdrawal drugs that require a physician's prescription. Over-the-counter nicotine patches and gums are not deductible.

**Exercise and weight-reduction programs.** If you incur costs for such programs to improve your general health, the costs are not deductible even if your doctor has recommended them. However, if your doctor has recommended a program as treatment for a specific condition, such as heart disease or hypertension, the IRS allows a deduction for the cost.

The IRS considers obesity a disease. If a physician has made a diagnosis of obesity, the costs of joining a weight-loss program and additional fees for meetings are eligible medical expenses. However, reduced-calorie diet foods that are substitutes for foods normally consumed are not deductible even if they are part of the program; *see* "Special foods" below.

**Special foods.** The IRS position on deducting the cost of "special foods" is unclear. The IRS has long taken the position in Publication 502 that the excess cost of special foods or beverages over a regular diet is not a deductible medical expense if the special foods "satisfy normal nutritional needs", even if a physician substantiates that a special diet is needed to alleviate or treat an illness. This IRS position not only bars a deduction for low-calorie foods, on the grounds that they substitute for a "normal" diet, but it could also block a deduction for diets required to deal with conditions such as Celiac disease. Although gluten-free foods may have a clear medical purpose as diagnosed by a physician, such foods obviously "satisfy normal nutritional needs" and so for that reason the IRS could deny a deduction for the excess cost.

In response to public pressure, the IRS informally suggested that it might change the language of Publication 502 and follow the standard used by the Tax Court, which allows a deduction for the excess cost of a special diet over ordinary food provided the medical need for it is established by a physician; *see* the Examples below. However, when this book was completed, the IRS had not eliminated its "normal nutritional needs" restriction.

**Caution**

**Over-the-Counter Drugs**

OTC drugs, even if prescribed by a doctor, are not deductible with the exception of insulin. Legislation has been proposed to eliminate the restriction for OTC drugs, but Congress has not enacted the proposals into law; *see* the *e-Supplement* at *jklasser.com* for an update, if any.

**IRS Alert**

**Breast Pumps and Lactation Supplies Deductible**

Breast pumps and supplies that assist lactation are treated by the IRS as medical expenses because, like obstetric care costs, they affect the structure or function of the lactating woman's body.

**IRS Alert**

**Weight-Loss Program for Obesity**

The IRS allows a deduction for the costs of joining a weight-loss program and fees for follow-up meetings if a physician has made a diagnosis of obesity.

**Caution**

**Deducting Costs of Health Improvement Programs**

Exercise and weight-reduction programs are deductible as treatments for specific conditions, but not as ways to improve your general health, even if your doctor has recommended them *(17.2)*.

*Filing Tip*

**Childbirth Classes**

A mother-to-be may deduct the cost of classes instructing her in Lamaze breathing and relaxation techniques, stages of labor, and delivery procedures. If her husband or other childbirth "coach" also attends the classes, the portion of the fee allocable to the coach is not deductible. Costs of classes on early pregnancy, fetal development, or caring for newborns also are not deductible.

---

### EXAMPLES

1. To alleviate an ulcer, your doctor puts you on a special diet. According to the IRS, the cost of your food and beverages is not deductible. The special diet replaces the food you normally eat.

   Under the Tax Court test, the extra costs of the special diet would be deductible given the medical purpose of the diet.

2. Anna Von Kalb suffered from hypoglycemia and her physician prescribed a special high protein diet, which required her to consume twice as much protein as an average person and exclude all processed foods and carbohydrates. She spent $3,483 for food, and deducted 30%, or $1,045, as the extra cost of her high protein diet. The IRS disallowed the deduction, claiming that the protein supplements were a substitute for foods normally consumed. The Tax Court disagreed. The high protein food did not substitute for her usual diet but helped alleviate her hypoglycemia. Thus, she may deduct its additional expense.

3. The Bechers suffered from allergies and were advised by a physician to eat organically grown food to avoid the chemicals in commercial food. The Bechers claimed a medical expense deduction of $2,255, the extra cost of buying organic food.

   The IRS disallowed the deduction and the Tax Court agreed. They did not present evidence that their allergies could be cured by limiting their diet to organic food. That the food was beneficial to their general health and was prescribed by a doctor is not sufficient for a deduction.

---

**Infant formula.** Applying its "nutritional needs" test, the IRS in a private ruling denied a mother's deduction for the cost of infant formula for her healthy child. Although the mother had a medical reason for buying the formula—she was unable to breastfeed her baby following a double mastectomy—the formula was food satisfying the child's ordinary nutritional needs, and therefore was a nondeductible personal expense.

**Portion of monthly service fees paid to retirement community.** The portion of the monthly fees that is allocable to medical care is a deductible medical expense *(34.9)*.

**Advance payment for lifetime care in retirement community.** If you pay a life-care fee or "founder's fee" either monthly or in a lump sum to a retirement community, the portion allocable to future medical care may be included as a current medical expense *(34.9)*.

**Advance payments for lifetime care of disabled dependent.** You can treat as a current medical expense a nonrefundable advance payment to a private institution for the lifetime care and treatment of your physically or mentally impaired child upon your death or when you become unable to provide care. The nonrefundable payment must be a condition for the institution's future acceptance of your child.

---

### EXAMPLE

Parents contracted with an institution to care for their handicapped child after their death. The contract provided for payments as follows: 20% on signing, 10% within 12 months, 10% within 24 months, and the balance when the child enters. Payment of specified amounts at specified intervals was a condition imposed by the institution for its agreement to accept the child for lifetime care. Since the obligation to pay was incurred at the time payments were made, the IRS held that they were deductible as medical expenses, although the medical services were not to be performed until a future time, if at all.

---

## Table 17-1 Deductible Medical Expenses

### Professional Services

| | | | |
|---|---|---|---|
| Chiropodist | Ophthalmologist | Podiatrist | Psychiatrist |
| Chiropractor | Optician | Practical or other nonprofessional | Psychoanalyst |
| Christian Science practitioner | Optometrist | nurse for medical services | Psychologist |
| Dermatologist | Orthopedist | only, not for care of a healthy | Registered nurse |
| Dentist | Osteopath | person or a child who is not ill. | Surgeon |
| Gynecologist | Pediatrician | Costs for medical care of elderly | Unlicensed practitioner services are |
| Neurologist | Physician | person unable to get about or | deductible if the type and quality |
| Obstetrician | Physiotherapist | person subject to spells are | of the services are not illegal. |
| | Plastic surgeon; but see 17.3. | deductible (17.12). | |

### Dental Services

| | | | |
|---|---|---|---|
| Artificial teeth | Dental X-rays | Filling teeth | Oral surgery |
| Cleaning teeth | Extracting teeth | Gum treatment | Straightening teeth |

### Equipment and Supplies

| | | | |
|---|---|---|---|
| Abdominal supports | Braces | Hearing aids | Repair of special telephone |
| Air conditioner where necessary | Breast pumps and lactation | Heating devices | equipment for the deaf |
| for relief from an allergy | supplies | Invalid chair | Sacroiliac belt |
| or for relieving difficulty in | Contact lenses and solutions | Iron lung | Special mattress and plywood bed |
| breathing (17.13). | Cost of installing stair-seat | Orthopedic shoes—excess cost | boards for relief of arthritis or |
| Ambulance hire | elevator for person with heart | over cost of regular shoes | spine |
| Arches | condition (17.13). | Oxygen or oxygen equipment | Splints |
| Artificial eyes, limbs | Crutches | to relieve breathing problems | Truss |
| Autoette (auto device for | Elastic hosiery | caused by a medical condition | Wheelchair |
| handicapped person) | Eyeglasses | Reclining chair if prescribed by | Wig advised by doctor as essential |
| Back supports | Fluoridation unit in home | doctor | to mental health of person who |
| | | | lost all hair from disease |

### Medical Treatments

| | | | |
|---|---|---|---|
| Abortion | Hydrotherapy (water treatments) | Navajo healing ceremonies | Radial keratotomy |
| Acupuncture | In vitro fertilization for a female | ("sings") | Radium therapy |
| Blood transfusion | otherwise unable to conceive | Nursing | Ultraviolet ray treatments |
| Childbirth delivery | Injections | Organ transplant | Vasectomy |
| Diathermy | Insulin treatments | Prenatal and postnatal treatments | Whirlpool baths |
| Electric shock treatments | Laser eye surgery or radial | Psychotherapy | X-ray treatments |
| Hearing services | keratotomy to improve vision | Sterilization | |

### Medicines and Drugs

Cost of prescriptions only;
over-the-counter medicine is
not deductible.

### Laboratory Examinations and Tests

| | | | |
|---|---|---|---|
| Blood tests | Spinal fluid tests | X-ray examinations | Oxygen mask, tent |
| Cardiographs | Sputum tests | Hospital Services | Use of operating room |
| Metabolism tests | Stool examinations | Anesthetist | Vaccines |
| | Urine analyses | Hospital bills | X-ray technician |

### Premiums for Medical Care Policies (17.5)

| | | | |
|---|---|---|---|
| Blue Cross and Blue Shield | supplemental insurance, and | Health insurance covering hospital, | Membership in medical service |
| Contact lens replacement insurance | Medicare D prescription drug | surgical, and other medical | cooperative |
| Medicare A (if not covered by | coverage | expenses | |
| Social Security), Medicare B | | | |

**Miscellaneous**

Alcoholic inpatient care costs

Birth control pills or other birth control items prescribed by your doctor

Braille books—excess cost of Braille works over cost of regular editions

Childbirth classes for expectant mother

Clarinet lessons advised by dentist for treatment of tooth defects

Convalescent home—for medical treatment only

Drug treatment center—inpatient care costs

Fees paid to health institute where the exercises, rubdowns, etc., taken there are prescribed by a physician as treatments necessary to alleviate a physical or mental defect or illness

Kidney donor's or possible kidney donor's expenses

Lead-based paint removal to prevent a child who has had lead poisoning from eating the paint. Repainting the scraped area is not deductible.

Legal fees for guardianship of mentally ill spouse where commitment was necessary for medical treatment

Lifetime care—advance payments made either monthly or as a lump sum under an agreement with a retirement home (34.10).

Long-term care costs for chronically ill (17.15).

Nurse's board and wages, including Social Security taxes paid on wages

Pregnancy test kit

Remedial reading for child suffering from dyslexia

School—payments to a special school for a mentally or physically impaired person if the main reason for using the school is its resources for relieving the disability (17.10).

"Seeing-eye" dog and its maintenance

Smoking cessation programs

Special school costs for physically and mentally handicapped children (17.10).

Telephone-teletype costs and television adapter for closed caption service for deaf person

Travel to obtain medical care (17.9).

Wages of guide for a blind person

Weight-loss program to treat obesity or other specific disease (17.2).

**Table 17-2 Nondeductible Medical Expenses**

Antiseptic diaper service

Athletic club expenses

Babysitting fees to enable you to make doctor's visits

Boarding school fees paid for healthy child while parent is recuperating from illness

Bottled water bought to avoid drinking fluoridated city water

Cost of divorce recommended by a psychiatrist

Cost of hotel room suggested for sex therapy

Cost of moving away from airport noise by person suffering a nervous breakdown

Cost of trips prescribed by a doctor for a "change of environment" to boost an ailing person's morale

Dance lessons advised by a doctor as general physical and mental therapy

Divorced spouse's medical bills

Domestic help; but see 17.12 if nursing duties are performed.

Ear piercing

Funeral, cremation, burial, cemetery plot, monument, or mausoleum

Health programs offered by resort hotels, health clubs, and gyms

Illegal operations and drugs

Marijuana, even if prescribed by a physician in a state permitting the prescription

Marriage counseling fees

Massages recommended by physician for general stress reduction

Maternity clothes

Premiums on policies guaranteeing you a specified amount of money each week in the event hospitalization

Scientology fees

Special food or beverage substitutes; but see 17.2.

Tattooing

Teeth whitening to reverse age-related discoloration

Toothpaste

Transportation costs of a disabled person to and from work

Travel costs to favorable climate when you can live there permanently

Travel costs to look for a new place to live—on a doctor's advice

Tuition and travel expenses to send a problem child to a particular school for a beneficial change in environment (17.10).

Weight-loss program to improve general health (17.2).

## 17.3 Nondeductible Medical Expenses

The most common nondeductible medical expense is the cost of over-the-counter medicines and drugs, such as aspirin and other cold remedies. A deduction for over-the-counter medicines is disallowed even if you have a doctor's prescription (17.2). Expenses incurred to improve your general health, such as exercise programs not related to a specific condition, are not deductible (17.2 and *Table 17-2*).

**Cosmetic procedures.** A medical expense deduction is allowed for cosmetic surgery if it is necessary to improve a disfigurement related to a congenital abnormality, disfiguring disease, or an accidental injury. For example, a deduction is allowed for breast reconstruction surgery, as well as breast prosthesis, following a mastectomy as part of a treatment for cancer.

You may not deduct the cost of cosmetic surgery or other procedures that do not have a medical purpose. Thus, face lifts, hair transplants, electrolysis, teeth-whitening procedures, and liposuction intended to improve appearance are generally not deductible. However, in one case, the Tax Court allowed an exotic dancer to claim a depreciation deduction for breast implants essential for her business (19.10).

**Future medical care.** Generally, you cannot include as a current medical expense payment for medical care that is to be provided substantially beyond the end of the year. However, advance payments for the care of a disabled dependent or the portion of a life-care fee or "founder's fee" to a retirement community that is allocable to future medical care is a currently deductible expense (17.2).

# 17.4 Reimbursements Reduce Deductible Expenses

Insurance or other reimbursements of your medical costs reduce your potential medical deduction. Reimbursements for loss of earnings or damages for personal injuries and mental suffering do not have to be taken into account. A reimbursement first reduces the medical expense for which it is paid. The excess is then applied to your other deductible medical costs. See Example 1 below.

**Personal injury settlements or awards.** Generally, a cash settlement recovered in a personal injury suit does not reduce your medical expense deduction. The settlement is not treated as reimbursement of your medical bills. But when part of the settlement is specifically earmarked by a court or by law for payment of hospital bills, the medical expense deduction is reduced.

If you receive a settlement for a personal injury that is partly allocable to future medical expenses, you reduce medical expenses for these injuries by the allocated amount until it is used up.

**Fake claims.** Medical reimbursements for fake injury claims are treated as taxable income; *see* Example 2 below.

### EXAMPLES

1. In 2018, Gail Hurz paid $2,400 in medical insurance premiums, $1,200 for doctor and hospital bills and $750 for prescription drugs. She received reimbursements of $1,175 from group hospitalization insurance ($800 for the doctor and hospital bills and $375 for the drugs.) Her adjusted gross income for 2018 is $32,100. If Gail itemizes, she can claim a medical expense deduction of $767, after taking into account the 7.5% AGI floor.

   | | |
   |---|---|
   | Prescription drugs | $750 |
   | Medical care expenses | 1,200 |
   | Premiums | 2,400 |
   | Total | $4,350 |
   | Less reimbursement | 1,175 |
   | Unreimbursed costs | $3,175 |
   | Less: 7.5% of $32,100 | 2,408 |
   | Medical expense deduction for 2018 | $767 |

2. Dodge, with the aid of a "friendly" doctor, arranged to be hospitalized for alleged back injuries and realized over $200,000 from HIP policies. The IRS charged that the insurance proceeds were taxable income. Dodge argued they were tax-free reimbursements of medical costs.

   The Tax Court sided with the IRS. The tax-free rules cover the payment of legitimate medical costs. Here there were no legitimate medical costs of actual injuries. Dodge took out the policies in a scam arrangement with the doctor.

**Reimbursements in excess of your medical expenses.** If you paid the entire premium for health insurance, you are not taxed on payments from the plan even if they exceed your medical expenses for the year. If you and your employer each contributed to the policy, you generally have to include in income that part of the excess reimbursement that is attributable to employer premium contributions not included in your gross income; *see* Examples 2–4 below. The taxable excess reimbursement must be reported as "Other income" on Line 21 of Form 1040.

However, you do not have to report any excess reimbursements that are tax-free payments for permanent disfigurement or loss of bodily functions *(3.2)*.

If your employer paid the total cost of the policy and the contributions were not taxed to you, you report as income all of your excess reimbursement, unless it covers payment for permanent injury or disfigurement *(3.2)*.

For the treatment of insurance reimbursements of long-term care costs, *see 17.15*.

*Court Decision*

### Sex Reassignment Surgery Is Deductible Expense

The IRS has agreed to follow a 2010 decision in which a Tax Court majority held, over a rigorous dissent, that Gender Identity Disorder (GID) is a disease for medical deduction purposes. A taxpayer, born male, was allowed to deduct expenses for cross-gender hormone therapy and sex reassignment surgery (SRS). Expert testimony confirmed that the taxpayer suffered from severe GID, and hormone therapy and SRS are essential elements of a widely accepted treatment protocol for that condition. The cost of breast augmentation surgery was potentially deductible, but under the facts here, the procedure was not shown to be medically necessary under accepted treatment protocols.

The IRS acquiescence to the decision means that it will no longer dispute that GID is a disease and that expenses for its treatment, including sex reassignment surgery and hormone therapy, are deductible medical expenses where there is medical documentation of GID.

*Caution*

### Reimbursements Exceeding Expenses

If you have more than one policy and receive reimbursements that exceed your total medical expenses for the year, you must pay tax on all or part of the reimbursement where your employer paid premiums on the policies; *see* Examples 1–4 in this section.

## EXAMPLES

1. Henry Knight pays the premiums for two personal health insurance policies. His total medical expenses are $900. He receives $700 from one insurance company and $500 from the other. The excess reimbursement of $300 ($1,200 − $900) is not taxable because he paid the entire premiums on the policies.

2. Lionel Guest's employer paid premiums of $1,800 for two employee health insurance policies covering medical expenses. Guest's medical expenses in one year are $900. He receives $1,200 from the two companies. The entire $300 excess is taxable because Guest's employer paid the total cost of the policies and the contributions were not taxed to him.

3. Kay Brown's employer paid a premium of $1,000 for a group health policy covering Brown, and Brown herself paid $300 for a personal health policy. Her medical expenses are $900. She receives reimbursements of $1,200, $700 under her employer's policy and $500 under her own policy. Brown's reimbursements exceed expenses by $300, but the taxable portion attributed to her employer's premium contribution is $175, computed this way:

| | |
|---|---|
| Reimbursement allocated to Brown's policy | |
| ($500 ÷ $1,200) × $900 | $375 |
| Reimbursement allocated to employer's policy | |
| ($700 ÷ $1,200) × $900 | $525 |
| Taxable excess allocated to employer's policy | |
| ($700 − $525) | $175 |

4. Mike Green's employer paid $1,200 for a health insurance policy but contributed only $450 and deducted $750 from Green's wages. Green also paid $300 for a personal health insurance policy. His medical expenses are $900. He recovered $700 from the employer's policy and $500 from his personal policy. The excess attributable to the employer's policy is $175 (computed as in Example 3 above). However, the taxable portion is only $65.63. Both Green and his employer contributed to the cost of the employer's policy and a further allocation is necessary:

| | |
|---|---|
| Green's contribution | $750 |
| Employer's contribution | 450 |
| Total cost of policy | $1,200 |
| Ratio of employer's contribution to annual cost of policy (450 ÷ 1,200, or 37.50%) | |
| Taxable portion: 37.50% of excess reimbursement of $175 | $65.63 |

**Reimbursement in a later year may be taxed.** If you took a medical expense deduction in one year and are reimbursed for all or part of the expense in a later year, the reimbursement may be taxed in the year received. The reimbursement is generally taxable income to the extent the deduction reduced your tax in the prior year. *See* the details for figuring taxable income on a recovery of a prior deduction in *Chapter 11 (11.6)*.

## EXAMPLES

1. In 2017, Anna Gurchani had adjusted gross income of $32,000. She claimed itemized deductions that exceeded her allowable standard deduction by $1,000; on her Schedule A, Gurchani listed medical expenses of $3,800. She deducted $1,400 for 2017, computed as follows:

| | |
|---|---|
| Medical expenses | $3,800 |
| Less: 7.5% of $32,000 | 2,400 |
| Allowable deduction | $1,400 |

In 2018, she collects $300 from insurance, reimbursing part of her 2017 medical expenses. If she had collected that amount in 2017, her medical expenses would have been $3,500 and her deduction would have been $1,100. The entire reimbursement of $300 is includible as taxable income for 2018. It is the amount by which the 2017 deduction of $1,400 exceeds the deduction of $1,100 that would have been allowed if the reimbursement had been received in 2017.

2. Same facts as in Example 1 above, but Anna did not deduct medical expenses in 2017 because she did not itemize deductions. The reimbursement in 2018 is not taxable.

## 17.5 Expenses of Your Spouse

Subject to the AGI floor *(17.1)*, you may deduct as medical expenses your payments of medical bills for your spouse if you were married either when your spouse received the medical services or at the time you paid the expenses. That is, you may deduct your payment of your spouse's medical bills even though you are divorced or widowed, if, at the time the expenses were incurred, you were married. Furthermore, if your spouse incurred medical expenses before you married and you pay the bills after you marry, you may deduct the expense.

### EXAMPLES

1. You got married in 2018. After the marriage, you pay your spouse's outstanding medical bills from 2017. You may claim the payment as a medical expense for 2018 on a joint return or on your own return if you and your spouse file separately.

2. In October 2017, your spouse had dental work done. In February 2018, you are divorced and in April 2018, you pay your former spouse's dental bills. You may deduct the payment on your 2018 tax return.

3. In 2018, you pay medical expenses for your spouse who died in 2017. In 2018 you remarry and file a joint 2018 return with your new spouse. On the 2018 joint return, you may deduct your payment of your deceased spouse's medical expenses.

**Filing separately in community property states.** If you and your spouse file separately and live in a community property state, any medical expenses paid out of community funds are treated as paid 50% by each of you. Medical expenses paid out of separate funds of one spouse can be deducted only by that spouse.

## 17.6 Expenses of Your Dependents

You may deduct your payment of medical bills for your children or other dependents, subject to the AGI floor *(17.1)*. You may deduct the expenses of a person who was your dependent (your qualifying child or qualifying relative; *21.1*) either at the time the medical services were provided or at the time you paid the expenses. That person must have been a U.S. citizen or national, or a resident of the United States, Canada, or Mexico, but this test does not apply to an adopted child who lived with you.

In determining whether a person is your "dependent" for medical expense purposes, you may be able to claim the expenses of someone who does not meet all of the regular tests for being your qualifying child or qualifying relative *(21.1)*. Specifically, you may deduct your payment of medical costs for a person who cannot be treated as your dependent for one of the following reasons: (1) the person is your child who is treated as a dependent of the other parent under the special rules *(21.7)* for divorced/separated parents; *see* below, (2) the person has gross income exceeding the limit for qualifying relatives ($4,150 for 2018), (3) the person files a joint return with their spouse, or (4) you are the dependent of another taxpayer and thus are barred from claiming any dependents on your return.

The other dependent tests for a qualifying child or a qualifying relative must be met. For example, to claim your payment of medical expenses for your parent, or for your child who is not your qualifying child *(21.3)*, you must pay over 50% of his or her support under the qualifying relative rules. *See* Examples 1–3 below. A child may not deduct medical expenses paid with his or her parent's welfare payments; *see* Example 4 below.

 *Filing Tip*

**Should Spouses File Separately?**

If you are married and both you and your spouse have separate incomes, and one of you has substantial medical expenses for 2018, consider filing separate returns. This way the AGI floor *(17.1)* will apply separately to your individual incomes, not to the higher joint income. To make sure which option to take—filing jointly or separately—you compute your tax on both types of returns and choose the one giving the lower overall tax *(1.3)* .

On a separate return, only include the expenses you paid. If you paid medical expenses out of a joint checking account in which you and your spouse have an equal interest, then each of you are considered to have paid half of the medical expenses unless you show otherwise.

**Divorced and separated parents.** You may be able to deduct your payment of your child's medical costs, even though your ex-spouse is entitled to treat the child as a dependent *(21.7)*. For purposes of a 2018 medical deduction, the child is considered to be the dependent of both you and the child's other parent if (1) you are divorced or legally separated under a court agreement, separated under a written agreement, or married but living apart during the last six months of 2018; (2) the child was in the custody of one or both of you for more than half of 2018; and (3) together you provided more than half of the child's 2018 support.

### EXAMPLES

1. You contribute more than half of your married son's support in 2018, including a payment of a medical expense of $800. Because your son filed a joint return with his wife for 2018, you may not claim him as a dependent *(21.1)*. But you still may include your payment of the $800 medical expense with your other qualifying medical expenses since you contributed more than half of his support.

2. Your mother, a U.S. citizen, underwent an operation in November 2017. You paid for the operation in February 2018. You may deduct the cost of the operation in 2018 if you furnished more than one-half of your mother's support in either 2017 or 2018.

3. Same facts as Example 2, except your mother is a citizen and resident of Italy. You may not deduct the cost of the operation. She is not a U.S. citizen or a resident of the United States, Canada, or Mexico and thus does not qualify as a dependent for exemption purposes *(21.8)* or for medical deduction purposes.

4. A son is the legal guardian of his mother who is mentally incompetent. As guardian, he received his mother's state welfare and Social Security benefits, which he deposited in his personal bank account and used to pay part of his mother's medical expenses. On his tax return, he claimed a deduction for the total medical expenses paid on behalf of his mother. The court held that he could deduct only medical expenses in excess of the amounts received as welfare and Social Security payments. The benefits, to the extent used to pay medical expenses, represented the mother's payments in her own behalf.

**Adopted children.** You may deduct medical expenses of an adopted child if you may claim the child as a dependent either when the medical services are rendered or when you pay the expenses. An adopted child is treated as your child for dependent purposes when a court has approved the adoption or the child is lawfully placed with you for legal adoption.

If you reimburse an adoption agency for medical expenses it paid under an agreement with you, you are considered to have paid the expenses. But if the reimbursement is for medical services that were provided and paid for before you began your adoption negotiations, you may not deduct your payment.

You may not deduct medical expenses for services rendered to the natural mother of the child you adopt.

**Multiple support agreements.** If you have the right to treat a person as your dependent under a multiple support agreement *(21.6)*, you may claim your unreimbursed payments of that person's medical expenses. Even if the person has a gross income of $4,150 or more, and therefore cannot be considered your qualifying child for other tax purposes, you may still deduct your 2018 payments of his or her medical expenses provided the other multiple support agreement tests *(21.6)* are met.

### EXAMPLE

Ingrid Fromm and her brother and sister share equally in the support of their mother. Part of their mother's support includes medical expenses. Should the three of them share in the payment of the bills or should only one of them pay the bills? The answer: Payment should be made by the person who may claim the mother as a dependent under a multiple support agreement. Only that person may deduct the payment. If Ingrid is going to claim her as an exemption, she should pay the bill. She may deduct the payment although she did not contribute more than half of her mother's support. If her brother and sister reimburse her for part of the bill, she may include only the unreimbursed portion in her medical expenses. Neither Ingrid's brother nor her sister may deduct this share. Thus, a deduction is lost for these amounts.

*Filing Instruction*

**Multiple Support Agreement**

If you may claim a person as your dependent under a multiple support agreement, include with your medical expenses only the amount you actually pay for the dependent's medical expenses. If you are reimbursed by others who signed the multiple support agreement, you must reduce your deduction by the amount of reimbursement.

## 17.7 Decedent's Medical Expenses

If you pay the medical expenses of your deceased spouse or dependent *(17.6)*, you may claim the payment as a medical expense in the year you pay the expenses, whether that is before or after the person's death.

If the executor or administrator of the estate pays the decedent's medical expenses within one year after the date of death, an election may be made to treat the expenses as if the deceased had paid them in the year the medical services were provided. The executor or administrator may file an amended return for the year the services were provided and claim them as a medical deduction for that year, assuming the period for filing the amended return *(47.2)* has not passed.

If the election is made by the executor to claim the expenses as an income tax deduction, and an estate tax return is filed, the expenses may not also be claimed as a deduction on the estate tax return. The executor must file a statement with the decedent's income tax return that the expenses have not been deducted on the estate tax return and the estate waives its right to deduct them for estate tax purposes.

If medical expenses are claimed as an income tax deduction, the portion of the expenses that are not allowed because they are below the AGI floor *(17.1)* may not be claimed as an estate tax deduction if an estate tax return is filed. Although the expenses were not actually deducted, the IRS considers them to be part of the overall income tax deduction.

> **EXAMPLE**
>
> Oscar Reyes incurred medical expenses of $5,000 in 2017 and $3,000 in 2018. He timely filed (by April 15, 2019) his 2018 return and died June 1, 2019, without having paid the $8,000 of medical expenses. In August 2019 his executor pays the medical expenses. The executor may file an amended return for 2017, claim a medical expense deduction for the $5,000 of 2017 expenses, and get a refund for the increased deductions. The executor may claim the remaining $3,000 as a medical expense deduction on an amended final return for 2018.

## 17.8 Premiums for Health Insurance

Unless you are self-employed and qualify for the 100% above-the-line deduction (discussed below), health insurance premiums are deductible only as an itemized medical expense on Schedule A (Form 1040), subject to the AGI floor *(17.1)*. Include premiums you paid for health insurance that covers hospital, surgical, drug costs, and other medical expenses for you, your spouse *(17.6)*, and your dependents *(17.7)*. Also deductible are premiums paid for contact lens replacement insurance. Deductions may be claimed for membership payments in associations furnishing cooperative or free-choice medical services, group hospitalization, or clinical care policies, including HMOs (health maintenance organizations) and medical care premiums paid to colleges as part of a tuition bill, if the amount is separately stated in the bill.

You may deduct premiums for Medicare Part B supplemental insurance and Medicare Part D prescription drug insurance. Payroll withholdings for Medicare Part A are not medical expenses, but premiums for voluntary coverage under Medicare (Part A) are deductible by those over age 65 who are not covered by Social Security.

Premiums paid before you reach age 65 for medical care insurance for protection after you reach age 65 are deductible in the year paid if they are payable on a level payment basis under the contract (1) for a period of 10 years or more or (2) until the year you reach age 65 (but in no case for a period of less than five years).

Premiums for qualifying long-term care policies are deductible subject to limitations *(17.15)*.

**Nondeductible premiums.** You may not deduct premiums for a policy guaranteeing you a specified amount each week (not to exceed a specified number of weeks) in the event you are hospitalized. Also, no deduction may be claimed for premiums paid for a policy that compensates you for loss of earnings while ill or injured, or for loss of life, limb, or sight. If your policy covers both medical care and loss of income or loss of life, limb, or sight, no part of the premium is deductible unless (1) the contract or separate statement from the

*Filing Instruction*

**Long-Term Care Premiums**

The amount of deductible premiums for a qualifying long-term care policy depends on your age *(17.15)*.

insurance company states what part of the premium is allocated to medical care and (2) the premium allocated to medical care is reasonable.

You may not deduct part of the car insurance premiums for medical insurance coverage for persons injured by or in your car where the premium covering you, your spouse *(17.6)*, or your dependents *(17.7)* is not stated separately from the premium covering medical care for others.

You generally cannot deduct premiums you pay for covering someone who is not your dependent, even if that person is your child (such as your non-dependent child under age 27 who is included on your policy). However, if that person is not your dependent only for the reasons specified in *17.7*, you may deduct the premiums paid for that person.

**Self-employed deduction.** If you were self-employed in 2017 you may claim a special deduction on Schedule 1 of Form 1040 for 100% of health insurance premiums you paid for yourself, your spouse, and your dependents. The deduction is also allowed if you received wages from an S corporation in which you were more than a 2% shareholder, you were a general partner, or you were a limited partner who received guaranteed payments.

The above-the-line deduction *(12.2)* may not be claimed for any month that you were eligible for coverage under an employer's subsidized health plan, including a plan of your spouse's employer. Also, the deduction may not exceed your net earnings from the business under which the health premiums are paid.

Any balance of premiums not deductible because you had coverage under a subsidized employer health plan may be claimed as an itemized medical expense subject to the AGI floor *(17.1)*.

## 17.9 Travel Costs May Be Medical Deductions

Travel costs to a doctor's office, hospital, or clinic where you, your spouse, or your dependents receive medical care are deductible medical expenses, subject to the AGI floor *(17.1)*. Commuting to work is not a medical expense, even if your condition requires you to make special travel arrangements.

Deductible travel includes fares for buses, taxis or trains, and the costs of hiring a car service or ambulance to obtain medical care. Plane fares to another city are allowed by the IRS so long as obtaining medical care is the primary purpose of the trip; *see* below for lodging expense rule.

*Filing Tip*

**Deductible Travel Costs**

The costs of trips to receive medical treatment are deductible as medical expenses subject to the AGI floor. The costs of a trip to a conference to learn about medical treatment may be deductible if recommended by a doctor.

> **EXAMPLE**
>
> In 2018, you drove your car to a doctor's office for treatment 40 times. Each round trip was 25 miles. If you use the IRS' flat mileage rate, you treat $180 (1,000 miles × 18 cents), plus any parking fees or tolls you paid on the doctor visits, as 2018 medical expenses.

If you used your automobile in 2018 to obtain medical care, you may include in your medical expenses a flat IRS rate of 18 cents a mile. In addition, you may deduct parking fees and tolls. If, however, auto expenses exceed this standard mileage rate, you may deduct your actual out-of-pocket costs for gas, oil, repairs, tolls, and parking fees. Do not include depreciation, general maintenance, or car insurance. The cost, as well as the operating and repair costs, of a wheelchair, autoette, or special auto device for a handicapped person is deductible if not used mainly for commuting.

**Medical conferences.** Travel costs and admission fees to a medical conference are deductible medical expenses if an illness suffered by you, your spouse, or your dependents is the subject of the conference. For example, the IRS allowed a parent to deduct the registration fees and cost of traveling to a medical conference dealing with treatment options for a disease suffered by her dependent child. The child's doctor had recommended the conference. During the conference, most of the parent's time was spent attending sessions on her child's condition. Any recreational activities were secondary. If the parent had attended the conference because of her own condition the same deductions would have been allowed.

Lodging and meals while attending the conference are not deductible; these are allowed only if treatment is received at a licensed hospital or similar facility, as discussed below.

**Lodging expenses.** If you are receiving inpatient care at a hospital or similar facility, your expenses, including lodging and meals, are deductible. If you are not an inpatient, lodging expenses while away from home are deductible as medical expenses if the trip is primarily to receive treatment from a doctor in a licensed hospital, hospital-related outpatient facility, or a facility equivalent to a hospital. Meal expenses are not deductible unless they are paid as part of inpatient care.

The deduction for lodging while receiving treatment as an outpatient at a licensed hospital, clinic, or hospital-equivalent facility is limited to $50 per night per person. For example, the limit is $100 if a parent travels with a sick child. The IRS ruled that the $50 allowance could be claimed by a parent for a six-week hotel stay while her eight-year-old daughter was treated in a nearby hospital for serious injuries received in an automobile accident. The mother's presence was necessary so that she could sign release forms.

## Deductible Transportation Costs

Examples of travel costs that have been treated as medical expenses by IRS rulings or court decisions are:

- Nurse's fare if nurse is required on trip
- Parent's fare if parent is needed to accompany child who requires medical care
- Parent's fare to visit his child at an institution where the visits are prescribed by a doctor
- Trip to visit specialist in another city
- Airplane fare to a distant city in which a patient used to live to have a checkup by a family doctor living there. That he could have received the same examination in the city in which he presently lived did not bar his deduction.
- Trip to escape a climate that is bad for a specific condition. For example, the cost of a trip from a northern state to Florida during the winter on the advice of a doctor to relieve a chronic heart condition is deductible. The cost of a trip made solely to improve a post-operative condition by a person recovering from a throat operation was ruled deductible.
- Travel to an Alcoholics Anonymous club meeting if membership in the group has been advised by a doctor
- Disabled veteran's commuting expenses where a doctor prescribed work and driving as therapy
- Wife's trip to provide nursing care for an ailing husband in a distant city. The trip was ordered by her husband's doctor as a necessity.
- Driving prescribed as therapy
- Travel costs of kidney transplant donor or prospective donor

## Nondeductible Transportation Costs

- Commuting to work
- Trip for the general improvement of your health
- Traveling to areas of favorable climates during the year for general health reasons, rather than living permanently in a locality suitable for your health Meals while on a trip for outpatient medical treatment—even if cost of transportation is a valid medical cost. However, a court has allowed the deduction of the extra cost of specially prepared food.
- Trip to get "spiritual" rather than medical aid. For example, the cost of a trip to the Shrine of Our Lady of Lourdes is not deductible.
- Moving a family to a climate more suitable to an ill mother's condition. Only the mother's travel costs are deductible.
- Moving household furnishings to area advised by physician
- Operating an auto or special vehicle to go to work because of a disability
- Convalescence cruise advised by a doctor for a patient recovering from pneumonia
- Loss on sale of car bought for medical travel
- Medical seminar cruise taken by patient whose condition was reviewed by physicians taking the cruise

 *Caution*

**Meal Costs of Medical Trip**

While transportation to receive medical care is a deductible medical expense subject to the AGI floor, meals while on a trip for medical treatment are not deductible. They simply replace the meals you normally would eat. However, if you are hospitalized, the cost of meals while an inpatient is a deductible expense.

## 17.10  Schooling for the Mentally or Physically Disabled

You may include as medical expenses subject to the AGI floor *(17.1)* the costs of sending on a doctor's recommendation a mentally or physically disabled dependent to a school or institution with special programs to overcome or alleviate his or her disability. Such costs may cover:

- Teaching of Braille or lip reading
- Training, caring for, supervising, and treating a mentally retarded person
- Training for a child with dyslexia
- Cost of meals and lodgings, if boarding is required at the school
- Costs of regular education courses also taught at the school, provided they are incidental to the special courses and services provided to overcome the disability

The school must have professional staff competent to design and supervise a program for helping your dependent overcome his or her disability. The fact that a particular school or camp is recommended for an emotionally disturbed child by a psychiatrist will not qualify the tuition as a deduction if the school or camp has no special program geared to the child's specific personal problem. The IRS allows a deduction for the costs of maintaining a mentally handicapped person in a home specially selected to meet the standards set by a psychiatrist to aid in an adjustment from life in a mental hospital to community living.

Payment for future medical care expenses is deductible if immediate payment is required by contract.

*Caution*

**Counseling at a Private School**

The parent of a child with psychological problems may deduct only that part of a private school fee directly related to psychological aid given to the child.

## 17.11  Nursing Homes

Your payment for medical services, meals, and lodging to a nursing home, convalescent home, home for the aged, or similar facility is treated as a medical expense subject to the AGI floor *(17.1)* if you, your spouse, or dependent is confined for medical treatment.

If obtaining medical care is not the main reason for admission, but you can show the part of the cost covering actual medical and nursing care, that amount is deductible, but not the cost of meals and lodging.

**Establishing medical purpose.** The following facts are helpful in establishing the full deductibility of payments to a nursing home, convalescent home, home for the aged, or sanitarium:

- The patient entered the institution on the direction or suggestion of a doctor.
- Attendance or treatment at the institution had a direct therapeutic effect on the condition suffered by the patient.
- The attendance at the institution was for a specific ailment rather than for a "general" health condition. Simply showing that the patient suffers from an ailment is not sufficient proof that he or she is in the home for treatment.

In an unusual case, a court allowed a medical expense deduction for apartment rent of an aged parent; *see* the following Example.

*Filing Tip*

**Meal Costs at a Nursing Home**

If the patient entered a nursing home to receive medical care, a deduction may be taken for meals and lodging while there, in addition to medical care costs.

> ### EXAMPLE
>
> A doctor recommended to Ungar that his 90-year-old mother, convalescing from a brain hemorrhage, could receive better care at less expense in accommodations away from a hospital. A two-room apartment was rented, hospital equipment installed, and nurses engaged for seven months. The rent totaled $1,400. Ungar's sister, who worked in her husband's shoe store, nursed her mother for six weeks. Ungar paid the wages of a clerk who was hired to substitute for his sister in the store. Ungar deducted both the rent and wages as medical expenses. The IRS disallowed them; a Tax Court reversed the IRS' decision. The apartment rent was no less a medical expense than the cost of a hospital room. As for the clerk's wages, they too were deductible medical costs. The clerk was hired specifically to allow the daughter to nurse her mother, thereby avoiding the larger, though more direct, medical expense of hiring a nurse.

## 17.12 Nurses' Wages

Wages or fees paid for nursing services are medical expenses subject to the AGI floor *(17.1)*. Include any Social Security or Medicare (FICA) tax, federal unemployment (FUTA) and state unemployment tax that you pay for the nurse. A nurse does not have to be registered or licensed so long as he or she provides you with nursing services. Nursing services include giving medications, changing dressings, and bathing and grooming the patient. If the nurse also performs personal or household services, you generally can deduct only that part of the pay attributable to nursing services for the patient. However, if the patient is considered chronically ill, certain maintenance or personal care services are deductible as long-term care services *(17.15)*.

The cost of an attendant's meals is included in your medical expenses. Divide total food costs among the household members to determine the attendant's share.

The salary of a clerk hired specifically to relieve a wife from working in her husband's store in order to care for her ill mother was allowed as a medical expense; *see* the Ungar Example *(17.11)*.

*Caution*

**Nurse's Services**

The cost of a nurse's services is a deductible medical expense, even if the nurse is not licensed or registered, so long as he or she provides the patient with nursing services. If household services are also provided, only the portion of the nurse's pay attributable to the provision of nursing services qualifies.

> ### EXAMPLE
>
> Dodge's wife was arthritic. He was advised by her doctor to have someone take care of her to prevent her from falling. He moved her to his daughter's home and paid the daughter to care for her mother. He deducted the payments to his daughter. The IRS disallowed the deduction, claiming that the daughter was not a trained nurse. The Tax Court allowed that part of the deduction specifically attributed to nursing aid. Whether a medical service has been rendered depends on the nature of the services rendered, not on the qualifications or title of the person who renders them. Here, the daughter's services, following the doctor's advice, qualify as medical care.

*Caution*

**Does Equipment Increase Value of Home?**

When special equipment is installed in your home to alleviate a disease or ailment, you must determine if it increases the value of your home. You generally may claim a medical deduction only to the extent that the cost of the equipment exceeds the increase in value. However, if you install a ramp or railing, widen doorways or hallways, or add similar improvements to cope with a disability, these are usually treated by the IRS as not adding to the value of the home.

**Costs eligible for dependent tax credit.** If, in order to work, you pay a nurse to look after a physically or mentally disabled dependent, you may be able to claim a credit for all or part of the nurse's wages as a dependent care expense *(25.4)*. You may not, however, claim both a credit and a medical expense deduction. First, you claim the nurse's wages as a dependent care cost. If not all of the wages are allowed as dependent care costs because of the expense limits *(25.5)*, the remaining balance is deductible as a medical expense.

## 17.13 Home Improvements as Medical Expenses

A disease or ailment may require the construction or installation of special equipment or facilities in a home: A heart patient may need an elevator to carry him or her upstairs; a polio patient, a pool; and an asthmatic patient, an air cleaning system.

Subject to the AGI floor *(17.1)*, you may deduct the full cost of equipment installed for a medical reason if it does not increase the value of your property, as, for example, the cost of a detachable window air conditioner. Where equipment or home improvement increases the value of your property, only the cost in excess of the increase in value to the home may be treated as a medical expense. This increased-value test does not apply to certain structural changes to a residence made to accommodate a disabling condition, as discussed below. If the equipment does not increase the value of the property, its entire cost is deductible, even though it is permanently fixed to the property.

The expense of maintaining and operating equipment installed for medical reasons may be claimed as a medical expense. This is true even if some or all of the cost does not qualify for a deduction because it must be reduced by the increase in value to your home. For example, if a heart patient installs an elevator in his home on the advice of his doctor, but an appraisal shows that the elevator increased the value of the home by more than the cost of the elevator, the cost would not be a medical expense. However, the cost of electricity to operate it and any maintenance costs are medical expenses as long as the medical reason for the elevator continues.

> **EXAMPLE**
>
> Mike Gerard's daughter suffered from cystic fibrosis. While there is no known cure for the disease, doctors attempt to prolong life by preventing pulmonary infection. One approach is to maintain a constant temperature and high humidity. A doctor recommended that Gerard install a central air-conditioning unit in his home for his daughter. It cost $1,300 and increased the value of his home by $800. The $500 balance was a deductible medical expense.

**Certain structural improvements to accommodate disability fully taken into account.** The increased-value test does not apply to structural changes made to a residence to accommodate your disabled condition, or the condition of your spouse or dependents who live with you. Eligible expenses include adding ramps, modifying doorways and stairways, installing railings and support bars, and altering cabinets, outlets, fixtures, and warning systems. Such improvements are treated for medical deduction purposes as not increasing the value of the home. Lifts, but not elevators, also are in this category. The full cost of such improvements is added to other deductible expenses and the total is deductible to the extent that it exceeds the AGI floor.

**Prepaid home construction costs.** Zipkin suffered from multiple chemical sensitivity syndrome and built a house with special filtering and ventilation systems. The cost of the special features exceeded the fair market value of the home by $645,000. She claimed a deduction for the full amount when the house was completed. The IRS disallowed the deduction for the construction costs incurred in the years before the home was completed. Zipkin successfully argued before a federal district court that the construction costs should be treated as prepaid medical expenses that are deductible in the year medical benefits are received. The federal court allowed Zipkin to deduct the full amount in the year the home became habitable.

**Deducting the cost of a swimming pool.** If swimming is prescribed as physical therapy, the cost of constructing a home swimming pool may be partly deductible as a medical expense but only to the extent the cost exceeds the increase in value to the house. However, the

IRS is likely to question any deduction because of the possibility that the pool may be used for recreation. If you can show that the pool is specially equipped to alleviate your condition and is not generally suited for recreation, the IRS will allow the deduction unless the expense is considered to be "lavish or extravagant." For example, the IRS allowed a deduction for a pool constructed by an osteoarthritis patient. His physician prescribed swimming several times a day as treatment. He built an indoor lap pool with specially designed stairs and a hydrotherapy device. Given these features, the IRS concluded that the pool was specially designed to provide medical treatment.

### EXAMPLES

1. Ken Cherry was advised by his doctor to swim to relieve his severe emphysema and bronchitis. He could not swim at local health spas; they did not open early enough or stay open late enough to allow him to swim before or after work. His home was too small for a pool. He bought a lot and built a new house with an indoor pool. He used the pool several times a day, and swimming improved his condition; if he did not swim, his symptoms returned. Cherry deducted pool operating costs of $4,000 for fuel, electricity, insurance, and repairs. The IRS disallowed the deductions, claiming that the pool was used for personal recreation. Besides, it did not have special medical equipment. The Tax Court allowed the deduction. Cherry built the pool to swim in order to exercise his lungs. That there was no special equipment is irrelevant; Cherry did not need special ramps, railings, a shallow floor, or whirlpool. Finally, his family rarely used the pool.

2. Doug Haines broke his leg in a skiing accident and underwent various forms of physical therapy, including swimming. To aid his recovery, his physician recommended that he install a swimming pool at his home. The Tax Court agreed with the IRS that the cost of the pool was not deductible. Although swimming was beneficial to his condition, he needed special therapy only for a limited period of time, and he could have gotten it at less cost at a nearby public pool. Finally, because of weather conditions, the pool could not be used for about half of the year.

In one case the IRS tried to limit the cost of a luxury indoor pool built for therapeutic reasons to the least expensive construction. The Tax Court rejected the IRS position, holding that a medical expense is not to be limited to the cheapest form of treatment; on appeal, the IRS position was adopted.

If, instead of building a pool, you buy a home with a pool, can you deduct the part of the purchase price allocated to the pool? The Tax Court said no. The purchase price of the house includes the fair market value of the pool. Therefore, there is no extra cost above the increase in the home's value that would support a medical expense deduction.

The operating costs of an indoor pool were allowed by the Tax Court as a deduction to an emphysema sufferer.

A deduction is barred where the primary purpose of the improvement is for personal convenience rather than medical necessity.

## 17.14 Costs Deductible as Business Expenses

In some cases, expenses may be deductible as business expenses rather than as medical expenses. Claiming a business deduction is preferable because the deduction is not subject to the adjusted gross income floor *(17.1)*. However, under the Tax Cuts and Jobs Act, the cost of a checkup required by your employer is no longer deductible as a miscellaneous itemized deduction for 2018 through 2025 *(19.1)*.

The Tax Court allowed a licensed social worker working as a therapist to deduct psychoanalysis costs as an education expense; *see 33.15.*

### EXAMPLE

In 2018, an airline pilot is required by his company to take a semi-annual physical exam at his own expense. If he fails to produce a resultant certificate of good health, he is subject to discharge. The cost of such checkups certifying physical fitness for a job is an ordinary and necessary business expense but employee job costs are

*Filing Tip*

**Disability-Related Job Costs**

If you are disabled and incur costs to enable you to work, the payments may be treated as a deductible business expense rather than as a medical expense.

not deductible as a miscellaneous itemized deduction for years after 2017. *(19.1)*. If the doctor prescribes a treatment or further examinations to maintain the pilot's physical condition, the cost of these subsequent treatments or examinations may be deducted only as medical expenses, even though they are needed to maintain the physical standards required by the job. Thus, a professional singer who consults a throat specialist may not deduct the fee as a business expense. The fee is a medical expense subject to the AGI floor.

**Impairment-related work expenses.** Some expenses incurred by a physically or mentally disabled person may be deductible as business expenses rather than as medical expenses. A business expense deduction may be allowed if the expense is necessary for you to satisfactorily perform your job and is not required or used, except incidentally, for personal purposes.

If you are self-employed, claim the deduction on Schedule C *(40.6)*.

If you are an employee, the expenses are listed on Form 2106 and if not reimbursed, entered on Schedule A as a fully deductible miscellaneous itemized deduction; *see 19.1*.

### EXAMPLES

1. A professor is paralyzed from the waist down and confined to a wheelchair. When he attends out-of-town business meetings, he has his wife, a friend, or a colleague accompany him to help him with baggage, stairs, narrow doors, and to sit with him on airplanes when airlines will not allow wheelchair passengers without an attendant. While he does not pay them a salary, he does pay their travel costs. He may deduct these costs as business expenses. They are incurred solely because of his occupation.

2. An attorney uses prostheses due to bilateral amputation of his legs and takes medication several times a day for other ailments. On both personal and business trips, his wife or a neighbor accompanies him to help him travel and receive medication. He may deduct the out-of-town expenses paid for his neighbor only as a medical expense. The neighbor's services are not business expenses because assistance in personal activities is regularly provided. When his wife accompanies him, he may deduct her transportation costs as a medical expense; her food and lodging are nondeductible ordinary living expenses.

## 17.15 Long-Term Care Premiums and Services

A qualified long-term care policy provides only for long-term-care services for the "chronically ill" (see below). If you pay premiums for a qualified long-term care policy, you may treat a fixed amount that depends on your age as medical expenses (subject to the AGI floor *(17.1)*).

If you, your spouse, or your dependent is chronically ill, you may include as medical expenses your unreimbursed expenses for qualifying long-term-care services.

**Did you pay qualifying long-term care services for a chronically ill individual?** A chronically ill person is someone who has been certified by a licensed health-care practitioner within the preceding 12 months as being unable to perform for a period of at least 90 days at least two of the following activities without substantial assistance: eating, toileting, dressing, bathing, continence, or transferring. Also qualifying as chronically ill is someone who requires substantial supervision because of severe cognitive impairment, such as from Alzheimer's disease.

Qualifying long-term-care services for a chronically ill individual are broadly defined as necessary diagnostic, preventive, therapeutic, curing, treating, mitigation, and rehabilitative services, and also maintenance or personal care services. The services must be provided under a plan of care prescribed by a licensed health-care practitioner, who may be a physician, a registered nurse, a licensed social worker, or other individual meeting Treasury requirements. Services provided by a spouse or relative are deductible only if that person is a licensed professional; services provided by a related corporation or partnership do not qualify.

*Filing Tip*

**Long-Term Care Insurance**

Unreimbursed expenses for long-term care services to care for a chronically ill patient are deductible medical expenses subject to the AGI floor. Premiums paid for a qualifying policy are includible in your medical expenses subject to a limit based on your age.

**Deductible premium costs of long-term-care policies.** Depending on your age at the end of the year, all or part of your premium payments for a qualified long-term-care policy may be included as deductible medical expenses, subject to the AGI floor *(17.1)*.

For 2018, the maximum deductible premium for each person covered under a qualifying policy is: $420 for covered persons age 40 or younger at the end of 2018; $780 for those age 41 through 50; $1,560 for those age 51 through 60; $4,160 for those age 61 through 70; and $5,200 for those over age 70. These limits will likely be increased for 2019 by an inflation factor; *see* the *e-Supplement* at *jklasser.com*.

If you are considering purchase of a long-term-care insurance policy, make sure that it qualifies for the tax treatment explained in this section. A qualified contract must provide only for coverage of qualified long-term-care services for the chronically ill (*see* above) and be guaranteed renewable; it may not provide for a cash surrender value or money that can be assigned, pledged, or borrowed; it may not reimburse expenses covered by Medicare except where Medicare is a secondary payer or the contract makes per diem payments without regard to expenses.

**Benefits paid by qualified long-term-care policies.** Benefits from a qualified long-term-care insurance contract (other than dividends) are generally excludable from income. If payments are made on a per diem or other periodic basis, meaning that they are made without regard to actual expenses incurred, there is an annual limitation on the amount that can be excluded. For 2018, per diem payments of up to $360 per day are tax free. If per diem payments exceed the $360 limit, the excess is tax free only to the extent of unreimbursed expenses for qualified long-term-care services. The per diem limit must be allocated among all policyholders who own qualified long-term-care insurance contracts for the same insured.

You should receive a Form 1099-LTC showing any payments to you from a long-term-care insurance contract. Box 3 of Form 1099-LTC should indicate whether the payments were made on a per diem basis or were reimbursements of actual long-term-care expenses. Per diem payments and reimbursements must be reported on Form 8853 to determine if any of the per diem payments are taxable.

## 17.16 Life Insurance Used by Chronically ill or Terminally ill Person

A person who is terminally ill may be forced to cash in a life insurance policy to pay medical bills and other living expenses. Insurance companies have developed life insurance policies with accelerated death benefit clauses to help terminally ill patients meet the high cost of medical care. Where a policy lacks an accelerated payment clause, it is also possible to sell a life insurance policy to a viatical settlement company that specializes in buying policies from ill persons who require funds to pay expenses.

Accelerated death benefits and viatical settlement proceeds received by terminally ill individuals are not taxed.

**Accelerated benefits from chronically ill person's life insurance contract.** A chronically ill *(17.15)* individual may sell a life insurance policy to a viatical settlement company to pay for long-term-care costs. However, if accelerated benefits are received on a per diem (or other periodic basis), the rules applied to long-term-care policies *(17.15)* determine if the proceeds are taxed. Thus, if the proceeds exceed the $360 per diem limit for 2018 and also exceed actual long-term care costs, the excess is taxable on Form 8853. Accelerated life insurance proceeds paid under a long-term-care rider are also subject to these rules *(17.15)*.

 *Filing Instruction*

**Form 8853**

If you received payments in 2018 from a qualified long-term care policy, you must figure the amount of taxable payments, if any, on Form 8853.

# CHAPTER 18

# Casualty and Theft Losses and Involuntary Conversions

Starting in 2018, if you itemize deductions, the deduction for casualty and theft losses of personal-use property is allowed only if the losses are attributed to federally declared disasters. Such losses are claimed on Form 4684 and the allowable amount is entered on Schedule A, Form 1040. If you have a "qualified 2017 disaster loss" that was not "sustained" until 2018 *(18.2)*, you can claim the loss as part of your 2018 standard deduction *(13.1)* even if you do not itemize other deductions on Schedule A for 2018.

A loss of property held for:

- Personal purposes must be attributable to a federally declared disaster *(18.1)* and the loss is subject to a dollar floor that reduces the deduction by $100, or by $500 for a qualified 2017 disaster loss *(18.8)*. In addition, net losses for personal-use assets are reduced by 10% of your adjusted gross income on Form 4684, unless the loss is a qualified 2017 disaster loss *(18.8)*.

- Income-producing purposes, such as negotiable securities, should be claimed on Form 4684 and then entered on Line 16 of Schedule A as an "other itemized deduction" *(19.1)*.

- Business or rental purposes is claimed on Form 4684 and then as a loss on Form 4797. It is not subject to any floor. Follow the instructions to Form 4684.

If you have realized a gain, you may defer tax by replacing or repairing the property *(18.14)*.

## 18.1 Casualty or Theft Losses for Personal-Use Property Must be Due to a Federally Declared Disaster

Under the Tax Cuts and Jobs Act, the itemized deduction for personal casualty and theft losses is restricted, starting with 2018 returns. A casualty is damage to or destruction of property due to a sudden event such as a flood, storm (including hurricanes and tornadoes), or wildfire.

Under the new law, a casualty or theft loss of personal-use property is deductible only if the loss is attributable to a federally declared disaster. A federally declared disaster is a disaster in an area determined by the President as warranting federal assistance (under the Robert T. Stafford Disaster Relief and Emergency Assistance Act or successor law).

If you have a loss to personal-use property as the result of any other type of casualty, such as damage to or destruction of your home in a fire, flood, or storm that is not a federally declared disaster, or your car is destroyed in an accident, or your property is stolen and the theft is unrelated to a federally declared disaster, the loss is not deductible for 2018 and later years, but there is this exception: If you have any gains from casualties or thefts of personal-use property, losses that are not attributable to a federally declared disaster offset the gains on Form 4684 *(18.9)*. You have a gain from a casualty or theft if you receive an insurance reimbursement that exceeds your adjusted basis for the property *(18.2, 18.9)*.

Gains and losses from casualties and thefts of personal-use property are reported on Section A of Form 4684 (Personal Use Property). Each casualty or theft loss of personal-use property (figured under the steps at *18.9*) must be reduced by insurance or other reimbursements *(18.2, 18.9)* and then by a $100 floor *(18.8)*. A net loss, if any, for all allowable personal casualty and theft losses during the year is further reduced by 10% of your adjusted gross income *(18.8)*. All or a substantial part of your potential deduction may be eliminated by the 10% floor; *see 18.8* and 18.9 for details on the $100 and 10% floors. The allowable loss from Form 4684 is entered as your casualty or theft loss deduction on Line 15 of Schedule A (Form 1040).

The IRS provides a list of federally declared disasters and tax relief information to disaster victims; go to https://www.irs.gov./newsroom/tax-relief-presidentially-declared-disaster-areas.

**If you are forced to relocate because your home was made unsafe by a federally declared disaster.** If your home was located in a federally declared disaster area, your state or local government may order you to demolish it or relocate it because it was rendered unsafe by the disaster, even though the actual damage from the disaster itself was minor. This could happen, for example, if a severe storm created a danger of mudslides to area homes. In this situation, the loss in value to your home is treated as a disaster loss so that you may elect to deduct the loss either for the year the loss was sustained (the year of the demolition or relocation order) or for the prior taxable year *(18.2)*. Disaster loss treatment applies if the order to demolish or relocate the home was issued within 120 days of the President's determination that the area warranted federal disaster assistance. The home could be your principal residence, vacation home, or rental property. In figuring the amount of the loss *(18.9)*, compare the fair market value of the home immediately before the disaster with the value after the disaster and prior to the demolition or relocation.

**Casualty or theft gains and losses for business and investment property.** Casualty and theft losses for business or income-producing property are figured in Section B of Form 1040. A gain is reported on Form 4684 only if you do not elect to defer it under the involuntary conversion rules *(18.14)*.

Losses do not have to be attributable to a federally declared disaster to be deductible (as do losses to personal-use property for 2018 and later years). Business and investment property losses (following steps 1-4 at *18.9*) are not subject to the $100 and 10% of adjusted gross income floors. For investment property, a loss from Form 4684 is entered as an "other itemized deduction" on Line 16 of Schedule A (Form 1040), not on Line 15 for "casualty and theft losses." For business property, a loss from Form 4684 is entered as a loss on Form 4797. Follow the Form 4684 instructions.

 *Law Alert*

**Deduction for Many Personal Casualties and Thefts Eliminated**

Starting with 2018 returns, a casualty or theft loss for personal-use property is allowed only if the loss is attributable to a federally declared disaster. However, if you have gains from personal casualties (because of generous insurance settlements or otherwise), losses from personal casualties and thefts that are not otherwise deductible (because they are not attributable to a federally declared disaster) can offset the gains.

**Tax-Free Disaster Relief Payments to Individuals**

You are not taxed on disaster relief payments from any source that reimburses or pays you for unreimbursed costs of repairing or rehabilitating your personal residence (whether you own or rent it), or replacing its contents, as a result of a federally declared disaster.

You are not taxed on payments, regardless of the source, that cover reasonable and necessary personal, family, living, or funeral expenses as a result of a federally declared disaster, so long as they are not otherwise paid by insurance or other reimbursement. The exclusion also applies to payments made by the federal, state, or local government to individuals affected by a federally declared disaster where the payments are based on need.

*Planning Reminder*

**IRS Interest Abatement**

If the IRS extends the due date to file tax returns and pay taxes for a person in an area declared to be a disaster area by the President, the IRS will abate interest on past-due taxes for the period covered by the extension.

*Caution*

**Are You Uncertain About Whether You Will Be Reimbursed?**

If you think you might be reimbursed for part of your casualty loss in a later year but are not sure, the IRS says to delay taking the deduction for that part until the year you become reasonably certain that it will not be reimbursed.

**Disaster relief payments are not taxable.** If you receive qualified disaster relief payments, the payments are not taxable so long as you have not otherwise been reimbursed for the expenses covered; *see* the nearby Law Alert on disaster relief payments.

**Disaster relief grants and loan cancellations.** Cancellation of part of a federal disaster loan under the Robert T. Stafford Disaster Relief and Emergency Assistance Act is treated as a reimbursement that reduces your loss *(18.2,18.9)*. If you receive a post-disaster grant under the Disaster Relief Act to help you meet medical, dental, housing, transportation, personal property, or funeral expenses, the grant is excludable from income. However, to the extent the grant specifically reimburses a medical expense, the payment is treated as a reimbursement that offsets the expense *(17.4)*. Similarly, if a casualty loss is specifically reimbursed by a grant, treat the grant as a reimbursement in figuring your disaster loss *(18.2, 18.9)*. Unemployment assistance payments under the Disaster Relief Act are taxable unemployment benefits *(2.6)*.

**Disaster grants for business property losses.** Payments by the federal government or a state or local government to a business for property losses may not be excluded from business gross income. The IRS has ruled that the disaster relief exclusion that applies to government payments made to individuals to promote the general welfare does not apply to business property losses. The business realizes a taxable gain to the extent the grant exceeds the adjusted basis in the damaged or destroyed property, but that gain can be deferred under the involuntary conversion rules *(18.14)* by making a timely reinvestment of the payments in qualified replacement property. The replacement period for damaged or destroyed business property is two years *(18.18)*.

**IRS interest abatement.** For declared disasters, the IRS will abate interest on taxes due for the period covered by an extension to file tax returns and pay taxes.

## 18.2 When To Deduct a Disaster Loss

A casualty or theft loss attributable to a federally declared disaster is deductible for the year the loss is "sustained." This is generally the year in which the disaster occurs, but the situation is more complicated when you have a pending claim for insurance or other reimbursement. According to the IRS, when a claim for reimbursement exists and there is a reasonable prospect of recovery as of the end of the year in which the disaster occurs, the loss is considered sustained in the year that the reimbursement claim is settled or in which there is no longer a reasonable prospect that reimbursement will be received. The Examples below illustrate how a loss can be sustained in a year after the year in which a federally declared disaster occurs.

Determining the year in which the loss is sustained is crucial for the "prior-year election" discussed in *18.3*. You can elect to deduct a loss attributable to a federally declared disaster either for the year in which it is sustained or for the year immediately preceding the year in which the loss is sustained; *see* *18.3* for election details.

Note that you must file a timely insurance claim if your property is covered by insurance. Otherwise, the amount covered by the insurance cannot be taken into account when figuring your deductible casualty loss; *see 18.9*. In addition to insurance, the IRS says that if you have a reasonable prospect of receiving federal or state benefits to restore your property, you must take those benefits into account as potential reimbursements.

**If you reasonably expect partial or complete reimbursement in a later year.** For the year the disaster occurred, you should deduct only that part of your loss, after applying the personal property floors *(18.8)* for which you do not expect reimbursement. For example, if your property was damaged in a 2018 federally declared disaster but you expect a full insurance recovery in 2019, you would not take any deduction on your 2018 return. If you are not sure if part of your loss will be reimbursed, the IRS advises you not to claim a deduction for that part until the year you become reasonably certain that it will not be reimbursed.

**If you deduct a loss and then are reimbursed for it.** If you deduct a loss on your 2018 return for a federally declared disaster occurring in 2018 because you do not expect any reimbursement, but you receive an insurance settlement or other reimbursement in 2019, the reimbursement is taxable in 2019 to the extent that the 2018 deduction gave you a tax benefit by reducing your 2018 taxable income *(11.6)*. You cannot avoid this income for 2019 by amending your 2018 tax return to reduce or eliminate the 2018 loss by the 2019 reimbursement.

---

**EXAMPLES**

1. In 2018, severe flooding destroyed your car and caused major damage to your home in an area that the President determined warranted federal disaster assistance. You filed a reimbursement claim with your insurance company but at the end of 2018, it was not clear how much reimbursement you would receive. In January 2019, your insurance company settles your claim and reimburses you for only half of your loss. For deduction purposes, the unreimbursed disaster loss is "sustained" in 2019, not 2018, because 2019 is when it became reasonably certain how much you would be reimbursed for. You can deduct the unreimbursed loss, subject to the personal property floors *(18.8)*, on your return for 2019, the year in which the loss is sustained, or you can make the prior-year election *(18.3)* and claim the deduction on your 2018 return.

2. Same facts as in Example 1 but in 2019 the insurance company completely denies your claim. You sue the insurance company and at the end of 2019, the case is still pending and you have a reasonable prospect of winning your claim. However, in 2020, the court rules against you. Your unreimbursed loss is considered sustained in 2020. You can deduct the unreimbursed loss, subject to the personal property floors *(18.8)*, on your return for 2020, the year in which the loss is sustained, or you can make the prior-year election *(18.3)* and claim the deduction on your 2019 return.

---

**Theft losses.** A theft loss attributable to a federally declared disaster is deductible for the year the theft is discovered *(18.7)*.

**You have a gain if reimbursements exceed your adjusted basis for the property.** Receiving reimbursements in excess of adjusted basis generally results in a gain that you must report on your return. The gain may be minimized by special rules where your principal residence is damaged or destroyed in a federally declared disaster *(18.4)*. The recognized gain must be reported unless you acquire qualifying replacement property and elect to defer the gain, or, if the gain is due to reimbursements for a destroyed principal residence, the gain is not taxable under the home sale exclusion *(18.14)*.

If a loss is claimed in one year and in a later year you receive reimbursements that exceed your adjusted basis, the gain is included in income for the later year to the extent the original deduction reduced your taxable income *(11.6)*. The remainder of the gain is taxable unless you buy replacement property that enables you to defer the gain *(18.14)*.

## 18.3 Prior-Year Election for Disaster Losses

If you suffer a loss from a disaster in an area determined by the President as warranting federal assistance (under the Robert T. Stafford Disaster Relief and Emergency Assistance Act or successor law), you may deduct the loss (figured on Form 4684 under the steps at *18.9*) either on your return for the year in which the loss is sustained or on the return for the year immediately preceding the year in which the loss is sustained. As discussed in *18.2*, if there is a pending claim for reimbursement as of the end of the year in which the disaster occurs, the loss is not considered sustained until the year in which it can be ascertained with reasonable certainty whether the reimbursement will be received. In the Form 4684 instructions, the IRS also refers to the year in which the loss is sustained as "the disaster year." Thus, the "prior year" for which the prior-year election may be made is the year preceding the disaster year.

**How and when to make the prior-year election.** You have time to decide whether it is more advantageous for you to deduct a disaster loss for the disaster year (the year in which the loss is sustained) or make the election to deduct it for the year preceding the disaster year. The deadline for making the prior-year election is the date that is six months after the original due date (without extensions) for your return for the disaster year. Thus, if the

*IRS Alert*

**IRS Deadline for Election to Claim Disaster Loss in Prior Year**

An election to deduct a disaster loss for the year preceding the year in which the loss is sustained can accelerate your loss deduction, generating an immediate tax refund for the prior year that you can use to recover from the disaster. The IRS gives you time to consider whether to claim the disaster loss for the year in which the loss is sustained or for the preceding year. The deadline for making the prior-year election is six months after the original due date (without extensions) for the return for the year in which the loss is sustained, generally October 15. If you make the election, you may revoke it on or before the date that is 90 days after the due date for making the election (T.D. 9789, 2016-44 IRB 527).

disaster year for a federally declared disaster is 2018 (meaning you sustain the loss in 2018) you have until October 15, 2019, to elect to claim the loss for 2017 (the year before the disaster year). The prior-year election is made on Part 1 of Section D on the 2017 Form 4684. By October 15, 2019, complete the Section D and attach it with the rest of Form 4684 to an amended return (Form 1040X) for 2017, assuming you have filed an original 2017 return.

If the disaster year is 2019, the prior-year election to claim the loss for 2018 is made on Part 1 of Section D on the 2018 Form 4684. Attach it to an original or amended return for 2018 by October 15, 2020.

**Revoking prior-year election.** If you make the prior-year election, you may revoke it in order to deduct the loss on your return for the disaster year (the year in which the loss is sustained). You must file the revocation with an amended return for the prior year to remove the disaster loss deduction. Your amended return eliminating the election must be filed (1) on or before the date that is 90 days after the due date for making the prior-year election (*see* above), and also (2) on or before the date on which you file the return or amended return for the disaster year on which you are going to claim the loss.

If 2018 is the disaster year and you made the prior-year election to deduct the loss on your 2017 return, you revoke the election by completing Part II of Section D and attaching it to an amended return for 2017 (the prior year for which the election was made). As a result of the revocation, the amended return will show a higher tax liability for 2017.

## 18.4 Gain Realized From Insurance Proceeds for Damaged or Destroyed Principal Residence

Generally, you have a taxable gain if you receive insurance proceeds in excess of your adjusted basis for damaged or destroyed property *(18.2, 18.14)*. However, if a principal residence is destroyed, the home sale exclusion may be available. Other special rules may allow you to avoid or minimize the gain, or make it easier to defer gain by purchasing replacement property, when the insurance proceeds are for a principal residence damaged or destroyed in a federally declared disaster area.

**Destruction of principal residence and contents.** If your principal residence is destroyed, and you receive insurance proceeds that exceed your adjusted basis in the property, you may be able to exclude the gain from your gross income under the $250,000 ($500,000 if married filing jointly) home sale exclusion *(29.1)*. The destruction does not have to be attributable to a federally declared disaster; thus, destruction of a home due to a fire that is not a federally declared disaster could qualify. For the exclusion to apply, you generally must have owned and lived in the home for at least two out of the five years ending on the date of destruction, the same ownership and use test that applies to a sale *(29.2)*. According to the IRS, a principal residence must be completely destroyed to qualify for the home sale exclusion; a partial destruction does not qualify. If a residence is damaged to the extent that the remaining structure must be deconstructed in order to rebuild, or the costs of repair substantially exceed the pre-disaster value of the home, the home is considered to have been completely destroyed, allowing the gain to be excluded from income subject to the $250,000/$500,000 exclusion limit. If the home sale exclusion is not available to you or if the gain exceeds your exclusion, the nonexcludable gain may be reduced under the gain minimization rules discussed next, and the balance deferred under the involuntary conversion rules if you buy a replacement residence *(18.14)*.

**Gain may be minimized by special computation rules.** Where your principal residence is damaged or destroyed in a federally declared disaster, favorable involuntary conversion rules eliminate tax on some of the gain and make it easier to defer the balance. These rules apply to renters as well as home owners.

1. Any gain on insurance proceeds received for "unscheduled" personal property in your principal residence (rented or owned) is not "recognized" by the tax law, so it is not taxable. Personal property is unscheduled if it is not separately listed on a schedule or rider to the basic insurance policy.

*Filing Tip*

**Nontaxable Disaster Mitigation Payments**

Property owners are not taxed on qualified disaster mitigation payments from FEMA (Federal Emergency Management Agency) to elevate or relocate flood-prone homes and businesses or build hurricane shelters.

2. Insurance proceeds received for the home itself or for scheduled property are treated as received for a single item of property. Gain on this combined insurance pool may be deferred by reinvesting in replacement property that is similar or related in service or use to either the damaged residence or its contents *(18.14)*. If the cost of a new principal residence and/or contents equals or exceeds the combined insurance pool, you may elect to defer any gain attributable to the insurance recovery *(18.19)*. The deferred gain reduces your basis in the replacement property. The period for purchasing replacement property ends four years after the end of the first tax year in which any part of your gain is realized *(18.18)*. If the cost of the replacement property is less than the combined insurance pool, your gain is taxed to the extent of the unspent reimbursement *(18.19)*.

---

**EXAMPLE**

You rent an apartment as your principal residence. Your apartment and its contents were completely destroyed by a hurricane in 2018; the county in which your apartment was located was in a federally declared disaster area. Later in 2018, you received insurance proceeds of $25,000 for unscheduled personal property in your apartment. The $25,000 proceeds are not taxable. Assume that in addition to the $25,000 for unscheduled property, you received in 2018 insurance proceeds of $200,000 for the home itself, and also $10,000 for jewelry and $5,000 for a stamp collection that were listed on a rider to your policy. If you invest the combined $215,000 of proceeds (for the home, jewelry, and stamps) in a replacement residence, scheduled or unscheduled property, or any combination thereof, you can elect to defer any gain ($215,000 minus adjusted basis) realized from the insurance proceeds. If you reinvest less than $215,000, your gain is taxable only to the extent that $215,000 exceeds the reinvestment (whether in a home, scheduled or unscheduled property). To defer gain, you must buy replacement property by the end of 2022, four years after the end of 2018, the year in which gain was realized on the receipt of the insurance. If gain is deferred, basis in the replacement property equals its cost minus the deferred gain.

---

**Sale of land underlying destroyed principal residence or second home.** If your principal residence is destroyed in a federally declared disaster, and you decide to relocate elsewhere and sell the underlying land, the IRS treats the sale and the destruction as a single involuntary conversion. If you have a gain that is not excludable under the home sale exclusion rules *(Chapter 29)*, the land sale proceeds are combined with your insurance recovery for purposes of figuring deferrable gain under the involuntary conversion replacement rules *(18.14)*. All of the gain resulting from the insurance recovery may be deferred if a new principal residence is purchased within the four-year replacement period and it costs at least as much as the combined insurance and sales proceeds. The replacement period ends four years after the close of the first year in which any part of your gain is realized.

The destroyed home does not have to be your principal residence or even be located in a federal disaster area for the above "single conversion" rule to apply. The rule applies to the destruction of a second residence such as a vacation home that qualifies for a mortgage interest deduction *(15.1)*, However, the replacement period *(18.18)* for a second home is two years, whether or not it was in a federal disaster area. The two-year replacement period also applies for principal residences that were not located in a federal disaster area (rather than the four-year period allowed for principal residences within federal disaster areas).

## 18.5 Who May Deduct a Disaster Loss

A casualty loss deduction may be claimed only by the owner of the property. For example, in 2018 a federally declared disaster destroys a car owned solely by one spouse. If the spouses file separate returns, the other spouse may not deduct the loss because he or she does not have an ownership interest; only the spouse who owned the car may deduct the loss on a separate return.

On jointly owned property, the loss is divided among the owners. If you and your spouse own the property jointly, you deduct the entire loss on a joint return. If you file separately, each owner deducts his or her share of the loss on each separate return.

If you have a legal life estate in the property, the loss is apportioned between yourself and those who will get the property after your death. The apportionment may be based on actuarial tables that consider your life expectancy.

**Lessee.** A person leasing property may be allowed to deduct payments to a lessor that are required under the lease to compensate for a casualty loss.

**Caution**

**Damage to Nearby Property**

The casualty must have caused damage to your property. Damage to a nearby area that lowered the value of your property does not give you a loss deduction.

> **EXAMPLE**
>
> You buy or lease a lot on which to build a cottage. Along with your purchase or lease, you have the privilege of using a nearby lake. The lake is later destroyed by a storm that is declared to be a federal disaster and the value of your property drops. You may not deduct the loss. The lake is not your property. You only had a privilege to use it, and this is not an ownership right that supports a casualty loss deduction.

## 18.6 Proving a Casualty Loss

If your return is audited, you will have to prove that the casualty occurred and the amount of the loss. For personal-use property, you must be prepared to show that your claimed loss is attributable to a federally declared disaster *(18.1)*. The time to collect your evidence is as soon after the casualty as possible. *Table 18-1*, Proving a Casualty Loss, indicates the information that you will need when computing your loss *(18.9)*.

## 18.7 Theft Losses

Starting with 2018 returns, a theft of personal-use property (not used in a business or held for investment) can be deducted only if the theft is attributable to a federally declared disaster *(18.1)*. This may be difficult to prove. For example, if you are forced to leave your home during a federally declared disaster and later find that property is missing, this by itself is not sufficient evidence that there was a theft, or that the theft was attributable to the disaster. There may be police records or news reports that could document that there were break-ins in your area following the disaster.

**Filing Instruction**

**If Stolen Property Is Recovered**

If you claim a theft loss and in a later year the property is returned to you, you must refigure your loss deduction. If the refigured deduction is lower than the amount you claimed, the difference must be reported as income in the year of the recovery. To recalculate the loss, follow the steps for figuring deductible losses *(18.9)*, but in Step 1, compute the loss in fair market value from the time the property was stolen until you recovered it. The lower of this loss in value, if any, or your adjusted basis for the property, is then reduced by insurance reimbursements and the personal-use floors *(18.8)* to get the recalculated loss.

If you can establish that a theft of your personal-use property was attributable to a federally declared disaster, take into account expected and actual reimbursements in determining the timing *(18.2)* and amount *(18.9)* of the deductible loss.

If personal-use property, such as your car, is stolen, and the theft is unrelated to a federally declared disaster, your loss is not deductible, but there is an exception if you also have any gains from personal casualties or thefts. In this case, you may reduce the gain (or gains) by theft or casualty loss losses that are not attributable to a federally declared disaster. See the instructions to Form 4684 for making this offset.

**Theft of business or investment property.** A theft of property used in your business or which you held for investment may be claimed in Section B of Form 4684. A loss for the unreimbursed value of the property is allowed; *see* steps 1-4 at *18.9* and follow the instructions to Section B of Form 4684.

An embezzlement from a business or investment account qualifies as a theft, but if you report on the cash basis, you may not take a deduction for the embezzlement of income you have not reported. For example, an agent embezzled royalties of $46,000 due an author. The author's theft deduction was disallowed. The author had not previously reported the royalties as income; therefore, she could not get the deduction.

See below for special rules that apply to fraudulent Ponzi-type investment schemes.

**Stock bought on the open market.** The IRS does not allow a theft loss deduction if you buy stock on the open market and some or all of your investment is lost because of the fraudulent activities of corporate officers or directors. Your loss is a capital loss *(5.4)*, not a theft loss. There is no theft in this situation because there is no direct connection between the corporate wrongdoers and the investors, and the officers and directors lacked a specific criminal intent to take the shareholders' funds.

The IRS contrasts such open market transactions with Ponzi-type fraudulent schemes, in which it holds there is a criminal intent to target the investors, and thus a theft loss is allowed for such Ponzi-scheme losses; *see* below.

### Deduction allowed to victims of Ponzi schemes and similar fraudulent schemes. The IRS allows investors who fall victim to fraudulent investment arrangements, including Ponzi schemes, to claim a theft loss deduction under special rules (Revenue Ruling 2009-9). A theft loss is deductible for the year the loss is discovered. The loss is considered a "theft," not a capital loss, as it is the result of a criminal fraudulent scheme intended to deprive investors of the funds they invested. Since the loss is to their investment account (transaction entered into for profit), the floors for personal-use property in *18.8* do not apply. The deductible theft loss includes the investments made in the fraudulent arrangement and any interest, dividends and capital gains from the scheme that were reported on prior-year tax returns and reinvested, minus any withdrawals. If in the year the loss is discovered the investor has a reasonable prospect of reimbursement, the deductible amount is reduced by the expected reimbursement.

Recognizing that it could be difficult to determine when and how much to deduct as a Ponzi-scheme loss, the IRS provides certain taxpayers with an optional safe harbor method, discussed below, for computing and reporting the theft loss (Revenue Procedure 2009-20).

If you are eligible for and choose to use the IRS safe harbor, first complete Section C of Form 4684, and then enter the deductible amount from Section C on Section B. If you cannot use the safe harbor, or choose not to, just complete Section B of Form 4684.

*Safe harbor.* The safe harbor allows eligible investors to deduct either 75% or 95% of their "qualified investment," less any actual or projected recovery from insurance, loss-protection arrangement, or the SIPC (Securities Investor Protection Corporation). The 75% deduction applies if the investor intends to pursue a third-party recovery, and the 95% deduction applies if a third-party recovery will not be pursued. If in a later year there is a recovery that exceeds the non-deducted 5% or 25% portion of the loss, the recovery is taxable under the tax benefit rule *(11.6)* to the extent of the safe harbor deduction (Revenue Procedure 2009-20).

Eligibility for the safe harbor is limited to investors who had a taxable investment account in the fraudulent arrangement and the investment must have been made directly, not through a fund, partnership, or other entity. Losses in IRAs or other tax-deferred retirement plans invested with the scheme do not qualify for the safe harbor.

A loss is eligible for safe harbor relief only if (1) the "lead figure" in the scheme was charged under federal or state law (by way of indictment or information) with fraud, embezzlement, or a similar crime, or (2) in response to a federal or state criminal complaint, the lead figure admitted guilt or a receiver or trustee was appointed or the assets were frozen, or (3) the assets of the investment scheme were frozen or a receiver or trustee was appointed after a state or federal agency filed a civil complaint in a court or administrative proceeding alleging a fraudulent arrangement conducted by the lead figure, and the lead figure died before being charged with criminal theft.

The loss is deductible for the taxable year in which the theft was discovered (the "discovery year"). Generally, this is the year in which the indictment, information, or complaint against the lead figure was filed. However, if the lead figure died before being charged with criminal theft and a civil complaint under (3) above was filed, the discovery year is the year of the lead figure's death where that is later than the year that the civil complaint was filed (Revenue Procedure 2011-58). In one case, a civil complaint under (3) above was filed against several lead figures, and in that same year, a receiver was appointed and one of the lead figures died before being criminally charged. In the following year, criminal charges were brought against another lead figure. The IRS ruled that the "year of discovery" for claiming the safe harbor loss was the first year, the year in which the civil complaint was filed, one of the lead figures died before being criminally charged, and a receiver was appointed, rather than in the second year in which criminal charges were brought against one of the lead figures.

 *Caution*

### Stock Devaluation Due to Corporate Misconduct

The IRS has warned shareholders who suffer a loss in the value of their stock due to the fraud, misappropriation, or other misconduct of corporate officers or directors that their loss is not a deductible theft loss. A decline in stock value is not a theft if the stock was purchased on the open market rather than directly from the corporate officials accused of misconduct. The loss for stock bought on the open market is deductible only as a capital loss when the stock is sold or becomes worthless *(5.4)*.

The Tax Court took the same approach in holding that a taxpayer who bought stock on the open market could not support a theft loss under California law because there was no "privity" relationship between the taxpayer and the corporate officers accused of wrong-doing, and so it could not be shown that there was intent to obtain the taxpayer's property.

| Table 18-1 Proving a Casualty Loss | |
|---|---|
| **To prove—** | **You need this information—** |
| That a casualty actually occurred | With a federally declared disaster, , you will have no difficulty proving the disaster occurred, but you must prove it affected your property. On Form 4684 for 2018, you must enter the FEMA disaster declaration number for the disaster.<br><br>Videos or photographs of the area where your property was located, before and after, and newspaper or online stories placing the damage in your neighborhood are helpful. |
| The cost of repairing the property | Cost of repairs is allowed as a measure of loss of repairing the property if the cost is not excessive and the repair merely restored your property to its condition immediately before the casualty. Save canceled checks, bills, receipts, and vouchers for expenses of clearing debris and restoring the property to its condition before the casualty. |
| The value immediately before and after the casualty | Appraisals by a competent expert are important. Get them in writing—in the form of an affidavit, deposition, estimate, appraisal, etc. The expert—an appraiser, engineer, or architect—should be qualified to judge local values. Any records of offers to buy your property, either before or after the casualty, are helpful. Automobile "blue books" may be used as guides in fixing the value of a car. But an amount offered for your car as a trade-in on a new car is not usually an acceptable measure of value. |
| Cost or other basis of your property—the deductible loss cannot be more than that | A deed, contract, bill of sale, or other document probably shows your original cost. Bills, receipts, and canceled checks probably show the cost of improvements. One court refused to allow a deduction because an owner failed to prove the original cost of a destroyed house and its value before the fire. In another case, estimates were allowed where a fire destroyed records of cost. A court held that the homeowner could not be expected to prove cost by documents lost in the fire that destroyed her property. She made inventories after the fire and again at a later date. Her reliance on memory to establish cost, even though inflated, was no bar to the deduction. The court estimated the market value based on her inventories. If you acquired the property by gift or inheritance, you must establish an adjusted basis in the property from records of the donor or the executor of the estate; *see* 5.17 and 5.18. |

*Law Alert*

### Losses from Hurricanes Harvey, Irma and Maria and California Wildfires

A net personal casualty or theft loss attributable to Hurricane Harvey, Irma, or Maria, or to the 2017 California wildfires, is not subject to the 10% AGI floor on Form 4684. However, the per-casualty event floor for such losses is increased from $100 to $500. If you are claiming the standard deduction and not itemizing deductions, you apply the $500 floor in figuring the allowable loss on Form 4684 and then add that loss to your regular standard deduction. The increased standard deduction is claimed as an "other itemized deduction" on Line 16 of Schedule A (Form 1040).

These rules can apply on 2018 returns to qualified 2017 disaster losses that were "sustained" in 2018 *(18.2)*. See Form 4684 and the instructions to Form 4684 and Schedule A for applying these special rules for qualified 2017 disaster losses.

Congress may add certain 2018 disasters to this list; any update will be in the *e-Supplement* at *jklasser.com*.

## 18.8 Floors for Personal-Use Property Losses

For years after 2017, a casualty or theft loss of personal-use property is deductible only if the loss is attributable to a federally declared disaster *(18.1)*. Allowable losses are subject to "floors" that will reduce, and in some cases eliminate, your deduction on Form 4684. Each casualty or theft loss for personal-use property, after taking into account reimbursements (Steps 1–4 at *18.9*), must be reduced by $100, and then the net loss for the year on all items of personal-use property is further reduced by 10% of your adjusted gross income (Step 5 at *18.9*). However, different rules apply to qualified 2017 disaster losses (losses from Hurricanes Harvey, Irma, and Maria and the 2017 California wildfires); *see* the Law Alert on this page.

**$100 floor for each loss.** Each casualty or theft loss of property used for personal purposes is reduced by $100. The $100 floor is applied after taking into account insurance proceeds received and insurance you expect to receive in a later year *(18.2)*.

The $100 floor does not apply to losses of business property or property held for the production of income such as securities. If property used in personal activities as well as for business or investment is damaged, the $100 offset applies only to the loss allocated to personal use.

For each personal casualty or theft, a separate $100 reduction applies. For example, if you suffer losses to personal-use property in two different federally declared disasters during 2018, there will be a separate $100 offset applied to each of the losses. But when two or more items of property are destroyed in one event, only one $100 offset is applied to the total loss. For example, a severe storm (designated as a federally declared disaster) damages your residence and also your car parked in the driveway. You figure the loss on the residence and car separately on Form 4684, but only one $100 offset applies to the total loss (*see* Example 1 in *18.9*).

Where a federally declared disaster damages property owned by two or more individuals, the $100 floor applies separately to the loss of each co-owner. The only exception is for a married couple filing jointly who apply only one $100 floor to their losses from a single casualty.

### EXAMPLES

1. Two sisters own and occupy a house that in 2018 is damaged in a federally declared disaster. Each sister applies the $100 floor to figure her separate deduction on Form 4684 for 2018.

2. In 2018, a federally declared disaster damages your house and also the personal property of a houseguest. You are subject to one $100 floor and the houseguest is subject to a separate $100 floor.

**10% AGI floor.** The 10% adjusted gross income (AGI) floor reduces your deduction for net casualty and theft losses realized during the year on personal-use property. In some cases the potential deduction will be completely eliminated by the 10% of AGI floor. The Example below illustrates the application of the $100 and 10% AGI floors.

If you have gains from casualties and thefts on personal-use property and also have losses that are attributable to federally declared disasters, and the total loss (after the $100 floor reduces each casualty/theft loss) exceeds the total gain, the net loss is reduced by 10% of your AGI; *see* Step 5 in *18.9*.

### EXAMPLE

In June 2018, your car, which was worth $28,000, was completely destroyed by a severe flood that was declared a federal disaster. You received insurance reimbursement of $14,000, so your unreimbursed loss was $14,000. In October 2018, another federally declared disaster floods your basement and causes $5,000 of damage to appliances and furniture stored there. You received insurance reimbursement of $2,700 so your loss was $2,300. Your adjusted gross income is $85,000. If you itemize deductions for 2018, use a separate Form 4684 to figure the allowable loss for each casualty. On the separate Forms 4684, calculate each loss through Line 10. On Line 11, you enter the $100 floor and on Line 12 you subtract the $100 floor from the loss on Line 10. Then combine the two losses (from Line 12 of each form) on a single Form 4684 and apply the 10% AGI floor on Line 17. Your deductible loss for 2018 is $7,600, figured as follows:

| | | |
|---|---:|---:|
| Loss on car (after reimbursement) | $14,000 | |
| Less $100 floor | 100 | $13,900 |
| Loss on basement (after reimbursement) | $2,300 | |
| Less $100 floor | 100 | 2,200 |
| Total loss ($13,900 + $2,200) | | 16,100 |
| Less 10% of $85,000 AGI | | 8,500 |
| Deductible loss | | $7,600 |

## 18.9 Figuring Your Loss on Form 4684

Form 4684 is used to report casualties or thefts of personal-use property, business property, or income-producing property. Starting in 2018, a loss to personal-use property is deductible only if the loss is attributable to a federally declared disaster *(18.1)*. However, if you have casualty or theft losses of personal-use property that are not attributable to federally declared disasters, and also have gains from casualties and thefts of personal-use property, whether or not the gains are attributable to federally declared disasters, the gains are offset by the losses, but a deduction for an excess loss is not allowed. *See* the Form 4684 instructions on offsetting the losses against the gains.

On Form 4684, a deductible loss is usually the difference between the fair market value of the property before the casualty or theft and the fair market value after the casualty or theft but this loss in value must be reduced by (1) reimbursements received for the loss and (2) if the property was used for personal purposes, by the $100 floor *(18.8)*. However, the loss may not exceed your adjusted basis *(5.20)* for the property, which for many items will be your cost. If your adjusted basis is less than the loss in value, your deduction is limited to basis, less reimbursements and the $100 floor for each personal-use asset. After figuring all allowable casualty and theft losses and gains for personal-use property, the net loss (losses in excess of gains if any) is deductible as an itemized deduction on Schedule A (Form 1040) only to the extent it exceeds the 10% adjusted gross income (AGI) floor *(18.8)*. A net loss from business property is not claimed as an itemized deduction; the loss from Form 4684 is entered on Form 4797.

**Steps for calculating your deductible loss for 2018.** The following five steps reflect the procedure on Form 4684 for computing a casualty or theft loss. If your loss is to business inventory, you do not have to use Form 4684, but may take the loss into account when figuring the cost of goods sold; see "Inventory losses" later in this section.

To figure your deductible loss, follow these five steps:

1. Step 1. Compute the loss in fair market value of the property. This is the difference between the fair market value immediately before and immediately after the casualty. You do not have to compute the loss in fair market value for business or income-producing property (such as a rental property) that has been completely destroyed or stolen; go to Step 2. *See* the IRS Alert on the next page for safe harbors that can be used to determine the loss in value of personal residential property.

   You will need written appraisals to support your claim for loss of value. You may not claim sentimental or aesthetic values or a fluctuation in property values caused by a casualty; you must deal with cost or market values of what has been lost. If the value of your property has been lowered because of damage to a nearby area, you do not have a deductible loss since your own property has not been damaged. No deduction may be claimed for estimated decline in value based on buyer resistance in an area subject to landslides.

   For household items, the Tax Court has allowed losses based on cost less depreciation, rather than on the decrease in fair market value.

2. Step 2. Compute your adjusted basis *(5.20)* for the property. This is usually the cost of the property plus the cost of improvements, less previous casualty loss deductions and depreciation if the property is used in business or for income-producing purposes. Unadjusted basis of property acquired other than by purchase is explained at *5.16*.

3. Step 3. Take the lower amount of Step 1 or 2. For business or income-producing property that was stolen or completely destroyed, reduce adjusted basis from Step 2 by any salvage value.

4. Step 4 Reduce the loss in Step 3 by the insurance proceeds or other reimbursements you receive for the loss. This is your deductible loss for business or income-producing property. If the loss was on property used for personal purposes, apply the reductions in Step 5.

   In addition to insurance proceeds, reimbursement includes property cleanup, repair, and restoration services you receive from relief agencies such as the Red Cross. However, cash gifts, donations, or grants you receive from relatives, friends, or organizations to help you recover are not treated as reimbursements if there are no conditions on your use of the money. Even if you actually use the money for repairs, it is not considered a reimbursement unless you were required to use it to repair or replace the property. If you successfully sue for damages for your loss, the net award you collect (after lawyer's fees and other expenses) is included as a reimbursement. If part of a disaster loan is canceled, the canceled part is a reimbursement. If your employer has an emergency disaster fund and you receive amounts from that fund that must be used to repair or replace your property, the amount you use is treated as a reimbursement.

   Insurance payments for the cost of additional living expenses you incur because of damage to your home are not treated as reimbursements. The payments are treated as separate and apart from payments for property damage. Insurance payments for excess living costs are not taxable if they are qualified disaster relief payments *(18.1)*; in other cases, some payments may be taxed *(18.12)*.

   If the insurance or other compensation exceeds your adjusted basis for the property, you have a taxable gain rather than a deductible loss. You may be able to defer the gain by buying replacement property *(18.14)*. If you have purchased replacement property or plan to do so within the replacement period, you elect deferral by filing a statement with your return; *see 18.16* for the required statement. If the election to defer is made, do not report the gain on Form 4684.

*Caution*

**Failure To Make an Insurance Claim**

If you have insurance coverage but do not file a claim because you do not want to risk cancellation of your policy, you may not claim a deduction for the part of your loss that is covered by the policy. The instructions to Form 4684 require you to report as a reimbursement the amount that would have been covered by insurance after taking into account the "deductible" under your policy. This means that the only part of the loss that is potentially deductible on your return (subject to the $100 and 10% of AGI floors) is the part not covered by the insurance. For example, assume your car worth $30,000 is completely destroyed in a federally declared disaster and your car insurance policy has a $2,500 deductible. If you do not file an insurance claim, you must report $27,500, the loss covered by the policy, as a reimbursement on Form 4684. The $2,500 not covered under the insurance policy, the amount equal to the plan deductible, is reduced by the $100 floor and the $2,400 balance is deductible only to the extent it exceeds 10% of your adjusted gross income, which means no deduction at all is allowed if AGI is $24,000 or more; *see* Step 5 below.

5. Step 5. If you had only one 2018 casualty or theft loss and the property was used for personal purposes, the loss from Step 4 must be reduced by the $100 floor and any balance is deductible only to the extent it exceeds 10% of your adjusted gross income. If you have more than one casualty or theft loss of personal-use property, you must reduce each loss by the $100 floor and then the total loss (after the $100 floor reduces each casualty/theft loss) is deductible only to the extent it exceeds the 10% AGI floor.

However, for a "qualified 2017 disaster loss"--a loss due to Hurricane Harvey, Irma, or Maria, or the 2017 California wildfires--the floor is $500 instead of $100, but the regular 10% AGI floor does not apply; *see* the Form 4684 instructions.

If you report gains from casualties and thefts on personal-use property (you do not elect deferral *(18.14)*) and also have losses for personal-use property that are attributable to federally declared disasters, and the total loss (after the $100 floor reduces each casualty/theft loss) exceeds the total gain, the net loss is reduced by 10% of your AGI and the excess if any is the deductible loss. For example, if you have a $12,700 loss attributable to a federally declared disaster (after reducing it by reimbursements and by the $100 floor) and a $6,700 casualty gain for a personal-use asset, the net loss of $6,000 ($12,700-$6,700) is deductible only to the extent it exceeds the 10% AGI floor. If the gain was $12,700 and the loss $6,700, the net gain of $6,000 is reported as capital gain income (either short-term or long-term) on Schedule D (Form 1040).

If you had casualty or theft gains on personal-use property (that are not deferred *(18.14)*) and also casualty or theft losses on personal-use property, some of which were attributable to federally declared disasters and some of which were not attributable to federally declared disasters, the gains are offset first by the losses that are not attributable to federally declared disasters. See the Form 4684 instructions on how to offset the gains by the losses not attributable to federally declared disasters, and how, if there are gains remaining, they are offset against the losses that are attributable to federally declared disasters.

## EXAMPLES

1. Your home, which cost $76,000 in 1979, was damaged by a storm that was declared a federal disaster in August 2018. The value of the house before the fire was $247,500, but afterwards, $202,500. Furniture that cost $5,000 in 1990 and was valued at $2,500 before the storm was totally destroyed. In September 2018, the insurance company reimbursed you $25,000 for your house damage and $1,000 for your furnishings. This was the only casualty for the year. Your adjusted gross income is $88,000. You figure your loss for the furniture separately from the loss on the house but apply only one $100 floor because the damage was from a single casualty.

| | | |
|---|---|---|
| 1. | Decrease in home's fair market value: | |
| | Value of house before fire | $247,500 |
| | Value of house after fire | 202,500 |
| | Decrease in value | $45,000 |
| 2. | Adjusted basis: | $76,000 |
| 3. | Loss sustained (lower of 1 or 2) | $45,000 |
| | Less: Insurance | 25,000 |
| | Loss on house | $20,000 |
| 4. | Loss on furnishings (decreased value)* | $2,500 |
| | Less: Insurance | 1,000 |
| | Loss on furnishings | $1,500 |
| 5. | Total loss ($20,000 and $1,500) | $21,500 |
| | Less: $100 floor | 100 |
| | Casualty loss (subject to 10% floor) | $21,400 |
| 6. | 10% AGI floor (10% of $88,000 AGI) | $8,800 |
| 7. | Casualty loss ($21,400 – $8,800) | $12,600 |

*The loss for the furnishings on Line 4 is $2,500, the decrease in fair market value, as this is lower than the $5,000 basis.

*IRS Alert*

### Safe Harbors for Figuring Loss in Value to Home

The IRS has provided an optional safe harbor method in Revenue Procedure 2018-8 that taxpayers can use to determine the decrease in fair market value of personal-use residential property and personal belongings as the result of a casualty or theft. If the taxpayer qualifies for and uses one of the safe harbors, that would establish the decrease in fair market value required under Step 1 of *18.9*; the IRS will not challenge that amount. Revenue Procedure 2018-9 provides an additional safe harbor based on cost indexes that can be used to determine the amount of loss to a home resulting from Hurricane and Tropical Storm Harvey, Hurricane Irma and Hurricane Maria. See the instructions to Form 4684 and Publication 547 for further details.

*Filing Instruction*

### Reporting Gains and Losses From Personal-Use Property on Form 4684

If you have a casualty or theft loss for personal-use property, use Section A on page 1 of Form 4684. If you suffered more than one casualty or theft of personal-use property during the year, use a separate Form 4684 for each one and make the calculations through Line 12. The amounts from the separate Forms 4684 should be combined on a single Form 4684.

If you have one or more gains from casualties or thefts of personal-use property, you report them on Section A of Form 4684 unless you elect to defer the gains; you can elect to defer if you have replaced the property or intend to buy a replacement within the replacement period *(18.14)*. If you report the gains on Section A and also report losses attributable to federally declared disasters, compare the gains (whether or not attributable to federally declared disasters) to the losses after reducing each loss by the $100 floor. If the losses are more than the gains, reduce the net loss (losses minus gains) by the 10% AGI floor (on Line 17 of the combined Form 4684) and if the net loss exceeds the 10% floor, the excess (on Line 18 of Form 4684) is entered on Line 15, Schedule A (Form 1040) as your casualty/theft loss deduction. If your gains exceed your losses, the excess is treated as capital gain on Schedule D.

2. Your depreciable business property with a fair market value of $3,500 and an adjusted basis of $4,000 is totally destroyed in a federally declared disaster. Because property used in your business was totally destroyed (see Step 3 *(18.9)*), your loss is measured by your adjusted basis of $4,000, which is larger than the $3,500 loss in fair market value. Salvage value, if any, reduces your deduction, but you disregard the $100 floor which applies only to casualty losses on personal property. If the property was used for personal purposes, the loss would have been limited to the $3,500 loss in market value less $100, leaving a loss of $3,400 before applying the 10% adjusted gross income floor.

**Business losses.** Losses from business property are generally netted against gains from casualties or thefts on Form 4684 and the net gain or loss is entered on Form 4797. Follow the instructions to Form 4684.

**Inventory losses.** A casualty or theft loss of inventory is automatically reflected on Schedule C in the cost of goods sold, which includes the lost items as part of your opening inventory. Any insurance or other reimbursement received for the loss must be included as sales income.

You may separately claim the inventory loss as a casualty or theft loss on Form 4684 instead of automatically claiming it as part of the cost of goods sold. If you do this, you must eliminate the items from inventory by lowering either opening inventory or purchases when figuring the cost of goods sold.

## 18.10 Personal and Business Use of Property

For property held partly for personal use and partly for business or income-producing purposes, a casualty or theft loss deduction is computed as if two separate pieces of property were damaged, destroyed, or stolen. Follow the steps for figuring the allowable loss *(18.9)*, but apply the $100 and 10% of adjusted gross income floors only to the personal part of the loss.

**Business or Income-Producing Property**

If you are claiming a loss for property used in your business or income-producing activity, use Section B on page 2 of Form 4684 to figure the allowable loss. Losses from income-producing property are entered on Line 16 of Schedule A as "other itemized deductions". Losses from business property are entered on Form 4797.

**Incidental Expenses**

Expenses that are incidental to a casualty or theft, such as medical treatment for personal injury, temporary housing, fuel, moving, or rentals for temporary living quarters, are not deductible as casualty losses.

### EXAMPLE

A building with two apartments, one used by the owner as his home and the other rented to a tenant, is damaged by a storm that is a federal declared disaster. The fair market value of the building before the fire was $169,000 and it was $136,000 after the fire, which damaged both apartments equally. Cost basis of the building was $120,000. Depreciation taken before the fire was $14,000. The insurance company paid $20,000. The owner has adjusted gross income of $40,000. This is his only loss this year. He has a business casualty loss of $6,500 and a deductible personal casualty loss of $2,400 figured as follows:

|  | Business | Personal |
|---|---|---|
| 1. Decrease in value of building: |  |  |
| Value before fire ($169,000) | $84,500 | $84,500 |
| Value after fire ($136,000) | (68,000) | (68,000) |
| Decrease in value | $16,500 | $16,500 |
| 2. Adjusted basis of building: | $60,000 | $60,000 |
| Less: Depreciation | (14,000) |  |
| Adjusted basis | $46,000 | $60,000 |
| 3. Loss sustained (lower of 1 or 2) | $16,500 | $16,500 |
| Less: Insurance (total $20,000) | ($10,000) | ($10,000) |
| 4. Loss | $6,500 | $6,500 |
| Less: $100 floor and 10% of adjusted gross income ($4,000) | — | (4,100) |
| Deductible casualty loss | $6,500 | $2,400 |

## 18.11 Repairs May Be a "Measure of Loss"

The cost of repairs may be treated as evidence of the loss of value (Step 1 in *18.9*), if the amount is not excessive and the repairs do nothing more than restore the property to its condition before the casualty. An estimate for repairs will not suffice; only actual repairs may be used as a measure of loss. However, where you measure your loss by comparing appraisals of value for before and after the casualty, repairs may be considered in arriving at a post-casualty value even though no actual repairs are made.

**Deduction not limited to repairs.** A casualty loss deduction is not limited to repair expenses where the decline in market value is greater, according to a federal appeals court; *see* the following Example.

*Planning Reminder*

**Keep Records of Deductible Losses**

If your property is damaged, you must reduce the basis of the damaged property by the casualty loss deduction and compensation received for the loss *(5.20)*. When you later sell the property, gain or loss is the difference between the selling price and the reduced basis.

> **EXAMPLE**
>
> Connor claimed that the market value of his house dropped $93,000 after it was damaged by fire. His $52,000 cash outlay in repairing the house was reimbursed by insurance. He claimed a casualty loss of approximately $40,000, the uncompensated drop in market value. The IRS barred the deduction. The house was restored to pre-casualty condition. The cost of the repairs is a realistic measure of the loss, and, as the expense was fully compensated by insurance, Connor suffered no loss. A federal appeals court disagreed. The house dropped $70,000 in market value, of which $20,000 was uncompensated by insurance. The deduction is measured by the uncompensated difference in value before and after the casualty. It is not limited to the cost of repairs, even where the repair expense is less than the difference in fair market values. Had the repairs cost more than this difference, the IRS would not have allowed a larger deduction.

## 18.12 Excess Living Costs Paid by Insurance Are Not Taxable

Your insurance contract may reimburse you for excess living costs when a casualty or a threat of casualty forces you to vacate your house. The insurance payments are completely tax free if the temporary increase in your living costs was due to a casualty (storm, flood, wildfire) in a federal disaster area; they are treated as qualified disaster area relief payments *(18.1)*.

If the casualty that forces you to vacate your home is not a federally declared disaster, some of the insurance payments may be taxable. These rules apply if:

1. Your principal residence is damaged or destroyed by fire, storm, or other casualty that is not a federally declared disaster or you are denied access to your home by a governmental order because of the occurrence or threat of the casualty.

2. You are paid under an insurance contract for living expenses resulting from the loss of occupancy or use of the residence.

**Tax-free reimbursements.** Whether you have a taxable or tax-free reimbursement is figured at the end of the period you were unable to use your residence. Thus, if the dislocation covers more than one taxable year, the taxable income, if any, will be reported in the taxable year in which the dislocation ended.

The tax-free amount is limited to the excess living costs paid by the insurance company. The excess is the difference between (1) the actual living expenses incurred during the time you could not use or occupy your house and (2) the normal living expenses that you would have incurred for yourself and members of your household during the period. Insurance payments that exceed (1) minus (2) are generally taxable; *see* the Examples below.

Living expenses during the period may include the cost of renting suitable housing and extraordinary expenses for transportation, food, utilities, and miscellaneous services. The expenses must be incurred for items and services (such as laundry) needed to maintain your standard of living that you enjoyed before the loss and must be covered by the policy.

Where a lump-sum settlement does not identify the amount covering living expenses, an allocation is required to determine the tax-free portion. In the case of uncontested claims, the tax-free portion is that part of the settlement that bears the same ratio to total recovery as increased living expense bears to total loss and expense. If your claim is contested, you must show the amount reasonably allocable to increased living expenses consistent with the terms of the insurance contract, but not in excess of coverage limitations specified in the contract.

The exclusion from income does not cover insurance reimbursements for loss of rental income or for loss of or damage to real or personal property; such reimbursements for property damage reduce your casualty loss *(18.9)*.

If your home is used for both residential and business purposes, the exclusion does not apply to insurance proceeds and expenses attributable to the nonresidential portion of the house. There is no exclusion for insurance recovered for expenses resulting from governmental condemnation or order unrelated to a casualty or threat of casualty.

The insurance reimbursement may cover part of your normal living expenses as well as the excess expenses due to the casualty. The part covering normal expenses is income; it does not reduce your casualty loss.

### EXAMPLES

1. On March 1, your home was damaged by fire. While it was being repaired, you and your spouse lived at a motel for a month and ate meals at restaurants. Costs are $1,200 at the motel, $1,000 for meals, and $75 for laundry services. You make the required March payment of $790 on your home mortgage. Your customary $40 commuting expense is $20 less for the month because the motel is closer to your work. Your usual commuting expense is therefore treated as not being incurred to the extent of the $20 decrease. Furthermore, you do not incur your customary $700 food expense for meals at home, $75 for utilities, and $60 for laundry at home. Your insurance company pays you $1,700 for expenses. The tax-free exclusion for insurance payments is limited to $1,420, computed in the third column below. On Line 21 of Schedule 1 (Form 1040) ("Other income") you must report $280 ($1,700 – $1,420) as "other income."

| | Expenses from casualty | Expenses not incurred | Increase (Decrease) |
|---|---|---|---|
| Housing | $1,200 | | $1,200 |
| Utilities | | $75 | (75) |
| Meals | 1,000 | 700 | 300 |
| Transportation | | 20 | (20) |
| Laundry | 75 | 60 | 15 |
| Total | $2,275 | $855 | $1,420 |

2. Same facts as in Example 1 except that you rented the residence for $400 per month and the risk of loss was to the landlord. You did not pay the March rent. The excludable amount is $1,020 ($1,420 less $400 normal rent not incurred). You would have to report as income the excess of the insurance received over the $1,020 exclusion.

---

*Filing Tip*

**Involuntary Conversion of Personal Residence**

Gain on the destruction or condemnation of your principal residence may escape tax under the home sale exclusion rules discussed in *Chapter 29*. If the exclusion is not available or the gain exceeds the excludable amount, but you buy a replacement residence, gain may be deferred under the involuntary conversion replacement rules *(18.14)*. Special rules apply if your principal residence was damaged or destroyed in a federally declared disaster: gain on insurance proceeds received for unscheduled personal property in the home is not taxable, and insurance proceeds for the home itself and scheduled personal property are combined for purposes of making a reinvestment in replacement property that qualifies for deferral *(18.4)*.

## 18.13 Do Your Casualty or Theft Losses Exceed Your Income?

If your 2018 casualty or theft losses exceed your income for the year, you pay no tax for 2018. Under the net operating loss (NOL) rules *(40.18)*, you may carry forward the excess casualty or theft loss.

The $100 floor *(18.8)* and the 10% of adjusted gross income floor *(18.8)* for personal casualty or theft losses apply only in the year of the loss; you do not again reduce your loss in the carryforward years.

## 18.14 Defer Gain from Involuntary Conversion by Replacing Property

If your property is destroyed, damaged, stolen, or seized or condemned by a government authority, this is considered to be an involuntary conversion for tax purposes *(18.15)*. If upon an involuntary conversion you receive insurance or other compensation (reduced by expenses in obtaining reimbursement) that exceeds the adjusted basis of the property, you realize a gain that is taxable unless you elect to defer (postpone) the gain or, in the case of a principal residence, it is gain that you may exclude from income under the rules in *Chapter 29*.

You may elect to postpone tax on the full gain provided you invest the proceeds in replacement property the cost of which is equal to or exceeds the net proceeds from the conversion *(18.19)*. Buying a replacement from a related party generally qualifies only if your gains from involuntary conversions are $100,000 or less *(18.17)*. Gain realized on a destroyed or condemned principal residence that exceeds the allowable exclusion under the rules in *Chapter 29* may be postponed if the cost of a replacement residence at least equals the conversion proceeds minus the excluded gain *(18.19)*.

The replacement period *(18.18)* is two years for personal-use property; for business and investment property it is two or three years depending on the type of involuntary conversion; for a principal residence and its contents involuntarily converted due to a federally declared disaster it is four years. If you find that you cannot buy a replacement by the end of the period, ask the IRS for an extension of time. *See 18.18* for replacement period details.

**Insurance proceeds may have to be allocated to determine if you have a gain.** If property used in your business is involuntarily converted, make a distinction between insurance proceeds compensating you for the loss of your property and any insurance that compensates you for loss of profits because of business interruption. Business interruption proceeds are fully taxed as ordinary income and may not be treated as proceeds of an involuntary conversion. Only take into account the insurance for the loss of property in figuring if you have a gain from the involuntary conversion.

A single standard fire insurance policy may cover several assets. Assume a fire occurs, and in a settlement the proceeds are allocated to each destroyed item according to its fair market value before the fire. In comparing the allocated proceeds to the adjusted basis of each item, you find that on some items, you have realized a gain; that is, the proceeds exceed basis. On the other items, you have a loss; the proceeds are less than basis. According to the IRS, you may elect to defer tax on the gain items by buying replacement property. You do not treat the proceeds paid under the single policy as a unit, but as separate payments made for each covered item.

**Election to defer reporting of a gain.** To defer reporting of your gain, do not report the gain on your return for the year it is realized. Make the election to defer on a statement attached to your return that provides details of the involuntary conversion and computation of the gain, and which describes the replacement property if you have already acquired it or states your intention to buy a replacement if you have not yet done so. Details on the required statement or statements you must file are at *18.16*.

**Basis of replacement property.** Your basis for the replacement property is its replacement cost, minus any postponed gain. This is the actual mechanism of deferral. By reducing basis of the replacement property by the amount of the deferred gain, tax on that gain is postponed until the replacement property is disposed of.

Should you elect to postpone gain? An election to defer your gain gives an immediate advantage: tax on gain is postponed and the funds that would have been spent to pay the tax may be used for other investments.

However, as a condition of deferring the gain, your basis for the replacement property equals its cost minus the deferred gain. If your reinvestment matches the insurance or other compensation, your basis for the new property will be the same as the basis for the converted property. If your reinvestment exceeds the compensation, the excess increases the basis of the replacement property. As long as the value of the replacement property does not decline, tax on the original gain is finally incurred when the property is sold.

 *Planning Reminder*

**Basis Reduction**

Consider whether postponement of gain at the expense of a reduced basis for property is advisable, compared with the tax consequences of reporting the gain in the year it is realized.

---

### EXAMPLE

Your rental building is destroyed by fire and after taking into account insurance payments, you have a gain (excess of insurance over adjusted basis for building) that is taxable as capital gain if you do not elect to defer the gain. Assume that you reinvest the reimbursement in replacement property so you qualify to make the election. Should you do so? An election to defer the gain is generally not advisable if you have capital losses to offset the gain. However, even if you have no capital losses, you may still decide to pay tax on the gain now and not make the election to defer. Reporting the gain now would allow you treat the purchase price of the new building as its basis for depreciation purposes. This can be an advantage if you anticipate that future depreciation deductions will offset income that will be taxed at a higher rate than the rate you are subject to currently. Of course, it may turn out that there will be little or no difference between your current tax rate and your future rate, so that a net after-tax benefit from the depreciation would not arise.

Ultimately, projecting future consequences may not be your key concern. You may decide to elect to defer the gain simply because you want to postpone the payment of tax.

## 18.15 Involuntary Conversions Qualifying for Tax Deferral

For purposes of an election to defer tax on gains, "involuntary conversion" is broadly defined. You have an involuntary conversion when your property is:

**Damaged or destroyed by some outside force, such as a storm, fire, or car accident, or it is stolen.**

**Seized, requisitioned, or condemned by a governmental authority.** If you voluntarily sell land made useless to you by the condemnation of your adjacent land, the sale may also qualify as a conversion. Condemnation of property as unfit for human habitation does not qualify. Condemnation, as used by the tax law, refers to the taking of private property for public use, not to the condemnation of property for noncompliance with housing and health regulations. Similarly, a tax sale to pay delinquent taxes is not an involuntary conversion. See condemnation awards below.

**Sold under a threat of seizure, condemnation, or requisition.** The threat must be made by an authority qualified to take property for public use. A sale following a threat of condemnation made by a government employee is a conversion if you reasonably believe he or she speaks with authority and could and would carry out the threat to have your property condemned. If you learn of the plan of an imminent condemnation from the news media, the IRS requires you to confirm the report from a government official before you act on the news.

**Condemnation awards.** You have a gain if your net condemnation award exceeds your adjusted basis in the condemned property. The net award is the total award reduced by expenses of getting the award such as legal, engineering, and appraisal fees. The treatment of special assessments and severance damages received when part of your property is condemned is explained in *18.20*.

Payments made directly by the condemning authority to your mortgagee do not reduce the gross award. For example, your condemnation award is set at $200,000 but you are paid only $148,000 because $52,000 was paid to your mortgage holder, including $2,000 to cover accrued real estate taxes. The entire $200,000 is treated as your condemnation award.

Do not include as part of the award interest paid on the award for delay in its payment; you separately report the interest as interest income. The IRS may treat as interest part of an award paid late, even though the award does not make any allocation for interest.

Relocation payments are not considered part of the condemnation award and are not treated as taxable income to the extent that they are spent for purposes of relocation; they increase basis of the newly acquired property.

**Farmers.** In addition to the above types of involuntary conversions, farmers also have involuntary conversions when:

- Land is sold within an irrigation project to meet federal acreage limitations;
- Cattle are destroyed by disease or sold because of disease; or
- Draft, breeding, or dairy livestock is sold because of drought. The election to treat the sale as a conversion is limited to livestock sold over the number that would have been sold but for the drought.

In some cases, livestock may be replaced with other farm property where there has been soil or other environmental contamination.

 *Filing Tip*

**Sale of Property Under Hazard Mitigation Program**

A sale or other transfer of vulnerable property to federal, state, or local authorities (or Indian tribal governments) under a hazard mitigation program is treated as an involuntary conversion, thereby allowing a gain to be deferred if a qualifying replacement *(18.17, 18.19)* is made.

## 18.16 How to Elect to Defer Gain

To defer reporting a gain, include your election on a statement attached to your return for the year the gain is realized. For example, for a gain realized in 2018 from an involuntary conversion, attach a statement to your 2018 return that provides details of the involuntary conversion, including reimbursements you received and how you figured the gain. If you have purchased replacement property *(18.17)* by the time you file your 2018 return, your statement should describe the replacement property and its cost, the amount of gain that can be deferred, which depends on the cost of the replacement *(18.19)*, the basis of the replacement property (cost minus deferred gain), and if not all of the gain is deferred, the gain being reported as income.

If you intend to purchase the replacement property after you file your 2018 return, the statement filed with the 2018 return should describe the conversion and the computation of gain and indicate that you intend to buy a replacement within the replacement period *(18.18)*. Then, when you file your return for the year you buy the replacement property, attach a statement to that return giving the details of the replacement property. Providing this statement starts the running of the three-year period of limitations during which the IRS can assess tax on the gain. Failure to give notice keeps the period open. Similarly, a failure to give notice of an intention not to replace also keeps the period open.

If you make an election to postpone the gain but do not buy replacement property within the replacement period (plus extensions if any; *see 18.18*), you must file an amended return for the year in which gain was realized to report the gain and pay the tax (if any) on the gain. Similarly, if you elect to defer gain and buy replacement property that costs less than the amount realized from the conversion *(18.19)*, you must file an amended return to report the gain that cannot be deferred and pay any additional tax due. Also *see* the Caution titled "Nullifying Deferral Election on Amended Return."

Assume you have a gain from an involuntary conversion and do not expect to reinvest the proceeds. You report the gain and pay the tax due. In a later year, but within the prescribed time limits, you buy qualifying replacement property. On an amended return for the year of the conversion, you may make an election to defer the gain and claim a refund for the tax paid in the earlier year on the gain.

**Deferring a gain from condemnation.** To defer reporting a gain from a condemnation, the replacement rules and required statement requirements discussed in the preceding paragraph generally apply.

However, if your property is condemned and the government authority gives you property that is similar or related in use to the condemned property, no election is necessary. You do not have to report the gain on your return; postponement of tax on the gain is required. For example, your local government condemns the building in which you operate your retail business and gives you a similar building, the value of which exceeds the adjusted basis of the old one. The gain is not taxed, and your basis for the new building is the same as your basis in the condemned building.

**Partnerships.** The election to defer gain must be made at the partnership level. Individual partners may not make separate elections unless the partnership has terminated, with all partnership affairs wound up. Dissolution under state law is not a termination for tax purposes.

## 18.17 Types of Qualifying Replacement Property

Under the deferral rules *(18.14)*, replacement property generally must be similar or related in service or use to the property that was involuntarily converted in order to defer tax. Where real property held for productive use in a business or for investment is converted through a condemnation or threat of condemnation, the replacement test is more liberal. A replacement merely has to be of a like kind to the converted property.

Under the like-kind test for condemned real estate, a replacement with other real estate qualifies. Improved real property may be replaced by unimproved real property *(6.1)*. Foreign and U.S. real property are considered to be of like kind for purposes of replacing

**Caution**

**Nullifying Deferral Election on Amended Return**

If you elect to defer a gain, intending to buy replacement property, but you fail to make a replacement within the time limit, you must file an amended return for the year of the gain and pay the tax that you had elected to defer. You also must file an amended return and report the gain not eligible for deferral if you invest in property that does not qualify as a replacement, or which costs less than the amount realized from the involuntary conversion.

However, if you elect to defer and make a timely qualifying replacement, you may not change your mind and pay tax on the gain in order to obtain a higher basis *(18.14)* for the replacement property. The Tax Court has agreed with the IRS that the election to defer is irrevocable once a qualified replacement is made within the time limits. Similarly, once you acquire qualified replacement property and designate it as such in a statement attached to your tax return, you may not substitute other replacement property, even if the replacement period has not yet expired.

*Filing Instruction*

**Attach Statement to Your Return to Defer Gain**

To defer reporting a gain when you receive re-imbursements that exceed your adjusted basis for the involuntarily converted property, you must attach a statement to your return that provides details of the involuntary conversion and that describes replacement property that you have already acquired or which states your intention to buy a replacement within the replacement period; *see 18.16* for details.

*Filing Instruction*

**Reporting a Condemnation Gain On Your Return**

Gain from a condemnation of personal-use property is reported on Forms 8949 and Schedule D *(5.8)* if it cannot be excluded from income (if a principal residence; *see 18.14*) or you do not elect to defer the gain. Gain from a condemnation of business property or investment property that is not deferred is generally reported on Form 4797.

Note: A loss on condemned business or investment property (net condemnation award is less than adjusted basis) is also reported on Form 4797.

**Caution**

**Loss on Condemned Residence Not Deductible**

If your principal residence or vacation home is condemned and the net condemnation award is less than your adjusted basis in the residence, you have a loss. The loss is not deductible, but if you received a Form 1099-S, you must report the condemnation on Form 8949 and Schedule D; *see 5.8.*

**Caution**

**Buying Replacement From Relative**

Buying a replacement from a relative or related business organization will not defer gain unless total gains from involuntary conversions for the year are $100,000 or less.

condemned property, even though under the like-kind exchange rules *(6.1)*, U.S. real estate and foreign real estate are not considered like-kind property.

Under the related in service or use test, the replacement of unimproved land for improved land does not qualify. A replacement generally must be closely related in function to the destroyed property. For example, a condemned personal residence must be replaced with another personal residence. The replacement of a house rented to a tenant with a house used as a personal residence does not qualify for tax deferral; the new house is not being used for the same purpose as the condemned one. This functional test, however, is not strictly applied to conversions of rental property. Here, the role of the owner toward the properties, rather than the functional use of the buildings, is reviewed. If an owner held both properties as investments and offered similar services and took similar business risks in both, the replacement may qualify.

You may own several parcels of property, one of which is condemned. You may want to use the condemnation award to make improvements on the other land such as drainage and grading. The IRS generally will not accept the improvements as a qualified replacement. However, an appeals court has rejected the IRS approach in one case.

If it is not feasible to reinvest the proceeds from the conversion of livestock because of soil contamination or other environmental contamination, then other property (including real property) used for farming purposes is treated as similar or related and qualifies as replacement property.

**Deferral may be barred when buying a replacement from a relative.** The gain deferral rules do not apply if you buy a replacement from a close relative or a related business organization unless the total gain you realized for the year on all involuntary conversions on which there are realized gains is $100,000 or less. In determining whether gains exceed $100,000, gains are not offset by losses. Affected related parties are the same as defined for loss transactions discussed in *5.6.*

**Buying controlling interest in a corporation.** The replacement test is satisfied by purchasing a controlling interest (80%) in a corporation owning property that is similar or related in service or use to the converted property.

**Business and investment property in a disaster area.** The similar or related-use tests do not have to be met when replacing business or investment property damaged or destroyed in a federally declared disaster area, provided you use the new property for business. You may make a qualified replacement by buying any tangible property held for business use; the replacement does not have to be in the federally declared disaster area.

## 18.18 Time Period for Buying Replacement Property

To defer tax, you generally must buy property similar or related in use *(18.17)* to the converted property within a fixed time period. The replacement period is either two, three, or four years:

1. A two-year replacement period applies for destroyed, damaged, or stolen property, whether used for business, investment, or personal purposes, but there is a four-year period for principal residences in federally declared disaster areas *(18.3)*. The two-year period for damaged, destroyed, and stolen property starts on the date the property was destroyed, damaged, or stolen, and ends two years after the end of the first year in which any part of your gain is realized. A two-year period also applies to a condemned residence.

2. A three-year replacement period applies for condemned business or investment real estate, excluding inventory. However, the two-year and not the three-year period applies if the condemned business or investment real estate is replaced by your acquiring control of a corporation that owns the replacement property.

3. A four-year replacement period applies for a principal residence or its contents involuntarily converted as a result of a federally declared disaster *(18.3)*. The four-year replacement period starts on the date the residence is involuntarily converted and ends four years after the end of the first taxable year in which any part of the gain is realized.

4. A four-year replacement period for farmers and ranchers who are forced to sell livestock due to drought, flooding, or other weather conditions in areas eligible for federal assistance. Gain on such a forced sale may be deferred by buying replacement livestock within four years after the end of the first taxable year in which any part of the gain is realized. The IRS may extend the four-year replacement period on a regional basis if the weather conditions persist for more than three years. If the IRS allows an extension, it is announced in a Notice that lists the qualifying counties.

**Giving IRS notice of replacement.** On your return for the year you realize the gain, you must attach a statement that describes the involuntary conversion and notifies the IRS either that you have acquired replacement property, or that you plan to do so within the replacement period, in which case another statement must be filed with your return for the year of the replacement. Details on these required statements are in *18.16*.

**Replacing condemned property.** For condemnations, the replacement period starts on the earlier of (1) the date you receive notification of the condemnation threat or (2) the date you dispose of the condemned property. Depending on the replacement period (*see* above), the period ends two, three, or four years after the end of the first year in which any part of the gain on the condemnation is realized. You may make a replacement after a threat of condemnation. If you buy property before the actual threat, it will not qualify as a replacement even though you still own it at the time of the actual condemnation.

**Advance payment of award.** Gain is realized in the year compensation for the converted property exceeds the basis of the converted property. An advance payment of an award that exceeds the adjusted basis of the property starts the running of the replacement period.

An award is treated as received in the year that it is made available to you without restrictions, even if you contest the amount.

**Replacement by an estate.** A person whose property was involuntarily converted may die before he or she makes a replacement. According to the IRS, his or her estate may not reinvest the proceeds within the allowed time and postpone tax on the gain. The Tax Court rejects the IRS position and has allowed tax deferral where the replacement was made by the deceased owner's estate. However, the Tax Court agreed with the IRS that a surviving spouse's investment in land did not defer tax on gain realized by her deceased husband on an involuntary conversion of his land. She had received his property as survivor of joint tenancy and could not, in making the investment, be considered as acting for his estate.

---

### EXAMPLES

1. On January 17, 2018, your parcel of investment real estate is condemned; the parcel cost $150,000. On March 26, 2018, you received a check for $230,500 from the state. Your expenses in obtaining the award were $10,000, so the net condemnation award is $220,500. You may defer the tax on the gain of $70,500 ($220,500-$150,000 basis) if you invest at least the net award *(18.19)*, or $220,500, in other real estate not later than December 31, 2021, the end of the three-year replacement period.

2. Business property was contaminated by dangerous chemicals, and after the Environmental Protection Agency ordered businesses and residents to relocate, the property was sold to the local government under a threat of condemnation. The owner was paid the full pre-contamination fair market value for the property. The owner wanted to defer gain under the three-year replacement rule for condemnations. However, the IRS said that part of the gain was deferrable under the two-year rule and part under the three-year rule. There were two conversions: (1) the contamination, subject to the two-year replacement rule; and (2) the later condemnation, subject to the three-year rule.

   To determine the amount eligible for deferral for each period, an allocation must be made between the proceeds allocable to the destruction of the property and the proceeds allocable to the condemnation.

   According to the IRS, the burden for making the allocation between the two conversions rests with the owner. The government's payments are allocable to the condemnation and, therefore, eligible for the three-year replacement rule, only to the extent of the post-contamination value. Practically speaking, it may be advisable in a case like this to make the replacement within the two-year period, as it may be difficult to show the contaminated land had any value after the contamination.

---

## 18.19 Cost of Replacement Property Determines Postponed Gain

To defer tax on the full gain realized on an involuntary conversion *(18.15)*, the cost of replacement property *(18.17)* must be equal to or exceed the net proceeds from the conversion (amount received minus your expenses). If replacement cost is no more than the adjusted basis of the converted property, you must include the entire gain in your income. If replacement cost is less than the net proceeds on the conversion but more than the basis of the converted property, the difference between the net proceeds and the cost of the replacement must be reported as a taxable gain; you may elect to postpone tax on the balance of the gain. See Examples 1–4 below.

### EXAMPLES

1. The adjusted basis of the apartment house that you rent out to tenants is $175,000. It is condemned to make way for a new street. You receive a condemnation award from the state of $305,000. Your legal expenses in obtaining the award were $5,000, so the net award is $300,000. Your gain is $125,000 ($300,000 net award – $175,000 adjusted basis). If you buy a similar apartment house for $175,000 or less, you must report the entire $125,000 gain.

2. Same facts as in Example 1, except that you buy an apartment house for $250,000. Of the gain of $125,000, you must report $50,000 as taxable gain ($300,000 – $250,000). You may elect to postpone the tax on the balance of the gain, or $75,000. If you elect deferral, your basis for the new building is $175,000 ($250,000 – $75,000 postponed gain).

3. Same facts as in Example 1, but you buy an apartment house for $300,000 or more. You may elect to postpone tax on the entire gain because you have invested the entire net award in replacement property. If the cost of the new building is $325,000 and you elect deferral, your basis for the new building is $200,000 ($325,000 – $125,000 postponed gain).

4. You bought a vacation home 20 years ago for $150,000 and over the years made capital improvements of $30,000, giving you an adjusted basis of $180,000. In January 2018, when the home was worth $350,000, it was destroyed in a storm. In May, you received $284,000 from the insurance company. You have a gain of $104,000 ($284,000 – $180,000). In October, you bought a new vacation home for $250,000. Since the cost of the replacement property was less than the $284,000 insurance proceeds, you must include in your income the unspent amount, or $34,000 ($284,000 – $250,000).

## 18.20 Special Assessments and Severance Damages from Condemnation

When only part of a property parcel is condemned for a public improvement, the condemning authority may:

1. Levy a special assessment against the remaining property, claiming that it is benefited by the improvement. The authority usually deducts the assessment from the condemnation award.

2. Grant an award for severance damages if the condemnation of part of your property causes a loss in value or damage to the remaining property that you keep.

A special assessment that is taken out of the award reduces the amount of the gross condemnation award. An assessment levied after the award is made may not be deducted from the award.

## EXAMPLE

Two acres of a 10-acre tract are condemned for a new highway. The adjusted basis of the land is $30,000, or $3,000 per acre. The condemnation award is $11,000; you incurred expenses of $1,000 to get the award. A special assessment against the remaining eight acres of $2,500 is withheld from the award. The net gain on the condemnation is $1,500:

| | |
|---|---|
| Condemnation award minus your expenses ($11,000 award – $1,000 expenses) | $10,000 |
| Less: Special assessment withheld from award | 2,500 |
| Net condemnation award | 7,500 |
| Basis of two condemned acres | 6,000 |
| Net gain (net award minus basis) | $1,500 |

When both the condemnation award and severance damages are received, the condemnation is treated as two separate involuntary conversions: (1) A conversion of the condemned land. Here, the condemnation award is applied against the basis of the condemned land to determine gain or loss on its conversion; and (2) a conversion of part of the remaining land in the sense that its utility has been reduced by condemnation, for which severance damages are paid.

Net severance damages reduce the basis of the retained property. Net severance damages are the total severance damages, reduced by expenses in obtaining the damages and by any special assessment withheld from the condemnation award. If the damages exceed basis, gain is realized. Tax may be deferred on the gain through the purchase of replacement property under the "similar or related in service or use" test *(18.17)*, such as adjacent land or restoration of the property to its original condition.

Allocating the proceeds between the condemnation award and severance damages will either reduce the gain or increase the loss realized on the condemned land. The IRS will allow such a division only when the condemnation authority specifically identifies part of the award as severance damage in the contract or in an itemized statement or closing sheet. The Tax Court, however, has allowed an allocation in the absence of earmarking where the state considered severance damages, and the value of the condemned land was small in comparison to the damages suffered by the remaining property. To avoid a dispute with the IRS, make sure the authority makes this breakdown. Without such identification, the IRS will treat the entire proceeds as consideration for the condemned property.

# CHAPTER 19

# Other Itemized Deductions

Apart from the expenses listed in Chapters 14 through 18, there are only a few expenses that can be claimed as itemized deductions on Schedule A (Form 1040) for 2018 and later years. These include casualty and theft losses of income-producing property, gambling losses to the extent of reported gambling winnings, and impairment-related job expenses *(19.1)*.

The law no longer allows any itemized deduction for a wide-ranging list of expenses that were deductible before 2018 to the extent that the total exceeded 2% of adjusted gross income, including unreimbursed employee expenses (employee travel expenses, work clothes, union and professional dues, education expenses and home office expenses), investment expenses, legal expenses, and tax preparation expenses.

## 19.1   Only a Few Expenses Are Allowed as "Other" Itemized Deductions

If you itemize deductions on Schedule A, the following expenses may be claimed as "Other Itemized Deductions":

**Impairment-related work expenses.** If you have a physical or mental disability that substantially limits your ability to walk, speak, breathe, or perform manual tasks and which limits your ability to work, you can deduct unreimbursed ordinary and necessary expenses that enable you to work. This includes attendant care services at your place of work and similar expenses.

If you are an employee, enter the impairment-related work expenses as well as any employer reimbursements on Form 2106. Then enter the unreimbursed amount on Line 16 (Other Itemized Deductions) of Schedule A.

If you are self-employed, the impairment-related expenses are reported as business expenses on Schedule C *(40.6)* and not as an itemized deduction.

**Casualty and theft losses of property held for investment.** If your investment property (work of art, rental property, stocks, bonds, precious metals) was stolen or damaged in a storm or other casualty, figure your allowable loss on Section B of Form 4684 *(18.7, 18.9)*. If you are a victim of a Ponzi or Ponzi-type scheme, your loss is treated as a theft loss of investment property; *see 18.7.*

**Gambling losses up to reported gambling winnings.** As discussed at *11.3*, gambling losses are deductible only up to the amount of gambling winnings reported as "other income" on Schedule 1, Form 1040.

**Repayment of more than $3,000 that you previously included in income under a claim of right.** Instead of claiming the repayment as an itemized deduction, you may recompute your tax for the year you reported the income and claim a tax credit for the year you repay it *(2.8)*.

**Estate tax attributable to income in respect of a decedent (IRD).** If federal estate tax was paid on IRD that you include on your return, the estate tax attributable to that IRD is deductible *(11.17)*.

**Amortizable bond premium in excess of interest on taxable bond.** If the allocable amortizable premium exceeds the interest income for the year, the excess premium is deductible *(4.17)*.

**Unrecovered investment in employee annuity.** If the last surviving annuitant of an employee annuity dies before the retiree's entire investment is recovered tax free, the balance is deductible on the final income tax return of the last annuitant; *see* the Example in *7.25*.

## 19.2 Deductions for Job Costs and Other Miscellaneous Expenses No Longer Allowed

The Tax Cuts and Jobs Act suspended, starting with 2018 returns, all the miscellaneous itemized deductions that were deductible for 2017 and prior years to the extent they exceeded 2% of adjusted gross income. The 2% floor had the effect of substantially reducing or eliminating the deduction for these expenses, but now an itemized deduction for these expenses is completely disallowed regardless of amount.

In general, three categories of expenses are no longer deductible: (1) unreimbursed employee expenses, (2) tax preparation expenses and practitioner fees for representing you in a tax dispute before the IRS or a court, and (3) fees to produce or collect taxable income and costs of managing or protecting investment property.

Here is a more specific list of expenses that are no longer deductible itemized deductions:

- Unreimbursed employee expenses. This includes employee travel and meals expenses on trips away from home *(20.6)*, local transportation costs to *see* clients or customers, union dues, professional and business association dues, uniforms and work clothes, costs of looking for a new job in the same line of work, employee home office expenses, job-related education costs, and business bad debt on a loan made to your employer to protect your job.

  As noted in *12.2*, an above-the-line deduction (an "adjustment to income" allowed whether the standard deduction or itemized deductions claimed) is allowed for certain unreimbursed employee expenses, including educator expenses up to $250, qualifying travel costs of Armed Forces Reservists, costs of state or local government officials paid on a fee basis, and expenses of qualifying performing artists. The above-the-line deduction for these expenses is not affected by the Tax Cuts and Jobs Act.

- General tax advice and tax return preparation fees. If you are self-employed, a tax practitioner's fee for preparing your Schedule C and related schedules, or Schedule F (farming) and related schedules, is a business expense deductible on the Schedule C or F. Similarly, a tax preparation fee allocable to reporting rental or royalty income on Schedule E is deduced on that form.

- Fees to a tax practitioner to represent you at an IRS examination, trial, or hearing involving any tax.

- Appraisal fees related to casualty losses and charitable property contributions.

- Investment costs, e.g., IRA custodial fees, safe-deposit rentals, subscriptions to investment services, fees to investment counselors, and travel costs of a trip away from home *(20.6)* to look after investment property or confer with an attorney, accountant, or financial advisor about managing your investments.

- Legal fees for recovering taxable job-related damages or personal damages. If you are self -employed, legal fees relating to your business are deductible on Schedule C (Schedule F for farming).

# CHAPTER 20

# Travel and Meal Expense Deductions

Unreimbursed employee travel expenses are no longer deductible, except for a very limited number of employees who may claim their expenses on Form 2106 *(20.1)*. Under an "accountable plan" arrangement, an employer's expense allowance for travel costs is not reported as income on Form W-2 if you substantiated the expenses to your employer and returned any unsubstantiated portion of the allowance *(20.18)*. If you are self-employed, travel expenses are claimed on Schedule C *(40.6)*.

The types of deductible travel expenses are highlighted in *Table 20-1*. You must be away from home to deduct travel expenses on overnight business trips. Meal costs on overnight trips away from home are subject to restrictions, including a 50% deduction limit (80% for certain transportation workers; *20.15*). On one-day business trips within the general area of your employment, only transportation costs may be deducted; meals may not.

To support your travel expense deductions, keep records that comply with IRS rules *(20.16)*.

You may no longer deduct entertainment expenses. Although deductions for entertainment have been eliminated, a 50% deduction may still be claimed for business meals provided that IRS requirements are satisfied *(20.13, 20.14)*.

## 20.1 Who May Deduct Travel and Transportation Expenses

Due to the repeal of miscellaneous itemized deductions subject to the 2% floor *(19.2)*, the only employees who may deduct unreimbursed travel and transportation costs for 2018 and later years are those in the following limited categories: (1) Armed Forces reservists who have reserves-related expenses for trips away from home *(20.6)* of more than 100 miles *(35.8)*, (2) fee-basis state or local government officials *(12.2)*, and (3) qualifying performing artists (see requirements at *12.2*)

Employees in these three categories use Form 2106 to report their eligible business expenses and employer reimbursements if any. Meals on business trips away from home are reduced by 50% on Form 2106. The qualifying portion of their unreimbursed expenses from Form 2106 is entered as an above-the-line deduction ("adjustment to income") on Line 24 of Schedule 1 (Form 1040), so it is allowed whether the standard deduction is claimed or deductions are itemized on Schedule A *(12.2)*.

Employees who are not within categories (1) through (3) may not use Form 2106 and may not deduct unreimbursed travel and transportation costs, starting with 2018 returns.

Self-employed individuals and employees in categories (1) through (3) should *see Table 20-1*, which summarizes the rules for deducting local business transportation costs and travel expenses while "away from home" *(20.6)* on business trips. Generally, commuting expenses from your home to your place of business when you are not away from home are not deductible *(20.2)*. However, you may be able to claim a deduction for daily transportation expenses incurred in commuting *(20.2)* to a temporary job location; *see Table 20-1*.

If you are self-employed, claim your deductible transportation and travel costs on Schedule C *(40.6)*.

## 20.2 Commuting Expenses

The cost of travel between your home and place of work is generally not deductible, even if the work location is in a remote area not serviced by public transportation. Nor can you justify the deduction by showing you need a car for faster trips to work or for emergency trips. Travel from a union hall to an assigned job is also considered commuting. If you join a car pool, you may not deduct expenses of gasoline, repairs, or other costs of driving you and your passengers to work.

According to the IRS, if you use your cell phone to make calls to clients or business associates while driving to your office, you are still commuting and your expenses are not deductible. Similarly, the deduction is not allowed if you drive passengers to work and discuss business.

**Deductible commuting expenses.** The IRS allows these exceptions to its blanket ban on commuting expense deductions.

*If you are on a business trip out of town,* you may deduct taxi fares or other transportation costs from your hotel to the first business call of the day and all other transportation costs between business calls.

*If you use your car to carry tools to work,* you may deduct transportation costs where you can prove that they were incurred in addition to the ordinary, nondeductible commuting expenses. The deduction will be allowed even if you would use a car in any event to commute; *see* the Examples below.

**Commuting to a temporary place of work.** Whether you can deduct commuting expenses to a temporary place of work may depend on the location of the temporary assignment and whether you have a regular place of business or a home office that is your principal place of business. According to the IRS, if you have a regular place of work outside of your home, or you have a home office that is your principal place of business, you may deduct the cost of commuting between your home and a temporary (see below) work location, regardless of where the temporary location is.

If you do not have a regular place of work but normally work at several locations in the metropolitan area where you live, you may deduct the costs of commuting to a temporary location that is outside that metropolitan area, but not to a temporary location within

*Court Decision*

**Self-Employed Person's Office at Home**

If you are self-employed and your regular office is outside your home, you may not deduct the cost of commuting to the office or from that office to your home even if you work at home at a second job. However, if your home office is your principal place of business *(40.12)*, you can deduct travel costs between the home office and the offices or worksites of your clients or customers.

the metropolitan area. If you do not have a regular place of work and all of your work assignments are outside the metropolitan area where you live, none of your commuting costs are deductible under the IRS rule.

### EXAMPLES

1. Jones commuted to and from work by public transportation before he had to carry tools. Public transportation cost $5 per day to commute to and from work. When he had to use the car to carry the tools, the cost of driving was $12 a day and $35 a day to rent a trailer to carry the tools. Jones may deduct only the cost of renting the trailer. The IRS does not allow a deduction for the additional $7 a day cost of operating the car. It is not considered related to the carrying of the tools. It is treated as part of the cost of commuting, which is not deductible.

2. Same facts as above, but Jones does not rent a trailer. He uses the car trunk to store his tools. He may not claim a deduction because he incurs no additional cost for carrying the tools.

3. Smith uses his car regardless of the need to transport tools. He rents a trailer for $35 a day to carry tools. He may deduct $35 a day under the "additional-cost" rule.

**What is a temporary place of work?** A temporary work location is one at which your assignment is realistically expected to last, and actually does last, for one year or less. If at first you realistically expect an assignment to last for no more than one year but that expectation changes, the IRS will generally treat the assignment as temporary until the date that it became realistic to expect that the work would exceed one year.

Accountants, architects, engineers, and other professionals often have to travel to job sites of their clients. If such work at the site is temporary and they can show they also have a regular work office, they may deduct commuting expenses from their homes to their work sites.

## 20.3 Overnight-Sleep Test Limits Deduction of Meal Costs

The overnight-sleep rule prevents the deduction of meal costs on one-day business trips. To be deductible, meal costs must be incurred while "away from home" and this test requires that they be on a business trip that lasts longer than a regular working day (but not necessarily 24 hours) and requires time off to sleep (not just to eat or rest) before returning home. Meal costs while away from home are subject to the 50% deduction limit *(20.15)*. Taking a nap in a parked car off the road does not meet the overnight-sleep test.

### EXAMPLES

1. A New York business owner flies to Washington, D.C., which is about 250 miles away, to *see* a client. He arrives at noon, eats lunch, and then visits the client. He flies back to New York that evening. He may deduct the cost of the plane fare, but not the cost of his lunch. He was not away overnight nor was he required to take time out to sleep before returning home.

2. Same facts as above except the business owner sleeps overnight in a Washington hotel. He eats breakfast there, and then sees another client and returns home to New York in the afternoon. He may deduct not only the cost of the plane fare but also the cost of his meals while on the trip and the cost of the hotel, since he was away overnight.

Several courts held that the IRS rule was unreasonable and outdated in the world of supersonic travel, and they would have allowed the New Yorker on the one-day trip to Washington, D.C., to deduct the cost of his lunch. The Supreme Court disagreed and upheld the IRS rule as a fair administrative approach.

**Meal costs during overtime.** Such costs are not deductible if you are not away from your place of business. Thus, for example, a resident physician could not deduct the cost of meals and sleeping quarters at the hospital during overnight or weekend duty.

 *Caution*

**IRS Definition of "Temporary"**

The IRS considers a work location temporary if the period of work is realistically expected to last, and actually does last, one year or less. If you take an assignment expected to last more than a year but it actually lasts less than a year, your assignment is not considered temporary and commuting costs are not deductible.

### Table 20-1    Deductible Travel and Transportation Expenses

**Caution:** For 2018 and later years, employees may not deduct unreimbursed employee travel and transportation costs unless they are fee-basis state or local government officials, certain Armed Forces reservists, or qualifying performing artists; *see 20.1.*

| Your Travel Status— | Tax Rule— |
| --- | --- |
| Local trips to *see* customers and client | You may deduct your transportation expenses but not the cost of personal meals on one-day business trips within the general area of your tax home. |
| Overnight trips away from home | You may deduct the cost of travel between your home and business destination lodging, on business trips "away from home", as well as transportation expenses when you arrive *(20.5)*. |
| Work in an area other than where you have your residence. EXAMPLE: You live with your family in Chicago, but work in Milwaukee where your business is located. During the week, you stay in a hotel in Milwaukee and eat meals in a restaurant. You return to your family in Chicago every weekend. | Milwaukee is your "home" for tax purposes; *see 20.6.* Thus, your expenses for traveling to Milwaukee and your meals and lodging there are personal, nondeductible expenses. |
| Temporary assignment in an area other than where you have your residence. EXAMPLE: You live in and operate your business in Kansas City. To supervise a project in Omaha, you travel to Omaha where you stay for 60 days. Occasionally, you return to Kansas City on your days off, and the rest of the time you stay in Omaha. | You may deduct the necessary expenses for traveling away from home from Kansas City to Omaha and returning to Kansas City after your temporary assignment is completed. You may also deduct expenses for meals and lodging (even for your days off) while you are in Omaha. As discussed at *20.8*, deductions are not allowed on temporary assignments that are expected to last more than one year. |
| Weekend trip home from temporary assignment. EXAMPLE: Same facts as in the Example above except that you return home to Kansas City on weekends. | You are not "away from home" while you are in Kansas City on your days off and your meals and lodging while you are there are not deductible. However, you may deduct your traveling expenses (including meals and lodging, if any) from Omaha to Kansas City and back if they are no more than the amount it would have cost you for your meals and lodging if you had stayed in Omaha. If they are more, your deduction is limited to the amount you would have spent in Omaha. If you retain your room in Omaha while in Kansas City, your expenses of returning to Kansas City on days off are deductible only to the extent of the amount you would have spent for your meals had you stayed in Omaha. |
| Seasonal work in different areas. EXAMPLE: You live in Cincinnati, where you work for eight months each year. You earn the greater share of your annual income from that work. For the remaining four months of the year, you work in Miami. When in Miami, you eat and sleep in a hotel. You have been working in both of these cities for several years and expect to continue to do so. | You have two recurring seasonal places of business. Cincinnati is your principal place of business. You may deduct the costs of your traveling expenses while away from Cincinnati working at your minor place of business in Miami, including meals and lodging in Miami. |
| Convention trip | You may deduct costs of travel to a business convention under the rules in *20.11*. If you are a delegate to a charitable or veterans' convention, you may claim a charitable deduction for the travel costs *(14.4)*. |
| Trip for health reasons | If you claim itemized expenses on Schedule A, you may deduct the cost of the trip as a medical expense if you meet the rules at *17.9*. |

## 20.4    IRS Meal Allowance

If you find it difficult to keep records of meal costs while away from home *(20.3)* on business trips, you may prefer to claim an IRS meal allowance. In government tables, the allowance is referred to as the "M&IE" rate (rate for meals and incidental expenses), the amount of which depends on where you travel. In addition to meals and tips for food servers, the allowance (M&IE rate) covers a limited amount of "incidental" expenses such as fees and tips for porters, baggage carriers, hotel maids, or room stewards. Self-employed individuals may claim the M&IE allowance *(40.6)* as well as employees listed in *20.1* who have qualifying expenses that are not reimbursed under an "accountable" plan *(20.18)*.

You must keep a record of the time, place, and business purpose of the trips. As long as you have this proof, you may claim the allowance even if your actual costs for meals and incidental expenses are less than the allowance.

If you are self-employed, the allowance is claimed on Schedule C, where the deductible amount must be reduced by 50%, unless the 80% deduction for transportation workers subject to the Department of Transportation hours of service limits applies *(40.6)*.

Employees eligible to deduct travel costs (only if they are listed at *20.1*) claim the meal allowance, reduced by 50%, on Form 2106; *see 20.1*.

**Meal allowance on 2018 tax returns.** The M&IE rates are determined by the federal government's General Services Administration (GSA) for travel within the continental U.S. (referred to as CONUS locations), for each fiscal year, effective October 1; the per locality rate is in effect for that entire fiscal year. Thus, the M&IE rates for travel within CONUS during the first nine months of 2018 are the rates for the government's fiscal year 2018 that began October 1, 2017, and ended September 30, 2018. For the first nine months of 2018, the standard meal allowance (standard M&IE), the amount allowed for most locations, is $51 per day, but higher rates of $54, $59, $64, $69, or $74 apply in major cities and other high-cost locations (such as resort areas) designated by the government. Effective October 1, 2018, new M&IE rates (the fiscal year 2019 rates) took effect. For travel in the last three months of 2018, the standard meal allowance (M&IE) is $55, with higher rates of $56, $61, $66, $71, and $76 for high-cost localities. The location-specific CONUS M&IE rates can be obtained from the GSA website at Gsa.gov/ perdiem. If you travel to more than one area on a given day, use the M&IE rate for the area where you stop for sleep. A special M&IE rule applies to workers in the transportation industry, as discussed below.

If you traveled away from home *(20.3)* in the first nine months of 2018 as well as in the last three months, you have the option of using the M&IE rates in effect for the first nine months for all your 2018 business trips. For travel in the last three months (October 1-December 31, 2018), you must consistently use either the rates for the first nine months or the new rates for the last three months.

The $55, $56, $61, $66, $71, and $76 M&IE rates applicable to the last three months of 2018 also will apply to travel in the first nine months of 2019.

**Travel outside the continental United States.** Different rates apply for travel in Alaska, Hawaii, Puerto Rico, and U.S. possessions, as well as for travel to foreign countries. These rates (OCONUS) are set by the Defense Department and there is a link to the DoD site from the GSA website at Gsa.gov/perdiem.

**Transportation industry workers.** Employees or self-employed persons in the transportation industry may elect to claim a special M&IE rate. For the first nine months of 2018, the rate is $63 per day for any CONUS location and $68 per day for any OCONUS location. For the last three months of 2018 and the first nine months of 2019, the rate increases to $66 per day for any CONUS location and $71 per day for any OCONUS location. The special rate avoids the need to apply the CONUS or OCONUS rates on a locality-by-locality basis. You cannot combine the two methods. If the special rate is used for one trip, it must be used for all trips during the same year.

**Allowance must be reduced.** The allowance is prorated for the first and last day of a trip. You may claim 75% of the allowance for the days you depart and return. Alternatively, you may claim 100% of the allowance if you are away for a regular "9-to-5" business day.

## 20.5 Business Trip Deductions

If you are self employed or an employee listed in *20.1*, the following expenses of a business trip away from home *(20.6)* are deductible:

- Plane, railroad, taxi, and other transportation fares between your home and your business destination
- Hotel and other lodging expenses. You need receipts or similar evidence for lodging expenses; there is no IRS standard lodging allowance as there is for meals *(20.4)*.

 *IRS Alert*

**Incidental Expenses**

The IRS standard meal allowance (M&IE rate) does not include laundry, cleaning, and pressing of clothing. If you have receipts to substantiate laundry and cleaning costs, you may deduct them separately from the M&IE allowance, which includes as incidental expenses fees and tips for porters, baggage carriers, hotel maids, and room stewards.

If you do not pay or incur any meal expenses for a particular day on a trip away from home but you do have qualifying incidental expenses on that day, you have the option of deducting the actual costs or an allowance of $5 per day for the incidental expenses. The $5-per-day allowance must be prorated for the first and last days of the trip.

*Filing Tip*

**How Much To Deduct for Spouse**

If your spouse accompanied you on a business trip, your bills will probably show costs for both of you. These usually are less than twice the cost for a single person. To find what you may deduct where your spouse's presence is for personal and not qualifying business reasons, do not divide the bill in half. Figure what accommodations and transportation would have cost you alone and deduct that. The excess over the single person's costs is not deductible.

- Meal costs. You may claim your actual meal costs if you maintain records, or you may use the standard meal allowance *(20.4)*. Whichever method you use, only 50% of the unreimbursed meal costs are deductible unless the 80% limit for workers subject to Department of transportation limits applies *(20.15)*.
- Tips, telephone, and telegraph costs
- Laundry and cleaning expenses
- Baggage charges (including insurance)
- Cab fares or other costs of transportation to and from the airport or station and your hotel. Also deductible are cab fares or other transportation costs, beginning with your first business call of the day, of getting from one customer to another, or from one place of business to another.

**Travel costs of a spouse, dependent, or business associate.** Travel costs of a spouse, dependent, or any other individual who accompanies you on a business trip are not deductible unless that person is also your employee or your business associate (partner, agent, advisor, client, customer, supplier) who has a bona fide business reason for taking the trip that would justify claiming a deduction if the person took the trip on his or her own.

> **EXAMPLES**
>
> 1. You and your spouse travel by car to a convention. You pay $200 a day for a double room. A single room would have cost $150 a day. Your spouse's presence at the convention was for social reasons. You may deduct the total cost of operating your car to and from the convention city. You may deduct $150 a day for your room. If you traveled by plane or railroad, you would deduct only your own fare.
>
> 2. Connie worked with her husband operating a home improvement contracting business. With him, she attended trade shows and conventions, where they ran a display booth. There, she talked about their company's services and solicited new business. The IRS disallowed the company's deduction of her travel expenses as having no business purpose. The Tax Court disagreed. Both Connie and her husband were officers and employees of the company. They attended the conferences together. As the IRS allowed her husband's expenses, it should have also allowed expenses attributed to her participation, especially as they were incurred together as employees.

**Cruise ship.** If you travel by cruise ship on a business trip, your deductible cruise costs are limited to twice the highest federal per diem rate for travel in the United States on that date multiplied by the number of days in transit.

> **EXAMPLE**
>
> You sail to Europe on business. While you are away, the highest per diem federal rate is $375 and the trip lasts six days. The maximum deduction for the cost of the trip is $4,500 (2 × $375 × 6). The double per diem rule applies without regard to the 50% limit on meal costs if meals are not separately stated in your bill. If a separate amount for meals or entertainment is included, such amount must be reduced by 50%.
>
> The double per diem rule does not apply to cruise ship convention costs that are deductible up to $2,000 a year if all the ports of call are in the U.S. or U.S. possessions and if the ship is registered in the United States *(20.19)*.

*Important: Recordkeeping requirements.* See the section for recordkeeping rules to support a deduction for unreimbursed travel expenses or to avoid being taxed on employer reimbursements *(20.16)*.

## 20.6 When Are You Away From Home?

You have to meet the "away from home" test to deduct the cost of meals (usually only 50% deductible) and lodging while traveling *(20.5)*. You have to be away from your tax home and satisfy the overnight-sleep rule *(20.3)* to be "away from home." In general, your tax home is the city or general area in which your regular place of business or post of duty is located, regardless of where your family is.

*Law Alert*

**Tax Home Defined**

For travel expense purposes, your home is your place of business, employment, or post of duty, regardless of where you maintain your family residence. This tax home includes the entire city or general area of your business premises or place of employment. The area of your residence may be your tax home if your job requires you to work at widely scattered locations, you have no fixed place of work, and your residence is in a location economically suited to your work.

**Do you regularly work at more than one location?** If you regularly work in two or more separate locations, your tax home is the area of your principal place of business or employment. You are away from home when you are away from the area of your principal place of business or employment. Therefore, you may deduct your transportation costs to and from your minor place of business and your living costs there.

---

### EXAMPLES

1. Sherman lived in Worcester, Mass., where he managed a factory. He opened his own sales agency in New York. He continued to manage the factory and spent considerable time in Worcester. The larger part of his income came from the New York business. However, he was allowed to treat New York as his minor place of business and to deduct his travel expenses to New York and his living expenses there because he spent most of his time in Worcester and his income there was substantial.

2. Benson, a consulting engineer, maintained a combination residence-business office in a home he owned in New York. He also taught four days a week at a Technological Institute in West Virginia under a temporary nine-month appointment. He spent three-day weekends, holidays, and part of the summer at his New York address. At the Institute, he rented a room in the student union building. The IRS disallowed transportation expenses between New York and West Virginia and meals and lodging there as not incurred while away from home. The Tax Court disagreed. A taxpayer may have more than one occupation in more than one city. When his occupations require him to spend a substantial amount of time in each place, he may deduct his travel expenses, including meals and lodging, at the place away from his permanent residence. That Benson's teaching salary happened to exceed his income from his private practice does not change the result.

---

**Are you constantly on the road?** If you do not work within any particular locality, an IRS agent may disallow your travel deductions on the grounds that your tax home is wherever you work; thus, you are never "away from home." You are considered a transient worker.

If your deduction is questioned because you have no regular or main place of business, you may be able to show that your tax home is the area of your residence. If you meet the following three tests, the IRS will treat your residence as your tax home: (1) you do some work in the vicinity of your residence, house, apartment, or room and live there while performing services in the area; (2) you have mortgage expenses or pay rent for the residence while away on the road; and (3) the residence is in an area where you were raised or lived for a long time, or a member of your immediate family such as your parent or child lives in the residence, or you frequently return there.

According to the IRS, if you meet only two of these three tests, it will decide on a case-by-case basis if your residence is your tax home. If you meet less than two of the tests, the IRS will not allow a deduction; each of your work locations is treated as your tax home.

If you live in a trailer at each work location and have no other home, each location is your principal place of business and you are not "away from home."

---

### EXAMPLES

1. Your residence is in a suburb within commuting distance of New York City where you do freelance work full time. Your personal home and tax home are the same, that is, within the metropolitan area of New York City. You are away from home when you leave this area, say, for Philadelphia. Meals and lodging are deductible only if you meet the overnight-sleep test *(20.3)*.

2. Your residence is in New York City, but you work in Baltimore. Your tax home is Baltimore; you may not deduct living expenses there. But you may deduct travel expenses on a temporary assignment to New York City even while living at your home there.

---

**Permanent duty station of service members.** The Supreme Court held that a member of the Armed Forces is not away from home when he or she is at a permanent duty station. This is true even if the service member has to maintain a separate home for family members who are not permitted to live at the duty station.

*Planning Reminder*

**Determining Your Principal Place of Business**

If you have more than one regular place of business, your tax home is your principal place of business. Your principal place of business or employment is determined by comparing: (1) the time ordinarily spent working in each area; (2) the degree of your business activity in each area; (3) the amount of your income from each area; (4) the taxpayer's permanent residence; and (5) whether employment at one location is temporary or indefinite.

No single factor is determinative. The relative importance of each factor will vary depending on the facts of a particular case. For example, where there are no substantial differences between incomes earned in two places of employment, your tax home is probably the area in which you spend more of your time. Where there are substantial income differences, your tax home is probably the area in which you earn more of your income.

## 20.7 Tax Home of Married Couple Working in Different Cities

When a husband and wife work and live in different cities during the week, one of them may seek to deduct travel expenses away from home. Such deductions have generally been disallowed, but courts have allowed some exceptions. Each spouse may have a separate tax home.

### EXAMPLES

1. Robert worked in Wilmington, Delaware; his wife, Margaret, worked in New York City. During the weekend, she traveled to Wilmington and deducted, as travel expenses away from home, her living costs in New York and weekend travel expenses to Wilmington. She argued that because she and her husband filed a joint return, they were a single taxable unit, and the tax home of this unit was Wilmington where her husband lived. The deduction was disallowed. That a couple can file a joint return does not give them deductions that are not otherwise available to them as individuals. Margaret's tax home was New York, where she worked. Therefore, her expenses there are not deductible. And, as the weekend trips to Wilmington had no relationship to her job, they, too, were not deductible.

2. Hundt and his wife lived in Arlington, Va., but he wrote and directed films in various parts of the country. He wrote screenplays either at his Arlington home or on location, but most of his business came from New York City, where he lived in hotels. One year, he spent 175 days in New York City on business and rented an apartment for $1,200 because it was cheaper than a hotel. He deducted half the annual rent for the New York apartment, the costs of traveling between Arlington and New York, and the cost of meals in New York. The IRS disallowed the expenses, finding New York to be his tax home. The Tax Court disagreed. Arlington was Hundt's tax home because (1) part of his income came from his creative writing in Arlington; and (2) his travel to other parts of the country was temporary. The fact that most of his income came from New York did not make New York his tax home.

## 20.8 Deducting Living Costs on Temporary Assignment

A business trip away from home (20.6) at a single location may last a few days, weeks, or months. If your assignment is considered temporary, you may deduct travel costs (see below) while there because your tax home has not changed. The IRS considers an assignment to be temporary if you realistically expect it to last for one year or less and it actually does last no more than one year. If an assignment is realistically expected to last more than a year it is considered indefinite, and you cannot deduct your living costs at the area of the assignment because that location becomes your tax home. This is true even if the assignment actually lasts only a year or less. That is, you can be away for a year or less and still be barred from claiming a deduction if at the time you started the assignment you realistically expected it to last for more than a year. Likewise, employment that is initially temporary may become indefinite due to changed circumstances; *see* the Examples below.

### EXAMPLES

1. You are on an assignment away from home in a single location that is expected to last (and it does in fact last) for one year or less. The IRS will treat the assignment as temporary, unless facts and circumstances indicate otherwise. Expenses are deductible.

2. You are on an assignment away from home at a single location. You expect that the job will last 18 months. However, due to financial difficulties the assignment ends after 11 months. Even though your assignment actually lasted for less than one year the IRS treats it as indefinite because you realistically expected it to last more than one year. Thus, your travel and living expenses while away from home are not deductible.

3. You are on an assignment away from home at a single location. You expect that it will last only nine months. However, due to changed circumstances occurring after eight months, you remain on the assignment for six more months. The IRS treats the assignment as temporary for eight months, and indefinite for the remaining time you are away from home. Thus, travel and living expenses you pay or incur during the first eight months are deductible; expenses paid or incurred thereafter are not.

*Planning Reminder*

**Federal Crime Investigations**

Federal employees such as FBI agents and prosecutors who are certified by the Attorney General as traveling on behalf of the federal government in a temporary duty status to investigate, prosecute, or provide support services for the investigation or prosecution of a federal crime are not subject to the one-year limitation on deductibility of expenses while away from home on temporary assignments.

**Deductible travel costs on temporary trip.** While on a temporary assignment expected to last a year or less, you may deduct the cost of meals and lodging there, even for your days off. If you return home, say for weekends, your living expenses at home are not deductible. You may deduct travel expenses, meals, and lodging en route between your home and your assignment location provided they do not exceed your living expenses had you stayed at the temporary location. If you keep a hotel room at the temporary location while you return home, you may deduct your round-trip expenses for the trip home only up to the amount you would have spent had you stayed at the temporary workplace.

> **EXAMPLE**
>
> Michaels, a cost analyst for Boeing, lived in Seattle. He traveled for Boeing, but was generally not away from home for more than five weeks. Michaels agreed to go to Los Angeles for a year to service Boeing's suppliers in that area. He rented his Seattle house and brought his family with him to Los Angeles. Ten months later, Boeing opened a permanent office in Los Angeles and asked Michaels to remain there permanently. Michaels argued that his expenses for food and lodging during the 10-month period were deductible as "away from home" expenses. The IRS contended that the Los Angeles assignment was for an indefinite period.
>
> The Tax Court sided with Michaels. He was told that the stay was for a year only. He leased his Seattle house to a tenant for one year, planning to return to it. He regarded his work in Los Angeles as temporary until Boeing changed its plans. The one-year period justified his taking the family but did not alter the temporary nature of the assignment.

**Separate assignments over a period over a year.** Where over a period of years you work on several separate assignments for one client, the IRS may attempt to treat the separate assignments as amounting to a permanent assignment and disallow living costs away from home, as in the Mitchell example below.

> **EXAMPLE**
>
> Mitchell, a publishing consultant who lived and worked out of his home in Illinois, advised a publisher of a magazine with offices in California. Over a five-year period, from 1991 to 1995, he worked on short job assignments that averaged 130 days a year for the magazine. Some assignments arose because of unforeseen events, such as the abrupt firing of a novice editor, the hiring of a new editor, and the editor's later absence because of cancer and her death. In 1994 and 1995, when working in California, he rented an apartment because it was cheaper than a hotel. He claimed lodging and meal expenses in California that the IRS disallowed on the grounds that his employment in California was not temporary; it lasted more than one year.
>
> The Tax Court disagreed. Just because an independent contractor returns to the same general location in more than one year does not mean that he is employed there on an indefinite basis. Mitchell's work followed an on again, off again pattern. Each job assignment that lasted less than a year ended with no expectation of future employment. Throughout the five-year period, his consultancy services were required by unexpected events.

## 20.9 Business-Vacation Trips Within the United States

On a business trip to a resort area, you may also spend time vacationing. If the primary purpose of the trip is to transact business and the area is within the United States (50 states and the District of Columbia) you may deduct all of the costs of your transportation to and from the area, lodging, and 50% of meal expenses, even if you do spend time vacationing. If the main purpose of the trip is personal, you may not deduct any part of your travel costs to and from the area. The amount of time spent on business as opposed to sightseeing or personal visits is the most important issue in determining your primary purpose. Regardless of the primary purpose of your trip, you are allowed to deduct expenses related to the business you transacted while in the area.

No deductions will be allowed if you attend a convention or seminar where you are given videotapes to view at your own convenience and no other business-related activities or lectures occur during the convention. The trip is considered a vacation.

 *Caution*

**Taking Your Family With You**

If you take your family with you to a temporary job site, an IRS agent may argue that this is evidence that you considered the assignment to be indefinite. In the Michaels Example in this section, however, such a move was not considered detrimental to a deduction of living expenses at the job location.

 *Caution*

**Primary Business Purpose**

If your return is examined, proving the business purpose of your trip depends on presenting evidence to convince an examining agent that the trip, despite your vacationing, was planned primarily to transact business. Keep a log or diary to substantiate business activities.

If your trip is primarily for business, and while at the business destination you extend your stay for a few days for nonbusiness reasons, such as to visit relatives, you deduct travel expenses to and from the business destination.

> **EXAMPLE**
>
> You work in Atlanta and make a business trip to New Orleans. You stay in New Orleans for six days and your total costs, including round-trip transportation to and from New Orleans, meals, and lodging, is $1,800, which you may deduct subject to the 50% limit for meals. If, on your way home, you spend three days in Mobile visiting relatives and incur an additional $600 in travel costs, your deduction is limited to the $1,800 (less 50% of meals) you would have spent had you gone home directly from New Orleans.

**Caution**

**Vacation Areas**

If the IRS determines that you were primarily on vacation, it will disallow all travel costs except for costs directly related to your business in the area such as registration fees at a foreign business convention *(20.12)*.

## 20.10 Business-Vacation Trips Outside the United States

On a business trip abroad, you may deduct your travel expenses (the 50% limit applies for meals), even though you take time out to vacation, provided you can prove: (1) the primary purpose of the trip was business and (2) you did not have control over arranging the trip.

If you are an employee, selecting the date of the trip does not mean that you had control over the assignment. IRS regulations assume that when you travel for your company under a reimbursement or allowance arrangement, you do not control the trip arrangements, provided also that you are not: (1) a managing executive of the company; (2) related to your employer *(20.4)*; or (3) have more than a 10% stock interest in the company. You are considered a managing executive if you are authorized without effective veto procedures to decide on the necessity of the trip. You are related to your employer if the employer is your spouse, parent, child, brother, sister, grandparent, or grandchild.

**Rule for managing executives and self-employed persons.** If you are a managing executive, self-employed, related to your employer, or have a more-than-10% stock interest, you are treated as having control over arranging the trip and your deduction for transportation costs to and from your business destination may be limited. However, a full deduction for transportation costs is allowed if:

1. The trip outside the United States took a week (7 consecutive days) or less, not counting the day you left the U.S. but counting the day you returned,

2. If the trip abroad lasted more than a week, you spent less than 25% of your time, counting the days your trip began and ended, on vacation or other personal activities, or

3. In planning the trip you did not place a major emphasis on taking a vacation.

If the vacationing and other personal activities took up 25% or more of your time on a trip lasting more than one week, and you cannot prove that the vacation was a minor consideration in planning the trip, you must allocate travel expenses between the time spent on business and that spent on personal affairs. The part allocated to business is deductible; the balance is not. To allocate, count the number of days spent on the trip outside the United States, including the day you leave the U.S. and the day you return. Then divide this total into the number of days on which you had business activities; include days of travel to and from a business destination.

If you vacation at, near, or beyond the city in which you do business, the expense subject to allocation is the cost of travel from the place of departure to the business destination and back. For example, you travel from New York to London on business and then vacation in Paris before returning to New York. The expense subject to allocation is the cost of traveling from New York to London and back; *see* Example 2 below. However, if from London you vacationed in Dublin before returning to New York, you would allocate the round-trip fare between New York and Dublin and also deduct the difference between that round-trip fare and the fare between New York and London; *see* Example 3 below.

## EXAMPLES

1. You fly from New York to Paris to attend a business meeting for one day. You spend the next two days sightseeing and then fly back to New York. The entire trip, including two days for travel en route, took five days. The plane fare is deductible. The trip did not exceed one week.

2. You fly from Chicago to New York, where you spend six days on business. You then fly to London, where you conduct business for two days. You then fly to Paris for a five-day vacation after which you fly back to Chicago. You would not have made the trip except for the business that you had to transact in London. The nine days of travel outside the United States away from home, including two days for travel en route, exceeded a week, and the five days devoted to vacationing were not less than 25% of the total travel time outside the U.S. The two days spent traveling between Chicago and New York, and the six days spent in New York, are not counted in determining whether the travel outside the United States exceeded a week and whether the time devoted to personal activities was less than 25%.

   Assume you are unable to prove either that you did not have substantial control over the arrangements of the trip or that an opportunity for taking a personal vacation was not a major consideration in your decision to take the trip. Thus, 5/9 (five nonbusiness days out of nine days outside the U.S.) of the plane fare from New York to London and from London to New York is not deductible. You may deduct 4/9 of the New-York-to-London round-trip fare, plus lodging, 50% of meals, and other allowable travel costs while in London. No deduction is allowed for any part of the costs of the trip from London to Paris.

3. Same facts as in Example 2, except that the vacation is in Dublin, which is closer to the U.S. than London. The allocation is based on the round-trip fare between New York and Dublin. Thus, 4/9 of the New York to Dublin fare is deductible and 5/9 is not deductible. Further, the IRS allows a deduction for the excess of the New-York-to-London fare over the New-York-to-Dublin fare.

**Weekends, holidays, and business standby days.** If you have business meetings scheduled before and after a weekend or holiday, the days in between the meetings are treated as days spent on business for purposes of the 25% business test discussed above. This is true although you spend the days for sightseeing or other personal travel. A similar rule applies if you have business meetings on Friday and the next scheduled meeting is the following Tuesday; Saturday through Monday are treated as business days. If your trip is extended over a weekend to take advantage of reduced airfares, the additional expense of meals, lodging, and other incidental expenses is deductible *(20.10)*.

## 20.11 Deducting Expenses of Business Conventions

Conventions and seminars at resort areas usually combine business with pleasure. Therefore, the IRS scrutinizes deductions claimed for attending a business convention where opportunities exist for vacationing. Especially questioned are trips where you are accompanied by your spouse and other members of your family. Deducting expenses of foreign conventions is subject to restrictions *(20.12)*.

You may not deduct expenses of attending investment conventions and seminars *(19.2)*. You also may not deduct the costs of business conventions or seminars where you merely receive a video or download of business lectures to be viewed at your convenience and no other business-related activities occur during the event.

In claiming a deduction for convention expenses, be prepared to show that your attendance at the convention benefitted your business. Cases and IRS rulings have upheld deductions for doctors, lawyers, and dentists attending professional conventions. One case allowed a deduction to a legal secretary for her costs at a secretaries' convention. If you are a delegate to a business convention, make sure you prove you attended to serve primarily your own business interests, not those of the association. However, it is not necessary for you to show that the convention dealt specifically with your business. It is sufficient that attendance at the convention may advance or benefit your business. If you fail to prove business purpose, the IRS will allocate your expenses between the time spent on your business and the time spent as a delegate. You then deduct only the expenses attributed to your business activities.

 *Filing Tip*

**Weekend Expenses**

If your business trip is extended over a weekend to take advantage of reduced airfares, the additional cost of meals, lodging, and other incidental expenses is deductible.

> **EXAMPLE**
>
> An attorney with a general law practice was interested in international law and relations. He was appointed a delegate to represent the American branch of the International Law Association at a convention in Paris. The attorney deducted the cost of the trip and convention as business expenses which the IRS and a court disallowed. He failed to prove that attending the conference on international law helped his general practice. He did not get any business referrals as a result of his attendance at the convention. Nor did he prove the chance of getting any potential business from the conference.

**Caution**

**Substantiate Convention Business**

Keep a copy of the convention program and a record of the business sessions you attend. If the convention provides a sign-in book, sign it. In addition, keep a record of all of your business expenses *(20.16)*.

**What expenses are deductible?** If the convention trip is primarily for business, you may deduct travel costs both to and from the convention, food costs, tips, display expenses (such as sample room costs), and hotel bills. If you entertain business clients or customers, you may deduct these amounts too.

Food and beverage costs are subject to the 50% cost limitation rule *(20.15)*.

Keep records of your payments identifying expenses directly connected with your business dealings at the convention and those that are part of your personal activity, such as sightseeing, social visiting, and entertaining. Recreation costs are not deductible even though a part of your overall convention costs.

> **EXAMPLE**
>
> You attend a business convention held in a coastal resort city primarily for business reasons. During the convention period, you do some local sightseeing, social entertaining, and visiting—all unrelated to your business. You may deduct your traveling expenses to and from the resort, your living expenses at the resort, and other expenses such as business entertaining, sample displays, etc. But you may not deduct the cost of sightseeing, personal entertaining, and social visiting.

**Fraternal organizations.** You may not deduct expenses at conventions held by fraternal organizations, such as the American Legion, Shriners, etc., even though incidental business was carried on. However, delegates to fraternal conventions may in some instances deduct expenses as charitable contributions *(14.4)*.

## 20.12 Restrictions on Foreign Conventions and Cruises

You may not deduct expenses at a foreign convention outside the North American area unless you satisfy the general deduction rules *(20.10)* and also can show the convention is directly related to your business and it was as reasonable for the meeting to be held outside the North American area as within it.

Apart from the United States, the North American area includes Mexico, Canada, Puerto Rico, U.S. Virgin Islands, American Samoa, Northern Mariana Islands, Guam, Marshall and Midway Islands, Micronesia, Palau and U.S. island possessions.

Conventions may also be held in eligible Caribbean countries that agree to exchange certain data with the U.S. and do not discriminate against conventions held in the United States. Antigua and Barbuda, Aruba, Bahamas, Barbados, Bermuda, Costa Rica, Curacao, Dominica, Dominican Republic, Grenada, Guyana, Honduras, Jamaica, Panama, Saint Lucia, and Trinidad and Tobago have qualified and are considered to be within the North American area.

Check with the convention operator about whether the country in which your convention is being held has qualified.

**Limited cruise ship deduction.** Up to $2,000 a year is allowed for attending cruise ship conventions if all the ports of call are in the U.S. or U.S. possessions and if the ship is registered in the United States. A deduction is allowed only if you attach to your return statements signed by you and by an officer of the convention sponsor that detail the daily schedule of business activities, the number of hours you attended these activities, and the total days of the trip. Do not confuse the $2,000 limitation with the per diem limitation for cruise ship costs *(20.5)*. The per diem limitation does not apply to cruises that meet the tests for the up-to-$2,000 deduction.

## 20.13 Entertainment Expenses No Longer Deductible

Under the Tax Cuts and Jobs Act, a business expense deduction is no longer allowed for most entertainment expenses after 2017. The new law repeals the rule that allowed a deduction for entertainment expenses that were "directly related to" or "associated with" the active conduct of a business. The repeal of the "directly related to" or "associated with" tests had caused doubt as to whether business meals for clients, customers, vendors, and other business associates would still be deductible, but the IRS responded with guidelines that allow a 50% deduction for business meals provided certain conditions are met; *see 20.14*.

**Some entertainment-related costs that were deductible under prior law remain deductible.** The new law does not change deductions allowed for reimbursed meal costs that are ordinary and necessary business expenses and treated as compensation paid. For example, a full deduction is still allowed if you reimburse an employee for client business meals and the expense is reported as taxable wages (subject to withholding) to the employee on Form W-2 because the employee does not adequately account for the expenses; you deduct the payment as compensation paid. Similarly, if you reimburse client meal expenses of a nonemployee who does not adequately account for the costs, the expenses are treated as as gross income for that person (generally reported on Form 1099-MISC); you deduct that amount as compensation paid.

The new law also does not change the rule that allows employers to fully deduct the costs of providing food and beverages at a holiday party or picnic for employees. Other fully deductible expenses are at *20.15*; *see* "Exceptions to 50% cost limitation."

Snacks, beverages, and on-premises meals provided to employees that qualify as *de minimis* fringe benefits *(3.10)* remain deductible but are now subject to the 50% deduction limit for meal expenses under the Tax Cuts and Jobs Act, instead of being fully deductible as under prior law *(20.15)*.

**Club dues and membership fees still nondeductible.** The Tax Cuts and Jobs Act does not change the prior law rule disallowing a deduction for dues or membership fees for country clubs, golf and athletic clubs, airline clubs, hotel clubs, business luncheon clubs, and other clubs organized for business, pleasure, recreation, or other social purposes. However, an IRS regulation has allowed a deduction for dues paid to (1) civic or public service organizations such as Kiwanis, Lions, and Rotary clubs; (2) professional organizations such as medical or bar associations; and (3) chambers of commerce, trade associations, business leagues, real estate boards, and boards of trade. The regulation allows the deduction for dues provided that the organization in (1)–(3) does not have a principal purpose of providing entertainment for members or their guests. The IRS has not yet indicated if this regulation still applies in light of the Tax Cuts and Jobs Act.

**Operating costs of entertainment facilities still nondeductible.** The Tax Cuts and Jobs Act does not change the prior law rule disallowing a deduction for the expenses of maintaining and operating facilities used to entertain clients and customers. Examples of entertainment facilities include yachts, hunting lodges, fishing camps, swimming pools, tennis courts, automobiles, airplanes, apartments, hotel suites, or homes in a vacation area. The disallowance rule applies to operating expenses such as rent, utilities, and security, and also to depreciation, but not to such expenses as interest, taxes, and casualty losses that are deductible without having to show business purpose.

## 20.14 Client Business Meals Still Generally Deductible

When the Tax Cuts and Jobs Act eliminated the deduction for entertainment expenses after 2017 *(20.13)*, without specifically addressing the deductibility of business meals, there was concern that the law change endangered deductions for wining and dining current and prospective clients, customers, and vendors. However, the IRS has released guidance that allows taxpayers to continue to deduct 50% of the cost of business meals, so long as the taxpayer (or an employee) is present during the meal, the cost of the food and beverages is not lavish or extravagant, and, when food and beverages is provided during an entertainment event, the cost is separately billed; *see* below (Notice 2018-76).

The IRS will issue proposed regulations that clarify when business meal expenses are deductible and when they are nondeductible entertainment expenses. Until the proposed regulations are issued, taxpayers may rely on the rules in Notice 2018-76; any updated guidance from the IRS will be in the *e-Supplement at jklasser.com*.

As provided in Notice 2018-76, a deduction is allowed for 50% of an otherwise allowable business meal expense if all of the following conditions are met:

1. The expense is an ordinary and necessary business expense paid or incurred during the taxable year;

2. The expense is not lavish or extravagant under the circumstances;

3. The taxpayer, or an employee of the taxpayer, is present at the furnishing of the food or beverages;

4. The food and beverages are provided to a current or potential business customer, client, consultant, or similar business contact; and

5. For food and beverages provided during or at an entertainment activity, the food and beverages are purchased separately from the entertainment, or the cost of the food and beverages is stated separately from the cost of the entertainment on a bill, invoice, or receipt.

The following examples from Notice 2018-76 illustrate the application of the above requirements, particularly requirement 5, which requires a separate purchase of or separate billing for the cost of food and beverages at an entertainment event.

### EXAMPLES

In these examples, the IRS assumes that the food and beverages are ordinary and necessary business expenses and the cost is not lavish or extravagant.

1. A taxpayer takes a business client to a baseball game. The game is entertainment so the cost of the tickets is not deductible. However, the taxpayer may deduct 50% of the cost of hot dogs and drinks purchased during the game, as they are purchased separately from the tickets and therefore not considered an entertainment expense.

2. A taxpayer takes a business customer to a basketball game. They watch the game in a suite that provides food and beverages. The invoice for the tickets includes the food and beverages. The taxpayer cannot deduct either the cost of the tickets or the cost of the food and beverages. The tickets are a nondeductible entertainment expense, and the food and beverages are also treated as entertainment and thus not deductible because they were not purchased separately or stated separately on the invoice.

3. Same facts as Example 2 except that the cost of food and beverages is stated separately on the invoice. As in Example 2, the cost of the game tickets themselves is a nondeductible entertainment expense. However, since the food and beverages are stated separately on the invoice, 50% of their cost is deductible.

## 20.15 50% Cost Limitation on Most Deductible Meals

You can generally only deduct 50% of meal expenses on business trips away from home *(20.6)*. However, the deductible percentage for workers subject to the Department of Transportation's "hours of service" limits is 80% rather than 50%. If you are self-employed and claim expenses for business travel while away from home, the 50% deduction limitation for meals (or 80% if you qualify) is taken into account on Line 24b of Schedule C *(40.6)*, whether you claim the IRS meal allowance *(20.4)* or actual meal expenses (including taxes and tips).

As discussed at *20.1*, most employees are no longer able to deduct business travel expenses, including meals away from home, because miscellaneous itemized deductions are no longer allowed. Only employees listed at *20.1* can deduct business travel expenses, subject to the 50% deduction limit on meals.

**50% of client meals generally deductible.** As discussed at *20.14*, the IRS has announced requirements for deducting 50% of the cost of business meals in light of the elimination of deductions for entertainment expenses by the Tax Cuts and Jobs Act.

**80% limit for certain transportation workers.** The deductible percentage for meals on business trips away from home *(20.6)* is 80% instead of 50% where the meals are consumed "during or incident to" any period of duty for which the Department of Transportation (DOT) hours of service limits are in effect. Individuals subject to the DOT hours of service limits include interstate truck and bus operators, pilots and other air transportation workers drivers, and certain merchant mariners.

**Food and beverages provided on premises to employees.** The Tax Cuts and Jobs Act did not change the law that allows a deduction for food or beverages provided to your employees as a tax-free *de minimis* fringe benefit *(3.10)*, but the deduction is now subject to the 50% deduction limit. This includes snacks and drinks you provide in a pantry or similar area for your employees. It also includes a cafeteria on your premises for employees where meal charges cover the direct operating cost of the cafeteria. Where the meals are furnished for your convenience (you have a substantial noncompensatory business purpose), the employees are deemed to have paid the "direct operating cost" attributable to their meals, so those meals are a tax-free *de minimis* fringe benefit *(3.10)*. In addition, if more than half the employees for whom meals are provided have the meals provided for your convenience, the employer convenience test is considered met for all of the on-premises meals, and the *de minimis* benefit exclusion applies to all the employees.

Under prior law, there was an exception to the 50% deduction limit that allowed a 100% deduction for food and beverages qualifying as a tax-free *de minimis* fringe benefit. However, the Tax Cuts and Jobs Act repealed this exception, so only 50% of the costs are now deductible.

Note: When the IRS announced guidelines for deducting 50% of the cost of client business meals in Notice 2018-76 *(20.14)*, it stated that it will issue separate guidance concerning employer deductions for food and beverages provided to employees on business premises; we will report any update from the IRS in the *e-Supplement* at *jklasser.com*.

**Exceptions to 50% cost limitation.** In the following cases, a full deduction for meals is allowed; the 50% limitation does not apply:

1. As an employer, you can deduct 100% of a reimbursement to an employee for meal costs that have not been adequately accounted for. You treat the reimbursement as taxable wages subject to withholding of income tax on the employee's Form W-2, which you deduct as compensation paid.

2. You reimburse an independent contractor for meal expenses he or she incurs on your behalf and the contractor does not adequately account for the expenses. You should report the reimbursements as compensation to the contractor, and you may claim a full deduction for the compensation, assuming the reimbursements are ordinary and necessary business expenses.

3. As an employer, you incur food and beverage expenses for recreational, social, or similar activities (including facilities) primarily for the benefit of employees who are not highly compensated employees. For example, the expenses of food and beverages for a company picnic or holiday party are not subject to the 50% limit.

4. Expenses for free meals made available to the general public for advertising or goodwill purposes.

5. Expenses for meals sold to the public in your business, such as food costs if you run a restaurant.

## 20.16 Substantiating Travel Expenses

To meet IRS substantiation requirements for travel cost deductions (including meals) in the event of an audit, you need two types of records:

1. A computer log, diary, account book, or similar record to list the time, place, and business purpose of your travel and entertainment expenses; and

2. Receipts, itemized paid bills, or similar statements for lodging regardless of the amount, and for other expenses of $75 or more. But note these exceptions:

- A receipt for transportation expenses of $75 or more is required only when it is readily obtainable.

 *Law Alert*

**Transportation Industry Workers**

Individuals subject to Department of Transportation limitations on hours of service, such as interstate truck and bus drivers, pilots and other air transportation workers, and train crews, may claim a higher deductible percentage of food and beverage costs when working away from home. The deductible amount is 80% rather than 50%.

- A canceled check by itself is not an acceptable voucher. If you cannot produce a bill or voucher, you may have to present other evidence such as a statement in writing from witnesses to prove business purpose of the expense.
- A receipted bill or voucher must show (1) the amount of the expense; (2) the date the expense was incurred; (3) where the expense was incurred; and (4) the nature of the expense.

A hotel bill must show the name, location, date, and separate amounts for charges such as lodgings, meals, and telephone calls. A receipt for meals or lodging is not needed if its cost is covered by a per diem allowance *(20.19)*. The IRS will not allow a credit card statement to substitute for a lodging receipt. The IRS wants detailed receipts to catch personal items such as personal phone calls or the purchase of gifts.

A restaurant bill must show the restaurant's name and location, the date and amount of the expense, and, when a charge is made for items other than meals or beverages, a description of the charge.

**Account book or computer entries.** Your records do not have to duplicate data recorded on a receipt, provided that a notation in your record is connected to the receipt. You are also not required to record amounts your company pays directly for any ticket or fare. Credit card charges should be recorded.

## Excuses for Inadequate Records

**Substantial compliance.** If you have made a "good faith" effort to comply with the IRS rules, you will not be penalized if your records do not satisfy every requirement. For example, you would not automatically be denied a deduction merely because you did not keep a receipt.

**Accidental destruction of records.** If receipts or records are lost or destroyed through circumstances beyond your control, such as in a flood or fire, you may substantiate deductions by reasonable reconstruction of your expenditures.

**Exceptional circumstances.** If, by reason of the "inherent nature of the situation," you are unable to keep adequate records, you may substantially comply by presenting the best evidence possible given the circumstances. IRS regulations do not explain the meaning of "inherent nature of the situation."

## 20.17 Employee Reporting of Unreimbursed Expenses

If you are paid a salary with the understanding that you will pay all of your travel expenses without reimbursement, you report all of your salary or commission income as shown on Form W-2. Under the Tax Cuts and Jobs Act, you may not claim a deduction for the expenses, because the itemized deduction for unreimbursed job expenses is suspended *(19.2)*. However, if you are an employee within one of the limited employee categories discussed at *20.1*, you may be able to deduct travel costs.

The result is the same if your employer has a reimbursement plan but the rules for accountable plans are not met; the reimbursements are treated as part of your taxable pay and you may not claim an offsetting deduction *(20.18)*.

## 20.18 Are You Reimbursed Under an Accountable Plan?

A reimbursement or allowance arrangement is an accountable plan if you must:

- Adequately account to your employer for your job expenses; and
- Return to your employer any excess reimbursement or allowance that you do not show was spent for ordinary and necessary business expenses.

If these requirements are not met, the plan is treated as a nonaccountable plan, and all reimbursements are reported as wages on your Form W-2 *(20.17)*.

If these requirements are met, the plan is treated as an accountable plan, and reimbursements made to you by the plan are not reported as taxable wages on your Form W-2. However, if the reimbursement is less than your expenses, you may not claim a deduction for the difference, except in the unlikely case that you are an employee listed at **20.1**. Under prior law, employees who itemized deductions could use Form 2106 to report their expenses and the reimbursement, and then enter the unreimbursed amount on Schedule A, where a deduction was limited by the 2% of AGI floor applicable to total miscellaneous itemized deductions. Starting in 2018, this limited deduction opportunity is no longer an option, as the deduction for unreimbursed job expenses, as well as other miscellaneous deductions, has been suspended by the Tax Cuts and Jobs Act *(19.2)*.

For employees listed at **20.1**, Form 2016 may be used to report unreimbursed job expenses (meals on business trips away from home are subject to a 50% reduction), and an above-the-line deduction for eligible amounts may be claimed; *see 20.1*.

**What is an adequate accounting?** You adequately account to your employer by submitting receipts and an account book, diary, or similar record in which you entered each expense at or near the time you had it. You must account to your employer for all amounts received as advances, reimbursements, or allowances, including amounts charged on a company credit card. Your records and supporting information must meet IRS rules *(20.16)*. You must also pay back reimbursements or allowances that exceed the expenses that you adequately accounted for, or the nonreturned excess will be taxable under the rules for non-accountable plans *(20.21)*.

The accounting requirements are eased if you are reimbursed under a per diem arrangement covering meals, lodging, and incidental expenses *(20.19)* or you receive a flat mileage allowance *(20.20)*.

*Planning Reminder*

**Importance of Adequate Accounting**

If you adequately report expenses to your employer and return excess reimbursements, you are treated as being reimbursed under an accountable plan and generally do not have to report the reimbursed amount as income on your return.

> **EXAMPLE**
>
> Your adjusted gross income is $85,000, and you incur travel expenses of $1,600, all of which are reimbursed by your company. If your reimbursement arrangement qualified as an accountable plan, and you made an adequate reporting to your employer, the $1,600 would not be reported as income on your Form W-2. You receive the equivalent of a full deduction by substantiating the expenses to your employer and not having the reimbursement included as income on your Form W-2.

**Time limits for receiving advances, substantiating expenses, and returning excess payments.** The general rule is that these events must occur within a reasonable time. Under an IRS "safe harbor," the following payments are considered to be within a reasonable time:

- Advance payments—if given to you within 30 days before you reasonably anticipate to pay or incur expenses;
- Substantiation of expenses—if provided to your employer within 60 days after the expense is paid or incurred; and
- Return of excess—if done within 120 days after you pay or incur expense.

An employer may set up a "periodic statement method" to meet IRS rules. Here, an employer gives each employee periodic statements (at least quarterly) that list the amounts paid in excess of expenses substantiated by the employee and request substantiation of the additional amounts paid, or a return of the excess, within 120 days of the date of the statement. Substantiation or return within the 120-day period satisfies the reasonable time test.

*Filing Tip*

**Failure To Timely Return Excess**

If you fail to return excess payments within a reasonable time but you meet all of the other tests applied to an accountable plan, such as providing proof of the expenses, only the retained excess is taxed to you as if paid outside of an accountable plan.

## 20.19 *Per Diem* Travel Allowance Under Accountable Plans

Instead of providing a straight reimbursement for substantiated out-of-pocket travel expenses, an employer may use a per diem allowance to cover meals, lodging, and incidental *(20.4)* expenses of employees on business trips away from home. If you are not related to the employer, you do not have to give your employer proof of your actual expenses if you receive a per diem allowance or reimbursement that is equal to or less than the federal travel rate for the particular area. You do have to account for the time, place, and business purpose of your travel. If you do not provide such an accounting for some travel days, you must be required to return the per diem allowance received for such days in order for the employer's plan to qualify. If these tests are met, the allowance satisfies the accountable plan *(20.18)* requirements and it does not have to be reported as income on your Form W-2.

**Federal travel rate.** Tables published by the government show the federal travel rate for areas within the continental U.S. (called CONUS locations) and for areas outside the continental U.S., including Hawaii and Alaska (called OCONUS locations). New CONUS tables are released every October, effective for the government's October 1– September 30 fiscal year *(20.4)*. You can obtain the CONUS per diem rates from the General Services Administration website at www.gsa.gov. The OCONUS rates can also be accessed from the GSA website.

If an employer uses the CONUS per diem rates to reimburse employees in the first nine months of the year, the CONUS per diem method must also be used for those employees for the last three months of the year; the "high-low" method (see below) may not be used for those employees until the following calendar year. Where employees are reimbursed in the first nine months using the CONUS per diem rates, the employer may reimburse their travel during the last three months using the per diem rates for the first nine months, or may use the new per diem rates taking effect October 1.

**High-low method.** For business trips within the continental United States (CONUS), employers may use the IRS' "high-low" method to reimburse employees for lodging, meals, and incidental expenses instead of using the locality-by-locality per diem CONUS rates set by the General Services Administration (GSA) for federal government workers. For each employee, either the federal per diem rates or the high-low method has to be used for the entire year.

There is a high-cost area rate and a rate for all other areas within CONUS. The rates are announced by the IRS in an annual notice that lists the areas qualifying for the high-cost rate as well as the months for which the high-cost rate may be used if the area qualifies for less than the full year. For the period beginning October 1, 2017, and ending September 30, 2018, the rate for designated high-cost areas within CONUS was $284 per day, and the rate for all other areas within CONUS, the "low" rate, was $191 per day (IRS Notice 2017-54). For the period beginning October 1, 2018, and ending September 30, 2019, the rate for designated high-cost areas increases to $287 and the rate for other areas increases to $195 per day (IRS Notice 2018-77).

For employer deduction purposes, $68 of the $284 high-cost-area rate (pre-October 1, 2018) and $71 of the $287 high-cost-area rate (effective October 1, 2018) must be allocated to meals, and $57 of the $191 low-cost area rate (pre-October 1, 2018) and $60 of the $195 low-cost area rate (effective October 1, 2018) is allocable to meals. Only 50% of the allocated meals portion is generally deductible *(20.15)*. The meal deduction percentage is 80% for meal costs of transportation workers such as pilots and interstate truck/bus drivers who are subject to Department of Transportation limits on service hours.

Transition rules require employers that used the high-low rates for a particular employee during the first nine months of a year to continue to use the high-low method for that employee for the remainder of that calendar year. If an employer used the high-low method for business trips during the first nine months of 2018, then for the last three months, the employer may use the new high-low rates ($287 or $195) along with the list of high-cost localities that took effect October 1, 2018 (as shown in Notice 2018-77). Alternatively, the employer may use the pre-October high-low rates ($284 or $191) and pre-October high-cost localities (from Notice 2017-54) for the last three months provided that those pre-October rates and localities are used for all employees who are reimbursed under the high-low method. An employer may not use the high-low method until 2019 for an employee whose expenses within CONUS for January through September 2018 were reimbursed using the locality-by-locality per diem CONUS rates set by the General Services Administration (GSA) for federal government workers.

**Employees related to the employer.** The IRS per diem rules that allow you to avoid accounting for actual expenses do not apply if you work for a brother, sister, spouse, parent, child, grandparent, or grandchild. They also do not apply if you are an employee-stockholder who owns more than 10% of the company's stock.

**Reporting a per diem allowance.** If the allowance does not exceed the federal travel rate or IRS high-low rate, the reimbursement is not reported on Form W-2. You do not have to report the expenses or the reimbursement on your tax return; *see* Example 1 below. If your expenses exceed the allowance, you may not deduct the excess by reporting the expenses and reimbursement on Form 2106, unless you are an eligible employee listed at *20.1*; *see* Examples 2 and 3 below.

If the allowance exceeds the federal rate, the allowance up to the federal rate is reported by the employer in Box 12 of your Form W-2, using Code L. This amount is not taxable. However, the excess allowance will be included as wages in Box 1 of your Form W-2; *see* Example 4 below.

*Caution*

**Excess Per Diem Allowances**

If a per diem allowance exceeds the federal travel rate or the IRS high-low rate, the excess will be reported as income on your Form W-2, unless you return the excess. The excess reportable on Form W-2 is also subject to income tax and FICA tax withholding.

---

### EXAMPLES

1. You take a three-day business trip to a locality at a time when the federal travel rate for the area is $149 per day. You account for the date, place, and business purpose of the trip. Your employer reimburses you at the federal rate of $149 a day for lodging, meals, and incidental expenses, for a total of $447. Your actual expenses do not exceed this amount. Your employer does not report the reimbursement on your Form W-2. You do not have to report the reimbursement on your return.

2. Same facts as in Example 1, except that the reimbursement is less than your actual expenses of $700. Even if you have records that substantiate your expenses, you cannot claim a deduction for any part of the nonreimbursed expenses.

3. Same facts as in Example 2, except that you are a fee-basis state or local government official eligible to file Form 2106 *(20.1)*. On Form 2106, you report the $447 reimbursement and your $700 of expenses and also must allocate part of the allowance to your meals expenses to apply the 50% deduction limit *(20.15)*. The instructions to Form 2106 have a worksheet for making the allocation. The net amount from Form 2106 is deductible as an above-the-line deduction on Line 24 of Schedule 1 (Form 1040).

4. Same facts as in Example 1, except that you receive a per diem allowance of $169 per day, or $20 per day more than the federal travel rate. If you do not return the excess of $60 ($20 × 3 days) within a reasonable time *(20.18)*, your employer must report the $60 as income in Box 1 of your Form W-2. The amount up to the federal travel rate, or $447, will be reported in Box 12 of Form W-2 with Code L, but not included as income.

---

**Allowance covering only meals and incidentals.** If your employer gives you a per diem allowance covering only meals and incidental expenses, it is not taxable to you if you are not related to the employer and the allowance does not exceed the IRS meal allowance rate for that locality (M&IE rate; *see 20.4*). Alternatively, for travel within CONUS, your employer may use the meals rate under the high-low method to substantiate the allowance. For the first nine months of 2018, the amount allocable to meals under the high-low method is $68 for high-cost localities and $57 for other areas; for the final three months, the amount allocable to meals under the high-low method is $71 for high cost localities and $60 for other areas (*see* "High-low method" above). Thus, an allowance for meals and incidental expenses for 2018 travel within CONUS is not be taxable to you if it does not exceed the applicable meals rate. However, your employer may choose to use the rates in effect for the first nine months as the reimbursement amount for the last three months, so check with your employer.

## 20.20 Automobile Mileage Allowance

If your employer paid you a fixed mileage allowance for business miles driven in 2018 of up to 54.5 cents per mile (the IRS standard mileage rate), the amount of your driving costs is treated as substantiated under the accountable plan rules *(20.18)*, provided you show the time, place, and business purpose of your travel. If the allowance is in the form of an advance, it must be given within a reasonable period before the anticipated travel and you must also be required to return within a reasonable period *(20.18)* any portion of the allowance that covers mileage that you have not substantiated.

If these tests are met, the allowance will not be reported as income on Form W-2, and you will not have to report the allowance or expenses on your return; *see* Example 1 below. If you do not prove to your employer the time, place, and purpose of your travel, the entire reimbursement is treated as paid from a non-accountable plan and will be reported as income on your Form W-2.

Your employer may reimburse you for any parking fees and tolls in addition to the mileage allowance.

---

**EXAMPLES**

1. In 2018 you drove 12,000 miles for business. You accounted to your employer for the time, place, and business purpose of each trip. Your employer reimbursed you at the IRS rate of 54.5 cents per mile. None of the reimbursements will be reported as income on your 2018 Form W-2, and you do not have to report the reimbursement on your return.

2. Same facts as in Example 1, except that your employer reimbursed you at a rate of 60 cents per mile. The amount using the IRS rate, or $6,540 (.545 × 12,000 miles), is $660 less than the reimbursement of $7,200 (.60 × 12,000) The $660 excess reimbursement over the IRS rate will be reported as wages on your 2018 Form W-2.

   Even if you have records substantiating expenses over the IRS rate of 54.5 cents per mile, you cannot claim the excess costs on Form 2106 because the miscellaneous itemized deduction for unreimbursed job costs has been repealed *(20.1)*.

3. Same facts as in Example 1, except that you were reimbursed only 50 cents per mile for all your business driving, for a total reimbursement of $6,000 (.50 × 12,000 miles). The reimbursements will not be reported as income on your Form W-2. You may not use the standard mileage rate to claim a deduction for expenses up to the IRS rate because the miscellaneous itemized deduction for unreimbursed job costs has been repealed *(20.1)*.

4. Same facts as Example 3, except you are a fee-basis state or local government official eligible to file Form 2106 *(20.1)*. The amount allowed by the IRS rate, or $6,540 (.545 × 12,000 miles), is $540 more than your $6,000 reimbursement. You can report the excess $540 on Form 2106 and claim it as an as an above-the-line deduction on Line 24 of Schedule 1 (Form 1040).

---

If you are not reimbursed for your business driving costs, or you are given a mileage allowance that is less than the expenses that you can substantiate, you may not use the 54.5 cents per mile allowance to claim a deduction for the unreimbursed costs unless you are an eligible employee described in *20.1*.

**Fixed and variable rate allowance (FAVR).** In lieu of setting the allowance at the IRS standard mileage rate, an employer may use a fixed and variable rate allowance, called a FAVR, that gives employees a cents-per-mile rate to cover gas and other operating costs, plus a flat amount to cover fixed costs such as depreciation or lease payments, insurance, and registration. A FAVR allowance must reflect local driving costs and allows employers to set reimbursements at a rate that more closely approximates employee expenses. If your employer sets up a qualifying FAVR under IRS guidelines, you will be required to provide records substantiating your mileage and certain car ownership information. Expenses up to the FAVR limits are deemed substantiated and will not be reported as wages on your Form W-2.

## 20.21 Reimbursements Under Non-Accountable Plans

A non-accountable plan is one that either does not require you to adequately account for your expenses or allows you to keep any excess reimbursement or allowances over the expenses for which you did adequately account.

Your employer reports allowances or reimbursements for a non-accountable plan as part of your salary income in Box 1 of your Form W-2. The allowance or reimbursement is also subject to income tax and FICA tax (Social Security and Medicare) withholding. You cannot deduct your expenses to offset the reimbursement (or allowance) included in your income, unless you are eligible to file Form 2106 and claim an above-the-line deduction as explained at *20.1*.

# PART 4

# Personal Tax Computations

In this part, you will learn how to:

- Figure your regular tax. After reducing adjusted gross income *(12.1)* by the standard deduction or itemized deductions *(13.1)* and, if applicable, the qualified business income deduction *(40.24)*, you figure your 2018 regular tax by looking up the tax in the Tax Table or by figuring the tax using the Tax Computation Worksheet or special capital gain worksheets *(22.1)*.

- Apply the alternative minimum tax. If you have reduced your taxable income by certain deductions and tax benefits, you may be subject to the AMT *(23.1)*.

- Reduce your tax liability with tax credits. You may be entitled to tax credits *(22.7)* that lower your regular tax as well as any AMT.

- Figure estimated tax payments. If you have investment and self-employment income, you generally have to pay quarterly estimated tax *(27.1)*.

- Compute the "kiddie tax." If your child under age 18 has investment income for 2018 exceeding $2,100, you must compute tax on it using the tax rates applicable to trusts and estates. The "kiddie tax" rules also apply if at the end of 2018 your child is age 18 or a full-time student under age 24, unless the child's earned income for 2018 exceeds 50% of his or her total support for the year *(24.2)*.

- Apply the Additional Medicare Tax and the Net Investment Income Tax. There is an 0.9% additional Medicare tax on earnings exceeding $200,000 if you are single or $250,000 if married filing jointly. Also, if modified adjusted gross income exceeds the $200,000 or $250,000 threshold, a 3.8% tax applies to the lesser of your net investment income or the MAGI exceeding the threshold. *See Chapter 28* for details on these additional taxes.

# Dependents

The deduction for personal exemptions has been suspended for 2018 through 2025 by the Tax Cuts and Jobs Act. Although a personal exemption deduction cannot be claimed for a dependent in 2018, the definition of a dependent is still important for purposes of claiming the child tax credit *(25.1)*, the new credit for other dependents *(25.4)*, claiming medical expenses of a dependent *(17.6)*, and qualifying for head of household status *(1.12)*.

To treat someone as your dependent, that person must be your qualifying child or qualifying relative, as explained in this chapter.

## 21.1 New Law Suspends Exemption Deductions for You, Your Spouse, and Your Dependents

The Tax Cuts and Jobs Act suspended the deduction for exemptions for 2018 through 2025. You can no longer claim exemptions for yourself, your spouse (on a joint return), or your dependents. For 2017, each exemption provided a deduction of $4,050, assuming the deduction was not subject to the phaseout rule that applied under the prior rules for high-income taxpayers.

**Definition of dependent still important.** Although you can no longer deduct exemptions for your dependents, being able to treat someone as your dependent is still important for purposes of qualifying for several tax benefits, such as the child tax credit *(25.2)*, the new $500 credit for other dependents *(25.4)*, the child and dependent care credit *(25.5)*, the earned income credit *(25.7)*, and eligibility to file as a head of household *(1.12)*. If you itemize deductions and are claiming medical expenses, you may include expenses you pay for your dependents *(17.6)*.

In addition, the health care mandate for 2018 requires you to have minimum essential coverage for you and your dependents unless you qualify for an exemption; otherwise, you are subject to a penalty *(38.5)*.

## 21.2 How Many Dependents Do You Have?

To claim someone as your dependent, he or she must be either your qualifying child or your qualifying relative. You must have a qualifying child under age 17 to claim the child tax credit or the additional child tax credit *(25.2)*. You must have a qualifying child over age 16 or a qualifying relative to claim the new $500 credit for dependents who do not qualify for the child tax credit *(25.4)*. To file as a head of household, you must maintain a home for a dependent (qualifying child or qualifying relative; *see 1.12* for relaxation of some of the dependent tests). Similarly, for qualifying widow/widower status, you must maintain a home for a dependent child who lives with you *(1.11)*.

In addition to meeting the tests for a qualifying child or qualifying relative, a child/relative can be your dependent only if he or she meets a citizen or resident test, and if married, generally must file separately Finally, even if a person meets the tests for being your dependent, you cannot claim anyone as your dependent if you, or your spouse if filing jointly, can be claimed as a dependent by another taxpayer. *See* "Additional tests for treating someone as your dependent" for further details.

**Do you have a qualifying child for 2018?** In addition to a biological child, a qualifying child can include your stepchild, adopted child, foster child, sibling, half-sibling, or step-sibling, and the descendants of any of these, such as your grandchild, niece, or nephew, provided all of the following tests are met:

1. The child had the same principal place of abode (residence) as you did for more than half of 2018. Temporary absences are disregarded.

2. The child is under age 19 at the end of 2018, or under age 24 at the end of 2018 if a full-time student during any part of at least five months during the year. In addition, the child must be younger than you are, or younger than your spouse if you file jointly. However, there is no age limit if the child is permanently and totally disabled at any time during the year.

3. The child did not provide more than half of his or her own support *(21.3)* for 2018.

4. If married, the child does not file a joint return for 2018, unless the return is only a claim for a refund.

*See 21.3* for further details on the qualifying child rules, including the tie-breaker rules that determine who can claim the child as a dependent when the child is a qualifying child of more than one person.

Keep in mind that for your child to be a qualifying child for purposes of the child tax credit and the additional child tax credit *(25.1)*, the above tests apply with one major exception: your child must be under age 17 for you to claim the credit *(25.1)*.

**Do you have a qualifying relative for 2018?.** An individual is your qualified relative for 2018 if the following three tests are met:

1. The individual is your relative or member of your household *(21.4)*, but that person must not be your qualifying child or the qualifying child of any other taxpayer. That person also cannot be your spouse, as a spouse cannot be your dependent for tax purposes.

2. The individual had gross income for 2018 of under $4,150.

3. You contributed over half of the individual's support for 2018, or you contributed more than 10% of his or her support under the multiple support test *(21.6)*.

*See 21.4* for the broad category of relatives that can meet the relationship test, and for further details on the other qualifying relative tests.

For each of your qualifying relatives, you generally may claim the $500 credit allowed by the Tax Cuts and Jobs Act for dependents who do not qualify for the child tax credit *(25.4)*.

**Additional tests for treating someone as your dependent.** Even if a person is your qualifying child or relative, you cannot claim that person as your dependent if any of the following apply:

1. You, or your spouse if filing jointly, could be claimed as a dependent by another taxpayer for the taxable year. You are not considered another person's dependent if that person is not required to file a return and either does not file or files solely to claim a refund for withheld taxes or estimated tax payments.

2. The child/relative is not a U.S. citizen or U.S. national, a U.S. resident alien, or a resident of Canada or Mexico for at least some part of the year; *see* below for an exception for certain adopted children. A U.S. national is one who owes permanent allegiance to the U.S., principally, a person born in American Samoa or the Northern Mariana Islands who has not become a naturalized American citizen.

   However, for purposes of the child tax credit and additional child tax credit *(25.1)*, a qualifying child does not include a resident of Canada or Mexico. Similarly, for purposes of the credit for dependents who do not qualify for the child tax credit *(25.4)*, a qualifying dependent does not include a resident of Canada or Mexico.

   If you are a U.S. citizen or U.S. national, and you legally adopted a child who is not a U.S. citizen, U.S. resident alien, or U.S. national, or the child was placed with you for legal adoption, your adopted child is treated as a U.S. citizen if the child lived with you as a member of your household for the entire year.

3. If married, the child/relative files a joint return, unless the joint return is only a claim for refund and neither spouse would owe tax on a separate return, as where the return is filed merely to obtain a refund of withheld taxes or of estimated tax payments. In this situation, the return is treated as a refund claim and not as a joint return that blocks dependent status.

**Special rules for divorced or separated parents.** The custodial parent generally may claim the child tax credit, additional child tax credit, and in some cases the credit for other dependents for the children, but special rules allow the custodial parent to waive the right to these benefits in favor of the noncustodial parent *(21.7)*.

**Death of dependent during the year.** If a dependent who otherwise met the tests for a qualifying child or relative died during the year, you can claim an exemption for that dependent.

## 21.3 Qualifying Children

Qualifying children include your children, siblings, and their descendants (*see* the relationship test below) if a residence test and age or student test are also met. If the relationship, residence, and age/student tests are met, you do not have to show that you provided more than half of the child's support, as is required for a qualifying relative *(21.4)*. However, a child is not a qualifying child if he or she provides over half of his or her own support. A married child who files a joint return also cannot be your qualifying child, unless the joint return is filed solely to obtain a refund. For a qualifying child, there is no gross income test; he or she may earn any amount and still be claimed as your dependent. Even if a child is not your

*Caution*

**Should Married Dependents File Separately?**

When a married dependent files a joint return, the dependent's parent cannot claim an exemption for him or her. The loss of the exemption may cost a parent more than the joint return saves the couple. In such a case, it may be advisable for the couple to file separate returns so that the parent may benefit from the larger tax saving.

If the couple decides to revoke their election to file jointly and then file separately in order to preserve the exemption for a parent, they must do so before the filing date for the return. Once a joint return is filed, the couple may not, after the filing deadline, file separate returns for the same year.

*Planning Reminder*

**Qualifying Children**

There is no gross income test for your child or your sibling (or descendant of your child or sibling) if the qualifying child rules under *21.3* are met. Nor do you have to provide over half of the child's support. However, *see* the "additional tests for claiming dependents" in *21.1*.

qualifying child, as where the age/student test or place of abode test is not met, you may still treat the child as your "qualifying relative," provided he or she has little or no income (no more than $4,150 for 2018) and you meet the support test *(21.4)*.

**Relationship test.** Your children, stepchildren, and their descendants (your grandchildren and great-grandchildren), and your siblings, including step- and half-brothers and -sisters and their descendants (your nieces and nephews), meet the relationship test. A legally adopted child or a child lawfully placed with you for adoption is treated as your child, as is a foster child placed with you by a court order or by an authorized placement agency.

**Residence test (abode test).** The qualifying child must have the same principal place of abode as you for more than half the year. You do not have to own the home or pay the maintenance costs, but the child must live with you for over half the year.

*Temporary absences disregarded.* In applying the residence test, your child is considered to be living with you while either of you is temporarily absent (or you both are) due to special circumstances. This includes temporary absences while away at school or on business, while obtaining medical treatment or institutional care, taking vacations, serving in the military, or while incarcerated.

*Kidnapped child.* The principal place of abode test is considered met for a child under age 18 who met the test prior to being kidnapped by a non–family member.

**Birth or death of child during the year.** The principal place of abode test is considered met for a child who died during the year if the child lived with you while alive. Similarly, the principal place of abode test is considered met for a newborn child who lives with you after birth for over half of the rest of the year, apart from required hospital stays. A child born alive but who dies shortly thereafter is considered your dependent.

**Age or student test.** Your qualifying child must either be: (1) under age 19 at the end of the year, (2) a full-time student under age 24 at the end of the year, or (3) permanently and totally disabled, regardless of age.

In addition, to qualify under Test 1 or 2, a child who is not permanently and totally disabled must be younger than you. If you are married and file jointly, the child must be younger than you or your spouse. For example, you are age 21 and you file jointly with your 25-year-old spouse. Your 23-year-old brother, a non-disabled full-time student, lives with you and your spouse. On your joint return, you can claim your brother as a qualifying child because he is younger than your spouse although older than you.

*Qualifying as a full-time student.* A full-time student is one who attends school full time during at least five calendar months in the tax year. For example: attendance from February through some part of June—or from February through May and then at least one month from September through December—qualifies. The five months do not have to run consecutively. Attendance at a vocational, trade, or technical school for the five-month period qualifies, but not correspondence schools or on-the-job training courses. Your child who attends school at night is considered a full-time student only if he or she is enrolled for the number of hours or classes that is considered full-time attendance.

**Child's self-support test.** You do not have to contribute over 50% of a qualifying child's support to claim an exemption. This is required for a qualifying relative *(21.4)* but not for a qualifying child. However, if a child contributes over half of his or her own support, he or she cannot be claimed as your qualifying child, even if the other tests are met (the relationship, residence, and age/student tests). *See 21.5* for a list of items (such as food, lodging and clothing) that count as support.

**Tie-breaker rules.** The law provides tie-breaker rules to determine who can treat a child as a qualifying child when the qualifying child tests are met by more than one taxpayer.

If only one of the eligible taxpayers is the parent of the child, the child is treated as the qualifying child of that parent. This situation could arise, for example, where a parent and infant child live with the child's grandparent for more than half the year. Both the child's parent and grandparent would meet the principal place of abode test and relationship test with respect to the child, but under the tie-breaker rule, the child is treated as the qualifying child of the parent. However, the parent can choose not to claim the child, and allow the grandparent to claim the exemption, provided the grandparent's adjusted gross income (AGI) exceeds his or her own AGI. If the parent's AGI equals or is higher than the grandparent's AGI, the grandparent cannot claim the exemption; only the parent can. If the parent or grandparent files a joint return, the total AGI on the joint return is taken into account in determining which of them has the higher AGI.

If the parents file separate returns and both meet the tests for treating the child as a qualifying child, they may be unable to agree on which of them should claim the child. If they each claim the child on a separate return, the IRS will first determine if the noncustodial parent is entitled to the exemption under the special rule for divorced or separated parents *(21.7)*. If the special rule applies, the tie-breaker rules do not apply. If the special rule does not apply and the child is a qualifying child of both parents under the above tests, the tie-breaker rule deems the child to be the qualifying child of the parent with whom the child has resided for the longer period during the year. If the residency period with both parents is the same, the parent with the higher adjusted gross income is entitled to treat the child as a qualifying child.

If no parent meets the tests for claiming the child and more than one non-parent meets the tests, the non-parent with the highest adjusted gross income is entitled to claim the child as a qualifying child.

## 21.4  Qualifying Relatives

You may claim an exemption for a person as your qualifying relative if:

1. the relationship, gross income, and support tests described below are met, and
2. the individual is not your qualifying child *(21.3)* nor the qualifying child of any other taxpayer, and
3. the individual meets the citizenship/resident test and joint return test required of all dependents (see "Additional tests for treating someone as your dependent", in *21.2*), and
4. you cannot be claimed as a dependent (nor your spouse if you file jointly) by another taxpayer (see "Additional tests for treating someone as your dependent", in *21.2*),

If the member-of-household test described below is met, it may be possible to claim an individual as your qualifying relative even if he or she is "technically" the qualifying child of another taxpayer.

**Relationship test.**  Relatives listed below meet the relationship test; they do not have to live with you. Unrelated or distantly related persons not on this list meet the relationship test if they live with you as discussed below under the member-of-household test.

*Children, grandchildren, and great-grandchildren who are not qualifying children.* Your children, grandchildren, and great-grandchildren can meet the relationship test for a qualifying relative only if they are not your qualifying children or the qualifying children of any other taxpayer under the rules for qualifying children *(21.3)*. For example, if your child is not your qualifying child for 2018 because he or she does not meet the age/student test or the principal place of abode test *(21.3)*, that child may be treated as your qualifying relative, but only if his or her gross income for 2018 is under $4,150 and you provide over 50% of his or her support for the year.

*Brothers, sisters, and their children.* The same considerations discussed above for children, grandchildren, and great-grandchildren apply for your siblings (including half- or step-siblings) and their children (your nieces and nephews). They can be your qualifying relatives only if they are not your qualifying children *(21.3)* or the qualifying children of anyone else.

*Parents, grandparents, and other relatives.* The following individuals also meet the relationship test: your parent, grandparent, great-grandparent, step-parent, son- or daughter-in-law, father- or mother-in-law, and brother- or sister-in-law. If related by blood, aunts and uncles also qualify.

*Stepchild's husband or wife or child.* Your stepchild's spouse does not meet the relationship test. Nor may you treat a step-grandchild as your qualifying relative if you file a separate return. But you may treat them on a joint return as qualifying relatives

 *Filing Tip*

**Nephew, Niece, Uncle, and Aunt**

Nephews, nieces, uncles, and aunts must be your blood relatives to qualify under the relationship test. For example, the brother or sister of your father or mother qualifies as your relative; their spouses do not. You may not claim your spouse's nephews, nieces, uncles, or aunts as your qualifying relatives unless you file a joint return.

**Caution**

**Qualifying Relationship Not Enough**

Assuming a person meets the relationship test *(21.4)*, you must provide over 50% of his or her support and his or her gross income for 2018 must be under $4,150 for you to claim that person as your qualifying relative for 2018.

if the other exemption tests are met. On a joint return, it is not necessary that the close relationship exist between the dependent and the spouse who furnishes the chief support. It is sufficient that the relationship exists with either spouse.

> **EXAMPLE**
>
> You contribute more than half of the support of the sister of your wife's mother (your wife's aunt). If you and your wife file a joint return, her aunt meets the relationship test. But your wife's aunt's husband is not related by blood to you or your wife. You cannot claim an exemption for him, even on a joint return, unless he is a member of your household under the rules discussed below and other exemption tests are met.
>
> In-laws. Brother-in-law, sister-in-law, father-in-law, mother-in-law, son-in-law, and daughter-in-law are relatives by marriage. They meet the relationship test and you may claim them as exemptions if the other tests for qualifying relatives are satisfied.

An in-law who was related to you by marriage and whom you continue to support after divorce or the death of your spouse meets the relationship test.

> **EXAMPLE**
>
> For many years, Allen has contributed all the support of his father-in-law, Jerry, who has no gross income. Allen's wife died in 2014. Allen has continued to be Jerry's sole source of support. Allen may claim Jerry as a qualifying relative for 2018.

*Death during the year.* If a person who meets the relationship test died during 2018 but was supported by you while alive, and the other tests are met, you may claim that person as your qualifying relative.

> **EXAMPLE**
>
> On January 21, 2018, your father died. Until that date, you contributed all of his support. He had no gross income for 2018. You may treat him as your qualifying relative for 2018.

*Member-of-household test for unrelated or distantly related dependents living with you.* A relative not listed above, such as a cousin, meets the relationship test if he or she lives with you all year as a member of your household, except for temporary absences due to schooling, vacationing, being away on business, serving in the military, or being confined to a hospital. A friend or live-in mate can also qualify, except in those few states where cohabitation is illegal.

The "all-year" test can prevent you from treating someone as your qualifying relative, despite the level of your support. For example, in one case, a taxpayer let his cousin and her children move in with him in May because the cousin feared her estranged husband. The Tax Court held that he could not claim the children as dependents under the member-of-household test because they did not live with him for the whole year, but only from May through December.

*Under the tax law, one spouse is not considered a dependent of the other (21.2).* If you are divorced or legally separated during the year, your former spouse cannot be your qualifying relative even if he or she is a member of your household for the whole year.

*Special exception for child of unmarried cohabitant.* If a taxpayer lives with and supports a mate and the mate's child, an exemption for the child may or may not be allowed to the taxpayer under the member-of-household test. For example, if a taxpayer supports his girlfriend and her child as members of his household, he "technically" cannot claim the child as his qualifying relative because the child is the mother's qualifying child *(21.3)* and a qualifying child cannot be the qualifying relative of someone else. However, the IRS allows a limited exception. The exemption for the child can be claimed if the child's mother (for whom the child is a qualifying child) is not required to file a tax return because of low income, and she does not file a return or files solely to get a refund of withheld income taxes. If the mother files a return to claim the earned income credit as well as to obtain a refund for withheld income taxes, the exception does not apply and the taxpayer cannot treat the child as his qualifying relative.

The mother can also be the qualifying relative of the taxpayer under the member-of-household test, provided that their relationship is not illegal under local law.

**Gross income limit.** A person meeting the above relationship test cannot be claimed as your qualifying relative for 2018 if he or she had gross income of $4,150 or more; gross income must be under $4,150. This gross income test applies even if you provide most or all of that person's support. The gross income limit may be raised for 2019 by an inflation adjustment.

Keep in mind that the gross income test does not apply to children who meet the tests for a qualifying child *(21.3)*. However, if a child does not meet the age/student test or principal place of abode test, and thus is not a qualifying child *(21.3)*, he or she must have gross income under the annual limit ($4,150 for 2018) to be claimed as a dependent under the qualifying relative rules.

Gross income here means taxable income items includible in the dependent's tax return. It does not include nontaxable items such as gifts and tax-exempt bond interest. Gross income for a service-type business is gross receipts without deductions of expenses and for a manufacturing or merchandising business is total sales less cost of goods sold. A partner's share of partnership gross income, not the share of net income, is treated as gross income.

Social Security benefits are treated as gross income only to the extent they are taxable *(34.3)*.

Exception for disabled student working at sheltered workshop. For purposes of the gross income test gross income does not include income earned by a totally and permanently disabled individual at a school operated by a government agency or tax-exempt organization, if the school provides special instruction for alleviating the disability and the income is incidental to medical care received.

**Support test.** A person cannot be your qualifying relative unless you provide over half of his or her total support for the year. The support test applies to a child who does not meet the tests for a qualifying child *(21.3)*. See *21.5* for how to count total support and your contribution to the total.

## 21.5 Meeting the Support Test for a Qualifying Relative

To claim a dependent as your qualifying relative *(21.4)*, you must contribute more than 50% of the dependent's total support for the year. You do not have to meet this support test to claim a child as your dependent under the qualifying child rules *(21.3)*, but qualifying child status is denied if a child provides over half of his or her own support, and the support items listed below count when making that determination.

**Meeting the support test.** Follow these steps to figure support: (1) Total the value of the support contributed by you, by the dependent, and by others for the dependent. Use the checklists later in this section for determining what to include in total support and what to exclude. (2) Determine your share of the total. If your share is more than 50% of the dependent's total support, you meet the support test. It does not matter how many months or days you provided the support; only the total cost of the support is considered. You may not take the exemption if the dependent contributed 50% or more of his or her own support or 50% or more was contributed by others, including government sources.

*Multiple support agreement.* If the dependent or someone else did not contribute 50% or more of the support, and you contributed more than 10% of the total support, you may be able to claim the exemption under a multiple support agreement *(21.6)*.

*Divorced or separated parents contributing to support of their children should follow a special rule (21.7).*

---

> ### EXAMPLE
> Eric Hill receives Social Security benefits of $9,000 and also $300 in bank interest in 2018. He has no other income. Eric spends $4,400 on food, clothes, transportation, and recreation. The $4,400 spent is his contribution to his own support. Eric's rent, utilities, unreimbursed medical expenses, and other necessities are paid by his son, Mike. If Mike's payments exceed $4,400, and no one else contributes to Eric's support, Mike may claim Eric as a dependent.

*Caution*

**Students Age 24 or Older**

The gross income test does not apply to qualifying children *(21.3)*, including full-time students who are under age 24 as of the end of the year. However, if your child was a student age 24 or older at the end of 2018 and had gross income of $4,150 or more, he or she cannot be your qualifying relative and you may not claim him or her as a dependent for 2018.

## Checklist of Support Items

- Food and lodging; *see* below.
- Clothing
- Medical and dental expenses, including premiums paid for health insurance policies and Medicare coverage (premiums paid for Medicare Parts A (if any), B, C, or D).
- Education expenses such as tuition, books, and supplies. If your child receives a student loan and is the primary obligor, the loan proceeds are considered his or her own support contribution. This is true even if you are a guarantor of the loan. Scholarships received by full-time students are not treated as support; *see* the checklist of nonsupport items in this section.
- Cars and transportation expenses. Include the cost of a car bought for a dependent as support. If you buy a car but register it in your own name, the cost of the car is not support provided by you, but any out-of-pocket expenses you have for operating the car are part of your support contribution.
- Recreation and entertainment. A computer or TV set bought for your child or other dependent is support. Also include costs of summer camp, singing and dancing lessons, and musical instruments, as well as wedding expenses.

**Planning Reminder**

### Savings and Investments as Support

Income that is invested is not treated as support. However, personal savings are treated as support if they are used for food, clothing, lodging, or other support items.

**Dependent's income and personal savings may be support.** In figuring a person's total support, include his or her taxable and tax-exempt income and personal savings if actually used for support items such as food, lodging, or clothing. Also include support items that are financed by loans. Income that is invested and not actually spent for support is not included in the earner's total support.

*Social Security.* Social Security benefits (whether taxable or tax-exempt) received by your dependent are included in his or her total support only if they are actually spent on support items and not invested.

Social Security benefits paid to children of deceased workers that are used for their support are treated as the children's contribution to their own support. Follow this rule even though benefits are paid to you as the child's parent or custodian. If the Social Security benefits used for a child's support are more than half of the child's total support, no one may claim the child as a dependent.

Where spouses are paid Social Security benefits in one check made out in their joint names, 50% is considered to be used by each spouse unless shown otherwise.

*Government benefits.* In figuring whether you have provided more than 50% of the dependent's support, you have to consider certain government benefits as support provided by a third party to the dependent. For example, Supplemental Security Income (SSI), welfare, food stamps, or housing payments based on need are support payments from the government if they are used for support of the dependent. G.I. Bill education assistance is support provided by the government.

Foster care payments by a child placement agency to parents are support provided by the agency and not by the parents. The value of board, lodging, and education provided to a child in a state juvenile home is treated as support provided by the state.

When a person joins the Armed Forces, the value of board, lodging, and clothing he or she receives is treated as the government's support contribution. However, if you are in the Armed Forces, dependency allotments withheld from your pay and used to support your dependents are included in your support contributions for them. Also included in your support contribution is a military quarters allowance covering a dependent.

**Planning Reminder**

### Dependents in the Armed Forces

If your dependent joins the military, the value of food, lodging, clothing, and educational assistance provided by the government constitutes government support.

**Lodging and food as support.** The dependent's total support includes the fair rental value of a room, apartment, or house in which the dependent lives. In your estimate of fair retail value, include a reasonable allowance for the rental value of furnishings and appliances, and for heat and other utilities. You do not add payments of rent, taxes, interest, depreciation, paint, insurance, and utilities. These are presumed to be accounted for in the fair rental estimate. The fair rental value of lodging you furnish a dependent is the amount you could reasonably expect to receive from a stranger for the lodging.

*Does dependent live in his or her own home?* If a dependent lives in his or her own home, treat the total fair rental value as his or her own contribution to support. However, if you help maintain the home by giving cash, or you directly pay such expenses as the mortgage, real estate taxes, fire insurance premiums, and repairs, you reduce the total fair rental value of the home by the amount you contributed when figuring his or her own support contributions; *see* the Example below.

If you lived with your dependent rent-free in his or her home, the fair rental value of lodging furnished to you must be offset against the amounts you spent for your dependent in determining the net amount of your contribution to the dependent's support.

 *Planning Reminder*

**Lump-Sum Payment to Care Facilities**

A lump-sum contribution covering a relative's lifetime care in a long-term care facility is prorated over the relative's life expectancy to determine your current support contribution.

---

### EXAMPLE

You contribute $7,000 as support to your father who lives in his own home, which has a fair rental value of $8,000 a year. He uses $4,600 of the money you give him to pay real estate taxes and $2,400 for food. He spends $3,000 of his Social Security for recreation and invests the rest. He has no gross income *(21.4)* and receives no other support. Your father's contribution to his own support is $6,400:

| | |
|---|---|
| Fair rental value of house | |
| ($8,000 less $4,600 you gave for taxes) | 3,400 |
| Social Security spent | 3,000 |
| Father's contribution to his own support | $6,400 |

You may claim your father as a dependent because your contribution of $7,000 exceeds half of his total support of $13,400 (your $7,000 contribution and his $6,400 contribution).

---

*Food and other similar household expenses.* If the dependent lives with you, you divide your total food expenses equally among all the members of your household, unless you have records showing the exact amount spent on the dependent; *see* the Examples at the end of this section. If he or she does not live with you, you count the actual amount of food expenses spent by or for that dependent.

*Do you pay for a relative's care in a health facility?* If you pay part of a relative's expenses for care in a nursing home or other facility, your payment is a support contribution. If you make a lump-sum contribution covering a relative's stay in an old-age home or other care facility, you prorate your payment over the relative's life expectancy to determine the current support contribution.

## Checklist of Items Not Counted as Support of Dependent

- Federal, state, and local income taxes and Social Security taxes paid by the dependent from his or her own income
- Funeral expenses
- Life insurance premiums
- Medicare benefits or proceeds under Medicare Parts A, B, C, or D. Note that the rule is different for Medicare premiums: Medicare premiums are treated as support, but Medicare benefits are disregarded in determining a person's support. In one case the IRS argued that Medicaid benefits were includible in total support but the Tax Court disagreed, holding that Medicaid is similar to excludable Medicare benefits.
- Medical insurance benefits received by the dependent
- Scholarships received by your child, stepchild, or legally adopted child who is a full-time student for at least five calendar months during the year. Scholarship aid is counted as support contributed by the child if he or she is not a full-time student for at least five months. Naval R.O.T.C. payments and payments made under the War Orphans Educational Assistance Act are scholarships that are not counted as support. State aid to a disabled child for education or training, including room and board, is a scholarship.

*Planning Reminder*

**Households with Several Dependents**

If your contribution does not exceed 50% of total household support, earmark contributions to at least one of the dependents. This will allow you to claim at least one exemption. Without proper records, however, the IRS treats your contributions as divided among the members of the household.

## Allocating Support

The Examples below illustrate how you should allocate various support items when your contributions benefit more than one person or when your dependent provides part of his or her own support.

**Earmarking support to one dependent.** If you are contributing funds to a household consisting of several persons and the amount you contribute does not exceed 50% of the total household support, you may be able to claim an exemption for at least one dependent by earmarking your support to his or her use. Your earmarked contributions must exceed 50% of this dependent's support costs. Mark your checks for the benefit of the dependent, or provide the dependents with a written statement of your support arrangement at the time you start your payments. If you do not designate for whom you are providing support, your contribution is allocated equally among all members of a household.

### EXAMPLES

1. Your father lives in your home with you, your spouse, and your three children. He receives Social Security benefits of $9,800, which are not subject to tax *(34.3)* and half of which ($4,900) he spends for his own clothing, travel, and recreation. You spend $6,600 for food during the year. You also paid his dental bill of $500. You estimate the annual fair rental value of the room furnished him as $3,600. Your father's total support is:

   | | |
   |---|---|
   | Social Security used for support | $4,900 |
   | Share of food costs (1/6 of $6,600) | 1,100 |
   | Dental bill paid by you | 500 |
   | Rental value of room | 3,600 |
   | | $10,100 |

   You meet the support test. You contributed more than half his total support, or $5,200 ($3,600 for lodging, $500 for the dental bill, and $1,100 for food).

2. Your parents live with you, your spouse, and your two children in a house you rent. The annual fair rental value of their room is $3,000. Your father receives a tax-free government pension of $5,200, all of which he spent equally for your mother and himself for clothing and recreation. Your parents' only other income was $500 of tax-exempt interest. They did not make any other contributions toward their own support. Your total expense in providing food for the household is $6,000. You pay heat and utility bills of $1,200. You paid your mother's medical expenses of $600. Your father's total support from all sources is $5,100 and your mother's is $5,700, figured as follows:

   | | Father | Mother |
   |---|---|---|
   | Fair rental value of room | $1,500 | $1,500 |
   | Pension used for their support | 2,600 | 2,600 |
   | Share of food costs (1/6 of $6,000) | 1,000 | 1,000 |
   | Medical expenses for mother | | 600 |
   | | $5,100 | $5,700 |

   In figuring your parents' total support, you do not include the cost of heat and utilities, because these are presumed to be included in the fair rental value of the room ($3,000). The support you furnish your father, $2,500 (lodging, $1,500; food, $1,000), is not over half of his total support of $5,100. The support you furnish your mother, $3,100 (lodging, $1,500; food, $1,000; medical, $600), is over half of her total support of $5,700. You meet the support test for your mother but not your father. Since she did not have taxable income, the gross income test *(21.4)* is satisfied.

## 21.6 Multiple Support Agreements

Are you and others sharing the support of one person, but with no one individual providing more than 50% *(21.5)* of his or her total support? You are treated as meeting the support test for a qualifying relative *(21.4)* if:

1. You gave more than 10% of the support;
2. The amount contributed by you and others to the dependent's support equals more than half the support;
3. Each contributor could have claimed the exemption—except that he or she gave less than half the support; and
4. Each contributor who gave more than 10% agrees to let you take the exemption. Each signs a Form 2120, "Multiple Support Declaration." You then attach the forms to your return.

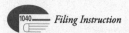

### EXAMPLES

1. You and your two brothers contribute $2,000 each toward the support of your mother. She contributes $1,000 of her own to support herself. Your two sisters contribute $500 each. Thus, the total support comes to $8,000. Of this, you and your brothers each gave 25% ($2,000 ÷ $8,000), for a total of 75%. Each sister gave 6¼% ($500 ÷ $8,000). You or one of your brothers may claim the exemption, assuming the other tests for a qualifying relative *(21.4)* are met. Since each of you contributed more than 10% and the total of your contributions is more than half of your mother's support, you may decide among yourselves which of the three of you will claim the exemption. If you claim the exemption, your brothers must sign Forms 2120, which you attach to your return. If one of your brothers claims the exemption, you sign a Form 2120, which is attached to the return of the brother who claims the exemption. Since neither of your sisters furnished more than 10%, neither can claim the exemption; they need not sign Forms 2120.

2. Your mother's support totals $10,000; you contribute $3,000; your brother, $2,000; your father, $1,600; and your mother from her savings contributes $3,400. Assume your father does not file a tax return claiming your mother as an exemption. You and your brother cannot use your father's contribution to meet the more than 50% test required by Rule 2 above. Your father may not join in a multiple support agreement because your mother is not his dependent for tax purposes, although an exemption may be claimed for a wife on the basis of the marital relationship *(21.2)*.

## 21.7 Special Rule for Divorced or Separated Parents

Although a deduction for personal exemptions is not allowed for 2018 through 2025 *(21.1)*, the right to claim an exemption still matters to divorced or separated parents because the right to claim the exemption for a child also determines which parent may claim the child tax credit and additional child tax credit, and perhaps the credit for other dependents. A child is generally treated as the qualifying child of the custodial parent, the parent with whom the child lives for the greater part of the year, because of the residence test *(21.3)*. Thus, for 2017 and prior years, the right to the exemption deduction for the child, and with it, the right to claim the child tax credit and possibly the additional child tax credit, belonged to the custodial parent, unless the custodial parent waived that right in favor of the noncustodial parent on Form 8332 (or similar statement).

This waiver rule still applies, despite the fact that there is no deduction for the exemption under the Tax Cuts and Jobs Act. For 2018 and later years, a waiver by the custodial parent of the right to the exemption for a child has the effect of allowing the noncustodial parent to claim the child tax credit and additional child tax credit, or if applicable, the new credit for other dependents, for that child.

For the waiver rule to apply, the threshold conditions listed below must be present.

Note that even if the custodial parent agrees to waive the right to the exemption on Form 8332, this waiver does not apply to the earned income credit *(25.7)*, child and dependent care credit *(25.5)*, or the exclusion for dependent care benefits *(3.5)*, which may be claimed, if at all, only by the custodial parent. Similarly, only a custodial parent can file as a head of household *(1.12)*.

*Planning Reminder*

**Form 8332 Waiver Applies to Child Tax Credit**

If a custodial parent releases the right to claim a dependency exemption for his or her child on Form 8332 (or substitute statement), the release gives the noncustodial parent the right to claim the child tax credit and the additional child tax credit, assuming the credits are not phased out; *see 25.2*.

**Threshold conditions for special rule.** The special rule applies only if the following threshold conditions are met: (1) the child receives over one-half of his or her total support for the year from one or both parents, (2) the parents are divorced or legally separated under a decree of divorce or separate maintenance, separated under a written separation agreement, or live apart at all times during the last six months of the year (this includes parents who were never married to each other), and (3) the child is in the custody of one or both parents for more than half the year.

The first condition is not met, and the special rule does not apply, if a parent and other individuals contributing more than 10% of the child's support enter into a multiple support agreement *(21.6)* authorizing the parent to claim the exemption.

**Custodial parent and noncustodial parent.** For purposes of the special rule, the custodial parent is the parent with whom the child resides for the greater number of nights during the year. The other parent is the noncustodial parent. A child who is temporarily absent is treated as residing with the parent with whom the child would otherwise have resided on that night. If during the year the child resides with both parents for an equal number of nights, the parent with the higher adjusted gross income is treated as the custodial parent.

**Custodial parent's waiver of exemption on Form 8332 or similar statement.** If the above threshold conditions are met, the custodial parent may provide a written waiver on Form 8332 (or similar statement) releasing the exemption for a named child to the noncustodial parent. If the noncustodial parent attaches the waiver to his or her return, the child is treated as the qualifying child or qualifying relative of the noncustodial parent for purposes of the dependency exemption deduction (for 2017 and earlier), the child tax credit, the additional child tax credit, and the credit for other dependents (for 2018 and later).

Under proposed regulations, the noncustodial parent can attach the waiver to an original or amended return, but a waiver attached to an amended return will not qualify if (1) the custodial parent filed a return claiming the child as an exemption before signing the waiver, and (2) the custodial parent has not filed an amended return to remove his or her claim to the exemption.

A waiver on Form 8332 (or similar written release) by the custodial parent must specify the year or years for which it is effective. Part I of Form 8332 is completed to waive the exemption for the current tax year, and Part II is used to waive the exemption for specific future years or all future years. If Part II provides a release for "all future years," IRS regulations treat this as referring to the first taxable year after the year of execution and all taxable years after that. The waiver cannot be conditioned on the payment of support, or the meeting of some other obligation, by the noncustodial parent.

If a post-1984 decree or agreement executed before 2009 states that the noncustodial parent has the unconditional right to claim the exemption for the child, and that the custodial parent is waiving the exemption for a specified year or years, the noncustodial parent can attach to his or her return the relevant pages from the decree or agreement instead of attaching Form 8332. The attachment must include the page that gives the noncustodial parent the unconditional right to the exemption, the page showing the custodial parent's waiver, the cover page, on which the custodial parent's Social Security number should be written, and the signature page showing the custodial parent's signature and date of the agreement.

The option to attach pages from a decree or agreement is not available if the decree/agreement was executed after 2008. The noncustodial parent may only by obtaining the custodial parent's waiver on Form 8332 (or similar written release) and attaching that to his or her return.

Note: A noncustodial parent who is given the right to claim the exemption under a pre-1985 agreement for a disabled child who has reached the age of majority may continue to treat the child as a dependent by providing at least $600 of the child's support for the year; *see* Publication 501 for details.

**Custodial parent may revoke waiver.** A custodial parent who has waived the exemption in favor of the noncustodial parent can revoke the waiver. The revocation can be made in Part III of Form 8332.

However, a revocation has a delayed effect. It does not apply until the year after the year in which you give a copy of it to the noncustodial parent or make a reasonable attempt to do so. For example, you are the custodial parent of your daughter and on Form 8332 you waived your right to the exemption for the years 2012 through 2020. In 2017 you revoked your waiver on Form 8332 and gave a copy of it to the noncustodial parent. You can treat your daughter as your dependent on your 2018 return, assuming the other qualifying child *(21.3)* or qualifying relative *(21.4)* tests are met, as well as on your 2019 and 2020 returns. However, if you did not give the copy of the revocation to the noncustodial parent until 2018, the revocation is not effective until 2019. You must attach a copy of the revocation to your return for each year that you claim the child as your dependent.

## 21.8  Reporting Social Security Numbers of Dependents

On your return, you must list the Social Security number (SSN) of each dependent you claim. Include the SSNs of parents or other adults you claim as dependents, as well as those of children.

An SSN may be obtained from the Social Security Administration for U.S. citizens and aliens who have been lawfully admitted for permanent residence or employment. If a dependent is a resident alien or nonresident alien ineligible to obtain an SSN, an individual taxpayer identification number (ITIN) must be obtained from the IRS by filing Form W-7.

If you are in the process of legally adopting a U.S. citizen or resident child who has been placed in your home by an authorized placement agency, and you cannot obtain a Social Security number for the child in time to file your tax return, you may use Form W-7A to apply to the IRS for a temporary adoption taxpayer identification number (ATIN).

If you fail to include a correct SSN or ITIN for a dependent claimed on your return, the IRS may disallow dependent treatment, although it may contact you and give you an opportunity to provide the number. If an exemption is disallowed, the IRS may assess the extra tax using a summary assessment procedure if you fail to request abatement of the assessment within 60 days of receiving notice; this procedure does not require issuance of a deficiency notice, so there is no appeal to the Tax Court.

To obtain a Social Security number for a dependent child, file Form SS-5 with your local Social Security Administration office. Parents of newborn children may request a number when filling out hospital birth-registration records.

**Religious beliefs.**  Religious beliefs against applying for and using SSN numbers for their children do not excuse taxpayers from the obligation to provide them. That's what the Tax Court told the Millers, who had refused to use SSN numbers for claiming their two children as exemptions. They argued that SSNs are universal numerical identifiers equal to the "mark of the Beast," as described in the New Testament. However, they were willing to use Individual Taxpayer Identification Numbers (ITINs).

The Court held that the IRS properly refused to issue ITINs in this case because ITINs are issued only to taxpayers who are ineligible to receive SSNs, which are issued by the Social Security Administration. The couple had argued that the requirement to use SSNs "substantially burdened" their First Amendment right to free exercise of religion, which entitled them to relief under the Religious Freedom Restoration Act of 1993. The Court held that it did not have to decide the "burden-on-religion" issue because the IRS was able to show that the SSN requirement furthers a compelling governmental interest and is the least restrictive means of achieving this interest. Here, the Government has a compelling interest in effectively tracking claimed dependency exemptions and administering the tax system in a uniform and mandatory way. Moreover, the requirement to supply SSNs for dependent children has significantly reduced the improper claiming of dependents. Allowing the use of ITINs would be a less effective means of detecting fraud than requiring SSNs. If an individual entitled to an SSN was issued an ITIN, an SSN could later be obtained, allowing duplicate exemption claims to be made.

 *Caution*

**Child Must Have SSN for You to Claim Child Tax Credit**

For 2018 and later years, you cannot claim the child tax credit or the additional child tax credit for a qualified child unless the child has been issued a Social Security number by the due date of your return *(25.1)*.

# CHAPTER 22

# Figuring Your Regular Income Tax Liability

There are two types of income tax rates: (1) regular rates, which apply to all taxpayers, and (2) alternative minimum tax (AMT) rates, which apply only if certain tax benefits, when added back to your income, result in an AMT tax that exceeds your regular tax.

Most taxpayers do not have to compute the regular tax. They find the tax for their income and filing status in the IRS Tax Table if their taxable income is less than $100,000 *(22.2)*. The Tax Computation Worksheet must be used to figure your regular income tax if taxable income is $100,000 or more *(22.3)*. However, if you have net capital gain or qualified dividends, do not use the Tax Table or the Tax Computation Worksheet. Instead, figure your regular tax liability on the applicable capital gains worksheet in the IRS instructions *(22.4)*. Use the Foreign Earned Income Tax Worksheet to figure your regular tax if you are claiming the foreign earned income exclusion or foreign housing exclusion *(22.5)*.

To determine if you owe alternative minimum tax *(23.1)*, you have to complete Form 6251.

## 22.1 Taxable Income and Regular Income Tax Liability

The way you determine your regular tax liability depends on the amount of your taxable income and in some cases the type of income you have. If your taxable income is less than $100,000, you generally must use the IRS Tax Table to look up your tax *(22.2)*. If your taxable income is $100,000 or more, you use the Tax Computation Worksheet to determine the tax *(22.3)*. However, if you have net capital gain or qualified dividends, you generally figure your tax on the Qualified Dividends and Capital Gain Tax Worksheet in the IRS instructions for Form 1040 *(22.4)*. Tax is figured on the Foreign Earned Income Tax Worksheet if you claim the foreign earned income or housing exclusion, or on Form 8615 if the "kiddie tax" computation *(24.3)* must be made. For 2018, all taxpayers will use Form 1040 and its schedules; Forms 1040A and Form 1040EZ have been eliminated *(page 8)*.

For 2018, taxable income is your adjusted gross income *(12.1)* minus: (1) your standard deduction or itemized deductions, whichever you claim *(13.1)*, and (2) the new deduction for qualified business income *(40.24)*. For 2017 and earlier years, personal exemptions were subtracted from adjusted gross income to figure taxable income, but exemptions are no longer deductible *(21.1)*.

*Separate self-employment tax computation.* If you have net self-employment earnings, figure your self-employment tax under the rules at *45.3*. Half of the self-employment tax is deductible as an above-the-line deduction from gross income when figuring your regular tax *(12.2)*. The self-employment tax figured on Schedule SE (Form 1040) is entered as an "other tax" on Schedule 4 (Form 1040), and then the total "other taxes" are added to your regular income tax liability on Form 1040.

*AMT computation.* Regardless of how your regular tax liability is determined, you may also be liable for alternative minimum tax (AMT), which is figured on Form 6251 *(23.1)*. If the tentative AMT figured on Form 6251 exceeds your regular tax (less any foreign tax credit and special averaging tax *(7.3)* on a lump-sum distribution if born before January 1, 1936), the excess is your AMT liability, which must be reported as an additional tax on Schedule 2 (Form 1040).

*Health care individual responsibility penalty.* You must pay a penalty for 2018 if you do not have minimum essential coverage, unless you qualify for an exemption; *see 38.5*. If you owe the penalty, it is reported as an "other tax" on Schedule 4 (Form 1040).

## 22.2 Using the Tax Table

You must use the Tax Table (shown in Part 8 of this book) to look up your regular income tax liability unless you have taxable income of $100,000 or more, you have net capital gain or qualified dividends *(22.4)*, or you are claiming the foreign earned income or housing exclusion *(22.5)*. If your taxable income is $100,000 or more, you use the Tax Computation Worksheet *(22.3)*. In the Tax Table, the tax for your taxable income amount will be shown in the column corresponding to your filing status. Filing status (single, married filing jointly, head of household, married filing separately, and qualifying widow/widower) is discussed in *Chapter 1*.

---

**EXAMPLES**

1. You are single, under age 65, and have adjusted gross income for 2018 of $59,595, consisting solely of salary and interest income. You claim the standard deduction *(13.1)*.

| | |
|---|---|
| Adjusted gross income | $59,595 |
| Less: Standard deduction | $12,000 |
| Taxable income | $47,595 |

Your 2018 tax liability from the Tax Table is $6,406, as shown in the column for single persons with taxable income of at least $47,550 but less than $47,600.

2. You are married filing jointly and have 2018 adjusted gross income of $86,190, consisting of salary, pensions and interest. You are over age 65 and your spouse is under age 65. Your standard deduction is $25,300 *(13.4)*, but this is less than your itemized deductions of $26,200, so you claim the itemized deductions.

| | | |
|---|---|---|
| Adjusted gross income | | $86,190 |
| Less: Itemized deductions | $26,200 | |
| Taxable income | | $59,990 |

Your 2018 tax liability from the Tax Table is $6,816, as shown in the column for taxpayers who are married filing jointly with taxable income of at least $59,950 but less than $60,000.

## 22.3 Tax Computation Worksheet

If your taxable income is $100,000 or more and you do not have net capital gain or qualified dividends *(22.4)*, or claim the foreign earned income or housing exclusion *(22.5)*, you must figure your 2018 regular tax liability on Form 1040 using the IRS' Tax Computation Worksheet, which is shown in Part 8 of this book.

Since the Tax Computation Worksheet is used only by taxpayers with taxable incomes of $100,000 or more, it only shows the tax rate brackets that a taxpayer with taxable income of at least $100,000 can be subject to. The Worksheet has four sections (A, B, C, D), one for each filing status. To figure your regular income tax liability using the Tax Computation Worksheet, follow the column-by-column instructions in the section for your filing status. The following Example and *Table 22-1* illustrates the computation for a married couple filing jointly.

**EXAMPLE**

You and your spouse file a joint return reporting taxable income of $142,274 for 2018. You do not have qualified dividends or capital gains or losses to report, so your regular tax liability is figured on the Tax Computation Worksheet. Following the column instructions for Section B of the Worksheet (for joint filers), as shown in *Table 22-1*, you figure a tax of $23,179:

| | |
|---|---|
| $142,274 × 22% rate from column (b) | $ 31,300.28 |
| Less: subtraction amount from column (d) | 8,121.00 |
| Tax | $ 23,179.28 |

**Table 22-1   Sample Section from 2018 Tax Computation Worksheet**
(Section B—Use If your filing status is married filing jointly or qualifying widow(er).
Complete the row below that applies to you, based on your 2018 taxable income.)

| If Taxable Income is— | (a) Enter taxable income— | (b) Multiplication amount— | (c) Multiply (a) by (b)— | (d) Subtraction Amount— | Tax Subtract (d) from (c)— |
|---|---|---|---|---|---|
| At least $100,000 but not over $165,000 | $142,274.00 | × 22% (.22) | $ 31,300.28 | $ 8,121.00 | $ 23,179.28 |
| Over $165,000 but not over $315,000 | | × 24% (.24) | | 11,421.00 | |
| Over $315,000 but not over $400,000 | | × 32% (.32) | | 36,621.00 | |
| Over $400,000 but not over $600,000 | | × 35% (.35) | | 48,621.00 | |
| Over $600,000 | | × 37% (.37) | | 60,621.00 | |

## 22.4 Tax Calculation If You Have Net Capital Gain or Qualified Dividends

If a portion of your taxable income consists of net capital gain (net long-term capital gain in excess of net short-term capital loss *(5.3)*) or qualified dividends *(4.1)*, you should figure your regular tax liability on the Qualified Dividends and Capital Gain Tax Worksheet in the IRS instruction booklet for Form 1040. On the Worksheet, you can apply the favorable capital gain rates *(5.3)* to your net gain and qualified dividends. An example of how to report transactions on Form 8949 and Schedule D (Form 1040) and a filled-in sample of the Qualified Dividends and Capital Gain Tax Worksheet is shown in *5.8*. You may be able to figure your liability on the Qualified Dividends and Capital Gain Tax Worksheet without having to file form 8949 and Schedule D if you have capital gain distributions from Box 2a of Form 1099-DIV *(32.8)* and/or qualified dividends from Box 1b of Form 1099-DIV and no other capital gains or losses.

However, you use a different worksheet if you report any 28% rate gains or unrecaptured Section 1250 gain on Schedule D. In this case, you must use the Schedule D Tax Worksheet *(5.3)* in the Schedule D instructions to figure tax liability.

## 22.5 Foreign Earned Income Tax Worksheet

If you claim the foreign earned income exclusion *(36.1)* on Form 2555 or Form 2555-EZ, or the foreign housing exclusion on Form 2555, you must figure your regular tax liability using the Foreign Earned Income Tax Worksheet in the Form 1040 instructions. The worksheet computation must be used because of the rule requiring non-excluded income to be "stacked" on top of the excluded income, so that the non-excluded income is subject to the same tax rate or rates that would have applied had the foreign exclusions not been elected.

## 22.6 Income Averaging for Farmers and Fishermen

A farmer or fisherman may elect to average 2018 farm or fishing income over three years on Schedule J of Form 1040. On Schedule J, one-third of elected farm or fishing income is allocated to each of 2015, 2016, and 2017. The tax for 2018 equals the tax liability figured without elected farm or fishing income plus increases in tax liability for the three prior years by including allocated elected farm or fishing income. Income averaging is available only to individual farmers or fishermen and may not be elected by estates or trusts engaged in the farming or fishing business. When computing potential AMT on Form 6251 *(23.1)*, regular tax liability is determined without regard to Schedule J averaging. Since AMT liability is based on the excess of tentative AMT over regular tax, ignoring the Schedule J reduction to the regular tax limits or eliminates the AMT.

Elected farm or fishing income is taxable income attributable to a farming or fishing business. A farming business is generally any business that involves cultivating land or raising or harvesting agricultural or horticultural commodities. A fishing business is generally any business involving the actual or attempted catching, taking, or harvesting of fish. See the Schedule J instructions.

A previous election to average farm income may by revoked or the elected farm income may be changed by filing an amended return within the period of limitations for a refund claim *(47.2)*.

## 22.7 Tax Credits

After figuring your 2018 regular tax liability, you may be able to reduce that liability as well as AMT liability *(23.1)* by claiming tax credits. The child tax credit, credit for other dependents, credit for child and dependent care, earned income credit, adoption credit, credit for retirement savings contributions, residential energy credit, plug-in electric drive motor vehicle credit, mortgage interest credit, the premium tax credit, and the health coverage credit are discussed in *Chapter 25*. The education tax credits are discussed in *Chapter 33*. The credit for the elderly is discussed in *Chapter 34* and the foreign tax credit in *Chapter 36*. The business tax credits are discussed in *Chapter 40*. The credit for prior year AMT liability is discussed at *23.5*.

If you worked for more than one employer in 2018 and Social Security taxes of more than $7,960.80 were withheld from your wages, the excess may be claimed as a credit on Schedule 5 (Form 1040) *(26.10)*.

## 22.8    Additional Medicare Tax and Net Investment Income Tax

There is an *0.9%* additional Medicare tax on wages and self-employment income exceeding $250,000 if married filing jointly; $200,000, if single, head of household, or a qualifying widow/widower; or $125,000, if married filing separately. To the extent the tax was not withheld *(26.8)* from your wages, you will have to pay it when you file Form 1040 *(28.2)*.

If you have net investment income (NII), some or all of it will be subject to a *3.8%* tax if you have modified adjusted gross income (MAGI) exceeding the applicable threshold. The same $250,000, $200,000 or $125,000 threshold shown above for the 0.9% tax also applies to the tax on NII except for qualifying widows/widowers, who are treated as married persons filing jointly for purposes of the 3.8% tax. If MAGI exceeds the threshold, the 3.8% tax applies to the lesser of your NII or the MAGI exceeding the threshold *(28.3)*.

# CHAPTER 23

# Alternative Minimum Tax (AMT)

The purpose of AMT is to effectively take back some of the tax breaks allowed for regular tax purposes. The AMT is an additional tax that you may owe if for regular tax purposes you claimed:

- Itemized deductions for taxes or investment expenses.
- Certain tax-exempt interest, accelerated depreciation, and incentive stock option benefits.

There are no specific tests to determine whether or not you are liable for AMT. You must first figure your regular income tax and then *see* whether tax benefit items must be added back to taxable income to figure alternative minimum taxable income, on which the AMT is figured. If after claiming the AMT exemption and applying the AMT rates of 26% and 28% the tentative alternative minimum tax exceeds your regular income tax, the excess is your AMT liability, which is added to the regular tax on your return. In other words, your tax liability for the year will be the greater of your regular tax or your AMT.

AMT liability is figured on Form 6251 and is attached to Form 1040.

## Table 23-1  Key to AMT Rules for 2018

| Item— | AMT Rule— |
|---|---|
| AMT exemptions and tax rates | The exemption shields an equivalent amount of alternative minimum taxable income (AMTI) from the AMT. For 2018, the AMT exemption amounts are $109,400 for married couples filing jointly and qualifying widows/widowers, $70,300 for single taxpayers and heads of households, and $54,700 for married persons filing separately. The exemption amounts are subject to a phaseout, but only if AMTI exceeds $1,000,000 for joint filers and qualifying widows/widowers, or $500,000 for all others *(23.1)*. |
| | AMTI in excess of the exemption (after phaseout if any) is subject to an AMT tax rate of 26% or 28% on Form 6251. For 2017, the 26% rate applies to a balance of $191,100 or less, $95,550 or less if married filing separately. A 28% rate applies to amounts exceeding the $191,100 or $95,550 ceiling for the 26% rate. However, net capital gain and qualified dividends are taxable for AMT at the same capital gain rates (0%, 15%, and 20%) used to figure regular income tax liability *(5.3)*. The resulting tax, reduced by any AMT foreign tax credit, is your tentative AMT liability, but you will have to pay it only to the extent that it exceeds your regular income tax liability |
| AMT taxable income (AMTI) | On Form 6251, you start with your regular Form 1040 taxable income, and then increase (or sometimes decrease) that amount by AMT adjustments and preferences to figure alternative minimum taxable income (AMTI). |
| AMT adjustments and preference items | Itemized deductions for taxes, and in some cases investment interest deductions are not allowed. |
| | The standard deduction is not an allowable AMT deduction. |
| | Tax-exempt interest from certain private activity bonds is taxable for the AMT. |
| | MACRS depreciation is figured under the alternative MACRS system for real estate using 40-year straight-line recovery, and, for personal property, the 150% declining balance method. |
| | For incentive stock options; *see 23.2*. |
| | If you sell qualified small business stock that qualifies for an exclusion *(5.7)*, 7% of the exclusion is a preference item. |
| | Mining exploration and development costs are allowable costs amortized over 10 years. |
| | For long-term contracts, income is generally figured under the percentage-of-completion method. |
| | Pollution control facilities amortization is figured under alternate MACRS. |
| | Alternative tax net operating loss is allowed with adjustments. |
| | Circulation expenditures must be amortized ratably over three years. |
| | Research and experimental expenditures must be amortized ratably over 10 years. |
| | Passive activity losses are recomputed; certain tax-shelter farm losses may not be allowed. |
| Adjusted gross income | In making AMT computations involving adjusted gross income limitations, use adjusted gross income as computed for regular tax purposes. |
| Partnership AMT | If you are a partner, include for AMT your distributive share of the partnership's adjustments and tax preference items. These are reported on Schedule K-1 (Form 1065). The partnership itself does not pay alternative minimum tax. |
| Trust or estate AMT | If you are a beneficiary of an estate or trust, consider for AMT your share of distributable net alternative minimum taxable income shown on Schedule K-1 (Form 1041). The estate or trust must pay tax on any remaining alternative minimum taxable income. |
| S corporation stockholder | If you are a shareholder, consider for AMT your share of the adjustments and tax preference items reported on Schedule K-1 (Form 1120S). |
| Children subject to "kiddie tax" | Children under age 24 who are subject to the "kiddie tax" *(24.3)* for 2018 may have to compute AMT liability on Form 6251. The 2018 AMT exemption for a child subject to the "kiddie tax" generally equals the child's earned income plus $7,650. |

## 23.1 Computing Alternative Minimum Tax on Form 6251

In addition to regular income tax, you might have to pay alternative minimum tax (AMT). To the extent that your tentative AMT figured on Form 6251 exceeds your regular tax liability, the excess is the AMT that you are liable for.

Fewer taxpayers are likely to be subject to the AMT because of the increases to the exemption amount and the phaseout threshold enacted by the Tax Cuts and Jobs Act; *see* below.

If you claim any of the items on the list below, you should complete Form 6251 to determine if you are liable for AMT. The starting point for calculating alternative minimum taxable income (AMTI) on Form 6251 is generally taxable income. Note that the standard deduction is not allowed for AMT purposes; it must be added back to regular taxable income when figuring AMTI. Similarly, the other items on the list below are AMT adjustments and preferences and, generally, some or all of the amount allowed for regular tax purposes must be added back to regular taxable income to calculate AMTI. The item that most commonly gets added back to income when calculating AMTI is state and local taxes. *See* **23.2** for details on the AMT adjustments and preference items.

 *Law Alert*

**Increased AMT Exemptions and Higher Phaseout Thresholds**

The AMT exemption amounts and phaseout thresholds have been increased for 2018 and later years by the Tax Cuts and Jobs Act. For 2018, the exemption amount is $109,400 if you are married filing jointly or a qualifying widow/widower, $70,300 if single or head of household, or $54,700 if married filing separately. The exemption does not begin to phase out until alternative minimum taxable income exceeds $1million if married filing jointly or a qualifying widow/widower, or $500,000 for all others. The exemptions and phaseout thresholds are subject to inflation adjustments for 2019.

### Items subject to AMT:

|     |                                                                              | Check: √ |
| --- | ---------------------------------------------------------------------------- | -------- |
| 1.  | Standard deduction                                                           | ☐        |
| 2.  | Itemized deductions for taxes and investment interest                        | ☐        |
| 3.  | Accelerated depreciation in excess of straight line                          | ☐        |
| 4.  | Income from the exercise of incentive stock options                          | ☐        |
| 5.  | Tax-exempt interest from private activity bonds                              | ☐        |
| 6.  | Intangible drilling costs                                                     | ☐        |
| 7.  | Depletion                                                                     | ☐        |
| 8.  | Circulation expenses                                                          | ☐        |
| 9.  | Mining exploration and development costs                                      | ☐        |
| 10. | Research and experimental costs                                              | ☐        |
| 11. | Pollution control facility amortization                                      | ☐        |
| 12. | Tax-shelter farm income or loss                                              | ☐        |
| 13. | Passive income or loss                                                        | ☐        |
| 14. | Certain installment sale income                                              | ☐        |
| 15. | Income from long-term contracts computed under percentage-of-income method   | ☐        |
| 16. | Net operating loss deduction                                                 | ☐        |
| 17. | Foreign tax credit                                                           | ☐        |
| 18. | Gain on small business stock qualifying for exclusion                         | ☐        |

**Higher AMT exemption amounts for 2018.** The Tax Cuts and Jobs Act substantially raises the AMT exemptions for 2018, compared with what they were for 2017. The 2018 exemptions are $109,400 for married couples filing jointly and qualifying widows/widowers (was $84,500 for 2017), $70,300 for single persons and heads of households (was $54,300 for 2017), and $54,700 for married persons filing separately (was $42,250 for 2017).

The exemption amounts may be reduced under the phaseout rule, but only for taxpayers with very high AMTI as discussed next.

For 2019, the exemption amounts will likely be increased for inflation; *see* the *e-Supplement at jklasser.com*.

**Much higher exemption phaseout thresholds for 2018.** The AMT exemptions are subject to a phaseout rule, but for 2018, most taxpayers will not be subject to the phaseout because of the much higher phaseout thresholds provided by the Tax Cuts and Jobs Act. For 2018, the phaseout threshold is $1 million for married couples filing jointly and qualifying widows/widowers (threshold for 2017 was $160,900) and for all others, the threshold is $500,000 (for 2017 it was $120,700 for single taxpayers and heads of household, and $80,450 for married persons filing separately).

For 2019, the phaseout thresholds will likely be increased for inflation; *see* the *e-Supplement at jklasser.com*.

Under the phaseout formula, the exemption amount is phased out by 25 cents for every dollar of AMTI in excess of the phaseout threshold. This means that the exemption for 2018 is completely phased out when AMTI equals or exceeds: $1,437,600 for married couples filing jointly and qualifying widows/widowers, $781,200 for single taxpayers and heads of household, and $718,800 for married persons filing separately. The Form 6251 instructions have a worksheet for figuring the phaseout.

If a married person filing separately has AMTI exceeding the $718,800 phaseout endpoint, 25% of the excess over $718,800, but no more than $54,700 (the full exemption amount), must be added to the AMTI before applying the AMT rates.

**AMT calculation.** After reducing AMTI by the allowable exemption, the 26% and possibly 28% AMT rate is applied. For 2018, the 26% AMT rate generally applies to the first $191,100 of AMTI, or $95,550 if married filing separately. The 28% rate applies to any balance of the AMTI over $191,100 or $95,550. However, if you had net capital gain or qualified dividends that qualify for reduced capital gains rates (5.3), you apply the same capital gains rate for AMT purposes as for regular income tax purposes; the capital gains calculation is made on page 2 of Form 6251. The boundary between the 26% and 28% brackets will likely be increased for 2019 by an inflation adjustment; *see* the *e-Supplement* at *jklasser.com*.

The resulting tax, less any AMT foreign tax credit, is the tentative AMT, which applies only to the extent it *exceeds* your regular income tax. For this purpose, regular income tax is the tax on Line 11a of Form 1040, *plus* any repayment of advances of the premium tax credit (25.12), with no reduction for tax credits other than the foreign tax credit, *minus* any special averaging tax on a lump-sum distribution (available only if you were born before January 2, 1936 (7.3)). If income averaging was used on Schedule J to figure the regular tax for farm or fishing income (22.6), that tax must be refigured without using averaging for purposes of determining AMT.

The excess, if any, of tentative AMT over the regular tax (modified as required by the Form 6251 instructions) is the AMT liability that you must report as an additional tax on Schedule 2 of Form 1040. You do not have to pay the AMT if your regular tax (adjusted as required) equals or exceeds the tentative AMT.

Follow the line-by-line instructions to Form 6251 to figure your AMT liability, if any.

## 23.2 Adjustments and Preferences for AMT

You have to add back to your income certain tax breaks allowed for regular tax purposes, as described below. In some cases, a negative adjustment reduces AMTI. Some of the items discussed below are technically "preference items" under the Internal Revenue

Code (such as interest from private activity bonds), rather than "adjustments", but the IRS lists them together on Part I of Form 6251 as items that increase or decrease AMTI.

**Taxes.** State, local, and foreign taxes deducted on Schedule A *(16.1)* must be added back to income in figuring alternative minimum taxable income (AMTI).

If you received in 2018 a refund of state or local taxes deducted in a prior year and the refund is reported as income on your 2018 Form 1040 *(11.5–11.6)*, you enter the refund on Form 6251 as a *negative* adjustment that reduces AMTI.

**Investment interest.** If for regular tax purposes you claimed an itemized deduction (Schedule A) for investment interest on Form 4952, or if you deducted investment interest for rental property on Schedule E, you must complete a second Form 4952 to determine if your allowable deduction for AMT is more or less than the itemized deduction, taking into account AMT adjustments and preferences. The difference between the regular tax deduction and the allowable AMT deduction is entered on Form 6251 as a positive adjustment if the regular tax deduction is more, or as a negative adjustment if the AMT amount is more.

**Net operating losses.** A net operating loss (NOL) claimed for regular tax purposes must be recomputed for AMT. The recomputed loss, or ATNOLD (alternative tax net operating loss deduction), is generally the excess of the deductions allowed in figuring AMTI (alternative minimum taxable income) over the income included in AMTI. For example, the nonbusiness deduction adjustment *(40.19)* must be separately figured for the ATNOLD, taking into account only nonbusiness income and deductions included in AMTI. Thus, state and local taxes that are not allowable AMT deductions *(23.2)* do not reduce nonbusiness income in figuring the ATNOLD.

The ATNOLD generally is limited to 90% of AMTI but certain losses (such as qualified disaster losses) are not subject to the 90% limit; *see* the instructions to Form 6251 for further details.

**Tax-exempt interest on private activity bonds.** You generally must increase alternative minimum taxable income (AMTI) by tax-exempt interest on private activity bonds issued after August 7, 1986 and before 2009, and on such bonds issued after 2010, but this does not include qualified 501(3) bonds, New York Liberty bonds, Gulf Opportunity Zone bonds, and Midwestern disaster area bonds. Also, if issued after July 30, 2008, qualified mortgage bonds, veterans' mortgage bonds, and exempt-facility bonds that have at least 95% of the net proceeds going to fund qualified residential rental projects are not treated as private activity bonds for AMT purposes.

Any bonds issued in 2009 and 2010 that would otherwise be treated as private activity bonds are not considered private activity bonds, so the interest on the 2009/2010 bonds does not get added back to AMTI.

**Exclusion on qualifying small business stock.** If you claim an exclusion for gain on the sale of qualified small business stock that you bought before September 28, 2010 *(5.7)*, 7% of the excluded gain must be added as a positive adjustment to AMTI.

**Incentive stock option (ISO) exercised.** For regular tax purposes, you are not taxed when you exercise an incentive stock option (ISO) *(2.16)*. If you acquire stock by exercising an ISO and you dispose of that stock in the same year, the tax treatment under the regular tax and the AMT is the same. No AMT adjustment is required. However, if you do not sell the stock in the same year that the option is exercised, the exercise of an ISO can result in a substantial AMT liability. You generally must increase AMT income by including on Form 6251 the excess, if any, of:

1. The fair market value of the stock acquired through exercise of the option (determined without regard to any lapse restriction) when your rights in the acquired stock first become transferable or when these rights are no longer subject to a substantial risk of forfeiture, over

2. The amount you paid for the stock, including any amount you paid for the ISO used to acquire the stock.

You should have received a Form 3921 from your employer that indicates the number of shares you acquired when you exercised the ISO, the exercise price you paid for each acquired share, and the fair market value of each share on the exercise date. You can use

**Caution**

**Standard Deduction Disallowed for AMT**

If you claimed the standard deduction instead of itemizing deductions (Schedule A, Form 1040),, the standard deduction is not allowed as an AMT deduction.

*Filing Instruction*

**Private Activity Bond Interest**

Private activity bond interest that is subject to AMT is reported in Box 9 of Form 1099-INT.

**Caution**

### Gain on Sale of Incentive Stock Option Stock

Your AMT basis in stock acquired through the exercise of an ISO is increased by the amount of the required AMT adjustment. Keep basis records for both AMT and regular tax purposes, since in the year the stock is sold, the higher AMT basis will reduce (or even eliminate in some cases) the gain reportable for AMT purposes.

these Form 3921 entries to figure the AMT adjustment (fair market value of acquired shares minus the amount you paid).

If in the year you exercise the ISO your rights in the acquired ISO stock are *not* transferable and *are* subject to a substantial risk of forfeiture, you do not report the AMT adjustment until the year your rights become transferable or are no longer forfeitable. However, within 30 days of the transfer to you of the stock acquired through exercise of the ISO, you may elect to include in AMT income for that year the excess of the stock's fair market value (determined without regard to any lapse restriction) over the exercise price; *see* the discussion of the Section 83(b) election at *2.17*.

If you report an AMT adjustment for stock acquired through the exercise of an ISO, increase the AMT basis of the stock by the amount of the adjustment. Since the AMT basis in stock acquired through an ISO is likely to be significantly higher than your regular tax basis, you may have a larger gain for regular tax purposes and a larger loss for AMT purposes in the year you sell the stock. This would produce a negative adjustment for AMT. Follow the Form 6251 instructions to the line for "Dispositions of Property".

**MACRS depreciation.** Depreciation allowed for AMT may differ from that allowed for regular tax purposes. For example, if for regular tax purposes you use the 200% declining balance method to depreciate business equipment with a recovery period of three, five, seven, or 10 years *(42.5)*, the difference between the regular depreciation and the 150% declining balance rate method allowed for AMT is generally an adjustment that increases alternative minimum taxable income, but there is an exception for property eligible for bonus depreciation *(42.20)*; *see* the Form 6251 instructions.

There is no AMT adjustment for real estate placed in service after 1999. For real estate placed in service before 1999, the adjustment is the difference between the straight-line depreciation claimed for regular tax purposes using the recovery period discussed in *42.12* and the straight-line recovery over the AMT 40-year recovery period.

The adjustment for MACRS may result in providing more depreciation for AMT purposes where the AMT depreciation computation towards the latter part of the useful life of the property provides larger deductions than the regular MACRS deduction. If the AMT deduction exceeds the regular tax deduction, the difference is entered as a negative adjustment that reduces alternative minimum taxable income.

**Basis adjustment affects AMT gain or loss.** When post-1986 depreciable assets are sold, gain for AMT purposes is figured on the basis of the property as adjusted by depreciation claimed for AMT purposes. This gain or loss will be different from the gain or loss figured for regular tax purposes where regular MACRS depreciation was used.

**Oil and gas costs.** Independent oil and gas producers and royalty owners do not have to refigure depletion deductions for the AMT. Excess intangible drilling costs (IDC) are generally not treated as a preference item unless they exceed 40% of AMT income; *see* the instructions to Form 6251.

**Mining exploration and development costs.** Unless the optional 10-year deduction was elected for regular tax purposes for mining exploration and development costs, the costs must be amortized ratably over a 10-year period for AMT purposes. The difference between the regular tax deduction and AMT deduction is entered on Form 6251 as an adjustment (positive or negative).

If a mine is abandoned as worthless, all mining exploration and development costs that have not been written off are deductible in the year of abandonment.

**Circulation costs.** If circulation costs were deducted in full for regular tax purposes (instead of using the optional three-year write-off), they must be amortized over three years for the AMT. The difference between the two allowable deductions must be reported as an adjustment on Form 6251, as either a positive or negative amount.

**Long-term contracts.** The use of the completed contract method of accounting or certain other methods of accounting for long-term contracts is generally not allowable for AMT. The percentage of completion method must be used to figure the AMT income from a long-term contract. However, there is an exception for home construction contracts.

The difference between the regular tax and AMT income is an AMT adjustment, either positive or negative.

**Research and experimental expenditures.** Costs must be amortized over 10 years for AMT purposes if incurred in a business in which you are not a material participant. The difference between the regular tax and AMT deductions must be entered as an adjustment (positive or negative) on Form 6251.

**Passive tax-shelter farm losses.** Generally, no AMT loss is deductible for any tax-shelter farm activity. A tax-shelter farm activity is any farming syndicate or any farming activity in which you do not materially participate. You may be treated as a material participant if a member of your family materially participates or you meet certain retirement or disability tests discussed at *10.6*.

Gains and losses reported for regular tax purposes from tax-shelter farm activities must be refigured by taking into account any AMT adjustments and preferences. However, a refigured loss is not allowed for AMT purposes except to the extent that you are insolvent at the end of the year. This means that you deduct the loss to the extent of your insolvency. Insolvency is the excess of liabilities over fair market value of assets. Any AMT-disallowed loss is carried forward to later years in which there is gain from that same activity, or until you dispose of the activity.

**Passive losses from nonfarming activities.** The passive losses are reduced by preference or adjustment items not allowed for AMT purposes. For example, an adjustment for MACRS depreciation is made directly against the passive loss and is not treated as a separate AMT adjustment item. The loss allowed for AMT purposes is increased by the amount by which you are insolvent at the end of the year. See the instructions to Form 6251, which suggest that you figure the AMT adjustment of passive losses on a separate Form 8582 that you do not file.

## 23.3 Tax Credits Allowed Against AMT

The only tax credit allowed in computing tentative alternative minimum tax liability on Form 6251 is a revised version of the foreign tax credit allowed for regular tax purposes. The allowable credit is generally based on foreign source AMT income. If the AMT foreign tax credit exceeds the limits detailed in the Form 6251 instructions, the unused amount generally may be carried back or forward; follow the Form 6251 instructions.

The AMT foreign tax credit reduces the tentative AMT figured on Form 6251 before comparing it to your regular tax liability. You subtract your regular tax from the tentative AMT, and if the result is more than zero, that is your actual AMT liability.

If there is an AMT liability on Form 6251, you enter the AMT as a separate tax on Schedule 2 of Form 1040. If you are entitled to any nonrefundable personal tax credits (including the child tax credit, dependent care credit, education credits, adoption credit, saver's credit; *see 25.1*), you may use them to offset your AMT as well as your regular tax liability.

## 23.4 Regular Tax Credit for Prior-Year AMT

You may be able to reduce your regular 2018 tax liability by a tax credit based on AMT incurred in prior years. The prior-year AMT had to be attributable to "deferral items" such as the ISO adjustment or depreciation that provide only a temporary difference to taxable income. Use Form 8801 to figure the credit. The credit is not allowed for 2018 unless your regular tax liability (as reduced by allowable tax credits) for 2018 exceeds your tentative alternative minimum tax liability for 2018 as shown on Form 6251.

## 23.5 Avoiding AMT

If you are within the range of the AMT tax, review periodically your income and expenses to determine whether to postpone or accelerate income, defer the payment of expenses, and/or make certain tax elections.

There are elections, such as the election of alternative straight-line MACRS depreciation, that may avoid AMT adjustments. However, such elections will increase your regular tax. Similarly, adjustment treatment for mining exploration and development costs, circulation expenses, and research expenses can be avoided by elections to amortize *(23.2)*.

If you are on the verge of becoming subject to the AMT, or are already subject to the AMT, and the 26% or 28% AMT rate exceeds your top rate for regular tax purposes you might want to consider the following steps:

- Postpone income that could trigger AMT by pushing your income over the AMT exemption. On a sale of property, an installment sale *(5.21)* can spread gain over a number of years.

- Do not prepay state or local income taxes or property taxes, as these are not deductible under the AMT.

- Spread out the exercise of incentive stock options (ISOs) over more than one year to limit the AMT adjustment for the bargain element (the difference between the option price and the fair market value of the stock on the date of exercise). If you exercise an ISO and hold the acquired stock beyond the end of the year, the bargain element is subject to AMT *(23.2)*. You may find yourself with an unexpected tax liability and if the stock has depreciated in value since the date of exercise, you may find yourself short of funds to pay the liability even after selling the stock. To limit the AMT adjustment, you can stagger the exercise of options over more than one year. You can avoid the adjustment completely by selling the stock in the same year that the option was exercised, but if you do, any gain on the sale will be taxed as ordinary income and not at the favorable rate for long-term capital gains.

**Accelerating income.** If you are generally in a tax bracket higher than the 26% or 28% AMT rate and project that you will be subject to AMT in a current year, you may want to subject additional income in that year to the 26% or 28% AMT tax rate. In such a case, consider accelerating the receipt of income to that year. If you are in business, you might ask for earlier payments from customers or clients. If you control a small corporation, you might prepay your salary or pay yourself a larger bonus, but be careful in the subsequent year not to run afoul of the reasonable compensation rule.

# CHAPTER 24

# Computing the "Kiddie Tax" on Your Child's Unearned Income

If the "kiddie tax" applies to a child, the child's 2018 investment income in excess of $2,100 is taxed at the tax rates for estates and trusts. Under the Tax Cuts and Jobs Act, the kiddie tax computation is no longer based on the tax rate of the parents or affected by the unearned income of siblings.

The kiddie tax applies not only to children under age 18, but also to children who are age 18 or full-time students age 19–23 who do not have earned income exceeding half of their support (24.2). Only investment income of a child over $2,100 is subject to the kiddie tax, not wages or self-employment earnings.

The kiddie tax is generally figured on Form 8615 as part of the computation of the child's regular tax liability for the year. The liability from Form 8615 is then entered on the child's tax return, and Form 8615 is attached. Instead of completing Form 8615, the parent of a child under age 19 (or under 24 if a full-time student) may elect on Form 8814 to report the child's investment income on the parent's own return, provided the child received only interest and dividend income. If the parent elects on Form 8814 to report the child's investment income, the tax on the child's income could be higher than if a separate return for the child was filed (24.4).

## 24.1 Filing Your Child's Return

To discourage substantial income splitting of investment income between parents and minor children, the tax law has complicated income reporting for parents and children by:

1. Imposing a "kiddie tax" that taxes a child's investment income over an annual floor ($2,100 for 2018) at the tax rates and brackets for estates and trusts (24.3). The kiddie tax applies not only to children under age 18, but also to most 18-year-olds and students under age 24 (24.2).

2. Barring a child who is treated as another taxpayer's dependent (21.1) from treating some other person as a dependent on his or her own tax return.

3. Limiting the standard deduction for a dependent child who has only investment income. For 2018 the deduction is $1,050 (13.5).

**Does your child have to file?** For a child who can be claimed as a dependent either as a qualifying child or a qualifying relative (21.1), the income filing threshold for 2018 is generally $1,050. If your dependent child has gross income (earned and investment income) of $1,050 or less for 2018, he or she is not subject to tax and does not have to file a tax return.

A 2018 return must be filed for a dependent child with investment income exceeding $350 and gross income of more than $1,050. If a dependent child has salary or other earned income but no investment income, a return does not have to be filed unless such earned income exceeds $12,000 for 2018. If your child's only income is from interest and dividends, you may be able to make an election to report the income on your own return, but this generally is not advisable (24.4).

A dependent child is allowed to claim at least a $1,050 standard deduction. A dependent child with earned income over $1,050 may claim a standard deduction up to those earnings plus an additional $350, but no more than the basic standard deduction, which is generally $12,000 (13.1).

### EXAMPLES

1. Your 14-year-old son, whom you claim as your dependent, has interest and dividend income of $480 and no other income for 2018. He has no income tax liability and does not have to file a return.

| | |
|---|---|
| Interest and dividend income | $480 |
| Less: standard deduction (13.5) | 1,050 |
| Tax liability | 0 |

2. In 2018, your 17-year-old daughter, whom you claim as your dependent, has interest income of $500 and qualified dividends (4.2) of $750. Her taxable income is $200.

| | |
|---|---|
| Interest income | $500 |
| Qualified dividends | 750 |
| | $1,250 |
| Less: standard deduction | 1,050 |
| Taxable income | $200 |

**How to file a 2018 return for your child.** If your child is not subject to the "kiddie tax" under the rules at 24.2, follow the regular filing rules and report the child's income and deductions on Form 1040. Since the "kiddie tax" computation does not apply, all of the child's income will be taxed at his or her own tax rate. If your child is unable to sign his or her tax return, you must do so (1.13).

If the kiddie tax computation applies (24.2), Form 8615 must be filed to compute the kiddie tax unless your child's only income is interest and dividends and you elect to report your child's investment earnings on your own return *(24.4)*. On Form 8615 you must provide your Social Security number and taxable income. Form 8615 is attached to the child's tax return *(24.3)*.

**Child's AMT liability.** A child who has substantial tax-exempt interest, tax preferences, or tax adjustments subject to the alternative minimum tax must compute tentative AMT liability on Form 6251; *see Chapter 23.*

You must file a 2018 Form 1040 for your daughter because she has taxable income, but the kiddie tax computation does not apply because her investment income does not exceed $2,100. On the Qualified Dividends and Capital Gain Tax Worksheet in the Form 1040 instructions, the $200 of taxable income will be attributed to the interest income and subject to your daughter's 10% tax rate and the qualified dividends will not be taxed at all because the 0% rate for qualified dividends and capital gains applies *(4.2)*.

## 24.2 Children Subject to "Kiddie Tax" for 2018

Form 8615 for 2018 must be filed for your child if all of the following conditions are met:

- Your child either (1) was under age 18 at the end of 2018, (2) was age 18 at the end of 2018 and did not have earned income exceeding half of his or her support for the year, or (3) was a full-time student during 2018 who at the end of the year was age 19 through 23 and did not have earned income exceeding half of his or her support for the year.

- For children born on January 1, the IRS treats the child's birthday as being on the last day of the prior year. Thus, a child who attains age 24 on January 1, 2019, is considered to be age 24, not 23, on December 31, 2018, and so the kiddie tax does not apply to the child's 2018 investment income under test (3) above for full-time students.

- For purposes of determining if the kiddie tax applies under tests (2) or (3) above, use the dependent rules for figuring full-time student status *(21.3)* and support *(21.5)*.

- Your child had more than $2,100 of investment income for 2018. The $2,100 floor is increased, as discussed below, if the child has itemized deductions exceeding $1,050 that are directly connected to the production of investment income.

- If married, your child files a separate 2018 return from his or her spouse.

If both of a child's parents were deceased at the end of 2018, the kiddie tax computation does not apply regardless of the above tests, and the child's tax is figured under the regular rules.

**Exceptions for children filing jointly and distributions from qualified disability trusts.** A married child can be subject to the kiddie tax only if he or she files separately; kiddie tax does not apply if a joint return is filed.

If a child is a beneficiary of a qualified disability trust (see the Form 8615 instructions), distributions of investment income from the trust are treated as earned income and thus not subject to the kiddie tax rules.

**Reporting child's unearned income on child's or parent's return.** The kiddie tax computation is generally made on Form 8615, which must be attached to your child's return. However, if your child is under age 19 or a full-time student under age 24 and his or her only income is interest and dividends and other tests are met, you may elect on Form 8814 to include your child's unearned income on your own tax return, instead of computing the kiddie tax on Form 8615 *(24.4)*.

**Kiddie tax on Form 8615 applies to investment income exceeding $2,100 floor.** If your child files his or her own 2018 return, the "kiddie tax" computation on Form 8615 applies to the child's net unearned income. For purposes of this rule, net unearned income equals gross unearned income minus $2,100 if your child does not itemize deductions on Schedule A. Thus, if your child does not itemize, the first $2,100 of unearned income is exempt from the kiddie tax. Unearned income exceeding $2,100 is considered net unearned income subject to the kiddie tax; *see* Example 1 below.

Unearned income includes all taxable income that is not earned income (compensation for personal services). Include taxable interest income (but not tax-exempt interest), dividends, capital gain distributions and capital gains on the sale of property, royalties, rents, and taxable pension payments. Payments from a trust are generally included to the extent of distributable net income, but, as noted earlier, there is an exception for distributions from qualified disability trusts, which are treated as earned income and thus not subject to the kiddie tax. Income in custodial accounts is treated as the child's income and is subject to the kiddie tax computation. Capital losses first offset capital gains, and any excess loss offsets up to $3,000 of other investment income.

Unearned income on all of your child's property must be considered, even if the property was a gift from you or someone else, or if the property was produced from your child's wages, such as a bank account into which the wages were deposited. The wages themselves, or self-employment earnings, are not considered.

If your child does itemize deductions on Schedule A (Form 1040) and has more than $1,050 of deductions that are directly connected to the production of investment income, the $2,100 floor is increased. The floor is $1,050 plus the directly connected deductions. If the directly connected deductions are $1,050 or less, the regular $2,100 kiddie tax exemption applies, as in Example 2 below. Directly connected itemized deductions are expenses paid to produce the unearned income. If, after you subtract the itemized deductions, your child's net unearned income exceeds his or her taxable income, you apply the kiddie tax to the lower taxable income, rather than to the net unearned income.

---

### EXAMPLE

For 2018, your 16-year- old son who qualifies as your dependent has dividend income of $2,750. After taking into account a standard deduction of $1,050, his taxable income is $1,700, of which $650 is subject to the kiddie tax computation on Form 8615.

| Figuring taxable income: | |
|---|---|
| Dividend income | $2,750 |
| Less: standard deduction | 1,050 |
| Taxable income | $1,700 |
| Income subject to kiddie tax on Form 8615: | |
| Investment income | $2,750 |
| Less: $2,100 floor | $2,100 |
| Subject to kiddie tax | $650 |

---

## 24.3 Computing "Kiddie Tax" on Child's Return

If your child is subject to the "kiddie tax" *(24.2)* for 2018, your child's regular income tax liability is computed on Form 8615, which is attached to his or her return, unless you make the parent's election to report the child's dividends and interest income on your own return *(24.4)*.

On Form 8615 (*see* sample below), your child's unearned income over the $2,100 floor *(24.2)* is taxed using the tax brackets and rates for trusts and estates. The tax computation is no longer based on the tax rate of the child's parents, as it was before 2018.

If none of the child's taxable income is from qualified dividends or net capital gain (such as where it includes only taxable interest, ordinary dividends that are not qualified dividends, rental income, or royalties), the regular income tax rates and brackets for trusts and estates apply. For 2018, the rates are: 10% on the first $2,550 of taxable income, 24% on taxable income over $2,550 and up to $9,150, 35% on taxable income over $9,150 and up to $12,500, and 37% on taxable income over $12,500. These rates are applied on the "2018 Line 7 Tax Computation Worksheet" in the instructions to Form 8615.

If taxable income includes any qualified dividends or net capital gain, a modified version of the Qualified Dividends and Capital Gain Tax Worksheet in the Form 1040 instructions (*see* sample at *5.8*) must be used to figure the tax on the taxable income. In general, the trust and estate rate brackets for qualified dividends/net capital gain are: 0% if taxable income does not exceed $2,600, 15% if taxable income is over $2,600 and up to $12,700, or 20% if taxable income exceeds $12,700. However, to take into account these rates for qualified dividends/net capital gain, as well as the rates for the portion of taxable income attributable to other types of unearned income, you must follow the Form 8615 worksheet instructions.

**Estimating the kiddie tax in case of filing delay.** If the child's taxable income, net unearned income, or filing status for 2018 is not known by the filing due date of April 15, 2019, reasonable estimates may be used on a timely filed Form 8615. When the correct details become available, an amended return for the child should be filed on Form 1040X.

Instead of estimating the kiddie tax, you may file Form 4868 to get a six-month extension *(46.3)* for the child's return on which the kiddie tax is included. However, interest will be charged on any tax due that was not paid by the original filing date, and late payment penalties may also apply *(46.3)*.

## 24.4 Parent's Election To Report Child's Dividends and Interest

Instead of filing a separate return for your child *(24.3)* whose income is subject to the "kiddie tax," you may elect on Form 8814 to report your child's income and compute the kiddie tax on your own 2018 return if all of the following tests are met:

- The child was under age 19, or under age 24 if a full-time student *(24.2)* at the end of 2018;
- The child's only 2018 income is from interest and dividends (including mutual fund capital gain distributions and Alaska Permanent Fund dividends);
- The total interest, dividends, and capital gain distributions are over $1,050 but less than $10,500;
- Estimated tax payments were not made in the child's name and Social Security number for 2018 and there was no overpayment from the child's 2017 return applied to his or her 2018 estimated tax; and
- The child was not subject to 2018 backup withholding.

On Form 8814, you determine the portion of the child's qualified dividends and capital gain distributions that you report on your own return, where they are eligible for the preferential rates *(5.3)* for qualified dividends/net capital gains. You report the balance of the child's investment income over $2,100 as "other income" on Line 21 of Schedule 1 (Form 1040). You also figure an additional tax equal to the smaller of $105 or 10% of your child's income over $1,050, which is included in the regular income tax liability you enter on Line 11 of your Form 1040.

If the parents are married filing separately, or are divorced, separated, or living apart for the last six months of the year, the custodial parent (with whom child lived with most of the year) is the parent who may make the election on Form 8814. If unmarried parents lived together with the child, the parent with the higher taxable income may make the election.

**The election can have major disadvantages.** For most taxpayers, the only advantage in making the election is to skip the paperwork involved in preparing a return in the child's name or returns in the children's names. This could save you money in the form of reduced tax preparation costs. In some cases, the increase in your income could allow you to deduct more charitable contributions *(14.17)*. Reporting your child's interest or dividends increases your net investment income, which may allow you to claim a larger deduction for investment interest *(15.10)*, but if you are close to or already over the threshold for the additional 3.8% tax on net investment income *(28.3)*, making the election could subject you to or increase your liability for the 3.8% tax.

There is a distinct disadvantage to the election if your child's investment income consists of qualified dividends or capital gain distributions. With the election, there is a 10% tax on the child's income between $1,050 and $2,100 (the income not subject to kiddie tax), whereas if a separate return is filed for the child, it is highly likely that the qualified dividends and capital gain distributions will escape tax entirely under the zero percent rate *(5.3, 24.3)*.

If you elect to report the child's interest and dividends on your own return, you may not claim any deductions that your child would have been able to claim on his or her own return such as the additional standard deduction for blindness, itemized deductions such as charitable donations or investment interest, or the above-the-line deduction for the penalty on premature withdrawals from a savings account.

Finally, including the child's investment income as your own may create these disadvantages by increasing your AGI:

- Make it more difficult to deduct medical deductions because of the AGI floor *(17.1)*.

- Reduce tax credits subject to income limits, such as the child tax credit *(25.2)*, the dependent care credit *(25.5)*, or the education tax credits *(33.7)*.

- Limit a deduction for IRA contributions under the phaseout rules *(8.4)*.

- Limit a deduction for student loan interest *(33.13)*.

- Limit your ability to claim the special $25,000 rental loss allowance under the passive activity rules *(10.2)*.

- Increase local and state tax liability.

- As noted earlier, subject you to or increase your liability for the additional 3.8% tax on net investment income *(28.3)*.

- Increase liability for the alternative minimum tax. In figuring whether you owe alternative minimum tax (AMT) on Form 6251, you must include, as a tax preference item, interest income your child receives from specified private activity bonds *(23.3)*; *see* the Form 6251 instructions.

- Subject you to an estimated tax penalty *(27.1)*. If you did not account for the child's income when planning your 2018 withholdings or estimated tax installments, you could face an estimated tax penalty if you make the election on Form 8814 for 2018. If you plan to report your child's income on your 2019 return, provide for the tax in your estimated tax payments or withholdings during 2019.

**!** *Caution*

**Reporting Child's Income on Your Return**

Including the child's income on your return could be disadvantageous not only by subjecting the income to a higher tax rate (than on the child's own return), but also by making it more difficult for you to claim certain deductions and tax credits and raising your state and local taxes.

---

## Sample Form 8615—Tax for Certain Children Who Have Unearned Income

| Form **8615** | **Tax for Certain Children Who Have Unearned Income** | OMB No. 1545-0074 |
|---|---|---|
| Department of the Treasury Internal Revenue Service (99) | ▶ Attach to your Form 1040 or Form 1040NR. ▶ Go to *www.irs.gov/Form8615* for instructions and the latest information. | 20**18** Attachment Sequence No. **33** |

| Name shown on return | Your social security number |
|---|---|

**Before you begin:** If you must use the Schedule D Tax Worksheet or have income from farming or fishing, see the instructions. Also see **Pub. 929,** Tax Rules for Children and Dependents. It explains how to figure your tax using the **Schedule D Tax Worksheet** or **Schedule J** (Form 1040).

| A Parent's name (first, initial, and last). **Caution:** See instructions before completing. | B Parent's social security number |
|---|---|

**Part I  Net Unearned Income**

| | | | |
|---|---|---|---|
| 1 | Enter your unearned income (see instructions) . . . . . . . . . . . . . . . . | **1** | |
| 2 | If you **did not** itemize deductions on **Schedule A** (Form 1040 or Form 1040NR), enter $2,100. Otherwise, see instructions . . . . . . . . . . . . . . . . . . . . | **2** | |
| 3 | Subtract line 2 from line 1. If zero or less, **stop;** do not complete the rest of this form but **do** attach it to your return . . . . . . . . . . . . . . . . . . . . . | **3** | |
| 4 | Enter your **taxable income** from Form 1040, line 10, or Form 1040NR, line 41. If you file Form 2555 or 2555-EZ, see the instructions | **4** | |
| 5 | Enter the **smaller** of line 3 or line 4. If zero, **stop;** do not complete the rest of this form but **do** attach it to your return . . . . . . . . . . . . . . . . | **5** | |

**Part II  Tax**

| | | | |
|---|---|---|---|
| 6 | Subtract line 5 from line 4 . . . . . . . . . . . . . . . | **6** | |
| 7 | Enter the tax on the amount on line 4 (see instructions). If the Qualified Dividends and Capital Gain Tax Worksheet, Schedule D Tax Worksheet, or Schedule J (Form 1040) is used to figure the tax, check here. If applicable, include this amount on your Form 1040, line 11, or Form 1040NR, line 42 (see instructions). If you file Form 2555 or 2555-EZ, see the instructions . . . . . . . ▶ ☐ | **7** | |

For Paperwork Reduction Act Notice, see your tax return instructions.          Cat. No. 64113U          Form **8615** (2018)

# CHAPTER 25

# Personal Tax Credits Reduce Your Tax Liability

In this chapter you will find discussions of the child tax credit, dependent care credit, earned income credit (EIC), adoption credit, retirement savings credit, mortgage interest credit, credit for plug-in electric vehicles, the premium tax credit, the residential energy credits and the health coverage credit for displaced workers. Education tax credits are discussed in *Chapter 33*.

The child tax credit is $2,000 for each qualifying dependent child under age 17. There is also a new $500 credit for other dependents. To claim these credits, you must follow the steps on the "Child Tax Credit and Credit for Other Dependents Worksheet" in the Form 1040 instructions. Both credits are subject to the same phaseout rule *(25.3, 25.4)*. If the child tax credit exceeds your tax liability, you may be entitled to a refundable credit called the "additional child tax credit" *(25.3)*.

Depending on your income, the child and dependent care credit is 20% to 35% of up to $3,000 of care expenses for one dependent and up to $6,000 of expenses for two or more dependents. If your adjusted gross income exceeds $43,000, the maximum credit is $600 for one dependent and $1,200 for two or more dependents *(25.5)*.

The earned income credit (EIC) is provided to low-income workers who support children, and a limited credit is allowed to certain workers without qualifying children *(25.6)*.

An adoption credit of up to $13,810 may be claimed on your 2018 return for costs of adopting a child under the age of 18 or a disabled person incapable of self-care *(25.8)*.

The premium tax credit applies to taxpayers with income within specified limits who obtain health coverage through a government Marketplace (also called exchange). Taxpayers who received an advance of the credit during 2018 to help pay their premiums must reconcile, on Form 8962, the advanced amount with the actual credit allowed for the year *(25.12)*.

## 25.1 Overview of Personal Tax Credits

After you determine your regular tax liability using the tax table *(22.2)*, Tax Computation Worksheet *(22.3)*, or capital gain worksheets *(22.4)*, and your AMT liability if any *(23.1)*, you may be able to reduce that liability by one or more tax credits. Most tax credits are nonrefundable, meaning that they are limited by your tax liability. All nonrefundable personal credits, including the child tax credit, dependent care credit, education credits, saver's credit and the adoption credit, may be claimed to the full extent of regular tax liability plus alternative minimum tax (AMT) liability.

The additional child tax credit, the net premium tax credit, the earned income credit, and in part, the American Opportunity credit, are refundable, meaning that if the credit exceeds your tax liability you will receive a refund for the excess.

Eligibility rules and credit limitations for many of the personal credits are discussed in this chapter, while some are discussed in other chapters as shown below. Business tax credits are in *Chapter 40*.

Child tax credit and additional child tax credit (25.2–25.3).

Credit for other dependents (25.4)

Child and dependent care credit *(25.5–25.6)*.

Earned income credit *(25.7–25.8)*.

Adoption credit *(25.9–25.10)*.

Qualified retirement savings contributions credit *(25.11–25.12)*.

Premium tax credit (25.13).

Health coverage credit (25.14).

Mortgage interest credit (25.15).

Residential energy tax credits (25.16).

Plug-in electric vehicle credit (25.17).

Repayment of the first-time homebuyer credit (25.18).

Education credits (American Opportunity and Lifetime Learning credits) *(33.7–33.9)*.

Credit for elderly or disabled *(34.7–34.9)*.

Foreign tax credit (36.13).

Prior-year AMT credit (23.4).

Credit for excess Social Security or Railroad Retirement withholdings (26.8).

Credit for tax on mutual fund undistributed capital gain (32.6).

## 25.2 Child Tax Credit for Children Under Age 17

For 2018 through 2025, the Tax Cuts and Jobs Act doubles the amount of the child tax credit to $2,000 per qualifying child. As under prior law, the credit may only be claimed for a qualifying child who is under age 17 at the end of the year (see "qualifying child" below). Under the new law, the credit is now available to many more taxpayers than previously because the threshold for phasing out the credit has been substantially raised: the credit will not begin to phase out until modified adjusted gross income (MAGI) exceeds $400,000 if married filing jointly, or $200,000 for all others *(25.3)*.

To figure the exact amount of your child tax credit on your 2018 return, you must complete the "Child Tax Credit and Credit for Other Dependents Worksheet" in the IRS instructions to Form 1040 *(see* sample Worksheet on page 810). On the IRS worksheet, you determine if the potential credit ($2,000 × number of qualifying children) is limited by the phaseout rule *(25.3)*. Whether or not the phaseout applies, the tentative credit (either full credit or reduced amount after phaseout) is compared with your tax liability (regular tax plus AMT minus specified credits), and the smaller amount is the allowable child tax credit. However, if your child tax credit is limited to your tax liability, part or all of the excess credit may be refundable as an additional credit (ACTC) if your earned income exceeds $2,500 or you have three or more children *(25.3)*.

If you are eligible for the credit for other dependents *(25.4)* as well as for the child tax credit, both credits are combined on the "Child Tax Credit and Credit for Other Dependents Worksheet" and the same phaseout rule and liability limitation applies to both credits.

*Law Alert*

**Valid SSN for Child Needed by Due Date of Return**

You (and your spouse if filing jointly) must have a valid Social Security number (SSN) by the due date for filing your 2018 return (plus extensions if any) to claim the child tax credit or the additional child tax credit (ACTC) *(25.3)* for 2018. If you are not eligible for a SSN, you must have an ITIN by the return due date (with extensions). If the SSN or ITIN has not been issued by the due date (with extensions), you cannot claim the child tax credit or the ACTC on your original return, or on an amended return if you get the number later.

In addition, under The Tax Cuts and Jobs Act, each qualifying child must have a SSN (that is valid for employment) issued before the due date of your return (with extensions). If the required SSN is not obtained by the due date (with extensions), you cannot claim the child tax credit or ACTC for that child, either on your original return, or on an amended return if you get the number later. However, if a qualifying child does not have the required SSN by your filing due date, you may treat that child as your dependent for purposes of claiming the credit for other dependents *(25.4)*.

**Qualifying child.** You can claim the child tax credit (and, if applicable, the ACTC) for a child who is under age 17 at the end of 2018 if the child is your "qualifying child" under the rules for dependents (*21.2* and *21.3*), and you are not disqualified from claiming that child as your dependent (see "Additional tests for treating someone as your dependent" in *21.2*). Note that the age test for the child tax credit is lower than the age test under the general definition of qualifying child (*21.2* and *21.3*). If the child is age 17 or older at the end of 2018, you cannot claim the child tax credit (or ACTC) for that child, even if he or she is your qualifying child for other purposes (*21.2*), such as to claim head of household status or the itemized deduction for medical expenses of dependents.

The qualifying child rules require the child to live with you for over half the year and not provide over half of his or her own support (*21.2*). The child may be your child, stepchild, grandchild, great-grandchild, brother, sister, stepbrother, stepsister, half-brother or -sister, or the descendant of any of these. An adopted child qualifies for a 2018 credit if placed with you by an authorized agency for legal adoption, even if the adoption is not final by the end of 2018. A foster child placed with you by a court or an authorized agency qualifies.

For purposes of the child tax credit and the ACTC (*25.3*), the child must be a U.S. citizen, U.S. resident alien (*1.18*), or U.S. national. An adopted child who would not otherwise meet this test is treated as a U.S. citizen if you are a U.S. citizen or national and he or she lived with you all year.

The child must have a Social Security number (SSN) that was issued before the due date of your return (including extensions). The SSN must be valid for employment; this test is automatically met if the child was a U.S. citizen when receiving the SSN. If the child is a qualifying child but lacks the required SSN, you cannot claim the child tax credit or the additional child tax credit (ACTC) for that child, but you may claim the credit for other dependents for the child (*25.4*).

**Did the IRS reduce or deny your 2016 or 2017 credit?** If the IRS reduced or disallowed your 2017 child tax credit or additional child tax credit (*25.3*) for any reason other than a math or clerical error on your part, you must complete and attach Form 8862 to your 2018 return to document your eligibility to claim a credit for 2018. If your 2016 credit was reduced or disallowed, file Form 8862 with your 2018 return unless you filed it with your 2017 return and the IRS allowed your 2017 credit.

If the child tax credit or ACTC is disallowed because you recklessly or intentionally disregarded the rules, you will not be allowed to claim the credit for the next two years, and if you fraudulently claimed it, the disallowance period increases to 10 years.

## 25.3 Figuring the Child Tax Credit and Additional Child Tax Credit

You use the Child Tax Credit and Credit for Other Dependents Worksheet in the IRS Form 1040 instructions or in Publication 972 (if required by the Form 1040 instructions) to figure the credit. You do not attach the worksheet to your return.

**Phaseout formula.** The $2,000 per qualifying child credit for 2018 is phased out if your modified adjusted gross income (MAGI) exceeds the phaseout threshold, which is:

- $200,000 if your filing status is single, head of household, qualifying widow/widower, or married filing separately, or
- $400,000 if you are married filing jointly

*Note that these thresholds will not be indexed after 2018 for inflation.*

The maximum credit of $2,000 per qualifying child is reduced by 5%, or $50 for each $1,000 (or fraction of $1,000) that your MAGI exceeds the phaseout threshold. In most cases, MAGI is the same as the AGI reported on your Form 1040 (Line 7). However, if you claim the foreign earned income exclusion, foreign housing exclusion or deduction, or possession exclusion for American Samoa residents, these amounts must be added back to AGI to get MAGI for credit purposes.

Since the phaseout percentage is 5%, one $2,000 credit is generally completely phased out when MAGI exceeds the phaseout threshold by $40,000 ($2,000 credit/.05 = $40,000 phaseout range). However, because of the "round up" rule for excess amounts that are not a multiple of $1,000, any excess of more than $39,000 but less than $40,000 ($39,001 through $39,999) will be rounded up to $40,000 and the $2,000 credit will be completely phased out. Thus, for a parent who is single, the phaseout of one $2,000 credit will be complete when MAGI is $239,001 or more. For married persons filing jointly, the phaseout of one $2,000 credit will be complete when MAGI is $439,001 or more.

If there are two qualifying children, both $2,000 credits ($4,000 total) are completely phased out when MAGI exceeds the phaseout threshold by $80,000 (2 × $40,000), but because of the "round up " rule, an excess of $79,001 through $79,999 is treated the same as an excess of $80,000. Thus, if you are married filing jointly with two qualifying children, the credits for both of them are completely phased out when MAGI is  $479,001 or more.

If your MAGI exceeds your phaseout threshold, follow the steps of the Child Tax Credit and Credit for Other Dependents Worksheet to figure how much of your credit is phased out. *See* Examples 2 and 3 below.

After applying the phaseout rule, you must apply the liability limitation discussed next.

**Liability limitation.**  On the Child Tax Credit and Credit for Other Dependents Worksheet, the child tax credit is limited to your tax liability where the liability is less than the otherwise allowable credit (either the full credit or reduced credit if part is phased out). Your tax liability is the regular tax plus alternative minimum tax and repayment of excess advance payment of the premium tax credit, if any,, reduced on the worksheet by certain other credits that you claim. If your liability equals or exceeds the otherwise allowable credit, the liability limit does not reduce the allowable credit. If your child tax credit is limited to your tax liability, you may be able to claim the "additional child tax credit" (ACTC), which is refundable up to a limit of $1,400 per qualifying child; *see* below.

The allowable child tax credit from the Child Tax Credit and Credit for Other Dependents Worksheet is entered on Line 12a of Form 1040.

---

### EXAMPLES—

*Assume that MAGI is the same as the taxpayer's AGI in these examples*

1. Carl and Abby's only children, twin daughters, were born in 2018. Carl and Abby file a joint return for 2018. Their MAGI is $88,000, and they claim the standard deduction. Their MAGI is well below the $400,000 phaseout threshold for the child tax credit *(25.3)*. They may claim the full child tax credit of $4,000 ($2,000 per child), as the $4,000 credit does not exceed their tax liability.

2. Same as Example 1, except that Carl and Abby's MAGI for 2018 is $438,650. Their potential child tax credit of $4,000 is partially phased out since MAGI exceeds the $400,000 phaseout threshold. The excess AGI of $38,650 ($438,650 – $400,000) is rounded up to $39,000 (next multiple of $1,000) and that is multiplied by 5% (the phaseout percentage), resulting in a phaseout of $1,950 ($39,000 × 5%). The non-phased portion of the credit is $2,050 ($4,000 – $1,950), and this is Carl and Abby's allowable child tax credit for 2018, as $2,050 is much lower than their tax liability.

3. Jane is single and has two dependent children, ages six and three. She files her 2018 return as head of household and claims the standard deduction. Her 2018 MAGI is $217,500. Because her AGI exceeds the $200,000 phaseout threshold for a head of household, her child tax credit for 2018 is reduced. The excess MAGI of $$17,500 is rounded up to $18,000 (next multiple of $1,000) and that is multiplied by the phaseout percentage of 5%, resulting in a $900 phaseout ($18,000 × 5%). Jane may claim a child tax credit of $3,100 ($4,000 – $900) on her 2018 return, as the $3,100 credit is well below her tax liability.

---

**The additional child tax credit (ACTC) on Schedule 8812.**  If the full amount of the child tax credit cannot be claimed on the Child Tax Credit Worksheet because of the tax liability limitation, you may be able to obtain a refund for the balance in the form of the additional child tax credit (ACTC). For 2018, the child tax credit  is refundable to the extent of 15% of your taxable earned income plus tax-free combat pay *(35.4)* in excess of $2,500, but the refundable amount cannot exceed $1,400 per qualifying child. There is an alternative formula for figuring the ACTC if you have three or more qualifying children and you paid Social Security and Medicare taxes that exceed your earned income credit, if any. Follow the IRS instructions to Schedule 8812 for figuring the ACTC. Any portion of the credit that is phased out as discussed above is "lost" and is not eligible for the ACTC on Schedule 8812. The allowable ACTC from Schedule 8812 is entered on Line 17b of Form 1040.

The ACTC is not allowed if you claim the exclusion for foreign earned income *(36.1)* or employer-financed foreign housing costs *(36.4)*, or if self-employed, the deduction for foreign housing costs *(36.4)*.

If the ACTC is claimed on a return filed at the very beginning of the tax filing season in late January, your anticipated refund may be delayed. The IRS cannot issue a refund before February 15 if the return includes the AOTC. The same rule applies to the earned income credit *(25.6)*. The entire refund must be withheld until February 15 and not just the portion of the refund attributable to the refundable child tax credit. The delay in issuing these very early refund claims is intended to give the IRS some extra time to review the returns and reduce improper refund payments.

## 25.4 New Credit for Other Dependents

Starting with 2018 returns, you can claim a $500 nonrefundable credit for each eligible dependent for whom the child tax credit *(25.2)* cannot be claimed. The credit for "other" dependents is figured together with the child tax credit on the Child Tax Credit and Credit for Other Dependents Worksheet in the Form 1040 instructions (*see* sample Worksheet on page 810).

You can claim the credit for each of the following dependents:

1. Your qualifying relative (meeting the tests at *21.4*), provided he or she is a U.S. citizen, U.S. national, or U.S. resident alien, and has a Social Security number (SSN), an ITIN (if a resident alien not eligible for a SSN), or adoption taxpayer identification number (ATIN) that is issued on or before the due date of your 2018 return (including extensions). If you apply for an ITIN or ATIN by the return due date (with extensions), the number is considered issued by the due date. Note that for other tax purposes, such as claiming head of household status, a qualifying relative can be a resident of Canada or Mexico, but to claim the credit for other dependents, the qualifying relative must be a a U.S. citizen, U.S. national, or U.S. resident alien.

2. Your qualifying child (meeting the tests at *21.3*) who is age 17 or older at the end of 2018 and therefore cannot be claimed for the child tax credit *(25.2)*, and

3. Your qualifying child (meeting the tests at *21.3*) who is under age 17 at the end of 2018 but who did not have a SSN valid for employment issued before the due date of your 2018 return (including extensions). Because the SSN is lacking, you cannot claim the child tax credit *(25.2)* for that child, but you can claim the credit for other dependents.

For each of the above dependents, figure your credit on the Child Tax Credit and Credit for Other Dependents Worksheet. On the Worksheet, the $500 credit per qualifying dependent may be reduced under the same phaseout rule and liability limitation discussed above for the child tax credit *(25.3)*. If you can claim both credits, the computation of both is combined on the Worksheet. The allowable credit for other dependents is entered on Line 12a of Form 1040 (together with the child tax credit if any).

## 25.5 Qualifying for the Child and Dependent Care Credit

Did you hire someone to care for your children under age 13 or other dependents while you work? If so, you may qualify for a tax credit for the expenses. The credit is generally available to the extent you have earnings from employment. You may claim the credit even if you work part time. You may claim the credit if you work from home and pay someone to care for your child while you are there. Your employer may have a plan qualifying for tax-free child care and, if you are covered, you may be unable to claim a tax credit *(25.6)*.

 *Law Alert*

**ACTC Is a Refundable Credit**

The refundable portion of the child tax credit (called the "Additional Child Tax Credit", or ACTC, on Form 8812) is 15% of taxable earned income in excess of $2,500, but no more than $1,400 per qualifying child. Combat pay that is otherwise excluded from income *(35.4)* is treated as taxable earned income for purposes of figuring the refundable amount.

**Credit requirements.** To qualify for the child and dependent care credit, you must:

1. Incur qualifying expenses to care for a qualifying person (see below), so that you can work. Expenses that you incur while looking for work qualify for the credit, but you must have earnings for the year; *see* Test 2 below. Qualifying expenses must be reduced by tax-free reimbursements received from your employer. Qualifying care expenses and dollar limits are discussed in *25.6*.

2. Have earned income for the year. If married, both you and your spouse generally must work, but there is an exception if one of you is a full-time student or is incapacitated; *see 25.6* for the exception details ("Earned income rule for married couples").

3. File jointly if you are married, unless you are separated under the rules discussed below.

4. Hire a care provider other than a person you may claim as your dependent *(21.1)*. Thus, if you pay your mother to care for your child and you cannot claim your mother as a dependent, such payments qualify for the credit, but if you can claim her as your dependent you cannot claim the credit. In addition, no credit may be claimed for payments made to (1) your child who is under 19 years of age at the close of the tax year, whether or not you may claim the child as a dependent, (2) your spouse, or (3) the other parent (who is not your spouse) of your child under age 13 whom you are claiming as your qualifying person.

5. Report on your tax return the name, address, and taxpayer identification number (Social Security number for individuals) of the child-care provider; *see* below.

*Caution*

**Nonrefundable Credit**

The dependent care credit is limited to your tax liability. In other words, if the credit amount exceeds the tax that you owe, you will not be given a refund of the difference.

**Where to claim the credit.** The credit is claimed on Form 2441 and entered on Line 49 of Schedule 3 (Form 1040). The size of the credit depends on the amount of your care expenses, number of dependents, and income. Depending on your adjusted gross income, the credit is 20% to 35% of up to $3,000 of care expenses for one dependent and up to $6,000 of expenses for two or more dependents. The minimum credit percentage of 20% applies if your adjusted gross income exceeds $43,000; there is no maximum income for the credit. See *Table 25-1 (25.6)*.

**Identifying care provider on your return.** On Form 2441, you must list the name, address, and taxpayer identification number of the person you paid to care for your dependent. If the care provider is an individual, his or her Social Security number is required. If the provider is a business, enter its employer identification number (EIN), but you do need to enter a taxpayer identification number if the care provider is a tax-exempt organization. Failure to list the correct name, address, and identifying number may result in a disallowance of the credit. To avoid this possibility, ask the provider to fill out Form W-10 or get the identifying information from a Social Security card, driver's license, or business letterhead or invoice. If a household employee has filled out Form W-4 for you, this may act as a backup record.

**Withholding tax for a housekeeper.** Where you employ help to care for your dependent in your home, you may be liable for FICA (Social Security) and FUTA (unemployment) taxes *(38.3)*.

**Are you married but separated from your spouse?** If you are married at the end of the year, you generally must file a joint return to claim the dependent care credit, but you are treated as unmarried and may claim the credit when you file as married filing separately, provided you meet all of the following tests:

1. You lived apart from your spouse during the last six months of the year;

2. Your home was the home of the qualifying person (see below) for more than half the year, and

3. You paid over half the cost of maintaining the household for the entire year.

If you satisfy these three tests, you do not have to take your spouse's income into account when applying the credit percentage shown at *25.5*.

**If you are divorced or separated and are the custodial parent.** If you are the custodial parent of your child who was under age 13 or physically or mentally incapable of caring for himself or herself, you may claim the credit even though you waived the right to claim an exemption for your child in favor of the noncustodial parent on Form 8332 (or equivalent) under the special rules for divorced or separated parents at *21.7*. You are the custodial parent if your child lived with you for more nights during the year than with his or her other parent. If your child stayed with each of you an equal number of nights, you are treated as the custodial parent if your adjusted gross income is higher than the other parent's adjusted gross income *(21.7)*. The noncustodial parent cannot treat the child as a qualifying person even though he or she claims the exemption under the special rules.

## Who is a Qualifying Person for Credit Purposes?

To claim the dependent care credit, you must incur employment-related expenses *(25.6)* for at least one of the following qualifying persons who lives with you more than half the year:

1. A dependent under the age of 13 who is your "qualifying child" under 21.3. If you are divorced or separated, and you resided with the child for a longer time during the year than the other parent, you may be able to claim the credit even if the other parent is entitled to claim the child as a dependent; *see* above.

   If your child becomes age 13 during the year, take into account expenses incurred for his or her care prior to the 13th birthday. However, you do not prorate the $3,000 limitation on expenses *(25.5)*. For example, if your child had her 13th birthday on May 1, 2018, and you incurred $3,000 or more in care expenses between January 1 and April 30, the entire $3,000 qualifies for the 2018 credit.

2. Your spouse, if physically or mentally incapable of caring for him- or herself.

3. A dependent, regardless of age, who is physically or mentally incapable of caring for himself or herself. For example, he or she needs help to dress or to take care of personal hygiene or nutritional needs, or requires constant attention to avoid hurting him- or herself or others. Generally, you must be able to claim the person as a dependent, either as your qualifying child *(21.3)* or qualifying relative *(21.4)*, but even if the person cannot be claimed as your qualifying relative because he or she has gross income of $4,150 or more for 2018, you may still claim a credit for his or her care costs. Also, if you cannot treat a person as your dependent because he or she filed a joint return, or because you (or your spouse if you file jointly) can be claimed as a dependent by another taxpayer *(21.2)*, you can still claim the credit for care costs that otherwise qualify.

> **EXAMPLE**
>
> You live with your mother, who is physically incapable of caring for herself. You hire a practical nurse to care for her in the home while you are at work. Payments to the nurse qualify as care costs. However, if you placed her in a nursing home, the cost of the nursing home would not qualify as a dependent care cost, but a medical expense deduction may be available *(17.11)*.

## 25.6 Figuring the Child and Dependent Care Credit

In figuring the credit on Form 2441, you may take into account up to $3,000 of the following types of expenses when figuring the credit for one dependent, or up to $6,000 for two or more dependents. If you receive employer-financed dependent care, tax-free reimbursements reduce the $3,000 or $6,000 base.

1. Costs of caring for your qualifying child under age 13, incapacitated spouse, or incapacitated dependent (of any age) in your home *(25.5)*. If you pay FICA or FUTA taxes on your housekeeper's wages *(38.3)*, you may include your share of the tax (employer) as part of the wages when entering your qualifying expenses. Also include your housekeeper's share of FICA tax if you pay it. Note that these taxes may more than offset your allowable credit.

   The manner of care need not be the least expensive alternative. For example, where a grandparent resides with you and may provide adequate care for your child to enable you to work, the cost of hiring someone to care for the child is still eligible for the credit.

2. Ordinary domestic services in your home, such as laundry, cleaning, and cooking (but not payments to a gardener or chauffeur) that are partly for the care of the qualifying person. Expenses for the dependent's food, clothing, or entertainment do not qualify. Food costs for a housekeeper who eats in your home may be added to qualifying expenses. Extra expenses for a housekeeper's lodging (extra rent or utilities) also qualify.

### Filing Tip

**Day-Care Center or Nursery School**

The amount you pay to a day-care center or nursery school for a dependent child under age 13 is eligible for the credit, even if it covers such incidental benefits as lunch. However, tuition for a child in kindergarten or higher is not taken into account. If the dependent is not your child, costs for care outside the home qualify only if the dependent regularly spends at least eight hours per day in your home. Up to $3,000 a year of outside-the-home care expenses may be taken into account in figuring the credit for one dependent, and up to $6,000 for two or more.

### Filing Instruction

**Credit Limited if One Spouse Is a Student or Disabled**

If one spouse works and the other is a full-time student and has no earned income for the year, the student-spouse is considered to have earned income of $250 ($500 if caring for more than one qualified person) for each month he or she is a student. Their credit base is limited to the deemed income amount for the student, assuming that is less than the working spouse's earnings. The same $250/$500 rule applies for each month one of the spouses is incapable of self-care.

3. Outside-the-home care costs for a child under age 13, as in a day-care center (must meet all state and local regulations and provide care services for over 6 persons), a day camp (including a specialty camp such as a computer or soccer camp), nursery school, or in the home of a babysitter. Outside-the-home care costs also qualify if incurred for a handicapped dependent, regardless of age, provided he or she regularly spends at least eight hours per day in your home. However, the cost of schooling in kindergarten or higher does not qualify for the credit. Costs for sleep-away camp also do not qualify for the credit.

You may not take into account your transportation costs in taking your qualifying person to and from a care center, or your payment of a care provider's transportation to and from your home.

## Limits on Eligible Expenses

In figuring the credit, you take into account qualifying expenses up to a limit of $3,000 for one qualifying person, or $6,000 for two or more qualifying persons. The $3,000 or $6,000 limit applies even if your actual expenses are much greater. Further, the $3,000 or $6,000 limit must be reduced by tax-free benefits received from an employer's dependent care plan, as discussed below. Finally, if your earned income is less than the $3,000 or $6,000 limit, your credit is figured on the lower income amount; *see* the earned income rule for married couples below.

**Earned income rule for married couples.** Generally, both spouses must work (wages, salary, or self-employment) at least part time to claim the credit, unless one is incapable of self-care or is a full-time student. If either you or your spouse earns less than the maximum $3,000 or $6,000 credit base, the base is limited to the smaller earned income. However, for each month you or your spouse is a full-time student or is disabled, that spouse is considered to have earned income of $250 if care expenses are incurred for one dependent, or $500 for two or more dependents, even if the spouse had no earnings or earnings under $250/$500 for the month. A full-time student is one who attends school full time during each of five calendar months during the year, whether or not the months are consecutive. A spouse who is incapable of self-care is considered disabled for purposes of the $250/$500 rule.

> ### EXAMPLES
>
> 1. John and Mary are married. In 2018, John earns $5,300. Mary earns $33,000. They incur care costs of $6,200 for their two children, ages 5 and 7. Their adjusted gross income including interest earnings is $38,575. As shown in *Table 25-1* below, the credit percentage for their adjusted gross income is 23%. The maximum $6,000 credit base (for two or more dependents) is limited to John's lower income of $5,300. They may claim a credit of $1,219 ($5,300 × 23%).
>
> 2. Same facts as in Example 1, except John was a full-time student for nine months and earned no income for the year. John is considered to have earned income of $500 for each month he was a full-time student since he and Mary had care costs for more than one qualifying child. The credit base is limited to $4,500 ($500 × 9 months). Their credit is $1,035 ($4,500 × 23%).

**Employer-financed dependent care reduces credit base.** Tax-free reimbursements under an employer's dependent care program *(3.5)* reduce the $3,000 or $6,000 credit base. For example, if you have one child and you receive a $1,500 reimbursement of child-care costs from your company's plan, the amount eligible for the tax credit is reduced to $1,500 ($3,000 – $1,500). A reimbursement of $3,000 or more would bar any credit. The $6,000 credit expense limit for two or more dependents is similarly reduced by dependent care benefits from your employer. On your Form W-2, your employer will report the amount of tax-free reimbursement *(3.4)*.

If your employer's plan allows you to fund a reimbursement account with salary-reduction contributions that are excluded from taxable pay *(3.14)*, reimbursements from the account are considered employer-financed payments that reduce the $3,000 or $6,000 credit base. In deciding whether to make salary-reduction contributions, you should determine whether the tax-free salary reduction will provide a larger tax savings than that provided by the credit. You may find that the salary reduction provides the larger tax savings, taking into consideration not only the decrease in federal income tax, but also the Social Security tax and state and local taxes avoided by using the salary reduction. Further, by lowering your adjusted gross income, a salary reduction may enable you to claim a larger IRA deduction if you are subject to the deduction phaseout rule *(8.4)*.

**How to treat prepayments and payments of prior year expenses.** Your credit for 2018 generally must be based on payments you made in 2018 for qualifying care services provided in 2018. There is an exception if in 2017 you prepaid for 2018 qualifying services; claim the 2017 prepayment as a qualifying expense paid in 2018 when you figure your 2018 credit on Form 2441.

If you paid for 2017 services in 2018, you may be able to claim an additional credit on your 2018 return, but only in limited circumstances. Specifically, payments made in 2018 for 2017 services may be eligible for an additional credit on your 2018 return but only if you did not use up the $3,000 or $6,000 expense limit that applied for the 2017 credit. Follow the instructions for Form 2441 to figure the additional credit.

If in 2018 you prepaid for 2019 services, you must allocate your payment. Only 2018 payments for 2018 services should be counted toward the $3,000 or $6,000 limit when figuring your 2018 credit; the prepayment for 2019 services will count as a 2019 expense in figuring the credit for 2019.

**Allocating expenses when employed less than an entire year.** If your dependent care expenses covered a period in which you worked or looked for work only part of the time, you must allocate the expenses on a daily basis to determine the work-related portion. However, if you were away on vacation or missed work due to illness for a short period, this is treated as a temporary absence from work and the expenses incurred during the absence qualify for the credit. The IRS considers an absence from work of two weeks or less as temporary; an absence of more than two weeks may be temporary depending on the facts and circumstances.

---

> **EXAMPLE**
>
> For the year, you are employed or look for work for only two months and 10 days. Monthly care expenses are $300. Eligible care expenses amount to $700 ($300 × 2 months, plus 1/3 of $300).

---

**Allocation if expenses cover noncare services.** If a portion of expenses is for other than dependent care or household services, only the portion allocable to dependent care or household services qualifies. No allocation is required if the non–dependent care services are minimal.

---

> **EXAMPLES**
>
> 1. A person accepts a full-time position and sends his 12-year-old child to boarding school. The expenses paid to the school must be allocated. The part representing care of the child qualifies; the part representing tuition does not.
>
> 2. A full-time housekeeper is hired to care for two children, ages 9 and 12. The housekeeper also drives the mother to and from work each day. The driving takes no longer than 30 minutes. No allocation is required because the non–dependent care driving services are minimal.

---

## Credit percentage

Depending on your adjusted gross income (AGI), a credit percentage of 20% to 35% applies to your expenses up to the $3,000 (one dependent) or $6,000 (two or more dependents) limit. The maximum credit is 35% for families with AGI of $15,000 or less. The 35% maximum credit percentage is reduced by 1% for each $2,000 of AGI or fraction of $2,000 over $15,000, but not below 20%. The minimum credit percentage of 20% applies where AGI exceeds $43,000, regardless of how high AGI is.

The dependent care credit is nonrefundable. It is limited to your tax liability; follow the IRS instructions.

**Filing Tip**

**Employer Reimbursements Reduce Credit**

Expenses qualifying for the dependent care credit are reduced by any tax-free reimbursements under a qualified employer dependent care program. That is, the reimbursements reduce the expense limit of $3,000 for one dependent, or the $6,000 expense limit for two or more qualifying dependents. Your employer will report reimbursements in Box 10 of your Form W-2. On Form 2441, you figure the tax-free portion of the reimbursement and any reduction to the credit expense base.

**Filing Tip**

**Care Costs Qualifying as Medical Expenses**

Care costs, such as a nurse's wages, may also qualify as medical expenses, but you may not claim both the dependent care credit and the medical expense deduction. If you use the expenses to figure the credit and your care costs exceed the amount allowed as dependent care costs, the excess, to the extent it qualifies as a medical expense *(17.12)*, may be added to other deductible medical costs.

### Table 25-1 Allowable Dependent Care Credit*

| Adjusted gross income | Credit percentage | Maximum credit for one dependent* | Maximum credit for two or more dependents* |
|---|---|---|---|
| $15,000 or less | 35% | $1,050 | $2,100 |
| 15,001–17,000 | 34 | 1,020 | 2,040 |
| 17,001–19,000 | 33 | 990 | 1,980 |
| 19,001–21,000 | 32 | 960 | 1,920 |
| 21,001–23,000 | 31 | 930 | 1,860 |
| 23,001–25,000 | 30 | 900 | 1,800 |
| 25,001–27,000 | 29 | 870 | 1,740 |
| 27,001–29,000 | 28 | 840 | 1,680 |
| 29,001–31,000 | 27 | 810 | 1,620 |
| 31,001–33,000 | 26 | 780 | 1,560 |
| 33,001–35,000 | 25 | 750 | 1,500 |
| 35,001–37,000 | 24 | 720 | 1,440 |
| 37,001–39,000 | 23 | 690 | 1,380 |
| 39,001–41,000 | 22 | 660 | 1,320 |
| 41,001–43,000 | 21 | 630 | 1,260 |
| 43,001 and over | 20 | 600 | 1,200 |

*Maximum credit assumes qualifying expenses are at least $3,000 for one dependent, or $6,000 for two or more dependents. If qualifying expenses are less than the $3,000/$6,000 maximum, your credit is the credit percentage multiplied by the expenses.

### EXAMPLES

1. You pay $6,500 in 2018 to a neighbor to care for your two children while you work. Your adjusted gross income is $34,824. The credit percentage of 25% is applied to the maximum expense limit of $6,000, giving you a credit of $1,500.

2. Same facts as in Example 1, except you receive a tax-free reimbursement of $2,500 from your employer's plan. The reimbursement reduces the $6,000 expense limit to $3,500 ($6,000 − $2,500). Your credit is $875 (25% of $3,500). If the tax-free reimbursement was $5,000 ($5,000 is the maximum allowable exclusion (3.5)), the credit would be $250 (25% × $1,000 ($6,000 − $5,000)).

## 25.7 Qualifying Tests for EIC

The earned income credit (EIC) is generally claimed by workers with qualifying children who meet the tests below, but in limited cases the credit is allowed to childless workers. Taxpayers with three or more qualifying children get a higher credit rate than taxpayers with fewer children. Also, a more favorable phaseout range is allowed for married couples filing jointly.

For 2018, the maximum EIC is $3,461 if you have one qualifying child, $5,716 if you have two qualifying children, $6,431 if you have three or more qualifying children, and $519 if you do not have a qualifying child. However, the maximum credit is subject to a phaseout based on income (25.8). The allowable credit is "refundable," meaning that you will receive a refund from the IRS if the credit exceeds your tax liability.

**Earliest refund claims delayed until February 15.** Taxpayers who claim the earned income credit and file their returns as soon as the tax filing season begins in January may face a slight delay in getting a refund. The IRS cannot issue a refund before February 15 if the return includes the earned income credit. The same rule applies to returns claiming the refundable child tax credit (ACTC, 25.3). The entire refund must be withheld until February 15 and not just the portion of the refund attributable to the earned income credit or the refundable child tax credit. The delay in issuing these very early refund claims is intended to give the IRS some extra time to review the returns and reduce improper refund payments.

## Claiming the EIC for 2018 if You Have One or More Qualifying Children

You may claim the EIC on a 2018 return if you:

- Are single, head of household, or a qualifying widow/widower with earned income, such as wages and self-employment earnings, and also adjusted gross income (AGI), under $40,320 if you have one qualifying child, $45,802 if two qualifying children, or $49,194 if you have three or more qualifying children.
- If you are married filing jointly, earned income and AGI must be less than $46,010 if you have one qualifying child, $51,492 if you have two qualifying children; or $54,884 if you have three or more qualifying children.
- If both your earned income and AGI equals or exceeds the applicable amount, the credit is completely phased out, so if your income is close to these amounts your credit will be low. The credit begins to phase out at much lower income levels *(25.8)*.
- Have a qualifying child who lived with you in your main home in the U.S. for more than six months in 2018; *see* below.
- File a joint return if married. Married persons filing separately may not claim the EIC. If you lived apart from your spouse for the last half of the year, you may be able to claim the credit as a head of household.
- File Schedule EIC with your Form 1040. On Schedule EIC, you identify and provide information about a qualifying child. Your child's Social Security number must be entered on Schedule EIC.
- Are not a qualifying child of another person.
- Include on your return your Social Security number and, if married, that of your spouse.

To claim the credit, your Social Security number (and if married, your spouse's) and the Social Security numbers of your qualifying children must be obtained by the due date of your return, including any extension; *see* the Law Alert in this section.

**A qualifying child.** A qualifying child is your son, daughter, adopted child, stepchild, grandchild or other descendent of any of these (your great-grandchild) who at the end of the year is under age 19 or under age 24 and a full-time student (enrolled full time during any five months), or any age if permanently and totally disabled. The qualifying person must live with you for over half the year. Your brother, sister, step- or half-brother or step- or half-sister, or their descendants (your niece or nephew), who meets the age 19 or 24 test and lives with you more than half the year also qualifies if he/she is younger than you (or your spouse if you file jointly) or is permanently and totally disabled. A foster child who lives with you for more than half the year qualifies if the child was placed with you by a court order or by an authorized placement agency.

The child must have a valid Social Security number to be treated as a qualifying child; *see* the Law Alert in this section.

**Household requirement.** The qualifying child must have lived with you in your main home in the U.S. for more than six months. Temporary absences for school, vacation, medical care, or detention in a juvenile facility count as time lived at home.

A person in the U.S. Armed Forces who is stationed outside the U.S. on extended active duty is treated as maintaining a main residence within the U.S.

If you are married, you must file a joint return with your spouse to claim the credit. However, if your spouse did not live in your household for the last six months of the year, and you maintained a home for a child who lived with you for more than half of the year, you may claim the credit as a head of household *(1.12)* .

*Caution*

**Recertification Required if EIC Denied**

If the IRS denies an EIC by issuing a deficiency notice, the credit may not be claimed in a future tax year unless you show on Form 8862 that you are eligible to take the credit. If the IRS recertifies eligibility, Form 8862 does not have to be filed again in subsequent tax years unless the IRS again denies the EIC in a deficiency proceeding.

*Law Alert*

**Valid SSN Needed by Due Date of Return to Claim EIC**

You (and if married your spouse) must have a valid Social Security number (SSN) by the due date for your 2018 return (April 15, 2019, or April 17 if a resident of Maine or Massachusetts), plus extensions if any) to claim the EIC for 2018. If you claim the EIC for qualifying children, they also must have a valid SSN by the return due date (including extensions). If you do not have a SSN by the return due date (with extensions), you cannot claim the credit on your original return and you cannot claim it on an amended return if you later obtain a SSN. Similarly, you cannot treat a child as a qualifying child on either your original return or on an amended return if that child did not have a SSN by the return due date (with extensions), even if the child later obtains the SSN.

*Caution*

**Denial of Future Credits for Recklessness or Fraud**

A taxpayer who negligently or fraudulently claims the EIC is prohibited from claiming future credits over a period of several years. The credit is disallowed for two years from the tax year for which it is determined that the EIC claim was claimed with reckless or intentional disregard of the rules. The disallowance period increases to 10 years from the most recent tax year for which it is found that the EIC was claimed fraudulently.

**Permanently and totally disabled.** A person is permanently and totally disabled if: (1) he or she cannot engage in any substantial gainful activity because of a physical or mental condition and (2) a physician determines that the condition has lasted or is expected to last for at least a year or lead to death.

**Qualifying child of two or more people.** "Tie-breaking" rules determine who can take the EIC if a child is a qualifying child of more than one person.

If both parents are eligible to claim the credit for the same qualifying child and they do not file a joint return, the custodial parent, the parent with whom the child resided for the longer period during the year, may claim the child. If the child lived with each parent for the same amount of time, the child will be treated as the qualifying child of the parent who had the higher adjusted gross income (AGI).

If a parent and one or more nonparents, such as a grandparent, are otherwise entitled to claim the child as a qualifying child, only the parent may claim the credit for the child. However, in this situation the parent can decline to claim the child as a qualifying child in order to allow the grandparent to claim the child, but only if the grandparent's AGI is more than the parent's AGI. If none of the persons otherwise entitled to treat the child as a qualifying child are the child's parent, the child will be treated as the qualifying child of the person who had the highest AGI for the year.

A taxpayer who "loses" under the tie-breaker rule, and who thus cannot claim a child as his or her qualifying child for EIC purposes, may still be allowed to claim the EIC under the rules below for taxpayers without a qualifying child (the childless EIC). The IRS instructions follow a 2017 proposed regulation that allows the childless EIC to be claimed by a taxpayer who otherwise qualifies; this reverses an earlier IRS position that prevented the childless EIC to be claimed in this situation. For example, a baby lives with her mother and grandmother in the grandmother's home. The baby "could be" the qualifying child of both the mother and the grandmother, but under the tie-breaker rule, the mother is entitled to treat the baby as her qualifying child, so she can claim the EIC for one qualifying child. Under the new IRS rule, the grandmother can claim the childless EIC if she meets the tests below ("Claiming the Childless EIC if You Have No Qualifying Children").

**Married child.** If your child was married at the end of the year, he or she is your qualifying child only if your child is your dependent under the rules at *21.3*, or the custodial parent waived the dependency exemption under the rules at *21.7*. However, if your child files a joint return, he or she is not your qualifying child unless the joint return is filed only as a refund claim.

**Nonresident aliens.** An individual who is a nonresident alien for any part of the year is not eligible for the credit unless he or she is married and an election is made by the couple to have all of their worldwide income subject to U.S. tax.

## Claiming the Childless EIC for 2018 if You Have No Qualifying Children

If you do not have a qualifying child, you may claim the childless EIC on a 2018 return if you:

- Have earned income, such as wages and self-employment earnings and also adjusted gross income under $15,270 ($20,950 if married filing jointly). These are the amounts at which the credit is completely phased out. The phaseout threshold is considerably lower *(25.7)*.
- Have your main home in the U.S. for more than six months in 2018.
- Are at least 25 but under age 65 at the end of 2018. If filing a joint return, either you or your spouse must satisfy this age test.
- File a joint return if married, unless you lived apart for the last six months and qualify to file as a head of household.
- Are not a dependent of another taxpayer. If filing jointly, your spouse also must not be another taxpayer's dependent.
- Are not a qualifying child of another taxpayer. If filing jointly, your spouse also must not be another taxpayer's qualifying child.
- Include your Social Security number on your return, and, if married, that of your spouse. You must have the Social Security number by the due date of your return, including extensions; *see* the Law Alert at the beginning of *25.7*.

## 25.8 Income Tests for Earned Income Credit (EIC)

For purposes of the credit, earned income includes wages, salary, tips, commissions, jury duty pay, union strike benefits, and net earnings from self-employment. If you retired on disability and you receive payments from the employer's plan that are reported as taxable wages, such disability benefits are considered earned income for EIC purposes until you reach minimum retirement age under the employer's plan. Once you reach minimum retirement age, the payments are treated as a pension and not earned income.

An election may be made to include combat pay that is otherwise excluded from income *(35.4)* as earned income for EIC purposes. The IRS cautions that electing to include combat pay may sometimes decrease, rather than increase, the allowable EIC; you can figure the credit with and without the combat pay on the IRS worksheet (see below) before deciding whether to make the election. Apart from such combat pay, nontaxable employee compensation, such as salary deferrals, or excludable dependent care benefits, is not considered when computing the credit.

**Figure the EIC on IRS worksheet.** A worksheet in the Form 1040 instructions is used to figure the EIC. Self-employed individuals have a separate worksheet. On the worksheet, you first look up the credit allowed based on your earned income (*see* above for combat pay election) in the EIC Table. If your earned income and adjusted gross income (AGI) are the same, the credit based on earned income is the allowable EIC. That amount (credit based on earned income) is also the allowable EIC if AGI is different than earned income and the AGI is under the phaseout threshold (*see* below). However, if AGI is at least as much as the phaseout threshold, you look up the credit based on the AGI in the EIC Table and the smaller of that amount and the amount based on earned income is the allowable EIC, which you enter on Line 17a of Form 1040.

The EIC Table will appear in the *e-Supplement* at *jklasser.com*.

**Disqualifying income.** For 2018, an individual is not eligible for the earned income credit if he or she has "disqualified income" exceeding $3,500. Disqualified income includes interest (taxable and tax-exempt), dividends, net rent and royalty income, net capital gain income, and net passive income that is not self-employment income.

**Credit phases out with income.** The phaseout range for married couples filing jointly is different from single taxpayers, heads of household, or qualifying widows/widowers.

If your filing status is single, head of household, or qualifying widow/widower, and you have qualifying children, your 2018 credit begins to phase out in the EIC Table if either earned income or adjusted gross income is at least $18,700, regardless of the number of children. The phaseout endpoint depends on the number of children. The credit is completely phased out if earned income or adjusted gross income is at least $40,320 for one child, $45,802 for two children, and $49,194 for three or more children.

If you are married filing jointly and have qualifying children, the 2018 credit begins to phase out in the EIC Table if either earned income or adjusted gross income is at least $24,350, regardless of the number of children. The phaseout endpoint depends on the number of children. The credit is completely phased out if earned income or adjusted gross income is at least $46,010 for one child, $51,492 for two children, and $54,884 for three or more children.

If you do not have any qualifying children, the phaseout of the childless EIC begins in the EIC Table when either earned income or AGI is at least $8,500, or $14,200 if married filing jointly, and the credit is completely phased out if either amount is $15,270 or more, or $20,950 or more if married filing jointly.

**Self-employed.** If you were self-employed in 2018, you figure your earned income for EIC purposes on the worksheet in the IRS instructions. Generally, your earned income for EIC purposes is the net earnings shown on Schedule SE, less the income tax deduction for 50% of self-employment tax. If your net earnings were less than $400, the net amount is your earned income for purposes of the credit. If you had a net loss, the loss is subtracted from any wages or other employee earned income. If you are a statutory employee, the income reported on Schedule C qualifies for the credit.

**Foreign earned income.** If you work abroad and claim the foreign earned income exclusion, you may not take the EIC.

 *Filing Tip*

**Definition of Earned Income for EIC Purposes**

Earned income includes tax free combat pay *(35.4)*, but does not include other nontaxable employee compensation such as salary deferrals and reductions, excludable dependent care benefits, and excludable education assistance.

## 25.9 Qualifying for the Adoption Credit

A tax credit of up to $13,810 may be available on your 2018 return for the qualifying costs of adopting an eligible child. An eligible child is a child under age 18, or any person who is physically and mentally incapable of self-care. The credit is phased out ratably for those with modified adjusted gross income between $207,140 and $247,140.

The credit is claimed on Form 8839. Special credit timing rules apply. If you paid qualifying adoption costs in 2018 but the adoption was not final at the end of the year, the credit may not be claimed on your 2018 return *(25.10)*.

If you are married, you generally must file a joint return to take the adoption credit or exclusion, even if only one spouse is adopting the child. You may take the credit or exclusion on a separate return if you are legally separated under a decree of divorce or separate maintenance, or if you lived apart from your spouse for the last six months of the tax year and (1) your home is the eligible child's home for more than half the year and (2) you pay more than half the cost of keeping up your home for the year.

**Qualified adoption expenses.** Qualifying adoption expenses are reasonable and necessary adoption fees, court costs, attorney fees, travel expenses away from home, and other expenses directly related to, and whose principal purpose is for, the legal adoption of an eligible child. Do not include expenses paid or reimbursed by your employer or any other person or organization. You may not claim a credit for the costs of a surrogate parenting arrangement or for adopting your spouse's child.

**Employer plans.** As discussed in *3.6*, an exclusion from income is also available to employees if adoption expenses are paid through a qualifying employer program, subject to rules similar to that of the credit. If you receive employer adoption benefits that are less than your qualifying adoption expenses, you may be able to claim the credit on Form 8839.

## 25.10 Claiming the Adoption Credit on Form 8839

The fact that you paid qualified adoption expenses during 2018 does not mean that you can claim a credit for those costs on your 2018 return. A 2018 credit is not allowed for 2018 expenses unless the adoption was finalized by the end of the year. Under the credit timing rules discussed below, you may claim a 2018 credit for expenses incurred in 2017 if the eligible child was a U.S. citizen or resident when the adoption effort began, even if the adoption is still not final at the end of 2018. If the child was not a U.S. citizen or resident when the adoption effort began, a credit is not allowed until the year the adoption is finalized even if you incurred expenses in one or more previous years.

If a credit is allowed for 2018, figure it on Form 8839 and attach the form to your Form 1040. You must enter an identification number for the child on Form 8839. Generally this is a Social Security number (SSN), but if you are in the process of adopting a child who is U.S. citizen or resident and you cannot get an SSN for the child before you file your return, you should apply for an adoption taxpayer identification number (ATIN) on IRS Form W-7A. If the child is not eligible for an SSN, apply for an individual identification number (ITIN) on Form W-7.

**When to claim the adoption credit for a child who is a U.S.** citizen or resident (U.S. child). If at the time the adoption effort begins the child is a U.S. citizen or resident and you pay qualifying expenses in any year before the year the adoption becomes final, the credit is delayed one year. The credit is allowed in the year after the year of the payment, whether or not the adoption is final in that year. If you pay qualifying expenses in the year the adoption becomes final, the credit for those expenses is claimed in that year. If qualifying expenses are paid in any year after the year in which the adoption becomes final, the credit is claimed in the year of payment.

**When to claim the adoption credit for a child who is not a U.S.** citizen or resident (foreign child). If you pay qualifying expenses to adopt a child who is not a U.S. citizen or resident at the time the adoption effort begins, a credit may not be claimed until the year the adoption becomes final. If adoption expenses are paid after the tax year in which the adoption became finalized, a credit for such expenses is allowed for the tax year of payment.

*Law Alert*

**Adoption Credit Limited by Tax Liability with Carryover for Excess**

The maximum 2018 credit is $13,810, but even if you would be entitled to the full amount, you may be unable to claim it because it is nonrefundable, meaning that it is limited to your tax liability. If the allowable credit exceeds your tax liability, the excess can be carried forward for up to five years.

The IRS has released safe harbors for determining the finality of an adoption of a foreign-born child and thereby the timing of a credit. These safe harbors apply only to adoptions of foreign-born children who receive an "immediate relative" (IR) visa from the State Department. IR visas are issued to a foreign-born child entering the U.S. after a foreign court or government agency (with authority over child welfare) has granted an adoption or guardianship decree.

If there is an adoption proceeding in a foreign country that is not a party to the Hague Adoption Convention, and the adopting parents bring a foreign-born child into the U.S. with an IR-2 visa, an IR-3 visa, or an IR-4 visa (if a "simple" adoption), the parents may treat the adoption as final in either (1) the taxable year in which the foreign court or agency enters the adoption decree or, (2) the taxable year in which a court in the parents' home state enters a decree of "re-adoption" or the home state otherwise recognizes the foreign adoption decree, provided this occurs in one of the two years after the year in which the foreign court or agency enters its decree. If the child receives an IR-4 visa under a guardianship or legal custody arrangement, the adoption may not be treated as final for tax purposes until the year in which a court in the parents' home state enters a decree of adoption (Rev. Proc. 2005-31, 2005-26 IRB 1374).

For a foreign adoption finalized abroad that is governed by the Hague Adoption Convention, the adoption may be treated as final in either the year the foreign country entered the final decree of adoption, or the year the U.S. Secretary of State issued a Hague Adoption Certificate (IHAC) (Rev. Proc. 2010-31, 2010-40 IRB 413).

**Credit limit and phaseout.** The maximum adoption credit on a 2018 return is $13,810 per child, before application of the phaseout rule. The limit is per child, not per taxpayer. If the parents are not spouses filing a joint return, and, to adopt the same child, each parent paid expenses that are allowed in 2018 under the credit timing rules, the parents must divide the $13,810 limit between them.

If under the credit timing rules you are claiming adoption expenses for a child on Form 8839 for 2018, but you claimed expenses for the same child in an earlier year, the earlier expenses reduce the $13,810 maximum credit for 2018. If under the credit timing rules you are allowed a 2018 credit for more than one child, a separate $13,810 limit applies for each. However, if an adoption of a child with special needs is finalized in 2018, the maximum $13,810 credit is allowed even if this amount exceeds your qualified adoption expenses; *see* below.

The credit may be reduced or eliminated on Form 8839 by a phaseout rule based on modified adjusted gross income (MAGI). For 2018, the phaseout applies if MAGI exceeds $207,140. The phaseout range is $40,000, so the credit for 2018 is completely phased out if MAGI is $247,140 or more.

After application of the phaseout rule, you also must apply the liability limit. The credit cannot exceed your tax liability (regular tax plus AMT if any), reduced by various other tax credits. There is a worksheet in the instructions to Form 8839 for figuring the liability limit. If you are unable to use the full credit because it exceeds the liability limit, the excess credit can be carried forward for up to five years.

The allowable credit for 2018 from Form 8839 is entered on Line 54 of Schedule 3 (Form 1040).

**Special needs adoption.** A special rule allows qualifying expenses to be grossed up to the maximum credit in the year the adoption is finalized where the aggregate of qualifying expenses for that year and all prior years is under the maximum. For example, if a special needs adoption is initiated in 2017 and finalized in 2018 and actual qualifying expenses for both years are $9,020, a $13,810 credit may be claimed for 2018, subject to the phaseout rule and liability limit. Total expenses are deemed to be the $13,810 maximum, so the credit for 2018 includes not only the $9,020 of actual expenses, but also an additional $4,790, the excess of $13,810 over the actual expenses. This special rule applies only to finalized special needs adoptions.

An adoption is considered a "special needs" adoption if the child is a U.S. citizen or resident when the adoption process begins, and a state (or District of Columbia) determines that the child cannot or should not be returned to his or her parents and that because of special factors, assistance is required to place the child with adoptive parents. Without a formal determination by the state that the child has special needs that justify providing financial assistance to the adoptive parents, the adoption is not treated as a special needs adoption. In one case, adoptive parents claimed that the fact that they had adopted a biracial child automatically entitled them to use the full credit amount allowed for finalized special needs adoptions, but a federal district court disagreed. There was no state determination of special needs, so the special needs credit rule did not apply.

## 25.11 Eligibility for the Saver's Credit

You may be able to claim the retirement savings contributions credit (saver's credit) on your 2018 return if you, or your spouse if filing jointly, made contributions *(25.12)* to a retirement plan for 2018. This includes a contribution made to a traditional IRA or Roth IRA for 2018 by April 15, 2019.

Eligibility for the saver's credit is restricted. You cannot claim the credit for 2018 contributions you made if any of the following are true:

1. Your adjusted gross income exceeds $63,000 if married filing jointly, $47,250 if a head of household, or $31,500 if single, married filing separately, or a qualifying widow or widower, adjusted gross income is increased by any exclusion for foreign earned income or income from Puerto Rico or American Samoa, or the foreign housing exclusion or deduction.

2. You were born after January 1, 2001. That is, you must be age 18 or older on January 1, 2019, to claim the credit for 2018.

3. You are claimed as a dependent on another taxpayer's 2018 return.

4. You were a full-time student during any part of five or more months in 2018.

If you are not disqualified from claiming the credit under tests 1-4 above, you generally may claim a credit on Form 8880 based on the first $2,000 of your retirement contributions, but only after contributions are reduced by recent retirement plan withdrawals *(25.12)*. As shown in *Table 25-2*, the credit percentage declines from 50% to 20% to 10% as income approaches the applicable $63,000, $47,250, or $31,500 limit.

Details on figuring the credit are in *25.12*. Any allowable credit is in addition to other tax breaks you may receive for making the contribution, such as the exclusion for elective salary deferrals to a 401(k) plan, or a deduction for a traditional IRA contribution.

## 25.12 Figuring the Saver's Credit

You figure your saver's credit on Form 8880. The maximum credit for 2018 equals the applicable income-dependent rate shown in *Table 25-2* (50%, 20%, or 10%) multiplied by the first $2,000 of eligible retirement contributions made for the year. If you are married filing jointly, you and your spouse may each take into account up to $2,000 of eligible contributions. Eligible contributions include: (1) contributions to a traditional IRA or Roth IRA, (2) salary-reduction contributions to a 401(k) plan (including a SIMPLE 401(k)), 403(b) plan, SIMPLE IRA, governmental Section 457 plan, or salary-reduction SEP, (3) contributions to your ABLE account *(34.12)*, or (4) voluntary after-tax contributions to a qualified plan or 403(b) plan.

Note in *Table 25-2* that the 20% credit bracket is extremely narrow, so as a practical matter, most eligible taxpayers will qualify for either the 50% or 10% credit percentage.

**Withdrawals can eliminate the credit.** A credit can be lost because you have withdrawn money from a retirement plan. In figuring a credit for 2018, your eligible contributions for 2018 must be reduced by the total of distributions you received (and also your spouse if filing jointly) after 2015 and before the due date of your 2018 return (including extensions) from traditional IRAs and Roth IRAs, ABLE accounts, 401(k) plans, SEPs, SIMPLE plans, 403(b) plans, the Federal Thrift Savings Plan, and other qualified retirement plans. Do not count tax-free rollovers, direct transfers (trustee-to-trustee), conversions of a traditional IRA to a Roth IRA, in-plan rollovers from a 401(k) plan to a designated Roth account, distributions of excess contributions or deferrals, IRA contributions returned by the due date; *see* the instructions to Form 8880 for other disregarded distributions.

**Tax liability limit.** The credit is not refundable. It is limited to your tax liability (regular tax plus AMT, if any), reduced by certain other nonrefundable credits such as the child and dependent care credit or the American Opportunity or Lifetime Learning credits.

*Law Alert*

**ABLE Account Beneficiaries**

Starting in 2018, the designated beneficiary of an ABLE account *(34.12)* may base the saver's credit on contributions he or she makes to that ABLE account.

### Table 25-2  Saver's Credit Based on AGI for 2018

| Credit Rate | Married Filing Jointly | Head of Household | Single, Married Filing Separately, or Qualifying Widow/Widower |
|---|---|---|---|
| 50% | up to $38,000 | up to $28,500 | up to $19,000 |
| 20% | $ 38,001 – $41,000 | $28,501 – $30,750 | $19,001 – $20,500 |
| 10% | $ 41,001 – $63,000 | $30,751 – $47,250 | $20,501 – $31,500 |
| 0% | over $63,000 | over $47,250 | over $31,500 |

For 2019, the income limits may be increased by an inflation adjustment; *see* the *e-Supplement at jklasser.com* for an update.

## 25.13  Premium Tax Credit

If you bought health care coverage in 2018 through a government exchange (also called "The Health Insurance Marketplace") and your household income is between 100% and 400% of the federal poverty line, you may be able to claim a tax credit on Form 8962 when you file your 2018 return. *See* the Sample Form 8962 below. If, like most Marketplace applicants, you received an advance of the credit that went right to your insurance company and was applied to your monthly premiums, you will have to reconcile the advance payments you received with the actual credit that you are entitled to on Form 8962. The advance payments may have been too much or too little, depending on changes to your income or family composition between the time you received the advance payments and when you file your 2018 return.

If your allowable credit on Form 8962 exceeds the advance payments, the excess, called the "Net Premium Tax Credit," can be claimed as a refundable credit on Line 70 of Schedule 5 (Form 1040).As a refundable credit, it will be paid to you even if it exceeds your tax liability.

However, if your advance payments exceed the allowable credit, you must pay back the excess, but there is a limit on the required repayment (shown below). The repayment is an additional tax that must be reported on Line 46 of Schedule 2 (Form 1040).

To complete Form 8962, you will need to enter amounts shown on Form 1095-A, which you will receive from the Marketplace through which you obtained coverage. Form 1095-A will provide a month-by-month breakdown of the coverage premiums for you and your family and show the advance payments you received.

**Eligibility for the premium tax credit.** You must have purchased health coverage through the Marketplace and must meet these requirements to be eligible for a 2019 premium tax credit:

1. Your household income for 2019 is at least 100% and no more than 400% of the poverty level for your family size. Household income is the modified adjusted gross income (MAGI) for you, your spouse, (if filing jointly) and your dependents who are required to file a tax return. MAGI is regular AGI increased by tax-exempt interest, the nontaxable part of Social Security benefits, and excluded foreign earned income. The Form 8962 instructions have worksheets for figuring MAGI and federal poverty tables that show the federal poverty line for your family size, depending on whether you live in the 48 contiguous states (and Washington DC), Alaska, or Hawaii.

2. You are not eligible for coverage from an employer plan or from a government plan (including Medicaid or Medicare). If you were offered employer plan coverage, but it was unaffordable or did not provide minimum value, the offered coverage does not block eligibility for the credit. The employer coverage is considered "unaffordable" for 2018 if the premium for self-only coverage exceeds 9.56% of your household income. You also remain eligible if the employer plan does not cover at least 60% of the cost of covered services; your employer must provide you with a plan summary that indicates if the plan meets the 60% test.

 *Caution*

**Report Changes to Marketplace That Could Affect Credit for 2019**

If you obtain coverage for 2019 through the Marketplace, your right to advance payments of the premium tax credit for 2019 will be based on the information you provide concerning your family composition and projected income. When you file your 2019 return, your actual credit will be based on the income and family size reported on Form 8962. If the advance payments are too high, you will have to make a repayment to the government. This could substantially reduce your expected refund or increase the balance due on your 2019 return. If you want to reduce the chances of having to make a repayment when you file, notify the Marketplace about increases in your household income or decreases in your family size. Also notify the Marketplace if you become eligible for employer-sponsored coverage or government sponsored coverage, as this will usually make you ineligible for the credit.

Similarly, notify the Marketplace about changed circumstances that could increase your advance payments, such as where you get married, have a child, or your household income drops below your initial estimate. If your advance payments are not adjusted to account for such changes, you will be entitled to a larger credit when you file.

3. If married, you must file jointly. However, if you have been the victim of domestic abuse or abandoned by your spouse, and you live apart when you file your 2018 return, you can claim the credit as a married person filing separately. Alternatively, you can claim the credit if you lived apart for the last six months of 2018 and can file as a head of household *(1.12)*.

4. You cannot be claimed as a dependent by another taxpayer.

5. You bought your coverage through the Marketplace. Purchasing identical coverage directly from the insurer disqualifies you from claiming the credit.

**Figuring the credit on Form 8962.** In Part I of Form 8962 (*see* the Sample form below), you compare your household income to the applicable federal poverty line. If the combined MAGI for you, your spouse (if filing jointly) and your dependents (who are required to file) is no more than four times larger (400%) than the applicable federal poverty line, you are eligible for a credit. If your income exceeds 400% of the poverty line, you are not entitled to any credit and must repay any advance payments you received.

If eligible, you figure your credit based on the premiums for your policy, your contribution amount, and the Marketplace premium for the second lowest cost silver plan (SLCSP) for your family in your local area.

**Contribution amount.** Your contribution amount is the amount you are required by law to contribute toward your coverage. Your annual contribution amount is your household income multiplied by the "applicable percentage" for your income level, shown in the "applicable figure" table in the Form 8962 instructions. As the percentage of household income to the federal poverty line increases (from 100% of the federal poverty line to 400%), your contribution percentage increases. For 2018, the contribution percentages range from a low of 2.01% to a high of 9.56%; the maximum percentage of 9.56% applies when household income is 300% through 400% of the federal poverty line.

**Premium amount for SLCSP.** The Form 1095-A you get from the Marketplace will give you the monthly premium for the second lowest cost silver plan (SLCSP) for your family in your local area. The SLCSP is referred to as the "reference" or "benchmark" plan and the SLCSP premium is used to calculate the monthly advance payments as well as the allowable credit on Form 8962, regardless of what coverage plan you actually have.

**Credit figured on annual or monthly basis.** In Part II of Form 8962, the maximum full-year credit is the lesser of (1) the annual premium for your policy, or (2) the excess of the annual SLCSP premium over your annual contribution amount. However, if Form 1095-A shows that you did not have Marketplace coverage for the whole year, or there were monthly changes to your premiums or to the SLCSP premiums, you have to figure your credit on a monthly basis. That is, for each month, you get a credit equal to the lesser of (1) the monthly premium amount for your coverage, or (2) the excess of the monthly SLCSP premium over your monthly contribution amount (1/12 of the annual contribution amount described above). Your Form 1095-A has the annual and monthly premium and SLCSP amounts; you enter these on Part II of your Form 8962.

You must then compare the allowable credit, either the annual amount or the total of the monthly amounts, to your advance payments. The advance payments, which are shown on Form 1095-A, must be entered in Part II of Form 8962. If the credit exceeds the advance payments, the excess is the "net premium tax credit" you are entitled to claim on Schedule 5, Line 70 (Form 1040). However, if the advance payments exceed the credit, you must make a repayment; *see* below.

**Repayment of excess advance payments.** If the advance payments you received in 2018 exceed your allowable credit for 2018, the excess must be repaid with your 2018 Form 1040; report the repayment on Line 46 of Schedule 2 (Form 1040). There is a cap on the required repayment based on filing status and income, provided your household income is under 400% of the federal poverty line for your family size.

If you are married at the end of 2018 but your filing status is married filing separately, you are allowed a credit only if you are a victim of spousal abuse or abandonment (see requirement 3 under "Eligibility for the premium tax credit" above). In that case, the repayment limitation in *Table 25-3* applies separately to you and your spouse based on the household income reported on your respective returns. If you are not a victim of spousal abuse or abandonment, you are not allowed any credit and must repay all or half of the advance payments you received, depending on who was covered by the policy; *see* the Form 8962 repayment instructions.

For 2019, the repayment limits may be increased by an inflation adjustment; *see* the *e-Supplement* at *jklasser.com*.

### Table 25-3 Repayment Limit on Excess Advances for 2018

| Household income as a percentage of federal poverty line | Limit for filing status of single | Limit for any other filing status |
| --- | --- | --- |
| Under 200% | $ 300 | $ 600 |
| At least 200%, but under 300% | 775 | 1,550 |
| At least 300%, but under 400% | 1,300 | 2,600 |
| 400% or more | Full repayment required | Full repayment required |

## 25.14 Health Coverage Credit

The Health Coverage Tax Credit (HCTC) provides a 72.5% credit on Form 8885 to a relatively small number of eligible individuals for premiums paid on qualifying health insurance that covers them, their spouse, and qualifying family members. Advance monthly payments of the credit are available; *see* below.

Eligible individuals are: displaced workers who have lost jobs due to foreign competition and are receiving Trade Adjustment Assistance (TAA) benefits, older workers receiving wage subsidies under an alternative trade adjustment assistance (ATAA) program or reemployment trade adjustment assistance (RTAA) program established by the Department of Labor, and Pension Benefit Guaranty Corporation (PBGC) pension beneficiaries age 55 to 65 who are not enrolled in Medicare.

The HCTC applies to premiums you paid for coverage under an individual (non-group) health insurance plan purchased from an insurance company, agent or broker. The HCTC does not apply to coverage purchased through the Health Insurance Marketplace (federally-administered or state exchange), but the premium tax credit may be available *(25.13)*.

In addition to individual health plan coverage (non-Marketplace), the HCTC applies to premiums for COBRA continuing coverage and coverage under a spouse's employer-sponsored plan, provided that your former employer or your spouse's employer did not pay 50% or more of the cost. Coverage through certain state-sponsored plans also qualify.

The HCTC may not be claimed for any month that you are enrolled in Medicare (Part A, B, or C), Medicaid, CHIP, FEHBP, or TRICARE and coverage for family members does not qualify if they are enrolled in such plans. However, once you enroll in Medicare, the HCTC generally can be claimed for eligible coverage of your qualified family members for 24 months.

Credit eligibility is determined on a month-by-month basis on Form 8885. If an "advance" of the credit was received (see below) and applied to the premiums for a month, no further credit for that month is allowed on Form 8885. The advance monthly payments are shown in Box 1 of Form 1099-H. The credit from Form 8885 if any is entered as a refundable credit (not limited by tax liability) on line 74 of Schedule 5 (Form 1040).

**Advance monthly payments of the HCTC.** You can receive the benefit of the HCTC on a monthly basis by enrolling on Form 13441-A ("Health Coverage Tax Credit (HCTC) Monthly Registration and Update"). After the IRS informs you that your registration is confirmed and you have been certified for advance monthly payments, you must pay 27.5% of your health insurance premiums to "US Treasury-HCTC" and the Treasury will then add the 72.5% advance portion and forward the entire amount to your health plan administrator each month.

## 25.15 Mortgage Interest Credit

Under special state and local programs, you may obtain a "mortgage credit certificate" to finance the purchase of a principal residence or to borrow funds for certain home improvements. Generally, a qualifying principal residence may not cost more than 90% of the average area purchase price, 110% in certain targeted areas. A tax credit for interest paid on the mortgage may be claimed. The credit is computed on Form 8396. The credit equals the interest paid multiplied by the certificate rate set by the governmental authority, but if the credit rate is over 20%, the credit is limited to $2,000.

**Liability limit and carryover.** The mortgage interest credit is subject to a tax liability limit and any excess is nonrefundable. The tax liability limitation is figured on Form 8396. The allowable credit from Form 8396 is entered on Line 54 of Schedule 3 (Form 1040). However, if your allowable credit exceeds the liability limitation, the unused credit can be carried forward for up to three years; *see* Part II of Form 8396.

**Mortgage interest deduction must be reduced.** If you itemize deductions, you must reduce your home mortgage interest deduction *(15.1)* by the tentative (prior to liability limit) mortgage interest credit shown on Line 3 of Form 8396 (certificate credit rate multiplied by interest paid, subject to the $2,000 limit). The reduction to the mortgage interest deduction applies even if part of the Line 3 credit is carried forward to the next tax year.

## 25.16 Residential Energy Credits

On Form 5695 for 2018, you can claim the residential energy efficient property credit (REEP) if you installed in your home qualifying solar panels, solar water heating equipment, small wind turbines, geothermal heat pumps, and residential fuel cells.

The nonbusiness energy property credit, which in prior years covered energy-efficient insulation, storm windows, furnaces, heaters, boilers, and central air conditioners, expired at the end of 2017. At the time this book was completed, it did not appear likely that Congress would retroactively restore these credits for property placed in service in 2018; an update, if any, will be in the *e-Supplement* at *jklasser.com*.

**Residential energy efficient property (REEP).** For 2018, a 30% credit is allowed on Form 5695 for the cost of qualified residential solar panels, solar water heating equipment, small wind turbines, geothermal heat pumps, and fuel cells that you installed in a home located in the United States.

The residence does not have to be your principal residence and the credit can apply to a home under construction. If you own a condominium or are a tenant-stockholder in a cooperative housing corporation, you are treated as having paid your share of qualifying costs paid by the condominium management association or cooperative housing corporation. The credit includes the cost of labor for onsite preparation, assembly, and installation. There is no dollar limit on the 30% credit. However, no credit is allowed for costs allocable to heating a swimming pool or hot tub. Any subsidy that you (or your contractor on your behalf) received from a public utility for qualified costs reduces your costs on Form 5695 unless you included the subsidy in your gross income.

A separate 30% credit is allowed on Form 5695 for qualified fuel cell property installed in your main home located in the United States. The fuel cell property must have a capacity of at least one-half kilowatt of electricity credit, and the credit cannot exceed the kilowatt capacity multiplied by $1,000.

You may rely on a manufacturer's written certification that a product meets the energy efficiency standards required for a credit. Keep the certification as part of your tax records. You do not have to attach the certification to Form 5695.

The overall credit on Form 5695 cannot exceed your tax liability, as reduced by various other tax credits; the Form 5695 instructions have a worksheet for figuring the liability limitation.

Phasedown of REEP for years after 2019: The REEP credit percentage will drop from 30% to 26% for 2020 and to 22% for 2021, and no credit will be allowed for property placed in service after 2021.

**Caution**

**Recapture of Mortgage Subsidy**

If within nine years of receiving a mortgage credit certificate you sell or dispose of your home at a gain, the mortgage subsidy you received generally must be recaptured as income. See Form 8828 for details.

**Law Alert**

**Home Energy Credits Expired at End of 2017**

Without a retroactive extension from Congress, you may not claim a 2018 tax credit for installing qualifying insulation, storm windows, furnaces, heaters, boilers, or central air conditioners in your principal residence; *see* the *e-Supplement* at *jklasser.com* for an update.

## Sample Form 8962—Premium Tax Credit (PTC)
### (This sample is subject to change; *see* the *e-Supplement* at jklasser.com)

| Form **8962** | **Premium Tax Credit (PTC)** | OMB No. 1545-0074 |
|---|---|---|
| Department of the Treasury Internal Revenue Service | ▶ **Attach to Form 1040 or Form 1040NR.** <br> ▶ **Go to www.irs.gov/Form8962 for instructions and the latest information.** | 20**18** <br> Attachment Sequence No. **73** |

Name shown on your return | Your social security number

You cannot take the PTC if your filing status is married filing separately unless you qualify for an exception (see instructions). If you qualify, check the box . . . ▶ ☐

### Part I    Annual and Monthly Contribution Amount

**1**   Tax family size. Enter your tax family size (see instructions) . . . . . . . . . . . . . . .   **1**

**2a**   Modified AGI. Enter your modified AGI (see instructions) . . . . . . . . .   **2a**

**b**   Enter the total of your dependents' modified AGI (see instructions)   **2b**

**3**   Household income. Add the amounts on lines 2a and 2b (see instructions) . . . . . . . . .   **3**

**4**   Federal poverty line. Enter the federal poverty line amount from Table 1-1, 1-2, or 1-3 (see instructions). Check the appropriate box for the federal poverty table used.   **a** ☐ Alaska   **b** ☐ Hawaii   **c** ☐ Other 48 states and DC   **4**

**5**   Household income as a percentage of federal poverty line (see instructions) . . . . . . . . .   **5**   %

**6**   Did you enter 401% on line 5? (See instructions if you entered less than 100%.)

    ☐ **No.** Continue to line 7.

    ☐ **Yes.** You are not eligible to take the PTC. If advance payment of the PTC was made, see the instructions for how to report your excess advance PTC repayment amount.

**7**   Applicable Figure. Using your line 5 percentage, locate your "applicable figure" on the table in the instructions . .   **7**

**8a**   Annual contribution amount. Multiply line 3 by line 7. Round to nearest whole dollar amount   **8a**   |   **b** Monthly contribution amount. Divide line 8a by 12. Round to nearest whole dollar amount   **8b**

### Part II    Premium Tax Credit Claim and Reconciliation of Advance Payment of Premium Tax Credit

**9**   Are you allocating policy amounts with another taxpayer or do you want to use the alternative calculation for year of marriage (see instructions)?

    ☐ **Yes.** Skip to Part IV, Allocation of Policy Amounts, or Part V, Alternative Calculation for Year of Marriage.   ☐ **No.** Continue to line 10.

**10**   See the instructions to determine if you can use line 11 or must complete lines 12 through 23.

    ☐ **Yes.** Continue to line 11. Compute your annual PTC. Then skip lines 12–23 and continue to line 24.   ☐ **No.** Continue to lines 12–23. Compute your monthly PTC and continue to line 24.

| Annual Calculation | (a) Annual enrollment premiums (Form(s) 1095-A, line 33A) | (b) Annual applicable SLCSP premium (Form(s) 1095-A, line 33B) | (c) Annual contribution amount (line 8a) | (d) Annual maximum premium assistance (subtract (c) from (b), if zero or less, enter -0-) | (e) Annual premium tax credit allowed (smaller of (a) or (d)) | (f) Annual advance payment of PTC (Form(s) 1095-A, line 33C) |
|---|---|---|---|---|---|---|
| **11**   Annual Totals | | | | | | |

| Monthly Calculation | (a) Monthly enrollment premiums (Form(s) 1095-A, lines 21–32, column A) | (b) Monthly applicable SLCSP premium (Form(s) 1095-A, lines 21–32, column B) | (c) Monthly contribution amount (amount from line 8b or alternative marriage monthly calculation) | (d) Monthly maximum premium assistance (subtract (c) from (b), if zero or less, enter -0-) | (e) Monthly premium tax credit allowed (smaller of (a) or (d)) | (f) Monthly advance payment of PTC (Form(s) 1095-A, lines 21–32, column C) |
|---|---|---|---|---|---|---|
| **12**   January | | | | | | |
| **13**   February | | | | | | |
| **14**   March | | | | | | |
| **15**   April | | | | | | |
| **16**   May | | | | | | |
| **17**   June | | | | | | |
| **18**   July | | | | | | |
| **19**   August | | | | | | |
| **20**   September | | | | | | |
| **21**   October | | | | | | |
| **22**   November | | | | | | |
| **23**   December | | | | | | |

**24**   Total premium tax credit. Enter the amount from line 11(e) or add lines 12(e) through 23(e) and enter the total here   **24**

**25**   Advance payment of PTC. Enter the amount from line 11(f) or add lines 12(f) through 23(f) and enter the total here   **25**

**26**   Net premium tax credit. If line 24 is greater than line 25, subtract line 25 from line 24. Enter the difference here and on Schedule 5 (Form 1040), line 70, or Form 1040NR, line 65. If line 24 equals line 25, enter -0-. Stop here. If line 25 is greater than line 24, leave this line blank and continue to line 27 . . . . . . . . . . . . . .   **26**

### Part III    Repayment of Excess Advance Payment of the Premium Tax Credit

**27**   Excess advance payment of PTC. If line 25 is greater than line 24, subtract line 24 from line 25. Enter the difference here   **27**

**28**   Repayment limitation (see instructions) . . . . . . . . . . . . . . . . . .   **28**

**29**   Excess advance premium tax credit repayment. Enter the smaller of line 27 or line 28 here and on Schedule 2 (Form 1040), line 46, or Form 1040NR, line 44 . . . . . . . . . . . . . . . . .   **29**

**For Paperwork Reduction Act Notice, see your tax return instructions.**    Cat. No. 37784Z    Form **8962** (2018)

## Sample Form 8962—Premium Tax Credit (PTC)

**(This sample is subject to change; *see* the *e-Supplement at jklasser.com*)**

Form 8962 (2018)                                                                                                                                   Page **2**

### Part IV    Allocation of Policy Amounts

Complete the following information for up to four policy amount allocations. See instructions for allocation details.

**Allocation 1**

| 30 | **(a)** Policy Number (Form 1095-A, line 2) | **(b)** SSN of other taxpayer | **(c)** Allocation start month | **(d)** Allocation stop month |
|---|---|---|---|---|
| | **Allocation percentage applied to monthly amounts** | **(e)** Premium Percentage | **(f)** SLCSP Percentage | **(g)** Advance Payment of the PTC Percentage |

**Allocation 2**

| 31 | **(a)** Policy Number (Form 1095-A, line 2) | **(b)** SSN of other taxpayer | **(c)** Allocation start month | **(d)** Allocation stop month |
|---|---|---|---|---|
| | **Allocation percentage applied to monthly amounts** | **(e)** Premium Percentage | **(f)** SLCSP Percentage | **(g)** Advance Payment of the PTC Percentage |

**Allocation 3**

| 32 | **(a)** Policy Number (Form 1095-A, line 2) | **(b)** SSN of other taxpayer | **(c)** Allocation start month | **(d)** Allocation stop month |
|---|---|---|---|---|
| | **Allocation percentage applied to monthly amounts** | **(e)** Premium Percentage | **(f)** SLCSP Percentage | **(g)** Advance Payment of the PTC Percentage |

**Allocation 4**

| 33 | **(a)** Policy Number (Form 1095-A, line 2) | **(b)** SSN of other taxpayer | **(c)** Allocation start month | **(d)** Allocation stop month |
|---|---|---|---|---|
| | **Allocation percentage applied to monthly amounts** | **(e)** Premium Percentage | **(f)** SLCSP Percentage | **(g)** Advance Payment of the PTC Percentage |

34  Have you completed all policy amount allocations?

☐ **Yes.** Multiply the amounts on Form 1095-A by the allocation percentages entered by policy. Add all allocated policy amounts and non-allocated policy amounts from Forms 1095-A, if any, to compute a combined total for each month. Enter the combined total for each month on lines 12–23, columns (a), (b), and (f). Compute the amounts for lines 12–23, columns (c)–(e), and continue to line 24.

☐ **No.** See the instructions to report additional policy amount allocations.

### Part V    Alternative Calculation for Year of Marriage

Complete line(s) 35 and/or 36 to elect the alternative calculation for year of marriage. For eligibility to make the election, see the instructions for line 9. To complete line(s) 35 and/or 36 and compute the amounts for lines 12–23, see the instructions for this Part V.

| 35 | **Alternative entries for your SSN** | **(a)** Alternative family size | **(b)** Alternative monthly contribution amount | **(c)** Alternative start month | **(d)** Alternative stop month |
|---|---|---|---|---|---|
| 36 | **Alternative entries for your spouse's SSN** | **(a)** Alternative family size | **(b)** Alternative monthly contribution amount | **(c)** Alternative start month | **(d)** Alternative stop month |

Form **8962** (2018)

## 25.17 Credit for Qualified Plug-in Electric and Fuel Cell Vehicles

For 2018, you can claim a credit for a qualified plug-in electric vehicle with at least four wheels on Form 8936; *see* below.

Both the credit for qualified fuel cell vehicles, which had been allowed on Form 8910, and the credit for qualified two-wheeled plug-in electric vehicles (electric motorcycles), which had been claimed on Form 8936, expired for vehicles purchased after 2017. However, these credits may be claimed for 2018 if a qualifying vehicle was purchased in 2017 but not placed in service until 2018; *see* the Form 8910 and Form 8936 instructions. When this book was completed, it appeared unlikely that Congress would extend these credits for purchases after 2017; an update, if any, will be in the *e-Supplement* at *jklasser.com*.

**Qualified plug-in electric-drive motor vehicle credit on Form 8936.** The credit for 2018 applies to a qualifying four- (or more) wheel vehicle that you purchased new and which is propelled to a significant extent by a rechargeable battery with a capacity of at least 4 kilowatt hours. The vehicle must have a gross vehicle weight of less than 14,000 pounds to qualify for the credit. The minimum credit is $2,500, and depending on battery capacity the credit is increased, up to a maximum credit of $7,500. You may rely on the manufacturer's certification that a vehicle qualifies for the credit and on the amount of the credit so certified, assuming the IRS does not withdraw the certification prior to your purchase.

You must be the original purchaser of a new qualifying vehicle to claim the credit. A credit is not allowed for a used vehicle. If you lease a qualifying vehicle, only the leasing company (and not you) may claim the credit. The vehicle must be manufactured primarily for use on public roads and you must use it primarily within the United States.

The personal use portion of the credit on Form 8936 is limited to tax liability (regular tax plus AMT) reduced by various nonrefundable personal credits. If the vehicle is used for business, the credit for business use figured on Form 8936 is entered on Form 3800 as part of the general business credit *(40.26)*.

*Credit phaseout based on manufacturer sales:* The credit for a particular manufacturer's plug-in electric drive motor vehicles begins to phase out starting in the second calendar quarter following the quarter in which the manufacturer has sold its 200,000th qualifying vehicle in the U.S. (cumulative sales after 2009). For that quarter and the next quarter, 50% of the full credit will be allowed, then 25% of the full credit will be allowed for two more quarters, after which no credits will be allowed.

Tesla announced that its sales exceeded the 200,000 mark in the third quarter of 2018 and that the $7,500 credit that has been allowed for its electric vehicles will begin to phase out two quarters later, starting January 1, 2019. For vehicles purchased in the first two quarters of 2019 (January 1 through June 30, 2019), the credit for Tesla electric vehicles will be $3,750 (50% of the full $7,500 credit), and the credit will fall to $1,875 for vehicles purchased from July 1 through December 31, 2019, after which no other credits will be allowed, assuming current law is not changed.

See the *e-Supplement* at *jklasser.com* for an update on whether other manufacturers announce the start of a phaseout of the credit for their electric vehicles.

## 25.18 Repayment of the First-Time Homebuyer Credit

For 2018 there is a repayment requirement only if a credit was claimed for a home purchased in 2008. The repayment requirement has expired for homes purchased in 2009-2011.

If you claimed the credit for a 2008 home purchase and you continued to own and use it as your principal residence for all of 2018, continue to repay at least 1/15th of the credit with your 2018 return, as you have been required to do starting with your 2010 return. Your repayment installment for 2018 should be entered on Line 60b of Schedule 4 (Form 1040) as an "Other Tax." You do not have to attach Form 5405 to report the repayment.

 *Law Alert*

**Credits for Fuel Cell Vehicles and Electric Motorcycles Expired at End of 2017**

Without a retroactive extension from Congress, you may not claim a tax credit for a fuel cell vehicle or two-wheeled plug-in electric vehicle (electric motorcycle) purchased after 2017; *see* the *e-Supplement* at *jklasser.com* for an update if any.

However, if you sold your home or converted your entire residence to rental or business use during 2018, repayment of the rest of the 2008 credit is generally accelerated, meaning that the balance must be reported on Form 5405 and repaid with your 2018 return. But there are exceptions that limit or eliminate the accelerated repayment requirement. For example, if you sold the home in 2018 to an unrelated party at a loss, no repayment of the credit is required. If you sold the home in 2018 for a gain to an unrelated party and the gain is less than the credit balance (the 2008 credit minus repayments made for 2010 through 2017), the 2018 repayment is limited to the gain.

If in 2018 your home was destroyed, condemned, or sold to an unrelated person through condemnation or threat of condemnation and you had a loss on the disposition, you do not have to repay any of the credit. If there was a gain on the 2018 disposition, repayment over the rest of the 15-year period is limited to the gain if the gain is less than the un-repaid balance of the credit. In that case, the minimum repayment for 2018 is one-seventh of the total gain, as there are seven years left (starting with 2018) on the original 15-year repayment period ending with 2024; for 2019, the minimum repayment will be one-sixth of the gain, and so on. But if you do not acquire a new principal residence within two years of the 2018 home destruction, condemnation, or condemnation-related sale, then in 2020 you will have to repay all of the remaining gain. See the Form 5405 instructions for details on the exceptions to the accelerated repayment rule.

If you were repaying the 2008 credit, got divorced, and ownership of the home was transferred to your spouse as part of the divorce settlement, your spouse becomes responsible for repaying 1/15 of the credit while he or she continues to use it as a principal residence, or if he or she stops using it as a principal residence, accelerated repayment could be required under the regular rules.

# CHAPTER 26

# Tax Withholdings

Withholding taxes gives the Government part of your income before you have a chance to use it. Withholding tax is imposed on salary and wage income, tip income, certain gambling winnings, pensions, and retirement distributions, but you may avoid withholding on retirement payments *(26.10)*. Withholding is also imposed on interest and dividends if you do not give your taxpayer identification number to a payer of interest or dividend income.

You may increase or decrease withholdings on your wages by submitting a new Form W-4 to your employer. Withholdings may be reduced by claiming allowances based on tax deductions and credits.

Make sure that tax withholdings meet or help you meet the estimated tax rules that require withholdings plus estimated tax payments to equal 90% of your current year liability or the required percentage of the prior year's liability; *see Chapter 27*.

A mandatory 20% withholding rate applies to eligible rollover distributions that are paid to you from an employer retirement plan. You may avoid the withholding by instructing your employer to directly transfer the funds to an IRA or the plan of a new employer *(26.9)*.

## 26.1 Withholdings Should Cover Estimated Tax

In fixing the rate of withholding on your wages, pay attention to the tests for determining whether sufficient income taxes have been withheld from your pay. A penalty will apply if your wage withholdings plus estimated tax payments (including prior year overpayments credited to current estimated tax) do not equal the lesser of 90% of your current tax liability or the required percentage of the prior year's tax *(27.1)*.

Taxes are withheld from payments made to you for services that you perform as an employee, subject to certain exceptions *(26.2)*. On Form W-4, you can claim allowances on Line 5 for yourself, your spouse, and dependents, as well as withholding allowances for itemized deductions and tax credits such as the child tax credit and the child and dependent care credit. The number of allowances claimed will either decrease or increase the amount of withholding.

If you need to increase your withholding, such as to cover investment or self-employment income, you can choose not to claim all of the allowances allowed on Form W-4 or increase withholdings even more by claiming "0" (zero) allowances on Line 5. If married, you can select on Line 3 for withholding to be at the higher rate for single persons. You can also direct your employer to withhold an additional flat amount from each paycheck on Line 6 of Form W-4.

You can change your withholdings, either increasing or decreasing them, if your financial or family situation changes *(26.4)*.

## 26.2 Income Taxes Withheld on Wages

The amount of income tax withheld for your wage bracket depends on your marital status and the number of allowances you claim. You file a withholding certificate, Form W-4, with your employer, indicating your status and allowances. Without a Form W-4, your employer must withhold tax as if you are a single person with no exemptions.

Cash payments or the cash value of benefits paid to an employee by an employer are subject to withholding, unless the payments are specifically excluded.

### Income Taxes Are Withheld on:

- Payments by your employer for salaries, wages, fees, commissions, vacation allowances, severance pay, and other payments for services performed (whether paid in cash or goods). You generally may elect to avoid withholding on pensions and retirement annuities *(26.10)*. If supplemental wages (payments that are not regular wages) such as bonuses, commissions, overtime pay, accumulated leave, or taxable expense allowances (under nonaccountable plans) are separately identified from regular wages, an employer may withhold at a flat rate of 25% for the supplemental wages instead of using the regular withholding tables.
- Sick pay paid by your employer. If a third party pays you sick pay on a plan funded by your employer, you may request withholding by filing Form W-4S.
- Taxable group insurance coverage over $50,000.
- Reimbursements of expenses that do not meet qualifying rules of accountable plans discussed in *20.31*. Also, reimbursements from accountable plans that exceed federal rates if the employee does not return the reimbursement or show that it is substantiated by proof of expenses.
- Pay to members of the U.S. Armed Forces. Differential wages paid by an employer to a former employee while on active military duty are subject to withholding.
- Prize awarded to a salesperson in a contest run by his or her employer.
- Retroactive pay and overtime under the Fair Labor Standards Act.
- Taxable supplemental unemployment compensation benefits.

### Income Taxes Are Not Withheld on:

- Earnings of self-employed persons; they may pay estimated tax installments throughout the year *(27.2)*.
- Payments to household workers. However, although income tax withholding is not required, the worker and the employer may make a voluntary withholding agreement; *see Chapter 38*.

**Planning Reminder**

**Adjust Withholdings**

If you do not expect withholdings to meet your final tax liability, ask your employer to withhold a greater amount of tax *(26.1)*. On the other hand, if the withholding rate applied to your wages results in overwithholding, you may claim extra withholding allowances to reduce withholding during the year *(26.4–26.5)*.

*Law Alert*

**Differential Wages Paid to Workers Joining Military**

Employees who enlist or are called up to active military service may receive "differential wages" from their former employer to cover the difference between their military pay and the wages that were being received prior to joining the military. Income tax must be withheld from the differential wages, but not FICA tax (Social Security and Medicare).

- Value of tax-free board and lodging furnished by an employer.
- Fringe benefits not subject to tax.
- Substantiated reimbursements for deductible moving expenses or medical care benefits under a self-insured medical reimbursement plan.
- Advances for traveling expenses if the employee substantiates expenses to the employer and if the employee returns any unsubstantiated amount *(20.31)*.
- Pay for U.S. citizen working abroad or in U.S. possessions to the extent that the pay is tax free *(36.1)*.
- Payments to agricultural workers, ministers of the gospel (except chaplains in the Armed Forces), nonresident aliens, public officials who receive fees directly from the public, notaries, jurors, witnesses, precinct workers, etc.
- Pay for newspaper home delivery by children under age 18.
- Death benefit payments to beneficiary of employee; wages due but unpaid at employee's death and paid to estate or beneficiary.

**Form W-2.** By January 31, 2019, your employer must give you duplicate copies of your 2018 Form W-2, which is a record of your pay and the withheld income tax, Social Security and Medicare taxes. If you leave your job or your employment is terminated and you request a Form W-2 from the employer, you should receive it within 30 days of the request or, if later, within 30 days of your final wage payment.

## 26.3  Low Earners May Be Exempt From Withholding

If you had no income tax liability in 2018 and expect none for 2019, you may be exempt from income tax withholdings on your 2019 wages. If eligible for an exemption, students working for the summer, retired persons working part time, and other part-time workers do not have to wait for a refund of withheld taxes they do not owe. The exemption applies only to income tax withholding, not to withholdings for Social Security and Medicare *(26.8)*.

If you cannot be claimed as a dependent by another person, you can claim the exemption from withholding if last year you had no tax liability and this year your total income is expected to be no more than t the standard deduction for your filing status. However, if you can be claimed as a dependent on another person's tax return and are under age 65, the exemption from withholding is not allowed if your expected total income (wages and investments) and investment income exceeds annual limits. For 2018, the total income limit was $1,050 and the investment income limit was $350. These amounts may be increased by an inflation adjustment for 2019, and if so, the revised amounts will be on the Form W-4 for 2019.

To claim an exemption for 2019, you must file Form W-4 with your employer and certify your eligibility on Line 7. If you will file a joint return for 2019, do not claim an exemption on Form W-4 if the joint return will show a tax liability. An exemption claimed during 2018 expires February 15, 2019.

## 26.4  Are You Withholding the Right Amount?

You do not want to withhold too little from your pay and you do not want to withhold too much. You may need to withhold more to avoid a large tax payment or an estimated tax penalty *(26.1)* when you file your return, especially if you have substantial income from investments or a business.

On the other hand, if you have been receiving large refunds from the IRS, you may want to consider reducing your Form W-4 allowances to avoid over-withholding. Balance the loss of the use of your earnings during the year against the value of receiving a substantial refund check from the IRS after you file your return.

If you are starting a new job or if you have not changed your withholding allowances in several years, review the Form W-4 worksheets to help you determine if you are withholding the right amount.

If you work for only one employer and are unmarried, you may claim an additional withholding allowance on the "Personal Allowances Worksheet." If you are married, you may claim the additional allowance if you work for only one employer and your spouse

*Planning Reminder*

**When to Change Withholdings**

Adjust the withholdings that were in effect during 2018 if you expect there to be a significant change in the tax you owe for 2019. For example, if you expect to have lower income, you can reduce your withholdings to increase your take home pay. On the other hand, a withholding increase may be advisable if previously claimed deductions or credits will not be available to you, or if you expect an increase in nonwage income such as capital gains. Check the instructions to Forms W-4 and 1040-ES for 2019 to help you adjust your withholdings for 2019.

## Part-Year Employees May Avoid Over-withholding

Starting a new job in the middle of a year presents a withholding problem. The amount of tax withheld from your paycheck is figured by taking your weekly pay and multiplying this by a 52-week pay period. For example, if as a recent graduate you start a job on July 1 and your weekly pay is $1,000 for 26 weeks (July 1–December 31), your withholding will be based on an annual income of $52,000 ($1,000 × 52 weeks) and not the $26,000 you will actually earn that year. This will result in over-withholding. To alleviate this problem, you may ask your employer to calculate withholdings on what is known as the "part year" method if your work days during the year are expected to be 245 or fewer. This formula calculates withholding based on actual earnings rather than expected earnings over a full year of employment. As an alternative, you may elect to claim extra exemptions on Form W-4, which has the same effect of reducing the amount withheld each week from your paycheck.

does not work, or your wages from a second job or your spouse's wages do not exceed the amount specified on the Worksheet.

If you work for two or more employers at the same time, or you are married filing jointly and you and your spouse both work, and the combined earnings from all jobs exceed the amount shown at the bottom of the Personal Allowances Worksheet, use the "Two-Earners/Multiple Jobs Worksheet" to figure how many withholding allowances you should claim. The purpose of this Worksheet is to ensure that you do not have too little tax withheld.

The Form W-4 instructions recommend that where both you and your spouse work, the total allowances for both of you should be claimed on the Form W-4 for the highest-paying job, and zero allowances should be claimed on the Forms W-4 for the other jobs.

File a new Form W-4 each year for withholding allowances based on your anticipated deductions and credits. Furthermore, you may have to file a new form to increase your withholding if withholding allowances you had been claiming are no longer allowed.

**IRS review of Form W-4.** Employers are not required to submit Forms W-4 to the IRS for review unless the IRS sends written notice directing the employer to provide the W-4 forms of specified employees. The IRS uses the information on Form W-2 wage statements to spot employees who are not withholding enough federal income tax from their income. If the IRS determines that too many withholding allowances are being claimed, the IRS can issue a "lock-in letter" requiring your employer to limit the number of allowances to a specified maximum. You will receive a copy of the "lock-in letter" and be given an opportunity to dispute the IRS determination before your employer adjusts your withholding.

The IRS may impose a $500 civil penalty if you did not have a reasonable basis for claiming allowances that reduced your withholding on Form W-4. There is also a criminal penalty for willfully supplying false information on Form W-4. Upon conviction, there could be a fine of up to $1,000, a jail sentence of up to a year, or both.

**When to file a new Form W-4.** You should file a new Form W-4 any time the withholding allowances increases or decreases, such as when a child is born or adopted, you marry, you get a divorce, or your deductible expenses change.

Your employer may make the new Form W-4 effective with the next payment of wages. However, an employer may postpone the new withholding rate until the start of the first payroll period ending on or after the 30th day from the day you submit the revised form.

## 26.5 Voluntary Withholding on Government Payments

You can choose to have federal income tax withheld from Social Security benefits (and equivalent tier 1 Railroad Retirement benefits), unemployment compensation, crop disaster payments, distributions from Alaska Native Corporations, and Commodity Credit Corporation loans. The withholding request is made on Form W-4V. Electing to have tax withheld may eliminate the need to make estimated tax installments *(27.2)*.

For unemployment compensation you may choose a withholding rate of 10%; this is the only rate you can choose. For Social Security and the other payments, you may select a withholding rate of 7%, 10%, 12%, or 22%. If you elect withholding and later decide to stop it, you can do so on a new Form W-4V.

## 26.6 When Tips Are Subject to Withholding

Tips are subject to income tax and FICA (Social Security and Medicare) withholdings. If you receive cash tips amounting to $20 or more in a month, you must report the total amount of tips received during the month to your employer on Form 4070 (or a similar written report). Include cash tips paid to you in your own behalf. If you "split" or share tips with others, you include in your report only your share. You do not include tips received in the form of merchandise or your share of service charges turned over to you by your employer. Make the report on or before the 10th day after the end of the month in which the tips are received. (If the 10th day is a Saturday, Sunday, or legal holiday, you must submit the report by the next business day.) For example, tips amounting to $20 or more that are received during January 2019 are reported by February 10, 2019. Your employer may require more frequent reporting.

You are considered to have income from tips when you receive the tips, even if they are not reported to the employer.

Your employer withholds the Social Security, Medicare, and income tax due on the tips from your wages or from funds you give him or her for withholding purposes. If the taxes due cannot be collected on the tips, either from your wages or from voluntary contributions, by the 10th day after the end of the month in which tips are reported, you have to pay the tax when you file your income tax return.

**Penalty for failure to report tips.** Failure to report tip income of $20 or more received during the month to your employer may subject you to a penalty of 50% of the Social Security and Medicare tax due on the unreported tips, unless your failure was due to reasonable cause rather than to willful neglect.

Tips of less than $20 per month are taxable but not subject to withholding.

**Tip allocation reporting by large restaurants.** To help the IRS audit the reporting of tip income, restaurants employing more than 10 people on a typical business day must make a special report of income and allocate tips based on gross receipts. For purposes of the allocation, the law assumes tip income of at least 8%. If you voluntarily report tips equal to your allocable share of 8% of the restaurant's gross receipts, no allocation will be made to you. However, if the total tips reported by all employees is less than 8% of gross receipts and you do not report your share of the 8%, your employer must make an allocation based on the difference between the amount you reported and your share of the 8% amount. The allocated amount is shown in Box 8 of your Form W-2. However, taxes are not withheld on the allocated amount. Taxes are withheld only on amounts actually reported by employees. An employer or majority of employees may ask the IRS to apply a tip percentage of less than 8%, but no lower than 2%.

**Reporting allocated tips.** Your employer will show allocated tips in Box 8 of your Form W-2. However, this amount will not be included in Box 1 wages and you must add it to income yourself by reporting it on Line 1 of Form 1040. You also must compute Social Security and Medicare tax on the allocated tips on Form 4137 and enter the tax from Form 4137 on Schedule 4 of Form 1040.

## 26.7 Withholding on Gambling Winnings

Gambling winnings are generally reported by the payer to the IRS and to the winner on Form W-2G if the amount paid is $600 or more and at least 300 times the amount of the wager. The payer has the option of reducing the amount paid by the wager in applying the $600 test.

Different reporting rules apply to winnings from poker tournaments, keno, bingo, and slot machines. Winnings from slot machines or bingo games of $1,200 or more, *not* reduced by the wager, are reported on Form W-2G. Poker tournament winnings are reported on Form W-2G if they exceed $5,000, *reduced* by the wager or buy-in. Keno winnings are reported on Form W-2G if they are $1,500 or more, *reduced* by the wager.

**Withholding.** Your winnings from gambling are subject to 24% withholding if your winnings minus the wager exceed:

1. $5,000 from lotteries, sweepstakes, and wagering pools, whether or not state-conducted, including church raffles and charity drawings, or
2. $5,000 from pari-mutuel pool wagers on horse races, dog races, or jai alai if the proceeds are at least 300 times as large as the amount wagered.

Winnings from slot machines, bingo, keno, or poker tournaments are exempt from the 24% withholding rule. However, "backup" withholding at 24% applies to reportable slot, keno, bingo, or tournament poker winnings if you do not provide a taxpayer identification number (TIN) to the payer; *see* the **Caution** on this page.

If your winnings exceed the $5,000 threshold, 24% withholding applies to your gross winnings less your wagers, and not just the amounts over $5,000. Any withholdings will be shown on Form W-2G.

**Filing Instruction**

**Tip Reporting**

If you have not reported tips of $20 or more in any month, or tips are allocated to you under the special tip allocation rules, you must compute Social Security and Medicare tax on that amount on Form 4137 and enter it as a tax due on Schedule 4 of Form 1040; attach Form 4137 to Form 1040. The unreported tips must be included as wages on Line 1 of Form 1040.

**Filing Instruction**

**Uncollected Social Security and Medicare Taxes on Tips**

If your employer is unable to collect enough money from your wages during the year to cover the Social Security or Medicare tax on the tips you reported, the uncollected amount is shown on your Form W-2 in Box 12 with Code A next to it for Social Security or Code B for Medicare. You must report the uncollected amount on Schedule 4 of Form 1040 as an additional tax due; enter code "UT".

**Caution**

**Backup Gambling Withholding**

Winnings from bingo, keno, and slot machines are not subject to 24% income tax withholding. However, if your slots or bingo winnings are $1,200 or more, keno winnings are $1,500 or more, or tournament poker winnings are over $5,000, and you do not provide a taxpayer identification number, the payer will withhold tax at the 24% backup withholding rate *(26.10)* on the winnings reduced, at the payer's option, by the wager.

The IRS requires you to tell the payers of gambling winnings if you are also receiving winnings from identical wagers; winnings from identical wagers must be added together to determine if withholding is required.

If you have agreed to share your winnings with another person, give the payer a Form 5754. The payer will then prepare separate Forms W-2G for each of you.

## 26.8 FICA Withholdings

FICA withholdings are employee contributions for Social Security and Medicare coverage. Your employer is liable for the tax if he or she fails to make proper withholdings. The amount withheld is figured on your wages and is not affected by your marital status, number of exemptions, or the fact that you may be collecting Social Security benefits. On Form W-2, Social Security withholdings are shown in Box 4 and Medicare withholdings in Box 6.

Subject to FICA tax are your regular salary, commissions, bonuses, vacation pay, cash tips, group-term insurance coverage over $50,000, the first six months of sick pay, and contributions to cash or deferred (401(k)) pay plans or salary-reduction contributions to a simplified employee pension (SEP), SIMPLE IRA, or tax-sheltered annuity. Severance pay to laid-off employees is also subject to FICA tax (the U.S. Supreme Court held this in 2014).

FICA tax does not apply to the value of tax-free meals and lodgings *(3.12)* or to reimbursements for substantiated travel or entertainment expenses or moving expenses.

**Excess Social Security and Railroad Retirement withholding.** If you have worked for more than one employer during 2018, attach all Copies B of Form W-2 to your return. Withholdings for Social Security taxes are shown in Box 4 of Form W-2. Check to *see* that the total withheld in 2018 by all your employers does not exceed the annual limit for Social Security taxes. The maximum 2018 liability for Social Security is $7,960.80, 6.2% of the first $128,400 of salary income. If too much was withheld, claim the excess as a credit against the tax you owe on Schedule 5 of your 2018 Form 1040.

Employees covered by the Railroad Retirement Tax Act (RRTA) receive Form W-2, which lists total wages paid and withholdings of income and Railroad Retirement taxes. Follow tax form instructions for claiming a credit for excess Railroad Retirement withholding.

If any one employer withheld too much Social Security or Railroad Retirement tax, you cannot claim the excess on your income tax return. You must ask that employer for a refund of the excess and if the employer refuses, get a record of the overpayment and file for a refund on Form 843.

**Medicare tax withholding.** Medicare tax is withheld at a rate of 1.45% on all salary and wage income; the amount is shown in Box 6 of Form W-2. In addition, if you had wages exceeding $200,000, your employer withheld the 0.9% Additional Medicare Tax on the excess, and this withholding is included in Box 6. *See 28.2* for further details on the 0.9% Additional Medicare Tax.

**Wages you pay to your spouse or child.** Wages you pay to your spouse for working in your business are subject to FICA tax and income tax withholding. Wages you pay to your child are subject to income tax withholding but if your child is under age 18 and your business is a sole proprietorship or a partnership in which the only partners are you and the child's other parent, the wages are exempt from FICA taxes. Wages you pay to your child under age 21 or to your spouse for domestic work or child care in your own home are exempt from FICA.

## 26.9 Withholding on Distributions from Retirement Plans and Commercial Annuities

Retirement plan and commercial annuity distributions are subject to withholding taxes, but you may choose to avoid withholdings. The method of avoiding withholding varies with the type of payment.

*Law Alert*

**Additional Medicare Tax May Be Shown on W-2**

Your employer must withhold the 0.9% Additional Medicare from your wages once the total exceeds $200,000 in a calendar year. Any withheld Additional Medicare Tax on the excess over $200,000 will be reported in Box 6 of your Form W-2, along with the regular 1.45% Medicare tax withholding on all the wages. Even if the Additional Medicare tax is not withheld from your pay, you must pay it when you file your Form 1040 if your wages for the year exceeded $200,000 if single, $ 250,000 if married filing jointly, or $125,000 if married filing separately. Self-employed individuals are also subject to the additional 0.9% Medicare tax. *See* 28.2 for further details.

*Planning Reminder*

**Wages Paid to Household Employees**

*See* Chapter 38 for FICA withholding on wages paid to household employees.

**Periodic payments.** If you receive periodic payments from a pension or an annuity (employee annuity or commercial annuity) in regular installments over more than one year (installments could be monthly, quarterly, semi-annually, or annually), withholding is required unless you elect to avoid withholding on Form W-4P, or on a substitute form furnished by the payer. If you are a U.S. citizen or resident alien, withholding may not be avoided on pensions or other distributions paid outside the U.S. or U.S. possessions. Payment must be to your home address within the U.S. (or in a U.S. possession) to avoid withholding.

The payer of a pension or annuity will use the regular wage withholding tables to figure withholdings on periodic payments as if you were married and claiming three withholding exemptions, unless on Form W-4P you elect to avoid withholding or you claim a different number of allowances and marital status. Withholding allowances may be claimed on Form W-4P for estimated itemized deductions, tax credits and adjustments to income such as alimony payments, student loan interest, and deductible IRA contributions.

You cannot designate the specific dollar amount that you would like to have withheld, but after selecting the number of withholding allowances and marital status on Form W-4P, you may request that the payer withhold a specific amount of additional tax from each payment.

**Nonperiodic payments.** Nonperiodic payments that are not eligible rollover distributions (*see* the next paragraph) are subject to withholding at a flat 10% rate unless you elect to avoid withholding on Form W-4P (or substitute form). IRA distributions that are payable upon demand are considered nonperiodic and, thus, subject to the 10% withholding rule. If you want more than 10% withheld, you can enter an additional amount on Form W-4P. As with periodic distributions (*see* above), the election to avoid withholding cannot be made for a nonperiodic distribution if you are a U.S. citizen or resident alien and payment is made to you outside the United States or its possessions.

**Eligible rollover distributions from qualified employer plans.** Employers must withhold 20% from nonperiodic payments, such as lump-sum distributions, that are eligible for tax-free rollover but which are paid directly to you. To avoid withholding you must direct your employer to make a direct rollover *(7.6)* of the funds to an IRA or to a qualified plan of your new employer. If you do not instruct your employer to make the direct transfer and elect to personally receive the distribution, 20% will be withheld before payment is made to you. The 20% withholding rule does not apply to qualifying hardship distributions or payments that are part of a series of substantially equal payments, as these are not eligible for rollover *(7.5)*.

See 7.6 for a further explanation and the "John Anderson" example showing the effects of the withholding rule where you receive the distribution and then decide to make a rollover yourself.

 *Planning Reminder*

**Direct Rollover from Employer Plan Avoids Withholding**

Your employer must withhold 20% from a distribution paid to you if the distribution was eligible for tax-free rollover *(7.6)*. Withholding does not apply if you have the employer make a direct rollover to a qualified plan or IRA.

## 26.10 Backup Withholding

Backup withholding is designed to pressure taxpayers to report interest and dividend income. You may be subject to backup withholding if you do not give your taxpayer identification number to parties paying you interest or dividend income, you give an incorrect number, or you ignore IRS notices stating that you have underreported interest or dividends. Your taxpayer identification number generally is your Social Security number or your employer identification number. The backup withholding rate is 24%.

Backup withholding will apply to fees of $600 or more (Form 1099-MISC) for work you do as an independent contractor, payments from brokers (Form 1099-B), royalty payments (Form 1099-MISC), and certain gambling winnings *(26.7)* if you do not give the payer your taxpayer identification number.

If you provide false information to avoid backup withholding, you could face a civil penalty of $500 or, if convicted of a willful violation, a criminal penalty of up to a $1,000 fine or imprisonment of up to one year or both.

# CHAPTER 27

# Estimated Tax Payments

Income taxes are collected on a pay-as-you-go basis through withholding on wages and pensions, as well as quarterly estimated tax payments on other income. Where all or most of your income is from wages, pensions, and annuities, you will generally not have to pay estimated tax, because your estimated tax liability has been satisfied by withholding. But do not assume you are not required to pay simply because taxes have been withheld from your wages. Always check your estimated tax liability. Withholding may not cover your tax; the withholding tax rate may be below your actual tax rate when considering other income such as interest, dividends, business income, and capital gains.

Your withholdings and estimated tax payments must also cover any liability for self-employment tax, alternative minimum tax (AMT), the additional 0.9% Medicare tax on earnings, the 3.8% tax on net investment income, and FICA withholding tax for household employees.

If you expect your 2019 tax liability to be $1,000 or more after taking into account withheld taxes and refundable credits, you should make quarterly estimated tax payments unless you expect the withholdings and credits to be at least 90% of your 2019 total tax, or, if less, 100% or 110% of your total tax for 2018. The 100% test applies if your 2018 adjusted gross income (AGI) was $150,000 or less, $75,000 or less if for 2019 you will file as married filing separately. The 110% test applies if your 2018 AGI exceeded the $150,000 or $75,000 threshold.

Failure to pay a required estimated tax installment will subject you to a penalty based on the prevailing IRS interest rate applied to tax deficiencies, unless the IRS waives the penalty.

## 27.1 Do You Owe an Estimated Tax Penalty for 2018?

When you have computed the exact amount of your tax liability on your 2018 return, you can determine whether you are subject to an estimated tax penalty. If you owe less than $1,000 on your 2018 return after taking into account withheld taxes and refundable credits, you are not subject to a penalty. If the tax owed after withholdings is $1,000 or more, you will not owe a penalty if your 2018 withholdings plus refundable credits and estimated tax installments were at least 90% (66 $^2/_3$ % for farmers and fishermen) of your 2018 total tax.

Total tax here means not only your 2018 regular income tax and alternative minimum tax (AMT) liability after credits, but also other taxes such as self-employment tax, the additional 0.9% Medicare tax on earnings *(28.2)*, the 3.8% tax on net investment income *(28.3)*, household employment taxes, penalty taxes (such as penalties on early retirement plan distributions, on distributions from qualified tuition programs not used for education), and taxes from recaptured credits. The individual shared responsibility payment for not having minimum essential coverage *(38.5)* is not included in the "total tax" for estimated tax purposes. However, the total tax does include any excess advanced premium tax credit that you received in 2018 and have to repay with your 2018 return when you reconcile your advanced credit with the credit you are actually entitled to *(25.12)*.

Even if the 90% test was not met, you may be able to avoid a penalty if your 2018 withholdings, refundable credits and estimated tax installments were at least 100% of the total tax *(see* above) shown on your 2017 return. This exception requires that the 2017 return covered all 12 months. However, if your 2017 adjusted gross income exceeded $150,000 ($75,000 if you are married filing separately for 2018), your withholdings plus estimated tax installments for 2018 had to be at least 110% of your 2017 total tax (not 100%) to qualify for this prior-year liability exception. The 110% rule does not apply to farmers and fishermen.

Note that to completely avoid a penalty for 2018 under either the 90% current year exception or the 100%/110% prior-year exception, you must have paid at least 25% of the amount required under the applicable exception by each of the four payment dates in 2018. The penalty is figured separately for each payment period; *see* below.

You are not subject to an estimated tax penalty for 2018 if you did not have to file a 2017 return or your 2017 total tax was zero. This is so even if you owe $1,000 or more (after withholdings) on your 2018 return and you do not qualify for either the 90% current-year exception, or the 100%/110% prior-year exception. This exception applies only if you were a U.S. citizen or resident for all of 2017 and your 2017 tax year included 12 full months.

If you underestimated your 2018 liability because of an unexpected increase in income during 2018, or if you did not earn income evenly throughout 2018, such as where you operated a seasonal business, you may be able to lower or eliminate the penalty by using the annualized income installment method. Under this exception, your required installment for one or more payment periods could be reduced below 25% of the required annual payment by figuring the installment that would be due if the income (and deductions) earned before the date for the installment were annualized. The computation is quite complicated; *see* the Form 2210 instructions and the worksheets in IRS Publication 505 for the details of applying the annualized income exception.

**Penalties are figured separately for each payment period.** Separate penalty determinations must be made for each of the four 2018 estimated tax payment periods, as of the applicable installment dates: April 17, June 15, and September 17 in 2018, and January 15, 2019. This means that if, after taking into account withholdings from your pay, you underpaid an installment, you may owe a penalty for that period even though you overpaid later installments to make up the difference. However, withholdings towards the end of the year can eliminate an underpayment for an earlier period. In applying withholdings, the total withholdings of the year are divided equally between each installment period unless you elect on Form 2210 to apply them to the periods in which they were actually withheld. An overpayment for a period carries over to the next period.

*Planning Reminder*

## Withholdings Cover Prior Underpayment

You have a choice in allocating withholdings from pay or other income that is subject to withholding: (1) You may treat your entire year's withholdings as having been withheld in equal amounts for each of the four payment periods or (2) you may allocate to each payment period the actual withholdings paid for that period. If toward the end of the year you find that you have underestimated for an earlier period, ask your employer to withhold an extra amount that may be allocated equally over the four periods. This way, you may eliminate the underestimate for the earlier periods under the equal allocation method.

*Filing Reminder*

## Penalty Waiver

From time to time, the IRS may waive estimated tax penalties resulting from law changes. For example, it announced in Notice 2018-26 that it will waive estimated penalties on the transition tax imposed on U.S. shareholders of foreign corporations (essentially a tax on repatriating offshore profits). If there is any penalty waiver for individuals, it will be discussed in the *e-Supplement* at *jklasser.com*.

The penalty for each period, which is based on the prevailing IRS interest rate for deficiencies *(46.7)*, runs from the installment due date until the amount is paid or until the regular filing date for the final tax return, whichever is earlier.

**Figure the 2018 penalty for yourself on Form 2210 or let the IRS do it.** In most cases you do not have to file Form 2210 to figure an estimated tax penalty; the IRS prefers to figure it and send you a bill if a penalty is due.

However, you must figure your penalty and file Form 2210 if (1) you request a partial waiver of your penalty (see below for waiver rules), (2) you use the annualized income method (Schedule AI of Form 2210) to reduce or eliminate your penalty, or (3) you elect to treat your withholdings as paid on the dates withheld rather than in equal amounts on the four installment dates.

In the following situations, the IRS requires you to file only page 1 of Form 2210 but not the rest of the form (Parts III and IV) on which the penalty computation is made: (1) you request a waiver for your entire penalty, or (2) you filed a joint return for either 2017 or 2018 (not both) and your required annual payment for 2018 was based on the 100% or 110% prior-year safe harbor (because it was less than the amount required by the 90% current-year test). If you are requesting a waiver, attach a statement to page 1 of Form 2210 that explains the grounds for the request (*see* the waiver rules below). For situations (1) or (2), you must file only page 1 (Parts I and II) of Form 2210 and are not required to figure your penalty, but you may use Part III or Part IV of Form 2210 as a worksheet to figure the penalty and enter it on your return.

If you use Part IV to figure the penalty under the regular method, an underpayment for any payment period reduces the payments made in the following period. That is, an underpayment of one period is carried over to succeeding periods on Form 2210. If you underpay for a period, any payment you make after that installment date will be applied first to the earlier underpayment. Thus, even if you make the required payment for a period, you could still be subject to a penalty for that period because your payment is applied to a prior underpayment.

If you overpaid for any period, the excess carries over to the next period. The excess cannot be used to make up for an underpayment of the prior period if the earlier payments were made online, by phone, or with Form 1040-ES vouchers. However, withholdings are allocated equally over the year so that withholdings late in the year can reduce an underpayment for an earlier payment period.

**Waiver of penalty for hardship, retirement, or disability.** The IRS may waive the penalty if you can show you failed to pay the estimated tax because of casualty, disaster, or other unusual circumstances.

The IRS may also waive a penalty for a 2018 underpayment if in 2017 or 2018 you retired after reaching age 62 or became disabled, and you failed to make a payment due to reasonable cause and not due to willful neglect.

To apply for the waiver, attach an explanation to Form 2210 that documents the circumstances supporting your waiver request. For a waiver due to retirement or disability, show your retirement date and age or disability date. If an underpayment was due to a federally declared disaster, you do not have to request a waiver on Form 2210 because the IRS allows an automatic postponement following such a disaster. When you file your return, the IRS should identify your residence as being in a federally declared disaster area and if you still owe a penalty following the end of the disaster waiver period, the IRS will send you a bill. If you are requesting a waiver due to a disaster other than a federally declared disaster, other casualty, or unusual circumstance, attach documentation of the event, including police and insurance company reports, and an explanation as to how it prevented you from making estimated tax payments.

**Farmers and fishermen.** Farmers or fishermen who earned at least ⅔ of their 2017 or 2018 gross income from farming or fishing can use Form 2210-F to determine whether they owe an estimated penalty for 2018, but generally the form does not have to be filed because the IRS will figure any penalty; *see* the Form 2210-F instructions.

## 27.2 Planning Estimated Tax Payments for 2019

In planning your payments for 2019, you may not want to pay any more than is necessary to avoid a penalty. You can avoid a penalty for 2019 by planning payments in 2019 that meet the 90% current-year test or the 100%/110% prior-year safe harbor.

**90% current-year test.** If you expect your income, deductions, and tax credits for 2019 to be about the same as they were for 2018, and you will not have any additional liabilities for 2019 that you did not have for 2018, you can base your 2019 withholdings and quarterly estimated tax installments on 90% of your projected 2019 total tax. In projecting your tax liability for 2019, take into account possible liability for the alternative minimum tax (AMT), self-employment tax, the 0.9% additional Medicare tax on earnings, the 3.8% tax on net investment income, household employee taxes, penalty taxes, and recapture taxes, including a repayment of advance payments of the premium tax credit.

If you expect your 2019 total tax to be lower than your 2018 total tax, such as where your income has dropped, you can base your 2019 withholdings and estimated tax installments on 90% of the estimated 2019 total tax.

You can use the 2019 Estimated Tax Worksheet in the instructions to Form 1040-ES for 2019 to figure the required annual payment under the 90% test, as well as under the prior-year safe harbor test discussed next.

**Safe harbor for 2019 based on 2018 tax.** If you cannot make a precise projection of your 2019 income and deductions, you can play it safe and avoid a possible penalty for 2019 by planning withholdings and quarterly estimated tax installments in 2019 that equal your 2018 total tax if your 2018 adjusted gross income is $150,000 or less ($75,000 or less if married filing separately for 2019), provided you filed a 2018 return covering a full 12 months. If your 2018 AGI exceeds the $150,000 (or $75,000) threshold, your payments for 2019 must be at least 110% of your 2018 tax under the prior-year safe harbor.

If an accurate estimate for 2019 is possible, it is generally advantageous to base your estimated payments on the 90% test rather than the 100%/110% prior year test, as using this prior year test will probably result in an overestimation of your liability unless the 2019 tax turns out to be substantially larger than the 2018 tax.

You may use the worksheet and the tax rate schedule included in the 2019 Form 1040-ES to figure your estimated tax liability and the required annual payment to avoid a penalty under either the 90% current-year or the 100%/110% prior-year liability tests.

**Making estimated tax payments.** Reduce your 2019 estimated tax liability by expected withholdings from wages, pensions, and annuities. If after withholdings and expected refundable credits your estimated tax is $1,000 or more, you must make estimated tax payments unless the withholdings and refundable credits will cover at least 90% of your estimated 2019 liability or 100%/110% of your 2018 liability. If the projected withholdings and credits will not cover the amount required under the 90% or 100%/110% tests, you may pay the balance of the estimated tax with Form 1040-ES vouchers, by credit card or debit card (online or by phone), online by direct transfer from your bank account ("Direct Pay"), or by scheduling payments from your bank account using the Electronic Federal Tax Payment System (EFTPS). *See* www.irs.gov/payments for details on the electronic payment options.

**Planning Reminder**

**Take COLAs and Law Changes into Account**

Numerous Cost-of-Living Adjustments (COLAs) are made annually to specified provisions in the tax law, including the tax brackets, standard deduction amounts, and the earned income tax credit. There are also law changes taking effect (e.g., the adjusted gross income threshold for itemizing medical expenses in 2019 is 10%, instead of the 7.5% in 2018). Be sure to review all the new amounts in estimating taxes for 2019.

**Planning Reminder**

**Annualized Income Method**

If your income typically fluctuates throughout the year, or if your income unexpectedly changes during the year, you may base installment payments on the annualized income method. This method allows you to avoid a penalty for installment periods during which less income is earned by reducing the required estimated tax payment for such periods. To figure your installment payments, use the Annualized Estimated Tax Worksheet in IRS Publication 505. If you base installment payments on the annualized method, you must file Form 2210 with your return to determine if you are subject to an estimated tax penalty.

**Planning Reminder**

**Estimate May Have to Include Additional Medicare Tax and NII Tax**

In planning your estimated tax payments, take into account possible liability for the 0.9% additional Medicare tax on wages and self-employment earnings in excess of the threshold amount for your filing status *(28.2)*. Also project possible liability for the 3.8% tax on net investment income (NII) tax if modified adjusted gross income exceeds the threshold amount *(28.3)*.

**Planning Reminder**

**Credit Card or Electronic Payments**

You can make estimated tax payments by check or money order with the Form 1040-ES vouchers, use a credit card, authorize withdrawals from your checking or savings account, or schedule payments through EFTPS (Electronic Federal Tax Payment System); *see* www.irs.gov/payments.

**Crediting 2018 refund to 2019 estimated tax.** If you are due a refund when you file your 2018 return, it may be credited to your 2019 estimated tax. You may also split up the amount due you. You may take part of the overpayment as a refund. The other part may be credited to your estimate of 2019 taxes. The IRS will credit the refund to the April installment of 2019 estimated tax unless you attach a statement to your return instructing the IRS to apply the refund to later installments.

Check your arithmetic before you apply an overpayment as a credit on your next year's estimate. If you apply too much, the amount credited may not be used to offset any additional tax due that the IRS determines you owe. For example, your 2018 return shows a $500 refund due, and you apply it towards your 2019 estimated tax. However, the IRS determines that you overpaid only $200 for 2018, not $500. You will be billed for the additional $300 tax, plus interest due; you may not offset the extra tax with the amount credited to 2019.

**Farmers or fishermen.** In figuring the required annual payment to avoid a penalty for 2019, a farmer or fisherman has to pay only 66⅔% of the 2019 estimated liability, rather than 90%. A penalty may also be avoided by paying 100% of the 2018 tax, provided a tax return covering a 12-month period was filed for 2018; the 110% test for higher-income taxpayers does not apply to a farmer or fisherman. To qualify as a farmer or fisherman for 2019 under these rules, at least two-thirds of gross income for 2018 or 2019 must be from farming or fishing.

## 27.3 Dates for Paying Estimated Tax Installments for 2019

The four installment dates for 2019 estimated tax are: April 15, 2019; June 17, 2019; September 16, 2019; and January 15, 2020. Later installments may be used to amend earlier ones *(27.1)*. You do not have to make the payment due January 15, 2020, if you file your 2019 tax return and pay the balance of tax due by January 31, 2020.

**If you use a fiscal year.** A fiscal year is any year other than the calendar year. If you file using a fiscal year, your first estimated installment is due on or before the 15th day of the fourth month of your fiscal year, assuming the 15th day. The second and third installments are due on or before the 15th day of the sixth and ninth months of your fiscal year with the final installment due by the 15th day of the first month of your next fiscal year. If any of these days are on the weekend or a legal holiday, the due date is the next business day.

**Farmers and fishermen.** Farmers only have to make one installment payment, generally by January 15 of the following year. Instead of making the estimated tax payment for 2019 by January 15, 2020, farmers may file their 2019 returns and pay the total tax due by March 2, 2020. To qualify under these rules, a farmer must receive two-thirds of his or her 2018 or 2019 gross income from farming.

Fishermen who expect to receive at least two-thirds of their gross income from fishing pay estimated taxes as farmers do.

## 27.4 Estimates by Married Taxpayers

A married couple may pay joint or separate estimated taxes. The joint or separate nature of the estimated tax does not control the kind of final return you can file.

Where a joint estimated tax is paid but separate tax returns are filed, you and your spouse can decide on how to divide the estimated payments between you. Either one of you can claim the whole amount, or you can agree to divide it in any way you choose. If you cannot agree, the IRS will allocate the estimated taxes proportionally according to the percentage of total tax each spouse owes.

If separate estimated taxes are paid, overpayment by one spouse is not applied against an underpayment by the other when separate final returns are filed.

Spouses may make joint estimated tax payments only if they are both citizens or residents of the United States. Both must have the same taxable year. A joint estimate may not be made if they are divorced or legally separated under a decree. If a joint estimate is made and the spouses are divorced or legally separated later in that year, they may divide the joint payments between them under the above rule for spouses who file separately.

*Prior-year safe harbor.* If you and your spouse file separately for 2018 (as single, head of household, or married filing separately) but expect to file a joint 2019 return, your 2018 total tax for purposes of determining the required 2019 annual payment under the prior-year safe harbor *(27.2)* is the total tax for both of you on the 2018 separate returns.

If you and your spouse file jointly for 2018 but expect to file separately for 2019, you must figure your share of the 2018 joint return tax to apply the prior-year safe harbor. Figure the tax that each of you would have paid on separate returns for 2018 using your 2019 filing status (single, head of household, or married filing separately). Then divide your separate return tax by the total tax for both separate returns. For example, if you would have paid tax of $7,000 on a separate 2018 return and your spouse would have paid $3,000 on a separate return, your 70% share ($7,000/$10,000) is the share of the 2018 joint return tax that you take into account in applying the prior-year safe harbor. Your spouse's share of the 2018 joint return tax is 30%.

## 27.5 Adjusting Your Payments During the Year

If, during the year, your income, expenses, or exemptions change, refigure your estimated tax liability and adjust your payment schedule as shown in the following Examples. Increasing an installment payment cannot make up for an underpayment in a prior period; *see* Example 2 below. However, withholdings from pay, pensions, and IRA withdrawals can be allocated equally over all four periods, so if you increase withholding at the end of the year you may apply it to earlier periods.

If taxes paid in the previous installments total more than your revised estimate, you cannot obtain a refund at that time. You must wait until you file your final return showing that a refund is due.

### EXAMPLES

1. Smith, who is self-employed, figures that to avoid a penalty for 2019 under the rules at *27.2*, he must make estimated tax installments of $6,000. By April 15, 2019, he pays an installment of $1,500. In June, he amends his estimate, showing a tax of $3,000 instead of $6,000. He refigures the installment schedule by dividing $3,000 by 4, which gives a payment rate of $750 for each period. As he paid $1,500 in April, the $750 overpayment covers his June obligation. By September 16, 2019, he pays $750; by January 15, 2020, he makes the last $750 payment.

2. In August 2019, Jones realizes that his estimated 2019 tax liability should be $25,000 rather than his original estimate of $20,000. He paid $5,000 as his April and June installments ($10,000 total). Under the amended schedule, he should have paid $6,250 per period ($25,000 ÷ 4), $6,250 by April 15 and $6,250 by June 17. Thus, there is a $2,500 underpayment ($12,500 − 10,000) for the first two periods.

   To cover the underpayment of $2,500, which carries over to the third payment period (June 1 through August 31), Jones's installment by September 16, 2019 must be at least $8,750 ($6,250 + $2,500). If less than $8,750 is paid, there will be an underpayment for the third payment period, as payments in that period are applied first to the carried-over underpayment of $2,500. If at least $8,750 is paid by September 16, there is no third period underpayment to be carried over, so the required installment for the fourth period (September 1 through December 31), due by January 15, 2020, will be $6,250. Unless an exception *(27.1)* applies, the underpayments for the first two periods will be subject to a penalty.

# CHAPTER 28

# Additional Medicare Tax and Net Investment Income Tax

An Additional Medicare Tax of 0.9% applies to wages, other employee compensation, and self-employment income to the extent such income exceeds a threshold of $250,000 for married persons filing jointly, $200,000 if single, head of household, or a qualifying widow/widower, or $125,000 if married filing separately. Figure liability for the additional tax on Form 8959. If the tax was withheld from your 2018 wages, you show the amount on Form 8959 and add it to your regular withholdings on Form 1040. *See 28.2* for details on the 0.9% tax.

A 3.8% tax (Net Investment Income Tax) applies to some or all of your net investment income if your modified adjusted gross income exceeds the applicable threshold of $250,000 for joint filers and qualifying widows/widowers, $200,000 if single or head of household, or $125,000 if married filing separately. The 3.8% tax is figured on Form 8960. *See 28.3* for details on the 3.8% tax.

In your planning for 2019, you may need to increase your withholdings or estimated tax installments to account for these taxes.

## 28.1 Higher-Income Taxpayers May be Subject to Additional Taxes

Higher-income taxpayers may be subject to one or both of two taxes that took effect in 2013 to help pay for health care reform, one on earned income and the other on investment income.

If you have wages and/or self-employed earnings over $200,000 if single, or $250,000 if married filing jointly, you are subject to the 0.9% Additional Medicare Tax on the earnings over the threshold. If you have modified adjusted gross income over the $200,000 or $250,000 thresholds, you are subject to a 3.8% tax on some or all of your net investment income (Net Investment Income Tax (NIIT)). The 0.9% Additional Medicare Tax is computed on Form 8959 and the 3.8% NIIT tax is computed on Form 8960.

Details on the thresholds and tax computations are in *28.2* for the 0.9% Additional Medicare Tax and in *28.3* for the 3.8% NIIT. Note that the thresholds for both of these taxes are fixed by statute; there is no annual cost-of-living adjustment for the thresholds. Take this into account in estimating your tax liability for 2019. The lack of an inflation adjustment means that taxpayers who are now slightly below the thresholds may become subject to the taxes in upcoming years.

If withholdings or estimated tax payments were not made in 2018 to cover these taxes, you could be subject to an estimated tax penalty *(27.1)*. The 0.9% tax may have been withheld from your 2018 wages, but as discussed in *28.2*, you may not be subject to the tax even though the tax was withheld, or you may not have been subject to withholding but may still owe the tax when you file your 2018 return.

## 28.2 Additional 0.9% Medicare Tax on Earnings

Wages, other employee compensation (tips, taxable fringe benefits), and net earnings from self-employment are combined to determine if you exceed the threshold for the 0.9% Additional Medicare Tax. The 0.9% tax, if applicable, is on top of the basic Medicare tax otherwise due (1.45% on all wages and salary; 2.90% on net self-employment earnings). Liability for the 0.9% tax does not depend on your adjusted gross income but only on your earnings. The 0.9% tax applies only to earnings above the following thresholds:

- $250,000 for married persons filing jointly
- $200,000 for single persons, heads of households and qualifying widows/widowers
- $125,000 for married persons filing separately

The tax is figured on Form 8959. If in 2018 you had wages (and tips or other taxable employee compensation treated as wages) but not self-employment earnings, the 0.9% tax applies on Part 1 of Form 8959 to the excess of the wages over your filing threshold. For example, if your 2018 wages are $225,000 and you are single, the tax applies to the $25,000 of wages over the $200,000 threshold, for a tax of $225 ($25,000 excess wages × 0.9% (0.009)). The $225 tax must be entered on Schedule 4 of Form 1040. Even if withholdings were taken from your pay to cover the 0.9% tax, they do not reduce liability for the tax on Form 8959. In the previous example, the $225 tax is reported as an additional tax whether or not your employer withheld the 0.9% tax. Withholdings for the 0.9% tax are separated out from regular Medicare withholdings on Part V of Form 8959 and then added to your federal income tax withholdings on Schedule 4 of Form 1040.

**Self-employed.** If you had only self-employment earnings in 2018, and no wages, you would figure liability for the 0.9% tax on Part II of Form 8959. If you had wages and also net self-employment earnings in 2018, you first determine if the 0.9% tax applies to your wages (Part I of Form 8959), and then you reduce your threshold amount by your wages to get a reduced threshold that is used to determine if the tax applies to the self-employment income; *see* the Examples below. A net loss from self-employment does not offset wages. The above-the-line deduction for 50% of self-employment tax liability *(45.3-45.4)* does not apply to the 0.9% Additional Medicare Tax.

*Caution*

**Withholdings May Not Cover 0.9% Additional Medicare Tax**

Employees who have more than one job and married couples where both spouses have wages may be subject to the 0.9% Additional Medicare Tax because the combined wages exceed the floor for the tax, but the tax will not be withheld from their pay because an employer will not withhold it unless the employee's wages exceed $200,000. *See 28.2* for withholding rule details. If you expect to have wages exceeding the tax threshold but not to have the tax withheld, you may need to increase your regular income tax withholding or make estimated tax installments to avoid an estimated tax penalty when you file your return.

**Employer withholding for the 0.9% tax.** Although the additional tax applies to the portion of earnings over the threshold ($250,000, $200,000, or $125,000), an employer will only withhold the additional Medicare tax once wages for the year (including tips, bonuses, and other taxable compensation) exceed $200,000. This means that some taxpayers will be subject to withholding but not owe the tax, while others will owe the tax but not be subject to withholding.

For example, assume that the combined wages of a married couple filing jointly do not exceed the $250,000 threshold, but one of the spouses has wages from one employer exceeding $200,000, In that case, the employer of the higher-earning spouse will withhold the 0.9% tax from the wages over $200,000. On Form 8959, there will be no liability for the tax because total wages do not exceed the threshold, but Form 8959 will have to be filed to show the additional withholding so it can be claimed on Form 1040.

On the other hand, an unmarried employee with several jobs could have wages well over the $200,000 threshold but not have the tax withheld by any employer because the wages from each job do not exceed $200,000. Similarly, for a married couple filing jointly, combined wages may exceed the $250,000 threshold but unless one spouse has wages exceeding $200,000 from a single employer, the additional tax will not be withheld from either spouse's pay. Thus, if one spouse has wages of $180,000 and the other has wages of $170,000, the 0.9% tax will not be withheld from either of them although their combined wages are $100,000 over the $250,000 threshold and they will owe additional tax of $900 (0.9% × $100,000 excess) on Form 8959. Finally, a married person filing separately with wages between $125,000 and $200,000 will not have the 0.9% tax withheld from his or her pay, but the tax will apply on Form 8959 to the wages over $125,000, the threshold for married persons filing separately.

If you (or you and your spouse on a joint return) owe the 0.9% but it is not withheld from your wages, you could face an estimated tax penalty *(27.2)* if the liability is not covered by regular income tax withholdings (Form W-4) or estimated tax installments.

### EXAMPLES

1. For 2018, you have wages of $150,000 and your spouse has $175,000 of net self-employment earnings (as reported on Schedule SE, Line 4). You file a 2018 joint return. Your threshold for figuring the 0.9% tax is $250,000. Because you and spouse do not have wages over $250,000, the 0.9% tax does not apply to your wages on Part I of Form 8959. On Part II of Form 8959, the $250,000 threshold is reduced by your $150,000 of wages, giving you a reduced self-employment income threshold of $100,000. Since the self-employment earnings of $175,000 exceed the reduced threshold of $100,000 by $75,000, there is a Part II tax of $675 on the excess self-employment income (0.9% (.009) × $75,000 = $675).

2. For 2018, you file as a head of household. You have wages of $235,000 from one employer, and net self-employment earnings of $50,000. In addition to regular Medicare withholding, your employer withheld an additional $315, the amount of the 0.9% tax on the $35,000 of wages exceeding $200,000 ($235,000 wages − $200,000 threshold). On Part I of Form 8959, you figure the $315 Additional Medicare Tax on the excess $35,000 of wages (0.9% × $35,000). On Part II of Form 8959, the total wages are subtracted from the threshold, leaving you with a zero threshold ($200,000 threshold − $235,000 wages). Since the threshold is zero, the 0.9% tax applies to the entire $50,000 of self-employment income ($50,000 − $0 reduced threshold), for a tax of $450 (0.9% × $50,000). The total tax on Form 8959 is $765 ($315 + $450). Add the $315 of additional Medicare tax withheld by your employer to your federal income tax withholdings on Line 16 of Form 1040. In other words, the $315 withheld to cover the 0.9% tax does not directly offset the $765 liability for the tax on Form 8959, but rather is applied against all of the taxes you are liable for on Form 1040, including the 0.9% tax.

## 28.3  Additional 3.8% Tax on Net Investment Income

If you have net investment income and you have modified adjusted gross income (MAGI) exceeding the applicable threshold for your filing status, some or all of the net investment income will be subject to a 3.8% tax on Form 8960. The tax is called the Net Investment Income Tax (NIIT) on Form 8960. The thresholds for the tax are:

- $250,000 for married persons filing jointly and qualifying widows/widowers
- $200,000 for single persons and heads of households
- $125,000 for married persons filing separately

If your MAGI exceeds the applicable threshold, the 3.8% tax applies to the *lesser* of (1) your net investment income, or (2) your MAGI exceeding the threshold. Thus, if you have net investment income of $50,000, but your MAGI exceeds your threshold by only $20,000, the 3.8% tax applies to the lesser amount of $20,000. Also *see* the Examples below.

Estates and trusts may also be subject to the net investment income tax; *see* below.

**MAGI thresholds.** The thresholds are based on modified adjusted gross income, which is the same as adjusted gross income (AGI) unless the foreign earned income exclusion *(36.1)* is claimed. If the foreign earned income exclusion is claimed, add back the excluded income (minus any above-the-line deductions or exclusions that were disallowed as allocable to the excluded foreign earned income) to get modified adjusted gross income.

**Investment income and net investment income.** Investment income subject to the 3.8% tax is entered on Part I of Form 8960. Investment income includes taxable interest, dividends, payments from commercial annuities (but not employee annuities), rents and royalties, capital gains from sales of stocks, bonds, mutual funds, or investment real estate including a vacation home, capital gain distributions from mutual funds, and passive income from partnerships and S corporations, including gain from the sale of a partnership or S corporation interest if you were a passive owner.

Do not count as investment income the following: tax-exempt interest, distributions from traditional IRAs, Roth IRAs, 401(k) plans and other qualified retirement plans such as pension plans, 403(b) plans and qualified annuity plans, and income from businesses, including partnerships and S corporations, in which you materially participate. Also excluded are Social Security benefits, life insurance, alimony and nontaxable veterans benefits.

A homeowner who sells his or her principal residence at a gain treats the gain as investment income for purposes of the 3.8% tax only to the extent that it exceeds the applicable home sale exclusion (usually $250,000 for singles and $500,000 for joint filers; *see 29.1*). If the gain is excluded from income, it is not subject to the 3.8% tax; *see* Examples 2 and 3 below.

Check the instructions to Form 8960 for further exceptions to the investment income category and details on items includible as investment income.

Note that a taxable distribution from a traditional IRA *(8.8)* or a qualified retirement plan, although excluded from the investment income category, is part of your MAGI, and the distribution, by increasing your MAGI, could push you over the threshold for the 3.8% tax or increase the tax if you are already over the threshold. This would not be true for a qualified Roth IRA distribution *(8.24)*, tax-exempt interest, or other item excluded from MAGI.

Investment expenses that are allocable to investment income are entered on Part II of Form 8960 and subtracted from investment income in Part III to arrive at net investment income. Allocable investment expenses include investment interest, depreciation or depletion, investment expenses reported on Schedule K-1 from a partnership or S corporation if not already included in Part I, and state and local income taxes allocable to items included as investment income: *see* the Form 8960 instructions for details on qualifying investment expenses.

 *Law Alert*

**Excludable Home Sale Gain Not Subject to 3.8% Tax**

Gain on the sale of a principal residence is not treated as investment income subject to the 3.8% tax to the extent it is tax free under the home sale exclusion rules *(29.1)*. See Examples 2 and 3 in *28.3*.

**QBI Deduction Does not Impact the 3.8% Tax**

The qualified business income (QBI) deduction (*see* 40.24) does not reduce net investment income for purposes of the 3.8% net investment income tax. And because the QBI deduction is subtracted from adjusted gross income, it has no impact on MAGI.

## EXAMPLES

1. John Smith, who is single, has $180,000 of wages in 2018, $20,000 of interest and dividends, and $80,000 of income from a passive partnership interest. John's MAGI is $280,000. His investment income is $100,000, which he reports on Part I of Form 8960. John's MAGI exceeds the $200,000 threshold for the 3.8% tax by $80,000, so in Part III of Form 8960, he figures the tax on the $80,000 excess MAGI, as it is less than the $100,000 of net investment income. John is liable for a tax of $3,040 ($80,000 × 3.8%). He must add the $3,040 to his other tax liability on Schedule 4 of Form 1040.

2. Donna Jones, who is single, earns wages of $45,000 in 2018. She also sells her principal residence, which she has owned and lived in since 2002, for $1 million. The home cost her $600,000, so her gain is $400,000. After claiming the $250,000 home sale exclusion *(29.1)*, her taxable gain on the sale is $150,000 ($400,000 − $250,000). The $150,000 gain is net investment income. However, since her MAGI of $195,000 ($45,000 wages plus $150,000 taxed gain) is under the $200,000 threshold amount for the 3.8% tax, Donna does not owe the tax.

3. Bob and Carol Wilson file a joint return. Together they have $75,000 of wages, and $125,000 of interest, dividends, and capital gains in 2018. They also sell their principal residence, which they owned and lived in since 1998, for $1.3 million. The house cost them $700,000, so their profit is $600,000. After claiming the $500,000 home sale exclusion *(29.3)*, their taxable gain from the sale is $100,000. Adding the $100,000 gain to the other $125,000 of investment income in Part I of Form 8960, Bob and Carol's net investment income is $225,000. Their MAGI is $300,000 ($75,000 wages plus $225,000 net investment income), $50,000 over the $250,000 threshold for the 3.8% tax. The tax applies to the $50,000 of excess MAGI, as it is less than the net investment income of $225,000. Bob and Carol's tax on Form 8960 is $1,900 ($50,000 × 3.8%).

**Estates and trusts may also be subject to the 3.8% tax.** For an estate or trust, the 3.8% tax generally applies to the lesser of its undistributed net investment income for the year or the excess of its AGI over the annual threshold for the 37% bracket for an estate or trust. For 2018, the 37% bracket threshold is $12,500. Grantor trusts and certain charitable trusts are exempt from the 3.8% tax. *See* the Form 8960 instructions for details.

## Sample Form 8959—Additional Medicare Tax
### (This sample is subject to change; see the *e-Supplement* at *jklasser.com*)

**Form 8959**

Department of the Treasury
Internal Revenue Service

**Additional Medicare Tax**

▶ If any line does not apply to you, leave it blank. See separate instructions.

▶ Attach to Form 1040, 1040NR, 1040-PR, or 1040-SS.

▶ Go to *www.irs.gov/Form8959* for instructions and the latest information.

OMB No. 1545-0074

**2018**

Attachment
Sequence No. **71**

Name(s) shown on return

Your social security number

**Part I  Additional Medicare Tax on Medicare Wages**

| | | | |
|---|---|---|---|
| 1 | Medicare wages and tips from Form W-2, box 5. If you have more than one Form W-2, enter the total of the amounts from box 5 . . . . . . . . . . . . | **1** | |
| 2 | Unreported tips from Form 4137, line 6 . . . . . . . . | **2** | |
| 3 | Wages from Form 8919, line 6 . . . . . . . . | **3** | |
| 4 | Add lines 1 through 3 . . . . . . . . | **4** | |
| 5 | Enter the following amount for your filing status: | | |
| | Married filing jointly . . . . . . . . $250,000 | | |
| | Married filing separately . . . . . . . . $125,000 | | |
| | Single, Head of household, or Qualifying widow(er) $200,000 | **5** | |
| 6 | Subtract line 5 from line 4. If zero or less, enter -0- . . . . . . . . | **6** | |
| 7 | Additional Medicare Tax on Medicare wages. Multiply line 6 by 0.9% (0.009). Enter here and go to Part II . . . . . . . . | **7** | |

**Part II  Additional Medicare Tax on Self-Employment Income**

| | | | |
|---|---|---|---|
| 8 | Self-employment income from Schedule SE (Form 1040), Section A, line 4, or Section B, line 6. If you had a loss, enter -0- (Form 1040-PR and Form 1040-SS filers, see instructions.) | **8** | |
| 9 | Enter the following amount for your filing status: | | |
| | Married filing jointly. . . . . . . . . $250,000 | | |
| | Married filing separately . . . . . . . . $125,000 | | |
| | Single, Head of household, or Qualifying widow(er) $200,000 | **9** | |
| 10 | Enter the amount from line 4 . . . . . . . . | **10** | |
| 11 | Subtract line 10 from line 9. If zero or less, enter -0- . . . . | **11** | |
| 12 | Subtract line 11 from line 8. If zero or less, enter -0- . . . . . | **12** | |
| 13 | Additional Medicare Tax on self-employment income. Multiply line 12 by 0.9% (0.009). Enter here and go to Part III . . . . . . . . | **13** | |

**Part III  Additional Medicare Tax on Railroad Retirement Tax Act (RRTA) Compensation**

| | | | |
|---|---|---|---|
| 14 | Railroad retirement (RRTA) compensation and tips from Form(s) W-2, box 14 (see instructions) . . . . . . . . | **14** | |
| 15 | Enter the following amount for your filing status: | | |
| | Married filing jointly. . . . . . . . . $250,000 | | |
| | Married filing separately . . . . . . . . $125,000 | | |
| | Single, Head of household, or Qualifying widow(er) $200,000 | **15** | |
| 16 | Subtract line 15 from line 14. If zero or less, enter -0- . . . . . . . . | **16** | |
| 17 | Additional Medicare Tax on railroad retirement (RRTA) compensation. Multiply line 16 by 0.9% (0.009). Enter here and go to Part IV . . . . . . . . | **17** | |

**Part IV  Total Additional Medicare Tax**

| | | | |
|---|---|---|---|
| 18 | Add lines 7, 13, and 17. Also include this amount on Schedule 4 (Form 1040), line 62 (check box a) (Form 1040NR, 1040-PR, and 1040-SS filers, see instructions), and go to Part V . . | **18** | |

**Part V  Withholding Reconciliation**

| | | | |
|---|---|---|---|
| 19 | Medicare tax withheld from Form W-2, box 6. If you have more than one Form W-2, enter the total of the amounts from box 6 . . . . . . . . . . | **19** | |
| 20 | Enter the amount from line 1 . . . . . . . . . | **20** | |
| 21 | Multiply line 20 by 1.45% (0.0145). This is your regular Medicare tax withholding on Medicare wages . . . . . | **21** | |
| 22 | Subtract line 21 from line 19. If zero or less, enter -0-. This is your Additional Medicare Tax withholding on Medicare wages | **22** | |
| 23 | Additional Medicare Tax withholding on railroad retirement (RRTA) compensation from Form W-2, box 14 (see instructions) . . . . . . . . | **23** | |
| 24 | **Total Additional Medicare Tax withholding.** Add lines 22 and 23. Also include this amount with federal income tax withholding on Form 1040, line 16 (Form 1040NR, 1040-PR, and 1040-SS filers, see instructions) | **24** | |

**For Paperwork Reduction Act Notice, see your tax return instructions.**          Cat. No. 59475X          Form **8959** (2018)

Additional 3.8% Tax on Net Investment Income

| Form **8960** | **Net Investment Income Tax—Individuals, Estates, and Trusts** | OMB No. 1545-2227 |
|---|---|---|
| Department of the Treasury Internal Revenue Service (99) | ► Attach to your tax return. ► Go to *www.irs.gov/Form8960* for instructions and the latest information. | **20**18 Attachment Sequence No. **72** |

| Name(s) shown on your tax return | | | Your social security number or EIN |
|---|---|---|---|

**Part I**    **Investment Income**    ☐ Section 6013(g) election (see instructions)
☐ Section 6013(h) election (see instructions)
☐ Regulations section 1.1411-10(g) election (see instructions)

| | | | |
|---|---|---|---|
| **1** | Taxable interest (see instructions) | **1** | |
| **2** | Ordinary dividends (see instructions) | **2** | |
| **3** | Annuities (see instructions) | **3** | |
| **4a** | Rental real estate, royalties, partnerships, S corporations, trusts, etc. (see instructions) | **4a** | |
| **b** | Adjustment for net income or loss derived in the ordinary course of a non-section 1411 trade or business (see instructions) | **4b** | |
| **c** | Combine lines 4a and 4b | **4c** | |
| **5a** | Net gain or loss from disposition of property (see instructions) | **5a** | |
| **b** | Net gain or loss from disposition of property that is not subject to net investment income tax (see instructions) | **5b** | |
| **c** | Adjustment from disposition of partnership interest or S corporation stock (see instructions) | **5c** | |
| **d** | Combine lines 5a through 5c | **5d** | |
| **6** | Adjustments to investment income for certain CFCs and PFICs (see instructions) | **6** | |
| **7** | Other modifications to investment income (see instructions) | **7** | |
| **8** | Total investment income. Combine lines 1, 2, 3, 4c, 5d, 6, and 7 | **8** | |

**Part II**    **Investment Expenses Allocable to Investment Income and Modifications**

| | | | |
|---|---|---|---|
| **9a** | Investment interest expenses (see instructions) | **9a** | |
| **b** | State, local, and foreign income tax (see instructions) | **9b** | |
| **c** | Miscellaneous investment expenses (see instructions) | **9c** | |
| **d** | Add lines 9a, 9b, and 9c | **9d** | |
| **10** | Additional modifications (see instructions) | **10** | |
| **11** | Total deductions and modifications. Add lines 9d and 10 | **11** | |

**Part III**    **Tax Computation**

| | | | |
|---|---|---|---|
| **12** | Net investment income. Subtract Part II, line 11, from Part I, line 8. Individuals, complete lines 13–17. Estates and trusts, complete lines 18a–21. If zero or less, enter -0- | **12** | |
| | **Individuals:** | | |
| **13** | Modified adjusted gross income (see instructions) | **13** | |
| **14** | Threshold based on filing status (see instructions) | **14** | |
| **15** | Subtract line 14 from line 13. If zero or less, enter -0- | **15** | |
| **16** | Enter the smaller of line 12 or line 15 | **16** | |
| **17** | Net investment income tax for individuals. Multiply line 16 by 3.8% (0.038). **Enter here and include on your tax return** (see instructions) | **17** | |
| | **Estates and Trusts:** | | |
| **18a** | Net investment income (line 12 above) | **18a** | |
| **b** | Deductions for distributions of net investment income and deductions under section 642(c) (see instructions) | **18b** | |
| **c** | Undistributed net investment income. Subtract line 18b from 18a (see instructions). If zero or less, enter -0- | **18c** | |
| **19a** | Adjusted gross income (see instructions) | **19a** | |
| **b** | Highest tax bracket for estates and trusts for the year (see instructions) | **19b** | |
| **c** | Subtract line 19b from line 19a. If zero or less, enter -0- | **19c** | |
| **20** | Enter the smaller of line 18c or line 19c | **20** | |
| **21** | Net investment income tax for estates and trusts. Multiply line 20 by 3.8% (0.038). **Enter here and include on your tax return** (see instructions) | **21** | |

For Paperwork Reduction Act Notice, see your tax return instructions.     Cat. No. 59474M     Form **8960** (2018)

# PART 5

# Tax Planning

The chapters in this part will alert you to special tax situations. They will point out tax-saving opportunities and show you how to take advantage of tax-saving ideas and planning strategies.

# CHAPTER 29

# Tax Savings for Residence Sales

You may avoid tax on gain on the sale of a principal residence if you owned and used it for at least two years during the five-year period ending on the date of sale. If you are single, you may avoid tax on up to $250,000 of gain, $500,000 if you are married and file jointly. However, gain attributable to nonqualified use after 2008 is not excludable *(29.2)*.

If you used the residence for less than two years, you may avoid tax if you sold because of a change of job location, poor health or unforeseen circumstance *(29.4)*.

You may not deduct a loss on the sale of a personal residence. Losses on the sale of property devoted to personal use are nondeductible *(29.8)*. However, there are circumstances under which you may claim a loss deduction on the sale of a residence *(29.9–29.10)*.

If you rent out a residential property and you or family members also use the residence during the year, rental expenses are subject to special restrictions *(9.7)*.

*Filing Instruction*

## Reporting Home Sale Gain or Loss on Your Return

If you have a gain on the sale of your principal residence and the entire gain is excludable from income under the rules discussed in this chapter *(29.1–29.7)*, you do not have to report the sale at all on your return unless you received a Form 1099-S from the settlement agent reporting the sale. If you have a taxable gain and did not receive Form 1099-S, or you received Form 1099-S and have any gain that cannot be excluded, or you decide not to claim the exclusion for excludable gain, report the transaction on Form 8949 *(5.8)*. If you can exclude all or part of your gain, you claim the allowable exclusion by entering code "H" in column (f) of Form 8949 and entering the exclusion as a negative adjustment in column (g). *See* the IRS instructions for Form 8949 for further details.

If you have gain that cannot be excluded, the taxable gain is subject to the 3.8% Net Investment Income Tax (NIIT), provided your income exceeds the applicable threshold for the NIIT *(28.3)*.

If you had a loss on the sale of your home, the loss is not deductible, but if you received a Form 1099-S, you must report the sale on Form 8949 *(29.8)*.

*Planning Reminder*

## Form 1099-S

The settlement agent responsible for closing the sale of your principal residence must report the sale to the IRS on Form 1099-S if the sales price exceeded $250,000, or $500,000 if you are married filing jointly. If the price was $250,000/$500,000 or less and you provide a written, signed certification that the full amount of your gain qualifies for the exclusion, the settlement agent may rely on the certification and not file the Form 1099-S or may choose to file the form anyway. IRS Revenue Procedure 2007-12 has a sample certification form, but certain required assurances that are not included in Revenue Procedure 2007-12 must be added to your certification; *see* the Form 1099-S instructions.

## 29.1 Avoiding Tax on Sale of Principal Residence

If you sell (or exchange) your principal residence at a gain *(29.5)*, up to $250,000 of the gain may be excluded from income if you owned and occupied it as a principal residence for an aggregate of at least two years in the five-year period ending on the date of sale and did not claim an exclusion on another sale within the prior two years. See the discussion of the two-out-of-five-year ownership and use tests in the following section *(29.2)*. If you are married filing jointly, you may be able to exclude up to $500,000 of gain *(29.3)*. Even if you do not meet the two-out-of-five-year ownership and use tests, you are entitled to a reduced maximum exclusion limit if the primary reason for your sale was a change in the place of employment, health reasons, or unforeseen circumstances *(29.4)*.

*Caution: If you use a residence as a vacation home or rental property after 2008, an allocable part of your gain may not qualify for the exclusion, even if you meet the two-out-of-five-year ownership and use tests (29.2).*

**Frequency of exclusion.** If you meet the ownership and use tests for a principal residence *(29.2)*, you may claim the exclusion when you sell it although you previously claimed the exclusion for another residence, provided that the sales are more than two years apart. If you claim the exclusion on a sale and within two years of the first sale you sell another principal residence, an exclusion may not be claimed on the second sale even if you meet the ownership and use tests for that residence. There is an exception if the second sale was due to a change in employment, health reasons, or unforeseen circumstances. In that case, a prorated exclusion limit is allowed *(29.4)*.

**Principal residence.** A principal residence is not restricted to one-family houses but includes a mobile home, trailer, houseboat, and condominium apartment used as a principal residence. An investment in a retirement community does not qualify as a principal residence unless you receive equity in the property. In the case of a tenant-stockholder of a cooperative housing corporation, the residence ownership requirement applies to the ownership of the stock and the use requirement applies to the house or apartment that the stockholder occupies *(29.2)*.

**If you have multiple homes.** If you have more than one home, you may exclude gain only on the sale of your principal residence and only if you meet the ownership and use tests *(29.2)* for that residence. Your "principal residence" is determined on a year-to-year basis, based primarily on where you live most of the time. However, the IRS may also consider such factors as the primary residence of your family members, your place of employment, mailing address, the address listed on your tax returns, driver's license and automobile and voter registration, and the location of your bank.

**Vacant land.** Vacant land owned and used as part of a taxpayer's principal residence may qualify for the exclusion. The vacant land must be adjacent to the residence and the sale of the residence must be within two years before or after the sale of the land. Qualifying sales of land and residence are treated as one sale, so the $250,000 exclusion limit ($500,000 for qualifying joint filers) applies to the combined sales. If the sales occur in different years, the exclusion limit applies first to the residence sale.

**Business or rental use.** If part of your home was rented out or used for business, *see* the rules for determining whether you can exclude all or some of the gain on a sale *(29.7)*. Also *see* the rules for deducting a loss where your residence was converted to rental property *(29.9)*.

**Home destroyed or condemned.** If your home is destroyed or condemned, this is treated as a sale, so any gain realized on the conversion may qualify for the exclusion. If vacant land used as part of your home is sold within two years of the conversion, the sale of the land may be combined with the sale of the residence for exclusion purposes; *see* the vacant land rule earlier. Any part of the gain that may not be excluded (because it exceeds the limit) may be postponed under the rules explained in *18.15*.

**Sale of remainder interest.** You may choose to exclude gain from the sale of a remainder interest in your home. If you do, you may not choose to exclude gain from your sale of any other interest in the home that you sell separately. Also, you may not exclude gain from the sale of a remainder interest to a related party. Related parties include your brothers and sisters, half-brothers and half-sisters, spouse, ancestors (parents, grandparents, etc.), and lineal descendants (children, grandchildren, etc.). Related parties also include certain corporations, partnerships, trusts, and exempt organizations.

**Expatriates.** You cannot claim the home sale exclusion if the expatriation tax *(1.20)* applies to you. The expatriation tax applies to U.S. citizens who have renounced their citizenship (and long-term residents who have ended their residency) if one of their principal purposes was to avoid U.S. taxes.

**The exclusion is not mandatory.** You do not have to apply the exclusion to a particular qualifying sale. For example, you are unable to sell a residence when you acquire a new residence. When you finally are able to find a buyer for the first home, you also decide to sell the second residence. Assume both sales may qualify for the exclusion, but the potential gain on the first house will be less than the potential gain on the sale of the second home. You will not want to apply the exclusion to the sale of the first home if doing so will prevent you from applying the exclusion to the second sale because of the rule allowing an exclusion for only one sale every two years.

**Federal subsidy recapture.** If your home was financed with the proceeds of a tax-exempt bond or a qualified mortgage credit certificate *(15.1)* and you sell or dispose of the home within nine years of the financing, you may have to recapture the federal subsidy received even if the sale qualifies for the home sale exclusion. Use Form 8828 to figure the amount of the recapture tax, which is reported on Form 1040 as a separate tax.

## 29.2  Meeting the Ownership and Use Tests for Exclusion

To qualify for the up-to-$250,000 exclusion, you must have owned and occupied a home as your principal residence for at least two years during the five-year period ending on the date of sale. The periods of ownership and use do not have to be continuous. The ownership and use tests may be met in different two-year periods, provided both tests are met during the five-year period ending on the date of sale (as in Example 3 below). You qualify if you can show that you owned the home and lived in it as your principal residence for 24 full months or for 730 days (365 × 2) during the five-year period ending on the date of sale. However, even you meet the two-out-of-five-year ownership and use tests, some of your gain will be taxable if you use the residence after 2008 as a second home or rental property, unless an exception applies; *see* the discussion of the nonqualified use rule at the end of this section.

If you or your spouse serve on qualified official extended duty as a member of the uniformed services, Foreign Service of the United States, intelligence community, or Peace Corps, you can suspend the five-year test period for the years of qualified service; *see* below.

If you are a joint owner of the residence and file a separate return, the up-to-$250,000 exclusion applies to your share of the gain, assuming you meet the ownership and use tests.

If you are married and file a joint return, you may claim an exclusion of up to $500,000 if one of you meets the ownership test and both of you meet the use test *(29.3)*.

If the ownership and use tests are not met but the primary reason for the sale was a change in the place of employment, health reasons, or unforeseen circumstances, an exclusion is allowed under the reduced maximum exclusion rules *(29.4)*.

Even if the ownership and use tests are met, the exclusion is not allowed for a sale if within the two-year period ending on the date of sale, you sold another principal residence for which you claimed the exclusion. However, a reduced exclusion limit may be available *(29.4)*.

**Short Absences**

Short temporary absences for vacations count as time you used the residence.

**Use Test Must be Met for Newly Built Home Replacing Demolished Home**

If a new house is built on the site of a former residence, the period of use of the old house does not count towards meeting the two-year use test for the new house. A couple wanted to remodel their home but, because of building code and permit restrictions, decided to demolish the old house and build a new one on the site. Once the new house was completed, they sold it for $1.1 million, which resulted in a $600,000 gain. On their joint return, they excluded $500,000 of the gain from their income. They had lived in the demolished home for a number of years but never lived in the newly constructed home.

The Tax Court agreed with the IRS that they did not qualify for the exclusion. The exclusion applies only if the dwelling sold was actually used by the taxpayer as a principal residence for the required two-out-of-five years before the sale. In this case, while the demolished home was used as a principal residence for the requisite period, the newly built home was not.

**EXAMPLES**

1. From 2003 through August 2017, Janet lived with her parents in a house that her parents owned. In September 2017, she bought this house from her parents. She continued to live there until December 18, 2018, when she sold it at a gain. Although Janet lived in the home for more than two years, she did not own it for at least two years. She may not exclude any part of her gain on the sale, unless she sold because of a change in her place of employment, health reasons, or unforeseen circumstances *(29.4)*.

2. John bought and moved into a house on July 9, 2016. He lived in it as his principal residence continuously until October 1, 2017, when he went abroad for a one-year sabbatical leave. After returning from the leave, he sold the house on November 6, 2018. He does not meet the two-year use test. Because his sabbatical was not a short, temporary absence, he may not include the period of leave in his period of use in order to meet the two-year use test. He may avoid tax on gain if he sold because of a changed job location unforeseen circumstances, or poor health (29.4).

3. Since 1992, Jonah lived in an apartment building that was changed to a condominium. He bought the apartment on December 3, 2014. In February 2016, he became ill and on April 16, 2016, he moved into his son's home. On July 16, 2018, while still living with his son, he sold the apartment.

   He may exclude gain on the sale of the apartment because he met the ownership and use tests. The five-year period is from July 17, 2013, to July 16, 2018, the date of the sale of the apartment. He owned the apartment from December 3, 2014, to July 16, 2018 (over two years). He lived in the apartment from July 17, 2013 (the beginning of the five-year period) to April 16, 2016, a period of use of over two years.

4. In 2006, Carol bought a house and lived in it until January 31, 2015, when she moved and put it up for rent. The house was rented from March 1, 2015, until May 31, 2018. Carol moved back into the house on June 1, 2018, and lived there until she sold it on October 30, 2018. During the five-year period ending on the date of the sale (November 1, 2013 – October 30, 2018), Carol lived in the house for less than two years.

| Five-year period— | Home use (months)— | Rental use (months)— |
|---|---|---|
| 10/1/13–1/31/15 | 16 | |
| 3/1/15–5/31/18 | | 39 |
| 6/1/18–10/30/18 | 5 | |
| Total | 21 | 39 |

Carol may not exclude any of the gain on the sale, unless she sold the house for health or employment reasons or due to unforeseen circumstances (29.4).

**Military and Foreign Service personnel, intelligence officers, and Peace Corps workers can suspend five-year period.** You may elect to suspend the running of the five-year ownership and use period while you or your spouse is on qualified official extended duty as a member of the uniformed services or Foreign Service of the United States. The suspension can be for up to 10 years. It is allowed for only one residence at a time. By making the election and disregarding up to 10 years of qualifying service, you can claim an exclusion where the two-year use test is met before you began the qualifying service and after your return; see the Example below. Qualified official extended duty means active duty for over 90 days or for an indefinite period with a branch of the U.S. Armed Forces at a duty station at least 50 miles from your principal residence or in Government-mandated quarters. Members of the Foreign Service, commissioned corps of the National Oceanic and Atmospheric Administration, and commissioned corps of the Public Health Service who meet the active duty tests also qualify.

Similarly, the five-year testing period is suspended for up to 10 years for intelligence community employees (specified national agencies and departments) and Peace Corps workers. The suspension rule for Peace Corps workers applies to Peace Corps employees, enrolled volunteers, or volunteer leaders for periods during which they are on qualified official extended duty outside the United States.

**Cooperative apartments.** If you sell your stock in a cooperative housing corporation, you meet the ownership and use tests if, during the five-year period ending on the date of sale, you:

1. Owned stock for at least two years, and
2. Used the house or apartment that the stock entitles you to occupy as your principal residence for at least two years.

*Caution*

**Residence Acquired in Like-Kind Exchange**

A residence acquired in a like-kind exchange must be owned for at least five years before gain on its sale can qualify for the exclusion.

**Incapacitated homeowner.** A homeowner who becomes physically or mentally incapable of self-care is deemed to use a residence as a principal residence during the time in which the individual owns the residence and resides in a licensed care facility. For this rule to apply, the homeowner must have owned and used the residence as a principal residence for an aggregate period of at least one year during the five years preceding the sale.

If you meet this disability exception, you still have to meet the two-out-of-five-year ownership test to claim the exclusion.

**Previous home destroyed or condemned.** For the ownership and use tests, you may add time you owned and lived in a previous home that was destroyed or condemned if any part of the basis of the current home sold depended on the basis of the destroyed or condemned home under the involuntary conversion rules *(18.15)*.

> ### EXAMPLE
>
> Michael bought a home in Maryland in March 2005 that he lived in before moving to Brazil in November 2009 as a member of the Foreign Service of the United States. He served there on qualified official extended duty for eight years, until the end of 2017. In January 2018, he sells the Maryland home at a gain. He did not use the home as his principal residence for two out of the five years preceding the sale and so does not qualify for an exclusion under the regular rule. However, Michael can exclude gain of up to $250,000 by electing to suspend the running of the five-year test period while he was abroad with the Foreign Service. Under the election, his eight years of service are disregarded and his years of use from March 2005—November 2009 are considered to be within the five-year period preceding the sale. He thus meets the two-out-of-five-year test and can claim the exclusion.

## No Exclusion for Nonqualified Use After 2008

Even if the two-out-of-five-year test for an exclusion is met, gain attributable to "nonqualified" use after 2008 is not eligible for the exclusion. The primary intent of the rule is apparently to deny an exclusion for some of the gain realized by taxpayers who convert a vacation home or rented residence to their principal residence and live in it for a few years before selling. However, the law as written is broader, generally treating any period after 2008 in which the home is not used as a principal residence by you, your spouse, or former spouse as "nonqualified use." Despite the broad wording of the law, there are exceptions (below) that lessen the potential impact of the nonqualified use rule. In particular, exception 1 allows many home sellers to avoid nonqualified use treatment where they move out and rent the home before selling it; *see* Example 2 below.

**Exceptions to nonqualified use.** There are exceptions that limit the impact of the nonqualified use rule. The law specifically exempts the following from the definition of post-2008 "nonqualified use": (1) the period after you, or your spouse, last use the home as your principal residence, so long as it is within the five years ending on the date of sale; *see* Example 2 below, (2) temporary absences from the residence, not to exceed two years in total, due to a change in employment, health reasons (such as time in a hospital or nursing home), or other unforeseen circumstances to be specified by the IRS, and (3) periods of up to 10 years (in aggregate) during which you, or your spouse, are on qualified official extended duty (duty station at least 50 miles from residence) as a member of the uniformed services, as a Foreign Service officer, or as an employee of the intelligence community.

The IRS has not released formal guidelines on "nonqualified use," including any other possible exceptions, such as whether short-term rental periods will be disregarded. However, in Publication 523 it takes the position that where rental or business space is physically part of the living area of your home, such as a home office or a spare bedroom that you rent out as part of a bed-and-breakfast business, that use is treated as residential use. Although the IRS does not specifically say so, such home office or rental space within the home is apparently not considered "nonqualified use" in applying the fractional computation below.

 *Court Decision*

### Co-Owner Can Claim Full $250,000 Exclusion

A single taxpayer who sells her home at a gain after owning and using it for at least two of the five years preceding the date of sale can exclude up to $250,000 of gain from income. What if there are two co-owners: do they have to split the $250,000 exclusion? Yes, argued the IRS in a 2010 case, the $250,000 exclusion has to be shared, but the Tax Court allowed a full exclusion. The taxpayer owned a 50% interest in a home she used as her principal residence since February 1997. When the home was sold in 2005, her share of the gain was $264,644.50 (half of the $529,289 total gain). She excluded $250,000 of her gain on her 2005 return, but the IRS said she was only entitled to half of the full exclusion, or $125,000.

The Tax Court allowed the full $250,000 exclusion. The statute (Code Section 121) does not limit the exclusion for partial owners of a principal residence. In fact, an example in the IRS regulations specifically allows unmarried joint owners holding 50% interests in a home to each exclude up to the full $250,000 limit for their shares of the gain on a sale so long as they each meet the ownership and use tests and have not excluded gain from another home sale within the prior two-year period.

**Figuring the excludable and nonexcludable gain.** To figure the exclusion on a sale where there is nonqualified use after 2008, the gain equal to post–May 6, 1997 depreciation (allowed or allowable *(29.7)*) is taken into account first. No exclusion is allowed for this depreciation amount *(29.7)*; this is a long-standing rule that is not changed by the nonqualified use calculation.

After taking into account post-May 6, 1997 depreciation, the portion of the remaining gain that is allocable to nonqualified use must be figured; this amount also is not eligible for the exclusion. The allocation is made by multiplying the gain by the following fraction:

$$\frac{\text{Total days of nonqualified use after 2008}}{\text{Total days of ownership of the home}}$$

You can use Worksheet 29-3 later in this chapter to make the allocation and figure your excludable and taxable gain.

---

### EXAMPLES

1. Martin bought his home on April 23, 2012, and lived in it until June 30, 2014 when he moved out. He rented the home from July 1, 2014, to June 30, 2016, and claimed depreciation deductions of $10,000 for that period. Martin moved back into the house July 1, 2016, and lived there until he sold it on January 31, 2018, for a gain of $310,000. In the five-year period ending on the date of sale (February 1, 2013 –January 31, 2018), Martin met the ownership and use test for an exclusion: he owned the home and used it for more than two years in the five-year period. He owned it for the entire five years and used it as his home for 36 months (17 months from February 1, 2013–June 30, 2014, and 19 months from July 1, 2016–January 31, 2018), while renting it for the other 24 months (July 1, 2014–June 30, 2016). The rental period is nonqualified use.

   Using Worksheet 29-3, Martin figures his exclusion and taxable gain. The $10,000 of gain allocable to depreciation cannot be excluded. Of the remaining $300,000 gain ($310,000 gain -$10,000 depreciation), Martin figures that $103,800 is allocable to nonqualified use and thus not eligible for an exclusion. Martin owned the home for 2,110 days (beginning with April 24, 2012, the day after he bought it, and ending on January 31, 2018, the date of sale). Of his 2,110 ownership days, 730 days (the rental days, July 1, 2014 through June 30, 2016) were nonqualified use. The allocation to nonqualified use is 730/ 2,110, or 34.6%, and 34.6% × $300,000 is $103,800. Martin may exclude $196,200 of the gain from income ($300,000-$103,800).

   On Form 8949 and Schedule D *(5.8)*, Martin will report taxable gain of $113,800 ($10,000 gain allocable to depreciation + $103,800 gain allocable to nonqualified use), and also will report the exclusion of $196,200. The $10,000 gain from depreciation is unrecaptured Section 1250 gain, which Martin will enter on the Unrecaptured Section 1250 Gain Worksheet in the Schedule D instructions *(5.3)*.

   Keep in mind that even without the nonqualified use rule, only $250,000 of Martin's $300,000 gain (after depreciation is recaptured) would have been excludable. The effect of the nonqualified use rule under these facts is to increase the taxed (nonexcludable) gain by an additional $53,800, from $50,000 ($300,000 – $250,000) to $103,800 under the allocation formula.

2. Andrea owned and lived in her principal residence from 2012 through 2015 and then moved to another state. She rented the home from January 1, 2016, until April 30, 2018, when she sold it. Andrea met the ownership and use test: she owned and lived in the house for more than two years in the five-year period ending on the date of sale (May 1, 2013 – April 30, 2018). Although Andrea rented out the home after 2009, the rental period (January 1, 2016–April 30, 2018) is not considered nonqualified use because it was after she moved out of the home and was within the five-year period ending on the sale date (Exception 1 under "Exceptions to nonqualified use" on the previous page). Andrea may exclude gain of up to $250,000, but not gain equal to the depreciation she claimed (or could have claimed) while the house was rented. Because the property was rented at the time of sale, the IRS requires the sale to be reported and the exclusion claimed on form 4797.

---

## 29.3 Home Sales by Married Persons

Where a married couple owned and lived in their principal residence for at least two years during the five-year period ending on the date of sale, they may claim an exclusion of up to $500,000 of gain on a joint return. Under the law, the up-to-$500,000 exclusion may be claimed on a joint return provided that during the five-year period ending on the date of sale: (1) either spouse owned the residence for at least two years, (2) both spouses lived in the house as their principal residence for at least two years, and (3) neither spouse is ineligible to claim the exclusion because an exclusion was previously claimed on a sale of a principal residence within the two-year period ending on the date of this sale. If Tests 1 and 3 are met but only one of you meets Test 2, your exclusion limit on a joint return is $250,000. However, even if the two-out-of-five-year use test is met, "nonqualified use" after 2008 may limit the exclusion you can claim; see 29.2.

**Death of spouse before sale.** If your spouse died and you inherit the house and later sell it, you are considered to have owned and used the property during any period of time when your spouse owned and used it as a principal home, provided you did not remarry before your sale. This rule can enable you to satisfy the two-out-of-five-year ownership and use tests where your spouse met the tests but you on your own did not. It may also enable you to claim the $500,000 exclusion if you sell the house in the year your spouse died or within the next two years, as discussed in the next two paragraphs.

If you and your spouse each met the use test and at least one of you met the ownership test as of the date of your spouse's death, and you sell the residence in the year he or she dies, you may use the $500,000 exclusion limit, assuming you file a joint return for the year of your spouse's death and neither of you claimed the exclusion for another home sale in the two years before your spouse died.

You are also entitled to use the $500,000 exclusion limit on a sale that is within two years of your spouse's death, provided you have not remarried and you and your spouse would have qualified for the $500,000 limit on a sale immediately before his or her death under Tests 1–3 at the beginning of 29.3.

 *Caution*

**Exclusion for Married Couple**

For a recently married couple, the exclusion limit on a joint return is $250,000, not $500,000, where one of the spouses has satisfied both the ownership test and the use test before a sale and the other spouse has not met the use test. Gain in excess of the $250,000 exclusion is reported on Form 8949 (5.8).

### EXAMPLES

1. You and your spouse owned and occupied your principal residence for 20 years. In December 2018, you sell the house for a gain of $450,000. If you file jointly, none of the gain is taxable as the up-to-$500,000 exclusion applies.

2. After your spouse died, you owned and lived in your principal residence from June 2013 through the end of 2017. In January 2018 you remarried and you and your wife lived in the house for nine months. In October 2018, you sold the house and realized a gain of $350,000. On a joint return for 2018, you may claim an exclusion of $250,000; the balance of $100,000 is taxable. You meet the exclusion tests, but your wife does not. Thus, the exclusion is limited to $250,000.

**Divorce.** If a residence is transferred to you incident to divorce, the time during which your former spouse owned the residence is added to your period of ownership. If pursuant to a divorce or separation decree or agreement you move out of a home that you own or jointly own with your spouse or former spouse, you are treated as having used the home for any period that you retain an ownership interest in the residence while the other spouse or former spouse continues to use it as a principal residence under the terms of the divorce or separation agreement.

**Separate residences.** Where a husband and wife own and live in separate residences, each spouse is entitled to a separate exclusion limit of $250,000 on the sale of his or her residence. If both residences are sold in the same year and each spouse met the ownership and use test for his or her separate residence, two exclusions may be claimed (up to $250,000 each), either on a joint return or on separate returns.

## 29.4 Reduced Maximum Exclusion

Generally, no exclusion is allowed on a sale of a principal residence if you owned or used the home for less than two of the five years preceding the sale *(29.2)*. Similarly, an exclusion is generally disallowed if within the two-year period ending on the date of sale, you sold another home at a gain that was wholly or partially excluded from your income.

However, even if a sale of a principal residence is made before meeting the ownership and use tests or it is within two years of a prior sale for which an exclusion was claimed, a partial exclusion is available if the primary reason for the sale is: (1) a change in the place of employment, (2) health, or (3) unforeseen circumstances. If the sale is for one of these qualifying reasons, you are entitled to a prorated portion of the regular $250,000 or $500,000 exclusion limit. The employment change, health problem, or unforeseen circumstance can be attributable to you or another "qualified individual," as defined below.

You automatically qualify for the reduced exclusion if your sale is within a safe harbor established by the IRS. If a safe harbor is not available, you may qualify by showing that the "facts and circumstances" of your situation establish that the primary reason for the sale was a change in the place of employment, health problem or unforeseen circumstances.

When you fall within a safe harbor or meet the primary reason test, you are allowed an allocable percentage of the regular $250,000 or $500,000 exclusion limit, depending on how much of the regular two-year ownership and use test was satisfied, or the time between this sale and a sale within the prior two years. For example, if you owned and lived in your home for 438 days before selling it to take a new job, you are entitled to 60% of the regular exclusion limit, which is based on 730 qualifying days (438/730 = 60%). Use Worksheet 29-1 to figure your reduced exclusion limit. Although the maximum exclusion is reduced, this may not disadvantage you. If the reduced exclusion limit equals or exceeds your gain, none of your gain is subject to tax.

---

### Worksheet 29-1    Reduced Maximum Exclusion

| | | | (a)<br>You | (b)<br>Your Spouse |
|---|---|---|---|---|
| **Caution:** Complete this worksheet only if you qualify for a reduced maximum exclusion (under the rules at 29.4). | | | | |
| 1. | Maximum amount | 1. | $250,000 | $250,000 |
| 2a. | Enter the number of days (or months) that you used the property as a main home during the 5-year period* ending on the date of sale | 2a. | | |
| b. | Enter the number of days (or months) that you owned the property during the 5-year period* ending on the date of sale. If you used days on line 2a, you also must use days on this line and on lines 3 and 5. If you used months on line 2a, you also must use months on this line and on lines 3 and 5. (If married filing jointly and one spouse owned the property longer than the other spouse, both spouses are treated as owning the property for the longer period.) | b. | | |
| c. | Enter the smaller of line 2a or 2b | c. | | |
| 3. | Have you (or your spouse, if filing jointly) excluded gain from the sale of another home during the 2-year period ending on the date of this sale?<br><br>☐ **No.** Skip line 3 and enter the number of days (or months) from line 2c on line 4.<br>☐ **Yes.** Enter the number of days (or months) between the date of the most recent sale of another home on which you excluded gain and the date of sale of this home | 3. | | |
| 4. | Enter the smaller of line 2c or 3 | 4. | | |
| 5. | Divide the amount on line 4 by 730 days (or 24 months). Enter the result as a decimal (rounded to at least 3 places). But do not enter an amount greater than 1.000 | 5. | | |
| 6. | Multiply the amount on line 1 by the decimal amount on line 5 | 6. | | |
| 7. | **Reduced maximum exclusion.** Add the amounts in columns (a) and (b) of line 6. Enter it here and on Worksheet 29-3, Line 13 | 7. | | |

*If you were a member of the uniformed services or Foreign Service, an employee of the intelligence community, or an employee or volunteer of the Peace Corps during the time you owned the home, see 29.2 to determine your 5-year period.

**Qualified individual.** In addition to yourself, the following persons are considered qualified individuals for purposes of qualifying for the reduced maximum exclusion: your spouse, a co-owner of the residence, or any person whose main home was your principal residence.

For purposes of the "health reasons" category, qualified individuals include not only the above individuals but also their family members: parents or step-parents, grandparents, children, stepchildren, adopted children, grandchildren, siblings (including step- or half-siblings), in-laws (mother/father, brother/sister, son/daughter), uncles, aunts, nephews, or nieces.

> **EXAMPLE**
>
> You bought and moved into your residence on April 4, 2018, so your holding period begins on April 5, 2018. In 2019 you move to a new job location in another state and sell your house at a gain of $50,000 on April 4, 2019. Since you owned and used your home for 12 months (365 days), your exclusion limit is reduced by 50% (365/730 days). You are single. Your reduced exclusion limit is $125,000 (50% of $250,000) and since the gain of $50,000 is totally covered by the $125,000 exclusion it is not taxable.

**Sale due to change in place of employment.** The reduced exclusion limit applies if the primary reason for your sale is a change in the location of a qualified individual's employment; *see* the above definition of qualified individual. "Employment" includes working for the same employer at a different location or starting with a new employer. It also includes the commencement of self-employment or the continuation of self-employment at a new location.

The IRS provides a safe harbor based on distance. If a qualified individual's new place of employment is at least 50 miles farther from the sold home than the old place of employment was, the reduced exclusion limit is allowed so long as the change in employment occurred while you owned and used the home as your principal residence. If an unemployed qualified person obtains employment, the safe harbor applies if the sold home is at least 50 miles from the place of employment.

If the 50-mile safe harbor cannot be met, the facts and circumstances may indicate that a change in the place of employment was the primary reason for the sale, thereby allowing the reduced exclusion limit.

> **EXAMPLE**
>
> An emergency room physician buys a condominium in March 2018 that is five miles from the hospital where she works. In November 2018, she takes a new job at a hospital 51 miles away from her home. She sells her home in December 2018 and buys a townhouse that is four miles away from the new hospital. The sale does not qualify for the 50-mile safe harbor since the new hospital is only 46 miles further from the old home than the first hospital was. However, given the doctor's need to work unscheduled hours and to get to work quickly, the IRS allows the reduced exclusion limit; the facts show that her change in place of employment was the primary reason for the home sale.

**Sale due to health problems.** The reduced exclusion limit applies if a principal residence is sold primarily to obtain or facilitate the diagnosis, treatment, or mitigation of a qualified person's disease, illness or injury, or to obtain or provide medical or personal care for a qualified individual suffering from a disease, illness, or injury. A sale does not qualify if it is merely to improve general health. Note that for "health sales," the definition of qualified individual is broadened to include family members; *see* above.

A physician's recommendation of a change in residence for health reasons automatically qualifies under an IRS safe harbor.

 *IRS Alert*

**Amended Return to Claim Reduced Maximum Exclusion**

If you reported gain on a sale that can be avoided under the reduced maximum exclusion rules for sales due to a change in place of employment, health, or unforeseen circumstances, a refund claim can be made on an amended return, provided the prior year is not closed by the statute of limitations (*47.2*).

**EXAMPLES**

1. One year after purchasing a home in Michigan, Smith is told by his doctor that moving to a warm, dry climate would mitigate his chronic asthma symptoms. Smith takes the advice, selling the house and moving to Arizona. The sale is within the doctor recommendation safe harbor and Smith may claim a reduced maximum exclusion for gain on the sale of the Michigan home.

2. In 2018, Mike and Kathy Anderson sell the house they bought in 2017 so they can move in with Kathy's father, who is chronically ill and unable to care for himself. The IRS allows the Andersons to claim a reduced maximum exclusion, as the primary reason for the sale is to provide care for Kathy's father, a qualified individual.

**Sale due to unforeseen circumstances.** A sale of a principal residence due to any of the following events fits within an IRS safe harbor for unforeseen circumstances and automatically qualifies for a reduced maximum exclusion:

1. The involuntary conversion of the home (condemnation or destruction of house in a storm or fire);

2. Damage to the residence from a natural or man-made disaster, war, or act of terrorism;

3. Any of the following events involving a qualified individual (*see* above): death, divorce or legal separation, becoming eligible for unemployment compensation, a change in employment or self-employment status that left the qualified individual unable to pay housing costs and reasonable basic household expenses, or multiple births resulting from the same pregnancy.

The IRS may expand the list of safe harbors in generally applicable revenue rulings or in private rulings requested by individual taxpayers.

Sales not covered by a safe harbor can qualify if the facts and circumstances indicate that the home was sold primarily because of an event that could not have been reasonably anticipated before the residence was purchased and occupied. The IRS in private letter rulings has been quite liberal in allowing the reduced maximum exclusion for unforeseen sales; *see* the examples below. Even the birth of a second child has been held to be an unforeseen circumstance (Example 5). However, an improvement in financial circumstances does not qualify under IRS regulations, even if the improvement is the result of unforeseen events, such as receiving a promotion and a large salary increase that would allow the purchase of a bigger home.

**EXAMPLES**

1. Three months after Jones buys a condominium as his principal residence, the condominium association replaces the roof and heating system and a few months later the monthly condominium fees are doubled. If Jones sells the condo because he cannot pay the higher fees and his monthly mortgage payment, the sale is considered to be due to unforeseen circumstances and Jones may claim a reduced maximum exclusion.

2. Tom and his fiancée, Alice, buy a house and live in it as their principal residence. The next year they break up and Tom moves out. The house is sold because Alice cannot afford to make the monthly payments alone. According to the IRS, the sale is due to unforeseen circumstances and Alice and Tom may each claim a reduced maximum exclusion.

3. A married couple purchased a home in a retirement community that had minimum age requirements for residents. Shortly after they moved in, their daughter lost her job and was in the process of getting a divorce. The daughter and her child wanted to move in but could not because of the community's age requirements. The couple sold the home and bought a new one in which their daughter and grandchild lived while the daughter looked for full-time employment. The IRS privately ruled that the sale of the retirement community home was due to unforeseen circumstances and the reduced maximum exclusion could be claimed.

4. A single mother bought a home and lived in it with her two daughters as their principal residence. One of the daughters was subjected to unruly behavior, verbal abuse, and sexual assault on the school bus. As a result, the daughter suffered from persistent fear and her school performance seriously declined. Her behavior was noticed by the school and brought to the mother's attention. She tried to work with the school district to resolve the problem, but when attempts failed, she sold her home and moved. The mother had not owned the home for two full years and asked the IRS whether she qualified for a partial exclusion. The IRS said yes. The primary reason for the sale prior to satisfying the two-year test was an unforeseen circumstance—the extreme bullying suffered by her daughter. Therefore, she can prorate the home sale exclusion for the part of the two years that she owned and lived in the home.

5. A married couple with one child bought a condominium with two small bed rooms and two baths. The child's bedroom was also used as the husband's home office and a guest room. After the wife gave birth to a second child, they moved out of the condo and later sold it at a gain. The IRS in a private ruling concluded that the birth of a second child was an unforeseen circumstance that rendered the condo unsuitable as a residence. Therefore, the couple could claim the reduced maximum exclusion.

## 29.5　Figuring Gain or Loss

To figure the gain or loss on the sale of your principal residence, you must determine the selling price, the amount realized, and the adjusted basis. Worksheet 29-3 may be used to figure gain or loss on the sale of a principal residence.

**Gain or loss.** The difference between the amount realized and adjusted basis is your gain or loss. If the amount realized exceeds the adjusted basis, the difference is a gain that may be excluded *(29.1)*. If amount realized is less than adjusted basis, the difference is a loss. A loss on the sale of your main home may not be deducted *(29.8)*.

**Foreclosure or repossession.** If your home was foreclosed on or repossessed, you have a sale. See Chapter 31.

**Selling price.** This is the total amount received for your home. It includes money, all notes, mortgages, or other debts assumed by the buyer as part of the sale, and the fair market value of any other property or any services received. The selling price does not include receipts for personal property sold with your home. Personal property is property that is not a permanent part of the home, such as furniture, draperies, and lawn equipment.

If your employer pays you for a loss on the sale or for your selling expenses, do not include the payment as part of the selling price. Include the payment as wages on Line 1 of Form 1040. (Your employer includes the payment with the rest of your wages in Box 1 of your Form W-2.)

If you grant an option to buy your home and the option is exercised, add the amount received for the option to the selling price of your home. If the option is not exercised, you report the amount as ordinary income in the year the option expires. Report the amount on Schedule 1 of Form 1040.

**Amount realized.** This is the selling price minus selling expenses, including commissions, advertising fees, legal fees, and loan charges paid by the seller (e.g., loan placement fees or "points").

**Adjusted basis.** This is the cost basis of your home increased by the cost of improvements and decreased by deducted casualty losses, if any *(29.6)*. Cost basis is generally what you paid for the residence. If you obtained possession through other means, such as a gift or inheritance, *see* the special basis rules for gifts and inheritances *(5.17)*.

**Seller-paid points.** If the person who sold you your residence paid points on your loan, you may have to reduce your basis in the home by the amount of the points. If you bought your residence after 1990 but before April 4, 1994, you reduce basis by the points only if you chose to deduct them as home mortgage interest in the year paid. If you bought the residence after April 3, 1994, you reduce basis by the points even if you did not deduct the points.

*Filing Tip*

**Form 1099-S**

If you received Form 1099-S, Box 2 should show the gross proceeds from the sale of your home. However, Box 2 does not include the fair market value of any property other than cash or notes, or any services you received or will receive. For these, Box 4 will be checked. If the sales price of your home does not exceed $250,000 or $500,000 (if filing jointly) and you certify to the person responsible for closing the sale that your entire gain is excludable from your gross income, that person does not have to report the sale on Form 1099-S but may choose to do so.

*Filing Tip*

**Jointly Owned Home**

If you and your spouse sell your jointly owned home and file a joint return, you figure your gain or loss as one taxpayer. If you file separate returns, each of you must figure your own gain or loss according to your ownership interest in the home. Your ownership interest is determined by state law.

If you and a joint owner other than your spouse sell your jointly owned home, each of you must figure your own gain or loss according to your ownership interest in the home.

 *Caution*

**Repairs**

These maintain your home in good condition but do not add to its value or prolong its life. You do not add their cost to the basis of your property. Examples of repairs include repainting your house inside or outside, fixing gutters or floors, repairing leaks or plastering, and replacing broken window panes. However, repairs made as part of a larger remodeling or restoration project are treated by the IRS as capital improvements that increase basis *(9.3)*.

**Settlement fees or closing costs.** When buying your home, you may have to pay settlement fees or closing costs in addition to the contract price of the property. You may include in basis fees and closing costs that are for buying the home. You may not include in your basis the fees and costs of getting a mortgage loan. Settlement fees also do not include amounts placed in escrow for the future payment of items such as taxes and insurance.

Examples of the settlement fees or closing costs that you may include in the basis of your property are: (1) abstract fees (sometimes called abstract of title fees), (2) charges for installing utility services, (3) legal fees (including fees for the title search and preparing the sales contract and deed), (4) recording fees, (5) survey fees, (6) transfer taxes, (7) owner's title insurance, and (8) any amounts the seller owes that you agree to pay, such as certain real estate taxes, back interest, recording or mortgage fees, charges for improvements or repairs, and sales commissions.

Examples of settlement fees and closing costs not included in your basis are: (1) fire insurance premiums, (2) rent for occupancy of the home before closing, (3) charges for utilities or other services relating to occupancy of the home before closing, (4) any fee or cost that you deducted as a moving expense before 1994, (5) charges connected with getting a mortgage loan, such as mortgage insurance premiums (including VA funding fees), loan assumption fees, cost of a credit report, and fee for an appraisal required by a lender, and (6) fees for refinancing a mortgage.

**Construction.** If you contracted to have your residence built on land you own, your basis is the cost of the land plus the cost of building the home, including the cost of labor and materials, payments to a contractor, architect's fees, building permit charges, utility meter and connection charges, and legal fees directly connected with building the home.

**Cooperative apartment.** Your basis in the apartment is usually the cost of your stock in the co-op housing corporation, which may include your share of a mortgage on the apartment building.

## 29.6　Figuring Adjusted Basis

Adjusted basis in your home is cost basis *(29.5)* adjusted for items discussed below. Worksheet 29-2 may be used to figure adjusted basis.

*Increases to cost basis include:* improvements with a useful life of more than one year, special assessments for local improvements, and amounts spent after a casualty to restore damaged property.

*Decreases to cost basis include:* gain you postponed from the sale of a previous home before May 7, 1997, deductible casualty losses not covered by insurance, insurance payments you received or expect to receive for casualty losses, itemized deductions claimed for general sales taxes on the purchase of a houseboat or a mobile home, payments you received for granting an easement or right-of-way, depreciation allowed or allowable if you used your home for business or rental purposes, any allowable tax credit after 2005 for a home energy improvement *(25.15)* that increases the basis of the home, residential energy credit (generally allowed from 1977 through 1987 and 2009 through 2017) claimed for the cost of energy improvements added to the basis of your home, adoption credit you claimed for improvements added to the basis of your home, nontaxable payments from an adoption assistance program of your employer that you used for improvements added to the basis of your home, District of Columbia first-time homebuyers credit (allowed to qualifying first-time homebuyers for purchase after August 4, 1997 and before 2012), and an energy conservation subsidy excluded from your gross income because you received it (directly or indirectly) from a public utility after 1992 to buy or install any energy conservation measure. An energy conservation measure is an installation or modification that is primarily designed either to reduce consumption of electricity or natural gas or to improve the management of energy demand for a home.

**Improvements.** Improvements add to the value of your home, prolong its useful life, or adapt it to new uses. You add the cost of improvements to the basis of your property.

Examples of improvements include: bedroom, bathroom, deck, garage, porch, and patio additions, landscaping, paving driveway, walkway, fencing, retaining wall, sprinkler system, swimming pool, storm windows and doors, new roof, wiring upgrades, satellite dish, security system, heating system, central air conditioning, furnace, duct work, central humidifier, filtration system, septic system, water heater, soft water system, built-in appliances, kitchen modernization, flooring, wall-to-wall carpeting, attic, walls, and pipes.

Adjusted basis does not include the cost of any improvements that are no longer part of the home.

> **EXAMPLE**
>
> You installed wall-to-wall carpeting in your home 15 years ago. In 2018, you replace that carpeting with new wall-to-wall carpeting. The cost of the new carpeting increases your basis, but the cost of the old carpeting is no longer part of adjusted basis.

**Recordkeeping.** Ordinarily, you must keep records for three years after the due date for filing your return for the tax year in which you sold your home. But you should keep home records as long as they are needed for tax purposes to prove adjusted basis. These include: (1) proof of the home's purchase price and purchase expenses, (2) receipts and other records for all improvements, additions, and other items that affect the home's adjusted basis, (3) any worksheets you used to figure the adjusted basis of the home you sold, the gain or loss on the sale, the exclusion, and the taxable gain, and (4) any Form 2119 that you filed to postpone gain from a home sale before May 7, 1997.

## 29.7 Personal and Business Use of a Home

If in 2018 you sold a home that was used for business or rental as well as residential purposes, you may be able to exclude part or all of any gain realized on the sale. The excludable amount depends on whether the non-residential and residential areas were part of the same dwelling unit, whether the ownership and use tests *(29.2)* were met, whether depreciation was allowable after May 6, 1997, and whether the non-residential use was before 2009 or after 2008.

**Nonqualified use after 2008.** Gain allocable to periods of "nonqualified" use (not used as principal residence) after 2008 is not excludable from income *(29.2)*, but certain nonresidential periods are excluded from the definition of nonqualified use. For example, renting your home after you (and your spouse) move out is not nonqualified use if the rental occurs within the five-year period ending on the date of sale (see Example 2 (Andrea) at the end of *29.2*).

The IRS does not treat home office use or rental of a spare room after 2008 as nonqualified use; *see* below.

**Home office or rental space within your principal residence.** The IRS takes the position that gain does not have to be allocated between the residential and business use portions of your home where both are within the same dwelling unit. This rule allows a home office to be considered part of your residential property for purposes of the home sale exclusion. Similarly, the IRS considers renting a spare room as a bed-and-breakfast bedroom to be residential use. If the two-out-of-five-year ownership and use test *(29.2)* is met for the regular residential portion, you are also treated as meeting the two-year residential use test for the home office or rental space, even if you used the area as a business office or rented room for your entire period of ownership. As a result, the gain on the entire residence is eligible for the exclusion, except for the gain equal to depreciation for periods after May 6, 1997. The gain equal to post–May 6, 1997, depreciation is never excludable; it must be reported on Schedule D (Form 1040) as unrecaptured Section 1250 gain *(5.3)*.

 *Planning Reminder*

**Gains Postponed Under Prior Law Rules**

Gain on a previous home sale that you postponed under the prior law rollover rules reduces the basis of your current home if your current home was a qualifying replacement residence for the previous home. Postponed gains on several earlier sales may have to be taken into account under the basis reduction rule. The basis reduction will increase the gain on the sale of your current home.

 *Law Alert*

**Nonqualified Use After 2008 May Limit Exclusion**

Unless an exception applies *(29.7)*, any period after 2008 that a home is not used as your principal residence is considered a period of "nonqualified use," and gain allocable to the nonqualified use is taxable, even if the two-year residential use test for an exclusion is otherwise met *(29.2)*.

**Depreciation allowed or allowable.** Under IRS rules, you must reduce your basis *(29.6)* in the home for purposes of figuring gain on a sale by any depreciation you were entitled to deduct, even if you did not deduct it. Furthermore, you cannot exclude the gain equal to the depreciation allowed or allowable for periods after May 6, 1997. This means that if you were entitled to take depreciation deductions for periods after May 6, 1997, but did not do so, the gain equal to the allowable depreciation is generally not excludable. However, if you have records showing that you claimed less depreciation than was allowable, the IRS will reduce the excludable gain only by the claimed (allowed) depreciation.

> **EXAMPLE**
>
> Alice bought a house in March 2012 that she lived in as her principal residence. She used one room as a law office from May 2014 until September 2017, and claimed depreciation deductions of $2,500 for the office space during that period. She sells the home in 2018. Assume that gain on the sale is $24,000. Since the office and residential area were in the same dwelling unit, Alice does not have to allocate gain to the office. Since she meets the ownership and use tests for the residential part, the tests are also considered met for the office space, She may exclude $21,500 of the $24,000 gain from her 2018 income. The $2,500 of gain equal to depreciation cannot be excluded. Alice reports her $24,000 gain and the $21,500 exclusion in Part II of Form 8949 *(5.8)*. The $2,500 gain attributable to the depreciation is unrecaptured Section 1250 gain, which Alice enters on the Unrecaptured Section 1250 Gain Worksheet in the Schedule D instructions *(5.3)*.

**Business or rental area separate from your dwelling unit.** If you sell property that was partly your home and partly business or rental property separate from your dwelling unit, and the business/rental use of the separate part exceeded three years during the five years before the sale, the gain allocable to the separate part is not eligible for an exclusion (since the two-year use test *(29.2)* has not been met for that part) and must be reported as taxable income on Form 4797. This could be the case if you lived in one apartment and rented out other apartments in the same building, you rented out an unattached garage or building elsewhere on your property, your apartment was upstairs from your business, you operated a business from a barn or other structure separate from your business, or your home was located on a working farm. The gain allocable to the part used as your home and any exclusion allowed for that part is reported on Form 8949 and Schedule D *(29.2)*. *See* IRS Publication 523 for reporting details.

## 29.8 No Loss Allowed on Personal Residence

A loss on the sale of your principal residence is not deductible. You do not have to report the sale on your return unless you received a Form 1099-S. If you received Form 1099-S, you must report the sale on Form 8949 *(5.8)* even though the loss is not deductible. Code "L" must be entered in column (f) of Form 8949 to indicate that the loss is not deductible, and the nondeductible loss must be entered as a positive adjustment in column (g). These are the same reporting rules as for a second home or vacation home discussed below.

If part of the sold property was a business or rental area separate from your principal residence and you did not meet the two-year residential use test *(29.2)* for that separate part, treat the sale as if two pieces of property were sold (*see* last paragraph of *29.7*). Report the personal part on Form 8949 and the business part on Form 4797. A loss is deductible only on the business part.

**Second home or vacation home.** If you sell at a loss a second home or vacation home that was used entirely for personal purposes and the sale was reported on Form 1099-S, you report the sale on Form 8949 and Schedule D, even though the loss is not deductible. On Form 8949 *(5.8)*, report the proceeds in column (d) and your basis in column (e). The loss (excess of basis over proceeds) is not deductible, so code "L" must be entered in column (f) and the amount of the loss entered as a positive amount in column (g). The positive adjustment in column (g) negates the loss, so the gain or loss in column (h) will be "0" *(5.8)*. If in the year of sale part of the home was rented out or used for business, allocate the sale between the personal part and the rental or business part; report the personal part on Form 8949 *(5.8)* and the rental or business part on Form 4797.

## 29.9 Loss on Residence Converted to Rental Property

You are not allowed to deduct a loss on the sale of your personal residence. If you convert the house from personal use to rental use you may claim a loss on a sale if the value has declined below the basis fixed for the residence as rental property.

To determine if you have a loss for tax purposes, you need to know the conversion date basis. This is the lower of (1) your adjusted basis *(29.6)* for the house at the time of conversion or (2) the fair market value at the time of conversion. Add to the lower amount the cost of capital improvements made after the conversion, and subtract depreciation and casualty loss deductions claimed after the conversion. To deduct a loss, you have to be able to show that this basis exceeds the sales price. For example, if you paid $200,000 for your home and convert it to rental property when the value has declined to $150,000, your conversion date basis for the rental property is $150,000. If the property continues to decline in value, and you sell for $125,000 after having deducted $10,000 for depreciation, you may claim a loss of $15,000 ($140,000 (conversion date basis of $150,000 reduced by $10,000 depreciation) – $125,000 sales price). Your loss deduction will not reflect the $50,000 loss occurring before the conversion.

> ### EXAMPLE
>
> In 1988, Adams bought a house in Fort Worth, Texas. He paid $124,000, put in capital improvements, and lived there until he was forced to put it on the market when he lost his job. In 1989, he listed the house with a broker for $145,000. After receiving no offers, he decided to lease the house through 1990. By October of 1990 Adams owed $4,551 in property taxes and was three months behind on his mortgage payments. Fearing foreclosure, he sold the house for $130,000.
>
> For purposes of figuring a loss, Adams assumed that the fair market value at the time of conversion was equal to the $145,000 list price. The adjusted basis of the house was $141,026. As this was less than the estimated fair market value of $145,000, he used the $141,026 adjusted basis to figure a loss of $11,026 ($130,000 – $141,026). The IRS claimed the fair market value at the time of conversion was equal to the actual sale price of $130,000. Since basis for the converted property is the lesser of fair market value ($130,000) or adjusted basis ($141,026), Adams had no loss on the sale.
>
> However, the Tax Court allowed a $5,000 loss by fixing the fair market value at the time of conversion at $135,000. It held that Adams sold at a lower price because of his weak financial position of which the buyer took advantage. The court figured the $135,000 as follows: $129,000 fair market value in 1988 (based on an appraisal report, which both parties agree was correct), plus $6,000 of appreciation attributable to the capital improvements made to the property after it was converted.

**Partially rented home.** If you rented part of your home for over three years during the five years preceding the sale, you must allocate the basis and amount realized between the portion used as your home and the rented portion *(29.7)*. A loss on a sale is allowable on the rented portion, which is reported on Form 4797.

**Profit-making purposes.** Renting a residence is a changeover from personal to profit-making purposes. If a house is merely put up for rent such as by listing it with a realty company but little else is done to obtain tenants and the property is in fact not rented, the IRS is likely to conclude that it was not converted to property held for the production of income and a loss on the sale will be treated as a nondeductible personal loss; *see* Example 1 in *9.10*.

Similarly, where a house is only rented for several months prior to a sale, the IRS may not treat this as a conversion to rental property and may disallow a loss deduction claimed on the sale.

**Filing Tip**

**Loss Allowed**

If you sell a house that has been converted from personal to rental use, and the sales price is less than the conversion date basis, a loss on the sale is deductible *(29.9)*.

*Caution*

**Temporary Rental Before Sale**

A rental loss may be barred on a temporary rental before sale. The IRS and Tax Court held that where a principal residence was rented for several months while being offered for sale, the rental did not convert the home to rental property. Deductions for rental expenses were limited to rental income; no loss could be claimed. A federal appeals court disagreed and allowed a rental loss deduction; also *see 9.7*.

**Loss allowed on house bought for resale.** A loss deduction may also be allowed where you acquired the house as an investment with the intention of selling it at a profit, even though you occupied it incidentally as a residence prior to sale. In an unusual case, an owner bought a house with the intention of selling it. He lived in it for six years, but during that period it was for sale. The Tax Court allowed him to deduct the loss on its sale by proving he lived in it to protect it from vandalism and to keep it in good condition so that it would attract possible buyers.

In another case, an architect and builder built a house and offered it for sale through an agent and advertisements. He had a home and no intention to occupy the new house. On a realtor's advice, he moved into the house to make it more saleable. Ten months later, he sold the house at a loss of $4,065 and promptly moved out. The loss was allowed on proof that his main purpose in building and occupying the house was to realize a profit by a sale; the residential use was incidental.

**Gain on rented residence.** You have a gain on the sale of rental property if you sell for more than your adjusted basis at the time of conversion, plus subsequent capital improvements, and minus depreciation and casualty loss deductions. The sale is subject to the rules in *Chapter 44* for depreciable property.

## 29.10 Loss on Residence Acquired by Gift or Inheritance

You may deduct a loss on the sale of a house received as an inheritance or gift if you personally did not use it and offered it for sale or rental immediately or within a few weeks after acquisition.

*Planning Reminder*

**Inherited Residence**

If you inherit a residence in which you do not intend to live, it may be advisable to put it up for rent to allow for an ordinary loss deduction on a later sale. If you merely try to sell, and you finally do so at a loss, you are limited to a capital loss.

> **EXAMPLES**
>
> 1. A couple owned a winter vacation home in Florida. When the husband died, his wife immediately put the house up for sale and never lived in it. It was sold at a loss. The IRS disallowed her capital loss deduction, claiming it was personal and nondeductible. The wife argued that her case was no different from the case of an heir inheriting and selling a home, since at the death of her husband her interest in the property was increased. The Tax Court agreed with her reasoning and allowed the capital loss deduction.
>
> 2. A widow inherited a house owned by her late husband and rented out by his estate. Shortly after getting title to the house, she sold it at a loss that she deducted as an ordinary loss. The IRS limited her to a capital loss deduction. The Tax Court agreed. She could not show any business activity. She did not negotiate the lease with the tenant who was in the house when she received title. She never arranged any maintenance or repairs for the building. Moreover, she sold the property shortly after receiving title, which indicates she viewed the house as investment, not rental, property.
>
> 3. An inherited residence was rented out by the owner to her brother for $500 a month when the fair market rental value was $700 to $750 per month. When she sold the residence at a loss, the IRS disallowed the loss, and the Tax Court agreed. The below-market rental was treated as evidence that she held the property for personal purposes, not as rental property or as investment property held for appreciation in value.

## Worksheet 29-2    Adjusted Basis of Home Sold

**Caution:** *See 29.6 before you use this worksheet.*

1. Enter the purchase price of the home sold. (If you filed Form 2119 when you originally acquired that home to postpone gain on the sale of a previous home before May 7, 1997, enter the adjusted basis of the new home from that Form 2119.) ........................................................ **1.** _____

2. Seller-paid points for home bought after 1990 (see 29.5). Do not include any seller-paid points you already subtracted to arrive at the amount entered on line 1 .................................... **2.** _____

3. Subtract line 2 from line 1 ............................................................................ **3.** _____

4. Settlement fees or closing costs (see 29.5). If line 1 includes the adjusted basis of the new home from Form 2119, skip lines 4a–4g and 5; go to line 6.

   a. Abstract and recording fees ........................................... **4a.** _____

   b. Legal fees (including fees for title search and preparing documents) .............. **4b.** _____

   c. Survey fees ............................................................ **4c.** _____

   d. Title insurance ........................................................ **4d.** _____

   e. Transfer or stamp taxes ............................................... **4e.** _____

   f. Amounts that the seller owed that you agreed to pay (back taxes or interest, recording or mortgage fees, and sales commissions) ......................... **4f.** _____

   g. Other .................................................................. **4g.** _____

5. Add lines 4a through 4g .............................................................. **5.** _____

6. Cost of additions and improvements. Do not include any additions and improvements included on line 1 ....... **6.** _____

7. Special tax assessments paid for local improvements, such as streets and sidewalks ................... **7.** _____

8. Other increases to basis ............................................................. **8.** _____

9. Add lines 3, 5, 6, 7, and 8 .......................................................... **9.** _____

10. Depreciation allowed or allowable, related to the business use or rental of the home ...... **10.** _____

11. Other decreases to basis (see 29.6) .................................... **11.** _____

12. Add lines 10 and 11 ................................................................. **12.** _____

13. **Adjusted basis of home sold.** Subtract line 12 from line 9. Enter here and on Worksheet 29-3, line 4 ....... **13.** _____

## Worksheet 29-3    Gain (or Loss), Exclusion, and Taxable Gain

**Part 1. Gain or (Loss) on Sale**

1. Selling price of home ................................................................. **1.** _____

2. Selling expenses (including commissions, advertising and legal fees, and seller-paid loan charges) ............ **2.** _____

3. Subtract line 2 from line 1. This is the amount realized ................................... **3.** _____

4. Adjusted basis of home sold (from Worksheet 29-2, line 13) ................................ **4.** _____

5. **Gain or (loss)** on the sale. Subtract line 4 from line 3. If this is a loss, stop here ................. **5.** _____

**Part 2. Exclusion and Taxable Gain**

6. Enter any depreciation allowed or allowable on the property for periods after May 6, 1997. If none, enter -0- ............................................................... **6.** _____

7. Subtract line 6 from line 5. If the result is less than zero, enter -0- ........................... **7.** _____

8. Aggregate number of days of nonqualified use after 12/31/2008 ............................. **8.** _____

9. Number of days taxpayer owned the property ........................................... **9.** _____

10. Divide the amount on line 8 by the amount on line 9. Enter the result as a decimal (rounded to at least 3 places). But do not enter an amount greater than 1.00 ............................................... **10.** _____

11. Gain allocated to nonqualified use. (Line 7 multiplied by line 10) ............................ **11.** _____

12. Gain eligible for exclusion. Subtract line 11 from line 7. ................................... **12.** _____

13. If you qualify to exclude gain on the sale, enter your maximum exclusion (see 29.2 – 29.4). If you qualify for a reduced maximum exclusion, enter the amount from Worksheet 29-1, line 7. If you do not qualify to exclude gain, enter -0- .............................................. **13.** _____

14. **Exclusion.** Enter the smaller of line 12 or line 13 ....................................... **14.** _____

15. **Taxable gain.** Subtract line 14 from line 5. Report this taxable gain and the exclusion from line 14 on Form 8949 and Schedule D as required by the instructions for those forms. Use Form 6252 if reporting the gain on the installment sale method (5.21) and enter the exclusion from line 14 on line 15 of Form 6252. ..................................... **15.** _____

16. Enter the **smaller** of line 6 or line 15. Enter this amount on line 12 of the Unrecaptured Section 1250 Gain Worksheet in the instructions for Schedule D (Form 1040) ................................... **16.** _____

# CHAPTER 30

# Tax Rules for Investors in Securities

You have the opportunity to control the taxable year in which to realize gains and losses. Gains and losses are realized when you sell, and if there are no market pressures, you can time sales to your advantage.

If you sell securities at a gain in 2018, and you held the securities more than one year, you can benefit from the 0%,15% or 20% rate for long-term capital gains.

The $3,000 limitation ($1,500 if married filing separately) on deducting capital losses from other types of income is a substantial restriction. If you have capital losses exceeding the $3,000 (or $1,500) limit, it is advisable to realize capital gains income that can be offset by the losses.

Investors who have multiple or numerous transactions throughout the year generally need not manually enter each transaction on self-prepared returns or provide details to a tax return preparer. Tax return preparation software allows transactions through brokerage firms and mutual fund companies to be imported to your tax return by a simple keystroke. The information contained in this chapter is intended to provide general information on the underlying tax implications of securities.

## 30.1 Planning Year-End Securities Transactions

First establish your current gain and loss position for the year. List gains and losses already realized from completed transactions. Then review the records of earlier years to find any carryover capital losses. Include nonbusiness bad debts as short-term capital losses. Then review your paper gains and losses and determine what losses might now be realized to offset realized gains or what gains might be realized to be offset by realized losses.

If you have already realized net capital losses exceeding $3,000 ($1,500 if married filing separately), you may want to realize capital gains that will be absorbed by the excess loss. Remember, only up to $3,000 (or $1,500) of capital losses exceeding net capital gain may be deducted from other income such as salary, interest, and dividends.

**Planning for losses.** Realizing losses may pose a problem if you believe the security is due to increase in value sometime in the near future. Although the wash sale rule *(30.6)* prevents you from taking the loss if you buy the security 30 days before or after the sale, the following possibilities are open to you.

- If you believe the security will go up, but not immediately, you can sell now, realize your loss, wait 31 days, and then recover your position by repurchasing before the expected rise.

- You can hedge by repurchasing similar securities immediately after the sale provided they are not substantially identical. They can be in the same industry and of the same quality without being considered substantially identical. Check with your broker to *see* if you can use a loss and still maintain your position. Some brokerage firms maintain recommended "switch" lists and suggest a practice of "doubling up"—that is, buying the stock of the same company and then 31 days later selling the original shares. Doubling up has disadvantages: It requires additional funds for the purchase of the second lot, exposes you to additional risks should the stock price fall, and the new shares take a new holding period.

> **EXAMPLE**
>
> You own 100 shares of Steel Co. stock that cost you $10,000. In mid-November 2018, the stock is selling at $6,000 ($60 a share × 100 shares). You would like to realize the $4,000 loss but, at the same time, you want to hold on to the investment. You buy 100 shares at a market price of $60 a share (total investment $6,000) and 31 days later sell your original 100 shares, realizing a loss for 2018 so long as the sales price is under $100 a share. You retain your investment in the new lot.

## 30.2 Earmarking Stock Lots

Keep a record of all your stock transactions, especially when you buy the stock of one company at varying prices. By keeping a record of each stock lot, you may control the amount of gain or loss on a sale of a part of your holdings. If you do not make an adequate identification, the IRS will treat the shares you bought first as the shares being sold under a first-in, first-out (FIFO) rule.

You may not average the cost of stock lots; averaging is generally allowed only for mutual fund shares *(32.10)*. However, under the basis reporting rules *(5.8)* for "covered" securities acquired after 2011, averaging is allowed for most ETFs structured as regulated investment companies, and for shares acquired through a qualifying dividend reinvestment plan (DRIP).

If your stock is held by your broker, the IRS considers that an adequate identification is made if you give instructions to your broker about which particular shares are to be sold, and you receive a written confirmation of your instructions from the broker or transfer agent within a reasonable time.

> **EXAMPLE**
>
> Over a three-year period, you bought the following shares of Acme Steel stock: In 2002, 100 shares at $77 per share; in 2003, 200 shares at $84 per share; and in 2004, 100 shares at $105 per share. When the stock is selling at $90, you plan to sell 100 shares. You may use the cost of your 2004 lot and get a $1,500 loss if, for example, you want to offset some gains or other income you have already earned this year. Or you may get capital gains by selling the 2002 lot or part of the 2003 lot.

 *Planning Reminder*

**December 31 Deadline for 2018 Gains and Losses**

If you want to realize gains on publicly traded securities for 2018, you have until Monday, December 31, 2018, to transact the sale. Gain is reported in 2018, although payment is not received until the settlement date in 2019. If you do not want to realize the gain in 2018, delay the trade date until 2019.

Losses are also realized as of the trade date; a loss on a sale made by December 31, 2018, is reported on your 2018 return.

You must clearly identify the lot you want to sell. Say you want a loss and sell the 2004 lot. Unless you identify it as the lot sold, the IRS will hold that you sold the 2002 lot under the "first-in, first-out" rule. This rule assumes that, when you have a number of identical items that you bought at different times, your sale of any of them is automatically the sale of the first you bought. So the cost of your first purchase is what you match against your selling price to find your gain or loss. Here is what to do to counteract the first-in, first-out rule: If you have stock certificates registered in your name, show that you delivered the 2004 stock certificates. If the broker is holding the stock, specifically identify the 2004 lot in your selling instructions and get a written confirmation.

On the sale of mutual fund shares, you have the option of using an average cost basis *(32.10)*.

## 30.3 Sale of Stock Dividends

A sale of stock originally received as a dividend is treated as any other sale of stock. The holding period of a taxable stock dividend *(4.8)* begins on the date of distribution. The holding period of a tax-free stock dividend or stock received in a split *(4.6)* begins on the same date as the holding period of the original stock.

> **EXAMPLE**
>
> You bought 100 shares of X Co. stock on December 3, 2004. On August 7, 2018, you receive 10 shares of X Co. stock as a tax-free stock dividend. On December 18, 2018, you sell the 10 shares at a profit. You report the sale as long-term capital gain because the holding period of the 10 shares begins December 4, 2004 (day after original purchase), not August 7, 2018.

**Basis of tax-free dividend in the same class of stock.** Assume you receive a common stock dividend on common stock. You divide the original cost by the total number of old shares and new shares to find the new basis per share.

> **EXAMPLE**
>
> You bought 100 shares of common stock for $1,000, so that each share has a basis of $10. You receive 100 shares of common stock as a tax-free stock dividend. The basis of your 200 shares remains $1,000. The new cost basis of each share is now $5 ($1,000 ÷ 200 shares). You sell 50 shares for $560. Your profit is $310 ($560 − $250).

**Basis of tax-free dividend in a different class of stock.** Assume you receive preferred stock dividends on common stock. You divide the basis of the old shares over the two classes in the ratio of their values at the time the stock dividend was distributed.

> **EXAMPLE**
>
> You bought 100 shares of common stock for $1,000. You receive a tax-free dividend of 10 shares of preferred stock. On the date of distribution, the market value of the common stock is $9 a share and that of the preferred stock is $30. That makes the market value of your common stock $900 and your preferred stock $300. So you allocate 75% ($900 ÷ $1,200) of your $1,000 original cost, or $750, to your common stock and 25% ($300 ÷ $1,200) of your cost to the preferred stock.

**Basis of taxable stock dividend.** The basis of a taxable stock dividend *(4.6)* is its fair market value at the time of the distribution. Its holding period begins on the date of distribution. The basis of the old stock remains unchanged.

> **EXAMPLE**
>
> You bought 1,000 shares of stock for $10,000. The company gives you a choice of a cash dividend or stock (one share for every hundred held). You elect the stock. On the date of the distribution, its market value was $15 a share. The basis of the new stock is $150 (10 × $15), the amount of the taxable dividend. The basis of the old stock remains $10,000.

## 30.4 Stock Rights

The tax consequences of the receipt of stock rights are discussed at *4.6*. The following is an explanation of how to treat the sale, exercise, or expiration of nontaxable stock rights. The basis of taxable rights is their fair market value at the time of distribution.

**Expiration of nontaxable distributed stock rights.** When you allow nontaxable rights to expire, you do not have a deductible loss; you have no basis in the rights.

**Sale of nontaxable distributed stock rights.** If you sell stock rights distributed on your stock, you treat the sale as the sale of a capital asset. The holding period begins from the date you acquired the original stock on which the rights were distributed.

**Purchased rights.** If you buy stock rights, your holding period starts the day after the date of the purchase. Your basis for the rights is the price paid; this basis is used in computing your capital gain or loss on the sale.

If you allow purchased rights to expire without sale or exercise, you realize a capital loss. The rights are treated as having been sold on the day of expiration. When purchased rights become worthless during the year prior to the year they lapse, you have a capital loss that is treated as having occurred on the last day of the year in which they became worthless.

**Figuring the basis of nontaxable stock rights.** Whether rights received by you as a stockholder have a basis depends on their fair market value when distributed. If the market value of rights is less than 15% of the market value of your old stock, the basis of your rights is zero, unless you elect to allocate the basis between the rights and your original stock. You make the election on your tax return for the year the rights are received by attaching to your return a statement that you are electing to divide basis. Keep a copy of the election and the return.

If the market value of the rights is 15% or more of the market value of your old stock, you must divide the basis of the stock between the old stock and the rights, according to their respective values on the date of distribution.

No basis adjustment is required for stock rights that become worthless during the year of issue.

## 30.5 Short Sales of Stock

A short sale is a sale of stock borrowed from a broker. The short sale is closed when you replace the borrowed stock by buying substantially identical stock and delivering it to the broker or by delivering stock that you held at the time of the short sale. One objective of a short sale is to profit from an anticipated drop in the market price of the stock; another objective may be to use the short sale as a hedge.

Tax rules applied to short sales are designed to prevent you from:

- Postponing gain to a later year when you sell short while holding an appreciated position in the same or substantially identical stock. This type of short sale is called "a sale against the box."
- Converting short-term gains to long-term gains.
- Converting long-term losses to short-term losses.

**Year in which gain on short sale is realized.** Generally, you report gain on a short sale on Form 8949 and Schedule D for the year in which you close the short sale by delivering replacement stock. However, if you execute a short sale while holding an appreciated position in the same stock (short sale against the box) or substantially identical stock is acquired to close an appreciated short position, the short sale or acquisition of substantially identical stock is treated as a constructive sale of an appreciated financial position *(30.9)* and you must report the transaction in the year of the constructive sale, even though delivery of replacement stock is made in a later year; *see* Examples below.

There is this exception to the constructive sale rule: The short sale is reported in the year of delivery of the replacement stock if (1) you close the short sale before the end of the 30th day of the next year, (2) you continue to hold a similar position in the stock for at least 60 days after the closing of the short sale, and (3) your risk of loss during the 60-day period was not reduced by other positions. *See* Example 3 below and *30.9* for further details on constructive sales.

 *Planning Reminder*

**Exercise of Stock Rights**

You realize no taxable income on the exercise of stock rights. Capital gain or loss on the new stock is recognized when you later sell the stock. The holding period of the new stock begins on the date you exercised the rights. Your basis for the new stock is the subscription price you paid plus your basis for the rights exercised.

If the stock sold short becomes worthless before you close the short sale, you recognize taxable gain in the year the shares became worthless.

---

**EXAMPLES**

1. On May 2, 2018, you buy 100 shares of Auto Corp. stock for $1,000. On September 7, 2018, you borrow 100 shares of Auto Corp. from your broker and sell them short for $1,600. You make no subsequent transactions involving Auto Corp. stock. The short sale is treated as a constructive sale of an appreciated financial position because a sale of your Auto Corp. stock on September 7, the date of the short sale, would have resulted in a gain. You have a $600 short-term capital gain from the constructive sale and you have a new holding period for your Auto Corp. stock that begins on September 7, 2018.

2. In January 2018 you buy 100 shares of Steel Co. stock for $1,000 (100 × $10). In November 2018 when the stock is selling at $50, you execute a short sale of 100 shares (100 × $50 = $5,000). In February 2019, you deliver your shares to close the short sale. The tax law treats the short sale as a constructive sale of an appreciated financial position because a sale of your Steel Co. stock on the date of the short sale would have resulted in a gain. You report the gain of $4,000 ($5,000 − $1,000) in 2018, the year of the short sale, not in 2019 when you close the sale. To shift tax reporting to 2019, you would have had to close the short sale by the 30th of January and obtain similar stock, which you would have had to hold for at least 60 days after the closing of the short sale; *see* Example 3.

3. On October 3, 2018, you buy 100 shares of Oil Co. for $60 a share. On December 11, 2018, you sell short 100 shares of Oil Co. for $80 a share. On January 18, 2019, you buy 100 shares of Oil Co. for $75 a share to close the short sale. You hold the October lot for over 60 days after January 18, 2019. The December 2018 short sale is not treated as a constructive sale in 2018 because you closed the short sale by January 30th and you held the October lot for at least 60 days after the short sale was closed. You have a loss of $5 per share when you close the short sale in January 2019.

4. A taxpayer who does not own any shares of XYZ stock directs his broker in January of Year 1 to sell short borrowed XYZ shares. On December 31 of Year 1, when the value of XYZ shares has decreased, the taxpayer directs the broker to close the short sale by purchasing XYZ shares in a "regular-way" sale, with actual delivery of the shares taking place at the beginning of Year 2. The IRS ruled that the short position is an appreciated financial position as of December 31, given the decrease in the stock price since the short sale. The purchase of replacement shares on December 31 is a constructive sale of the appreciated position. Gain is taxable in Year 1, not in Year 2 when the shares were delivered.

---

**Short-term or long-term gain or loss.** Whether you have short-term or long-term capital gain or loss generally depends on your holding period for the property delivered to the broker to close the short sale. Furthermore, you must apply Rules 1 and 2 below if you answer "yes" to either of the following questions:

- When you sold short, did you or your spouse hold for one year or less securities substantially identical to the securities sold short? (Substantially identical securities are described at *30.6*.)
- After the short sale, did you or your spouse acquire substantially identical securities on or before the date of the closing of the short sale?

*Rule 1.* Gain realized on the closing of the short sale is short term. The gain is short term regardless of the period of time you have held the securities as of the closing date of the short sale.

*Rule 2.* The beginning date of the holding period of substantially identical stock is suspended. The holding period of substantially identical securities owned or bought under the facts of question (1) or (2) does not begin until the date of the closing of the short sale (or the date of the sale, gift, or other disposition of the securities, whichever date occurs first). But note that this rule applies only to the number of securities that do not exceed the quantity sold short.

**Losses.** A loss on a short sale is not deductible until shares closing the short sale are delivered to the broker. You may not realize a short-term loss on the closing of a short sale if you held substantially identical securities long term (that is, for more than a year) on the date of the short sale. The loss is long term even if the securities used to close the sale were held for one year or less. This rule prevents you from creating short-term losses when you held the covering stock long term. Loss deductions on short sales may be disallowed under the wash sale rules in *30.6*.

---

### EXAMPLES

1. On February 2, 2018, the stock of Oil Co., which you do not own, is selling at $90 per share. You expect the price to fall over the next year and sell short 500 shares borrowed from your broker for $45,000 (500 × $ 90). However, 13 months later, on March 14, 2019, after the price has risen to $110, you close the short sale by buying 500 shares of Oil Co. stock ($500 × $110 = $55,000 cost) and immediately delivering them to your broker. Your loss of $10,000 ($55,000 – $45,000) is treated as a short-term capital loss because your holding period for the delivered stock is less than one day.

2. On February 13, 2018, you buy 100 shares of Tech Corp. stock for $1,000. On July 13, 2018, you sell short 100 shares of Tech Corp. for $1,600. You close the short sale on November 9, 2018, by buying 100 shares for $1,800 and delivering them to your broker. On the short sale, you realize a $200 short-term capital loss.

    On February 26, 2019, you sell for $1,900 your original lot of Tech Corp. stock bought on February 13, 2018. Although you have held these shares for more than one year, the $900 gain realized on the sale is treated as a short-term capital gain under Rule 2 above. Rule 2 applies because on the date of the short sale (July 13, 2018), the February 13 shares were held short term (one year or less). Under Rule 2, the holding period of the February 13 lot is considered to begin on November 9, 2018, the date the short sale was closed.

---

**Expenses of short sales.** Before you buy stock to close out a short sale, you pay the broker for dividends paid on stock you have sold short. If you itemize deductions, you may treat your payment as investment interest *(15.10)*, provided the short sale is held open at least 46 days, or more than a year in the case of extraordinary dividends. If the 46-day (or one-year) test is not met, the payment is generally not deductible and is added to basis; in counting the short-sale period, do not count any period during which you have an option to buy or are obligated to buy substantially identical securities, or are protected from the risk of loss from the short sale by a substantially similar position.

Under an exception to the 46-day test, if you receive compensation from the lender of the stock for the use of collateral and you report the compensation as ordinary income, your payment for dividends is deductible to the extent of the compensation; only the excess of your payment over the compensation is disallowed. This exception does not apply to payments with respect to extraordinary dividends.

An extraordinary dividend is generally a dividend that equals or exceeds the amount realized on the short sale by 10% for any common stock or by 5% for any preferred stock dividends. For purposes of this test, dividends on stock received within an 85-day period are aggregated; a one-year aggregation period applies if dividends exceed 20% of the adjusted basis in the stock.

## 30.6  Wash Sales

The objective of the wash sale rule is to disallow a loss deduction where you recover your market position in a security within a short period of time after the sale. Under the wash sale rule, which applies to investors and traders (but not dealers), your loss deduction is barred if within 30 days of the sale you buy substantially identical stock or securities, you buy a "call" option on such securities, or you sell a "put" option on the securities that is "deep-in-the-money". The wash sale period is 61 days—running from 30 days before to 30 days after the date of sale. The end of a taxable year during this 61-day period does not affect the wash sale rule. The loss is still denied. If you sell at a loss and your spouse buys substantially identical stock within this period, the loss is also barred. The disallowed loss is added to the basis of the replacement stock.

*Caution*

**Wash Sale Rule Applies If Replacement Bought in IRA**

The IRS has ruled that a loss on the sale of stock is disallowed by the wash sale rule if within 30 days before or after the sale replacement shares are bought through a traditional IRA or Roth IRA.

*Planning Reminder*

**Tax Advantage of Wash Sale Rule**

Sometimes the wash sale rule can work to your advantage. Assume that during December you are negotiating a sale of real estate that will bring you a large capital gain. You want to offset a part of that gain by selling certain securities at a loss. You are unsure just when the gain transaction will go through. It may be on the last day of the year, at which point it may be too late to sell the loss securities before the end of the same year.

You can do this: Sell the loss securities during the last week of December. If the profitable deal goes through before the end of the year, you need not do anything further. If it does not, buy back the loss securities early in January. The December sale will be a wash sale and the loss disallowed. When the profitable real estate sale occurs next year, you can sell the loss securities again. This time the loss will be allowed and will offset the gain.

The wash sale rule does not apply to gains. It also does not apply to acquisitions by gift, inheritance, or tax-free exchange.

### EXAMPLES

1. You bought common stock of Appliance Co. for $10,000 in 1996. On June 25, 2018, you sold the stock for $8,000, incurring a $2,000 loss. A week later, you repurchased the same number of shares of Appliance stock for $9,000. Your loss of $2,000 on the sale is disallowed because of the wash sale rule. The basis of the new lot becomes $11,000, equal to the cost of the new shares ($9,000) plus the disallowed loss ($2,000).

2. Assume the same facts as in Example 1, except that you repurchase the stock for $7,000. The basis of the new lot is $9,000, the cost of the new shares ($7,000) plus the disallowed loss ($2,000).

3. Assume that in February 2019 you sell the new lot of stock acquired in Example 1 above for $9,000 and do not run afoul of the wash sale rule. On the sale, you realize a loss of $2,000 ($11,000 basis – $9,000 sales price).

**Buying replacement shares through IRA.** The IRS has ruled that buying replacement shares in a traditional IRA or Roth IRA triggers the wash sale rule. Some commentators had suggested that the wash sale rule should not apply because the seller and the IRA, although "related," are different entities for tax purposes. The IRS disagrees. Although the IRA is a separate tax-exempt trust, the seller of the loss shares is treated as acquiring the replacement shares through the IRA.

There is an additional penalty for using an IRA to acquire replacement shares. The increase to basis that would have applied if the replacement shares had been bought in a taxable account is lost. When the replacement is made in a taxable account, the basis increase preserves for future use the economic value of the disallowed loss by allowing gain to be reduced, or loss to be increased, on a later sale of the replacement shares. However, there is no basis increase for the shares held in the IRA and the wash sale loss is permanently disallowed, making this a worse result than if the replacement had been made in a taxable account.

**Loss on the sale of part of a stock lot bought less than 30 days ago.** If you buy stock and then, within 30 days, sell some of those shares, a loss on the sale is deductible; the wash sale disallowance rule does not apply.

### EXAMPLE

You buy 200 shares of stock. Within 30 days, you sell 100 shares at a loss. The loss is not disallowed by the wash sale rule. The wash sale rule does not apply to a loss sustained in a bona fide sale made to reduce your market position. It does apply when you sustain a loss for tax purposes with the intent of recovering your position in the security within a short period. Thus if, after selling the 100 shares, you repurchase 100 shares of the same stock within 30 days after the sale, the loss is disallowed.

**Oral sale-repurchase agreement.** The wash sale rule applies to an oral sale-repurchase agreement between business associates.

**Defining "substantially identical."** What is substantially identical stock or securities? Buying and selling General Motors stock is dealing in an identical security. Selling General Motors and buying Fiat Chrysler stock is not dealing in substantially identical securities.

Bonds of the same obligor are substantially identical if they carry the same rate of interest; that they have different issue dates and interest payment dates will not remove them from the wash sale provisions. Different maturity dates will have no effect, unless the difference is economically significant. Where there is a long time span between the purchase date and the maturity date, a difference of several years between maturity dates may be considered insignificant. A difference of three years between maturity dates was held to be insignificant where the maturity dates of the bonds, measured from the time of purchase, were 45 and 48 years away. There was no significant difference where the maturity dates differed by less than one year, and the remaining life, measured from the time of purchase, was more than 15 years.

The wash sale rules do not apply if you buy bonds of the same company with substantially different interest rates, buy bonds of a different company, or buy substantially identical bonds outside of the wash sale period.

**Warrants.** A warrant falls within the wash sale rule if it is an option to buy substantially identical stock. Consequently, a loss on the sale of common stocks of a corporation is disallowed when warrants for the common stock of the same corporation are bought within the period 30 days before or after the sale. But if the timing is reversed—that is, you sell warrants at a loss and simultaneously buy common stock of the same corporation—the wash sale rules may or may not apply depending on whether the warrants are substantially identical to the purchased stock. This is determined by comparing the relative values of the stock and warrants. The wash sale rule will apply only if the relative values and price changes are so similar that the warrants become fully convertible securities.

**Repurchasing fewer shares.** If the number of shares of stock reacquired in a wash sale is less than the amount sold, only a proportionate part of the loss is disallowed.

> **EXAMPLE**
>
> On August 20, 2018, you bought 100 shares of Stock A for $10,000. On December 10, 2018, you sell the lot for $8,000, incurring a loss of $2,000. On January 14, 2019, you repurchase 75 shares of Stock A for $6,000. Three-quarters (75/100) of your loss is disallowed, or $1,500 (¾ of $2,000). You deduct the remaining loss of $500 on your return for 2018. The basis of the new shares is $7,500 ($6,000 cost plus $1,500 disallowed loss).

**Holding period of new stock.** After a wash sale, the holding period of the new stock includes the holding period of the old lots. If you sold more than one old lot in wash sales, you add the holding periods of all the old lots to the holding period of the new lot. You do this even if your holding periods overlapped as you purchased another lot before you sold the first. You do not count the periods between the sale and purchase when you have no stock.

**Losses on short sales.** Losses incurred on short sales are subject to the wash sale rules. A loss on the closing of a short sale is denied if you sell the stock or enter into a second short sale within the period beginning 30 days before and ending 30 days after the closing of the short sale. Furthermore, you cannot deduct a loss on the closing of a short sale if within 30 days of the short sale you bought substantially identical stock.

## 30.7 Convertible Stocks and Bonds

You realize no gain or loss when you convert a bond into stock, or preferred stock into common stock of the same corporation, provided the conversion privilege was allowed by the bond or preferred stock certificate.

**Holding period.** Stock acquired through the conversion of bonds or preferred stock takes the same holding period as the securities exchanged. However, where the new stock is acquired partly for cash and partly by tax-free exchange, each new share of stock has a split holding period. The portion of each new share allocable to the ownership of the converted bonds (or preferred stock) includes the holding period of the bonds (or preferred stock). The portion of the new stock allocable to the cash purchase takes a holding period beginning with the day after acquisition of the stock.

**Basis.** Securities acquired through the conversion of bonds or preferred stock into common take the same basis as the securities exchanged. Where there is a partial cash payment, the basis of the portion of the stock attributable to the cash is the amount of cash paid; *see* Examples 1 and 2 below.

 *Planning Reminder*

**Basis Adjusted for New Stock**

Although the loss deduction is barred if the wash-sale rule applies, the economic loss is not forfeited for tax purposes. The loss might be realized at a later date when the repurchased stock is sold, because after the disallowance of the loss, the cost basis of the new lot is increased by the disallowed loss. However, the basis increase is not allowed by the IRS if the shares are purchased by your IRA rather than by you individually.

If you paid a premium for a convertible bond, you may not amortize the amount of the premium that is attributable to the conversion feature.

### EXAMPLES

1. On January 5, you paid $100 for a bond of A Co. Your holding period for the bond begins on January 6 *(5.9)*. The bond provides that the holder may receive one share of A Co. common stock upon surrender of the bond and the payment of $50. On October 19, you convert the bond to stock on payment of $50. For tax purposes, you realize no gain or loss upon the conversion regardless of whether the fair market value of the stock is more or less than $150 on the date of the conversion. The basis and holding period for the stock is as follows: $100 basis for the portion attributed to the ownership of the bond with the holding period beginning January 6; and $50 basis attributed to the cash payment with the holding period for this portion beginning October 20.

2. Same facts as in the above Example, but you acquired the bond on January 5 through the exercise of rights on that date. Since the holding period for the bond includes the date of exercise of the rights *(5.10)*, the portion of the stock allocable to the bond takes a holding period beginning on January 5.

## 30.8  Stock Options

Stock options are contracts to buy or sell a fixed number of shares by a set date (called the expiration date). Stock options are purchased from public exchanges. If you are buying an option, you are a holder; if you are selling an option, you are a writer. Writers receive a cash premium from the holder. While there are numerous variations on how stock options can be used as investment strategies, the basic ones include the following.

**Calls.** Buying a call gives the holder the right to buy a specified number of shares of the underlying stock at a given exercise price on or before the option expiration date. Selling a call gives the seller, called the writer, the obligation to sell shares to the holder at the agreed upon price on or before the option expiration date. The holder pays a premium to the writer for the right to buy the shares. If the price of the stock rises above the agreed-upon price (the strike or exercise price), the holder exercises the buy option and acquires the shares. If not, the holder lets the options expire. The holder can sell the call prior to the expiration date.

**Puts.** Buying a put gives the holder the right, but not the obligation, to sell a specified number of shares of the underlying stock at the given exercise price on or before the option expiration date. Selling a put gives the seller, called the writer, the obligation to buy shares from the holder at the agreed upon price (the strike or exercise price). The writer receives a premium for this obligation. If the stock price rises above the strike price, the holder does not exercise the put option. The holder may sell the put option before the expiration date.

*Planning Pointer*

**Employee Stock Options**

Different tax rules apply to incentive stock options and nonqualified stock options obtained in connection with employment (*see 2.16*).

*Planning Reminder*

**Speculate with Puts and Calls**

Puts and calls allow you to speculate at the expense of a small investment—a call by the holder, for expected price rises, and a put by the holder, for expected price declines. They may also be used to protect paper profits or fix the amount of your losses on securities you own.

| *Table 30-1*  Tax results from calls: | | |
| --- | --- | --- |
| The call— | The holder— | The writer— |
| Is exercised | Add the cost of the call to your basis in the stock | Increase the amount realized on the sale of the stock by the amount you received for the call |
| Expires | Report the cost of the call as a capital loss on the date it expires | Report the amount you received for the call as a short-term capital gain |
| Is sold by the holder | Report as capital gain or loss the difference between the cost of the call and the amount you receive for it | N/A |

| *Table 30-2*    Tax results from puts: | | |
|---|---|---|
| **The put—** | **The holder—** | **The writer—** |
| Is exercised | Reduce the amount realized from the sale of the underlying stock by the cost of the put | Reduce your basis in the stock that you acquire as a result of the put by the amount you received for the put |
| Expires | Report the cost of the put as a capital loss on the date it expires | Report the amount you received for the call as a short-term capital gain |
| Is sold by the holder | Report as capital gain or loss the difference between the cost of the put and the amount you receive for it | N/A |

## 30.9   Sophisticated Financial Transactions

Some individuals may engage in certain complicated and risky financial transactions in the stock market. These activities are not for the average investor, and the tax treatment of these transactions can be complex. The following is a brief overview of some of these transactions and where you can find more information if necessary.

**Arbitrage transactions.** These are transactions in which an investor simultaneously buys and sells securities, currency, or commodities in different markets to benefit from differing prices for the same asset. Special holding period rules apply to short sales involved in identifying arbitrage transactions in convertible securities and stocks into which the securities are convertible (see Treasury regulations under Internal Revenue Code 1233).

**Constructive sales of appreciated financial positions.** You have made a constructive sale of an appreciated financial position if you:

1. Enter into a short sale of the same or substantially identical property *(30.5)*,
2. Enter into an offsetting notional principal contract relating to the same or substantially identical property,
3. Enter into a futures or forward contract to deliver the same or substantially identical property, or
4. Acquire the same or substantially identical property (if the appreciated financial position is a short sale, an offsetting notional principal contract, or a futures or forward contract).

You are also treated as having made a constructive sale of an appreciated financial position if a person related to you enters into any of the above transactions.

A contract for sale of any stock, debt instrument, or partnership interest that is not a marketable security is not a constructive sale if it settles within one year of the date you enter into it.

If you are considered to have transacted a constructive sale, you must report as taxable income gain on the financial position as if the position was sold at its fair market value on the date of the constructive sale. The property held by you receives a new holding period starting on the date of the constructive sale and its basis is the fair market value at that date. Thus, under the constructive sale rule you are also treated as immediately repurchasing the position as of the date of the constructive sale.

**Straddle losses.** Commodities and stock options can be used to straddle positions that an investor holds to effectively hedge his or her bets against future price changes. Generally, under tax accounting rules, losses are used to match unrealized gains. Find more information in the instructions to Form 6781 and in IRS Publication 550.

*Caution*

**Get Professional Help**

Anyone engaging in any sophisticated financial transaction should fully understand the nature of the transaction and the risk, and would be well advised to work with a financial advisor and a tax professional.

*Planning Reminder*

**Avoiding Constructive Sale Treatment**

Certain actions (e.g., closing a transaction before a set time; holding a position through a set time) can be employed to avoid the constructive sale rules.

**Regulated futures contracts.** These are contracts to buy or sell commodities or currency on a futures exchange (e.g., the Chicago Board of Trade). Gain or loss is reported annually under the marked-to-market accounting system. Find more information in the instructions to Form 6781 and in IRS Publication 550.

**Conversion transactions.** A conversion transaction is one involving two or more positions taken with regard to the same or similar property. The investor is in the economic position of a lender who expects to receive income while undertaking no significant risks other than those of a lender. Conversion transactions are reported on Form 6781. However, the ordinary income element from a conversion transaction is not reported as interest; it is treated as ordinary gain on Form 4797.

## 30.10 Investing in Tax-Exempts

Interest on state and local obligations is not subject to federal income tax. It is also exempt from the tax of the state in which the obligations are issued. In comparing the interest return of a tax-exempt with that of a taxable bond, you figure the taxable return that is equivalent to the tax-free yield of the tax-exempt. This amount depends on your marginal tax bracket (your top tax rate). For example, a tax-exempt municipal bond yielding 3% is the equivalent of a taxable yield of 3.95% subject to a marginal tax rate of 24%.

You can compare the value of tax-exempt interest to taxable interest for your tax bracket by using this formula:

$$\frac{\text{Tax-exempt interest rate}}{1 \text{ minus your marginal tax bracket}}$$

The denominator of the above fraction is:

0.88 if your marginal tax bracket is 12%
0.78 if your marginal tax bracket is 22%
0.76 if your marginal tax bracket is 24%
0.68 if your marginal tax bracket is 32%
0.65 if your marginal tax bracket is 35%
0.63 if your marginal tax bracket is 37%

*Planning Reminder*

**Municipal Bond Funds**

Instead of purchasing tax-exempts directly, you may consider investing in municipal bond funds. The funds invest in various municipal bonds and, thus, offer the safety of diversity. The value of fund shares will fluctuate with the bond markets. Also, an investment in the fund may be as small as $1,000 compared with the typical $5,000 municipal bond. Check on fees and other restrictions in municipal bond funds.

> **EXAMPLE**
>
> You are deciding between a tax-exempt bond and a taxable bond. You want to find which will give you more income after taxes. You have a choice between a tax-exempt bond paying 2.5% and a taxable bond paying 3.25%. Your marginal tax bracket is 32%.
>
> You find that the tax-exempt bond is a slightly better buy in your tax bracket as it is the equivalent of a taxable bond paying nearly 3.68%.
>
> $$\text{Taxable Equivalent Rate (T)} = \frac{0.025}{0.68\,(1.00 - 0.32)}$$
>
> $$T = .03676, \text{ or } 3.676\%$$

**AMT and other restrictions.** In buying state or local bonds, check the prospectus for the issue date and tax status of the bond. The tax law treats bonds issued after August 7, 1986, as follows:

1. "Public-purpose" bonds. These include bonds issued directly by state or local governments or their agencies to meet essential government functions, such as highway construction and school financing. These bonds are generally tax exempt.

2. "Qualified private activity" bonds. Interest on private activity bonds is taxable unless the bond is a qualified bond. Qualified bonds generally finance housing, student loans, or redevelopment, or they benefit tax-exempt organizations. Interest on qualified private activity bonds issued after August 7, 1986, although tax free for regular income tax purposes, is a tax preference item for purposes of computing alternative minimum tax *(23.3)* unless an exception applies. Because of the AMT, these private activity bonds may pay slightly higher interest than public-purpose bonds.

Several types of bonds have been excluded from private activity bond treatment so the interest is not treated as an AMT preference item, including qualified Section 501(c) (3) bonds, Gulf Opportunity Zone bonds, Midwestern disaster area bonds, most New York Liberty bonds, and qualified mortgage bonds issued after July 30, 2008. In addition, any bonds issued in 2009 and 2010 that would otherwise be considered private activity bonds are not treated as private activity bonds, so the interest on the 2009/2010 bonds is not a tax preference item.

Your broker can help you identify bonds subject to and exempt from AMT preference item treatment.

3. "Taxable" municipals. These are bonds issued for nonqualifying private purposes. They are subject to federal income tax, but may be exempt from state and local taxes in the states in which they are issued.

## 30.11 Ordinary Loss for Small Business Stock (Section 1244)

Shareholders of qualifying "small" corporations may claim within limits an ordinary loss, rather than a capital loss, on the sale or worthlessness of Section 1244 stock. An ordinary loss up to $50,000, or $100,000 on a joint return, may be claimed on Form 4797. On a joint return, the $100,000 limit applies even if only one spouse has a Section 1244 loss. Losses in excess of these limits are deductible as capital losses on Form 8949. Any gains on Section 1244 stock are reported as capital gain on Form 8949.

An ordinary loss may be claimed only by the original owner of the stock. If a partnership sells Section 1244 stock at a loss, an ordinary loss deduction may be claimed by individuals who were partners when the stock was issued. If a partnership distributes the Section 1244 stock to the partners, the partners may not claim an ordinary loss on their disposition of the stock.

If an S corporation sells Section 1244 stock at a loss, S corporation shareholders may not claim an ordinary loss deduction. The IRS with Tax Court approval limits shareholders' deductions to capital losses, which are deductible only against capital gains plus $3,000 ($1,500 if married filing separately) (5.4).

To qualify as Section 1244 stock:

1. The corporation's equity may not exceed $1,000,000 at the time the stock is issued, including amounts received for the stock to be issued. Thus, if the corporation already has $600,000 equity from stock previously issued, it may not designate more than $400,000 worth of additional stock as Section 1244 stock.

   If the $1,000,000 equity limit is exceeded, the corporation follows an IRS procedure for designating which shares qualify as Section 1244 stock.

   Preferred stock issued after July 18, 1984, may qualify for Section 1244 loss treatment, as well as common stock.

2. The stock must be issued for money or property (other than stock and securities).

3. The corporation for the five years preceding your loss must generally have derived more than half of its gross receipts from business operations and not from passive income such as rents, royalties, dividends, interest, annuities, or gains from the sales or exchanges of stock or securities. The five-year requirement is waived if the corporation's deductions (other than for dividends received or net operating losses) exceed gross income. If the corporation has not been in existence for the five years before your loss, then generally the period for which the corporation has been in existence is examined for the gross receipts test.

## 30.12 Series EE Bonds

Series EE savings bonds give you an opportunity to defer tax; see below. EE bonds may only be purchased online from Treasury Direct at www.treasurydirect.gov. They must be held 12 months from the issue date before they can be redeemed. Bonds cashed in any time before five years are subject to a three-month interest penalty; see the Example below.

Series EE savings bonds with an issue date on or after May 1, 2005, earn a fixed rate of interest. The Treasury announces the fixed rate that will apply to new bonds every May 1 and November 1. Interest accrues monthly and is compounded semiannually. EE bonds issued from May 1997 through April 2005 continue to earn market-based interest rates set at 90% of the average five-year Treasury securities yields for the preceding six months; these rates change every May 1 and November 1. EE bonds issued before May 1997 earn various rates depending on the date of issue.

**Filing Instruction**

**Interest Subject to AMT**

Interest on qualified private activity bonds issued after August 7, 1986, is tax free for regular tax purposes but may be a tax preference item for alternative minimum tax (AMT) purposes (23.2).

**Planning Reminder**

**Recordkeeping for Section 1244 Stock**

You must keep records that distinguish between Section 1244 stock and other stock interests. Your records must show that the corporation qualified as a small business corporation when the stock was issued, you are the original holder of the Section 1244 stock, and it was issued for money or property. Stock issued for services does not qualify. In addition, the records should also show the amount paid for the stock, information relating to any property transferred for the stock, any tax-free stock dividends issued on the stock, and the corporation's gross receipts data for the most recent five-year period.

You do not attach the records to the return, but should attach a computation of the loss to Form 4797. However, the failure to keep these records will be grounds for disallowing a loss that is claimed on Section 1244 stock.

**Caution**

**Timing Redemptions of Older EE Bonds**

In the year you cash in a Series EE savings bond you could lose interest by cashing it in too soon. Interest accrues only twice a year on EE bonds issued prior to May 1, 1997. The accrual months depend on the month of issue. If you cash pre–May 1997 bonds before the accrual month that applies to your bond, you will lose interest, as explained in 30.12.

**Deferring tax on savings bond interest.** Unless you report the interest annually, Series EE bond interest is deferred *(4.29)* until the year you redeem the bond or it reaches final maturity. When you redeem the bond, the accumulated interest is taxable on your federal return but not taxable on your state and local income tax return. If in the year of redemption you use the proceeds to pay for higher education or vocational school costs, the accumulated interest may be tax free for federal tax purposes *(33.4)*.

**Interest accrual dates for Series EE savings bonds.** For EE bonds issued after April 1997, interest accrues on the first day of every month. For EE bonds issued before May 1, 1997, interest generally accrues twice a year: on the first day of the issue month and first day of the sixth month after the issue month. For example, if you own an EE bond issued in August 1995, interest accrues every August 1 (month of issue) and every February 1 (six months after the August issue month). There is an exception for EE bonds issued from March 1993 through April 1995; these bonds accrue interest monthly (not just twice-a-year) to guarantee a 4% return.

When you cash a bond, you receive the value of the bond as of the last date that interest was added. If you cash a bond in between accrual months, you will not receive interest for the partial period. For example, if interest on a bond issued before May 1, 1997, accrues in February and August, and you cash a bond in during July, you would earn interest only through February. By waiting until August 1 to cash the bond, you would earn another six months of interest.

**Final maturity for savings bonds.** Do not neglect the final maturity date for older bonds. After the final maturity date, no further interest will accrue. No E bonds are still accruing interest. The last issued E bonds, those from June 1980, reached final maturity after 30 years in June 2010 and thus they, as well as all older E bonds, have ceased earning interest.

EE bonds issued in 1980 (the first year available) reached final maturity in 2010, 30 years after issue, after which no further interest has accrued. All EE bonds have 30-year maturities, so EE bonds issued in 1988 stopped earning interest in 2018 after they earned interest for 30 years, and EE bonds issued in 1989 will stop earning interest after the month in 2019 that is 30 years after issue.

**Series HH bonds.** HH bonds obtained before September 1, 2004, in exchange for savings bonds or savings notes pay taxable interest every six months at a fixed rate. Currently, all HH bonds are paying 1.5% per year. Interest is paid until final maturity is reached 20 years after issue.

*Caution*

**All E Bonds and Some EE Bonds Have Reached Final Maturity**

The last outstanding E bonds reached their 30-year final maturity by June 2010 and are no longer earning additional interest. If you are still holding any E bonds, you can redeem them for their value as of the final maturity date.

EE bonds that have reached final maturity after 30 years have also stopped earning interest *(30.12)*.

| Table 30-3 | Savings Bond Maturity Dates | |
|---|---|---|
| **Bond** | **Issue Date** | **Final Maturity** |
| Series E | May 1941–November 1965 | 40 years after issue |
| | December 1965–June 1980 | 30 years after issue |
| Series EE | January 1980 or later | 30 years after issue |
| Savings notes (Freedom Shares) | May 1967–October 1970 | 30 years after issue |
| H bonds | February 1957–December 1979 | 30 years after issue |
| HH bonds | January 1980–August 2004 | 20 years after issue |
| I bonds | September 1998 or later | 30 years after issue |

## 30.13  I Bonds

Treasury "I bonds" provide a return that rises and falls with inflation. I bonds may only be purchased online from TreasuryDirect at www.treasurydirect.gov. However, you can ask the IRS on Form 8888 to use your federal tax refund to buy I bonds, either by directly depositing the refund into your TreasuryDirect account if you have one, or to buy paper bonds if you do not have a TreasuryDirect account; *see* the Form 8888 instructions.

I bonds earn interest for 30 years. Interest is credited to a bond on the first day of every month and paid when the bond is redeemed.

I bonds are not redeemable within the first 12 months. You forfeit the last three months of interest if you redeem an I bond within the first five years, the same rule as for EE bonds *(30.12)*.

**Rates.** Interest on an I bond is determined by two rates. One rate, set by the Treasury Department, remains constant for the life of the bond. The second rate is a variable inflation rate announced each May and November by the Treasury Department to reflect changes reported by the Bureau of Labor Statistics in the Consumer Price Index. If deflation sets in, the variable rate will be negative for a six-month period and the negative rate will reduce the fixed rate, but not below zero, so, even if the negative variable rate exceeds the fixed rate, the redemption value of the bond is not reduced.

**Income tax reporting.** Investors may defer paying federal income taxes on I bond interest, which is automatically reinvested and added to the principal. Deferral applies to the fixed rate interest as well as the variable inflation rate interest. You may defer federal tax on the interest until you redeem the bond or the bond reaches maturity in 30 years *(4.29)*. You may report the interest each year as it accrues instead of deferring the interest. I bond interest is exempt from state and local income taxes.

If an I bond is redeemed to pay for college tuition or other college fees, all or part of the interest may be excludable from income under the rules discussed in *33.4*.

## 30.14  Trader, Dealer, or Investor?

The tax law recognizes three types of individuals who may sell and buy securities. They are:

**Investor.** You are an investor if you buy and sell securities for long-term capital gains and to earn dividends and interest.

**Trader.** You may be a trader if you buy and sell securities to profit from daily market movements in the prices of securities and not from dividends, interest, or capital appreciation. Your buy and sell orders must be frequent, continuous, and substantial. There are at present no clear-cut tests to determine the amount of sales volume that qualifies a person as a trader. The term "trader" is not defined in the Internal Revenue Code or Treasury regulations. The IRS has not issued rulings for determining trader status. The Tax Court has held that sporadic trading does not qualify; *see* the Examples below.

**Dealer.** You are a dealer if you hold an inventory of securities to sell to others. Dealers report their profits and losses as business income and losses under special tax rules not discussed in this book.

### EXAMPLES

1. After he retired, Holsinger began buying and selling stocks. In 2001, he made 289 trades over 63 days, and had losses of almost $179,000, which he reported as ordinary losses. In 2002, he made 372 trades over 110 days, and reported trading losses of just over $11,000 as an ordinary loss.

   The Tax Court held that Holsinger was an investor, not a trader. His trading losses were capital losses, and as such they could be deducted only to the extent of capital gains and then $3,000 of ordinary income. The Court held that the level of Holsinger's trading activities was not substantial enough to constitute a business. In addition, his trades were not aimed at catching the swings in daily market movements and profiting from these short-term changes, as evidenced by the fact that a significant amount of his positions were held more than 31 days. Since Holsinger failed to establish that he was in business as a trader, he could not make a mark-to-market election.

2. While holding a full-time job as a computer chip engineer in 1999, Chen made 323 transactions, 94 percent of which occurred in February, March, and April; he did no trading in June or August through December. Most of the securities were held for less than a month. He had losses of nearly $85,000, which he reported as ordinary losses.

The Tax Court held that Chen was not a trader in securities and was limited to deducting $3,000 of his net 1999 loss against ordinary income. To be considered a trader, the purchases and sales of securities must amount to a trade or business. There is no exact number of trades or other clear standard used to make this determination. Rather, it is based on the taxpayer's intent, the nature of the income derived from trading, and the frequency, extent, and regularity of the transactions. During three months of the year, Chen bought and sold with frequency, but he failed to achieve trader status because, overall, his activities were not frequent, regular, and continuous. In prior cases, trader status has been found where such activities usually were frequent, regular, and continuous for a period of more than a single year. Because Chen could not claim trader status, he was ineligible to make a mark-to-market election.

**Tax treatment of traders.** The tax rules applied to traders are a hybrid of tax rules applied to investors and business persons, as discussed in the following paragraphs.

**Reporting trader gains and losses.** Unless a trader previously made a mark-to-market election, gains and losses are reported as capital gains and losses on Form 8949 and Schedule D. As almost all or substantially all of a trader's sales are short-term, such gains are reported as short-term gains and losses as short-term losses. A net profit from Schedule D is not subject to self-employment tax *(45.1)*. Substantial losses subject to capital loss treatment are a tax disadvantage because capital losses in excess of capital gains are deductible only up to $3,000 of ordinary income in one tax year. True, carryover capital losses may offset capital gains in the next year, but your inability to deduct them immediately may subject you to paying a tax liability that might have been reduced or eliminated if the losses had been deductible for the year of the sale. If you are concerned about incurring substantial short-term capital losses that would be limited by capital loss treatment, you may consider a mark-to-market election *(30.15)*, which would allow you to treat your security gains and losses as ordinary income and loss.

**Deducting trader expenses.** Although a trader does not sell to customers but for his or her own account, a trader is considered to be in business. Expenses such as subscriptions and margin interest may be deducted as ordinary business losses on Schedule C of Form 1040. Home office expenses are deductible if the office is regularly and exclusively used as the principal place of conducting the trading business *(40.12)*.

An investor, on the other hand, may deduct margin interest only as an itemized deduction to the extent of net investment income *(15.10)*. Other investment expenses are not deductible in 2018 through 2025 due to the suspension of miscellaneous itemized costs in excess of the 2% of adjusted gross income floor *(19.1)*. An investor may not deduct home office expenses since investment activities, no matter how extensive, are not considered a business; *see* the Moller decision discussed in *40.16*.

## 30.15 Mark-to-Market Election for Traders

A trader in securities may elect to have his gains and losses treated as ordinary gains and losses by making a mark-to-market election. As explained below, it is too late to make an election for 2018. In the absence of an election, gains and losses of a trader are treated as capital gains and losses on Form 8949 and Schedule D.

If the mark-to-market election is made, you report trading gains and losses on closed transactions plus unrealized gains and losses on securities held in your trading business at the end of your taxable year as ordinary gains and losses on Form 4797. Trader profits are not subject to self-employment tax *(45.1)*, whether or not the mark-to-market election is made. The unrealized gain or loss on a security that is reported on Form 4797 increases or reduces the basis of the security. For example, if you report an unrealized gain of $50 on stock with a cost of $100, you increase the basis of the stock to $150. If you later sell the stock for $90, you report a loss of $60 in the year of the sale. The requirement to report unrealized gains and losses at the end of the year and to adjust basis of shares is an automatic change in accounting method that requires you to file Form 3115 with the IRS National Office. On Form 3115, use code #64 (the designated automatic accounting method change number), and report required adjustments; *see* IRS Publication 550 for details. The failure to file Form 3115 does not invalidate a timely and valid election.

Once the mark-to-market election is made, it applies to all future years unless the IRS agrees in writing to a revocation.

Making the election is not proof that you are actually a trader in securities. If you are audited by the IRS, you must be able to prove that your activities are such that you are in the business of making money by buying and selling over short periods of time. As mentioned in *30.14*, there are no hard and fast rules that specify how many daily or short-term trades qualify you as a trader.

The mark-to-market election does not apply to the securities you hold for investment. Sales of your investment securities are reported on Form 8949 and Schedule D, not Form 4797.

**When to make the mark-to-market election.** The IRS requires you to make the election by the due date (without extensions) of the tax return for the year prior to the year for which the election is to be effective. Under this due date rule, it is too late to make an election for 2018, as this had to be done by April 17, 2018, the due date for your 2017 return. The election for 2019 must be filed by April 15, 2019.

A regulation gives the IRS authority to grant an extension of time to file the mark-to-market election if the taxpayer has acted reasonably and in good faith and allowing relief does not prejudice the interests of the government. However, the IRS has refused to allow such extensions, claiming that a late election invariably results in prejudice to the interests of the government.

The Tax Court has supported the IRS in cases where the taxpayers, in filing their elections several years late, were relying on hindsight to try to gain a tax advantage from ordinary loss treatment.

The Ninth Circuit Court of Appeals has also refused to allow a late election where the taxpayer was relying on hindsight to try to gain a tax advantage. On his 1999 return, Acar reported over $950,000 in losses from trading securities, treating them as capital losses. In early 2002, he filed an amended return and tried to make a retroactive mark-to-market election beginning with 1999 so he could treat his 1999 losses as ordinary losses and claim a refund. The IRS disallowed the late election and a federal district court and the Ninth Circuit affirmed. Allowing the late election would give Acar an advantage that was not available on April 15, 1999, the due date for making the election for 1999 under Revenue Procedure 99-17. When the late election was made, Acar knew that he had incurred losses and, with that hindsight, was trying to convert what had been capital losses on his original return into ordinary losses. It does not matter that any advantage from a late election for 1999 could be outweighed if Acar in later years realized trading gains that under the irrevocable election would have to be treated as ordinary rather than capital gains. That a taxpayer might come to regret an election in later years does not mean that hindsight was not used to gain an advantage at the time of the retroactive election.

In another case, the Tax Court was more sympathetic, allowing an extension to a taxpayer who filed his election for 2000 on July 21, 2000, three months after the IRS deadline of April 17, 2000. He had left his law practice and became a trader in January 2000. The accountant who prepared his 1999 return did not know about the mark-to-mark election but a friend told him about it in June 2000 and in July the taxpayer hired a law firm, which filed the election for him and asked the IRS to allow the extension. The taxpayer did not conduct any trading activities between the date he should have filed the election and the date he actually filed it. Over IRS objection, the Tax Court allowed the late election on the grounds that the taxpayer had acted reasonably and in good faith by promptly employing the law firm after learning about the availability of the election. Since the taxpayer did not realize any further gains or losses between the date he should have filed the election and when he actually did so, the Court held that the interests of the government were not prejudiced.

 *Planning Reminder*

**Wash Sale Rule Does Not Apply**

If you make a mark-to-market election, the wash sale rule does not apply; all losses are reported as ordinary losses under the mark-to-market rules

**How to make the mark-to-market election.** The election for 2019 is made by attaching a statement to your 2018 return by April 15, 2019, and by filing Form 3115 for an accounting method change with the return; enter code #64 (the designated automatic accounting method change number) on the Form 3115 (Section *23.01* of Revenue Procedure 2017-30). The statement with your return must specify that effective for the taxable year starting January 1, 2019, you are electing to report gains and losses from your trading business under the mark-to-market rules of Section 475(f). However, if you are not required to file a 2018 return, make the election for 2019 by placing a statement of election in your books and records no later than March 15, 2019. A copy of the statement must be attached to your original 2019 return.

One of the conditions of the election is that you must clearly distinguish between securities held for investment and trading purposes. The election applies only to the securities held in your trading business, not to the securities held for investment. Holding investment securities in a separate account is advisable.

*See* IRS Revenue Procedure 99-17 and the instructions to Form 3115 for further details on making the mark-to-market election. In light of the accounting requirements and the overall effect of reporting unrealized gains and losses, before making the election you should consult a professional experienced in the use of mark-to-market accounting.

**Revoking the election.** An election can only be revoked as an automatic change in accounting method (code #218 is the designated automatic accounting method change number). Details about the revocation procedure are in Revenue Procedure 2017-30 (Section *23.02*).

# CHAPTER 31

# Tax Savings for Investors in Real Estate

Real estate investors may take advantage of the following tax benefits:

- Gains on the sale of investment property may be taxed at capital gain rates.
- Depreciation can provide a source of temporary tax-free income *(31.1)*.
- Rental income can be used to offset passive losses Chapter 10.
- Tax-free exchanges make it possible to defer tax on exchanges of real estate held for investment *(31.3)*.

However, real estate gains may be subject to the 3.8% net investment income tax *(28.3)*.

Losses on real estate transactions may be subject to the following disadvantages:

- Rental losses may not be deductible from other income such as salary, interest, and dividends unless you qualify as a real estate professional or for the special $25,000 rental loss allowance under the passive loss rules Chapter 10.
- Compromises of mortgage liability may subject you to tax *(31.10)*.
- A foreclosure or repossession is treated as a sale on which you realize gain or loss. In addition, if you are personally liable on the loan and the amount of debt canceled in the foreclosure exceeds the fair market value of the transferred property, you will owe tax on cancellation of debt income unless an exception is available *(31.9)*.
- Certain dividends from REITs are eligible for the qualified business income (QBI) deduction *(31.16)*.

## 31.1 Real Estate Ventures

A real estate investment should provide a current income return and an appreciation in the value of the original investment. As an additional incentive, a real estate investment may in the early years of the investment return income subject to little or no tax. That may happen when depreciation and other expense deductions reduce taxable income without reducing the amount of cash available for distribution. This tax savings is temporary and limited by the terms and the amount of the mortgage debt on the property. Payments allocated to amortization of mortgage principal reduce the amount of cash available to investors without an offsetting tax deduction. Thus, the amount of tax-free return depends on the extent to which depreciation deductions exceed the amortization payments.

To provide a higher return of tax-free income, at least during the early years of its operations, a venture must obtain a constant payment mortgage that provides for the payment of fixed annual amounts that are allocated to continually decreasing amounts of interest and increasing amounts of amortization payments. Consequently, in the early years, a tax-free return of income is high while the amortization payments are low, but as the amortization payments increase, nontaxable income decreases. When this tax-free return has been substantially reduced, a partnership must refinance the mortgage to reduce the amortization payments and once again increase the tax-free return; *see* Examples 1 and 2 below.

In the case of a building, the tax-free return is based on the assumption that the building does not actually depreciate at as fast a rate as the tax depreciation rate being claimed by the investors. If the building is depreciating physically at a faster rate, the so-called tax-free return on investment is illusory. There is no tax-free return because the distributions to investors (over and above current income return) are, in fact, a return of the investor's own capital.

*Caution*

**NII Tax on Rental Income**

Rental income and expenses are taken into account in figuring the 3.8% net investment income tax for high-income taxpayers *(28.3)*.

---

### EXAMPLES

1. A limited partnership of 100 investors owns a building that returns an annual income of $100,000 after a deduction of operating expenses, but before a depreciation deduction of $80,000. Thus, taxable income is $20,000 ($100,000 − $80,000). Assuming that there is no mortgage on the building, all of the $100,000 is available for distribution. (Since the depreciation requires no cash outlay, it does not reduce the cash available for distribution.) Each investor receives $1,000. Taxable income being $20,000, only 20% ($20,000 ÷ $100,000) of the distribution is taxable. Thus, each investor reports as income only $200 of his or her $1,000 distribution; $800 is tax free.

2. Same facts as in Example 1, except that the building is mortgaged, and an annual amortization payment of $40,000 is being made. Consequently, only $60,000 is available for distribution, of which $20,000 is taxable. Each investor receives $600, of which 1/3 ($20,000 ÷ $60,000), or $200, is taxed, and $400 is tax free. In other words, the $60,000 distribution is tax free to the extent that the depreciation deduction of $80,000 exceeds the amortization of $40,000—namely $40,000. If the amortization payment were increased to $50,000, only $30,000 of the distribution would be tax free ($80,000 − $50,000).

---

**Real estate investment trusts (REITs).** The tax treatment of real estate investment trusts resembles that of open-end mutual funds. Distributions generally are reported to the investors on Form 1099-DIV as dividend income. However, distributions generally do not qualify for the reduced tax rate on qualified dividends *(4.1)* but may be eligible for the qualified business income (QBI) deduction *(31.16)*. A distribution qualifies for the reduced rate (but not the QBI deduction) only to the extent it represents previously taxed undistributed income or qualifying dividends received by the REIT (from stock investments) that are passed through to the investors. Capital gain distributions reported on Form 1099-DIV must be reported as long-term capital gains regardless of how long the REIT shares have been held *(4.4)*. If the trust operates at a loss, the loss may not be passed on to the investors.

**REMICs.** A real estate mortgage investment company (REMIC) holds a fixed pool of mortgages. Investors are treated as holding a regular or residual interest. A REMIC is not a taxable entity for federal income tax purposes. It is generally treated as a partnership, with the residual interest holders as partners.

Investors with regular REMIC interests are treated as holding debt obligations. Interest income is reported to them by the REMIC on Form 1099-INT and original issue discount (OID) on Form 1099-OID.

The net income of the REMIC, after payments to regular interest holders, is passed through to the holders of residual interests. A residual interest holder's share of the REMIC's taxable income or loss is reported by the REMIC to the interest holder each quarter on Schedule Q of Form 1066, and the investor reports his or her total share of the year in Part IV of Schedule E.

## 31.2  Sales of Subdivided Land—Dealer or Investor?

An investor faces a degree of uncertainty in determining the tax treatment of sales of subdivided realty. In some situations, investor status may be preferred, and in others, dealer status.

**Capital gain on sale.**  Investor status allows capital gain treatment. Capital losses may offset the gains. For capital gain, an investor generally has to show that his or her activities were not those of a dealer but were steps taken in a liquidation of the investment. To convince an IRS agent or a court of investment activity, this type of evidence may present a favorable argument for capital gain treatment:

- The property was bought as an investment, to build a residence, or received as a gift or inheritance.
- No substantial improvements were added to the tract.
- The property was subdivided to liquidate the investment.
- Sales came through unsolicited offers. There was no advertising or agents.
- Sales were infrequent.
- There were no previous activities as a real estate dealer.
- The seller was in a business unrelated to real estate.
- The property was held for a long period of time.
- Sales proceeds were invested in other investment property.

 *Planning Reminder*

**Installment Sales**

The distinction between an investor and dealer is significant if land is sold on the installment basis. Investor status is preferable if you want to elect the installment method. Dealers may not elect installment sale treatment *(5.21)*.

> ### EXAMPLE
>
> Morley was interested in buying farm acreage to resell at a profit. Two and a half million dollars was set as the purchase price. To swing the deal, Morley borrowed $600,000. A short time later, his attempts to resell the property failed, and he allowed the property to be foreclosed. While he held the property he incurred interest costs of over $400,000, which he deducted. The IRS held the interest was not fully deductible. It claimed the interest was investment interest subject to investment interest restrictions. That is, the debt was incurred to purchase and carry investment property. The IRS position was based on the so-called "one-bite" rule, which holds that a taxpayer who engages in only one venture may not under any circumstances be held to be in a business as to that venture. Morley argued that he bought the property not as an investment property but as business property for immediate resale.
>
> The Tax Court sided with Morley, holding that he held the acreage as ordinary business property. The court rejected the "one-bite" rule. The fact that he had not previously sold business property did not mean that he could not prove that he held acreage for resale. Here, he intended promptly to resell it, and the facts supported his intention.

**Section 1237 capital gain opportunity.**  Section 1237 is a limited tax provision that provides a capital gain opportunity for subdivided lots only if arbitrary holding period rules and restrictions on substantial improvements are complied with. For example, the lots must generally be held at least five years before sale unless they were inherited. If the lots were previously held for sale to customers, or if other lots are so held in the year of sale, Section 1237 does not apply. Furthermore, substantial improvements must not have been made to the lots. According to the IRS, a disqualifying substantial improvement is one that increases the value of the property by more than 10%. The IRS considers buildings, hard surface roads, or utilities, such as sewers, water, gas, or electric lines, as substantial improvements.

**Interest expense deductions.** The distinction between an investor in land and a dealer is also important in the case of interest expenses. Dealer status is usually preferable here. Interest expenses incurred by an investor are subject to investment interest deduction limitations; *see Chapter 15.* On the other hand, interest expenses of a dealer in the course of business activities are fully deductible (subject to the limitation for large dealers (*see 40.6*); *see* the Morley Example below.

**Passive activity.** Income from sales of lots is not considered passive activity income. Thus, losses from sales of land may offset salary and other investment income. If you hold rental property and also sell land, make sure that your accounts distinguish between and separate each type of income. This way income and losses from land sales will not be commingled with rent income subject to the passive activity restrictions discussed in *Chapter 10.* Your activity in real property development counts towards qualifying you as a real estate professional who may deduct rental losses from nonpassive income if material participation tests are met *(10.3).*

## 31.3 Exchanging Real Estate Without Tax

You may exchange real estate held for investment for other investment real estate and incur no immediate tax consequences. On a fully tax-free exchange of "like-kind" property, you do not recognize any gain realized on the exchange and you cannot deduct any loss. If you had a gain, the potential tax on the gain is postponed until you sell the new property for more than your basis. A tax-free exchange may also defer a potential tax due on gain from depreciation recapture and might be considered where the depreciable basis of a building has been substantially written off. Here, the building may be exchanged for other property that will give larger tax deductions.

**Fully tax-free exchanges.** To transact a fully tax-free exchange, you must satisfy these conditions:

- The property traded must be solely for property of a "like kind." The words like kind are liberally interpreted. They refer to the nature or character of the property, not its grade, quality, or use. Some examples of like-kind exchanges are: farm or ranch for city property; unimproved land for improved real estate; rental house for a store building; and fee in business property for 30-year or more leasehold in the same type of property *(6.1).* However, you may not make a tax-free exchange of U.S. real estate for real estate in foreign countries; your gain or loss on the exchange must be recognized.
- The property exchanged must have been held for productive use in your business or for investment and traded for property to be held for productive use in business or investment. Therefore, trades of property used, or to be used, for personal purposes, such as exchanging a residence for rental property, cannot receive tax-free treatment. However, if you rent out your vacation home and meet the conditions of an IRS safe harbor *(6.1),* the residence is treated as investment property rather than personal-use property, so it can be part of a like-kind exchange for other investment property.
- If you trade your principal residence for another principal residence, gain may be tax free under the home sale exclusion rules *(29.2).*
- The trade must generally occur within a 180-day period, and property identification must occur within 45 days of the first transfer *(6.4).*

A real estate dealer cannot transact a tax-free exchange of property held for sale to customers. Also, an exchange is not tax free if the property received is held for immediate resale.

Tax-free exchanges between related parties are subject to tax if either party disposes of the exchanged property within a two-year period *(6.6).*

**Disadvantage of tax-free exchange.** Although the postponement of tax on gain from a tax-free exchange is equivalent to an interest-free loan from the government equal to the amount you would have owed in taxes had you sold the property, this tax advantage is offset by a disadvantage in the case of an exchange of depreciable real estate. You must carry over the basis of the old property to the new property; *see* the following Example.

*Planning Reminder*

**Exchanging a Building for Land**

A tax-free exchange may be advantageous in the case of land. Land is not depreciable, but it may be exchanged for a depreciable rental building. The exchange is tax free and depreciation may be claimed on the building. However, be aware of a possible tax trap if you exchange rental property for land and the building was subject to depreciation recapture: The recapture provisions override the tax-free exchange rules. The "recapture element" will be taxable as ordinary income.

*Planning Reminder*

**Loss Deduction**

A tax-free exchange is not desirable if the transaction will result in a loss, since you may not deduct a loss in a tax-free exchange. To ensure the loss deduction, first sell the property and then buy new property with the proceeds.

*EXAMPLE*

You have property with a basis of $25,000, now valued at $50,000, that you exchange for another property worth $50,000. Your basis for depreciation for the new property is $25,000.

If—instead of making an exchange—you sell the old property and use the proceeds to buy similarly valued property, the tax basis for depreciation would be $50,000, giving you larger depreciation deductions than you would get in the exchange transaction. If increased depreciation deductions are desirable, then it may pay to sell the property and purchase new property. Tax may be spread by transacting an installment sale. Project the tax consequences of a sale and an exchange and choose the one giving the greater overall tax benefits. You may find it preferable to sell the property and purchase new property on which MACRS depreciation may be claimed.

**Partially tax-free exchanges.** To be completely tax free, the exchange must be solely an exchange of like-kind properties. If you receive "boot," such as cash or property that is not of like kind, gain is taxed up to the amount of the boot.

If you trade mortgaged property, the mortgage released is treated as boot *(6.3)*. When there are mortgages on both properties, the mortgages are netted. The party giving up the larger mortgage and getting the smaller mortgage treats the excess as boot. Taxable boot cannot exceed the amount of your gain. *See* the Example below and also the Example in *6.3*, which illustrates how to report an exchange on Form 8824.

*EXAMPLE*

You own a small office building with a fair market value of $170,000, and an adjusted basis of $150,000. There is a $130,000 mortgage on the building. You exchange it for Low's building valued at $155,000, having a $120,000 mortgage, and you also get $5,000 in cash. You compute your gain in this way:

| What you received | | |
|---|---|---|
| Fair market value of Low's property | | $155,000 |
| Cash | | 5,000 |
| Mortgage assumed by Low on building you traded | | 130,000 |
| Total received | | $290,000 |
| Less: | | |
| Adjusted basis of building you traded | $150,000 | |
| Mortgage assumed by you | 120,000 | 270,000 |
| Actual gain on the exchange | | $20,000 |

However, your actual gain of $20,000 is taxed only up to the amount of boot, $15,000.

| Figuring boot | | |
|---|---|---|
| Cash received | | $5,000 |
| Mortgage assumed by Low on building you traded | $130,000 | |
| Less: | | |
| Mortgage you assumed on Low's property | 120,000 | 10,000 |
| Gain taxed to the extent of boot | | $15,000 |

## 31.4 Timing Your Real Property Sales

Generally, a taxable transaction occurs in the year in which title or possession to property passes to the buyer. By controlling the year title and possession pass, you may select the year in which to report profit or loss. For example, you intend to sell property this year, but you estimate that reporting the sale next year will incur less in taxes. You can postpone the transfer of title and possession to next year. Alternatively, you can transact an installment sale, giving title and possession this year but delaying the receipt of all or most of the sale proceeds until next year *(5.21)*.

## 31.5 Cancellation of a Lease

Payments received by the tenant on the cancellation of a business lease held long term are treated as proceeds received in a Section 1231 transaction *(44.8)*. Payments received by the tenant on cancellation of a lease on a personal residence or apartment are treated as proceeds of a capital asset transaction. Gain is long-term capital gain if the lease was held long term; losses are not deductible.

Payments received by a landlord from a tenant for canceling a lease or modifying lease terms are reported as rental income when received *(9.1)*.

Cancellation of a distributor's agreement is treated as a sale if you made a substantial capital investment in the distributorship. For example, you own facilities for storage, transporting, processing, or dealing with the physical product covered by the franchise. If you have an office mainly for clerical work, or where you handle just a small part of the goods covered by the franchise, the cancellation is not treated as a sale. Your gain or loss is ordinary income or loss. If the cancellation is treated as a sale, the sale is subject to Section 1231 treatment *(44.8)*.

## 31.6 Sale of an Option

The tax treatment of the sale of an option to buy property depends on the tax classification of the property to which the option relates.

If the option is for the purchase of property that would be a capital asset in your hands, profit on the sale of the option is treated as capital gain. A loss is treated as a capital loss if the property subject to the option was investment property; if the property was personal property, the loss is not deductible. Whether the gain or loss is long term or short term depends on your holding period.

> **EXAMPLES**
>
> 1. You pay $500 for an option to purchase a house. After holding the option for five months, you sell the option for $750. Your profit of $250 is short-term capital gain.
> 2. The same facts as in Example 1 above, except that you sell the option for $300. The loss is not deductible because the option is related to a sale of a personal residence.

If the option is for a "Section 1231 asset" *(44.8)*, gain or loss on the sale of the option is combined with other Section 1231 asset transactions to determine if there is capital gain or ordinary loss.

If the option relates to an ordinary income asset in your hands, then gain or loss would be ordinary income or loss.

If you fail to exercise an option and allow it to lapse, the option is considered to have been sold on the expiration date. Gain or loss is computed according to the rules just discussed.

The party granting the option realizes ordinary income on its expiration, regardless of the nature of the underlying property. If the option is exercised, the option payment is added to the selling price of the property when figuring gain or loss.

## 31.7 Granting of an Easement

Granting an easement presents a practical problem of determining whether all or part of the basis of the property is allocable to the easement proceeds. This requires an opinion as to whether the easement affects the entire property or just a part of the property. There is no hard and fast rule to determine whether an easement affects all or part of the property. The issue is factual. For example, an easement for electric lines will generally affect only the area over which the lines are suspended and for which the right of way is granted. In such a case, an allocation may be required; *see* Example 1 below. If the entire property is affected, no allocation is required and the proceeds reduce the basis of the property. If only part of the property is affected, then the proceeds are applied to the cost allocated to the area affected by the easement. If the proceeds exceed the amount allocated to basis, a gain is realized. Capital gain treatment generally applies to grants of easements. The granting of a perpetual easement that requires you to give up all or substantially all of a beneficial use of the area affected by the easement is treated as a sale. The contribution to a government body of a scenic easement in perpetuity is a charitable contribution *(14.10)*, not a sale.

**Condemnation.** If you realize a gain on a grant of an easement under a condemnation or threat of condemnation, you may defer tax by investing in replacement property *(18.19)*.

**Basis Allocation**

In reviewing an easement, the IRS will generally try to find grounds for allocating part of a property owner's basis to easement proceeds, especially where the allocation will result in a taxable gain. In opposition, a property owner will generally argue that the easement affects the entire property or that it is impossible to make an allocation because of the nature of the easement or the particular nature of the property. If he or she can sustain that argument, the proceeds for granting the easement reduce the basis of the entire property; *see* the Examples in *31.7*.

> **EXAMPLES**
>
> 1. The owner of a 600-acre farm was paid $5,000 by a power company for the right to put up poles and power lines. The right of way covered 20 acres along one boundary that the owner continued to farm. The cost basis of the farm was $60,000, or $100 an acre. The IRS ruled that he had to allocate the basis. At $100 an acre, the allocated basis for the 20 acres was $2,000. Thus, a gain of $3,000 was realized ($5,000 − $2,000).
>
> 2. The owner of a tract of unimproved land gave a state highway department a perpetual easement affecting only part of the land. He wanted to treat the payment as a reduction of the basis of the entire tract and so report no gain. The IRS ruled that he had to allocate basis to the portion affected by the road.
>
> 3. The owner of farmland gave a transmission company a 50-foot right of way for an underground pipeline that did not interfere with farming. During construction, the right of way was 150 feet. The owner received payments for damages covering loss of rental income during construction and for the 50-foot permanent right of way. The IRS ruled that the damage payment was taxable as ordinary income; the payment for the right of way was a taxable gain to the extent that it exceeded the basis allocated to the acreage within the 50-foot strip.

**Release of a restrictive covenant.** A payment received for a release of a restrictive covenant is treated as a capital gain if the release involves property held for investment.

> **EXAMPLE**
>
> You sell several acres of land held for investment to a construction company subject to a covenant that restricts construction to residential dwellings. Later, the company wants to erect structures other than individual homes and pays you for the release of the restrictive covenant in the deed. You realize capital gain on receipt of the payment. The restrictive covenant is a property interest and a capital asset in your hands.

## 31.8   Special Tax Credits for Real Estate Investments

To encourage certain real estate investments, the tax law offers the following tax credits:

**Low-income housing credit.** Qualifying investors are allowed to claim a tax credit in annual installments over 10 years for qualifying newly constructed low-income housing and certain existing structures that are substantially rehabilitated. The amount of the credit depends on whether the building is new and whether federal subsidies are received. If you are the building owner, you must receive a certification from an authorized housing credit agency on Form 8609. Individual investors who get their share of the credit from a pass-through entity (from a partnership, S corporation, estate, or trust) may claim their credit directly on Form 3800 (General Business Credit) and do not have to complete Form 8586, which otherwise must be used; *see* the Form 8586 instructions.

Building owners are subject to a 15-year compliance period during which recapture of the credit may be required (on Form 8611) if the building is disposed of or the qualified basis of the building is reduced. Owners must file Form 8609-A for each year of the compliance period.

**Rehabilitation credit for certified historic structures.** On Form 3468, you may claim a 20% credit for rehabilitating certified historic structures. To claim the credit, you must generally incur rehabilitation expenses that exceed the greater of $5,000 or your adjusted basis in the building. For purposes of figuring depreciation deductions, you must reduce basis by the full amount of the rehabilitation credit.

The credit is subject to recapture if you dispose of the property within five years after it was placed in service or you change use of the property within the five-year period so it no longer qualifies for the credit; *see* Form 4255 for recapture details.

**Certified historic structure.** A certified historic structure may be used for residential or nonresidential purposes. The National Park Service must certify that a planned rehabilitation is in keeping with the building's historic status designation for the credit to be available.

In one case, a developer who rehabilitated a certified historic structure and donated a conservation easement to a historic society in the same year was required to base the credit computation on the rehabilitation expenses minus the charitable deduction claimed. If the donation had been made in a later year, a portion of the original credit claimed would be subject to recapture.

**Tax credit limitations.** Tax credits for low-income housing and rehabilitating historic or pre-1936 buildings may be limited by passive activity restrictions on Form 8582-CR *(Chapter 10)* and by tax liability limits for the general business credit on Form 3800 *(Chapter 40)*.

## 31.9 Foreclosures, Repossessions, Short Sales, and Voluntary Conveyances to Creditors

If you are unable to meet payments on a debt secured by property, the creditor may foreclose on the loan or repossess the property. A foreclosure sale or repossession, including a voluntary return by you of the property to the creditor, is treated as a sale of the property on which you must figure gain or loss. Similarly, if the lender agrees to a "short sale" for less than the outstanding mortgage balance in which it accepts the sales proceeds in satisfaction of the mortgage, you must figure gain or loss. A loss on a principal residence or other personal real estate is not deductible. If you were personally liable on the debt, then in addition to realizing gain or loss on the transfer, you also have debt forgiveness income from the cancellation of the debt to the extent the canceled debt exceeds the value of the property, unless an exception *(11.8)* applies. For example, if you were insolvent at the time of the debt discharge, the debt forgiveness is not taxable. In the case of a principal residence, a special exclusion for up to $2 million of forgiven debt *(11.8)* was allowed through 2017; *see* the *e-Supplement* at *jklasser.com* for an update on a possible extension of the exclusion to 2018.

**Figuring gain or loss and income from cancellation of debt on a foreclosure, short sale, or repossession.** You have gain or loss equal to the difference between your adjusted basis *(5.20)* in the property and the amount realized on the foreclosure, short sale, or repossession. The amount realized depends on whether or not you are personally liable for the debt that secures the property, as discussed below. Note that if the property was your home or other personal-use property and a loss is realized on the foreclosure or repossession, the loss is nondeductible. If the property was your principal residence and you realize a gain on a foreclosure, short sale, or repossession, you may be able to exclude from income up to $250,000 of the gain, or $500,000 on a joint return, under the home sale exclusion rules *(29.1)*.

In addition to realizing gain or loss on the transfer of the property to the lender, you may also have to report income from the cancellation of the debt if you are personally liable for the debt *(11.8)*.

*Filing Instruction*

**Donating Easement After Claiming Rehabilitation Credit**

The charitable deduction for a historic building easement *(14.10)* must be reduced if a rehabilitation credit was claimed for the building in the five years preceding the donation.

*Caution*

**Form 1099-A Notifies IRS**

If your mortgaged property is foreclosed or repossessed, and the bank or other lender reacquires it, or if the lender knows that you have abandoned the property, you should receive from the lender Form 1099-A, which indicates the fair market value of the property (generally the foreclosure bid price), the amount of your unpaid debt, and whether you were personally liable. The IRS may compare its copy of Form 1099-A with your return to check whether you have reported income from the foreclosure or abandonment.

If the lender also cancels your debt of $600 or more, you may instead receive Form 1099-C, on which the information about the foreclosure or repossession will be included.

**Amount realized if you are not personally liable (nonrecourse debt).** If you are not personally liable on the debt secured by the property, the amount realized on the foreclosure, short sale, or repossession includes, in addition to any sale proceeds you receive, the full amount of the debt that is canceled as part of the transfer to the lender, even if the fair market value of the property is less than the canceled debt.

You do not realize income from the cancellation of nonrecourse debt upon a foreclosure, short sale, or repossession. However, if in lieu of foreclosure (or repossession) the lender offers a discount for early repayment or agrees to a loan modification ("workout") in which the principal balance of the nonrecourse loan is reduced, and you retain the collateral, the debt reduction results in income from the cancellation of debt even where you are not personally liable on the loan *(31.10)*.

**Amount realized if you are personally liable (recourse debt).** If you are personally liable on the debt secured by the property, the amount realized includes the smaller of the canceled debt or the fair market value of the property transferred to the lender. This is in addition to any sale proceeds received.

Where the canceled debt exceeds the fair market value of the transferred property, the excess must be reported as ordinary income from the cancellation of debt, unless the law allows it to be excluded. Exclusions that may be available are the exclusions for insolvency, bankruptcy, or qualified farm debt, discussed in *11.8*, or the exclusion for qualified business real estate debt discussed in *31.10*. See the *e-Supplement at jklasser. com* for an update on whether the exclusion for qualified principal residence indebtedness, which expired at the end of 2017 *(11.8)*, is extended to 2018.

> ### *EXAMPLE*
>
> Jones could not meet the mortgage payments on a vacation home that cost him $185,000. He had paid cash of $20,000 and taken a mortgage loan of $165,000 on which he was personally liable. In 2018, when the remaining balance of the loan was $162,000, he defaulted, and the bank accepted his voluntary conveyance of the unit, canceling the loan. Similar units at the time were selling for $150,000. Because Jones was personally liable for the debt, he is deemed to have an amount realized of $150,000, the fair market value of the property, as this is less than the $162,000 canceled loan. Jones incurred a loss of $35,000: the difference between his adjusted basis of $185,000 and the $150,000 fair market value of the unit. The loss is not deductible because the unit was held for personal purposes. Jones also recognizes income on the cancellation of the loan because the amount of the debt ($162,000) exceeded the fair market value of the unit ($150,000) by $12,000. This amount is taxable, unless Jones can show he was insolvent at the time of the transfer to the bank; *see 11.8.*

## 31.10 Restructuring Mortgage Debt

Rather than foreclose on a mortgage, a lender (mortgagee) may be willing to restructure the mortgage debt by canceling either all or part of the debt. As a borrower (mortgagor), do not overlook the tax consequences of the new debt arrangement. If the lender agrees to a "workout," under which part of your loan principal is reduced as part of a loan modification, or if you pay off the loan early in return for a "discount" that reduces the debt, and you keep the collateral, the reduction or discount is canceled debt, reportable as ordinary income (cancellation of debt income) unless an exception applies. This is true whether or not you are personally liable for the debt. However, if you were not personally liable (nonrecourse debt) and do not keep the collateral, there is no cancellation of debt income.

You may be able to avoid the ordinary income from the cancellation of the debt by taking advantage of one of the exclusions in the law, such as the exclusions for insolvency, bankruptcy, qualified business real estate debt (see below), or qualified farm debt. Details of these exclusions are discussed in *11.8*. The Jones example in *11.8* illustrates the IRS approach to figuring insolvency upon a reduction of a nonrecourse debt.

In the case of partnership property, tax consequences of the restructuring of a third-party loan are determined at the partner level. This means that if you are a partner and are solvent *(11.8)*, you may not avoid tax on the transaction, even if the partnership is insolvent.

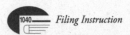 *Filing Instruction*

### Reporting a Foreclosure or Voluntary Conveyance

You generally report a foreclosure sale or voluntary conveyance in 2018 to a creditor on Form 8949 and Schedule D if the property was held for personal or investment purposes. However, if the property was your principal residence and you have a gain, the foreclosure or voluntary conveyance does not have to be reported at all if you can exclude all of it under the home sale exclusion rules *(29.1)*.

Foreclosures and reconveyances of business assets are reported on Form 4797.

If income from cancellation of indebtedness is realized and it is not excludable under the rules discussed at *11.8*, you report the taxable amount on Schedule 1 of Form 1040.

 *Caution*

### Form 1099-C

If your lender agrees to a "workout" that reduces the principal balance of your loan, the canceled debt will be reported on Form 1099-C in Box 2. This amount must be included in your income unless one of the exclusion rules *(11.8)* applies.

**Restructuring debt on business real estate.** A solvent taxpayer may avoid tax on a restructuring of qualifying business real estate debt *(11.8)* by electing to reduce the basis of depreciable real property by the amount of the tax-free debt discharge. The election to reduce basis is made on Form 982.

---

### EXAMPLE

Grant, who is solvent, owns a building worth $150,000 used in his business. It is subject to a first mortgage of $110,000 and a second mortgage of $90,000. Grant's basis in the building is $120,000. On July 13, 2018, the second mortgagee agrees to reduce the second mortgage to $30,000. This results in debt discharge of $60,000 ($90,000 – $30,000). The $60,000 is considered debt discharge income. But Grant may elect to exclude $50,000. He reports the remaining $10,000 of discharged debt as taxable income. The exclusion limit is the excess of (1) the pre-discharge mortgage balance, over (2) the pre-discharge fair market value of the building, minus the pre-discharge balance of the other mortgage *(11.8)*, calculated as follows:

| | |
|---|---|
| 2nd mortgage before discharge | $90,000 |
| Less: Fair market value of building reduced by first mortgage ($150,000 – $110,000) | 40,000 |
| Excludable amount | $50,000 |

On Form 982, Grant may elect to exclude $50,000 from income because the basis of the building is sufficient to absorb a basis reduction of $50,000.

---

## 31.11 Abandonments

To abandon property, you must terminate your ownership by voluntarily and permanently giving up possession and use of the property without passing it on to someone else. On an abandonment of mortgaged real estate (whether held for business, investment, or personal use), the type of debt determines if there is gain or loss on the abandonment. If you are personally liable for the debt (recourse debt), there is no gain or loss until a later foreclosure or repossession. If you are not personally liable (nonrecourse debt), the IRS treats the abandonment itself as a sale on which gain or loss is realized.

For example, if in 2018 you abandon investment real estate that secures your recourse debt, you do not have gain or loss for 2018, but if the lender forecloses on the loan in 2019, you will have a gain or loss in 2019. Under the foreclosure sale rules for recourse debt property *(31.9)*, the amount realized in 2019 will include the smaller of the canceled debt or the fair market value of the property. In addition, if the canceled recourse debt exceeds the fair market value, the excess is ordinary income from cancellation of debt *(31.9)*. On the other hand, if you were not personally liable for the debt securing the property (nonrecourse debt), then an abandonment in 2018 would be treated by the IRS as a 2018 sale, and the full outstanding debt would be treated as the amount realized in figuring gain or loss; there would not be any cancellation of debt income *(31.9)*.

If the abandoned property was held for personal use, any loss on the abandonment or on a foreclosure or repossession is not deductible. If recourse debt is canceled in a foreclosure or repossession, you will realize ordinary income from cancellation of the debt if the canceled amount exceeds the value of the transferred property *(31.9)*.

**Abandoning a partnership interest.** Where real estate values have sharply declined, partnerships may be holding realty subject to mortgage debt that exceeds the current value of the property. Some investors in such partnerships have claimed that they can abandon their partnership interests and claim abandonment losses. In one case, an investor in a partnership holding land in Houston, Texas, argued that he abandoned his partnership interest by making an abandonment declaration at a meeting of partners, and also declaring that he would make no further payments. He offered his interest to the others, who refused his offer. The IRS held that he failed to prove abandonment of his partnership interest or that the partnership abandoned the land. The Tax Court sided with the IRS, emphasizing his failure to show that the partnership abandoned the land. However, the appeals court for the Fifth Circuit reversed and allowed the abandonment loss. It held that the emphasis should be on the partner's actions, not the actions of the partnership. Although neither state law nor the IRS regulations described how a partnership interest is to be abandoned, the appeals court held that the partner's acts and declaration were sufficient to effect an abandonment of his partnership interest. The appeals court also held that the loss on the partnership interest could have been sustained on the basis of the worthlessness of his interest. The partnership was insolvent beyond hope of rehabilitation: (1) the partnership's only asset was land with a fair market value less than the mortgage debt; (2) the partnership had no source of income; and (3) the partners refused to contribute more funds to keep the partnership afloat.

In a subsequent case, the Tax Court held that a doctor had abandoned a movie production partnership interest when he refused to advance any more money or to participate in the venture because he disapproved of the content of the film being produced and feared it might jeopardize his position at a hospital operated by a religious organization. Also, the limited partners had voted to dissolve.

## 31.12 Seller's Repossession After Buyer's Default on Mortgage

When you, as a seller, repossess realty on the buyer's default of a debt that the realty secures, you may realize gain or loss. (If the realty was a personal residence, the loss is not deductible.) A debt is secured by real property whenever you have the right to take title or possession or both in the event the buyer defaults on his or her obligation under the contract.

Figuring gain on the repossession. Gain on the repossession is the excess of: (1) payments received on the original sales contract prior to and on the repossession, including payments made by the buyer for your benefit to another party, over (2) the amount of taxable gain previously reported prior to the repossession.

Gain computed under these two steps may not be fully taxable. Taxable gain is limited to (1) the amount of original profit less gain on the sale already reported as income for periods prior to the repossession, plus (2) your repossession costs.

The limitation on gain does not apply if the selling price cannot be computed at the time of sale as, for example, where the selling price is stated as a percentage of the profits to be realized from the development of the property sold.

These repossession gain rules do not apply if you repurchase the property by paying the buyer a sum in addition to the discharge of the debt, unless the repurchase and payment was provided for in the original sale contract, or the buyer has defaulted on his or her obligation, or default is imminent. In such cases, gain or loss on the repossession, and basis in the repossessed property, must be determined under the different rules for personal property; *see* IRS Publication 537 for details.

**The basis of repossessed property.** This is the adjusted basis of the debt (face value of the debt less the unreported profits) secured by the property, figured as of the date of repossession, increased by (1) the taxable gain on repossession and (2) the legal fees and other repossession costs you paid.

If you treated the debt as having become worthless or partially worthless before repossession, you are considered to receive, upon the repossession of the property securing the debt, an amount equal to the amount of the debt treated as worthless. You report as income the amount of any prior bad debt deduction and increase the basis of the debt by an amount equal to the amount reported as income.

If your debt is not fully discharged as a result of the repossession, the basis of the undischarged debt is zero. No loss may be claimed if the obligations subsequently become worthless. This rule applies to undischarged debts on the original obligation of the purchaser, a substituted obligation of the purchaser, a deficiency judgment entered in a court of law into which the purchaser's obligation was merged, and any other obligations arising from the transaction.

 *Caution*

**Character of Gain**

The gain limitation rules *(31.12)* do not affect the character of the gain. Thus, if you repossess property as a dealer, the gain is subject to ordinary income rates. If you, as an investor, repossess a tract originally held long term whose gain was reported on the installment method, the gain is capital gain.

**EXAMPLE**

Assume you sell land for $25,000. You take a $5,000 down payment plus a $20,000 mortgage, secured by the property, from the buyer, with principal payable at the rate of $4,000 annually plus 9% interest. The adjusted basis of the land was $20,000 and you elected to report the transaction on the installment basis. Your gross profit percentage is 20% ($5,000 profit divided by $25,000 selling price). In the year of sale, you include $1,000 in your income on the installment basis (20% of $5,000 down payment). The next year you reported profit of $800 (20% of $4,000 annual installment). In the third year, the buyer defaults, and you repossess the property. Your repossession costs are $500. The amount of gain on repossession is computed as follows:

1. Compute gain:

| | | |
|---|---|---|
| Amount of money received before repossession ($5,000 plus $4,000) | | $9,000 |
| Less: Amount of gain taxed in prior years ($1,000 plus $800) | | 1,800 |
| Gain | | $7,200 |

2. Compute limit on taxable gain:

| | | |
|---|---|---|
| Original profit | | $5,000 |
| Less: | | |
| Gain reported as income | $1,800 | |
| Repossession costs | 500 | 2,300 |
| Taxable gain on repossession | | $2,700 |

**Principal residence.** Special rules apply to repossessions and resales of a principal residence if you excluded all or part of the gain on your original sale of the residence *(29.1)*, and you resell it within a year after you repossess it.

The original sale and resale is treated as one transaction. You refigure the amount realized on the sale. You combine the selling price of the resale with the selling price of the original sale. From this total, you subtract selling expenses for both sales, the part of the original installment obligation that remains unpaid at the time of repossession, and repossession costs. The net is the amount realized on the combined sale-resale. Subtracting basis in the home from the amount realized gives the gain on the combined sale-resale before taking into account the home sale exclusion *(29.1)* rules. *See* Treasury Regulation Section *1.1038*-2 for further details.

If the repossessed principal residence is not sold within one year, the combined sale-resale rule does not apply. The seller must report as income previously received payments that were not taxed (they were excluded under the home sale exclusion).

**EXAMPLE**

Same facts as in the previous Example. The basis of the repossessed property is computed as follows:

| | | | |
|---|---|---|---|
| 1. | Unpaid debt ($20,000 note less $4,000 payment) | | $16,000 |
| 2. | Less: Unreported profit (20% of the $16,000 still due on the note) | | 3,200 |
| 3. | Adjusted basis in installment obligation at date of repossession | | $12,800 |
| 4. | Plus: Gain on repossession | $2,700 | |
| | Repossession costs | 500 | 3,200 |
| 5. | Basis of repossessed property | | $16,000 |

## 31.13 Foreclosure on Mortgages Other Than Purchase Money

If you, as a mortgagee (lender), bid in on a foreclosure sale to pay off a mortgage that is not a purchase money mortgage, your actual financial loss is the difference between the unpaid mortgage debt and the value of the property. For tax purposes, however, you may realize a capital gain or loss and a bad debt loss that are reportable in the year of the foreclosure sale.

Your bid is treated as consisting of two distinct transactions:

1. The repayment of your loan. To determine whether this results in a bad debt, the bid price is matched against the face amount of the mortgage.

2. A taxable exchange of your mortgage note for the foreclosed property, which may result in a capital gain or loss. This is determined by matching the bid price against the fair market value of the property.

Where the bid price equals the mortgage debt plus unreported but accrued interest, you report the interest as income. But where the accrued interest has been reported, the unpaid amount is added to the collection expenses.

---

### EXAMPLES

1. **Mortgagee's bid less than market value.** You hold a $40,000 mortgage on property having a fair market value of $30,000. You bid on the property at the foreclosure sale at $28,000. The expenses of the sale are $2,000, reducing the bid price to $26,000. The mortgagor is insolvent, so you have a bad debt loss of $14,000 ($40,000 − $26,000). You also have a $4,000 capital gain (the fair market value of the property of $30,000 − $26,000 net bid price).

2. **Mortgagee's bid equal to market value.** Suppose your bid was $32,000, and you had $2,000 in expenses. The difference between the net bid price of $30,000 and the mortgage of $40,000 is $10,000. As the mortgagor is insolvent, there is a bad debt loss of $10,000. Since the net bid price equals the fair market value, there is neither capital gain nor loss.

3. **Mortgagee's bid greater than market value.** Suppose your bid was $36,000 and you had $2,000 in expenses. Your bad debt deduction is $6,000—the difference between the mortgage debt of $40,000 and the net bid price of $34,000. You also had a capital loss of $4,000 (the difference between the net bid price of $34,000 and the fair market value of $30,000).

---

## 31.14 Foreclosure Sale to Third Party

When a third party buys the property in a foreclosure, you, as the mortgagee, receive the purchase price to apply against the mortgage debt. If it is less than the debt, and the mortgagor was personally liable, you may proceed against the mortgagor for the difference. Foreclosure expenses are treated as offsets against the foreclosure proceeds and increase the loss.

---

### EXAMPLE

You hold a $30,000 note and mortgage that are in default. You foreclose, and a third party buys the property for $20,000. Foreclosure expenses amount to $2,000. The deficiency is uncollectible. Your $12,000 loss is figured as follows:

| | | |
|---|---|---|
| Unpaid mortgage debt | | $30,000 |
| Foreclosure proceeds | $20,000 | |
| Less: Expenses | 2,000 | |
| Net proceeds | | 18,000 |
| Bad debt loss | | $12,000 |

---

You deduct your loss as a bad debt. The law distinguishes between two types of bad debt deductions: business bad debts and nonbusiness bad debts. A business bad debt is fully deductible. A nonbusiness bad debt is a short-term capital loss that can be offset only against capital gains, plus a limited amount of ordinary income (5.33). In addition, you may deduct a partially worthless business bad debt, but you may not deduct a partially

*Planning Reminder*

**Voluntary Conveyance**

Instead of forcing you to foreclose, the mortgagor may voluntarily convey the property to you in consideration for your canceling the mortgage debt. Your loss is the amount by which the mortgage debt plus accrued interest exceeds the fair market value of the property. If, however, the fair market value exceeds the mortgage debt plus accrued interest, the difference is taxable gain. The gain or loss is reportable in the year you receive the property. Your basis in the property is its fair market value when you receive it.

**Planning Reminder**

**Keep Records**

Preserve evidence of the property's fair market value. At a later date, the IRS may claim that the property was worth more than your bid and may tax you for the difference. Furthermore, be prepared to prove the worthlessness of the debt in order to support the bad debt deduction.

worthless nonbusiness bad debt. Remember this distinction if you are thinking of forgiving part of the mortgage debt as a settlement. If the debt is a nonbusiness bad debt, you will not be able to take a deduction until the entire debt proves to be worthless. But whether you are deducting a business or a nonbusiness bad debt, your deduction will be allowed only if you show the debt to be uncollectible—for example, because a deficiency judgment is worthless or because the mortgagor is declared bankrupt.

## 31.15 Transferring Mortgaged Realty

Mortgaging realty that has appreciated in value is one way of realizing cash on the appreciation without current tax consequences. The receipt of cash by mortgaging the property is not taxed; tax will generally be imposed only when the property is sold. However, there is a possible tax where the mortgage exceeds the adjusted basis of the property and the property is given away or transferred to a controlled corporation. Where the property is transferred to a controlled corporation, the excess is taxable gain. Further, if the IRS successfully charges that the transfer is part of a tax avoidance scheme, the taxable gain may be as high as the amount of the mortgage liability.

**Charitable donations.** The IRS holds that a donation of mortgaged property to a charity is a part-sale, part-gift, and the donor has taxable gain to the extent the mortgage liability exceeds the portion of the donor's basis allocable to the sale part of the transaction *(14.8)*.

## 31.16 QBI Deduction for REIT Dividends

If you own an interest in a real estate investment trust (REIT), you can take a deduction (a subtraction from adjusted gross income) of up to 20% of combined qualified REIT dividends and publicly-traded partnership (PTP) income. This deduction applies whether you hold the interest directly or through a pass-through entity (including a trust).

Qualified REIT dividends for purposes of the QBI deduction means dividends from REITs that do not qualify for preferential tax rates (i.e., ordinary dividends).

The qualified REIT dividend component of the qualified business income (QBI) deduction (*see 40.29*) is not limited by W-2 wages or the unadjusted basis immediately after acquisition (UBIA) of qualified property. But the total QBI deduction is the lesser of the sum of combined amounts of the deduction from pass-through businesses plus amounts from REITs and PTPs, or 20% of the excess of taxable income over net capital gains for the year.

If your taxable income in 2018 is not more than $157,500 ($315,000 if married filing jointly), you figure this deduction on the 2018 Qualified Business Income Deduction—Simplified Worksheet in the instructions to Form 1040. If your taxable income is higher, use the worksheet in IRS Publication 535.

# CHAPTER 32

# Tax Rules for Investors in Mutual Funds

As a mutual fund shareholder, you may receive several types of distributions, such as ordinary dividends, capital gain distributions, exempt-interest dividends, and return of capital distributions. The rules for reporting the different types of distributions are discussed in this chapter.

The tax law provides different methods of identifying the particular shares being sold when you sell a portion of your mutual fund holdings and of determining the cost basis of those shares. You may be able to use these methods to obtain a preferred tax result on the sale.

## 32.1 Timing of Your Investment Can Affect Your Taxes

You may buy a tax liability if you invest in a mutual fund that has already realized significant capital gains during the year. For example, if a fund is about to make a year-end capital gain distribution and you invest shortly before that, you will in effect have to pay tax on the return of your recently invested money.

You will be eligible to receive a forthcoming dividend or capital gain distribution if you are a shareholder of record on the "record date" set by the fund. On the "ex-dividend date," the net asset value per share will be reduced by the distribution amount per share. If you buy before the record date, the higher cost for your shares will be offset by the distributions you receive, but you will have to pay tax on the distributions. On the other hand, because you paid the higher pre-distribution price, your higher basis will reduce any capital gain on a later sale, or increase any capital loss.

If you want to limit your current tax and forego the basis increase, postpone your investment until after the record date for distributions. By that time, the value per share that determines the price will have been reduced by the distribution. Before investing, you may be able to find out from the fund when distributions for the year are expected; call the fund or check the fund's website for an estimate of projected distributions.

## 32.2 Reinvestment Plans

A mutual fund will allow you to reinvest dividends and capital gain distributions from the fund in new fund shares instead of receiving cash. You report reinvested distributions as if you received them in cash. Form 1099-DIV sent to you by a fund reports the gross amount of taxable distributions that you must report on your return *(32.3)*.

**Keep track of reinvested distributions.** If you reinvest your mutual fund distributions instead of taking them in cash, you will need a record of the distributions and of the shares purchased with the reinvestment; your fund can likely provide you with a history of your reinvestments. The reinvested distributions are considered your cost basis for the acquired shares. You need a record of reinvestments to figure your cost when you sell your shares; *see* below *(32.8)* for calculating gain on the sale of mutual fund shares.

**Reinvested distribution can trigger wash sale.** If you redeem fund shares at a loss within 30 days before or after a dividend distribution is reinvested into your account, a "wash sale" results, and the portion of the loss allocable to the reinvestment is not deductible *(30.6)*. The allocable loss is disallowed even though the wash sale was inadvertently caused by the reinvestment. The disallowed loss is actually deferred, as it is added to the cost basis of the replacement shares and will affect the computation of gain or loss on a later sale.

## 32.3 Mutual Fund Distributions Reported on Form 1099-DIV

Mutual fund distributions are reported to you and the IRS by the fund on Form 1099-DIV or substitute statement. Distributions that you reinvested to acquire additional shares are reported and taxed in the same way as distributions that are actually paid out to you.

**Types of distributions.** The Form 1099-DIV (or substitute statement) from your fund for 2018 may show several kinds of distributions. Distributions that you reinvested *(32.2)* instead of receiving in cash are included on the Form 1099-DIV.

- Ordinary dividends—are the most common type of dividend, payable out of the fund's earnings and profits. They are shown in Box 1a of Form 1099-DIV. Short-term capital gain distributions are reported as ordinary dividends.
- Qualified dividends—shown in Box 1b, are your share of the ordinary dividends (Box 1a) that are qualified dividends *(4.2)* from the fund's investments in U.S. corporations and qualified foreign corporations. This amount is eligible for the zero, 15%, or 20% capital gain rate *(5.3)*, but only if you held your fund shares for at least 61 days during the 121-day period beginning 60 days before the ex-dividend date *(4.2)*.
- Capital gain distributions—shown in Box 2a of Form 1099-DIV, are your share of the net long-term capital gains realized by the fund on sales of securities in its portfolio. These are taxable to you as long-term capital gain *(5.3)* regardless of how long you have owned your fund shares.

- If the fund retained long-term capital gains and paid tax on them, your share will be reported to you on Form 2439, rather than Form 1099-DIV *(32.6)*.
- Return of capital (nontaxable) distributions—shown in Box 3 of Form 1099-DIV, are a return of your investment that reduce your basis in your shares and are not taxed until basis has been reduced to zero. If basis has been reduced to zero, you report the excess amount on Form 8949 as either short-term or long-term gain (depending on your holding period for the shares) by reporting the excess as the sales price in column (d), and reporting a zero basis in column (f). See the Form 8949 instructions for further details.

*See Table 32-1* for details on how to report these and other distributions on your tax return.

**Year-end dividends.** Mutual funds sometimes declare dividends at the end of a calendar year but do not pay them until January of the following year. If the dividend is declared in October, November, or December, and paid in the following January, the fund will report the distribution as taxable in the year it is declared.

## 32.4 Tax-Exempt Bond Funds

Dividends from a bond fund that represent tax-exempt interest earned by the fund are not subject to regular income tax, but capital gain distributions are taxable. The exempt-interest dividends are shown by the fund in Box 10 of Form 1099-DIV. You report exempt-interest dividends along with your other tax-exempt interest on Line 2a of Form 1040. The amount on Line 2a is not taxable, but if you receive Social Security benefits, it could increase the amount of taxable benefits *(34.3)*. If part of the exempt-interest dividends is attributable to private activity bonds, that amount may be a preference item subject to alternative minimum tax (AMT) *(23.3)*. The amount subject to AMT is shown in Box 12 of Form 1099-DIV.

Capital gain distributions are shown on Form 1099-DIV and must be reported on your return; *see Table 32-1*.

When you redeem your shares in a tax-exempt bond fund or exchange the fund shares for other shares in a different fund, you realize taxable capital gain or deductible loss.

If you received exempt-interest dividends on mutual fund shares held for six months or less and sold those shares at a loss, the amount of your loss is reduced by the exempt-interest dividend. To reflect this adjustment, on Part I (short-term gains and losses) of Form 8949, you increase the sales price in column (d) by the exempt-interest dividend.

> **EXAMPLE**
>
> In January 2018, you bought a mutual fund share for $40. In February 2018, the mutual fund paid a $5 dividend from tax-exempt interest, which is not taxable to you. In March 2018, you sold the share for $34. If it were not for the tax-exempt dividend, your loss would be $6 ($40 − 34). However, you may deduct only $1, the part of the loss that exceeds the exempt-interest dividend ($6 − 5). On Form 8949, increase the sales price in column (d) of Part I by $5 (the $5 nondeductible loss), to $39 from $34, thereby reducing your short-term capital loss to $1 ($40 − 39).

## 32.5 Fund Expenses

If you own shares in a publicly offered mutual fund, you do not pay tax on your share of the fund expenses. There should be no entry in Box 6 of your Form 1099-DIV. However, expenses of a non–publicly offered fund are included in Box 6 of Form 1099-DIV and must be reported as a taxable dividend, even though the amount has not actually been distributed to you. This amount is included as a fully taxable ordinary dividend in Box 1 of Form 1099-DIV. And because of the suspension of miscellaneous itemized deductions subject to the 2% of adjusted gross income floor for 2018 through 2025, an offsetting deduction is not permissible.

 *Filing Tip*

**Reduced Rate Qualified Dividends**

Box 1b of Form 1099-DIV for 2018 shows your qualified dividends, the portion of the amount in Box 1a (total ordinary dividends) that is eligible for the 0%, 15% or 20% capital gain rate.

 *Filing Tip*

**Tax-exempt Interest Impacts Premium Tax Credit**

Tax-exempt interest is taken into account in determining household income, which is the amount on which eligibility for the premium tax credit hinges. *See 25.12.*

 *Filing Tip*

**Undistributed Capital Gains From REITs**

The capital gain reporting and credit rules for mutual funds *(32.6)* also apply if you own shares in a REIT that has retained its long-term capital gains.

## 32.6 Tax Credits From Mutual Funds

**Undistributed capital gains.** Some mutual funds retain their long-term capital gains and pay capital gains tax on those amounts. Even though not actually received by you, you include as a capital gain distribution on your return the amount of the undistributed capital gain allocated to you by the fund. If the mutual fund paid a tax on the undistributed capital gain, you are entitled to a tax credit.

To claim the credit, check the Form 2439 sent to you by your fund, which lists your share of undistributed capital gain and the amount of tax paid on it by the fund. Enter your share of the tax the fund paid on this gain as a tax payment on Schedule 5 of Form 1040, and check box "a" for Form 2439. Attach Copy B of Form 2439 to your return to support your tax credit. Increase the basis of your shares by the excess of the undistributed capital gain over the amount of tax paid by the mutual fund, as reported on Form 2439.

**Foreign tax credit or deduction.** You may be able to claim a foreign tax credit (on Form 1116) or a deduction on Schedule A for your share of the fund's foreign taxes. In Box 6 of Form 1099-DIV, the fund will report your share of the foreign taxes paid by the fund. The fund should give you instructions for claiming the foreign tax credit or deduction *(36.13)* .

## 32.7 How to Report Mutual Fund Distributions

Report an undistributed capital gain on Schedule D or a return of capital distribution on Form 8949 and Schedule D because your basis in your fund shares has been reduced to zero.

Check *Table 32-1* below for details on reporting distributions on your return.

## 32.8 Redemptions and Exchanges of Fund Shares

When you ask the fund to redeem all or part of your shares, you have transacted a sale subject to capital gain or loss rules explained in *Chapter 5* . Exchanges of shares of one fund for shares of another fund within the same fund "family" are treated as sales. If you owned the shares for more than one year, your gain or loss is long term; if you held them for a year or less, your gain or loss is short term. However, if you received a capital gain distribution before selling shares held six months or less at a loss, your loss must be reported as a long-term capital loss to the extent of the capital gain distribution attributable to the sold shares. Any excess loss is reported as a short-term capital loss. This restriction does not apply to dispositions under periodic redemption plans.

 *Planning Reminder*

**Keeping Track of Cost Basis**

Keep confirmation statements for purchases of shares as well as a record of distributions that are automatically reinvested in your account. These will show the cost basis for your shares. Your basis is increased by amounts reported to you by the fund on Form 2439, representing the difference between your share of undistributed capital gains that you were required to report as income and your share of the tax paid by the fund on undistributed gains. Your basis is reduced by nontaxable dividends that are a return of your investment. Keep copies of Form 2439 and information returns showing nontaxable dividends.

> **EXAMPLE**
>
> In June 2018, you bought mutual fund shares for $1,000. In August, you received a capital gain distribution of $50, and in September you sold the shares for $850. Instead of reporting a $150 short-term capital loss ($1,000 cost – $850 proceeds), you must report a long-term capital loss of $50, the amount of the capital gain distribution; the remaining $100 of the loss is a short-term capital loss.

**Identifying the shares you sell.** Determining which mutual funds shares are being sold is necessary to figure your gain or loss and whether the gain or loss is short term or long term *(32.9)* .

**Holding period of fund shares.** You determine your holding period by using the trade dates. The trade date is the date on which you buy or redeem the mutual fund shares. Do not confuse the trade date with the settlement date, which is the date by which the mutual fund shares must be delivered and payment must be made. Most mutual funds will show the trade date on your purchase and redemption confirmation statements.

Your holding period starts on the day after the day you bought the shares (the trade date). This same date of each succeeding month is the start of a new month regardless of the number of days in the month before. The day you dispose of the shares (trade date) is also part of your holding period.

## *Table 32-1*  Reporting Mutual Fund Distributions for 2018

| Type of Distribution | Shown by the Fund in | How To Report |
|---|---|---|
| Ordinary dividends and short-term capital gain distributions. | Box 1a, Form 1099-DIV | Box 1a of Form 1099-DIV shows taxable ordinary dividends. The total includes ordinary dividends and short-term capital gain distributions, which are taxed as ordinary income, and also qualified dividends, if any, which are taxable at the applicable capital gain rate *(5.3)* . The Box 1a total must be entered on Line 3b of Form 1040. If your total ordinary dividends from all sources exceed $1,500 or if you received as a nominee ordinary dividends on behalf of another taxpayer, you must itemize the ordinary dividends on Line 5 of Schedule B (Form 1040). |
| Qualified dividends (eligible for capital gain rate if you held shares at least 61 days during the 121-day period beginning 60 days before the ex-dividend date). | Box 1b, Form 1099-DIV | Box 1b shows the portion of the Box 1a amount that is eligible for the 0%, 15% or 20% capital gain rate *(5.3)* . Report these qualified dividends on Line 3a of Form 1040. Unless you have 28% rate gains or unrecaptured Section 1250 gains that have to be reported on the "Schedule D Tax Worksheet" in the Schedule D instructions, you may use the "Qualified Dividends and Capital Gain Tax Worksheet'" in the Form 1040 instructions to figure your regular tax liability using the capital gain rates. |
| Capital gain distributions. (This represents your share of net long-term gains realized by a fund on sales made from its portfolio.) | Boxes 2a–2d, Form 1099-DIV | Box 2a of Form 1099-DIV shows your total capital gain distributions. If your only capital gains are capital gain distributions, you do not have capital losses, and no amount is shown in Boxes 2b–2d of all your Forms 1099-DIV, you generally do not have to complete Schedule D (Form 1040) and may report the capital gain distributions from Box 2a directly on Schedule 1 of Form 1040. In that case, you use the Qualified Dividends and Capital Gain Tax Worksheet in the Form 1040 instructions to figure your tax using the capital gain rates. If Schedule D is required, the total capital gain distributions from Box 2a must be reported on Line 13 of Schedule D and the rest of Schedule D completed. Box 2b shows the part of Box 2a that is unrecaptured Section 1250 gain from the sale of depreciable buildings. Box 2c shows the part of Box 2a that is Section 1202 gain eligible for an exclusion *(5.7)* . Box 2d shows the amount of Box 2a that is 28% rate gain from sales of collectibles. If you have an amount in Box 2b, 2c, or 2d, you must complete Schedule D. |
| Return of capital distributions (nontaxable) | Box 3, Form 1099-DIV | A return of capital distribution is not taxable income. However, if your basis for your shares has been reduced to zero by return of capital gain distributions, report additional nontaxable distributions as either long-term or short-term capital gain on Form 8949, depending on how long you held the shares *(32.3)* . |
| Exempt-interest dividends | Box 11, Form 1099-DIV | Report along with other tax-exempt interest on Line 2a of Form 1040. The portion of the exempt-interest dividends that is attributable to private activity bonds subject to AMT *(23.3)*  is shown in Box 12 of Form 1099-DIV |
| Undistributed capital gains | Undistributed gains shown on Form 2439, Box 1a<br><br>Tax paid by fund shown on Form 2439, Box 2 | Box 1a of Form 2439 shows your total share of undistributed long-term capital gains. The undistributed gains are reported on Line 11 of Schedule D. To get a tax credit for the tax paid by the fund, enter the tax as a payment on Schedule 5 of Form 1040. Increase the basis of your mutual fund shares by the excess of the undistributed gains included on Schedule D over the tax credit claimed on Form 1040. |
| Foreign taxes | Box 6, Form 1099-DIV. | The foreign taxes may be claimed as a tax credit on Form 1116 or as an itemized deduction on Schedule A of Form 1040 *(36.13)* . |
| Federal income tax withheld | Box 4, Form 1099-DIV. Box 4 Form 1099-INT. | If you are subject to back-up withholding, the amount of federal income tax withheld should be included on Schedule 5 of Form 1040. |

**Caution**

**Wash Sale Loss Disallowance**

A loss on the redemption of fund shares is disallowed to the extent that within 30 days before or after the sale, you buy shares in the same fund. The wash sale rule *(30.6)* is triggered even when the acquisition of new shares occurs automatically (within the 61-day period) under a dividend reinvestment plan.

**Planning Reminder**

**Inherited Shares**

If you inherit shares of a decedent and an estate tax return was filed after July 31, 2015, the executor of the estate must provide you with a statement that shows the date-of-death value of the property you received, and if the property increased the estate tax liability, you are required to use that value as your basis when you sell. For further inherited property basis rules, *see 5.17.*

**Caution**

**Basis of Shares Acquired After 2011 Reported to the IRS**

When you sell mutual fund shares that you acquired after 2011 in a nonretirement account, the fund will report the cost basis of the shares to both the IRS and you on Form 1099-B.

## 32.9 Basis of Redeemed Shares

To figure gain or loss, you need to know the basis per share. Generally, your basis is the purchase price of the shares, including shares acquired by reinvesting distributions back into the fund, plus commission or load charges.

**Load charges.** Basis does not include load charges (acquisition fees) on the purchase of mutual fund shares if you held the shares for 90 days or less and then exchanged them for shares in a different fund in the same family of funds for which the load charge is reduced or waived.

> **EXAMPLE**
>
> You pay a $200 load charge on purchasing shares for $10,000 in Fund A. Within 90 days, you exchange the Fund A shares for Fund B shares. Because Fund A and Fund B are in the same family of funds, the $200 load charge that would otherwise be due on the purchase of the Fund B shares is waived. For purposes of figuring your gain or loss on the exchange of Fund A shares, your basis is $10,000, not $10,200. The disallowed $200 is added to the basis of the new Fund B shares, provided those shares are held more than 90 days. If the waived load charge on Fund B shares had been $100, basis for the original Fund A shares would be increased by $100, the excess of the original $200 load charge over the amount waived on the reinvestment.

**Cost basis of sold shares.** If you are selling your entire mutual fund account, you need to know your total basis for all the shares. If your shares in the fund were acquired at different times, and you are selling only some of the shares in your account, you need to know which shares are being sold and the basis of those shares to determine gain or loss. In general, you can choose between at least three basis methods: the average cost method, the specific identification method, and the first- in, first-out method. These methods are discussed below. When you sell shares that you acquired after 2011, your cost basis for those shares will be reported to both you and the IRS; *see* below.

**Basis will be reported to the IRS when you sell shares acquired after 2011.** Mutual fund shares acquired after 2011 are considered "covered shares." When you sell covered shares, the fund will report your cost basis for the shares in Box 1e of Form 1099-B sent to both you and the IRS.

When you sell shares acquired before 2012, or "noncovered shares," your mutual fund will not report cost basis on the Form 1099-B it sends to the IRS. On the Form 1099-B it sends to you, the fund will probably report basis using the average cost method, but this does not require you to use the average cost method on your tax return and the basis information will not be reported to the IRS.

If you acquired shares both before 2012 and after 2011, a sale may involve noncovered shares, covered shares, or both, depending on the basis method you select and the number of shares sold. For example, if you use the average cost method, noncovered shares will be considered redeemed first in the order you acquired them, before covered shares are considered sold. The fund will separately figure the average cost for your noncovered and covered shares.

Whether the sold shares are covered or noncovered, you are responsible for reporting your cost basis and calculating your gain or loss on Form 8949 and Schedule D (Form 1040). For covered shares, the IRS can match the basis reported by the fund on Form 1099-B with the basis you report on your return.

**Basis methods you can select.** To identify the shares you are selling, you can choose between the average cost method, the specific identification method, the first in, first out method, or some other variation of the specification method. Check with the fund for its rules on selecting a preferred basis method for covered shares and its rules for changing the basis method.

If you sell covered shares without having designated a cost basis method, the fund will likely use average cost as its "default" method for reporting basis on the Forms 1099-B (in Box 1e, with Box 3 checked) it sends to you and the IRS. If average cost is the fund's default method, and you want to use another basis method for your first sale of covered shares, such as the specific identification method, you must select that method online or on a paper form you mail to the fund before the fund will complete your transaction. Once specific identification is selected, you can identify the specific shares you want to sell by phone (if allowed by the fund), online, or in writing. If you initially use the average cost method, either as the default or because you selected it, and you want to change to another method, or you initially choose another method and want to change to average cost, you must make the change from or to average cost online or in writing, not by phone. If you sell covered shares using the average cost method and then elect another basis method, the new method will apply only to shares purchased after the date that the change request is processed.

If you plan to sell noncovered shares and want to use the specific identification method when you report basis on Form 8949 and Schedule D, you must select that method prior to the sale (online or in writing) and must keep for your records a confirmation from the fund showing that you selected specific shares to be sold. You will need purchase records to substantiate the basis you report on your return for the specifically identified shares.

Here is a summary of the basis methods.

- Average Cost Method—averages your cost for all shares in the fund regardless of when they were acquired. You do not have to identify the exact shares being sold. The average cost for each share is the total cost for all shares, including those acquired by reinvesting dividends and capital gain distributions, divided by the number of shares. For holding period purposes when you file your return (long- or short-term treatment on Form 8949/Schedule D), shares sold under the average cost method are considered sold in the order you acquired them (FIFO). Your fund will calculate average cost separately for your covered and noncovered shares.

- Specific Identification Method—allows you to select exactly which shares are being sold, enabling you to determine your gain or loss and achieve a desired tax result. Check with your fund for its procedures in selecting the specific identification method and for identifying the shares to be sold using the method.

- First-in, first-out (FIFO) Method—treats shares as sold in the order that they were acquired.

Your fund may also offer variations of the above methods, such as highest in, first out (HIFO), which treats the highest cost shares as sold first, or last in, first out (LIFO), which treats the most recently acquired shares as sold first. Check with your fund for the available methods and selection procedures.

---

**EXAMPLE**

You bought 160 shares of the XYZ Mutual Fund on February 7, 2008, for $4,000. On August 14, 2008, you bought another 240 shares for $4,800. You obtained an additional 10 shares on December 18, 2008, when you reinvested a $300 dividend. On December 22, 2009, you obtained an additional 20 shares when you reinvested a $750 dividend. This was your last investment in the fund. Since then, you have taken distributions in cash rather than reinvesting them. You sell 200 shares of the fund on September 24, 2018, for $8,000.

As all of the sold shares were acquired before 2012, they are considered noncovered shares. The XYZ Fund provides your average cost basis on the Form 1099-B it sends to you. The Form 1099-B sent to the IRS does not include basis.

Using the average cost method, your average basis is $22.91 per share. Your total cost basis for all 430 shares is $9,850. Dividing $9,850 by 430 gives you an average basis per share of $22.91. Thus, your basis for the 200 sold shares is $4,582 (200 × $22.91 = $4,582).

For holding period purposes, shares sold under the average cost method are deemed sold in the order they were acquired (FIFO). Thus, you are deemed to have sold the 160 shares bought on February 7, 2008, and 40 of the 240 shares bought on August 14, 2008. The sold shares were held long term on the sale date of September 24, 2018. You have a $3,418 long-term capital gain on the sale: $8,000 proceeds less $4,582 basis figured under the average cost method.

---

 *Planning Reminder*

**Shares Received as Gift**

To determine your original basis of mutual fund shares you acquired by gift, you must know the donor's adjusted basis, the date of the gift, the fair market value of the shares at the time of the gift, and whether any gift tax was paid on the shares (5.17).

## 32.10 Comparison of Basis Methods

Your choice of basis method can have a significant effect on the computation of capital gains and losses when you sell a portion of your shares in a mutual fund *(32.9)*. The following example compares the average cost method to the specific identification and FIFO methods.

**Transaction history.** Assume that on February 7, 1997, you made an initial investment of $4,500 for 375 shares in ABC Mutual Fund at $12 per share. Under the dividend reinvestment plan, you received a $400 dividend on December 19, 1997, that you reinvested for an additional 40 shares at $10 per share. On June 12, 1998, you bought 350 shares at $15 per share. On December 22, 1998, you reinvested your dividend, this time for 25 shares at $12 per share. On September 9, 1999, you bought 200 shares at $16 per share. On August 17, 2010, you bought 200 shares at $25 per share. You did not reinvest your dividends received after 1998 and did not buy any more shares after August 17, 2010 or sell any of the shares.

Now assume that you are planning to redeem some of your shares in 2019 and are trying to decide whether to use the average cost, specific identification, or FIFO method for figuring basis. Since all of your shares have been held long term, capital gain or loss will be long term regardless of which basis method is used.

You decide to redeem 200 shares on October 15, 2019, when shares are selling at $20 per share. The table below shows your transaction history and following that is a comparison of how the three basis methods would work given these facts.

**Specific identification method.** If you identify the particular shares you are selling, you can use the basis of those shares to figure your gain or loss. You must specifically tell the funds the particular shares you want to be redeemed prior to the time of the sale, and must receive a written confirmation of your specification within a reasonable time. Depending on your situation, you may want to either maximize or minimize your gain or loss on the sale.

Assume that under the transaction facts above, you want to realize a loss on the redemption that can be used to offset other gains. You would specify the 200 shares purchased at $25 per share on August 17, 2010, as the shares sold. Since the sales price on October 15, 2019, was $20 per share, the loss would be $5 per share, for an overall long-term capital loss of $1,000 ($4,000 – $5,000).

On the other hand, if you realized a gain, you could offset some capital losses that you realized earlier in the year, but you want to minimize the gain. You would specify the 200 shares bought at $16 per share on September 9, 1999, as the shares sold. Since the shares were sold for $20 per share, the gain would be $4 per share, for an overall $800 long-term capital gain ($4,000 – $3,200).

**FIFO (first-in, first-out).** Under the FIFO method, the oldest shares, the February 7, 1997 shares, are considered sold first. Thus, the basis of the 200 shares sold would be $12 per share. Your long-term capital gain is $1,600 ($4,000 – $2,400).

**Average cost.** Assume that the ABC Mutual Fund has calculated your average basis and provides it on your account statements. Your average cost is $15.67. This is your total investment of $18,650 divided by the 1,190 total shares. At $15.67 per share, the total cost is $3,134 for the 200 redeemed shares. Your long-term capital gain is $866 ($4,000 – $3,134). The shares sold are considered to be from the earliest lot in 1997.

**Conclusion.** Given this transaction history and preferred gain or loss objective, the specific identification method is advantageous. It allows you to realize a loss if that is your preferred tax result, or to realize the lowest capital gain if that is your preferred tax result.

*Caution*

**Get Written Confirmation for Specific Identification Method**

If you want to take advantage of the specific identification method, make sure the fund sends you a written confirmation of your selling instructions.

The specific identification method allows you to designate specific shares as the shares sold, allowing you to minimize a gain on the sale or to select shares that, because of their basis, would give you a loss.

| Transaction History | | | | |
| --- | --- | --- | --- | --- |
| Date | Action | Share Price | No. of Shares | Shares Owned |
| 2/7/1997 | Invest $4,500 | $12 | 375 | 375 |
| 12/19/1997 | Reinvest $400 dividend | $10 | 40 | 415 |
| 6/12/1998 | Invest $5,250 | $15 | 350 | 765 |
| 12/22/1998 | Reinvest $300 dividend | $12 | 25 | 790 |
| 9/9/1999 | Invest $3,200 | $16 | 200 | 990 |
| 8/17/2010 | Invest $5,000 | $25 | 200 | 1,190 |
| 10/15/2019 | Redeem $4,000 | $20 | 200 | 990 |

## 32.11 Mutual Funds Compared to Exchange-Traded Funds

From an investment perspective, mutual funds are similar to exchange traded funds (ETFs); both offer a bundle of underlying investments providing diversity that reduces the risk of loss. If there are any dividends from these investments, both permit dividend reinvestment in most cases. However, there are significant differences in tax treatment.

**Tax efficiency.** Mutual funds may generate tax consequences for investors because fund managers trade and re-balance the funds' holdings to satisfy shareholder redemptions. In effect, there may be capital gains for shareholders even though such shareholders have unrealized losses on their holdings (i.e., the value of their investment may have declined even though they are required to report gains). In contrast, ETFs generally do not generate gains from underlying investments while shareholders hold their positions; shareholders only realize gain or loss when they sell their ETF shares. However, certain ETFs offer less tax efficiency (check with a financial/tax advisor for guidance on the tax ramifications of a particular ETF).

**Dividends.** Dividends paid from ETFs may be treated as qualified dividends, which are subject to favorable tax treatment *(4.2)*. These dividends cannot offset capital losses. Capital gain distributions from mutual funds are considered long-term capital gains; they are taxed at favorable capital gain rates *(32.3)*. They can also be used to offset capital losses and a limited amount of ordinary income *(5.4)*.

**Identifying shares sold.** If you acquire shares at different times and sell less than your entire holdings, you may take action to minimize gain or maximize loss (depending on your overall tax position for the year). If no action is taken, you are treated as selling the first shares acquired (first-in, first-out). For ETFs, which are treated like stock, you can choose to use the specific identification method *(32.10)* to select those shares that produce the desired tax results. For mutual fund shares, you can use the specific identification method or an averaging method *(32.10)*. You cannot use the averaging method for shares in ETFs.

# CHAPTER 33

# Educational Tax Benefits

The tax law provides several tax benefits for people attending school. If you can take advantage of them, you are in effect receiving a government subsidy that lowers the cost of education.

Qualified tuition programs (529 plans), which are designed primarily to cover higher education costs, can be used, starting in 2018, to pay tuition up to $10,000 for elementary and secondary school.

The American Opportunity Tax Credit, the Lifetime Learning credit, the student loan interest deduction, and Coverdell ESAs can also provide substantial tax savings. The above-the-line deduction for higher education tuition and fees may be available if it is extended for 2018 and you do not claim an American Opportunity or Lifetime Learning credit. However, these tax benefit provisions are hedged with restrictions, such as income-based limitations, that may bar or limit their availability.

## 33.1 Scholarships and Grants

Scholarships and fellowships of a degree candidate are tax free to the extent that the grants pay for tuition and course-related fees, books, supplies, and equipment that are required for courses. Amounts for room, board, travel, and incidental expenses do not qualify and must be reported as income. If you are not a candidate for a degree (see the degree test below), your entire grant is taxable.

Generally, you must pay tax on grants or tuition reductions that pay for teaching, research, or other services required as a condition of receiving the grant. This is true even if all degree candidates are required to perform the services. Thus, if you are a graduate student and receive a stipend for teaching, those payments are taxable, subject to withholding, and reported by the school on Form W-2. Similarly, no tax-free exclusion is allowed for federal grants where the recipient agrees to do future work with the federal government. However, a grant or tuition reduction that represents payment for teaching, research, or other services is not taxable if it is paid under the National Health Services Corps Scholarship Program or the Armed Forces Health Professions Scholarship and Financial Assistance Program.

**Degree test.** Scholarships given to students attending a primary or secondary school, or to those pursuing a degree at a college or university, meet the degree test. Also qualifying are full-time or part-time scholarships for study at an educational institution that (1) provides an educational program acceptable for full-time credit towards a higher degree or offers a program of training to prepare students for gainful employment in a recognized occupation and (2) is authorized under federal or state law to provide such a program and is accredited by a nationally recognized accreditation agency.

**Pell grants.** Pell grants are need-based grants that are subject to the above rules for scholarships. Thus, they are tax free to the extent they are used for tuition and course-related fees, books, supplies, and equipment that are required for courses.

## 33.2 Tuition Reductions for College Employees

Free or partially free tuition for undergraduate studies provided to a faculty member or school employee is generally not taxable. The tuition reduction may be for education at his or her own school or at another school. Tuition benefits may be taxable to highly compensated employees if the tuition plan discriminates in their favor. Tuition reductions that represent compensation for services are taxable unless paid under the National Health Services Corps Scholarship Program or the Armed Forces Health Professions Scholarship and Financial Assistance Program.

Tax-free tuition benefits may also be provided to the employee's spouse, dependent child, a former employee who retired or left on disability, a widow or widower of an individual who died while employed by the school, or a widow or widower of a retired or disabled employee.

A child under the age of 25 qualifies for a tax-free tuition reduction if both parents have died and one of the parents qualified for tax-free tuition benefits. If the child is age 25 or over, tuition reductions are taxed even if both parents are deceased.

A tuition reduction for graduate studies may also be tax free; *see* the Caution on this page.

*Caution*

**Graduate Teaching and Research Assistants**

If you must teach, do research, or provide other services to obtain a tuition reduction for graduate studies, a tuition reduction from the school is tax free if it is in addition to regular pay for the services. If the tuition reduction is your compensation, it is taxable, unless it is paid under the National Health Services Corps Scholarship Program or the Armed Forces Health Professions Scholarship and Financial Assistance Program.

## 33.3 How Fulbright Awards Are Taxed

Most Fulbright awards are treated as taxable wages for teaching, lecturing, or research. If you are abroad over a year, you may be able to claim the foreign earned income exclusion to avoid tax on the grant *(Chapter 36)* . Foreign income taxes paid on taxable Fulbright wages are eligible for the foreign tax credit *(36.12)* .

## 33.4 United States Savings Bond Tuition Plans

Consider the use of Series EE bonds *(30.12)* or I bonds *(30.13)* to fund part of a college savings program. You can defer the interest income until final maturity (30 years) or report the interest annually. At redemption, the interest is not subject to state or local tax. For bonds purchased in your child's name, having your child report the interest annually may be advisable where it can be offset by the child's standard deduction or itemized deductions. To the extent interest is offset each year, it escapes tax *(4.29)*.

**Interest exclusion may be available if you redeem EE bonds issued in your own name after 1989 or I bonds.** If you purchased I bonds *(30.13)* or post-1989 EE bonds *(30.12)* in your own name or jointly with your spouse and have been deferring the reporting of interest income, you may be able to exclude accumulated interest from federal tax in the year you redeem the bonds if in that year you pay tuition and enrollment education fees or you contribute to a Coverdell ESA *(33.11)* or qualified tuition program (QTP) *(33.5)*. The exclusion, claimed on Form 8815, is subject to several limitations as discussed in the following paragraphs.

**Who qualifies for the exclusion.** You must have been age 24 or over before the month in which the qualified bonds were purchased, and the bonds must have been issued solely in your name or in the joint names of you and your spouse. You may not claim the exclusion for bonds bought in your child's name or owned jointly with your child. In the year the bonds are redeemed you must pay tuition and enrollment fees or contribute to a Coverdell ESA or QTP for yourself, your spouse, or your dependents *(21.2)*. Thus, grandparents who redeem bonds that they bought to fund the college education of their grandchildren may not claim the exclusion unless the grandchildren are their dependents in the year the bonds are redeemed. If you are married, you must file a joint return for the year you redeem the bonds; married persons filing separately are not eligible for the exclusion.

If these tests are met, and your income does not exceed the annual limit for the exclusion, you may claim a full or partial exclusion, depending on whether your qualified education expenses exceed the bond redemption proceeds, as discussed in the following paragraphs.

**Excludable amount and phaseout rule.** The tax-free amount of EE or I bond interest is figured on Form 8815. Even if you pay qualified higher educational expenses in the year you redeem the bond, your potential interest exclusion may be limited or barred because: (1) the qualified expenses must be reduced by nontaxable educational benefits received in the year the bond is redeemed, (2) your potential exclusion is reduced or eliminated under the phaseout rule based on modified adjusted gross income (MAGI), or (3) you are married filing separately, in which case you are not allowed an exclusion regardless of your income or amount of expenses.

Qualified higher education expenses include the following expenses that you pay in the year of redemption for yourself, your spouse, or your dependents *(21.2)*: (1) tuition and fees required for enrollment at a college, university, or vocational school that meets federal financial aid standards, and (2) contributions to a Coverdell. ESA or QTP. Room and board are not eligible expenses.

On Form 8815, qualified expenses must be reduced by the amount of any nontaxable scholarship or fellowship grant, tax-free employer-provided educational assistance, educational expenses taken into account when figuring the American Opportunity credit or Lifetime Learning credit *(33.7)*, and educational expenses taken into account when figuring the tax-free portion of a distribution from a qualified tuition plan *(33.6)* or a Coverdell ESA *(33.11)*.

If after the required reductions, qualified expenses equal or exceed the redemption proceeds, 100% of the interest is potentially excludable, subject to the phaseout based on MAGI. If the redeemed amount exceeds the amount of educational expenses (after any required reduction), the excludable amount is based on the ratio of expenses to the redemption amount and the phaseout computation.

A full interest exclusion is allowed only to persons with MAGI below a phaseout threshold. For 2018, the MAGI phaseout ranges are:

- $79,550 to $94,550 for single persons, heads of household, and qualifying widows/ widowers
- $119,300 to $149,300 for married persons filing jointly

No exclusion is allowed if MAGI equals or exceeds the $94,550 or $149,300 limit. For purposes of applying the phaseout, MAGI is generally your regular adjusted gross income plus the interest on the redeemed EE or I bonds, student loan interest *(33.14)*, or tuition and fees *(33.13)* that you deduct, and foreign income items and employer-provided adoption assistance that you excluded from income. See the Form 8815 instructions.

> **EXAMPLE**
>
> In November 2018, you redeem an I bond that in September 2001 cost you $10,000 (face value). On the redemption you receive $24,096 of which $10,000 is the return of your investment and $14,096 is interest. In 2018, you paid qualified higher education expenses of $19,250 for your daughter, who you claim as your dependent. After taking into account $4,000 of expenses used to figure an American Opportunity credit *(33.8)*, you show $15,250 of qualified higher education expenses on Form 8815. Prior to application of the phaseout rule, the excludable percentage of interest is 63.3% ($15,250 education expenses divided by $24,096 redemption proceeds). Thus, $8,923 of the interest (63.3% × $14,096) is potentially excludable from income, pending application of the phaseout rule.
>
> Assume that you are married filing jointly and have MAGI for 2018 of $130,372, which exceeds the phaseout threshold of $119,300 by $11,072. On Form 8815, you divide your excess MAGI of $11,072 by the $30,000 phaseout range to get a phaseout percentage of 36.9%. Thus, 36.9% of the potential $8,923 exclusion, or $3,293, is phased out. The excludable I bond interest is limited to $5,630 ($8,923 – $3,293).

## 33.5 Contributing to a Qualified Tuition Program (Section 529 Plan)

Qualified tuition programs (QTPs), also known as Section 529 plans, allow you to either prepay a designated beneficiary's future qualified higher education expenses or to establish a savings plan from which such expenses can be paid. States can sponsor savings plans and prepayment plans. Private colleges, universities, and vocational schools can set up prepayment plans only. Distributions are generally tax free to the extent of qualified higher education expenses; and, starting in 2018, distributions of up to $10,000 to pay tuition for elementary or secondary school also qualify *(33.6)* .

In a college prepayment plan, a parent or other relative can purchase tuition credits or certificates as a prepayment of a child's future college costs. Where the child will not start college for many years, prepaying tuition according to a set schedule can avoid higher inflation-based tuition costs down the road. In a state-sponsored savings plan, annual contributions are made to an account for the benefit of the designated beneficiary, earnings accumulate tax-free, and withdrawals can later be made to pay the beneficiary's qualified higher education costs.

Contribution details and other plan terms including investment options can vary greatly from plan to plan. If you are considering an investment, you should contact the state or educational institution maintaining the plan for details.

Contributions are not deductible for federal tax purposes. However, a state income tax deduction may be available to residents who contribute to a state-sponsored QTP.

You may contribute to both a QTP and a Coverdell ESA *(33.11)* in the same year on behalf of the same beneficiary.

**Gift tax consequences.** A contribution to a QTP is treated as a completed gift of a present interest passed from the contributor to the beneficiary at the time of contribution. Contributions are eligible for the annual gift tax exclusion, which applies separately to each individual to whom you make gifts during a year. For 2018, you can make gifts of up to $15,000 per person that are free from gift tax under the annual exclusion, but if you are married and your spouse elects to split your gift on Form 709, the per-donee exclusion doubles to $30,000 *(39.2)* . If your gift exceeds the annual exclusion, a special gift tax rule allows you to elect on Form 709 (annual gift tax and generation-skipping transfer tax return) to treat contributions of up to five times the annual exclusion as if they were made over five years. Thus, for 2018, you can elect to treat QTP contributions of up to $75,000

 *Legislative Alert*

**Tuition for Elementary and Secondary School**

For 2018, a distribution from a 529 plan to pay tuition up to $10,000 per beneficiary for public, private, or religious elementary or secondary school is tax free.

(five times the $15,000 exclusion) as if the contributions were made ratably over five years, and this is doubled to $150,000 if your spouse elects to split your gifts. If the election is made, the reportable gift on Form 709 for 2018 is (1) 20% of the QTP contributions up to the $75,000/$150,000 limit, allowing that amount to be offset by the annual exclusion, plus (2) the amount of any contribution exceeding the $75,000/$150,000 limit.

## 33.6 Distributions From Qualified Tuition Programs (Section 529 Plans)

The portion of a QTP distribution that is allocable to a recovery of contributions to the plan (basis) is not taxable. This is true whether the plan is a state QTP or a private educational institution QTP. A beneficiary who receives a distribution of earnings from a state or private QTP to pay qualified education costs does not have to include the earnings in income if the total distribution does not exceed "adjusted qualified education expenses" for the year, as discussed below in "Figuring the taxable portion of a distribution from a QTP."

On Form 1099-Q, which you should receive from the plan paying the distribution, the gross distribution in Box 1 is divided between earnings in Box 2 and the return of investment (or basis) in Box 3.

**Qualified higher education expenses.** For purposes of figuring if part of a distribution from a QTP is taxable (*see* below), qualified higher education costs are tuition, fees, books, supplies, and equipment required for enrollment or attendance at an eligible educational institution, which is any college, university, vocational school, or other postsecondary school eligible to participate in federal student aid programs. Qualified expenses also include the purchase of computer or peripheral equipment, software, and internet access.

Reasonable room and board costs for a designated beneficiary who is at least a half-time student also qualify. The limit that is considered reasonable for room and board expenses is the greater of the room and board allowance determined by the eligible institution for federal financial aid purposes or the actual amount charged for a student residing in housing that is owned and operated by the eligible educational institution. In the case of a special needs beneficiary, the definition of qualifying expenses includes all expenses that are necessary for that person's enrollment or attendance at an eligible institution.

**Qualified elementary and secondary school tuition.** The amount of qualified expenses is limited to tuition at a public, private, or religious elementary or secondary school (K-12). The $10,000 cap applies per beneficiary, not per account. So if a child is a beneficiary of more than one 529 plan, only a maximum of $10,000 can be excluded from gross income in 2018 (assuming that tuition is at least equal to the distribution).

**Figuring the taxable portion of a distribution from a QTP.** Whether or not a distribution of earnings from a QTP is taxable depends on whether the distribution exceeds adjusted qualified education expenses. The qualified education expenses paid during the year must be reduced by any tax-free assistance such as scholarships, Pell grants, veterans' assistance, and employer-paid expenses. If an American Opportunity or Lifetime Learning credit is claimed for the year of the distribution, the expenses taken into account in determining the credit also reduce qualified education expenses. If after the reductions the resulting adjusted qualified education expenses equal or exceed the total QTP distribution, the entire distribution is tax free. If after the reductions the resulting adjusted qualified education costs are less than the total QTP distribution, part of the earnings (shown in Box 2 of Form 1099-Q) is taxable. The Example below illustrates the computation of the taxable amount.

If earnings are taxable, a 10% "additional tax" may also be due, but there are exceptions for distributions that are taxable merely because qualified expenses had to be reduced by tax-free education assistance or expenses taken into account in figuring an American Opportunity or Lifetime Learning credit. The additional tax is figured on Form 5329.

**Coordination with Coverdell ESA distributions.** If distributions from both a QTP and a Coverdell ESA *(33.11)* are received in the same year and the total distributions exceed the adjusted qualified education expenses, the expenses must be allocated between the distributions. Assume that in the example below Marta had withdrawn $3,000 from her QTP and $600 from her Coverdell ESA instead of taking the entire amount from her QTP. Marta would allocate $1,250 of the expenses to the QTP distribution ($3,000 QTP / $3,600 total distribution × $1,500 expenses = $1,250), and $250 of the expenses to the ESA ($600 ESA/$3,600 distribution × $1,500 expenses = $250). She would then figure the taxable portion of earnings from each distribution based on the allocable $1,250 or $250 of expenses.

**Contributor's loss on QTP investment.** If the entire account is distributed and the total investment in the account has not been recovered, the contributor cannot claim a loss because of the suspension of the miscellaneous itemized deduction subject to the 2% of AGI floor for 2018 through 2025.

Changing the designated beneficiary or rollover of QTP distribution. The QTP owner can instruct the trustee of the account to change the designated beneficiary with no tax consequences. Similarly, a distribution from a 529 plan can be rolled over tax free to a different plan for the same beneficiary within 60 days after receipt of the distribution, or the rollover can be to a QTP for a member of the original beneficiary's family, including his or her spouse. For each beneficiary, only one rollover is allowed within a 12-month period.

*Planning Reminder*

**Rollover to ABLE Account Barred**

You can now make a tax-free rollover from a 529 plan to an ABLE account if the ABLE account is owned by the same designated beneficiary of the 529 plan.

---

### EXAMPLE

In 2010, Marta's parents opened a savings QTP maintained by their state government. Over the years they contributed $18,000 to the account. The total balance in the account is $27,000 in June 2018 when a $3,600 distribution from the plan is made to Marta. In the summer of 2018, Marta enrolled in college and had $8,500 of qualified education expenses for the rest of the year. Marta was awarded a $3,000 scholarship. On their 2018 return, Marta's parents claimed an American Opportunity credit of $2,500 (the maximum credit per student *(33.8)*.

Before Marta can determine the taxable portion of her withdrawal, she must reduce her total qualified education expenses. Note that the reduction for the American Opportunity credit is $4,000, as $4,000 of expenses are taken into account in figuring a $2,500 credit *(33.8)*.

| | |
|---|---|
| Total qualified education expenses | $8,500 |
| *Less:* Tax-free scholarship | – 3,000 |
| *Less:* Expenses taken into account in figuring American Opportunity credit | – 4,000 |
| Equals: Adjusted qualified education expenses (AQEE) | $1,500 |

Since Marta's adjusted qualified expenses of $1,500 are less than the $3,600 QTP distribution, she must pay tax on the part of the distributed earnings that is not allocable to the expenses. She received a Form 1099-Q that showed that $2,400 of the QTP distribution was a recovery of basis and $1,200 was earnings. Marta figures the taxable part of distributed earnings as follows:

1. The tax-free portion of the earnings is $500: $1,200 distributed earnings × $1,500 (AQEE)/ $3,600 distribution.

2. The balance of the earnings, or $700 ($1,200 – $500), is taxable. Marta must report it as "other income" on Schedule 1 of Form 1040.

---

## 33.7 Education Tax Credits

There are two tax credits for higher education tuition and qualified fees: The American Opportunity credit and the Lifetime Learning credit. Both credits are figured on Form 8863. You may not claim both credits for the same student for the same year.

The maximum American Opportunity credit is $2,500 per eligible student for qualified expenses in the first four years of post-secondary education. 40% of the credit is generally refundable, meaning that it is allowed even if it exceeds your tax liability. *See 33.8* for details on the American Opportunity credit.

*Law Alert*

### Form 1098-T Needed to Claim Education Credit

Form 1098-T is required to support any claim for the American Opportunity credit *(33.8)* or Lifetime Learning credit *(33.9)*, unless the IRS provides an exception; *see* the Form 8863 instructions. However, as the text below points out *(see* "Form 1098-T" on this page), Form 1098-T may not provide you with all the information you need to figure a credit on Form 8863.

Unlike the American Opportunity credit, the Lifetime Learning credit may be claimed for higher education costs beyond the fourth year of post-secondary education and for non-degree courses that enable the student to acquire or improve job skills. Only tuition and fees/expenses required for enrollment or attendance qualify. The maximum Lifetime Learning credit is $2,000 annually, regardless of how many students you pay expenses for. *See 33.9* for details on the Lifetime Learning credit.

A phaseout rule based on modified adjusted gross income (MAGI), may limit or even eliminate both credits. However, the American Opportunity credit phases out over a higher MAGI range *(33.8)* than the Lifetime Learning credit *(33.9)*.

Some of the qualification rules for the American Opportunity and Lifetime Learning credits are the same and these are discussed below.

## Rules Applicable to Both the American Opportunity Credit and Lifetime Learning Credit

**Married persons filing separately are not eligible.** If you are married at the end of the year, you must file jointly to claim either the American Opportunity credit or the Lifetime Learning credit.

**Borrowed funds used to pay expenses.** You can claim either the American Opportunity credit or the Lifetime Learning credit for eligible expenses paid with loan proceeds. If loan proceeds are sent directly to the educational institution, they are not considered paid until the institution credits the student's account.

**Prepaid expenses.** Your American Opportunity or Lifetime Learning credit for 2018 is based on qualified expenses you paid in 2018 for academic periods beginning in 2018, as well as 2018 payments of qualified expenses for academic periods beginning in the first three months of 2018. If you made a payment in 2018 for academic periods beginning after March 2019, the payment is not eligible for a 2018 credit and it also will not be eligible for a 2019 credit.

**Eligible students at eligible educational institutions.** To claim an American Opportunity credit or a Lifetime Learning credit you must pay qualified expenses for yourself, your spouse, or dependents claimed as exemptions on your return. The expenses must be for courses at eligible educational institutions. Specific student eligibility requirements for the American Opportunity credit are discussed at *33.8*. An eligible educational institution is any accredited public, nonprofit, or proprietary college, university, vocational school, or other postsecondary institution eligible to participate in the student aid programs administered by the U.S. Department of Education.

**Qualified expenses.** For both credits, qualified expenses include tuition, student activity fees that are required of all students for enrollment or attendance, and course-related books, supplies, and equipment that must be purchased from the educational institution as a condition of enrollment or attendance. Other required course materials, such as books or equipment bought privately, qualify for the American Opportunity credit but not the Lifetime Learning credit. Expenses for sports or hobby-related courses that are not part of the student's degree program do not qualify for the American Opportunity credit but such non-degree courses qualify for the Lifetime Learning credit if they help the student acquire or improve job skills. Room and board, insurance, medical expenses, transportation, and other personal expenses are not qualified expenses for either credit.

For purposes of figuring either credit, qualified expenses must be reduced by tax-free scholarships, Pell grants, educational assistance from the VA (Department of Veterans Affairs) or employer-provided educational assistance *(3.7)*.

**Form 1098-T.** On Form 1098-T for 2018, the educational institution must report to the enrolled student the total payments received in 2018 for qualified tuition and related expenses (Box 1). The Box 1 amount is after any reduction for reimbursements or refunds made in 2018. Any scholarships or grants that could reduce the allowable credit are shown in Box 5. Your credit for 2018 must be based on payments you actually made in 2018, or payments made by your child or a third party that you are deemed to have paid (*see* next paragraph), which may *not* be reflected on Form 1098-T. For years before 2018, educational institutions could report on Form 1098-T the total amounts billed for qualified expenses instead of the total payments received; but starting in 2018, the option to report the amounts billed is no longer allowed, and educational institutions that do not provide in Box 1 the total payments received will be subject to a penalty.

**Who can claim a credit for expenses paid by your child or by a third party?** Before 2018, a dependent's expenses were treated as the expenses of the taxpayer who claimed an exemption for the dependent. Although exemptions are not deductible for 2018 through 2025 *(21.1)*, the student's qualified expenses are still treated as having been paid by the taxpayer who claims the student as a dependent *(21.2)*.

For example, if your child is an eligible student and pays qualified expenses in 2018 or the expenses are paid by a third party (such as by the child's grandparent or under a court-approved divorce decree) you are treated as paying the expenses if you claim the student as your dependent and only you can claim a credit for those expenses. If no one claims the student as a dependent, only the student can claim the credit.

**Double benefits not allowed.** You may not claim an American Opportunity credit and the Lifetime Learning credit for the same student for the same year. If you claim either credit, you may not claim the above-the-line tuition and fees deduction (assuming it is extended for 2018) *(33.12)* for the same student for the same year.

You may be able to receive a tax-free distribution from either a Coverdell ESA or a state qualified tuition program (QTP) in the same year that you claim an American Opportunity credit or Lifetime Learning credit. The expenses taken into account as the basis of an American Opportunity or Lifetime Learning credit reduce eligible expenses for purposes of figuring the tax-free part of an ESA or state QTP distribution.

**Recapture of credit.** If you claim a credit and after you file your return for that year you receive tax-free educational assistance for the prior year or receive a refund of an expense used to figure the prior-year credit, you have to refigure the original credit. If the refund or assistance would have reduced the original credit, the amount of the reduction must be added to your tax liability for the year you receive the refund or assistance; *see* the Form 8863 instructions.

## 33.8 American Opportunity Credit

You may claim an American Opportunity credit on Form 8863 if you pay qualified tuition and fees for an eligible student in the first four years of college or other post-secondary institution and the credit is not barred by the phaseout rule (see below).

A student is an eligible student for purposes of the credit only if all of the following requirements are met: (1) the student must be enrolled in one of the first four years of postsecondary education, (2) the student is enrolled in a program that leads to a degree, certificate, or other recognized educational credential, (3) the student is taking at least one-half of the normal full-time workload for his or her course of study for at least one academic period beginning during the calendar year, (4) both the taxpayer claiming the credit and the student have a TIN by the due date of the return (see the Law Alert on this page), and (5) the student does not have any felony conviction (state or federal) for possessing or distributing a controlled substance as of the end of the tax year.

Even if the above five requirements are met, a student is not eligible for the American Opportunity credit if the credit, together with its predecessor the Hope Scholarship credit, was claimed for any four years preceding the current year. For example, a 2018 American Opportunity credit cannot be claimed by anyone for a student if the American Opportunity credit and/or the Hope Scholarship was claimed for that student for any four tax years before 2018.

To claim the maximum credit of $2,500 for an eligible student, you must pay at least $4,000 in qualified expenses for that student. For each eligible student, the American Opportunity credit is 100% of the first $2,000 and 25% of the next $2,000 (for a maximum of $2,500) of tuition, student-activity fees that are required as a condition

*Law Alert*

**TIN Needed by Filer and Student by Return Due Date**

The American Opportunity credit cannot be claimed by a taxpayer who does not have a taxpayer identification number (TIN) by the due date of the return including extensions. This is your Social Security number, or an ITIN if not eligible for a Social Security number. The student also must have a TIN by the due date of the return (with extensions).

*Law Alert*

**Preparer's Due Diligence Requirement**

Paid preparers must complete Form 8867, which is a due diligence checklist, to ensure that a taxpayer is eligible for the American Opportunity credit.

of enrollment or attendance, and books, supplies, and equipment needed for courses. The books, supplies, and equipment qualify for the credit whether or not they had to be purchased from the educational institution.

Keep in mind that the qualified expenses eligible for the credit are reduced by tax-free educational assistance, including the tax-free part of a Pell grant or other scholarship or fellowship, tax-free employer-provided assistance *(3.7)*, and VA educational assistance. The reduction of the expenses by the tax-free educational assistance could eliminate much or all of the credit. You have the option of allocating part of a Pell grant to room and board, or other education costs that do not qualify for the credit. The amount allocated to the room and board would be included in the student's gross income rather than be a tax-free scholarship, but the allocated amount would not reduce the expenses eligible for the credit. *See* the instructions to Form 8863 for further details.

**Phaseout of credit depends on MAGI.** The tentative credit (100% of the first $2,000 and 25% of the next $2,000 of qualified expenses) is phased out over a modified adjusted gross income (MAGI) range of $80,000–$90,000 if you are single, head of household, or a qualifying widow/widower, or $160,000–$180,000 if married filing jointly. You are not allowed any credit if your MAGI is $90,000 or more, or $180,000 or more on a joint return. The example below illustrates the application of the phaseout.

Modified adjusted gross income is the same as adjusted gross income (AGI) unless you are claiming the foreign earned income exclusion *(36.3)* or foreign housing exclusion or deduction *(36.4)*, or the exclusions for income from Puerto Rico *(36.10)* or American Samoa *(36.9)*. If so, adjusted gross income is increased by such amounts on Form 8863.

**Refundable and nonrefundable parts of the credit.** After applying the phaseout rule, 40% of the allowable credit is refundable, meaning that you claim it on your return as if it were a tax payment, like withholding, that you get back even if it exceeds your tax liability for the year. However, none of the credit is refundable if you are under age 24 with investment income subject to the kiddie tax *(24.2)*.

The balance of the credit (60% unless the kiddie tax applies) is a nonrefundable credit that offsets your regular tax plus AMT (minus certain credits). The Form 8863 instructions have a credit limit worksheet for applying the tax liability limitation.

For example, assume that after applying the phaseout rule, you are allowed a $2,500 credit. 40% of the $2,500, or $1,000, is a refundable credit. The $1,500 balance is a nonrefundable credit that offsets your total tax liability but may not exceed that liability. Assume your regular tax plus AMT liabilities total $1,300. Your nonrefundable credit is reduced from $1,500 to $1,300. You may claim a $1,000 refundable credit and a $1,300 nonrefundable credit. Also *see* the following example for how the refundable and nonrefundable portions of the credit are figured after application of the phaseout rule.

> **EXAMPLE**
>
> Ron and Jackie are married and file jointly. In 2018, they pay $7,000 in qualifying college tuition and fees for their son Leo, and $8,500 for their daughter Ally. Leo and Ally both meet the tests for eligible students, and both are claimed as dependents on Ron and Jackie's joint return for 2018. Their joint return MAGI for 2017 is $163,000. A tentative American Opportunity credit of $5,000, $2,500 for each child *(33.8)*, is allowed on Form 8863 prior to application of the phaseout rule. The phaseout rule reduces their credit to $4,250. Their excess MAGI of $3,000 ($163,000 MAGI − $160,000 phaseout threshold on joint return) is 15% of the $20,000 phaseout range, so 15% of the tentative $5,000 credit, or $750, is phased out, and 85%, or $4,250 (85% of $5,000), is allowed.
>
> Of the $4,250 allowed by the phaseout rule, 40%, or $1,700, is a refundable credit, which Ron and Jackie enter on Line 17c of Form 1040. The $2,550 credit balance ($4,250 − $1,700) is allowed as a nonrefundable credit on Schedule 3 of Form 1040, assuming their tax liability is at least much, as figured in the credit limit worksheet in the Form 8863 instructions.

# 33.9 Lifetime Learning Credit

You may claim on Form 8863 a Lifetime Learning credit of up to $2,000 for the total qualified expenses paid for yourself, your spouse, or your dependents enrolled in eligible educational institutions *(33.7)* during the year, subject to the income phaseout (see below). The credit is nonrefundable, meaning that it cannot exceed your regular tax plus AMT liability. In addition to tuition, the only qualified expenses are student activity fees and course-related books, supplies, and equipment that must be paid to the educational institution as a condition of enrollment or attendance.

In contrast to the American Opportunity credit, the Lifetime Learning credit does not have a degree requirement or a workload requirement. The credit may be claimed for one or more courses at an eligible educational institution that are either part of a post-secondary degree program or part of a nondegree program taken to acquire or improve job skills. The Lifetime Learning credit is not limited to students in the first four years of postsecondary education, as is the American Opportunity credit. There is no limit on the number of years for which the Lifetime Learning credit can be claimed.

The Lifetime Learning credit for any year is 20% of the first $10,000 paid in that year for qualified expenses for all eligible students. Thus, the maximum Lifetime Learning credit you may claim for 2018 is $2,000 (20% of $10,000), even if you paid qualified expenses for more than one eligible student. The $2,000 maximum may be reduced because of the income-based phaseout or because the allowable credit (after the phaseout) exceeds your tax liability. Under current law, both the credit percentage (20%) and the expense limit ($10,000) are fixed and not eligible for an inflation adjustment.

For students within the first four years of post-secondary education in 2018, both the Lifetime Learning credit and the American Opportunity credit are potentially available, but you cannot elect both credits for the same student and the American Opportunity credit is more advantageous. For one student, the maximum Lifetime Learning credit is $2,000 and the maximum American Opportunity credit is $2,500, and if you paid qualified expenses for more than one eligible student, the overall Lifetime Learning credit you may claim remains $2,000 regardless of the number of students, whereas the American Opportunity credit is up to $2,500 per eligible student *(33.8)*. In addition, a more favorable phaseout range applies to the American Opportunity credit and 40% of the American Opportunity credit is refundable *(33.8)*, whereas the Lifetime Learning credit is nonrefundable.

**Phaseout of credit for 2018.** The tentative Lifetime Learning credit (20% of the first $10,000 of qualified expenses) is phased out for 2018 if modified adjusted gross income (MAGI; same definition as at *33.8*) is between $57,000 and $67,000 and you file as single, head of household, or qualifying widow/widower, or between $114,000 and $134,000 on a joint return. No credit is allowed for 2018 once MAGI reaches $67,000, or $137,000 on a joint return. The example below illustrates the application of the phaseout.

**Tax liability limitation.** The Lifetime Learning credit allowed after applying the phaseout rule is a nonrefundable credit that is allowed only to the extent of your regular tax and AMT liability (minus certain credits). The Form 8863 instructions have a credit limit worksheet for applying the tax liability limitation.

 *Law Alert*

**Credit Denial Could Lead to Future Disallowance**

If the American Opportunity credit is denied by the IRS, you may have to recertify on Form 8862 your eligibility for future credits. However, if the credit is denied because you recklessly or intentionally disregarded the rules, you will not be allowed to claim the credit for the next two years, and if you fraudulently claimed it, the disallowance period increases to 10 years.

---

### EXAMPLE

John, unmarried, pays $6,400 in qualified tuition and fees in 2018 for courses to improve his job skills. His MAGI for 2018 is $59,000. His tentative Lifetime Learning credit *(33.9)* before taking into account the phaseout is $1,280 (20% of $6,400). After applying the phaseout rule on Form 8863, John is allowed a Lifetime Learning credit of $1,024. His excess MAGI of $2,000 ($59,000 MAGI – $57,000 phaseout threshold for single filer) is 20% of the $10,000 phaseout range, so 20% of the tentative $1,280 credit, or $256, is phased out. The other 80%, or $1,024, is allowed as a nonrefundable credit on Schedule 3 of Form 1040, assuming it is less than his tax liability as figured in the credit limit worksheet in the Form 8863 instructions.

## 33.10 Contributing to a Coverdell Education Savings Account (ESA)

A Coverdell Education Savings Account, or ESA, is a trust or custodial account set up specifically for the purpose of paying the qualified education expenses of the designated beneficiary of the account. A contribution cannot be made for a beneficiary after he or she reaches age 18 unless the beneficiary is a special needs beneficiary, as discussed below. Contributions must be in cash. Coverdell Education Savings Accounts were formerly known as Education IRAs.

**Contribution deadline.** The deadline for making a contribution for any year is the due date of your return for that year (not including extensions). You can make a contribution to a Coverdell ESA up until April 15, 2019, and designate it as a contribution for 2018.

**Two annual contribution limits.** The maximum annual cash contribution that can be made for a designated beneficiary is $2,000. The $2,000 limit applies to the total contributions for each designated beneficiary for the year. For example, if you and several family members would each like to contribute to a Coverdell ESA for your child, the total amount of 2018 contributions that can be made for your child is $2,000, no matter how many Coverdell ESAs have been set up or how many persons contribute.

Each contributor is also subject to a $2,000 annual contribution limit for each beneficiary, but the $2,000 limit can be reduced by the phaseout rule. The $2,000 per beneficiary limit is reduced if your modified adjusted gross income (MAGI) is between $95,000 and $110,000, or between $190,000 and $220,000 if you are married filing jointly. You may not contribute to any beneficiary's Coverdell ESA if your MAGI is $110,000 or more, or $220,000 or more if filing a joint return. These phaseout ranges are not adjusted for inflation. For most individuals, MAGI is the same as adjusted gross income (AGI), but if the foreign earned income exclusion or an exclusion of income from Puerto Rico or American Samoa is claimed, the exclusion is added back to AGI.

For example, assume you are single and have MAGI of $96,500 for 2018. Since your MAGI exceeds the phaseout threshold of $95,000 by $1,500 and the phaseout range is $15,000, 10% ($1,500/$15,000) of your contribution limit or $200 (10% of $2,000) is phased out. For 2018, you may contribute up to $1,800 for each Coverdell ESA beneficiary. If you contribute $1,800 for a beneficiary, others can contribute no more than $200 for that beneficiary for that year, as contributions for a beneficiary may not exceed $2,000 from all sources.

The Coverdell ESA beneficiary must pay a 6% excise tax on Form 5329 if total contributions to his or her ESAs for the year exceed $2,000, or the contributions exceed the reduced limits allowed to contributors under the phaseout rule. The penalty is imposed on the beneficiary and not the contributors. The excise tax does not apply if the excess contributions (and any earnings) are withdrawn before the first day of the sixth month (June 1) of the following year. The withdrawn earnings are taxable to the beneficiary for the year in which the excess contribution was made.

**Special needs beneficiary.** Contributions to a Coverdell ESA for a special needs beneficiary may be made even if he or she is over age 18.

## 33.11 Distributions From Coverdell ESAs

A designated beneficiary of a Coverdell ESA is not taxed on withdrawals that do not exceed qualified education expenses for that year. If withdrawals were made in 2018 and the total exceeds the qualified education expenses (*see* below) for 2018, a portion of the withdrawals is taxable to the beneficiary. The distribution will be reported to the beneficiary and the IRS on Form 1099-Q. The taxable portion is the amount of the excess withdrawal allocable to earnings; *see* the Example below and the worksheet in IRS Publication 970.

**Qualified education expenses.** In addition to qualified higher education expenses (as defined at *33.6* for QTPs), qualified expenses for ESA distribution purposes include contributions to a QTP *(33.5)* on behalf of the ESA beneficiary. Also qualifying are elementary and secondary education expenses, kindergarten through grade 12. The elementary or secondary school may be a public, private, or religious school. Eligible expenses for elementary and secondary school students include tuition, fees, academic tutoring, books, supplies, special services for special needs beneficiaries, computers and peripheral equipment, Internet access, and software. Software designed for sports or hobbies must be predominately educational in nature. Qualified expenses also include room and board, uniforms, transportation, and supplementary items and services including extended day programs required or provided by the school.

**Coordination with education credits.** If an American Opportunity credit or Lifetime Learning credit is claimed for 2018, then in figuring the tax-free portion of a 2018 Coverdell ESA distribution, qualified Coverdell ESA expenses must be reduced by the expenses taken into account when figuring the credit.

Figuring the tax-free and taxable part of a distribution. If the adjusted qualified education expenses (AQEE) of the beneficiary equal or exceed the distribution, the entire distribution is tax free. If a distribution exceeds the AQEE, then part of the earnings included in the distribution is taxable. To determine the amount of AQEE, reduce the total qualified education expenses (defined above) by any tax-free educational assistance such as excludable scholarships, Pell grants, veteran's educational assistance or employer-provided educational assistance. Any expenses taken into account when figuring an American Opportunity credit or Lifetime Learning credit further reduce qualified expenses. The balance of qualifying expenses after subtracting tax-free educational assistance and credit-related expenses is the beneficiary's AQEE. The Example below shows how the taxable portion of the distribution is determined when the total distribution exceeds the AQEE.

**Additional tax on taxable distributions.** Generally, a taxable distribution is subject to a 10% additional tax, which is figured on Form 5329. However, the 10% additional tax does not apply to distributions that are: (1) made to a beneficiary (or to the estate of the designated beneficiary) on or after the death of the designated beneficiary, (2) made because the designated beneficiary is disabled, (3) taxable because the designated beneficiary received a tax-free scholarship or educational assistance allowance that equals or exceeds the distribution, or (4) taxable only because the qualified ESA education expenses were reduced by expenses used in figuring an American Opportunity or Lifetime Learning credit.

The 10% additional tax also does not apply to the withdrawal of an excess contribution (and allocable earnings before June 1 of the following year.

**Age 30 duration rule.** If there are assets remaining in a Coverdell ESA when the designated beneficiary reaches age 30, the beneficiary must withdraw the assets within 30 days, unless he or she is a special needs beneficiary. The duration of the account can be extended by changing the designated beneficiary or rolling over the account to a member of the beneficiary's family who is under age 30; *see* below.

**Rollovers and other transfers.** Withdrawn assets may be rolled over tax free from one Coverdell ESA to another for the benefit of the same beneficiary or a member of the beneficiary's family if the recipient is under age 30. For example, if a beneficiary still has money in his or her account upon graduation from college, the Coverdell ESA can be rolled over tax free to the Coverdell ESA of a younger sibling. The withdrawal is considered rolled over if it is paid to another Coverdell ESA within 60 days. Only one rollover per Coverdell ESA is allowed during the 12-month period ending on the date of the payment or withdrawal. For rollover purposes, members of the beneficiary's family include the beneficiary's spouse, child, grandchild, stepchild, brother, sister (and a sibling's son or daughter), half-sister, half-brother, stepbrother, stepsister, father, mother (and siblings of parents), grandfather, grandmother, stepfather, stepmother, in-laws, the spouses of any of the above, and first cousins.

The designated beneficiary can be changed to a member of the beneficiary's family (included in the above list) with no tax consequences if the new beneficiary is under age 30. The new beneficiary will have to withdraw the account balance no later than 30 days after reaching age 30, unless he or she is a special needs beneficiary.

**Filing Tip**

**Coordination with Education Credits**

An American Opportunity credit or Lifetime Learning credit may be claimed for 2018 even if you exclude from 2018 income a Coverdell ESA distribution, as long as the distribution does not cover the same expenses for which a credit is claimed.

*Law Alert*

**Additional Tax Exception for Service Academy Appointees**

If a designated beneficiary is appointed to the U.S. Military Academy, Naval Academy, Air Force Academy, Coast Guard Academy, or Merchant Marine Academy, a distribution is not subject to the 10% additional tax to the extent of the costs of "advanced education" at such academy (as defined by Section 2005(d)(3) of Title 10, United States Code).

If the beneficiary dies before age 30, the account balance generally must be distributed to the beneficiary's estate within 30 days of the date of death. However, if the Coverdell ESA is transferred to a surviving spouse or other family member (defined above) who is under age 30, the account may be maintained until he or she reaches age 30. The age 30 limitation will not apply if the new beneficiary is a special needs beneficiary.

---

### EXAMPLE

Bianca Jane had $6,200 of qualified higher education expenses in 2018, her first year of college. She paid her college expenses from a variety of sources: a partial scholarship (excluded from gross income) of $1,500, a $1,000 Coverdell ESA withdrawal, a $1,500 gift from her parents, and $2,200 of earnings from a part-time job.

Of her $6,200 of qualified expenses, $4,300 was tuition and required fees that also qualified for an American Opportunity credit. Bianca Jane's parents claimed the maximum $2,500 American Opportunity credit on their 2018 tax return *(33.8)*.

Before Bianca Jane can determine the taxable portion of her ESA withdrawal, she must reduce her total qualified higher education expenses. Note that the reduction for the American Opportunity credit is $4,000, as $4,000 of expenses are taken into account in figuring a $2,500 credit *(33.8)*.

| | |
|---|---|
| Total qualified higher education expenses | $6,200 |
| *Less:* Tax-free education benefits | − 1,500 |
| *Less:* Expenses taken into account in figuring American Opportunity credit | − 4,000 |
| Equals: Adjusted qualified education expenses (AQEE) | $700 |

Since Bianca Jane's AQEE of $700 are less than the $1,000 Coverdell ESA withdrawal, part of the withdrawal will be taxable. The balance in Bianca Jane's account at the end of 2018 was $1,800. Total contributions were $2,500. The Form 1099-Q sent to Bianca Jane shows that $893 of the $1,000 withdrawal is allocable to contributions (basis) and $107 to earnings. She must include $32 of the $107 earnings in her income, figured as follows:

1. The tax-free portion of the earnings used for qualified expenses is $75: $107 earnings × ($700 AQEE ÷ $1,000 distribution).
2. The balance of the earnings, or $32 ($107 − $75), is taxable, and must be reported as "other income" on Schedule 1 of Form 1040.

If Form 1099-Q had not provided Bianca with the breakdown between earnings and basis, she would need to rely on records showing her unrecovered contributions (basis) in order to figure the taxable part of the distribution. For example, Bianca's records show that total contributions to her account (none of which have previously been distributed) were $2,500. Dividing the $2,500 contributions by $2,800 (the $1,800 year-end account balance plus the $1,000 distribution) and multiplying the result by the $1,000 distribution gives the $893 basis portion of the distribution ($1,000 × $2,500 ÷ $2,800 = $893). The balance of the distribution, or $107 ($1,000 − $893), is the earnings portion of the distribution.

---

## 33.12 Tuition and Fees Deduction

*Caution*: **The deduction for tuition and fees expired at the end of 2017.** When this book was completed, it was unclear if Congress would extend the deduction to 2018. Given the possibility that there will be an extension, we are providing below the pre-2018 rules for the deduction on the assumption that those same rules will apply if the deduction is extended. *See* the *e-Supplement* at *jklasser.com* for a legislation update.

If the deduction is extended to 2018, then depending on your income, you may be able to deduct up to $2,000 or $4,000 of qualifying higher education tuition and fees paid during 2018. The deduction is figured on Form 8917 and claimed directly from gross income on Form 1040, whether or not you itemize deductions. You generally must have received a Form 1098-T from an eligible educational institution in order to claim the deduction.

You may not claim the deduction for expenses of a dependent for whom an American Opportunity credit or Lifetime Learning credit is claimed, even if the credit is claimed by someone else. You may not claim the credit for some of an eligible student's expenses and the deduction for the balance. If you qualify for both, you must choose between the credit and the deduction. Generally, a credit provides a larger tax savings than a deduction, but if you would be allowed only a partial credit because of the income-based phaseout *(33.8, 33.9)*, you may be able to obtain a larger tax benefit from the tuition and fees deduction.

**Deduction amount based on income.** If you are single, head of household, or a qualifying widow/widower, your maximum tuition and fees deduction is $4,000 if your 2018 modified adjusted gross income (MAGI) does not exceed $65,000, and your maximum deduction is $2,000 if your MAGI is over $65,000 but not more than $80,000. No deduction is allowed if your MAGI is over $80,000.

If you are married filing jointly, your maximum tuition and fees deduction is $4,000 if your MAGI is no more than $130,000, and your maximum deduction is $2,000 if MAGI exceeds $130,000 but is no more than $160,000. No deduction is allowed if MAGI exceeds $160,000.

For purposes of the deduction limitation, MAGI is generally the same as the AGI shown on your return, figured without taking into account the deduction for domestic production activities. You must add back to AGI any exclusion for foreign earned income or income from Puerto Rico or American Samoa, or the foreign housing exclusion or deduction.

**Ineligible taxpayers.** You may not claim the deduction if you are married filing separately. You are also ineligible if you may be claimed as a dependent on another taxpayer's return, whether or not you are actually so claimed.

**Qualified higher education expenses.** Expenses eligible for the deduction are the same as those qualifying for the Lifetime Learning credit *(33.9)*. That is, the deduction is generally limited to tuition and enrollment fees paid to an eligible educational institution for yourself, your spouse or your dependents. Student activity fees and course-related books, supplies and equipment are included only if they must be paid to the school as a condition of enrollment or attendance. Eligible expenses paid in 2018 for an academic period starting in 2018 or in the first three months of 2019 are deductible for 2018. Eligible educational institutions include any college, university, vocational school, or other postsecondary institution eligible to participate in the financial aid programs of the Department of Education.

**Claiming a dependent's expenses.** You can deduct your dependent's eligible expenses if you paid them . You cannot claim the deduction for expenses paid by the dependent or by a third party on behalf of the dependent.

**Deduction affected by excludable education benefits.** Expenses eligible for the deduction are reduced by tax-free scholarships *(33.1)* and other tax-free educational assistance. If you receive tax-free interest from an EE or I savings bond used for tuition *(33.4)*, the excludable interest reduces the expenses eligible for the deduction. A tax-free distribution of earnings from a Coverdell ESA *(33.12)* or a QTP *(33.6)* reduces the deduction-eligible expenses.

**Recapture of deduction.** If after you file your return on which the deduction was claimed you receive tax-free educational assistance for that year or receive a refund of an expense used to figure the deduction, you may have to repay (recapture) all or part of the original deduction. You recapture the deduction to the extent it gave you a tax benefit by reducing your tax. Refigure the original deduction by reducing it by the refunded amount and also refigure tax liability for that year. To the extent of the increase in tax liability, you must include the refunded amount as "Other income" for the year you receive it; *see* IRS Publication 970 for further details.

*Filing Tip*

**Credit or Deduction?**

Assuming that Congress extends the tuition and fees deduction to 2018, you may not claim a tax credit and also the deduction for the same student for 2018. If you paid qualifying education expenses for 2018, check to determine whether or not you can claim either the American Opportunity or Lifetime Learning credit. A credit produces a dollar-for-dollar reduction of your tax liability, while a deduction only reduces your taxable income. Claim the credit if it provides you with a larger tax benefit.

# 33.13 Student Loan Interest Deduction

If you paid interest on a qualified student loan in 2018, you may be able to claim an above-the-line (directly from gross income) deduction of up to $2,500. You should receive a Form 1098-E (or substitute statement) from each lender that received interest payments of $600 or more from you during the year.

**Forgiveness of Student Loans**

Federal student loan debt may be forgiven after 20 or 25 years, depending on when the loan was taken. Public service workers (e.g., teachers, nurses, police) may receive loan forgiveness after 10 years. Loan forgiveness is taxable unless a special exception applies; *see 11.8.*

*Caution*

**Deduction Lost for Student Dependent's Loan**

If your parent or someone else claims you as a dependent on his or her return, you may not deduct interest on your return for student loan interest you paid. Furthermore, the person who claims you as a dependent may not deduct the interest where you are the borrower legally obligated to repay the loan.

Eligibility for the deduction is phased out for 2018 if you have modified adjusted gross income (MAGI, *see* below) between $65,000 and $80,000, or between $135,000 and $165,000 if married filing a 2018 joint return. On a joint return, the deduction limit remains $2,500 even if you and your spouse each pay interest on a qualified student loan. The $2,500 deduction limit is set by statute and is not subject to annual inflation adjustments. If you are claimed as a dependent by another taxpayer, or you are married filing separately, you may not claim the deduction regardless of your income. The deduction is claimed on Schedule 1 of Form 1040 as an above-the-line deduction available even if you do not claim itemized deductions.

**Qualified loans and expenses.** A qualified student loan is one taken out to pay qualified higher education expenses (defined below) for you, your spouse, or a person who was your dependent when you took out the loan. The education expenses must be paid or incurred within a reasonable time before or after the loan was taken out, and the funds obtained must be used toward education furnished while the student is enrolled at least half-time in a program leading to a degree or other recognized educational credential at an eligible educational institution. Eligible institutions are colleges, universities, vocational schools, and other post-secondary educational institutions eligible to participate in Department of Education student aid programs. Graduate school programs are included. Also included are medical internships or residency programs leading to a degree or certificate from an educational institution or hospital offering postgraduate training.

Qualified higher education expenses include tuition, fees, room and board (within the limits at *33.6*), books, equipment, and other necessary expenses such as transportation. These costs must be reduced by:

1. Nontaxable employer-provided educational assistance benefits.
2. Nontaxable Coverdell ESA or QTP distributions.
3. U.S. Savings Bond interest excluded from income because it is used to pay higher education expenses.
4. Qualified tax-free scholarships.
5. Veterans' educational assistance benefits.

Loan origination fees and capitalized interest (unpaid interest that accrues and is added by the lender to the outstanding balance of the loan principal) can be counted as interest. In general, a payment, regardless of its label, is treated first as a payment of interest to the extent that accrued interest remains unpaid, second as a payment of any loan origination fees or capitalized interest, until such amounts are reduced to zero, and, third as a payment of principal.

**Voluntary interest payments are deductible.** You can deduct voluntary payments of interest made before your loan has entered repayment status or while you have a repayment deferment.

**Dependents and married persons filing separately are ineligible.** You may not claim a student loan interest deduction during any year in which someone claims you as a dependent. However, you may deduct interest payments made in a later year when you are no longer claimed as a dependent.

You may not claim a student loan interest deduction for any year in which you are married and file a separate tax return.

**Loans that do not qualify for deduction.** You may not deduct interest paid on a loan from a relative as student loan interest *(5.6)*.

You may not deduct interest on a loan from a qualified employer plan.

You may not treat interest paid on a revolving line of credit as qualified student loan debt unless you use the funds solely to pay qualified higher education costs.

You may not claim a student loan interest deduction for any amount you may deduct under any other tax law provision, for example home mortgage interest. You also cannot use the deduction if you use part of the borrowed money for purposes other than education, for instance to make improvements to your house.

**Phaseout for 2018.** The student loan interest deduction is reduced or eliminated if your modified adjusted gross income (MAGI) exceeds phaseout limits. For 2018, the reduction applies if your MAGI is more than $65,000, or more than $135,000 on a joint return. If MAGI is $80,000 or more, or $165,000 or more on a joint return, you may not claim any deduction for 2018; the deduction is completely phased out. MAGI is the same as the adjusted gross income shown on your return (disregarding student loan interest) unless you claim a deduction for tuition and fees *(33.13)*, the exclusion for foreign earned income *(Chapter 36)*, the domestic production activities deduction *(40.23)*, or certain other items of foreign income or expenses were excluded or deducted from your income. Such items generally must be added back to adjusted gross income.

If your MAGI is within the phaseout range, the phased out amount is figured by multiplying your deductible interest (up to the $2,500 limit) by a fraction, the numerator of which is your MAGI minus the phaseout threshold ($65,000, or $135,000 if married filing jointly), and the denominator of which is the phaseout range of $15,000, or $30,000 if married filing jointly. The result is subtracted from the qualifying student loan interest to get the deductible amount; *see* the Examples below for the computation.

The student loan deduction worksheet in the Form 1040 instructions can be used to figure the phaseout reduction and the amount of your deduction.

---

**EXAMPLES**

1. In 2018 you paid $900 interest on a qualified student loan. You file a joint return and have MAGI of $140,000. Your deduction for 2018 is reduced by $150 under the phaseout rule. You can deduct $750 ($900 – $150).

$$\$900 \times \frac{\$140,000 \text{ MAGI} - \$135,000 \text{ phaseout threshold}}{\$30,000 \text{ phaseout range}} = \$150 \text{ reduction}$$

2. The same facts as in Example 1, except you paid $2,600 interest. The maximum deduction of $2,500 is reduced by $417. You can deduct $2,083 ($2,500 – $417).

$$\$2,500 \times \frac{\$140,000 \text{ MAGI} - \$135,000 \text{ phaseout threshold}}{\$30,000 \text{ phaseout range}} = \$417 \text{ reduction}$$

---

## 33.14 Types of Deductible Work-Related Costs

If you improve your professional skills by attending continuing education or refresher classes, advanced academic courses, or vocational training, you may be able to treat your expenses as a business expense deduction. As a self-employed business owner or professional, allowable expenses are deductible on Schedule C and reduce income subject to self-employment tax *(45.1)* as well as income tax liability. However, as an employee, for 2018 through 2025, no deduction can be claimed for work-related education costs because of the suspension of the miscellaneous itemized deduction for costs exceeding 2% of your adjusted gross income; *see 19.1*.

Keep in mind that tuition and fees (but not transportation and usually not books or supplies) for work-related educational courses may also qualify for the Lifetime Learning credit *(33.9)* or the tuition and fees deduction, assuming the deduction is extended by Congress *(33.12)*. The Lifetime Learning credit, by reducing tax liability rather than taxable income, is more valuable than a deduction for education costs. However, you may be unable to claim the credit because your income exceeds the phaseout limit for the credit *(33.9)*. The tuition and fees deduction, if available *(33.12)*, is an above-the-line deduction that is allowed even if you do not claim itemized deductions.

To deduct education costs on Schedule C (self-employed), you must show that the following conditions are met:

1. You are self-employed;
2. You already meet the minimum requirements of your business or profession;
3. The course maintains or improves your professional skills, or you are required by law to take the course to keep your present salary or position; and
4. The course does not lead to qualification for a new profession or business. The cost of courses preparing you for a new profession is not deductible, even if you take them to improve your skills. This rule prevents the deduction of law school costs. Furthermore, the cost of a bar review course or CPA review course is not deductible because it leads to a new profession as an attorney or CPA. If courses lead to qualification for a new business or profession, no deduction is allowed even if you keep your current position.

If your courses meet the above requirements you may deduct the following education costs on Schedule C if self-employed :

1. Tuition, textbooks, fees, equipment, and supplies required by the courses.
2. Local transportation costs *(33.16)*.
3. Travel to and from a school away from home, and lodging and 50% of meals while at school away from home *(33.16)*. The IRS will not disallow traveling expenses to attend a school away from home or in a foreign country merely because you could have taken the course in a local school. But it may disallow your board and lodging and expenses at the school if your stay lasts longer than a year.

Further details of the deduction requirements are provided in *33.15*.

## 33.15 Work-Related Tests for Education Costs

Educational costs are not deductible on Schedule C (self-employed) if you are inactive in a business or profession. The cost of "brush-up" courses taken in anticipation of resuming work is also not deductible.

You are not considered unemployed when you take courses during a temporary leave of absence lasting one year or less.

**Course must not meet minimum standards.** You may not deduct the cost of courses taken to meet the minimum requirements of your work. The minimum requirements of a position are based on a review of the laws and regulations of the state you live in and the standards of your profession or business.

If minimum standards change after you enter a profession, courses you take to meet the new standards are deductible.

**Course must maintain or improve work skills.** To be deductible, the education must maintain or improve your current work skills. That you are established in your position and that persons in similar positions usually pursue such education indicates that the courses are taken to maintain and improve work skills. However, the IRS may not allow a deduction for a general education course that is a prerequisite for a work-related course.

If the courses lead to a change of your line of work within the same occupation, a deduction for their cost will usually be allowed if your new duties involve the same general type of work. However, if the course leads to qualification for a new profession, the IRS will disallow a deduction even if the course also improves current work skills.

**Courses must not lead to qualification for a new profession.** If a course improves your current work skills but leads to qualification for a new profession, the course is not deductible, even if you have no intention of entering that business or profession. For example, a deduction is not allowed for the cost of law school or medical school courses since they prepare you for a new profession. This is true even if you do not intend to practice medicine or law. The IRS with Tax Court approval has also held that a deduction is not allowed for the cost of college courses that are part of a degree program, such as a bachelor of arts or science degree.

 *Filing Tip*

**Lifetime Learning Credit or Tuition and Fees Deduction**

If you have qualifying work-related education costs, you should determine whether you can claim the Lifetime Learning credit *(33.9)*. Also check to *see* if you are eligible for the above-the-line deduction for tuition and fees *(33.12)*. These tax breaks may be more valuable to you than a business deduction.

If you are practicing your profession, the cost of courses leading to a specialty within that profession is deductible. For example, a practicing attorney may deduct the cost of a master's of law degree program (LLM).

---

### EXAMPLES

1. A practicing dentist returned to school full time to study orthodontics while continuing his practice on a part-time basis. When he finished his training, he limited his work to orthodontics. The IRS ruled he could deduct the cost of his studies. His post-graduate schooling improved his professional skills as a dentist. It did not qualify him for a new profession.

2. A practicing psychiatrist may deduct the cost of attending an accredited psychoanalytic institute to qualify to practice psychoanalysis. A social worker has also been allowed a deduction for the cost of learning psychoanalysis. In one case, the Tax Court allowed a psychiatrist to deduct the cost of personal therapy sessions conducted through telephone conversations and tape cassettes. The court was convinced that the therapy improved his job skills by eliminating psychological blind spots that prevented him from understanding his patients' problems.

3. A licensed practical nurse may not deduct the costs of a college program that qualifies him or her as a "physician's assistant," which is a new business. Physicians' assistants and practical nurses are subject to different registration and certification requirements under state law, and, more importantly, the physician's assistant may perform duties, such as physical examinations and minor surgery, which go beyond practical nursing duties.

4. Edward, a self-employed golf instructor without an undergraduate degree, earned an associate's degree in business from the Golf Academy of the South. The IRS and Tax Court disallowed his deduction for tuition and fees. It does not matter that the courses may have improved his skills as a golf instructor. No deduction was allowed because completing the associate's program was a first step in acquiring a basic undergraduate degree that would qualify Edward for a variety of trades or businesses other than that of a golf instructor.

---

## 33.16 Local Transportation and Travel Away From Home To Take Courses

If you are self-employed and your courses meet the requirements in the preceding two sections *(33.14, 33.15)*, costs of local transportation and travel away from home may be included in the business expense deduction.

**Local transportation expenses.** If your courses qualify for a deduction under *33.15*, you may deduct transportation costs of going from work directly to school. Transportation costs include the actual costs of bus, subway, cab, or other fares, as well as the costs of using your car. According to the IRS, the return trip from school to home is also deductible if you are regularly employed and going to school on a temporary basis. According to the IRS, you are going to school on a temporary basis if your courses are realistically expected to last for one year or less and actually do last no more than one year. This is the same one-year test for determining whether you can deduct the cost of commuting to a "temporary" work location *(20.2)* or living costs while away from home on a "temporary" assignment *(20.9)*. The IRS position is illustrated in the following Examples.

**Using your car.** If you use your own car for transportation to school, you may deduct your actual expenses or use the standard business mileage rate to figure the deductible amount. The standard mileage rate for 2018 is 54.5 cents per mile. Whether you deduct the standard mileage rate or actual expenses, you may also deduct parking fees and tolls.

**Travel and living expenses away from home.** "Away from home" has a special tax meaning *(20.7)*. You are not away from home unless you are away overnight. If you are away from home to attend a qualifying course, you may deduct the cost of travel to and from the site of the course, plus lodging and 50% of meals while you are there.

Expenses of sightseeing, social visiting, and entertaining while taking courses are not deductible. If personal reasons are your main purpose in going to the vicinity of the school, such as to take a vacation, you may deduct only the cost of the courses and your living expenses while attending school. You may not deduct the rest of your travel costs.

To determine the purpose of your trip, an IRS agent will pay close attention to the amount of time devoted to personal activities relative to the time devoted to the courses.

---

### EXAMPLES

1. You drive home from work, and two nights a week for one month you drive from home to attend a refresher course. The course is considered temporary. You may deduct the round-trip transportation costs between home and school. The deduction is allowed regardless of how far you travel.

   If you went directly from work to the school, you may deduct transportation from work to school, and from school to home.

2. On six consecutive Saturdays, which are nonworkdays for you, you drive from home to attend a qualifying course. This is considered a temporary course. You are allowed a deduction for round-trip transportation between home and school, even though you are traveling on a nonworkday.

3. Assume that in Example 1, you took classes twice a week for 15 months instead of one month. The IRS does not consider the course to be temporary. You may deduct the cost of going directly from work to school, but the costs of going between home and school are nondeductible to the extent they exceed the cost of going to school directly from work.

---

**Is travel itself a form of education?** You generally may not deduct the cost of an "educational" trip to another state or country. Although a trip may have educational value, the IRS position is that a specific statute, Code Section 274(m)(2), bars a deduction for travel as a form of education. For example, an architect who travels to Rome to look at buildings usually cannot deduct travel costs as an education expense.

There may be exceptions where specific research can only be accomplished at a particular location, but a trip for "general" educational purposes does not qualify according to the IRS. For example, if the architect takes a course on architecture at a university in Rome (and otherwise meets the requirements outlined earlier in this chapter), then education costs (e.g., tuition, travel costs) may be deductible.

# CHAPTER 34

# Special Tax Rules for Senior Citizens and the Disabled

All of your Social Security benefits are tax free if your "provisional income," explained in *34.3*, is $25,000 or less if you are single, or $32,000 or less if you are married and file a joint return. No more than 50% of your benefits are subject to tax if you file a joint return and your provisional income is over $32,000 but no more than $44,000, or if you are single and your provisional income is over $25,000 but no more than $34,000. When provisional income exceeds $34,000 or $44,000 (depending on your filing status), no more than 85% of your benefits are subject to tax. If you are married and filing separately, and did not live apart for the whole year, you must apply the 85% rate without considering the base amounts. If you are married filing separately and you lived apart the entire year, are a head of household, or are a qualifying widow/widower, use the $25,000 and $34,000 amounts for single persons.

If you are receiving Social Security benefits but continue to earn wages or self-employed income, you must pay FICA taxes or self-employment tax on that income regardless of your age.

If you are on Medicare, be sure you understand the impact of adjusted gross income on your premiums *(34.10)*.

If you are disabled, you may be receiving Social Security and other benefits. The tax rules for Social Security disability payments are the same as for Social Security retirement payments. Other government benefits may be tax free *(34.11)*.

Those who become disabled at a young age may be able to have a special savings account, called an ABLE account, which does not prevent eligibility for government programs, such as Medicaid *(34.12)*.

## 34.1 Senior Citizens Get Certain Filing Breaks

The following special tax rules favor senior citizens:

- **Higher filing thresholds.** If you are single and age 65 or older on or before January 1, 2019, you do not have to file a 2018 return unless your gross income is over $13,600. This is $1,600 more than for younger taxpayers. If you are married and you and your spouse are both age 65 or older, a joint return does not have to be filed unless your gross income is over $26,600, or $25,300 or over if only one of you is age 65 or older; *see* the chart on page 2 for further details.

- **Higher standard deduction.** If you are age 65 or older on or before January 1, 2019, you receive an additional standard deduction allowance if you do not itemize deductions. If you are single you get an additional $1,600 on your 2018 return, or $1,300 if you are married or a qualifying widow/widower *(13.4)*. Your 2018 standard deduction is $13,600 if you are single. If married filing jointly, it is $25,300 if one of you is age 65 or over, or $26,600 if both of you are *(13.4)*.

- **Social Security benefits may be exempt from tax.** The taxable portion of your Social Security benefits may vary from year to year because it depends on an amount called "provisional income" *(34.3)*. If you are married and file jointly, none of your net Social Security benefits are taxable if your provisional income is not more than a base amount of $32,000. The base amount is $25,000 if your filing status is single, head of household, qualifying widow/widower, or you are married filing separately and did not live with your spouse at any time during the year. Married persons who file separately and live together at any time during the year are not allowed any base amount; *see 34.3* for computing taxable Social Security benefits.

- **Tax credit if age 65 or older.** This is a minimal tax credit for taxpayers age 65 or older who receive little or no Social Security or Railroad Retirement benefits and for individuals under age 65 who are totally disabled with extremely low incomes *(34.7)*. If you are single, or married but only you are eligible, and receive more than $416 each month from Social Security, you may not claim the credit. If you are married and both you and your spouse are eligible for the credit and file a joint return, you may not claim the credit if you receive more than $625 each month from Social Security.

## 34.2 Social Security Benefits Subject to Tax

If you received or repaid Social Security benefits in 2018, you will receive Form SSA-1099 from the Social Security Administration, showing the total benefits paid to you and any benefits you repaid to the government in 2018. Box 3 of Form SSA-1099 shows the total benefits paid to you in 2018. This may include, in addition to Social Security retirement benefits, survivor and disability benefits, which are subject to the same tax rules as retirement benefits. Also included in the Box 3 total are amounts withheld from your benefits for Medicare premiums, workers' compensation offset, or attorneys' fees for handling your Social Security claim; these and other withholdings are itemized in the "description" section below Box 3. However, Box 3 does not include Supplemental Security Income (SSI), which is not taxable.

The net benefit shown in Box 5 of Form SSA-1099 (benefits paid less benefits repaid) is the benefit amount used to determine the taxable portion of your benefits (if any) *(34.3)*. Keep Form SSA-1099 for your records; do not attach it to your return.

**Railroad Retirement benefits.** The portion of your Tier 1 Railroad Retirement benefits that is equivalent to Social Security retirement benefits is subject to the computation for determining taxable benefits *(34.3)*. If any part of your 2018 Tier 1 benefits is equivalent to Social Security benefits, you will receive Form RRB-1099 from the government. The net Social Security Equivalent Benefit shown on Form RRB-1099 is the amount used to determine taxable benefits *(34.3)*. Other Tier 1 Railroad Retirement benefits, as well as Tier 2 benefits, are treated as pension income and not as Social Security benefits for tax purposes.

**Benefits paid on behalf of child or incompetent.** If a child is entitled to Social Security benefits, such as after the death of a parent, the benefit is considered to be the child's regardless of who actually receives the payment. Whether the child's benefit is subject to tax will depend on the amount of the child's income.

*Planning Reminder*

**Voluntary Withholding on Social Security Benefits**

You can use your Social Security benefits to meet your estimated and final tax liability by electing on Form W-4V to have tax withheld from benefits at a 7%, 10%, 12%, or 22% rate.

**Medicare premiums deducted from benefits.** The Medicare premiums deducted from your benefits are included in the total for benefits paid in Box 3 of Form SSA-1099. This includes premiums for Medicare Parts B, C and D. The premiums do not reduce the net benefits in Box 5 used to figure taxable benefits *(34.3)*.

**Workers' compensation.** If you are receiving Social Security disability payments and workers' compensation for the same disability, your Social Security benefits may be reduced in order for the total benefits to stay within an overall limit. The combined monthly total of the workers' compensation and Social Security disability cannot exceed 80% of your "average current earnings" before you became disabled. If the total exceeds 80%, your Social Security disability benefits are reduced by the excess amount. The reduction continues until you reach your full retirement age *(34.5)*.

However, when your Social Security disability benefits are reduced under the 80% rule, the amount reported to you in Box 3 of Form SSA-1099 as "benefits paid" includes the reduction. Box 3 will include the reduction (it will be labeled as "workers' compensation offset" in the description section below Box 3) as a "benefit paid" to you although you did not receive it. For purposes of the computation steps to determine taxability of benefits *(34.3)*, you treat the full amount shown in Box 3 as your Social Security benefits.

In several cases, disabled workers whose Social Security disability benefits were reduced because they received workers' compensation argued that since the workers' compensation payments are tax free *(2.13)*, the portion of Social Security benefits not paid to them because of the overall limit should also be tax free. The Tax Court however agreed with the IRS that for purposes of figuring the tax on benefits *(34.3)*, the specific terms of the tax code include the reduction for workers' compensation as a Social Security benefit that must be taken into account.

**Net benefits.** The net benefit shown in Box 5 of Form SSA-1099 is the amount used to determine the taxable portion of your benefits. If Box 5 shows a negative amount (a figure in parentheses), none of your benefits are taxable. If the negative amount is related to Social Security benefits included in gross income in a prior year, you may be entitled to a deduction or a credit; *see* IRS Publication 915 for further instructions on how to figure the deduction or credit when your repayments exceed your gross benefits.

Taxable Social Security benefits are not considered earnings and therefore may not be the basis of an IRA contribution *(8.2)*, earned income credit *(25.6)*, or foreign earned income exclusion *(36.2)*.

**Nonresident aliens.** Unless provided otherwise by tax treaty, 85% of a nonresident alien's Social Security benefits will be subject to the 30% withholding tax imposed on U.S. source income that is not connected with a U.S. trade or business. See IRS Publication 915 for further details.

## 34.3 Computing Taxable Social Security Benefits

To calculate the taxable part of your Social Security benefits you must determine your provisional income (see Worksheet 34-1) and compare it to the base amount and adjusted base amount allowed for your filing status (see *Table 34-1*). Provisional income is not an amount you find on your tax return; it is only relevant to the computation of your Social Security benefits. As detailed below in Worksheet 34-1, provisional income will always be more than the "total income" reported on your return because you have to increase your reported income by 50% of your net Social Security benefits, tax-exempt interest if any, and certain other fringe benefits and above-the-line adjustments claimed on your return.

**Overview of rules for taxation of Social Security benefits.** The benefits that are potentially subject to tax are your net benefits, shown in Box 5 of Form SSA-1099 (or Form RRB-1099). If your provisional income (figured on Worksheet 34-1 below) does not exceed your base amount (from *Table 34-1* below), none of your benefits are taxable. Thus, if you are single and your provisional income does not exceed $25,000, or you are married filing jointly and your provisional income does not exceed $32,000, you are not taxed on any of your Social Security benefits. However, you cannot avoid tax on your benefits if you are married filing separately and you lived with your spouse at any time during the year, because the law does not allow you any base amount or adjusted base amount.

If your provisional income exceeds your $25,000 or $32,000 base amount but does not exceed your $34,000 or $44,000 adjusted base amount *(Table 34-1)*, the taxable amount of benefits will generally equal 50% of the excess of your provisional income over the base amount, and in no event can the taxable amount be more than 50% of your net benefits. Use Worksheet 34-2 to figure the exact amount of your taxable benefits. Example 3 illustrates the computation.

If your provisional income exceeds your $34,000 or $44,000 adjusted base amount, the taxable portion of your benefits depends on the excess, but in no event can the taxable amount exceed 85% of your net benefits. Use Worksheet 34-3 to figure the exact amount of your taxable benefits. Examples 2 and 4 illustrate the computation.

If you are married filing separately and you lived with your spouse at any time during the year, your base amount and adjusted base amount is $0, and you are subject to the most disadvantageous rule for figuring taxable benefits. You must include in your taxable income the lesser of (1) 85% of your net Social Security benefits, or (2) 85% of your provisional income. Use Worksheet 34-4 to figure the exact amount of taxable benefits.

**IRA contributions.** Do not use Worksheet 34-2, Worksheet 34-3 or Worksheet 34-4 to figure your taxable Social Security benefits for 2018 if (1) you made or are planning to make a contribution to a traditional IRA *(8.4)* for 2018, and (2) you or your spouse is an active participant *(8.5)* in an employer plan for 2018. In that case, you must use three worksheets in Appendix B of IRS Publication 590-A. The first worksheet is used to determine the amount of Social Security benefits that would be subject to tax if no IRA deduction were claimed. That taxable Social Security amount (if any) is included in MAGI on the second worksheet in order to figure if your IRA deduction is affected by the deduction phaseout rules *(8.4)* for active plan participants. Finally, the allowable IRA deduction from the second worksheet is included in the third worksheet to compute the taxable portion of your Social Security benefits.

*Caution*

**Married Filing Separately**

If you are married filing separately and you lived with your spouse at any time during the year, you must include in your taxable income the lesser of (1) 85% of your net Social Security benefits, or (2) 85% of your provisional income.

### Table 34-1  Base Amount and Adjusted Base Amount

| Filing Status | Base Amount | Adjusted Base Amount |
| --- | --- | --- |
| Single, head of household, qualifying widow/widower, or married filing separately and you lived apart from your spouse for the entire year | $25,000 | $34,000 |
| Married filing jointly | $32,000 | $44,000 |
| Married filing separately and you lived with your spouse at any time during the year | $0 | $0 |

## Worksheet 34-1 Figure Your Provisional Income

**Figure Your Provisional Income**

1. Enter your net Social Security benefits, the amount shown in Box 5 of all of your Forms SSA-1099 and RRB-1099. If married filing jointly, total the Box 5 amounts for you and your spouse.  1. _____

2. Enter one-half of the net benefits on Line 1 (50% × Line 1).  2. _____

3. Enter the "total income" from your return, shown on Line 6 of Form 1040.  3. _____

4. Enter the tax-exempt interest received for the year, if any (should be included on Line 2a of Form 1040).  4. _____

5. Enter the following amounts, if any: adoption benefits excluded from income (Form 8839), Series EE or I Savings Bond interest excluded from income (Form 8815), foreign earned income exclusion, foreign housing exclusion, foreign housing deduction (from Form 2555), excludable income from Puerto Rico or American Samoa (Form 4563)  5. _____

6. Add Lines 2, 3, 4 and 5. The total is your provisional income if you did not claim any above-the-line deductions on your return (deductions that reduce total income to arrive at adjusted gross income *(12.2)* ). If you claimed above-the-line deductions on Form 1040, go to Line 7.  6. _____

7. Enter the total above-the-line deductions that you claimed on Line 36, Schedule 1 of Form 1040 but do not include (1) the student loan interest deduction, or (2) the tuition and fees deduction if it is extended to 2018 by Congress.  7. _____

8. If there is an amount on Line 7, subtract Line 7 from Line 6. If Line 7 is blank, enter the amount from Line 6. This is your provisional income.  8. _____

## Worksheet 34-2 Figure Your Taxable Benefits if

*Your Provisional Income Exceeds the $25,000 or $32,000 Base Amount But Not the $34,000 or $44,000 Adjusted Base Amount*

1. Subtract your base amount ($25,000 or $32,000; *see Table 34-1*) from your provisional income (Line 8 of Worksheet 34-1) and enter the excess provisional income here.  1. _____

2. Multiply Line 1 by 50%.  2. _____

3. Enter 50% of your net Social Security benefits (Line 2 of Worksheet 34-1).  3. _____

4. The smaller of Line 2 or Line 3 is taxable. Enter the smaller amount as your taxable Social Security benefits here and on Line 5b of Form 1040.  4. _____

## Worksheet 34-3　Figure Your Taxable Benefits if

### Your Provisional Income Exceeds the $34,000 or $44,000 Adjusted Base Amount

1. Subtract your adjusted base amount ($34,000 or $44,000; *see Table 34-1*) from your provisional income (Line 8 of Worksheet 34-1) and enter the excess provisional income here · · · · · · · · 1. _____

2. Multiply Line 1 by 85%. · · · · · · · · 2. _____

3. Enter your net Social Security benefits (Line 1 of Worksheet 34-1). · · · · · · · · 3. _____

4. Multiply Line 3 by 85%. · · · · · · · · 4. _____

5. If Line 4 is more than Line 2, go to Line 6; leave this line blank. If Line 4 is less than or equal to Line 2, 85% of your net Social Security benefits, shown on Line 4, is taxable. This is the maximum amount of benefits that can be taxed under the law. Enter the Line 4 amount as your taxable Social Security benefits here and on Line 5b of Form 1040. Do not complete Lines 6-8. · · · · · · · · 5. _____

6. If Line 5 is blank, enter the smaller of (a) or (b):
   (a) $6,000 if your adjusted base amount is $44,000, or $4,500 if your adjusted base amount is $34,000 (see *Table 34-1*),
   OR
   (b) 50% of your net Social Security benefits (Line 2 of Worksheet 34-1) · · · · · · · · 6. _____

7. Add Line 2 and Line 6. · · · · · · · · 7. _____

8. The smaller of Line 4 or Line 7 is taxable. Enter the smaller amount as your taxable Social Security benefits here and on Line 5b of Form 1040. · · · · · · · · 8. _____

## Worksheet 34-4　Figure Your Taxable Benefits if

### You Are Married Filing Separately and You Lived With Your Spouse at Any Time During the Year

1. Enter your net Social Security benefits (Line 1 of Worksheet 34-1). · · · · · · · · 1. _____

2. Multiply Line 1 by 85%. · · · · · · · · 2. _____

3. Enter your provisional income (Line 8 of Worksheet 34-1). · · · · · · · · 3. _____

4. Multiply Line 3 by 85%. · · · · · · · · 4. _____

5. The smaller of Line 2 or Line 4 is taxable. Enter the smaller amount as your taxable Social Security benefits here and on Line 5b of Form 1040. · · · · · · · · 5. _____

## EXAMPLES

1. Frank Adams, who is single, has 2018 earnings of $14,000 from a part-time job, $500 of interest income, and $1,700 of dividends. He also receives $15,800 of net Social Security benefits (Box 5 of Form SSA-1099). Frank's provisional income, figured on Worksheet 34-1, is $24,100 ($14,000 + $500+ $1,700 + $7,900 (50% of the $15,800 net Social Security benefits)). Since provisional income of $24,100 does not exceed the base amount of $25,000 for single taxpayers *(Table 34-1)*, none of Frank's Social Security benefits are taxable.

2. Same facts as Example 1 except that Frank also has a pension of $24,950. This raises his provisional income from $24,100 to $49,050 ($24,950 + $14,000 + $500+ $1,700 + $7,900 (50% of the $15,800 net Social Security benefits)). His provisional income exceeds the adjusted base amount for single taxpayers of $34,000 *(Table 34-1)*. On Worksheet 34-3, he figures that $ 13,430 of his $15,800 of net benefits are subject to tax. Here are Frank's line entries on Worksheet 34-3:

| | | |
|---|---|---|
| 1. | Provisional income in excess of $34,000 adjusted base amount ($49,050 – $34,000) | $ 15,050 |
| 2. | 85% of Line 1 | 12,793 |
| 3. | Net Social Security benefits | 15,800 |
| 4. | 85% of Line 3 | 13,430 |
| 5. | Leave blank because Line 4 is more than Line 2 | |
| 6. | Smaller of (a) $4,500 (because adjusted base amount is $34,000), or (b) $7,900 (50% of $15,800 net benefits) | 4,500 |
| 7. | Add Lines 2 and 6 | 17,293 |
| 8. | Smaller of Line 4 or Line 7 is taxable | $13,430 |

Given these facts, 85% of Frank's net Social Security benefits, or $13,430, is taxable. Since 85% is the maximum taxable percentage under the law, the result would be the same even if Frank's provisional income was much higher. The taxable amount of benefits would still be $13,430, equal to 85% of Frank's net benefits.

3. Sam and Fran Baker are both retired. In 2018, they receive net Social Security benefits (Box 5 of Form SSA-1099) of $27,600 between them. They have taxable pensions of $24,000, interest income of $300, dividends of $750 and tax-exempt interest of $1,200. They file a joint return on Form 1040. Their provisional income, figured on Worksheet 34-1, is $40,050 ($24,000 + $300 + 750 + $1,200 + $13,800 (50% of the $27,600 net Social Security benefits)). Their provisional income exceeds the base amount of $32,000 for married persons filing jointly *(Table 34-1)*, but not the adjusted base amount of $44,000 *(Table 34-1)*. On Worksheet 34-2, Sam and Fran determine that $4,025 of their benefits are subject to tax. Here are Sam and Fran's line entries on Worksheet 34-2:

| | | |
|---|---|---|
| 1. | Provisional income in excess of $32,000 base amount ($40,050 – $32,000) | $ 8,050 |
| 2. | 50% of Line 1 | 4,025 |
| 3. | 50% of net Social Security benefits | 13,800 |
| 4. | Smaller of Line 2 or Line 3 is taxable | 4,025 |

Note that the taxable amount of $4,025 represents only 14.58% of Sam and Fran's net benefits ($4,025/$27,600).

4. Same facts as Example 3 except that Sam and Fran have taxable pensions of $60,000 instead of $24,000. This raises their provisional income by $36,000 to $76,050 ($60,000+ $300+750+$1,200 + $13,800 (50% of the $27,600 net Social Security benefits)). Since their provisional income exceeds their adjusted base amount of $44,000 *(Table 34-1)*, they use Worksheet 34-3 to figure the amount of their taxable benefits and determine that 85% of their $27,600 net benefits, or $23,460, is subject to tax. 85% is the maximum taxable percentage under the law.

Here are Sam and Fran's line entries on Worksheet 34-3:

| | | |
|---|---|---|
| 1. | Provisional income in excess of $44,000 adjusted base amount ($76,050-$44,000) | $ 32,050 |
| 2. | 85% of Line 1 | 27,243 |
| 3. | Net Social Security benefits | 27,600 |
| 4. | 85% of Line 3 | 23,460 |
| 5. | Line 4 is taxable because it is less than Line 2. Lines 6-8 of Worksheet 34-3 do not have to be completed | 23,460 |

Given these facts, 85% of Sam and Fran's net Social Security benefits, or $23,460, is taxable. Since 85% is the maximum taxable percentage under the law, the result would be the same even if Sam and Fran's provisional income was much higher. The taxable amount of benefits would still be $23,460, equal to 85% of their net benefits.

## 34.4 Election for Lump-Sum Social Security Benefit Payment

If in 2018 you receive a lump-sum payment of Social Security benefits (whether retirement or disability benefits) covering prior years, you have a choice as to how to determine the taxable portion of the benefits: (1) You may treat the entire payment as a 2018 benefit taxable under the regular rules *(34.3)*, or (2) you may allocate the benefits between 2018 and the earlier years. Choose the method that provides the lowest required increase to income in the current year. For example, if you receive a 2018 lump-sum payment that includes benefits for 2017, you may find that an allocation of benefits is advantageous where your income over the two-year period has fluctuated and benefits allocated to 2017 would be subject to a lower taxable percentage than if they were treated as 2018 benefits.

When you elect to allocate benefits to a prior year, you do not amend the return for that year. You compute the increase in income (if any) that would have resulted if the Social Security benefits had been received in that year. You then add that amount to the income of the current year.

*See* IRS Publication 915 for instructions and worksheets for making the allocation and figuring the amount to be reported on your return.

## 34.5 Retiring on Social Security Benefits

Retirement benefits are not paid automatically. You should file for Social Security retirement benefits three months before you want to start receiving benefits. The age for receiving full Social Security benefits, traditionally 65, was increased for those born after 1937. For those born in 1943–1954, you must be age 66 to receive full benefits; *see* the Law Alert on this page. Reduced benefits may be elected if you are at least age 62. The reduction for starting benefits early depends on the number of months between the start date and your full Social Security retirement age. For example, if you were born in 1957 and elect benefits at age 62 in 2019, the benefit is 72.5% of what could be claimed at full retirement (age 66 and 6 months). Even though your full Social Security retirement age is over 65, you should register with the Social Security Administration three months before the month in which you turn age 65 to ensure Medicare coverage.

If you were born in 1943 or later and delay benefits beyond full Social Security retirement age, your Social Security benefit increases 8% for each year you delay retirement. The increase for delaying benefits no longer applies once you reach age 70.

**Benefits before reaching full retirement age may be reduced because of earnings.** If you are under full retirement age and are receiving benefits, $1 of benefits will be deducted for each $2 earned above an annual limit. In 2018, the limit was $17,040 (the 2019 limit will be listed in the *e-Supplement* at *jklasser.com*). For the year you reach full retirement age, $1 of benefits is deducted for each $3 earned over a different limit. For example, if in 2018 you reached the full Social Security retirement age of 66, benefits were reduced $1 for every $3 of earnings over $45,360, but only earnings before the month in which you reached age 66 are counted. Starting with the month in which you reach full retirement age, you are entitled to full benefits with no limit on how much you may earn.

There is also a favorable rule for the first year of retirement. A full benefit may be received for any month in which your earnings do not exceed 1/12 of the annual limit, even if the yearly limit is exceeded. However, this special rule does not apply for any month in which you are self-employed and devote over 45 hours to the business, or between 15 and 45 hours if your business involves a highly skilled profession.

So long as you continue to work, you pay Social Security taxes on your earnings, regardless of your age, so the additional earnings can increase your benefits. In addition, after you reach full retirement age, you will be given credit for any months in which you did not receive a benefit because of your earnings.

Regardless of your age, you may receive any amount of income from sources other than work—for example, pensions or investments—without affecting the amount of Social Security retirement benefits.

 *Law Alert*

**Social Security Retirement Age**

The retirement age for receiving full Social Security benefits is gradually increasing under current law to 67, as shown below. If you were born on the first of the month, Social Security treats your birthday as if it were in the previous month.

| Birth year— | Full Social Security retirement age— |
|---|---|
| 1943–1954 | 66 |
| 1955 | 66 and 2 months |
| 1956 | 66 and 4 months |
| 1957 | 66 and 6 months |
| 1958 | 66 and 8 months |
| 1959 | 66 and 10 months |
| 1960 and after | 67 |

### EXAMPLES

1. Jones retires and begins receiving reduced Social Security benefits in January 2018 at age 62. Without regard to earnings, he is entitled to receive $975 a month ($11,700 annually). He takes a part time job in May and for the year earns $24,560, which is $7,520 over the $17,040 limit for 2018. Under the regular benefit reduction rule, Jones would lose $3,760 of benefits ($1 for every $2 of earnings over $17,040). However, since this is his first year of retirement, a full benefit is paid for any month in which earnings were $1,420 (1/12 of $17,040) or less.

2. Smith, who began receiving benefits before 2018, reaches full retirement age of 66 in August 2018. Without regard to earnings, he would be entitled to monthly benefits of $1,850. He was fully employed during the year, earning $46,440 before August and $22,500 for the remainder of the year. The benefit reduction applies to his pre-August benefits. He earned $1,080 over the $45,360 limit and loses $360 of benefits ($1 for every $3 earned over $45,360). Starting in August, he begins to receive his full benefits regardless of the amount of his earnings.

## 34.6 How Tax on Social Security Reduces Your Earnings

There is an added tax cost of earning income if the earnings will subject your Social Security benefits to tax. Therefore, if your benefits are not currently exposed to tax, you have to figure not only the tax on the extra income but also the amount of Social Security benefits subjected to tax by those earnings. If the additional earnings will put you over the base amount *(34.3)*, then you will not only have to pay tax on the additional earnings but also on the Social Security benefits that will be subject to tax.

### EXAMPLES

1. You are over full Social Security retirement age *(34.5)* and you and your spouse receive net Social Security benefits of $18,000. You file jointly. You have pension income of $21,900, taxable interest of $500 and $400 in tax-exempt interest. Your provisional income *(34.3)* is $31,800. No part of your Social Security benefits is taxable because your provisional income of $31,800 does not exceed the $32,000 base amount for married persons filing jointly.

2. Same facts as in Example 1, except that you take a part-time job paying $7,000. This increases your provisional income to $38,800 and subjects $3,400 of Social Security benefits to tax.

| | |
|---|---|
| Provisional income | $38,800 |
| Less: Base amount | 32,000 |
| Excess | $6,800 |
| 50% of excess taxable (34.3) | $3,400 |

The $7,000 of additional earnings increases your taxable income by $10,400, which is the $7,000 of earnings plus the $3,400 of Social Security benefits made taxable because of the increase in provisional income.

## 34.7   Eligibility for the Credit for the Elderly or the Disabled

The tax credit for the elderly or disabled can be claimed by very few taxpayers. You can qualify for a 2018 credit only if your income is quite low and you meet one of the following conditions:

- Your 65th birthday is on or before January 1, 2019; or
- You were under age 65 at the end of 2018, you retired before the end of 2018 because of permanent and total disability, you received taxable disability income in 2018 from your former employer's disability plan, and you had not reached mandatory retirement age from the employer plan as of January 1, 2018. Disability income is taxable wages or payments in lieu of wages paid to you while you are absent from work because of permanent and total disability.

You will not be able to claim any credit if your Social Security benefits or adjusted gross income is "too high", or if you have no tax liability *(34.8)* .

**Disabled.** You are considered permanently and totally disabled if you are unable to engage in any substantial gainful activity by reason of any medically determinable physical or mental impairment that can be expected to result in death or that has lasted or can be expected to last for a continuous period of not less than 12 months.

For the first year you claim the credit, you need a physician's certification of your disability. For later years, new certifications are generally not required.

**Married couples.** If you are married, the credit generally may be claimed only if you file jointly. However, if you and your spouse live apart at all times during the taxable year, a qualifying spouse may claim the credit on a separate return.

**Nonresident aliens.** You may not claim the credit if you are a nonresident alien at any time during the year, unless you are married to a citizen or resident and you have elected to be treated as a resident *(1.5)* .

## 34.8   Figuring the Credit for the Elderly or Disabled

The credit is figured on Schedule R, which you attach to Form 1040 if any amount is allowed. The law specifies an initial base amount for figuring the credit. This base amount is reduced by nontaxable Social Security and other tax-free pensions, as well as by adjusted gross income exceeding specific limits. The 15% credit amount applies to the reduced base amount, but the resulting credit is allowed only to the extent it does not exceed your tax liability. These limitations are discussed below.

The initial base amount is:

- $5,000, if you are single, head of household, or are a qualifying widow/widower age 65 or over. If you are under age 65 and retired on permanent and total disability, the base amount is the lower of your taxable disability income or $5,000.
- $5,000, if you file a joint return and only one spouse is eligible for the credit (the eligible spouse is either age 65 or older or under 65 but retired on permanent and total disability).
- $7,500, if you file a joint return and both spouses are 65 or over. The credit is figured solely on this base; a separate computation is not made for each spouse. If one of you is age 65 or over and the other is under age 65 and retired on total disability, the initial base amount is the lesser of (1) $7,500 or (2) $5,000 plus the taxable disability income of the spouse under age 65. If both of you are under age 65 and retired on permanent and total disability, the initial base amount is the lower of your combined taxable disability income or $7,500.
- $3,750, if you are married filing a separate return and you lived apart from your spouse the entire year, and you are either age 65 or older or under 65 but retired on permanent and total disability.

**Nontaxable Social Security and pensions reduce the base amount.** The base amount is reduced by:

- Social Security and Railroad Retirement benefits that are not taxable *(34.3)* ; and
- Tax-free pension, annuity, or disability income paid under a law administered by the Veterans Administration (but not military disability pensions) or under other federal laws.

*Law Alert*

**Lack of Inflation Adjustment Severely Limits Credit**

Since 1983, the base amounts and AGI phaseout thresholds *(34.8)* for figuring the credit for the elderly or disabled have remained the same while inflation adjustments and tax law changes have reduced tax liability. Since the credit cannot exceed tax liability, the number of taxpayers able to claim the credit has dropped drastically and continues to decline annually.

*Caution*

**Low Social Security Benefits Required for Credit**

The tax credit for the elderly or disabled is not available to an unmarried individual who receives $5,000 or more of nontaxable Social Security benefits or nontaxable federal pensions such as from the Veterans Administration. The $5,000 limit also applies if you are married filing jointly and only one spouse qualifies for the credit. The limit is $7,500 if you file a joint return and both spouses qualify for the credit.

The base amount is not reduced by military disability pensions received for active service in the armed forces of any country, disability pensions for active service in the National Oceanic and Atmospheric Administration or Public Health Service, certain disability annuities paid under the Foreign Service Act of 1980, and workers' compensation benefits. However, if Social Security benefits are reduced by workers' compensation benefits, the amount of workers' compensation benefits is treated as Social Security benefits that reduce the base.

---

### EXAMPLE

John Andrews is 58 years old and single. In 2010, he retired on permanent and total disability. In 2018, he receives a taxable disability pension of $12,250, nontaxable Social Security disability benefits of $1,800, and taxable interest of $100. Adjusted gross income (AGI) is $12,350 ($12,250 + $100). His taxable income after claiming the standard deduction ($12,000) is only $350. As shown below, the credit formula would allow a credit of $116, but the credit cannot exceed John's 2018 tax liability, which is $36 (based on taxable income of $350).

| | |
|---|---:|
| Initial base amount | $5,000 |
| Less: nontaxable Social Security disability | 1,800 |
| Less: 50% of AGI over $7,500 (50% of $4,850 excess AGI ($12,350 AGI minus $7,500)) | 2,425 |
| Credit base amount | $775 |
| Credit (15% of credit base amount) | $116 |
| Tax liability limitation | $ 36 |

---

**Excess adjusted gross income reduces the base amount.** You reduce the base amount by one-half of adjusted gross income (AGI) exceeding: $7,500 if you are single, head of household, or a qualifying widow/widower; $10,000 if you are married filing a joint return; or $5,000 if you are married, live apart from your spouse for the entire year, and file a separate return. Because of these income reductions, the credit is not available to a single person (or head of household or qualifying widow/widower) when AGI reaches $17,500, $20,000 on a joint return where one spouse is eligible for the credit, $25,000 on a joint return where both spouses are eligible for the credit, and $12,500 where a married person files separately.

**15% credit limited by tax liability.** After reducing the credit base amount as just discussed for nontaxable Social Security and pensions and excess AGI, the remaining credit base is multiplied by 15%. This is the maximum credit but where this amount exceeds tax liability, the credit is limited to the lesser liability, as in the Example above.

## 34.9 Tax Effects of Moving to a Continuing Care Facility

Senior citizens who move into "continuing care" or "life-care" facilities pay large upfront entrance fees upon admittance, as well as monthly fees thereafter in return for a residence, meals, and lifetime health care, including long-term skilled nursing care, should that become necessary.

**Portion of monthly fees deductible as medical expense.** Part of the monthly fees to a life-care community are allocable to health care. If you itemize deductions on Schedule A (Form 1040), you may include the allocable fee in your medical expenses (subject to the AGI floor, 17.1). Continuing care facilities generally send a statement to the residents specifying the portion of their monthly service fees that went towards health care.

The IRS and Tax Court have approved the use of a "percentage method" for allocating the community's medical expenses among the residents. In general, the annual medical expenses of the community are divided by total operating expenses to get the medical care allocation percentage. In a particular case, the IRS could contest how the allocation is figured or how the allocated amount is divided among the residents.

For example, in a 2004 case (Baker, 122 TC 143), the IRS contested a couple's medical expense deduction for a portion of the monthly service fees paid for their two-bedroom duplex apartment, categorized as an "independent living unit" (ILU). Using a percentage method computation supplied by the resident council of their continuing care retirement community, the Bakers deducted $6,557 of their 1997 monthly service fees and $9,891 of their 1998 monthly fees as medical expenses. The IRS initially allowed a deduction for $4,488 of the 1997 fees and $5,142 of the 1998 fees using a different percentage method. Then, when the Bakers appealed to the Tax Court, the IRS argued that the deductible part of the service fees should be figured using an "actuarial method," which would increase the Bakers' two-year deduction by a few hundred dollars over what the examining agent had allowed.

However, the Tax Court refused to require use of the actuarial method, which requires projections of longevity and lifetime utilization of health-care services, and is so complicated that the IRS could not fully explain the method to the Court. The Court held that the percentage method is appropriate, noting that the IRS has approved use of the percentage method in rulings since 1967. However, in applying the percentage method to determine the Bakers' deductions, the Court had to resolve disputes over how certain expenses should be treated and how the allocated medical care percentage, once determined, should be split among the residents. For example, the Court held that the community's interest expenses, depreciation and amortization allowances should be included in both the numerator and denominator when dividing medical costs by operating costs to determine the medical care allocation percentage.

The Court calculated that 27.93% of the community's 1997 total costs and 30.07% of the 1998 costs were allocable to medical care. The Court then held that the Bakers could not simply multiply these percentages by the fees they paid to get their deductions. The same medical expense amount must be allocated to each ILU resident by multiplying the allocation percentage by a weighted average of the service fees paid each year by the ILU residents. The weighted average annual service fee for 1997 paid by the ILU residents was $13,902, which when multiplied by the allocation percentage of 27.93%, gave a medical care allocation of $3,883 per resident. For 1998, the weighted average annual service fee for ILU residents was $14,093, which when multiplied by the allocation percentage of 30.07%, gave a medical care allocation of $4,238 per resident. On their joint returns, the Bakers could treat double the per resident amounts as medical expenses; that is, $7,766 for 1997 and $8,476 for 1998.

**Portion of nonrefundable entrance fee deductible as medical expense.** What about the upfront payments required by life-care communities? If an entrance fee or founder's fee for lifetime care is nonrefundable, part may be treated as a medical expense *(17.1)* if you can prove what part of the lump sum is allocable to future medical coverage. The IRS recognizes that a deduction may be based on a showing that the life-care facility historically allocates a specified percentage of the fee to future medical care. With such proof there is a current obligation to pay and the allocable amount is treated as a deductible medical expense when the lump sum is paid. The same rules apply if the life-care or founder's fee is paid monthly rather than as a lump sum.

**Separate sponsorship gift.** In one case, an individual was allowed by the Tax Court and an appeals court to claim a charitable contribution deduction for a "sponsorship gift" paid to a life-care retirement facility where she and her husband were residents. The sponsorship gift was entirely separate from her entrance fee; it was not required for admission and did not entitle her to reduced monthly payments. She did not receive any extra benefit from her gift and was not entitled to a refund of any part of it.

## 34.10 Medicare Part B and Part D Premiums for 2019

At the time this book was completed, the Medicare Part B monthly premiums for 2019 had not yet been announced. Individuals with modified adjusted gross income (MAGI) over $85,000, and married couples filing jointly with MAGI over $170,000, must pay a surcharge in addition to the basic Part B premium. The surcharges for 2019 are generally based on MAGI for 2017 (two years prior to the 2019 premium year). Individuals subject to the Part B surcharges also must pay a surcharge in addition to their regular Medicare Part D prescription drug plan premiums. See the *e-Supplement* at *jklasser.com* for a table showing the 2019 Part B premium amounts, and the Part B and D surcharges.

*Caution*

**Charitable Contribution Deductions**

Payments you make to a tax-exempt organization that operates a life-care community are generally not deductible as a charitable contribution if you are a resident receiving services in exchange for the payments. If you donate amounts over and above your regular monthly fees and do not receive any extra benefit as a result, you may deduct the excess payment as a charitable contribution *(14.3)*.

## 34.11 Special Tax Rules for the Disabled

The following special tax rules apply for disabled individuals:

- Higher standard deduction for the blind. If you are completely blind, or partially blind with a note from an ophthalmologist or optometrist that vision is no better than 20/200 in the better eye with corrective lenses or that the field of vision is 20 degrees or less, you can claim an additional standard deduction amount if you do not itemize personal deductions *(13.4)*. The additional amount for 2018 is $1,600 if you are single or head of household, or $1,300 if you are married filing jointly, married filing separately, or a qualifying widow(er).
- Workers' compensation. This benefit, which is paid because of an injury or illness sustained on a job, is usually tax free *(2.13)*.
- Social Security disability benefits. If you are a worker receiving Social Security benefits on account of disability, the benefits are taxed in the same way as benefits received by retirees *(34.3)*. If you also receive workers' compensation that reduces Social Security benefits, all of the benefits are treated as Social Security benefits, which may be partially includible in gross income.
- Tax credit for the permanently disabled. The limited tax credit for seniors (age 65 and older) who receive little or no Social Security or Railroad Retirement benefits also applies for those who are under age 65 and who receive disability income for being permanently and totally disabled *(34.7)*.
- ABLE accounts. A special savings account can be used to pay for an array of qualified disability expenses *(34.12)*.
- Impairment-related work expenses. Unreimbursed work-related expenses incurred because of a disability are deductible on Schedule A (Form 1040) if you itemize deductions *(19.1)*.
- Penalty-free distributions from qualified retirement plans and IRAs. The 10% early distribution penalty does not apply for withdrawals made by someone who is disabled *(7.13; 8.12)*.
- Extended period for refund claims. The usual period for claiming a tax refund is suspended for someone unable to manage his or her financial affairs due to a disability *(47.2)*.
- Those who care for a disabled individual may qualify for special tax rules:
- Dependent care credit. Those who work and care for a spouse or child of any age who is physically or mentally incapable of self care may claim a dependent care credit *(25.4)*.
- Earned income credit. When claiming an earned income credit, a disabled child is a qualifying child, regardless of age *(25.6)*.
- Medical expenses. Various costs for the care of a disabled person may qualify as a deductible medical expense *(17.1)*, including special schooling for a physically or mentally handicapped child.

## 34.12 ABLE Accounts

ABLE accounts (authorized by the Stephen Beck Jr. Achieving a Better Life Experience Act of 2014) allow contributions (nondeductible) to be made to tax-favored accounts for certain disabled individuals without causing them to lose eligibility for government programs, such as Medicaid. Earnings in an ABLE account are not taxed unless a distribution exceeds the beneficiary's qualified disability expenses for that year.

**Setting up an ABLE account.** Each state can establish ABLE accounts for its residents or for nonresidents. The person holding the disabled individual's power of attorney may establish an ABLE account if the beneficiary cannot do so, or the beneficiary's parent or guardian may do so if no one has power of attorney.

At the time an ABLE account is set up, evidence must be presented to the state that the beneficiary became blind or disabled before age 26 and is entitled to Social Security disability benefits; otherwise a disability certification, signed under penalties of perjury, and accompanied by a physician's diagnosis, must be submitted. Annual recertifications of disability must be made; check with the plan administrator for details because "deemed recertifications" may be permissible.

A beneficiary can have only one ABLE account, and when establishing an ABLE account, the beneficiary must check a box or otherwise verify, under penalties of perjury, that the account being established is his or her only ABLE account.

 *Caution*

**Disabled Person Must Be the Account Owner**

A person other than the beneficiary who has signature authority over the ABLE account cannot have any interest in the account and must administer it for the benefit of the beneficiary.

If a beneficiary establishes an ABLE account in a state and then moves to another state, the ABLE account can remain with the state in which the account was created although the beneficiary is no longer a resident. However, a program-to-program transfer or a 60-day rollover of a distribution to another state program is allowed; such transfers do not violate the rule prohibiting multiple ABLE accounts. A program-to-program transfer is not treated as a taxable distribution; a rollover is not taxable unless it is within 12 months of a prior ABLE account rollover.

**Contributions.** Nondeductible cash contributions can be made to an ABLE account by anyone, but the combined contributions for the year (not counting rollovers or program-to-program transfers) from all contributors generally may not exceed the annual gift tax exclusion, currently $15,000. However, the Tax Cuts and Jobs Act allows an additional annual contribution to be made for working beneficiaries starting in 2018, provided no contribution has been made for the beneficiary to a qualified retirement plan (401(k) plan, 403(a) qualified annuity plan, 403(b) plan, or 457(b) deferred compensation plan) for the year. The additional contribution can be up to the lesser of (1) the beneficiary's compensation for the year, or (2) the amount of the federal poverty line for a one-person household for the preceding year. The designated beneficiary, or a person acting on behalf of the designated beneficiary, is responsible for maintaining records regarding the beneficiary's compensation to ensure that the limit on the additional contribution is not exceeded.

The Tax Cuts and Jobs Act also allows a rollover to be made to an ABLE account from a Section 529 qualified tuition plan *(33.5)* , so long as the designated beneficiary of both accounts is the same, or the ABLE account owner is a family member of the Section 529 account designated beneficiary. However, the rollover is subject to the regular annual ABLE contribution limit, equal to the annual gift tax exclusion ($15,000 for 2018).

Contributions in excess of the annual contribution limit, plus earnings on the excess, must be returned by the administrator of the ABLE program to the contributors by the beneficiary's filing due date (including extensions) in order for the contributors to avoid a 6% penalty; the penalty is figured on Form 5329.

Contributions will be reported to the beneficiary and to the IRS on Form 5498-QA. Form 5498-QA will be issued even for years for which no contributions are made; the fair market value of the account as of the end of the year will be reported, and a code showing the basis of the beneficiary's eligibility will be included.

There is also an overall limit on contributions: aggregate contributions on behalf of an ABLE account beneficiary cannot exceed the state's limit for a Section 529 qualified tuition program *(33.5)* .

**Distributions.** ABLE account distributions are reported to the beneficiary (and the IRS) on Form 1099-QA. If the distributions for a year do not exceed the beneficiary's annual qualified disability expenses, they are not taxed. If the distributions exceed the qualifying expenses, the portion of the distributions allocable to earnings that are not attributable to qualifying expenses are taxable and also subject to a 10% penalty figured on Form 5329. For example, if the qualified disability expenses for the year are 70% of the ABLE account distributions, then 70% of the earnings portion of the distribution will be tax free and 30% of the earnings portion will be taxable and subject to the 10% penalty.

Form 1099-QA will show the gross distribution, the earnings portion of the distribution, and the basis (total contributions) allocable to the distribution. A box will be checked if a program-to-program transfer was made or if the ABLE account was terminated.

The IRS broadly defines the term "qualified disability expenses" in order to carry out Congress's intent to assist the beneficiaries in maintaining or improving their "health, independence, or quality of life." Thus, qualified disability expenses are not limited to medically necessary items, but may also include basic living costs. This includes education, housing, transportation, employment training and support, assistive technology, personal support services, wellness programs, financial management, and legal fees. An IRS example indicates that buying and maintaining a smart phone would be a qualified expense for a child with autism where it helps the child navigate and communicate more safely and effectively.

 *Law Alert*

**Increased Contribution Limit and Rollover from 529 Plan Allowed**

Starting in 2018, the Tax Cuts and Jobs Act increases the ABLE account contribution limit for beneficiaries with compensation, but only if they are not covered by a qualified employer retirement plan. For eligible beneficiaries, the regular contribution limit, equal to the annual gift tax exclusion ($15,000 in 2018), may be increased by up to the lesser of the beneficiary's compensation for the year, or the prior year federal poverty line amount for a one-person household.

The Tax Cuts and Jobs Act also allows the designated beneficiary of a Section 529 plan *(33.5)* to make a rollover to his or her ABLE account, or to the ABLE account of a family member, subject to the contribution limit based on the annual gift tax exclusion.

# CHAPTER 35

# Members of the Armed Forces

Special tax benefits are provided to Armed Forces personnel. A major tax-free benefit is the combat pay exclusion. Under this exclusion, members of the Armed Forces, including active duty reservists, may exclude from gross income all compensation for active service received for any month in which they served in a combat zone or were hospitalized as a result of any wound, injury, or disease incurred while serving in a combat zone. Commissioned officers are allowed an exclusion equal to the highest rate of basic pay at the top pay level for enlisted personnel, plus any hostile fire/imminent danger pay received for the month.

Other pay benefits may be tax free, and you may be able to get filing extensions and time extensions for home residence replacements. A list of tax-free benefits may be found in *35.2*. Filing extensions are discussed in *35.5*.

Combat zone designations apply to Iraq and neighboring areas in the "Arabian Peninsula," Afghanistan, and the Balkans Kosovo area *(35.4)*. The Sinai Peninsula of Egypt is a qualified hazardous duty area and is treated the same as a combat zone.

## 35.1 Taxable Armed Forces Pay and Benefits

Armed Forces personnel report as taxable pay the following items:

- Basic pay for active duty, attendance at a designated service school, back wages, drills, reserve training, and training duty.
- Special pay for hazardous duty, hostile fire or imminent danger, aviation career incentives, diving duty, foreign duty (for serving outside the 48 contiguous states and the District of Columbia), medical and dental officers, nuclear-qualified officers, and special duty assignments.
- Enlistment and reenlistment bonuses.
- Payments for accrued leave, and personal money allowances paid to high-ranking officers.
- Student loan repayment from programs such as the Department of Defense Educational Loan Repayment Program when year's service is not attributable to a combat zone.

**State income tax withholding.** A state that makes a withholding agreement with the Secretary of the Treasury may subject members of the Armed Forces regularly stationed within that state to its payroll withholding provisions. National Guard members and reservists are not considered to be members of the Armed Forces for purposes of this section.

**Where and when to file.** If you file a paper return, mail it to the Internal Revenue Service Center for the place you are stationed. For example, you are stationed in Arizona but have a permanent home address in Missouri; you send your return to the Service Center for Arizona. For filing extensions on entering the service*(35.7)* .

## 35.2 Tax Breaks for Armed Forces Members

Military personnel and their families may qualify for numerous tax benefits. Here is a summary of some key tax breaks. For further details, *see* IRS Publication 3 (Armed Forces' Tax Guide).

The following payments or allowances are not subject to tax:

- Combat pay*(35.4)* . Although qualifying combat pay is not taxed, an election may be made to treat nontaxable combat pay*(35.4)* as earned income for purposes of the earned income tax credit*(25.6)* .
- Living allowances for BAH (Basic Allowance for Housing). You may deduct mortgage interest and real estate taxes on your home even if you pay these expenses with BAH funds.
- BAS (Basic Allowance for Subsistence) living allowances.
- Housing and cost-of-living allowances abroad, whether paid by the U.S. Government or by a foreign government.
- VHA (Variable Housing Allowance).
- Family allowances for educational expenses for dependents, emergencies, evacuation to a place of safety, and separation.
- Death allowances for burial services, death gratuity payments to eligible survivors, and travel of dependents to burial site.
- Dislocation allowance, intended to partially reimburse expenses such as lease forfeitures, temporary living charges in hotels, and other expenses incurred in relocating a household.
- Temporary lodging expense allowance intended to partially offset the added living expenses of temporary lodging within the United States for up to 10 days and up to 60 days abroad.
- A moving-in housing allowance, intended to defray costs, such as for rental agent fees, home-security improvements, and supplemental heating equipment, associated with occupying leased space outside the United States.
- Travel allowances for annual round trip for dependent students, leave between consecutive overseas tours, reassignment in a dependent-restricted status, and transportation for you or your dependents during ship overhaul or inactivation.

*Caution*

**Community Property**

If you are married and your domicile (permanent home to which you intend to return) is in one of the following states, your military pay is subject to community property laws of that state: Arizona, California, Idaho, Louisiana, Nevada, New Mexico, Texas, Washington, and Wisconsin (and Alaska for couples who opt in to make their property community property). *See 1.6* for community property reporting rules.

- Defense counseling payments.
- ROTC educational and subsistence allowances.
- Survivor and retirement protection plan premium payments.
- Uniform allowances paid to officers and uniforms furnished to enlisted personnel.
- Medical or hospital treatment provided by the United States in government hospitals.
- Pay forfeited on order of a court martial.
- Education, training, or subsistence allowances paid under any law administered by the Department of Veterans Affairs (VA). However, deductible education costs must be reduced by the VA allowance.
- Adjustments in pay to compensate for losses resulting from inflated foreign currency.
- Payments to former prisoners of war from the U.S. Government in compensation for inhumane treatment suffered at the hands of an enemy government.
- Benefits under Servicemembers' Group Life Insurance.
- Dividends on GI insurance. These are a tax-free return of premiums paid.
- Interest on dividends left on deposit with the Department of Veterans Affairs (VA).

**Distributions to reservists.** Reservists called to active duty for at least 180 days are not subject to the general 10% penalty for distributions before age 59½ from retirement plans and IRAs. They also are allowed in some cases to make withdrawals of unused benefits from a health flexible spending account. These rules are discussed further at *35.8* .

**State and local bonuses may be tax free.** Some states and municipalities pay bonuses to active or former military personnel or their dependents because of service in a combat zone. Such payments may be excludable from gross income under the combat pay rules at *35.4* .

**Extended statute of limitations for disability determinations.** Usually, a taxpayer must file for a refund claim *(47.2)* within three years of the due date of the return on which the income was reported. Payments from the government based on a service-connected disability are tax free, while payments based on length of service are taxable. The Department of Veterans Affairs may take a long time to make a disability determination, with the result that taxpayers may include the payments as income. Then, when they receive a favorable determination, they can file an amended return to receive a tax refund. A law allows the refund claim to be filed until one year after the date of a disability determination to file a refund claim if this date is later than the end of the three-year period of limitation.

**Death benefits.** Beneficiaries who receive military death gratuities or payments from the Servicemembers' Group Life Insurance (SGLI) program can roll these amounts over to a Roth IRA or Coverdell education savings account (ESA) within one year of receipt. The usual limits on contribution amounts and income limitations for Roth IRAs *(8.20)* and Coverdell ESAs *(33.11)* do not apply to these rollovers.

**Veterans not taxed on payments from Compensated Work Therapy program.** In response to a 2007 Tax Court decision that held that payments made by the U.S. Department of Veterans Affairs (VA) to disabled veterans under the Compensated Work Therapy (CWT) program are tax-free veterans' benefits, the IRS reversed position and announced that it no longer treats CWT payments as taxable pay for services. Under the CWT program, the VA provides vocational rehabilitation services to veterans who have been unable to work and support themselves. The VA contracts with private industry and government agencies to provide these veterans with therapeutic work that emphasizes work skills training.

**Disability retirement pay.** Your disability retirement pay may be tax free if you are a former member of the Armed Forces of any country, the Foreign Service, the Coast Guard, the National Oceanic and Atmospheric Administration, or the Public Health Service *(2.14)* . Tax-free treatment of disability retirement pay is retroactive to the date of the application for benefits. But Social Security disability payments made on account of a combat-related injury are taxable to the same extent as Social Security retirement payments *(34.3)* .

*Caution*

**Withholding on Differential Wages Paid to Workers Joining Military**

Employees who enlist or are called up to active military service for over 30 days may receive "differential wages" from their former employer to cover some or all of the difference between their military pay and the wages that were being received prior to joining the military. The differential wages are taxable and cannot be excluded as combat pay *(35.4)* . Income tax must be withheld from the differential wages, but not FICA tax (Social Security and Medicare). If the active duty is for 30 days or less, differential wages are subject to FICA tax withholding as well as to income tax withholding

## 35.3  Deductions for Armed Forces Personnel

For 2018 through 2025, members of the Armed Forces cannot deduct certain unreimbursed business expenses as miscellaneous itemized deductions subject to the 2% of adjusted gross income (AGI) floor because of the suspension of this deduction *(19.1)*. Such expenses had included:

- Board and lodging costs over those paid to you by the government while on temporary duty away from your home base.
- Costs of rank insignia, collar devices, gold braids, etc., and the cost of altering rank insignia when promoted or demoted.
- Contributions to a "Company" fund made according to Service regulations. But personal contributions made to stimulate interest and morale in a unit are not deductible.
- Court martial legal expenses in successfully defending against the charge of conduct unbecoming an officer.
- Dues to professional societies. But you may not deduct dues for officers' and noncommissioned officers' clubs.
- Expense of obtaining increased retirement pay.
- Subscriptions to professional journals.
- Transportation, food, and lodging expenses while on official travel status. But you are taxed on mileage and per diem subsistence allowance.
- Uniforms. The cost and cleaning of uniforms are deductible if: (1) they must be worn on duty; (2) they cannot under military regulations be worn off duty; and (3) the cost exceeds any tax-free clothing allowance.

However, there are two types of expenses you can deduct from gross income (no itemizing is required):

- Moving expenses. If you are on active duty and move pursuant to a military order and incident to a permanent change of station, you can deduct your moving expenses. This includes a deduction for driving your vehicle at the 2018 rate of 18¢ per mile. You can also exclude from your income any in-kind moving and storage expenses you receive.
- Reservists expenses. If you travel overnight more than 100 miles from home in connection with your performance of services as a member of the reserves, you can deduct your travel costs. If you use your vehicle for this travel, you can deduct your mileage at the 2018 rate of 54.5 cents per mile. You can also deduct the cost of lodging and 50% of meal costs.

## 35.4  Tax-Free Pay for Service in Combat Zone

If your grade is below commissioned officer (you are an enlisted member, warrant officer or commissioned warrant officer) and you serve in a designated combat zone during any part of a month, all of your qualifying military pay (see below) for that month is excluded from your taxable income. You may also exclude military pay earned during any part of a month that you are hospitalized as a result of wounds, disease, or injury incurred in a combat zone. The exclusion for military pay while hospitalized does not apply to any month that begins more than two years after the end of combat activities in that combat zone. Your hospitalization does not have to be in the combat zone.

**Officers.**  If you are a commissioned officer, you may exclude up to the highest rate of basic pay at the highest pay grade that enlisted personnel receive per month plus any hostile fire/imminent danger pay received for each month during any part of which you served in a combat zone or were hospitalized as a result of the combat zone service.

If you are a commissioned warrant officer, you are considered an enlisted person.

**What is included as tax-free combat pay?**  The following pay received as a member of the U.S. Armed Forces qualifies for tax-free treatment: (1) active duty pay earned in any month you served in a combat zone; (2) imminent danger / hostile fire pay; (3) a reenlistment bonus if the voluntary extension or reenlistment occurs in a month you served in a combat zone; (4) pay for accrued leave earned in any month you served in a combat zone (the Department of Defense must determine that the unused leave was earned during that

*Filing Tip*

**Who Qualifies for Exclusion?**

Members of the U.S. Armed Forces qualifying for the exclusion include commissioned officers and enlisted personnel in all regular and reserve units under control of the Secretaries of Defense, Army, Navy, and Air Force, and the Coast Guard. Members of the U.S. Merchant Marines or the American Red Cross are not included.

period); (5) pay received for duties as a member of the Armed Forces in clubs, messes, post and station theaters, and other nonappropriated fund activities. The pay must be earned in a month you served in a combat zone; (6) awards for suggestions, inventions, or scientific achievements you are entitled to because of a submission you made in a month you served in a combat zone; and (7) student loan repayments earned for military service. For each month of combat zone service during the year, 1/12 of the repayment for that year is considered tax-free combat zone pay.

Service in the combat zone includes any periods you are absent from duty because of sickness, wounds, or leave. If, as a result of serving in a combat zone, you become a prisoner of war or missing in action, you are considered to be serving in the combat zone as long as you keep that status for military pay purposes.

Retirement pay and pensions do not qualify for the combat zone exclusion. According to a Fourth Circuit Court of Appeals decision, a Navy severance pay package was taxable although the recipient became entitled to the payment while on active duty in the Persian Gulf. The court differentiated the package, which was provided in order to entice the man to leave the service, from a reenlistment bonus provided as compensation for active service.

**Combat zones.** A combat zone is any area the President of the United States designates by Executive Order as an area in which the U.S. Armed Forces are or have engaged in combat. An area becomes and ceases to be a combat zone on the dates designated by the President. When this book was completed, there were three designated combat zones: (1) the Afghanistan area, including countries in which military service has been certified by the Defense Department as in direct support of the operations in Afghanistan, (2) the Arabian Peninsula area, and (3) the Kosovo area. The Sinai Peninsula in Egypt is a qualified hazardous duty area that is effectively treated the same as a combat zone. IRS Publication 3 has the full list of countries in each of these areas.

**Qualifying service outside a combat zone considered combat zone service.** Military service outside a combat zone is considered to be performed in a combat zone if: (1) the service is designated by the Defense Department to be in direct support of military operations in the combat zone, and (2) the service qualifies you for special military pay for duty subject to hostile fire or imminent danger. Military pay received for this service will qualify for the combat zone exclusion if the other requirements are met.

**Nonqualifying service.** The following military service does not qualify as service in a combat zone: (1) presence in a combat zone while on leave from a duty station located outside the combat zone; (2) passage over or through a combat zone during a trip between two points that are outside a combat zone; and (3) presence in a combat zone solely for your personal convenience. Such service will not qualify you for the pay exclusion.

**Hospitalized while serving in a combat zone or after leaving a combat zone.** If you are hospitalized while serving in a combat zone, the wound, disease, or injury that is the reason for the hospitalization will be presumed to have been incurred while serving in the combat zone unless there is clear evidence to the contrary. The presumption may also apply if you were hospitalized after leaving a combat zone.

 *Law Alert*

**IRA Contributions Based on Tax-Free Combat Pay**

Members of the armed services serving in a combat zone may base contributions to either a traditional IRA *(8.2)* or a Roth IRA *(8.20)* on their tax-free combat pay.

---

### EXAMPLES

1. You are hospitalized for a specific disease after serving in a combat zone for three weeks, and the disease for which you are hospitalized has an incubation period of two to four weeks. The disease is presumed to have been incurred while you were serving in the combat zone. On the other hand, if the incubation period of the disease is one year, the disease would not have been incurred while you were serving in the combat zone.

2. You were hospitalized for a specific disease three weeks after you left the combat zone. The incubation period of the disease is from two to four weeks. The disease is considered to have been incurred while serving in the combat zone.

---

**Form W-2.** The wages shown in Box 1 of your Form W-2 should not include combat pay. Retirement pay is not combat pay.

*Filing Tip*

**Spouses of Combat Zone Personnel**

If your spouse serves in a combat zone or contingency operation, you are generally entitled to the same deadline extension as he or she is. However, any extra extension for your spouse's hospitalization within the United States is not available to you. Further, a spouse's extension does not apply to any year beginning more than two years after the area ceases to be a combat zone or the operation ceases to be a contingency operation.

## 35.5 Tax Deadlines Extended for Combat Zone or Contingency Operation Service

You are allowed an extension of at least 180 days (see below) to take care of tax matters if you are a member of the Armed Forces who served in a combat zone or in a contingency operation. The extension applies to filing tax returns, paying taxes, filing a Tax Court petition, filing refund claims, and making an IRA contribution. The time allowed for the IRS to begin an audit or take collection actions is also extended. *See* IRS Publication 3 for details on the extension rules.

**Support personnel.** The deadline extension also applies if you are serving in a combat zone or contingency operation in support of the Armed Forces. This includes Red Cross personnel, accredited correspondents, and civilian personnel acting under the direction of the Armed Forces in support of those forces.

**Extension is a minimum of 180 days.** Your deadline for taking actions with the IRS is extended for at least 180 days after the later of: (1) the last day you are in a combat zone or serving in a contingency operation (or the last day the area qualifies as a combat zone or the operation qualifies as a contingency operation), or (2) the last day of any continuous qualified hospitalization for injury from service in the combat zone or contingency operation. Hospitalization may be outside the United States, or up to five years of hospitalization in the United States.

Time in a missing status (missing in action or prisoner of war) counts as time in a combat zone or contingency operation.

In addition to the 180 days, a filing deadline is also extended by the number of days you had left to file with the IRS when you entered a combat zone or began serving in a contingency operation. If you entered the combat zone or began contingency operation service before the time to file began, the deadline is extended by the entire filing time.

## 35.6 Tax Forgiveness for Combat Zone or Terrorist or Military Action Deaths

If a member of the Armed Forces is killed in a combat zone or dies from wounds or disease incurred while actively serving in a combat zone, any income tax liability for the year of death and any earlier year in which he or she actively served in a combat zone is waived. In addition, the service member's estate is entitled to a refund for income tax paid while serving there.

If a member of the Armed Forces was a resident of a community property state and his or her spouse reported half of the military pay on a separate return, the spouse may get a refund of taxes paid on his or her share of the combat zone pay.

Forgiveness benefits apply to an Armed Forces member serving outside the zone if service: (1) was in direct support of military operations there, and (2) qualified the member for special military pay for duty subject to hostile fire or imminent danger.

**Missing status.** The date of death for a member of the Armed Forces who was in a missing status (missing in action or prisoner of war) is the date his or her name is removed from missing status for military pay purposes. This is true even if death occurred earlier.

**Tax forgiveness for civilian or military personnel killed in terroristic or military action.** Tax liability is waived for civilian or military U.S. government employees killed in terroristic or military actions, even if the President has not designated the area as a combat zone. The individual must be a U.S. government employee both on the date of injury and date of death. Tax liability is waived for the period beginning with the taxable year before the year in which the injuries were incurred and ending with the year of death. Refund claims for prior years must generally be filed on Form 1040X by the later of three years from the time the original return was filed or two years from the time the tax was paid. However, if death occurred in a combat zone, the filing period is extended by the time served in the combat zone, plus the period of continuous hospitalization outside the U.S., plus an additional 180 days.

*Caution*

**Training Exercises**

Tax forgiveness for personnel killed in a "military action" does not apply to a U.S. civilian or military employee who dies as a result of a training exercise.

**How tax forgiveness is claimed.** If the individual died in a combat zone or in a terroristic or military action, you file as the individual's representative: (1) Form 1040 if a U.S. individual income tax return has not been filed for the tax year. Form W-2, Wage and Tax Statement, must accompany the return. (2) Form 1040X if a U.S. individual income tax return has been filed. A separate Form 1040X must be filed for each year in question. *See* IRS Publication 3 for how to identify the military or terrorist action in which the death occurred.

An attachment should accompany any return or claim and should include a computation of the decedent's tax liability before any amount is forgiven and the amount that is to be forgiven.

The following documents must also accompany all returns and claims for refund: (1) Form 1310, "Statement of Person Claiming Refund Due a Deceased Taxpayer"; and (2) a certification from the Department of Defense. Department of State certification is required if the decedent was a civilian employee of an agency other than the Department of Defense. *See* IRS Publication 3 for the IRS address where the tax forgiveness claim and documents must be filed.

## 35.7 Extension To Pay Your Tax When Entering the Service

If you are unable to pay your income taxes when you enter the Armed Forces (whether they became due before or during your military service), you may get an extension until 180 days after leaving the military to pay the tax, provided that you apply for the extension after receiving a notice from the IRS asking for payment. Your request must show that your ability to pay has been materially affected because of your military service. If the request is granted and you pay the entire tax due by the end of the postponement period, no interest or penalties will be charged for that period.

The extension does not cover your spouse, who must file a separate return and pay the tax due. But you and your spouse may file a joint return before the postponement period expires even though your spouse filed a separate return for that particular year.

**Automatic extension of time to file your return.** If you are on duty outside the U.S. or Puerto Rico on April 15, 2019, you get an automatic two-month extension to file your 2018 return; *see* page 6.

**Interest charged on back taxes.** If you do not show hardship qualifying you for the above interest-free payment extension, the maximum interest rate the IRS may charge while you are on active duty for taxes incurred prior to your entry into active service is 6%, provided your service affected your ability to pay. This is the maximum rate; in recent years the regular interest rate has been 4% *(46.8)*, so the 6% rule has not been a benefit.

## 35.8 Tax Information for Reservists

Transportation costs to reservist meetings may or may not be deductible, following the regular rules for transportation and commuting *(20.2)*. A deduction would ordinarily be allowed if on a regular workday you travel from your regular job location to a reserve unit meeting, as the meeting is considered a second workplace. But due to the suspension of miscellaneous itemized deductions subject to the 2% of adjusted gross income (AGI) floor from 2018 through 2025, no current write-off is allowed.

If you travel overnight more than 100 miles away from your tax home to a meeting or training camp, these costs can still be taken as an above-the-line deduction *(35.3)*

**Deferring tax payments and reduction of IRS interest rate.** If you owed a tax deficiency to the IRS before being called to active duty, the IRS may defer payment, without interest, if your ability to pay has been severely impaired by your call-up *(35.7)*.

**Penalty-free withdrawal and repayment of qualified reservist retirement distribution.** If you are called to active military duty for over 179 days or indefinitely, and during the active duty period you receive a distribution from a traditional IRA or a distribution attributable to elective deferrals (from a 401(k) or 403(b) plan), the distribution is considered a qualified reservist distribution. If you are under age 59½ when you receive a qualified reservist distribution, you are not subject to the 10% penalty for early distributions *(7.15, 8.12)*.

Furthermore, you can recontribute a qualified reservist distribution to a traditional IRA within two years after the end of the active duty period. Repayment must be made to a traditional IRA even if the distribution was from a 401(k) or 403(b) plan. The repayment should be reported on Form 8606 (Line 1) as a nondeductible contribution to the traditional IRA.

**Distributions of unused balance from health flexible spending arrangement (HFSA).** If you contribute to a health flexible spending arrangement *(3.15)*, but before you can use up your HFSA balance to reimburse your medical expenses you are called to active military duty for over 179 days, or indefinitely, you can withdraw the funds and use them for any purpose if your employer allows "qualified reservist distributions" and you withdraw the balance by the regular plan deadline for receiving reimbursements. If your employer allows employees to obtain reimbursements of medical expenses within a 2½-month grace period after the end of the plan year *(3.15)*, you have the same deadline to receive a distribution of your HFSA balance, but it does not have to be used to pay medical expenses.

# CHAPTER 36

# How To Treat Foreign Earned Income

There is a tax incentive for working abroad—in 2018 up to $103,900 of income earned abroad may escape U.S. income taxes and you may be entitled to an exclusion or deduction for certain housing costs. In measuring the economic value of this tax savings, consider the extra cost of living abroad. In some areas, the high cost of living and currency exchange rates will erode your tax savings.

The exclusion does not apply to investment income or to any other earned income that does not meet the exclusion tests.

To claim a foreign income exclusion you must satisfy a foreign residence or physical presence test *(36.5)*.

Employees of the U.S. government may not claim an exclusion based on the government pay earned abroad.

If you keep income in a foreign bank or other financial accounts, you may have special reporting requirements for the accounts *(4.12, 48.7)*.

## 36.1    Claiming the Foreign Earned Income Exclusion

If your tax home is in a foreign country and you meet either the foreign residence test or physical presence test *(36.3)*, you may exclude up to $103,900 of foreign earned income earned in 2018. You must file a U.S. return if your gross income exceeds the filing threshold for your personal status, even though all or part of your foreign earned income may be tax free. For years after 2018, the maximum $103,900 exclusion may be increased by an inflation adjustment. The exclusion is not automatic; you must elect it. You elect the foreign earned income exclusion on Form 2555, which you attach to Form 1040. The housing cost exclusion *(36.4)* is also elected on Form 2555.

You may file simplified Form 2555-EZ if your 2018 foreign wages are $103,900 or less, you do not have self-employment income, and you do not claim the foreign housing exclusion, housing deduction, business expenses, or moving expenses.

A separate exclusion is allowed for the value of meals and lodging received by employees living in qualified camps; *see 36.8*.

If you claim the foreign income exclusion of $103,900, you may not:

- Claim business deductions allocable to the excluded income;
- Make a deductible traditional IRA contribution, or a Roth IRA contribution, based on the excluded income; or
- Claim foreign taxes paid on excluded income as a credit or deduction.

In deciding whether to claim the exclusion, compare the overall tax (1) with the exclusion and (2) without the exclusion but with the full foreign tax credit and allocable deductions. Choose whichever gives you the lower tax; *see 36.3* and *36.6*.

Keep in mind that if you claim the exclusion, any taxable income not subject to the earned income and housing exclusions will be taxed at the same rates that would have applied had no exclusions been allowed. To apply this "stacking" rule, you must figure your regular tax liability using the Foreign Earned Income Tax Worksheet in the instructions to Form 1040. Also, to figure AMT liability, use the Foreign Earned Income Tax Worksheet in the instructions to Form 6251.

**Election applies until revoked.** Once you elect the exclusion, that election remains in effect for all future years unless you revoke it. If you revoke the election, you cannot elect the exclusion again during the next five years without IRS consent. A revocation is made in a statement attached to your return for the year you want it to take effect. The foreign earned income exclusion and the housing cost exclusion must be revoked separately.

The IRS may consent to a reinstatement of the exclusion following a revocation under the following circumstances: you return for a period of time to the United States, you move to another foreign country with different tax rates, you change employers, or there has been substantial change in the tax law of the foreign country of residence or physical presence.

> **EXAMPLE**
>
> A U.S. citizen living abroad asked the IRS if the declaration of a tax holiday by a foreign country in 1999 was a substantial change of law. Prior to 1996, while working abroad he had claimed the foreign income exclusion. But in 1996 and 1997, he revoked the election and claimed a foreign tax credit for taxes paid on his foreign earnings. In 1999, he wanted to resume claiming the income exclusion due to the declaration of a tax holiday in the country in which he was employed. The IRS ruled that he can claim the exclusion. The declaration of a tax holiday is considered a substantial change of law because he went from being taxed to being exempt from tax.

## 36.2    What Is Foreign Earned Income?

For exclusion purposes, foreign earned income includes salaries, wages, commissions, professional fees, and bonuses for personal services performed while your tax home is in a foreign country and you meet either the foreign residence test or the physical presence test; *see 36.3*. Earned income also includes allowances from your employer for housing or other expenses, as well as the value of housing or a car provided by the employer. It

*Caution*

**Claiming Foreign Tax Credit Revokes Prior Election**

If you have been claiming the exclusion and decide that it would be advantageous this year to forego the exclusion and instead claim the foreign tax credit for foreign earned income, be aware that claiming the credit is treated by the IRS as a revocation of the prior exclusion election. You may not claim an exclusion for the next five years unless the IRS allows you to reelect the exclusion.

Claiming a foreign tax credit also may revoke a prior election to claim the housing cost exclusion. Depending on the foreign earned income in the year the credit is claimed, the credit may be considered a revocation of a prior earned income exclusion election and also a prior housing cost exclusion election, or as a revocation of only one of the elections.

A good faith error in calculating foreign earned income that leads to claiming a foreign credit will not be treated as a revocation of prior elections.

may also include business profits, royalties, and rents, provided this income is tied to the performance of services. Earned income does not include pension or annuity income, payments for nonqualified employee trusts or nonqualified annuities, dividends, interest, capital gains, gambling winnings, alimony, or the value of tax-free meals or lodging under the rules in *3.13*.

Foreign earned income does not include amounts earned in countries subject to U.S. government travel restrictions.

Courts have agreed with the IRS that income earned in Antarctica, in international waters, and in international airspace is not earned in a foreign country and thus cannot qualify for the exclusion.

**United States government pay ineligible.** If you are an employee of the U.S. government or its agencies, you may not exclude any part of your pay from your government employer. Courts have agreed with the IRS that U.S. government workers were U.S. employees even though they were paid from sources other than Congressionally appropriated funds. If you are not an employee of the U.S. government or any of its agencies, your pay is excludable even if paid by a government source. You are not considered a U.S. government employee if you work for a private employer that has contracted with the government, provided you are under the employer's control and supervision, you are paid by the employer, and no U.S. government agency would be liable for your salary if your employer defaulted.

Under a special law, tax liability is waived for a civilian or military employee of the U.S. government killed in a military action overseas; *see 35.6.*

> ### EXAMPLES
>
> 1. A U.S. citizen resides in England. He invests in an English partnership that sells manufactured goods outside the U.S. He performs no services for the business. His share of net profits does not qualify as earned income.
>
> 2. Same facts as in Example 1, except he devotes his full time to the partnership business. Then up to 30% of his share of the net profits may qualify as earned income. Thus, if his share of profits is $50,000, earned income is $15,000 (30% of $50,000), assuming the value of his services is at least $15,000.
>
> 3. You and another person are consultants, operating as a partnership in Europe. Since capital is not an income-producing element, the entire gross income of the business is earned income.
>
>    The partnership agreement generally determines the tax status of partnership income in a U.S. partnership with a foreign branch. Thus, if the partnership agreement allocates foreign earnings to partners abroad, the allocation will be recognized unless it lacks substantial economic effect.

**Profits from sole proprietorship or partnership.** If your business consists solely of services (no capital investment), 100% of gross income is considered earned income. If services and capital are both income-producing factors, the value of your personal services, but no more than 30% of your share of the net profit, is considered earned income. Net profit is reduced by the deduction for the employer-equivalent portion of self-employment tax *(12.2)* before figuring your 30% share.

If you do not contribute any services to a business (for example, you are a "silent partner"), your share of the net profits is not earned income.

If you do not have a net profit, the portion of your gross profit that represents a reasonable allowance for personal services is considered earned income.

**Fringe benefits.** The value of fringe benefits, such as the right to use company property and facilities, is added to your compensation when figuring the amount of your earned income.

**Royalties.** Royalties from articles or books are earned income if you receive them for transferring all of your rights to your work, or you have contracted to write the articles or book for an amount in cash plus a royalty on sales.

Royalties from the leasing of oil and mineral lands and from patents are not earned income.

 *Caution*

**Qualified Business Income Deduction Barred**

The 20% deduction for qualified business income does not apply to foreign income. That deduction is limited to income effectively connected with the conduct of a trade or business within the U.S. and that is includible in taxable income.

**Caution**

**Rental Income**

Rental income is generally not earned income. However, if you perform personal services, for example as an owner-manager of a hotel or rooming house in a foreign country, then up to 30% of your net rents may be earned income.

**Reimbursement of employee expenses.** Do not include reimbursement of expenses as earned income to the extent they equal expenses that you adequately accounted for to your employer; *see 20.31*. If your expenses exceed reimbursements, the excess is allocated according to the rules in *36.6*. If reimbursements exceed expenses, the excess is treated as earned income.

Straight commission salespersons or other employees who arrange with their employers, for withholding purposes, to consider a percentage of their commissions as attributable to their expenses treat such amounts as earned income.

## 36.3 Qualifying for the Foreign Earned Income Exclusion

You may elect the exclusion for foreign earned income (*see 36.2*, including the rule that denies eligibility for U.S. government pay) only if your tax home is in a foreign country and you meet either the foreign residence test or the foreign physical presence test of 330 days. The foreign residence and physical presence tests are discussed in *36.5*. Tax home is discussed at *20.7–20.9*. If your tax home is in the U.S., you may not claim the exclusion but may claim the foreign tax credit and your living expenses while away from home if you meet the rules in *20.9* for temporary assignments that are expected to last, and actually do last, for one year or less. Starting in 2018, contractors and their employees who support U.S. Armed Forces in designated combat zones *(35.4)* are treated as meeting the foreign tax home test even if they have an abode in the United States.

**Exclusion prorated on a daily basis.** If you qualify under the foreign residence or physical presence test for only part of 2018, the $103,900 exclusion limit is reduced on a daily basis.

> **EXAMPLES**
>
> 1. You were a resident of France from February 20, 2016, until July 1, 2018. On July 2, 2018, you returned to the U.S. Since your period of foreign residency included all of 2017, thereby satisfying the foreign residence test, you may claim a prorated exclusion for 2018. As you were abroad for 182 of the 365 days in 2018 (January 1 through July 1), you can exclude earnings up to $51,808, or 182/365 of the $103,900 maximum exclusion. If you earned more than $51,808, the exclusion is limited to $51,808.
> 2. You worked in France from June 1, 2017, through September 30, 2018. Your only days outside France were a 15-day vacation to the U.S. in December 2017. You do not qualify for an exclusion under the foreign residence test because you were not abroad for a full taxable year; you were not abroad for either the full year of 2017 or 2018. However, you do qualify under the physical presence test; you were physically present abroad for at least 330 full days during a 12-month period. The 12-month period giving you the largest 2018 exclusion is the 12-month period starting October 21, 2017, and ending October 20, 2018. See 36.5 for figuring the 12-month period. Since you were abroad for at least 330 full days during that 12-month period, you may claim an exclusion. In 2018, you were abroad for 293 days within the 12-month period (January 1 through October 20, 2018, is 293 days). Thus, you exclude earnings up to $83,405 ($103,900 × 293/365). Earnings exceeding $83,405 are not excludable.

**Caution**

**Countries Subject to Travel Restrictions**

You may not claim the foreign earned income exclusion, or the housing exclusion or deduction, if you work in a country subject to U.S. government travel restrictions, such as Cuba (not including non-government workers at Guantanamo Bay). You are not treated as a bona fide resident of, or as present in, a country subject to the travel ban. *See* Publication 54 and the Form 2555 instructions for a list of countries subject to travel restrictions.

If you are married and you and your spouse each have foreign earned income and meet the foreign residence or physical presence test, you may each claim a separate exclusion. If your permanent home is in a community property state, your earned income is not considered community property for purposes of the exclusion.

**Foreign earnings from a prior year.** Foreign income earned in a prior year but paid in 2018 does not qualify for the 2018 exclusion. However, if the income was attributable to foreign services performed in 2017, the pay is tax free in 2018 to the extent that you did not use the full 2017 exclusion of $102,100. Under another exception, payments received in 2018 for 2017 services are treated as 2018 income if the payment was within a normal payroll period of 16 days or less that included the last day of 2017. If the services were performed before 2017, no exclusion is available to shelter the pay. You cannot exclude income that you receive after the end of the year following the year in which you provide the services.

Income for services performed in the U.S. does not qualify for the exclusion, even though it is paid to you while you are abroad.

**Foreign tax credit.** Foreign taxes paid on tax-free foreign earned income do not qualify for a credit or deduction. But if your foreign pay for 2018 exceeds $103,900, you may claim a foreign tax credit or deduction for the foreign taxes allocated to taxable income. The instructions to Form 1116 and IRS Publication 514 provide details for making the computation.

## 36.4　How To Treat Housing Costs

The housing costs of employees and self-employed persons are treated differently by the tax law. Employees get a housing exclusion; self-employed persons get a deduction from taxable foreign earned income. If you live in a special camp provided by your employer, all housing costs are excluded; *see 36.8*.

**Exclusion for employer-financed housing costs.** The housing exclusion is the excess of the employer-financed reasonable housing expenses (see below) over a "base housing amount." The daily base housing amount is 16% of the maximum foreign earned income exclusion, prorated for the number of your qualifying days of foreign residence or presence for the year. Thus, for 2018, the base housing amount is $16,624 ($103,900 maximum foreign earned income exclusion × 16%) if you qualify under the foreign residence or physical presence test for the entire year. If you qualify under the residence or presence test for only part of the year, the $16,624 maximum base amount is prorated on a daily basis, so $45.55 ($16,624 ÷ 365) is allowed for each qualifying day in 2018.

In figuring housing expenses in excess of the base housing amount, there is a limit on the expenses that can be taken into account. Generally, the housing expenses cannot exceed 30% of the maximum earned income exclusion, prorated as applicable by the number of qualifying days of foreign residence or presence for the year. Thus, for 2018, the limit on housing expenses is generally $31,170 (30% × $103,900), or $85.40 per day, and the maximum housing exclusion is generally $14,546 ($31,170 – $16,624 maximum base amount). However, the expense limit, and thus the exclusion, may be significantly more than this if you work in a high cost locality. The IRS raises the annual limit for housing expenses in expensive foreign areas. The adjusted limits for high cost areas are provided in a table included in the instructions to Form 2555. In addition, when the IRS announces the high cost area limits for 2019 (in a notice likely to be released in March or April 2019), it is likely that it will allow taxpayers to use those 2019 limits to figure their housing exclusion for 2018 if the 2019 limit for housing expenses (full-year or daily) is higher than the amount allowed by the high cost area table in the 2018 Form 2555 instructions.

On Form 2555, your foreign earned income exclusion is limited to the excess of your foreign earned income (including employer-financed housing costs) over your housing exclusion.

**Reasonable housing expenses.** Include your rent, utilities other than telephone costs, insurance, parking, furniture rentals, and household repairs. The following expenses do not qualify: cost of purchasing a home, furniture, or accessories; pay television, home improvements; payments of mortgage principal; domestic labor; and depreciation on a home or on improvements to leased housing. Furthermore, interest and taxes that are otherwise deductible do not qualify for the exclusion.

You may include the costs of a separate household that you maintain outside the U.S. for your spouse and dependents because living conditions at your foreign home are adverse.

**Self-employed persons.** On Form 2555, self-employed individuals may claim a limited deduction (but not an exclusion) for housing costs exceeding the base housing amount. You may claim this deduction only to the extent it offsets taxable foreign earned income. The deduction is claimed "above-the-line" on Form 1040, even if you do not itemize deductions.

 *Filing Tip*

**Claiming the Housing Exclusion**

On Form 2555, you figure the housing exclusion before the foreign income exclusion. The income exclusion is limited to the excess of foreign earned income over the housing exclusion.

Where you may not deduct expenses because you do not have taxable foreign earned income, expenses may be carried forward to the next year and deducted in that year to the extent of taxable foreign earned income. Only a one-year carryover is allowed. If you have a carryover from 2018 to 2019 that cannot be claimed for 2019, that amount is lost.

**If you are an employee and self-employed during the same year.** Housing expenses above the base amount are partly excludable and partly deductible. For example, if half of your foreign earned income is from services as an employee, half of the excess housing expenses over the base amount are excludable. The remaining excess housing costs are deductible to the extent you have taxable foreign earned income after reducing it by the total of your allowable earned income exclusion plus your housing exclusion. Follow the instructions to Form 2555.

**Countries ineligible for tax benefits.** Housing expenses incurred in a country subject to a U.S. government travel restriction are not eligible for the tax benefits explained in this section. See Form 2555 instructions for a list of countries to which travel restrictions apply.

## 36.5 Meeting the Foreign Residence or Physical Presence Test

To qualify for the foreign earned income exclusion, you must be (1) a U.S. citizen (or U.S. resident alien who is a citizen or national of a country with which the U.S. has a tax treaty) who meets the foreign residence test, or (2) a U.S. citizen or resident alien meeting the physical presence test in a foreign country. The following areas are not considered foreign countries: Puerto Rico, Virgin Islands, Guam, Commonwealth of the Northern Mariana Islands, American Samoa, or the Antarctic region. The Tax Court has held that income earned in international airspace (by a flight attendant, for example) or in international waters (by a ship officer, for example) is not earned in a foreign country and thus does not qualify for the foreign earned income exclusion.

If, by the due date of your 2018 return (April 15, 2019), you have not yet satisfied the foreign residence or physical presence test, but you expect to meet either test after the filing date, you may either file on the due date and report your earnings or ask for a filing extension under the rules at *36.7.*

**Waiver of time test.** If war or civil unrest prevented you from meeting the foreign residence or physical presence test, you may claim the exclusion for the period you actually were a resident or physically present abroad. Foreign locations and the time periods that qualify for the waiver of the 2018 residency and physical presence tests will be listed in the Internal Revenue Bulletin early in 2019.

**Planning Reminder**

**Claiming Exemption From Withholding for Excludable Income**

You can file Form 673 with your U.S. employer to claim an exemption from withholding on wages to the extent of your expected foreign earned income exclusion and foreign housing exclusion. You must certify, under penalty of perjury, that you have good reason to believe that you will qualify under the foreign residence or physical presence test and also must certify your estimated foreign housing costs.

**Caution**

**Residence or Domicile?**

Residence does not have the same meaning as domicile. Your domicile is a permanent place of abode; it is the place to which you eventually plan to return wherever you go. You may have a residence in a place other than your domicile. Thus, you may go, say, to Amsterdam, and take up residence there and still intend to return to your domicile in the U.S. But leaving your domicile does not, by itself, establish a bona fide residence in a new place. You must intend to make a new place your residence.

> **EXAMPLE**
>
> You are a bona fide foreign resident from September 30, 2017, to March 25, 2019. The period includes your entire 2018 tax year. Therefore, up to $103,900 of your 2018 earnings is excludable. Your overseas earnings in 2017 and 2019 qualify for a proportionate part of the maximum exclusion allowed for those years.

**Foreign residence test.** You must be a U.S. citizen who is a bona fide resident of a foreign country for an uninterrupted period that includes one full tax year; a full tax year is from January 1 through December 31 for individuals who file on a calendar-year basis. A U.S. resident alien who is a citizen or national of a country with which the U.S. has an income tax treaty and meets the full-year foreign residence test also qualifies. Business or vacation trips to the U.S. or another country will not disqualify you from satisfying the foreign residence test. If you are abroad more than one year but less than two, the entire period qualifies if it includes one full tax year.

To prove you are a foreign resident, you must show your intention to be a resident of the foreign country. Evidence tending to confirm your intention to stay in a foreign country includes: (1) your family accompanies you; (2) you buy a house or rent an apartment rather than a hotel room; (3) you participate in the foreign community activities; (4) you can speak the foreign language; (5) you have a permanent foreign address; (6) you join clubs there; or (7) you open charge accounts in stores in the foreign country.

You will not qualify if you take inconsistent positions toward your foreign residency. That is, you will not be treated as a bona fide resident of a foreign country if you have earned income from sources within that country, filed a statement with the authorities of that country that you are not a resident there, and have been held not subject to the income tax of that country. However, this rule does not prevent you from qualifying under the physical presence test.

If you cannot prove that you are a resident, check to determine if your stay qualifies under the physical presence test.

**Physical presence test.** To qualify under this test, you must show you were on foreign soil 330 full days (about 11 months) during a 12-month period. Whether you were a resident or a transient is of no importance. You have to show you were physically present in a foreign country or countries for 330 full days during any 12-consecutive-month period. The 330 qualifying days do not have to be consecutive. The 12-month period may begin with any day. There is no requirement that it begin with your first full day abroad. It may begin before or after arrival in a foreign country and may end before or after departure from a foreign country. A full day is from midnight to midnight (24 consecutive hours). You must spend each of the 330 days on foreign soil. In departing from U.S. soil to go directly to the foreign country, or in returning directly to the U.S. from a foreign country, the time you spend on or over international waters does not count toward the 330-day total.

---

### EXAMPLES

1. On August 9, you fly from New York City to London. You arrive there at 10 a.m. August 10. Your first full qualifying day toward the 330-day period is August 11.

   You may count in your 330-day period:

2. Time spent traveling between foreign countries.

3. Time spent on a vacation in foreign countries. There is no requirement that the 330 days must be spent on a job.

4. Time spent in a foreign country while employed by the U.S. government counts towards the 330-day test, even though pay from the government does not qualify for the earned income exclusion.

5. Time in foreign countries, territorial waters, or travel in the air over a foreign country. However, you will lose qualifying days if any part of such travel is on or over international waters and takes 24 hours or more, or any part of such travel is within the U.S. or its possessions.

6. You depart from Naples, Italy, by ship on June 10 at 6:00 p.m. and arrive at Haifa, Israel, at 7:00 a.m. on June 14. The trip exceeded 24 hours and passed through international waters. Therefore, you lose as qualifying days June 10, 11, 12, 13, and 14. Assuming you remain in Haifa, Israel, the next qualifying day is June 15.

---

**Choosing the 12-month period.** You qualify under the physical presence test if you were on foreign soil 330 days during any period of 12 consecutive months. Since there may be several 12-month periods during which you meet the 330-day test, you should choose the 12-month period allowing you the largest possible exclusion if you qualify under the physical presence test for only part of 2018.

---

### EXAMPLE

You worked in France from June 1, 2017, through September 30, 2018, and the next day you left the country. During this period, you left France only for a 15-day vacation to the U.S. during December 2017. You earned $100,000 for your work in France during 2018. Your maximum 2018 exclusion is figured as follows:

1. Start with your last full day, September 30, 2018, and count back 330 full days during which you were abroad. Not counting the 15 vacation days in the U.S., the 330th day is October 21, 2017. This is the first day of your 12-month period.

2. From October 21, 2017, count forward 12 months to October 20, 2018, which is the last day of your 12-month period.

---

3. Count the number of days in 2018 that fall within the 12-month period ending October 20, 2018. Here, the number of qualifying days is 293, from January 1 through October 20, 2018.

4. The maximum 2018 exclusion is $103,900 × 293/365, or $83,405. You may exclude $83,405, the lesser of the maximum exclusion or your actual earnings of $100,000.

## 36.6 Claiming Deductions

You may not deduct expenses that are allocable to the foreign earned income and housing exclusions. If you elect the earned income exclusion, you deduct expenses as follows:

Personal or nonbusiness deductions, such as medical expenses, mortgage interest, and real estate taxes paid on a personal residence, are deductible if you itemize deductions. Business expenses from self-employment that are attributable to earning excludable income are not deductible. Job-related business expenses attributable to non-excludable earnings are in any case not deductible from 2018 through 2025 due to the suspension of miscellaneous itemized deductions subject to the 2% of adjusted gross income floor.

If your foreign earnings exceed the exclusion ceiling, you allocate expenses between taxable and excludable income and deduct the amount allocated to taxable earned income; *see* Example 2 below.

### EXAMPLES

1. You were a resident of Denmark and elect to exclude your self-employment earnings of $70,000 from income. You also incurred unreimbursed travel expenses of $2,000. You may not deduct the travel expenses, since the amount is attributable to the earning of tax-free income.

2. You have self-employment earnings of $128,875 in Germany and satisfy the physical presence test. Your unreimbursed travel expenses for 2018 are $5,000, after reducing meal costs by 50%. If you elect the $103,900 exclusion (80% of your foreign earnings), 20% of the travel expenses, or $1,000, attributable to the taxable 20% of earnings, may be claimed as a business deduction on Schedule C.

**Filing Tip**

**Extension of Time To File**

If you are living and working abroad on April 15, 2019, you have an automatic extension to June 17, 2019. For an additional four months, file Form 4868 by June 17, 2019, and pay the estimated tax to limit interest and late payment penalties. For a longer extension, in anticipation of owing no tax on your foreign income, you may file Form 2350 either with the Internal Revenue Service Center in Austin, TX 73301-0045, or with a local IRS representative. File Form 2350 by the due date for filing your 2018 return, which is June 17, 2019, if you are abroad and are on a calendar year. Generally, you will be granted an extension for a period ending 30 days after the date you reasonably expect to qualify for the foreign earned income exclusion.

If your job expenses are reimbursed and the expenses are adequately accounted for to your employer *(20.30)*, the reimbursements are not reported as income on your Form W-2. You may have to allocate state income taxes paid on your income.

If either you or your spouse elects the earned income or housing exclusion, you may not claim an IRA deduction based on excluded income.

If you were reimbursed by your employer under a non-accountable plan, or if the reimbursement is for expenses that you deducted in an earlier year, the reimbursement is considered earned income in the year of receipt and is added to other earned income before taking the exclusion and making the allocation.

**Compulsory home leave.** Foreign service officers stationed abroad must periodically return to the U.S. Because the home leave is compulsory, foreign service officers may deduct their travel expenses; travel expenses of the officer's family are not deductible.

## 36.7 Exclusion Not Established When Your Return Is Due

When your 2018 return is due, you may not have been abroad long enough to qualify for the exclusion. If you expect to qualify under either the residence or physical presence test after the due date for your 2018 return, you may either (1) ask for an extension of time for filing your return on Form 2350 until after you qualify under either rule or (2) file your return on the due date, reporting the foreign income on the return, pay the full tax, and then file for a refund when you qualify.

If you will have tax to pay even after qualifying for the exclusion—for example, your earned income exceeds the exclusion—you may file for an extension to file but you will owe interest on the tax due. To avoid interest charges on the tax, you may take one of the following steps:

1. File a timely return and pay the total tax due without the application of the exclusion. When you do qualify, make sure you file a timely *(47.2)* refund claim; or

2. Pay the estimated tax liability when you apply for the extension to file on Form 2350. If the extension is granted, the payment is applied to the tax shown on your return when you file.

## 36.8 Tax-Free Meals and Lodging for Workers in Camps

If you must live in a camp provided by your employer, you may exclude from income *(3.13)* the value of the lodging and meals furnished to you if the camp is (1) provided because you work in a remote area where satisfactory housing is not available; (2) located as near as is practical to the worksite; and (3) in an enclave that normally houses at least 10 employees and in which lodgings are not offered to the general public.

You also may qualify for the earned income exclusion; *see 36.1.*

## 36.9 U. S. Virgin Islands, Samoa, Guam, and Northern Marianas

The U.S. Virgin Islands, Puerto Rico, Guam, American Samoa, and the Commonwealth of the Northern Mariana Islands have their own independent tax departments. Therefore, contact the particular tax authority for the proper treatment of your income and obtain a copy of IRS Publication 570, Tax Guide for Individuals With Income From U.S. Possessions, which provides phone, mail, and internet contact information.

**Possession exclusion.** A possession exclusion applies to bona fide residents of American Samoa for the entire year. On Form 4563, such residents may exclude for U.S. tax purposes their income from sources in American Samoa and income effectively connected with a business in American Samoa. The exclusion applies to amounts earned for services as an employee of the American Samoan government or its agencies but does not apply to pay as an employee, whether civilian or military, of the U.S. government or its agencies.

## 36.10 Earnings in Puerto Rico

If you are a U.S. citizen or resident alien who is also a resident of Puerto Rico for the entire year, you generally report all of your income on your Puerto Rico tax return. Where you report income from U.S. sources on the Puerto Rico tax return, a credit against the Puerto Rico tax may be claimed for income taxes paid to the United States.

If you are not a resident of Puerto Rico, you report on a Puerto Rico return only income from Puerto Rico sources. Wages earned for services performed in Puerto Rico for the U.S. government or for private employers are treated as income from Puerto Rico sources.

**United States· tax returns.** As a U.S. citizen, you must file a U.S. tax return reporting income from all sources. But if you are a bona fide resident of Puerto Rico for an entire tax year, you do not report on a U.S. tax return any income earned in Puerto Rico during your residence there, except amounts received for services performed in Puerto Rico as an employee of the U.S. government. Similar rules apply if you have been a bona fide resident of Puerto Rico for at least two years before changing your residence from Puerto Rico. On a U.S. tax return, you may not deduct expenses or claim tax credits allocable to the excludable income. Personal exemptions are fully deductible.

If you are not a bona fide resident of Puerto Rico for the entire tax year, or were not a bona fide resident for two years prior to the tax year, you report on your U.S. tax return all income you earned in Puerto Rico, as well as all income from other sources. If you are required to report income earned in Puerto Rico on your U.S. tax return, you may claim a credit for income tax paid to Puerto Rico. You figure the credit on Form 1116.

**Caution**

**Form 8898 To Report Change of Residence**

You generally must file Form 8898 for a tax year in which you have worldwide income of over $75,000 and in which you become or cease to be a bona fide resident of a U.S. possession. The test is for each person, so if you and your spouse each meet the test, each of you must file a Form 8898. A $1,000 penalty may be imposed for failure to file a required Form 8898.

**Planning Reminder**

**Information for Puerto Rico Filing**

Information on Puerto Rico tax returns may be obtained at www.hacienda.gobierno.pr. The phone number is 787-622-0123. Written requests may be sent to the Departamento de Hacienda, Negociado de Asistencia Contributiva, P.O. Box 9024140, San Juan, Puerto Rico, 00902-4140.

**Caution**

**Earnings Subject to Self-Employment Tax**

Even if you have net self-employment earnings from Puerto Rico sources and do not have to file a U.S. return, you must still report the earnings and pay U.S. self-employment tax on Form 1040-SS.

*See* IRS Publication 570, Tax Guide for Individuals With Income from U.S. Possessions, for further information on filing U.S. and Puerto Rico tax returns.

## 36.11 Tax Treaties With Foreign Countries

Tax treaties between the United States and foreign countries modify some of the rules discussed in this chapter. The purpose of the treaties is to avoid double taxation. Consult your tax advisor about the effect of these treaties on your income. IRS Publications 54 and 901 have information about the tax treaties the U.S. maintains with foreign countries; also find information at www.irs.gov/Businesses/International-Businesses/United-States-Income-Tax-Treaties — A-to-Z.

## 36.12 Exchange Rates and Blocked Currency

Income reported on your federal income tax return must be stated in U.S. dollars. Where you are paid in foreign currency, you report your pay in U.S. dollars on the basis of the exchange rates prevailing at the time the income is actually or constructively received. You use the rate that most closely reflects the value of the foreign currency. Be prepared to justify the rate you use.

**Fulbright grants.** If 70% or more of a Fulbright grant is paid in nonconvertible foreign currency, U.S. tax may be paid in the foreign currency. *See* IRS Publication 54 for details.

**Blocked currency.** A citizen or resident alien may be paid in a foreign currency that cannot be converted into American dollars and removed from the foreign country. If your income is in blocked currency, you may elect to defer the reporting of that income until: (1) the currency becomes convertible into dollars, (2) you actually convert it into dollars, or (3) you use it for personal expenses. Purchase of a business or investment in the foreign country is not the kind of use that is treated as a conversion. (4) You make a gift of it or leave it in your will. (5) You are a resident alien and you give up your U.S. residence.

If you use this method to defer the income, you may not deduct the expenses of earning it until you report it. You must continue to use this method after you choose it. You may only change with permission of the IRS.

You do not defer the reporting of capital losses incurred in a country having a blocked currency.

There may be these disadvantages in deferring income:

- Many years' income may accumulate and all be taxed in one year.
- You have no control over the year in which the blocked income becomes taxable. You usually cannot control the events that cause the income to become unblocked.

**Filing Tip**

**Choosing Credit or Deduction**

If you qualify for a credit or deduction for foreign income taxes, you will generally receive a larger tax reduction by claiming a tax credit rather than a deduction. A deduction is only a partial offset against your tax, whereas a credit is deducted in full from your tax. Also, taking a deduction may bar you from carrying back an excess credit from a later year. However, a deduction for foreign income taxes may give you a larger tax saving if the foreign tax is levied at a high rate and the proportion of foreign income to U.S. income is small. Compute your tax under both methods and choose the one providing the larger tax reduction.

You choose to defer income in blocked currency by filing a tentative tax return reporting your blocked taxable income and explaining that you are deferring the payment of income tax because your income is not in dollars or in property or currency that is readily convertible into dollars. You must attach to your tentative return a regular return, reporting any unblocked taxable income received during the year or taxable income that became unblocked during the year. When the currency finally becomes unblocked or convertible into a currency or property convertible to dollars, you pay tax on the earnings at the rate prevailing in the year the currency became unblocked or convertible. On the tentative return, note at the top: "Report of Deferrable Foreign Income, pursuant to Revenue Ruling 74-351." File separate returns for each country from which blocked currency is received. The election must be made by the due date for filing a return for the year in which an election is sought.

## 36.13 Foreign Tax Credit or Deduction for Foreign Taxes Paid

You do not have to live abroad to have paid foreign taxes; the taxes may result from having foreign investments. You may claim an itemized deduction (Schedule A, Form 1040) for qualified foreign income taxes or you may claim a foreign tax credit. You must file Form 1116 to compute your credit unless the *de minimis* exception applies; *see* below. You may not claim a foreign tax credit or deduction for taxes paid on income not subject to U.S. tax. If all of your foreign earned income is excluded, none of the foreign taxes paid on such income may be taken as a credit or deduction on your U.S. return. If you exclude only part of your foreign pay, you determine which foreign taxes are attributable to excluded income and thus barred as foreign tax credits by applying the fractional computation provided in the instructions to Form 1116 and IRS Publication 514.

For any tax year, you may not elect to deduct some foreign taxes and claim others as a credit. One method must be applied to all taxes paid or accrued during the tax year. If you are a cash-basis taxpayer, you may claim a credit for accrued foreign taxes, but you must consistently follow this method once elected.

**Exemption from credit limit for de minimis foreign taxes.** If you have $300 or less of creditable foreign taxes, $600 or less if married filing jointly, you may elect to be exempt from the overall limitation on the credit, provided that your only foreign source income is qualified passive income and all the income and any foreign taxes paid on it were reported to you on a qualified payee statement such as Form 1099-DIV, Form 1099-INT, or Schedule K-1 of Form 1041, 1065, 1065-B, or 1120S. If the election is made, a foreign tax credit may be claimed without filing Form 1116. See the instructions to Form 1116 for rules on making this election.

**Credit disallowed.** The credit may not be claimed if:

- You are a nonresident alien. However, under certain circumstances, if you are a bona fide resident for an entire taxable year in Puerto Rico you may be able to claim the credit. Also, a nonresident alien engaged in a U.S. trade or business may be able to claim a credit for foreign taxes paid on foreign source income effectively connected to that U.S. business.
- You are a citizen of a U.S. possession (except Puerto Rico) but not a U.S. citizen or resident.

No credit is allowed for taxes imposed by a country designated by the government as engaging in terroristic activities; *see* IRS Publication 514 for a list of these countries.

**Taxes qualifying for the credit.** The credit is allowed only for foreign income tax, excess profits taxes, and similar taxes in the nature of an income tax. It is not allowed for any taxes paid to foreign countries on sales, gross receipts, production, the privilege to do business, personal property, or export of capital. *See* the instructions to Form 1116 and IRS Publication 514 for other taxes that may qualify for the credit.

**Reporting foreign income on your return.** You report the gross amount of your foreign income in terms of United States currency. You also attach a schedule showing how you figured the foreign income in United States currency.

**Limit on credit.** Your credit for foreign income taxes paid or accrued is subject to a limitation on Form 1116 unless you qualify for and elect the exemption for *de minimis* taxes discussed above. The limitation is your total U.S. regular tax liability multiplied by a fraction: the numerator is your net foreign source taxable income (after required adjustments), and the denominator is your total taxable income from all sources. To determine the limit, you must separate your foreign source income into either the passive income category or the general income category. If you have both categories of foreign source income, you must figure the credit limit for each category on a separate Form 1116. If you have income from activities in sanctioned countries, or certain income re-sourced by treaty as foreign source income, or you paid taxes on a foreign source lump-sum distribution from a pension plan, a separate Form 1116 must be used to figure the limit for these categories as well. If you have more than one category of income, you combine the credits for the separate categories on Part IV of the Form 1116 with the largest credit. Part IV is not completed on the other Forms 1116, which are filed as attachments. See IRS Publication 514 and the instructions to Form 1116 for the details on these computations.

**Carryback and carryover of excess foreign tax credit.** If you are unable to claim all of the qualified foreign taxes paid or accrued during the year because of the limit on the credit, the balance may be carried back one year and then carried forward 10 years. For further details, *see* IRS Publication 514 and the instructions to Form 1116.

*Caution*

**Foreign Accounts May Be Reportable**
If you have foreign financial accounts, you may have to report them annually; *see 4.12*, 48.7.

# CHAPTER 37

# Planning Alimony and Marital Settlements

The tax treatment of alimony payments is changing for amounts pursuant to decrees and agreements finalized after December 31, 2018. But the tax rules in this chapter apply for 2018 returns. Payments under decrees and agreements finalized before 2019 that meet the tax law tests for alimony are deductible if you pay them, and taxable if you receive them. Payments are not deductible by the payer unless taxable to the recipient.

You claim a deduction for deductible alimony that you pay on Form 1040. You deduct the payments even if you claim the standard deduction rather than itemizing deductions. You must enter the Social Security number of your ex-spouse. Otherwise, your deduction may be disallowed and you may have to pay a $50 penalty. If you pay deductible alimony to more than one ex-spouse, enter the Social Security number of one of them and provide similar information for the others on a separate statement attached to your return.

If you receive taxable alimony, report the payments on Form 1040. You must give your ex-spouse your Social Security number and could be subject to a $50 penalty if you fail to do so.

Transfers of property between spouses during marriage, as well as transfers incident to divorce, are generally treated as tax-free exchanges. The transferor-spouse does not realize gain or loss and the transferee takes the transferor's basis in the property (6.7).

*Note: The discussion below in 37.1 through 37.7 explains the tax rules applicable to qualifying alimony payments made under pre-2019 agreements. For agreements finalized after 2018, see 37.9.*

## 37.1 Rules for Pre-2019 Alimony Agreements

Under alimony agreements entered into before 2019, it was important for both spouses to recognize that they may have had a common financial interest.

For example, assume that after a divorce in 2018 one spouse is to make payments to the other spouse. If tax planning is approached from the viewpoint of each spouse separately, the tax deduction is an advantage for the payer-spouse, while the payee-spouse would prefer the payments to be tax free. However, both advantages could not be achieved, and the couple had to face the reality of the tax law, which allowed the payer-spouse to deduct payments only if they were taxed as alimony to the payee-spouse. The spouses had to compromise by setting amounts and tax consequences that balanced their interests. The projected tax brackets of the parties may have been an important factor, especially where the payer expected to be in a high bracket. For example, if the payer-spouse expected to be in a higher tax bracket during the payout period than the payee-spouse, the tax savings that the payer-spouse would receive from an agreement that qualifies the alimony as deductible by that spouse and taxable to the other spouse could conserve more of the payer-spouse's assets while the payee-spouse receives payments.

**Alimony requirements.** For payments under a pre-2019 agreement to be alimony that is deductible by the payer and taxable to the recipient, separate returns must be filed if you are still married at the end of the year, and these rules must be met:

- The alimony must be paid under a decree of divorce or legal separation, a written separation agreement or decree of support *(37.2)*. Payments may be called alimony, spousal support, spousal maintenance, or another term required by local law.

- The agreement must provide for cash payments *(37.3)*. A noncash property settlement is not alimony. There is no minimum payout period for annual cash alimony payments of $15,000 or less. One payment of $15,000 can qualify as deductible and taxable alimony. There is also no minimum payout period for annual alimony payments exceeding $15,000. However, recapture of alimony deductions claimed in the first or second year may occur where annual payments of over $15,000 are scheduled and paid, but in the second or third year a reduced payment is made. To avoid recapture of deductions for payments over $15,000, carefully plan schedules of declining payments within the rules discussed at *37.7*.

- In providing for the support of children, a specific allocation to their support or the setting of certain contingencies disqualifies payments as alimony, so such payments are not deductible by the payer and not taxable to the recipient *(37.5)*.

- Divorced and legally separated parties must not live in the same household when payments are made. If they live in the same household, alimony payments are not deductible or taxable. However, there are these exceptions: A spouse who makes payments while preparing to leave the common residence may deduct payments made within one month before the departure. Also, where the spouses are separated under a written agreement, but not legally separated under a decree of divorce or separate maintenance, payments can be alimony even if they are members of the same household when the payments are made.

- The payer spouse's liability to pay alimony must end on the death of the payee-spouse. The alimony agreement does not have to state expressly that payments end on death if liability ends under state law *(37.4)*.

**Qualifying payments can be designated as "not alimony."** You may specifically state in the decree or agreement that payments that otherwise would be alimony are not. A provision stating that the payments are neither taxable to the payee-spouse (under IRC Section 71) nor deductible by the payer-spouse (under IRC Section 215) effectively disqualifies the payments from alimony treatment. A copy of the agreement that contains the statement must be attached to the tax return of the payee-spouse for each year the statement is applicable.

## 37.2 Decree or Agreement Required

To be deductible and taxable as alimony, payments must be required by one of the following divorce or separation instruments: (1) a decree of divorce or legal separation; (2) a written separation agreement; or (3) a decree of support. Voluntary payments are not deductible or taxable.

When a decree of divorce or separate maintenance fails to mention alimony, payments qualify as long as they are made under a written agreement considered "incident to" the decree.

Payments made under an agreement amended after a divorce or legal separation may also qualify, if the amendment is considered "incident" to the divorce or separation. For example, the IRS agrees that a written amendment changing the amount of alimony payments is incident to the divorce where the legal obligation to support under the original agreement survived the divorce. However, payments under an amended agreement did not qualify where the original agreement settled all rights between the parties and made no provision for future support. The legal obligation to support the former spouse did not survive the divorce and could not be revived by the new agreement.

**Divorced or legally separated.** The obligation to pay alimony must be imposed by the decree of divorce or separate maintenance or a written agreement incident to the divorce or separation.

Alimony paid under a Mexican divorce decree qualifies. Payments under a Mexican or state decree declared invalid by another jurisdiction do not qualify according to the IRS. Two appeals courts have rejected the IRS position.

Support payments ordered by a court in a spouse's home state qualify as alimony, even though not provided for by an ex parte divorce decree obtained by the other spouse in another state. Similarly, payments qualified when a state court increased support originally ordered before the husband obtained an uncontested Mexican divorce.

Payments made under a separation approved by a Roman Catholic ecclesiastical board do not qualify.

**Annulments.** Payments made under an annulment decree qualify as deductible (and taxable) alimony.

**Separated from spouse.** Where spouses are separated and living apart, alimony is deductible by the payer-spouse and taxable to the payee-spouse provided it is paid under either a written separation agreement or decree of support.

**A decree of support.** Any court decree or order requiring support payments qualifies, including alimony pendente lite (temporary alimony while the action is pending) and an interlocutory (not final) divorce decree.

In certain community property states, payments under a decree of alimony pendente lite which do not exceed the spouse's interest in community income are neither deductible by one spouse nor taxable to the other spouse; payments exceeding a spouse's interest are taxable to that spouse and deductible by the other spouse.

## 37.3 Cash Payments Required

Only payments of cash, checks, and money orders payable on demand qualify as taxable and deductible alimony. Your cash payment to a third party for a spouse qualifies if made under the terms of a divorce decree or separation instrument. For example, as required by your divorce decree, you pay your former spouse's mortgage payments and real estate taxes on a home he or she owns, as well as his or her medical costs and tuition expenses. Assuming the other alimony tests *(37.1)* are met, you may deduct the payments as alimony and your former spouse must report them as alimony received. Your former spouse may

**Reporting Alimony**

If you paid alimony in 2018 meeting the deductible tests, you must report the recipient's Social Security number.

**Property Transfers**

A property transfer to a former spouse that is incident to a divorce is generally treated as a tax-free exchange *(6.7)*.

deduct the real estate taxes, mortgage interest, medical and tuition costs as if he or she had paid them directly, subject to the regular deduction limits.

You may not deduct payments to maintain property owned by you but used by your spouse. For example, you pay the mortgage expenses, real estate taxes, and insurance premiums for a house that you own and in which your former spouse lives. You may not deduct those payments as alimony even if they are required by a decree or agreement.

Providing services or transferring or providing property does not qualify. For example, you may not deduct as alimony your note, the assignment of a third party note, or an annuity contract.

Premiums paid for term or whole life insurance on your life made under a divorce or separation instrument qualify as deductible alimony to the extent your former spouse owns the policy.

## 37.4 Payments Must Stop at Death

Liability for a payment must end on the death of the payee-spouse. If all the payments must continue after the death of the payee-spouse, none of the payments, whether made before or after the payee's death, qualify as taxable (to payee-spouse) or deductible (by payer-spouse) alimony. If some payments must continue after the payee's death, that amount is not alimony regardless of when paid.

Note that these rules do not just prevent a deduction for payments made to the payee-spouse's estate or heirs after the payee's death, but may also have the surprising result of disallowing an alimony deduction for otherwise qualifying payments actually made to the payee-spouse. The issue is a hypothetical one: would the payment have to be made after the payee-spouse's death?

If the answer is yes, the payment is not deductible, regardless of when made.

The divorce decree or separation agreement does not have to specifically state that payments end at death, if under state law the liability to pay ends on the death of the payee-spouse.

 *Planning Reminder*

**Payments to a Third Party**

Cash payments to a third party may be deducted as alimony if they are under the terms of a divorce decree or separation instrument. You may also deduct as alimony payments made to a third party at the written request of the payee-spouse. For example, your former spouse asks you to make a cash donation to a charitable organization instead of paying alimony installments to her. Her request must be in writing and state that both she and you intend the payment to be treated as alimony. You must receive the written request before you file your return for the taxable year in which the payment was made. Your former spouse may deduct the payment as a charitable contribution if she claims itemized deductions.

### EXAMPLES

1. Under the terms of a divorce decree, Smith is obligated to make annual alimony payments of $30,000, terminating on the earlier of the end of six years or the death of Mrs. Smith. She also is to keep custody of their two minor children. The decree also provides that if on her death the children are still minors, Smith is to pay annually $10,000 to a trust each year. The trust income and corpus are to be used for the children until the youngest child reaches the age of majority. Under these facts, Smith's possible liability to make annual $10,000 payments to the trust is treated as a substitute for $10,000 of the $30,000 annual payments. $10,000 of each of the $30,000 annual payments does not qualify as alimony.

2. Same facts as in Example 1, but the alimony is to end on the earlier of the expiration of 15 years or the death of Mrs. Smith. Further, if Mrs. Smith dies before the end of the 15-year period, Smith will pay her estate the difference between the total amount that he would have paid had she survived and the amount actually paid. For example, if she dies at the end of the tenth year, he will pay her estate $150,000 ($450,000 − $300,000). Under these facts, his liability to make a lump-sum payment to her estate is a substitute for the full amount of each of the annual $30,000 payments. Accordingly, none of the annual $30,000 payments qualify as alimony.

To the extent that one or more payments are to begin, increase in amount, or accelerate after the death of the payee-spouse, such payments may be treated as a substitute for continuing payments after the death of the payee-spouse. Such substitute payments will be denied alimony treatment.

**Attorneys' fees.** Under the laws of many states, a court award of attorneys' fees remains enforceable after the death of the payee-spouse, thereby disqualifying a payer's alimony deduction for the payment and making it nontaxable to the payee-spouse. For example, a husband who was ordered by an Oklahoma court to pay his wife $154,000 for her attorneys' fees prior to the entry of a final divorce decree was unable to deduct his payment. The Tax Court and the Tenth Circuit Court of Appeals agreed with the IRS that under Oklahoma law, the husband's liability to pay the attorneys' fees would not have ended, as a hypothetical matter, had the wife died before the final decree was entered. The policy reason for the state law is to assure that attorneys get paid for their services, which will enable indigent clients to retain counsel in divorce actions.

In this situation, the payer can obtain a deduction if the attorneys' fees remain the liability of the payee-spouse and the court decree increases the amount of cash alimony to cover the fees, rather than having them paid separately. The cash alimony would be taxable to the payee-spouse. The payee-spouse's payment of the fees to the attorneys may be deductible, but only as a miscellaneous expense subject to the 2% of AGI floor.

## 37.5 Child Support Payments Are Not Alimony

A payment that is specifically designated as child support in the divorce or separation instrument (37.2) is not deductible by the payer or taxable as alimony to the payee.

Even if there is not a specific allocation to child support, a payment will be presumed by the IRS to be payable for child support if it is to be reduced on the happening of a contingency relating to the child, such as: the child reaches a specific age or income level, or the child leaves school, marries, leaves the parent's household, or begins to work.

If a divorce or separation instrument requires both alimony and child support payments, and child support payments for a prior year were missed, or current-year child support payments are less than the required amount, an expected alimony deduction for current-year payments can be lost because the payments are applied first to the child support obligations, including any arrearage. For example, a taxpayer paid $17,963 to his ex-spouse in 2004. His total child support obligation in 2004 for his two children was $23,147, of which $12,000 was for 2004 child support, $5,125 for past-due child support, and $6,022 to reimburse his ex-spouse for her payment of health insurance premiums and medical expenses for the children that he was obligated to pay. Since his total payments in 2004 of $17,963 were less than the total child support owed for 2004, the Tax Court held that all of the payments were allocable to the child support and not deductible as alimony.

**Tax refund diversion for delinquent child support.** The IRS can give your tax refund to a state that is paying support to your child if you fail to make support payments. The IRS will not notify you of the diversion until it is made to the state. However, the state agency must provide prior notice of the proposed offset and procedures for contesting it.

*Caution*

**Alimony Reductions Tied to Child's Age**

If a reduction in your payments is not specifically tied to your child's reaching majority age but the scheduled date for the reduction is within six months before or after your child reaches age 18 or 21 (or other age of majority under local law), the IRS holds that the reduction is tied to the child's age. The reduction amount will be treated as child support unless you can prove that the reduction is for some other purpose. The IRS makes the same presumption if you have more than one child and your alimony payments are to be reduced at least twice and each reduction is within one year of a different child's reaching a particular age between ages 18 and 24; *see* the Example in *37.5*.

> ### EXAMPLE
>
> On March 1, 2018, Thomas and Tina were divorced when their children, John (born July 15, 2004), and Jane (born September 23, 2006), are ages 13 and 11. Under the divorce decree, Thomas is to make monthly alimony payments of $2,000. The monthly payments are to be reduced to $1,500 on January 1, 2025, and to $1,000 on January 1, 2029. On January 1, 2025, the date of the first reduction, John will be 20 years, 5 months, and 17 days old. On January 1, 2029, the date of the second reduction, Jane will be 22 years, 3 months, and 9 days old. As each reduction is to occur not more than one year before or after each child reaches the age of 21 years and four months, the IRS will presume that the reductions are associated with the happening of a contingency relating to the children. The two reductions total $1,000 per month and are treated as the amount fixed for the support of the children. Thus, $1,000 of the $2,000 monthly payment does not qualify as alimony. To avoid this result, Thomas must prove that the reductions were not related to the support of the children.

## 37.6 No Minimum Payment Period for Alimony

There is no minimum payment period, but a recapture rule applies where payments fall by more than $15,000 within the first three years (37.7).

## 37.7 3rd Year Recapture If Alimony Drops by More Than $15,000

The recapture rules are designed to prevent the so-called "front loading" of property settlement payments disguised as alimony. However, the rules apply even where no property settlement was intended if you come within their terms. For example, the recapture rules may be triggered where several scheduled payments in the first year are missed and paid in the second year.

In general, deductible payments you make in the first year or second year are recaptured (that is, reported as income) in the third year where payments within the first three years decline by more than $15,000. The three years are called "post-separation years." The first post-separation year is the first calendar year in which you make a payment qualifying as alimony under a decree of divorce or separate maintenance or a separation agreement. The period does not begin with the year of the decree or agreement if no payments are made. Recapture does not apply to temporary support payments made before the final decree or agreement. The second and third post-separation years are the next two calendar years after the first post-separation year whether or not payments are made during those years.

### The steps of recapture are:

1. Step 1. Recapture for the second-year payment is computed first. This is the excess, if any, of the second-year payment over the third-year payment, minus $15,000.

2. Step 2. Recapture for the first-year payment is computed next. There is recapture if the first-year payment exceeds by more than $15,000 the average payment made in the second and third years. In figuring the average payment, reduce the second-year payment by any recapture amount for the second year figured under Step 1.

The Examples below illustrate how to make these computations.

 *Filing Tip*

**Reporting Recapture on Your Return**

The payer-spouse reports the recaptured amount as income in the third year and the payee-spouse claims a deduction for the same amount. The payer reports the recaptured amount on Form 1040.

The payee-spouse deducts the recaptured amount on Form 1040.

### EXAMPLES

1. In 2016, Jones obtains a divorce and pays deductible alimony of $50,000. His ex-spouse reports $50,000 as income. In 2017 and 2018, he makes no payments. On his 2018 return, $35,000 of the first year (2016) deduction is recaptured ($50,000 – $15,000) and reported as income by Jones. His ex-spouse deducts the recaptured $35,000 on her 2018 return.

2. In 2016, Smith makes his first alimony payment of $50,000; in 2017 he pays $20,000 and in 2018 he pays nothing. On his 2018 return, $32,500 is recaptured as follows:

| | | |
|---|---|---|
| Recapture of second-year payment: | | |
| Payment in 2nd year | | $20,000 |
| Less: 3rd-year payment | $0 | |
| Less: Allowance | 15,000 | 15,000 |
| Recapture for second year | | $ 5,000 |
| Recapture of first-year payment: | | |
| Average calculation: | | |
| Payment over the 2nd and 3rd years | $20,000 | |
| Less: recapture for the 2nd year | $ 5,000 | |
| | $15,000 | |
| Average ($15,000 ÷ 2) | $ 7,500 | |
| Payment in first year | | $50,000 |
| Less: Average | $ 7,500 | |
| Less: Allowance | 15,000 | 22,500 |
| Recapture for first year | | $27,500 |
| Total recaptured in 2018: | | |
| For second year | | $ 5,000 |
| For first year | | $27,500 |
| Total: | | $32,500 |

**When recapture does not apply.** Recapture is not triggered if payments in both the first and second post-separation years do not exceed $15,000. Recapture also does not apply to:

- Payments made under a continuing liability to pay for at least three years a fixed part of your income from a business or property or from a job or self-employed business or profession, or

- Payments that end because of your death or the death of your former spouse or the remarriage of your former spouse at any time before the end of the third post-separation year.

## 37.8 Legal Fees of Marital Settlements

Until now, legal fees allocable to the receipt of taxable alimony were deductible as a miscellaneous itemized deduction subject to the 2% of adjusted gross income floor. However, due to the suspension of this deduction for 2018 through 2025, no write-off can be taken for legal fees related to marital settlements.

## 37.9 Alimony Rules for 2019

If you have a divorce decree or separation agreement that is finalized before January 1, 2019, then all of the rules in this chapter continue to apply to alimony payments. However, for decrees and agreements finalized after December 31, 2018, new rules will apply going forward.

Under the new rules, no deduction is allowed for alimony payments and the receipt of alimony payments is not taxable. There are no exceptions.

**Modifications of earlier decrees.** If you executed a divorce or separation instrument before January 1, 2019, but it is modified on or after this date, the new rules apply if the modification expressly states that alimony will not be deductible by the payer or taxable to the recipient.

# CHAPTER 38

# Other Taxes

The regular income tax figured on taxable income may not be the net amount of taxes you owe for the year. There are additional taxes that may apply to you. For example, if you employ a household worker, such as a nanny, you may owe employment taxes for this worker *(38.1–38.4)*. If you fail to have minimum essential health coverage for 2018 and are not exempt, there is a penalty tax *(38.5–38.6)*.

Most additional taxes are listed in Schedule 4 of Form 1040; the alternative minimum tax entered in Schedule 2 of Form 1040. Some of these other taxes are covered in this chapter; others are covered in other chapters as noted in *Table 38-1*.

Estimated taxes *(27.1–27.5)* are not a separate tax liability; they are merely a way in which to pay taxes where income tax withholding does not cover the expected tax bill for the year.

## 38.1 Overview of Household Employment Taxes

If you hired someone to do household work in or around your home and you were able to control what work he or she did and how it was done, you had a household employee. This could include a babysitter, house cleaner, cook, nanny, yard worker, maid, driver, health aide, or private nurse. Unless an exception applies (*see* below), such a worker is your employee regardless of whether the work is full or part time or whether you hired the worker through an agency or from a list provided by an agency or association. Also, it does not matter if the wages were paid for work done on an hourly, daily, weekly, or per-job basis.

If a worker is your household employee, you may have to withhold and pay Social Security and Medicare taxes (FICA, *38.2*) and pay federal unemployment tax (FUTA, *38.4*).

**Workers who are not your employees.** Workers you hire through an agency are not your employees if the agency is responsible for who does the work and how it is done. If you use a placement agency that exercises control over what work is done and how it is done, the worker is not your employee. Self-employed workers are also not your employees; in addition to maintaining control over how their work is done, self-employed workers usually provide their own tools and offer services to the general public. For example, you need work done on your lawn and you hire the self-employed owner of a lawn care business, who provides his own tools and supplies and hires and pays any other workers as needed. He and his workers are not your household employees.

**Notable exceptions to the household employee definition.** You do not have to file a Schedule H and pay Social Security, Medicare, or federal unemployment taxes if the household employee was your spouse, your child who was under age 21, or, in most cases, your parent. However, for Social Security and Medicare tax *(38.2)* purposes, you must treat your parent as your household employee if he or she takes care of your child in your home and (1) the child is either under age 18 or has a physical or mental condition that requires personal care by a adult for at least four continuous weeks in a calendar quarter, and (2) you are divorced and not remarried, widowed, or are living with a spouse whose physical or mental condition prevents him or her from caring for your child for at least four continuous weeks in a calendar quarter.

For Social Security and Medicare tax purposes, you do not have to include wages paid to an individual who is under age 18 at any point during the year so long as his or her principal occupation is not providing household services; a student under age 18 qualifies for this exception and is not considered a household employee.

**Verifying employment status.** It is unlawful to employ an alien who cannot legally work in the United States. If you hire a household employee to work for you on a regular basis, you and the employee must each complete part of the U.S. Citizenship and Immigration Services (USCIS) Form I-9, "Employment Eligibility Verification." By looking at documents that the employee shows you, you must verify that he or she is either a U.S. citizen or an alien who can legally work in the U.S. and you must keep Form I-9 for your records. The form and a USCIS Handbook for Employers can be obtained at www.uscis. gov or by calling (800) 870-3676. For answers to other questions about the employment eligibility verification process or other immigration-related matters, contact the USCIS Office of Business Liaison at (800) 357-2099.

**Employee's Social Security number.** You are required to get each employee's name and Social Security number and enter them on Form W-2. This applies to both resident and nonresident alien employees. You may not accept an individual taxpayer identification number (ITIN) in place of an SSN. An ITIN is only available to resident and nonresident aliens who are ineligible to work in the U.S. and need identification for tax purposes. You may verify up to 10 names and numbers by calling the Social Security Administration and registering for automated telephone access at

(800) 772-6270, or by getting online access at www.socialsecurity.gov/employer.

## Table 38-1    Key to Other Taxes

| Item— | Comments— |
|---|---|
| Alternative minimum tax | If you are able to reduce your regular tax bill through allowable deductions and other tax breaks, you may still owe tax through a shadow tax system called the alternative minimum tax (AMT). This applies when your income figured in a special way (with certain adjustments from the regular tax) exceeds an exemption based on your filing status *(23.1–23.5)*. |
| Household employment taxes | If you employ someone to care for your children or elderly parent in your home, clean your residence, cook, or provide personal services in or around your home, you may be obligated to pay and withhold Social Security and Medicare taxes, as well as federal unemployment (FUTA) taxes *(38.1–38.4)*. |
| Shared responsibility tax | If you fail to have certain health coverage for yourself and family and are not exempt from the shared responsibility requirement under the Affordable Care Act, you must figure a penalty tax *(38.5–38.6)*. |
| Self-employment tax | If you have net earnings from an unincorporated business, such as a sole proprietorship, partnership, or limited liability company of $400 or more, you must figure Social Security and Medicare taxes on the net earnings; this is called self-employment tax *(45.1–45.6)*. If you also have wages and other taxable compensation, some or all of the Social Security portion of self-employment tax may be satisfied by FICA. |
| Additional tax on IRAs and other benefit plans | Certain actions with respect to various benefit plans results in a penalty. These include taking early distributions from IRAs and qualified retirement plans *(7.15, 7.19, 8.12)*, failing to take required minimum distributions from IRAs and qualified retirement plans *(7.13, 8.13)*, making contributions to IRAs and qualified retirement plans over allowable limits *(7.18, 8.7)*, taking withdrawals from health savings accounts for nonmedical purposes *(41.12)*, and taking distributions from Coverdell education savings accounts for nonqualified purposes *(33.11)*. These penalties are figured on Form 5329. |
| Kiddie tax | If you have a child under a certain age with investment income over $2,100 in 2018, you may have to figure the child's income tax using tax rates for trusts and estates for such income over this threshold amount; the tax is imposed on the child. *(24.1–24.4)*. |
| Repayment of the first-time homebuyer credit | If you purchased a home in 2008 and qualified for the first-time homebuyer credit of up to $7,500, you must report 1/15th of the credit as an additional tax until it is fully recaptured *(25.17)*. |
| Additional Medicare tax on earned income | If you have earned income from a job or self-employment exceeding a threshold amount for your filing status, you must pay 0.9% on any excess earned income *(28.1–28.2)*. |
| Net Investment Income tax | If you have net investment income and your modified adjusted gross income is over a threshold amount for your filing status, you must pay 3.8% on the lesser of your net investment income or your MAGI over the threshold amount *(28.1 and 28.3)*. |

## 38.2    Social Security and Medicare (FICA) Taxes for Household Employees

Income tax withholding is not required for a household employee *(38.3)*, but generally you must withhold Social Security and Medicare (FICA) taxes from the employee's cash wages and also pay the employer share of FICA yourself, unless the wages are below an annual threshold, which for 2018 is $2,100. You report and pay the FICA taxes on Schedule H, which you must attach to your Form 1040; *see 38.3*. If you pay the household employee cash wages of less than $2,100, the wages are not subject to FICA taxes.

Once payments to a household employee (*see 38.1* for employee exceptions) equal or exceed $2,100 in 2018, the entire amount, including the first $2,100, is subject to FICA taxes. The $2,100 threshold may be increased for 2019 by an inflation adjustment.

**Tax rates.**  If in 2018 you pay your household employee cash wages of $2,100 or more, you are liable for: (1) Social Security taxes at the rate of 12.4% (6.2% for you and also 6.2% for your employee) on wages up to the annual Social Security wage base, which for 2018 is $128,400, and (2) Medicare taxes at a rate of 2.9% (1.45% for each of you) on all wages with no limit.

 *Caution*

**W-2 Distribution Deadline**

Even if you request an extension to file copies of Form W-2 with the Social Security Administration, you must still furnish Form W-2 for 2018 to each employee by January 31, 2019.

You are responsible for paying your employee's share of Social Security and Medicare taxes as well as your own share. You must either withhold your employee's share from his or her wages or pay it from your own funds. On Schedule H, you are liable for the total tax, both your share and the employee's share *(38.3)*. If you decide to pay the employee's share of the Social Security and Medicare taxes from your own funds rather than withholding the taxes from the employee's pay, you must treat your payment as additional wages when you report the employee's wages on his or her Form W-2, but the payment is not considered wages for purposes of figuring your FICA or FUTA liability on Schedule H; *see* the Example in *38.3*.

***Withholding requirement for Additional Medicare Tax if employee paid over $200,000.*** In the unlikely situation where wages paid to a household employee exceed $200,000 for the year, you must withhold from your employee's pay, in addition to the 1.45% Medicare tax, the 0.9% Additional Medicare Tax from the wages exceeding $200,000 *(28.2)*. The 0.9% tax is imposed only on the employee; there is no separate employer share.

**Estimated taxes.** To cover the household employment taxes that you owe, you may need to increase the federal income tax withheld from your pay or pay estimated taxes to avoid an estimated tax penalty *(27.1)*.

**Reporting options for self-employed persons who have regular business employees as well as household employees.** Self-employed persons who have business employees in addition to household employees may use one of the following reporting options:

1. Report FICA and FUTA taxes and any income tax withholding for household employees annually on Schedule H, and report FICA taxes and any income tax withholding for other employees quarterly on Form 941 and FUTA taxes annually on Form 940; or

2. Report FICA taxes and any income tax withholding for all employees (household employees as well as other employees) quarterly on Form 941 and report FUTA taxes annually on Form 940.

Small employers whose annual liability for Social Security, Medicare, and withheld federal income tax is $1,000 or less may be notified by the IRS that they must file Form 944 to report and pay the taxes only once a year, instead of quarterly on Form 941. If you are a new employer filing Form SS-4 to get an EIN *(38.3)* and expect to have $1,000 or less of employment tax liability, you may tell the IRS on the Form SS-4 that you would like to file Form 944. You may also make a request to use Form 944 if you have used Form 941 but expect to have employment tax liability of $1,000 or less for the upcoming calendar year; you must make the request by the deadline specified in the Form 944 instructions. If you receive a notification from the IRS that you must file Form 944, you may request a change to Form 941 filing; *see* the Form 944 instructions.

Employers of household employees must also give copies of Form W-2 ("Wage and Tax Statement") to each employee and to the Social Security Administration, as discussed in *38.3*.

## 38.3 Filing Schedule H To Report Household Employment Taxes

You must file Schedule H with your 2018 Form 1040 if you paid any one household employee cash wages of $2,100 or more in 2018, or withheld federal income tax during 2018 for a household employee, or paid cash wages totaling $1,000 or more in any calendar quarter during 2017 or 2018 to all household employees. On Schedule H, you report the Social Security and Medicare taxes *(38.2)*, federal income taxes withheld, if any (see below), and federal unemployment taxes *(38.4)* for your household employees. Total household employment taxes from Schedule H are entered as an "Other tax" on Line 60a of your Form 1040.

If you get an extension to file your return, file Schedule H with the return by the extended due date. If you are not required to file a 2018 tax return, you may file Schedule H by itself by the filing deadline, April 15, 2019. The completed Schedule H should be mailed to the same address that you would use for filing a return, along with a check or money order for the total household employment taxes due.

**Withholding federal income taxes.** Income tax withholding is not required for a household employee, but if the employee requests withholding and you agree to do it, the employee must furnish you with a complete Form W-4, "Employee's Withholding Allowance Certificate." Use the income tax withholding tables in IRS Publication 15 (Circular E, Employer's Tax Guide), which has detailed instructions.

**The earned income credit (EIC).** Copy B of Form W-2 has a notice about the EIC. If you do not give Copy B (or a substitute with similar EIC information) to your household employee by January 31, 2019, you must provide equivalent EIC notice on Notice 797 or your own written equivalent statement by the January 31 deadline. If you agreed to withhold federal income taxes from the employee's 2018 wages, but a Form W-2 is not required (under the Form W-2 instructions), the EIC notice should be given to the employee by February 7, 2019.

**Fringe benefits.** All or part of the value of certain fringe benefits is specifically excluded from a household employee's taxable wages. If you provide a household employee with lodging or meals on your premises, the benefits are not taxable if furnished for your convenience as a condition of employment. You may also provide tax-free transportation assistance to an employee. The tax-free limit for transportation fringe benefits in 2018 is $260 per month for transit passes you give to your household employee, and $260 per month for reimbursements you provide for your employee's parking costs near your home or near a mass transit location from which your employee commutes to your home.

---

### EXAMPLE

On February 25, 2018, Nancy Nixon hired Eleanor Edwards to clean her house every Wednesday. She paid Eleanor $50 every Wednesday and did not withhold Eleanor's share of Social Security and Medicare (FICA) taxes from her wages. Instead, Nancy will pay Eleanor's share of Social Security and Medicare taxes out of pocket when she files Schedule H with her 2018 Form 1040. Nancy also did not withhold any federal income taxes because Eleanor did not give her a W-4 or in any other way request that income taxes be withheld. Nancy has never had any other household employee.

Eleanor worked for a total of 44 Wednesdays and received $2,200 (44 × $50) in total compensation from Nancy.

Eleanor's total cash wages $2,200 ($50 × 44 weeks)
Eleanor's share of employment taxes paid by Nancy:
Social security tax $136.40 ($2,200 × 6.2%)
Medicare tax $31.90 ($2,200 × 1.45%)
Wages included in Box 1 of Eleanor's Form W-2 and Nancy's Form W-3:

| | |
|---|---|
| Cash wages | $2,200.00 |
| Eleanor's share of Social Security tax paid by Nancy | 136.40 |
| Eleanor's share of Medicare tax paid by Nancy | 31.90 |
| Total wages for Eleanor on Form W-2 | $2,368.30 |

Although the taxable wages that Nancy reports for Eleanor in Box 1 of Form W-2 ($2,368.30) includes her payment of Eleanor's share of FICA taxes (Social Security and Medicare) in addition to the cash wages, only the cash wages of $2,200 are reported as Social Security and Medicare wages in Boxes 3 and 5 of Eleanor's Form W-2. When Nancy computes her liability for Social Security and Medicare taxes in Part I of Schedule H, she pays the combined employer/employee rate of 12.4% for Social Security and also the combined employer/employee Medicare rate of 2.9% on the cash wages of $2,200.

Nancy is not liable for FUTA tax *(38.4)* in Part II of Schedule H because she did not pay household employee wages of $1,000 or more in any quarter of 2017 (no household employees in 2017) or in any calendar quarter of 2018 to Eleanor.

**Check State Requirements for Employers**

You may have to register and pay state unemployment tax for a household employee. Contact your state unemployment tax agency; IRS Publication 926 has contact information. You should also contact the state labor department to determine if you need to carry workers' compensation insurance or pay other state employment taxes.

**Employer identification number (EIN).** If you have a household employee, you will need an employer identification number (EIN) to report employment taxes on Schedule H. You can obtain an EIN by completing Form SS-4, Application for an Employer Identification Number. The number can be obtained immediately by phone, over the Internet, or in four weeks if you apply by mail. If you applied for an EIN and are still waiting for it when filing Schedule H, do not enter your Social Security number as a substitute. Instead, enter "Applied For" and the date you applied for the EIN in the space provided for the number on Schedule H.

Forms W-2 and W-3. You need an EIN in order to properly file the necessary W-2 and W-3 forms. You must file a Form W-2 for each household employee to whom you paid $2,100 or more of cash wages in 2018 that are subject to Social Security and Medicare (FICA) taxes. You also must file Form W-2 for an employee whose wages were not subject to FICA taxes *(38.1)* but for whom you withheld income taxes. Furnish copies B, C, and 2 of Form W-2 to your household employee by January 31, 2018.

If you file one or more Forms W-2 for 2018, you must also file a Form W-3, Transmittal of Wage and Tax Statement. You must send Copy A of all Forms W-2 together with Form W-3 to the Social Security Administration (SSA) by January 31, 2019, whether you submit Forms W-2 and W-3 on paper or file electronically.

## 38.4 Federal Unemployment Taxes (FUTA) for Household Employees

As an employer, you are also liable for FUTA (federal unemployment taxes) for 2018 in Part II of Schedule H if you paid cash wages of $1,000 or more for household services (by all household employees) during any calendar quarter of 2018 or in any calendar quarter of 2017. Your employee is not liable for FUTA. You must pay it with your own funds. You do not pay FUTA on wages paid to your spouse, your parents, or your children under age 21. Schedule H is attached to your Form 1040. If you have regular business employees, *see 38.2* for more reporting options.

**Reduced Credit for Some States**

If you are in a state that owes money to the federal unemployment fund, your FUTA credit for state unemployment taxes is reduced on Schedule H. Credit reduction states, if any, are listed in Schedule A of Form 940 and in the Schedule H instructions.

The FUTA rate is 6% of the first $7,000 of cash wages paid to each household employee in 2018. However, there is a credit of up to 5.4% for state unemployment taxes that reduces FUTA liability, resulting in a net tax of 0.6% where the full 5.4% credit is available. Only employers that pay all the required state unemployment fund contributions for 2018 by April 15, 2019, will receive the full credit; the credit for contributions made after this date, is limited to 90% of the pre-deadline credit.

Employers in some states will not be entitled to the full 5.4% credit because the state owes money to the federal unemployment fund. A worksheet in the Schedule H instructions shows the reduced credit rate allowed in the affected states.

## 38.5 Individual Responsibility Penalty

If you fail to have minimum essential health coverage for you and your dependents and you are not exempt from this mandate *(38.6)*, you owe a penalty tax called the shared responsibility payment. While the penalty is repealed as of 2019, it continues to apply for 2018. If you are married filing jointly, you and your spouse are jointly liable for the penalty.

For 2018, the shared responsibility payment is the *greater* of:

- Alternative 1: 2.5% of your household income in excess of the 2018 filing threshold for your filing status (page 3), or
- Alternative 2: $695 per adult in your household and $347.50 for a dependent child under age 18, but no more than $2,085

There is also a cap on the penalty (greater of Alternative 1 or Alternative 2) that applies only in cases of extremely high incomes: the penalty tax cannot be more than the national average premium for a bronze level policy offered through the exchange (Marketplace). For 2018, this is $3,396 per individual ($283 per month × 12 months), limited to $16,980 for a family of five or more ($283 × 5 = $1,415 per month × 12 months = $16,980).

If you lack minimum essential coverage (defined below) for three months or more and do not have an exemption, figure the penalty for 2018 by dividing the amount found above by 1/12 and then multiply it by the number of months with neither coverage nor an exemption. As long as you have minimum essential coverage for at least one day during a month, you are considered to have coverage for that entire month. The instructions for Form 8965 ("Health Coverage Exemptions") have a flowchart and worksheets you can use to figure your penalty.

---

**EXAMPLES**

1. You and your spouse (both under age 65) file jointly for 2018. You have two dependent children under age 18 and household income in 2018 of $75,000. None of you has minimum essential coverage at any time during the year and no family member qualifies for an exemption. Your penalty, based on Alternative 2, is $2,085. Alternative 2 applies because it is more than Alternative 1 ($1,275) and it is less than the national average for a bronze plan for a family of four, or $13,584 (4 × $3,396).

   *Alternative 1:* 2.5% of household income of $75,000 in excess of the filing threshold for joint filers ($24,000) is $1,275 ($75,000 − $24,000 = $51,000 × 2.5% = $1,275).

   *Alternative 2:* $695 × 2 adults, plus $347.50 × 2 children = $2,085.

2. In 2018, you are single, age 32, with no dependents, and you did not have coverage for January through May. You began a job on June 1 from which you had minimum essential coverage for the balance of the year. Assume that your household income for the year is $35,000. Your penalty for 2018 is $290. Under Alternative 1, the penalty is $575 ($35,000 − $12,000 filing threshold for single person × 2.5%). As that is less than the $695 amount under Alternative 2, $695 becomes the applicable alternative. Therefore, the penalty for five months is 5/12ths of Alternative 2, or $290 ([$695 ÷ 12] × 5).

---

**Minimum essential coverage.** The shared responsibility provision of the Affordable Care Act requires you to have minimum essential coverage for yourself, your spouse and your dependents unless you or they have an exemption *(38.6)* from the requirement. Minimum essential coverage is a medical plan that provides health insurance coverage as required by the Affordable Care Act. The plan may be:

- Individual coverage purchased through a government exchange (the federal or your state's marketplace) or directly from an insurance company
- An employer plan (including COBRA and retiree coverage)
- A government plan (e.g., Medicare, Medicaid, the Children's Health Insurance Program (CHIP), TRICARE, veterans health care programs)
- Peace Corps volunteer programs
- Self-funded health coverage of universities for their students
- Department of Defense Nonappropriated Fund Health Benefits Program
- Refugee medical assistance
- Coverage through a Basic Health Program (BHP) standard health plan

You can be covered under a different health plan than your spouse and dependent children, so long as you each have minimum essential coverage (or have an exemption).

Not all types of coverage are treated as minimum essential coverage. For example, dental and vision coverage, worker's compensation, and coverage for a specific disease or condition, such as cancer, do not qualify as minimum essential coverage.

**Household income.** Household income is a new term in the tax law. The starting point is your adjusted gross income, plus the adjusted gross income of your dependents for whom you may claim a personal exemption if they are required to file a tax return, increased by any excludable foreign earned income and tax-exempt interest for you and your dependents.

**Report the penalty tax on Form 1040.** Enter the penalty tax on Schedule 4 of Form 1040. You should receive a Form 1095-B or Form 1095-C that reports the months of coverage for each covered individual if you have minimum essential coverage from an employer or government plan, or a policy purchased on the individual market (but not through a government exchange, which will send you a Form 1095-A).

## 38.6 Exemption from Individual Responsibility Payment

Even if you do not have minimum essential health coverage, you do not owe a penalty tax if you qualify for a coverage exemption and file Form 8965 ("Health Coverage Exemptions") with your tax return. Exemptions available for 2018 include:

- You lack minimum essential coverage for less than three months in 2018
- The lowest-priced coverage available to you through an exchange costs more than 8.05% of your household income (household income is defined in *38.5*)
- Your household income or your gross income is below your tax filing threshold (page 3)
- You are a member of a federally recognized Native American tribe or are eligible for services through an Indian Health Services provider
- You are a member of a recognized health care sharing ministry
- You are a member of a recognized religious sect with religious objections to insurance, including Social Security and Medicare
- You are incarcerated
- You are not lawfully in the U.S.
- You claim hardship

**Hardship.** There are currently more than a dozen recognized hardship situations that entitle you to be exempt from the individual mandate and avoid the penalty tax. More situations may be added to this list; *see* the *e-Supplement* at *jklasser.com*.

- You are homeless
- You were evicted in the past six months or are facing eviction or foreclosure
- You received a shut-off notice from a utility company
- You recently experienced domestic violence
- You recently experienced the death of a close family member
- You experienced a fire, flood, or other disaster that caused substantial damage to your property
- You filed for bankruptcy within the last 6 months
- You had medical expenses you couldn't pay in the last 24 months which resulted in substantial debt
- You experienced unexpected increases in necessary expenses due to caring for an ill, disabled, or aging family member
- Your child, who is your dependent, has been denied coverage in Medicaid and CHIP, and another person is required by court order to give medical support to the child; you are exempt from the penalty for this child
- You become eligible for enrollment in a qualified health plan (QHP) through an exchange as a result of an eligibility appeals decision (this enrollment now entitles you to lower month premiums or cost-sharing reductions)
- You are ineligible for Medicaid because your state did not expand its eligibility rules under the Affordable Care Act
- Your health care policy was canceled and you believe other plans offered through the exchange are unaffordable
- You were eligible for the health coverage tax credit but failed to obtain coverage
- You experienced another hardship in obtaining health coverage (something you'll need to explain)

Some of the exemptions are available only through the exchange, some only from the IRS, and some from either. If you are claiming any of these exemptions, you must file Form 8965, "Health Coverage Exemptions," with your return. If you obtained an exemption from an exchange (Marketplace) when applying for coverage, complete Part I of Form 8965 and enter the Exemption Certificate Number (ECN) received from the Marketplace (or indicate that the Marketplace was still processing your request when you filed your return). If you are claiming an exemption when you file your return, complete Part II or Part III of Form 8965. Instructions for Form 8965 list a code for each exemption option.

*Filing Tip*

**Proof of Coverage**

You should receive Form 1095-B or 1095-C from your employer showing the amount of coverage for 2018. This gives you proof of your coverage for the year.

# CHAPTER 39

# Gift and Estate Tax Planning Basics

Gift planning can be an important part of estate planning. This chapter provides an overview of the federal gift tax and estate tax, which is separate and apart from income tax. Developing an estate plan for your assets requires professional assistance, but the basic guidelines in this chapter can help you begin to estimate your potential estate and start thinking about property transfers that may reduce or avoid the estate tax.

Relatively small gifts can completely avoid gift tax (39.2) because of the annual gift tax exclusion, which for 2018 is $15,000 per donee. Gifts to a spouse and certain gifts to pay educational or medical expenses also are not subject to the gift tax.

Gift tax (39.4) generally does not have to be paid even on very substantial taxable gifts because the tax is offset by a tax credit that for 2018 effectively exempts up to $11.18 million of taxable gifts from the tax.

The credit for gift and estate taxes is unified, so the same exemption of $11.18 million applies to the estates of those dying in 2018, to the extent that the exemption was not used to offset lifetime taxable gifts. An unlimited estate tax marital deduction is allowed for transfers to a citizen spouse. The estate of a married individual can make a portability election that allows any portion of the decedent's unused exemption amount to pass to the surviving spouse.

## 39.1 Gifts of Appreciated Property

Making a gift of appreciated property to a family member in advance of an anticipated sale can reduce the income tax liability for the family as a whole. By making a gift of interests in the property to several family members, it may be possible to spread the profit and the tax among a number of taxpayers in low tax brackets. Depending on the value of the property, you may or may not have to file a gift tax return *(39.2)*.

However, the tax benefit of making gifts of property to younger family members is limited by the "kiddie tax." The kiddie tax *(24.2)* covers most 18-year-olds and college students age 19 to 23.

Do not make a gift of investment property such as stock that has decreased in value if you want a deduction for the loss. Once you give the property away, the loss deduction for income tax purposes is gone forever. Neither you nor your donee can ever take advantage of it. The better way is first to sell the property, get a loss deduction, and then make a gift of the proceeds.

Warning: The IRS may claim that the gift was never completed if, after sale by the donee, you control the sales proceeds or have the use of them.

## 39.2 Gift Tax Basics

You can make substantial gifts of cash or property without incurring gift tax liability because of exclusions allowed by the tax law. Even where a gift exceeds the available exclusions and is technically subject to the gift tax, liability computed on Form 709 can generally be avoided by applying the lifetime credit, which for 2018 effectively exempts up to $11.18 million of taxable gifts from the tax *(39.4)*.

**The annual exclusion and other tax-free gifts.** Gift tax liability may be avoided by making gifts that do not exceed the annual exclusion. The annual exclusion applies separately to each donee to whom you make gifts during a calendar year. For gifts made in 2018, the per-donee exclusion is $15,000, or $30,000 if your spouse consents on Form 709 to "split" your gifts. The annual exclusion is allowed only for cash gifts or gifts of present interests in property; gifts of future interests do not qualify. For gifts made in 2019, the annual exclusion might be increased above $15,000 by an inflation adjustment; *see* the *e-Supplement at jklasser.com* for an update.

Gifts to your spouse are completely tax free under the gift tax marital deduction if your spouse is a U.S. citizen at the time of the gift. For gifts to a spouse who is not a U.S. citizen, there is an annual exclusion, which for 2018 gifts is $152,000, provided that the $137,000 excess over the basic $15,000 annual exclusion otherwise qualifies for the marital deduction.

There is an unlimited gift tax exclusion for payments of another person's tuition or medical expenses, if you make the payment directly to the educational organization or care provider. The medical and educational exclusions are allowed without regard to the relationship between you and the donee for whom you are making the payments. The exclusion for directly paid educational expenses applies only to tuition, not to room and board, books, or supplies.

Contributions to a qualified tuition program (QTP; *see* **33.5**) on behalf of a designated beneficiary do not qualify for the educational exclusion, but do qualify for an enhanced annual exclusion. You can elect to treat a QTP contribution over the basic annual exclusion as if it were made ratably over a five-year period, but only up to five times the annual exclusion. For example, a QTP contribution made in 2018 of up to $75,000 may be treated as if 1/5 , or $15,000, had been contributed in 2017 and in each of the next four years. Thus, the entire gift up to $75,000 can avoid gift tax and if your spouse consents to split the gift on Form 709 *(39.3)* the exclusion increases to $150,000. If you make QTP contributions for more than one person in the same year, you can make the special QTP election for each of them.

Taxable gifts. If you make a gift that exceeds the allowable annual exclusion and which is not otherwise exempt from the gift tax, you must report the gift on Form 709 *(39.3)*. *Table 39-1 (39.9)* shows the tax rates applicable to taxable gifts made in 2018 and later years. However, the tax as computed using the rate table can be offset by the allowable credit *(39.4)*.

**Basis for property received as gift.** The basis for appreciated property received as a gift is generally the same as the donor's basis. If gift tax was paid by the donor, basis is increased. The basis computation is explained in *5.17*.

*Planning Reminder*

**Annual Gift Tax Exclusion**

For 2018, the annual gift tax exclusion *(39.2)* exempts from gift tax the first $15,000 of cash gifts and/or gifts of present interests made to each donee. If your spouse consents on Form 709 to split your 2018 gifts, the exclusion for each donee doubles to $30,000. Any change to the exclusion amount for gifts made in 2019 will be reported in the *e-Supplement* at *jklasser.com*.

If you make gifts of present interests in trust for more than one beneficiary, each beneficiary is treated separately for purposes of the annual exclusion. Also, if you give a present interest in property to more than one person as joint tenants, the annual exclusion can be claimed for each donee.

*Caution*

**Gifts to ABLE Accounts not QTP Contributions**

While contributions to a QTP qualify for five times the annual gift tax exclusion in one year, there is no comparable rule for contributions to ABLE accounts *(34.12)*; tax-free contributions in 2018 to ABLE accounts generally are limited to $15,000 (but can be higher through 2025 for contributions made by a designated beneficiary).

## 39.3    Filing a Gift Tax Return

A gift tax return generally must be filed on Form 709 for a gift made during 2018 to an individual other than your spouse if it exceeds $15,000 or is a gift of a future interest (regardless of value). A return does not have to be filed for gifts qualifying for the tuition or medical expense exclusion discussed in *39.2*.

Married couples who want to split gifts of over $15,000 in 2018 to any one person must report the gifts to the IRS on Form 709 and the consenting spouse must sign the consent in Part I. No gift tax is due under the annual exclusion if the "split" gift is $30,000 or less.

Form 709 for 2018 generally must be filed by April 15, 2019. If you get a filing extension (Form 4868) for your income tax return, the extension also applies to the gift tax return. If you do not request an extension for your income tax return, you can use Form 8892 to request a filing extension for your gift tax return.

> **EXAMPLES**
>
> 1. On July 18, 2018, Randall Johnson makes a gift of publicly traded stock to his son, Philip. He gives Philip 1,000 shares of stock valued at $20,000 ($20 per share). His cost basis for the 1,000 shares was $15,000. On Randall's Form 709, Randall's wife, Claire, consents to split the gift, thereby doubling the $15,000 annual exclusion for the gift. Neither Randall nor Claire made any other gifts during 2018 and neither had made a taxable gift before 2018. As a result of the gift splitting, Randall and Claire are each considered to have made a gift of $10,000 that is offset by the annual exclusion. No gift tax is due.
>
> 2. Same facts as in Example 1 except that the value of the stock given to Philip was $40,000 instead of $20,000. After Claire consents to split Randall's gift, there is a taxable gift of $10,000 ($40,000 − $30,000 annual exclusion), of which half, or $5,000, is attributed to each of them. They each must file their own Form 709. They will each figure a gift tax of $900 on their $5,000 gift *(Table 39-1)*, but no tax is due because it is offset by the credit *(39.4)*.

**Caution**

**Gift Disclosure Starts Running of Statute of Limitations**

To begin the running of the statute of limitations on gift valuation, the gift must be adequately disclosed on Form 709 filed for the year of the gift. Follow the gift reporting instructions for Schedule A of Form 709. Given this statute of limitations consideration, even donors of property valued at under the annual exclusion ($15,000 for 2018) may want to report the gift on Form 709 in order to start the clock running on how long the IRS has to challenge valuation of the gift.

## 39.4    Gift Tax Credit

On Form 709, any gift tax that you otherwise would owe is eliminated or reduced by a tax credit. The credit applies to lifetime gifts, so any credit that was used to offset gift tax in prior years reduces the credit available for taxable gifts made in 2018 or later years. The amount of the gifts that can pass tax free depends on the applicable credit amount allowed for the year. For 2018, the maximum credit against taxable gifts is $4,417,800, unless it is increased for a surviving spouse because a portability election (*see* below) was made. The $4,417,800 applicable credit amount offsets the tax (figured under *Table 39-1*) on the basic exclusion amount of $11.18 million for 2018. The "exclusion amount" is often referred to as the "exemption" from tax. Since the basic exclusion amount (exemption) is subject to annual inflation increases and the credit is based on the basic exclusion amount, both amounts may increase for 2019; any increase will be in the *e-Supplement* at *jklasser.com*.

If your spouse died after 2010 and your spouse's estate made the "portability" election on a timely filed Form 706 to transfer to you his or her unused basic exclusion amount *(39.9)*, your maximum gift tax exclusion is increased by the unused exclusion amount from your spouse, thereby increasing your available tax credit; *see* the Form 709 instructions.

The basic exclusion amount and credit are "unified" for gift tax and estate tax purposes, so any basic exclusion amount/credit used to offset lifetime taxable gifts reduces the estate tax basic exclusion amount/credit that may be used by your estate *(39.9)*.

## 39.5    Custodial Accounts for Minors

A minor generally lacks the ability to manage property. You could create a formal trust, but this step may be costly. A practical alternative may be a custodial account under the Uniform Gifts to Minors Act (UGMA), or the Uniform Transfers to Minors Act (UTMA), which has replaced the UGMA in practically every state.

Custodial accounts set up in a bank, mutual fund, or brokerage firm can achieve income splitting; the tax consequences discussed below generally apply to such accounts. Trust accounts that are considered revocable under state law are ineffective in splitting income.

Although custodial accounts may be opened anywhere in the United States, the rules governing the accounts may vary from state to state. The differences between the laws of the states generally do not affect federal tax consequences.

There are limitations placed on the custodian. Proceeds from the sale of an investment or income from an investment may not be used to buy additional securities on margin. While a custodian should prudently seek reasonable income and capital preservation, he or she generally is not liable for losses unless they result from bad faith, intentional wrongdoing, or gross negligence.

When the minor reaches majority age (depending on state law), property in the custodial account is turned over to him or her. No formal accounting is required. The child, now an adult, may sign a simple release freeing the custodian from any liability. But on reaching majority, the child may request a formal accounting if there are any doubts as to the propriety of the custodian's actions while acting as custodian. For this reason, and also for tax recordkeeping purposes, a separate bank account should be opened in which proceeds from sales of investments and investment income are deposited pending reinvestment on behalf of the child. Such an account will furnish a convenient record of sales proceeds, investment income, and reinvestment of the same.

Income tax treatment of custodian account. Income from a custodian account is generally taxable to the child. However, if the "kiddie tax" applies *(24.2)*, taxable income from a custodial account in excess of the annual "kiddie" tax floor ($2,100 in 2018) is taxed to the child using the tax rates for trusts and estates.

If a parent is the donor of the custodial property or the custodian of the account and income from the account is used to discharge the parent's legal obligation to support the child, the account income is taxed to the parent.

**Gift tax treatment of custodial account.** When setting up a custodial account, you may have to pay a gift tax. A transfer of cash or securities to a custodial account is a gift. But you are not subject to a gift tax if you properly plan the cash contributions or purchase of securities for your children's accounts. You may make gifts that are shielded from gift tax by the annual exclusion. The exclusion applies each year to each person to whom you make a gift. If your spouse consents to join with you in the gift, the annual exclusion is doubled. For gifts in 2018, the per-donee exclusion is $15,000, $30,000 if your spouse consents to split the gift *(39.2)*.

If the custodial account is set up at the end of December, another tax-free transfer of up to the annual exclusion may be made in the first days of January of the following year. Assuming the annual exclusion in each year is $15,000, a total of $60,000 can be shifted within the two-month period with spousal consent.

Even if gifts exceeding the annual exclusion are made, gift tax liability may be offset by the unified credit *(39.4)*.

**Estate tax treatment of custodial account.** The value of a custodial account will be taxed in your estate if you die while acting as custodian of an account before your child reaches his or her majority. However, you may avoid the problem by naming someone other than yourself as custodian. If you should decide to act as custodian, taking the risk that the account will be taxed in your estate, remember that no estate tax is incurred if the tax on your estate is offset by the estate tax credit.

If you act as custodian and decide to terminate the custodianship, care should be taken to formally close the account. Otherwise, if you die while retaining power over the account, the IRS may try to tax the account in your estate.

## 39.6    Trusts in Family Planning

You establish a trust by transferring legal title to property to a trustee who manages the property for one or more beneficiaries. As the one who sets up the trust, you are called the grantor or settlor of the trust. The trustee may be one or more individuals or an institution such as a bank or a trust company.

You can create a trust during your lifetime or by your will. A trust created during your lifetime is called an inter vivos trust; one established in your will is a testamentary trust. An inter vivos trust can be revocable or irrevocable. An irrevocable trust does not

**Planning Reminder**

**529 Plans an Alternative to UTMAs**

These education plans can be used in lieu of UTMAs to save money for children's education. UTMAs can be rolled into 529 plans (*see 33.6*).

**Planning Reminder**

**Custodial Securities Account**

Purchase of securities through custodial accounts provides a practical method for making a gift of securities to a minor child, eliminating the need for a trust. The mechanics of opening a custodial account are simple. An adult opens a stock brokerage account for a minor child and registers the securities in the name of a custodian for the benefit of the child. The custodian may be a parent, a child's guardian, grandparent, brother, sister, uncle, or aunt. In some states, the custodian may be any adult or a bank or trust company. The custodian has the right to sell securities in the account and collect sales proceeds and investment income, and use them for the child's benefit or reinvestment. Tax treatment of custodial accounts is discussed in *39.5*.

allow for changes of heart; it requires a complete surrender of property. By conveying property irrevocably to a trust, you may relieve yourself of tax on the income from the trust principal. Furthermore, the property in trust usually is not subject to estate tax, although it may be subject to gift tax. A trust should be made irrevocable only if you are certain you will not need the trust property in a financial emergency.

Consult with an experienced tax professional if you are considering the use of a trust.

**Trust income.** Where a child is a trust beneficiary, the child reports distributable net trust income as taxable income. Distributable net income may be subject to the "kiddie tax" *(24.2)*. Income that is accumulated for the benefit of a minor child is generally not taxable and, thus, not subject to the kiddie tax.

**Grantor trusts.** The grantor of a grantor trust is taxed on the income of the trust. A trust is treated as a grantor trust where the grantor has a reversionary interest (at the time of the transfer) of more than 5% of the value of the property transferred to the trust. Under an exception, a grantor is not treated as having a reversionary interest if that interest can take effect only upon the death before age 21 of a beneficiary who is a lineal descendant of the grantor. The beneficiary must have the entire present interest in the trust or trust portion for this exception to apply.

Given the highly compressed tax brackets for trust income, a grantor may intentionally retain an interest in the trust property so that he or she will be taxed under the grantor trust rules. By setting up such a "defective" grantor trust, trust income may be subject to lower tax at the grantor's tax bracket than under the trust rate schedule.

## 39.7 What is the Estate Tax?

The estate you built up may not be entirely yours to give away. If your estate is substantial enough, the federal government and, in most cases, at least one state government stand ready to claim their shares. The federal estate tax is a tax on the act of transferring property at death. It is not a tax on the right of the beneficiary to receive the property. If tax is due, the estate and the estate alone pays the tax, although the property passing to individual beneficiaries may be diminished by the tax.

You may not have to be concerned about a future federal estate tax liability because of the large exemption (also called the basic exclusion amount) allowed under the tax law. Current law allows a basic exclusion amount (exemption) of up to $11.18 million for 2018 estates *(39.9)*, and the basic exclusion amount will increase in future years with inflation adjustments (at least through 2025). However, your potential taxable estate may be larger than you realize. The estate includes not only your business interests, real estate holdings (foreign and domestic), bank accounts, retirement accounts, stocks and bonds, mutual funds, and personal property such as art objects, but can also include life insurance, your interest in trusts or jointly held property, and certain interests you have in other estates. *See 39.8* for estimating the value of your potential estate.

You will need to consult with an experienced estate tax planning professional, who can explain the potential extent of estate tax costs and help you develop a plan that can avoid or reduce those costs.

## 39.8 Take Inventory and Estimate the Value of Your Potential Estate

The first step in estate tax planning requires taking inventory of everything you own. Include your cash, real estate (here and abroad), securities, retirement accounts, mortgages, rights in property, trust accounts, personal effects, collections, and art works. Life insurance is includible if: (1) it is payable to your estate; (2) it is payable to others and you have kept "incidents of ownership" such as the right to change beneficiaries, surrender or assign the policy, or pledge it for a loan; or (3) you assign the policy and die within three years.

If you own property jointly with your spouse, your estate includes only one-half its value.

If you had appraisals made of specially treasured items or collections, or property of substantial value, file such appraisals with your estate papers and then enter the value on your inventory.

*Planning Reminder*

**Revocable Trusts**

In a revocable trust, you retain control over the property by reserving the right to revoke the trust. As such, it is considered an incomplete gift and offers no present income tax savings. Furthermore, the trust property will be included as part of your estate. But a revocable trust minimizes delay in passing property to beneficiaries if you die while the trust is in force. When you transfer property to a trust, the property is generally not subject to probate, administration expenses, delays attendant on distributions of estates, or claims of creditors. The interests of trust beneficiaries are generally more secure than those of heirs under a will because a will may be denied probate if found invalid.

*Planning Reminder*

**Life Insurance**

If you are buying a new policy with yourself as the insured, and you want to keep the proceeds out of your gross estate, set up an irrevocable trust to buy the policy or have the individual beneficiary buy the policy. For example, a daughter applies for a $1 million policy on her father's life and is the policy owner under the terms of the policy. If the father pays the premiums, his payments are treated as gifts, but the proceeds paid at his death are not subject to estate tax because he never had ownership rights in the policy.

If you have an existing policy, you may assign your ownership rights, such as the right to change beneficiaries, the right to surrender or cancel the policy, the right to assign it, and the right to borrow against it, but the assignment must occur more than three years before death to exclude the proceeds from your estate.

**Retirement benefits.** The gross estate includes benefits payable at your death from any of the following retirement plans: corporate or self-employed pension and profit-sharing plans, traditional IRAs, Roth IRAs, or annuities. The fact that your account balance in an IRA, 401(k), or other retirement plan is a nonprobate asset that passes outside of the estate to the beneficiaries designated by the terms of the plan does not change the fact that these assets are included in the gross estate.

**Estimating the value of your assets.** When you have completed your inventory, assign to each asset what you consider to be its fair market value. This may be difficult to do for some assets. Resist the tendency to overvalue articles that arouse feelings of pride or sentiment and undervalue some articles of great intrinsic worth. For purposes of your initial estimate, it is better to err on the side of overvaluation. You can list ordinary personal effects at nominal value.

If you have a family business, your idea of its value and that of the IRS may vary greatly. Estate plans have been upset by the higher value placed on such a business by the IRS. You can protect your estate by anticipating this problem in consultation with your business associates and counselors.

If your business is owned by a closely held corporation, and there is no ready or open market in which the stock can be valued, get some factual basis for a figure that will be reported on the estate tax return. One of the ways to do this is by arranging a buy-sell agreement with a potential purchaser. This agreement must fix the value of the stock. Generally, an agreement that binds both the estate and the purchaser and restricts lifetime sales of the stock will effectively fix the value of the stock for estate tax purposes. Another way would be to make a gift of some shares to a family member and have value established in gift tax proceedings.

If a substantial part of your estate is real estate used in farming or a closely held business, your executor may be able to elect, with the consent of heirs having an interest in the property, to value the property on the basis of its farming or business use, rather than its highest and best use.

## 39.9 Estate Tax for 2018

The estate tax is figured by the executor on Form 706, "United States Estate (and Generation-Skipping Transfer) Tax Return." The executor must file Form 706 for the estate of an individual dying in 2018 if the gross estate, plus adjusted taxable gifts made after 1976, is more than $11.18 million, the basic estate tax exclusion amount for 2018; the term "exemption" is often used interchangably with "exclusion amount". A timely Form 706 also must be filed, regardless of the size of the decedent's gross estate, if the executor wants to make the portability election (*see* below) to permit the decedent's surviving spouse to use the decedent's unused basic exclusion amount. Form 706 must be filed within nine months after the date of death; an automatic six-month filing extension can be obtained by filing Form 4768.

On Form 706, the gross estate is reduced by allowable deductions. On the schedules of Form 706, deductions are allowed for funeral expenses, executor commissions, costs of preserving and distributing estate assets including attorney, accountant, and appraiser fees and court costs, debts owed by the decedent, bequests to a surviving spouse that qualify for the marital deduction, and charitable transfers. A deduction on Form 706 is also allowed for state death taxes (state estate, inheritance, legacy, or succession taxes) paid to any state or the District of Columbia on account of the decedent's death.

The estate tax rates from *Table 39-1* are applied to the taxable estate, the gross estate minus allowable deductions. If taxable gifts (over the annual gift tax exclusion) were made after 1976, the gifts are added to the taxable estate and the tax is figured on the total. The tentative tax from the rate table is reduced by the gift taxes paid or payable on the post-1976 gifts (see the Form 706 instructions). The practical effect of making the adjustments for prior taxable gifts is to reduce the basic exclusion amount and tax credit available to the estate by the basic exclusion amount and credit amounts used to offset the taxable gifts.

*Planning Reminder*

**Executor Must Report Property Values to Heirs**

If an estate tax return is required to be filed because the value of the gross estate is more than $11.18 million in 2018, the executor must tell the heirs (and the IRS) the estate tax value of property items. This value becomes the heirs' tax basis in the property for income tax purposes *(5.17)*.

After making the required adjustments for lifetime gifts on Form 706, the resulting gross estate tax is then reduced by the applicable credit. The credit equals the tax on the basic exclusion amount (exemption). The basic exclusion amount for 2018 is $11.18 million, so the 2018 applicable credit is $4,417,800, the tax on a net estate of $11.18 million (see *Table 39-1*). The basic exclusion amount is increased above $11.18 million if the decedent is the surviving spouse of a predeceased spouse who died after 2010 and the executor of the earlier estate made the portability election on Form 706. If the basic exclusion amount is increased by the portability election, the applicable credit is also increased, so that it equals the tax on the increased basic exclusion amount.

If there is any estate tax due on Form 706 after subtracting the applicable credit (and any other available credits), the balance must be paid within nine months after the date of death, but if it is impossible or impractical to meet the deadline, a request for a payment extension may be made on Form 4768; a detailed explanation must be attached to justify the request.

**Portability election.** The estate of a married individual dying after 2010 can make a special portability election to benefit a surviving spouse. The election allows any part of the basic exclusion amount that was unused by the deceased spouse for gift or estate tax purposes to be left to the surviving spouse. The portable amount is called the "deceased spousal unused exclusion," or DSUE.

The estate of a 2018 decedent makes the portability election on Part 6 of Form 706. The election is made by completing and timely filing the Form 706, including Sections B and C of Part 6. In Section C of Part 6, the estate computes the unused exclusion (DSUE) that is being transferred to the surviving spouse. The Form 706 must be timely filed (including extensions) to make the election, even if the assets of the estate are below the filing threshold of $11.18 million for 2018. If the estate is below the filing threshold, the executor may estimate the value of the gross estate on Form 706 based on a good faith determination; *see* the Form 706 instructions. If an estate below the filing threshold does not file Form 706, this is treated as opting out of the election.

If the estate of a decedent with a surviving spouse is required to file Form 706 and does not want to elect portability, check the box in Section A of Part 6 to opt out.

The surviving spouse on whose behalf the portability election is made may increase his or her lifetime gift tax exemption (basic exclusion amount) by the transferred DSUE, or it will increase the basic exclusion amount available to his or her estate. If the surviving spouse who received the DSUE from a predeceased spouse died in 2018, the basic exclusion amount allowed to his or her estate on Form 706 is increased by the DSUE that was not applied against lifetime gifts. On the 2018 Form 706, the available DSUE is entered on Line 9b of Part II, and is added to the basic exclusion amount of $11.18 million shown on Line 9a.

 *Filing Tip*

**Portability Election for Small Estates**

For estates of decedents dying after 2010 where the value of the estate is below the basic exclusion amount, Form 706 must be filed nonetheless to make the portability election.

## 39.10 Planning for a Potential Estate Tax

If you have substantial assets that forseeably may exceed the basic exclusion amount (exemption) available to your estate, there are general approaches that you can take to reduce or eliminate a potential estate tax.

You can make direct lifetime gifts. Any appreciation on the property transferred will be removed from your estate. Furthermore, each gift, to the extent of the annual per donee exclusion *(39.2)*, reduces your gross estate *(39.9)*. Life insurance can be assigned to avoid estate tax, provided the assignment takes place more than three years before death *(39.8)*. You can provide in your will for bequests that will qualify for the marital and charitable deductions.

**The marital deduction.** An unlimited marital deduction is available for property passing to a spouse who is a U.S. citizen. What should be done if you believe your spouse cannot manage property? The law permits you to put the property in certain trust arrangements that provide the surviving spouse with ownership rights sufficient to allow the marital deduction. An estate tax attorney can explain how you can protect your spouse's interest and qualify the trust property for the marital deduction.

Life insurance proceeds may qualify as marital deduction property. Name your spouse the unconditional beneficiary of the proceeds with unrestricted control over any unpaid proceeds. If your spouse is not given this control or general power of appointment, and there is no requirement that proceeds remaining on your spouse's death be payable to his or her estate, the insurance proceeds will not qualify for the marital deduction.

**Marital deduction restrictions for noncitizen spouses.** A marital deduction may not be claimed for property passing outright to a surviving spouse who is not a U.S. citizen. However, the marital deduction is allowed if the surviving spouse's interest is in a qualifying domestic trust (QDOT). At least one trustee must be an individual U.S. citizen or domestic corporation with power to withhold estate tax due from distributions of trust corpus. The trust must maintain sufficient assets as required by IRS regulations. For the marital deduction to apply, the executor must make an irrevocable election on the decedent's estate tax return. On Form 706-QDT, estate tax will apply to certain distributions of trust corpus made prior to the surviving spouse's death, and to the value of the QDOT property remaining at the surviving spouse's death. You should consult an experienced tax practitioner to set up a QDOT trust and plan for distribution provisions.

The estate of a nonresident alien is subject to estate tax only to the extent that the estate is located in the United States. A marital deduction may be claimed by the estate of a nonresident alien for property passing to a surviving spouse who is a U.S. citizen. If the surviving spouse is not a U.S. citizen, then the transferred interest must be in the form of a QDOT.

**Periodically review your estate plan.** No estate plan is ever really final. Economic conditions and inflation constantly change values. For this reason, your plan must be reviewed periodically as changes occur in your family and business, as when a birth or death occurs; when you receive a substantial increase or decrease in income; when you enter a new business venture or resign from an old one; or when you sell, retire from, or bring new persons into your business. A member of your family may no longer need any part of your estate, while others may need more. Material changes may occur in the health or life expectancy of one of your beneficiaries. Furthermore, tax law changes may require you to adjust your estate planning,

**Caution**

**Generation-Skipping Transfer Tax**

Tax may not be avoided by having a grandparent transfer property to a grandchild, skipping the child's generation. A special tax, called the generation-skipping transfer (GST) tax, may apply in this case (whether the transfer is made during life or at death). The GST exemption amount for 2018 is $11.18 million (the basic estate tax exclusion amount). The GST rules are complicated and you should consult an experienced tax professional if you are contemplating a generation-skipping transfer.

### Table 39-1 Unified Estate and Gift Tax Schedule for 2018 and Later Years

| If taxable amount is: over— | But not over— | The tax is— | Plus %— | Of the amount over— |
|---|---|---|---|---|
| $0 | $10,000 | $0 | 18 | $0 |
| 10,000 | 20,000 | 1,800 | 20 | 10,000 |
| 20,000 | 40,000 | 3,800 | 22 | 20,000 |
| 40,000 | 60,000 | 8,200 | 24 | 40,000 |
| 60,000 | 80,000 | 13,000 | 26 | 60,000 |
| 80,000 | 100,000 | 18,200 | 28 | 80,000 |
| 100,000 | 150,000 | 23,800 | 30 | 100,000 |
| 150,000 | 250,000 | 38,800 | 32 | 150,000 |
| 250,000 | 500,000 | 70,800 | 34 | 250,000 |
| 500,000 | 750,000 | 155,800 | 37 | 500,000 |
| 750,000 | 1,000,000 | 248,300 | 39 | 750,000 |
| 1,000,000 | | 345,800 | 40 | 1,000,000 |

# PART 6

# Business Tax Planning

In this part, you will learn how to report your income from a business or profession, and how to reduce your tax liability by claiming expense deductions. Pay special attention to—

- Reporting rules for income and expenses on Schedule C *(Chapter 40)*.
- Restrictions on deducting home office expenses. Your deduction may be limited by a restrictive income test *(Chapter 40)*.
- The new 20% deduction for qualified business income (QBI) *(Chapter 40)*.
- The increased deduction for qualified domestic production activities income *(Chapter 40)*.
- SEP, and SIMPLE, and qualified retirement plan rules if you are self-employed. These plans offer tax deductions for contributions and tax-free accumulation of income within the plan.
- Health savings accounts and other medical plans *(Chapter 41)*.
- First-year expensing and depreciation write-offs for business assets *(Chapter 42)*.
- The IRS mileage allowance as an alternative to claiming actual expenses for your business automobile *(Chapter 43)*.
- Reporting sales of business property on Form 4797 *(Chapter 44)*.
- Computing and paying self-employment tax on self-employment earnings from a business or profession *(Chapter 45)*.

# CHAPTER 40

# Income or Loss From Your Business or Profession

As a self-employed person, you report income and expenses from your business or profession separately from your other income, such as income from wages. On Schedule C, you report your business income and itemize your expenses. Any net profit is subject to self-employment tax, as well as regular tax. A net profit can also be the basis of deductible contributions to a SEP or qualified retirement plan, as discussed in *Chapter 41*.

If you work out of your home, you may deduct home office expenses *(40.12)*.

If you claim a loss on Schedule C, be prepared to show that you regularly and substantially participate in the business. Otherwise, your loss may be considered a passive loss deductible only from passive income, as discussed in *Chapter 10*.

If you have no employees and business expenses of $5,000 or less, you may be able to file a simplified schedule called Schedule C-EZ *(40.6)*.

If you show a profit, you may be eligible for a personal deduction of 20% of qualified business income *(40.29)*. If you have a loss that you can't fully use on your 2018 return, you may be able to carry it forward and use it in future years *(40.18)*.

## 40.1 Forms of Doing Business

The legal form of your business determines the way you report business income and loss, the taxes you pay, the ability of the business to accumulate capital, the extent of your personal liability, and whether you qualify to take a 20% qualified business income (QBI) deduction off your taxable income. It is beyond the scope of this book to discuss the pros and cons of each form. The decision should be made with the services of a professional experienced in both the legal and tax consequences of doing business in a particular form as it applies to your current and future business prospects, especially in light of the 21% tax rate on regular corporations.

If you are going into business alone, your choices are: operating as a sole proprietor, incorporating, and forming a limited liability company (LLC). If you are going to operate with associates, you may choose to operate as a partnership, a corporation, or an LLC. If you are concerned with limiting your personal liability, your choice is between a corporation or an LLC. An LLC gives you the advantage of limited liability without having to incorporate.

As a sole proprietor, you report business profit or loss on your personal tax return, as explained in this chapter. If you are a partner, you report your share of partnership profit and loss as explained in *Chapter 11*. If you incorporate, the corporation pays tax on business income. You are taxable on salaries and dividends paid to you by the corporation. You may avoid this double corporate tax by making an S corporation election, which allows you to report corporate income and loss *(11.14)*.

If you operate through an LLC with no co-owners, you report income and loss as a sole proprietor. If you operate an LLC with associates, the LLC reports as a partnership and you report your share of income and loss. However, under check-the-box rules, the LLC may elect on Form 8832 to report as an association taxable as a corporation.

## 40.2 Reporting Self-Employed Income

You file a Schedule C along with Form 1040 if you are a sole proprietor of a business or a professional in your own practice. If you do freelance work as an independent contractor, you are self-employed and use Schedule C. If you are an employee with a sideline business (e.g., you work for Uber, or TaskRabbit, or Lyft, or Upwork), report the self-employment income and expenses from that business on Schedule C. File a separate Schedule C for each different business you run (e.g., one for being a freelance writer and another for running a boutique). Do not file Schedule C if your business is operated through a partnership or corporation. *See* the guide to Schedule C in *40.6*.

On Schedule C, you deduct your allowable business expenses from your business income. Net business profit (or loss) figured on Schedule C is entered on Line 12, Page 1 of Form 1040. Thus, business profit (or loss) is added to (or subtracted from) nonbusiness income on Form 1040 to compute adjusted gross income. This procedure gives you the chance to deduct your business expenses, whether you claim itemized deductions on Schedule A, such as charitable contributions, taxes up to $10,000, and medical expenses, or you claim the standard deduction where it exceeds your allowable itemized deductions *(13.2)*.

You may be able to file a simplified schedule, Schedule C-EZ, if your income and expenses are below certain limits *(40.6)*.

**Passive loss restrictions.** Pay special attention to the passive loss restrictions discussed in *Chapter 10*. Generally, if you do not regularly and substantially participate in your business, losses are considered passive and are deductible only against other passive income.

**Recordkeeping.** You are required to keep books and records for your business activities, tracking your income and expenses carefully so you can report them accurately on your return. You enter this information according to your method of accounting *(40.3)*.

The tax law does not determine the way in which you must keep these records; today most self-employed taxpayers use computer-based or cloud-based recordkeeping systems.

**Schedule F for Farming Business**

If you are self-employed and your business involves farming, you report on Schedule F instead of Schedule C. However, much of the information contained in Chapters 40 through 45 applies to you as well.

**Did You Suffer a Loss?**

Business persons and professionals with a loss that can't be fully deducted in 2018 can carry a net operating loss forward indefinitely to offset 80% of taxable income in future years *(40.18)*.

**Spouses Can File on Schedule C for Jointly Owned Business**

Instead of having to file a partnership return, spouses can elect qualified joint venture status and file as sole proprietors on Schedule C if they are the sole owners of their business, they both materially participate in the business, and they file a joint return; *see 40.6* for details.

**Tax ID number.** As a sole proprietor, you usually do not need a separate tax ID number for Schedule C; you can use your Social Security number as your tax ID number. However, you must obtain an employer identification number if you have any employees and/or maintain a qualified retirement plan (you may also need one to open a business bank account). You can obtain your employer identification number online at https://www.irs.gov/businesses/small-businesses-self-employed/employer-id-numbers.

| *Table 40-1* Key to Reporting Business and Professional Income and Loss | |
|---|---|
| Item— | Comments— |
| Tax return to file | If you are self-employed, prepare Schedule C to report business or professional income. If your business expenses are $5,000 or less, and you have no employees, you may be able to file a simplified Schedule C-EZ *(40.6)*. If you are a farmer, use Schedule F. You attach Schedule C and/or F to Form 1040. If you operate as a partnership, use Form 1065; if you operate as a corporation, use Form 1120S or Form 1120. If you are a one-member limited liability company that has not elected to be taxed as a corporation, file Schedule C. |
| Method of reporting income | The cash or accrual accounting rules determine when you report income and expenses. You must use the accrual basis if you sell a product that must be inventoried unless you meet a new gross receipts test. The cash-basis and accrual-basis methods are discussed at *40.3*. |
| Tax reporting year | There are two general tax reporting years: calendar years that end on December 31 and fiscal years that end on the last day of any month other than December. Your taxable year must be the same for both your business and nonbusiness income. Most business income must be reported on a calendar-year basis. If, as a self-employed person, you report your business income on a fiscal-year basis, you must also report your nonbusiness income on a fiscal-year basis. Use of a fiscal year is restricted for partnerships and S corporations. |
| Office in home | To claim home office expenses as a self-employed person, you must use the home area exclusively and on a regular basis either as a place of business to meet or deal with patients, clients, or customers in the normal course of your business or as your principal place of business *(40.12)*. You may claim a standard amount (simplified method) on Schedule C or use Form 8829 to compute the deduction based on actual expenses *(40.13)*. |
| Social Security coverage | If you have self-employment income, you may have to pay self-employment tax, which goes to financing Social Security and Medicare benefits; *see Chapter 45*. |
| Passive participation in a business | If you do not regularly, continuously, and substantially participate in the business, your business income or loss is subject to passive activity restrictions. A loss is deductible only against other passive activity income. The passive activity restrictions are discussed in detail in *Chapter 10*. |
| Self-employed retirement plan | You may set up a retirement plan based on business or professional income. Individuals who are self-employed may contribute to a self-employed retirement plan, according to the rules in *Chapter 41*. |
| Health insurance | You may deduct 100% of premiums paid for health insurance coverage for yourself, spouse, and dependents. This deduction is claimed directly from gross income on Schedule 1 of Form 1040. You may also take advantage of a health savings account plan; *see Chapter 41*. |
| Depreciation | Under the first-year expensing deduction, you generally may deduct up to $1 million for equipment placed in service in 2018 *(42.3)*. Depreciation rules for assets not deducted under first-year expensing are in *Chapter 42*. Cars and trucks are subject to special depreciation limits; *see* Chapter 43. |
| Net operating losses | A loss incurred in your profession or business is deducted from other income reported on Form 1040. If the loss exceeds income, the excess is carried forward indefinitely until it is used up (a 2-year carryback and indefinite carryforward is available to farming businesses) *(40.18)*.<br>For NOLs arising after 2017, the carryforward can offset up to 80% of taxable income. And excess business losses are not currently allowed; they're treated as NOLs *(40.20)*. |
| Sideline business | You report business income of a sideline business following the rules that apply to full-time business. For example, if you are self-employed, you report business income on Schedule C or C-EZ. You may also have to pay self-employment tax on this income; *see* Chapter 45. You may also set up a self-employment retirement plan based on such income; *see* Chapter 41.<br>If you incur losses over several years, the hobby loss rules *(40.10)* may limit your loss deduction. |
| Qualified business income deduction | If your business is profitable, you may qualify for a personal deduction of 20% of your profits reported on Schedule C. The deduction does not reduce your business income; it is a subtraction from taxable income on Form 1040 *(40.24)*. |

## 40.3 Accounting Methods for Reporting Business Income

Business income is reported on either the accrual or cash basis. If you have more than one business, you may have a different accounting method for each business.

**Inventories.** Unless the gross receipts test (discussed below) applies, the IRS requires inventories at the beginning and end of every taxable year in which the production, purchase, or sale of merchandise is an income-producing factor. If you must keep inventories, you must use the accrual basis unless you meet the gross receipts test.

**Cash method.** You report income items in the taxable year in which they are received; you deduct all expenses in the taxable year in which they are paid. Under the cash method, income is also reported if it is "constructively" received. You have "constructively" received income when an amount is credited to your account, subject to your control, or set apart for you and may be drawn by you at any time. For example, in 2018 you receive a check in payment of services, but you do not cash it until 2019. You have constructively received the income in 2018, and it is taxable in 2018.

On the cash basis, you deduct expenses in the year of payment. Expenses paid by credit card are deducted in the year they are charged. Expenses paid through a "pay by phone" account with a bank are deducted in the year the bank sends the payment. This date is reported by the bank on your account statements.

**Advance payments.** Generally, no immediate deduction can be claimed for advance rent or premium covering charges of a later year. However, under a "12-month rule," you can claim an immediate deduction for prepayments that create rights or benefits that do not extend beyond the earlier of: (1) 12 months after the first date on which the taxpayer realizes rights or benefits attributable to the expenditure, or (2) the end of the taxable year following the taxable year in which the payment is made. However, prepayments of rent remain nondeductible for accrual-method taxpayers under the economic performance rules.

**Cash method of accounting limited.** The following may not use the cash method: a regular C corporation, a partnership with a C corporation as a partner, a tax shelter, or a tax-exempt trust with unrelated business income. Exceptions: A farming or tree-raising business may use the cash method even if it operates as a C corporation or a partnership with a C corporation as a partner. The cash method may also be used by personal service corporations in the fields of medicine, law, engineering, accounting, architecture, performing arts, actuarial science, or consulting. To qualify, substantially all of the stock must be owned directly or indirectly (through partnerships, S corporations, or personal service corporations) by employees.

If the production, purchase, or sale of merchandise is not an income-producing factor, the cash method may be used by a C corporation or a partnership with a C corporation as a partner if the average annual gross receipts over the prior three-year period were $5 million or less.

**Cash method for small businesses (gross receipts test).** Business owners with average annual gross receipts of $25 million or less in the three prior years ("gross receipts test") can use the cash method, even if the business owner would otherwise have to account for inventories under the accrual method. A qualifying taxpayer may not deduct items purchased for resale to customers or used as raw materials for producing finished goods until the year the items are provided to customers if that is later than the year the items were purchased. A qualifying small business that used the accrual method in 2017 and wants to change to the cash method in 2018 must file for an accounting method change as explained in the instructions to Form 3115.

**Accrual method.** On the accrual method, report income that has been earned, whether or not received, unless your right to collect the income is unsure because a substantial contingency may prevent payment; *see* the Example below.

Where you are prepaid for services to be performed in a later year, you usually can elect to defer income for only one year. However, this election does not apply to prepaid rents and certain other items. Because this is a new rule created by the Tax Cuts and Jobs Act, IRS guidance is needed to know which items are or are not subject to the deferral election; *see* the *e-Supplement* for any update.

*Law Alert*

**Cash Method for Small Businesses**

Businesses with average annual gross receipts of $25 million or less in the three prior years are eligible to use a cash method ("gross receipts test").

*Planning Reminder*

**Advantage of Cash Basis Accounting**

The cash basis has this advantage over other accounting methods: You may defer reporting income by postponing the receipt of income. But make certain that you avoid the constructive receipt rule. For example, if 2018 is a high income year or you might drop to a lower tax bracket in 2019, you might delay mailing some of your customers' bills so they do not receive them until 2019. You may also postpone the payment of presently due expenses to a year in which the deduction gives you a greater tax savings.

*Filing Tip*

**Changing to Cash Method**

A change to the cash method under the gross receipts test is an automatic change in accounting method. See Rev. Proc. 2018-31.

Expenses under the accrual method are deductible in the year your liability for payment is fixed, even though payment is made in a later year. To prevent manipulation of expense deductions, there are tax law tests for fixing the timing of accrual method expense deductions. The tests generally require that economic performance must occur before a deduction may be claimed, but there are exceptions, such as for "recurring expenses." These rules are discussed in IRS Publication 538.

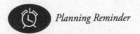

**Planning Reminder**

**Advantage of Accrual-Method Accounting**

The accrual method has this advantage over the cash basis: It generally gives a more even and balanced financial report.

> **EXAMPLE**
>
> You report business income as a calendar-year accrual taxpayer. You sell several products on December 27, 2018, and bill the customer in January 2019. You report the sales income on your 2018 Schedule C, even though payment is not made until 2019. Under the accrual method, you are considered to earn the income when the products are sold and delivered to the customer.

**Expenses owed by an accrual method business owner to a related cash basis taxpayer.** A business expense owed to your spouse, brother, sister, parent, child, grandparent, or grandchild who reports on the cash basis may not be deducted by you until you make the payment and the relative includes it as income. The same rule applies to amounts owed to a controlled corporation (more than 50% ownership) and other related entities.

**Long-term contracts.** Section 460 of the Internal Revenue Code has a special percentage of completion method of accounting for long-term construction contractors.

**Capitalize costs of business property you produce or buy for resale.** A complicated statute (Code Section 263A) generally requires manufacturers and builders to capitalize certain indirect costs (such as administrative costs, interest expenses, storage fees, and insurance), as well as direct production expenses, by including them in inventory costs; *see* IRS Publication 538, Form 3115, and the regulations to Code Section 263A.

**Non-accrual experience method (NAE) for deferring service income.** Taxpayers using the accrual method who either provide services in the fields of health, law, accounting, actuarial science, engineering, architecture, performing arts, or consulting, or who meet a $5 million annual gross receipts test, can use the non-accrual experience method (NAE). If you qualify, you do not have to accrue amounts that on the basis of your experience will not be collected. However, if interest or a penalty is charged for a failure to make a timely payment for the services, income is reported when the amount is billed. Furthermore, if discounts for early payments are offered, the full amount of the bill must be accrued; the discount for early payment is treated as an adjustment to income in the year payment is made.

Regulation Section *1.448*-2T allows four safe harbor NAE methods.

## 40.4 Tax Reporting Year for Self-Employed

Your taxable year must be the same for both your business and nonbusiness income. If you report your business income on a fiscal year basis, you must also report your nonbusiness income on a fiscal year basis.

Generally, you report the tax consequences of transactions that have occurred during a 12-month period. If the period ends on December 31, it is called a calendar year. If it ends on the last day of any month other than December, it is called a fiscal year. A reporting period, technically called a taxable year, can never be longer than 12 months unless you report on a 52-to-53-week fiscal year basis, details of which can be found in IRS Publication 538. A reporting period may be less than 12 months whenever you start or end your business in the middle of your regular taxable year, or change your taxable year.

To change from a calendar year to fiscal year reporting for self-employment income, you must ask the IRS for permission by filing Form 1128. Support your request with a business reason such as that the use of the fiscal year coincides with your business cycle. To use a fiscal year basis, you must keep your books and records following that fiscal year period.

**Fiscal year restrictions.** Restrictions on fiscal years for partnerships, personal service corporations, and S corporations are discussed in *11.11* and IRS Publication 538.

**Reporting Requirements for Merchant Transactions**

Banks and credit card processors report to the IRS all credit card and electronic payments (including PayPal, Google Checkout, and Amazon Pay) of merchants. Exempt from reporting are "small" merchants (those with no more than $20,000 in total payments or 200 or fewer transactions). If you do receive Form 1099-K, you are not required to reconcile amounts reported on the form with your income. Report your gross receipts in the usual way, taking into account returns, allowances, and other adjustments (not reflected on Form 1099-K).

*Law Alert*

**Increased Penalties**

The penalties for late or non-filing can be increased for inflation annually. One of the basic penalty amounts has changed for 2018, and the maximum penalty amounts have increased.

*Filing Tip*

**Penalty Relief Program for Form 5500-EZ Late Filers**

Delinquent returns can be submitted without penalty, although there is a $500 filing fee. Details are in Revenue Procedure 2015-32.

## 40.5 Reporting Certain Payments and Receipts to the IRS

In certain situations, you are required to report payments and receipts to the IRS. If you fail to comply with this reporting, you can be penalized.

**Payments to independent contractors.** If you pay independent contractors, freelancers, or subcontractors a total of $600 or more within the year, you must report all payments to the IRS and the contractors on Form 1099-MISC. For 2018 payments, furnish the contractor with the form and provide a copy to the IRS by January 31, 2019, whether you file by paper or electronically.

The penalty for not filing or filing late depends on the extent of tardiness. For example, the penalty is only $50 per information return if you miss the due date but then file correctly within 30 days. The maximum penalty for 2018 returns filed in 2019 can go as high as $191,000 for a small business, which includes a self-employed individual with average annual gross receipts for three years of $5 million or less.

**Receipts of cash payments over $10,000.** If you are paid more than $10,000 in cash in one or more related transactions in the course of your business, you must report the transaction to the IRS. "Cash" includes currency, cashier's checks, money orders, bank drafts, and traveler's checks having a face amount of $10,000 or less received in a transaction used to avoid this reporting requirement. File Form 8300 with the IRS no later than the 15th day after the date the cash was received. For example, if you receive a $12,000 cash payment on May 1, 2019, you must report it by May 16, 2019.

You have until January 31 of the year following the year of the transaction to give a written statement to the party that paid you. In the example above, this means giving the statement to the party that paid you on May 1, 2019, by January 31, 2020.

There can be civil and even criminal penalties for not filing this return.

**Pension distributions to employees.** If your business maintains a qualified retirement plan and makes distributions from the plan to you or any employee, you must report the distributions to the IRS on Form 1099-R and furnish a copy to the recipient.

Furnish each contractor and the IRS with a Form 1099-R by January 31, 2019, for 2018 payments.

The penalty is $50, $100, or $270 per return for late filing, depending on the lateness of the return (see the general instructions for Forms 1099).

**Retirement plans.** If you maintain a qualified retirement plan (other than a SEP or SIMPLE-IRA), you must file an annual information return with the Department of Labor unless your plan is exempt.

No return is required if you (or you and your spouse) are the only participant(s) and plan assets at the end of 2018 do not exceed $250,000. However, regardless of the amount of plan assets, a return is required in the final year of the plan.

File Form 5500-EZ if you (or you and your spouse) are the only participant(s). If your plan covers employees, file Form 5500. The form is an IRS form, but it is filed with the Employee Benefits Security Administration of the U.S. Department of Labor. The due date for the form is the last day of the seventh month after the close of the plan year (e.g., July 31, 2019, for 2018 calendar-year plans).

The late filing penalty is $25 per day (up to $15,000).

**Small cash transactions.** If you are in a business, such as a convenience store, liquor store, or gas station, that sells or redeems money orders or traveler's checks in excess of $1,000 per customer per day or issues your own value cards, the government asks that you report any suspicious transactions that exceed $2,000. While this filing isn't mandatory (there is no penalty for non-filing), the Treasury Department asks that you report when someone provides false or expired identification, buys multiple money orders in even hundred-dollar denominations or in unusual quantities, attempts to bribe or threaten you or your employee, or does anything else suspicious.

File FinCEN Form 109, "Suspicious Activity Report by Money Services Business," with the Treasury Department within 30 days of the suspicious activity (it is filed electronically by submitting a "Registration of Money Service Business (RMSB)" form through the BSA e-filing system at https://bsaefiling.fincen.treas.gov/main.html). Under federal law, you are protected from civil liability so the person you report cannot sue for damages.

**Wages to employees.** If you have any employees, including your spouse or child, you must report wages for the year to the Social Security Administration and the employee. Furnish the employee with Form W-2 and a copy plus a transmittal form with the Social Security Administration by January 31 of the year following the year in which the wages were paid.

## 40.6  Filing Schedule C

In this section are explanations of how a sole proprietor reports income and expenses on Schedule C, a sample of which is on page 684. If you have more than one sole proprietorship, use a separate Schedule C for each business.

**Schedule C-EZ.** This simple form is designed for persons on the cash basis who do not have a net business loss and have:

- Business expenses of $5,000 or less;
- No inventory at any time during the year;
- Only one sole proprietorship;
- No employees;
- No home office expense deduction;
- No prior year suspended passive activity losses from this business; and
- No depreciation to be reported on Form 4562.

**Statutory employees.** Statutory employees report income and expenses on Schedule C. Thus, expenses may be deducted in full on Schedule C. Statutory employees are full-time life insurance salespersons, agent or commission drivers distributing certain foods and beverages, pieceworkers, and full-time traveling or city salespersons who solicit on behalf of and transmit to their principals orders from wholesalers and retailers for merchandise for resale or for supplies.

The term full time refers to an exclusive or principal business activity for a single company or person and not to the time spent on the job. If your principal activity is soliciting orders for one company, but you also solicit incidental orders for another company, you are a full-time salesperson for the primary company. Solicitations of orders are considered incidental to a principal business activity if you devote 20% or less of your time to the solicitation activity. A city or traveling salesperson is presumed to meet the principal business activity test in a calendar year in which he or she devotes 80% or more of working time to soliciting orders for one principal.

IRS regulations give this example: A salesperson's principal activity is getting orders from retail pharmacies for a wholesale drug company called Que Company. He occasionally takes orders for two other companies. He is a statutory employee only for Que Company.

If you are a statutory employee, your company checks Box 13 on Form W-2, identifying you as a statutory employee. Although a statutory employee may treat job expenses as business expenses, the employer withholds FICA (Social Security and Medicare) taxes on wages and commissions.

If you received a Form W-2 with "Statutory employee" checked in Box 13, include the income from Box 1 of the W-2 on Line 1 of Schedule C (or C-EZ) and check the box on that line. If you also have self-employment earnings from another business, you must report the self-employment earnings and statutory employee income on separate Schedules C. If both types of income are earned in the same business, allocate the expenses between the two activities on the separate schedules.

**Gross receipts or sales on Schedule C.** Your gross receipts are reported on Line 1 of Schedule C.

 *Filing Tip*

**Spouses Can Elect Qualified Joint Venture Status for Their Business**

Instead of having to file a partnership return, spouses can elect qualified joint venture status, which allows them to file as sole proprietors on Schedule C, provided they are the sole owners of their business, they both materially participate in the business, and they file a joint return.

To make the election, each spouse must file a separate Schedule C (or C-EZ), and report his or her respective share of the income and expenses from the business. For a rental real estate business, Schedule E is used instead of Schedule C.

If the election is made, each spouse's share of the net profit is considered to be his or her self-employment earnings for purposes of figuring self-employment tax *(45.1)* and for crediting Social Security and Medicare benefits.

 *Filing Tip*

**Health Insurance Premiums**

As a sole proprietor, you do not deduct your health insurance premiums on Schedule C. Instead, you deduct 100% of health insurance costs for yourself, your spouse, and your dependents on Schedule 1 (Form 1040).

Claim health savings account contributions also on Schedule 1 (Form 1040) *(41.11)*.

| SCHEDULE C (Form 1040) | **Profit or Loss From Business** | OMB No. 1545-0074 |
|---|---|---|

**SCHEDULE C**
**(Form 1040)**

Department of the Treasury
Internal Revenue Service (99)

**Profit or Loss From Business**
(Sole Proprietorship)

▶ Go to *www.irs.gov/ScheduleC* for instructions and the latest information.
▶ **Attach to Form 1040, 1040NR, or 1041; partnerships generally must file Form 1065.**

OMB No. 1545-0074

**2018**

Attachment
Sequence No. **09**

Name of proprietor

Social security number (SSN)

| A | Principal business or profession, including product or service (see instructions) | B Enter code from instructions ▶ |
| C | Business name. If no separate business name, leave blank. | D Employer ID number (EIN) (see instr.) |
| E | Business address (including suite or room no.) ▶ | |
| | City, town or post office, state, and ZIP code | |

F Accounting method: **(1)** ☐ Cash **(2)** ☐ Accrual **(3)** ☐ Other (specify) ▶
G Did you "materially participate" in the operation of this business during 2018? If "No," see instructions for limit on losses . ☐ Yes ☐ No
H If you started or acquired this business during 2018, check here . . . . . . . . . . . . . ▶ ☐
I Did you make any payments in 2018 that would require you to file Form(s) 1099? (see instructions) . . . . . ☐ Yes ☐ No
J If "Yes," did you or will you file required Forms 1099? . . . . . . . . . . . . . . . . ☐ Yes ☐ No

**Part I   Income**

| 1 | Gross receipts or sales. See instructions for line 1 and check the box if this income was reported to you on Form W-2 and the "Statutory employee" box on that form was checked . . . . . . . . . ▶ ☐ | 1 | |
| 2 | Returns and allowances . . . . . . . . . . . . . . . . . . . . . . . | 2 | |
| 3 | Subtract line 2 from line 1 . . . . . . . . . . . . . . . . . . . . . | 3 | |
| 4 | Cost of goods sold (from line 42) . . . . . . . . . . . . . . . . . . . | 4 | |
| 5 | **Gross profit.** Subtract line 4 from line 3 . . . . . . . . . . . . . . . . | 5 | |
| 6 | Other income, including federal and state gasoline or fuel tax credit or refund (see instructions) . . . . | 6 | |
| 7 | **Gross income.** Add lines 5 and 6 . . . . . . . . . . . . . . . . . . ▶ | 7 | |

**Part II   Expenses.** Enter expenses for business use of your home **only** on line 30.

| 8 | Advertising . . . . . | 8 | | | 18 | Office expense (see instructions) | 18 | |
| 9 | Car and truck expenses (see instructions) . . . . . . | 9 | | | 19 | Pension and profit-sharing plans . | 19 | |
| | | | | | 20 | Rent or lease (see instructions): | | |
| 10 | Commissions and fees . | 10 | | | a | Vehicles, machinery, and equipment | 20a | |
| 11 | Contract labor (see instructions) | 11 | | | b | Other business property . . . | 20b | |
| 12 | Depletion . . . . . | 12 | | | 21 | Repairs and maintenance . . | 21 | |
| 13 | Depreciation and section 179 expense deduction (not included in Part III) (see instructions) . . . . . | 13 | | | 22 | Supplies (not included in Part III) | 22 | |
| | | | | | 23 | Taxes and licenses . . . . . | 23 | |
| | | | | | 24 | Travel and meals: | | |
| 14 | Employee benefit programs (other than on line 19) . . | 14 | | | a | Travel . . . . . . . . | 24a | |
| 15 | Insurance (other than health) | 15 | | | b | Deductible meals (see instructions) . . . . . . | 24b | |
| 16 | Interest (see instructions): | | | | 25 | Utilities . . . . . . . | 25 | |
| a | Mortgage (paid to banks, etc.) | 16a | | | 26 | Wages (less employment credits) . | 26 | |
| b | Other . . . . . . . | 16b | | | 27a | Other expenses (from line 48) . . | 27a | |
| 17 | Legal and professional services | 17 | | | b | **Reserved for future use** . . . | 27b | |

| 28 | **Total expenses** before expenses for business use of home. Add lines 8 through 27a . . . . . . ▶ | 28 | |
| 29 | Tentative profit or (loss). Subtract line 28 from line 7 . . . . . . . . . . . . . . . | 29 | |
| 30 | Expenses for business use of your home. Do not report these expenses elsewhere. Attach Form 8829 unless using the simplified method (see instructions). **Simplified method filers only:** enter the total square footage of: (a) your home: _____ and (b) the part of your home used for business: _____ . Use the Simplified Method Worksheet in the instructions to figure the amount to enter on line 30 . . . . . . . . . | 30 | |
| 31 | **Net profit or (loss).** Subtract line 30 from line 29. • If a profit, enter on both **Schedule 1 (Form 1040), line 12** (or **Form 1040NR, line 13**) and on **Schedule SE, line 2**. (If you checked the box on line 1, see instructions). Estates and trusts, enter on **Form 1041, line 3**. • If a loss, you **must** go to line 32. | 31 | |
| 32 | If you have a loss, check the box that describes your investment in this activity (see instructions). • If you checked 32a, enter the loss on both **Schedule 1 (Form 1040), line 12** (or **Form 1040NR, line 13**) and on **Schedule SE, line 2**. (If you checked the box on line 1, see the line 31 instructions). Estates and trusts, enter on **Form 1041, line 3**. • If you checked 32b, you **must** attach **Form 6198.** Your loss may be limited. | 32a ☐ All investment is at risk. 32b ☐ Some investment is not at risk. |

For Paperwork Reduction Act Notice, see the separate instructions.    Cat. No. 11334P    Schedule C (Form 1040) 2018

## Sample Schedule C—Profit or Loss From Business
*(This sample is subject to change; see the e-Supplement at www.jklasser.com)*

Schedule C (Form 1040) 2018                                                                 Page **2**

**Part III**    **Cost of Goods Sold** (see instructions)

**33**  Method(s) used to
value closing inventory:    **a** ☐ Cost    **b** ☐ Lower of cost or market    **c** ☐ Other (attach explanation)

**34**  Was there any change in determining quantities, costs, or valuations between opening and closing inventory?
If "Yes," attach explanation . . . . . . . . . . . . . . . . . . . . . . . . . . . . . . .  ☐ Yes    ☐ No

| | | |
|---|---|---|
| **35**  Inventory at beginning of year. If different from last year's closing inventory, attach explanation . . . | **35** | |
| **36**  Purchases less cost of items withdrawn for personal use . . . . . . . . . | **36** | |
| **37**  Cost of labor. Do not include any amounts paid to yourself . . . . . . . . | **37** | |
| **38**  Materials and supplies . . . . . . . . . . . . . | **38** | |
| **39**  Other costs . . . . . . . . . . . . . . | **39** | |
| **40**  Add lines 35 through 39 . . . . . . . . . | **40** | |
| **41**  Inventory at end of year . . . . . . . . . | **41** | |
| **42**  **Cost of goods sold.** Subtract line 41 from line 40. Enter the result here and on line 4 . . . . . . | **42** | |

**Part IV**    **Information on Your Vehicle.**  Complete this part **only** if you are claiming car or truck expenses on line 9 and are not required to file Form 4562 for this business. See the instructions for line 13 to find out if you must file Form 4562.

**43**  When did you place your vehicle in service for business purposes? (month, day, year) ▶ _____ / _____ / _____

**44**  Of the total number of miles you drove your vehicle during 2018, enter the number of miles you used your vehicle for:

**a**  Business _____    **b** Commuting (see instructions) _____    **c** Other _____

**45**  Was your vehicle available for personal use during off-duty hours? . . . . . . . . . . . . . . . .  ☐ Yes    ☐ No

**46**  Do you (or your spouse) have another vehicle available for personal use?. . . . . . . . . . . . .  ☐ Yes    ☐ No

**47a**  Do you have evidence to support your deduction? . . . . . . . . . . . . . . . . . . .  ☐ Yes    ☐ No

**b**  If "Yes," is the evidence written? . . . . . . . . . . . . . . . . . . . . . . . . . .  ☐ Yes    ☐ No

**Part V**    **Other Expenses.**  List below business expenses not included on lines 8–26 or line 30.

| | |
|---|---|
| _____ | |
| _____ | |
| _____ | |
| _____ | |
| _____ | |
| _____ | |
| _____ | |
| _____ | |
| **48**  **Total other expenses.** Enter here and on line 27a . . . . . . . . . . . . . . | **48** |

Schedule C (Form 1040) 2018

If you received business payments through merchant credit cards and third party networks such as PayPal, Amazon Pay, and Google Checkout, such payments should have been reported to you by banks and third party network payers in Box 1 of Form 1099-K if your total transactions exceeded $20,000 and the number of transactions exceeded 200 for the year. No special reporting on Schedule C is required; report gross receipts as you would whether or not you receive Form 1099-K. As discussed above, "statutory employee" income from Form W-2 is entered on Line 1.

Do not report as receipts on Schedule C the following items:

- Gains or losses on the sale of property used in your business or profession. These transactions are reported on Schedule D and Form 4797.
- Dividends from stock held in the ordinary course of your business. These are reported as dividends from stocks that are held for investment.

**Deductions on Schedule C.** You can usually deduct most expenses incurred in your business, although there may be limits on the amount or timing of deductions. The basic requirement for deductibility is that expenses must be ordinary and necessary to your business. An ordinary expense is one that is common and accepted in your business; a necessary expense is one that is helpful and appropriate to your business.

Deductible business expenses are claimed in Part II; the descriptive breakdown of items is generally self-explanatory. However, note these points:

*Car and truck expenses (Line 9): In the year you place a car in service, you may choose between the IRS mileage allowance and deducting actual expenses, plus depreciation.* You must also attach Form 4562 to support a depreciation deduction; *see **Chapter 43**.*

*Depreciation (Line 13): Enter here the amount of your annual depreciation deduction or Section 179 expensing.* A complete discussion of depreciation may be found in **Chapter 42**. You must figure your deduction on Form 4562 for assets placed in service in 2018, or for cars or other "listed property," regardless of when the assets were placed in service.

*Employee benefit programs including health insurance (Line 14):* Enter your cost for the following programs you provide for your employees: accident or health plans; group-term life insurance; long-term care insurance coverage; wage continuation; self-insured medical reimbursement plans; dependent care assistance; educational assistance programs; supplemental unemployment benefits; and prepaid legal expenses. Retirement plan contributions for employees, such as to pension and profit-sharing plans, are reported separately on Line 19.

*Insurance other than health insurance (Line 15):* Insurance policy premiums for the protection of your business, such as accident, burglary, embezzlement, marine risks, plate glass, public liability, workers' compensation, fire, storm, or theft, and indemnity bonds upon employees, are deductible. State unemployment insurance payments are deducted here or as taxes if they are considered taxes under state law.

Premiums paid on an insurance policy on the life of an employee or one financially interested in a business, for the purpose of protecting you from loss in the event of the death of the insured, are not deductible.

Under a "12-month" rule, prepaid premiums can be deducted in the year paid if the coverage term does not extend more than 12 months beyond the first date coverage is received, and also does not extend beyond the taxable year following the year in which the premium is paid.

Premiums for disability insurance to cover loss of earnings when out ill or injured are nondeductible personal expenses. But you may deduct premiums covering business overhead expenses.

*Interest (Line 16):* While large businesses have a limitation on how much interest they can deduct, small businesses (the same $25 gross receipts test for using the cash method explained earlier in this chapter) can deduct all business interest unless other limitations apply. Include interest on business debts, but prepaid interest that applies to future years is not deductible.

Deductible interest on an insurance loan is limited if you borrow against a life insurance policy covering yourself as an employee or the life of any other employee, officer, or other person financially interested in your business. Interest on such a loan is deductible only if the policy covers an officer or 20% owner (no more than five such "key persons" can be

*Filing Tip*

**Security Trader's Operating Expenses**

A security trader may deduct expenses of trading on Schedule C; for further details *(30.14)*.

counted) and the loan is no more than $50,000 per person. If you own policies covering the same employees (or other persons) in more than one business, the $50,000 limit applies on an aggregate basis to all the policies. The interest deduction limit applies even if a sole proprietor borrows against a policy on his or her own life and uses the proceeds in a business; interest is not deductible to the extent the loan exceeds $50,000.

*Pension and profit-sharing plans (Line 19):* SEP, SIMPLE, or qualified retirement plan contributions made for your employees are entered here; contributions made for your account are entered directly on Form 1040 (Line 28) as an adjustment to income. In addition, you may have to file an information return by the last day of the seventh month following the end of the plan year *(41.8)*.

*Rent on business property (Line 20):* Rent paid for the use of lofts, buildings, trucks, and other equipment is deductible. Prepaid rents can be deducted by cash-method taxpayers in the year of payment if the rent term does not extend more than 12 months beyond the first day of the lease and also not beyond the end of the taxable year following the taxable year in which the prepayment is made. However, the economic performance rules prevent accrual-method taxpayers from deducting prepaid rent; economic performance occurs only ratably over the lease term.

Taxes on leased property that you pay to the lessor are deductible as additional rent.

*Repairs (Line 21):* The cost of repairs and maintenance generally is deductible. Expenses of repairs or replacements that increase the value of property, make it more useful, or lengthen its life are capitalized and their cost recovered through depreciation unless safe harbors or *de minimis* rules under final repair regulations are used.

*Taxes (Line 23):* Deduct real estate and personal property taxes on business assets here. Also deduct your share of Social Security and Medicare taxes paid on behalf of employees and payments of federal unemployment tax. Federal highway use tax is deductible. Federal import duties and excise and stamp taxes normally not deductible as itemized deductions are deductible as business taxes if incurred by the business. Taxes on business property, such as an ad valorem tax, must be deducted here; they are not to be treated as itemized deductions. However, the IRS holds that you may not deduct state income taxes on business income as a business expense. Its reasoning: Income taxes are personal taxes even when paid on business income. As such, you may deduct state income tax only as an itemized deduction on Schedule A, subject to the $10,000 limit on personal state and local taxes. The Tax Court supports the IRS rule on the grounds that it reflects Congressional intent toward the treatment of state income taxes in figuring taxable income.

For purposes of computing a net operating loss, state income tax on business income is treated as a business deduction.

If you pay or accrue sales tax on the purchase of nondepreciable business property, the sales tax is a deductible business expense. If the property is depreciable, add the sales tax to the cost basis for purposes of computing depreciation deductions.

*Travel and meals (Line 24):* Travel expenses on overnight business trips while "away from home" *(20.5)* are claimed on Line 24a. Total meals expenses on travel away from home, reduced by 50%, are claimed on Line 24b. The 50% limit for meals is increased to 80% for transportation industry workers subject to the Department of Transportation hours of service limits. Wining and dining customers, vendors and other business associates is also 50% deductible, provided the meals are not lavish or extravagant under the circumstances and the owner or an employee is present *(20.14)*.

Self-employed persons may use the IRS meal allowance rates *(20.4)*, instead of claiming actual expenses. Recordkeeping requirements for travel expenses are discussed in **Chapter 20 (20.26–20.28)**.

*Utilities (Line 25):* Deduct utilities such as gas, electric, and telephone expenses incurred in your business. However, if you have a home office *(40.12)*, you may not deduct the base rate (including taxes) of the first phone line into your home *(19.15)*.

*Wages (Line 26):* You do not deduct wages paid to yourself. You may deduct reasonable wages paid to family members who work for you. If you have an employee who works in your office and also in your home, such as a domestic worker, you deduct that part of the salary allocated to the work in your office. If you claim any employment-related tax credit *(40.26)*, the wage deduction is reduced by the credit.

**Interest on Business Tax Deficiency**

Interest on a tax deficiency based on business income reporting is not a deductible business expense; interest on a tax deficiency is always nondeductible personal interest.

**Tax Advice and Tax Preparation Costs**

On Line 17 of Schedule C, you deduct the portion of tax preparation costs allocable to preparing Schedule C and related tax forms. Also deduct on Line 17 fees for tax advice related to the business.

**Employment Tax Responsibilities**

If you have employees, you must comply with employment tax responsibilities, such as collecting and paying to the government income tax withholding from employee wages. For details, *see* IRS Publication 15, Circular E, Employer's Tax Guide.

**Caution**

### Deduction for Commercial Buildings

Owners and leaseholders of commercial buildings that are certified to meet certain energy-efficiency standards were able to qualify for a deduction of up to $1.80 per square foot. This provision expired at the end of 2017 but could be extended by Congress; *see* the *e-Supplement* at *jklasser.com*.

*Other expenses (Line 27):* In Part V of Schedule C, you list deductible expenses not reported in Part II, such as amortizable business start-up costs *(40.11)*, business-related education *(33.15)*, subscriptions, and professional dues, and enter the total on Line 27.

*Home office deduction (Line 30):* If you qualify for this deduction, it is first figured separately on Form 8829 if you use the actual expense method, or multiply your square footage (up to 300 square feet) by $5; the deductible amount is then entered here *(40.12)*.

*Net profit (or loss) (Line 31):* The net results of your entries on lines 1 through 30 will produce a profit (or loss). A profit, called net earnings from self-employment, is subject to self-employment tax *(45.1–45.6)*. It may also be subject to a 0.9% additional Medicare tax *(28.2)*. But a profit may entitle you to a 20% deduction *(40.24)*.

**Limited deduction for business gifts.** Your deduction for gifts to business customers and clients is limited to $25 per person per year. You and your spouse are treated as one person in figuring this limitation even if you do not file a joint return and even if you have separate business connections with the recipient. The $25 limitation also applies to partnerships; thus a gift by the partnership to one person may not exceed $25, regardless of the number of partners. Gifts not coming within the $25 limit are: (1) scholarships that are tax free under the rules in *Chapter 33*; (2) prizes and awards that are tax free under the rules in *11.1*; and (3) awards to employees, discussed below.

If you made a gift to the spouse of a business associate, it is considered as made to the associate. If the spouse has an independent bona fide business connection with you, the gift is not considered as made to the associate unless it is intended for the associate's eventual use. If you made a gift to a corporation or other business group intended for the personal use of an employee, stockholder, or other owner of the corporation, the gift generally is considered as made to that individual.

Packaged food or drink given to a business associate is a gift if it is to be consumed at a later time. Theater or sporting event tickets given to business associates are entertainment, not gift, expenses if you accompany them, and under the Tax Cuts and Jobs Act, entertainment expenses after 2017 are not deductible *(20.13)*. If you do not accompany them, you may treat the tickets as gifts, subject to the $25 limitation.

In figuring the $25 limitation to each business associate, do not include the following items:

1. A gift of a specialty advertising item that costs $4 or less on which your name is clearly and permanently imprinted. This exception saves you the trouble of having to keep records of such items as pens, desk sets, plastic bags, and cases on which you have your name imprinted for business promotion.

2. Signs, displays, racks, or other promotional material that is used on business premises by the person to whom you gave the material.

3. Incidental costs of wrapping, insuring, mailing, or delivering the gift. However, the cost of an ornamental basket or container must be included if it has a substantial value in relation to the goods it contains.

**Deducting length of service or safety achievement awards to employees.** There is an exception to the $25 gift deduction limitation for achievement awards of tangible personal property given to your employees in recognition of length of service or safety achievement, provided they are given as part of a presentation under circumstances indicating that they are not a form of disguised compensation. The Tax Cuts and Jobs Act clarified that these rules do not apply to cash awards, gift cards, gift certificates (unless they entitle the employee to select from an approved employer list of items of tangible personal property), vacations, meals, lodging, tickets to sports or theater events, stocks, bonds, other securities, or similar items.

The amount of your deduction for the cost of a length of service or safety achievement award depends on whether it is considered a qualified plan award. To be a qualified plan award, the award must be given under an established written plan or program that does not discriminate in favor of highly compensated employees. The average cost of all awards under the plan for the year (to all employees) must not exceed $400. In determining this $400 average cost, awards of nominal value are not to be taken into account. You may deduct up to $1,600 for all qualified plan awards (safety and length of service) given to the same employee during the taxable year. If the award is not a qualified plan award, the annual deduction ceiling for each employee is $400. The $1,600 overall limit applies if the same employee receives some qualified plan awards and some non-qualified awards during the same year. Claim the deduction as a non-wage expense on your Schedule C. In a partnership, the deduction limitation applies to the partnership as well as to each partner.

A length of service award does not qualify as an employee achievement award if it is given during the employee's first five years or if another length of service was received in the current year or previous four years..

A safety award granted to managers, administrators, clerical employees, or professional employees are not considered employee achievement awards. Furthermore, if during the year more than 10% of other employees (not counting managers, administrators, clerical employees, or professional employees) previously received safety awards, none of the later awards are subject to the employee achievement award rules.

The amount that you deduct (up to the $400 or $1600 limit) for an employee achievement award is tax free to the employee *(3.12)*. For example, you give a qualified plan award costing $2,000 to an employee. You may deduct only $1,600. The employee is not taxed on the award up to $1,600; the $400 balance is taxable.

## 40.7 Deductions for Professionals

The following expenses incurred by self-employed professionals in the course of their work are generally allowed as deductions from income when figuring profit (or loss) from their professional practices on Schedule C:

- Dues to professional societies.
- Operating expenses and repairs of car used on professional calls.
- Supplies.
- Subscriptions to professional journals.
- Rent for office space.
- Cost of fuel, light, water, and telephone used in the office.
- Salaries of assistants.
- Malpractice insurance *(40.6)*.
- Cost of books, information services, professional instruments, and equipment with a useful life of one year or less. Professional libraries are depreciable if their value decreases with time. Depreciation rules are discussed in *42.1*.
- Fees paid to a tax preparer for preparing Schedule C and related business forms.

**Professionals as employees.** Professionals who are not in their own practice may not deduct professional expenses on Schedule C. Salaried professionals may not deduct professional expenses, which previously were claimed as miscellaneous itemized deductions on Schedule A, subject to the 2% of adjusted gross income (AGI) floor *(19.1)*, because this deduction has been suspended for 2018 though 2025. However, "statutory" employees may use Schedule C *(40.6)*.

**The cost of preparing for a profession.** You may not deduct the cost of a professional education *(33.16)*.

The IRS does not allow a deduction for the cost of a license to practice. However, the Tax Court has allowed attorneys to amortize over their life expectancy bar admission fees paid to state authorities.

**Payment of clients' expenses.** An attorney may follow a practice of paying his or her clients' expenses in pending cases. The IRS will disallow a deduction claimed for these payments on the grounds that the expenses are those of the client, not the attorney. The courts agree with the IRS position where there is a net fee agreement. In a net fee agreement, expenses first reduce the recovery before the attorney takes a fee. However, where the attorney is paid under a gross fee agreement, an appeals court has reversed a Tax Court decision that disallowed the deduction of the attorney's payment of client expenses. Under a gross fee agreement, the attorney's fee is based on the gross award; the prior payment of expenses does not enter into the fee agreement and so is not reimbursed. Because he would not be reimbursed, an attorney claimed his payment of client expenses was deductible. An appeals court accepted this argument and allowed the deduction. The court allowed the deduction although California law disapproved of the practice of paying

*Caution*

**Employee Bonuses**

Employee bonuses should not be labeled as gifts. An IRS agent examining your records may, with this description, limit the deduction to $25 unless you can prove the excess over $25 was compensation. By describing the payment as a gift, you are inviting an IRS disallowance of the excess over $25. This was the experience of an attorney who gave his secretary $200 at Christmas. The IRS disallowed $175 of his deduction. The Tax Court refused to reverse the IRS. The attorney could not prove that the payment was for services.

client expenses without a right of reimbursement. The court believed that there is no ethical difficulty with the practice and other jurisdictions approve of it. It is necessary for and it is the practice of personal injury firms to pay the costs of many of their clients.

If you are not allowed a current deduction for payment of clients' expenses, you may deduct your advance as a bad debt if the claim is worthless in another year *(40.6)*.

An attorney might deduct a payment to a client reimbursing the client for a bad investment recommended by the attorney. A court upheld the deduction on the grounds that the reimbursement was required to protect the reputation of an established law practice. However, no deduction is allowed when malpractice insurance reimbursement is available but the attorney fails to make a claim.

## 40.8 Nondeductible Expense Items

Capital expenditures may not be deducted. Generally, the cost of acquiring an asset or of prolonging its life is a capital expenditure that must be amortized over its expected life. If the useful life of an item is less than a year, its cost, including sales tax on the purchase, is deductible. Otherwise, you generally may recover your cost only through depreciation except to the extent first-year expensing *(42.3)* or bonus depreciation *(42.30)* applies. IRS regulations provide safe harbors, including a "12-month" rule, for expenditures relating to intangible assets or benefits *(40.3)*.

**Expenses while you are not in business.** You are not allowed to deduct business expenses incurred during the time you are not engaged in your business or profession.

> **EXAMPLE**
>
> A lawyer continued to maintain his office while he was employed by the government. During that time he did no private law work. He only kept the office to have it ready at such time as he quit the government job and returned to practice. His costs of keeping up his office while he was working for the government were not deductible.

**Bribes and kickbacks.** Bribes and kickbacks are not deductible if they are illegal under a federal or a generally enforced state law that subjects the payer to a criminal penalty or provides for the loss of license or privilege to engage in business. A kickback, even if not illegal, is not deductible by a physician or other person who has furnished items or services that are payable under the Medicare or Medicaid programs. A kickback includes payments for referral of a client, patient, or customer.

In one case, the IRS, with support from the Tax Court and a federal appeals court, disallowed a deduction for legal kickbacks paid by a subcontractor. The courts held that the kickbacks were not a "necessary" business expense because the contractor had obtained nearly all of its other contracts without paying kickbacks, including contracts from the same general contractor bribed here.

**Sexual harassment settlements subject to confidentiality agreements.** The cost of settlements, including legal fees, paid or incurred after December 31, 2017, are not deductible if subject to a nondisclosure agreement.

## 40.9 How Authors and Artists May Write Off Expenses

Self-employed authors, artists, photographers, and other qualifying creative professionals may write off business expenses as they are paid. The law (Code Section 263A) that requires expenses to be amortized over the period income is received does not apply to freelancers who personally create literary manuscripts, musical or dance scores, paintings, pictures, sculptures, drawings, cartoons, graphic designs, original print editions, photographs, or photographic negatives or transparencies. Furthermore, expenses of a personal service corporation do not have to be amortized if they directly relate to expenses of a qualifying author, artist, or photographer who owns (or whose relatives own) substantially all of the corporation's stock.

Current deductions generally are not allowed for expenses relating to motion picture films, videotapes, printing, photographic plates, or similar items. However, bonus

**Penalties and Fines**

Penalties or fines paid to a government agency because of a violation of any law are not deductible. You may deduct penalties imposed by a business contract for late performance or nonperformance.

**No Deductions for Cannibis Businesses**

Even though the sale of marijuana for medical or recreational purposes is legal in about half the states, it remains contraband under federal law. As such no business deductions are allowed because of Code Sec. 280E. However, the IRS allows cannabis businesses to take the cost of cannabis into account in figuring the cost of goods sold (Chief Counsel Memorandum 201504011).

depreciation is allowed for film and television productions and live theatrical productions placed in service after September 17, 2017.

An author or artist with expenses exceeding income may be barred by the IRS from claiming a loss under a profit motive test; in that case, the profit-presumption rule *(40.10)* may allow a deduction of the loss.

## 40.10 Deducting Expenses of a Sideline Business or Hobby

There is a one-way tax rule for hobbies: Income from a hobby is taxable as "other income" on Form 1040; expenses (other than amounts allowed without regard to whether the activity is engaged in for profit, such as mortgage interest) are not deductible. In the past, hobby expenses could be deducted to the extent of income from the activity, but due to the suspension of miscellaneous itemized deductions subject to the 2%-of-AGI floor, there are no write-offs permitted for 2018 through 2025. A profitable sale of a hobby collection or activity held long term is taxable as capital gain; losses are not deductible.

**Presumption of profit-seeking motive.** You are presumed to be engaged in an activity for profit if you can show a profit in at least three of the last five years, including the current year. If the activity is horse breeding, training, racing, or showing, the profit presumption applies if you show profits in two of the last seven (including current) years. The presumption does not necessarily mean that losses will automatically be allowed; the IRS may try to rebut the presumption. You would then have to prove a profit motive by showing these types of facts: You spend considerable time in the activity; you keep businesslike records; you have a written business plan showing how you plan to make a profit; you relied on expert advice; you expect the assets to appreciate in value; and losses are common in the start-up phase of your type of business.

**Election postpones determination of profit presumption.** If you have losses in the first few years of an activity and the IRS tries to disallow them as hobby losses, you have this option: You may make an election on Form 5213 to postpone the determination of whether the above profit presumption applies. The postponement is until after the end of the fourth taxable year (sixth year for a horse breeding, training, showing, or racing activity) following the first year of the activity. For example, if you enter a farming activity in 2018, you can elect to postpone the profit motive determination until after the end of 2022. Then, if you have realized profits in at least three of the five years (2018–2022), the profit presumption applies. When you make the election on Form 5213, you agree to waive the statute of limitations for all activity-related items in the taxable years involved. The waiver generally gives the IRS an additional two years after the filing due date for the last year in the presumption period to issue deficiencies related to the activity.

To make the election, you must file Form 5213 within three years of the due date of the return for the year you started the activity. If before the end of this three-year period you receive a deficiency notice from the IRS disallowing a loss from the activity and you have not yet made the election, you can still do so within 60 days of receiving the notice. These election rules apply to individuals, partnerships, and S corporations. An election by a partnership or S corporation is binding on all partners or S corporation shareholders holding interests during the presumption period.

## 40.11 Deducting Expenses of Looking for a New Business

When you are planning to invest in a business, you may incur preliminary expenses for traveling to look at the property and for legal or accounting advice. Expenses incurred during a general search or preliminary investigation of a business are not deductible, including expenses related to the decision whether or not to enter a transaction. However, when you go beyond a general search and actually go into business, you may elect to deduct or amortize your start-up costs.

**Deductible or amortizable start-up costs.** If you began your business in 2018, up to $5,000 of eligible start-up expenses is allowed. The limit is reduced by the amount of start-up costs exceeding $50,000. Start-up costs over the first-year deduction limit may be

*Planning Reminder*

**Hobby or Sideline Business**

The question of whether an activity, such as dog breeding or collecting and selling coins and stamps, is a hobby or sideline business arises when losses are incurred. As long as you show a profit, you may deduct the expenses of the activity. If your return is examined, you may be able to take advantage of a "profit presumption" *(40.10)*, or you may have to prove that you are engaged in the activity to make a profit. If you have more than one business activity, you may be able to aggregate them to show that you have an overall profit motive.

*Filing Tip*

**Aggregating Activities**

If you have two or more activities, they can be grouped together to determine an overall profit motive based on the degree of organization and economic interrelationship of the various undertakings, the business purpose of carrying them on together or separately, and the similarity of various undertakings.

**Remember Amortized Startup Costs from Previous Years**

If you started your business and did not fully deduct your start up costs in your first year, you may have an amortized amount that is deductible on this year's return. Check prior tax returns for any unamortized amount that can be deducted in 2018.

amortized over 15 years. An election to amortize is made by claiming the deduction on Form 4562, and it is then entered in Part V ("Other Expenses") of Schedule C.

Eligible costs include investigating and setting up the business, such as expenses of surveying potential markets, products, labor supply, and transportation facilities; travel and other expenses incurred in lining up prospective distributors, suppliers, or customers; salaries or fees paid to consultants or attorneys, and fees for similar professional services. The business may be one you acquire from someone else or a new business you create.

**Organizational costs for a partnership or corporation.** Costs incident to the creation of a partnership or corporation are also deductible or amortizable under the rules for start-up costs discussed above. For a partnership, qualifying expenses include legal fees for negotiating and preparing a partnership agreement, and management, consulting, or accounting fees in setting up the partnership. No deduction or amortization is allowed for syndication costs of issuing and marketing partnership interests such as brokerage and registration fees, fees of an underwriter, and costs of preparing a prospectus.

For a corporation, qualifying expenses include the cost of organizational meetings, incorporation fees, and accounting and legal fees for drafting corporate documents. Costs of selling stock or securities, such as commissions, do not qualify.

An election to amortize is made on Part VI of Form 4562 for the first year the partnership or corporation is in business. The election on Form 4562 and the required statement must be filed no later than the return due date, including extensions, for the year in which the business begins.

**Nonqualifying expenses.** Deductible and amortizable expenses are restricted to expenses incurred in investigating the acquisition or creation of an active business, and setting up such an active business. They do not include taxes or interest. Research and experimental costs are not start-up costs, but are separately deductible or amortizable; *see* IRS Publication 535 and Code Section 174. For rental activities to qualify as an active business, there must be significant furnishing of services incident to the rentals. For example, the operation of an apartment complex, an office building, or a shopping center would generally be considered an active business.

If you do not elect to deduct or amortize qualifying start-up costs, you treat the expenses as follows:

- Costs connected with the acquisition of capital assets are capitalized and depreciated; and
- Costs related to assets with unlimited or indeterminable useful lives are recovered only on the future sale or liquidation of the business.

**Nonqualifying Costs**

You may not deduct or amortize the expenses incurred in acquiring or selling securities or partnership interests such as securities registration expenses or underwriters' commissions.

If the acquisition fails. Where you have gone beyond a general search and have focused on the acquisition of a particular business, but the acquisition falls through, you may deduct the expenses as a capital loss.

> **EXAMPLES**
>
> 1. In search of a business, you place newspaper advertisements and travel to investigate various prospective ventures. You pay for audits to evaluate the potential of some of the ventures. You then decide to purchase a specific business and hire a law firm to draft necessary documents. However, you change your mind and later abandon your plan to acquire the business. According to the IRS, you may not deduct the related expenses for advertisements, travel, and audits. These are considered investigatory. You may deduct the expense of hiring the law firm.
> 2. Domenie left his job to invest in a business. He advertised and was contacted by a party who wished to sell. He agreed to buy, hired an attorney, transferred funds to finance the business, and worked a month with the company manager to familiarize himself with the business. Discovering misrepresentations, he refused to buy the company and deducted over $5,000 for expenses, including travel and legal fees. The IRS disallowed the deduction as incurred in a business search. The Tax Court disagreed. Domenie thought he had found a business and acted as such in transferring funds and drawing legal papers for a takeover.

# 40.12 Home Office Deduction

If you operate your business from your home, using a room or other space as an office or area to assemble or prepare items for sale, you may be able to deduct expenses such as utilities, insurance, repairs, and depreciation allocated to your business use of the area. Collectively, these expenses are deducted as a single write-off, called the home office deduction. There are now two ways to figure the deduction: using your actual expenses or relying on an IRS-set standard amount *(40.13)*.

**Exclusive and regular use.** To deduct home office expenses, you must prove that you use the home area exclusively and on a regular basis either as:

1. A place of business to meet or deal with patients, clients, or customers in the normal course of your business (incidental or occasional meetings do not meet this test), or

2. Your principal place of business. Your home office will qualify as your principal place of business if you spend most of your working time there and most of your business income is attributable to your activities there.

**Administrative (recordkeeping) activity.** A home office meets the principal place of business test (Test 2), even if you spend most of your working time providing services at outside locations, if: (1) you use it regularly and exclusively for administrative or management activities of your business and (2) you have no other fixed location where you do a substantial amount of such administrative work. Self-employed persons are the beneficiaries of this administrative/management rule. Examples of administrative and management activities include billing customers, clients, or patients; keeping books and records; ordering supplies; setting up appointments; forwarding orders; and writing reports.

According to the IRS, performance of management or administrative activities under the following conditions do not disqualify a home office as a principal place of business:

- You have a company send out your bills from its place of business (*see* Example 1 below).

- You do administrative or management activities at times from a hotel or automobile (*see* Example 2 below).

- You occasionally conduct minimal administrative or management activities at a fixed location outside your home.

- You have suitable space to do administrative or management work outside your home but choose to use your home office for such activities (see Example 3 below).

## EXAMPLES

1. A self-employed plumber does all of his repair and installation services outside of his home where he has a small office used to phone customers, order supplies, and keep his books. However, he uses a local bookkeeping service to bill his customers. He has no other fixed location for doing his administrative work. That he uses an outside billing service does not disqualify his home office as a principal place of business.

2. A self-employed sales representative for several products uses a home office to set up appointments and write up orders. When she is out of town, she writes up such orders from a hotel room. The occasional use of a hotel room to write up orders does not disqualify the home office as a principal place of business that otherwise meets the new tests.

3. A self-employed anesthesiologist spends most of his professional time at three local hospitals. One of the hospitals provides him with a small shared office where he could do administrative and management work; however, he does not use this space. He uses his home as an office to: contact patients, surgeons, and hospitals regarding schedules; prepare presentations; keep billing records and patient logs; and read medical journals and books. His use of the home office for administrative activities satisfies the principal place of business test. His choice to use his home office instead of the one provided by one hospital does not disqualify his home office as the principal place of business.

 *Filing Tip*

**Incidental Personal Use of a Home Office**

Merely walking through a home office area to get to personal use space in a small apartment or storing some personal papers in the home office does not violate the exclusive use test.

*Caution*

**Principal Place of Business Test**

The tests for deducting office expenses will generally not present problems where the home area is the principal place of business or professional activity. For example, you are a doctor and *see* most of your patients at an office set aside in your home. A tax dispute may arise where you have a principal place of business elsewhere and use a part of your home for occasional work or administrative paperwork. Occasional use is not sufficient. If your deduction is questioned, you must prove that the area is used regularly and exclusively to meet with customers, clients, or patients or that the home office is the only place where administrative/management activities for the business are conducted. Have evidence that you have actual office facilities. Furnish the room as an office—with a desk, files, and a phone used only for business calls. Also keep a record of work done and business visitors.

*Filing Tip*

**Mobile Offices**

If you use a recreational vehicle (RV) as your office, you may be able to deduct some related costs, provided you can document business use.

If you work at home and also outside of your home at other locations and you do not meet the administrative/management rule, deductions of home office expenses should be supported by evidence that your activities at home are relatively more important or time consuming than those outside your home.

**Exclusive and regular business use of home area required.** If you use a room, such as a den, both for business and family purposes, be prepared to show that a specific section of the den is used exclusively as office space. For example, a real estate operator was not allowed to deduct the cost of a home office, on evidence that he also used the office area for nonbusiness purposes. A partition or other physical separation of the office area is helpful but not required.

Under the regular basis test, expenses attributable to incidental or occasional trade or business use are not deductible, even if the room is used for no other purpose but business.

Even if you meet these tests, your deduction for allocable office expenses may be substantially limited or barred by a restrictive rule that limits deductions to the income from the office activity. This computation is made on Form 8829 *(40.15)*.

**Multiple business use of home office.** If you use a home office for more than one business, make sure that the home office tests are met for all businesses before you claim deductions. If one business use qualifies and another use does not, the IRS will disallow deductions even for the qualifying use.

**Separate structure.** If in your business you use a separate structure not attached to your home, such as a studio adjacent but unattached to your home, the expenses are generally deductible if you satisfy the exclusive use and regular basis tests discussed earlier. A separate structure does not have to qualify as your principal place of business or a place for meeting patients, clients, or customers.

However, an income limitation *(40.15)* applies. In one case, a taxpayer argued that an office located in a separate building in his backyard was not subject to the exclusive and regular business use tests and the gross income limitation. However, the IRS and Tax Court held that it was. The office building was "appurtenant" to the home and thus part of it, based on these facts: The office building was 12 feet away from the house and within the same fenced-in residential area; it did not have a separate address; it was included in the same title and subject to the same mortgage as the house; and all taxes, utilities, and insurance were paid as a unit for both buildings.

**Day-care services.** The exclusive-use test does not have to be met for business use of a home to provide day-care services for children and handicapped persons, or persons age 65 or older, provided certain state licensing requirements are met. If part of your home is regularly but not exclusively used to provide day-care services, you may deduct an allocable part of your home expenses. You allocate expenses by multiplying the total costs by two fractions: (1) The total square footage in the home that is available for day-care use throughout each business day and regularly so used, divided by the total square footage for the home. (2) The total hours of business operation divided by the total number of hours in the year (8,760 in 2018).

If the area is exclusively used for day-care services, only fraction (1) applies.

> **EXAMPLE**
>
> In 2018, Alice Jones operates a day-care center at home from 7 a.m. to 6 p.m., five days a week for 50 weeks, for a total of 2,750 business-use hours during the year. Her family uses the area the rest of the time. Annual home expenses total $10,000 ($5,000 for interest and taxes; $4,000 for electricity, gas, water, trash collection, maintenance, and insurance; and $1,000 for depreciation). The total floor area of the home is 2,000 square feet; 1,500 square feet are used for day-care purposes. Alice multiplies her $10,000 of expenses by 75%, the part of the home used for day-care purposes (1,500 square feet ÷ 2,000 square feet), and also by 31.39%, the percentage of business-use time (2,750 hours ÷ 8,760 hours). Thus, she may deduct $2,354: $10,000 × 75% × 31.39%. The full $2,354 is deductible only if net income generated from the day-care facility is at least that much.

In one case, the Tax Court held that utility rooms, such as a laundry and storage room and garage, may be counted as part of the day-care business area. The IRS had argued that because the children were not allowed in these areas, the space could not be considered as used for business. The Tax Court disagreed. The laundry room was used to wash the children's clothes; the storage room and garage were used to store play items and equipment. Thus, the space was considered as used for child care even though the rooms were off limits to the children.

**Storage space and inventory.** If your home is the only location of a business selling products (wholesale or retail), you may deduct expenses allocated to space regularly used for inventory storage, including product samples, if the space is separately identifiable and suitable for storage. The space does not have to be used exclusively for business.

## 40.13 Write-Off Methods for Home Office Expenses

There are two ways in which you can figure your home office deduction: deduct your actual expenses or rely on an IRS-set standard deduction (simplified method). The two methods are explained below.

**Simplified method.** As long as the use of a portion of your home qualifies as a home office *(40.12)*, you can choose to use a standard home office deduction (safe harbor) amount. For 2018, the amount is $5 per square foot for up to 300 of square feet of office space (maximum deduction is $1,500). Figure the deduction using a worksheet in the instructions for line 30 of Schedule C.

You can decide whether to use the safe harbor method from year to year. In making your choice, keep in mind that the portion of the safe harbor amount that is not deductible because of the gross income limit *(40.15)* cannot be carried over and is lost forever. However, if in 2016 you deducted actual costs and switched to the simplified method for 2017 and for 2018 you are going back to deducting actual expenses, any unallowed expenses from 2016 may be deducted on your 2018 Form 8829.

When you opt for the safe harbor amount, no additional depreciation allowance can be claimed. If, in a future year you deduct your actual costs, ignore the year or years in which depreciation was not claimed and figure depreciation accordingly.

### EXAMPLE

You started claiming a home office deduction in 2014 based on your actual expenses but decided to use the safe harbor allowance for 2018. In 2019, you again deduct your actual costs, including depreciation. For 2019, you are now in year 5 (2014, 2015, 2016, 2017, and 2019) for purposes of figuring depreciation.

**Actual expense method.** For a qualifying home office *(40.12)* for which the actual expense method is used, deductible costs may include real estate taxes, mortgage interest, operating expenses (such as home insurance premiums and utility costs), and depreciation allocated to the area used for business. The deduction figured on Form 8829 may not exceed the net income derived from the business *(40.15)*.

The deduction from Form 8829 is entered on Line 30 of Schedule C.

Expenses that affect only the business part of your home, such as repairs or painting of the home office only, are entered on Form 8829 as "direct" expenses. Expenses for running the entire home, including mortgage interest, taxes, utilities, and insurance, are deductible as "indirect" expenses to the extent of your business-use percentage *(40.14)*.

Household expenses and repairs that do not benefit the office space are not deductible. However, a pro rata share of the cost of painting the outside of a house or repairing a roof is deductible. Costs of a new roof and landscaping are capital improvements according to the IRS, and so are not deductible immediately but may be recovered through depreciation.

If you install a security system for all your home's windows and doors, the portion of your monthly maintenance fee that is allocable to the office area is a deductible operating expense. Furthermore, the business portion of your cost for the system is depreciable.

*Caution*

**No Home Office Deduction for Records Storage**

The exception to the exclusive use test for storing inventory and supplies does not extend to storing records. This is so even if storage is required by state law and doing this in the home is the most convenient and least expensive option.

*Filing Instruction*

**Form 8829**

If using the actual expense method, you must report deductible home office expenses on Form 8829. Part I is used for showing the space allocated to business use *(40.14)*; Part II for reporting deductible expenses allocated to business use *(40.14)*; Part III for figuring depreciation on the business area *(40.13)*; and Part IV for carryover to 2019 of expenses not allowed in 2018 because of income limitations applied in Part II *(40.15)*. A sample copy of Form 8829 is on page 700.

*Filing Instruction*

### When To Figure Depreciation on a Home Office Using 27.5 Year Recovery

While depreciation of a home office usually is figured using a 39-year recovery period, a *27.5* year recovery period can be used by an on-site landlord of a building in which at least one dwelling unit is rented out and 80% or more of the gross rental income is rental income from dwelling units within the building. In applying the 80% test, the rental value of the entire landlord's unit is treated as gross rental income and the rental value of the landlord's residential space (but not the home office) is treated as rental income from a dwelling unit.

For example, where a landlord lived in one unit of his eight-unit building and used a room in his unit for a home office, the IRS allowed the home office to be depreciated over 27.5 years as residential rental property.

Thus, if the office takes up 20% of your home *(40.14)* you may deduct, subject to an income limitation *(40.15)*, 20% of the maintenance fee and a depreciation deduction for 20% of the cost.

> **EXAMPLE**
>
> In April 2018, you start to use one room in your single-family house exclusively and on a regular basis to meet with clients. This room is 10% of the square footage of your home. In 2000, you bought the property for $100,000, of which $90,000 was allocated to the house. The house has a fair market value of $185,000 in April 2018. You compute depreciation on the cost basis of $90,000, which is lower than the value. You multiply $90,000 by 10% (business-use percentage), which gives you $9,000 as the depreciable basis of the business part of the house. As you started business use in the fourth month of 2018, you multiply the depreciable basis of $9,000 by 1.819%. This percentage is listed for the fourth month in *Table 40-2*. Your depreciation deduction is $163.71 (9,000 × 1.819%).

**Figuring depreciation.** Even though a home is a residence, depreciation on a home office usually is figured as if it were commercial property using a 39-year recovery period (see *Table 40-2*). For depreciation purposes, the cost basis of the house is the lower of the fair market value of the house at the time you started to use a part of it for business or its adjusted basis, exclusive of the land. Only that part of the cost basis allocated to the office is depreciable. Form 8829 has a special section, Part III, for making this computation.

## 40.14 Allocating Expenses to Business Use

Allocate to home office use qualifying operating expenses *(40.13)* as follows: If the rooms are not equal or approximately equal in size, compare the number of square feet of space used for business with the total number of square feet in the home and then apply the resulting percentage to the total deductible expenses.

If all rooms in your home are approximately the same size, you may base the allocation on a comparison of the number of rooms used as an office to the total number of rooms.

> **EXAMPLE**
>
> A doctor rents the ground floor of a home and uses three rooms for his office and seven rooms for his residence. The rooms are not equal in size. The entire area has 2,000 square feet; the office has 699. He allocates 30% (600/2,000) of the following expenses to his office:
>
> | | Total | Office | Residence |
> |---|---|---|---|
> | Rent | $7,200 | $2,160 | $5,040 |
> | Light | 600 | 180 | 420 |
> | Heat | 1,000 | 300 | 700 |
> | Wages of domestic | 2,000 | 600 | 1,400 |
> | | $10,800 | $3,240 | $7,560 |
>
> The $3,240 of office expenses are deductible as indirect expenses on Form 8829, subject to an income limitation *(40.15)*.

## Table 40-2 Nonresidential Real Property
### (39 years—Property placed in service after May 12, 1993)
#### Use the column for the month of taxable year placed in service.

| | 1 | 2 | 3 | 4 | 5 | 6 | 7 | 8 | 9 | 10 | 11 | 12 |
|---|---|---|---|---|---|---|---|---|---|---|---|---|
| **Year** | | | | | | | | | | | | |
| 1 | 2.461% | 2.247% | 2.033% | 1.819% | 1.605% | 1.391% | 1.177% | 0.963% | 0.749% | 0.535% | 0.321% | 0.107% |
| 2–39 | 2.564 | 2.564 | 2.564 | 2.564 | 2.564 | 2.564 | 2.564 | 2.564 | 2.564 | 2.564 | 2.564 | 2.564 |
| 40 | 0.107 | 0.321 | 0.535 | 0.749 | 0.963 | 1.177 | 1.391 | 1.605 | 1.819 | 2.033 | 2.247 | 2.461 |

## 40.15 Business Income May Limit Home Office Deductions

Even if your home business use satisfies the deduction tests *(40.12)*, deductions for the business portion *(40.14)* of utilities, maintenance, and insurance costs, as well as depreciation or rent deductions, may not exceed net business income after reducing the tentative profit from Schedule C by allocable mortgage interest, real estate taxes, and federally-declared disaster losses. To make sure that deductible expenses do not exceed income, the IRS requires you to use Form 8829. If you do not realize income during the year, no deduction is allowed. For example, you are a full-time writer and use an office in your home. You do not sell any of your work this year or receive any advances or royalties. Therefore, you may not claim a home office deduction for this year. See also the rules for writers and artists earlier in this chapter *(40.9)*.

Part II of Form 8829 limits the deduction of home office expenses to net income derived from office use. You start with the tentative profit from Schedule C. If you sold your home during the year, increase the tentative profit by any net gain (or decrease tentative profit by any net loss) that is allocable to the office area and reported on Schedule D or Form 4797. The following expenses are listed first in Part II of Form 8829 for purposes of applying the income limit: Disaster losses affecting the residence, deductible mortgage interest, and real estate taxes. If there is income remaining after these expenses are subtracted from the Schedule C tentative profit, then home insurance premiums, repair and maintenance expenses for the residence, utility expenses, and rent are claimed against the remaining income. Depreciation is taken into account last, in Part III of Form 8829.

Business expenses not related to the home are deducted on the appropriate lines of Schedule C. For example, a salary paid to a secretary is deducted on Line 26 of Schedule C; the cost of depreciable business equipment used in your home is deducted on Line 13 of Schedule C.

The amount of real estate taxes, mortgage interest, or federally-declared disaster losses not allocated to home office use may be claimed as itemized deductions on Schedule A.

### EXAMPLE

In April 2018, Samuel Brown starts to use a room in his single-family house regularly and exclusively as a home office for his sideline consulting business. The office space takes up 20% of the area of his home. His gross income in 2018 from consulting services is $12,400. He paid $7,600 for a photocopy machine and a computer, and had office telephone expenses of $600 and office supply costs of $800.

In addition, his home costs are:

| | |
|---|---|
| Mortgage interest | $10,000 |
| Real estate taxes | 4,000 |
| Insurance | 1,200 |
| Utilities | 1,800 |

 *Planning Reminder*

**Carryover Allowed**

Expenses disallowed under the actual expense method because of the income limitation may be carried forward and treated as home office expenses in a later tax year (Part IV, Form 8829). The carryover, as well as the expenses of the later year, are subject to the income limitation of that year. For example, tentative profit for 2018 on Line 29 of Schedule C is $1,000. Expenses allocated to the home office are $2,000. Only $1,000 of the expenses are deductible; $1,000 is carried over to 2019.

On Schedule C he claims first-year expensing *(42.3)* for the copier and the computer, and also deducts the office phone costs and supplies. This gives a tentative profit of $3,400 ($12,400 – $9,000) on Line 29, Schedule C.

In Part I of Form 8829, he lists the total area of the home and the area used for business, showing 20% business use.

In Part II, he enters the home costs listed above.

In Part III, Samuel figures depreciation on the cost basis of his home of $188,975 (excluding the land), as this is less than its value in April 2018 when his home office use began. Taking into account that the office is 20% of the home area, his depreciable basis is $37,795 (20% × $188,975), and using a depreciation rate of 1.819% for the fourth month from *Table 40-2*, he figures depreciation allocated to business use of $687.

Samuel Brown's Form 8829 is on page 700. Here are the entries from the relevant lines of the Form 8829 to illustrate the computation of his home office deduction.

Form 8829, Part II, Line—

| Line | Description | Amount |
|---|---|---|
| 8. | Tentative profit from Schedule C, Line 29 | $3,400 |
| 10b. | Mortgage interest | $10,000 |
| 11b. | Real estate taxes | 4,000 |
| 12b. | Total | $14,000 |
| 13 & 14. | Business portion of Line 12 | 2,800 |
| 15. | Remaining tentative profit | 600 |
| 17b. | Insurance | 1,200 |
| 20b. | Utilities | 1,800 |
| 22b. | Total | 3,000 |
| 23, 25, & 26. | Business portion of Line | 22 600 |
| 27. | Remaining tentative profit | 0 |

No depreciation is deductible on Line 32 because there is no remaining business income and excess home office expenses may not generate a loss deduction. The depreciation of $687, shown on Lines 29 and 41, is carried over to 2019 on Line 43. Home office expenses of $3,400 from Lines 14 and 26 are allowed on Line 35 of Form 8829 and entered as a deduction on Line 30, Schedule C.

## 40.16  Home Office for Sideline Business

You may have an occupation and also run a sideline business from an office in your home. The home office expenses for the sideline business are deductible on Form 8829 if the office is a principal place of operating the business or a place to meet with clients, customers, or patients. See the deduction tests *(40.12)* and the income limit computation *(40.15)* for home office deductions. Managing rental property may qualify as a business.

**Managing your own securities portfolio.** Investors managing their own securities portfolios may find it difficult to convince a court that investment management is a business activity. According to Congressional committee reports, a home office deduction should be denied to an investor who uses a home office to read financial periodicals and reports, clip bond coupons, and perform similar activities. In one case, the Claims Court allowed a deduction to Moller, who spent about 40 hours a week at a home office managing a substantial stock portfolio. The Claims Court held these activities amounted to a business. However, an appeals court reversed the decision. According to the appeals court, the test is whether or not a person is a trader. A trader is in a business; an investor is not. A trader buys and sells frequently to catch daily market swings. An investor buys securities for capital appreciation and income without regard to daily market developments. Therefore, to be a trader, one's activities must be directed to short-term trading, not the long-term holding of investments. Here,

Moller was an investor; he was primarily interested in the long-term growth potential of stock. He did not earn his income from the short-term turnovers of stocks. He had no significant trading profits. His interest and dividend income was 98% of his income. See the discussion of trader expenses in *30.15*.

> **EXAMPLE**
>
> A doctor was employed full time by a hospital. He also owned six rental properties that he personally managed. He sought new tenants, supplied furnishings, and cleaned and prepared the units for tenants. He used one bedroom in his two-bedroom home exclusively as an office to manage the properties. The room was furnished with a desk, bookcase, filing cabinet, calculators, and answering service; furnishings and other materials for preparing rental units for tenants were stored there. According to the Tax Court, the doctor's efforts in managing the rental properties constituted a business; he could deduct expenses allocable to the home office.

## 40.17 Depreciation of Office in Cooperative Apartment

If your home office meets the tests discussed in *40.12*, you may deduct depreciation on your stock interest in the cooperative. The basis for depreciation may be your share of the cooperative corporation's basis for the building or an amount computed from the price you paid for the stock. The method you use depends on whether you are the first or a later owner of the stock.

**You are the first owner.** In figuring your depreciation, you start with the cooperative's depreciable basis of the building. You then take your share of depreciation according to the percentage of stock interest you own. The cooperative can provide the details needed for the computation.

If space in the building is rented to commercial tenants who do not have stock interests in the corporation, the total allowable depreciation is reduced by the amount allocated to the space used by the commercial tenants.

**You are a later owner of the cooperative's stock.** When you buy stock from a prior owner, your depreciable basis is determined by the price of your stock and your share of the co-op's outstanding mortgage, reduced by amounts allocable to land and to commercial space.

## 40.18 Net Operating Losses (NOLs)

A loss incurred in your profession or unincorporated business is deducted from other income reported on Form 1040. If the loss exceeds your other income, you may have a net operating loss (NOL). An NOL can be used to offset income in other years. More specifically, for NOLs arising in 2018, you can carry the loss forward indefinitely to offset income until the NOL is used up. There is no carryback for a 2018 NOL, although those engaged in farming (Schedule F filers) have a two-year carryback (which can be waived so the NOL is only carried forward).

**80% offset.** For NOLs in 2018, only 80% can be used to offset taxable income in the carryforward (or in the case of farming losses, the carryback) year.

**Carryover of loss from prior year to 2018.** If you had a net operating loss in an earlier year that is being carried forward to 2018, the loss carryover is reported as a minus figure on the line for "other income" on Schedule 1 of Form 1040. You must attach a detailed statement showing how you figured the carryover.

**Change in marital status.** If you incur a net operating loss while single but are married filing jointly in a carryback or carryforward year, the loss may be used only to offset your own income on the joint return.

If the net operating loss was claimed on a joint return and in the carryback or carryforward year you are not filing jointly with the same spouse, only your allocable share of the original loss may be claimed; *see* IRS Publication 536.

 *Planning Reminder*

**Substantiating the Sideline Business**

In claiming home office expenses of a sideline business, it is important to be ready to prove that you are actually in business *(40.10)*. In the case cited in the Example in *40.16*, the Tax Court held that the doctor's personal efforts in managing the six units for tenants were sufficiently systematic and continuous to put him in the rental real estate business. In some cases, the rental of even a single piece of real property may be a business if additional services are provided such as cleaning or maid service.

## Sample Form 8829—Expenses for Business Use of Your Home
*(This sample is subject to change; see the e-Supplement at www.jklasser.com)*

| Form **8829** | **Expenses for Business Use of Your Home** | OMB No. 1545-0074 |
|---|---|---|
| Department of the Treasury Internal Revenue Service (99) | ▶ File only with Schedule C (Form 1040). Use a separate Form 8829 for each home you used for business during the year. ▶ Go to *www.irs.gov/Form8829* for instructions and the latest information. | **2018** Attachment Sequence No. **176** |

| Name(s) of proprietor(s) | Your social security number |
|---|---|
| Samuel Brown | X1X-01-1111 |

**Part I  Part of Your Home Used for Business**

| | | | |
|---|---|---|---|
| 1 | Area used regularly and exclusively for business, regularly for daycare, or for storage of inventory or product samples (see instructions) | 1 | 500 |
| 2 | Total area of home | 2 | 2,500 sq. ft. |
| 3 | Divide line 1 by line 2. Enter the result as a percentage | 3 | 20 % |

**For daycare facilities not used exclusively for business, go to line 4. All others, go to line 7.**

| | | | | |
|---|---|---|---|---|
| 4 | Multiply days used for daycare during year by hours used per day | 4 | | hr. |
| 5 | Total hours available for use during the year (365 days x 24 hours) (see instructions) | 5 | 8,760 hr. | |
| 6 | Divide line 4 by line 5. Enter the result as a decimal amount | 6 | . | |
| 7 | Business percentage. For daycare facilities not used exclusively for business, multiply line 6 by line 3 (enter the result as a percentage). All others, enter the amount from line 3 ▶ | 7 | 20 % | |

**Part II  Figure Your Allowable Deduction**

| | | | | | |
|---|---|---|---|---|---|
| 8 | Enter the amount from Schedule C, line 29, **plus** any gain derived from the business use of your home, **minus** any loss from the trade or business not derived from the business use of your home (see instructions) | | 8 | 3,400 | |

See instructions for columns (a) and (b) before completing lines 9–22.

| | | | (a) Direct expenses | (b) Indirect expenses | | |
|---|---|---|---|---|---|---|
| 9 | Casualty losses (see instructions) | 9 | | | | |
| 10 | Deductible mortgage interest (see instructions) | 10 | | 10,000 | | |
| 11 | Real estate taxes (see instructions) | 11 | | 4,000 | | |
| 12 | Add lines 9, 10, and 11 | 12 | | 14,000 | | |
| 13 | Multiply line 12, column (b), by line 7 | 13 | | 2,800 | | |
| 14 | Add line 12, column (a), and line 13 | | | | 14 | 2,800 |
| 15 | Subtract line 14 from line 8. If zero or less, enter -0- | | | | 15 | 600 |
| 16 | Excess mortgage interest (see instructions) | 16 | | | | |
| 17 | Excess real estate taxes (see instructions) | 17 | | 1,200 | | |
| 18 | Insurance | 18 | | | | |
| 19 | Rent | 19 | | | | |
| 20 | Repairs and maintenance | 20 | | 1,800 | | |
| 21 | Utilities | 21 | | | | |
| 22 | Other expenses (see instructions) | 22 | | | | |
| 23 | Add lines 16 through 22 | 23 | | 3,000 | | |
| 24 | Multiply line 23, column (b), by line 7 | 24 | 600 | | | |
| 25 | Carryover of prior year operating expenses (see instructions) | 25 | | | | |
| 26 | Add line 23, column (a), line 24, and line 25 | | | | 26 | 600 |
| 27 | Allowable operating expenses. Enter the **smaller** of line 15 or line 26 | | | | 27 | 600 |
| 28 | Limit on excess casualty losses and depreciation. Subtract line 27 from line 15 | | | | 28 | - 0 - |
| 29 | Excess casualty losses (see instructions) | 29 | | | | |
| 30 | Depreciation of your home from line 42 below | 30 | 687 | | | |
| 31 | Carryover of prior year excess casualty losses and depreciation (see instructions) | 31 | | | | |
| 32 | Add lines 29 through 31 | | | | 32 | 687 |
| 33 | Allowable excess casualty losses and depreciation. Enter the **smaller** of line 28 or line 32 | | | | 33 | - 0 - |
| 34 | Add lines 14, 27, and 33 | | | | 34 | 3,400 |
| 35 | Casualty loss portion, if any, from lines 14 and 33. Carry amount to **Form 4684** (see instructions) | | | | 35 | |
| 36 | **Allowable expenses for business use of your home.** Subtract line 35 from line 34. Enter here and on Schedule C, line 30. If your home was used for more than one business, see instructions ▶ | | | | 36 | 3,400 |

**Part III  Depreciation of Your Home**

| | | | |
|---|---|---|---|
| 37 | Enter the **smaller** of your home's adjusted basis or its fair market value (see instructions) | 37 | 283,975 |
| 38 | Value of land included on line 37 | 38 | 50,000 |
| 39 | Basis of building. Subtract line 38 from line 37 | 39 | 188,975 |
| 40 | Business basis of building. Multiply line 39 by line 7 | 40 | 37,795 |
| 41 | Depreciation percentage (see instructions) | 41 | 1.819 % |
| 42 | Depreciation allowable (see instructions). Multiply line 40 by line 41. Enter here and on line 30 above | 42 | 687 |

**Part IV  Carryover of Unallowed Expenses to 2019**

| | | | |
|---|---|---|---|
| 43 | Operating expenses. Subtract line 27 from line 26. If less than zero, enter -0- | 43 | - 0 - |
| 44 | Excess casualty losses and depreciation. Subtract line 33 from line 32. If less than zero, enter -0- | 44 | 687 |

For Paperwork Reduction Act Notice, see your tax return instructions.     Cat. No. 13232M     Form **8829** (2018)

**Passive activity limitation.** Losses subject to passive activity rules of *Chapter 10* are not deductible as net operating losses. However, losses of rental operations coming within the $25,000 allowance *(10.2)* may be treated as net operating loss if the loss exceeds passive and other income.

**Figuring an NOL.** A net operating loss is generally the excess of deductible business expenses over business income. The net operating loss may also include the following losses and deductions:

- Your share of a partnership or S corporation operating loss.
- Loss on the sale of small business investment company (SBIC) stock.
- Loss incurred on Section 1244 stock.

An operating loss may not include:

- Net operating loss carryback or carryover from any year.
- Capital losses that exceed capital gain.
- Excess of nonbusiness deductions over nonbusiness income plus nonbusiness net capital gain.
- A self-employed person's contribution to a qualified retirement plan or SEP.
- An IRA deduction.

Income from other sources may eliminate or reduce your net operating loss.

> **EXAMPLE**
>
> You are self-employed and incur a business loss of $10,000. Your spouse earns a salary of $10,000. When you file a joint return, your business loss will be eliminated by your spouse's salary. Similarly, if you also had salary from another position, the salary would reduce your business loss.

## 40.19 How To Report a Net Operating Loss

You compute your net operating loss deduction on Schedule A of Form 1045 *(40.21)*. You start with adjusted gross income and personal deductions shown on your tax return. As these figures include items not allowed for net operating loss purposes, you follow the line-by-line steps of Schedule A (Form 1045) to eliminate them. That is, you reduce the loss by the nonallowed items such as deductions for personal exemptions, net capital loss, and nonbusiness deductions exceeding nonbusiness income. The Example at the end of this section illustrates the steps in the schedule.

**Adjustment for nonbusiness deductions.** Nonbusiness deductions that exceed nonbusiness income may not be included in a net operating loss deduction. Nonbusiness deductions include deductions for IRA and qualified retirement plans and itemized deductions such as charitable contributions, interest expense, state taxes, and medical expenses. Do not include in this non-allowed group deductible casualty and theft losses, which for net operating loss purposes are treated as business losses. If you do not claim itemized deductions in the year of the loss, you must treat the standard deduction as a nonbusiness deduction.

Nonbusiness income is income that is not from a trade or business—such as dividends, interest, and annuity income. The excess of nonbusiness capital gains over nonbusiness capital losses is also treated as part of nonbusiness income that offsets nonbusiness deductions.

> **EXAMPLE**
>
> Income from dividends and interest is $6,000 and nonbusiness deductions are $6,500. The excess deduction of $500 is an adjustment that reduces your loss on Form 1045.

**At-risk loss limitations.** The loss used to figure your net operating loss deduction is subject to the at-risk rules *(10.17)*. If part of your investment is in nonrecourse loans or is otherwise not at risk, you must compute your deductible loss on Form 6198, which you attach to Form 1040. The deductible loss from Form 6198 is reflected in the income and deduction figures you enter on the Form 1045 schedule to compute your net operating loss deduction.

*Filing Instruction*

**Adjustment for Capital Losses**

A net nonbusiness capital loss may not be included in a net operating loss. If nonbusiness capital losses exceed nonbusiness capital gains, the excess is an adjustment that reduces your loss on Schedule A of Form 1045. In figuring your loss, you may take into account business capital losses only up to the total of business capital gains plus any nonbusiness capital gains remaining after the adjustment for nonbusiness deductions.

### EXAMPLE

You are single and in 2018 you have a salary of $3,000, interest of $1,200, a net business loss of $10,000 (income of $50,000 and expenses of $60,000), itemized Schedule A deductions of $15,000, and a net nonbusiness capital gain of $1,000. After the required addbacks and adjustments are made, your net operating loss is $7,000. The following computation approximates the steps of the computation on Schedule A, Form 1045.

| | |
|---|---:|
| Salary | $3,000 |
| Interest | 1,200 |
| Capital gain income | 1,000 |
| Business loss | ($10,000) |
| Adjusted gross income | ($4,800) |
| Itemized deductions | (15,000) |
| | (19,800) |
| Adjustments: | |
| Excess nonbusiness deduction* | 12,800 |
| Net operating loss | ($7,000) |

*The excess nonbusiness expenses deduction was figured as follows:

| | | |
|---|---:|---:|
| Itemized deductions | | $15,000 |
| Net capital gain income | $1,000 | |
| Interest income | 1,200 | 2,200 |
| Excess | | $12,800 |

**Reporting NOLs.** NOLs carried forward from prior years are reported on the line for "other income" on Schedule 1 of Form 1040 as "other income." The NOL is entered as a negative amount.

## 40.20 Excess Business Losses

Noncorporate taxpayers, such as Schedule C and Schedule F filers, have a special rule for losses in 2018 through 2025. Excess business losses cannot be claimed in the current year. They are treated as a net operating loss carryover *(40.18)*.

**Excess business losses.** This is the excess, if any, of:

- Your aggregate deductions for your business, determined without regard to whether or not such deductions are disallowed for the year because of the excess business loss limitation, over
- The sum of (1) your gross income or gain from your trades or businesses, plus (2) $250,000 ($500,000 if you are married filing jointly. The $250,000/$500,000 amounts will be adjusted for inflation after 2018.

The passive activity loss rules are taken into account before the excess business loss limitation.

### Example

In 2018, you are single and have gross income on Schedule C of $1 million and deductions from the business of $1.3 million. Your excess business loss is $50,000 ($1.3 million − [$1 million + $250,000]), The excess business loss of $50,000 is an NOL carryover to 2019.

The limitation on excess business losses is figured on Form 461, "Limitation on Business Losses."

## 40.21 Business Credits

You may be eligible to reduce your tax liability by credits related to your business. Unlike personal credits, however, many business-related credits are subject to a special limitation, called the general business credit. The general business credit is not a separate credit; it is a compilation of one or more separate business-related credits that are specifically included by law within the general business credit. The reason for grouping the credits as one is to impose an overall limitation, explained below.

The general business credit for 2018 includes the following credits (credits followed by an asterisk expired at the end of 2017 but could be extended by Congress, so check the *e-Supplement* at *jklasser.com*):

- The investment credit on Form 3468, consisting of the rehabilitation property credit (*see 31.8*), the energy credit, and the reforestation credit;
- The research credit on Form 6765;
- The low-income housing credit on Form 8586 *(31.8)*;
- The disabled access credit on Form 8826;
- The renewable electricity production credit on Form 8835;
- The credit for small employer pension plan startup costs on Form 8881;
- The credit for employer-provided child-care facilities and services on Form 8882;
- The Indian employment credit on Form 8845; *
- The orphan drug credit on Form 8820;
- The credit for employer-paid Social Security and Medicare taxes on certain tips received by employees of food and beverage establishments on Form 8846;
- The credit for contributions to certain community development corporations on Form 8847;
- The new markets credit on Form 8874;
- The railroad track maintenance credit on Form 8900; *
- The biodiesel and renewable fuels credit on Form 8864; *
- The low sulfur diesel fuel production on Form 8896;
- The energy efficient home credit on Form 8908; *
- The alternative motor vehicle credit (fuel cell vehicles) on Form 8910; *
- The alternative fuel vehicle refueling property credit on Form 8911; *
- The credit for employer differential wage payments to activated military personnel on Form 8932;
- The distilled spirits credit on Form 8906;
- The carbon dioxide sequestration credit on Form 8923;
- The qualified plug-in electric drive motor vehicle credit on Form 8936 (for the portion of an electric vehicle used for business);
- Work opportunity credit on Form 5884
- Credit for small employer health insurance premiums (Form 8941) (*see 41.14*)
- Empowerment zone employment credit,* and
- Credit for paid family and medical leave on Form 8994.

**Computing the general business credit.** You compute each credit separately. If you claim only one credit, that credit is considered your general business credit for 2018. The credit is subject to a limitation based on tax liability that is figured on the form used to compute that particular credit. You then enter the allowable credit as your general business credit on Form 1040.

If you claim more than one credit, each of the credits is first computed separately. Most of the credits are then listed on Form 3800 but some of the credits, which have special tax liability limitations, are not entered on Form 3800. For the credits entered on Form 3800, you must figure an overall tax liability limitation. You must compute tentative alternative minimum tax (AMT) on Form 6251 even if the complete computation on Form 6251 shows that you do not have an actual AMT liability for the year. Your limit for the general business credit on Form 3800 is your regular tax liability (after tax credits other than the general business credit), plus actual AMT liability from Form 6251 (if any), minus whichever of the following is larger: either (1) tentative AMT from Form 6251 or (2) 25% of your regular income tax liability (after other credits) over $25,000.

 *Filing Tip*

**Plug-in Vehicle**

If you buy a plug-in electric vehicle, only the portion of the applicable credit related to business driving is part of the general business credit. For example, in 2018 you buy an electric vehicle for which there is a $7,000 credit. You use the car 60% for business and 40% for personal driving. Only $4,200 (60% of $7,000) is part of the general business credit *(25.16)*.

 *Planning Reminder*

**Small Business Health Care Credit**

If you pay at least half the cost of coverage for your staff, purchase the coverage through a government Marketplace, and meet certain eligibility tests, you can claim a tax credit for your payments. *See 41.14*.

 *Planning Reminder*

**Fuel-Related Credits**

For a qualified business use, a refundable credit may be claimed for gasoline or special fuels. For example, a credit applies for fuel used in non-highway vehicles (other than motorboats), including generators, compressors, fork-lift trucks, and bulldozers. A credit may also be claimed for aviation fuel used for farming or commercial aviation. Different credit rates apply depending on the type of fuel. You must claim the credit on a timely filed income tax return, including extensions. You compute the credit on Form 4136, which you attach to Form 1040. For further details, *see* IRS Publication 378; farmers should *see* IRS Publication 225.

Keep separate records of each of the component credits making up the general business credit. The credits are considered to be used up in a specific order; *see* the instructions to Form 3800.

General business credits in excess of the liability limitation could be carried back one year and then forward for up to 20 years.

If you have business credits from a passive activity under the rules discussed in *Chapter 10*, you must figure the credits on Form 8582-CR; generally, the credits are limited to the tax liability from passive activities.

## 40.22 Filing Schedule F

The designation "farm" includes stock, dairy, poultry, fruit, and truck farms, plantations, ranches, and all lands used for farming operations. A fish farm where fish are specially fed and raised, and not just caught, is a farm. So too are animal breeding farms, such as mink, fox, and chinchilla farms.

A farmer who is a sole proprietor files Schedule F along with his or her Form 1040. This schedule is similar to Schedule C for sole proprietors other than farmers; it reports income and expenses related to farming activities.

The same rules for accounting, the reporting period, and for income and expenses to Schedule C apply for farmers filing Schedule F. However, there are some key exceptions designed to provide special breaks for farmers. Since most farmers report on the cash basis and use a calendar year for tax reporting, the following information is limited to these farmers.

**Special income treatment.** Certain types of farm-related income enjoy special tax treatment:

- Sales of livestock (including poultry) and produce can receive Section 1231 treatment. If crops are sold on a deferred payment contract, report the income when payment is received.
- Sales of livestock caused by drought, flood, or other weather conditions can be reported in the following year if you can show that the sale would not have occurred but for the weather condition and you are eligible for federal assistance because of the weather condition.
- Rents, including crop shares, are treated as rental income, rather than as farm income, and are not part of farm net income or loss.

## 40.23 Farming Expenses

Certain types of expenses related to farmers enjoy special tax treatment. Here are some key rules unique to farmers:

**Depreciation.** There are special recovery periods for certain farm animals and equipment, including farm buildings and agricultural structures (*see* IRS Publication 225).

**Prepaid farm supplies.** While cash method farmers usually can deduct expenses in the year they are paid, prepaid farm supplies must be deducted ratably over the period in which they are used. However, there is a special exception that allows them to be deducted in the year of payment if they do not exceed 50% of other deductible farm expenses (including depreciation and amortization); any prepaid expenses in excess of this limit are deductible in the following year.

**Livestock feed.** While the cost of feed usually is deductible in the year it is consumed, it can be deducted in the year of payment if:

1. The expense is a payment for the purchase of food (and not a deposit).
2. The prepayment has a business, and not merely a tax avoidance, purpose.
3. The deduction of feed costs does not result in a material distortion of income.

**Breeding fees.** A cash basis farmer can deduct breeding fees as a business expense; an accrual method farmer must capitalize the fees and allocate them to the cost basis of the calf, foal, or other animal to which they relate.

**Filing Tip**

**Figuring Tax on Farm Income**

Farmers and commercial fisherman can use income averaging to figure the tax on their business income *(22.6)*.

**Filing Tip**

**Livestock Sales Due to Drought Have 4-Year Replacement Period**

Farmers and ranchers forced to sell livestock who are in areas specified by the IRS as eligible for special drought relief have four years in which to defer gain from the sale; *see* the *e-Supplement* at *jklasser.com* for the 2018 designations.

**Fertilizer and lime.** You can deduct the cost of fertilizer and lime in the year of payment or you can capitalize the cost and deduct a part of it each year in which the benefit lasts as long as the benefit lasts more than one year.

**Soil and water conservation expenses.** Usually, these expenses must be capitalized. However, you can elect to deduct them within limits (the deduction cannot be more than 25% of gross income from farming).

**Reforestation expenses.** You can deduct up to $5,000 ($10,000 if married filing jointly). Costs in excess of this dollar limit can be amortized over 84 months.

**Conservation easement.** Farmers and ranchers can claim a full deduction for a donation of a conservation easement without regard to their adjusted gross income *(14.10)*.

## 40.24 Qualified Business Income Deduction

If your business shows a profit on Schedule C, you may be eligible for a personal deduction of up to 20% of that profit (with some adjustments). The rules are complicated and 2018 is the first year that the deduction is in effect. The deduction generally equals 20% of qualified business income (QBI), which is essentially an owner's share of profits with some adjustments (see the definition of QBI below). The deduction is subtracted from adjusted gross income (not from business income or as an adjustment to gross income) but not as an itemized deduction, so the deduction is available to those claiming the standard deduction as well as those who itemize. If your taxable income does not exceed $157,500 ($315,000 if you file jointly), the deduction is 20% of QBI. You may also be entitled to add to the QBI deduction up to 20% of combined qualified REIT dividends *(see 4.4)* and qualified publicly traded partnership (PTP) income *(see 31.6)*.

**QBI.** Your qualified business income (QBI) is the net amount of items of income, gain, deduction, or loss from your business. It does not include any capital gain (including Section 1231 gain) or loss, dividends, or interest income (other than interest properly allocable to your business). It does not include any net operating loss carryovers (other than those attributable to excess business losses of noncorporate taxpayers as explained in *40.19*).

**Limitations.** If your taxable income in 2018 is above $157,500 ($315,000 if you file jointly), special limitations to the 20% deduction apply. Your deduction is the lesser of 20% of QBI or (1) the greater of 50% of the total W-2 wages paid by the business to employees, or (2) 25% of W-2 wages plus 2.5% of the unadjusted basis immediately after acquisition (UBIA) of depreciable tangible property owned by the business. "Qualified property" is depreciable business property for which the "depreciable period" has not ended before the close of the year. The depreciable period is the period beginning on the date the property is placed in service and ends on the later of 10 years after this date or the last day of the full year of the applicable recovery period. The component of the deduction for REIT dividends and PTP income is not limited by W-2 wages or the UBIA of qualified property.

**Specified service business.** If you are in "specified service business" and your taxable income exceeds the applicable threshold ($157,500 for singles; $315,000 for joint filers), the amount of qualified business income that can be taken into account for purposes of figuring the limitation on the deduction phases out over the first $100,000 of taxable income exceeding the $315,000 threshold for joint filers, or over the first $50,000 exceeding the $157,500 threshold for others. Thus, doctors, lawyers, accountants, consultants, financial advisors, actuaries, athletes, and performing artists, as well as owners of other businesses where the reputation or skill of the employees is "the principal asset of the business," cannot claim any deduction once 2018 taxable income reaches $415,000 on a joint return, or $207,500 for singles.

If your taxable income is no more than $157,500 ($315,000 on a joint return), you figure the deduction using the Qualified Business Income Deduction—Simplified Worksheet (see page 706).

If taxable income is greater, then use the worksheet found in Publication 535.

*Filing Tip*

**Farm-Related Net Operating Losses**

When expenses exceed farm income, a net operating loss may result. Unlike most business net operating losses arising in 2018 and later that cannot be carried back, farm net operating losses can be carried back for two years *(40.21)*.

*Caution*

**Guidance on the QBI deduction**

The IRS has issued proposed regulations clarifying some of the rules for the QBI deduction, including when businesses can be aggregated for purposes of figuring limitations.

## Sample Qualified Business Income Deduction—Simplified Worksheet
*(This sample is subject to change; see the e-Supplement at www.jklasser.com)*

**Before you begin:** This worksheet is for taxpayers who:

- ✓ Have qualified business income.
- ✓ Are not a patron in a specified agricultural or horticultural cooperative.
- ✓ Have taxable income less than $157,500 ($315,000 if married filing jointly).

1.

| (a) Trade or business name | (b) Employer identification number | (c) Qualified business income or (loss) |
|---|---|---|
| | | |
| | | |
| | | |
| | | |

2.  Total qualified business income or (loss). Add the amounts in column 1(c) ..... **2.** _____

   *Note. If reporting qualified business income or (loss) from more than four trades or businesses, see the instructions for line 2 of this worksheet.*

3.  Qualified business loss carryforward from the prior year. Enter as a negative number .............. **3.** _____

4.  Total qualified business income. Combine lines 2 and 3. If zero or less, enter -0- ................ **4.** _____

5.  Qualified business income component. Multiply line 4 by 20% (0.20) ......................... **5.** _____

6.  Qualified REIT dividends and PTP income or (loss) ........................ **6.** _____

7.  Qualified REIT and PTP loss carryforward from the prior year. Enter as a negative number ........ **7.** ( _____ )

8.  Total qualified REIT and PTP income. Add lines 6 and 7. If zero or less, enter -0- ................ **8.** _____

9.  Multiply line 8 by 20% (0.20) ............................................ **9.** _____

10. Qualified business income deduction before the income limitation. Add lines 5 and 9 ............. **10.** _____

11. Income before qualified business income deduction ........................ **11.** _____

12. Net capital gains (see instructions) ................................... **12.** _____

13. Subtract line 12 from line 11. If zero or less, enter -0- ...................... **13.** _____

14. Income limitation. Multiply line 13 by 20% (0.20) ............................ **14.** _____

15. Qualified business income deduction. Enter the smaller of line 10 or line 14 .................... **15.** _____

16. Total qualified business loss carryforward. Add lines 2 and 3. If more than zero, enter -0- .......... **16.** ( _____ )

17. Total qualified REIT income and PTP loss carryforward. Add lines 6 and 7. If more than zero, enter -0- ................................................................... **17.** ( _____ )

# CHAPTER 41

# Retirement and Medical Plans for Self-Employed

Self-employed persons and partners can take advantage of tax-sheltered retirement plans or simplified employee pension plans (SEPs) *(41.2)*.

Advantages flow from: (1) tax deductions allowed for contributions to the plan (a form of forced savings); (2) tax-free accumulations of income earned on assets held by the plan; and (3) in limited cases, special averaging for lump-sum benefits paid from a qualified retirement plan on retirement.

If you have employees, you must consider the cost of covering them when setting up your plan.

If you do not have any other retirement plan and have no more than 100 employees, you may set up a salary-reduction SIMPLE plan.

Sole proprietors must have minimum essential health coverage. Those who want to buy it through a government exchange must use the Marketplace for individuals, not the SHOPs for small businesses. Self-employed persons can pay for their health coverage on a more advantageous basis than other individuals. They can also use special health-related plans to further lower out-of-pocket medical costs while obtaining tax breaks. If you pay a certain amount for coverage of employees, you may be entitled to a tax credit *(41.14)*.

*Planning Reminder*

**Employees Who Are Self-Employed on the Side**

If you are an employee-member of a company retirement plan, you may set up a qualified retirement plan if you carry on a self-employed enterprise or profession on the side. For example, you are employed by a company that has a qualified 401(k) plan to which you make salary deferrals. At the same time, you have a sideline consulting business. You may set up a retirement plan based on your consultant earnings. Each plan is independent of the other. As an alternative to a retirement plan, you may contribute to a simplified employee pension plan (SEP), *(41.3)*, or a SIMPLE IRA *(41.9)*.

*Planning Reminder*

**One-Person 401(k) Plan**

If you have no employees other than your spouse, you may want to consider a "one-person" 401(k) plan, which allows you to contribute more than to a SEP. For example, for 2018, elective deferrals of up to $18,500 could be made, or $24,500 if age 50 or older during the year (up to $6,000 in "catch-up" contributions). In addition to the deferrals, a contribution of up to 20% of net earnings (reduced by the deductible portion of self-employment tax liability *(41.4)*) can be made to your account, subject to the overall limit, which for 2018 is $55,000, or $61,000 if age 50 or older. You can add a Roth 401(k) option to your plan, allowing after-tax contributions to produce tax-free distributions *(7.18)*). The income limitation on eligibility to contribute to a Roth IRA does not apply to a Roth 401(k). *See* the *e-Supplement* at *jklasser.com* for the 2018 overall limit.

## 41.1 Overview of Retirement and Medical Plans

Self-employed individuals can shelter income and obtain desired retirement savings and health coverage using various plans. While the plans are tied to being in business, the deductions for them are not business write-offs. Instead, deductions for the self-employed person's own coverage are claimed directly on page 1 of Form 1040. For example, a self-employed person's deductions for contributions to his or her own account in a qualified retirement plan *(41.2)*, SEP *(41.3)*, or SIMPLE IRA *(41.9)* are claimed on Line 28 of Schedule 1 (Form 1040). If the plans also cover employees of the self-employed person, deductions related to employees are claimed on Schedule C.

Self-employed individuals who obtain their own health insurance can deduct the premiums from gross income, rather than as an itemized medical expense *(12.2)*. They may be able to cut the high cost of health coverage by using a high-deductible health plan, combined with a health savings account (HSA) *(41.10)*. Contributions to the HSA are also deductible from gross income *(41.11)*. Alternatively, self-employed individuals who have previously set up Archer MSAs can continue to use these tax-advantaged accounts to pay for medical costs not covered by insurance *(41.13)*.

## 41.2 Choosing a Qualified Retirement Plan

You may set up a self-employed retirement plan if you have net earnings (gross business or professional income less allowable business deductions) from your sole proprietorship or partnership for which the plan is established. If you are an inactive owner, such as a limited partner, you do not qualify to set up a qualified plan—unless you receive guaranteed payments for services that are treated as earnings from self-employment.

**Set-up deadline.** To deduct contributions for a tax year, your qualified plan must be adopted by the last day of that year (December 31 if you report on a calendar year basis). If it is, contributions can be made up to the due date of your return for that year, plus extensions.

**Partnership plans.** An individual partner or partners, although self-employed, may not set up a qualified plan. The plan must be established by the partnership. Partnership deductions for contributions to an individual partner's account are reported on the partner's Schedule K-1 (Form 1065) and deducted by the partner as an adjustment to income on Line 28 of Schedule 1 (Form 1040).

**Including employees in your plan.** You must include in your plan all employees who have reached age 21 with at least one year of service. An employee may be required to complete two years of service before participating if your plan provides for full and immediate vesting after no more than two years. You generally are not required to cover seasonal or part-time employees who work less than 1,000 hours during a 12-month period.

A minimum coverage rule requires that a defined benefit plan must include at least 40% of all employees, or 50 employees if that is less.

Your plan may not exclude employees who are over a certain age.

A plan may not discriminate in favor of officers or other highly compensated personnel. Benefits must be for the employees and their beneficiaries, and their plan rights may not be subject to forfeiture. A plan may not allow any of its funds to be diverted for purposes other than pension benefits. Contributions made on your behalf may not exceed the ratio of contributions made on behalf of employees.

**Types of qualified plans.** There are two types of qualified plans: defined benefit plans and defined contribution plans, and different rules apply to each. A defined benefit plan provides in advance for a specific retirement benefit funded by quarterly contributions based on an IRS formula and actuarial assumptions. A defined contribution plan does not fix a specific retirement benefit, but rather sets the amount of annual contributions so that the amount of retirement benefits depends on contributions and income earned on those contributions. If contributions are geared to profits, the plan is a profit-sharing plan, but fixed annual contributions are not required. A plan that requires fixed contributions regardless of profits is a money purchase plan. If you have a profit-sharing plan, a 401(k) plan arrangement can be included to allow you (and other participants) to make elective deferral contributions of before-tax compensation to the plan.

A defined benefit plan may prove costly if you have older employees who also must be provided with proportionate defined benefits. Furthermore, a defined benefit plan requires you to contribute to their accounts even if you do not have profits. For 2018, the benefit limit is the lesser of (a) 100% of the participant's average compensation for the three consecutive years of highest compensation as an active participant or (b) $220,000. This dollar limit is reduced if benefits begin before age 62 and increased if benefits begin after age 65. The $220,000 limit is subject to cost-of-living increases; *see* the *e-Supplement* at *jklasser.com* for the 2019 limit.

For defined contribution plans, the 2018 limit on annual contributions and other additions (excluding earnings) was the lesser of 100% of compensation or $55,000. For 2019, the $55,000 limit may be adjusted for inflation; *see* the *e-Supplement* at *jklasser.com*.

## 41.3 Choosing a SEP

Under a SEP (simplified employee pension plan), you may contribute to a special type of IRA more than is allowed under the regular IRA rules. Contributions do not have to be made every year. When you do make contributions, they must be based on a written allocation formula and must not discriminate in favor of yourself, other owners with more than a 5% interest, or highly compensated employees. Coverage requirements for employees are in *8.15*. A salary-reduction arrangement for employees may be provided under a qualifying SEP established before 1997 or under a SIMPLE IRA plan established after 1996 *(8.17)*.

The deadline for both setting up and contributing to a SEP is the due date for your return, including extensions. Thus, if you have not set up a qualified plan by the end of the taxable year *(41.2)*, you may still make a deductible retirement contribution for the year by contributing to a SEP by the due date of your return.

## 41.4 Deductible Contributions

The deductible limit for a qualified retirement plan depends on whether you have a defined contribution plan (profit-sharing or money purchase pension plan) or a defined benefit plan. A SEP is treated as a profit-sharing plan subject to the defined contribution plan deduction limits explained below.

If you have a defined benefit plan, you generally may deduct contributions needed to produce the accrued benefits provided for by the plan, including any unfunded current liability. This is a complicated calculation requiring actuarial computations that call for the services of a pension expert.

**Deductible contribution to a defined contribution qualified retirement plan or a SEP.** Before figuring the deductible contribution you can make for 2018 to a profit-sharing plan or SEP account, or to a money purchase pension plan, you must first figure your self-employment tax liability on Schedule SE and your deduction for one-half of the self-employment tax to be claimed on Line 27 of Schedule 1 (Form 1040). In computing your deductible plan contribution, your net profit from Line 31 of Schedule C, Line 3 of Schedule C-EZ, or Line 34 of Schedule F is reduced by the deduction for one half of your self-employment tax; *see* the Example below.

As a self-employed person, you are not allowed to figure the deductible contribution for yourself by applying the contribution rate stated in your plan. The rate must be reduced, as required by law, to reflect the reduction of net earnings by the deductible contribution itself. If your plan rate is a whole number, the reduced percentage is shown in the Rate Table for Self-Employed *(Table 41-1)* below. If the plan rate is fractional, the reduced percentage is figured using the Fractional Rate Worksheet for Self-Employed (Worksheet 41-2).

**Figuring your maximum deductible contribution.** After figuring your net earnings and reducing that amount by one-half of your self-employment tax liability, you multiply the balance by the reduced rate from *Table 41-1* or *Worksheet 41-2*. This is generally your maximum deductible contribution to a profit-sharing qualified retirement plan or SEP. However, the maximum deductible contribution cannot exceed the annual limit on additions to a defined contribution plan. The annual limit for 2018 is the lesser of

*Planning Reminder*

**Small Employer Credit for Retirement Plan Startup Costs**

Employers with 100 or fewer employees that do not have a qualified retirement plan generally may claim a tax credit on Form 8881 for administrative costs of setting up a pension plan, profit-sharing plan, 401(k) plan, SEP, or SIMPLE plan. At least one non-highly-compensated employee must be covered. The maximum credit is $500, 50% of the first $1,000 of startup costs. The credit is allowed for costs incurred in the year in which the plan takes effect and in the next two years.

*Caution*

**Deadline for Setting Up Qualified Retirement Plan or SEP**

You must formally set up a qualified retirement plan in writing on or before the end of the taxable year in which you want the plan to be effective. For example, if you want to make a contribution for 2018, your plan must be set up on or before December 31, 2018, if you report on a calendar year basis. If a profit-sharing plan is established by the end of 2018, you have up until the due date for filing your 2018 return, plus any extension, to make a deductible contribution within the limits discussed in this section.

If you miss the deadline for setting up a qualified retirement plan, you may contribute to a simplified employee pension plan (SEP) set up by the filing deadline for Form 1040, including extensions *(41.4)*.

(1) $55,000, or (2) $275,000 (maximum compensation that can be taken into account) multiplied by the stated plan contribution rate, not the reduced rate. See the Deduction Worksheet for Self-Employed *(Worksheet 41-1)* below, which takes you through the steps of figuring your deductible contribution.

If elective deferrals were made during the year, extra steps are required to compute the maximum deductible contribution; *see* Step 9 of Worksheet 41-1, shown below. Any "catch-up" contributions are entered in Step 17 of the Worksheet.

**EXAMPLE**

You are a sole proprietor with no employees and have a profit-sharing plan that provides for a 25% contribution rate. You did not make any elective deferrals or catch-up contributions to your plan for 2018. Your net self-employment earnings for 2018 from Line 31 of Schedule C are $147,000. On Line 5 of Schedule SE, you figure your self-employment tax liability of $19,859, and on Line 6 of Schedule SE, you figure a deduction for self-employment tax of $9,930, which you claim on Line 27 of Schedule 1 of Form 1040. By completing the Deduction Worksheet for Self-Employed shown below, you figure your maximum deductible profit-sharing contribution for 2018 is $27,414.

### Table 41-1   Rate Table for Self-Employed

| If plan rate is— | Self-employed person's reduced rate is— |
|---|---|
| 1 % | .009901 |
| 2 | .019608 |
| 3 | .029126 |
| 4 | .038462 |
| 5 | .047619 |
| 6 | .056604 |
| 7 | .065421 |
| 8 | .074074 |
| 9 | .082569 |
| 10 | .090909 |
| 11 | .099099 |
| 12 | .107143 |
| 13 | .115044 |
| 14 | .122807 |
| 15 | .130435 |
| 16 | .137931 |
| 17 | .145299 |
| 18 | .152542 |
| 19 | .159664 |
| 20 | .166667 |
| 21 | .173554 |
| 22 | .180328 |
| 23 | .186992 |
| 24 | .193548 |
| 25* | .200000* |

\* The maximum deductible percentage for contributions (other than elective deferrals) to your own profit-sharing, money-purchase, or SEP is 20% and for your employees, 25%.

## Worksheet 41-1   Deduction for Self-Employed

**Step 1**   Enter your net profit from—
- line 31, Schedule C (Form 1040);
- line 3, Schedule C-EZ (Form 1040);
- line 34, Schedule F (Form 1040)*;
- or box 14, code A**, Schedule K1 (Form 1065)*.

For information on other income included in net profit from self-employment, *see* the Instructions for Schedule SE, Form 1040.

*Reduce this amount by any amount reported on Schedule SE (Form 1040), line 1b.

**General partners should reduce this amount by the same additional expenses subtracted from box 14, code A, to determine the amount on line 1 or 2 of Schedule SE.   $ 147,000

**Step 2**   Enter your deduction for self-employment tax from line 27.of Schedule 1 (Form 1040)   9,930

**Step 3**   Net earnings from self-employment.
Subtract step 2 from step 1.   137,070

**Step 4**   Enter your rate from the Rate Table for Self-Employed or Rate Worksheet for Self-Employed.   .20

**Step 5**   Multiply step 3 by step 4.   27,414

**Step 6**   Multiply $275,000 by your plan contribution rate (not the reduced rate).   68,750

**Step 7**   Enter the smaller of step 5 or step 6.   27,414

**Step 8**   Contribution dollar limit:
- If you made any elective deferrals to your self-employed plan, go to step 9.
- Otherwise, skip steps 9 through 20 and enter the smaller of step 7 or step 8 on step 21.   $ 55,000

**Step 9**   Enter your allowable elective deferrals (including designated Roth contributions) made to your self-employed plan during 2018. Do not enter more than $18,500.

**Step 10**   Subtract step 9 from step 8.

**Step 11**   Subtract step 9 from step 3.

**Step 12**   Enter one-half of step 11.

**Step 13**   Enter the smallest of steps 7, 10, or 12.

**Step 14**   Subtract step 13 from step 3.

**Step 15**   Enter the smaller of step 9 or step 14:
If you made catch-up contributions, go to step 16.
Otherwise, skip steps 16 through 18 and go to step 19.

**Step 16**   Subtract step 15 from step 14.

**Step 17**   Enter your catchup contributions (including designated Roth contributions), if any. Do not enter more than $6,000.

**Step 18**   Enter the smaller of step 16 or step 17.

**Step 19**   Add steps 13, 15, and 18.

**Step 20**   Enter the amount of designated Roth contributions included on lines 9 and 17.

**Step 21**   Subtract step 20 from step 19. This is your maximum deduction contribution.   $ 27,414

**Next:** Enter your actual contribution, not to exceed your maximum deductible contribution, on line 28 of Schedule 1 (Form 1040).

## Worksheet 41-2 Fractional Rate Worksheet for Self-Employed

If the plan rate is fractional and thus not listed in the table above, figure your deductible percentage this way:

1. Write the plan rate as a decimal. For example, if the plan rate is 10.5%, write .105 as the decimal amount.                                                          1. _____

2. Add 1 to the decimal rate. For example, if the rate is .105, the result is 1.105.                                                                                   2. _____

3. Divide Step 1 by Step 2. This gives you the deductible percentage. If the plan rate is .105, the deductible percentage is .0950 (.105 ÷ 1.105).                     3. _____

**Contributions for your employees.** The deduction complications that apply to your own contributions do not apply to contributions for employees. You make contributions for your employees at the rate specified in your plan, based upon their compensation, subject to the annual limit discussed above. Thus, if your plan contribution rate is 25%, you would contribute 25% of your employees' pay to the plan, even though your own contribution rate is reduced to 20% under the Rate Table for Self Employed shown above. You deduct contributions for employees when figuring your net earnings from self-employment on Schedule C or Schedule F before figuring your own deductible contribution using the steps shown in the Example above.

**Contributions allowed after age 70½.** You may continue to make contributions for yourself to a qualified retirement plan or SEP as long as you have self-employment income. However, you must begin to receive required minimum distributions from a SEP by April 1 of the year following the year in which you reach age 70½ *(8.15)*. This age 70½ required distribution beginning date also applies to a qualified retirement plan if you are a more-than-5% owner of the business *(7.11)*.

**Excess contributions.** Contributions to a plan exceeding the deduction ceiling may be carried over and deducted in later years subject to the ceiling for those years. However, if contributions exceed the deductible amount, you are generally subject to a 10% penalty on nondeductible contributions that are not returned by the end of your tax year. The penalty is computed on Form 5330, which must be filed with the IRS by the end of the seventh month following the end of the tax year.

## 41.5 How To Claim the Deduction for Contributions

Contributions made to your qualified or SEP account as a self-employed person are deducted as an adjustment to gross income on Line 28 of Schedule 1 (Form 1040). A deduction for a contribution made for your benefit may not be part of a net operating loss.

Contributions for your employees are entered as deductions on Schedule C (or Schedule F) for purposes of computing profit or loss from your business. Trustees' fees not provided for by contributions are deductible in addition to the maximum contribution deduction.

Deductible plan contributions may generally be made at any time up to the due date of your return, including any extension of time. However, the plan itself must be set up before the close of the taxable year for which the deduction is sought. If you miss the December 31 deadline for setting up a qualified plan, you have at least up to April 15, 2019, to set up a SEP for 2018. If you have a filing extension, you have until the extended due date to set up a SEP and make your contribution.

## 41.6 How To Qualify a Retirement Plan or SEP Plan

You may set up a qualified retirement plan and contribute to it without advance approval. But since advance approval is advisable, you may, in a determination letter, ask the IRS to review your plan. Approval requirements depend on whether you set up your own administered plan or join a master plan administered by a bank, insurance company, mutual fund, or a prototype plan sponsored by a trade or professional association. If you start your own individually designed plan, you pay the IRS a fee and request a determination letter; *see* IRS Publication 560.

If you join a master or prototype plan, the sponsoring organization applies to the IRS for approval of its plan. You should then be given a copy of the approved plan and copies of any subsequent amendments.

To set up a SEP with a bank, broker, or other financial institution, you do not need IRS approval. If you do not maintain any other qualified retirement plan apart from another SEP and other tests are met, a model SEP may be adopted using Form 5305-SEP.

## 41.7 Annual Qualified Retirement Plan Reporting

Partial relief from one burdensome IRS paperwork requirement may be available if your pension or profit-sharing plan covers only yourself, or you and your spouse, or you and your business partners and the spouses of the partners. Such plans are treated as one-participant plans by the IRS.

A one-participant plan does not file the extensive annual Form 5500 information return. A one-participant plan either files Form 5500-EZ on paper, or if eligible, it may file the form electronically. If a sole proprietor has a plan for employees, file Form 5500-SF.

Under an exception for small one-participant plans, Form 5500-EZ does not have to be filed if the value of plan assets at the end of the year is not more than $250,000. The exception applies if you have two or more one-participant plans that together have not exceeded the $250,000 asset threshold. All one-participant plans must file a Form 5500-EZ for their final plan year even if the plan assets have always been below $250,000.

The filing deadline for 5500 forms is the last day of the seventh month after the end of the plan year unless an extension is obtained; *see* the forms instructions for filing electronically or when a paper form can be used.

*Planning Reminder*

**No Annual Filing for SEPs and SIMPLE IRAs**

These plans do not have to file Form 5500-EZ or any other annual information return in the 5500 series.

## 41.8 How Qualified Retirement Plan Distributions Are Taxed

Distributions from a qualified retirement plan generally may not be received without penalty before age 59½ unless you are disabled or meet the other exceptions listed in *7.13*. If you are a more-than-5% owner, you must begin to receive minimum required distributions by April 1 of the year following the year in which you reach age 70½, even though you are not retired; penalties may apply if an insufficient distribution is received *(7.11)*.

A lump-sum and other eligible distributions *(7.5)* may be rolled over tax free to another employer plan or IRA. For participants born before January 2, 1936, 10-year averaging may be available *(7.3)*. Pension distributions from a defined benefit plan are taxed under the annuity rules discussed in *7.24–7.27*, but for purposes of figuring your cost investment, include only nondeductible voluntary contributions; deductible contributions made on your behalf are not part of your investment.

If you receive amounts in excess of the benefits provided for you under the plan formula and you own more than a 5% interest in the employer, the excess benefit is subject to a 10% penalty. The penalty also applies if you were a more-than-5% owner at any time during the five plan years preceding the plan year that ends within the year of an excess distribution.

Other rules discussed in *7.1–7.14* apply to self-employed qualified plans as well as qualified corporate plans.

After the death of a self-employed plan owner, distributions from the plan to beneficiaries may be spread over the periods discussed at *7.12* provided the plan covers more than one person. Distributions to a surviving spouse can be rolled over to that spouse's IRA *(7.4)*. Distributions to non-spouse beneficiaries can be directly rolled over in a trustee-to-trustee transfer to an IRA that is treated as an inherited IRA from which required minimum distributions must be received annually *(7.6, 8.14)*.

**SEP distributions.** Distributions from a SEP are subject to the IRA rules at *8.8*.

## 41.9 SIMPLE IRA Plans

If you do not maintain any other retirement plan and have 100 or fewer employees, you may set up a salary-reduction type of plan for yourself and your employees. The SIMPLE IRA contribution rules are discussed at *8.17*. A SIMPLE plan may also be made as part of a 401(k) plan *(7.15)*.

Under a SIMPLE IRA for 2018, you may contribute to your own account $12,500 of net earnings plus an additional $3,000 if age 50 or over by the end of the year. You may also make a "matching" contribution of up to 3% of your net earnings.

If you have employees, they generally could make elective salary-reduction contributions for 2017 up to $12,500 (plus $3,000 if age 50 or over). You must make a 3% matching contribution unless you choose to make a 2% non-elective contribution.

See Chapter 8 for further details on SIMPLE IRAs *(8.17 – 8.18)*.

## 41.10 Health Savings Account (HSA) Basics

Health savings accounts (HSAs) can be used by individuals covered by a high-deductible health plan (HDHP) to save for health-care costs on a tax-free basis in an IRA-like account. HSAs are intended to supplant Archer MSAs; *see* the discussion of Archer MSA rules later in this Chapter *(41.13)*.

The HSA provides a tax-sheltered account for paying routine medical expenses that fall below the deductible set by the HDHP. To contribute to an HSA, you must not be enrolled in Medicare Part A or Part B and you must not be a dependent of another taxpayer.

A qualifying HDHP must have a minimum annual deductible and a maximum annual limit on out-of-pocket costs (see below). HDHPs typically are bronze-level plans on the government marketplace, but not all marketplaces offer such plans (see HealthCare.gov).

Generally, contributions to an HSA are not allowed if the taxpayer has coverage under any health plan that does not meet the "high deductible" requirement of an HDHP, but there are exceptions. A plan that otherwise satisfies HDHP rules may provide preventive care benefits without a deductible or with a deductible below the minimum annual deductible. Benefits may also be provided under certain types of "permitted" coverage and insurance before the deductible of the HDHP is satisfied. Permitted coverage includes coverage for vision, dental or long-term care, accidents, and disability. Permitted insurance includes per diem insurance while hospitalized, insurance for a specific disease or illness (such as cancer, diabetes, asthma, or heart failure), and insurance relating to workers' compensation liability, tort liability, or liabilities relating to owning or using a car or other property.

**Qualifying HDHP for 2018.** For 2018, the minimum annual HDHP deductible is $1,350 for self-only coverage and $2,700 for family coverage. The limit on out-of-pocket costs for 2018 is $6,650 for self-only coverage and $13,300 for family coverage. The limit applies to co-payments, deductibles, and other payments but not premiums.

## 41.11 Limits on Deductible HSA Contributions

If you are an eligible individual *(41.10)*, you can set up an HSA with an insurance company, bank, or other financial institution that has been approved by the IRS for this purpose. Contributions can be made up until the due date for filing your tax return (without extensions). Thus, HSA contributions for 2018 can be made through April 15, 2019. HSA contributions are reported to the IRS on Form 5498-SA.

**Planning Reminder**

**HSA Limits for 2019**

The annual contribution limits for 2019 are slightly higher at $3,500 for self-only coverage and $7,000 for family coverage. If you are age 55 or older by the end of the year, you can contribute an additional $1,000, but the right to contribute ends once you enroll in Medicare.

**Filing Instruction**

**Report HSA Contributions and Distributions on Form 8889**

Report your HSA contributions on Form 8889 and follow the instructions to figure any limitations on the amount you may deduct. Also use Form 8889 to report an HSA distribution and figure the amount, if any, that is taxable. Form 8889 must be attached to your Form 1040.

The full contribution limit for 2018 (depending on your coverage; *see* below) is available regardless of when during the year you became eligible *(41.10)* for an HSA, so long as you were eligible on December 1, 2018; you are treated as if you were enrolled in the December 1 plan for the entire year. However, if you do not remain eligible for the next 12 months (December 1, 2018 through December 31, 2019), and are not disabled, you have to recapture as income on your 2019 return the contribution that could not have been made without the December 1 rule; *see* Publication 969 and the Form 8889 instructions for details on this recapture rule. If the December 1 rule does not apply, the contribution limit is figured on a monthly basis.

For 2018, the maximum deductible contribution limit for an individual with self-only HDHP coverage is $3,450. For an individual with family coverage, the maximum deductible contribution for 2018 is $6,900. If a married couple has family HDHP coverage and both spouses are eligible for an HSA, they can decide between themselves how to allocate HSA contributions.

The contribution limit is increased for an account owner who is at least age 55 by the end of the year and who has not enrolled in Medicare. The "catch-up" contribution limit is $1,000. If both spouses are age 55 or older and not yet on Medicare, each must make this catch-up contribution to separate HSAs.

However, starting with the month that an individual enrolls in Medicare Part A, B, or Medicare Advantage (generally at age 65), no further contributions, including catch-up contributions, can be made to his or her HSA. For example, if you turned age 65 and enrolled in Medicare in September 2018 and had been contributing to a HDHP with self-only coverage, you can make an HSA contribution for the eight months preceding the month of Medicare enrollment. Since the full-year contribution limit for 2018 would be $4,450 ($3,450 for self-only HDHP plus $1,000 additional for being at least age 55), your contribution limit for eight months (January through August) is $2,967 ($4,450 × 8/12).

You may have more than one HSA, but the above maximum annual contribution limit applies to the aggregate contributions to all of the HSAs.

If you are an employee eligible to contribute and your employer contributes to an HSA on your behalf, employer contributions within the limit are excludable from your income *(3.2)*. If your employer's contribution is below the applicable limit, you may contribute to your HSA but the totals of all the contributions cannot exceed the applicable limit.

Contributions exceeding your applicable HSA limit are not deductible and are subject to a 6% excise tax. Contributions by an employer to an employee's HSA in excess of the limit are includible in the employee's income and subject to the excise tax. However, the excise tax can be avoided by a timely withdrawal of the excess contribution and any allocable income. The withdrawal deadline is generally the filing due date including extensions, or April 15, 2019, for an excess 2018 contribution. However, if you timely file without making the withdrawal, you may do so by October 15, 2019. On a timely withdrawal, the income is taxed in the year withdrawn but the excise tax does not apply and the distribution of the excess contribution is not taxed. See the instructions to Form 5329 for further details.

**Use Form 8889 to report your HSA contributions and figure your deduction.** You must report your HSA contributions for 2018 and apply the deduction limits on Form 8889, which must be attached to Form 1040. The deduction from Form 8889 is entered on Line 25 of Schedule 1 (Form 1040), where it is deductible "above the line" from gross income.

## 41.12 Distributions From HSAs

Earnings accumulate tax free within an HSA, as with an IRA. Distributions from an HSA used exclusively to pay or reimburse qualified medical expenses of the account owner, his or her spouse, or dependents are not taxable. Distributions used for anything other than qualified medical expenses are taxable. Taxable distributions are also subject to a 20% penalty unless the distribution is made after the account owner becomes disabled, reaches age 65, or dies.

Distributions need not be taken in the year in which the expense is incurred to be tax free; they can be taken in the following year or in any later year. This may be necessary if there are insufficient funds to cover the expense at the time it is incurred. For example, an HSA account holder who incurs a $1,500 medical expense on December 1, 2018, can wait until 2019 (or later) when the account balance exceeds $1,500. The distribution is tax free so long as records are kept to show that the distribution was used to reimburse qualified medical expenses that were not covered by insurance or otherwise reimbursed and not claimed in a prior year as an itemized deduction. The HSA must have been set up before the expense was incurred.

For tax-free distribution purposes, a "qualified medical expense" is generally a non-reimbursed payment for medical care that would otherwise be eligible for an itemized deduction *(17.2)*. In addition, over-the-counter medications for which you get a doctor's prescription are qualified medical expenses for HSA purposes although they are not eligible for an itemized deduction. Health-care premiums generally do not qualify for HSA purposes, but there are exceptions. An HSA can pay for premiums for long-term-care insurance, COBRA health-care continuation coverage, health coverage while an individual is receiving unemployment compensation, and for individuals over age 65, Medicare Part A, B, or D, Medicare Advantage, and the employee share of premiums for employer-sponsored health insurance including retiree health insurance. HSA distributions used to pay or reimburse long-term-care premiums are tax free only to the extent of the age-based deductible limit for such premiums *(17.5)*. For example, if a person age 41 uses HSA funds to pay long-term-care premiums of $1,800 in 2018, only $780 (the deductible limit for those age 41 through 50 in 2018) is tax free. The balance of the distribution is taxable and subject to a 20% penalty for withdrawal of funds prior to age 65.

A qualified medical expense may be for the care of the account owner, his or her spouse, or dependents, without regard to whether they are eligible to make HSA contributions. In the case of a married couple where both spouses have HSAs, one spouse may use a distribution from his or her HSA to pay or reimburse the qualified medical costs of the other spouse. However, both HSAs may not reimburse the same expense.

If an HSA account holder mistakenly takes a distribution such as to reimburse an expense he or she reasonably but mistakenly believes is a qualified medical expense, the funds can be repaid to the HSA in order to avoid tax on the withdrawn amount, assuming the plan accepts a return of mistaken distributions. The funds must be returned by April 15 of the year following the first year that the account holder knew or should have known of the mistake.

**Inherited HSAs.** If the beneficiary of an HSA is the surviving spouse of the deceased account owner, the surviving spouse becomes the owner of the account and will be subject to tax only on distributions that are not used for qualified medical expenses. If the beneficiary is not the surviving spouse, the account ceases to be an HSA as of the date of the owner's death and the date-of-death value of the HSA assets must be included in the beneficiary's income. The beneficiary (other than the decedent's estate) may reduce the taxable amount by any HSA payments for the decedent's medical expenses made within one year after death. A beneficiary is not subject to the penalty for taxable distributions.

**Report HSA distributions on Form 8889.** You must report an HSA distribution on Part II of Form 8889, which must be attached to Form 1040. A taxable distribution, if any, from Form 8889 is reported on Line 21 of Schedule 1 of Form 1040 ("Other income"). On the dotted line next to Line 21 enter "HSA" and the amount. If there is a taxable distribution and no exception to the penalty is available, the 20% penalty is entered on Form 8889 and reported on Line 62 of Schedule 4 (Form 1040). On the dotted line next to Line 62, enter "HSA" and the amount. The HSA custodian or trustee will report the distribution to the IRS on Form 1099-SA.

## 41.13 Archer MSAs

Archer MSAs (medical savings accounts) have largely been replaced by health savings accounts (HSAs) *(3.2)*. The law authorizing the establishment of new Archer MSAs has expired. However, taxpayers who set up Archer MSAs before 2008 can continue to fund them.

*Caution*

**IRS Can Levy on HSAs**

The IRS can levy on an HSA to recover taxed owed. If the HSA owner is under age 65, there is a 20% penalty (there is no exception from this penalty for an involuntary distribution such as an IRS levy).

An Archer MSA can be rolled over to an HSA. Contributions may not be made to an Archer MSA or to an HSA after you become entitled to Medicare benefits.

For 2018, a high-deductible health plan for self-only coverage must have a deductible of at least $2,300 and no more than $3,450. For family coverage, the deductible must be at least $4,550 and no more than $6,850. The high-deductible plan must limit out-of-pocket costs (other than premiums) for 2018 to $4,550 for self-only coverage and $8,400 for family coverage. You generally may not have any other coverage in addition to the high-deductible plan, but separate policies are allowed for disability, vision or dental care, long-term care, accidental injuries, specific diseases or illnesses, fixed payments during hospitalization, workers' compensation liability, tort liability, and liabilities arising from the ownership or use of property.

**Deductible contribution limit.** If you are self-employed, the maximum deductible contribution is 65% of the annual policy deductible if you have self-only coverage under a high-deductible plan, and 75% of the annual policy deductible if you have family coverage. To deduct the maximum amount, you must have the policy for the entire year. Otherwise one-twelfth of the limit may be deducted for each full month of coverage. The deduction may not exceed your net self-employment income from the business through which you have the high-deductible insurance.

If you are an employee of an MSA-participating employer and your employer makes any contributions to your Archer MSA, you are barred from making a deductible contribution; also *see* the Caution on employer contributions to a spouse's Archer MSA. Your employer's contribution to your Archer MSA is not taxable to you if it is within the 65%/75% limit discussed above *(3.2)*.

Report contributions to your Archer MSA on Form 8853, which must be attached to your Form 1040. The deductible contribution shown on Form 8853 is entered on Line 36 of Schedule 1 (Form 1040); write "MSA" next to the entry.

**Report Archer MSA distributions on Form 8853.** Distributions used to pay for qualified medical expenses that are not reimbursable under your high-deductible plan are tax free. Qualifying exoenses and reporting taxable distributions are the same as for HSAs, except use code "MSA." *See 41.12* and the Form 8853 instructions.

# 41.14 Small Employer Health Insurance Credit

If you pay at least half of the premiums for your staff and you meet eligibility requirements, you can claim a tax credit of 50% of your eligible payments on Form 8941. The credit is highly complex.

**Eligibility.** You must meet these four tests for a 2018 credit:

1. You have fewer than 25 full-time equivalent employees (FTEs) for the tax year. Add up the hours per year (but not more than 2,080 hours per employee) that employees (other than owners, relatives, and seasonal workers) work and divide by 2,080 to find the number of full-time equivalents.
2. The average annual wages of its employees for the year is less than $53,200 per FTE.
3. You must pay the premiums under a "qualifying arrangement."
4. You purchase the coverage through a government Marketplace (SHOP). However, the IRS has provided relief to employers in counties that do not offer coverage; the credit can be claimed for coverage purchased directly outside of a SHOP (see Notice 2018-27).

**Credit amount.** A full credit applies if you have no more than 10 FTEs with average wages of $26,600 per FTE. The credit phases out for those with 10 to 25 FTEs and with wages of $26,600 to $53,200.

The credit is based on the lesser of actual payments or the average premium for the small group market in the states where your employees work. The 2018 average premiums will be listed on a county-by-county basis for each state in the Form 8941 instructions.

### Employer Contribution to Spouse's MSA

If you and your spouse are covered under a high-deductible health plan with family coverage, employer contributions to either of your Archer MSAs bar both of you from making Archer MSA contributions for that year. If you each have self-only coverage under a high-deductible health plan, employer contributions to one of your Archer MSAs do not prevent the other from making MSA contributions.

### MSA Contribution Deadline

You have until April 15, 2019, to make a deductible contribution to an Archer MSA for 2018.

### No Credit for Self-Employed Premiums

You cannot take a tax credit on Form 8941 for premiums you pay to cover yourself, your spouse, or your dependents.

### Credit for 2018?

The small employer health insurance credit can only be claimed for two consecutive years, so if you claimed it for 2016 and 2017, you cannot do so in 2018.

# CHAPTER 42

# Claiming Depreciation Deductions

There are several methods of claiming expense deductions for your purchases in 2018 of equipment, fixtures, autos, and trucks used in your business:

- First-year expensing (Section 179 deduction), which allows a deduction of up to $1 million (*42.3*).
- Bonus depreciation, which is another first-year deduction at 100% of cost for eligible property (*42.20*).
- Regular depreciation, which allows a prorated deduction over a period of years. Most business equipment is depreciable under MACRS (modified accelerated cost recovery system) over a six-year period. MACRS applies to new and used property. The objective of MACRS is to provide rapid depreciation and to eliminate disputes over useful life, salvage value, and depreciation methods. Useful life and depreciation methods are fixed by law; salvage value is treated as zero. If you do not want to use MACRS accelerated rates, you may elect the straight-line method.

Capital investments in buildings are depreciable using the straight-line method; residential buildings are depreciated over 27.5 years; nonresidential real property placed in service after May 12, 1993, is depreciated over 39 years (*42.12*). Specific annual rates for each class of property are provided by IRS tables.

Land is not depreciable.

## 42.1 What Property May Be Depreciated?

Depreciation deductions may be claimed only for property used in your business or other income-producing activity. If the primary purpose of the property is to produce income but it fails to yield any income, the property may still be depreciated.

Depreciation may not be claimed on property held for personal purposes such as a personal residence or pleasure car. If property, such as a car, is used both for business and pleasure, only the business portion may be depreciated.

> **EXAMPLES**
>
> 1. An anesthesiologist suspended his practice indefinitely because of malpractice premium rate increases. He continued to maintain his professional competence by taking courses and keeping up his equipment. The IRS ruled that he could not take depreciation on his equipment. Since he was no longer practicing, the depreciation did not relate to a current trade or business.
>
> 2. An electrician spent $1,325 on a trailer to carry his tools and protective clothing. Based on a useful life of three years less salvage value of $25, annual depreciation deductions came to $433. However, the IRS claimed that he could not claim depreciation during the months he was unemployed and the trailer was not used. The Tax Court disagreed. Depreciation is allowed as long as the asset is held for use in a trade or business, even though the asset is idle or its use is temporarily suspended due to business conditions.

**Nondepreciable assets.** Not all assets used in your business or for the production of income may be depreciable. Land is not depreciable, but the cost of landscaping business property may be depreciated if the landscaping is so closely associated with a building that it would have to be destroyed if the building were replaced. Qualifying trees and bushes are depreciable over 15 years.

Property held primarily for sale to customers or property includible in inventory is not depreciable, regardless of its useful life.

**Amortization for business intangibles.** The cost of goodwill, going concern value, and other intangibles including covenants not to compete, information bases, customer lists, franchises, licenses, and trademarks is amortizable over a 15-year period.

The amortization rule generally applies to property acquired after August 10, 1993 *(42.17)*.

**Residences.** For depreciation of rented residences, *see 9.5*. For depreciation of a home office, *see 40.13*. For depreciation of a sublet cooperative apartment or one used in business, *see 40.17*.

**Farm property.** Farmland is not depreciable; farm machinery and buildings are. Livestock acquired for work, breeding, or dairy purposes and not included in inventory may also be depreciated. For a detailed explanation of the highly technical rules for depreciating farm property and livestock, *see* IRS Publication 225, Farmer's Tax Guide.

**Relevance of useful life.** According to the Tax Court, under current MACRS law (as under prior ACRS rules for assets placed in service 1981-1986), useful life is irrelevant for claiming depreciation if you can show that an asset is subject to exhaustion, wear and tear, or obsolescence. Thus, in the case of antique musical instruments played by professional musicians, depreciation is allowable because of wear and tear, even though the instruments have an indeterminable useful life. Two federal appeals courts agreed, allowing professional violinists to deduct ACRS depreciation for their instruments.

In a case involving exotic cars that were not used for transportation but for exhibition, MACRS depreciation was allowed because the owner showed that they were subject to obsolescence. The autos were purchased solely for exhibition. The three state-of-the-art autos were a 1987 Lotus Pantera costing $63,000, a Lotus Espirit costing $48,000, and a Ferrari Testarossa costing $290,453. Over a four-year period, the owner deducted depreciation of over $298,000 while reporting gross income from exhibition fees of $96,630. The IRS disallowed the depreciation because the cars had no determinable useful

**Tangible Personal Property**

If you use the de minimis rule to deduct the cost of tangible personal property up to $2,500 per item or invoice, you do not depreciate the cost. *See 9.3*.

**Corrections to Prior Year Returns**

If you did not deduct the correct amount of depreciation for a prior year, you may be able to make a correction by filing an amended return. However, if you did not deduct the correct amount of depreciation for two or more consecutive years, you must request an accounting method change; *see* IRS Publication 946 for details. Adjustments to basis for unclaimed depreciation taken in prior years are discussed in *5.20*.

life. The Tax Court allowed the depreciation because such cars are subject to obsolescence in the car-show business when new models appear with newer designs and high-tech features. One witness testified this could occur in some cases within a year.

The Tax Court warned that such exotic cars should not be confused with museum pieces. If they had been museum pieces, such as antique cars, no depreciation would have been allowed. In the case of art objects and antiques used as business assets, the useful life requirement remains relevant because such assets are not subject to exhaustion, wear or tear, or obsolescence.

The IRS may continue to dispute and litigate cases in which depreciation is claimed on assets with indeterminable useful lives. For example, in a private ruling, the IRS did not allow a developer to depreciate street improvements that had been turned over to a city. The improvements were an intangible asset that improved the developer's access to its real estate projects, but this asset had an unlimited life. There was no determinable useful life because the city had agreed to maintain and replace the improvements as necessary, and there was no evidence that the city would ever assess the developer for replacement costs.

**Basis for depreciation.** Generally, the basis of the property on which you figure depreciation is its adjusted basis, which usually is its cost. To determine basis when property is acquired other than by purchase, *see 5.16 through 5.20.*

If you convert property from personal to business use, the basis for depreciation purposes is the lower of its adjusted basis or its fair market value at the time of the conversion.

*Planning Reminder*

**Allocating Basis between Land and Buildings**

The allocation should be made by relying on your county assessor's assessments or a sound appraisal.

> **EXAMPLE**
>
> In 2016, you bought a laptop for $2,400 for personal use. In 2018, when it is worth $800, you convert the computer to business use. The basis for depreciation is $800, the fair market value of the computer, which is lower than its adjusted basis of $2,400.

## 42.2 Claiming Depreciation on Your Tax Return

If you report business or professional self-employed income, use Form 4562 for assets placed in service during 2018; enter the total deduction on Line 13, Schedule C. For claiming depreciation on "listed property" such as cars, you use Form 4562, regardless of the year placed in service. See the explanation of listed property in this chapter *(42.10)*. If your only depreciation deduction is for pre-2018 assets, none of which is listed property, you do not need to use Form 4562; figure the deduction on your own worksheet, and enter it on Line 13, Schedule C.

If you are an employee claiming auto expenses, you must use Form 2106 to claim depreciation on an automobile used for business purposes.

If you claim a home office deduction using the actual expense method *(40.13)*, you must use Form 8829 to claim depreciation on the portion of your home used for business.

If you report rental income on Schedule E, you must use Form 4562 for claiming depreciation on buildings placed in service in 2018. For buildings placed in service before 2018, enter the depreciation deduction directly on Schedule E. If you have a rental loss on Schedule E, your deduction for depreciation and other expenses may have to be included on Form 8582 to figure net passive activity income or loss; *see Chapter 10.*

## 42.3 First-Year Expensing Deduction

The dollar limit on first-year expensing in 2018 is $1 million. The dollar limit is phased out if the cost of qualifying property placed in service during the year exceeds a set dollar limit ($2.5 million in 2018).

*Law Alert*

**First-Year Expensing Limit**

The $1 million limit applicable for 2018 may be indexed for inflation. *See* the *e-Supplement at jklasser.com* for an update on any increase for 2019.

**Costs eligible for expensing.** You may elect first-year expensing for tangible personal property bought for business use, such as machinery, equipment, or a car, truck or computer, provided the property is acquired from a non-related party. Qualified improvement property and certain improvements to nonresidential real property (e.g., roofs; heating, ventilation, and air-conditioning; fire protection and alarm systems; security systems) also qualify for expensing (42.14). Expensing is not allowed for property held for investment.

To elect the expensing deduction for the cost of qualifying property for 2018, the qualifying property must have been purchased and placed in service in 2018. You may not elect first-year expensing for property purchased before 2018 if 2018 is the first year you use it for business. For example, if you bought a laptop for family use in 2017 and in 2018 you converted it to business use, expensing is not allowed on your 2018 return. Vehicles are subject to special dollar limits (43.4).

The portion of cost not eligible for first-year expensing may be recovered by depreciation under the regular MACRS rules (42.4–42.5). The first-year expensing deduction is technically called the "Section 179 deduction."

**Electing first-year expensing.** You make the election simply by reporting on Form 4562 the assets for which the election applies. You are permitted to make an election or revoke an election (or change the amount of an election or the assets for which the election applies) on a timely filed amended return. You do not need IRS consent. A revocation, once made, is irrevocable.

**Partial business use.** If you use the equipment for both business and personal use, business use must exceed 50% in the year the equipment is first placed into service to claim a first-year expensing deduction. The expensing deduction may be claimed for the cost allocated to business use up to the dollar limit. For business vehicles, the deduction may not exceed the annual depreciation limit (43.4).

To elect first-year expensing for "listed property" such as a car or van (42.10), business use in the first year you use it must exceed 50%. If it does, you show the amount eligible for expensing in the section for "Listed Property" on Form 4562 and then transfer the amount to the part of Form 4562 where the expensing election is claimed.

**Figuring the deduction.** For business use of less than 100% (but more than 50%), the expensing deduction is limited to the business portion of the cost. As discussed below, the dollar limit may have to be reduced because your taxable income is lower than the applicable dollar limit ($1 million in 2018), eligible purchases exceed a set dollar amount ($2.5 million), or you are married filing separately.

If you qualify for expensing, you do not have to claim the entire amount. If in 2018 you place in service more than one item of property, you may allocate the dollar limit between the items. If you placed in service only one item of qualifying property that cost less than the dollar limit, your deduction is limited to that cost.

If you acquire property in a trade-in, the cost eligible for expensing is limited to the cash you paid. You may not include the adjusted basis of the property traded in, although your basis for the new property includes that amount.

**Limit reduced if taxable income is lower.** Your expensing deduction may not exceed net income from all your active businesses; *see* the Caution on this page.

**Limit reduced if qualifying purchases exceed threshold.** If the total cost of qualifying property placed in service during 2018 exceeds the purchase limit of $2.5 million, the dollar limit on expensing is reduced dollar for dollar by the cost of qualifying property exceeding the limit. For example, if in 2018 you place in service machinery costing $2.6, the $1 million limit is reduced by $100,000 ($2.6 million – $2.5 million). The reduced limit of $900,000 is shown on Form 4562 on Line 5 of Part I (labeled "Dollar limitation for tax year.") If the total cost is $3.5 million or more, no first-year expensing deduction is allowed for 2018.

**Limit reduced if married filing separately.** If you and your spouse file separate returns, the 2018 expensing limit for both of you is one-half the usual amount. Unless you agree to a different allocation, you are each allowed only one-half of the limit, or $500,000. The phaseout threshold for purchases also applies to both of you as a unit. Thus, the dollar limit is fully phased out when purchases exceed $3.5 million.

**Planning Reminder**

**Computer Software**

Software purchased "off the shelf" (*see* the Filing Tip in *42.16*) and used for business is eligible for first-year expensing (*42.3*) and also qualifies for bonus depreciation (*42.18*). Alternatively, if it has a useful life exceeding one year, it may be depreciated using the straight-line method over 36 months. If the useful life does not exceed one year (such as an annual tax program), the cost is deductible as a business expense for the year of purchase.

**Filing Tip**

**First-Year Expensing or Bonus Depreciation?**

If the property you place in service in 2018 qualifies for both types of write-offs, you may simply use bonus depreciation (*42.18*) and not elect first-year expensing.

**Caution**

**Losses and Low Income May Limit Deduction**

The expensing deduction may not exceed the net taxable income from all businesses that you actively conduct. Net income from active businesses is figured without regard to expensing, the deduction for the employer portion of self-employment liability, or any net operating loss carryback or carryforward. You may include wage or salary income as active business income and if you are married filing jointly, also include your spouse's net taxable income.

If you have an overall net loss from all actively conducted businesses, you may not claim an expensing deduction for 2018. If net income is less than the cost of qualifying assets, expensing is limited to the income. However, the cost over the income limit is carried forward to 2019 on Form 4562 provided you complete the expensing section of Form 4562 for 2018. You do not get a carryover unless the deduction is claimed on the return for the first year the property is placed in service. An expensing deduction cannot be used to create or increase a net operating loss.

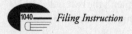

**Filing Instruction**

**Higher Expensing Limits**

Before 2018, the expensing limit was increased by $35,000 for qualified empowerment zone property, but the law authorizing empowerment zone designations expired at the end of 2017; *see* the *e-Supplement at jklasser.com* for an update on whether empowerment zone rules are extended by Congress for 2018.

*Planning Reminder*

**Year-End Purchases**

Equipment placed in service on the last day of the 2018 taxable year may qualify for the entire first-year expensing limit. You do not have to prorate the limit for the amount of time you held the property.

**Partners and S corporation stockholders.** For property bought by a partnership or an S corporation, the dollar limit and taxable income limit applies to the business, as well as the owners as individual taxpayers. The partnership or S corporation determines its expensing deduction subject to the limits and allocates the deduction, if any, among the partners or shareholders. The allocated deduction may not exceed the net taxable income of the partnership or S corporation from actively conducted businesses.

An individual partner's expensing deduction may not exceed dollar limit, regardless of how many partnership interests he or she has. However, the partner must reduce the basis of each partnership interest by the full allocable share of each partnership's expensing deduction, even if that amount is not deductible because of the dollar limit.

**Disqualified acquisitions from related parties.** Property does not qualify for the expense election if:

1. It is acquired from a spouse, ancestor, or lineal descendant, or from non–family-related parties subject to the loss disallowance rule *(5.6)*. For purposes of the expensing election, a corporation is controlled by you and thus subject to the loss disallowance rule *(5.6)* if 50% or more of the stock is owned by you, your spouse, your ancestors, or your descendants.

2. The property is acquired by a member of the same controlled group (using a 50% control test).

3. The basis of the property is determined in whole or in part (a) by reference to the adjusted basis of the property of the person from whom you acquired it or (b) under the stepped-up basis rules for inherited property.

**Recapture of expensing deduction.** Recapture of the first-year expensing deduction may occur on a disposition of the asset or if business use falls to 50% or less. If business use falls to 50% or less after the year the property is placed in service but before the end of the depreciable recovery period *(42.4, 42.10)*, you must "recapture" the benefit from the first-year expensing deduction. The amount recaptured is the excess of the expensing deduction over the amount of depreciation that would have been claimed (through the year of recapture) without expensing *(42.10)*. Recaptured amounts are reported as ordinary income on Form 4797.

When you sell or dispose of the property, the first-year expensing deduction is treated as depreciation for purposes of the recapture rules *(44.3)* that treat gain as ordinary income to the extent of depreciation claimed.

## 42.4 MACRS Recovery Periods

Depreciable assets other than buildings fall within a three-, five-, seven-, 10-, 15-, or 20-year recovery period under the general depreciation system (GDS).

Straight-line recovery for buildings is claimed over a period of *27.5* years for residential rental property or 39 years for nonresidential real property *(42.13)*.

Note: The actual write-off period of depreciation for an asset is one year longer than the class life because of the convention rules *(42.5–42.7)*.

**Three-year property.** This class includes property with a class life of four years or less, other than cars and light-duty trucks, which are in the five-year class.

This class includes: special handling devices for the manufacture of food and beverages; special tools and devices for the manufacture of rubber products; special tools for the manufacture of finished plastic products, fabricated metal products, or motor vehicles; and breeding hogs. By law, racehorses of any age and other horses more than 12 years old when placed in service are also in the three-year class. However, the three-year period will not apply to racehorses two years or younger in 2018 unless Congress extends the law. See the *e-Supplement* at *jklasser.com* for any update.

**Five-year property.** This class includes property with a class life of more than four years and less than 10 years such as computers *(42.10)*, typewriters, copiers, duplicating equipment, heavy general-purpose trucks, trailers, cargo containers, and trailer-mounted containers. Also included by law in the five-year class are cars, light-duty trucks (actual unloaded weight less than 13,000 pounds), taxis, buses, computer-based telephone central office switching equipment, computer-related peripheral equipment, semiconductor manufacturing equipment, and property used in research and experimentation. These leasehold improvements eligible for a five-year recovery period must be depreciated using the straight-line method. Farming equipment placed in service after 2017 is five-year property (formerly it had been seven-year property).

**Seven-year property.** This class includes any property with a class life of 10 years or more but less than 16 years. This is also a catch-all category for assets with no class life that have not been assigned by law to another class. Included in the seven-year class are: office furniture and fixtures, such as desks, safes, and files; cellular phones; fax machines; refrigerators; dishwashers; and machines used to produce jewelry, musical instruments, toys, and sporting goods. Qualified motor sports entertainment complexes were seven-year properties in 2017 but the law expired; *see* the *e-Supplement at jklasser.com* for any update on an extension.

**Ten-year property.** This includes property with a class life of 16 years or more and less than 20 years, such as vessels, barges, tugs, and water transportation equipment, and assets used in petroleum refining or in the manufacture of tobacco products and certain food products. The 10-year class also includes single-purpose agricultural and horticultural structures, and trees or vines bearing fruit or nuts.

**Fifteen-year property.** This includes land improvements such as fences, sidewalks, docks, shrubbery, roads, and bridges. It also includes other property with a class life of 20 years or more but less than 25 years, such as municipal sewage plants and telephone distribution plants. Gas station convenience stores are in the 15-year class if the property is no more than 1,400 square feet, or at least 50% of the floor space is devoted to selling petroleum products, or at least 50% of revenues are from petroleum sales. The owner of the gas station property does not have to be the operator of businesses on the property. Qualified improvement property *(42.14)* is 15-year property (assuming a technical correction is made by Congress for this purpose; *see* the *e-Supplement at jklasser.com*).

**Twenty-year property.** This class includes property with a class life of 25 years or more, such as farm buildings and municipal sewers, except that residential and nonresidential real estate is excluded *(42.13)*.

## 42.5    MACRS Rates

The MACRS rate under the general depreciation system depends on the recovery period *(42.4)* for the property and whether the half-year or mid-quarter convention applies. The 200% declining balance rate applies to three-year property, five-year property, seven-year property, and 10-year property. *See 42.8* for the 150% declining balance rate election. These rates are adjusted for the convention rules explained below. When the 200% declining balance rate provides a lower annual deduction than the straight-line rate, the 200% declining balance rate is replaced by the straight-line rate. The rates in the tables at the end of this section incorporate the applicable convention and the change from the 200% declining balance rate to a straight-line recovery. MACRS straight-line rates are discussed later in this Chapter *(42.9)*.

**Conventions.** Under the half-year convention, all property acquired during the year, regardless of when acquired during the year, is treated as acquired in the middle of the year. As a result, only one-half of the full first-year depreciation is deductible and in the year after the last class life year, the balance of the depreciation is written off. Furthermore, in the year property is sold, only half of the full depreciation for that year is deductible *(42.6)*.

The half-year convention applies unless the total cost bases of depreciable assets placed in service during the last three months of the taxable year exceed 40% of the total bases of all property placed in service during the entire year. If this 40% test applies, you must use a mid-quarter convention to figure your annual depreciation deduction *(42.7)*.

Buildings are depreciated using a mid-month convention *(42.12)*.

*Planning Reminder*

**Recovery Periods**

The depreciation recovery periods for different types of assets are generally fixed by law according to the rules on this page.

**Depreciation tables.** *Table 42-1* provides year-by-year rates for property in the three, five-, and seven-year classes. The rates incorporate the adjustment for the half-year or mid-quarter convention and the switch from the 200% declining balance rate to the straight-line method. Use the rate shown in the table under the convention for your asset. The rate is applied to original basis, minus any first-year expensing deduction *(42.3)* and bonus depreciation *(42.20)* you claimed. After applying the rate from the table to the basis, you claim the deduction on Form 4562, Part III, Section B, labeled "General Depreciation System" (GDS).

You use the tables for the entire recovery period unless you claim a deductible casualty loss that reduces your basis in the property. For the year of the casualty loss and later years, depreciation must be based on the adjusted basis of the property at the end of the year. The tables may no longer be used; *see* IRS Publication 946 for further details.

---

**EXAMPLE**

During June 2018, you place in business service a used machine costing $20,000. It is your only acquisition in 2018. (Assume you do not elect to expense the cost.) The machine is five-year property and is subject to the half-year convention. The depreciation rate for the first year is 20% (see the table below for five-year property). Your 2018 depreciation deduction is $4,000 ($20,000 × 20%). If you hold the machine for the entire six-year recovery period, your total deduction for all years will equal your $20,000 cost.

**Summary of Deductions**

| Year | Deduction |
|---|---|
| 1 (2018) | $4,000 |
| 2 (2019) | 6,400 |
| 3 (2020) | 3,840 |
| 4 (2021) | 2,304 |
| 5 (2022) | 2,304 |
| 6 (2023) | 1,152 |
| Total | $20,000 |

---

## 42.6 Half-Year Convention for MACRS

The half-year convention treats all business equipment placed in service during a tax year as placed in service in the midpoint of that tax year. The same rule applies in the year in which the property is disposed of. The effect of this rule is as follows: A half-year of depreciation is allowed in the first year property is placed in service, regardless of when the property is placed in service during the tax year. For each of the remaining years of the recovery period, a full year of depreciation is claimed. If you hold the property for the entire recovery period, a half-year of depreciation is claimed for the year following the end of the recovery period. If you dispose of the property before the end of the recovery period, a half-year of depreciation is allowable for the year of disposition.

*See Table 42-1(MACRS Depreciation Rates(42.5)) for year-by-year rates under the half-year convention.* Apply the rate from the table to the original basis, minus any first-year expensing *(42.3)* deduction and bonus depreciation *(42.20)* claimed. The Example in *42.5* shows the year-by-year deduction computation for five-year property under the half-year convention.

If you dispose of property before the end of its recovery period *(42.5)*, your deduction for the year of disposition is one-half of the deduction that would be allowed for the full year using the rate shown in the table. For example, if you sell the machine in the Example in *42.5* in year three, the deduction is $1,920 (½ of $3,840).

*Planning Reminder*

**Half-Year Convention**

The half-year convention applies unless the total cost basis of depreciable assets placed in service during the last three months of the year exceeds 40% of the total basis of all property placed in service during the year.

Under the half-year convention, all assets placed in service during the year are treated as placed in service at the midpoint of the year.

### Table 42-1   MACRS Depreciation Rates

| Year | Half-Year Convention | 1st (Quarter) | 2nd (Quarter) | 3rd (Quarter) | 4th (Quarter) |
|------|------|------|------|------|------|
| | | \-\-\-\-\-\-Mid-Quarter Convention\-\-\-\-\-\- | | | |

**3-Year Property**

| Year | Half-Year Convention | 1st (Quarter) | 2nd (Quarter) | 3rd (Quarter) | 4th (Quarter) |
|------|------|------|------|------|------|
| 1 | 33.33% | 58.33% | 41.67% | 25.00% | 8.33% |
| 2 | 44.45 | 27.78 | 38.89 | 50.00 | 61.11 |
| 3 | 14.81 | 12.35 | 14.14 | 16.67 | 20.37 |
| 4 | 7.41 | 1.54 | 5.30 | 8.33 | 10.19 |

**5-Year Property**

| Year | Half-Year Convention | 1st (Quarter) | 2nd (Quarter) | 3rd (Quarter) | 4th (Quarter) |
|------|------|------|------|------|------|
| 1 | 20.00% | 35.00% | 25.00% | 15.00% | 5.00% |
| 2 | 32.00 | 26.00 | 30.00 | 34.00 | 38.00 |
| 3 | 19.20 | 15.60 | 18.00 | 20.40 | 22.80 |
| 4 | 11.52 | 11.01 | 11.37 | 12.24 | 13.68 |
| 5 | 11.52 | 11.01 | 11.37 | 11.30 | 10.94 |
| 6 | 5.76 | 1.38 | 4.26 | 7.06 | 9.58 |

**7-Year Property**

| Year | Half-Year Convention | 1st (Quarter) | 2nd (Quarter) | 3rd (Quarter) | 4th (Quarter) |
|------|------|------|------|------|------|
| 1 | 14.29% | 25.00% | 17.85% | 10.71% | 3.57% |
| 2 | 24.49 | 21.43 | 23.47 | 25.51 | 27.55 |
| 3 | 17.49 | 15.31 | 16.76 | 18.22 | 19.68 |
| 4 | 12.49 | 10.93 | 11.97 | 13.02 | 14.06 |
| 5 | 8.93 | 8.75 | 8.87 | 9.30 | 10.04 |
| 6 | 8.92 | 8.74 | 8.87 | 8.85 | 8.73 |
| 7 | 8.93 | 8.75 | 8.87 | 8.86 | 8.73 |
| 8 | 4.46 | 1.09 | 3.33 | 5.53 | 7.64 |

## 42.7   Last Quarter Placements—Mid-Quarter Convention

A mid-quarter convention generally applies if the total cost basis of business equipment placed in service during the last three months of the tax year exceeds 40% of the total basis of all the property placed in service during the year. In applying the 40% rule, you do not count residential rental property, nonresidential realty, and assets that were placed in service and disposed of during the same year.

Under the mid-quarter convention, the first-year depreciation allowance for all property (other than nonresidential real property and residential rental property) placed in service during the year is based on the number of quarters that the asset was in service. Property placed in service at any time during a quarter is treated as having been placed in service in the middle of the quarter. The mid-quarter convention also applies to sales and disposals of property. The disposal is treated as occurring in the midpoint of the quarter.

**EXAMPLE**

During August 2018, you place in service office furniture costing $1,000, and in October, a computer costing $5,000. You are on the calendar year. The total basis of all property placed in service in 2018 is $6,000. As the $5,000 basis of the computer placed in service in the last quarter exceeds 40% of the total basis of all property placed in service during 2018, you must use the mid-quarter convention for the furniture and the computer. The office furniture, which is seven-year property, and the computer, which is five-year property, are depreciated using MACRS and a mid-quarter convention.

You first multiply the $1,000 basis of the furniture by 10.71%—the first-year mid-quarter convention rate for seven-year property placed in service in the third quarter (see *Table 42-1*). The depreciation deduction is $107. You then multiply the $5,000 basis of the computer by 5%—the five-year property mid-quarter convention rate for the fourth quarter of the first year (see *Table 42-1*). The deduction is $250. Total depreciation is $357.

If you dispose of property before the end of its recovery period *(42.5)*, your deduction for the year is figured by multiplying a full year of depreciation by the percentage listed in the following chart for the quarter in which you disposed of the property.

| *Quarter* | *Percentage* |
|-----------|--------------|
| First | 12.5% |
| Second | 37.5% |
| Third | 62.5% |
| Fourth | 87.5% |

**EXAMPLE**

On November 1, 2015, you placed in service a machine costing $10,000 with a five-year recovery period. You used the mid-quarter convention because it was the only item placed in service during the year. In May 2018, you sell the machine.

To determine depreciation for 2018, first figure the deduction for the full year (see *Table 42-1*). This is $1,368 (13.68% (rate for fourth year, fourth quarter) of $10,000). Since May, the month of disposition, is in the second quarter of the year, you multiply $1,368 by 37.5% to figure your depreciation deduction for 2018 of $513.

## 42.8  150% Rate Election

Instead of using the 200% declining balance rate for property in the three-, five-, seven-, and 10-year classes, you may elect a 150% declining balance rate. You may prefer the 150% rate when you are subject to the alternative minimum tax (AMT). For AMT purposes, you must use the 150% rate and adjust your taxable income if the 200% rate was used for regular tax purposes *(23.2)*. If for regular tax purposes you elect to apply the 150% rate, use the same recovery period *(42.4)* you would have used if you had claimed the 200% declining balance rate. Thus, the recovery period is five years for cars and computers and seven years for office furniture and fixtures. If the half-year convention applies, the first-year rate for the five-year class is 15%, and 10.71% for the seven-year class; *see* the table below. Apply the rate from the table to your original basis, minus any first-year expensing deduction and bonus depreciation claimed. If you are subject to the mid-quarter convention, *see* IRS Publication 946 for the tables showing mid-quarter convention rates.

The election to use the 150% rate must be made for all property within a given class placed in service in the same year. The election is irrevocable.

### Table 42-2 Half-Year Convention—150% Rate

| | Recovery Period | |
| --- | --- | --- |
| Year— | 5-Year— | 7-Year— |
| 1 | 15.00% | 10.71% |
| 2 | 25.50 | 19.13 |
| 3 | 17.85 | 15.03 |
| 4 | 16.66 | 12.25 |
| 5 | 16.66 | 12.25 |
| 6 | 8.33 | 12.25 |
| 7 | | 12.25 |
| 8 | | 6.13 |

## 42.9 Straight-Line Depreciation

You may not want an accelerated rate and may prefer to write off depreciation at an even pace. There are two straight-line methods. You may make an irrevocable election to use the straight-line method over the regular MACRS recovery period *(42.4)* under the general depreciation system (GDS). Alternatively, you may elect straight-line recovery over the designated recovery period for the class life under the alternative depreciation system (ADS). For some assets, such as cars, the GDS and ADS recovery periods are the same (five years for a car). In most cases, the ADS recovery period is longer than the GDS recovery period. For example, the recovery period for office furniture and fixtures is seven years under GDS and 10 years under ADS.

Half-year and quarter-year conventions apply to both straight-line methods *(42.6, 42.7)*. A mid-month convention applies under the straight-line rule for buildings *(42.12)*.

**Straight-line over regular recovery period (GDS).** You make this election on Form 4562, Part III, Section B, labeled "General Depreciation System". To elect this method for one asset, you must also use it for all other assets in the same class that are placed in service during the year. The straight-line election is irrevocable.

**Straight-line under the alternative depreciation system (ADS).** Under the alternative depreciation system (ADS), the straight-line recovery period is generally the same as the "class life" of the asset as determined by the IRS; the ADS recovery periods are shown in IRS Publication 946. The ADS recovery period for cars, light trucks, and computers is five years, the same as under the GDS. For business office furniture and fixtures, the ADS straight-line recovery period is 10 years. The ADS recovery period for personal property with no class life is 12 years. For nonresidential real property, the ADS recovery period is 40 years; for residential rental property, the ADS recovery period has been reduced from 40 years to 30 years for property placed in service after 2017. *See* IRS Publication 946 for other ADS class lives.

Except for real estate, the ADS election applies to all property within the same class placed in service during the taxable year. For real estate, the election to use the alternative depreciation method may be made on a property-by-property basis. The election is irrevocable. The deduction is claimed on Form 4562, Part III, Section C, labeled "Alternative Depreciation System,"

**Straight-line rate table.** The table below shows straight-line rates for five-year, seven-year, and 10-year property under the half-year convention. As discussed earlier, the recovery period depends on whether the GDS or ADS straight-line method is used. If you are subject to the mid-quarter convention *(42.7)*, *see* IRS Publication 946 for tables showing the applicable rates.

*Filing Tip*

**Should You Elect Straight-Line Recovery?**
Accelerated rates of MACRS merely give you an opportunity to advance the time of taking your deduction. This may be a decided advantage where the higher deductions in the first few years will provide you with cash for working capital or for investments in other income-producing sources. That is, by accelerating the deductions, you defer the payment of taxes that would be due if you claimed smaller depreciation deductions, using more conservative straight-line rates. The tax deferral lasts until the rapid method provides lower depreciation deductions than would the more conservative method. You are generally more likely to benefit from accelerated MACRS in an ongoing business.

If you are starting a new business in which you expect losses or low income at the start, accelerated MACRS may waste depreciation deductions that could be used in later years when your income increases. Therefore, before deciding to use accelerated MACRS rates, consider your income prospects.

### Table 42-3 Half-Year Convention—Straight-Line Rate

| Year— | Recovery Period | | |
| --- | --- | --- | --- |
| | 5-Year— | 7-Year— | 10-Year— |
| 1 | 10.00% | 7.14% | 5.00% |
| 2 | 20.00 | 14.29 | 10.00 |
| 3 | 20.00 | 14.29 | 10.00 |
| 4 | 20.00 | 14.28 | 10.00 |
| 5 | 20.00 | 14.29 | 10.00 |
| 6 | 10.00 | 14.28 | 10.00 |
| 7 | | 14.29 | 10.00 |
| 8 | | 7.14 | 10.00 |
| 9 | | | 10.00 |
| 10 | | | 10.00 |
| 11 | | | 5.00 |

**AMT depreciation.** There is no AMT adjustment for depreciation if for regular tax purposes straight-line depreciation is claimed on tangible personal property placed in service after 1998. Similarly, for real estate placed in service after 1998, the straight-line depreciation deduction claimed for regular tax purposes does not have to be refigured for AMT. For real property placed in service before 1999, regular tax straight-line depreciation is refigured for AMT purposes using the straight-line method over 40 years.

**Mandatory straight-line depreciation.** You are required to use the alternative depreciation system for automobiles *(43.3)* and certain computers *(42.10)* used 50% or less for business.

Alternative MACRS depreciation must also be used for:

- Figuring earnings and profits;
- Tangible property which, during the taxable year, is used predominantly outside the United States;
- Tax-exempt use property;
- Tax-exempt bond financed property; and
- Imported property covered by an executive order.

## 42.10 Listed Property

"Listed property" is a term applied to certain equipment that may be used for personal and business purposes. For such property, the law allows first-year expensing *(42.3)*, bonus depreciation *(42.20)*, or accelerated MACRS *(42.5)* deductions only if business use exceeds 50%. For business use of 50% or less, you must use ADS straight-line depreciation *(42.9)*. Deductions for listed property are claimed on Part V of Form 4562. If the more-than-50%-business-use test is met in the first year and first-year expensing or accelerated MACRS is claimed, but business use of listed property falls to 50% or less during the ADS straight-line recovery period *(42.9)*, you must "recapture" first-year expensing, bonus depreciation and accelerated MACRS deductions.

What is "listed property"? Listed property includes passenger autos and other transportation vehicles (*see* exceptions at *43.3*), boats, airplanes, and any photographic, sound, or video recording equipment that could be used for entertainment or recreational purposes. However, there is an exception for photographic, phonographic, communications, or video equipment used exclusively and regularly in your business or at your regular business establishment. A home office that meets the requirements for deducting home office expenses *(40.12)* is considered a regular business establishment.

Computers and peripheral equipment placed in service after 2017 have been removed from the category of listed property; *see* the Law Alert and Examples 1 and 2 on this page.

**Deductions for listed property subject to recapture.** If business use of listed property exceeds 50% in the first year but drops to 50% or less within the ADS recovery period *(Table 42-3)*, bonus depreciation, MACRS and any first-year expensing deduction are subject to "recapture." In the year in which business use drops to 50% or less, you recapture the excess of (1) the MACRS, bonus depreciation, and first-year expensing deductions claimed in prior years over (2) the deductions that would have been allowed using ADS straight-line depreciation *(42.9)*. For the rest of the recovery period, you continue to use the alternative straight-line rate.

Recapture is figured on Form 4797. The recapture computation follows the steps shown in *43.10* for recapture of excess depreciation on an automobile.

 *Law Alert*

**Computers and Peripheral Equipment**

Computers and peripheral equipment placed in service after 2017 are no longer treated as listed property. If placed in service before 2018, computers and peripheral equipment were generally treated as listed property, but there was an exception for equipment that a taxpayer owned or leased and used exclusively at a regular business establishment, including a qualifying home office. A pre-2018 computer that did not qualify for this exception is subject to the listed property recapture rule.

---

**EXAMPLES**

1. In 2018, you buy a computer that you use exclusively for business. The computer is not listed property because it is placed in service after 2017. You may claim bonus depreciation *(42.18)*, first-year expensing *(42.3)*, or accelerated MACRS *(42.5)* for your investment on Form 4562. If business use falls to 50% or less after 2018, the listed property recapture rule (*see* above) does not apply but a first-year expensing deduction would be subject to recapture under the expensing rules.

2. In 2017, you bought a computer to use in your work as a freelance consultant. You did not use it exclusively in a regular business office, so under the rules for computers placed in service before 2018 the computer was considered listed property (*see* the Law Alert on this page). As listed property, first-year expensing, bonus depreciation, or accelerated MACRS was allowed for 2017 only if you used the computer more than 50% for business. If business use in 2017 did exceed 50%, but it falls to 50% or less within the ADS recovery period *(42.9)*, you must recapture your prior-year deductions (*see* listed property recapture rule above). If business use in 2017 did not exceed 50%, ADS straight-line depreciation over 5 years must be used *(42.9)*.

---

**Leasing listed property.** You may deduct the portion of your lease payments attributable to business use. However, if business use is 50% or less for any year, you must report as income an amount based on the fair market value of the unit, the percentage of business plus investment use, and percentages from two IRS tables shown in Publication 946. Special rules apply for leasing cars, light trucks, and vans *(43.12)*.

## 42.11 Assets in Service Before 1987

Assets placed in service before 1987 were depreciated under a different recovery system called ACRS. Most of the assets have already been fully depreciated, although some assets, such as certain real estate placed in service before 1987, continue to be governed by these rules *(42.15)*.

## 42.12 MACRS for Real Estate Placed in Service After 1986

The recovery period for residential rental property placed in service after December 31, 1986, is 27.5 years. The recovery period for nonresidential real property is either 39 years or 31.5 years, depending on when the property was placed in service.

The method of recovery for nonresidential or residential property is the straight-line method using a mid-month convention. See *Table 42-4* for rate tables for each class of property.

## Table 42-4  MACRS Real Estate Depreciation

### Residential Rental Property (27.5 years; see 42.12)
Use the column for the month of taxable year placed in service.

| Year | Month property placed in service | | | | | | | | | | | |
|---|---|---|---|---|---|---|---|---|---|---|---|---|
| | 1 | 2 | 3 | 4 | 5 | 6 | 7 | 8 | 9 | 10 | 11 | 12 |
| 1 | 3.485% | 3.182% | 2.879% | 2.576% | 2.273% | 1.970% | 1.667% | 1.364% | 1.061% | 0.758% | 0.455% | 0.152% |
| 2–9 | 3.636 | 3.636 | 3.636 | 3.636 | 3.636 | 3.636 | 3.636 | 3.636 | 3.636 | 3.636 | 3.636 | 3.636 |
| 10 | 3.637 | 3.637 | 3.637 | 3.637 | 3.637 | 3.637 | 3.636 | 3.636 | 3.636 | 3.636 | 3.636 | 3.636 |
| 11 | 3.636 | 3.636 | 3.636 | 3.636 | 3.636 | 3.636 | 3.637 | 3.637 | 3.637 | 3.637 | 3.637 | 3.637 |
| 12 | 3.637 | 3.637 | 3.637 | 3.637 | 3.637 | 3.637 | 3.636 | 3.636 | 3.636 | 3.636 | 3.636 | 3.636 |
| 13 | 3.636 | 3.636 | 3.636 | 3.636 | 3.636 | 3.636 | 3.637 | 3.637 | 3.637 | 3.637 | 3.637 | 3.637 |
| 14 | 3.637 | 3.637 | 3.637 | 3.637 | 3.637 | 3.637 | 3.636 | 3.636 | 3.636 | 3.636 | 3.636 | 3.636 |
| 15 | 3.636 | 3.636 | 3.636 | 3.636 | 3.636 | 3.636 | 3.637 | 3.637 | 3.637 | 3.637 | 3.637 | 3.637 |
| 16 | 3.637 | 3.637 | 3.637 | 3.637 | 3.637 | 3.637 | 3.636 | 3.636 | 3.636 | 3.636 | 3.636 | 3.636 |
| 17 | 3.636 | 3.636 | 3.636 | 3.636 | 3.636 | 3.636 | 3.637 | 3.637 | 3.637 | 3.637 | 3.637 | 3.637 |
| 18 | 3.637 | 3.637 | 3.637 | 3.637 | 3.637 | 3.637 | 3.636 | 3.636 | 3.636 | 3.636 | 3.636 | 3.636 |
| 19 | 3.636 | 3.636 | 3.636 | 3.636 | 3.636 | 3.636 | 3.637 | 3.637 | 3.637 | 3.637 | 3.637 | 3.637 |
| 20 | 3.637 | 3.637 | 3.637 | 3.637 | 3.637 | 3.637 | 3.636 | 3.636 | 3.636 | 3.636 | 3.636 | 3.636 |
| 21 | 3.636 | 3.636 | 3.636 | 3.636 | 3.636 | 3.636 | 3.637 | 3.637 | 3.637 | 3.637 | 3.637 | 3.637 |
| 22 | 3.637 | 3.637 | 3.637 | 3.637 | 3.637 | 3.637 | 3.636 | 3.636 | 3.636 | 3.636 | 3.636 | 3.636 |
| 23 | 3.636 | 3.636 | 3.636 | 3.636 | 3.636 | 3.636 | 3.637 | 3.637 | 3.637 | 3.637 | 3.637 | 3.637 |
| 24 | 3.637 | 3.637 | 3.637 | 3.637 | 3.637 | 3.637 | 3.636 | 3.636 | 3.636 | 3.636 | 3.636 | 3.636 |
| 25 | 3.636 | 3.636 | 3.636 | 3.636 | 3.636 | 3.636 | 3.637 | 3.637 | 3.637 | 3.637 | 3.637 | 3.637 |
| 26 | 3.637 | 3.637 | 3.637 | 3.637 | 3.637 | 3.637 | 3.636 | 3.636 | 3.636 | 3.636 | 3.636 | 3.636 |
| 27 | 3.636 | 3.636 | 3.636 | 3.636 | 3.636 | 3.636 | 3.637 | 3.637 | 3.637 | 3.637 | 3.637 | 3.637 |
| 28 | 1.97 | 2.273 | 2.576 | 2.879 | 3.182 | 3.485 | 3.636 | 3.636 | 3.636 | 3.636 | 3.636 | 3.636 |
| 29 | | | | | | | 0.152 | 0.455 | 0.758 | 1.061 | 1.364 | 1.667 |

### Nonresidential Real Property (39 years—placed in service on or after May 13, 1993; see 42.12)
Use the column for the month of taxable year placed in service.

| Year \ Month | 1 | 2 | 3 | 4 | 5 | 6 | 7 | 8 | 9 | 10 | 11 | 12 |
|---|---|---|---|---|---|---|---|---|---|---|---|---|
| 1 | 2.461% | 2.247% | 2.033% | 1.819% | 1.605% | 1.391% | 1.177% | 0.963% | 0.749% | 0.535% | 0.321% | 0.107% |
| 2–39 | 2.564 | 2.564 | 2.564 | 2.564 | 2.564 | 2.564 | 2.564 | 2.564 | 2.564 | 2.564 | 2.564 | 2.564 |
| 40 | 0.107 | 0.321 | 0.535 | 0.749 | 0.963 | 1.177 | 1.391 | 1.605 | 1.819 | 2.033 | 2.247 | 2.461 |

### Nonresidential Real Property (31.5 years—placed in service before May 13, 1993; see 42.12)
Use the column for the month of taxable year placed in service

| Year \ Month | 1 | 2 | 3 | 4 | 5 | 6 | 7 | 8 | 9 | 10 | 11 | 12 |
|---|---|---|---|---|---|---|---|---|---|---|---|---|
| 20 | 3.175 | 3.174 | 3.175 | 3.174 | 3.175 | 3.174 | 3.175 | 3.174 | 3.175 | 3.174 | 3.175 | 3.174 |
| 21 | 3.174 | 3.175 | 3.174 | 3.175 | 3.174 | 3.175 | 3.174 | 3.175 | 3.174 | 3.175 | 3.174 | 3.175 |
| 22 | 3.175 | 3.174 | 3.175 | 3.174 | 3.175 | 3.174 | 3.175 | 3.174 | 3.175 | 3.174 | 3.175 | 3.174 |
| 23 | 3.174 | 3.175 | 3.174 | 3.175 | 3.174 | 3.175 | 3.174 | 3.175 | 3.174 | 3.175 | 3.174 | 3.175 |
| 24 | 3.175 | 3.174 | 3.175 | 3.174 | 3.175 | 3.174 | 3.175 | 3.174 | 3.175 | 3.174 | 3.175 | 3.174 |
| 25 | 3.174 | 3.175 | 3.174 | 3.175 | 3.174 | 3.175 | 3.174 | 3.175 | 3.174 | 3.175 | 3.174 | 3.175 |
| 26 | 3.175 | 3.174 | 3.175 | 3.174 | 3.175 | 3.174 | 3.175 | 3.174 | 3.175 | 3.174 | 3.175 | 3.174 |
| 27 | 3.174 | 3.175 | 3.174 | 3.175 | 3.174 | 3.175 | 3.174 | 3.175 | 3.174 | 3.175 | 3.174 | 3.175 |
| 28 | 3.175 | 3.174 | 3.175 | 3.174 | 3.175 | 3.174 | 3.175 | 3.174 | 3.175 | 3.174 | 3.175 | 3.174 |
| 29 | 3.174 | 3.175 | 3.174 | 3.175 | 3.174 | 3.175 | 3.174 | 3.175 | 3.174 | 3.175 | 3.174 | 3.175 |
| 30 | 3.175 | 3.174 | 3.175 | 3.174 | 3.175 | 3.174 | 3.175 | 3.174 | 3.175 | 3.174 | 3.175 | 3.174 |
| 31 | 3.174 | 3.175 | 3.174 | 3.175 | 3.174 | 3.175 | 3.174 | 3.175 | 3.174 | 3.175 | 3.174 | 3.175 |
| 32 | 1.720 | 1.984 | 2.249 | 2.513 | 2.778 | 3.042 | 3.175 | 3.174 | 3.175 | 3.174 | 3.175 | 3.174 |
| 33 | | | | | | | 0.132 | 0.397 | 0.661 | 0.926 | 1.190 | 1.455 |

*For nonresidential real property placed in service after December 31, 1986, but before May 13, 1993, the depreciation recovery period is 31.5 years.*

*For nonresidential real property placed in service after May 12, 1993, the recovery period is 39 years.* Under a transition rule, the 31.5-year recovery period rather than the 39-year recovery period applies to a building placed in service before 1994 if before May 13, 1993, you had entered into a binding, written contract to buy or build it, or if, before that date, you had begun construction. The transition rule also applies if you obtained the contract or property from someone else who satisfied the pre–May 13, 1993, contract or construction requirement, provided he or she never put the building in service and you did so before 1994.

However, *see 42.14* for qualified improvement property.

*Residential rental property subject to the 27.5 year recovery period is defined as a rental building or structure for which 80% or more of the gross rental income for the tax year is rental income from dwelling units.* If you occupy any part of the building, the gross rental income includes the fair rental value of the part you occupy.

A dwelling unit is a house or an apartment used to provide living accommodations in a building or structure, but not a unit in a hotel, motel, inn, or other establishment where more than one-half of the units are used on a transient basis.

**Mid-month convention.** Under a mid-month convention, all residential rental property and nonresidential real property placed in service or disposed of during any month is treated as placed in service or disposed of at the midpoint of that month. You may determine the first-year deduction for your property by applying the percentage from *Table 42-4* to the original depreciable basis. In later years, use the same column of the table to figure your deduction. If the property is disposed of before the end of the recovery period, the deduction for the year of disposition is figured by prorating the full-year deduction for the months the property was in service, treating the month of disposition as one-half of a month of use.

---

### EXAMPLES

1.  In February 2018, you buy an apartment building for $100,000 and place it in service. You use the calendar year. *Table 42-4* (preceding page) gives a first-year depreciation rate of 3.182% for 27.5-year residential rental property placed in service during February. Applying this rate, you get a deduction of $3,182.

    For 2019 (year 2), the rate will be 3.636%, for a deduction of $3,636.

2.  Assume that you sell the apartment building in Example 1 on March 7, 2020. A full year of depreciation for 2020 is $3,636 (3.636% rate for year 3 × $100,000). You are treated as using the property for 2.5 months in 2020, so your deduction is $757.50 ($3,636 ÷ 12 × 2.5).

---

**Additions or improvements to property.** The depreciation deduction for any additions to, or improvement of, any property is figured in the same way as the deduction for the property would be figured if the property had been placed in service at the same time as the addition or improvement. However, *see 42.14* for qualified improvement property.

## 42.13 Demolishing a Building

When you buy improved property, the purchase price is allocated between the land and the building; only the building may be depreciated. The land may not *(42.1)*. If you later demolish the building, you may not deduct the cost of the demolition or the undepreciated basis of the building as a loss in the year of demolition. Expenses or losses in connection with the demolition of any structure, including certified historic structures, are not deductible. They must be capitalized and added to the basis of the land on which the structure is located.

**Major rehabilitation.** Where you are considering a major rehabilitation of a building that involves some demolition of the building, IRS guidelines may allow you to deduct the costs of demolition and a removal of part of the structure. Under the IRS rules, the costs

*Filing Tip*

**Additions and Improvements**

The MACRS class for an addition or improvement is generally determined by the MACRS class of the property to which the addition or improvement is made. For example, if you put an addition on a rental home that you are depreciating over 27.5 years, the addition is depreciated as 27.5-year residential rental property. The period for figuring depreciation begins on the date that the addition or improvement is placed in service, or, if later, the date that the property to which the addition or improvement was made is placed in service.

of structural modification may avoid capitalization if 75% or more of the existing external walls are retained as internal or external walls and 75% or more of the existing internal framework is also retained. For certified historic structures, the modification must also be part of a certified rehabilitation.

## 42.14 Qualified Improvement Property

The cost of qualified improvement property can be expensed up to the overall first-year expensing limit of $1 million *(42.3)*. In addition, qualified improvement property is eligible for bonus depreciation *(42.18)*, or is depreciable under MACRS over a 15-year period using the straight-line method (assuming a technical correction is made by Congress to provide this treatment; *see* the *e-Supplement at jklasser.com*).

**Qualified improvement property.** Qualified improvement property is any improvement to an interior part of a building that is nonresidential realty and is made after the date the building was placed in service. However, any improvements for the enlargement of the building, an elevator or escalator, or changes to the internal framework of the building, are not qualified improvement property.

## 42.15 Depreciating Real Estate Placed in Service After 1980 and Before 1987

The ACRS recovery period of almost all buildings placed in service before 1987 has already ended. Some pre-1987 buildings are still being depreciated over a 35-year or 45-year period if the straight-line election discussed in the next paragraph was made.

**Election to use straight-line depreciation.** For 15-year, 18-year, or 19-year real property, you may have elected to use the straight-line method over 35 or 45 years. An election of the straight-line method for real property had to be made on a property-by-property basis, by the return due date, plus extensions, for the year the property was placed in service.

**Rate of recovery.** The rate of recovery is listed in Treasury tables that are available in IRS Publication 534.

**Substantial improvements.** Substantial improvements made after 1986 to an ACRS building are depreciable under MACRS *(42.13)*, not ACRS.

**Recapture.** *See 44.1* for recapture rules on the sale of ACRS property.

## 42.16 Amortizing Goodwill and Other Intangibles (Section 197)

The costs of intangibles coming within Section 197 are amortized over a 15-year period. The 15-year period applies regardless of the actual useful life of "Section 197 intangibles" acquired after August 10, 1993 (or after July 25, 1991, if elected), and held in connection with a business or income-producing activity.

Generally, the amount subject to amortization is cost. Annual amortization is reported on Form 4562. The 15-year period starts with the month the intangible was acquired.

A "Section 197 intangible" is: (1) goodwill; (2) going-concern value; (3) workforce in place; (4) information base; (5) know-how, but *see* exceptions below; (6) any customer-based intangible; (7) any supplier-based intangible; (8) any license, permit, or other right granted by a governmental unit or agency; (9) any covenant not to compete made in the acquisition of a business; and (10) any franchise, trademark, or trade name.

**Goodwill.** Goodwill is the value of a business attributable to the expectancy of continued customer patronage, due to the name or reputation of a business or any other factor.

**Franchises, trademarks, and trade names.** A franchise (excluding sports franchises), trademark, or trade name is a Section 197 intangible. Amounts, whether fixed or contingent, paid on the transfer of a trademark, trade name, or franchise are chargeable to capital account and must be ratably amortized over a 15-year period. The renewal of a franchise, trademark, or trade name is treated as an acquisition of the franchise, trademark, or trade name. Renewal costs are amortized over 15 years beginning in the month of renewal.

*Planning Reminder*

**Abandonment of Leasehold Improvements**

Upon the termination of a lease, the adjusted basis of a lessee's leasehold improvements that are abandoned may be claimed as a loss. A lessor may follow the rule applied to lessees if the improvements are irrevocably disposed of or abandoned at the termination of the lease. The lessor may recognize loss for the remaining adjusted basis of the improvements.

*See* the Form 4562 instructions for further details.

**Know-how.** A patent, copyright, formula, process, design, pattern, format, or similar item may be a Section 197 intangible. However, the following interests are not Section 197 intangibles unless acquired as part of the acquisition of a business: patents, copyrights, and interests in films, sound recordings, videotapes, books, or other similar property.

**Customer-based intangibles.** Customer-based intangibles include the portion of an acquired trade or business attributable to a customer base, circulation base, undeveloped market or market growth, insurance in force, investment management contracts, or other relationships with customers that involve the future provision of goods or services.

**Supplier-based intangibles.** The portion of the purchase price of an acquired business attributable to a favorable relationship with persons who provide distribution services, such as favorable shelf or display space at a retail outlet, the existence of a favorable credit rating, or the existence of favorable supply contracts, are Section 197 intangibles.

**Going-concern value.** This is the additional value that attaches to property because it is an integral part of a going concern. This includes the value attributable to the ability of a trade or business to continue to operate and generate sales without interruption in spite of a change in ownership.

**Workforce in place.** The portion of the purchase price of an acquired business attributable to a highly skilled workforce is amortizable over 15 years. Similarly, the cost of acquiring an existing employment contract is amortizable over 15 years.

**Information base.** This includes the cost of acquiring customer lists; subscription lists; insurance expirations; patient or client files; lists of newspaper, magazine, radio, or television advertisers; business books and records; and operating systems. The intangible value of technical manuals, training manuals or programs, data files, and accounting or inventory control systems is also a Section 197 intangible.

**Self-created intangibles.** A Section 197 intangible created by a taxpayer is generally not amortizable, unless created in connection with a transaction that involves the acquisition of assets of a business. However, this deduction bar for self-created intangibles does not apply to the following: (1) any license, permit, or other right granted by a governmental unit or agency; (2) a covenant not to compete entered into on the acquisition of a business; or (3) any franchise, trademark, or trade name. For example, the 15-year amortization period may apply to the capitalized costs of registering or developing a trademark or trade name.

A person who contracts for or renews a contract for the use of a Section 197 intangible may not be considered to have created that intangible. For example, a licensee who contracts for the use of know-how may amortize capitalized costs over 15 years.

**The following intangible assets are not Section 197 intangibles.** (1) interests in a corporation, partnership, trust, or estate; (2) interests under certain financial contracts; (3) interests in land; (4) certain computer software (*see* the Filing Tip on this page); (5) certain separately acquired rights and interests; (6) interests under existing leases of tangible property; (7) interests under existing indebtedness; (8) sports franchises; (9) certain residential mortgage servicing rights; and (10) certain corporate transaction costs.

**Loss limitations.** A person who disposes of an amortizable Section 197 intangible at a loss and at the same time retains other Section 197 intangibles acquired in the same transaction may not deduct the loss. The disallowed loss is added to the basis of the retained Section 197 intangibles. The same rule applies if a Section 197 intangible is abandoned or becomes worthless and other Section 197 intangibles acquired in the same transaction are kept. The basis of the remaining intangibles is increased by the disallowed loss.

You may not treat a covenant not to compete as worthless any earlier than the disposition or worthlessness of the entire interest in a business.

**Dispositions.** An amortizable Section 197 intangible is not a capital asset. It is treated as depreciable property, and if held for more than one year, it will generally qualify as a Section 1231 asset *(44.1)*. Amortization claimed on a Section 197 intangible is subject to recapture under Section 1245 and gain on its sale to certain related persons is subject to ordinary income treatment under Section 1239.

### *Planning Reminder*

### Covenants Not To Compete

A covenant not to compete is a Section 197 intangible if paid for in connection with the acquisition of a business. Excessive compensation or rental paid to a former owner of a business for continuing to perform services or provide the use of property is considered an amount paid for a covenant not to compete if the services or property benefits the trade or business. But an amount paid under a covenant not to compete that actually represents additional consideration for corporate stock is not a Section 197 intangible and must be added to the basis of the acquired stock.

### *Filing Tip*

### Computer Software Not Considered a Section 197 Intangible

Computer software is not a Section 197 intangible if it is readily available to the general public, is not subject to an exclusive license and has not been substantially changed. If this test is met, business software is treated as "off the shelf" software that is eligible for first-year expensing *(42.3)* or bonus depreciation *(42.18)*, or it may be depreciated over 36 months using the straight-line method if it has a useful life of over one year.

Even if the above test is not met, computer software is not a Section 197 intangible unless it is acquired in the acquisition of a business.

## 42.17 Amortizing Research and Experimentation Costs

If you have these costs, you can deduct them currently or elect to amortize them over a period of not less than 60 months. The election may be advisable if you do not have current income; the deductions may become more valuable to you in the future.

You may be eligible for a tax credit for increasing your R&D costs *(40.26)*. However, you cannot take a deduction and a credit with respect to the same costs.

## 42.18 Bonus Depreciation

Bonus depreciation is an additional first-year depreciation allowance equal to a set percentage of the adjusted basis of eligible property. The percentage for bonus depreciation for 2018 is 100%. Bonus depreciation is fully deductible for alternative minimum tax purposes *(23.2)*; no adjustment is required.

Bonus depreciation (also called a Section 168(k) allowance and a special depreciation allowance) can be claimed in addition to any first-year expensing. In figuring "adjusted basis" for purposes of bonus depreciation, any first-year expensing deduction is taken into account first. Then, you figure bonus depreciation on the cost of the property minus the first-year expensing allowance. *As a practical matter, for property placed in service in 2018 that is eligible for bonus depreciation, there is no need to elect first-year expensing; the entire cost can be written off using bonus depreciation.*

Under prior law, you had to be the original user of the property; but this rule no longer applies for property acquired after and placed in service after September 27, 2017.

Bonus depreciation cannot be claimed for property that must be depreciated under the ADS straight-line method *(42.9)*. For example, it may not be used for listed property used 50% or less for business *(42.10)* since such property must be depreciated under ADS.

Bonus depreciation allows the first-year dollar limit on write-offs for vehicles weighing less than 6,000 pounds to be increased by a fixed dollar amount reflecting bonus depreciation, provided that business use exceeds 50%. The bonus allowance increases the total dollar limit for such vehicles placed in service during 2018 by $8,000 *(43.4)*.

**Eligible property.** Bonus depreciation can be claimed for any property with a recovery period of 20 years or less, computer software that is not a Section 197 intangible (*see* the Filing Tip in *42.16*), and buildings that replace or rehabilitate property damaged, destroyed, or condemned as a result of a federally declared disaster.

Bonus depreciation is also allowed for "qualified improvement property," provided Congress enacts a technical correction to allow this (*see* the ***e-Supplement at jklasser. com***). Qualified improvements are improvements made to the interior of a nonresidential building after the building is placed in service, other than elevators, escalators, enlargements, or changes to the structural framework.

**Claiming bonus depreciation.** You report bonus depreciation in Part II of Form 4562 labeled "Special Depreciation Allowance," unless the property is "listed property" *(42.10)*. For listed property, use Part V of Form 4562.

**Election out of bonus depreciation.** Unlike regular depreciation, you are not required to use bonus depreciation and have the option of electing out of its use. If eligible for bonus depreciation, you can elect not to use it. The election out is made on a per-asset-class basis. Thus, for example, you can opt out of bonus depreciation for all five-year property while claiming it for seven-year property. To make the election out of claiming bonus depreciation, attach a statement to your return specifying the class of property for which the election not to claim additional depreciation is being made.

If you fail to make an election not to claim bonus depreciation, then you are deemed to have claimed it (even though you did not) and must reduce the basis of the property by the amount of bonus depreciation that could have been claimed.

*Law Alert*

**Bonus depreciation for new and pre-owned property**

Bonus depreciation can be claimed for eligible property whether it is new or used if acquired after and placed in service after September 27, 2017.

# CHAPTER 43

# Deducting Car and Truck Expenses

The costs of buying and operating a car, truck, or van for business are deductible under rules hedged with restrictions. Depreciation deductions for most cars, trucks, and vans are subject to annual ceilings, but for vehicles placed in service in 2018, they do not apply to those vehicles costing less than $90,000 in most cases. The cost of heavy SUVs used 100% for business that are placed in service in 2018 can be fully deducted in 2018.

To avoid accounting for actual vehicle expenses and depreciation, you may claim an IRS mileage allowance. The allowance for 2018 is 54.5 cents per mile. Keep a record of business trip mileage.

If you are self-employed, you deduct your vehicle expenses on Schedule C or Schedule C-EZ if eligible *(40.6)*. Use Form 4562 to compute depreciation if you claim actual operating costs instead of the IRS mileage allowance. If you are an employee, you cannot deduct your unreimbursed vehicle expenses because of the suspension of miscellaneous itemized deductions subject to the 2% of adjusted gross income floor for 2018 through 2025 *(19.2)*.

If you bought an electric vehicle in 2018 for business and/or personal use, you may be eligible for a tax credit *(25.16)*.

## First-Year Election Affects Later Years

In deciding whether to elect the allowance in the first year, consider not only whether you will get a bigger first-year deduction using the allowance, or deducting actual operating costs plus depreciation, but also project your mileage, operating expenses, and depreciation expenses over the years you expect to use the vehicle. If in the first year you elect to deduct actual costs, including MACRS or straight-line MACRS depreciation, you may not use the IRS auto allowance for that vehicle in a later year. On the other hand, claiming the IRS allowance in the first year you put a vehicle in service forfeits your privilege to use MACRS and first-year expensing. If you switch from the allowance to deducting actual expenses in later years, you may claim straight-line depreciation over the remaining estimated useful life of the vehicle if the vehicle is not considered fully depreciated.

## No Standard Mileage Rate for Fleets

IRS policy has not allowed use of the standard mileage rate if you use five or more automobiles simultaneously (such as in fleet operations), whether you own or lease the vehicles. You must use the actual expense method for all the vehicles (i.e., deduct the actual operating costs of the vehicles).If you alternate use among five (or more) vehicles, so they are not used in your business at the same time, you may use the standard mileage rate for all the vehicles.

# 43.1 Standard Mileage Rate

If you start to use your car for business in 2018, you have a choice of either deducting the actual operating costs of your car during business trips or deducting a flat IRS allowance. The allowance is 54.5 cents per mile. The mileage allowance also applies to business trips in a van or pickup or panel truck as if it were a car.

If you placed a car, van, pick-up, or panel truck in service before 2018 and have always used the IRS mileage allowance, you may apply the 54.5 cents-per-mile rate to your 2018 business mileage or deduct your actual operating costs plus straight-line depreciation over the remaining estimated useful life of the vehicle (assuming the vehicle is not considered fully depreciated).

The rate may not be used to deduct the costs of a vehicle used for nonbusiness income-producing activities such as looking after investment property.

**Allowance must be elected for the first year.** The choice of the allowance must be made in the first year you place the vehicle in service for business travel. If you do not use the allowance in the year you first use the vehicle for business, you may not use the allowance for that vehicle in any other year. Thus, if you bought a car for business in 2017 and on your 2017 return you deducted actual operating costs plus depreciation, you may not use the mileage allowance on your 2018 return or in any later year.

**Allowance takes the place of fixed operating costs plus depreciation.** If you claim the allowance, you cannot deduct your actual outlays for expenses such as gasoline (including state and local taxes), oil, repairs, license tags, or insurance, nor can you deduct depreciation (if you own the vehicle) or lease payments. Parking fees and tolls during business trips are deductible in addition to the mileage allowance. The IRS will not disallow a deduction based on the allowance even though it exceeds your actual vehicle costs. If you use more than one automobile in your business travel and elect the allowance, total the business mileage traveled in both cars.

> ### EXAMPLES
>
> 1. You buy a car in 2018 and drive it on business trips. You keep a record of your business mileage. You traveled 30,000 miles for business during the year. You may deduct $16,350 (30,000 × 54.5 cents). In addition to the $16,350 allowance, you may deduct your expenses for tolls and parking.
>
> 2. You use one car primarily for business and occasionally your spouse's car for business trips. In 2018, you drove your car on business trips 10,000 miles and your spouse's car 2,000 miles. Total business mileage is 12,000 miles for purposes of the cents-per-mile allowance.

**Records.** You may decide to use the allowance if you do not keep accurate records of operating costs. However, you must keep a record of your business trips, dates, customers or clients visited, business purpose of the trips, your total mileage during the year, and the number of miles traveled on business. An IRS agent may attempt to verify mileage by asking for repair bills near the beginning and end of the year if the bills note mileage readings.

**Mileage allowance for leased vehicle.** The IRS mileage allowance is also available for leased cars, vans, and pick-up or panel trucks, but it must be used for the entire lease period or not at all. For example, if in 2018 you leased a car for business purposes and you claim the cents-per-mile allowance, you will also have to use it for the remainder of the lease period, including renewals.

**Interest on a vehicle loan and taxes.** The deduction rules are discussed in the following section (43.2).

**Mileage allowance disallowed.** You may not claim the cents-per-mile allowance if:

- You have claimed depreciation, first-year expensing, or first-year bonus depreciation in the year the vehicle was placed in service.
- You use in your business five or more vehicles simultaneously, such as in a fleet operation.

**IRS allowance includes depreciation.** When you use the IRS mileage allowance, you may not claim a separate depreciation deduction. The IRS mileage allowance includes an estimate for depreciation. For purposes of figuring gain or loss on a disposition, you must reduce the basis of the vehicle by the following depreciation amounts: 23 cents per mile in 2010, 22 cents per mile in 2011, 23 cents per mile in 2012 and 2013, 22 cents per mile in 2014, 24 cents per mile in 2015 and 2016, and 25 cents per mile in 2017 and 2018.

**Depreciation when switching from allowance to actual costs.** If you use the IRS mileage allowance in the first year, you may switch to the actual-cost method in a later year, but depreciation must be based on the straight-line method over the remaining estimated useful life. However, no depreciation may be claimed if basis has been reduced to zero under the annual cents-per-mile reduction rule in the preceding paragraph.

## 43.2 Expense Allocations

If you do not claim the IRS mileage allowance, you may deduct car, truck, or van expenses on business trips such as the cost of gas and oil (including state and local taxes), repairs, parking, and tolls, in addition to depreciation for your car *(43.3–43.5)*.

If you use your vehicle exclusively for business, all of your operating expenses are deductible.

**Apportioning vehicle expenses between business and personal use.** For a vehicle used for business and personal purposes, deduct only the expenses and depreciation allocated to your business use of the vehicle.

The business portion of vehicle expenses is determined by the percentage of mileage driven on business trips during the year.

### Table 43-1 Deducting Car and Truck Expenses

| Item— | Tax Rule— |
|---|---|
| IRS mileage allowance | You may avoid the trouble of keeping a record of actual vehicle expenses and calculating depreciation by electing the IRS mileage allowance for a car, van, or pick-up or panel truck. However, to claim the allowance, you must be ready to prove business use of the vehicle and keep a record of your mileage. The allowance may give you a larger deduction than your actual outlays plus depreciation. You must elect the allowance in the first year you use the vehicle for business. If you do not, you may not use the allowance for that vehicle in any other year<br><br>If your actual operating costs plus depreciation exceed the allowance for the first year you place the vehicle in business service, you may claim your actual operating expenses and depreciation, but doing so will forfeit your right to elect the allowance for that vehicle in any later year. |
| Depreciation | If you claim actual operating expenses, such as gasoline, repairs, and insurance costs, you may also claim depreciation. There is a cap on the annual depreciation deduction. For a car placed in service in 2018, the first-year depreciation limit is $18,000 ($10,000 if bonus depreciation is not used). These limits must be reduced for personal use *(43.4)*. Electing first-year expensing or depreciation for a car, truck, or van placed in service in 2018 prevents you from using the IRS mileage allowance *(43.1)* for that car in later years.<br><br>For cars, trucks, and vans placed in business service in 2018 that are used 50% or less for business, you must use straight-line depreciation subject to the dollar limits *(43.6)*. If business use is initially over 50% but declines to 50% or less in a later year, prior year depreciation deductions, including bonus depreciation and first-year expensing, must be recaptured as income to the extent they exceeded straight-line deductions *(43.10)*.<br><br>For a vehicle placed in service before 2018, *see* Tables 43-2 and 43-3 for the maximum depreciation you can claim for 2018. |
| Vehicle used for business and personal driving | You may deduct only the amount allocated to business mileage. For example, total mileage is 20,000 in 2018 and your business mileage is 15,000. You may claim only 75% of your deductible costs (15,000 ÷ 20,000). |
| Tax return reporting | As a self-employed individual, you deduct business costs on Schedule C and use Form 4562 to compute depreciation if you claim actual operating costs. Employees cannot take a deduction for business driving as a miscellaneous itemized deduction; this deduction is suspended for 2018 through 2025 *(19.2)*. |

**EXAMPLE**

You have been deducting actual expenses plus depreciation each year for your car rather than the IRS mileage allowance *(43.1)*. In 2018, you drove your car 15,000 miles. Of this, 12,000 miles was on business trips. The percentage of business use is 80%:

$$\frac{\text{business mileage}}{\text{total mileage}} = \frac{12,000}{15,000} = 80\%$$

If your actual car expenses (gas, oil, repairs, etc.) for the year were $3,000, $2,400 ($3,000 × 80%) is deductible plus 80% of allowable depreciation.

**Interest on vehicle loan.** If you are self-employed, the allocated business percentage of the interest is fully deductible on Schedule C; the personal percentage is not deductible. If you are an employee, all of the interest is considered personal interest and is not deductible even if you use the vehicle 100% of the time for your job.

**Taxes paid on your car.** The business portion of sales taxes paid on your vehicle is not deductible whether you are an employee or self-employed; the tax is added to the basis of the vehicle for depreciation purposes *(43.3)*.

If you are an employee, state and local vehicle registration and license fees may be deducted as personal property taxes if you itemize deductions on Schedule A, but only if they are based on the value of the vehicle *(16.8)* (and subject to the $10,000 cap on state and local taxes *(16.1)*). If you are self-employed, deduct the business portion of the personal property taxes on Schedule C and the personal percentage on Schedule A if you itemize (subject to the $10,000 cap on state and local taxes).

**Leased vehicle.** If you lease a car, truck, or van for business use and do not claim the IRS mileage allowance *(43.1)*, you deduct the lease payments plus other costs of operating the vehicle. If the vehicle is also used for personal driving, the lease payments must be allocated between business and personal mileage. The rules requiring a reduction in the deduction for lease payments are discussed later in this chapter *(43.12)*.

## 43.3 Depreciation Restrictions on Cars, Trucks, and Vans

The law contains restrictions on so-called "listed property" that limit and, in some cases, deny depreciation deductions for a business car, truck, or van. Self-employed individuals must determine if they can use accelerated MACRS rates or must use straight-line rates. Finally, regardless of which depreciation method is used, the annual deduction may not exceed a ceiling set by law for passenger cars and certain light trucks and vans; details on the annual ceilings are in *43.4*.

**EXAMPLE**

Theodore bought a truck on March 4, 2018, for $40,000, which is used 100% for business. Theodore's MACRS deduction *(43.5)* using the 200% declining balance method and the half-year convention under *Table 43-4* is $8,000 ($40,000 × .20 first-year rate).

**More-than-50%-business-use test for claiming expensing or accelerated MACRS depreciation.** Automobiles and other vehicles used to transport persons or goods are considered "listed property" *(42.10)*, but there are exceptions for ambulances, hearses, and trucks or vans that are qualified non-personal-use vehicles *(43.4)*. Unless the vehicle is excepted from the listed property rules, you must use the vehicle more than 50% of the time for business in the year you place it in service in order to claim bonus depreciation, first-year expensing or accelerated MACRS *(43.5)*. The annual ceiling, if applicable *(43.4)*, applies to the total of any bonus allowance, first-year expensing and MACRS depreciation.

If you meet the more-than-50%-business-use test in the year you place the vehicle in service but in a later year within the recovery period your business use falls to 50% or less, you must use straight-line depreciation and recapture "excess" deductions for prior years; *see* the Caution on this page and *43.10*.

If business use is 50% or less in the year the vehicle is placed in service, bonus depreciation, first-year expensing and accelerated MACRS are barred; depreciation must be claimed over a six-year period under the straight-line method. Technically, the recovery period is five years but the period is extended to six years because, in the first year, a convention rule limits the deductible percentage. *See* Tables 43-6 and 43-7 *(43.6)*. The straight-line method must be used for the entire recovery period, even if business use in the years after the first year exceeds 50%.

---

**EXAMPLE**

Jeremy bought a truck on March 4, 2018, for $40,000, but business use is 40%. His basis for depreciation is $10,000 ($40,000 × 40% business use). Jeremy cannot use accelerated depreciation. His depreciation allowance for 2018 under the straight-line method is $1,000 ($10,000 × .10 first-year rate).

---

If a vehicle is used for both business and investment purposes, only business use is considered in determining whether you meet the more-than-50%-business-use test and therefore qualify for MACRS. However, investment use is added to business use in determining your actual deduction.

**Do your employees use the vehicle?** In certain cases, an employer who provides a vehicle to employees as part of their compensation may be unable to count the employee's use as qualified business use, thereby preventing the employer from meeting the more-than-50%-business-use test for claiming MACRS. An employer is allowed to treat the employee's use as qualified business use only if: (1) the employee is not a relative and does not own more than 5% of the business and (2) the employer treats the fair market value of the employee's personal use of the vehicle as wage income and withholds tax on that amount. If such income is reported, all of the employee's use, including personal use, may be counted by an employer as qualified business use.

If an employee owning more than a 5% interest is allowed use of a company-owned vehicle as part of his or her compensation, the employer may not count that use as qualified business use, even if the personal use is reported as income. The same strict rule applies if the vehicle is provided to a person who is related to the employer.

## 43.4 Annual Ceilings on Depreciation

Annual ceilings limit the amount of depreciation you may deduct for passenger cars, light trucks, and vans. As a result of the ceilings, the actual write-off period for your car may be several years longer than the MACRS recovery period of six years *(43.5)*.

Year-by-year limits for vehicles placed in service in 2018 and prior years can be found in *Table 43.2* (cars) and *Table 43-3* (trucks and vans).

**Vehicles weighing 6,000 pounds or less (cars, trucks, or vans).** The ceiling on depreciation for a vehicle placed in service in 2018 is generally $10,000, reduced by personal use. If the vehicle is used more than 50% for business in 2018, the first-year dollar limit is increased by the bonus depreciation allowance to $18,000, reduced by personal use. For purposes of the annual depreciation ceilings, a car is any four-wheeled vehicle that is manufactured primarily for use on public thoroughfares and that is weight-rated by the manufacturer at 6,000 pounds or less when unloaded (without passengers or cargo), or, in the case of trucks or vans, 6,000 pounds or less gross vehicle weight. However, the following vehicles are exempt from the annual depreciation limits: (1) an ambulance, hearse, or combination ambulance-hearse used directly in a business; (2) a vehicle such as a taxi cab used directly in the business of transporting persons or property for compensation or hire; and (3) qualified non-personal-use vehicles discussed below.

**Caution**

**Recapture of MACRS Deductions**

If you meet the more-than-50% test in the year the car or other vehicle is placed in service, which entitles you to claim bonus depreciation, first-year expensing, or accelerated MACRS, but business use falls to 50% or less in a later year within the recovery period, you become subject to straight-line depreciation and recapture rules *(43.10)* apply.

**Filing Tip**

**Claiming First-Year Expensing or Depreciation for Your Car**

First-year expensing or depreciation (under the 200% or 150% declining balance method, or the straight-line method) is claimed on Form 4562 and then entered on Schedule C of Form 1040 if you are self employed.

**Non-personal-use vehicles.** The depreciation limits do not apply to trucks and vans that are qualified non-personal-use vehicles. These include moving vans, flatbed trucks, and delivery trucks with seating only for the driver (or driver seat plus folding jump seat). Also included are specially modified trucks and vans that are unlikely to be used more than a minimal amount for personal purposes. An example would be a van that has been painted to display advertising or the company's name and which has permanent shelving for carrying merchandise or equipment.

**Heavy trucks, vans, and SUVs.** Trucks, vans, and SUVs built on a truck chassis that are weight-rated by the manufacturer at more than 6,000 pounds gross vehicle weight are not subject to the annual depreciation ceilings. However, first-year expensing *(42.3)* for the vehicle may be limited to $25,000 rather than the general expensing limit, which for 2018 is $1 million *(42.3)*. The vehicle must be used more than 50% for business to qualify for first-year expensing. If first-year expensing is not or cannot be elected *(42.3)*, a full depreciation deduction using the MACRS rate *(43.5)* is allowed with no dollar limit. *Further, if bought and placed in service in 2018 and used over 50% for business, 100% bonus depreciation can be used. In effect, the cost of a heavy SUV bought and placed in service in 2018 can be fully deducted.*

The $25,000 limit on first-year expensing applies to SUVs rated at more than 6,000 pounds but not more than 14,000 pounds gross vehicle weight. For purposes of the $25,000 expensing limit, an SUV means any four-wheeled vehicle primarily designed or which can be used to carry passengers over public thoroughfares. Trucks and vans as well as SUVs can be covered by this definition, but the law allows certain exceptions. Exceptions are allowed for vehicles with seating for more than nine passengers behind the driver, for pickup trucks with an interior cargo bed at least six feet long that is an open area or is enclosed by a cap and not readily accessible to passengers, and cargo vans without rear seating and with no body sections protruding more than 30 inches ahead of the windshield. For these excepted vehicles, the $25,000 limit on first-year expensing does not apply.

## 43.5 MACRS Rates for Cars, Trucks, and Vans

Business autos, trucks, and vans are technically in a five-year MACRS class *(42.4)*, but because of the half-year or mid-quarter convention, the MACRS recovery period for five-year property is six years, and because of the annual deduction ceilings *(43.4,* and *Tables 43-2* and *43-3* below), the actual write-off period may be years longer.

*Filing Tip*

**Capital Improvements**

A capital improvement to a business vehicle is depreciable under MACRS in the year the improvement is made. The MACRS deductions for the improvement and the vehicle are considered as a unit for purposes of applying the limits on the annual MACRS depreciation deduction.

**Accelerated MACRS rate allowed only if business use in the first year exceeds 50%.** To use accelerated MACRS rates, you must meet the more-than-50%-business-use test *(43.3)* in the year the vehicle is placed in business service. Generally, the accelerated MACRS rate is based on the 200% declining balance method, but as shown on *Table 43-4* (half-year convention) or *Table 43-5* (mid-quarter convention), a 150% declining balance rate may be elected, which may be advantageous when you are subject to the alternative minimum tax *(23.2)*.

The deduction allowed under *Table 43-4* or *Table 43-5* using accelerated MACRS rates applies only to the extent it does not exceed the annual depreciation ceiling shown in *Table 43-2* or *Table 43-3*. Bonus depreciation increases the first-year ceiling for vehicles that are used over 50% for business, unless you elect on your return not to claim bonus depreciation *(42.18)*; *see Table 43-2* and *Table 43-3*. The limits from the tables must be further reduced for personal use.

If you do not meet the more-than-50%-business-use test in the year the vehicle is placed in service, you must compute your depreciation deductions using the straight-line rates shown in *43.6*, subject to the annual depreciation limit.

**Deductions for later years in the recovery period.** For years two through six of the recovery period, the MACRS rate from *Table 43-4* or *Table 43-5* is used unless business use for a year falls to 50% or less *(43.10)*. However, the deduction figured under the MACRS table is allowed only if it does not exceed the annual depreciation ceiling *(43.4)* shown in *Table*

43-2 or *Table 43-3*; *see* the Bill Johnston Example at the end of this section. See below for details on using the MACRS tables.

*Caution:* If you used the 100% bonus depreciation rule for vehicles placed in service after September 8, 2010, and before 2012 to increase your first-year depreciation deduction and you still own this vehicle, you must use an IRS safe harbor to figure your deductions starting in the second recovery year, as explained in Revenue Procedure 2011-26. The same issue applies to vehicles placed in service after September 27, 2017, where the 100% bonus depreciation rule applies. The IRS is expected to issue the same safe harbor contained in Revenue Procedure 2011-26 but has yet to do so; *see* the *e-Supplement* at *jklasser.com* for any update.

**Deduction for year of disposition.** If you dispose of your vehicle before the end of the six-year MACRS recovery period, a partial-year deduction is allowed for the year of disposition under the half-year or mid-quarter convention *(43.7)*.

**Use of vehicle after end of recovery period.** If you continue to use the vehicle for business after the end of the recovery period, and the annual deduction ceilings prevented you from deducting your full unadjusted basis during the recovery period, you generally may deduct depreciation in the succeeding years up to the annual ceiling *(43.8)*.

**Business use falls to 50% or less after the first year.** What if business use exceeds 50% in the year the vehicle is placed in service but in a later year within the recovery period business use drops to 50% or lower? In that case, the right to use accelerated MACRS (200% or 150% declining balance method) terminates. You must use the straight-line method and recapture the benefit of the accelerated deductions claimed for the prior years *(43.10)*.

**Straight-line election for vehicle if business use exceeds 50%.** If business use of your vehicle exceeds 50% in the year you place it in service, you may elect to write off your cost under the straight-line method *(43.6)* instead of using the regular MACRS 200% declining balance method. The straight-line deduction is limited by the annual ceilings shown in Tables 43-2 and 43-3. By electing straight-line depreciation, you avoid the recapture of excess MACRS deductions if business use drops to 50% or less in a later year *(43.10)*. If the election is made, you must also use the straight-line method for all other five-year property placed in service during the same year as the vehicle.

**Electing 150% declining balance method.** Depreciation rates under the half-year and mid-quarter conventions are generally based on the 200% declining balance method. You may instead make an irrevocable election to apply the 150% declining balance method. The 150% method may be advantageous when you are subject to the alternative minimum tax. For alternative minimum tax (AMT) purposes *(23.2)*, vehicle depreciation is based on the 150% declining balance method unless you use the straight-line method for regular tax purposes. If you are subject to AMT and use the 150% declining balance method instead of the 200% declining balance method for regular tax purposes, you do not have to report an AMT adjustment on Form 6251.

An election to use the 150% declining balance method is irrevocable and must be applied to all depreciable assets placed in service in the same year, except for nonresidential real and residential rental property.

## MACRS Tables Applying the Half-Year Convention or Mid-Quarter Convention if Business Use Exceeds 50%

For the year you place the vehicle in service and the year (within the recovery period) you dispose of the property, you may not claim a full year's worth of depreciation. The deduction is limited by either the half-year convention or the mid-quarter convention, depending on the month in which the vehicle was placed in service and the other business assets, if any, placed in service during that year.

The applicable convention determines the rate table you will use to figure your depreciation deduction for the entire six-year recovery period, assuming that your business use each year exceeds 50%. The half-year and mid-quarter convention rates shown in *Table 43-4* or *Table 43-5* reflect the 200% or 150% declining balance method, with a switch to the straight-line method when that method provides a larger deduction; the switch to straight line is built into the tables.

**Rate applied to unadjusted basis.** For each year in the recovery period, the rate from MACRS *Table 43-4* or *Table 43-5* is applied against the business use percentage of your unadjusted basis for the vehicle. The deduction figured using the table rate may be claimed to the extent that it does not exceed the annual depreciation ceiling (*Table 43-2* or *Table 43-3*); *see* the Bill Johnston Example on the next page. Investment use may be added to the business use percentage, but keep in mind that the MACRS table may be used only if business use by itself exceeds 50% *(43.3)*.

Unadjusted basis is your cost minus any first-year expensing deduction as well as any special first-year bonus depreciation (for a vehicle placed into service after September 10, 2001, and before January 1, 2005, and during 2008 through September 27, 2017). The basis reduction for bonus depreciation applies if you were eligible for the special allowance (vehicle purchased new and used over 50% for business) even if you did not claim it, unless on your return you "elected out" of the special allowance for the vehicle and all other five-year property placed in service during the same year.

**Basis for vehicle converted from personal to business use.** The basis for depreciation is the lower of the fair market value of the vehicle at the time of conversion or its adjusted basis, which is your original cost plus any substantial improvements and minus any deductible casualty losses or diesel fuel tax credit claimed for the vehicle. In most cases, the value of the vehicle will be lower than adjusted basis, and thus the value will be your depreciable basis. For a vehicle converted to business use in 2018, the MACRS rate is applied to basis allocated to business travel. Unless you have mileage records for the entire year, you should base your business-use percentage on driving after the conversion. For example, in April 2018, you started to use your car for business and in the last nine months of the year you drove 10,000 miles, 8,000 of which were for business. This business percentage of 80% is multiplied by the fraction 9/12 (months used for business divided by 12) to give you a business-use percentage for the year of 60% (9/12 of 80%).

**Determining whether the half-year convention or mid-quarter convention applies.** If you bought a vehicle for use in your business in 2018, and it was the only business equipment placed in service during the year, then the half-year convention applies, unless you bought the vehicle in the last quarter of 2018 (October, November, or December). Under the half-year convention, the vehicle is treated as if it were placed in service in the middle of the year. Use *Table 43-4* below to determine your deduction under the half-year convention.

If the only business equipment bought in 2018 was a vehicle bought in the last quarter (October, November, or December), the mid-quarter convention applies. Under *Table 43-5* for the mid-quarter convention, a 5% rate applies under the 200% declining balance method for a vehicle purchased in the fourth quarter, subject to the deduction ceiling in 2018 (*Table 43-2* or *Table 43-3*).

If you bought other business equipment in addition to the vehicle, you must consider the total cost basis of property placed in service during the last quarter of 2018. If the total bases of such acquisitions (other than realty) exceed 40% of the total bases of all property placed in service during the year, then a mid-quarter rate applies to all of the property (other than realty). The mid-quarter rate for each asset then depends on the quarter the asset was placed in service, and that quarter determines the mid-quarter rates for each year of the recovery period; *see Table 43-5*. If the 40% test is not met, then the half-year convention *(Table 43-4)* applies to all the property acquisitions.

## Deduction from MACRS Tables Cannot Exceed Annual Ceiling

If the deduction figured under the half-year or mid-quarter convention MACRS table (*Table 43-4* or *43-5*), or the straight-line table (*Table 43-6* or *43-7*), exceeds the annual deduction ceiling (*Table 43-2* or *43-3*), your deduction is limited to the annual ceiling, reduced by the percentage of your personal use; *see* the Bill Johnston Example below.

Keep in mind that if you were eligible for the special first-year depreciation allowance (bonus depreciation) for a vehicle placed in service after September 10, 2001, and before January 1, 2005 and during 2008 through September 27, 2017, basis for MACRS purposes is reduced by the special allowance unless you elected on your return not to claim it.

If you used bonus depreciation for a vehicle placed in service after September 8, 2010, and before 2012, and you still own the vehicle, you cannot claim any deduction in years two through six unless you use an IRS safe harbor explained in Revenue Procedure 2011-26. The same is true for a vehicle placed in service after September 27, 2017, assuming the IRS agrees to have this safe harbor rule apply; *see* the *e-Supplement* at *jklasser.com* for any update.

---

**EXAMPLE**

On May 3, 2014, Bill Johnston placed in service a new car that cost $20,000, which he used 100% for business for the rest of 2014. He did not claim first-year expensing and "elected out" of bonus depreciation. Bill continued to use the car 100% for business through 2017. In 2018 and 2019, he uses it 75% of the time for business. Here is Bill's depreciation schedule for the six-year recovery period, using the 200% declining balance rate as limited by the annual ceilings.

For years after 2019, Bill can deduct his "unrecovered basis," but the amount of unrecovered basis is figured as if there had been 100% business use during the entire six-year recovery period (43.8).

| Year | Deduction from MACRS (Table 43-4) | Annual ceiling (Table 43-2) | Allowable deduction |
|------|-----------------------------------|-----------------------------|---------------------|
| 2014 | $ 4,000 (20% × $20,000) | $ 3,160 | $ 3,160 |
| 2015 | 6,400 (32% × $20,000) | 5,100 | 5,100 |
| 2016 | 3,840 (19.20% × $20,000) | 3,050 | 3,050 |
| 2017 | 2,304 (11.52% × $20,000) | 1,875 | 1,875 |
| 2018 | 1,728 (11.52% × $20,000) × 75%) | 1,406 ($1,875 × 75%) | 1,406 |
| 2019* | 864 (5.76% × $20,000 × 75%) | 1,406 ($1,875 × 75%) | 864 |

*Note that for the first five years (2014 – 2018), the allowable deduction is limited to the annual ceiling but for year six (2019), the deduction is based on the MACRS rate table because $864 (5.76% × $20,000 × 75% business use) is less than the $1,406 annual ceiling ($1,875 × 75% business use).

---

### Table 43-2  Maximum Depreciation Deduction for Cars
(The ceiling must be reduced for personal use.)

| Year Placed In Service | 1st Year | 2nd Year | 3rd Year | 4th and Later Years |
|------------------------|----------|----------|----------|---------------------|
| 2018 | $18,000[1] | $16,000 | $9,600 | $5,760 |
| 2012 – 2017 | 11,160[2] | 5,100 | 3,050 | 1,875 |
| 2010 and 2011 | 11,060[3] | 4,900 | 2,950 | 1,775 |

[1] $10,000 if the car does not qualify for the bonus allowance, or if you elect not to claim bonus depreciation.
[2] $3,160 if the car does not qualify for the bonus allowance, or if you elect not to claim bonus depreciation.
[3] $3,060 if the car does not qualify for the bonus allowance, or if you elect not to claim bonus depreciation.

## Table 43-3 Maximum Depreciation Deduction for Trucks and Vans
### (The ceiling must be reduced for personal use.)

| Year Placed In Service | 1st Year | 2nd Year | 3rd Year | 4th and Later Years |
|---|---|---|---|---|
| 2018 | $18,000[1] | $16,000 | $9,600 | $5,760 |
| 2017 | 11,560[2] | 5,700 | 3,450 | 2,075 |
| 2016 | 11,560[2] | 5,700 | 3,350 | 2,075 |
| 2015 | 11,460[3] | 5,600 | 3,350 | 1,975 |
| 2014 | 11,460[3] | 5,500 | 3,350 | 1,975 |
| 2013 | 11,360[4] | 5,400 | 3,250 | 1,975 |
| 2012 | 11,360[4] | 5,300 | 3,150 | 1,875 |
| 2011 | 11,260[5] | 5,200 | 3,150 | 1,875 |
| 2010 | 11,160[6] | 5,100 | 3,050 | 1,875 |

[1] $10,000 if the vehicle does not qualify for the bonus allowance, or if you elect not to claim bonus depreciation.
[2] $3,560 if the vehicle does not qualify for the bonus allowance, or if you elect not to claim bonus depreciation.
[3] $3,460 if the vehicle does not qualify for the bonus allowance, or if you elect not to claim bonus depreciation.
[4] $3,360 if the vehicle does not qualify for the bonus allowance, or if you elect not to claim bonus depreciation.
[5] $3,260 if the vehicle does not qualify for the bonus allowance, or if you elect not to claim bonus depreciation.
[6] $3,160 if the vehicle does not qualify for the bonus allowance, or if you elect not to claim bonus depreciation.

## Table 43-4 MACRS Deduction: Half-Year Convention

| Year— | 200% Rate | 150% Rate |
|---|---|---|
| 1 | 20.00% | 15.00% |
| 2 | 32.00 | 25.50 |
| 3 | 19.20 | 17.85 |
| 4 | 11.52 | 16.66 |
| 5 | 11.52 | 16.66 |
| 6 | 5.76 | 8.33 |

## Table 43-5 MACRS Deduction: Mid-Quarter Convention

Placed in service in—

| Year— | First Quarter | | Second Quarter | | Third Quarter | | Fourth Quarter | |
|---|---|---|---|---|---|---|---|---|
| | 200% Rate | 150% Rate | 200% Rate | 150% Rate | 200% Rate | 150% Rate | 200% Rate | 150% Rate |
| 1 | 35.00% | 26.25% | 25.00% | 18.75% | 15.00% | 11.25% | 5.00% | 3.75% |
| 2 | 26.00 | 22.13 | 30.00 | 24.38 | 34.00 | 26.63 | 38.00 | 28.88 |
| 3 | 15.60 | 16.52 | 18.00 | 17.06 | 20.40 | 18.64 | 22.80 | 20.21 |
| 4 | 11.01 | 16.52 | 11.37 | 16.76 | 12.24 | 16.56 | 13.68 | 16.40 |
| 5 | 11.01 | 16.52 | 11.37 | 16.76 | 11.30 | 16.57 | 10.94 | 16.41 |
| 6 | 1.38 | 2.06 | 4.26 | 6.29 | 7.06 | 10.35 | 9.58 | 14.35 |

## 43.6 Straight-Line Method

You may not use first-year expensing (Section 179 deduction), bonus depreciation, or accelerated MACRS *(43.5)* if your business use of your car, truck, or van is 50% or less in the year you place it in service; only business use is considered here, not investment use. Mandatory straight-line recovery rates for business use of 50% or less using the half-year or mid-quarter convention are shown below. These straight-line rates are also used if your business use exceeds 50% and you elect straight-line recovery instead of the regular MACRS method. *See* the preceding section *(43.5)* for determining whether the half-year or mid-quarter convention applies.

For each year of the six-year recovery period, apply the straight-line rate from the applicable table against your unadjusted basis, which is the business part of your cost minus any first-year expensing deduction or special bonus depreciation allowance *(43.5)*. Investment use may be added to the business use part of cost when figuring the straight-line deduction for each year. The deduction from the table is allowed only to the extent that it does not exceed the annual deduction ceiling (*Table 43-2* or *Table 43-3*).

If business use initially exceeds 50% and accelerated MACRS is claimed but business use drops to 50% or less before the end of the six-year recovery period, a recapture rule applies a straight-line computation retroactively *(43.10)*.

### Table 43-6 Straight-Line Half-Year Convention*

| Straight-line year— | Half-year convention rate— |
|---|---|
| 1 | 10% |
| 2 | 20 |
| 3 | 20 |
| 4 | 20 |
| 5 | 20 |
| 6 | 10 |

*The deduction may not exceed the annual deduction ceiling (*Table 43-2* or *43-3*).

**EXAMPLE**

In April 2018, you place in service a used automobile which cost $24,000. You used it 40% for business. The depreciable basis is $9,600 (40% of $24,000). The straight-line depreciation deduction for 2018 is $960 (10% of $9,600) if the half-year convention applies. It is less than the annual deduction ceiling of $7,200 (40% of the $18,000 first-year ceiling for 2018; *see Table 43-2*).

### Table 43-7 Straight-Line Mid-Quarter Convention*

Placed in service in—

| Year | First Quarter | Second Quarter | Third Quarter | Fourth Quarter |
|---|---|---|---|---|
| 1 | 17.50% | 12.50% | 7.50% | 2.50% |
| 2 | 20.00 | 20.00 | 20.00 | 20.00 |
| 3 | 20.00 | 20.00 | 20.00 | 20.00 |
| 4 | 20.00 | 20.00 | 20.00 | 20.00 |
| 5 | 20.00 | 20.00 | 20.00 | 20.00 |
| 6 | 2.50 | 7.50 | 12.50 | 17.50 |

*The deduction may not exceed the annual deduction ceiling (*Table 43-2 or 43-3*).

> **EXAMPLE**
>
> In 2018, you place in service a used car costing $15,000 that you used 40% for business. Assume the mid-quarter convention applies. Depending on the quarter placed in service, the deduction is listed below, figured on a basis of $6,000 ($15,000 × 40%). The first-year depreciation ceiling (see *Table 43-2*) at 40% business use is $4,000 ($10,000 × 40%). The $4,000 ceiling does not apply because the mid-quarter rates provide a lower deduction.
>
> | Quarter | Deduction |
> |---------|-----------|
> | 1 | $1,050 ($6,000 × 17.5%) |
> | 2 | 750 ($6,000 × 12.5%) |
> | 3 | 450 ($6,000 × 7.5%) |
> | 4 | 150 ($6,000 × 2.5%) |

## 43.7 Depreciation for Year Vehicle Is Disposed of

If you dispose of your car, truck, or van before the end of the six-year recovery period, you are allowed a partial depreciation deduction for the year of disposition. The deduction depends on the depreciation method and convention being used.

If you were depreciating the vehicle under the half-year convention *(43.5)*, you may claim for the year of disposition 50% of the deduction that would be allowed for the full year under the 200% or 150% declining balance method *(Table 43-4)*, or the straight-line method *(Table 43-6)*.

If you were depreciating the vehicle under the mid-quarter convention *(43.5)*, your deduction for the year of disposition depends on the month of disposition. You deduct 87.5% of the full-year mid-quarter convention deduction (from *Table 43-5* or *Table 43-7*) if the disposition occurred in October–December. If the disposition is in July–September, 62.5% of the full year's deduction is allowed. Your deduction is 37.5% of the full-year deduction if the disposition is in April–June, or 12.5% of the full-year deduction if the disposition is in January–March.

> **EXAMPLE**
>
> In December 2014 you bought a used car costing $20,000 that you used exclusively for business until you sold it in April 2018. You depreciated the car under the mid-quarter convention and the 200% rate *(Table 43-5)*.
>
> For 2018, the year of disposition, the full-year deduction would be $1,875, the annual ceiling for the fifth year under *Table 43-2* for a car placed in service in 2014. The annual ceiling of $1,875 applies because it is less than the $2,188 deduction (10.94% × $20,000) allowed for the fifth year under the mid-quarter convention table *(Table 43-5)* for fourth quarter property using the 200% rate. Since the car was disposed of in April, you may deduct 37.5% of $1,875, or $703, on your 2018 return.

## 43.8 Depreciation After Recovery Period Ends

If your business use of a car, truck, or van throughout the six-year recovery period is 100% and your deductions are limited by the annual ceilings *(43.4)*, any remaining basis that was not deducted because of the ceilings, called "unrecovered basis", may be depreciated in the years after the end of the recovery period. The maximum you can deduct each year will be the deduction ceiling for that year multiplied by your business use percentage.

If the vehicle was used less than 100% for business during the recovery period, your "unrecovered basis" is deductible in later years, but to determine unrecovered basis, original basis must be reduced by the depreciation that would have been allowed had the vehicle been used 100% for business.

## EXAMPLE

In January 2012 you bought a used car costing $28,600 that you used 100% for business every year from 2012 through 2017. You elected not to claim first-year expensing for 2012 and bonus depreciation was not available because the car was used. Your depreciation deductions for the six-year recovery period under the 200% declining balance method *(Table 43-4)* were limited because of the annual deduction ceilings *(Table 43-2)*. For 2012 through 2016, you deducted the annual ceiling amounts. For 2017, your deduction ($1,647) was based on the MACRS half-year convention rate table *(Table 43-4)* because this amount was less than the annual ceiling ($1,875). Total allowable depreciation deductions for 2012–2017 were $16,707 as shown below.

| Year | 200% rate deduction (Table 43-4) | Annual ceiling (Table 43-2) | Allowable deduction |
|------|----------------------------------|-----------------------------|---------------------|
| 2012 | $5,720 (20% × $28,600) | $ 3,160 | $ 3,160 |
| 2013 | 9,152 (32% × $28,600) | 5,100 | 5,100 |
| 2014 | 5,491 (19.20% × $28,600) | 3,050 | 3,050 |
| 2015 | 3,295 (11.52% × $28,600) | 1,875 | 1,875 |
| 2016 | 3,295 (11.52% × $28,600) | 1,875 | 1,875 |
| 2017 | 1,647 (5.76% × $28,600) | 1,875 | 1,647 |

At the beginning of 2018, your unrecovered basis in the car is $11,893 (the original basis of $28,600 minus the $16,707 of depreciation deductions allowed from 2012 through 2017). If you continue to use the car 100% for business in 2018 and later years, you can deduct $1,875 in 2018 and also in later years until the $11,893 of unrecovered basis is used up. In years of partial business use, the deduction will be limited to $1,875 multiplied by the business-use percentage.

If your business use percentage was not 100% for the entire six-year recovery period, your unrecovered basis as of the beginning of 2018 would still be $11,893. That is because for purposes of figuring unrecovered basis, you must reduce original basis by the depreciation that would have been allowed based on 100% business use. Even if you actually deducted less than $16,707 from 2012 through 2017, you still must reduce your $28,600 basis by $16,707, leaving you with an unrecovered basis of $11,893 that can be depreciated starting in 2018.

## 43.9 Trade-in of Business Vehicle

For trade-ins before 2018, you were able to avoid recognition of gain, but this rule no longer applies. If you trade in your business vehicle in 2018, you must figure gain on the trade-in. In effect, whether you sell or trade in your old vehicle, the tax result is the same. This is the difference between what you receive (an allowance toward the purchase of a new vehicle) and the adjusted basis of the vehicle you trade in.

### Example

In 2018, you trade in a truck that you bought for $32,000 for which you've claimed depreciation totaling $22,285. Your adjusted basis is $9,715 ($32,000 - $22,285). If the allowance toward the purchase of a new truck is $12,000, you must report a gain of $2,285 ($12,000 - $9,715).

## 43.10 Recapture of Deductions on Business Car, Truck, or Van

If you use your car, truck, or van more than 50% for business in the year you place it in service, you may use MACRS accelerated rates *(43.5)*. If business use drops to 50% or less in the second, third, fourth, fifth, or sixth year, earlier MACRS deductions must be

 *Planning Pointer*

**Sell the vehicle rather than trade it in**

You get the same tax treatment whether you sell the vehicle or trade it in. But you may be able to receive more through a sale to a third party than the trade-in allowance from a car dealer.

recaptured and reported as ordinary income. In the year in which business use drops to 50% or less, you must recapture excess depreciation for all prior years. Excess depreciation is the difference between: (1) the MACRS deductions allowed in previous years, including the first-year expensing deduction and bonus first-year depreciation allowance *(43.4)*, if any, and (2) the amount of depreciation that would have been allowed if you claimed straight-line depreciation *(43.6)* based on a six-year recovery period.

---

### EXAMPLE

On June 28, 2014, you bought a used car for $11,000 that you used exclusively for business in 2014, 2015, 2016, and 2017. The half-year convention applied to your MACRS deductions *(43.5)*. The deductions figured under the half-year convention table *(Table 43-4)* were $2,200 for 2014 (20% rate), $3,520 for 2015 (32% rate), $2,112 for 2016 (19.20% rate), and $1,267 for 2017 (11.52% rate). These were the allowable amounts because they were less than the annual ceilings for those years ($3,160, $5,100, $3,050, and $1,875, respectively under *Table 43-2*). During 2018, you used the car 40% for business and 60% for personal purposes. As you did not meet the more-than-50%-business-use test in 2018, excess depreciation of $1,724 is recaptured and reported on Form 4797 for 2018:

| | | |
|---|---|---|
| Total MACRS depreciation claimed (2014–2017) | | $9,099 |
| Total straight-line depreciation (*Table 43-6* at *43.6*) allowable: | | |
| 2014—lesser of 10% of $11,000 or annual ceiling of $3,160 = | $1,100 | |
| 2015—lesser of 20% of $11,000 or annual ceiling of $5,100 = | $2,200 | |
| 2016—lesser of 20% of $11,000 or annual ceiling of $3,050 = | $2,200 | |
| 2017—lesser of 20% of $11,000 or annual ceiling of $1,875 = | $1,875 | |
| | | $7,375 |
| Excess depreciation recaptured ($9,099 – $7,375) | | $1,724 |

Your 2018 depreciation deduction is $710. The straight-line deduction from *Table 43-6* would be $880 ($11,000 × 20% straight-line rate in fifth year × 40% business use). However, the deduction is limited to the reduced annual ceiling of $750 ($1,875 ceiling × 40% business use).

The amount of recaptured depreciation increases the adjusted basis for purposes of computing gain or loss on a disposition of the automobile.

---

The recapture rules do not apply if you elected straight-line recovery instead of applying accelerated MACRS rates.

Recapture is reported on Form 4797, which must be attached to Form 1040. Under the listed property rules, the 50%-business-use test and recapture rule apply to cars, trucks, vans, boats, airplanes, motorcycles, and other vehicles used to transport persons or goods, but there are exceptions for ambulances, hearses, and other trucks and vans that are considered qualified non-personal-use vehicles *(43.4)*.

Any recaptured amount increases the adjusted basis of the property for purposes of figuring gain or loss when you dispose of the vehicle. To compute depreciation for the year in which business use drops to 50% or less and for later years within the six-year straight-line recovery period, you apply the straight-line rates *(43.6)* to your original cost (unadjusted basis) and business use percentage, but the deduction may be limited by the annual ceiling for that year (*Table 43-2* or *Table 43-3*); *see* the Example above in this section.

## 43.11  Keeping Records of Business Use

Keep a log or diary or similar record of the business use of a car. You can also find an app for your smartphone or other mobile device to keep track of your business mileage. Record the purpose of the business trips and mileage covered for business travel. In the record book or electronic record, also note the odometer reading for the beginning and end of the taxable year. You need this data to prove business use. If you do not keep written records of business mileage and your return is examined, you will have to convince an IRS agent of your business mileage through oral testimony. Without written evidence, you may be unable to convince an IRS agent that you use the car for business travel or that you meet the business-use tests for claiming MACRS. You may also be subject to general negligence penalties for claiming deductions that you cannot prove you incurred.

Unless you are electing the standard mileage rate *(43.1)*, mileage records are not required for vehicles that are unlikely to be used for personal purposes, such as delivery trucks with seating only for the driver.

## 43.12  Leased Business Vehicles: Deductions and Income

If you lease rather than purchase a car, truck, or van for business use, you may deduct the lease charges as a business expense deduction if you use the vehicle exclusively for business. If you also use the vehicle for personal driving, you may deduct only the lease payments allocated to business travel. Also keep a record of business use; *see 43.11*.

**Inclusion amount.** If in 2018 you lease a vehicle for 30 days or more, you may have to reduce the deduction for the lease payment based on an IRS table. This rule applies if you deduct the business portion of your lease payments plus other operating costs; it does not apply if you claim the standard mileage allowance *(43.1)*. On Schedule C (if self-employed), the inclusion amount reduces your deduction for lease payments similar to the way your depreciation deductions would have been limited if you had bought the vehicle outright. The income amount is reduced where you leased the vehicle for less than the entire year or business use is less than 100%. For vehicles first leased in 2018, there's no inclusion amount if the fair market value of the vehicle at the start of the lease is $50,000 or less.

The lease tables, which are in IRS Publication 463, show income amounts for each year of the lease. Publication 463 also has tables showing income amounts for vehicles leased before 2018.

*Planning Pointer*

**Apps for Tracking Mileage**

There are a number of free or low-cost apps for smartphones and tablets that can be used to record the necessary information for business driving.

*Caution*

**Leased Vehicle**

If in 2018 you leased a car, truck, or van for at least 30 days and you deduct the lease charges as a business expense *(43.12)*, you generally must reduce the deduction by an "income inclusion amount" based on an IRS table. If you claim the standard mileage allowance *(43.1)*, the income inclusion rule does not apply. *See* IRS Publication 463 for details.

# CHAPTER 44

# Sales of Business Property

On the sale of business assets, the tax treatment depends on the type of asset sold.

*Inventory items:* Profits are taxable as ordinary income; losses are fully deductible. Sales of merchandise are reported on Schedule C if you are self-employed or Schedule F if you are a farmer.

*Depreciable property, such as buildings, machinery, and equipment:* If you sell at a gain, the gain is taxable as ordinary income to the extent depreciation is recaptured *(44.1–44.2)*. Any remaining gain may be treated as capital gain or ordinary income, depending on the Section 1231 computation *(44.8)*. Losses may be deductible as ordinary losses *(44.8)*. Sales are reported on Form 4797. Depreciable business equipment subject to recapture is described as a Section 1245 asset. Depreciable livestock is also a Section 1245 asset. Depreciable realty is generally described as a Section 1250 asset.

*Land:* If used in your business, capital gain or ordinary income may be realized under the rules of Section 1231 *(44.8)*. If land owned by your business is held for investment, gain or loss is subject to capital gain treatment. Schedule D is used to report the sale of capital assets.

## 44.1 Depreciation Recaptured as Ordinary Income on Sale of Personal Property

On Form 4797, you report gain or loss on the sale of depreciable property. Gain realized on the sale of depreciable personal property (Section 1245 property) is treated as ordinary income to the extent the gain is attributed to depreciation deductions that reduced basis. In other words, the depreciation deductions are "recaptured" as ordinary income. If gain exceeds the amount of depreciation subject to recapture, the excess may be capital gain under Section 1231 *(44.8)*.

Gain on the sale of real estate placed in service before 1987 may be subject to depreciation recapture *(44.2)*.

Gain subject to recapture for Section 1245 property is limited to the lower of (1) the amount of gain on the sale (amount realized less adjusted basis) or (2) the depreciation allowed or allowable while you held the property. Generally, the depreciation deduction taken into account for each year is the amount allowed or allowable, whichever is greater. However, for purposes of figuring what portion of the gain is treated as ordinary income under the recapture rules (but not for purposes of figuring gain or loss), the depreciation taken into account for any year will be the amount actually "allowed" on your prior returns under a proper depreciation method, rather than the amount "allowable," if the allowed deduction is smaller and you can prove its amount.

The adjusted basis of personal property depreciable under ACRS, such as business equipment and machinery, is fixed as of the beginning of the year of disposition. However, property depreciated under MACRS is subject to the convention rules so that partial depreciation under the applicable convention is allowed in the year of sale; this year of sale depreciation reduces adjusted basis.

> **EXAMPLE**
>
> In March 2016, you bought and placed in service a light truck (five-year property) at a cost of $10,000. You used the truck 100% for business. You deducted depreciation under the half-year convention of $2,000 for 2016 and $3,200 for 2017; *see* the MACRS and dollar limits on depreciation for light trucks in *43.5.* In January 2018, you sold the truck for $6,000. For 2018, you are allowed an MACRS deduction of one-half of the full year deduction, or $960 (19.20% × $10,000 ÷ 2). Your adjusted basis is $3,840 ($10,000 cost – $6,160 total depreciation). Your gain on the sale is $2,160 ($6,000 proceeds – $3,840 adjusted basis). You must recapture the entire $2,160 gain as ordinary income, as it is less than the $6,160 depreciation.

## 44.2 Depreciation Recaptured as Ordinary Income on Sale of Real Estate

All or part of gain on the sale of depreciable real property may be attributable to depreciation deductions that reduced the basis of the property. On Form 4797, gain attributable to depreciation on Section 1250 realty placed in service before 1987 is subject to recapture as ordinary income unless straight-line depreciation was used. The amount of depreciation recapture depends on when the building was placed in service and whether it was residential or nonresidential; *see* below.

There is no ordinary income recapture for residential rental and nonresidential real property placed in service after 1986 because such properties are depreciated using the straight-line MACRS method *(42.13)*. Previously claimed bonus depreciation is subject to recapture.

To the extent depreciation is not subject to ordinary income recapture, the gain on the sale is subject to the Section 1231 netting rules *(44.8)*. If there is a net Section 1231 gain, the gain attributed to the depreciation is entered on the Unrecaptured Section 1250 Gain Worksheet in the Schedule D (Form 1040) instructions. The unrecaptured Section 1250 gain from that worksheet is subject to a top rate of 25% on the Schedule D Tax Worksheet included in the Schedule D instructions.

*Caution*

**Dispositions Other Than Sales**

Recapture rules affect gifts, charitable donations, and inheritances of depreciable property *(44.4)*, as well as like-kind exchanges and involuntary conversions *(44.5)*.

**Recaptured depreciation.** Ordinary income recapture may apply to Section 1250 realty placed in service before 1987. Section 1250 property includes buildings and structural components, except for elevators and escalators or other tangible property used as an integral part of manufacturing, production, or extraction, or of furnishing transportation, electrical energy, water, gas, sewage disposal services, or communications. Property may initially be Section 1250 property and then, on a change of use, become Section 1245 property *(44.1)*. Such property may not be reconverted to Section 1250 property.

**Depreciation claimed on realty placed in service after 1980 and before 1987.** For real property placed in service after 1980 and before 1987 that was subject to ACRS, adjusted basis for computing gain or loss is the adjusted basis at the start of the year reduced by the ACRS deduction, if any, allowed for the year of disposition (based on number of months the realty is in service in disposition year; *see 42.15*). The recapture rules distinguish between residential and nonresidential property.

If the prescribed accelerated method is used to recover the cost of nonresidential property, all gain on the disposition of the realty is recaptured as ordinary income to the extent of recovery allowances previously taken. Thus, nonresidential realty will be treated in the same way as personal property *(44.1)* for purposes of recapture if the accelerated recovery allowance was claimed. If the straight-line method was elected, there is no recapture; all gain is subject to the netting rules of Section 1231 *(44.8)*.

If accelerated cost recovery is used for a nonresidential building and straight-line depreciation is used for a substantial improvement to that building that you are allowed to depreciate separately *(42.15)*, all gain on a disposition of the entire building is treated as ordinary income to the extent of the accelerated cost recovery claimed. Remaining gain is subject to the rules for Section 1231 assets *(44.8)*.

For residential real estate, 100% of the excess depreciation claimed is subject to recapture. That is, there is ordinary income recapture to the extent the depreciation allowed under the prescribed accelerated method exceeds the recovery that would have been allowable if the straight-line method over the ACRS recovery period had been used. If the straight-line method was elected, there is no recapture. All gain is subject to Section 1231 netting *(44.8)*.

For low-income rental housing, the percentage of excess depreciation (over straight-line) subject to recapture is 100% minus 1% for each full month the property was held over 100 months, so there is no recapture of cost recovery deductions once the property was held at least 200 months (16 years and 8 months). If you dispose of low-income housing with separate improvements, or with units placed in service at different times, the amount of excess depreciation must be computed separately for each element. See IRS Publication 544 for details on the recapture rules for low-income housing.

Different recapture rules applied to depreciation on realty placed in service before 1981.

## 44.3 Recapture of First-Year Expensing

On Form 4797, the first-year expensing deduction (Section 179 deduction *(42.3)*) is treated as depreciation for purposes of recapture. When expensed property is sold or exchanged, gain is recaptured as ordinary income *(44.1)* to the extent of the first-year expense deduction plus ACRS or MACRS deductions and bonus depreciation *(42.20)*, if any. If the entire cost of the property was expensed, adjusted basis will generally be reduced to zero, gain on a sale or exchange will equal the sales price (less expenses), and the entire gain will be recaptured as ordinary income.

Expensing deductions are also subject to recapture if property placed in service after 1986 is not used more than 50% of the time for business in any year before the end of the recovery period. The amount recaptured is the excess of the first-year expensing deduction over the amount of depreciation that would have been claimed in prior years and in the recapture year without expensing.

**Automobiles and other "listed property."** If the more-than-50%-business-use test for a business automobile or other "listed property" *(42.10)* is not met in a year after the auto or other "listed property" is placed in service and before the end of the recovery period, any first-year expensing deduction is subject to recapture on Form 4797; *see* the Example at *43.10*.

## 44.4   Gifts and Inheritances of Depreciable Property

Gifts and charitable donations of depreciable property may be affected by the recapture rules. On the gift of depreciable property, the ordinary income potential of the depreciation carries over into the hands of the donee (the person who received the gift). When the donee later sells the property at a profit, he or she will realize ordinary income *(44.1)*.

On the donation of depreciable property, the amount of the charitable contribution deduction is reduced by the amount that would be taxed as ordinary income had the donor sold the equipment at its fair market value.

The transfer of depreciable property to an heir through inheritance is not a taxable event for recapture purposes. The ordinary income potential does not carry over to the heir because his or her basis is usually fixed as of the date of the decedent's death.

Important: A gift of depreciable property subject to a mortgage may be taxed to the extent that the liability exceeds the basis of the property *(14.6, 31.15)*.

## 44.5   Involuntary Conversions and Tax-Free Exchanges

**Involuntary conversions.**   Gain may be taxed as ordinary income in either of the following two cases: (1) you do not buy qualified replacement property or (2) you buy a qualified replacement, but the cost of the replacement is less than the amount realized on the conversion *(18.19)*. The amount taxable as ordinary income may not exceed the amount of gain that is normally taxed under involuntary conversion rules when the replacement cost is less than the amount realized on the conversion. Also, the amount of ordinary income is increased by the value of any nondepreciable property that is bought as qualified replacement property, such as the purchase of 80% or more of stock in a company that owns property similar to the converted property.

**Distributions by a partnership to a partner.**   A distribution of depreciable property by a partnership to a partner does not result in ordinary income to the distributee at the time of the distribution. But the partner assumes the ordinary income potential of the depreciation deduction taken by the partnership on the property. When he or she later disposes of the property, ordinary income may be realized.

## 44.6   Installment Sale of Depreciable Property

All depreciation recapture income (including the first-year expensing deduction) is fully taxable in the year of sale, without regard to the time of payment. Recapture is figured on Form 4797. On Form 6252, the gain in excess of the recapture income is reported under the installment method *(5.21)*.

## 44.7   Sale of a Proprietorship

The sale of a sole proprietorship is not considered as the sale of a business unit but as sales of individual business assets. Each sale is reported separately on your tax return.

A purchase of a business involves the purchase of various individual business assets of the business. To force buyers and sellers to follow the same allocation rules, current law requires both the buyer and the seller to allocate the purchase price of a business among the transferred assets using a residual method formula. Allocations are based on the proportion of sales price to an asset's fair market value and they are made in a specific order set out on Form 8594.

Caution

**Installment Sale**

If you sell property on the installment basis, the first-year expensing deduction claimed for the property in a prior year is recaptured in the year of sale on Form 4797. An installment sale does not defer recapture of the first-year deduction *(44.6)*.

Caution

**Tax–Free Exchanges**

Ordinary income generally is not realized on a tax-free exchange (unless some gain is taxed because the exchange is accompanied by "boot" *(6.3)* such as money). The ordinary income potential is assumed in the basis of the new property. However, where depreciable realty acquired before 1987 is exchanged for land, the amount of any depreciation recapture is immediately taxable in the year of the exchange.

## 44.8 Property Used in a Business (Section 1231 Assets)

Form 4797 is used to report the sale or exchange of Section 1231 assets. The following properties used in a business are considered "Section 1231 assets":

- Depreciable assets such as buildings, machinery, and other equipment held more than one year. Depreciable rental property and royalty property fits in this category if held more than one year.
- Land (including growing crops and water rights underlying farmland) held more than one year.
- Timber, coal, or domestic iron ore subject to special capital gain treatment.
- Leaseholds held more than one year.
- An unharvested crop on farmlands, if the crop and land are sold, exchanged, or involuntarily converted at the same time and to the same person and the land has been held more than one year. Such property is not included here if you retain an option to reacquire the land.
- Cattle and horses held for draft, breeding, dairy, or sporting purposes for at least 24 months.
- Livestock (other than cattle and horses) held for draft, breeding, dairy, or sporting purposes for at least 12 months. Poultry is not treated as livestock for purposes of Section 1231.

**Section 1231 netting.** On Form 4797, you combine all losses and gains, except gains allocated to depreciation recapture, from:

- The sale of Section 1231 assets (from the list at the beginning of this section).
- The involuntary conversion of Section 1231 assets and capital assets held for more than one year for business or investment purposes. You include casualty and theft losses incurred on business or investment property held for more than one year. However, there is an exception if losses exceed gains from casualties or thefts in one taxable year.
- Involuntary conversions of capital assets held for personal purposes are not subject to a Section 1231 computation but are subject to a separate computation; *see* 18.25.

**Result of netting.** A net gain on Section 1231 assets from Form 4797 is entered on Schedule D as a long-term capital gain unless the recapture rule (*see* the second Caution on this page) for net ordinary losses applies. A net loss on Section 1231 assets is treated as an ordinary loss that is combined on Form 4797 with ordinary income from depreciation recapture *(44.1)* and with ordinary gains and losses from the sale of business property that does not qualify for Section 1231 netting.

**Installment sale.** Gain realized on the installment sale of business or income-producing property held for more than a year may be capital gain one year and ordinary income another year. Actual treatment in each year depends on the net result of all sales, including installment payments received in that year *(44.6)*.

> **EXAMPLE**
>
> You suffer an uninsured fire loss of $2,000 on business equipment and gain of $1,000 on other insured investment property damaged by a storm. All of the property was held more than one year. Because loss exceeds gain, neither transaction enters into a Section 1231 computation. The gain is reported as ordinary income and the loss is deducted as an ordinary loss. The effect is a net $1,000 loss deduction. If the figures were reversed, that is, if the gain were $2,000 and the loss $1,000, both assets would enter into the Section 1231 computation. If only the fire loss occurred, the loss would be treated as a casualty loss and would not enter into the Section 1231 computation.

**Losses exceed gains from casualties or thefts.** On Form 4684, you must compute the net financial result from all involuntary conversions arising from fire, storm, or other casualty or theft of assets used in your business and capital assets held for business or income-producing purposes and held more than one year. The purpose of the computation is to determine whether these involuntary conversions enter into the above Section 1231

**Caution**

### Capital Gain or Ordinary Loss

Profitable sales and involuntary conversions of Section 1231 assets are generally treated as capital gain, except for profits on equipment *(44.1)* and real estate allocated to recaptured depreciation *(44.2)*, and losses are deducted as ordinary loss. However, the exact tax result depends on the net profit and loss realized for all sales of such property made during the tax year. Under the netting rules *(44.8)*, the net result of these sales determines the tax treatment of each individual sale. In making the computation on Form 4797, you must also consider losses and gains from casualty, theft, and other involuntary conversions involving business and investment property held more than one year. Follow the Form 4797 instructions.

**Caution**

### Recapture of Net Ordinary Losses

Net Section 1231 gain is not treated as capital gain but as ordinary income to the extent of net Section 1231 losses realized in the five most recent prior taxable years. Losses in the five preceding years that have not yet been applied against net Section 1231 gains are recaptured in chronological order on Line 8 of Form 4797. Losses that have already been "recaptured" under this rule in prior years are not taken into account.

computation. If the net result is a gain, all of the assets enter into the Section 1231 computation. If the net result is a loss, then these assets do not enter into the computation; the losses are deducted separately as casualty losses, and the gains reported separately as ordinary income. If you incur only losses, the losses similarly do not enter into the Section 1231 computation.

## 44.9 Sale of Property Used for Business and Personal Purposes

One sale will be reported as two separate sales for tax purposes when you sell a car or any other equipment used for business and personal purposes, or in some cases where a sold residence *(29.7)* was used partly as a residence and partly as a place of business or to produce rent income.

You allocate the sales price and the basis of the property between the business portion and the personal portion. The allocation is based on use. For example, with a car, the allocation is based on mileage used in business and personal driving.

### EXAMPLE

Two partners bought an airplane for about $54,000. They used approximately 75% of its flying time for personal flights and 25% for business flights. After using the plane for eight years, they sold it for about $35,000. Depreciation taken on the business part of the plane amounted to $13,000. The partners figured they incurred a loss of $6,000 on the sale. The IRS, allocating the proceeds and basis between business and personal use, claimed they realized a profit of $8,250 on the business part of the plane and a nondeductible loss of $14,250 on the personal part. The allocation was as follows:

|  | Partners' claim | IRS Position Business (25%) | Personal (75%) |
|---|---|---|---|
| Original cost | $54,000 | $13,500 | $40,500 |
| Depreciation | 13,000 | 13,000 | |
| Adjusted basis | 41,000 | 500 | 40,500 |
| Selling price | 35,000 | 8,750 | 26,250 |
| Gain (Nondeductible loss) | ($6,000) | $8,250 | ($14,250) |

The partners argued that the IRS could not split the sale into two separate sales. They sold only one airplane and therefore there was only one sale. A federal district court and appeals court disagreed and held that the IRS method of allocation is practical and fair.

## 44.10 Should You Trade in Business Equipment?

The purchase of new business equipment is often partially financed by trading in old equipment. For tax purposes, after 2017 a trade-in of equipment, including business vehicles, is treated as a sale. Gain on the sale must be immediately recognized. It may be preferable to sell the equipment and then use the proceeds to buy new equipment if you can get more on this sale to a third party.

## 44.11 Corporate Liquidation

Liquidation of a corporation and distribution of its assets for your stock is generally subject to capital gain or loss treatment. For example, on a corporate liquidation, you receive property worth $10,000 from the corporation. Assume the basis of your shares, which you have held long term, is $6,000. You have realized a long-term gain of $4,000.

If you incur legal expenses in pressing payment of a claim, you treat the fee as a capital expense, according to the IRS. The Tax Court and an appeals court have held that the fee is an expense incurred to produce income and is deductible as a miscellaneous itemized deduction subject to the 2% of adjusted gross income (AGI) floor. However, the deduction cannot be claimed in 2018 through 2025 due to the suspension of this deduction *(19.2)*.

If you recover a judgment against the liquidator of a corporation for misuse of corporate funds, the judgment is considered part of the amount you received on liquidation and gives you capital gain, not ordinary income.

If you paid a corporate debt after liquidation, the payment reduces the gain realized on the corporate liquidation in the earlier year; thus, in effect, it is a capital loss.

If the corporation distributes liquidating payments over a period of years, gain is not reported until the distributions exceed the adjusted basis of your stock.

## 44.12 Additional Taxes on Higher-Income Taxpayers

Self-employed individuals who sell business property and who have "high-income" may be subject to additional taxes that are intended to help pay for health care reform. If your income exceeds the applicable threshold for your filing status, you may be subject to either or both of these taxes:

- An additional 0.9% Medicare tax on net earnings from self-employment *(28.2)*.
- An additional 3.8% tax on net investment income (NII tax) *(28.3)*.

When are sales of business property treated as earned income (for the 0.9% tax) or investment income (for the 3.8% tax)? The following guidance should be applied to determine whether the additional taxes apply:

- *Active businesses.* Self-employed people who are active in their businesses do not treat gains from the sale of business assets as subject to either the 0.9% tax (the gains are not part of net earnings from self-employment) or the 3.8% tax (the gains are from a business, not an investment).
- *Passive activities.* Those who are not active in their businesses (i.e., they are passive investors) treat taxable gains from the sales of business property as investment income for purposes of the 3.8% tax. This assumes that the business is a passive activity because the self-employed person does not meet the material participation tests *(10.6)*; *see Chapter 10* for details on the passive activity rules.

 *Caution*

**No Deduction for Additional Medicare Tax**

While self-employed individuals can deduct one-half of the Medicare tax that applies to their net earnings from self employment *(45.3)*, no deduction is allowed for any portion of the 0.9% additional Medicare tax.

# CHAPTER 45

# Figuring Self-Employment Tax

Self-employment tax provides funds for Social Security and Medicare benefits. The self-employment tax is calculated on Schedule SE. You are required to prepare Schedule SE if you have self-employment net earnings of $400 or more in 2018, but you will not incur the tax unless your net self-employment earnings exceed $433.13. The tax is added to your income tax liability. When preparing your estimated tax liability, you must also include an estimate of self-employment tax; *see Chapter 27*.

On Schedule SE, self-employment income is reduced by a deduction reflected in the decimal of .9235 listed on the form. You also deduct the employer-equivalent portion of the self-employment tax on Line 27 of Form 1040.

For 2018, the self-employment tax of 15.3% consists of the following two rates: 12.4% for Social Security and 2.9% for Medicare. After multiplying the net earnings by .9235, the combined 15.3% rate applies to a taxable earnings base of $128,400 or less; the 2.9% rate applies to all taxable earnings exceeding $128,400.

You are required to pay self-employment tax on self-employment income even after you retire and receive Social Security benefits.

## 45.1 What Is Self-Employment Income?

On Schedule SE, you generally figure self-employment tax on the net profit from your business or profession whether you participate in its activities full or part time. Net profit is generally the amount shown on Line 31 of Schedule C (or Line 3 of Schedule C-EZ) if you are a sole proprietor. If you are a partner, net earnings subject to self-employment tax are taken from Box 14, Schedule K-1, of Form 1065. If you are a farmer, net farm profit is shown on Line 34, Schedule F.

If you have more than one self-employed operation, your net profit from all the operations is combined. A loss in one self-employed business will reduce the income from another business. You file separate Schedules C for each operation and one Schedule SE showing the combined income (less losses, if any).

For self-employment tax purposes, net earnings are not reduced by deductible contributions to your own SEP or self-employed qualified retirement plan *(41.4)*.

**Married couples.** Where you and your spouse each have self-employment income, each spouse must figure separate self-employment income on a separate Schedule SE. Each pays the tax on the separate self-employment income. Both schedules are attached to the joint return.

If you live in a community property state, business income is not treated as community property for self-employment tax purposes. The spouse who is actually carrying on the business is subject to self-employment tax on the earnings.

**Qualified joint venture election by spouses.** If you and your spouse are the only members of a business that you jointly own and operate, you each materially participate in the business, and you file a joint return, you can make a joint election to file as sole proprietors on Schedule C ("qualified joint venture election") instead of as a partnership. You make the joint venture election by filing separate Schedule Cs or C-EZs on which you each report your respective share (according to respective ownership interests) of the business income, gains, losses, deductions, and credits. If you make the election, each of you must file a separate Schedule SE to figure self-employment tax on your share of the joint venture income.

However, the reporting rule is different if you are making the election for a rental real estate business. In that case, use Schedule E instead of Schedule C. On one Schedule E, you each report your respective interests in the qualified joint venture and divide the income, gains, losses, deductions, and credits between you; check the "QJV" box on Schedule E and *see* the instructions. Since rental real estate income is generally not subject to self-employment tax (see exception 1 below), you do not have to file Schedule SE unless you have other income that is subject to self-employment tax.

**Exceptions to self-employment tax.** The following types of income or payments are not included as self-employment income on Schedule SE:

1. Rent from real estate is generally not self-employment income. However, self-employment tax applies to the business income of a real estate dealer or income in a rental business where substantial services are rendered to the occupant, as in the leasing of—
   - Rooms in a hotel or in a boarding house.
   - Apartments, but only if extra services for the occupants' convenience, such as maid service or changing linens, are provided.
   - Cabins or cabanas in tourist camps where you provide maid services, linens, utensils, and swimming, boating, fishing, and other facilities, for which you do not charge separately.
   - Farmland in which the landlord materially participates in the actual production of the farm or in the management of production. For purposes of "material participation," the activities of a landlord's agent are not counted, only the landlord's actual participation.
2. Capital gains are not self-employment income. Self-employment income does not include gains from the sale of property unless it is inventory or held for sale to

**Caution**

**Self-employment in Puerto Rico**

Even though residents of Puerto Rico are exempt from federal income tax, self-employed individuals still owe self-employment tax on net earnings earned in Puerto Rico.

**Caution**

**Freelancer Fees**

Fees you earn for freelance work as an independent contractor are business earnings reportable on Schedule C, and if you have a net profit, they are subject to self-employment tax on Schedule SE.

**Filing Tip**

**Real Estate Investor**

The owner of one office building who holds it for investment (rather than for sale in the ordinary course of business) is not a real estate dealer, but a real estate investor. If the only tenant services provided are heat, light, water, and trash collection, report the rental income and expenses on Schedule E. The activity is not a Schedule C business subject to self-employment tax.

customers in the ordinary course of business. Thus, traders in securities *(30.14)* who buy and sell securities for their own account do not treat net gains or losses from the sales as self-employment income or loss. Dealers in commodities and options are subject to self-employment tax *see* Table 45.1.

3. Dividends and interest. Generally, dividends and interest are not self-employment income. However, dividends earned by a dealer in securities and interest on accounts receivable are treated as self-employment income if the securities are not being held for investment. A dealer is one who buys stock as inventory to sell to customers.

4. Conservation Reserve Program payments received by farmers receiving Social Security retirement or disability benefits. These payments reduce net farm profit reported on Schedule SE.

5. Certain family-related compensation. Payments you receive from an insurance company or government program as a family caregiver are not treated as self-employment income unless you are in the trade or business of being a caregiver. Similarly, executor fees for handling an estate are not considered self-employment income unless you are in the business of regularly acting as an executor for estates.

**Net operating loss deduction.** A loss carryover from past years does not reduce business income for self-employment tax purposes.

**Statutory employees.** Wages of a statutory employee, such as a full-time life insurance salesperson *(40.6)*, are not subject to self-employment tax because Social Security and Medicare tax have been withheld.

**Farmers.** A share farmer's part of the profit from crops on land owned by another is self-employment income.

**Business interruption proceeds.** The IRS and the Tax Court disagree over whether business interruption insurance proceeds must be reported as earnings subject to self-employment tax. The Tax Court held that insurance payments made to a grocer as compensation for lost earnings due to a fire were not subject to self-employment tax because the payment was not for actual services. The IRS refuses to follow the decision, holding that such payments represented income that would have been earned had business operations not been interrupted.

## 45.2 Partners Pay Self-Employment Tax

A general partner includes his or her share of partnership income or loss in net earnings from self-employment, including guaranteed payments. If your personal tax year is different from the partnership's tax year, you include your share of partnership income or loss for the partnership tax year ending within 2018.

A limited partner is not subject to self-employment tax on his or her share of partnership income except for guaranteed payments for services performed, which are subject to the tax.

If a general partner dies within the partnership's tax year, self-employment income includes his or her distributive share of the income earned by the partnership through the end of the month in which the death occurs. This is true even though his or her heirs or estate succeeds to the partnership rights. For this purpose, partnership income for the year is considered to be earned ratably each month.

**Retirement payments from partnership.** Retirement payments you receive from your partnership are not subject to self-employment tax if the following conditions are met:

1. The payments are made under a qualified written plan providing for periodic payments on retirement of partners with payments to continue until death.

2. You rendered no services in any business conducted by the partnership during the tax year of the partnership ending within or with your tax year.

3. By the end of the partnership's tax year, your share in the partnership's capital has been paid to you in full, and there is no obligation from the other partners to you other than with respect to the retirement payments under the plan.

 *Filing Tip*

**Trader in Securities**

If you are a trader in securities *(30.14)*, gains or losses from your trading business are not subject to self-employment tax.

**IRS Alert**

### IRS Guidance on LLC Members

The IRS has indicated it will issue guidance on whether and to what extent LLC members are subject to self-employment tax; *see the e-Supplement* at *jklasser.com* for any update.

**Filing Tip**

### Deduction for Self-Employment Tax

You can deduct one-half of the self-employment tax, representing the so-called "employer share," as an above-the-line deduction on Schedule 1 of Form 1040.

**Limited liability company (LLC) members.** Are LLC members treated as general or limited partners for purposes of self-employment tax? The matter is not completely settled, but it appears that members owe self-employment tax when they perform services for their business, participate in management activities, and are not mere investors.

## 45.3 Schedule SE

Schedule SE has an introductory "road map" designed to lead you to either the short or long version of Schedule SE. Once you pass through the road map, the preparation of either the short or long schedule for 2018 is not difficult. On both schedules, you reduce your net profit by .9235 to get your net earnings from self-employment. In other words, only 92.35% of the net earnings is subject to self-employment tax. The .9235 adjustment is the equivalent of a 7.65% reduction to net earnings, which, along with the income tax deduction for one-half of self-employment tax on Schedule 1 of Form 1040, attempts to place self-employed individuals on the same level as employees subject to FICA taxes.

The .9235 adjustment is made on Line 4 of either the short or long Schedule SE. After the .9235 adjustment is made, net earnings are subject to the 12.4% and 2.9% rates, assuming the resulting net earnings are $400 or more. For 2018, the 12.4% Social Security rate applies to the first $128,400 of net earnings and the 2.9% Medicare rate applies to all of the net earnings.

> **EXAMPLE**
>
> Your 2018 net profit from Schedule C is $130,000. As shown in the filled-in Short Schedule SE below, your net earnings subject to self-employment tax are $120,055 after the .9235 adjustment. Your self-employment tax is $18,368. You may deduct $9,184 of the tax on Schedule 1 of Form 1040.

## Worksheet—Short Schedule SE

**Section A—Short Schedule SE.** Caution: Read above to see if you can use Short Schedule SE.

| | | | |
|---|---|---|---|
| **1a** | Net farm profit or (loss) from Schedule F, line 34, and farm partnerships, Schedule K-1 (Form 1065), box 14, code A . . . . . . . . . . . . . . . . . . . . | **1a** | |
| **b** | If you received social security retirement or disability benefits, enter the amount of Conservation Reserve Program payments included on Schedule F, line 4b, or listed on Schedule K-1 (Form 1065), box 20, code AH | **1b** ( | ) |
| **2** | Net profit or (loss) from Schedule C, line 31; Schedule C-EZ, line 3; Schedule K-1 (Form 1065), box 14, code A (other than farming); and Schedule K-1 (Form 1065-B), box 9, code J1. Ministers and members of religious orders, see instructions for types of income to report on this line. See instructions for other income to report . . . . . . . . . . . . | **2** | 130,000 |
| **3** | Combine lines 1a, 1b, and 2 . . . . . . . . . . . . . . . . | **3** | 130,000 |
| **4** | Multiply line 3 by 92.35% (0.9235). If less than $400, you don't owe self-employment tax; **don't** file this schedule unless you have an amount on line 1b. . . . . . . . . . . . ▶ | **4** | 120,055 |
| | **Note:** If line 4 is less than $400 due to Conservation Reserve Program payments on line 1b, see instructions. | | |
| **5** | **Self-employment tax.** If the amount on line 4 is: | | |
| | • $128,400 or less, multiply line 4 by 15.3% (0.153). Enter the result here and on **Schedule 4 (Form 1040), line 57,** or **Form 1040NR, line 55** | | |
| | • More than $128,400, multiply line 4 by 2.9% (0.029). Then, add $15,921.60 to the result. Enter the total here and on **Schedule 4 (Form 1040), line 57,** or **Form 1040NR, line 55** . . | **5** | 18,368 |
| **6** | **Deduction for one-half of self-employment tax.** | | |
| | Multiply line 5 by 50% (0.50). Enter the result here and on **Schedule 1 (Form 1040), line 27,** or **Form 1040NR, line 27** . .  **6**  9,184 | | |

**For Paperwork Reduction Act Notice, see your tax return instructions.**   Cat. No. 11358Z   **Schedule SE (Form 1040) 2018**

## 45.4 How Wages Affect Self-Employment Tax

If you have both net earnings from self-employment and also wage and/or tip income subject to FICA taxes (Social Security and Medicare), the amount of such FICA earnings may affect your self-employment tax liability.

If your 2018 FICA wages or tips were $128,400 or over, your net self-employment earnings (after the .9235 adjustment) are subject only to the 2.9% Medicare rate. If the total of your 2018 FICA wages (and tips) and net self-employment earnings was $128,400 or less, all of your net earnings are subject to the 12.4% Social Security rate and the 2.9% Medicare rate.

If your 2018 FICA wages or tips were under $128,400, but the total of the wages and tips plus your 2018 net earnings was over the $128,400 limit for the 12.4% Social Security rate, the 12.4% rate applies to the lesser of: (1) Line 6 of the Long Schedule SE, which shows your net self-employment earnings (after the .9235 adjustment), or (2) Line 9 of the Long Schedule SE, which shows the excess of $128,400 over the FICA wages and tips. The 2.9% Medicare rate applies to the entire amount of net self-employment earnings. *See* the following Example and the filled-in long Schedule SE worksheet below.

*Caution*

**Foreign Earned Income**

If you are self employed and living outside the United States and qualify for the 2018 foreign earned income exclusion of up to $103,900 *(36.3)*, you are still subject to self-employment tax on all of your earnings, unless an exception is allowed under a social security agreement between the United States and the government of the country you are living in.

### Worksheet—Long Schedule SE

**Part I    Self-Employment Tax**

**Note:** If your only income subject to self-employment tax is **church employee income,** see instructions. Also see instructions for the definition of church employee income.

| | | | | |
|---|---|---|---|---|
| **A** | If you are a minister, member of a religious order, or Christian Science practitioner **and** you filed Form 4361, but you had $400 or more of **other** net earnings from self-employment, check here and continue with Part I . . . . . . . ▶ ☐ | | | |
| **1a** | Net farm profit or (loss) from Schedule F, line 34, and farm partnerships, Schedule K-1 (Form 1065), box 14, code A. **Note:** Skip lines 1a and 1b if you use the farm optional method (see instructions) | **1a** | | |
| **b** | If you received social security retirement or disability benefits, enter the amount of Conservation Reserve Program payments included on Schedule F, line 4b, or listed on Schedule K-1 (Form 1065), box 20, code AH | **1b** | ( | ) |
| **2** | Net profit or (loss) from Schedule C, line 31; Schedule C-EZ, line 3; Schedule K-1 (Form 1065), box 14, code A (other than farming); and Schedule K-1 (Form 1065-B), box 9, code J1. Ministers and members of religious orders, see instructions for types of income to report on this line. See instructions for other income to report. **Note:** Skip this line if you use the nonfarm optional method (see instructions) . . . . . . . . . . | **2** | 82,228 | |
| **3** | Combine lines 1a, 1b, and 2 . . . . . . . . . . | **3** | 82,228 | |
| **4a** | If line 3 is more than zero, multiply line 3 by 92.35% (0.9235). Otherwise, enter amount from line 3 | **4a** | 75,938 | |
| | **Note:** If line 4a is less than $400 due to Conservation Reserve Program payments on line 1b, see instructions. | | | |
| **b** | If you elect one or both of the optional methods, enter the total of lines 15 and 17 here . . | **4b** | | |
| **c** | Combine lines 4a and 4b. If less than $400, **stop;** you don't owe self-employment tax. **Exception:** If less than $400 and you had **church employee income,** enter -0- and continue ▶ | **4c** | 75,938 | |
| **5a** | Enter your **church employee income** from Form W-2. See instructions for definition of church employee income . . .   **5a** | | | |
| **b** | Multiply line 5a by 92.35% (0.9235). If less than $100, enter -0- . . . . . . . . . . | **5b** | | |
| **6** | Add lines 4c and 5b . . . . . . . . . . . . . | **6** | 75,938 | |
| **7** | Maximum amount of combined wages and self-employment earnings subject to social security tax or the 6.2% portion of the 7.65% railroad retirement (tier 1) tax for 2018 . . . . . . | **7** | 128,400 | 00 |
| **8a** | Total social security wages and tips (total of boxes 3 and 7 on Form(s) W-2) and railroad retirement (tier 1) compensation. If $128,400 or more, skip lines 8b through 10, and go to line 11   **8a**   66,450 | | | |
| **b** | Unreported tips subject to social security tax (from Form 4137, line 10)   **8b** | | | |
| **c** | Wages subject to social security tax (from Form 8919, line 10)   **8c** | | | |
| **d** | Add lines 8a, 8b, and 8c . . . . . . . . . . . | **8d** | 66,450 | |
| **9** | Subtract line 8d from line 7. If zero or less, enter -0- here and on line 10 and go to line 11 . ▶ | **9** | 61,950 | |
| **10** | Multiply the **smaller** of line 6 or line 9 by 12.4% (0.124) . . . . . . . . . . . | **10** | 7,682 | |
| **11** | Multiply line 6 by 2.9% (0.029) . . . . . . . . . . . . . . . . | **11** | 2,202 | |
| **12** | **Self-employment tax.** Add lines 10 and 11. Enter here and on **Schedule 4 (Form 1040), line 57,** or **Form 1040NR, line 55** | **12** | 9,884 | |
| **13** | **Deduction for one-half of self-employment tax.** Multiply line 12 by 50% (0.50). Enter the result here and on **Schedule 1 (Form 1040), line 27,** or **Form 1040NR, line 27** .   **13**   4,942 | | | |

## 45.5 Optional Method If 2018 Was a Low-Income or Loss Year

The law provides a small increased tax base for Social Security coverage if you have a low net profit or a net loss. The increased tax base is provided by an optional method and is figured in Part II of Section B of Schedule SE. One optional method is for nonfarm self-employment and another for farm income. You may not use the optional method to report an amount less than your actual net earnings from nonfarm self-employment.

**Nonfarm optional method.** You may use the nonfarm optional method for 2018 if you meet all the following tests:

1. Your net earnings (profit) from nonfarm self-employment on Line 31 of Schedule C, Line 3 of Schedule C-EZ, or Box 14 (Code A) of Schedule K-1 (Form 1065) are less than $5,717.

2. Your net nonfarm profits are less than 72.189% of your gross nonfarm income.

3. You had net earnings from self-employment of $400 or more in at least two of the following years: 2015, 2016 and 2017.

4. You have not previously used this method for more than four years. There is a five-year lifetime limit for use of the nonfarm optional base. The years do not have to be consecutive.

If your net profit from all nonfarm trades or businesses is less than $5,717 and also less than 72.189% of gross nonfarm income, and you have no gross farm income, you may report two-thirds of the gross income from your nonfarm business, but no more than $5,280, as net earnings from self-employment for 2018.

*Filing Tip*

**Optional Method**

Electing the optional method to increase the base for Social Security coverage may also increase earned income for purposes of the dependent care credit, the aditional child tax credit and the earned income credit.

**EXAMPLES**

1. Brown had net earnings from self-employment of $800 in 2016 and $900 in 2017 and so meets Test 3 above. In 2018, she has gross nonfarm self-employment income of $6,200 and net nonfarm self-employment earnings of $4,000. Net earnings from self-employment of $4,000 are less than $5,717 (Test 1 above) and also less than $4,476 (72.189% × $6,200) (Test 2). Brown may figure self-employment tax on $4,133 (2/3 of $6,200), as it is less than $5,280, which is the maximum income that can be used for the 2018 optional methods.

2. Same facts as in Example 1, but Brown has a net self-employment loss of $700. She may elect to report $4,133 (2/3 of $6,200) as net earnings under the optional method.

3. Smith had gross nonfarm income of $1,000 and net nonfarm self-employment earnings of $800. He may not use the optional method because net earnings of $800 are not less than 72.189% of $1,000 gross income, or $722.

4. Jones has gross nonfarm income of $525 and net nonfarm self-employment earnings of $175. Jones may not use the optional method because two-thirds of his gross income, or $350, is less than the minimum income of $400 required to be subject to the self-employment tax.

**Optional farm method.** If you have farming income (other than as a limited partner) you may use the farm optional method to figure your net earnings from farm self-employment.

You can use the farm optional method for 2018 only if your gross farm income was not more than $7,920 or your net farm profits were less than $5,717.

You may report the smaller of two-thirds of your gross income or $5,280 as your net earnings from farm self-employment.

Farm income includes income from cultivating the soil or harvesting any agricultural commodities. It also includes income from the operation of a livestock, dairy, poultry, bee, fish, fruit, or truck farm, or plantation, ranch, nursery, range, orchard, or oyster bed, as well as income in the form of crop shares if you materially participate in production or management of production.

## 45.6   Self-Employment Tax Rules for Certain Positions

| *Table 45-1*   Self-Employed or Employee? | |
|---|---|
| **If you are—** | **Tax rule—** |
| Babysitter | Where you perform services in your own home and determine the nature and manner of the services to be performed, you are considered to have self-employment income. However, where services are performed in the parent's home according to instructions by the parents, you are an employee of the parents and do not have self-employment earnings. |
| | In one case, the Tax Court held that grandparents who provided care only for their own grandchildren and received payments from a state-sponsored childcare assistance program had to pay income tax on the payments, but the payments were not subject to self-employment tax because the grandparents' primary purpose in providing the care was not to make a profit. |
| Clergy | If you are an ordained minister, priest, or rabbi, a member of a religious order who has not taken a vow of poverty, or a Christian Science practitioner, you are subject to self-employment tax, unless you elect not to be covered on the grounds of conscientious or religious objection to Social Security benefits. An application for exemption from Social Security coverage must be filed on Form 4361 by the due date, including extensions, of your income tax return for the second taxable year for which you have net earnings from services of $400 or more. An exemption, once granted, is irrevocable. |
| | Self-employment tax does not apply to the rental value of any parsonage or parsonage allowance provided after retirement. Other retirement benefits from a church plan are also exempted. |
| Consultant | The IRS generally takes the position that income earned by a consultant is subject to self-employment tax. The IRS has also held that a retired executive hired as a consultant by his former firm received self-employment income, even though he was subject to an agreement prohibiting him from giving advice to competing companies. According to the IRS, consulting for one firm is a business; it makes no difference that you act as a consultant only with your former company. The IRS has also imposed self-employment tax on consulting fees, although no services were performed for them. The courts have generally approved the IRS position. |
| Dealer in commodities and options | Registered options dealers and commodities dealers are subject to self-employment tax on net gains from trading in Section 1256 contracts, which include regulated futures contracts, foreign currency contracts, dealer equity options, and non-equity options. Self-employment tax also applies to net gains from trading property related to such contracts, like stock used to hedge options. |
| Director | You are taxed as a self-employed person if you are not an employee of the company. Fees for attendance at meetings are self-employment income. If the fees are not received until after the year you provide the services, you treat the fees as self-employment earnings in the year they are received. |
| Employee of foreign government or international organization | If you are a U.S. citizen and you work in the United States, Puerto Rico, the Virgin Islands, American Samoa, the Commonwealth of the Northern Mariana Islands, or Guam, for a foreign government or its wholly owned instrumentality, or an international organization, you pay self-employment tax on your earnings if Social Security and Medicare taxes are not withheld from your pay. |

Figuring Self-employment Tax | **763**

## Table 45-1  Self-Employed or Employee?

| If you are— | Tax rule— |
|---|---|
| Executor or guardian | If you are a professional fiduciary, your fees will always be treated as self-employment income, regardless of the assets held by the estate. But if you serve as a nonprofessional executor or administrator for the estate of a deceased friend or relative, your fees will not be treated as self-employment income unless all of the following tests are met: (1) the estate includes a business; (2) you actively participate in the operation of the business; and (3) all or part of your fee is related to your operation of the business. <br><br>The IRS applied similar business tests to deny self-employment treatment for a guardian who was appointed by a court to care for a disabled cousin. The guardian negotiated sales of the cousin's property and invested the proceeds, but these activities were not extensive enough to be considered management of a business. |
| Former insurance salespersons | Termination payments by a former insurance salesperson may be exempt from self-employment tax. They must be received from an insurance company after the termination of a services agreement. No services may be performed for the company after the agreement ends and before the end of the tax year. The payments must be conditioned on the salesperson's entering into a covenant not to compete with the company for at least one year after termination. The amount of the payment must be primarily based on policies sold by (or credited to) the salesperson during the last year of the services agreement or on the period for which such policies remain in force after the termination. |
| Lecturer | You are not taxed as a self-employed person if you give only occasional lectures. If, however, you seek lecture engagements and get them with reasonable regularity, your lecture fees are treated as self-employment income. |
| Nonresident alien | You generally do not pay Social Security tax on your self-employment income derived from a trade, business, or profession in the United States. This is so even though you pay income tax. However, an international agreement between the United States and another country might provide that you are covered under the U.S. Social Security system, in which case, you are subject to self-employment tax. In the absence of such an agreement, you are exempt from self-employment tax even if your business in the United States is carried on by an agent, employee, or partnership of which you are a member. However, if you live in Puerto Rico, the Virgin Islands, American Samoa, the Commonwealth of the Northern Mariana Islands, or Guam, you are not considered a nonresident alien and are subject to self-employment tax. |
| Nurse | If you are a registered nurse or licensed practical nurse who is hired directly by clients for private nursing services, you are considered self-employed. You are an employee if hired directly by a hospital or a private physician and work for a salary following a strict routine during fixed hours, or if you provide primarily domestic services in the home of a client. <br><br>Where registered or licensed practical nurses are assigned nursing jobs by an agency that pays them, the IRS, in several rulings, has treated such nurses as employees of the agency. <br><br>Nurses' aides, domestics, and other unlicensed individuals who classify themselves as practical nurses are treated by the IRS as employees, regardless of whether they work for a medical institution, a private physician, or a private household. |
| Real estate agent or door-to-door salesperson | Licensed real estate agents are considered self-employed if they have a contract specifying that they are not to be treated as employees and if substantially all of their pay is related to sales rather than number of hours worked. <br><br>The same rule also applies to door-to-door salespeople with similar contracts who work on a commission basis selling products in homes or other non-retail establishments. |
| Technical service contractor | Consulting engineers and computer technicians who receive assignments from technical service agencies are generally treated as employees and do not pay self-employment tax. The IRS distinguishes between (1) technicians who in three-party arrangements are assigned clients by a technical services agency and (2) those who directly enter into contracts with clients. Employee status covers only technicians in Group 1. <br><br>Technical specialists who contract directly with clients may be classified as independent contractors by showing that they have been consistently treated as independent contractors by the client, and that other workers in similar positions have also been treated as independent contractors. Thus, they may treat their income as self-employment income. <br><br>Firms that are treated as employers of technical specialists are responsible for withholding and payroll taxes. |
| Traders in securities | Gains and losses from a trading business are not subject to self-employment tax. |
| Writer | Royalties from writing books are self-employment income to a writer. Royalties on books by a professor employed by a university may also be self-employment income despite employment as a professor. |

# PART 7

# Filing Your Return and What Happens After You File

This part is designed to help you —

- Organize your tax data. Whether you plan to prepare your own tax return or have someone else prepare it, you must first gather and organize your tax information.
- Understand how the IRS reviews your return and initiates audit procedures, including information on how the IRS matches your return with reports of distributions to you from banks, corporations, and government agencies.
- Avoid penalties for underpaying your tax. You may avoid penalties for positions taken on your tax return by making certain disclosures, obtaining authoritative support for your position, or showing reasonable cause for a tax underpayment (48.6).
- Understand the factors that might lead to an audit. Your chances of being selected for an examination depend on your income, profession, deductions claimed, and even where you live (48.1).
- Prepare for an audit. Advance preparations and knowing your rights can help support your position (48.4).
- Dispute adverse IRS determinations. You can appeal within the IRS and go to court if you disagree with the IRS audit results. If you win, you may receive attorneys' fees and other expenses (48.8).
- File a timely refund claim if you have overpaid your tax (47.2).
- File an amended return if you omitted income or claimed excessive deductions on your original return (47.8).

# CHAPTER 46

# Filing Your Return

Whether you prepare your return yourself or retain a professional preparer, you must first collect and organize your tax records. You cannot prepare your return unless you get your personal tax data in order. Good records will help you figure your income and deductions and will serve as a written record to present to the IRS in the event that you are audited.

Review income statements from banks, employers, brokers, and governmental agencies on their respective Forms 1099. Check for miscalculations, additions, and omissions.

Survey *Chapters 12–20* of this book for deductions you can claim directly from gross income and itemized deductions you can claim on Schedule A of Form 1040.

Reviewing your tax return from prior years will help refresh your memory as to how you handled income and expenses in prior years. This review will also remind you of deductions, carryover losses, and other items you might otherwise have overlooked that you might be eligible for. If you self-prepare your return using the same software or an online solution as in the prior year, it will automatically display this information for your (as long as you import last year's return information). If your prior year returns were prepared by a professional, he or she can probably provide you with a copy of your returns if you do not have them. Otherwise, you may obtain copies of prior year tax returns by filing Form 4506 with the IRS and paying a fee.

In this chapter you will find a checklist of steps to take when preparing and checking your return. If you need an extension to file, *see 46.3.*

**Getting a Copy of an Old Tax Return**

You can obtain a copy of a prior year tax return from the IRS by filing Form 4506 and paying a $50 fee per return.

You can use Form 4506-T to order free of charge a transcript of tax return information that provides line entries from tax returns for the three prior years and a transcript of data from Forms W-2 and 1099 for up to 10 years in some cases.

You can obtain a transcript online using the IRS service "Get Transcript" (irs.gov/individuals/get-transcript). This involves a registration process in order to view your tax transcript.

*Planning Reminder*

**Keep Copies**

Make a copy of your signed return and keep it with copies of Form W-2 and other income statements, plus receipts, canceled checks, and other items to substantiate your deductions.

## 46.1  Keeping Tax Records

To maximize tax-savings opportunities, you must keep good records throughout the year. Good recordkeeping makes it easier to prepare your return, reduces errors, and provides a defense to any challenge from the IRS.

- Make a habit of jotting down deductible items as they come along.
- Keep a calender or diary of expenses to record deductible items.
- Keep a file of bills and receipts. This will remind you of deductible items and provide you with supporting evidence to present to the IRS if audited.
- Use your credit card receipts, online account statements, and checkbook stubs as a record. If you own a business, you must keep a complete set of account books for it.

**IRA records.** If you have made nondeductible contributions to a traditional IRA, keep a record of both your nondeductible and deductible contributions. This will help you when you withdraw IRA money to figure the tax-free and taxed parts of the withdrawal *(8.9)*. Also keep records of contributions and conversions to Roth IRA*s (8.20–8.22)*. For these purposes, you should keep copies of Form 8606 and Form 5498 *(8.8)*.

**Reinvested mutual fund or ETF distributions.** Keep a record of mutual fund or ETF distributions that you have reinvested in additional fund shares. The reinvested amounts are part of your cost basis in the fund. When you redeem your shares, you need to know your basis to compute gain or loss *(32.10)*. Your fund probably keeps track of basis for you, so you can get basis information from the fund when planning a sale.

**Passive losses.** If you have losses that are suspended and carried forward to future years under the passive loss restrictions *(10.13)*, keep the worksheets to Form 8582 as a record of the carry-forward losses. Also, if you deducted passive losses from rental real estate as an active participant or a real estate professional, retain records, such as a diary, showing your participation in rental activities.

**Home mortgage interest.** Keep your bank statements and canceled checks. If a loan secured by a first or second home is used to make substantial home improvements, keep records of the improvement costs to support your home interest deduction *(15.5)*.

**How long should you keep your records?** Your records should be kept for a minimum of three years after the year to which they are applicable, since the IRS generally has three years from the date your return is filed to audit your return. Some authorities advise keeping them for six years, since in some cases where income has not been reported, the IRS may go back as far as six years to question a tax return. In cases of suspected tax fraud, there is no time limitation at all.

Keep records of transactions relating to the basis of property for as long as they are important in figuring the basis of the original or replacement property. For example, records of the purchase of rental property or improvements thereto must be held as long as you own the property.

As mentioned above, if you have made any nondeductible IRA contributions, records of IRA contributions and distributions must be kept until all funds have been withdrawn. Similarly, you should save confirmations from stock dividend reinvestment plans and mutual funds, or other records showing reinvested dividends and cash purchases of shares; these are part of your cost basis and will reduce taxable gain when you sell shares in the fund.

## 46.2  Getting Ready To File Your Return

You must collect your tax records before you can start the preparation of your return. Even if you employ a tax professional to prepare your return, organizing your tax data is essential.

You may obtain IRS forms and publications online at IRS.gov. You can obtain forms by phone from the IRS by calling (800) 829-3676.

**Checking for possible errors.** After you have completed your return, put it aside and postpone checking your completed return for several hours or even a day so that you can review it in a fresh state of mind. See below for common errors that might delay a refund or result in a tax deficiency and interest costs.

**If filing electronically.** To do this, you need your prior-year adjusted gross income (AGI) to validate your signature. If your return is rejected, read the explanation (maybe you mis-entered your Social Security number). If you have further questions, call the IRS at (800) 829-1040. Find more information at E-File Options for Individuals at https://www. irs.gov/filing/e-file-options.

**If mailing your return.** If you are mailing your paper return to the IRS, first check it to ensure the following:

- Your arithmetic is correct.
- Your Social Security number, and that of your spouse if you are filing jointly, is recorded correctly on each form and schedule.
- You have filled in the proper boxes that state your filing status and your dependents, including their Social Security number and relationship to you *(21.8)*.
- You have claimed the full standard deduction you are entitled to if you are age 65 or older, or blind *(13.4)*.
- You have used the Tax Table, Tax Computation Worksheet, or special capital gain or foreign earned income worksheet applicable to your tax status. If you do not have net capital gain or qualified dividends, use the Tax Table if your taxable income is less than $100,000, or the Tax Computation Worksheet if your taxable income is $100,000 or more. *See 22.4* if you have net capital gain or qualified dividends. *See 22.5* if you claimed the foreign earned income exclusion or foreign housing exclusion.
- You have put the refund due you or your tax payable on the correct line.
- If you owe tax and are paying by check, your check should be made out to the "United States Treasury" for the correct amount due and your Social Security number should be on the check. Send payment voucher Form 1040-V along with your payment.
- You have signed your return and, if you are filing a joint return, your spouse has also signed *(1.4)*
- You have attached the correct copy of your Form W-2 and all appropriate forms and schedules to your return.
- If you have elected to have your refund directly deposited into your personal account, verify that you have provided the IRS with the correct routing information on Line20b of Form 1040.
- You have correctly addressed the envelope and affixed proper postage.
- You use certified or registered mail or an IRS-specified private delivery service to prove that your return was postmarked on or before the filing date. *See* the adjacent Planning Reminder for more details.

## 46.3 Applying for an Extension

If you cannot file your return on time, apply by the due date of the return for an extension of time to file. Send the extension request on Form 4868 to the Internal Revenue Service office with which you file your return.

**Automatic filing extension.** You may get an extension without waiting for the IRS to act on your request. You receive an automatic six-month extension for your 2018 return if you file Form 4868 by April 15, 2019 (or April 17 if you live in Maine or Massachusetts). The extension gives you until October 15, 2019, to file your 2018 return. A late filing penalty will not be imposed if you fail to submit a payment with Form 4868 provided you make a good faith estimate of your liability based upon available information at the time of filing. However, although the extension will be allowed without a payment, you will be subject to interest charges and possible penalties (discussed below) on 2018 taxes not paid by April 15 or 17, 2019.

You may e-file Form 4868 for free through the IRS Free File program (go to IRS.gov). You may also file Form 4868 electronically using tax preparation software or your tax

*Planning Reminder*

**Get Timely Postmark for Last Minute Mailing**

Last minute filers who do not e-file may use specified services from Federal Express, UPS, and DHL as well as the U.S. Postal Service. The IRS instructions to Form 1040 have a list of the eligible private delivery services. If using the U.S. Postal Service, send the return certified (or registered) mail and keep the postmark receipt. If you use a private delivery service, keep a copy of the mailing label or obtain a receipt to verify a timely postmark. If your return is postmarked before or at any time on the filing due date (April 15, 2019, or April 17 for residents of Maine or Massachusetts) for 2018 returns, it is considered timely filed under a "timely-mailing-is-timely-filing" rule, even if the IRS receives it after the due date.

The timely mailing rule also applies if you obtain a filing extension and are mailing your return on or before the extended due date.

A timely foreign postmark for a return filed from abroad will also be accepted by the IRS as proof of a timely filing.

preparer may file it electronically for you. To make a tax payment, you may use a credit card or debit card (a fee will be charged), you can authorize a payment from your savings or checking account through IRS Direct Pay at www.irs.gov/Payments/Direct-Pay, or you can make a payment through the Electronic Federal Tax Payment System (EFTPS); for details go to http://www.irs.gov/payments. When you make a payment with Direct Pay, a credit or debit card, or EFTPS, you get a confirmation number that you should keep for your records. You can pay cash using PayNearMe at a local 7-Eleven, which requires you to obtain an online confirmation code from the IRS.

When you file your return within the extension period, you enter on the appropriate line of the return any tax payment that you sent with your extension request, and include the balance of the unpaid tax, if any.

While the extension is automatically obtained by a proper filing on Form 4868, the IRS may terminate the extension by mailing you a notice at least 10 days prior to the termination date designated in the notice.

**Interest and penalty for late payment.** You have to pay interest on any 2018 tax not paid by April 15, 2019 (or April 17 for residents of Maine or Massachusetts), even if you obtain a filing extension. In addition, if the tax paid with Form 4868, plus withholdings and estimated tax payments for 2018, is less than 90% of the amount due, you will be subject to a late-payment penalty (usually one-half of 1% of the unpaid tax per month)—unless you can show reasonable cause.

**Abroad on April 15, 2019 (April 17 for Maine/Massachusetts residents).** You do not get an automatic extension for filing and paying your tax merely because you are out of the country on the filing due date. If you plan to be traveling abroad on April 15 or 17, 2019, you must either request the automatic six-month filing extension on Form 4868, or request an extension along with a payment made by EFTPS, account withdrawal, credit card or debit card (*see* above).

The only exception is for U.S. citizens or residents who live and have their main place of business outside the U.S. or Puerto Rico, or military personnel stationed outside the U.S. or Puerto Rico, on April 15 (or 17), 2019. If you qualify, you are allowed an automatic two-month extension without having to request it, until June 17, 2019. The two-month extension is for filing your return and also paying any tax due. However, the IRS will charge interest from the original April 15 (or 17) due date on any unpaid tax. If you cannot file within the two-month extension period, you can obtain an additional four-month extension by filing Form 4868 by June 17, 2019. This additional four-month extension is for filing only and not payment. In addition to interest, a late payment penalty may be imposed (*see* above) on any tax not paid by June 17, 2019.

If you are eligible for the two-month extension but expect to qualify for the foreign earned income exclusion *(36.3)* under the foreign residence or presence test after June 17, 2019, you can request on Form 2350 an extension until after the expected qualification date; *see 36.7*.

## 46.4 Getting Your Refund

If you show an overpayment of tax on your 2018 return, you can have a refund check mailed to you or have the IRS directly deposit the refund into as many as three bank, brokerage, or mutual fund accounts; *see* below. For a direct deposit you must provide the IRS with the correct routing information for your account. On your 2018 Form 1040, you can apply all or part of your refund to your 2019 estimated tax; this is an irrevocable election.

**Direct-deposit refund option.** If you want the IRS to directly deposit your refund into only one account, just give the IRS the appropriate routing and account numbers on the refund line of your return. If you want the refund to be directly deposited into two or three accounts, File Form 8888 with your Form 1040. You can have the refund directly deposited into a checking or savings account, an online Treasury Direct account, or even to a traditional IRA *(8.1)* Roth IRA *(8.19)*, or health savings account *(41.10)*. If you want the deposit to go into a traditional IRA or Roth IRA, you must establish the IRA

*Planning Reminder*

**You Can Get a Six-Month Filing Extension**

You can get an automatic six-month extension to file your 2018 return by filing Form 4868 by April 15, 2019 (April 17 for residents of Maine or Massachusetts). The extension is for filing only and does not extend the time to pay your taxes for 2018.

*Filing Tip*

**Certain Refunds Delayed**

No refund related to the earned income tax credit or the child tax credit can be issued before February 15, no matter how early you file your return.

before you request direct deposit. Make sure that you notify the IRA trustee if you want the deposit to count as an IRA contribution for 2018 (rather than for 2019 when the deposit is made). To count as a 2018 IRA contribution (traditional or Roth), the direct deposit must actually be made to the IRA by the April 15, 2019 (April 17 for Maine or Massachusetts residents) due date for your 2018 return (extensions are disregarded).

You can also request on Form 8888 for your refund (or part of it) to be invested in up to $5,000 of paper series I bonds *(30.15)*.

If you file Form 8379 *(see* below) for a refund as an injured spouse, you cannot use Form 8888.

**Checking refund status online or by phone.** You can check the status of your refund online at IRS.gov (click on "Where's My Refund"). You will need to provide the Social Security number shown on the return (or the first Social Security number if you filed a joint return), your filing status, and the amount of the refund. You also can check the status of your refund by downloading the IRS2Go app, by calling the automated refund information phone number (800) 829-1954, or by calling (800) 829-1040.

**Form 8379: Injured spouse may get refund that was withheld to pay spouse's debts.** If a refund was due on a joint return that you filed with a spouse who owed child or spousal support, federal student loans, or state income tax, the Treasury Department's Bureau of the Fiscal Service may have withheld payment of the refund to cover the obligations. If your spouse owed federal taxes, the refund may have been offset by the IRS. If you are not liable for the past-due payments, and your tax payments (withholdings or estimated tax installments) or refundable credits exceed your income reported on the joint return, you may file Form 8379 to get back your share of the refund.

**Penalty for filing excessive refund claim.** A 20% penalty can apply to an excessive claim for refund or credit on an original or on an amended return *(47.8)*. The penalty is 20% of the "excessive" amount, the excess of the refund or credit claimed over the amount allowed, unless there is a reasonable basis for the amount claimed.

The penalty does not apply to claims relating to the earned income credit *(25.6)*. It also does not apply to any portion of the excess that is subject to the accuracy-related penalties (including the penalty for understatements due to reportable or listed transactions), or the fraud penalty *(48.6)*.

## 46.5 Paying Taxes Due

If you owe tax on a return that you are mailing to the IRS, you may pay by check, money order, credit card, or debit card. Payments can also be made by direct debit from your bank account, either by phone or online using the IRS' Direct Pay or Electronic Federal Tax Payment System (EFTPS). For those who do not have a bank account or credit card, payment can also be made in cash, although it is not sent to the IRS or Treasury, as explained below.

If paying by check or money order, make it payable to the "United States Treasury." Write your Social Security number on the check or money order. Attach Form 1040-V along with your payment.

A credit card or debit card payment can be made by phone or over the Internet with a service provider that handles the transaction for the IRS. The service provider will impose a fee based on the amount you are paying. Go to www.irs.gov/payments.

**IRS online or phone option for making payments.** The IRS' Electronic Federal Tax Payment System (EFTPS) accepts online tax payments from individual as well as business taxpayers. You may use EFTPS to pay the balance due on your individual tax return or to pay estimated tax installments.

Payments are made by direct debit from an account that you designate when you enroll with EFTPS. Individual tax payments may be scheduled up to 365 days in advance and business taxes up to 120 days in advance. You can enroll online at www.eftps.gov.

Payments via EFTPS can also be made by phone after you enroll with EFTPS and set up a direct debit arrangement. Call (800) 555-4477 for enrollment information.

*Caution*

**Direct Deposit of Joint Refund**

If you are due a refund on a joint return, your financial institution may reject a request to have a direct deposit of the joint refund made to an individual account or IRA. If the direct deposit is rejected, the IRS will mail you a refund check.

*Planning Reminder*

**Interest Not Paid on Most Refunds**

If your 2018 return is filed on or before the April 15, 2019 (April 17 for residents of Maine or Massachusetts) filing deadline, the IRS does not have to pay interest if the refund is issued on or before May 30, 2019, which is the 45th day after April 15 (for Maine and Massachusetts residents, the 45th day would be June 1). If the return is filed after April 15 (or 17), 2019, with or without an extension, no interest is due on refunds issued within 45 days after the actual filing date. If the overpayment is not refunded within 45 days, interest is paid from the date the tax was overpaid up to a date determined by the IRS that can be as much as 30 days before the date of the refund check.

**Direct Pay.** Instead of registering to use EFTPS.gov or paying a convenience fee to charge your taxes (as explained below), you can use the free IRS online payment system at www.irs.gov/ Payments/Direct-Pay. You authorize the IRS to withdraw funds from your checking or savings account to pay your taxes, but bank account and other information is not stored.

**Pay in cash.** If you do not have a bank account or credit card to use for paying taxes, you can pay cash through the IRS' PayNearMe option at participating retailers, such as 7-Eleven stores. You must go to the Official Payments website and follow instructions to receive a confirmation of your information that will then be verified by the IRS. After you receive a payment code from the IRS via email, you can present it and make your payment in cash at your local store. This payment option costs $3.99 and is limited to $1,000 per day. Find details at https://www.irs.gov/payments/pay-with-cash-at-a-retail-partner.

**Paying electronically.** If you file electronically, you may pay taxes by authorizing a direct debit from your checking or savings account, or by using a credit or debit card. If you use a credit/debit card, the processing company will charge you a fee.

**Installment agreements.** If you cannot pay the full amount due on your return when you file, but will be able to pay the full amount within 120 days, you may ask the IRS for a short-term extension by calling (800) 829-1040. The IRS will not charge a fee for a 120-day extension, but interest will be charged and a late payment penalty *(46.9)* might be imposed.

If you need more than 120 days, you can request an installment agreement on Form 9465. If you owe $50,000 or less (tax, penalties and interest), you can apply online for a payment agreement instead of filing Form 9465; select "Payments" at IRS.gov. Even if the IRS agrees to an installment arrangement, you will be charged interest and may have to pay a late payment penalty *(46.9)* on any tax not paid by the due date.

If you owe $10,000 or less and agree to pay the full amount owed within three years, your request for an installment agreement cannot be turned down, provided that for the previous five years, you (and your spouse if currently filing jointly) timely filed and paid the taxes due and did not have an installment agreement during that period. Under such a "guaranteed installment agreement," you must timely file and pay any taxes due while the agreement is in effect.

If payments are not made under a three-year guaranteed installment agreement, you generally must pay the full balance due in no more than 72 monthly installments. If you owe over $25,000 but not over $50,000, you must disclose financial details to the IRS on Form 433-F ("Collection Information Statement") unless you agree to make payments by direct debit from your checking account or by payroll deduction. If you owe more than $50,000, you must complete Form 433-F as part of your application.

The IRS may approve a request to make installment payments for less than the full amount you owe, but only after a thorough review of your financial circumstances and after you have sold assets and used home equity to reduce the tax bill. If agreed to, the IRS will reevaluate a partial payment plan every two years.

The IRS will usually inform you within 30 days if your proposed payment plan is accepted. If it is, you will have to pay a processing fee. If payments are made by direct debit from your checking account, the fee is $107, if the agreement is set up by phone or mail, but only $31 for direct debit agreements set up online. For payment plans of more than 120 days, the fee is $225, or $149 if set up online.

A $43 fee generally applies for individuals whose income does not exceed 250% of the federal poverty guidelines, but this fee is waived if the taxpayer agrees to make direct debit payments from a checking account. If a taxpayer is unable to make direct debit payments and indicates this on the application (Line 13c of Form 9465), the $43 fee is reimbursed upon completion of the installment agreement. When you apply for an installment agreement, whether on Form 9465, online (at IRS.gov), by phone, or face-to-face with an IRS employee, the IRS will automatically review the income information from your return to determine eligibility for the reduced fee. If the IRS approves a monthly installment plan without granting a reduced user fee and you think you qualify, you can request the reduced fee by filing Form 13844 with the IRS within 30 days of receiving the IRS' acceptance notice.

If you are using an installment agreement to pay the tax due on a timely filed return (including extensions), the late payment penalty is reduced by half from .5% to .25% per month.

**Offer in Compromise.** If your financial circumstances are dire and you believe you will be unable to pay what you owe even with an installment agreement, you may make an offer to settle your tax debt for less than the full amount due on Form 656 ("Offer in Compromise"), as discussed in *48.10*.

## 46.6    Handling Identity Theft

Identity theft continues to proliferate, and annually makes the IRS' list of Dirty Dozen Tax Scams. If you know your personal information has been compromised, or suspect that it has, tell the IRS. File Form 14039, "Identity Theft Affidavit," at https://www.irs.gov/pub/irs-pdf/f14039.pdf), to put the IRS on alert immediately. Follow the instructions for mailing or faxing the form to the IRS. By filing this form, the IRS marks your tax account as "suspect." Unfortunately, this will not necessarily speed up the issuance of your tax refund, but it may ease filings going forward.

**Special tax identification number.** If someone else is using your Social Security number to file a bogus tax return, it interferes with your filings. You can obtain an Identity Protection Personal Identification Number (IP PIN), a six-digit number, to use in place of your Social Security number on future tax returns.

You must obtain an IP PIN if:

- You lost an IRS notice (CP01A) sent to you with an IP PIN.
- You had an IP PIN before but didn't receive a new one.
- Your e-filed return was rejected because your IP PIN was missing or incorrect.

You can choose to obtain an IP PIN if:

- You live in Florida, Georgia, or the District of Columbia, which are areas that are part of a pilot program on combating ID theft.
- You received an IRS letter inviting you to "opt-in" to get an IP PIN.

To obtain an IP PIN online, you must go through an authentication process called "Secure Access Steps." These steps are explained at the IRS' Secure Access page at https://www.irs.gov/individuals/secure-access-how-to-register-for-certain-online-self-help-tools.

**Learning more about tax-related ID theft.** Combating ID theft is a priority for the IRS, and toward this end it has many resources to help you.

- https://www.irs.gov/individuals/how-irs-id-theft-victim-assistance-works
- Publication 4524, Security Awareness to Taxpayers.
- Taxes. Security. Together. This is a joint campaign by the IRS, state tax administrators, and the private-sector tax industry to encourage taxpayers to protect personal and financial data online and offline.
- Taxpayer Guide to Identity Theft, which is a landing page at https://www.irs.gov/uac/taxpayer-guide-to-identity-theft that contains information and links.

## 46.7    Notify the IRS of Address Changes

If the IRS does not have your current address, payment of a refund due you may be delayed. If you owe taxes, the IRS may enforce a deficiency notice sent to the address on your most recently filed tax return, even if you never receive the IRS notice.

To avoid these problems, you can call the IRS to update your address at (800) 829-1040. You also may file Form 8822 with the IRS to provide notice of an address change, or send a signed written statement to the IRS Service Center covering your old residence. The statement should state the new and old address, your full name, and your Social Security or employer identification number.

If you and your spouse separate after filing a joint return, you should each notify the IRS of your current address.

If after you move you receive an IRS correspondence that has been forwarded by the Post Office, you may correct the address shown on the letter and mail it back to the IRS. Your correction is considered notice of an address change.

## 46.8  Interest on Tax Underpayments

You may be charged interest by the IRS if you have underpaid the tax due. The interest rate, which equals the federal short-term rate plus 3%, is determined every quarter. Interest begins to accrue from the due date of the return. Interest is compounded daily except for estimated tax penalties. If you relied on IRS assistance in preparing a return, and taxes are owed because of a mathematical or clerical error, interest does not begin to accrue until 30 days from a formal demand by the IRS for the payment of additional taxes.

IRS interest rates on taxes owed are as follows:

| Interest Rate on Underpayments | | |
| --- | --- | --- |
| From— | To— | Underpayment Rate— |
| 4/1/18 | 12/31/2018 | 5% |
| 4/1/2016 | 3/31/2018 | 4 |
| 10/1/2011 | 3/31/2016 | 3 |
| 4/1/2011 | 9/30/2011 | 4 |
| 1/1/2011 | 3/31/2011 | 3 |

## 46.9  Tax Penalties for Late Filing and Late Payment

**Late filing.** If your return is filed late without reasonable cause (illness, death in family, natural disaster, or other event beyond your control) and you owe tax, the IRS may impose a penalty of 5% of the net tax due for each month the return is late; *see* the Note below.

If your return is more than 60 days late, there is a minimum penalty, which for 2018 returns is equal to the smaller of $210 and 100% of the tax due; the $210 amount may be increased for 2019. In one case, the IRS tried to impose the minimum penalty on a taxpayer who did not owe any tax because her withholdings exceeded her liability. However, the Tax Court held that the minimum penalty does not apply unless tax is underpaid. The IRS has agreed to follow the decision.

If failure to file is fraudulent, the monthly penalty is 15% of the net tax due, with a maximum penalty of 75%.

Note: For months that you are subject to the 0.5% monthly penalty for late payment (described below) as well as the penalty for late filing, the late filing penalty is reduced by the late payment penalty, from 5% to 4.5% per month. Thus, the combined penalty for each of the first five months is 5% (4.5% + 0.5%), with the late filing penalty reaching its maximum of 22.5% in five months (4.5% × 5 = 22.5%). After five months, the 0.5% monthly late payment penalty can continue until the tax is paid but not beyond the 50th month when the 25% limit is reached (0.5% × 50 = 25%).

**Late payments.** If you are late in paying your taxes, a monthly penalty of 0.5% (½ of 1%) is imposed on the net amount of tax due and not paid by the due date. The maximum penalty is 25% of the tax due. The penalty is in addition to the regular interest charge. This penalty does not apply to the estimated tax *(27.1)*. The late payment penalty does not apply if you can show that the failure to pay is due to reasonable cause and not to willful neglect.

A special reasonable cause rule applies if you obtain a filing extension. If by the original due date you paid at least 90% of your total tax liability through withholdings, estimated tax installments, or payment with your extension request, reasonable cause is presumed and the penalty does not apply for the period covered by the extension.

Unless reasonable cause is shown, the 0.5% monthly penalty also applies for failure to pay a tax deficiency within 21 calendar days of the date of notice and demand for payment if the tax due is less than $100,000. If the tax is $100,000 or more, the penalty-free payment period is 10 business days.

The monthly penalty may be doubled to 1%, if, after repeated requests to pay and a notice of levy, you do not pay. The increased penalty applies starting in the month that begins after the earlier of the following IRS notices: (1) a notice that the IRS will levy upon your assets within 10 days unless payment is made or (2) a notice demanding immediate payment where the IRS believes collection of the tax is in jeopardy. If the tax is not paid after such a demand for immediate payment, the IRS may levy upon your assets without waiting 10 days.

# CHAPTER 47

# Filing Refund Claims, and Amended Returns

File a refund claim on Form 1040X if you want to take advantage of a retroactive change in the law, if you have overpaid your tax because you failed to take allowable deductions or credits, or overstated your income. You may use Form 1040X to correct your return if you underreported your income or improperly claimed deductions.

File a refund claim on time. The time limits discussed in *47.2* must be strictly observed; otherwise, even if you file a valid refund claim, it will be denied because of late filing.

You do not have to file a refund claim if you have overpaid your tax due to excessive withholding of taxes on your wages or salary, or if you have overpaid your estimated tax. You get a refund on these overpayments by filing your tax return and requesting a refund for these amounts. You must file your return within three years from the time the tax was paid to get the refund *(47.2)*.

For a refund of an overpayment of FICA taxes, *see 26.8* for how to claim a refund on your tax return. If you are not required to file a tax return, you file a refund claim on Form 843.

If you are entitled to a refund due to the earned income credit for certain low-income working families, you must file your tax return to get your refund, even though your income and filing status would not otherwise require that a return be filed. *See Chapter 25.*

## 47.1 Filing An Amended Return

You should file Form 1040X (Amended U.S. Individual Income Tax Return) to revise a previously filed return, either to claim a refund (see below) or to report additional tax owed *(47.8)*.

As a refund claim, Form 1040X can be filed if you overpaid your tax on your original return, such as where you failed to take allowable deductions or credits or overstated your income. You generally can use Form 1040X to change your filing status, such as where you were entitled to head of household status but filed as a single taxpayer. You can change your filing status from married filing separately to married filing jointly, but you cannot switch from a joint return to separate returns after the due date for the return.

If you are entitled to a refund, you will be sent a check. A refund on an amended return cannot be made by direct deposit to your bank account.

You do not have to file a refund claim if you have overpaid your tax due to excessive withholding of taxes on your wages or salary, or if you have overpaid your estimated tax. You will receive a refund on those overpayments by filing your tax return and requesting a refund at that time *(46.4)*.

Claiming an unwarranted refund can be costly. There is a 20% penalty for an excessive claim for refund or credit *(47.9)*.

**Married or divorced taxpayers.** If a joint return was filed for a year in which a refund is due, both spouses are entitled to recover jointly and both must file a joint refund claim. Where separate returns were filed, each spouse is a separate taxpayer and may not file a claim to recover a refund based on the other spouse's return, except if that spouse becomes the fiduciary when one spouse becomes incompetent or dies. If you are divorced and incur a net operating loss or credit that may be carried back to a year in which you were married, you may file a refund claim based on the carryback *(see 40.18)* with your signature alone and the refund check will be made out only to you.

## 47.2 When To File a Refund Claim

You may file a refund claim on Form 1040X within three years from the time your original return was filed, or within two years from the time you paid your tax, whichever is later. However, a refund claim on a late-filed return may be barred under a three-year "look back" rule; *see* below. A return filed before its due date is treated as having been filed on the due date. If you had a filing extension and filed before the extension deadline, your return is considered filed on the actual filing date. The filing deadlines are suspended if you are unable to manage your financial affairs; *see* the Planning Reminder on the next page.

A refund claim based on a bad debt or worthless securities may be made within seven years of the due date of the return for the year in which the debt or security became worthless.

The time for filing refund claims based on carrybacks of net operating losses or general business credits is within three years of the due date (including extensions) of the return for the year the loss or credit arose.

If you filed an agreement giving the IRS an extended period of time in which to assess a tax against you, you are allowed an additional period in which to file a claim for refund. The claim, up to certain amounts, may be filed through the extension period and for six months afterwards.

**Look-back rule may limit refund claim for withholdings and estimated tax on late-filed original return.** A refund for withheld income taxes or estimated tax installments can be lost if you delay filing your original return too long. The Supreme Court agrees with the IRS that the withholdings and estimated tax are considered to be paid on the original due date of the return. To obtain a refund of these taxes, you must file the return within three years of the due date, or within three years plus any extension period if a filing extension was obtained for the year the taxes were withheld or paid. If the return is filed after the end of this three-year (plus extension) "look-back" period, the withholdings and estimated taxes cannot be refunded.

*Caution*

**Time Limits Must Be Observed**

Failure to file a timely refund claim is fatal, regardless of its merits. Even if you expect that your claim will have to be pursued in court, you must still file a timely refund claim with the IRS. Mailing a refund claim so that it is postmarked by the due date (including extensions) qualifies as a timely filing if you use the U.S. Postal Service. The timely mailing rule also applies to refund claims that are timely deposited with private delivery services that have been designated by the IRS.

*Planning Reminder*

**Disability Suspends Limitation**

The limitations period for filing a refund claim is suspended during any period in which a person is unable to manage his or her financial affairs due to a physical or mental impairment that has lasted or is expected to last for at least one year or to result in death. The suspension does not apply during a period in which a guardian is authorized to handle the individual's financial affairs.

For example, if taxes were withheld from your 2015 wages and you are due a refund but have not yet filed your 2015 return, you must do so by April 15, 2019 (April 17 for residents of Maine or Massachusetts), to obtain a refund of the withholdings. If you had obtained an extension until October 17, 2016, to file your 2015 return, and still have not filed, the deadline for doing so and claiming the refund for the 2015 taxes will be October 15, 2019. What if you claim the refund for the withheld 2014 taxes on an original 2014 return mailed and postmarked on or slightly before the last day of the "three years plus extension" period, namely, April 15 (or 17), 2019, or October 15, 2019, if you had an extension for the 2015 return? Even if the mailing is not received until after the April 15 (or 17) or October 15 deadline, the timely mailing/timely filing rule applies, and the IRS treats the claim as filed on the date of mailing for purposes of applying the "three years plus extension" look-back rule.

**Armed Forces service members and veterans.** In determining the time limits within which a refund claim may be filed, you disregard intervening periods of service in a combat zone or in a contingency operation, plus periods of continuous hospitalization outside the United States as a result of combat zone injury, and the next 180 days thereafter *(35.5)*.

**Claiming refund for deceased taxpayer.** If you are a surviving spouse filing an amended joint return to claim a refund for you and your deceased spouse, you only need to file Form 1040X. A court-appointed personal representative must attach Form 1310 to Form 1040X to claim the refund.

## 47.3　Stating the Reasons for Refund Claim

After entering changes to your original return on Form 1040X, in Part III of the form you explain the changes and tell the IRS why you are claiming a refund. Where appropriate, you should attach a statement explaining:

- All the facts that support the claim. Attach all supporting documents and tax forms supporting your claim.
- All the grounds for the claim. If you are uncertain about the exact legal grounds, alternate and even inconsistent grounds may be given. For example: "The loss was incurred from an embezzlement; if not, from a bad debt." To protect against understating the amount of the claim, you might preface the claim with this phrase: "The following or such greater amounts as may be legally refunded."

If your refund claim is denied by the IRS, it may become the basis of a court suit. If you have not stated all the grounds on Form 1040X, you may not be allowed to argue them in court.

## 47.4　Quick Refund Claims

Form 1045 may be used for filing refunds due to carrybacks from net operating losses, the general business credit, and net Section 1256 contract losses. Form 1045 also may be used for a quick refund based on a repayment exceeding $3,000 of income reported in an earlier year. Form 1045 generally must be filed within 12 months after the end of the year in which the loss, credit, or repayment claim arose; *see* the Form 1045 instructions. The IRS will generally process your claim within 90 days, or if later, 90 days after the end of the month in which your return is due. Payment of quick refund claims is not a final settlement of your return; the IRS may still audit and then disallow the refund claim. Note that the filing of a quick refund, if rejected, may not be the basis of a suit for refund; a regular refund claim must be filed.

## 47.5　Interest Paid on Refund Claims

If a refund claim is filed within the time limits in *47.2* and the IRS pays the refund within 45 days, interest is paid from the date of overpayment to the date the claim was filed. If the refund is not made within the 45-day period, interest is paid from the date of overpayment to a date set by the IRS that is not more than 30 days before the date of the refund check.

The IRS does not have to pay interest on overpayments resulting from net operating loss carrybacks or business credit carrybacks if a refund is paid within 45 days of the filing of the refund claim. If a refund claim based on a loss or credit carryback is filed and subsequently a quick refund claim is filed on Form 1045 for the same refund, the 45-day period starts to run on the date Form 1045 is filed.

Interest rates applied to overpayments are as follows:

| Refund for — | Overpayment rate is— |
| --- | --- |
| 4/1/2018 – 12/31/2018 | 5% |
| 4/1/2016 – 3/31/2018 | 4 |
| 10/1/2011 – 3/31/2016 | 3 |
| 4/1/2011 – 9/30/2011 | 4 |
| 1/1/2011 – 3/31/2011 | 3 |

## 47.6  Refunds Withheld To Cover Debts

The IRS may withhold all or part of your refund if you owe federal taxes. Under the Treasury Offset Program (TOP), the IRS may withhold all or part of your refund if you owe child or spousal support or federal non-tax debts, such as student loans or state income taxes. If you file a joint return with a spouse who owes child support or federal debts, you may be able to obtain your share of a refund due on the joint return by filing Form 8379 *(46.4)*.

## 47.7  Amended Returns Showing Additional Tax

If, after filing your 2018 return, you find that you did not report some income or claimed excessive deductions, you should file an amended return on Form 1040X to limit interest charges and possible tax penalties.

If you filed early and then file an amended return by the filing due date (including any extensions) that shows additional tax due, you will not be charged interest or penalties based on the original return; the amended return is considered a substitute for the original.

You must pay the additional tax due as shown on Form 1040X. Even if you expect a refund on your original return, the IRS will not reduce the refund check to cover the additional tax. You must pay it and you will receive the original refund separately.

## 47.8  Penalty for Filing Excessive Refund Claim

A 20% penalty can apply to an excessive claim for refund or credit that you claim on an original return *(46.4)* or amended *(47.1)* return. The penalty is 20% of the "excessive" amount, the excess of the refund or credit claimed over the amount allowed. For example, assume that you mailed your 2017 Form 1040 to the IRS on April 11, 2018, and included a $400 check to cover the tax due. On June 12, 2019, you file an amended return and claim a $2,000 refund based on an increase in itemized deductions. The IRS reduces the refund to $1,000. If you cannot show that you had a reasonable basis for making the additional $1,000 claim, the IRS will assess a penalty of $200 (20% of the $1,000 excess).

There are exceptions. The penalty does not apply if the claim has a reasonable basis. It does not apply to claims relating to the earned income credit *(25.6)* or to any portion of the excess that is subject to the accuracy-related penalties (including the penalty for understatements due to reportable or listed transactions), or the fraud penalty, discussed at *48.6*.

*Caution*

**Refund Offset for Overdue State Taxes**
If you owe state income taxes, the state can refer the debt to the Treasury Department's Bureau of the Fiscal Service (BFS), which administers the Treasury Offset Program. The BFS can offset your federal tax refund by the state tax if your address on the return is within the state seeking the offset. The state must give you written notice that the debt is being referred to the BFS and provide an opportunity for disputing the liability.

# CHAPTER 48°

# If the IRS Examines Your Return

Because the IRS is only able to examine a very low percentage of returns, it follows a policy of examining returns which, upon preliminary inspection, indicate the largest possible source of potential tax deficiency. Various weights are assigned to separate items on each tax return, thus permitting the ranking of returns for the greatest potential error.

This chapter discusses what may trigger an audit and how you can handle an audit if your return is selected for examination.

Also discussed in this chapter are various penalties the IRS can assess if you file an inaccurate return, and the penalties for not reporting your foreign financial accounts.

## 48.1  Odds of Being Audited

The odds are quite low that your return will be picked for an audit. In Fiscal Year 2017 (October 2016 through September 2017), the overall audit rate for individual returns was only 0.60%, compared to an overall audit rate of 0.70% in FY 2016. The audit rates are higher for taxpayers with large adjusted gross incomes and sole proprietors with substantial total gross receipts. Budget pressures on the IRS suggest that low audit rates will continue for most income groups for the forseeable future.

Audit odds vary depending on your income, profession, type of return, type of transactions reported, and where you live. Individual returns are classified by all income items on the return without regard to losses. Professional or business income reported on Schedule C and farm income reported on Schedule F is classified by total gross receipts, and corporate returns are classified by total assets.

Your return may command special IRS scrutiny because of your profession, the type of transactions reported, or the deductions claimed. The chances of being audited are greater under the following circumstances:

- Your information reported on the tax return does not match information received from third-party documentation, such as Forms 1099 and W-2.
- Your itemized deductions exceed IRS targets.
- You claim tax-shelter losses.
- You report complex investment or business transactions without clear explanations.
- You receive cash payments in your work that the IRS thinks are easy to conceal, such as cash fees received by doctors or tips received by cab drivers and waiters.
- Business expenses are large in relation to income.
- Cash contributions to charity are large in relation to income.
- You are a shareholder of a closely held corporation whose return has been examined.
- A prior audit resulted in a tax deficiency.
- An informer gives the IRS grounds to believe that you are omitting income from your return.

**Itemized deductions.**  If your itemized deductions exceed target ranges set by the IRS, the chances of being audited increase. The IRS does not publicize its audit criteria for excessive deductions, but it does release statistics showing the average amount of deductions claimed according to reported income. *Table 48-1* shows the IRS figures based on deductions claimed on 2016 returns filed through September 2017.

**Taxpayer Bill of Rights.**  The "Taxpayer Bill of Rights" collectively refers to a series of laws that aim to protect taxpayers from mistreatment by IRS personnel and insure that they are treated fairly, professionally, promptly, and courteously by the IRS and its employees:

1. The right to be informed
2. The right to quality service
3. The right to pay no more than the correct amount of tax
4. The right to challenge the IRS' position and be heard
5. The right to appeal an IRS decision in an independent forum
6. The right to finality
7. The right to privacy
8. The right to confidentiality
9. The right to retain representation
10. The right to a fair and just tax system

These rights are listed in the IRS instructions for Forms 1040 and in IRS Publication 1.

If you have a dispute with the IRS, you should ask for an explanation of the procedural rules affecting your case, if these are not already included in the documents sent to you. For example, before the IRS may enforce a tax lien by seizing property by levy, the IRS must provide you with a notice of your right to a hearing before an appeals officer, an explanation of the levy procedures, the availability of administrative appeals and the appeals procedures, the alternatives to the proposed levy such as an installment agreement, and the

 *Caution*

**IRS Audits of High-Income Taxpayers**
Despite very low audit rates overall, the audit rate is higher for individuals with adjusted gross income over $200,000 and sole proprietors with over $25,000 in total gross receipts, compared to those with lesser incomes.

rules for obtaining the release of a lien. *See* IRS Publication 1, *Your Rights as a Taxpayer,* IRS Publication 556, *Examination of Returns, Appeal Rights, and Claims for Refund;* IRS Publication 594, *The IRS Collection Process;* and IRS Publication 5, *Your Appeal Rights and How to Prepare a Protest if You Don't Agree.*

**Taxpayer Advocate.** The Taxpayer Advocate Service (TAS) is an independent office within the IRS. The function of the TAS is to assist taxpayers in resolving problems with the IRS, propose changes in administrative practices of the IRS, and identify potential legislative changes that may mitigate problems and improve the tax system.

You may be able to receive TAS assistance if you have unsuccessfully tried to resolve your problem with the IRS and have not had your calls or letters returned. However, because of the demand on its resources, the TAS is most likely to provide assistance if you face a significant hardship because of an impending IRS action or lack of IRS response to your problem. If you qualify, you will be assigned a personal advocate to try to resolve your problem. Contact the TAS at its homepage at *www.taxpayeradvocate.irs.gov*. From the website, you can access a state-by-state list of addresses and phone numbers for TAS offices. The list is also in IRS Publication 1546. You can contact the TAS by calling 1-877-777-4778, or you may apply for assistance by filing Form 911 ("Request for Taxpayer Advocate Service Assistance (And Application for Taxpayer Assistance Order)").

| *Table 48-1* Average Itemized Deductions for 2016 | | | | |
|---|---|---|---|---|
| AGI (thousands) | Medical | Taxes | Interest | Charitable |
| Under $ 15 | $9,106 | $3,885 | $6,761 | $1,471 |
| 15 – <30 | $8,884 | $3,565 | $6,252 | $2,525 |
| 30 – <50 | $8,587 | $4,196 | $6,387 | $2,871 |
| 50 – <100 | $9,375 | $6,457 | $7,367 | $3,296 |
| 100 – <200 | $12,425 | $11,243 | $8,891 | $4,245 |
| 200 – <250 | $20,701 | $18,028 | $11,177 | $5,470 |
| 250 and over | $34,154 | $50,851 | $15,981 | $21,361 |

## 48.2 When the IRS Can Assess Additional Taxes

**Three-year statute of limitations.** The IRS has three years after the date on which your return is filed to assess additional taxes. When you file a return before the due date, however, the three-year period starts from the due date, generally April 15.

Where the due date of a return falls on a Saturday, Sunday, or legal holiday, the due date is postponed to the next business day.

> **EXAMPLES**
>
> 1. You filed your 2018 return on February 9, 2019. The last day on which the IRS can make an assessment on your 2018 return is April 15, 2022.
> 2. You filed your 2015 return on May 15, 2016. The IRS has until May 15, 2019, to assess a deficiency.

**Amended returns.** If you file an amended return shortly before the three-year limitations period is about to expire and the return shows that you owe additional tax, the IRS has 60 days from the date it receives the return to assess the additional tax, even though the regular limitations period would expire before the 60-day period.

**Six-year statute.** When you fail to report an item of gross income which is more than 25% of the gross income reported on your return, the IRS has six years after the return is

*Caution*

**No Limitation Period for Fraud**

There is no limitation on when tax may be assessed where a false or fraudulent return is filed with intent to evade tax, or where no return is filed.

filed to assess additional taxes. An item that is adequately disclosed is not considered an omission. An overstatement of basis that minimizes gain is an "omission" of gross income in determining if the 25% test for triggering the six-year statute of limitations is met.

**IRS request for audit extension.** If the IRS cannot complete an audit within three years, it may request that you sign Form 872 to extend the time for assessing the tax. However, where an individual was "scared" into signing such an agreement, it was held invalid. *See* the following Example.

---

**EXAMPLE**

Robertson, a plumber, won $30,000 in a sweepstakes. An IRS agent asked him to sign an agreement to extend the tax assessment deadline. Robertson never had any prior dealings with the IRS, he did not know that his return was under examination, and he was not in touch with the lawyer who prepared the return on which his sweepstakes winnings were averaged.

Robertson wanted to *see* his lawyer before signing Form 872, but the agent pressed hard for the signature, phoning him and his wife at home and at work 20 times in a week. The agent did not tell him the amount of additional tax that might be involved, or explain that if he refused to sign he would have an opportunity before the IRS and the courts to contest any additional tax. Instead, the agent's comments gave him the impression that his home could be confiscated if he refused to sign. Robertson signed and the IRS later increased his tax.

Robertson argued that the agreement was not valid. He signed under duress. The Tax Court agreed. He convinced the court that he really believed he could lose his house and property if he did not comply. No adequate explanation of the real consequences of refusal to sign was made, although Robertson asked. Since he signed Form 872 under duress, the IRS could not increase his tax after the three-year period.

---

## 48.3 Audit Overview

When you file, the IRS checks your return for computational accuracy and clerical errors, such as a missing signature or missing or inaccurate Social Security numbers. To check whether you have omitted income from your return, the IRS will match your return against the Forms W-2 and Forms 1099 it receives from employers, brokers, payers of interest and dividends, and others who have filed information returns reporting payments to you.

If an error is found, or you have not submitted required attachments, you will probably be advised by mail of the corrections and of additional tax due, or you may be asked to provide additional information to substantiate tax deductions or credits. If you disagree with an IRS assessment of additional tax, you may request an interview or submit additional information. For example, if you file early for 2018, are advised of an error, and the correction is made before April 15, 2019, interest is not charged.

If your refund is selected for a more thorough review, you will be notified by mail. This may not happen for a year or two; *see 48.2.*

**Types of audits.** An examination may be held by correspondence, at a local IRS office, at your tax preparer's office or your place of business, office, or home. Correspondence audits are by far the most common type of audit. An examination at an IRS office is called a desk or office examination. An examination at your office or your preparer's office, or your place of business or home, is called a field examination. When you are contacted by the IRS, you should receive an explanation of the examination process.

In a correspondence audit, the IRS sends you a letter asking for additional information about an item on your return. For example, the IRS may ask you to document a claimed deduction for charitable contributions or medical expenses. If the IRS is not satisfied with your response, you may be called in for an office audit. The IRS also notifies you by letter of mathematical or clerical errors you have made on your return, or if you have failed to report income, such as interest or dividends, that are shown by payers on information returns and matched to taxpayer returns by IRS computers.

**Authorize Someone To Represent You**

Just above the signature section of your Form 1040, you may consent to contacts between the IRS and your designee to resolve return processing issues such as mathematical errors, missing return information, or questions about refunds or payments. The designee can be a friend or relative and need not be a tax professional. If you want to authorize someone to represent you at an audit or appeals procedure, or to handle collection notices, you must give that person a power of attorney on Form 2848. However, preparers who are not attorneys, CPAs, or enrolled agents cannot represent you before the IRS with respect to a return they prepared after 2015 unless they participate in the IRS' Annual Filing Season Program.

*Planning Reminder*

**Audit Scheduling**

Make sure that the examination is scheduled far enough in advance for you to get ready. Do not let the IRS hurry you into an examination until you are prepared. In some localities, particularly rural areas, the IRS may give short notice in scheduling a field audit. An agent may even appear at your place of business and try to begin the audit immediately. Resist this pressure and reschedule the meeting at your convenience.

If the IRS wants to conduct an in-person audit, the complexity of the transactions reported on a return generally determines whether a return will be reviewed at an office or field examination.

Most in-person audits of individual returns, except for returns reporting self-employment income, are conducted at IRS offices. An office audit usually covers only a few specific issues which the IRS specifies in its notice to you. For example, the examining agent may only be interested in seeing proof for travel expense deductions or educational expenses.

Field audits generally involve business returns; they are more extensive and time-consuming than office audits and are handled by more experienced IRS agents. For self-employed individuals, most examinations are field audits at their place of business. It is advisable to have a tax professional go over the potential weak spots in your return and represent you at the examination.

## 48.4  Preparing for the Audit

After an office audit is scheduled, the first thing to do is look over your return. Refresh your memory. Examine the items the IRS questioned in its notice of audit, and organize your records accordingly. Also check the rest of your return and gather proof for items you are unsure of. At this point, you should take a broad view of your return to anticipate problems you may encounter. Before the actual examination begins, consider possible settlement terms. Assume that the agent will assess additional tax, but establish the range you will consider reasonable. You can always change your mind, but giving some thought beforehand to possible settlement terms will help you later when settlements are actually discussed.

You may authorize an attorney, CPA, enrolled agent, or other individual recognized to practice before the IRS to represent you at the examination without your being there. To do so, give your representative authorization on Form 2848. An attorney or other representative authorized on Form 2848 can perform any acts that you could, including entering into a binding settlement agreement. Caution: For returns prepared and signed after 2015, only attorneys, CPAs and enrolled agents have full representation rights for their clients before any IRS officer. A preparer who is not an attorney, CPA or enrolled agent cannot represent you at an audit with respect to a return prepared and signed after 2015 unless he or she has completed continuing education courses and received a Record of Completion as part of the IRS' Annual Filing Season Program (AFSP). Even with an AFSP Record of Completion, the preparer cannot represent you before IRS appeals or collection officers.

If you attend the audit, take only the records related to the items questioned in the IRS notice. Do not volunteer extra records; if the agent sees them, it might suggest new areas for investigation.

If you are concerned that there may be a problem of fraud, *see* a qualified attorney before you come into contact with an IRS official. The attorney can put your actions in perspective and help protect your legal rights. Besides, what you tell an attorney is privileged information; he or she cannot divulge or be forced to divulge data you have provided, other than data used to prepare your tax return.

A field audit of your business return is likely to involve a comprehensive examination and requires careful preparation. Together with your tax adviser, go over your return for potential areas of weakness. For example, the agent is likely to question deductions you have claimed for business travel. If you are an incorporated professional, the corporation's deductions for expenses of company-owned cars or planes will probably be reviewed. The agent may suspect that a portion of these business deductions are actually nondeductible personal travel costs; be prepared to substantiate the business portion of your total mileage and operating expenses.

The IRS is generally required to hold an office audit at the office located nearest to your home. The IRS generally may not conduct a field audit at the site of a small business if the audit would essentially require the shutting down of the business, unless a direct visit is necessary to determine inventory or verify assets.

## 48.5 Handling the Audit

If you have authorized someone to represent you at the examination, your representative may appear at the examination without you. If the IRS wants to question you, it must issue you an administrative summons. If you are present and questioned, you may stop the examination to consult with counsel, unless the examination is pursuant to an administrative summons.

Audits conducted at an IRS office may conclude quickly because they usually involve only a few specific issues. In some cases, the audit may take less than an hour. The key to handling the audit is advance preparation. When you arrive at the IRS office, be prepared to produce your records quickly. Records should be organized by topic so that you do not waste time leafing through pages for a receipt or other document.

If the agent decides to question an item not mentioned in the notice of audit, refuse politely but firmly to answer the questions. Tell the agent that you must first review your records. If the agent insists on pursuing the matter, another meeting will have to be scheduled. The agent might decide it is not worth the time and drop the issue.

Common sense rules of courtesy should be your guide in your contacts with the agent. Avoid personality clashes; they can only interfere with a speedy and fair resolution of the examination. However, be firm in your approach and, if the agent appears to be unreasonable in his or her approach, make it clear that—if necessary—you will go all the way to court to win your point. A vacillating approach may weaken your position in reaching a settlement.

If the IRS has scheduled a field audit, ask that the examination be held at your representative's office. If you have not retained professional help and the examination takes place on your business premises, do not allow the agent free run of the area: Provide the agent with a comfortable work area for examining your records. If possible, the workplace should be isolated so that the agent can concentrate on the examination without being distracted by office operations that might spark questions. Tell your employees not to answer questions about your business or engage in small talk with the agent. As with an office audit, help speed along the field examination by having prepared your records so that requested information can be quickly produced.

**Recording the examination.** You have the right to make an audio recording of any interview with an IRS official. Video recordings are not permitted. No later than 10 calendar days before the interview, give written notice to the agent conducting the interview that you will make a recording. Later requests are at the discretion of the IRS. You must pay for all recording expenses and supply the equipment. The IRS may also make a recording of the interview, upon giving notice of at least 10 calendar days. However, IRS notice is not necessary if you have already submitted a request to make a recording. You have the right to obtain a transcript, at your own expense, of any recording made by the IRS. Generally, a request for a copy must be received by the IRS agent within 30 calendar days after the recording, although later requests may be honored.

## 48.6 Tax Penalties for Inaccurate Returns

As discussed in this section, an "accuracy-related" penalty applies to the portion of any tax underpayment attributable to any of the following: (1) negligence or disregard of IRS rules and regulations; (2) substantial understatement of tax liability; (3) overvaluation of property; (4) undervaluation of property on a gift tax or estate tax return; (5) claim of benefits from a transaction lacking economic substance, (6) an undisclosed foreign financial asset, or (7) claiming a basis for property in excess of the amount reported on an estate tax return. There is no stacking of penalties. Only one penalty can be imposed on a portion of an underpayment, even if that portion is attributable to more than one of the above types of prohibited conduct.

The above accuracy-related penalties generally may be avoided by showing that you acted in good faith and with reasonable cause in underpaying the tax. Reliance on a tax preparer may constitute reasonable cause and good faith, but the reliance on the preparer must be reasonable. The Tax Court has held that reliance on a preparer is not reasonable if the taxpayer does not provide the preparer with the documents necessary to make a professional conclusion, or if the preparer lacks sufficient expertise to justify reliance.

A stricter reasonable cause exception applies to the penalty for overvaluing charitable donations or the basis of depreciable property; *see* below. There is no reasonable cause exception for penalties attributable to transactions lacking economic substance.

Also discussed below are penalties for (1) failing to disclose participation in "reportable" transactions, (2) understating tax liability on "listed" transactions or on other reportable transactions with a significant tax avoidance purpose, (3) filing an erroneous refund claim, and (4) filing a frivolous return.

**Negligence or disregard of IRS rules or regulations.** The 20% penalty applies to the portion of the underpayment attributable to negligence. Negligence is defined as failing to make a reasonable attempt to comply with the law. Failure to report income shown on an information return, such as interest or dividends, is considered strong evidence of negligence.

The 20% penalty may also apply if you take a position on a return which is contrary to IRS revenue rulings, notices, or regulations. This penalty for disregarding IRS rules or regulations may be avoided if you have a reasonable basis for your position and you disclose that position on Form 8275 or on Form 8275-R in the case of a good faith position contrary to a regulation. Thus, disclosure will not avoid a penalty for a position that does not have a reasonable basis.

**Substantial understatement of tax.** If you understate tax liability on a return by the greater of $5,000 or 10% of the proper tax, you may be subject to a penalty equal to 20% of the underpayment attributable to the understatement.

The penalty may be avoided if you have a reasonable basis for your position and you disclose the position to the IRS on Form 8275, or on Form 8275-R in the case of a position that is contrary to an IRS regulation.

The penalty also may be avoided if you can show that your position was supported by "substantial authority" such as statutes, court decisions, final, temporary, or proposed IRS regulations, IRS revenue rulings and procedures, and notices, announcements, and other administrative pronouncements published by the IRS in the weekly Internal Revenue Bulletin. You may also rely on IRS private letter rulings and technical advice memoranda, as well as IRS actions on decisions and general counsel memoranda. However, according to the IRS, such rulings and internal IRS memoranda that are more than 10 years old should be accorded very little weight. Congressional committee reports and the tax law explanations prepared by Congress's Joint Committee on Taxation, known as the "Blue Book," may be relied on as authority for your position.

However, the exceptions for disclosed positions (with a reasonable basis) and substantial authority do not apply to items attributable to a tax shelter, which for this purpose means any arrangement that has tax avoidance or evasion as a significant purpose. An understatement of tax due to tax shelter positions may be subject to the understatement penalty for "reportable" transactions discussed below; if the understatement penalty for "reportable" transactions does apply, the 20% penalty discussed above for substantial understatements of tax does not apply to the same understatement.

**Overvaluing donated property value or depreciable basis.** If the claimed value of property donated to charity is 150% or more of the correct value, resulting in a tax underpayment exceeding $5,000, a penalty equal to 20% of the underpayment applies, and the penalty is doubled to 40% if the overvaluation is 200% or more. The same penalty thresholds and rates apply where the basis of depreciable property has been inflated. A reasonable cause exception to the 20% penalty is available (but not for the 40% penalty) if you relied on a qualified appraisal and you investigated the value of the property in good faith *(14.16)*.

**Undervaluation on gift or estate tax return.** If the value of property reported on a gift tax or estate tax return is 65% or less of the correct value, and the resulting tax underpayment from the undervaluation exceeds $5,000, the penalty is 20% of the underpayment. The penalty doubles to 40% of the underpayment if the claimed value of the property is 40% or less of the correct value.

**Claiming benefits from transaction lacking economic substance.** If you claim tax benefits from a transaction lacking economic substance, the penalty is 20% of the resulting

**Caution**

**Too Good to Be True**

If you claim a deduction, credit, or exclusion on your return that would seem to a reasonable person to be "too good to be true" under the circumstances, the IRS is likely to consider you negligent unless you show you made an attempt to verify the correctness of the position.

underpayment. There is no reasonable cause exception for transactions lacking economic substance. The penalty doubles to 40% of the underpayment if the transaction is not adequately disclosed.

**Understatement due to undisclosed foreign financial asset.** A 40% accuracy-related penalty applies to the portion of a tax underpayment that is attributable to an undisclosed specified foreign financial asset. These are assets required to be reported on Form 8938, as discussed in *48.7*.

**Claiming basis higher than estate tax value.** As discussed in *5.17*, you are subject to a 20% penalty if you inherit property that increased the estate tax liability owed by the estate and you claim a basis for the property (such as when you sell or claim depreciation) that is higher than the estate tax value reported to you on Schedule A of Form 8971.

**Penalties relating to reportable transactions.** A penalty may be imposed on individuals and business entities who fail to adequately disclose a "reportable" transaction on Form 8886. This penalty is in addition to any other penalty that may be imposed. Some reportable transactions may fall into the category of "listed" transactions. The Form 8886 instructions explain the difference between listed transactions and other types of reportable transactions. The amount of the penalty for failure to disclose is generally 75% of the tax reduction claimed on the return as a result of the transaction, but there is a minimum penalty of $5,000 per reportable transaction (whether or not listed) for individuals ($10,000 for non-individual returns). There is also a maximum penalty. If the failure to disclose involves a reportable transaction that is not a listed transaction, the maximum penalty is $10,000 ($50,000 for non-individual returns). If the transaction is a listed transaction, the maximum penalty is $100,000 for individuals ($200,000 for non-individual returns).

There is a separate "accuracy-related" penalty for understating tax liability attributable to a listed transaction or to any reportable transaction (other than a listed transaction) with a significant tax avoidance purpose. The penalty is generally 20% of the understatement if the transaction was adequately disclosed on Form 8886. There is an exception for reasonable cause, but to qualify, stringent requirements must be met; *see* Code Section 6664(d). If the transaction was not adequately disclosed, the penalty increases to 30% of the understatement and there is no reasonable cause exception.

**Fraud penalty.** A 75% penalty applies to the portion of any tax underpayment due to fraud. If the IRS establishes that any part of an underpayment is due to fraud, the entire underpayment will be attributed to fraud, unless you prove otherwise.

**Interest on penalties.** A higher interest cost is imposed on individuals subject to the following penalties: failure to file a timely return *(46.9)*, negligence or fraud, overvaluation of property, undervaluation of gift or estate tax property, substantial understatement of tax liability, or understatements attributable to reportable transactions or undisclosed foreign financial assets. Interest starts to run on these penalties from the due date of the return (including extensions) until the date the penalty is paid. For other penalties, interest is imposed only if the penalty is not paid within 21 calendar days of an IRS demand for payment if the penalty is less than $100,000. The interest-free period is 10 business days after the IRS demand for payment if the penalty is $100,000 or more.

**Penalty for filing erroneous refund claim or tax credit claim.** A 20% penalty can apply to an erroneous tax credit or claim for refund on any original *(46.4)* or amended return *(47.8)*, but it does not apply to claims relating to the Earned Income Credit *(25.7)*. The penalty is 20% of the "excessive" amount, the excess of the refund or credit claimed over the amount allowed, unless there is a reasonable basis for the amount claimed. The penalty applies only where the IRS initially disallows part of the credit or refund at the time the return is processed. It does not apply to any portion of the excess that is subject to the accuracy-related penalties (including the penalty for understatements due to reportable or listed transactions), or the fraud penalty. If a refund is paid to a taxpayer and the IRS later determines that the refund was excessive, the accuracy-related or fraud penalty might apply, but the erroneous refund penalty would not apply since the IRS disallowance was after the issuance of the refund.

**Penalty for frivolous tax return or submission.** In addition to any other penalty, there is a $5,000 penalty for filing a frivolous tax return. A $5,000 penalty also applies to frivolous submissions, including requests for a collection due process hearing or an application for an installment agreement, offer-in-compromise, or Taxpayer Assistance Order based on a frivolous position. In Notice 2010-33, the IRS lists positions it considers frivolous. The IRS provides an in-depth rebuttal of frivolous positions at www.irs.gov/tax-professionals/the-truth-about-frivolous-tax-arguments-introduction.

**Acting on wrong IRS advice.** A penalty will not be imposed if you reasonably rely on erroneous advice provided in writing by IRS officials in response to your specific written request. It is necessary for you to show that you provided accurate information when asking for advice.

## 48.7 Penalties for Not Reporting Foreign Financial Accounts

If you have financial interests in foreign bank accounts or other foreign financial accounts or assets, you may be required to file a FBAR, Form 8938, or both. Depending on your holdings, you may be required to file both forms, so check the filing requirements for both. Failure to file a required form may result in substantial penalties.

**FBAR.** A Report of Foreign Bank and Financial Accounts, generally referred to as the "FBAR", must be filed if you have a financial interest in or signature authority over foreign bank or other financial accounts and the aggregate value of the accounts at any time during the year exceeds $10,000. The annual report is FinCEN Form 114, which is filed electronically with the Treasury Department. FinCEN is the Treasury's Financial Crimes Enforcement Network.

The FBAR, if required, is not filed with your income tax return. For 2018 foreign holdings, the FBAR report is due on April 15, 2019. The report is filed with the Treasury Department separately from the income tax return. There is an automatic 6-month filing extension for FinCEN Form 114; no form needs to be filed to obtain the extension.

In Part III of Schedule B (Form 1040) you must tell the IRS if you had a financial interest in or signature interest over a financial account located in a foreign country. If you answer yes, you are directed to the FBAR instructions to determine if you must file the form, and if you are required to file the FBAR, you are asked to enter the name of the foreign country where the financial account is located.

*Penalties.* If you are required to file a FBAR and fail to do so, a civil penalty of up to $12,459 per violation (this amount is subject to inflation adjustments) may be imposed if the violation was not willful. The penalty may be waived if there was reasonable cause for the failure and a FBAR is properly filed. For a willful failure to file, the civil penalty per violation can be up to the greater of $124,588 (this amount is subject to inflation adjustments) or 50% of the account balance at the time of the violation; criminal penalties may also apply.

**Form 8938.** Form 8938 must be filed with Form 1040 if you have specified foreign financial assets (SFFAs) at the end of the year in excess of the applicable threshold. SFFAs include, in addition to financial accounts maintained by foreign financial institutions, foreign stocks and securities, financial instruments or contracts issued by a foreign party, and interests in certain foreign estates, trusts, and partnerships. The Form 8938 instructions have detailed definitions of SFFAs and exceptions.

The reporting threshold depends on whether you live in the U.S. or abroad and whether you are married filing jointly. For example, unmarried taxpayers living in the U.S., and married taxpayers filing separately and living in the U.S., must file Form 8938 with their 2018 Form 1040 if the total value of their SFFAs on the last day of 2018 exceeded $50,000, or if the value exceeded $75,000 at any time in 2018. For married couples filing jointly and living in the U.S., reporting on Form 8938 is required if the year-end value of their SFFAs exceeded $100,000, or over $150,000 at any time during the year. For a U.S. citizen living abroad who has been a bona fide foreign resident for a full year or who meets a 330-day physical presence test, Form 8938 must be filed if the year-end value of SFFAs exceeded $200,000, or exceeded $300,000 at any time during the year; these thresholds are doubled to $400,000/$600,000 for married couples filing jointly. The Form 8938 instructions have examples of situations in which filing is and is not required.

*IRS Alert*

**Offshore Voluntary Disclosure Program (OVDP) discontinued**

The IRS has discontinued its Offshore Voluntary Disclosure Program (OVDP), effective September 28, 2018. This program enabled taxpayers with undisclosed offshore accounts to come into tax compliance, with the possibility of reduced penalties. For further details, *see* https://www.irs.gov/newsroom/irs-offshore-voluntary-compliance-program-to-end-sept-28.

*Penalties.* Failure to file Form 8938, or understating tax by omitting income attributable to an undisclosed SFFA, can result in substantial penalties.

There is a $10,000 penalty for not filing a complete and correct Form 8938 by the due date (including extensions) of your return, and a continuing failure to file within 90 days after receiving IRS notice to file may result in additional $10,000 penalties for each 30-day period, up to a maximum additional penalty of $50,000 (for a maximum penalty of $60,000). If you can show reasonable cause for not filing Form 8938 or not reporting one or more SFFAs, the penalty can be avoided.

As noted at *48.6*, an accuracy-related penalty may be imposed if you do not disclose an SFFA and income related to the undisclosed SFFA is not reported on your return. The penalty is 40% of the tax underpayment resulting from the omission of income. The penalty can be avoided if you can show reasonable cause for the underpayment. An underpayment due to fraud is subject to a 75% penalty.

## 48.8  Agreeing to the Audit Changes

After the audit, the agent will discuss proposed changes either with you or your representative.

If you agree with the agent's proposed changes, you will be asked to sign a Form 870, which, when signed, permits an immediate assessment of a deficiency plus penalties and interest, if due. The Form 870 is called "Waiver of Restrictions on Assessment and Collection of Deficiency in Tax and Acceptance of Overassessment."

If you believe that you have done as well or better than expected regarding the proposed deficiency, you can bring the case to a close by signing the Form 870, but the agent's supervisor must also approve the assessment.

By signing the form, you limit the amount of interest charges added to the deficiency. A signed Form 870 does not prevent the IRS from reopening the case to assess an additional deficiency. If on review the deficiency is increased, you will receive a revised Form 870. You can refuse to sign the form. The signed first form has the effect of stopping the interest on the original deficiency. As a matter of practice, however, waivers of acceptances ordinarily result in closing of the case.

It is possible, although unlikely, that upon examining your return, the agent will determine that you are due a refund. In this situation, a signed Form 870 is considered a valid refund claim. You should file a protective refund claim even if you sign the Form 870 acknowledging the overpayment. Generally, the agent will process the refund, but if he or she fails to do so or the review staff puts it aside for some reason and the limitations period expires, the refund will be lost. The refund claim will protect you from such a mishap.

The payment of tax before the deficiency notice (90-day letter) is mailed is, in effect, a waiver of the restrictions on assessment and collection. If the payment satisfies your entire tax liability for that year, you cannot appeal to the Tax Court. You must sue for a refund in either federal district court or the Court of Federal Claims.

## 48.9  Disputing the Audit Changes

If you disagree with the agent and the examination takes place in an IRS office, you may ask for an immediate meeting with a supervisor to argue your side of the dispute. If an agreement is not reached at this meeting or the audit is at your office or home, the agent prepares a report of the proposed adjustments. You will receive a 30-day letter in which you are given the opportunity to request a conference. You may decide not to ask for a conference and await a formal notice of deficiency (90-day letter).

**Appeals conference.** If your examination was conducted as an office audit or by correspondence, or the disputed amount does not exceed $25,000, you do not have to prepare a written protest for a conference with the IRS Appeals Office. The written protest is a detailed presentation of your reasons for disagreeing with the agent's report. Even where a formal written protest is not required, you must provide a brief written statement indicating your reasons for disagreeing with the agent when you request an appeals conference; you can use Form 12203 (Request for Appeals Review).

At the conference you may appear for yourself or be represented by an attorney or other agent, and you may bring witnesses. The conference is held in an informal manner and you are given ample opportunity to present your case.

 *Caution*

**Waiving Your Right To Appeal**
Before deciding whether to sign the Form 870, consider that, by signing, you are giving up your right of appeal to both the IRS Office of Appeals and the Tax Court. However, you may still file a refund suit in a federal district court or in the Court of Federal Claims unless you have agreed not to do so on the Form 870.

If you cannot reach a settlement, you will receive a Notice of Deficiency, commonly called a 90-day letter. In it, you are notified that at the end of 90 days from the date it was mailed, the government will assess the additional tax.

**Interest abatement.** An IRS delay in completing an audit increases the interest that you have to pay when a deficiency notice is eventually issued. You may ask the IRS on Form 843 for an abatement of interest charges that are attributable to unreasonable errors or delays by IRS employees in performing a ministerial or managerial act.

A ministerial act is defined as a procedural or mechanical act that does not involve the exercise of an IRS employee's discretion or judgment, such as the transfer of a taxpayer's case to a different IRS office after the transfer is approved by a group manager. A managerial act refers to the exercise of discretion or judgment by an IRS employee in managing personnel. Misplacing the taxpayer's case file is also a managerial act. General IRS administrative decisions, such as prioritizing the order of processing returns, or decisions on applying the tax law, that result in delay, are not ministerial or management acts for which interest abatement is available.

If you make a request on Form 843 for an abatement of interest and the IRS rejects your claim, you can petition the Tax Court within 180 days to review whether the IRS abused its discretion, provided that your net worth does not exceed $2 million ($7 million for businesses). The same net worth limit applies to recoveries of administrative and litigation costs; *see 48.10*. The Tax Court has exclusive jurisdiction to review the denial of the interest abatement request; an appeal of the IRS decision cannot be brought in a federal district court or the U.S. Court of Claims.

**Going to court.** Within 90 days from the date a 90-day letter (notice of deficiency) is mailed to you (150 days if it is addressed to you outside the United States), you may file a petition with the Tax Court without having to pay the tax. The Tax Court has a small tax case procedure for deficiencies of $50,000 or less. Such cases are handled expeditiously and informally. Cases may be heard by appointed special trial judges. A small claim case may be discontinued at any time before a decision, but the decision when made is final. No appeal may be taken by you or the IRS.

Instead of petitioning the Tax Court, you may pay the additional tax, file a refund claim for it, and—after the refund claim is denied—sue for a refund in a federal district court or the U.S. Court of Federal Claims.

You should consult with an experienced tax practitioner before deciding to litigate.

## 48.10 Offer in Compromise

If you are unable to pay a tax debt in full, you may be able to make an offer in compromise (OIC), but it should be considered a last resort. An OIC is an agreement between a taxpayer and the IRS in which the IRS accepts less than full payment of the outstanding tax liabilities as settlement of the tax debt.

However, the number of accepted offers has declined steadily, and the National Taxpayer Advocate believes that taxpayers are deterred from applying by the burdensome disclosure and other application requirements. There is generally a $186 application fee (some exceptions apply) that the IRS will keep unless the offer cannot be processed. There also is a requirement to submit a nonrefundable payment with the offer on Form 656, and this has been strongly criticized as a major reason for reducing access to the OIC program.

There are two payment options. You can make an up-front payment on Form 656 equal to 20% of a lump-sum offer, with the balance payable in five or fewer installments within five months of IRS acceptance. Alternatively, you may choose the periodic payment option, which requires you to submit the first proposed payment with Form 656 and pay the rest of your offer within 24 months. You must make regular payments in accordance with your proposed offer while the IRS considers your application. These upfront payments are not refundable even if you withdraw the offer prior to IRS acceptance or the IRS rejects the offer; they will be applied to your tax debt.

The only exceptions to the application fee and upfront payment requirements are for (1) low-income individuals who certify that their income is below poverty guidelines, and (2) taxpayers who file an offer on Form 656-L based on doubt as to liability. The IRS

**Caution**

**Penalty for Frivolous Tax Court Action**

If you bring a case to the Tax Court that the Court concludes is frivolous or brought primarily for delay, or you unreasonably failed to pursue IRS administrative remedies, the Tax Court may impose a penalty of up to $25,000. Furthermore, if you appeal a Tax Court decision and the federal appeals court or the Supreme Court finds that the appeal was frivolous or brought primarily for delay, the Court may impose a penalty.

as well as the Treasury Department and Taxpayer Advocate have called on Congress for legislation to eliminate mandatory upfront payments.

**Grounds for an Offer in Compromise.** The IRS has authority to settle or "compromise" for one of the following reasons: Doubt as to liability, doubt as to collectibility, and effective tax administration. Doubt as to liability means that doubt exists concerning the correctness of the IRS' tax assessment. Doubt as to collectibility means that you may never be able to pay the full amount of tax owed. Even where there is no doubt that you owe the tax and you could manage full repayment, you can apply for an OIC on "effective tax administration" grounds if collection of the full tax would cause you economic hardship or there are exceptional circumstances that would make full collection unfair and inequitable.

**Applying for an Offer in Compromise on Form 656 or 656-L.** You must submit an OIC on Form 656 where the offer is based on doubt as to collectibility or effective tax administration (exceptional circumstances). The IRS will consider the OIC only after other payment options have been exhausted, including an installment agreement. An OIC based on doubt as to liability must be filed on Form 656-L; there is no application fee or upfront payment requirement for an offer made on Form 656-L.

When you submit an OIC on Form 656, you must make an upfront payment unless the exception for low-income taxpayers applies as discussed above. Form 656-B, the OIC booklet, includes an explanation of the OIC program and instructions for completing Form 656. The booklet also includes financial disclosure statements that must be attached to support an OIC based on doubt as to collectibility or effective tax administration. Wage earners and self-employed individuals must use Form 433-A, while partnerships and corporations use Form 433-B. In some cases, the IRS may request Form 433-A from corporate officers or individual partners. Form 656-B is available online at *IRS.gov* or can be obtained by calling (800) 829-3676.

If your offer is rejected, you will be given an opportunity to appeal the decision and to amend the offer.

**Application fee.** An application fee must be paid with Form 656 unless you certify in Section 1 of Form 656 that your total monthly income is at or below federal poverty guidelines (Section 1 has a table showing the monthly income limits based on family size). The fee is $186. No fee is required for an offer made on Form 656-L based on doubt as to liability.

**Compliance conditions.** If the IRS accepts an OIC, you must pay the agreed-to amount in accordance with the acceptance agreement and must timely file and pay all required taxes for a period of five years from the acceptance date, or until the accepted amount is paid in full, whichever is longer. You may also be asked as part of the agreement to pay a percentage of your future earnings to the IRS. A failure to comply with the agreement causes default of the OIC and the reinstatement of the original liability.

 *Filing Tip*

**Appealing Rejected Offer**

You can appeal a rejection within 30 days by filing Form 13711, "Request for Appeal of Offer in Compromise."

## 48.11 Recovering Costs of a Tax Dispute

In a tax dispute, you may believe that the IRS has taken an unreasonable position, forcing you to incur legal fees and other expenses to win your case. You may be able to recover all or part of—

1. Reasonable administrative costs of proceedings within the IRS, and
2. Reasonable litigation costs in a court proceeding.

A judgment for reasonable litigation costs will *not* be awarded in any court proceeding if you did not exhaust all IRS administrative remedies. A refusal by the taxpayer to agree to an extension of time for a tax assessment is not a bar to an award, but unreasonably delaying the proceedings is.

You may *not* recover costs if your net worth at the time the action begins exceeds $2 million. The $2 million net worth limit applies separately to each spouse in determining whether a married couple filing jointly is entitled to recover legal fees. No recovery is allowed to sole proprietors, partnerships, and corporations if their net worth exceeds $7 million or they have more than 500 employees.

To receive an award, you must "substantially prevail" as to the key issues in the case or the amount of tax involved. If you do, you will be entitled to a recovery unless the IRS proves that it was "substantially justified" in maintaining the position that it did. You may be treated as the prevailing party if a court determines that your liability is equal to or less than an amount that you offered in settlement. The offer must be considered a qualified offer made during a period that begins on the date of the first letter of proposed deficiency allowing for an IRS administrative appeal and ends 30 days before the date first set for trial.

The Tax Court and other courts have interpreted "substantially justified" to be a reasonableness standard. The IRS is presumed not to be "substantially justified" if it does not follow its own published regulations, revenue rulings, procedures, notices, announcements, or a private ruling issued to the taxpayer. The IRS may try to rebut the presumption. A court may also consider whether an IRS position has been rejected by federal courts of appeal of other circuits in determining whether the IRS position was substantially justified.

Reasonable administrative costs include IRS fees, reasonable fees for witnesses and experts, and attorneys' fees subject to the annual limit; *see* below. The IRS determines the amount of such an award, which may include costs incurred from the date the IRS sent its first letter of a proposed deficiency allowing you to ask for an administrative appeal. For an award of administrative costs, you must file an application with the IRS before the 91st day after the date on which the IRS mailed you its final decision. To appeal a denial of your application, you must petition the Tax Court within 90 days from the date the IRS mailed the denial.

Reasonable litigation costs include reasonable court costs, fees of witnesses and experts, and attorneys' fees. Fees of witnesses may not exceed the rate paid by the U.S. government. For attorneys' fees incurred in 2015 through 2018, the limit is $200 per hour. The limit was $190 per hour for attorneys' fees incurred in 2013 and 2014 and $180 per hour for fees incurred in 2009-2012. The court may also increase the award for attorneys' fees to account for special factors, such as the difficulty of the issues and the availability of local tax expertise. However, an attorney's general expertise in tax law or experience in tax litigation is not in itself a special factor warranting a higher fee award.

You may *not* recover attorneys' fees if you represent yourself *(pro se)*. However, you are still entitled to recover fees for witnesses and experts. If you represent a prevailing taxpayer on a *pro bono* basis or for a nominal fee, a court may award you or your employer reasonable attorneys' fees.

## 48.12 Suing the IRS for Unauthorized Collection

If an IRS employee or officer recklessly, intentionally, or negligently disregards the law or IRS regulations when taking a collection action, you may sue the IRS in federal district court for actual economic damages resulting from the IRS employee's misconduct, plus certain costs of bringing the action. The lawsuit must be filed within two years of the date that the unauthorized collection action was taken.

For negligent IRS collection activities, you may sue for damages of up to $100,000, and for reckless or intentional misconduct, the maximum damage award is $1 million. Administrative remedies must be exhausted to obtain an award.

According to IRS regulations, actual economic damages that may be recovered are monetary losses you suffer as a direct result of the IRS' action. For example, a business may lose loyal customers and suffer an actual cash loss if the IRS' action damages the business's reputation. Other actual expenses could include the cost of renting a house or a car if the IRS puts a lien on or seizes your property, or loss of income due to the garnishment of your paycheck. Damages from the IRS for loss of reputation, inconvenience, or emotional distress are allowed only to the extent that they result in such actual monetary loss.

The IRS defines "costs of action" that you may recover as (1) fees of the clerk and marshall; (2) fees of the court reporter; (3) fees and disbursements for printing and witnesses; (4) copying fees; (5) docket fees; and (6) compensation for court-appointed experts and interpreters.

Litigation costs and administrative proceeding costs are not treated as "costs of the action." However, if the IRS denies your administrative claim for damages and you successfully sue in federal district court, you are considered a "prevailing party" and may recover attorneys' fees, related litigation expenses, and administrative costs before the IRS as discussed in *48.11*.

*Planning Reminder*

**Recovering Attorneys' Fees**

Attorneys' fees include the fees paid by a taxpayer for the services of anyone who is authorized to practice before the Tax Court or IRS.

*Caution*

**Penalty for Frivolous Action**

If you bring an action in federal district court for unauthorized collection activities that the court considers to be frivolous, it may impose a penalty of up to $10,000.

*Planning Reminder*

**IRS Failure To Release Lien**

A suit for damages may also be brought in federal district court against the IRS if IRS employees improperly fail to release a lien on your property. Before you sue, you must file an administrative claim for damages. The lawsuit must be filed within two years after your claim arose. You may sue for actual economic damages plus costs of the action; the types of damages that may be recovered are similar to those discussed for suing the IRS for unauthorized collection actions.

# PART 8

# 2018 Tax Forms

In the following pages, you will find Form 1040 and selected Schedules, which are subject to change. The final versions of these and other Forms and tax return-related materials will be available from the IRS website, IRS.gov, and in the *e-Supplement* at *jklasser.com*.

**Form 1040**
Department of the Treasury—Internal Revenue Service (99)
**U.S. Individual Income Tax Return**
**2018** OMB No. 1545-0074 | IRS Use Only—Do not write or staple in this space.

Filing status: ☐ Single ☐ Married filing jointly ☐ Married filing separately ☐ Head of household ☐ Qualifying widow(er)

| Your first name and initial | Last name | **Your social security number** |
|---|---|---|

Your standard deduction: ☐ Someone can claim you as a dependent ☐ You were born before January 2, 1954 ☐ You are blind

| If joint return, spouse's first name and initial | Last name | **Spouse's social security number** |
|---|---|---|

Spouse standard deduction: ☐ Someone can claim your spouse as a dependent ☐ Spouse was born before January 2, 1954
☐ Spouse is blind ☐ Spouse itemizes on a separate return or you were dual-status alien
☐ Full-year health care coverage or exempt (see inst.)

Home address (number and street). If you have a P.O. box, see instructions. | Apt. no.
**Presidential Election Campaign** (see inst.) ☐ You ☐ Spouse

City, town or post office, state, and ZIP code. If you have a foreign address, attach Schedule 6.
If more than four dependents, see inst. and ✓ here ▶ ☐

**Dependents** (see instructions):

| (1) First name          Last name | | | **(4)** ✓ if qualifies for (see inst.): | |
|---|---|---|---|---|
| | | | Child tax credit | Credit for other dependents |
| | | | ☐ | ☐ |
| | | | ☐ | ☐ |
| | | | ☐ | ☐ |
| | | | ☐ | ☐ |

**Sign Here**
Under penalties of perjury, I declare that I have examined this return and accompanying schedules and statements, and to the best of my knowledge and belief, they are true, correct, and complete. Declaration of preparer (other than taxpayer) is based on all information of which preparer has any knowledge.

Joint return? See instructions.
Keep a copy for your records.

| Your signature | Date | Your occupation | If the IRS sent you an Identity Protection PIN, enter it here (see inst.) |
|---|---|---|---|
| Spouse's signature. If a joint return, **both** must sign. | Date | Spouse's occupation | If the IRS sent you an Identity Protection PIN, enter it here (see inst.) |

**Paid Preparer Use Only**

| Preparer's name | Preparer's signature | PTIN | Firm's EIN | Check if: |
|---|---|---|---|---|
| | | | | ☐ 3rd Party Designee |
| Firm's name ▶ | | Phone no. | | ☐ Self-employed |
| Firm's address ▶ | | | | |

For Disclosure, Privacy Act, and Paperwork Reduction Act Notice, see separate instructions. Cat. No. 11320B Form **1040** (2018)

Form 1040

| | | | | | | |
|---|---|---|---|---|---|---|
| Attach Form(s) W-2. Also attach Form(s) W-2G and 1099-R if tax was withheld. | **1** | Wages, salaries, tips, etc. Attach Form(s) W-2 . . . . . . . . | | | **1** | |
| | **2a** | Tax-exempt interest . . . | **2a** | **b** Taxable interest . . . | **2b** | |
| | **3a** | Qualified dividends . . . | **3a** | **b** Ordinary dividends . . | **3b** | |
| | **4a** | IRAs, pensions, and annuities . | **4a** | **b** Taxable amount . . . . | **4b** | |
| | **5a** | Social security benefits . . | **5a** | **b** Taxable amount . . . . | **5b** | |
| | **6** | Total income. Add lines 1 through 5. Add any amount from Schedule 1, line 22 _____ . . . . . . | | | **6** | |
| **Standard Deduction for—** | **7** | Adjusted gross income. If you have no adjustments to income, enter the amount from line 6; otherwise, subtract Schedule 1, line 36, from line 6 . . . . . . . . | | | **7** | |
| • Single or married filing separately, $12,000 | **8** | **Standard deduction or itemized deductions** (from Schedule A) . . . . . . . | | | **8** | |
| | **9** | | | | **9** | |
| • Married filing jointly or Qualifying widow(er), $24,000 | **10** | Taxable income. Subtract lines 8 and 9 from line 7. If zero or less, enter -0- . . . . . . . . | | | **10** | |
| | **11** | **a** Tax (see inst) _____ (check if any from: **1** ☐ Form(s) 8814 **2** ☐ Form 4972 **3** ☐ _____ ) | | | | |
| • Head of household, $18,000 | | **b Add** any amount from Schedule 2 and check here . . . . . . . . . . . ▶ ☐ | | | **11** | |
| | **12** | **a** Child tax credit/credit for other dependents _____ **b Add** any amount from Schedule 3 and check here ▶ ☐ | | | **12** | |
| • If you checked any box under Standard deduction, see instructions. | **13** | | | | **13** | |
| | **14** | Other taxes. Attach Schedule 4 . . . . . . . . . . . . . . . . | | | **14** | |
| | **15** | Total tax. Add lines 13 and 14 . . . . . . . . . . . . . . | | | **15** | |
| | **16** | Federal income tax withheld from Forms W-2 and 1099 . . . . . . . . . . | | | **16** | |
| | **17** | Refundable credits: **a** EIC (see inst.) _____ **b** Sch 8812 _____ **c** Form 8863 _____ | | | | |
| | | **Add** any amount from Schedule 5 _____ . . . . . . . . . . . | | | **17** | |
| | **18** | | | | **18** | |
| **Refund** | **19** | If line 18 is more than line 15, subtract line 15 from line 18. This is the amount you **overpaid** . . . . | | | **19** | |
| | **20a** | Amount of line 19 you want **refunded to you.** If Form 8888 is attached, check here . . . . ▶ ☐ | | | **20a** | |
| Direct deposit? ▶ See instructions. | **b** | Routing number _____ ▶ **c** Type: ☐ Checking ☐ Savings | | | | |
| ▶ | **d** | Account number _____ | | | | |
| | **21** | Amount of line 19 you want **applied to your 2019 estimated tax** . . ▶ | **21** | | | |
| **Amount You Owe** | **22** | **Amount you owe.** Subtract line 18 from line 15. For details on how to pay, see instructions . . . ▶ | | | **22** | |
| | **23** | Estimated tax penalty (see instructions) . . . . . . . . . ▶ | **23** | | | |

Go to *www.irs.gov/Form1040* for instructions and the latest information.							Form **1040** (2018)

**SCHEDULE 1**
(Form 1040)

Department of the Treasury
Internal Revenue Service

# Additional Income and Adjustments to Income

▶ Attach to Form 1040.
▶ Go to *www.irs.gov/Form1040* for instructions and the latest information.

OMB No. 1545-0074

20**18**

Attachment
Sequence No. **01**

Name(s) shown on Form 1040

Your social security number

| | | | | |
|---|---|---|---|---|
| **Additional Income** | 1–9b | Reserved | 1–9b | |
| | 10 | Taxable refunds, credits, or offsets of state and local income taxes | 10 | |
| | 11 | Alimony received | 11 | |
| | 12 | Business income or (loss). Attach Schedule C or C-EZ | 12 | |
| | 13 | Capital gain or (loss). Attach Schedule D if required. If not required, check here ▶ ☐ | 13 | |
| | 14 | Other gains or (losses). Attach Form 4797 | 14 | |
| | 15a | Reserved | 15b | |
| | 16a | Reserved | 16b | |
| | 17 | Rental real estate, royalties, partnerships, S corporations, trusts, etc. Attach Schedule E | 17 | |
| | 18 | Farm income or (loss). Attach Schedule F | 18 | |
| | 19 | Unemployment compensation | 19 | |
| | 20a | Reserved | 20b | |
| | 21 | Other income. List type and amount ▶ _____ | 21 | |
| | 22 | Combine the amounts in the far right column. If you don't have any adjustments to income, enter here and include on Form 1040, line 6. Otherwise, go to line 23 | 22 | |
| **Adjustments to Income** | 23 | Educator expenses | 23 | |
| | 24 | Certain business expenses of reservists, performing artists, and fee-basis government officials. Attach Form 2106 | 24 | |
| | 25 | Health savings account deduction. Attach Form 8889 | 25 | |
| | 26 | Moving expenses for members of the Armed Forces. Attach Form 3903 | 26 | |
| | 27 | Deductible part of self-employment tax. Attach Schedule SE | 27 | |
| | 28 | Self-employed SEP, SIMPLE, and qualified plans | 28 | |
| | 29 | Self-employed health insurance deduction | 29 | |
| | 30 | Penalty on early withdrawal of savings | 30 | |
| | 31a | Alimony paid **b** Recipient's SSN ▶ | 31a | |
| | 32 | IRA deduction | 32 | |
| | 33 | Student loan interest deduction | 33 | |
| | 34 | Reserved | 34 | |
| | 35 | Reserved | 35 | |
| | 36 | Add lines 23 through 35 | 36 | |

For Paperwork Reduction Act Notice, see your tax return instructions.     Cat. No. 71479F     Schedule 1 (Form 1040) 2018

---

**SCHEDULE 2**
(Form 1040)

Department of the Treasury
Internal Revenue Service

# Tax

▶ Attach to Form 1040.
▶ Go to *www.irs.gov/Form1040* for instructions and the latest information.

OMB No. 1545-0074

20**18**

Attachment
Sequence No. **02**

Name(s) shown on Form 1040

Your social security number

| | | | | |
|---|---|---|---|---|
| **Tax** | 38–44 | Reserved | 38–44 | |
| | 45 | Alternative minimum tax. Attach Form 6251 | 45 | |
| | 46 | Excess advance premium tax credit repayment. Attach Form 8962 | 46 | |
| | 47 | Add the amounts in the far right column. Enter here and include on Form 1040, line 11 | 47 | |

For Paperwork Reduction Act Notice, see your tax return instructions.     Cat. No. 71478U     Schedule 2 (Form 1040) 2018

**SCHEDULE 3**
**(Form 1040)**

Department of the Treasury
Internal Revenue Service

**Nonrefundable Credits**

▶ Attach to Form 1040.
▶ Go to *www.irs.gov/Form1040* for instructions and the latest information.

OMB No. 1545-0074

**2018**

Attachment
Sequence No. **03**

Name(s) shown on Form 1040

Your social security number

| | | | | |
|---|---|---|---|---|
| **Nonrefundable Credits** | 48 | Foreign tax credit. Attach Form 1116 if required . . . . . . . . . . . . . . . | 48 | |
| | 49 | Credit for child and dependent care expenses. Attach Form 2441 . . . . . . . | 49 | |
| | 50 | Education credits from Form 8863, line 19 . . . . . . . . . . | 50 | |
| | 51 | Retirement savings contributions credit. Attach Form 8880 . . . . . . . . . | 51 | |
| | 52 | Reserved . . . . . . . . . . . . . . . . . . . . . . . . . | 52 | |
| | 53 | Residential energy credit. Attach Form 5695 . . . . . . . . . . . | 53 | |
| | 54 | Other credits from Form **a** ☐ 3800 **b** ☐ 8801 **c** ☐ _____ | 54 | |
| | 55 | Add the amounts in the far right column. Enter here and include on Form 1040, line 12 | 55 | |

For Paperwork Reduction Act Notice, see your tax return instructions.          Cat. No. 71480G          **Schedule 3 (Form 1040) 2018**

**SCHEDULE 4**
**(Form 1040)**

Department of the Treasury
Internal Revenue Service

**Other Taxes**

▶ Attach to Form 1040.
▶ Go to *www.irs.gov/Form1040* for instructions and the latest information.

OMB No. 1545-0074

**2018**

Attachment
Sequence No. **04**

Name(s) shown on Form 1040

Your social security number

| | | | | |
|---|---|---|---|---|
| **Other Taxes** | 57 | Self-employment tax. Attach Schedule SE . . . . . . . . . . . . . | 57 | |
| | 58 | Unreported social security and Medicare tax from: Form **a** ☐ 4137 **b** ☐ 8919 | 58 | |
| | 59 | Additional tax on IRAs, other qualified retirement plans, and other tax-favored accounts. Attach Form 5329 if required . . . . . . . . . . . . . | 59 | |
| | 60a | Household employment taxes. Attach Schedule H . . . . . . . . . . | 60a | |
| | **b** | Repayment of first-time homebuyer credit from Form 5405. Attach Form 5405 if required . . . . . . . . . . . . . . . . . . . . . . . | 60b | |
| | 61 | Health care: individual responsibility (see instructions) . . . . . . . . . . | 61 | |
| | 62 | Taxes from: **a** ☐ Form 8959 **b** ☐ Form 8960 **c** ☐ Instructions; enter code(s) _____ | 62 | |
| | 63 | Section 965 net tax liability installment from Form 965-A . . . . . . . . . | 63 | | | |
| | 64 | Add the amounts in the far right column. These are your **total other taxes**. Enter here and on Form 1040, line 14 . . . . . . . . . . . . . . . . | 64 | |

For Paperwork Reduction Act Notice, see your tax return instructions.          Cat. No. 71481R          **Schedule 4 (Form 1040) 2018**

**SCHEDULE 5**
**(Form 1040)**

Department of the Treasury
Internal Revenue Service

# Other Payments and Refundable Credits

▶ Attach to Form 1040.
▶ Go to *www.irs.gov/Form1040* for instructions and the latest information.

OMB No. 1545-0074

**2018**

Attachment
Sequence No. **05**

Name(s) shown on Form 1040

Your social security number

| Other Payments and Refundable Credits | 65 | Reserved . . . . . . . . . . . . . . . . . . . . . . | 65 | |
|---|---|---|---|---|
| | 66 | 2018 estimated tax payments and amount applied from 2017 return . . . . | 66 | |
| | 67a | Reserved . . . . . . . . . . . . . . . . . . . . . . | 67a | |
| | b | Reserved . . . . . . . . . . . . . . . . . . . . . . | 67b | |
| | 68–69 | Reserved . . . . . . . . . . . . . . . . . . . . . . | 68–69 | |
| | 70 | Net premium tax credit. Attach Form 8962 . . . . . . . . . . | 70 | |
| | 71 | Amount paid with request for extension to file (see instructions) . . . . . | 71 | |
| | 72 | Excess social security and tier 1 RRTA tax withheld . . . . . . . . | 72 | |
| | 73 | Credit for federal tax on fuels. Attach Form 4136 . . . . . . . . | 73 | |
| | 74 | Credits from Form: **a** ☐ 2439 **b** ☐ Reserved **c** ☐ 8885 **d** ☐ _____ | 74 | |
| | 75 | Add the amounts in the far right column. These are your total **other payments and refundable credits.** Enter here and include on Form 1040, line 17 . . . | 75 | |

For Paperwork Reduction Act Notice, see your tax return instructions.　　　Cat. No. 71482C　　　Schedule 5 (Form 1040) 2018

---

**SCHEDULE 6**
**(Form 1040)**

Department of the Treasury
Internal Revenue Service

# Foreign Address and Third Party Designee

▶ Attach to Form 1040.
▶ Go to *www.irs.gov/Form1040* for instructions and the latest information.

OMB No. 1545-0074

**2018**

Attachment
Sequence No. **05A**

Name(s) shown on Form 1040

Your social security number

| Foreign Address | Foreign country name | Foreign province/county | Foreign postal code |
|---|---|---|---|

| Third Party Designee | Do you want to allow another person to discuss this return with the IRS (see instructions)? ☐ **Yes.** Complete below. ☐ **No** | | |
|---|---|---|---|
| | Designee's name ▶ | Phone no. ▶ | Personal identification number (PIN) ▶ ☐☐☐☐☐ |

For Paperwork Reduction Act Notice, see your tax return instructions.　　　Cat. No. 71483N　　　Schedule 6 (Form 1040) 2018

**SCHEDULE A**
**(Form 1040)**

Department of the Treasury
Internal Revenue Service (99)

# Itemized Deductions

▶ Go to *www.irs.gov/ScheduleA* for instructions and the latest information.
▶ Attach to Form 1040.

**Caution:** If you are claiming a net qualified disaster loss on Form 4684, see the instructions for line 16.

OMB No. 1545-0074

20**18**

Attachment
Sequence No. **07**

Name(s) shown on Form 1040 | Your social security number

| | | | | |
|---|---|---|---|---|
| **Medical and Dental Expenses** | **Caution:** Do not include expenses reimbursed or paid by others. | | | |
| | 1 Medical and dental expenses (see instructions) | **1** | | |
| | 2 Enter amount from Form 1040, line 7   **2** | | | |
| | 3 Multiply line 2 by 7.5% (0.075) | **3** | | |
| | 4 Subtract line 3 from line 1. If line 3 is more than line 1, enter -0- | | **4** | |
| **Taxes You Paid** | 5 State and local taxes | | | |
| | **a** State and local income taxes or general sales taxes. You may include either income taxes or general sales taxes on line 5a, but not both. If you elect to include general sales taxes instead of income taxes, check this box   ▶ ☐ | **5a** | | |
| | **b** State and local real estate taxes (see instructions) | **5b** | | |
| | **c** State and local personal property taxes | **5c** | | |
| | **d** Add lines 5a through 5c | **5d** | | |
| | **e** Enter the smaller of line 5d and $10,000 ($5,000 if married filing separately) | **5e** | | |
| | 6 Other taxes. List type and amount ▶ _____ | **6** | | |
| | 7 Add lines 5e and 6 | | **7** | |
| **Interest You Paid**<br>**Caution:** Your mortgage interest deduction may be limited (see instructions). | 8 Home mortgage interest and points. If you didn't use all of your home mortgage loan(s) to buy, build, or improve your home, see instructions and check this box   ▶ ☐ | | | |
| | **a** Home mortgage interest and points reported to you on Form 1098 | **8a** | | |
| | **b** Home mortgage interest not reported to you on Form 1098. If paid to the person from whom you bought the home, see instructions and show that person's name, identifying no., and address ▶ _____ | **8b** | | |
| | **c** Points not reported to you on Form 1098. See instructions for special rules | **8c** | | |
| | **d** Reserved | **8d** | | |
| | **e** Add lines 8a through 8c | **8e** | | |
| | 9 Investment interest. Attach Form 4952 if required. See instructions | **9** | | |
| | 10 Add lines 8e and 9 | | **10** | |
| **Gifts to Charity**<br>If you made a gift and got a benefit for it, see instructions. | 11 Gifts by cash or check. If you made any gift of $250 or more, see instructions | **11** | | |
| | 12 Other than by cash or check. If any gift of $250 or more, see instructions. You **must** attach Form 8283 if over $500 | **12** | | |
| | 13 Carryover from prior year | **13** | | |
| | 14 Add lines 11 through 13 | | **14** | |
| **Casualty and Theft Losses** | 15 Casualty and theft loss(es) from a federally declared disaster (other than net qualified disaster losses). Attach Form 4684 and enter the amount from line 18 of that form. See instructions | | **15** | |
| **Other Itemized Deductions** | 16 Other—from list in instructions. List type and amount ▶ _____ | | **16** | |
| **Total Itemized Deductions** | 17 Add the amounts in the far right column for lines 4 through 16. Also, enter this amount on Form 1040, line 8 | | **17** | |
| | 18 If you elect to itemize deductions even though they are less than your standard deduction, check here   ▶ ☐ | | | |

**For Paperwork Reduction Act Notice, see the Instructions for Form 1040.**     Cat. No. 17145C     **Schedule A (Form 1040) 2018**

**SCHEDULE B**
(Form 1040)

Department of the Treasury
Internal Revenue Service (99)

## Interest and Ordinary Dividends

▶ Go to *www.irs.gov/ScheduleB* for instructions and the latest information.
▶ Attach to Form 1040.

OMB No. 1545-0074

20**18**

Attachment
Sequence No. **08**

Name(s) shown on return

Your social security number

| Part I<br><br>**Interest**<br><br>(See instructions and the instructions for Form 1040, line 2b.)<br><br>**Note:** If you received a Form 1099-INT, Form 1099-OID, or substitute statement from a brokerage firm, list the firm's name as the payer and enter the total interest shown on that form. | 1 | List name of payer. If any interest is from a seller-financed mortgage and the buyer used the property as a personal residence, see the instructions and list this interest first. Also, show that buyer's social security number and address ▶ | | **Amount** |
|---|---|---|---|---|
| | | | 1 | |
| | 2 | Add the amounts on line 1 . . . . . . . . . . . . | 2 | |
| | 3 | Excludable interest on series EE and I U.S. savings bonds issued after 1989. Attach Form 8815 . . . . . . . . . . . . | 3 | |
| | 4 | Subtract line 3 from line 2. Enter the result here and on Form 1040, line 2b . . ▶ | 4 | |

**Note:** If line 4 is over $1,500, you must complete Part III.

| Part II<br><br>**Ordinary Dividends**<br><br>(See instructions and the instructions for Form 1040, line 3b.)<br><br>**Note:** If you received a Form 1099-DIV or substitute statement from a brokerage firm, list the firm's name as the payer and enter the ordinary dividends shown on that form. | 5 | List name of payer ▶ | | **Amount** |
|---|---|---|---|---|
| | | | 5 | |
| | 6 | Add the amounts on line 5. Enter the total here and on Form 1040, line 3b . . ▶ | 6 | |

**Note:** If line 6 is over $1,500, you must complete Part III.

| Part III<br><br>**Foreign Accounts and Trusts**<br><br>(See instructions.) | You must complete this part if you **(a)** had over $1,500 of taxable interest or ordinary dividends; **(b)** had a foreign account; or **(c)** received a distribution from, or were a grantor of, or a transferor to, a foreign trust. | | Yes | No |
|---|---|---|---|---|
| | 7a | At any time during 2018, did you have a financial interest in or signature authority over a financial account (such as a bank account, securities account, or brokerage account) located in a foreign country? See instructions . . . . . . . . . . | | |
| | | If "Yes," are you required to file FinCEN Form 114, Report of Foreign Bank and Financial Accounts (FBAR), to report that financial interest or signature authority? See FinCEN Form 114 and its instructions for filing requirements and exceptions to those requirements . . . . . . | | |
| | b | If you are required to file FinCEN Form 114, enter the name of the foreign country where the financial account is located ▶ | | |
| | 8 | During 2018, did you receive a distribution from, or were you the grantor of, or transferor to, a foreign trust? If "Yes," you may have to file Form 3520. See instructions . . . . . . . . . . | | |

**For Paperwork Reduction Act Notice, see your tax return instructions.**  Cat. No. 17146N  **Schedule B (Form 1040) 2018**

**SCHEDULE C**
**(Form 1040)**

Department of the Treasury
Internal Revenue Service (99)

# Profit or Loss From Business
(Sole Proprietorship)

▶ Go to *www.irs.gov/ScheduleC* for instructions and the latest information.
▶ **Attach to Form 1040, 1040NR, or 1041; partnerships generally must file Form 1065.**

OMB No. 1545-0074

**2018**

Attachment
Sequence No. **09**

Name of proprietor | Social security number (SSN)

**A** Principal business or profession, including product or service (see instructions)

**B** Enter code from instructions
▶

**C** Business name. If no separate business name, leave blank.

**D** Employer ID number (EIN) (see instr.)

**E** Business address (including suite or room no.) ▶
City, town or post office, state, and ZIP code

**F** Accounting method: **(1)** ☐ Cash **(2)** ☐ Accrual **(3)** ☐ Other (specify) ▶

**G** Did you "materially participate" in the operation of this business during 2018? If "No," see instructions for limit on losses . ☐ Yes ☐ No

**H** If you started or acquired this business during 2018, check here . . . . . . . . . . . ▶ ☐

**I** Did you make any payments in 2018 that would require you to file Form(s) 1099? (see instructions) . . . . . . . ☐ Yes ☐ No

**J** If "Yes," did you or will you file required Forms 1099? . . . . . . . . . . . . . . ☐ Yes ☐ No

## Part I Income

| | | | |
|---|---|---|---|
| 1 | Gross receipts or sales. See instructions for line 1 and check the box if this income was reported to you on Form W-2 and the "Statutory employee" box on that form was checked . . . . . . . . . ▶ ☐ | **1** | |
| 2 | Returns and allowances | **2** | |
| 3 | Subtract line 2 from line 1 | **3** | |
| 4 | Cost of goods sold (from line 42) | **4** | |
| 5 | **Gross profit.** Subtract line 4 from line 3 | **5** | |
| 6 | Other income, including federal and state gasoline or fuel tax credit or refund (see instructions) . . . | **6** | |
| 7 | **Gross income.** Add lines 5 and 6 . . . . . . . . . . . . . . . . . . . . ▶ | **7** | |

## Part II Expenses. Enter expenses for business use of your home **only** on line 30.

| | | | | | | | |
|---|---|---|---|---|---|---|---|
| 8 | Advertising . . . . . | **8** | | 18 | Office expense (see instructions) | **18** | |
| 9 | Car and truck expenses (see instructions) . . . . | **9** | | 19 | Pension and profit-sharing plans . | **19** | |
| | | | | 20 | Rent or lease (see instructions): | | |
| 10 | Commissions and fees . | **10** | | a | Vehicles, machinery, and equipment | **20a** | |
| 11 | Contract labor (see instructions) | **11** | | b | Other business property . . . | **20b** | |
| 12 | Depletion . . . . . | **12** | | 21 | Repairs and maintenance . . . | **21** | |
| 13 | Depreciation and section 179 expense deduction (not included in Part III) (see instructions) . . . . . | **13** | | 22 | Supplies (not included in Part III) . | **22** | |
| | | | | 23 | Taxes and licenses . . . . . | **23** | |
| | | | | 24 | Travel and meals: | | |
| 14 | Employee benefit programs (other than on line 19) . . | **14** | | a | Travel . . . . . . . . . | **24a** | |
| | | | | b | Deductible meals (see instructions) . . . . . . | **24b** | |
| 15 | Insurance (other than health) | **15** | | 25 | Utilities . . . . . . . . | **25** | |
| 16 | Interest (see instructions): | | | 26 | Wages (less employment credits) . | **26** | |
| a | Mortgage (paid to banks, etc.) | **16a** | | 27a | Other expenses (from line 48) . . | **27a** | |
| b | Other . . . . . . | **16b** | | b | **Reserved for future use** . . . | **27b** | |
| 17 | Legal and professional services | **17** | | | | | |

| | | | |
|---|---|---|---|
| 28 | **Total expenses** before expenses for business use of home. Add lines 8 through 27a . . . . . . ▶ | **28** | |
| 29 | Tentative profit or (loss). Subtract line 28 from line 7 . . . . . . . . . . . . . . | **29** | |
| 30 | Expenses for business use of your home. Do not report these expenses elsewhere. Attach Form 8829 unless using the simplified method (see instructions). **Simplified method filers only:** enter the total square footage of: (a) your home: _____ and (b) the part of your home used for business: _____ . Use the Simplified Method Worksheet in the instructions to figure the amount to enter on line 30 . . . . . . . . . | **30** | |
| 31 | **Net profit or (loss).** Subtract line 30 from line 29. • If a profit, enter on both **Schedule 1 (Form 1040), line 12** (or Form 1040NR, line 13) and on **Schedule SE, line 2.** (If you checked the box on line 1, see instructions). Estates and trusts, enter on **Form 1041, line 3.** • If a loss, you **must** go to line 32. | **31** | |
| 32 | If you have a loss, check the box that describes your investment in this activity (see instructions). • If you checked 32a, enter the loss on both **Schedule 1 (Form 1040), line 12** (or **Form 1040NR, line 13**) and on **Schedule SE, line 2.** (If you checked the box on line 1, see the line 31 instructions). Estates and trusts, enter on **Form 1041, line 3.** • If you checked 32b, you **must** attach **Form 6198.** Your loss may be limited. | **32a** ☐ All investment is at risk. **32b** ☐ Some investment is not at risk. | |

**For Paperwork Reduction Act Notice, see the separate instructions.** Cat. No. 11334P Schedule C (Form 1040) 2018

**Part III**    **Cost of Goods Sold**   (see instructions)

33    Method(s) used to
value closing inventory:    **a** ☐ Cost    **b** ☐ Lower of cost or market    **c** ☐ Other (attach explanation)

34    Was there any change in determining quantities, costs, or valuations between opening and closing inventory?
If "Yes," attach explanation . . . . . . . . . . . . . . . . . . . . . . . . . .    ☐ Yes    ☐ No

| | | | |
|---|---|---|---|
| 35 | Inventory at beginning of year. If different from last year's closing inventory, attach explanation . . . | **35** | |
| 36 | Purchases less cost of items withdrawn for personal use . . . . . . . . . . | **36** | |
| 37 | Cost of labor. Do not include any amounts paid to yourself . . . . . . . . . | **37** | |
| 38 | Materials and supplies . . . . . . . . . . . . . . . | **38** | |
| 39 | Other costs . . . . . . . . . . . . . . . | **39** | |
| 40 | Add lines 35 through 39 . . . . . . . . . . | **40** | |
| 41 | Inventory at end of year . . . . . . . . . . . | **41** | |
| 42 | **Cost of goods sold.** Subtract line 41 from line 40. Enter the result here and on line 4 . . . . . . | **42** | |

**Part IV**    **Information on Your Vehicle. Complete this part only if you are claiming car or truck expenses on line 9 and are not required to file Form 4562 for this business. See the instructions for line 13 to find out if you must file Form 4562.**

43    When did you place your vehicle in service for business purposes? (month, day, year)   ▶   ___/___/___

44    Of the total number of miles you drove your vehicle during 2018, enter the number of miles you used your vehicle for:

   **a**   Business _____    **b** Commuting (see instructions) _____    **c** Other _____

45    Was your vehicle available for personal use during off-duty hours? . . . . . . . . . . . .    ☐ Yes    ☐ No

46    Do you (or your spouse) have another vehicle available for personal use? . . . . . . . . . .    ☐ Yes    ☐ No

47a    Do you have evidence to support your deduction? . . . . . . . . . . . . . . .    ☐ Yes    ☐ No

   **b**   If "Yes," is the evidence written? . . . . . . . . . . . . . . . . . . . . .    ☐ Yes    ☐ No

**Part V**    **Other Expenses.**   List below business expenses not included on lines 8–26 or line 30.

| | | |
|---|---|---|
| _____ | | |
| _____ | | |
| _____ | | |
| _____ | | |
| _____ | | |
| _____ | | |
| _____ | | |
| _____ | | |
| 48   **Total other expenses.** Enter here and on line 27a . . . . . . . . . . . . . . . | **48** | |

**SCHEDULE D**
**(Form 1040)**

Department of the Treasury
Internal Revenue Service (99)

# Capital Gains and Losses

▶ Attach to Form 1040 or Form 1040NR.
▶ Go to *www.irs.gov/ScheduleD* for instructions and the latest information.
▶ Use Form 8949 to list your transactions for lines 1b, 2, 3, 8b, 9, and 10.

OMB No. 1545-0074

**2018**

Attachment
Sequence No. **12**

Name(s) shown on return

Your social security number

**Part I**    **Short-Term Capital Gains and Losses—Generally Assets Held One Year or Less** (see instructions)

| See instructions for how to figure the amounts to enter on the lines below.<br><br>This form may be easier to complete if you round off cents to whole dollars. | **(d)** Proceeds (sales price) | **(e)** Cost (or other basis) | **(g)** Adjustments to gain or loss from Form(s) 8949, Part I, line 2, column (g) | **(h) Gain or (loss)** Subtract column (e) from column (d) and combine the result with column (g) |
|---|---|---|---|---|
| **1a** Totals for all short-term transactions reported on Form 1099-B for which basis was reported to the IRS and for which you have no adjustments (see instructions). However, if you choose to report all these transactions on Form 8949, leave this line blank and go to line 1b . | | | | |
| **1b** Totals for all transactions reported on Form(s) 8949 with **Box A** checked . . . . . . . . . . . . . | | | | |
| **2** Totals for all transactions reported on Form(s) 8949 with **Box B** checked . . . . . . . . . . . . . | | | | |
| **3** Totals for all transactions reported on Form(s) 8949 with **Box C** checked . . . . . . . . . . . . . | | | | |

| | | |
|---|---|---|
| **4** Short-term gain from Form 6252 and short-term gain or (loss) from Forms 4684, 6781, and 8824 . . | **4** | |
| **5** Net short-term gain or (loss) from partnerships, S corporations, estates, and trusts from Schedule(s) K-1 . . . . . . . . . . . . . . . . . . . . | **5** | |
| **6** Short-term capital loss carryover. Enter the amount, if any, from line 8 of your **Capital Loss Carryover Worksheet** in the instructions . . . . . . . . . . . | **6** (       ) |
| **7** **Net short-term capital gain or (loss).** Combine lines 1a through 6 in column (h). If you have any long-term capital gains or losses, go to Part II below. Otherwise, go to Part III on the back . . . . . . | **7** | |

**Part II**    **Long-Term Capital Gains and Losses—Generally Assets Held More Than One Year** (see instructions)

| See instructions for how to figure the amounts to enter on the lines below.<br><br>This form may be easier to complete if you round off cents to whole dollars. | **(d)** Proceeds (sales price) | **(e)** Cost (or other basis) | **(g)** Adjustments to gain or loss from Form(s) 8949, Part II, line 2, column (g) | **(h) Gain or (loss)** Subtract column (e) from column (d) and combine the result with column (g) |
|---|---|---|---|---|
| **8a** Totals for all long-term transactions reported on Form 1099-B for which basis was reported to the IRS and for which you have no adjustments (see instructions). However, if you choose to report all these transactions on Form 8949, leave this line blank and go to line 8b . | | | | |
| **8b** Totals for all transactions reported on Form(s) 8949 with **Box D** checked . . . . . . . . . . . . . | | | | |
| **9** Totals for all transactions reported on Form(s) 8949 with **Box E** checked . . . . . . . . . . . . . | | | | |
| **10** Totals for all transactions reported on Form(s) 8949 with **Box F** checked. | | | | |

| | | |
|---|---|---|
| **11** Gain from Form 4797, Part I; long-term gain from Forms 2439 and 6252; and long-term gain or (loss) from Forms 4684, 6781, and 8824 . . . . . . . . . . . . . . . . . | **11** | |
| **12** Net long-term gain or (loss) from partnerships, S corporations, estates, and trusts from Schedule(s) K-1 | **12** | |
| **13** Capital gain distributions. See the instructions . . . . . . . . . . . . . . | **13** | |
| **14** Long-term capital loss carryover. Enter the amount, if any, from line 13 of your **Capital Loss Carryover Worksheet** in the instructions . . . . . . . . . . | **14** (       ) |
| **15** **Net long-term capital gain or (loss).** Combine lines 8a through 14 in column (h). Then go to Part III on the back . . . . . . . . . . . . . . . . . . . . . . . | **15** | |

For Paperwork Reduction Act Notice, see your tax return instructions.      Cat. No. 11338H      **Schedule D (Form 1040) 2018**

**Part III**    **Summary**

**16**    Combine lines 7 and 15 and enter the result . . . . . . . . . . . . . .    **16**

- If line 16 is a **gain,** enter the amount from line 16 on Schedule 1 (Form 1040), line 13, or Form 1040NR, line 14. Then go to line 17 below.
- If line 16 is a **loss,** skip lines 17 through 20 below. Then go to line 21. Also be sure to complete line 22.
- If line 16 is **zero,** skip lines 17 through 21 below and enter -0- on Schedule 1 (Form 1040), line 13, or Form 1040NR, line 14. Then go to line 22.

**17**    Are lines 15 and 16 **both** gains?
    ☐ **Yes.** Go to line 18.
    ☐ **No.** Skip lines 18 through 21, and go to line 22.

**18**    If you are required to complete the **28% Rate Gain Worksheet** (see instructions), enter the amount, if any, from line 7 of that worksheet . . . . . . . . . . . . ▶    **18**

**19**    If you are required to complete the **Unrecaptured Section 1250 Gain Worksheet** (see instructions), enter the amount, if any, from line 18 of that worksheet . . . . . . . . . ▶    **19**

**20**    Are lines 18 and 19 **both** zero or blank?
    ☐ **Yes.** Complete the **Qualified Dividends and Capital Gain Tax Worksheet** in the instructions for Form 1040, line 11a (or in the instructions for Form 1040NR, line 42). **Don't** complete lines 21 and 22 below.

    ☐ **No.** Complete the **Schedule D Tax Worksheet** in the instructions. **Don't** complete lines 21 and 22 below.

**21**    If line 16 is a loss, enter here and on Schedule 1 (Form 1040), line 13, or Form 1040NR, line 14, the **smaller** of:

- The loss on line 16; or         ⎫   . . . . . . . . . . . . . . . . .    **21** (                 )
- ($3,000), or if married filing separately, ($1,500)   ⎭

   **Note:** When figuring which amount is smaller, treat both amounts as positive numbers.

**22**    Do you have qualified dividends on Form 1040, line 3a, or Form 1040NR, line 10b?

    ☐ **Yes.** Complete the **Qualified Dividends and Capital Gain Tax Worksheet** in the instructions for Form 1040, line 11a (or in the instructions for Form 1040NR, line 42).

    ☐ **No.** Complete the rest of Form 1040 or Form 1040NR.

Schedule D (Form 1040) 2018

**SCHEDULE E**
**(Form 1040)**

Department of the Treasury
Internal Revenue Service (99)

**Supplemental Income and Loss**
(From rental real estate, royalties, partnerships, S corporations, estates, trusts, REMICs, etc.)
▶ **Attach to Form 1040, 1040NR, or Form 1041.**
▶ **Go to** *www.irs.gov/ScheduleE* **for instructions and the latest information.**

OMB No. 1545-0074

**2018**

Attachment
Sequence No. **13**

Name(s) shown on return

Your social security number

---

**Part I**    **Income or Loss From Rental Real Estate and Royalties**    **Note:** If you are in the business of renting personal property, use **Schedule C or C-EZ** (see instructions). If you are an individual, report farm rental income or loss from **Form 4835** on page 2, line 40.

**A** Did you make any payments in 2018 that would require you to file Form(s) 1099? (see instructions) . . . . . ☐ Yes ☐ No
**B** If "Yes," did you or will you file required Forms 1099? . . . . . . . . . . . . . . . . . . . ☐ Yes ☐ No

| 1a | Physical address of each property (street, city, state, ZIP code) |
|---|---|
| A | |
| B | |
| C | |

| 1b | Type of Property (from list below) | 2 | For each rental real estate property listed above, report the number of fair rental and personal use days. Check the **QJV** box only if you meet the requirements to file as a qualified joint venture. See instructions. | | Fair Rental Days | Personal Use Days | QJV |
|---|---|---|---|---|---|---|---|
| A | | | | A | | | ☐ |
| B | | | | B | | | ☐ |
| C | | | | C | | | ☐ |

**Type of Property:**

1 Single Family Residence    3 Vacation/Short-Term Rental   5 Land      7 Self-Rental
2 Multi-Family Residence     4 Commercial               6 Royalties    8 Other (describe)

| Income: | Properties: | | A | B | C |
|---|---|---|---|---|---|
| **3** Rents received . . . . . . . . . . . . . . | | 3 | | | |
| **4** Royalties received . . . . . . . . . . . . | | 4 | | | |
| **Expenses:** | | | | | |
| **5** Advertising . . . . . . . . . . . . . | | 5 | | | |
| **6** Auto and travel (see instructions) . . . . . . | | 6 | | | |
| **7** Cleaning and maintenance . . . . . . . . | | 7 | | | |
| **8** Commissions. . . . . . . . . . . . . | | 8 | | | |
| **9** Insurance . . . . . . . . . . . . . . | | 9 | | | |
| **10** Legal and other professional fees . . . . . . | | 10 | | | |
| **11** Management fees . . . . . . . . . . . | | 11 | | | |
| **12** Mortgage interest paid to banks, etc. (see instructions) | | 12 | | | |
| **13** Other interest. . . . . . . . . . . . | | 13 | | | |
| **14** Repairs. . . . . . . . . . . . . . | | 14 | | | |
| **15** Supplies . . . . . . . . . . . . . | | 15 | | | |
| **16** Taxes . . . . . . . . . . . . . . | | 16 | | | |
| **17** Utilities . . . . . . . . . . . . . | | 17 | | | |
| **18** Depreciation expense or depletion . . . . . | | 18 | | | |
| **19** Other (list) ▶ _____ | | 19 | | | |
| **20** Total expenses. Add lines 5 through 19 . . . . | | 20 | | | |
| **21** Subtract line 20 from line 3 (rents) and/or 4 (royalties). If result is a (loss), see instructions to find out if you must file **Form 6198** . . . . . . . . . . . . . | | 21 | | | |
| **22** Deductible rental real estate loss after limitation, if any, on **Form 8582** (see instructions) . . . . . . . | | 22 | ( ) | ( ) | ( ) |

| 23a | Total of all amounts reported on line 3 for all rental properties . . . | 23a | |
|---|---|---|---|
| b | Total of all amounts reported on line 4 for all royalty properties . . . . | 23b | |
| c | Total of all amounts reported on line 12 for all properties . . . . . | 23c | |
| d | Total of all amounts reported on line 18 for all properties . . . . . . | 23d | |
| e | Total of all amounts reported on line 20 for all properties . . . . . . | 23e | |
| **24** | **Income.** Add positive amounts shown on line 21. **Do not** include any losses . . . . . . . | **24** | |
| **25** | **Losses.** Add royalty losses from line 21 and rental real estate losses from line 22. Enter total losses here . | **25** | ( ) |
| **26** | **Total rental real estate and royalty income or (loss).** Combine lines 24 and 25. Enter the result here. If Parts II, III, IV, and line 40 on page 2 do not apply to you, also enter this amount on Schedule 1 (Form 1040), line 17, or Form 1040NR, line 18. Otherwise, include this amount in the total on line 41 on page 2. . . . . . . . . . . . . . . . . . . . . . . . | **26** | |

**For Paperwork Reduction Act Notice, see the separate instructions.**     Cat. No. 11344L     Schedule E (Form 1040) 2018

Name(s) shown on return. Do not enter name and social security number if shown on other side.     **Your social security number**

**Caution:** The IRS compares amounts reported on your tax return with amounts shown on Schedule(s) K-1.

**Part II**    **Income or Loss From Partnerships and S Corporations — Note:** If you report a loss, receive a distribution, dispose of stock, or receive a loan repayment from an S corporation, you **must** check the box in column **(e)** on line 28 and attach the required basis computation. If you report a loss from an at-risk activity for which **any** amount is **not** at risk, you **must** check the box in column **(f)** on line 28 and attach **Form 6198** (see instructions).

27    Are you reporting any loss not allowed in a prior year due to the at-risk, excess farm loss, or basis limitations, a prior year unallowed loss from a passive activity (if that loss was not reported on Form 8582), or unreimbursed partnership expenses? If you answered "Yes," see instructions before completing this section . . . . . . . . . . . . . . .  ☐ **Yes**   ☐ **No**

| 28 | (a) Name | (b) Enter **P** for partnership; **S** for S corporation | (c) Check if foreign partnership | (d) Employer identification number | (e) Check if basis computation is required | (f) Check if any amount is not at risk |
|---|---|---|---|---|---|---|
| **A** | | | ☐ | | ☐ | ☐ |
| **B** | | | ☐ | | ☐ | ☐ |
| **C** | | | ☐ | | ☐ | ☐ |
| **D** | | | ☐ | | ☐ | ☐ |

| | Passive Income and Loss | | Nonpassive Income and Loss | | |
|---|---|---|---|---|---|
| | (g) Passive loss allowed (attach **Form 8582** if required) | (h) Passive income from **Schedule K-1** | (i) Nonpassive loss from **Schedule K-1** | (j) Section 179 expense deduction from **Form 4562** | (k) Nonpassive income from **Schedule K-1** |
| **A** | | | | | |
| **B** | | | | | |
| **C** | | | | | |
| **D** | | | | | |
| **29a** Totals | | | | | |
| **b** Totals | | | | | |

| 30 | Add columns (h) and (k) of line 29a. . . . . . . . . . . | **30** | |
|---|---|---|---|
| 31 | Add columns (g), (i), and (j) of line 29b. . . . . . . . . | **31** | ( ) |
| 32 | **Total partnership and S corporation income or (loss).** Combine lines 30 and 31 . . . . . | **32** | |

**Part III**    **Income or Loss From Estates and Trusts**

| 33 | (a) Name | (b) Employer identification number |
|---|---|---|
| **A** | | |
| **B** | | |

| | Passive Income and Loss | | Nonpassive Income and Loss | |
|---|---|---|---|---|
| | (c) Passive deduction or loss allowed (attach **Form 8582** if required) | (d) Passive income from **Schedule K-1** | (e) Deduction or loss from **Schedule K-1** | (f) Other income from **Schedule K-1** |
| **A** | | | | |
| **B** | | | | |
| **34a** Totals | | | | |
| **b** Totals | | | | |

| 35 | Add columns (d) and (f) of line 34a . . . . . . . . . . . | **35** | |
|---|---|---|---|
| 36 | Add columns (c) and (e) of line 34b . . . . . . . . . . . | **36** | ( ) |
| 37 | **Total estate and trust income or (loss).** Combine lines 35 and 36 . . . . . . . . . | **37** | |

**Part IV**    **Income or Loss From Real Estate Mortgage Investment Conduits (REMICs)—Residual Holder**

| 38 | (a) Name | (b) Employer identification number | (c) Excess inclusion from **Schedules Q**, line 2c (see instructions) | (d) Taxable income (net loss) from **Schedules Q**, line 1b | (e) Income from **Schedules Q**, line 3b |
|---|---|---|---|---|---|
| | | | | | |

| 39 | Combine columns (d) and (e) only. Enter the result here and include in the total on line 41 below | **39** | |
|---|---|---|---|

**Part V**    **Summary**

| 40 | Net farm rental income or (loss) from **Form 4835.** Also, complete line 42 below . . . . . . | **40** | |
|---|---|---|---|
| 41 | **Total income or (loss).** Combine lines 26, 32, 37, 39, and 40. Enter the result here and on Schedule 1 (Form 1040), line 17, or Form 1040NR, line 18 ▶ | **41** | |

| 42 | **Reconciliation of farming and fishing income.** Enter your **gross** farming and fishing income reported on Form 4835, line 7; Schedule K-1 (Form 1065), box 14, code B; Schedule K-1 (Form 1120S), box 17, code AC; and Schedule K-1 (Form 1041), box 14, code F (see instructions) | **42** | |
|---|---|---|---|
| 43 | **Reconciliation for real estate professionals.** If you were a real estate professional (see instructions), enter the net income or (loss) you reported anywhere on Form 1040 or Form 1040NR from all rental real estate activities in which you materially participated under the passive activity loss rules . . | **43** | |

Schedule E (Form 1040) 2018

**SCHEDULE SE**
**(Form 1040)**

Department of the Treasury
Internal Revenue Service (99)

# Self-Employment Tax

▶ Go to *www.irs.gov/ScheduleSE* for instructions and the latest information.
▶ **Attach to Form 1040 or Form 1040NR.**

OMB No. 1545-0074

**2018**

Attachment
Sequence No. **17**

| Name of person with **self-employment** income (as shown on Form 1040 or Form 1040NR) | Social security number of person with **self-employment** income ▶ |
|---|---|

***Before you begin:*** To determine if you must file Schedule SE, see the instructions.

## May I Use Short Schedule SE or Must I Use Long Schedule SE?

**Note:** Use this flowchart **only if** you must file Schedule SE. If unsure, see *Who Must File Schedule SE* in the instructions.

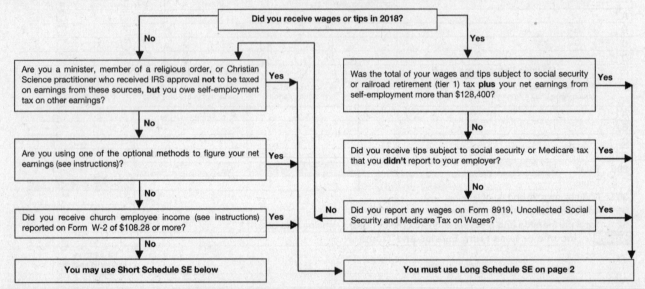

**Section A—Short Schedule SE.   Caution:** Read above to see if you can use Short Schedule SE.

| | | | | |
|---|---|---|---|---|
| **1a** | Net farm profit or (loss) from Schedule F, line 34, and farm partnerships, Schedule K-1 (Form 1065), box 14, code A . . . . . . . . . . . | **1a** | | |
| **b** | If you received social security retirement or disability benefits, enter the amount of Conservation Reserve Program payments included on Schedule F, line 4b, or listed on Schedule K-1 (Form 1065), box 20, code AH | **1b** | ( | ) |
| **2** | Net profit or (loss) from Schedule C, line 31; Schedule C-EZ, line 3; Schedule K-1 (Form 1065), box 14, code A (other than farming); and Schedule K-1 (Form 1065-B), box 9, code J1. Ministers and members of religious orders, see instructions for types of income to report on this line. See instructions for other income to report . . . . . . . . . . | **2** | | |
| **3** | Combine lines 1a, 1b, and 2   . . . . . . . . . . . . . . . . | **3** | | |
| **4** | Multiply line 3 by 92.35% (0.9235). If less than $400, you don't owe self-employment tax; **don't** file this schedule unless you have an amount on line 1b. . . . . . . . . . . . ▶ | **4** | | |
| | **Note:** If line 4 is less than $400 due to Conservation Reserve Program payments on line 1b, see instructions. | | | |
| **5** | **Self-employment tax.** If the amount on line 4 is: <br>• $128,400 or less, multiply line 4 by 15.3% (0.153). Enter the result here and on **Schedule 4 (Form 1040), line 57,** or **Form 1040NR, line 55** <br>• More than $128,400, multiply line 4 by 2.9% (0.029). Then, add $15,921.60 to the result. Enter the total here and on **Schedule 4 (Form 1040), line 57,** or **Form 1040NR, line 55** . . | **5** | | |
| **6** | **Deduction for one-half of self-employment tax.** <br>Multiply line 5 by 50% (0.50). Enter the result here and on **Schedule 1 (Form 1040), line 27,** or **Form 1040NR, line 27** . | **6** | | |

**For Paperwork Reduction Act Notice, see your tax return instructions.**          Cat. No. 11358Z          **Schedule SE (Form 1040) 2018**

Attachment Sequence No. **17** Page **2**

| Name of person with **self-employment** income (as shown on Form 1040 or Form 1040NR) | Social security number of person with **self-employment** income ▶ |
|---|---|

## Section B—Long Schedule SE

### Part I   Self-Employment Tax

**Note:** If your only income subject to self-employment tax is **church employee income,** see instructions. Also see instructions for the definition of church employee income.

**A**   If you are a minister, member of a religious order, or Christian Science practitioner **and** you filed Form 4361, but you had $400 or more of **other** net earnings from self-employment, check here and continue with Part I . . . . . . . ▶ ☐

**1a**   Net farm profit or (loss) from Schedule F, line 34, and farm partnerships, Schedule K-1 (Form 1065), box 14, code A. **Note:** Skip lines 1a and 1b if you use the farm optional method (see instructions) | **1a** |

**b**   If you received social security retirement or disability benefits, enter the amount of Conservation Reserve Program payments included on Schedule F, line 4b, or listed on Schedule K-1 (Form 1065), box 20, code AH | **1b** ( | )

**2**   Net profit or (loss) from Schedule C, line 31; Schedule C-EZ, line 3; Schedule K-1 (Form 1065), box 14, code A (other than farming); and Schedule K-1 (Form 1065-B), box 9, code J1. Ministers and members of religious orders, see instructions for types of income to report on this line. See instructions for other income to report. **Note:** Skip this line if you use the nonfarm optional method (see instructions) . . . . . . . . . . . | **2** |

**3**   Combine lines 1a, 1b, and 2 . . . . . . . . | **3** |

**4a**   If line 3 is more than zero, multiply line 3 by 92.35% (0.9235). Otherwise, enter amount from line 3 | **4a** |
   **Note:** If line 4a is less than $400 due to Conservation Reserve Program payments on line 1b, see instructions.

**b**   If you elect one or both of the optional methods, enter the total of lines 15 and 17 here . . | **4b** |

**c**   Combine lines 4a and 4b. If less than $400, **stop;** you don't owe self-employment tax. **Exception:** If less than $400 and you had **church employee income,** enter -0- and continue ▶ | **4c** |

**5a**   Enter your **church employee income** from Form W-2. See instructions for definition of church employee income . . . | **5a** | |

**b**   Multiply line 5a by 92.35% (0.9235). If less than $100, enter -0- . . . . . . . | **5b** |

**6**   Add lines 4c and 5b . . . . . . . . | **6** |

**7**   Maximum amount of combined wages and self-employment earnings subject to social security tax or the 6.2% portion of the 7.65% railroad retirement (tier 1) tax for 2018 . . . . . . | **7** | 128,400 | 00 |

**8a**   Total social security wages and tips (total of boxes 3 and 7 on Form(s) W-2) and railroad retirement (tier 1) compensation. If $128,400 or more, skip lines 8b through 10, and go to line 11 | **8a** |

**b**   Unreported tips subject to social security tax (from Form 4137, line 10) | **8b** |

**c**   Wages subject to social security tax (from Form 8919, line 10) | **8c** |

**d**   Add lines 8a, 8b, and 8c . . . . . . . . . . . . | **8d** |

**9**   Subtract line 8d from line 7. If zero or less, enter -0- here and on line 10 and go to line 11 . ▶ | **9** |

**10**   Multiply the **smaller** of line 6 or line 9 by 12.4% (0.124) . . . . . . | **10** |

**11**   Multiply line 6 by 2.9% (0.029) . . . . . . . . . | **11** |

**12**   **Self-employment tax.** Add lines 10 and 11. Enter here and on **Schedule 4 (Form 1040), line 57,** or **Form 1040NR, line 55** . . . . . . . . | **12** |

**13**   **Deduction for one-half of self-employment tax.**
   Multiply line 12 by 50% (0.50). Enter the result here and on **Schedule 1 (Form 1040), line 27,** or **Form 1040NR, line 27** . . . | **13** |

### Part II   Optional Methods To Figure Net Earnings (see instructions)

**Farm Optional Method.** You may use this method **only** if **(a)** your gross farm income[1] wasn't more than $7,920, **or (b)** your net farm profits[2] were less than $5,717.

**14**   Maximum income for optional methods . . . . . . . . . . . . | **14** | 5,280 | 00 |

**15**   Enter the **smaller** of: two-thirds (²/₃) of gross farm income[1] (not less than zero) or $5,280. Also include this amount on line 4b above . . . . . . . . . . . | **15** |

**Nonfarm Optional Method.** You may use this method **only** if **(a)** your net nonfarm profits[3] were less than $5,717 and also less than 72.189% of your gross nonfarm income,[4] **and (b)** you had net earnings from self-employment of at least $400 in 2 of the prior 3 years. **Caution:** You may use this method no more than five times.

**16**   Subtract line 15 from line 14 . . . . . . . . . . . . | **16** |

**17**   Enter the **smaller** of: two-thirds (²/₃) of gross nonfarm income[4] (not less than zero) **or** the amount on line 16. Also include this amount on line 4b above . . . . . . . . . . . | **17** |

[1] From Sch. F, line 9, and Sch. K-1 (Form 1065), box 14, code B.
[2] From Sch. F, line 34, and Sch. K-1 (Form 1065), box 14, code A—minus the amount you would have entered on line 1b had you not used the optional method.

[3] From Sch. C, line 31; Sch. C-EZ, line 3; Sch. K-1 (Form 1065), box 14, code A; and Sch. K-1 (Form 1065-B), box 9, code J1.
[4] From Sch. C, line 7; Sch. C-EZ, line 1; Sch. K-1 (Form 1065), box 14, code C; and Sch. K-1 (Form 1065-B), box 9, code J2.

Schedule SE (Form 1040) 2018

## 2018 Child Tax Credit and Credit for Other Dependents Worksheet—Line 12a

2018 Form 1040—Line 12a
*Keep for Your Records*

**CAUTION**

1. To be a qualifying child for the child tax credit, the child must be your dependent, **under age 17** at the end of 2018, and meet all the conditions in Steps 1 through 3 under *Who Qualifies as Your Dependent*. Make sure you checked the "child tax credit" box in column (4) of the *Dependents* section on Form 1040 for each qualifying child.

2. If you don't have a qualifying child, you can't claim the child tax credit; but you may be able to claim the credit for other dependents for that child, see Step 3 under *Who Qualifies as Your Dependent*.

3. To see if your qualifying relative qualifies you to take the credit for other dependents, see Step 5 under *Who Qualifies as Your Dependent*.

4. Be sure to see *Social security number* under *Who Qualifies as Your Dependent*.

5. Do **not** use this worksheet, but use Pub. 972 instead, if:

   **a.** You are claiming the adoption credit, mortgage interest credit, District of Columbia first-time homebuyer credit, or residential energy efficient property credit\*;

   **b.** You are excluding income from Puerto Rico; or

   **c.** You are filing Form 2555, 2555-EZ, or 4563.
   \*If applicable.

---

**Part 1**

1. Number of qualifying children under age 17 with the required social security number: _____ × $2,000. Enter the result. | **1** | |

2. Number of other dependents, including qualifying children without the required social security number: _____ × $500. Enter the result. | **2** | |

   **Caution.** Don't include yourself, your spouse, or anyone who is not a U.S. citizen, U.S. national, or U.S. resident alien. Also, don't include anyone you included on line 1.

3. Add lines 1 and 2. | **3** | |

4. Enter the amount from Form 1040, line 7. | **4** | |

5. Enter the amount shown below for your filing status.

   ● Married filing jointly — $400,000

   ● All other filing statuses — $200,000 | **5** | |

6. Is the amount on line 4 more than the amount on line 5?

   ☐ **No.** Leave line 6 blank. Enter -0- on line 7, and go to line 8.

   ☐ **Yes.** Subtract line 5 from line 4.
   If the result isn't a multiple of $1,000, increase it to the next multiple of $1,000. For example, increase $425 to $1,000, increase $1,025 to $2,000, etc. | **6** | |

7. Multiply the amount on line 6 by 5% (0.05). Enter the result. | **7** | |

8. Is the amount on line 3 more than the amount on line 7?

   ☐ **No.** **(STOP)**
   You can't take the child tax credit on Form 1040, line 12a. You also can't take the additional child tax credit on Form 1040, line 17b. Complete the rest of your Form 1040.

   ☐ **Yes.** Subtract line 7 from line 3. Enter the result.
   *Go to Part 2.* | **8** | |

---

## 2018 Child Tax Credit and Credit for Other Dependents Worksheet—*Continued*

2018 Form 1040—Line 12a

*Keep for Your Records*

**Before you begin Part 2:** ✓ Figure the amount of any credits you are claiming on Schedule 3; Form 5695, Part II*; Form 8910; Form 8936; or Schedule R.

**Part 2**

9. Enter the amount from Form 1040, line 11.

| 9 | |
|---|---|

10. Add any amounts from:

Schedule 3, line 48 _____

Schedule 3, line 49 + _____

Schedule 3, line 50 + _____

Schedule 3, line 51 + _____

Form 5695, line 30* + _____

Form 8910, line 15 + _____

Form 8936, line 23 + _____

Schedule R, line 22 + _____

Enter the total.

| 10 | |
|---|---|

11. Are the amounts on lines 9 and 10 the same?

☐ **Yes.** 🛑
You can't take this credit because there is no tax to reduce. However, you may be able to take the **additional child tax credit** if line 1 is more than zero. See the **TIP** below.

☐ **No.** Subtract line 10 from line 9.

| 11 | |
|---|---|

12. Is the amount on line 8 more than the amount on line 11?

☐ **Yes.** Enter the amount from line 11. Also, you may be able to take the **additional child tax credit** if line 1 is more than zero. See the **TIP** below.

☐ **No.** Enter the amount from line 8.

} **This is your child tax credit and credit for other dependents.**

| 12 | |
|---|---|

Enter this amount on Form 1040, line 12a.

**TIP** *You may be able to take the **additional child tax credit** on Form 1040, line 17b, if you answered "Yes" on line 11 **or** line 12 above.*

- *First, complete your Form 1040 through line 17a (also complete Schedule 5, line 72).*
- *Then, use Schedule 8812 to figure any additional child tax credit.*

**⚠ CAUTION** *If your child tax credit or additional child tax credit for a year after 2015 was reduced or disallowed, see Form 8862, who must file to find out if you must file Form 8862 to take the credit for 2018.*

*If applicable.

# 2018 Tax Table

See the instructions for line 11a to see if you must use the Tax Table below to figure your tax.

**Example.** Mr. and Mrs. Brown are filing a joint return. Their taxable income on Form 1040, line 10, is $25,300. First, they find the $25,300-25,350 taxable income line. Next, they find the column for married filing jointly and read down the column. The amount shown where the taxable income line and filing status column meet is $2,658. This is the tax amount they should enter in the entry space on Form 1040, line 11a.

## Sample Table

| At Least | But Less Than | Single | Married filing jointly* | Married filing separately | Head of a household |
|---|---|---|---|---|---|
| | | | **Your tax is—** | | |
| 25,200 | 25,250 | 2,837 | 2,646 | 2,837 | 2,755 |
| 25,250 | 25,300 | 2,843 | 2,652 | 2,843 | 2,761 |
| 25,300 | 25,350 | 2,849 | (2,658) | 2,849 | 2,767 |
| 25,350 | 25,400 | 2,855 | 2,664 | 2,855 | 2,773 |

| If line 10 (taxable income) is— At least | But less than | And you are— Single | Married filing jointly * | Married filing sepa-rately | Head of a house-hold |
|---|---|---|---|---|---|
| | | | **Your tax is—** | | |
| 0 | 5 | 0 | 0 | 0 | 0 |
| 5 | 15 | 1 | 1 | 1 | 1 |
| 15 | 25 | 2 | 2 | 2 | 2 |
| 25 | 50 | 4 | 4 | 4 | 4 |
| 50 | 75 | 6 | 6 | 6 | 6 |
| 75 | 100 | 9 | 9 | 9 | 9 |
| 100 | 125 | 11 | 11 | 11 | 11 |
| 125 | 150 | 14 | 14 | 14 | 14 |
| 150 | 175 | 16 | 16 | 16 | 16 |
| 175 | 200 | 19 | 19 | 19 | 19 |
| 200 | 225 | 21 | 21 | 21 | 21 |
| 225 | 250 | 24 | 24 | 24 | 24 |
| 250 | 275 | 26 | 26 | 26 | 26 |
| 275 | 300 | 29 | 29 | 29 | 29 |
| 300 | 325 | 31 | 31 | 31 | 31 |
| 325 | 350 | 34 | 34 | 34 | 34 |
| 350 | 375 | 36 | 36 | 36 | 36 |
| 375 | 400 | 39 | 39 | 39 | 39 |
| 400 | 425 | 41 | 41 | 41 | 41 |
| 425 | 450 | 44 | 44 | 44 | 44 |
| 450 | 475 | 46 | 46 | 46 | 46 |
| 475 | 500 | 49 | 49 | 49 | 49 |
| 500 | 525 | 51 | 51 | 51 | 51 |
| 525 | 550 | 54 | 54 | 54 | 54 |
| 550 | 575 | 56 | 56 | 56 | 56 |
| 575 | 600 | 59 | 59 | 59 | 59 |
| 600 | 625 | 61 | 61 | 61 | 61 |
| 625 | 650 | 64 | 64 | 64 | 64 |
| 650 | 675 | 66 | 66 | 66 | 66 |
| 675 | 700 | 69 | 69 | 69 | 69 |
| 700 | 725 | 71 | 71 | 71 | 71 |
| 725 | 750 | 74 | 74 | 74 | 74 |
| 750 | 775 | 76 | 76 | 76 | 76 |
| 775 | 800 | 79 | 79 | 79 | 79 |
| 800 | 825 | 81 | 81 | 81 | 81 |
| 825 | 850 | 84 | 84 | 84 | 84 |
| 850 | 875 | 86 | 86 | 86 | 86 |
| 875 | 900 | 89 | 89 | 89 | 89 |
| 900 | 925 | 91 | 91 | 91 | 91 |
| 925 | 950 | 94 | 94 | 94 | 94 |
| 950 | 975 | 96 | 96 | 96 | 96 |
| 975 | 1,000 | 99 | 99 | 99 | 99 |

### 1,000

| If line 10 (taxable income) is— At least | But less than | And you are— Single | Married filing jointly * | Married filing sepa-rately | Head of a house-hold |
|---|---|---|---|---|---|
| | | | **Your tax is—** | | |
| 1,000 | 1,025 | 101 | 101 | 101 | 101 |
| 1,025 | 1,050 | 104 | 104 | 104 | 104 |
| 1,050 | 1,075 | 106 | 106 | 106 | 106 |
| 1,075 | 1,100 | 109 | 109 | 109 | 109 |
| 1,100 | 1,125 | 111 | 111 | 111 | 111 |
| 1,125 | 1,150 | 114 | 114 | 114 | 114 |
| 1,150 | 1,175 | 116 | 116 | 116 | 116 |
| 1,175 | 1,200 | 119 | 119 | 119 | 119 |
| 1,200 | 1,225 | 121 | 121 | 121 | 121 |
| 1,225 | 1,250 | 124 | 124 | 124 | 124 |
| 1,250 | 1,275 | 126 | 126 | 126 | 126 |
| 1,275 | 1,300 | 129 | 129 | 129 | 129 |
| 1,300 | 1,325 | 131 | 131 | 131 | 131 |
| 1,325 | 1,350 | 134 | 134 | 134 | 134 |
| 1,350 | 1,375 | 136 | 136 | 136 | 136 |
| 1,375 | 1,400 | 139 | 139 | 139 | 139 |
| 1,400 | 1,425 | 141 | 141 | 141 | 141 |
| 1,425 | 1,450 | 144 | 144 | 144 | 144 |
| 1,450 | 1,475 | 146 | 146 | 146 | 146 |
| 1,475 | 1,500 | 149 | 149 | 149 | 149 |
| 1,500 | 1,525 | 151 | 151 | 151 | 151 |
| 1,525 | 1,550 | 154 | 154 | 154 | 154 |
| 1,550 | 1,575 | 156 | 156 | 156 | 156 |
| 1,575 | 1,600 | 159 | 159 | 159 | 159 |
| 1,600 | 1,625 | 161 | 161 | 161 | 161 |
| 1,625 | 1,650 | 164 | 164 | 164 | 164 |
| 1,650 | 1,675 | 166 | 166 | 166 | 166 |
| 1,675 | 1,700 | 169 | 169 | 169 | 169 |
| 1,700 | 1,725 | 171 | 171 | 171 | 171 |
| 1,725 | 1,750 | 174 | 174 | 174 | 174 |
| 1,750 | 1,775 | 176 | 176 | 176 | 176 |
| 1,775 | 1,800 | 179 | 179 | 179 | 179 |
| 1,800 | 1,825 | 181 | 181 | 181 | 181 |
| 1,825 | 1,850 | 184 | 184 | 184 | 184 |
| 1,850 | 1,875 | 186 | 186 | 186 | 186 |
| 1,875 | 1,900 | 189 | 189 | 189 | 189 |
| 1,900 | 1,925 | 191 | 191 | 191 | 191 |
| 1,925 | 1,950 | 194 | 194 | 194 | 194 |
| 1,950 | 1,975 | 196 | 196 | 196 | 196 |
| 1,975 | 2,000 | 199 | 199 | 199 | 199 |

### 2,000

| If line 10 (taxable income) is— At least | But less than | And you are— Single | Married filing jointly * | Married filing sepa-rately | Head of a house-hold |
|---|---|---|---|---|---|
| | | | **Your tax is—** | | |
| 2,000 | 2,025 | 201 | 201 | 201 | 201 |
| 2,025 | 2,050 | 204 | 204 | 204 | 204 |
| 2,050 | 2,075 | 206 | 206 | 206 | 206 |
| 2,075 | 2,100 | 209 | 209 | 209 | 209 |
| 2,100 | 2,125 | 211 | 211 | 211 | 211 |
| 2,125 | 2,150 | 214 | 214 | 214 | 214 |
| 2,150 | 2,175 | 216 | 216 | 216 | 216 |
| 2,175 | 2,200 | 219 | 219 | 219 | 219 |
| 2,200 | 2,225 | 221 | 221 | 221 | 221 |
| 2,225 | 2,250 | 224 | 224 | 224 | 224 |
| 2,250 | 2,275 | 226 | 226 | 226 | 226 |
| 2,275 | 2,300 | 229 | 229 | 229 | 229 |
| 2,300 | 2,325 | 231 | 231 | 231 | 231 |
| 2,325 | 2,350 | 234 | 234 | 234 | 234 |
| 2,350 | 2,375 | 236 | 236 | 236 | 236 |
| 2,375 | 2,400 | 239 | 239 | 239 | 239 |
| 2,400 | 2,425 | 241 | 241 | 241 | 241 |
| 2,425 | 2,450 | 244 | 244 | 244 | 244 |
| 2,450 | 2,475 | 246 | 246 | 246 | 246 |
| 2,475 | 2,500 | 249 | 249 | 249 | 249 |
| 2,500 | 2,525 | 251 | 251 | 251 | 251 |
| 2,525 | 2,550 | 254 | 254 | 254 | 254 |
| 2,550 | 2,575 | 256 | 256 | 256 | 256 |
| 2,575 | 2,600 | 259 | 259 | 259 | 259 |
| 2,600 | 2,625 | 261 | 261 | 261 | 261 |
| 2,625 | 2,650 | 264 | 264 | 264 | 264 |
| 2,650 | 2,675 | 266 | 266 | 266 | 266 |
| 2,675 | 2,700 | 269 | 269 | 269 | 269 |
| 2,700 | 2,725 | 271 | 271 | 271 | 271 |
| 2,725 | 2,750 | 274 | 274 | 274 | 274 |
| 2,750 | 2,775 | 276 | 276 | 276 | 276 |
| 2,775 | 2,800 | 279 | 279 | 279 | 279 |
| 2,800 | 2,825 | 281 | 281 | 281 | 281 |
| 2,825 | 2,850 | 284 | 284 | 284 | 284 |
| 2,850 | 2,875 | 286 | 286 | 286 | 286 |
| 2,875 | 2,900 | 289 | 289 | 289 | 289 |
| 2,900 | 2,925 | 291 | 291 | 291 | 291 |
| 2,925 | 2,950 | 294 | 294 | 294 | 294 |
| 2,950 | 2,975 | 296 | 296 | 296 | 296 |
| 2,975 | 3,000 | 299 | 299 | 299 | 299 |

*(Continued)*

\* This column must also be used by a qualifying widow(er).

## 3,000

| If line 10 (taxable income) is— At least | But less than | Single | Married filing jointly * | Married filing separately | Head of a household |
|---|---|---|---|---|---|
| 3,000 | 3,050 | 303 | 303 | 303 | 303 |
| 3,050 | 3,100 | 308 | 308 | 308 | 308 |
| 3,100 | 3,150 | 313 | 313 | 313 | 313 |
| 3,150 | 3,200 | 318 | 318 | 318 | 318 |
| 3,200 | 3,250 | 323 | 323 | 323 | 323 |
| 3,250 | 3,300 | 328 | 328 | 328 | 328 |
| 3,300 | 3,350 | 333 | 333 | 333 | 333 |
| 3,350 | 3,400 | 338 | 338 | 338 | 338 |
| 3,400 | 3,450 | 343 | 343 | 343 | 343 |
| 3,450 | 3,500 | 348 | 348 | 348 | 348 |
| 3,500 | 3,550 | 353 | 353 | 353 | 353 |
| 3,550 | 3,600 | 358 | 358 | 358 | 358 |
| 3,600 | 3,650 | 363 | 363 | 363 | 363 |
| 3,650 | 3,700 | 368 | 368 | 368 | 368 |
| 3,700 | 3,750 | 373 | 373 | 373 | 373 |
| 3,750 | 3,800 | 378 | 378 | 378 | 378 |
| 3,800 | 3,850 | 383 | 383 | 383 | 383 |
| 3,850 | 3,900 | 388 | 388 | 388 | 388 |
| 3,900 | 3,950 | 393 | 393 | 393 | 393 |
| 3,950 | 4,000 | 398 | 398 | 398 | 398 |

## 4,000

| At least | But less than | Single | Married filing jointly * | Married filing separately | Head of a household |
|---|---|---|---|---|---|
| 4,000 | 4,050 | 403 | 403 | 403 | 403 |
| 4,050 | 4,100 | 408 | 408 | 408 | 408 |
| 4,100 | 4,150 | 413 | 413 | 413 | 413 |
| 4,150 | 4,200 | 418 | 418 | 418 | 418 |
| 4,200 | 4,250 | 423 | 423 | 423 | 423 |
| 4,250 | 4,300 | 428 | 428 | 428 | 428 |
| 4,300 | 4,350 | 433 | 433 | 433 | 433 |
| 4,350 | 4,400 | 438 | 438 | 438 | 438 |
| 4,400 | 4,450 | 443 | 443 | 443 | 443 |
| 4,450 | 4,500 | 448 | 448 | 448 | 448 |
| 4,500 | 4,550 | 453 | 453 | 453 | 453 |
| 4,550 | 4,600 | 458 | 458 | 458 | 458 |
| 4,600 | 4,650 | 463 | 463 | 463 | 463 |
| 4,650 | 4,700 | 468 | 468 | 468 | 468 |
| 4,700 | 4,750 | 473 | 473 | 473 | 473 |
| 4,750 | 4,800 | 478 | 478 | 478 | 478 |
| 4,800 | 4,850 | 483 | 483 | 483 | 483 |
| 4,850 | 4,900 | 488 | 488 | 488 | 488 |
| 4,900 | 4,950 | 493 | 493 | 493 | 493 |
| 4,950 | 5,000 | 498 | 498 | 498 | 498 |

## 5,000

| At least | But less than | Single | Married filing jointly * | Married filing separately | Head of a household |
|---|---|---|---|---|---|
| 5,000 | 5,050 | 503 | 503 | 503 | 503 |
| 5,050 | 5,100 | 508 | 508 | 508 | 508 |
| 5,100 | 5,150 | 513 | 513 | 513 | 513 |
| 5,150 | 5,200 | 518 | 518 | 518 | 518 |
| 5,200 | 5,250 | 523 | 523 | 523 | 523 |
| 5,250 | 5,300 | 528 | 528 | 528 | 528 |
| 5,300 | 5,350 | 533 | 533 | 533 | 533 |
| 5,350 | 5,400 | 538 | 538 | 538 | 538 |
| 5,400 | 5,450 | 543 | 543 | 543 | 543 |
| 5,450 | 5,500 | 548 | 548 | 548 | 548 |
| 5,500 | 5,550 | 553 | 553 | 553 | 553 |
| 5,550 | 5,600 | 558 | 558 | 558 | 558 |
| 5,600 | 5,650 | 563 | 563 | 563 | 563 |
| 5,650 | 5,700 | 568 | 568 | 568 | 568 |
| 5,700 | 5,750 | 573 | 573 | 573 | 573 |
| 5,750 | 5,800 | 578 | 578 | 578 | 578 |
| 5,800 | 5,850 | 583 | 583 | 583 | 583 |
| 5,850 | 5,900 | 588 | 588 | 588 | 588 |
| 5,900 | 5,950 | 593 | 593 | 593 | 593 |
| 5,950 | 6,000 | 598 | 598 | 598 | 598 |

## 6,000

| At least | But less than | Single | Married filing jointly * | Married filing separately | Head of a household |
|---|---|---|---|---|---|
| 6,000 | 6,050 | 603 | 603 | 603 | 603 |
| 6,050 | 6,100 | 608 | 608 | 608 | 608 |
| 6,100 | 6,150 | 613 | 613 | 613 | 613 |
| 6,150 | 6,200 | 618 | 618 | 618 | 618 |
| 6,200 | 6,250 | 623 | 623 | 623 | 623 |
| 6,250 | 6,300 | 628 | 628 | 628 | 628 |
| 6,300 | 6,350 | 633 | 633 | 633 | 633 |
| 6,350 | 6,400 | 638 | 638 | 638 | 638 |
| 6,400 | 6,450 | 643 | 643 | 643 | 643 |
| 6,450 | 6,500 | 648 | 648 | 648 | 648 |
| 6,500 | 6,550 | 653 | 653 | 653 | 653 |
| 6,550 | 6,600 | 658 | 658 | 658 | 658 |
| 6,600 | 6,650 | 663 | 663 | 663 | 663 |
| 6,650 | 6,700 | 668 | 668 | 668 | 668 |
| 6,700 | 6,750 | 673 | 673 | 673 | 673 |
| 6,750 | 6,800 | 678 | 678 | 678 | 678 |
| 6,800 | 6,850 | 683 | 683 | 683 | 683 |
| 6,850 | 6,900 | 688 | 688 | 688 | 688 |
| 6,900 | 6,950 | 693 | 693 | 693 | 693 |
| 6,950 | 7,000 | 698 | 698 | 698 | 698 |

## 7,000

| At least | But less than | Single | Married filing jointly * | Married filing separately | Head of a household |
|---|---|---|---|---|---|
| 7,000 | 7,050 | 703 | 703 | 703 | 703 |
| 7,050 | 7,100 | 708 | 708 | 708 | 708 |
| 7,100 | 7,150 | 713 | 713 | 713 | 713 |
| 7,150 | 7,200 | 718 | 718 | 718 | 718 |
| 7,200 | 7,250 | 723 | 723 | 723 | 723 |
| 7,250 | 7,300 | 728 | 728 | 728 | 728 |
| 7,300 | 7,350 | 733 | 733 | 733 | 733 |
| 7,350 | 7,400 | 738 | 738 | 738 | 738 |
| 7,400 | 7,450 | 743 | 743 | 743 | 743 |
| 7,450 | 7,500 | 748 | 748 | 748 | 748 |
| 7,500 | 7,550 | 753 | 753 | 753 | 753 |
| 7,550 | 7,600 | 758 | 758 | 758 | 758 |
| 7,600 | 7,650 | 763 | 763 | 763 | 763 |
| 7,650 | 7,700 | 768 | 768 | 768 | 768 |
| 7,700 | 7,750 | 773 | 773 | 773 | 773 |
| 7,750 | 7,800 | 778 | 778 | 778 | 778 |
| 7,800 | 7,850 | 783 | 783 | 783 | 783 |
| 7,850 | 7,900 | 788 | 788 | 788 | 788 |
| 7,900 | 7,950 | 793 | 793 | 793 | 793 |
| 7,950 | 8,000 | 798 | 798 | 798 | 798 |

## 8,000

| At least | But less than | Single | Married filing jointly * | Married filing separately | Head of a household |
|---|---|---|---|---|---|
| 8,000 | 8,050 | 803 | 803 | 803 | 803 |
| 8,050 | 8,100 | 808 | 808 | 808 | 808 |
| 8,100 | 8,150 | 813 | 813 | 813 | 813 |
| 8,150 | 8,200 | 818 | 818 | 818 | 818 |
| 8,200 | 8,250 | 823 | 823 | 823 | 823 |
| 8,250 | 8,300 | 828 | 828 | 828 | 828 |
| 8,300 | 8,350 | 833 | 833 | 833 | 833 |
| 8,350 | 8,400 | 838 | 838 | 838 | 838 |
| 8,400 | 8,450 | 843 | 843 | 843 | 843 |
| 8,450 | 8,500 | 848 | 848 | 848 | 848 |
| 8,500 | 8,550 | 853 | 853 | 853 | 853 |
| 8,550 | 8,600 | 858 | 858 | 858 | 858 |
| 8,600 | 8,650 | 863 | 863 | 863 | 863 |
| 8,650 | 8,700 | 868 | 868 | 868 | 868 |
| 8,700 | 8,750 | 873 | 873 | 873 | 873 |
| 8,750 | 8,800 | 878 | 878 | 878 | 878 |
| 8,800 | 8,850 | 883 | 883 | 883 | 883 |
| 8,850 | 8,900 | 888 | 888 | 888 | 888 |
| 8,900 | 8,950 | 893 | 893 | 893 | 893 |
| 8,950 | 9,000 | 896 | 898 | 898 | 898 |

## 9,000

| At least | But less than | Single | Married filing jointly * | Married filing separately | Head of a household |
|---|---|---|---|---|---|
| 9,000 | 9,050 | 903 | 903 | 903 | 903 |
| 9,050 | 9,100 | 908 | 908 | 908 | 908 |
| 9,100 | 9,150 | 913 | 913 | 913 | 913 |
| 9,150 | 9,200 | 918 | 918 | 918 | 918 |
| 9,200 | 9,250 | 923 | 923 | 923 | 923 |
| 9,250 | 9,300 | 928 | 928 | 928 | 928 |
| 9,300 | 9,350 | 933 | 933 | 933 | 933 |
| 9,350 | 9,400 | 938 | 938 | 938 | 938 |
| 9,400 | 9,450 | 943 | 943 | 943 | 943 |
| 9,450 | 9,500 | 948 | 948 | 948 | 948 |
| 9,500 | 9,550 | 953 | 953 | 953 | 953 |
| 9,550 | 9,600 | 959 | 958 | 959 | 958 |
| 9,600 | 9,650 | 965 | 963 | 965 | 963 |
| 9,650 | 9,700 | 971 | 968 | 971 | 968 |
| 9,700 | 9,750 | 977 | 973 | 977 | 973 |
| 9,750 | 9,800 | 983 | 978 | 983 | 978 |
| 9,800 | 9,850 | 989 | 983 | 989 | 983 |
| 9,850 | 9,900 | 995 | 988 | 995 | 988 |
| 9,900 | 9,950 | 1,001 | 993 | 1,001 | 993 |
| 9,950 | 10,000 | 1,007 | 998 | 1,007 | 998 |

## 10,000

| At least | But less than | Single | Married filing jointly * | Married filing separately | Head of a household |
|---|---|---|---|---|---|
| 10,000 | 10,050 | 1,013 | 1,003 | 1,013 | 1,003 |
| 10,050 | 10,100 | 1,019 | 1,008 | 1,019 | 1,008 |
| 10,100 | 10,150 | 1,025 | 1,013 | 1,025 | 1,013 |
| 10,150 | 10,200 | 1,031 | 1,018 | 1,031 | 1,018 |
| 10,200 | 10,250 | 1,037 | 1,023 | 1,037 | 1,023 |
| 10,250 | 10,300 | 1,043 | 1,028 | 1,043 | 1,028 |
| 10,300 | 10,350 | 1,049 | 1,033 | 1,049 | 1,033 |
| 10,350 | 10,400 | 1,055 | 1,038 | 1,055 | 1,038 |
| 10,400 | 10,450 | 1,061 | 1,043 | 1,061 | 1,043 |
| 10,450 | 10,500 | 1,067 | 1,048 | 1,067 | 1,048 |
| 10,500 | 10,550 | 1,073 | 1,053 | 1,073 | 1,053 |
| 10,550 | 10,600 | 1,079 | 1,058 | 1,079 | 1,058 |
| 10,600 | 10,650 | 1,085 | 1,063 | 1,085 | 1,063 |
| 10,650 | 10,700 | 1,091 | 1,068 | 1,091 | 1,068 |
| 10,700 | 10,750 | 1,097 | 1,073 | 1,097 | 1,073 |
| 10,750 | 10,800 | 1,103 | 1,078 | 1,103 | 1,078 |
| 10,800 | 10,850 | 1,109 | 1,083 | 1,109 | 1,083 |
| 10,850 | 10,900 | 1,115 | 1,088 | 1,115 | 1,088 |
| 10,900 | 10,950 | 1,121 | 1,093 | 1,121 | 1,093 |
| 10,950 | 11,000 | 1,127 | 1,098 | 1,127 | 1,098 |

## 11,000

| At least | But less than | Single | Married filing jointly * | Married filing separately | Head of a household |
|---|---|---|---|---|---|
| 11,000 | 11,050 | 1,133 | 1,103 | 1,133 | 1,103 |
| 11,050 | 11,100 | 1,139 | 1,108 | 1,139 | 1,108 |
| 11,100 | 11,150 | 1,145 | 1,113 | 1,145 | 1,113 |
| 11,150 | 11,200 | 1,151 | 1,118 | 1,151 | 1,118 |
| 11,200 | 11,250 | 1,157 | 1,123 | 1,157 | 1,123 |
| 11,250 | 11,300 | 1,163 | 1,128 | 1,163 | 1,128 |
| 11,300 | 11,350 | 1,169 | 1,133 | 1,169 | 1,133 |
| 11,350 | 11,400 | 1,175 | 1,138 | 1,175 | 1,138 |
| 11,400 | 11,450 | 1,181 | 1,143 | 1,181 | 1,143 |
| 11,450 | 11,500 | 1,187 | 1,148 | 1,187 | 1,148 |
| 11,500 | 11,550 | 1,193 | 1,153 | 1,193 | 1,153 |
| 11,550 | 11,600 | 1,199 | 1,158 | 1,199 | 1,158 |
| 11,600 | 11,650 | 1,205 | 1,163 | 1,205 | 1,163 |
| 11,650 | 11,700 | 1,211 | 1,168 | 1,211 | 1,168 |
| 11,700 | 11,750 | 1,217 | 1,173 | 1,217 | 1,173 |
| 11,750 | 11,800 | 1,223 | 1,178 | 1,223 | 1,178 |
| 11,800 | 11,850 | 1,229 | 1,183 | 1,229 | 1,183 |
| 11,850 | 11,900 | 1,235 | 1,188 | 1,235 | 1,188 |
| 11,900 | 11,950 | 1,241 | 1,193 | 1,241 | 1,193 |
| 11,950 | 12,000 | 1,247 | 1,198 | 1,247 | 1,198 |

* This column must also be used by a qualifying widow(er).

*(Continued)*

## 12,000

| At least | But less than | Single | Married filing jointly * | Married filing separately | Head of a household |
|---|---|---|---|---|---|
| 12,000 | 12,050 | 1,253 | 1,203 | 1,253 | 1,203 |
| 12,050 | 12,100 | 1,259 | 1,208 | 1,259 | 1,208 |
| 12,100 | 12,150 | 1,265 | 1,213 | 1,265 | 1,213 |
| 12,150 | 12,200 | 1,271 | 1,218 | 1,271 | 1,218 |
| 12,200 | 12,250 | 1,277 | 1,223 | 1,277 | 1,223 |
| 12,250 | 12,300 | 1,283 | 1,228 | 1,283 | 1,228 |
| 12,300 | 12,350 | 1,289 | 1,233 | 1,289 | 1,233 |
| 12,350 | 12,400 | 1,295 | 1,238 | 1,295 | 1,238 |
| 12,400 | 12,450 | 1,301 | 1,243 | 1,301 | 1,243 |
| 12,450 | 12,500 | 1,307 | 1,248 | 1,307 | 1,248 |
| 12,500 | 12,550 | 1,313 | 1,253 | 1,313 | 1,253 |
| 12,550 | 12,600 | 1,319 | 1,258 | 1,319 | 1,258 |
| 12,600 | 12,650 | 1,325 | 1,263 | 1,325 | 1,263 |
| 12,650 | 12,700 | 1,331 | 1,268 | 1,331 | 1,268 |
| 12,700 | 12,750 | 1,337 | 1,273 | 1,337 | 1,273 |
| 12,750 | 12,800 | 1,343 | 1,278 | 1,343 | 1,278 |
| 12,800 | 12,850 | 1,349 | 1,283 | 1,349 | 1,283 |
| 12,850 | 12,900 | 1,355 | 1,288 | 1,355 | 1,288 |
| 12,900 | 12,950 | 1,361 | 1,293 | 1,361 | 1,293 |
| 12,950 | 13,000 | 1,367 | 1,298 | 1,367 | 1,298 |

## 13,000

| At least | But less than | Single | Married filing jointly * | Married filing separately | Head of a household |
|---|---|---|---|---|---|
| 13,000 | 13,050 | 1,373 | 1,303 | 1,373 | 1,303 |
| 13,050 | 13,100 | 1,379 | 1,308 | 1,379 | 1,308 |
| 13,100 | 13,150 | 1,385 | 1,313 | 1,385 | 1,313 |
| 13,150 | 13,200 | 1,391 | 1,318 | 1,391 | 1,318 |
| 13,200 | 13,250 | 1,397 | 1,323 | 1,397 | 1,323 |
| 13,250 | 13,300 | 1,403 | 1,328 | 1,403 | 1,328 |
| 13,300 | 13,350 | 1,409 | 1,333 | 1,409 | 1,333 |
| 13,350 | 13,400 | 1,415 | 1,338 | 1,415 | 1,338 |
| 13,400 | 13,450 | 1,421 | 1,343 | 1,421 | 1,343 |
| 13,450 | 13,500 | 1,427 | 1,348 | 1,427 | 1,348 |
| 13,500 | 13,550 | 1,433 | 1,353 | 1,433 | 1,353 |
| 13,550 | 13,600 | 1,439 | 1,358 | 1,439 | 1,358 |
| 13,600 | 13,650 | 1,445 | 1,363 | 1,445 | 1,363 |
| 13,650 | 13,700 | 1,451 | 1,368 | 1,451 | 1,369 |
| 13,700 | 13,750 | 1,457 | 1,373 | 1,457 | 1,375 |
| 13,750 | 13,800 | 1,463 | 1,378 | 1,463 | 1,381 |
| 13,800 | 13,850 | 1,469 | 1,383 | 1,469 | 1,387 |
| 13,850 | 13,900 | 1,475 | 1,388 | 1,475 | 1,393 |
| 13,900 | 13,950 | 1,481 | 1,393 | 1,481 | 1,399 |
| 13,950 | 14,000 | 1,487 | 1,398 | 1,487 | 1,405 |

## 14,000

| At least | But less than | Single | Married filing jointly * | Married filing separately | Head of a household |
|---|---|---|---|---|---|
| 14,000 | 14,050 | 1,493 | 1,403 | 1,493 | 1,411 |
| 14,050 | 14,100 | 1,499 | 1,408 | 1,499 | 1,417 |
| 14,100 | 14,150 | 1,505 | 1,413 | 1,505 | 1,423 |
| 14,150 | 14,200 | 1,511 | 1,418 | 1,511 | 1,429 |
| 14,200 | 14,250 | 1,517 | 1,423 | 1,517 | 1,435 |
| 14,250 | 14,300 | 1,523 | 1,428 | 1,523 | 1,441 |
| 14,300 | 14,350 | 1,529 | 1,433 | 1,529 | 1,447 |
| 14,350 | 14,400 | 1,535 | 1,438 | 1,535 | 1,453 |
| 14,400 | 14,450 | 1,541 | 1,443 | 1,541 | 1,459 |
| 14,450 | 14,500 | 1,547 | 1,448 | 1,547 | 1,465 |
| 14,500 | 14,550 | 1,553 | 1,453 | 1,553 | 1,471 |
| 14,550 | 14,600 | 1,559 | 1,458 | 1,559 | 1,477 |
| 14,600 | 14,650 | 1,565 | 1,463 | 1,565 | 1,483 |
| 14,650 | 14,700 | 1,571 | 1,468 | 1,571 | 1,489 |
| 14,700 | 14,750 | 1,577 | 1,473 | 1,577 | 1,495 |
| 14,750 | 14,800 | 1,583 | 1,478 | 1,583 | 1,501 |
| 14,800 | 14,850 | 1,589 | 1,483 | 1,589 | 1,507 |
| 14,850 | 14,900 | 1,595 | 1,488 | 1,595 | 1,513 |
| 14,900 | 14,950 | 1,601 | 1,493 | 1,601 | 1,519 |
| 14,950 | 15,000 | 1,607 | 1,498 | 1,607 | 1,525 |

## 15,000

| At least | But less than | Single | Married filing jointly * | Married filing separately | Head of a household |
|---|---|---|---|---|---|
| 15,000 | 15,050 | 1,613 | 1,503 | 1,613 | 1,531 |
| 15,050 | 15,100 | 1,619 | 1,508 | 1,619 | 1,537 |
| 15,100 | 15,150 | 1,625 | 1,513 | 1,625 | 1,543 |
| 15,150 | 15,200 | 1,631 | 1,518 | 1,631 | 1,549 |
| 15,200 | 15,250 | 1,637 | 1,523 | 1,637 | 1,555 |
| 15,250 | 15,300 | 1,643 | 1,528 | 1,643 | 1,561 |
| 15,300 | 15,350 | 1,649 | 1,533 | 1,649 | 1,567 |
| 15,350 | 15,400 | 1,655 | 1,538 | 1,655 | 1,573 |
| 15,400 | 15,450 | 1,661 | 1,543 | 1,661 | 1,579 |
| 15,450 | 15,500 | 1,667 | 1,548 | 1,667 | 1,585 |
| 15,500 | 15,550 | 1,673 | 1,553 | 1,673 | 1,591 |
| 15,550 | 15,600 | 1,679 | 1,558 | 1,679 | 1,597 |
| 15,600 | 15,650 | 1,685 | 1,563 | 1,685 | 1,603 |
| 15,650 | 15,700 | 1,691 | 1,568 | 1,691 | 1,609 |
| 15,700 | 15,750 | 1,697 | 1,573 | 1,697 | 1,615 |
| 15,750 | 15,800 | 1,703 | 1,578 | 1,703 | 1,621 |
| 15,800 | 15,850 | 1,709 | 1,583 | 1,709 | 1,627 |
| 15,850 | 15,900 | 1,715 | 1,588 | 1,715 | 1,633 |
| 15,900 | 15,950 | 1,721 | 1,593 | 1,721 | 1,639 |
| 15,950 | 16,000 | 1,727 | 1,598 | 1,727 | 1,645 |

## 16,000

| At least | But less than | Single | Married filing jointly * | Married filing separately | Head of a household |
|---|---|---|---|---|---|
| 16,000 | 16,050 | 1,733 | 1,603 | 1,733 | 1,651 |
| 16,050 | 16,100 | 1,739 | 1,608 | 1,739 | 1,657 |
| 16,100 | 16,150 | 1,745 | 1,613 | 1,745 | 1,663 |
| 16,150 | 16,200 | 1,751 | 1,618 | 1,751 | 1,669 |
| 16,200 | 16,250 | 1,757 | 1,623 | 1,757 | 1,675 |
| 16,250 | 16,300 | 1,763 | 1,628 | 1,763 | 1,681 |
| 16,300 | 16,350 | 1,769 | 1,633 | 1,769 | 1,687 |
| 16,350 | 16,400 | 1,775 | 1,638 | 1,775 | 1,693 |
| 16,400 | 16,450 | 1,781 | 1,643 | 1,781 | 1,699 |
| 16,450 | 16,500 | 1,787 | 1,648 | 1,787 | 1,705 |
| 16,500 | 16,550 | 1,793 | 1,653 | 1,793 | 1,711 |
| 16,550 | 16,600 | 1,799 | 1,658 | 1,799 | 1,717 |
| 16,600 | 16,650 | 1,805 | 1,663 | 1,805 | 1,723 |
| 16,650 | 16,700 | 1,811 | 1,668 | 1,811 | 1,729 |
| 16,700 | 16,750 | 1,817 | 1,673 | 1,817 | 1,735 |
| 16,750 | 16,800 | 1,823 | 1,678 | 1,823 | 1,741 |
| 16,800 | 16,850 | 1,829 | 1,683 | 1,829 | 1,747 |
| 16,850 | 16,900 | 1,835 | 1,688 | 1,835 | 1,753 |
| 16,900 | 16,950 | 1,841 | 1,693 | 1,841 | 1,759 |
| 16,950 | 17,000 | 1,847 | 1,698 | 1,847 | 1,765 |

## 17,000

| At least | But less than | Single | Married filing jointly * | Married filing separately | Head of a household |
|---|---|---|---|---|---|
| 17,000 | 17,050 | 1,853 | 1,703 | 1,853 | 1,771 |
| 17,050 | 17,100 | 1,859 | 1,708 | 1,859 | 1,777 |
| 17,100 | 17,150 | 1,865 | 1,713 | 1,865 | 1,783 |
| 17,150 | 17,200 | 1,871 | 1,718 | 1,871 | 1,789 |
| 17,200 | 17,250 | 1,877 | 1,723 | 1,877 | 1,795 |
| 17,250 | 17,300 | 1,883 | 1,728 | 1,883 | 1,801 |
| 17,300 | 17,350 | 1,889 | 1,733 | 1,889 | 1,807 |
| 17,350 | 17,400 | 1,895 | 1,738 | 1,895 | 1,813 |
| 17,400 | 17,450 | 1,901 | 1,743 | 1,901 | 1,819 |
| 17,450 | 17,500 | 1,907 | 1,748 | 1,907 | 1,825 |
| 17,500 | 17,550 | 1,913 | 1,753 | 1,913 | 1,831 |
| 17,550 | 17,600 | 1,919 | 1,758 | 1,919 | 1,837 |
| 17,600 | 17,650 | 1,925 | 1,763 | 1,925 | 1,843 |
| 17,650 | 17,700 | 1,931 | 1,768 | 1,931 | 1,849 |
| 17,700 | 17,750 | 1,937 | 1,773 | 1,937 | 1,855 |
| 17,750 | 17,800 | 1,943 | 1,778 | 1,943 | 1,861 |
| 17,800 | 17,850 | 1,949 | 1,783 | 1,949 | 1,867 |
| 17,850 | 17,900 | 1,955 | 1,788 | 1,955 | 1,873 |
| 17,900 | 17,950 | 1,961 | 1,793 | 1,961 | 1,879 |
| 17,950 | 18,000 | 1,967 | 1,798 | 1,967 | 1,885 |

## 18,000

| At least | But less than | Single | Married filing jointly * | Married filing separately | Head of a household |
|---|---|---|---|---|---|
| 18,000 | 18,050 | 1,973 | 1,803 | 1,973 | 1,891 |
| 18,050 | 18,100 | 1,979 | 1,808 | 1,979 | 1,897 |
| 18,100 | 18,150 | 1,985 | 1,813 | 1,985 | 1,903 |
| 18,150 | 18,200 | 1,991 | 1,818 | 1,991 | 1,909 |
| 18,200 | 18,250 | 1,997 | 1,823 | 1,997 | 1,915 |
| 18,250 | 18,300 | 2,003 | 1,828 | 2,003 | 1,921 |
| 18,300 | 18,350 | 2,009 | 1,833 | 2,009 | 1,927 |
| 18,350 | 18,400 | 2,015 | 1,838 | 2,015 | 1,933 |
| 18,400 | 18,450 | 2,021 | 1,843 | 2,021 | 1,939 |
| 18,450 | 18,500 | 2,027 | 1,848 | 2,027 | 1,945 |
| 18,500 | 18,550 | 2,033 | 1,853 | 2,033 | 1,951 |
| 18,550 | 18,600 | 2,039 | 1,858 | 2,039 | 1,957 |
| 18,600 | 18,650 | 2,045 | 1,863 | 2,045 | 1,963 |
| 18,650 | 18,700 | 2,051 | 1,868 | 2,051 | 1,969 |
| 18,700 | 18,750 | 2,057 | 1,873 | 2,057 | 1,975 |
| 18,750 | 18,800 | 2,063 | 1,878 | 2,063 | 1,981 |
| 18,800 | 18,850 | 2,069 | 1,883 | 2,069 | 1,987 |
| 18,850 | 18,900 | 2,075 | 1,888 | 2,075 | 1,993 |
| 18,900 | 18,950 | 2,081 | 1,893 | 2,081 | 1,999 |
| 18,950 | 19,000 | 2,087 | 1,898 | 2,087 | 2,005 |

## 19,000

| At least | But less than | Single | Married filing jointly * | Married filing separately | Head of a household |
|---|---|---|---|---|---|
| 19,000 | 19,050 | 2,093 | 1,903 | 2,093 | 2,011 |
| 19,050 | 19,100 | 2,099 | 1,908 | 2,099 | 2,017 |
| 19,100 | 19,150 | 2,105 | 1,914 | 2,105 | 2,023 |
| 19,150 | 19,200 | 2,111 | 1,920 | 2,111 | 2,029 |
| 19,200 | 19,250 | 2,117 | 1,926 | 2,117 | 2,035 |
| 19,250 | 19,300 | 2,123 | 1,932 | 2,123 | 2,041 |
| 19,300 | 19,350 | 2,129 | 1,938 | 2,129 | 2,047 |
| 19,350 | 19,400 | 2,135 | 1,944 | 2,135 | 2,053 |
| 19,400 | 19,450 | 2,141 | 1,950 | 2,141 | 2,059 |
| 19,450 | 19,500 | 2,147 | 1,956 | 2,147 | 2,065 |
| 19,500 | 19,550 | 2,153 | 1,962 | 2,153 | 2,071 |
| 19,550 | 19,600 | 2,159 | 1,968 | 2,159 | 2,077 |
| 19,600 | 19,650 | 2,165 | 1,974 | 2,165 | 2,083 |
| 19,650 | 19,700 | 2,171 | 1,980 | 2,171 | 2,089 |
| 19,700 | 19,750 | 2,177 | 1,986 | 2,177 | 2,095 |
| 19,750 | 19,800 | 2,183 | 1,992 | 2,183 | 2,101 |
| 19,800 | 19,850 | 2,189 | 1,998 | 2,189 | 2,107 |
| 19,850 | 19,900 | 2,195 | 2,004 | 2,195 | 2,113 |
| 19,900 | 19,950 | 2,201 | 2,010 | 2,201 | 2,119 |
| 19,950 | 20,000 | 2,207 | 2,016 | 2,207 | 2,125 |

## 20,000

| At least | But less than | Single | Married filing jointly * | Married filing separately | Head of a household |
|---|---|---|---|---|---|
| 20,000 | 20,050 | 2,213 | 2,022 | 2,213 | 2,131 |
| 20,050 | 20,100 | 2,219 | 2,028 | 2,219 | 2,137 |
| 20,100 | 20,150 | 2,225 | 2,034 | 2,225 | 2,143 |
| 20,150 | 20,200 | 2,231 | 2,040 | 2,231 | 2,149 |
| 20,200 | 20,250 | 2,237 | 2,046 | 2,237 | 2,155 |
| 20,250 | 20,300 | 2,243 | 2,052 | 2,243 | 2,161 |
| 20,300 | 20,350 | 2,249 | 2,058 | 2,249 | 2,167 |
| 20,350 | 20,400 | 2,255 | 2,064 | 2,255 | 2,173 |
| 20,400 | 20,450 | 2,261 | 2,070 | 2,261 | 2,179 |
| 20,450 | 20,500 | 2,267 | 2,076 | 2,267 | 2,185 |
| 20,500 | 20,550 | 2,273 | 2,082 | 2,273 | 2,191 |
| 20,550 | 20,600 | 2,279 | 2,088 | 2,279 | 2,197 |
| 20,600 | 20,650 | 2,285 | 2,094 | 2,285 | 2,203 |
| 20,650 | 20,700 | 2,291 | 2,100 | 2,291 | 2,209 |
| 20,700 | 20,750 | 2,297 | 2,106 | 2,297 | 2,215 |
| 20,750 | 20,800 | 2,303 | 2,112 | 2,303 | 2,221 |
| 20,800 | 20,850 | 2,309 | 2,118 | 2,309 | 2,227 |
| 20,850 | 20,900 | 2,315 | 2,124 | 2,315 | 2,233 |
| 20,900 | 20,950 | 2,321 | 2,130 | 2,321 | 2,239 |
| 20,950 | 21,000 | 2,327 | 2,136 | 2,327 | 2,245 |

*(Continued)*

* This column must also be used by a qualifying widow(er).

## 21,000

| At least | But less than | Single | Married filing jointly * | Married filing separately | Head of a household |
|---|---|---|---|---|---|
| 21,000 | 21,050 | 2,333 | 2,142 | 2,333 | 2,251 |
| 21,050 | 21,100 | 2,339 | 2,148 | 2,339 | 2,257 |
| 21,100 | 21,150 | 2,345 | 2,154 | 2,345 | 2,263 |
| 21,150 | 21,200 | 2,351 | 2,160 | 2,351 | 2,269 |
| 21,200 | 21,250 | 2,357 | 2,166 | 2,357 | 2,275 |
| 21,250 | 21,300 | 2,363 | 2,172 | 2,363 | 2,281 |
| 21,300 | 21,350 | 2,369 | 2,178 | 2,369 | 2,287 |
| 21,350 | 21,400 | 2,375 | 2,184 | 2,375 | 2,293 |
| 21,400 | 21,450 | 2,381 | 2,190 | 2,381 | 2,299 |
| 21,450 | 21,500 | 2,387 | 2,196 | 2,387 | 2,305 |
| 21,500 | 21,550 | 2,393 | 2,202 | 2,393 | 2,311 |
| 21,550 | 21,600 | 2,399 | 2,208 | 2,399 | 2,317 |
| 21,600 | 21,650 | 2,405 | 2,214 | 2,405 | 2,323 |
| 21,650 | 21,700 | 2,411 | 2,220 | 2,411 | 2,329 |
| 21,700 | 21,750 | 2,417 | 2,226 | 2,417 | 2,335 |
| 21,750 | 21,800 | 2,423 | 2,232 | 2,423 | 2,341 |
| 21,800 | 21,850 | 2,429 | 2,238 | 2,429 | 2,347 |
| 21,850 | 21,900 | 2,435 | 2,244 | 2,435 | 2,353 |
| 21,900 | 21,950 | 2,441 | 2,250 | 2,441 | 2,359 |
| 21,950 | 22,000 | 2,447 | 2,256 | 2,447 | 2,365 |

## 22,000

| At least | But less than | Single | Married filing jointly * | Married filing separately | Head of a household |
|---|---|---|---|---|---|
| 22,000 | 22,050 | 2,453 | 2,262 | 2,453 | 2,371 |
| 22,050 | 22,100 | 2,459 | 2,268 | 2,459 | 2,377 |
| 22,100 | 22,150 | 2,465 | 2,274 | 2,465 | 2,383 |
| 22,150 | 22,200 | 2,471 | 2,280 | 2,471 | 2,389 |
| 22,200 | 22,250 | 2,477 | 2,286 | 2,477 | 2,395 |
| 22,250 | 22,300 | 2,483 | 2,292 | 2,483 | 2,401 |
| 22,300 | 22,350 | 2,489 | 2,298 | 2,489 | 2,407 |
| 22,350 | 22,400 | 2,495 | 2,304 | 2,495 | 2,413 |
| 22,400 | 22,450 | 2,501 | 2,310 | 2,501 | 2,419 |
| 22,450 | 22,500 | 2,507 | 2,316 | 2,507 | 2,425 |
| 22,500 | 22,550 | 2,513 | 2,322 | 2,513 | 2,431 |
| 22,550 | 22,600 | 2,519 | 2,328 | 2,519 | 2,437 |
| 22,600 | 22,650 | 2,525 | 2,334 | 2,525 | 2,443 |
| 22,650 | 22,700 | 2,531 | 2,340 | 2,531 | 2,449 |
| 22,700 | 22,750 | 2,537 | 2,346 | 2,537 | 2,455 |
| 22,750 | 22,800 | 2,543 | 2,352 | 2,543 | 2,461 |
| 22,800 | 22,850 | 2,549 | 2,358 | 2,549 | 2,467 |
| 22,850 | 22,900 | 2,555 | 2,364 | 2,555 | 2,473 |
| 22,900 | 22,950 | 2,561 | 2,370 | 2,561 | 2,479 |
| 22,950 | 23,000 | 2,567 | 2,376 | 2,567 | 2,485 |

## 23,000

| At least | But less than | Single | Married filing jointly * | Married filing separately | Head of a household |
|---|---|---|---|---|---|
| 23,000 | 23,050 | 2,573 | 2,382 | 2,573 | 2,491 |
| 23,050 | 23,100 | 2,579 | 2,388 | 2,579 | 2,497 |
| 23,100 | 23,150 | 2,585 | 2,394 | 2,585 | 2,503 |
| 23,150 | 23,200 | 2,591 | 2,400 | 2,591 | 2,509 |
| 23,200 | 23,250 | 2,597 | 2,406 | 2,597 | 2,515 |
| 23,250 | 23,300 | 2,603 | 2,412 | 2,603 | 2,521 |
| 23,300 | 23,350 | 2,609 | 2,418 | 2,609 | 2,527 |
| 23,350 | 23,400 | 2,615 | 2,424 | 2,615 | 2,533 |
| 23,400 | 23,450 | 2,621 | 2,430 | 2,621 | 2,539 |
| 23,450 | 23,500 | 2,627 | 2,436 | 2,627 | 2,545 |
| 23,500 | 23,550 | 2,633 | 2,442 | 2,633 | 2,551 |
| 23,550 | 23,600 | 2,639 | 2,448 | 2,639 | 2,557 |
| 23,600 | 23,650 | 2,645 | 2,454 | 2,645 | 2,563 |
| 23,650 | 23,700 | 2,651 | 2,460 | 2,651 | 2,569 |
| 23,700 | 23,750 | 2,657 | 2,466 | 2,657 | 2,575 |
| 23,750 | 23,800 | 2,663 | 2,472 | 2,663 | 2,581 |
| 23,800 | 23,850 | 2,669 | 2,478 | 2,669 | 2,587 |
| 23,850 | 23,900 | 2,675 | 2,484 | 2,675 | 2,593 |
| 23,900 | 23,950 | 2,681 | 2,490 | 2,681 | 2,599 |
| 23,950 | 24,000 | 2,687 | 2,496 | 2,687 | 2,605 |

## 24,000

| At least | But less than | Single | Married filing jointly * | Married filing separately | Head of a household |
|---|---|---|---|---|---|
| 24,000 | 24,050 | 2,693 | 2,502 | 2,693 | 2,611 |
| 24,050 | 24,100 | 2,699 | 2,508 | 2,699 | 2,617 |
| 24,100 | 24,150 | 2,705 | 2,514 | 2,705 | 2,623 |
| 24,150 | 24,200 | 2,711 | 2,520 | 2,711 | 2,629 |
| 24,200 | 24,250 | 2,717 | 2,526 | 2,717 | 2,635 |
| 24,250 | 24,300 | 2,723 | 2,532 | 2,723 | 2,641 |
| 24,300 | 24,350 | 2,729 | 2,538 | 2,729 | 2,647 |
| 24,350 | 24,400 | 2,735 | 2,544 | 2,735 | 2,653 |
| 24,400 | 24,450 | 2,741 | 2,550 | 2,741 | 2,659 |
| 24,450 | 24,500 | 2,747 | 2,556 | 2,747 | 2,665 |
| 24,500 | 24,550 | 2,753 | 2,562 | 2,753 | 2,671 |
| 24,550 | 24,600 | 2,759 | 2,568 | 2,759 | 2,677 |
| 24,600 | 24,650 | 2,765 | 2,574 | 2,765 | 2,683 |
| 24,650 | 24,700 | 2,771 | 2,580 | 2,771 | 2,689 |
| 24,700 | 24,750 | 2,777 | 2,586 | 2,777 | 2,695 |
| 24,750 | 24,800 | 2,783 | 2,592 | 2,783 | 2,701 |
| 24,800 | 24,850 | 2,789 | 2,598 | 2,789 | 2,707 |
| 24,850 | 24,900 | 2,795 | 2,604 | 2,795 | 2,713 |
| 24,900 | 24,950 | 2,801 | 2,610 | 2,801 | 2,719 |
| 24,950 | 25,000 | 2,807 | 2,616 | 2,807 | 2,725 |

## 25,000

| At least | But less than | Single | Married filing jointly * | Married filing separately | Head of a household |
|---|---|---|---|---|---|
| 25,000 | 25,050 | 2,813 | 2,622 | 2,813 | 2,731 |
| 25,050 | 25,100 | 2,819 | 2,628 | 2,819 | 2,737 |
| 25,100 | 25,150 | 2,825 | 2,634 | 2,825 | 2,743 |
| 25,150 | 25,200 | 2,831 | 2,640 | 2,831 | 2,749 |
| 25,200 | 25,250 | 2,837 | 2,646 | 2,837 | 2,755 |
| 25,250 | 25,300 | 2,843 | 2,652 | 2,843 | 2,761 |
| 25,300 | 25,350 | 2,849 | 2,658 | 2,849 | 2,767 |
| 25,350 | 25,400 | 2,855 | 2,664 | 2,855 | 2,773 |
| 25,400 | 25,450 | 2,861 | 2,670 | 2,861 | 2,779 |
| 25,450 | 25,500 | 2,867 | 2,676 | 2,867 | 2,785 |
| 25,500 | 25,550 | 2,873 | 2,682 | 2,873 | 2,791 |
| 25,550 | 25,600 | 2,879 | 2,688 | 2,879 | 2,797 |
| 25,600 | 25,650 | 2,885 | 2,694 | 2,885 | 2,803 |
| 25,650 | 25,700 | 2,891 | 2,700 | 2,891 | 2,809 |
| 25,700 | 25,750 | 2,897 | 2,706 | 2,897 | 2,815 |
| 25,750 | 25,800 | 2,903 | 2,712 | 2,903 | 2,821 |
| 25,800 | 25,850 | 2,909 | 2,718 | 2,909 | 2,827 |
| 25,850 | 25,900 | 2,915 | 2,724 | 2,915 | 2,833 |
| 25,900 | 25,950 | 2,921 | 2,730 | 2,921 | 2,839 |
| 25,950 | 26,000 | 2,927 | 2,736 | 2,927 | 2,845 |

## 26,000

| At least | But less than | Single | Married filing jointly * | Married filing separately | Head of a household |
|---|---|---|---|---|---|
| 26,000 | 26,050 | 2,933 | 2,742 | 2,933 | 2,851 |
| 26,050 | 26,100 | 2,939 | 2,748 | 2,939 | 2,857 |
| 26,100 | 26,150 | 2,945 | 2,754 | 2,945 | 2,863 |
| 26,150 | 26,200 | 2,951 | 2,760 | 2,951 | 2,869 |
| 26,200 | 26,250 | 2,957 | 2,766 | 2,957 | 2,875 |
| 26,250 | 26,300 | 2,963 | 2,772 | 2,963 | 2,881 |
| 26,300 | 26,350 | 2,969 | 2,778 | 2,969 | 2,887 |
| 26,350 | 26,400 | 2,975 | 2,784 | 2,975 | 2,893 |
| 26,400 | 26,450 | 2,981 | 2,790 | 2,981 | 2,899 |
| 26,450 | 26,500 | 2,987 | 2,796 | 2,987 | 2,905 |
| 26,500 | 26,550 | 2,993 | 2,802 | 2,993 | 2,911 |
| 26,550 | 26,600 | 2,999 | 2,808 | 2,999 | 2,917 |
| 26,600 | 26,650 | 3,005 | 2,814 | 3,005 | 2,923 |
| 26,650 | 26,700 | 3,011 | 2,820 | 3,011 | 2,929 |
| 26,700 | 26,750 | 3,017 | 2,826 | 3,017 | 2,935 |
| 26,750 | 26,800 | 3,023 | 2,832 | 3,023 | 2,941 |
| 26,800 | 26,850 | 3,029 | 2,838 | 3,029 | 2,947 |
| 26,850 | 26,900 | 3,035 | 2,844 | 3,035 | 2,953 |
| 26,900 | 26,950 | 3,041 | 2,850 | 3,041 | 2,959 |
| 26,950 | 27,000 | 3,047 | 2,856 | 3,047 | 2,965 |

## 27,000

| At least | But less than | Single | Married filing jointly * | Married filing separately | Head of a household |
|---|---|---|---|---|---|
| 27,000 | 27,050 | 3,053 | 2,862 | 3,053 | 2,971 |
| 27,050 | 27,100 | 3,059 | 2,868 | 3,059 | 2,977 |
| 27,100 | 27,150 | 3,065 | 2,874 | 3,065 | 2,983 |
| 27,150 | 27,200 | 3,071 | 2,880 | 3,071 | 2,989 |
| 27,200 | 27,250 | 3,077 | 2,886 | 3,077 | 2,995 |
| 27,250 | 27,300 | 3,083 | 2,892 | 3,083 | 3,001 |
| 27,300 | 27,350 | 3,089 | 2,898 | 3,089 | 3,007 |
| 27,350 | 27,400 | 3,095 | 2,904 | 3,095 | 3,013 |
| 27,400 | 27,450 | 3,101 | 2,910 | 3,101 | 3,019 |
| 27,450 | 27,500 | 3,107 | 2,916 | 3,107 | 3,025 |
| 27,500 | 27,550 | 3,113 | 2,922 | 3,113 | 3,031 |
| 27,550 | 27,600 | 3,119 | 2,928 | 3,119 | 3,037 |
| 27,600 | 27,650 | 3,125 | 2,934 | 3,125 | 3,043 |
| 27,650 | 27,700 | 3,131 | 2,940 | 3,131 | 3,049 |
| 27,700 | 27,750 | 3,137 | 2,946 | 3,137 | 3,055 |
| 27,750 | 27,800 | 3,143 | 2,952 | 3,143 | 3,061 |
| 27,800 | 27,850 | 3,149 | 2,958 | 3,149 | 3,067 |
| 27,850 | 27,900 | 3,155 | 2,964 | 3,155 | 3,073 |
| 27,900 | 27,950 | 3,161 | 2,970 | 3,161 | 3,079 |
| 27,950 | 28,000 | 3,167 | 2,976 | 3,167 | 3,085 |

## 28,000

| At least | But less than | Single | Married filing jointly * | Married filing separately | Head of a household |
|---|---|---|---|---|---|
| 28,000 | 28,050 | 3,173 | 2,982 | 3,173 | 3,091 |
| 28,050 | 28,100 | 3,179 | 2,988 | 3,179 | 3,097 |
| 28,100 | 28,150 | 3,185 | 2,994 | 3,185 | 3,103 |
| 28,150 | 28,200 | 3,191 | 3,000 | 3,191 | 3,109 |
| 28,200 | 28,250 | 3,197 | 3,006 | 3,197 | 3,115 |
| 28,250 | 28,300 | 3,203 | 3,012 | 3,203 | 3,121 |
| 28,300 | 28,350 | 3,209 | 3,018 | 3,209 | 3,127 |
| 28,350 | 28,400 | 3,215 | 3,024 | 3,215 | 3,133 |
| 28,400 | 28,450 | 3,221 | 3,030 | 3,221 | 3,139 |
| 28,450 | 28,500 | 3,227 | 3,036 | 3,227 | 3,145 |
| 28,500 | 28,550 | 3,233 | 3,042 | 3,233 | 3,151 |
| 28,550 | 28,600 | 3,239 | 3,048 | 3,239 | 3,157 |
| 28,600 | 28,650 | 3,245 | 3,054 | 3,245 | 3,163 |
| 28,650 | 28,700 | 3,251 | 3,060 | 3,251 | 3,169 |
| 28,700 | 28,750 | 3,257 | 3,066 | 3,257 | 3,175 |
| 28,750 | 28,800 | 3,263 | 3,072 | 3,263 | 3,181 |
| 28,800 | 28,850 | 3,269 | 3,078 | 3,269 | 3,187 |
| 28,850 | 28,900 | 3,275 | 3,084 | 3,275 | 3,193 |
| 28,900 | 28,950 | 3,281 | 3,090 | 3,281 | 3,199 |
| 28,950 | 29,000 | 3,287 | 3,096 | 3,287 | 3,205 |

## 29,000

| At least | But less than | Single | Married filing jointly * | Married filing separately | Head of a household |
|---|---|---|---|---|---|
| 29,000 | 29,050 | 3,293 | 3,102 | 3,293 | 3,211 |
| 29,050 | 29,100 | 3,299 | 3,108 | 3,299 | 3,217 |
| 29,100 | 29,150 | 3,305 | 3,114 | 3,305 | 3,223 |
| 29,150 | 29,200 | 3,311 | 3,120 | 3,311 | 3,229 |
| 29,200 | 29,250 | 3,317 | 3,126 | 3,317 | 3,235 |
| 29,250 | 29,300 | 3,323 | 3,132 | 3,323 | 3,241 |
| 29,300 | 29,350 | 3,329 | 3,138 | 3,329 | 3,247 |
| 29,350 | 29,400 | 3,335 | 3,144 | 3,335 | 3,253 |
| 29,400 | 29,450 | 3,341 | 3,150 | 3,341 | 3,259 |
| 29,450 | 29,500 | 3,347 | 3,156 | 3,347 | 3,265 |
| 29,500 | 29,550 | 3,353 | 3,162 | 3,353 | 3,271 |
| 29,550 | 29,600 | 3,359 | 3,168 | 3,359 | 3,277 |
| 29,600 | 29,650 | 3,365 | 3,174 | 3,365 | 3,283 |
| 29,650 | 29,700 | 3,371 | 3,180 | 3,371 | 3,289 |
| 29,700 | 29,750 | 3,377 | 3,186 | 3,377 | 3,295 |
| 29,750 | 29,800 | 3,383 | 3,192 | 3,383 | 3,301 |
| 29,800 | 29,850 | 3,389 | 3,198 | 3,389 | 3,307 |
| 29,850 | 29,900 | 3,395 | 3,204 | 3,395 | 3,313 |
| 29,900 | 29,950 | 3,401 | 3,210 | 3,401 | 3,319 |
| 29,950 | 30,000 | 3,407 | 3,216 | 3,407 | 3,325 |

*(Continued)*

\* This column must also be used by a qualifying widow(er).

## 30,000

| At least | But less than | Single | Married filing jointly * | Married filing separately | Head of a household |
|---|---|---|---|---|---|
| | | | Your tax is— | | |
| 30,000 | 30,050 | 3,413 | 3,222 | 3,413 | 3,331 |
| 30,050 | 30,100 | 3,419 | 3,228 | 3,419 | 3,337 |
| 30,100 | 30,150 | 3,425 | 3,234 | 3,425 | 3,343 |
| 30,150 | 30,200 | 3,431 | 3,240 | 3,431 | 3,349 |
| 30,200 | 30,250 | 3,437 | 3,246 | 3,437 | 3,355 |
| 30,250 | 30,300 | 3,443 | 3,252 | 3,443 | 3,361 |
| 30,300 | 30,350 | 3,449 | 3,258 | 3,449 | 3,367 |
| 30,350 | 30,400 | 3,455 | 3,264 | 3,455 | 3,373 |
| 30,400 | 30,450 | 3,461 | 3,270 | 3,461 | 3,379 |
| 30,450 | 30,500 | 3,467 | 3,276 | 3,467 | 3,385 |
| 30,500 | 30,550 | 3,473 | 3,282 | 3,473 | 3,391 |
| 30,550 | 30,600 | 3,479 | 3,288 | 3,479 | 3,397 |
| 30,600 | 30,650 | 3,485 | 3,294 | 3,485 | 3,403 |
| 30,650 | 30,700 | 3,491 | 3,300 | 3,491 | 3,409 |
| 30,700 | 30,750 | 3,497 | 3,306 | 3,497 | 3,415 |
| 30,750 | 30,800 | 3,503 | 3,312 | 3,503 | 3,421 |
| 30,800 | 30,850 | 3,509 | 3,318 | 3,509 | 3,427 |
| 30,850 | 30,900 | 3,515 | 3,324 | 3,515 | 3,433 |
| 30,900 | 30,950 | 3,521 | 3,330 | 3,521 | 3,439 |
| 30,950 | 31,000 | 3,527 | 3,336 | 3,527 | 3,445 |

## 31,000

| At least | But less than | Single | Married filing jointly * | Married filing separately | Head of a household |
|---|---|---|---|---|---|
| 31,000 | 31,050 | 3,533 | 3,342 | 3,533 | 3,451 |
| 31,050 | 31,100 | 3,539 | 3,348 | 3,539 | 3,457 |
| 31,100 | 31,150 | 3,545 | 3,354 | 3,545 | 3,463 |
| 31,150 | 31,200 | 3,551 | 3,360 | 3,551 | 3,469 |
| 31,200 | 31,250 | 3,557 | 3,366 | 3,557 | 3,475 |
| 31,250 | 31,300 | 3,563 | 3,372 | 3,563 | 3,481 |
| 31,300 | 31,350 | 3,569 | 3,378 | 3,569 | 3,487 |
| 31,350 | 31,400 | 3,575 | 3,384 | 3,575 | 3,493 |
| 31,400 | 31,450 | 3,581 | 3,390 | 3,581 | 3,499 |
| 31,450 | 31,500 | 3,587 | 3,396 | 3,587 | 3,505 |
| 31,500 | 31,550 | 3,593 | 3,402 | 3,593 | 3,511 |
| 31,550 | 31,600 | 3,599 | 3,408 | 3,599 | 3,517 |
| 31,600 | 31,650 | 3,605 | 3,414 | 3,605 | 3,523 |
| 31,650 | 31,700 | 3,611 | 3,420 | 3,611 | 3,529 |
| 31,700 | 31,750 | 3,617 | 3,426 | 3,617 | 3,535 |
| 31,750 | 31,800 | 3,623 | 3,432 | 3,623 | 3,541 |
| 31,800 | 31,850 | 3,629 | 3,438 | 3,629 | 3,547 |
| 31,850 | 31,900 | 3,635 | 3,444 | 3,635 | 3,553 |
| 31,900 | 31,950 | 3,641 | 3,450 | 3,641 | 3,559 |
| 31,950 | 32,000 | 3,647 | 3,456 | 3,647 | 3,565 |

## 32,000

| At least | But less than | Single | Married filing jointly * | Married filing separately | Head of a household |
|---|---|---|---|---|---|
| 32,000 | 32,050 | 3,653 | 3,462 | 3,653 | 3,571 |
| 32,050 | 32,100 | 3,659 | 3,468 | 3,659 | 3,577 |
| 32,100 | 32,150 | 3,665 | 3,474 | 3,665 | 3,583 |
| 32,150 | 32,200 | 3,671 | 3,480 | 3,671 | 3,589 |
| 32,200 | 32,250 | 3,677 | 3,486 | 3,677 | 3,595 |
| 32,250 | 32,300 | 3,683 | 3,492 | 3,683 | 3,601 |
| 32,300 | 32,350 | 3,689 | 3,498 | 3,689 | 3,607 |
| 32,350 | 32,400 | 3,695 | 3,504 | 3,695 | 3,613 |
| 32,400 | 32,450 | 3,701 | 3,510 | 3,701 | 3,619 |
| 32,450 | 32,500 | 3,707 | 3,516 | 3,707 | 3,625 |
| 32,500 | 32,550 | 3,713 | 3,522 | 3,713 | 3,631 |
| 32,550 | 32,600 | 3,719 | 3,528 | 3,719 | 3,637 |
| 32,600 | 32,650 | 3,725 | 3,534 | 3,725 | 3,643 |
| 32,650 | 32,700 | 3,731 | 3,540 | 3,731 | 3,649 |
| 32,700 | 32,750 | 3,737 | 3,546 | 3,737 | 3,655 |
| 32,750 | 32,800 | 3,743 | 3,552 | 3,743 | 3,661 |
| 32,800 | 32,850 | 3,749 | 3,558 | 3,749 | 3,667 |
| 32,850 | 32,900 | 3,755 | 3,564 | 3,755 | 3,673 |
| 32,900 | 32,950 | 3,761 | 3,570 | 3,761 | 3,679 |
| 32,950 | 33,000 | 3,767 | 3,576 | 3,767 | 3,685 |

## 33,000

| At least | But less than | Single | Married filing jointly * | Married filing separately | Head of a household |
|---|---|---|---|---|---|
| | | | Your tax is— | | |
| 33,000 | 33,050 | 3,773 | 3,582 | 3,773 | 3,691 |
| 33,050 | 33,100 | 3,779 | 3,588 | 3,779 | 3,697 |
| 33,100 | 33,150 | 3,785 | 3,594 | 3,785 | 3,703 |
| 33,150 | 33,200 | 3,791 | 3,600 | 3,791 | 3,709 |
| 33,200 | 33,250 | 3,797 | 3,606 | 3,797 | 3,715 |
| 33,250 | 33,300 | 3,803 | 3,612 | 3,803 | 3,721 |
| 33,300 | 33,350 | 3,809 | 3,618 | 3,809 | 3,727 |
| 33,350 | 33,400 | 3,815 | 3,624 | 3,815 | 3,733 |
| 33,400 | 33,450 | 3,821 | 3,630 | 3,821 | 3,739 |
| 33,450 | 33,500 | 3,827 | 3,636 | 3,827 | 3,745 |
| 33,500 | 33,550 | 3,833 | 3,642 | 3,833 | 3,751 |
| 33,550 | 33,600 | 3,839 | 3,648 | 3,839 | 3,757 |
| 33,600 | 33,650 | 3,845 | 3,654 | 3,845 | 3,763 |
| 33,650 | 33,700 | 3,851 | 3,660 | 3,851 | 3,769 |
| 33,700 | 33,750 | 3,857 | 3,666 | 3,857 | 3,775 |
| 33,750 | 33,800 | 3,863 | 3,672 | 3,863 | 3,781 |
| 33,800 | 33,850 | 3,869 | 3,678 | 3,869 | 3,787 |
| 33,850 | 33,900 | 3,875 | 3,684 | 3,875 | 3,793 |
| 33,900 | 33,950 | 3,881 | 3,690 | 3,881 | 3,799 |
| 33,950 | 34,000 | 3,887 | 3,696 | 3,887 | 3,805 |

## 34,000

| At least | But less than | Single | Married filing jointly * | Married filing separately | Head of a household |
|---|---|---|---|---|---|
| 34,000 | 34,050 | 3,893 | 3,702 | 3,893 | 3,811 |
| 34,050 | 34,100 | 3,899 | 3,708 | 3,899 | 3,817 |
| 34,100 | 34,150 | 3,905 | 3,714 | 3,905 | 3,823 |
| 34,150 | 34,200 | 3,911 | 3,720 | 3,911 | 3,829 |
| 34,200 | 34,250 | 3,917 | 3,726 | 3,917 | 3,835 |
| 34,250 | 34,300 | 3,923 | 3,732 | 3,923 | 3,841 |
| 34,300 | 34,350 | 3,929 | 3,738 | 3,929 | 3,847 |
| 34,350 | 34,400 | 3,935 | 3,744 | 3,935 | 3,853 |
| 34,400 | 34,450 | 3,941 | 3,750 | 3,941 | 3,859 |
| 34,450 | 34,500 | 3,947 | 3,756 | 3,947 | 3,865 |
| 34,500 | 34,550 | 3,953 | 3,762 | 3,953 | 3,871 |
| 34,550 | 34,600 | 3,959 | 3,768 | 3,959 | 3,877 |
| 34,600 | 34,650 | 3,965 | 3,774 | 3,965 | 3,883 |
| 34,650 | 34,700 | 3,971 | 3,780 | 3,971 | 3,889 |
| 34,700 | 34,750 | 3,977 | 3,786 | 3,977 | 3,895 |
| 34,750 | 34,800 | 3,983 | 3,792 | 3,983 | 3,901 |
| 34,800 | 34,850 | 3,989 | 3,798 | 3,989 | 3,907 |
| 34,850 | 34,900 | 3,995 | 3,804 | 3,995 | 3,913 |
| 34,900 | 34,950 | 4,001 | 3,810 | 4,001 | 3,919 |
| 34,950 | 35,000 | 4,007 | 3,816 | 4,007 | 3,925 |

## 35,000

| At least | But less than | Single | Married filing jointly * | Married filing separately | Head of a household |
|---|---|---|---|---|---|
| 35,000 | 35,050 | 4,013 | 3,822 | 4,013 | 3,931 |
| 35,050 | 35,100 | 4,019 | 3,828 | 4,019 | 3,937 |
| 35,100 | 35,150 | 4,025 | 3,834 | 4,025 | 3,943 |
| 35,150 | 35,200 | 4,031 | 3,840 | 4,031 | 3,949 |
| 35,200 | 35,250 | 4,037 | 3,846 | 4,037 | 3,955 |
| 35,250 | 35,300 | 4,043 | 3,852 | 4,043 | 3,961 |
| 35,300 | 35,350 | 4,049 | 3,858 | 4,049 | 3,967 |
| 35,350 | 35,400 | 4,055 | 3,864 | 4,055 | 3,973 |
| 35,400 | 35,450 | 4,061 | 3,870 | 4,061 | 3,979 |
| 35,450 | 35,500 | 4,067 | 3,876 | 4,067 | 3,985 |
| 35,500 | 35,550 | 4,073 | 3,882 | 4,073 | 3,991 |
| 35,550 | 35,600 | 4,079 | 3,888 | 4,079 | 3,997 |
| 35,600 | 35,650 | 4,085 | 3,894 | 4,085 | 4,003 |
| 35,650 | 35,700 | 4,091 | 3,900 | 4,091 | 4,009 |
| 35,700 | 35,750 | 4,097 | 3,906 | 4,097 | 4,015 |
| 35,750 | 35,800 | 4,103 | 3,912 | 4,103 | 4,021 |
| 35,800 | 35,850 | 4,109 | 3,918 | 4,109 | 4,027 |
| 35,850 | 35,900 | 4,115 | 3,924 | 4,115 | 4,033 |
| 35,900 | 35,950 | 4,121 | 3,930 | 4,121 | 4,039 |
| 35,950 | 36,000 | 4,127 | 3,936 | 4,127 | 4,045 |

## 36,000

| At least | But less than | Single | Married filing jointly * | Married filing separately | Head of a household |
|---|---|---|---|---|---|
| | | | Your tax is— | | |
| 36,000 | 36,050 | 4,133 | 3,942 | 4,133 | 4,051 |
| 36,050 | 36,100 | 4,139 | 3,948 | 4,139 | 4,057 |
| 36,100 | 36,150 | 4,145 | 3,954 | 4,145 | 4,063 |
| 36,150 | 36,200 | 4,151 | 3,960 | 4,151 | 4,069 |
| 36,200 | 36,250 | 4,157 | 3,966 | 4,157 | 4,075 |
| 36,250 | 36,300 | 4,163 | 3,972 | 4,163 | 4,081 |
| 36,300 | 36,350 | 4,169 | 3,978 | 4,169 | 4,087 |
| 36,350 | 36,400 | 4,175 | 3,984 | 4,175 | 4,093 |
| 36,400 | 36,450 | 4,181 | 3,990 | 4,181 | 4,099 |
| 36,450 | 36,500 | 4,187 | 3,996 | 4,187 | 4,105 |
| 36,500 | 36,550 | 4,193 | 4,002 | 4,193 | 4,111 |
| 36,550 | 36,600 | 4,199 | 4,008 | 4,199 | 4,117 |
| 36,600 | 36,650 | 4,205 | 4,014 | 4,205 | 4,123 |
| 36,650 | 36,700 | 4,211 | 4,020 | 4,211 | 4,129 |
| 36,700 | 36,750 | 4,217 | 4,026 | 4,217 | 4,135 |
| 36,750 | 36,800 | 4,223 | 4,032 | 4,223 | 4,141 |
| 36,800 | 36,850 | 4,229 | 4,038 | 4,229 | 4,147 |
| 36,850 | 36,900 | 4,235 | 4,044 | 4,235 | 4,153 |
| 36,900 | 36,950 | 4,241 | 4,050 | 4,241 | 4,159 |
| 36,950 | 37,000 | 4,247 | 4,056 | 4,247 | 4,165 |

## 37,000

| At least | But less than | Single | Married filing jointly * | Married filing separately | Head of a household |
|---|---|---|---|---|---|
| 37,000 | 37,050 | 4,253 | 4,062 | 4,253 | 4,171 |
| 37,050 | 37,100 | 4,259 | 4,068 | 4,259 | 4,177 |
| 37,100 | 37,150 | 4,265 | 4,074 | 4,265 | 4,183 |
| 37,150 | 37,200 | 4,271 | 4,080 | 4,271 | 4,189 |
| 37,200 | 37,250 | 4,277 | 4,086 | 4,277 | 4,195 |
| 37,250 | 37,300 | 4,283 | 4,092 | 4,283 | 4,201 |
| 37,300 | 37,350 | 4,289 | 4,098 | 4,289 | 4,207 |
| 37,350 | 37,400 | 4,295 | 4,104 | 4,295 | 4,213 |
| 37,400 | 37,450 | 4,301 | 4,110 | 4,301 | 4,219 |
| 37,450 | 37,500 | 4,307 | 4,116 | 4,307 | 4,225 |
| 37,500 | 37,550 | 4,313 | 4,122 | 4,313 | 4,231 |
| 37,550 | 37,600 | 4,319 | 4,128 | 4,319 | 4,237 |
| 37,600 | 37,650 | 4,325 | 4,134 | 4,325 | 4,243 |
| 37,650 | 37,700 | 4,331 | 4,140 | 4,331 | 4,249 |
| 37,700 | 37,750 | 4,337 | 4,146 | 4,337 | 4,255 |
| 37,750 | 37,800 | 4,343 | 4,152 | 4,343 | 4,261 |
| 37,800 | 37,850 | 4,349 | 4,158 | 4,349 | 4,267 |
| 37,850 | 37,900 | 4,355 | 4,164 | 4,355 | 4,273 |
| 37,900 | 37,950 | 4,361 | 4,170 | 4,361 | 4,279 |
| 37,950 | 38,000 | 4,367 | 4,176 | 4,367 | 4,285 |

## 38,000

| At least | But less than | Single | Married filing jointly * | Married filing separately | Head of a household |
|---|---|---|---|---|---|
| 38,000 | 38,050 | 4,373 | 4,182 | 4,373 | 4,291 |
| 38,050 | 38,100 | 4,379 | 4,188 | 4,379 | 4,297 |
| 38,100 | 38,150 | 4,385 | 4,194 | 4,385 | 4,303 |
| 38,150 | 38,200 | 4,391 | 4,200 | 4,391 | 4,309 |
| 38,200 | 38,250 | 4,397 | 4,206 | 4,397 | 4,315 |
| 38,250 | 38,300 | 4,403 | 4,212 | 4,403 | 4,321 |
| 38,300 | 38,350 | 4,409 | 4,218 | 4,409 | 4,327 |
| 38,350 | 38,400 | 4,415 | 4,224 | 4,415 | 4,333 |
| 38,400 | 38,450 | 4,421 | 4,230 | 4,421 | 4,339 |
| 38,450 | 38,500 | 4,427 | 4,236 | 4,427 | 4,345 |
| 38,500 | 38,550 | 4,433 | 4,242 | 4,433 | 4,351 |
| 38,550 | 38,600 | 4,439 | 4,248 | 4,439 | 4,357 |
| 38,600 | 38,650 | 4,445 | 4,254 | 4,445 | 4,363 |
| 38,650 | 38,700 | 4,451 | 4,260 | 4,451 | 4,369 |
| 38,700 | 38,750 | 4,459 | 4,266 | 4,459 | 4,375 |
| 38,750 | 38,800 | 4,470 | 4,272 | 4,470 | 4,381 |
| 38,800 | 38,850 | 4,481 | 4,278 | 4,481 | 4,387 |
| 38,850 | 38,900 | 4,492 | 4,284 | 4,492 | 4,393 |
| 38,900 | 38,950 | 4,503 | 4,290 | 4,503 | 4,399 |
| 38,950 | 39,000 | 4,514 | 4,296 | 4,514 | 4,405 |

* This column must also be used by a qualifying widow(er).

*(Continued)*

## 39,000

| At least | But less than | Single | Married filing jointly * | Married filing separately | Head of a household |
|---|---|---|---|---|---|
| 39,000 | 39,050 | 4,525 | 4,302 | 4,525 | 4,411 |
| 39,050 | 39,100 | 4,536 | 4,308 | 4,536 | 4,417 |
| 39,100 | 39,150 | 4,547 | 4,314 | 4,547 | 4,423 |
| 39,150 | 39,200 | 4,558 | 4,320 | 4,558 | 4,429 |
| 39,200 | 39,250 | 4,569 | 4,326 | 4,569 | 4,435 |
| 39,250 | 39,300 | 4,580 | 4,332 | 4,580 | 4,441 |
| 39,300 | 39,350 | 4,591 | 4,338 | 4,591 | 4,447 |
| 39,350 | 39,400 | 4,602 | 4,344 | 4,602 | 4,453 |
| 39,400 | 39,450 | 4,613 | 4,350 | 4,613 | 4,459 |
| 39,450 | 39,500 | 4,624 | 4,356 | 4,624 | 4,465 |
| 39,500 | 39,550 | 4,635 | 4,362 | 4,635 | 4,471 |
| 39,550 | 39,600 | 4,646 | 4,368 | 4,646 | 4,477 |
| 39,600 | 39,650 | 4,657 | 4,374 | 4,657 | 4,483 |
| 39,650 | 39,700 | 4,668 | 4,380 | 4,668 | 4,489 |
| 39,700 | 39,750 | 4,679 | 4,386 | 4,679 | 4,495 |
| 39,750 | 39,800 | 4,690 | 4,392 | 4,690 | 4,501 |
| 39,800 | 39,850 | 4,701 | 4,398 | 4,701 | 4,507 |
| 39,850 | 39,900 | 4,712 | 4,404 | 4,712 | 4,513 |
| 39,900 | 39,950 | 4,723 | 4,410 | 4,723 | 4,519 |
| 39,950 | 40,000 | 4,734 | 4,416 | 4,734 | 4,525 |

## 40,000

| At least | But less than | Single | Married filing jointly * | Married filing separately | Head of a household |
|---|---|---|---|---|---|
| 40,000 | 40,050 | 4,745 | 4,422 | 4,745 | 4,531 |
| 40,050 | 40,100 | 4,756 | 4,428 | 4,756 | 4,537 |
| 40,100 | 40,150 | 4,767 | 4,434 | 4,767 | 4,543 |
| 40,150 | 40,200 | 4,778 | 4,440 | 4,778 | 4,549 |
| 40,200 | 40,250 | 4,789 | 4,446 | 4,789 | 4,555 |
| 40,250 | 40,300 | 4,800 | 4,452 | 4,800 | 4,561 |
| 40,300 | 40,350 | 4,811 | 4,458 | 4,811 | 4,567 |
| 40,350 | 40,400 | 4,822 | 4,464 | 4,822 | 4,573 |
| 40,400 | 40,450 | 4,833 | 4,470 | 4,833 | 4,579 |
| 40,450 | 40,500 | 4,844 | 4,476 | 4,844 | 4,585 |
| 40,500 | 40,550 | 4,855 | 4,482 | 4,855 | 4,591 |
| 40,550 | 40,600 | 4,866 | 4,488 | 4,866 | 4,597 |
| 40,600 | 40,650 | 4,877 | 4,494 | 4,877 | 4,603 |
| 40,650 | 40,700 | 4,888 | 4,500 | 4,888 | 4,609 |
| 40,700 | 40,750 | 4,899 | 4,506 | 4,899 | 4,615 |
| 40,750 | 40,800 | 4,910 | 4,512 | 4,910 | 4,621 |
| 40,800 | 40,850 | 4,921 | 4,518 | 4,921 | 4,627 |
| 40,850 | 40,900 | 4,932 | 4,524 | 4,932 | 4,633 |
| 40,900 | 40,950 | 4,943 | 4,530 | 4,943 | 4,639 |
| 40,950 | 41,000 | 4,954 | 4,536 | 4,954 | 4,645 |

## 41,000

| At least | But less than | Single | Married filing jointly * | Married filing separately | Head of a household |
|---|---|---|---|---|---|
| 41,000 | 41,050 | 4,965 | 4,542 | 4,965 | 4,651 |
| 41,050 | 41,100 | 4,976 | 4,548 | 4,976 | 4,657 |
| 41,100 | 41,150 | 4,987 | 4,554 | 4,987 | 4,663 |
| 41,150 | 41,200 | 4,998 | 4,560 | 4,998 | 4,669 |
| 41,200 | 41,250 | 5,009 | 4,566 | 5,009 | 4,675 |
| 41,250 | 41,300 | 5,020 | 4,572 | 5,020 | 4,681 |
| 41,300 | 41,350 | 5,031 | 4,578 | 5,031 | 4,687 |
| 41,350 | 41,400 | 5,042 | 4,584 | 5,042 | 4,693 |
| 41,400 | 41,450 | 5,053 | 4,590 | 5,053 | 4,699 |
| 41,450 | 41,500 | 5,064 | 4,596 | 5,064 | 4,705 |
| 41,500 | 41,550 | 5,075 | 4,602 | 5,075 | 4,711 |
| 41,550 | 41,600 | 5,086 | 4,608 | 5,086 | 4,717 |
| 41,600 | 41,650 | 5,097 | 4,614 | 5,097 | 4,723 |
| 41,650 | 41,700 | 5,108 | 4,620 | 5,108 | 4,729 |
| 41,700 | 41,750 | 5,119 | 4,626 | 5,119 | 4,735 |
| 41,750 | 41,800 | 5,130 | 4,632 | 5,130 | 4,741 |
| 41,800 | 41,850 | 5,141 | 4,638 | 5,141 | 4,747 |
| 41,850 | 41,900 | 5,152 | 4,644 | 5,152 | 4,753 |
| 41,900 | 41,950 | 5,163 | 4,650 | 5,163 | 4,759 |
| 41,950 | 42,000 | 5,174 | 4,656 | 5,174 | 4,765 |

## 42,000

| At least | But less than | Single | Married filing jointly * | Married filing separately | Head of a household |
|---|---|---|---|---|---|
| 42,000 | 42,050 | 5,185 | 4,662 | 5,185 | 4,771 |
| 42,050 | 42,100 | 5,196 | 4,668 | 5,196 | 4,777 |
| 42,100 | 42,150 | 5,207 | 4,674 | 5,207 | 4,783 |
| 42,150 | 42,200 | 5,218 | 4,680 | 5,218 | 4,789 |
| 42,200 | 42,250 | 5,229 | 4,686 | 5,229 | 4,795 |
| 42,250 | 42,300 | 5,240 | 4,692 | 5,240 | 4,801 |
| 42,300 | 42,350 | 5,251 | 4,698 | 5,251 | 4,807 |
| 42,350 | 42,400 | 5,262 | 4,704 | 5,262 | 4,813 |
| 42,400 | 42,450 | 5,273 | 4,710 | 5,273 | 4,819 |
| 42,450 | 42,500 | 5,284 | 4,716 | 5,284 | 4,825 |
| 42,500 | 42,550 | 5,295 | 4,722 | 5,295 | 4,831 |
| 42,550 | 42,600 | 5,306 | 4,728 | 5,306 | 4,837 |
| 42,600 | 42,650 | 5,317 | 4,734 | 5,317 | 4,843 |
| 42,650 | 42,700 | 5,328 | 4,740 | 5,328 | 4,849 |
| 42,700 | 42,750 | 5,339 | 4,746 | 5,339 | 4,855 |
| 42,750 | 42,800 | 5,350 | 4,752 | 5,350 | 4,861 |
| 42,800 | 42,850 | 5,361 | 4,758 | 5,361 | 4,867 |
| 42,850 | 42,900 | 5,372 | 4,764 | 5,372 | 4,873 |
| 42,900 | 42,950 | 5,383 | 4,770 | 5,383 | 4,879 |
| 42,950 | 43,000 | 5,394 | 4,776 | 5,394 | 4,885 |

## 43,000

| At least | But less than | Single | Married filing jointly * | Married filing separately | Head of a household |
|---|---|---|---|---|---|
| 43,000 | 43,050 | 5,405 | 4,782 | 5,405 | 4,891 |
| 43,050 | 43,100 | 5,416 | 4,788 | 5,416 | 4,897 |
| 43,100 | 43,150 | 5,427 | 4,794 | 5,427 | 4,903 |
| 43,150 | 43,200 | 5,438 | 4,800 | 5,438 | 4,909 |
| 43,200 | 43,250 | 5,449 | 4,806 | 5,449 | 4,915 |
| 43,250 | 43,300 | 5,460 | 4,812 | 5,460 | 4,921 |
| 43,300 | 43,350 | 5,471 | 4,818 | 5,471 | 4,927 |
| 43,350 | 43,400 | 5,482 | 4,824 | 5,482 | 4,933 |
| 43,400 | 43,450 | 5,493 | 4,830 | 5,493 | 4,939 |
| 43,450 | 43,500 | 5,504 | 4,836 | 5,504 | 4,945 |
| 43,500 | 43,550 | 5,515 | 4,842 | 5,515 | 4,951 |
| 43,550 | 43,600 | 5,526 | 4,848 | 5,526 | 4,957 |
| 43,600 | 43,650 | 5,537 | 4,854 | 5,537 | 4,963 |
| 43,650 | 43,700 | 5,548 | 4,860 | 5,548 | 4,969 |
| 43,700 | 43,750 | 5,559 | 4,866 | 5,559 | 4,975 |
| 43,750 | 43,800 | 5,570 | 4,872 | 5,570 | 4,981 |
| 43,800 | 43,850 | 5,581 | 4,878 | 5,581 | 4,987 |
| 43,850 | 43,900 | 5,592 | 4,884 | 5,592 | 4,993 |
| 43,900 | 43,950 | 5,603 | 4,890 | 5,603 | 4,999 |
| 43,950 | 44,000 | 5,614 | 4,896 | 5,614 | 5,005 |

## 44,000

| At least | But less than | Single | Married filing jointly * | Married filing separately | Head of a household |
|---|---|---|---|---|---|
| 44,000 | 44,050 | 5,625 | 4,902 | 5,625 | 5,011 |
| 44,050 | 44,100 | 5,636 | 4,908 | 5,636 | 5,017 |
| 44,100 | 44,150 | 5,647 | 4,914 | 5,647 | 5,023 |
| 44,150 | 44,200 | 5,658 | 4,920 | 5,658 | 5,029 |
| 44,200 | 44,250 | 5,669 | 4,926 | 5,669 | 5,035 |
| 44,250 | 44,300 | 5,680 | 4,932 | 5,680 | 5,041 |
| 44,300 | 44,350 | 5,691 | 4,938 | 5,691 | 5,047 |
| 44,350 | 44,400 | 5,702 | 4,944 | 5,702 | 5,053 |
| 44,400 | 44,450 | 5,713 | 4,950 | 5,713 | 5,059 |
| 44,450 | 44,500 | 5,724 | 4,956 | 5,724 | 5,065 |
| 44,500 | 44,550 | 5,735 | 4,962 | 5,735 | 5,071 |
| 44,550 | 44,600 | 5,746 | 4,968 | 5,746 | 5,077 |
| 44,600 | 44,650 | 5,757 | 4,974 | 5,757 | 5,083 |
| 44,650 | 44,700 | 5,768 | 4,980 | 5,768 | 5,089 |
| 44,700 | 44,750 | 5,779 | 4,986 | 5,779 | 5,095 |
| 44,750 | 44,800 | 5,790 | 4,992 | 5,790 | 5,101 |
| 44,800 | 44,850 | 5,801 | 4,998 | 5,801 | 5,107 |
| 44,850 | 44,900 | 5,812 | 5,004 | 5,812 | 5,113 |
| 44,900 | 44,950 | 5,823 | 5,010 | 5,823 | 5,119 |
| 44,950 | 45,000 | 5,834 | 5,016 | 5,834 | 5,125 |

## 45,000

| At least | But less than | Single | Married filing jointly * | Married filing separately | Head of a household |
|---|---|---|---|---|---|
| 45,000 | 45,050 | 5,845 | 5,022 | 5,845 | 5,131 |
| 45,050 | 45,100 | 5,856 | 5,028 | 5,856 | 5,137 |
| 45,100 | 45,150 | 5,867 | 5,034 | 5,867 | 5,143 |
| 45,150 | 45,200 | 5,878 | 5,040 | 5,878 | 5,149 |
| 45,200 | 45,250 | 5,889 | 5,046 | 5,889 | 5,155 |
| 45,250 | 45,300 | 5,900 | 5,052 | 5,900 | 5,161 |
| 45,300 | 45,350 | 5,911 | 5,058 | 5,911 | 5,167 |
| 45,350 | 45,400 | 5,922 | 5,064 | 5,922 | 5,173 |
| 45,400 | 45,450 | 5,933 | 5,070 | 5,933 | 5,179 |
| 45,450 | 45,500 | 5,944 | 5,076 | 5,944 | 5,185 |
| 45,500 | 45,550 | 5,955 | 5,082 | 5,955 | 5,191 |
| 45,550 | 45,600 | 5,966 | 5,088 | 5,966 | 5,197 |
| 45,600 | 45,650 | 5,977 | 5,094 | 5,977 | 5,203 |
| 45,650 | 45,700 | 5,988 | 5,100 | 5,988 | 5,209 |
| 45,700 | 45,750 | 5,999 | 5,106 | 5,999 | 5,215 |
| 45,750 | 45,800 | 6,010 | 5,112 | 6,010 | 5,221 |
| 45,800 | 45,850 | 6,021 | 5,118 | 6,021 | 5,227 |
| 45,850 | 45,900 | 6,032 | 5,124 | 6,032 | 5,233 |
| 45,900 | 45,950 | 6,043 | 5,130 | 6,043 | 5,239 |
| 45,950 | 46,000 | 6,054 | 5,136 | 6,054 | 5,245 |

## 46,000

| At least | But less than | Single | Married filing jointly * | Married filing separately | Head of a household |
|---|---|---|---|---|---|
| 46,000 | 46,050 | 6,065 | 5,142 | 6,065 | 5,251 |
| 46,050 | 46,100 | 6,076 | 5,148 | 6,076 | 5,257 |
| 46,100 | 46,150 | 6,087 | 5,154 | 6,087 | 5,263 |
| 46,150 | 46,200 | 6,098 | 5,160 | 6,098 | 5,269 |
| 46,200 | 46,250 | 6,109 | 5,166 | 6,109 | 5,275 |
| 46,250 | 46,300 | 6,120 | 5,172 | 6,120 | 5,281 |
| 46,300 | 46,350 | 6,131 | 5,178 | 6,131 | 5,287 |
| 46,350 | 46,400 | 6,142 | 5,184 | 6,142 | 5,293 |
| 46,400 | 46,450 | 6,153 | 5,190 | 6,153 | 5,299 |
| 46,450 | 46,500 | 6,164 | 5,196 | 6,164 | 5,305 |
| 46,500 | 46,550 | 6,175 | 5,202 | 6,175 | 5,311 |
| 46,550 | 46,600 | 6,186 | 5,208 | 6,186 | 5,317 |
| 46,600 | 46,650 | 6,197 | 5,214 | 6,197 | 5,323 |
| 46,650 | 46,700 | 6,208 | 5,220 | 6,208 | 5,329 |
| 46,700 | 46,750 | 6,219 | 5,226 | 6,219 | 5,335 |
| 46,750 | 46,800 | 6,230 | 5,232 | 6,230 | 5,341 |
| 46,800 | 46,850 | 6,241 | 5,238 | 6,241 | 5,347 |
| 46,850 | 46,900 | 6,252 | 5,244 | 6,252 | 5,353 |
| 46,900 | 46,950 | 6,263 | 5,250 | 6,263 | 5,359 |
| 46,950 | 47,000 | 6,274 | 5,256 | 6,274 | 5,365 |

## 47,000

| At least | But less than | Single | Married filing jointly * | Married filing separately | Head of a household |
|---|---|---|---|---|---|
| 47,000 | 47,050 | 6,285 | 5,262 | 6,285 | 5,371 |
| 47,050 | 47,100 | 6,296 | 5,268 | 6,296 | 5,377 |
| 47,100 | 47,150 | 6,307 | 5,274 | 6,307 | 5,383 |
| 47,150 | 47,200 | 6,318 | 5,280 | 6,318 | 5,389 |
| 47,200 | 47,250 | 6,329 | 5,286 | 6,329 | 5,395 |
| 47,250 | 47,300 | 6,340 | 5,292 | 6,340 | 5,401 |
| 47,300 | 47,350 | 6,351 | 5,298 | 6,351 | 5,407 |
| 47,350 | 47,400 | 6,362 | 5,304 | 6,362 | 5,413 |
| 47,400 | 47,450 | 6,373 | 5,310 | 6,373 | 5,419 |
| 47,450 | 47,500 | 6,384 | 5,316 | 6,384 | 5,425 |
| 47,500 | 47,550 | 6,395 | 5,322 | 6,395 | 5,431 |
| 47,550 | 47,600 | 6,406 | 5,328 | 6,406 | 5,437 |
| 47,600 | 47,650 | 6,417 | 5,334 | 6,417 | 5,443 |
| 47,650 | 47,700 | 6,428 | 5,340 | 6,428 | 5,449 |
| 47,700 | 47,750 | 6,439 | 5,346 | 6,439 | 5,455 |
| 47,750 | 47,800 | 6,450 | 5,352 | 6,450 | 5,461 |
| 47,800 | 47,850 | 6,461 | 5,358 | 6,461 | 5,467 |
| 47,850 | 47,900 | 6,472 | 5,364 | 6,472 | 5,473 |
| 47,900 | 47,950 | 6,483 | 5,370 | 6,483 | 5,479 |
| 47,950 | 48,000 | 6,494 | 5,376 | 6,494 | 5,485 |

* This column must also be used by a qualifying widow(er).

(Continued)

Header for each block:

If line 10 (taxable income) is— / And you are— : At least | But less than | Single | Married filing jointly * | Married filing separately | Head of a household — Your tax is—

## 48,000

| At least | But less than | Single | Married filing jointly * | Married filing separately | Head of a household |
|---|---|---|---|---|---|
| 48,000 | 48,050 | 6,505 | 5,382 | 6,505 | 5,491 |
| 48,050 | 48,100 | 6,516 | 5,388 | 6,516 | 5,497 |
| 48,100 | 48,150 | 6,527 | 5,394 | 6,527 | 5,503 |
| 48,150 | 48,200 | 6,538 | 5,400 | 6,538 | 5,509 |
| 48,200 | 48,250 | 6,549 | 5,406 | 6,549 | 5,515 |
| 48,250 | 48,300 | 6,560 | 5,412 | 6,560 | 5,521 |
| 48,300 | 48,350 | 6,571 | 5,418 | 6,571 | 5,527 |
| 48,350 | 48,400 | 6,582 | 5,424 | 6,582 | 5,533 |
| 48,400 | 48,450 | 6,593 | 5,430 | 6,593 | 5,539 |
| 48,450 | 48,500 | 6,604 | 5,436 | 6,604 | 5,545 |
| 48,500 | 48,550 | 6,615 | 5,442 | 6,615 | 5,551 |
| 48,550 | 48,600 | 6,626 | 5,448 | 6,626 | 5,557 |
| 48,600 | 48,650 | 6,637 | 5,454 | 6,637 | 5,563 |
| 48,650 | 48,700 | 6,648 | 5,460 | 6,648 | 5,569 |
| 48,700 | 48,750 | 6,659 | 5,466 | 6,659 | 5,575 |
| 48,750 | 48,800 | 6,670 | 5,472 | 6,670 | 5,581 |
| 48,800 | 48,850 | 6,681 | 5,478 | 6,681 | 5,587 |
| 48,850 | 48,900 | 6,692 | 5,484 | 6,692 | 5,593 |
| 48,900 | 48,950 | 6,703 | 5,490 | 6,703 | 5,599 |
| 48,950 | 49,000 | 6,714 | 5,496 | 6,714 | 5,605 |

## 49,000

| At least | But less than | Single | Married filing jointly * | Married filing separately | Head of a household |
|---|---|---|---|---|---|
| 49,000 | 49,050 | 6,725 | 5,502 | 6,725 | 5,611 |
| 49,050 | 49,100 | 6,736 | 5,508 | 6,736 | 5,617 |
| 49,100 | 49,150 | 6,747 | 5,514 | 6,747 | 5,623 |
| 49,150 | 49,200 | 6,758 | 5,520 | 6,758 | 5,629 |
| 49,200 | 49,250 | 6,769 | 5,526 | 6,769 | 5,635 |
| 49,250 | 49,300 | 6,780 | 5,532 | 6,780 | 5,641 |
| 49,300 | 49,350 | 6,791 | 5,538 | 6,791 | 5,647 |
| 49,350 | 49,400 | 6,802 | 5,544 | 6,802 | 5,653 |
| 49,400 | 49,450 | 6,813 | 5,550 | 6,813 | 5,659 |
| 49,450 | 49,500 | 6,824 | 5,556 | 6,824 | 5,665 |
| 49,500 | 49,550 | 6,835 | 5,562 | 6,835 | 5,671 |
| 49,550 | 49,600 | 6,846 | 5,568 | 6,846 | 5,677 |
| 49,600 | 49,650 | 6,857 | 5,574 | 6,857 | 5,683 |
| 49,650 | 49,700 | 6,868 | 5,580 | 6,868 | 5,689 |
| 49,700 | 49,750 | 6,879 | 5,586 | 6,879 | 5,695 |
| 49,750 | 49,800 | 6,890 | 5,592 | 6,890 | 5,701 |
| 49,800 | 49,850 | 6,901 | 5,598 | 6,901 | 5,707 |
| 49,850 | 49,900 | 6,912 | 5,604 | 6,912 | 5,713 |
| 49,900 | 49,950 | 6,923 | 5,610 | 6,923 | 5,719 |
| 49,950 | 50,000 | 6,934 | 5,616 | 6,934 | 5,725 |

## 50,000

| At least | But less than | Single | Married filing jointly * | Married filing separately | Head of a household |
|---|---|---|---|---|---|
| 50,000 | 50,050 | 6,945 | 5,622 | 6,945 | 5,731 |
| 50,050 | 50,100 | 6,956 | 5,628 | 6,956 | 5,737 |
| 50,100 | 50,150 | 6,967 | 5,634 | 6,967 | 5,743 |
| 50,150 | 50,200 | 6,978 | 5,640 | 6,978 | 5,749 |
| 50,200 | 50,250 | 6,989 | 5,646 | 6,989 | 5,755 |
| 50,250 | 50,300 | 7,000 | 5,652 | 7,000 | 5,761 |
| 50,300 | 50,350 | 7,011 | 5,658 | 7,011 | 5,767 |
| 50,350 | 50,400 | 7,022 | 5,664 | 7,022 | 5,773 |
| 50,400 | 50,450 | 7,033 | 5,670 | 7,033 | 5,779 |
| 50,450 | 50,500 | 7,044 | 5,676 | 7,044 | 5,785 |
| 50,500 | 50,550 | 7,055 | 5,682 | 7,055 | 5,791 |
| 50,550 | 50,600 | 7,066 | 5,688 | 7,066 | 5,797 |
| 50,600 | 50,650 | 7,077 | 5,694 | 7,077 | 5,803 |
| 50,650 | 50,700 | 7,088 | 5,700 | 7,088 | 5,809 |
| 50,700 | 50,750 | 7,099 | 5,706 | 7,099 | 5,815 |
| 50,750 | 50,800 | 7,110 | 5,712 | 7,110 | 5,821 |
| 50,800 | 50,850 | 7,121 | 5,718 | 7,121 | 5,827 |
| 50,850 | 50,900 | 7,132 | 5,724 | 7,132 | 5,833 |
| 50,900 | 50,950 | 7,143 | 5,730 | 7,143 | 5,839 |
| 50,950 | 51,000 | 7,154 | 5,736 | 7,154 | 5,845 |

## 51,000

| At least | But less than | Single | Married filing jointly * | Married filing separately | Head of a household |
|---|---|---|---|---|---|
| 51,000 | 51,050 | 7,165 | 5,742 | 7,165 | 5,851 |
| 51,050 | 51,100 | 7,176 | 5,748 | 7,176 | 5,857 |
| 51,100 | 51,150 | 7,187 | 5,754 | 7,187 | 5,863 |
| 51,150 | 51,200 | 7,198 | 5,760 | 7,198 | 5,869 |
| 51,200 | 51,250 | 7,209 | 5,766 | 7,209 | 5,875 |
| 51,250 | 51,300 | 7,220 | 5,772 | 7,220 | 5,881 |
| 51,300 | 51,350 | 7,231 | 5,778 | 7,231 | 5,887 |
| 51,350 | 51,400 | 7,242 | 5,784 | 7,242 | 5,893 |
| 51,400 | 51,450 | 7,253 | 5,790 | 7,253 | 5,899 |
| 51,450 | 51,500 | 7,264 | 5,796 | 7,264 | 5,905 |
| 51,500 | 51,550 | 7,275 | 5,802 | 7,275 | 5,911 |
| 51,550 | 51,600 | 7,286 | 5,808 | 7,286 | 5,917 |
| 51,600 | 51,650 | 7,297 | 5,814 | 7,297 | 5,923 |
| 51,650 | 51,700 | 7,308 | 5,820 | 7,308 | 5,929 |
| 51,700 | 51,750 | 7,319 | 5,826 | 7,319 | 5,935 |
| 51,750 | 51,800 | 7,330 | 5,832 | 7,330 | 5,941 |
| 51,800 | 51,850 | 7,341 | 5,838 | 7,341 | 5,950 |
| 51,850 | 51,900 | 7,352 | 5,844 | 7,352 | 5,961 |
| 51,900 | 51,950 | 7,363 | 5,850 | 7,363 | 5,972 |
| 51,950 | 52,000 | 7,374 | 5,856 | 7,374 | 5,983 |

## 52,000

| At least | But less than | Single | Married filing jointly * | Married filing separately | Head of a household |
|---|---|---|---|---|---|
| 52,000 | 52,050 | 7,385 | 5,862 | 7,385 | 5,994 |
| 52,050 | 52,100 | 7,396 | 5,868 | 7,396 | 6,005 |
| 52,100 | 52,150 | 7,407 | 5,874 | 7,407 | 6,016 |
| 52,150 | 52,200 | 7,418 | 5,880 | 7,418 | 6,027 |
| 52,200 | 52,250 | 7,429 | 5,886 | 7,429 | 6,038 |
| 52,250 | 52,300 | 7,440 | 5,892 | 7,440 | 6,049 |
| 52,300 | 52,350 | 7,451 | 5,898 | 7,451 | 6,060 |
| 52,350 | 52,400 | 7,462 | 5,904 | 7,462 | 6,071 |
| 52,400 | 52,450 | 7,473 | 5,910 | 7,473 | 6,082 |
| 52,450 | 52,500 | 7,484 | 5,916 | 7,484 | 6,093 |
| 52,500 | 52,550 | 7,495 | 5,922 | 7,495 | 6,104 |
| 52,550 | 52,600 | 7,506 | 5,928 | 7,506 | 6,115 |
| 52,600 | 52,650 | 7,517 | 5,934 | 7,517 | 6,126 |
| 52,650 | 52,700 | 7,528 | 5,940 | 7,528 | 6,137 |
| 52,700 | 52,750 | 7,539 | 5,946 | 7,539 | 6,148 |
| 52,750 | 52,800 | 7,550 | 5,952 | 7,550 | 6,159 |
| 52,800 | 52,850 | 7,561 | 5,958 | 7,561 | 6,170 |
| 52,850 | 52,900 | 7,572 | 5,964 | 7,572 | 6,181 |
| 52,900 | 52,950 | 7,583 | 5,970 | 7,583 | 6,192 |
| 52,950 | 53,000 | 7,594 | 5,976 | 7,594 | 6,203 |

## 53,000

| At least | But less than | Single | Married filing jointly * | Married filing separately | Head of a household |
|---|---|---|---|---|---|
| 53,000 | 53,050 | 7,605 | 5,982 | 7,605 | 6,214 |
| 53,050 | 53,100 | 7,616 | 5,988 | 7,616 | 6,225 |
| 53,100 | 53,150 | 7,627 | 5,994 | 7,627 | 6,236 |
| 53,150 | 53,200 | 7,638 | 6,000 | 7,638 | 6,247 |
| 53,200 | 53,250 | 7,649 | 6,006 | 7,649 | 6,258 |
| 53,250 | 53,300 | 7,660 | 6,012 | 7,660 | 6,269 |
| 53,300 | 53,350 | 7,671 | 6,018 | 7,671 | 6,280 |
| 53,350 | 53,400 | 7,682 | 6,024 | 7,682 | 6,291 |
| 53,400 | 53,450 | 7,693 | 6,030 | 7,693 | 6,302 |
| 53,450 | 53,500 | 7,704 | 6,036 | 7,704 | 6,313 |
| 53,500 | 53,550 | 7,715 | 6,042 | 7,715 | 6,324 |
| 53,550 | 53,600 | 7,726 | 6,048 | 7,726 | 6,335 |
| 53,600 | 53,650 | 7,737 | 6,054 | 7,737 | 6,346 |
| 53,650 | 53,700 | 7,748 | 6,060 | 7,748 | 6,357 |
| 53,700 | 53,750 | 7,759 | 6,066 | 7,759 | 6,368 |
| 53,750 | 53,800 | 7,770 | 6,072 | 7,770 | 6,379 |
| 53,800 | 53,850 | 7,781 | 6,078 | 7,781 | 6,390 |
| 53,850 | 53,900 | 7,792 | 6,084 | 7,792 | 6,401 |
| 53,900 | 53,950 | 7,803 | 6,090 | 7,803 | 6,412 |
| 53,950 | 54,000 | 7,814 | 6,096 | 7,814 | 6,423 |

## 54,000

| At least | But less than | Single | Married filing jointly * | Married filing separately | Head of a household |
|---|---|---|---|---|---|
| 54,000 | 54,050 | 7,825 | 6,102 | 7,825 | 6,434 |
| 54,050 | 54,100 | 7,836 | 6,108 | 7,836 | 6,445 |
| 54,100 | 54,150 | 7,847 | 6,114 | 7,847 | 6,456 |
| 54,150 | 54,200 | 7,858 | 6,120 | 7,858 | 6,467 |
| 54,200 | 54,250 | 7,869 | 6,126 | 7,869 | 6,478 |
| 54,250 | 54,300 | 7,880 | 6,132 | 7,880 | 6,489 |
| 54,300 | 54,350 | 7,891 | 6,138 | 7,891 | 6,500 |
| 54,350 | 54,400 | 7,902 | 6,144 | 7,902 | 6,511 |
| 54,400 | 54,450 | 7,913 | 6,150 | 7,913 | 6,522 |
| 54,450 | 54,500 | 7,924 | 6,156 | 7,924 | 6,533 |
| 54,500 | 54,550 | 7,935 | 6,162 | 7,935 | 6,544 |
| 54,550 | 54,600 | 7,946 | 6,168 | 7,946 | 6,555 |
| 54,600 | 54,650 | 7,957 | 6,174 | 7,957 | 6,566 |
| 54,650 | 54,700 | 7,968 | 6,180 | 7,968 | 6,577 |
| 54,700 | 54,750 | 7,979 | 6,186 | 7,979 | 6,588 |
| 54,750 | 54,800 | 7,990 | 6,192 | 7,990 | 6,599 |
| 54,800 | 54,850 | 8,001 | 6,198 | 8,001 | 6,610 |
| 54,850 | 54,900 | 8,012 | 6,204 | 8,012 | 6,621 |
| 54,900 | 54,950 | 8,023 | 6,210 | 8,023 | 6,632 |
| 54,950 | 55,000 | 8,034 | 6,216 | 8,034 | 6,643 |

## 55,000

| At least | But less than | Single | Married filing jointly * | Married filing separately | Head of a household |
|---|---|---|---|---|---|
| 55,000 | 55,050 | 8,045 | 6,222 | 8,045 | 6,654 |
| 55,050 | 55,100 | 8,056 | 6,228 | 8,056 | 6,665 |
| 55,100 | 55,150 | 8,067 | 6,234 | 8,067 | 6,676 |
| 55,150 | 55,200 | 8,078 | 6,240 | 8,078 | 6,687 |
| 55,200 | 55,250 | 8,089 | 6,246 | 8,089 | 6,698 |
| 55,250 | 55,300 | 8,100 | 6,252 | 8,100 | 6,709 |
| 55,300 | 55,350 | 8,111 | 6,258 | 8,111 | 6,720 |
| 55,350 | 55,400 | 8,122 | 6,264 | 8,122 | 6,731 |
| 55,400 | 55,450 | 8,133 | 6,270 | 8,133 | 6,742 |
| 55,450 | 55,500 | 8,144 | 6,276 | 8,144 | 6,753 |
| 55,500 | 55,550 | 8,155 | 6,282 | 8,155 | 6,764 |
| 55,550 | 55,600 | 8,166 | 6,288 | 8,166 | 6,775 |
| 55,600 | 55,650 | 8,177 | 6,294 | 8,177 | 6,786 |
| 55,650 | 55,700 | 8,188 | 6,300 | 8,188 | 6,797 |
| 55,700 | 55,750 | 8,199 | 6,306 | 8,199 | 6,808 |
| 55,750 | 55,800 | 8,210 | 6,312 | 8,210 | 6,819 |
| 55,800 | 55,850 | 8,221 | 6,318 | 8,221 | 6,830 |
| 55,850 | 55,900 | 8,232 | 6,324 | 8,232 | 6,841 |
| 55,900 | 55,950 | 8,243 | 6,330 | 8,243 | 6,852 |
| 55,950 | 56,000 | 8,254 | 6,336 | 8,254 | 6,863 |

## 56,000

| At least | But less than | Single | Married filing jointly * | Married filing separately | Head of a household |
|---|---|---|---|---|---|
| 56,000 | 56,050 | 8,265 | 6,342 | 8,265 | 6,874 |
| 56,050 | 56,100 | 8,276 | 6,348 | 8,276 | 6,885 |
| 56,100 | 56,150 | 8,287 | 6,354 | 8,287 | 6,896 |
| 56,150 | 56,200 | 8,298 | 6,360 | 8,298 | 6,907 |
| 56,200 | 56,250 | 8,309 | 6,366 | 8,309 | 6,918 |
| 56,250 | 56,300 | 8,320 | 6,372 | 8,320 | 6,929 |
| 56,300 | 56,350 | 8,331 | 6,378 | 8,331 | 6,940 |
| 56,350 | 56,400 | 8,342 | 6,384 | 8,342 | 6,951 |
| 56,400 | 56,450 | 8,353 | 6,390 | 8,353 | 6,962 |
| 56,450 | 56,500 | 8,364 | 6,396 | 8,364 | 6,973 |
| 56,500 | 56,550 | 8,375 | 6,402 | 8,375 | 6,984 |
| 56,550 | 56,600 | 8,386 | 6,408 | 8,386 | 6,995 |
| 56,600 | 56,650 | 8,397 | 6,414 | 8,397 | 7,006 |
| 56,650 | 56,700 | 8,408 | 6,420 | 8,408 | 7,017 |
| 56,700 | 56,750 | 8,419 | 6,426 | 8,419 | 7,028 |
| 56,750 | 56,800 | 8,430 | 6,432 | 8,430 | 7,039 |
| 56,800 | 56,850 | 8,441 | 6,438 | 8,441 | 7,050 |
| 56,850 | 56,900 | 8,452 | 6,444 | 8,452 | 7,061 |
| 56,900 | 56,950 | 8,463 | 6,450 | 8,463 | 7,072 |
| 56,950 | 57,000 | 8,474 | 6,456 | 8,474 | 7,083 |

* This column must also be used by a qualifying widow(er).

*(Continued)*

## 57,000

| At least | But less than | Single | Married filing jointly* | Married filing separately | Head of a household |
|---|---|---|---|---|---|
| 57,000 | 57,050 | 8,485 | 6,462 | 8,485 | 7,094 |
| 57,050 | 57,100 | 8,496 | 6,468 | 8,496 | 7,105 |
| 57,100 | 57,150 | 8,507 | 6,474 | 8,507 | 7,116 |
| 57,150 | 57,200 | 8,518 | 6,480 | 8,518 | 7,127 |
| 57,200 | 57,250 | 8,529 | 6,486 | 8,529 | 7,138 |
| 57,250 | 57,300 | 8,540 | 6,492 | 8,540 | 7,149 |
| 57,300 | 57,350 | 8,551 | 6,498 | 8,551 | 7,160 |
| 57,350 | 57,400 | 8,562 | 6,504 | 8,562 | 7,171 |
| 57,400 | 57,450 | 8,573 | 6,510 | 8,573 | 7,182 |
| 57,450 | 57,500 | 8,584 | 6,516 | 8,584 | 7,193 |
| 57,500 | 57,550 | 8,595 | 6,522 | 8,595 | 7,204 |
| 57,550 | 57,600 | 8,606 | 6,528 | 8,606 | 7,215 |
| 57,600 | 57,650 | 8,617 | 6,534 | 8,617 | 7,226 |
| 57,650 | 57,700 | 8,628 | 6,540 | 8,628 | 7,237 |
| 57,700 | 57,750 | 8,639 | 6,546 | 8,639 | 7,248 |
| 57,750 | 57,800 | 8,650 | 6,552 | 8,650 | 7,259 |
| 57,800 | 57,850 | 8,661 | 6,558 | 8,661 | 7,270 |
| 57,850 | 57,900 | 8,672 | 6,564 | 8,672 | 7,281 |
| 57,900 | 57,950 | 8,683 | 6,570 | 8,683 | 7,292 |
| 57,950 | 58,000 | 8,694 | 6,576 | 8,694 | 7,303 |

## 58,000

| At least | But less than | Single | Married filing jointly* | Married filing separately | Head of a household |
|---|---|---|---|---|---|
| 58,000 | 58,050 | 8,705 | 6,582 | 8,705 | 7,314 |
| 58,050 | 58,100 | 8,716 | 6,588 | 8,716 | 7,325 |
| 58,100 | 58,150 | 8,727 | 6,594 | 8,727 | 7,336 |
| 58,150 | 58,200 | 8,738 | 6,600 | 8,738 | 7,347 |
| 58,200 | 58,250 | 8,749 | 6,606 | 8,749 | 7,358 |
| 58,250 | 58,300 | 8,760 | 6,612 | 8,760 | 7,369 |
| 58,300 | 58,350 | 8,771 | 6,618 | 8,771 | 7,380 |
| 58,350 | 58,400 | 8,782 | 6,624 | 8,782 | 7,391 |
| 58,400 | 58,450 | 8,793 | 6,630 | 8,793 | 7,402 |
| 58,450 | 58,500 | 8,804 | 6,636 | 8,804 | 7,413 |
| 58,500 | 58,550 | 8,815 | 6,642 | 8,815 | 7,424 |
| 58,550 | 58,600 | 8,826 | 6,648 | 8,826 | 7,435 |
| 58,600 | 58,650 | 8,837 | 6,654 | 8,837 | 7,446 |
| 58,650 | 58,700 | 8,848 | 6,660 | 8,848 | 7,457 |
| 58,700 | 58,750 | 8,859 | 6,666 | 8,859 | 7,468 |
| 58,750 | 58,800 | 8,870 | 6,672 | 8,870 | 7,479 |
| 58,800 | 58,850 | 8,881 | 6,678 | 8,881 | 7,490 |
| 58,850 | 58,900 | 8,892 | 6,684 | 8,892 | 7,501 |
| 58,900 | 58,950 | 8,903 | 6,690 | 8,903 | 7,512 |
| 58,950 | 59,000 | 8,914 | 6,696 | 8,914 | 7,523 |

## 59,000

| At least | But less than | Single | Married filing jointly* | Married filing separately | Head of a household |
|---|---|---|---|---|---|
| 59,000 | 59,050 | 8,925 | 6,702 | 8,925 | 7,534 |
| 59,050 | 59,100 | 8,936 | 6,708 | 8,936 | 7,545 |
| 59,100 | 59,150 | 8,947 | 6,714 | 8,947 | 7,556 |
| 59,150 | 59,200 | 8,958 | 6,720 | 8,958 | 7,567 |
| 59,200 | 59,250 | 8,969 | 6,726 | 8,969 | 7,578 |
| 59,250 | 59,300 | 8,980 | 6,732 | 8,980 | 7,589 |
| 59,300 | 59,350 | 8,991 | 6,738 | 8,991 | 7,600 |
| 59,350 | 59,400 | 9,002 | 6,744 | 9,002 | 7,611 |
| 59,400 | 59,450 | 9,013 | 6,750 | 9,013 | 7,622 |
| 59,450 | 59,500 | 9,024 | 6,756 | 9,024 | 7,633 |
| 59,500 | 59,550 | 9,035 | 6,762 | 9,035 | 7,644 |
| 59,550 | 59,600 | 9,046 | 6,768 | 9,046 | 7,655 |
| 59,600 | 59,650 | 9,057 | 6,774 | 9,057 | 7,666 |
| 59,650 | 59,700 | 9,068 | 6,780 | 9,068 | 7,677 |
| 59,700 | 59,750 | 9,079 | 6,786 | 9,079 | 7,688 |
| 59,750 | 59,800 | 9,090 | 6,792 | 9,090 | 7,699 |
| 59,800 | 59,850 | 9,101 | 6,798 | 9,101 | 7,710 |
| 59,850 | 59,900 | 9,112 | 6,804 | 9,112 | 7,721 |
| 59,900 | 59,950 | 9,123 | 6,810 | 9,123 | 7,732 |
| 59,950 | 60,000 | 9,134 | 6,816 | 9,134 | 7,743 |

## 60,000

| At least | But less than | Single | Married filing jointly* | Married filing separately | Head of a household |
|---|---|---|---|---|---|
| 60,000 | 60,050 | 9,145 | 6,822 | 9,145 | 7,754 |
| 60,050 | 60,100 | 9,156 | 6,828 | 9,156 | 7,765 |
| 60,100 | 60,150 | 9,167 | 6,834 | 9,167 | 7,776 |
| 60,150 | 60,200 | 9,178 | 6,840 | 9,178 | 7,787 |
| 60,200 | 60,250 | 9,189 | 6,846 | 9,189 | 7,798 |
| 60,250 | 60,300 | 9,200 | 6,852 | 9,200 | 7,809 |
| 60,300 | 60,350 | 9,211 | 6,858 | 9,211 | 7,820 |
| 60,350 | 60,400 | 9,222 | 6,864 | 9,222 | 7,831 |
| 60,400 | 60,450 | 9,233 | 6,870 | 9,233 | 7,842 |
| 60,450 | 60,500 | 9,244 | 6,876 | 9,244 | 7,853 |
| 60,500 | 60,550 | 9,255 | 6,882 | 9,255 | 7,864 |
| 60,550 | 60,600 | 9,266 | 6,888 | 9,266 | 7,875 |
| 60,600 | 60,650 | 9,277 | 6,894 | 9,277 | 7,886 |
| 60,650 | 60,700 | 9,288 | 6,900 | 9,288 | 7,897 |
| 60,700 | 60,750 | 9,299 | 6,906 | 9,299 | 7,908 |
| 60,750 | 60,800 | 9,310 | 6,912 | 9,310 | 7,919 |
| 60,800 | 60,850 | 9,321 | 6,918 | 9,321 | 7,930 |
| 60,850 | 60,900 | 9,332 | 6,924 | 9,332 | 7,941 |
| 60,900 | 60,950 | 9,343 | 6,930 | 9,343 | 7,952 |
| 60,950 | 61,000 | 9,354 | 6,936 | 9,354 | 7,963 |

## 61,000

| At least | But less than | Single | Married filing jointly* | Married filing separately | Head of a household |
|---|---|---|---|---|---|
| 61,000 | 61,050 | 9,365 | 6,942 | 9,365 | 7,974 |
| 61,050 | 61,100 | 9,376 | 6,948 | 9,376 | 7,985 |
| 61,100 | 61,150 | 9,387 | 6,954 | 9,387 | 7,996 |
| 61,150 | 61,200 | 9,398 | 6,960 | 9,398 | 8,007 |
| 61,200 | 61,250 | 9,409 | 6,966 | 9,409 | 8,018 |
| 61,250 | 61,300 | 9,420 | 6,972 | 9,420 | 8,029 |
| 61,300 | 61,350 | 9,431 | 6,978 | 9,431 | 8,040 |
| 61,350 | 61,400 | 9,442 | 6,984 | 9,442 | 8,051 |
| 61,400 | 61,450 | 9,453 | 6,990 | 9,453 | 8,062 |
| 61,450 | 61,500 | 9,464 | 6,996 | 9,464 | 8,073 |
| 61,500 | 61,550 | 9,475 | 7,002 | 9,475 | 8,084 |
| 61,550 | 61,600 | 9,486 | 7,008 | 9,486 | 8,095 |
| 61,600 | 61,650 | 9,497 | 7,014 | 9,497 | 8,106 |
| 61,650 | 61,700 | 9,508 | 7,020 | 9,508 | 8,117 |
| 61,700 | 61,750 | 9,519 | 7,026 | 9,519 | 8,128 |
| 61,750 | 61,800 | 9,530 | 7,032 | 9,530 | 8,139 |
| 61,800 | 61,850 | 9,541 | 7,038 | 9,541 | 8,150 |
| 61,850 | 61,900 | 9,552 | 7,044 | 9,552 | 8,161 |
| 61,900 | 61,950 | 9,563 | 7,050 | 9,563 | 8,172 |
| 61,950 | 62,000 | 9,574 | 7,056 | 9,574 | 8,183 |

## 62,000

| At least | But less than | Single | Married filing jointly* | Married filing separately | Head of a household |
|---|---|---|---|---|---|
| 62,000 | 62,050 | 9,585 | 7,062 | 9,585 | 8,194 |
| 62,050 | 62,100 | 9,596 | 7,068 | 9,596 | 8,205 |
| 62,100 | 62,150 | 9,607 | 7,074 | 9,607 | 8,216 |
| 62,150 | 62,200 | 9,618 | 7,080 | 9,618 | 8,227 |
| 62,200 | 62,250 | 9,629 | 7,086 | 9,629 | 8,238 |
| 62,250 | 62,300 | 9,640 | 7,092 | 9,640 | 8,249 |
| 62,300 | 62,350 | 9,651 | 7,098 | 9,651 | 8,260 |
| 62,350 | 62,400 | 9,662 | 7,104 | 9,662 | 8,271 |
| 62,400 | 62,450 | 9,673 | 7,110 | 9,673 | 8,282 |
| 62,450 | 62,500 | 9,684 | 7,116 | 9,684 | 8,293 |
| 62,500 | 62,550 | 9,695 | 7,122 | 9,695 | 8,304 |
| 62,550 | 62,600 | 9,706 | 7,128 | 9,706 | 8,315 |
| 62,600 | 62,650 | 9,717 | 7,134 | 9,717 | 8,326 |
| 62,650 | 62,700 | 9,728 | 7,140 | 9,728 | 8,337 |
| 62,700 | 62,750 | 9,739 | 7,146 | 9,739 | 8,348 |
| 62,750 | 62,800 | 9,750 | 7,152 | 9,750 | 8,359 |
| 62,800 | 62,850 | 9,761 | 7,158 | 9,761 | 8,370 |
| 62,850 | 62,900 | 9,772 | 7,164 | 9,772 | 8,381 |
| 62,900 | 62,950 | 9,783 | 7,170 | 9,783 | 8,392 |
| 62,950 | 63,000 | 9,794 | 7,176 | 9,794 | 8,403 |

## 63,000

| At least | But less than | Single | Married filing jointly* | Married filing separately | Head of a household |
|---|---|---|---|---|---|
| 63,000 | 63,050 | 9,805 | 7,182 | 9,805 | 8,414 |
| 63,050 | 63,100 | 9,816 | 7,188 | 9,816 | 8,425 |
| 63,100 | 63,150 | 9,827 | 7,194 | 9,827 | 8,436 |
| 63,150 | 63,200 | 9,838 | 7,200 | 9,838 | 8,447 |
| 63,200 | 63,250 | 9,849 | 7,206 | 9,849 | 8,458 |
| 63,250 | 63,300 | 9,860 | 7,212 | 9,860 | 8,469 |
| 63,300 | 63,350 | 9,871 | 7,218 | 9,871 | 8,480 |
| 63,350 | 63,400 | 9,882 | 7,224 | 9,882 | 8,491 |
| 63,400 | 63,450 | 9,893 | 7,230 | 9,893 | 8,502 |
| 63,450 | 63,500 | 9,904 | 7,236 | 9,904 | 8,513 |
| 63,500 | 63,550 | 9,915 | 7,242 | 9,915 | 8,524 |
| 63,550 | 63,600 | 9,926 | 7,248 | 9,926 | 8,535 |
| 63,600 | 63,650 | 9,937 | 7,254 | 9,937 | 8,546 |
| 63,650 | 63,700 | 9,948 | 7,260 | 9,948 | 8,557 |
| 63,700 | 63,750 | 9,959 | 7,266 | 9,959 | 8,568 |
| 63,750 | 63,800 | 9,970 | 7,272 | 9,970 | 8,579 |
| 63,800 | 63,850 | 9,981 | 7,278 | 9,981 | 8,590 |
| 63,850 | 63,900 | 9,992 | 7,284 | 9,992 | 8,601 |
| 63,900 | 63,950 | 10,003 | 7,290 | 10,003 | 8,612 |
| 63,950 | 64,000 | 10,014 | 7,296 | 10,014 | 8,623 |

## 64,000

| At least | But less than | Single | Married filing jointly* | Married filing separately | Head of a household |
|---|---|---|---|---|---|
| 64,000 | 64,050 | 10,025 | 7,302 | 10,025 | 8,634 |
| 64,050 | 64,100 | 10,036 | 7,308 | 10,036 | 8,645 |
| 64,100 | 64,150 | 10,047 | 7,314 | 10,047 | 8,656 |
| 64,150 | 64,200 | 10,058 | 7,320 | 10,058 | 8,667 |
| 64,200 | 64,250 | 10,069 | 7,326 | 10,069 | 8,678 |
| 64,250 | 64,300 | 10,080 | 7,332 | 10,080 | 8,689 |
| 64,300 | 64,350 | 10,091 | 7,338 | 10,091 | 8,700 |
| 64,350 | 64,400 | 10,102 | 7,344 | 10,102 | 8,711 |
| 64,400 | 64,450 | 10,113 | 7,350 | 10,113 | 8,722 |
| 64,450 | 64,500 | 10,124 | 7,356 | 10,124 | 8,733 |
| 64,500 | 64,550 | 10,135 | 7,362 | 10,135 | 8,744 |
| 64,550 | 64,600 | 10,146 | 7,368 | 10,146 | 8,755 |
| 64,600 | 64,650 | 10,157 | 7,374 | 10,157 | 8,766 |
| 64,650 | 64,700 | 10,168 | 7,380 | 10,168 | 8,777 |
| 64,700 | 64,750 | 10,179 | 7,386 | 10,179 | 8,788 |
| 64,750 | 64,800 | 10,190 | 7,392 | 10,190 | 8,799 |
| 64,800 | 64,850 | 10,201 | 7,398 | 10,201 | 8,810 |
| 64,850 | 64,900 | 10,212 | 7,404 | 10,212 | 8,821 |
| 64,900 | 64,950 | 10,223 | 7,410 | 10,223 | 8,832 |
| 64,950 | 65,000 | 10,234 | 7,416 | 10,234 | 8,843 |

## 65,000

| At least | But less than | Single | Married filing jointly* | Married filing separately | Head of a household |
|---|---|---|---|---|---|
| 65,000 | 65,050 | 10,245 | 7,422 | 10,245 | 8,854 |
| 65,050 | 65,100 | 10,256 | 7,428 | 10,256 | 8,865 |
| 65,100 | 65,150 | 10,267 | 7,434 | 10,267 | 8,876 |
| 65,150 | 65,200 | 10,278 | 7,440 | 10,278 | 8,887 |
| 65,200 | 65,250 | 10,289 | 7,446 | 10,289 | 8,898 |
| 65,250 | 65,300 | 10,300 | 7,452 | 10,300 | 8,909 |
| 65,300 | 65,350 | 10,311 | 7,458 | 10,311 | 8,920 |
| 65,350 | 65,400 | 10,322 | 7,464 | 10,322 | 8,931 |
| 65,400 | 65,450 | 10,333 | 7,470 | 10,333 | 8,942 |
| 65,450 | 65,500 | 10,344 | 7,476 | 10,344 | 8,953 |
| 65,500 | 65,550 | 10,355 | 7,482 | 10,355 | 8,964 |
| 65,550 | 65,600 | 10,366 | 7,488 | 10,366 | 8,975 |
| 65,600 | 65,650 | 10,377 | 7,494 | 10,377 | 8,986 |
| 65,650 | 65,700 | 10,388 | 7,500 | 10,388 | 8,997 |
| 65,700 | 65,750 | 10,399 | 7,506 | 10,399 | 9,008 |
| 65,750 | 65,800 | 10,410 | 7,512 | 10,410 | 9,019 |
| 65,800 | 65,850 | 10,421 | 7,518 | 10,421 | 9,030 |
| 65,850 | 65,900 | 10,432 | 7,524 | 10,432 | 9,041 |
| 65,900 | 65,950 | 10,443 | 7,530 | 10,443 | 9,052 |
| 65,950 | 66,000 | 10,454 | 7,536 | 10,454 | 9,063 |

*This column must also be used by a qualifying widow(er).

(Continued)

**2018 Tax Table — *Continued***

| If line 10 (taxable income) is— At least | But less than | And you are— Single | Married filing jointly * | Married filing separately | Head of a household |
|---|---|---|---|---|---|
| | | Your tax is— | | | |
| **66,000** | | | | | |
| 66,000 | 66,050 | 10,465 | 7,542 | 10,465 | 9,074 |
| 66,050 | 66,100 | 10,476 | 7,548 | 10,476 | 9,085 |
| 66,100 | 66,150 | 10,487 | 7,554 | 10,487 | 9,096 |
| 66,150 | 66,200 | 10,498 | 7,560 | 10,498 | 9,107 |
| 66,200 | 66,250 | 10,509 | 7,566 | 10,509 | 9,118 |
| 66,250 | 66,300 | 10,520 | 7,572 | 10,520 | 9,129 |
| 66,300 | 66,350 | 10,531 | 7,578 | 10,531 | 9,140 |
| 66,350 | 66,400 | 10,542 | 7,584 | 10,542 | 9,151 |
| 66,400 | 66,450 | 10,553 | 7,590 | 10,553 | 9,162 |
| 66,450 | 66,500 | 10,564 | 7,596 | 10,564 | 9,173 |
| 66,500 | 66,550 | 10,575 | 7,602 | 10,575 | 9,184 |
| 66,550 | 66,600 | 10,586 | 7,608 | 10,586 | 9,195 |
| 66,600 | 66,650 | 10,597 | 7,614 | 10,597 | 9,206 |
| 66,650 | 66,700 | 10,608 | 7,620 | 10,608 | 9,217 |
| 66,700 | 66,750 | 10,619 | 7,626 | 10,619 | 9,228 |
| 66,750 | 66,800 | 10,630 | 7,632 | 10,630 | 9,239 |
| 66,800 | 66,850 | 10,641 | 7,638 | 10,641 | 9,250 |
| 66,850 | 66,900 | 10,652 | 7,644 | 10,652 | 9,261 |
| 66,900 | 66,950 | 10,663 | 7,650 | 10,663 | 9,272 |
| 66,950 | 67,000 | 10,674 | 7,656 | 10,674 | 9,283 |
| **67,000** | | | | | |
| 67,000 | 67,050 | 10,685 | 7,662 | 10,685 | 9,294 |
| 67,050 | 67,100 | 10,696 | 7,668 | 10,696 | 9,305 |
| 67,100 | 67,150 | 10,707 | 7,674 | 10,707 | 9,316 |
| 67,150 | 67,200 | 10,718 | 7,680 | 10,718 | 9,327 |
| 67,200 | 67,250 | 10,729 | 7,686 | 10,729 | 9,338 |
| 67,250 | 67,300 | 10,740 | 7,692 | 10,740 | 9,349 |
| 67,300 | 67,350 | 10,751 | 7,698 | 10,751 | 9,360 |
| 67,350 | 67,400 | 10,762 | 7,704 | 10,762 | 9,371 |
| 67,400 | 67,450 | 10,773 | 7,710 | 10,773 | 9,382 |
| 67,450 | 67,500 | 10,784 | 7,716 | 10,784 | 9,393 |
| 67,500 | 67,550 | 10,795 | 7,722 | 10,795 | 9,404 |
| 67,550 | 67,600 | 10,806 | 7,728 | 10,806 | 9,415 |
| 67,600 | 67,650 | 10,817 | 7,734 | 10,817 | 9,426 |
| 67,650 | 67,700 | 10,828 | 7,740 | 10,828 | 9,437 |
| 67,700 | 67,750 | 10,839 | 7,746 | 10,839 | 9,448 |
| 67,750 | 67,800 | 10,850 | 7,752 | 10,850 | 9,459 |
| 67,800 | 67,850 | 10,861 | 7,758 | 10,861 | 9,470 |
| 67,850 | 67,900 | 10,872 | 7,764 | 10,872 | 9,481 |
| 67,900 | 67,950 | 10,883 | 7,770 | 10,883 | 9,492 |
| 67,950 | 68,000 | 10,894 | 7,776 | 10,894 | 9,503 |
| **68,000** | | | | | |
| 68,000 | 68,050 | 10,905 | 7,782 | 10,905 | 9,514 |
| 68,050 | 68,100 | 10,916 | 7,788 | 10,916 | 9,525 |
| 68,100 | 68,150 | 10,927 | 7,794 | 10,927 | 9,536 |
| 68,150 | 68,200 | 10,938 | 7,800 | 10,938 | 9,547 |
| 68,200 | 68,250 | 10,949 | 7,806 | 10,949 | 9,558 |
| 68,250 | 68,300 | 10,960 | 7,812 | 10,960 | 9,569 |
| 68,300 | 68,350 | 10,971 | 7,818 | 10,971 | 9,580 |
| 68,350 | 68,400 | 10,982 | 7,824 | 10,982 | 9,591 |
| 68,400 | 68,450 | 10,993 | 7,830 | 10,993 | 9,602 |
| 68,450 | 68,500 | 11,004 | 7,836 | 11,004 | 9,613 |
| 68,500 | 68,550 | 11,015 | 7,842 | 11,015 | 9,624 |
| 68,550 | 68,600 | 11,026 | 7,848 | 11,026 | 9,635 |
| 68,600 | 68,650 | 11,037 | 7,854 | 11,037 | 9,646 |
| 68,650 | 68,700 | 11,048 | 7,860 | 11,048 | 9,657 |
| 68,700 | 68,750 | 11,059 | 7,866 | 11,059 | 9,668 |
| 68,750 | 68,800 | 11,070 | 7,872 | 11,070 | 9,679 |
| 68,800 | 68,850 | 11,081 | 7,878 | 11,081 | 9,690 |
| 68,850 | 68,900 | 11,092 | 7,884 | 11,092 | 9,701 |
| 68,900 | 68,950 | 11,103 | 7,890 | 11,103 | 9,712 |
| 68,950 | 69,000 | 11,114 | 7,896 | 11,114 | 9,723 |

| If line 10 (taxable income) is— At least | But less than | And you are— Single | Married filing jointly * | Married filing separately | Head of a household |
|---|---|---|---|---|---|
| | | Your tax is— | | | |
| **69,000** | | | | | |
| 69,000 | 69,050 | 11,125 | 7,902 | 11,125 | 9,734 |
| 69,050 | 69,100 | 11,136 | 7,908 | 11,136 | 9,745 |
| 69,100 | 69,150 | 11,147 | 7,914 | 11,147 | 9,756 |
| 69,150 | 69,200 | 11,158 | 7,920 | 11,158 | 9,767 |
| 69,200 | 69,250 | 11,169 | 7,926 | 11,169 | 9,778 |
| 69,250 | 69,300 | 11,180 | 7,932 | 11,180 | 9,789 |
| 69,300 | 69,350 | 11,191 | 7,938 | 11,191 | 9,800 |
| 69,350 | 69,400 | 11,202 | 7,944 | 11,202 | 9,811 |
| 69,400 | 69,450 | 11,213 | 7,950 | 11,213 | 9,822 |
| 69,450 | 69,500 | 11,224 | 7,956 | 11,224 | 9,833 |
| 69,500 | 69,550 | 11,235 | 7,962 | 11,235 | 9,844 |
| 69,550 | 69,600 | 11,246 | 7,968 | 11,246 | 9,855 |
| 69,600 | 69,650 | 11,257 | 7,974 | 11,257 | 9,866 |
| 69,650 | 69,700 | 11,268 | 7,980 | 11,268 | 9,877 |
| 69,700 | 69,750 | 11,279 | 7,986 | 11,279 | 9,888 |
| 69,750 | 69,800 | 11,290 | 7,992 | 11,290 | 9,899 |
| 69,800 | 69,850 | 11,301 | 7,998 | 11,301 | 9,910 |
| 69,850 | 69,900 | 11,312 | 8,004 | 11,312 | 9,921 |
| 69,900 | 69,950 | 11,323 | 8,010 | 11,323 | 9,932 |
| 69,950 | 70,000 | 11,334 | 8,016 | 11,334 | 9,943 |
| **70,000** | | | | | |
| 70,000 | 70,050 | 11,345 | 8,022 | 11,345 | 9,954 |
| 70,050 | 70,100 | 11,356 | 8,028 | 11,356 | 9,965 |
| 70,100 | 70,150 | 11,367 | 8,034 | 11,367 | 9,976 |
| 70,150 | 70,200 | 11,378 | 8,040 | 11,378 | 9,987 |
| 70,200 | 70,250 | 11,389 | 8,046 | 11,389 | 9,998 |
| 70,250 | 70,300 | 11,400 | 8,052 | 11,400 | 10,009 |
| 70,300 | 70,350 | 11,411 | 8,058 | 11,411 | 10,020 |
| 70,350 | 70,400 | 11,422 | 8,064 | 11,422 | 10,031 |
| 70,400 | 70,450 | 11,433 | 8,070 | 11,433 | 10,042 |
| 70,450 | 70,500 | 11,444 | 8,076 | 11,444 | 10,053 |
| 70,500 | 70,550 | 11,455 | 8,082 | 11,455 | 10,064 |
| 70,550 | 70,600 | 11,466 | 8,088 | 11,466 | 10,075 |
| 70,600 | 70,650 | 11,477 | 8,094 | 11,477 | 10,086 |
| 70,650 | 70,700 | 11,488 | 8,100 | 11,488 | 10,097 |
| 70,700 | 70,750 | 11,499 | 8,106 | 11,499 | 10,108 |
| 70,750 | 70,800 | 11,510 | 8,112 | 11,510 | 10,119 |
| 70,800 | 70,850 | 11,521 | 8,118 | 11,521 | 10,130 |
| 70,850 | 70,900 | 11,532 | 8,124 | 11,532 | 10,141 |
| 70,900 | 70,950 | 11,543 | 8,130 | 11,543 | 10,152 |
| 70,950 | 71,000 | 11,554 | 8,136 | 11,554 | 10,163 |
| **71,000** | | | | | |
| 71,000 | 71,050 | 11,565 | 8,142 | 11,565 | 10,174 |
| 71,050 | 71,100 | 11,576 | 8,148 | 11,576 | 10,185 |
| 71,100 | 71,150 | 11,587 | 8,154 | 11,587 | 10,196 |
| 71,150 | 71,200 | 11,598 | 8,160 | 11,598 | 10,207 |
| 71,200 | 71,250 | 11,609 | 8,166 | 11,609 | 10,218 |
| 71,250 | 71,300 | 11,620 | 8,172 | 11,620 | 10,229 |
| 71,300 | 71,350 | 11,631 | 8,178 | 11,631 | 10,240 |
| 71,350 | 71,400 | 11,642 | 8,184 | 11,642 | 10,251 |
| 71,400 | 71,450 | 11,653 | 8,190 | 11,653 | 10,262 |
| 71,450 | 71,500 | 11,664 | 8,196 | 11,664 | 10,273 |
| 71,500 | 71,550 | 11,675 | 8,202 | 11,675 | 10,284 |
| 71,550 | 71,600 | 11,686 | 8,208 | 11,686 | 10,295 |
| 71,600 | 71,650 | 11,697 | 8,214 | 11,697 | 10,306 |
| 71,650 | 71,700 | 11,708 | 8,220 | 11,708 | 10,317 |
| 71,700 | 71,750 | 11,719 | 8,226 | 11,719 | 10,328 |
| 71,750 | 71,800 | 11,730 | 8,232 | 11,730 | 10,339 |
| 71,800 | 71,850 | 11,741 | 8,238 | 11,741 | 10,350 |
| 71,850 | 71,900 | 11,752 | 8,244 | 11,752 | 10,361 |
| 71,900 | 71,950 | 11,763 | 8,250 | 11,763 | 10,372 |
| 71,950 | 72,000 | 11,774 | 8,256 | 11,774 | 10,383 |

| If line 10 (taxable income) is— At least | But less than | And you are— Single | Married filing jointly * | Married filing separately | Head of a household |
|---|---|---|---|---|---|
| | | Your tax is— | | | |
| **72,000** | | | | | |
| 72,000 | 72,050 | 11,785 | 8,262 | 11,785 | 10,394 |
| 72,050 | 72,100 | 11,796 | 8,268 | 11,796 | 10,405 |
| 72,100 | 72,150 | 11,807 | 8,274 | 11,807 | 10,416 |
| 72,150 | 72,200 | 11,818 | 8,280 | 11,818 | 10,427 |
| 72,200 | 72,250 | 11,829 | 8,286 | 11,829 | 10,438 |
| 72,250 | 72,300 | 11,840 | 8,292 | 11,840 | 10,449 |
| 72,300 | 72,350 | 11,851 | 8,298 | 11,851 | 10,460 |
| 72,350 | 72,400 | 11,862 | 8,304 | 11,862 | 10,471 |
| 72,400 | 72,450 | 11,873 | 8,310 | 11,873 | 10,482 |
| 72,450 | 72,500 | 11,884 | 8,316 | 11,884 | 10,493 |
| 72,500 | 72,550 | 11,895 | 8,322 | 11,895 | 10,504 |
| 72,550 | 72,600 | 11,906 | 8,328 | 11,906 | 10,515 |
| 72,600 | 72,650 | 11,917 | 8,334 | 11,917 | 10,526 |
| 72,650 | 72,700 | 11,928 | 8,340 | 11,928 | 10,537 |
| 72,700 | 72,750 | 11,939 | 8,346 | 11,939 | 10,548 |
| 72,750 | 72,800 | 11,950 | 8,352 | 11,950 | 10,559 |
| 72,800 | 72,850 | 11,961 | 8,358 | 11,961 | 10,570 |
| 72,850 | 72,900 | 11,972 | 8,364 | 11,972 | 10,581 |
| 72,900 | 72,950 | 11,983 | 8,370 | 11,983 | 10,592 |
| 72,950 | 73,000 | 11,994 | 8,376 | 11,994 | 10,603 |
| **73,000** | | | | | |
| 73,000 | 73,050 | 12,005 | 8,382 | 12,005 | 10,614 |
| 73,050 | 73,100 | 12,016 | 8,388 | 12,016 | 10,625 |
| 73,100 | 73,150 | 12,027 | 8,394 | 12,027 | 10,636 |
| 73,150 | 73,200 | 12,038 | 8,400 | 12,038 | 10,647 |
| 73,200 | 73,250 | 12,049 | 8,406 | 12,049 | 10,658 |
| 73,250 | 73,300 | 12,060 | 8,412 | 12,060 | 10,669 |
| 73,300 | 73,350 | 12,071 | 8,418 | 12,071 | 10,680 |
| 73,350 | 73,400 | 12,082 | 8,424 | 12,082 | 10,691 |
| 73,400 | 73,450 | 12,093 | 8,430 | 12,093 | 10,702 |
| 73,450 | 73,500 | 12,104 | 8,436 | 12,104 | 10,713 |
| 73,500 | 73,550 | 12,115 | 8,442 | 12,115 | 10,724 |
| 73,550 | 73,600 | 12,126 | 8,448 | 12,126 | 10,735 |
| 73,600 | 73,650 | 12,137 | 8,454 | 12,137 | 10,746 |
| 73,650 | 73,700 | 12,148 | 8,460 | 12,148 | 10,757 |
| 73,700 | 73,750 | 12,159 | 8,466 | 12,159 | 10,768 |
| 73,750 | 73,800 | 12,170 | 8,472 | 12,170 | 10,779 |
| 73,800 | 73,850 | 12,181 | 8,478 | 12,181 | 10,790 |
| 73,850 | 73,900 | 12,192 | 8,484 | 12,192 | 10,801 |
| 73,900 | 73,950 | 12,203 | 8,490 | 12,203 | 10,812 |
| 73,950 | 74,000 | 12,214 | 8,496 | 12,214 | 10,823 |
| **74,000** | | | | | |
| 74,000 | 74,050 | 12,225 | 8,502 | 12,225 | 10,834 |
| 74,050 | 74,100 | 12,236 | 8,508 | 12,236 | 10,845 |
| 74,100 | 74,150 | 12,247 | 8,514 | 12,247 | 10,856 |
| 74,150 | 74,200 | 12,258 | 8,520 | 12,258 | 10,867 |
| 74,200 | 74,250 | 12,269 | 8,526 | 12,269 | 10,878 |
| 74,250 | 74,300 | 12,280 | 8,532 | 12,280 | 10,889 |
| 74,300 | 74,350 | 12,291 | 8,538 | 12,291 | 10,900 |
| 74,350 | 74,400 | 12,302 | 8,544 | 12,302 | 10,911 |
| 74,400 | 74,450 | 12,313 | 8,550 | 12,313 | 10,922 |
| 74,450 | 74,500 | 12,324 | 8,556 | 12,324 | 10,933 |
| 74,500 | 74,550 | 12,335 | 8,562 | 12,335 | 10,944 |
| 74,550 | 74,600 | 12,346 | 8,568 | 12,346 | 10,955 |
| 74,600 | 74,650 | 12,357 | 8,574 | 12,357 | 10,966 |
| 74,650 | 74,700 | 12,368 | 8,580 | 12,368 | 10,977 |
| 74,700 | 74,750 | 12,379 | 8,586 | 12,379 | 10,988 |
| 74,750 | 74,800 | 12,390 | 8,592 | 12,390 | 10,999 |
| 74,800 | 74,850 | 12,401 | 8,598 | 12,401 | 11,010 |
| 74,850 | 74,900 | 12,412 | 8,604 | 12,412 | 11,021 |
| 74,900 | 74,950 | 12,423 | 8,610 | 12,423 | 11,032 |
| 74,950 | 75,000 | 12,434 | 8,616 | 12,434 | 11,043 |

*(Continued)*

* This column must also be used by a qualifying widow(er).

**Your tax is—** columns below apply to: Single | Married filing jointly* | Married filing separately | Head of a household

## 75,000

| At least | But less than | Single | Married filing jointly* | Married filing separately | Head of a household |
|---|---|---|---|---|---|
| 75,000 | 75,050 | 12,445 | 8,622 | 12,445 | 11,054 |
| 75,050 | 75,100 | 12,456 | 8,628 | 12,456 | 11,065 |
| 75,100 | 75,150 | 12,467 | 8,634 | 12,467 | 11,076 |
| 75,150 | 75,200 | 12,478 | 8,640 | 12,478 | 11,087 |
| 75,200 | 75,250 | 12,489 | 8,646 | 12,489 | 11,098 |
| 75,250 | 75,300 | 12,500 | 8,652 | 12,500 | 11,109 |
| 75,300 | 75,350 | 12,511 | 8,658 | 12,511 | 11,120 |
| 75,350 | 75,400 | 12,522 | 8,664 | 12,522 | 11,131 |
| 75,400 | 75,450 | 12,533 | 8,670 | 12,533 | 11,142 |
| 75,450 | 75,500 | 12,544 | 8,676 | 12,544 | 11,153 |
| 75,500 | 75,550 | 12,555 | 8,682 | 12,555 | 11,164 |
| 75,550 | 75,600 | 12,566 | 8,688 | 12,566 | 11,175 |
| 75,600 | 75,650 | 12,577 | 8,694 | 12,577 | 11,186 |
| 75,650 | 75,700 | 12,588 | 8,700 | 12,588 | 11,197 |
| 75,700 | 75,750 | 12,599 | 8,706 | 12,599 | 11,208 |
| 75,750 | 75,800 | 12,610 | 8,712 | 12,610 | 11,219 |
| 75,800 | 75,850 | 12,621 | 8,718 | 12,621 | 11,230 |
| 75,850 | 75,900 | 12,632 | 8,724 | 12,632 | 11,241 |
| 75,900 | 75,950 | 12,643 | 8,730 | 12,643 | 11,252 |
| 75,950 | 76,000 | 12,654 | 8,736 | 12,654 | 11,263 |

## 76,000

| At least | But less than | Single | Married filing jointly* | Married filing separately | Head of a household |
|---|---|---|---|---|---|
| 76,000 | 76,050 | 12,665 | 8,742 | 12,665 | 11,274 |
| 76,050 | 76,100 | 12,676 | 8,748 | 12,676 | 11,285 |
| 76,100 | 76,150 | 12,687 | 8,754 | 12,687 | 11,296 |
| 76,150 | 76,200 | 12,698 | 8,760 | 12,698 | 11,307 |
| 76,200 | 76,250 | 12,709 | 8,766 | 12,709 | 11,318 |
| 76,250 | 76,300 | 12,720 | 8,772 | 12,720 | 11,329 |
| 76,300 | 76,350 | 12,731 | 8,778 | 12,731 | 11,340 |
| 76,350 | 76,400 | 12,742 | 8,784 | 12,742 | 11,351 |
| 76,400 | 76,450 | 12,753 | 8,790 | 12,753 | 11,362 |
| 76,450 | 76,500 | 12,764 | 8,796 | 12,764 | 11,373 |
| 76,500 | 76,550 | 12,775 | 8,802 | 12,775 | 11,384 |
| 76,550 | 76,600 | 12,786 | 8,808 | 12,786 | 11,395 |
| 76,600 | 76,650 | 12,797 | 8,814 | 12,797 | 11,406 |
| 76,650 | 76,700 | 12,808 | 8,820 | 12,808 | 11,417 |
| 76,700 | 76,750 | 12,819 | 8,826 | 12,819 | 11,428 |
| 76,750 | 76,800 | 12,830 | 8,832 | 12,830 | 11,439 |
| 76,800 | 76,850 | 12,841 | 8,838 | 12,841 | 11,450 |
| 76,850 | 76,900 | 12,852 | 8,844 | 12,852 | 11,461 |
| 76,900 | 76,950 | 12,863 | 8,850 | 12,863 | 11,472 |
| 76,950 | 77,000 | 12,874 | 8,856 | 12,874 | 11,483 |

## 77,000

| At least | But less than | Single | Married filing jointly* | Married filing separately | Head of a household |
|---|---|---|---|---|---|
| 77,000 | 77,050 | 12,885 | 8,862 | 12,885 | 11,494 |
| 77,050 | 77,100 | 12,896 | 8,868 | 12,896 | 11,505 |
| 77,100 | 77,150 | 12,907 | 8,874 | 12,907 | 11,516 |
| 77,150 | 77,200 | 12,918 | 8,880 | 12,918 | 11,527 |
| 77,200 | 77,250 | 12,929 | 8,886 | 12,929 | 11,538 |
| 77,250 | 77,300 | 12,940 | 8,892 | 12,940 | 11,549 |
| 77,300 | 77,350 | 12,951 | 8,898 | 12,951 | 11,560 |
| 77,350 | 77,400 | 12,962 | 8,904 | 12,962 | 11,571 |
| 77,400 | 77,450 | 12,973 | 8,913 | 12,973 | 11,582 |
| 77,450 | 77,500 | 12,984 | 8,924 | 12,984 | 11,593 |
| 77,500 | 77,550 | 12,995 | 8,935 | 12,995 | 11,604 |
| 77,550 | 77,600 | 13,006 | 8,946 | 13,006 | 11,615 |
| 77,600 | 77,650 | 13,017 | 8,957 | 13,017 | 11,626 |
| 77,650 | 77,700 | 13,028 | 8,968 | 13,028 | 11,637 |
| 77,700 | 77,750 | 13,039 | 8,979 | 13,039 | 11,648 |
| 77,750 | 77,800 | 13,050 | 8,990 | 13,050 | 11,659 |
| 77,800 | 77,850 | 13,061 | 9,001 | 13,061 | 11,670 |
| 77,850 | 77,900 | 13,072 | 9,012 | 13,072 | 11,681 |
| 77,900 | 77,950 | 13,083 | 9,023 | 13,083 | 11,692 |
| 77,950 | 78,000 | 13,094 | 9,034 | 13,094 | 11,703 |

## 78,000

| At least | But less than | Single | Married filing jointly* | Married filing separately | Head of a household |
|---|---|---|---|---|---|
| 78,000 | 78,050 | 13,105 | 9,045 | 13,105 | 11,714 |
| 78,050 | 78,100 | 13,116 | 9,056 | 13,116 | 11,725 |
| 78,100 | 78,150 | 13,127 | 9,067 | 13,127 | 11,736 |
| 78,150 | 78,200 | 13,138 | 9,078 | 13,138 | 11,747 |
| 78,200 | 78,250 | 13,149 | 9,089 | 13,149 | 11,758 |
| 78,250 | 78,300 | 13,160 | 9,100 | 13,160 | 11,769 |
| 78,300 | 78,350 | 13,171 | 9,111 | 13,171 | 11,780 |
| 78,350 | 78,400 | 13,182 | 9,122 | 13,182 | 11,791 |
| 78,400 | 78,450 | 13,193 | 9,133 | 13,193 | 11,802 |
| 78,450 | 78,500 | 13,204 | 9,144 | 13,204 | 11,813 |
| 78,500 | 78,550 | 13,215 | 9,155 | 13,215 | 11,824 |
| 78,550 | 78,600 | 13,226 | 9,166 | 13,226 | 11,835 |
| 78,600 | 78,650 | 13,237 | 9,177 | 13,237 | 11,846 |
| 78,650 | 78,700 | 13,248 | 9,188 | 13,248 | 11,857 |
| 78,700 | 78,750 | 13,259 | 9,199 | 13,259 | 11,868 |
| 78,750 | 78,800 | 13,270 | 9,210 | 13,270 | 11,879 |
| 78,800 | 78,850 | 13,281 | 9,221 | 13,281 | 11,890 |
| 78,850 | 78,900 | 13,292 | 9,232 | 13,292 | 11,901 |
| 78,900 | 78,950 | 13,303 | 9,243 | 13,303 | 11,912 |
| 78,950 | 79,000 | 13,314 | 9,254 | 13,314 | 11,923 |

## 79,000

| At least | But less than | Single | Married filing jointly* | Married filing separately | Head of a household |
|---|---|---|---|---|---|
| 79,000 | 79,050 | 13,325 | 9,265 | 13,325 | 11,934 |
| 79,050 | 79,100 | 13,336 | 9,276 | 13,336 | 11,945 |
| 79,100 | 79,150 | 13,347 | 9,287 | 13,347 | 11,956 |
| 79,150 | 79,200 | 13,358 | 9,298 | 13,358 | 11,967 |
| 79,200 | 79,250 | 13,369 | 9,309 | 13,369 | 11,978 |
| 79,250 | 79,300 | 13,380 | 9,320 | 13,380 | 11,989 |
| 79,300 | 79,350 | 13,391 | 9,331 | 13,391 | 12,000 |
| 79,350 | 79,400 | 13,402 | 9,342 | 13,402 | 12,011 |
| 79,400 | 79,450 | 13,413 | 9,353 | 13,413 | 12,022 |
| 79,450 | 79,500 | 13,424 | 9,364 | 13,424 | 12,033 |
| 79,500 | 79,550 | 13,435 | 9,375 | 13,435 | 12,044 |
| 79,550 | 79,600 | 13,446 | 9,386 | 13,446 | 12,055 |
| 79,600 | 79,650 | 13,457 | 9,397 | 13,457 | 12,066 |
| 79,650 | 79,700 | 13,468 | 9,408 | 13,468 | 12,077 |
| 79,700 | 79,750 | 13,479 | 9,419 | 13,479 | 12,088 |
| 79,750 | 79,800 | 13,490 | 9,430 | 13,490 | 12,099 |
| 79,800 | 79,850 | 13,501 | 9,441 | 13,501 | 12,110 |
| 79,850 | 79,900 | 13,512 | 9,452 | 13,512 | 12,121 |
| 79,900 | 79,950 | 13,523 | 9,463 | 13,523 | 12,132 |
| 79,950 | 80,000 | 13,534 | 9,474 | 13,534 | 12,143 |

## 80,000

| At least | But less than | Single | Married filing jointly* | Married filing separately | Head of a household |
|---|---|---|---|---|---|
| 80,000 | 80,050 | 13,545 | 9,485 | 13,545 | 12,154 |
| 80,050 | 80,100 | 13,556 | 9,496 | 13,556 | 12,165 |
| 80,100 | 80,150 | 13,567 | 9,507 | 13,567 | 12,176 |
| 80,150 | 80,200 | 13,578 | 9,518 | 13,578 | 12,187 |
| 80,200 | 80,250 | 13,589 | 9,529 | 13,589 | 12,198 |
| 80,250 | 80,300 | 13,600 | 9,540 | 13,600 | 12,209 |
| 80,300 | 80,350 | 13,611 | 9,551 | 13,611 | 12,220 |
| 80,350 | 80,400 | 13,622 | 9,562 | 13,622 | 12,231 |
| 80,400 | 80,450 | 13,633 | 9,573 | 13,633 | 12,242 |
| 80,450 | 80,500 | 13,644 | 9,584 | 13,644 | 12,253 |
| 80,500 | 80,550 | 13,655 | 9,595 | 13,655 | 12,264 |
| 80,550 | 80,600 | 13,666 | 9,606 | 13,666 | 12,275 |
| 80,600 | 80,650 | 13,677 | 9,617 | 13,677 | 12,286 |
| 80,650 | 80,700 | 13,688 | 9,628 | 13,688 | 12,297 |
| 80,700 | 80,750 | 13,699 | 9,639 | 13,699 | 12,308 |
| 80,750 | 80,800 | 13,710 | 9,650 | 13,710 | 12,319 |
| 80,800 | 80,850 | 13,721 | 9,661 | 13,721 | 12,330 |
| 80,850 | 80,900 | 13,732 | 9,672 | 13,732 | 12,341 |
| 80,900 | 80,950 | 13,743 | 9,683 | 13,743 | 12,352 |
| 80,950 | 81,000 | 13,754 | 9,694 | 13,754 | 12,363 |

## 81,000

| At least | But less than | Single | Married filing jointly* | Married filing separately | Head of a household |
|---|---|---|---|---|---|
| 81,000 | 81,050 | 13,765 | 9,705 | 13,765 | 12,374 |
| 81,050 | 81,100 | 13,776 | 9,716 | 13,776 | 12,385 |
| 81,100 | 81,150 | 13,787 | 9,727 | 13,787 | 12,396 |
| 81,150 | 81,200 | 13,798 | 9,738 | 13,798 | 12,407 |
| 81,200 | 81,250 | 13,809 | 9,749 | 13,809 | 12,418 |
| 81,250 | 81,300 | 13,820 | 9,760 | 13,820 | 12,429 |
| 81,300 | 81,350 | 13,831 | 9,771 | 13,831 | 12,440 |
| 81,350 | 81,400 | 13,842 | 9,782 | 13,842 | 12,451 |
| 81,400 | 81,450 | 13,853 | 9,793 | 13,853 | 12,462 |
| 81,450 | 81,500 | 13,864 | 9,804 | 13,864 | 12,473 |
| 81,500 | 81,550 | 13,875 | 9,815 | 13,875 | 12,484 |
| 81,550 | 81,600 | 13,886 | 9,826 | 13,886 | 12,495 |
| 81,600 | 81,650 | 13,897 | 9,837 | 13,897 | 12,506 |
| 81,650 | 81,700 | 13,908 | 9,848 | 13,908 | 12,517 |
| 81,700 | 81,750 | 13,919 | 9,859 | 13,919 | 12,528 |
| 81,750 | 81,800 | 13,930 | 9,870 | 13,930 | 12,539 |
| 81,800 | 81,850 | 13,941 | 9,881 | 13,941 | 12,550 |
| 81,850 | 81,900 | 13,952 | 9,892 | 13,952 | 12,561 |
| 81,900 | 81,950 | 13,963 | 9,903 | 13,963 | 12,572 |
| 81,950 | 82,000 | 13,974 | 9,914 | 13,974 | 12,583 |

## 82,000

| At least | But less than | Single | Married filing jointly* | Married filing separately | Head of a household |
|---|---|---|---|---|---|
| 82,000 | 82,050 | 13,985 | 9,925 | 13,985 | 12,594 |
| 82,050 | 82,100 | 13,996 | 9,936 | 13,996 | 12,605 |
| 82,100 | 82,150 | 14,007 | 9,947 | 14,007 | 12,616 |
| 82,150 | 82,200 | 14,018 | 9,958 | 14,018 | 12,627 |
| 82,200 | 82,250 | 14,029 | 9,969 | 14,029 | 12,638 |
| 82,250 | 82,300 | 14,040 | 9,980 | 14,040 | 12,649 |
| 82,300 | 82,350 | 14,051 | 9,991 | 14,051 | 12,660 |
| 82,350 | 82,400 | 14,062 | 10,002 | 14,062 | 12,671 |
| 82,400 | 82,450 | 14,073 | 10,013 | 14,073 | 12,682 |
| 82,450 | 82,500 | 14,084 | 10,024 | 14,084 | 12,693 |
| 82,500 | 82,550 | 14,096 | 10,035 | 14,096 | 12,704 |
| 82,550 | 82,600 | 14,108 | 10,046 | 14,108 | 12,716 |
| 82,600 | 82,650 | 14,120 | 10,057 | 14,120 | 12,728 |
| 82,650 | 82,700 | 14,132 | 10,068 | 14,132 | 12,740 |
| 82,700 | 82,750 | 14,144 | 10,079 | 14,144 | 12,752 |
| 82,750 | 82,800 | 14,156 | 10,090 | 14,156 | 12,764 |
| 82,800 | 82,850 | 14,168 | 10,101 | 14,168 | 12,776 |
| 82,850 | 82,900 | 14,180 | 10,112 | 14,180 | 12,788 |
| 82,900 | 82,950 | 14,192 | 10,123 | 14,192 | 12,800 |
| 82,950 | 83,000 | 14,204 | 10,134 | 14,204 | 12,812 |

## 83,000

| At least | But less than | Single | Married filing jointly* | Married filing separately | Head of a household |
|---|---|---|---|---|---|
| 83,000 | 83,050 | 14,216 | 10,145 | 14,216 | 12,824 |
| 83,050 | 83,100 | 14,228 | 10,156 | 14,228 | 12,836 |
| 83,100 | 83,150 | 14,240 | 10,167 | 14,240 | 12,848 |
| 83,150 | 83,200 | 14,252 | 10,178 | 14,252 | 12,860 |
| 83,200 | 83,250 | 14,264 | 10,189 | 14,264 | 12,872 |
| 83,250 | 83,300 | 14,276 | 10,200 | 14,276 | 12,884 |
| 83,300 | 83,350 | 14,288 | 10,211 | 14,288 | 12,896 |
| 83,350 | 83,400 | 14,300 | 10,222 | 14,300 | 12,908 |
| 83,400 | 83,450 | 14,312 | 10,233 | 14,312 | 12,920 |
| 83,450 | 83,500 | 14,324 | 10,244 | 14,324 | 12,932 |
| 83,500 | 83,550 | 14,336 | 10,255 | 14,336 | 12,944 |
| 83,550 | 83,600 | 14,348 | 10,266 | 14,348 | 12,956 |
| 83,600 | 83,650 | 14,360 | 10,277 | 14,360 | 12,968 |
| 83,650 | 83,700 | 14,372 | 10,288 | 14,372 | 12,980 |
| 83,700 | 83,750 | 14,384 | 10,299 | 14,384 | 12,992 |
| 83,750 | 83,800 | 14,396 | 10,310 | 14,396 | 13,004 |
| 83,800 | 83,850 | 14,408 | 10,321 | 14,408 | 13,016 |
| 83,850 | 83,900 | 14,420 | 10,332 | 14,420 | 13,028 |
| 83,900 | 83,950 | 14,432 | 10,343 | 14,432 | 13,040 |
| 83,950 | 84,000 | 14,444 | 10,354 | 14,444 | 13,052 |

*(Continued)*

* This column must also be used by a qualifying widow(er).

## 84,000

| At least | But less than | Single | Married filing jointly * | Married filing separately | Head of a household |
|---|---|---|---|---|---|
| 84,000 | 84,050 | 14,456 | 10,365 | 14,456 | 13,064 |
| 84,050 | 84,100 | 14,468 | 10,376 | 14,468 | 13,076 |
| 84,100 | 84,150 | 14,480 | 10,387 | 14,480 | 13,088 |
| 84,150 | 84,200 | 14,492 | 10,398 | 14,492 | 13,100 |
| 84,200 | 84,250 | 14,504 | 10,409 | 14,504 | 13,112 |
| 84,250 | 84,300 | 14,516 | 10,420 | 14,516 | 13,124 |
| 84,300 | 84,350 | 14,528 | 10,431 | 14,528 | 13,136 |
| 84,350 | 84,400 | 14,540 | 10,442 | 14,540 | 13,148 |
| 84,400 | 84,450 | 14,552 | 10,453 | 14,552 | 13,160 |
| 84,450 | 84,500 | 14,564 | 10,464 | 14,564 | 13,172 |
| 84,500 | 84,550 | 14,576 | 10,475 | 14,576 | 13,184 |
| 84,550 | 84,600 | 14,588 | 10,486 | 14,588 | 13,196 |
| 84,600 | 84,650 | 14,600 | 10,497 | 14,600 | 13,208 |
| 84,650 | 84,700 | 14,612 | 10,508 | 14,612 | 13,220 |
| 84,700 | 84,750 | 14,624 | 10,519 | 14,624 | 13,232 |
| 84,750 | 84,800 | 14,636 | 10,530 | 14,636 | 13,244 |
| 84,800 | 84,850 | 14,648 | 10,541 | 14,648 | 13,256 |
| 84,850 | 84,900 | 14,660 | 10,552 | 14,660 | 13,268 |
| 84,900 | 84,950 | 14,672 | 10,563 | 14,672 | 13,280 |
| 84,950 | 85,000 | 14,684 | 10,574 | 14,684 | 13,292 |

## 85,000

| At least | But less than | Single | Married filing jointly * | Married filing separately | Head of a household |
|---|---|---|---|---|---|
| 85,000 | 85,050 | 14,696 | 10,585 | 14,696 | 13,304 |
| 85,050 | 85,100 | 14,708 | 10,596 | 14,708 | 13,316 |
| 85,100 | 85,150 | 14,720 | 10,607 | 14,720 | 13,328 |
| 85,150 | 85,200 | 14,732 | 10,618 | 14,732 | 13,340 |
| 85,200 | 85,250 | 14,744 | 10,629 | 14,744 | 13,352 |
| 85,250 | 85,300 | 14,756 | 10,640 | 14,756 | 13,364 |
| 85,300 | 85,350 | 14,768 | 10,651 | 14,768 | 13,376 |
| 85,350 | 85,400 | 14,780 | 10,662 | 14,780 | 13,388 |
| 85,400 | 85,450 | 14,792 | 10,673 | 14,792 | 13,400 |
| 85,450 | 85,500 | 14,804 | 10,684 | 14,804 | 13,412 |
| 85,500 | 85,550 | 14,816 | 10,695 | 14,816 | 13,424 |
| 85,550 | 85,600 | 14,828 | 10,706 | 14,828 | 13,436 |
| 85,600 | 85,650 | 14,840 | 10,717 | 14,840 | 13,448 |
| 85,650 | 85,700 | 14,852 | 10,728 | 14,852 | 13,460 |
| 85,700 | 85,750 | 14,864 | 10,739 | 14,864 | 13,472 |
| 85,750 | 85,800 | 14,876 | 10,750 | 14,876 | 13,484 |
| 85,800 | 85,850 | 14,888 | 10,761 | 14,888 | 13,496 |
| 85,850 | 85,900 | 14,900 | 10,772 | 14,900 | 13,508 |
| 85,900 | 85,950 | 14,912 | 10,783 | 14,912 | 13,520 |
| 85,950 | 86,000 | 14,924 | 10,794 | 14,924 | 13,532 |

## 86,000

| At least | But less than | Single | Married filing jointly * | Married filing separately | Head of a household |
|---|---|---|---|---|---|
| 86,000 | 86,050 | 14,936 | 10,805 | 14,936 | 13,544 |
| 86,050 | 86,100 | 14,948 | 10,816 | 14,948 | 13,556 |
| 86,100 | 86,150 | 14,960 | 10,827 | 14,960 | 13,568 |
| 86,150 | 86,200 | 14,972 | 10,838 | 14,972 | 13,580 |
| 86,200 | 86,250 | 14,984 | 10,849 | 14,984 | 13,592 |
| 86,250 | 86,300 | 14,996 | 10,860 | 14,996 | 13,604 |
| 86,300 | 86,350 | 15,008 | 10,871 | 15,008 | 13,616 |
| 86,350 | 86,400 | 15,020 | 10,882 | 15,020 | 13,628 |
| 86,400 | 86,450 | 15,032 | 10,893 | 15,032 | 13,640 |
| 86,450 | 86,500 | 15,044 | 10,904 | 15,044 | 13,652 |
| 86,500 | 86,550 | 15,056 | 10,915 | 15,056 | 13,664 |
| 86,550 | 86,600 | 15,068 | 10,926 | 15,068 | 13,676 |
| 86,600 | 86,650 | 15,080 | 10,937 | 15,080 | 13,688 |
| 86,650 | 86,700 | 15,092 | 10,948 | 15,092 | 13,700 |
| 86,700 | 86,750 | 15,104 | 10,959 | 15,104 | 13,712 |
| 86,750 | 86,800 | 15,116 | 10,970 | 15,116 | 13,724 |
| 86,800 | 86,850 | 15,128 | 10,981 | 15,128 | 13,736 |
| 86,850 | 86,900 | 15,140 | 10,992 | 15,140 | 13,748 |
| 86,900 | 86,950 | 15,152 | 11,003 | 15,152 | 13,760 |
| 86,950 | 87,000 | 15,164 | 11,014 | 15,164 | 13,772 |

## 87,000

| At least | But less than | Single | Married filing jointly * | Married filing separately | Head of a household |
|---|---|---|---|---|---|
| 87,000 | 87,050 | 15,176 | 11,025 | 15,176 | 13,784 |
| 87,050 | 87,100 | 15,188 | 11,036 | 15,188 | 13,796 |
| 87,100 | 87,150 | 15,200 | 11,047 | 15,200 | 13,808 |
| 87,150 | 87,200 | 15,212 | 11,058 | 15,212 | 13,820 |
| 87,200 | 87,250 | 15,224 | 11,069 | 15,224 | 13,832 |
| 87,250 | 87,300 | 15,236 | 11,080 | 15,236 | 13,844 |
| 87,300 | 87,350 | 15,248 | 11,091 | 15,248 | 13,856 |
| 87,350 | 87,400 | 15,260 | 11,102 | 15,260 | 13,868 |
| 87,400 | 87,450 | 15,272 | 11,113 | 15,272 | 13,880 |
| 87,450 | 87,500 | 15,284 | 11,124 | 15,284 | 13,892 |
| 87,500 | 87,550 | 15,296 | 11,135 | 15,296 | 13,904 |
| 87,550 | 87,600 | 15,308 | 11,146 | 15,308 | 13,916 |
| 87,600 | 87,650 | 15,320 | 11,157 | 15,320 | 13,928 |
| 87,650 | 87,700 | 15,332 | 11,168 | 15,332 | 13,940 |
| 87,700 | 87,750 | 15,344 | 11,179 | 15,344 | 13,952 |
| 87,750 | 87,800 | 15,356 | 11,190 | 15,356 | 13,964 |
| 87,800 | 87,850 | 15,368 | 11,201 | 15,368 | 13,976 |
| 87,850 | 87,900 | 15,380 | 11,212 | 15,380 | 13,988 |
| 87,900 | 87,950 | 15,392 | 11,223 | 15,392 | 14,000 |
| 87,950 | 88,000 | 15,404 | 11,234 | 15,404 | 14,012 |

## 88,000

| At least | But less than | Single | Married filing jointly * | Married filing separately | Head of a household |
|---|---|---|---|---|---|
| 88,000 | 88,050 | 15,416 | 11,245 | 15,416 | 14,024 |
| 88,050 | 88,100 | 15,428 | 11,256 | 15,428 | 14,036 |
| 88,100 | 88,150 | 15,440 | 11,267 | 15,440 | 14,048 |
| 88,150 | 88,200 | 15,452 | 11,278 | 15,452 | 14,060 |
| 88,200 | 88,250 | 15,464 | 11,289 | 15,464 | 14,072 |
| 88,250 | 88,300 | 15,476 | 11,300 | 15,476 | 14,084 |
| 88,300 | 88,350 | 15,488 | 11,311 | 15,488 | 14,096 |
| 88,350 | 88,400 | 15,500 | 11,322 | 15,500 | 14,108 |
| 88,400 | 88,450 | 15,512 | 11,333 | 15,512 | 14,120 |
| 88,450 | 88,500 | 15,524 | 11,344 | 15,524 | 14,132 |
| 88,500 | 88,550 | 15,536 | 11,355 | 15,536 | 14,144 |
| 88,550 | 88,600 | 15,548 | 11,366 | 15,548 | 14,156 |
| 88,600 | 88,650 | 15,560 | 11,377 | 15,560 | 14,168 |
| 88,650 | 88,700 | 15,572 | 11,388 | 15,572 | 14,180 |
| 88,700 | 88,750 | 15,584 | 11,399 | 15,584 | 14,192 |
| 88,750 | 88,800 | 15,596 | 11,410 | 15,596 | 14,204 |
| 88,800 | 88,850 | 15,608 | 11,421 | 15,608 | 14,216 |
| 88,850 | 88,900 | 15,620 | 11,432 | 15,620 | 14,228 |
| 88,900 | 88,950 | 15,632 | 11,443 | 15,632 | 14,240 |
| 88,950 | 89,000 | 15,644 | 11,454 | 15,644 | 14,252 |

## 89,000

| At least | But less than | Single | Married filing jointly * | Married filing separately | Head of a household |
|---|---|---|---|---|---|
| 89,000 | 89,050 | 15,656 | 11,465 | 15,656 | 14,264 |
| 89,050 | 89,100 | 15,668 | 11,476 | 15,668 | 14,276 |
| 89,100 | 89,150 | 15,680 | 11,487 | 15,680 | 14,288 |
| 89,150 | 89,200 | 15,692 | 11,498 | 15,692 | 14,300 |
| 89,200 | 89,250 | 15,704 | 11,509 | 15,704 | 14,312 |
| 89,250 | 89,300 | 15,716 | 11,520 | 15,716 | 14,324 |
| 89,300 | 89,350 | 15,728 | 11,531 | 15,728 | 14,336 |
| 89,350 | 89,400 | 15,740 | 11,542 | 15,740 | 14,348 |
| 89,400 | 89,450 | 15,752 | 11,553 | 15,752 | 14,360 |
| 89,450 | 89,500 | 15,764 | 11,564 | 15,764 | 14,372 |
| 89,500 | 89,550 | 15,776 | 11,575 | 15,776 | 14,384 |
| 89,550 | 89,600 | 15,788 | 11,586 | 15,788 | 14,396 |
| 89,600 | 89,650 | 15,800 | 11,597 | 15,800 | 14,408 |
| 89,650 | 89,700 | 15,812 | 11,608 | 15,812 | 14,420 |
| 89,700 | 89,750 | 15,824 | 11,619 | 15,824 | 14,432 |
| 89,750 | 89,800 | 15,836 | 11,630 | 15,836 | 14,444 |
| 89,800 | 89,850 | 15,848 | 11,641 | 15,848 | 14,456 |
| 89,850 | 89,900 | 15,860 | 11,652 | 15,860 | 14,468 |
| 89,900 | 89,950 | 15,872 | 11,663 | 15,872 | 14,480 |
| 89,950 | 90,000 | 15,884 | 11,674 | 15,884 | 14,492 |

## 90,000

| At least | But less than | Single | Married filing jointly * | Married filing separately | Head of a household |
|---|---|---|---|---|---|
| 90,000 | 90,050 | 15,896 | 11,685 | 15,896 | 14,504 |
| 90,050 | 90,100 | 15,908 | 11,696 | 15,908 | 14,516 |
| 90,100 | 90,150 | 15,920 | 11,707 | 15,920 | 14,528 |
| 90,150 | 90,200 | 15,932 | 11,718 | 15,932 | 14,540 |
| 90,200 | 90,250 | 15,944 | 11,729 | 15,944 | 14,552 |
| 90,250 | 90,300 | 15,956 | 11,740 | 15,956 | 14,564 |
| 90,300 | 90,350 | 15,968 | 11,751 | 15,968 | 14,576 |
| 90,350 | 90,400 | 15,980 | 11,762 | 15,980 | 14,588 |
| 90,400 | 90,450 | 15,992 | 11,773 | 15,992 | 14,600 |
| 90,450 | 90,500 | 16,004 | 11,784 | 16,004 | 14,612 |
| 90,500 | 90,550 | 16,016 | 11,795 | 16,016 | 14,624 |
| 90,550 | 90,600 | 16,028 | 11,806 | 16,028 | 14,636 |
| 90,600 | 90,650 | 16,040 | 11,817 | 16,040 | 14,648 |
| 90,650 | 90,700 | 16,052 | 11,828 | 16,052 | 14,660 |
| 90,700 | 90,750 | 16,064 | 11,839 | 16,064 | 14,672 |
| 90,750 | 90,800 | 16,076 | 11,850 | 16,076 | 14,684 |
| 90,800 | 90,850 | 16,088 | 11,861 | 16,088 | 14,696 |
| 90,850 | 90,900 | 16,100 | 11,872 | 16,100 | 14,708 |
| 90,900 | 90,950 | 16,112 | 11,883 | 16,112 | 14,720 |
| 90,950 | 91,000 | 16,124 | 11,894 | 16,124 | 14,732 |

## 91,000

| At least | But less than | Single | Married filing jointly * | Married filing separately | Head of a household |
|---|---|---|---|---|---|
| 91,000 | 91,050 | 16,136 | 11,905 | 16,136 | 14,744 |
| 91,050 | 91,100 | 16,148 | 11,916 | 16,148 | 14,756 |
| 91,100 | 91,150 | 16,160 | 11,927 | 16,160 | 14,768 |
| 91,150 | 91,200 | 16,172 | 11,938 | 16,172 | 14,780 |
| 91,200 | 91,250 | 16,184 | 11,949 | 16,184 | 14,792 |
| 91,250 | 91,300 | 16,196 | 11,960 | 16,196 | 14,804 |
| 91,300 | 91,350 | 16,208 | 11,971 | 16,208 | 14,816 |
| 91,350 | 91,400 | 16,220 | 11,982 | 16,220 | 14,828 |
| 91,400 | 91,450 | 16,232 | 11,993 | 16,232 | 14,840 |
| 91,450 | 91,500 | 16,244 | 12,004 | 16,244 | 14,852 |
| 91,500 | 91,550 | 16,256 | 12,015 | 16,256 | 14,864 |
| 91,550 | 91,600 | 16,268 | 12,026 | 16,268 | 14,876 |
| 91,600 | 91,650 | 16,280 | 12,037 | 16,280 | 14,888 |
| 91,650 | 91,700 | 16,292 | 12,048 | 16,292 | 14,900 |
| 91,700 | 91,750 | 16,304 | 12,059 | 16,304 | 14,912 |
| 91,750 | 91,800 | 16,316 | 12,070 | 16,316 | 14,924 |
| 91,800 | 91,850 | 16,328 | 12,081 | 16,328 | 14,936 |
| 91,850 | 91,900 | 16,340 | 12,092 | 16,340 | 14,948 |
| 91,900 | 91,950 | 16,352 | 12,103 | 16,352 | 14,960 |
| 91,950 | 92,000 | 16,364 | 12,114 | 16,364 | 14,972 |

## 92,000

| At least | But less than | Single | Married filing jointly * | Married filing separately | Head of a household |
|---|---|---|---|---|---|
| 92,000 | 92,050 | 16,376 | 12,125 | 16,376 | 14,984 |
| 92,050 | 92,100 | 16,388 | 12,136 | 16,388 | 14,996 |
| 92,100 | 92,150 | 16,400 | 12,147 | 16,400 | 15,008 |
| 92,150 | 92,200 | 16,412 | 12,158 | 16,412 | 15,020 |
| 92,200 | 92,250 | 16,424 | 12,169 | 16,424 | 15,032 |
| 92,250 | 92,300 | 16,436 | 12,180 | 16,436 | 15,044 |
| 92,300 | 92,350 | 16,448 | 12,191 | 16,448 | 15,056 |
| 92,350 | 92,400 | 16,460 | 12,202 | 16,460 | 15,068 |
| 92,400 | 92,450 | 16,472 | 12,213 | 16,472 | 15,080 |
| 92,450 | 92,500 | 16,484 | 12,224 | 16,484 | 15,092 |
| 92,500 | 92,550 | 16,496 | 12,235 | 16,496 | 15,104 |
| 92,550 | 92,600 | 16,508 | 12,246 | 16,508 | 15,116 |
| 92,600 | 92,650 | 16,520 | 12,257 | 16,520 | 15,128 |
| 92,650 | 92,700 | 16,532 | 12,268 | 16,532 | 15,140 |
| 92,700 | 92,750 | 16,544 | 12,279 | 16,544 | 15,152 |
| 92,750 | 92,800 | 16,556 | 12,290 | 16,556 | 15,164 |
| 92,800 | 92,850 | 16,568 | 12,301 | 16,568 | 15,176 |
| 92,850 | 92,900 | 16,580 | 12,312 | 16,580 | 15,188 |
| 92,900 | 92,950 | 16,592 | 12,323 | 16,592 | 15,200 |
| 92,950 | 93,000 | 16,604 | 12,334 | 16,604 | 15,212 |

*If line 10 (taxable income) is— / And you are— / Your tax is—*

* This column must also be used by a qualifying widow(er).

*(Continued)*

## 93,000

| At least | But less than | Single | Married filing jointly * | Married filing separately | Head of a household |
|---|---|---|---|---|---|
| | | | | | Your tax is— |
| 93,000 | 93,050 | 16,616 | 12,345 | 16,616 | 15,224 |
| 93,050 | 93,100 | 16,628 | 12,356 | 16,628 | 15,236 |
| 93,100 | 93,150 | 16,640 | 12,367 | 16,640 | 15,248 |
| 93,150 | 93,200 | 16,652 | 12,378 | 16,652 | 15,260 |
| 93,200 | 93,250 | 16,664 | 12,389 | 16,664 | 15,272 |
| 93,250 | 93,300 | 16,676 | 12,400 | 16,676 | 15,284 |
| 93,300 | 93,350 | 16,688 | 12,411 | 16,688 | 15,296 |
| 93,350 | 93,400 | 16,700 | 12,422 | 16,700 | 15,308 |
| 93,400 | 93,450 | 16,712 | 12,433 | 16,712 | 15,320 |
| 93,450 | 93,500 | 16,724 | 12,444 | 16,724 | 15,332 |
| 93,500 | 93,550 | 16,736 | 12,455 | 16,736 | 15,344 |
| 93,550 | 93,600 | 16,748 | 12,466 | 16,748 | 15,356 |
| 93,600 | 93,650 | 16,760 | 12,477 | 16,760 | 15,368 |
| 93,650 | 93,700 | 16,772 | 12,488 | 16,772 | 15,380 |
| 93,700 | 93,750 | 16,784 | 12,499 | 16,784 | 15,392 |
| 93,750 | 93,800 | 16,796 | 12,510 | 16,796 | 15,404 |
| 93,800 | 93,850 | 16,808 | 12,521 | 16,808 | 15,416 |
| 93,850 | 93,900 | 16,820 | 12,532 | 16,820 | 15,428 |
| 93,900 | 93,950 | 16,832 | 12,543 | 16,832 | 15,440 |
| 93,950 | 94,000 | 16,844 | 12,554 | 16,844 | 15,452 |

## 94,000

| At least | But less than | Single | Married filing jointly * | Married filing separately | Head of a household |
|---|---|---|---|---|---|
| 94,000 | 94,050 | 16,856 | 12,565 | 16,856 | 15,464 |
| 94,050 | 94,100 | 16,868 | 12,576 | 16,868 | 15,476 |
| 94,100 | 94,150 | 16,880 | 12,587 | 16,880 | 15,488 |
| 94,150 | 94,200 | 16,892 | 12,598 | 16,892 | 15,500 |
| 94,200 | 94,250 | 16,904 | 12,609 | 16,904 | 15,512 |
| 94,250 | 94,300 | 16,916 | 12,620 | 16,916 | 15,524 |
| 94,300 | 94,350 | 16,928 | 12,631 | 16,928 | 15,536 |
| 94,350 | 94,400 | 16,940 | 12,642 | 16,940 | 15,548 |
| 94,400 | 94,450 | 16,952 | 12,653 | 16,952 | 15,560 |
| 94,450 | 94,500 | 16,964 | 12,664 | 16,964 | 15,572 |
| 94,500 | 94,550 | 16,976 | 12,675 | 16,976 | 15,584 |
| 94,550 | 94,600 | 16,988 | 12,686 | 16,988 | 15,596 |
| 94,600 | 94,650 | 17,000 | 12,697 | 17,000 | 15,608 |
| 94,650 | 94,700 | 17,012 | 12,708 | 17,012 | 15,620 |
| 94,700 | 94,750 | 17,024 | 12,719 | 17,024 | 15,632 |
| 94,750 | 94,800 | 17,036 | 12,730 | 17,036 | 15,644 |
| 94,800 | 94,850 | 17,048 | 12,741 | 17,048 | 15,656 |
| 94,850 | 94,900 | 17,060 | 12,752 | 17,060 | 15,668 |
| 94,900 | 94,950 | 17,072 | 12,763 | 17,072 | 15,680 |
| 94,950 | 95,000 | 17,084 | 12,774 | 17,084 | 15,692 |

## 95,000

| At least | But less than | Single | Married filing jointly * | Married filing separately | Head of a household |
|---|---|---|---|---|---|
| 95,000 | 95,050 | 17,096 | 12,785 | 17,096 | 15,704 |
| 95,050 | 95,100 | 17,108 | 12,796 | 17,108 | 15,716 |
| 95,100 | 95,150 | 17,120 | 12,807 | 17,120 | 15,728 |
| 95,150 | 95,200 | 17,132 | 12,818 | 17,132 | 15,740 |
| 95,200 | 95,250 | 17,144 | 12,829 | 17,144 | 15,752 |
| 95,250 | 95,300 | 17,156 | 12,840 | 17,156 | 15,764 |
| 95,300 | 95,350 | 17,168 | 12,851 | 17,168 | 15,776 |
| 95,350 | 95,400 | 17,180 | 12,862 | 17,180 | 15,788 |
| 95,400 | 95,450 | 17,192 | 12,873 | 17,192 | 15,800 |
| 95,450 | 95,500 | 17,204 | 12,884 | 17,204 | 15,812 |
| 95,500 | 95,550 | 17,216 | 12,895 | 17,216 | 15,824 |
| 95,550 | 95,600 | 17,228 | 12,906 | 17,228 | 15,836 |
| 95,600 | 95,650 | 17,240 | 12,917 | 17,240 | 15,848 |
| 95,650 | 95,700 | 17,252 | 12,928 | 17,252 | 15,860 |
| 95,700 | 95,750 | 17,264 | 12,939 | 17,264 | 15,872 |
| 95,750 | 95,800 | 17,276 | 12,950 | 17,276 | 15,884 |
| 95,800 | 95,850 | 17,288 | 12,961 | 17,288 | 15,896 |
| 95,850 | 95,900 | 17,300 | 12,972 | 17,300 | 15,908 |
| 95,900 | 95,950 | 17,312 | 12,983 | 17,312 | 15,920 |
| 95,950 | 96,000 | 17,324 | 12,994 | 17,324 | 15,932 |

## 96,000

| At least | But less than | Single | Married filing jointly * | Married filing separately | Head of a household |
|---|---|---|---|---|---|
| 96,000 | 96,050 | 17,336 | 13,005 | 17,336 | 15,944 |
| 96,050 | 96,100 | 17,348 | 13,016 | 17,348 | 15,956 |
| 96,100 | 96,150 | 17,360 | 13,027 | 17,360 | 15,968 |
| 96,150 | 96,200 | 17,372 | 13,038 | 17,372 | 15,980 |
| 96,200 | 96,250 | 17,384 | 13,049 | 17,384 | 15,992 |
| 96,250 | 96,300 | 17,396 | 13,060 | 17,396 | 16,004 |
| 96,300 | 96,350 | 17,408 | 13,071 | 17,408 | 16,016 |
| 96,350 | 96,400 | 17,420 | 13,082 | 17,420 | 16,028 |
| 96,400 | 96,450 | 17,432 | 13,093 | 17,432 | 16,040 |
| 96,450 | 96,500 | 17,444 | 13,104 | 17,444 | 16,052 |
| 96,500 | 96,550 | 17,456 | 13,115 | 17,456 | 16,064 |
| 96,550 | 96,600 | 17,468 | 13,126 | 17,468 | 16,076 |
| 96,600 | 96,650 | 17,480 | 13,137 | 17,480 | 16,088 |
| 96,650 | 96,700 | 17,492 | 13,148 | 17,492 | 16,100 |
| 96,700 | 96,750 | 17,504 | 13,159 | 17,504 | 16,112 |
| 96,750 | 96,800 | 17,516 | 13,170 | 17,516 | 16,124 |
| 96,800 | 96,850 | 17,528 | 13,181 | 17,528 | 16,136 |
| 96,850 | 96,900 | 17,540 | 13,192 | 17,540 | 16,148 |
| 96,900 | 96,950 | 17,552 | 13,203 | 17,552 | 16,160 |
| 96,950 | 97,000 | 17,564 | 13,214 | 17,564 | 16,172 |

## 97,000

| At least | But less than | Single | Married filing jointly * | Married filing separately | Head of a household |
|---|---|---|---|---|---|
| 97,000 | 97,050 | 17,576 | 13,225 | 17,576 | 16,184 |
| 97,050 | 97,100 | 17,588 | 13,236 | 17,588 | 16,196 |
| 97,100 | 97,150 | 17,600 | 13,247 | 17,600 | 16,208 |
| 97,150 | 97,200 | 17,612 | 13,258 | 17,612 | 16,220 |
| 97,200 | 97,250 | 17,624 | 13,269 | 17,624 | 16,232 |
| 97,250 | 97,300 | 17,636 | 13,280 | 17,636 | 16,244 |
| 97,300 | 97,350 | 17,648 | 13,291 | 17,648 | 16,256 |
| 97,350 | 97,400 | 17,660 | 13,302 | 17,660 | 16,268 |
| 97,400 | 97,450 | 17,672 | 13,313 | 17,672 | 16,280 |
| 97,450 | 97,500 | 17,684 | 13,324 | 17,684 | 16,292 |
| 97,500 | 97,550 | 17,696 | 13,335 | 17,696 | 16,304 |
| 97,550 | 97,600 | 17,708 | 13,346 | 17,708 | 16,316 |
| 97,600 | 97,650 | 17,720 | 13,357 | 17,720 | 16,328 |
| 97,650 | 97,700 | 17,732 | 13,368 | 17,732 | 16,340 |
| 97,700 | 97,750 | 17,744 | 13,379 | 17,744 | 16,352 |
| 97,750 | 97,800 | 17,756 | 13,390 | 17,756 | 16,364 |
| 97,800 | 97,850 | 17,768 | 13,401 | 17,768 | 16,376 |
| 97,850 | 97,900 | 17,780 | 13,412 | 17,780 | 16,388 |
| 97,900 | 97,950 | 17,792 | 13,423 | 17,792 | 16,400 |
| 97,950 | 98,000 | 17,804 | 13,434 | 17,804 | 16,412 |

## 98,000

| At least | But less than | Single | Married filing jointly * | Married filing separately | Head of a household |
|---|---|---|---|---|---|
| 98,000 | 98,050 | 17,816 | 13,445 | 17,816 | 16,424 |
| 98,050 | 98,100 | 17,828 | 13,456 | 17,828 | 16,436 |
| 98,100 | 98,150 | 17,840 | 13,467 | 17,840 | 16,448 |
| 98,150 | 98,200 | 17,852 | 13,478 | 17,852 | 16,460 |
| 98,200 | 98,250 | 17,864 | 13,489 | 17,864 | 16,472 |
| 98,250 | 98,300 | 17,876 | 13,500 | 17,876 | 16,484 |
| 98,300 | 98,350 | 17,888 | 13,511 | 17,888 | 16,496 |
| 98,350 | 98,400 | 17,900 | 13,522 | 17,900 | 16,508 |
| 98,400 | 98,450 | 17,912 | 13,533 | 17,912 | 16,520 |
| 98,450 | 98,500 | 17,924 | 13,544 | 17,924 | 16,532 |
| 98,500 | 98,550 | 17,936 | 13,555 | 17,936 | 16,544 |
| 98,550 | 98,600 | 17,948 | 13,566 | 17,948 | 16,556 |
| 98,600 | 98,650 | 17,960 | 13,577 | 17,960 | 16,568 |
| 98,650 | 98,700 | 17,972 | 13,588 | 17,972 | 16,580 |
| 98,700 | 98,750 | 17,984 | 13,599 | 17,984 | 16,592 |
| 98,750 | 98,800 | 17,996 | 13,610 | 17,996 | 16,604 |
| 98,800 | 98,850 | 18,008 | 13,621 | 18,008 | 16,616 |
| 98,850 | 98,900 | 18,020 | 13,632 | 18,020 | 16,628 |
| 98,900 | 98,950 | 18,032 | 13,643 | 18,032 | 16,640 |
| 98,950 | 99,000 | 18,044 | 13,654 | 18,044 | 16,652 |

## 99,000

| At least | But less than | Single | Married filing jointly * | Married filing separately | Head of a household |
|---|---|---|---|---|---|
| 99,000 | 99,050 | 18,056 | 13,665 | 18,056 | 16,664 |
| 99,050 | 99,100 | 18,068 | 13,676 | 18,068 | 16,676 |
| 99,100 | 99,150 | 18,080 | 13,687 | 18,080 | 16,688 |
| 99,150 | 99,200 | 18,092 | 13,698 | 18,092 | 16,700 |
| 99,200 | 99,250 | 18,104 | 13,709 | 18,104 | 16,712 |
| 99,250 | 99,300 | 18,116 | 13,720 | 18,116 | 16,724 |
| 99,300 | 99,350 | 18,128 | 13,731 | 18,128 | 16,736 |
| 99,350 | 99,400 | 18,140 | 13,742 | 18,140 | 16,748 |
| 99,400 | 99,450 | 18,152 | 13,753 | 18,152 | 16,760 |
| 99,450 | 99,500 | 18,164 | 13,764 | 18,164 | 16,772 |
| 99,500 | 99,550 | 18,176 | 13,775 | 18,176 | 16,784 |
| 99,550 | 99,600 | 18,188 | 13,786 | 18,188 | 16,796 |
| 99,600 | 99,650 | 18,200 | 13,797 | 18,200 | 16,808 |
| 99,650 | 99,700 | 18,212 | 13,808 | 18,212 | 16,820 |
| 99,700 | 99,750 | 18,224 | 13,819 | 18,224 | 16,832 |
| 99,750 | 99,800 | 18,236 | 13,830 | 18,236 | 16,844 |
| 99,800 | 99,850 | 18,248 | 13,841 | 18,248 | 16,856 |
| 99,850 | 99,900 | 18,260 | 13,852 | 18,260 | 16,868 |
| 99,900 | 99,950 | 18,272 | 13,863 | 18,272 | 16,880 |
| 99,950 | 100,000 | 18,284 | 13,874 | 18,284 | 16,892 |

$100,000
or over
use the Tax
Computation
Worksheet

* This column must also be used by a qualifying widow(er).

# 2018 Tax Computation Worksheet—Line 11a

 *See the instructions for line 11a to see if you must use the worksheet below to figure your tax.*

**Note.** If you are required to use this worksheet to figure the tax on an amount from another form or worksheet, such as the Qualified Dividends and Capital Gain Tax Worksheet, the Schedule D Tax Worksheet, Schedule J, Form 8615, or the Foreign Earned Income Tax Worksheet, enter the amount from that form or worksheet in column (a) of the row that applies to the amount you are looking up. Enter the result on the appropriate line of the form or worksheet that you are completing.

**Section A**—Use if your filing status is **Single.** Complete the row below that applies to you.

| Taxable income. If line 10 is— | (a) Enter the amount from line 10 | (b) Multiplication amount | (c) Multiply (a) by (b) | (d) Subtraction amount | Tax. Subtract (d) from (c). Enter the result here and on the entry space on line 11a. |
|---|---|---|---|---|---|
| At least $100,000 but not over $157,500 | $ | × 24% (0.24) | $ | $ 5,710.50 | $ |
| Over $157,500 but not over $200,000 | $ | × 32% (0.32) | $ | $ 18,310.50 | $ |
| Over $200,000 but not over $500,000 | $ | × 35% (0.35) | $ | $ 24,310.50 | $ |
| Over $500,000 | $ | × 37% (0.37) | $ | $ 34,310.50 | $ |

**Section B**—Use if your filing status is **Married filing jointly** or **Qualifying widow(er).** Complete the row below that applies to you.

| Taxable income. If line 10 is— | (a) Enter the amount from line 10 | (b) Multiplication amount | (c) Multiply (a) by (b) | (d) Subtraction amount | Tax. Subtract (d) from (c). Enter the result here and on the entry space on line 11a. |
|---|---|---|---|---|---|
| At least $100,000 but not over $165,000 | $ | × 22% (0.22) | $ | $ 8,121.00 | $ |
| Over $165,000 but not over $315,000 | $ | × 24% (0.24) | $ | $ 11,421.00 | $ |
| Over $315,000 but not over $400,000 | $ | × 32% (0.32) | $ | $ 36,621.00 | $ |
| Over $400,000 but not over $600,000 | $ | × 35% (0.35) | $ | $ 48,621.00 | $ |
| Over $600,000 | $ | × 37% (0.37) | $ | $ 60,621.00 | $ |

**Section C**—Use if your filing status is **Married filing separately.** Complete the row below that applies to you.

| Taxable income. If line 10 is— | (a) Enter the amount from line 10 | (b) Multiplication amount | (c) Multiply (a) by (b) | (d) Subtraction amount | Tax. Subtract (d) from (c). Enter the result here and on the entry space on line 11a. |
|---|---|---|---|---|---|
| At least $100,000 but not over $157,500 | $ | × 24% (0.24) | $ | $ 5,710.50 | $ |
| Over $157,500 but not over $200,000 | $ | × 32% (0.32) | $ | $ 18,310.50 | $ |
| Over $200,000 but not over $300,000 | $ | × 35% (0.35) | $ | $ 24,310.50 | $ |
| Over $300,000 | $ | × 37% (0.37) | $ | $ 30,310.50 | $ |

**Section D**—Use if your filing status is **Head of household.** Complete the row below that applies to you.

| Taxable income. If line 10 is— | (a) Enter the amount from line 10 | (b) Multiplication amount | (c) Multiply (a) by (b) | (d) Subtraction amount | Tax. Subtract (d) from (c). Enter the result here and on the entry space on line 11a. |
|---|---|---|---|---|---|
| At least $100,000 but not over $157,500 | $ | × 24% (0.24) | $ | $ 7,102.00 | $ |
| Over $157,500 but not over $200,000 | $ | × 32% (0.32) | $ | $ 19,702.00 | $ |
| Over $200,000 but not over $500,000 | $ | × 35% (0.35) | $ | $ 25,702.00 | $ |
| Over $500,000 | $ | × 37% (0.37) | $ | $ 35,702.00 | $ |

## A

**ABLE account.** An account for a person who became disabled before age 26. Nondeductible annual contributions can be made up to a specified limit and distributions are tax free if used to pay qualified disability expenses; *see 34.12.*

**Accelerated cost recovery system (ACRS).** A statutory method –of depreciation allowing accelerated rates for most types of property used in business and income-producing activities during the years 1981 through 1986. It has been superseded by the modified accelerated cost recovery system (MACRS) for assets placed in service after 1986; *see 42.4* and *42.12.*

**Accelerated depreciation.** Depreciation methods that allow faster write-offs than straight-line rates in the earlier periods of the useful life of an asset. For example, in the first few years of recovery, MACRS allows a 200% double declining balance write-off, twice the straight-line rate; *see 42.5–42.8.*

**Accountable reimbursement plan.** An employer reimbursement or allowance arrangement that requires you to adequately substantiate business expenses to your employer, and to return any excess reimbursement; *see 20.32.*

**Accrual method of accounting.** A business method of accounting requiring income to be reported when earned and expenses to be deducted when incurred. However, deductions generally may not be claimed until economic performance has occurred; *see 40.3.*

**Acquisition debt.** Debt used to buy, build, or construct a principal residence or second home and that generally qualifies for a full interest expense deduction; *see 15.2.*

**Active participation.** Test for determining deductibility of IRA deductions. Active participants in employer retirement plans are subject to IRA deduction phaseout rules if adjusted gross income exceeds certain thresholds; *see 8.4.*

**Adjusted basis.** A statutory term describing the cost used to determine your profit or loss from a sale or exchange of property. It is generally your original cost, increased by capital improvements, and decreased by depreciation, depletion, and other capital write-offs; *see 5.20.*

**Adjusted gross income (AGI).** Gross income less allowable adjustments, such as deductions for IRAs, alimony, and self-employed retirement plans. AGI determines whether various tax benefits are phased out, such as the child tax credit, the earned income credit, and the rental loss allowance; *see 12.1* and modified adjusted gross income (MAGI).

**Alimony.** Payments made to a separated or divorced spouse as required by a decree or agreement. Qualifying payments are deductible by the payor and taxable to the payee; *see Chapter 37.*

**Alternative minimum tax (AMT).** A tax triggered if certain tax benefits reduce your regular income tax below the tax computed on Form 6251 for AMT purposes; *see Chapter 23.*

**Amended return.** On Form 1040X, you may file an amended return within a three-year period to claim a refund or correct a mistake made on an original or previously amended return; *see Chapter 47.*

**Amortizable bond premium.** The additional amount paid over the face amount of an obligation that may be deducted under the rules in *4.17.*

**Amortization of intangibles.** Writing off an investment in intangible assets over a specified period; *see 42.17–42.19.*

**Amount realized.** A statutory term used to figure your profit or loss on a sale or exchange. Generally, it is sales proceeds plus mortgages assumed or taken subject to, less transaction expenses, such as commissions and legal costs; *see 5.14.*

**Amount recognized.** The amount of gain reportable and subject to tax. On certain tax-free exchanges of property, gain is not recognized in the year it is realized; *see 6.1.*

**Annualized rate.** A rate for a period of less than a year computed as though for a full year.

**Annuity.** An annual payment of money by a company or individual to a person called the annuitant. Payment is for a fixed period or the life of the annuitant. Tax consequences depend on the type of contract and funding; *see 7.21–7.27.*

**Applicable federal rate.** Interest rate fixed by the Treasury for determining imputed interest; *see 4.30–4.32.*

**Appreciation in value.** Increase in value of property due to market conditions. When you sell appreciated property, you pay tax on the appreciation since the date of purchase. When you donate appreciated property held long term, you may generally deduct the appreciated value; *see 14.6.*

**Archer Medical Savings Account (MSA).** A type of medical plan combining high deductible medical insurance protection with an IRA-type savings account fund to pay unreimbursed medical expenses; *see 41.13.*

**Assessment.** The IRS action of fixing tax liability that sets in motion collection procedures, such as charging interest, imposing penalties, and, if necessary, seizing property; *see 48.2.*

**Assignment.** The legal transfer of property, rights, or interest to another person called an assignee. You cannot avoid tax on income by assigning the income to another person.

**At-risk rules.** Rules limiting loss deductions to cash investments and personal liability notes. An exception for real estate treats certain nonrecourse commercial loans as amounts "at risk"; *see 10.18.*

**Audit.** An IRS examination of your tax return, generally limited to a three-year period after you file; *see* Chapter 48.

**Away from home.** A tax requirement for deducting travel expenses on a business trip. Sleeping arrangements are required for at least one night before returning home; *see 20.3* and *20.5–20.7.*

## B

**Balloon.** A final payment on a loan in one lump sum.

**Basis.** Generally, the amount paid for property. You need to know your basis to figure gain or loss on a sale; *see 5.16.*

**Bonus depreciation.** An additional first-year depreciation allowance (100% for 2018) for qualifying property; *see 42.18.*

**Boot.** Generally, the receipt of cash or its equivalent accompanying an exchange of property. In a tax-free exchange, boot is subject to immediate tax; *see 6.3.*

# C

**Cancellation of debt.** Release of a debt without consideration by a creditor. Cancellations of debt are generally taxable; *see 11.8.*

**Capital.** The excess of assets over liabilities.

**Capital asset.** Property subject to capital gain or loss treatment. Almost all assets you own are considered capital assets except for certain business assets or works you created; *see 5.2.*

**Capital expenses.** Costs that are not currently deductible and that are added to the basis of property. A capital expense generally increases the value of property. When added to depreciable property, the cost is deductible over the life of the asset.

**Capital gain or loss.** The difference between amount realized and adjusted basis on the sale or exchange of capital assets. Long-term capital gains are taxed favorably, as explained in *Chapter 5.* Capital losses are deducted first against capital gains, and then again up to $3,000 of other income; *see 5.1–5.5.*

**Capital gain distribution.** A mutual fund distribution allocated to gains realized on the sale of fund portfolio assets. You report the distribution as long-term capital gain even if you held the fund shares short term; *see 32.3–32.4.*

**Capital loss carryover.** A capital loss that is not deductible because it exceeds the annual $3,000 capital loss ceiling. A carryover loss may be deducted from capital gains of later years plus up to $3,000 of ordinary income; *see 5.4.*

**Capitalization.** Adding a cost or expense to the basis of the property.

**Carryforward.** A tax technique of applying a loss or credit from a current year to a later year. For example, a business net operating loss may be carried forward 20 years; *see 40.18.*

**Cash method of accounting.** Reporting income when actually or constructively received and deducting expenses when paid. Certain businesses may not use the cash method; *see 40.3.*

**Casualty loss.** Loss from an unforeseen and sudden event that in the case of personal-use property is deductible only if attributable to a federally declared disaster, subject to a $100 per event floor and an overall 10% income floor; *see 18.1.*

**Child and dependent care credit.** A credit ranging from 20% to 35% based on certain care expenses incurred to allow you to work; *see 25.4.*

**Community income.** Income earned by persons domiciled in community property states and treated as belonging equally to husband and wife; *see 1.6.*

**Condemnation.** The seizure of property by a public authority for a public purpose. Tax on gain realized on many conversions may be deferred; *see 18.19–18.20.*

**Constructive receipt.** A tax rule that taxes income that is not received by you but that you may draw upon; *see 2.2.*

**Consumer interest.** Interest incurred on personal debt and consumer credit. Consumer interest is not deductible.

**Convention.** Rule for determining MACRS depreciation in the year property is placed in service. Either a half-year convention, mid-quarter convention, or mid-month convention applies; *see 42.5–42.7, 42.12.*

**Coverdell Education Savings Account.** A special account set up to fund education expenses of a student; *see 33.10–33.11.*

**Credit.** A tax credit directly reduces tax liability, as opposed to a deduction that reduces income subject to tax.

# D

**Declining balance method.** A rapid depreciation method determined by a constant percentage based on useful life and applied to the adjusted basis of the property; *see 42.5 and 42.8.*

**Deductions.** Items directly reducing income. Personal deductions such as for mortgage interest, state and local taxes, and charitable contributions are allowed only if deductions are itemized on Schedule A of form 1040, but deductions such as for alimony, capital losses, business losses, student loan interest, the deductible part of self-employment tax, and traditional IRA and self-employed retirement plan contributions are deducted from gross income even if itemized deductions are not claimed; *see Chapter 12.*

**Deferred compensation.** A portion of earnings withheld by an employer or put into a retirement plan for distribution to the employee at a later date. If certain legal requirements are met, the deferred amount is not taxable until actually paid, for example, after retirement; *see 2.7.*

**Deficiency.** The excess of the tax assessed by the IRS over the amount reported on your return; *see 48.8.*

**Defined benefit plan.** A retirement plan that pays fixed benefits based on actuarial projections; *see 41.2.*

**Defined contribution plan.** A retirement plan that pays benefits based on contributions to individual accounts, plus accumulated earnings. Contributions are generally based on a percentage of salary or earned income; *see 41.2.*

**Dependent.** A relative or household member for whom various tax benefits may be claimed; *see Chapter 21.*

**Depletion.** Deduction claimed for the use of mineral resources; *see 9.15.*

**Depreciable property.** A business or income-producing asset with a useful life exceeding one year; *see 42.1.*

**Depreciation.** Writing off the cost of depreciable property over a period of years, usually its class life or recovery period specified in the tax law; *see 42.4.*

**Depreciation recapture.** An amount of gain on the sale of certain depreciable property that is treated as ordinary income in the case of personal property. Recapture is computed on Form 4797; *see 44.1.* For recapture on the sale of realty, *see 44.2.*

**Disaster losses.** Casualty losses such as from a hurricane or severe flooding, in areas declared by the President to warrant federal assistance. An election may be made to deduct the loss in the year before the loss or the year of the loss; *see 18.3.*

**Dividend.** A distribution made by a corporation to its shareholders generally of company earnings or surplus. Most dividends are taxable but exceptions are explained in *Chapter 4.*

# E

**Earned income.** Compensation for performing personal services. You must have earned income for a deductible IRA, *see 8.2,* or to claim the earned income credit, *see 25.6.*

**Earned income credit.** A credit allowed to taxpayers with earned income or adjusted gross income (AGI) below certain thresholds; *see 25.6.*

**Education IRA.** See Coverdell Education Savings Account and *33.10–33.11.*

**Electronic Federal Tax Payment System (EFTPS).** An online and phone tax payment system available 24 hours a day. For enrollment information, call (800) 555-4477, or go to www.eftps.gov.

**Estimated tax.** Advance payment of current tax liability based either on wage withholdings or installment payments of your estimated tax liability. To avoid penalties, you generally must pay to the IRS either 90% of your final tax liability, or either 100% or 110% of the prior year's tax liability, depending on your adjusted gross income; see *Chapter 27*.

## F

**Fair market value.** What a willing buyer would pay to a willing seller when neither is under any compulsion to buy or sell.

**Fiduciary.** A person or corporation such as a trustee, executor, or guardian who manages property for another person.

**First-year expensing (or Section 179 deduction).** A deduction of the cost of business equipment in the year placed in service; see *42.3* for limitations.

**Fiscal year.** A 12-month period ending on the last day of any month other than December. Partnerships, S corporations, and personal service corporations are limited in their choice of fiscal years and face special restrictions.

**Flexible spending arrangement.** A salary reduction plan that allows employees to pay for enhanced medical coverage or dependent care expenses on a tax-free basis; see *3.16*.

**Foreign earned income exclusion.** For 2018, up to $103,900 of foreign earned income is exempt from tax if a foreign residence or physical presence test is met; see *36.1–36.2*.

**Foreign tax credit.** A credit for income taxes paid to a foreign country or U.S. possession; see *36.13*.

**401(k) plan.** A deferred pay plan, authorized by Section 401(k) of the Internal Revenue Code, under which a percentage of an employee's salary is withheld and placed in a savings account or the company's profit-sharing plan. Income accumulates on the deferred amount until withdrawn by the employee after reaching age 59½ or when the employee retires or leaves the company; see *7.15*.

## G

**Gift tax.** Gifts in excess of an per-donee annual exclusion ($15,000 for 2018) are subject to gift tax, but the tax may be offset by a gift tax credit; see *39.2*.

**Grantor trust rules.** Tax rules that tax the grantor of a trust on the trust income; see *39.6*.

**Gross income.** The total amount of income received from all sources before exclusions and deductions.

**Gross receipts.** Total business receipts reported on Schedule C or Schedule C-EZ before deducting adjustments for returns and allowances and cost of goods sold; see *40.6*.

**Group-term life insurance.** Employees are not taxed on up to $50,000 of group-term coverage; see *3.4*.

## H

**Head of household.** Generally, an unmarried person who maintains a household for dependents and is allowed to compute his or her tax based on head of household rates, which are more favorable than single person rates; see *1.12*.

**Health reimbursement arrangement (HRA).** An employer-established account that provides tax-free reimbursements to employees for deductibles and other medical expenses that could be taken as itemized deductions; see *3.3*.

**Health savings account.** For calendar year 2018, taxpayers covered by an HDHP may contribute up to $3,450 ($6,900 for family coverage) plus $1,000 extra if age 55 or older and not enrolled in Medicare; see *3.2* and *41.11*.

**High deductible health plan (HDHP).** For 2018, a high deductible health plan is a health plan with an annual deductible that is not less than $1,350 for self-only coverage or $2,700 for family coverage, and with annual out-of-pocket expenses that do not exceed $6,650 or $13,300, respectively.

**Hobby loss.** Hobby expenses are deductible only up to income from the activity; loss deductions are not allowed; see *40.10*.

**Holding period.** The length of time that an asset is owned and that generally determines long- or short-term capital gain treatment; see *5.3* and *5.9–5.12*.

**Household income.** This amount is used to determine eligibility for the premium tax credit (*25.12*) and the individual shared responsibility payment (*38.6*). It is AGI increased by excluded foreign income and tax-exempt interest.

## I

**Imputed interest.** Interest deemed earned on seller-financed sales or low-interest loans, where the parties' stated interest rate is below the applicable IRS federal rate; see *4.31* and *4.32*.

**Incentive stock option.** Option meeting tax law tests that defers tax on the option transaction until the obtained stock is sold; see *2.16*.

**Inclusion amount for leased cars.** Based on an IRS table, an amount that reduces a business deduction taken for payments on an auto leased for a minimum of 30 days; see *43.12*.

**Income in respect of a decedent.** Income earned by a person before death but taxable to an estate or heir who receives it; see *1.14* and *11.16*.

**Independent contractor.** One who controls his or her own work and reports as a self-employed person; see *Chapters 40* and *45*.

**Individual retirement account (IRA).** A retirement account to which up to $5,500 (or $6,500 if you are 50 or over) may be contributed for 2018, but deductions for contributions to a traditional IRA are restricted if you are covered by a company retirement plan. Earnings accumulate tax free; see *Chapter 8*.

**Installment payment agreement.** A formal arrangement with the IRS to pay taxes over time; see *46.5*.

**Installment sale.** A sale of property that allows for tax deferment if at least one payment is received after the end of the tax year in which the sale occurs. The installment method does not apply to year-end sales of publicly traded securities. Dealers may not use the installment method. Investors with very large installment balances could face a special tax; see *5.21*.

**Intangible assets.** Intangible assets that come within Section 197, such as goodwill, are amortizable over a 15-year period; see *42.17*.

**Inter vivos or lifetime trust.** A trust created during the lifetime of the person who created the trust. If irrevocable, income on the trust principal is generally shifted to the trust beneficiaries; see *39.6*.

**Investment in the contract.** The total cost investment in an annuity. When annuity payments are made, the portion allocable to the cost investment is tax free; see *7.21* and *7.24–7.27*.

**Investment interest.** Interest on debt used to carry investments, but not including interest expense from a passive activity. Deductions are limited to net investment income; see *15.10*.

**Involuntary conversion.** Forced disposition of property due to condemnation, theft, or casualty. Tax on gain from involuntary conversions may be deferred if replacement property is purchased; see *18.19-18.20*.

**Itemized deductions.** Items, such as interest, state and local income and sales taxes, charitable contributions, and medical deductions, claimed on Schedule A of Form 1040. Itemized deductions are subtracted from adjusted gross income to arrive at taxable income; see *Chapter 13*.

# J

**Joint return.** A return filed by a married couple reporting their combined income and deductions. Joint return status provides tax savings to many couples; see *1.4*.

**Joint tenants.** Ownership of property by two persons. When one dies, the decedent's interest passes to the survivor; see *5.18*.

# K

**Keogh plan.** A term that is sometimes used to describe a qualified retirement plan set up by a self-employed person, providing tax-deductible contributions, tax-free income accumulations until withdrawal, and favorable averaging for qualifying lump-sum distributions; see *Chapter 41*.

**Kiddie tax.** The tax on the investment income in excess of an annual floor ($2,100 for 2018) of a child under age 18, and many children age 18–23. The tax is based on the tax rates for trusts and estates and computed on Form 8615; see *24.2*.

# L

**Legally separated.** A husband and wife who are required to live apart from each other by the terms of a decree of separate maintenance. Payments under the decree are deductible by the payor and taxable to the payee as alimony; see *37.2*.

**Like-kind exchange.** An exchange of similar assets used in a business or held for investment on which gain may be deferred; see *6.1*.

**Lump-sum distribution.** Payments within one tax year of the entire amount due to a participant in a qualified retirement plan. Qualifying lump sums may be directly rolled over tax free. For participants born before January 2, 1936, a lump sum may be eligible for current tax under a favorable averaging method; see *7.2*.

# M

**Marital deduction.** An estate tax and gift tax deduction for assets passing to a spouse. It allows estate and gift transfers completely free of tax; see *39.10*.

**Market discount.** The difference between face value of a bond and lower market price, attributable to rising interest rates. On a sale, gain on the bond is generally taxed as ordinary income to the extent of the discount; see *4.20*.

**Material participation tests.** Rules for determining whether a person is active in a business activity for passive activity rule purposes. Unless the tests are met, passive loss limits apply; see *10.6*.

**Modified ACRS (MACRS).** Depreciation methods applied to assets placed in service after 1986.

**Modified adjusted gross income (MAGI).** This is generally adjusted gross income increased by certain items such as tax-free foreign earned income. MAGI usually is used to determine phaseouts of certain deductions and credits.

**Mortgage interest.** Interest on acquisition debt for up to two residences that is fully deductible if within debt ceilings; see *15.1*.

# N

**Net operating loss.** A business loss that exceeds current income may be carried forward as a deduction from future income until eliminated; see *40.18-40.20*.

**Nonperiodic distributions.** A 20% withholding rule applies to nonperiodic distributions, such as lump-sum distributions, paid directly to employees from an employer plan; see *7.6* and *26.9*.

**Nonrecourse financing.** Debt on which a person is not personally liable. In case of nonpayment, the creditor must foreclose on property securing the debt. At-risk rules generally bar losses where there is nonrecourse financing, but an exception applies to certain nonrecourse financing for real estate; see *10.18*.

# O

**Offer in compromise.** A proposal to the IRS that, if accepted, allows a taxpayer to pay less than the full amount of tax owed; see *48.10*.

**Ordinary and necessary.** A statutory requirement for the deductibility of a business expense.

**Ordinary income.** Income other than long-term capital gains or qualified dividends that are taxed the same as long-term capital gains; see *5.3*.

**Ordinary loss.** A loss other than a capital loss.

**Original issue discount (OID).** The difference between the face value of a bond and its original issue price. OID is reported on an annual basis as interest income; see *4.19*.

# P

**Partnership.** An unincorporated business or income-producing entity organized by two or more persons. A partnership is not subject to tax but passes through to the partners all income, deductions, and credits, according to the terms of the partnership agreement; see *11.9–11.13*.

**Passive activity loss rules.** Rules that limit the deduction of losses from passive activities to income from other passive activities. Passive activities include investment rental operations or businesses in which you do not materially participate; see *10.1*.

**Patronage dividend.** A taxable distribution made by a cooperative to its members or patrons.

**Percentage depletion.** A deduction method that applies a fixed percentage to the gross income generated by mineral property; see *9.15*.

**Personal interest.** Tax term for interest on personal loans and consumer purchases. Such interest is not deductible.

**Placed in service.** The time when a depreciable asset is ready to be used. The date fixes the beginning of the depreciation period.

**Points.** Charges to the homeowner at the time of the loan. A point is equal to 1 percent. Depending on the type of loan, points may be currently deductible or amortized over the life of the loan; see *15.8*.

**Premature distributions.** Withdrawals before age 59½ from qualified retirement plans are subject to penalties unless specific exceptions are met; see *7.13* and *8.12*.

**Principal residence.** On a sale of a principal residence, you may avoid tax under the rules explained in *Chapter 29*.

**Private letter ruling.** A written determination issued to a taxpayer by the IRS that interprets and applies the tax laws to the taxpayer's specific set of facts. A letter ruling advises the taxpayer regarding the tax treatment that can be expected from the IRS in the circumstances specified by the ruling. It may not be used or cited as precedent by another taxpayer.

**Probate estate.** Property held in a decedent's name passing by will; *see 39.7*.

**Profit-sharing plan.** A defined contribution plan under which the amount contributed to the employees' accounts is based on a percentage of the employer's profits; *see 7.15* and *41.2*.

**Provisional income.** If your provisional income exceeds a base amount, part of your Social Security benefits may be subject to tax. To figure provisional income, *see 34.3*.

**PTIN.** A preparer tax identification number required for tax professionals to prepare tax returns for compensation.

## Q

**Qualified business income deduction.** A deduction for 20% of qualified business income, subject to income limitations; *see 40.24*

**Qualified charitable organization.** A nonprofit philanthropic organization that is approved by the U.S. Treasury to receive charitable contribution deductions; *see 14.1*.

**Qualified dividends.** Dividends that are taxed at the long-term capital gain rate; *see 4.2*.

**Qualified domestic relations order (QDRO).** A specialized domestic relations court order that conforms to IRS regulations and provides instructions to pension plan administrators and IRA custodians as to how to pay benefits to a divorced spouse; *see 7.10* and *8.11*.

**Qualified plan.** A retirement plan that meets tax law tests and allows for tax deferment and tax-free accumulation of income until benefits are withdrawn. Pension, profit-sharing, stock bonus, employee stock ownership, and IRAs may be qualified plans; *see Chapters 7, 8, and 41*.

**Qualified tuition program (QTP).** A state-sponsored college savings plan or prepayment plan, or a prepayment plan established by a private college; *see 33.5*.

**Qualifying widow or widower.** A filing status entitling the taxpayer with dependents to use joint tax rates for up to two tax years after the death of a spouse; *see 1.11*.

## R

**Real estate investment trust (REIT).** An entity that invests primarily in real estate and mortgages and passes through income to investors; *see 31.1*.

**Real estate professional.** An individual who, because of his or her real estate activity, qualifies to deduct rental losses from nonpassive income; *see 10.3*.

**Real property.** Land and the buildings on land. Buildings are depreciable; *see 42.12* and *42.15*.

**Recognized gain or loss.** The amount of gain or loss to be reported on a tax return. Gain may not be recognized on certain exchanges of property; *see 6.1*.

**Recovery property.** Tangible depreciable property placed in service after 1980 and before 1987 and depreciable under ACRS; *see 42.11* and *42.15*.

**Refundable tax credit.** A credit that entitles you to a refund even if you owe no tax for the year.

**Required Minimum Distributions (RMDs).** Distributions that must be taken annually to avoid a 50% IRS penalty by a traditional IRA account owner starting with the year age 70½ is reached. For qualified plan participants the starting date may be delayed for employees working beyond age 70½. Minimum distribution rules also apply to beneficiaries of qualified plans, traditional IRAs, and Roth IRAs. See *7.11–7.12*, *8.13–8.14*, and *8.25*.

**Residence interest.** Term for deductible mortgage interest on a principal residence and a second home; *see 15.1–15.2*.

**Residential rental property.** Real property in which 80% or more of the gross income is from dwelling units. Under MACRS, depreciation is claimed over *27.5* years under the straight-line method; *see 42.12*.

**Retirement savers credit.** Eligible taxpayers may claim a tax credit for 10%, 20%, or 50% of up to $2,000 of retirement plan contributions; *see 25.10*.

**Return of capital.** A distribution of your investment that is not subject to tax unless the distribution exceeds your investment; *see 4.11*.

**Revenue ruling.** A revenue ruling is the Commissioner's "official interpretation of the interpretation of the law" and generally is binding on revenue agents and other IRS officials. Taxpayers generally may rely on published revenue rulings in determining the tax treatment of their own transactions that arise out of similar facts and circumstances.

**Revocable trust.** A trust that may be changed or terminated by its creator or another person. Such trusts do not provide an income tax savings to the creator; *see 39.6*.

**Rollover.** A tax-free reinvestment of a distribution from a qualified retirement plan into an IRA or other qualified plan, or from one IRA to another, within 60 days of the distribution; *see 7.2, 7.6,* and *8.10*.

**Roth IRA.** A nondeductible contributory IRA that allows for tax-free accumulation of income. Qualifying distributions are completely tax free. See *8.19–8.25*.

## S

**Salvage value.** The estimated value of an asset at the end of its useful life. Salvage value is ignored by ACRS and MACRS rules.

**S corporation.** A corporation that elects S status in order to receive tax treatment similar to that of a partnership; *see Chapter 11*.

**Section 179 deduction (or First-year expensing).** A deduction allowed for investments in depreciable business equipment in the year the property is placed in service; *see 42.3* for limitations.

**Section 457 plan.** Deferred compensation plan set up by a state or local government, or tax-exempt organization, which allows tax-free deferrals of salary; *see 7.20*.

**Section 1231 property.** Depreciable property used in a trade or business and held for more than a year. All Section 1231 gains and losses are netted; a net gain is treated as capital gain, a net loss as an ordinary loss; *see 44.8*.

**Section 1244 stock.** Stock in a closely-held corporation for which losses up to a dollar limit are treated as ordinary rather than capital losses; *see 30.11*.

**Self-employed person.** An individual who operates a business or profession as a proprietor or independent contractor and reports self-employment income on Schedule C; *see **Chapters 40** and **45**.*

**Self-employment tax.** Tax paid by self-employed persons to finance Social Security and Medicare coverage. For 2018, there are two rates. A 12.4% rate (for Social Security) applies to a taxable earnings base of $128,400 or less and a 2.9% rate (for Medicare) applies to all net earnings; *see **Chapter 45**.*

**Separate return.** Return filed by a married person who does not file a joint return. Filing separately may save taxes where each spouse has separate deductions, but certain tax benefits require a joint return; *see **1.3**.*

**Short sale.** Sale of borrowed securities made to freeze a paper profit or to gain from a declining market; *see **30.5**.*

**Short tax year.** A tax year of less than 12 months. May occur with the startup of a business or change in accounting method.

**Short-term capital gain or loss.** Gain or loss on the sale or exchange of a capital asset held one year or less; *see **5.1**, **5.3**, and **5.10**.*

**Simplified employee plan (SEP).** IRA-type plan set up by an employer, rather than the employee. Salary-reduction contributions may be allowed to plans of small employers set up before 1997; *see **8.15–8.16**.*

**Standard deduction.** A fixed deduction allowed to taxpayers who do not itemize deductions, based on filing status, plus an additional amount for those age 65 or older or blind; *see **13.1**.*

**Standard mileage rate.** A fixed rate allowed by the IRS for business auto expenses in place of deducting actual expenses; *see **43.1**.*

**Statutory employees.** Certain employees, such as full-time life insurance salespersons, who may report income and deductions on Schedule C, rather than on Schedule A as miscellaneous itemized deductions; *see **40.6**.*

**Stock dividend.** A distribution of additional shares of a corporation's stock to its shareholders; *see **4.6**.*

**Stock option.** A right to buy stock at a fixed price.

**Straddle.** Taking an offsetting investment position to reduce the risk of loss in a similar investment; *see **30.9**.*

**Straight-line method.** A method of depreciating the cost of a depreciable asset on a *pro rata* basis over its cost recovery period; *see **42.9**, **42.12**, **42.15**.*

# T

**Tangible personal property.** Movable property, such as desks, computers, machinery, and autos, depreciable over a five-year or seven-year period; *see **42.4**.*

**Taxable income.** Net income after claiming all deductions from gross income and adjusted gross income, such as IRA deductions, itemized deductions or the standard deduction, and the qualified business income deduction; *see **22.1**.*

**Tax attributes.** When debts are canceled in bankruptcy cases, the canceled amount is excluded from gross income. Tax attributes are certain losses, credits, and property basis that must be reduced to the extent of the exclusion; *see **11.8**.*

**Tax deferral.** Shifting income to a later year, such as where you defer taxable interest to the following year by purchasing a T-bill or savings certificate maturing after the end of the current year; *see* Chapter 4. Investments in qualified retirement plans provide tax deferral (***Chapters 7, 8,** and **41***).

**Tax home.** The area of your principal place of business or employment. You must be away from your tax home on a business trip to deduct travel expenses; *see **20.7–20.10**.*

**Tax identification number.** For an individual, his or her Social Security number; for businesses, fiduciaries, and other non-individual taxpayers, the employer identification number.

**Tax preference items.** Items that may subject a taxpayer to the alternative minimum tax (AMT); *see **23.2**.*

**Tax-sheltered annuity.** A type of retirement annuity offered to employees of charitable organizations and educational systems, generally funded by employee salary-reduction contributions; *see **7.19**.*

**Tax year.** A period (generally 12 months) for reporting income and expenses; *see **40.4**.*

**Tenancy by the entireties.** A joint tenancy in real property in the name of both husband and wife. On the death of one tenant, the survivor receives entire interest.

**Tenants in common.** Two or more persons who have undivided ownership rights in property. Upon death of a tenant, his or her share passes to his or her estate, rather than to the surviving tenants.

**Testamentary trust.** A trust established under a will.

**Trust.** An arrangement under which one person transfers legal ownership of assets to another person or corporation (the trustee) for the benefit of one or more third persons (beneficiaries).

# U

**Unrecaptured Section 1250 gain.** Long-term gain realized on the sale of depreciable realty attributed to depreciation deductions and subject to a 25% capital gain rate; *see **5.3** and **44.2**.*

**Useful life.** For property not depreciated under ACRS or MACRS, the estimate of time in which a depreciable asset will be used.

# W

**Wash sales.** Sales on which losses are disallowed because you recover your market position within a 61-day period; *see **30.6**.*

**Withholding.** An amount taken from income as a prepayment of an individual's tax liability for the year. In the case of wages, the employer withholds part of every wage payment. Backup withholding from dividend or interest income is required if you do not provide the payer with a correct taxpayer identification number. Withholding on pensions and IRAs is automatic unless you elect to waive withholding; *see **Chapter 26**.*